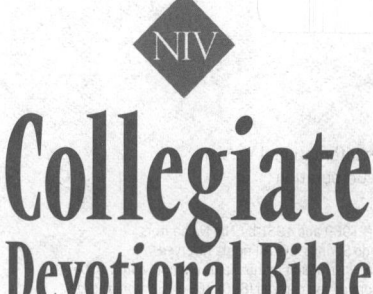

Collegiate
Devotional Bible

Devotions for Knowing God

and Discovering His Purpose

for Your Life

New International Version

Zondervan Publishing House
Grand Rapids, Michigan 49530, U.S.A.

*You will be pleased to know that a portion of the purchase price of your
new NIV Bible has been provided to International Bible Society to help
spread the gospel of Jesus Christ around the world!*

TABLE OF CONTENTS

Alphabetical List of Bible Books iv
The Navigators' Mission v
How to Use the Collegiate Devotional Bible vi
Preface to the NIV viii

Old Testament

Genesis ... 1	2 Chronicles ... 464	Daniel ... 966
Exodus ... 61	Ezra ... 504	Hosea ... 985
Leviticus ... 108	Nehemiah ... 517	Joel ... 997
Numbers ... 139	Esther ... 535	Amos ... 1003
Deuteronomy ... 184	Job ... 544	Obadiah ... 1012
Joshua ... 224	Psalms ... 582	Jonah ... 1015
Judges ... 254	Proverbs ... 691	Micah ... 1018
Ruth ... 283	Ecclesiastes ... 733	Nahum ... 1026
1 Samuel ... 289	Song of Songs ... 747	Habakkuk ... 1030
2 Samuel ... 325	Isaiah ... 755	Zephaniah ... 1035
1 Kings ... 358	Jeremiah ... 835	Haggai ... 1040
2 Kings ... 393	Lamentations ... 905	Zechariah ... 1043
1 Chronicles ... 427	Ezekiel ... 913	Malachi ... 1053

New Testament

Matthew ... 1059	Ephesians ... 1323	Hebrews ... 1377
Mark ... 1103	Philippians ... 1333	James ... 1392
Luke ... 1130	Colossians ... 1341	1 Peter ... 1399
John ... 1176	1 Thessalonians ... 1348	2 Peter ... 1406
Acts ... 1213	2 Thessalonians ... 1354	1 John ... 1411
Romans ... 1256	1 Timothy ... 1358	2 John ... 1418
1 Corinthians ... 1279	2 Timothy ... 1365	3 John ... 1420
2 Corinthians ... 1300	Titus ... 1372	Jude ... 1422
Galatians ... 1314	Philemon ... 1375	Revelation ... 1425

Weights and Measures 1449
One Month Reading Plan 1450
One Year Reading Plan 1451
Subject Index to Scripture 1457
Subject Index to Daily Devotions and Weekend Bible Studies .. 1479
Author Acknowledgments 1483

ALPHABETICAL LIST OF BIBLE BOOKS

The books of the New Testament are in *italic*.

Acts 1213	*James* 1392	Nehemiah 517
Amos 1003	Jeremiah 835	Numbers 139
1 Chronicles 427	Job 544	Obadiah 1012
2 Chronicles 464	Joel 997	*1 Peter* 1399
Colossians 1341	*John* 1176	*2 Peter* 1406
1 Corinthians 1279	*1 John* 1411	*Philemon* 1375
2 Corinthians 1300	*2 John* 1418	*Philippians* 1333
Daniel 966	*3 John* 1420	Proverbs 691
Deuteronomy 184	Jonah 1015	Psalms 582
Ecclesiastes 733	Joshua 224	*Revelation* 1425
Ephesians 1323	*Jude* 1422	*Romans* 1256
Esther 535	Judges 254	Ruth 283
Exodus 61	1 Kings 358	1 Samuel 289
Ezekiel 913	2 Kings 393	2 Samuel 325
Ezra 504	Lamentations 905	Song of Songs 747
Galatians 1314	Leviticus 108	*1 Thessalonians* 1348
Genesis 1	*Luke* 1130	*2 Thessalonians* 1354
Habakkuk 1030	Malachi 1053	*1 Timothy* 1358
Haggai 1040	*Mark* 1103	*2 Timothy* 1365
Hebrews 1377	*Matthew* 1059	*Titus* 1372
Hosea 985	Micah 1018	Zechariah 1043
Isaiah 755	Nahum 1026	Zephaniah 1035

Jesus Christ gave his followers the Great Commission—to go and make disciples (Matthew 28:19). The Navigators is an international Christian organization whose aim is to help fulfill that commission by multiplying laborers for Jesus Christ in every nation.

The mission of the US Navigators is to reach, disciple and equip people to know Christ and to make him known through successive generations, a mission which involves three essential elements:

- engaging people in the Scriptures so that they discover Jesus Christ and learn to apply his truth in every aspect of their lives
- discipling people life on life so that they come to trust and obey Jesus Christ
- equipping disciples to reproduce the life of Jesus Christ in others

We envision multitudes of diverse people throughout the world sharing a passionate love for Jesus Christ, living a lifestyle of sharing his love and multiplying spiritual laborers among those who do not know him.

The US Collegiate Ministries strategy is to carry out this vision and mission on the college and university campuses of America. Our primary mission is to develop spiritual laborers from among the student population, equipping and mobilizing them for a lifetime of laboring in their sphere of influence and beyond.

If you would like further information about The Navigators and its ministries (e.g. high school, collegiate, military, community, church discipleship) in your area, please write to: The Navigators, PO Box 6000, Colorado Springs, CO 80934.

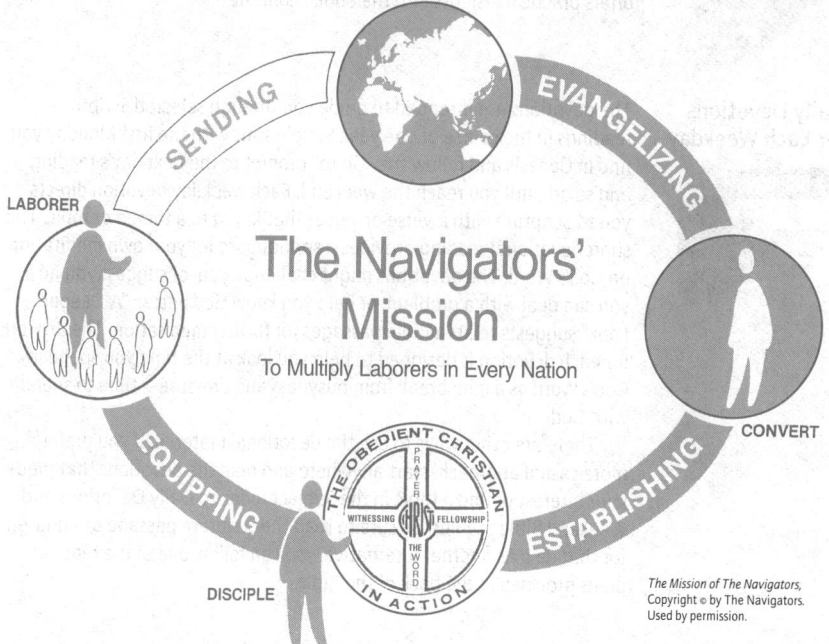

How to use the Collegiate Devotional Bible

You're at a crossroads in almost every aspect of your life. You're in the process of leaving behind the familiarity of your parents' home, and you wonder if you'll ever figure out how you're going to make sense of all the decisions and choices you have to make. You know you want to follow God's leading, but how are you going to find out what that is? You don't want an itinerary designed for anyone else. With God's guidance, you want to chart a course that is uniquely yours. And you want real answers and real direction. With that in mind, Navigator US Campus ministry staff and Zondervan Publishing House have teamed up to provide you with the *Collegiate Devotional Bible*, a map book for finding God's direction for your life. Finding your way through the *Collegiate Devotional Bible* is easy. Here are some features to help you:

Book Introductions

Each of the sixty-six books of the Bible begins with an introduction that highlights the theme of the book, provides background information and offers practical insights into the book's content.

Daily Devotions for Each Weekday

The devotions are arranged to guide you through selected Scripture readings in the course of one year. Simply start with the first Monday you find in Genesis and follow the "Go to" prompt to the next day's reading and so on until you reach the weekend. Each weekday devotion directs you to Scripture with a verse or verses that key in to a theme or topic. The short devotional reading provides a springboard for your own meditation on God's Word. The devotions might challenge you, or suggest you how you can deal with a problem, or help you know God better. "A Deeper Look" suggests related Bible passages for further meditation. The artwork for each devotion is designed to help you look at the time you spend in God's Word as a mini break from busyness and pressure—time to spend with God.

There are other ways to use the devotional material. If you prefer a more casual approach, start anywhere and read the devotions that pique your interest or find a topic in the Subject Index to Daily Devotions and Weekend Bible Studies. Be sure to read the Scripture passage designated for that day. As another alternative, you can follow one of the reading plans provided in the back of the Bible.

Mini Bible Studies for Each Weekend

Charting out your life's direction requires close attention to the "map" God has provided—his Word. Knowing how to study it is crucial. The *Collegiate Devotional Bible* can help. Friday's devotion will link you to a Weekend where you will find a change of pace in a mini Bible study. Each Weekend provides a passage to read, key verses and background information on a Biblical principle or theme. Each study also includes related passages that will help you discover firsthand what God has to say about the topic.

Point of Interest

As you explore the Bible, the "Points of Interest" are good places to stop and take special notice of a verse here and there. These short articles highlight archaeological facts, link you to other passages, or just challenge you to think through implications and applications.

Tools for Bible Study, Application and Evangelism

Check out the four-color pages placed throughout the Bible. Many of these are practical, time-tested Navigator tools for learning how to get to know God and his Word, how to really live out its truth and how to share the "Good News" with others.

The Word of God

Far more important than any of the tools we've provided, however, is the text itself, the Word of God. The Bible is a supernaturally powerful book. The life-giving truth it offers is startlingly simple, yet deeply layered. It takes only a moment to receive its grace but a lifetime to fathom its meaning. God's Word is always current and always dynamic, no matter how fast or how much the world changes. It is full of the energy of youth and the wisdom of the ages. Explore its many facets— the Word of God will continue to transform your heart and deepen your character while God unfolds the course of your life.

Preface to the niv

THE NEW INTERNATIONAL VERSION is a completely new translation of the Holy Bible made by over a hundred scholars working directly from the best available Hebrew, Aramaic and Greek texts. It had its beginning in 1965 when, after several years of exploratory study by committees from the Christian Reformed Church and the National Association of Evangelicals, a group of scholars met at Palos Heights, Illinois, and concurred in the need for a new translation of the Bible in contemporary English. This group, though not made up of official church representatives, was transdenominational. Its conclusion was endorsed by a large number of leaders from many denominations who met in Chicago in 1966.

Responsibility for the new version was delegated by the Palos Heights group to a self-governing body of fifteen, the Committee on Bible Translation, composed for the most part of biblical scholars from colleges, universities and seminaries. In 1967 the New York Bible Society (now the International Bible Society) generously undertook the financial sponsorship of the project—a sponsorship that made it possible to enlist the help of many distinguished scholars. The fact that participants from the United States, Great Britain, Canada, Australia and New Zealand worked together gave the project its international scope. That they were from many denominations—including Anglican, Assemblies of God, Baptist, Brethren, Christian Reformed, Church of Christ, Evangelical Free, Lutheran, Mennonite, Methodist, Nazarene, Presbyterian, Wesleyan and other churches—helped to safeguard the translation from sectarian bias.

How it was made helps to give the New International Version its distinctiveness. The translation of each book was assigned to a team of scholars. Next, one of the Intermediate Editorial Committees revised the initial translation, with constant reference to the Hebrew, Aramaic or Greek. Their work then went to one of the General Editorial Committees, which checked it in detail and made another thorough revision. This revision in turn was carefully reviewed by the Committee on Bible Translation, which made further changes and then released the final version for publication. In this way the entire Bible underwent three revisions, during each of which the translation was examined for its faithfulness to the original languages and for its English style.

All this involved many thousands of hours of research and discussion regarding the meaning of the texts and the precise way of putting them into English. It may well be that no other translation has been made by a more thorough process of review and revision from committee to committee than this one.

From the beginning of the project, the Committee on Bible Translation held to certain goals for the New International Version: that it would be an accurate translation and one that would have clarity and literary quality and so prove suitable for public and private reading, teaching, preaching, memorizing and liturgical use. The Committee also sought to preserve some measure of continuity with the long tradition of translating the Scriptures into English.

In working toward these goals, the translators were united in their commitment to the authority and infallibility of the Bible as God's Word in written form. They believe that it contains the divine answer to the deepest needs of humanity, that it sheds unique light on our path in a dark world, and that it sets forth the way to our eternal well-being.

The first concern of the translators has been the accuracy of the translation and its fidelity to the thought of the biblical writers. They have weighed the significance of the lexical and grammatical details of the Hebrew, Aramaic and Greek texts. At the same time, they have striven for more than a word-for-word translation. Because thought patterns and syntax differ from language to language, faithful communication of the meaning of the writers of the Bible demands frequent modifications in sentence structure and constant regard for the contextual meanings of words.

A sensitive feeling for style does not always accompany scholarship. Accordingly the Committee on Bible Translation submitted the developing version to a number of stylistic consultants. Two of them read every book of both Old and New Testaments twice—once before and once after the last major revision—and made invaluable suggestions. Samples of the translation were tested for clarity and ease of reading by various kinds of people—young and old, highly educated and less well educated, ministers and laymen.

Concern for clear and natural English—that the New International Version should be idiomatic but not idiosyncratic, contemporary but not dated—motivated the translators and consultants. At the same time, they tried to reflect the differing styles of the biblical writers. In view of the international use of English, the translators sought to avoid obvious Americanisms on the one hand and obvious Anglicisms on the other. A British edition reflects the comparatively few differences of significant idiom and of spelling.

As for the traditional pronouns "thou," "thee" and "thine" in reference to the Deity, the translators judged that to use these archaisms (along with the old verb forms such as "doest," "wouldest" and "hadst") would violate accuracy in translation. Neither Hebrew, Aramaic nor Greek uses special pronouns for the persons of the Godhead. A present-day translation is not enhanced by forms that in the time of the King James Version were used in everyday speech, whether referring to God or man.

For the Old Testament the standard Hebrew text, the Masoretic Text as published in the latest editions of *Biblia Hebraica,* was used throughout. The Dead Sea Scrolls contain material bearing on an earlier stage of the Hebrew text. They were consulted, as were the Samaritan Pentateuch and the ancient scribal traditions relating to textual changes. Sometimes a variant Hebrew reading in the margin of the Masoretic Text was followed instead of the text itself. Such instances, being variants within the Masoretic tradition, are not specified by footnotes. In rare cases, words in the consonantal text were divided differently from the way they appear in the Masoretic Text. Footnotes indicate this. The translators also consulted the more important early versions—the Septuagint; Aquila, Symmachus and Theodotion; the Vulgate; the Syriac Peshitta; the Targums; and for the Psalms the *Juxta Hebraica* of Jerome. Readings from these versions were occasionally followed where the Masoretic Text seemed doubtful and where accepted principles of textual criticism showed that one or more of these textual witnesses appeared to provide the correct reading. Such instances are footnoted. Sometimes vowel letters and vowel signs did not, in the judgment of the translators, represent the correct vowels for the original consonantal text. Accordingly some words were read with a different set of vowels. These instances are usually not indicated by footnotes.

The Greek text used in translating the New Testament was an eclectic one. No other piece of ancient literature has such an abundance of manuscript witnesses as does the New Testament. Where existing manuscripts differ, the translators made their choice of readings according to accepted principles of New Testament textual criticism. Footnotes call attention to places where there was uncertainty about what the original text was. The best current printed texts of the Greek New Testament were used.

There is a sense in which the work of translation is never wholly finished. This applies to all great literature and uniquely so to the Bible. In 1973 the New Testament in the New International Version was published. Since then, suggestions for corrections and revisions have been received from various sources. The Committee on Bible Translation carefully considered the suggestions and adopted a number of them. These were incorporated in the first printing of the entire Bible in 1978. Additional revisions were made by the Committee on Bible Translation in 1983 and appear in printings after that date.

As in other ancient documents, the precise meaning of the biblical texts is sometimes uncertain. This is more often the case with the Hebrew and Aramaic texts than with the Greek text. Although archaeological and linguistic discoveries in this century aid in understanding difficult passages, some uncertainties remain. The more significant of these have been called to the reader's attention in the footnotes.

In regard to the divine name *YHWH*, commonly referred to as the *Tetragrammaton,* the translators adopted the device used in most English versions of rendering that name as "Lord" in capital letters to distinguish it from *Adonai,* another Hebrew word rendered "Lord," for which small letters are used. Wherever the two names stand together in the Old Testament as a compound name of God, they are rendered "Sovereign Lord."

Because for most readers today the phrases "the Lord of hosts" and "God of hosts" have little meaning, this version renders them "the Lord Almighty" and "God Almighty." These renderings convey the sense of the Hebrew, namely, "he who is sovereign over all the 'hosts' (powers) in heaven and on earth, especially over the 'hosts' (armies) of Israel." For readers unacquainted with Hebrew this does not make clear the distinction between *Sabaoth* ("hosts" or "Almighty") and *Shaddai* (which can also be translated

"Almighty"), but the latter occurs infrequently and is always footnoted. When *Adonai* and *YHWH Sabaoth* occur together, they are rendered "the Lord, the Lᴏʀᴅ Almighty."

As for other proper nouns, the familiar spellings of the King James Version are generally retained. Names traditionally spelled with "ch," except where it is final, are usually spelled in this translation with "k" or "c," since the biblical languages do not have the sound that "ch" frequently indicates in English— for example, in *chant.* For well-known names such as Zechariah, however, the traditional spelling has been retained. Variation in the spelling of names in the original languages has usually not been indicated. Where a person or place has two or more different names in the Hebrew, Aramaic or Greek texts, the more familiar one has generally been used, with footnotes where needed.

To achieve clarity the translators sometimes supplied words not in the original texts but required by the context. If there was uncertainty about such material, it is enclosed in brackets. Also for the sake of clarity or style, nouns, including some proper nouns, are sometimes substituted for pronouns, and vice versa. And though the Hebrew writers often shifted back and forth between first, second and third personal pronouns without change of antecedent, this translation often makes them uniform, in accordance with English style and without the use of footnotes.

Poetical passages are printed as poetry, that is, with indentation of lines with separate stanzas. These are generally designed to reflect the structure of Hebrew poetry. This poetry is normally characterized by parallelism in balanced lines. Most of the poetry in the Bible is in the Old Testament, and scholars differ regarding the scansion of Hebrew lines. The translators determined the stanza divisions for the most part by analysis of the subject matter. The stanzas therefore serve as poetic paragraphs.

As an aid to the reader, italicized sectional headings are inserted in most of the books. They are not to be regarded as part of the NIV text, are not for oral reading, and are not intended to dictate the interpretation of the sections they head.

The footnotes in this version are of several kinds, most of which need no explanation. Those giving alternative translations begin with "Or" and generally introduce the alternative with the last word preceding it in the text, except when it is a single-word alternative; in poetry quoted in a footnote a slant mark indicates a line division. Footnotes introduced by "Or" do not have uniform significance. In some cases two possible translations were considered to have about equal validity. In other cases, though the translators were convinced that the translation in the text was correct, they judged that another interpretation was possible and of sufficient importance to be represented in a footnote.

In the New Testament, footnotes that refer to uncertainty regarding the original text are introduced by "Some manuscripts" or similar expressions. In the Old Testament, evidence for the reading chosen is given first and evidence for the alternative is added after a semicolon (for example: Septuagint; Hebrew *father*). In such notes the term "Hebrew" refers to the Masoretic Text.

It should be noted that minerals, flora and fauna, architectural details, articles of clothing and jewelry, musical instruments and other articles cannot always be identified with precision. Also measures of capacity in the biblical period are particularly uncertain (see the table of weights and measures following the text).

Like all translations of the Bible, made as they are by imperfect man, this one undoubtedly falls short of its goals. Yet we are grateful to God for the extent to which he has enabled us to realize these goals and for the strength he has given us and our colleagues to complete our task. We offer this version of the Bible to him in whose name and for whose glory it has been made. We pray that it will lead many into a better understanding of the Holy Scriptures and a fuller knowledge of Jesus Christ the incarnate Word, of whom the Scriptures so faithfully testify.

The Committee on Bible Translation

June 1978
(Revised August 1983)

Names of the translators and editors may be secured
from the International Bible Society,
translation sponsors of the New International Version,
1820 Jet Stream Drive, Colorado Springs, Colorado
80921-3696 U.S.A.

OLD TESTAMENT

The question of when and how the world began has intrigued us since, well, since the beginning. The book of Genesis is about many beginnings—the beginning of the universe, the beginning of humankind, the beginning of sin, and the beginning of God's promises and his plan for salvation. It's a book about why we began and where God wants to take us. It's about relationships—between God and his creation, between God and humankind and between one person and another. The book of Genesis recounts how God designed a covenant with his chosen people and how he pledged his love and faithfulness to them.

GENESIS

The Beginning

1 In the beginning God created the heavens and the earth. ²Now the earth was*ᵃ* formless and empty, darkness was over the surface of the deep, and the Spirit of God was hovering over the waters.

³And God said, "Let there be light," and there was light. ⁴God saw that the light was good, and he separated the light from the darkness. ⁵God called the light "day," and the darkness he called "night." And there was evening, and there was morning—the first day.

⁶And God said, "Let there be an expanse between the waters to separate water from water." ⁷So God made the expanse and separated the water under the expanse from the water above it. And it was so. ⁸God called the expanse "sky." And there was evening, and there was morning—the second day.

⁹And God said, "Let the water under the sky be gathered to one place, and let dry ground appear." And it was so. ¹⁰God called the dry ground "land," and the gathered waters he called

ᵃ2 Or possibly *became*

"seas." And God saw that it was good.

¹¹Then God said, "Let the land produce vegetation: seed-bearing plants and trees on the land that bear fruit with seed in it, according to their various kinds." And it was so. ¹²The land produced vegetation: plants bearing seed according to their kinds and trees bearing fruit with seed in it according to their kinds. And God saw that it was good. ¹³And there was evening, and there was morning—the third day.

¹⁴And God said, "Let there be lights in the expanse of the sky to separate the day from the night, and let them serve as signs to mark seasons and days and years, ¹⁵and let them be lights in the expanse of the sky to give light on the earth." And it was so. ¹⁶God made two great lights— the greater light to govern the day and the lesser light to govern the night. He also made the stars. ¹⁷God set them in the expanse of the sky to give light on the earth, ¹⁸to govern the day and the night, and to separate light from darkness. And God saw that it was good. ¹⁹And there was evening, and there was morning—the fourth day.

²⁰And God said, "Let the water teem with living creatures, and let birds fly above the earth across the expanse of the sky." ²¹So God created the great creatures of the sea and every living and moving thing with which the water teems, according to their kinds, and every winged bird according to its kind. And God saw that it was good. ²²God blessed them and said, "Be fruitful and increase in number and fill the water in the seas, and let the birds increase on the earth." ²³And there was evening, and there was morning—the fifth day.

²⁴And God said, "Let the land produce living creatures according to their kinds: livestock, creatures that move along the ground, and wild animals, each according to its kind." And it was so. ²⁵God made the wild animals according to their kinds, the livestock according to their kinds, and all the creatures that move along the ground according to their

kinds. And God saw that it was good.

²⁶Then God said, "Let us make man in our image, in our likeness, and let them rule over the fish of the sea and the birds of the air, over the livestock, over all the earth,ᵃ and over all the creatures that move along the ground."

²⁷So God created man in his own
    image,
in the image of God he created
    him;
male and female he created them.

²⁸God blessed them and said to them, "Be fruitful and increase in number; fill the earth and subdue it. Rule over the fish of the sea and the birds of the air and over every living creature that moves on the ground."

²⁹Then God said, "I give you every seed-bearing plant on the face of the whole earth and every tree that has fruit with seed in it. They will be yours for food. ³⁰And to all the beasts of the earth and all the birds of the air and all the creatures that move on the ground—everything that has the breath of life in it—I give every green plant for food." And it was so.

³¹God saw all that he had made, and it was very good. And there was evening, and there was morning— the sixth day.

2 Thus the heavens and the earth were completed in all their vast array.

²By the seventh day God had finished the work he had been doing; so on the seventh day he restedᵇ from all his work. ³And God blessed the seventh day and made it holy, because on it he rested from all the work of creating that he had done.

Adam and Eve

⁴This is the account of the heavens and the earth when they were created.

When the LORD God made the earth and the heavens— ⁵and no shrub of the field had yet appeared on the earthᶜ and

ᵃ26 Hebrew; Syriac *all the wild animals*   ᵇ2 Or *ceased*; also in verse 3   ᶜ5 Or *land*; also in verse 6 no plant of the field had yet sprung up, for the LORD God had not sent rain on the earth[a] and there was no man to work the ground, [6]but streams[b] came up from the earth and watered the whole surface of the ground— [7]the LORD God formed the man[c] from the dust of the ground and breathed into his nostrils the breath of life, and the man became a living being.

[8]Now the LORD God had planted a gar-

[a]5 Or land; also in verse 6   [b]6 Or mist
[c]7 The Hebrew for man (adam) sounds like and may be related to the Hebrew for ground (adamah); it is also the name Adam (see Gen. 2:20).

MONDAY

Read Genesis 1:1–31
Key Verses Genesis 1:27–28

Why Have Children? – Randy C. Johnson

Why would I want to bring children into the world? How can such a question be answered? Every day the news media remind us of just how troubled the world is. Television brings pictures of natural catastrophes, famines and war, environmental crises, and reports of social and economic problems. Newspapers and magazines publish articles about the increasing incidence of pregnancy, sexually transmitted diseases, drug use and suicide among our nation's children. So why would anyone want to bring kids into a mixed-up world like ours?

God commands us to "be fruitful and increase in number" (Genesis 1:28). No other act in all of our human experience identifies us more closely with the creative power of God than conceiving and bearing children. This same God who formed us in his image, "male and female," made it possible for us, through the miracle of procreation, to give life to another human being.

Children are gifts from God–his blessing to us (see Psalm 127:3). Children are a source of joy, hope and renewal for all of society. Even those who have no children benefit from the energy and fresh perspective of youth. Watch what happens the next time someone brings a newborn to church for the first time.

Raising caring and responsible children is an investment in God's kingdom. We pass on to them not only our possessions but also our dreams, values and beliefs. They are the ones who will carry on God's work in the world as the next leaders, educators and parents.

It would be wonderful to be able to provide our children with a trouble-free future. Who wouldn't like to guarantee their offspring a lifetime of health, happiness and prosperity? The truth is , we cannot promise them paradise here on earth. As long as they are in this world, they will face problems, temptations and heartaches—the same as everyone else. But we can instill within our children the Biblical promises that keep us going in troubled times. Our God is in control and "in keeping with his promise we are looking forward to a new heaven and a new earth, the home of righteousness" (2 Peter 3:13).

A Deeper Look
Proverbs 14:26; Zechariah 10:6–12; Luke 18:16

Go to page 6 for your next devotional reading.

den in the east, in Eden; and there he put the man he had formed. ⁹And the LORD God made all kinds of trees grow out of the ground—trees that were pleasing to the eye and good for food. In the middle of the garden were the tree of life and the tree of the knowledge of good and evil.

¹⁰A river watering the garden flowed from Eden; from there it was separated into four headwaters. ¹¹The name of the first is the Pishon; it winds through the entire land of Havilah, where there is gold. ¹²(The gold of that land is good; aromatic resin*a* and onyx are also there.) ¹³The name of the second river is the Gihon; it winds through the entire land of Cush.*b* ¹⁴The name of the third river is the Tigris; it runs along the east side of Asshur. And the fourth river is the Euphrates.

¹⁵The LORD God took the man and put him in the Garden of Eden to work it and take care of it. ¹⁶And the LORD God commanded the man, "You are free to eat from any tree in the garden; ¹⁷but you must not eat from the tree of the knowledge of good and evil, for when you eat of it you will surely die."

¹⁸The LORD God said, "It is not good for the man to be alone. I will make a helper suitable for him."

¹⁹Now the LORD God had formed out of the ground all the beasts of the field and all the birds of the air. He brought them to the man to see what he would name them; and whatever the man called each living creature, that was its name. ²⁰So the man gave names to all the livestock, the birds of the air and all the beasts of the field.

But for Adam*c* no suitable helper was found. ²¹So the LORD God caused the man to fall into a deep sleep; and while he was sleeping, he took one of the man's ribs*d* and closed up the place with flesh. ²²Then the LORD God made a woman from the rib*e* he had taken out of the man, and he brought her to the man.

²³The man said,

"This is now bone of my bones
    and flesh of my flesh;
she shall be called 'woman,*f*'
    for she was taken out of man."

²⁴For this reason a man will leave his father and mother and be united to his wife, and they will become one flesh.

²⁵The man and his wife were both naked, and they felt no shame.

The Fall of Man

3 Now the serpent was more crafty than any of the wild animals the LORD God had made. He said to the woman, "Did God really say, 'You must not eat from any tree in the garden'?"

²The woman said to the serpent, "We may eat fruit from the trees in the garden, ³but God did say, 'You must not eat fruit from the tree that is in the middle of the garden, and you must not touch it, or you will die.' "

⁴"You will not surely die," the serpent said to the woman. ⁵"For God knows that when you eat of it your eyes will be opened, and you will be like God, knowing good and evil."

⁶When the woman saw that the fruit of the tree was good for food and pleasing to the eye, and also desirable for gaining wisdom, she took some and ate it. She also gave some to her husband, who was with her, and he ate it. ⁷Then the eyes of both of them were opened, and they realized they were naked; so they sewed fig leaves together and made coverings for themselves.

⁸Then the man and his wife heard the sound of the LORD God as he was walking in the garden in the cool of the day, and they hid from the LORD God among the trees of the garden. ⁹But the LORD God called to the man, "Where are you?"

¹⁰He answered, "I heard you in the garden, and I was afraid because I was naked; so I hid."

¹¹And he said, "Who told you that you were naked? Have you eaten from the tree that I commanded you not to eat from?"

¹²The man said, "The woman you put here with me—she gave me some fruit from the tree, and I ate it."

¹³Then the LORD God said to the woman, "What is this you have done?"

The woman said, "The serpent deceived me, and I ate."

¹⁴So the LORD God said to the serpent, "Because you have done this,

"Cursed are you above all the
            livestock
    and all the wild animals!
You will crawl on your belly

---

*a*12 Or *good; pearls*   *b*13 Possibly southeast Mesopotamia   *c*20 Or *the man*   *d*21 Or *took part of the man's side*   *e*22 Or *part*   *f*23 The Hebrew for *woman* sounds like the Hebrew for *man.*

and you will eat dust
　　all the days of your life.
¹⁵And I will put enmity
　　between you and the woman,
　　and between your offspring^a and
　　　hers;
　he will crush^b your head,
　　and you will strike his heel."

¹⁶To the woman he said,

"I will greatly increase your pains in
　　childbearing;
　with pain you will give birth to
　　children.
Your desire will be for your husband,
　　and he will rule over you."

¹⁷To Adam he said, "Because you listened to your wife and ate from the tree about which I commanded you, 'You must not eat of it,'

"Cursed is the ground because of
　　you;
　through painful toil you will eat of
　　it
　all the days of your life.
¹⁸It will produce thorns and thistles for
　　you,
　and you will eat the plants of the
　　field.
¹⁹By the sweat of your brow
　　you will eat your food
　until you return to the ground,
　　since from it you were taken;
　for dust you are
　　and to dust you will return."

²⁰Adam^c named his wife Eve,^d because she would become the mother of all the living.
²¹The Lord God made garments of skin for Adam and his wife and clothed them. ²²And the Lord God said, "The man has now become like one of us, knowing good and evil. He must not be allowed to reach out his hand and take also from the tree of life and eat, and live forever." ²³So the Lord God banished him from the Garden of Eden to work the ground from which he had been taken. ²⁴After he drove the man out, he placed on the east side^e of the Garden of Eden cherubim and a flaming sword flashing back and forth to guard the way to the tree of life.

Cain and Abel

4 Adam^c lay with his wife Eve, and she became pregnant and gave birth to Cain.^f She said, "With the help of the Lord I have brought forth^g a man." ²Later she gave birth to his brother Abel.

Now Abel kept flocks, and Cain worked the soil. ³In the course of time Cain brought some of the fruits of the soil as an offering to the Lord. ⁴But Abel brought fat portions from some of the firstborn of his flock. The Lord looked with favor on Abel and his offering, ⁵but on Cain and his offering he did not look with favor. So Cain was very angry, and his face was downcast.

⁶Then the Lord said to Cain, "Why are you angry? Why is your face downcast? ⁷If you do what is right, will you not be accepted? But if you do not do what is right, sin is crouching at your door; it desires to have you, but you must master it."

⁸Now Cain said to his brother Abel, "Let's go out to the field."^h And while they were in the field, Cain attacked his brother Abel and killed him.

⁹Then the Lord said to Cain, "Where is your brother Abel?"

"I don't know," he replied. "Am I my brother's keeper?"

¹⁰The Lord said, "What have you done? Listen! Your brother's blood cries out to me from the ground. ¹¹Now you are under a curse and driven from the ground, which opened its mouth to receive your brother's blood from your hand. ¹²When you work the ground, it will no longer yield its crops for you. You will be a restless wanderer on the earth."

¹³Cain said to the Lord, "My punishment is more than I can bear. ¹⁴Today you are driving me from the land, and I will be hidden from your presence; I will be a restless wanderer on the earth, and whoever finds me will kill me."

¹⁵But the Lord said to him, "Not soⁱ; if anyone kills Cain, he will suffer vengeance seven times over." Then the Lord put a mark on Cain so that no one who found him would kill him. ¹⁶So Cain went out from the Lord's presence and lived in the land of Nod,^j east of Eden.

¹⁷Cain lay with his wife, and she be-

^a15 Or *seed*　　^b15 Or *strike*　　^c20,1 Or *The man*　　^d20 *Eve* probably means *living.*
^e24 Or *placed in front*　　^f1 *Cain* sounds like the Hebrew for *brought forth* or *acquired.*　　^g1 Or *have acquired*　　^h8 Samaritan Pentateuch, Septuagint, Vulgate and Syriac; Masoretic Text does not have "Let's go out to the field."
ⁱ15 Septuagint, Vulgate and Syriac; Hebrew *Very well*　　^j16 *Nod* means *wandering* (see verses 12 and 14).

came pregnant and gave birth to Enoch. Cain was then building a city, and he named it after his son Enoch. ¹⁸To Enoch was born Irad, and Irad was the father of Mehujael, and Mehujael was the father of Methushael, and Methushael was the father of Lamech.

¹⁹Lamech married two women, one named Adah and the other Zillah. ²⁰Adah gave birth to Jabal; he was the father of those who live in tents and raise livestock. ²¹His brother's name was Jubal; he was the father of all who play the harp and flute. ²²Zillah also had a son, Tubal-Cain, who forged all kinds of tools out of*ᵃ* bronze and iron. Tubal-Cain's sister was Naamah.

²³Lamech said to his wives,

"Adah and Zillah, listen to me;
    wives of Lamech, hear my words.
I have killed*ᵇ* a man for wounding
    me,

a young man for injuring me.
²⁴If Cain is avenged seven times,
    then Lamech seventy-seven times."

²⁵Adam lay with his wife again, and she gave birth to a son and named him Seth,*ᶜ* saying, "God has granted me another child in place of Abel, since Cain killed him." ²⁶Seth also had a son, and he named him Enosh.

At that time men began to call on*ᵈ* the name of the LORD.

From Adam to Noah

5 This is the written account of Adam's line.

When God created man, he made him in the likeness of God. ²He created them male and female and blessed them. And

ᵃ22 Or *who instructed all who work in*   *ᵇ23* Or *I will kill*   *ᶜ25* *Seth* probably means *granted.*   *ᵈ26* Or *to proclaim*

TUESDAY

Read *Genesis 3:1–24*
Key Verses *Genesis 3:22–23*

The Fall — Dennis Stokes

As my friend Ron was riding down the steep hill in front of me, his horse tripped, rolling headlong down the hill. When I saw the horse somersault on top of him, I called for help, but none was really needed. Ron recovered within a few minutes without lasting injury.

That wasn't the case when humankind fell. The lasting impact from that moment thousands of years ago still plagues you and me. Sin distorts our perspective and holds us in a prison whether or not we are conscious of it. Our relationships, decisions, goals, abilities—even our environment and our communities—are affected by the inevitable disintegration caused by sin's entrance into the world. According to Romans 5:12 sin entered the world through one person, but its result, death, came to all people, because all have sinned.

If that sounds a little bleak, take heart. Before Adam and Eve made that fatal decision to disobey, God already had plans to rescue us. Because of Jesus Christ's death and resurrection, we have been set free from sin's crippling effects: "How much more, then, will the blood of Christ, who through the eternal Spirit offered himself unblemished to God, cleanse our consciences from acts that lead to death, so that we may serve the living God!" (Hebrews 9:14).

A Deeper Look
Ecclesiastes 7:20; Romans 3:23–26

Go to page 9 for your next devotional reading.

when they were created, he called them "man.ᵃ"

³When Adam had lived 130 years, he had a son in his own likeness, in his own image; and he named him Seth. ⁴After Seth was born, Adam lived 800 years and had other sons and daughters. ⁵Altogether, Adam lived 930 years, and then he died.

⁶When Seth had lived 105 years, he became the fatherᵇ of Enosh. ⁷And after he became the father of Enosh, Seth lived 807 years and had other sons and daughters. ⁸Altogether, Seth lived 912 years, and then he died.

⁹When Enosh had lived 90 years, he became the father of Kenan. ¹⁰And after he became the father of Kenan, Enosh lived 815 years and had other sons and daughters. ¹¹Altogether, Enosh lived 905 years, and then he died.

¹²When Kenan had lived 70 years, he became the father of Mahalalel. ¹³And after he became the father of Mahalalel, Kenan lived 840 years and had other sons and daughters. ¹⁴Altogether, Kenan lived 910 years, and then he died.

¹⁵When Mahalalel had lived 65 years, he became the father of Jared. ¹⁶And after he became the father of Jared, Mahalalel lived 830 years and had other sons and daughters. ¹⁷Altogether, Mahalalel lived 895 years, and then he died.

¹⁸When Jared had lived 162 years, he became the father of Enoch. ¹⁹And after he became the father of Enoch, Jared lived 800 years and had other sons and daughters. ²⁰Altogether, Jared lived 962 years, and then he died.

²¹When Enoch had lived 65 years, he became the father of Methuselah. ²²And after he became the father of Methuselah, Enoch walked with God 300 years and had other sons and daughters. ²³Altogether, Enoch lived 365 years. ²⁴Enoch walked with God; then he was no more, because God took him away.

²⁵When Methuselah had lived 187 years, he became the father of Lamech. ²⁶And after he became the father of Lamech, Methuselah lived 782 years and had other sons and daughters. ²⁷Altogether, Methuselah lived 969 years, and then he died.

²⁸When Lamech had lived 182 years, he had a son. ²⁹He named him Noahᶜ and said, "He will comfort us in the labor and painful toil of our hands caused by the ground the LORD has cursed." ³⁰After Noah was born, Lamech lived 595 years and had other sons and daughters. ³¹Altogether, Lamech lived 777 years, and then he died.

³²After Noah was 500 years old, he became the father of Shem, Ham and Japheth.

The Flood

6 When men began to increase in number on the earth and daughters were born to them, ²the sons of God saw that the daughters of men were beautiful, and they married any of them they chose. ³Then the LORD said, "My Spirit will not contend withᵈ man forever, for he is mortalᵉ; his days will be a hundred and twenty years."

⁴The Nephilim were on the earth in those days—and also afterward—when the sons of God went to the daughters of men and had children by them. They were the heroes of old, men of renown.

⁵The LORD saw how great man's wickedness on the earth had become, and that every inclination of the thoughts of his heart was only evil all the time. ⁶The LORD was grieved that he had made man on the earth, and his heart was filled with pain. ⁷So the LORD said, "I will wipe mankind, whom I have created, from the face of the earth—men and animals, and creatures that move along the ground, and birds of the air—for I am grieved that I have

ᵃ2 Hebrew adam   ᵇ6 Father may mean ancestor; also in verses 7-26.   ᶜ29 Noah sounds like the Hebrew for comfort.   ᵈ3 Or My spirit will not remain in   ᵉ3 Or corrupt

POINT OF INTEREST   Genesis 5:27

Before the flood of Genesis 6, a life span was measured in centuries rather than decades. After the flood, life spans gradually decreased until by Moses' time they were about the same length as ours today. Could the flood have created climatic or environmental changes that shortened human life spans? Could sin's effects have influenced genetic potential? What do you think? (See Genesis 6:3 and Psalm 90:10.)

made them." **8**But Noah found favor in the eyes of the LORD.

9This is the account of Noah.

Noah was a righteous man, blameless among the people of his time, and he walked with God. **10**Noah had three sons: Shem, Ham and Japheth.

11Now the earth was corrupt in God's sight and was full of violence. **12**God saw how corrupt the earth had become, for all the people on earth had corrupted their ways. **13**So God said to Noah, "I am going to put an end to all people, for the earth is filled with violence because of them. I am surely going to destroy both them and the earth. **14**So make yourself an ark of cypress*a* wood; make rooms in it and coat it with pitch inside and out. **15**This is how you are to build it: The ark is to be 450 feet long, 75 feet wide and 45 feet high.*b* **16**Make a roof for it and finish*c* the ark to within 18 inches*d* of the top. Put a door in the side of the ark and make lower, middle and upper decks. **17**I am going to bring floodwaters on the earth to destroy all life under the heavens, every creature that has the breath of life in it. Everything on earth will perish. **18**But I will establish my covenant with you, and you will enter the ark—you and your sons and your wife and your sons' wives with you. **19**You are to bring into the ark two of all living creatures, male and female, to keep them alive with you. **20**Two of every kind of bird, of every kind of animal and of every kind of creature that moves along the ground will come to you to be kept alive. **21**You are to take every kind of food that is to be eaten and store it away as food for you and for them."

22Noah did everything just as God commanded him.

7 The LORD then said to Noah, "Go into the ark, you and your whole family, because I have found you righteous in this generation. **2**Take with you seven*e* of every kind of clean animal, a male and its mate, and two of every kind of unclean animal, a male and its mate, **3**and also seven of every kind of bird, male and female, to keep their various kinds alive throughout the earth. **4**Seven days from now I will send rain on the earth for forty days and forty nights, and I will wipe from the face of the earth every living creature I have made."

5And Noah did all that the LORD commanded him.

6Noah was six hundred years old when the floodwaters came on the earth. **7**And Noah and his sons and his wife and his sons' wives entered the ark to escape the waters of the flood. **8**Pairs of clean and unclean animals, of birds and of all creatures that move along the ground, **9**male and female, came to Noah and entered the ark, as God had commanded Noah. **10**And after the seven days the floodwaters came on the earth.

11In the six hundredth year of Noah's life, on the seventeenth day of the second month—on that day all the springs of the great deep burst forth, and the floodgates of the heavens were opened. **12**And rain fell on the earth forty days and forty nights.

13On that very day Noah and his sons, Shem, Ham and Japheth, together with his wife and the wives of his three sons, entered the ark. **14**They had with them every wild animal according to its kind, all livestock according to their kinds, every creature that moves along the ground according to its kind and every bird according to its kind, everything with wings. **15**Pairs of all creatures that have the breath of life in them came to Noah and entered the ark. **16**The animals going in were male and female of every living thing, as God had commanded Noah. Then the LORD shut him in.

17For forty days the flood kept coming on the earth, and as the waters increased they lifted the ark high above the earth. **18**The waters rose and increased greatly on the earth, and the ark floated on the surface of the water. **19**They rose greatly on the earth, and all the high mountains under the entire heavens were covered. **20**The waters rose and covered the mountains to a depth of more than twenty feet.*f, g* **21**Every living thing that moved on the earth perished—birds, livestock, wild animals, all the creatures that swarm over the earth, and all mankind. **22**Everything on dry land that had the breath of life in its nostrils died. **23**Every living thing on the face of the earth was wiped out; men and animals and the

---

a14 The meaning of the Hebrew for this word is uncertain. *b15* Hebrew *300 cubits long, 50 cubits wide and 30 cubits high* (about 140 meters long, 23 meters wide and 13.5 meters high) *c16* Or *Make an opening for light by finishing* *d16* Hebrew *a cubit* (about 0.5 meter) *e2* Or *seven pairs*; also in verse 3 *f20* Hebrew *fifteen cubits* (about 6.9 meters) *g20* Or *rose more than twenty feet, and the mountains were covered* creatures that move along the ground and the birds of the air were wiped from the earth. Only Noah was left, and those with him in the ark.

²⁴The waters flooded the earth for a hundred and fifty days.

8 But God remembered Noah and all the wild animals and the livestock that were with him in the ark, and he sent a wind over the earth, and the waters receded. ²Now the springs of the deep and the floodgates of the heavens had been closed, and the rain had stopped falling from the sky. ³The water receded steadily from the earth. At the end of the hundred and fifty days the water had gone down, ⁴and on the seventeenth day of the seventh month the ark came to rest on the

---

WEDNESDAY

Read Genesis 6:5—7:6
Key Verses Genesis 7:6

Instantly Is Too Slow – Dr. Tom Yeakley

We have ten-minute oil changes, five-minute microwave popcorn, three-minute ATM transactions, and one-minute news breaks. Fast food has to be ready when we place our order, or we begin to get impatient. Any line longer than two people is intolerable. Customer service representatives often hear, "I want it yesterday!" We feel so pressured to have it all and do it all that we don't want to wait for anything. Instantly is too slow!

Often we're impatient even when we pray. If the answer isn't on our doorstep within a day or two we give up or conclude that God hasn't heard us. Our faith is far less sturdy than that of the psalmist who declared, "Be still before the LORD and wait patiently for him" (Psalm 37:7).

Compare our "instant" mind-set with God's eternal perspective. Noah had to wait a long time before he saw God act. From the time Noah was given the promise concerning the flood, until the rain began to fall, perhaps as many as one hundred and twenty years had elapsed (compare Genesis 5:32; 6:3 and 7:6). From the time the rain started until his family left the ark, Noah waited another year inside the closed ark (compare Genesis 7:11 and 8:14). As Noah waited those many years for the first raindrops to fall, it's very likely he was subject to times of doubt. But he remained obedient to all God had told him (Genesis 7:5). God had promised, and Noah took him at his word. It was not a matter of *if*, but *when*.

Noah wasn't the only one who waited. Abraham waited twenty-five years for his promised son to be born. The people of Israel waited for centuries for the promised Messiah. And the church of Jesus Christ has been waiting two thousand years for his second coming.

What answers to prayer are you waiting for? Does God seem to take intolerably long to show you that he has heard? Don't give up. God will answer in his perfect timing. "You need to persevere so that when you have done the will of God, you will receive what he has promised" (Hebrews 10:36).

A Deeper Look
Psalm 38:15; Luke 18:1; Romans 8:25

Go to page 14 for your next devotional reading.

mountains of Ararat. ⁵The waters continued to recede until the tenth month, and on the first day of the tenth month the tops of the mountains became visible.

⁶After forty days Noah opened the window he had made in the ark ⁷and sent out a raven, and it kept flying back and forth until the water had dried up from the earth. ⁸Then he sent out a dove to see if the water had receded from the surface of the ground. ⁹But the dove could find no place to set its feet because there was water over all the surface of the earth; so it returned to Noah in the ark. He reached out his hand and took the dove and brought it back to himself in the ark. ¹⁰He waited seven more days and again sent out the dove from the ark. ¹¹When the dove returned to him in the evening, there in its beak was a freshly plucked olive leaf! Then Noah knew that the water had receded from the earth. ¹²He waited seven more days and sent the dove out again, but this time it did not return to him.

¹³By the first day of the first month of Noah's six hundred and first year, the water had dried up from the earth. Noah then removed the covering from the ark and saw that the surface of the ground was dry. ¹⁴By the twenty-seventh day of the second month the earth was completely dry.

¹⁵Then God said to Noah, ¹⁶"Come out of the ark, you and your wife and your sons and their wives. ¹⁷Bring out every kind of living creature that is with you—the birds, the animals, and all the creatures that move along the ground—so they can multiply on the earth and be fruitful and increase in number upon it."

¹⁸So Noah came out, together with his sons and his wife and his sons' wives. ¹⁹All the animals and all the creatures that move along the ground and all the birds—everything that moves on the earth—came out of the ark, one kind after another.

²⁰Then Noah built an altar to the LORD and, taking some of all the clean animals and clean birds, he sacrificed burnt offerings on it. ²¹The LORD smelled the pleasing aroma and said in his heart: "Never again will I curse the ground because of man, even though[a] every inclination of his heart is evil from childhood. And never again will I destroy all living creatures, as I have done.

²²"As long as the earth endures,
   seedtime and harvest,
   cold and heat,
   summer and winter,
   day and night
   will never cease."

God's Covenant With Noah

9 Then God blessed Noah and his sons, saying to them, "Be fruitful and increase in number and fill the earth. ²The fear and dread of you will fall upon all the beasts of the earth and all the birds of the air, upon every creature that moves along the ground, and upon all the fish of the sea; they are given into your hands. ³Everything that lives and moves will be food for you. Just as I gave you the green plants, I now give you everything.

⁴"But you must not eat meat that has its lifeblood still in it. ⁵And for your lifeblood I will surely demand an accounting. I will demand an accounting from every animal. And from each man, too, I will demand an accounting for the life of his fellow man.

⁶"Whoever sheds the blood of man,
   by man shall his blood be shed;
   for in the image of God
   has God made man.

⁷As for you, be fruitful and increase in number; multiply on the earth and increase upon it."

⁸Then God said to Noah and to his sons with him: ⁹"I now establish my covenant with you and with your descendants after you ¹⁰and with every living creature that was with you—the birds, the livestock and all the wild animals, all those that came out of the ark with you—every living creature on earth. ¹¹I establish my covenant with you: Never again

a21 Or man, for

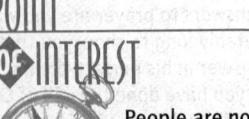

POINT OF INTEREST

Genesis 9:2

People are not among the most physically intimidating creatures in the world. We don't have fangs, claws or fur. We are neither particularly large nor very powerful. So why are animals innately afraid of human beings?

will all life be cut off by the waters of a flood; never again will there be a flood to destroy the earth."

¹²And God said, "This is the sign of the covenant I am making between me and you and every living creature with you, a covenant for all generations to come: ¹³I have set my rainbow in the clouds, and it will be the sign of the covenant between me and the earth. ¹⁴Whenever I bring clouds over the earth and the rainbow appears in the clouds, ¹⁵I will remember my covenant between me and you and all living creatures of every kind. Never again will the waters become a flood to destroy all life. ¹⁶Whenever the rainbow appears in the clouds, I will see it and remember the everlasting covenant between God and all living creatures of every kind on the earth."

¹⁷So God said to Noah, "This is the sign of the covenant I have established between me and all life on the earth."

The Sons of Noah

¹⁸The sons of Noah who came out of the ark were Shem, Ham and Japheth. (Ham was the father of Canaan.) ¹⁹These were the three sons of Noah, and from them came the people who were scattered over the earth.

²⁰Noah, a man of the soil, proceeded*a* to plant a vineyard. ²¹When he drank some of its wine, he became drunk and lay uncovered inside his tent. ²²Ham, the father of Canaan, saw his father's nakedness and told his two brothers outside. ²³But Shem and Japheth took a garment and laid it across their shoulders; then they walked in backward and covered their father's nakedness. Their faces were turned the other way so that they would not see their father's nakedness.

²⁴When Noah awoke from his wine and found out what his youngest son had done to him, ²⁵he said,

"Cursed be Canaan!
    The lowest of slaves
    will he be to his brothers."

²⁶He also said,

"Blessed be the LORD, the God of Shem!
    May Canaan be the slave of Shem.*b*

²⁷May God extend the territory of Japheth*c*;

may Japheth live in the tents of Shem,
    and may Canaan be his*d* slave."

²⁸After the flood Noah lived 350 years. ²⁹Altogether, Noah lived 950 years, and then he died.

The Table of Nations

10 This is the account of Shem, Ham and Japheth, Noah's sons, who themselves had sons after the flood.

The Japhethites

²The sons*e* of Japheth:
    Gomer, Magog, Madai, Javan, Tubal, Meshech and Tiras.
³The sons of Gomer:
    Ashkenaz, Riphath and Togarmah.
⁴The sons of Javan:
    Elishah, Tarshish, the Kittim and the Rodanim.*f* ⁵(From these the maritime peoples spread out into their territories by their clans within their nations, each with its own language.)

The Hamites

⁶The sons of Ham:
    Cush, Mizraim,*g* Put and Canaan.
⁷The sons of Cush:
    Seba, Havilah, Sabtah, Raamah and Sabteca.
  The sons of Raamah:
    Sheba and Dedan.

⁸Cush was the father*h* of Nimrod, who grew to be a mighty warrior on the earth. ⁹He was a mighty hunter before the LORD; that is why it is said, "Like Nimrod, a mighty hunter before the LORD." ¹⁰The first centers of his kingdom were Babylon, Erech, Akkad and Calneh, in*i* Shinar.*j* ¹¹From that land he went to Assyria, where he built Nineveh, Rehoboth Ir,*k* Calah ¹²and Resen, which is be-

---

a20 Or *soil, was the first*   *b26* Or *be his slave*
c27 Japheth sounds like the Hebrew for *extend.*
d27 Or *their*   *e2 Sons* may mean *descendants* or *successors* or *nations*; also in verses 3, 4, 6, 7, 20-23, 29 and 31.   *f4* Some manuscripts of the Masoretic Text and Samaritan Pentateuch (see also Septuagint and 1 Chron. 1:7); most manuscripts of the Masoretic Text *Dodanim*   *g6* That is, Egypt; also in verse 13   *h8 Father* may mean *ancestor* or *predecessor* or *founder*; also in verses 13, 15, 24 and 26.   *i10 Erech and Akkad—all of them in* *j10* That is, Babylonia   *k11* Or *Nineveh with its city squares*

tween Nineveh and Calah; that is the great city.

13Mizraim was the father of
the Ludites, Anamites, Leha-bites, Naphtuhites, 14Pathru-sites, Casluhites (from whom the Philistines came) and Caph-torites.

15Canaan was the father of
Sidon his firstborn,a and of the Hittites, 16Jebusites, Amorites, Girgashites, 17Hivites, Arkites, Sinites, 18Arvadites, Zemarites and Hamathites.

Later the Canaanite clans scattered 19and the borders of Canaan reached from Sidon toward Gerar as far as Gaza, and then toward Sodom, Gomorrah, Ad-mah and Zeboiim, as far as Lasha.

20These are the sons of Ham by their clans and languages, in their territories and nations.

The Semites

21Sons were also born to Shem, whose older brother wasb Japheth; Shem was the ancestor of all the sons of Eber.

22The sons of Shem:
Elam, Asshur, Arphaxad, Lud and Aram.

23The sons of Aram:
Uz, Hul, Gether and Meshech.c

24Arphaxad was the father ofd She-lah,
and Shelah the father of Eber.

25Two sons were born to Eber:
One was named Peleg,e be-cause in his time the earth was divided; his brother was named Joktan.

26Joktan was the father of
Almodad, Sheleph, Hazarma-veth, Jerah, 27Hadoram, Uzal, Diklah, 28Obal, Abimael, Sheba, 29Ophir, Havilah and Jobab. All these were sons of Joktan.

30The region where they lived stretched from Mesha toward Sephar, in the east-ern hill country.

31These are the sons of Shem by their clans and languages, in their territories and nations.

32These are the clans of Noah's sons, according to their lines of descent, within their nations. From these the nations spread out over the earth after the flood.

The Tower of Babel

11 Now the whole world had one lan-guage and a common speech. 2As men moved eastward,f they found a plain in Shinarg and settled there.

3They said to each other, "Come, let's make bricks and bake them thoroughly." They used brick instead of stone, and tar for mortar. 4Then they said, "Come, let us build ourselves a city, with a tower that reaches to the heavens, so that we may make a name for ourselves and not be scattered over the face of the whole earth."

5But the LORD came down to see the city and the tower that the men were building. 6The LORD said, "If as one peo-ple speaking the same language they have begun to do this, then nothing they plan to do will be impossible for them. 7Come, let us go down and confuse their language so they will not understand each other."

8So the LORD scattered them from there over all the earth, and they stopped building the city. 9That is why it was called Babelh—because there the LORD confused the language of the whole world. From there the LORD scattered them over the face of the whole earth.

From Shem to Abram

10This is the account of Shem.

Two years after the flood, when Shem was 100 years old, he became the fa-theri of Arphaxad. 11And after he be-came the father of Arphaxad, Shem lived 500 years and had other sons and daugh-ters.

12When Arphaxad had lived 35 years, he became the father of Shelah. 13And after he became the father of Shelah, Ar-phaxad lived 403 years and had other sons and daughters.j

a15 Or of the Sidonians, the foremost   b21 Or Shem, the older brother of   c23 See Septuagint and 1 Chron. 1:17; Hebrew Mash   d24 Hebrew; Septuagint father of Cainan, and Cainan was the father of   e25 Peleg means division.   f2 Or from the east; or in the east   g2 That is, Babylonia   h9 That is, Babylon; Babel sounds like the Hebrew for confused.   i10 Father may mean ancestor; also in verses 11-25.   j12,13 Hebrew; Septuagint (see also Luke 3:35, 36 and note at Gen. 10:24) 35 years, he became the father of Cainan. 13And after he became the father of Cainan, Arphaxad lived 430 years and had other sons and daughters, and then he died. When Cainan had lived 130 years, he became the father of Shelah. And after he became the father of Shelah, Cainan lived 330 years and had other sons and daughters

¹⁴When Shelah had lived 30 years, he became the father of Eber. ¹⁵And after he became the father of Eber, Shelah lived 403 years and had other sons and daughters.

¹⁶When Eber had lived 34 years, he became the father of Peleg. ¹⁷And after he became the father of Peleg, Eber lived 430 years and had other sons and daughters.

¹⁸When Peleg had lived 30 years, he became the father of Reu. ¹⁹And after he became the father of Reu, Peleg lived 209 years and had other sons and daughters.

²⁰When Reu had lived 32 years, he became the father of Serug. ²¹And after he became the father of Serug, Reu lived 207 years and had other sons and daughters.

²²When Serug had lived 30 years, he became the father of Nahor. ²³And after he became the father of Nahor, Serug lived 200 years and had other sons and daughters.

²⁴When Nahor had lived 29 years, he became the father of Terah. ²⁵And after he became the father of Terah, Nahor lived 119 years and had other sons and daughters.

²⁶After Terah had lived 70 years, he became the father of Abram, Nahor and Haran.

²⁷This is the account of Terah.

Terah became the father of Abram, Nahor and Haran. And Haran became the father of Lot. ²⁸While his father Terah was still alive, Haran died in Ur of the Chaldeans, in the land of his birth. ²⁹Abram and Nahor both married. The name of Abram's wife was Sarai, and the name of Nahor's wife was Milcah; she was the daughter of Haran, the father of both Milcah and Iscah. ³⁰Now Sarai was barren; she had no children.

³¹Terah took his son Abram, his grandson Lot son of Haran, and his daughter-in-law Sarai, the wife of his son Abram, and together they set out from Ur of the Chaldeans to go to Canaan. But when they came to Haran, they settled there.

³²Terah lived 205 years, and he died in Haran.

The Call of Abram

12 The LORD had said to Abram, "Leave your country, your people and your father's household and go to the land I will show you.

²"I will make you into a great nation
     and I will bless you;
I will make your name great,
     and you will be a blessing.
³I will bless those who bless you,
     and whoever curses you I will
          curse;
and all peoples on earth
     will be blessed through you."

⁴So Abram left, as the LORD had told him; and Lot went with him. Abram was seventy-five years old when he set out from Haran. ⁵He took his wife Sarai, his nephew Lot, all the possessions they had accumulated and the people they had acquired in Haran, and they set out for the land of Canaan, and they arrived there.

⁶Abram traveled through the land as far as the site of the great tree of Moreh at Shechem. At that time the Canaanites were in the land. ⁷The LORD appeared to Abram and said, "To your offspring[a] I will give this land." So he built an altar there to the LORD, who had appeared to him.

⁸From there he went on toward the hills east of Bethel and pitched his tent, with Bethel on the west and Ai on the east. There he built an altar to the LORD and called on the name of the LORD. ⁹Then Abram set out and continued toward the Negev.

Abram in Egypt

¹⁰Now there was a famine in the land, and Abram went down to Egypt to live there for a while because the famine was severe. ¹¹As he was about to enter Egypt, he said to his wife Sarai, "I know what a beautiful woman you are. ¹²When the Egyptians see you, they will say, 'This is his wife.' Then they will kill me but will let you live. ¹³Say you are my sister, so that I will be treated well for your sake and my life will be spared because of you."

¹⁴When Abram came to Egypt, the Egyptians saw that she was a very beautiful woman. ¹⁵And when Pharaoh's officials saw her, they praised her to Pharaoh, and she was taken into his palace. ¹⁶He treated Abram well for her sake, and Abram acquired sheep and cattle, male and female donkeys, menservants and maidservants, and camels.

¹⁷But the LORD inflicted serious diseases on Pharaoh and his household be-

a7 Or seed

cause of Abram's wife Sarai. [18]So Pharaoh summoned Abram. "What have you done to me?" he said. "Why didn't you tell me she was your wife? [19]Why did you say, 'She is my sister,' so that I took her to be my wife? Now then, here is your wife. Take her and go!" [20]Then Pharaoh gave orders about Abram to his men, and they sent him on his way, with his wife and everything he had.

Abram and Lot Separate

13 So Abram went up from Egypt to the Negev, with his wife and everything he had, and Lot went with him. [2]Abram had become very wealthy in livestock and in silver and gold.

[3]From the Negev he went from place to place until he came to Bethel, to the place between Bethel and Ai where his tent had been earlier [4]and where he had first built an altar. There Abram called on the name of the LORD.

[5]Now Lot, who was moving about with Abram, also had flocks and herds and tents. [6]But the land could not support them while they stayed together, for their possessions were so great that they were not able to stay together. [7]And quarreling arose between Abram's herdsmen and the herdsmen of Lot. The Canaanites and Perizzites were also living in the land at that time.

[8]So Abram said to Lot, "Let's not have any quarreling between you and me, or between your herdsmen and mine, for

---

THURSDAY

Read Genesis 12:1–20
Key Verses Genesis 12:1–3

Stay or Obey? – Sheri Platt

"Estonia . . . where is Estonia? You want me to move there for a whole year? This is crazy! Not me! No way!"

Estonia was definitely not a part of my plans. After my senior year in college, I could not imagine leaving everything I had ever known to go to a country I knew nothing about. I struggled—I wanted to be obedient, but I feared the unknown. I thought God would certainly understand that I was uncomfortable raising financial support, leaving my family and friends and going to a foreign land where I didn't even know the language. "Please God, not me! Ask someone else!"

But God wouldn't take no for an answer. He reassured me that he did care about my fears, family, friends and finances! He promised to meet my needs, but he still wanted me to go to Estonia.

John 14:21 tells us that as God's children we will obey him if we love him. So I went to Estonia, and I am so glad I did. God helped me raise the finances; he blessed the people who supported me. God blessed me through the lives I saw him change, including my own! He taught me about faith and dependence on him as I saw my needs being met one after another. It was difficult, but it was worth it.

Sometimes following God is like walking into a room with automatic lighting. The room is very dark until we step through the door and trigger the sensor to give us light. Come on in! If you don't you could be missing out on an incredible blessing! Trust him, obey him and experience God in a great, new way!

A Deeper Look
Exodus 4:10–11; Isaiah 6:8; John 15:16

Go to page 19 for your next devotional reading.

we are brothers. ⁹Is not the whole land before you? Let's part company. If you go to the left, I'll go to the right; if you go to the right, I'll go to the left."

¹⁰Lot looked up and saw that the whole plain of the Jordan was well watered, like the garden of the Lord, like the land of Egypt, toward Zoar. (This was before the Lord destroyed Sodom and Gomorrah.) ¹¹So Lot chose for himself the whole plain of the Jordan and set out toward the east. The two men parted company: ¹²Abram lived in the land of Canaan, while Lot lived among the cities of the plain and pitched his tents near Sodom. ¹³Now the men of Sodom were wicked and were sinning greatly against the Lord.

¹⁴The Lord said to Abram after Lot had parted from him, "Lift up your eyes from where you are and look north and south, east and west. ¹⁵All the land that you see I will give to you and your offspringᵃ forever. ¹⁶I will make your offspring like the dust of the earth, so that if anyone could count the dust, then your offspring could be counted. ¹⁷Go, walk through the length and breadth of the land, for I am giving it to you."

¹⁸So Abram moved his tents and went to live near the great trees of Mamre at Hebron, where he built an altar to the Lord.

Abram Rescues Lot

14 At this time Amraphel king of Shinar,ᵇ Arioch king of Ellasar, Kedorlaomer king of Elam and Tidal king of Goiim ²went to war against Bera king of Sodom, Birsha king of Gomorrah, Shinab king of Admah, Shemeber king of Zeboiim, and the king of Bela (that is, Zoar). ³All these latter kings joined forces in the Valley of Siddim (the Salt Seaᶜ). ⁴For twelve years they had been subject to Kedorlaomer, but in the thirteenth year they rebelled.

⁵In the fourteenth year, Kedorlaomer and the kings allied with him went out and defeated the Rephaites in Ashteroth Karnaim, the Zuzites in Ham, the Emites in Shaveh Kiriathaim ⁶and the Horites in the hill country of Seir, as far as El Paran near the desert. ⁷Then they turned back and went to En Mishpat (that is, Kadesh), and they conquered the whole territory of the Amalekites, as well as the Amorites who were living in Hazazon Tamar.

⁸Then the king of Sodom, the king of Gomorrah, the king of Admah, the king of Zeboiim and the king of Bela (that is, Zoar) marched out and drew up their battle lines in the Valley of Siddim ⁹against Kedorlaomer king of Elam, Tidal king of Goiim, Amraphel king of Shinar and Arioch king of Ellasar—four kings against five. ¹⁰Now the Valley of Siddim was full of tar pits, and when the kings of Sodom and Gomorrah fled, some of the men fell into them and the rest fled to the hills. ¹¹The four kings seized all the goods of Sodom and Gomorrah and all their food; then they went away. ¹²They also carried off Abram's nephew Lot and his possessions, since he was living in Sodom.

¹³One who had escaped came and reported this to Abram the Hebrew. Now Abram was living near the great trees of Mamre the Amorite, a brotherᵈ of Eshcol and Aner, all of whom were allied with Abram. ¹⁴When Abram heard that his relative had been taken captive, he called out the 318 trained men born in his household and went in pursuit as far as Dan. ¹⁵During the night Abram divided his men to attack them and he routed them, pursuing them as far as Hobah, north of Damascus. ¹⁶He recovered all the goods and brought back his relative Lot and his possessions, together with the women and the other people.

¹⁷After Abram returned from defeating Kedorlaomer and the kings allied with him, the king of Sodom came out to meet him in the Valley of Shaveh (that is, the King's Valley).

¹⁸Then Melchizedek king of Salemᵉ brought out bread and wine. He was priest of God Most High, ¹⁹and he blessed Abram, saying,

"Blessed be Abram by God Most
      High,
   Creatorᶠ of heaven and earth.
²⁰And blessed beᵍ God Most High,
   who delivered your enemies into
      your hand."

Then Abram gave him a tenth of everything.

²¹The king of Sodom said to Abram, "Give me the people and keep the goods for yourself."

²²But Abram said to the king of Sod-

ᵃ15 Or seed; also in verse 16   ᵇ1 That is, Babylonia; also in verse 9   ᶜ3 That is, the Dead Sea   ᵈ13 Or a relative; or an ally   ᵉ18 That is, Jerusalem   ᶠ19 Or Possessor; also in verse 22   ᵍ20 Or And praise be to om, "I have raised my hand to the LORD, God Most High, Creator of heaven and earth, and have taken an oath ²³that I will accept nothing belonging to you, not even a thread or the thong of a sandal, so that you will never be able to say, 'I made Abram rich.' ²⁴I will accept nothing but what my men have eaten and the share that belongs to the men who went with me—to Aner, Eshcol and Mamre. Let them have their share."

God's Covenant With Abram

15 After this, the word of the LORD came to Abram in a vision:

"Do not be afraid, Abram.
　I am your shield,ᵃ
　your very great reward.ᵇ"

²But Abram said, "O Sovereign LORD, what can you give me since I remain childless and the one who will inheritᶜ my estate is Eliezer of Damascus?" ³And Abram said, "You have given me no children; so a servant in my household will be my heir."

⁴Then the word of the LORD came to him: "This man will not be your heir, but a son coming from your own body will be your heir." ⁵He took him outside and said, "Look up at the heavens and count the stars—if indeed you can count them." Then he said to him, "So shall your offspring be."

⁶Abram believed the LORD, and he credited it to him as righteousness.

⁷He also said to him, "I am the LORD, who brought you out of Ur of the Chaldeans to give you this land to take possession of it."

⁸But Abram said, "O Sovereign LORD, how can I know that I will gain possession of it?"

⁹So the LORD said to him, "Bring me a heifer, a goat and a ram, each three years old, along with a dove and a young pigeon."

¹⁰Abram brought all these to him, cut them in two and arranged the halves opposite each other; the birds, however, he did not cut in half. ¹¹Then birds of prey came down on the carcasses, but Abram drove them away.

¹²As the sun was setting, Abram fell into a deep sleep, and a thick and dreadful darkness came over him. ¹³Then the LORD said to him, "Know for certain that your descendants will be strangers in a country not their own, and they will be enslaved and mistreated four hundred years. ¹⁴But I will punish the nation they serve as slaves, and afterward they will come out with great possessions. ¹⁵You, however, will go to your fathers in peace and be buried at a good old age. ¹⁶In the fourth generation your descendants will come back here, for the sin of the Amorites has not yet reached its full measure."

¹⁷When the sun had set and darkness had fallen, a smoking firepot with a blazing torch appeared and passed between the pieces. ¹⁸On that day the LORD made a covenant with Abram and said, "To your descendants I give this land, from the riverᵈ of Egypt to the great river, the Euphrates— ¹⁹the land of the Kenites, Kenizzites, Kadmonites, ²⁰Hittites, Perizzites, Rephaites, ²¹Amorites, Canaanites, Girgashites and Jebusites."

Hagar and Ishmael

16 Now Sarai, Abram's wife, had borne him no children. But she had an Egyptian maidservant named Hagar; ²so she said to Abram, "The LORD has kept me from having children. Go, sleep with my maidservant; perhaps I can build a family through her."

Abram agreed to what Sarai said. ³So after Abram had been living in Canaan ten years, Sarai his wife took her Egyptian maidservant Hagar and gave her to her husband to be his wife. ⁴He slept with Hagar, and she conceived.

When she knew she was pregnant, she began to despise her mistress. ⁵Then Sarai said to Abram, "You are responsible

---

ᵃ1 Or *sovereign*　　ᵇ1 Or *shield; / your reward will be very great*　　ᶜ2 The meaning of the Hebrew for this phrase is uncertain.　　ᵈ18 Or *Wadi*

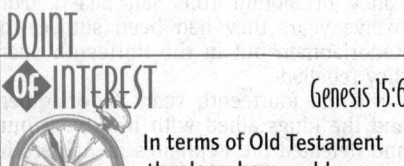

POINT OF INTEREST

Genesis 15:6

In terms of Old Testament theology, how could a person be credited as righteous? By believing God's promises. God made a promise and Abram believed him. Based on that step of faith alone, God declared Abram righteous. Having faith is so important to being righteous that God reminds us of it in Romans 4:3.

for the wrong I am suffering. I put my servant in your arms, and now that she knows she is pregnant, she despises me. May the Lord judge between you and me."

⁶"Your servant is in your hands," Abram said. "Do with her whatever you think best." Then Sarai mistreated Hagar; so she fled from her.

⁷The angel of the Lord found Hagar near a spring in the desert; it was the spring that is beside the road to Shur. ⁸And he said, "Hagar, servant of Sarai, where have you come from, and where are you going?"

"I'm running away from my mistress Sarai," she answered.

⁹Then the angel of the Lord told her, "Go back to your mistress and submit to her." ¹⁰The angel added, "I will so increase your descendants that they will be too numerous to count."

¹¹The angel of the Lord also said to her:

"You are now with child
  and you will have a son.
You shall name him Ishmael,ᵃ
  for the Lord has heard of your
    misery.
¹²He will be a wild donkey of a man;
  his hand will be against everyone
    and everyone's hand against him,
and he will live in hostility
  towardᵇ all his brothers."

¹³She gave this name to the Lord who spoke to her: "You are the God who sees me," for she said, "I have now seenᶜ the One who sees me." ¹⁴That is why the well was called Beer Lahai Roiᵈ; it is still there, between Kadesh and Bered.

¹⁵So Hagar bore Abram a son, and Abram gave the name Ishmael to the son she had borne. ¹⁶Abram was eighty-six years old when Hagar bore him Ishmael.

The Covenant of Circumcision

17 When Abram was ninety-nine years old, the Lord appeared to him and said, "I am God Almightyᵉ; walk before me and be blameless. ²I will confirm my covenant between me and you and will greatly increase your numbers."

³Abram fell facedown, and God said to him, ⁴"As for me, this is my covenant with you: You will be the father of many nations. ⁵No longer will you be called Abramᶠ; your name will be Abraham,ᵍ for I have made you a father of many nations. ⁶I will make you very fruitful; I

will make nations of you, and kings will come from you. ⁷I will establish my covenant as an everlasting covenant between me and you and your descendants after you for the generations to come, to be your God and the God of your descendants after you. ⁸The whole land of Canaan, where you are now an alien, I will give as an everlasting possession to you and your descendants after you; and I will be their God."

⁹Then God said to Abraham, "As for you, you must keep my covenant, you and your descendants after you for the generations to come. ¹⁰This is my covenant with you and your descendants after you, the covenant you are to keep: Every male among you shall be circumcised. ¹¹You are to undergo circumcision, and it will be the sign of the covenant between me and you. ¹²For the generations to come every male among you who is eight days old must be circumcised, including those born in your household or bought with money from a foreigner— those who are not your offspring. ¹³Whether born in your household or bought with your money, they must be circumcised. My covenant in your flesh is to be an everlasting covenant. ¹⁴Any uncircumcised male, who has not been circumcised in the flesh, will be cut off from his people; he has broken my covenant."

¹⁵God also said to Abraham, "As for Sarai your wife, you are no longer to call her Sarai; her name will be Sarah. ¹⁶I will bless her and will surely give you a son by her. I will bless her so that she will be the mother of nations; kings of peoples will come from her."

¹⁷Abraham fell facedown; he laughed and said to himself, "Will a son be born to a man a hundred years old? Will Sarah bear a child at the age of ninety?" ¹⁸And Abraham said to God, "If only Ishmael might live under your blessing!"

¹⁹Then God said, "Yes, but your wife Sarah will bear you a son, and you will call him Isaac.ʰ I will establish my covenant with him as an everlasting covenant for his descendants after him. ²⁰And as for Ishmael, I have heard you: I

ᵃ11 *Ishmael* means *God hears.*   ᵇ12 Or *live to the east / of*   ᶜ13 Or *seen the back of*   ᵈ14 *Beer Lahai Roi* means *well of the Living One who sees me.*   ᵉ1 Hebrew *El-Shaddai*   ᶠ5 *Abram* means *exalted father.*   ᵍ5 *Abraham* means *father of many.*   ʰ19 *Isaac* means *he laughs.*

will surely bless him; I will make him fruitful and will greatly increase his numbers. He will be the father of twelve rulers, and I will make him into a great nation. ²¹But my covenant I will establish with Isaac, whom Sarah will bear to you by this time next year." ²²When he had finished speaking with Abraham, God went up from him.

²³On that very day Abraham took his son Ishmael and all those born in his household or bought with his money, every male in his household, and circumcised them, as God told him. ²⁴Abraham was ninety-nine years old when he was circumcised, ²⁵and his son Ishmael was thirteen; ²⁶Abraham and his son Ishmael were both circumcised on that same day. ²⁷And every male in Abraham's household, including those born in his household or bought from a foreigner, was circumcised with him.

The Three Visitors

18 The LORD appeared to Abraham near the great trees of Mamre while he was sitting at the entrance to his tent in the heat of the day. ²Abraham looked up and saw three men standing nearby. When he saw them, he hurried from the entrance of his tent to meet them and bowed low to the ground.

³He said, "If I have found favor in your eyes, my lord,ᵃ do not pass your servant by. ⁴Let a little water be brought, and then you may all wash your feet and rest under this tree. ⁵Let me get you something to eat, so you can be refreshed and then go on your way—now that you have come to your servant."

"Very well," they answered, "do as you say."

⁶So Abraham hurried into the tent to Sarah. "Quick," he said, "get three seahsᵇ of fine flour and knead it and bake some bread."

⁷Then he ran to the herd and selected a choice, tender calf and gave it to a servant, who hurried to prepare it. ⁸He then brought some curds and milk and the calf that had been prepared, and set these before them. While they ate, he stood near them under a tree.

⁹"Where is your wife Sarah?" they asked him.

"There, in the tent," he said.

¹⁰Then the LORDᶜ said, "I will surely return to you about this time next year, and Sarah your wife will have a son."

Now Sarah was listening at the entrance to the tent, which was behind him. ¹¹Abraham and Sarah were already old and well advanced in years, and Sarah was past the age of childbearing. ¹²So Sarah laughed to herself as she thought, "After I am worn out and my masterᵈ is old, will I now have this pleasure?"

¹³Then the LORD said to Abraham, "Why did Sarah laugh and say, 'Will I really have a child, now that I am old?' ¹⁴Is anything too hard for the LORD? I will return to you at the appointed time next year and Sarah will have a son."

¹⁵Sarah was afraid, so she lied and said, "I did not laugh."

But he said, "Yes, you did laugh."

Abraham Pleads for Sodom

¹⁶When the men got up to leave, they looked down toward Sodom, and Abraham walked along with them to see them on their way. ¹⁷Then the LORD said, "Shall I hide from Abraham what I am about to do? ¹⁸Abraham will surely become a great and powerful nation, and all nations on earth will be blessed through him. ¹⁹For I have chosen him, so that he will direct his children and his household after him to keep the way of the LORD by doing what is right and just, so that the LORD will bring about for Abraham what he has promised him."

²⁰Then the LORD said, "The outcry against Sodom and Gomorrah is so great and their sin so grievous ²¹that I will go down and see if what they have done is as bad as the outcry that has reached me. If not, I will know."

²²The men turned away and went to-

ᵃ3 Or O Lord   ᵇ6 That is, probably about 20 quarts (about 22 liters)   ᶜ10 Hebrew *Then he*   ᵈ12 Or *husband*

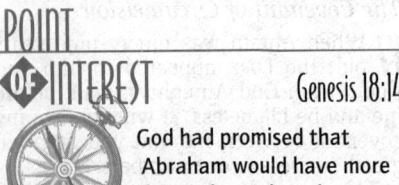

POINT OF INTEREST

Genesis 18:14

God had promised that Abraham would have more descendants than the stars in the sky (see Genesis 15:5), but both Sarah and Abraham found it difficult to take God literally. Here God renewed his promise by attaching a timetable.

ward Sodom, but Abraham remained standing before the LORD.*a* 23Then Abraham approached him and said: "Will you sweep away the righteous with the wicked? 24What if there are fifty righteous people in the city? Will you really sweep it away and not spare*b* the place for the sake of the fifty righteous people in it? 25Far be it from you to do such a thing— to kill the righteous with the wicked, treating the righteous and the wicked alike. Far be it from you! Will not the Judge*c* of all the earth do right?"

26The LORD said, "If I find fifty righteous people in the city of Sodom, I will spare the whole place for their sake."

27Then Abraham spoke up again: "Now that I have been so bold as to speak to the Lord, though I am nothing but dust and ashes, 28what if the number of the righteous is five less than fifty? Will you destroy the whole city because of five people?"

"If I find forty-five there," he said, "I will not destroy it."

29Once again he spoke to him, "What if only forty are found there?"

He said, "For the sake of forty, I will not do it."

30Then he said, "May the Lord not be angry, but let me speak. What if only thirty can be found there?"

a22 Masoretic Text; an ancient Hebrew scribal tradition *but the LORD remained standing before Abraham*   *b24* Or *forgive*; also in verse 26   *c25* Or *Ruler*

FRIDAY

Read *Genesis 18:1–33*
Key Verse *Genesis 18:25*

Why Did God Allow It? — Julie Bundt

I arrived at our Bible study a little late that night. Immediately I sensed the heaviness in the room. The agony in my friends' faces confirmed that something was very wrong. In that one night our idealistic view of the world was shattered. Our friend was dead; she had been stabbed to death in her apartment.

All the old doubts I had had about God suddenly resurfaced. I'd come to believe that God was good, just and sovereign, but how could a loving and powerful God allow some drug addict to brutally murder my friend? I cried for her, I cried for myself, and I cried because all my doubts and fears remained unanswered.

In spite of my doubts, to think that God was *not* good or sovereign was too frightening. I couldn't face contemplating that God was not in control of the world or that evil was as powerful as good. I started reading the Old Testament, and the truth about God's character confronted me at every turn—how he loved to keep forgiving and showing mercy to the Israelites when they showed even a spark of obedience! How carefully he worked out his plan to save them through Moses and many other leaders as well!

God didn't answer my specific questions about my friend's death. I still don't understand why she died. Maybe I won't understand in my lifetime why it happened or see how in my friend's death "God [worked] for the good of those who love him" (Romans 8:28). But I know I can trust him to do it. I believe by faith that he is sovereign and that his plans are good. I'll rest in that until I can ask him face to face!

A Deeper Look
Psalm 27:13; Isaiah 55:8–9

Go to page 24 for your next devotional reading.

He answered, "I will not do it if I find thirty there."

³¹Abraham said, "Now that I have been so bold as to speak to the Lord, what if only twenty can be found there?"

He said, "For the sake of twenty, I will not destroy it."

³²Then he said, "May the Lord not be angry, but let me speak just once more. What if only ten can be found there?"

He answered, "For the sake of ten, I will not destroy it."

³³When the LORD had finished speaking with Abraham, he left, and Abraham returned home.

Sodom and Gomorrah Destroyed

19 The two angels arrived at Sodom in the evening, and Lot was sitting in the gateway of the city. When he saw them, he got up to meet them and bowed down with his face to the ground. ²"My lords," he said, "please turn aside to your servant's house. You can wash your feet and spend the night and then go on your way early in the morning."

"No," they answered, "we will spend the night in the square."

³But he insisted so strongly that they did go with him and entered his house. He prepared a meal for them, baking bread without yeast, and they ate. ⁴Before they had gone to bed, all the men from every part of the city of Sodom—both young and old—surrounded the house. ⁵They called to Lot, "Where are the men who came to you tonight? Bring them out to us so that we can have sex with them."

⁶Lot went outside to meet them and shut the door behind him ⁷and said, "No, my friends. Don't do this wicked thing. ⁸Look, I have two daughters who have never slept with a man. Let me bring them out to you, and you can do what you like with them. But don't do anything to these men, for they have come under the protection of my roof."

⁹"Get out of our way," they replied. And they said, "This fellow came here as an alien, and now he wants to play the judge! We'll treat you worse than them." They kept bringing pressure on Lot and moved forward to break down the door.

¹⁰But the men inside reached out and pulled Lot back into the house and shut the door. ¹¹Then they struck the men who were at the door of the house, young and old, with blindness so that they could not find the door.

¹²The two men said to Lot, "Do you have anyone else here—sons-in-law, sons or daughters, or anyone else in the city who belongs to you? Get them out of here, ¹³because we are going to destroy this place. The outcry to the LORD against its people is so great that he has sent us to destroy it."

¹⁴So Lot went out and spoke to his sons-in-law, who were pledged to marryᵃ his daughters. He said, "Hurry and get out of this place, because the LORD is about to destroy the city!" But his sons-in-law thought he was joking.

¹⁵With the coming of dawn, the angels urged Lot, saying, "Hurry! Take your wife and your two daughters who are here, or you will be swept away when the city is punished."

¹⁶When he hesitated, the men grasped his hand and the hands of his wife and of his two daughters and led them safely out of the city, for the LORD was merciful to them. ¹⁷As soon as they had brought them out, one of them said, "Flee for your lives! Don't look back, and don't stop anywhere in the plain! Flee to the mountains or you will be swept away!"

¹⁸But Lot said to them, "No, my lords,ᵇ please! ¹⁹Yourᶜ servant has found favor in yourᶜ eyes, and youᶜ have shown great kindness to me in sparing my life. But I can't flee to the mountains; this disaster will overtake me, and I'll die. ²⁰Look, here is a town near enough to run to, and it is small. Let me flee to it—it is very small, isn't it? Then my life will be spared."

²¹He said to him, "Very well, I will grant this request too; I will not overthrow the town you speak of. ²²But flee there quickly, because I cannot do anything until you reach it." (That is why the town was called Zoar.ᵈ)

²³By the time Lot reached Zoar, the sun had risen over the land. ²⁴Then the LORD rained down burning sulfur on Sodom and Gomorrah—from the LORD out of the heavens. ²⁵Thus he overthrew those cities and the entire plain, including all those living in the cities—and also the vegetation in the land. ²⁶But Lot's wife

---

ᵃ14 Or were married to   ᵇ18 Or No, Lord; or No, my lord   ᶜ19 The Hebrew is singular.
ᵈ22 Zoar means small.

looked back, and she became a pillar of salt.

²⁷Early the next morning Abraham got up and returned to the place where he had stood before the LORD. ²⁸He looked down toward Sodom and Gomorrah, toward all the land of the plain, and he saw dense smoke rising from the land, like smoke from a furnace.

²⁹So when God destroyed the cities of the plain, he remembered Abraham, and he brought Lot out of the catastrophe that overthrew the cities where Lot had lived.

Lot and His Daughters

³⁰Lot and his two daughters left Zoar and settled in the mountains, for he was afraid to stay in Zoar. He and his two daughters lived in a cave. ³¹One day the older daughter said to the younger, "Our father is old, and there is no man around here to lie with us, as is the custom all over the earth. ³²Let's get our father to drink wine and then lie with him and preserve our family line through our father."

³³That night they got their father to drink wine, and the older daughter went in and lay with him. He was not aware of it when she lay down or when she got up.

³⁴The next day the older daughter said to the younger, "Last night I lay with my father. Let's get him to drink wine again tonight, and you go in and lie with him so we can preserve our family line through our father." ³⁵So they got their father to drink wine that night also, and the younger daughter went and lay with him. Again he was not aware of it when she lay down or when she got up.

³⁶So both of Lot's daughters became pregnant by their father. ³⁷The older daughter had a son, and she named him Moab[a]; he is the father of the Moabites of today. ³⁸The younger daughter also had a son, and she named him Ben-Ammi[b]; he is the father of the Ammonites of today.

Abraham and Abimelech

20 Now Abraham moved on from there into the region of the Negev and lived between Kadesh and Shur. For a while he stayed in Gerar, ²and there Abraham said of his wife Sarah, "She is my sister." Then Abimelech king of Gerar sent for Sarah and took her.

³But God came to Abimelech in a dream one night and said to him, "You are as good as dead because of the woman you have taken; she is a married woman."

⁴Now Abimelech had not gone near her, so he said, "Lord, will you destroy an innocent nation? ⁵Did he not say to me, 'She is my sister,' and didn't she also say, 'He is my brother'? I have done this with a clear conscience and clean hands."

⁶Then God said to him in the dream, "Yes, I know you did this with a clear conscience, and so I have kept you from sinning against me. That is why I did not let you touch her. ⁷Now return the man's wife, for he is a prophet, and he will pray for you and you will live. But if you do not return her, you may be sure that you and all yours will die."

⁸Early the next morning Abimelech summoned all his officials, and when he told them all that had happened, they were very much afraid. ⁹Then Abimelech called Abraham in and said, "What have you done to us? How have I wronged you that you have brought such great guilt upon me and my kingdom? You have done things to me that should not be done." ¹⁰And Abimelech asked Abraham, "What was your reason for doing this?"

¹¹Abraham replied, "I said to myself, 'There is surely no fear of God in this place, and they will kill me because of my wife.' ¹²Besides, she really is my sister, the daughter of my father though not of my mother; and she became my wife. ¹³And when God had me wander from my father's household, I said to her, 'This is how you can show your love to me: Everywhere we go, say of me, "He is my brother."'"

¹⁴Then Abimelech brought sheep and cattle and male and female slaves and gave them to Abraham, and he returned Sarah his wife to him. ¹⁵And Abimelech said, "My land is before you; live wherever you like."

¹⁶To Sarah he said, "I am giving your brother a thousand shekels[c] of silver. This is to cover the offense against you before all who are with you; you are completely vindicated."

¹⁷Then Abraham prayed to God, and God healed Abimelech, his wife and his slave girls so they could have children

---

[a]37 Moab sounds like the Hebrew for from father.
[b]38 Ben-Ammi means son of my people.
[c]16 That is, about 25 pounds (about 11.5 kilograms)

again, ¹⁸for the LORD had closed up every womb in Abimelech's household because of Abraham's wife Sarah.

The Birth of Isaac

21 Now the LORD was gracious to Sarah as he had said, and the LORD did for Sarah what he had promised. ²Sarah became pregnant and bore a son to Abraham in his old age, at the very time God had promised him. ³Abraham gave the name Isaac*a* to the son Sarah bore him. ⁴When his son Isaac was eight days old, Abraham circumcised him, as God commanded him. ⁵Abraham was a hundred years old when his son Isaac was born to him.

⁶Sarah said, "God has brought me laughter, and everyone who hears about this will laugh with me." ⁷And she added, "Who would have said to Abraham that Sarah would nurse children? Yet I have borne him a son in his old age."

Hagar and Ishmael Sent Away

⁸The child grew and was weaned, and on the day Isaac was weaned Abraham held a great feast. ⁹But Sarah saw that the son whom Hagar the Egyptian had borne to Abraham was mocking, ¹⁰and she said to Abraham, "Get rid of that slave woman and her son, for that slave woman's son will never share in the inheritance with my son Isaac."

¹¹The matter distressed Abraham greatly because it concerned his son. ¹²But God said to him, "Do not be so distressed about the boy and your maidservant. Listen to whatever Sarah tells you, because it is through Isaac that your offspring*b* will be reckoned. ¹³I will make the son of the maidservant into a nation also, because he is your offspring."

¹⁴Early the next morning Abraham took some food and a skin of water and gave them to Hagar. He set them on her shoulders and then sent her off with the boy. She went on her way and wandered in the desert of Beersheba.

¹⁵When the water in the skin was gone, she put the boy under one of the bushes. ¹⁶Then she went off and sat down nearby, about a bowshot away, for she thought, "I cannot watch the boy die." And as she sat there nearby, she*c* began to sob.

¹⁷God heard the boy crying, and the angel of God called to Hagar from heaven and said to her, "What is the matter, Hagar? Do not be afraid; God has heard the boy crying as he lies there. ¹⁸Lift the boy up and take him by the hand, for I will make him into a great nation."

¹⁹Then God opened her eyes and she saw a well of water. So she went and filled the skin with water and gave the boy a drink.

²⁰God was with the boy as he grew up. He lived in the desert and became an archer. ²¹While he was living in the Desert of Paran, his mother got a wife for him from Egypt.

The Treaty at Beersheba

²²At that time Abimelech and Phicol the commander of his forces said to Abraham, "God is with you in everything you do. ²³Now swear to me here before God that you will not deal falsely with me or my children or my descendants. Show to me and the country where you are living as an alien the same kindness I have shown to you."

²⁴Abraham said, "I swear it."

²⁵Then Abraham complained to Abimelech about a well of water that Abimelech's servants had seized. ²⁶But Abimelech said, "I don't know who has done this. You did not tell me, and I heard about it only today."

²⁷So Abraham brought sheep and cattle and gave them to Abimelech, and the two men made a treaty. ²⁸Abraham set apart seven ewe lambs from the flock, ²⁹and Abimelech asked Abraham, "What is the meaning of these seven ewe lambs you have set apart by themselves?"

³⁰He replied, "Accept these seven lambs from my hand as a witness that I dug this well."

³¹So that place was called Beersheba,*d* because the two men swore an oath there.

³²After the treaty had been made at Beersheba, Abimelech and Phicol the commander of his forces returned to the land of the Philistines. ³³Abraham planted a tamarisk tree in Beersheba, and there he called upon the name of the LORD, the Eternal God. ³⁴And Abraham stayed in the land of the Philistines for a long time.

Abraham Tested

22 Some time later God tested Abraham. He said to him, "Abraham!"

---

*a*3 Isaac means he laughs.   *b*12 Or seed
*c*16 Hebrew; Septuagint the child   *d*31 Beersheba can mean well of seven or well of the oath.

"Here I am," he replied.

²Then God said, "Take your son, your only son, Isaac, whom you love, and go to the region of Moriah. Sacrifice him there as a burnt offering on one of the mountains I will tell you about."

³Early the next morning Abraham got up and saddled his donkey. He took with him two of his servants and his son Isaac. When he had cut enough wood for the burnt offering, he set out for the place God had told him about. ⁴On the third day Abraham looked up and saw the place in the distance. ⁵He said to his servants, "Stay here with the donkey while I and the boy go over there. We will worship and then we will come back to you."

⁶Abraham took the wood for the burnt offering and placed it on his son Isaac, and he himself carried the fire and the knife. As the two of them went on together, ⁷Isaac spoke up and said to his father Abraham, "Father?"

"Yes, my son?" Abraham replied.

"The fire and wood are here," Isaac said, "but where is the lamb for the burnt offering?"

⁸Abraham answered, "God himself will provide the lamb for the burnt offering, my son." And the two of them went on together.

⁹When they reached the place God had told him about, Abraham built an altar there and arranged the wood on it. He bound his son Isaac and laid him on the altar, on top of the wood. ¹⁰Then he reached out his hand and took the knife to slay his son. ¹¹But the angel of the LORD called out to him from heaven, "Abraham! Abraham!"

"Here I am," he replied.

¹²"Do not lay a hand on the boy," he said. "Do not do anything to him. Now I know that you fear God, because you have not withheld from me your son, your only son."

¹³Abraham looked up and there in a thicket he saw a ram*a* caught by its horns. He went over and took the ram and sacrificed it as a burnt offering instead of his son. ¹⁴So Abraham called that place The LORD Will Provide. And to this day it is said, "On the mountain of the LORD it will be provided."

¹⁵The angel of the LORD called to Abraham from heaven a second time ¹⁶and said, "I swear by myself, declares the LORD, that because you have done this and have not withheld your son, your only son, ¹⁷I will surely bless you and make your descendants as numerous as the stars in the sky and as the sand on the seashore. Your descendants will take possession of the cities of their enemies, ¹⁸and through your offspring*b* all nations on earth will be blessed, because you have obeyed me."

¹⁹Then Abraham returned to his servants, and they set off together for Beersheba. And Abraham stayed in Beersheba.

Nahor's Sons

²⁰Some time later Abraham was told, "Milcah is also a mother; she has borne sons to your brother Nahor: ²¹Uz the firstborn, Buz his brother, Kemuel (the father of Aram), ²²Kesed, Hazo, Pildash, Jidlaph and Bethuel." ²³Bethuel became the father of Rebekah. Milcah bore these eight sons to Abraham's brother Nahor. ²⁴His concubine, whose name was Reumah, also had sons: Tebah, Gaham, Tahash and Maacah.

The Death of Sarah

23 Sarah lived to be a hundred and twenty-seven years old. ²She died at Kiriath Arba (that is, Hebron) in the land of Canaan, and Abraham went to mourn for Sarah and to weep over her.

³Then Abraham rose from beside his dead wife and spoke to the Hittites.*c* He said, ⁴"I am an alien and a stranger among you. Sell me some property for a burial site here so I can bury my dead."

⁵The Hittites replied to Abraham, ⁶"Sir, listen to us. You are a mighty prince among us. Bury your dead in the choicest of our tombs. None of us will refuse you his tomb for burying your dead."

⁷Then Abraham rose and bowed down before the people of the land, the Hittites. ⁸He said to them, "If you are willing to let me bury my dead, then listen to me and intercede with Ephron son of Zohar on my behalf ⁹so he will sell me the cave of Machpelah, which belongs to him and is at the end of his field. Ask him to sell it to me for the full price as a burial site among you."

¹⁰Ephron the Hittite was sitting among

---

*a13 Many manuscripts of the Masoretic Text, Samaritan Pentateuch, Septuagint and Syriac; most manuscripts of the Masoretic Text a ram behind him   *b18 Or seed   *c3 Or the sons of Heth; also in verses 5, 7, 10, 16, 18 and 20

Read Genesis 22:1–19
Key Verse Genesis 22:8

Trusting God

Entrusting God with our future can be terrifying. We don't know what he holds in store for us or what path he will lead us down. But consider this: A future *not* trusting God isn't a walk in the park either! Living by faith in God means trusting him for the unseen and the unknown. That kind of faith is a lifelong process—as we trust him for each small step along the way, we discover we can trust him for the giant leaps too.

God asked Abraham to do the unthinkable and to trust him for the unseen. Although it was perhaps the hardest challenge he'd ever encountered, Abraham passed the test because he trusted God rather than the things he could see with his eyes and understand with his finite mind. Abraham showed by example that "the righteous will live by faith," a truth we read four times in the Bible—(Habakkuk 2:4; Romans 1:17; Galatians 3:11; Hebrews 10:38).

Digging Into the Word
1. God's command to Abraham required an act of obedience (Genesis 22:1–2). Abraham responded by doing as God had asked (Genesis 22:3–11). How are faith and obedience linked together?—*Mark 1:14–20; Hebrews 11:8–10*
2. God's clear answer often comes at the last minute (Genesis 22:12). What do the following passages teach you about God's timing and your faith?—*Joshua 3:14–16; Daniel 10:1–14*

Personal Reflection
Is there some area in your life you need to submit to God by faith? Maybe it seems too hard—maybe it does not make sense to you—but you know that God is calling you to obedience. What do you need to change to walk by faith in this area of your life?

One Step Deeper
Romans 4:20–21; 2 Corinthians 1:8–11

Go to page 31 for your next devotional reading.

his people and he replied to Abraham in the hearing of all the Hittites who had come to the gate of his city. [11]"No, my lord," he said. "Listen to me; I give[a] you the field, and I give[a] you the cave that is in it. I give[a] it to you in the presence of my people. Bury your dead."

[12]Again Abraham bowed down before the people of the land [13]and he said to Ephron in their hearing, "Listen to me, if you will. I will pay the price of the field. Accept it from me so I can bury my dead there."

[14]Ephron answered Abraham, [15]"Listen to me, my lord; the land is worth four hundred shekels[b] of silver, but what is that between me and you? Bury your dead."

[16]Abraham agreed to Ephron's terms and weighed out for him the price he had named in the hearing of the Hittites: four hundred shekels of silver, according to the weight current among the merchants.

[17]So Ephron's field in Machpelah near Mamre—both the field and the cave in it, and all the trees within the borders of the field—was deeded [18]to Abraham as his property in the presence of all the Hittites who had come to the gate of the city. [19]Afterward Abraham buried his wife Sarah in the cave in the field of Machpelah near Mamre (which is at Hebron) in the land of Canaan. [20]So the field and the cave in it were deeded to Abraham by the Hittites as a burial site.

Isaac and Rebekah

24 Abraham was now old and well advanced in years, and the LORD had blessed him in every way. [2]He said to the chief[c] servant in his household, the one in charge of all that he had, "Put your hand under my thigh. [3]I want you to swear by the LORD, the God of heaven and the God of earth, that you will not get a wife for my son from the daughters of the Canaanites, among whom I am living, [4]but will go to my country and my own relatives and get a wife for my son Isaac."

[5]The servant asked him, "What if the woman is unwilling to come back with me to this land? Shall I then take your son back to the country you came from?"

[6]"Make sure that you do not take my son back there," Abraham said. [7]"The LORD, the God of heaven, who brought me out of my father's household and my native land and who spoke to me and promised me on oath, saying, 'To your off-spring[d] I will give this land'—he will send his angel before you so that you can get a wife for my son from there. [8]If the woman is unwilling to come back with you, then you will be released from this oath of mine. Only do not take my son back there." [9]So the servant put his hand under the thigh of his master Abraham and swore an oath to him concerning this matter.

[10]Then the servant took ten of his master's camels and left, taking with him all kinds of good things from his master. He set out for Aram Naharaim[e] and made his way to the town of Nahor. [11]He had the camels kneel down near the well outside the town; it was toward evening, the time the women go out to draw water.

[12]Then he prayed, "O LORD, God of my master Abraham, give me success today, and show kindness to my master Abraham. [13]See, I am standing beside this spring, and the daughters of the townspeople are coming out to draw water. [14]May it be that when I say to a girl, 'Please let down your jar that I may have a drink,' and she says, 'Drink, and I'll water your camels too'—let her be the one you have chosen for your servant Isaac. By this I will know that you have shown kindness to my master."

[15]Before he had finished praying, Rebekah came out with her jar on her shoulder. She was the daughter of Bethuel son of Milcah, who was the wife of Abraham's brother Nahor. [16]The girl was very beautiful, a virgin; no man had ever lain with her. She went down to the spring, filled her jar and came up again.

[17]The servant hurried to meet her and said, "Please give me a little water from your jar."

[18]"Drink, my lord," she said, and quickly lowered the jar to her hands and gave him a drink.

[19]After she had given him a drink, she said, "I'll draw water for your camels too, until they have finished drinking." [20]So she quickly emptied her jar into the trough, ran back to the well to draw more water, and drew enough for all his camels. [21]Without saying a word, the man watched her closely to learn whether or not the LORD had made his journey successful.

---

[a]11 Or sell   [b]15 That is, about 10 pounds (about 4.5 kilograms)   [c]2 Or oldest   [d]7 Or seed   [e]10 That is, Northwest Mesopotamia

²²When the camels had finished drinking, the man took out a gold nose ring weighing a beka*a* and two gold bracelets weighing ten shekels. *b* ²³Then he asked, "Whose daughter are you? Please tell me, is there room in your father's house for us to spend the night?"

²⁴She answered him, "I am the daughter of Bethuel, the son that Milcah bore to Nahor." ²⁵And she added, "We have plenty of straw and fodder, as well as room for you to spend the night."

²⁶Then the man bowed down and worshiped the LORD, ²⁷saying, "Praise be to the LORD, the God of my master Abraham, who has not abandoned his kindness and faithfulness to my master. As for me, the LORD has led me on the journey to the house of my master's relatives."

²⁸The girl ran and told her mother's household about these things. ²⁹Now Rebekah had a brother named Laban, and he hurried out to the man at the spring. ³⁰As soon as he had seen the nose ring, and the bracelets on his sister's arms, and had heard Rebekah tell what the man said to her, he went out to the man and found him standing by the camels near the spring. ³¹"Come, you who are blessed by the LORD," he said. "Why are you standing out here? I have prepared the house and a place for the camels."

³²So the man went to the house, and the camels were unloaded. Straw and fodder were brought for the camels, and water for him and his men to wash their feet. ³³Then food was set before him, but he said, "I will not eat until I have told you what I have to say."

"Then tell us," ⌊Laban⌋ said.

³⁴So he said, "I am Abraham's servant. ³⁵The LORD has blessed my master abundantly, and he has become wealthy. He has given him sheep and cattle, silver and gold, menservants and maidservants, and camels and donkeys. ³⁶My master's wife Sarah has borne him a son in her*c* old age, and he has given him everything he owns. ³⁷And my master made me swear an oath, and said, 'You must not get a wife for my son from the daughters of the Canaanites, in whose land I live, ³⁸but go to my father's family and to my own clan, and get a wife for my son.'

³⁹"Then I asked my master, 'What if the woman will not come back with me?'

⁴⁰"He replied, 'The LORD, before whom I have walked, will send his angel with you and make your journey a success, so that you can get a wife for my son from my own clan and from my father's family. ⁴¹Then, when you go to my clan, you will be released from my oath even if they refuse to give her to you—you will be released from my oath.'

⁴²"When I came to the spring today, I said, 'O LORD, God of my master Abraham, if you will, please grant success to the journey on which I have come. ⁴³See, I am standing beside this spring; if a maiden comes out to draw water and I say to her, "Please let me drink a little water from your jar," ⁴⁴and if she says to me, "Drink, and I'll draw water for your camels too," let her be the one the LORD has chosen for my master's son.'

⁴⁵"Before I finished praying in my heart, Rebekah came out, with her jar on her shoulder. She went down to the spring and drew water, and I said to her, 'Please give me a drink.'

⁴⁶"She quickly lowered her jar from her shoulder and said, 'Drink, and I'll water your camels too.' So I drank, and she watered the camels also.

⁴⁷"I asked her, 'Whose daughter are you?'

"She said, 'The daughter of Bethuel son of Nahor, whom Milcah bore to him.'

"Then I put the ring in her nose and the bracelets on her arms, ⁴⁸and I bowed down and worshiped the LORD. I praised the LORD, the God of my master Abraham, who had led me on the right road to get the granddaughter of my master's brother for his son. ⁴⁹Now if you will show kindness and faithfulness to my master, tell me; and if not, tell me, so I may know which way to turn."

⁵⁰Laban and Bethuel answered, "This is from the LORD; we can say nothing to you one way or the other. ⁵¹Here is Rebekah; take her and go, and let her become the wife of your master's son, as the LORD has directed."

⁵²When Abraham's servant heard what they said, he bowed down to the ground before the LORD. ⁵³Then the servant brought out gold and silver jewelry and articles of clothing and gave them to Rebekah; he also gave costly gifts to her brother and to her mother. ⁵⁴Then he and

---

a22 That is, about 1/5 ounce (about 5.5 grams)
b22 That is, about 4 ounces (about 110 grams)
c36 Or *his*

the men who were with him ate and drank and spent the night there.

When they got up the next morning, he said, "Send me on my way to my master."

⁵⁵But her brother and her mother replied, "Let the girl remain with us ten days or so; then you*a* may go."

⁵⁶But he said to them, "Do not detain me, now that the LORD has granted success to my journey. Send me on my way so I may go to my master."

⁵⁷Then they said, "Let's call the girl and ask her about it." ⁵⁸So they called Rebekah and asked her, "Will you go with this man?"

"I will go," she said.

⁵⁹So they sent their sister Rebekah on her way, along with her nurse and Abraham's servant and his men. ⁶⁰And they blessed Rebekah and said to her,

"Our sister, may you increase
  to thousands upon thousands;
may your offspring possess
  the gates of their enemies."

⁶¹Then Rebekah and her maids got ready and mounted their camels and went back with the man. So the servant took Rebekah and left.

⁶²Now Isaac had come from Beer Lahai Roi, for he was living in the Negev. ⁶³He went out to the field one evening to meditate,*b* and as he looked up, he saw camels approaching. ⁶⁴Rebekah also looked up and saw Isaac. She got down from her camel ⁶⁵and asked the servant, "Who is that man in the field coming to meet us?"

"He is my master," the servant answered. So she took her veil and covered herself.

⁶⁶Then the servant told Isaac all he had done. ⁶⁷Isaac brought her into the tent of his mother Sarah, and he married Rebekah. So she became his wife, and he loved her; and Isaac was comforted after his mother's death.

The Death of Abraham

25 Abraham took*c* another wife, whose name was Keturah. ²She bore him Zimran, Jokshan, Medan, Midian, Ishbak and Shuah. ³Jokshan was the father of Sheba and Dedan; the descendants of Dedan were the Asshurites, the Letushites and the Leummites. ⁴The sons of Midian were Ephah, Epher, Hanoch, Abida and

Eldaah. All these were descendants of Keturah.

⁵Abraham left everything he owned to Isaac. ⁶But while he was still living, he gave gifts to the sons of his concubines and sent them away from his son Isaac to the land of the east.

⁷Altogether, Abraham lived a hundred and seventy-five years. ⁸Then Abraham breathed his last and died at a good old age, an old man and full of years; and he was gathered to his people. ⁹His sons Isaac and Ishmael buried him in the cave of Machpelah near Mamre, in the field of Ephron son of Zohar the Hittite, ¹⁰the field Abraham had bought from the Hittites.*d* There Abraham was buried with his wife Sarah. ¹¹After Abraham's death, God blessed his son Isaac, who then lived near Beer Lahai Roi.

Ishmael's Sons

¹²This is the account of Abraham's son Ishmael, whom Sarah's maidservant, Hagar the Egyptian, bore to Abraham.

¹³These are the names of the sons of Ishmael, listed in the order of their birth: Nebaioth the firstborn of Ishmael, Kedar, Adbeel, Mibsam, ¹⁴Mishma, Dumah, Massa, ¹⁵Hadad, Tema, Jetur, Naphish and Kedemah. ¹⁶These were the sons of Ishmael, and these are the names of the twelve tribal rulers according to their settlements and camps. ¹⁷Altogether, Ishmael lived a hundred and thirty-seven years. He breathed his last and died, and he was gathered to his people. ¹⁸His descendants settled in the area from Havilah to Shur, near the border of Egypt, as you go toward Asshur. And they lived in hostility toward*e* all their brothers.

Jacob and Esau

¹⁹This is the account of Abraham's son Isaac.

Abraham became the father of Isaac, ²⁰and Isaac was forty years old when he married Rebekah daughter of Bethuel the Aramean from Paddan Aram*f* and sister of Laban the Aramean.

²¹Isaac prayed to the LORD on behalf of his wife, because she was barren. The LORD answered his prayer, and his wife Rebekah became pregnant. ²²The babies

---

*a*55 Or *she*   *b*63 The meaning of the Hebrew for this word is uncertain.   *c*1 Or *had taken*
*d*10 Or *the sons of Heth*   *e*18 Or *lived to the east of*   *f*20 That is, Northwest Mesopotamia

jostled each other within her, and she said, "Why is this happening to me?" So she went to inquire of the LORD.

²³The LORD said to her,

"Two nations are in your womb,
    and two peoples from within you
        will be separated;
one people will be stronger than the
        other,
    and the older will serve the
        younger."

²⁴When the time came for her to give birth, there were twin boys in her womb. ²⁵The first to come out was red, and his whole body was like a hairy garment; so they named him Esau.ᵃ ²⁶After this, his brother came out, with his hand grasping Esau's heel; so he was named Jacob.ᵇ Isaac was sixty years old when Rebekah gave birth to them.

²⁷The boys grew up, and Esau became a skillful hunter, a man of the open country, while Jacob was a quiet man, staying among the tents. ²⁸Isaac, who had a taste for wild game, loved Esau, but Rebekah loved Jacob.

²⁹Once when Jacob was cooking some stew, Esau came in from the open country, famished. ³⁰He said to Jacob, "Quick, let me have some of that red stew! I'm famished!" (That is why he was also called Edom.ᶜ)

³¹Jacob replied, "First sell me your birthright."

³²"Look, I am about to die," Esau said. "What good is the birthright to me?"

³³But Jacob said, "Swear to me first." So he swore an oath to him, selling his birthright to Jacob.

³⁴Then Jacob gave Esau some bread and some lentil stew. He ate and drank, and then got up and left.

So Esau despised his birthright.

Isaac and Abimelech

26 Now there was a famine in the land—besides the earlier famine of Abraham's time—and Isaac went to Abimelech king of the Philistines in Gerar. ²The LORD appeared to Isaac and said, "Do not go down to Egypt; live in the land where I tell you to live. ³Stay in this land for a while, and I will be with you and will bless you. For to you and your descendants I will give all these lands and will confirm the oath I swore to your father Abraham. ⁴I will make your descendants as numerous as the stars in

the sky and will give them all these lands, and through your offspringᵈ all nations on earth will be blessed, ⁵because Abraham obeyed me and kept my requirements, my commands, my decrees and my laws." ⁶So Isaac stayed in Gerar.

⁷When the men of that place asked him about his wife, he said, "She is my sister," because he was afraid to say, "She is my wife." He thought, "The men of this place might kill me on account of Rebekah, because she is beautiful."

⁸When Isaac had been there a long time, Abimelech king of the Philistines looked down from a window and saw Isaac caressing his wife Rebekah. ⁹So Abimelech summoned Isaac and said, "She is really your wife! Why did you say, 'She is my sister'?"

Isaac answered him, "Because I thought I might lose my life on account of her."

¹⁰Then Abimelech said, "What is this you have done to us? One of the men might well have slept with your wife, and you would have brought guilt upon us."

¹¹So Abimelech gave orders to all the people: "Anyone who molests this man or his wife shall surely be put to death."

¹²Isaac planted crops in that land and the same year reaped a hundredfold, because the LORD blessed him. ¹³The man became rich, and his wealth continued to grow until he became very wealthy. ¹⁴He had so many flocks and herds and servants that the Philistines envied him. ¹⁵So all the wells that his father's servants had dug in the time of his father Abraham, the Philistines stopped up, filling them with earth.

¹⁶Then Abimelech said to Isaac, "Move away from us; you have become too powerful for us."

¹⁷So Isaac moved away from there and encamped in the Valley of Gerar and settled there. ¹⁸Isaac reopened the wells that had been dug in the time of his father Abraham, which the Philistines had stopped up after Abraham died, and he gave them the same names his father had given them.

¹⁹Isaac's servants dug in the valley and discovered a well of fresh water there. ²⁰But the herdsmen of Gerar quarreled with Isaac's herdsmen and said, "The

---

ᵃ25 *Esau* may mean *hairy*; he was also called Edom, which means *red*.   ᵇ26 *Jacob* means *he grasps the heel* (figuratively, *he deceives*).   ᶜ30 *Edom* means *red*.   ᵈ4 Or *seed* water is ours!" So he named the well Esek,*a* because they disputed with him. 21Then they dug another well, but they quarreled over that one also; so he named it Sitnah.*b* 22He moved on from there and dug another well, and no one quarreled over it. He named it Rehoboth,*c* saying, "Now the LORD has given us room and we will flourish in the land."

23From there he went up to Beersheba. 24That night the LORD appeared to him and said, "I am the God of your father Abraham. Do not be afraid, for I am with you; I will bless you and will increase the number of your descendants for the sake of my servant Abraham."

25Isaac built an altar there and called on the name of the LORD. There he pitched his tent, and there his servants dug a well.

26Meanwhile, Abimelech had come to him from Gerar, with Ahuzzath his personal adviser and Phicol the commander of his forces. 27Isaac asked them, "Why have you come to me, since you were hostile to me and sent me away?"

28They answered, "We saw clearly that the LORD was with you; so we said, 'There ought to be a sworn agreement between us'—between us and you. Let us make a treaty with you 29that you will do us no harm, just as we did not molest you but always treated you well and sent you away in peace. And now you are blessed by the LORD."

30Isaac then made a feast for them, and they ate and drank. 31Early the next morning the men swore an oath to each other. Then Isaac sent them on their way, and they left him in peace.

32That day Isaac's servants came and told him about the well they had dug. They said, "We've found water!" 33He called it Shibah,*d* and to this day the name of the town has been Beersheba.*e*

34When Esau was forty years old, he married Judith daughter of Beeri the Hittite, and also Basemath daughter of Elon the Hittite. 35They were a source of grief to Isaac and Rebekah.

Jacob Gets Isaac's Blessing

27 When Isaac was old and his eyes were so weak that he could no longer see, he called for Esau his older son and said to him, "My son."

"Here I am," he answered.

2Isaac said, "I am now an old man and don't know the day of my death. 3Now then, get your weapons—your quiver and bow—and go out to the open country to hunt some wild game for me. 4Prepare me the kind of tasty food I like and bring it to me to eat, so that I may give you my blessing before I die."

5Now Rebekah was listening as Isaac spoke to his son Esau. When Esau left for the open country to hunt game and bring it back, 6Rebekah said to her son Jacob, "Look, I overheard your father say to your brother Esau, 7'Bring me some game and prepare me some tasty food to eat, so that I may give you my blessing in the presence of the LORD before I die.' 8Now, my son, listen carefully and do what I tell you: 9Go out to the flock and bring me two choice young goats, so I can prepare some tasty food for your father, just the way he likes it. 10Then take it to your father to eat, so that he may give you his blessing before he dies."

11Jacob said to Rebekah his mother, "But my brother Esau is a hairy man, and I'm a man with smooth skin. 12What if my father touches me? I would appear to be tricking him and would bring down a curse on myself rather than a blessing."

13His mother said to him, "My son, let the curse fall on me. Just do what I say; go and get them for me."

14So he went and got them and brought them to his mother, and she prepared some tasty food, just the way his father liked it. 15Then Rebekah took the best clothes of Esau her older son, which she had in the house, and put them on her younger son Jacob. 16She also covered his hands and the smooth part of his neck with the goatskins. 17Then she handed to her son Jacob the tasty food and the bread she had made.

18He went to his father and said, "My father."

"Yes, my son," he answered. "Who is it?"

19Jacob said to his father, "I am Esau your firstborn. I have done as you told me. Please sit up and eat some of my game so that you may give me your blessing."

20Isaac asked his son, "How did you find it so quickly, my son?"

---

a20 Esek means *dispute.*   *b21 Sitnah* means *opposition.*   *c22 Rehoboth* means *room.*
d33 Shibah can mean *oath* or *seven.*
e33 Beersheba can mean *well of the oath* or *well of seven.*

"The LORD your God gave me success," he replied.

²¹Then Isaac said to Jacob, "Come near so I can touch you, my son, to know whether you really are my son Esau or not."

²²Jacob went close to his father Isaac, who touched him and said, "The voice is the voice of Jacob, but the hands are the hands of Esau." ²³He did not recognize him, for his hands were hairy like those of his brother Esau; so he blessed him. ²⁴"Are you really my son Esau?" he asked.

"I am," he replied.

²⁵Then he said, "My son, bring me some of your game to eat, so that I may give you my blessing."

Jacob brought it to him and he ate; and he brought some wine and he drank. ²⁶Then his father Isaac said to him, "Come here, my son, and kiss me."

²⁷So he went to him and kissed him. When Isaac caught the smell of his clothes, he blessed him and said,

"Ah, the smell of my son
     is like the smell of a field
     that the LORD has blessed.
²⁸May God give you of heaven's dew
     and of earth's richness—
     an abundance of grain and new
          wine.
²⁹May nations serve you
     and peoples bow down to you.
Be lord over your brothers,
     and may the sons of your mother
          bow down to you.
May those who curse you be cursed
     and those who bless you be
          blessed."

³⁰After Isaac finished blessing him and Jacob had scarcely left his father's presence, his brother Esau came in from hunting. ³¹He too prepared some tasty food and brought it to his father. Then he said to him, "My father, sit up and eat some of my game, so that you may give me your blessing."

³²His father Isaac asked him, "Who are you?"

"I am your son," he answered, "your firstborn, Esau."

³³Isaac trembled violently and said, "Who was it, then, that hunted game and brought it to me? I ate it just before you came and I blessed him—and indeed he will be blessed!"

³⁴When Esau heard his father's words, he burst out with a loud and bitter cry and said to his father, "Bless me—me too, my father!"

³⁵But he said, "Your brother came deceitfully and took your blessing."

³⁶Esau said, "Isn't he rightly named Jacob*a*? He has deceived me these two times: He took my birthright, and now he's taken my blessing!" Then he asked, "Haven't you reserved any blessing for me?"

³⁷Isaac answered Esau, "I have made him lord over you and have made all his relatives his servants, and I have sustained him with grain and new wine. So what can I possibly do for you, my son?"

³⁸Esau said to his father, "Do you have only one blessing, my father? Bless me too, my father!" Then Esau wept aloud.

³⁹His father Isaac answered him,

"Your dwelling will be
     away from the earth's richness,
     away from the dew of heaven
          above.
⁴⁰You will live by the sword
     and you will serve your brother.
But when you grow restless,
     you will throw his yoke
     from off your neck."

Jacob Flees to Laban

⁴¹Esau held a grudge against Jacob because of the blessing his father had given him. He said to himself, "The days of mourning for my father are near; then I will kill my brother Jacob."

⁴²When Rebekah was told what her older son Esau had said, she sent for her younger son Jacob and said to him, "Your brother Esau is consoling himself with the thought of killing you. ⁴³Now then, my son, do what I say: Flee at once to my brother Laban in Haran. ⁴⁴Stay with him for a while until your brother's fury subsides. ⁴⁵When your brother is no longer angry with you and forgets what you did to him, I'll send word for you to come back from there. Why should I lose both of you in one day?"

⁴⁶Then Rebekah said to Isaac, "I'm disgusted with living because of these Hittite women. If Jacob takes a wife from among the women of this land, from Hittite women like these, my life will not be worth living."

a36 *Jacob* means *he grasps the heel* (figuratively, *he deceives*).

28 So Isaac called for Jacob and blessed[a] him and commanded him: "Do not marry a Canaanite woman. ²Go at once to Paddan Aram,[b] to the house of your mother's father Bethuel. Take a wife for yourself there, from among the daughters of Laban, your mother's brother. ³May God Almighty[c] bless you and make you fruitful and increase your numbers until you become a community of peoples. ⁴May he give you and your descendants the blessing given to Abraham, so that you may take possession of the land where you now live as an alien, the land God gave to Abraham." ⁵Then Isaac sent Jacob on his way, and he went to Paddan Aram, to Laban son of Bethuel

[a]1 Or *greeted*   [b]2 That is, Northwest Mesopotamia; also in verses 5, 6 and 7
[c]3 Hebrew *El-Shaddai*

MONDAY

Read Genesis 27:1–46
Key Verses Genesis 27:41–46

Anger – A Choice We Make – Craig Parker

In an argument we often lash out with the line, "*You* make me angry!" Sometimes we soften it to say, "*That* makes me angry!" Honesty tells us that what we should really say is, "*I* make me angry!" because anger is really a choice we make.

Anger is an emotion and, like all emotions, it is morally neutral. But if we don't handle anger correctly, it can lead to sin. In Genesis 27:41–46 we see how Esau holds a grudge against his brother, Jacob, because Jacob has tricked Esau out of their father's blessing. Esau's temper burned out of control at his brother's trickery, so much so that he swore to kill Jacob and made a poor choice in marriage just to spite his parents.

To avoid letting anger rule our lives, we would do well to step back whenever we get angry and look at the emotions that might underlie our anger:

- a sense of loss or grief (as in a lost possession or relationship)
- frustration when an important goal or desire is blocked
- misunderstanding resulting from our limited view of what really happened
- a sense of injustice when people take advantage of our kindness or attack us with untruth

Understanding the emotions that trigger our anger helps us to bite our tongues, step back and consider how to allow God's Spirit to guide our response. We can say, "No one can make me angry but me, and I choose not to let my anger control me." We can choose to remember Ephesians 4:26–27: "In your anger do not sin: Do not let the sun go down while you are still angry, and do not give the devil a foothold."

By the way, Esau's story has a happy ending; though the brothers were estranged for many years, it seems that God understood the pain underlying Esau's anger and blessed him. With God's grace Esau graciously and willingly forgave his brother (see Genesis 33:4–15).

A Deeper Look
Psalm 37:7–8; Ecclesiastes 7:8–9

Go to page 35 for your next devotional reading.

the Aramean, the brother of Rebekah, who was the mother of Jacob and Esau.

⁶Now Esau learned that Isaac had blessed Jacob and had sent him to Paddan Aram to take a wife from there, and that when he blessed him he commanded him, "Do not marry a Canaanite woman," ⁷and that Jacob had obeyed his father and mother and had gone to Paddan Aram. ⁸Esau then realized how displeasing the Canaanite women were to his father Isaac; ⁹so he went to Ishmael and married Mahalath, the sister of Nebaioth and daughter of Ishmael son of Abraham, in addition to the wives he already had.

Jacob's Dream at Bethel

¹⁰Jacob left Beersheba and set out for Haran. ¹¹When he reached a certain place, he stopped for the night because the sun had set. Taking one of the stones there, he put it under his head and lay down to sleep. ¹²He had a dream in which he saw a stairway[a] resting on the earth, with its top reaching to heaven, and the angels of God were ascending and descending on it. ¹³There above it[b] stood the LORD, and he said: "I am the LORD, the God of your father Abraham and the God of Isaac. I will give you and your descendants the land on which you are lying. ¹⁴Your descendants will be like the dust of the earth, and you will spread out to the west and to the east, to the north and to the south. All peoples on earth will be blessed through you and your offspring. ¹⁵I am with you and will watch over you wherever you go, and I will bring you back to this land. I will not leave you until I have done what I have promised you."

¹⁶When Jacob awoke from his sleep, he thought, "Surely the LORD is in this place, and I was not aware of it." ¹⁷He was afraid and said, "How awesome is this place! This is none other than the house of God; this is the gate of heaven."

¹⁸Early the next morning Jacob took the stone he had placed under his head and set it up as a pillar and poured oil on top of it. ¹⁹He called that place Bethel,[c] though the city used to be called Luz.

²⁰Then Jacob made a vow, saying, "If God will be with me and will watch over me on this journey I am taking and will give me food to eat and clothes to wear ²¹so that I return safely to my father's house, then the LORD[d] will be my God ²²and[e] this stone that I have set up as a

pillar will be God's house, and of all that you give me I will give you a tenth."

Jacob Arrives in Paddan Aram

29 Then Jacob continued on his journey and came to the land of the eastern peoples. ²There he saw a well in the field, with three flocks of sheep lying near it because the flocks were watered from that well. The stone over the mouth of the well was large. ³When all the flocks were gathered there, the shepherds would roll the stone away from the well's mouth and water the sheep. Then they would return the stone to its place over the mouth of the well.

⁴Jacob asked the shepherds, "My brothers, where are you from?"

"We're from Haran," they replied.

⁵He said to them, "Do you know Laban, Nahor's grandson?"

"Yes, we know him," they answered.

⁶Then Jacob asked them, "Is he well?"

"Yes, he is," they said, "and here comes his daughter Rachel with the sheep."

⁷"Look," he said, "the sun is still high; it is not time for the flocks to be gathered. Water the sheep and take them back to pasture."

⁸"We can't," they replied, "until all the flocks are gathered and the stone has been rolled away from the mouth of the well. Then we will water the sheep."

⁹While he was still talking with them, Rachel came with her father's sheep, for she was a shepherdess. ¹⁰When Jacob saw Rachel daughter of Laban, his mother's brother, and Laban's sheep, he went over and rolled the stone away from the mouth of the well and watered his uncle's sheep. ¹¹Then Jacob kissed Rachel and began to weep aloud. ¹²He had told Rachel that he was a relative of her father and a son of Rebekah. So she ran and told her father.

¹³As soon as Laban heard the news about Jacob, his sister's son, he hurried to meet him. He embraced him and kissed him and brought him to his home, and there Jacob told him all these things. ¹⁴Then Laban said to him, "You are my own flesh and blood."

---

*a*12 Or *ladder*   *b*13 Or *There beside him*
*c*19 *Bethel* means *house of God.*   *d*20,21 Or
Since God . . . father's house, the LORD   *e*21,22 Or
house, and the LORD will be my God, 22*then*

Jacob Marries Leah and Rachel

After Jacob had stayed with him for a whole month, ¹⁵Laban said to him, "Just because you are a relative of mine, should you work for me for nothing? Tell me what your wages should be."

¹⁶Now Laban had two daughters; the name of the older was Leah, and the name of the younger was Rachel. ¹⁷Leah had weak[a] eyes, but Rachel was lovely in form, and beautiful. ¹⁸Jacob was in love with Rachel and said, "I'll work for you seven years in return for your younger daughter Rachel."

¹⁹Laban said, "It's better that I give her to you than to some other man. Stay here with me." ²⁰So Jacob served seven years to get Rachel, but they seemed like only a few days to him because of his love for her.

²¹Then Jacob said to Laban, "Give me my wife. My time is completed, and I want to lie with her."

²²So Laban brought together all the people of the place and gave a feast. ²³But when evening came, he took his daughter Leah and gave her to Jacob, and Jacob lay with her. ²⁴And Laban gave his servant girl Zilpah to his daughter as her maidservant.

²⁵When morning came, there was Leah! So Jacob said to Laban, "What is this you have done to me? I served you for Rachel, didn't I? Why have you deceived me?"

²⁶Laban replied, "It is not our custom here to give the younger daughter in marriage before the older one. ²⁷Finish this daughter's bridal week; then we will give you the younger one also, in return for another seven years of work."

²⁸And Jacob did so. He finished the week with Leah, and then Laban gave him his daughter Rachel to be his wife. ²⁹Laban gave his servant girl Bilhah to his daughter Rachel as her maidservant. ³⁰Jacob lay with Rachel also, and he loved Rachel more than Leah. And he worked for Laban another seven years.

Jacob's Children

³¹When the LORD saw that Leah was not loved, he opened her womb, but Rachel was barren. ³²Leah became pregnant and gave birth to a son. She named him Reuben,[b] for she said, "It is because the LORD has seen my misery. Surely my husband will love me now."

³³She conceived again, and when she gave birth to a son she said, "Because the LORD heard that I am not loved, he gave me this one too." So she named him Simeon.[c]

³⁴Again she conceived, and when she gave birth to a son she said, "Now at last my husband will become attached to me, because I have borne him three sons." So he was named Levi.[d]

³⁵She conceived again, and when she gave birth to a son she said, "This time I will praise the LORD." So she named him Judah.[e] Then she stopped having children.

30 When Rachel saw that she was not bearing Jacob any children, she became jealous of her sister. So she said to Jacob, "Give me children, or I'll die!"

²Jacob became angry with her and said, "Am I in the place of God, who has kept you from having children?"

³Then she said, "Here is Bilhah, my maidservant. Sleep with her so that she can bear children for me and that through her I too can build a family."

⁴So she gave him her servant Bilhah as a wife. Jacob slept with her, ⁵and she became pregnant and bore him a son. ⁶Then Rachel said, "God has vindicated me; he has listened to my plea and given me a son." Because of this she named him Dan.[f]

⁷Rachel's servant Bilhah conceived again and bore Jacob a second son. ⁸Then Rachel said, "I have had a great struggle with my sister, and I have won." So she named him Naphtali.[g]

⁹When Leah saw that she had stopped having children, she took her maidservant Zilpah and gave her to Jacob as a wife. ¹⁰Leah's servant Zilpah bore Jacob a son. ¹¹Then Leah said, "What good fortune!"[h] So she named him Gad.[i]

¹²Leah's servant Zilpah bore Jacob a second son. ¹³Then Leah said, "How happy I am! The women will call me happy." So she named him Asher.[j]

¹⁴During wheat harvest, Reuben went

---

[a] 17 Or *delicate*   [b] 32 *Reuben* sounds like the Hebrew for *he has seen my misery*; the name means *see, a son*.   [c] 33 *Simeon* probably means *one who hears*.   [d] 34 *Levi* sounds like and may be derived from the Hebrew for *attached*.   [e] 35 *Judah* sounds like and may be derived from the Hebrew for *praise*.   [f] 6 *Dan* here means *he has vindicated*.   [g] 8 *Naphtali* means *my struggle*.   [h] 11 Or *"A troop is coming!"*   [i] 11 *Gad* can mean *good fortune* or *a troop*.   [j] 13 *Asher* means *happy*.

out into the fields and found some mandrake plants, which he brought to his mother Leah. Rachel said to Leah, "Please give me some of your son's mandrakes."

¹⁵But she said to her, "Wasn't it enough that you took away my husband? Will you take my son's mandrakes too?"

"Very well," Rachel said, "he can sleep with you tonight in return for your son's mandrakes."

¹⁶So when Jacob came in from the fields that evening, Leah went out to meet him. "You must sleep with me," she said. "I have hired you with my son's mandrakes." So he slept with her that night.

¹⁷God listened to Leah, and she became pregnant and bore Jacob a fifth son. ¹⁸Then Leah said, "God has rewarded me for giving my maidservant to my husband." So she named him Issachar.ᵃ

¹⁹Leah conceived again and bore Jacob a sixth son. ²⁰Then Leah said, "God has presented me with a precious gift. This time my husband will treat me with honor, because I have borne him six sons." So she named him Zebulun.ᵇ

²¹Some time later she gave birth to a daughter and named her Dinah.

²²Then God remembered Rachel; he listened to her and opened her womb. ²³She became pregnant and gave birth to a son and said, "God has taken away my disgrace." ²⁴She named him Joseph,ᶜ and said, "May the LORD add to me another son."

Jacob's Flocks Increase

²⁵After Rachel gave birth to Joseph, Jacob said to Laban, "Send me on my way so I can go back to my own homeland. ²⁶Give me my wives and children, for whom I have served you, and I will be on my way. You know how much work I've done for you."

²⁷But Laban said to him, "If I have found favor in your eyes, please stay. I have learned by divination thatᵈ the LORD has blessed me because of you." ²⁸He added, "Name your wages, and I will pay them."

²⁹Jacob said to him, "You know how I have worked for you and how your livestock has fared under my care. ³⁰The little you had before I came has increased greatly, and the LORD has blessed you wherever I have been. But now, when

may I do something for my own household?"

³¹"What shall I give you?" he asked.

"Don't give me anything," Jacob replied. "But if you will do this one thing for me, I will go on tending your flocks and watching over them: ³²Let me go through all your flocks today and remove from them every speckled or spotted sheep, every dark-colored lamb and every spotted or speckled goat. They will be my wages. ³³And my honesty will testify for me in the future, whenever you check on the wages you have paid me. Any goat in my possession that is not speckled or spotted, or any lamb that is not dark-colored, will be considered stolen."

³⁴"Agreed," said Laban. "Let it be as you have said." ³⁵That same day he removed all the male goats that were streaked or spotted, and all the speckled or spotted female goats (all that had white on them) and all the dark-colored lambs, and he placed them in the care of his sons. ³⁶Then he put a three-day journey between himself and Jacob, while Jacob continued to tend the rest of Laban's flocks.

³⁷Jacob, however, took fresh-cut branches from poplar, almond and plane trees and made white stripes on them by peeling the bark and exposing the white inner wood of the branches. ³⁸Then he placed the peeled branches in all the watering troughs, so that they would be directly in front of the flocks when they came to drink. When the flocks were in heat and came to drink, ³⁹they mated in front of the branches. And they bore young that were streaked or speckled or spotted. ⁴⁰Jacob set apart the young of the flock by themselves, but made the rest face the streaked and dark-colored animals that belonged to Laban. Thus he made separate flocks for himself and did not put them with Laban's animals. ⁴¹Whenever the stronger females were in heat, Jacob would place the branches in the troughs in front of the animals so they would mate near the branches, ⁴²but if the animals were weak, he would not place them there. So the weak animals went to Laban and the strong ones to Jacob. ⁴³In this way the man grew exceedingly prosperous and came to own large

---

ᵃ18 Issachar sounds like the Hebrew for reward.
ᵇ20 Zebulun probably means honor. ᶜ24 Joseph means may he add. ᵈ27 Or possibly have become rich and

flocks, and maidservants and menservants, and camels and donkeys.

Jacob Flees From Laban

31 Jacob heard that Laban's sons were saying, "Jacob has taken everything our father owned and has gained all this wealth from what belonged to our father." ²And Jacob noticed that Laban's attitude toward him was not what it had been.

³Then the LORD said to Jacob, "Go back to the land of your fathers and to your relatives, and I will be with you."

⁴So Jacob sent word to Rachel and Leah to come out to the fields where his flocks were. ⁵He said to them, "I see that your father's attitude toward me is not what it was before, but the God of my father has been with me. ⁶You know that I've worked for your father with all my strength, ⁷yet your father has cheated me by changing my wages ten times. However-

er, God has not allowed him to harm me. ⁸If he said, 'The speckled ones will be your wages,' then all the flocks gave birth to speckled young; and if he said, 'The streaked ones will be your wages,' then all the flocks bore streaked young. ⁹So God has taken away your father's livestock and has given them to me.

¹⁰"In breeding season I once had a dream in which I looked up and saw that the male goats mating with the flock were streaked, speckled or spotted. ¹¹The angel of God said to me in the dream, 'Jacob.' I answered, 'Here I am.' ¹²And he said, 'Look up and see that all the male goats mating with the flock are streaked, speckled or spotted, for I have seen all that Laban has been doing to you. ¹³I am the God of Bethel, where you anointed a pillar and where you made a vow to me. Now leave this land at once and go back to your native land.' "

¹⁴Then Rachel and Leah replied, "Do

TUESDAY

Read Genesis 31:1–55
Key Verse Genesis 31:7

Cheated? —Dean Storelli

"What?" In disbelief and growing anger I asked again why the school that had just offered me a job suddenly had no hours for me on their teaching schedule.

"You called and said you didn't want any hours!" the secretary explained, passing on a lie that only later made sense. I discovered that my former boss had called my new school and had me "unhired." He promised to meet the new offer, but the "offer" involved working longer hours.

Looking back, I saw that just as God had worked in Jacob's life, so he had worked in mine. My old boss treated me poorly, but by continuing to work for him, I learned skills that I later used on the mission field. Jacob was cheated when Laban changed his wages ten times; my schedule was changed almost "ten times," but the Lord did not allow my boss to hurt me.

When people cheat us or lie to us, there's no denying that our pain is real. But there's another reality, and that's that we are loved and ultimately protected: "Who shall separate us from the love of Christ? Shall trouble or hardship or persecution or famine or nakedness or danger or sword? No, in all these things we are more than conquerors through him who loved us" (Romans 8:35,37).

A Deeper Look
Malachi 3:5; Matthew 10:30–31; Luke 18:7–8

Go to page 39 for your next devotional reading.

we still have any share in the inheritance of our father's estate? **15**Does he not regard us as foreigners? Not only has he sold us, but he has used up what was paid for us. **16**Surely all the wealth that God took away from our father belongs to us and our children. So do whatever God has told you."

17Then Jacob put his children and his wives on camels, **18**and he drove all his livestock ahead of him, along with all the goods he had accumulated in Paddan Aram,*a* to go to his father Isaac in the land of Canaan.

19When Laban had gone to shear his sheep, Rachel stole her father's household gods. **20**Moreover, Jacob deceived Laban the Aramean by not telling him he was running away. **21**So he fled with all he had, and crossing the River,*b* he headed for the hill country of Gilead.

Laban Pursues Jacob

22On the third day Laban was told that Jacob had fled. **23**Taking his relatives with him, he pursued Jacob for seven days and caught up with him in the hill country of Gilead. **24**Then God came to Laban the Aramean in a dream at night and said to him, "Be careful not to say anything to Jacob, either good or bad."

25Jacob had pitched his tent in the hill country of Gilead when Laban overtook him, and Laban and his relatives camped there too. **26**Then Laban said to Jacob, "What have you done? You've deceived me, and you've carried off my daughters like captives in war. **27**Why did you run off secretly and deceive me? Why didn't you tell me, so I could send you away with joy and singing to the music of tambourines and harps? **28**You didn't even let me kiss my grandchildren and my daughters good-by. You have done a foolish thing. **29**I have the power to harm you; but last night the God of your father said to me, 'Be careful not to say anything to Jacob, either good or bad.' **30**Now you have gone off because you longed to return to your father's house. But why did you steal my gods?"

31Jacob answered Laban, "I was afraid, because I thought you would take your daughters away from me by force. **32**But if you find anyone who has your gods, he shall not live. In the presence of our relatives, see for yourself whether there is anything of yours here with me;

and if so, take it." Now Jacob did not know that Rachel had stolen the gods.

33So Laban went into Jacob's tent and into Leah's tent and into the tent of the two maidservants, but he found nothing. After he came out of Leah's tent, he entered Rachel's tent. **34**Now Rachel had taken the household gods and put them inside her camel's saddle and was sitting on them. Laban searched through everything in the tent but found nothing.

35Rachel said to her father, "Don't be angry, my lord, that I cannot stand up in your presence; I'm having my period." So he searched but could not find the household gods.

36Jacob was angry and took Laban to task. "What is my crime?" he asked Laban. "What sin have I committed that you hunt me down? **37**Now that you have searched through all my goods, what have you found that belongs to your household? Put it here in front of your relatives and mine, and let them judge between the two of us.

38"I have been with you for twenty years now. Your sheep and goats have not miscarried, nor have I eaten rams from your flocks. **39**I did not bring you animals torn by wild beasts; I bore the loss myself. And you demanded payment from me for whatever was stolen by day or night. **40**This was my situation: The heat consumed me in the daytime and the cold at night, and sleep fled from my eyes. **41**It was like this for the twenty years I was in your household. I worked for you fourteen years for your two daughters and six years for your flocks, and you changed my wages ten times. **42**If the God of my father, the God of Abraham and the Fear of Isaac, had not been with me, you would surely have sent me away empty-handed. But God has seen my hardship and the toil of my hands, and last night he rebuked you."

43Laban answered Jacob, "The women are my daughters, the children are my children, and the flocks are my flocks. All you see is mine. Yet what can I do today about these daughters of mine, or about the children they have borne? **44**Come now, let's make a covenant, you and I, and let it serve as a witness between us."

45So Jacob took a stone and set it up as a pillar. **46**He said to his relatives, "Gather

a 18 That is, Northwest Mesopotamia   *b 21* That is, the Euphrates some stones." So they took stones and piled them in a heap, and they ate there by the heap. 47Laban called it Jegar Sahadutha,*a* and Jacob called it Galeed.*b*

48Laban said, "This heap is a witness between you and me today." That is why it was called Galeed. 49It was also called Mizpah,*c* because he said, "May the LORD keep watch between you and me when we are away from each other. 50If you mistreat my daughters or if you take any wives besides my daughters, even though no one is with us, remember that God is a witness between you and me."

51Laban also said to Jacob, "Here is this heap, and here is this pillar I have set up between you and me. 52This heap is a witness, and this pillar is a witness, that I will not go past this heap to your side to harm you and that you will not go past this heap and pillar to my side to harm me. 53May the God of Abraham and the God of Nahor, the God of their father, judge between us."

So Jacob took an oath in the name of the Fear of his father Isaac. 54He offered a sacrifice there in the hill country and invited his relatives to a meal. After they had eaten, they spent the night there.

55Early the next morning Laban kissed his grandchildren and his daughters and blessed them. Then he left and returned home.

Jacob Prepares to Meet Esau

32 Jacob also went on his way, and the angels of God met him. 2When Jacob saw them, he said, "This is the camp of God!" So he named that place Mahanaim.*d*

3Jacob sent messengers ahead of him to his brother Esau in the land of Seir, the country of Edom. 4He instructed them: "This is what you are to say to my master Esau: 'Your servant Jacob says, I have been staying with Laban and have remained there till now. 5I have cattle and donkeys, sheep and goats, menservants and maidservants. Now I am sending this message to my lord, that I may find favor in your eyes.'"

6When the messengers returned to Jacob, they said, "We went to your brother Esau, and now he is coming to meet you, and four hundred men are with him."

7In great fear and distress Jacob divided the people who were with him into two groups,*e* and the flocks and herds and camels as well. 8He thought, "If Esau comes and attacks one group,*f* the group*f* that is left may escape."

9Then Jacob prayed, "O God of my father Abraham, God of my father Isaac, O LORD, who said to me, 'Go back to your country and your relatives, and I will make you prosper,' 10I am unworthy of all the kindness and faithfulness you have shown your servant. I had only my staff when I crossed this Jordan, but now I have become two groups. 11Save me, I pray, from the hand of my brother Esau, for I am afraid he will come and attack me, and also the mothers with their children. 12But you have said, 'I will surely make you prosper and will make your descendants like the sand of the sea, which cannot be counted.'"

13He spent the night there, and from what he had with him he selected a gift for his brother Esau: 14two hundred female goats and twenty male goats, two hundred ewes and twenty rams, 15thirty female camels with their young, forty cows and ten bulls, and twenty female donkeys and ten male donkeys. 16He put them in the care of his servants, each herd by itself, and said to his servants, "Go ahead of me, and keep some space between the herds."

17He instructed the one in the lead: "When my brother Esau meets you and asks, 'To whom do you belong, and where are you going, and who owns all these animals in front of you?' 18then you are to say, 'They belong to your servant

a47 The Aramaic *Jegar Sahadutha* means *witness heap.*   *b47* The Hebrew *Galeed* means *witness heap.*   *c49* *Mizpah* means *watchtower.*
d2 *Mahanaim* means *two camps.*   *e7* Or *camps; also in verse 10*   *f8* Or *camp*

POINT OF INTEREST

Genesis 32:1-2

Jacob was fearful of seeing his brother Esau again. They had been bitter enemies when they had last talked. But God's angels appeared to Jacob. Jacob called the place "the camp of God"; the angels' appearance encouraged Jacob to go to his brother, and as he went forward in faith, he triumphed in faith.

Jacob. They are a gift sent to my lord Esau, and he is coming behind us.' "

¹⁹He also instructed the second, the third and all the others who followed the herds: "You are to say the same thing to Esau when you meet him. ²⁰And be sure to say, 'Your servant Jacob is coming behind us.' " For he thought, "I will pacify him with these gifts I am sending on ahead; later, when I see him, perhaps he will receive me." ²¹So Jacob's gifts went on ahead of him, but he himself spent the night in the camp.

Jacob Wrestles With God

²²That night Jacob got up and took his two wives, his two maidservants and his eleven sons and crossed the ford of the Jabbok. ²³After he had sent them across the stream, he sent over all his possessions. ²⁴So Jacob was left alone, and a man wrestled with him till daybreak. ²⁵When the man saw that he could not overpower him, he touched the socket of Jacob's hip so that his hip was wrenched as he wrestled with the man. ²⁶Then the man said, "Let me go, for it is daybreak."

But Jacob replied, "I will not let you go unless you bless me."

²⁷The man asked him, "What is your name?"

"Jacob," he answered.

²⁸Then the man said, "Your name will no longer be Jacob, but Israel,ᵃ because you have struggled with God and with men and have overcome."

²⁹Jacob said, "Please tell me your name."

But he replied, "Why do you ask my name?" Then he blessed him there.

³⁰So Jacob called the place Peniel,ᵇ saying, "It is because I saw God face to face, and yet my life was spared."

³¹The sun rose above him as he passed Peniel,ᶜ and he was limping because of his hip. ³²Therefore to this day the Israelites do not eat the tendon attached to the socket of the hip, because the socket of Jacob's hip was touched near the tendon.

Jacob Meets Esau

33 Jacob looked up and there was Esau, coming with his four hundred men; so he divided the children among Leah, Rachel and the two maidservants. ²He put the maidservants and their children in front, Leah and her children next, and Rachel and Joseph in the rear. ³He himself went on ahead and bowed down to the ground seven times as he approached his brother.

⁴But Esau ran to meet Jacob and embraced him; he threw his arms around his neck and kissed him. And they wept. ⁵Then Esau looked up and saw the women and children. "Who are these with you?" he asked.

Jacob answered, "They are the children God has graciously given your servant."

⁶Then the maidservants and their children approached and bowed down. ⁷Next, Leah and her children came and bowed down. Last of all came Joseph and Rachel, and they too bowed down.

⁸Esau asked, "What do you mean by all these droves I met?"

"To find favor in your eyes, my lord," he said.

⁹But Esau said, "I already have plenty, my brother. Keep what you have for yourself."

¹⁰"No, please!" said Jacob. "If I have found favor in your eyes, accept this gift from me. For to see your face is like seeing the face of God, now that you have received me favorably. ¹¹Please accept the present that was brought to you, for God has been gracious to me and I have all I need." And because Jacob insisted, Esau accepted it.

¹²Then Esau said, "Let us be on our way; I'll accompany you."

¹³But Jacob said to him, "My lord knows that the children are tender and that I must care for the ewes and cows that are nursing their young. If they are driven hard just one day, all the animals will die. ¹⁴So let my lord go on ahead of his servant, while I move along slowly at the pace of the droves before me and that of the children, until I come to my lord in Seir."

¹⁵Esau said, "Then let me leave some of my men with you."

"But why do that?" Jacob asked. "Just let me find favor in the eyes of my lord."

¹⁶So that day Esau started on his way back to Seir. ¹⁷Jacob, however, went to Succoth, where he built a place for himself and made shelters for his livestock. That is why the place is called Succoth.ᵈ

¹⁸After Jacob came from Paddan

ᵃ28 *Israel* means *he struggles with God.*
ᵇ30 *Peniel* means *face of God.*   ᶜ31 Hebrew *Penuel,* a variant of *Peniel*   ᵈ17 *Succoth* means *shelters.*

Aram,[a] he arrived safely at the[b] city of Shechem in Canaan and camped within sight of the city. [19]For a hundred pieces of silver,[c] he bought from the sons of Hamor, the father of Shechem, the plot of ground where he pitched his tent. [20]There he set up an altar and called it El Elohe Israel.[d]

Dinah and the Shechemites

34 Now Dinah, the daughter Leah had borne to Jacob, went out to visit the women of the land. [2]When Shechem son of Hamor the Hivite, the ruler of that area, saw her, he took her and violated her. [3]His heart was drawn to Dinah daughter of Jacob, and he loved the girl

and spoke tenderly to her. [4]And Shechem said to his father Hamor, "Get me this girl as my wife."

[5]When Jacob heard that his daughter Dinah had been defiled, his sons were in the fields with his livestock; so he kept quiet about it until they came home.

[6]Then Shechem's father Hamor went out to talk with Jacob. [7]Now Jacob's sons had come in from the fields as soon as they heard what had happened. They were filled with grief and fury, because

[a]18 That is, Northwest Mesopotamia   [b]18 Or *arrived at Shalem, a*   [c]19 Hebrew *hundred kesitahs*; a kesitah was a unit of money of unknown weight and value.   [d]20 *El Elohe Israel* can mean *God, the God of Israel* or *mighty is the God of Israel.*

WEDNESDAY

Read Genesis 33:1–20
Key Verse Genesis 33:10

The First Step – Vollie Sanders

Who takes the first step toward forgiveness? Me? Or the one who has offended me? It seems only fair that our offenders should take the first step. After all, they are the ones who have caused us the pain. And it's hard to forgive someone who doesn't seem sorry, or who might just turn around and hurt us again. But Jesus set a high standard of forgiveness—he died for us while we were still sinners, even before we asked for his forgiveness (see Romans 5:8).

The two brothers, Jacob and Esau, had a huge quarrel. First, Jacob took advantage of his brother's weaknesses and swindled him out of his birthright. Later, Jacob tricked their father into giving the blessing of the firstborn to him instead of Esau (Genesis 25, 27). Jacob stole his brother's entire inheritance!

After years of separation, Esau and Jacob encountered each other again. Knowing full well that he could expect retaliation from Esau, Jacob was prepared to fight in order to defend his family. But that didn't happen. Instead Esau ran out to meet Jacob, embracing and kissing the very same brother who had hurt him.

How was it possible? Esau was the offended one, yet by God's grace he was able to forgive his brother. His forgiveness reminded Jacob of the forgiveness he had received from God. Jacob said, "to see your face is like seeing the face of God, now that you have received me favorably" (Genesis 33:10).

Many times, when someone has hurt us, we wait for the offender to come and ask for forgiveness. But the ball of forgiveness is always in *our* court. Reconciliation occurs when we take the first step. That's when others see the face of God reflected in us.

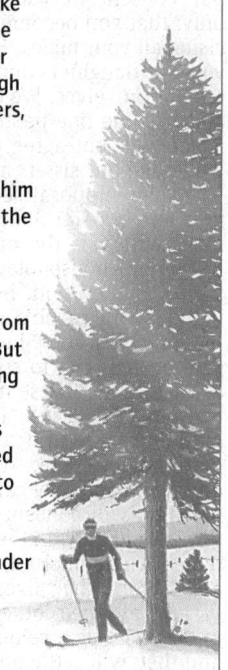

A Deeper Look
Matthew 5:23–24; 18:21–22; Romans 12:18–21

Go to page 46 for your next devotional reading.

Shechem had done a disgraceful thing in[a] Israel by lying with Jacob's daughter—a thing that should not be done.

8But Hamor said to them, "My son Shechem has his heart set on your daughter. Please give her to him as his wife. 9Intermarry with us; give us your daughters and take our daughters for yourselves. 10You can settle among us; the land is open to you. Live in it, trade[b] in it, and acquire property in it."

11Then Shechem said to Dinah's father and brothers, "Let me find favor in your eyes, and I will give you whatever you ask. 12Make the price for the bride and the gift I am to bring as great as you like, and I'll pay whatever you ask me. Only give me the girl as my wife."

13Because their sister Dinah had been defiled, Jacob's sons replied deceitfully as they spoke to Shechem and his father Hamor. 14They said to them, "We can't do such a thing; we can't give our sister to a man who is not circumcised. That would be a disgrace to us. 15We will give our consent to you on one condition only: that you become like us by circumcising all your males. 16Then we will give you our daughters and take your daughters for ourselves. We'll settle among you and become one people with you. 17But if you will not agree to be circumcised, we'll take our sister[c] and go."

18Their proposal seemed good to Hamor and his son Shechem. 19The young man, who was the most honored of all his father's household, lost no time in doing what they said, because he was delighted with Jacob's daughter. 20So Hamor and his son Shechem went to the gate of their city to speak to their fellow townsmen. 21"These men are friendly toward us," they said. "Let them live in our land and trade in it; the land has plenty of room for them. We can marry their daughters and they can marry ours. 22But the men will consent to live with us as one people only on the condition that our males be circumcised, as they themselves are. 23Won't their livestock, their property and all their other animals become ours? So let us give our consent to them, and they will settle among us."

24All the men who went out of the city gate agreed with Hamor and his son Shechem, and every male in the city was circumcised.

25Three days later, while all of them were still in pain, two of Jacob's sons, Simeon and Levi, Dinah's brothers, took their swords and attacked the unsuspecting city, killing every male. 26They put Hamor and his son Shechem to the sword and took Dinah from Shechem's house and left. 27The sons of Jacob came upon the dead bodies and looted the city where[d] their sister had been defiled. 28They seized their flocks and herds and donkeys and everything else of theirs in the city and out in the fields. 29They carried off all their wealth and all their women and children, taking as plunder everything in the houses.

30Then Jacob said to Simeon and Levi, "You have brought trouble on me by making me a stench to the Canaanites and Perizzites, the people living in this land. We are few in number, and if they join forces against me and attack me, I and my household will be destroyed."

31But they replied, "Should he have treated our sister like a prostitute?"

Jacob Returns to Bethel

35 Then God said to Jacob, "Go up to Bethel and settle there, and build an altar there to God, who appeared to you when you were fleeing from your brother Esau."

2So Jacob said to his household and to all who were with him, "Get rid of the foreign gods you have with you, and purify yourselves and change your clothes. 3Then come, let us go up to Bethel, where I will build an altar to God, who answered me in the day of my distress and who has been with me wherever I have

---

[a]7 Or *against*   [b]10 Or *move about freely;* also in verse 21   [c]17 Hebrew *daughter*   [d]27 Or *because*

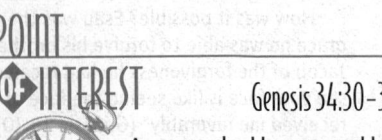

POINT OF INTEREST

Genesis 34:30-31

A woman had been raped by a local prince, and her brothers, in retribution, had murdered the entire male population of her village. Now her whole family was in mortal danger. Who was to blame for this mess? Not Dinah. The Bible assigns no blame to innocent victims. Are you that compassionate?

gone." ⁴So they gave Jacob all the foreign gods they had and the rings in their ears, and Jacob buried them under the oak at Shechem. ⁵Then they set out, and the terror of God fell upon the towns all around them so that no one pursued them.

⁶Jacob and all the people with him came to Luz (that is, Bethel) in the land of Canaan. ⁷There he built an altar, and he called the place El Bethel,ᵃ because it was there that God revealed himself to him when he was fleeing from his brother.

⁸Now Deborah, Rebekah's nurse, died and was buried under the oak below Bethel. So it was named Allon Bacuth.ᵇ

⁹After Jacob returned from Paddan Aram,ᶜ God appeared to him again and blessed him. ¹⁰God said to him, "Your name is Jacob,ᵈ but you will no longer be called Jacob; your name will be Israel.ᵉ" So he named him Israel.

¹¹And God said to him, "I am God Almightyᶠ; be fruitful and increase in number. A nation and a community of nations will come from you, and kings will come from your body. ¹²The land I gave to Abraham and Isaac I also give to you, and I will give this land to your descendants after you." ¹³Then God went up from him at the place where he had talked with him.

¹⁴Jacob set up a stone pillar at the place where God had talked with him, and he poured out a drink offering on it; he also poured oil on it. ¹⁵Jacob called the place where God had talked with him Bethel.ᵍ

The Deaths of Rachel and Isaac

¹⁶Then they moved on from Bethel. While they were still some distance from Ephrath, Rachel began to give birth and had great difficulty. ¹⁷And as she was having great difficulty in childbirth, the midwife said to her, "Don't be afraid, for you have another son." ¹⁸As she breathed her last—for she was dying—she named her son Ben-Oni.ʰ But his father named him Benjamin.ⁱ

¹⁹So Rachel died and was buried on the way to Ephrath (that is, Bethlehem). ²⁰Over her tomb Jacob set up a pillar, and to this day that pillar marks Rachel's tomb.

²¹Israel moved on again and pitched his tent beyond Migdal Eder. ²²While Israel was living in that region, Reuben went in and slept with his father's concubine Bilhah, and Israel heard of it.

Jacob had twelve sons:

²³The sons of Leah:

Reuben the firstborn of Jacob,
Simeon, Levi, Judah, Issachar and Zebulun.

²⁴The sons of Rachel:

Joseph and Benjamin.

²⁵The sons of Rachel's maidservant Bilhah:

Dan and Naphtali.

²⁶The sons of Leah's maidservant Zilpah:

Gad and Asher.

These were the sons of Jacob, who were born to him in Paddan Aram.

²⁷Jacob came home to his father Isaac in Mamre, near Kiriath Arba (that is, Hebron), where Abraham and Isaac had stayed. ²⁸Isaac lived a hundred and eighty years. ²⁹Then he breathed his last and died and was gathered to his people, old and full of years. And his sons Esau and Jacob buried him.

Esau's Descendants

36 This is the account of Esau (that is, Edom).

²Esau took his wives from the women of Canaan: Adah daughter of Elon the Hittite, and Oholibamah daughter of Anah and granddaughter of Zibeon the Hivite— ³also Basemath daughter of Ishmael and sister of Nebaioth.

⁴Adah bore Eliphaz to Esau, Basemath bore Reuel, ⁵and Oholibamah bore Jeush, Jalam and Korah. These were the sons of Esau, who were born to him in Canaan.

⁶Esau took his wives and sons and daughters and all the members of his household, as well as his livestock and all his other animals and all the goods he had acquired in Canaan, and moved to a land some distance from his brother Jacob. ⁷Their possessions were too great

---

ᵃ7 *El Bethel* means *God of Bethel.*   ᵇ8 *Allon Bacuth* means *oak of weeping.*   ᶜ9 That is, Northwest Mesopotamia; also in verse 26
ᵈ10 *Jacob* means *he grasps the heel* (figuratively, *he deceives*).   ᵉ10 *Israel* means *he struggles with God.*   ᶠ11 Hebrew *El-Shaddai*   ᵍ15 *Bethel* means *house of God.*   ʰ18 *Ben-Oni* means *son of my trouble.*   ⁱ18 *Benjamin* means *son of my right hand.*

for them to remain together; the land where they were staying could not support them both because of their livestock. ⁸So Esau (that is, Edom) settled in the hill country of Seir.

⁹This is the account of Esau the father of the Edomites in the hill country of Seir.

¹⁰These are the names of Esau's sons:
Eliphaz, the son of Esau's wife Adah, and Reuel, the son of Esau's wife Basemath.
¹¹The sons of Eliphaz:
Teman, Omar, Zepho, Gatam and Kenaz.
¹²Esau's son Eliphaz also had a concubine named Timna, who bore him Amalek. These were grandsons of Esau's wife Adah.
¹³The sons of Reuel:
Nahath, Zerah, Shammah and Mizzah. These were grandsons of Esau's wife Basemath.
¹⁴The sons of Esau's wife Oholibamah daughter of Anah and granddaughter of Zibeon, whom she bore to Esau:
Jeush, Jalam and Korah.

¹⁵These were the chiefs among Esau's descendants:
The sons of Eliphaz the firstborn of Esau:
Chiefs Teman, Omar, Zepho, Kenaz, ¹⁶Korah,*a* Gatam and Amalek. These were the chiefs descended from Eliphaz in Edom; they were grandsons of Adah.
¹⁷The sons of Esau's son Reuel:
Chiefs Nahath, Zerah, Shammah and Mizzah. These were the chiefs descended from Reuel in Edom; they were grandsons of Esau's wife Basemath.
¹⁸The sons of Esau's wife Oholibamah:
Chiefs Jeush, Jalam and Korah. These were the chiefs descended from Esau's wife Oholibamah daughter of Anah.
¹⁹These were the sons of Esau (that is, Edom), and these were their chiefs.

²⁰These were the sons of Seir the Horite, who were living in the region:
Lotan, Shobal, Zibeon, Anah, ²¹Dishon, Ezer and Dishan.

These sons of Seir in Edom were Horite chiefs.
²²The sons of Lotan:
Hori and Homam.*b* Timna was Lotan's sister.
²³The sons of Shobal:
Alvan, Manahath, Ebal, Shepho and Onam.
²⁴The sons of Zibeon:
Aiah and Anah. This is the Anah who discovered the hot springs*c* in the desert while he was grazing the donkeys of his father Zibeon.
²⁵The children of Anah:
Dishon and Oholibamah daughter of Anah.
²⁶The sons of Dishon*d*:
Hemdan, Eshban, Ithran and Keran.
²⁷The sons of Ezer:
Bilhan, Zaavan and Akan.
²⁸The sons of Dishan:
Uz and Aran.
²⁹These were the Horite chiefs:
Lotan, Shobal, Zibeon, Anah, ³⁰Dishon, Ezer and Dishan. These were the Horite chiefs, according to their divisions, in the land of Seir.

The Rulers of Edom

³¹These were the kings who reigned in Edom before any Israelite king reigned*e*:
³²Bela son of Beor became king of Edom. His city was named Dinhabah.
³³When Bela died, Jobab son of Zerah from Bozrah succeeded him as king.
³⁴When Jobab died, Husham from the land of the Temanites succeeded him as king.
³⁵When Husham died, Hadad son of Bedad, who defeated Midian in the country of Moab, succeeded him as king. His city was named Avith.
³⁶When Hadad died, Samlah from Masrekah succeeded him as king.
³⁷When Samlah died, Shaul from Re-

a16 Masoretic Text; Samaritan Pentateuch (see also Gen. 36:11 and 1 Chron. 1:36) does not have *Korah.* *b22* Hebrew *Hemam,* a variant of *Homam* (see 1 Chron. 1:39) *c24* Vulgate; Syriac *discovered water;* the meaning of the Hebrew for this word is uncertain. *d26* Hebrew *Dishan,* a variant of *Dishon* *e31* Or *before an Israelite king reigned over them* hoboth on the river[a] succeeded him as king.

³⁸When Shaul died, Baal-Hanan son of Acbor succeeded him as king.

³⁹When Baal-Hanan son of Acbor died, Hadad[b] succeeded him as king. His city was named Pau, and his wife's name was Mehetabel daughter of Matred, the daughter of Me-Zahab.

⁴⁰These were the chiefs descended from Esau, by name, according to their clans and regions:

Timna, Alvah, Jetheth, ⁴¹Oholibamah, Elah, Pinon, ⁴²Kenaz, Teman, Mibzar, ⁴³Magdiel and Iram. These were the chiefs of Edom, according to their settlements in the land they occupied.

This was Esau the father of the Edomites.

Joseph's Dreams

37 Jacob lived in the land where his father had stayed, the land of Canaan.

²This is the account of Jacob.

Joseph, a young man of seventeen, was tending the flocks with his brothers, the sons of Bilhah and the sons of Zilpah, his father's wives, and he brought their father a bad report about them. ³Now Israel loved Joseph more than any of his other sons, because he had been born to him in his old age; and he made a richly ornamented[c] robe for him. ⁴When his brothers saw that their father loved him more than any of them, they hated him and could not speak a kind word to him.

⁵Joseph had a dream, and when he told it to his brothers, they hated him all the more. ⁶He said to them, "Listen to this dream I had: ⁷We were binding sheaves of grain out in the field when suddenly my sheaf rose and stood upright, while your sheaves gathered around mine and bowed down to it."

⁸His brothers said to him, "Do you intend to reign over us? Will you actually rule us?" And they hated him all the more because of his dream and what he had said.

⁹Then he had another dream, and he told it to his brothers. "Listen," he said, "I had another dream, and this time the sun and moon and eleven stars were bowing down to me."

¹⁰When he told his father as well as his brothers, his father rebuked him and said, "What is this dream you had? Will your mother and I and your brothers actually come and bow down to the ground before you?" ¹¹His brothers were jealous of him, but his father kept the matter in mind.

Joseph Sold by His Brothers

¹²Now his brothers had gone to graze their father's flocks near Shechem, ¹³and Israel said to Joseph, "As you know, your brothers are grazing the flocks near Shechem. Come, I am going to send you to them."

"Very well," he replied.

¹⁴So he said to him, "Go and see if all is well with your brothers and with the flocks, and bring word back to me." Then he sent him off from the Valley of Hebron.

When Joseph arrived at Shechem, ¹⁵a man found him wandering around in the fields and asked him, "What are you looking for?"

¹⁶He replied, "I'm looking for my brothers. Can you tell me where they are grazing their flocks?"

¹⁷"They have moved on from here," the man answered. "I heard them say, 'Let's go to Dothan.'"

So Joseph went after his brothers and found them near Dothan. ¹⁸But they saw him in the distance, and before he reached them, they plotted to kill him.

¹⁹"Here comes that dreamer!" they said to each other. ²⁰"Come now, let's kill

---

a 37 Possibly the Euphrates　　*b 39* Many manuscripts of the Masoretic Text, Samaritan Pentateuch and Syriac (see also 1 Chron. 1:50); most manuscripts of the Masoretic Text *Hadar*　*c 3* The meaning of the Hebrew for *richly ornamented* is uncertain; also in verses 23 and 32.

POINT OF INTEREST

Genesis 37:2

What was Joseph like at age seventeen? Would you have hung out with him? Draw your conclusions as you read on and see how God directed Joseph's circumstances. The story of Joseph's life demonstrates that there are no shortcuts to a mature faith.

him and throw him into one of these cisterns and say that a ferocious animal devoured him. Then we'll see what comes of his dreams."

²¹When Reuben heard this, he tried to rescue him from their hands. "Let's not take his life," he said. ²²"Don't shed any blood. Throw him into this cistern here in the desert, but don't lay a hand on him." Reuben said this to rescue him from them and take him back to his father.

²³So when Joseph came to his brothers, they stripped him of his robe—the richly ornamented robe he was wearing— ²⁴and they took him and threw him into the cistern. Now the cistern was empty; there was no water in it.

²⁵As they sat down to eat their meal, they looked up and saw a caravan of Ishmaelites coming from Gilead. Their camels were loaded with spices, balm and myrrh, and they were on their way to take them down to Egypt.

²⁶Judah said to his brothers, "What will we gain if we kill our brother and cover up his blood? ²⁷Come, let's sell him to the Ishmaelites and not lay our hands on him; after all, he is our brother, our own flesh and blood." His brothers agreed.

²⁸So when the Midianite merchants came by, his brothers pulled Joseph up out of the cistern and sold him for twenty shekels[a] of silver to the Ishmaelites, who took him to Egypt.

²⁹When Reuben returned to the cistern and saw that Joseph was not there, he tore his clothes. ³⁰He went back to his brothers and said, "The boy isn't there! Where can I turn now?"

³¹Then they got Joseph's robe, slaughtered a goat and dipped the robe in the blood. ³²They took the ornamented robe back to their father and said, "We found this. Examine it to see whether it is your son's robe."

³³He recognized it and said, "It is my son's robe! Some ferocious animal has devoured him. Joseph has surely been torn to pieces."

³⁴Then Jacob tore his clothes, put on sackcloth and mourned for his son many days. ³⁵All his sons and daughters came to comfort him, but he refused to be comforted. "No," he said, "in mourning will I go down to the grave[b] to my son." So his father wept for him.

³⁶Meanwhile, the Midianites[c] sold Joseph in Egypt to Potiphar, one of Pharaoh's officials, the captain of the guard.

Judah and Tamar

38 At that time, Judah left his brothers and went down to stay with a man of Adullam named Hirah. ²There Judah met the daughter of a Canaanite man named Shua. He married her and lay with her; ³she became pregnant and gave birth to a son, who was named Er. ⁴She conceived again and gave birth to a son and named him Onan. ⁵She gave birth to still another son and named him Shelah. It was at Kezib that she gave birth to him.

⁶Judah got a wife for Er, his firstborn, and her name was Tamar. ⁷But Er, Judah's firstborn, was wicked in the LORD's sight; so the LORD put him to death.

⁸Then Judah said to Onan, "Lie with your brother's wife and fulfill your duty to her as a brother-in-law to produce offspring for your brother." ⁹But Onan knew that the offspring would not be his; so whenever he lay with his brother's wife, he spilled his semen on the ground to keep from producing offspring for his brother. ¹⁰What he did was wicked in the LORD's sight; so he put him to death also.

¹¹Judah then said to his daughter-in-law Tamar, "Live as a widow in your father's house until my son Shelah grows up." For he thought, "He may die too, just like his brothers." So Tamar went to live in her father's house.

¹²After a long time Judah's wife, the daughter of Shua, died. When Judah had recovered from his grief, he went up to Timnah, to the men who were shearing his sheep, and his friend Hirah the Adullamite went with him.

¹³When Tamar was told, "Your father-in-law is on his way to Timnah to shear his sheep," ¹⁴she took off her widow's clothes, covered herself with a veil to disguise herself, and then sat down at the entrance to Enaim, which is on the road to Timnah. For she saw that, though Shelah had now grown up, she had not been given to him as his wife.

¹⁵When Judah saw her, he thought she was a prostitute, for she had covered her face. ¹⁶Not realizing that she was his daughter-in-law, he went over to her by

---

a28 That is, about 8 ounces (about 0.2 kilogram)
b35 Hebrew *Sheol*   *c36* Samaritan Pentateuch, Septuagint, Vulgate and Syriac (see also verse 28); Masoretic Text *Medanites*

the roadside and said, "Come now, let me sleep with you."

"And what will you give me to sleep with you?" she asked.

¹⁷"I'll send you a young goat from my flock," he said.

"Will you give me something as a pledge until you send it?" she asked.

¹⁸He said, "What pledge should I give you?"

"Your seal and its cord, and the staff in your hand," she answered. So he gave them to her and slept with her, and she became pregnant by him. ¹⁹After she left, she took off her veil and put on her widow's clothes again.

²⁰Meanwhile Judah sent the young goat by his friend the Adullamite in order to get his pledge back from the woman, but he did not find her. ²¹He asked the men who lived there, "Where is the shrine prostitute who was beside the road at Enaim?"

"There hasn't been any shrine prostitute here," they said.

²²So he went back to Judah and said, "I didn't find her. Besides, the men who lived there said, 'There hasn't been any shrine prostitute here.' "

²³Then Judah said, "Let her keep what she has, or we will become a laughingstock. After all, I did send her this young goat, but you didn't find her."

²⁴About three months later Judah was told, "Your daughter-in-law Tamar is guilty of prostitution, and as a result she is now pregnant."

Judah said, "Bring her out and have her burned to death!"

²⁵As she was being brought out, she sent a message to her father-in-law. "I am pregnant by the man who owns these," she said. And she added, "See if you recognize whose seal and cord and staff these are."

²⁶Judah recognized them and said, "She is more righteous than I, since I wouldn't give her to my son Shelah." And he did not sleep with her again.

²⁷When the time came for her to give birth, there were twin boys in her womb. ²⁸As she was giving birth, one of them put out his hand; so the midwife took a scarlet thread and tied it on his wrist and said, "This one came out first." ²⁹But when he drew back his hand, his brother came out, and she said, "So this is how you have broken out!" And he was

named Perez.ᵃ ³⁰Then his brother, who had the scarlet thread on his wrist, came out and he was given the name Zerah.ᵇ

Joseph and Potiphar's Wife

39 Now Joseph had been taken down to Egypt. Potiphar, an Egyptian who was one of Pharaoh's officials, the captain of the guard, bought him from the Ishmaelites who had taken him there.

²The LORD was with Joseph and he prospered, and he lived in the house of his Egyptian master. ³When his master saw that the LORD was with him and that the LORD gave him success in everything he did, ⁴Joseph found favor in his eyes and became his attendant. Potiphar put him in charge of his household, and he entrusted to his care everything he owned. ⁵From the time he put him in charge of his household and of all that he owned, the LORD blessed the household of the Egyptian because of Joseph. The blessing of the LORD was on everything Potiphar had, both in the house and in the field. ⁶So he left in Joseph's care everything he had; with Joseph in charge, he did not concern himself with anything except the food he ate.

Now Joseph was well-built and handsome, ⁷and after a while his master's wife took notice of Joseph and said, "Come to bed with me!"

⁸But he refused. "With me in charge," he told her, "my master does not concern himself with anything in the house; everything he owns he has entrusted to my care. ⁹No one is greater in this house than I am. My master has withheld nothing from me except you, because you are his wife. How then could I do such a wicked thing and sin against God?" ¹⁰And though she spoke to Joseph day after day, he refused to go to bed with her or even be with her.

¹¹One day he went into the house to attend to his duties, and none of the household servants was inside. ¹²She caught him by his cloak and said, "Come to bed with me!" But he left his cloak in her hand and ran out of the house.

¹³When she saw that he had left his cloak in her hand and had run out of the house, ¹⁴she called her household servants. "Look," she said to them, "this Hebrew has been brought to us to make

---

ᵃ29 *Perez* means *breaking out.*   ᵇ30 *Zerah* can mean *scarlet* or *brightness.*

sport of us! He came in here to sleep with me, but I screamed. [15]When he heard me scream for help, he left his cloak beside me and ran out of the house."

[16]She kept his cloak beside her until his master came home. [17]Then she told him this story: "That Hebrew slave you brought us came to me to make sport of me. [18]But as soon as I screamed for help, he left his cloak beside me and ran out of the house."

[19]When his master heard the story his wife told him, saying, "This is how your slave treated me," he burned with anger.

[20]Joseph's master took him and put him in prison, the place where the king's prisoners were confined.

But while Joseph was there in the prison, [21]the LORD was with him; he showed him kindness and granted him favor in the eyes of the prison warden. [22]So the warden put Joseph in charge of all those held in the prison, and he was made responsible for all that was done there. [23]The warden paid no attention to anything under Joseph's care, because the LORD was with Joseph and gave him success in whatever he did.

THURSDAY

Read Genesis 39:1–23
Key Verses Genesis 39:9–10

An Enticing Situation – Steve Rugg

Joseph found himself in an enticing situation. Potiphar had fully trusted Joseph and had put him in charge of all of his household. But now Potiphar's wife was making a pass at the young Hebrew. There she was, tempting him day after day. One day she even caught him by the cloak and begged him to come to bed with her! Joseph already had fame and fortune, and now he had an opportunity to "get the girl" as well. No one was around, no one would ever have to know . . .

Joseph, however, realized that even though he might "get away" with the affair, he would still be sinning against God. Joseph knew that nothing he had ever done, whether good or bad, had escaped the eyes of the Lord, and that reality gave him perspective. Joseph resolved in his heart that he would maintain purity in this situation even though "she spoke to Joseph day after day" (Genesis 39:10). Not only did Joseph refuse to go to bed with her, he refused even to be in the same room with her! He firmly put his desire to please and to serve God above any of his own sinful cravings.

We can learn a lot from Joseph's example. It seems clear that he had made a commitment to purity long before he found himself in a tempting situation. He had decided what his boundaries were. So when the tempting situation presented itself, he was able to turn away from it without hesitation. Purity began in Joseph's heart and mind—before he was tempted—and he was ready to make purity a verb.

How would each of us react in Joseph's situation? If we make a decision to live purely—thinking through and setting boundaries for our behavior *before* we encounter temptation—and then ask God to provide us with the strength to stick to it, we are ready to face those tempting situations when no one is looking.

A Deeper Look
1 Corinthians 10:13; 2 Corinthians 7:1; Ephesians 5:3–4

Go to page 50 for your next devotional reading.

The Cupbearer and the Baker

40 Some time later, the cupbearer and the baker of the king of Egypt offended their master, the king of Egypt. ²Pharaoh was angry with his two officials, the chief cupbearer and the chief baker, ³and put them in custody in the house of the captain of the guard, in the same prison where Joseph was confined. ⁴The captain of the guard assigned them to Joseph, and he attended them.

After they had been in custody for some time, ⁵each of the two men—the cupbearer and the baker of the king of Egypt, who were being held in prison—had a dream the same night, and each dream had a meaning of its own.

⁶When Joseph came to them the next morning, he saw that they were dejected. ⁷So he asked Pharaoh's officials who were in custody with him in his master's house, "Why are your faces so sad today?"

⁸"We both had dreams," they answered, "but there is no one to interpret them."

Then Joseph said to them, "Do not interpretations belong to God? Tell me your dreams."

⁹So the chief cupbearer told Joseph his dream. He said to him, "In my dream I saw a vine in front of me, ¹⁰and on the vine were three branches. As soon as it budded, it blossomed, and its clusters ripened into grapes. ¹¹Pharaoh's cup was in my hand, and I took the grapes, squeezed them into Pharaoh's cup and put the cup in his hand."

¹²"This is what it means," Joseph said to him. "The three branches are three days. ¹³Within three days Pharaoh will lift up your head and restore you to your position, and you will put Pharaoh's cup in his hand, just as you used to do when you were his cupbearer. ¹⁴But when all goes well with you, remember me and show me kindness; mention me to Pharaoh and get me out of this prison. ¹⁵For I was forcibly carried off from the land of the Hebrews, and even here I have done nothing to deserve being put in a dungeon."

¹⁶When the chief baker saw that Joseph had given a favorable interpretation, he said to Joseph, "I too had a dream: On my head were three baskets of bread.ᵃ ¹⁷In the top basket were all kinds of baked goods for Pharaoh, but the birds were eating them out of the basket on my head."

¹⁸"This is what it means," Joseph said. "The three baskets are three days. ¹⁹Within three days Pharaoh will lift off your head and hang you on a tree.ᵇ And the birds will eat away your flesh."

²⁰Now the third day was Pharaoh's birthday, and he gave a feast for all his officials. He lifted up the heads of the chief cupbearer and the chief baker in the presence of his officials: ²¹He restored the chief cupbearer to his position, so that he once again put the cup into Pharaoh's hand, ²²but he hangedᶜ the chief baker, just as Joseph had said to them in his interpretation.

²³The chief cupbearer, however, did not remember Joseph; he forgot him.

Pharaoh's Dreams

41 When two full years had passed, Pharaoh had a dream: He was standing by the Nile, ²when out of the river there came up seven cows, sleek and fat, and they grazed among the reeds. ³After them, seven other cows, ugly and gaunt, came up out of the Nile and stood beside those on the riverbank. ⁴And the cows that were ugly and gaunt ate up the seven sleek, fat cows. Then Pharaoh woke up.

⁵He fell asleep again and had a second dream: Seven heads of grain, healthy and good, were growing on a single stalk. ⁶After them, seven other heads of grain sprouted—thin and scorched by the east wind. ⁷The thin heads of grain swallowed up the seven healthy, full heads. Then Pharaoh woke up; it had been a dream.

⁸In the morning his mind was troubled, so he sent for all the magicians and wise men of Egypt. Pharaoh told them his dreams, but no one could interpret them for him.

⁹Then the chief cupbearer said to Pharaoh, "Today I am reminded of my shortcomings. ¹⁰Pharaoh was once angry with his servants, and he imprisoned me and the chief baker in the house of the captain of the guard. ¹¹Each of us had a dream the same night, and each dream had a meaning of its own. ¹²Now a young Hebrew was there with us, a servant of the captain of the guard. We told him our dreams, and he interpreted them for us, giving each man the interpretation of his

ᵃ16 Or *three wicker baskets*   ᵇ19 Or *and impale you on a pole*   ᶜ22 Or *impaled* dream. ¹³And things turned out exactly as he interpreted them to us: I was restored to my position, and the other man was hanged.ᵃ"

¹⁴So Pharaoh sent for Joseph, and he was quickly brought from the dungeon. When he had shaved and changed his clothes, he came before Pharaoh.

¹⁵Pharaoh said to Joseph, "I had a dream, and no one can interpret it. But I have heard it said of you that when you hear a dream you can interpret it."

¹⁶"I cannot do it," Joseph replied to Pharaoh, "but God will give Pharaoh the answer he desires."

¹⁷Then Pharaoh said to Joseph, "In my dream I was standing on the bank of the Nile, ¹⁸when out of the river there came up seven cows, fat and sleek, and they grazed among the reeds. ¹⁹After them, seven other cows came up—scrawny and very ugly and lean. I had never seen such ugly cows in all the land of Egypt. ²⁰The lean, ugly cows ate up the seven fat cows that came up first. ²¹But even after they ate them, no one could tell that they had done so; they looked just as ugly as before. Then I woke up.

²²"In my dreams I also saw seven heads of grain, full and good, growing on a single stalk. ²³After them, seven other heads sprouted—withered and thin and scorched by the east wind. ²⁴The thin heads of grain swallowed up the seven good heads. I told this to the magicians, but none could explain it to me."

²⁵Then Joseph said to Pharaoh, "The dreams of Pharaoh are one and the same. God has revealed to Pharaoh what he is about to do. ²⁶The seven good cows are seven years, and the seven good heads of grain are seven years; it is one and the same dream. ²⁷The seven lean, ugly cows that came up afterward are seven years, and so are the seven worthless heads of grain scorched by the east wind: They are seven years of famine.

²⁸"It is just as I said to Pharaoh: God has shown Pharaoh what he is about to do. ²⁹Seven years of great abundance are coming throughout the land of Egypt, ³⁰but seven years of famine will follow them. Then all the abundance in Egypt will be forgotten, and the famine will ravage the land. ³¹The abundance in the land will not be remembered, because the famine that follows it will be so severe. ³²The reason the dream was given to Pharaoh in two forms is that the matter

has been firmly decided by God, and God will do it soon.

³³"And now let Pharaoh look for a discerning and wise man and put him in charge of the land of Egypt. ³⁴Let Pharaoh appoint commissioners over the land to take a fifth of the harvest of Egypt during the seven years of abundance. ³⁵They should collect all the food of these good years that are coming and store up the grain under the authority of Pharaoh, to be kept in the cities for food. ³⁶This food should be held in reserve for the country, to be used during the seven years of famine that will come upon Egypt, so that the country may not be ruined by the famine."

³⁷The plan seemed good to Pharaoh and to all his officials. ³⁸So Pharaoh asked them, "Can we find anyone like this man, one in whom is the spirit of Godᵇ?"

³⁹Then Pharaoh said to Joseph, "Since God has made all this known to you, there is no one so discerning and wise as you. ⁴⁰You shall be in charge of my palace, and all my people are to submit to your orders. Only with respect to the throne will I be greater than you."

Joseph in Charge of Egypt

⁴¹So Pharaoh said to Joseph, "I hereby put you in charge of the whole land of Egypt." ⁴²Then Pharaoh took his signet ring from his finger and put it on Joseph's finger. He dressed him in robes of fine linen and put a gold chain around his neck. ⁴³He had him ride in a chariot as his second-in-command,ᶜ and men shouted before him, "Make wayᵈ!" Thus he put him in charge of the whole land of Egypt.

⁴⁴Then Pharaoh said to Joseph, "I am Pharaoh, but without your word no one will lift hand or foot in all Egypt." ⁴⁵Pharaoh gave Joseph the name Zaphenath-Paneah and gave him Asenath daughter of Potiphera, priest of On,ᵉ to be his wife. And Joseph went throughout the land of Egypt.

⁴⁶Joseph was thirty years old when he entered the service of Pharaoh king of Egypt. And Joseph went out from Pharaoh's presence and traveled throughout Egypt. ⁴⁷During the seven years of abun-

ᵃ13 Or *impaled*   ᵇ38 Or *of the gods*   ᶜ43 Or *in the chariot of his second-in-command*; or *in his second chariot*   ᵈ43 Or *Bow down*   ᵉ45 That is, Heliopolis; also in verse 50 dance the land produced plentifully. **48**Joseph collected all the food produced in those seven years of abundance in Egypt and stored it in the cities. In each city he put the food grown in the fields surrounding it. **49**Joseph stored up huge quantities of grain, like the sand of the sea; it was so much that he stopped keeping records because it was beyond measure.

50Before the years of famine came, two sons were born to Joseph by Asenath daughter of Potiphera, priest of On. **51**Joseph named his firstborn Manasseh*a* and said, "It is because God has made me forget all my trouble and all my father's household." **52**The second son he named Ephraim*b* and said, "It is because God has made me fruitful in the land of my suffering."

53The seven years of abundance in Egypt came to an end, **54**and the seven years of famine began, just as Joseph had said. There was famine in all the other lands, but in the whole land of Egypt there was food. **55**When all Egypt began to feel the famine, the people cried to Pharaoh for food. Then Pharaoh told all the Egyptians, "Go to Joseph and do what he tells you."

56When the famine had spread over the whole country, Joseph opened the storehouses and sold grain to the Egyptians, for the famine was severe throughout Egypt. **57**And all the countries came to Egypt to buy grain from Joseph, because the famine was severe in all the world.

Joseph's Brothers Go to Egypt

42 When Jacob learned that there was grain in Egypt, he said to his sons, "Why do you just keep looking at each other?" **2**He continued, "I have heard that there is grain in Egypt. Go down there and buy some for us, so that we may live and not die."

3Then ten of Joseph's brothers went down to buy grain from Egypt. **4**But Jacob did not send Benjamin, Joseph's brother, with the others, because he was afraid that harm might come to him. **5**So Israel's sons were among those who went to buy grain, for the famine was in the land of Canaan also.

6Now Joseph was the governor of the land, the one who sold grain to all its people. So when Joseph's brothers arrived, they bowed down to him with their faces to the ground. **7**As soon as Joseph saw his brothers, he recognized them, but he pretended to be a stranger and spoke harshly to them. "Where do you come from?" he asked.

"From the land of Canaan," they replied, "to buy food."

8Although Joseph recognized his brothers, they did not recognize him. **9**Then he remembered his dreams about them and said to them, "You are spies! You have come to see where our land is unprotected."

10"No, my lord," they answered. "Your servants have come to buy food. **11**We are all the sons of one man. Your servants are honest men, not spies."

12"No!" he said to them. "You have come to see where our land is unprotected."

13But they replied, "Your servants were twelve brothers, the sons of one man, who lives in the land of Canaan. The youngest is now with our father, and one is no more."

14Joseph said to them, "It is just as I told you: You are spies! **15**And this is how you will be tested: As surely as Pharaoh lives, you will not leave this place unless your youngest brother comes here. **16**Send one of your number to get your brother; the rest of you will be kept in prison, so that your words may be tested to see if you are telling the truth. If you are not, then as surely as Pharaoh lives, you are spies!" **17**And he put them all in custody for three days.

18On the third day, Joseph said to them, "Do this and you will live, for I fear God: **19**If you are honest men, let one of your brothers stay here in prison, while the rest of you go and take grain back for your starving households. **20**But you must bring your youngest brother to me, so that your words may be verified and that you may not die." This they proceeded to do.

21They said to one another, "Surely we are being punished because of our brother. We saw how distressed he was when he pleaded with us for his life, but we would not listen; that's why this distress has come upon us."

22Reuben replied, "Didn't I tell you not to sin against the boy? But you wouldn't listen! Now we must give an accounting

---

a 51 Manasseh sounds like and may be derived from the Hebrew for *forget.*   *b 52 Ephraim* sounds like the Hebrew for *twice fruitful.*

for his blood." ²³They did not realize that Joseph could understand them, since he was using an interpreter.

²⁴He turned away from them and began to weep, but then turned back and spoke to them again. He had Simeon taken from them and bound before their eyes.

²⁵Joseph gave orders to fill their bags with grain, to put each man's silver back in his sack, and to give them provisions for their journey. After this was done for them, ²⁶they loaded their grain on their donkeys and left.

²⁷At the place where they stopped for the night one of them opened his sack to get feed for his donkey, and he saw his silver in the mouth of his sack. ²⁸"My silver has been returned," he said to his brothers. "Here it is in my sack."

Their hearts sank and they turned to each other trembling and said, "What is this that God has done to us?"

²⁹When they came to their father Jacob in the land of Canaan, they told him all that had happened to them. They said, ³⁰"The man who is lord over the land spoke harshly to us and treated us as though we were spying on the land. ³¹But we said to him, 'We are honest men; we are not spies. ³²We were twelve brothers, sons of one father. One is no more, and

FRIDAY

Read Genesis 42:1–38
Key Verse Genesis 42:28

Looking Over My Shoulder — Shaunda McQueeney

I wonder if, after selling their brother Joseph to slave traders, Jacob's sons lived in agony. Maybe they looked anxiously over their shoulders for years, watching for God to come and strike them down. Or maybe they stuffed their fear deep inside. In any case, the fear that raced through them when Pharaoh's men uncovered silver in their sacks stemmed from guilt: "Surely we are being punished because of our brother" (Genesis 42:21). God had finally caught up with them!

Sometimes I, too, worry about God's judgment. There are Bible passages that thunder with judgment (see Isaiah 30:30; Lamentations 2:2; Ezekiel 7:3). God takes sin seriously, and he deals with sinners in serious ways. His holiness is awesome, majestic and totally without compromise.

But what I need to remember, and what Jacob's sons didn't yet understand about God, is that although he is infinitely holy, he is also infinitely good. While the sons of Jacob thought God was waiting to punish them, in reality he was waiting patiently for them to face their wrongdoing and admit it honestly. He yearned to shower his love and forgiveness on them if they just would ask for it.

God could destroy me in a moment if he wished. But he doesn't. I don't have to look over my shoulder waiting for God to punish me for deceit or meanness, jealousy or even selling my little brother to slave traders (as tempting as that sometimes seems). God has already punished someone—Jesus—for those sins. He just wants me to stop looking over my shoulder and believe that he forgives me and wants me to live in him day by day.

A Deeper Look
Psalm 103:9–12; Matthew 23:37; 1 John 1:9

Go to page 59 for your next devotional reading.

the youngest is now with our father in Canaan.'

33"Then the man who is lord over the land said to us, 'This is how I will know whether you are honest men: Leave one of your brothers here with me, and take food for your starving households and go. 34But bring your youngest brother to me so I will know that you are not spies but honest men. Then I will give your brother back to you, and you can trade*a* in the land.' "

35As they were emptying their sacks, there in each man's sack was his pouch of silver! When they and their father saw the money pouches, they were frightened. 36Their father Jacob said to them, "You have deprived me of my children. Joseph is no more and Simeon is no more, and now you want to take Benjamin. Everything is against me!"

37Then Reuben said to his father, "You may put both of my sons to death if I do not bring him back to you. Entrust him to my care, and I will bring him back."

38But Jacob said, "My son will not go down there with you; his brother is dead and he is the only one left. If harm comes to him on the journey you are taking, you will bring my gray head down to the grave*b* in sorrow."

The Second Journey to Egypt

43 Now the famine was still severe in the land. 2So when they had eaten all the grain they had brought from Egypt, their father said to them, "Go back and buy us a little more food."

3But Judah said to him, "The man warned us solemnly, 'You will not see my face again unless your brother is with you.' 4If you will send our brother along with us, we will go down and buy food for you. 5But if you will not send him, we will not go down, because the man said to us, 'You will not see my face again unless your brother is with you.' "

6Israel asked, "Why did you bring this trouble on me by telling the man you had another brother?"

7They replied, "The man questioned us closely about ourselves and our family. 'Is your father still living?' he asked us. 'Do you have another brother?' We simply answered his questions. How were we to know he would say, 'Bring your brother down here'?"

8Then Judah said to Israel his father, "Send the boy along with me and we will go at once, so that we and you and our children may live and not die. 9I myself will guarantee his safety; you can hold me personally responsible for him. If I do not bring him back to you and set him here before you, I will bear the blame before you all my life. 10As it is, if we had not delayed, we could have gone and returned twice."

11Then their father Israel said to them, "If it must be, then do this: Put some of the best products of the land in your bags and take them down to the man as a gift—a little balm and a little honey, some spices and myrrh, some pistachio nuts and almonds. 12Take double the amount of silver with you, for you must return the silver that was put back into the mouths of your sacks. Perhaps it was a mistake. 13Take your brother also and go back to the man at once. 14And may God Almighty*c* grant you mercy before the man so that he will let your other brother and Benjamin come back with you. As for me, if I am bereaved, I am bereaved."

15So the men took the gifts and double the amount of silver, and Benjamin also. They hurried down to Egypt and presented themselves to Joseph. 16When Joseph saw Benjamin with them, he said to the steward of his house, "Take these men to my house, slaughter an animal and prepare dinner; they are to eat with me at noon."

17The man did as Joseph told him and took the men to Joseph's house. 18Now the men were frightened when they were taken to his house. They thought, "We were brought here because of the silver that was put back into our sacks the first time. He wants to attack us and overpower us and seize us as slaves and take our donkeys."

19So they went up to Joseph's steward and spoke to him at the entrance to the house. 20"Please, sir," they said, "we came down here the first time to buy food. 21But at the place where we stopped for the night we opened our sacks and each of us found his silver—the exact weight—in the mouth of his sack. So we have brought it back with us. 22We have also brought additional silver with us to buy food. We don't know who put our silver in our sacks."

---

*a*34 Or *move about freely*   *b*38 Hebrew *Sheol*
*c*14 Hebrew *El-Shaddai*

²³"It's all right," he said. "Don't be afraid. Your God, the God of your father, has given you treasure in your sacks; I received your silver." Then he brought Simeon out to them.

²⁴The steward took the men into Joseph's house, gave them water to wash their feet and provided fodder for their donkeys. ²⁵They prepared their gifts for Joseph's arrival at noon, because they had heard that they were to eat there.

²⁶When Joseph came home, they presented to him the gifts they had brought into the house, and they bowed down before him to the ground. ²⁷He asked them how they were, and then he said, "How is your aged father you told me about? Is he still living?"

²⁸They replied, "Your servant our father is still alive and well." And they bowed low to pay him honor.

²⁹As he looked about and saw his brother Benjamin, his own mother's son, he asked, "Is this your youngest brother, the one you told me about?" And he said, "God be gracious to you, my son." ³⁰Deeply moved at the sight of his brother, Joseph hurried out and looked for a place to weep. He went into his private room and wept there.

³¹After he had washed his face, he came out and, controlling himself, said, "Serve the food."

³²They served him by himself, the brothers by themselves, and the Egyptians who ate with him by themselves, because Egyptians could not eat with Hebrews, for that is detestable to Egyptians. ³³The men had been seated before him in the order of their ages, from the firstborn to the youngest; and they looked at each other in astonishment. ³⁴When portions were served to them from Joseph's table, Benjamin's portion was five times as much as anyone else's. So they feasted and drank freely with him.

A Silver Cup in a Sack

44 Now Joseph gave these instructions to the steward of his house: "Fill the men's sacks with as much food as they can carry, and put each man's silver in the mouth of his sack. ²Then put my cup, the silver one, in the mouth of the youngest one's sack, along with the silver for his grain." And he did as Joseph said.

³As morning dawned, the men were sent on their way with their donkeys. ⁴They had not gone far from the city when Joseph said to his steward, "Go after those men at once, and when you catch up with them, say to them, 'Why have you repaid good with evil? ⁵Isn't this the cup my master drinks from and also uses for divination? This is a wicked thing you have done.' "

⁶When he caught up with them, he repeated these words to them. ⁷But they said to him, "Why does my lord say such things? Far be it from your servants to do anything like that! ⁸We even brought back to you from the land of Canaan the silver we found inside the mouths of our sacks. So why would we steal silver or gold from your master's house? ⁹If any of your servants is found to have it, he will die; and the rest of us will become my lord's slaves."

¹⁰"Very well, then," he said, "let it be as you say. Whoever is found to have it will become my slave; the rest of you will be free from blame."

¹¹Each of them quickly lowered his sack to the ground and opened it. ¹²Then the steward proceeded to search, beginning with the oldest and ending with the youngest. And the cup was found in Benjamin's sack. ¹³At this, they tore their clothes. Then they all loaded their donkeys and returned to the city.

¹⁴Joseph was still in the house when Judah and his brothers came in, and they threw themselves to the ground before him. ¹⁵Joseph said to them, "What is this you have done? Don't you know that a man like me can find things out by divination?"

¹⁶"What can we say to my lord?" Judah replied. "What can we say? How can we prove our innocence? God has uncovered your servants' guilt. We are now my lord's slaves—we ourselves and the one who was found to have the cup."

¹⁷But Joseph said, "Far be it from me to do such a thing! Only the man who was found to have the cup will become my slave. The rest of you, go back to your father in peace."

¹⁸Then Judah went up to him and said: "Please, my lord, let your servant speak a word to my lord. Do not be angry with your servant, though you are equal to Pharaoh himself. ¹⁹My lord asked his servants, 'Do you have a father or a brother?' ²⁰And we answered, 'We have an aged father, and there is a young son born to him in his old age. His brother is dead, and he is the only one of his moth-

er's sons left, and his father loves him.'
21"Then you said to your servants,
'Bring him down to me so I can see him
for myself.' 22And we said to my lord,
'The boy cannot leave his father; if he
leaves him, his father will die.' 23But you
told your servants, 'Unless your youngest
brother comes down with you, you will
not see my face again.' 24When we went
back to your servant my father, we told
him what my lord had said.

25"Then our father said, 'Go back and
buy a little more food.' 26But we said,
'We cannot go down. Only if our youngest brother is with us will we go. We
cannot see the man's face unless our
youngest brother is with us.'

27"Your servant my father said to us,
'You know that my wife bore me two
sons. 28One of them went away from me,
and I said, "He has surely been torn to
pieces." And I have not seen him since.
29If you take this one from me too and
harm comes to him, you will bring my
gray head down to the grave*a* in misery.'

30"So now, if the boy is not with us
when I go back to your servant my father
and if my father, whose life is closely
bound up with the boy's life, 31sees that
the boy isn't there, he will die. Your servants will bring the gray head of our father down to the grave in sorrow. 32Your
servant guaranteed the boy's safety to my
father. I said, 'If I do not bring him back
to you, I will bear the blame before you,
my father, all my life!'

33"Now then, please let your servant
remain here as my lord's slave in place of
the boy, and let the boy return with his
brothers. 34How can I go back to my father if the boy is not with me? No! Do not
let me see the misery that would come
upon my father."

Joseph Makes Himself Known

45 Then Joseph could no longer control
himself before all his attendants, and
he cried out, "Have everyone leave my
presence!" So there was no one with Joseph when he made himself known to his
brothers. 2And he wept so loudly that the
Egyptians heard him, and Pharaoh's
household heard about it.

3Joseph said to his brothers, "I am Joseph! Is my father still living?" But his
brothers were not able to answer him,
because they were terrified at his presence.

4Then Joseph said to his brothers,
"Come close to me." When they had
done so, he said, "I am your brother Joseph, the one you sold into Egypt! 5And
now, do not be distressed and do not be
angry with yourselves for selling me
here, because it was to save lives that
God sent me ahead of you. 6For two years
now there has been famine in the land,
and for the next five years there will not
be plowing and reaping. 7But God sent
me ahead of you to preserve for you a
remnant on earth and to save your lives
by a great deliverance.*b*

8"So then, it was not you who sent me
here, but God. He made me father to
Pharaoh, lord of his entire household and
ruler of all Egypt. 9Now hurry back to my
father and say to him, 'This is what your
son Joseph says: God has made me lord
of all Egypt. Come down to me; don't delay. 10You shall live in the region of Goshen and be near me—you, your children and grandchildren, your flocks and
herds, and all you have. 11I will provide
for you there, because five years of famine are still to come. Otherwise you and
your household and all who belong to
you will become destitute.'

12"You can see for yourselves, and so
can my brother Benjamin, that it is really
I who am speaking to you. 13Tell my father about all the honor accorded me in
Egypt and about everything you have
seen. And bring my father down here
quickly."

14Then he threw his arms around his
brother Benjamin and wept, and Benjamin embraced him, weeping. 15And he
kissed all his brothers and wept over
them. Afterward his brothers talked with
him.

16When the news reached Pharaoh's
palace that Joseph's brothers had come,
Pharaoh and all his officials were
pleased. 17Pharaoh said to Joseph, "Tell
your brothers, 'Do this: Load your animals and return to the land of Canaan,
18and bring your father and your families
back to me. I will give you the best of the
land of Egypt and you can enjoy the fat of
the land.'

19"You are also directed to tell them,
'Do this: Take some carts from Egypt for
your children and your wives, and get
your father and come. 20Never mind

---

*a29 Hebrew Sheol; also in verse 31   b7 Or save
you as a great band of survivors*

about your belongings, because the best of all Egypt will be yours.' "

²¹So the sons of Israel did this. Joseph gave them carts, as Pharaoh had commanded, and he also gave them provisions for their journey. ²²To each of them he gave new clothing, but to Benjamin he gave three hundred shekels*a* of silver and five sets of clothes. ²³And this is what he sent to his father: ten donkeys loaded with the best things of Egypt, and ten female donkeys loaded with grain and bread and other provisions for his journey. ²⁴Then he sent his brothers away, and as they were leaving he said to them, "Don't quarrel on the way!"

²⁵So they went up out of Egypt and came to their father Jacob in the land of Canaan. ²⁶They told him, "Joseph is still alive! In fact, he is ruler of all Egypt." Jacob was stunned; he did not believe them. ²⁷But when they told him everything Joseph had said to them, and when he saw the carts Joseph had sent to carry him back, the spirit of their father Jacob revived. ²⁸And Israel said, "I'm convinced! My son Joseph is still alive. I will go and see him before I die."

Jacob Goes to Egypt

46 So Israel set out with all that was his, and when he reached Beersheba, he offered sacrifices to the God of his father Isaac.

²And God spoke to Israel in a vision at night and said, "Jacob! Jacob!"

"Here I am," he replied.

³"I am God, the God of your father," he said. "Do not be afraid to go down to Egypt, for I will make you into a great nation there. ⁴I will go down to Egypt with you, and I will surely bring you back again. And Joseph's own hand will close your eyes."

⁵Then Jacob left Beersheba, and Israel's sons took their father Jacob and their children and their wives in the carts that Pharaoh had sent to transport him. ⁶They also took with them their livestock and the possessions they had acquired in Canaan, and Jacob and all his offspring went to Egypt. ⁷He took with him to Egypt his sons and grandsons and his daughters and granddaughters—all his offspring.

⁸These are the names of the sons of Israel (Jacob and his descendants) who went to Egypt:

Reuben the firstborn of Jacob.
⁹The sons of Reuben:
  Hanoch, Pallu, Hezron and Carmi.
¹⁰The sons of Simeon:
  Jemuel, Jamin, Ohad, Jakin, Zohar and Shaul the son of a Canaanite woman.
¹¹The sons of Levi:
  Gershon, Kohath and Merari.
¹²The sons of Judah:
  Er, Onan, Shelah, Perez and Zerah (but Er and Onan had died in the land of Canaan).
  The sons of Perez:
  Hezron and Hamul.
¹³The sons of Issachar:
  Tola, Puah,*b* Jashub*c* and Shimron.
¹⁴The sons of Zebulun:
  Sered, Elon and Jahleel.
¹⁵These were the sons Leah bore to Jacob in Paddan Aram,*d* besides his daughter Dinah. These sons and daughters of his were thirty-three in all.

¹⁶The sons of Gad:
  Zephon,*e* Haggi, Shuni, Ezbon, Eri, Arodi and Areli.
¹⁷The sons of Asher:
  Imnah, Ishvah, Ishvi and Beriah.

a22 That is, about 7 1/2 pounds (about 3.5 kilograms)   *b13* Samaritan Pentateuch and Syriac (see also 1 Chron. 7:1); Masoretic Text *Puvah*   *c13* Samaritan Pentateuch and some Septuagint manuscripts (see also Num. 26:24 and 1 Chron. 7:1); Masoretic Text *Iob*   *d15* That is, Northwest Mesopotamia   *e16* Samaritan Pentateuch and Septuagint (see also Num. 26:15); Masoretic Text *Ziphion*

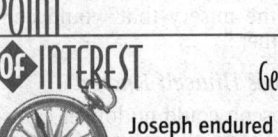

POINT OF INTEREST

Genesis 45:14-15

Joseph endured many injustices. He was sold into slavery, falsely accused by Potiphar's wife, forgotten and left in jail—all because of his brothers' jealousy. But Joseph was able to forgive them because he viewed these events from a faith-filled perspective. We are able to forgive others when we know that God is at work in all of our circumstances (see Romans 8:28).

Their sister was Serah.
The sons of Beriah:
  Heber and Malkiel.
18These were the children born to Jacob by Zilpah, whom Laban had given to his daughter Leah—sixteen in all.

19The sons of Jacob's wife Rachel:
  Joseph and Benjamin. **20**In Egypt, Manasseh and Ephraim were born to Joseph by Asenath daughter of Potiphera, priest of On.*ᵃ*
21The sons of Benjamin:
  Bela, Beker, Ashbel, Gera, Naaman, Ehi, Rosh, Muppim, Huppim and Ard.
22These were the sons of Rachel who were born to Jacob—fourteen in all.

23The son of Dan:
  Hushim.
24The sons of Naphtali:
  Jahziel, Guni, Jezer and Shillem.
25These were the sons born to Jacob by Bilhah, whom Laban had given to his daughter Rachel—seven in all.

26All those who went to Egypt with Jacob—those who were his direct descendants, not counting his sons' wives—numbered sixty-six persons. **27**With the two sons*ᵇ* who had been born to Joseph in Egypt, the members of Jacob's family, which went to Egypt, were seventy*ᶜ* in all.

28Now Jacob sent Judah ahead of him to Joseph to get directions to Goshen. When they arrived in the region of Goshen, **29**Joseph had his chariot made ready and went to Goshen to meet his father Israel. As soon as Joseph appeared before him, he threw his arms around his father*ᵈ* and wept for a long time.
30Israel said to Joseph, "Now I am ready to die, since I have seen for myself that you are still alive."
31Then Joseph said to his brothers and to his father's household, "I will go up and speak to Pharaoh and will say to him, 'My brothers and my father's household, who were living in the land of Canaan, have come to me. **32**The men are shepherds; they tend livestock, and they have brought along their flocks and herds and everything they own.' **33**When Pharaoh calls you in and asks, 'What is your occupation?' **34**you should answer, 'Your servants have tended livestock from our boyhood on, just as our fathers did.'

Then you will be allowed to settle in the region of Goshen, for all shepherds are detestable to the Egyptians."

47 Joseph went and told Pharaoh, "My father and brothers, with their flocks and herds and everything they own, have come from the land of Canaan and are now in Goshen." **2**He chose five of his brothers and presented them before Pharaoh.

3Pharaoh asked the brothers, "What is your occupation?"

"Your servants are shepherds," they replied to Pharaoh, "just as our fathers were." **4**They also said to him, "We have come to live here awhile, because the famine is severe in Canaan and your servants' flocks have no pasture. So now, please let your servants settle in Goshen."

5Pharaoh said to Joseph, "Your father and your brothers have come to you, **6**and the land of Egypt is before you; settle your father and your brothers in the best part of the land. Let them live in Goshen. And if you know of any among them with special ability, put them in charge of my own livestock."

7Then Joseph brought his father Jacob in and presented him before Pharaoh. After Jacob blessed*ᵉ* Pharaoh, **8**Pharaoh asked him, "How old are you?"

9And Jacob said to Pharaoh, "The years of my pilgrimage are a hundred and thirty. My years have been few and difficult, and they do not equal the years of the pilgrimage of my fathers." **10**Then Jacob blessed*ᶠ* Pharaoh and went out from his presence.

11So Joseph settled his father and his brothers in Egypt and gave them property in the best part of the land, the district of Rameses, as Pharaoh directed. **12**Joseph also provided his father and his brothers and all his father's household with food, according to the number of their children.

Joseph and the Famine

13There was no food, however, in the whole region because the famine was severe; both Egypt and Canaan wasted away because of the famine. **14**Joseph collected all the money that was to be

---

ᵃ20 That is, Heliopolis   *ᵇ27* Hebrew; Septuagint *the nine children*   *ᶜ27* Hebrew (see also Exodus 1:5 and footnote); Septuagint (see also Acts 7:14) *seventy-five*   *ᵈ29* Hebrew *around him*   *ᵉ7* Or *greeted*   *ᶠ10* Or *said farewell to* found in Egypt and Canaan in payment for the grain they were buying, and he brought it to Pharaoh's palace. ¹⁵When the money of the people of Egypt and Canaan was gone, all Egypt came to Joseph and said, "Give us food. Why should we die before your eyes? Our money is used up."

¹⁶"Then bring your livestock," said Joseph. "I will sell you food in exchange for your livestock, since your money is gone." ¹⁷So they brought their livestock to Joseph, and he gave them food in exchange for their horses, their sheep and goats, their cattle and donkeys. And he brought them through that year with food in exchange for all their livestock.

¹⁸When that year was over, they came to him the following year and said, "We cannot hide from our lord the fact that since our money is gone and our livestock belongs to you, there is nothing left for our lord except our bodies and our land. ¹⁹Why should we perish before your eyes—we and our land as well? Buy us and our land in exchange for food, and we with our land will be in bondage to Pharaoh. Give us seed so that we may live and not die, and that the land may not become desolate."

²⁰So Joseph bought all the land in Egypt for Pharaoh. The Egyptians, one and all, sold their fields, because the famine was too severe for them. The land became Pharaoh's, ²¹and Joseph reduced the people to servitude,ᵃ from one end of Egypt to the other. ²²However, he did not buy the land of the priests, because they received a regular allotment from Pharaoh and had food enough from the allotment Pharaoh gave them. That is why they did not sell their land.

²³Joseph said to the people, "Now that I have bought you and your land today for Pharaoh, here is seed for you so you can plant the ground. ²⁴But when the crop comes in, give a fifth of it to Pharaoh. The other four-fifths you may keep as seed for the fields and as food for yourselves and your households and your children."

²⁵"You have saved our lives," they said. "May we find favor in the eyes of our lord; we will be in bondage to Pharaoh."

²⁶So Joseph established it as a law concerning land in Egypt—still in force today—that a fifth of the produce belongs to Pharaoh. It was only the land of the priests that did not become Pharaoh's.

²⁷Now the Israelites settled in Egypt in the region of Goshen. They acquired property there and were fruitful and increased greatly in number.

²⁸Jacob lived in Egypt seventeen years, and the years of his life were a hundred and forty-seven. ²⁹When the time drew near for Israel to die, he called for his son Joseph and said to him, "If I have found favor in your eyes, put your hand under my thigh and promise that you will show me kindness and faithfulness. Do not bury me in Egypt, ³⁰but when I rest with my fathers, carry me out of Egypt and bury me where they are buried."

"I will do as you say," he said.

³¹"Swear to me," he said. Then Joseph swore to him, and Israel worshiped as he leaned on the top of his staff.ᵇ

Manasseh and Ephraim

48 Some time later Joseph was told, "Your father is ill." So he took his two sons Manasseh and Ephraim along with him. ²When Jacob was told, "Your son Joseph has come to you," Israel rallied his strength and sat up on the bed.

³Jacob said to Joseph, "God Almightyᶜ appeared to me at Luz in the land of Canaan, and there he blessed me ⁴and said to me, 'I am going to make you fruitful and will increase your numbers. I will make you a community of peoples, and I will give this land as an everlasting possession to your descendants after you.'

⁵"Now then, your two sons born to you in Egypt before I came to you here will be reckoned as mine; Ephraim and Manasseh will be mine, just as Reuben and Simeon are mine. ⁶Any children born to you after them will be yours; in the territory they inherit they will be reckoned under the names of their brothers. ⁷As I was returning from Paddan,ᵈ to my sorrow Rachel died in the land of Canaan while we were still on the way, a little distance from Ephrath. So I buried her there beside the road to Ephrath" (that is, Bethlehem).

⁸When Israel saw the sons of Joseph, he asked, "Who are these?"

ᵃ21 Samaritan Pentateuch and Septuagint (see also Vulgate); Masoretic Text *and he moved the people into the cities*   ᵇ31 Or *Israel bowed down at the head of his bed*   ᶜ3 Hebrew *El-Shaddai*   ᵈ7 That is, Northwest Mesopotamia

9"They are the sons God has given me here," Joseph said to his father.

Then Israel said, "Bring them to me so I may bless them."

10Now Israel's eyes were failing because of old age, and he could hardly see. So Joseph brought his sons close to him, and his father kissed them and embraced them.

11Israel said to Joseph, "I never expected to see your face again, and now God has allowed me to see your children too."

12Then Joseph removed them from Israel's knees and bowed down with his face to the ground. 13And Joseph took both of them, Ephraim on his right toward Israel's left hand and Manasseh on his left toward Israel's right hand, and brought them close to him. 14But Israel reached out his right hand and put it on Ephraim's head, though he was the younger, and crossing his arms, he put his left hand on Manasseh's head, even though Manasseh was the firstborn.

15Then he blessed Joseph and said,

"May the God before whom my
     fathers
    Abraham and Isaac walked,
the God who has been my shepherd
    all my life to this day,
16the Angel who has delivered me from
     all harm
—may he bless these boys.
May they be called by my name
    and the names of my fathers
     Abraham and Isaac,
and may they increase greatly
    upon the earth."

17When Joseph saw his father placing his right hand on Ephraim's head he was displeased; so he took hold of his father's hand to move it from Ephraim's head to Manasseh's head. 18Joseph said to him, "No, my father, this one is the firstborn; put your right hand on his head."

19But his father refused and said, "I know, my son, I know. He too will become a people, and he too will become great. Nevertheless, his younger brother will be greater than he, and his descendants will become a group of nations." 20He blessed them that day and said,

"In your*a* name will Israel
    pronounce this blessing:
    'May God make you like Ephraim
     and Manasseh.' "

So he put Ephraim ahead of Manasseh.

21Then Israel said to Joseph, "I am about to die, but God will be with you*b* and take you*b* back to the land of your*b* fathers. 22And to you, as one who is over your brothers, I give the ridge of land*c* I took from the Amorites with my sword and my bow."

Jacob Blesses His Sons

49 Then Jacob called for his sons and said: "Gather around so I can tell you what will happen to you in days to come.

2"Assemble and listen, sons of Jacob;
    listen to your father Israel.

3"Reuben, you are my firstborn,
    my might, the first sign of my
     strength,
    excelling in honor, excelling in
     power.
4Turbulent as the waters, you will no
     longer excel,
    for you went up onto your father's
     bed,
    onto my couch and defiled it.

5"Simeon and Levi are brothers—
    their swords*d* are weapons of
     violence.
6Let me not enter their council,
    let me not join their assembly,
for they have killed men in their
     anger
    and hamstrung oxen as they
     pleased.
7Cursed be their anger, so fierce,
    and their fury, so cruel!
I will scatter them in Jacob
    and disperse them in Israel.

8"Judah,*e* your brothers will praise
     you;
    your hand will be on the neck of
     your enemies;
    your father's sons will bow down
     to you.
9You are a lion's cub, O Judah;
    you return from the prey, my son.
Like a lion he crouches and lies
     down,
    like a lioness—who dares to rouse
     him?
10The scepter will not depart from
     Judah,

a20 The Hebrew is singular.   b21 The Hebrew is plural.   c22 Or And to you I give one portion more than to your brothers—the portion d5 The meaning of the Hebrew for this word is uncertain.   e8 Judah sounds like and may be derived from the Hebrew for praise.

nor the ruler's staff from between
his feet,
until he comes to whom it belongs[a]
and the obedience of the nations is
his.
11He will tether his donkey to a vine,
his colt to the choicest branch;
he will wash his garments in wine,
his robes in the blood of grapes.
12His eyes will be darker than wine,
his teeth whiter than milk.[b]

13"Zebulun will live by the seashore
and become a haven for ships;
his border will extend toward
Sidon.

14"Issachar is a rawboned[c] donkey
lying down between two
saddlebags.[d]
15When he sees how good is his resting
place
and how pleasant is his land,
he will bend his shoulder to the
burden
and submit to forced labor.

16"Dan[e] will provide justice for his
people
as one of the tribes of Israel.
17Dan will be a serpent by the
roadside,
a viper along the path,
that bites the horse's heels
so that its rider tumbles backward.

18"I look for your deliverance, O LORD.

19"Gad[f] will be attacked by a band of
raiders,
but he will attack them at their
heels.

20"Asher's food will be rich;
he will provide delicacies fit for a
king.

21"Naphtali is a doe set free
that bears beautiful fawns.[g]

22"Joseph is a fruitful vine,
a fruitful vine near a spring,
whose branches climb over a
wall.[h]
23With bitterness archers attacked him;
they shot at him with hostility.
24But his bow remained steady,
his strong arms stayed[i] limber,
because of the hand of the Mighty
One of Jacob,
because of the Shepherd, the Rock
of Israel,

25because of your father's God, who
helps you,
because of the Almighty,[j] who
blesses you
with blessings of the heavens above,
blessings of the deep that lies
below,
blessings of the breast and womb.
26Your father's blessings are greater
than the blessings of the ancient
mountains,
than[k] the bounty of the age-old
hills.
Let all these rest on the head of
Joseph,
on the brow of the prince among[l]
his brothers.

27"Benjamin is a ravenous wolf;
in the morning he devours the
prey,
in the evening he divides the
plunder."

28All these are the twelve tribes of Israel, and this is what their father said to
them when he blessed them, giving each
the blessing appropriate to him.

The Death of Jacob

29Then he gave them these instructions: "I am about to be gathered to my
people. Bury me with my fathers in the
cave in the field of Ephron the Hittite,
30the cave in the field of Machpelah, near
Mamre in Canaan, which Abraham
bought as a burial place from Ephron the
Hittite, along with the field. 31There
Abraham and his wife Sarah were buried,
there Isaac and his wife Rebekah were
buried, and there I buried Leah. 32The
field and the cave in it were bought from
the Hittites.[m] "

33When Jacob had finished giving instructions to his sons, he drew his feet up
into the bed, breathed his last and was
gathered to his people.

50 Joseph threw himself upon his father
and wept over him and kissed him.

a10 Or until Shiloh comes; or until he comes to
whom tribute belongs   b12 Or will be dull from
wine, / his teeth white from milk   c14 Or strong
d14 Or campfires   e16 Dan here means he
provides justice.   f19 Gad can mean attack
and band of raiders.   g21 Or free; / he utters
beautiful words   h22 Or Joseph is a wild colt, / a
wild colt near a spring, / a wild donkey on a
terraced hill   i23,24 Or archers will attack . . .
will shoot . . . will remain . . . will stay
j25 Hebrew Shaddai   k26 Or of my progenitors,
/ as great as   l26 Or the one separated from
m32 Or the sons of Heth

Read Genesis 49:29—50:26
Key Verse Genesis 50:20

A Different Look at Life's Struggles

Joseph knew the pain of life firsthand. Think about it . . . he was hated by his brothers, sold into slavery, imprisoned for rejecting the sexual advances of his master's wife and left to rot in jail. He had every reason to be angry with God, but he wasn't. Instead, he saw God working out his purposes in the unexplainable events of life. By the end of Joseph's story, we learn that God saved his people from starvation through Joseph's presence and position in Egypt. Joseph learned in a big way that God can take a terrible situation and make something good out of it!

Just as God was in control of all that happened to Joseph, he is in control of what happens to you. One key to gaining perspective on life's struggles is to grow in your understanding of God's character. Then, although you may not understand why you face the pain and struggles of daily life, you can trust in God's power, love and goodness. That was Joseph's anchor in his turbulent life, and it can also be yours!

Digging Into the Word
1. When tragedies strike close to home, we sometimes question why God would allow such things. How can what you read in Romans 8:28 strengthen you when something unexpected and difficult comes your way?
2. What impresses you about God's character as you read the following passages?—*Psalm 115:3; Psalm 119:68; 1 John 4:8*

Commit to Pray
Think of one person you know who is going through a time of struggle and pain. Pray that this person will be able to focus on the unchanging character of God. Let them know you are praying for them and, if appropriate, tell them what you learned about God's character from this study.

One Step Deeper
1 Samuel 2:6–8; 1 Chronicles 29:10–13

Go to page 64 for your next devotional reading.

²Then Joseph directed the physicians in his service to embalm his father Israel. So the physicians embalmed him, ³taking a full forty days, for that was the time required for embalming. And the Egyptians mourned for him seventy days.

⁴When the days of mourning had passed, Joseph said to Pharaoh's court, "If I have found favor in your eyes, speak to Pharaoh for me. Tell him, ⁵'My father made me swear an oath and said, "I am about to die; bury me in the tomb I dug for myself in the land of Canaan." Now let me go up and bury my father; then I will return.' "

⁶Pharaoh said, "Go up and bury your father, as he made you swear to do."

⁷So Joseph went up to bury his father. All Pharaoh's officials accompanied him—the dignitaries of his court and all the dignitaries of Egypt— ⁸besides all the members of Joseph's household and his brothers and those belonging to his father's household. Only their children and their flocks and herds were left in Goshen. ⁹Chariots and horsemen*a* also went up with him. It was a very large company.

¹⁰When they reached the threshing floor of Atad, near the Jordan, they lamented loudly and bitterly; and there Joseph observed a seven-day period of mourning for his father. ¹¹When the Canaanites who lived there saw the mourning at the threshing floor of Atad, they said, "The Egyptians are holding a solemn ceremony of mourning." That is why that place near the Jordan is called Abel Mizraim.*b*

¹²So Jacob's sons did as he had commanded them: ¹³They carried him to the land of Canaan and buried him in the cave in the field of Machpelah, near Mamre, which Abraham had bought as a burial place from Ephron the Hittite, along with the field. ¹⁴After burying his father, Joseph returned to Egypt, together with his brothers and all the others who had gone with him to bury his father.

Joseph Reassures His Brothers

¹⁵When Joseph's brothers saw that their father was dead, they said, "What if Joseph holds a grudge against us and pays us back for all the wrongs we did to him?" ¹⁶So they sent word to Joseph, saying, "Your father left these instructions before he died: ¹⁷'This is what you are to say to Joseph: I ask you to forgive your brothers the sins and the wrongs they committed in treating you so badly.' Now please forgive the sins of the servants of the God of your father." When their message came to him, Joseph wept.

¹⁸His brothers then came and threw themselves down before him. "We are your slaves," they said.

¹⁹But Joseph said to them, "Don't be afraid. Am I in the place of God? ²⁰You intended to harm me, but God intended it for good to accomplish what is now being done, the saving of many lives. ²¹So then, don't be afraid. I will provide for you and your children." And he reassured them and spoke kindly to them.

The Death of Joseph

²²Joseph stayed in Egypt, along with all his father's family. He lived a hundred and ten years ²³and saw the third generation of Ephraim's children. Also the children of Makir son of Manasseh were placed at birth on Joseph's knees.*c*

²⁴Then Joseph said to his brothers, "I am about to die. But God will surely come to your aid and take you up out of this land to the land he promised on oath to Abraham, Isaac and Jacob." ²⁵And Joseph made the sons of Israel swear an oath and said, "God will surely come to your aid, and then you must carry my bones up from this place."

²⁶So Joseph died at the age of a hundred and ten. And after they embalmed him, he was placed in a coffin in Egypt.

---

*a*9 Or *charioteers*   *b*11 *Abel Mizraim* means *mourning of the Egyptians.*   *c*23 That is, were counted as his

Ever wonder what it would be like to witness the parting of the Red Sea? To hear God speak from a burning bush? To see the glory of the Lord? Moses and the Israelites experience this and more in Exodus. The author Moses narrates these incredible stories and tells how God frees the Israelites from Egyptian slavery. He tells how God reveals himself to the people he loves and establishes his law—our foundation for worship and life. As you read Exodus, pay special attention to God's constant care for his people, and see how they respond.

EXODUS

The Israelites Oppressed

1 These are the names of the sons of Israel who went to Egypt with Jacob, each with his family: ²Reuben, Simeon, Levi and Judah; ³Issachar, Zebulun and Benjamin; ⁴Dan and Naphtali; Gad and Asher. ⁵The descendants of Jacob numbered seventy[a] in all; Joseph was already in Egypt.

⁶Now Joseph and all his brothers and all that generation died, ⁷but the Israelites were fruitful and multiplied greatly and became exceedingly numerous, so that the land was filled with them.

⁸Then a new king, who did not know about Joseph, came to power in Egypt. ⁹"Look," he said to his people, "the Israelites have become much too numerous for us. ¹⁰Come, we must deal shrewdly with them or they will become even more numerous and, if war breaks out, will join our enemies, fight against us and leave the country."

¹¹So they put slave masters over them to oppress them with forced labor, and they built Pithom and Rameses as store cities for Pharaoh. ¹²But the more they were oppressed, the more they multiplied and spread; so the Egyptians came to dread the Israelites ¹³and worked them ruthlessly. ¹⁴They made their lives bitter with hard labor in brick and mortar and

a5 Masoretic Text (see also Gen. 46:27); Dead Sea Scrolls and Septuagint (see also Acts 7:14 and note at Gen. 46:27) *seventy-five* with all kinds of work in the fields; in all their hard labor the Egyptians used them ruthlessly.

¹⁵The king of Egypt said to the Hebrew midwives, whose names were Shiphrah and Puah, ¹⁶"When you help the Hebrew women in childbirth and observe them on the delivery stool, if it is a boy, kill him; but if it is a girl, let her live." ¹⁷The midwives, however, feared God and did not do what the king of Egypt had told them to do; they let the boys live. ¹⁸Then the king of Egypt summoned the midwives and asked them, "Why have you done this? Why have you let the boys live?"

¹⁹The midwives answered Pharaoh, "Hebrew women are not like Egyptian women; they are vigorous and give birth before the midwives arrive."

²⁰So God was kind to the midwives and the people increased and became even more numerous. ²¹And because the midwives feared God, he gave them families of their own.

²²Then Pharaoh gave this order to all his people: "Every boy that is born*ᵃ* you must throw into the Nile, but let every girl live."

The Birth of Moses

2 Now a man of the house of Levi married a Levite woman, ²and she became pregnant and gave birth to a son. When she saw that he was a fine child, she hid him for three months. ³But when she could hide him no longer, she got a papyrus basket for him and coated it with tar and pitch. Then she placed the child in it and put it among the reeds along the bank of the Nile. ⁴His sister stood at a distance to see what would happen to him.

⁵Then Pharaoh's daughter went down to the Nile to bathe, and her attendants were walking along the river bank. She saw the basket among the reeds and sent her slave girl to get it. ⁶She opened it and saw the baby. He was crying, and she felt sorry for him. "This is one of the Hebrew babies," she said.

⁷Then his sister asked Pharaoh's daughter, "Shall I go and get one of the Hebrew women to nurse the baby for you?"

⁸"Yes, go," she answered. And the girl went and got the baby's mother. ⁹Pharaoh's daughter said to her, "Take this baby and nurse him for me, and I will pay

you." So the woman took the baby and nursed him. ¹⁰When the child grew older, she took him to Pharaoh's daughter and he became her son. She named him Moses,*ᵇ* saying, "I drew him out of the water."

Moses Flees to Midian

¹¹One day, after Moses had grown up, he went out to where his own people were and watched them at their hard labor. He saw an Egyptian beating a Hebrew, one of his own people. ¹²Glancing this way and that and seeing no one, he killed the Egyptian and hid him in the sand. ¹³The next day he went out and saw two Hebrews fighting. He asked the one in the wrong, "Why are you hitting your fellow Hebrew?"

¹⁴The man said, "Who made you ruler and judge over us? Are you thinking of killing me as you killed the Egyptian?" Then Moses was afraid and thought, "What I did must have become known."

¹⁵When Pharaoh heard of this, he tried to kill Moses, but Moses fled from Pharaoh and went to live in Midian, where he sat down by a well. ¹⁶Now a priest of Midian had seven daughters, and they came to draw water and fill the troughs to water their father's flock. ¹⁷Some shepherds came along and drove them away, but Moses got up and came to their rescue and watered their flock.

¹⁸When the girls returned to Reuel their father, he asked them, "Why have you returned so early today?"

ᵃ22 Masoretic Text; Samaritan Pentateuch, Septuagint and Targums *born to the Hebrews*
ᵇ10 Moses sounds like the Hebrew for *draw out.*

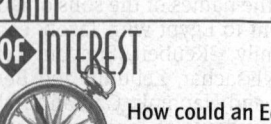

POINT OF INTEREST

Exodus 1:8

How could an Egyptian king not know who Joseph was? Long chronological gaps sometimes occur between significant events in the Biblical account. In this case, four hundred years pass between Exodus 1:6 (the end of the Joseph era) and Exodus 1:8. By that time, Joseph's amazing life had been relegated to an easily overlooked historical footnote, too small for this king to notice.

[19]They answered, "An Egyptian rescued us from the shepherds. He even drew water for us and watered the flock."

[20]"And where is he?" he asked his daughters. "Why did you leave him? Invite him to have something to eat."

[21]Moses agreed to stay with the man, who gave his daughter Zipporah to Moses in marriage. [22]Zipporah gave birth to a son, and Moses named him Gershom,[a] saying, "I have become an alien in a foreign land."

[23]During that long period, the king of Egypt died. The Israelites groaned in their slavery and cried out, and their cry for help because of their slavery went up to God. [24]God heard their groaning and he remembered his covenant with Abraham, with Isaac and with Jacob. [25]So God looked on the Israelites and was concerned about them.

Moses and the Burning Bush

3 Now Moses was tending the flock of Jethro his father-in-law, the priest of Midian, and he led the flock to the far side of the desert and came to Horeb, the mountain of God. [2]There the angel of the LORD appeared to him in flames of fire from within a bush. Moses saw that though the bush was on fire it did not burn up. [3]So Moses thought, "I will go over and see this strange sight—why the bush does not burn up."

[4]When the LORD saw that he had gone over to look, God called to him from within the bush, "Moses! Moses!"

And Moses said, "Here I am."

[5]"Do not come any closer," God said. "Take off your sandals, for the place where you are standing is holy ground." [6]Then he said, "I am the God of your father, the God of Abraham, the God of Isaac and the God of Jacob." At this, Moses hid his face, because he was afraid to look at God.

[7]The LORD said, "I have indeed seen the misery of my people in Egypt. I have heard them crying out because of their slave drivers, and I am concerned about their suffering. [8]So I have come down to rescue them from the hand of the Egyptians and to bring them up out of that land into a good and spacious land, a land flowing with milk and honey—the home of the Canaanites, Hittites, Amorites, Perizzites, Hivites and Jebusites. [9]And now the cry of the Israelites has reached me, and I have seen the way the Egyptians are oppressing them. [10]So now, go. I am sending you to Pharaoh to bring my people the Israelites out of Egypt."

[11]But Moses said to God, "Who am I, that I should go to Pharaoh and bring the Israelites out of Egypt?"

[12]And God said, "I will be with you. And this will be the sign to you that it is I who have sent you: When you have brought the people out of Egypt, you[b] will worship God on this mountain."

[13]Moses said to God, "Suppose I go to the Israelites and say to them, 'The God of your fathers has sent me to you,' and they ask me, 'What is his name?' Then what shall I tell them?"

[14]God said to Moses, "I AM WHO I AM.[c] This is what you are to say to the Israelites: 'I AM has sent me to you.' "

[15]God also said to Moses, "Say to the Israelites, 'The LORD,[d] the God of your fathers—the God of Abraham, the God of Isaac and the God of Jacob—has sent me to you.' This is my name forever, the name by which I am to be remembered from generation to generation.

[16]"Go, assemble the elders of Israel and say to them, 'The LORD, the God of your fathers—the God of Abraham, Isaac and Jacob—appeared to me and said: I have watched over you and have seen what has been done to you in Egypt. [17]And I have promised to bring you up out of your misery in Egypt into the land of the Canaanites, Hittites, Amorites, Perizzites, Hivites and Jebusites—a land flowing with milk and honey.'

---

[a]22 *Gershom* sounds like the Hebrew for *an alien there.*   [b]12 The Hebrew is plural.   [c]14 Or *I WILL BE WHAT I WILL BE*   [d]15 The Hebrew for LORD sounds like and may be derived from the Hebrew for *I AM* in verse 14.

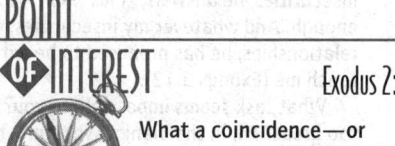

POINT OF INTEREST

Exodus 2:7

What a coincidence—or was it? Look again and see how God delivered Moses at the perfect moment through the careful planning of Moses' mother and the kindness of Pharaoh's daughter. All such perfect moments are God's.

18"The elders of Israel will listen to you. Then you and the elders are to go to the king of Egypt and say to him, 'The LORD, the God of the Hebrews, has met with us. Let us take a three-day journey into the desert to offer sacrifices to the LORD our God.' 19But I know that the king of Egypt will not let you go unless a mighty hand compels him. 20So I will stretch out my hand and strike the Egyptians with all the wonders that I will perform among them. After that, he will let you go.

21"And I will make the Egyptians favorably disposed toward this people, so that when you leave you will not go empty-handed. 22Every woman is to ask her neighbor and any woman living in her house for articles of silver and gold and for clothing, which you will put on your sons and daughters. And so you will plunder the Egyptians."

Signs for Moses

4 Moses answered, "What if they do not believe me or listen to me and say, 'The LORD did not appear to you'?"

2Then the LORD said to him, "What is that in your hand?"

"A staff," he replied.

3The LORD said, "Throw it on the ground."

Moses threw it on the ground and it became a snake, and he ran from it. 4Then the LORD said to him, "Reach out your hand and take it by the tail." So Moses reached out and took hold of the snake and it turned back into a staff in his hand. 5"This," said the LORD, "is so that they may believe that the LORD, the God of their fathers—the God of Abraham, the God of Isaac and the God of Jacob—has appeared to you."

6Then the LORD said, "Put your hand inside your cloak." So Moses put his

---

MONDAY

Read Exodus 3:1–4:17
Key Verse Exodus 3:14

Who Am I . . . ? —Christy Haley

For the last several weeks my journal could have been titled "Woe Is Me." I knew God had given me work to do but I was convinced I had nothing to offer. My skills were deficient and I was bound to fail, or so I thought. I filled my journal with phrases like "Why, God?" and "I can't, God!" or "Don't make me try again, God!"

My lack of confidence was sapping my faith and my enthusiasm—until I read Exodus 3 and 4. I realized that Moses also felt inadequate and had little confidence in himself. He did not want to try what God was proposing. I noticed that in the interaction between Moses and God, the focus of all Moses' questions was "Who am I?" But God always responded with who *he* was, not who *Moses* was.

That day I realized that the answer isn't to be found within myself; it's found in God's nature and being. To my doubts, fears and insecurities, he answers, "I AM WHO I AM" (Exodus 3:14). He is enough. And whatever my insecurities, whether in ministry, work or relationships, he has promised to be with me, to help me and to teach me (Exodus 3:12).

What task seems impossible to you? What challenge seems just too great? Fill in the blank: "Who am I, that I should _____?" God answers: "I AM WHO I AM" and "I will be with you, no matter what."

A Deeper Look
Exodus 4:11–12; Proverbs 2:2–6; Isaiah 41:10

Go to page 68 for your next devotional reading.

hand into his cloak, and when he took it out, it was leprous,[a] like snow.

⁷"Now put it back into your cloak," he said. So Moses put his hand back into his cloak, and when he took it out, it was restored, like the rest of his flesh.

⁸Then the LORD said, "If they do not believe you or pay attention to the first miraculous sign, they may believe the second. ⁹But if they do not believe these two signs or listen to you, take some water from the Nile and pour it on the dry ground. The water you take from the river will become blood on the ground."

¹⁰Moses said to the LORD, "O Lord, I have never been eloquent, neither in the past nor since you have spoken to your servant. I am slow of speech and tongue."

¹¹The LORD said to him, "Who gave man his mouth? Who makes him deaf or mute? Who gives him sight or makes him blind? Is it not I, the LORD? ¹²Now go; I will help you speak and will teach you what to say."

¹³But Moses said, "O Lord, please send someone else to do it."

¹⁴Then the LORD's anger burned against Moses and he said, "What about your brother, Aaron the Levite? I know he can speak well. He is already on his way to meet you, and his heart will be glad when he sees you. ¹⁵You shall speak to him and put words in his mouth; I will help both of you speak and will teach you what to do. ¹⁶He will speak to the people for you, and it will be as if he were your mouth and as if you were God to him. ¹⁷But take this staff in your hand so you can perform miraculous signs with it."

Moses Returns to Egypt

¹⁸Then Moses went back to Jethro his father-in-law and said to him, "Let me go back to my own people in Egypt to see if any of them are still alive."

Jethro said, "Go, and I wish you well."

¹⁹Now the LORD had said to Moses in Midian, "Go back to Egypt, for all the men who wanted to kill you are dead." ²⁰So Moses took his wife and sons, put them on a donkey and started back to Egypt. And he took the staff of God in his hand.

²¹The LORD said to Moses, "When you return to Egypt, see that you perform before Pharaoh all the wonders I have given you the power to do. But I will harden his heart so that he will not let the people go.

²²Then say to Pharaoh, 'This is what the LORD says: Israel is my firstborn son, ²³and I told you, "Let my son go, so he may worship me." But you refused to let him go; so I will kill your firstborn son.' "

²⁴At a lodging place on the way, the LORD met ⌐Moses¬[b] and was about to kill him. ²⁵But Zipporah took a flint knife, cut off her son's foreskin and touched ⌐Moses'¬ feet with it.[c] "Surely you are a bridegroom of blood to me," she said. ²⁶So the LORD let him alone. (At that time she said "bridegroom of blood," referring to circumcision.)

²⁷The LORD said to Aaron, "Go into the desert to meet Moses." So he met Moses at the mountain of God and kissed him. ²⁸Then Moses told Aaron everything the LORD had sent him to say, and also about all the miraculous signs he had commanded him to perform.

²⁹Moses and Aaron brought together all the elders of the Israelites, ³⁰and Aaron told them everything the LORD had said to Moses. He also performed the signs before the people, ³¹and they believed. And when they heard that the LORD was concerned about them and had seen their misery, they bowed down and worshiped.

Bricks Without Straw

5 Afterward Moses and Aaron went to Pharaoh and said, "This is what the LORD, the God of Israel, says: 'Let my people go, so that they may hold a festival to me in the desert.' "

²Pharaoh said, "Who is the LORD, that I should obey him and let Israel go? I do not know the LORD and I will not let Israel go."

³Then they said, "The God of the Hebrews has met with us. Now let us take a three-day journey into the desert to offer sacrifices to the LORD our God, or he may strike us with plagues or with the sword."

⁴But the king of Egypt said, "Moses and Aaron, why are you taking the people away from their labor? Get back to your work!" ⁵Then Pharaoh said, "Look, the people of the land are now numerous, and you are stopping them from working."

⁶That same day Pharaoh gave this or-

---

a6 The Hebrew word was used for various diseases affecting the skin—not necessarily leprosy. *b24* Or ⌐Moses' son⌐; Hebrew *him*   *c25* Or *and drew near ⌐Moses'⌐ feet* der to the slave drivers and foremen in charge of the people: [7]"You are no longer to supply the people with straw for making bricks; let them go and gather their own straw. [8]But require them to make the same number of bricks as before; don't reduce the quota. They are lazy; that is why they are crying out, 'Let us go and sacrifice to our God.' [9]Make the work harder for the men so that they keep working and pay no attention to lies."

[10]Then the slave drivers and the foremen went out and said to the people, "This is what Pharaoh says: 'I will not give you any more straw. [11]Go and get your own straw wherever you can find it, but your work will not be reduced at all.' " [12]So the people scattered all over Egypt to gather stubble to use for straw. [13]The slave drivers kept pressing them, saying, "Complete the work required of you for each day, just as when you had straw." [14]The Israelite foremen appointed by Pharaoh's slave drivers were beaten and were asked, "Why didn't you meet your quota of bricks yesterday or today, as before?"

[15]Then the Israelite foremen went and appealed to Pharaoh: "Why have you treated your servants this way? [16]Your servants are given no straw, yet we are told, 'Make bricks!' Your servants are being beaten, but the fault is with your own people."

[17]Pharaoh said, "Lazy, that's what you are—lazy! That is why you keep saying, 'Let us go and sacrifice to the LORD.' [18]Now get to work. You will not be given any straw, yet you must produce your full quota of bricks."

[19]The Israelite foremen realized they were in trouble when they were told, "You are not to reduce the number of bricks required of you for each day." [20]When they left Pharaoh, they found Moses and Aaron waiting to meet them, [21]and they said, "May the LORD look upon you and judge you! You have made us a stench to Pharaoh and his officials and have put a sword in their hand to kill us."

God Promises Deliverance

[22]Moses returned to the LORD and said, "O Lord, why have you brought trouble upon this people? Is this why you sent me? [23]Ever since I went to Pharaoh to speak in your name, he has brought trouble upon this people, and you have not rescued your people at all."

6 Then the LORD said to Moses, "Now you will see what I will do to Pharaoh: Because of my mighty hand he will let them go; because of my mighty hand he will drive them out of his country."

[2]God also said to Moses, "I am the LORD. [3]I appeared to Abraham, to Isaac and to Jacob as God Almighty,[a] but by my name the LORD[b] I did not make myself known to them.[c] [4]I also established my covenant with them to give them the land of Canaan, where they lived as aliens. [5]Moreover, I have heard the groaning of the Israelites, whom the Egyptians are enslaving, and I have remembered my covenant.

[6]"Therefore, say to the Israelites: 'I am the LORD, and I will bring you out from under the yoke of the Egyptians. I will free you from being slaves to them, and I will redeem you with an outstretched arm and with mighty acts of judgment. [7]I will take you as my own people, and I will be your God. Then you will know that I am the LORD your God, who brought you out from under the yoke of the Egyptians. [8]And I will bring you to the land I swore with uplifted hand to give to Abraham, to Isaac and to Jacob. I will give it to you as a possession. I am the LORD.' "

[9]Moses reported this to the Israelites, but they did not listen to him because of their discouragement and cruel bondage.

[10]Then the LORD said to Moses, [11]"Go, tell Pharaoh king of Egypt to let the Israelites go out of his country."

[12]But Moses said to the LORD, "If the

---

[a]3 Hebrew *El-Shaddai*   [b]3 See note at Exodus 3:15.   [c]3 Or *Almighty, and by my name the LORD did I not let myself be known to them?*

POINT OF INTEREST

Exodus 5:7

Archaeological excavations at the ancient Egyptian city of Pithom (see Exodus 1:11) revealed a brick wall in which the bottom bricks contained straw. The middle bricks were made with stubble, and the upper courses of bricks contained no binding material. Do you think these could be the bricks described in this passage?

Israelites will not listen to me, why would Pharaoh listen to me, since I speak with faltering lips*ª*?"

Family Record of Moses and Aaron

¹³Now the LORD spoke to Moses and Aaron about the Israelites and Pharaoh king of Egypt, and he commanded them to bring the Israelites out of Egypt.

¹⁴These were the heads of their families*ᵇ*:

The sons of Reuben the firstborn son of Israel were Hanoch and Pallu, Hezron and Carmi. These were the clans of Reuben.

¹⁵The sons of Simeon were Jemuel, Jamin, Ohad, Jakin, Zohar and Shaul the son of a Canaanite woman. These were the clans of Simeon.

¹⁶These were the names of the sons of Levi according to their records: Gershon, Kohath and Merari. Levi lived 137 years.

¹⁷The sons of Gershon, by clans, were Libni and Shimei.

¹⁸The sons of Kohath were Amram, Izhar, Hebron and Uzziel. Kohath lived 133 years.

¹⁹The sons of Merari were Mahli and Mushi.

These were the clans of Levi according to their records.

²⁰Amram married his father's sister Jochebed, who bore him Aaron and Moses. Amram lived 137 years.

²¹The sons of Izhar were Korah, Nepheg and Zicri.

²²The sons of Uzziel were Mishael, Elzaphan and Sithri.

²³Aaron married Elisheba, daughter of Amminadab and sister of Nahshon, and she bore him Nadab and Abihu, Eleazar and Ithamar.

²⁴The sons of Korah were Assir, Elkanah and Abiasaph. These were the Korahite clans.

²⁵Eleazar son of Aaron married one of the daughters of Putiel, and she bore him Phinehas.

These were the heads of the Levite families, clan by clan.

²⁶It was this same Aaron and Moses to whom the LORD said, "Bring the Israelites out of Egypt by their divisions." ²⁷They were the ones who spoke to Pharaoh king of Egypt about bringing the Israelites out

of Egypt. It was the same Moses and Aaron.

Aaron to Speak for Moses

²⁸Now when the LORD spoke to Moses in Egypt, ²⁹he said to him, "I am the LORD. Tell Pharaoh king of Egypt everything I tell you."

³⁰But Moses said to the LORD, "Since I speak with faltering lips, why would Pharaoh listen to me?"

7 Then the LORD said to Moses, "See, I have made you like God to Pharaoh, and your brother Aaron will be your prophet. ²You are to say everything I command you, and your brother Aaron is to tell Pharaoh to let the Israelites go out of his country. ³But I will harden Pharaoh's heart, and though I multiply my miraculous signs and wonders in Egypt, ⁴he will not listen to you. Then I will lay my hand on Egypt and with mighty acts of judgment I will bring out my divisions, my people the Israelites. ⁵And the Egyptians will know that I am the LORD when I stretch out my hand against Egypt and bring the Israelites out of it."

⁶Moses and Aaron did just as the LORD commanded them. ⁷Moses was eighty years old and Aaron eighty-three when they spoke to Pharaoh.

Aaron's Staff Becomes a Snake

⁸The LORD said to Moses and Aaron, ⁹"When Pharaoh says to you, 'Perform a miracle,' then say to Aaron, 'Take your staff and throw it down before Pharaoh,' and it will become a snake."

¹⁰So Moses and Aaron went to Pharaoh and did just as the LORD commanded. Aaron threw his staff down in front of Pharaoh and his officials, and it became a snake. ¹¹Pharaoh then summoned wise men and sorcerers, and the Egyptian magicians also did the same things by their secret arts: ¹²Each one threw down his staff and it became a snake. But Aaron's staff swallowed up their staffs. ¹³Yet Pharaoh's heart became hard and he would not listen to them, just as the LORD had said.

The Plague of Blood

¹⁴Then the LORD said to Moses, "Pharaoh's heart is unyielding; he refuses to let the people go. ¹⁵Go to Pharaoh in the

---

ª12 Hebrew I am uncircumcised of lips; also in verse 30   ᵇ14 The Hebrew for families here and in verse 25 refers to units larger than clans.

morning as he goes out to the water. Wait on the bank of the Nile to meet him, and take in your hand the staff that was changed into a snake. ¹⁶Then say to him, 'The LORD, the God of the Hebrews, has sent me to say to you: Let my people go, so that they may worship me in the desert. But until now you have not listened. ¹⁷This is what the LORD says: By this you will know that I am the LORD: With the staff that is in my hand I will strike the water of the Nile, and it will be changed into blood. ¹⁸The fish in the Nile will die, and the river will stink; the Egyptians will not be able to drink its water.' "

¹⁹The LORD said to Moses, "Tell Aaron, 'Take your staff and stretch out your hand over the waters of Egypt—over the streams and canals, over the ponds and all the reservoirs'—and they will turn to blood. Blood will be everywhere in Egypt, even in the wooden buckets and stone jars."

²⁰Moses and Aaron did just as the LORD had commanded. He raised his staff in the presence of Pharaoh and his officials and struck the water of the Nile, and all

---

TUESDAY

Read *Exodus 5:22—7:5*
Key Verses *Exodus 7:2–5*

On Grasshoppers and Grace – Phil Lewis

If you were asked to name one of the plagues God sent on the Egyptians, which one would you recall? The most memorable for many people is the plague of locusts—maybe because we can imagine what it must have been like for the Egyptians to have insects creeping and crawling all over their clay pots and papyrus and getting crunched beneath their sandals. The ground was *black* with locusts. Yuck!

The interesting thing about locusts is that normally they're just ordinary grasshoppers, eating a few leaves and not causing much trouble. However, if conditions are right and there is an abundance of food and water, these grasshoppers will transform at their last molt into migratory locusts. Then they fly in tremendous swarms and devour anything edible.

Sin is sort of like grasshoppers. Sometimes we allow certain sins to grow so that they eat at our relationships with God and with those around us. We let them grow instead of stamping on them immediately, and soon they're out of control and begin to devour our lives like a plague. But sin won't cause widespread destruction if it's killed quickly by repentance and confession: "If we confess our sins, he is faithful and just and will forgive us our sins and purify us from all unrighteousness" (1 John 1:8–9). Instead, "from the fullness of his grace we have all received one blessing after another" (John 1:16).

Pharaoh's heart was hard; his mind was made up; he was resistant to God's Word. So the plagues kept coming. Don't be like him. Let God's word sink in. When the Holy Spirit shows you something you need to change, do it. There's no future in letting grasshoppers—or sin—get out of control. Let God send you grace instead of grasshoppers!

A Deeper Look
2 Chronicles 7:14; Proverbs 28:13–14; 1 John 1:8–9

Go to page 76 for your next devotional reading.

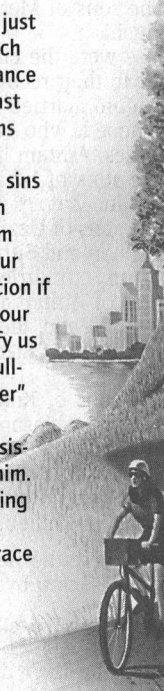

the water was changed into blood. ²¹The fish in the Nile died, and the river smelled so bad that the Egyptians could not drink its water. Blood was everywhere in Egypt.

²²But the Egyptian magicians did the same things by their secret arts, and Pharaoh's heart became hard; he would not listen to Moses and Aaron, just as the LORD had said. ²³Instead, he turned and went into his palace, and did not take even this to heart. ²⁴And all the Egyptians dug along the Nile to get drinking water, because they could not drink the water of the river.

The Plague of Frogs

²⁵Seven days passed after the LORD struck the Nile. ¹Then the LORD said to Moses, "Go to Pharaoh and say to him, 'This is what the LORD says: Let my people go, so that they may worship me. ²If you refuse to let them go, I will plague your whole country with frogs. ³The Nile will teem with frogs. They will come up into your palace and your bedroom and onto your bed, into the houses of your officials and on your people, and into your ovens and kneading troughs. ⁴The frogs will go up on you and your people and all your officials.' "

⁵Then the LORD said to Moses, "Tell Aaron, 'Stretch out your hand with your staff over the streams and canals and ponds, and make frogs come up on the land of Egypt.' "

⁶So Aaron stretched out his hand over the waters of Egypt, and the frogs came up and covered the land. ⁷But the magicians did the same things by their secret arts; they also made frogs come up on the land of Egypt.

⁸Pharaoh summoned Moses and Aaron and said, "Pray to the LORD to take the frogs away from me and my people, and I will let your people go to offer sacrifices to the LORD."

⁹Moses said to Pharaoh, "I leave to you the honor of setting the time for me to pray for you and your officials and your people that you and your houses may be rid of the frogs, except for those that remain in the Nile."

¹⁰"Tomorrow," Pharaoh said.

Moses replied, "It will be as you say, so that you may know there is no one like the LORD our God. ¹¹The frogs will leave you and your houses, your officials and

your people; they will remain only in the Nile."

¹²After Moses and Aaron left Pharaoh, Moses cried out to the LORD about the frogs he had brought on Pharaoh. ¹³And the LORD did what Moses asked. The frogs died in the houses, in the courtyards and in the fields. ¹⁴They were piled into heaps, and the land reeked of them. ¹⁵But when Pharaoh saw that there was relief, he hardened his heart and would not listen to Moses and Aaron, just as the LORD had said.

The Plague of Gnats

¹⁶Then the LORD said to Moses, "Tell Aaron, 'Stretch out your staff and strike the dust of the ground,' and throughout the land of Egypt the dust will become gnats." ¹⁷They did this, and when Aaron stretched out his hand with the staff and struck the dust of the ground, gnats came upon men and animals. All the dust throughout the land of Egypt became gnats. ¹⁸But when the magicians tried to produce gnats by their secret arts, they could not. And the gnats were on men and animals.

¹⁹The magicians said to Pharaoh, "This is the finger of God." But Pharaoh's heart was hard and he would not listen, just as the LORD had said.

The Plague of Flies

²⁰Then the LORD said to Moses, "Get up early in the morning and confront Pharaoh as he goes to the water and say to him, 'This is what the LORD says: Let my people go, so that they may worship me. ²¹If you do not let my people go, I will send swarms of flies on you and your

POINT OF INTEREST

Exodus 8:19

Some of the plagues were environmental phenomena (hail, frogs, insects, darkness). Some people contend these were only natural occurrences, not miracles. However, this view cannot explain why the Hebrews were exempt from these calamities. Pharaoh's advisers recognized the true source of the plagues: "This is the finger of God."

officials, on your people and into your houses. The houses of the Egyptians will be full of flies, and even the ground where they are.

22" 'But on that day I will deal differently with the land of Goshen, where my people live; no swarms of flies will be there, so that you will know that I, the LORD, am in this land. 23I will make a distinction[a] between my people and your people. This miraculous sign will occur tomorrow.' "

24And the LORD did this. Dense swarms of flies poured into Pharaoh's palace and into the houses of his officials, and throughout Egypt the land was ruined by the flies.

25Then Pharaoh summoned Moses and Aaron and said, "Go, sacrifice to your God here in the land."

26But Moses said, "That would not be right. The sacrifices we offer the LORD our God would be detestable to the Egyptians. And if we offer sacrifices that are detestable in their eyes, will they not stone us? 27We must take a three-day journey into the desert to offer sacrifices to the LORD our God, as he commands us."

28Pharaoh said, "I will let you go to offer sacrifices to the LORD your God in the desert, but you must not go very far. Now pray for me."

29Moses answered, "As soon as I leave you, I will pray to the LORD, and tomorrow the flies will leave Pharaoh and his officials and his people. Only be sure that Pharaoh does not act deceitfully again by not letting the people go to offer sacrifices to the LORD."

30Then Moses left Pharaoh and prayed to the LORD, 31and the LORD did what Moses asked: The flies left Pharaoh and his officials and his people; not a fly remained. 32But this time also Pharaoh hardened his heart and would not let the people go.

The Plague on Livestock

9 Then the LORD said to Moses, "Go to Pharaoh and say to him, 'This is what the LORD, the God of the Hebrews, says: "Let my people go, so that they may worship me." 2If you refuse to let them go and continue to hold them back, 3the hand of the LORD will bring a terrible plague on your livestock in the field—on your horses and donkeys and camels and on your cattle and sheep and goats. 4But

the LORD will make a distinction between the livestock of Israel and that of Egypt, so that no animal belonging to the Israelites will die.' "

5The LORD set a time and said, "Tomorrow the LORD will do this in the land." 6And the next day the LORD did it: All the livestock of the Egyptians died, but not one animal belonging to the Israelites died. 7Pharaoh sent men to investigate and found that not even one of the animals of the Israelites had died. Yet his heart was unyielding and he would not let the people go.

The Plague of Boils

8Then the LORD said to Moses and Aaron, "Take handfuls of soot from a furnace and have Moses toss it into the air in the presence of Pharaoh. 9 It will become fine dust over the whole land of Egypt, and festering boils will break out on men and animals throughout the land."

10So they took soot from a furnace and stood before Pharaoh. Moses tossed it into the air, and festering boils broke out on men and animals. 11The magicians could not stand before Moses because of the boils that were on them and on all the Egyptians. 12But the LORD hardened Pharaoh's heart and he would not listen to Moses and Aaron, just as the LORD had said to Moses.

The Plague of Hail

13Then the LORD said to Moses, "Get up early in the morning, confront Pharaoh and say to him, 'This is what the LORD, the God of the Hebrews, says: Let my people go, so that they may worship me, 14or this time I will send the full force of my plagues against you and against your officials and your people, so you may know that there is no one like me in all the earth. 15For by now I could have stretched out my hand and struck you and your people with a plague that would have wiped you off the earth. 16But I have raised you up[b] for this very purpose, that I might show you my power and that my name might be proclaimed in all the earth. 17You still set yourself against my people and will not let them go. 18Therefore, at this time tomorrow I will send the worst hailstorm that has ever fallen on Egypt, from the day it was founded till

---

a23 Septuagint and Vulgate; Hebrew *will put a deliverance*   b16 Or *have spared you* now. ¹⁹Give an order now to bring your livestock and everything you have in the field to a place of shelter, because the hail will fall on every man and animal that has not been brought in and is still out in the field, and they will die.' "

²⁰Those officials of Pharaoh who feared the word of the LORD hurried to bring their slaves and their livestock inside. ²¹But those who ignored the word of the LORD left their slaves and livestock in the field.

²²Then the LORD said to Moses, "Stretch out your hand toward the sky so that hail will fall all over Egypt—on men and animals and on everything growing in the fields of Egypt." ²³When Moses stretched out his staff toward the sky, the LORD sent thunder and hail, and lightning flashed down to the ground. So the LORD rained hail on the land of Egypt; ²⁴hail fell and lightning flashed back and forth. It was the worst storm in all the land of Egypt since it had become a nation. ²⁵Throughout Egypt hail struck everything in the fields—both men and animals; it beat down everything growing in the fields and stripped every tree. ²⁶The only place it did not hail was the land of Goshen, where the Israelites were.

²⁷Then Pharaoh summoned Moses and Aaron. "This time I have sinned," he said to them. "The LORD is in the right, and I and my people are in the wrong. ²⁸Pray to the LORD, for we have had enough thunder and hail. I will let you go; you don't have to stay any longer."

²⁹Moses replied, "When I have gone out of the city, I will spread out my hands in prayer to the LORD. The thunder will stop and there will be no more hail, so you may know that the earth is the LORD's. ³⁰But I know that you and your officials still do not fear the LORD God."

³¹(The flax and barley were destroyed, since the barley had headed and the flax was in bloom. ³²The wheat and spelt, however, were not destroyed, because they ripen later.)

³³Then Moses left Pharaoh and went out of the city. He spread out his hands toward the LORD; the thunder and hail stopped, and the rain no longer poured down on the land. ³⁴When Pharaoh saw that the rain and hail and thunder had stopped, he sinned again: He and his officials hardened their hearts. ³⁵So Pharaoh's heart was hard and he would not let the Israelites go, just as the LORD had said through Moses.

The Plague of Locusts

10 Then the LORD said to Moses, "Go to Pharaoh, for I have hardened his heart and the hearts of his officials so that I may perform these miraculous signs of mine among them ²that you may tell your children and grandchildren how I dealt harshly with the Egyptians and how I performed my signs among them, and that you may know that I am the LORD."

³So Moses and Aaron went to Pharaoh and said to him, "This is what the LORD, the God of the Hebrews, says: 'How long will you refuse to humble yourself before me? Let my people go, so that they may worship me. ⁴If you refuse to let them go, I will bring locusts into your country tomorrow. ⁵They will cover the face of the ground so that it cannot be seen. They will devour what little you have left after the hail, including every tree that is growing in your fields. ⁶They will fill your houses and those of all your officials and all the Egyptians—something neither your fathers nor your forefathers have ever seen from the day they settled in this land till now.' " Then Moses turned and left Pharaoh.

⁷Pharaoh's officials said to him, "How long will this man be a snare to us? Let the people go, so that they may worship the LORD their God. Do you not yet realize that Egypt is ruined?"

⁸Then Moses and Aaron were brought back to Pharaoh. "Go, worship the LORD your God," he said. "But just who will be going?"

⁹Moses answered, "We will go with our young and old, with our sons and daughters, and with our flocks and herds, because we are to celebrate a festival to the LORD."

¹⁰Pharaoh said, "The LORD be with you—if I let you go, along with your women and children! Clearly you are bent on evil.ᵃ ¹¹No! Have only the men go; and worship the LORD, since that's what you have been asking for." Then Moses and Aaron were driven out of Pharaoh's presence.

¹²And the LORD said to Moses, "Stretch out your hand over Egypt so that locusts will swarm over the land and devour ev-

---

ᵃ 10 Or Be careful, trouble is in store for you!

erything growing in the fields, everything left by the hail."

¹³So Moses stretched out his staff over Egypt, and the Lord made an east wind blow across the land all that day and all that night. By morning the wind had brought the locusts; ¹⁴they invaded all Egypt and settled down in every area of the country in great numbers. Never before had there been such a plague of locusts, nor will there ever be again. ¹⁵They covered all the ground until it was black. They devoured all that was left after the hail—everything growing in the fields and the fruit on the trees. Nothing green remained on tree or plant in all the land of Egypt.

¹⁶Pharaoh quickly summoned Moses and Aaron and said, "I have sinned against the Lord your God and against you. ¹⁷Now forgive my sin once more and pray to the Lord your God to take this deadly plague away from me."

¹⁸Moses then left Pharaoh and prayed to the Lord. ¹⁹And the Lord changed the wind to a very strong west wind, which caught up the locusts and carried them into the Red Sea.ᵃ Not a locust was left anywhere in Egypt. ²⁰But the Lord hardened Pharaoh's heart, and he would not let the Israelites go.

The Plague of Darkness

²¹Then the Lord said to Moses, "Stretch out your hand toward the sky so that darkness will spread over Egypt— darkness that can be felt." ²²So Moses stretched out his hand toward the sky, and total darkness covered all Egypt for three days. ²³No one could see anyone else or leave his place for three days. Yet all the Israelites had light in the places where they lived.

²⁴Then Pharaoh summoned Moses and said, "Go, worship the Lord. Even your women and children may go with you; only leave your flocks and herds behind."

²⁵But Moses said, "You must allow us to have sacrifices and burnt offerings to present to the Lord our God. ²⁶Our livestock too must go with us; not a hoof is to be left behind. We have to use some of them in worshiping the Lord our God, and until we get there we will not know what we are to use to worship the Lord."

²⁷But the Lord hardened Pharaoh's heart, and he was not willing to let them go. ²⁸Pharaoh said to Moses, "Get out of

my sight! Make sure you do not appear before me again! The day you see my face you will die."

²⁹"Just as you say," Moses replied, "I will never appear before you again."

The Plague on the Firstborn

11 Now the Lord had said to Moses, "I will bring one more plague on Pharaoh and on Egypt. After that, he will let you go from here, and when he does, he will drive you out completely. ²Tell the people that men and women alike are to ask their neighbors for articles of silver and gold." ³(The Lord made the Egyptians favorably disposed toward the people, and Moses himself was highly regarded in Egypt by Pharaoh's officials and by the people.)

⁴So Moses said, "This is what the Lord says: 'About midnight I will go throughout Egypt. ⁵Every firstborn son in Egypt will die, from the firstborn son of Pharaoh, who sits on the throne, to the firstborn son of the slave girl, who is at her hand mill, and all the firstborn of the cattle as well. ⁶There will be loud wailing throughout Egypt—worse than there has ever been or ever will be again. ⁷But among the Israelites not a dog will bark at any man or animal.' Then you will know that the Lord makes a distinction between Egypt and Israel. ⁸All these officials of yours will come to me, bowing down before me and saying, 'Go, you and all the people who follow you!' After that I will leave." Then Moses, hot with anger, left Pharaoh.

⁹The Lord had said to Moses, "Pharaoh will refuse to listen to you—so that my wonders may be multiplied in Egypt." ¹⁰Moses and Aaron performed all these wonders before Pharaoh, but the Lord hardened Pharaoh's heart, and he would not let the Israelites go out of his country.

The Passover

12 The Lord said to Moses and Aaron in Egypt, ²"This month is to be for you the first month, the first month of your year. ³Tell the whole community of Israel that on the tenth day of this month each man is to take a lambᵇ for his family, one for each household. ⁴If any household is too small for a whole lamb, they must share one with their nearest neigh-

---

ᵃ19 Hebrew *Yam Suph*; that is, Sea of Reeds
ᵇ3 The Hebrew word can mean *lamb* or *kid*; also in verse 4.

bor, having taken into account the number of people there are. You are to determine the amount of lamb needed in accordance with what each person will eat. ⁵The animals you choose must be year-old males without defect, and you may take them from the sheep or the goats. ⁶Take care of them until the fourteenth day of the month, when all the people of the community of Israel must slaughter them at twilight. ⁷Then they are to take some of the blood and put it on the sides and tops of the doorframes of the houses where they eat the lambs. ⁸That same night they are to eat the meat roasted over the fire, along with bitter herbs, and bread made without yeast. ⁹Do not eat the meat raw or cooked in water, but roast it over the fire—head, legs and inner parts. ¹⁰Do not leave any of it till morning; if some is left till morning, you must burn it. ¹¹This is how you are to eat it: with your cloak tucked into your belt, your sandals on your feet and your staff in your hand. Eat it in haste; it is the LORD's Passover.

¹²"On that same night I will pass through Egypt and strike down every firstborn—both men and animals—and I will bring judgment on all the gods of Egypt. I am the LORD. ¹³The blood will be a sign for you on the houses where you are; and when I see the blood, I will pass over you. No destructive plague will touch you when I strike Egypt.

¹⁴"This is a day you are to commemorate; for the generations to come you shall celebrate it as a festival to the LORD—a lasting ordinance. ¹⁵For seven days you are to eat bread made without yeast. On the first day remove the yeast from your houses, for whoever eats anything with yeast in it from the first day through the seventh must be cut off from Israel. ¹⁶On the first day hold a sacred assembly, and another one on the seventh day. Do no work at all on these days, except to prepare food for everyone to eat—that is all you may do.

¹⁷"Celebrate the Feast of Unleavened Bread, because it was on this very day that I brought your divisions out of Egypt. Celebrate this day as a lasting ordinance for the generations to come. ¹⁸In the first month you are to eat bread made without yeast, from the evening of the fourteenth day until the evening of the twenty-first day. ¹⁹For seven days no yeast is to be found in your houses. And whoever eats anything with yeast in it must be cut off from the community of Israel, whether he is an alien or native-born. ²⁰Eat nothing made with yeast. Wherever you live, you must eat unleavened bread."

²¹Then Moses summoned all the elders of Israel and said to them, "Go at once and select the animals for your families and slaughter the Passover lamb. ²²Take a bunch of hyssop, dip it into the blood in the basin and put some of the blood on the top and on both sides of the doorframe. Not one of you shall go out the door of his house until morning. ²³When the LORD goes through the land to strike down the Egyptians, he will see the blood on the top and sides of the doorframe and will pass over that doorway, and he will not permit the destroyer to enter your houses and strike you down.

²⁴"Obey these instructions as a lasting ordinance for you and your descendants. ²⁵When you enter the land that the LORD will give you as he promised, observe this ceremony. ²⁶And when your children ask you, 'What does this ceremony mean to you?' ²⁷then tell them, 'It is the Passover sacrifice to the LORD, who passed over the houses of the Israelites in Egypt and spared our homes when he struck down the Egyptians.' " Then the people bowed down and worshiped. ²⁸The Israelites did just what the LORD commanded Moses and Aaron.

²⁹At midnight the LORD struck down all the firstborn in Egypt, from the firstborn of Pharaoh, who sat on the throne, to the firstborn of the prisoner, who was in the dungeon, and the firstborn of all the livestock as well. ³⁰Pharaoh and all his offi-

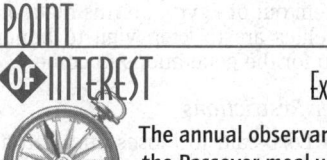

POINT OF INTEREST

Exodus 12:11

The annual observance of the Passover meal was ordained in Israel to commemorate the Israelites' deliverance from Egyptian slavery. This celebration foreshadowed Jesus' death; he is our Passover lamb (see 1 Corinthians 5:7). Read Matthew 26:17–29 to see how Jesus celebrated the Passover with his disciples.

cials and all the Egyptians got up during the night, and there was loud wailing in Egypt, for there was not a house without someone dead.

The Exodus

³¹During the night Pharaoh summoned Moses and Aaron and said, "Up! Leave my people, you and the Israelites! Go, worship the LORD as you have requested. ³²Take your flocks and herds, as you have said, and go. And also bless me."

³³The Egyptians urged the people to hurry and leave the country. "For otherwise," they said, "we will all die!" ³⁴So the people took their dough before the yeast was added, and carried it on their shoulders in kneading troughs wrapped in clothing. ³⁵The Israelites did as Moses instructed and asked the Egyptians for articles of silver and gold and for clothing. ³⁶The LORD had made the Egyptians favorably disposed toward the people, and they gave them what they asked for; so they plundered the Egyptians.

³⁷The Israelites journeyed from Rameses to Succoth. There were about six hundred thousand men on foot, besides women and children. ³⁸Many other people went up with them, as well as large droves of livestock, both flocks and herds. ³⁹With the dough they had brought from Egypt, they baked cakes of unleavened bread. The dough was without yeast because they had been driven out of Egypt and did not have time to prepare food for themselves.

⁴⁰Now the length of time the Israelite people lived in Egypt^a was 430 years. ⁴¹At the end of the 430 years, to the very day, all the LORD's divisions left Egypt. ⁴²Because the LORD kept vigil that night to bring them out of Egypt, on this night all the Israelites are to keep vigil to honor the LORD for the generations to come.

Passover Restrictions

⁴³The LORD said to Moses and Aaron, "These are the regulations for the Passover:

"No foreigner is to eat of it. ⁴⁴Any slave you have bought may eat of it after you have circumcised him, ⁴⁵but a temporary resident and a hired worker may not eat of it.

⁴⁶"It must be eaten inside one house; take none of the meat outside the house. Do not break any of the bones. ⁴⁷The whole community of Israel must celebrate it.

⁴⁸"An alien living among you who wants to celebrate the LORD's Passover must have all the males in his household circumcised; then he may take part like one born in the land. No uncircumcised male may eat of it. ⁴⁹The same law applies to the native-born and to the alien living among you."

⁵⁰All the Israelites did just what the LORD had commanded Moses and Aaron. ⁵¹And on that very day the LORD brought the Israelites out of Egypt by their divisions.

Consecration of the Firstborn

13 The LORD said to Moses, ²"Consecrate to me every firstborn male. The first offspring of every womb among the Israelites belongs to me, whether man or animal."

³Then Moses said to the people, "Commemorate this day, the day you came out of Egypt, out of the land of slavery, because the LORD brought you out of it with a mighty hand. Eat nothing containing yeast. ⁴Today, in the month of Abib, you are leaving. ⁵When the LORD brings you into the land of the Canaanites, Hittites, Amorites, Hivites and Jebusites— the land he swore to your forefathers to give you, a land flowing with milk and honey—you are to observe this ceremony in this month: ⁶For seven days eat bread made without yeast and on the seventh day hold a festival to the LORD. ⁷Eat unleavened bread during those seven days; nothing with yeast in it is to be seen among you, nor shall any yeast be seen anywhere within your borders. ⁸On that day tell your son, 'I do this because of what the LORD did for me when I came out of Egypt.' ⁹This observance will be for you like a sign on your hand and a reminder on your forehead that the law of the LORD is to be on your lips. For the LORD brought you out of Egypt with his mighty hand. ¹⁰You must keep this ordinance at the appointed time year after year.

¹¹"After the LORD brings you into the land of the Canaanites and gives it to you, as he promised on oath to you and your forefathers, ¹²you are to give over to the LORD the first offspring of every

ᵃ40 Masoretic Text; Samaritan Pentateuch and Septuagint *Egypt and Canaan* womb. All the firstborn males of your livestock belong to the LORD. ¹³Redeem with a lamb every firstborn donkey, but if you do not redeem it, break its neck. Redeem every firstborn among your sons.

¹⁴"In days to come, when your son asks you, 'What does this mean?' say to him, 'With a mighty hand the LORD brought us out of Egypt, out of the land of slavery. ¹⁵When Pharaoh stubbornly refused to let us go, the LORD killed every firstborn in Egypt, both man and animal. This is why I sacrifice to the LORD the first male offspring of every womb and redeem each of my firstborn sons.' ¹⁶And it will be like a sign on your hand and a symbol on your forehead that the LORD brought us out of Egypt with his mighty hand."

Crossing the Sea

¹⁷When Pharaoh let the people go, God did not lead them on the road through the Philistine country, though that was shorter. For God said, "If they face war, they might change their minds and return to Egypt." ¹⁸So God led the people around by the desert road toward the Red Sea.ᵃ The Israelites went up out of Egypt armed for battle.

¹⁹Moses took the bones of Joseph with him because Joseph had made the sons of Israel swear an oath. He had said, "God will surely come to your aid, and then you must carry my bones up with you from this place."ᵇ

²⁰After leaving Succoth they camped at Etham on the edge of the desert. ²¹By day the LORD went ahead of them in a pillar of cloud to guide them on their way and by night in a pillar of fire to give them light, so that they could travel by day or night. ²²Neither the pillar of cloud by day nor the pillar of fire by night left its place in front of the people.

14 Then the LORD said to Moses, ²"Tell the Israelites to turn back and encamp near Pi Hahiroth, between Migdol and the sea. They are to encamp by the sea, directly opposite Baal Zephon. ³Pharaoh will think, 'The Israelites are wandering around the land in confusion, hemmed in by the desert.' ⁴And I will harden Pharaoh's heart, and he will pursue them. But I will gain glory for myself through Pharaoh and all his army, and the Egyptians will know that I am the LORD." So the Israelites did this.

⁵When the king of Egypt was told that the people had fled, Pharaoh and his officials changed their minds about them and said, "What have we done? We have let the Israelites go and have lost their services!" ⁶So he had his chariot made ready and took his army with him. ⁷He took six hundred of the best chariots, along with all the other chariots of Egypt, with officers over all of them. ⁸The LORD hardened the heart of Pharaoh king of Egypt, so that he pursued the Israelites, who were marching out boldly. ⁹The Egyptians—all Pharaoh's horses and chariots, horsemenᶜ and troops—pursued the Israelites and overtook them as they camped by the sea near Pi Hahiroth, opposite Baal Zephon.

¹⁰As Pharaoh approached, the Israelites looked up, and there were the Egyptians, marching after them. They were terrified and cried out to the LORD. ¹¹They said to Moses, "Was it because there were no graves in Egypt that you brought us to the desert to die? What have you done to us by bringing us out of Egypt? ¹²Didn't we say to you in Egypt, 'Leave us alone; let us serve the Egyptians'? It would have been better for us to serve the Egyptians than to die in the desert!"

¹³Moses answered the people, "Do not be afraid. Stand firm and you will see the deliverance the LORD will bring you today. The Egyptians you see today you will never see again. ¹⁴The LORD will fight for you; you need only to be still."

¹⁵Then the LORD said to Moses, "Why are you crying out to me? Tell the Israelites to move on. ¹⁶Raise your staff and stretch out your hand over the sea to divide the water so that the Israelites can go through the sea on dry ground. ¹⁷I will harden the hearts of the Egyptians so that they will go in after them. And I will gain glory through Pharaoh and all his army, through his chariots and his horsemen. ¹⁸The Egyptians will know that I am the LORD when I gain glory through Pharaoh, his chariots and his horsemen."

¹⁹Then the angel of God, who had been traveling in front of Israel's army, withdrew and went behind them. The pillar of cloud also moved from in front and stood behind them, ²⁰coming between the armies of Egypt and Israel. Throughout the night the cloud brought

ᵃ18 Hebrew *Yam Suph*; that is, Sea of Reeds
ᵇ19 See Gen. 50:25.   ᶜ9 Or *charioteers*; also in verses 17, 18, 23, 26 and 28

darkness to the one side and light to the other side; so neither went near the other all night long. ²¹Then Moses stretched out his hand over the sea, and all that night the LORD drove the sea back with a strong east wind and turned it into dry land. The waters were divided, ²²and the Israelites went through the sea on dry ground, with a wall of water on their right and on their left.

²³The Egyptians pursued them, and all Pharaoh's horses and chariots and horsemen followed them into the sea. ²⁴During the last watch of the night the LORD looked down from the pillar of fire and cloud at the Egyptian army and threw it into confusion. ²⁵He made the wheels of their chariots come off*a* so that they had difficulty driving. And the Egyptians said, "Let's get away from the Israelites! The LORD is fighting for them against Egypt."

²⁶Then the LORD said to Moses, "Stretch out your hand over the sea so that the waters may flow back over the Egyptians and their chariots and horsemen." ²⁷Moses stretched out his hand over the sea, and at daybreak the sea went back to its place. The Egyptians were fleeing toward*b* it, and the LORD swept them into the sea. ²⁸The water flowed back and covered the chariots and horsemen—the entire army of Pharaoh that had followed the Israelites into the sea. Not one of them survived.

²⁹But the Israelites went through the sea on dry ground, with a wall of water on their right and on their left. ³⁰That day the LORD saved Israel from the hands of

a25 Or *He jammed the wheels of their chariots* (see Samaritan Pentateuch, Septuagint and Syriac) *b27* Or *from*

Read Exodus 14:1–31
Key Verses Exodus 14:13–14

Strength in Due Time – Sharla Walstrom

Have you ever taken a class that just naturally suited you? It was that way with a computer programming class I took. I loved learning the new language. There was a problem though—a very popular, great-looking guy in my class was acting very friendly toward me. That's a problem, you ask? It was, because although I really liked the attention he gave me, I knew what he really wanted—someone to do his homework.

When our first programming assignment was due, he asked me for "help." I tried to give him a little tutoring but quickly found out he wanted me to print two copies of my program and put his name on one of them. He was really charming and I almost buckled, but I told him I needed to think about it. His face changed and he walked away.

"Lord, what do I do?" I asked. I didn't want to totally turn this guy off, but I knew I would be aiding and abetting a cheater. It was as risky as it was wrong. And it was tempting—almost too tempting. So I prayed, "Lord, help me to be holy before you and not weak before this temptation."

The next day I shakily told "Kyle" I wouldn't give him a copy of my program. At first he tried to charm me into it; then he stormed off in a huff. I was especially satisfied with that programming assignment as I turned it in to the professor.

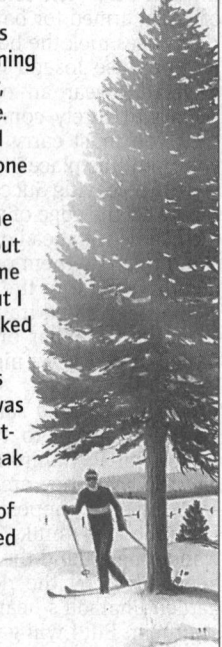

A Deeper Look
Psalm 27:5; Psalm 50:15; Matthew 10:29–31

Go to page 83 for your next devotional reading.

the Egyptians, and Israel saw the Egyptians lying dead on the shore. ³¹And when the Israelites saw the great power the LORD displayed against the Egyptians, the people feared the LORD and put their trust in him and in Moses his servant.

The Song of Moses and Miriam

15 Then Moses and the Israelites sang this song to the LORD:

"I will sing to the LORD,
  for he is highly exalted.
The horse and its rider
  he has hurled into the sea.
²The LORD is my strength and my song;
  he has become my salvation.
He is my God, and I will praise him,
  my father's God, and I will exalt
    him.
³The LORD is a warrior;
  the LORD is his name.
⁴Pharaoh's chariots and his army
  he has hurled into the sea.
The best of Pharaoh's officers
  are drowned in the Red Sea.ᵃ
⁵The deep waters have covered them;
  they sank to the depths like a
    stone.

⁶"Your right hand, O LORD,
  was majestic in power.
Your right hand, O LORD,
  shattered the enemy.
⁷In the greatness of your majesty
  you threw down those who
    opposed you.
You unleashed your burning anger;
  it consumed them like stubble.
⁸By the blast of your nostrils
  the waters piled up.
The surging waters stood firm like a
    wall;
  the deep waters congealed in the
    heart of the sea.

⁹"The enemy boasted,
  'I will pursue, I will overtake
    them.
I will divide the spoils;
  I will gorge myself on them.
I will draw my sword
  and my hand will destroy them.'
¹⁰But you blew with your breath,
  and the sea covered them.
They sank like lead
  in the mighty waters.

¹¹"Who among the gods is like you,
    O LORD?
Who is like you—

majestic in holiness,
  awesome in glory,
  working wonders?
¹²You stretched out your right hand
  and the earth swallowed them.

¹³"In your unfailing love you will lead
  the people you have redeemed.
In your strength you will guide them
  to your holy dwelling.
¹⁴The nations will hear and tremble;
  anguish will grip the people of
    Philistia.
¹⁵The chiefs of Edom will be terrified,
  the leaders of Moab will be seized
    with trembling,
the peopleᵇ of Canaan will melt
    away;
¹⁶   terror and dread will fall upon
      them.
By the power of your arm
  they will be as still as a stone—
until your people pass by, O LORD,
  until the people you boughtᶜ pass
    by.
¹⁷You will bring them in and plant
    them
  on the mountain of your
    inheritance—
the place, O LORD, you made for your
    dwelling,
  the sanctuary, O Lord, your hands
    established.
¹⁸The LORD will reign
  for ever and ever."

¹⁹When Pharaoh's horses, chariots and horsemenᵈ went into the sea, the LORD brought the waters of the sea back

ᵃ4 Hebrew *Yam Suph*; that is, Sea of Reeds; also in verse 22   ᵇ15 Or *rulers*   ᶜ16 Or *created*
ᵈ19 Or *charioteers*

POINT OF INTEREST

Exodus 14:22

No one knows precisely where the Israelites crossed the Red Sea. But we do know that the sea at that place was wide enough and deep enough to initially prevent them from crossing and to eventually drown the Egyptians. The God who brought the plagues down on the Egyptians parted the water and led the Israelites to safety. Another miracle!

over them, but the Israelites walked through the sea on dry ground. ²⁰Then Miriam the prophetess, Aaron's sister, took a tambourine in her hand, and all the women followed her, with tambourines and dancing. ²¹Miriam sang to them:

"Sing to the LORD,
  for he is highly exalted.
The horse and its rider
  he has hurled into the sea."

The Waters of Marah and Elim

²²Then Moses led Israel from the Red Sea and they went into the Desert of Shur. For three days they traveled in the desert without finding water. ²³When they came to Marah, they could not drink its water because it was bitter. (That is why the place is called Marah.ᵃ) ²⁴So the people grumbled against Moses, saying, "What are we to drink?"

²⁵Then Moses cried out to the LORD, and the LORD showed him a piece of wood. He threw it into the water, and the water became sweet.

There the LORD made a decree and a law for them, and there he tested them. ²⁶He said, "If you listen carefully to the voice of the LORD your God and do what is right in his eyes, if you pay attention to his commands and keep all his decrees, I will not bring on you any of the diseases I brought on the Egyptians, for I am the LORD, who heals you."

²⁷Then they came to Elim, where there were twelve springs and seventy palm trees, and they camped there near the water.

Manna and Quail

16 The whole Israelite community set out from Elim and came to the Desert of Sin, which is between Elim and Sinai, on the fifteenth day of the second month after they had come out of Egypt. ²In the desert the whole community grumbled against Moses and Aaron. ³The Israelites said to them, "If only we had died by the LORD's hand in Egypt! There we sat around pots of meat and ate all the food we wanted, but you have brought us out into this desert to starve this entire assembly to death."

⁴Then the LORD said to Moses, "I will rain down bread from heaven for you. The people are to go out each day and gather enough for that day. In this way I will test them and see whether they will follow my instructions. ⁵On the sixth day they are to prepare what they bring in, and that is to be twice as much as they gather on the other days."

⁶So Moses and Aaron said to all the Israelites, "In the evening you will know that it was the LORD who brought you out of Egypt, ⁷and in the morning you will see the glory of the LORD, because he has heard your grumbling against him. Who are we, that you should grumble against us?" ⁸Moses also said, "You will know that it was the LORD when he gives you meat to eat in the evening and all the bread you want in the morning, because he has heard your grumbling against him. Who are we? You are not grumbling against us, but against the LORD."

⁹Then Moses told Aaron, "Say to the entire Israelite community, 'Come before the LORD, for he has heard your grumbling.'"

¹⁰While Aaron was speaking to the whole Israelite community, they looked toward the desert, and there was the glory of the LORD appearing in the cloud.

¹¹The LORD said to Moses, ¹²"I have heard the grumbling of the Israelites. Tell them, 'At twilight you will eat meat, and in the morning you will be filled with bread. Then you will know that I am the LORD your God.'"

¹³That evening quail came and covered the camp, and in the morning there was a layer of dew around the camp. ¹⁴When the dew was gone, thin flakes like frost on the ground appeared on the desert floor. ¹⁵When the Israelites saw it,

---

ᵃ23 *Marah* means *bitter*.

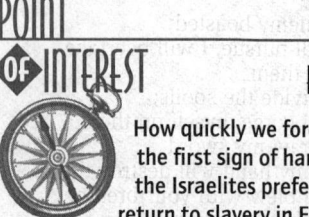

POINT OF INTEREST

Exodus 16:3

How quickly we forget! At the first sign of hardship, the Israelites preferred to return to slavery in Egypt rather than trust in God and walk in freedom. We struggle with the same tendency in the Christian life (see Galatians 5:1). When we trust God, we're better prepared to see him working in our lives.

they said to each other, "What is it?" For they did not know what it was.

Moses said to them, "It is the bread the LORD has given you to eat. [16]This is what the LORD has commanded: 'Each one is to gather as much as he needs. Take an omer[a] for each person you have in your tent.' "

[17]The Israelites did as they were told; some gathered much, some little. [18]And when they measured it by the omer, he who gathered much did not have too much, and he who gathered little did not have too little. Each one gathered as much as he needed.

[19]Then Moses said to them, "No one is to keep any of it until morning."

[20]However, some of them paid no attention to Moses; they kept part of it until morning, but it was full of maggots and began to smell. So Moses was angry with them.

[21]Each morning everyone gathered as much as he needed, and when the sun grew hot, it melted away. [22]On the sixth day, they gathered twice as much—two omers[b] for each person—and the leaders of the community came and reported this to Moses. [23]He said to them, "This is what the LORD commanded: 'Tomorrow is to be a day of rest, a holy Sabbath to the LORD. So bake what you want to bake and boil what you want to boil. Save whatever is left and keep it until morning.' "

[24]So they saved it until morning, as Moses commanded, and it did not stink or get maggots in it. [25]"Eat it today," Moses said, "because today is a Sabbath to the LORD. You will not find any of it on the ground today. [26]Six days you are to gather it, but on the seventh day, the Sabbath, there will not be any."

[27]Nevertheless, some of the people went out on the seventh day to gather it, but they found none. [28]Then the LORD said to Moses, "How long will you[c] refuse to keep my commands and my instructions? [29]Bear in mind that the LORD has given you the Sabbath; that is why on the sixth day he gives you bread for two days. Everyone is to stay where he is on the seventh day; no one is to go out." [30]So the people rested on the seventh day.

[31]The people of Israel called the bread manna.[d] It was white like coriander seed and tasted like wafers made with honey. [32]Moses said, "This is what the LORD has commanded: 'Take an omer of manna and keep it for the generations to come, so they can see the bread I gave you to eat in the desert when I brought you out of Egypt.' "

[33]So Moses said to Aaron, "Take a jar and put an omer of manna in it. Then place it before the LORD to be kept for the generations to come."

[34]As the LORD commanded Moses, Aaron put the manna in front of the Testimony, that it might be kept. [35]The Israelites ate manna forty years, until they came to a land that was settled; they ate manna until they reached the border of Canaan. [36](An omer is one tenth of an ephah.)

Water From the Rock

17 The whole Israelite community set out from the Desert of Sin, traveling from place to place as the LORD commanded. They camped at Rephidim, but there was no water for the people to drink. [2]So they quarreled with Moses and said, "Give us water to drink."

Moses replied, "Why do you quarrel with me? Why do you put the LORD to the test?"

[3]But the people were thirsty for water there, and they grumbled against Moses. They said, "Why did you bring us up out of Egypt to make us and our children and livestock die of thirst?"

[4]Then Moses cried out to the LORD, "What am I to do with these people? They are almost ready to stone me."

[5]The LORD answered Moses, "Walk on ahead of the people. Take with you some of the elders of Israel and take in your hand the staff with which you struck the Nile, and go. [6]I will stand there before you by the rock at Horeb. Strike the rock, and water will come out of it for the people to drink." So Moses did this in the sight of the elders of Israel. [7]And he called the place Massah[e] and Meribah[f] because the Israelites quarreled and because they tested the LORD saying, "Is the LORD among us or not?"

The Amalekites Defeated

[8]The Amalekites came and attacked the Israelites at Rephidim. [9]Moses said to

---

[a]16 That is, probably about 2 quarts (about 2 liters); also in verses 18, 32, 33 and 36
[b]22 That is, probably about 4 quarts (about 4.5 liters)   [c]28 The Hebrew is plural.
[d]31 Manna means What is it? (see verse 15).
[e]7 Massah means testing.   [f]7 Meribah means quarreling.

Joshua, "Choose some of our men and go out to fight the Amalekites. Tomorrow I will stand on top of the hill with the staff of God in my hands."

¹⁰So Joshua fought the Amalekites as Moses had ordered, and Moses, Aaron and Hur went to the top of the hill. ¹¹As long as Moses held up his hands, the Israelites were winning, but whenever he lowered his hands, the Amalekites were winning. ¹²When Moses' hands grew tired, they took a stone and put it under him and he sat on it. Aaron and Hur held his hands up—one on one side, one on the other—so that his hands remained steady till sunset. ¹³So Joshua overcame the Amalekite army with the sword.

¹⁴Then the LORD said to Moses, "Write this on a scroll as something to be remembered and make sure that Joshua hears it, because I will completely blot out the memory of Amalek from under heaven."

¹⁵Moses built an altar and called it The LORD is my Banner. ¹⁶He said, "For hands were lifted up to the throne of the LORD. The*a* LORD will be at war against the Amalekites from generation to generation."

Jethro Visits Moses

18 Now Jethro, the priest of Midian and father-in-law of Moses, heard of everything God had done for Moses and for his people Israel, and how the LORD had brought Israel out of Egypt.

²After Moses had sent away his wife Zipporah, his father-in-law Jethro received her ³and her two sons. One son was named Gershom,*b* for Moses said, "I have become an alien in a foreign land"; ⁴and the other was named Eliezer,*c* for he said, "My father's God was my helper; he saved me from the sword of Pharaoh."

⁵Jethro, Moses' father-in-law, together with Moses' sons and wife, came to him in the desert, where he was camped near the mountain of God. ⁶Jethro had sent word to him, "I, your father-in-law Jethro, am coming to you with your wife and her two sons."

⁷So Moses went out to meet his father-in-law and bowed down and kissed him. They greeted each other and then went into the tent. ⁸Moses told his father-in-law about everything the LORD had done to Pharaoh and the Egyptians for Israel's sake and about all the hardships they had met along the way and how the LORD had saved them.

⁹Jethro was delighted to hear about all the good things the LORD had done for Israel in rescuing them from the hand of the Egyptians. ¹⁰He said, "Praise be to the LORD, who rescued you from the hand of the Egyptians and of Pharaoh, and who rescued the people from the hand of the Egyptians. ¹¹Now I know that the LORD is greater than all other gods, for he did this to those who had treated Israel arrogantly." ¹²Then Jethro, Moses' father-in-law, brought a burnt offering and other sacrifices to God, and Aaron came with all the elders of Israel to eat bread with Moses' father-in-law in the presence of God.

¹³The next day Moses took his seat to serve as judge for the people, and they stood around him from morning till evening. ¹⁴When his father-in-law saw all that Moses was doing for the people, he said, "What is this you are doing for the people? Why do you alone sit as judge, while all these people stand around you from morning till evening?"

¹⁵Moses answered him, "Because the people come to me to seek God's will. ¹⁶Whenever they have a dispute, it is brought to me, and I decide between the parties and inform them of God's decrees and laws."

¹⁷Moses' father-in-law replied, "What you are doing is not good. ¹⁸You and these people who come to you will only wear yourselves out. The work is too heavy for you; you cannot handle it alone. ¹⁹Listen now to me and I will give you some advice, and may God be with

---

*a*16 Or *"Because a hand was against the throne of the* LORD, *the*   *b*3 *Gershom sounds like the Hebrew for an alien there.*   *c*4 *Eliezer means my God is helper.*

POINT OF INTEREST

Exodus 17:11

Moses held in his hands the staff he had used to inaugurate the plagues and that he had held over the water when God parted the Red Sea. The staff represented God's power; when Moses held it over his head, it symbolized the people's dependence on God.

you. You must be the people's representative before God and bring their disputes to him. ²⁰Teach them the decrees and laws, and show them the way to live and the duties they are to perform. ²¹But select capable men from all the people—men who fear God, trustworthy men who hate dishonest gain—and appoint them as officials over thousands, hundreds, fifties and tens. ²²Have them serve as judges for the people at all times, but have them bring every difficult case to you; the simple cases they can decide themselves. That will make your load lighter, because they will share it with you. ²³If you do this and God so commands, you will be able to stand the strain, and all these people will go home satisfied."

²⁴Moses listened to his father-in-law and did everything he said. ²⁵He chose capable men from all Israel and made them leaders of the people, officials over thousands, hundreds, fifties and tens. ²⁶They served as judges for the people at all times. The difficult cases they brought to Moses, but the simple ones they decided themselves.

²⁷Then Moses sent his father-in-law on his way, and Jethro returned to his own country.

At Mount Sinai

19 In the third month after the Israelites left Egypt—on the very day—they came to the Desert of Sinai. ²After they set out from Rephidim, they entered the Desert of Sinai, and Israel camped there in the desert in front of the mountain. ³Then Moses went up to God, and the LORD called to him from the mountain and said, "This is what you are to say to the house of Jacob and what you are to tell the people of Israel: ⁴'You yourselves have seen what I did to Egypt, and how I carried you on eagles' wings and brought you to myself. ⁵Now if you obey me fully and keep my covenant, then out of all nations you will be my treasured possession. Although the whole earth is mine, ⁶you*ᵃ* will be for me a kingdom of priests and a holy nation.' These are the words you are to speak to the Israelites."

⁷So Moses went back and summoned the elders of the people and set before them all the words the LORD had commanded him to speak. ⁸The people all responded together, "We will do every-

thing the LORD has said." So Moses brought their answer back to the LORD.

⁹The LORD said to Moses, "I am going to come to you in a dense cloud, so that the people will hear me speaking with you and will always put their trust in you." Then Moses told the LORD what the people had said.

¹⁰And the LORD said to Moses, "Go to the people and consecrate them today and tomorrow. Have them wash their clothes ¹¹and be ready by the third day, because on that day the LORD will come down on Mount Sinai in the sight of all the people. ¹²Put limits for the people around the mountain and tell them, 'Be careful that you do not go up the mountain or touch the foot of it. Whoever touches the mountain shall surely be put to death. ¹³He shall surely be stoned or shot with arrows; not a hand is to be laid on him. Whether man or animal, he shall not be permitted to live.' Only when the ram's horn sounds a long blast may they go up to the mountain."

¹⁴After Moses had gone down the mountain to the people, he consecrated them, and they washed their clothes. ¹⁵Then he said to the people, "Prepare yourselves for the third day. Abstain from sexual relations."

¹⁶On the morning of the third day there was thunder and lightning, with a thick cloud over the mountain, and a very loud trumpet blast. Everyone in the camp trembled. ¹⁷Then Moses led the people out of the camp to meet with God, and they stood at the foot of the mountain. ¹⁸Mount Sinai was covered with smoke, because the LORD descended on it in fire. The smoke billowed up from it like smoke from a furnace, the whole

ᵃ5,6 Or possession, for the whole earth is mine.
⁶You

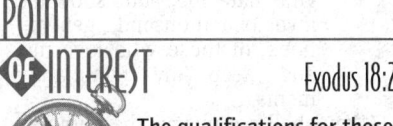

POINT OF INTEREST

Exodus 18:21

The qualifications for those who would help Moses lead the people were quite demanding. Compare these standards with those listed for church leaders in 1 Timothy 3:2–7. How are they the same? How are they different?

mountain*a* trembled violently, ¹⁹and the sound of the trumpet grew louder and louder. Then Moses spoke and the voice of God answered him.*b*

²⁰The LORD descended to the top of Mount Sinai and called Moses to the top of the mountain. So Moses went up ²¹and the LORD said to him, "Go down and warn the people so they do not force their way through to see the LORD and many of them perish. ²²Even the priests, who approach the LORD, must consecrate themselves, or the LORD will break out against them."

²³Moses said to the LORD, "The people cannot come up Mount Sinai, because you yourself warned us, 'Put limits around the mountain and set it apart as holy.' "

²⁴The LORD replied, "Go down and bring Aaron up with you. But the priests and the people must not force their way through to come up to the LORD, or he will break out against them."

²⁵So Moses went down to the people and told them.

The Ten Commandments

20 And God spoke all these words:

²"I am the LORD your God, who brought you out of Egypt, out of the land of slavery.

³"You shall have no other gods before*c* me.

⁴"You shall not make for yourself an idol in the form of anything in heaven above or on the earth beneath or in the waters below. ⁵You shall not bow down to them or worship them; for I, the LORD your God, am a jealous God, punishing the children for the sin of the fathers to the third and fourth generation of those who hate me, ⁶but showing love to a thousand ⌐generations⌐ of those who love me and keep my commandments.

⁷"You shall not misuse the name of the LORD your God, for the LORD will not hold anyone guiltless who misuses his name.

⁸"Remember the Sabbath day by keeping it holy. ⁹Six days you shall labor and do all your work, ¹⁰but the seventh day is a Sabbath to the LORD your God. On it you shall not do any work, neither you, nor your son or daughter, nor your manservant or maidservant, nor your animals, nor the alien within your gates. ¹¹For in six days the LORD made the heavens and the earth, the sea, and all that is in them, but he rested on the seventh day. Therefore the LORD blessed the Sabbath day and made it holy.

¹²"Honor your father and your mother, so that you may live long in the land the LORD your God is giving you.

¹³"You shall not murder.

¹⁴"You shall not commit adultery.

¹⁵"You shall not steal.

¹⁶"You shall not give false testimony against your neighbor.

¹⁷"You shall not covet your neighbor's house. You shall not covet your neighbor's wife, or his manservant or maidservant, his ox or donkey, or anything that belongs to your neighbor."

¹⁸When the people saw the thunder and lightning and heard the trumpet and saw the mountain in smoke, they trembled with fear. They stayed at a distance ¹⁹and said to Moses, "Speak to us yourself and we will listen. But do not have God speak to us or we will die."

²⁰Moses said to the people, "Do not be afraid. God has come to test you, so that the fear of God will be with you to keep you from sinning."

²¹The people remained at a distance, while Moses approached the thick darkness where God was.

Idols and Altars

²²Then the LORD said to Moses, "Tell the Israelites this: 'You have seen for yourselves that I have spoken to you from heaven: ²³Do not make any gods to be alongside me; do not make for yourselves gods of silver or gods of gold.

a 18 Most Hebrew manuscripts; a few Hebrew manuscripts and Septuagint *all the people*
b 19 Or *and God answered him with thunder*
c 3 Or *besides*

²⁴" 'Make an altar of earth for me and sacrifice on it your burnt offerings and fellowship offerings,ᵃ your sheep and goats and your cattle. Wherever I cause my name to be honored, I will come to you and bless you. ²⁵If you make an altar of stones for me, do not build it with dressed stones, for you will defile it if you use a tool on it. ²⁶And do not go up to my altar on steps, lest your nakedness be exposed on it.'

21 "These are the laws you are to set before them:

Hebrew Servants

²"If you buy a Hebrew servant, he is to serve you for six years. But in the seventh year, he shall go free, without paying anything. ³If he comes alone, he is to go free alone; but if he has a wife when he

ᵃ24 Traditionally *peace offerings*

Read Exodus 20:1–26
Key Verses Exodus 20:3–17

Religion ... or Relationship? — Jim Lett

The Ten Commandments are not just ten religious rules! They are more than ten good suggestions to live by. The beauty of the "Ten Words from God," as they are known to the Hebrew people, is in their wisdom and truthfulness and their intention to set apart God's people as a holy nation and to preserve them emotionally, physically and spiritually. They are a gift from a gracious God for all our relationships:

The first four commandments (Exodus 20:3–11), guide our relationship with the God who created, loves and cares for us. Our relationship with God is primary to all other relationships.

The fifth commandment (Exodus 20:12), directing children to honor their parents, is a transition to the remaining five. Parents, whether they do their job well or not, are representatives to the family on God's behalf. Giving parents honor and respect for their God-given role was essential for preserving the important family structure of the Israelites, and it is just as important for giving the family stability in our times. Honoring our parents trains and shapes our wills to honor God as well.

Commandments six through ten (Exodus 20:13–17) focus on our relationships with others. When applied to all of our human relationships, these commandments are designed to preserve and protect us and our communities and to help us live in harmony and contentment.

"Ten Words from God" are the basis for all the laws that follow in Exodus and the rest of Scripture. As you read them, look beyond the laws and look for the positive principles on which they are based. Ask the question, "What does this tell me about how to 'love the Lord [my] God with all [my] heart and with all [my] soul and with all [my] mind,' " and, "What does this tell me about how to 'love [my] neighbor as [myself]?' " (Matthew 22:37–39).

A Deeper Look
Matthew 22:34–40; John 13:34–35

Go to page 86 for your next devotional reading.

comes, she is to go with him. ⁴If his master gives him a wife and she bears him sons or daughters, the woman and her children shall belong to her master, and only the man shall go free.

⁵"But if the servant declares, 'I love my master and my wife and children and do not want to go free,' ⁶then his master must take him before the judges.ᵃ He shall take him to the door or the doorpost and pierce his ear with an awl. Then he will be his servant for life.

⁷"If a man sells his daughter as a servant, she is not to go free as menservants do. ⁸If she does not please the master who has selected her for himself,ᵇ he must let her be redeemed. He has no right to sell her to foreigners, because he has broken faith with her. ⁹If he selects her for his son, he must grant her the rights of a daughter. ¹⁰If he marries another woman, he must not deprive the first one of her food, clothing and marital rights. ¹¹If he does not provide her with these three things, she is to go free, without any payment of money.

Personal Injuries

¹²"Anyone who strikes a man and kills him shall surely be put to death. ¹³However, if he does not do it intentionally, but God lets it happen, he is to flee to a place I will designate. ¹⁴But if a man schemes and kills another man deliberately, take him away from my altar and put him to death.

¹⁵"Anyone who attacksᶜ his father or his mother must be put to death.

¹⁶"Anyone who kidnaps another and either sells him or still has him when he is caught must be put to death.

¹⁷"Anyone who curses his father or mother must be put to death.

¹⁸"If men quarrel and one hits the other with a stone or with his fistᵈ and he does not die but is confined to bed, ¹⁹the one who struck the blow will not be held responsible if the other gets up and walks around outside with his staff; however, he must pay the injured man for the loss of his time and see that he is completely healed.

²⁰"If a man beats his male or female slave with a rod and the slave dies as a direct result, he must be punished, ²¹but he is not to be punished if the slave gets up after a day or two, since the slave is his property.

²²"If men who are fighting hit a pregnant woman and she gives birth prematurelyᵉ but there is no serious injury, the offender must be fined whatever the woman's husband demands and the court allows. ²³But if there is serious injury, you are to take life for life, ²⁴eye for eye, tooth for tooth, hand for hand, foot for foot, ²⁵burn for burn, wound for wound, bruise for bruise.

²⁶"If a man hits a manservant or maidservant in the eye and destroys it, he must let the servant go free to compensate for the eye. ²⁷And if he knocks out the tooth of a manservant or maidservant, he must let the servant go free to compensate for the tooth.

²⁸"If a bull gores a man or a woman to death, the bull must be stoned to death, and its meat must not be eaten. But the owner of the bull will not be held responsible. ²⁹If, however, the bull has had the habit of goring and the owner has been warned but has not kept it penned up and it kills a man or woman, the bull must be stoned and the owner also must be put to death. ³⁰However, if payment is demanded of him, he may redeem his life by paying whatever is demanded. ³¹This law also applies if the bull gores a son or daughter. ³²If the bull gores a male or female slave, the owner must pay thirty shekelsᶠ of silver to the master of the slave, and the bull must be stoned.

³³"If a man uncovers a pit or digs one and fails to cover it and an ox or a donkey falls into it, ³⁴the owner of the pit must pay for the loss; he must pay its owner, and the dead animal will be his.

ᵃ6 Or *before God*   ᵇ8 Or *master so that he does not choose her*   ᶜ15 Or *kills*   ᵈ18 Or *with a tool*   ᵉ22 Or *she has a miscarriage*   ᶠ32 That is, about 12 ounces (about 0.3 kilogram)

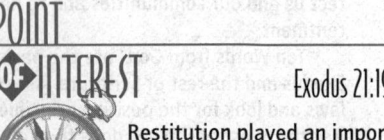

POINT OF INTEREST

Exodus 21:19

Restitution played an important part in Old Testament law. In dealing with crimes between individuals, the principle of restitution held that an individual was responsible for his or her actions and was required to restore what was taken or damaged. What impact might restitution have on both the criminal and the victim?

³⁵"If a man's bull injures the bull of another and it dies, they are to sell the live one and divide both the money and the dead animal equally. ³⁶However, if it was known that the bull had the habit of goring, yet the owner did not keep it penned up, the owner must pay, animal for animal, and the dead animal will be his.

Protection of Property

22 "If a man steals an ox or a sheep and slaughters it or sells it, he must pay back five head of cattle for the ox and four sheep for the sheep.

²"If a thief is caught breaking in and is struck so that he dies, the defender is not guilty of bloodshed; ³but if it happens*a* after sunrise, he is guilty of bloodshed.

"A thief must certainly make restitution, but if he has nothing, he must be sold to pay for his theft.

⁴"If the stolen animal is found alive in his possession—whether ox or donkey or sheep—he must pay back double.

⁵"If a man grazes his livestock in a field or vineyard and lets them stray and they graze in another man's field, he must make restitution from the best of his own field or vineyard.

⁶"If a fire breaks out and spreads into thornbushes so that it burns shocks of grain or standing grain or the whole field, the one who started the fire must make restitution.

⁷"If a man gives his neighbor silver or goods for safekeeping and they are stolen from the neighbor's house, the thief, if he is caught, must pay back double. ⁸But if the thief is not found, the owner of the house must appear before the judges*b* to determine whether he has laid his hands on the other man's property. ⁹In all cases of illegal possession of an ox, a donkey, a sheep, a garment, or any other lost property about which somebody says, 'This is mine,' both parties are to bring their cases before the judges. The one whom the judges declare*c* guilty must pay back double to his neighbor.

¹⁰"If a man gives a donkey, an ox, a sheep or any other animal to his neighbor for safekeeping and it dies or is injured or is taken away while no one is looking, ¹¹the issue between them will be settled by the taking of an oath before the LORD that the neighbor did not lay hands on the other person's property. The owner is to accept this, and no restitution is re-quired. ¹²But if the animal was stolen from the neighbor, he must make restitution to the owner. ¹³If it was torn to pieces by a wild animal, he shall bring in the remains as evidence and he will not be required to pay for the torn animal.

¹⁴"If a man borrows an animal from his neighbor and it is injured or dies while the owner is not present, he must make restitution. ¹⁵But if the owner is with the animal, the borrower will not have to pay. If the animal was hired, the money paid for the hire covers the loss.

Social Responsibility

¹⁶"If a man seduces a virgin who is not pledged to be married and sleeps with her, he must pay the bride-price, and she shall be his wife. ¹⁷If her father absolutely refuses to give her to him, he must still pay the bride-price for virgins.

¹⁸"Do not allow a sorceress to live.

¹⁹"Anyone who has sexual relations with an animal must be put to death.

²⁰"Whoever sacrifices to any god other than the LORD must be destroyed.*d*

²¹"Do not mistreat an alien or oppress him, for you were aliens in Egypt.

²²"Do not take advantage of a widow or an orphan. ²³If you do and they cry out to me, I will certainly hear their cry. ²⁴My anger will be aroused, and I will kill you with the sword; your wives will become widows and your children fatherless.

²⁵"If you lend money to one of my people among you who is needy, do not be like a moneylender; charge him no interest.*e* ²⁶If you take your neighbor's cloak as a pledge, return it to him by sunset, ²⁷because his cloak is the only covering he has for his body. What else will he sleep in? When he cries out to me, I will hear, for I am compassionate.

²⁸"Do not blaspheme God*f* or curse the ruler of your people.

²⁹"Do not hold back offerings from your granaries or your vats.*g*

"You must give me the firstborn of your sons. ³⁰Do the same with your cattle and your sheep. Let them stay with their mothers for seven days, but give them to me on the eighth day.

---

a3 Or *if he strikes him*   *b8* Or *before God*; also in verse 9   *c9* Or *whom God declares*
d20 The Hebrew term refers to the irrevocable giving over of things or persons to the LORD, often by totally destroying them.   *e25* Or *excessive interest*   *f28* Or *Do not revile the judges*
g29 The meaning of the Hebrew for this phrase is uncertain.

³¹"You are to be my holy people. So do not eat the meat of an animal torn by wild beasts; throw it to the dogs.

Laws of Justice and Mercy

23 "Do not spread false reports. Do not help a wicked man by being a malicious witness.

²"Do not follow the crowd in doing wrong. When you give testimony in a lawsuit, do not pervert justice by siding with the crowd, ³and do not show favoritism to a poor man in his lawsuit.

⁴"If you come across your enemy's ox or donkey wandering off, be sure to take it back to him. ⁵If you see the donkey of someone who hates you fallen down under its load, do not leave it there; be sure you help him with it.

⁶"Do not deny justice to your poor people in their lawsuits. ⁷Have nothing to do with a false charge and do not put an innocent or honest person to death, for I will not acquit the guilty.

⁸"Do not accept a bribe, for a bribe blinds those who see and twists the words of the righteous.

⁹"Do not oppress an alien; you yourselves know how it feels to be aliens, because you were aliens in Egypt.

FRIDAY

Read Exodus 23:1–33
Key Verse Exodus 23:2

Following the Crowd — Bill Gensky

A few years ago a study was conducted to measure the influence students have on each other in forming opinions. All the members of the class but one were aware of the object of the test. When various questions were asked of the students, they all gave correct answers.

Then the students were shown two lines, one obviously longer than the other, and asked to identify the longer line. The students who were "in" on the test each said the shorter line was the longer of the two. The one student who didn't know he was being tested sided with each of his peers more than 75 percent of the time. This student could plainly see the other line was longer, but because everyone said otherwise, the tested student followed the majority.

The desire to belong to the group can strongly influence our decisions. Even when we're faced with choices we know are not the best, we often choose what will make us look like we fit in. We've all been faced with this situation at one time or another, but does peer acceptance really give our lives meaning? Does it make us feel fulfilled? Does it mean more to us than wisdom or truth?

Or does that kind of meaning come from following the God who loves and cares for us more than anyone else—friends, teammates, professors, parents—possibly can? He tells us, "I have loved you with an everlasting love; I have drawn you with loving-kindness" (Jeremiah 31:3). Through Jesus we all fit in: "And you also were included in Christ when you heard the word of truth, the gospel of your salvation. Having believed, you were marked in him with a seal, the promised Holy Spirit" (Ephesians 1:13). It is God who draws us into the greatest peer group we could ever have—"a chosen people, a royal priesthood, a holy nation" (1 Peter 2:9).

A Deeper Look
1 Corinthians 15:33; 2 Corinthians 6:14–18

Go to page 98 for your next devotional reading.

Sabbath Laws

¹⁰"For six years you are to sow your fields and harvest the crops, ¹¹but during the seventh year let the land lie unplowed and unused. Then the poor among your people may get food from it, and the wild animals may eat what they leave. Do the same with your vineyard and your olive grove.

¹²"Six days do your work, but on the seventh day do not work, so that your ox and your donkey may rest and the slave born in your household, and the alien as well, may be refreshed.

¹³"Be careful to do everything I have said to you. Do not invoke the names of other gods; do not let them be heard on your lips.

The Three Annual Festivals

¹⁴"Three times a year you are to celebrate a festival to me.

¹⁵"Celebrate the Feast of Unleavened Bread; for seven days eat bread made without yeast, as I commanded you. Do this at the appointed time in the month of Abib, for in that month you came out of Egypt.

"No one is to appear before me empty-handed.

¹⁶"Celebrate the Feast of Harvest with the firstfruits of the crops you sow in your field.

"Celebrate the Feast of Ingathering at the end of the year, when you gather in your crops from the field.

¹⁷"Three times a year all the men are to appear before the Sovereign LORD.

¹⁸"Do not offer the blood of a sacrifice to me along with anything containing yeast.

"The fat of my festival offerings must not be kept until morning.

¹⁹"Bring the best of the firstfruits of your soil to the house of the LORD your God.

"Do not cook a young goat in its mother's milk.

God's Angel to Prepare the Way

²⁰"See, I am sending an angel ahead of you to guard you along the way and to bring you to the place I have prepared. ²¹Pay attention to him and listen to what he says. Do not rebel against him; he will not forgive your rebellion, since my Name is in him. ²²If you listen carefully to what he says and do all that I say, I will be an enemy to your enemies and will oppose those who oppose you. ²³My angel will go ahead of you and bring you into the land of the Amorites, Hittites, Perizzites, Canaanites, Hivites and Jebusites, and I will wipe them out. ²⁴Do not bow down before their gods or worship them or follow their practices. You must demolish them and break their sacred stones to pieces. ²⁵Worship the LORD your God, and his blessing will be on your food and water. I will take away sickness from among you, ²⁶and none will miscarry or be barren in your land. I will give you a full life span.

²⁷"I will send my terror ahead of you and throw into confusion every nation you encounter. I will make all your enemies turn their backs and run. ²⁸I will send the hornet ahead of you to drive the Hivites, Canaanites and Hittites out of your way. ²⁹But I will not drive them out in a single year, because the land would become desolate and the wild animals too numerous for you. ³⁰Little by little I will drive them out before you, until you have increased enough to take possession of the land.

³¹"I will establish your borders from the Red Sea[a] to the Sea of the Philistines,[b] and from the desert to the River.[c] I will hand over to you the people who live in the land and you will drive them out before you. ³²Do not make a covenant with them or with their gods. ³³Do not let them live in your land, or they will cause you to sin against me, because the worship of their gods will certainly be a snare to you."

The Covenant Confirmed

24 Then he said to Moses, "Come up to the LORD, you and Aaron, Nadab and Abihu, and seventy of the elders of Israel. You are to worship at a distance, ²but Moses alone is to approach the LORD; the others must not come near. And the people may not come up with him."

³When Moses went and told the people all the LORD's words and laws, they responded with one voice, "Everything the LORD has said we will do." ⁴Moses then wrote down everything the LORD had said.

He got up early the next morning and built an altar at the foot of the mountain

---

a31 Hebrew *Yam Suph*; that is, Sea of Reeds
b31 That is, the Mediterranean   c31 That is, the Euphrates

and set up twelve stone pillars representing the twelve tribes of Israel. ⁵Then he sent young Israelite men, and they offered burnt offerings and sacrificed young bulls as fellowship offerings*a* to the LORD. ⁶Moses took half of the blood and put it in bowls, and the other half he sprinkled on the altar. ⁷Then he took the Book of the Covenant and read it to the people. They responded, "We will do everything the LORD has said; we will obey."

⁸Moses then took the blood, sprinkled it on the people and said, "This is the blood of the covenant that the LORD has made with you in accordance with all these words."

⁹Moses and Aaron, Nadab and Abihu, and the seventy elders of Israel went up ¹⁰and saw the God of Israel. Under his feet was something like a pavement made of sapphire,*b* clear as the sky itself. ¹¹But God did not raise his hand against these leaders of the Israelites; they saw God, and they ate and drank.

¹²The LORD said to Moses, "Come up to me on the mountain and stay here, and I will give you the tablets of stone, with the law and commands I have written for their instruction."

¹³Then Moses set out with Joshua his aide, and Moses went up on the mountain of God. ¹⁴He said to the elders, "Wait here for us until we come back to you. Aaron and Hur are with you, and anyone involved in a dispute can go to them."

¹⁵When Moses went up on the mountain, the cloud covered it, ¹⁶and the glory of the LORD settled on Mount Sinai. For six days the cloud covered the mountain, and on the seventh day the LORD called to Moses from within the cloud. ¹⁷To the Israelites the glory of the LORD looked like a consuming fire on top of the mountain. ¹⁸Then Moses entered the cloud as he went on up the mountain. And he stayed on the mountain forty days and forty nights.

Offerings for the Tabernacle

25 The LORD said to Moses, ²"Tell the Israelites to bring me an offering. You are to receive the offering for me from each man whose heart prompts him to give. ³These are the offerings you are to receive from them: gold, silver and bronze; ⁴blue, purple and scarlet yarn and fine linen; goat hair; ⁵ram skins dyed red and hides of sea cows*c*; acacia wood; ⁶olive oil for the light; spices for the anointing oil and for the fragrant incense; ⁷and onyx stones and other gems to be mounted on the ephod and breastpiece.

⁸"Then have them make a sanctuary for me, and I will dwell among them. ⁹Make this tabernacle and all its furnishings exactly like the pattern I will show you.

The Ark

¹⁰"Have them make a chest of acacia wood—two and a half cubits long, a cubit and a half wide, and a cubit and a half high.*d* ¹¹Overlay it with pure gold, both inside and out, and make a gold molding around it. ¹²Cast four gold rings for it and fasten them to its four feet, with two rings on one side and two rings on the other. ¹³Then make poles of acacia wood and overlay them with gold. ¹⁴Insert the poles into the rings on the sides of the chest to carry it. ¹⁵The poles are to remain in the rings of this ark; they are not to be removed. ¹⁶Then put in the ark the Testimony, which I will give you.

¹⁷"Make an atonement cover*e* of pure gold—two and a half cubits long and a cubit and a half wide.*f* ¹⁸And make two cherubim out of hammered gold at the ends of the cover. ¹⁹Make one cherub on one end and the second cherub on the other; make the cherubim of one piece with the cover, at the two ends. ²⁰The cherubim are to have their wings spread upward, overshadowing the cover with them. The cherubim are to face each oth-

a5 Traditionally *peace offerings*   *b10* Or *lapis lazuli*   *c5* That is, dugongs   *d10* That is, about 3 3/4 feet (about 1.1 meters) long and 2 1/4 feet (about 0.7 meter) wide and high   *e17* Traditionally *a mercy seat*   *f17* That is, about 3 3/4 feet (about 1.1 meters) long and 2 1/4 feet (about 0.7 meter) wide

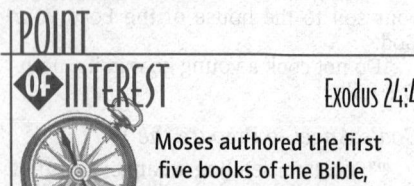

POINT OF INTEREST

Exodus 24:4

Moses authored the first five books of the Bible, called the "Pentateuch." Jesus himself referred to these books as the Law of Moses (see Luke 24:44). Raised in Pharaoh's house, Moses very likely would have been literate while most Hebrew slaves were not.

er, looking toward the cover. ²¹Place the cover on top of the ark and put in the ark the Testimony, which I will give you. ²²There, above the cover between the two cherubim that are over the ark of the Testimony, I will meet with you and give you all my commands for the Israelites.

The Table

²³"Make a table of acacia wood—two cubits long, a cubit wide and a cubit and a half high.*a* ²⁴Overlay it with pure gold and make a gold molding around it. ²⁵Also make around it a rim a handbreadth*b* wide and put a gold molding on the rim. ²⁶Make four gold rings for the table and fasten them to the four corners, where the four legs are. ²⁷The rings are to be close to the rim to hold the poles used in carrying the table. ²⁸Make the poles of acacia wood, overlay them with gold and carry the table with them. ²⁹And make its plates and dishes of pure gold, as well as its pitchers and bowls for the pouring out of offerings. ³⁰Put the bread of the Presence on this table to be before me at all times.

The Lampstand

³¹"Make a lampstand of pure gold and hammer it out, base and shaft; its flower-like cups, buds and blossoms shall be of one piece with it. ³²Six branches are to extend from the sides of the lampstand—three on one side and three on the other. ³³Three cups shaped like almond flowers with buds and blossoms are to be on one branch, three on the next branch, and the same for all six branches extending from the lampstand. ³⁴And on the lampstand there are to be four cups shaped like almond flowers with buds and blossoms. ³⁵One bud shall be under the first pair of branches extending from the lampstand, a second bud under the second pair, and a third bud under the third pair—six branches in all. ³⁶The buds and branches shall all be of one piece with the lampstand, hammered out of pure gold.

³⁷"Then make its seven lamps and set them up on it so that they light the space in front of it. ³⁸Its wick trimmers and trays are to be of pure gold. ³⁹A talent*c* of pure gold is to be used for the lampstand and all these accessories. ⁴⁰See that you make them according to the pattern shown you on the mountain.

The Tabernacle

26 "Make the tabernacle with ten curtains of finely twisted linen and blue, purple and scarlet yarn, with cherubim worked into them by a skilled craftsman. ²All the curtains are to be the same size— twenty-eight cubits long and four cubits wide.*d* ³Join five of the curtains together, and do the same with the other five. ⁴Make loops of blue material along the edge of the end curtain in one set, and do the same with the end curtain in the other set. ⁵Make fifty loops on one curtain and fifty loops on the end curtain of the other set, with the loops opposite each other. ⁶Then make fifty gold clasps and use them to fasten the curtains together so that the tabernacle is a unit.

⁷"Make curtains of goat hair for the tent over the tabernacle—eleven altogether. ⁸All eleven curtains are to be the same size—thirty cubits long and four cubits wide.*e* ⁹Join five of the curtains together into one set and the other six into another set. Fold the sixth curtain double at the front of the tent. ¹⁰Make fifty loops along the edge of the end curtain in one set and also along the edge of the end curtain in the other set. ¹¹Then make fifty bronze clasps and put them in the loops to fasten the tent together as a unit. ¹²As for the additional length of the tent curtains, the half curtain that is left over is to hang down at the rear of the tabernacle. ¹³The tent curtains will be a

---

a23 That is, about 3 feet (about 0.9 meter) long and 1 1/2 feet (about 0.5 meter) wide and 2 1/4 feet (about 0.7 meter) high   b25 That is, about 3 inches (about 8 centimeters)   c39 That is, about 75 pounds (about 34 kilograms)   d2 That is, about 42 feet (about 12.5 meters) long and 6 feet (about 1.8 meters) wide   e8 That is, about 45 feet (about 13.5 meters) long and 6 feet (about 1.8 meters) wide

POINT OF INTEREST

Exodus 25:32

Modern Judaism can trace its customs for worship back to these instructions for tabernacle construction given over 3,400 years ago. In fact, the seven-branched lampstand, called the "menorah," is still one of the major symbols of Judaism today.

cubit*a* longer on both sides; what is left will hang over the sides of the tabernacle so as to cover it. **14**Make for the tent a covering of ram skins dyed red, and over that a covering of hides of sea cows.*b*

15"Make upright frames of acacia wood for the tabernacle. **16**Each frame is to be ten cubits long and a cubit and a half wide,*c* **17**with two projections set parallel to each other. Make all the frames of the tabernacle in this way. **18**Make twenty frames for the south side of the tabernacle **19**and make forty silver bases to go under them—two bases for each frame, one under each projection. **20**For the other side, the north side of the tabernacle, make twenty frames **21**and forty silver bases—two under each frame. **22**Make six frames for the far end, that is, the west end of the tabernacle, **23**and make two frames for the corners at the far end. **24**At these two corners they must be double from the bottom all the way to the top, and fitted into a single ring; both shall be like that. **25**So there will be eight frames and sixteen silver bases—two under each frame.

26"Also make crossbars of acacia wood: five for the frames on one side of the tabernacle, **27**five for those on the other side, and five for the frames on the west, at the far end of the tabernacle. **28**The center crossbar is to extend from end to end at the middle of the frames. **29**Overlay the frames with gold and make gold rings to hold the crossbars. Also overlay the crossbars with gold.

30"Set up the tabernacle according to the plan shown you on the mountain.

31"Make a curtain of blue, purple and scarlet yarn and finely twisted linen, with cherubim worked into it by a skilled craftsman. **32**Hang it with gold hooks on four posts of acacia wood overlaid with gold and standing on four silver bases. **33**Hang the curtain from the clasps and place the ark of the Testimony behind the curtain. The curtain will separate the Holy Place from the Most Holy Place. **34**Put the atonement cover on the ark of the Testimony in the Most Holy Place. **35**Place the table outside the curtain on the north side of the tabernacle and put the lampstand opposite it on the south side.

36"For the entrance to the tent make a curtain of blue, purple and scarlet yarn and finely twisted linen—the work of an embroiderer. **37**Make gold hooks for this

curtain and five posts of acacia wood overlaid with gold. And cast five bronze bases for them.

The Altar of Burnt Offering

27 "Build an altar of acacia wood, three cubits*d* high; it is to be square, five cubits long and five cubits wide.*e* **2**Make a horn at each of the four corners, so that the horns and the altar are of one piece, and overlay the altar with bronze. **3**Make all its utensils of bronze—its pots to remove the ashes, and its shovels, sprinkling bowls, meat forks and firepans. **4**Make a grating for it, a bronze network, and make a bronze ring at each of the four corners of the network. **5**Put it under the ledge of the altar so that it is halfway up the altar. **6**Make poles of acacia wood for the altar and overlay them with bronze. **7**The poles are to be inserted into the rings so they will be on two sides of the altar when it is carried. **8**Make the altar hollow, out of boards. It is to be made just as you were shown on the mountain.

The Courtyard

9"Make a courtyard for the tabernacle. The south side shall be a hundred cubits*f* long and is to have curtains of finely twisted linen, **10**with twenty posts and twenty bronze bases and with silver hooks and bands on the posts. **11**The north side shall also be a hundred cubits long and is to have curtains, with twenty posts and twenty bronze bases and with silver hooks and bands on the posts.

12"The west end of the courtyard shall be fifty cubits*g* wide and have curtains, with ten posts and ten bases. **13**On the east end, toward the sunrise, the courtyard shall also be fifty cubits wide. **14**Curtains fifteen cubits*h* long are to be on one side of the entrance, with three posts and three bases, **15**and curtains fifteen cubits long are to be on the other side, with three posts and three bases.

16"For the entrance to the courtyard,

---

a13 That is, about 1 1/2 feet (about 0.5 meter)
b14 That is, dugongs   *c16* That is, about 15 feet (about 4.5 meters) long and 2 1/4 feet (about 0.7 meter) wide   *d1* That is, about 4 1/2 feet (about 1.3 meters)   *e1* That is, about 7 1/2 feet (about 2.3 meters) long and wide   *f9* That is, about 150 feet (about 46 meters); also in verse 11
g12 That is, about 75 feet (about 23 meters); also in verse 13   *h14* That is, about 22 1/2 feet (about 6.9 meters); also in verse 15

provide a curtain twenty cubits*a* long, of blue, purple and scarlet yarn and finely twisted linen—the work of an embroiderer—with four posts and four bases. [17]All the posts around the courtyard are to have silver bands and hooks, and bronze bases. [18]The courtyard shall be a hundred cubits long and fifty cubits wide,*b* with curtains of finely twisted linen five cubits*c* high, and with bronze bases. [19]All the other articles used in the service of the tabernacle, whatever their function, including all the tent pegs for it and those for the courtyard, are to be of bronze.

Oil for the Lampstand

[20]"Command the Israelites to bring you clear oil of pressed olives for the light so that the lamps may be kept burning. [21]In the Tent of Meeting, outside the curtain that is in front of the Testimony, Aaron and his sons are to keep the lamps burning before the LORD from evening till morning. This is to be a lasting ordinance among the Israelites for the generations to come.

The Priestly Garments

28 "Have Aaron your brother brought to you from among the Israelites, along with his sons Nadab and Abihu, Eleazar and Ithamar, so they may serve me as priests. [2]Make sacred garments for your brother Aaron, to give him dignity and honor. [3]Tell all the skilled men to whom I have given wisdom in such matters that they are to make garments for Aaron, for his consecration, so he may serve me as priest. [4]These are the garments they are to make: a breastpiece, an ephod, a robe, a woven tunic, a turban and a sash. They are to make these sacred garments for your brother Aaron and his sons, so they may serve me as priests. [5]Have them use gold, and blue, purple and scarlet yarn, and fine linen.

The Ephod

[6]"Make the ephod of gold, and of blue, purple and scarlet yarn, and of finely twisted linen—the work of a skilled craftsman. [7]It is to have two shoulder pieces attached to two of its corners, so it can be fastened. [8]Its skillfully woven waistband is to be like it—of one piece with the ephod and made with gold, and with blue, purple and scarlet yarn, and with finely twisted linen.

[9]"Take two onyx stones and engrave on them the names of the sons of Israel [10]in the order of their birth—six names on one stone and the remaining six on the other. [11]Engrave the names of the sons of Israel on the two stones the way a gem cutter engraves a seal. Then mount the stones in gold filigree settings [12]and fasten them on the shoulder pieces of the ephod as memorial stones for the sons of Israel. Aaron is to bear the names on his shoulders as a memorial before the LORD. [13]Make gold filigree settings [14]and two braided chains of pure gold, like a rope, and attach the chains to the settings.

The Breastpiece

[15]"Fashion a breastpiece for making decisions—the work of a skilled craftsman. Make it like the ephod: of gold, and of blue, purple and scarlet yarn, and of finely twisted linen. [16]It is to be square—a span*d* long and a span wide—and folded double. [17]Then mount four rows of precious stones on it. In the first row there shall be a ruby, a topaz and a beryl; [18]in the second row a turquoise, a sapphire*e* and an emerald; [19]in the third row a jacinth, an agate and an amethyst; [20]in the fourth row a chrysolite, an onyx and a jasper.*f* Mount them in gold filigree settings. [21]There are to be twelve stones, one for each of the names of the sons of Israel, each engraved like a seal with the name of one of the twelve tribes.

[22]"For the breastpiece make braided

a16 That is, about 30 feet (about 9 meters)
b18 That is, about 150 feet (about 46 meters) long and 75 feet (about 23 meters) wide   *c18* That is, about 7 1/2 feet (about 2.3 meters)   *d16* That is, about 9 inches (about 22 centimeters)   *e18* Or lapis lazuli   *f20* The precise identification of some of these precious stones is uncertain.

POINT OF INTEREST

Exodus 28:2

God designed the priest's clothing as a visual aid for the Israelites. As God's representative to the people, the high priest needed to embody purity in everything, including his dress. This holiness contrasted sharply with the lewd pagan practices the Israelites later encountered in Canaan.

chains of pure gold, like a rope. 23Make two gold rings for it and fasten them to two corners of the breastpiece. 24Fasten the two gold chains to the rings at the corners of the breastpiece, 25and the other ends of the chains to the two settings, attaching them to the shoulder pieces of the ephod at the front. 26Make two gold rings and attach them to the other two corners of the breastpiece on the inside edge next to the ephod. 27Make two more gold rings and attach them to the bottom of the shoulder pieces on the front of the ephod, close to the seam just above the waistband of the ephod. 28The rings of the breastpiece are to be tied to the rings of the ephod with blue cord, connecting it to the waistband, so that the breastpiece will not swing out from the ephod.

29"Whenever Aaron enters the Holy Place, he will bear the names of the sons of Israel over his heart on the breastpiece of decision as a continuing memorial before the LORD. 30Also put the Urim and the Thummim in the breastpiece, so they may be over Aaron's heart whenever he enters the presence of the LORD. Thus Aaron will always bear the means of making decisions for the Israelites over his heart before the LORD.

Other Priestly Garments

31"Make the robe of the ephod entirely of blue cloth, 32with an opening for the head in its center. There shall be a woven edge like a collar*a* around this opening, so that it will not tear. 33Make pomegranates of blue, purple and scarlet yarn around the hem of the robe, with gold bells between them. 34The gold bells and the pomegranates are to alternate around the hem of the robe. 35Aaron must wear it when he ministers. The sound of the bells will be heard when he enters the Holy Place before the LORD and when he comes out, so that he will not die.

36"Make a plate of pure gold and engrave on it as on a seal: HOLY TO THE LORD. 37Fasten a blue cord to it to attach it to the turban; it is to be on the front of the turban. 38It will be on Aaron's forehead, and he will bear the guilt involved in the sacred gifts the Israelites consecrate, whatever their gifts may be. It will be on Aaron's forehead continually so that they will be acceptable to the LORD.

39"Weave the tunic of fine linen and make the turban of fine linen. The sash is to be the work of an embroiderer. 40Make tunics, sashes and headbands for Aaron's sons, to give them dignity and honor. 41After you put these clothes on your brother Aaron and his sons, anoint and ordain them. Consecrate them so they may serve me as priests.

42"Make linen undergarments as a covering for the body, reaching from the waist to the thigh. 43Aaron and his sons must wear them whenever they enter the Tent of Meeting or approach the altar to minister in the Holy Place, so that they will not incur guilt and die.

"This is to be a lasting ordinance for Aaron and his descendants.

Consecration of the Priests

29 "This is what you are to do to consecrate them, so they may serve me as priests: Take a young bull and two rams without defect. 2And from fine wheat flour, without yeast, make bread, and cakes mixed with oil, and wafers spread with oil. 3Put them in a basket and present them in it—along with the bull and the two rams. 4Then bring Aaron and his sons to the entrance to the Tent of Meeting and wash them with water. 5Take the garments and dress Aaron with the tunic, the robe of the ephod, the ephod itself and the breastpiece. Fasten the ephod on him by its skillfully woven waistband. 6Put the turban on his head and attach the sacred diadem to the turban. 7Take the anointing oil and anoint him by pouring it on his head. 8Bring his sons and dress them in tunics 9and put headbands on them. Then tie sashes on Aaron and his sons.*b* The priesthood is theirs by a lasting ordinance. In this way you shall ordain Aaron and his sons.

10"Bring the bull to the front of the Tent of Meeting, and Aaron and his sons shall lay their hands on its head. 11Slaughter it in the LORD's presence at the entrance to the Tent of Meeting. 12Take some of the bull's blood and put it on the horns of the altar with your finger, and pour out the rest of it at the base of the altar. 13Then take all the fat around the inner parts, the covering of the liver, and both kidneys with the fat on them, and burn them on the altar. 14But burn the bull's flesh and its hide and its offal outside the camp. It is a sin offering.

15"Take one of the rams, and Aaron

a32 The meaning of the Hebrew for this word is uncertain.   *b9* Hebrew; Septuagint *on them* and his sons shall lay their hands on its head. ¹⁶Slaughter it and take the blood and sprinkle it against the altar on all sides. ¹⁷Cut the ram into pieces and wash the inner parts and the legs, putting them with the head and the other pieces. ¹⁸Then burn the entire ram on the altar. It is a burnt offering to the LORD, a pleasing aroma, an offering made to the LORD by fire.

¹⁹"Take the other ram, and Aaron and his sons shall lay their hands on its head. ²⁰Slaughter it, take some of its blood and put it on the lobes of the right ears of Aaron and his sons, on the thumbs of their right hands, and on the big toes of their right feet. Then sprinkle blood against the altar on all sides. ²¹And take some of the blood on the altar and some of the anointing oil and sprinkle it on Aaron and his garments and on his sons and their garments. Then he and his sons and their garments will be consecrated.

²²"Take from this ram the fat, the fat tail, the fat around the inner parts, the covering of the liver, both kidneys with the fat on them, and the right thigh. (This is the ram for the ordination.) ²³From the basket of bread made without yeast, which is before the LORD, take a loaf, and a cake made with oil, and a wafer. ²⁴Put all these in the hands of Aaron and his sons and wave them before the LORD as a wave offering. ²⁵Then take them from their hands and burn them on the altar along with the burnt offering for a pleasing aroma to the LORD, an offering made to the LORD by fire. ²⁶After you take the breast of the ram for Aaron's ordination, wave it before the LORD as a wave offering, and it will be your share.

²⁷"Consecrate those parts of the ordination ram that belong to Aaron and his sons: the breast that was waved and the thigh that was presented. ²⁸This is always to be the regular share from the Israelites for Aaron and his sons. It is the contribution the Israelites are to make to the LORD from their fellowship offerings.ᵃ

²⁹"Aaron's sacred garments will belong to his descendants so that they can be anointed and ordained in them. ³⁰The son who succeeds him as priest and comes to the Tent of Meeting to minister in the Holy Place is to wear them seven days.

³¹"Take the ram for the ordination and cook the meat in a sacred place. ³²At the entrance to the Tent of Meeting, Aaron and his sons are to eat the meat of the ram and the bread that is in the basket. ³³They are to eat these offerings by which atonement was made for their ordination and consecration. But no one else may eat them, because they are sacred. ³⁴And if any of the meat of the ordination ram or any bread is left over till morning, burn it up. It must not be eaten, because it is sacred.

³⁵"Do for Aaron and his sons everything I have commanded you, taking seven days to ordain them. ³⁶Sacrifice a bull each day as a sin offering to make atonement. Purify the altar by making atonement for it, and anoint it to consecrate it. ³⁷For seven days make atonement for the altar and consecrate it. Then the altar will be most holy, and whatever touches it will be holy.

³⁸"This is what you are to offer on the altar regularly each day: two lambs a year old. ³⁹Offer one in the morning and the other at twilight. ⁴⁰With the first lamb offer a tenth of an ephahᵇ of fine flour mixed with a quarter of a hinᶜ of oil from pressed olives, and a quarter of a hin of wine as a drink offering. ⁴¹Sacrifice the other lamb at twilight with the same grain offering and its drink offering as in the morning—a pleasing aroma, an offering made to the LORD by fire.

⁴²"For the generations to come this burnt offering is to be made regularly at the entrance to the Tent of Meeting before the LORD. There I will meet you and speak to you; ⁴³there also I will meet with

ᵃ28 Traditionally *peace offerings*   ᵇ40 That is, probably about 2 quarts (about 2 liters)
ᶜ40 That is, probably about 1 quart (about 1 liter)

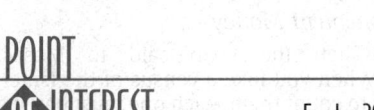

POINT OF INTEREST

Exodus 29:10

The sacrificial animal's blood served as a substitute for the blood of the sinner. A priest placed his hand on the head of the animal to indicate that this animal was the atonement or substitutionary payment for the people's sin. Jesus is called "the Lamb of God, who takes away the sin of the world!" (John 1:29).

the Israelites, and the place will be consecrated by my glory.

44"So I will consecrate the Tent of
Meeting and the altar and will consecrate
Aaron and his sons to serve me as priests.
45Then I will dwell among the Israelites
and be their God. 46They will know that
I am the LORD their God, who brought
them out of Egypt so that I might dwell
among them. I am the LORD their God.

The Altar of Incense

30 "Make an altar of acacia wood for
burning incense. 2It is to be square, a
cubit long and a cubit wide, and two cubits high*a*—its horns of one piece with
it. 3Overlay the top and all the sides and
the horns with pure gold, and make a
gold molding around it. 4Make two gold
rings for the altar below the molding—
two on opposite sides—to hold the poles
used to carry it. 5Make the poles of acacia
wood and overlay them with gold. 6Put
the altar in front of the curtain that is
before the ark of the Testimony—before
the atonement cover that is over the
Testimony—where I will meet with you.

7"Aaron must burn fragrant incense on
the altar every morning when he tends
the lamps. 8He must burn incense again
when he lights the lamps at twilight so
incense will burn regularly before the
LORD for the generations to come. 9Do not
offer on this altar any other incense or
any burnt offering or grain offering, and
do not pour a drink offering on it. 10Once
a year Aaron shall make atonement on its
horns. This annual atonement must be
made with the blood of the atoning sin
offering for the generations to come. It is
most holy to the LORD."

Atonement Money

11Then the LORD said to Moses,
12"When you take a census of the Israelites to count them, each one must pay the
LORD a ransom for his life at the time he is
counted. Then no plague will come on
them when you number them. 13Each
one who crosses over to those already
counted is to give a half shekel,*b* according to the sanctuary shekel, which
weighs twenty gerahs. This half shekel
is an offering to the LORD. 14All who cross
over, those twenty years old or more, are
to give an offering to the LORD. 15The rich
are not to give more than a half shekel
and the poor are not to give less when
you make the offering to the LORD to

atone for your lives. 16Receive the atonement money from the Israelites and use it
for the service of the Tent of Meeting. It
will be a memorial for the Israelites before the LORD, making atonement for your
lives."

Basin for Washing

17Then the LORD said to Moses,
18"Make a bronze basin, with its bronze
stand, for washing. Place it between the
Tent of Meeting and the altar, and put
water in it. 19Aaron and his sons are to
wash their hands and feet with water
from it. 20Whenever they enter the Tent
of Meeting, they shall wash with water so
that they will not die. Also, when they
approach the altar to minister by presenting an offering made to the LORD by fire,
21they shall wash their hands and feet so
that they will not die. This is to be a lasting ordinance for Aaron and his descendants for the generations to come."

Anointing Oil

22Then the LORD said to Moses, 23"Take
the following fine spices: 500 shekels*c*
of liquid myrrh, half as much (that is, 250
shekels) of fragrant cinnamon, 250 shekels of fragrant cane, 24500 shekels of
cassia—all according to the sanctuary
shekel—and a hin*d* of olive oil. 25Make
these into a sacred anointing oil, a fragrant blend, the work of a perfumer. It
will be the sacred anointing oil. 26Then
use it to anoint the Tent of Meeting, the
ark of the Testimony, 27the table and all
its articles, the lampstand and its accessories, the altar of incense, 28the altar of
burnt offering and all its utensils, and the
basin with its stand. 29You shall consecrate them so they will be most holy, and
whatever touches them will be holy.

30"Anoint Aaron and his sons and consecrate them so they may serve me as
priests. 31Say to the Israelites, 'This is to
be my sacred anointing oil for the generations to come. 32Do not pour it on men's
bodies and do not make any oil with the
same formula. It is sacred, and you are to
consider it sacred. 33Whoever makes perfume like it and whoever puts it on any-

---

a2 That is, about 1 1/2 feet (about 0.5 meter) long
and wide and about 3 feet (about 0.9 meter) high
b13 That is, about 1/5 ounce (about 6 grams); also
in verse 15   *c23* That is, about 12 1/2 pounds
(about 6 kilograms)   *d24* That is, probably
about 4 quarts (about 4 liters)

one other than a priest must be cut off from his people.' "

Incense

³⁴Then the LORD said to Moses, "Take fragrant spices—gum resin, onycha and galbanum—and pure frankincense, all in equal amounts, ³⁵and make a fragrant blend of incense, the work of a perfumer. It is to be salted and pure and sacred. ³⁶Grind some of it to powder and place it in front of the Testimony in the Tent of Meeting, where I will meet with you. It shall be most holy to you. ³⁷Do not make any incense with this formula for yourselves; consider it holy to the LORD. ³⁸Whoever makes any like it to enjoy its fragrance must be cut off from his people."

Bezalel and Oholiab

31 Then the LORD said to Moses, ²"See, I have chosen Bezalel son of Uri, the son of Hur, of the tribe of Judah, ³and I have filled him with the Spirit of God, with skill, ability and knowledge in all kinds of crafts— ⁴to make artistic designs for work in gold, silver and bronze, ⁵to cut and set stones, to work in wood, and to engage in all kinds of craftsmanship. ⁶Moreover, I have appointed Oholiab son of Ahisamach, of the tribe of Dan, to help him. Also I have given skill to all the craftsmen to make everything I have commanded you: ⁷the Tent of Meeting, the ark of the Testimony with the atonement cover on it, and all the other furnishings of the tent— ⁸the table and its articles, the pure gold lampstand and all its accessories, the altar of incense, ⁹the altar of burnt offering and all its utensils, the basin with its stand— ¹⁰and also the woven garments, both the sacred garments for Aaron the priest and the garments for his sons when they serve as priests, ¹¹and the anointing oil and fragrant incense for the Holy Place. They are to make them just as I commanded you."

The Sabbath

¹²Then the LORD said to Moses, ¹³"Say to the Israelites, 'You must observe my Sabbaths. This will be a sign between me and you for the generations to come, so you may know that I am the LORD, who makes you holy.[a]

¹⁴" 'Observe the Sabbath, because it is holy to you. Anyone who desecrates it must be put to death; whoever does any work on that day must be cut off from his people. ¹⁵For six days, work is to be done, but the seventh day is a Sabbath of rest, holy to the LORD. Whoever does any work on the Sabbath day must be put to death. ¹⁶The Israelites are to observe the Sabbath, celebrating it for the generations to come as a lasting covenant. ¹⁷It will be a sign between me and the Israelites forever, for in six days the LORD made the heavens and the earth, and on the seventh day he abstained from work and rested.' "

¹⁸When the LORD finished speaking to Moses on Mount Sinai, he gave him the two tablets of the Testimony, the tablets of stone inscribed by the finger of God.

The Golden Calf

32 When the people saw that Moses was so long in coming down from the mountain, they gathered around Aaron and said, "Come, make us gods[b] who will go before us. As for this fellow Moses who brought us up out of Egypt, we don't know what has happened to him."

²Aaron answered them, "Take off the gold earrings that your wives, your sons and your daughters are wearing, and bring them to me." ³So all the people took off their earrings and brought them to Aaron. ⁴He took what they handed him and made it into an idol cast in the shape of a calf, fashioning it with a tool. Then they said, "These are your gods,[c] O Israel, who brought you up out of Egypt."

⁵When Aaron saw this, he built an al-

---

[a]13 Or *who sanctifies you;* or *who sets you apart as holy*   [b]1 Or *a god;* also in verses 23 and 31   [c]4 Or *This is your god;* also in verse 8

---

tar in front of the calf and announced, "Tomorrow there will be a festival to the LORD." ⁶So the next day the people rose early and sacrificed burnt offerings and presented fellowship offerings.ª Afterward they sat down to eat and drink and got up to indulge in revelry.

⁷Then the LORD said to Moses, "Go down, because your people, whom you brought up out of Egypt, have become corrupt. ⁸They have been quick to turn away from what I commanded them and have made themselves an idol cast in the shape of a calf. They have bowed down to it and sacrificed to it and have said, 'These are your gods, O Israel, who brought you up out of Egypt.'

⁹"I have seen these people," the LORD said to Moses, "and they are a stiff-necked people. ¹⁰Now leave me alone so that my anger may burn against them and that I may destroy them. Then I will make you into a great nation."

¹¹But Moses sought the favor of the LORD his God. "O LORD," he said, "why should your anger burn against your people, whom you brought out of Egypt with great power and a mighty hand? ¹²Why should the Egyptians say, 'It was with evil intent that he brought them out, to kill them in the mountains and to wipe them off the face of the earth'? Turn from your fierce anger; relent and do not bring disaster on your people. ¹³Remember your servants Abraham, Isaac and Israel, to whom you swore by your own self: 'I will make your descendants as numerous as the stars in the sky and I will give your descendants all this land I promised them, and it will be their inheritance forever.' " ¹⁴Then the LORD relented and did not bring on his people the disaster he had threatened.

¹⁵Moses turned and went down the mountain with the two tablets of the Testimony in his hands. They were inscribed on both sides, front and back. ¹⁶The tablets were the work of God; the writing was the writing of God, engraved on the tablets.

¹⁷When Joshua heard the noise of the people shouting, he said to Moses, "There is the sound of war in the camp."

¹⁸Moses replied:

"It is not the sound of victory,
   it is not the sound of defeat;
   it is the sound of singing that I
     hear."

¹⁹When Moses approached the camp and saw the calf and the dancing, his anger burned and he threw the tablets out of his hands, breaking them to pieces at the foot of the mountain. ²⁰And he took the calf they had made and burned it in the fire; then he ground it to powder, scattered it on the water and made the Israelites drink it.

²¹He said to Aaron, "What did these people do to you, that you led them into such great sin?"

²²"Do not be angry, my lord," Aaron answered. "You know how prone these people are to evil. ²³They said to me, 'Make us gods who will go before us. As for this fellow Moses who brought us up out of Egypt, we don't know what has happened to him.' ²⁴So I told them, 'Whoever has any gold jewelry, take it off.' Then they gave me the gold, and I threw it into the fire, and out came this calf!"

²⁵Moses saw that the people were running wild and that Aaron had let them get out of control and so become a laughing-stock to their enemies. ²⁶So he stood at the entrance to the camp and said, "Whoever is for the LORD, come to me." And all the Levites rallied to him.

²⁷Then he said to them, "This is what the LORD, the God of Israel, says: 'Each man strap a sword to his side. Go back and forth through the camp from one end to the other, each killing his brother and friend and neighbor.' " ²⁸The Levites did as Moses commanded, and that day about three thousand of the people died.

ª6 Traditionally *peace offerings*

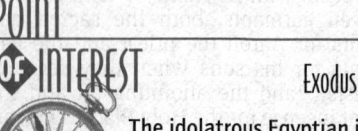

POINT OF INTEREST

Exodus 32:1

The idolatrous Egyptian influence had not yet been purged from God's people. They wanted a god they could touch and see, preferring to believe by sight instead of by faith. It's ironic that as their leader met with and received commandments from the one true God, the people created a substitute god and violated the second commandment (see Exodus 20:4).

29Then Moses said, "You have been set apart to the LORD today, for you were against your own sons and brothers, and he has blessed you this day."

30The next day Moses said to the people, "You have committed a great sin. But now I will go up to the LORD; perhaps I can make atonement for your sin."

31So Moses went back to the LORD and said, "Oh, what a great sin these people have committed! They have made themselves gods of gold. **32**But now, please forgive their sin—but if not, then blot me out of the book you have written."

33The LORD replied to Moses, "Whoever has sinned against me I will blot out of my book. **34**Now go, lead the people to the place I spoke of, and my angel will go before you. However, when the time comes for me to punish, I will punish them for their sin."

35And the LORD struck the people with a plague because of what they did with the calf Aaron had made.

33 Then the LORD said to Moses, "Leave this place, you and the people you brought up out of Egypt, and go up to the land I promised on oath to Abraham, Isaac and Jacob, saying, 'I will give it to your descendants.' **2**I will send an angel before you and drive out the Canaanites, Amorites, Hittites, Perizzites, Hivites and Jebusites. **3**Go up to the land flowing with milk and honey. But I will not go with you, because you are a stiff-necked people and I might destroy you on the way."

4When the people heard these distressing words, they began to mourn and no one put on any ornaments. **5**For the LORD had said to Moses, "Tell the Israelites, 'You are a stiff-necked people. If I were to go with you even for a moment, I might destroy you. Now take off your ornaments and I will decide what to do with you.'" **6**So the Israelites stripped off their ornaments at Mount Horeb.

The Tent of Meeting

7Now Moses used to take a tent and pitch it outside the camp some distance away, calling it the "tent of meeting." Anyone inquiring of the LORD would go to the tent of meeting outside the camp. **8**And whenever Moses went out to the tent, all the people rose and stood at the entrances to their tents, watching Moses until he entered the tent. **9**As Moses went into the tent, the pillar of cloud would come down and stay at the entrance, while the LORD spoke with Moses. **10**Whenever the people saw the pillar of cloud standing at the entrance to the tent, they all stood and worshiped, each at the entrance to his tent. **11**The LORD would speak to Moses face to face, as a man speaks with his friend. Then Moses would return to the camp, but his young aide Joshua son of Nun did not leave the tent.

Moses and the Glory of the LORD

12Moses said to the LORD, "You have been telling me, 'Lead these people,' but you have not let me know whom you will send with me. You have said, 'I know you by name and you have found favor with me.' **13**If you are pleased with me, teach me your ways so I may know you and continue to find favor with you. Remember that this nation is your people."

14The LORD replied, "My Presence will go with you, and I will give you rest."

15Then Moses said to him, "If your Presence does not go with us, do not send us up from here. **16**How will anyone know that you are pleased with me and with your people unless you go with us? What else will distinguish me and your people from all the other people on the face of the earth?"

17And the LORD said to Moses, "I will do the very thing you have asked, because I am pleased with you and I know you by name."

18Then Moses said, "Now show me your glory."

19And the LORD said, "I will cause all my goodness to pass in front of you, and I will proclaim my name, the LORD, in your presence. I will have mercy on whom I will have mercy, and I will have compassion on whom I will have compassion. **20**But," he said, "you cannot see my face, for no one may see me and live."

21Then the LORD said, "There is a place near me where you may stand on a rock. **22**When my glory passes by, I will put you in a cleft in the rock and cover you with my hand until I have passed by. **23**Then I will remove my hand and you will see my back; but my face must not be seen."

The New Stone Tablets

34 The LORD said to Moses, "Chisel out two stone tablets like the first ones, and I will write on them the words that

Read Exodus 33:7–23
Key Verse Exodus 33:11

Becoming God's Friend

Picture a solitary tent pitched out in the desert, far from the noise and bustle of the camp. When Moses went into the tent, God came down in a pillar of cloud and talked to him face to face. He talked to Moses as a "man speaks with his friend" (Exodus 33:11). The relationship between the man and God grew deep and personal.

God wants to be your friend too. It may be hard to believe, but it's true—the One who made heaven and earth, the giver of life, the most powerful being in all the universe, wants to hang out with you and be your friend! He really does. But as with every other good relationship, you'll have to spend time together. You'll find that when you take yourself out of the hustle of life to be with God, he'll respond: "Come near to God and he will come near to you" (James 4:8).

Digging Into the Word
1. Eternal life is not something that we have to wait to experience until after we die. Rather, it is a personal relationship with God that begins the moment we believe in Jesus Christ and then continues for eternity. What do the following passages tell you about your relationship with God?—*John 1:12–13; John 17:3, 20–26*
2. How can you model the example of Jesus as you learn how he related to his Father?—*Mark 1:35; Luke 5:15–16*

Action Challenge
Commit to spend a set amount of time with God each day, talking with him as your friend. Listen to him as you read his Word; talk to him about who he is and what he means to you. Ask him questions. Tell him about your joys, dreams and fears.

One Step Deeper
Psalm 5:3; Matthew 6:6

Go to page 106 for your next devotional reading.

were on the first tablets, which you broke. ²Be ready in the morning, and then come up on Mount Sinai. Present yourself to me there on top of the mountain. ³No one is to come with you or be seen anywhere on the mountain; not even the flocks and herds may graze in front of the mountain."

⁴So Moses chiseled out two stone tablets like the first ones and went up Mount Sinai early in the morning, as the LORD had commanded him; and he carried the two stone tablets in his hands. ⁵Then the LORD came down in the cloud and stood there with him and proclaimed his name, the LORD. ⁶And he passed in front of Moses, proclaiming, "The LORD, the LORD, the compassionate and gracious God, slow to anger, abounding in love and faithfulness, ⁷maintaining love to thousands, and forgiving wickedness, rebellion and sin. Yet he does not leave the guilty unpunished; he punishes the children and their children for the sin of the fathers to the third and fourth generation."

⁸Moses bowed to the ground at once and worshiped. ⁹"O Lord, if I have found favor in your eyes," he said, "then let the Lord go with us. Although this is a stiff-necked people, forgive our wickedness and our sin, and take us as your inheritance."

¹⁰Then the LORD said: "I am making a covenant with you. Before all your people I will do wonders never before done in any nation in all the world. The people you live among will see how awesome is the work that I, the LORD, will do for you. ¹¹Obey what I command you today. I will drive out before you the Amorites, Canaanites, Hittites, Perizzites, Hivites and Jebusites. ¹²Be careful not to make a treaty with those who live in the land where you are going, or they will be a snare among you. ¹³Break down their altars, smash their sacred stones and cut down their Asherah poles.ᵃ ¹⁴Do not worship any other god, for the LORD, whose name is Jealous, is a jealous God.

¹⁵"Be careful not to make a treaty with those who live in the land; for when they prostitute themselves to their gods and sacrifice to them, they will invite you and you will eat their sacrifices. ¹⁶And when you choose some of their daughters as wives for your sons and those daughters prostitute themselves to their gods, they will lead your sons to do the same.

¹⁷"Do not make cast idols.

¹⁸"Celebrate the Feast of Unleavened Bread. For seven days eat bread made without yeast, as I commanded you. Do this at the appointed time in the month of Abib, for in that month you came out of Egypt.

¹⁹"The first offspring of every womb belongs to me, including all the firstborn males of your livestock, whether from herd or flock. ²⁰Redeem the firstborn donkey with a lamb, but if you do not redeem it, break its neck. Redeem all your firstborn sons.

"No one is to appear before me empty-handed.

²¹"Six days you shall labor, but on the seventh day you shall rest; even during the plowing season and harvest you must rest.

²²"Celebrate the Feast of Weeks with the firstfruits of the wheat harvest, and the Feast of Ingathering at the turn of the year.ᵇ ²³Three times a year all your men are to appear before the Sovereign LORD, the God of Israel. ²⁴I will drive out nations before you and enlarge your territory, and no one will covet your land when you go up three times each year to appear before the LORD your God.

²⁵"Do not offer the blood of a sacrifice to me along with anything containing yeast, and do not let any of the sacrifice from the Passover Feast remain until morning.

²⁶"Bring the best of the firstfruits of your soil to the house of the LORD your God.

"Do not cook a young goat in its mother's milk."

ᵃ13 That is, symbols of the goddess Asherah
ᵇ22 That is, in the fall

POINT OF INTEREST   Exodus 33:21

Moses wanted to see God's divine glory. It was a bold request. No sinful creature can behold God's unfiltered holiness, look upon God's *face* and live (see verse 20). But the compassionate, gracious Creator provided a safe place for Moses to see his *back* and glimpse the lingering afterglow of God's glory.

27Then the LORD said to Moses, "Write down these words, for in accordance with these words I have made a covenant with you and with Israel." 28Moses was there with the LORD forty days and forty nights without eating bread or drinking water. And he wrote on the tablets the words of the covenant—the Ten Commandments.

The Radiant Face of Moses

29When Moses came down from Mount Sinai with the two tablets of the Testimony in his hands, he was not aware that his face was radiant because he had spoken with the LORD. 30When Aaron and all the Israelites saw Moses, his face was radiant, and they were afraid to come near him. 31But Moses called to them; so Aaron and all the leaders of the community came back to him, and he spoke to them. 32Afterward all the Israelites came near him, and he gave them all the commands the LORD had given him on Mount Sinai.

33When Moses finished speaking to them, he put a veil over his face. 34But whenever he entered the LORD's presence to speak with him, he removed the veil until he came out. And when he came out and told the Israelites what he had been commanded, 35they saw that his face was radiant. Then Moses would put the veil back over his face until he went in to speak with the LORD.

Sabbath Regulations

35 Moses assembled the whole Israelite community and said to them, "These are the things the LORD has commanded you to do: 2For six days, work is to be done, but the seventh day shall be your holy day, a Sabbath of rest to the LORD. Whoever does any work on it must be put to death. 3Do not light a fire in any of your dwellings on the Sabbath day."

Materials for the Tabernacle

4Moses said to the whole Israelite community, "This is what the LORD has commanded: 5From what you have, take an offering for the LORD. Everyone who is willing is to bring to the LORD an offering of gold, silver and bronze; 6blue, purple and scarlet yarn and fine linen; goat hair; 7ram skins dyed red and hides of sea cows*a*; acacia wood; 8olive oil for the light; spices for the anointing oil and for the fragrant incense; 9and onyx stones and other gems to be mounted on the ephod and breastpiece.

10"All who are skilled among you are to come and make everything the LORD has commanded: 11the tabernacle with its tent and its covering, clasps, frames, crossbars, posts and bases; 12the ark with its poles and the atonement cover and the curtain that shields it; 13the table with its poles and all its articles and the bread of the Presence; 14the lampstand that is for light with its accessories, lamps and oil for the light; 15the altar of incense with its poles, the anointing oil and the fragrant incense; the curtain for the doorway at the entrance to the tabernacle; 16the altar of burnt offering with its bronze grating, its poles and all its utensils; the bronze basin with its stand; 17the curtains of the courtyard with its posts and bases, and the curtain for the entrance to the courtyard; 18the tent pegs for the tabernacle and for the courtyard, and their ropes; 19the woven garments worn for ministering in the sanctuary—both the sacred garments for Aaron the priest and the garments for his sons when they serve as priests."

20Then the whole Israelite community withdrew from Moses' presence, 21and everyone who was willing and whose heart moved him came and brought an offering to the LORD for the work on the Tent of Meeting, for all its service, and for the sacred garments. 22All who were willing, men and women alike, came and brought gold jewelry of all kinds: brooches, earrings, rings and ornaments. They all presented their gold as a wave offering to the LORD. 23Everyone who had

*a*7 That is, dugongs; also in verse 23

POINT OF INTEREST

Exodus 35:10

God often endowed common people with special gifts that enabled them to participate in his work. Seeing God's gifts at work was an encouragement to others to develop their own talents and contributions to God's work. See this principle applied in a different context in Ephesians 4:11–16.

blue, purple or scarlet yarn or fine linen, or goat hair, ram skins dyed red or hides of sea cows brought them. 24Those presenting an offering of silver or bronze brought it as an offering to the LORD, and everyone who had acacia wood for any part of the work brought it. 25Every skilled woman spun with her hands and brought what she had spun—blue, purple or scarlet yarn or fine linen. 26And all the women who were willing and had the skill spun the goat hair. 27The leaders brought onyx stones and other gems to be mounted on the ephod and breastpiece. 28They also brought spices and olive oil for the light and for the anointing oil and for the fragrant incense. 29All the Israelite men and women who were willing brought to the LORD freewill offerings for all the work the LORD through Moses had commanded them to do.

Bezalel and Oholiab

30Then Moses said to the Israelites, "See, the LORD has chosen Bezalel son of Uri, the son of Hur, of the tribe of Judah, 31and he has filled him with the Spirit of God, with skill, ability and knowledge in all kinds of crafts— 32to make artistic designs for work in gold, silver and bronze, 33to cut and set stones, to work in wood and to engage in all kinds of artistic craftsmanship. 34And he has given both him and Oholiab son of Ahisamach, of the tribe of Dan, the ability to teach others. 35He has filled them with skill to do all kinds of work as craftsmen, designers, embroiderers in blue, purple and scarlet yarn and fine linen, and weavers— all of them master craftsmen and designers. **36** 1So Bezalel, Oholiab and every skilled person to whom the LORD has given skill and ability to know how to carry out all the work of constructing the sanctuary are to do the work just as the LORD has commanded."

2Then Moses summoned Bezalel and Oholiab and every skilled person to whom the LORD had given ability and who was willing to come and do the work. 3They received from Moses all the offerings the Israelites had brought to carry out the work of constructing the sanctuary. And the people continued to bring freewill offerings morning after morning. 4So all the skilled craftsmen who were doing all the work on the sanctuary left their work 5and said to Moses, "The people are bringing more than enough for doing the work the LORD commanded to be done."

6Then Moses gave an order and they sent this word throughout the camp: "No man or woman is to make anything else as an offering for the sanctuary." And so the people were restrained from bringing more, 7because what they already had was more than enough to do all the work.

The Tabernacle

8All the skilled men among the workmen made the tabernacle with ten curtains of finely twisted linen and blue, purple and scarlet yarn, with cherubim worked into them by a skilled craftsman. 9All the curtains were the same size— twenty-eight cubits long and four cubits wide.a 10They joined five of the curtains together and did the same with the other five. 11Then they made loops of blue material along the edge of the end curtain in one set, and the same was done with the end curtain in the other set. 12They also made fifty loops on one curtain and fifty loops on the end curtain of the other set, with the loops opposite each other. 13Then they made fifty gold clasps and used them to fasten the two sets of curtains together so that the tabernacle was a unit.

14They made curtains of goat hair for the tent over the tabernacle—eleven altogether. 15All eleven curtains were the same size—thirty cubits long and four cubits wide.b 16They joined five of the curtains into one set and the other six into another set. 17Then they made fifty loops along the edge of the end curtain in one set and also along the edge of the end curtain in the other set. 18They made fifty bronze clasps to fasten the tent together as a unit. 19Then they made for the tent a covering of ram skins dyed red, and over that a covering of hides of sea cows.c

20They made upright frames of acacia wood for the tabernacle. 21Each frame was ten cubits long and a cubit and a half wide,d 22with two projections set parallel to each other. They made all the frames of the tabernacle in this way. 23They made twenty frames for the south side of the tabernacle 24and made forty

a9 That is, about 42 feet (about 12.5 meters) long and 6 feet (about 1.8 meters) wide   b15 That is, about 45 feet (about 13.5 meters) long and 6 feet (about 1.8 meters) wide   c19 That is, dugongs   d21 That is, about 15 feet (about 4.5 meters) long and 2 1/4 feet (about 0.7 meter) wide silver bases to go under them—two bases for each frame, one under each projection. ²⁵For the other side, the north side of the tabernacle, they made twenty frames ²⁶and forty silver bases—two under each frame. ²⁷They made six frames for the far end, that is, the west end of the tabernacle, ²⁸and two frames were made for the corners of the tabernacle at the far end. ²⁹At these two corners the frames were double from the bottom all the way to the top and fitted into a single ring; both were made alike. ³⁰So there were eight frames and sixteen silver bases—two under each frame.

³¹They also made crossbars of acacia wood: five for the frames on one side of the tabernacle, ³²five for those on the other side, and five for the frames on the west, at the far end of the tabernacle. ³³They made the center crossbar so that it extended from end to end at the middle of the frames. ³⁴They overlaid the frames with gold and made gold rings to hold the crossbars. They also overlaid the crossbars with gold.

³⁵They made the curtain of blue, purple and scarlet yarn and finely twisted linen, with cherubim worked into it by a skilled craftsman. ³⁶They made four posts of acacia wood for it and overlaid them with gold. They made gold hooks for them and cast their four silver bases. ³⁷For the entrance to the tent they made a curtain of blue, purple and scarlet yarn and finely twisted linen—the work of an embroiderer; ³⁸and they made five posts with hooks for them. They overlaid the tops of the posts and their bands with gold and made their five bases of bronze.

The Ark

37 Bezalel made the ark of acacia wood—two and a half cubits long, a cubit and a half wide, and a cubit and a half high.ᵃ ²He overlaid it with pure gold, both inside and out, and made a gold molding around it. ³He cast four gold rings for it and fastened them to its four feet, with two rings on one side and two rings on the other. ⁴Then he made poles of acacia wood and overlaid them with gold. ⁵And he inserted the poles into the rings on the sides of the ark to carry it.

⁶He made the atonement cover of pure gold—two and a half cubits long and a cubit and a half wide.ᵇ ⁷Then he made two cherubim out of hammered gold at the ends of the cover. ⁸He made one cherub on one end and the second cherub on the other; at the two ends he made them of one piece with the cover. ⁹The cherubim had their wings spread upward, overshadowing the cover with them. The cherubim faced each other, looking toward the cover.

The Table

¹⁰Theyᶜ made the table of acacia wood—two cubits long, a cubit wide, and a cubit and a half high.ᵈ ¹¹Then they overlaid it with pure gold and made a gold molding around it. ¹²They also made around it a rim a handbreadthᵉ wide and put a gold molding on the rim. ¹³They cast four gold rings for the table and fastened them to the four corners, where the four legs were. ¹⁴The rings were put close to the rim to hold the poles used in carrying the table. ¹⁵The poles for carrying the table were made of acacia wood and were overlaid with gold. ¹⁶And they made from pure gold the articles for the table—its plates and dishes and bowls and its pitchers for the pouring out of drink offerings.

The Lampstand

¹⁷They made the lampstand of pure gold and hammered it out, base and shaft; its flowerlike cups, buds and blossoms were of one piece with it. ¹⁸Six branches extended from the sides of the lampstand—three on one side and three on the other. ¹⁹Three cups shaped like almond flowers with buds and blossoms were on one branch, three on the next branch and the same for all six branches extending from the lampstand. ²⁰And on the lampstand were four cups shaped like almond flowers with buds and blossoms. ²¹One bud was under the first pair of branches extending from the lampstand, a second bud under the second pair, and a third bud under the third pair—six branches in all. ²²The buds and the branches were all of one piece with the lampstand, hammered out of pure gold.

²³They made its seven lamps, as well as its wick trimmers and trays, of pure

---

ᵃ1 That is, about 3 3/4 feet (about 1.1 meters) long and 2 1/4 feet (about 0.7 meter) wide and high
ᵇ6 That is, about 3 3/4 feet (about 1.1 meters) long and 2 1/4 feet (about 0.7 meter) wide   ᶜ10 Or *He*; also in verses 11-29   ᵈ10 That is, about 3 feet (about 0.9 meter) long, 1 1/2 feet (about 0.5 meter) wide, and 2 1/4 feet (about 0.7 meter) high
ᵉ12 That is, about 3 inches (about 8 centimeters)

gold. ²⁴They made the lampstand and all its accessories from one talent^a of pure gold.

The Altar of Incense

²⁵They made the altar of incense out of acacia wood. It was square, a cubit long and a cubit wide, and two cubits high^b—its horns of one piece with it. ²⁶They overlaid the top and all the sides and the horns with pure gold, and made a gold molding around it. ²⁷They made two gold rings below the molding—two on opposite sides—to hold the poles used to carry it. ²⁸They made the poles of acacia wood and overlaid them with gold.

²⁹They also made the sacred anointing oil and the pure, fragrant incense—the work of a perfumer.

The Altar of Burnt Offering

38 They^c built the altar of burnt offering of acacia wood, three cubits^d high; it was square, five cubits long and five cubits wide.^e ²They made a horn at each of the four corners, so that the horns and the altar were of one piece, and they overlaid the altar with bronze. ³They made all its utensils of bronze—its pots, shovels, sprinkling bowls, meat forks and firepans. ⁴They made a grating for the altar, a bronze network, to be under its ledge, halfway up the altar. ⁵They cast bronze rings to hold the poles for the four corners of the bronze grating. ⁶They made the poles of acacia wood and overlaid them with bronze. ⁷They inserted the poles into the rings so they would be on the sides of the altar for carrying it. They made it hollow, out of boards.

Basin for Washing

⁸They made the bronze basin and its bronze stand from the mirrors of the women who served at the entrance to the Tent of Meeting.

The Courtyard

⁹Next they made the courtyard. The south side was a hundred cubits^f long and had curtains of finely twisted linen, ¹⁰with twenty posts and twenty bronze bases, and with silver hooks and bands on the posts. ¹¹The north side was also a hundred cubits long and had twenty posts and twenty bronze bases, with silver hooks and bands on the posts. ¹²The west end was fifty cubits^g wide and had curtains, with ten posts and ten bases, with silver hooks and bands on the posts. ¹³The east end, toward the sunrise, was also fifty cubits wide. ¹⁴Curtains fifteen cubits^h long were on one side of the entrance, with three posts and three bases, ¹⁵and curtains fifteen cubits long were on the other side of the entrance to the courtyard, with three posts and three bases. ¹⁶All the curtains around the courtyard were of finely twisted linen. ¹⁷The bases for the posts were bronze. The hooks and bands on the posts were silver, and their tops were overlaid with silver; so all the posts of the courtyard had silver bands.

¹⁸The curtain for the entrance to the courtyard was of blue, purple and scarlet yarn and finely twisted linen—the work of an embroiderer. It was twenty cubitsⁱ long and, like the curtains of the courtyard, five cubits^j high, ¹⁹with four posts and four bronze bases. Their hooks and bands were silver, and their tops were overlaid with silver. ²⁰All the tent pegs of the tabernacle and of the surrounding courtyard were bronze.

The Materials Used

²¹These are the amounts of the materials used for the tabernacle, the tabernacle of the Testimony, which were recorded at Moses' command by the Levites under the direction of Ithamar son of Aaron, the priest. ²²(Bezalel son of Uri, the son of Hur, of the tribe of Judah, made everything the LORD commanded Moses; ²³with him was Oholiab son of Ahisamach, of the tribe of Dan—a craftsman and designer, and an embroiderer in blue, purple and scarlet yarn and fine linen.) ²⁴The total amount of the gold from the wave offering used for all the work on the sanctuary was 29 talents and 730 shekels,^k according to the sanctuary shekel.

²⁵The silver obtained from those of the community who were counted in the cen-

^a24 That is, about 75 pounds (about 34 kilograms)
^b25 That is, about 1 1/2 feet (about 0.5 meter) long and wide, and about 3 feet (about 0.9 meter) high
^c1 Or He; also in verses 2-9   ^d1 That is, about 4 1/2 feet (about 1.3 meters)   ^e1 That is, about 7 1/2 feet (about 2.3 meters) long and wide
^f9 That is, about 150 feet (about 46 meters)
^g12 That is, about 75 feet (about 23 meters)
^h14 That is, about 22 1/2 feet (about 6.9 meters)
ⁱ18 That is, about 30 feet (about 9 meters)
^j18 That is, about 7 1/2 feet (about 2.3 meters)
^k24 The weight of the gold was a little over one ton (about 1 metric ton).

sus was 100 talents and 1,775 shekels,[a] according to the sanctuary shekel— [26]one beka per person, that is, half a shekel,[b] according to the sanctuary shekel, from everyone who had crossed over to those counted, twenty years old or more, a total of 603,550 men. [27]The 100 talents[c] of silver were used to cast the bases for the sanctuary and for the curtain—100 bases from the 100 talents, one talent for each base. [28]They used the 1,775 shekels[d] to make the hooks for the posts, to overlay the tops of the posts, and to make their bands.

[29]The bronze from the wave offering was 70 talents and 2,400 shekels.[e] [30]They used it to make the bases for the entrance to the Tent of Meeting, the bronze altar with its bronze grating and all its utensils, [31]the bases for the surrounding courtyard and those for its entrance and all the tent pegs for the tabernacle and those for the surrounding courtyard.

The Priestly Garments

39 From the blue, purple and scarlet yarn they made woven garments for ministering in the sanctuary. They also made sacred garments for Aaron, as the LORD commanded Moses.

The Ephod

[2]They[f] made the ephod of gold, and of blue, purple and scarlet yarn, and of finely twisted linen. [3]They hammered out thin sheets of gold and cut strands to be worked into the blue, purple and scarlet yarn and fine linen—the work of a skilled craftsman. [4]They made shoulder pieces for the ephod, which were attached to two of its corners, so it could be fastened. [5]Its skillfully woven waistband was like it—of one piece with the ephod and made with gold, and with blue, purple and scarlet yarn, and with finely twisted linen, as the LORD commanded Moses.

[6]They mounted the onyx stones in gold filigree settings and engraved them like a seal with the names of the sons of Israel. [7]Then they fastened them on the shoulder pieces of the ephod as memorial stones for the sons of Israel, as the LORD commanded Moses.

The Breastpiece

[8]They fashioned the breastpiece—the work of a skilled craftsman. They made it like the ephod: of gold, and of blue, purple and scarlet yarn, and of finely twisted linen. [9]It was square—a span[g] long and a span wide—and folded double. [10]Then they mounted four rows of precious stones on it. In the first row there was a ruby, a topaz and a beryl; [11]in the second row a turquoise, a sapphire[h] and an emerald; [12]in the third row a jacinth, an agate and an amethyst; [13]in the fourth row a chrysolite, an onyx and a jasper.[i] They were mounted in gold filigree settings. [14]There were twelve stones, one for each of the names of the sons of Israel, each engraved like a seal with the name of one of the twelve tribes.

[15]For the breastpiece they made braided chains of pure gold, like a rope. [16]They made two gold filigree settings and two gold rings, and fastened the rings to two of the corners of the breastpiece. [17]They fastened the two gold chains to the rings at the corners of the breastpiece, [18]and the other ends of the chains to the two settings, attaching them to the shoulder pieces of the ephod at the front. [19]They made two gold rings and attached them to the other two corners of the breastpiece on the inside edge next to the ephod. [20]Then they made two more gold rings and attached them to the bottom of the shoulder pieces on the front of the ephod, close to the seam just above the waistband of the ephod. [21]They tied

[a]25 The weight of the silver was a little over 3 3/4 tons (about 3.4 metric tons).   [b]26 That is, about 1/5 ounce (about 5.5 grams)   [c]27 That is, about 3 3/4 tons (about 3.4 metric tons)   [d]28 That is, about 45 pounds (about 20 kilograms)
[e]29 The weight of the bronze was about 2 1/2 tons (about 2.4 metric tons).   [f]2 Or *He*; also in verses 7, 8 and 22   [g]9 That is, about 9 inches (about 22 centimeters)   [h]11 Or *lapis lazuli*
[i]13 The precise identification of some of these precious stones is uncertain.

POINT OF INTEREST

Exodus 38:28

The people contributed more than a ton of gold and more than three tons of silver. Where did these former slaves get that much wealth? Before they left Egypt, God commanded the Hebrews to ask the Egyptians for gold and silver (see Exodus 12:35–36). These offerings represent a portion of the treasure.

the rings of the breastpiece to the rings of the ephod with blue cord, connecting it to the waistband so that the breastpiece would not swing out from the ephod—as the LORD commanded Moses.

Other Priestly Garments

²²They made the robe of the ephod entirely of blue cloth—the work of a weaver— ²³with an opening in the center of the robe like the opening of a collar,ᵃ and a band around this opening, so that it would not tear. ²⁴They made pomegranates of blue, purple and scarlet yarn and finely twisted linen around the hem of the robe. ²⁵And they made bells of pure gold and attached them around the hem between the pomegranates. ²⁶The bells and pomegranates alternated around the hem of the robe to be worn for ministering, as the LORD commanded Moses.

²⁷For Aaron and his sons, they made tunics of fine linen—the work of a weaver— ²⁸and the turban of fine linen, the linen headbands and the undergarments of finely twisted linen. ²⁹The sash was of finely twisted linen and blue, purple and scarlet yarn—the work of an embroiderer—as the LORD commanded Moses.

³⁰They made the plate, the sacred diadem, out of pure gold and engraved on it, like an inscription on a seal: HOLY TO THE LORD. ³¹Then they fastened a blue cord to it to attach it to the turban, as the LORD commanded Moses.

Moses Inspects the Tabernacle

³²So all the work on the tabernacle, the Tent of Meeting, was completed. The Israelites did everything just as the LORD commanded Moses. ³³Then they brought the tabernacle to Moses: the tent and all its furnishings, its clasps, frames, crossbars, posts and bases; ³⁴the covering of ram skins dyed red, the covering of hides of sea cowsᵇ and the shielding curtain; ³⁵the ark of the Testimony with its poles and the atonement cover; ³⁶the table with all its articles and the bread of the Presence; ³⁷the pure gold lampstand with its row of lamps and all its accessories, and the oil for the light; ³⁸the gold altar, the anointing oil, the fragrant incense, and the curtain for the entrance to the tent; ³⁹the bronze altar with its bronze grating, its poles and all its utensils; the basin with its stand; ⁴⁰the curtains of the court-

yard with its posts and bases, and the curtain for the entrance to the courtyard; the ropes and tent pegs for the courtyard; all the furnishings for the tabernacle, the Tent of Meeting; ⁴¹and the woven garments worn for ministering in the sanctuary, both the sacred garments for Aaron the priest and the garments for his sons when serving as priests.

⁴²The Israelites had done all the work just as the LORD had commanded Moses. ⁴³Moses inspected the work and saw that they had done it just as the LORD had commanded. So Moses blessed them.

Setting Up the Tabernacle

40 Then the LORD said to Moses: ²"Set up the tabernacle, the Tent of Meeting, on the first day of the first month. ³Place the ark of the Testimony in it and shield the ark with the curtain. ⁴Bring in the table and set out what belongs on it. Then bring in the lampstand and set up its lamps. ⁵Place the gold altar of incense in front of the ark of the Testimony and put the curtain at the entrance to the tabernacle.

⁶"Place the altar of burnt offering in front of the entrance to the tabernacle, the Tent of Meeting; ⁷place the basin between the Tent of Meeting and the altar and put water in it. ⁸Set up the courtyard around it and put the curtain at the entrance to the courtyard.

⁹"Take the anointing oil and anoint the tabernacle and everything in it; consecrate it and all its furnishings, and it will be holy. ¹⁰Then anoint the altar of burnt offering and all its utensils; consecrate the altar, and it will be most holy. ¹¹Anoint the basin and its stand and consecrate them.

¹²"Bring Aaron and his sons to the entrance to the Tent of Meeting and wash them with water. ¹³Then dress Aaron in the sacred garments, anoint him and consecrate him so he may serve me as priest. ¹⁴Bring his sons and dress them in tunics. ¹⁵Anoint them just as you anointed their father, so they may serve me as priests. Their anointing will be to a priesthood that will continue for all generations to come." ¹⁶Moses did everything just as the LORD commanded him.

¹⁷So the tabernacle was set up on the first day of the first month in the second

year. ¹⁸When Moses set up the tabernacle, he put the bases in place, erected the frames, inserted the crossbars and set up the posts. ¹⁹Then he spread the tent over the tabernacle and put the covering over the tent, as the LORD commanded him.

²⁰He took the Testimony and placed it in the ark, attached the poles to the ark and put the atonement cover over it. ²¹Then he brought the ark into the tabernacle and hung the shielding curtain and shielded the ark of the Testimony, as the LORD commanded him.

²²Moses placed the table in the Tent of Meeting on the north side of the tabernacle outside the curtain ²³and set out the bread on it before the LORD, as the LORD commanded him.

²⁴He placed the lampstand in the Tent of Meeting opposite the table on the south side of the tabernacle ²⁵and set up the lamps before the LORD, as the LORD commanded him.

²⁶Moses placed the gold altar in the Tent of Meeting in front of the curtain ²⁷and burned fragrant incense on it, as the LORD commanded him. ²⁸Then he put up the curtain at the entrance to the tabernacle.

²⁹He set the altar of burnt offering near the entrance to the tabernacle, the Tent of Meeting, and offered on it burnt offerings and grain offerings, as the LORD commanded him.

³⁰He placed the basin between the Tent of Meeting and the altar and put water in it for washing, ³¹and Moses and Aaron and his sons used it to wash their hands and feet. ³²They washed whenever they entered the Tent of Meeting or approached the altar, as the LORD commanded Moses.

³³Then Moses set up the courtyard around the tabernacle and altar and put up the curtain at the entrance to the courtyard. And so Moses finished the work.

The Glory of the LORD

³⁴Then the cloud covered the Tent of Meeting, and the glory of the LORD filled the tabernacle. ³⁵Moses could not enter

---

MONDAY

Read Exodus 40:1–38
Key Verses Exodus 40:36–38

Our Own Cloud of God — Jena Borah

Life would be so much easier if we, like the Israelites, could wake up every morning, look out the window and see a cloud of God telling us to stay or go. Go where? That would be simple—just follow the cloud!

While we may wish to have our own personal "cloud of God," in reality it's already ours! We have God's personal presence in our lives—his Holy Spirit. Jesus said that the Holy Spirit teaches us all things and reminds us of everything he has said (see John 14:26). And Paul urges us in Galatians 5:25 to "keep in step with the Spirit." That means that he's moving, and we need to be paying attention and moving with him!

We follow the Holy Spirit when we read the Bible and find a command to obey, a sin to avoid or a promise to rely on, and then act on what we've read. Or the Holy Spirit may speak through godly counselors or through circumstances that clearly and Biblically lead us.

So the next time the Spirit leads, don't hesitate . . . follow that cloud!

A Deeper Look
Psalm 32:8; John 16:13

Go to page 116 for your next devotional reading.

the Tent of Meeting because the cloud had settled upon it, and the glory of the LORD filled the tabernacle.

36In all the travels of the Israelites, whenever the cloud lifted from above the tabernacle, they would set out; 37but if the cloud did not lift, they did not set out—until the day it lifted. 38So the cloud of the LORD was over the tabernacle by day, and fire was in the cloud by night, in the sight of all the house of Israel during all their travels.

At first Leviticus may seem like an endless list of rules and regulations. The book catalogues the instructions God gave to Moses for the Israelites, including such things as sacrifices, moral laws and special holidays. The book of Leviticus isn't about rules but about holiness—God's holiness—as it is unveiled in his name, his attributes and his redemptive work. As you read, don't miss God's heart for the Israelites—and for all his followers today: "Be holy, because I am holy" (11:45).

LEVITICUS

The Burnt Offering

1 The LORD called to Moses and spoke to him from the Tent of Meeting. He said, ²"Speak to the Israelites and say to them: 'When any of you brings an offering to the LORD, bring as your offering an animal from either the herd or the flock.

³" 'If the offering is a burnt offering from the herd, he is to offer a male without defect. He must present it at the entrance to the Tent of Meeting so that it*a* will be acceptable to the LORD. ⁴He is to lay his hand on the head of the burnt offering, and it will be accepted on his behalf to make atonement for him. ⁵He is to slaughter the young bull before the LORD, and then Aaron's sons the priests shall bring the blood and sprinkle it against the altar on all sides at the entrance to the Tent of Meeting. ⁶He is to skin the burnt offering and cut it into

pieces. ⁷The sons of Aaron the priest are to put fire on the altar and arrange wood on the fire. ⁸Then Aaron's sons the priests shall arrange the pieces, including the head and the fat, on the burning wood that is on the altar. ⁹He is to wash the inner parts and the legs with water, and the priest is to burn all of it on the altar. It is a burnt offering, an offering made by fire, an aroma pleasing to the LORD.

¹⁰" 'If the offering is a burnt offering from the flock, from either the sheep or the goats, he is to offer a male without defect. ¹¹He is to slaughter it at the north side of the altar before the LORD, and Aaron's sons the priests shall sprinkle its blood against the altar on all sides. ¹²He is to cut it into pieces, and the priest shall

a3 Or he

arrange them, including the head and the fat, on the burning wood that is on the altar. ¹³He is to wash the inner parts and the legs with water, and the priest is to bring all of it and burn it on the altar. It is a burnt offering, an offering made by fire, an aroma pleasing to the LORD.

¹⁴" 'If the offering to the LORD is a burnt offering of birds, he is to offer a dove or a young pigeon. ¹⁵The priest shall bring it to the altar, wring off the head and burn it on the altar; its blood shall be drained out on the side of the altar. ¹⁶He is to remove the crop with its contentsᵃ and throw it to the east side of the altar, where the ashes are. ¹⁷He shall tear it open by the wings, not severing it completely, and then the priest shall burn it on the wood that is on the fire on the altar. It is a burnt offering, an offering made by fire, an aroma pleasing to the LORD.

The Grain Offering

2 " 'When someone brings a grain offering to the LORD, his offering is to be of fine flour. He is to pour oil on it, put incense on it ²and take it to Aaron's sons the priests. The priest shall take a handful of the fine flour and oil, together with all the incense, and burn this as a memorial portion on the altar, an offering made by fire, an aroma pleasing to the LORD. ³The rest of the grain offering belongs to Aaron and his sons; it is a most holy part of the offerings made to the LORD by fire.

⁴" 'If you bring a grain offering baked in an oven, it is to consist of fine flour: cakes made without yeast and mixed with oil, orᵇ wafers made without yeast and spread with oil. ⁵If your grain offering is prepared on a griddle, it is to be made of fine flour mixed with oil, and without yeast. ⁶Crumble it and pour oil on it; it is a grain offering. ⁷If your grain offering is cooked in a pan, it is to be made of fine flour and oil. ⁸Bring the grain offering made of these things to the LORD; present it to the priest, who shall take it to the altar. ⁹He shall take out the memorial portion from the grain offering and burn it on the altar as an offering made by fire, an aroma pleasing to the LORD. ¹⁰The rest of the grain offering belongs to Aaron and his sons; it is a most holy part of the offerings made to the LORD by fire.

¹¹" 'Every grain offering you bring to the LORD must be made without yeast, for you are not to burn any yeast or honey in an offering made to the LORD by fire. ¹²You may bring them to the LORD as an offering of the firstfruits, but they are not to be offered on the altar as a pleasing aroma. ¹³Season all your grain offerings with salt. Do not leave the salt of the covenant of your God out of your grain offerings; add salt to all your offerings.

¹⁴" 'If you bring a grain offering of firstfruits to the LORD, offer crushed heads of new grain roasted in the fire. ¹⁵Put oil and incense on it; it is a grain offering. ¹⁶The priest shall burn the memorial portion of the crushed grain and the oil, together with all the incense, as an offering made to the LORD by fire.

The Fellowship Offering

3 " 'If someone's offering is a fellowship offering,ᶜ and he offers an animal from the herd, whether male or female, he is to present before the LORD an animal without defect. ²He is to lay his hand on the head of his offering and slaughter it at the entrance to the Tent of Meeting. Then Aaron's sons the priests shall sprinkle the blood against the altar on all sides. ³From the fellowship offering he is to bring a sacrifice made to the LORD by fire: all the fat that covers the inner parts or is connected to them, ⁴both kidneys with the fat on them near the loins, and the covering of the liver, which he will remove with the kidneys. ⁵Then Aaron's sons are to burn it on the altar on top of the burnt offering that is on the burning wood, as an offering made by fire, an aroma pleasing to the LORD.

⁶" 'If he offers an animal from the flock as a fellowship offering to the LORD,

ᵃ16 Or crop and the feathers; the meaning of the Hebrew for this word is uncertain.   ᵇ4 Or and   ᶜ1 Traditionally peace offering; also in verses 3, 6 and 9

POINT OF INTEREST

Leviticus 2:1

The grain offering had a practical as well as a religious use. Only part of the grain offering was given to God. The remainder was given to the priests as part of their food allotment.

he is to offer a male or female without defect. [7]If he offers a lamb, he is to present it before the LORD. [8]He is to lay his hand on the head of his offering and slaughter it in front of the Tent of Meeting. Then Aaron's sons shall sprinkle its blood against the altar on all sides. [9]From the fellowship offering he is to bring a sacrifice made to the LORD by fire: its fat, the entire fat tail cut off close to the backbone, all the fat that covers the inner parts or is connected to them, [10]both kidneys with the fat on them near the loins, and the covering of the liver, which he will remove with the kidneys. [11]The priest shall burn them on the altar as food, an offering made to the LORD by fire.

[12]" 'If his offering is a goat, he is to present it before the LORD. [13]He is to lay his hand on its head and slaughter it in front of the Tent of Meeting. Then Aaron's sons shall sprinkle its blood against the altar on all sides. [14]From what he offers he is to make this offering to the LORD by fire: all the fat that covers the inner parts or is connected to them, [15]both kidneys with the fat on them near the loins, and the covering of the liver, which he will remove with the kidneys. [16]The priest shall burn them on the altar as food, an offering made by fire, a pleasing aroma. All the fat is the LORD's.

[17]" 'This is a lasting ordinance for the generations to come, wherever you live: You must not eat any fat or any blood.' "

The Sin Offering

4 The LORD said to Moses, [2]"Say to the Israelites: 'When anyone sins unintentionally and does what is forbidden in any of the LORD's commands—

[3]" 'If the anointed priest sins, bringing guilt on the people, he must bring to the LORD a young bull without defect as a sin offering for the sin he has committed. [4]He is to present the bull at the entrance to the Tent of Meeting before the LORD. He is to lay his hand on its head and slaughter it before the LORD. [5]Then the anointed priest shall take some of the bull's blood and carry it into the Tent of Meeting. [6]He is to dip his finger into the blood and sprinkle some of it seven times before the LORD, in front of the curtain of the sanctuary. [7]The priest shall then put some of the blood on the horns of the altar of fragrant incense that is before the LORD in the Tent of Meeting. The rest of the bull's blood he

shall pour out at the base of the altar of burnt offering at the entrance to the Tent of Meeting. [8]He shall remove all the fat from the bull of the sin offering—the fat that covers the inner parts or is connected to them, [9]both kidneys with the fat on them near the loins, and the covering of the liver, which he will remove with the kidneys— [10]just as the fat is removed from the ox[a] sacrificed as a fellowship offering.[b] Then the priest shall burn them on the altar of burnt offering. [11]But the hide of the bull and all its flesh, as well as the head and legs, the inner parts and offal— [12]that is, all the rest of the bull—he must take outside the camp to a place ceremonially clean, where the ashes are thrown, and burn it in a wood fire on the ash heap.

[13]" 'If the whole Israelite community sins unintentionally and does what is forbidden in any of the LORD's commands, even though the community is unaware of the matter, they are guilty. [14]When they become aware of the sin they committed, the assembly must bring a young bull as a sin offering and present it before the Tent of Meeting. [15]The elders of the community are to lay their hands on the bull's head before the LORD, and the bull shall be slaughtered before the LORD. [16]Then the anointed priest is to take some of the bull's blood into the Tent of Meeting. [17]He shall dip his finger into the blood and sprinkle it before the LORD seven times in front of the curtain. [18]He is to put some of the blood on the horns of the

[a]10 The Hebrew word can include both male and female.   [b]10 Traditionally *peace offering*; also in verses 26, 31 and 35

POINT OF INTEREST

Leviticus 4:2

The sin offering was given for unintentionally committed sins. It did not cover premeditated, rebellious acts. We often overlook unintentional sins with an "I didn't mean to do it" attitude. But Jewish law attributed the guilt to the action rather than the intention. If a person violated God's law, that person was guilty whether he or she meant to do it or not.

altar that is before the Lord in the Tent of Meeting. The rest of the blood he shall pour out at the base of the altar of burnt offering at the entrance to the Tent of Meeting. ¹⁹He shall remove all the fat from it and burn it on the altar, ²⁰and do with this bull just as he did with the bull for the sin offering. In this way the priest will make atonement for them, and they will be forgiven. ²¹Then he shall take the bull outside the camp and burn it as he burned the first bull. This is the sin offering for the community.

²²" 'When a leader sins unintentionally and does what is forbidden in any of the commands of the Lord his God, he is guilty. ²³When he is made aware of the sin he committed, he must bring as his offering a male goat without defect. ²⁴He is to lay his hand on the goat's head and slaughter it at the place where the burnt offering is slaughtered before the Lord. It is a sin offering. ²⁵Then the priest shall take some of the blood of the sin offering with his finger and put it on the horns of the altar of burnt offering and pour out the rest of the blood at the base of the altar. ²⁶He shall burn all the fat on the altar as he burned the fat of the fellowship offering. In this way the priest will make atonement for the man's sin, and he will be forgiven.

²⁷" 'If a member of the community sins unintentionally and does what is forbidden in any of the Lord's commands, he is guilty. ²⁸When he is made aware of the sin he committed, he must bring as his offering for the sin he committed a female goat without defect. ²⁹He is to lay his hand on the head of the sin offering and slaughter it at the place of the burnt offering. ³⁰Then the priest is to take some of the blood with his finger and put it on the horns of the altar of burnt offering and pour out the rest of the blood at the base of the altar. ³¹He shall remove all the fat, just as the fat is removed from the fellowship offering, and the priest shall burn it on the altar as an aroma pleasing to the Lord. In this way the priest will make atonement for him, and he will be forgiven.

³²" 'If he brings a lamb as his sin offering, he is to bring a female without defect. ³³He is to lay his hand on its head and slaughter it for a sin offering at the place where the burnt offering is slaughtered. ³⁴Then the priest shall take some of the blood of the sin offering with his finger and put it on the horns of the altar of burnt offering and pour out the rest of blood at the base of the altar. ³⁵He shall remove all the fat, just as the fat is removed from the lamb of the fellowship offering, and the priest shall burn it on the altar on top of the offerings made to the Lord by fire. In this way the priest will make atonement for him for the sin he has committed, and he will be forgiven.

5 " 'If a person sins because he does not speak up when he hears a public charge to testify regarding something he has seen or learned about, he will be held responsible.

²" 'Or if a person touches anything ceremonially unclean—whether the carcasses of unclean wild animals or of unclean livestock or of unclean creatures that move along the ground—even though he is unaware of it, he has become unclean and is guilty.

³" 'Or if he touches human uncleanness—anything that would make him unclean—even though he is unaware of it, when he learns of it he will be guilty.

⁴" 'Or if a person thoughtlessly takes an oath to do anything, whether good or evil—in any matter one might carelessly swear about—even though he is unaware of it, in any case when he learns of it he will be guilty.

⁵" 'When anyone is guilty in any of these ways, he must confess in what way he has sinned ⁶and, as a penalty for the sin he has committed, he must bring to the Lord a female lamb or goat from the flock as a sin offering; and the priest shall make atonement for him for his sin.

⁷" 'If he cannot afford a lamb, he is to bring two doves or two young pigeons to the Lord as a penalty for his sin—one for a sin offering and the other for a burnt offering. ⁸He is to bring them to the priest, who shall first offer the one for the sin offering. He is to wring its head from its neck, not severing it completely, ⁹and is to sprinkle some of the blood of the sin offering against the side of the altar; the rest of the blood must be drained out at the base of the altar. It is a sin offering. ¹⁰The priest shall then offer the other as a burnt offering in the prescribed way and make atonement for him for the sin he has committed, and he will be forgiven.

¹¹" 'If, however, he cannot afford two

doves or two young pigeons, he is to bring as an offering for his sin a tenth of an ephah*a* of fine flour for a sin offering. He must not put oil or incense on it, because it is a sin offering. ¹²He is to bring it to the priest, who shall take a handful of it as a memorial portion and burn it on the altar on top of the offerings made to the LORD by fire. It is a sin offering. ¹³In this way the priest will make atonement for him for any of these sins he has committed, and he will be forgiven. The rest of the offering will belong to the priest, as in the case of the grain offering.' "

The Guilt Offering

¹⁴The LORD said to Moses: ¹⁵"When a person commits a violation and sins unintentionally in regard to any of the LORD's holy things, he is to bring to the LORD as a penalty a ram from the flock, one without defect and of the proper value in silver, according to the sanctuary shekel.*b* It is a guilt offering. ¹⁶He must make restitution for what he has failed to do in regard to the holy things, add a fifth of the value to that and give it all to the priest, who will make atonement for him with the ram as a guilt offering, and he will be forgiven.

¹⁷"If a person sins and does what is forbidden in any of the LORD's commands, even though he does not know it, he is guilty and will be held responsible. ¹⁸He is to bring to the priest as a guilt offering a ram from the flock, one without defect and of the proper value. In this way the priest will make atonement for him for the wrong he has committed unintentionally, and he will be forgiven. ¹⁹It is a guilt offering; he has been guilty of*c* wrongdoing against the LORD."

6 The LORD said to Moses: ²"If anyone sins and is unfaithful to the LORD by deceiving his neighbor about something entrusted to him or left in his care or stolen, or if he cheats him, ³or if he finds lost property and lies about it, or if he swears falsely, or if he commits any such sin that people may do— ⁴when he thus sins and becomes guilty, he must return what he has stolen or taken by extortion, or what was entrusted to him, or the lost property he found, ⁵or whatever it was he swore falsely about. He must make restitution in full, add a fifth of the value to it and give it all to the owner on the day he presents his guilt offering. ⁶And as a penalty he must bring to the priest, that is, to

the LORD, his guilt offering, a ram from the flock, one without defect and of the proper value. ⁷In this way the priest will make atonement for him before the LORD, and he will be forgiven for any of these things he did that made him guilty."

The Burnt Offering

⁸The LORD said to Moses: ⁹"Give Aaron and his sons this command: 'These are the regulations for the burnt offering: The burnt offering is to remain on the altar hearth throughout the night, till morning, and the fire must be kept burning on the altar. ¹⁰The priest shall then put on his linen clothes, with linen undergarments next to his body, and shall remove the ashes of the burnt offering that the fire has consumed on the altar and place them beside the altar. ¹¹Then he is to take off these clothes and put on others, and carry the ashes outside the camp to a place that is ceremonially clean. ¹²The fire on the altar must be kept burning; it must not go out. Every morning the priest is to add firewood and arrange the burnt offering on the fire and burn the fat of the fellowship offerings*d* on it. ¹³The fire must be kept burning on the altar continuously; it must not go out.

The Grain Offering

¹⁴" 'These are the regulations for the grain offering: Aaron's sons are to bring it before the LORD, in front of the altar. ¹⁵The priest is to take a handful of fine flour and oil, together with all the incense on the grain offering, and burn the memorial portion on the altar as an aroma pleasing to the LORD. ¹⁶Aaron and his sons shall eat the rest of it, but it is to be eaten without yeast in a holy place; they are to eat it in the courtyard of the Tent of Meeting. ¹⁷It must not be baked with yeast; I have given it as their share of the offerings made to me by fire. Like the sin offering and the guilt offering, it is most holy. ¹⁸Any male descendant of Aaron may eat it. It is his regular share of the offerings made to the LORD by fire for the generations to come. Whatever touches them will become holy.*e* '"

¹⁹The LORD also said to Moses, ²⁰"This

a11 That is, probably about 2 quarts (about 2 liters)   *b15* That is, about 2/5 ounce (about 11.5 grams)   *c19* Or *has made full expiation for his*   *d12* Traditionally *peace offerings*   *e18* Or *Whoever touches them must be holy*; similarly in verse 27 is the offering Aaron and his sons are to bring to the LORD on the day he*a* is anointed: a tenth of an ephah*b* of fine flour as a regular grain offering, half of it in the morning and half in the evening. ²¹Prepare it with oil on a griddle; bring it well-mixed and present the grain offering broken*c* in pieces as an aroma pleasing to the LORD. ²²The son who is to succeed him as anointed priest shall prepare it. It is the LORD's regular share and is to be burned completely. ²³Every grain offering of a priest shall be burned completely; it must not be eaten."

The Sin Offering

²⁴The LORD said to Moses, ²⁵"Say to Aaron and his sons: 'These are the regulations for the sin offering: The sin offering is to be slaughtered before the LORD in the place the burnt offering is slaughtered; it is most holy. ²⁶The priest who offers it shall eat it; it is to be eaten in a holy place, in the courtyard of the Tent of Meeting. ²⁷Whatever touches any of the flesh will become holy, and if any of the blood is spattered on a garment, you must wash it in a holy place. ²⁸The clay pot the meat is cooked in must be broken; but if it is cooked in a bronze pot, the pot is to be scoured and rinsed with water. ²⁹Any male in a priest's family may eat it; it is most holy. ³⁰But any sin offering whose blood is brought into the Tent of Meeting to make atonement in the Holy Place must not be eaten; it must be burned.

The Guilt Offering

7 " 'These are the regulations for the guilt offering, which is most holy: ²The guilt offering is to be slaughtered in the place where the burnt offering is slaughtered, and its blood is to be sprinkled against the altar on all sides. ³All its fat shall be offered: the fat tail and the fat that covers the inner parts, ⁴both kidneys with the fat on them near the loins, and the covering of the liver, which is to be removed with the kidneys. ⁵The priest shall burn them on the altar as an offering made to the LORD by fire. It is a guilt offering. ⁶Any male in a priest's family may eat it, but it must be eaten in a holy place; it is most holy.

⁷" 'The same law applies to both the sin offering and the guilt offering: They belong to the priest who makes atonement with them. ⁸The priest who offers a burnt offering for anyone may keep its hide for himself. ⁹Every grain offering baked in an oven or cooked in a pan or on a griddle belongs to the priest who offers it, ¹⁰and every grain offering, whether mixed with oil or dry, belongs equally to all the sons of Aaron.

The Fellowship Offering

¹¹" 'These are the regulations for the fellowship offering*d* a person may present to the LORD:

¹²" 'If he offers it as an expression of thankfulness, then along with this thank offering he is to offer cakes of bread made without yeast and mixed with oil, wafers made without yeast and spread with oil, and cakes of fine flour well-kneaded and mixed with oil. ¹³Along with his fellowship offering of thanksgiving he is to present an offering with cakes of bread made with yeast. ¹⁴He is to bring one of each kind as an offering, a contribution to the LORD; it belongs to the priest who sprinkles the blood of the fellowship offerings. ¹⁵The meat of his fellowship offering of thanksgiving must be eaten on the day it is offered; he must leave none of it till morning.

¹⁶" 'If, however, his offering is the result of a vow or is a freewill offering, the sacrifice shall be eaten on the day he offers it, but anything left over may be eaten on the next day. ¹⁷Any meat of the sacrifice left over till the third day must be burned up. ¹⁸If any meat of the fellowship offering is eaten on the third day, it will not be accepted. It will not be credited to the one who offered it, for it is impure; the person who eats any of it will be held responsible.

¹⁹" 'Meat that touches anything ceremonially unclean must not be eaten; it must be burned up. As for other meat, anyone ceremonially clean may eat it. ²⁰But if anyone who is unclean eats any meat of the fellowship offering belonging to the LORD, that person must be cut off from his people. ²¹If anyone touches something unclean—whether human uncleanness or an unclean animal or any unclean, detestable thing—and then eats any of the meat of the fellowship offering

---

a 20 Or *each*　*b 20* That is, probably about 2 quarts (about 2 liters)　*c 21* The meaning of the Hebrew for this word is uncertain.
d 11 Traditionally *peace offering*; also in verses 13-37

belonging to the LORD, that person must be cut off from his people.' "

Eating Fat and Blood Forbidden

22The LORD said to Moses, 23"Say to the Israelites: 'Do not eat any of the fat of cattle, sheep or goats. 24The fat of an animal found dead or torn by wild animals may be used for any other purpose, but you must not eat it. 25Anyone who eats the fat of an animal from which an offering by fire may be*a* made to the LORD must be cut off from his people. 26And wherever you live, you must not eat the blood of any bird or animal. 27If anyone eats blood, that person must be cut off from his people.' "

The Priests' Share

28The LORD said to Moses, 29"Say to the Israelites: 'Anyone who brings a fellowship offering to the LORD is to bring part of it as his sacrifice to the LORD. 30With his own hands he is to bring the offering made to the LORD by fire; he is to bring the fat, together with the breast, and wave the breast before the LORD as a wave offering. 31The priest shall burn the fat on the altar, but the breast belongs to Aaron and his sons. 32You are to give the right thigh of your fellowship offerings to the priest as a contribution. 33The son of Aaron who offers the blood and the fat of the fellowship offering shall have the right thigh as his share. 34From the fellowship offerings of the Israelites, I have taken the breast that is waved and the thigh that is presented and have given them to Aaron the priest and his sons as their regular share from the Israelites.' "

35This is the portion of the offerings made to the LORD by fire that were allotted to Aaron and his sons on the day they were presented to serve the LORD as priests. 36On the day they were anointed, the LORD commanded that the Israelites give this to them as their regular share for the generations to come.

37These, then, are the regulations for the burnt offering, the grain offering, the sin offering, the guilt offering, the ordination offering and the fellowship offering, 38which the LORD gave Moses on Mount Sinai on the day he commanded the Israelites to bring their offerings to the LORD, in the Desert of Sinai.

The Ordination of Aaron and His Sons

8 The LORD said to Moses, 2"Bring Aaron and his sons, their garments, the anointing oil, the bull for the sin offering, the two rams and the basket containing bread made without yeast, 3and gather the entire assembly at the entrance to the Tent of Meeting." 4Moses did as the LORD commanded him, and the assembly gathered at the entrance to the Tent of Meeting.

5Moses said to the assembly, "This is what the LORD has commanded to be done." 6Then Moses brought Aaron and his sons forward and washed them with water. 7He put the tunic on Aaron, tied the sash around him, clothed him with the robe and put the ephod on him. He also tied the ephod to him by its skillfully woven waistband; so it was fastened on him. 8He placed the breastpiece on him and put the Urim and Thummim in the breastpiece. 9Then he placed the turban on Aaron's head and set the gold plate, the sacred diadem, on the front of it, as the LORD commanded Moses.

10Then Moses took the anointing oil and anointed the tabernacle and everything in it, and so consecrated them. 11He sprinkled some of the oil on the altar seven times, anointing the altar and all its utensils and the basin with its stand, to consecrate them. 12He poured some of the anointing oil on Aaron's head and anointed him to consecrate him. 13Then he brought Aaron's sons forward, put tunics on them, tied sashes around them and put headbands on them, as the LORD commanded Moses.

14He then presented the bull for the sin offering, and Aaron and his sons laid their hands on its head. 15Moses slaughtered the bull and took some of the blood, and with his finger he put it on all the horns of the altar to purify the altar. He poured out the rest of the blood at the base of the altar. So he consecrated it to make atonement for it. 16Moses also took all the fat around the inner parts, the covering of the liver, and both kidneys and their fat, and burned it on the altar. 17But the bull with its hide and its flesh and its offal he burned up outside the camp, as the LORD commanded Moses.

18He then presented the ram for the burnt offering, and Aaron and his sons

a25 Or fire is

laid their hands on its head. ¹⁹Then Moses slaughtered the ram and sprinkled the blood against the altar on all sides. ²⁰He cut the ram into pieces and burned the head, the pieces and the fat. ²¹He washed the inner parts and the legs with water and burned the whole ram on the altar as a burnt offering, a pleasing aroma, an offering made to the LORD by fire, as the LORD commanded Moses.

²²He then presented the other ram, the ram for the ordination, and Aaron and his sons laid their hands on its head. ²³Moses slaughtered the ram and took some of its blood and put it on the lobe of Aaron's right ear, on the thumb of his right hand and on the big toe of his right foot. ²⁴Moses also brought Aaron's sons forward and put some of the blood on the lobes of their right ears, on the thumbs of their right hands and on the big toes of their right feet. Then he sprinkled blood against the altar on all sides. ²⁵He took the fat, the fat tail, all the fat around the inner parts, the covering of the liver, both kidneys and their fat and the right thigh. ²⁶Then from the basket of bread made without yeast, which was before the LORD, he took a cake of bread, and one made with oil, and a wafer; he put these on the fat portions and on the right thigh. ²⁷He put all these in the hands of Aaron and his sons and waved them before the LORD as a wave offering. ²⁸Then Moses took them from their hands and burned them on the altar on top of the burnt offering as an ordination offering, a pleasing aroma, an offering made to the LORD by fire. ²⁹He also took the breast—Moses' share of the ordination ram—and waved it before the LORD as a wave offering, as the LORD commanded Moses.

³⁰Then Moses took some of the anointing oil and some of the blood from the altar and sprinkled them on Aaron and his garments and on his sons and their garments. So he consecrated Aaron and his garments and his sons and their garments.

³¹Moses then said to Aaron and his sons, "Cook the meat at the entrance to the Tent of Meeting and eat it there with the bread from the basket of ordination offerings, as I commanded, saying,ᵃ 'Aaron and his sons are to eat it.' ³²Then burn up the rest of the meat and the bread. ³³Do not leave the entrance to the Tent of Meeting for seven days, until the days of your ordination are complet-

ed, for your ordination will last seven days. ³⁴What has been done today was commanded by the LORD to make atonement for you. ³⁵You must stay at the entrance to the Tent of Meeting day and night for seven days and do what the LORD requires, so you will not die; for that is what I have been commanded." ³⁶So Aaron and his sons did everything the LORD commanded through Moses.

The Priests Begin Their Ministry

9 On the eighth day Moses summoned Aaron and his sons and the elders of Israel. ²He said to Aaron, "Take a bull calf for your sin offering and a ram for your burnt offering, both without defect, and present them before the LORD. ³Then say to the Israelites: 'Take a male goat for a sin offering, a calf and a lamb—both a year old and without defect—for a burnt offering, ⁴and an oxᵇ and a ram for a fellowship offeringᶜ to sacrifice before the LORD, together with a grain offering mixed with oil. For today the LORD will appear to you.' "

⁵They took the things Moses commanded to the front of the Tent of Meeting, and the entire assembly came near and stood before the LORD. ⁶Then Moses said, "This is what the LORD has commanded you to do, so that the glory of the LORD may appear to you."

⁷Moses said to Aaron, "Come to the altar and sacrifice your sin offering and your burnt offering and make atonement for yourself and the people; sacrifice the offering that is for the people and make atonement for them, as the LORD has commanded."

⁸So Aaron came to the altar and slaughtered the calf as a sin offering for himself. ⁹His sons brought the blood to him, and he dipped his finger into the blood and put it on the horns of the altar; the rest of the blood he poured out at the base of the altar. ¹⁰On the altar he burned the fat, the kidneys and the covering of the liver from the sin offering, as the LORD commanded Moses; ¹¹the flesh and the hide he burned up outside the camp.

¹²Then he slaughtered the burnt offering. His sons handed him the blood, and he sprinkled it against the altar on all sides. ¹³They handed him the burnt offer-

---

ᵃ31 Or *I was commanded:*   ᵇ4 The Hebrew word can include both male and female; also in verses 18 and 19.   ᶜ4 Traditionally *peace offering*; also in verses 18 and 22 ing piece by piece, including the head, and he burned them on the altar. ¹⁴He washed the inner parts and the legs and burned them on top of the burnt offering on the altar.

¹⁵Aaron then brought the offering that was for the people. He took the goat for the people's sin offering and slaughtered it and offered it for a sin offering as he did with the first one.

¹⁶He brought the burnt offering and offered it in the prescribed way. ¹⁷He also brought the grain offering, took a handful of it and burned it on the altar in addition to the morning's burnt offering.

¹⁸He slaughtered the ox and the ram as the fellowship offering for the people. His sons handed him the blood, and he sprinkled it against the altar on all sides. ¹⁹But the fat portions of the ox and the ram— the fat tail, the layer of fat, the kidneys and the covering of the liver— ²⁰these they laid on the breasts, and then Aaron burned the fat on the altar. ²¹Aaron waved the breasts and the right thigh be-

fore the LORD as a wave offering, as Moses commanded.

²²Then Aaron lifted his hands toward the people and blessed them. And having sacrificed the sin offering, the burnt offering and the fellowship offering, he stepped down.

²³Moses and Aaron then went into the Tent of Meeting. When they came out, they blessed the people; and the glory of the LORD appeared to all the people. ²⁴Fire came out from the presence of the LORD and consumed the burnt offering and the fat portions on the altar. And when all the people saw it, they shouted for joy and fell facedown.

The Death of Nadab and Abihu

10 Aaron's sons Nadab and Abihu took their censers, put fire in them and added incense; and they offered unauthorized fire before the LORD, contrary to his command. ²So fire came out from the presence of the LORD and consumed them, and they died before the LORD. ³Mo-

---

TUESDAY

Read Leviticus 9:1–24
Key Verse Leviticus 9:6

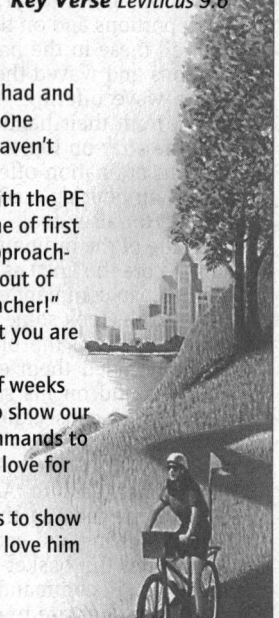

Show Him – Sherie Falkenstine

Remember PE class in elementary school—all the fun you had and how much you loved your teacher? Your PE coach was the one teacher that never gave homework or tests! Well, things haven't changed much.

While student teaching, I was walking down the hall with the PE teacher during a break. Straight ahead came an orderly line of first graders. As we got closer, the students saw the teacher approaching. In their excitement at seeing her, most of them broke out of line. They ran up and hugged her, saying, "We love you, teacher!"

Her response to them was this: "If you love me, do what you are supposed to do and get back into line."

I didn't think much about her response until a couple of weeks later when I realized that that's what God wants of us—to show our love by doing what he wants us to do. He has given us commands to follow, and as we obey them we are actually revealing our love for him!

God doesn't just want to hear, "I love you." He wants us to show him our love by our obedience. How can you show him you love him right now?

A Deeper Look
Luke 6:46–49; John 14:21

Go to page 129 for your next devotional reading.

ses then said to Aaron, "This is what the LORD spoke of when he said:

" 'Among those who approach me
    I will show myself holy;
in the sight of all the people
    I will be honored.' "

Aaron remained silent.

⁴Moses summoned Mishael and Elzaphan, sons of Aaron's uncle Uzziel, and said to them, "Come here; carry your cousins outside the camp, away from the front of the sanctuary." ⁵So they came and carried them, still in their tunics, outside the camp, as Moses ordered.

⁶Then Moses said to Aaron and his sons Eleazar and Ithamar, "Do not let your hair become unkempt,ᵃ and do not tear your clothes, or you will die and the LORD will be angry with the whole community. But your relatives, all the house of Israel, may mourn for those the LORD has destroyed by fire. ⁷Do not leave the entrance to the Tent of Meeting or you will die, because the LORD's anointing oil is on you." So they did as Moses said.

⁸Then the LORD said to Aaron, ⁹"You and your sons are not to drink wine or other fermented drink whenever you go into the Tent of Meeting, or you will die. This is a lasting ordinance for the generations to come. ¹⁰You must distinguish between the holy and the common, between the unclean and the clean, ¹¹and you must teach the Israelites all the decrees the LORD has given them through Moses."

¹²Moses said to Aaron and his remaining sons, Eleazar and Ithamar, "Take the grain offering left over from the offerings made to the LORD by fire and eat it prepared without yeast beside the altar, for it is most holy. ¹³Eat it in a holy place, because it is your share and your sons' share of the offerings made to the LORD by fire; for so I have been commanded. ¹⁴But you and your sons and your daughters may eat the breast that was waved and the thigh that was presented. Eat them in a ceremonially clean place; they have been given to you and your children as your share of the Israelites' fellowship offerings.ᵇ ¹⁵The thigh that was presented and the breast that was waved must be brought with the fat portions of the offerings made by fire, to be waved before the LORD as a wave offering. This will be the regular share for you and your children, as the LORD has commanded."

¹⁶When Moses inquired about the goat of the sin offering and found that it had been burned up, he was angry with Eleazar and Ithamar, Aaron's remaining sons, and asked, ¹⁷"Why didn't you eat the sin offering in the sanctuary area? It is most holy; it was given to you to take away the guilt of the community by making atonement for them before the LORD. ¹⁸Since its blood was not taken into the Holy Place, you should have eaten the goat in the sanctuary area, as I commanded."

¹⁹Aaron replied to Moses, "Today they sacrificed their sin offering and their burnt offering before the LORD, but such things as this have happened to me. Would the LORD have been pleased if I had eaten the sin offering today?" ²⁰When Moses heard this, he was satisfied.

Clean and Unclean Food

11 The LORD said to Moses and Aaron, ²"Say to the Israelites: 'Of all the animals that live on land, these are the ones you may eat: ³You may eat any animal that has a split hoof completely divided and that chews the cud.

⁴" 'There are some that only chew the cud or only have a split hoof, but you must not eat them. The camel, though it chews the cud, does not have a split hoof; it is ceremonially unclean for you. ⁵The coney,ᶜ though it chews the cud, does not have a split hoof; it is unclean for you. ⁶The rabbit, though it chews the cud, does not have a split hoof; it is unclean for you. ⁷And the pig, though it has a split hoof completely divided, does not chew the cud; it is unclean for you. ⁸You

ᵃ6 Or *Do not uncover your heads*
ᵇ14 Traditionally *peace offerings*   ᶜ5 That is, the hyrax or rock badger

POINT OF INTEREST

Leviticus 10:1

Aaron's two oldest sons attempted to worship God on their own terms. In practicing pagan religions, in which deities exemplified all the finite frailties of humanity, these men seriously defiled God's sovereign nature. God's response to Aaron's sons was immediate.

must not eat their meat or touch their carcasses; they are unclean for you.

9" 'Of all the creatures living in the water of the seas and the streams, you may eat any that have fins and scales. 10But all creatures in the seas or streams that do not have fins and scales—whether among all the swarming things or among all the other living creatures in the water—you are to detest. 11And since you are to detest them, you must not eat their meat and you must detest their carcasses. 12Anything living in the water that does not have fins and scales is to be detestable to you.

13" 'These are the birds you are to detest and not eat because they are detestable: the eagle, the vulture, the black vulture, 14the red kite, any kind of black kite, 15any kind of raven, 16the horned owl, the screech owl, the gull, any kind of hawk, 17the little owl, the cormorant, the great owl, 18the white owl, the desert owl, the osprey, 19the stork, any kind of heron, the hoopoe and the bat.*a*

20" 'All flying insects that walk on all fours are to be detestable to you. 21There are, however, some winged creatures that walk on all fours that you may eat: those that have jointed legs for hopping on the ground. 22Of these you may eat any kind of locust, katydid, cricket or grasshopper. 23But all other winged creatures that have four legs you are to detest.

24" 'You will make yourselves unclean by these; whoever touches their carcasses will be unclean till evening. 25Whoever picks up one of their carcasses must wash his clothes, and he will be unclean till evening.

26" 'Every animal that has a split hoof not completely divided or that does not chew the cud is unclean for you; whoever touches ⌊the carcass of⌋ any of them will be unclean. 27Of all the animals that walk on all fours, those that walk on their paws are unclean for you; whoever touches their carcasses will be unclean till evening. 28Anyone who picks up their carcasses must wash his clothes, and he will be unclean till evening. They are unclean for you.

29" 'Of the animals that move about on the ground, these are unclean for you: the weasel, the rat, any kind of great lizard, 30the gecko, the monitor lizard, the wall lizard, the skink and the chameleon. 31Of all those that move along the

ground, these are unclean for you. Whoever touches them when they are dead will be unclean till evening. 32When one of them dies and falls on something, that article, whatever its use, will be unclean, whether it is made of wood, cloth, hide or sackcloth. Put it in water; it will be unclean till evening, and then it will be clean. 33If one of them falls into a clay pot, everything in it will be unclean, and you must break the pot. 34Any food that could be eaten but has water on it from such a pot is unclean, and any liquid that could be drunk from it is unclean. 35Anything that one of their carcasses falls on becomes unclean; an oven or cooking pot must be broken up. They are unclean, and you are to regard them as unclean. 36A spring, however, or a cistern for collecting water remains clean, but anyone who touches one of these carcasses is unclean. 37If a carcass falls on any seeds that are to be planted, they remain clean. 38But if water has been put on the seed and a carcass falls on it, it is unclean for you.

39" 'If an animal that you are allowed to eat dies, anyone who touches the carcass will be unclean till evening. 40Anyone who eats some of the carcass must wash his clothes, and he will be unclean till evening. Anyone who picks up the carcass must wash his clothes, and he will be unclean till evening.

41" 'Every creature that moves about on the ground is detestable; it is not to be eaten. 42You are not to eat any creature that moves about on the ground, whether it moves on its belly or walks on all fours or on many feet; it is detestable. 43Do not defile yourselves by any of these creatures. Do not make yourselves unclean by means of them or be made unclean by them. 44I am the LORD your God; consecrate yourselves and be holy, because I am holy. Do not make yourselves unclean by any creature that moves about on the ground. 45I am the LORD who brought you up out of Egypt to be your God; therefore be holy, because I am holy.

46" 'These are the regulations concerning animals, birds, every living thing that moves in the water and every creature that moves about on the ground. 47You must distinguish between the unclean

---

a19 The precise identification of some of the birds, insects and animals in this chapter is uncertain.

and the clean, between living creatures that may be eaten and those that may not be eaten.' "

Purification After Childbirth

12 The LORD said to Moses, ²"Say to the Israelites: 'A woman who becomes pregnant and gives birth to a son will be ceremonially unclean for seven days, just as she is unclean during her monthly period. ³On the eighth day the boy is to be circumcised. ⁴Then the woman must wait thirty-three days to be purified from her bleeding. She must not touch anything sacred or go to the sanctuary until the days of her purification are over. ⁵If she gives birth to a daughter, for two weeks the woman will be unclean, as during her period. Then she must wait sixty-six days to be purified from her bleeding.

⁶" 'When the days of her purification for a son or daughter are over, she is to bring to the priest at the entrance to the Tent of Meeting a year-old lamb for a burnt offering and a young pigeon or a dove for a sin offering. ⁷He shall offer them before the LORD to make atonement for her, and then she will be ceremonially clean from her flow of blood.

" 'These are the regulations for the woman who gives birth to a boy or a girl. ⁸If she cannot afford a lamb, she is to bring two doves or two young pigeons, one for a burnt offering and the other for a sin offering. In this way the priest will make atonement for her, and she will be clean.' "

Regulations About Infectious Skin Diseases

13 The LORD said to Moses and Aaron, ²"When anyone has a swelling or a rash or a bright spot on his skin that may become an infectious skin disease,ᵃ he must be brought to Aaron the priest or to one of his sonsᵇ who is a priest. ³The priest is to examine the sore on his skin, and if the hair in the sore has turned white and the sore appears to be more than skin deep,ᶜ it is an infectious skin disease. When the priest examines him, he shall pronounce him ceremonially unclean. ⁴If the spot on his skin is white but does not appear to be more than skin deep and the hair in it has not turned white, the priest is to put the infected person in isolation for seven days. ⁵On the seventh day the priest is to examine him,

and if he sees that the sore is unchanged and has not spread in the skin, he is to keep him in isolation another seven days. ⁶On the seventh day the priest is to examine him again, and if the sore has faded and has not spread in the skin, the priest shall pronounce him clean; it is only a rash. The man must wash his clothes, and he will be clean. ⁷But if the rash does spread in his skin after he has shown himself to the priest to be pronounced clean, he must appear before the priest again. ⁸The priest is to examine him, and if the rash has spread in the skin, he shall pronounce him unclean; it is an infectious disease.

⁹"When anyone has an infectious skin disease, he must be brought to the priest. ¹⁰The priest is to examine him, and if there is a white swelling in the skin that has turned the hair white and if there is raw flesh in the swelling, ¹¹it is a chronic skin disease and the priest shall pronounce him unclean. He is not to put him in isolation, because he is already unclean.

¹²"If the disease breaks out all over his skin and, so far as the priest can see, it covers all the skin of the infected person from head to foot, ¹³the priest is to examine him, and if the disease has covered his whole body, he shall pronounce that person clean. Since it has all turned white, he is clean. ¹⁴But whenever raw flesh appears on him, he will be unclean. ¹⁵When the priest sees the raw flesh, he

ᵃ2 Traditionally *leprosy*; the Hebrew word was used for various diseases affecting the skin—not necessarily leprosy; also elsewhere in this chapter.
ᵇ2 Or *descendants*   ᶜ3 Or *be lower than the rest of the skin*; also elsewhere in this chapter

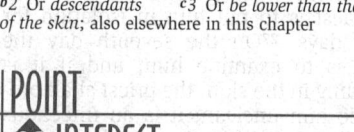

POINT OF INTEREST   Leviticus 11:45

Holiness is one of God's essential characteristics. God is uniquely pure and separate from evil. For us to "be holy" as God is holy doesn't mean perfect behavior on our part; it means complete dedication to God and dependence on his saving power. Peter reminds us of this absolute standard for our behavior in 1 Peter 1:16.

shall pronounce him unclean. The raw flesh is unclean; he has an infectious disease. [16]Should the raw flesh change and turn white, he must go to the priest. [17]The priest is to examine him, and if the sores have turned white, the priest shall pronounce the infected person clean; then he will be clean.

[18]"When someone has a boil on his skin and it heals, [19]and in the place where the boil was, a white swelling or reddish-white spot appears, he must present himself to the priest. [20]The priest is to examine it, and if it appears to be more than skin deep and the hair in it has turned white, the priest shall pronounce him unclean. It is an infectious skin disease that has broken out where the boil was. [21]But if, when the priest examines it, there is no white hair in it and it is not more than skin deep and has faded, then the priest is to put him in isolation for seven days. [22]If it is spreading in the skin, the priest shall pronounce him unclean; it is infectious. [23]But if the spot is unchanged and has not spread, it is only a scar from the boil, and the priest shall pronounce him clean.

[24]"When someone has a burn on his skin and a reddish-white or white spot appears in the raw flesh of the burn, [25]the priest is to examine the spot, and if the hair in it has turned white, and it appears to be more than skin deep, it is an infectious disease that has broken out in the burn. The priest shall pronounce him unclean; it is an infectious skin disease. [26]But if the priest examines it and there is no white hair in the spot and if it is not more than skin deep and has faded, then the priest is to put him in isolation for seven days. [27]On the seventh day the priest is to examine him, and if it is spreading in the skin, the priest shall pronounce him unclean; it is an infectious skin disease. [28]If, however, the spot is unchanged and has not spread in the skin but has faded, it is a swelling from the burn, and the priest shall pronounce him clean; it is only a scar from the burn.

[29]"If a man or woman has a sore on the head or on the chin, [30]the priest is to examine the sore, and if it appears to be more than skin deep and the hair in it is yellow and thin, the priest shall pronounce that person unclean; it is an itch, an infectious disease of the head or chin. [31]But if, when the priest examines this kind of sore, it does not seem to be more than skin deep and there is no black hair in it, then the priest is to put the infected person in isolation for seven days. [32]On the seventh day the priest is to examine the sore, and if the itch has not spread and there is no yellow hair in it and it does not appear to be more than skin deep, [33]he must be shaved except for the diseased area, and the priest is to keep him in isolation another seven days. [34]On the seventh day the priest is to examine the itch, and if it has not spread in the skin and appears to be no more than skin deep, the priest shall pronounce him clean. He must wash his clothes, and he will be clean. [35]But if the itch does spread in the skin after he is pronounced clean, [36]the priest is to examine him, and if the itch has spread in the skin, the priest does not need to look for yellow hair; the person is unclean. [37]If, however, in his judgment it is unchanged and black hair has grown in it, the itch is healed. He is clean, and the priest shall pronounce him clean.

[38]"When a man or woman has white spots on the skin, [39]the priest is to examine them, and if the spots are dull white, it is a harmless rash that has broken out on the skin; that person is clean.

[40]"When a man has lost his hair and is bald, he is clean. [41]If he has lost his hair from the front of his scalp and has a bald forehead, he is clean. [42]But if he has a reddish-white sore on his bald head or forehead, it is an infectious disease breaking out on his head or forehead. [43]The priest is to examine him, and if the swollen sore on his head or forehead is reddish-white like an infectious skin disease, [44]the man is diseased and is unclean. The priest shall pronounce him unclean because of the sore on his head.

[45]"The person with such an infectious disease must wear torn clothes, let his hair be unkempt,[a] cover the lower part of his face and cry out, 'Unclean! Unclean!' [46]As long as he has the infection he remains unclean. He must live alone; he must live outside the camp.

Regulations About Mildew

[47]"If any clothing is contaminated with mildew—any woolen or linen clothing, [48]any woven or knitted material of linen or wool, any leather or anything made of leather— [49]and if the contamination in

[a]45 Or *clothes, uncover his head*

the clothing, or leather, or woven or knitted material, or any leather article, is greenish or reddish, it is a spreading mildew and must be shown to the priest. [50]The priest is to examine the mildew and isolate the affected article for seven days. [51]On the seventh day he is to examine it, and if the mildew has spread in the clothing, or the woven or knitted material, or the leather, whatever its use, it is a destructive mildew; the article is unclean. [52]He must burn up the clothing, or the woven or knitted material of wool or linen, or any leather article that has the contamination in it, because the mildew is destructive; the article must be burned up.

[53]"But if, when the priest examines it, the mildew has not spread in the clothing, or the woven or knitted material, or the leather article, [54]he shall order that the contaminated article be washed. Then he is to isolate it for another seven days. [55]After the affected article has been washed, the priest is to examine it, and if the mildew has not changed its appearance, even though it has not spread, it is unclean. Burn it with fire, whether the mildew has affected one side or the other. [56]If, when the priest examines it, the mildew has faded after the article has been washed, he is to tear the contaminated part out of the clothing, or the leather, or the woven or knitted material. [57]But if it reappears in the clothing, or in the woven or knitted material, or in the leather article, it is spreading, and whatever has the mildew must be burned with fire. [58]The clothing, or the woven or knitted material, or any leather article that has been washed and is rid of the mildew, must be washed again, and it will be clean."

[59]These are the regulations concerning contamination by mildew in woolen or linen clothing, woven or knitted material, or any leather article, for pronouncing them clean or unclean.

Cleansing From Infectious Skin Diseases

14 The LORD said to Moses, [2]"These are the regulations for the diseased person at the time of his ceremonial cleansing, when he is brought to the priest: [3]The priest is to go outside the camp and examine him. If the person has been healed of his infectious skin disease,[a]

[4]the priest shall order that two live clean birds and some cedar wood, scarlet yarn and hyssop be brought for the one to be cleansed. [5]Then the priest shall order that one of the birds be killed over fresh water in a clay pot. [6]He is then to take the live bird and dip it, together with the cedar wood, the scarlet yarn and the hyssop, into the blood of the bird that was killed over the fresh water. [7]Seven times he shall sprinkle the one to be cleansed of the infectious disease and pronounce him clean. Then he is to release the live bird in the open fields.

[8]"The person to be cleansed must wash his clothes, shave off all his hair and bathe with water; then he will be ceremonially clean. After this he may come into the camp, but he must stay outside his tent for seven days. [9]On the seventh day he must shave off all his hair; he must shave his head, his beard, his eyebrows and the rest of his hair. He must wash his clothes and bathe himself with water, and he will be clean.

[10]"On the eighth day he must bring two male lambs and one ewe lamb a year old, each without defect, along with three-tenths of an ephah[b] of fine flour mixed with oil for a grain offering, and one log[c] of oil. [11]The priest who pronounces him clean shall present both the one to be cleansed and his offerings be-

---

[a]3 Traditionally *leprosy*; the Hebrew word was used for various diseases affecting the skin—not necessarily leprosy; also elsewhere in this chapter. [b]10 That is, probably about 6 quarts (about 6.5 liters)   [c]10 That is, probably about 2/3 pint (about 0.3 liter); also in verses 12, 15, 21 and 24

POINT OF INTEREST

Leviticus 13:51

Why all these rules about mildew? God dwelt in the Israelite camp much like the Holy Spirit resides in believers' hearts today (see 1 Corinthians 3:16). Aside from the physically destructive aspects of mildew, taking precautions against its spread served as an illustration of purity in the camp. Sin, like mildew, ruins whatever it touches and must be cleaned away whenever it shows up in our lives.

fore the LORD at the entrance to the Tent of Meeting.

¹²"Then the priest is to take one of the male lambs and offer it as a guilt offering, along with the log of oil; he shall wave them before the LORD as a wave offering. ¹³He is to slaughter the lamb in the holy place where the sin offering and the burnt offering are slaughtered. Like the sin offering, the guilt offering belongs to the priest; it is most holy. ¹⁴The priest is to take some of the blood of the guilt offering and put it on the lobe of the right ear of the one to be cleansed, on the thumb of his right hand and on the big toe of his right foot. ¹⁵The priest shall then take some of the log of oil, pour it in the palm of his own left hand, ¹⁶dip his right forefinger into the oil in his palm, and with his finger sprinkle some of it before the LORD seven times. ¹⁷The priest is to put some of the oil remaining in his palm on the lobe of the right ear of the one to be cleansed, on the thumb of his right hand and on the big toe of his right foot, on top of the blood of the guilt offering. ¹⁸The rest of the oil in his palm the priest shall put on the head of the one to be cleansed and make atonement for him before the LORD.

¹⁹"Then the priest is to sacrifice the sin offering and make atonement for the one to be cleansed from his uncleanness. After that, the priest shall slaughter the burnt offering ²⁰and offer it on the altar, together with the grain offering, and make atonement for him, and he will be clean.

²¹"If, however, he is poor and cannot afford these, he must take one male lamb as a guilt offering to be waved to make atonement for him, together with a tenth of an ephah[a] of fine flour mixed with oil for a grain offering, a log of oil, ²²and two doves or two young pigeons, which he can afford, one for a sin offering and the other for a burnt offering.

²³"On the eighth day he must bring them for his cleansing to the priest at the entrance to the Tent of Meeting, before the LORD. ²⁴The priest is to take the lamb for the guilt offering, together with the log of oil, and wave them before the LORD as a wave offering. ²⁵He shall slaughter the lamb for the guilt offering and take some of its blood and put it on the lobe of the right ear of the one to be cleansed, on the thumb of his right hand and on the big toe of his right foot. ²⁶The priest is to

pour some of the oil into the palm of his own left hand, ²⁷and with his right forefinger sprinkle some of the oil from his palm seven times before the LORD. ²⁸Some of the oil in his palm he is to put on the same places he put the blood of the guilt offering—on the lobe of the right ear of the one to be cleansed, on the thumb of his right hand and on the big toe of his right foot. ²⁹The rest of the oil in his palm the priest shall put on the head of the one to be cleansed, to make atonement for him before the LORD. ³⁰Then he shall sacrifice the doves or the young pigeons, which the person can afford, ³¹one[b] as a sin offering and the other as a burnt offering, together with the grain offering. In this way the priest will make atonement before the LORD on behalf of the one to be cleansed."

³²These are the regulations for anyone who has an infectious skin disease and who cannot afford the regular offerings for his cleansing.

Cleansing From Mildew

³³The LORD said to Moses and Aaron, ³⁴"When you enter the land of Canaan, which I am giving you as your possession, and I put a spreading mildew in a house in that land, ³⁵the owner of the house must go and tell the priest, 'I have seen something that looks like mildew in my house.' ³⁶The priest is to order the house to be emptied before he goes in to examine the mildew, so that nothing in the house will be pronounced unclean. After this the priest is to go in and inspect the house. ³⁷He is to examine the mildew on the walls, and if it has greenish or reddish depressions that appear to be deeper than the surface of the wall, ³⁸the priest shall go out the doorway of the house and close it up for seven days. ³⁹On the seventh day the priest shall return to inspect the house. If the mildew has spread on the walls, ⁴⁰he is to order that the contaminated stones be torn out and thrown into an unclean place outside the town. ⁴¹He must have all the inside walls of the house scraped and the material that is scraped off dumped into an unclean place outside the town. ⁴²Then they are to take other stones to replace these and take new clay and plaster the house.

---

a21 That is, probably about 2 quarts (about 2 liters)   *b31* Septuagint and Syriac; Hebrew *31such as the person can afford, one*

43"If the mildew reappears in the house after the stones have been torn out and the house scraped and plastered, 44the priest is to go and examine it and, if the mildew has spread in the house, it is a destructive mildew; the house is unclean. 45It must be torn down—its stones, timbers and all the plaster—and taken out of the town to an unclean place.

46"Anyone who goes into the house while it is closed up will be unclean till evening. 47Anyone who sleeps or eats in the house must wash his clothes.

48"But if the priest comes to examine it and the mildew has not spread after the house has been plastered, he shall pronounce the house clean, because the mildew is gone. 49To purify the house he is to take two birds and some cedar wood, scarlet yarn and hyssop. 50He shall kill one of the birds over fresh water in a clay pot. 51Then he is to take the cedar wood, the hyssop, the scarlet yarn and the live bird, dip them into the blood of the dead bird and the fresh water, and sprinkle the house seven times. 52He shall purify the house with the bird's blood, the fresh water, the live bird, the cedar wood, the hyssop and the scarlet yarn. 53Then he is to release the live bird in the open fields outside the town. In this way he will make atonement for the house, and it will be clean."

54These are the regulations for any infectious skin disease, for an itch, 55for mildew in clothing or in a house, 56and for a swelling, a rash or a bright spot, 57to determine when something is clean or unclean.

These are the regulations for infectious skin diseases and mildew.

Discharges Causing Uncleanness

15 The LORD said to Moses and Aaron, 2"Speak to the Israelites and say to them: 'When any man has a bodily discharge, the discharge is unclean. 3Whether it continues flowing from his body or is blocked, it will make him unclean. This is how his discharge will bring about uncleanness:

4" 'Any bed the man with a discharge lies on will be unclean, and anything he sits on will be unclean. 5Anyone who touches his bed must wash his clothes and bathe with water, and he will be unclean till evening. 6Whoever sits on anything that the man with a discharge sat on must wash his clothes and bathe with water, and he will be unclean till evening.

7" 'Whoever touches the man who has a discharge must wash his clothes and bathe with water, and he will be unclean till evening.

8" 'If the man with the discharge spits on someone who is clean, that person must wash his clothes and bathe with water, and he will be unclean till evening.

9" 'Everything the man sits on when riding will be unclean, 10and whoever touches any of the things that were under him will be unclean till evening; whoever picks up those things must wash his clothes and bathe with water, and he will be unclean till evening.

11" 'Anyone the man with a discharge touches without rinsing his hands with water must wash his clothes and bathe with water, and he will be unclean till evening.

12" 'A clay pot that the man touches must be broken, and any wooden article is to be rinsed with water.

13" 'When a man is cleansed from his discharge, he is to count off seven days for his ceremonial cleansing; he must wash his clothes and bathe himself with fresh water, and he will be clean. 14On the eighth day he must take two doves or two young pigeons and come before the LORD to the entrance to the Tent of Meeting and give them to the priest. 15The priest is to sacrifice them, the one for a sin offering and the other for a burnt offering. In this way he will make atonement before the LORD for the man because of his discharge.

16" 'When a man has an emission of semen, he must bathe his whole body with water, and he will be unclean till evening. 17Any clothing or leather that has semen on it must be washed with water, and it will be unclean till evening. 18When a man lies with a woman and there is an emission of semen, both must bathe with water, and they will be unclean till evening.

19" 'When a woman has her regular flow of blood, the impurity of her monthly period will last seven days, and anyone who touches her will be unclean till evening.

20" 'Anything she lies on during her period will be unclean, and anything she sits on will be unclean. 21Whoever touches her bed must wash his clothes and bathe with water, and he will be unclean till evening. 22Whoever touches anything she sits on must wash his clothes and bathe with water, and he will be unclean till evening. 23Whether it is the bed or anything she was sitting on, when anyone touches it, he will be unclean till evening.

24" 'If a man lies with her and her monthly flow touches him, he will be unclean for seven days; any bed he lies on will be unclean.

25" 'When a woman has a discharge of blood for many days at a time other than her monthly period or has a discharge that continues beyond her period, she will be unclean as long as she has the discharge, just as in the days of her period. 26Any bed she lies on while her discharge continues will be unclean, as is her bed during her monthly period, and anything she sits on will be unclean, as during her period. 27Whoever touches them will be unclean; he must wash his clothes and bathe with water, and he will be unclean till evening.

28" 'When she is cleansed from her discharge, she must count off seven days, and after that she will be ceremonially clean. 29On the eighth day she must take two doves or two young pigeons and bring them to the priest at the entrance to the Tent of Meeting. 30The priest is to sacrifice one for a sin offering and the other for a burnt offering. In this way he will make atonement for her before the LORD for the uncleanness of her discharge.

31" 'You must keep the Israelites separate from things that make them unclean, so they will not die in their uncleanness for defiling my dwelling place,*a* which is among them.' "

32These are the regulations for a man with a discharge, for anyone made unclean by an emission of semen, 33for a woman in her monthly period, for a man or a woman with a discharge, and for a man who lies with a woman who is ceremonially unclean.

The Day of Atonement

16 The LORD spoke to Moses after the death of the two sons of Aaron who died when they approached the LORD. 2The LORD said to Moses: "Tell your brother Aaron not to come whenever he chooses into the Most Holy Place behind the curtain in front of the atonement cover on the ark, or else he will die, because I appear in the cloud over the atonement cover.

3"This is how Aaron is to enter the sanctuary area: with a young bull for a sin offering and a ram for a burnt offering. 4He is to put on the sacred linen tunic, with linen undergarments next to his body; he is to tie the linen sash around him and put on the linen turban. These are sacred garments; so he must bathe himself with water before he puts them on. 5From the Israelite community he is to take two male goats for a sin offering and a ram for a burnt offering.

6"Aaron is to offer the bull for his own sin offering to make atonement for himself and his household. 7Then he is to take the two goats and present them before the LORD at the entrance to the Tent of Meeting. 8He is to cast lots for the two goats—one lot for the LORD and the other for the scapegoat.*b* 9Aaron shall bring the goat whose lot falls to the LORD and sacrifice it for a sin offering. 10But the goat chosen by lot as the scapegoat shall be presented alive before the LORD to be used for making atonement by sending it into the desert as a scapegoat.

11"Aaron shall bring the bull for his own sin offering to make atonement for himself and his household, and he is to slaughter the bull for his own sin offering. 12He is to take a censer full of burning coals from the altar before the LORD and two handfuls of finely ground fragrant incense and take them behind the curtain. 13He is to put the incense on the fire before the LORD, and the smoke of the incense will conceal the atonement cover above the Testimony, so that he will not die. 14He is to take some of the bull's blood and with his finger sprinkle it on the front of the atonement cover; then he shall sprinkle some of it with his finger seven times before the atonement cover.

15"He shall then slaughter the goat for the sin offering for the people and take its blood behind the curtain and do with it as he did with the bull's blood: He shall sprinkle it on the atonement cover and in front of it. 16In this way he will make atonement for the Most Holy Place because of the uncleanness and rebellion of the Israelites, whatever their sins have

---

a31 Or *my tabernacle*   *b8* That is, the goat of removal; Hebrew *azazel*; also in verses 10 and 26 been. He is to do the same for the Tent of Meeting, which is among them in the midst of their uncleanness. [17]No one is to be in the Tent of Meeting from the time Aaron goes in to make atonement in the Most Holy Place until he comes out, having made atonement for himself, his household and the whole community of Israel.

[18]"Then he shall come out to the altar that is before the LORD and make atonement for it. He shall take some of the bull's blood and some of the goat's blood and put it on all the horns of the altar. [19]He shall sprinkle some of the blood on it with his finger seven times to cleanse it and to consecrate it from the uncleanness of the Israelites.

[20]"When Aaron has finished making atonement for the Most Holy Place, the Tent of Meeting and the altar, he shall bring forward the live goat. [21]He is to lay both hands on the head of the live goat and confess over it all the wickedness and rebellion of the Israelites—all their sins—and put them on the goat's head. He shall send the goat away into the desert in the care of a man appointed for the task. [22]The goat will carry on itself all their sins to a solitary place; and the man shall release it in the desert.

[23]"Then Aaron is to go into the Tent of Meeting and take off the linen garments he put on before he entered the Most Holy Place, and he is to leave them there. [24]He shall bathe himself with water in a holy place and put on his regular garments. Then he shall come out and sacrifice the burnt offering for himself and the burnt offering for the people, to make atonement for himself and for the people. [25]He shall also burn the fat of the sin offering on the altar.

[26]"The man who releases the goat as a scapegoat must wash his clothes and bathe himself with water; afterward he may come into the camp. [27]The bull and the goat for the sin offerings, whose blood was brought into the Most Holy Place to make atonement, must be taken outside the camp; their hides, flesh and offal are to be burned up. [28]The man who burns them must wash his clothes and bathe himself with water; afterward he may come into the camp.

[29]"This is to be a lasting ordinance for you: On the tenth day of the seventh month you must deny yourselves[a] and not do any work—whether native-born or an alien living among you— [30]because on this day atonement will be made for you, to cleanse you. Then, before the LORD, you will be clean from all your sins. [31]It is a sabbath of rest, and you must deny yourselves; it is a lasting ordinance. [32]The priest who is anointed and ordained to succeed his father as high priest is to make atonement. He is to put on the sacred linen garments [33]and make atonement for the Most Holy Place, for the Tent of Meeting and the altar, and for the priests and all the people of the community.

[34]"This is to be a lasting ordinance for you: Atonement is to be made once a year for all the sins of the Israelites."

And it was done, as the LORD commanded Moses.

Eating Blood Forbidden

17 The LORD said to Moses, [2]"Speak to Aaron and his sons and to all the Israelites and say to them: 'This is what the LORD has commanded: [3]Any Israelite who sacrifices an ox,[b] a lamb or a goat in the camp or outside of it [4]instead of bringing it to the entrance to the Tent of Meeting to present it as an offering to the LORD in front of the tabernacle of the LORD—that man shall be considered guilty of bloodshed; he has shed blood and must be cut off from his people. [5]This is so the Israelites will bring to the LORD the sacrifices they are now making in the open fields. They must bring them to the priest, that is, to the LORD, at the entrance to the Tent

---

[a]29 Or *must fast*; also in verse 31   [b]3 The Hebrew word can include both male and female.

POINT OF INTEREST

Leviticus 16:30

Israel celebrated the Day of Atonement annually. On that day the high priest made sacrifices both for himself and for the nation. At the end of the ceremony, a live goat was released into the desert, figuratively carrying with it the confessed sins of Israel (Leviticus 16:10, 22). What a visual reminder of the need for atonement and God's complete forgiveness!

of Meeting and sacrifice them as fellowship offerings.*a* 6The priest is to sprinkle the blood against the altar of the Lord at the entrance to the Tent of Meeting and burn the fat as an aroma pleasing to the Lord. 7They must no longer offer any of their sacrifices to the goat idols*b* to whom they prostitute themselves. This is to be a lasting ordinance for them and for the generations to come.'

8"Say to them: 'Any Israelite or any alien living among them who offers a burnt offering or sacrifice 9and does not bring it to the entrance to the Tent of Meeting to sacrifice it to the Lord—that man must be cut off from his people.

10" 'Any Israelite or any alien living among them who eats any blood—I will set my face against that person who eats blood and will cut him off from his people. 11For the life of a creature is in the blood, and I have given it to you to make atonement for yourselves on the altar; it is the blood that makes atonement for one's life. 12Therefore I say to the Israelites, "None of you may eat blood, nor may an alien living among you eat blood."

13" 'Any Israelite or any alien living among you who hunts any animal or bird that may be eaten must drain out the blood and cover it with earth, 14because the life of every creature is its blood. That is why I have said to the Israelites, "You must not eat the blood of any creature, because the life of every creature is its blood; anyone who eats it must be cut off."

15" 'Anyone, whether native-born or alien, who eats anything found dead or torn by wild animals must wash his clothes and bathe with water, and he will be ceremonially unclean till evening; then he will be clean. 16But if he does not wash his clothes and bathe himself, he will be held responsible.' "

Unlawful Sexual Relations

18 The Lord said to Moses, 2"Speak to the Israelites and say to them: 'I am the Lord your God. 3You must not do as they do in Egypt, where you used to live, and you must not do as they do in the land of Canaan, where I am bringing you. Do not follow their practices. 4You must obey my laws and be careful to follow my decrees. I am the Lord your God. 5Keep my decrees and laws, for the man who obeys them will live by them. I am the Lord.

6" 'No one is to approach any close relative to have sexual relations. I am the Lord.

7" 'Do not dishonor your father by having sexual relations with your mother. She is your mother; do not have relations with her.

8" 'Do not have sexual relations with your father's wife; that would dishonor your father.

9" 'Do not have sexual relations with your sister, either your father's daughter or your mother's daughter, whether she was born in the same home or elsewhere.

10" 'Do not have sexual relations with your son's daughter or your daughter's daughter; that would dishonor you.

11" 'Do not have sexual relations with the daughter of your father's wife, born to your father; she is your sister.

12" 'Do not have sexual relations with your father's sister; she is your father's close relative.

13" 'Do not have sexual relations with your mother's sister, because she is your mother's close relative.

14" 'Do not dishonor your father's brother by approaching his wife to have sexual relations; she is your aunt.

15" 'Do not have sexual relations with your daughter-in-law. She is your son's wife; do not have relations with her.

16" 'Do not have sexual relations with your brother's wife; that would dishonor your brother.

17" 'Do not have sexual relations with both a woman and her daughter. Do not have sexual relations with either her son's daughter or her daughter's daughter; they are her close relatives. That is wickedness.

18" 'Do not take your wife's sister as a rival wife and have sexual relations with her while your wife is living.

19" 'Do not approach a woman to have sexual relations during the uncleanness of her monthly period.

20" 'Do not have sexual relations with your neighbor's wife and defile yourself with her.

21" 'Do not give any of your children to be sacrificed*c* to Molech, for you must not profane the name of your God. I am the Lord.

---

a5 Traditionally *peace offerings*   *b7* Or *demons*
c21 Or *to be passed through ⌊the fire⌋*

²²" 'Do not lie with a man as one lies with a woman; that is detestable.

²³" 'Do not have sexual relations with an animal and defile yourself with it. A woman must not present herself to an animal to have sexual relations with it; that is a perversion.

²⁴" 'Do not defile yourselves in any of these ways, because this is how the nations that I am going to drive out before you became defiled. ²⁵Even the land was defiled; so I punished it for its sin, and the land vomited out its inhabitants. ²⁶But you must keep my decrees and my laws. The native-born and the aliens living among you must not do any of these detestable things, ²⁷for all these things were done by the people who lived in the land before you, and the land became defiled. ²⁸And if you defile the land, it will vomit you out as it vomited out the nations that were before you.

²⁹" 'Everyone who does any of these detestable things—such persons must be cut off from their people. ³⁰Keep my requirements and do not follow any of the detestable customs that were practiced before you came and do not defile yourselves with them. I am the LORD your God.' "

Various Laws

19 The LORD said to Moses, ²"Speak to the entire assembly of Israel and say to them: 'Be holy because I, the LORD your God, am holy.

³" 'Each of you must respect his mother and father, and you must observe my Sabbaths. I am the LORD your God.

⁴" 'Do not turn to idols or make gods of cast metal for yourselves. I am the LORD your God.

⁵" 'When you sacrifice a fellowship offering^a to the LORD, sacrifice it in such a way that it will be accepted on your behalf. ⁶It shall be eaten on the day you sacrifice it or on the next day; anything left over until the third day must be burned up. ⁷If any of it is eaten on the third day, it is impure and will not be accepted. ⁸Whoever eats it will be held responsible because he has desecrated what is holy to the LORD; that person must be cut off from his people.

⁹" 'When you reap the harvest of your land, do not reap to the very edges of your field or gather the gleanings of your harvest. ¹⁰Do not go over your vineyard a second time or pick up the grapes that

have fallen. Leave them for the poor and the alien. I am the LORD your God.

¹¹" 'Do not steal.

" 'Do not lie.

" 'Do not deceive one another.

¹²" 'Do not swear falsely by my name and so profane the name of your God. I am the LORD.

¹³" 'Do not defraud your neighbor or rob him.

" 'Do not hold back the wages of a hired man overnight.

¹⁴" 'Do not curse the deaf or put a stumbling block in front of the blind, but fear your God. I am the LORD.

¹⁵" 'Do not pervert justice; do not show partiality to the poor or favoritism to the great, but judge your neighbor fairly.

¹⁶" 'Do not go about spreading slander among your people.

" 'Do not do anything that endangers your neighbor's life. I am the LORD.

¹⁷" 'Do not hate your brother in your heart. Rebuke your neighbor frankly so you will not share in his guilt.

¹⁸" 'Do not seek revenge or bear a grudge against one of your people, but love your neighbor as yourself. I am the LORD.

¹⁹" 'Keep my decrees.

" 'Do not mate different kinds of animals.

" 'Do not plant your field with two kinds of seed.

" 'Do not wear clothing woven of two kinds of material.

²⁰" 'If a man sleeps with a woman who is a slave girl promised to another man but who has not been ransomed or given her freedom, there must be due punishment. Yet they are not to be put to death, because she had not been freed. ²¹The

^a5 Traditionally *peace offering*

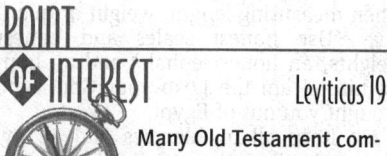

POINT OF INTEREST   Leviticus 19:11

Many Old Testament commands are repeated in the New Testament. Colossians 3:9 exhorts believers not to "lie to each other, since you have taken off your old self with its practices." Why do you think we need to hear it twice?

man, however, must bring a ram to the entrance to the Tent of Meeting for a guilt offering to the LORD. ²²With the ram of the guilt offering the priest is to make atonement for him before the LORD for the sin he has committed, and his sin will be forgiven.

²³" 'When you enter the land and plant any kind of fruit tree, regard its fruit as forbidden.ᵃ For three years you are to consider it forbiddenᵃ; it must not be eaten. ²⁴In the fourth year all its fruit will be holy, an offering of praise to the LORD. ²⁵But in the fifth year you may eat its fruit. In this way your harvest will be increased. I am the LORD your God.

²⁶" 'Do not eat any meat with the blood still in it.

" 'Do not practice divination or sorcery.

²⁷" 'Do not cut the hair at the sides of your head or clip off the edges of your beard.

²⁸" 'Do not cut your bodies for the dead or put tattoo marks on yourselves. I am the LORD.

²⁹" 'Do not degrade your daughter by making her a prostitute, or the land will turn to prostitution and be filled with wickedness.

³⁰" 'Observe my Sabbaths and have reverence for my sanctuary. I am the LORD.

³¹" 'Do not turn to mediums or seek out spiritists, for you will be defiled by them. I am the LORD your God.

³²" 'Rise in the presence of the aged, show respect for the elderly and revere your God. I am the LORD.

³³" 'When an alien lives with you in your land, do not mistreat him. ³⁴The alien living with you must be treated as one of your native-born. Love him as yourself, for you were aliens in Egypt. I am the LORD your God.

³⁵" 'Do not use dishonest standards when measuring length, weight or quantity. ³⁶Use honest scales and honest weights, an honest ephahᵇ and an honest hin.ᶜ I am the LORD your God, who brought you out of Egypt.

³⁷" 'Keep all my decrees and all my laws and follow them. I am the LORD.' "

Punishments for Sin

20 The LORD said to Moses, ²"Say to the Israelites: 'Any Israelite or any alien living in Israel who givesᵈ any of his children to Molech must be put to death. The people of the community are to stone him. ³I will set my face against that man and I will cut him off from his people; for by giving his children to Molech, he has defiled my sanctuary and profaned my holy name. ⁴If the people of the community close their eyes when that man gives one of his children to Molech and they fail to put him to death, ⁵I will set my face against that man and his family and will cut off from their people both him and all who follow him in prostituting themselves to Molech.

⁶" 'I will set my face against the person who turns to mediums and spiritists to prostitute himself by following them, and I will cut him off from his people.

⁷" 'Consecrate yourselves and be holy, because I am the LORD your God. ⁸Keep my decrees and follow them. I am the LORD, who makes you holy.ᵉ

⁹" 'If anyone curses his father or mother, he must be put to death. He has cursed his father or his mother, and his blood will be on his own head.

¹⁰" 'If a man commits adultery with another man's wife—with the wife of his neighbor—both the adulterer and the adulteress must be put to death.

¹¹" 'If a man sleeps with his father's wife, he has dishonored his father. Both the man and the woman must be put to death; their blood will be on their own heads.

¹²" 'If a man sleeps with his daughter-in-law, both of them must be put to death. What they have done is a perversion; their blood will be on their own heads.

¹³" 'If a man lies with a man as one lies with a woman, both of them have done what is detestable. They must be put to death; their blood will be on their own heads.

¹⁴" 'If a man marries both a woman and her mother, it is wicked. Both he and they must be burned in the fire, so that no wickedness will be among you.

¹⁵" 'If a man has sexual relations with an animal, he must be put to death, and you must kill the animal.

¹⁶" 'If a woman approaches an animal to have sexual relations with it, kill both the woman and the animal. They must be

---

ᵃ23 Hebrew *uncircumcised*   ᵇ36 An ephah was a dry measure.   ᶜ36 A hin was a liquid measure.   ᵈ2 Or *sacrifices*; also in verses 3 and 4   ᵉ8 Or *who sanctifies you*; or *who sets you apart as holy* put to death; their blood will be on their own heads.

¹⁷ 'If a man marries his sister, the daughter of either his father or his mother, and they have sexual relations, it is a disgrace. They must be cut off before the eyes of their people. He has dishonored his sister and will be held responsible.

¹⁸ 'If a man lies with a woman during her monthly period and has sexual relations with her, he has exposed the source of her flow, and she has also uncovered it. Both of them must be cut off from their people.

¹⁹ 'Do not have sexual relations with the sister of either your mother or your father, for that would dishonor a close relative; both of you would be held responsible.

²⁰ 'If a man sleeps with his aunt, he has dishonored his uncle. They will be held responsible; they will die childless.

²¹ " 'If a man marries his brother's wife, it is an act of impurity; he has dishonored his brother. They will be childless.

²² " 'Keep all my decrees and laws and follow them, so that the land where I am bringing you to live may not vomit you out. ²³You must not live according to the customs of the nations I am going to drive out before you. Because they did all these things, I abhorred them. ²⁴But I said to you, "You will possess their land; I will

---

WEDNESDAY

Read *Leviticus 20:1–27*
Key Verse *Leviticus 20:13*

Hope for the Homosexual — Kenneth G. Tussey

Wow! Leviticus 20:13 is a tough verse for someone like me, a former practicing homosexual. Many people in our culture consider homosexuality a viable alternative lifestyle. Yet the Word of God doesn't present it that way. God's Word clearly restricts sexual activity to a heterosexual marriage relationship. As strict as God's laws are concerning homosexual activity, there is hope for the homosexual for God's grace is big enough for any sin, including this one. Romans 6:23 says, "For the wages of sin is death, but the gift of God is eternal life in Christ Jesus our Lord."

In contrast to Leviticus 20:13, which says, "their blood will be on their own heads," Romans 5:8–9 highlights God's grace and forgiveness: "But God demonstrates his own love for us in this: While we were still sinners, Christ died for us. Since we have now been justified by his blood, how much more shall we be saved from God's wrath through him!" We are reassured that hope isn't lost; the blood of Jesus covers us and purifies us from all sin, even homosexuality, and satisfies God's standard of perfect holiness.

Not only does Jesus Christ provide forgiveness and salvation for sexual sin, but he also provides the hope for healing. After listing several sins Paul says in 1 Corinthians 6:11: "And that is what some of you were. But you were washed, you were sanctified, you were justified in the name of the Lord Jesus Christ and by the Spirit of our God." Jesus not only paid the price for our sin, but he also emptied sin of its power in our lives.

God offers hope, love, healing, forgiveness and a renewed life! Thank you, Lord Jesus, for paying the price for my sin.

A Deeper Look
Romans 1:24–27; 1 Corinthians 6:18–20

Go to page 132 for your next devotional reading.

give it to you as an inheritance, a land flowing with milk and honey." I am the LORD your God, who has set you apart from the nations.

²⁵" 'You must therefore make a distinction between clean and unclean animals and between unclean and clean birds. Do not defile yourselves by any animal or bird or anything that moves along the ground—those which I have set apart as unclean for you. ²⁶You are to be holy to me*ᵃ* because I, the LORD, am holy, and I have set you apart from the nations to be my own.

²⁷" 'A man or woman who is a medium or spiritist among you must be put to death. You are to stone them; their blood will be on their own heads.' "

Rules for Priests

21 The LORD said to Moses, "Speak to the priests, the sons of Aaron, and say to them: 'A priest must not make himself ceremonially unclean for any of his people who die, ²except for a close relative, such as his mother or father, his son or daughter, his brother, ³or an unmarried sister who is dependent on him since she has no husband—for her he may make himself unclean. ⁴He must not make himself unclean for people related to him by marriage,*ᵇ* and so defile himself.

⁵" 'Priests must not shave their heads or shave off the edges of their beards or cut their bodies. ⁶They must be holy to their God and must not profane the name of their God. Because they present the offerings made to the LORD by fire, the food of their God, they are to be holy.

⁷" 'They must not marry women defiled by prostitution or divorced from their husbands, because priests are holy to their God. ⁸Regard them as holy, because they offer up the food of your God. Consider them holy, because I the LORD am holy—I who make you holy.*ᶜ*

⁹" 'If a priest's daughter defiles herself by becoming a prostitute, she disgraces her father; she must be burned in the fire.

¹⁰" 'The high priest, the one among his brothers who has had the anointing oil poured on his head and who has been ordained to wear the priestly garments, must not let his hair become unkempt*ᵈ* or tear his clothes. ¹¹He must not enter a place where there is a dead body. He must not make himself unclean, even for his father or mother, ¹²nor leave the sanctuary of his God or desecrate it, because

he has been dedicated by the anointing oil of his God. I am the LORD.

¹³" 'The woman he marries must be a virgin. ¹⁴He must not marry a widow, a divorced woman, or a woman defiled by prostitution, but only a virgin from his own people, ¹⁵so he will not defile his offspring among his people. I am the LORD, who makes him holy.*ᵉ* "

¹⁶The LORD said to Moses, ¹⁷"Say to Aaron: 'For the generations to come none of your descendants who has a defect may come near to offer the food of his God. ¹⁸No man who has any defect may come near: no man who is blind or lame, disfigured or deformed; ¹⁹no man with a crippled foot or hand, ²⁰or who is hunchbacked or dwarfed, or who has any eye defect, or who has festering or running sores or damaged testicles. ²¹No descendant of Aaron the priest who has any defect is to come near to present the offerings made to the LORD by fire. He has a defect; he must not come near to offer the food of his God. ²²He may eat the most holy food of his God, as well as the holy food; ²³yet because of his defect, he must not go near the curtain or approach the altar, and so desecrate my sanctuary. I am the LORD, who makes them holy.*ᶠ* "

²⁴So Moses told this to Aaron and his sons and to all the Israelites.

22 The LORD said to Moses, ²"Tell Aaron and his sons to treat with respect the sacred offerings the Israelites consecrate to me, so they will not profane my holy name. I am the LORD.

³"Say to them: 'For the generations to come, if any of your descendants is ceremonially unclean and yet comes near the sacred offerings that the Israelites consecrate to the LORD, that person must be cut off from my presence. I am the LORD.

⁴" 'If a descendant of Aaron has an infectious skin disease*ᵍ* or a bodily discharge, he may not eat the sacred offerings until he is cleansed. He will also be unclean if he touches something defiled by a corpse or by anyone who has an emission of semen, ⁵or if he touches

---

ᵃ26 Or *be my holy ones*   *ᵇ4* Or *unclean as a leader among his people*   *ᶜ8* Or *who sanctify you; or who set you apart as holy*   *ᵈ10* Or *not uncover his head*   *ᵉ15* Or *who sanctifies him; or who sets him apart as holy*   *ᶠ23* Or *who sanctifies them; or who sets them apart as holy*
ᵍ4 Traditionally *leprosy;* the Hebrew word was used for various diseases affecting the skin—not necessarily leprosy.

any crawling thing that makes him unclean, or any person who makes him unclean, whatever the uncleanness may be. 6The one who touches any such thing will be unclean till evening. He must not eat any of the sacred offerings unless he has bathed himself with water. 7When the sun goes down, he will be clean, and after that he may eat the sacred offerings, for they are his food. 8He must not eat anything found dead or torn by wild animals, and so become unclean through it. I am the LORD.

9" 'The priests are to keep my requirements so that they do not become guilty and die for treating them with contempt. I am the LORD, who makes them holy.a

10" 'No one outside a priest's family may eat the sacred offering, nor may the guest of a priest or his hired worker eat it. 11But if a priest buys a slave with money, or if a slave is born in his household, that slave may eat his food. 12If a priest's daughter marries anyone other than a priest, she may not eat any of the sacred contributions. 13But if a priest's daughter becomes a widow or is divorced, yet has no children, and she returns to live in her father's house as in her youth, she may eat of her father's food. No unauthorized person, however, may eat any of it.

14" 'If anyone eats a sacred offering by mistake, he must make restitution to the priest for the offering and add a fifth of the value to it. 15The priests must not desecrate the sacred offerings the Israelites present to the LORD 16by allowing them to eat the sacred offerings and so bring upon them guilt requiring payment. I am the LORD, who makes them holy.' "

Unacceptable Sacrifices

17The LORD said to Moses, 18"Speak to Aaron and his sons and to all the Israelites and say to them: 'If any of you— either an Israelite or an alien living in Israel—presents a gift for a burnt offering to the LORD, either to fulfill a vow or as a freewill offering, 19you must present a male without defect from the cattle, sheep or goats in order that it may be accepted on your behalf. 20Do not bring anything with a defect, because it will not be accepted on your behalf. 21When anyone brings from the herd or flock a fellowship offeringb to the LORD to fulfill a special vow or as a freewill offering, it must be without defect or blemish to be acceptable. 22Do not offer to the LORD the

blind, the injured or the maimed, or anything with warts or festering or running sores. Do not place any of these on the altar as an offering made to the LORD by fire. 23You may, however, present as a freewill offering an oxc or a sheep that is deformed or stunted, but it will not be accepted in fulfillment of a vow. 24You must not offer to the LORD an animal whose testicles are bruised, crushed, torn or cut. You must not do this in your own land, 25and you must not accept such animals from the hand of a foreigner and offer them as the food of your God. They will not be accepted on your behalf, because they are deformed and have defects.' "

26The LORD said to Moses, 27"When a calf, a lamb or a goat is born, it is to remain with its mother for seven days. From the eighth day on, it will be acceptable as an offering made to the LORD by fire. 28Do not slaughter a cow or a sheep and its young on the same day.

29"When you sacrifice a thank offering to the LORD, sacrifice it in such a way that it will be accepted on your behalf. 30It must be eaten that same day; leave none of it till morning. I am the LORD.

31"Keep my commands and follow them. I am the LORD. 32Do not profane my holy name. I must be acknowledged as holy by the Israelites. I am the LORD, who makesd you holye 33and who brought you out of Egypt to be your God. I am the LORD."

23 The LORD said to Moses, 2"Speak to the Israelites and say to them: 'These are my appointed feasts, the appointed feasts of the LORD, which you are to proclaim as sacred assemblies.

The Sabbath

3" 'There are six days when you may work, but the seventh day is a Sabbath of rest, a day of sacred assembly. You are not to do any work; wherever you live, it is a Sabbath to the LORD.

The Passover and Unleavened Bread

4" 'These are the LORD's appointed feasts, the sacred assemblies you are to proclaim at their appointed times: 5The

---

a9 Or who sanctifies them; or who sets them apart as holy; also in verse 16   b21 Traditionally peace offering   c23 The Hebrew word can include both male and female.   d32 Or made   e32 Or who sanctifies you; or who sets you apart as holy

LORD's Passover begins at twilight on the fourteenth day of the first month. ⁶On the fifteenth day of that month the LORD's Feast of Unleavened Bread begins; for seven days you must eat bread made without yeast. ⁷On the first day hold a sacred assembly and do no regular work. ⁸For seven days present an offering made to the LORD by fire. And on the seventh day hold a sacred assembly and do no regular work.' "

Firstfruits

⁹The LORD said to Moses, ¹⁰"Speak to the Israelites and say to them: 'When you enter the land I am going to give you and you reap its harvest, bring to the priest a sheaf of the first grain you harvest. ¹¹He is to wave the sheaf before the LORD so it will be accepted on your behalf; the priest is to wave it on the day after the Sabbath. ¹²On the day you wave the sheaf, you must sacrifice as a burnt offering to the LORD a lamb a year old without defect, ¹³together with its grain offering of two-tenths of an ephah*ᵃ* of fine flour mixed with oil—an offering made to the LORD by fire, a pleasing aroma—and its drink offering of a quarter of a hin*ᵇ* of wine. ¹⁴You must not eat any bread, or roasted or new grain, until the very day you bring this offering to your God. This is to be a lasting ordinance for the generations to come, wherever you live.

Feast of Weeks

¹⁵ 'From the day after the Sabbath, the day you brought the sheaf of the wave offering, count off seven full weeks. ¹⁶Count off fifty days up to the day after the seventh Sabbath, and then present an offering of new grain to the

ᵃ13 That is, probably about 4 quarts (about 4.5 liters); also in verse 17   ᵇ13 That is, probably about 1 quart (about 1 liter)

THURSDAY

Read Leviticus 23:1–44
Key Verse Leviticus 23:3

Don't Forget Rest! — Shannon Gayk

My first year at college was really rough. It was difficult being away from home where everything was familiar. Instead I found myself in a strange place where I was expected to perform academically in ways I hadn't even known existed. I hadn't studied very much in high school and was shocked to find out that I was going to have to study here—a lot!

My life soon became an endless cycle of sleepless nights, hours in the library and meals eaten on the run. My body was telling me that I needed to rest, but I ignored it's warnings most of the time. One day, in a rare moment, I looked at the sky and saw how peaceful the clouds looked. I had to stop and rejoice that God had created such beauty. That great view of the sky brought perspective back to my life. In the frantic rush of school, I'd forgotten that God knows us better than we know ourselves—he knows that we need a rest. As a matter of fact, it's so important that it's in his Word!

God has been really working in me this past year, teaching me how to slow down and rest in him. When I stop being busy long enough to focus on him, I gain peace in the midst of a crazy world. And who knows—maybe in the long run I get more done that way anyhow.

A Deeper Look
Psalm 46:10; Matthew 11:29–30; Luke 5:16

Go to page 157 for your next devotional reading.

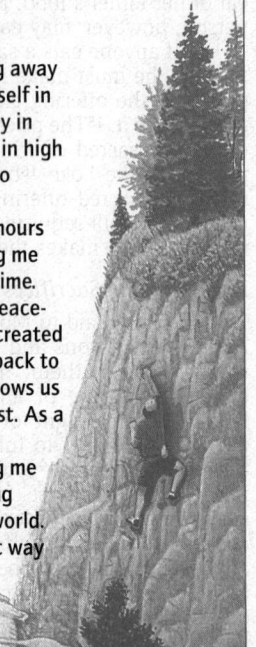

LORD. ¹⁷From wherever you live, bring two loaves made of two-tenths of an ephah of fine flour, baked with yeast, as a wave offering of firstfruits to the LORD. ¹⁸Present with this bread seven male lambs, each a year old and without defect, one young bull and two rams. They will be a burnt offering to the LORD, together with their grain offerings and drink offerings—an offering made by fire, an aroma pleasing to the LORD. ¹⁹Then sacrifice one male goat for a sin offering and two lambs, each a year old, for a fellowship offering.^a ²⁰The priest is to wave the two lambs before the LORD as a wave offering, together with the bread of the firstfruits. They are a sacred offering to the LORD for the priest. ²¹On that same day you are to proclaim a sacred assembly and do no regular work. This is to be a lasting ordinance for the generations to come, wherever you live.

²²" 'When you reap the harvest of your land, do not reap to the very edges of your field or gather the gleanings of your harvest. Leave them for the poor and the alien. I am the LORD your God.' "

Feast of Trumpets

²³The LORD said to Moses, ²⁴"Say to the Israelites: 'On the first day of the seventh month you are to have a day of rest, a sacred assembly commemorated with trumpet blasts. ²⁵Do no regular work, but present an offering made to the LORD by fire.' "

Day of Atonement

²⁶The LORD said to Moses, ²⁷"The tenth day of this seventh month is the Day of Atonement. Hold a sacred assembly and deny yourselves,^b and present an offering made to the LORD by fire. ²⁸Do no work on that day, because it is the Day of Atonement, when atonement is made for you before the LORD your God. ²⁹Anyone who does not deny himself on that day must be cut off from his people. ³⁰I will destroy from among his people anyone who does any work on that day. ³¹You shall do no work at all. This is to be a lasting ordinance for the generations to come, wherever you live. ³²It is a sabbath of rest for you, and you must deny yourselves. From the evening of the ninth day of the month until the following evening you are to observe your sabbath."

Feast of Tabernacles

³³The LORD said to Moses, ³⁴"Say to the Israelites: 'On the fifteenth day of the seventh month the LORD's Feast of Tabernacles begins, and it lasts for seven days. ³⁵The first day is a sacred assembly; do no regular work. ³⁶For seven days present offerings made to the LORD by fire, and on the eighth day hold a sacred assembly and present an offering made to the LORD by fire. It is the closing assembly; do no regular work.

³⁷(" 'These are the LORD's appointed feasts, which you are to proclaim as sacred assemblies for bringing offerings made to the LORD by fire—the burnt offerings and grain offerings, sacrifices and drink offerings required for each day. ³⁸These offerings are in addition to those for the LORD's Sabbaths and^c in addition to your gifts and whatever you have vowed and all the freewill offerings you give to the LORD.)

³⁹" 'So beginning with the fifteenth day of the seventh month, after you have gathered the crops of the land, celebrate the festival to the LORD for seven days; the first day is a day of rest, and the eighth day also is a day of rest. ⁴⁰On the first day you are to take choice fruit from the trees, and palm fronds, leafy branches and poplars, and rejoice before the LORD your God for seven days. ⁴¹Celebrate this as a festival to the LORD for seven days each year. This is to be a lasting ordinance for the generations to come; celebrate it in the seventh month. ⁴²Live in booths for seven days: All native-born Israelites are to live in booths ⁴³so your descendants will know that I had the Israelites live in booths when I brought them out of Egypt. I am the LORD your God.' "

⁴⁴So Moses announced to the Israelites the appointed feasts of the LORD.

Oil and Bread Set Before the LORD

24 The LORD said to Moses, ²"Command the Israelites to bring you clear oil of pressed olives for the light so that the lamps may be kept burning continually. ³Outside the curtain of the Testimony in the Tent of Meeting, Aaron is to tend the lamps before the LORD from evening till

---

^a19 Traditionally *peace offering*   ^b27 Or *and fast*; also in verses 29 and 32   ^c38 Or *These feasts are in addition to the LORD's Sabbaths, and these offerings are*

morning, continually. This is to be a lasting ordinance for the generations to come. ⁴The lamps on the pure gold lampstand before the LORD must be tended continually.

⁵"Take fine flour and bake twelve loaves of bread, using two-tenths of an ephah*ᵃ* for each loaf. ⁶Set them in two rows, six in each row, on the table of pure gold before the LORD. ⁷Along each row put some pure incense as a memorial portion to represent the bread and to be an offering made to the LORD by fire. ⁸This bread is to be set out before the LORD regularly, Sabbath after Sabbath, on behalf of the Israelites, as a lasting covenant. ⁹It belongs to Aaron and his sons, who are to eat it in a holy place, because it is a most holy part of their regular share of the offerings made to the LORD by fire."

A Blasphemer Stoned

¹⁰Now the son of an Israelite mother and an Egyptian father went out among the Israelites, and a fight broke out in the camp between him and an Israelite. ¹¹The son of the Israelite woman blasphemed the Name with a curse; so they brought him to Moses. (His mother's name was Shelomith, the daughter of Dibri the Danite.) ¹²They put him in custody until the will of the LORD should be made clear to them.

¹³Then the LORD said to Moses: ¹⁴"Take the blasphemer outside the camp. All those who heard him are to lay their hands on his head, and the entire assembly is to stone him. ¹⁵Say to the Israelites: 'If anyone curses his God, he will be held responsible; ¹⁶anyone who blasphemes the name of the LORD must be put to death. The entire assembly must stone him. Whether an alien or native-born, when he blasphemes the Name, he must be put to death.

¹⁷"'If anyone takes the life of a human being, he must be put to death. ¹⁸Anyone who takes the life of someone's animal must make restitution—life for life. ¹⁹If anyone injures his neighbor, whatever he has done must be done to him: ²⁰fracture for fracture, eye for eye, tooth for tooth. As he has injured the other, so he is to be injured. ²¹Whoever kills an animal must make restitution, but whoever kills a man must be put to death. ²²You are to have the same law for the alien and the native-born. I am the LORD your God.' "

²³Then Moses spoke to the Israelites,

and they took the blasphemer outside the camp and stoned him. The Israelites did as the LORD commanded Moses.

The Sabbath Year

25 The LORD said to Moses on Mount Sinai, ²"Speak to the Israelites and say to them: 'When you enter the land I am going to give you, the land itself must observe a sabbath to the LORD. ³For six years sow your fields, and for six years prune your vineyards and gather their crops. ⁴But in the seventh year the land is to have a sabbath of rest, a sabbath to the LORD. Do not sow your fields or prune your vineyards. ⁵Do not reap what grows of itself or harvest the grapes of your untended vines. The land is to have a year of rest. ⁶Whatever the land yields during the sabbath year will be food for you—for yourself, your manservant and maidservant, and the hired worker and temporary resident who live among you, ⁷as well as for your livestock and the wild animals in your land. Whatever the land produces may be eaten.

The Year of Jubilee

⁸"'Count off seven sabbaths of years—seven times seven years—so that the seven sabbaths of years amount to a period of forty-nine years. ⁹Then have the trumpet sounded everywhere on the tenth day of the seventh month; on the Day of Atonement sound the trumpet throughout your land. ¹⁰Consecrate the fiftieth year and proclaim liberty throughout the land to all its inhabitants. It shall be a jubilee for you; each one of you is to return to his family property and each to his own clan. ¹¹The fiftieth year shall be a jubilee for you; do not sow and do not reap what grows of itself or harvest the untended vines. ¹²For it is a jubilee and is

ᵃ5 That is, probably about 4 quarts (about 4.5 liters)

POINT OF INTEREST

Leviticus 24:21

Why is killing a person more serious than killing an animal? See Genesis 9:6 for the answer.

to be holy for you; eat only what is taken directly from the fields.

¹³ " 'In this Year of Jubilee everyone is to return to his own property.

¹⁴ " 'If you sell land to one of your countrymen or buy any from him, do not take advantage of each other. ¹⁵You are to buy from your countryman on the basis of the number of years since the Jubilee. And he is to sell to you on the basis of the number of years left for harvesting crops. ¹⁶When the years are many, you are to increase the price, and when the years are few, you are to decrease the price, because what he is really selling you is the number of crops. ¹⁷Do not take advantage of each other, but fear your God. I am the LORD your God.

¹⁸ " 'Follow my decrees and be careful to obey my laws, and you will live safely in the land. ¹⁹Then the land will yield its fruit, and you will eat your fill and live there in safety. ²⁰You may ask, "What will we eat in the seventh year if we do not plant or harvest our crops?" ²¹I will send you such a blessing in the sixth year that the land will yield enough for three years. ²²While you plant during the eighth year, you will eat from the old crop and will continue to eat from it until the harvest of the ninth year comes in.

²³ " 'The land must not be sold permanently, because the land is mine and you are but aliens and my tenants. ²⁴Throughout the country that you hold as a possession, you must provide for the redemption of the land.

²⁵ " 'If one of your countrymen becomes poor and sells some of his property, his nearest relative is to come and redeem what his countryman has sold. ²⁶If, however, a man has no one to redeem it for him but he himself prospers and acquires sufficient means to redeem it, ²⁷he is to determine the value for the years since he sold it and refund the balance to the man to whom he sold it; he can then go back to his own property. ²⁸But if he does not acquire the means to repay him, what he sold will remain in the possession of the buyer until the Year of Jubilee. It will be returned in the Jubilee, and he can then go back to his property.

²⁹ " 'If a man sells a house in a walled city, he retains the right of redemption a full year after its sale. During that time he may redeem it. ³⁰If it is not redeemed before a full year has passed, the house in the walled city shall belong permanently to the buyer and his descendants. It is not to be returned in the Jubilee. ³¹But houses in villages without walls around them are to be considered as open country. They can be redeemed, and they are to be returned in the Jubilee.

³² " 'The Levites always have the right to redeem their houses in the Levitical towns, which they possess. ³³So the property of the Levites is redeemable—that is, a house sold in any town they hold—and is to be returned in the Jubilee, because the houses in the towns of the Levites are their property among the Israelites. ³⁴But the pastureland belonging to their towns must not be sold; it is their permanent possession.

³⁵ " 'If one of your countrymen becomes poor and is unable to support himself among you, help him as you would an alien or a temporary resident, so he can continue to live among you. ³⁶Do not take interest of any kind[a] from him, but fear your God, so that your countryman may continue to live among you. ³⁷You must not lend him money at interest or sell him food at a profit. ³⁸I am the LORD your God, who brought you out of Egypt to give you the land of Canaan and to be your God.

³⁹ " 'If one of your countrymen becomes poor among you and sells himself to you, do not make him work as a slave. ⁴⁰He is to be treated as a hired worker or a temporary resident among you; he is to work for you until the Year of Jubilee. ⁴¹Then he and his children are to be released, and he will go back to his own clan and to the property of his forefathers. ⁴²Because the Israelites are my servants, whom I brought out of Egypt, they must not be sold as slaves. ⁴³Do not rule over them ruthlessly, but fear your God.

⁴⁴ " 'Your male and female slaves are to come from the nations around you; from them you may buy slaves. ⁴⁵You may also buy some of the temporary residents living among you and members of their clans born in your country, and they will become your property. ⁴⁶You can will them to your children as inherited property and can make them slaves for life, but you must not rule over your fellow Israelites ruthlessly.

⁴⁷ " 'If an alien or a temporary resident among you becomes rich and one of your

---

a36 Or *take excessive interest*; similarly in verse 37

countrymen becomes poor and sells himself to the alien living among you or to a member of the alien's clan, **48**he retains the right of redemption after he has sold himself. One of his relatives may redeem him: **49**An uncle or a cousin or any blood relative in his clan may redeem him. Or if he prospers, he may redeem himself. **50**He and his buyer are to count the time from the year he sold himself up to the Year of Jubilee. The price for his release is to be based on the rate paid to a hired man for that number of years. **51**If many years remain, he must pay for his redemption a larger share of the price paid for him. **52**If only a few years remain until the Year of Jubilee, he is to compute that and pay for his redemption accordingly. **53**He is to be treated as a man hired from year to year; you must see to it that his owner does not rule over him ruthlessly.

54" 'Even if he is not redeemed in any of these ways, he and his children are to be released in the Year of Jubilee, **55**for the Israelites belong to me as servants. They are my servants, whom I brought out of Egypt. I am the LORD your God.

Reward for Obedience

26 " 'Do not make idols or set up an image or a sacred stone for yourselves, and do not place a carved stone in your land to bow down before it. I am the LORD your God.

2" 'Observe my Sabbaths and have reverence for my sanctuary. I am the LORD.

3" 'If you follow my decrees and are careful to obey my commands, **4**I will send you rain in its season, and the ground will yield its crops and the trees of the field their fruit. **5**Your threshing will continue until grape harvest and the grape harvest will continue until planting, and you will eat all the food you want and live in safety in your land.

6" 'I will grant peace in the land, and you will lie down and no one will make you afraid. I will remove savage beasts from the land, and the sword will not pass through your country. **7**You will pursue your enemies, and they will fall by the sword before you. **8**Five of you will chase a hundred, and a hundred of you will chase ten thousand, and your enemies will fall by the sword before you.

9" 'I will look on you with favor and make you fruitful and increase your numbers, and I will keep my covenant with you. **10**You will still be eating last year's harvest when you will have to move it out to make room for the new. **11**I will put my dwelling place*a* among you, and I will not abhor you. **12**I will walk among you and be your God, and you will be my people. **13**I am the LORD your God, who brought you out of Egypt so that you would no longer be slaves to the Egyptians; I broke the bars of your yoke and enabled you to walk with heads held high.

Punishment for Disobedience

14" 'But if you will not listen to me and carry out all these commands, **15**and if you reject my decrees and abhor my laws and fail to carry out all my commands and so violate my covenant, **16**then I will do this to you: I will bring upon you sudden terror, wasting diseases and fever that will destroy your sight and drain away your life. You will plant seed in vain, because your enemies will eat it. **17**I will set my face against you so that you will be defeated by your enemies; those who hate you will rule over you, and you will flee even when no one is pursuing you.

18" 'If after all this you will not listen to me, I will punish you for your sins seven times over. **19**I will break down your stubborn pride and make the sky above you like iron and the ground beneath you like bronze. **20**Your strength will be spent in vain, because your soil will not yield its crops, nor will the trees of the land yield their fruit.

21" 'If you remain hostile toward me and refuse to listen to me, I will multiply your afflictions seven times over, as your sins deserve. **22**I will send wild animals against you, and they will rob you of your children, destroy your cattle and make you so few in number that your roads will be deserted.

23" 'If in spite of these things you do not accept my correction but continue to be hostile toward me, **24**I myself will be hostile toward you and will afflict you for your sins seven times over. **25**And I will bring the sword upon you to avenge the breaking of the covenant. When you withdraw into your cities, I will send a plague among you, and you will be given into enemy hands. **26**When I cut off your supply of bread, ten women will be able

a 11 Or my tabernacle

to bake your bread in one oven, and they will dole out the bread by weight. You will eat, but you will not be satisfied.

²⁷" 'If in spite of this you still do not listen to me but continue to be hostile toward me, ²⁸then in my anger I will be hostile toward you, and I myself will punish you for your sins seven times over. ²⁹You will eat the flesh of your sons and the flesh of your daughters. ³⁰I will destroy your high places, cut down your incense altars and pile your dead bodies on the lifeless forms of your idols, and I will abhor you. ³¹I will turn your cities into ruins and lay waste your sanctuaries, and I will take no delight in the pleasing aroma of your offerings. ³²I will lay waste the land, so that your enemies who live there will be appalled. ³³I will scatter you among the nations and will draw out my sword and pursue you. Your land will be laid waste, and your cities will lie in ruins. ³⁴Then the land will enjoy its sabbath years all the time that it lies desolate and you are in the country of your enemies; then the land will rest and enjoy its sabbaths. ³⁵All the time that it lies desolate, the land will have the rest it did not have during the sabbaths you lived in it.

³⁶" 'As for those of you who are left, I will make their hearts so fearful in the lands of their enemies that the sound of a windblown leaf will put them to flight. They will run as though fleeing from the sword, and they will fall, even though no one is pursuing them. ³⁷They will stumble over one another as though fleeing from the sword, even though no one is pursuing them. So you will not be able to stand before your enemies. ³⁸You will perish among the nations; the land of your enemies will devour you. ³⁹Those of you who are left will waste away in the lands of their enemies because of their sins; also because of their fathers' sins they will waste away.

⁴⁰" 'But if they will confess their sins and the sins of their fathers—their treachery against me and their hostility toward me, ⁴¹which made me hostile toward them so that I sent them into the land of their enemies—then when their uncircumcised hearts are humbled and they pay for their sin, ⁴²I will remember my covenant with Jacob and my covenant with Isaac and my covenant with Abraham, and I will remember the land. ⁴³For the land will be deserted by them and will enjoy its sabbaths while it lies

desolate without them. They will pay for their sins because they rejected my laws and abhorred my decrees. ⁴⁴Yet in spite of this, when they are in the land of their enemies, I will not reject them or abhor them so as to destroy them completely, breaking my covenant with them. I am the LORD their God. ⁴⁵But for their sake I will remember the covenant with their ancestors whom I brought out of Egypt in the sight of the nations to be their God. I am the LORD.' "

⁴⁶These are the decrees, the laws and the regulations that the LORD established on Mount Sinai between himself and the Israelites through Moses.

Redeeming What Is the LORD's

27 The LORD said to Moses, ²"Speak to the Israelites and say to them: 'If anyone makes a special vow to dedicate persons to the LORD by giving equivalent values, ³set the value of a male between the ages of twenty and sixty at fifty shekels*a* of silver, according to the sanctuary shekel*b*; ⁴and if it is a female, set her value at thirty shekels.*c* ⁵If it is a person between the ages of five and twenty, set the value of a male at twenty shekels*d* and of a female at ten shekels.*e* ⁶If it is a person between one month and five years, set the value of a male at five shekels*f* of silver and that of a female at three shekels*g* of silver. ⁷If it is a person sixty years old or more, set the value of a male at fifteen shekels*h* and of a female at ten shekels. ⁸If anyone making the vow is too poor to pay the specified amount, he is to present the person to the priest, who will set the value for him according to what the man making the vow can afford.

⁹" 'If what he vowed is an animal that is acceptable as an offering to the LORD, such an animal given to the LORD becomes holy. ¹⁰He must not exchange it or substitute a good one for a bad one, or a bad one for a good one; if he should substitute one animal for another, both it and the substitute become holy. ¹¹If what

---

*a*3 That is, about 1 1/4 pounds (about 0.6 kilogram); also in verse 16   *b*3 That is, about 2/5 ounce (about 11.5 grams); also in verse 25   *c*4 That is, about 12 ounces (about 0.3 kilogram)   *d*5 That is, about 8 ounces (about 0.2 kilogram)   *e*5 That is, about 4 ounces (about 110 grams); also in verse 7   *f*6 That is, about 2 ounces (about 55 grams)   *g*6 That is, about 1 1/4 ounces (about 35 grams)   *h*7 That is, about 6 ounces (about 170 grams) he vowed is a ceremonially unclean animal—one that is not acceptable as an offering to the LORD—the animal must be presented to the priest, 12who will judge its quality as good or bad. Whatever value the priest then sets, that is what it will be. 13If the owner wishes to redeem the animal, he must add a fifth to its value.

14" 'If a man dedicates his house as something holy to the LORD, the priest will judge its quality as good or bad. Whatever value the priest then sets, so it will remain. 15If the man who dedicates his house redeems it, he must add a fifth to its value, and the house will again become his.

16" 'If a man dedicates to the LORD part of his family land, its value is to be set according to the amount of seed required for it—fifty shekels of silver to a homer*a* of barley seed. 17If he dedicates his field during the Year of Jubilee, the value that has been set remains. 18But if he dedicates his field after the Jubilee, the priest will determine the value according to the number of years that remain until the next Year of Jubilee, and its set value will be reduced. 19If the man who dedicates the field wishes to redeem it, he must add a fifth to its value, and the field will again become his. 20If, however, he does not redeem the field, or if he has sold it to someone else, it can never be redeemed. 21When the field is released in the Jubilee, it will become holy, like a field devoted to the LORD; it will become the property of the priests.*b*

22" 'If a man dedicates to the LORD a field he has bought, which is not part of his family land, 23the priest will determine its value up to the Year of Jubilee, and the man must pay its value on that day as something holy to the LORD. 24In the Year of Jubilee the field will revert to the person from whom he bought it, the one whose land it was. 25Every value is to be set according to the sanctuary shekel, twenty gerahs to the shekel.

26" 'No one, however, may dedicate the firstborn of an animal, since the firstborn already belongs to the LORD; whether an ox*c* or a sheep, it is the LORD's. 27If it is one of the unclean animals, he may buy it back at its set value, adding a fifth of the value to it. If he does not redeem it, it is to be sold at its set value.

28" 'But nothing that a man owns and devotes*d* to the LORD—whether man or animal or family land—may be sold or redeemed; everything so devoted is most holy to the LORD.

29" 'No person devoted to destruction*e* may be ransomed; he must be put to death.

30" 'A tithe of everything from the land, whether grain from the soil or fruit from the trees, belongs to the LORD; it is holy to the LORD. 31If a man redeems any of his tithe, he must add a fifth of the value to it. 32The entire tithe of the herd and flock—every tenth animal that passes under the shepherd's rod—will be holy to the LORD. 33He must not pick out the good from the bad or make any substitution. If he does make a substitution, both the animal and its substitute become holy and cannot be redeemed.' "

34These are the commands the LORD gave Moses on Mount Sinai for the Israelites.

a16 That is, probably about 6 bushels (about 220 liters)   *b21* Or *priest*   *c26* The Hebrew word can include both male and female.   *d28* The Hebrew term refers to the irrevocable giving over of things or persons to the LORD.
e29 The Hebrew term refers to the irrevocable giving over of things or persons to the LORD, often by totally destroying them.

We might think of the book of Numbers as a census, a Gallup poll and a social commentary all rolled into one. The Israelites were counted twice during their thirty-eight years of wandering in the desert, hence the book's name. Numbers describes the complaining and rebellion of the Israelites, and how their attitude resulted in punishment—a life of exile in the desert—rather than enjoyment of God's promised blessings. But throughout the desert years, it becomes clear to Israel that God is always with his people, and that he loves, forgives and provides for them—even when they wander.

NUMBERS

The Census

1 The LORD spoke to Moses in the Tent of Meeting in the Desert of Sinai on the first day of the second month of the second year after the Israelites came out of Egypt. He said: ²"Take a census of the whole Israelite community by their clans and families, listing every man by name, one by one. ³You and Aaron are to number by their divisions all the men in Israel twenty years old or more who are able to serve in the army. ⁴One man from each tribe, each the head of his family, is to help you. ⁵These are the names of the men who are to assist you:

from Reuben, Elizur son of Shedeur;
⁶from Simeon, Shelumiel son of Zurishaddai;
⁷from Judah, Nahshon son of Amminadab;
⁸from Issachar, Nethanel son of Zuar;
⁹from Zebulun, Eliab son of Helon;
¹⁰from the sons of Joseph:
from Ephraim, Elishama son of Ammihud;
from Manasseh, Gamaliel son of Pedahzur;
¹¹from Benjamin, Abidan son of Gideoni;

¹²from Dan, Ahiezer son of Ammi-shaddai;
¹³from Asher, Pagiel son of Ocran;
¹⁴from Gad, Eliasaph son of Deuel;
¹⁵from Naphtali, Ahira son of Enan."

¹⁶These were the men appointed from the community, the leaders of their ancestral tribes. They were the heads of the clans of Israel.

¹⁷Moses and Aaron took these men whose names had been given, ¹⁸and they called the whole community together on the first day of the second month. The people indicated their ancestry by their clans and families, and the men twenty years old or more were listed by name, one by one, ¹⁹as the LORD commanded Moses. And so he counted them in the Desert of Sinai:

²⁰From the descendants of Reuben the firstborn son of Israel:
All the men twenty years old or more who were able to serve in the army were listed by name, one by one, according to the records of their clans and families. ²¹The number from the tribe of Reuben was 46,500.

²²From the descendants of Simeon:
All the men twenty years old or more who were able to serve in the army were counted and listed by name, one by one, according to the records of their clans and families. ²³The number from the tribe of Simeon was 59,300.

²⁴From the descendants of Gad:
All the men twenty years old or more who were able to serve in the army were listed by name, according to the records of their clans and families. ²⁵The number from the tribe of Gad was 45,650.

²⁶From the descendants of Judah:
All the men twenty years old or more who were able to serve in the army were listed by name, according to the records of their clans and families. ²⁷The number from the tribe of Judah was 74,600.

²⁸From the descendants of Issachar:
All the men twenty years old or more who were able to serve in the army were listed by name, according to the records of their clans and families. ²⁹The number from the tribe of Issachar was 54,400.

³⁰From the descendants of Zebulun:
All the men twenty years old or more who were able to serve in the army were listed by name, according to the records of their clans and families. ³¹The number from the tribe of Zebulun was 57,400.

³²From the sons of Joseph:
From the descendants of Ephraim:
All the men twenty years old or more who were able to serve in the army were listed by name, according to the records of their clans and families. ³³The number from the tribe of Ephraim was 40,500.

³⁴From the descendants of Manasseh:
All the men twenty years old or more who were able to serve in the army were listed by name, according to the records of their clans and families. ³⁵The number from the tribe of Manasseh was 32,200.

³⁶From the descendants of Benjamin:
All the men twenty years old or more who were able to serve in the army were listed by name, according to the records of their clans and families. ³⁷The number from the tribe of Benjamin was 35,400.

³⁸From the descendants of Dan:
All the men twenty years old or more who were able to serve in the army were listed by name, according to the records of their clans and families. ³⁹The number from the tribe of Dan was 62,700.

⁴⁰From the descendants of Asher:
All the men twenty years old or more who were able to serve in the army were listed by name, according to the records of their clans and families. ⁴¹The number from the tribe of Asher was 41,500.

⁴²From the descendants of Naphtali:
All the men twenty years old or

more who were able to serve in the army were listed by name, according to the records of their clans and families. ⁴³The number from the tribe of Naphtali was 53,400.

⁴⁴These were the men counted by Moses and Aaron and the twelve leaders of Israel, each one representing his family. ⁴⁵All the Israelites twenty years old or more who were able to serve in Israel's army were counted according to their families. ⁴⁶The total number was 603,550. ⁴⁷The families of the tribe of Levi, however, were not counted along with the others. ⁴⁸The LORD had said to Moses: ⁴⁹"You must not count the tribe of Levi or include them in the census of the other Israelites. ⁵⁰Instead, appoint the Levites to be in charge of the tabernacle of the Testimony—over all its furnishings and everything belonging to it. They are to carry the tabernacle and all its furnishings; they are to take care of it and encamp around it. ⁵¹Whenever the tabernacle is to move, the Levites are to take it down, and whenever the tabernacle is to be set up, the Levites shall do it. Anyone else who goes near it shall be put to death. ⁵²The Israelites are to set up their tents by divisions, each man in his own camp under his own standard. ⁵³The Levites, however, are to set up their tents around the tabernacle of the Testimony so that wrath will not fall on the Israelite community. The Levites are to be responsible for the care of the tabernacle of the Testimony." ⁵⁴The Israelites did all this just as the LORD commanded Moses.

The Arrangement of the Tribal Camps

2 The LORD said to Moses and Aaron: ²"The Israelites are to camp around the Tent of Meeting some distance from it, each man under his standard with the banners of his family."

³On the east, toward the sunrise, the divisions of the camp of Judah are to encamp under their standard. The leader of the people of Judah is Nahshon son of Amminadab. ⁴His division numbers 74,600.

⁵The tribe of Issachar will camp next to them. The leader of the people of Issachar is Nethanel son of Zuar. ⁶His division numbers 54,400.

⁷The tribe of Zebulun will be next. The leader of the people of Zebulun is Eliab son of Helon. ⁸His division numbers 57,400.

⁹All the men assigned to the camp of Judah, according to their divisions, number 186,400. They will set out first.

¹⁰On the south will be the divisions of the camp of Reuben under their standard. The leader of the people of Reuben is Elizur son of Shedeur. ¹¹His division numbers 46,500.

¹²The tribe of Simeon will camp next to them. The leader of the people of Simeon is Shelumiel son of Zurishaddai. ¹³His division numbers 59,300.

¹⁴The tribe of Gad will be next. The leader of the people of Gad is Eliasaph son of Deuel.^a ¹⁵His division numbers 45,650.

¹⁶All the men assigned to the camp of Reuben, according to their divisions, number 151,450. They will set out second.

¹⁷Then the Tent of Meeting and the camp of the Levites will set out in the middle of the camps. They will set out in the same order as they encamp, each in his own place under his standard.

¹⁸On the west will be the divisions of the camp of Ephraim under their standard. The leader of the people of Ephraim is Elishama son of Ammihud. ¹⁹His division numbers 40,500.

²⁰The tribe of Manasseh will be next to them. The leader of the people of Manasseh is Gamaliel son of Pedahzur. ²¹His division numbers 32,200.

²²The tribe of Benjamin will be next. The leader of the people of Benjamin is Abidan son of Gideoni. ²³His division numbers 35,400.

²⁴All the men assigned to the camp of Ephraim, according to their divisions, number 108,100. They will set out third.

^a14 Many manuscripts of the Masoretic Text, Samaritan Pentateuch and Vulgate (see also Num. 1:14); most manuscripts of the Masoretic Text *Reuel*

²⁵On the north will be the divisions of the camp of Dan, under their standard. The leader of the people of Dan is Ahiezer son of Ammishaddai. ²⁶His division numbers 62,700.

²⁷The tribe of Asher will camp next to them. The leader of the people of Asher is Pagiel son of Ocran. ²⁸His division numbers 41,500.

²⁹The tribe of Naphtali will be next. The leader of the people of Naphtali is Ahira son of Enan. ³⁰His division numbers 53,400.

³¹All the men assigned to the camp of Dan number 157,600. They will set out last, under their standards.

³²These are the Israelites, counted according to their families. All those in the camps, by their divisions, number 603,550. ³³The Levites, however, were not counted along with the other Israelites, as the LORD commanded Moses.

³⁴So the Israelites did everything the LORD commanded Moses; that is the way they encamped under their standards, and that is the way they set out, each with his clan and family.

The Levites

3 This is the account of the family of Aaron and Moses at the time the LORD talked with Moses on Mount Sinai.

²The names of the sons of Aaron were Nadab the firstborn and Abihu, Eleazar and Ithamar. ³Those were the names of Aaron's sons, the anointed priests, who were ordained to serve as priests. ⁴Nadab and Abihu, however, fell dead before the LORD when they made an offering with unauthorized fire before him in the Desert of Sinai. They had no sons; so only Eleazar and Ithamar served as priests during the lifetime of their father Aaron.

⁵The LORD said to Moses, ⁶"Bring the tribe of Levi and present them to Aaron the priest to assist him. ⁷They are to perform duties for him and for the whole community at the Tent of Meeting by doing the work of the tabernacle. ⁸They are to take care of all the furnishings of the Tent of Meeting, fulfilling the obligations of the Israelites by doing the work of the tabernacle. ⁹Give the Levites to Aaron and his sons; they are the Israelites who

are to be given wholly to him.ᵃ ¹⁰Appoint Aaron and his sons to serve as priests; anyone else who approaches the sanctuary must be put to death."

¹¹The LORD also said to Moses, ¹²"I have taken the Levites from among the Israelites in place of the first male offspring of every Israelite woman. The Levites are mine, ¹³for all the firstborn are mine. When I struck down all the firstborn in Egypt, I set apart for myself every firstborn in Israel, whether man or animal. They are to be mine. I am the LORD."

¹⁴The LORD said to Moses in the Desert of Sinai, ¹⁵"Count the Levites by their families and clans. Count every male a month old or more." ¹⁶So Moses counted them, as he was commanded by the word of the LORD.

¹⁷These were the names of the sons of Levi:
Gershon, Kohath and Merari.
¹⁸These were the names of the Gershonite clans:
Libni and Shimei.
¹⁹The Kohathite clans:
Amram, Izhar, Hebron and Uzziel.
²⁰The Merarite clans:
Mahli and Mushi.
These were the Levite clans, according to their families.

²¹To Gershon belonged the clans of the Libnites and Shimeites; these were the Gershonite clans. ²²The number of all the males a month old or more who

ᵃ9 Most manuscripts of the Masoretic Text; some manuscripts of the Masoretic Text, Samaritan Pentateuch and Septuagint (see also Num. 8:16) *to me*

POINT OF INTEREST

Numbers 2:32

This numbering does not include women, young children or teenagers. Israel's total population could have been more than two million people. How did the seventy people who had journeyed to Egypt 430 years earlier become so many? Exodus 1:7 says that God blessed the Israelites with fruitfulness and the nation experienced supernatural multiplication.

were counted was 7,500. ²³The Gershonite clans were to camp on the west, behind the tabernacle. ²⁴The leader of the families of the Gershonites was Eliasaph son of Lael. ²⁵At the Tent of Meeting the Gershonites were responsible for the care of the tabernacle and tent, its coverings, the curtain at the entrance to the Tent of Meeting, ²⁶the curtains of the courtyard, the curtain at the entrance to the courtyard surrounding the tabernacle and altar, and the ropes—and everything related to their use.

²⁷To Kohath belonged the clans of the Amramites, Izharites, Hebronites and Uzzielites; these were the Kohathite clans. ²⁸The number of all the males a month old or more was 8,600.ᵃ The Kohathites were responsible for the care of the sanctuary. ²⁹The Kohathite clans were to camp on the south side of the tabernacle. ³⁰The leader of the families of the Kohathite clans was Elizaphan son of Uzziel. ³¹They were responsible for the care of the ark, the table, the lampstand, the altars, the articles of the sanctuary used in ministering, the curtain, and everything related to their use. ³²The chief leader of the Levites was Eleazar son of Aaron, the priest. He was appointed over those who were responsible for the care of the sanctuary.

³³To Merari belonged the clans of the Mahlites and the Mushites; these were the Merarite clans. ³⁴The number of all the males a month old or more who were counted was 6,200. ³⁵The leader of the families of the Merarite clans was Zuriel son of Abihail; they were to camp on the north side of the tabernacle. ³⁶The Merarites were appointed to take care of the frames of the tabernacle, its crossbars, posts, bases, all its equipment, and everything related to their use, ³⁷as well as the posts of the surrounding courtyard with their bases, tent pegs and ropes.

³⁸Moses and Aaron and his sons were to camp to the east of the tabernacle, toward the sunrise, in front of the Tent of Meeting. They were responsible for the care of the sanctuary on behalf of the Israelites. Anyone else who approached the sanctuary was to be put to death.

³⁹The total number of Levites counted at the LORD's command by Moses and Aaron according to their clans, including every male a month old or more, was 22,000.

⁴⁰The LORD said to Moses, "Count all the firstborn Israelite males who are a month old or more and make a list of their names. ⁴¹Take the Levites for me in place of all the firstborn of the Israelites, and the livestock of the Levites in place of all the firstborn of the livestock of the Israelites. I am the LORD."

⁴²So Moses counted all the firstborn of the Israelites, as the LORD commanded him. ⁴³The total number of firstborn males a month old or more, listed by name, was 22,273.

⁴⁴The LORD also said to Moses, ⁴⁵"Take the Levites in place of all the firstborn of Israel, and the livestock of the Levites in place of their livestock. The Levites are to be mine. I am the LORD. ⁴⁶To redeem the 273 firstborn Israelites who exceed the number of the Levites, ⁴⁷collect five shekelsᵇ for each one, according to the sanctuary shekel, which weighs twenty gerahs. ⁴⁸Give the money for the redemption of the additional Israelites to Aaron and his sons."

⁴⁹So Moses collected the redemption money from those who exceeded the number redeemed by the Levites. ⁵⁰From the firstborn of the Israelites he collected silver weighing 1,365 shekels,ᶜ according to the sanctuary shekel. ⁵¹Moses gave the redemption money to Aaron and his sons, as he was commanded by the word of the LORD.

The Kohathites

4 The LORD said to Moses and Aaron: ²"Take a census of the Kohathite branch of the Levites by their clans and families. ³Count all the men from thirty to fifty years of age who come to serve in the work in the Tent of Meeting.

⁴"This is the work of the Kohathites in the Tent of Meeting: the care of the most holy things. ⁵When the camp is to move, Aaron and his sons are to go in and take down the shielding curtain and cover the ark of the Testimony with it. ⁶Then they are to cover this with hides of sea

ᵃ28 Hebrew; some Septuagint manuscripts 8,300
ᵇ47 That is, about 2 ounces (about 55 grams)
ᶜ50 That is, about 35 pounds (about 15.5 kilograms)

cows,[a] spread a cloth of solid blue over that and put the poles in place.

[7]"Over the table of the Presence they are to spread a blue cloth and put on it the plates, dishes and bowls, and the jars for drink offerings; the bread that is continually there is to remain on it. [8]Over these they are to spread a scarlet cloth, cover that with hides of sea cows and put its poles in place.

[9]"They are to take a blue cloth and cover the lampstand that is for light, together with its lamps, its wick trimmers and trays, and all its jars for the oil used to supply it. [10]Then they are to wrap it and all its accessories in a covering of hides of sea cows and put it on a carrying frame.

[11]"Over the gold altar they are to spread a blue cloth and cover that with hides of sea cows and put its poles in place.

[12]"They are to take all the articles used for ministering in the sanctuary, wrap them in a blue cloth, cover that with hides of sea cows and put them on a carrying frame.

[13]"They are to remove the ashes from the bronze altar and spread a purple cloth over it. [14]Then they are to place on it all the utensils used for ministering at the altar, including the firepans, meat forks, shovels and sprinkling bowls. Over it they are to spread a covering of hides of sea cows and put its poles in place.

[15]"After Aaron and his sons have finished covering the holy furnishings and all the holy articles, and when the camp is ready to move, the Kohathites are to come to do the carrying. But they must not touch the holy things or they will die. The Kohathites are to carry those things that are in the Tent of Meeting.

[16]"Eleazar son of Aaron, the priest, is to have charge of the oil for the light, the fragrant incense, the regular grain offering and the anointing oil. He is to be in charge of the entire tabernacle and everything in it, including its holy furnishings and articles."

[17]The LORD said to Moses and Aaron, [18]"See that the Kohathite tribal clans are not cut off from the Levites. [19]So that they may live and not die when they come near the most holy things, do this for them: Aaron and his sons are to go into the sanctuary and assign to each man his work and what he is to carry. [20]But the Kohathites must not go in to look at the holy things, even for a moment, or they will die."

The Gershonites

[21]The LORD said to Moses, [22]"Take a census also of the Gershonites by their families and clans. [23]Count all the men from thirty to fifty years of age who come to serve in the work at the Tent of Meeting.

[24]"This is the service of the Gershonite clans as they work and carry burdens: [25]They are to carry the curtains of the tabernacle, the Tent of Meeting, its covering and the outer covering of hides of sea cows, the curtains for the entrance to the Tent of Meeting, [26]the curtains of the courtyard surrounding the tabernacle and altar, the curtain for the entrance, the ropes and all the equipment used in its service. The Gershonites are to do all that needs to be done with these things. [27]All their service, whether carrying or doing other work, is to be done under the direction of Aaron and his sons. You shall assign to them as their responsibility all they are to carry. [28]This is the service of the Gershonite clans at the Tent of Meeting. Their duties are to be under the direction of Ithamar son of Aaron, the priest.

The Merarites

[29]"Count the Merarites by their clans and families. [30]Count all the men from thirty to fifty years of age who come to serve in the work at the Tent of Meeting.

[a]6 That is, dugongs; also in verses 8, 10, 11, 12, 14 and 25

³¹This is their duty as they perform service at the Tent of Meeting: to carry the frames of the tabernacle, its crossbars, posts and bases, ³²as well as the posts of the surrounding courtyard with their bases, tent pegs, ropes, all their equipment and everything related to their use. Assign to each man the specific things he is to carry. ³³This is the service of the Merarite clans as they work at the Tent of Meeting under the direction of Ithamar son of Aaron, the priest."

The Numbering of the Levite Clans

³⁴Moses, Aaron and the leaders of the community counted the Kohathites by their clans and families. ³⁵All the men from thirty to fifty years of age who came to serve in the work in the Tent of Meeting, ³⁶counted by clans, were 2,750. ³⁷This was the total of all those in the Kohathite clans who served in the Tent of Meeting. Moses and Aaron counted them according to the LORD's command through Moses.

³⁸The Gershonites were counted by their clans and families. ³⁹All the men from thirty to fifty years of age who came to serve in the work at the Tent of Meeting, ⁴⁰counted by their clans and families, were 2,630. ⁴¹This was the total of those in the Gershonite clans who served at the Tent of Meeting. Moses and Aaron counted them according to the LORD's command.

⁴²The Merarites were counted by their clans and families. ⁴³All the men from thirty to fifty years of age who came to serve in the work at the Tent of Meeting, ⁴⁴counted by their clans, were 3,200. ⁴⁵This was the total of those in the Merarite clans. Moses and Aaron counted them according to the LORD's command through Moses.

⁴⁶So Moses, Aaron and the leaders of Israel counted all the Levites by their clans and families. ⁴⁷All the men from thirty to fifty years of age who came to do the work of serving and carrying the Tent of Meeting ⁴⁸numbered 8,580. ⁴⁹At the LORD's command through Moses, each was assigned his work and told what to carry.

Thus they were counted, as the LORD commanded Moses.

The Purity of the Camp

5 The LORD said to Moses, ²"Command the Israelites to send away from the camp anyone who has an infectious skin disease*ᵃ* or a discharge of any kind, or who is ceremonially unclean because of a dead body. ³Send away male and female alike; send them outside the camp so they will not defile their camp, where I dwell among them." ⁴The Israelites did this; they sent them outside the camp. They did just as the LORD had instructed Moses.

Restitution for Wrongs

⁵The LORD said to Moses, ⁶"Say to the Israelites: 'When a man or woman wrongs another in any way*ᵇ* and so is unfaithful to the LORD, that person is guilty ⁷and must confess the sin he has committed. He must make full restitution for his wrong, add one fifth to it and give it all to the person he has wronged. ⁸But if that person has no close relative to whom restitution can be made for the wrong, the restitution belongs to the LORD and must be given to the priest, along with the ram with which atonement is made for him. ⁹All the sacred contributions the Israelites bring to a priest will belong to him. ¹⁰Each man's sacred gifts are his own, but what he gives to the priest will belong to the priest.' "

The Test for an Unfaithful Wife

¹¹Then the LORD said to Moses, ¹²"Speak to the Israelites and say to them: 'If a man's wife goes astray and is unfaithful to him ¹³by sleeping with another man, and this is hidden from her husband and her impurity is undetected (since there is no witness against her and she has not been caught in the act), ¹⁴and if feelings of jealousy come over her husband and he suspects his wife and she is impure—or if he is jealous and suspects her even though she is not impure—¹⁵then he is to take his wife to the priest. He must also take an offering of a tenth of an ephah*ᶜ* of barley flour on her behalf. He must not pour oil on it or put incense on it, because it is a grain offering for jealousy, a reminder offering to draw attention to guilt.

¹⁶" 'The priest shall bring her and have her stand before the LORD. ¹⁷Then he shall take some holy water in a clay jar

---

ᵃ2 Traditionally *leprosy*; the Hebrew word was used for various diseases affecting the skin—not necessarily leprosy.   *ᵇ6* Or *woman commits any wrong common to mankind*   *ᶜ15* That is, probably about 2 quarts (about 2 liters) and put some dust from the tabernacle floor into the water. ¹⁸After the priest has had the woman stand before the LORD, he shall loosen her hair and place in her hands the reminder offering, the grain offering for jealousy, while he himself holds the bitter water that brings a curse. ¹⁹Then the priest shall put the woman under oath and say to her, "If no other man has slept with you and you have not gone astray and become impure while married to your husband, may this bitter water that brings a curse not harm you. ²⁰But if you have gone astray while married to your husband and you have defiled yourself by sleeping with a man other than your husband"— ²¹here the priest is to put the woman under this curse of the oath—"may the LORD cause your people to curse and denounce you when he causes your thigh to waste away and your abdomen to swell.ᵃ ²²May this water that brings a curse enter your body so that your abdomen swells and your thigh wastes away.ᵇ"

" 'Then the woman is to say, "Amen. So be it."

²³" 'The priest is to write these curses on a scroll and then wash them off into the bitter water. ²⁴He shall have the woman drink the bitter water that brings a curse, and this water will enter her and cause bitter suffering. ²⁵The priest is to take from her hands the grain offering for jealousy, wave it before the LORD and bring it to the altar. ²⁶The priest is then to take a handful of the grain offering as a memorial offering and burn it on the altar; after that, he is to have the woman drink the water. ²⁷If she has defiled herself and been unfaithful to her husband, then when she is made to drink the water that brings a curse, it will go into her and cause bitter suffering; her abdomen will swell and her thigh waste away,ᶜ and she will become accursed among her people. ²⁸If, however, the woman has not defiled herself and is free from impurity, she will be cleared of guilt and will be able to have children.

²⁹" 'This, then, is the law of jealousy when a woman goes astray and defiles herself while married to her husband, ³⁰or when feelings of jealousy come over a man because he suspects his wife. The priest is to have her stand before the LORD and is to apply this entire law to her. ³¹The husband will be innocent of any

wrongdoing, but the woman will bear the consequences of her sin.' "

The Nazirite

6 The LORD said to Moses, ²"Speak to the Israelites and say to them: 'If a man or woman wants to make a special vow, a vow of separation to the LORD as a Nazirite, ³he must abstain from wine and other fermented drink and must not drink vinegar made from wine or from other fermented drink. He must not drink grape juice or eat grapes or raisins. ⁴As long as he is a Nazirite, he must not eat anything that comes from the grapevine, not even the seeds or skins.

⁵" 'During the entire period of his vow of separation no razor may be used on his head. He must be holy until the period of his separation to the LORD is over; he must let the hair of his head grow long. ⁶Throughout the period of his separation to the LORD he must not go near a dead body. ⁷Even if his own father or mother or brother or sister dies, he must not make himself ceremonially unclean on account of them, because the symbol of his separation to God is on his head. ⁸Throughout the period of his separation he is consecrated to the LORD.

⁹" 'If someone dies suddenly in his presence, thus defiling the hair he has dedicated, he must shave his head on the day of his cleansing—the seventh day. ¹⁰Then on the eighth day he must bring

ᵃ21 Or causes you to have a miscarrying womb and barrenness   ᵇ22 Or body and cause you to be barren and have a miscarrying womb   ᶜ27 Or suffering; she will have barrenness and a miscarrying womb

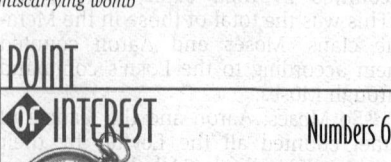

POINT OF INTEREST

Numbers 6:2

Throughout Israel's history, a certain group of people dedicated themselves to God in a special way—either for a specified period of time or for life. Such people were called Nazirites. Numbers 6 lists the regulations governing Nazirite vows. Three well-known Biblical Nazirites were Samson (see Judges 13), Samuel (see 1 Samuel 1) and John the Baptist (see Luke 1).

two doves or two young pigeons to the priest at the entrance to the Tent of Meeting. ¹¹The priest is to offer one as a sin offering and the other as a burnt offering to make atonement for him because he sinned by being in the presence of the dead body. That same day he is to consecrate his head. ¹²He must dedicate himself to the LORD for the period of his separation and must bring a year-old male lamb as a guilt offering. The previous days do not count, because he became defiled during his separation.

¹³" 'Now this is the law for the Nazirite when the period of his separation is over. He is to be brought to the entrance to the Tent of Meeting. ¹⁴There he is to present his offerings to the LORD: a year-old male lamb without defect for a burnt offering, a year-old ewe lamb without defect for a sin offering, a ram without defect for a fellowship offering,ᵃ ¹⁵together with their grain offerings and drink offerings, and a basket of bread made without yeast—cakes made of fine flour mixed with oil, and wafers spread with oil.

¹⁶" 'The priest is to present them before the LORD and make the sin offering and the burnt offering. ¹⁷He is to present the basket of unleavened bread and is to sacrifice the ram as a fellowship offering to the LORD, together with its grain offering and drink offering.

¹⁸" 'Then at the entrance to the Tent of Meeting, the Nazirite must shave off the hair that he dedicated. He is to take the hair and put it in the fire that is under the sacrifice of the fellowship offering.

¹⁹" 'After the Nazirite has shaved off the hair of his dedication, the priest is to place in his hands a boiled shoulder of the ram, and a cake and a wafer from the basket, both made without yeast. ²⁰The priest shall then wave them before the LORD as a wave offering; they are holy and belong to the priest, together with the breast that was waved and the thigh that was presented. After that, the Nazirite may drink wine.

²¹" 'This is the law of the Nazirite who vows his offering to the LORD in accordance with his separation, in addition to whatever else he can afford. He must fulfill the vow he has made, according to the law of the Nazirite.' "

The Priestly Blessing

²²The LORD said to Moses, ²³"Tell Aar-

on and his sons, 'This is how you are to bless the Israelites. Say to them:

²⁴" ' "The LORD bless you
    and keep you;
²⁵the LORD make his face shine upon
    you
    and be gracious to you;
²⁶the LORD turn his face toward you
    and give you peace." '

²⁷"So they will put my name on the Israelites, and I will bless them."

Offerings at the Dedication of the Tabernacle

7 When Moses finished setting up the tabernacle, he anointed it and consecrated it and all its furnishings. He also anointed and consecrated the altar and all its utensils. ²Then the leaders of Israel, the heads of families who were the tribal leaders in charge of those who were counted, made offerings. ³They brought as their gifts before the LORD six covered carts and twelve oxen—an ox from each leader and a cart from every two. These they presented before the tabernacle.

⁴The LORD said to Moses, ⁵"Accept these from them, that they may be used in the work at the Tent of Meeting. Give them to the Levites as each man's work requires."

⁶So Moses took the carts and oxen and gave them to the Levites. ⁷He gave two carts and four oxen to the Gershonites, as their work required, ⁸and he gave four carts and eight oxen to the Merarites, as their work required. They were all under the direction of Ithamar son of Aaron, the priest. ⁹But Moses did not give any to the Kohathites, because they were to carry on their shoulders the holy things, for which they were responsible.

¹⁰When the altar was anointed, the leaders brought their offerings for its dedication and presented them before the altar. ¹¹For the LORD had said to Moses, "Each day one leader is to bring his offering for the dedication of the altar."

¹²The one who brought his offering on the first day was Nahshon son of Amminadab of the tribe of Judah.

¹³His offering was one silver plate weighing a hundred and thirty shekels,ᵇ and one silver sprinkling

---

ᵃ14 Traditionally *peace offering*; also in verses 17 and 18   ᵇ13 That is, about 3 1/4 pounds (about 1.5 kilograms); also elsewhere in this chapter bowl weighing seventy shekels,[a] both according to the sanctuary shekel, each filled with fine flour mixed with oil as a grain offering; [14]one gold dish weighing ten shekels,[b] filled with incense; [15]one young bull, one ram and one male lamb a year old, for a burnt offering; [16]one male goat for a sin offering; [17]and two oxen, five rams, five male goats and five male lambs a year old, to be sacrificed as a fellowship offering.[c] This was the offering of Nahshon son of Amminadab.

[18]On the second day Nethanel son of Zuar, the leader of Issachar, brought his offering.

[19]The offering he brought was one silver plate weighing a hundred and thirty shekels, and one silver sprinkling bowl weighing seventy shekels, both according to the sanctuary shekel, each filled with fine flour mixed with oil as a grain offering; [20]one gold dish weighing ten shekels, filled with incense; [21]one young bull, one ram and one male lamb a year old, for a burnt offering; [22]one male goat for a sin offering; [23]and two oxen, five rams, five male goats and five male lambs a year old, to be sacrificed as a fellowship offering. This was the offering of Nethanel son of Zuar.

[24]On the third day, Eliab son of Helon, the leader of the people of Zebulun, brought his offering.

[25]His offering was one silver plate weighing a hundred and thirty shekels, and one silver sprinkling bowl weighing seventy shekels, both according to the sanctuary shekel, each filled with fine flour mixed with oil as a grain offering; [26]one gold dish weighing ten shekels, filled with incense; [27]one young bull, one ram and one male lamb a year old, for a burnt offering; [28]one male goat for a sin offering; [29]and two oxen, five rams, five male goats and five male lambs a year old, to be sacrificed as a fellowship offering. This was the offering of Eliab son of Helon.

[30]On the fourth day Elizur son of Shedeur, the leader of the people of Reuben, brought his offering.

[31]His offering was one silver plate weighing a hundred and thirty shekels, and one silver sprinkling bowl weighing seventy shekels, both according to the sanctuary shekel, each filled with fine flour mixed with oil as a grain offering; [32]one gold dish weighing ten shekels, filled with incense; [33]one young bull, one ram and one male lamb a year old, for a burnt offering; [34]one male goat for a sin offering; [35]and two oxen, five rams, five male goats and five male lambs a year old, to be sacrificed as a fellowship offering. This was the offering of Elizur son of Shedeur.

[36]On the fifth day Shelumiel son of Zurishaddai, the leader of the people of Simeon, brought his offering.

[37]His offering was one silver plate weighing a hundred and thirty shekels, and one silver sprinkling bowl weighing seventy shekels, both according to the sanctuary shekel, each filled with fine flour mixed with oil as a grain offering; [38]one gold dish weighing ten shekels, filled with incense; [39]one young bull, one ram and one male lamb a year old, for a burnt offering; [40]one male goat for a sin offering; [41]and two oxen, five rams, five male goats and five male lambs a year old, to be sacrificed as a fellowship offering. This was the offering of Shelumiel son of Zurishaddai.

[42]On the sixth day Eliasaph son of Deuel, the leader of the people of Gad, brought his offering.

[43]His offering was one silver plate weighing a hundred and thirty shekels, and one silver sprinkling bowl weighing seventy shekels, both according to the sanctuary shekel, each filled with fine flour mixed with oil as a grain offering; [44]one gold dish weighing ten shekels, filled with incense; [45]one young bull, one ram and one male lamb a year old, for a burnt offering; [46]one male goat for a sin offering; [47]and two oxen, five rams, five male goats

---

a 13 That is, about 1 3/4 pounds (about 0.8 kilogram); also elsewhere in this chapter
b 14 That is, about 4 ounces (about 110 grams); also elsewhere in this chapter   *c 17* Traditionally *peace offering*; also elsewhere in this chapter

and five male lambs a year old, to be sacrificed as a fellowship offering. This was the offering of Eliasaph son of Deuel.

48On the seventh day Elishama son of Ammihud, the leader of the people of Ephraim, brought his offering. 49His offering was one silver plate weighing a hundred and thirty shekels, and one silver sprinkling bowl weighing seventy shekels, both according to the sanctuary shekel, each filled with fine flour mixed with oil as a grain offering; 50one gold dish weighing ten shekels, filled with incense; 51one young bull, one ram and one male lamb a year old, for a burnt offering; 52one male goat for a sin offering; 53and two oxen, five rams, five male goats and five male lambs a year old, to be sacrificed as a fellowship offering. This was the offering of Elishama son of Ammihud.

54On the eighth day Gamaliel son of Pedahzur, the leader of the people of Manasseh, brought his offering. 55His offering was one silver plate weighing a hundred and thirty shekels, and one silver sprinkling bowl weighing seventy shekels, both according to the sanctuary shekel, each filled with fine flour mixed with oil as a grain offering; 56one gold dish weighing ten shekels, filled with incense; 57one young bull, one ram and one male lamb a year old, for a burnt offering; 58one male goat for a sin offering; 59and two oxen, five rams, five male goats and five male lambs a year old, to be sacrificed as a fellowship offering. This was the offering of Gamaliel son of Pedahzur.

60On the ninth day Abidan son of Gideoni, the leader of the people of Benjamin, brought his offering. 61His offering was one silver plate weighing a hundred and thirty shekels, and one silver sprinkling bowl weighing seventy shekels, both according to the sanctuary shekel, each filled with fine flour mixed with oil as a grain offering; 62one gold dish weighing ten shekels, filled with incense; 63one young bull, one ram and one male lamb a

year old, for a burnt offering; 64one male goat for a sin offering; 65and two oxen, five rams, five male goats and five male lambs a year old, to be sacrificed as a fellowship offering. This was the offering of Abidan son of Gideoni.

66On the tenth day Ahiezer son of Ammishaddai, the leader of the people of Dan, brought his offering. 67His offering was one silver plate weighing a hundred and thirty shekels, and one silver sprinkling bowl weighing seventy shekels, both according to the sanctuary shekel, each filled with fine flour mixed with oil as a grain offering; 68one gold dish weighing ten shekels, filled with incense; 69one young bull, one ram and one male lamb a year old, for a burnt offering; 70one male goat for a sin offering; 71and two oxen, five rams, five male goats and five male lambs a year old, to be sacrificed as a fellowship offering. This was the offering of Ahiezer son of Ammishaddai.

72On the eleventh day Pagiel son of Ocran, the leader of the people of Asher, brought his offering. 73His offering was one silver plate weighing a hundred and thirty shekels, and one silver sprinkling bowl weighing seventy shekels, both according to the sanctuary shekel, each filled with fine flour mixed with oil as a grain offering; 74one gold dish weighing ten shekels, filled with incense; 75one young bull, one ram and one male lamb a year old, for a burnt offering; 76one male goat for a sin offering; 77and two oxen, five rams, five male goats and five male lambs a year old, to be sacrificed as a fellowship offering. This was the offering of Pagiel son of Ocran.

78On the twelfth day Ahira son of Enan, the leader of the people of Naphtali, brought his offering. 79His offering was one silver plate weighing a hundred and thirty shekels, and one silver sprinkling bowl weighing seventy shekels, both according to the sanctuary shekel, each filled with fine flour mixed with oil as a grain offering;

80one gold dish weighing ten shekels, filled with incense; 81one young bull, one ram and one male lamb a year old, for a burnt offering; 82one male goat for a sin offering; 83and two oxen, five rams, five male goats and five male lambs a year old, to be sacrificed as a fellowship offering. This was the offering of Ahira son of Enan.

84These were the offerings of the Israelite leaders for the dedication of the altar when it was anointed: twelve silver plates, twelve silver sprinkling bowls and twelve gold dishes. 85Each silver plate weighed a hundred and thirty shekels, and each sprinkling bowl seventy shekels. Altogether, the silver dishes weighed two thousand four hundred shekels,*a* according to the sanctuary shekel. 86The twelve gold dishes filled with incense weighed ten shekels each, according to the sanctuary shekel. Altogether, the gold dishes weighed a hundred and twenty shekels.*b* 87The total number of animals for the burnt offering came to twelve young bulls, twelve rams and twelve male lambs a year old, together with their grain offering. Twelve male goats were used for the sin offering. 88The total number of animals for the sacrifice of the fellowship offering came to twenty-four oxen, sixty rams, sixty male goats and sixty male lambs a year old. These were the offerings for the dedication of the altar after it was anointed.

89When Moses entered the Tent of Meeting to speak with the LORD, he heard the voice speaking to him from between the two cherubim above the atonement cover on the ark of the Testimony. And he spoke with him.

Setting Up the Lamps

8 The LORD said to Moses, 2"Speak to Aaron and say to him, 'When you set up the seven lamps, they are to light the area in front of the lampstand.' "

3Aaron did so; he set up the lamps so that they faced forward on the lampstand, just as the LORD commanded Moses. 4This is how the lampstand was made: It was made of hammered gold—from its base to its blossoms. The lampstand was made exactly like the pattern the LORD had shown Moses.

The Setting Apart of the Levites

5The LORD said to Moses: 6"Take the Levites from among the other Israelites and make them ceremonially clean. 7To purify them, do this: Sprinkle the water of cleansing on them; then have them shave their whole bodies and wash their clothes, and so purify themselves. 8Have them take a young bull with its grain offering of fine flour mixed with oil; then you are to take a second young bull for a sin offering. 9Bring the Levites to the front of the Tent of Meeting and assemble the whole Israelite community. 10You are to bring the Levites before the LORD, and the Israelites are to lay their hands on them. 11Aaron is to present the Levites before the LORD as a wave offering from the Israelites, so that they may be ready to do the work of the LORD.

12"After the Levites lay their hands on the heads of the bulls, use the one for a sin offering to the LORD and the other for a burnt offering, to make atonement for the Levites. 13Have the Levites stand in front of Aaron and his sons and then present them as a wave offering to the LORD. 14In this way you are to set the Levites apart from the other Israelites, and the Levites will be mine.

15"After you have purified the Levites and presented them as a wave offering, they are to come to do their work at the Tent of Meeting. 16They are the Israelites who are to be given wholly to me. I have taken them as my own in place of the firstborn, the first male offspring from every Israelite woman. 17Every firstborn male in Israel, whether man or animal, is

*a85 That is, about 60 pounds (about 28 kilograms)
*b86 That is, about 3 pounds (about 1.4 kilograms)

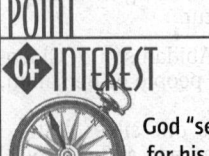

POINT OF INTEREST

Numbers 8:14

God "set the Levites apart" for his service. He himself was their inheritance (see Numbers 18:20–21). In the New Testament also, God set aside believers for his service (see Acts 13:2) and does the same for believers today. Trust him to set you apart for his service and to shape you for the task.

mine. When I struck down all the first-born in Egypt, I set them apart for myself. [18]And I have taken the Levites in place of all the firstborn sons in Israel. [19]Of all the Israelites, I have given the Levites as gifts to Aaron and his sons to do the work at the Tent of Meeting on behalf of the Israelites and to make atonement for them so that no plague will strike the Israelites when they go near the sanctuary."

[20]Moses, Aaron and the whole Israelite community did with the Levites just as the LORD commanded Moses. [21]The Levites purified themselves and washed their clothes. Then Aaron presented them as a wave offering before the LORD and made atonement for them to purify them. [22]After that, the Levites came to do their work at the Tent of Meeting under the supervision of Aaron and his sons. They did with the Levites just as the LORD commanded Moses.

[23]The LORD said to Moses, [24]"This applies to the Levites: Men twenty-five years old or more shall come to take part in the work at the Tent of Meeting, [25]but at the age of fifty, they must retire from their regular service and work no longer. [26]They may assist their brothers in performing their duties at the Tent of Meeting, but they themselves must not do the work. This, then, is how you are to assign the responsibilities of the Levites."

The Passover

9 The LORD spoke to Moses in the Desert of Sinai in the first month of the second year after they came out of Egypt. He said, [2]"Have the Israelites celebrate the Passover at the appointed time. [3]Celebrate it at the appointed time, at twilight on the fourteenth day of this month, in accordance with all its rules and regulations."

[4]So Moses told the Israelites to celebrate the Passover, [5]and they did so in the Desert of Sinai at twilight on the fourteenth day of the first month. The Israelites did everything just as the LORD commanded Moses.

[6]But some of them could not celebrate the Passover on that day because they were ceremonially unclean on account of a dead body. So they came to Moses and Aaron that same day [7]and said to Moses, "We have become unclean because of a dead body, but why should we be kept from presenting the LORD's offering with

the other Israelites at the appointed time?"

[8]Moses answered them, "Wait until I find out what the LORD commands concerning you."

[9]Then the LORD said to Moses, [10]"Tell the Israelites: 'When any of you or your descendants are unclean because of a dead body or are away on a journey, they may still celebrate the LORD's Passover. [11]They are to celebrate it on the fourteenth day of the second month at twilight. They are to eat the lamb, together with unleavened bread and bitter herbs. [12]They must not leave any of it till morning or break any of its bones. When they celebrate the Passover, they must follow all the regulations. [13]But if a man who is ceremonially clean and not on a journey fails to celebrate the Passover, that person must be cut off from his people because he did not present the LORD's offering at the appointed time. That man will bear the consequences of his sin.

[14]"'An alien living among you who wants to celebrate the LORD's Passover must do so in accordance with its rules and regulations. You must have the same regulations for the alien and the native-born.'"

The Cloud Above the Tabernacle

[15]On the day the tabernacle, the Tent of the Testimony, was set up, the cloud covered it. From evening till morning the cloud above the tabernacle looked like fire. [16]That is how it continued to be; the cloud covered it, and at night it looked like fire. [17]Whenever the cloud lifted from above the Tent, the Israelites set out; wherever the cloud settled, the Israelites encamped. [18]At the LORD's command the Israelites set out, and at his command they encamped. As long as the cloud stayed over the tabernacle, they remained in camp. [19]When the cloud remained over the tabernacle a long time, the Israelites obeyed the LORD's order and did not set out. [20]Sometimes the cloud was over the tabernacle only a few days; at the LORD's command they would encamp, and then at his command they would set out. [21]Sometimes the cloud stayed only from evening till morning, and when it lifted in the morning, they set out. Whether by day or by night, whenever the cloud lifted, they set out. [22]Whether the cloud stayed over the tabernacle for two days or a month or a year,

the Israelites would remain in camp and not set out; but when it lifted, they would set out. 23At the LORD's command they encamped, and at the LORD's command they set out. They obeyed the LORD's order, in accordance with his command through Moses.

The Silver Trumpets

10 The LORD said to Moses: 2"Make two trumpets of hammered silver, and use them for calling the community together and for having the camps set out. 3When both are sounded, the whole community is to assemble before you at the entrance to the Tent of Meeting. 4If only one is sounded, the leaders—the heads of the clans of Israel—are to assemble before you. 5When a trumpet blast is sounded, the tribes camping on the east are to set out. 6At the sounding of a second blast, the camps on the south are to set out. The blast will be the signal for setting out. 7To gather the assembly, blow the trumpets, but not with the same signal.

8"The sons of Aaron, the priests, are to blow the trumpets. This is to be a lasting ordinance for you and the generations to come. 9When you go into battle in your own land against an enemy who is oppressing you, sound a blast on the trumpets. Then you will be remembered by the LORD your God and rescued from your enemies. 10Also at your times of rejoicing—your appointed feasts and New Moon festivals—you are to sound the trumpets over your burnt offerings and fellowship offerings,a and they will be a memorial for you before your God. I am the LORD your God."

The Israelites Leave Sinai

11On the twentieth day of the second month of the second year, the cloud lifted from above the tabernacle of the Testimony. 12Then the Israelites set out from the Desert of Sinai and traveled from place to place until the cloud came to rest in the Desert of Paran. 13They set out, this first time, at the LORD's command through Moses. 14The divisions of the camp of Judah went first, under their standard. Nahshon son of Amminadab was in command. 15Nethanel son of Zuar was over the division of the tribe of Issachar, 16and Eliab son of Helon was over the division of the tribe of Zebulun. 17Then the tabernacle

was taken down, and the Gershonites and Merarites, who carried it, set out.

18The divisions of the camp of Reuben went next, under their standard. Elizur son of Shedeur was in command. 19Shelumiel son of Zurishaddai was over the division of the tribe of Simeon, 20and Eliasaph son of Deuel was over the division of the tribe of Gad. 21Then the Kohathites set out, carrying the holy things. The tabernacle was to be set up before they arrived.

22The divisions of the camp of Ephraim went next, under their standard. Elishama son of Ammihud was in command. 23Gamaliel son of Pedahzur was over the division of the tribe of Manasseh, 24and Abidan son of Gideoni was over the division of the tribe of Benjamin.

25Finally, as the rear guard for all the units, the divisions of the camp of Dan set out, under their standard. Ahiezer son of Ammishaddai was in command. 26Pagiel son of Ocran was over the division of the tribe of Asher, 27and Ahira son of Enan was over the division of the tribe of Naphtali. 28This was the order of march for the Israelite divisions as they set out.

29Now Moses said to Hobab son of Reuel the Midianite, Moses' father-inlaw, "We are setting out for the place about which the LORD said, 'I will give it to you.' Come with us and we will treat you well, for the LORD has promised good things to Israel."

30He answered, "No, I will not go; I am going back to my own land and my own people."

31But Moses said, "Please do not leave us. You know where we should camp in the desert, and you can be our eyes. 32If you come with us, we will share with you whatever good things the LORD gives us."

33So they set out from the mountain of the LORD and traveled for three days. The ark of the covenant of the LORD went before them during those three days to find them a place to rest. 34The cloud of the LORD was over them by day when they set out from the camp.

35Whenever the ark set out, Moses said,

"Rise up, O LORD!
    May your enemies be scattered;
    may your foes flee before you."

a 10 Traditionally peace offerings

³⁶Whenever it came to rest, he said,

"Return, O LORD,
    to the countless thousands of
      Israel."

Fire From the LORD

11 Now the people complained about their hardships in the hearing of the LORD, and when he heard them his anger was aroused. Then fire from the LORD burned among them and consumed some of the outskirts of the camp. ²When the people cried out to Moses, he prayed to the LORD and the fire died down. ³So that place was called Taberah,ᵃ because fire from the LORD had burned among them.

Quail From the LORD

⁴The rabble with them began to crave other food, and again the Israelites started wailing and said, "If only we had meat to eat! ⁵We remember the fish we ate in Egypt at no cost—also the cucumbers, melons, leeks, onions and garlic. ⁶But now we have lost our appetite; we never see anything but this manna!"

⁷The manna was like coriander seed and looked like resin. ⁸The people went around gathering it, and then ground it in a handmill or crushed it in a mortar. They cooked it in a pot or made it into cakes. And it tasted like something made with olive oil. ⁹When the dew settled on the camp at night, the manna also came down.

¹⁰Moses heard the people of every family wailing, each at the entrance to his tent. The LORD became exceedingly angry, and Moses was troubled. ¹¹He asked the LORD, "Why have you brought this trouble on your servant? What have I done to displease you that you put the burden of all these people on me? ¹²Did I conceive all these people? Did I give them birth? Why do you tell me to carry them in my arms, as a nurse carries an infant, to the land you promised on oath to their forefathers? ¹³Where can I get meat for all these people? They keep wailing to me, 'Give us meat to eat!' ¹⁴I cannot carry all these people by myself; the burden is too heavy for me. ¹⁵If this is how you are going to treat me, put me to death right now—if I have found favor in your eyes—and do not let me face my own ruin."

¹⁶The LORD said to Moses: "Bring me seventy of Israel's elders who are known to you as leaders and officials among the people. Have them come to the Tent of Meeting, that they may stand there with you. ¹⁷I will come down and speak with you there, and I will take of the Spirit that is on you and put the Spirit on them. They will help you carry the burden of the people so that you will not have to carry it alone.

¹⁸"Tell the people: 'Consecrate yourselves in preparation for tomorrow, when you will eat meat. The LORD heard you when you wailed, "If only we had meat to eat! We were better off in Egypt!" Now the LORD will give you meat, and you will eat it. ¹⁹You will not eat it for just one day, or two days, or five, ten or twenty days, ²⁰but for a whole month—until it comes out of your nostrils and you loathe it—because you have rejected the LORD, who is among you, and have wailed before him, saying, "Why did we ever leave Egypt?" ' "

²¹But Moses said, "Here I am among six hundred thousand men on foot, and you say, 'I will give them meat to eat for a whole month!' ²²Would they have enough if flocks and herds were slaughtered for them? Would they have enough if all the fish in the sea were caught for them?"

²³The LORD answered Moses, "Is the LORD's arm too short? You will now see whether or not what I say will come true for you."

²⁴So Moses went out and told the people what the LORD had said. He brought together seventy of their elders and had them stand around the Tent. ²⁵Then the

---

ᵃ3 *Taberah* means *burning.*

POINT OF INTEREST

Numbers 11:9

God provided food for the Israelites every day for forty years. The food was called "manna." It tasted like wafers made with honey (see Exodus 16:31). It wasn't unpleasant, but the menu was identical, day after day, month after month. Listen to the Israelites' complaints after only one year. What was the result of their ingratitude? How would you have responded?

LORD came down in the cloud and spoke with him, and he took of the Spirit that was on him and put the Spirit on the seventy elders. When the Spirit rested on them, they prophesied, but they did not do so again.ᵃ

²⁶However, two men, whose names were Eldad and Medad, had remained in the camp. They were listed among the elders, but did not go out to the Tent. Yet the Spirit also rested on them, and they prophesied in the camp. ²⁷A young man ran and told Moses, "Eldad and Medad are prophesying in the camp."

²⁸Joshua son of Nun, who had been Moses' aide since youth, spoke up and said, "Moses, my lord, stop them!"

²⁹But Moses replied, "Are you jealous for my sake? I wish that all the LORD's people were prophets and that the LORD would put his Spirit on them!" ³⁰Then Moses and the elders of Israel returned to the camp.

³¹Now a wind went out from the LORD and drove quail in from the sea. It brought themᵇ down all around the camp to about three feetᶜ above the ground, as far as a day's walk in any direction. ³²All that day and night and all the next day the people went out and gathered quail. No one gathered less than ten homers.ᵈ Then they spread them out all around the camp. ³³But while the meat was still between their teeth and before it could be consumed, the anger of the LORD burned against the people, and he struck them with a severe plague. ³⁴Therefore the place was named Kibroth Hattaavah,ᵉ because there they buried the people who had craved other food.

³⁵From Kibroth Hattaavah the people traveled to Hazeroth and stayed there.

Miriam and Aaron Oppose Moses

12 Miriam and Aaron began to talk against Moses because of his Cushite wife, for he had married a Cushite. ²"Has the LORD spoken only through Moses?" they asked. "Hasn't he also spoken through us?" And the LORD heard this.

³(Now Moses was a very humble man, more humble than anyone else on the face of the earth.)

⁴At once the LORD said to Moses, Aaron and Miriam, "Come out to the Tent of Meeting, all three of you." So the three of them came out. ⁵Then the LORD came down in a pillar of cloud; he stood at the entrance to the Tent and summoned Aar-on and Miriam. When both of them stepped forward, ⁶he said, "Listen to my words:

"When a prophet of the LORD is
    among you,
I reveal myself to him in visions,
I speak to him in dreams.
⁷But this is not true of my servant
    Moses;
he is faithful in all my house.
⁸With him I speak face to face,
    clearly and not in riddles;
he sees the form of the LORD.
Why then were you not afraid
to speak against my servant
    Moses?"

⁹The anger of the LORD burned against them, and he left them.

¹⁰When the cloud lifted from above the Tent, there stood Miriam—leprous,ᶠ like snow. Aaron turned toward her and saw that she had leprosy; ¹¹and he said to Moses, "Please, my lord, do not hold against us the sin we have so foolishly committed. ¹²Do not let her be like a stillborn infant coming from its mother's womb with its flesh half eaten away."

¹³So Moses cried out to the LORD, "O God, please heal her!"

¹⁴The LORD replied to Moses, "If her father had spit in her face, would she not have been in disgrace for seven days? Confine her outside the camp for seven days; after that she can be brought back." ¹⁵So Miriam was confined outside the camp for seven days, and the people did not move on till she was brought back. ¹⁶After that, the people left Hazeroth and encamped in the Desert of Paran.

Exploring Canaan

13 The LORD said to Moses, ²"Send some men to explore the land of Canaan, which I am giving to the Israelites. From each ancestral tribe send one of its leaders."

³So at the LORD's command Moses sent them out from the Desert of Paran. All of them were leaders of the Israelites. ⁴These are their names:

ᵃ25 Or *prophesied and continued to do so*
ᵇ31 Or *They flew*   ᶜ31 Hebrew *two cubits* (about 1 meter)   ᵈ32 That is, probably about 60 bushels (about 2.2 kiloliters)   ᵉ34 *Kibroth Hattaavah* means *graves of craving*.
ᶠ10 The Hebrew word was used for various diseases affecting the skin—not necessarily leprosy.

from the tribe of Reuben, Shammua son of Zaccur;
⁵from the tribe of Simeon, Shaphat son of Hori;
⁶from the tribe of Judah, Caleb son of Jephunneh;
⁷from the tribe of Issachar, Igal son of Joseph;
⁸from the tribe of Ephraim, Hoshea son of Nun;
⁹from the tribe of Benjamin, Palti son of Raphu;
¹⁰from the tribe of Zebulun, Gaddiel son of Sodi;
¹¹from the tribe of Manasseh (a tribe of Joseph), Gaddi son of Susi;
¹²from the tribe of Dan, Ammiel son of Gemalli;
¹³from the tribe of Asher, Sethur son of Michael;
¹⁴from the tribe of Naphtali, Nahbi son of Vophsi;
¹⁵from the tribe of Gad, Geuel son of Maki.

¹⁶These are the names of the men Moses sent to explore the land. (Moses gave Hoshea son of Nun the name Joshua.)

¹⁷When Moses sent them to explore Canaan, he said, "Go up through the Negev and on into the hill country. ¹⁸See what the land is like and whether the people who live there are strong or weak, few or many. ¹⁹What kind of land do they live in? Is it good or bad? What kind of towns do they live in? Are they unwalled or fortified? ²⁰How is the soil? Is it fertile or poor? Are there trees on it or not? Do your best to bring back some of the fruit of the land." (It was the season for the first ripe grapes.)

²¹So they went up and explored the land from the Desert of Zin as far as Rehob, toward Lebo*ᵃ* Hamath. ²²They went up through the Negev and came to Hebron, where Ahiman, Sheshai and Talmai, the descendants of Anak, lived. (Hebron had been built seven years before Zoan in Egypt.) ²³When they reached the Valley of Eshcol,*ᵇ* they cut off a branch bearing a single cluster of grapes. Two of them carried it on a pole between them, along with some pomegranates and figs. ²⁴That place was called the Valley of Eshcol because of the cluster of grapes the Israelites cut off there. ²⁵At the end of forty days they returned from exploring the land.

Report on the Exploration

²⁶They came back to Moses and Aaron and the whole Israelite community at Kadesh in the Desert of Paran. There they reported to them and to the whole assembly and showed them the fruit of the land. ²⁷They gave Moses this account: "We went into the land to which you sent us, and it does flow with milk and honey! Here is its fruit. ²⁸But the people who live there are powerful, and the cities are fortified and very large. We even saw descendants of Anak there. ²⁹The Amalekites live in the Negev; the Hittites, Jebusites and Amorites live in the hill country; and the Canaanites live near the sea and along the Jordan."

³⁰Then Caleb silenced the people before Moses and said, "We should go up and take possession of the land, for we can certainly do it."

³¹But the men who had gone up with him said, "We can't attack those people; they are stronger than we are." ³²And they spread among the Israelites a bad report about the land they had explored. They said, "The land we explored devours those living in it. All the people we saw there are of great size. ³³We saw the Nephilim there (the descendants of Anak come from the Nephilim). We seemed like grasshoppers in our own eyes, and we looked the same to them."

The People Rebel

14 That night all the people of the community raised their voices and

ᵃ21 Or *toward the entrance to*   *ᵇ23 Eshcol* means *cluster; also in verse 24.*

POINT OF INTEREST

Numbers 13:2

God had promised Abraham three things: a son, a nation and a homeland (see Genesis 21:2; 12:2; 13:14–15). God kept his promises. Isaac was born, Abraham's descendants became the nation of Israel and the people were poised to occupy their promised homeland. But some of Abraham's descendants entered the land while others did not. Did God break his promise?

wept aloud. ²All the Israelites grumbled against Moses and Aaron, and the whole assembly said to them, "If only we had died in Egypt! Or in this desert! ³Why is the LORD bringing us to this land only to let us fall by the sword? Our wives and children will be taken as plunder. Wouldn't it be better for us to go back to Egypt?" ⁴And they said to each other, "We should choose a leader and go back to Egypt."

⁵Then Moses and Aaron fell facedown in front of the whole Israelite assembly gathered there. ⁶Joshua son of Nun and Caleb son of Jephunneh, who were among those who had explored the land, tore their clothes ⁷and said to the entire Israelite assembly, "The land we passed through and explored is exceedingly good. ⁸If the LORD is pleased with us, he will lead us into that land, a land flowing with milk and honey, and will give it to us. ⁹Only do not rebel against the LORD. And do not be afraid of the people of the land, because we will swallow them up. Their protection is gone, but the LORD is with us. Do not be afraid of them."

¹⁰But the whole assembly talked about stoning them. Then the glory of the LORD appeared at the Tent of Meeting to all the Israelites. ¹¹The LORD said to Moses, "How long will these people treat me with contempt? How long will they refuse to believe in me, in spite of all the miraculous signs I have performed among them? ¹²I will strike them down with a plague and destroy them, but I will make you into a nation greater and stronger than they."

¹³Moses said to the LORD, "Then the Egyptians will hear about it! By your power you brought these people up from among them. ¹⁴And they will tell the inhabitants of this land about it. They have already heard that you, O LORD, are with these people and that you, O LORD, have been seen face to face, that your cloud stays over them, and that you go before them in a pillar of cloud by day and a pillar of fire by night. ¹⁵If you put these people to death all at one time, the nations who have heard this report about you will say, ¹⁶'The LORD was not able to bring these people into the land he promised them on oath; so he slaughtered them in the desert.'

¹⁷"Now may the Lord's strength be displayed, just as you have declared: ¹⁸'The LORD is slow to anger, abounding in love and forgiving sin and rebellion. Yet he does not leave the guilty unpunished; he punishes the children for the sin of the fathers to the third and fourth generation.' ¹⁹In accordance with your great love, forgive the sin of these people, just as you have pardoned them from the time they left Egypt until now."

²⁰The LORD replied, "I have forgiven them, as you asked. ²¹Nevertheless, as surely as I live and as surely as the glory of the LORD fills the whole earth, ²²not one of the men who saw my glory and the miraculous signs I performed in Egypt and in the desert but who disobeyed me and tested me ten times— ²³not one of them will ever see the land I promised on oath to their forefathers. No one who has treated me with contempt will ever see it. ²⁴But because my servant Caleb has a different spirit and follows me wholeheartedly, I will bring him into the land he went to, and his descendants will inherit it. ²⁵Since the Amalekites and Canaanites are living in the valleys, turn back tomorrow and set out toward the desert along the route to the Red Sea.ᵃ"

²⁶The LORD said to Moses and Aaron: ²⁷"How long will this wicked community grumble against me? I have heard the complaints of these grumbling Israelites. ²⁸So tell them, 'As surely as I live, declares the LORD, I will do to you the very things I heard you say: ²⁹In this desert your bodies will fall—every one of you twenty years old or more who was counted in the census and who has grumbled against me. ³⁰Not one of you will enter the land I swore with uplifted hand to make your home, except Caleb son of Jephunneh and Joshua son of Nun. ³¹As for your children that you said would be taken as plunder, I will bring them in to enjoy the land you have rejected. ³²But you—your bodies will fall in this desert. ³³Your children will be shepherds here for forty years, suffering for your unfaithfulness, until the last of your bodies lies in the desert. ³⁴For forty years—one year for each of the forty days you explored the land—you will suffer for your sins and know what it is like to have me against you.' ³⁵I, the LORD, have spoken, and I will surely do these things to this whole wicked community, which has banded together against me. They will

---

ᵃ25 Hebrew *Yam Suph*; that is, Sea of Reeds

meet their end in this desert; here they will die."

³⁶So the men Moses had sent to explore the land, who returned and made the whole community grumble against him by spreading a bad report about it— ³⁷these men responsible for spreading the bad report about the land were struck down and died of a plague before the LORD. ³⁸Of the men who went to explore the land, only Joshua son of Nun and Caleb son of Jephunneh survived.

³⁹When Moses reported this to all the Israelites, they mourned bitterly. ⁴⁰Early the next morning they went up toward the high hill country. "We have sinned," they said. "We will go up to the place the LORD promised."

⁴¹But Moses said, "Why are you disobeying the LORD's command? This will

FRIDAY

Read Numbers 13:26—14:24
Key Verse Numbers 14:24

A Different Spirit —Mike Edsall

I can remember the first day of high school. I had carefully selected my shirt, pants, shoes and even my socks. But I was uncharacteristically quiet as I slipped into my seat. Somewhere between getting out of the car and walking into my first period class I had been horrified to discover what almost everyone else had already noticed: My clothes were too "new." At this rate, I would *never* be cool!

One of the great terrors of youth is to be ostracized for being "different." We dress like our friends. We want to be noticed, but not for something that makes us a target for the ridicule of others. Standing out is risky. Fitting in feels safer.

Caleb was different for sure! Caleb had such confidence in God that he wasn't afraid to stand out in the crowd. Caleb was one of twelve spies whom God told Moses to send into the promised land in preparation for Israel's invasion. When they returned, all of the spies agreed on the bounty of the land, but ten of them had taken one look at the formidable inhabitants and had immediately concluded that Israel could not overcome "the giants." As they gave Moses their pessimistic report, Caleb jumped up, crying, "We should go up . . . we can certainly do it" (Numbers 13:30). His opinion was dismissed, but he didn't let it go at that. As the discouraged ex-slaves planned to return to Egypt, Caleb, now joined by Joshua, tore his clothes and shouted, "If the LORD is pleased with us, he will lead us into that land . . . and will give it to us" (Numbers 14:8–9). Caleb and Joshua were standing firm, but they were standing alone.

Where did Caleb's confidence come from? Caleb knew God's track record. God had delivered Israel from Egypt with many signs and wonders. Caleb knew that if God said something it was as good as accomplished.

Like Caleb, we too can dare to be different because we know that we do not stand alone, but that we stand with Christ Jesus, "who is able to do immeasurably more than all we ask or imagine, according to his power that is at work within us" (Ephesians 3:20).

A Deeper Look
2 Kings 18:5–6; Philippians 1:27–28

Go to page 160 for your next devotional reading.

not succeed! **42**Do not go up, because the LORD is not with you. You will be defeated by your enemies, **43**for the Amalekites and Canaanites will face you there. Because you have turned away from the LORD, he will not be with you and you will fall by the sword."

44Nevertheless, in their presumption they went up toward the high hill country, though neither Moses nor the ark of the LORD's covenant moved from the camp. **45**Then the Amalekites and Canaanites who lived in that hill country came down and attacked them and beat them down all the way to Hormah.

Supplementary Offerings

15 The LORD said to Moses, **2**"Speak to the Israelites and say to them: 'After you enter the land I am giving you as a home **3**and you present to the LORD offerings made by fire, from the herd or the flock, as an aroma pleasing to the LORD— whether burnt offerings or sacrifices, for special vows or freewill offerings or festival offerings— **4**then the one who brings his offering shall present to the LORD a grain offering of a tenth of an ephah*a* of fine flour mixed with a quarter of a hin*b* of oil. **5**With each lamb for the burnt offering or the sacrifice, prepare a quarter of a hin of wine as a drink offering.

6" 'With a ram prepare a grain offering of two-tenths of an ephah*c* of fine flour mixed with a third of a hin*d* of oil, **7**and a third of a hin of wine as a drink offering. Offer it as an aroma pleasing to the LORD.

8" 'When you prepare a young bull as a burnt offering or sacrifice, for a special vow or a fellowship offering*e* to the LORD, **9**bring with the bull a grain offering of three-tenths of an ephah*f* of fine flour mixed with half a hin*g* of oil. **10**Also bring half a hin of wine as a drink offering. It will be an offering made by fire, an aroma pleasing to the LORD. **11**Each bull or ram, each lamb or young goat, is to be prepared in this manner. **12**Do this for each one, for as many as you prepare.

13" 'Everyone who is native-born must do these things in this way when he brings an offering made by fire as an aroma pleasing to the LORD. **14**For the generations to come, whenever an alien or anyone else living among you presents an offering made by fire as an aroma pleasing to the LORD, he must do exactly as you do. **15**The community is to have the same rules for you and for the alien living among you; this is a lasting ordinance for the generations to come. You and the alien shall be the same before the LORD: **16**The same laws and regulations will apply both to you and to the alien living among you.' "

17The LORD said to Moses, **18**"Speak to the Israelites and say to them: 'When you enter the land to which I am taking you **19**and you eat the food of the land, present a portion as an offering to the LORD. **20**Present a cake from the first of your ground meal and present it as an offering from the threshing floor. **21**Throughout the generations to come you are to give this offering to the LORD from the first of your ground meal.

Offerings for Unintentional Sins

22" 'Now if you unintentionally fail to keep any of these commands the LORD gave Moses— **23**any of the LORD's commands to you through him, from the day the LORD gave them and continuing through the generations to come— **24**and if this is done unintentionally without the community being aware of it, then the whole community is to offer a young bull for a burnt offering as an aroma pleasing to the LORD, along with its prescribed grain offering and drink offering, and a male goat for a sin offering. **25**The priest is to make atonement for the whole Israelite community, and they will be forgiven, for it was not intentional and they have brought to the LORD for their wrong an offering made by fire and a sin offering. **26**The whole Israelite community and the aliens living among them will be forgiven, because all the people were involved in the unintentional wrong.

27" 'But if just one person sins unintentionally, he must bring a year-old female goat for a sin offering. **28**The priest is to make atonement before the LORD for the one who erred by sinning unintentionally, and when atonement has been made for him, he will be forgiven. **29**One and the same law applies to everyone

a4 That is, probably about 2 quarts (about 2 liters)
b4 That is, probably about 1 quart (about 1 liter); also in verse 5   c6 That is, probably about 4 quarts (about 4.5 liters)   d6 That is, probably about 1 1/4 quarts (about 1.2 liters); also in verse 7   e8 Traditionally peace offering   f9 That is, probably about 6 quarts (about 6.5 liters)   g9 That is, probably about 2 quarts (about 2 liters); also in verse 10

who sins unintentionally, whether he is a native-born Israelite or an alien.

30 "'But anyone who sins defiantly, whether native-born or alien, blasphemes the Lord, and that person must be cut off from his people. 31Because he has despised the Lord's word and broken his commands, that person must surely be cut off; his guilt remains on him.' "

The Sabbath-Breaker Put to Death

32While the Israelites were in the desert, a man was found gathering wood on the Sabbath day. 33Those who found him gathering wood brought him to Moses and Aaron and the whole assembly, 34and they kept him in custody, because it was not clear what should be done to him. 35Then the Lord said to Moses, "The man must die. The whole assembly must stone him outside the camp." 36So the assembly took him outside the camp and stoned him to death, as the Lord commanded Moses.

Tassels on Garments

37The Lord said to Moses, 38"Speak to the Israelites and say to them: 'Throughout the generations to come you are to make tassels on the corners of your garments, with a blue cord on each tassel. 39You will have these tassels to look at and so you will remember all the commands of the Lord, that you may obey them and not prostitute yourselves by going after the lusts of your own hearts and eyes. 40Then you will remember to obey all my commands and will be consecrated to your God. 41I am the Lord your God, who brought you out of Egypt to be your God. I am the Lord your God.' "

Korah, Dathan and Abiram

16 Korah son of Izhar, the son of Kohath, the son of Levi, and certain Reubenites—Dathan and Abiram, sons of Eliab, and On son of Peleth—became insolent*a* 2and rose up against Moses. With them were 250 Israelite men, well-known community leaders who had been appointed members of the council. 3They came as a group to oppose Moses and Aaron and said to them, "You have gone too far! The whole community is holy, every one of them, and the Lord is with them. Why then do you set yourselves above the Lord's assembly?"

4When Moses heard this, he fell facedown. 5Then he said to Korah and all his followers: "In the morning the Lord will show who belongs to him and who is holy, and he will have that person come near him. The man he chooses he will cause to come near him. 6You, Korah, and all your followers are to do this: Take censers 7and tomorrow put fire and incense in them before the Lord. The man the Lord chooses will be the one who is holy. You Levites have gone too far!"

8Moses also said to Korah, "Now listen, you Levites! 9Isn't it enough for you that the God of Israel has separated you from the rest of the Israelite community and brought you near himself to do the work at the Lord's tabernacle and to stand before the community and minister to them? 10He has brought you and all your fellow Levites near himself, but now you are trying to get the priesthood too. 11It is against the Lord that you and all your followers have banded together. Who is Aaron that you should grumble against him?"

12Then Moses summoned Dathan and Abiram, the sons of Eliab. But they said, "We will not come! 13Isn't it enough that you have brought us up out of a land flowing with milk and honey to kill us in the desert? And now you also want to lord it over us? 14Moreover, you haven't brought us into a land flowing with milk and honey or given us an inheritance of fields and vineyards. Will you gouge out the eyes of*b* these men? No, we will not come!"

15Then Moses became very angry and said to the Lord, "Do not accept their of-

a1 Or Peleth—took ⌐men⌐ *b14 Or you make slaves of; or you deceive*

POINT OF INTEREST

Numbers 16:3

Discontent can spread like gangrene throughout any group. One envious, rebellious individual can stir up several others who can, in turn, infect hundreds. The Israelites were not immune to the spread of discontentment. God's response to Korah and his co-conspirators underscores the destructive evil of a rebellious spirit.

Read Numbers 16:1–50
Key Verse Numbers 16:11

Attitude and Authority

Authority is not PC—a Popular Concept—these days. Mention the word, and people have an instant negative reaction. We often submit to, and even acknowledge, authority figures out of expediency rather than on principle. But really, resistance to authority is nothing new; it has been the status quo throughout history—take this story about Moses and Aaron, for example.

Although we are often inclined to resist and resent appointed leaders, we must recognize that God has established relationships that involve both authority and submission—relationships that are meant to maintain order, justice and peace. An authority figure is "God's servant to do you good" (Romans 13:4). Government has authority over citizens, and employers have authority over employees. We have spiritual leaders in the church and in the home. When a person is placed in a position of leadership, it doesn't imply that he or she is superior; it only indicates that that person holds a different role in the relationship—a role with responsibility and accountability to God.

God takes rebellion against authority very seriously. This story challenges us to willingly submit to the authorities God has placed in our lives, knowing that *he* is the final authority over all people.

Digging Into the Word
1. How did Daniel and his friends respond to the ungodly authority over them? What was the response of Daniel's three friends when they faced another difficult decision about submission to authorities?—*Daniel 1:1–16; Daniel 3:1–30*
2. Read Esther 4—7. How does Esther respond to authority in an unjust situation?

Personal Reflection
What should your attitude and actions be when under an ungodly authority? Make this question a discussion starter with a group of friends.

One Step Deeper
Matthew 27:11–14; Romans 13:1–7

Go to page 169 for your next devotional reading.

fering. I have not taken so much as a donkey from them, nor have I wronged any of them."

¹⁶Moses said to Korah, "You and all your followers are to appear before the LORD tomorrow—you and they and Aaron. ¹⁷Each man is to take his censer and put incense in it—250 censers in all—and present it before the LORD. You and Aaron are to present your censers also." ¹⁸So each man took his censer, put fire and incense in it, and stood with Moses and Aaron at the entrance to the Tent of Meeting. ¹⁹When Korah had gathered all his followers in opposition to them at the entrance to the Tent of Meeting, the glory of the LORD appeared to the entire assembly. ²⁰The LORD said to Moses and Aaron, ²¹"Separate yourselves from this assembly so I can put an end to them at once."

²²But Moses and Aaron fell facedown and cried out, "O God, God of the spirits of all mankind, will you be angry with the entire assembly when only one man sins?"

²³Then the LORD said to Moses, ²⁴"Say to the assembly, 'Move away from the tents of Korah, Dathan and Abiram.' "

²⁵Moses got up and went to Dathan and Abiram, and the elders of Israel followed him. ²⁶He warned the assembly, "Move back from the tents of these wicked men! Do not touch anything belonging to them, or you will be swept away because of all their sins." ²⁷So they moved away from the tents of Korah, Dathan and Abiram. Dathan and Abiram had come out and were standing with their wives, children and little ones at the entrances to their tents.

²⁸Then Moses said, "This is how you will know that the LORD has sent me to do all these things and that it was not my idea: ²⁹If these men die a natural death and experience only what usually happens to men, then the LORD has not sent me. ³⁰But if the LORD brings about something totally new, and the earth opens its mouth and swallows them, with everything that belongs to them, and they go down alive into the grave,ᵃ then you will know that these men have treated the LORD with contempt."

³¹As soon as he finished saying all this, the ground under them split apart ³²and the earth opened its mouth and swallowed them, with their households and all Korah's men and all their possessions. ³³They went down alive into the grave,

with everything they owned; the earth closed over them, and they perished and were gone from the community. ³⁴At their cries, all the Israelites around them fled, shouting, "The earth is going to swallow us too!"

³⁵And fire came out from the LORD and consumed the 250 men who were offering the incense.

³⁶The LORD said to Moses, ³⁷"Tell Eleazar son of Aaron, the priest, to take the censers out of the smoldering remains and scatter the coals some distance away, for the censers are holy— ³⁸the censers of the men who sinned at the cost of their lives. Hammer the censers into sheets to overlay the altar, for they were presented before the LORD and have become holy. Let them be a sign to the Israelites."

³⁹So Eleazar the priest collected the bronze censers brought by those who had been burned up, and he had them hammered out to overlay the altar, ⁴⁰as the LORD directed him through Moses. This was to remind the Israelites that no one except a descendant of Aaron should come to burn incense before the LORD, or he would become like Korah and his followers.

⁴¹The next day the whole Israelite community grumbled against Moses and Aaron. "You have killed the LORD's people," they said.

⁴²But when the assembly gathered in opposition to Moses and Aaron and turned toward the Tent of Meeting, suddenly the cloud covered it and the glory of the LORD appeared. ⁴³Then Moses and Aaron went to the front of the Tent of Meeting, ⁴⁴and the LORD said to Moses, ⁴⁵"Get away from this assembly so I can put an end to them at once." And they fell facedown.

⁴⁶Then Moses said to Aaron, "Take your censer and put incense in it, along with fire from the altar, and hurry to the assembly to make atonement for them. Wrath has come out from the LORD; the plague has started." ⁴⁷So Aaron did as Moses said, and ran into the midst of the assembly. The plague had already started among the people, but Aaron offered the incense and made atonement for them. ⁴⁸He stood between the living and the dead, and the plague stopped. ⁴⁹But 14,700 people died from the plague, in addition to those who had died because

---

ᵃ30 Hebrew *Sheol*; also in verse 33

of Korah. [50]Then Aaron returned to Moses at the entrance to the Tent of Meeting, for the plague had stopped.

The Budding of Aaron's Staff

17 The LORD said to Moses, [2]"Speak to the Israelites and get twelve staffs from them, one from the leader of each of their ancestral tribes. Write the name of each man on his staff. [3]On the staff of Levi write Aaron's name, for there must be one staff for the head of each ancestral tribe. [4]Place them in the Tent of Meeting in front of the Testimony, where I meet with you. [5]The staff belonging to the man I choose will sprout, and I will rid myself of this constant grumbling against you by the Israelites."

[6]So Moses spoke to the Israelites, and their leaders gave him twelve staffs, one for the leader of each of their ancestral tribes, and Aaron's staff was among them. [7]Moses placed the staffs before the LORD in the Tent of the Testimony.

[8]The next day Moses entered the Tent of the Testimony and saw that Aaron's staff, which represented the house of Levi, had not only sprouted but had budded, blossomed and produced almonds. [9]Then Moses brought out all the staffs from the LORD's presence to all the Israelites. They looked at them, and each man took his own staff.

[10]The LORD said to Moses, "Put back Aaron's staff in front of the Testimony, to be kept as a sign to the rebellious. This will put an end to their grumbling against me, so that they will not die." [11]Moses did just as the LORD commanded him.

[12]The Israelites said to Moses, "We will die! We are lost, we are all lost! [13]Anyone who even comes near the tabernacle of the LORD will die. Are we all going to die?"

Duties of Priests and Levites

18 The LORD said to Aaron, "You, your sons and your father's family are to bear the responsibility for offenses against the sanctuary, and you and your sons alone are to bear the responsibility for offenses against the priesthood. [2]Bring your fellow Levites from your ancestral tribe to join you and assist you when you and your sons minister before the Tent of the Testimony. [3]They are to be responsible to you and are to perform all the duties of the Tent, but they must not go near the furnishings of the sanctu-

ary or the altar, or both they and you will die. [4]They are to join you and be responsible for the care of the Tent of Meeting—all the work at the Tent—and no one else may come near where you are.

[5]"You are to be responsible for the care of the sanctuary and the altar, so that wrath will not fall on the Israelites again. [6]I myself have selected your fellow Levites from among the Israelites as a gift to you, dedicated to the LORD to do the work at the Tent of Meeting. [7]But only you and your sons may serve as priests in connection with everything at the altar and inside the curtain. I am giving you the service of the priesthood as a gift. Anyone else who comes near the sanctuary must be put to death."

Offerings for Priests and Levites

[8]Then the LORD said to Aaron, "I myself have put you in charge of the offerings presented to me; all the holy offerings the Israelites give me I give to you and your sons as your portion and regular share. [9]You are to have the part of the most holy offerings that is kept from the fire. From all the gifts they bring me as most holy offerings, whether grain or sin or guilt offerings, that part belongs to you and your sons. [10]Eat it as something most holy; every male shall eat it. You must regard it as holy.

[11]"This also is yours: whatever is set aside from the gifts of all the wave offerings of the Israelites. I give this to you and your sons and daughters as your regular share. Everyone in your household who is ceremonially clean may eat it.

[12]"I give you all the finest olive oil and all the finest new wine and grain they give the LORD as the firstfruits of their harvest. [13]All the land's firstfruits that they bring to the LORD will be yours. Everyone in your household who is ceremonially clean may eat it.

[14]"Everything in Israel that is devoted[a] to the LORD is yours. [15]The first offspring of every womb, both man and animal, that is offered to the LORD is yours. But you must redeem every firstborn son and every firstborn male of unclean animals. [16]When they are a month old, you must redeem them at the redemption price set at five shekels[b] of

---

[a]14 The Hebrew term refers to the irrevocable giving over of things or persons to the LORD.
[b]16 That is, about 2 ounces (about 55 grams)

silver, according to the sanctuary shekel, which weighs twenty gerahs.

[17]"But you must not redeem the firstborn of an ox, a sheep or a goat; they are holy. Sprinkle their blood on the altar and burn their fat as an offering made by fire, an aroma pleasing to the LORD. [18]Their meat is to be yours, just as the breast of the wave offering and the right thigh are yours. [19]Whatever is set aside from the holy offerings the Israelites present to the LORD I give to you and your sons and daughters as your regular share. It is an everlasting covenant of salt before the LORD for both you and your offspring."

[20]The LORD said to Aaron, "You will have no inheritance in their land, nor will you have any share among them; I am your share and your inheritance among the Israelites.

[21]"I give to the Levites all the tithes in Israel as their inheritance in return for the work they do while serving at the Tent of Meeting. [22]From now on the Israelites must not go near the Tent of Meeting, or they will bear the consequences of their sin and will die. [23]It is the Levites who are to do the work at the Tent of Meeting and bear the responsibility for offenses against it. This is a lasting ordinance for the generations to come. They will receive no inheritance among the Israelites. [24]Instead, I give to the Levites as their inheritance the tithes that the Israelites present as an offering to the LORD. That is why I said concerning them: 'They will have no inheritance among the Israelites.' "

[25]The LORD said to Moses, [26]"Speak to the Levites and say to them: 'When you receive from the Israelites the tithe I give you as your inheritance, you must present a tenth of that tithe as the LORD's offering. [27]Your offering will be reckoned to you as grain from the threshing floor or juice from the winepress. [28]In this way you also will present an offering to the LORD from all the tithes you receive from the Israelites. From these tithes you must give the LORD's portion to Aaron the priest. [29]You must present as the LORD's portion the best and holiest part of everything given to you.'

[30]"Say to the Levites: 'When you present the best part, it will be reckoned to you as the product of the threshing floor or the winepress. [31]You and your households may eat the rest of it anywhere, for it is your wages for your work at the Tent of Meeting. [32]By presenting the best part of it you will not be guilty in this matter; then you will not defile the holy offerings of the Israelites, and you will not die.' "

The Water of Cleansing

19 The LORD said to Moses and Aaron: [2]"This is a requirement of the law that the LORD has commanded: Tell the Israelites to bring you a red heifer without defect or blemish and that has never been under a yoke. [3]Give it to Eleazar the priest; it is to be taken outside the camp and slaughtered in his presence. [4]Then Eleazar the priest is to take some of its blood on his finger and sprinkle it seven times toward the front of the Tent of Meeting. [5]While he watches, the heifer is to be burned—its hide, flesh, blood and offal. [6]The priest is to take some cedar wood, hyssop and scarlet wool and throw them onto the burning heifer. [7]After that, the priest must wash his clothes and bathe himself with water. He may then come into the camp, but he will be ceremonially unclean till evening. [8]The man who burns it must also wash his clothes and bathe with water, and he too will be unclean till evening.

[9]"A man who is clean shall gather up the ashes of the heifer and put them in a ceremonially clean place outside the camp. They shall be kept by the Israelite community for use in the water of cleansing; it is for purification from sin. [10]The man who gathers up the ashes of the heifer must also wash his clothes, and he too will be unclean till evening. This will be a lasting ordinance both for the Israelites and for the aliens living among them.

[11]"Whoever touches the dead body of anyone will be unclean for seven days. [12]He must purify himself with the water on the third day and on the seventh day; then he will be clean. But if he does not purify himself on the third and seventh days, he will not be clean. [13]Whoever touches the dead body of anyone and fails to purify himself defiles the LORD's tabernacle. That person must be cut off from Israel. Because the water of cleansing has not been sprinkled on him, he is unclean; his uncleanness remains on him.

[14]"This is the law that applies when a person dies in a tent: Anyone who enters the tent and anyone who is in it will be

unclean for seven days, 15and every open container without a lid fastened on it will be unclean.

16"Anyone out in the open who touches someone who has been killed with a sword or someone who has died a natural death, or anyone who touches a human bone or a grave, will be unclean for seven days.

17"For the unclean person, put some ashes from the burned purification offering into a jar and pour fresh water over them. 18Then a man who is ceremonially clean is to take some hyssop, dip it in the water and sprinkle the tent and all the furnishings and the people who were there. He must also sprinkle anyone who has touched a human bone or a grave or someone who has been killed or someone who has died a natural death. 19The man who is clean is to sprinkle the unclean person on the third and seventh days, and on the seventh day he is to purify him. The person being cleansed must wash his clothes and bathe with water, and that evening he will be clean. 20But if a person who is unclean does not purify himself, he must be cut off from the community, because he has defiled the sanctuary of the LORD. The water of cleansing has not been sprinkled on him, and he is unclean. 21This is a lasting ordinance for them.

"The man who sprinkles the water of cleansing must also wash his clothes, and anyone who touches the water of cleansing will be unclean till evening. 22Anything that an unclean person touches becomes unclean, and anyone who touches it becomes unclean till evening."

Water From the Rock

20 In the first month the whole Israelite community arrived at the Desert of Zin, and they stayed at Kadesh. There Miriam died and was buried.

2Now there was no water for the community, and the people gathered in opposition to Moses and Aaron. 3They quarreled with Moses and said, "If only we had died when our brothers fell dead before the LORD! 4Why did you bring the LORD's community into this desert, that we and our livestock should die here? 5Why did you bring us up out of Egypt to this terrible place? It has no grain or figs, grapevines or pomegranates. And there is no water to drink!"

6Moses and Aaron went from the assembly to the entrance to the Tent of Meeting and fell facedown, and the glory of the LORD appeared to them. 7The LORD said to Moses, 8"Take the staff, and you and your brother Aaron gather the assembly together. Speak to that rock before their eyes and it will pour out its water. You will bring water out of the rock for the community so they and their livestock can drink."

9So Moses took the staff from the LORD's presence, just as he commanded him. 10He and Aaron gathered the assembly together in front of the rock and Moses said to them, "Listen, you rebels, must we bring you water out of this rock?" 11Then Moses raised his arm and struck the rock twice with his staff. Water gushed out, and the community and their livestock drank.

12But the LORD said to Moses and Aaron, "Because you did not trust in me enough to honor me as holy in the sight of the Israelites, you will not bring this community into the land I give them."

13These were the waters of Meribah,*a* where the Israelites quarreled with the LORD and where he showed himself holy among them.

Edom Denies Israel Passage

14Moses sent messengers from Kadesh to the king of Edom, saying:

"This is what your brother Israel says: You know about all the hardships that have come upon us. 15Our forefathers went down into Egypt, and we lived there many years. The Egyptians mistreated us and our fathers, 16but when we

a13 Meribah means *quarreling.*

cried out to the LORD, he heard our cry and sent an angel and brought us out of Egypt.

"Now we are here at Kadesh, a town on the edge of your territory. ¹⁷Please let us pass through your country. We will not go through any field or vineyard, or drink water from any well. We will travel along the king's highway and not turn to the right or to the left until we have passed through your territory."

¹⁸But Edom answered:

"You may not pass through here; if you try, we will march out and attack you with the sword."

¹⁹The Israelites replied:

"We will go along the main road, and if we or our livestock drink any of your water, we will pay for it. We only want to pass through on foot— nothing else."

²⁰Again they answered:

"You may not pass through."

Then Edom came out against them with a large and powerful army. ²¹Since Edom refused to let them go through their territory, Israel turned away from them.

The Death of Aaron

²²The whole Israelite community set out from Kadesh and came to Mount Hor. ²³At Mount Hor, near the border of Edom, the LORD said to Moses and Aaron, ²⁴"Aaron will be gathered to his people. He will not enter the land I give the Israelites, because both of you rebelled against my command at the waters of Meribah. ²⁵Get Aaron and his son Eleazar and take them up Mount Hor. ²⁶Remove Aaron's garments and put them on his son Eleazar, for Aaron will be gathered to his people; he will die there."

²⁷Moses did as the LORD commanded: They went up Mount Hor in the sight of the whole community. ²⁸Moses removed Aaron's garments and put them on his son Eleazar. And Aaron died there on top of the mountain. Then Moses and Eleazar came down from the mountain, ²⁹and when the whole community learned that Aaron had died, the entire house of Israel mourned for him thirty days.

Arad Destroyed

21 When the Canaanite king of Arad, who lived in the Negev, heard that Israel was coming along the road to Atharim, he attacked the Israelites and captured some of them. ²Then Israel made this vow to the LORD: "If you will deliver these people into our hands, we will totally destroy*a* their cities." ³The LORD listened to Israel's plea and gave the Canaanites over to them. They completely destroyed them and their towns; so the place was named Hormah.*b*

The Bronze Snake

⁴They traveled from Mount Hor along the route to the Red Sea,*c* to go around Edom. But the people grew impatient on the way; ⁵they spoke against God and against Moses, and said, "Why have you brought us up out of Egypt to die in the desert? There is no bread! There is no water! And we detest this miserable food!"

⁶Then the LORD sent venomous snakes among them; they bit the people and many Israelites died. ⁷The people came to Moses and said, "We sinned when we spoke against the LORD and against you. Pray that the LORD will take the snakes away from us." So Moses prayed for the people.

⁸The LORD said to Moses, "Make a snake and put it up on a pole; anyone who is bitten can look at it and live." ⁹So Moses made a bronze snake and put it up on a pole. Then when anyone was bitten by a snake and looked at the bronze snake, he lived.

The Journey to Moab

¹⁰The Israelites moved on and camped at Oboth. ¹¹Then they set out from Oboth and camped in Iye Abarim, in the desert that faces Moab toward the sunrise. ¹²From there they moved on and camped in the Zered Valley. ¹³They set out from there and camped alongside the Arnon, which is in the desert extending into Amorite territory. The Arnon is the border of Moab, between Moab and the Amorites. ¹⁴That is why the Book of the Wars of the LORD says:

a2 The Hebrew term refers to the irrevocable giving over of things or persons to the LORD, often by totally destroying them; also in verse 3.   *b3* *Hormah* means *destruction.*   *c4* Hebrew *Yam Suph*; that is, Sea of Reeds

". . . Waheb in Suphah[a] and the
        ravines,
    the Arnon [15]and[b] the slopes of the
        ravines
that lead to the site of Ar
    and lie along the border of Moab."

[16]From there they continued on to Beer,
the well where the LORD said to Moses,
"Gather the people together and I will
give them water."
    [17]Then Israel sang this song:

"Spring up, O well!
    Sing about it,
[18]about the well that the princes dug,
    that the nobles of the people
        sank—
    the nobles with scepters and
        staffs."

Then they went from the desert to Mattanah, [19]from Mattanah to Nahaliel, from
Nahaliel to Bamoth, [20]and from Bamoth
to the valley in Moab where the top of
Pisgah overlooks the wasteland.

Defeat of Sihon and Og

[21]Israel sent messengers to say to Sihon king of the Amorites:

    [22]"Let us pass through your
    country. We will not turn aside into
    any field or vineyard, or drink water
    from any well. We will travel along
    the king's highway until we have
    passed through your territory."

[23]But Sihon would not let Israel pass
through his territory. He mustered his entire army and marched out into the desert
against Israel. When he reached Jahaz,
he fought with Israel. [24]Israel, however,
put him to the sword and took over his
land from the Arnon to the Jabbok, but
only as far as the Ammonites, because
their border was fortified. [25]Israel captured all the cities of the Amorites and
occupied them, including Heshbon and
all its surrounding settlements. [26]Hesh-
bon was the city of Sihon king of the Amorites, who had fought against the former
king of Moab and had taken from him all
his land as far as the Arnon.
    [27]That is why the poets say:

"Come to Heshbon and let it be
        rebuilt;
    let Sihon's city be restored.

[28]"Fire went out from Heshbon,
    a blaze from the city of Sihon.

It consumed Ar of Moab,
    the citizens of Arnon's heights.
[29]Woe to you, O Moab!
    You are destroyed, O people of
        Chemosh!
He has given up his sons as fugitives
    and his daughters as captives
    to Sihon king of the Amorites.

[30]"But we have overthrown them;
    Heshbon is destroyed all the way
        to Dibon.
We have demolished them as far as
        Nophah,
    which extends to Medeba."

[31]So Israel settled in the land of the
Amorites.
    [32]After Moses had sent spies to Jazer,
the Israelites captured its surrounding
settlements and drove out the Amorites
who were there. [33]Then they turned and
went up along the road toward Bashan,
and Og king of Bashan and his whole
army marched out to meet them in battle
at Edrei.
    [34]The LORD said to Moses, "Do not be
afraid of him, for I have handed him over
to you, with his whole army and his land.
Do to him what you did to Sihon king of
the Amorites, who reigned in Heshbon."
    [35]So they struck him down, together
with his sons and his whole army, leaving them no survivors. And they took
possession of his land.

Balak Summons Balaam

22 Then the Israelites traveled to the
plains of Moab and camped along the
Jordan across from Jericho.[c]
    [2]Now Balak son of Zippor saw all that
Israel had done to the Amorites, [3]and
Moab was terrified because there were so
many people. Indeed, Moab was filled
with dread because of the Israelites.
    [4]The Moabites said to the elders of
Midian, "This horde is going to lick up
everything around us, as an ox licks up
the grass of the field."

So Balak son of Zippor, who was king
of Moab at that time, [5]sent messengers to
summon Balaam son of Beor, who was at
Pethor, near the River,[d] in his native
land. Balak said:

[a]14 The meaning of the Hebrew for this phrase is
uncertain.   [b]14,15 Or "I have been given from
Suphah and the ravines / of the Arnon [15]to
[c]1 Hebrew Jordan of Jericho; possibly an ancient
name for the Jordan River   [d]5 That is, the
Euphrates

"A people has come out of Egypt; they cover the face of the land and have settled next to me. ⁶Now come and put a curse on these people, because they are too powerful for me. Perhaps then I will be able to defeat them and drive them out of the country. For I know that those you bless are blessed, and those you curse are cursed."

⁷The elders of Moab and Midian left, taking with them the fee for divination. When they came to Balaam, they told him what Balak had said.

⁸"Spend the night here," Balaam said to them, "and I will bring you back the answer the Lord gives me." So the Moabite princes stayed with him.

⁹God came to Balaam and asked, "Who are these men with you?"

¹⁰Balaam said to God, "Balak son of Zippor, king of Moab, sent me this message: ¹¹'A people that has come out of Egypt covers the face of the land. Now come and put a curse on them for me. Perhaps then I will be able to fight them and drive them away.'"

¹²But God said to Balaam, "Do not go with them. You must not put a curse on those people, because they are blessed."

¹³The next morning Balaam got up and said to Balak's princes, "Go back to your own country, for the Lord has refused to let me go with you."

¹⁴So the Moabite princes returned to Balak and said, "Balaam refused to come with us."

¹⁵Then Balak sent other princes, more numerous and more distinguished than the first. ¹⁶They came to Balaam and said:

"This is what Balak son of Zippor says: Do not let anything keep you from coming to me, ¹⁷because I will reward you handsomely and do whatever you say. Come and put a curse on these people for me."

¹⁸But Balaam answered them, "Even if Balak gave me his palace filled with silver and gold, I could not do anything great or small to go beyond the command of the Lord my God. ¹⁹Now stay here tonight as the others did, and I will find out what else the Lord will tell me."

²⁰That night God came to Balaam and said, "Since these men have come to summon you, go with them, but do only what I tell you."

Balaam's Donkey

²¹Balaam got up in the morning, saddled his donkey and went with the princes of Moab. ²²But God was very angry when he went, and the angel of the Lord stood in the road to oppose him. Balaam was riding on his donkey, and his two servants were with him. ²³When the donkey saw the angel of the Lord standing in the road with a drawn sword in his hand, she turned off the road into a field. Balaam beat her to get her back on the road.

²⁴Then the angel of the Lord stood in a narrow path between two vineyards, with walls on both sides. ²⁵When the donkey saw the angel of the Lord, she pressed close to the wall, crushing Balaam's foot against it. So he beat her again.

²⁶Then the angel of the Lord moved on ahead and stood in a narrow place where there was no room to turn, either to the right or to the left. ²⁷When the donkey saw the angel of the Lord, she lay down under Balaam, and he was angry and beat her with his staff. ²⁸Then the Lord opened the donkey's mouth, and she said to Balaam, "What have I done to you to make you beat me these three times?"

²⁹Balaam answered the donkey, "You have made a fool of me! If I had a sword in my hand, I would kill you right now."

³⁰The donkey said to Balaam, "Am I not your own donkey, which you have always ridden, to this day? Have I been in the habit of doing this to you?"

"No," he said.

³¹Then the Lord opened Balaam's eyes, and he saw the angel of the Lord standing

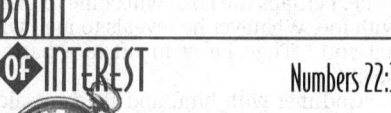

POINT OF INTEREST   Numbers 22:3

Moab was situated on the east bank of the Dead Sea in what is now the land of Jordan. Israel had been ordered not to attack Moab (see Deuteronomy 2:18) and had camped to the north, across the river from Jericho.

in the road with his sword drawn. So he bowed low and fell facedown.

³²The angel of the LORD asked him, "Why have you beaten your donkey these three times? I have come here to oppose you because your path is a reckless one before me.ᵃ ³³The donkey saw me and turned away from me these three times. If she had not turned away, I would certainly have killed you by now, but I would have spared her."

³⁴Balaam said to the angel of the LORD, "I have sinned. I did not realize you were standing in the road to oppose me. Now if you are displeased, I will go back."

³⁵The angel of the LORD said to Balaam, "Go with the men, but speak only what I tell you." So Balaam went with the princes of Balak.

³⁶When Balak heard that Balaam was coming, he went out to meet him at the Moabite town on the Arnon border, at the edge of his territory. ³⁷Balak said to Balaam, "Did I not send you an urgent summons? Why didn't you come to me? Am I really not able to reward you?"

³⁸"Well, I have come to you now," Balaam replied. "But can I say just anything? I must speak only what God puts in my mouth."

³⁹Then Balaam went with Balak to Kiriath Huzoth. ⁴⁰Balak sacrificed cattle and sheep, and gave some to Balaam and the princes who were with him. ⁴¹The next morning Balak took Balaam up to Bamoth Baal, and from there he saw part of the people.

Balaam's First Oracle

23 Balaam said, "Build me seven altars here, and prepare seven bulls and seven rams for me." ²Balak did as Balaam said, and the two of them offered a bull and a ram on each altar.

³Then Balaam said to Balak, "Stay here beside your offering while I go aside. Perhaps the LORD will come to meet with me. Whatever he reveals to me I will tell you." Then he went off to a barren height.

⁴God met with him, and Balaam said, "I have prepared seven altars, and on each altar I have offered a bull and a ram."

⁵The LORD put a message in Balaam's mouth and said, "Go back to Balak and give him this message."

⁶So he went back to him and found him standing beside his offering, with all

the princes of Moab. ⁷Then Balaam uttered his oracle:

"Balak brought me from Aram,
    the king of Moab from the eastern mountains.
'Come,' he said, 'curse Jacob for me;
    come, denounce Israel.'
⁸How can I curse
    those whom God has not cursed?
How can I denounce
    those whom the LORD has not denounced?
⁹From the rocky peaks I see them,
    from the heights I view them.
I see a people who live apart
    and do not consider themselves
        one of the nations.
¹⁰Who can count the dust of Jacob
    or number the fourth part of Israel?
Let me die the death of the righteous,
    and may my end be like theirs!"

¹¹Balak said to Balaam, "What have you done to me? I brought you to curse my enemies, but you have done nothing but bless them!"

¹²He answered, "Must I not speak what the LORD puts in my mouth?"

Balaam's Second Oracle

¹³Then Balak said to him, "Come with me to another place where you can see them; you will see only a part but not all of them. And from there, curse them for me." ¹⁴So he took him to the field of Zophim on the top of Pisgah, and there he built seven altars and offered a bull and a ram on each altar.

¹⁵Balaam said to Balak, "Stay here beside your offering while I meet with him over there."

¹⁶The LORD met with Balaam and put a message in his mouth and said, "Go back to Balak and give him this message."

¹⁷So he went to him and found him standing beside his offering, with the princes of Moab. Balak asked him, "What did the LORD say?"

¹⁸Then he uttered his oracle:

"Arise, Balak, and listen;
    hear me, son of Zippor.
¹⁹God is not a man, that he should lie,
    nor a son of man, that he should change his mind.
Does he speak and then not act?
    Does he promise and not fulfill?

ᵃ32 The meaning of the Hebrew for this clause is uncertain.

²⁰I have received a command to bless;
  he has blessed, and I cannot
    change it.
²¹"No misfortune is seen in Jacob,
  no misery observed in Israel.ᵃ
 The LORD their God is with them;
  the shout of the King is among
    them.
²²God brought them out of Egypt;
  they have the strength of a wild
    ox.
²³There is no sorcery against Jacob,

no divination against Israel.
 It will now be said of Jacob
  and of Israel, 'See what God has
    done!'
²⁴The people rise like a lioness;
  they rouse themselves like a lion
 that does not rest till he devours his
    prey
  and drinks the blood of his
    victims."

ᵃ21 Or *He has not looked on Jacob's offenses / or
on the wrongs found in Israel.*

MONDAY

Read *Numbers 23:1–26*
Key Verse *Numbers 23:19*

Always Faithful – Lynn Feldner

God's faithfulness is sometimes hard for us to comprehend. After all, our own fickle tendencies provide the most observable models of fidelity that we have. We make promises we can't keep, begin tasks we never finish, and make decisions we don't stand by.

At the beginning of every semester in college, I would make a resolution to stick to the class syllabus so that I wouldn't spend hours the night before a test catching up on a month's worth of reading. Yet two months into each semester I would find myself cramming the night before exams. Other times I've made commitments to get in shape. I would decide to get up early each morning to run or swim, only to find myself within a matter of weeks sleeping in on a daily basis.

Over the years I haven't changed much. True, I have to be faithful to get to work by eight every morning and to pay my bills on time. But although the affected areas of my life have changed, I still struggle with lack of faithfulness.

The comforting thing is that God never changes. Just as he was faithful to the Israelites in spite of their unfaithfulness to him, he is faithful to me. He is trustworthy, reliable, constant. "Does he promise and not fulfill?" (Numbers 23:19). Not a chance. His love is enduring: "The LORD is faithful to all his promises and loving toward all he has made" (Psalm 145:13).

How do I know? When I have asked him to fulfill his promises in my life, I have *seen* his faithfulness, although I have learned that sometimes I need to be patient, to "be strong and take heart and wait for the LORD" (Psalm 27:14). Too often I pray over a promise from God but take things into my own hands when things don't happen according to my timetable. But when I do wait for him, I see and know the God who is "abounding in love and faithfulness" (Exodus 34:6).

A Deeper Look
Deuteronomy 7:9; 1 Corinthians 1:9

Go to page 193 for your next devotional reading.

²⁵Then Balak said to Balaam, "Neither curse them at all nor bless them at all!"

²⁶Balaam answered, "Did I not tell you I must do whatever the LORD says?"

Balaam's Third Oracle

²⁷Then Balak said to Balaam, "Come, let me take you to another place. Perhaps it will please God to let you curse them for me from there." ²⁸And Balak took Balaam to the top of Peor, overlooking the wasteland.

²⁹Balaam said, "Build me seven altars here, and prepare seven bulls and seven rams for me." ³⁰Balak did as Balaam had said, and offered a bull and a ram on each altar.

24 Now when Balaam saw that it pleased the LORD to bless Israel, he did not resort to sorcery as at other times, but turned his face toward the desert. ²When Balaam looked out and saw Israel encamped tribe by tribe, the Spirit of God came upon him ³and he uttered his oracle:

"The oracle of Balaam son of Beor,
    the oracle of one whose eye sees
        clearly,
⁴the oracle of one who hears the
        words of God,
    who sees a vision from the
        Almighty,ᵃ
    who falls prostrate, and whose
        eyes are opened:

⁵"How beautiful are your tents,
        O Jacob,
    your dwelling places, O Israel!

⁶"Like valleys they spread out,
    like gardens beside a river,
like aloes planted by the LORD,
    like cedars beside the waters.
⁷Water will flow from their buckets;
    their seed will have abundant
        water.

"Their king will be greater than Agag;
    their kingdom will be exalted.

⁸"God brought them out of Egypt;
    they have the strength of a wild
        ox.
They devour hostile nations
    and break their bones in pieces;
    with their arrows they pierce them.
⁹Like a lion they crouch and lie down,
    like a lioness—who dares to rouse
        them?

"May those who bless you be blessed

and those who curse you be
        cursed!"

¹⁰Then Balak's anger burned against Balaam. He struck his hands together and said to him, "I summoned you to curse my enemies, but you have blessed them these three times. ¹¹Now leave at once and go home! I said I would reward you handsomely, but the LORD has kept you from being rewarded."

¹²Balaam answered Balak, "Did I not tell the messengers you sent me, ¹³'Even if Balak gave me his palace filled with silver and gold, I could not do anything of my own accord, good or bad, to go beyond the command of the LORD—and I must say only what the LORD says'? ¹⁴Now I am going back to my people, but come, let me warn you of what this people will do to your people in days to come."

Balaam's Fourth Oracle

¹⁵Then he uttered his oracle:

"The oracle of Balaam son of Beor,
    the oracle of one whose eye sees
        clearly,
¹⁶the oracle of one who hears the
        words of God,
    who has knowledge from the Most
        High,
    who sees a vision from the Almighty,
    who falls prostrate, and whose
        eyes are opened:

¹⁷"I see him, but not now;
    I behold him, but not near.
A star will come out of Jacob;
    a scepter will rise out of Israel.
He will crush the foreheads of Moab,
    the skullsᵇ ofᶜ all the sons of
        Sheth.ᵈ
¹⁸Edom will be conquered;
    Seir, his enemy, will be conquered,
    but Israel will grow strong.
¹⁹A ruler will come out of Jacob
    and destroy the survivors of the
        city."

Balaam's Final Oracles

²⁰Then Balaam saw Amalek and uttered his oracle:

ᵃ4 Hebrew *Shaddai*; also in verse 16
ᵇ17 Samaritan Pentateuch (see also Jer. 48:45); the meaning of the word in the Masoretic Text is uncertain.   ᶜ17 Or possibly *Moab, / batter*
ᵈ17 Or *all the noisy boasters*

"Amalek was first among the nations,
but he will come to ruin at last."

²¹Then he saw the Kenites and uttered
his oracle:

"Your dwelling place is secure,
your nest is set in a rock;
²²yet you Kenites will be destroyed
when Asshur takes you captive."

²³Then he uttered his oracle:

"Ah, who can live when God does
this?ᵃ
²⁴   Ships will come from the shores of
Kittim;
they will subdue Asshur and Eber,
but they too will come to ruin."

²⁵Then Balaam got up and returned
home and Balak went his own way.

Moab Seduces Israel

25 While Israel was staying in Shittim,
the men began to indulge in sexual
immorality with Moabite women, ²who
invited them to the sacrifices to their
gods. The people ate and bowed down
before these gods. ³So Israel joined in
worshiping the Baal of Peor. And the
LORD's anger burned against them.

⁴The LORD said to Moses, "Take all the
leaders of these people, kill them and expose them in broad daylight before the
LORD, so that the LORD's fierce anger may
turn away from Israel."

⁵So Moses said to Israel's judges,
"Each of you must put to death those of
your men who have joined in worshiping
the Baal of Peor."

⁶Then an Israelite man brought to his
family a Midianite woman right before
the eyes of Moses and the whole assembly of Israel while they were weeping at
the entrance to the Tent of Meeting.
⁷When Phinehas son of Eleazar, the son
of Aaron, the priest, saw this, he left the
assembly, took a spear in his hand ⁸and
followed the Israelite into the tent. He
drove the spear through both of them—
through the Israelite and into the woman's body. Then the plague against the
Israelites was stopped; ⁹but those who
died in the plague numbered 24,000.

¹⁰The LORD said to Moses, ¹¹"Phinehas
son of Eleazar, the son of Aaron, the
priest, has turned my anger away from
the Israelites; for he was as zealous as I
am for my honor among them, so that in
my zeal I did not put an end to them.

¹²Therefore tell him I am making my covenant of peace with him. ¹³He and his
descendants will have a covenant of a
lasting priesthood, because he was zealous for the honor of his God and made
atonement for the Israelites."

¹⁴The name of the Israelite who was
killed with the Midianite woman was
Zimri son of Salu, the leader of a Simeon-
ite family. ¹⁵And the name of the Midianite woman who was put to death was
Cozbi daughter of Zur, a tribal chief of a
Midianite family.

¹⁶The LORD said to Moses, ¹⁷"Treat the
Midianites as enemies and kill them,
¹⁸because they treated you as enemies
when they deceived you in the affair of
Peor and their sister Cozbi, the daughter
of a Midianite leader, the woman who
was killed when the plague came as a
result of Peor."

The Second Census

26 After the plague the LORD said to Moses and Eleazar son of Aaron, the
priest, ²"Take a census of the whole Israelite community by families—all those
twenty years old or more who are able to
serve in the army of Israel." ³So on the
plains of Moab by the Jordan across from
Jericho,ᵇ Moses and Eleazar the priest
spoke with them and said, ⁴"Take a census of the men twenty years old or more,
as the LORD commanded Moses."

These were the Israelites who came
out of Egypt:

⁵The descendants of Reuben, the firstborn son of Israel, were:

ᵃ23 Masoretic Text; with a different word division
of the Hebrew *A people will gather from the north.*
ᵇ3 Hebrew *Jordan of Jericho*; possibly an ancient
name for the Jordan River; also in verse 63

POINT OF INTEREST   Numbers 25:3

The Moabite women invited
the Israelite men to join
their Baal worship. These
temptresses were more pow-
erful than an army in bringing about the
downfall of the Israelites. Where open battle failed, idolatrous seduction won—for
the moment.

through Hanoch, the Hanochite
clan;
through Pallu, the Palluite clan;
⁶through Hezron, the Hezronite
clan;
through Carmi, the Carmite clan.
⁷These were the clans of Reuben; those
numbered were 43,730.

⁸The son of Pallu was Eliab, ⁹and the
sons of Eliab were Nemuel, Dathan and
Abiram. The same Dathan and Abiram
were the community officials who rebelled against Moses and Aaron and were
among Korah's followers when they rebelled against the LORD. ¹⁰The earth
opened its mouth and swallowed them
along with Korah, whose followers died
when the fire devoured the 250 men. And
they served as a warning sign. ¹¹The line
of Korah, however, did not die out.

¹²The descendants of Simeon by their
clans were:
through Nemuel, the Nemuelite
clan;
through Jamin, the Jaminite clan;
through Jakin, the Jakinite clan;
¹³through Zerah, the Zerahite clan;
through Shaul, the Shaulite clan.
¹⁴These were the clans of Simeon; there
were 22,200 men.

¹⁵The descendants of Gad by their clans
were:
through Zephon, the Zephonite
clan;
through Haggi, the Haggite clan;
through Shuni, the Shunite clan;
¹⁶through Ozni, the Oznite clan;
through Eri, the Erite clan;
¹⁷through Arodi,ᵃ the Arodite clan;
through Areli, the Arelite clan.
¹⁸These were the clans of Gad; those
numbered were 40,500.

¹⁹Er and Onan were sons of Judah, but
they died in Canaan.
²⁰The descendants of Judah by their clans
were:
through Shelah, the Shelanite clan;
through Perez, the Perezite clan;
through Zerah, the Zerahite clan.
²¹The descendants of Perez were:
through Hezron, the Hezronite
clan;
through Hamul, the Hamulite
clan.
²²These were the clans of Judah; those
numbered were 76,500.

²³The descendants of Issachar by their
clans were:
through Tola, the Tolaite clan;
through Puah, the Puiteᵇ clan;
²⁴through Jashub, the Jashubite
clan;
through Shimron, the Shimronite
clan.
²⁵These were the clans of Issachar; those
numbered were 64,300.

²⁶The descendants of Zebulun by their
clans were:
through Sered, the Seredite clan;
through Elon, the Elonite clan;
through Jahleel, the Jahleelite clan.
²⁷These were the clans of Zebulun; those
numbered were 60,500.

²⁸The descendants of Joseph by their
clans through Manasseh and Ephraim
were:
²⁹The descendants of Manasseh:
through Makir, the Makirite clan
(Makir was the father of Gilead);
through Gilead, the Gileadite clan.
³⁰These were the descendants of Gilead:
through Iezer, the Iezerite clan;
through Helek, the Helekite
clan;
³¹through Asriel, the Asrielite
clan;
through Shechem, the Shechem-
ite clan;
³²through Shemida, the Shemida-
ite clan;
through Hepher, the Hepherite
clan.
³³(Zelophehad son of Hepher had
no sons; he had only daughters,
whose names were Mahlah,
Noah, Hoglah, Milcah and Tirzah.)
³⁴These were the clans of Manasseh;
those numbered were 52,700.

³⁵These were the descendants of Ephraim
by their clans:
through Shuthelah, the Shuthela-
hite clan;
through Beker, the Bekerite clan;
through Tahan, the Tahanite clan.
³⁶These were the descendants of
Shuthelah:

ᵃ17 Samaritan Pentateuch and Syriac (see also Gen.
46:16); Masoretic Text *Arod*   ᵇ23 Samaritan
Pentateuch, Septuagint, Vulgate and Syriac (see also
1 Chron. 7:1); Masoretic Text *through Puvah, the
Punite*

through Eran, the Eranite clan.
37These were the clans of Ephraim; those numbered were 32,500.

These were the descendants of Joseph by their clans.

38The descendants of Benjamin by their clans were:
  through Bela, the Belaite clan;
  through Ashbel, the Ashbelite clan;
  through Ahiram, the Ahiramite clan;
  39through Shupham,*a* the Shuphamite clan;
  through Hupham, the Huphamite clan.
40The descendants of Bela through Ard and Naaman were:
  through Ard,*b* the Ardite clan;
  through Naaman, the Naamite clan.
41These were the clans of Benjamin; those numbered were 45,600.

42These were the descendants of Dan by their clans:
  through Shuham, the Shuhamite clan.
These were the clans of Dan: 43All of them were Shuhamite clans; and those numbered were 64,400.

44The descendants of Asher by their clans were:
  through Imnah, the Imnite clan;
  through Ishvi, the Ishvite clan;
  through Beriah, the Beriite clan;
  45and through the descendants of Beriah:
  through Heber, the Heberite clan;
  through Malkiel, the Malkielite clan.
46(Asher had a daughter named Serah.)
47These were the clans of Asher; those numbered were 53,400.

48The descendants of Naphtali by their clans were:
  through Jahzeel, the Jahzeelite clan;
  through Guni, the Gunite clan;
  49through Jezer, the Jezerite clan;
  through Shillem, the Shillemite clan.
50These were the clans of Naphtali; those numbered were 45,400.

51The total number of the men of Israel was 601,730.

52The LORD said to Moses, 53"The land is to be allotted to them as an inheritance based on the number of names. 54To a larger group give a larger inheritance, and to a smaller group a smaller one; each is to receive its inheritance according to the number of those listed. 55Be sure that the land is distributed by lot. What each group inherits will be according to the names for its ancestral tribe. 56Each inheritance is to be distributed by lot among the larger and smaller groups."

57These were the Levites who were counted by their clans:
  through Gershon, the Gershonite clan;
  through Kohath, the Kohathite clan;
  through Merari, the Merarite clan.
58These also were Levite clans:
  the Libnite clan,
  the Hebronite clan,
  the Mahlite clan,
  the Mushite clan,
  the Korahite clan.
(Kohath was the forefather of Amram; 59the name of Amram's wife was Jochebed, a descendant of Levi, who was born to the Levites*c* in Egypt. To Amram she bore Aaron, Moses and their sister Miriam. 60Aaron was the father of Nadab and Abihu, Eleazar and Ithamar. 61But Nadab and Abihu died when they made an offering before the LORD with unauthorized fire.)

62All the male Levites a month old or more numbered 23,000. They were not counted along with the other Israelites because they received no inheritance among them.

63These are the ones counted by Moses and Eleazar the priest when they counted the Israelites on the plains of Moab by the Jordan across from Jericho. 64Not one of them was among those counted by Moses and Aaron the priest when they counted the Israelites in the Desert of Sinai. 65For

---

a39 A few manuscripts of the Masoretic Text, Samaritan Pentateuch, Vulgate and Syriac (see also Septuagint); most manuscripts of the Masoretic Text *Shephupham*   *b40* Samaritan Pentateuch and Vulgate (see also Septuagint); Masoretic Text does not have *through Ard.*   *c59* Or *Jochebed, a daughter of Levi, who was born to Levi* the LORD had told those Israelites they would surely die in the desert, and not one of them was left except Caleb son of Jephunneh and Joshua son of Nun.

Zelophehad's Daughters

27 The daughters of Zelophehad son of Hepher, the son of Gilead, the son of Makir, the son of Manasseh, belonged to the clans of Manasseh son of Joseph. The names of the daughters were Mahlah, Noah, Hoglah, Milcah and Tirzah. They approached ²the entrance to the Tent of Meeting and stood before Moses, Eleazar the priest, the leaders and the whole assembly, and said, ³"Our father died in the desert. He was not among Korah's followers, who banded together against the LORD, but he died for his own sin and left no sons. ⁴Why should our father's name disappear from his clan because he had no son? Give us property among our father's relatives."

⁵So Moses brought their case before the LORD ⁶and the LORD said to him, ⁷"What Zelophehad's daughters are saying is right. You must certainly give them property as an inheritance among their father's relatives and turn their father's inheritance over to them.

⁸"Say to the Israelites, 'If a man dies and leaves no son, turn his inheritance over to his daughter. ⁹If he has no daughter, give his inheritance to his brothers. ¹⁰If he has no brothers, give his inheritance to his father's brothers. ¹¹If his father had no brothers, give his inheritance to the nearest relative in his clan, that he may possess it. This is to be a legal requirement for the Israelites, as the LORD commanded Moses.' "

Joshua to Succeed Moses

¹²Then the LORD said to Moses, "Go up this mountain in the Abarim range and see the land I have given the Israelites. ¹³After you have seen it, you too will be gathered to your people, as your brother Aaron was, ¹⁴for when the community rebelled at the waters in the Desert of Zin, both of you disobeyed my command to honor me as holy before their eyes." (These were the waters of Meribah Kadesh, in the Desert of Zin.)

¹⁵Moses said to the LORD, ¹⁶"May the LORD, the God of the spirits of all mankind, appoint a man over this community ¹⁷to go out and come in before them, one who will lead them out and bring them in, so the LORD's people will not be like sheep without a shepherd."

¹⁸So the LORD said to Moses, "Take Joshua son of Nun, a man in whom is the spirit,ᵃ and lay your hand on him. ¹⁹Have him stand before Eleazar the priest and the entire assembly and commission him in their presence. ²⁰Give him some of your authority so the whole Israelite community will obey him. ²¹He is to stand before Eleazar the priest, who will obtain decisions for him by inquiring of the Urim before the LORD. At his command he and the entire community of the Israelites will go out, and at his command they will come in."

²²Moses did as the LORD commanded him. He took Joshua and had him stand before Eleazar the priest and the whole assembly. ²³Then he laid his hands on him and commissioned him, as the LORD instructed through Moses.

Daily Offerings

28 The LORD said to Moses, ²"Give this command to the Israelites and say to them: 'See that you present to me at the appointed time the food for my offerings made by fire, as an aroma pleasing to me.' ³Say to them: 'This is the offering made by fire that you are to present to the LORD: two lambs a year old without defect, as a regular burnt offering each day. ⁴Prepare one lamb in the morning and the other at twilight, ⁵together with a grain offering of a tenth of an ephahᵇ of fine flour mixed with a quarter of a hinᶜ

ᵃ18 Or *Spirit* ᵇ5 That is, probably about 2 quarts (about 2 liters); also in verses 13, 21 and 29 ᶜ5 That is, probably about 1 quart (about 1 liter); also in verses 7 and 14

POINT OF INTEREST

Numbers 27:23

Strong leadership is important in any group. Joshua was not selected arbitrarily from the crowd. He had proven his character earlier at Kadesh Barnea, where he encouraged the people to trust God and enter the land (see Numbers 14:6–9). Joshua's resulting forty-year apprenticeship as Moses' personal aide had honed his executive ability.

of oil from pressed olives. ⁶This is the regular burnt offering instituted at Mount Sinai as a pleasing aroma, an offering made to the Lord by fire. ⁷The accompanying drink offering is to be a quarter of a hin of fermented drink with each lamb. Pour out the drink offering to the Lord at the sanctuary. ⁸Prepare the second lamb at twilight, along with the same kind of grain offering and drink offering that you prepare in the morning. This is an offering made by fire, an aroma pleasing to the Lord.

Sabbath Offerings

⁹" 'On the Sabbath day, make an offering of two lambs a year old without defect, together with its drink offering and a grain offering of two-tenths of an ephah*a* of fine flour mixed with oil. ¹⁰This is the burnt offering for every Sabbath, in addition to the regular burnt offering and its drink offering.

Monthly Offerings

¹¹" 'On the first of every month, present to the Lord a burnt offering of two young bulls, one ram and seven male lambs a year old, all without defect. ¹²With each bull there is to be a grain offering of three-tenths of an ephah*b* of fine flour mixed with oil; with the ram, a grain offering of two-tenths of an ephah of fine flour mixed with oil; ¹³and with each lamb, a grain offering of a tenth of an ephah of fine flour mixed with oil. This is for a burnt offering, a pleasing aroma, an offering made to the Lord by fire. ¹⁴With each bull there is to be a drink offering of half a hin*c* of wine; with the ram, a third of a hin*d*; and with each lamb, a quarter of a hin. This is the monthly burnt offering to be made at each new moon during the year. ¹⁵Besides the regular burnt offering with its drink offering, one male goat is to be presented to the Lord as a sin offering.

The Passover

¹⁶" 'On the fourteenth day of the first month the Lord's Passover is to be held. ¹⁷On the fifteenth day of this month there is to be a festival; for seven days eat bread made without yeast. ¹⁸On the first day hold a sacred assembly and do no regular work. ¹⁹Present to the Lord an offering made by fire, a burnt offering of two young bulls, one ram and seven male lambs a year old, all without defect.

²⁰With each bull prepare a grain offering of three-tenths of an ephah of fine flour mixed with oil; with the ram, two-tenths; ²¹and with each of the seven lambs, one-tenth. ²²Include one male goat as a sin offering to make atonement for you. ²³Prepare these in addition to the regular morning burnt offering. ²⁴In this way prepare the food for the offering made by fire every day for seven days as an aroma pleasing to the Lord; it is to be prepared in addition to the regular burnt offering and its drink offering. ²⁵On the seventh day hold a sacred assembly and do no regular work.

Feast of Weeks

²⁶" 'On the day of firstfruits, when you present to the Lord an offering of new grain during the Feast of Weeks, hold a sacred assembly and do no regular work. ²⁷Present a burnt offering of two young bulls, one ram and seven male lambs a year old as an aroma pleasing to the Lord. ²⁸With each bull there is to be a grain offering of three-tenths of an ephah of fine flour mixed with oil; with the ram, two-tenths; ²⁹and with each of the seven lambs, one-tenth. ³⁰Include one male goat to make atonement for you. ³¹Prepare these together with their drink offerings, in addition to the regular burnt offering and its grain offering. Be sure the animals are without defect.

Feast of Trumpets

29 " 'On the first day of the seventh month hold a sacred assembly and do no regular work. It is a day for you to sound the trumpets. ²As an aroma pleasing to the Lord, prepare a burnt offering of one young bull, one ram and seven male lambs a year old, all without defect. ³With the bull prepare a grain offering of three-tenths of an ephah*e* of fine flour mixed with oil; with the ram, two-tenths*f*; ⁴and with each of the seven lambs, one-tenth.*g* ⁵Include one male goat as a sin offering to make atonement

a9 That is, probably about 4 quarts (about 4.5 liters); also in verses 12, 20 and 28   *b12* That is, probably about 6 quarts (about 6.5 liters); also in verses 20 and 28   *c14* That is, probably about 2 quarts (about 2 liters)   *d14* That is, probably about 1 1/4 quarts (about 1.2 liters)   *e3* That is, probably about 6 quarts (about 6.5 liters); also in verses 9 and 14   *f3* That is, probably about 4 quarts (about 4.5 liters); also in verses 9 and 14   *g4* That is, probably about 2 quarts (about 2 liters); also in verses 10 and 15 for you. ⁶These are in addition to the monthly and daily burnt offerings with their grain offerings and drink offerings as specified. They are offerings made to the LORD by fire—a pleasing aroma.

Day of Atonement

⁷" 'On the tenth day of this seventh month hold a sacred assembly. You must deny yourselves*a* and do no work. ⁸Present as an aroma pleasing to the LORD a burnt offering of one young bull, one ram and seven male lambs a year old, all without defect. ⁹With the bull prepare a grain offering of three-tenths of an ephah of fine flour mixed with oil; with the ram, two-tenths; ¹⁰and with each of the seven lambs, one-tenth. ¹¹Include one male goat as a sin offering, in addition to the sin offering for atonement and the regular burnt offering with its grain offering, and their drink offerings.

Feast of Tabernacles

¹²" 'On the fifteenth day of the seventh month, hold a sacred assembly and do no regular work. Celebrate a festival to the LORD for seven days. ¹³Present an offering made by fire as an aroma pleasing to the LORD, a burnt offering of thirteen young bulls, two rams and fourteen male lambs a year old, all without defect. ¹⁴With each of the thirteen bulls prepare a grain offering of three-tenths of an ephah of fine flour mixed with oil; with each of the two rams, two-tenths; ¹⁵and with each of the fourteen lambs, one-tenth. ¹⁶Include one male goat as a sin offering, in addition to the regular burnt offering with its grain offering and drink offering.

¹⁷" 'On the second day prepare twelve young bulls, two rams and fourteen male lambs a year old, all without defect. ¹⁸With the bulls, rams and lambs, prepare their grain offerings and drink offerings according to the number specified. ¹⁹Include one male goat as a sin offering, in addition to the regular burnt offering with its grain offering, and their drink offerings.

²⁰" 'On the third day prepare eleven bulls, two rams and fourteen male lambs a year old, all without defect. ²¹With the bulls, rams and lambs, prepare their grain offerings and drink offerings according to the number specified. ²²Include one male goat as a sin offering, in addition to the regular burnt offering with its grain offering and drink offering.

²³" 'On the fourth day prepare ten bulls, two rams and fourteen male lambs a year old, all without defect. ²⁴With the bulls, rams and lambs, prepare their grain offerings and drink offerings according to the number specified. ²⁵Include one male goat as a sin offering, in addition to the regular burnt offering with its grain offering and drink offering.

²⁶" 'On the fifth day prepare nine bulls, two rams and fourteen male lambs a year old, all without defect. ²⁷With the bulls, rams and lambs, prepare their grain offerings and drink offerings according to the number specified. ²⁸Include one male goat as a sin offering, in addition to the regular burnt offering with its grain offering and drink offering.

²⁹" 'On the sixth day prepare eight bulls, two rams and fourteen male lambs a year old, all without defect. ³⁰With the bulls, rams and lambs, prepare their grain offerings and drink offerings according to the number specified. ³¹Include one male goat as a sin offering, in addition to the regular burnt offering with its grain offering and drink offering.

³²" 'On the seventh day prepare seven bulls, two rams and fourteen male lambs a year old, all without defect. ³³With the bulls, rams and lambs, prepare their grain offerings and drink offerings according to the number specified. ³⁴Include one male goat as a sin offering, in addition to the regular burnt offering with its grain offering and drink offering.

³⁵" 'On the eighth day hold an assembly and do no regular work. ³⁶Present an offering made by fire as an aroma pleasing to the LORD, a burnt offering of one bull, one ram and seven male lambs a year old, all without defect. ³⁷With the bull, the ram and the lambs, prepare their grain offerings and drink offerings according to the number specified. ³⁸Include one male goat as a sin offering, in addition to the regular burnt offering with its grain offering and drink offering.

³⁹" 'In addition to what you vow and your freewill offerings, prepare these for the LORD at your appointed feasts: your burnt offerings, grain offerings, drink offerings and fellowship offerings.*b* ' "

⁴⁰Moses told the Israelites all that the LORD commanded him.

---

a7 Or *must fast*　　*b39* Traditionally *peace offerings*

Vows

30 Moses said to the heads of the tribes of Israel: "This is what the LORD commands: ²When a man makes a vow to the LORD or takes an oath to obligate himself by a pledge, he must not break his word but must do everything he said.

³"When a young woman still living in her father's house makes a vow to the LORD or obligates herself by a pledge ⁴and her father hears about her vow or pledge but says nothing to her, then all her vows and every pledge by which she obligated herself will stand. ⁵But if her father forbids her when he hears about it, none of her vows or the pledges by which she obligated herself will stand; the LORD will release her because her father has forbidden her.

⁶"If she marries after she makes a vow or after her lips utter a rash promise by which she obligates herself ⁷and her husband hears about it but says nothing to her, then her vows or the pledges by which she obligated herself will stand. ⁸But if her husband forbids her when he hears about it, he nullifies the vow that obligates her or the rash promise by which she obligates herself, and the LORD will release her.

⁹"Any vow or obligation taken by a widow or divorced woman will be binding on her.

¹⁰"If a woman living with her husband makes a vow or obligates herself by a pledge under oath ¹¹and her husband hears about it but says nothing to her and does not forbid her, then all her vows or the pledges by which she obligated herself will stand. ¹²But if her husband nullifies them when he hears about them, then none of the vows or pledges that came from her lips will stand. Her husband has nullified them, and the LORD will release her. ¹³Her husband may confirm or nullify any vow she makes or any sworn pledge to deny herself. ¹⁴But if her husband says nothing to her about it from day to day, then he confirms all her vows or the pledges binding on her. He confirms them by saying nothing to her when he hears about them. ¹⁵If, however, he nullifies them some time after he hears about them, then he is responsible for her guilt."

¹⁶These are the regulations the LORD gave Moses concerning relationships between a man and his wife, and between a father and his young daughter still living in his house.

Vengeance on the Midianites

31 The LORD said to Moses, ²"Take vengeance on the Midianites for the Israelites. After that, you will be gathered to your people."

³So Moses said to the people, "Arm some of your men to go to war against the Midianites and to carry out the LORD's vengeance on them. ⁴Send into battle a thousand men from each of the tribes of Israel." ⁵So twelve thousand men armed for battle, a thousand from each tribe, were supplied from the clans of Israel. ⁶Moses sent them into battle, a thousand from each tribe, along with Phinehas son of Eleazar, the priest, who took with him articles from the sanctuary and the trumpets for signaling.

⁷They fought against Midian, as the LORD commanded Moses, and killed every man. ⁸Among their victims were Evi, Rekem, Zur, Hur and Reba—the five kings of Midian. They also killed Balaam son of Beor with the sword. ⁹The Israelites captured the Midianite women and children and took all the Midianite herds, flocks and goods as plunder. ¹⁰They burned all the towns where the Midianites had settled, as well as all their camps. ¹¹They took all the plunder and spoils, including the people and animals, ¹²and brought the captives, spoils and plunder to Moses and Eleazar the priest and the Israelite assembly at their camp on the plains of Moab, by the Jordan across from Jericho.ᵃ

¹³Moses, Eleazar the priest and all the leaders of the community went to meet them outside the camp. ¹⁴Moses was angry with the officers of the army—the commanders of thousands and commanders of hundreds—who returned from the battle.

¹⁵"Have you allowed all the women to live?" he asked them. ¹⁶"They were the ones who followed Balaam's advice and were the means of turning the Israelites away from the LORD in what happened at Peor, so that a plague struck the LORD's people. ¹⁷Now kill all the boys. And kill every woman who has slept with a man, ¹⁸but save for yourselves every girl who has never slept with a man.

ᵃ12 Hebrew *Jordan of Jericho*; possibly an ancient name for the Jordan River

¹⁹"All of you who have killed anyone or touched anyone who was killed must stay outside the camp seven days. On the third and seventh days you must purify yourselves and your captives. ²⁰Purify every garment as well as everything made of leather, goat hair or wood."

²¹Then Eleazar the priest said to the soldiers who had gone into battle, "This is the requirement of the law that the LORD gave Moses: ²²Gold, silver, bronze, iron, tin, lead ²³and anything else that can withstand fire must be put through the fire, and then it will be clean. But it must also be purified with the water of cleansing. And whatever cannot withstand fire must be put through that water. ²⁴On the seventh day wash your clothes and you will be clean. Then you may come into the camp."

Dividing the Spoils

²⁵The LORD said to Moses, ²⁶"You and Eleazar the priest and the family heads of the community are to count all the people and animals that were captured. ²⁷Divide the spoils between the soldiers who took part in the battle and the rest of the community. ²⁸From the soldiers who fought in the battle, set apart as tribute for the LORD one out of every five hundred, whether persons, cattle, donkeys, sheep or goats. ²⁹Take this tribute from their half share and give it to Eleazar the priest as the LORD's part. ³⁰From the Israelites' half, select one out of every fifty, whether persons, cattle, donkeys, sheep, goats or other animals. Give them to the Levites, who are responsible for the care of the LORD's tabernacle." ³¹So Moses and Eleazar the priest did as the LORD commanded Moses.

³²The plunder remaining from the spoils that the soldiers took was 675,000 sheep, ³³72,000 cattle, ³⁴61,000 donkeys ³⁵and 32,000 women who had never slept with a man.

³⁶The half share of those who fought in the battle was:

337,500 sheep, ³⁷of which the tribute for the LORD was 675;
³⁸36,000 cattle, of which the tribute for the LORD was 72;
³⁹30,500 donkeys, of which the tribute for the LORD was 61;
⁴⁰16,000 people, of which the tribute for the LORD was 32.

⁴¹Moses gave the tribute to Eleazar the priest as the LORD's part, as the LORD commanded Moses.

⁴²The half belonging to the Israelites, which Moses set apart from that of the fighting men— ⁴³the community's half—was 337,500 sheep, ⁴⁴36,000 cattle, ⁴⁵30,500 donkeys ⁴⁶and 16,000 people. ⁴⁷From the Israelites' half, Moses selected one out of every fifty persons and animals, as the LORD commanded him, and gave them to the Levites, who were responsible for the care of the LORD's tabernacle.

⁴⁸Then the officers who were over the units of the army—the commanders of thousands and commanders of hundreds—went to Moses ⁴⁹and said to him, "Your servants have counted the soldiers under our command, and not one is missing. ⁵⁰So we have brought as an offering to the LORD the gold articles each of us acquired—armlets, bracelets, signet rings, earrings and necklaces—to make atonement for ourselves before the LORD."

⁵¹Moses and Eleazar the priest accepted from them the gold—all the crafted articles. ⁵²All the gold from the commanders of thousands and commanders of hundreds that Moses and Eleazar presented as a gift to the LORD weighed 16,750 shekels.ᵃ ⁵³Each soldier had taken plunder for himself. ⁵⁴Moses and Eleazar the priest accepted the gold from the commanders of thousands and commanders of hundreds and brought it into the Tent of Meeting as a memorial for the Israelites before the LORD.

The Transjordan Tribes

32 The Reubenites and Gadites, who had very large herds and flocks, saw that the lands of Jazer and Gilead were suitable for livestock. ²So they came to Moses and Eleazar the priest and to the leaders of the community, and said, ³"Ataroth, Dibon, Jazer, Nimrah, Heshbon, Elealeh, Sebam, Nebo and Beon— ⁴the land the LORD subdued before the people of Israel—are suitable for livestock, and your servants have livestock. ⁵If we have found favor in your eyes," they said, "let this land be given to your servants as our possession. Do not make us cross the Jordan."

⁶Moses said to the Gadites and Reu-

ᵃ52 That is, about 420 pounds (about 190 kilograms)

benites, "Shall your countrymen go to war while you sit here? ⁷Why do you discourage the Israelites from going over into the land the LORD has given them? ⁸This is what your fathers did when I sent them from Kadesh Barnea to look over the land. ⁹After they went up to the Valley of Eshcol and viewed the land, they discouraged the Israelites from entering the land the LORD had given them. ¹⁰The LORD's anger was aroused that day and he swore this oath: ¹¹'Because they have not followed me wholeheartedly, not one of the men twenty years old or more who came up out of Egypt will see the land I promised on oath to Abraham, Isaac and Jacob— ¹²not one except Caleb son of Jephunneh the Kenizzite and Joshua son of Nun, for they followed the LORD wholeheartedly.' ¹³The LORD's anger burned against Israel and he made them wander in the desert forty years, until the whole generation of those who had done evil in his sight was gone.

¹⁴"And here you are, a brood of sinners, standing in the place of your fathers and making the LORD even more angry with Israel. ¹⁵If you turn away from following him, he will again leave all this people in the desert, and you will be the cause of their destruction."

¹⁶Then they came up to him and said, "We would like to build pens here for our livestock and cities for our women and children. ¹⁷But we are ready to arm ourselves and go ahead of the Israelites until we have brought them to their place. Meanwhile our women and children will live in fortified cities, for protection from the inhabitants of the land. ¹⁸We will not return to our homes until every Israelite has received his inheritance. ¹⁹We will not receive any inheritance with them on the other side of the Jordan, because our inheritance has come to us on the east side of the Jordan."

²⁰Then Moses said to them, "If you will do this—if you will arm yourselves before the LORD for battle, ²¹and if all of you will go armed over the Jordan before the LORD until he has driven his enemies out before him— ²²then when the land is subdued before the LORD, you may return and be free from your obligation to the LORD and to Israel. And this land will be your possession before the LORD.

²³"But if you fail to do this, you will be sinning against the LORD; and you may be sure that your sin will find you out.

²⁴Build cities for your women and children, and pens for your flocks, but do what you have promised."

²⁵The Gadites and Reubenites said to Moses, "We your servants will do as our lord commands. ²⁶Our children and wives, our flocks and herds will remain here in the cities of Gilead. ²⁷But your servants, every man armed for battle, will cross over to fight before the LORD, just as our lord says."

²⁸Then Moses gave orders about them to Eleazar the priest and Joshua son of Nun and to the family heads of the Israelite tribes. ²⁹He said to them, "If the Gadites and Reubenites, every man armed for battle, cross over the Jordan with you before the LORD, then when the land is subdued before you, give them the land of Gilead as their possession. ³⁰But if they do not cross over with you armed, they must accept their possession with you in Canaan."

³¹The Gadites and Reubenites answered, "Your servants will do what the LORD has said. ³²We will cross over before the LORD into Canaan armed, but the property we inherit will be on this side of the Jordan."

³³Then Moses gave to the Gadites, the Reubenites and the half-tribe of Manasseh son of Joseph the kingdom of Sihon king of the Amorites and the kingdom of Og king of Bashan—the whole land with its cities and the territory around them.

³⁴The Gadites built up Dibon, Ataroth, Aroer, ³⁵Atroth Shophan, Jazer, Jogbehah, ³⁶Beth Nimrah and Beth Haran as fortified cities, and built pens for their flocks. ³⁷And the Reubenites rebuilt Heshbon, Elealeh and Kiriathaim, ³⁸as

POINT OF INTEREST

Numbers 32:5

The tribes of Reuben and Gad desired a different inheritance than the other ten tribes of Israel, and they submitted their request to the Israelite leaders for approval. Permission was granted, but with several conditions. Take a moment to read the rest of this chapter. What were these conditions, and why were they a good idea?

well as Nebo and Baal Meon (these names were changed) and Sibmah. They gave names to the cities they rebuilt.

³⁹The descendants of Makir son of Manasseh went to Gilead, captured it and drove out the Amorites who were there. ⁴⁰So Moses gave Gilead to the Makirites, the descendants of Manasseh, and they settled there. ⁴¹Jair, a descendant of Manasseh, captured their settlements and called them Havvoth Jair.ᵃ ⁴²And Nobah captured Kenath and its surrounding settlements and called it Nobah after himself.

Stages in Israel's Journey

33 Here are the stages in the journey of the Israelites when they came out of Egypt by divisions under the leadership of Moses and Aaron. ²At the LORD's command Moses recorded the stages in their journey. This is their journey by stages:

³The Israelites set out from Rameses on the fifteenth day of the first month, the day after the Passover. They marched out boldly in full view of all the Egyptians, ⁴who were burying all their firstborn, whom the LORD had struck down among them; for the LORD had brought judgment on their gods.

⁵The Israelites left Rameses and camped at Succoth.

⁶They left Succoth and camped at Etham, on the edge of the desert.

⁷They left Etham, turned back to Pi Hahiroth, to the east of Baal Zephon, and camped near Migdol.

⁸They left Pi Hahirothᵇ and passed through the sea into the desert, and when they had traveled for three days in the Desert of Etham, they camped at Marah.

⁹They left Marah and went to Elim, where there were twelve springs and seventy palm trees, and they camped there.

¹⁰They left Elim and camped by the Red Sea.ᶜ

¹¹They left the Red Sea and camped in the Desert of Sin.

¹²They left the Desert of Sin and camped at Dophkah.

¹³They left Dophkah and camped at Alush.

¹⁴They left Alush and camped at Rephidim, where there was no water for the people to drink.

¹⁵They left Rephidim and camped in the Desert of Sinai.

¹⁶They left the Desert of Sinai and camped at Kibroth Hattaavah.

¹⁷They left Kibroth Hattaavah and camped at Hazeroth.

¹⁸They left Hazeroth and camped at Rithmah.

¹⁹They left Rithmah and camped at Rimmon Perez.

²⁰They left Rimmon Perez and camped at Libnah.

²¹They left Libnah and camped at Rissah.

²²They left Rissah and camped at Kehelathah.

²³They left Kehelathah and camped at Mount Shepher.

²⁴They left Mount Shepher and camped at Haradah.

²⁵They left Haradah and camped at Makheloth.

²⁶They left Makheloth and camped at Tahath.

²⁷They left Tahath and camped at Terah.

²⁸They left Terah and camped at Mithcah.

²⁹They left Mithcah and camped at Hashmonah.

³⁰They left Hashmonah and camped at Moseroth.

³¹They left Moseroth and camped at Bene Jaakan.

³²They left Bene Jaakan and camped at Hor Haggidgad.

³³They left Hor Haggidgad and camped at Jotbathah.

³⁴They left Jotbathah and camped at Abronah.

³⁵They left Abronah and camped at Ezion Geber.

³⁶They left Ezion Geber and camped at Kadesh, in the Desert of Zin.

³⁷They left Kadesh and camped at Mount Hor, on the border of Edom. ³⁸At the LORD's command Aaron the priest went up Mount Hor, where he died on the first day of the fifth month of the fortieth year after the Israelites came out of Egypt. ³⁹Aaron was a hundred and

ᵃ41 Or *them the settlements of Jair*   ᵇ8 Many manuscripts of the Masoretic Text, Samaritan Pentateuch and Vulgate; most manuscripts of the Masoretic Text *left from before Hahiroth*
ᶜ10 Hebrew *Yam Suph*; that is, Sea of Reeds; also in verse 11

twenty-three years old when he died on Mount Hor.

⁴⁰The Canaanite king of Arad, who lived in the Negev of Canaan, heard that the Israelites were coming.

⁴¹They left Mount Hor and camped at Zalmonah.

⁴²They left Zalmonah and camped at Punon.

⁴³They left Punon and camped at Oboth.

⁴⁴They left Oboth and camped at Iye Abarim, on the border of Moab.

⁴⁵They left Iyim*a* and camped at Dibon Gad.

⁴⁶They left Dibon Gad and camped at Almon Diblathaim.

⁴⁷They left Almon Diblathaim and camped in the mountains of Abarim, near Nebo.

⁴⁸They left the mountains of Abarim and camped on the plains of Moab by the Jordan across from Jericho.*b* ⁴⁹There on the plains of Moab they camped along the Jordan from Beth Jeshimoth to Abel Shittim.

⁵⁰On the plains of Moab by the Jordan across from Jericho the LORD said to Moses, ⁵¹"Speak to the Israelites and say to them: 'When you cross the Jordan into Canaan, ⁵²drive out all the inhabitants of the land before you. Destroy all their carved images and their cast idols, and demolish all their high places. ⁵³Take possession of the land and settle in it, for I have given you the land to possess. ⁵⁴Distribute the land by lot, according to your clans. To a larger group give a larger inheritance, and to a smaller group a smaller one. Whatever falls to them by lot will be theirs. Distribute it according to your ancestral tribes.

⁵⁵" 'But if you do not drive out the inhabitants of the land, those you allow to remain will become barbs in your eyes and thorns in your sides. They will give you trouble in the land where you will live. ⁵⁶And then I will do to you what I plan to do to them.' "

Boundaries of Canaan

34 The LORD said to Moses, ²"Command the Israelites and say to them: 'When you enter Canaan, the land that will be allotted to you as an inheritance will have these boundaries:

³" 'Your southern side will include some of the Desert of Zin along the border of Edom. On the east, your southern boundary will start from the end of the Salt Sea,*c* ⁴cross south of Scorpion*d* Pass, continue on to Zin and go south of Kadesh Barnea. Then it will go to Hazar Addar and over to Azmon, ⁵where it will turn, join the Wadi of Egypt and end at the Sea.*e*

⁶" 'Your western boundary will be the coast of the Great Sea. This will be your boundary on the west.

⁷" 'For your northern boundary, run a line from the Great Sea to Mount Hor ⁸and from Mount Hor to Lebo*f* Hamath. Then the boundary will go to Zedad, ⁹continue to Ziphron and end at Hazar Enan. This will be your boundary on the north.

¹⁰" 'For your eastern boundary, run a line from Hazar Enan to Shepham. ¹¹The boundary will go down from Shepham to Riblah on the east side of Ain and continue along the slopes east of the Sea of Kinnereth.*g* ¹²Then the boundary will go down along the Jordan and end at the Salt Sea.

" 'This will be your land, with its boundaries on every side.' "

¹³Moses commanded the Israelites: "Assign this land by lot as an inheritance. The LORD has ordered that it be given to the nine and a half tribes, ¹⁴because the families of the tribe of Reuben, the tribe of Gad and the half-tribe of Manasseh have received their inheritance. ¹⁵These two and a half tribes have received their inheritance on the east side of the Jordan of Jericho,*h* toward the sunrise."

¹⁶The LORD said to Moses, ¹⁷"These are the names of the men who are to assign the land for you as an inheritance: Eleazar the priest and Joshua son of Nun. ¹⁸And appoint one leader from each tribe to help assign the land. ¹⁹These are their names:

Caleb son of Jephunneh,
    from the tribe of Judah;
²⁰Shemuel son of Ammihud,
    from the tribe of Simeon;

---

a45 That is, Iye Abarim   *b48* Hebrew *Jordan of Jericho*; possibly an ancient name for the Jordan River; also in verse 50   *c3* That is, the Dead Sea; also in verse 12   *d4* Hebrew *Akrabbim*   *e5* That is, the Mediterranean; also in verses 6 and 7   *f8* Or *to the entrance to*   *g11* That is, Galilee   *h15* *Jordan of Jericho* was possibly an ancient name for the Jordan River.

21Elidad son of Kislon,
from the tribe of Benjamin;
22Bukki son of Jogli,
the leader from the tribe of Dan;
23Hanniel son of Ephod,
the leader from the tribe of Manasseh son of Joseph;
24Kemuel son of Shiphtan,
the leader from the tribe of Ephraim son of Joseph;
25Elizaphan son of Parnach,
the leader from the tribe of Zebulun;
26Paltiel son of Azzan,
the leader from the tribe of Issachar;
27Ahihud son of Shelomi,
the leader from the tribe of Asher;
28Pedahel son of Ammihud,
the leader from the tribe of Naphtali."
29These are the men the LORD commanded to assign the inheritance to the Israelites in the land of Canaan.

Towns for the Levites

35 On the plains of Moab by the Jordan across from Jericho,*a* the LORD said to Moses, 2"Command the Israelites to give the Levites towns to live in from the inheritance the Israelites will possess. And give them pasturelands around the towns. 3Then they will have towns to live in and pasturelands for their cattle, flocks and all their other livestock.

4"The pasturelands around the towns that you give the Levites will extend out fifteen hundred feet*b* from the town wall. 5Outside the town, measure three thousand feet*c* on the east side, three thousand on the south side, three thousand on the west and three thousand on the north, with the town in the center. They will have this area as pastureland for the towns.

Cities of Refuge

6"Six of the towns you give the Levites will be cities of refuge, to which a person who has killed someone may flee. In addition, give them forty-two other towns. 7In all you must give the Levites forty-eight towns, together with their pasturelands. 8The towns you give the Levites from the land the Israelites possess are to be given in proportion to the inheritance of each tribe: Take many towns from a tribe that has many, but few from one that has few."

9Then the LORD said to Moses: 10"Speak to the Israelites and say to them: 'When you cross the Jordan into Canaan, 11select some towns to be your cities of refuge, to which a person who has killed someone accidentally may flee. 12They will be places of refuge from the avenger, so that a person accused of murder may not die before he stands trial before the assembly. 13These six towns you give will be your cities of refuge. 14Give three on this side of the Jordan and three in Canaan as cities of refuge. 15These six towns will be a place of refuge for Israelites, aliens and any other people living among them, so that anyone who has killed another accidentally can flee there.

16" 'If a man strikes someone with an iron object so that he dies, he is a murderer; the murderer shall be put to death. 17Or if anyone has a stone in his hand that could kill, and he strikes someone so that he dies, he is a murderer; the murderer shall be put to death. 18Or if anyone has a wooden object in his hand that could kill, and he hits someone so that he dies, he is a murderer; the murderer shall be put to death. 19The avenger of blood shall put the murderer to death; when he meets him, he shall put him to death. 20If anyone with malice aforethought shoves another or throws something at him intentionally so that he dies 21or if in hostility he hits him with his fist so that he dies, that person shall be put to death; he is a murderer. The avenger of blood shall put the murderer to death when he meets him.

22" 'But if without hostility someone suddenly shoves another or throws something at him unintentionally 23or, without seeing him, drops a stone on him that could kill him, and he dies, then since he was not his enemy and he did not intend to harm him, 24the assembly must judge between him and the avenger of blood according to these regulations. 25The assembly must protect the one accused of murder from the avenger of blood and send him back to the city of refuge to which he fled. He must stay there until the death of the high priest, who was anointed with the holy oil.

a 1 Hebrew Jordan of Jericho; possibly an ancient name for the Jordan River   b 4 Hebrew a thousand cubits (about 450 meters)   c 5 Hebrew two thousand cubits (about 900 meters)

²⁶" 'But if the accused ever goes outside the limits of the city of refuge to which he has fled ²⁷and the avenger of blood finds him outside the city, the avenger of blood may kill the accused without being guilty of murder. ²⁸The accused must stay in his city of refuge until the death of the high priest; only after the death of the high priest may he return to his own property.

²⁹" 'These are to be legal requirements for you throughout the generations to come, wherever you live.

³⁰" 'Anyone who kills a person is to be put to death as a murderer only on the testimony of witnesses. But no one is to be put to death on the testimony of only one witness.

³¹" 'Do not accept a ransom for the life of a murderer, who deserves to die. He must surely be put to death.

³²" 'Do not accept a ransom for anyone who has fled to a city of refuge and so allow him to go back and live on his own land before the death of the high priest.

³³" 'Do not pollute the land where you are. Bloodshed pollutes the land, and atonement cannot be made for the land on which blood has been shed, except by the blood of the one who shed it. ³⁴Do not defile the land where you live and where I dwell, for I, the LORD, dwell among the Israelites.' "

Inheritance of Zelophehad's Daughters

36 The family heads of the clan of Gilead son of Makir, the son of Manasseh, who were from the clans of the descendants of Joseph, came and spoke before Moses and the leaders, the heads of the Israelite families. ²They said, "When the LORD commanded my lord to give the land as an inheritance to the Israelites by lot, he ordered you to give the inheritance of our brother Zelophehad to his daughters. ³Now suppose they marry men from other Israelite tribes; then their inheritance will be taken from our ancestral inheritance and added to that of the tribe they marry into. And so part of the inheritance allotted to us will be taken away. ⁴When the Year of Jubilee for the Israelites comes, their inheritance will be added to that of the tribe into which they marry, and their property will be taken from the tribal inheritance of our forefathers."

⁵Then at the LORD's command Moses gave this order to the Israelites: "What the tribe of the descendants of Joseph is saying is right. ⁶This is what the LORD commands for Zelophehad's daughters: They may marry anyone they please as long as they marry within the tribal clan of their father. ⁷No inheritance in Israel is to pass from tribe to tribe, for every Israelite shall keep the tribal land inherited from his forefathers. ⁸Every daughter who inherits land in any Israelite tribe must marry someone in her father's tribal clan, so that every Israelite will possess the inheritance of his fathers. ⁹No inheritance may pass from tribe to tribe, for each Israelite tribe is to keep the land it inherits."

¹⁰So Zelophehad's daughters did as the LORD commanded Moses. ¹¹Zelophehad's daughters—Mahlah, Tirzah, Hoglah, Milcah and Noah—married their cousins on their father's side. ¹²They married within the clans of the descendants of Manasseh son of Joseph, and their inheritance remained in their father's clan and tribe.

¹³These are the commands and regulations the LORD gave through Moses to the Israelites on the plains of Moab by the Jordan across from Jericho.ᵃ

ᵃ 13 Hebrew *Jordan of Jericho*; possibly an ancient name for the Jordan River

POINT OF INTEREST

Numbers 35:25

In ancient times, the family or clan of an injured party dispensed justice and often exacted revenge far in excess of the crime. Because cities of refuge offered protection from retribution and an opportunity for trial, they were a compassionate innovation in a land of unbridled vengeance.

Reminders. We all need them,

and the most important ones often come at crossroads in

our lives. In Deuteronomy, Moses and the people of Israel

are at a crossroads. Behind them are forty years of desert

wandering. Before them stretches a land of promise and

opportunity. At this key moment, Moses reminds them to

obey the laws God has established. He reminds them how

God has loved and cared for them and

that they are to return the love

of the awesome God they serve.

DEUTERONOMY

The Command to Leave Horeb

These are the words Moses spoke to all Israel in the desert east of the Jordan— that is, in the Arabah—opposite Suph, between Paran and Tophel, Laban, Hazeroth and Dizahab. ²(It takes eleven days to go from Horeb to Kadesh Barnea by the Mount Seir road.)

³In the fortieth year, on the first day of the eleventh month, Moses proclaimed to the Israelites all that the LORD had commanded him concerning them. ⁴This was after he had defeated Sihon king of the Amorites, who reigned in Heshbon, and at Edrei had defeated Og king of Bashan, who reigned in Ashtaroth.

⁵East of the Jordan in the territory of Moab, Moses began to expound this law, saying:

⁶The LORD our God said to us at Horeb, "You have stayed long enough at this mountain. ⁷Break camp and advance into the hill country of the Amorites; go to all the neighboring peoples in the Arabah, in the mountains, in the western foothills, in the Negev and along the coast, to the land of the Canaanites and to Lebanon, as far as the great river, the Euphrates. ⁸See, I have given you this land. Go in and take possession of the land that the LORD swore he would give to your fathers—to Abraham, Isaac and Jacob— and to their descendants after them."

The Appointment of Leaders

⁹At that time I said to you, "You are too heavy a burden for me to carry alone. ¹⁰The LORD your God has increased your numbers so that today you are as many as the stars in the sky. ¹¹May the LORD, the God of your fathers, increase you a thousand times and bless you as he has promised! ¹²But how can I bear your problems and your burdens and your disputes all by myself? ¹³Choose some wise, understanding and respected men from

each of your tribes, and I will set them over you."

¹⁴You answered me, "What you propose to do is good."

¹⁵So I took the leading men of your tribes, wise and respected men, and appointed them to have authority over you—as commanders of thousands, of hundreds, of fifties and of tens and as tribal officials. ¹⁶And I charged your judges at that time: Hear the disputes between your brothers and judge fairly, whether the case is between brother Israelites or between one of them and an alien. ¹⁷Do not show partiality in judging; hear both small and great alike. Do not be afraid of any man, for judgment belongs to God. Bring me any case too hard for you, and I will hear it. ¹⁸And at that time I told you everything you were to do.

Spies Sent Out

¹⁹Then, as the LORD our God commanded us, we set out from Horeb and went toward the hill country of the Amorites through all that vast and dreadful desert that you have seen, and so we reached Kadesh Barnea. ²⁰Then I said to you, "You have reached the hill country of the Amorites, which the LORD our God is giving us. ²¹See, the LORD your God has given you the land. Go up and take possession of it as the LORD, the God of your fathers, told you. Do not be afraid; do not be discouraged."

²²Then all of you came to me and said, "Let us send men ahead to spy out the land for us and bring back a report about the route we are to take and the towns we will come to."

²³The idea seemed good to me; so I selected twelve of you, one man from each tribe. ²⁴They left and went up into the hill country, and came to the Valley of Eshcol and explored it. ²⁵Taking with them some of the fruit of the land, they brought it down to us and reported, "It is a good land that the LORD our God is giving us."

Rebellion Against the LORD

²⁶But you were unwilling to go up; you rebelled against the command of the LORD your God. ²⁷You grumbled in your tents and said, "The LORD hates us; so he brought us out of Egypt to deliver us into the hands of the Amorites to destroy us. ²⁸Where can we go? Our brothers have made us lose heart. They say, 'The peo-

ple are stronger and taller than we are; the cities are large, with walls up to the sky. We even saw the Anakites there.' "

²⁹Then I said to you, "Do not be terrified; do not be afraid of them. ³⁰The LORD your God, who is going before you, will fight for you, as he did for you in Egypt, before your very eyes, ³¹and in the desert. There you saw how the LORD your God carried you, as a father carries his son, all the way you went until you reached this place."

³²In spite of this, you did not trust in the LORD your God, ³³who went ahead of you on your journey, in fire by night and in a cloud by day, to search out places for you to camp and to show you the way you should go.

³⁴When the LORD heard what you said, he was angry and solemnly swore: ³⁵"Not a man of this evil generation shall see the good land I swore to give your forefathers, ³⁶except Caleb son of Jephunneh. He will see it, and I will give him and his descendants the land he set his feet on, because he followed the LORD wholeheartedly."

³⁷Because of you the LORD became angry with me also and said, "You shall not enter it, either. ³⁸But your assistant, Joshua son of Nun, will enter it. Encourage him, because he will lead Israel to inherit it. ³⁹And the little ones that you said would be taken captive, your children who do not yet know good from bad—they will enter the land. I will give it to them and they will take possession of it. ⁴⁰But as for you, turn around and set out toward the desert along the route to the Red Sea.ᵃ"

⁴¹Then you replied, "We have sinned against the LORD. We will go up and fight, as the LORD our God commanded us." So every one of you put on his weapons, thinking it easy to go up into the hill country.

⁴²But the LORD said to me, "Tell them, 'Do not go up and fight, because I will not be with you. You will be defeated by your enemies.' "

⁴³So I told you, but you would not listen. You rebelled against the LORD's command and in your arrogance you marched up into the hill country. ⁴⁴The Amorites who lived in those hills came out against you; they chased you like a swarm of bees and beat you down from

ᵃ40 Hebrew *Yam Suph*; that is, Sea of Reeds

Seir all the way to Hormah. ⁴⁵You came back and wept before the LORD, but he paid no attention to your weeping and turned a deaf ear to you. ⁴⁶And so you stayed in Kadesh many days—all the time you spent there.

Wanderings in the Desert

2 Then we turned back and set out toward the desert along the route to the Red Sea,ᵃ as the LORD had directed me. For a long time we made our way around the hill country of Seir.

²Then the LORD said to me, ³"You have made your way around this hill country long enough; now turn north. ⁴Give the people these orders: 'You are about to pass through the territory of your brothers the descendants of Esau, who live in Seir. They will be afraid of you, but be very careful. ⁵Do not provoke them to war, for I will not give you any of their land, not even enough to put your foot on. I have given Esau the hill country of Seir as his own. ⁶You are to pay them in silver for the food you eat and the water you drink.' "

⁷The LORD your God has blessed you in all the work of your hands. He has watched over your journey through this vast desert. These forty years the LORD your God has been with you, and you have not lacked anything.

⁸So we went on past our brothers the descendants of Esau, who live in Seir. We turned from the Arabah road, which comes up from Elath and Ezion Geber, and traveled along the desert road of Moab.

⁹Then the LORD said to me, "Do not harass the Moabites or provoke them to war, for I will not give you any part of their land. I have given Ar to the descendants of Lot as a possession."

¹⁰(The Emites used to live there—a people strong and numerous, and as tall as the Anakites. ¹¹Like the Anakites, they too were considered Rephaites, but the Moabites called them Emites. ¹²Horites used to live in Seir, but the descendants of Esau drove them out. They destroyed the Horites from before them and settled in their place, just as Israel did in the land the LORD gave them as their possession.)

¹³And the LORD said, "Now get up and cross the Zered Valley." So we crossed the valley.

¹⁴Thirty-eight years passed from the time we left Kadesh Barnea until we crossed the Zered Valley. By then, that entire generation of fighting men had perished from the camp, as the LORD had sworn to them. ¹⁵The LORD's hand was against them until he had completely eliminated them from the camp.

¹⁶Now when the last of these fighting men among the people had died, ¹⁷the LORD said to me, ¹⁸"Today you are to pass by the region of Moab at Ar. ¹⁹When you come to the Ammonites, do not harass them or provoke them to war, for I will not give you possession of any land belonging to the Ammonites. I have given it as a possession to the descendants of Lot."

²⁰(That too was considered a land of the Rephaites, who used to live there; but the Ammonites called them Zamzummites. ²¹They were a people strong and numerous, and as tall as the Anakites. The LORD destroyed them from before the Ammonites, who drove them out and settled in their place. ²²The LORD had done the same for the descendants of Esau, who lived in Seir, when he destroyed the Horites from before them. They drove them out and have lived in their place to this day. ²³And as for the Avvites who lived in villages as far as Gaza, the Caphtorites coming out from Caphtorᵇ destroyed them and settled in their place.)

Defeat of Sihon King of Heshbon

²⁴"Set out now and cross the Arnon Gorge. See, I have given into your hand Sihon the Amorite, king of Heshbon, and his country. Begin to take possession of it and engage him in battle. ²⁵This very day I will begin to put the terror and fear of you on all the nations under heaven. They will hear reports of you and will tremble and be in anguish because of you."

²⁶From the desert of Kedemoth I sent messengers to Sihon king of Heshbon offering peace and saying, ²⁷"Let us pass through your country. We will stay on the main road; we will not turn aside to the right or to the left. ²⁸Sell us food to eat and water to drink for their price in silver. Only let us pass through on foot— ²⁹as the descendants of Esau, who live in Seir, and the Moabites, who live in Ar, did for us—until we cross the Jordan into the land the LORD our God is giving us."

ᵃ1 Hebrew *Yam Suph*; that is, Sea of Reeds
ᵇ23 That is, Crete

30But Sihon king of Heshbon refused to let us pass through. For the LORD your God had made his spirit stubborn and his heart obstinate in order to give him into your hands, as he has now done.

31The LORD said to me, "See, I have begun to deliver Sihon and his country over to you. Now begin to conquer and possess his land."

32When Sihon and all his army came out to meet us in battle at Jahaz, **33**the LORD our God delivered him over to us and we struck him down, together with his sons and his whole army. **34**At that time we took all his towns and completely destroyed[a] them—men, women and children. We left no survivors. **35**But the livestock and the plunder from the towns we had captured we carried off for ourselves. **36**From Aroer on the rim of the Arnon Gorge, and from the town in the gorge, even as far as Gilead, not one town was too strong for us. The LORD our God gave us all of them. **37**But in accordance with the command of the LORD our God, you did not encroach on any of the land of the Ammonites, neither the land along the course of the Jabbok nor that around the towns in the hills.

Defeat of Og King of Bashan

3 Next we turned and went up along the road toward Bashan, and Og king of Bashan with his whole army marched out to meet us in battle at Edrei. **2**The LORD said to me, "Do not be afraid of him, for I have handed him over to you with his whole army and his land. Do to him what you did to Sihon king of the Amorites, who reigned in Heshbon."

3So the LORD our God also gave into our hands Og king of Bashan and all his army. We struck them down, leaving no survivors. **4**At that time we took all his cities. There was not one of the sixty cities that we did not take from them—the whole region of Argob, Og's kingdom in Bashan. **5**All these cities were fortified with high walls and with gates and bars, and there were also a great many unwalled villages. **6**We completely destroyed[a] them, as we had done with Sihon king of Heshbon, destroying[a] every city—men, women and children. **7**But all the livestock and the plunder from their cities we carried off for ourselves.

8So at that time we took from these two kings of the Amorites the territory east of the Jordan, from the Arnon Gorge as far as Mount Hermon. **9**(Hermon is called Sirion by the Sidonians; the Amorites call it Senir.) **10**We took all the towns on the plateau, and all Gilead, and all Bashan as far as Salecah and Edrei, towns of Og's kingdom in Bashan. **11**(Only Og king of Bashan was left of the remnant of the Rephaites. His bed[b] was made of iron and was more than thirteen feet long and six feet wide.[c] It is still in Rabbah of the Ammonites.)

Division of the Land

12Of the land that we took over at that time, I gave the Reubenites and the Gadites the territory north of Aroer by the Arnon Gorge, including half the hill country of Gilead, together with its towns. **13**The rest of Gilead and also all of Bashan, the kingdom of Og, I gave to the half tribe of Manasseh. (The whole region of Argob in Bashan used to be known as a land of the Rephaites. **14**Jair, a descendant of Manasseh, took the whole region of Argob as far as the border of the Geshurites and the Maacathites; it was named after him, so that to this day Bashan is called Havvoth Jair.[d]) **15**And I gave Gilead to Makir. **16**But to the Reubenites and the Gadites I gave the territory extending from Gilead down to the Arnon Gorge (the middle of the gorge being the border) and out to the Jabbok River, which is the border of the Ammonites. **17**Its western border was

---

a 34,6 The Hebrew term refers to the irrevocable giving over of things or persons to the LORD, often by totally destroying them.   *b 11* Or *sarcophagus*   *c 11* Hebrew *nine cubits long and four cubits wide* (about 4 meters long and 1.8 meters wide)   *d 14* Or *called the settlements of Jair*

POINT OF INTEREST

Deuteronomy 3:10

This reference to Og highlights three facts: (1) Huge warriors lived in Canaan (see Numbers 13:33); (2) these giants were significant enough for special mention; (3) they were no match for the armies of God! God is still in control. He can turn our defeats into victory in a split second when we trust him to.

the Jordan in the Arabah, from Kinnereth to the Sea of the Arabah (the Salt Sea*ª*), below the slopes of Pisgah.

¹⁸I commanded you at that time: "The LORD your God has given you this land to take possession of it. But all your able-bodied men, armed for battle, must cross over ahead of your brother Israelites. ¹⁹However, your wives, your children and your livestock (I know you have much livestock) may stay in the towns I have given you, ²⁰until the LORD gives rest to your brothers as he has to you, and they too have taken over the land that the LORD your God is giving them, across the Jordan. After that, each of you may go back to the possession I have given you."

Moses Forbidden to Cross the Jordan

²¹At that time I commanded Joshua: "You have seen with your own eyes all that the LORD your God has done to these two kings. The LORD will do the same to all the kingdoms over there where you are going. ²²Do not be afraid of them; the LORD your God himself will fight for you."

²³At that time I pleaded with the LORD: ²⁴"O Sovereign LORD, you have begun to show to your servant your greatness and your strong hand. For what god is there in heaven or on earth who can do the deeds and mighty works you do? ²⁵Let me go over and see the good land beyond the Jordan—that fine hill country and Lebanon."

²⁶But because of you the LORD was angry with me and would not listen to me. "That is enough," the LORD said. "Do not speak to me anymore about this matter. ²⁷Go up to the top of Pisgah and look west and north and south and east. Look at the land with your own eyes, since you are not going to cross this Jordan. ²⁸But commission Joshua, and encourage and strengthen him, for he will lead this people across and will cause them to inherit the land that you will see." ²⁹So we stayed in the valley near Beth Peor.

Obedience Commanded

4 Hear now, O Israel, the decrees and laws I am about to teach you. Follow them so that you may live and may go in and take possession of the land that the LORD, the God of your fathers, is giving you. ²Do not add to what I command you and do not subtract from it, but keep the commands of the LORD your God that I give you.

³You saw with your own eyes what the LORD did at Baal Peor. The LORD your God destroyed from among you everyone who followed the Baal of Peor, ⁴but all of you who held fast to the LORD your God are still alive today.

⁵See, I have taught you decrees and laws as the LORD my God commanded me, so that you may follow them in the land you are entering to take possession of it. ⁶Observe them carefully, for this will show your wisdom and understanding to the nations, who will hear about all these decrees and say, "Surely this great nation is a wise and understanding people." ⁷What other nation is so great as to have their gods near them the way the LORD our God is near us whenever we pray to him? ⁸And what other nation is so great as to have such righteous decrees and laws as this body of laws I am setting before you today?

⁹Only be careful, and watch yourselves closely so that you do not forget the things your eyes have seen or let them slip from your heart as long as you live. Teach them to your children and to their children after them. ¹⁰Remember the day you stood before the LORD your God at Horeb, when he said to me, "Assemble the people before me to hear my words so that they may learn to revere me as long as they live in the land and may teach them to their children." ¹¹You came near and stood at the foot of the mountain while it blazed with fire to the very heavens, with black clouds and deep darkness. ¹²Then the LORD spoke to you out of the fire. You heard the sound of words but saw no form; there was only a voice. ¹³He declared to you his covenant, the Ten Commandments, which he commanded you to follow and then wrote them on two stone tablets. ¹⁴And the LORD directed me at that time to teach you the decrees and laws you are to follow in the land that you are crossing the Jordan to possess.

Idolatry Forbidden

¹⁵You saw no form of any kind the day the LORD spoke to you at Horeb out of the fire. Therefore watch yourselves very carefully, ¹⁶so that you do not become corrupt and make for yourselves an idol, an image of any shape, whether formed like a man or a woman, ¹⁷or like any ani-

ª17 That is, the Dead Sea

mal on earth or any bird that flies in the air, ¹⁸or like any creature that moves along the ground or any fish in the waters below. ¹⁹And when you look up to the sky and see the sun, the moon and the stars—all the heavenly array—do not be enticed into bowing down to them and worshiping things the LORD your God has apportioned to all the nations under heaven. ²⁰But as for you, the LORD took you and brought you out of the iron-smelting furnace, out of Egypt, to be the people of his inheritance, as you now are.

²¹The LORD was angry with me because of you, and he solemnly swore that I would not cross the Jordan and enter the good land the LORD your God is giving you as your inheritance. ²²I will die in this land; I will not cross the Jordan; but you are about to cross over and take possession of that good land. ²³Be careful not to forget the covenant of the LORD your God that he made with you; do not make for yourselves an idol in the form of anything the LORD your God has forbidden. ²⁴For the LORD your God is a consuming fire, a jealous God.

²⁵After you have had children and grandchildren and have lived in the land a long time—if you then become corrupt and make any kind of idol, doing evil in the eyes of the LORD your God and provoking him to anger, ²⁶I call heaven and earth as witnesses against you this day that you will quickly perish from the land that you are crossing the Jordan to possess. You will not live there long but will certainly be destroyed. ²⁷The LORD will scatter you among the peoples, and only a few of you will survive among the nations to which the LORD will drive you. ²⁸There you will worship man-made gods of wood and stone, which cannot see or hear or eat or smell. ²⁹But if from there you seek the LORD your God, you will find him if you look for him with all your heart and with all your soul. ³⁰When you are in distress and all these things have happened to you, then in later days you will return to the LORD your God and obey him. ³¹For the LORD your God is a merciful God; he will not abandon or destroy you or forget the covenant with your forefathers, which he confirmed to them by oath.

The LORD Is God

³²Ask now about the former days, long before your time, from the day God creat-ed man on the earth; ask from one end of the heavens to the other. Has anything so great as this ever happened, or has anything like it ever been heard of? ³³Has any other people heard the voice of God*a* speaking out of fire, as you have, and lived? ³⁴Has any god ever tried to take for himself one nation out of another nation, by testings, by miraculous signs and wonders, by war, by a mighty hand and an outstretched arm, or by great and awesome deeds, like all the things the LORD your God did for you in Egypt before your very eyes?

³⁵You were shown these things so that you might know that the LORD is God; besides him there is no other. ³⁶From heaven he made you hear his voice to discipline you. On earth he showed you his great fire, and you heard his words from out of the fire. ³⁷Because he loved your forefathers and chose their descendants after them, he brought you out of Egypt by his Presence and his great strength, ³⁸to drive out before you nations greater and stronger than you and to bring you into their land to give it to you for your inheritance, as it is today.

³⁹Acknowledge and take to heart this day that the LORD is God in heaven above and on the earth below. There is no other. ⁴⁰Keep his decrees and commands, which I am giving you today, so that it may go well with you and your children after you and that you may live long in the land the LORD your God gives you for all time.

Cities of Refuge

⁴¹Then Moses set aside three cities east of the Jordan, ⁴²to which anyone who had killed a person could flee if he had unintentionally killed his neighbor without malice aforethought. He could flee into one of these cities and save his life. ⁴³The cities were these: Bezer in the desert plateau, for the Reubenites; Ramoth in Gilead, for the Gadites; and Golan in Bashan, for the Manassites.

Introduction to the Law

⁴⁴This is the law Moses set before the Israelites. ⁴⁵These are the stipulations, decrees and laws Moses gave them when they came out of Egypt ⁴⁶and were in the valley near Beth Peor east of the Jordan, in the land of Sihon king of the Amorites,

a33 Or *of a god*

who reigned in Heshbon and was defeated by Moses and the Israelites as they came out of Egypt. ⁴⁷They took possession of his land and the land of Og king of Bashan, the two Amorite kings east of the Jordan. ⁴⁸This land extended from Aroer on the rim of the Arnon Gorge to Mount Siyon*ᵃ* (that is, Hermon), ⁴⁹and included all the Arabah east of the Jordan, as far as the Sea of the Arabah,*ᵇ* below the slopes of Pisgah.

The Ten Commandments

5 Moses summoned all Israel and said: Hear, O Israel, the decrees and laws I declare in your hearing today. Learn them and be sure to follow them. ²The LORD our God made a covenant with us at Horeb. ³It was not with our fathers that the LORD made this covenant, but with us, with all of us who are alive here today. ⁴The LORD spoke to you face to face out of the fire on the mountain. ⁵(At that time I stood between the LORD and you to declare to you the word of the LORD, because you were afraid of the fire and did not go up the mountain.) And he said:

⁶"I am the LORD your God, who brought you out of Egypt, out of the land of slavery.

⁷"You shall have no other gods before*ᶜ* me.

⁸"You shall not make for yourself an idol in the form of anything in heaven above or on the earth beneath or in the waters below. ⁹You shall not bow down to them or worship them; for I, the LORD your God, am a jealous God, punishing the children for the sin of the fathers to the third and fourth generation of those who hate me, ¹⁰but showing love to a thousand ⌐generations⌐ of those who love me and keep my commandments.

¹¹"You shall not misuse the name of the LORD your God, for the LORD will not hold anyone guiltless who misuses his name.

¹²"Observe the Sabbath day by keeping it holy, as the LORD your God has commanded you. ¹³Six days you shall labor and do all your work, ¹⁴but the seventh day is a Sabbath to the LORD your God. On it you shall not do any work, neither you, nor your son or daughter, nor your manservant or maidservant, nor your ox, your donkey or any of your animals, nor the alien within your gates, so that your manservant and maidservant may rest, as you do. ¹⁵Remember that you were slaves in Egypt and that the LORD your God brought you out of there with a mighty hand and an outstretched arm. Therefore the LORD your God has commanded you to observe the Sabbath day.

¹⁶"Honor your father and your mother, as the LORD your God has commanded you, so that you may live long and that it may go well with you in the land the LORD your God is giving you.

¹⁷"You shall not murder.

¹⁸"You shall not commit adultery.

¹⁹"You shall not steal.

²⁰"You shall not give false testimony against your neighbor.

²¹"You shall not covet your neighbor's wife. You shall not set your desire on your neighbor's house or land, his manservant or maidservant, his ox or donkey, or anything that belongs to your neighbor."

ᵃ48 Hebrew; Syriac (see also Deut. 3:9) *Sirion*
ᵇ49 That is, the Dead Sea   *ᶜ7* Or *besides*

POINT OF INTEREST

Deuteronomy 5:1

If a police officer stops you for a traffic violation, will your offense be overlooked if you can accurately quote the traffic code? Of course not. Laws are made to be obeyed. God's laws must be obeyed too. Jesus put it this way: "Why do you call me, 'Lord, Lord,' and do not do what I say?" (Luke 6:46).

²²These are the commandments the LORD proclaimed in a loud voice to your whole assembly there on the mountain from out of the fire, the cloud and the deep darkness; and he added nothing more. Then he wrote them on two stone tablets and gave them to me.

²³When you heard the voice out of the darkness, while the mountain was ablaze with fire, all the leading men of your tribes and your elders came to me. ²⁴And you said, "The LORD our God has shown us his glory and his majesty, and we have heard his voice from the fire. Today we have seen that a man can live even if God speaks with him. ²⁵But now, why should we die? This great fire will consume us, and we will die if we hear the voice of the LORD our God any longer. ²⁶For what mortal man has ever heard the voice of the living God speaking out of fire, as we have, and survived? ²⁷Go near and listen to all that the LORD our God says. Then tell us whatever the LORD our God tells you. We will listen and obey."

²⁸The LORD heard you when you spoke to me and the LORD said to me, "I have heard what this people said to you. Everything they said was good. ²⁹Oh, that their hearts would be inclined to fear me and keep all my commands always, so that it might go well with them and their children forever!

³⁰"Go, tell them to return to their tents. ³¹But you stay here with me so that I may give you all the commands, decrees and laws you are to teach them to follow in the land I am giving them to possess."

³²So be careful to do what the LORD your God has commanded you; do not turn aside to the right or to the left. ³³Walk in all the way that the LORD your God has commanded you, so that you may live and prosper and prolong your days in the land that you will possess.

Love the LORD Your God

6 These are the commands, decrees and laws the LORD your God directed me to teach you to observe in the land that you are crossing the Jordan to possess, ²so that you, your children and their children after them may fear the LORD your God as long as you live by keeping all his decrees and commands that I give you, and so that you may enjoy long life. ³Hear, O Israel, and be careful to obey so that it may go well with you and that you may increase greatly in a land flowing with milk and honey, just as the LORD, the God of your fathers, promised you.

⁴Hear, O Israel: The LORD our God, the LORD is one.ᵃ ⁵Love the LORD your God with all your heart and with all your soul and with all your strength. ⁶These commandments that I give you today are to be upon your hearts. ⁷Impress them on your children. Talk about them when you sit at home and when you walk along the road, when you lie down and when you get up. ⁸Tie them as symbols on your hands and bind them on your foreheads. ⁹Write them on the doorframes of your houses and on your gates.

¹⁰When the LORD your God brings you into the land he swore to your fathers, to Abraham, Isaac and Jacob, to give you—a land with large, flourishing cities you did not build, ¹¹houses filled with all kinds of good things you did not provide, wells you did not dig, and vineyards and olive groves you did not plant—then when you eat and are satisfied, ¹²be careful that you do not forget the LORD, who brought you out of Egypt, out of the land of slavery.

¹³Fear the LORD your God, serve him only and take your oaths in his name. ¹⁴Do not follow other gods, the gods of the peoples around you; ¹⁵for the LORD your God, who is among you, is a jealous God and his anger will burn against you, and he will destroy you from the face of the land. ¹⁶Do not test the LORD your God as you did at Massah. ¹⁷Be sure to keep the commands of the LORD your God and the stipulations and decrees he has given you. ¹⁸Do what is right and good in the LORD's sight, so that it may go well with you and you may go in and take over the

ᵃ4 Or *The LORD our God is one LORD*; or *The LORD is our God, the LORD is one*; or *The LORD is our God, the LORD alone*

POINT OF INTEREST

Deuteronomy 6:4

The words of this verse constitute the ancient *shema*, the daily declaration of the Hebrew faith. When asked in Matthew 22:36 to identify the greatest commandment, Jesus began here with Deuteronomy 6:5.

good land that the LORD promised on oath to your forefathers, ¹⁹thrusting out all your enemies before you, as the LORD said.

²⁰In the future, when your son asks you, "What is the meaning of the stipulations, decrees and laws the LORD our God has commanded you?" ²¹tell him: "We were slaves of Pharaoh in Egypt, but the LORD brought us out of Egypt with a mighty hand. ²²Before our eyes the LORD sent miraculous signs and wonders— great and terrible—upon Egypt and Pharaoh and his whole household. ²³But he brought us out from there to bring us in and give us the land that he promised on oath to our forefathers. ²⁴The LORD commanded us to obey all these decrees and to fear the LORD our God, so that we might always prosper and be kept alive, as is the case today. ²⁵And if we are careful to obey all this law before the LORD our God, as he has commanded us, that will be our righteousness."

Driving Out the Nations

7 When the LORD your God brings you into the land you are entering to possess and drives out before you many nations—the Hittites, Girgashites, Amorites, Canaanites, Perizzites, Hivites and Jebusites, seven nations larger and stronger than you— ²and when the LORD your God has delivered them over to you and you have defeated them, then you must destroy them totally.ᵃ Make no treaty with them, and show them no mercy. ³Do not intermarry with them. Do not give your daughters to their sons or take their daughters for your sons, ⁴for they will turn your sons away from following me to serve other gods, and the LORD's anger will burn against you and will quickly destroy you. ⁵This is what you are to do to them: Break down their altars, smash their sacred stones, cut down their Asherah polesᵇ and burn their idols in the fire. ⁶For you are a people holy to the LORD your God. The LORD your God has chosen you out of all the peoples on the face of the earth to be his people, his treasured possession.

⁷The LORD did not set his affection on you and choose you because you were more numerous than other peoples, for you were the fewest of all peoples. ⁸But it was because the LORD loved you and kept the oath he swore to your forefathers that he brought you out with a mighty hand

and redeemed you from the land of slavery, from the power of Pharaoh king of Egypt. ⁹Know therefore that the LORD your God is God; he is the faithful God, keeping his covenant of love to a thousand generations of those who love him and keep his commands. ¹⁰But

those who hate him he will repay to
their face by destruction;
he will not be slow to repay to
their face those who hate
him.

¹¹Therefore, take care to follow the commands, decrees and laws I give you today.

¹²If you pay attention to these laws and are careful to follow them, then the LORD your God will keep his covenant of love with you, as he swore to your forefathers. ¹³He will love you and bless you and increase your numbers. He will bless the fruit of your womb, the crops of your land—your grain, new wine and oil—the calves of your herds and the lambs of your flocks in the land that he swore to your forefathers to give you. ¹⁴You will be blessed more than any other people; none of your men or women will be childless, nor any of your livestock without young. ¹⁵The LORD will keep you free from every disease. He will not inflict on you the horrible diseases you knew in Egypt, but he will inflict them on all who hate you. ¹⁶You must destroy all the peoples the LORD your God gives over to you. Do not look on them with pity and do not serve their gods, for that will be a snare to you.

¹⁷You may say to yourselves, "These nations are stronger than we are. How can we drive them out?" ¹⁸But do not be afraid of them; remember well what the LORD your God did to Pharaoh and to all Egypt. ¹⁹You saw with your own eyes the great trials, the miraculous signs and wonders, the mighty hand and outstretched arm, with which the LORD your God brought you out. The LORD your God will do the same to all the peoples you now fear. ²⁰Moreover, the LORD your God will send the hornet among them until even the survivors who hide from you have perished. ²¹Do not be terrified by

---

ᵃ2 The Hebrew term refers to the irrevocable giving over of things or persons to the LORD, often by totally destroying them; also in verse 26.
ᵇ5 That is, symbols of the goddess Asherah; here and elsewhere in Deuteronomy

them, for the LORD your God, who is among you, is a great and awesome God. ²²The LORD your God will drive out those nations before you, little by little. You will not be allowed to eliminate them all at once, or the wild animals will multiply around you. ²³But the LORD your God will deliver them over to you, throwing them into great confusion until they are destroyed. ²⁴He will give their kings into your hand, and you will wipe out their names from under heaven. No one will be able to stand up against you; you will destroy them. ²⁵The images of their gods

---

TUESDAY

Read Deuteronomy 7:1–26
Key Verse Deuteronomy 7:22

Little by Little – Terry Cook

I was embarrassed—so much so that I kept avoiding my turn in the rotation. Every guy my age in the weight room was bench-pressing at least 115 pounds. At my best, I could lift only 85 pounds. "I'll never be able to catch up," I thought. The standard was just too high.

Then the thought occurred to me that I probably couldn't make up a 30-pound difference overnight, but I could work on five pounds at a time. So I began the slow process of lowering the weight bar to 90 pounds and working hard until I could easily lift it.

Success! I pressed 90 pounds, then raised my goal to 95. It was hard work, but after awhile I reached that goal too. I was motivated to raise my goal again, and again, and again. After months of inching my way along, little by little, I found that I was bench pressing 200 pounds! All those seemingly insignificant increments added up over time.

I was surprised to read later in Deuteronomy 7:22 that this "little by little" principle of overcoming obstacles is one that God initiated centuries ago. The Israelites weren't allowed to drive out all the nations at once, lest "the wild animals . . . multiply around [them]." It was for their protection that the obstacles facing them were not eliminated immediately. They had to do it little by little.

Our Christian lives are like that too. We face many obstacles that God uses for our growth: "Consider it pure joy, my brothers, whenever you face trials of many kinds, because you know that the testing of your faith develops perseverance. Perseverance must finish its work so that you may be mature and complete, not lacking anything" (James 1:2–4).

Our growth as Christians is also incremental. Like adding weight to a bench press, we are to "make every effort to add to [our] faith goodness; and to goodness, knowledge; and to knowledge, self-control; and to self-control, perseverance; and to perseverance, godliness; and to godliness, brotherly kindness; and to brotherly kindness, love. For if you possess these qualities in increasing measure, they will keep you from being ineffective and unproductive in your knowledge of our Lord Jesus Christ" (2 Peter 1:5–8).

A Deeper Look
Psalm 128:1–2; Proverbs 13:11; 1 Corinthians 15:58

Go to page 197 for your next devotional reading.

you are to burn in the fire. Do not covet the silver and gold on them, and do not take it for yourselves, or you will be ensnared by it, for it is detestable to the LORD your God. 26Do not bring a detestable thing into your house or you, like it, will be set apart for destruction. Utterly abhor and detest it, for it is set apart for destruction.

Do Not Forget the LORD

8 Be careful to follow every command I am giving you today, so that you may live and increase and may enter and possess the land that the LORD promised on oath to your forefathers. 2Remember how the LORD your God led you all the way in the desert these forty years, to humble you and to test you in order to know what was in your heart, whether or not you would keep his commands. 3He humbled you, causing you to hunger and then feeding you with manna, which neither you nor your fathers had known, to teach you that man does not live on bread alone but on every word that comes from the mouth of the LORD. 4Your clothes did not wear out and your feet did not swell during these forty years. 5Know then in your heart that as a man disciplines his son, so the LORD your God disciplines you.

6Observe the commands of the LORD your God, walking in his ways and revering him. 7For the LORD your God is bringing you into a good land—a land with streams and pools of water, with springs flowing in the valleys and hills; 8a land with wheat and barley, vines and fig trees, pomegranates, olive oil and honey; 9a land where bread will not be scarce and you will lack nothing; a land where the rocks are iron and you can dig copper out of the hills.

10When you have eaten and are satisfied, praise the LORD your God for the good land he has given you. 11Be careful that you do not forget the LORD your God, failing to observe his commands, his laws and his decrees that I am giving you this day. 12Otherwise, when you eat and are satisfied, when you build fine houses and settle down, 13and when your herds and flocks grow large and your silver and gold increase and all you have is multiplied, 14then your heart will become proud and you will forget the LORD your God, who brought you out of Egypt, out of the land of slavery. 15He led you

through the vast and dreadful desert, that thirsty and waterless land, with its venomous snakes and scorpions. He brought you water out of hard rock. 16He gave you manna to eat in the desert, something your fathers had never known, to humble and to test you so that in the end it might go well with you. 17You may say to yourself, "My power and the strength of my hands have produced this wealth for me." 18But remember the LORD your God, for it is he who gives you the ability to produce wealth, and so confirms his covenant, which he swore to your forefathers, as it is today.

19If you ever forget the LORD your God and follow other gods and worship and bow down to them, I testify against you today that you will surely be destroyed. 20Like the nations the LORD destroyed before you, so you will be destroyed for not obeying the LORD your God.

Not Because of Israel's Righteousness

9 Hear, O Israel. You are now about to cross the Jordan to go in and dispossess nations greater and stronger than you, with large cities that have walls up to the sky. 2The people are strong and tall—Anakites! You know about them and have heard it said: "Who can stand up against the Anakites?" 3But be assured today that the LORD your God is the one who goes across ahead of you like a devouring fire. He will destroy them; he will subdue them before you. And you will drive them out and annihilate them quickly, as the LORD has promised you.

4After the LORD your God has driven them out before you, do not say to yourself, "The LORD has brought me here to take possession of this land because of my righteousness." No, it is on account of the wickedness of these nations that the LORD is going to drive them out before you. 5It is not because of your righteousness or your integrity that you are going in to take possession of their land; but on account of the wickedness of these nations, the LORD your God will drive them out before you, to accomplish what he swore to your fathers, to Abraham, Isaac and Jacob. 6Understand, then, that it is not because of your righteousness that the LORD your God is giving you this good land to possess, for you are a stiff-necked people.

The Golden Calf

⁷Remember this and never forget how you provoked the LORD your God to anger in the desert. From the day you left Egypt until you arrived here, you have been rebellious against the LORD. ⁸At Horeb you aroused the LORD's wrath so that he was angry enough to destroy you. ⁹When I went up on the mountain to receive the tablets of stone, the tablets of the covenant that the LORD had made with you, I stayed on the mountain forty days and forty nights; I ate no bread and drank no water. ¹⁰The LORD gave me two stone tablets inscribed by the finger of God. On them were all the commandments the LORD proclaimed to you on the mountain out of the fire, on the day of the assembly.

¹¹At the end of the forty days and forty nights, the LORD gave me the two stone tablets, the tablets of the covenant. ¹²Then the LORD told me, "Go down from here at once, because your people whom you brought out of Egypt have become corrupt. They have turned away quickly from what I commanded them and have made a cast idol for themselves."

¹³And the LORD said to me, "I have seen this people, and they are a stiff-necked people indeed! ¹⁴Let me alone, so that I may destroy them and blot out their name from under heaven. And I will make you into a nation stronger and more numerous than they."

¹⁵So I turned and went down from the mountain while it was ablaze with fire. And the two tablets of the covenant were in my hands.ᵃ ¹⁶When I looked, I saw that you had sinned against the LORD your God; you had made for yourselves an idol cast in the shape of a calf. You had turned aside quickly from the way that the LORD had commanded you. ¹⁷So I took the two tablets and threw them out of my hands, breaking them to pieces before your eyes.

¹⁸Then once again I fell prostrate before the LORD for forty days and forty nights; I ate no bread and drank no water, because of all the sin you had committed, doing what was evil in the LORD's sight and so provoking him to anger. ¹⁹I feared the anger and wrath of the LORD, for he was angry enough with you to destroy you. But again the LORD listened to me. ²⁰And the LORD was angry enough with Aaron to destroy him, but at that time I prayed for Aaron too. ²¹Also I took that sinful thing of yours, the calf you had made, and burned it in the fire. Then I crushed it and ground it to powder as fine as dust and threw the dust into a stream that flowed down the mountain.

²²You also made the LORD angry at Taberah, at Massah and at Kibroth Hattaavah.

²³And when the LORD sent you out from Kadesh Barnea, he said, "Go up and take possession of the land I have given you." But you rebelled against the command of the LORD your God. You did not trust him or obey him. ²⁴You have been rebellious against the LORD ever since I have known you.

²⁵I lay prostrate before the LORD those forty days and forty nights because the LORD had said he would destroy you. ²⁶I prayed to the LORD and said, "O Sovereign LORD, do not destroy your people, your own inheritance that you redeemed by your great power and brought out of Egypt with a mighty hand. ²⁷Remember your servants Abraham, Isaac and Jacob. Overlook the stubbornness of this people, their wickedness and their sin. ²⁸Otherwise, the country from which you brought us will say, 'Because the LORD was not able to take them into the land he had promised them, and because he hated them, he brought them out to put them to death in the desert.' ²⁹But they are your people, your inheritance that you brought out by your great power and your outstretched arm."

ᵃ15 Or *And I had the two tablets of the covenant with me, one in each hand*

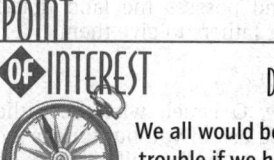

POINT OF INTEREST

Deuteronomy 9:6

We all would be in serious trouble if we had to be perfect in order to deserve God's love. But being perfect wasn't God's requirement for Israel. God chose his people in spite of their sinfulness, and he does the same for us. How does Romans 5:8 describe our standing with God?

Tablets Like the First Ones

10 At that time the LORD said to me, "Chisel out two stone tablets like the first ones and come up to me on the mountain. Also make a wooden chest.*a* ²I will write on the tablets the words that were on the first tablets, which you broke. Then you are to put them in the chest."

³So I made the ark out of acacia wood and chiseled out two stone tablets like the first ones, and I went up on the mountain with the two tablets in my hands. ⁴The LORD wrote on these tablets what he had written before, the Ten Commandments he had proclaimed to you on the mountain, out of the fire, on the day of the assembly. And the LORD gave them to me. ⁵Then I came back down the mountain and put the tablets in the ark I had made, as the LORD commanded me, and they are there now.

⁶(The Israelites traveled from the wells of the Jaakanites to Moserah. There Aaron died and was buried, and Eleazar his son succeeded him as priest. ⁷From there they traveled to Gudgodah and on to Jotbathah, a land with streams of water. ⁸At that time the LORD set apart the tribe of Levi to carry the ark of the covenant of the LORD, to stand before the LORD to minister and to pronounce blessings in his name, as they still do today. ⁹That is why the Levites have no share or inheritance among their brothers; the LORD is their inheritance, as the LORD your God told them.)

¹⁰Now I had stayed on the mountain forty days and nights, as I did the first time, and the LORD listened to me at this time also. It was not his will to destroy you. ¹¹"Go," the LORD said to me, "and lead the people on their way, so that they may enter and possess the land that I swore to their fathers to give them."

Fear the LORD

¹²And now, O Israel, what does the LORD your God ask of you but to fear the LORD your God, to walk in all his ways, to love him, to serve the LORD your God with all your heart and with all your soul, ¹³and to observe the LORD's commands and decrees that I am giving you today for your own good?

¹⁴To the LORD your God belong the heavens, even the highest heavens, the earth and everything in it. ¹⁵Yet the LORD set his affection on your forefathers and loved them, and he chose you, their descendants, above all the nations, as it is today. ¹⁶Circumcise your hearts, therefore, and do not be stiff-necked any longer. ¹⁷For the LORD your God is God of gods and Lord of lords, the great God, mighty and awesome, who shows no partiality and accepts no bribes. ¹⁸He defends the cause of the fatherless and the widow, and loves the alien, giving him food and clothing. ¹⁹And you are to love those who are aliens, for you yourselves were aliens in Egypt. ²⁰Fear the LORD your God and serve him. Hold fast to him and take your oaths in his name. ²¹He is your praise; he is your God, who performed for you those great and awesome wonders you saw with your own eyes. ²²Your forefathers who went down into Egypt were seventy in all, and now the LORD your God has made you as numerous as the stars in the sky.

Love and Obey the LORD

11 Love the LORD your God and keep his requirements, his decrees, his laws and his commands always. ²Remember today that your children were not the ones who saw and experienced the discipline of the LORD your God: his majesty, his mighty hand, his outstretched arm; ³the signs he performed and the things he did in the heart of Egypt, both to Pharaoh king of Egypt and to his whole country; ⁴what he did to the Egyptian army, to its horses and chariots, how he overwhelmed them with the waters of the Red Sea*b* as they were pursuing you, and how the LORD brought lasting ruin on them. ⁵It was not your children who saw what he did for you in the desert until you arrived at this place, ⁶and what he did to Dathan and Abiram, sons of Eliab the Reubenite, when the earth opened its mouth right in the middle of all Israel and swallowed them up with their households, their tents and every living thing that belonged to them. ⁷But it was your own eyes that saw all these great things the LORD has done.

⁸Observe therefore all the commands I am giving you today, so that you may have the strength to go in and take over the land that you are crossing the Jordan to possess, ⁹and so that you may live long

---

a1 That is, an ark   *b4* Hebrew *Yam Suph*; that is, Sea of Reeds in the land that the LORD swore to your forefathers to give to them and their descendants, a land flowing with milk and honey. ¹⁰The land you are entering to take over is not like the land of Egypt, from which you have come, where you planted your seed and irrigated it by foot as in a vegetable garden. ¹¹But the land you are crossing the Jordan to take possession of is a land of mountains and valleys that drinks rain from heaven. ¹²It is a land the LORD your God cares for; the eyes of the LORD your God are continually on it from the beginning of the year to its end.

¹³So if you faithfully obey the commands I am giving you today—to love the LORD your God and to serve him with all your heart and with all your soul— ¹⁴then I will send rain on your land in its season, both autumn and spring rains, so that you may gather in your grain, new wine and oil. ¹⁵I will provide grass in the fields for your cattle, and you will eat and be satisfied.

¹⁶Be careful, or you will be enticed to turn away and worship other gods and bow down to them. ¹⁷Then the LORD's anger will burn against you, and he will shut the heavens so that it will not rain and the ground will yield no produce, and you will soon perish from the good land the LORD is giving you. ¹⁸Fix these words of mine in your hearts and minds; tie them as symbols on your hands and bind them on your foreheads. ¹⁹Teach

WEDNESDAY

Read Deuteronomy 10:1–22
Key Verses Deuteronomy 10:18–19

Entertaining Angels – Vic Black

My apartment complex was in the older part of town. It was part of a strange, elaborate maze of buildings. Everything looked ancient, sort of medieval. I suppose it could have been mistaken for a church. That's probably why the homeless old man knocked at my door. He was looking for the priest.

Normally I would have said that he had the wrong building, and maybe I would have even helped him find the priest. But something inside me said to invite him in. "I'm not the priest, but could I help you?" I couldn't believe those words were coming from my mouth. After all, I was in the middle of studying. And what could *I* do?

The winter had taken its toll on the old man. I offered him something to eat. Soup was all he could handle due to his chronic stomach problems. While he ate, we chatted about life. I was a struggling college student. He was down on his luck. As he prepared to leave, I couldn't help noticing his threadbare winter clothing. The new fleece-lined gloves Mom had given me for Christmas would serve him well. Besides, I had an older pair. Tears welled up in his eyes as he put on the gloves, and I got a big lump in my throat. I told him to come back anytime for another cup of soup, but I never saw him again.

The Bible says we sometimes entertain angels and aren't even aware of it (see Hebrews 13:2). Jesus said when we've fed and clothed the least of his people, we've done it for him (see Matthew 25:40). I don't know if that old man was an angel or not, but it sure gave me deep pleasure to share my food and clothes with him.

A Deeper Look
Luke 6:38; 1 John 3:16–18

Go to page 204 for your next devotional reading.

them to your children, talking about them when you sit at home and when you walk along the road, when you lie down and when you get up. ²⁰Write them on the doorframes of your houses and on your gates, ²¹so that your days and the days of your children may be many in the land that the LORD swore to give your forefathers, as many as the days that the heavens are above the earth.

²²If you carefully observe all these commands I am giving you to follow—to love the LORD your God, to walk in all his ways and to hold fast to him— ²³then the LORD will drive out all these nations before you, and you will dispossess nations larger and stronger than you. ²⁴Every place where you set your foot will be yours: Your territory will extend from the desert to Lebanon, and from the Euphrates River to the western sea.ᵃ ²⁵No man will be able to stand against you. The LORD your God, as he promised you, will put the terror and fear of you on the whole land, wherever you go.

²⁶See, I am setting before you today a blessing and a curse— ²⁷the blessing if you obey the commands of the LORD your God that I am giving you today; ²⁸the curse if you disobey the commands of the LORD your God and turn from the way that I command you today by following other gods, which you have not known. ²⁹When the LORD your God has brought you into the land you are entering to possess, you are to proclaim on Mount Gerizim the blessings, and on Mount Ebal the curses. ³⁰As you know, these mountains are across the Jordan, west of the road,ᵇ toward the setting sun, near the great trees of Moreh, in the territory of those Canaanites living in the Arabah in the vicinity of Gilgal. ³¹You are about to cross the Jordan to enter and take possession of the land the LORD your God is giving you. When you have taken it over and are living there, ³²be sure that you obey all the decrees and laws I am setting before you today.

The One Place of Worship

12 These are the decrees and laws you must be careful to follow in the land that the LORD, the God of your fathers, has given you to possess—as long as you live in the land. ²Destroy completely all the places on the high mountains and on the hills and under every spreading tree where the nations you are dispossessing

worship their gods. ³Break down their altars, smash their sacred stones and burn their Asherah poles in the fire; cut down the idols of their gods and wipe out their names from those places.

⁴You must not worship the LORD your God in their way. ⁵But you are to seek the place the LORD your God will choose from among all your tribes to put his Name there for his dwelling. To that place you must go; ⁶there bring your burnt offerings and sacrifices, your tithes and special gifts, what you have vowed to give and your freewill offerings, and the firstborn of your herds and flocks. ⁷There, in the presence of the LORD your God, you and your families shall eat and shall rejoice in everything you have put your hand to, because the LORD your God has blessed you.

⁸You are not to do as we do here today, everyone as he sees fit, ⁹since you have not yet reached the resting place and the inheritance the LORD your God is giving you. ¹⁰But you will cross the Jordan and settle in the land the LORD your God is giving you as an inheritance, and he will give you rest from all your enemies around you so that you will live in safety. ¹¹Then to the place the LORD your God will choose as a dwelling for his Name—there you are to bring everything I command you: your burnt offerings and sacrifices, your tithes and special gifts, and all the choice possessions you have vowed to the LORD. ¹²And there rejoice before the LORD your God, you, your sons and daughters, your menservants and maidservants, and the Levites from your towns, who have no allotment or inheritance of their own. ¹³Be careful not to sacrifice your burnt offerings anywhere you please. ¹⁴Offer them only at the place the LORD will choose in one of your tribes, and there observe everything I command you.

¹⁵Nevertheless, you may slaughter your animals in any of your towns and eat as much of the meat as you want, as if it were gazelle or deer, according to the blessing the LORD your God gives you. Both the ceremonially unclean and the clean may eat it. ¹⁶But you must not eat the blood; pour it out on the ground like water. ¹⁷You must not eat in your own towns the tithe of your grain and new

ᵃ24 That is, the Mediterranean   ᵇ30 Or *Jordan, westward*

wine and oil, or the firstborn of your herds and flocks, or whatever you have vowed to give, or your freewill offerings or special gifts. ¹⁸Instead, you are to eat them in the presence of the LORD your God at the place the LORD your God will choose—you, your sons and daughters, your menservants and maidservants, and the Levites from your towns—and you are to rejoice before the LORD your God in everything you put your hand to. ¹⁹Be careful not to neglect the Levites as long as you live in your land.

²⁰When the LORD your God has enlarged your territory as he promised you, and you crave meat and say, "I would like some meat," then you may eat as much of it as you want. ²¹If the place where the LORD your God chooses to put his Name is too far away from you, you may slaughter animals from the herds and flocks the LORD has given you, as I have commanded you, and in your own towns you may eat as much of them as you want. ²²Eat them as you would gazelle or deer. Both the ceremonially unclean and the clean may eat. ²³But be sure you do not eat the blood, because the blood is the life, and you must not eat the life with the meat. ²⁴You must not eat the blood; pour it out on the ground like water. ²⁵Do not eat it, so that it may go well with you and your children after you, because you will be doing what is right in the eyes of the LORD.

²⁶But take your consecrated things and whatever you have vowed to give, and go to the place the LORD will choose. ²⁷Present your burnt offerings on the altar of the LORD your God, both the meat and the blood. The blood of your sacrifices must be poured beside the altar of the LORD your God, but you may eat the meat. ²⁸Be careful to obey all these regulations I am giving you, so that it may always go well with you and your children after you, because you will be doing what is good and right in the eyes of the LORD your God.

²⁹The LORD your God will cut off before you the nations you are about to invade and dispossess. But when you have driven them out and settled in their land, ³⁰and after they have been destroyed before you, be careful not to be ensnared by inquiring about their gods, saying, "How do these nations serve their gods? We will do the same." ³¹You must not worship the LORD your God in their way, be-

cause in worshiping their gods, they do all kinds of detestable things the LORD hates. They even burn their sons and daughters in the fire as sacrifices to their gods.

³²See that you do all I command you; do not add to it or take away from it.

Worshiping Other Gods

13 If a prophet, or one who foretells by dreams, appears among you and announces to you a miraculous sign or wonder, ²and if the sign or wonder of which he has spoken takes place, and he says, "Let us follow other gods" (gods you have not known) "and let us worship them," ³you must not listen to the words of that prophet or dreamer. The LORD your God is testing you to find out whether you love him with all your heart and with all your soul. ⁴It is the LORD your God you must follow, and him you must revere. Keep his commands and obey him; serve him and hold fast to him. ⁵That prophet or dreamer must be put to death, because he preached rebellion against the LORD your God, who brought you out of Egypt and redeemed you from the land of slavery; he has tried to turn you from the way the LORD your God commanded you to follow. You must purge the evil from among you.

⁶If your very own brother, or your son or daughter, or the wife you love, or your closest friend secretly entices you, saying, "Let us go and worship other gods" (gods that neither you nor your fathers have known, ⁷gods of the peoples around you, whether near or far, from one end of the land to the other), ⁸do not yield to him or listen to him. Show him no pity. Do not spare him or shield him. ⁹You must certainly put him to death. Your hand must be the first in putting him to

POINT OF INTEREST   Deuteronomy 12:32

Believers can err with respect to God's Word in two ways: They attempt to expand on God's law with additions, or they shorten God's words to more comfortable proportions. God specifically warns against either tendency.

death, and then the hands of all the people. [10]Stone him to death, because he tried to turn you away from the LORD your God, who brought you out of Egypt, out of the land of slavery. [11]Then all Israel will hear and be afraid, and no one among you will do such an evil thing again.

[12]If you hear it said about one of the towns the LORD your God is giving you to live in [13]that wicked men have arisen among you and have led the people of their town astray, saying, "Let us go and worship other gods" (gods you have not known), [14]then you must inquire, probe and investigate it thoroughly. And if it is true and it has been proved that this detestable thing has been done among you, [15]you must certainly put to the sword all who live in that town. Destroy it completely,[a] both its people and its livestock. [16]Gather all the plunder of the town into the middle of the public square and completely burn the town and all its plunder as a whole burnt offering to the LORD your God. It is to remain a ruin forever, never to be rebuilt. [17]None of those condemned things[a] shall be found in your hands, so that the LORD will turn from his fierce anger; he will show you mercy, have compassion on you, and increase your numbers, as he promised on oath to your forefathers, [18]because you obey the LORD your God, keeping all his commands that I am giving you today and doing what is right in his eyes.

Clean and Unclean Food

14 You are the children of the LORD your God. Do not cut yourselves or shave the front of your heads for the dead, [2]for you are a people holy to the LORD your God. Out of all the peoples on the face of the earth, the LORD has chosen you to be his treasured possession.

[3]Do not eat any detestable thing. [4]These are the animals you may eat: the ox, the sheep, the goat, [5]the deer, the gazelle, the roe deer, the wild goat, the ibex, the antelope and the mountain sheep.[b] [6]You may eat any animal that has a split hoof divided in two and that chews the cud. [7]However, of those that chew the cud or that have a split hoof completely divided you may not eat the camel, the rabbit or the coney.[c] Although they chew the cud, they do not have a split hoof; they are ceremonially unclean for you. [8]The pig is also unclean;

although it has a split hoof, it does not chew the cud. You are not to eat their meat or touch their carcasses.

[9]Of all the creatures living in the water, you may eat any that has fins and scales. [10]But anything that does not have fins and scales you may not eat; for you it is unclean.

[11]You may eat any clean bird. [12]But these you may not eat: the eagle, the vulture, the black vulture, [13]the red kite, the black kite, any kind of falcon, [14]any kind of raven, [15]the horned owl, the screech owl, the gull, any kind of hawk, [16]the little owl, the great owl, the white owl, [17]the desert owl, the osprey, the cormorant, [18]the stork, any kind of heron, the hoopoe and the bat.

[19]All flying insects that swarm are unclean to you; do not eat them. [20]But any winged creature that is clean you may eat.

[21]Do not eat anything you find already dead. You may give it to an alien living in any of your towns, and he may eat it, or you may sell it to a foreigner. But you are a people holy to the LORD your God.

Do not cook a young goat in its mother's milk.

Tithes

[22]Be sure to set aside a tenth of all that your fields produce each year. [23]Eat the tithe of your grain, new wine and oil, and the firstborn of your herds and flocks in the presence of the LORD your God at the place he will choose as a dwelling for his Name, so that you may learn to revere the LORD your God always. [24]But if that place is too distant and you have been blessed by the LORD your God and cannot carry your tithe (because the place where the LORD will choose to put his Name is so far away), [25]then exchange your tithe for silver, and take the silver with you and go to the place the LORD your God will choose. [26]Use the silver to buy whatever you like: cattle, sheep, wine or other fermented drink, or anything you wish. Then you and your household shall eat there in the presence of the LORD your God and rejoice. [27]And do not neglect the Levites living in your towns, for they

---

[a]15,17 The Hebrew term refers to the irrevocable giving over of things or persons to the LORD, often by totally destroying them.   [b]5 The precise identification of some of the birds and animals in this chapter is uncertain.   [c]7 That is, the hyrax or rock badger

have no allotment or inheritance of their own.

²⁸At the end of every three years, bring all the tithes of that year's produce and store it in your towns, ²⁹so that the Levites (who have no allotment or inheritance of their own) and the aliens, the fatherless and the widows who live in your towns may come and eat and be satisfied, and so that the LORD your God may bless you in all the work of your hands.

The Year for Canceling Debts

15 At the end of every seven years you must cancel debts. ²This is how it is to be done: Every creditor shall cancel the loan he has made to his fellow Israelite. He shall not require payment from his fellow Israelite or brother, because the LORD's time for canceling debts has been proclaimed. ³You may require payment from a foreigner, but you must cancel any debt your brother owes you. ⁴However, there should be no poor among you, for in the land the LORD your God is giving you to possess as your inheritance, he will richly bless you, ⁵if only you fully obey the LORD your God and are careful to follow all these commands I am giving you today. ⁶For the LORD your God will bless you as he has promised, and you will lend to many nations but will borrow from none. You will rule over many nations but none will rule over you.

⁷If there is a poor man among your brothers in any of the towns of the land that the LORD your God is giving you, do not be hardhearted or tightfisted toward your poor brother. ⁸Rather be openhanded and freely lend him whatever he needs. ⁹Be careful not to harbor this wicked thought: "The seventh year, the year for canceling debts, is near," so that you do not show ill will toward your needy brother and give him nothing. He may then appeal to the LORD against you, and you will be found guilty of sin. ¹⁰Give generously to him and do so without a grudging heart; then because of this the LORD your God will bless you in all your work and in everything you put your hand to. ¹¹There will always be poor people in the land. Therefore I command you to be openhanded toward your brothers and toward the poor and needy in your land.

Freeing Servants

¹²If a fellow Hebrew, a man or a woman, sells himself to you and serves you six years, in the seventh year you must let him go free. ¹³And when you release him, do not send him away empty-handed. ¹⁴Supply him liberally from your flock, your threshing floor and your winepress. Give to him as the LORD your God has blessed you. ¹⁵Remember that you were slaves in Egypt and the LORD your God redeemed you. That is why I give you this command today.

¹⁶But if your servant says to you, "I do not want to leave you," because he loves you and your family and is well off with you, ¹⁷then take an awl and push it through his ear lobe into the door, and he will become your servant for life. Do the same for your maidservant.

¹⁸Do not consider it a hardship to set your servant free, because his service to you these six years has been worth twice as much as that of a hired hand. And the LORD your God will bless you in everything you do.

The Firstborn Animals

¹⁹Set apart for the LORD your God every firstborn male of your herds and flocks. Do not put the firstborn of your oxen to work, and do not shear the firstborn of your sheep. ²⁰Each year you and your family are to eat them in the presence of the LORD your God at the place he will choose. ²¹If an animal has a defect, is lame or blind, or has any serious flaw, you must not sacrifice it to the LORD your God. ²²You are to eat it in your own towns. Both the ceremonially unclean and the clean may eat it, as if it were gazelle or deer. ²³But you must not eat

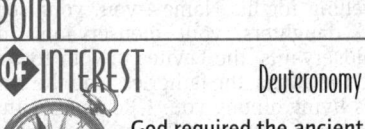

POINT OF INTEREST

Deuteronomy 15:2

God required the ancient Hebrews to forgive all outstanding debts every seven years. His desire was that none of his children be permanently trapped in the downward spiral of increasing debt. What would be the result of such debt cancellation in a modern economy?

the blood; pour it out on the ground like water.

Passover

16 Observe the month of Abib and celebrate the Passover of the LORD your God, because in the month of Abib he brought you out of Egypt by night. ²Sacrifice as the Passover to the LORD your God an animal from your flock or herd at the place the LORD will choose as a dwelling for his Name. ³Do not eat it with bread made with yeast, but for seven days eat unleavened bread, the bread of affliction, because you left Egypt in haste—so that all the days of your life you may remember the time of your departure from Egypt. ⁴Let no yeast be found in your possession in all your land for seven days. Do not let any of the meat you sacrifice on the evening of the first day remain until morning.

⁵You must not sacrifice the Passover in any town the LORD your God gives you ⁶except in the place he will choose as a dwelling for his Name. There you must sacrifice the Passover in the evening, when the sun goes down, on the anniversary*a* of your departure from Egypt. ⁷Roast it and eat it at the place the LORD your God will choose. Then in the morning return to your tents. ⁸For six days eat unleavened bread and on the seventh day hold an assembly to the LORD your God and do no work.

Feast of Weeks

⁹Count off seven weeks from the time you begin to put the sickle to the standing grain. ¹⁰Then celebrate the Feast of Weeks to the LORD your God by giving a freewill offering in proportion to the blessings the LORD your God has given you. ¹¹And rejoice before the LORD your God at the place he will choose as a dwelling for his Name—you, your sons and daughters, your menservants and maidservants, the Levites in your towns, and the aliens, the fatherless and the widows living among you. ¹²Remember that you were slaves in Egypt, and follow carefully these decrees.

Feast of Tabernacles

¹³Celebrate the Feast of Tabernacles for seven days after you have gathered the produce of your threshing floor and your winepress. ¹⁴Be joyful at your Feast—you, your sons and daughters,

your menservants and maidservants, and the Levites, the aliens, the fatherless and the widows who live in your towns. ¹⁵For seven days celebrate the Feast to the LORD your God at the place the LORD will choose. For the LORD your God will bless you in all your harvest and in all the work of your hands, and your joy will be complete.

¹⁶Three times a year all your men must appear before the LORD your God at the place he will choose: at the Feast of Unleavened Bread, the Feast of Weeks and the Feast of Tabernacles. No man should appear before the LORD empty-handed: ¹⁷Each of you must bring a gift in proportion to the way the LORD your God has blessed you.

Judges

¹⁸Appoint judges and officials for each of your tribes in every town the LORD your God is giving you, and they shall judge the people fairly. ¹⁹Do not pervert justice or show partiality. Do not accept a bribe, for a bribe blinds the eyes of the wise and twists the words of the righteous. ²⁰Follow justice and justice alone, so that you may live and possess the land the LORD your God is giving you.

Worshiping Other Gods

²¹Do not set up any wooden Asherah pole*b* beside the altar you build to the LORD your God, ²²and do not erect a sacred stone, for these the LORD your God hates.

17 Do not sacrifice to the LORD your God an ox or a sheep that has any defect or flaw in it, for that would be detestable to him.

²If a man or woman living among you in one of the towns the LORD gives you is found doing evil in the eyes of the LORD your God in violation of his covenant, ³and contrary to my command has worshiped other gods, bowing down to them or to the sun or the moon or the stars of the sky, ⁴and this has been brought to your attention, then you must investigate it thoroughly. If it is true and it has been proved that this detestable thing has been done in Israel, ⁵take the man or woman who has done this evil deed to your city gate and stone that person to death. ⁶On the testimony of two or three witnesses a

---

a6 Or down, at the time of day   b21 Or Do not plant any tree dedicated to Asherah man shall be put to death, but no one shall be put to death on the testimony of only one witness. [7]The hands of the witnesses must be the first in putting him to death, and then the hands of all the people. You must purge the evil from among you.

Law Courts

[8]If cases come before your courts that are too difficult for you to judge—whether bloodshed, lawsuits or assaults—take them to the place the LORD your God will choose. [9]Go to the priests, who are Levites, and to the judge who is in office at that time. Inquire of them and they will give you the verdict. [10]You must act according to the decisions they give you at the place the LORD will choose. Be careful to do everything they direct you to do. [11]Act according to the law they teach you and the decisions they give you. Do not turn aside from what they tell you, to the right or to the left. [12]The man who shows contempt for the judge or for the priest who stands ministering there to the LORD your God must be put to death. You must purge the evil from Israel. [13]All the people will hear and be afraid, and will not be contemptuous again.

The King

[14]When you enter the land the LORD your God is giving you and have taken possession of it and settled in it, and you say, "Let us set a king over us like all the nations around us," [15]be sure to appoint over you the king the LORD your God chooses. He must be from among your own brothers. Do not place a foreigner over you, one who is not a brother Israelite. [16]The king, moreover, must not acquire great numbers of horses for himself or make the people return to Egypt to get more of them, for the LORD has told you, "You are not to go back that way again." [17]He must not take many wives, or his heart will be led astray. He must not accumulate large amounts of silver and gold.

[18]When he takes the throne of his kingdom, he is to write for himself on a scroll a copy of this law, taken from that of the priests, who are Levites. [19]It is to be with him, and he is to read it all the days of his life so that he may learn to revere the LORD his God and follow carefully all the words of this law and these decrees [20]and not consider himself better than his brothers and turn from the law to the right or to the left. Then he and his descendants will reign a long time over his kingdom in Israel.

Offerings for Priests and Levites

18 The priests, who are Levites—indeed the whole tribe of Levi—are to have no allotment or inheritance with Israel. They shall live on the offerings made to the LORD by fire, for that is their inheritance. [2]They shall have no inheritance among their brothers; the LORD is their inheritance, as he promised them.

[3]This is the share due the priests from the people who sacrifice a bull or a sheep: the shoulder, the jowls and the inner parts. [4]You are to give them the firstfruits of your grain, new wine and oil, and the first wool from the shearing of your sheep, [5]for the LORD your God has chosen them and their descendants out of all your tribes to stand and minister in the LORD's name always.

[6]If a Levite moves from one of your towns anywhere in Israel where he is living, and comes in all earnestness to the place the LORD will choose, [7]he may minister in the name of the LORD his God like all his fellow Levites who serve there in the presence of the LORD. [8]He is to share equally in their benefits, even though he has received money from the sale of family possessions.

Detestable Practices

[9]When you enter the land the LORD your God is giving you, do not learn to imitate the detestable ways of the nations there. [10]Let no one be found among you who sacrifices his son or daughter in[a] the fire, who practices divination or sorcery, interprets omens, engages in witchcraft, [11]or casts spells, or who is a medium or spiritist or who consults the dead. [12]Anyone who does these things is detestable to the LORD, and because of these detestable practices the LORD your God will drive out those nations before you. [13]You must be blameless before the LORD your God.

The Prophet

[14]The nations you will dispossess listen to those who practice sorcery or divination. But as for you, the LORD your God

---

[a] 10 Or *who makes his son or daughter pass through*

has not permitted you to do so. ¹⁵The LORD your God will raise up for you a prophet like me from among your own brothers. You must listen to him. ¹⁶For this is what you asked of the LORD your God at Horeb on the day of the assembly when you said, "Let us not hear the voice of the LORD our God nor see this great fire anymore, or we will die."

¹⁷The LORD said to me: "What they say is good. ¹⁸I will raise up for them a prophet like you from among their brothers; I will put my words in his mouth, and he will tell them everything I command him. ¹⁹If anyone does not listen to my words

that the prophet speaks in my name, I myself will call him to account. ²⁰But a prophet who presumes to speak in my name anything I have not commanded him to say, or a prophet who speaks in the name of other gods, must be put to death."

²¹You may say to yourselves, "How can we know when a message has not been spoken by the LORD?" ²²If what a prophet proclaims in the name of the LORD does not take place or come true, that is a message the LORD has not spoken. That prophet has spoken presumptuously. Do not be afraid of him.

THURSDAY

Read *Deuteronomy 17:1–20*
Key Verses *Deuteronomy 17:16–17*

A Material Guy – Scott L. Moore

Me? No, I'm not very materialistic. Sure, I enjoy a few toys here and there—electronic equipment, clothes, CDs. But everybody knows that it's not a good thing to be materialistic. No one wants to be thought of as greedy. No, I don't really struggle much with this problem. Really!

What's that you say? Your homeless friend could use my jacket? Yeah, I've got two other coats that keep me just as warm, but I really like this one. I worked hard to pay for it. And besides, I give to the church. Don't they provide for the homeless with their shelters and soup kitchens? I'm sure they've got a nice coat for him, if he'll only put forth the effort to walk to the shelter. Those people can be pretty lazy, you know. (Boy, that was close. I thought I was going to have to give up my jacket there for a second.)

Like I said, I don't struggle much with materialism. I'm really not trying to make tons of money so I can drive a Rolls Royce, for crying out loud. I just like my stuff—that's all. Just don't ask me to give up any of it for some lazy bum. He must have done something wrong to get into his situation. You have to be a wise steward of God's wealth, you know. It's not like I'm worshiping golden calves or something.

What's this? Lord, are you trying to tell me something? *"No one can serve two masters. Either he will hate the one and love the other, or he will be devoted to the one and despise the other. You cannot serve both God and Money"* (Matthew 6:24) . . . *"I tell you the truth, whatever you did not do for one of the least of these, you did not do for me"* (Matthew 25:45) . . . *"For we brought nothing into the world, and we can take nothing out of it . . . for the love of money is a root of all kinds of evil"* (1 Timothy 6:7,10).

A Deeper Look
Luke 12:14–21; 1 Timothy 6:17–19

Go to page 206 for your next devotional reading.

Cities of Refuge

19 When the LORD your God has destroyed the nations whose land he is giving you, and when you have driven them out and settled in their towns and houses, ²then set aside for yourselves three cities centrally located in the land the LORD your God is giving you to possess. ³Build roads to them and divide into three parts the land the LORD your God is giving you as an inheritance, so that anyone who kills a man may flee there.

⁴This is the rule concerning the man who kills another and flees there to save his life—one who kills his neighbor unintentionally, without malice aforethought. ⁵For instance, a man may go into the forest with his neighbor to cut wood, and as he swings his ax to fell a tree, the head may fly off and hit his neighbor and kill him. That man may flee to one of these cities and save his life. ⁶Otherwise, the avenger of blood might pursue him in a rage, overtake him if the distance is too great, and kill him even though he is not deserving of death, since he did it to his neighbor without malice aforethought. ⁷This is why I command you to set aside for yourselves three cities.

⁸If the LORD your God enlarges your territory, as he promised on oath to your forefathers, and gives you the whole land he promised them, ⁹because you carefully follow all these laws I command you today—to love the LORD your God and to walk always in his ways—then you are to set aside three more cities. ¹⁰Do this so that innocent blood will not be shed in your land, which the LORD your God is giving you as your inheritance, and so that you will not be guilty of bloodshed.

¹¹But if a man hates his neighbor and lies in wait for him, assaults and kills him, and then flees to one of these cities, ¹²the elders of his town shall send for him, bring him back from the city, and hand him over to the avenger of blood to die. ¹³Show him no pity. You must purge from Israel the guilt of shedding innocent blood, so that it may go well with you.

¹⁴Do not move your neighbor's boundary stone set up by your predecessors in the inheritance you receive in the land the LORD your God is giving you to possess.

Witnesses

¹⁵One witness is not enough to convict a man accused of any crime or offense he may have committed. A matter must be established by the testimony of two or three witnesses.

¹⁶If a malicious witness takes the stand to accuse a man of a crime, ¹⁷the two men involved in the dispute must stand in the presence of the LORD before the priests and the judges who are in office at the time. ¹⁸The judges must make a thorough investigation, and if the witness proves to be a liar, giving false testimony against his brother, ¹⁹then do to him as he intended to do to his brother. You must purge the evil from among you. ²⁰The rest of the people will hear of this and be afraid, and never again will such an evil thing be done among you. ²¹Show no pity: life for life, eye for eye, tooth for tooth, hand for hand, foot for foot.

Going to War

20 When you go to war against your enemies and see horses and chariots and an army greater than yours, do not be afraid of them, because the LORD your God, who brought you up out of Egypt, will be with you. ²When you are about to go into battle, the priest shall come forward and address the army. ³He shall say: "Hear, O Israel, today you are going into battle against your enemies. Do not be fainthearted or afraid; do not be terrified or give way to panic before them. ⁴For the LORD your God is the one who goes with you to fight for you against your enemies to give you victory."

⁵The officers shall say to the army: "Has anyone built a new house and not dedicated it? Let him go home, or he may die in battle and someone else may dedicate it. ⁶Has anyone planted a vineyard and not begun to enjoy it? Let him go home, or he may die in battle and someone else enjoy it. ⁷Has anyone become pledged to a woman and not married her? Let him go home, or he may die in battle and someone else marry her." ⁸Then the officers shall add, "Is any man afraid or fainthearted? Let him go home so that his brothers will not become disheartened too." ⁹When the officers have finished speaking to the army, they shall appoint commanders over it.

¹⁰When you march up to attack a city, make its people an offer of peace. ¹¹If they accept and open their gates, all the people in it shall be subject to forced labor and shall work for you. ¹²If they re-

fuse to make peace and they engage you in battle, lay siege to that city. ¹³When the LORD your God delivers it into your hand, put to the sword all the men in it. ¹⁴As for the women, the children, the livestock and everything else in the city, you may take these as plunder for yourselves. And you may use the plunder the LORD your God gives you from your enemies. ¹⁵This is how you are to treat all the cities that are at a distance from you and do not belong to the nations nearby.

¹⁶However, in the cities of the nations the LORD your God is giving you as an inheritance, do not leave alive anything that breathes. ¹⁷Completely destroy*ᵃ* them—the Hittites, Amorites, Canaan-

---

*ᵃ*17 The Hebrew term refers to the irrevocable giving over of things or persons to the LORD, often by totally destroying them.

FRIDAY

Read *Deuteronomy 20:1–20*
Key Verses *Deuteronomy 20:3–4*

Courage! — Jena Borah

God had planted a dream in my husband Bernard's heart—to buy an old church building and turn it into a hangout for high school and college students. But a local youth worker ominously predicted that the neighbors would take us to court or blackball us in our small town. Bernard doesn't care much for conflict, but he knew that God's hand was in this idea. So he gathered his courage, picked up the phone and dialed the number of the "hangout's" closest neighbor. Bernard asked, "What is your reaction to this idea and how do you think the other neighbors will take it?" The man's answer was a complete shock to us. "I have no problems with it at all," he said. "In fact, I will be your advocate with the other neighbors!" Bernard nearly passed out with relief!

Why such an unexpected, positive response? The Lord had gone before us to fight our battle. This neighbor was a professor in the math department on our local college campus. The previous semester he had had a graduate student who was in one of Bernard's Bible studies. The student had spoken favorably about Bernard, so this neighbor was ready to work with us! God had gone ahead and prepared the way.

After this experience, our faith increased all the more. After overcoming a few more obstacles, we won the war. God gave us the church building and the courage to implement Bernard's dream!

Have you ever tried to do something for God only to be paralyzed by the obstacles and opposition and the discouragement of the people who thought it wouldn't work? Deuteronomy 20:8 offers you one option: If you are afraid—go home! If you would rather be doing something else—go home! Your lack of courage will rub off on everyone else. Here's another option: Take courage, because God says, "Do not be fainthearted or afraid; do not be terrified or give way to panic before them. For the LORD your God is the one who goes with you to fight for you against your enemies to give you victory" (Deuteronomy 20:3–4).

A Deeper Look
Isaiah 41:11–13; Ephesians 6:10–13

Go to page 221 for your next devotional reading.

ites, Perizzites, Hivites and Jebusites—as the LORD your God has commanded you. ¹⁸Otherwise, they will teach you to follow all the detestable things they do in worshiping their gods, and you will sin against the LORD your God.

¹⁹When you lay siege to a city for a long time, fighting against it to capture it, do not destroy its trees by putting an ax to them, because you can eat their fruit. Do not cut them down. Are the trees of the field people, that you should besiege them?ᵃ ²⁰However, you may cut down trees that you know are not fruit trees and use them to build siege works until the city at war with you falls.

Atonement for an Unsolved Murder

21 If a man is found slain, lying in a field in the land the LORD your God is giving you to possess, and it is not known who killed him, ²your elders and judges shall go out and measure the distance from the body to the neighboring towns. ³Then the elders of the town nearest the body shall take a heifer that has never been worked and has never worn a yoke ⁴and lead her down to a valley that has not been plowed or planted and where there is a flowing stream. There in the valley they are to break the heifer's neck. ⁵The priests, the sons of Levi, shall step forward, for the LORD your God has chosen them to minister and to pronounce blessings in the name of the LORD and to decide all cases of dispute and assault. ⁶Then all the elders of the town nearest the body shall wash their hands over the heifer whose neck was broken in the valley, ⁷and they shall declare: "Our hands did not shed this blood, nor did our eyes see it done. ⁸Accept this atonement for your people Israel, whom you have redeemed, O LORD, and do not hold your people guilty of the blood of an innocent man." And the bloodshed will be atoned for. ⁹So you will purge from yourselves the guilt of shedding innocent blood, since you have done what is right in the eyes of the LORD.

Marrying a Captive Woman

¹⁰When you go to war against your enemies and the LORD your God delivers them into your hands and you take captives, ¹¹if you notice among the captives a beautiful woman and are attracted to her, you may take her as your wife. ¹²Bring her into your home and have her shave her head, trim her nails ¹³and put aside the clothes she was wearing when captured. After she has lived in your house and mourned her father and mother for a full month, then you may go to her and be her husband and she shall be your wife. ¹⁴If you are not pleased with her, let her go wherever she wishes. You must not sell her or treat her as a slave, since you have dishonored her.

The Right of the Firstborn

¹⁵If a man has two wives, and he loves one but not the other, and both bear him sons but the firstborn is the son of the wife he does not love, ¹⁶when he wills his property to his sons, he must not give the rights of the firstborn to the son of the wife he loves in preference to his actual firstborn, the son of the wife he does not love. ¹⁷He must acknowledge the son of his unloved wife as the firstborn by giving him a double share of all he has. That son is the first sign of his father's strength. The right of the firstborn belongs to him.

A Rebellious Son

¹⁸If a man has a stubborn and rebellious son who does not obey his father and mother and will not listen to them when they discipline him, ¹⁹his father and mother shall take hold of him and bring him to the elders at the gate of his town. ²⁰They shall say to the elders, "This son of ours is stubborn and rebellious. He will not obey us. He is a profligate and a drunkard." ²¹Then all the men of his town shall stone him to death. You must purge the evil from among you. All Israel will hear of it and be afraid.

Various Laws

²²If a man guilty of a capital offense is put to death and his body is hung on a tree, ²³you must not leave his body on the tree overnight. Be sure to bury him that same day, because anyone who is hung on a tree is under God's curse. You must not desecrate the land the LORD your God is giving you as an inheritance.

22 If you see your brother's ox or sheep straying, do not ignore it but be sure to take it back to him. ²If the brother does not live near you or if you do not know who he is, take it home with you and

---

ᵃ19 Or down to use in the siege, for the fruit trees are for the benefit of man.

keep it until he comes looking for it. Then give it back to him. ³Do the same if you find your brother's donkey or his cloak or anything he loses. Do not ignore it.

⁴If you see your brother's donkey or his ox fallen on the road, do not ignore it. Help him get it to its feet.

⁵A woman must not wear men's clothing, nor a man wear women's clothing, for the LORD your God detests anyone who does this.

⁶If you come across a bird's nest beside the road, either in a tree or on the ground, and the mother is sitting on the young or on the eggs, do not take the mother with the young. ⁷You may take the young, but be sure to let the mother go, so that it may go well with you and you may have a long life.

⁸When you build a new house, make a parapet around your roof so that you may not bring the guilt of bloodshed on your house if someone falls from the roof.

⁹Do not plant two kinds of seed in your vineyard; if you do, not only the crops you plant but also the fruit of the vineyard will be defiled.ᵃ

¹⁰Do not plow with an ox and a donkey yoked together.

¹¹Do not wear clothes of wool and linen woven together.

¹²Make tassels on the four corners of the cloak you wear.

Marriage Violations

¹³If a man takes a wife and, after lying with her, dislikes her ¹⁴and slanders her and gives her a bad name, saying, "I married this woman, but when I approached her, I did not find proof of her virginity," ¹⁵then the girl's father and mother shall bring proof that she was a virgin to the town elders at the gate. ¹⁶The girl's father will say to the elders, "I gave my daughter in marriage to this man, but he dislikes her. ¹⁷Now he has slandered her and said, 'I did not find your daughter to be a virgin.' But here is the proof of my daughter's virginity." Then her parents shall display the cloth before the elders of the town, ¹⁸and the elders shall take the man and punish him. ¹⁹They shall fine him a hundred shekels of silverᵇ and give them to the girl's father, because this man has given an Israelite virgin a bad name. She shall continue to be his wife; he must not divorce her as long as he lives.

²⁰If, however, the charge is true and no proof of the girl's virginity can be found, ²¹she shall be brought to the door of her father's house and there the men of her town shall stone her to death. She has done a disgraceful thing in Israel by being promiscuous while still in her father's house. You must purge the evil from among you.

²²If a man is found sleeping with another man's wife, both the man who slept with her and the woman must die. You must purge the evil from Israel.

²³If a man happens to meet in a town a virgin pledged to be married and he sleeps with her, ²⁴you shall take both of them to the gate of that town and stone them to death—the girl because she was in a town and did not scream for help, and the man because he violated another man's wife. You must purge the evil from among you.

²⁵But if out in the country a man happens to meet a girl pledged to be married and rapes her, only the man who has done this shall die. ²⁶Do nothing to the girl; she has committed no sin deserving death. This case is like that of someone who attacks and murders his neighbor, ²⁷for the man found the girl out in the country, and though the betrothed girl screamed, there was no one to rescue her.

²⁸If a man happens to meet a virgin who is not pledged to be married and rapes her and they are discovered, ²⁹he shall pay the girl's father fifty shekels of silver.ᶜ He must marry the girl, for he

---

ᵃ9 Or be forfeited to the sanctuary   ᵇ19 That is, about 2 1/2 pounds (about 1 kilogram)   ᶜ29 That is, about 1 1/4 pounds (about 0.6 kilogram)

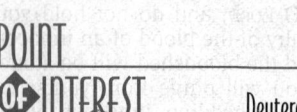

POINT OF INTEREST

Deuteronomy 22:22

Marriage was intended as a sacred union between a man and a woman. In a case of adultery, both individuals were equally guilty, and the threat of the death penalty functioned as a strong deterrent to family breakdown. What makes Jesus' response to the woman caught in adultery in John 8:3–11 so noteworthy?

has violated her. He can never divorce her as long as he lives.

³⁰A man is not to marry his father's wife; he must not dishonor his father's bed.

Exclusion From the Assembly

23 No one who has been emasculated by crushing or cutting may enter the assembly of the LORD.

²No one born of a forbidden marriage*a* nor any of his descendants may enter the assembly of the LORD, even down to the tenth generation.

³No Ammonite or Moabite or any of his descendants may enter the assembly of the LORD, even down to the tenth generation. ⁴For they did not come to meet you with bread and water on your way when you came out of Egypt, and they hired Balaam son of Beor from Pethor in Aram Naharaim*b* to pronounce a curse on you. ⁵However, the LORD your God would not listen to Balaam but turned the curse into a blessing for you, because the LORD your God loves you. ⁶Do not seek a treaty of friendship with them as long as you live.

⁷Do not abhor an Edomite, for he is your brother. Do not abhor an Egyptian, because you lived as an alien in his country. ⁸The third generation of children born to them may enter the assembly of the LORD.

Uncleanness in the Camp

⁹When you are encamped against your enemies, keep away from everything impure. ¹⁰If one of your men is unclean because of a nocturnal emission, he is to go outside the camp and stay there. ¹¹But as evening approaches he is to wash himself, and at sunset he may return to the camp.

¹²Designate a place outside the camp where you can go to relieve yourself. ¹³As part of your equipment have something to dig with, and when you relieve yourself, dig a hole and cover up your excrement. ¹⁴For the LORD your God moves about in your camp to protect you and to deliver your enemies to you. Your camp must be holy, so that he will not see among you anything indecent and turn away from you.

Miscellaneous Laws

¹⁵If a slave has taken refuge with you, do not hand him over to his master. ¹⁶Let him live among you wherever he likes and in whatever town he chooses. Do not oppress him.

¹⁷No Israelite man or woman is to become a shrine prostitute. ¹⁸You must not bring the earnings of a female prostitute or of a male prostitute*c* into the house of the LORD your God to pay any vow, because the LORD your God detests them both.

¹⁹Do not charge your brother interest, whether on money or food or anything else that may earn interest. ²⁰You may charge a foreigner interest, but not a brother Israelite, so that the LORD your God may bless you in everything you put your hand to in the land you are entering to possess.

²¹If you make a vow to the LORD your God, do not be slow to pay it, for the LORD your God will certainly demand it of you and you will be guilty of sin. ²²But if you refrain from making a vow, you will not be guilty. ²³Whatever your lips utter you must be sure to do, because you made your vow freely to the LORD your God with your own mouth.

²⁴If you enter your neighbor's vineyard, you may eat all the grapes you want, but do not put any in your basket. ²⁵If you enter your neighbor's grainfield, you may pick kernels with your hands, but you must not put a sickle to his standing grain.

24 If a man marries a woman who becomes displeasing to him because he finds something indecent about her, and he writes her a certificate of divorce, gives it to her and sends her from his house, ²and if after she leaves his house she becomes the wife of another man, ³and her second husband dislikes her and writes her a certificate of divorce, gives it to her and sends her from his house, or if he dies, ⁴then her first husband, who divorced her, is not allowed to marry her again after she has been defiled. That would be detestable in the eyes of the LORD. Do not bring sin upon the land the LORD your God is giving you as an inheritance.

⁵If a man has recently married, he must not be sent to war or have any other duty laid on him. For one year he is to be free to stay at home and bring happiness to the wife he has married.

---

*a*2 Or *one of illegitimate birth*　　*b*4 That is, Northwest Mesopotamia　　*c*18 Hebrew *of a dog*

⁶Do not take a pair of millstones—not even the upper one—as security for a debt, because that would be taking a man's livelihood as security.

⁷If a man is caught kidnapping one of his brother Israelites and treats him as a slave or sells him, the kidnapper must die. You must purge the evil from among you.

⁸In cases of leprous*a* diseases be very careful to do exactly as the priests, who are Levites, instruct you. You must follow carefully what I have commanded them. ⁹Remember what the LORD your God did to Miriam along the way after you came out of Egypt.

¹⁰When you make a loan of any kind to your neighbor, do not go into his house to get what he is offering as a pledge. ¹¹Stay outside and let the man to whom you are making the loan bring the pledge out to you. ¹²If the man is poor, do not go to sleep with his pledge in your possession. ¹³Return his cloak to him by sunset so that he may sleep in it. Then he will thank you, and it will be regarded as a righteous act in the sight of the LORD your God.

¹⁴Do not take advantage of a hired man who is poor and needy, whether he is a brother Israelite or an alien living in one of your towns. ¹⁵Pay him his wages each day before sunset, because he is poor and is counting on it. Otherwise he may cry to the LORD against you, and you will be guilty of sin.

¹⁶Fathers shall not be put to death for their children, nor children put to death for their fathers; each is to die for his own sin.

¹⁷Do not deprive the alien or the fatherless of justice, or take the cloak of the widow as a pledge. ¹⁸Remember that you were slaves in Egypt and the LORD your God redeemed you from there. That is why I command you to do this.

¹⁹When you are harvesting in your field and you overlook a sheaf, do not go back to get it. Leave it for the alien, the fatherless and the widow, so that the LORD your God may bless you in all the work of your hands. ²⁰When you beat the olives from your trees, do not go over the branches a second time. Leave what remains for the alien, the fatherless and the widow. ²¹When you harvest the grapes in your vineyard, do not go over the vines again. Leave what remains for the alien, the fatherless and the widow.

²²Remember that you were slaves in Egypt. That is why I command you to do this.

25 When men have a dispute, they are to take it to court and the judges will decide the case, acquitting the innocent and condemning the guilty. ²If the guilty man deserves to be beaten, the judge shall make him lie down and have him flogged in his presence with the number of lashes his crime deserves, ³but he must not give him more than forty lashes. If he is flogged more than that, your brother will be degraded in your eyes.

⁴Do not muzzle an ox while it is treading out the grain.

⁵If brothers are living together and one of them dies without a son, his widow must not marry outside the family. Her husband's brother shall take her and marry her and fulfill the duty of a brother-in-law to her. ⁶The first son she bears shall carry on the name of the dead brother so that his name will not be blotted out from Israel.

⁷However, if a man does not want to marry his brother's wife, she shall go to the elders at the town gate and say, "My husband's brother refuses to carry on his brother's name in Israel. He will not fulfill the duty of a brother-in-law to me." ⁸Then the elders of his town shall summon him and talk to him. If he persists in saying, "I do not want to marry her," ⁹his brother's widow shall go up to him in the presence of the elders, take off one of his sandals, spit in his face and say, "This is what is done to the man who will not build up his brother's family line." ¹⁰That man's line shall be known in Israel as The Family of the Unsandaled.

a8 The Hebrew word was used for various diseases affecting the skin—not necessarily leprosy.

POINT OF INTEREST

Deuteronomy 24:16

In ancient cultures, one family member's offense put entire families at risk of being slaughtered. The idea that only the perpetrator be held responsible for a crime was a breakthrough in justice and compassion that reflected God's unconditional love.

¹¹If two men are fighting and the wife of one of them comes to rescue her husband from his assailant, and she reaches out and seizes him by his private parts, ¹²you shall cut off her hand. Show her no pity.

¹³Do not have two differing weights in your bag—one heavy, one light. ¹⁴Do not have two differing measures in your house—one large, one small. ¹⁵You must have accurate and honest weights and measures, so that you may live long in the land the LORD your God is giving you. ¹⁶For the LORD your God detests anyone who does these things, anyone who deals dishonestly.

¹⁷Remember what the Amalekites did to you along the way when you came out of Egypt. ¹⁸When you were weary and worn out, they met you on your journey and cut off all who were lagging behind; they had no fear of God. ¹⁹When the LORD your God gives you rest from all the enemies around you in the land he is giving you to possess as an inheritance, you shall blot out the memory of Amalek from under heaven. Do not forget!

Firstfruits and Tithes

26 When you have entered the land the LORD your God is giving you as an inheritance and have taken possession of it and settled in it, ²take some of the firstfruits of all that you produce from the soil of the land the LORD your God is giving you and put them in a basket. Then go to the place the LORD your God will choose as a dwelling for his Name ³and say to the priest in office at the time, "I declare today to the LORD your God that I have come to the land the LORD swore to our forefathers to give us." ⁴The priest shall take the basket from your hands and set it down in front of the altar of the LORD your God. ⁵Then you shall declare before the LORD your God: "My father was a wandering Aramean, and he went down into Egypt with a few people and lived there and became a great nation, powerful and numerous. ⁶But the Egyptians mistreated us and made us suffer, putting us to hard labor. ⁷Then we cried out to the LORD, the God of our fathers, and the LORD heard our voice and saw our misery, toil and oppression. ⁸So the LORD brought us out of Egypt with a mighty hand and an outstretched arm, with great terror and with miraculous signs and wonders. ⁹He brought us to this place and gave us

this land, a land flowing with milk and honey; ¹⁰and now I bring the firstfruits of the soil that you, O LORD, have given me." Place the basket before the LORD your God and bow down before him. ¹¹And you and the Levites and the aliens among you shall rejoice in all the good things the LORD your God has given to you and your household.

¹²When you have finished setting aside a tenth of all your produce in the third year, the year of the tithe, you shall give it to the Levite, the alien, the fatherless and the widow, so that they may eat in your towns and be satisfied. ¹³Then say to the LORD your God: "I have removed from my house the sacred portion and have given it to the Levite, the alien, the fatherless and the widow, according to all you commanded. I have not turned aside from your commands nor have I forgotten any of them. ¹⁴I have not eaten any of the sacred portion while I was in mourning, nor have I removed any of it while I was unclean, nor have I offered any of it to the dead. I have obeyed the LORD my God; I have done everything you commanded me. ¹⁵Look down from heaven, your holy dwelling place, and bless your people Israel and the land you have given us as you promised on oath to our forefathers, a land flowing with milk and honey."

Follow the LORD's Commands

¹⁶The LORD your God commands you this day to follow these decrees and laws; carefully observe them with all your heart and with all your soul. ¹⁷You have declared this day that the LORD is your God and that you will walk in his ways,

POINT OF INTEREST   Deuteronomy 26:12

Giving! This passage explains the distribution of tithes. First in line were the Levites who served at the tabernacle. Then came the destitute foreigners, most likely driven from their homelands by famine or war. Not to be forgotten were the orphans and widows. Giving to any of these individuals was the same as giving to God.

that you will keep his decrees, commands and laws, and that you will obey him. [18]And the LORD has declared this day that you are his people, his treasured possession as he promised, and that you are to keep all his commands. [19]He has declared that he will set you in praise, fame and honor high above all the nations he has made and that you will be a people holy to the LORD your God, as he promised.

The Altar on Mount Ebal

27 Moses and the elders of Israel commanded the people: "Keep all these commands that I give you today. [2]When you have crossed the Jordan into the land the LORD your God is giving you, set up some large stones and coat them with plaster. [3]Write on them all the words of this law when you have crossed over to enter the land the LORD your God is giving you, a land flowing with milk and honey, just as the LORD, the God of your fathers, promised you. [4]And when you have crossed the Jordan, set up these stones on Mount Ebal, as I command you today, and coat them with plaster. [5]Build there an altar to the LORD your God, an altar of stones. Do not use any iron tool upon them. [6]Build the altar of the LORD your God with fieldstones and offer burnt offerings on it to the LORD your God. [7]Sacrifice fellowship offerings[a] there, eating them and rejoicing in the presence of the LORD your God. [8]And you shall write very clearly all the words of this law on these stones you have set up."

Curses From Mount Ebal

[9]Then Moses and the priests, who are Levites, said to all Israel, "Be silent, O Israel, and listen! You have now become the people of the LORD your God. [10]Obey the LORD your God and follow his commands and decrees that I give you today."

[11]On the same day Moses commanded the people:

[12]When you have crossed the Jordan, these tribes shall stand on Mount Gerizim to bless the people: Simeon, Levi, Judah, Issachar, Joseph and Benjamin. [13]And these tribes shall stand on Mount Ebal to pronounce curses: Reuben, Gad, Asher, Zebulun, Dan and Naphtali.

[14]The Levites shall recite to all the people of Israel in a loud voice:

[15]"Cursed is the man who carves an image or casts an idol—a thing detestable to the LORD, the work of the craftsman's hands—and sets it up in secret."

Then all the people shall say,
"Amen!"

[16]"Cursed is the man who dishonors his father or his mother."

Then all the people shall say,
"Amen!"

[17]"Cursed is the man who moves his neighbor's boundary stone."

Then all the people shall say,
"Amen!"

[18]"Cursed is the man who leads the blind astray on the road."

Then all the people shall say,
"Amen!"

[19]"Cursed is the man who withholds justice from the alien, the fatherless or the widow."

Then all the people shall say,
"Amen!"

[20]"Cursed is the man who sleeps with his father's wife, for he dishonors his father's bed."

Then all the people shall say,
"Amen!"

[21]"Cursed is the man who has sexual relations with any animal."

Then all the people shall say,
"Amen!"

[22]"Cursed is the man who sleeps with his sister, the daughter of his father or the daughter of his mother."

Then all the people shall say,
"Amen!"

[23]"Cursed is the man who sleeps with his mother-in-law."

Then all the people shall say,
"Amen!"

[24]"Cursed is the man who kills his neighbor secretly."

Then all the people shall say,
"Amen!"

[25]"Cursed is the man who accepts a bribe to kill an innocent person."

Then all the people shall say,
"Amen!"

[26]"Cursed is the man who does not uphold the words of this law by carrying them out."

Then all the people shall say,
"Amen!"

---

[a]7 Traditionally *peace offerings*

Blessings for Obedience

28 If you fully obey the LORD your God and carefully follow all his commands I give you today, the LORD your God will set you high above all the nations on earth. ²All these blessings will come upon you and accompany you if you obey the LORD your God:

³You will be blessed in the city and blessed in the country.

⁴The fruit of your womb will be blessed, and the crops of your land and the young of your livestock— the calves of your herds and the lambs of your flocks.

⁵Your basket and your kneading trough will be blessed.

⁶You will be blessed when you come in and blessed when you go out.

⁷The LORD will grant that the enemies who rise up against you will be defeated before you. They will come at you from one direction but flee from you in seven.

⁸The LORD will send a blessing on your barns and on everything you put your hand to. The LORD your God will bless you in the land he is giving you.

⁹The LORD will establish you as his holy people, as he promised you on oath, if you keep the commands of the LORD your God and walk in his ways. ¹⁰Then all the peoples on earth will see that you are called by the name of the LORD, and they will fear you. ¹¹The LORD will grant you abundant prosperity—in the fruit of your womb, the young of your livestock and the crops of your ground—in the land he swore to your forefathers to give you.

¹²The LORD will open the heavens, the storehouse of his bounty, to send rain on your land in season and to bless all the work of your hands. You will lend to many nations but will borrow from none. ¹³The LORD will make you the head, not the tail. If you pay attention to the commands of the LORD your God that I give you this day and carefully follow them, you will always be at the top, never at the bottom. ¹⁴Do not turn aside from any of the commands I give you today, to the right or to the left, following other gods and serving them.

Curses for Disobedience

¹⁵However, if you do not obey the LORD your God and do not carefully follow all his commands and decrees I am giving you today, all these curses will come upon you and overtake you:

¹⁶You will be cursed in the city and cursed in the country.

¹⁷Your basket and your kneading trough will be cursed.

¹⁸The fruit of your womb will be cursed, and the crops of your land, and the calves of your herds and the lambs of your flocks.

¹⁹You will be cursed when you come in and cursed when you go out.

²⁰The LORD will send on you curses, confusion and rebuke in everything you put your hand to, until you are destroyed and come to sudden ruin because of the evil you have done in forsaking him.ᵃ ²¹The LORD will plague you with diseases until he has destroyed you from the land you are entering to possess. ²²The LORD will strike you with wasting disease, with fever and inflammation, with scorching heat and drought, with blight and mildew, which will plague you until you perish. ²³The sky over your head will be bronze, the ground beneath you iron. ²⁴The LORD will turn the rain of your country into dust and powder; it will come down from the skies until you are destroyed.

²⁵The LORD will cause you to be defeated before your enemies. You will come at them from one direction but flee from them in seven, and you will become a thing of horror to all the kingdoms on earth. ²⁶Your carcasses will be food for all the birds of the air and the beasts of the earth, and there will be no one to frighten them away. ²⁷The LORD will afflict you with the boils of Egypt and with tumors, festering sores and the itch, from which

ᵃ20 Hebrew me

POINT OF INTEREST

Deuteronomy 28:15

There are two sides to every question, two faces to every coin. So it is with God's law. Obedience brought blessings; disobedience brought curses. There was no middle ground.

you cannot be cured. 28The LORD will afflict you with madness, blindness and confusion of mind. 29At midday you will grope about like a blind man in the dark. You will be unsuccessful in everything you do; day after day you will be oppressed and robbed, with no one to rescue you.

30You will be pledged to be married to a woman, but another will take her and ravish her. You will build a house, but you will not live in it. You will plant a vineyard, but you will not even begin to enjoy its fruit. 31Your ox will be slaughtered before your eyes, but you will eat none of it. Your donkey will be forcibly taken from you and will not be returned. Your sheep will be given to your enemies, and no one will rescue them. 32Your sons and daughters will be given to another nation, and you will wear out your eyes watching for them day after day, powerless to lift a hand. 33A people that you do not know will eat what your land and labor produce, and you will have nothing but cruel oppression all your days. 34The sights you see will drive you mad. 35The LORD will afflict your knees and legs with painful boils that cannot be cured, spreading from the soles of your feet to the top of your head.

36The LORD will drive you and the king you set over you to a nation unknown to you or your fathers. There you will worship other gods, gods of wood and stone. 37You will become a thing of horror and an object of scorn and ridicule to all the nations where the LORD will drive you.

38You will sow much seed in the field but you will harvest little, because locusts will devour it. 39You will plant vineyards and cultivate them but you will not drink the wine or gather the grapes, because worms will eat them. 40You will have olive trees throughout your country but you will not use the oil, because the olives will drop off. 41You will have sons and daughters but you will not keep them, because they will go into captivity. 42Swarms of locusts will take over all your trees and the crops of your land.

43The alien who lives among you will rise above you higher and higher, but you will sink lower and lower. 44He will lend to you, but you will not lend to him. He will be the head, but you will be the tail.

45All these curses will come upon you. They will pursue you and overtake you until you are destroyed, because you did not obey the LORD your God and observe the commands and decrees he gave you. 46They will be a sign and a wonder to you and your descendants forever. 47Because you did not serve the LORD your God joyfully and gladly in the time of prosperity, 48therefore in hunger and thirst, in nakedness and dire poverty, you will serve the enemies the LORD sends against you. He will put an iron yoke on your neck until he has destroyed you.

49The LORD will bring a nation against you from far away, from the ends of the earth, like an eagle swooping down, a nation whose language you will not understand, 50a fierce-looking nation without respect for the old or pity for the young. 51They will devour the young of your livestock and the crops of your land until you are destroyed. They will leave you no grain, new wine or oil, nor any calves of your herds or lambs of your flocks until you are ruined. 52They will lay siege to all the cities throughout your land until the high fortified walls in which you trust fall down. They will besiege all the cities throughout the land the LORD your God is giving you.

53Because of the suffering that your enemy will inflict on you during the siege, you will eat the fruit of the womb, the flesh of the sons and daughters the LORD your God has given you. 54Even the most gentle and sensitive man among you will have no compassion on his own brother or the wife he loves or his surviving children, 55and he will not give to one of them any of the flesh of his children that he is eating. It will be all he has left because of the suffering your enemy will inflict on you during the siege of all your cities. 56The most gentle and sensitive woman among you—so sensitive and gentle that she would not venture to touch the ground with the sole of her foot—will begrudge the husband she loves and her own son or daughter 57the afterbirth from her womb and the children she bears. For she intends to eat them secretly during the siege and in the distress that your enemy will inflict on you in your cities.

58If you do not carefully follow all the words of this law, which are written in this book, and do not revere this glorious and awesome name—the LORD your God— 59the LORD will send fearful plagues on you and your descendants, harsh and prolonged disasters, and severe and lingering illnesses. 60He will bring upon you all the diseases of Egypt that you dreaded, and they will cling to you. 61The LORD will also bring on you every kind of sickness and disaster not recorded in this Book of the Law, until you are destroyed. 62You who were as numerous as the stars in the sky will be left but few in number, because you did not obey the LORD your God. 63Just as it pleased the LORD to make you prosper and increase in number, so it will please him to ruin and destroy you. You will be uprooted from the land you are entering to possess.

64Then the LORD will scatter you among all nations, from one end of the earth to the other. There you will worship other gods—gods of wood and stone, which neither you nor your fathers have known. 65Among those nations you will find no repose, no resting place for the sole of your foot. There the LORD will give you an anxious mind, eyes weary with longing, and a despairing heart. 66You will live in constant suspense, filled with dread both night and day, never sure of your life. 67In the morning you will say, "If only it were evening!" and in the evening, "If only it were morning!"—because of the terror that will fill your hearts and the sights that your eyes will see. 68The LORD will send you back in ships to Egypt on a journey I said you should never make again. There you will offer yourselves for sale to your enemies as male and female slaves, but no one will buy you.

Renewal of the Covenant

29 These are the terms of the covenant the LORD commanded Moses to make with the Israelites in Moab, in addition to the covenant he had made with them at Horeb.

2Moses summoned all the Israelites and said to them:

Your eyes have seen all that the LORD did in Egypt to Pharaoh, to all his officials and to all his land. 3With your own eyes you saw those great trials, those miraculous signs and great wonders. 4But to this day the LORD has not given you a mind that understands or eyes that see or ears that hear. 5During the forty years that I led you through the desert, your clothes did not wear out, nor did the sandals on your feet. 6You ate no bread and drank no wine or other fermented drink. I did this so that you might know that I am the LORD your God.

7When you reached this place, Sihon king of Heshbon and Og king of Bashan came out to fight against us, but we defeated them. 8We took their land and gave it as an inheritance to the Reubenites, the Gadites and the half-tribe of Manasseh.

9Carefully follow the terms of this covenant, so that you may prosper in everything you do. 10All of you are standing today in the presence of the LORD your God—your leaders and chief men, your elders and officials, and all the other men of Israel, 11together with your children and your wives, and the aliens living in your camps who chop your wood and carry your water. 12You are standing here in order to enter into a covenant with the LORD your God, a covenant the LORD is making with you this day and sealing with an oath, 13to confirm you this day as his people, that he may be your God as he promised you and as he swore to your fathers, Abraham, Isaac and Jacob. 14I am making this covenant, with its oath, not only with you 15who are standing here with us today in the presence of the LORD our God but also with those who are not here today.

16You yourselves know how we lived in Egypt and how we passed through the countries on the way here. 17You saw among them their detestable images and idols of wood and stone, of silver and gold. 18Make sure there is no man or woman, clan or tribe among you today whose heart turns away from the LORD

POINT OF INTEREST

Deuteronomy 29:1

Forty years earlier God had formed a covenant relationship with Israel. After the rebellion at Kadesh Barnea (see Numbers 14), the rebel Israelites were forced to wander in the desert until all the insurgents had died. Now a new generation needed to renew the covenant with God prior to entering the promised land.

our God to go and worship the gods of those nations; make sure there is no root among you that produces such bitter poison.

¹⁹When such a person hears the words of this oath, he invokes a blessing on himself and therefore thinks, "I will be safe, even though I persist in going my own way." This will bring disaster on the watered land as well as the dry.ᵃ ²⁰The LORD will never be willing to forgive him; his wrath and zeal will burn against that man. All the curses written in this book will fall upon him, and the LORD will blot out his name from under heaven. ²¹The LORD will single him out from all the tribes of Israel for disaster, according to all the curses of the covenant written in this Book of the Law.

²²Your children who follow you in later generations and foreigners who come from distant lands will see the calamities that have fallen on the land and the diseases with which the LORD has afflicted it. ²³The whole land will be a burning waste of salt and sulfur—nothing planted, nothing sprouting, no vegetation growing on it. It will be like the destruction of Sodom and Gomorrah, Admah and Zeboiim, which the LORD overthrew in fierce anger. ²⁴All the nations will ask: "Why has the LORD done this to this land? Why this fierce, burning anger?"

²⁵And the answer will be: "It is because this people abandoned the covenant of the LORD, the God of their fathers, the covenant he made with them when he brought them out of Egypt. ²⁶They went off and worshiped other gods and bowed down to them, gods they did not know, gods he had not given them. ²⁷Therefore the LORD's anger burned against this land, so that he brought on it all the curses written in this book. ²⁸In furious anger and in great wrath the LORD uprooted them from their land and thrust them into another land, as it is now."

²⁹The secret things belong to the LORD our God, but the things revealed belong to us and to our children forever, that we may follow all the words of this law.

Prosperity After Turning to the LORD

30 When all these blessings and curses I have set before you come upon you and you take them to heart wherever the LORD your God disperses you among the nations, ²and when you and your chil-

dren return to the LORD your God and obey him with all your heart and with all your soul according to everything I command you today, ³then the LORD your God will restore your fortunesᵇ and have compassion on you and gather you again from all the nations where he scattered you. ⁴Even if you have been banished to the most distant land under the heavens, from there the LORD your God will gather you and bring you back. ⁵He will bring you to the land that belonged to your fathers, and you will take possession of it. He will make you more prosperous and numerous than your fathers. ⁶The LORD your God will circumcise your hearts and the hearts of your descendants, so that you may love him with all your heart and with all your soul, and live. ⁷The LORD your God will put all these curses on your enemies who hate and persecute you. ⁸You will again obey the LORD and follow all his commands I am giving you today. ⁹Then the LORD your God will make you most prosperous in all the work of your hands and in the fruit of your womb, the young of your livestock and the crops of your land. The LORD will again delight in you and make you prosperous, just as he delighted in your fathers, ¹⁰if you obey the LORD your God and keep his commands and decrees that are written in this Book of the Law and turn to the LORD your God with all your heart and with all your soul.

The Offer of Life or Death

¹¹Now what I am commanding you today is not too difficult for you or beyond your reach. ¹²It is not up in heaven, so that you have to ask, "Who will ascend

ᵃ19 Or *way, in order to add drunkenness to thirst.*"
ᵇ3 Or *will bring you back from captivity*

POINT OF INTEREST   Deuteronomy 30:3

God's chosen people were scattered throughout the world in 722 B.C., 586 B.C. and A.D. 70. Centuries later, in 1948, they returned to Israel to become a nation again. Why? Because God made a promise, and God never fails to fulfill his promises.

into heaven to get it and proclaim it to us so we may obey it?" ¹³Nor is it beyond the sea, so that you have to ask, "Who will cross the sea to get it and proclaim it to us so we may obey it?" ¹⁴No, the word is very near you; it is in your mouth and in your heart so you may obey it.

¹⁵See, I set before you today life and prosperity, death and destruction. ¹⁶For I command you today to love the LORD your God, to walk in his ways, and to keep his commands, decrees and laws; then you will live and increase, and the LORD your God will bless you in the land you are entering to possess.

¹⁷But if your heart turns away and you are not obedient, and if you are drawn away to bow down to other gods and worship them, ¹⁸I declare to you this day that you will certainly be destroyed. You will not live long in the land you are crossing the Jordan to enter and possess.

¹⁹This day I call heaven and earth as witnesses against you that I have set before you life and death, blessings and curses. Now choose life, so that you and your children may live ²⁰and that you may love the LORD your God, listen to his voice, and hold fast to him. For the LORD is your life, and he will give you many years in the land he swore to give to your fathers, Abraham, Isaac and Jacob.

Joshua to Succeed Moses

31 Then Moses went out and spoke these words to all Israel: ²"I am now a hundred and twenty years old and I am no longer able to lead you. The LORD has said to me, 'You shall not cross the Jordan.' ³The LORD your God himself will cross over ahead of you. He will destroy these nations before you, and you will take possession of their land. Joshua also will cross over ahead of you, as the LORD said. ⁴And the LORD will do to them what he did to Sihon and Og, the kings of the Amorites, whom he destroyed along with their land. ⁵The LORD will deliver them to you, and you must do to them all that I have commanded you. ⁶Be strong and courageous. Do not be afraid or terrified because of them, for the LORD your God goes with you; he will never leave you nor forsake you."

⁷Then Moses summoned Joshua and said to him in the presence of all Israel, "Be strong and courageous, for you must go with this people into the land that the LORD swore to their forefathers to give

them, and you must divide it among them as their inheritance. ⁸The LORD himself goes before you and will be with you; he will never leave you nor forsake you. Do not be afraid; do not be discouraged."

The Reading of the Law

⁹So Moses wrote down this law and gave it to the priests, the sons of Levi, who carried the ark of the covenant of the LORD, and to all the elders of Israel. ¹⁰Then Moses commanded them: "At the end of every seven years, in the year for canceling debts, during the Feast of Tabernacles, ¹¹when all Israel comes to appear before the LORD your God at the place he will choose, you shall read this law before them in their hearing. ¹²Assemble the people—men, women and children, and the aliens living in your towns—so they can listen and learn to fear the LORD your God and follow carefully all the words of this law. ¹³Their children, who do not know this law, must hear it and learn to fear the LORD your God as long as you live in the land you are crossing the Jordan to possess."

Israel's Rebellion Predicted

¹⁴The LORD said to Moses, "Now the day of your death is near. Call Joshua and present yourselves at the Tent of Meeting, where I will commission him." So Moses and Joshua came and presented themselves at the Tent of Meeting.

¹⁵Then the LORD appeared at the Tent in a pillar of cloud, and the cloud stood over the entrance to the Tent. ¹⁶And the LORD said to Moses: "You are going to rest with your fathers, and these people will soon prostitute themselves to the foreign gods of the land they are entering. They will forsake me and break the covenant I made with them. ¹⁷On that day I will become angry with them and forsake them; I will hide my face from them, and they will be destroyed. Many disasters and difficulties will come upon them, and on that day they will ask, 'Have not these disasters come upon us because our God is not with us?' ¹⁸And I will certainly hide my face on that day because of all their wickedness in turning to other gods.

¹⁹"Now write down for yourselves this song and teach it to the Israelites and have them sing it, so that it may be a witness for me against them. ²⁰When I have brought them into the land flowing with milk and honey, the land I promised

on oath to their forefathers, and when they eat their fill and thrive, they will turn to other gods and worship them, rejecting me and breaking my covenant. ²¹And when many disasters and difficulties come upon them, this song will testify against them, because it will not be forgotten by their descendants. I know what they are disposed to do, even before I bring them into the land I promised them on oath." ²²So Moses wrote down this song that day and taught it to the Israelites.

²³The LORD gave this command to Joshua son of Nun: "Be strong and courageous, for you will bring the Israelites into the land I promised them on oath, and I myself will be with you."

²⁴After Moses finished writing in a book the words of this law from beginning to end, ²⁵he gave this command to the Levites who carried the ark of the covenant of the LORD: ²⁶"Take this Book of the Law and place it beside the ark of the covenant of the LORD your God. There it will remain as a witness against you. ²⁷For I know how rebellious and stiffnecked you are. If you have been rebellious against the LORD while I am still alive and with you, how much more will you rebel after I die! ²⁸Assemble before me all the elders of your tribes and all your officials, so that I can speak these words in their hearing and call heaven and earth to testify against them. ²⁹For I know that after my death you are sure to become utterly corrupt and to turn from the way I have commanded you. In days to come, disaster will fall upon you because you will do evil in the sight of the LORD and provoke him to anger by what your hands have made."

The Song of Moses

³⁰And Moses recited the words of this song from beginning to end in the hearing of the whole assembly of Israel:

32 Listen, O heavens, and I will speak;
　　hear, O earth, the words of my
　　　　mouth.
²Let my teaching fall like rain
　　and my words descend like dew,
　like showers on new grass,
　　like abundant rain on tender
　　　　plants.
³I will proclaim the name of the LORD.
　　Oh, praise the greatness of our
　　　　God!

⁴He is the Rock, his works are perfect,
　　and all his ways are just.
A faithful God who does no wrong,
　　upright and just is he.

⁵They have acted corruptly toward
　　　　him;
　　to their shame they are no longer
　　　　his children,
　　but a warped and crooked
　　　　generation. ᵃ
⁶Is this the way you repay the LORD,
　　O foolish and unwise people?
Is he not your Father, your Creator, ᵇ
　　who made you and formed you?

⁷Remember the days of old;
　　consider the generations long past.
Ask your father and he will tell you,
　　your elders, and they will explain
　　　　to you.
⁸When the Most High gave the nations
　　　　their inheritance,
　　when he divided all mankind,
　he set up boundaries for the peoples
　　according to the number of the
　　　　sons of Israel. ᶜ
⁹For the LORD's portion is his people,
　　Jacob his allotted inheritance.

¹⁰In a desert land he found him,
　　in a barren and howling waste.
He shielded him and cared for him;
　　he guarded him as the apple of his
　　　　eye,
¹¹like an eagle that stirs up its nest
　　and hovers over its young,
　　that spreads its wings to catch them

ᵃ5 Or *Corrupt are they and not his children, / a generation warped and twisted to their shame*
ᵇ6 Or *Father, who bought you*　ᶜ8 Masoretic Text; Dead Sea Scrolls (see also Septuagint) *sons of God*

POINT OF INTEREST

Deuteronomy 31:24

You've been typing on your keyboard for hours when suddenly your computer screen freezes up. You realize the danger that, upon restarting, you may lose everything you have been working on. The question flashes across your mind, *Did I save my work?* Moses didn't have this problem. He wrote, then the Levites saved his work. What a great back-up system!

and carries them on its pinions.
¹²The LORD alone led him;
  no foreign god was with him.

¹³He made him ride on the heights of
    the land
  and fed him with the fruit of the
    fields.
He nourished him with honey from
    the rock,
  and with oil from the flinty crag,
¹⁴with curds and milk from herd and
    flock
  and with fattened lambs and goats,
with choice rams of Bashan
  and the finest kernels of wheat.
You drank the foaming blood of the
    grape.

¹⁵Jeshurun*ᵃ* grew fat and kicked;
  filled with food, he became heavy
    and sleek.
He abandoned the God who made
    him
  and rejected the Rock his Savior.
¹⁶They made him jealous with their
    foreign gods
  and angered him with their
    detestable idols.
¹⁷They sacrificed to demons, which are
    not God—
  gods they had not known,
  gods that recently appeared,
  gods your fathers did not fear.
¹⁸You deserted the Rock, who fathered
    you;
  you forgot the God who gave you
    birth.

¹⁹The LORD saw this and rejected them
  because he was angered by his
    sons and daughters.
²⁰"I will hide my face from them," he
    said,
  "and see what their end will be;
for they are a perverse generation,
  children who are unfaithful.
²¹They made me jealous by what is no
    god
  and angered me with their
    worthless idols.
I will make them envious by those
    who are not a people;
  I will make them angry by a nation
    that has no understanding.
²²For a fire has been kindled by my
    wrath,
  one that burns to the realm of
    death*ᵇ* below.

It will devour the earth and its
    harvests
  and set afire the foundations of the
    mountains.

²³"I will heap calamities upon them
  and spend my arrows against
    them.
²⁴I will send wasting famine against
    them,
  consuming pestilence and deadly
    plague;
I will send against them the fangs of
    wild beasts,
  the venom of vipers that glide in
    the dust.
²⁵In the street the sword will make
    them childless;
  in their homes terror will reign.
Young men and young women will
    perish,
  infants and gray-haired men.
²⁶I said I would scatter them
  and blot out their memory from
    mankind,
²⁷but I dreaded the taunt of the enemy,
  lest the adversary misunderstand
and say, 'Our hand has triumphed;
  the LORD has not done all this.' "

²⁸They are a nation without sense,
  there is no discernment in them.
²⁹If only they were wise and would
    understand this
  and discern what their end will be!
³⁰How could one man chase a
    thousand,
  or two put ten thousand to flight,
unless their Rock had sold them,
  unless the LORD had given them
    up?
³¹For their rock is not like our Rock,
  as even our enemies concede.
³²Their vine comes from the vine of
    Sodom
  and from the fields of Gomorrah.
Their grapes are filled with poison,
  and their clusters with bitterness.
³³Their wine is the venom of serpents,
  the deadly poison of cobras.

³⁴"Have I not kept this in reserve
  and sealed it in my vaults?
³⁵It is mine to avenge; I will repay.
  In due time their foot will slip;
their day of disaster is near
  and their doom rushes upon
    them."

ᵃ15 Jeshurun means *the upright one*, that is, Israel.
ᵇ22 Hebrew *to Sheol*

³⁶The Lᴏʀᴅ will judge his people
　　and have compassion on his
　　　servants
　when he sees their strength is gone
　　and no one is left, slave or free.
³⁷He will say: "Now where are their
　　　gods,
　　the rock they took refuge in,
³⁸the gods who ate the fat of their
　　　sacrifices
　　and drank the wine of their drink
　　　offerings?
　Let them rise up to help you!
　　Let them give you shelter!

³⁹"See now that I myself am He!
　　There is no god besides me.
　I put to death and I bring to life,
　　I have wounded and I will heal,
　　and no one can deliver out of my
　　　hand.
⁴⁰I lift my hand to heaven and declare:
　　As surely as I live forever,
⁴¹when I sharpen my flashing sword
　　and my hand grasps it in
　　　judgment,
　I will take vengeance on my
　　　adversaries
　　and repay those who hate me.
⁴²I will make my arrows drunk with
　　　blood,
　　while my sword devours flesh:
　the blood of the slain and the
　　　captives,
　　the heads of the enemy leaders."

⁴³Rejoice, O nations, with his
　　　people,ᵃ, ᵇ
　for he will avenge the blood of his
　　　servants;
　he will take vengeance on his
　　　enemies
　　and make atonement for his land
　　　and people.

⁴⁴Moses came with Joshuaᶜ son of
Nun and spoke all the words of this song
in the hearing of the people. ⁴⁵When Moses finished reciting all these words to all
Israel, ⁴⁶he said to them, "Take to heart
all the words I have solemnly declared to
you this day, so that you may command
your children to obey carefully all the
words of this law. ⁴⁷They are not just idle
words for you—they are your life. By
them you will live long in the land you
are crossing the Jordan to possess."

Moses to Die on Mount Nebo

⁴⁸On that same day the Lᴏʀᴅ told Moses, ⁴⁹"Go up into the Abarim Range to
Mount Nebo in Moab, across from Jericho, and view Canaan, the land I am giving the Israelites as their own possession.
⁵⁰There on the mountain that you have
climbed you will die and be gathered to
your people, just as your brother Aaron
died on Mount Hor and was gathered to
his people. ⁵¹This is because both of you
broke faith with me in the presence of the
Israelites at the waters of Meribah Kadesh in the Desert of Zin and because you
did not uphold my holiness among the
Israelites. ⁵²Therefore, you will see the
land only from a distance; you will not
enter the land I am giving to the people
of Israel."

Moses Blesses the Tribes

33 This is the blessing that Moses the
man of God pronounced on the Israelites before his death. ²He said:

"The Lᴏʀᴅ came from Sinai
　　and dawned over them from Seir;
　　he shone forth from Mount Paran.
He came withᵈ myriads of holy ones
　　from the south, from his mountain
　　　slopes.ᵉ
³Surely it is you who love the people;
　　all the holy ones are in your hand.
At your feet they all bow down,
　　and from you receive instruction,
⁴the law that Moses gave us,
　　the possession of the assembly of
　　　Jacob.
⁵He was king over Jeshurunᶠ

ᵃ43 Or *Make his people rejoice, O nations*
ᵇ43 Masoretic Text; Dead Sea Scrolls (see also
Septuagint) *people, / and let all the angels worship
him /*　ᶜ44 Hebrew *Hoshea*, a variant of *Joshua*
ᵈ2 Or *from*　ᵉ2 The meaning of the Hebrew for
this phrase is uncertain.　ᶠ5 *Jeshurun* means *the
upright one,* that is, Israel; also in verse 26.

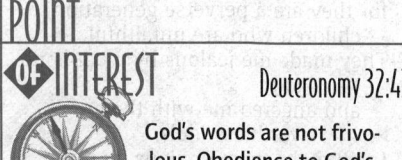

POINT OF INTEREST

Deuteronomy 32:47

God's words are not frivo-
lous. Obedience to God's
words meant life for the
Israelites and means life and
strength for us today too (see 2 Timothy
3:16–17). For a New Testament perspective, compare this verse with John 6:63–
69.

Read Deuteronomy 32:1–52
Key Verses Deuteronomy 32:46–47

God's Word—Your Life!

A compass needle always points north. From it you can get your bearings . . . even when the trail isn't marked and the path is hard to follow. In fact, if you're lost in the woods, a compass can save your life!

Just as the compass needle points north, the Bible always points to God. When we're lost in the dark paths of life, it points us to the truth, to the light of God's will. Every day we face worries and temptations. We have to make important decisions that will set a course for the rest of our lives.

A compass isn't much good if you don't trust it and follow its direction. Likewise, knowledge of the Bible is great, but if you don't trust it and obey what it says, you'll still be lost in the dark. God's words are different from the words in any other book you'll ever read. The Bible points from the darkness to the light, from death to life!

Digging Into the Word
1. According to these passages, why is God's Word so important?— *Matthew 4:4; Acts 20:32*
2. Why is obeying God's Word essential for a joy-filled life?— *Matthew 7:24–27; John 15:9–11*

Action Challenge
Commit to one practical action that will grow out of your Bible study on a daily basis. Be very specific: What will you do? When will you do it? How will you know you have done it? Who will pray for you and hold you accountable?

One Step Deeper
Isaiah 55:10–11; 2 Timothy 3:16–17

Go to page 225 for your next devotional reading.

when the leaders of the people
assembled,
along with the tribes of Israel.

6"Let Reuben live and not die,
nor[a] his men be few."

7And this he said about Judah:

"Hear, O LORD, the cry of Judah;
bring him to his people.
With his own hands he defends his
cause.
Oh, be his help against his foes!"

8About Levi he said:

"Your Thummim and Urim belong
to the man you favored.
You tested him at Massah;
you contended with him at the
waters of Meribah.
9He said of his father and mother,
'I have no regard for them.'
He did not recognize his brothers
or acknowledge his own children,
but he watched over your word
and guarded your covenant.
10He teaches your precepts to Jacob
and your law to Israel.
He offers incense before you
and whole burnt offerings on your
altar.
11Bless all his skills, O LORD,
and be pleased with the work of
his hands.
Smite the loins of those who rise up
against him;
strike his foes till they rise no
more."

12About Benjamin he said:

"Let the beloved of the LORD rest
secure in him,
for he shields him all day long,
and the one the LORD loves rests
between his shoulders."

13About Joseph he said:

"May the LORD bless his land
with the precious dew from heaven
above
and with the deep waters that lie
below;
14with the best the sun brings forth
and the finest the moon can yield;
15with the choicest gifts of the ancient
mountains
and the fruitfulness of the
everlasting hills;

16with the best gifts of the earth and its
fullness
and the favor of him who dwelt in
the burning bush.
Let all these rest on the head of
Joseph,
on the brow of the prince among[b]
his brothers.
17In majesty he is like a firstborn bull;
his horns are the horns of a wild
ox.
With them he will gore the nations,
even those at the ends of the earth.
Such are the ten thousands of
Ephraim;
such are the thousands of
Manasseh."

18About Zebulun he said:

"Rejoice, Zebulun, in your going out,
and you, Issachar, in your tents.
19They will summon peoples to the
mountain
and there offer sacrifices of
righteousness;
they will feast on the abundance of
the seas,
on the treasures hidden in the
sand."

20About Gad he said:

"Blessed is he who enlarges Gad's
domain!
Gad lives there like a lion,
tearing at arm or head.
21He chose the best land for himself;
the leader's portion was kept for
him.
When the heads of the people
assembled,
he carried out the LORD's righteous
will,
and his judgments concerning
Israel."

22About Dan he said:

"Dan is a lion's cub,
springing out of Bashan."

23About Naphtali he said:

"Naphtali is abounding with the favor
of the LORD
and is full of his blessing;
he will inherit southward to the
lake."

24About Asher he said:

a6 Or but let   b16 Or of the one separated from

"Most blessed of sons is Asher;
  let him be favored by his brothers,
  and let him bathe his feet in oil.
25The bolts of your gates will be iron
    and bronze,
  and your strength will equal your
    days.

26"There is no one like the God of
    Jeshurun,
  who rides on the heavens to help
    you
  and on the clouds in his majesty.
27The eternal God is your refuge,
  and underneath are the everlasting
    arms.
He will drive out your enemy before
    you,
  saying, 'Destroy him!'
28So Israel will live in safety alone;
  Jacob's spring is secure
in a land of grain and new wine,
  where the heavens drop dew.
29Blessed are you, O Israel!
  Who is like you,
  a people saved by the LORD?
He is your shield and helper
  and your glorious sword.
Your enemies will cower before you,
  and you will trample down their
    high places.a"

The Death of Moses

34 Then Moses climbed Mount Nebo
from the plains of Moab to the top of
Pisgah, across from Jericho. There the
LORD showed him the whole land—from
Gilead to Dan, 2all of Naphtali, the territory of Ephraim and Manasseh, all the
land of Judah as far as the western sea,b
3the Negev and the whole region from the
Valley of Jericho, the City of Palms, as
far as Zoar. 4Then the LORD said to him,
"This is the land I promised on oath to
Abraham, Isaac and Jacob when I said, 'I
will give it to your descendants.' I have
let you see it with your eyes, but you will
not cross over into it."

5And Moses the servant of the LORD
died there in Moab, as the LORD had said.
6He buried himc in Moab, in the valley
opposite Beth Peor, but to this day no one
knows where his grave is. 7Moses was a
hundred and twenty years old when he
died, yet his eyes were not weak nor his
strength gone. 8The Israelites grieved for
Moses in the plains of Moab thirty days,
until the time of weeping and mourning
was over.

9Now Joshua son of Nun was filled
with the spiritd of wisdom because Moses had laid his hands on him. So the
Israelites listened to him and did what
the LORD had commanded Moses.

10Since then, no prophet has risen in
Israel like Moses, whom the LORD knew
face to face, 11who did all those miraculous signs and wonders the LORD sent him
to do in Egypt—to Pharaoh and to all his
officials and to his whole land. 12For no
one has ever shown the mighty power or
performed the awesome deeds that Moses did in the sight of all Israel.

---

a29 Or *will tread upon their bodies*   b2 That is,
the Mediterranean   c6 Or *He was buried*
d9 Or *Spirit*

POINT OF INTEREST

Deuteronomy 34:9

Moses spent forty years
herding sheep before God
called him to oversee the rebellious Israelites in the
desert. Joshua served Moses throughout
this forty-year exile, observing and learning, until it was his turn to assume the
leadership role. Forty years of waiting requires patience!

Joshua documents one of the greatest periods in the history of Israel—the establishment of the nation in the land God had promised them. If you're into war stories, this book is full of them. But you won't find what many would consider brilliant examples of military genius. What you will see is the power of the God who not only promised victory, but made it happen in ways that defy human understanding. Behind all the accounts of battles and conquests is the story of a people who believe God and experience the blessings that come from obedience to him.

JOSHUA

The Lord Commands Joshua

1 After the death of Moses the servant of the Lord, the Lord said to Joshua son of Nun, Moses' aide: 2"Moses my servant is dead. Now then, you and all these people, get ready to cross the Jordan River into the land I am about to give to them—to the Israelites. 3I will give you every place where you set your foot, as I promised Moses. 4Your territory will extend from the desert to Lebanon, and from the great river, the Euphrates—all the Hittite country—to the Great Sea[a] on the west. 5No one will be able to stand up against you all the days of your life. As I was with Moses, so I will be with you; I will never leave you nor forsake you.

6"Be strong and courageous, because you will lead these people to inherit the land I swore to their forefathers to give them. 7Be strong and very courageous. Be careful to obey all the law my servant Moses gave you; do not turn from it to the right or to the left, that you may be successful wherever you go. 8Do not let this Book of the Law depart from your mouth; meditate on it day and night, so that you may be careful to do everything written in it. Then you will be prosperous and successful. 9Have I not commanded you? Be strong and courageous. Do not be terrified; do not be discouraged, for the Lord your God will be with you wherever you go."

10So Joshua ordered the officers of the

a 4 That is, the Mediterranean

people: ¹¹"Go through the camp and tell the people, 'Get your supplies ready. Three days from now you will cross the Jordan here to go in and take possession of the land the LORD your God is giving you for your own.' "

¹²But to the Reubenites, the Gadites and the half-tribe of Manasseh, Joshua said, ¹³"Remember the command that Moses the servant of the LORD gave you: 'The LORD your God is giving you rest and has granted you this land.' ¹⁴Your wives, your children and your livestock may stay in the land that Moses gave you east of the Jordan, but all your fighting men, fully armed, must cross over ahead of your brothers. You are to help your brothers ¹⁵until the LORD gives them rest, as he has done for you, and until they too have taken possession of the land that the LORD your God is giving them. After that, you may go back and occupy your own land, which Moses the servant of the LORD gave you east of the Jordan toward the sunrise."

¹⁶Then they answered Joshua, "What-

MONDAY

Read *Joshua 1:1–18*
Key Verse *Joshua 1:8*

Spelling Success – Kent Walstrom

How do you spell success? The culture we live in spells it academic achievement, money, fame, popularity or security. Success is when we get that scholastic prize, buy the big house, sell our paintings in a high-end gallery, or make it on Wall Street. The emphasis is on the end result of all of our work and ambition. It becomes a problem when we give so much significance to the goal that we tend to get there by any means we can: If we're happy with the end result, who cares about ethics or morals or integrity? If I get an A on an exam, does it matter whether I did the work myself? As long as nobody gets hurt, does it make a difference if I lie a little to get the job?

In God's definition of success, the means and the end are synonymous. God wanted Joshua to live so intimately attuned to his voice that the Israelite leader would *be* what God wanted him to be, would *know* what God wanted him to do and would *do* it fully believing that God would protect and bless him. Joshua's motives, thoughts and decisions would grow out of his relationship with God. Then he would be successful in the battles he would fight and in his leadership, and his prosperity would be the *shalom*, the spiritual well-being that would flourish out of his relationship with God.

God is concerned with the end results of our living and working; he wants us to become successful in what he gives us to do. But he is also concerned about the means: He wants us to prosper by loving him, talking to him and delighting in his Word.

"'For I know the plans I have for you,' declares the LORD, "'plans to prosper you and not to harm you, plans to give you hope and a future. Then you will call upon me and come and pray to me, and I will listen to you. You will seek me and find me when you seek me with all your heart'" (Jeremiah 29:11–13).

A Deeper Look
1 Kings 2:3–4; Psalm 1:2–3; Proverbs 16:3

Go to page 228 for your next devotional reading.

ever you have commanded us we will do, and wherever you send us we will go. [17]Just as we fully obeyed Moses, so we will obey you. Only may the LORD your God be with you as he was with Moses. [18]Whoever rebels against your word and does not obey your words, whatever you may command them, will be put to death. Only be strong and courageous!"

Rahab and the Spies

2 Then Joshua son of Nun secretly sent two spies from Shittim. "Go, look over the land," he said, "especially Jericho." So they went and entered the house of a prostitute[a] named Rahab and stayed there.

[2]The king of Jericho was told, "Look! Some of the Israelites have come here tonight to spy out the land." [3]So the king of Jericho sent this message to Rahab: "Bring out the men who came to you and entered your house, because they have come to spy out the whole land."

[4]But the woman had taken the two men and hidden them. She said, "Yes, the men came to me, but I did not know where they had come from. [5]At dusk, when it was time to close the city gate, the men left. I don't know which way they went. Go after them quickly. You may catch up with them." [6](But she had taken them up to the roof and hidden them under the stalks of flax she had laid out on the roof.) [7]So the men set out in pursuit of the spies on the road that leads to the fords of the Jordan, and as soon as the pursuers had gone out, the gate was shut.

[8]Before the spies lay down for the night, she went up on the roof [9]and said to them, "I know that the LORD has given this land to you and that a great fear of you has fallen on us, so that all who live in this country are melting in fear because of you. [10]We have heard how the LORD dried up the water of the Red Sea[b] for you when you came out of Egypt, and what you did to Sihon and Og, the two kings of the Amorites east of the Jordan, whom you completely destroyed.[c] [11]When we heard of it, our hearts melted and everyone's courage failed because of you, for the LORD your God is God in heaven above and on the earth below. [12]Now then, please swear to me by the LORD that you will show kindness to my family, because I have shown kindness to you. Give me a sure sign [13]that you will

spare the lives of my father and mother, my brothers and sisters, and all who belong to them, and that you will save us from death."

[14]"Our lives for your lives!" the men assured her. "If you don't tell what we are doing, we will treat you kindly and faithfully when the LORD gives us the land."

[15]So she let them down by a rope through the window, for the house she lived in was part of the city wall. [16]Now she had said to them, "Go to the hills so the pursuers will not find you. Hide yourselves there three days until they return, and then go on your way."

[17]The men said to her, "This oath you made us swear will not be binding on us [18]unless, when we enter the land, you have tied this scarlet cord in the window through which you let us down, and unless you have brought your father and mother, your brothers and all your family into your house. [19]If anyone goes outside your house into the street, his blood will be on his own head; we will not be responsible. As for anyone who is in the house with you, his blood will be on our head if a hand is laid on him. [20]But if you tell what we are doing, we will be released from the oath you made us swear."

[21]"Agreed," she replied. "Let it be as you say." So she sent them away and they departed. And she tied the scarlet cord in the window.

---

a 1 Or possibly *an innkeeper*   *b 10* Hebrew *Yam Suph*; that is, Sea of Reeds   *c 10* The Hebrew term refers to the irrevocable giving over of things or persons to the LORD, often by totally destroying them.

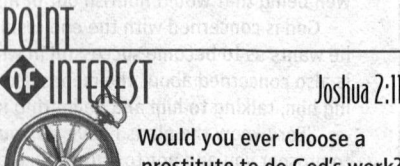

POINT OF INTEREST

Joshua 2:11

Would you ever choose a prostitute to do God's work? God did. Despite her occupational background, Rahab understood that God was the God of heaven and earth. Rahab feared him. As a result, she and her family were saved from annihilation. God's hand reached out to her at her point of need. Background never limits God's saving grace.

²²When they left, they went into the hills and stayed there three days, until the pursuers had searched all along the road and returned without finding them. ²³Then the two men started back. They went down out of the hills, forded the river and came to Joshua son of Nun and told him everything that had happened to them. ²⁴They said to Joshua, "The LORD has surely given the whole land into our hands; all the people are melting in fear because of us."

Crossing the Jordan

3 Early in the morning Joshua and all the Israelites set out from Shittim and went to the Jordan, where they camped before crossing over. ²After three days the officers went throughout the camp, ³giving orders to the people: "When you see the ark of the covenant of the LORD your God, and the priests, who are Levites, carrying it, you are to move out from your positions and follow it. ⁴Then you will know which way to go, since you have never been this way before. But keep a distance of about a thousand yards[a] between you and the ark; do not go near it."

⁵Joshua told the people, "Consecrate yourselves, for tomorrow the LORD will do amazing things among you."

⁶Joshua said to the priests, "Take up the ark of the covenant and pass on ahead of the people." So they took it up and went ahead of them.

⁷And the LORD said to Joshua, "Today I will begin to exalt you in the eyes of all Israel, so they may know that I am with you as I was with Moses. ⁸Tell the priests who carry the ark of the covenant: 'When you reach the edge of the Jordan's waters, go and stand in the river.' "

⁹Joshua said to the Israelites, "Come here and listen to the words of the LORD your God. ¹⁰This is how you will know that the living God is among you and that he will certainly drive out before you the Canaanites, Hittites, Hivites, Perizzites, Girgashites, Amorites and Jebusites. ¹¹See, the ark of the covenant of the Lord of all the earth will go into the Jordan ahead of you. ¹²Now then, choose twelve men from the tribes of Israel, one from each tribe. ¹³And as soon as the priests who carry the ark of the LORD—the Lord of all the earth—set foot in the Jordan, its waters flowing downstream will be cut off and stand up in a heap."

¹⁴So when the people broke camp to cross the Jordan, the priests carrying the ark of the covenant went ahead of them. ¹⁵Now the Jordan is at flood stage all during harvest. Yet as soon as the priests who carried the ark reached the Jordan and their feet touched the water's edge, ¹⁶the water from upstream stopped flowing. It piled up in a heap a great distance away, at a town called Adam in the vicinity of Zarethan, while the water flowing down to the Sea of the Arabah (the Salt Sea[b]) was completely cut off. So the people crossed over opposite Jericho. ¹⁷The priests who carried the ark of the covenant of the LORD stood firm on dry ground in the middle of the Jordan, while all Israel passed by until the whole nation had completed the crossing on dry ground.

4 When the whole nation had finished crossing the Jordan, the LORD said to Joshua, ²"Choose twelve men from among the people, one from each tribe, ³and tell them to take up twelve stones from the middle of the Jordan from right where the priests stood and to carry them over with you and put them down at the place where you stay tonight."

⁴So Joshua called together the twelve men he had appointed from the Israelites, one from each tribe, ⁵and said to them, "Go over before the ark of the LORD your God into the middle of the Jordan. Each of you is to take up a stone on his shoulder, according to the number of the tribes of the Israelites, ⁶to serve as a sign among you. In the future, when your children ask you, 'What do these stones mean?' ⁷tell them that the flow of the Jordan was cut off before the ark of the covenant of the LORD. When it crossed the Jordan, the waters of the Jordan were cut off. These stones are to be a memorial to the people of Israel forever."

⁸So the Israelites did as Joshua commanded them. They took twelve stones from the middle of the Jordan, according to the number of the tribes of the Israelites, as the LORD had told Joshua; and they carried them over with them to their camp, where they put them down. ⁹Joshua set up the twelve stones that had been[c] in the middle of the Jordan at the

---

[a]4 Hebrew about two thousand cubits (about 900 meters)   [b]16 That is, the Dead Sea   [c]9 Or Joshua also set up twelve stones

spot where the priests who carried the ark of the covenant had stood. And they are there to this day.

¹⁰Now the priests who carried the ark remained standing in the middle of the Jordan until everything the LORD had commanded Joshua was done by the people, just as Moses had directed Joshua. The people hurried over, ¹¹and as soon as all of them had crossed, the ark of the LORD and the priests came to the other side while the people watched. ¹²The men of Reuben, Gad and the half-tribe of Manasseh crossed over, armed, in front of the Israelites, as Moses had directed them. ¹³About forty thousand armed for battle crossed over before the LORD to the plains of Jericho for war.

¹⁴That day the LORD exalted Joshua in the sight of all Israel; and they revered him all the days of his life, just as they had revered Moses.

¹⁵Then the LORD said to Joshua, ¹⁶"Command the priests carrying the ark of the Testimony to come up out of the Jordan."

¹⁷So Joshua commanded the priests, "Come up out of the Jordan."

¹⁸And the priests came up out of the river carrying the ark of the covenant of

---

TUESDAY

Read Joshua 3:1–17
Key Verses Joshua 3:15–16

Stepping into the Water — Cathy Bowman

I wonder whether the priests in this account were afraid they would drown. They were, after all, stepping into a swollen, raging river. Yet God let them take that first step of faith before he parted the water.

A few years ago, God prompted me to take a big step of faith. I felt he wanted me to switch jobs so that I'd have more time to minister to people. "Cathy, you're crazy!" was my boss's reaction. I enjoyed what I was doing, I was up for a promotion, and the area was saturated with consultants in my field. Jobs were scarce. Maybe I *was* crazy!

I like feeling secure; I like knowing that I will be able to pay my bills. Yet God asked me to leave the dry land and follow him into waters of uncertainty, and he wanted me to take the first step by faith. He kept prompting me, and even though the waters ahead looked deep and murky, I decided to step in and switch to consulting.

Once the decision was made, God began parting the waters for me. Two weeks before I needed a new job, I discovered that three consultants in my field had just left their jobs, and before I knew it I had more offers than I could accept. Then I was able to rent the last apartment in a complex. On top of that, the manager reluctantly agreed to let three of us live in the apartment instead of two. I was overwhelmed by God's timing, provision and faithfulness.

Jesus himself told us that if we ask in his name he will do great things through us. I found him faithful to that promise! "I tell you the truth, anyone who has faith in me will do what I have been doing . . . You may ask me for anything in my name, and I will do it" (John 14:12–14).

A Deeper Look
1 Kings 17:7–16; Hebrews 11

Go to page 232 for your next devotional reading.

the LORD. No sooner had they set their feet on the dry ground than the waters of the Jordan returned to their place and ran at flood stage as before.

¹⁹On the tenth day of the first month the people went up from the Jordan and camped at Gilgal on the eastern border of Jericho. ²⁰And Joshua set up at Gilgal the twelve stones they had taken out of the Jordan. ²¹He said to the Israelites, "In the future when your descendants ask their fathers, 'What do these stones mean?' ²²tell them, 'Israel crossed the Jordan on dry ground.' ²³For the LORD your God dried up the Jordan before you until you had crossed over. The LORD your God did to the Jordan just what he had done to the Red Sea*a* when he dried it up before us until we had crossed over. ²⁴He did this so that all the peoples of the earth might know that the hand of the LORD is powerful and so that you might always fear the LORD your God."

Circumcision at Gilgal

5 Now when all the Amorite kings west of the Jordan and all the Canaanite kings along the coast heard how the LORD had dried up the Jordan before the Israelites until we had crossed over, their hearts melted and they no longer had the courage to face the Israelites.

²At that time the LORD said to Joshua, "Make flint knives and circumcise the Israelites again." ³So Joshua made flint knives and circumcised the Israelites at Gibeath Haaraloth.*b*

⁴Now this is why he did so: All those who came out of Egypt—all the men of military age—died in the desert on the way after leaving Egypt. ⁵All the people that came out had been circumcised, but all the people born in the desert during the journey from Egypt had not. ⁶The Israelites had moved about in the desert forty years until all the men who were of military age when they left Egypt had died, since they had not obeyed the LORD. For the LORD had sworn to them that they would not see the land that he had solemnly promised their fathers to give us, a land flowing with milk and honey. ⁷So he raised up their sons in their place, and these were the ones Joshua circumcised. They were still uncircumcised because they had not been circumcised on the way. ⁸And after the whole nation had been circumcised, they remained where they were in camp until they were healed.

⁹Then the LORD said to Joshua, "Today I have rolled away the reproach of Egypt from you." So the place has been called Gilgal*c* to this day.

¹⁰On the evening of the fourteenth day of the month, while camped at Gilgal on the plains of Jericho, the Israelites celebrated the Passover. ¹¹The day after the Passover, that very day, they ate some of the produce of the land: unleavened bread and roasted grain. ¹²The manna stopped the day after*d* they ate this food from the land; there was no longer any manna for the Israelites, but that year they ate of the produce of Canaan.

The Fall of Jericho

¹³Now when Joshua was near Jericho, he looked up and saw a man standing in front of him with a drawn sword in his hand. Joshua went up to him and asked, "Are you for us or for our enemies?"

¹⁴"Neither," he replied, "but as commander of the army of the LORD I have now come." Then Joshua fell facedown to the ground in reverence, and asked him, "What message does my Lord*e* have for his servant?"

¹⁵The commander of the LORD's army replied, "Take off your sandals, for the place where you are standing is holy." And Joshua did so.

6 Now Jericho was tightly shut up because of the Israelites. No one went out and no one came in.

²Then the LORD said to Joshua, "See, I have delivered Jericho into your hands, along with its king and its fighting men. ³March around the city once with all the armed men. Do this for six days. ⁴Have seven priests carry trumpets of rams' horns in front of the ark. On the seventh day, march around the city seven times, with the priests blowing the trumpets. ⁵When you hear them sound a long blast on the trumpets, have all the people give a loud shout; then the wall of the city will collapse and the people will go up, every man straight in."

⁶So Joshua son of Nun called the priests and said to them, "Take up the ark of the covenant of the LORD and have

---

a23 Hebrew *Yam Suph*; that is, Sea of Reeds
b3 Gibeath Haaraloth means *hill of foreskins.*
c9 Gilgal sounds like the Hebrew for *roll.*
d12 Or *the day*   *e14* Or *lord*

seven priests carry trumpets in front of it." ⁷And he ordered the people, "Advance! March around the city, with the armed guard going ahead of the ark of the LORD."

⁸When Joshua had spoken to the people, the seven priests carrying the seven trumpets before the LORD went forward, blowing their trumpets, and the ark of the LORD's covenant followed them. ⁹The armed guard marched ahead of the priests who blew the trumpets, and the rear guard followed the ark. All this time the trumpets were sounding. ¹⁰But Joshua had commanded the people, "Do not give a war cry, do not raise your voices, do not say a word until the day I tell you to shout. Then shout!" ¹¹So he had the ark of the LORD carried around the city, circling it once. Then the people returned to camp and spent the night there.

¹²Joshua got up early the next morning and the priests took up the ark of the LORD. ¹³The seven priests carrying the seven trumpets went forward, marching before the ark of the LORD and blowing the trumpets. The armed men went ahead of them and the rear guard followed the ark of the LORD, while the trumpets kept sounding. ¹⁴So on the second day they marched around the city once and returned to the camp. They did this for six days.

¹⁵On the seventh day, they got up at daybreak and marched around the city seven times in the same manner, except that on that day they circled the city seven times. ¹⁶The seventh time around, when the priests sounded the trumpet blast, Joshua commanded the people, "Shout! For the LORD has given you the city! ¹⁷The city and all that is in it are to be devoted*ᵃ* to the LORD. Only Rahab the prostitute*ᵇ* and all who are with her in her house shall be spared, because she hid the spies we sent. ¹⁸But keep away from the devoted things, so that you will not bring about your own destruction by taking any of them. Otherwise you will make the camp of Israel liable to destruction and bring trouble on it. ¹⁹All the silver and gold and the articles of bronze and iron are sacred to the LORD and must go into his treasury."

²⁰When the trumpets sounded, the people shouted, and at the sound of the trumpet, when the people gave a loud shout, the wall collapsed; so every man charged straight in, and they took the city. ²¹They devoted the city to the LORD and destroyed with the sword every living thing in it—men and women, young and old, cattle, sheep and donkeys.

²²Joshua said to the two men who had spied out the land, "Go into the prostitute's house and bring her out and all who belong to her, in accordance with your oath to her." ²³So the young men who had done the spying went in and brought out Rahab, her father and mother and brothers and all who belonged to her. They brought out her entire family and put them in a place outside the camp of Israel.

²⁴Then they burned the whole city and everything in it, but they put the silver and gold and the articles of bronze and iron into the treasury of the LORD's house. ²⁵But Joshua spared Rahab the prostitute, with her family and all who belonged to her, because she hid the men Joshua had sent as spies to Jericho—and she lives among the Israelites to this day.

²⁶At that time Joshua pronounced this solemn oath: "Cursed before the LORD is the man who undertakes to rebuild this city, Jericho:

"At the cost of his firstborn son
    will he lay its foundations;
at the cost of his youngest
    will he set up its gates."

²⁷So the LORD was with Joshua, and his fame spread throughout the land.

ᵃ17 The Hebrew term refers to the irrevocable giving over of things or persons to the LORD, often by totally destroying them; also in verses 18 and 21. *ᵇ17* Or possibly *innkeeper*; also in verses 22 and 25

POINT OF INTEREST

Joshua 6:20

A mound of dirt marks the site of Old Testament Jericho. Hiel the Bethelite tried to resurrect the city 550 years after its destruction, and the death of his sons fulfilled Joshua's ancient curse. First excavated in 1868, most of the remains of the city have been lost to erosion.

Achan's Sin

7 But the Israelites acted unfaithfully in regard to the devoted things[a]; Achan son of Carmi, the son of Zimri,[b] the son of Zerah, of the tribe of Judah, took some of them. So the LORD's anger burned against Israel.

²Now Joshua sent men from Jericho to Ai, which is near Beth Aven to the east of Bethel, and told them, "Go up and spy out the region." So the men went up and spied out Ai.

³When they returned to Joshua, they said, "Not all the people will have to go up against Ai. Send two or three thousand men to take it and do not weary all the people, for only a few men are there." ⁴So about three thousand men went up; but they were routed by the men of Ai, ⁵who killed about thirty-six of them. They chased the Israelites from the city gate as far as the stone quarries[c] and struck them down on the slopes. At this the hearts of the people melted and became like water.

⁶Then Joshua tore his clothes and fell facedown to the ground before the ark of the LORD, remaining there till evening. The elders of Israel did the same, and sprinkled dust on their heads. ⁷And Joshua said, "Ah, Sovereign LORD, why did you ever bring this people across the Jordan to deliver us into the hands of the Amorites to destroy us? If only we had been content to stay on the other side of the Jordan! ⁸O Lord, what can I say, now that Israel has been routed by its enemies? ⁹The Canaanites and the other people of the country will hear about this and they will surround us and wipe out our name from the earth. What then will you do for your own great name?"

¹⁰The LORD said to Joshua, "Stand up! What are you doing down on your face? ¹¹Israel has sinned; they have violated my covenant, which I commanded them to keep. They have taken some of the devoted things; they have stolen, they have lied, they have put them with their own possessions. ¹²That is why the Israelites cannot stand against their enemies; they turn their backs and run because they have been made liable to destruction. I will not be with you anymore unless you destroy whatever among you is devoted to destruction.

¹³"Go, consecrate the people. Tell them, 'Consecrate yourselves in prepara-

tion for tomorrow; for this is what the LORD, the God of Israel, says: That which is devoted is among you, O Israel. You cannot stand against your enemies until you remove it.

¹⁴"'In the morning, present yourselves tribe by tribe. The tribe that the LORD takes shall come forward clan by clan; the clan that the LORD takes shall come forward family by family; and the family that the LORD takes shall come forward man by man. ¹⁵He who is caught with the devoted things shall be destroyed by fire, along with all that belongs to him. He has violated the covenant of the LORD and has done a disgraceful thing in Israel!'"

¹⁶Early the next morning Joshua had Israel come forward by tribes, and Judah was taken. ¹⁷The clans of Judah came forward, and he took the Zerahites. He had the clan of the Zerahites come forward by families, and Zimri was taken. ¹⁸Joshua had his family come forward man by man, and Achan son of Carmi, the son of Zimri, the son of Zerah, of the tribe of Judah, was taken.

¹⁹Then Joshua said to Achan, "My son, give glory to the LORD,[d] the God of Israel, and give him the praise.[e] Tell me what you have done; do not hide it from me."

²⁰Achan replied, "It is true! I have sinned against the LORD, the God of Israel. This is what I have done: ²¹When I saw in the plunder a beautiful robe from Babylonia,[f] two hundred shekels[g] of silver and a wedge of gold weighing fifty shekels,[h] I coveted them and took them. They are hidden in the ground inside my tent, with the silver underneath."

²²So Joshua sent messengers, and they ran to the tent, and there it was, hidden in his tent, with the silver underneath. ²³They took the things from the tent, brought them to Joshua and all the Israelites and spread them out before the LORD.

²⁴Then Joshua, together with all Israel, took Achan son of Zerah, the silver,

---

a 1 The Hebrew term refers to the irrevocable giving over of things or persons to the LORD, often by totally destroying them; also in verses 11, 12, 13 and 15.   *b 1* See Septuagint and 1 Chron. 2:6; Hebrew *Zabdi*; also in verses 17 and 18.   *c 5* Or *as far as Shebarim*   *d 19* A solemn charge to tell the truth   *e 19* Or *and confess to him*   *f 21* Hebrew *Shinar*   *g 21* That is, about 5 pounds (about 2.3 kilograms)   *h 21* That is, about 1 1/4 pounds (about 0.6 kilogram) the robe, the gold wedge, his sons and daughters, his cattle, donkeys and sheep, his tent and all that he had, to the Valley of Achor. 25Joshua said, "Why have you brought this trouble on us? The LORD will bring trouble on you today."

Then all Israel stoned him, and after they had stoned the rest, they burned them. 26Over Achan they heaped up a large pile of rocks, which remains to this day. Then the LORD turned from his fierce anger. Therefore that place has been called the Valley of Achor*a* ever since.

Ai Destroyed

8 Then the LORD said to Joshua, "Do not be afraid; do not be discouraged. Take the whole army with you, and go up and attack Ai. For I have delivered into your hands the king of Ai, his people, his city and his land. 2You shall do to Ai and its king as you did to Jericho and its king, except that you may carry off their plunder and livestock for yourselves. Set an ambush behind the city."

a26 Achor means trouble.

Read *Joshua 7:1–26*
Key Verse *Joshua 7:21*

Where's the Battle? — John Carroll

Maybe it would be easy to blame Achan's failure on his circumstances, which were probably unavoidable. He was surrounded by all that glittering, shiny stuff—bronze and silver and gold. His fingers began to itch; he wanted to own the treasure from a fallen city—treasure that was already devoted to God. The robe, the silver and the gold belonged in the Lord's treasury. Achan knew it was wrong to keep them for himself—Joshua had made that clear from the beginning (see Joshua 6:18–19). But Achan ignored the warning and helped himself. He tried to hide his guilty conscience along with the loot. He couldn't even enjoy the stuff. He couldn't show it off to anyone; he couldn't use the robe, the gold or the silver without being found out.

Rather than facing what he'd done and confessing his sin, he continued to pretend that all was well. But soon Achan's sin brought suffering upon others as well (see Joshua 7:4–5). After the defeat at Ai, God told Joshua what Achan had done. Then everyone knew that Achan was responsible. Sin never stays hidden: "You may be sure that your sin will find you out" (Numbers 32:23). And Achan didn't pay for his sin alone; he dragged his household down with him. Achan's seemingly small but bad choice to covet something beautiful and valuable led to disaster.

The battle with temptation is fought first in the mind. It begins with a choice—a choice that seems small but may be loaded with consequences. But the battle is "winnable" when we rely on God's grace to help. He has given us his word to fortify us: "No temptation has seized you except what is common to man. And God is faithful; he will not let you be tempted beyond what you can bear. But when you are tempted, he will also provide a way out so that you can stand up under it" (1 Corinthians 10:13).

A Deeper Look
Psalm 119:9–11; Romans 13:9–10; 1 Timothy 6:11–13

Go to page 235 for your next devotional reading.

³So Joshua and the whole army moved out to attack Ai. He chose thirty thousand of his best fighting men and sent them out at night ⁴with these orders: "Listen carefully. You are to set an ambush behind the city. Don't go very far from it. All of you be on the alert. ⁵I and all those with me will advance on the city, and when the men come out against us, as they did before, we will flee from them. ⁶They will pursue us until we have lured them away from the city, for they will say, 'They are running away from us as they did before.' So when we flee from them, ⁷you are to rise up from ambush and take the city. The Lord your God will give it into your hand. ⁸When you have taken the city, set it on fire. Do what the Lord has commanded. See to it; you have my orders."

⁹Then Joshua sent them off, and they went to the place of ambush and lay in wait between Bethel and Ai, to the west of Ai—but Joshua spent that night with the people.

¹⁰Early the next morning Joshua mustered his men, and he and the leaders of Israel marched before them to Ai. ¹¹The entire force that was with him marched up and approached the city and arrived in front of it. They set up camp north of Ai, with the valley between them and the city. ¹²Joshua had taken about five thousand men and set them in ambush between Bethel and Ai, to the west of the city. ¹³They had the soldiers take up their positions—all those in the camp to the north of the city and the ambush to the west of it. That night Joshua went into the valley.

¹⁴When the king of Ai saw this, he and all the men of the city hurried out early in the morning to meet Israel in battle at a certain place overlooking the Arabah. But he did not know that an ambush had been set against him behind the city. ¹⁵Joshua and all Israel let themselves be driven back before them, and they fled toward the desert. ¹⁶All the men of Ai were called to pursue them, and they pursued Joshua and were lured away from the city. ¹⁷Not a man remained in Ai or Bethel who did not go after Israel. They left the city open and went in pursuit of Israel.

¹⁸Then the Lord said to Joshua, "Hold out toward Ai the javelin that is in your hand, for into your hand I will deliver the city." So Joshua held out his javelin toward Ai. ¹⁹As soon as he did this, the men in the ambush rose quickly from their position and rushed forward. They entered the city and captured it and quickly set it on fire.

²⁰The men of Ai looked back and saw the smoke of the city rising against the sky, but they had no chance to escape in any direction, for the Israelites who had been fleeing toward the desert had turned back against their pursuers. ²¹For when Joshua and all Israel saw that the ambush had taken the city and that smoke was going up from the city, they turned around and attacked the men of Ai. ²²The men of the ambush also came out of the city against them, so that they were caught in the middle, with Israelites on both sides. Israel cut them down, leaving them neither survivors nor fugitives. ²³But they took the king of Ai alive and brought him to Joshua.

²⁴When Israel had finished killing all the men of Ai in the fields and in the desert where they had chased them, and when every one of them had been put to the sword, all the Israelites returned to Ai and killed those who were in it. ²⁵Twelve thousand men and women fell that day— all the people of Ai. ²⁶For Joshua did not draw back the hand that held out his javelin until he had destroyed[a] all who lived in Ai. ²⁷But Israel did carry off for themselves the livestock and plunder of this city, as the Lord had instructed Joshua.

²⁸So Joshua burned Ai and made it a permanent heap of ruins, a desolate place to this day. ²⁹He hung the king of Ai on a tree and left him there until evening. At sunset, Joshua ordered them to take his body from the tree and throw it down at the entrance of the city gate. And they raised a large pile of rocks over it, which remains to this day.

The Covenant Renewed at Mount Ebal

³⁰Then Joshua built on Mount Ebal an altar to the Lord, the God of Israel, ³¹as Moses the servant of the Lord had commanded the Israelites. He built it according to what is written in the Book of the Law of Moses—an altar of uncut stones, on which no iron tool had been used.

a26 The Hebrew term refers to the irrevocable giving over of things or persons to the Lord, often by totally destroying them.

On it they offered to the LORD burnt offerings and sacrificed fellowship offerings.*a*
32There, in the presence of the Israelites, Joshua copied on stones the law of Moses, which he had written. 33All Israel, aliens and citizens alike, with their elders, officials and judges, were standing on both sides of the ark of the covenant of the LORD, facing those who carried it— the priests, who were Levites. Half of the people stood in front of Mount Gerizim and half of them in front of Mount Ebal, as Moses the servant of the LORD had formerly commanded when he gave instructions to bless the people of Israel.

34Afterward, Joshua read all the words of the law—the blessings and the curses—just as it is written in the Book of the Law. 35There was not a word of all that Moses had commanded that Joshua did not read to the whole assembly of Israel, including the women and children, and the aliens who lived among them.

The Gibeonite Deception

9 Now when all the kings west of the Jordan heard about these things— those in the hill country, in the western foothills, and along the entire coast of the Great Sea*b* as far as Lebanon (the kings of the Hittites, Amorites, Canaanites, Perizzites, Hivites and Jebusites)— 2they came together to make war against Joshua and Israel.

3However, when the people of Gibeon heard what Joshua had done to Jericho and Ai, 4they resorted to a ruse: They went as a delegation whose donkeys were loaded*c* with worn-out sacks and old wineskins, cracked and mended. 5The men put worn and patched sandals on their feet and wore old clothes. All the bread of their food supply was dry and moldy. 6Then they went to Joshua in the camp at Gilgal and said to him and the men of Israel, "We have come from a distant country; make a treaty with us."

7The men of Israel said to the Hivites, "But perhaps you live near us. How then can we make a treaty with you?"

8"We are your servants," they said to Joshua.

But Joshua asked, "Who are you and where do you come from?"

9They answered: "Your servants have come from a very distant country because of the fame of the LORD your God.

For we have heard reports of him: all that he did in Egypt, 10and all that he did to the two kings of the Amorites east of the Jordan—Sihon king of Heshbon, and Og king of Bashan, who reigned in Ashtaroth. 11And our elders and all those living in our country said to us, 'Take provisions for your journey; go and meet them and say to them, "We are your servants; make a treaty with us." ' 12This bread of ours was warm when we packed it at home on the day we left to come to you. But now see how dry and moldy it is. 13And these wineskins that we filled were new, but see how cracked they are. And our clothes and sandals are worn out by the very long journey."

14The men of Israel sampled their provisions but did not inquire of the LORD. 15Then Joshua made a treaty of peace with them to let them live, and the leaders of the assembly ratified it by oath.

16Three days after they made the treaty with the Gibeonites, the Israelites heard that they were neighbors, living near them. 17So the Israelites set out and on the third day came to their cities: Gibeon, Kephirah, Beeroth and Kiriath Jearim. 18But the Israelites did not attack them, because the leaders of the assembly had sworn an oath to them by the LORD, the God of Israel.

The whole assembly grumbled against the leaders, 19but all the leaders answered, "We have given them our oath by the LORD, the God of Israel, and we cannot touch them now. 20This is what we will do to them: We will let them live, so that wrath will not fall on us for breaking the oath we swore to them." 21They continued, "Let them live, but let them be woodcutters and water carriers for the entire community." So the leaders' promise to them was kept.

22Then Joshua summoned the Gibeonites and said, "Why did you deceive us by saying, 'We live a long way from you,' while actually you live near us? 23You are now under a curse: You will never cease to serve as woodcutters and water carriers for the house of my God."

24They answered Joshua, "Your servants were clearly told how the LORD your God had commanded his servant Moses

---

*a*31 Traditionally *peace offerings*   *b*1 That is, the Mediterranean   *c*4 Most Hebrew manuscripts; some Hebrew manuscripts, Vulgate and Syriac (see also Septuagint) *They prepared provisions and loaded their donkeys* to give you the whole land and to wipe out all its inhabitants from before you. So we feared for our lives because of you, and that is why we did this. ²⁵We are now in your hands. Do to us whatever seems good and right to you."

²⁶So Joshua saved them from the Israelites, and they did not kill them. ²⁷That day he made the Gibeonites woodcutters and water carriers for the community and for the altar of the LORD at the place the LORD would choose. And that is what they are to this day.

The Sun Stands Still

10 Now Adoni-Zedek king of Jerusalem heard that Joshua had taken Ai and totally destroyed[a] it, doing to Ai and its

*a*1 The Hebrew term refers to the irrevocable giving over of things or persons to the LORD, often by totally destroying them; also in verses 28, 35, 37, 39 and 40.

THURSDAY

Read *Joshua 9:1–27*
Key Verse *Joshua 9:14*

Check with God First — Tony Cammarota

The great reformer Martin Luther once commented about the extra load of activities he had to accomplish for the day and said, "Work, work, from early till late. In fact, I have so much to do that I shall spend the first three hours in prayer." Luther depended on God— not on his own strength. He understood that if he consulted with God before his day began, it would go more smoothly; he would avoid obstacles and pitfalls.

This passage in Joshua illustrates the same principle but in a negative way. Knowing that the Israelites had been commanded to conquer all the people of Canaan, the Gibeonites feared that they would soon be wiped out like their neighbors. So they pulled a fast one on the Israelites by telling them that they had come from far away—and that they were not one of Israel's soon-to-be-conquered neighbors. They offered to work as servants in exchange for a treaty that provided them with immunity from the Israelite swords. Without asking God about it, Joshua and the elders made and ratified a peace treaty. Because they did not check with the Lord *first*, the Israelites were deceived by the Gibeonites. When the Israelites found out that the Gibeonites were neighbors, their hands were tied. They even had to go out and fight against the Gibeonites' enemies.

Let's be honest—it might *seem* easier to rely on our intelligence and common sense. When we carry on for awhile without seeking out God's viewpoint, we might think we are doing all right, but we have no way of seeing the pitfalls and deceptions that might be waiting for us. The only way to gain that kind of vision and wisdom is to ask God. Who knows better than the All-knowing? Who guides better than The Way? Who counsels better than the Wonderful Counselor? His thoughts are higher than our thoughts, his ways are higher than our ways (see Isaiah 55:9). He promises to give us counsel if only we look to him (see Isaiah 48:17–18).

A Deeper Look
Psalm 32:8; Proverbs 3:5–6; Jeremiah 33:2–3

Go to page 241 for your next devotional reading.

king as he had done to Jericho and its king, and that the people of Gibeon had made a treaty of peace with Israel and were living near them. ²He and his people were very much alarmed at this, because Gibeon was an important city, like one of the royal cities; it was larger than Ai, and all its men were good fighters. ³So Adoni-Zedek king of Jerusalem appealed to Hoham king of Hebron, Piram king of Jarmuth, Japhia king of Lachish and Debir king of Eglon. ⁴"Come up and help me attack Gibeon," he said, "because it has made peace with Joshua and the Israelites."

⁵Then the five kings of the Amorites— the kings of Jerusalem, Hebron, Jarmuth, Lachish and Eglon—joined forces. They moved up with all their troops and took up positions against Gibeon and attacked it.

⁶The Gibeonites then sent word to Joshua in the camp at Gilgal: "Do not abandon your servants. Come up to us quickly and save us! Help us, because all the Amorite kings from the hill country have joined forces against us."

⁷So Joshua marched up from Gilgal with his entire army, including all the best fighting men. ⁸The LORD said to Joshua, "Do not be afraid of them; I have given them into your hand. Not one of them will be able to withstand you."

⁹After an all-night march from Gilgal, Joshua took them by surprise. ¹⁰The LORD threw them into confusion before Israel, who defeated them in a great victory at Gibeon. Israel pursued them along the road going up to Beth Horon and cut them down all the way to Azekah and Makkedah. ¹¹As they fled before Israel on the road down from Beth Horon to Azekah, the LORD hurled large hailstones down on them from the sky, and more of them died from the hailstones than were killed by the swords of the Israelites.

¹²On the day the LORD gave the Amorites over to Israel, Joshua said to the LORD in the presence of Israel:

"O sun, stand still over Gibeon,
    O moon, over the Valley of
        Aijalon."
¹³So the sun stood still,
    and the moon stopped,
    till the nation avenged itself on*ᵃ
        its enemies,

as it is written in the Book of Jashar. The sun stopped in the middle of the sky and delayed going down about a full day. ¹⁴There has never been a day like it before or since, a day when the LORD listened to a man. Surely the LORD was fighting for Israel!

¹⁵Then Joshua returned with all Israel to the camp at Gilgal.

Five Amorite Kings Killed

¹⁶Now the five kings had fled and hidden in the cave at Makkedah. ¹⁷When Joshua was told that the five kings had been found hiding in the cave at Makkedah, ¹⁸he said, "Roll large rocks up to the mouth of the cave, and post some men there to guard it. ¹⁹But don't stop! Pursue your enemies, attack them from the rear and don't let them reach their cities, for the LORD your God has given them into your hand."

²⁰So Joshua and the Israelites destroyed them completely—almost to a man—but the few who were left reached their fortified cities. ²¹The whole army then returned safely to Joshua in the camp at Makkedah, and no one uttered a word against the Israelites.

²²Joshua said, "Open the mouth of the cave and bring those five kings out to me." ²³So they brought the five kings out of the cave—the kings of Jerusalem, Hebron, Jarmuth, Lachish and Eglon. ²⁴When they had brought these kings to Joshua, he summoned all the men of Israel and said to the army commanders who had come with him, "Come here and put your feet on the necks of these kings." So

ᵃ13 Or nation triumphed over

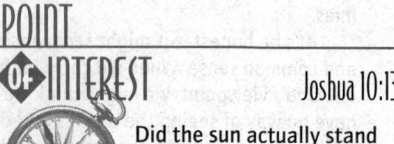

POINT OF INTEREST   Joshua 10:13

Did the sun actually stand still? Scientists and theologians have debated the answer to this question for centuries. Ask yourself these questions: Could the Creator of the universe stop the earth's rotation so that the sun appeared to stand still? Could this passage refer to an eclipse? Was this a prayer for God to delay the sunrise so that the day would be cooler for battle? What do you think?

they came forward and placed their feet on their necks.

²⁵Joshua said to them, "Do not be afraid; do not be discouraged. Be strong and courageous. This is what the LORD will do to all the enemies you are going to fight." ²⁶Then Joshua struck and killed the kings and hung them on five trees, and they were left hanging on the trees until evening.

²⁷At sunset Joshua gave the order and they took them down from the trees and threw them into the cave where they had been hiding. At the mouth of the cave they placed large rocks, which are there to this day.

²⁸That day Joshua took Makkedah. He put the city and its king to the sword and totally destroyed everyone in it. He left no survivors. And he did to the king of Makkedah as he had done to the king of Jericho.

Southern Cities Conquered

²⁹Then Joshua and all Israel with him moved on from Makkedah to Libnah and attacked it. ³⁰The LORD also gave that city and its king into Israel's hand. The city and everyone in it Joshua put to the sword. He left no survivors there. And he did to its king as he had done to the king of Jericho.

³¹Then Joshua and all Israel with him moved on from Libnah to Lachish; he took up positions against it and attacked it. ³²The LORD handed Lachish over to Israel, and Joshua took it on the second day. The city and everyone in it he put to the sword, just as he had done to Libnah. ³³Meanwhile, Horam king of Gezer had come up to help Lachish, but Joshua defeated him and his army—until no survivors were left.

³⁴Then Joshua and all Israel with him moved on from Lachish to Eglon; they took up positions against it and attacked it. ³⁵They captured it that same day and put it to the sword and totally destroyed everyone in it, just as they had done to Lachish.

³⁶Then Joshua and all Israel with him went up from Eglon to Hebron and attacked it. ³⁷They took the city and put it to the sword, together with its king, its villages and everyone in it. They left no survivors. Just as at Eglon, they totally destroyed it and everyone in it.

³⁸Then Joshua and all Israel with him turned around and attacked Debir. ³⁹They took the city, its king and its villages, and put them to the sword. Everyone in it they totally destroyed. They left no survivors. They did to Debir and its king as they had done to Libnah and its king and to Hebron.

⁴⁰So Joshua subdued the whole region, including the hill country, the Negev, the western foothills and the mountain slopes, together with all their kings. He left no survivors. He totally destroyed all who breathed, just as the LORD, the God of Israel, had commanded. ⁴¹Joshua subdued them from Kadesh Barnea to Gaza and from the whole region of Goshen to Gibeon. ⁴²All these kings and their lands Joshua conquered in one campaign, because the LORD, the God of Israel, fought for Israel.

⁴³Then Joshua returned with all Israel to the camp at Gilgal.

Northern Kings Defeated

11 When Jabin king of Hazor heard of this, he sent word to Jobab king of Madon, to the kings of Shimron and Acshaph, ²and to the northern kings who were in the mountains, in the Arabah south of Kinnereth, in the western foothills and in Naphoth Dorᵃ on the west; ³to the Canaanites in the east and west; to the Amorites, Hittites, Perizzites and Jebusites in the hill country; and to the Hivites below Hermon in the region of Mizpah. ⁴They came out with all their troops and a large number of horses and chariots—a huge army, as numerous as the sand on the seashore. ⁵All these kings joined forces and made camp together at the Waters of Merom, to fight against Israel.

⁶The LORD said to Joshua, "Do not be afraid of them, because by this time tomorrow I will hand all of them over to Israel, slain. You are to hamstring their horses and burn their chariots."

⁷So Joshua and his whole army came against them suddenly at the Waters of Merom and attacked them, ⁸and the LORD gave them into the hand of Israel. They defeated them and pursued them all the way to Greater Sidon, to Misrephoth Maim, and to the Valley of Mizpah on the east, until no survivors were left. ⁹Joshua did to them as the LORD had directed: He

ᵃ2 Or in the heights of Dor

hamstrung their horses and burned their chariots.

[10]At that time Joshua turned back and captured Hazor and put its king to the sword. (Hazor had been the head of all these kingdoms.) [11]Everyone in it they put to the sword. They totally destroyed[a] them, not sparing anything that breathed, and he burned up Hazor itself.

[12]Joshua took all these royal cities and their kings and put them to the sword. He totally destroyed them, as Moses the servant of the LORD had commanded. [13]Yet Israel did not burn any of the cities built on their mounds—except Hazor, which Joshua burned. [14]The Israelites carried off for themselves all the plunder and livestock of these cities, but all the people they put to the sword until they completely destroyed them, not sparing anyone that breathed. [15]As the LORD commanded his servant Moses, so Moses commanded Joshua, and Joshua did it; he left nothing undone of all that the LORD commanded Moses.

[16]So Joshua took this entire land: the hill country, all the Negev, the whole region of Goshen, the western foothills, the Arabah and the mountains of Israel with their foothills, [17]from Mount Halak, which rises toward Seir, to Baal Gad in the Valley of Lebanon below Mount Hermon. He captured all their kings and struck them down, putting them to death. [18]Joshua waged war against all these kings for a long time. [19]Except for the Hivites living in Gibeon, not one city made a treaty of peace with the Israelites, who took them all in battle. [20]For it was the LORD himself who hardened their hearts to wage war against Israel, so that he might destroy them totally, exterminating them without mercy, as the LORD had commanded Moses.

[21]At that time Joshua went and destroyed the Anakites from the hill country: from Hebron, Debir and Anab, from all the hill country of Judah, and from all the hill country of Israel. Joshua totally destroyed them and their towns. [22]No Anakites were left in Israelite territory; only in Gaza, Gath and Ashdod did any survive. [23]So Joshua took the entire land, just as the LORD had directed Moses, and he gave it as an inheritance to Israel according to their tribal divisions.

Then the land had rest from war.

List of Defeated Kings

[12] These are the kings of the land whom the Israelites had defeated and whose territory they took over east of the Jordan, from the Arnon Gorge to Mount Hermon, including all the eastern side of the Arabah:

[2]Sihon king of the Amorites,
who reigned in Heshbon. He ruled from Aroer on the rim of the Arnon Gorge—from the middle of the gorge—to the Jabbok River, which is the border of the Ammonites. This included half of Gilead. [3]He also ruled over the eastern Arabah from the Sea of Kinnereth[b] to the Sea of the Arabah (the Salt Sea[c]), to Beth Jeshimoth, and then southward below the slopes of Pisgah.

[4]And the territory of Og king of Bashan, one of the last of the Rephaites, who reigned in Ashtaroth and Edrei. [5]He ruled over Mount Hermon, Salecah, all of Bashan to the border of the people of Geshur and Maacah, and half of Gilead to the border of Sihon king of Heshbon.

[6]Moses, the servant of the LORD, and the Israelites conquered them. And Moses the servant of the LORD gave their land to the Reubenites, the Gadites and the half-tribe of Manasseh to be their possession.

---

[a]11 The Hebrew term refers to the irrevocable giving over of things or persons to the LORD, often by totally destroying them; also in verses 12, 20 and 21.   [b]3 That is, Galilee   [c]3 That is, the Dead Sea

POINT OF INTEREST

Joshua 11:15

God trusted Moses, and Moses proved faithful. Moses trusted Joshua, and Joshua delivered. Identify a task that is so important to you that you always do it yourself. Now imagine that you *must,* for whatever reason, entrust this task to another person. Whom would you choose? Whom could you trust? Could other people count on you to take over their important work?

7These are the kings of the land that Joshua and the Israelites conquered on the west side of the Jordan, from Baal Gad in the Valley of Lebanon to Mount Halak, which rises toward Seir (their lands Joshua gave as an inheritance to the tribes of Israel according to their tribal divisions— 8the hill country, the western foothills, the Arabah, the mountain slopes, the desert and the Negev—the lands of the Hittites, Amorites, Canaanites, Perizzites, Hivites and Jebusites):

9the king of Jericho	one
the king of Ai (near Bethel)	one
10the king of Jerusalem	one
the king of Hebron	one
11the king of Jarmuth	one
the king of Lachish	one
12the king of Eglon	one
the king of Gezer	one
13the king of Debir	one
the king of Geder	one
14the king of Hormah	one
the king of Arad	one
15the king of Libnah	one
the king of Adullam	one
16the king of Makkedah	one
the king of Bethel	one
17the king of Tappuah	one
the king of Hepher	one
18the king of Aphek	one
the king of Lasharon	one
19the king of Madon	one
the king of Hazor	one
20the king of Shimron Meron	one
the king of Acshaph	one
21the king of Taanach	one
the king of Megiddo	one
22the king of Kedesh	one
the king of Jokneam in Carmel	one
23the king of Dor (in Naphoth Dora)	one
the king of Goyim in Gilgal	one
24the king of Tirzah	one

thirty-one kings in all.

Land Still to Be Taken

13 When Joshua was old and well advanced in years, the LORD said to him, "You are very old, and there are still very large areas of land to be taken over.

2"This is the land that remains: all the regions of the Philistines and Geshurites: 3from the Shihor River on the east of Egypt to the territory of Ekron on the north, all of it counted as Canaanite (the territory of the five Philistine rulers in Gaza, Ashdod, Ashkelon, Gath and Ekron—that of the Avvites); 4from the south, all the land of the Canaanites, from Arah of the Sidonians as far as Aphek, the region of the Amorites, 5the area of the Gebalitesb; and all Lebanon to the east, from Baal Gad below Mount Hermon to Leboc Hamath.

6"As for all the inhabitants of the mountain regions from Lebanon to Misrephoth Maim, that is, all the Sidonians, I myself will drive them out before the Israelites. Be sure to allocate this land to Israel for an inheritance, as I have instructed you, 7and divide it as an inheritance among the nine tribes and half of the tribe of Manasseh."

Division of the Land East of the Jordan

8The other half of Manasseh,d the Reubenites and the Gadites had received the inheritance that Moses had given them east of the Jordan, as he, the servant of the LORD, had assigned it to them.

9It extended from Aroer on the rim of the Arnon Gorge, and from the town in the middle of the gorge, and included the whole plateau of Medeba as far as Dibon, 10and all the towns of Sihon king of the Amorites, who ruled in Heshbon, out to the border of the Ammonites. 11It also included Gilead, the territory of the people of Geshur and Maacah, all of Mount Hermon and all Bashan as far as Salecah— 12that is, the whole kingdom of Og in Bashan, who had reigned in Ashtaroth and Edrei and had survived as one of the last of the Rephaites. Moses had defeated them and taken over their land. 13But the Israelites did not drive out the people of Geshur and Maacah, so they continue to live among the Israelites to this day.

14But to the tribe of Levi he gave no inheritance, since the offerings made by fire to the LORD, the God of Israel, are their inheritance, as he promised them.

a23 Or in the heights of Dor   b5 That is, the area of Byblos   c5 Or to the entrance to   d8 Hebrew With it (that is, with the other half of Manasseh)

¹⁵This is what Moses had given to the tribe of Reuben, clan by clan:

¹⁶The territory from Aroer on the rim of the Arnon Gorge, and from the town in the middle of the gorge, and the whole plateau past Medeba ¹⁷to Heshbon and all its towns on the plateau, including Dibon, Bamoth Baal, Beth Baal Meon, ¹⁸Jahaz, Kedemoth, Mephaath, ¹⁹Kiriathaim, Sibmah, Zereth Shahar on the hill in the valley, ²⁰Beth Peor, the slopes of Pisgah, and Beth Jeshimoth ²¹—all the towns on the plateau and the entire realm of Sihon king of the Amorites, who ruled at Heshbon. Moses had defeated him and the Midianite chiefs, Evi, Rekem, Zur, Hur and Reba—princes allied with Sihon—who lived in that country. ²²In addition to those slain in battle, the Israelites had put to the sword Balaam son of Beor, who practiced divination. ²³The boundary of the Reubenites was the bank of the Jordan. These towns and their villages were the inheritance of the Reubenites, clan by clan.

²⁴This is what Moses had given to the tribe of Gad, clan by clan:

²⁵The territory of Jazer, all the towns of Gilead and half the Ammonite country as far as Aroer, near Rabbah; ²⁶and from Heshbon to Ramath Mizpah and Betonim, and from Mahanaim to the territory of Debir; ²⁷and in the valley, Beth Haram, Beth Nimrah, Succoth and Zaphon with the rest of the realm of Sihon king of Heshbon (the east side of the Jordan, the territory up to the end of the Sea of Kinnereth*ᵃ). ²⁸These towns and their villages were the inheritance of the Gadites, clan by clan.

²⁹This is what Moses had given to the half-tribe of Manasseh, that is, to half the family of the descendants of Manasseh, clan by clan:

³⁰The territory extending from Mahanaim and including all of Bashan, the entire realm of Og king of Bashan—all the settlements of Jair in Bashan, sixty towns, ³¹half of Gilead, and Ashtaroth and Edrei (the royal cities of Og in Bashan). This was for the descendants of Makir son of Manasseh—for half of the sons of Makir, clan by clan.

³²This is the inheritance Moses had given when he was in the plains of Moab across the Jordan east of Jericho. ³³But to the tribe of Levi, Moses had given no inheritance; the LORD, the God of Israel, is their inheritance, as he promised them.

Division of the Land West of the Jordan

14 Now these are the areas the Israelites received as an inheritance in the land of Canaan, which Eleazar the priest, Joshua son of Nun and the heads of the tribal clans of Israel allotted to them. ²Their inheritances were assigned by lot to the nine-and-a-half tribes, as the LORD had commanded through Moses. ³Moses had granted the two-and-a-half tribes their inheritance east of the Jordan but had not granted the Levites an inheritance among the rest, ⁴for the sons of Joseph had become two tribes—Manasseh and Ephraim. The Levites received no share of the land but only towns to live in, with pasturelands for their flocks and herds. ⁵So the Israelites divided the land, just as the LORD had commanded Moses.

Hebron Given to Caleb

⁶Now the men of Judah approached Joshua at Gilgal, and Caleb son of Jephunneh the Kenizzite said to him, "You know what the LORD said to Moses the man of God at Kadesh Barnea about you and me. ⁷I was forty years old when Moses the servant of the LORD sent me from Kadesh Barnea to explore the land. And I

ᵃ27 That is, Galilee

POINT OF INTEREST

Joshua 13:14

The whole nation of Israel was responsible to support the Levites. The amount of that support was contingent on Israel's giving as God had commanded. God still wants his children to be cheerful and generous in their giving (see 2 Corinthians 9:6–9).

brought him back a report according to my convictions, **8**but my brothers who went up with me made the hearts of the people melt with fear. I, however, followed the LORD my God wholeheartedly. **9**So on that day Moses swore to me, 'The land on which your feet have walked will be your inheritance and that of your children forever, because you have followed the LORD my God wholeheartedly.'*a*

10"Now then, just as the LORD promised, he has kept me alive for forty-five years since the time he said this to Moses, while Israel moved about in the desert.

So here I am today, eighty-five years old! **11**I am still as strong today as the day Moses sent me out; I'm just as vigorous to go out to battle now as I was then. **12**Now give me this hill country that the LORD promised me that day. You yourself heard then that the Anakites were there and their cities were large and fortified, but, the LORD helping me, I will drive them out just as he said."

13Then Joshua blessed Caleb son of Jephunneh and gave him Hebron as his in-

*a*9 Deut. 1:36

FRIDAY

Read Joshua 14:6–15
Key Verse Joshua 14:12

Fighting Giants – Roger Hamilton

Sometimes life seems like a series of giant battles: final exams and financial challenges, family and peer pressures, finding and keeping a decent job.

Caleb could relate. God had graciously promised to give his people a land rich beyond their wildest dreams. But in Numbers 14 Caleb and his fellow Israelites faced an overwhelming obstacle: This land was home to people much bigger and stronger than the Israelites. Only Caleb and Joshua believed they could conquer the "giants" and take the land.

Even 45 years after that incident, Caleb, at age 85, was still eager to take on the remaining giants. He readily admitted the job wouldn't be easy, but rather than quaking with fear at the battles ahead, he couldn't wait to get out to Hebron and take on the giants. What long-term motivation kept Caleb going in his twilight years?

First, Caleb's understanding of God gave him the ability to see obstacles as opportunities. He remembered, "the LORD promised me," and he knew God was faithful to keep all his promises. If God had said something, it would happen! Caleb also understood that success was a result of cooperating with God—"the LORD helping me." This old man with a young heart wasn't willing to sit on the sidelines while God worked on his behalf. He had a job to do, but he could do it only with God's help. What a great picture of how to work together with God to bring about his plans. I suspect Caleb also recalled another key promise that had been given to Joshua: "Be strong and courageous . . . for the LORD your God will be with you wherever you go" (Joshua 1:9).

What obstacles are you facing? Who or what are the giants in your life? Let wise old Joshua teach you. God promises that he will be with those who trust him.

A Deeper Look
1 Samuel 17:38–50; Psalm 107:15–16; Isaiah 42:16

Go to page 249 for your next devotional reading.

heritance. [14]So Hebron has belonged to Caleb son of Jephunneh the Kenizzite ever since, because he followed the LORD, the God of Israel, wholeheartedly. [15](Hebron used to be called Kiriath Arba after Arba, who was the greatest man among the Anakites.)

Then the land had rest from war.

Allotment for Judah

15 The allotment for the tribe of Judah, clan by clan, extended down to the territory of Edom, to the Desert of Zin in the extreme south.

[2]Their southern boundary started from the bay at the southern end of the Salt Sea,[a] [3]crossed south of Scorpion[b] Pass, continued on to Zin and went over to the south of Kadesh Barnea. Then it ran past Hezron up to Addar and curved around to Karka. [4]It then passed along to Azmon and joined the Wadi of Egypt, ending at the sea. This is their[c] southern boundary.

[5]The eastern boundary is the Salt Sea as far as the mouth of the Jordan.

The northern boundary started from the bay of the sea at the mouth of the Jordan, [6]went up to Beth Hoglah and continued north of Beth Arabah to the Stone of Bohan son of Reuben. [7]The boundary then went up to Debir from the Valley of Achor and turned north to Gilgal, which faces the Pass of Adummim south of the gorge. It continued along to the waters of En Shemesh and came out at En Rogel. [8]Then it ran up the Valley of Ben Hinnom along the southern slope of the Jebusite city (that is, Jerusalem). From there it climbed to the top of the hill west of the Hinnom Valley at the northern end of the Valley of Rephaim. [9]From the hilltop the boundary headed toward the spring of the waters of Nephtoah, came out at the towns of Mount Ephron and went down toward Baalah (that is, Kiriath Jearim). [10]Then it curved westward from Baalah to Mount Seir, ran along the northern slope of Mount Jearim (that is, Kesalon), continued down to Beth Shemesh and crossed to Timnah. [11]It went to the northern slope of Ekron, turned toward Shikkeron, passed along to Mount Baalah and reached Jabneel. The boundary ended at the sea.

[12]The western boundary is the coastline of the Great Sea.[d]

These are the boundaries around the people of Judah by their clans.

[13]In accordance with the LORD's command to him, Joshua gave to Caleb son of Jephunneh a portion in Judah—Kiriath Arba, that is, Hebron. (Arba was the forefather of Anak.) [14]From Hebron Caleb drove out the three Anakites—Sheshai, Ahiman and Talmai—descendants of Anak. [15]From there he marched against the people living in Debir (formerly called Kiriath Sepher). [16]And Caleb said, "I will give my daughter Acsah in marriage to the man who attacks and captures Kiriath Sepher." [17]Othniel son of Kenaz, Caleb's brother, took it; so Caleb gave his daughter Acsah to him in marriage.

[18]One day when she came to Othniel, she urged him[e] to ask her father for a field. When she got off her donkey, Caleb asked her, "What can I do for you?"

[19]She replied, "Do me a special favor. Since you have given me land in the Negev, give me also springs of water." So Caleb gave her the upper and lower springs.

[20]This is the inheritance of the tribe of Judah, clan by clan:

[21]The southernmost towns of the tribe of Judah in the Negev toward the boundary of Edom were:

Kabzeel, Eder, Jagur, [22]Kinah, Dimonah, Adadah, [23]Kedesh, Hazor, Ithnan, [24]Ziph, Telem, Bealoth, [25]Hazor Hadattah, Kerioth Hezron (that is, Hazor), [26]Amam, Shema, Moladah, [27]Hazar Gaddah, Heshmon, Beth Pelet, [28]Hazar Shual, Beersheba, Biziothiah, [29]Baalah, Iim, Ezem, [30]Eltolad, Kesil, Hormah, [31]Ziklag, Madmannah, Sansannah, [32]Lebaoth, Shilhim, Ain and Rimmon—a total of twenty-nine towns and their villages.

---

[a]2 That is, the Dead Sea; also in verse 5
[b]3 Hebrew *Akrabbim*   [c]4 Hebrew *your*
[d]12 That is, the Mediterranean; also in verse 47
[e]18 Hebrew and some Septuagint manuscripts; other Septuagint manuscripts (see also note at Judges 1:14) *Othniel, he urged her*

33In the western foothills:

Eshtaol, Zorah, Ashnah, **34**Zanoah, En Gannim, Tappuah, Enam, **35**Jarmuth, Adullam, Socoh, Azekah, **36**Shaaraim, Adithaim and Gederah (or Gederothaim)*a*—fourteen towns and their villages.

37Zenan, Hadashah, Migdal Gad, **38**Dilean, Mizpah, Joktheel, **39**Lachish, Bozkath, Eglon, **40**Cabbon, Lahmas, Kitlish, **41**Gederoth, Beth Dagon, Naamah and Makkedah—sixteen towns and their villages.

42Libnah, Ether, Ashan, **43**Iphtah, Ashnah, Nezib, **44**Keilah, Aczib and Mareshah—nine towns and their villages.

45Ekron, with its surrounding settlements and villages; **46**west of Ekron, all that were in the vicinity of Ashdod, together with their villages; **47**Ashdod, its surrounding settlements and villages; and Gaza, its settlements and villages, as far as the Wadi of Egypt and the coastline of the Great Sea.

48In the hill country:

Shamir, Jattir, Socoh, **49**Dannah, Kiriath Sannah (that is, Debir), **50**Anab, Eshtemoh, Anim, **51**Goshen, Holon and Giloh—eleven towns and their villages.

52Arab, Dumah, Eshan, **53**Janim, Beth Tappuah, Aphekah, **54**Humtah, Kiriath Arba (that is, Hebron) and Zior—nine towns and their villages.

55Maon, Carmel, Ziph, Juttah, **56**Jezreel, Jokdeam, Zanoah, **57**Kain, Gibeah and Timnah—ten towns and their villages.

58Halhul, Beth Zur, Gedor, **59**Maarath, Beth Anoth and Eltekon—six towns and their villages.

60Kiriath Baal (that is, Kiriath Jearim) and Rabbah—two towns and their villages.

61In the desert:

Beth Arabah, Middin, Secacah, **62**Nibshan, the City of Salt and En Gedi—six towns and their villages.

63Judah could not dislodge the Jebusites, who were living in Jerusalem; to this day the Jebusites live there with the people of Judah.

Allotment for Ephraim and Manasseh

16 The allotment for Joseph began at the Jordan of Jericho,*b* east of the waters of Jericho, and went up from there through the desert into the hill country of Bethel. **2**It went on from Bethel (that is, Luz),*c* crossed over to the territory of the Arkites in Ataroth, **3**descended westward to the territory of the Japhletites as far as the region of Lower Beth Horon and on to Gezer, ending at the sea.

4So Manasseh and Ephraim, the descendants of Joseph, received their inheritance.

5This was the territory of Ephraim, clan by clan:

The boundary of their inheritance went from Ataroth Addar in the east to Upper Beth Horon **6**and continued to the sea. From Micmethath on the north it curved eastward to Taanath Shiloh, passing by it to Janoah on the east. **7**Then it went down from Janoah to Ataroth and Naarah, touched Jericho and came out at the Jordan. **8**From Tappuah the border went west to the Kanah Ravine and ended at the sea. This was the inheritance of the tribe of the Ephraimites, clan by clan. **9**It also included all the towns and their villages that were set aside for the Ephraimites within the inheritance of the Manassites.

10They did not dislodge the Canaanites living in Gezer; to this day the Canaanites live among the people of Ephraim but are required to do forced labor.

17 This was the allotment for the tribe of Manasseh as Joseph's firstborn, that is, for Makir, Manasseh's firstborn. Makir was the ancestor of the Gileadites, who had received Gilead and Bashan because the Makirites were great soldiers. **2**So this allotment was for the rest of the people of Manasseh—the clans of Abiezer, Helek, Asriel, Shechem, Hepher and Shemida. These are the other male descendants of Manasseh son of Joseph by their clans.

3Now Zelophehad son of Hepher, the son of Gilead, the son of Makir, the son of Manasseh, had no sons but only daugh-

---

a36 Or *Gederah and Gederothaim*   *b1 Jordan of Jericho* was possibly an ancient name for the Jordan River.   *c2* Septuagint; Hebrew *Bethel to Luz* ters, whose names were Mahlah, Noah, Hoglah, Milcah and Tirzah. [4]They went to Eleazar the priest, Joshua son of Nun, and the leaders and said, "The LORD commanded Moses to give us an inheritance among our brothers." So Joshua gave them an inheritance along with the brothers of their father, according to the LORD's command. [5]Manasseh's share consisted of ten tracts of land besides Gilead and Bashan east of the Jordan, [6]because the daughters of the tribe of Manasseh received an inheritance among the sons. The land of Gilead belonged to the rest of the descendants of Manasseh.

[7]The territory of Manasseh extended from Asher to Micmethath east of Shechem. The boundary ran southward from there to include the people living at En Tappuah. [8](Manasseh had the land of Tappuah, but Tappuah itself, on the boundary of Manasseh, belonged to the Ephraimites.) [9]Then the boundary continued south to the Kanah Ravine. There were towns belonging to Ephraim lying among the towns of Manasseh, but the boundary of Manasseh was the northern side of the ravine and ended at the sea. [10]On the south the land belonged to Ephraim, on the north to Manasseh. The territory of Manasseh reached the sea and bordered Asher on the north and Issachar on the east. [11]Within Issachar and Asher, Manasseh also had Beth Shan, Ibleam and the people of Dor, Endor, Taanach and Megiddo, together with their surrounding settlements (the third in the list is Naphoth[a]).

[12]Yet the Manassites were not able to occupy these towns, for the Canaanites were determined to live in that region. [13]However, when the Israelites grew stronger, they subjected the Canaanites to forced labor but did not drive them out completely.

[14]The people of Joseph said to Joshua, "Why have you given us only one allotment and one portion for an inheritance? We are a numerous people and the LORD has blessed us abundantly."

[15]"If you are so numerous," Joshua answered, "and if the hill country of Ephraim is too small for you, go up into the forest and clear land for yourselves there in the land of the Perizzites and Rephaites."

[16]The people of Joseph replied, "The hill country is not enough for us, and all the Canaanites who live in the plain have iron chariots, both those in Beth Shan and its settlements and those in the Valley of Jezreel."

[17]But Joshua said to the house of Joseph—to Ephraim and Manasseh— "You are numerous and very powerful. You will have not only one allotment [18]but the forested hill country as well. Clear it, and its farthest limits will be yours; though the Canaanites have iron chariots and though they are strong, you can drive them out."

Division of the Rest of the Land

18 The whole assembly of the Israelites gathered at Shiloh and set up the Tent of Meeting there. The country was brought under their control, [2]but there were still seven Israelite tribes who had not yet received their inheritance.

[3]So Joshua said to the Israelites: "How long will you wait before you begin to take possession of the land that the LORD, the God of your fathers, has given you? [4]Appoint three men from each tribe. I will send them out to make a survey of the land and to write a description of it, according to the inheritance of each. Then they will return to me. [5]You are to divide the land into seven parts. Judah is to remain in its territory on the south and the house of Joseph in its territory on the north. [6]After you have written descriptions of the seven parts of the land, bring them here to me and I will cast lots for you in the presence of the LORD our God.

[a] 11 That is, Naphoth Dor

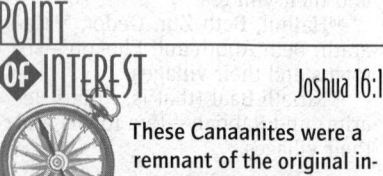

POINT OF INTEREST   Joshua 16:10

These Canaanites were a remnant of the original inhabitants of the promised land. The Israelites chose to exploit them as slaves rather than wipe them out as God had directed (see Deuteronomy 12:2–3). But the Canaanites' idolatrous worship proved to be a stumbling block to Israel and helped bring about its ultimate destruction.

HOW TO HAVE A DAILY QUIET TIME

Eternal life is knowing God and Jesus Christ (see John 17:3). It is a personal relationship that grows when we talk with him and listen to him through his Word. God has promised that he will be available to anyone who looks for him: "If . . . you seek the LORD your God, you will find him if you look for him with all your heart and with all your soul" (Deuteronomy 4:29). Here are a few suggestions to guide you in your daily quiet time with him.

Before You Begin

- Decide to begin meeting with God daily.

- Set aside a time and find a place that will be free from distractions.

- Decide on a plan so that you will know how much you will read each day.

- Use a notebook or journal to record your thoughts and observations.

Components of a Daily Quiet Time

◼ Pray

- Focus your mind on God.

- Praise and thank God.

- Ask God to speak to you through his Word.

◼ Read

- Read your predetermined amount of Scripture.

- Read thoughtfully and look for a thought about God; a promise from God; a directive to obey, or some other insight.

◼ Meditate/Reflect

- Ask God to show you how his Word applies to you that day.

- Ask yourself these questions about the passage you read:

    What does it say?

    What does it mean?

    How does it apply?

◼ Record in your notebook:

- thoughts about God or from God

- any insights, applications or questions

◼ Pray

- Thank God for what he has said to you.

- Pray over any applications from your reading.

- Include various kinds of prayer such as adoration, thanksgiving, confession and intercession for yourself and others.

HOW TO MEMORIZE SCRIPTURE

Memorizing passages of Scripture is one of the best ways to assimilate God's Word so that we can grow spiritually. When we store Scripture verses in our hearts, the Holy Spirit can bring them to mind to help us to avoid sin (see Psalm 119:11), guide us in decision making (see Psalm 119:9–10), and be a powerful witness to unbelievers (see Romans 10:17). Scripture memory takes discipline and work, but the benefits far outweigh the costs. The Holy Spirit helps us in this process, "The Counselor, the Holy Spirit, whom the Father will send in my name, will teach you all things and will remind you of everything I have said to you" (John 14:26). Here's how to begin:

■ As you read and study your Bible, keep a running list of passages you would like to memorize.

■ Establish a goal. Two verses each week is a good start. Decide which passage you want to memorize and assign a topic to that passage. A topic will help you remember the passage (e.g. Assurance of Salvation— 1 John 5:13).

■ Write out the topic and passage on a small card and carry it with you so you can review it often.

■ Know the context of the verses you are memorizing. Reading the verses in several Bible translations can deepen your understanding of the meaning of the passage.

■ Read the passage aloud several times to help you understand it as a whole.

■ Start to memorize. Learn the topic and reference first.

■ Next learn the passage phrase by phrase, always beginning with the topic and reference and ending with the reference as you recite it to yourself. Every time you review the verse, begin with the topic, reference and verse and then repeat the reference again to help firmly fix it in your mind.

CONTINUED ON NEXT PAGE

CONTINUED FROM PREVIOUS PAGE

■ Review the verse often. Repetition is the key to memory work!

■ Always try to memorize the passage accurately. It is very difficult to unlearn mistakes, so be sure that the first impression on your mind is correct.

■ Select a time for your memory work when you are free from distractions. Many people like to include their memory work as part of their daily devotional time.

■ As you memorize and review the passage, think about how God would want you to apply it. The goal in Scripture memory is not only additional knowledge but the application of God's Word to your life.

■ Ask a friend to help you review your memory verses.

THE HAND ILLUSTRATION

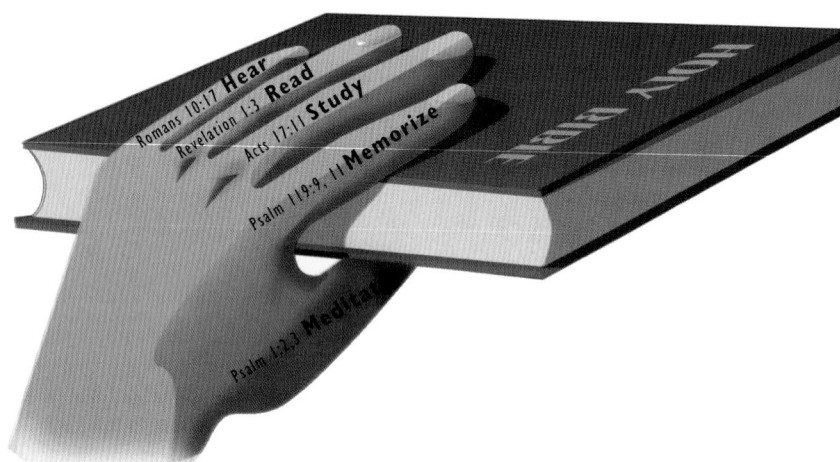

The Hand Illustration shows the various ways a person can take in the Word of God.

█ HEAR   Listening to a taped message or to a sermon in church

█ READ   Reading through the entire Bible in one year

█ STUDY   Studying in preparation for a weekly small group Bible study

█ MEMORIZE   Memorizing Scripture verses and reviewing the verses you've already memorized

█ MEDITATE   Thinking about Scripture with a view toward personal application

Meditation is used in conjunction with the other four means of taking in God's Word. Meditation is the "thumb" that allows us a firm grasp of the Bible.

The Hand Illustration, Copyright by The Navigators. Used by permission of NavPress

7The Levites, however, do not get a portion among you, because the priestly service of the LORD is their inheritance. And Gad, Reuben and the half-tribe of Manasseh have already received their inheritance on the east side of the Jordan. Moses the servant of the LORD gave it to them."

8As the men started on their way to map out the land, Joshua instructed them, "Go and make a survey of the land and write a description of it. Then return to me, and I will cast lots for you here at Shiloh in the presence of the LORD." **9**So the men left and went through the land. They wrote its description on a scroll, town by town, in seven parts, and returned to Joshua in the camp at Shiloh. **10**Joshua then cast lots for them in Shiloh in the presence of the LORD, and there he distributed the land to the Israelites according to their tribal divisions.

Allotment for Benjamin

11The lot came up for the tribe of Benjamin, clan by clan. Their allotted territory lay between the tribes of Judah and Joseph:

12On the north side their boundary began at the Jordan, passed the northern slope of Jericho and headed west into the hill country, coming out at the desert of Beth Aven. **13**From there it crossed to the south slope of Luz (that is, Bethel) and went down to Ataroth Addar on the hill south of Lower Beth Horon.

14From the hill facing Beth Horon on the south the boundary turned south along the western side and came out at Kiriath Baal (that is, Kiriath Jearim), a town of the people of Judah. This was the western side.

15The southern side began at the outskirts of Kiriath Jearim on the west, and the boundary came out at the spring of the waters of Nephtoah. **16**The boundary went down to the foot of the hill facing the Valley of Ben Hinnom, north of the Valley of Rephaim. It continued down the Hinnom Valley along the southern slope of the Jebusite city and so to En Rogel. **17**It then curved north, went to En Shemesh, continued to Geliloth, which faces the Pass of Adummim, and ran down to the Stone of Bohan son of Reuben. **18**It continued to the northern slope of Beth Arabah*a* and on down into the Arabah. **19**It then went to the northern slope of Beth Hoglah and came out at the northern bay of the Salt Sea,*b* at the mouth of the Jordan in the south. This was the southern boundary.

20The Jordan formed the boundary on the eastern side.

These were the boundaries that marked out the inheritance of the clans of Benjamin on all sides.

21The tribe of Benjamin, clan by clan, had the following cities:

Jericho, Beth Hoglah, Emek Keziz, **22**Beth Arabah, Zemaraim, Bethel, **23**Avvim, Parah, Ophrah, **24**Kephar Ammoni, Ophni and Geba—twelve towns and their villages.

25Gibeon, Ramah, Beeroth, **26**Mizpah, Kephirah, Mozah, **27**Rekem, Irpeel, Taralah, **28**Zelah, Haeleph, the Jebusite city (that is, Jerusalem), Gibeah and Kiriath—fourteen towns and their villages.

This was the inheritance of Benjamin for its clans.

Allotment for Simeon

19 The second lot came out for the tribe of Simeon, clan by clan. Their inheritance lay within the territory of Judah. **2**It included:

Beersheba (or Sheba),*c* Moladah, **3**Hazar Shual, Balah, Ezem, **4**Eltolad, Bethul, Hormah, **5**Ziklag, Beth Marcaboth, Hazar Susah, **6**Beth Lebaoth and Sharuhen—thirteen towns and their villages;

7Ain, Rimmon, Ether and Ashan—four towns and their villages— **8**and all the villages around these towns as far as Baalath Beer (Ramah in the Negev).

This was the inheritance of the tribe of the Simeonites, clan by clan. **9**The inheritance of the Simeonites was taken from the share of Judah, because Judah's portion was more than they needed. So the Simeonites received their inheritance within the territory of Judah.

---

a 18 Septuagint; Hebrew *slope facing the Arabah*   *b 19* That is, the Dead Sea   *c 2* Or *Beersheba, Sheba;* 1 Chron. 4:28 does not have *Sheba.*

Allotment for Zebulun

¹⁰The third lot came up for Zebulun, clan by clan:

The boundary of their inheritance went as far as Sarid. ¹¹Going west it ran to Maralah, touched Dabbesheth, and extended to the ravine near Jokneam. ¹²It turned east from Sarid toward the sunrise to the territory of Kisloth Tabor and went on to Daberath and up to Japhia. ¹³Then it continued eastward to Gath Hepher and Eth Kazin; it came out at Rimmon and turned toward Neah. ¹⁴There the boundary went around on the north to Hannathon and ended at the Valley of Iphtah El. ¹⁵Included were Kattath, Nahalal, Shimron, Idalah and Bethlehem. There were twelve towns and their villages.

¹⁶These towns and their villages were the inheritance of Zebulun, clan by clan.

Allotment for Issachar

¹⁷The fourth lot came out for Issachar, clan by clan. ¹⁸Their territory included:

Jezreel, Kesulloth, Shunem, ¹⁹Hapharaim, Shion, Anaharath, ²⁰Rabbith, Kishion, Ebez, ²¹Remeth, En Gannim, En Haddah and Beth Pazzez. ²²The boundary touched Tabor, Shahazumah and Beth Shemesh, and ended at the Jordan. There were sixteen towns and their villages.

²³These towns and their villages were the inheritance of the tribe of Issachar, clan by clan.

Allotment for Asher

²⁴The fifth lot came out for the tribe of Asher, clan by clan. ²⁵Their territory included:

Helkath, Hali, Beten, Acshaph, ²⁶Allammelech, Amad and Mishal. On the west the boundary touched Carmel and Shihor Libnath. ²⁷It then turned east toward Beth Dagon, touched Zebulun and the Valley of Iphtah El, and went north to Beth Emek and Neiel, passing Cabul on the left. ²⁸It went to Abdon,ᵃ Rehob, Hammon and Kanah, as far as Greater Sidon. ²⁹The boundary then turned back toward Ramah and went to the fortified city of Tyre, turned toward Hosah and came out at the sea in the region of Aczib, ³⁰Ummah, Aphek and Rehob. There were twenty-two towns and their villages.

³¹These towns and their villages were the inheritance of the tribe of Asher, clan by clan.

Allotment for Naphtali

³²The sixth lot came out for Naphtali, clan by clan:

³³Their boundary went from Heleph and the large tree in Zaanannim, passing Adami Nekeb and Jabneel to Lakkum and ending at the Jordan. ³⁴The boundary ran west through Aznoth Tabor and came out at Hukkok. It touched Zebulun on the south, Asher on the west and the Jordanᵇ on the east. ³⁵The fortified cities were Ziddim, Zer, Hammath, Rakkath, Kinnereth, ³⁶Adamah, Ramah, Hazor, ³⁷Kedesh, Edrei, En Hazor, ³⁸Iron, Migdal El, Horem, Beth Anath and Beth Shemesh. There were nineteen towns and their villages.

³⁹These towns and their villages were the inheritance of the tribe of Naphtali, clan by clan.

Allotment for Dan

⁴⁰The seventh lot came out for the tribe of Dan, clan by clan. ⁴¹The territory of their inheritance included:

Zorah, Eshtaol, Ir Shemesh, ⁴²Shaalabbin, Aijalon, Ithlah, ⁴³Elon, Timnah, Ekron, ⁴⁴Eltekeh, Gibbethon, Baalath, ⁴⁵Jehud, Bene Berak, Gath Rimmon, ⁴⁶Me Jarkon and Rakkon, with the area facing Joppa.

⁴⁷(But the Danites had difficulty taking possession of their territory, so they went up and attacked Leshem, took it, put it to the sword and occupied it. They settled in Leshem and named it Dan after their forefather.)

⁴⁸These towns and their villages were the inheritance of the tribe of Dan, clan by clan.

Allotment for Joshua

⁴⁹When they had finished dividing the land into its allotted portions, the Israel-

---

ᵃ28 Some Hebrew manuscripts (see also Joshua 21:30); most Hebrew manuscripts *Ebron*
ᵇ34 Septuagint; Hebrew *west, and Judah, the Jordan,*

ites gave Joshua son of Nun an inheritance among them, **50**as the LORD had commanded. They gave him the town he asked for—Timnath Serah*a* in the hill country of Ephraim. And he built up the town and settled there.

51These are the territories that Eleazar the priest, Joshua son of Nun and the heads of the tribal clans of Israel assigned by lot at Shiloh in the presence of the LORD at the entrance to the Tent of Meeting. And so they finished dividing the land.

Cities of Refuge

20 Then the LORD said to Joshua: **2**"Tell the Israelites to designate the cities of refuge, as I instructed you through Moses, **3**so that anyone who kills a person accidentally and unintentionally may flee there and find protection from the avenger of blood.

4"When he flees to one of these cities, he is to stand in the entrance of the city gate and state his case before the elders of that city. Then they are to admit him into their city and give him a place to live with them. **5**If the avenger of blood pursues him, they must not surrender the one accused, because he killed his neighbor unintentionally and without malice aforethought. **6**He is to stay in that city until he has stood trial before the assembly and until the death of the high priest who is serving at that time. Then he may go back to his own home in the town from which he fled."

7So they set apart Kedesh in Galilee in the hill country of Naphtali, Shechem in the hill country of Ephraim, and Kiriath Arba (that is, Hebron) in the hill country of Judah. **8**On the east side of the Jordan of Jericho*b* they designated Bezer in the desert on the plateau in the tribe of Reuben, Ramoth in Gilead in the tribe of Gad, and Golan in Bashan in the tribe of Manasseh. **9**Any of the Israelites or any alien living among them who killed someone accidentally could flee to these designated cities and not be killed by the avenger of blood prior to standing trial before the assembly.

Towns for the Levites

21 Now the family heads of the Levites approached Eleazar the priest, Joshua son of Nun, and the heads of the other tribal families of Israel **2**at Shiloh in Canaan and said to them, "The LORD com-

manded through Moses that you give us towns to live in, with pasturelands for our livestock." **3**So, as the LORD had commanded, the Israelites gave the Levites the following towns and pasturelands out of their own inheritance:

4The first lot came out for the Kohathites, clan by clan. The Levites who were descendants of Aaron the priest were allotted thirteen towns from the tribes of Judah, Simeon and Benjamin. **5**The rest of Kohath's descendants were allotted ten towns from the clans of the tribes of Ephraim, Dan and half of Manasseh.

6The descendants of Gershon were allotted thirteen towns from the clans of the tribes of Issachar, Asher, Naphtali and the half-tribe of Manasseh in Bashan.

7The descendants of Merari, clan by clan, received twelve towns from the tribes of Reuben, Gad and Zebulun.

8So the Israelites allotted to the Levites these towns and their pasturelands, as the LORD had commanded through Moses.

9From the tribes of Judah and Simeon they allotted the following towns by name **10**(these towns were assigned to the descendants of Aaron who were from the Kohathite clans of the Levites, because the first lot fell to them):

11They gave them Kiriath Arba (that is, Hebron), with its surrounding pastureland, in the hill country of Judah. (Arba was the forefather of Anak.) **12**But the fields and vil-

---

a50 Also known as *Timnath Heres* (see Judges 2:9)
b8 Jordan of Jericho was possibly an ancient name for the Jordan River.

POINT OF INTEREST

Joshua 20:6

In ancient societies, relatives of an injured party meted out justice. This practice frequently resulted in revenge and fostered blood feuds between families. The Old Testament institution of legal trials, including examination of the facts before an impartial audience, was a judiciary milestone. What might have been the effects of such trials on the ancient community at large?

lages around the city they had given to Caleb son of Jephunneh as his possession.

13So to the descendants of Aaron the priest they gave Hebron (a city of refuge for one accused of murder), Libnah, 14Jattir, Eshtemoa, 15Holon, Debir, 16Ain, Juttah and Beth Shemesh, together with their pasturelands—nine towns from these two tribes.

17And from the tribe of Benjamin they gave them Gibeon, Geba, 18Anathoth and Almon, together with their pasturelands—four towns.

19All the towns for the priests, the descendants of Aaron, were thirteen, together with their pasturelands.

20The rest of the Kohathite clans of the Levites were allotted towns from the tribe of Ephraim:

21In the hill country of Ephraim they were given Shechem (a city of refuge for one accused of murder) and Gezer, 22Kibzaim and Beth Horon, together with their pasturelands—four towns.

23Also from the tribe of Dan they received Eltekeh, Gibbethon, 24Aijalon and Gath Rimmon, together with their pasturelands—four towns.

25From half the tribe of Manasseh they received Taanach and Gath Rimmon, together with their pasturelands—two towns.

26All these ten towns and their pasturelands were given to the rest of the Kohathite clans.

27The Levite clans of the Gershonites were given:
from the half-tribe of Manasseh,
Golan in Bashan (a city of refuge for one accused of murder) and Be Eshtarah, together with their pasturelands—two towns;
28from the tribe of Issachar,
Kishion, Daberath, 29Jarmuth and En Gannim, together with their pasturelands—four towns;
30from the tribe of Asher,
Mishal, Abdon, 31Helkath and Rehob, together with their pasturelands—four towns;
32from the tribe of Naphtali,
Kedesh in Galilee (a city of refuge for one accused of murder), Hammoth Dor and Kartan, together with their pasturelands—three towns.

33All the towns of the Gershonite clans were thirteen, together with their pasturelands.

34The Merarite clans (the rest of the Levites) were given:
from the tribe of Zebulun,
Jokneam, Kartah, 35Dimnah and Nahalal, together with their pasturelands—four towns;
36from the tribe of Reuben,
Bezer, Jahaz, 37Kedemoth and Mephaath, together with their pasturelands—four towns;
38from the tribe of Gad,
Ramoth in Gilead (a city of refuge for one accused of murder), Mahanaim, 39Heshbon and Jazer, together with their pasturelands—four towns in all.

40All the towns allotted to the Merarite clans, who were the rest of the Levites, were twelve.

41The towns of the Levites in the territory held by the Israelites were forty-eight in all, together with their pasturelands. 42Each of these towns had pasturelands surrounding it; this was true for all these towns.

43So the LORD gave Israel all the land he had sworn to give their forefathers, and they took possession of it and settled there. 44The LORD gave them rest on every side, just as he had sworn to their forefathers. Not one of their enemies withstood them; the LORD handed all their enemies over to them. 45Not one of all the LORD's good promises to the house of Israel failed; every one was fulfilled.

Eastern Tribes Return Home

22 Then Joshua summoned the Reubenites, the Gadites and the half-tribe of Manasseh 2and said to them, "You have done all that Moses the servant of the LORD commanded, and you have obeyed me in everything I commanded. 3For a long time now—to this very day—you have not deserted your brothers but have carried out the mission the LORD your God gave you. 4Now that the LORD your God has given your brothers rest as he promised, return to your homes in the land that Moses the servant of the LORD gave you on the other side of the Jordan. 5But be very careful to keep the commandment and the law that Moses the servant

Read Joshua 21:43—22:34
Key Verse Joshua 21:45

And *That's* a Promise!

Remember Mary Poppins saying, "That's a pie-crust promise—lightly made and easily broken"? We all have felt the bitter disappointment of a broken promise. At the same time, we know what it is like to make a promise to someone else, even with the best of intentions, and fail to follow through. Let's face it, because we are imperfect human beings, we can never keep one hundred percent of the promises we've made. Promises are only as good as the character and as strong as the power of the one who makes them. But here's the good news: When God makes a promise, his perfect character and limitless power guarantee that it will always be kept.

Our lives as Christians begin when we believe God's promise that our sins are forgiven through the shed blood of Jesus Christ, that we can live abundant lives in him. This is no pie-crust promise! We can stake our lives on it. It cost Jesus his life to make it!

Digging Into the Word
1. What does God promise in the following passages?—*John 5:24; John 6:40*
2. What promises does God make about prayer in the following passages?—*Psalm 50:15; Luke 11:9–10*

Action Challenge
Begin a journal of God's promises. Over the coming weeks and months as you continue studying your Bible on a regular basis, write down each promise you discover in your studies. Go back to this journal often and read through the promises of God. Remember, his character and power stand behind every promise he makes.

One Step Deeper
John 16:24; 1 John 2:25

Go to page 258 for your next devotional reading.

of the LORD gave you: to love the LORD your God, to walk in all his ways, to obey his commands, to hold fast to him and to serve him with all your heart and all your soul."

⁶Then Joshua blessed them and sent them away, and they went to their homes. ⁷(To the half-tribe of Manasseh Moses had given land in Bashan, and to the other half of the tribe Joshua gave land on the west side of the Jordan with their brothers.) When Joshua sent them home, he blessed them, ⁸saying, "Return to your homes with your great wealth—with large herds of livestock, with silver, gold, bronze and iron, and a great quantity of clothing—and divide with your brothers the plunder from your enemies."

⁹So the Reubenites, the Gadites and the half-tribe of Manasseh left the Israelites at Shiloh in Canaan to return to Gilead, their own land, which they had acquired in accordance with the command of the LORD through Moses.

¹⁰When they came to Geliloth near the Jordan in the land of Canaan, the Reubenites, the Gadites and the half-tribe of Manasseh built an imposing altar there by the Jordan. ¹¹And when the Israelites heard that they had built the altar on the border of Canaan at Geliloth near the Jordan on the Israelite side, ¹²the whole assembly of Israel gathered at Shiloh to go to war against them.

¹³So the Israelites sent Phinehas son of Eleazar, the priest, to the land of Gilead—to Reuben, Gad and the half-tribe of Manasseh. ¹⁴With him they sent ten of the chief men, one for each of the tribes of Israel, each the head of a family division among the Israelite clans.

¹⁵When they went to Gilead—to Reuben, Gad and the half-tribe of Manasseh—they said to them: ¹⁶"The whole assembly of the LORD says: 'How could you break faith with the God of Israel like this? How could you turn away from the LORD and build yourselves an altar in rebellion against him now? ¹⁷Was not the sin of Peor enough for us? Up to this very day we have not cleansed ourselves from that sin, even though a plague fell on the community of the LORD! ¹⁸And are you now turning away from the LORD?

" 'If you rebel against the LORD today, tomorrow he will be angry with the whole community of Israel. ¹⁹If the land

you possess is defiled, come over to the LORD's land, where the LORD's tabernacle stands, and share the land with us. But do not rebel against the LORD or against us by building an altar for yourselves, other than the altar of the LORD our God. ²⁰When Achan son of Zerah acted unfaithfully regarding the devoted things,ᵃ did not wrath come upon the whole community of Israel? He was not the only one who died for his sin.' "

²¹Then Reuben, Gad and the half-tribe of Manasseh replied to the heads of the clans of Israel: ²²"The Mighty One, God, the LORD! The Mighty One, God, the LORD! He knows! And let Israel know! If this has been in rebellion or disobedience to the LORD, do not spare us this day. ²³If we have built our own altar to turn away from the LORD and to offer burnt offerings and grain offerings, or to sacrifice fellowship offeringsᵇ on it, may the LORD himself call us to account.

²⁴"No! We did it for fear that some day your descendants might say to ours, 'What do you have to do with the LORD, the God of Israel? ²⁵The LORD has made the Jordan a boundary between us and you—you Reubenites and Gadites! You have no share in the LORD.' So your descendants might cause ours to stop fearing the LORD.

²⁶"That is why we said, 'Let us get ready and build an altar—but not for burnt offerings or sacrifices.' ²⁷On the contrary, it is to be a witness between us and you and the generations that follow,

ᵃ20 The Hebrew term refers to the irrevocable giving over of things or persons to the LORD, often by totally destroying them.   ᵇ23 Traditionally *peace offerings*; also in verse 27

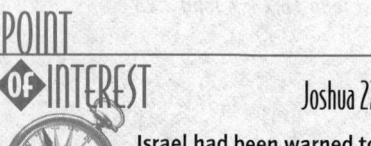

POINT OF INTEREST

Joshua 22:16

Israel had been warned to avoid the idolatrous practices that took place at the pagan hilltop shrines. When the western clans of Israel saw the hilltop altar of the clans on the eastern side of the Jordan, they assumed the worst and were ready to attack their eastern cousins. But jumping to conclusions is dangerous. Read on for the rest of the story.

that we will worship the LORD at his sanctuary with our burnt offerings, sacrifices and fellowship offerings. Then in the future your descendants will not be able to say to ours, 'You have no share in the LORD.'

28"And we said, 'If they ever say this to us, or to our descendants, we will answer: Look at the replica of the LORD's altar, which our fathers built, not for burnt offerings and sacrifices, but as a witness between us and you.'

29"Far be it from us to rebel against the LORD and turn away from him today by building an altar for burnt offerings, grain offerings and sacrifices, other than the altar of the LORD our God that stands before his tabernacle."

30When Phinehas the priest and the leaders of the community—the heads of the clans of the Israelites—heard what Reuben, Gad and Manasseh had to say, they were pleased. 31And Phinehas son of Eleazar, the priest, said to Reuben, Gad and Manasseh, "Today we know that the LORD is with us, because you have not acted unfaithfully toward the LORD in this matter. Now you have rescued the Israelites from the LORD's hand."

32Then Phinehas son of Eleazar, the priest, and the leaders returned to Canaan from their meeting with the Reubenites and Gadites in Gilead and reported to the Israelites. 33They were glad to hear the report and praised God. And they talked no more about going to war against them to devastate the country where the Reubenites and the Gadites lived.

34And the Reubenites and the Gadites gave the altar this name: A Witness Between Us that the LORD is God.

Joshua's Farewell to the Leaders

23 After a long time had passed and the LORD had given Israel rest from all their enemies around them, Joshua, by then old and well advanced in years, 2summoned all Israel—their elders, leaders, judges and officials—and said to them: "I am old and well advanced in years. 3You yourselves have seen everything the LORD your God has done to all these nations for your sake; it was the LORD your God who fought for you. 4Remember how I have allotted as an inheritance for your tribes all the land of the nations that remain—the nations I conquered—between the Jordan and the Great Sea[a] in the west. 5The LORD your God himself will drive them out of your way. He will push them out before you, and you will take possession of their land, as the LORD your God promised you.

6"Be very strong; be careful to obey all that is written in the Book of the Law of Moses, without turning aside to the right or to the left. 7Do not associate with these nations that remain among you; do not invoke the names of their gods or swear by them. You must not serve them or bow down to them. 8But you are to hold fast to the LORD your God, as you have until now.

9"The LORD has driven out before you great and powerful nations; to this day no one has been able to withstand you. 10One of you routs a thousand, because the LORD your God fights for you, just as he promised. 11So be very careful to love the LORD your God.

12"But if you turn away and ally yourselves with the survivors of these nations that remain among you and if you intermarry with them and associate with them, 13then you may be sure that the LORD your God will no longer drive out these nations before you. Instead, they will become snares and traps for you, whips on your backs and thorns in your eyes, until you perish from this good land, which the LORD your God has given you.

14"Now I am about to go the way of all the earth. You know with all your heart and soul that not one of all the good promises the LORD your God gave you has failed. Every promise has been fulfilled; not one has failed. 15But just as every good promise of the LORD your God has come true, so the LORD will bring on you all the evil he has threatened, until he has destroyed you from this good land he has given you. 16If you violate the covenant of the LORD your God, which he commanded you, and go and serve other gods and bow down to them, the LORD's anger will burn against you, and you will quickly perish from the good land he has given you."

The Covenant Renewed at Shechem

24 Then Joshua assembled all the tribes of Israel at Shechem. He summoned the elders, leaders, judges and officials of

a4 That is, the Mediterranean

Israel, and they presented themselves before God.

²Joshua said to all the people, "This is what the LORD, the God of Israel, says: 'Long ago your forefathers, including Terah the father of Abraham and Nahor, lived beyond the River[a] and worshiped other gods. ³But I took your father Abraham from the land beyond the River and led him throughout Canaan and gave him many descendants. I gave him Isaac, ⁴and to Isaac I gave Jacob and Esau. I assigned the hill country of Seir to Esau, but Jacob and his sons went down to Egypt.

⁵" 'Then I sent Moses and Aaron, and I afflicted the Egyptians by what I did there, and I brought you out. ⁶When I brought your fathers out of Egypt, you came to the sea, and the Egyptians pursued them with chariots and horsemen[b] as far as the Red Sea.[c] ⁷But they cried to the LORD for help, and he put darkness between you and the Egyptians; he brought the sea over them and covered them. You saw with your own eyes what I did to the Egyptians. Then you lived in the desert for a long time.

⁸" 'I brought you to the land of the Amorites who lived east of the Jordan. They fought against you, but I gave them into your hands. I destroyed them from before you, and you took possession of their land. ⁹When Balak son of Zippor, the king of Moab, prepared to fight against Israel, he sent for Balaam son of Beor to put a curse on you. ¹⁰But I would not listen to Balaam, so he blessed you again and again, and I delivered you out of his hand.

¹¹" 'Then you crossed the Jordan and came to Jericho. The citizens of Jericho fought against you, as did also the Amorites, Perizzites, Canaanites, Hittites, Girgashites, Hivites and Jebusites, but I gave them into your hands. ¹²I sent the hornet ahead of you, which drove them out before you—also the two Amorite kings. You did not do it with your own sword and bow. ¹³So I gave you a land on which you did not toil and cities you did not build; and you live in them and eat from vineyards and olive groves that you did not plant.'

¹⁴"Now fear the LORD and serve him with all faithfulness. Throw away the gods your forefathers worshiped beyond the River and in Egypt, and serve the LORD. ¹⁵But if serving the LORD seems undesirable to you, then choose for yourselves this day whom you will serve, whether the gods your forefathers served beyond the River, or the gods of the Amorites, in whose land you are living. But as for me and my household, we will serve the LORD."

¹⁶Then the people answered, "Far be it from us to forsake the LORD to serve other gods! ¹⁷It was the LORD our God himself who brought us and our fathers up out of Egypt, from that land of slavery, and performed those great signs before our eyes. He protected us on our entire journey and among all the nations through which we traveled. ¹⁸And the LORD drove out before us all the nations, including the Amorites, who lived in the land. We too will serve the LORD, because he is our God."

¹⁹Joshua said to the people, "You are not able to serve the LORD. He is a holy God; he is a jealous God. He will not forgive your rebellion and your sins. ²⁰If you forsake the LORD and serve foreign gods, he will turn and bring disaster on you and make an end of you, after he has been good to you."

²¹But the people said to Joshua, "No! We will serve the LORD."

²²Then Joshua said, "You are witnesses against yourselves that you have chosen to serve the LORD."

"Yes, we are witnesses," they replied.

²³"Now then," said Joshua, "throw away the foreign gods that are among you and yield your hearts to the LORD, the God of Israel."

---

[a]2 That is, the Euphrates; also in verses 3, 14 and 15   [b]6 Or *charioteers*   [c]6 Hebrew *Yam Suph*; that is, Sea of Reeds

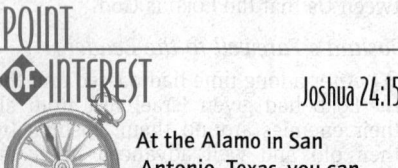

POINT OF INTEREST

Joshua 24:15

At the Alamo in San Antonio, Texas, you can hear the story of Colonel Travis, who supposedly drew his sword through the sand and summoned his men to cross the drawn line and courageously give their lives to defend the fortress. Joshua's challenge to Israel is no less powerful. This old general's voice reverberates down through the centuries as he calls out, "Choose!"

²⁴And the people said to Joshua, "We will serve the LORD our God and obey him."

²⁵On that day Joshua made a covenant for the people, and there at Shechem he drew up for them decrees and laws. ²⁶And Joshua recorded these things in the Book of the Law of God. Then he took a large stone and set it up there under the oak near the holy place of the LORD.

²⁷"See!" he said to all the people. "This stone will be a witness against us. It has heard all the words the LORD has said to us. It will be a witness against you if you are untrue to your God."

Buried in the Promised Land

²⁸Then Joshua sent the people away, each to his own inheritance.

²⁹After these things, Joshua son of Nun, the servant of the LORD, died at the age of a hundred and ten. ³⁰And they bur-ied him in the land of his inheritance, at Timnath Serah*a* in the hill country of Ephraim, north of Mount Gaash.

³¹Israel served the LORD throughout the lifetime of Joshua and of the elders who outlived him and who had experienced everything the LORD had done for Israel.

³²And Joseph's bones, which the Israelites had brought up from Egypt, were buried at Shechem in the tract of land that Jacob bought for a hundred pieces of silver*b* from the sons of Hamor, the father of Shechem. This became the inheritance of Joseph's descendants.

³³And Eleazar son of Aaron died and was buried at Gibeah, which had been allotted to his son Phinehas in the hill country of Ephraim.

a30 Also known as *Timnath Heres* (see Judges 2:9)
b32 Hebrew *hundred kesitahs*; a kesitah was a unit of money of unknown weight and value.

If Joshua recounts an "up" time for the people of Israel, then Judges recounts some of the "down" times. In fact, this period in Israel's history is like a roller coaster ride. Israel repeatedly falls away from God, a situation where "Israel had no king; everyone did as he saw fit" (17:6). Eventually the Israelites become desperate and beg God to save them. God sends a judge to lead them out of trouble, things go better for a while, then the cycle starts again. This book clearly shows what happens when we try to get along without God—and what can happen when we turn around and trust God again.

JUDGES

Israel Fights the Remaining Canaanites

1 After the death of Joshua, the Israelites asked the LORD, "Who will be the first to go up and fight for us against the Canaanites?"

2The LORD answered, "Judah is to go; I have given the land into their hands."

3Then the men of Judah said to the Simeonites their brothers, "Come up with us into the territory allotted to us, to fight against the Canaanites. We in turn will go with you into yours." So the Simeonites went with them.

4When Judah attacked, the LORD gave the Canaanites and Perizzites into their hands and they struck down ten thousand men at Bezek. 5It was there that they found Adoni-Bezek and fought against him, putting to rout the Canaanites and Perizzites. 6Adoni-Bezek fled, but they chased him and caught him, and cut off his thumbs and big toes.

7Then Adoni-Bezek said, "Seventy kings with their thumbs and big toes cut off have picked up scraps under my table. Now God has paid me back for what I did to them." They brought him to Jerusalem, and he died there.

8The men of Judah attacked Jerusalem also and took it. They put the city to the sword and set it on fire.

⁹After that, the men of Judah went down to fight against the Canaanites living in the hill country, the Negev and the western foothills. ¹⁰They advanced against the Canaanites living in Hebron (formerly called Kiriath Arba) and defeated Sheshai, Ahiman and Talmai. ¹¹From there they advanced against the people living in Debir (formerly called Kiriath Sepher). ¹²And Caleb said, "I will give my daughter Acsah in marriage to the man who attacks and captures Kiriath Sepher." ¹³Othniel son of Kenaz, Caleb's younger brother, took it; so Caleb gave his daughter Acsah to him in marriage.

¹⁴One day when she came to Othniel, she urged himᵃ to ask her father for a field. When she got off her donkey, Caleb asked her, "What can I do for you?"

¹⁵She replied, "Do me a special favor. Since you have given me land in the Negev, give me also springs of water." Then Caleb gave her the upper and lower springs.

¹⁶The descendants of Moses' father-in-law, the Kenite, went up from the City of Palmsᵇ with the men of Judah to live among the people of the Desert of Judah in the Negev near Arad.

¹⁷Then the men of Judah went with the Simeonites their brothers and attacked the Canaanites living in Zephath, and they totally destroyedᶜ the city. Therefore it was called Hormah.ᵈ ¹⁸The men of Judah also tookᵉ Gaza, Ashkelon and Ekron—each city with its territory.

¹⁹The Lᴏʀᴅ was with the men of Judah. They took possession of the hill country, but they were unable to drive the people from the plains, because they had iron chariots. ²⁰As Moses had promised, Hebron was given to Caleb, who drove from it the three sons of Anak. ²¹The Benjamites, however, failed to dislodge the Jebusites, who were living in Jerusalem; to this day the Jebusites live there with the Benjamites.

²²Now the house of Joseph attacked Bethel, and the Lᴏʀᴅ was with them. ²³When they sent men to spy out Bethel (formerly called Luz), ²⁴the spies saw a man coming out of the city and they said to him, "Show us how to get into the city and we will see that you are treated well." ²⁵So he showed them, and they put the city to the sword but spared the man and his whole family. ²⁶He then went to the land of the Hittites, where he built a city and called it Luz, which is its name to this day.

²⁷But Manasseh did not drive out the people of Beth Shan or Taanach or Dor or Ibleam or Megiddo and their surrounding settlements, for the Canaanites were determined to live in that land. ²⁸When Israel became strong, they pressed the Canaanites into forced labor but never drove them out completely. ²⁹Nor did Ephraim drive out the Canaanites living in Gezer, but the Canaanites continued to live there among them. ³⁰Neither did Zebulun drive out the Canaanites living in Kitron or Nahalol, who remained among them; but they did subject them to forced labor. ³¹Nor did Asher drive out those living in Acco or Sidon or Ahlab or Aczib or Helbah or Aphek or Rehob, ³²and because of this the people of Asher lived among the Canaanite inhabitants of the land. ³³Neither did Naphtali drive out those living in Beth Shemesh or Beth Anath; but the Naphtalites too lived among the Canaanite inhabitants of the land, and those living in Beth Shemesh and Beth Anath became forced laborers for them. ³⁴The Amorites confined the Danites to the hill country, not allowing them to come down into the plain. ³⁵And the Amorites were determined also to hold out in Mount Heres, Aijalon and Shaalbim, but when the power of the house of Joseph increased, they too were pressed into forced labor. ³⁶The boundary of the Amorites was from Scorpionᶠ Pass to Sela and beyond.

The Angel of the Lᴏʀᴅ at Bokim

2 The angel of the Lᴏʀᴅ went up from Gilgal to Bokim and said, "I brought you up out of Egypt and led you into the land that I swore to give to your forefathers. I said, 'I will never break my covenant with you, ²and you shall not make a covenant with the people of this land, but you shall break down their altars.' Yet you have disobeyed me. Why have you done this? ³Now therefore I tell you that I will not drive them out before you; they will be ⌞thorns⌟ in your sides and their gods will be a snare to you."

ᵃ14 Hebrew; Septuagint and Vulgate *Othniel, he urged her*   ᵇ16 That is, Jericho
ᶜ17 The Hebrew term refers to the irrevocable giving over of things or persons to the Lᴏʀᴅ, often by totally destroying them.   ᵈ17 *Hormah* means *destruction.*   ᵉ18 Hebrew; Septuagint *Judah did not take*   ᶠ36 Hebrew *Akrabbim*

⁴When the angel of the Lord had spoken these things to all the Israelites, the people wept aloud, ⁵and they called that place Bokim.ᵃ There they offered sacrifices to the Lord.

Disobedience and Defeat

⁶After Joshua had dismissed the Israelites, they went to take possession of the land, each to his own inheritance. ⁷The people served the Lord throughout the lifetime of Joshua and of the elders who outlived him and who had seen all the great things the Lord had done for Israel.

⁸Joshua son of Nun, the servant of the Lord, died at the age of a hundred and ten. ⁹And they buried him in the land of his inheritance, at Timnath Heresᵇ in the hill country of Ephraim, north of Mount Gaash.

¹⁰After that whole generation had been gathered to their fathers, another generation grew up, who knew neither the Lord nor what he had done for Israel. ¹¹Then the Israelites did evil in the eyes of the Lord and served the Baals. ¹²They forsook the Lord, the God of their fathers, who had brought them out of Egypt. They followed and worshiped various gods of the peoples around them. They provoked the Lord to anger ¹³because they forsook him and served Baal and the Ashtoreths. ¹⁴In his anger against Israel the Lord handed them over to raiders who plundered them. He sold them to their enemies all around, whom they were no longer able to resist. ¹⁵Whenever Israel went out to fight, the hand of the Lord was against them to defeat them, just as he had sworn to them. They were in great distress.

¹⁶Then the Lord raised up judges,ᶜ who saved them out of the hands of these raiders. ¹⁷Yet they would not listen to their judges but prostituted themselves to other gods and worshiped them. Unlike their fathers, they quickly turned from the way in which their fathers had walked, the way of obedience to the Lord's commands. ¹⁸Whenever the Lord raised up a judge for them, he was with the judge and saved them out of the hands of their enemies as long as the judge lived; for the Lord had compassion on them as they groaned under those who oppressed and afflicted them. ¹⁹But when the judge died, the people returned to ways even more corrupt than those of their fathers, following other gods and serving and worshiping them. They refused to give up their evil practices and stubborn ways.

²⁰Therefore the Lord was very angry with Israel and said, "Because this nation has violated the covenant that I laid down for their forefathers and has not listened to me, ²¹I will no longer drive out before them any of the nations Joshua left when he died. ²²I will use them to test Israel and see whether they will keep the way of the Lord and walk in it as their forefathers did." ²³The Lord had allowed those nations to remain; he did not drive them out at once by giving them into the hands of Joshua.

3 These are the nations the Lord left to test all those Israelites who had not experienced any of the wars in Canaan ²(he did this only to teach warfare to the descendants of the Israelites who had not had previous battle experience): ³the five rulers of the Philistines, all the Canaanites, the Sidonians, and the Hivites living in the Lebanon mountains from Mount Baal Hermon to Leboᵈ Hamath. ⁴They were left to test the Israelites to see whether they would obey the Lord's commands, which he had given their forefathers through Moses.

⁵The Israelites lived among the Canaanites, Hittites, Amorites, Perizzites, Hivites and Jebusites. ⁶They took their daughters in marriage and gave their own daughters to their sons, and served their gods.

Othniel

⁷The Israelites did evil in the eyes of the Lord; they forgot the Lord their God and served the Baals and the Asherahs.

ᵃ5 *Bokim* means *weepers.*   ᵇ9 Also known as *Timnath Serah* (see Joshua 19:50 and 24:30)   ᶜ16 Or *leaders;* similarly in verses 17-19   ᵈ3 Or *to the entrance to*

POINT OF INTEREST

Judges 2:16

Where do leaders come from? Genuine spiritual leaders aren't self-appointed; God "raises them up." What insight does Psalm 75:6–7 add about this subject?

[8]The anger of the LORD burned against Israel so that he sold them into the hands of Cushan-Rishathaim king of Aram Naharaim,[a] to whom the Israelites were subject for eight years. [9]But when they cried out to the LORD, he raised up for them a deliverer, Othniel son of Kenaz, Caleb's younger brother, who saved them. [10]The Spirit of the LORD came upon him, so that he became Israel's judge[b] and went to war. The LORD gave Cushan-Rishathaim king of Aram into the hands of Othniel, who overpowered him. [11]So the land had peace for forty years, until Othniel son of Kenaz died.

Ehud

[12]Once again the Israelites did evil in the eyes of the LORD, and because they did this evil the LORD gave Eglon king of Moab power over Israel. [13]Getting the Ammonites and Amalekites to join him, Eglon came and attacked Israel, and they took possession of the City of Palms.[c] [14]The Israelites were subject to Eglon king of Moab for eighteen years.

[15]Again the Israelites cried out to the LORD, and he gave them a deliverer—Ehud, a left-handed man, the son of Gera the Benjamite. The Israelites sent him with tribute to Eglon king of Moab. [16]Now Ehud had made a double-edged sword about a foot and a half[d] long, which he strapped to his right thigh under his clothing. [17]He presented the tribute to Eglon king of Moab, who was a very fat man. [18]After Ehud had presented the tribute, he sent on their way the men who had carried it. [19]At the idols[e] near Gilgal he himself turned back and said, "I have a secret message for you, O king."

The king said, "Quiet!" And all his attendants left him.

[20]Ehud then approached him while he was sitting alone in the upper room of his summer palace[f] and said, "I have a message from God for you." As the king rose from his seat, [21]Ehud reached with his left hand, drew the sword from his right thigh and plunged it into the king's belly. [22]Even the handle sank in after the blade, which came out his back. Ehud did not pull the sword out, and the fat closed in over it. [23]Then Ehud went out to the porch[g]; he shut the doors of the upper room behind him and locked them.

[24]After he had gone, the servants came and found the doors of the upper room locked. They said, "He must be relieving himself in the inner room of the house." [25]They waited to the point of embarrassment, but when he did not open the doors of the room, they took a key and unlocked them. There they saw their lord fallen to the floor, dead.

[26]While they waited, Ehud got away. He passed by the idols and escaped to Seirah. [27]When he arrived there, he blew a trumpet in the hill country of Ephraim, and the Israelites went down with him from the hills, with him leading them.

[28]"Follow me," he ordered, "for the LORD has given Moab, your enemy, into your hands." So they followed him down and, taking possession of the fords of the Jordan that led to Moab, they allowed no one to cross over. [29]At that time they struck down about ten thousand Moabites, all vigorous and strong; not a man escaped. [30]That day Moab was made subject to Israel, and the land had peace for eighty years.

Shamgar

[31]After Ehud came Shamgar son of Anath, who struck down six hundred Philistines with an oxgoad. He too saved Israel.

Deborah

4 After Ehud died, the Israelites once again did evil in the eyes of the LORD. [2]So the LORD sold them into the hands of Jabin, a king of Canaan, who reigned in Hazor. The commander of his army was Sisera, who lived in Harosheth Haggoyim. [3]Because he had nine hundred iron chariots and had cruelly oppressed the Israelites for twenty years, they cried to the LORD for help.

[4]Deborah, a prophetess, the wife of Lappidoth, was leading[h] Israel at that time. [5]She held court under the Palm of Deborah between Ramah and Bethel in the hill country of Ephraim, and the Israelites came to her to have their disputes decided. [6]She sent for Barak son of Abinoam from Kedesh in Naphtali and said to him, "The LORD, the God of Israel, commands you: 'Go, take with you ten thousand men of Naphtali and Zebulun and lead the way to Mount Tabor. [7]I will lure

---

[a]8 That is, Northwest Mesopotamia   [b]10 Or leader   [c]13 That is, Jericho   [d]16 Hebrew a cubit (about 0.5 meter)   [e]19 Or the stone quarries; also in verse 26   [f]20 The meaning of the Hebrew for this phrase is uncertain.   [g]23 The meaning of the Hebrew for this word is uncertain.   [h]4 Traditionally judging

Sisera, the commander of Jabin's army, with his chariots and his troops to the Kishon River and give him into your hands.' "

⁸Barak said to her, "If you go with me, I will go; but if you don't go with me, I won't go."

⁹"Very well," Deborah said, "I will go with you. But because of the way you are going about this,ᵃ the honor will not be yours, for the LORD will hand Sisera over to a woman." So Deborah went with Barak to Kedesh, ¹⁰where he summoned Zebulun and Naphtali. Ten thousand men followed him, and Deborah also went with him.

¹¹Now Heber the Kenite had left the other Kenites, the descendants of Hobab, Moses' brother-in-law,ᵇ and pitched his tent by the great tree in Zaanannim near Kedesh.

¹²When they told Sisera that Barak son of Abinoam had gone up to Mount Tabor, ¹³Sisera gathered together his nine hundred iron chariots and all the men with him, from Harosheth Haggoyim to the Kishon River.

¹⁴Then Deborah said to Barak, "Go! This is the day the LORD has given Sisera

ᵃ9 Or But on the expedition you are undertaking
ᵇ11 Or father-in-law

Read Judges 3:12–31
Key Verse Judges 3:31

Use What You Have — Louise B. Wyly

Do you have much money? Do you have many assets? Many of us would say "no" to both questions. But what about the little things in our lives that we often overlook? It might be a talent for whistling, running a fast mile or adding up a long column of figures. Or maybe it's having a handy little pocketknife or a mini-calculator. If we think we have nothing to offer, it may be that we need to remember that "little is much when God is in it." We never know when God might want to use the "little" things he's given us.

Consider the following:
—David killed the giant Goliath with a slingshot.
—Rahab saved two spies with a piece of rope.
—Shamgar killed six hundred Philistines with an oxgoad.

These heroes accomplished great things for God. How? Look at their hearts. Without a willing heart, Shamgar might never have been included in the Bible. Yet there's his name in black and white for all posterity.

Why were these incidents included in Scripture? Perhaps it was to show us that we should use what we have with the right attitude. Shamgar was probably a humble farmer plowing his field when the Philistines invaded the Israelite land. He miraculously killed the enemy with his oxgoad and saved Israel.

When we use what we have, God can greatly multiply it. Look at how Jesus fed a crowd of people with five loaves of bread and two fish that a small boy was willing to share (see John 6:8–13).

Are you ready to give what you have to God? Can he count on your willing heart?

A Deeper Look
Matthew 25:14–30; Mark 6:37–44

Go to page 259 for your next devotional reading.

into your hands. Has not the LORD gone ahead of you?" So Barak went down Mount Tabor, followed by ten thousand men. ¹⁵At Barak's advance, the LORD routed Sisera and all his chariots and army by the sword, and Sisera abandoned his chariot and fled on foot. ¹⁶But Barak pursued the chariots and army as far as Harosheth Haggoyim. All the troops of Sisera fell by the sword; not a man was left.

¹⁷Sisera, however, fled on foot to the tent of Jael, the wife of Heber the Kenite, because there were friendly relations between Jabin king of Hazor and the clan of Heber the Kenite.

¹⁸Jael went out to meet Sisera and said to him, "Come, my lord, come right in. Don't be afraid." So he entered her tent, and she put a covering over him.

¹⁹"I'm thirsty," he said. "Please give me some water." She opened a skin of

---

TUESDAY

Read Judges 4:1–24
Key Verse Judges 4:8

Barak: A Reluctant Hero — Dana Yeakley

Amazingly, we find Barak's name listed among the great heroes of the faith in Hebrews 11:32–33: "And what more shall I say? I do not have time to tell about Gideon, Barak, Samson, Jepthah, David, Samuel and the prophets who through faith conquered kingdoms . . ." David? Yes. The prophets? Yes. But Barak? When we read the account of Barak in Judges 4 and 5, Barak seems a reluctant hero at best.

True, life was extremely difficult and unstable in Barak's time. It was a period of Israel's history when "everyone did as he saw fit" (Judges 21:25). It was also a time when "village life in Israel [had] ceased" (Judges 5:7). Many had fled to walled towns for protection. The Israelites were crying out to God for deliverance from the oppression of Sisera's army.

In the midst of these circumstances God raised up a great woman of faith, Deborah, a prophetess, and through her God's word came to Barak, "The LORD, the God of Israel, commands you: 'Go, take with you ten thousand men . . . I will lure Sisera . . . and give him into your hands' " (Judges 4:6–7).

Barak responded to God's command reluctantly. He requested that Deborah accompany him into the battle, needing the reassurance that God was with them. She agreed to go with him, yet admonished him, declaring that because of his reluctance a woman would receive the honor for the victory (see Judges 5:24).

With Deborah's encouragement and support, Barak did lead the Israelites into battle, and God kept his promise: "All the troops of Sisera fell by the sword; not a man was left" (Judges 4:15–16). Even though he was reluctant and fearful, Barak chose to follow God by faith, and God endorsed him as a hero.

Sometimes we're reluctant to follow God's leading, or we doubt that God will keep his promises to us. Sometimes we need encouragement from others who have the gift of faith. Even so, God is looking for men and women of faith, such as Barak, who will follow him, regardless of their fears. The true heroes of the faith are those who find God's strong support as they obey him.

A Deeper Look
2 Chronicles 16:9; Matthew 8:23–27; Hebrews 11:6

Go to page 264 for your next devotional reading.

milk, gave him a drink, and covered him up.

²⁰"Stand in the doorway of the tent," he told her. "If someone comes by and asks you, 'Is anyone here?' say 'No.' "

²¹But Jael, Heber's wife, picked up a tent peg and a hammer and went quietly to him while he lay fast asleep, exhausted. She drove the peg through his temple into the ground, and he died.

²²Barak came by in pursuit of Sisera, and Jael went out to meet him. "Come," she said, "I will show you the man you're looking for." So he went in with her, and there lay Sisera with the tent peg through his temple—dead.

²³On that day God subdued Jabin, the Canaanite king, before the Israelites. ²⁴And the hand of the Israelites grew stronger and stronger against Jabin, the Canaanite king, until they destroyed him.

The Song of Deborah

5 On that day Deborah and Barak son of Abinoam sang this song:

²"When the princes in Israel take the
        lead,
    when the people willingly offer
        themselves—
    praise the LORD!

³"Hear this, you kings! Listen, you
        rulers!
    I will sing toᵃ the LORD, I will
        sing;
    I will make music toᵇ the LORD,
        the God of Israel.

⁴"O LORD, when you went out from
        Seir,
    when you marched from the land
        of Edom,
    the earth shook, the heavens poured,
        the clouds poured down water.
⁵The mountains quaked before the
        LORD, the One of Sinai,
    before the LORD, the God of Israel.

⁶"In the days of Shamgar son of
        Anath,
    in the days of Jael, the roads were
        abandoned;
    travelers took to winding paths.
⁷Village lifeᶜ in Israel ceased,
    ceased until I,ᵈ Deborah, arose,
    arose a mother in Israel.
⁸When they chose new gods,
    war came to the city gates,
    and not a shield or spear was seen

among forty thousand in Israel.
⁹My heart is with Israel's princes,
    with the willing volunteers among
        the people.
    Praise the LORD!

¹⁰"You who ride on white donkeys,
    sitting on your saddle blankets,
    and you who walk along the road,
    consider ¹¹the voice of the singersᵉ
        at the watering places.
    They recite the righteous acts of
        the LORD,
    the righteous acts of his warriorsᶠ
        in Israel.

"Then the people of the LORD
        went down to the city gates.
¹²'Wake up, wake up, Deborah!
    Wake up, wake up, break out in
        song!
    Arise, O Barak!
    Take captive your captives, O son
        of Abinoam.'

¹³"Then the men who were left
        came down to the nobles;
    the people of the LORD
        came to me with the mighty.
¹⁴Some came from Ephraim, whose
        roots were in Amalek;
    Benjamin was with the people who
        followed you.
    From Makir captains came down,
        from Zebulun those who bear a
        commander's staff.
¹⁵The princes of Issachar were with
        Deborah;
    yes, Issachar was with Barak,
        rushing after him into the valley.
    In the districts of Reuben
        there was much searching of heart.
¹⁶Why did you stay among the
        campfiresᵍ
    to hear the whistling for the flocks?
    In the districts of Reuben
        there was much searching of heart.
¹⁷Gilead stayed beyond the Jordan.
    And Dan, why did he linger by the
        ships?
    Asher remained on the coast
        and stayed in his coves.
¹⁸The people of Zebulun risked their
        very lives;

ᵃ3 Or of   ᵇ3 Or / with song I will praise
ᶜ7 Or Warriors   ᵈ7 Or you   ᵉ11 Or archers;
the meaning of the Hebrew for this word is
uncertain.   ᶠ11 Or villagers   ᵍ16 Or
saddlebags

so did Naphtali on the heights of
the field.

¹⁹"Kings came, they fought;
the kings of Canaan fought
at Taanach by the waters of Megiddo,
but they carried off no silver, no
plunder.
²⁰From the heavens the stars fought,
from their courses they fought
against Sisera.
²¹The river Kishon swept them away,
the age-old river, the river Kishon.
March on, my soul; be strong!
²²Then thundered the horses' hoofs—
galloping, galloping go his mighty
steeds.
²³'Curse Meroz,' said the angel of the
LORD.
'Curse its people bitterly,
because they did not come to help
the LORD,
to help the LORD against the
mighty.'

²⁴"Most blessed of women be Jael,
the wife of Heber the Kenite,
most blessed of tent-dwelling
women.
²⁵He asked for water, and she gave him
milk;
in a bowl fit for nobles she brought
him curdled milk.
²⁶Her hand reached for the tent peg,
her right hand for the workman's
hammer.
She struck Sisera, she crushed his
head,
she shattered and pierced his
temple.
²⁷At her feet he sank,
he fell; there he lay.
At her feet he sank, he fell;
where he sank, there he fell—
dead.

²⁸"Through the window peered Sisera's
mother;
behind the lattice she cried out,
'Why is his chariot so long in
coming?
Why is the clatter of his chariots
delayed?'
²⁹The wisest of her ladies answer her;
indeed, she keeps saying to herself,
³⁰'Are they not finding and dividing the
spoils:
a girl or two for each man,
colorful garments as plunder for
Sisera,
colorful garments embroidered,
highly embroidered garments for
my neck—
all this as plunder?'

³¹"So may all your enemies perish,
O LORD!
But may they who love you be like
the sun
when it rises in its strength."

Then the land had peace forty years.

Gideon

6 Again the Israelites did evil in the eyes
of the LORD, and for seven years he
gave them into the hands of the Midianites. ²Because the power of Midian was
so oppressive, the Israelites prepared
shelters for themselves in mountain
clefts, caves and strongholds. ³Whenever
the Israelites planted their crops, the Midianites, Amalekites and other eastern
peoples invaded the country. ⁴They
camped on the land and ruined the crops
all the way to Gaza and did not spare a
living thing for Israel, neither sheep nor
cattle nor donkeys. ⁵They came up with
their livestock and their tents like
swarms of locusts. It was impossible to
count the men and their camels; they invaded the land to ravage it. ⁶Midian so
impoverished the Israelites that they
cried out to the LORD for help.

⁷When the Israelites cried to the LORD
because of Midian, ⁸he sent them a
prophet, who said, "This is what the
LORD, the God of Israel, says: I brought
you up out of Egypt, out of the land of
slavery. ⁹I snatched you from the power
of Egypt and from the hand of all your
oppressors. I drove them from before you
and gave you their land. ¹⁰I said to you, 'I
am the LORD your God; do not worship
the gods of the Amorites, in whose land
you live.' But you have not listened
to me."

¹¹The angel of the LORD came and sat
down under the oak in Ophrah that belonged to Joash the Abiezrite, where his
son Gideon was threshing wheat in a
winepress to keep it from the Midianites.
¹²When the angel of the LORD appeared to
Gideon, he said, "The LORD is with you,
mighty warrior."

¹³"But sir," Gideon replied, "if the
LORD is with us, why has all this happened to us? Where are all his wonders
that our fathers told us about when they

said, 'Did not the LORD bring us up out of Egypt?' But now the LORD has abandoned us and put us into the hand of Midian."

¹⁴The LORD turned to him and said, "Go in the strength you have and save Israel out of Midian's hand. Am I not sending you?"

¹⁵"But Lord,ᵃ" Gideon asked, "how can I save Israel? My clan is the weakest in Manasseh, and I am the least in my family."

¹⁶The LORD answered, "I will be with you, and you will strike down all the Midianites together."

¹⁷Gideon replied, "If now I have found favor in your eyes, give me a sign that it is really you talking to me. ¹⁸Please do not go away until I come back and bring my offering and set it before you."

And the LORD said, "I will wait until you return."

¹⁹Gideon went in, prepared a young goat, and from an ephahᵇ of flour he made bread without yeast. Putting the meat in a basket and its broth in a pot, he brought them out and offered them to him under the oak.

²⁰The angel of God said to him, "Take the meat and the unleavened bread, place them on this rock, and pour out the broth." And Gideon did so. ²¹With the tip of the staff that was in his hand, the angel of the LORD touched the meat and the unleavened bread. Fire flared from the rock, consuming the meat and the bread. And the angel of the LORD disappeared. ²²When Gideon realized that it was the angel of the LORD, he exclaimed, "Ah, Sovereign LORD! I have seen the angel of the LORD face to face!"

²³But the LORD said to him, "Peace! Do not be afraid. You are not going to die."

²⁴So Gideon built an altar to the LORD there and called it The LORD is Peace. To this day it stands in Ophrah of the Abiezrites.

²⁵That same night the LORD said to him, "Take the second bull from your father's herd, the one seven years old.ᶜ Tear down your father's altar to Baal and cut down the Asherah poleᵈ beside it. ²⁶Then build a proper kind ofᵉ altar to the LORD your God on the top of this height. Using the wood of the Asherah pole that you cut down, offer the secondᶠ bull as a burnt offering."

²⁷So Gideon took ten of his servants and did as the LORD told him. But because he was afraid of his family and the men

of the town, he did it at night rather than in the daytime.

²⁸In the morning when the men of the town got up, there was Baal's altar, demolished, with the Asherah pole beside it cut down and the second bull sacrificed on the newly built altar!

²⁹They asked each other, "Who did this?"

When they carefully investigated, they were told, "Gideon son of Joash did it."

³⁰The men of the town demanded of Joash, "Bring out your son. He must die, because he has broken down Baal's altar and cut down the Asherah pole beside it."

³¹But Joash replied to the hostile crowd around him, "Are you going to plead Baal's cause? Are you trying to save him? Whoever fights for him shall be put to death by morning! If Baal really is a god, he can defend himself when someone breaks down his altar." ³²So that day they called Gideon "Jerub-Baal,ᵍ" saying, "Let Baal contend with him," because he broke down Baal's altar.

³³Now all the Midianites, Amalekites and other eastern peoples joined forces and crossed over the Jordan and camped in the Valley of Jezreel. ³⁴Then the Spirit of the LORD came upon Gideon, and he blew a trumpet, summoning the Abiezrites to follow him. ³⁵He sent messengers throughout Manasseh, calling them to arms, and also into Asher, Zebulun and Naphtali, so that they too went up to meet them.

ᵃ15 Or sir   ᵇ19 That is, probably about 3/5 bushel (about 22 liters)   ᶜ25 Or Take a full-grown, mature bull from your father's herd ᵈ25 That is, a symbol of the goddess Asherah; here and elsewhere in Judges   ᵉ26 Or build with layers of stone an   ᶠ26 Or full-grown; also in verse 28   ᵍ32 Jerub-Baal means let Baal contend.

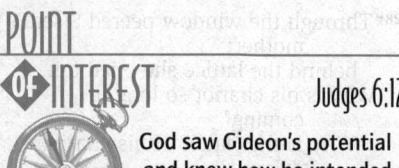

POINT OF INTEREST

Judges 6:12

God saw Gideon's potential and knew how he intended to appoint the young farmer as a warrior and the defender of Israel. What do you see when you look in the mirror? God will give you the resources to accomplish every task he asks you to do. Watch and wait for his leading.

³⁶Gideon said to God, "If you will save Israel by my hand as you have promised— ³⁷look, I will place a wool fleece on the threshing floor. If there is dew only on the fleece and all the ground is dry, then I will know that you will save Israel by my hand, as you said." ³⁸And that is what happened. Gideon rose early the next day; he squeezed the fleece and wrung out the dew—a bowlful of water. ³⁹Then Gideon said to God, "Do not be angry with me. Let me make just one more request. Allow me one more test with the fleece. This time make the fleece dry and the ground covered with dew." ⁴⁰That night God did so. Only the fleece was dry; all the ground was covered with dew.

Gideon Defeats the Midianites

7 Early in the morning, Jerub-Baal (that is, Gideon) and all his men camped at the spring of Harod. The camp of Midian was north of them in the valley near the hill of Moreh. ²The LORD said to Gideon, "You have too many men for me to deliver Midian into their hands. In order that Israel may not boast against me that her own strength has saved her, ³announce now to the people, 'Anyone who trembles with fear may turn back and leave Mount Gilead.' " So twenty-two thousand men left, while ten thousand remained.

⁴But the LORD said to Gideon, "There are still too many men. Take them down to the water, and I will sift them for you there. If I say, 'This one shall go with you,' he shall go; but if I say, 'This one shall not go with you,' he shall not go." ⁵So Gideon took the men down to the water. There the LORD told him, "Separate those who lap the water with their tongues like a dog from those who kneel down to drink." ⁶Three hundred men lapped with their hands to their mouths. All the rest got down on their knees to drink.

⁷The LORD said to Gideon, "With the three hundred men that lapped I will save you and give the Midianites into your hands. Let all the other men go, each to his own place." ⁸So Gideon sent the rest of the Israelites to their tents but kept the three hundred, who took over the provisions and trumpets of the others.

Now the camp of Midian lay below him in the valley. ⁹During that night the LORD said to Gideon, "Get up, go down against the camp, because I am going to give it into your hands. ¹⁰If you are afraid to attack, go down to the camp with your servant Purah ¹¹and listen to what they are saying. Afterward, you will be encouraged to attack the camp." So he and Purah his servant went down to the outposts of the camp. ¹²The Midianites, the Amalekites and all the other eastern peoples had settled in the valley, thick as locusts. Their camels could no more be counted than the sand on the seashore.

¹³Gideon arrived just as a man was telling a friend his dream. "I had a dream," he was saying. "A round loaf of barley bread came tumbling into the Midianite camp. It struck the tent with such force that the tent overturned and collapsed."

¹⁴His friend responded, "This can be nothing other than the sword of Gideon son of Joash, the Israelite. God has given the Midianites and the whole camp into his hands."

¹⁵When Gideon heard the dream and its interpretation, he worshiped God. He returned to the camp of Israel and called out, "Get up! The LORD has given the Midianite camp into your hands." ¹⁶Dividing the three hundred men into three companies, he placed trumpets and empty jars in the hands of all of them, with torches inside.

¹⁷"Watch me," he told them. "Follow my lead. When I get to the edge of the camp, do exactly as I do. ¹⁸When I and all who are with me blow our trumpets, then from all around the camp blow yours and shout, 'For the LORD and for Gideon.' "

¹⁹Gideon and the hundred men with him reached the edge of the camp at the beginning of the middle watch, just after they had changed the guard. They blew their trumpets and broke the jars that were in their hands. ²⁰The three companies blew the trumpets and smashed the jars. Grasping the torches in their left hands and holding in their right hands the trumpets they were to blow, they shouted, "A sword for the LORD and for Gideon!" ²¹While each man held his position around the camp, all the Midianites ran, crying out as they fled.

²²When the three hundred trumpets sounded, the LORD caused the men throughout the camp to turn on each other with their swords. The army fled to Beth Shittah toward Zererah as far as the border of Abel Meholah near Tabbath.

23Israelites from Naphtali, Asher and all Manasseh were called out, and they pursued the Midianites. 24Gideon sent messengers throughout the hill country of Ephraim, saying, "Come down against the Midianites and seize the waters of the Jordan ahead of them as far as Beth Barah."

So all the men of Ephraim were called out and they took the waters of the Jordan as far as Beth Barah. 25They also captured two of the Midianite leaders, Oreb and Zeeb. They killed Oreb at the rock of Oreb, and Zeeb at the winepress of Zeeb. They pursued the Midianites and brought the heads of Oreb and Zeeb to Gideon, who was by the Jordan.

Zebah and Zalmunna

8 Now the Ephraimites asked Gideon, "Why have you treated us like this? Why didn't you call us when you went to fight Midian?" And they criticized him sharply.

2But he answered them, "What have I accomplished compared to you? Aren't the gleanings of Ephraim's grapes better than the full grape harvest of Abiezer? 3God gave Oreb and Zeeb, the Midianite leaders, into your hands. What was I able to do compared to you?" At this, their resentment against him subsided.

4Gideon and his three hundred men, exhausted yet keeping up the pursuit, came to the Jordan and crossed it. 5He

---

WEDNESDAY

Read Judges 8: 1–12
Key Verse Judges 8:4

Exhausted? Persevere! —Mistie Hutchison

I once heard a missionary describe his work like this: "When I lie down at night, I'm tired. But it's a good tired." His words have stuck with me over the years, because I often need encouragement to keep on with what God has called me to do—especially when I feel exhausted.

I've noticed that when we're exhausted we're most likely to abandon godly pursuits; we're more vulnerable to feelings of discouragement and uselessness. But even though we're exhausted, God wants us to continue to love him and others. Sometimes he wants us to keep going, relying on him for strength. The apostle Paul conveyed something of this when he wrote, "We proclaim him, admonishing and teaching everyone with all wisdom, so that we may present everyone perfect in Christ. To this end I labor, struggling with all his energy, which so powerfully works in me" (Colossians 1:28–29). The word translated "labor" literally means to work to the point of exhaustion. Perhaps Paul would have felt at home with Gideon and his men. Paul's words and life illustrate perseverance and highlight its source—Christ's energy.

Certainly we need to be smart about using our time and energy so that we don't become depleted by trivial activities. And there are times when God calls us to rest and to be quiet. But if we feel drained, and God is asking us to keep going, then we can look to the examples of Gideon and Paul. We may learn the value of exhaustion for the cause of Jesus Christ: "That is why, for Christ's sake, I delight in weaknesses, in insults, in hardships, in persecutions, in difficulties. For when I am weak, then I am strong" (2 Corinthians 12:10).

A Deeper Look
1 Corinthians 15:58; Hebrews 12:1–3

Go to page 275 for your next devotional reading.

said to the men of Succoth, "Give my troops some bread; they are worn out, and I am still pursuing Zebah and Zalmunna, the kings of Midian."

⁶But the officials of Succoth said, "Do you already have the hands of Zebah and Zalmunna in your possession? Why should we give bread to your troops?"

⁷Then Gideon replied, "Just for that, when the LORD has given Zebah and Zalmunna into my hand, I will tear your flesh with desert thorns and briers."

⁸From there he went up to Peniel*ᵃ* and made the same request of them, but they answered as the men of Succoth had. ⁹So he said to the men of Peniel, "When I return in triumph, I will tear down this tower."

¹⁰Now Zebah and Zalmunna were in Karkor with a force of about fifteen thousand men, all that were left of the armies of the eastern peoples; a hundred and twenty thousand swordsmen had fallen. ¹¹Gideon went up by the route of the nomads east of Nobah and Jogbehah and fell upon the unsuspecting army. ¹²Zebah and Zalmunna, the two kings of Midian, fled, but he pursued them and captured them, routing their entire army.

¹³Gideon son of Joash then returned from the battle by the Pass of Heres. ¹⁴He caught a young man of Succoth and questioned him, and the young man wrote down for him the names of the seventy-seven officials of Succoth, the elders of the town. ¹⁵Then Gideon came and said to the men of Succoth, "Here are Zebah and Zalmunna, about whom you taunted me by saying, 'Do you already have the hands of Zebah and Zalmunna in your possession? Why should we give bread to your exhausted men?' " ¹⁶He took the elders of the town and taught the men of Succoth a lesson by punishing them with desert thorns and briers. ¹⁷He also pulled down the tower of Peniel and killed the men of the town.

¹⁸Then he asked Zebah and Zalmunna, "What kind of men did you kill at Tabor?"

"Men like you," they answered, "each one with the bearing of a prince."

¹⁹Gideon replied, "Those were my brothers, the sons of my own mother. As surely as the LORD lives, if you had spared their lives, I would not kill you." ²⁰Turning to Jether, his oldest son, he said, "Kill them!" But Jether did not draw his sword, because he was only a boy and was afraid.

²¹Zebah and Zalmunna said, "Come, do it yourself. 'As is the man, so is his strength.' " So Gideon stepped forward and killed them, and took the ornaments off their camels' necks.

Gideon's Ephod

²²The Israelites said to Gideon, "Rule over us—you, your son and your grandson—because you have saved us out of the hand of Midian."

²³But Gideon told them, "I will not rule over you, nor will my son rule over you. The LORD will rule over you." ²⁴And he said, "I do have one request, that each of you give me an earring from your share of the plunder." (It was the custom of the Ishmaelites to wear gold earrings.)

²⁵They answered, "We'll be glad to give them." So they spread out a garment, and each man threw a ring from his plunder onto it. ²⁶The weight of the gold rings he asked for came to seventeen hundred shekels,*ᵇ* not counting the ornaments, the pendants and the purple garments worn by the kings of Midian or the chains that were on their camels' necks. ²⁷Gideon made the gold into an ephod, which he placed in Ophrah, his town. All Israel prostituted themselves by worshiping it there, and it became a snare to Gideon and his family.

Gideon's Death

²⁸Thus Midian was subdued before the Israelites and did not raise its head again.

ᵃ8 Hebrew *Penuel*, a variant of *Peniel*; also in verses 9 and 17   *ᵇ26* That is, about 43 pounds (about 19.5 kilograms)

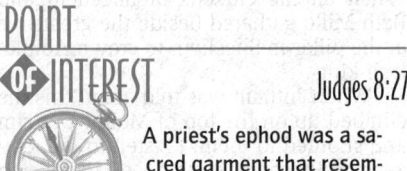

POINT OF INTEREST

Judges 8:27

A priest's ephod was a sacred garment that resembled an apron. Gideon wanted to memorialize the victory God had granted by creating this replica of an ephod. But a well-worn pattern reemerges: The people's worship subtly shifted from devotion to God to glorifying the object itself. At that point the memorial became an idol.

During Gideon's lifetime, the land enjoyed peace forty years.

²⁹Jerub-Baal son of Joash went back home to live. ³⁰He had seventy sons of his own, for he had many wives. ³¹His concubine, who lived in Shechem, also bore him a son, whom he named Abimelech. ³²Gideon son of Joash died at a good old age and was buried in the tomb of his father Joash in Ophrah of the Abiezrites.

³³No sooner had Gideon died than the Israelites again prostituted themselves to the Baals. They set up Baal-Berith as their god and ³⁴did not remember the LORD their God, who had rescued them from the hands of all their enemies on every side. ³⁵They also failed to show kindness to the family of Jerub-Baal (that is, Gideon) for all the good things he had done for them.

Abimelech

9 Abimelech son of Jerub-Baal went to his mother's brothers in Shechem and said to them and to all his mother's clan, ²"Ask all the citizens of Shechem, 'Which is better for you: to have all seventy of Jerub-Baal's sons rule over you, or just one man?' Remember, I am your flesh and blood."

³When the brothers repeated all this to the citizens of Shechem, they were inclined to follow Abimelech, for they said, "He is our brother." ⁴They gave him seventy shekels*ᵃ* of silver from the temple of Baal-Berith, and Abimelech used it to hire reckless adventurers, who became his followers. ⁵He went to his father's home in Ophrah and on one stone murdered his seventy brothers, the sons of Jerub-Baal. But Jotham, the youngest son of Jerub-Baal, escaped by hiding. ⁶Then all the citizens of Shechem and Beth Millo gathered beside the great tree at the pillar in Shechem to crown Abimelech king.

⁷When Jotham was told about this, he climbed up on the top of Mount Gerizim and shouted to them, "Listen to me, citizens of Shechem, so that God may listen to you. ⁸One day the trees went out to anoint a king for themselves. They said to the olive tree, 'Be our king.'

⁹"But the olive tree answered, 'Should I give up my oil, by which both gods and men are honored, to hold sway over the trees?'

¹⁰"Next, the trees said to the fig tree, 'Come and be our king.'

¹¹"But the fig tree replied, 'Should I give up my fruit, so good and sweet, to hold sway over the trees?'

¹²"Then the trees said to the vine, 'Come and be our king.'

¹³"But the vine answered, 'Should I give up my wine, which cheers both gods and men, to hold sway over the trees?'

¹⁴"Finally all the trees said to the thornbush, 'Come and be our king.'

¹⁵"The thornbush said to the trees, 'If you really want to anoint me king over you, come and take refuge in my shade; but if not, then let fire come out of the thornbush and consume the cedars of Lebanon!'

¹⁶"Now if you have acted honorably and in good faith when you made Abimelech king, and if you have been fair to Jerub-Baal and his family, and if you have treated him as he deserves— ¹⁷and to think that my father fought for you, risked his life to rescue you from the hand of Midian ¹⁸(but today you have revolted against my father's family, murdered his seventy sons on a single stone, and made Abimelech, the son of his slave girl, king over the citizens of Shechem because he is your brother)— ¹⁹if then you have acted honorably and in good faith toward Jerub-Baal and his family today, may Abimelech be your joy, and may you be his, too! ²⁰But if you have not, let fire come out from Abimelech and consume you, citizens of Shechem and Beth Millo, and let fire come out from you, citizens of Shechem and Beth Millo, and consume Abimelech!"

²¹Then Jotham fled, escaping to Beer, and he lived there because he was afraid of his brother Abimelech.

²²After Abimelech had governed Israel three years, ²³God sent an evil spirit between Abimelech and the citizens of Shechem, who acted treacherously against Abimelech. ²⁴God did this in order that the crime against Jerub-Baal's seventy sons, the shedding of their blood, might be avenged on their brother Abimelech and on the citizens of Shechem, who had helped him murder his brothers. ²⁵In opposition to him these citizens of Shechem set men on the hilltops to ambush and rob everyone who passed by, and this was reported to Abimelech.

²⁶Now Gaal son of Ebed moved with

ᵃ4 That is, about 1 3/4 pounds (about 0.8 kilogram)

his brothers into Shechem, and its citizens put their confidence in him. ²⁷After they had gone out into the fields and gathered the grapes and trodden them, they held a festival in the temple of their god. While they were eating and drinking, they cursed Abimelech. ²⁸Then Gaal son of Ebed said, "Who is Abimelech, and who is Shechem, that we should be subject to him? Isn't he Jerub-Baal's son, and isn't Zebul his deputy? Serve the men of Hamor, Shechem's father! Why should we serve Abimelech? ²⁹If only this people were under my command! Then I would get rid of him. I would say to Abimelech, 'Call out your whole army!'" *a*

³⁰When Zebul the governor of the city heard what Gaal son of Ebed said, he was very angry. ³¹Under cover he sent messengers to Abimelech, saying, "Gaal son of Ebed and his brothers have come to Shechem and are stirring up the city against you. ³²Now then, during the night you and your men should come and lie in wait in the fields. ³³In the morning at sunrise, advance against the city. When Gaal and his men come out against you, do whatever your hand finds to do."

³⁴So Abimelech and all his troops set out by night and took up concealed positions near Shechem in four companies. ³⁵Now Gaal son of Ebed had gone out and was standing at the entrance to the city gate just as Abimelech and his soldiers came out from their hiding place.

³⁶When Gaal saw them, he said to Zebul, "Look, people are coming down from the tops of the mountains!"

Zebul replied, "You mistake the shadows of the mountains for men."

³⁷But Gaal spoke up again: "Look, people are coming down from the center of the land, and a company is coming from the direction of the soothsayers' tree."

³⁸Then Zebul said to him, "Where is your big talk now, you who said, 'Who is Abimelech that we should be subject to him?' Aren't these the men you ridiculed? Go out and fight them!"

³⁹So Gaal led out*b* the citizens of Shechem and fought Abimelech. ⁴⁰Abimelech chased him, and many fell wounded in the flight—all the way to the entrance to the gate. ⁴¹Abimelech stayed in Arumah, and Zebul drove Gaal and his brothers out of Shechem.

⁴²The next day the people of Shechem went out to the fields, and this was reported to Abimelech. ⁴³So he took his men, divided them into three companies and set an ambush in the fields. When he saw the people coming out of the city, he rose to attack them. ⁴⁴Abimelech and the companies with him rushed forward to a position at the entrance to the city gate. Then two companies rushed upon those in the fields and struck them down. ⁴⁵All that day Abimelech pressed his attack against the city until he had captured it and killed its people. Then he destroyed the city and scattered salt over it.

⁴⁶On hearing this, the citizens in the tower of Shechem went into the stronghold of the temple of El-Berith. ⁴⁷When Abimelech heard that they had assembled there, ⁴⁸he and all his men went up Mount Zalmon. He took an ax and cut off some branches, which he lifted to his shoulders. He ordered the men with him, "Quick! Do what you have seen me do!" ⁴⁹So all the men cut branches and followed Abimelech. They piled them against the stronghold and set it on fire over the people inside. So all the people in the tower of Shechem, about a thousand men and women, also died.

⁵⁰Next Abimelech went to Thebez and besieged it and captured it. ⁵¹Inside the city, however, was a strong tower, to which all the men and women—all the people of the city—fled. They locked themselves in and climbed up on the tower roof. ⁵²Abimelech went to the tower and stormed it. But as he approached the entrance to the tower to set it on fire, ⁵³a woman dropped an upper millstone on his head and cracked his skull.

⁵⁴Hurriedly he called to his armorbearer, "Draw your sword and kill me, so that they can't say, 'A woman killed him.'" So his servant ran him through, and he died. ⁵⁵When the Israelites saw that Abimelech was dead, they went home.

⁵⁶Thus God repaid the wickedness that Abimelech had done to his father by murdering his seventy brothers. ⁵⁷God also made the men of Shechem pay for all their wickedness. The curse of Jotham son of Jerub-Baal came on them.

Tola

10 After the time of Abimelech a man of Issachar, Tola son of Puah, the son of Dodo, rose to save Israel. He lived in Sha-

---

a29 Septuagint; Hebrew *him." Then he said to Abimelech, "Call out your whole army!"* *b39* Or *Gaal went out in the sight of* mir, in the hill country of Ephraim. ²He led*a* Israel twenty-three years; then he died, and was buried in Shamir.

Jair

³He was followed by Jair of Gilead, who led Israel twenty-two years. ⁴He had thirty sons, who rode thirty donkeys. They controlled thirty towns in Gilead, which to this day are called Havvoth Jair.*b* ⁵When Jair died, he was buried in Kamon.

Jephthah

⁶Again the Israelites did evil in the eyes of the LORD. They served the Baals and the Ashtoreths, and the gods of Aram, the gods of Sidon, the gods of Moab, the gods of the Ammonites and the gods of the Philistines. And because the Israelites forsook the LORD and no longer served him, ⁷he became angry with them. He sold them into the hands of the Philistines and the Ammonites, ⁸who that year shattered and crushed them. For eighteen years they oppressed all the Israelites on the east side of the Jordan in Gilead, the land of the Amorites. ⁹The Ammonites also crossed the Jordan to fight against Judah, Benjamin and the house of Ephraim; and Israel was in great distress. ¹⁰Then the Israelites cried out to the LORD, "We have sinned against you, forsaking our God and serving the Baals."

¹¹The LORD replied, "When the Egyptians, the Amorites, the Ammonites, the Philistines, ¹²the Sidonians, the Amalekites and the Maonites*c* oppressed you and you cried to me for help, did I not save you from their hands? ¹³But you have forsaken me and served other gods, so I will no longer save you. ¹⁴Go and cry out to the gods you have chosen. Let them save you when you are in trouble!"

¹⁵But the Israelites said to the LORD, "We have sinned. Do with us whatever you think best, but please rescue us now." ¹⁶Then they got rid of the foreign gods among them and served the LORD. And he could bear Israel's misery no longer.

¹⁷When the Ammonites were called to arms and camped in Gilead, the Israelites assembled and camped at Mizpah. ¹⁸The leaders of the people of Gilead said to each other, "Whoever will launch the attack against the Ammonites will be the head of all those living in Gilead."

11 Jephthah the Gileadite was a mighty warrior. His father was Gilead; his mother was a prostitute. ²Gilead's wife also bore him sons, and when they were grown up, they drove Jephthah away. "You are not going to get any inheritance in our family," they said, "because you are the son of another woman." ³So Jephthah fled from his brothers and settled in the land of Tob, where a group of adventurers gathered around him and followed him.

⁴Some time later, when the Ammonites made war on Israel, ⁵the elders of Gilead went to get Jephthah from the land of Tob. ⁶"Come," they said, "be our commander, so we can fight the Ammonites."

⁷Jephthah said to them, "Didn't you hate me and drive me from my father's house? Why do you come to me now, when you're in trouble?"

⁸The elders of Gilead said to him, "Nevertheless, we are turning to you now; come with us to fight the Ammonites, and you will be our head over all who live in Gilead."

⁹Jephthah answered, "Suppose you take me back to fight the Ammonites and the LORD gives them to me—will I really be your head?"

¹⁰The elders of Gilead replied, "The LORD is our witness; we will certainly do as you say." ¹¹So Jephthah went with the elders of Gilead, and the people made him head and commander over them. And he repeated all his words before the LORD in Mizpah.

¹²Then Jephthah sent messengers to

---

a2 Traditionally *judged*; also in verse 3   *b4* Or *called the settlements of Jair*   *c12* Hebrew; some Septuagint manuscripts *Midianites*

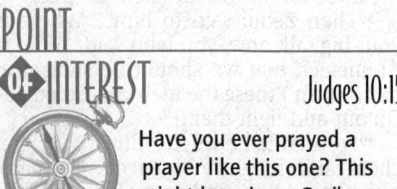

POINT OF INTEREST

Judges 10:15

Have you ever prayed a prayer like this one? This might have been God's moment to abandon the Israelites forever. But he didn't. We can find encouragement in God's long-suffering response to their short-sighted request. God didn't abandon the Israelites at their point of need, and he won't abandon us either.

the Ammonite king with the question: "What do you have against us that you have attacked our country?" ¹³The king of the Ammonites answered Jephthah's messengers, "When Israel came up out of Egypt, they took away my land from the Arnon to the Jabbok, all the way to the Jordan. Now give it back peaceably."

¹⁴Jephthah sent back messengers to the Ammonite king, ¹⁵saying:

"This is what Jephthah says: Israel did not take the land of Moab or the land of the Ammonites. ¹⁶But when they came up out of Egypt, Israel went through the desert to the Red Sea*ᵃ* and on to Kadesh. ¹⁷Then Israel sent messengers to the king of Edom, saying, 'Give us permission to go through your country,' but the king of Edom would not listen. They sent also to the king of Moab, and he refused. So Israel stayed at Kadesh.

¹⁸"Next they traveled through the desert, skirted the lands of Edom and Moab, passed along the eastern side of the country of Moab, and camped on the other side of the Arnon. They did not enter the territory of Moab, for the Arnon was its border.

¹⁹"Then Israel sent messengers to Sihon king of the Amorites, who ruled in Heshbon, and said to him, 'Let us pass through your country to our own place.' ²⁰Sihon, however, did not trust Israel*ᵇ* to pass through his territory. He mustered all his men and encamped at Jahaz and fought with Israel.

²¹"Then the LORD, the God of Israel, gave Sihon and all his men into Israel's hands, and they defeated them. Israel took over all the land of the Amorites who lived in that country, ²²capturing all of it from the Arnon to the Jabbok and from the desert to the Jordan.

²³"Now since the LORD, the God of Israel, has driven the Amorites out before his people Israel, what right have you to take it over? ²⁴Will you not take what your god Chemosh gives you? Likewise, whatever the LORD our God has given us, we will possess. ²⁵Are you better than Balak son of Zippor, king of Moab? Did he ever quarrel with Israel or fight with them? ²⁶For three hundred years Israel occupied Heshbon, Aroer, the surrounding settlements and all the towns along the Arnon. Why didn't you retake them during that time? ²⁷I have not wronged you, but you are doing me wrong by waging war against me. Let the LORD, the Judge,*ᶜ* decide the dispute this day between the Israelites and the Ammonites."

²⁸The king of Ammon, however, paid no attention to the message Jephthah sent him.

²⁹Then the Spirit of the LORD came upon Jephthah. He crossed Gilead and Manasseh, passed through Mizpah of Gilead, and from there he advanced against the Ammonites. ³⁰And Jephthah made a vow to the LORD: "If you give the Ammonites into my hands, ³¹whatever comes out of the door of my house to meet me when I return in triumph from the Ammonites will be the LORD's, and I will sacrifice it as a burnt offering."

³²Then Jephthah went over to fight the Ammonites, and the LORD gave them into his hands. ³³He devastated twenty towns from Aroer to the vicinity of Minnith, as far as Abel Keramim. Thus Israel subdued Ammon.

³⁴When Jephthah returned to his home in Mizpah, who should come out to meet him but his daughter, dancing to the sound of tambourines! She was an only child. Except for her he had neither son nor daughter. ³⁵When he saw her, he tore his clothes and cried, "Oh! My daughter! You have made me miserable and wretched, because I have made a vow to the LORD that I cannot break."

³⁶"My father," she replied, "you have given your word to the LORD. Do to me just as you promised, now that the LORD has avenged you of your enemies, the Ammonites. ³⁷But grant me this one request," she said. "Give me two months to roam the hills and weep with my friends, because I will never marry."

³⁸"You may go," he said. And he let her go for two months. She and the girls went into the hills and wept because she would never marry. ³⁹After the two months, she returned to her father and he

---

*ᵃ*16 Hebrew *Yam Suph*; that is, Sea of Reeds
*ᵇ*20 Or *however, would not make an agreement for Israel*   *ᶜ*27 Or *Ruler*

did to her as he had vowed. And she was a virgin.

From this comes the Israelite custom ⁴⁰that each year the young women of Israel go out for four days to commemorate the daughter of Jephthah the Gileadite.

Jephthah and Ephraim

12 The men of Ephraim called out their forces, crossed over to Zaphon and said to Jephthah, "Why did you go to fight the Ammonites without calling us to go with you? We're going to burn down your house over your head."

²Jephthah answered, "I and my people were engaged in a great struggle with the Ammonites, and although I called, you didn't save me out of their hands. ³When I saw that you wouldn't help, I took my life in my hands and crossed over to fight the Ammonites, and the LORD gave me the victory over them. Now why have you come up today to fight me?"

⁴Jephthah then called together the men of Gilead and fought against Ephraim. The Gileadites struck them down because the Ephraimites had said, "You Gileadites are renegades from Ephraim and Manasseh." ⁵The Gileadites captured the fords of the Jordan leading to Ephraim, and whenever a survivor of Ephraim said, "Let me cross over," the men of Gilead asked him, "Are you an Ephraimite?" If he replied, "No," ⁶they said, "All right, say 'Shibboleth.'" If he said, "Sibboleth," because he could not pronounce the word correctly, they seized him and killed him at the fords of the Jordan. Forty-two thousand Ephraimites were killed at that time.

⁷Jephthah led*ᵃ* Israel six years. Then Jephthah the Gileadite died, and was buried in a town in Gilead.

Ibzan, Elon and Abdon

⁸After him, Ibzan of Bethlehem led Israel. ⁹He had thirty sons and thirty daughters. He gave his daughters away in marriage to those outside his clan, and for his sons he brought in thirty young women as wives from outside his clan. Ibzan led Israel seven years. ¹⁰Then Ibzan died, and was buried in Bethlehem.

¹¹After him, Elon the Zebulunite led Israel ten years. ¹²Then Elon died, and was buried in Aijalon in the land of Zebulun.

¹³After him, Abdon son of Hillel, from Pirathon, led Israel. ¹⁴He had forty sons and thirty grandsons, who rode on seventy donkeys. He led Israel eight years. ¹⁵Then Abdon son of Hillel died, and was buried at Pirathon in Ephraim, in the hill country of the Amalekites.

The Birth of Samson

13 Again the Israelites did evil in the eyes of the LORD, so the LORD delivered them into the hands of the Philistines for forty years.

²A certain man of Zorah, named Manoah, from the clan of the Danites, had a wife who was sterile and remained childless. ³The angel of the LORD appeared to her and said, "You are sterile and childless, but you are going to conceive and have a son. ⁴Now see to it that you drink no wine or other fermented drink and that you do not eat anything unclean, ⁵because you will conceive and give birth to a son. No razor may be used on his head, because the boy is to be a Nazirite, set apart to God from birth, and he will begin the deliverance of Israel from the hands of the Philistines."

⁶Then the woman went to her husband and told him, "A man of God came to me. He looked like an angel of God, very awesome. I didn't ask him where he came from, and he didn't tell me his name. ⁷But he said to me, 'You will conceive and give birth to a son. Now then, drink no wine or other fermented drink and do not eat anything unclean, because the boy will be a Nazirite of God from birth until the day of his death.'"

⁸Then Manoah prayed to the LORD: "O Lord, I beg you, let the man of God you sent to us come again to teach us

a7 Traditionally *judged*; also in verses 8-14

POINT OF INTEREST

Judges 11:39

Even though God had specifically forbidden human sacrifice (see Deuteronomy 12:31), Jephthah didn't want to renege on his promise. Caught between the proverbial "rock and a hard place," Jephthah's bargain for God's blessing resulted in horrifying grief for a whole family.

how to bring up the boy who is to be born."

⁹God heard Manoah, and the angel of God came again to the woman while she was out in the field; but her husband Manoah was not with her. ¹⁰The woman hurried to tell her husband, "He's here! The man who appeared to me the other day!"

¹¹Manoah got up and followed his wife. When he came to the man, he said, "Are you the one who talked to my wife?"

"I am," he said.

¹²So Manoah asked him, "When your words are fulfilled, what is to be the rule for the boy's life and work?"

¹³The angel of the LORD answered, "Your wife must do all that I have told her. ¹⁴She must not eat anything that comes from the grapevine, nor drink any wine or other fermented drink nor eat anything unclean. She must do everything I have commanded her."

¹⁵Manoah said to the angel of the LORD, "We would like you to stay until we prepare a young goat for you."

¹⁶The angel of the LORD replied, "Even though you detain me, I will not eat any of your food. But if you prepare a burnt offering, offer it to the LORD." (Manoah did not realize that it was the angel of the LORD.)

¹⁷Then Manoah inquired of the angel of the LORD, "What is your name, so that we may honor you when your word comes true?"

¹⁸He replied, "Why do you ask my name? It is beyond understanding.ᵃ"

¹⁹Then Manoah took a young goat, together with the grain offering, and sacrificed it on a rock to the LORD. And the LORD did an amazing thing while Manoah and his wife watched: ²⁰As the flame blazed up from the altar toward heaven, the angel of the LORD ascended in the flame. Seeing this, Manoah and his wife fell with their faces to the ground. ²¹When the angel of the LORD did not show himself again to Manoah and his wife, Manoah realized that it was the angel of the LORD.

²²"We are doomed to die!" he said to his wife. "We have seen God!"

²³But his wife answered, "If the LORD had meant to kill us, he would not have accepted a burnt offering and grain offering from our hands, nor shown us all these things or now told us this."

²⁴The woman gave birth to a boy and named him Samson. He grew and the LORD blessed him, ²⁵and the Spirit of the LORD began to stir him while he was in Mahaneh Dan, between Zorah and Eshtaol.

Samson's Marriage

14 Samson went down to Timnah and saw there a young Philistine woman. ²When he returned, he said to his father and mother, "I have seen a Philistine woman in Timnah; now get her for me as my wife."

³His father and mother replied, "Isn't there an acceptable woman among your relatives or among all our people? Must you go to the uncircumcised Philistines to get a wife?"

But Samson said to his father, "Get her for me. She's the right one for me." ⁴(His parents did not know that this was from the LORD, who was seeking an occasion to confront the Philistines; for at that time they were ruling over Israel.) ⁵Samson went down to Timnah together with his father and mother. As they approached the vineyards of Timnah, suddenly a young lion came roaring toward him. ⁶The Spirit of the LORD came upon him in power so that he tore the lion apart with his bare hands as he might have torn a young goat. But he told neither his father nor his mother what he had done. ⁷Then he went down and talked with the woman, and he liked her.

⁸Some time later, when he went back to marry her, he turned aside to look at the lion's carcass. In it was a swarm of bees and some honey, ⁹which he scooped

ᵃ18 Or *is wonderful*

out with his hands and ate as he went along. When he rejoined his parents, he gave them some, and they too ate it. But he did not tell them that he had taken the honey from the lion's carcass.

¹⁰Now his father went down to see the woman. And Samson made a feast there, as was customary for bridegrooms. ¹¹When he appeared, he was given thirty companions.

¹²"Let me tell you a riddle," Samson said to them. "If you can give me the answer within the seven days of the feast, I will give you thirty linen garments and thirty sets of clothes. ¹³If you can't tell me the answer, you must give me thirty linen garments and thirty sets of clothes."

"Tell us your riddle," they said. "Let's hear it."

¹⁴He replied,

"Out of the eater, something to eat;
  out of the strong, something
    sweet."

For three days they could not give the answer.

¹⁵On the fourth[a] day, they said to Samson's wife, "Coax your husband into explaining the riddle for us, or we will burn you and your father's household to death. Did you invite us here to rob us?"

¹⁶Then Samson's wife threw herself on him, sobbing, "You hate me! You don't really love me. You've given my people a riddle, but you haven't told me the answer."

"I haven't even explained it to my father or mother," he replied, "so why should I explain it to you?" ¹⁷She cried the whole seven days of the feast. So on the seventh day he finally told her, because she continued to press him. She in turn explained the riddle to her people.

¹⁸Before sunset on the seventh day the men of the town said to him,

"What is sweeter than honey?
  What is stronger than a lion?"

Samson said to them,

"If you had not plowed with my
  heifer,
    you would not have solved my
      riddle."

¹⁹Then the Spirit of the LORD came upon him in power. He went down to Ashkelon, struck down thirty of their men, stripped them of their belongings and gave their clothes to those who had explained the riddle. Burning with anger, he went up to his father's house. ²⁰And Samson's wife was given to the friend who had attended him at his wedding.

Samson's Vengeance on the Philistines

15 Later on, at the time of wheat harvest, Samson took a young goat and went to visit his wife. He said, "I'm going to my wife's room." But her father would not let him go in.

²"I was so sure you thoroughly hated her," he said, "that I gave her to your friend. Isn't her younger sister more attractive? Take her instead."

³Samson said to them, "This time I have a right to get even with the Philistines; I will really harm them." ⁴So he went out and caught three hundred foxes and tied them tail to tail in pairs. He then fastened a torch to every pair of tails, ⁵lit the torches and let the foxes loose in the standing grain of the Philistines. He burned up the shocks and standing grain, together with the vineyards and olive groves.

⁶When the Philistines asked, "Who did this?" they were told, "Samson, the Timnite's son-in-law, because his wife was given to his friend."

So the Philistines went up and burned her and her father to death. ⁷Samson said to them, "Since you've acted like this, I won't stop until I get my revenge on you." ⁸He attacked them viciously and slaughtered many of them. Then he went down and stayed in a cave in the rock of Etam.

⁹The Philistines went up and camped in Judah, spreading out near Lehi. ¹⁰The men of Judah asked, "Why have you come to fight us?"

"We have come to take Samson prisoner," they answered, "to do to him as he did to us."

¹¹Then three thousand men from Judah went down to the cave in the rock of Etam and said to Samson, "Don't you realize that the Philistines are rulers over us? What have you done to us?"

He answered, "I merely did to them what they did to me."

¹²They said to him, "We've come to tie

---

[a] 15 Some Septuagint manuscripts and Syriac; Hebrew *seventh*

you up and hand you over to the Philistines."

Samson said, "Swear to me that you won't kill me yourselves."

¹³"Agreed," they answered. "We will only tie you up and hand you over to them. We will not kill you." So they bound him with two new ropes and led him up from the rock. ¹⁴As he approached Lehi, the Philistines came toward him shouting. The Spirit of the LORD came upon him in power. The ropes on his arms became like charred flax, and the bindings dropped from his hands. ¹⁵Finding a fresh jawbone of a donkey, he grabbed it and struck down a thousand men.

¹⁶Then Samson said,

"With a donkey's jawbone
    I have made donkeys of them.ᵃ
With a donkey's jawbone
    I have killed a thousand men."

¹⁷When he finished speaking, he threw away the jawbone; and the place was called Ramath Lehi.ᵇ

¹⁸Because he was very thirsty, he cried out to the LORD, "You have given your servant this great victory. Must I now die of thirst and fall into the hands of the uncircumcised?" ¹⁹Then God opened up the hollow place in Lehi, and water came out of it. When Samson drank, his strength returned and he revived. So the spring was called En Hakkore,ᶜ and it is still there in Lehi.

²⁰Samson ledᵈ Israel for twenty years in the days of the Philistines.

Samson and Delilah

16 One day Samson went to Gaza, where he saw a prostitute. He went in to spend the night with her. ²The people of Gaza were told, "Samson is here!" So they surrounded the place and lay in wait for him all night at the city gate. They made no move during the night, saying, "At dawn we'll kill him."

³But Samson lay there only until the middle of the night. Then he got up and took hold of the doors of the city gate, together with the two posts, and tore them loose, bar and all. He lifted them to his shoulders and carried them to the top of the hill that faces Hebron.

⁴Some time later, he fell in love with a woman in the Valley of Sorek whose name was Delilah. ⁵The rulers of the Philistines went to her and said, "See if you can lure him into showing you the secret of his great strength and how we can overpower him so we may tie him up and subdue him. Each one of us will give you eleven hundred shekelsᵉ of silver."

⁶So Delilah said to Samson, "Tell me the secret of your great strength and how you can be tied up and subdued."

⁷Samson answered her, "If anyone ties me with seven fresh thongsᶠ that have not been dried, I'll become as weak as any other man."

⁸Then the rulers of the Philistines brought her seven fresh thongs that had not been dried, and she tied him with them. ⁹With men hidden in the room, she called to him, "Samson, the Philistines are upon you!" But he snapped the thongs as easily as a piece of string snaps when it comes close to a flame. So the secret of his strength was not discovered.

¹⁰Then Delilah said to Samson, "You have made a fool of me; you lied to me. Come now, tell me how you can be tied."

¹¹He said, "If anyone ties me securely with new ropes that have never been used, I'll become as weak as any other man."

¹²So Delilah took new ropes and tied him with them. Then, with men hidden in the room, she called to him, "Samson, the Philistines are upon you!" But he snapped the ropes off his arms as if they were threads.

¹³Delilah then said to Samson, "Until now, you have been making a fool of me and lying to me. Tell me how you can be tied."

He replied, "If you weave the seven braids of my head into the fabric ˻on the loom˼ and tighten it with the pin, I'll become as weak as any other man." So while he was sleeping, Delilah took the seven braids of his head, wove them into the fabric ¹⁴andᵍ tightened it with the pin.

Again she called to him, "Samson, the Philistines are upon you!" He awoke from his sleep and pulled up the pin and the loom, with the fabric. ¹⁵Then she said to him, "How can you

---

ᵃ16 Or *made a heap or two*; the Hebrew for *donkey* sounds like the Hebrew for *heap*.   ᵇ17 *Ramath Lehi* means *jawbone hill*.   ᶜ19 *En Hakkore* means *caller's spring*.   ᵈ20 Traditionally *judged*   ᵉ5 That is, about 28 pounds (about 13 kilograms)   ᶠ7 Or *bowstrings*; also in verses 8 and 9   ᵍ13,14 Some Septuagint manuscripts; Hebrew "˻I can˼ *if you weave the seven braids of my head into the fabric ˻on the loom˼.*" ¹⁴*So she* say, 'I love you,' when you won't confide in me? This is the third time you have made a fool of me and haven't told me the secret of your great strength." 16With such nagging she prodded him day after day until he was tired to death.

17So he told her everything. "No razor has ever been used on my head," he said, "because I have been a Nazirite set apart to God since birth. If my head were shaved, my strength would leave me, and I would become as weak as any other man."

18When Delilah saw that he had told her everything, she sent word to the rulers of the Philistines, "Come back once more; he has told me everything." So the rulers of the Philistines returned with the silver in their hands. 19Having put him to sleep on her lap, she called a man to shave off the seven braids of his hair, and so began to subdue him.a And his strength left him.

20Then she called, "Samson, the Philistines are upon you!"

He awoke from his sleep and thought, "I'll go out as before and shake myself free." But he did not know that the LORD had left him.

21Then the Philistines seized him, gouged out his eyes and took him down to Gaza. Binding him with bronze shackles, they set him to grinding in the prison. 22But the hair on his head began to grow again after it had been shaved.

The Death of Samson

23Now the rulers of the Philistines assembled to offer a great sacrifice to Dagon their god and to celebrate, saying, "Our god has delivered Samson, our enemy, into our hands."

24When the people saw him, they praised their god, saying,

"Our god has delivered our enemy
    into our hands,
the one who laid waste our land
    and multiplied our slain."

25While they were in high spirits, they shouted, "Bring out Samson to entertain us." So they called Samson out of the prison, and he performed for them.

When they stood him among the pillars, 26Samson said to the servant who held his hand, "Put me where I can feel the pillars that support the temple, so that I may lean against them." 27Now the temple was crowded with men and wom-

en; all the rulers of the Philistines were there, and on the roof were about three thousand men and women watching Samson perform. 28Then Samson prayed to the LORD, "O Sovereign LORD, remember me. O God, please strengthen me just once more, and let me with one blow get revenge on the Philistines for my two eyes." 29Then Samson reached toward the two central pillars on which the temple stood. Bracing himself against them, his right hand on the one and his left hand on the other, 30Samson said, "Let me die with the Philistines!" Then he pushed with all his might, and down came the temple on the rulers and all the people in it. Thus he killed many more when he died than while he lived.

31Then his brothers and his father's whole family went down to get him. They brought him back and buried him between Zorah and Eshtaol in the tomb of Manoah his father. He had ledb Israel twenty years.

Micah's Idols

17 Now a man named Micah from the hill country of Ephraim 2said to his mother, "The eleven hundred shekelsc of silver that were taken from you and about which I heard you utter a curse—I have that silver with me; I took it."

Then his mother said, "The LORD bless you, my son!"

3When he returned the eleven hundred shekels of silver to his mother, she said, "I solemnly consecrate my silver to the LORD for my son to make a carved image and a cast idol. I will give it back to you."

4So he returned the silver to his mother, and she took two hundred shekelsd of silver and gave them to a silversmith, who made them into the image and the idol. And they were put in Micah's house.

5Now this man Micah had a shrine, and he made an ephod and some idols and installed one of his sons as his priest. 6In those days Israel had no king; everyone did as he saw fit.

7A young Levite from Bethlehem in Judah, who had been living within the clan of Judah, 8left that town in search of

---

a19 Hebrew; some Septuagint manuscripts and he began to weaken   b31 Traditionally judged
c2 That is, about 28 pounds (about 13 kilograms)
d4 That is, about 5 pounds (about 2.3 kilograms)

some other place to stay. On his way[a] he came to Micah's house in the hill country of Ephraim.

[9]Micah asked him, "Where are you from?"

"I'm a Levite from Bethlehem in Judah," he said, "and I'm looking for a place to stay."

[10]Then Micah said to him, "Live with me and be my father and priest, and I'll give you ten shekels[b] of silver a year, your clothes and your food." [11]So the Levite agreed to live with him, and the young man was to him like one of his

[a]8 Or *To carry on his profession*   [b]10 That is, about 4 ounces (about 110 grams)

THURSDAY

Read Judges 16:1–31
Key Verses Judges 16:28–30

Who Are Your Heroes? —Eileen Anderson

We expect a lot from our heroes. The media highlight people who have been blessed with notable accomplishments, stunning beauty or exceptional skills. It's easy to admire them, to wish we could be like them. But as time goes on, we often see our heroes fail: Musicians do drugs; movie stars commit suicide; even religious or political leaders break the law. It's hard to handle the disappointment when our heroes fall, especially when they had such great potential. But maybe we can learn from them.

Judges 16 gives us an example of such a hero gone bad. Samson started out with a promising future. The angel of the Lord had told Samson's mother that Samson would begin Israel's deliverance from the Philistines (see Judges 13:5). God had great plans for Samson; he set Samson apart from the crowd with a special blessing and gave him an awesome physical strength (see Judges 13:7, 24–25; 14:6).

But Samson didn't fulfill his potential because he let his weaknesses take over his life. Samson was the strongest man alive, yet he couldn't control his own desires. He was a "he-man" with a "she-problem." Samson's first recorded words reveal the true condition of his heart, which was demanding, arrogant and lustful: "I have seen a Philistine woman in Timnah; now get her for me as my wife" (Judges 14:2). Later, Samson slept with a prostitute and then fell in love with Delilah, who single-handedly brought Samson to his knees.

In spite of the fact that Samson was anointed by God, his life was characterized by cruelty, violence, deceit, lies and self-indulgence. Vengeance incited his final act, which resulted in death for himself as well as many Philistines. Samson may have accomplished God's purposes, but sadly, his poor choices also resulted in suffering, bloodshed, and shame for himself and many others.

Physical beauty, strength, athletic prowess and talent are often the hallmarks of a hero, but if not used according to God's will they can be the very qualities that lead to a tragic downfall. The person who loves the Lord with a whole heart and follows him in humility and obedience is the real hero in God's eyes.

A Deeper Look
1 Samuel 16:7; Isaiah 66:2

Go to page 276 for your next devotional reading.

sons. ¹²Then Micah installed the Levite, and the young man became his priest and lived in his house. ¹³And Micah said, "Now I know that the LORD will be good to me, since this Levite has become my priest."

Danites Settle in Laish

18 In those days Israel had no king.
And in those days the tribe of the Danites was seeking a place of their own where they might settle, because they had not yet come into an inheritance among the tribes of Israel. ²So the Danites sent five warriors from Zorah and Eshtaol to spy out the land and explore it. These men represented all their clans. They told them, "Go, explore the land."

The men entered the hill country of Ephraim and came to the house of Micah, where they spent the night. ³When they

were near Micah's house, they recognized the voice of the young Levite; so they turned in there and asked him, "Who brought you here? What are you doing in this place? Why are you here?"

⁴He told them what Micah had done for him, and said, "He has hired me and I am his priest."

⁵Then they said to him, "Please inquire of God to learn whether our journey will be successful."

⁶The priest answered them, "Go in peace. Your journey has the LORD's approval."

⁷So the five men left and came to Laish, where they saw that the people were living in safety, like the Sidonians, unsuspecting and secure. And since their land lacked nothing, they were prosperous.ᵃ

ᵃ7 The meaning of the Hebrew for this clause is uncertain.

FRIDAY

Read Judges 17:1—18:31
Key Verses Judges 17:1–4

Micah – Son of a Permissive Parent — Dana Yeakley

Can you imagine stealing a large sum of money from your mother? Can you imagine that when you confess to her what you have done, she shows no anger and doesn't even punish you? What a mom! Or is she?

This is exactly what happened to Micah. After stealing eleven hundred shekels of silver from his mother, he returns it, and she exclaims, "The LORD bless you, my son!" (Micah 17:2). No doubt she was pleased with his confession, but where was the discipline for stealing?

Many people have had parents like Micah's. Without parental involvement and discipline they may have grown up with an underdeveloped sense of right and wrong. Parents who let their children have their way, without disciplining them when they do wrong, are letting their children wander into a lifestyle without boundaries or any sense of moral or ethical code—a lifestyle that is self-centered and haphazard. Not a very secure or satisfying way to live!

Think about how your parents disciplined you as you grew up. Did you get away with everything? How are you doing now that you are an adult? If you realize that your parents were like Micah's mom, look to your heavenly Father for loving discipline and fair boundaries; look to him to give you a sense of purpose, self-respect, a good reputation and joy!

A Deeper Look
Proverbs 3:11–18; Hebrews 12:5–6

Go to page 281 for your next devotional reading.

Also, they lived a long way from the Sidonians and had no relationship with anyone else.[a]

8When they returned to Zorah and Eshtaol, their brothers asked them, "How did you find things?"

9They answered, "Come on, let's attack them! We have seen that the land is very good. Aren't you going to do something? Don't hesitate to go there and take it over. 10When you get there, you will find an unsuspecting people and a spacious land that God has put into your hands, a land that lacks nothing whatever."

11Then six hundred men from the clan of the Danites, armed for battle, set out from Zorah and Eshtaol. 12On their way they set up camp near Kiriath Jearim in Judah. This is why the place west of Kiriath Jearim is called Mahaneh Dan[b] to this day. 13From there they went on to the hill country of Ephraim and came to Micah's house.

14Then the five men who had spied out the land of Laish said to their brothers, "Do you know that one of these houses has an ephod, other household gods, a carved image and a cast idol? Now you know what to do." 15So they turned in there and went to the house of the young Levite at Micah's place and greeted him. 16The six hundred Danites, armed for battle, stood at the entrance to the gate. 17The five men who had spied out the land went inside and took the carved image, the ephod, the other household gods and the cast idol while the priest and the six hundred armed men stood at the entrance to the gate.

18When these men went into Micah's house and took the carved image, the ephod, the other household gods and the cast idol, the priest said to them, "What are you doing?"

19They answered him, "Be quiet! Don't say a word. Come with us, and be our father and priest. Isn't it better that you serve a tribe and clan in Israel as priest rather than just one man's household?" 20Then the priest was glad. He took the ephod, the other household gods and the carved image and went along with the people. 21Putting their little children, their livestock and their possessions in front of them, they turned away and left.

22When they had gone some distance from Micah's house, the men who lived near Micah were called together and overtook the Danites. 23As they shouted after them, the Danites turned and said to Micah, "What's the matter with you that you called out your men to fight?"

24He replied, "You took the gods I made, and my priest, and went away. What else do I have? How can you ask, 'What's the matter with you?' "

25The Danites answered, "Don't argue with us, or some hot-tempered men will attack you, and you and your family will lose your lives." 26So the Danites went their way, and Micah, seeing that they were too strong for him, turned around and went back home.

27Then they took what Micah had made, and his priest, and went on to Laish, against a peaceful and unsuspecting people. They attacked them with the sword and burned down their city. 28There was no one to rescue them because they lived a long way from Sidon and had no relationship with anyone else. The city was in a valley near Beth Rehob.

The Danites rebuilt the city and settled there. 29They named it Dan after their forefather Dan, who was born to Israel—though the city used to be called Laish. 30There the Danites set up for themselves the idols, and Jonathan son of Gershom, the son of Moses,[c] and his sons were priests for the tribe of Dan until the time of the captivity of the land. 31They continued to use the idols Micah had made, all the time the house of God was in Shiloh.

a7 Hebrew; some Septuagint manuscripts *with the Arameans*   b12 *Mahaneh Dan* means *Dan's camp.*   c30 An ancient Hebrew scribal tradition, some Septuagint manuscripts and Vulgate; Masoretic Text *Manasseh*

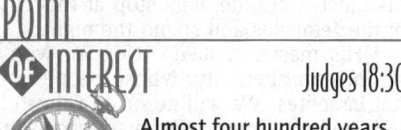

POINT OF INTEREST

Judges 18:30

Almost four hundred years had passed since Joshua had led Israel across the Jordan River. Throughout those years Israel had repeatedly fallen into the spiritual abyss of idolatry and reaped the inevitable destruction. Here we see this pattern emerging again.

A Levite and His Concubine

19 In those days Israel had no king. Now a Levite who lived in a remote area in the hill country of Ephraim took a concubine from Bethlehem in Judah. ²But she was unfaithful to him. She left him and went back to her father's house in Bethlehem, Judah. After she had been there four months, ³her husband went to her to persuade her to return. He had with him his servant and two donkeys. She took him into her father's house, and when her father saw him, he gladly welcomed him. ⁴His father-in-law, the girl's father, prevailed upon him to stay; so he remained with him three days, eating and drinking, and sleeping there.

⁵On the fourth day they got up early and he prepared to leave, but the girl's father said to his son-in-law, "Refresh yourself with something to eat; then you can go." ⁶So the two of them sat down to eat and drink together. Afterward the girl's father said, "Please stay tonight and enjoy yourself." ⁷And when the man got up to go, his father-in-law persuaded him, so he stayed there that night. ⁸On the morning of the fifth day, when he rose to go, the girl's father said, "Refresh yourself. Wait till afternoon!" So the two of them ate together.

⁹Then when the man, with his concubine and his servant, got up to leave, his father-in-law, the girl's father, said, "Now look, it's almost evening. Spend the night here; the day is nearly over. Stay and enjoy yourself. Early tomorrow morning you can get up and be on your way home." ¹⁰But, unwilling to stay another night, the man left and went toward Jebus (that is, Jerusalem), with his two saddled donkeys and his concubine.

¹¹When they were near Jebus and the day was almost gone, the servant said to his master, "Come, let's stop at this city of the Jebusites and spend the night." ¹²His master replied, "No. We won't go into an alien city, whose people are not Israelites. We will go on to Gibeah." ¹³He added, "Come, let's try to reach Gibeah or Ramah and spend the night in one of those places." ¹⁴So they went on, and the sun set as they neared Gibeah in Benjamin. ¹⁵There they stopped to spend the night. They went and sat in the city square, but no one took them into his home for the night.

¹⁶That evening an old man from the hill country of Ephraim, who was living in Gibeah (the men of the place were Benjamites), came in from his work in the fields. ¹⁷When he looked and saw the traveler in the city square, the old man asked, "Where are you going? Where did you come from?"

¹⁸He answered, "We are on our way from Bethlehem in Judah to a remote area in the hill country of Ephraim where I live. I have been to Bethlehem in Judah and now I am going to the house of the LORD. No one has taken me into his house. ¹⁹We have both straw and fodder for our donkeys and bread and wine for ourselves your servants—me, your maidservant, and the young man with us. We don't need anything."

²⁰"You are welcome at my house," the old man said. "Let me supply whatever you need. Only don't spend the night in the square." ²¹So he took him into his house and fed his donkeys. After they had washed their feet, they had something to eat and drink.

²²While they were enjoying themselves, some of the wicked men of the city surrounded the house. Pounding on the door, they shouted to the old man who owned the house, "Bring out the man who came to your house so we can have sex with him."

²³The owner of the house went outside and said to them, "No, my friends, don't be so vile. Since this man is my guest, don't do this disgraceful thing. ²⁴Look, here is my virgin daughter, and his concubine. I will bring them out to you now, and you can use them and do to them whatever you wish. But to this man, don't do such a disgraceful thing."

²⁵But the men would not listen to him. So the man took his concubine and sent her outside to them, and they raped her and abused her throughout the night, and at dawn they let her go. ²⁶At daybreak the woman went back to the house where her master was staying, fell down at the door and lay there until daylight.

²⁷When her master got up in the morning and opened the door of the house and stepped out to continue on his way, there lay his concubine, fallen in the doorway of the house, with her hands on the threshold. ²⁸He said to her, "Get up; let's go." But there was no answer. Then the man put her on his donkey and set out for home.

²⁹When he reached home, he took a

knife and cut up his concubine, limb by limb, into twelve parts and sent them into all the areas of Israel. ³⁰Everyone who saw it said, "Such a thing has never been seen or done, not since the day the Israelites came up out of Egypt. Think about it! Consider it! Tell us what to do!"

Israelites Fight the Benjamites

20 Then all the Israelites from Dan to Beersheba and from the land of Gilead came out as one man and assembled before the LORD in Mizpah. ²The leaders of all the people of the tribes of Israel took their places in the assembly of the people of God, four hundred thousand soldiers armed with swords. ³(The Benjamites heard that the Israelites had gone up to Mizpah.) Then the Israelites said, "Tell us how this awful thing happened."

⁴So the Levite, the husband of the murdered woman, said, "I and my concubine came to Gibeah in Benjamin to spend the night. ⁵During the night the men of Gibeah came after me and surrounded the house, intending to kill me. They raped my concubine, and she died. ⁶I took my concubine, cut her into pieces and sent one piece to each region of Israel's inheritance, because they committed this lewd and disgraceful act in Israel. ⁷Now, all you Israelites, speak up and give your verdict."

⁸All the people rose as one man, saying, "None of us will go home. No, not one of us will return to his house. ⁹But now this is what we'll do to Gibeah: We'll go up against it as the lot directs. ¹⁰We'll take ten men out of every hundred from all the tribes of Israel, and a hundred from a thousand, and a thousand from ten thousand, to get provisions for the army. Then, when the army arrives at Gibeah^a in Benjamin, it can give them what they deserve for all this vileness done in Israel." ¹¹So all the men of Israel got together and united as one man against the city.

¹²The tribes of Israel sent men throughout the tribe of Benjamin, saying, "What about this awful crime that was committed among you? ¹³Now surrender those wicked men of Gibeah so that we may put them to death and purge the evil from Israel."

But the Benjamites would not listen to their fellow Israelites. ¹⁴From their towns they came together at Gibeah to fight against the Israelites. ¹⁵At once the Benja-

mites mobilized twenty-six thousand swordsmen from their towns, in addition to seven hundred chosen men from those living in Gibeah. ¹⁶Among all these soldiers there were seven hundred chosen men who were left-handed, each of whom could sling a stone at a hair and not miss.

¹⁷Israel, apart from Benjamin, mustered four hundred thousand swordsmen, all of them fighting men.

¹⁸The Israelites went up to Bethel^b and inquired of God. They said, "Who of us shall go first to fight against the Benjamites?"

The LORD replied, "Judah shall go first."

¹⁹The next morning the Israelites got up and pitched camp near Gibeah. ²⁰The men of Israel went out to fight the Benjamites and took up battle positions against them at Gibeah. ²¹The Benjamites came out of Gibeah and cut down twenty-two thousand Israelites on the battlefield that day. ²²But the men of Israel encouraged one another and again took up their positions where they had stationed themselves the first day. ²³The Israelites went up and wept before the LORD until evening, and they inquired of the LORD. They said, "Shall we go up again to battle against the Benjamites, our brothers?"

The LORD answered, "Go up against them."

²⁴Then the Israelites drew near to Benjamin the second day. ²⁵This time, when the Benjamites came out from Gibeah to oppose them, they cut down another

^a10 One Hebrew manuscript; most Hebrew manuscripts *Geba*, a variant of *Gibeah*   ^b18 Or *to the house of God*; also in verse 26

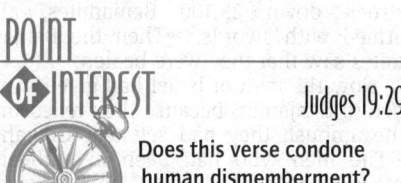

POINT OF INTEREST

Judges 19:29

Does this verse condone human dismemberment? Had Israel fallen so far that dismemberment was an acceptable response to societal decay? The fact that Biblical chroniclers reported such events does not mean they condoned them. Such honesty adds credibility to the entire Biblical record, for who could fictionalize anything this brutal?

eighteen thousand Israelites, all of them armed with swords.

²⁶Then the Israelites, all the people, went up to Bethel, and there they sat weeping before the LORD. They fasted that day until evening and presented burnt offerings and fellowship offerings^a to the LORD. ²⁷And the Israelites inquired of the LORD. (In those days the ark of the covenant of God was there, ²⁸with Phinehas son of Eleazar, the son of Aaron, ministering before it.) They asked, "Shall we go up again to battle with Benjamin our brother, or not?"

The LORD responded, "Go, for tomorrow I will give them into your hands."

²⁹Then Israel set an ambush around Gibeah. ³⁰They went up against the Benjamites on the third day and took up positions against Gibeah as they had done before. ³¹The Benjamites came out to meet them and were drawn away from the city. They began to inflict casualties on the Israelites as before, so that about thirty men fell in the open field and on the roads—the one leading to Bethel and the other to Gibeah.

³²While the Benjamites were saying, "We are defeating them as before," the Israelites were saying, "Let's retreat and draw them away from the city to the roads."

³³All the men of Israel moved from their places and took up positions at Baal Tamar, and the Israelite ambush charged out of its place on the west^b of Gibeah.^c ³⁴Then ten thousand of Israel's finest men made a frontal attack on Gibeah. The fighting was so heavy that the Benjamites did not realize how near disaster was. ³⁵The LORD defeated Benjamin before Israel, and on that day the Israelites struck down 25,100 Benjamites, all armed with swords. ³⁶Then the Benjamites saw that they were beaten.

Now the men of Israel had given way before Benjamin, because they relied on the ambush they had set near Gibeah. ³⁷The men who had been in ambush made a sudden dash into Gibeah, spread out and put the whole city to the sword. ³⁸The men of Israel had arranged with the ambush that they should send up a great cloud of smoke from the city, ³⁹and then the men of Israel would turn in the battle.

The Benjamites had begun to inflict casualties on the men of Israel (about thirty), and they said, "We are defeating them as in the first battle." ⁴⁰But when the column of smoke began to rise from the city, the Benjamites turned and saw the smoke of the whole city going up into the sky. ⁴¹Then the men of Israel turned on them, and the men of Benjamin were terrified, because they realized that disaster had come upon them. ⁴²So they fled before the Israelites in the direction of the desert, but they could not escape the battle. And the men of Israel who came out of the towns cut them down there. ⁴³They surrounded the Benjamites, chased them and easily^d overran them in the vicinity of Gibeah on the east. ⁴⁴Eighteen thousand Benjamites fell, all of them valiant fighters. ⁴⁵As they turned and fled toward the desert to the rock of Rimmon, the Israelites cut down five thousand men along the roads. They kept pressing after the Benjamites as far as Gidom and struck down two thousand more.

⁴⁶On that day twenty-five thousand Benjamite swordsmen fell, all of them valiant fighters. ⁴⁷But six hundred men turned and fled into the desert to the rock of Rimmon, where they stayed four months. ⁴⁸The men of Israel went back to Benjamin and put all the towns to the sword, including the animals and everything else they found. All the towns they came across they set on fire.

Wives for the Benjamites

21 The men of Israel had taken an oath at Mizpah: "Not one of us will give his daughter in marriage to a Benjamite."

²The people went to Bethel,^e where they sat before God until evening, raising their voices and weeping bitterly. ³"O LORD, the God of Israel," they cried, "why has this happened to Israel? Why should one tribe be missing from Israel today?"

⁴Early the next day the people built an altar and presented burnt offerings and fellowship offerings.^a

⁵Then the Israelites asked, "Who from all the tribes of Israel has failed to assemble before the LORD?" For they had taken a solemn oath that anyone who failed to

---

^a26,4 Traditionally *peace offerings*   ^b33 Some Septuagint manuscripts and Vulgate; the meaning of the Hebrew for this word is uncertain.
^c33 Hebrew *Geba*, a variant of *Gibeah*
^d43 The meaning of the Hebrew for this word is uncertain.   ^e2 Or *to the house of God*

Read Judges 21:1–25
Key Verse Judges 21:25

On Solid Ground

Human moral and ethical standards tend to wax and wane with every generation. Rigidity is replaced with permissiveness, and then the pendulum swings back again. Sometimes it feels as though truth is up for grabs and standards are a matter of opinion. In other words, everyone does as he or she sees fit. While we might sometimes enjoy the "anything goes" mentality, if we're honest we have to admit that our human spirits cry out for standards that do not change with every new trend or belief system.

God has an answer for that hunger for permanence. In a world that drifts in a sea of relativism, he has established an island of stability—his revealed truth. If we saturate our minds with God's truth, we will learn to think God's thoughts and be discerning and wise. Through the Scriptures the Holy Spirit anchors us to the truth and keeps us from floating adrift on our own imperfect understanding.

Digging Into the Word
1. God's truth never changes. What do you learn about truth in the following passages?—John 14:1,6, 16–17; John 16:13–15
2. What do you learn in the following passages about salvation and truth?—John 3:21; John 8:32; Ephesians 1:13

Discussion Starter
Fire up a conversation with friends by asking: What is one thing you believe with absolute conviction and confidence? Why do you believe this to be true?

One Step Deeper
Psalm 43:3; Proverbs 23:23

Go to page 284 for your next devotional reading.

assemble before the LORD at Mizpah should certainly be put to death.

⁶Now the Israelites grieved for their brothers, the Benjamites. "Today one tribe is cut off from Israel," they said. ⁷"How can we provide wives for those who are left, since we have taken an oath by the LORD not to give them any of our daughters in marriage?" ⁸Then they asked, "Which one of the tribes of Israel failed to assemble before the LORD at Mizpah?" They discovered that no one from Jabesh Gilead had come to the camp for the assembly. ⁹For when they counted the people, they found that none of the people of Jabesh Gilead were there.

¹⁰So the assembly sent twelve thousand fighting men with instructions to go to Jabesh Gilead and put to the sword those living there, including the women and children. ¹¹"This is what you are to do," they said. "Kill every male and every woman who is not a virgin." ¹²They found among the people living in Jabesh Gilead four hundred young women who had never slept with a man, and they took them to the camp at Shiloh in Canaan.

¹³Then the whole assembly sent an offer of peace to the Benjamites at the rock of Rimmon. ¹⁴So the Benjamites returned at that time and were given the women of Jabesh Gilead who had been spared. But there were not enough for all of them.

¹⁵The people grieved for Benjamin, because the LORD had made a gap in the tribes of Israel. ¹⁶And the elders of the assembly said, "With the women of Benjamin destroyed, how shall we provide wives for the men who are left? ¹⁷The Benjamite survivors must have heirs," they said, "so that a tribe of Israel will not be wiped out. ¹⁸We can't give them our daughters as wives, since we Israelites have taken this oath: 'Cursed be anyone who gives a wife to a Benjamite.' ¹⁹But

look, there is the annual festival of the LORD in Shiloh, to the north of Bethel, and east of the road that goes from Bethel to Shechem, and to the south of Lebonah."

²⁰So they instructed the Benjamites, saying, "Go and hide in the vineyards ²¹and watch. When the girls of Shiloh come out to join in the dancing, then rush from the vineyards and each of you seize a wife from the girls of Shiloh and go to the land of Benjamin. ²²When their fathers or brothers complain to us, we will say to them, 'Do us a kindness by helping them, because we did not get wives for them during the war, and you are innocent, since you did not give your daughters to them.' "

²³So that is what the Benjamites did. While the girls were dancing, each man caught one and carried her off to be his wife. Then they returned to their inheritance and rebuilt the towns and settled in them.

²⁴At that time the Israelites left that place and went home to their tribes and clans, each to his own inheritance.

²⁵In those days Israel had no king; everyone did as he saw fit.

POINT OF INTEREST

Judges 21:25

The rallying cry of the 1960s generation was, "If it feels good, do it!" and that philosophy remains with us today. Many of the stories in this book read like a page from any modern, big-city newspaper. When people act on this rebellious, self-seeking mentality, chilling commentaries similar to those recorded in the book of Judges are sure to result.

God often uses difficult or confusing times in our lives to fulfill his purposes, and he often goes about his work in ways that surprise us. Take Ruth's story for example. This short book allows us an intimate glimpse into the lives of Ruth, Naomi and Boaz. We see how, in the midst of grief and loss, their true faith and devotion to God leads them into self-giving love for each other. In this ancient love story, God responds to the needs of ordinary people as he unfolds his extraordinary design for salvation.

RUTH

Naomi and Ruth

In the days when the judges ruled,*a* there was a famine in the land, and a man from Bethlehem in Judah, together with his wife and two sons, went to live for a while in the country of Moab. ²The man's name was Elimelech, his wife's name Naomi, and the names of his two sons were Mahlon and Kilion. They were Ephrathites from Bethlehem, Judah. And they went to Moab and lived there.

³Now Elimelech, Naomi's husband, died, and she was left with her two sons. ⁴They married Moabite women, one named Orpah and the other Ruth. After they had lived there about ten years, ⁵both Mahlon and Kilion also died, and Naomi was left without her two sons and her husband.

⁶When she heard in Moab that the LORD had come to the aid of his people by providing food for them, Naomi and her daughters-in-law prepared to return home from there. ⁷With her two daughters-in-law she left the place where she had been living and set out on the road that would take them back to the land of Judah.

⁸Then Naomi said to her two daughters-in-law, "Go back, each of you, to your mother's home. May the LORD show kindness to you, as you have shown to your dead and to me. ⁹May the LORD grant that each of you will find rest in the home of another husband."

Then she kissed them and they wept aloud ¹⁰and said to her, "We will go back with you to your people."

¹¹But Naomi said, "Return home, my daughters. Why would you come with

a1 Traditionally judged

me? Am I going to have any more sons, who could become your husbands? ¹²Return home, my daughters; I am too old to have another husband. Even if I thought there was still hope for me—even if I had a husband tonight and then gave birth to sons— ¹³would you wait until they grew up? Would you remain unmarried for them? No, my daughters. It is more bitter for me than for you, because the LORD's hand has gone out against me!"

¹⁴At this they wept again. Then Orpah kissed her mother-in-law good-by, but Ruth clung to her.

¹⁵"Look," said Naomi, "your sister-in-law is going back to her people and her gods. Go back with her."

¹⁶But Ruth replied, "Don't urge me to leave you or to turn back from you. Where you go I will go, and where you stay I will stay. Your people will be my people and your God my God. ¹⁷Where you die I will die, and there I will be buried. May the LORD deal with me, be it ever so severely, if anything but death separates you and me." ¹⁸When Naomi realized that Ruth was determined to go with her, she stopped urging her.

¹⁹So the two women went on until they came to Bethlehem. When they ar-

---

MONDAY

Read Ruth 1:1–22
Key Verses Ruth 1:16–17

A Loyalty Born of Love – Steve Draper

Bob was a lanky southern Texan with a Master's degree from Yale. Alice was a short, intense young woman from Ohio. They were both in China. His job was to recruit and train Chinese men to lead a YMCA in the south. She taught English at a school for the blind in northern China.

They met at a summer camp in the Gooling Mountains, and God began to draw them together. Returning to their separate jobs, they continued to communicate in spite of poor mail delivery and civil war. Enough of Alice's letters made it through for Bob to sense her soul, and he began to think about marriage. He wrote regularly and prayed diligently throughout the winter, finally deciding that God was pleased with their relationship.

Bob worked up his courage and proposed to Alice via telegram. She was thrilled to receive his message—but, due to the public nature of the telegraph system, everyone else in her missionary compound received it too! Alice wanted to answer Bob in a way that was both private and respectful. All that Bob received in response was the reference, "Ruth 1:16–17." He scrambled to find the nearest Bible. There he read, "Where you go I will go . . ."

And those verses continued to describe the love and loyalty between my grandparents. How often I, too, say these words to God—but fail to follow through on them. Then I realize with thankfulness that this is the very commitment that God makes to us! The psalmist writes: "Where can I go from your Spirit? Where can I flee from your presence? If I go up to the heavens, you are there; if I make my bed in the depths, you are there. If I rise on the wings of the dawn, if I settle on the far side of the sea, even there your hand will guide me, your right hand will hold me fast" (Psalm 139:7–10).

A Deeper Look
John 14:15–17; Hebrews 13:5

Go to page 286 for your next devotional reading.

rived in Bethlehem, the whole town was stirred because of them, and the women exclaimed, "Can this be Naomi?"

20"Don't call me Naomi,*a* " she told them. "Call me Mara,*b* because the Almighty*c* has made my life very bitter. 21I went away full, but the LORD has brought me back empty. Why call me Naomi? The LORD has afflicted*d* me; the Almighty has brought misfortune upon me."

22So Naomi returned from Moab accompanied by Ruth the Moabitess, her daughter-in-law, arriving in Bethlehem as the barley harvest was beginning.

Ruth Meets Boaz

2 Now Naomi had a relative on her husband's side, from the clan of Elimelech, a man of standing, whose name was Boaz.

2And Ruth the Moabitess said to Naomi, "Let me go to the fields and pick up the leftover grain behind anyone in whose eyes I find favor."

Naomi said to her, "Go ahead, my daughter." 3So she went out and began to glean in the fields behind the harvesters. As it turned out, she found herself working in a field belonging to Boaz, who was from the clan of Elimelech.

4Just then Boaz arrived from Bethlehem and greeted the harvesters, "The LORD be with you!"

"The LORD bless you!" they called back.

5Boaz asked the foreman of his harvesters, "Whose young woman is that?"

6The foreman replied, "She is the Moabitess who came back from Moab with Naomi. 7She said, 'Please let me glean and gather among the sheaves behind the harvesters.' She went into the field and has worked steadily from morning till now, except for a short rest in the shelter."

8So Boaz said to Ruth, "My daughter, listen to me. Don't go and glean in another field and don't go away from here. Stay here with my servant girls. 9Watch the field where the men are harvesting, and follow along after the girls. I have told the men not to touch you. And whenever you are thirsty, go and get a drink from the water jars the men have filled."

10At this, she bowed down with her face to the ground. She exclaimed, "Why have I found such favor in your eyes that you notice me—a foreigner?"

11Boaz replied, "I've been told all about what you have done for your mother-in-law since the death of your husband—how you left your father and mother and your homeland and came to live with a people you did not know before. 12May the LORD repay you for what you have done. May you be richly rewarded by the LORD, the God of Israel, under whose wings you have come to take refuge."

13"May I continue to find favor in your eyes, my lord," she said. "You have given me comfort and have spoken kindly to your servant—though I do not have the standing of one of your servant girls."

14At mealtime Boaz said to her, "Come over here. Have some bread and dip it in the wine vinegar."

When she sat down with the harvesters, he offered her some roasted grain. She ate all she wanted and had some left over. 15As she got up to glean, Boaz gave orders to his men, "Even if she gathers among the sheaves, don't embarrass her. 16Rather, pull out some stalks for her from the bundles and leave them for her to pick up, and don't rebuke her."

17So Ruth gleaned in the field until evening. Then she threshed the barley she had gathered, and it amounted to about an ephah.*e* 18She carried it back to town, and her mother-in-law saw how much she had gathered. Ruth also brought out and gave her what she had left over after she had eaten enough.

19Her mother-in-law asked her, "Where did you glean today? Where did you work? Blessed be the man who took notice of you!"

Then Ruth told her mother-in-law about the one at whose place she had been working. "The name of the man I worked with today is Boaz," she said.

20"The LORD bless him!" Naomi said to her daughter-in-law. "He has not stopped showing his kindness to the living and the dead." She added, "That man is our close relative; he is one of our kinsman-redeemers."

21Then Ruth the Moabitess said, "He even said to me, 'Stay with my workers until they finish harvesting all my grain.' "

---

a20 Naomi means *pleasant;* also in verse 21.
b20 Mara means *bitter.*　*c20* Hebrew *Shaddai;* also in verse 21　*d21* Or *has testified against*
e17 That is, probably about 3/5 bushel (about 22 liters)

²²Naomi said to Ruth her daughter-in-law, "It will be good for you, my daughter, to go with his girls, because in someone else's field you might be harmed."

²³So Ruth stayed close to the servant girls of Boaz to glean until the barley and wheat harvests were finished. And she lived with her mother-in-law.

Ruth and Boaz at the Threshing Floor

3 One day Naomi her mother-in-law said to her, "My daughter, should I not try to find a home*a* for you, where you will be well provided for? ²Is not Boaz, with whose servant girls you have been, a kinsman of ours? Tonight he will be winnowing barley on the threshing floor. ³Wash and perfume yourself, and put on your best clothes. Then go down to the threshing floor, but don't let him know you are there until he has finished eating and drinking. ⁴When he lies down, note the place where he is lying. Then go and uncover his feet and lie down. He will tell you what to do."

⁵"I will do whatever you say," Ruth answered. ⁶So she went down to the threshing floor and did everything her mother-in-law told her to do.

⁷When Boaz had finished eating and drinking and was in good spirits, he went over to lie down at the far end of the grain pile. Ruth approached quietly, uncovered his feet and lay down. ⁸In the middle of the night something startled the man, and he turned and discovered a woman lying at his feet.

⁹"Who are you?" he asked.

*a*1 Hebrew *find rest* (see Ruth 1:9)

TUESDAY

Read *Ruth 2:1–20*
Key Verse *Ruth 2:20*

An Act of Kindness – Julie Bundt

Boaz did not perform a "random" act of kindness when he stepped forward and asked Ruth, the daughter-in-law of a destitute kinswoman, Naomi, to be his wife. In doing so he acted as kinsman-redeemer, ensuring that their land and lineage would stay intact. The concept of a kinsman-redeemer was a common theme in family law in the Israelite culture. Each member of a clan or family was obligated to defend and provide for those who were economically or physically unable to provide for themselves. Although Boaz was not the next in line as Naomi and Ruth's kinsman-redeemer, he took the role upon himself and asked for permission to buy the land on their behalf and marry Ruth.

What makes this story really shine is that Boaz was not only being faithful to the law, but he was also acting out of love for the faithful Ruth and on behalf of the "Lord, the God of Israel, under whose wings you have come to take refuge" (Ruth 2:12).

Boaz's action as a gracious kinsman-redeemer gave the Israelites a glimpse of what Jesus Christ would do for us. Because of sin we lost our place in God's kingdom, yet out of love and kindness Jesus bought us back. Because of his great love for us, he was glad to sacrifice himself to redeem us. Jesus restored each of us to a place in God's family. Jesus calls us his brothers and sisters. He is our ultimate kinsman-redeemer.

A Deeper Look
Isaiah 53:10–11; Titus 2:14

Go to page 293 for your next devotional reading.

"I am your servant Ruth," she said. "Spread the corner of your garment over me, since you are a kinsman-redeemer."

[10]"The LORD bless you, my daughter," he replied. "This kindness is greater than that which you showed earlier: You have not run after the younger men, whether rich or poor. [11]And now, my daughter, don't be afraid. I will do for you all you ask. All my fellow townsmen know that you are a woman of noble character. [12]Although it is true that I am near of kin, there is a kinsman-redeemer nearer than I. [13]Stay here for the night, and in the morning if he wants to redeem, good; let him redeem. But if he is not willing, as surely as the LORD lives I will do it. Lie here until morning."

[14]So she lay at his feet until morning, but got up before anyone could be recognized; and he said, "Don't let it be known that a woman came to the threshing floor."

[15]He also said, "Bring me the shawl you are wearing and hold it out." When she did so, he poured into it six measures of barley and put it on her. Then he[a] went back to town.

[16]When Ruth came to her mother-in-law, Naomi asked, "How did it go, my daughter?"

Then she told her everything Boaz had done for her [17]and added, "He gave me these six measures of barley, saying, 'Don't go back to your mother-in-law empty-handed.' "

[18]Then Naomi said, "Wait, my daughter, until you find out what happens. For the man will not rest until the matter is settled today."

Boaz Marries Ruth

4 Meanwhile Boaz went up to the town gate and sat there. When the kinsman-redeemer he had mentioned came along, Boaz said, "Come over here, my friend, and sit down." So he went over and sat down.

[2]Boaz took ten of the elders of the town and said, "Sit here," and they did so. [3]Then he said to the kinsman-redeemer, "Naomi, who has come back from Moab, is selling the piece of land that belonged to our brother Elimelech. [4]I thought I should bring the matter to your attention and suggest that you buy it in the presence of these seated here and in the presence of the elders of my people. If you will redeem it, do so. But if you[b]

will not, tell me, so I will know. For no one has the right to do it except you, and I am next in line."

"I will redeem it," he said.

[5]Then Boaz said, "On the day you buy the land from Naomi and from Ruth the Moabitess, you acquire[c] the dead man's widow, in order to maintain the name of the dead with his property."

[6]At this, the kinsman-redeemer said, "Then I cannot redeem it because I might endanger my own estate. You redeem it yourself. I cannot do it."

[7](Now in earlier times in Israel, for the redemption and transfer of property to become final, one party took off his sandal and gave it to the other. This was the method of legalizing transactions in Israel.)

[8]So the kinsman-redeemer said to Boaz, "Buy it yourself." And he removed his sandal.

[9]Then Boaz announced to the elders and all the people, "Today you are witnesses that I have bought from Naomi all the property of Elimelech, Kilion and Mahlon. [10]I have also acquired Ruth the Moabitess, Mahlon's widow, as my wife, in order to maintain the name of the dead with his property, so that his name will not disappear from among his family or from the town records. Today you are witnesses!"

[11]Then the elders and all those at the gate said, "We are witnesses. May the LORD make the woman who is coming into your home like Rachel and Leah, who together built up the house of Israel. May you have standing in Ephrathah and be famous in Bethlehem. [12]Through the offspring the LORD gives you by this young woman, may your family be like that of Perez, whom Tamar bore to Judah."

The Genealogy of David

[13]So Boaz took Ruth and she became his wife. Then he went to her, and the LORD enabled her to conceive, and she gave birth to a son. [14]The women said to Naomi: "Praise be to the LORD, who this day has not left you without a kinsman-redeemer. May he become famous

a15 Most Hebrew manuscripts; many Hebrew manuscripts, Vulgate and Syriac she   b4 Many Hebrew manuscripts, Septuagint, Vulgate and Syriac; most Hebrew manuscripts he
c5 Hebrew; Vulgate and Syriac Naomi, you acquire Ruth the Moabitess,

throughout Israel! **15**He will renew your life and sustain you in your old age. For your daughter-in-law, who loves you and who is better to you than seven sons, has given him birth."

16Then Naomi took the child, laid him in her lap and cared for him. **17**The women living there said, "Naomi has a son." And they named him Obed. He was the father of Jesse, the father of David.

18This, then, is the family line of Perez:

Perez was the father of Hezron,
19Hezron the father of Ram,
Ram the father of Amminadab,
20Amminadab the father of Nahshon,
Nahshon the father of Salmon,[a]
21Salmon the father of Boaz,
Boaz the father of Obed,
22Obed the father of Jesse,
and Jesse the father of David.

[a]20 A few Hebrew manuscripts, some Septuagint manuscripts and Vulgate (see also verse 21 and Septuagint of 1 Chron. 2:11); most Hebrew manuscripts Salma

first Samuel is a story of contrast between a man who abandons God and a man who abandons his life to God. Written by the prophet Samuel, the book focuses on Israel's first two kings, Saul and David. Saul, the first anointed king of Israel, decides to disobey God's directions. Tormented by his sin, he is finally rejected as ruler of Israel. In contrast, his successor David dedicates himself one hundred percent to the Lord, and God rewards him accordingly. As you read 1 Samuel, allow the stirring stories of David and Saul to inspire you to follow God wholeheartedly.

1 SAMUEL

The Birth of Samuel

1 There was a certain man from Ramathaim, a Zuphite*a* from the hill country of Ephraim, whose name was Elkanah son of Jeroham, the son of Elihu, the son of Tohu, the son of Zuph, an Ephraimite. ²He had two wives; one was called Hannah and the other Peninnah. Peninnah had children, but Hannah had none.

³Year after year this man went up from his town to worship and sacrifice to the LORD Almighty at Shiloh, where Hophni and Phinehas, the two sons of Eli, were priests of the LORD. ⁴Whenever the day came for Elkanah to sacrifice, he would give portions of the meat to his wife Peninnah and to all her sons and daughters. ⁵But to Hannah he gave a double portion because he loved her, and the LORD had closed her womb. ⁶And because the LORD had closed her womb, her rival kept provoking her in order to irritate her. ⁷This went on year after year. Whenever Hannah went up to the house of the LORD, her rival provoked her till she wept and would not eat. ⁸Elkanah her husband would say to her, "Hannah, why are you weeping? Why don't you eat? Why are you downhearted? Don't I mean more to you than ten sons?"

⁹Once when they had finished eating and drinking in Shiloh, Hannah stood up. Now Eli the priest was sitting on a chair by the doorpost of the LORD's temple.*b*

a1 Or *from Ramathaim Zuphim*   *b9* That is, tabernacle

¹⁰In bitterness of soul Hannah wept much and prayed to the LORD. ¹¹And she made a vow, saying, "O LORD Almighty, if you will only look upon your servant's misery and remember me, and not forget your servant but give her a son, then I will give him to the LORD for all the days of his life, and no razor will ever be used on his head."

¹²As she kept on praying to the LORD, Eli observed her mouth. ¹³Hannah was praying in her heart, and her lips were moving but her voice was not heard. Eli thought she was drunk ¹⁴and said to her, "How long will you keep on getting drunk? Get rid of your wine."

¹⁵"Not so, my lord," Hannah replied, "I am a woman who is deeply troubled. I have not been drinking wine or beer; I was pouring out my soul to the LORD. ¹⁶Do not take your servant for a wicked woman; I have been praying here out of my great anguish and grief."

¹⁷Eli answered, "Go in peace, and may the God of Israel grant you what you have asked of him."

¹⁸She said, "May your servant find favor in your eyes." Then she went her way and ate something, and her face was no longer downcast.

¹⁹Early the next morning they arose and worshiped before the LORD and then went back to their home at Ramah. Elkanah lay with Hannah his wife, and the LORD remembered her. ²⁰So in the course of time Hannah conceived and gave birth to a son. She named him Samuel,ᵃ saying, "Because I asked the LORD for him."

Hannah Dedicates Samuel

²¹When the man Elkanah went up with all his family to offer the annual sacrifice to the LORD and to fulfill his vow, ²²Hannah did not go. She said to her husband, "After the boy is weaned, I will take him and present him before the LORD, and he will live there always."

²³"Do what seems best to you," Elkanah her husband told her. "Stay here until you have weaned him; only may the LORD make good hisᵇ word." So the woman stayed at home and nursed her son until she had weaned him.

²⁴After he was weaned, she took the boy with her, young as he was, along with a three-year-old bull,ᶜ an ephahᵈ of flour and a skin of wine, and brought him to the house of the LORD at Shiloh. ²⁵When they had slaughtered the bull,

they brought the boy to Eli, ²⁶and she said to him, "As surely as you live, my lord, I am the woman who stood here beside you praying to the LORD. ²⁷I prayed for this child, and the LORD has granted me what I asked of him. ²⁸So now I give him to the LORD. For his whole life he will be given over to the LORD." And he worshiped the LORD there.

Hannah's Prayer

2 Then Hannah prayed and said:

"My heart rejoices in the LORD;
    in the LORD my hornᵉ is lifted
        high.
My mouth boasts over my enemies,
    for I delight in your deliverance.

²"There is no one holyᶠ like the LORD;
    there is no one besides you;
    there is no Rock like our God.

³"Do not keep talking so proudly
    or let your mouth speak such
        arrogance,
for the LORD is a God who knows,
    and by him deeds are weighed.

⁴"The bows of the warriors are
        broken,
    but those who stumbled are armed
        with strength.
⁵Those who were full hire themselves
        out for food,

ᵃ20 *Samuel* sounds like the Hebrew for *heard of
God.*   ᵇ23 Masoretic Text; Dead Sea Scrolls,
Septuagint and Syriac *your*   ᶜ24 Dead Sea
Scrolls, Septuagint and Syriac; Masoretic Text *with
three bulls*   ᵈ24 That is, probably about 3/5
bushel (about 22 liters)   ᵉ1 *Horn* here
symbolizes strength; also in verse 10.   ᶠ2 Or *no
Holy One*

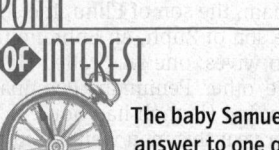

POINT OF INTEREST

1 Samuel 1:20

The baby Samuel was God's answer to one godly woman's prayers. When Samuel became the last judge of Israel, he anointed Saul, Israel's first king, and David, Israel's greatest earthly king. Samuel's life stood as a mighty oak of faith in a barren desert of unbelief.

but those who were hungry hunger
no more.
She who was barren has borne seven
children,
but she who has had many sons
pines away.

6"The Lord brings death and makes
alive;
he brings down to the grave*a* and
raises up.
7The Lord sends poverty and wealth;
he humbles and he exalts.
8He raises the poor from the dust
and lifts the needy from the ash
heap;
he seats them with princes
and has them inherit a throne of
honor.

"For the foundations of the earth are
the Lord's;
upon them he has set the world.
9He will guard the feet of his saints,
but the wicked will be silenced in
darkness.

"It is not by strength that one
prevails;
10   those who oppose the Lord will be
shattered.
He will thunder against them from
heaven;
the Lord will judge the ends of the
earth.

"He will give strength to his king
and exalt the horn of his
anointed."

11Then Elkanah went home to Ramah,
but the boy ministered before the Lord
under Eli the priest.

Eli's Wicked Sons

12Eli's sons were wicked men; they
had no regard for the Lord. 13Now it was
the practice of the priests with the people
that whenever anyone offered a sacrifice
and while the meat was being boiled, the
servant of the priest would come with a
three-pronged fork in his hand. 14He
would plunge it into the pan or kettle or
caldron or pot, and the priest would take
for himself whatever the fork brought up.
This is how they treated all the Israelites
who came to Shiloh. 15But even before
the fat was burned, the servant of the
priest would come and say to the man
who was sacrificing, "Give the priest

some meat to roast; he won't accept
boiled meat from you, but only raw."
16If the man said to him, "Let the fat be
burned up first, and then take whatever
you want," the servant would then answer, "No, hand it over now; if you
don't, I'll take it by force."
17This sin of the young men was very
great in the Lord's sight, for they*b* were
treating the Lord's offering with contempt.
18But Samuel was ministering before
the Lord—a boy wearing a linen ephod.
19Each year his mother made him a little
robe and took it to him when she went up
with her husband to offer the annual sacrifice. 20Eli would bless Elkanah and his
wife, saying, "May the Lord give you children by this woman to take the place of
the one she prayed for and gave to the
Lord." Then they would go home. 21And
the Lord was gracious to Hannah; she
conceived and gave birth to three sons
and two daughters. Meanwhile, the boy
Samuel grew up in the presence of the
Lord.
22Now Eli, who was very old, heard
about everything his sons were doing to
all Israel and how they slept with the
women who served at the entrance to the
Tent of Meeting. 23So he said to them,
"Why do you do such things? I hear from
all the people about these wicked deeds
of yours. 24No, my sons; it is not a good
report that I hear spreading among the
Lord's people. 25If a man sins against another man, God*c* may mediate for him;
but if a man sins against the Lord, who
will intercede for him?" His sons, however, did not listen to their father's rebuke,
for it was the Lord's will to put them to
death.
26And the boy Samuel continued to
grow in stature and in favor with the Lord
and with men.

Prophecy Against the House of Eli

27Now a man of God came to Eli and
said to him, "This is what the Lord says:
'Did I not clearly reveal myself to your
father's house when they were in Egypt
under Pharaoh? 28I chose your father out
of all the tribes of Israel to be my priest,
to go up to my altar, to burn incense, and
to wear an ephod in my presence. I also
gave your father's house all the offerings

a6 Hebrew *Sheol*   *b17* Or *men*   *c25* Or *the
judges*

made with fire by the Israelites. ²⁹Why do you*a* scorn my sacrifice and offering that I prescribed for my dwelling? Why do you honor your sons more than me by fattening yourselves on the choice parts of every offering made by my people Israel?'

³⁰"Therefore the Lᴏʀᴅ, the God of Israel, declares: 'I promised that your house and your father's house would minister before me forever.' But now the Lᴏʀᴅ declares: 'Far be it from me! Those who honor me I will honor, but those who despise me will be disdained. ³¹The time is coming when I will cut short your strength and the strength of your father's house, so that there will not be an old man in your family line ³²and you will see distress in my dwelling. Although good will be done to Israel, in your family line there will never be an old man. ³³Every one of you that I do not cut off from my altar will be spared only to blind your eyes with tears and to grieve your heart, and all your descendants will die in the prime of life.

³⁴" 'And what happens to your two sons, Hophni and Phinehas, will be a sign to you—they will both die on the same day. ³⁵I will raise up for myself a faithful priest, who will do according to what is in my heart and mind. I will firmly establish his house, and he will minister before my anointed one always. ³⁶Then everyone left in your family line will come and bow down before him for a piece of silver and a crust of bread and plead, "Appoint me to some priestly office so I can have food to eat." ' "

The Lᴏʀᴅ Calls Samuel

3 The boy Samuel ministered before the Lᴏʀᴅ under Eli. In those days the word of the Lᴏʀᴅ was rare; there were not many visions.

²One night Eli, whose eyes were becoming so weak that he could barely see, was lying down in his usual place. ³The lamp of God had not yet gone out, and Samuel was lying down in the temple*b* of the Lᴏʀᴅ, where the ark of God was. ⁴Then the Lᴏʀᴅ called Samuel.

Samuel answered, "Here I am." ⁵And he ran to Eli and said, "Here I am; you called me."

But Eli said, "I did not call; go back and lie down." So he went and lay down. ⁶Again the Lᴏʀᴅ called, "Samuel!" And

Samuel got up and went to Eli and said, "Here I am; you called me."

"My son," Eli said, "I did not call; go back and lie down."

⁷Now Samuel did not yet know the Lᴏʀᴅ: The word of the Lᴏʀᴅ had not yet been revealed to him.

⁸The Lᴏʀᴅ called Samuel a third time, and Samuel got up and went to Eli and said, "Here I am; you called me."

Then Eli realized that the Lᴏʀᴅ was calling the boy. ⁹So Eli told Samuel, "Go and lie down, and if he calls you, say, 'Speak, Lᴏʀᴅ, for your servant is listening.' " So Samuel went and lay down in his place.

¹⁰The Lᴏʀᴅ came and stood there, calling as at the other times, "Samuel! Samuel!"

Then Samuel said, "Speak, for your servant is listening."

¹¹And the Lᴏʀᴅ said to Samuel: "See, I am about to do something in Israel that will make the ears of everyone who hears of it tingle. ¹²At that time I will carry out against Eli everything I spoke against his family—from beginning to end. ¹³For I told him that I would judge his family forever because of the sin he knew about; his sons made themselves contemptible,*c* and he failed to restrain them. ¹⁴Therefore, I swore to the house of Eli, 'The guilt of Eli's house will never be atoned for by sacrifice or offering.' "

¹⁵Samuel lay down until morning and then opened the doors of the house of the Lᴏʀᴅ. He was afraid to tell Eli the vision, ¹⁶but Eli called him and said, "Samuel, my son."

Samuel answered, "Here I am."

¹⁷"What was it he said to you?" Eli asked. "Do not hide it from me. May God deal with you, be it ever so severely, if you hide from me anything he told you." ¹⁸So Samuel told him everything, hiding nothing from him. Then Eli said, "He is the Lᴏʀᴅ; let him do what is good in his eyes."

¹⁹The Lᴏʀᴅ was with Samuel as he grew up, and he let none of his words fall to the ground. ²⁰And all Israel from Dan to Beersheba recognized that Samuel was attested as a prophet of the Lᴏʀᴅ. ²¹The Lᴏʀᴅ continued to appear at Shiloh, and

---

a29 The Hebrew is plural.　　*b3* That is, tabernacle　　*c13* Masoretic Text; an ancient Hebrew scribal tradition and Septuagint *sons blasphemed God* there he revealed himself to Samuel through his word.

4 And Samuel's word came to all Israel.

The Philistines Capture the Ark

Now the Israelites went out to fight against the Philistines. The Israelites camped at Ebenezer, and the Philistines at Aphek. ²The Philistines deployed their forces to meet Israel, and as the battle spread, Israel was defeated by the Philistines, who killed about four thousand of them on the battlefield. ³When the soldiers returned to camp, the elders of Israel asked, "Why did the LORD bring defeat upon us today before the Philistines? Let us bring the ark of the LORD's covenant

from Shiloh, so that it*ª* may go with us and save us from the hand of our enemies."

⁴So the people sent men to Shiloh, and they brought back the ark of the covenant of the LORD Almighty, who is enthroned between the cherubim. And Eli's two sons, Hophni and Phinehas, were there with the ark of the covenant of God.

⁵When the ark of the LORD's covenant came into the camp, all Israel raised such a great shout that the ground shook. ⁶Hearing the uproar, the Philistines asked, "What's all this shouting in the Hebrew camp?"

ª3 Or *he*

WEDNESDAY

Read *1 Samuel 3:1–21*
Key Verse *1 Samuel 3:10*

Listen Up! –Bill Gensky

How would you rate yourself as a listener? The dictionary defines listening like this: "to hear with thoughtful attention." When you're with your friends, do you "hear with thoughtful attention" as they speak, or are you like many of us—half listening, letting your mind drift away, thinking about homework or the movie you saw last night, or trying to figure out if your money supply will last all month?

Our communication with God can end up the same way. We barely give a thought to the fact that the Creator of the world may be trying to get our attention, that he may have something to say to us. Yes, God wants to speak to each of us! He wants an intimate relationship with us so he can guide, counsel and love us. Like Samuel, though, we need to be awake and aware, for the voice of God may call us at any time.

Listening to God takes practice. Jesus said in John 10:4 that "his sheep follow him because they know his voice." A man who has cared for sheep explained that when a new shepherd comes, sheep are often confused by his voice and listen for the one they are accustomed to hearing. But after time passes, the sheep calm down as they learn to distinguish the new shepherd's voice. Listening to God may require a similar "transition" time—but it's well worth the effort.

1 Corinthians 2:11–13 tells us that God has given us his Spirit to tell us his very thoughts, to teach us things that only he can teach. So as you read God's Word and learn of his heart, stay awake—listen for his voice!

A Deeper Look
Proverbs 8:32–34; Luke 8:15; John 10:27

Go to page 303 for your next devotional reading.

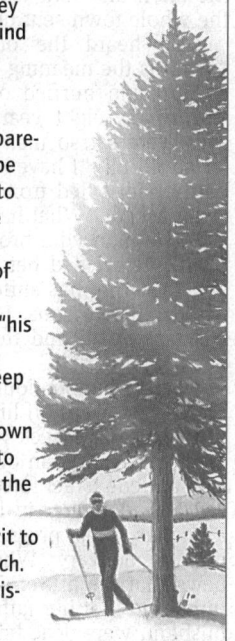

When they learned that the ark of the LORD had come into the camp, 7the Philistines were afraid. "A god has come into the camp," they said. "We're in trouble! Nothing like this has happened before. 8Woe to us! Who will deliver us from the hand of these mighty gods? They are the gods who struck the Egyptians with all kinds of plagues in the desert. 9Be strong, Philistines! Be men, or you will be subject to the Hebrews, as they have been to you. Be men, and fight!"

10So the Philistines fought, and the Israelites were defeated and every man fled to his tent. The slaughter was very great; Israel lost thirty thousand foot soldiers. 11The ark of God was captured, and Eli's two sons, Hophni and Phinehas, died.

Death of Eli

12That same day a Benjamite ran from the battle line and went to Shiloh, his clothes torn and dust on his head. 13When he arrived, there was Eli sitting on his chair by the side of the road, watching, because his heart feared for the ark of God. When the man entered the town and told what had happened, the whole town sent up a cry.

14Eli heard the outcry and asked, "What is the meaning of this uproar?"

The man hurried over to Eli, 15who was ninety-eight years old and whose eyes were set so that he could not see. 16He told Eli, "I have just come from the battle line; I fled from it this very day."

Eli asked, "What happened, my son?"

17The man who brought the news replied, "Israel fled before the Philistines, and the army has suffered heavy losses. Also your two sons, Hophni and Phinehas, are dead, and the ark of God has been captured."

18When he mentioned the ark of God, Eli fell backward off his chair by the side of the gate. His neck was broken and he died, for he was an old man and heavy. He had led*a* Israel forty years.

19His daughter-in-law, the wife of Phinehas, was pregnant and near the time of delivery. When she heard the news that the ark of God had been captured and that her father-in-law and her husband were dead, she went into labor and gave birth, but was overcome by her labor pains. 20As she was dying, the women attending her said, "Don't despair; you have given birth to a son." But she did not respond or pay any attention.

21She named the boy Ichabod,*b* saying, "The glory has departed from Israel"—because of the capture of the ark of God and the deaths of her father-in-law and her husband. 22She said, "The glory has departed from Israel, for the ark of God has been captured."

The Ark in Ashdod and Ekron

5 After the Philistines had captured the ark of God, they took it from Ebenezer to Ashdod. 2Then they carried the ark into Dagon's temple and set it beside Dagon. 3When the people of Ashdod rose early the next day, there was Dagon, fallen on his face on the ground before the ark of the LORD! They took Dagon and put him back in his place. 4But the following morning when they rose, there was Dagon, fallen on his face on the ground before the ark of the LORD! His head and hands had been broken off and were lying on the threshold; only his body remained. 5That is why to this day neither the priests of Dagon nor any others who enter Dagon's temple at Ashdod step on the threshold.

6The LORD's hand was heavy upon the people of Ashdod and its vicinity; he brought devastation upon them and afflicted them with tumors.*c* 7When the men of Ashdod saw what was happening, they said, "The ark of the god of Israel must not stay here with us, because his hand is heavy upon us and upon Dagon our god." 8So they called together all the

---

a 18 Traditionally *judged*   *b 21 Ichabod* means *no glory.*   *c 6* Hebrew; Septuagint and Vulgate *tumors. And rats appeared in their land, and death and destruction were throughout the city*

POINT OF INTEREST

1 Samuel 5:3

This passage highlights the difference between Yahweh, the one true God, and the false gods that humans create. Some inscriptions depict Dagon as a statue with the head of a fish. God presents himself to us in the Bible as the Creator who is able to move mountains—or in this case, to crush worthless statues. Everything in heaven and on earth is subject to our all-powerful Creator God.

rulers of the Philistines and asked them, "What shall we do with the ark of the god of Israel?"

They answered, "Have the ark of the god of Israel moved to Gath." So they moved the ark of the God of Israel.

⁹But after they had moved it, the LORD's hand was against that city, throwing it into a great panic. He afflicted the people of the city, both young and old, with an outbreak of tumors.ᵃ ¹⁰So they sent the ark of God to Ekron.

As the ark of God was entering Ekron, the people of Ekron cried out, "They have brought the ark of the god of Israel around to us to kill us and our people." ¹¹So they called together all the rulers of the Philistines and said, "Send the ark of the god of Israel away; let it go back to its own place, or itᵇ will kill us and our people." For death had filled the city with panic; God's hand was very heavy upon it. ¹²Those who did not die were afflicted with tumors, and the outcry of the city went up to heaven.

The Ark Returned to Israel

6 When the ark of the LORD had been in Philistine territory seven months, ²the Philistines called for the priests and the diviners and said, "What shall we do with the ark of the LORD? Tell us how we should send it back to its place."

³They answered, "If you return the ark of the god of Israel, do not send it away empty, but by all means send a guilt offering to him. Then you will be healed, and you will know why his hand has not been lifted from you."

⁴The Philistines asked, "What guilt offering should we send to him?"

They replied, "Five gold tumors and five gold rats, according to the number of the Philistine rulers, because the same plague has struck both you and your rulers. ⁵Make models of the tumors and of the rats that are destroying the country, and pay honor to Israel's god. Perhaps he will lift his hand from you and your gods and your land. ⁶Why do you harden your hearts as the Egyptians and Pharaoh did? When heᶜ treated them harshly, did they not send the Israelites out so they could go on their way?

⁷"Now then, get a new cart ready, with two cows that have calved and have never been yoked. Hitch the cows to the cart, but take their calves away and pen them up. ⁸Take the ark of the LORD and put it on the cart, and in a chest beside it put the gold objects you are sending back to him as a guilt offering. Send it on its way, ⁹but keep watching it. If it goes up to its own territory, toward Beth Shemesh, then the LORD has brought this great disaster on us. But if it does not, then we will know that it was not his hand that struck us and that it happened to us by chance."

¹⁰So they did this. They took two such cows and hitched them to the cart and penned up their calves. ¹¹They placed the ark of the LORD on the cart and along with it the chest containing the gold rats and the models of the tumors. ¹²Then the cows went straight up toward Beth Shemesh, keeping on the road and lowing all the way; they did not turn to the right or to the left. The rulers of the Philistines followed them as far as the border of Beth Shemesh.

¹³Now the people of Beth Shemesh were harvesting their wheat in the valley, and when they looked up and saw the ark, they rejoiced at the sight. ¹⁴The cart came to the field of Joshua of Beth Shemesh, and there it stopped beside a large rock. The people chopped up the wood of the cart and sacrificed the cows as a burnt offering to the LORD. ¹⁵The Levites took down the ark of the LORD, together with the chest containing the gold objects, and placed them on the large rock. On that day the people of Beth Shemesh offered burnt offerings and made sacrifices to the LORD. ¹⁶The five rulers of the Philistines saw all this and then returned that same day to Ekron.

¹⁷These are the gold tumors the Philistines sent as a guilt offering to the LORD— one each for Ashdod, Gaza, Ashkelon, Gath and Ekron. ¹⁸And the number of the gold rats was according to the number of Philistine towns belonging to the five rulers—the fortified towns with their country villages. The large rock, on whichᵈ they set the ark of the LORD, is a witness to this day in the field of Joshua of Beth Shemesh.

¹⁹But God struck down some of the men of Beth Shemesh, putting seventyᵉ of them to death because they had looked

---

ᵃ9 Or *with tumors in the groin* (see Septuagint)   ᵇ11 Or *he*   ᶜ6 That is, God   ᵈ18 A few Hebrew manuscripts (see also Septuagint); most Hebrew manuscripts *villages as far as Greater Abel, where*   ᵉ19 A few Hebrew manuscripts; most Hebrew manuscripts and Septuagint 50,070 into the ark of the LORD. The people mourned because of the heavy blow the LORD had dealt them, 20and the men of Beth Shemesh asked, "Who can stand in the presence of the LORD, this holy God? To whom will the ark go up from here?"

21Then they sent messengers to the people of Kiriath Jearim, saying, "The Philistines have returned the ark of the LORD. Come down and take it up to your place." 1So the men of Kiriath Jearim came and took up the ark of the LORD. They took it to Abinadab's house on the hill and consecrated Eleazar his son to guard the ark of the LORD.

Samuel Subdues the Philistines at Mizpah

2It was a long time, twenty years in all, that the ark remained at Kiriath Jearim, and all the people of Israel mourned and sought after the LORD. 3And Samuel said to the whole house of Israel, "If you are returning to the LORD with all your hearts, then rid yourselves of the foreign gods and the Ashtoreths and commit yourselves to the LORD and serve him only, and he will deliver you out of the hand of the Philistines." 4So the Israelites put away their Baals and Ashtoreths, and served the LORD only.

5Then Samuel said, "Assemble all Israel at Mizpah and I will intercede with the LORD for you." 6When they had assembled at Mizpah, they drew water and poured it out before the LORD. On that day they fasted and there they confessed, "We have sinned against the LORD." And Samuel was leader*a* of Israel at Mizpah.

7When the Philistines heard that Israel had assembled at Mizpah, the rulers of the Philistines came up to attack them. And when the Israelites heard of it, they were afraid because of the Philistines. 8They said to Samuel, "Do not stop crying out to the LORD our God for us, that he may rescue us from the hand of the Philistines." 9Then Samuel took a suckling lamb and offered it up as a whole burnt offering to the LORD. He cried out to the LORD on Israel's behalf, and the LORD answered him.

10While Samuel was sacrificing the burnt offering, the Philistines drew near to engage Israel in battle. But that day the LORD thundered with loud thunder against the Philistines and threw them into such a panic that they were routed before the Israelites. 11The men of Israel

rushed out of Mizpah and pursued the Philistines, slaughtering them along the way to a point below Beth Car.

12Then Samuel took a stone and set it up between Mizpah and Shen. He named it Ebenezer,*b* saying, "Thus far has the LORD helped us." 13So the Philistines were subdued and did not invade Israelite territory again.

Throughout Samuel's lifetime, the hand of the LORD was against the Philistines. 14The towns from Ekron to Gath that the Philistines had captured from Israel were restored to her, and Israel delivered the neighboring territory from the power of the Philistines. And there was peace between Israel and the Amorites.

15Samuel continued as judge over Israel all the days of his life. 16From year to year he went on a circuit from Bethel to Gilgal to Mizpah, judging Israel in all those places. 17But he always went back to Ramah, where his home was, and there he also judged Israel. And he built an altar there to the LORD.

Israel Asks for a King

8 When Samuel grew old, he appointed his sons as judges for Israel. 2The name of his firstborn was Joel and the name of his second was Abijah, and they served at Beersheba. 3But his sons did not walk in his ways. They turned aside after dishonest gain and accepted bribes and perverted justice.

4So all the elders of Israel gathered together and came to Samuel at Ramah. 5They said to him, "You are old, and your sons do not walk in your ways; now appoint a king to lead*c* us, such as all the other nations have."

6But when they said, "Give us a king to lead us," this displeased Samuel; so he prayed to the LORD. 7And the LORD told him: "Listen to all that the people are saying to you; it is not you they have rejected, but they have rejected me as their king. 8As they have done from the day I brought them up out of Egypt until this day, forsaking me and serving other gods, so they are doing to you. 9Now listen to them; but warn them solemnly and let them know what the king who will reign over them will do."

10Samuel told all the words of the LORD to the people who were asking him for a

---

a6 Traditionally *judge*　　*b12 Ebenezer* means *stone of help.*　　*c5* Traditionally *judge*; also in verses 6 and 20 king. ¹¹He said, "This is what the king who will reign over you will do: He will take your sons and make them serve with his chariots and horses, and they will run in front of his chariots. ¹²Some he will assign to be commanders of thousands and commanders of fifties, and others to plow his ground and reap his harvest, and still others to make weapons of war and equipment for his chariots. ¹³He will take your daughters to be perfumers and cooks and bakers. ¹⁴He will take the best of your fields and vineyards and olive groves and give them to his attendants. ¹⁵He will take a tenth of your grain and of your vintage and give it to his officials and attendants. ¹⁶Your menservants and maidservants and the best of your cattle*ᵃ* and donkeys he will take for his own use. ¹⁷He will take a tenth of your flocks, and you yourselves will become his slaves. ¹⁸When that day comes, you will cry out for relief from the king you have chosen, and the Lord will not answer you in that day."

¹⁹But the people refused to listen to Samuel. "No!" they said. "We want a king over us. ²⁰Then we will be like all the other nations, with a king to lead us and to go out before us and fight our battles."

²¹When Samuel heard all that the people said, he repeated it before the Lord. ²²The Lord answered, "Listen to them and give them a king."

Then Samuel said to the men of Israel, "Everyone go back to his town."

Samuel Anoints Saul

9 There was a Benjamite, a man of standing, whose name was Kish son of Abiel, the son of Zeror, the son of Becorath, the son of Aphiah of Benjamin. ²He had a son named Saul, an impressive young man without equal among the Israelites—a head taller than any of the others.

³Now the donkeys belonging to Saul's father Kish were lost, and Kish said to his son Saul, "Take one of the servants with you and go and look for the donkeys." ⁴So he passed through the hill country of Ephraim and through the area around Shalisha, but they did not find them. They went on into the district of Shaalim, but the donkeys were not there. Then he passed through the territory of Benjamin, but they did not find them.

⁵When they reached the district of Zuph, Saul said to the servant who was with him, "Come, let's go back, or my father will stop thinking about the donkeys and start worrying about us."

⁶But the servant replied, "Look, in this town there is a man of God; he is highly respected, and everything he says comes true. Let's go there now. Perhaps he will tell us what way to take."

⁷Saul said to his servant, "If we go, what can we give the man? The food in our sacks is gone. We have no gift to take to the man of God. What do we have?"

⁸The servant answered him again. "Look," he said, "I have a quarter of a shekel*ᵇ* of silver. I will give it to the man of God so that he will tell us what way to take." ⁹(Formerly in Israel, if a man went to inquire of God, he would say, "Come, let us go to the seer," because the prophet of today used to be called a seer.)

¹⁰"Good," Saul said to his servant. "Come, let's go." So they set out for the town where the man of God was.

¹¹As they were going up the hill to the town, they met some girls coming out to draw water, and they asked them, "Is the seer here?"

¹²"He is," they answered. "He's ahead of you. Hurry now; he has just come to our town today, for the people have a sacrifice at the high place. ¹³As soon as you enter the town, you will find him before he goes up to the high place to eat. The people will not begin eating until he comes, because he must bless the sacrifice; afterward, those who are invited will eat. Go up now; you should find him about this time."

¹⁴They went up to the town, and as they were entering it, there was Samuel,

---

ᵃ16 Septuagint; Hebrew *young men*   *ᵇ8* That is, about 1/10 ounce (about 3 grams)

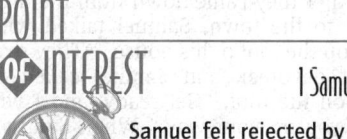

POINT OF INTEREST   1 Samuel 8:7

Samuel felt rejected by the people when they challenged his leadership. But the people were actually rejecting *God's* leadership. As the following verses illustrate, they would soon learn the consequences of that rejection.

coming toward them on his way up to the high place.

[15]Now the day before Saul came, the LORD had revealed this to Samuel: [16]"About this time tomorrow I will send you a man from the land of Benjamin. Anoint him leader over my people Israel; he will deliver my people from the hand of the Philistines. I have looked upon my people, for their cry has reached me."

[17]When Samuel caught sight of Saul, the LORD said to him, "This is the man I spoke to you about; he will govern my people."

[18]Saul approached Samuel in the gateway and asked, "Would you please tell me where the seer's house is?"

[19]"I am the seer," Samuel replied. "Go up ahead of me to the high place, for today you are to eat with me, and in the morning I will let you go and will tell you all that is in your heart. [20]As for the donkeys you lost three days ago, do not worry about them; they have been found. And to whom is all the desire of Israel turned, if not to you and all your father's family?"

[21]Saul answered, "But am I not a Benjamite, from the smallest tribe of Israel, and is not my clan the least of all the clans of the tribe of Benjamin? Why do you say such a thing to me?"

[22]Then Samuel brought Saul and his servant into the hall and seated them at the head of those who were invited—about thirty in number. [23]Samuel said to the cook, "Bring the piece of meat I gave you, the one I told you to lay aside."

[24]So the cook took up the leg with what was on it and set it in front of Saul. Samuel said, "Here is what has been kept for you. Eat, because it was set aside for you for this occasion, from the time I said, 'I have invited guests.'" And Saul dined with Samuel that day.

[25]After they came down from the high place to the town, Samuel talked with Saul on the roof of his house. [26]They rose about daybreak and Samuel called to Saul on the roof, "Get ready, and I will send you on your way." When Saul got ready, he and Samuel went outside together. [27]As they were going down to the edge of the town, Samuel said to Saul, "Tell the servant to go on ahead of us"—and the servant did so—"but you stay here awhile, so that I may give you a message from God."

10 Then Samuel took a flask of oil and poured it on Saul's head and kissed him, saying, "Has not the LORD anointed you leader over his inheritance?[a] [2]When you leave me today, you will meet two men near Rachel's tomb, at Zelzah on the border of Benjamin. They will say to you, 'The donkeys you set out to look for have been found. And now your father has stopped thinking about them and is worried about you. He is asking, "What shall I do about my son?"'

[3]"Then you will go on from there until you reach the great tree of Tabor. Three men going up to God at Bethel will meet you there. One will be carrying three young goats, another three loaves of bread, and another a skin of wine. [4]They will greet you and offer you two loaves of bread, which you will accept from them.

[5]"After that you will go to Gibeah of God, where there is a Philistine outpost. As you approach the town, you will meet a procession of prophets coming down from the high place with lyres, tambourines, flutes and harps being played before them, and they will be prophesying. [6]The Spirit of the LORD will come upon you in power, and you will prophesy with them; and you will be changed into a different person. [7]Once these signs are fulfilled, do whatever your hand finds to do, for God is with you.

[8]"Go down ahead of me to Gilgal. I will surely come down to you to sacrifice burnt offerings and fellowship offerings,[b] but you must wait seven days until I come to you and tell you what you are to do."

Saul Made King

[9]As Saul turned to leave Samuel, God changed Saul's heart, and all these signs were fulfilled that day. [10]When they arrived at Gibeah, a procession of prophets met him; the Spirit of God came upon him in power, and he joined in their prophesying. [11]When all those who had formerly known him saw him prophesying with the prophets, they asked each other, "What is this that has happened to the son of Kish? Is Saul also among the prophets?"

[a]1 Hebrew; Septuagint and Vulgate *over his people Israel? You will reign over the LORD's people and save them from the power of their enemies round about. And this will be a sign to you that the LORD has anointed you leader over his inheritance:*
[b]8 Traditionally *peace offerings*

¹²A man who lived there answered, "And who is their father?" So it became a saying: "Is Saul also among the prophets?" ¹³After Saul stopped prophesying, he went to the high place.

¹⁴Now Saul's uncle asked him and his servant, "Where have you been?"

"Looking for the donkeys," he said. "But when we saw they were not to be found, we went to Samuel."

¹⁵Saul's uncle said, "Tell me what Samuel said to you."

¹⁶Saul replied, "He assured us that the donkeys had been found." But he did not tell his uncle what Samuel had said about the kingship.

¹⁷Samuel summoned the people of Israel to the LORD at Mizpah ¹⁸and said to them, "This is what the LORD, the God of Israel, says: 'I brought Israel up out of Egypt, and I delivered you from the power of Egypt and all the kingdoms that oppressed you.' ¹⁹But you have now rejected your God, who saves you out of all your calamities and distresses. And you have said, 'No, set a king over us.' So now present yourselves before the LORD by your tribes and clans."

²⁰When Samuel brought all the tribes of Israel near, the tribe of Benjamin was chosen. ²¹Then he brought forward the tribe of Benjamin, clan by clan, and Matri's clan was chosen. Finally Saul son of Kish was chosen. But when they looked for him, he was not to be found. ²²So they inquired further of the LORD, "Has the man come here yet?"

And the LORD said, "Yes, he has hidden himself among the baggage."

²³They ran and brought him out, and as he stood among the people he was a head taller than any of the others. ²⁴Samuel said to all the people, "Do you see the man the LORD has chosen? There is no one like him among all the people."

Then the people shouted, "Long live the king!"

²⁵Samuel explained to the people the regulations of the kingship. He wrote them down on a scroll and deposited it before the LORD. Then Samuel dismissed the people, each to his own home.

²⁶Saul also went to his home in Gibeah, accompanied by valiant men whose hearts God had touched. ²⁷But some troublemakers said, "How can this fellow save us?" They despised him and brought him no gifts. But Saul kept silent.

Saul Rescues the City of Jabesh

11 Nahash the Ammonite went up and besieged Jabesh Gilead. And all the men of Jabesh said to him, "Make a treaty with us, and we will be subject to you."

²But Nahash the Ammonite replied, "I will make a treaty with you only on the condition that I gouge out the right eye of every one of you and so bring disgrace on all Israel."

³The elders of Jabesh said to him, "Give us seven days so we can send messengers throughout Israel; if no one comes to rescue us, we will surrender to you."

⁴When the messengers came to Gibeah of Saul and reported these terms to the people, they all wept aloud. ⁵Just then Saul was returning from the fields, behind his oxen, and he asked, "What is wrong with the people? Why are they weeping?" Then they repeated to him what the men of Jabesh had said.

⁶When Saul heard their words, the Spirit of God came upon him in power, and he burned with anger. ⁷He took a pair of oxen, cut them into pieces, and sent the pieces by messengers throughout Israel, proclaiming, "This is what will be done to the oxen of anyone who does not follow Saul and Samuel." Then the terror of the LORD fell on the people, and they turned out as one man. ⁸When Saul mustered them at Bezek, the men of Israel numbered three hundred thousand and the men of Judah thirty thousand.

⁹They told the messengers who had come, "Say to the men of Jabesh Gilead, 'By the time the sun is hot tomorrow, you will be delivered.' " When the messengers went and reported this to the men of Jabesh, they were elated. ¹⁰They said to the Ammonites, "Tomorrow we will surrender to you, and you can do to us whatever seems good to you."

¹¹The next day Saul separated his men into three divisions; during the last watch of the night they broke into the camp of the Ammonites and slaughtered them until the heat of the day. Those who survived were scattered, so that no two of them were left together.

Saul Confirmed as King

¹²The people then said to Samuel, "Who was it that asked, 'Shall Saul reign

over us?' Bring these men to us and we will put them to death."

13But Saul said, "No one shall be put to death today, for this day the LORD has rescued Israel."

14Then Samuel said to the people, "Come, let us go to Gilgal and there reaffirm the kingship." 15So all the people went to Gilgal and confirmed Saul as king in the presence of the LORD. There they sacrificed fellowship offerings*a* before the LORD, and Saul and all the Israelites held a great celebration.

Samuel's Farewell Speech

12 Samuel said to all Israel, "I have listened to everything you said to me and have set a king over you. 2Now you have a king as your leader. As for me, I am old and gray, and my sons are here with you. I have been your leader from my youth until this day. 3Here I stand. Testify against me in the presence of the LORD and his anointed. Whose ox have I taken? Whose donkey have I taken? Whom have I cheated? Whom have I oppressed? From whose hand have I accepted a bribe to make me shut my eyes? If I have done any of these, I will make it right."

4"You have not cheated or oppressed us," they replied. "You have not taken anything from anyone's hand."

5Samuel said to them, "The LORD is witness against you, and also his anointed is witness this day, that you have not found anything in my hand."

"He is witness," they said.

6Then Samuel said to the people, "It is the LORD who appointed Moses and Aaron and brought your forefathers up out of Egypt. 7Now then, stand here, because I am going to confront you with evidence before the LORD as to all the righteous acts performed by the LORD for you and your fathers.

8"After Jacob entered Egypt, they cried to the LORD for help, and the LORD sent Moses and Aaron, who brought your forefathers out of Egypt and settled them in this place.

9"But they forgot the LORD their God; so he sold them into the hand of Sisera, the commander of the army of Hazor, and into the hands of the Philistines and the king of Moab, who fought against them. 10They cried out to the LORD and said, 'We have sinned; we have forsaken the LORD and served the Baals and the

Ashtoreths. But now deliver us from the hands of our enemies, and we will serve you.' 11Then the LORD sent Jerub-Baal,*b* Barak,*c* Jephthah and Samuel,*d* and he delivered you from the hands of your enemies on every side, so that you lived securely.

12"But when you saw that Nahash king of the Ammonites was moving against you, you said to me, 'No, we want a king to rule over us'—even though the LORD your God was your king. 13Now here is the king you have chosen, the one you asked for; see, the LORD has set a king over you. 14If you fear the LORD and serve and obey him and do not rebel against his commands, and if both you and the king who reigns over you follow the LORD your God—good! 15But if you do not obey the LORD, and if you rebel against his commands, his hand will be against you, as it was against your fathers.

16"Now then, stand still and see this great thing the LORD is about to do before your eyes! 17Is it not wheat harvest now? I will call upon the LORD to send thunder and rain. And you will realize what an evil thing you did in the eyes of the LORD when you asked for a king."

18Then Samuel called upon the LORD, and that same day the LORD sent thunder and rain. So all the people stood in awe of the LORD and of Samuel.

19The people all said to Samuel, "Pray to the LORD your God for your servants so that we will not die, for we have added to all our other sins the evil of asking for a king."

20"Do not be afraid," Samuel replied. "You have done all this evil; yet do not turn away from the LORD, but serve the LORD with all your heart. 21Do not turn away after useless idols. They can do you no good, nor can they rescue you, because they are useless. 22For the sake of his great name the LORD will not reject his people, because the LORD was pleased to make you his own. 23As for me, far be it from me that I should sin against the LORD by failing to pray for you. And I will teach you the way that is good and right. 24But be sure to fear the LORD and serve him faithfully with all your heart; consider what great things he has done for you.

---

a 15 Traditionally *peace offerings*   *b 11* Also called *Gideon*   *c 11* Some Septuagint manuscripts and Syriac; Hebrew *Bedan*   *d 11* Hebrew; some Septuagint manuscripts and Syriac *Samson*

²⁵Yet if you persist in doing evil, both you and your king will be swept away."

Samuel Rebukes Saul

13 Saul was ⌐thirty⌐ᵃ years old when he became king, and he reigned over Israel ⌐forty-⌐ᵇ two years.

²Saulᶜ chose three thousand men from Israel; two thousand were with him at Micmash and in the hill country of Bethel, and a thousand were with Jonathan at Gibeah in Benjamin. The rest of the men he sent back to their homes.

³Jonathan attacked the Philistine outpost at Geba, and the Philistines heard about it. Then Saul had the trumpet blown throughout the land and said, "Let the Hebrews hear!" ⁴So all Israel heard the news: "Saul has attacked the Philistine outpost, and now Israel has become a stench to the Philistines." And the people were summoned to join Saul at Gilgal.

⁵The Philistines assembled to fight Israel, with three thousandᵈ chariots, six thousand charioteers, and soldiers as numerous as the sand on the seashore. They went up and camped at Micmash, east of Beth Aven. ⁶When the men of Israel saw that their situation was critical and that their army was hard pressed, they hid in caves and thickets, among the rocks, and in pits and cisterns. ⁷Some Hebrews even crossed the Jordan to the land of Gad and Gilead.

Saul remained at Gilgal, and all the troops with him were quaking with fear. ⁸He waited seven days, the time set by Samuel; but Samuel did not come to Gilgal, and Saul's men began to scatter. ⁹So he said, "Bring me the burnt offering and the fellowship offerings.ᵉ" And Saul offered up the burnt offering. ¹⁰Just as he finished making the offering, Samuel arrived, and Saul went out to greet him.

¹¹"What have you done?" asked Samuel.

Saul replied, "When I saw that the men were scattering, and that you did not come at the set time, and that the Philistines were assembling at Micmash, ¹²I thought, 'Now the Philistines will come down against me at Gilgal, and I have not sought the LORD's favor.' So I felt compelled to offer the burnt offering."

¹³"You acted foolishly," Samuel said. "You have not kept the command the LORD your God gave you; if you had, he would have established your kingdom over Israel for all time. ¹⁴But now your kingdom will not endure; the LORD has sought out a man after his own heart and appointed him leader of his people, because you have not kept the LORD's command."

¹⁵Then Samuel left Gilgalᶠ and went up to Gibeah in Benjamin, and Saul counted the men who were with him. They numbered about six hundred.

Israel Without Weapons

¹⁶Saul and his son Jonathan and the men with them were staying in Gibeahᵍ in Benjamin, while the Philistines camped at Micmash. ¹⁷Raiding parties went out from the Philistine camp in three detachments. One turned toward Ophrah in the vicinity of Shual, ¹⁸another toward Beth Horon, and the third toward the borderland overlooking the Valley of Zeboim facing the desert.

¹⁹Not a blacksmith could be found in the whole land of Israel, because the Philistines had said, "Otherwise the Hebrews will make swords or spears!" ²⁰So all Israel went down to the Philistines to have their plowshares, mattocks, axes and sicklesʰ sharpened. ²¹The price was two thirds of a shekelⁱ for sharpening plowshares and mattocks, and a third of a shekelʲ for sharpening forks and axes and for repointing goads.

ᵃ1 A few late manuscripts of the Septuagint; Hebrew does not have *thirty*.   ᵇ1 See the round number in Acts 13:21; Hebrew does not have *forty-*.   ᶜ1,2 Or *and when he had reigned over Israel two years,* ²*he*   ᵈ5 Some Septuagint manuscripts and Syriac; Hebrew *thirty thousand*   ᵉ9 Traditionally *peace offerings*   ᶠ15 Hebrew; Septuagint *Gilgal and went his way; the rest of the people went after Saul to meet the army, and they went out of Gilgal*   ᵍ16 Two Hebrew manuscripts; most Hebrew manuscripts *Geba*, a variant of *Gibeah*   ʰ20 Septuagint; Hebrew *plowshares*   ⁱ21 Hebrew *pim*; that is, about 1/4 ounce (about 8 grams)   ʲ21 That is, about 1/8 ounce (about 4 grams)

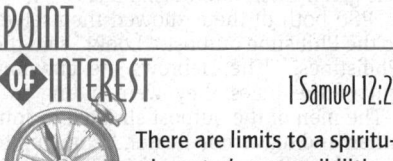

POINT OF INTEREST

1 Samuel 12:23

There are limits to a spiritual mentor's responsibilities. While a mentor can pray, teach or serve as a role model, obeying God is the responsibility of the one being mentored. Not one person will ever get to heaven on someone else's "coattails"!

²²So on the day of the battle not a soldier with Saul and Jonathan had a sword or spear in his hand; only Saul and his son Jonathan had them.

Jonathan Attacks the Philistines

²³Now a detachment of Philistines had gone out to the pass at Micmash. **14** ¹One day Jonathan son of Saul said to the young man bearing his armor, "Come, let's go over to the Philistine outpost on the other side." But he did not tell his father.

²Saul was staying on the outskirts of Gibeah under a pomegranate tree in Migron. With him were about six hundred men, ³among whom was Ahijah, who was wearing an ephod. He was a son of Ichabod's brother Ahitub son of Phinehas, the son of Eli, the LORD's priest in Shiloh. No one was aware that Jonathan had left.

⁴On each side of the pass that Jonathan intended to cross to reach the Philistine outpost was a cliff; one was called Bozez, and the other Seneh. ⁵One cliff stood to the north toward Micmash, the other to the south toward Geba.

⁶Jonathan said to his young armor-bearer, "Come, let's go over to the outpost of those uncircumcised fellows. Perhaps the LORD will act in our behalf. Nothing can hinder the LORD from saving, whether by many or by few."

⁷"Do all that you have in mind," his armor-bearer said. "Go ahead; I am with you heart and soul."

⁸Jonathan said, "Come, then; we will cross over toward the men and let them see us. ⁹If they say to us, 'Wait there until we come to you,' we will stay where we are and not go up to them. ¹⁰But if they say, 'Come up to us,' we will climb up, because that will be our sign that the LORD has given them into our hands."

¹¹So both of them showed themselves to the Philistine outpost. "Look!" said the Philistines. "The Hebrews are crawling out of the holes they were hiding in." ¹²The men of the outpost shouted to Jonathan and his armor-bearer, "Come up to us and we'll teach you a lesson."

So Jonathan said to his armor-bearer, "Climb up after me; the LORD has given them into the hand of Israel."

¹³Jonathan climbed up, using his hands and feet, with his armor-bearer right behind him. The Philistines fell before Jonathan, and his armor-bearer followed and killed behind him. ¹⁴In that first attack Jonathan and his armor-bearer killed some twenty men in an area of about half an acre.*ᵃ*

Israel Routs the Philistines

¹⁵Then panic struck the whole army—those in the camp and field, and those in the outposts and raiding parties—and the ground shook. It was a panic sent by God.*ᵇ*

¹⁶Saul's lookouts at Gibeah in Benjamin saw the army melting away in all directions. ¹⁷Then Saul said to the men who were with him, "Muster the forces and see who has left us." When they did, it was Jonathan and his armor-bearer who were not there.

¹⁸Saul said to Ahijah, "Bring the ark of God." (At that time it was with the Israelites.)*ᶜ* ¹⁹While Saul was talking to the priest, the tumult in the Philistine camp increased more and more. So Saul said to the priest, "Withdraw your hand."

²⁰Then Saul and all his men assembled and went to the battle. They found the Philistines in total confusion, striking each other with their swords. ²¹Those Hebrews who had previously been with the Philistines and had gone up with them to their camp went over to the Israelites who were with Saul and Jonathan. ²²When all the Israelites who had hidden in the hill country of Ephraim heard that the Philistines were on the run, they joined the battle in hot pursuit. ²³So the LORD rescued Israel that day, and the battle moved on beyond Beth Aven.

Jonathan Eats Honey

²⁴Now the men of Israel were in distress that day, because Saul had bound the people under an oath, saying, "Cursed be any man who eats food before evening comes, before I have avenged myself on my enemies!" So none of the troops tasted food.

²⁵The entire army*ᵈ* entered the woods, and there was honey on the ground. ²⁶When they went into the woods, they saw the honey oozing out, yet no one put his hand to his mouth, because they feared the oath. ²⁷But Jona-

---

ᵃ14 Hebrew *half a yoke*; a "yoke" was the land plowed by a yoke of oxen in one day.   *ᵇ15* Or *a terrible panic*   *ᶜ18* Hebrew; Septuagint *"Bring the ephod." (At that time he wore the ephod before the Israelites.)*   *ᵈ25* Or *Now all the people of the land* than had not heard that his father had bound the people with the oath, so he reached out the end of the staff that was in his hand and dipped it into the honeycomb. He raised his hand to his mouth, and his eyes brightened.[a] 28Then one of the soldiers told him, "Your father bound the army under a strict oath, saying, 'Cursed be any man who eats food today!' That is why the men are faint."

29Jonathan said, "My father has made trouble for the country. See how my eyes brightened[b] when I tasted a little of this honey. 30How much better it would have been if the men had eaten today some of the plunder they took from their enemies. Would not the slaughter of the Philistines have been even greater?"

31That day, after the Israelites had struck down the Philistines from Micmash to Aijalon, they were exhausted. 32They pounced on the plunder and, taking sheep, cattle and calves, they butchered them on the ground and ate them, together with the blood. 33Then someone said to Saul, "Look, the men are sinning

---

a27 Or his strength was renewed   b29 Or my strength was renewed

---

THURSDAY

Read 1 Samuel 13:23—14:23
Key Verse 1 Samuel 14:7

Follow Wholeheartedly – Joe Bernardy

"You want me to do *what*?"

That's one way to respond when a pastor, elder or spiritual leader gives you an assignment or makes a suggestion to you.

Jonathan made a decision that was potentially life-threatening to himself and his armor-bearer. His idea was simple: The two of them would walk into the Philistine camp and see what God would do. "Perhaps the Lord will act in our behalf. Nothing can hinder the Lord from saving, whether by many or by few" (1 Samuel 14:6). They went up, showed themselves to the Philistines, and routed them! The two of them killed some twenty men, causing the rest of the Philistines to panic and giving Israel a great victory.

Jonathan was clearly a man of faith with a vision. God's Word urges us to imitate the faith of our leaders and to obey them and submit to their authority (see Hebrews 13:17). Jonathan's armor-bearer did just that. If his armor-bearer had balked, reminding him of their statistical disadvantage and questioning his wisdom, this great victory might never have occurred.

How would you have responded if you had been the armor-bearer? We must choose carefully the spiritual leaders we will support— and then follow them wholeheartedly. We can make their jobs easier or more difficult by our attitudes. We can encourage them to be people of faith, or we can opt to be discouraging, questioning every move they make or whining about difficulties. And the kingdom of God may be advanced or hindered by our choice of attitudes.

So the next time your leader talks about taking a Christ-led step—or even a leap of faith—be like Jonathan's armor-bearer: "Do all that you have in mind . . . Go ahead; I am with you heart and soul" (1 Samuel 14:7). Then watch God do some God-sized things!

A Deeper Look
Romans 13:1–7; Ephesians 5:21

Go to page 306 for your next devotional reading.

against the LORD by eating meat that has blood in it."

"You have broken faith," he said. "Roll a large stone over here at once." **34**Then he said, "Go out among the men and tell them, 'Each of you bring me your cattle and sheep, and slaughter them here and eat them. Do not sin against the LORD by eating meat with blood still in it.' "

So everyone brought his ox that night and slaughtered it there. **35**Then Saul built an altar to the LORD; it was the first time he had done this.

36Saul said, "Let us go down after the Philistines by night and plunder them till dawn, and let us not leave one of them alive."

"Do whatever seems best to you," they replied.

But the priest said, "Let us inquire of God here."

37So Saul asked God, "Shall I go down after the Philistines? Will you give them into Israel's hand?" But God did not answer him that day.

38Saul therefore said, "Come here, all you who are leaders of the army, and let us find out what sin has been committed today. **39**As surely as the LORD who rescues Israel lives, even if it lies with my son Jonathan, he must die." But not one of the men said a word.

40Saul then said to all the Israelites, "You stand over there; I and Jonathan my son will stand over here."

"Do what seems best to you," the men replied.

41Then Saul prayed to the LORD, the God of Israel, "Give me the right answer."*a* And Jonathan and Saul were taken by lot, and the men were cleared. **42**Saul said, "Cast the lot between me and Jonathan my son." And Jonathan was taken.

43Then Saul said to Jonathan, "Tell me what you have done."

So Jonathan told him, "I merely tasted a little honey with the end of my staff. And now must I die?"

44Saul said, "May God deal with me, be it ever so severely, if you do not die, Jonathan."

45But the men said to Saul, "Should Jonathan die—he who has brought about this great deliverance in Israel? Never! As surely as the LORD lives, not a hair of his head will fall to the ground, for he did this today with God's help." So the men

rescued Jonathan, and he was not put to death.

46Then Saul stopped pursuing the Philistines, and they withdrew to their own land.

47After Saul had assumed rule over Israel, he fought against their enemies on every side: Moab, the Ammonites, Edom, the kings*b* of Zobah, and the Philistines. Wherever he turned, he inflicted punishment on them.*c* **48**He fought valiantly and defeated the Amalekites, delivering Israel from the hands of those who had plundered them.

Saul's Family

49Saul's sons were Jonathan, Ishvi and Malki-Shua. The name of his older daughter was Merab, and that of the younger was Michal. **50**His wife's name was Ahinoam daughter of Ahimaaz. The name of the commander of Saul's army was Abner son of Ner, and Ner was Saul's uncle. **51**Saul's father Kish and Abner's father Ner were sons of Abiel.

52All the days of Saul there was bitter war with the Philistines, and whenever Saul saw a mighty or brave man, he took him into his service.

The LORD Rejects Saul as King

15 Samuel said to Saul, "I am the one the LORD sent to anoint you king over his people Israel; so listen now to the message from the LORD. **2**This is what the LORD Almighty says: 'I will punish the Amalekites for what they did to Israel when they waylaid them as they came up from Egypt. **3**Now go, attack the Amalekites and totally destroy*d* everything that belongs to them. Do not spare them; put to death men and women, children and infants, cattle and sheep, camels and donkeys.' "

4So Saul summoned the men and mustered them at Telaim—two hundred thousand foot soldiers and ten thousand men from Judah. **5**Saul went to the city of Amalek and set an ambush in the ravine. **6**Then he said to the Kenites, "Go away,

---

a41 Hebrew; Septuagint *"Why have you not answered your servant today? If the fault is in me or my son Jonathan, respond with Urim, but if the men of Israel are at fault, respond with Thummim."* *b47* Masoretic Text; Dead Sea Scrolls and Septuagint *king* *c47* Hebrew; Septuagint *he was victorious* *d3* The Hebrew term refers to the irrevocable giving over of things or persons to the LORD, often by totally destroying them; also in verses 8, 9, 15, 18, 20 and 21.

leave the Amalekites so that I do not destroy you along with them; for you showed kindness to all the Israelites when they came up out of Egypt." So the Kenites moved away from the Amalekites.

⁷Then Saul attacked the Amalekites all the way from Havilah to Shur, to the east of Egypt. ⁸He took Agag king of the Amalekites alive, and all his people he totally destroyed with the sword. ⁹But Saul and the army spared Agag and the best of the sheep and cattle, the fat calves*ᵃ* and lambs—everything that was good. These they were unwilling to destroy completely, but everything that was despised and weak they totally destroyed.

¹⁰Then the word of the LORD came to Samuel: ¹¹"I am grieved that I have made Saul king, because he has turned away from me and has not carried out my instructions." Samuel was troubled, and he cried out to the LORD all that night.

¹²Early in the morning Samuel got up and went to meet Saul, but he was told, "Saul has gone to Carmel. There he has set up a monument in his own honor and has turned and gone on down to Gilgal."

¹³When Samuel reached him, Saul said, "The LORD bless you! I have carried out the LORD's instructions."

¹⁴But Samuel said, "What then is this bleating of sheep in my ears? What is this lowing of cattle that I hear?"

¹⁵Saul answered, "The soldiers brought them from the Amalekites; they spared the best of the sheep and cattle to sacrifice to the LORD your God, but we totally destroyed the rest."

¹⁶"Stop!" Samuel said to Saul. "Let me tell you what the LORD said to me last night."

"Tell me," Saul replied.

¹⁷Samuel said, "Although you were once small in your own eyes, did you not become the head of the tribes of Israel? The LORD anointed you king over Israel. ¹⁸And he sent you on a mission, saying, 'Go and completely destroy those wicked people, the Amalekites; make war on them until you have wiped them out.' ¹⁹Why did you not obey the LORD? Why did you pounce on the plunder and do evil in the eyes of the LORD?"

²⁰"But I did obey the LORD," Saul said. "I went on the mission the LORD assigned me. I completely destroyed the Amalekites and brought back Agag their king. ²¹The soldiers took sheep and cattle from the plunder, the best of what was devoted to God, in order to sacrifice them to the LORD your God at Gilgal."

²²But Samuel replied:

"Does the LORD delight in burnt
    offerings and sacrifices
  as much as in obeying the voice of
    the LORD?
To obey is better than sacrifice,
  and to heed is better than the fat
    of rams.
²³For rebellion is like the sin of
    divination,
  and arrogance like the evil of
    idolatry.
Because you have rejected the word
    of the LORD,
  he has rejected you as king."

²⁴Then Saul said to Samuel, "I have sinned. I violated the LORD's command and your instructions. I was afraid of the people and so I gave in to them. ²⁵Now I beg you, forgive my sin and come back with me, so that I may worship the LORD."

²⁶But Samuel said to him, "I will not go back with you. You have rejected the word of the LORD, and the LORD has rejected you as king over Israel!"

²⁷As Samuel turned to leave, Saul caught hold of the hem of his robe, and it tore. ²⁸Samuel said to him, "The LORD has torn the kingdom of Israel from you today and has given it to one of your neighbors—to one better than you. ²⁹He who is the Glory of Israel does not lie or change his mind; for he is not a man, that he should change his mind."

³⁰Saul replied, "I have sinned. But please honor me before the elders of my people and before Israel; come back with me, so that I may worship the LORD your God." ³¹So Samuel went back with Saul, and Saul worshiped the LORD.

³²Then Samuel said, "Bring me Agag king of the Amalekites."

Agag came to him confidently,*ᵇ* thinking, "Surely the bitterness of death is past."

³³But Samuel said,

"As your sword has made women
    childless,
  so will your mother be childless
    among women."

ᵃ9 Or the grown bulls; the meaning of the Hebrew for this phrase is uncertain.   ᵇ32 Or him trembling, yet

And Samuel put Agag to death before the LORD at Gilgal.

³⁴Then Samuel left for Ramah, but Saul went up to his home in Gibeah of Saul. ³⁵Until the day Samuel died, he did not go to see Saul again, though Samuel mourned for him. And the LORD was grieved that he had made Saul king over Israel.

Samuel Anoints David

16 The LORD said to Samuel, "How long will you mourn for Saul, since I have rejected him as king over Israel? Fill your horn with oil and be on your way; I am sending you to Jesse of Bethlehem. I have chosen one of his sons to be king."

²But Samuel said, "How can I go? Saul will hear about it and kill me."

The LORD said, "Take a heifer with you and say, 'I have come to sacrifice to the LORD.' ³Invite Jesse to the sacrifice, and I will show you what to do. You are to anoint for me the one I indicate."

⁴Samuel did what the LORD said. When he arrived at Bethlehem, the elders of the town trembled when they met him. They asked, "Do you come in peace?"

⁵Samuel replied, "Yes, in peace; I have come to sacrifice to the LORD. Consecrate yourselves and come to the sacrifice with me." Then he consecrated Jesse and his sons and invited them to the sacrifice.

⁶When they arrived, Samuel saw Eliab and thought, "Surely the LORD's anointed stands here before the LORD."

⁷But the LORD said to Samuel, "Do not consider his appearance or his height, for I have rejected him. The LORD does not look at the things man looks at. Man

---

FRIDAY

Read 1 Samuel 16:1–13
Key Verse 1 Samuel 16:7

Is Image Everything ? —Lynn M. Hamilton

Life is a stage for super models, professional athletes, politicians . . . and for you and me. Because so many in our culture judge us according to physical appearance—because "image is everything"—we work hard to make that first impression just right. Everywhere we turn we are told to look a certain way—to "dress for success." Our culture screams, "change how you look and you will be accepted!"

But God has a different way. God says he accepts us fully in Jesus Christ (see Romans 15:7). God looks at the heart, and that can't be camouflaged by a cool earring or the right brand of jeans. He is not impressed by the clearness of our complexion or the whiteness of our teeth or by whether or not our clothes come from the most in-style stores. He is concerned, however, with the development of our character and our faith. Our main concern should be feeding our souls, grooming our minds and examining our hearts. And the apostle Paul tells us that as "God's chosen people" we are to "clothe [ourselves] with compassion, kindness, humility, gentleness and patience" (Colossians 3:12). You can't buy those at the mall!

We are made in God's image (see Genesis 1:27). Although sin has tarnished and muddied that image, in Christ we are to "put on the new self, which is being renewed in knowledge in the image of its Creator" (Colossians 3:10). Image *is* everything—God's image!

A Deeper Look
Proverbs 4:23; Philippians 1:6

Go to page 313 for your next devotional reading.

looks at the outward appearance, but the LORD looks at the heart."

⁸Then Jesse called Abinadab and had him pass in front of Samuel. But Samuel said, "The LORD has not chosen this one either." ⁹Jesse then had Shammah pass by, but Samuel said, "Nor has the LORD chosen this one." ¹⁰Jesse had seven of his sons pass before Samuel, but Samuel said to him, "The LORD has not chosen these." ¹¹So he asked Jesse, "Are these all the sons you have?"

"There is still the youngest," Jesse answered, "but he is tending the sheep."

Samuel said, "Send for him; we will not sit down*a* until he arrives."

¹²So he sent and had him brought in. He was ruddy, with a fine appearance and handsome features.

Then the LORD said, "Rise and anoint him; he is the one."

¹³So Samuel took the horn of oil and anointed him in the presence of his brothers, and from that day on the Spirit of the LORD came upon David in power. Samuel then went to Ramah.

David in Saul's Service

¹⁴Now the Spirit of the LORD had departed from Saul, and an evil*b* spirit from the LORD tormented him.

¹⁵Saul's attendants said to him, "See, an evil spirit from God is tormenting you. ¹⁶Let our lord command his servants here to search for someone who can play the harp. He will play when the evil spirit from God comes upon you, and you will feel better."

¹⁷So Saul said to his attendants, "Find someone who plays well and bring him to me."

¹⁸One of the servants answered, "I have seen a son of Jesse of Bethlehem who knows how to play the harp. He is a brave man and a warrior. He speaks well and is a fine-looking man. And the LORD is with him."

¹⁹Then Saul sent messengers to Jesse and said, "Send me your son David, who is with the sheep." ²⁰So Jesse took a donkey loaded with bread, a skin of wine and a young goat and sent them with his son David to Saul.

²¹David came to Saul and entered his service. Saul liked him very much, and David became one of his armor-bearers. ²²Then Saul sent word to Jesse, saying, "Allow David to remain in my service, for I am pleased with him."

²³Whenever the spirit from God came upon Saul, David would take his harp and play. Then relief would come to Saul; he would feel better, and the evil spirit would leave him.

David and Goliath

17 Now the Philistines gathered their forces for war and assembled at Socoh in Judah. They pitched camp at Ephes Dammim, between Socoh and Azekah. ²Saul and the Israelites assembled and camped in the Valley of Elah and drew up their battle line to meet the Philistines. ³The Philistines occupied one hill and the Israelites another, with the valley between them.

⁴A champion named Goliath, who was from Gath, came out of the Philistine camp. He was over nine feet*c* tall. ⁵He had a bronze helmet on his head and wore a coat of scale armor of bronze weighing five thousand shekels*d*; ⁶on his legs he wore bronze greaves, and a bronze javelin was slung on his back. ⁷His spear shaft was like a weaver's rod, and its iron point weighed six hundred shekels.*e* His shield bearer went ahead of him.

⁸Goliath stood and shouted to the ranks of Israel, "Why do you come out and line up for battle? Am I not a Philistine, and are you not the servants of Saul? Choose a man and have him come down to me. ⁹If he is able to fight and kill me, we will become your subjects; but if I overcome him and kill him, you will become our subjects and serve us." ¹⁰Then the Philistine said, "This day I defy the ranks of Israel! Give me a man and let us fight each other." ¹¹On hearing the Philistine's words, Saul and all the Israelites were dismayed and terrified.

¹²Now David was the son of an Ephrathite named Jesse, who was from Bethlehem in Judah. Jesse had eight sons, and in Saul's time he was old and well advanced in years. ¹³Jesse's three oldest sons had followed Saul to the war: The firstborn was Eliab; the second, Abinadab; and the third, Shammah. ¹⁴David was the youngest. The three oldest followed Saul, ¹⁵but David went back and

a 11 Some Septuagint manuscripts; Hebrew *not gather around*   *b 14* Or *injurious*; also in verses 15, 16 and 23   *c 4* Hebrew *was six cubits and a span* (about 3 meters)   *d 5* That is, about 125 pounds (about 57 kilograms)   *e 7* That is, about 15 pounds (about 7 kilograms) forth from Saul to tend his father's sheep at Bethlehem.

¹⁶For forty days the Philistine came forward every morning and evening and took his stand.

¹⁷Now Jesse said to his son David, "Take this ephah*ᵃ* of roasted grain and these ten loaves of bread for your brothers and hurry to their camp. ¹⁸Take along these ten cheeses to the commander of their unit.*ᵇ* See how your brothers are and bring back some assurance*ᶜ* from them. ¹⁹They are with Saul and all the men of Israel in the Valley of Elah, fighting against the Philistines."

²⁰Early in the morning David left the flock with a shepherd, loaded up and set out, as Jesse had directed. He reached the camp as the army was going out to its battle positions, shouting the war cry. ²¹Israel and the Philistines were drawing up their lines facing each other. ²²David left his things with the keeper of supplies, ran to the battle lines and greeted his brothers. ²³As he was talking with them, Goliath, the Philistine champion from Gath, stepped out from his lines and shouted his usual defiance, and David heard it. ²⁴When the Israelites saw the man, they all ran from him in great fear.

²⁵Now the Israelites had been saying, "Do you see how this man keeps coming out? He comes out to defy Israel. The king will give great wealth to the man who kills him. He will also give him his daughter in marriage and will exempt his father's family from taxes in Israel."

²⁶David asked the men standing near him, "What will be done for the man who kills this Philistine and removes this disgrace from Israel? Who is this uncircumcised Philistine that he should defy the armies of the living God?"

²⁷They repeated to him what they had been saying and told him, "This is what will be done for the man who kills him."

²⁸When Eliab, David's oldest brother, heard him speaking with the men, he burned with anger at him and asked, "Why have you come down here? And with whom did you leave those few sheep in the desert? I know how conceited you are and how wicked your heart is; you came down only to watch the battle."

²⁹"Now what have I done?" said David. "Can't I even speak?" ³⁰He then turned away to someone else and brought up the same matter, and the men

answered him as before. ³¹What David said was overheard and reported to Saul, and Saul sent for him.

³²David said to Saul, "Let no one lose heart on account of this Philistine; your servant will go and fight him."

³³Saul replied, "You are not able to go out against this Philistine and fight him; you are only a boy, and he has been a fighting man from his youth."

³⁴But David said to Saul, "Your servant has been keeping his father's sheep. When a lion or a bear came and carried off a sheep from the flock, ³⁵I went after it, struck it and rescued the sheep from its mouth. When it turned on me, I seized it by its hair, struck it and killed it. ³⁶Your servant has killed both the lion and the bear; this uncircumcised Philistine will be like one of them, because he has defied the armies of the living God. ³⁷The LORD who delivered me from the paw of the lion and the paw of the bear will deliver me from the hand of this Philistine."

Saul said to David, "Go, and the LORD be with you."

³⁸Then Saul dressed David in his own tunic. He put a coat of armor on him and a bronze helmet on his head. ³⁹David fastened on his sword over the tunic and tried walking around, because he was not used to them.

"I cannot go in these," he said to Saul, "because I am not used to them." So he took them off. ⁴⁰Then he took his staff in his hand, chose five smooth stones from the stream, put them in the pouch of his

ᵃ17 That is, probably about 3/5 bushel (about 22 liters) ᵇ18 Hebrew thousand ᶜ18 Or some token; or some pledge of spoils

POINT OF INTEREST

1 Samuel 17:36

David's confidence was not based on a youthful feeling of invincibility, but rather stemmed from a reliance on God's power. God had delivered David from danger before, and David believed God would do it again. God's past mercies became David's guarantees for future deliverance. What mercies in your past can become your guarantees for the future?

shepherd's bag and, with his sling in his hand, approached the Philistine. ⁴¹Meanwhile, the Philistine, with his shield bearer in front of him, kept coming closer to David. ⁴²He looked David over and saw that he was only a boy, ruddy and handsome, and he despised him. ⁴³He said to David, "Am I a dog, that you come at me with sticks?" And the Philistine cursed David by his gods. ⁴⁴"Come here," he said, "and I'll give your flesh to the birds of the air and the beasts of the field!"

⁴⁵David said to the Philistine, "You come against me with sword and spear and javelin, but I come against you in the name of the LORD Almighty, the God of the armies of Israel, whom you have defied. ⁴⁶This day the LORD will hand you over to me, and I'll strike you down and cut off your head. Today I will give the carcasses of the Philistine army to the birds of the air and the beasts of the earth, and the whole world will know that there is a God in Israel. ⁴⁷All those gathered here will know that it is not by sword or spear that the LORD saves; for the battle is the LORD's, and he will give all of you into our hands."

⁴⁸As the Philistine moved closer to attack him, David ran quickly toward the battle line to meet him. ⁴⁹Reaching into his bag and taking out a stone, he slung it and struck the Philistine on the forehead. The stone sank into his forehead, and he fell facedown on the ground.

⁵⁰So David triumphed over the Philistine with a sling and a stone; without a sword in his hand he struck down the Philistine and killed him.

⁵¹David ran and stood over him. He took hold of the Philistine's sword and drew it from the scabbard. After he killed him, he cut off his head with the sword.

When the Philistines saw that their hero was dead, they turned and ran. ⁵²Then the men of Israel and Judah surged forward with a shout and pursued the Philistines to the entrance of Gath*a* and to the gates of Ekron. Their dead were strewn along the Shaaraim road to Gath and Ekron. ⁵³When the Israelites returned from chasing the Philistines, they plundered their camp. ⁵⁴David took the Philistine's head and brought it to Jerusalem, and he put the Philistine's weapons in his own tent.

⁵⁵As Saul watched David going out to meet the Philistine, he said to Abner, commander of the army, "Abner, whose son is that young man?"

Abner replied, "As surely as you live, O king, I don't know."

⁵⁶The king said, "Find out whose son this young man is."

⁵⁷As soon as David returned from killing the Philistine, Abner took him and brought him before Saul, with David still holding the Philistine's head.

⁵⁸"Whose son are you, young man?" Saul asked him.

David said, "I am the son of your servant Jesse of Bethlehem."

Saul's Jealousy of David

18 After David had finished talking with Saul, Jonathan became one in spirit with David, and he loved him as himself. ²From that day Saul kept David with him and did not let him return to his father's house. ³And Jonathan made a covenant with David because he loved him as himself. ⁴Jonathan took off the robe he was wearing and gave it to David, along with his tunic, and even his sword, his bow and his belt.

⁵Whatever Saul sent him to do, David did it so successfully*b* that Saul gave him a high rank in the army. This pleased all the people, and Saul's officers as well.

⁶When the men were returning home after David had killed the Philistine, the women came out from all the towns of Israel to meet King Saul with singing and dancing, with joyful songs and with tambourines and lutes. ⁷As they danced, they sang:

"Saul has slain his thousands,
and David his tens of thousands."

⁸Saul was very angry; this refrain galled him. "They have credited David with tens of thousands," he thought, "but me with only thousands. What more can he get but the kingdom?" ⁹And from that time on Saul kept a jealous eye on David.

¹⁰The next day an evil*c* spirit from God came forcefully upon Saul. He was prophesying in his house, while David was playing the harp, as he usually did. Saul had a spear in his hand ¹¹and he hurled it, saying to himself, "I'll pin David to the wall." But David eluded him twice.

---

a52 Some Septuagint manuscripts; Hebrew *a valley*
b5 Or *wisely*   *c10* Or *injurious*

¹²Saul was afraid of David, because the LORD was with David but had left Saul. ¹³So he sent David away from him and gave him command over a thousand men, and David led the troops in their campaigns. ¹⁴In everything he did he had great success,ᵃ because the LORD was with him. ¹⁵When Saul saw how successfulᵇ he was, he was afraid of him. ¹⁶But all Israel and Judah loved David, because he led them in their campaigns.

¹⁷Saul said to David, "Here is my older daughter Merab. I will give her to you in marriage; only serve me bravely and fight the battles of the LORD." For Saul said to himself, "I will not raise a hand against him. Let the Philistines do that!"

¹⁸But David said to Saul, "Who am I, and what is my family or my father's clan in Israel, that I should become the king's son-in-law?" ¹⁹Soᶜ when the time came for Merab, Saul's daughter, to be given to David, she was given in marriage to Adriel of Meholah.

²⁰Now Saul's daughter Michal was in love with David, and when they told Saul about it, he was pleased. ²¹"I will give her to him," he thought, "so that she may be a snare to him and so that the hand of the Philistines may be against him." So Saul said to David, "Now you have a second opportunity to become my son-in-law."

²²Then Saul ordered his attendants: "Speak to David privately and say, 'Look, the king is pleased with you, and his attendants all like you; now become his son-in-law.' "

²³They repeated these words to David. But David said, "Do you think it is a small matter to become the king's son-in-law? I'm only a poor man and little known."

²⁴When Saul's servants told him what David had said, ²⁵Saul replied, "Say to David, 'The king wants no other price for the bride than a hundred Philistine foreskins, to take revenge on his enemies.' " Saul's plan was to have David fall by the hands of the Philistines.

²⁶When the attendants told David these things, he was pleased to become the king's son-in-law. So before the allotted time elapsed, ²⁷David and his men went out and killed two hundred Philistines. He brought their foreskins and presented the full number to the king so that he might become the king's son-in-law.

Then Saul gave him his daughter Michal in marriage.

²⁸When Saul realized that the LORD was with David and that his daughter Michal loved David, ²⁹Saul became still more afraid of him, and he remained his enemy the rest of his days.

³⁰The Philistine commanders continued to go out to battle, and as often as they did, David met with more successᵈ than the rest of Saul's officers, and his name became well known.

Saul Tries to Kill David

19 Saul told his son Jonathan and all the attendants to kill David. But Jonathan was very fond of David ²and warned him, "My father Saul is looking for a chance to kill you. Be on your guard tomorrow morning; go into hiding and stay there. ³I will go out and stand with my father in the field where you are. I'll speak to him about you and will tell you what I find out."

⁴Jonathan spoke well of David to Saul his father and said to him, "Let not the king do wrong to his servant David; he has not wronged you, and what he has done has benefited you greatly. ⁵He took his life in his hands when he killed the Philistine. The LORD won a great victory for all Israel, and you saw it and were glad. Why then would you do wrong to an innocent man like David by killing him for no reason?"

⁶Saul listened to Jonathan and took this oath: "As surely as the LORD lives, David will not be put to death."

⁷So Jonathan called David and told him the whole conversation. He brought

---

ᵃ14 Or *he was very wise*   ᵇ15 Or *wise*
ᶜ19 Or *However,*   ᵈ30 Or *David acted more wisely*

POINT OF INTEREST

1 Samuel 18:29

Is a comfortable life of love and approval a sign that you have God's blessing? Not necessarily. Jesus said that if you are God's servant, you can expect opposition from those who are at odds with God (see John 15:18).

him to Saul, and David was with Saul as before.

⁸Once more war broke out, and David went out and fought the Philistines. He struck them with such force that they fled before him.

⁹But an evil*a* spirit from the LORD came upon Saul as he was sitting in his house with his spear in his hand. While David was playing the harp, ¹⁰Saul tried to pin him to the wall with his spear, but David eluded him as Saul drove the spear into the wall. That night David made good his escape.

¹¹Saul sent men to David's house to watch it and to kill him in the morning. But Michal, David's wife, warned him, "If you don't run for your life tonight, tomorrow you'll be killed." ¹²So Michal let David down through a window, and he fled and escaped. ¹³Then Michal took an idol*b* and laid it on the bed, covering it with a garment and putting some goats' hair at the head.

¹⁴When Saul sent the men to capture David, Michal said, "He is ill."

¹⁵Then Saul sent the men back to see David and told them, "Bring him up to me in his bed so that I may kill him." ¹⁶But when the men entered, there was the idol in the bed, and at the head was some goats' hair.

¹⁷Saul said to Michal, "Why did you deceive me like this and send my enemy away so that he escaped?"

Michal told him, "He said to me, 'Let me get away. Why should I kill you?' "

¹⁸When David had fled and made his escape, he went to Samuel at Ramah and told him all that Saul had done to him. Then he and Samuel went to Naioth and stayed there. ¹⁹Word came to Saul: "David is in Naioth at Ramah"; ²⁰so he sent men to capture him. But when they saw a group of prophets prophesying, with Samuel standing there as their leader, the Spirit of God came upon Saul's men and they also prophesied. ²¹Saul was told about it, and he sent more men, and they prophesied too. Saul sent men a third time, and they also prophesied. ²²Finally, he himself left for Ramah and went to the great cistern at Secu. And he asked, "Where are Samuel and David?"

"Over in Naioth at Ramah," they said.

²³So Saul went to Naioth at Ramah. But the Spirit of God came even upon him, and he walked along prophesying until he came to Naioth. ²⁴He stripped off

his robes and also prophesied in Samuel's presence. He lay that way all that day and night. This is why people say, "Is Saul also among the prophets?"

David and Jonathan

20 Then David fled from Naioth at Ramah and went to Jonathan and asked, "What have I done? What is my crime? How have I wronged your father, that he is trying to take my life?"

²"Never!" Jonathan replied. "You are not going to die! Look, my father doesn't do anything, great or small, without confiding in me. Why would he hide this from me? It's not so!"

³But David took an oath and said, "Your father knows very well that I have found favor in your eyes, and he has said to himself, 'Jonathan must not know this or he will be grieved.' Yet as surely as the LORD lives and as you live, there is only a step between me and death."

⁴Jonathan said to David, "Whatever you want me to do, I'll do for you."

⁵So David said, "Look, tomorrow is the New Moon festival, and I am supposed to dine with the king; but let me go and hide in the field until the evening of the day after tomorrow. ⁶If your father misses me at all, tell him, 'David earnestly asked my permission to hurry to Bethlehem, his hometown, because an annual sacrifice is being made there for his whole clan.' ⁷If he says, 'Very well,' then your servant is safe. But if he loses his temper, you can be sure that he is determined to harm me. ⁸As for you, show kindness to your servant, for you have brought him into a covenant with you before the LORD. If I am guilty, then kill me yourself! Why hand me over to your father?"

⁹"Never!" Jonathan said. "If I had the least inkling that my father was determined to harm you, wouldn't I tell you?"

¹⁰David asked, "Who will tell me if your father answers you harshly?"

¹¹"Come," Jonathan said, "let's go out into the field." So they went there together.

¹²Then Jonathan said to David: "By the LORD, the God of Israel, I will surely sound out my father by this time the day after tomorrow! If he is favorably disposed toward you, will I not send you

a9 Or injurious   *b13 Hebrew teraphim; also in verse 16* word and let you know? ¹³But if my father is inclined to harm you, may the LORD deal with me, be it ever so severely, if I do not let you know and send you away safely. May the LORD be with you as he has been with my father. ¹⁴But show me unfailing kindness like that of the LORD as long as I live, so that I may not be killed, ¹⁵and do not ever cut off your kindness from my family—not even when the LORD has cut off every one of David's enemies from the face of the earth."

¹⁶So Jonathan made a covenant with the house of David, saying, "May the LORD call David's enemies to account." ¹⁷And Jonathan had David reaffirm his oath out of love for him, because he loved him as he loved himself.

¹⁸Then Jonathan said to David: "Tomorrow is the New Moon festival. You will be missed, because your seat will be empty. ¹⁹The day after tomorrow, toward evening, go to the place where you hid when this trouble began, and wait by the stone Ezel. ²⁰I will shoot three arrows to the side of it, as though I were shooting at a target. ²¹Then I will send a boy and say, 'Go, find the arrows.' If I say to him, 'Look, the arrows are on this side of you; bring them here,' then come, because, as surely as the LORD lives, you are safe; there is no danger. ²²But if I say to the boy, 'Look, the arrows are beyond you,' then you must go, because the LORD has sent you away. ²³And about the matter you and I discussed—remember, the LORD is witness between you and me forever."

²⁴So David hid in the field, and when the New Moon festival came, the king sat down to eat. ²⁵He sat in his customary place by the wall, opposite Jonathan,ᵃ and Abner sat next to Saul, but David's place was empty. ²⁶Saul said nothing that day, for he thought, "Something must have happened to David to make him ceremonially unclean—surely he is unclean." ²⁷But the next day, the second day of the month, David's place was empty again. Then Saul said to his son Jonathan, "Why hasn't the son of Jesse come to the meal, either yesterday or today?"

²⁸Jonathan answered, "David earnestly asked me for permission to go to Bethlehem. ²⁹He said, 'Let me go, because our family is observing a sacrifice in the town

and my brother has ordered me to be there. If I have found favor in your eyes, let me get away to see my brothers.' That is why he has not come to the king's table."

³⁰Saul's anger flared up at Jonathan and he said to him, "You son of a perverse and rebellious woman! Don't I know that you have sided with the son of Jesse to your own shame and to the shame of the mother who bore you? ³¹As long as the son of Jesse lives on this earth, neither you nor your kingdom will be established. Now send and bring him to me, for he must die!"

³²"Why should he be put to death? What has he done?" Jonathan asked his father. ³³But Saul hurled his spear at him to kill him. Then Jonathan knew that his father intended to kill David.

³⁴Jonathan got up from the table in fierce anger; on that second day of the month he did not eat, because he was grieved at his father's shameful treatment of David.

³⁵In the morning Jonathan went out to the field for his meeting with David. He had a small boy with him, ³⁶and he said to the boy, "Run and find the arrows I shoot." As the boy ran, he shot an arrow beyond him. ³⁷When the boy came to the place where Jonathan's arrow had fallen, Jonathan called out after him, "Isn't the arrow beyond you?" ³⁸Then he shouted, "Hurry! Go quickly! Don't stop!" The boy picked up the arrow and returned to his master. ³⁹(The boy knew nothing of all this; only Jonathan and David knew.) ⁴⁰Then Jonathan gave his weapons to the boy and said, "Go, carry them back to town."

⁴¹After the boy had gone, David got up from the south side ⌊of the stone⌋ and bowed down before Jonathan three times, with his face to the ground. Then they kissed each other and wept together—but David wept the most.

⁴²Jonathan said to David, "Go in peace, for we have sworn friendship with each other in the name of the LORD, saying, 'The LORD is witness between you and me, and between your descendants and my descendants forever.' " Then David left, and Jonathan went back to town.

ᵃ25 Septuagint; Hebrew *wall. Jonathan arose*

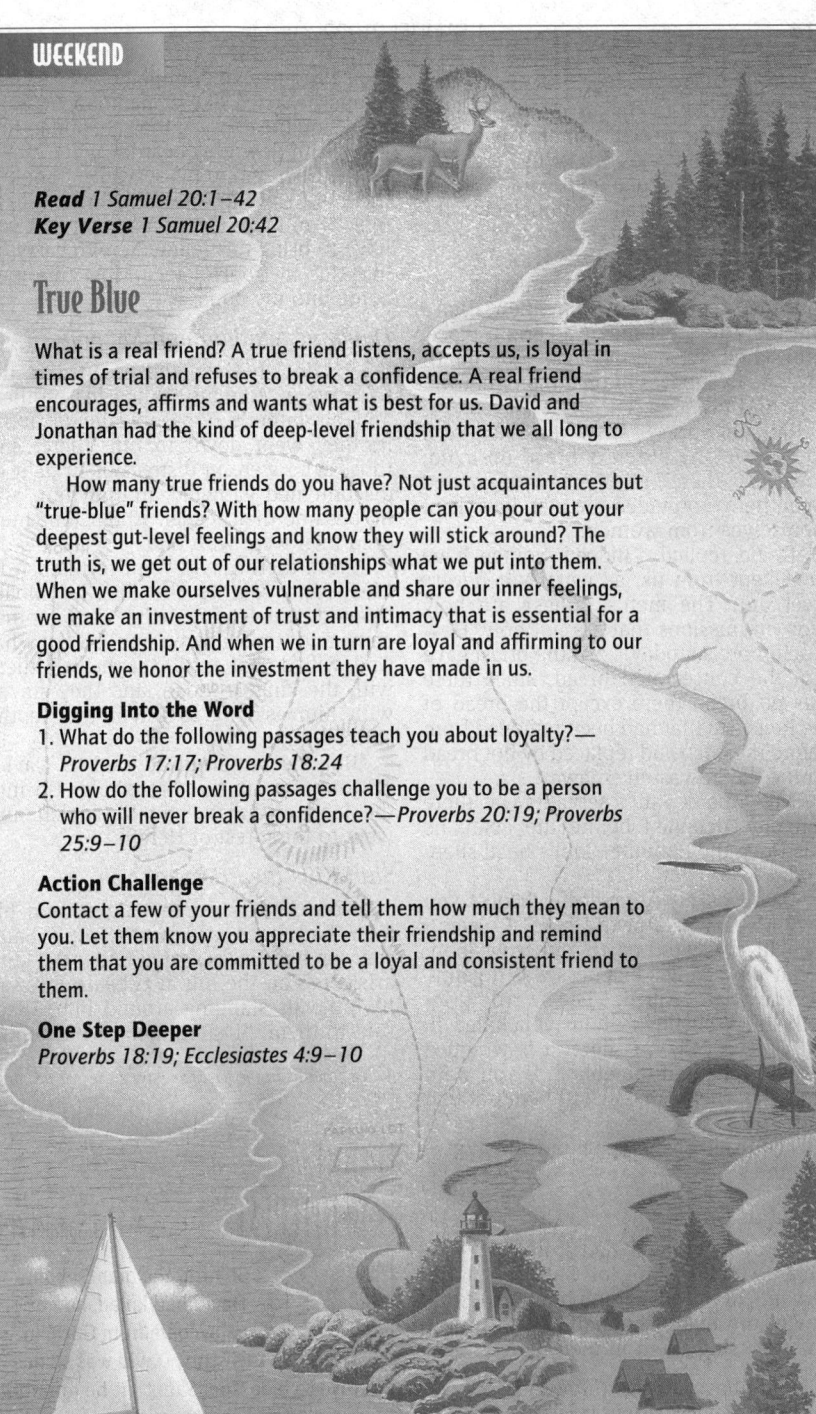

Read *1 Samuel 20:1–42*
Key Verse *1 Samuel 20:42*

True Blue

What is a real friend? A true friend listens, accepts us, is loyal in times of trial and refuses to break a confidence. A real friend encourages, affirms and wants what is best for us. David and Jonathan had the kind of deep-level friendship that we all long to experience.

How many true friends do you have? Not just acquaintances but "true-blue" friends? With how many people can you pour out your deepest gut-level feelings and know they will stick around? The truth is, we get out of our relationships what we put into them. When we make ourselves vulnerable and share our inner feelings, we make an investment of trust and intimacy that is essential for a good friendship. And when we in turn are loyal and affirming to our friends, we honor the investment they have made in us.

Digging Into the Word
1. What do the following passages teach you about loyalty?— *Proverbs 17:17; Proverbs 18:24*
2. How do the following passages challenge you to be a person who will never break a confidence?—*Proverbs 20:19; Proverbs 25:9–10*

Action Challenge
Contact a few of your friends and tell them how much they mean to you. Let them know you appreciate their friendship and remind them that you are committed to be a loyal and consistent friend to them.

One Step Deeper
Proverbs 18:19; Ecclesiastes 4:9–10

Go to page 323 for your next devotional reading.

David at Nob

21 David went to Nob, to Ahimelech the priest. Ahimelech trembled when he met him, and asked, "Why are you alone? Why is no one with you?"

²David answered Ahimelech the priest, "The king charged me with a certain matter and said to me, 'No one is to know anything about your mission and your instructions.' As for my men, I have told them to meet me at a certain place. ³Now then, what do you have on hand? Give me five loaves of bread, or whatever you can find."

⁴But the priest answered David, "I don't have any ordinary bread on hand; however, there is some consecrated bread here—provided the men have kept themselves from women."

⁵David replied, "Indeed women have been kept from us, as usual whenever*a* I set out. The men's things*b* are holy even on missions that are not holy. How much more so today!" ⁶So the priest gave him the consecrated bread, since there was no bread there except the bread of the Presence that had been removed from before the LORD and replaced by hot bread on the day it was taken away.

⁷Now one of Saul's servants was there that day, detained before the LORD; he was Doeg the Edomite, Saul's head shepherd.

⁸David asked Ahimelech, "Don't you have a spear or a sword here? I haven't brought my sword or any other weapon, because the king's business was urgent."

⁹The priest replied, "The sword of Goliath the Philistine, whom you killed in the Valley of Elah, is here; it is wrapped in a cloth behind the ephod. If you want it, take it; there is no sword here but that one."

David said, "There is none like it; give it to me."

David at Gath

¹⁰That day David fled from Saul and went to Achish king of Gath. ¹¹But the servants of Achish said to him, "Isn't this David, the king of the land? Isn't he the one they sing about in their dances:

" 'Saul has slain his thousands,
     and David his tens of thousands'?"

¹²David took these words to heart and was very much afraid of Achish king of Gath. ¹³So he pretended to be insane in their presence; and while he was in their hands he acted like a madman, making marks on the doors of the gate and letting saliva run down his beard.

¹⁴Achish said to his servants, "Look at the man! He is insane! Why bring him to me? ¹⁵Am I so short of madmen that you have to bring this fellow here to carry on like this in front of me? Must this man come into my house?"

David at Adullam and Mizpah

22 David left Gath and escaped to the cave of Adullam. When his brothers and his father's household heard about it, they went down to him there. ²All those who were in distress or in debt or discontented gathered around him, and he became their leader. About four hundred men were with him.

³From there David went to Mizpah in Moab and said to the king of Moab, "Would you let my father and mother come and stay with you until I learn what God will do for me?" ⁴So he left them with the king of Moab, and they stayed with him as long as David was in the stronghold.

⁵But the prophet Gad said to David, "Do not stay in the stronghold. Go into the land of Judah." So David left and went to the forest of Hereth.

Saul Kills the Priests of Nob

⁶Now Saul heard that David and his men had been discovered. And Saul, spear in hand, was seated under the tamarisk tree on the hill at Gibeah, with all his officials standing around him. ⁷Saul said to them, "Listen, men of Benjamin!

---

*a*5 Or *from us in the past few days since*   *b*5 Or *bodies*

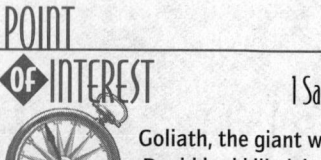

POINT OF INTEREST

1 Samuel 21:10

Goliath, the giant whom David had killed, had originally come from Gath. In this story, David was so desperate to hide from Saul that he ran right into Goliath's hometown. When he realized his tactical error, David pretended insanity and escaped. Through it all, God kept David safe.

Will the son of Jesse give all of you fields and vineyards? Will he make all of you commanders of thousands and commanders of hundreds? ⁸Is that why you have all conspired against me? No one tells me when my son makes a covenant with the son of Jesse. None of you is concerned about me or tells me that my son has incited my servant to lie in wait for me, as he does today."

⁹But Doeg the Edomite, who was standing with Saul's officials, said, "I saw the son of Jesse come to Ahimelech son of Ahitub at Nob. ¹⁰Ahimelech inquired of the LORD for him; he also gave him provisions and the sword of Goliath the Philistine."

¹¹Then the king sent for the priest Ahimelech son of Ahitub and his father's whole family, who were the priests at Nob, and they all came to the king. ¹²Saul said, "Listen now, son of Ahitub."

"Yes, my lord," he answered.

¹³Saul said to him, "Why have you conspired against me, you and the son of Jesse, giving him bread and a sword and inquiring of God for him, so that he has rebelled against me and lies in wait for me, as he does today?"

¹⁴Ahimelech answered the king, "Who of all your servants is as loyal as David, the king's son-in-law, captain of your bodyguard and highly respected in your household? ¹⁵Was that day the first time I inquired of God for him? Of course not! Let not the king accuse your servant or any of his father's family, for your servant knows nothing at all about this whole affair."

¹⁶But the king said, "You will surely die, Ahimelech, you and your father's whole family."

¹⁷Then the king ordered the guards at his side: "Turn and kill the priests of the LORD, because they too have sided with David. They knew he was fleeing, yet they did not tell me."

But the king's officials were not willing to raise a hand to strike the priests of the LORD.

¹⁸The king then ordered Doeg, "You turn and strike down the priests." So Doeg the Edomite turned and struck them down. That day he killed eighty-five men who wore the linen ephod. ¹⁹He also put to the sword Nob, the town of the priests, with its men and women, its children and infants, and its cattle, donkeys and sheep.

²⁰But Abiathar, a son of Ahimelech son of Ahitub, escaped and fled to join David. ²¹He told David that Saul had killed the priests of the LORD. ²²Then David said to Abiathar: "That day, when Doeg the Edomite was there, I knew he would be sure to tell Saul. I am responsible for the death of your father's whole family. ²³Stay with me; don't be afraid; the man who is seeking your life is seeking mine also. You will be safe with me."

David Saves Keilah

23 When David was told, "Look, the Philistines are fighting against Keilah and are looting the threshing floors," ²he inquired of the LORD, saying, "Shall I go and attack these Philistines?"

The LORD answered him, "Go, attack the Philistines and save Keilah."

³But David's men said to him, "Here in Judah we are afraid. How much more, then, if we go to Keilah against the Philistine forces!"

⁴Once again David inquired of the LORD, and the LORD answered him, "Go down to Keilah, for I am going to give the Philistines into your hand." ⁵So David and his men went to Keilah, fought the Philistines and carried off their livestock. He inflicted heavy losses on the Philistines and saved the people of Keilah. ⁶(Now Abiathar son of Ahimelech had brought the ephod down with him when he fled to David at Keilah.)

Saul Pursues David

⁷Saul was told that David had gone to Keilah, and he said, "God has handed him over to me, for David has imprisoned himself by entering a town with gates and bars." ⁸And Saul called up all his forces for battle, to go down to Keilah to besiege David and his men.

POINT OF INTEREST

1 Samuel 23:2

A spiritual leader rarely follows public opinion, but instead seeks godly advice, follows God in obedient faith and leads others to do the same. What leadership qualities did David show in this situation?

⁹When David learned that Saul was plotting against him, he said to Abiathar the priest, "Bring the ephod." ¹⁰David said, "O LORD, God of Israel, your servant has heard definitely that Saul plans to come to Keilah and destroy the town on account of me. ¹¹Will the citizens of Keilah surrender me to him? Will Saul come down, as your servant has heard? O LORD, God of Israel, tell your servant."

And the LORD said, "He will."

¹²Again David asked, "Will the citizens of Keilah surrender me and my men to Saul?"

And the LORD said, "They will."

¹³So David and his men, about six hundred in number, left Keilah and kept moving from place to place. When Saul was told that David had escaped from Keilah, he did not go there.

¹⁴David stayed in the desert strongholds and in the hills of the Desert of Ziph. Day after day Saul searched for him, but God did not give David into his hands.

¹⁵While David was at Horesh in the Desert of Ziph, he learned that Saul had come out to take his life. ¹⁶And Saul's son Jonathan went to David at Horesh and helped him find strength in God. ¹⁷"Don't be afraid," he said. "My father Saul will not lay a hand on you. You will be king over Israel, and I will be second to you. Even my father Saul knows this." ¹⁸The two of them made a covenant before the LORD. Then Jonathan went home, but David remained at Horesh.

¹⁹The Ziphites went up to Saul at Gibeah and said, "Is not David hiding among us in the strongholds at Horesh, on the hill of Hakilah, south of Jeshimon? ²⁰Now, O king, come down whenever it pleases you to do so, and we will be responsible for handing him over to the king."

²¹Saul replied, "The LORD bless you for your concern for me. ²²Go and make further preparation. Find out where David usually goes and who has seen him there. They tell me he is very crafty. ²³Find out about all the hiding places he uses and come back to me with definite information.ᵃ Then I will go with you; if he is in the area, I will track him down among all the clans of Judah."

²⁴So they set out and went to Ziph ahead of Saul. Now David and his men were in the Desert of Maon, in the Arabah south of Jeshimon. ²⁵Saul and his men began the search, and when David was told about it, he went down to the rock and stayed in the Desert of Maon. When Saul heard this, he went into the Desert of Maon in pursuit of David.

²⁶Saul was going along one side of the mountain, and David and his men were on the other side, hurrying to get away from Saul. As Saul and his forces were closing in on David and his men to capture them, ²⁷a messenger came to Saul, saying, "Come quickly! The Philistines are raiding the land." ²⁸Then Saul broke off his pursuit of David and went to meet the Philistines. That is why they call this place Sela Hammahlekoth.ᵇ ²⁹And David went up from there and lived in the strongholds of En Gedi.

David Spares Saul's Life

24 After Saul returned from pursuing the Philistines, he was told, "David is in the Desert of En Gedi." ²So Saul took three thousand chosen men from all Israel and set out to look for David and his men near the Crags of the Wild Goats.

³He came to the sheep pens along the way; a cave was there, and Saul went in to relieve himself. David and his men were far back in the cave. ⁴The men said, "This is the day the LORD spoke of when he saidᶜ to you, 'I will give your enemy into your hands for you to deal with as you wish.' " Then David crept up unnoticed and cut off a corner of Saul's robe.

⁵Afterward, David was conscience-stricken for having cut off a corner of his robe. ⁶He said to his men, "The LORD forbid that I should do such a thing to my master, the LORD's anointed, or lift my hand against him; for he is the anointed

---

ᵃ23 Or me at Nacon   ᵇ28 Sela Hammahlekoth
means rock of parting.   ᶜ4 Or "Today the LORD is
saying

POINT
OF INTEREST   1 Samuel 23:16

How does your relationship with your friends affect you? What effect do you have on the lives of your friends? What can you do to help others find strength in God?

of the LORD." 7With these words David rebuked his men and did not allow them to attack Saul. And Saul left the cave and went his way.

8Then David went out of the cave and called out to Saul, "My lord the king!" When Saul looked behind him, David bowed down and prostrated himself with his face to the ground. 9He said to Saul, "Why do you listen when men say, 'David is bent on harming you'? 10This day you have seen with your own eyes how the LORD delivered you into my hands in the cave. Some urged me to kill you, but I spared you; I said, 'I will not lift my hand against my master, because he is the LORD's anointed.' 11See, my father, look at this piece of your robe in my hand! I cut off the corner of your robe but did not kill you. Now understand and recognize that I am not guilty of wrongdoing or rebellion. I have not wronged you, but you are hunting me down to take my life. 12May the LORD judge between you and me. And may the LORD avenge the wrongs you have done to me, but my hand will not touch you. 13As the old saying goes, 'From evildoers come evil deeds,' so my hand will not touch you.

14"Against whom has the king of Israel come out? Whom are you pursuing? A dead dog? A flea? 15May the LORD be our judge and decide between us. May he consider my cause and uphold it; may he vindicate me by delivering me from your hand."

16When David finished saying this, Saul asked, "Is that your voice, David my son?" And he wept aloud. 17"You are more righteous than I," he said. "You have treated me well, but I have treated you badly. 18You have just now told me of the good you did to me; the LORD delivered me into your hands, but you did not kill me. 19When a man finds his enemy, does he let him get away unharmed? May the LORD reward you well for the way you treated me today. 20I know that you will surely be king and that the kingdom of Israel will be established in your hands. 21Now swear to me by the LORD that you will not cut off my descendants or wipe out my name from my father's family."

22So David gave his oath to Saul. Then Saul returned home, but David and his men went up to the stronghold.

David, Nabal and Abigail

25 Now Samuel died, and all Israel assembled and mourned for him; and they buried him at his home in Ramah.

Then David moved down into the Desert of Maon.*a* 2A certain man in Maon, who had property there at Carmel, was very wealthy. He had a thousand goats and three thousand sheep, which he was shearing in Carmel. 3His name was Nabal and his wife's name was Abigail. She was an intelligent and beautiful woman, but her husband, a Calebite, was surly and mean in his dealings.

4While David was in the desert, he heard that Nabal was shearing sheep. 5So he sent ten young men and said to them, "Go up to Nabal at Carmel and greet him in my name. 6Say to him: 'Long life to you! Good health to you and your household! And good health to all that is yours!

7" 'Now I hear that it is sheep-shearing time. When your shepherds were with us, we did not mistreat them, and the whole time they were at Carmel nothing of theirs was missing. 8Ask your own servants and they will tell you. Therefore be favorable toward my young men, since we come at a festive time. Please give your servants and your son David whatever you can find for them.' "

9When David's men arrived, they gave Nabal this message in David's name. Then they waited.

10Nabal answered David's servants, "Who is this David? Who is this son of Jesse? Many servants are breaking away from their masters these days. 11Why should I take my bread and water, and the meat I have slaughtered for my shearers, and give it to men coming from who knows where?"

12David's men turned around and went back. When they arrived, they reported every word. 13David said to his men, "Put on your swords!" So they put on their swords, and David put on his. About four hundred men went up with David, while two hundred stayed with the supplies.

14One of the servants told Nabal's wife Abigail: "David sent messengers from the desert to give our master his greetings, but he hurled insults at them. 15Yet these men were very good to us. They did not mistreat us, and the whole time we were out in the fields near them nothing was

a 1 Some Septuagint manuscripts; Hebrew Paran

missing. ¹⁶Night and day they were a wall around us all the time we were herding our sheep near them. ¹⁷Now think it over and see what you can do, because disaster is hanging over our master and his whole household. He is such a wicked man that no one can talk to him."

¹⁸Abigail lost no time. She took two hundred loaves of bread, two skins of wine, five dressed sheep, five seahs*ᵃ* of roasted grain, a hundred cakes of raisins and two hundred cakes of pressed figs, and loaded them on donkeys. ¹⁹Then she told her servants, "Go on ahead; I'll follow you." But she did not tell her husband Nabal.

²⁰As she came riding her donkey into a mountain ravine, there were David and his men descending toward her, and she met them. ²¹David had just said, "It's been useless—all my watching over this fellow's property in the desert so that nothing of his was missing. He has paid me back evil for good. ²²May God deal with David,*ᵇ* be it ever so severely, if by morning I leave alive one male of all who belong to him!"

²³When Abigail saw David, she quickly got off her donkey and bowed down before David with her face to the ground. ²⁴She fell at his feet and said: "My lord, let the blame be on me alone. Please let your servant speak to you; hear what your servant has to say. ²⁵May my lord pay no attention to that wicked man Nabal. He is just like his name—his name is Fool, and folly goes with him. But as for me, your servant, I did not see the men my master sent.

²⁶"Now since the LORD has kept you, my master, from bloodshed and from avenging yourself with your own hands, as surely as the LORD lives and as you live, may your enemies and all who intend to harm my master be like Nabal. ²⁷And let this gift, which your servant has brought to my master, be given to the men who follow you. ²⁸Please forgive your servant's offense, for the LORD will certainly make a lasting dynasty for my master, because he fights the LORD's battles. Let no wrongdoing be found in you as long as you live. ²⁹Even though someone is pursuing you to take your life, the life of my master will be bound securely in the bundle of the living by the LORD your God. But the lives of your enemies he will hurl away as from the pocket of a sling. ³⁰When the LORD has done for my master

every good thing he promised concerning him and has appointed him leader over Israel, ³¹my master will not have on his conscience the staggering burden of needless bloodshed or of having avenged himself. And when the LORD has brought my master success, remember your servant."

³²David said to Abigail, "Praise be to the LORD, the God of Israel, who has sent you today to meet me. ³³May you be blessed for your good judgment and for keeping me from bloodshed this day and from avenging myself with my own hands. ³⁴Otherwise, as surely as the LORD, the God of Israel, lives, who has kept me from harming you, if you had not come quickly to meet me, not one male belonging to Nabal would have been left alive by daybreak."

³⁵Then David accepted from her hand what she had brought him and said, "Go home in peace. I have heard your words and granted your request."

³⁶When Abigail went to Nabal, he was in the house holding a banquet like that of a king. He was in high spirits and very drunk. So she told him nothing until daybreak. ³⁷Then in the morning, when Nabal was sober, his wife told him all these things, and his heart failed him and he became like a stone. ³⁸About ten days later, the LORD struck Nabal and he died.

³⁹When David heard that Nabal was dead, he said, "Praise be to the LORD, who has upheld my cause against Nabal for treating me with contempt. He has kept his servant from doing wrong and has brought Nabal's wrongdoing down on his own head."

Then David sent word to Abigail, ask-

ᵃ18 That is, probably about a bushel (about 37 liters)   *ᵇ22* Some Septuagint manuscripts; Hebrew *with David's enemies*

POINT OF INTEREST

1 Samuel 25:18

Most people waste time just trying to begin a task. Abigail didn't waste a moment. Her insight, determination and initiative averted disaster and saved the lives of many people. Is there anything you need to begin today?

ing her to become his wife. ⁴⁰His servants went to Carmel and said to Abigail, "David has sent us to you to take you to become his wife."

⁴¹She bowed down with her face to the ground and said, "Here is your maidservant, ready to serve you and wash the feet of my master's servants." ⁴²Abigail quickly got on a donkey and, attended by her five maids, went with David's messengers and became his wife. ⁴³David had also married Ahinoam of Jezreel, and they both were his wives. ⁴⁴But Saul had given his daughter Michal, David's wife, to Paltiel*a* son of Laish, who was from Gallim.

David Again Spares Saul's Life

26 The Ziphites went to Saul at Gibeah and said, "Is not David hiding on the hill of Hakilah, which faces Jeshimon?" ²So Saul went down to the Desert of Ziph, with his three thousand chosen men of Israel, to search there for David. ³Saul made his camp beside the road on the hill of Hakilah facing Jeshimon, but David stayed in the desert. When he saw that Saul had followed him there, ⁴he sent out scouts and learned that Saul had definitely arrived.*b*

⁵Then David set out and went to the place where Saul had camped. He saw where Saul and Abner son of Ner, the commander of the army, had lain down. Saul was lying inside the camp, with the army encamped around him. ⁶David then asked Ahimelech the Hittite and Abishai son of Zeruiah, Joab's brother, "Who will go down into the camp with me to Saul?"

"I'll go with you," said Abishai.

⁷So David and Abishai went to the army by night, and there was Saul, lying asleep inside the camp with his spear stuck in the ground near his head. Abner and the soldiers were lying around him. ⁸Abishai said to David, "Today God has delivered your enemy into your hands. Now let me pin him to the ground with one thrust of my spear; I won't strike him twice."

⁹But David said to Abishai, "Don't destroy him! Who can lay a hand on the LORD's anointed and be guiltless? ¹⁰As surely as the LORD lives," he said, "the LORD himself will strike him; either his time will come and he will die, or he will go into battle and perish. ¹¹But the LORD forbid that I should lay a hand on the

LORD's anointed. Now get the spear and water jug that are near his head, and let's go."

¹²So David took the spear and water jug near Saul's head, and they left. No one saw or knew about it, nor did anyone wake up. They were all sleeping, because the LORD had put them into a deep sleep.

¹³Then David crossed over to the other side and stood on top of the hill some distance away; there was a wide space between them. ¹⁴He called out to the army and to Abner son of Ner, "Aren't you going to answer me, Abner?"

Abner replied, "Who are you who calls to the king?"

¹⁵David said, "You're a man, aren't you? And who is like you in Israel? Why didn't you guard your lord the king? Someone came to destroy your lord the king. ¹⁶What you have done is not good. As surely as the LORD lives, you and your men deserve to die, because you did not guard your master, the LORD's anointed. Look around you. Where are the king's spear and water jug that were near his head?"

¹⁷Saul recognized David's voice and said, "Is that your voice, David my son?"

David replied, "Yes it is, my lord the king." ¹⁸And he added, "Why is my lord pursuing his servant? What have I done, and what wrong am I guilty of? ¹⁹Now let my lord the king listen to his servant's words. If the LORD has incited you against me, then may he accept an offering. If, however, men have done it, may they be cursed before the LORD! They have now driven me from my share in the LORD's

---

a44 Hebrew Palti, *a variant of* Paltiel   *b4 Or had come to Nacon*

POINT OF INTEREST

1 Samuel 26:18

David was in his late teens when Samuel anointed him to be the next king of Israel. But he did not become king until he had spent the next twenty years either serving King Saul or running away from him. David learned that God's will and timing are not always the same as ours.

inheritance and have said, 'Go, serve other gods.' ²⁰Now do not let my blood fall to the ground far from the presence of the LORD. The king of Israel has come out to look for a flea—as one hunts a partridge in the mountains."

²¹Then Saul said, "I have sinned. Come back, David my son. Because you considered my life precious today, I will not try to harm you again. Surely I have acted like a fool and have erred greatly."

²²"Here is the king's spear," David answered. "Let one of your young men come over and get it. ²³The LORD rewards every man for his righteousness and faithfulness. The LORD delivered you into my hands today, but I would not lay a hand on the LORD's anointed. ²⁴As surely as I valued your life today, so may the LORD value my life and deliver me from all trouble."

²⁵Then Saul said to David, "May you be blessed, my son David; you will do great things and surely triumph."

So David went on his way, and Saul returned home.

David Among the Philistines

27 But David thought to himself, "One of these days I will be destroyed by the hand of Saul. The best thing I can do is to escape to the land of the Philistines. Then Saul will give up searching for me anywhere in Israel, and I will slip out of his hand."

²So David and the six hundred men with him left and went over to Achish son of Maoch king of Gath. ³David and his men settled in Gath with Achish. Each man had his family with him, and David had his two wives: Ahinoam of Jezreel and Abigail of Carmel, the widow of Nabal. ⁴When Saul was told that David had fled to Gath, he no longer searched for him.

⁵Then David said to Achish, "If I have found favor in your eyes, let a place be assigned to me in one of the country towns, that I may live there. Why should your servant live in the royal city with you?"

⁶So on that day Achish gave him Ziklag, and it has belonged to the kings of Judah ever since. ⁷David lived in Philistine territory a year and four months.

⁸Now David and his men went up and raided the Geshurites, the Girzites and the Amalekites. (From ancient times these peoples had lived in the land extending to Shur and Egypt.) ⁹Whenever David attacked an area, he did not leave a man or woman alive, but took sheep and cattle, donkeys and camels, and clothes. Then he returned to Achish.

¹⁰When Achish asked, "Where did you go raiding today?" David would say, "Against the Negev of Judah" or "Against the Negev of Jerahmeel" or "Against the Negev of the Kenites." ¹¹He did not leave a man or woman alive to be brought to Gath, for he thought, "They might inform on us and say, 'This is what David did.'" And such was his practice as long as he lived in Philistine territory. ¹²Achish trusted David and said to himself, "He has become so odious to his people, the Israelites, that he will be my servant forever."

Saul and the Witch of Endor

28 In those days the Philistines gathered their forces to fight against Israel. Achish said to David, "You must understand that you and your men will accompany me in the army."

²David said, "Then you will see for yourself what your servant can do."

Achish replied, "Very well, I will make you my bodyguard for life."

³Now Samuel was dead, and all Israel had mourned for him and buried him in his own town of Ramah. Saul had expelled the mediums and spiritists from the land.

⁴The Philistines assembled and came and set up camp at Shunem, while Saul gathered all the Israelites and set up camp at Gilboa. ⁵When Saul saw the Philistine army, he was afraid; terror filled his heart. ⁶He inquired of the LORD, but the LORD did not answer him by dreams or Urim or prophets. ⁷Saul then said to his attendants, "Find me a woman who is a medium, so I may go and inquire of her."

"There is one in Endor," they said.

⁸So Saul disguised himself, putting on other clothes, and at night he and two men went to the woman. "Consult a spirit for me," he said, "and bring up for me the one I name."

⁹But the woman said to him, "Surely you know what Saul has done. He has cut off the mediums and spiritists from the land. Why have you set a trap for my life to bring about my death?"

¹⁰Saul swore to her by the LORD, "As surely as the LORD lives, you will not be punished for this."

¹¹Then the woman asked, "Whom shall I bring up for you?"

"Bring up Samuel," he said.

¹²When the woman saw Samuel, she cried out at the top of her voice and said to Saul, "Why have you deceived me? You are Saul!"

¹³The king said to her, "Don't be afraid. What do you see?"

The woman said, "I see a spirit*a* coming up out of the ground."

¹⁴"What does he look like?" he asked.

"An old man wearing a robe is coming up," she said.

Then Saul knew it was Samuel, and he bowed down and prostrated himself with his face to the ground.

¹⁵Samuel said to Saul, "Why have you disturbed me by bringing me up?"

"I am in great distress," Saul said. "The Philistines are fighting against me, and God has turned away from me. He no longer answers me, either by prophets or by dreams. So I have called on you to tell me what to do."

¹⁶Samuel said, "Why do you consult me, now that the LORD has turned away from you and become your enemy? ¹⁷The LORD has done what he predicted through me. The LORD has torn the kingdom out of your hands and given it to one of your neighbors—to David. ¹⁸Because you did not obey the LORD or carry out his fierce wrath against the Amalekites, the LORD has done this to you today. ¹⁹The LORD will hand over both Israel and you to the Philistines, and tomorrow you and your sons will be with me. The LORD will also hand over the army of Israel to the Philistines."

²⁰Immediately Saul fell full length on the ground, filled with fear because of Samuel's words. His strength was gone, for he had eaten nothing all that day and night.

²¹When the woman came to Saul and saw that he was greatly shaken, she said, "Look, your maidservant has obeyed you. I took my life in my hands and did what you told me to do. ²²Now please listen to your servant and let me give you some food so you may eat and have the strength to go on your way."

²³He refused and said, "I will not eat."

But his men joined the woman in urging him, and he listened to them. He got up from the ground and sat on the couch.

²⁴The woman had a fattened calf at the house, which she butchered at once. She took some flour, kneaded it and baked bread without yeast. ²⁵Then she set it before Saul and his men, and they ate. That same night they got up and left.

Achish Sends David Back to Ziklag

29 The Philistines gathered all their forces at Aphek, and Israel camped by the spring in Jezreel. ²As the Philistine rulers marched with their units of hundreds and thousands, David and his men were marching at the rear with Achish. ³The commanders of the Philistines asked, "What about these Hebrews?"

Achish replied, "Is this not David, who was an officer of Saul king of Israel? He has already been with me for over a year, and from the day he left Saul until now, I have found no fault in him."

⁴But the Philistine commanders were angry with him and said, "Send the man back, that he may return to the place you assigned him. He must not go with us into battle, or he will turn against us during the fighting. How better could he regain his master's favor than by taking the heads of our own men? ⁵Isn't this the David they sang about in their dances:

" 'Saul has slain his thousands,
    and David his tens of thousands'?"

⁶So Achish called David and said to him, "As surely as the LORD lives, you have been reliable, and I would be pleased to have you serve with me in the army. From the day you came to me until now, I have found no fault in you, but the rulers don't approve of you. ⁷Turn back

---

a13 Or see spirits; or see gods

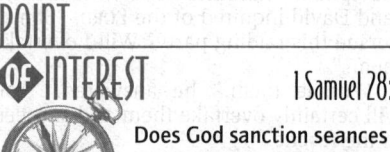

POINT OF INTEREST

1 Samuel 28:7

Does God sanction seances and consulting with spirits of the dead? The answer is an emphatic *No!* Deuteronomy 18:10–11 clearly forbids these practices. Saul's action was the desperate behavior of a person whom God had already abandoned.

and go in peace; do nothing to displease the Philistine rulers."

⁸"But what have I done?" asked David. "What have you found against your servant from the day I came to you until now? Why can't I go and fight against the enemies of my lord the king?"

⁹Achish answered, "I know that you have been as pleasing in my eyes as an angel of God; nevertheless, the Philistine commanders have said, 'He must not go up with us into battle.' ¹⁰Now get up early, along with your master's servants who have come with you, and leave in the morning as soon as it is light."

¹¹So David and his men got up early in the morning to go back to the land of the Philistines, and the Philistines went up to Jezreel.

David Destroys the Amalekites

30 David and his men reached Ziklag on the third day. Now the Amalekites had raided the Negev and Ziklag. They had attacked Ziklag and burned it, ²and had taken captive the women and all who were in it, both young and old. They killed none of them, but carried them off as they went on their way.

³When David and his men came to Ziklag, they found it destroyed by fire and their wives and sons and daughters taken captive. ⁴So David and his men wept aloud until they had no strength left to weep. ⁵David's two wives had been captured—Ahinoam of Jezreel and Abigail, the widow of Nabal of Carmel. ⁶David was greatly distressed because the men were talking of stoning him; each one was bitter in spirit because of his sons and daughters. But David found strength in the LORD his God.

⁷Then David said to Abiathar the priest, the son of Ahimelech, "Bring me the ephod." Abiathar brought it to him, ⁸and David inquired of the LORD, "Shall I pursue this raiding party? Will I overtake them?"

"Pursue them," he answered. "You will certainly overtake them and succeed in the rescue."

⁹David and the six hundred men with him came to the Besor Ravine, where some stayed behind, ¹⁰for two hundred men were too exhausted to cross the ravine. But David and four hundred men continued the pursuit.

¹¹They found an Egyptian in a field and brought him to David. They gave him water to drink and food to eat— ¹²part of a cake of pressed figs and two cakes of raisins. He ate and was revived, for he had not eaten any food or drunk any water for three days and three nights.

¹³David asked him, "To whom do you belong, and where do you come from?"

He said, "I am an Egyptian, the slave of an Amalekite. My master abandoned me when I became ill three days ago. ¹⁴We raided the Negev of the Kerethites and the territory belonging to Judah and the Negev of Caleb. And we burned Ziklag."

¹⁵David asked him, "Can you lead me down to this raiding party?"

He answered, "Swear to me before God that you will not kill me or hand me over to my master, and I will take you down to them."

¹⁶He led David down, and there they were, scattered over the countryside, eating, drinking and reveling because of the great amount of plunder they had taken from the land of the Philistines and from Judah. ¹⁷David fought them from dusk until the evening of the next day, and none of them got away, except four hundred young men who rode off on camels and fled. ¹⁸David recovered everything the Amalekites had taken, including his two wives. ¹⁹Nothing was missing: young or old, boy or girl, plunder or anything else they had taken. David brought everything back. ²⁰He took all the flocks and herds, and his men drove them ahead of the other livestock, saying, "This is David's plunder."

²¹Then David came to the two hundred men who had been too exhausted to follow him and who were left behind at the Besor Ravine. They came out to meet David and the people with him. As David and his men approached, he greeted them. ²²But all the evil men and troublemakers among David's followers said, "Because they did not go out with us, we will not share with them the plunder we recovered. However, each man may take his wife and children and go."

²³David replied, "No, my brothers, you must not do that with what the LORD has given us. He has protected us and handed over to us the forces that came against us. ²⁴Who will listen to what you say? The share of the man who stayed with the supplies is to be the same as that of him who went down to the battle. All will

share alike." ²⁵David made this a statute and ordinance for Israel from that day to this.

²⁶When David arrived in Ziklag, he sent some of the plunder to the elders of Judah, who were his friends, saying, "Here is a present for you from the plunder of the LORD's enemies."

²⁷He sent it to those who were in Bethel, Ramoth Negev and Jattir; ²⁸to those in Aroer, Siphmoth, Eshtemoa ²⁹and Racal; to those in the towns of the Jerahmeelites and the Kenites; ³⁰to those in Hormah, Bor Ashan, Athach ³¹and Hebron; and to those in all the other places where David and his men had roamed.

Saul Takes His Life

31 Now the Philistines fought against Israel; the Israelites fled before them, and many fell slain on Mount Gilboa. ²The Philistines pressed hard after Saul and his sons, and they killed his sons Jonathan, Abinadab and Malki-Shua. ³The fighting grew fierce around Saul, and when the archers overtook him, they wounded him critically.

⁴Saul said to his armor-bearer, "Draw

MONDAY

Read *1 Samuel 30:1–31*
Key Verse *1 Samuel 30:24*

All Will Share Alike – Phil Ward

Mention the words "group project" and you'll get a variety of responses. Some love the interaction, while others dread the seemingly endless meetings preceding the final product. A lot of us remember group projects as studies in frustration. There always seemed to be certain members who didn't pull their own weight and who became the undeserving beneficiaries of the good grade. That's when the "they-don't-deserve-it" attitude reared its ugly head in me. Instead of enjoying the A we had earned, I would sulk about the lack of fairness. What I lacked was a sense of graciousness such as King David clearly exemplified.

Imagine pursuing a vast army with just six hundred men, and then having one-third of your forces drop out due to exhaustion! Had it not been for the promise of God, even David might have abandoned the attack. The battle was won and the plunder recovered through the efforts of four hundred men. But what of the tuckered-out two hundred? I probably would have joined with those who said, "Because they did not go out with us, we will not share with them the plunder we recovered" (1 Samuel 30:22). David firmly stated, "All will share alike" (1 Samuel 30:24). David understood that *God* had won the victory. So the entire army—not just those who had abandoned the chase—received what they did not deserve.

How often we seek justice for ourselves rather than mercy for others! "I deserved an A, but he only earned a C," was my common reaction on group projects. My bad attitude reflected a failure on my part to realize that none of us deserves anything apart from God's grace. When we feel used, the choice is ours. If we're grace-givers, not "sulkers," we'll be amazed at how God will use our lives.

A Deeper Look
Matthew 5:43–48; Matthew 20:1–16

Go to page 333 for your next devotional reading.

your sword and run me through, or these uncircumcised fellows will come and run me through and abuse me."

But his armor-bearer was terrified and would not do it; so Saul took his own sword and fell on it. ⁵When the armor-bearer saw that Saul was dead, he too fell on his sword and died with him. ⁶So Saul and his three sons and his armor-bearer and all his men died together that same day.

⁷When the Israelites along the valley and those across the Jordan saw that the Israelite army had fled and that Saul and his sons had died, they abandoned their towns and fled. And the Philistines came and occupied them.

⁸The next day, when the Philistines came to strip the dead, they found Saul and his three sons fallen on Mount Gilboa. ⁹They cut off his head and stripped off his armor, and they sent messengers throughout the land of the Philistines to proclaim the news in the temple of their idols and among their people. ¹⁰They put his armor in the temple of the Ashtoreths and fastened his body to the wall of Beth Shan.

¹¹When the people of Jabesh Gilead heard of what the Philistines had done to Saul, ¹²all their valiant men journeyed through the night to Beth Shan. They took down the bodies of Saul and his sons from the wall of Beth Shan and went to Jabesh, where they burned them. ¹³Then they took their bones and buried them under a tamarisk tree at Jabesh, and they fasted seven days.

What does it mean to be a person "after [God's] own heart" (1 Samuel 13:14)? To find out, look at David's life. David's greatness resided in his response to his failures as well as in his many successes. Even after he had sinned terribly, David turned back to God with honesty and humility. From David we learn that God's favor doesn't depend on our perfection but on his. As you read 2 Samuel, follow David's example: Go to the Lord, regardless of the imperfect condition of your life, and lay it down before him—watch his redeeming power work in you.

2 SAMUEL

David Hears of Saul's Death

1 After the death of Saul, David returned from defeating the Amalekites and stayed in Ziklag two days. ²On the third day a man arrived from Saul's camp, with his clothes torn and with dust on his head. When he came to David, he fell to the ground to pay him honor.

³"Where have you come from?" David asked him.

He answered, "I have escaped from the Israelite camp."

⁴"What happened?" David asked. "Tell me."

He said, "The men fled from the battle. Many of them fell and died. And Saul and his son Jonathan are dead."

⁵Then David said to the young man who brought him the report, "How do you know that Saul and his son Jonathan are dead?"

⁶"I happened to be on Mount Gilboa," the young man said, "and there was Saul, leaning on his spear, with the chariots and riders almost upon him. ⁷When he turned around and saw me, he called out to me, and I said, 'What can I do?'

⁸"He asked me, 'Who are you?'

" 'An Amalekite,' I answered.

⁹"Then he said to me, 'Stand over me and kill me! I am in the throes of death, but I'm still alive.'

¹⁰"So I stood over him and killed him, because I knew that after he had fallen he could not survive. And I took the crown that was on his head and the band on his

arm and have brought them here to my lord."

¹¹Then David and all the men with him took hold of their clothes and tore them. ¹²They mourned and wept and fasted till evening for Saul and his son Jonathan, and for the army of the LORD and the house of Israel, because they had fallen by the sword.

¹³David said to the young man who brought him the report, "Where are you from?"

"I am the son of an alien, an Amalekite," he answered.

¹⁴David asked him, "Why were you not afraid to lift your hand to destroy the LORD's anointed?"

¹⁵Then David called one of his men and said, "Go, strike him down!" So he struck him down, and he died. ¹⁶For David had said to him, "Your blood be on your own head. Your own mouth testified against you when you said, 'I killed the LORD's anointed.' "

David's Lament for Saul and Jonathan

¹⁷David took up this lament concerning Saul and his son Jonathan, ¹⁸and ordered that the men of Judah be taught this lament of the bow (it is written in the Book of Jashar):

¹⁹"Your glory, O Israel, lies slain on
     your heights.
  How the mighty have fallen!

²⁰"Tell it not in Gath,
     proclaim it not in the streets of
        Ashkelon,
  lest the daughters of the Philistines be
     glad,
  lest the daughters of the
     uncircumcised rejoice.

²¹"O mountains of Gilboa,
  may you have neither dew nor
     rain,
  nor fields that yield offerings ⌊of
     grain⌋.
  For there the shield of the mighty
     was defiled,
  the shield of Saul—no longer
     rubbed with oil.
²²From the blood of the slain,
  from the flesh of the mighty,
  the bow of Jonathan did not turn
     back,
  the sword of Saul did not return
     unsatisfied.

²³"Saul and Jonathan—
  in life they were loved and
     gracious,
  and in death they were not parted.
  They were swifter than eagles,
  they were stronger than lions.

²⁴"O daughters of Israel,
  weep for Saul,
  who clothed you in scarlet and finery,
  who adorned your garments with
     ornaments of gold.

²⁵"How the mighty have fallen in
     battle!
  Jonathan lies slain on your heights.
²⁶I grieve for you, Jonathan my
     brother;
  you were very dear to me.
  Your love for me was wonderful,
  more wonderful than that of
     women.

²⁷"How the mighty have fallen!
  The weapons of war have
     perished!"

David Anointed King Over Judah

2 In the course of time, David inquired of the LORD. "Shall I go up to one of the towns of Judah?" he asked.

The LORD said, "Go up."

David asked, "Where shall I go?"

"To Hebron," the LORD answered.

²So David went up there with his two wives, Ahinoam of Jezreel and Abigail, the widow of Nabal of Carmel. ³David also took the men who were with him, each with his family, and they settled in Hebron and its towns. ⁴Then the men of Judah came to Hebron and there they anointed David king over the house of Judah.

When David was told that it was the

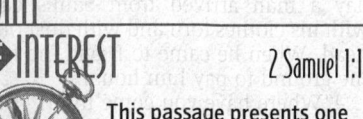

POINT OF INTEREST   2 Samuel 1:17

This passage presents one of the most poignant eulogies ever delivered. Read verses 19 through 27 in three different ways: (1) silently, to familiarize yourself with the passage, (2) aloud normally, so that your ears hear the words, (3) aloud dramatically, to experience the emotion of David's broken heart.

men of Jabesh Gilead who had buried Saul, ⁵he sent messengers to the men of Jabesh Gilead to say to them, "The LORD bless you for showing this kindness to Saul your master by burying him. ⁶May the LORD now show you kindness and faithfulness, and I too will show you the same favor because you have done this. ⁷Now then, be strong and brave, for Saul your master is dead, and the house of Judah has anointed me king over them."

War Between the Houses of David and Saul

⁸Meanwhile, Abner son of Ner, the commander of Saul's army, had taken Ish-Bosheth son of Saul and brought him over to Mahanaim. ⁹He made him king over Gilead, Ashuriᵃ and Jezreel, and also over Ephraim, Benjamin and all Israel.

¹⁰Ish-Bosheth son of Saul was forty years old when he became king over Israel, and he reigned two years. The house of Judah, however, followed David. ¹¹The length of time David was king in Hebron over the house of Judah was seven years and six months.

¹²Abner son of Ner, together with the men of Ish-Bosheth son of Saul, left Mahanaim and went to Gibeon. ¹³Joab son of Zeruiah and David's men went out and met them at the pool of Gibeon. One group sat down on one side of the pool and one group on the other side.

¹⁴Then Abner said to Joab, "Let's have some of the young men get up and fight hand to hand in front of us."

"All right, let them do it," Joab said.

¹⁵So they stood up and were counted off—twelve men for Benjamin and Ish-Bosheth son of Saul, and twelve for David. ¹⁶Then each man grabbed his opponent by the head and thrust his dagger into his opponent's side, and they fell down together. So that place in Gibeon was called Helkath Hazzurim.ᵇ

¹⁷The battle that day was very fierce, and Abner and the men of Israel were defeated by David's men.

¹⁸The three sons of Zeruiah were there: Joab, Abishai and Asahel. Now Asahel was as fleet-footed as a wild gazelle. ¹⁹He chased Abner, turning neither to the right nor to the left as he pursued him. ²⁰Abner looked behind him and asked, "Is that you, Asahel?"

"It is," he answered.

²¹Then Abner said to him, "Turn aside to the right or to the left; take on one of the young men and strip him of his weapons." But Asahel would not stop chasing him.

²²Again Abner warned Asahel, "Stop chasing me! Why should I strike you down? How could I look your brother Joab in the face?"

²³But Asahel refused to give up the pursuit; so Abner thrust the butt of his spear into Asahel's stomach, and the spear came out through his back. He fell there and died on the spot. And every man stopped when he came to the place where Asahel had fallen and died.

²⁴But Joab and Abishai pursued Abner, and as the sun was setting, they came to the hill of Ammah, near Giah on the way to the wasteland of Gibeon. ²⁵Then the men of Benjamin rallied behind Abner. They formed themselves into a group and took their stand on top of a hill.

²⁶Abner called out to Joab, "Must the sword devour forever? Don't you realize that this will end in bitterness? How long before you order your men to stop pursuing their brothers?"

²⁷Joab answered, "As surely as God lives, if you had not spoken, the men would have continued the pursuit of their brothers until morning.ᶜ"

²⁸So Joab blew the trumpet, and all the men came to a halt; they no longer pursued Israel, nor did they fight anymore.

²⁹All that night Abner and his men

ᵃ9 Or *Asher*   ᵇ16 *Helkath Hazzurim* means *field of daggers* or *field of hostilities.*   ᶜ27 Or *spoken this morning, the men would not have taken up the pursuit of their brothers*; or *spoken, the men would have given up the pursuit of their brothers by morning*

POINT OF INTEREST

2 Samuel 2:10

Tribal loyalty was important in David's time. David was from the tribe of Judah, so Judah supported him as king. Saul was from the tribe of Benjamin, so the Benjamites aligned with Ish-Bosheth. The war that ensued between Judah and Benjamin affected the allegiance of the remaining ten tribes (see 2 Samuel 5:1–5).

marched through the Arabah. They crossed the Jordan, continued through the whole Bithron*a* and came to Mahanaim.

³⁰Then Joab returned from pursuing Abner and assembled all his men. Besides Asahel, nineteen of David's men were found missing. ³¹But David's men had killed three hundred and sixty Benjamites who were with Abner. ³²They took Asahel and buried him in his father's tomb at Bethlehem. Then Joab and his men marched all night and arrived at Hebron by daybreak.

3 The war between the house of Saul and the house of David lasted a long time. David grew stronger and stronger, while the house of Saul grew weaker and weaker.

²Sons were born to David in Hebron:

His firstborn was Amnon the son of Ahinoam of Jezreel;

³his second, Kileab the son of Abigail the widow of Nabal of Carmel;

the third, Absalom the son of Maacah daughter of Talmai king of Geshur;

⁴the fourth, Adonijah the son of Haggith;

the fifth, Shephatiah the son of Abital;

⁵and the sixth, Ithream the son of David's wife Eglah.

These were born to David in Hebron.

Abner Goes Over to David

⁶During the war between the house of Saul and the house of David, Abner had been strengthening his own position in the house of Saul. ⁷Now Saul had had a concubine named Rizpah daughter of Aiah. And Ish-Bosheth said to Abner, "Why did you sleep with my father's concubine?"

⁸Abner was very angry because of what Ish-Bosheth said and he answered, "Am I a dog's head—on Judah's side? This very day I am loyal to the house of your father Saul and to his family and friends. I haven't handed you over to David. Yet now you accuse me of an offense involving this woman! ⁹May God deal with Abner, be it ever so severely, if I do not do for David what the LORD promised him on oath ¹⁰and transfer the kingdom from the house of Saul and establish David's throne over Israel and Judah from Dan to Beersheba." ¹¹Ish-Bosheth did not dare to say another word to Abner, because he was afraid of him.

¹²Then Abner sent messengers on his behalf to say to David, "Whose land is it? Make an agreement with me, and I will help you bring all Israel over to you."

¹³"Good," said David. "I will make an agreement with you. But I demand one thing of you: Do not come into my presence unless you bring Michal daughter of Saul when you come to see me." ¹⁴Then David sent messengers to Ish-Bosheth son of Saul, demanding, "Give me my wife Michal, whom I betrothed to myself for the price of a hundred Philistine foreskins."

¹⁵So Ish-Bosheth gave orders and had her taken away from her husband Paltiel son of Laish. ¹⁶Her husband, however, went with her, weeping behind her all the way to Bahurim. Then Abner said to him, "Go back home!" So he went back.

¹⁷Abner conferred with the elders of Israel and said, "For some time you have wanted to make David your king. ¹⁸Now do it! For the LORD promised David, 'By my servant David I will rescue my people Israel from the hand of the Philistines and from the hand of all their enemies.' "

¹⁹Abner also spoke to the Benjamites in person. Then he went to Hebron to tell David everything that Israel and the whole house of Benjamin wanted to do. ²⁰When Abner, who had twenty men with him, came to David at Hebron, David prepared a feast for him and his men. ²¹Then Abner said to David, "Let me go at once and assemble all Israel for my lord the king, so that they may make a compact with you, and that you may rule over all that your heart desires." So David sent Abner away, and he went in peace.

Joab Murders Abner

²²Just then David's men and Joab returned from a raid and brought with them a great deal of plunder. But Abner was no longer with David in Hebron, because David had sent him away, and he had gone in peace. ²³When Joab and all the soldiers with him arrived, he was told that Abner son of Ner had come to the

a29 Or morning; or ravine; the meaning of the Hebrew for this word is uncertain.

king and that the king had sent him away and that he had gone in peace.

²⁴So Joab went to the king and said, "What have you done? Look, Abner came to you. Why did you let him go? Now he is gone! ²⁵You know Abner son of Ner; he came to deceive you and observe your movements and find out everything you are doing."

²⁶Joab then left David and sent messengers after Abner, and they brought him back from the well of Sirah. But David did not know it. ²⁷Now when Abner returned to Hebron, Joab took him aside into the gateway, as though to speak with him privately. And there, to avenge the blood of his brother Asahel, Joab stabbed him in the stomach, and he died.

²⁸Later, when David heard about this, he said, "I and my kingdom are forever innocent before the Lord concerning the blood of Abner son of Ner. ²⁹May his blood fall upon the head of Joab and upon all his father's house! May Joab's house never be without someone who has a running sore or leprosy*ᵃ* or who leans on a crutch or who falls by the sword or who lacks food."

³⁰(Joab and his brother Abishai murdered Abner because he had killed their brother Asahel in the battle at Gibeon.)

³¹Then David said to Joab and all the people with him, "Tear your clothes and put on sackcloth and walk in mourning in front of Abner." King David himself walked behind the bier. ³²They buried Abner in Hebron, and the king wept aloud at Abner's tomb. All the people wept also.

³³The king sang this lament for Abner:

"Should Abner have died as the
　　lawless die?
³⁴　Your hands were not bound,
　　your feet were not fettered.
You fell as one falls before wicked
　　men."

And all the people wept over him again.

³⁵Then they all came and urged David to eat something while it was still day; but David took an oath, saying, "May God deal with me, be it ever so severely, if I taste bread or anything else before the sun sets!"

³⁶All the people took note and were pleased; indeed, everything the king did pleased them. ³⁷So on that day all the people and all Israel knew that the king

had no part in the murder of Abner son of Ner.

³⁸Then the king said to his men, "Do you not realize that a prince and a great man has fallen in Israel this day? ³⁹And today, though I am the anointed king, I am weak, and these sons of Zeruiah are too strong for me. May the Lord repay the evildoer according to his evil deeds!"

Ish-Bosheth Murdered

4 When Ish-Bosheth son of Saul heard that Abner had died in Hebron, he lost courage, and all Israel became alarmed. ²Now Saul's son had two men who were leaders of raiding bands. One was named Baanah and the other Recab; they were sons of Rimmon the Beerothite from the tribe of Benjamin—Beeroth is considered part of Benjamin, ³because the people of Beeroth fled to Gittaim and have lived there as aliens to this day.

⁴(Jonathan son of Saul had a son who was lame in both feet. He was five years old when the news about Saul and Jonathan came from Jezreel. His nurse picked him up and fled, but as she hurried to leave, he fell and became crippled. His name was Mephibosheth.)

⁵Now Recab and Baanah, the sons of Rimmon the Beerothite, set out for the house of Ish-Bosheth, and they arrived there in the heat of the day while he was taking his noonday rest. ⁶They went into the inner part of the house as if to get some wheat, and they stabbed him in the stomach. Then Recab and his brother Baanah slipped away.

⁷They had gone into the house while he was lying on the bed in his bedroom. After they stabbed and killed him, they cut off his head. Taking it with them, they traveled all night by way of the Arabah. ⁸They brought the head of Ish-Bosheth to David at Hebron and said to the king, "Here is the head of Ish-Bosheth son of Saul, your enemy, who tried to take your life. This day the Lord has avenged my lord the king against Saul and his offspring."

⁹David answered Recab and his brother Baanah, the sons of Rimmon the Beerothite, "As surely as the Lord lives, who has delivered me out of all trouble, ¹⁰when a man told me, 'Saul is dead,' and thought he was bringing good news, I

ᵃ29 The Hebrew word was used for various diseases affecting the skin—not necessarily leprosy.

seized him and put him to death in Ziklag. That was the reward I gave him for his news! ¹¹How much more—when wicked men have killed an innocent man in his own house and on his own bed— should I not now demand his blood from your hand and rid the earth of you!"

¹²So David gave an order to his men, and they killed them. They cut off their hands and feet and hung the bodies by the pool in Hebron. But they took the head of Ish-Bosheth and buried it in Abner's tomb at Hebron.

David Becomes King Over Israel

5 All the tribes of Israel came to David at Hebron and said, "We are your own flesh and blood. ²In the past, while Saul was king over us, you were the one who led Israel on their military campaigns. And the LORD said to you, 'You will shepherd my people Israel, and you will become their ruler.' "

³When all the elders of Israel had come to King David at Hebron, the king made a compact with them at Hebron before the LORD, and they anointed David king over Israel.

⁴David was thirty years old when he became king, and he reigned forty years. ⁵In Hebron he reigned over Judah seven years and six months, and in Jerusalem he reigned over all Israel and Judah thirty-three years.

David Conquers Jerusalem

⁶The king and his men marched to Jerusalem to attack the Jebusites, who lived there. The Jebusites said to David, "You will not get in here; even the blind and the lame can ward you off." They thought, "David cannot get in here." ⁷Nevertheless, David captured the fortress of Zion, the City of David.

⁸On that day, David said, "Anyone who conquers the Jebusites will have to use the water shaft[a] to reach those 'lame and blind' who are David's enemies.[b] " That is why they say, "The 'blind and lame' will not enter the palace."

⁹David then took up residence in the fortress and called it the City of David. He built up the area around it, from the supporting terraces[c] inward. ¹⁰And he became more and more powerful, because the LORD God Almighty was with him.

¹¹Now Hiram king of Tyre sent messengers to David, along with cedar logs and carpenters and stonemasons, and they built a palace for David. ¹²And David knew that the LORD had established him as king over Israel and had exalted his kingdom for the sake of his people Israel.

¹³After he left Hebron, David took more concubines and wives in Jerusalem, and more sons and daughters were born to him. ¹⁴These are the names of the children born to him there: Shammua, Shobab, Nathan, Solomon, ¹⁵Ibhar, Elishua, Nepheg, Japhia, ¹⁶Elishama, Eliada and Eliphelet.

David Defeats the Philistines

¹⁷When the Philistines heard that David had been anointed king over Israel, they went up in full force to search for him, but David heard about it and went down to the stronghold. ¹⁸Now the Philistines had come and spread out in the Valley of Rephaim; ¹⁹so David inquired of the LORD, "Shall I go and attack the Philistines? Will you hand them over to me?"

The LORD answered him, "Go, for I will surely hand the Philistines over to you."

²⁰So David went to Baal Perazim, and there he defeated them. He said, "As waters break out, the LORD has broken out against my enemies before me." So that place was called Baal Perazim.[d] ²¹The Philistines abandoned their idols there, and David and his men carried them off.

²²Once more the Philistines came up and spread out in the Valley of Rephaim; ²³so David inquired of the LORD, and he answered, "Do not go straight up, but circle around behind them and attack them

---

[a]8 Or *use scaling hooks*   [b]8 Or *are hated by David*   [c]9 Or *the Millo*   [d]20 *Baal Perazim* means *the lord who breaks out.*

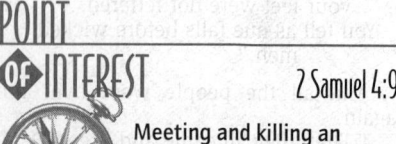

POINT OF INTEREST

2 Samuel 4:9

Meeting and killing an enemy in open battle was considered honorable in ancient Israel. However, killing by deceit or under the guise of friendship was considered murder. David demonstrated his integrity by his unwillingness to let the murder of an enemy and rival go unpunished.

in front of the balsam trees. ²⁴As soon as you hear the sound of marching in the tops of the balsam trees, move quickly, because that will mean the Lord has gone out in front of you to strike the Philistine army." ²⁵So David did as the Lord commanded him, and he struck down the Philistines all the way from Gibeon*a* to Gezer.

The Ark Brought to Jerusalem

6 David again brought together out of Israel chosen men, thirty thousand in all. ²He and all his men set out from Baalah of Judah*b* to bring up from there the ark of God, which is called by the Name,*c* the name of the Lord Almighty, who is enthroned between the cherubim that are on the ark. ³They set the ark of God on a new cart and brought it from the house of Abinadab, which was on the hill. Uzzah and Ahio, sons of Abinadab, were guiding the new cart ⁴with the ark of God on it,*d* and Ahio was walking in front of it. ⁵David and the whole house of Israel were celebrating with all their might before the Lord, with songs*e* and with harps, lyres, tambourines, sistrums and cymbals.

⁶When they came to the threshing floor of Nacon, Uzzah reached out and took hold of the ark of God, because the oxen stumbled. ⁷The Lord's anger burned against Uzzah because of his irreverent act; therefore God struck him down and he died there beside the ark of God.

⁸Then David was angry because the Lord's wrath had broken out against Uzzah, and to this day that place is called Perez Uzzah.*f*

⁹David was afraid of the Lord that day and said, "How can the ark of the Lord ever come to me?" ¹⁰He was not willing to take the ark of the Lord to be with him in the City of David. Instead, he took it aside to the house of Obed-Edom the Gittite. ¹¹The ark of the Lord remained in the house of Obed-Edom the Gittite for three months, and the Lord blessed him and his entire household.

¹²Now King David was told, "The Lord has blessed the household of Obed-Edom and everything he has, because of the ark of God." So David went down and brought up the ark of God from the house of Obed-Edom to the City of David with rejoicing. ¹³When those who were carrying the ark of the Lord had taken six steps, he sacrificed a bull and a fattened calf. ¹⁴David, wearing a linen ephod, danced before the Lord with all his might, ¹⁵while he and the entire house of Israel brought up the ark of the Lord with shouts and the sound of trumpets.

¹⁶As the ark of the Lord was entering the City of David, Michal daughter of Saul watched from a window. And when she saw King David leaping and dancing before the Lord, she despised him in her heart.

¹⁷They brought the ark of the Lord and set it in its place inside the tent that David had pitched for it, and David sacrificed burnt offerings and fellowship offerings*g* before the Lord. ¹⁸After he had finished sacrificing the burnt offerings and fellowship offerings, he blessed the people in the name of the Lord Almighty. ¹⁹Then he gave a loaf of bread, a cake of dates and a cake of raisins to each person in the whole crowd of Israelites, both men and women. And all the people went to their homes.

²⁰When David returned home to bless his household, Michal daughter of Saul came out to meet him and said, "How the king of Israel has distinguished himself today, disrobing in the sight of the slave girls of his servants as any vulgar fellow would!"

²¹David said to Michal, "It was before the Lord, who chose me rather than your father or anyone from his house when he appointed me ruler over the Lord's people Israel—I will celebrate before the Lord. ²²I will become even more undignified than this, and I will be humiliated in my own eyes. But by these slave girls you spoke of, I will be held in honor."

²³And Michal daughter of Saul had no children to the day of her death.

God's Promise to David

7 After the king was settled in his palace and the Lord had given him rest from all his enemies around him, ²he said to Nathan the prophet, "Here I am, living in

---

a25 Septuagint (see also 1 Chron. 14:16); Hebrew *Geba*   *b2* That is, Kiriath Jearim; Hebrew *Baale Judah*, a variant of *Baalah of Judah*   *c2* Hebrew; Septuagint and Vulgate do not have *the Name*. *d3,4* Dead Sea Scrolls and some Septuagint manuscripts; Masoretic Text *cart* ⁴*and they brought it with the ark of God from the house of Abinadab, which was on the hill*   *e5* See Dead Sea Scrolls, Septuagint and 1 Chronicles 13:8; Masoretic Text *celebrating before the Lord with all kinds of instruments made of pine.*   *f8* *Perez Uzzah* means *outbreak against Uzzah.* *g17* Traditionally *peace offerings*; also in verse 18 a palace of cedar, while the ark of God remains in a tent."

³Nathan replied to the king, "Whatever you have in mind, go ahead and do it, for the LORD is with you."

⁴That night the word of the LORD came to Nathan, saying:

⁵"Go and tell my servant David, 'This is what the LORD says: Are you the one to build me a house to dwell in? ⁶I have not dwelt in a house from the day I brought the Israelites up out of Egypt to this day. I have been moving from place to place with a tent as my dwelling. ⁷Wherever I have moved with all the Israelites, did I ever say to any of their rulers whom I commanded to shepherd my people Israel, "Why have you not built me a house of cedar?"'

⁸"Now then, tell my servant David, 'This is what the LORD Almighty says: I took you from the pasture and from following the flock to be ruler over my people Israel. ⁹I have been with you wherever you have gone, and I have cut off all your enemies from before you. Now I will make your name great, like the names of the greatest men of the earth. ¹⁰And I will provide a place for my people Israel and will plant them so that they can have a home of their own and no longer be disturbed. Wicked people will not oppress them anymore, as they did at the beginning ¹¹and have done ever since the time I appointed leaders*a* over my people Israel. I will also give you rest from all your enemies.

" 'The LORD declares to you that the LORD himself will establish a house for you: ¹²When your days are over and you rest with your fathers, I will raise up your offspring to succeed you, who will come from your own body, and I will establish his kingdom. ¹³He is the one who will build a house for my Name, and I will establish the throne of his kingdom forever. ¹⁴I will be his father, and he will be my son. When he does wrong, I will punish him with the rod of men, with floggings inflicted by men. ¹⁵But my love will never be taken away from him, as I took it away from Saul, whom I re-

moved from before you. ¹⁶Your house and your kingdom will endure forever before me*b*; your throne will be established forever.' "

¹⁷Nathan reported to David all the words of this entire revelation.

David's Prayer

¹⁸Then King David went in and sat before the LORD, and he said:

"Who am I, O Sovereign LORD, and what is my family, that you have brought me this far? ¹⁹And as if this were not enough in your sight, O Sovereign LORD, you have also spoken about the future of the house of your servant. Is this your usual way of dealing with man, O Sovereign LORD?

²⁰"What more can David say to you? For you know your servant, O Sovereign LORD. ²¹For the sake of your word and according to your will, you have done this great thing and made it known to your servant.

²²"How great you are, O Sovereign LORD! There is no one like you, and there is no God but you, as we have heard with our own ears. ²³And who is like your people Israel—the one nation on earth that God went out to redeem as a people for himself, and to make a name for himself, and to perform great and awesome wonders by driving out nations and their gods from before your people, whom you redeemed from Egypt?*c* ²⁴You have established your people Israel as your very own forever, and you, O LORD, have become their God.

²⁵"And now, LORD God, keep forever the promise you have made concerning your servant and his house. Do as you promised, ²⁶so that your name will be great forever. Then men will say, 'The LORD Almighty is God over Israel!' And the house of your servant David will be established before you.

²⁷"O LORD Almighty, God of Isra-

---

a 11 Traditionally *judges*   *b 16* Some Hebrew manuscripts and Septuagint; most Hebrew manuscripts *you*   *c 23* See Septuagint and 1 Chron. 17:21; Hebrew *wonders for your land and before your people, whom you redeemed from Egypt, from the nations and their gods.*

el, you have revealed this to your servant, saying, 'I will build a house for you.' So your servant has found courage to offer you this prayer. **28**O Sovereign LORD, you are God! Your words are trustworthy, and you have promised these good things to your servant. **29**Now be pleased to bless the house of your servant, that it may continue forever in your sight; for you, O Sovereign LORD, have spoken, and with your blessing the house of your servant will be blessed forever."

David's Victories

8 In the course of time, David defeated the Philistines and subdued them, and he took Metheg Ammah from the control of the Philistines.

2David also defeated the Moabites. He made them lie down on the ground and measured them off with a length of cord. Every two lengths of them were put to death, and the third length was allowed to live. So the Moabites became subject to David and brought tribute.

3Moreover, David fought Hadadezer son of Rehob, king of Zobah, when he went to restore his control along the Euphrates River. **4**David captured a thousand of his chariots, seven thousand charioteers*a* and twenty thousand foot soldiers. He hamstrung all but a hundred of the chariot horses.

5When the Arameans of Damascus came to help Hadadezer king of Zobah, David struck down twenty-two thousand of them. **6**He put garrisons in the Aramean kingdom of Damascus, and the Arameans became subject to him and

a4 Septuagint (see also Dead Sea Scrolls and 1 Chron. 18:4); Masoretic Text *captured seventeen hundred of his charioteers*

TUESDAY

Read *2 Samuel 7:1–29*
Key Verses *2 Samuel 7:18–29*

"No" –Ellen B. Susman

Have you ever received a "no" from God? I waited for what seemed a very long time before I found the man I married. I hated being without a boyfriend or even any possibilities. I had begun to think that God either wanted me to be single or was teaching me some difficult lesson. I concluded that God was teaching me to trust him with a "no" to my prayer. I stopped praying for a guy to come my way and started praying for contentment in my single status. God gave me contentment, and only later did he give me the guy.

David also received a "no" from God. He wanted to build a house for God, but God said "no." That didn't seem very fair—David only wanted to do something good for God.

So what did David do? Right away he thanked God for answering him, and he didn't complain. In fact, David praised God for all he had done. David didn't question God's judgment but remembered his faithfulness.

Are you frustrated with God's answer? Are you impatiently waiting for a wedding ring? The right job? Does it seem that God doesn't understand? That he's not paying attention?

Like David, we can respond to God's "no" by remembering what he's done for us in the past and thanking him for his love for us. Then he'll replace our impatience with contentment.

A Deeper Look
Luke 22:39–44; 2 Corinthians 12:7–10

Go to page 336 for your next devotional reading.

brought tribute. The LORD gave David victory wherever he went.

⁷David took the gold shields that belonged to the officers of Hadadezer and brought them to Jerusalem. ⁸From Tebahᵃ and Berothai, towns that belonged to Hadadezer, King David took a great quantity of bronze.

⁹When Touᵇ king of Hamath heard that David had defeated the entire army of Hadadezer, ¹⁰he sent his son Joramᶜ to King David to greet him and congratulate him on his victory in battle over Hadadezer, who had been at war with Tou. Joram brought with him articles of silver and gold and bronze.

¹¹King David dedicated these articles to the LORD, as he had done with the silver and gold from all the nations he had subdued: ¹²Edomᵈ and Moab, the Ammonites and the Philistines, and Amalek. He also dedicated the plunder taken from Hadadezer son of Rehob, king of Zobah.

¹³And David became famous after he returned from striking down eighteen thousand Edomitesᵉ in the Valley of Salt.

¹⁴He put garrisons throughout Edom, and all the Edomites became subject to David. The LORD gave David victory wherever he went.

David's Officials

¹⁵David reigned over all Israel, doing what was just and right for all his people. ¹⁶Joab son of Zeruiah was over the army; Jehoshaphat son of Ahilud was recorder; ¹⁷Zadok son of Ahitub and Ahimelech son of Abiathar were priests; Seraiah was secretary; ¹⁸Benaiah son of Jehoiada was over the Kerethites and Pelethites; and David's sons were royal advisers.ᶠ

David and Mephibosheth

9 David asked, "Is there anyone still left of the house of Saul to whom I can show kindness for Jonathan's sake?"

²Now there was a servant of Saul's household named Ziba. They called him to appear before David, and the king said to him, "Are you Ziba?"

"Your servant," he replied.

³The king asked, "Is there no one still left of the house of Saul to whom I can show God's kindness?"

Ziba answered the king, "There is still a son of Jonathan; he is crippled in both feet."

⁴"Where is he?" the king asked.

Ziba answered, "He is at the house of Makir son of Ammiel in Lo Debar."

⁵So King David had him brought from Lo Debar, from the house of Makir son of Ammiel.

⁶When Mephibosheth son of Jonathan, the son of Saul, came to David, he bowed down to pay him honor.

David said, "Mephibosheth!"

"Your servant," he replied.

⁷"Don't be afraid," David said to him, "for I will surely show you kindness for the sake of your father Jonathan. I will restore to you all the land that belonged to your grandfather Saul, and you will always eat at my table."

⁸Mephibosheth bowed down and said, "What is your servant, that you should notice a dead dog like me?"

⁹Then the king summoned Ziba, Saul's servant, and said to him, "I have given your master's grandson everything that belonged to Saul and his family. ¹⁰You and your sons and your servants are to farm the land for him and bring in the crops, so that your master's grandson may be provided for. And Mephibosheth, grandson of your master, will always eat at my table." (Now Ziba had fifteen sons and twenty servants.)

¹¹Then Ziba said to the king, "Your servant will do whatever my lord the king commands his servant to do." So

---

ᵃ8 See some Septuagint manuscripts (see also 1 Chron. 18:8); Hebrew *Betah.*   ᵇ9 Hebrew *Toi,* a variant of *Tou*; also in verse 10   ᶜ10 A variant of *Hadoram*   ᵈ12 Some Hebrew manuscripts, Septuagint and Syriac (see also 1 Chron. 18:11); most Hebrew manuscripts *Aram*   ᵉ13 A few Hebrew manuscripts, Septuagint and Syriac (see also 1 Chron. 18:12); most Hebrew manuscripts *Aram* (that is, Arameans)   ᶠ18 Or *were priests*

POINT OF INTEREST

2 Samuel 9:7

Think about David's actions toward Mephibosheth. David's faith in God empowered him to live differently from many other rulers. His actions in this passage demonstrate that David was a man of integrity and a faithful friend. He remembered his promise to Jonathan (see 1 Samuel 20:15, 42) and acted upon it.

Mephibosheth ate at David's*a* table like one of the king's sons.

¹²Mephibosheth had a young son named Mica, and all the members of Ziba's household were servants of Mephibosheth. ¹³And Mephibosheth lived in Jerusalem, because he always ate at the king's table, and he was crippled in both feet.

David Defeats the Ammonites

10 In the course of time, the king of the Ammonites died, and his son Hanun succeeded him as king. ²David thought, "I will show kindness to Hanun son of Nahash, just as his father showed kindness to me." So David sent a delegation to express his sympathy to Hanun concerning his father.

When David's men came to the land of the Ammonites, ³the Ammonite nobles said to Hanun their lord, "Do you think David is honoring your father by sending men to you to express sympathy? Hasn't David sent them to you to explore the city and spy it out and overthrow it?" ⁴So Hanun seized David's men, shaved off half of each man's beard, cut off their garments in the middle at the buttocks, and sent them away.

⁵When David was told about this, he sent messengers to meet the men, for they were greatly humiliated. The king said, "Stay at Jericho till your beards have grown, and then come back."

⁶When the Ammonites realized that they had become a stench in David's nostrils, they hired twenty thousand Aramean foot soldiers from Beth Rehob and Zobah, as well as the king of Maacah with a thousand men, and also twelve thousand men from Tob.

⁷On hearing this, David sent Joab out with the entire army of fighting men. ⁸The Ammonites came out and drew up in battle formation at the entrance to their city gate, while the Arameans of Zobah and Rehob and the men of Tob and Maacah were by themselves in the open country.

⁹Joab saw that there were battle lines in front of him and behind him; so he selected some of the best troops in Israel and deployed them against the Arameans. ¹⁰He put the rest of the men under the command of Abishai his brother and deployed them against the Ammonites. ¹¹Joab said, "If the Arameans are too

strong for me, then you are to come to my rescue; but if the Ammonites are too strong for you, then I will come to rescue you. ¹²Be strong and let us fight bravely for our people and the cities of our God. The LORD will do what is good in his sight."

¹³Then Joab and the troops with him advanced to fight the Arameans, and they fled before him. ¹⁴When the Ammonites saw that the Arameans were fleeing, they fled before Abishai and went inside the city. So Joab returned from fighting the Ammonites and came to Jerusalem.

¹⁵After the Arameans saw that they had been routed by Israel, they regrouped. ¹⁶Hadadezer had Arameans brought from beyond the River*b*; they went to Helam, with Shobach the commander of Hadadezer's army leading them.

¹⁷When David was told of this, he gathered all Israel, crossed the Jordan and went to Helam. The Arameans formed their battle lines to meet David and fought against him. ¹⁸But they fled before Israel, and David killed seven hundred of their charioteers and forty thousand of their foot soldiers.*c* He also struck down Shobach the commander of their army, and he died there. ¹⁹When all the kings who were vassals of Hadadezer saw that they had been defeated by Israel, they made peace with the Israelites and became subject to them.

So the Arameans were afraid to help the Ammonites anymore.

David and Bathsheba

11 In the spring, at the time when kings go off to war, David sent Joab out with the king's men and the whole Israelite army. They destroyed the Ammonites and besieged Rabbah. But David remained in Jerusalem.

²One evening David got up from his bed and walked around on the roof of the palace. From the roof he saw a woman bathing. The woman was very beautiful, ³and David sent someone to find out about her. The man said, "Isn't this Bathsheba, the daughter of Eliam and the wife of Uriah the Hittite?" ⁴Then David sent messengers to get her. She came to him,

a 11 Septuagint; Hebrew *my*   *b 16* That is, the Euphrates   *c 18* Some Septuagint manuscripts (see also 1 Chron. 19:18); Hebrew *horsemen* and he slept with her. (She had purified herself from her uncleanness.) Then*a* she went back home. *⁵*The woman conceived and sent word to David, saying, "I am pregnant."

*⁶*So David sent this word to Joab: "Send me Uriah the Hittite." And Joab sent him to David. *⁷*When Uriah came to him, David asked him how Joab was, how the soldiers were and how the war was going. *⁸*Then David said to Uriah, "Go down to your house and wash your feet." So Uriah left the palace, and a gift from the king was sent after him. *⁹*But Uriah slept at the entrance to the palace

a4 Or with her. When she purified herself from her uncleanness,

---

WEDNESDAY

Read 2 Samuel 11:1–27
Key Verses 2 Samuel 11:1–5

Create in Us Pure Hearts – Dennis Stokes

Even though King David was called "a man after God's own heart," he made a series of amazingly bad decisions that spiraled into a cycle of events resulting in suffering and ruined lives. And it all began with a disastrous gaze . . .

About halfway through his forty-year reign, David decided to stay home from the war, choosing not to go to battle. He saw Bathsheba, decided he wanted her and sent a servant to invite her up to his place and into his bed. To cover up the scandal he arranged to have her husband murdered on the battlefield.

Though David sought and received forgiveness from God (see 2 Samuel 12), he still had to live a long time with the consequences of his poor choices. The child born to David and Bathsheba died soon after birth, and during the last twenty years of David's reign he encountered struggles and difficulties very unlike his first twenty years.

Statistics reveal that over eighty percent of North American teens have sex before marriage. The pressure to become sexually active can be intense, especially in a college setting where it may seem as though premarital sex is the norm rather than the exception. But, as David's situation illustrates, giving in to temptation, even a little, can snowball into consequences that last a long time.

If you're thinking about becoming sexually involved, think again about David. If you have sinned sexually, ask God for forgiveness and thank him for the grace to start anew. If through a series of bad decisions you have found yourself saddled with the consequences of sexual sin, take that to God, too, and pray as David did: "Have mercy on me, O God, according to your unfailing love; according to your great compassion blot out my transgressions. Wash away all my iniquity and cleanse me from my sin . . . Cleanse me with hyssop, and I will be clean; wash me, and I will be whiter than snow. Let me hear joy and gladness; let the bones you have crushed rejoice. Hide your face from my sins and blot out all my iniquity. Create in me a pure heart, O God, and renew a steadfast spirit within me" (Psalm 51:1–2, 7–10).

A Deeper Look
Isaiah 1:18; 1 Timothy 4:12; Hebrews 13:4

Go to page 342 for your next devotional reading.

with all his master's servants and did not go down to his house. ¹⁰When David was told, "Uriah did not go home," he asked him, "Haven't you just come from a distance? Why didn't you go home?"

¹¹Uriah said to David, "The ark and Israel and Judah are staying in tents, and my master Joab and my lord's men are camped in the open fields. How could I go to my house to eat and drink and lie with my wife? As surely as you live, I will not do such a thing!"

¹²Then David said to him, "Stay here one more day, and tomorrow I will send you back." So Uriah remained in Jerusalem that day and the next. ¹³At David's invitation, he ate and drank with him, and David made him drunk. But in the evening Uriah went out to sleep on his mat among his master's servants; he did not go home.

¹⁴In the morning David wrote a letter to Joab and sent it with Uriah. ¹⁵In it he wrote, "Put Uriah in the front line where the fighting is fiercest. Then withdraw from him so he will be struck down and die."

¹⁶So while Joab had the city under siege, he put Uriah at a place where he knew the strongest defenders were. ¹⁷When the men of the city came out and fought against Joab, some of the men in David's army fell; moreover, Uriah the Hittite died.

¹⁸Joab sent David a full account of the battle. ¹⁹He instructed the messenger: "When you have finished giving the king this account of the battle, ²⁰the king's anger may flare up, and he may ask you, 'Why did you get so close to the city to fight? Didn't you know they would shoot arrows from the wall? ²¹Who killed Abimelech son of Jerub-Besheth*? Didn't a woman throw an upper millstone on him from the wall, so that he died in Thebez? Why did you get so close to the wall?' If he asks you this, then say to him, 'Also, your servant Uriah the Hittite is dead.' "

²²The messenger set out, and when he arrived he told David everything Joab had sent him to say. ²³The messenger said to David, "The men overpowered us and came out against us in the open, but we drove them back to the entrance to the city gate. ²⁴Then the archers shot arrows at your servants from the wall, and

some of the king's men died. Moreover, your servant Uriah the Hittite is dead."

²⁵David told the messenger, "Say this to Joab: 'Don't let this upset you; the sword devours one as well as another. Press the attack against the city and destroy it.' Say this to encourage Joab."

²⁶When Uriah's wife heard that her husband was dead, she mourned for him. ²⁷After the time of mourning was over, David had her brought to his house, and she became his wife and bore him a son. But the thing David had done displeased the LORD.

Nathan Rebukes David

12 The LORD sent Nathan to David. When he came to him, he said, "There were two men in a certain town, one rich and the other poor. ²The rich man had a very large number of sheep and cattle, ³but the poor man had nothing except one little ewe lamb he had bought. He raised it, and it grew up with him and his children. It shared his food, drank from his cup and even slept in his arms. It was like a daughter to him.

⁴"Now a traveler came to the rich man, but the rich man refrained from taking one of his own sheep or cattle to prepare a meal for the traveler who had come to him. Instead, he took the ewe lamb that belonged to the poor man and prepared it for the one who had come to him."

⁵David burned with anger against the man and said to Nathan, "As surely as the LORD lives, the man who did this deserves to die! ⁶He must pay for that lamb four times over, because he did such a thing and had no pity."

⁷Then Nathan said to David, "You are the man! This is what the LORD, the God of Israel, says: 'I anointed you king over Israel, and I delivered you from the hand of Saul. ⁸I gave your master's house to you, and your master's wives into your arms. I gave you the house of Israel and Judah. And if all this had been too little, I would have given you even more. ⁹Why did you despise the word of the LORD by doing what is evil in his eyes? You struck down Uriah the Hittite with the sword and took his wife to be your own. You killed him with the sword of the Ammonites. ¹⁰Now, therefore, the sword will never depart from your house, because

*21 Also known as *Jerub-Baal* (that is, Gideon)

you despised me and took the wife of Uriah the Hittite to be your own.'

11 "This is what the LORD says: 'Out of your own household I am going to bring calamity upon you. Before your very eyes I will take your wives and give them to one who is close to you, and he will lie with your wives in broad daylight. 12 You did it in secret, but I will do this thing in broad daylight before all Israel.' "

13 Then David said to Nathan, "I have sinned against the LORD."

Nathan replied, "The LORD has taken away your sin. You are not going to die. 14 But because by doing this you have made the enemies of the LORD show utter contempt,ᵃ the son born to you will die."

15 After Nathan had gone home, the LORD struck the child that Uriah's wife had borne to David, and he became ill. 16 David pleaded with God for the child. He fasted and went into his house and spent the nights lying on the ground. 17 The elders of his household stood beside him to get him up from the ground, but he refused, and he would not eat any food with them.

18 On the seventh day the child died. David's servants were afraid to tell him that the child was dead, for they thought, "While the child was still living, we spoke to David but he would not listen to us. How can we tell him the child is dead? He may do something desperate."

19 David noticed that his servants were whispering among themselves and he realized the child was dead. "Is the child dead?" he asked.

"Yes," they replied, "he is dead."

20 Then David got up from the ground. After he had washed, put on lotions and changed his clothes, he went into the house of the LORD and worshiped. Then he went to his own house, and at his request they served him food, and he ate.

21 His servants asked him, "Why are you acting this way? While the child was alive, you fasted and wept, but now that the child is dead, you get up and eat!"

22 He answered, "While the child was still alive, I fasted and wept. I thought, 'Who knows? The LORD may be gracious to me and let the child live.' 23 But now that he is dead, why should I fast? Can I bring him back again? I will go to him, but he will not return to me."

24 Then David comforted his wife Bathsheba, and he went to her and lay with her. She gave birth to a son, and they named him Solomon. The LORD loved him; 25 and because the LORD loved him, he sent word through Nathan the prophet to name him Jedidiah.ᵇ

26 Meanwhile Joab fought against Rabbah of the Ammonites and captured the royal citadel. 27 Joab then sent messengers to David, saying, "I have fought against Rabbah and taken its water supply. 28 Now muster the rest of the troops and besiege the city and capture it. Otherwise I will take the city, and it will be named after me."

29 So David mustered the entire army and went to Rabbah, and attacked and captured it. 30 He took the crown from the head of their kingᶜ—its weight was a talentᵈ of gold, and it was set with precious stones—and it was placed on David's head. He took a great quantity of plunder from the city 31 and brought out the people who were there, consigning them to labor with saws and with iron picks and axes, and he made them work at brickmaking.ᵉ He did this to all the Ammonite towns. Then David and his entire army returned to Jerusalem.

Amnon and Tamar

13 In the course of time, Amnon son of David fell in love with Tamar, the beautiful sister of Absalom son of David.

2 Amnon became frustrated to the point of illness on account of his sister Tamar, for she was a virgin, and it seemed impossible for him to do anything to her.

3 Now Amnon had a friend named Jonadab son of Shimeah, David's brother. Jonadab was a very shrewd man. 4 He asked Amnon, "Why do you, the king's son, look so haggard morning after morning? Won't you tell me?"

Amnon said to him, "I'm in love with Tamar, my brother Absalom's sister."

5 "Go to bed and pretend to be ill," Jonadab said. "When your father comes to see you, say to him, 'I would like my sister Tamar to come and give me something to eat. Let her prepare the food in

---

ᵃ14 Masoretic Text; an ancient Hebrew scribal tradition *this you have shown utter contempt for the* LORD   ᵇ25 *Jedidiah* means *loved by the* LORD.   ᶜ30 Or *of Milcom* (that is, Molech)   ᵈ30 That is, about 75 pounds (about 34 kilograms)   ᵉ31 The meaning of the Hebrew for this clause is uncertain.

my sight so I may watch her and then eat it from her hand.' "

⁶So Amnon lay down and pretended to be ill. When the king came to see him, Amnon said to him, "I would like my sister Tamar to come and make some special bread in my sight, so I may eat from her hand."

⁷David sent word to Tamar at the palace: "Go to the house of your brother Amnon and prepare some food for him." ⁸So Tamar went to the house of her brother Amnon, who was lying down. She took some dough, kneaded it, made the bread in his sight and baked it. ⁹Then she took the pan and served him the bread, but he refused to eat.

"Send everyone out of here," Amnon said. So everyone left him. ¹⁰Then Amnon said to Tamar, "Bring the food here into my bedroom so I may eat from your hand." And Tamar took the bread she had prepared and brought it to her brother Amnon in his bedroom. ¹¹But when she took it to him to eat, he grabbed her and said, "Come to bed with me, my sister."

¹²"Don't, my brother!" she said to him. "Don't force me. Such a thing should not be done in Israel! Don't do this wicked thing. ¹³What about me? Where could I get rid of my disgrace? And what about you? You would be like one of the wicked fools in Israel. Please speak to the king; he will not keep me from being married to you." ¹⁴But he refused to listen to her, and since he was stronger than she, he raped her.

¹⁵Then Amnon hated her with intense hatred. In fact, he hated her more than he had loved her. Amnon said to her, "Get up and get out!"

¹⁶"No!" she said to him. "Sending me away would be a greater wrong than what you have already done to me."

But he refused to listen to her. ¹⁷He called his personal servant and said, "Get this woman out of here and bolt the door after her." ¹⁸So his servant put her out and bolted the door after her. She was wearing a richly ornamented[a] robe, for this was the kind of garment the virgin daughters of the king wore. ¹⁹Tamar put ashes on her head and tore the ornamented[b] robe she was wearing. She put her hand on her head and went away, weeping aloud as she went.

²⁰Her brother Absalom said to her, "Has that Amnon, your brother, been with you? Be quiet now, my sister; he is your brother. Don't take this thing to heart." And Tamar lived in her brother Absalom's house, a desolate woman.

²¹When King David heard all this, he was furious. ²²Absalom never said a word to Amnon, either good or bad; he hated Amnon because he had disgraced his sister Tamar.

Absalom Kills Amnon

²³Two years later, when Absalom's sheepshearers were at Baal Hazor near the border of Ephraim, he invited all the king's sons to come there. ²⁴Absalom went to the king and said, "Your servant has had shearers come. Will the king and his officials please join me?"

²⁵"No, my son," the king replied. "All of us should not go; we would only be a burden to you." Although Absalom urged him, he still refused to go, but gave him his blessing.

²⁶Then Absalom said, "If not, please let my brother Amnon come with us."

The king asked him, "Why should he go with you?" ²⁷But Absalom urged him, so he sent with him Amnon and the rest of the king's sons.

²⁸Absalom ordered his men, "Listen! When Amnon is in high spirits from drinking wine and I say to you, 'Strike Amnon down,' then kill him. Don't be afraid. Have not I given you this order? Be strong and brave." ²⁹So Absalom's men did to Amnon what Absalom had ordered. Then all the king's sons got up, mounted their mules and fled.

---

a18 The meaning of the Hebrew for this phrase is uncertain.   *b19* The meaning of the Hebrew for this word is uncertain.

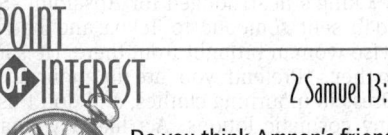

POINT OF INTEREST   2 Samuel 13:5

Do you think Amnon's friend Jonadab believed that members of the king's family were above the law? Many commentators see a connection between David's sin with Bathsheba, Amnon's violation of Tamar, the subsequent murder of Amnon and Absalom's rebellion. What might have happened if David had dealt quickly and justly with Amnon's sin?

³⁰While they were on their way, the report came to David: "Absalom has struck down all the king's sons; not one of them is left." ³¹The king stood up, tore his clothes and lay down on the ground; and all his servants stood by with their clothes torn.

³²But Jonadab son of Shimeah, David's brother, said, "My lord should not think that they killed all the princes; only Amnon is dead. This has been Absalom's expressed intention ever since the day Amnon raped his sister Tamar. ³³My lord the king should not be concerned about the report that all the king's sons are dead. Only Amnon is dead."

³⁴Meanwhile, Absalom had fled.

Now the man standing watch looked up and saw many people on the road west of him, coming down the side of the hill. The watchman went and told the king, "I see men in the direction of Horonaim, on the side of the hill."*ᵃ*

³⁵Jonadab said to the king, "See, the king's sons are here; it has happened just as your servant said."

³⁶As he finished speaking, the king's sons came in, wailing loudly. The king, too, and all his servants wept very bitterly.

³⁷Absalom fled and went to Talmai son of Ammihud, the king of Geshur. But King David mourned for his son every day.

³⁸After Absalom fled and went to Geshur, he stayed there three years. ³⁹And the spirit of the king*ᵇ* longed to go to Absalom, for he was consoled concerning Amnon's death.

Absalom Returns to Jerusalem

14 Joab son of Zeruiah knew that the king's heart longed for Absalom. ²So Joab sent someone to Tekoa and had a wise woman brought from there. He said to her, "Pretend you are in mourning. Dress in mourning clothes, and don't use any cosmetic lotions. Act like a woman who has spent many days grieving for the dead. ³Then go to the king and speak these words to him." And Joab put the words in her mouth.

⁴When the woman from Tekoa went*ᶜ* to the king, she fell with her face to the ground to pay him honor, and she said, "Help me, O king!"

⁵The king asked her, "What is troubling you?"

She said, "I am indeed a widow; my husband is dead. ⁶I your servant had two sons. They got into a fight with each other in the field, and no one was there to separate them. One struck the other and killed him. ⁷Now the whole clan has risen up against your servant; they say, 'Hand over the one who struck his brother down, so that we may put him to death for the life of his brother whom he killed; then we will get rid of the heir as well.' They would put out the only burning coal I have left, leaving my husband neither name nor descendant on the face of the earth."

⁸The king said to the woman, "Go home, and I will issue an order in your behalf."

⁹But the woman from Tekoa said to him, "My lord the king, let the blame rest on me and on my father's family, and let the king and his throne be without guilt."

¹⁰The king replied, "If anyone says anything to you, bring him to me, and he will not bother you again."

¹¹She said, "Then let the king invoke the LORD his God to prevent the avenger of blood from adding to the destruction, so that my son will not be destroyed."

"As surely as the LORD lives," he said, "not one hair of your son's head will fall to the ground."

¹²Then the woman said, "Let your servant speak a word to my lord the king."

"Speak," he replied.

¹³The woman said, "Why then have you devised a thing like this against the people of God? When the king says this, does he not convict himself, for the king has not brought back his banished son? ¹⁴Like water spilled on the ground, which cannot be recovered, so we must die. But God does not take away life; instead, he devises ways so that a banished person may not remain estranged from him.

¹⁵"And now I have come to say this to my lord the king because the people have made me afraid. Your servant thought, 'I will speak to the king; perhaps he will do what his servant asks. ¹⁶Perhaps the king will agree to deliver his servant from the hand of the man who is trying to cut off both me and my son from the inheritance God gave us.'

ᵃ34 Septuagint; Hebrew does not have this sentence.   *ᵇ39* Dead Sea Scrolls and some Septuagint manuscripts; Masoretic Text *But ʟthe spirit of⌐ David the king*   *ᶜ4* Many Hebrew manuscripts, Septuagint, Vulgate and Syriac; most Hebrew manuscripts *spoke*

17"And now your servant says, 'May the word of my lord the king bring me rest, for my lord the king is like an angel of God in discerning good and evil. May the LORD your God be with you.' "

18Then the king said to the woman, "Do not keep from me the answer to what I am going to ask you."

"Let my lord the king speak," the woman said.

19The king asked, "Isn't the hand of Joab with you in all this?"

The woman answered, "As surely as you live, my lord the king, no one can turn to the right or to the left from anything my lord the king says. Yes, it was your servant Joab who instructed me to do this and who put all these words into the mouth of your servant. **20**Your servant Joab did this to change the present situation. My lord has wisdom like that of an angel of God—he knows everything that happens in the land."

21The king said to Joab, "Very well, I will do it. Go, bring back the young man Absalom."

22Joab fell with his face to the ground to pay him honor, and he blessed the king. Joab said, "Today your servant knows that he has found favor in your eyes, my lord the king, because the king has granted his servant's request."

23Then Joab went to Geshur and brought Absalom back to Jerusalem. **24**But the king said, "He must go to his own house; he must not see my face." So Absalom went to his own house and did not see the face of the king.

25In all Israel there was not a man so highly praised for his handsome appearance as Absalom. From the top of his head to the sole of his foot there was no blemish in him. **26**Whenever he cut the hair of his head—he used to cut his hair from time to time when it became too heavy for him—he would weigh it, and its weight was two hundred shekels[a] by the royal standard.

27Three sons and a daughter were born to Absalom. The daughter's name was Tamar, and she became a beautiful woman.

28Absalom lived two years in Jerusalem without seeing the king's face. **29**Then Absalom sent for Joab in order to send him to the king, but Joab refused to come to him. So he sent a second time, but he refused to come. **30**Then he said to his servants, "Look, Joab's field is next to mine, and he has barley there. Go and set it on fire." So Absalom's servants set the field on fire.

31Then Joab did go to Absalom's house and he said to him, "Why have your servants set my field on fire?"

32Absalom said to Joab, "Look, I sent word to you and said, 'Come here so I can send you to the king to ask, "Why have I come from Geshur? It would be better for me if I were still there!" ' Now then, I want to see the king's face, and if I am guilty of anything, let him put me to death."

33So Joab went to the king and told him this. Then the king summoned Absalom, and he came in and bowed down with his face to the ground before the king. And the king kissed Absalom.

Absalom's Conspiracy

15 In the course of time, Absalom provided himself with a chariot and horses and with fifty men to run ahead of him. **2**He would get up early and stand by the side of the road leading to the city gate. Whenever anyone came with a complaint to be placed before the king for a decision, Absalom would call out to him, "What town are you from?" He would answer, "Your servant is from one of the tribes of Israel." **3**Then Absalom would say to him, "Look, your claims are valid and proper, but there is no representative of the king to hear you." **4**And Absalom would add, "If only I were appointed judge in the land! Then everyone who has a complaint or case could come to me and I would see that he gets justice."

5Also, whenever anyone approached him to bow down before him, Absalom would reach out his hand, take hold of him and kiss him. **6**Absalom behaved in this way toward all the Israelites who came to the king asking for justice, and so he stole the hearts of the men of Israel.

7At the end of four[b] years, Absalom said to the king, "Let me go to Hebron and fulfill a vow I made to the LORD. **8**While your servant was living at Geshur in Aram, I made this vow: 'If the LORD takes me back to Jerusalem, I will worship the LORD in Hebron.[c] ' "

---

a26 That is, about 5 pounds (about 2.3 kilograms)
b7 Some Septuagint manuscripts, Syriac and Josephus; Hebrew *forty*   *c8* Some Septuagint manuscripts; Hebrew does not have *in Hebron.*

⁹The king said to him, "Go in peace." So he went to Hebron.

¹⁰Then Absalom sent secret messengers throughout the tribes of Israel to say, "As soon as you hear the sound of the trumpets, then say, 'Absalom is king in Hebron.' " ¹¹Two hundred men from Jerusalem had accompanied Absalom. They had been invited as guests and went quite innocently, knowing nothing about the matter. ¹²While Absalom was offering sacrifices, he also sent for Ahithophel the Gilonite, David's counselor, to come from Giloh, his hometown. And so the conspiracy gained strength, and Absalom's following kept on increasing.

David Flees

¹³A messenger came and told David, "The hearts of the men of Israel are with Absalom."

¹⁴Then David said to all his officials who were with him in Jerusalem, "Come! We must flee, or none of us will escape from Absalom. We must leave immediately, or he will move quickly to overtake us and bring ruin upon us and put the city to the sword."

¹⁵The king's officials answered him, "Your servants are ready to do whatever our lord the king chooses."

¹⁶The king set out, with his entire

THURSDAY

Read *2 Samuel 15:1–26*
Key Verses *2 Samuel 15:5–6*

Seeking God's Favor — Vollie Sanders

What do student body presidents, company CEOs and spiritual leaders have in common? Power would likely be on the list as well as competition for power from those who want more of it. Power, as well as ambition, can be used positively or negatively. People in power, as well as those who want power, can have pure or impure motives. How should we understand ambition and keep the desire for power in check?

Absalom, King David's son, wanted to take the throne from his father and claim it for himself: "Look, your claims are valid and proper, but there is no representative of the king to hear you. . . . If only I were appointed judge in the land!" (2 Samuel 15:3–4). Absalom's true motives are revealed in 2 Samuel 15:6: "So he stole the hearts of the men of Israel."

King David, although far from perfect, was considered a man after God's own heart (see Acts 13:22). He wanted no part of the kingdom if this was not God's perfect will for him. Contrast Absalom's words and motivations with David's: "If I find favor in the LORD's eyes, he will bring me back and let me see [the ark] and his dwelling place again. But if he says, 'I am not pleased with you,' then I am ready; let him do to me whatever seems good to him" (2 Samuel 15:25–26).

Some of us are like Absalom, stealing from another through flattery or criticism. Often there is no limit to what we will do or say to get what we want. But instead of valuing power and prestige, we are called to be like David, to accept the positions of authority God has designed for us and to prefer his will, even if that means taking a more humble role.

A Deeper Look
Daniel 5:18–21; Matthew 23:11; Romans 2:8

Go to page 344 for your next devotional reading.

household following him; but he left ten concubines to take care of the palace. ¹⁷So the king set out, with all the people following him, and they halted at a place some distance away. ¹⁸All his men marched past him, along with all the Kerethites and Pelethites; and all the six hundred Gittites who had accompanied him from Gath marched before the king.

¹⁹The king said to Ittai the Gittite, "Why should you come along with us? Go back and stay with King Absalom. You are a foreigner, an exile from your homeland. ²⁰You came only yesterday. And today shall I make you wander about with us, when I do not know where I am going? Go back, and take your countrymen. May kindness and faithfulness be with you."

²¹But Ittai replied to the king, "As surely as the LORD lives, and as my lord the king lives, wherever my lord the king may be, whether it means life or death, there will your servant be."

²²David said to Ittai, "Go ahead, march on." So Ittai the Gittite marched on with all his men and the families that were with him.

²³The whole countryside wept aloud as all the people passed by. The king also crossed the Kidron Valley, and all the people moved on toward the desert.

²⁴Zadok was there, too, and all the Levites who were with him were carrying the ark of the covenant of God. They set down the ark of God, and Abiathar offered sacrifices^a until all the people had finished leaving the city.

²⁵Then the king said to Zadok, "Take the ark of God back into the city. If I find favor in the LORD's eyes, he will bring me back and let me see it and his dwelling place again. ²⁶But if he says, 'I am not pleased with you,' then I am ready; let him do to me whatever seems good to him."

²⁷The king also said to Zadok the priest, "Aren't you a seer? Go back to the city in peace, with your son Ahimaaz and Jonathan son of Abiathar. You and Abiathar take your two sons with you. ²⁸I will wait at the fords in the desert until word comes from you to inform me." ²⁹So Zadok and Abiathar took the ark of God back to Jerusalem and stayed there.

³⁰But David continued up the Mount of Olives, weeping as he went; his head was covered and he was barefoot. All the people with him covered their heads too and were weeping as they went up. ³¹Now David had been told, "Ahithophel is among the conspirators with Absalom." So David prayed, "O LORD, turn Ahithophel's counsel into foolishness."

³²When David arrived at the summit, where people used to worship God, Hushai the Arkite was there to meet him, his robe torn and dust on his head. ³³David said to him, "If you go with me, you will be a burden to me. ³⁴But if you return to the city and say to Absalom, 'I will be your servant, O king; I was your father's servant in the past, but now I will be your servant,' then you can help me by frustrating Ahithophel's advice. ³⁵Won't the priests Zadok and Abiathar be there with you? Tell them anything you hear in the king's palace. ³⁶Their two sons, Ahimaaz son of Zadok and Jonathan son of Abiathar, are there with them. Send them to me with anything you hear."

³⁷So David's friend Hushai arrived at Jerusalem as Absalom was entering the city.

David and Ziba

16 When David had gone a short distance beyond the summit, there was Ziba, the steward of Mephibosheth, waiting to meet him. He had a string of donkeys saddled and loaded with two hundred loaves of bread, a hundred cakes of raisins, a hundred cakes of figs and a skin of wine.

²The king asked Ziba, "Why have you brought these?"

Ziba answered, "The donkeys are for the king's household to ride on, the bread and fruit are for the men to eat, and the wine is to refresh those who become exhausted in the desert."

³The king then asked, "Where is your master's grandson?"

Ziba said to him, "He is staying in Jerusalem, because he thinks, 'Today the house of Israel will give me back my grandfather's kingdom.'"

⁴Then the king said to Ziba, "All that belonged to Mephibosheth is now yours."

"I humbly bow," Ziba said. "May I find favor in your eyes, my lord the king."

Shimei Curses David

⁵As King David approached Bahurim,

---

^a24 Or *Abiathar went up*

a man from the same clan as Saul's family came out from there. His name was Shimei son of Gera, and he cursed as he came out. 6He pelted David and all the king's officials with stones, though all the troops and the special guard were on David's right and left. 7As he cursed, Shimei said, "Get out, get out, you man of blood, you scoundrel! 8The LORD has repaid you for all the blood you shed in the household of Saul, in whose place you have reigned. The LORD has handed the kingdom over to your son Absalom. You have come to ruin because you are a man of blood!"

9Then Abishai son of Zeruiah said to the king, "Why should this dead dog curse my lord the king? Let me go over and cut off his head."

10But the king said, "What do you and I have in common, you sons of Zeruiah? If he is cursing because the LORD said to him, 'Curse David,' who can ask, 'Why do you do this?' "

11David then said to Abishai and all his officials, "My son, who is of my own flesh, is trying to take my life. How much more, then, this Benjamite! Leave him alone; let him curse, for the LORD has told him to. 12It may be that the LORD will see my distress and repay me with good for the cursing I am receiving today."

13So David and his men continued along the road while Shimei was going along the hillside opposite him, cursing as he went and throwing stones at him and showering him with dirt. 14The king and all the people with him arrived at their destination exhausted. And there he refreshed himself.

FRIDAY

Read 2 Samuel 16:1–23
Key Verses 2 Samuel 16:9–12

"Repay Me with Good" — Julie Bundt

I was in that half-conscious mental state. It was seven in the morning, and I was mindlessly swimming laps. The pool was a little crowded, but I was able to make my turns in spite of the guys hanging around at the end of the lane.

In the midst of a turn, one of the guys stopped me. He then told me in curt language that he and his friends thought I was cutting them off. He said I was rude and told me to either shape up or move to another lane. I couldn't believe it, especially when they all started mocking me.

I was so angry. My adrenaline was flowing. I was sure they were just acting out of pride because a girl kept passing them. But after the anger wore off, I just felt humiliated and hoped I never ran into them again. On the other hand, I thought, it would be fun to run into them in a situation where I had the upper hand and could ridicule them.

Then God doused me with conviction. I remembered clearly that two weeks before I'd passed a guy just to show him up because I thought he was in my way. I'd also recently asked God to convict me of sin and to do whatever it took to break me of that sin.

I think God used those guys at the pool to "repay me with good" (2 Samuel 16:12)—to humble me and expose my petty attitude, rid me of my own pride and teach me to let him take care of the way people treated me in the future. He was successful!

A Deeper Look
Psalm 9:4; 1 Peter 2:23

Go to page 354 for your next devotional reading.

The Advice of Hushai and Ahithophel

[15]Meanwhile, Absalom and all the men of Israel came to Jerusalem, and Ahithophel was with him. [16]Then Hushai the Arkite, David's friend, went to Absalom and said to him, "Long live the king! Long live the king!"

[17]Absalom asked Hushai, "Is this the love you show your friend? Why didn't you go with your friend?"

[18]Hushai said to Absalom, "No, the one chosen by the LORD, by these people, and by all the men of Israel—his I will be, and I will remain with him. [19]Furthermore, whom should I serve? Should I not serve the son? Just as I served your father, so I will serve you."

[20]Absalom said to Ahithophel, "Give us your advice. What should we do?"

[21]Ahithophel answered, "Lie with your father's concubines whom he left to take care of the palace. Then all Israel will hear that you have made yourself a stench in your father's nostrils, and the hands of everyone with you will be strengthened." [22]So they pitched a tent for Absalom on the roof, and he lay with his father's concubines in the sight of all Israel.

[23]Now in those days the advice Ahithophel gave was like that of one who inquires of God. That was how both David and Absalom regarded all of Ahithophel's advice.

17 Ahithophel said to Absalom, "I would[a] choose twelve thousand men and set out tonight in pursuit of David. [2]I would[b] attack him while he is weary and weak. I would[b] strike him with terror, and then all the people with him will flee. I would[b] strike down only the king [3]and bring all the people back to you. The death of the man you seek will mean the return of all; all the people will be unharmed." [4]This plan seemed good to Absalom and to all the elders of Israel.

[5]But Absalom said, "Summon also Hushai the Arkite, so we can hear what he has to say." [6]When Hushai came to him, Absalom said, "Ahithophel has given this advice. Should we do what he says? If not, give us your opinion."

[7]Hushai replied to Absalom, "The advice Ahithophel has given is not good this time. [8]You know your father and his men; they are fighters, and as fierce as a wild bear robbed of her cubs. Besides, your father is an experienced fighter; he will not spend the night with the troops. [9]Even now, he is hidden in a cave or some other place. If he should attack your troops first,[c] whoever hears about it will say, 'There has been a slaughter among the troops who follow Absalom.' [10]Then even the bravest soldier, whose heart is like the heart of a lion, will melt with fear, for all Israel knows that your father is a fighter and that those with him are brave.

[11]"So I advise you: Let all Israel, from Dan to Beersheba—as numerous as the sand on the seashore—be gathered to you, with you yourself leading them into battle. [12]Then we will attack him wherever he may be found, and we will fall on him as dew settles on the ground. Neither he nor any of his men will be left alive. [13]If he withdraws into a city, then all Israel will bring ropes to that city, and we will drag it down to the valley until not even a piece of it can be found."

[14]Absalom and all the men of Israel said, "The advice of Hushai the Arkite is better than that of Ahithophel." For the LORD had determined to frustrate the good advice of Ahithophel in order to bring disaster on Absalom.

[15]Hushai told Zadok and Abiathar, the priests, "Ahithophel has advised Absalom and the elders of Israel to do such and such, but I have advised them to do so and so. [16]Now send a message immediately and tell David, 'Do not spend the night at the fords in the desert; cross over without fail, or the king and all the people with him will be swallowed up.'"

[17]Jonathan and Ahimaaz were staying at En Rogel. A servant girl was to go and inform them, and they were to go and tell King David, for they could not risk being seen entering the city. [18]But a young man saw them and told Absalom. So the two of them left quickly and went to the house of a man in Bahurim. He had a well in his courtyard, and they climbed down into it. [19]His wife took a covering and spread it out over the opening of the well and scattered grain over it. No one knew anything about it.

[20]When Absalom's men came to the woman at the house, they asked, "Where are Ahimaaz and Jonathan?"

The woman answered them, "They

---

a 1 Or Let me   b 2 Or will   c 9 Or When some of the men fall at the first attack crossed over the brook."*a* The men searched but found no one, so they returned to Jerusalem.

²¹After the men had gone, the two climbed out of the well and went to inform King David. They said to him, "Set out and cross the river at once; Ahithophel has advised such and such against you." ²²So David and all the people with him set out and crossed the Jordan. By daybreak, no one was left who had not crossed the Jordan.

²³When Ahithophel saw that his advice had not been followed, he saddled his donkey and set out for his house in his hometown. He put his house in order and then hanged himself. So he died and was buried in his father's tomb.

²⁴David went to Mahanaim, and Absalom crossed the Jordan with all the men of Israel. ²⁵Absalom had appointed Amasa over the army in place of Joab. Amasa was the son of a man named Jether,*b* an Israelite*c* who had married Abigail,*d* the daughter of Nahash and sister of Zeruiah the mother of Joab. ²⁶The Israelites and Absalom camped in the land of Gilead.

²⁷When David came to Mahanaim, Shobi son of Nahash from Rabbah of the Ammonites, and Makir son of Ammiel from Lo Debar, and Barzillai the Gileadite from Rogelim ²⁸brought bedding and bowls and articles of pottery. They also brought wheat and barley, flour and roasted grain, beans and lentils,*e* ²⁹honey and curds, sheep, and cheese from cows' milk for David and his people to eat. For they said, "The people have become hungry and tired and thirsty in the desert."

Absalom's Death

18 David mustered the men who were with him and appointed over them commanders of thousands and commanders of hundreds. ²David sent the troops out—a third under the command of Joab, a third under Joab's brother Abishai son of Zeruiah, and a third under Ittai the Gittite. The king told the troops, "I myself will surely march out with you."

³But the men said, "You must not go out; if we are forced to flee, they won't care about us. Even if half of us die, they won't care; but you are worth ten thousand of us.*f* It would be better now for you to give us support from the city."

⁴The king answered, "I will do whatever seems best to you."

So the king stood beside the gate while all the men marched out in units of hundreds and of thousands. ⁵The king commanded Joab, Abishai and Ittai, "Be gentle with the young man Absalom for my sake." And all the troops heard the king giving orders concerning Absalom to each of the commanders.

⁶The army marched into the field to fight Israel, and the battle took place in the forest of Ephraim. ⁷There the army of Israel was defeated by David's men, and the casualties that day were great—twenty thousand men. ⁸The battle spread out over the whole countryside, and the forest claimed more lives that day than the sword.

⁹Now Absalom happened to meet David's men. He was riding his mule, and as the mule went under the thick branches of a large oak, Absalom's head got caught in the tree. He was left hanging in midair, while the mule he was riding kept on going.

¹⁰When one of the men saw this, he told Joab, "I just saw Absalom hanging in an oak tree."

¹¹Joab said to the man who had told him this, "What! You saw him? Why didn't you strike him to the ground right there? Then I would have had to give you ten shekels*g* of silver and a warrior's belt."

¹²But the man replied, "Even if a thousand shekels*h* were weighed out into my hands, I would not lift my hand against the king's son. In our hearing the king commanded you and Abishai and Ittai, 'Protect the young man Absalom for my sake.'*i* ¹³And if I had put my life in jeopardy*j*—and nothing is hidden from the king—you would have kept your distance from me."

a20 Or *"They passed by the sheep pen toward the water."* *b25* Hebrew *Ithra,* a variant of *Jether* *c25* Hebrew and some Septuagint manuscripts; other Septuagint manuscripts (see also 1 Chron. 2:17) *Ishmaelite* or *Jezreelite* *d25* Hebrew *Abigal,* a variant of *Abigail* *e28* Most Septuagint manuscripts and Syriac; Hebrew *lentils, and roasted grain* *f3* Two Hebrew manuscripts, some Septuagint manuscripts and Vulgate; most Hebrew manuscripts *care; for now there are ten thousand like us* *g11* That is, about 4 ounces (about 115 grams) *h12* That is, about 25 pounds (about 11 kilograms) *i12* A few Hebrew manuscripts, Septuagint, Vulgate and Syriac; most Hebrew manuscripts may be translated *Absalom, whoever you may be.* *j13* Or *Otherwise, if I had acted treacherously toward him*

14Joab said, "I'm not going to wait like this for you." So he took three javelins in his hand and plunged them into Absalom's heart while Absalom was still alive in the oak tree. **15**And ten of Joab's armor-bearers surrounded Absalom, struck him and killed him.

16Then Joab sounded the trumpet, and the troops stopped pursuing Israel, for Joab halted them. **17**They took Absalom, threw him into a big pit in the forest and piled up a large heap of rocks over him. Meanwhile, all the Israelites fled to their homes.

18During his lifetime Absalom had taken a pillar and erected it in the King's Valley as a monument to himself, for he thought, "I have no son to carry on the memory of my name." He named the pillar after himself, and it is called Absalom's Monument to this day.

David Mourns

19Now Ahimaaz son of Zadok said, "Let me run and take the news to the king that the LORD has delivered him from the hand of his enemies."

20"You are not the one to take the news today," Joab told him. "You may take the news another time, but you must not do so today, because the king's son is dead."

21Then Joab said to a Cushite, "Go, tell the king what you have seen." The Cushite bowed down before Joab and ran off.

22Ahimaaz son of Zadok again said to Joab, "Come what may, please let me run behind the Cushite."

But Joab replied, "My son, why do you want to go? You don't have any news that will bring you a reward."

23He said, "Come what may, I want to run."

So Joab said, "Run!" Then Ahimaaz ran by way of the plain*a* and outran the Cushite.

24While David was sitting between the inner and outer gates, the watchman went up to the roof of the gateway by the wall. As he looked out, he saw a man running alone. **25**The watchman called out to the king and reported it.

The king said, "If he is alone, he must have good news." And the man came closer and closer.

26Then the watchman saw another man running, and he called down to the gatekeeper, "Look, another man running alone!"

The king said, "He must be bringing good news, too."

27The watchman said, "It seems to me that the first one runs like Ahimaaz son of Zadok."

"He's a good man," the king said. "He comes with good news."

28Then Ahimaaz called out to the king, "All is well!" He bowed down before the king with his face to the ground and said, "Praise be to the LORD your God! He has delivered up the men who lifted their hands against my lord the king."

29The king asked, "Is the young man Absalom safe?"

Ahimaaz answered, "I saw great confusion just as Joab was about to send the king's servant and me, your servant, but I don't know what it was."

30The king said, "Stand aside and wait here." So he stepped aside and stood there.

31Then the Cushite arrived and said, "My lord the king, hear the good news! The LORD has delivered you today from all who rose up against you."

32The king asked the Cushite, "Is the young man Absalom safe?"

The Cushite replied, "May the enemies of my lord the king and all who rise up to harm you be like that young man."

33The king was shaken. He went up to the room over the gateway and wept. As he went, he said: "O my son Absalom! My son, my son Absalom! If only I had died instead of you—O Absalom, my son, my son!"

19 Joab was told, "The king is weeping and mourning for Absalom." **2**And for the whole army the victory that day

a23 That is, the plain of the Jordan

POINT
OF INTEREST   2 Samuel 18:12

David, with a father's heart, had expressly commanded his army to spare his son Absalom. Though Joab's motive in killing Absalom was the defense of David's monarchy, Joab's disobedient and ruthless methods made him a villain rather than a hero. Good motives never justify evil actions.

was turned into mourning, because on that day the troops heard it said, "The king is grieving for his son." ³The men stole into the city that day as men steal in who are ashamed when they flee from battle. ⁴The king covered his face and cried aloud, "O my son Absalom! O Absalom, my son, my son!"

⁵Then Joab went into the house to the king and said, "Today you have humiliated all your men, who have just saved your life and the lives of your sons and daughters and the lives of your wives and concubines. ⁶You love those who hate you and hate those who love you. You have made it clear today that the commanders and their men mean nothing to you. I see that you would be pleased if Absalom were alive today and all of us were dead. ⁷Now go out and encourage your men. I swear by the LORD that if you don't go out, not a man will be left with you by nightfall. This will be worse for you than all the calamities that have come upon you from your youth till now."

⁸So the king got up and took his seat in the gateway. When the men were told, "The king is sitting in the gateway," they all came before him.

David Returns to Jerusalem

Meanwhile, the Israelites had fled to their homes. ⁹Throughout the tribes of Israel, the people were all arguing with each other, saying, "The king delivered us from the hand of our enemies; he is the one who rescued us from the hand of the Philistines. But now he has fled the country because of Absalom; ¹⁰and Absalom, whom we anointed to rule over us, has died in battle. So why do you say nothing about bringing the king back?"

¹¹King David sent this message to Zadok and Abiathar, the priests: "Ask the elders of Judah, 'Why should you be the last to bring the king back to his palace, since what is being said throughout Israel has reached the king at his quarters? ¹²You are my brothers, my own flesh and blood. So why should you be the last to bring back the king?' ¹³And say to Amasa, 'Are you not my own flesh and blood? May God deal with me, be it ever so severely, if from now on you are not the commander of my army in place of Joab.'"

¹⁴He won over the hearts of all the men of Judah as though they were one man. They sent word to the king, "Return, you and all your men." ¹⁵Then the king returned and went as far as the Jordan.

Now the men of Judah had come to Gilgal to go out and meet the king and bring him across the Jordan. ¹⁶Shimei son of Gera, the Benjamite from Bahurim, hurried down with the men of Judah to meet King David. ¹⁷With him were a thousand Benjamites, along with Ziba, the steward of Saul's household, and his fifteen sons and twenty servants. They rushed to the Jordan, where the king was. ¹⁸They crossed at the ford to take the king's household over and to do whatever he wished.

When Shimei son of Gera crossed the Jordan, he fell prostrate before the king ¹⁹and said to him, "May my lord not hold me guilty. Do not remember how your servant did wrong on the day my lord the king left Jerusalem. May the king put it out of his mind. ²⁰For I your servant know that I have sinned, but today I have come here as the first of the whole house of Joseph to come down and meet my lord the king."

²¹Then Abishai son of Zeruiah said, "Shouldn't Shimei be put to death for this? He cursed the LORD's anointed."

²²David replied, "What do you and I have in common, you sons of Zeruiah? This day you have become my adversaries! Should anyone be put to death in Israel today? Do I not know that today I am king over Israel?" ²³So the king said to Shimei, "You shall not die." And the king promised him on oath.

²⁴Mephibosheth, Saul's grandson, also went down to meet the king. He had not taken care of his feet or trimmed his mustache or washed his clothes from the day the king left until the day he returned safely. ²⁵When he came from Jerusalem to meet the king, the king asked him, "Why didn't you go with me, Mephibosheth?"

²⁶He said, "My lord the king, since I your servant am lame, I said, 'I will have my donkey saddled and will ride on it, so I can go with the king.' But Ziba my servant betrayed me. ²⁷And he has slandered your servant to my lord the king. My lord the king is like an angel of God; so do whatever pleases you. ²⁸All my grandfather's descendants deserved nothing but death from my lord the king, but you gave your servant a place among

those who eat at your table. So what right do I have to make any more appeals to the king?" ²⁹The king said to him, "Why say more? I order you and Ziba to divide the fields."

³⁰Mephibosheth said to the king, "Let him take everything, now that my lord the king has arrived home safely."

³¹Barzillai the Gileadite also came down from Rogelim to cross the Jordan with the king and to send him on his way from there. ³²Now Barzillai was a very old man, eighty years of age. He had provided for the king during his stay in Mahanaim, for he was a very wealthy man. ³³The king said to Barzillai, "Cross over with me and stay with me in Jerusalem, and I will provide for you."

³⁴But Barzillai answered the king, "How many more years will I live, that I should go up to Jerusalem with the king? ³⁵I am now eighty years old. Can I tell the difference between what is good and what is not? Can your servant taste what he eats and drinks? Can I still hear the voices of men and women singers? Why should your servant be an added burden to my lord the king? ³⁶Your servant will cross over the Jordan with the king for a short distance, but why should the king reward me in this way? ³⁷Let your servant return, that I may die in my own town near the tomb of my father and mother. But here is your servant Kimham. Let him cross over with my lord the king. Do for him whatever pleases you."

³⁸The king said, "Kimham shall cross over with me, and I will do for him whatever pleases you. And anything you desire from me I will do for you."

³⁹So all the people crossed the Jordan, and then the king crossed over. The king kissed Barzillai and gave him his blessing, and Barzillai returned to his home.

⁴⁰When the king crossed over to Gilgal, Kimham crossed with him. All the troops of Judah and half the troops of Israel had taken the king over. ⁴¹Soon all the men of Israel were coming to the king and saying to him, "Why did our brothers, the men of Judah, steal the king away and bring him and his household across the Jordan, together with all his men?"

⁴²All the men of Judah answered the men of Israel, "We did this because the king is closely related to us. Why are you angry about it? Have we eaten any of the king's provisions? Have we taken anything for ourselves?"

⁴³Then the men of Israel answered the men of Judah, "We have ten shares in the king; and besides, we have a greater claim on David than you have. So why do you treat us with contempt? Were we not the first to speak of bringing back our king?"

But the men of Judah responded even more harshly than the men of Israel.

Sheba Rebels Against David

20 Now a troublemaker named Sheba son of Bicri, a Benjamite, happened to be there. He sounded the trumpet and shouted,

"We have no share in David,
    no part in Jesse's son!
Every man to his tent, O Israel!"

²So all the men of Israel deserted David to follow Sheba son of Bicri. But the men of Judah stayed by their king all the way from the Jordan to Jerusalem.

³When David returned to his palace in Jerusalem, he took the ten concubines he had left to take care of the palace and put them in a house under guard. He provided for them, but did not lie with them. They were kept in confinement till the day of their death, living as widows.

⁴Then the king said to Amasa, "Summon the men of Judah to come to me within three days, and be here yourself." ⁵But when Amasa went to summon Judah, he took longer than the time the king had set for him.

⁶David said to Abishai, "Now Sheba son of Bicri will do us more harm than Absalom did. Take your master's men and pursue him, or he will find fortified cities and escape from us." ⁷So Joab's men and the Kerethites and Pelethites and all the mighty warriors went out under the command of Abishai. They marched out from Jerusalem to pursue Sheba son of Bicri.

⁸While they were at the great rock in Gibeon, Amasa came to meet them. Joab was wearing his military tunic, and strapped over it at his waist was a belt with a dagger in its sheath. As he stepped forward, it dropped out of its sheath.

⁹Joab said to Amasa, "How are you, my brother?" Then Joab took Amasa by the beard with his right hand to kiss him. ¹⁰Amasa was not on his guard against the dagger in Joab's hand, and Joab plunged

it into his belly, and his intestines spilled out on the ground. Without being stabbed again, Amasa died. Then Joab and his brother Abishai pursued Sheba son of Bicri.

¹¹One of Joab's men stood beside Amasa and said, "Whoever favors Joab, and whoever is for David, let him follow Joab!" ¹²Amasa lay wallowing in his blood in the middle of the road, and the man saw that all the troops came to a halt there. When he realized that everyone who came up to Amasa stopped, he dragged him from the road into a field and threw a garment over him. ¹³After Amasa had been removed from the road, all the men went on with Joab to pursue Sheba son of Bicri.

¹⁴Sheba passed through all the tribes of Israel to Abel Beth Maacah*a* and through the entire region of the Berites, who gathered together and followed him. ¹⁵All the troops with Joab came and besieged Sheba in Abel Beth Maacah. They built a siege ramp up to the city, and it stood against the outer fortifications. While they were battering the wall to bring it down, ¹⁶a wise woman called from the city, "Listen! Listen! Tell Joab to come here so I can speak to him." ¹⁷He went toward her, and she asked, "Are you Joab?"

"I am," he answered.

She said, "Listen to what your servant has to say."

"I'm listening," he said.

¹⁸She continued, "Long ago they used to say, 'Get your answer at Abel,' and that settled it. ¹⁹We are the peaceful and faithful in Israel. You are trying to destroy a city that is a mother in Israel. Why do you want to swallow up the LORD's inheritance?"

²⁰"Far be it from me!" Joab replied, "Far be it from me to swallow up or destroy! ²¹That is not the case. A man named Sheba son of Bicri, from the hill country of Ephraim, has lifted up his hand against the king, against David. Hand over this one man, and I'll withdraw from the city."

The woman said to Joab, "His head will be thrown to you from the wall."

²²Then the woman went to all the people with her wise advice, and they cut off the head of Sheba son of Bicri and threw it to Joab. So he sounded the trumpet, and his men dispersed from the city, each

returning to his home. And Joab went back to the king in Jerusalem.

²³Joab was over Israel's entire army; Benaiah son of Jehoiada was over the Kerethites and Pelethites; ²⁴Adoniram*b* was in charge of forced labor; Jehoshaphat son of Ahilud was recorder; ²⁵Sheva was secretary; Zadok and Abiathar were priests; ²⁶and Ira the Jairite was David's priest.

The Gibeonites Avenged

21 During the reign of David, there was a famine for three successive years; so David sought the face of the LORD. The LORD said, "It is on account of Saul and his blood-stained house; it is because he put the Gibeonites to death."

²The king summoned the Gibeonites and spoke to them. (Now the Gibeonites were not a part of Israel but were survivors of the Amorites; the Israelites had sworn to ⌊spare⌋ them, but Saul in his zeal for Israel and Judah had tried to annihilate them.) ³David asked the Gibeonites, "What shall I do for you? How shall I make amends so that you will bless the LORD's inheritance?"

⁴The Gibeonites answered him, "We have no right to demand silver or gold from Saul or his family, nor do we have the right to put anyone in Israel to death."

"What do you want me to do for you?" David asked.

⁵They answered the king, "As for the man who destroyed us and plotted against us so that we have been decimated and have no place anywhere in Israel, ⁶let seven of his male descendants be given to us to be killed and exposed before the LORD at Gibeah of Saul—the LORD's chosen one."

So the king said, "I will give them to you."

⁷The king spared Mephibosheth son of Jonathan, the son of Saul, because of the oath before the LORD between David and Jonathan son of Saul. ⁸But the king took Armoni and Mephibosheth, the two sons of Aiah's daughter Rizpah, whom she had borne to Saul, together with the five sons of Saul's daughter Merab,*c* whom

---

a14 Or *Abel, even Beth Maacah*; also in verse 15
b24 Some Septuagint manuscripts (see also 1 Kings 4:6 and 5:14); Hebrew *Adoram*   *c8* Two Hebrew manuscripts, some Septuagint manuscripts and Syriac (see also 1 Samuel 18:19); most Hebrew and Septuagint manuscripts *Michal*

she had borne to Adriel son of Barzillai the Meholathite. ⁹He handed them over to the Gibeonites, who killed and exposed them on a hill before the LORD. All seven of them fell together; they were put to death during the first days of the harvest, just as the barley harvest was beginning.

¹⁰Rizpah daughter of Aiah took sackcloth and spread it out for herself on a rock. From the beginning of the harvest till the rain poured down from the heavens on the bodies, she did not let the birds of the air touch them by day or the wild animals by night. ¹¹When David was told what Aiah's daughter Rizpah, Saul's concubine, had done, ¹²he went and took the bones of Saul and his son Jonathan from the citizens of Jabesh Gilead. (They had taken them secretly from the public square at Beth Shan, where the Philistines had hung them after they struck Saul down on Gilboa.) ¹³David brought the bones of Saul and his son Jonathan from there, and the bones of those who had been killed and exposed were gathered up.

¹⁴They buried the bones of Saul and his son Jonathan in the tomb of Saul's father Kish, at Zela in Benjamin, and did everything the king commanded. After that, God answered prayer in behalf of the land.

Wars Against the Philistines

¹⁵Once again there was a battle between the Philistines and Israel. David went down with his men to fight against the Philistines, and he became exhausted. ¹⁶And Ishbi-Benob, one of the descendants of Rapha, whose bronze spearhead weighed three hundred shekels[a] and who was armed with a new ⌊sword⌋, said he would kill David. ¹⁷But Abishai son of Zeruiah came to David's rescue; he struck the Philistine down and killed him. Then David's men swore to him, saying, "Never again will you go out with us to battle, so that the lamp of Israel will not be extinguished."

¹⁸In the course of time, there was another battle with the Philistines, at Gob. At that time Sibbecai the Hushathite killed Saph, one of the descendants of Rapha.

¹⁹In another battle with the Philistines at Gob, Elhanan son of Jaare-Oregim[b] the Bethlehemite killed Goliath[c] the Gittite, who had a spear with a shaft like a weaver's rod.

²⁰In still another battle, which took place at Gath, there was a huge man with six fingers on each hand and six toes on each foot—twenty-four in all. He also was descended from Rapha. ²¹When he taunted Israel, Jonathan son of Shimeah, David's brother, killed him.

²²These four were descendants of Rapha in Gath, and they fell at the hands of David and his men.

David's Song of Praise

22 David sang to the LORD the words of this song when the LORD delivered him from the hand of all his enemies and from the hand of Saul. ²He said:

"The LORD is my rock, my fortress
 and my deliverer;
³ my God is my rock, in whom I
  take refuge,
 my shield and the horn[d] of my
  salvation.
He is my stronghold, my refuge and
 my savior—
 from violent men you save me.
⁴I call to the LORD, who is worthy of
 praise,
 and I am saved from my enemies.

---

a16 That is, about 7 1/2 pounds (about 3.5 kilograms)   b19 Or son of Jair the weaver   c19 Hebrew and Septuagint; 1 Chron. 20:5 son of Jair killed Lahmi the brother of Goliath   d3 Horn here symbolizes strength.

POINT OF INTEREST

2 Samuel 21:20

Until Roger Bannister's breakthrough in 1954, no one had run a mile in under four minutes, but today running a sub four-minute mile is common in the world of track and field. Until David killed Goliath, giant killers were nonexistent in Israel. But here the writer lists several giant killers. Why? Was it because David broke the giant-killing barrier? What seemingly insurmountable tasks do you face? Meet them head on in God's name and watch what happens.

5"The waves of death swirled about
     me;
   the torrents of destruction
     overwhelmed me.
6The cords of the grave*a* coiled
     around me;
   the snares of death confronted me.
7In my distress I called to the LORD;
   I called out to my God.
 From his temple he heard my voice;
   my cry came to his ears.

8"The earth trembled and quaked,
   the foundations of the heavens*b*
     shook;
   they trembled because he was
     angry.
9Smoke rose from his nostrils;
   consuming fire came from his
     mouth,
   burning coals blazed out of it.
10He parted the heavens and came
     down;
   dark clouds were under his feet.
11He mounted the cherubim and flew;
   he soared*c* on the wings of the
     wind.
12He made darkness his canopy around
     him—
   the dark*d* rain clouds of the sky.
13Out of the brightness of his presence
   bolts of lightning blazed forth.
14The LORD thundered from heaven;
   the voice of the Most High
     resounded.
15He shot arrows and scattered ⌊the
     enemies⌋,
   bolts of lightning and routed them.
16The valleys of the sea were exposed
   and the foundations of the earth
     laid bare
 at the rebuke of the LORD,
   at the blast of breath from his
     nostrils.

17"He reached down from on high and
     took hold of me;
   he drew me out of deep waters.
18He rescued me from my powerful
     enemy,
   from my foes, who were too strong
     for me.
19They confronted me in the day of my
     disaster,
   but the LORD was my support.
20He brought me out into a spacious
     place;
   he rescued me because he
     delighted in me.

21"The LORD has dealt with me
     according to my
     righteousness;
   according to the cleanness of my
     hands he has rewarded me.
22For I have kept the ways of the LORD;
   I have not done evil by turning
     from my God.
23All his laws are before me;
   I have not turned away from his
     decrees.
24I have been blameless before him
   and have kept myself from sin.
25The LORD has rewarded me according
     to my righteousness,
   according to my cleanness*e* in his
     sight.

26"To the faithful you show yourself
     faithful,
   to the blameless you show yourself
     blameless,
27to the pure you show yourself pure,
   but to the crooked you show
     yourself shrewd.
28You save the humble,
   but your eyes are on the haughty
     to bring them low.
29You are my lamp, O LORD;
   the LORD turns my darkness into
     light.
30With your help I can advance against
     a troop*f*;
   with my God I can scale a wall.

31"As for God, his way is perfect;
   the word of the LORD is flawless.
 He is a shield
   for all who take refuge in him.
32For who is God besides the LORD?
   And who is the Rock except our
     God?
33It is God who arms me with
     strength*g*
   and makes my way perfect.
34He makes my feet like the feet of a
     deer;
   he enables me to stand on the
     heights.
35He trains my hands for battle;

---

a6 Hebrew *Sheol*   *b8* Hebrew; Vulgate and
Syriac (see also Psalm 18:7) *mountains*
c11 Many Hebrew manuscripts (see also Psalm
18:10); most Hebrew manuscripts *appeared*
d12 Septuagint and Vulgate (see also Psalm 18:11);
Hebrew *massed*   *e25* Hebrew; Septuagint and
Vulgate (see also Psalm 18:24) *to the cleanness of
my hands*   *f30* Or *can run through a barricade*
g33 Dead Sea Scrolls, some Septuagint manuscripts,
Vulgate and Syriac (see also Psalm 18:32);
Masoretic Text *who is my strong refuge*

my arms can bend a bow of
    bronze.
³⁶You give me your shield of victory;
    you stoop down to make me great.
³⁷You broaden the path beneath me,
    so that my ankles do not turn.

³⁸"I pursued my enemies and crushed
        them;
    I did not turn back till they were
        destroyed.
³⁹I crushed them completely, and they
        could not rise;
    they fell beneath my feet.
⁴⁰You armed me with strength for
        battle;
    you made my adversaries bow at
        my feet.
⁴¹You made my enemies turn their
        backs in flight,
    and I destroyed my foes.
⁴²They cried for help, but there was no
        one to save them—
    to the LORD, but he did not answer.
⁴³I beat them as fine as the dust of the
        earth;
    I pounded and trampled them like
        mud in the streets.

⁴⁴"You have delivered me from the
        attacks of my people;
    you have preserved me as the head
        of nations.
People I did not know are subject to
        me,
⁴⁵   and foreigners come cringing to
        me;
    as soon as they hear me, they obey
        me.
⁴⁶They all lose heart;
    they come trembling*a* from their
        strongholds.

⁴⁷"The LORD lives! Praise be to my
        Rock!
    Exalted be God, the Rock, my
        Savior!
⁴⁸He is the God who avenges me,
    who puts the nations under me,
⁴⁹   who sets me free from my
        enemies.
You exalted me above my foes;
    from violent men you rescued me.
⁵⁰Therefore I will praise you, O LORD,
        among the nations;
    I will sing praises to your name.
⁵¹He gives his king great victories;
    he shows unfailing kindness to his
        anointed,

to David and his descendants
    forever."

The Last Words of David

23 These are the last words of David:

"The oracle of David son of Jesse,
    the oracle of the man exalted by
        the Most High,
the man anointed by the God of
        Jacob,
    Israel's singer of songs*b*:

²"The Spirit of the LORD spoke through
        me;
    his word was on my tongue.
³The God of Israel spoke,
    the Rock of Israel said to me:
'When one rules over men in
        righteousness,
    when he rules in the fear of God,
⁴he is like the light of morning at
        sunrise
on a cloudless morning,
    like the brightness after rain
    that brings the grass from the
        earth.'

⁵"Is not my house right with God?
    Has he not made with me an
        everlasting covenant,
    arranged and secured in every
        part?
Will he not bring to fruition my
        salvation
    and grant me my every desire?
⁶But evil men are all to be cast aside
        like thorns,
    which are not gathered with the
        hand.
⁷Whoever touches thorns
    uses a tool of iron or the shaft of a
        spear;
    they are burned up where they
        lie."

David's Mighty Men

⁸These are the names of David's
mighty men:

Josheb-Basshebeth,*c* a Tahkemonite,*d*
was chief of the Three; he raised his

---

a46 Some Septuagint manuscripts and Vulgate (see
also Psalm 18:45); Masoretic Text *they arm
themselves.*   *b1* Or *Israel's beloved singer*
c8 Hebrew; some Septuagint manuscripts suggest
Ish-Bosheth, that is, *Esh-Baal* (see also 1 Chron.
11:11 *Jashobeam*).   *d8* Probably a variant of
Hacmonite (see 1 Chron. 11:11)

Read 2 Samuel 22:1–51
Key Verse 2 Samuel 22:47

A Sacrifice of Praise

To praise God is to worship, honor and exalt him as we acknowledge our total dependency on him. Our praise can be lifted up in song or in prayer or expressed through writing, performing or visual arts. It can be done individually or in a group. However we express our praise, it is a deep response from our inner being to the greatness and power of our Creator.

Sometimes our prayers are self-centered rather than God-centered. Although God is worthy of our adoration, we are consumed with the "needs" right in front of our noses, and we forget to spend time praising God. But when we put aside our needs, our wants, our concerns, and focus instead on God's attributes, power and perfection, we offer him a "sacrifice of praise—the fruit of lips that confess his name" (Hebrews 13:15).

Digging Into the Word
1. What do the following passages teach you about God's rule and reign?—*Psalm 47:1–9; Psalm 103:19–22*
2. What do the following passages communicate to you about God's goodness and his awesome works?—*Psalm 119:68; Nahum 1:7*

Action Challenge
Praise God by making a list of how he has been good to you in the past week. Write down as many praises as you can think of, big or small.

One Step Deeper
Nehemiah 9:5–6; Revelation 4:9–11

Go to page 363 for your next devotional reading.

spear against eight hundred men, whom he killed*a* in one encounter. **9**Next to him was Eleazar son of Dodai the Ahohite. As one of the three mighty men, he was with David when they taunted the Philistines gathered ⌞at Pas Dammim⌟*b* for battle. Then the men of Israel retreated, **10**but he stood his ground and struck down the Philistines till his hand grew tired and froze to the sword. The LORD brought about a great victory that day. The troops returned to Eleazar, but only to strip the dead.

11Next to him was Shammah son of Agee the Hararite. When the Philistines banded together at a place where there was a field full of lentils, Israel's troops fled from them. **12**But Shammah took his stand in the middle of the field. He defended it and struck the Philistines down, and the LORD brought about a great victory.

13During harvest time, three of the thirty chief men came down to David at the cave of Adullam, while a band of Philistines was encamped in the Valley of Rephaim. **14**At that time David was in the stronghold, and the Philistine garrison was at Bethlehem. **15**David longed for water and said, "Oh, that someone would get me a drink of water from the well near the gate of Bethlehem!" **16**So the three mighty men broke through the Philistine lines, drew water from the well near the gate of Bethlehem and carried it back to David. But he refused to drink it; instead, he poured it out before the LORD. **17**"Far be it from me, O LORD, to do this!" he said. "Is it not the blood of men who went at the risk of their lives?" And David would not drink it.

Such were the exploits of the three mighty men.

18Abishai the brother of Joab son of Zeruiah was chief of the Three.*c* He raised his spear against three hundred men, whom he killed, and so he became as famous as the Three. **19**Was he not held in greater honor than the Three? He became their commander, even though he was not included among them.

20Benaiah son of Jehoiada was a valiant fighter from Kabzeel, who performed great exploits. He struck down two of Moab's best men. He also went down into a pit on a snowy day and killed a lion. **21**And he struck down a huge Egyptian. Although the Egyptian had a spear in his hand, Benaiah went against him with a club. He snatched the spear from the Egyptian's hand and killed him with his own spear. **22**Such were the exploits of Benaiah son of Jehoiada; he too was as famous as the three mighty men. **23**He was held in greater honor than any of the Thirty, but he was not included among the Three. And David put him in charge of his bodyguard.

24Among the Thirty were:
Asahel the brother of Joab,
Elhanan son of Dodo from Bethlehem,
25Shammah the Harodite,
Elika the Harodite,
26Helez the Paltite,
Ira son of Ikkesh from Tekoa,
27Abiezer from Anathoth,
Mebunnai*d* the Hushathite,
28Zalmon the Ahohite,
Maharai the Netophathite,
29Heled*e* son of Baanah the Netophathite,
Ithai son of Ribai from Gibeah in Benjamin,
30Benaiah the Pirathonite,
Hiddai*f* from the ravines of Gaash,
31Abi-Albon the Arbathite,
Azmaveth the Barhumite,
32Eliahba the Shaalbonite,
the sons of Jashen,
Jonathan **33**son of*g* Shammah the Hararite,
Ahiam son of Sharar*h* the Hararite,
34Eliphelet son of Ahasbai the Maacathite,
Eliam son of Ahithophel the Gilonite,
35Hezro the Carmelite,
Paarai the Arbite,
36Igal son of Nathan from Zobah, the son of Hagri,*i*

a8 Some Septuagint manuscripts (see also 1 Chron. 11:11); Hebrew and other Septuagint manuscripts *Three; it was Adino the Eznite who killed eight hundred men* *b9* See 1 Chron. 11:13; Hebrew *gathered there.* *c18* Most Hebrew manuscripts (see also 1 Chron. 11:20); two Hebrew manuscripts and Syriac *Thirty* *d27* Hebrew; some Septuagint manuscripts (see also 1 Chron. 11:29) *Sibbecai* *e29* Some Hebrew manuscripts and Vulgate (see also 1 Chron. 11:30); most Hebrew manuscripts *Heleb* *f30* Hebrew; some Septuagint manuscripts (see also 1 Chron. 11:32) *Hurai* *g33* Some Septuagint manuscripts (see also 1 Chron. 11:34); Hebrew does not have *son of.* *h33* Hebrew; some Septuagint manuscripts (see also 1 Chron. 11:35) *Sacar* *i36* Some Septuagint manuscripts (see also 1 Chron. 11:38); Hebrew *Haggadi*

³⁷Zelek the Ammonite,
  Naharai the Beerothite, the armor-bearer of Joab son of Zeruiah,
³⁸Ira the Ithrite,
  Gareb the Ithrite
³⁹and Uriah the Hittite.
  There were thirty-seven in all.

David Counts the Fighting Men

24 Again the anger of the LORD burned against Israel, and he incited David against them, saying, "Go and take a census of Israel and Judah."

²So the king said to Joab and the army commanders*ᵃ* with him, "Go throughout the tribes of Israel from Dan to Beersheba and enroll the fighting men, so that I may know how many there are."

³But Joab replied to the king, "May the LORD your God multiply the troops a hundred times over, and may the eyes of my lord the king see it. But why does my lord the king want to do such a thing?"

⁴The king's word, however, overruled Joab and the army commanders; so they left the presence of the king to enroll the fighting men of Israel.

⁵After crossing the Jordan, they camped near Aroer, south of the town in the gorge, and then went through Gad and on to Jazer. ⁶They went to Gilead and the region of Tahtim Hodshi, and on to Dan Jaan and around toward Sidon. ⁷Then they went toward the fortress of Tyre and all the towns of the Hivites and Canaanites. Finally, they went on to Beersheba in the Negev of Judah.

⁸After they had gone through the entire land, they came back to Jerusalem at the end of nine months and twenty days.

⁹Joab reported the number of the fighting men to the king: In Israel there were eight hundred thousand able-bodied men who could handle a sword, and in Judah five hundred thousand.

¹⁰David was conscience-stricken after he had counted the fighting men, and he said to the LORD, "I have sinned greatly in what I have done. Now, O LORD, I beg you, take away the guilt of your servant. I have done a very foolish thing."

¹¹Before David got up the next morning, the word of the LORD had come to Gad the prophet, David's seer: ¹²"Go and tell David, 'This is what the LORD says: I am giving you three options. Choose one of them for me to carry out against you.'"

¹³So Gad went to David and said to him, "Shall there come upon you three*ᵇ* years of famine in your land? Or three months of fleeing from your enemies while they pursue you? Or three days of plague in your land? Now then, think it over and decide how I should answer the one who sent me."

¹⁴David said to Gad, "I am in deep distress. Let us fall into the hands of the LORD, for his mercy is great; but do not let me fall into the hands of men."

¹⁵So the LORD sent a plague on Israel from that morning until the end of the time designated, and seventy thousand of the people from Dan to Beersheba died. ¹⁶When the angel stretched out his hand to destroy Jerusalem, the LORD was grieved because of the calamity and said to the angel who was afflicting the people, "Enough! Withdraw your hand." The angel of the LORD was then at the threshing floor of Araunah the Jebusite.

¹⁷When David saw the angel who was striking down the people, he said to the LORD, "I am the one who has sinned and done wrong. These are but sheep. What have they done? Let your hand fall upon me and my family."

David Builds an Altar

¹⁸On that day Gad went to David and said to him, "Go up and build an altar to the LORD on the threshing floor of Araunah the Jebusite." ¹⁹So David went up, as the LORD had commanded through Gad. ²⁰When Araunah looked and saw the king and his men coming toward him, he went out and bowed down before the king with his face to the ground.

²¹Araunah said, "Why has my lord the king come to his servant?"

"To buy your threshing floor," David answered, "so I can build an altar to the LORD, that the plague on the people may be stopped."

²²Araunah said to David, "Let my lord the king take whatever pleases him and offer it up. Here are oxen for the burnt offering, and here are threshing sledges and ox yokes for the wood. ²³O king, Araunah gives all this to the king." Araunah also said to him, "May the LORD your God accept you."

²⁴But the king replied to Araunah,

ᵃ2 Septuagint (see also verse 4 and 1 Chron. 21:2); Hebrew *Joab the army commander*
ᵇ13 Septuagint (see also 1 Chron. 21:12); Hebrew *seven*

"No, I insist on paying you for it. I will not sacrifice to the LORD my God burnt offerings that cost me nothing."

So David bought the threshing floor and the oxen and paid fifty shekels*a* of silver for them. 25David built an altar to the LORD there and sacrificed burnt offerings and fellowship offerings.*b* Then the LORD answered prayer in behalf of the land, and the plague on Israel was stopped.

a24 That is, about 1 1/4 pounds (about 0.6 kilogram)   *b25* Traditionally *peace offerings*

first Kings evaluates the kings of Israel and Judah and how faithfully they serve God. Some of them worship the Lord faithfully; others disregard him completely. Probably the highest standards for leadership are set by King Solomon and the prophet Elijah. Solomon is known as the wisest man who ever lived; in 1 Kings we see the impact of his leadership on the entire ancient world. And Elijah's total dedication to God distinguishes him as a model leader for all times. Consider their positive examples as you serve God in your own life.

1 KINGS

Adonijah Sets Himself Up as King

1 When King David was old and well advanced in years, he could not keep warm even when they put covers over him. ²So his servants said to him, "Let us look for a young virgin to attend the king and take care of him. She can lie beside him so that our lord the king may keep warm."

³Then they searched throughout Israel for a beautiful girl and found Abishag, a Shunammite, and brought her to the king. ⁴The girl was very beautiful; she took care of the king and waited on him, but the king had no intimate relations with her.

⁵Now Adonijah, whose mother was Haggith, put himself forward and said, "I will be king." So he got chariots and horses*a* ready, with fifty men to run ahead of him. ⁶(His father had never interfered with him by asking, "Why do you behave as you do?" He was also very handsome and was born next after Absalom.)

⁷Adonijah conferred with Joab son of Zeruiah and with Abiathar the priest, and they gave him their support. ⁸But Zadok the priest, Benaiah son of Jehoiada, Nathan the prophet, Shimei and Rei*b* and David's special guard did not join Adonijah.

⁹Adonijah then sacrificed sheep, cattle and fattened calves at the Stone of Zoheleth near En Rogel. He invited all his

a5 Or charioteers   *b8 Or and his friends*

brothers, the king's sons, and all the men of Judah who were royal officials, [10]but he did not invite Nathan the prophet or Benaiah or the special guard or his brother Solomon.

[11]Then Nathan asked Bathsheba, Solomon's mother, "Have you not heard that Adonijah, the son of Haggith, has become king without our lord David's knowing it? [12]Now then, let me advise you how you can save your own life and the life of your son Solomon. [13]Go in to King David and say to him, 'My lord the king, did you not swear to me your servant: "Surely Solomon your son shall be king after me, and he will sit on my throne"? Why then has Adonijah become king?' [14]While you are still there talking to the king, I will come in and confirm what you have said."

[15]So Bathsheba went to see the aged king in his room, where Abishag the Shunammite was attending him. [16]Bathsheba bowed low and knelt before the king.

"What is it you want?" the king asked.

[17]She said to him, "My lord, you yourself swore to me your servant by the LORD your God: 'Solomon your son shall be king after me, and he will sit on my throne.' [18]But now Adonijah has become king, and you, my lord the king, do not know about it. [19]He has sacrificed great numbers of cattle, fattened calves, and sheep, and has invited all the king's sons, Abiathar the priest and Joab the commander of the army, but he has not invited Solomon your servant. [20]My lord the king, the eyes of all Israel are on you, to learn from you who will sit on the throne of my lord the king after him. [21]Otherwise, as soon as my lord the king is laid to rest with his fathers, I and my son Solomon will be treated as criminals."

[22]While she was still speaking with the king, Nathan the prophet arrived. [23]And they told the king, "Nathan the prophet is here." So he went before the king and bowed with his face to the ground.

[24]Nathan said, "Have you, my lord the king, declared that Adonijah shall be king after you, and that he will sit on your throne? [25]Today he has gone down and sacrificed great numbers of cattle, fattened calves, and sheep. He has invited all the king's sons, the commanders of the army and Abiathar the priest. Right now they are eating and drinking with him and saying, 'Long live King Adonijah!' [26]But me your servant, and Zadok the priest, and Benaiah son of Jehoiada, and your servant Solomon he did not invite. [27]Is this something my lord the king has done without letting his servants know who should sit on the throne of my lord the king after him?"

David Makes Solomon King

[28]Then King David said, "Call in Bathsheba." So she came into the king's presence and stood before him.

[29]The king then took an oath: "As surely as the LORD lives, who has delivered me out of every trouble, [30]I will surely carry out today what I swore to you by the LORD, the God of Israel: Solomon your son shall be king after me, and he will sit on my throne in my place."

[31]Then Bathsheba bowed low with her face to the ground and, kneeling before the king, said, "May my lord King David live forever!"

[32]King David said, "Call in Zadok the priest, Nathan the prophet and Benaiah son of Jehoiada." When they came before the king, [33]he said to them: "Take your lord's servants with you and set Solomon my son on my own mule and take him down to Gihon. [34]There have Zadok the priest and Nathan the prophet anoint him king over Israel. Blow the trumpet and shout, 'Long live King Solomon!' [35]Then you are to go up with him, and he is to come and sit on my throne and reign in my place. I have appointed him ruler over Israel and Judah."

[36]Benaiah son of Jehoiada answered the king, "Amen! May the LORD, the God of my lord the king, so declare it. [37]As the LORD was with my lord the king, so may he be with Solomon to make his throne

POINT OF INTEREST   1 Kings 1:11

Bathsheba was now an old woman. As the queen mother, she had become an influential member of the court. In spite of her adultery with David and the sin surrounding it, God had granted her forgiveness. And God would eventually elevate her son to the throne. Our God is a God of grace.

even greater than the throne of my lord King David!"

³⁸So Zadok the priest, Nathan the prophet, Benaiah son of Jehoiada, the Kerethites and the Pelethites went down and put Solomon on King David's mule and escorted him to Gihon. ³⁹Zadok the priest took the horn of oil from the sacred tent and anointed Solomon. Then they sounded the trumpet and all the people shouted, "Long live King Solomon!" ⁴⁰And all the people went up after him, playing flutes and rejoicing greatly, so that the ground shook with the sound.

⁴¹Adonijah and all the guests who were with him heard it as they were finishing their feast. On hearing the sound of the trumpet, Joab asked, "What's the meaning of all the noise in the city?"

⁴²Even as he was speaking, Jonathan son of Abiathar the priest arrived. Adonijah said, "Come in. A worthy man like you must be bringing good news."

⁴³"Not at all!" Jonathan answered. "Our lord King David has made Solomon king. ⁴⁴The king has sent with him Zadok the priest, Nathan the prophet, Benaiah son of Jehoiada, the Kerethites and the Pelethites, and they have put him on the king's mule, ⁴⁵and Zadok the priest and Nathan the prophet have anointed him king at Gihon. From there they have gone up cheering, and the city resounds with it. That's the noise you hear. ⁴⁶Moreover, Solomon has taken his seat on the royal throne. ⁴⁷Also, the royal officials have come to congratulate our lord King David, saying, 'May your God make Solomon's name more famous than yours and his throne greater than yours!' And the king bowed in worship on his bed ⁴⁸and said, 'Praise be to the LORD, the God of Israel, who has allowed my eyes to see a successor on my throne today.'"

⁴⁹At this, all Adonijah's guests rose in alarm and dispersed. ⁵⁰But Adonijah, in fear of Solomon, went and took hold of the horns of the altar. ⁵¹Then Solomon was told, "Adonijah is afraid of King Solomon and is clinging to the horns of the altar. He says, 'Let King Solomon swear to me today that he will not put his servant to death with the sword.'"

⁵²Solomon replied, "If he shows himself to be a worthy man, not a hair of his head will fall to the ground; but if evil is found in him, he will die." ⁵³Then King Solomon sent men, and they brought him down from the altar. And Adonijah came

and bowed down to King Solomon, and Solomon said, "Go to your home."

David's Charge to Solomon

2 When the time drew near for David to die, he gave a charge to Solomon his son.

²"I am about to go the way of all the earth," he said. "So be strong, show yourself a man, ³and observe what the LORD your God requires: Walk in his ways, and keep his decrees and commands, his laws and requirements, as written in the Law of Moses, so that you may prosper in all you do and wherever you go, ⁴and that the LORD may keep his promise to me: 'If your descendants watch how they live, and if they walk faithfully before me with all their heart and soul, you will never fail to have a man on the throne of Israel.'

⁵"Now you yourself know what Joab son of Zeruiah did to me—what he did to the two commanders of Israel's armies, Abner son of Ner and Amasa son of Jether. He killed them, shedding their blood in peacetime as if in battle, and with that blood stained the belt around his waist and the sandals on his feet. ⁶Deal with him according to your wisdom, but do not let his gray head go down to the grave*ᵃ* in peace.

⁷"But show kindness to the sons of Barzillai of Gilead and let them be among those who eat at your table. They stood by me when I fled from your brother Absalom.

⁸"And remember, you have with you Shimei son of Gera, the Benjamite from

ᵃ6 Hebrew Sheol; *also in verse 9*

POINT OF INTEREST

1 Kings 2:2

When David told Solomon to "be strong," he wasn't telling his son to work out at the gym. David was challenging Solomon to walk in God's ways and "keep his decrees and commands" (verse 3). David said that if Solomon developed spiritual maturity, he would be prosperous in everything. How can you become more spiritually mature?

Bahurim, who called down bitter curses on me the day I went to Mahanaim. When he came down to meet me at the Jordan, I swore to him by the LORD: 'I will not put you to death by the sword.' ⁹But now, do not consider him innocent. You are a man of wisdom; you will know what to do to him. Bring his gray head down to the grave in blood."

¹⁰Then David rested with his fathers and was buried in the City of David. ¹¹He had reigned forty years over Israel—seven years in Hebron and thirty-three in Jerusalem. ¹²So Solomon sat on the throne of his father David, and his rule was firmly established.

Solomon's Throne Established

¹³Now Adonijah, the son of Haggith, went to Bathsheba, Solomon's mother. Bathsheba asked him, "Do you come peacefully?"

He answered, "Yes, peacefully." ¹⁴Then he added, "I have something to say to you."

"You may say it," she replied.

¹⁵"As you know," he said, "the kingdom was mine. All Israel looked to me as their king. But things changed, and the kingdom has gone to my brother; for it has come to him from the LORD. ¹⁶Now I have one request to make of you. Do not refuse me."

"You may make it," she said.

¹⁷So he continued, "Please ask King Solomon—he will not refuse you—to give me Abishag the Shunammite as my wife."

¹⁸"Very well," Bathsheba replied, "I will speak to the king for you."

¹⁹When Bathsheba went to King Solomon to speak to him for Adonijah, the king stood up to meet her, bowed down to her and sat down on his throne. He had a throne brought for the king's mother, and she sat down at his right hand.

²⁰"I have one small request to make of you," she said. "Do not refuse me."

The king replied, "Make it, my mother; I will not refuse you."

²¹So she said, "Let Abishag the Shunammite be given in marriage to your brother Adonijah."

²²King Solomon answered his mother, "Why do you request Abishag the Shunammite for Adonijah? You might as well request the kingdom for him—after all, he is my older brother—yes, for him and

for Abiathar the priest and Joab son of Zeruiah!"

²³Then King Solomon swore by the LORD: "May God deal with me, be it ever so severely, if Adonijah does not pay with his life for this request! ²⁴And now, as surely as the LORD lives—he who has established me securely on the throne of my father David and has founded a dynasty for me as he promised—Adonijah shall be put to death today!" ²⁵So King Solomon gave orders to Benaiah son of Jehoiada, and he struck down Adonijah and he died.

²⁶To Abiathar the priest the king said, "Go back to your fields in Anathoth. You deserve to die, but I will not put you to death now, because you carried the ark of the Sovereign LORD before my father David and shared all my father's hardships." ²⁷So Solomon removed Abiathar from the priesthood of the LORD, fulfilling the word the LORD had spoken at Shiloh about the house of Eli.

²⁸When the news reached Joab, who had conspired with Adonijah though not with Absalom, he fled to the tent of the LORD and took hold of the horns of the altar. ²⁹King Solomon was told that Joab had fled to the tent of the LORD and was beside the altar. Then Solomon ordered Benaiah son of Jehoiada, "Go, strike him down!"

³⁰So Benaiah entered the tent of the LORD and said to Joab, "The king says, 'Come out!' "

But he answered, "No, I will die here." Benaiah reported to the king, "This is how Joab answered me."

³¹Then the king commanded Benaiah, "Do as he says. Strike him down and bury him, and so clear me and my father's house of the guilt of the innocent blood that Joab shed. ³²The LORD will repay him for the blood he shed, because without the knowledge of my father David he attacked two men and killed them with the sword. Both of them—Abner son of Ner, commander of Israel's army, and Amasa son of Jether, commander of Judah's army—were better men and more upright than he. ³³May the guilt of their blood rest on the head of Joab and his descendants forever. But on David and his descendants, his house and his throne, may there be the LORD's peace forever."

³⁴So Benaiah son of Jehoiada went up and struck down Joab and killed him,

and he was buried on his own land*a* in the desert. ³⁵The king put Benaiah son of Jehoiada over the army in Joab's position and replaced Abiathar with Zadok the priest.

³⁶Then the king sent for Shimei and said to him, "Build yourself a house in Jerusalem and live there, but do not go anywhere else. ³⁷The day you leave and cross the Kidron Valley, you can be sure you will die; your blood will be on your own head."

³⁸Shimei answered the king, "What you say is good. Your servant will do as my lord the king has said." And Shimei stayed in Jerusalem for a long time.

³⁹But three years later, two of Shimei's slaves ran off to Achish son of Maacah, king of Gath, and Shimei was told, "Your slaves are in Gath." ⁴⁰At this, he saddled his donkey and went to Achish at Gath in search of his slaves. So Shimei went away and brought the slaves back from Gath.

⁴¹When Solomon was told that Shimei had gone from Jerusalem to Gath and had returned, ⁴²the king summoned Shimei and said to him, "Did I not make you swear by the LORD and warn you, 'On the day you leave to go anywhere else, you can be sure you will die'? At that time you said to me, 'What you say is good. I will obey.' ⁴³Why then did you not keep your oath to the LORD and obey the command I gave you?"

⁴⁴The king also said to Shimei, "You know in your heart all the wrong you did to my father David. Now the LORD will repay you for your wrongdoing. ⁴⁵But King Solomon will be blessed, and David's throne will remain secure before the LORD forever."

⁴⁶Then the king gave the order to Benaiah son of Jehoiada, and he went out and struck Shimei down and killed him.

The kingdom was now firmly established in Solomon's hands.

Solomon Asks for Wisdom

3 Solomon made an alliance with Pharaoh king of Egypt and married his daughter. He brought her to the City of David until he finished building his palace and the temple of the LORD, and the wall around Jerusalem. ²The people, however, were still sacrificing at the high places, because a temple had not yet been built for the Name of the LORD. ³Solomon showed his love for the LORD by walking according to the statutes of his father David, except that he offered sacrifices and burned incense on the high places.

⁴The king went to Gibeon to offer sacrifices, for that was the most important high place, and Solomon offered a thousand burnt offerings on that altar. ⁵At Gibeon the LORD appeared to Solomon during the night in a dream, and God said, "Ask for whatever you want me to give you."

⁶Solomon answered, "You have shown great kindness to your servant, my father David, because he was faithful to you and righteous and upright in heart. You have continued this great kindness to him and have given him a son to sit on his throne this very day.

⁷"Now, O LORD my God, you have made your servant king in place of my father David. But I am only a little child and do not know how to carry out my duties. ⁸Your servant is here among the people you have chosen, a great people, too numerous to count or number. ⁹So give your servant a discerning heart to govern your people and to distinguish between right and wrong. For who is able to govern this great people of yours?"

¹⁰The Lord was pleased that Solomon had asked for this. ¹¹So God said to him, "Since you have asked for this and not for long life or wealth for yourself, nor have asked for the death of your enemies but for discernment in administering justice, ¹²I will do what you have asked. I will give you a wise and discerning heart, so that there will never have been anyone like you, nor will there ever be. ¹³Moreover, I will give you what you have not asked for—both riches and honor—so that in your lifetime you will have no equal among kings. ¹⁴And if you walk in my ways and obey my statutes and commands as David your father did, I will give you a long life." ¹⁵Then Solomon awoke—and he realized it had been a dream.

He returned to Jerusalem, stood before the ark of the Lord's covenant and sacrificed burnt offerings and fellowship offerings.*b* Then he gave a feast for all his court.

---

*a*34 Or *buried in his tomb*   *b*15 Traditionally *peace offerings*

A Wise Ruling

¹⁶Now two prostitutes came to the king and stood before him. ¹⁷One of them said, "My lord, this woman and I live in the same house. I had a baby while she was there with me. ¹⁸The third day after my child was born, this woman also had a baby. We were alone; there was no one in the house but the two of us.

¹⁹"During the night this woman's son died because she lay on him. ²⁰So she got up in the middle of the night and took my son from my side while I your servant was asleep. She put him by her breast

---

MONDAY

Read 1 Kings 3:1–28
Key Verse 1 Kings 3:9

Making God's Mark—or Missing It? – Julie Bundt

Life was full of possibilities for the young king Solomon—the son of David, raised in the royal palace and chosen by God to build the temple. Solomon had everything going for him; he had the potential to make God's mark in the world like no other before him.

Solomon was humble enough to know that he needed the Lord to help and guide him. When the Lord appeared to Solomon in a dream, Solomon pleased the Lord by asking for wisdom and a discerning heart. He realized that he needed the ability to judge between good and evil. He had to be able to see the truth in the midst of complex circumstances in order to rule his people with justice.

God was so pleased with Solomon's humility that he gave Solomon "a wise and discerning heart, so that there will never have been anyone like you, nor will there ever be." Not only that, but he expanded Solomon's prospects even more: "Moreover, I will give you what you have not asked for—both riches and honor—so that in your lifetime you will have no equal among kings." Then God added both a guarantee and a warning: "And if you walk in my ways and obeys my statutes and commands as David your father did, I will give you a long life" (1 Kings 3:13–14). God's caveat underlined this truth: that the gift of wisdom was dependent on Solomon's dependence on the One who had given it to him.

At first Solomon did depend on God. He made his mark on the world—the "wisdom of Solomon" and the "wealth of Solomon" are legendary. But gradually Solomon slid into self-sufficiency; he forgot who had given him his kingdom and ability to rule well. He began to disobey God's commands and acquired wealth for his kingdom though harmful alliances (see Deuteronomy 17:16). Rather than making his mark, he began missing it, and his actions were to reap unfortunate results for a long time.

God has often granted extraordinary gifts of wisdom to leaders, leaders whom he has used to make his mark on the world. God can use us too—when we ask him for wisdom and then depend on him.

A Deeper Look
1 Kings 2:3; Proverbs 2:1–11; James 1:5

Go to page 371 for your next devotional reading.

and put her dead son by my breast. ²¹The next morning, I got up to nurse my son—and he was dead! But when I looked at him closely in the morning light, I saw that it wasn't the son I had borne."

²²The other woman said, "No! The living one is my son; the dead one is yours."

But the first one insisted, "No! The dead one is yours; the living one is mine." And so they argued before the king.

²³The king said, "This one says, 'My son is alive and your son is dead,' while that one says, 'No! Your son is dead and mine is alive.'"

²⁴Then the king said, "Bring me a sword." So they brought a sword for the king. ²⁵He then gave an order: "Cut the living child in two and give half to one and half to the other."

²⁶The woman whose son was alive was filled with compassion for her son and said to the king, "Please, my lord, give her the living baby! Don't kill him!"

But the other said, "Neither I nor you shall have him. Cut him in two!"

²⁷Then the king gave his ruling: "Give the living baby to the first woman. Do not kill him; she is his mother."

²⁸When all Israel heard the verdict the king had given, they held the king in awe, because they saw that he had wisdom from God to administer justice.

Solomon's Officials and Governors

4 So King Solomon ruled over all Israel. ²And these were his chief officials:

Azariah son of Zadok—the priest;
³Elihoreph and Ahijah, sons of Shisha—secretaries;
Jehoshaphat son of Ahilud—recorder;
⁴Benaiah son of Jehoiada—commander in chief;
Zadok and Abiathar—priests;
⁵Azariah son of Nathan—in charge of the district officers;
Zabud son of Nathan—a priest and personal adviser to the king;
⁶Ahishar—in charge of the palace;
Adoniram son of Abda—in charge of forced labor.

⁷Solomon also had twelve district governors over all Israel, who supplied provisions for the king and the royal household. Each one had to provide supplies for one month in the year. ⁸These are their names:

Ben-Hur—in the hill country of Ephraim;
⁹Ben-Deker—in Makaz, Shaalbim, Beth Shemesh and Elon Bethhanan;
¹⁰Ben-Hesed—in Arubboth (Socoh and all the land of Hepher were his);
¹¹Ben-Abinadab—in Naphoth Dorᵃ (he was married to Taphath daughter of Solomon);
¹²Baana son of Ahilud—in Taanach and Megiddo, and in all of Beth Shan next to Zarethan below Jezreel, from Beth Shan to Abel Meholah across to Jokmeam;
¹³Ben-Geber—in Ramoth Gilead (the settlements of Jair son of Manasseh in Gilead were his, as well as the district of Argob in Bashan and its sixty large walled cities with bronze gate bars);
¹⁴Ahinadab son of Iddo—in Mahanaim;
¹⁵Ahimaaz—in Naphtali (he had married Basemath daughter of Solomon);
¹⁶Baana son of Hushai—in Asher and in Aloth;
¹⁷Jehoshaphat son of Paruah—in Issachar;
¹⁸Shimei son of Ela—in Benjamin;
¹⁹Geber son of Uri—in Gilead (the country of Sihon king of the Amorites and the country of Og king of Bashan). He was the only governor over the district.

Solomon's Daily Provisions

²⁰The people of Judah and Israel were as numerous as the sand on the seashore; they ate, they drank and they were happy. ²¹And Solomon ruled over all the kingdoms from the Riverᵇ to the land of the Philistines, as far as the border of Egypt. These countries brought tribute and were Solomon's subjects all his life.

²²Solomon's daily provisions were thirty corsᶜ of fine flour and sixty corsᵈ of meal, ²³ten head of stall-fed cattle, twenty of pasture-fed cattle and a hundred sheep and goats, as well as deer, gazelles, roebucks and choice fowl. ²⁴For he ruled over all the kingdoms west of

---

ᵃ11 Or *in the heights of Dor*   ᵇ21 That is, the Euphrates; also in verse 24   ᶜ22 That is, probably about 185 bushels (about 6.6 kiloliters)   ᵈ22 That is, probably about 375 bushels (about 13.2 kiloliters) the River, from Tiphsah to Gaza, and had peace on all sides. [25]During Solomon's lifetime Judah and Israel, from Dan to Beersheba, lived in safety, each man under his own vine and fig tree.

[26]Solomon had four[a] thousand stalls for chariot horses, and twelve thousand horses.[b]

[27]The district officers, each in his month, supplied provisions for King Solomon and all who came to the king's table. They saw to it that nothing was lacking. [28]They also brought to the proper place their quotas of barley and straw for the chariot horses and the other horses.

Solomon's Wisdom

[29]God gave Solomon wisdom and very great insight, and a breadth of understanding as measureless as the sand on the seashore. [30]Solomon's wisdom was greater than the wisdom of all the men of the East, and greater than all the wisdom of Egypt. [31]He was wiser than any other man, including Ethan the Ezrahite—wiser than Heman, Calcol and Darda, the sons of Mahol. And his fame spread to all the surrounding nations. [32]He spoke three thousand proverbs and his songs numbered a thousand and five. [33]He described plant life, from the cedar of Lebanon to the hyssop that grows out of walls. He also taught about animals and birds, reptiles and fish. [34]Men of all nations came to listen to Solomon's wisdom, sent by all the kings of the world, who had heard of his wisdom.

Preparations for Building the Temple

5 When Hiram king of Tyre heard that Solomon had been anointed king to succeed his father David, he sent his envoys to Solomon, because he had always been on friendly terms with David. [2]Solomon sent back this message to Hiram:

[3]"You know that because of the wars waged against my father David from all sides, he could not build a temple for the Name of the LORD his God until the LORD put his enemies under his feet. [4]But now the LORD my God has given me rest on every side, and there is no adversary or disaster. [5]I intend, therefore, to build a temple for the Name of the LORD my God, as the LORD told my father David, when he said, 'Your son whom I will put on the throne in your place will build the temple for my Name.'

[6]"So give orders that cedars of Lebanon be cut for me. My men will work with yours, and I will pay you for your men whatever wages you set. You know that we have no one so skilled in felling timber as the Sidonians."

[7]When Hiram heard Solomon's message, he was greatly pleased and said, "Praise be to the LORD today, for he has given David a wise son to rule over this great nation."

[8]So Hiram sent word to Solomon:

"I have received the message you sent me and will do all you want in providing the cedar and pine logs. [9]My men will haul them down from Lebanon to the sea, and I will float them in rafts by sea to the place you specify. There I will separate them and you can take them away. And you are to grant my wish by providing food for my royal household."

[10]In this way Hiram kept Solomon supplied with all the cedar and pine logs he wanted, [11]and Solomon gave Hiram twenty thousand cors[c] of wheat as food for his household, in addition to twenty thousand baths[d,e] of pressed olive oil. Solomon continued to do this for Hiram year after year. [12]The LORD gave Solomon wisdom, just as he had promised him. There were peaceful relations between

---

[a]26 Some Septuagint manuscripts (see also 2 Chron. 9:25); Hebrew *forty*   [b]26 Or *charioteers*   [c]11 That is, probably about 125,000 bushels (about 4,400 kiloliters)   [d]11 Septuagint (see also 2 Chron. 2:10); Hebrew *twenty cors*   [e]11 That is, about 115,000 gallons (about 440 kiloliters)

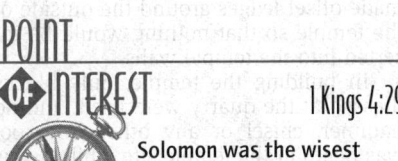

POINT OF INTEREST

1 Kings 4:29

Solomon was the wisest man who ever lived. He was a prolific writer and musician, a botanist and zoologist, a statesman and philosopher, and an acclaimed orator. As you read through verse 34, take note of how Solomon used his extraordinary gifts. What would you do if you possessed these gifts?

Hiram and Solomon, and the two of them made a treaty.

[13]King Solomon conscripted laborers from all Israel—thirty thousand men. [14]He sent them off to Lebanon in shifts of ten thousand a month, so that they spent one month in Lebanon and two months at home. Adoniram was in charge of the forced labor. [15]Solomon had seventy thousand carriers and eighty thousand stonecutters in the hills, [16]as well as thirty-three hundred[a] foremen who supervised the project and directed the workmen. [17]At the king's command they removed from the quarry large blocks of quality stone to provide a foundation of dressed stone for the temple. [18]The craftsmen of Solomon and Hiram and the men of Gebal[b] cut and prepared the timber and stone for the building of the temple.

Solomon Builds the Temple

6 In the four hundred and eightieth[c] year after the Israelites had come out of Egypt, in the fourth year of Solomon's reign over Israel, in the month of Ziv, the second month, he began to build the temple of the LORD.

[2]The temple that King Solomon built for the LORD was sixty cubits long, twenty wide and thirty high.[d] [3]The portico at the front of the main hall of the temple extended the width of the temple, that is twenty cubits,[e] and projected ten cubits[f] from the front of the temple. [4]He made narrow clerestory windows in the temple. [5]Against the walls of the main hall and inner sanctuary he built a structure around the building, in which there were side rooms. [6]The lowest floor was five cubits[g] wide, the middle floor six cubits[h] and the third floor seven.[i] He made offset ledges around the outside of the temple so that nothing would be inserted into the temple walls.

[7]In building the temple, only blocks dressed at the quarry were used, and no hammer, chisel or any other iron tool was heard at the temple site while it was being built.

[8]The entrance to the lowest[j] floor was on the south side of the temple; a stairway led up to the middle level and from there to the third. [9]So he built the temple and completed it, roofing it with beams and cedar planks. [10]And he built the side rooms all along the temple. The height of each was five cubits, and they

were attached to the temple by beams of cedar.

[11]The word of the LORD came to Solomon: [12]"As for this temple you are building, if you follow my decrees, carry out my regulations and keep all my commands and obey them, I will fulfill through you the promise I gave to David your father. [13]And I will live among the Israelites and will not abandon my people Israel."

[14]So Solomon built the temple and completed it. [15]He lined its interior walls with cedar boards, paneling them from the floor of the temple to the ceiling, and covered the floor of the temple with planks of pine. [16]He partitioned off twenty cubits[e] at the rear of the temple with cedar boards from floor to ceiling to form within the temple an inner sanctuary, the Most Holy Place. [17]The main hall in front of this room was forty cubits[k] long. [18]The inside of the temple was cedar, carved with gourds and open flowers. Everything was cedar; no stone was to be seen.

[19]He prepared the inner sanctuary within the temple to set the ark of the covenant of the LORD there. [20]The inner sanctuary was twenty cubits long, twenty wide and twenty high.[l] He overlaid the inside with pure gold, and he also overlaid the altar of cedar. [21]Solomon covered the inside of the temple with pure gold, and he extended gold chains across the front of the inner sanctuary, which was overlaid with gold. [22]So he overlaid the whole interior with gold. He also overlaid with gold the altar that belonged to the inner sanctuary.

[23]In the inner sanctuary he made a pair of cherubim of olive wood, each ten cubits[f] high. [24]One wing of the first cherub was five cubits long, and the other wing five cubits—ten cubits from wing tip to wing tip. [25]The second cherub also mea-

---

a 16 Hebrew; some Septuagint manuscripts (see also 2 Chron. 2:2, 18) *thirty-six hundred*　　*b 18* That is, Byblos　　*c 1* Hebrew; Septuagint *four hundred and fortieth*　　*d 2* That is, about 90 feet (about 27 meters) long and 30 feet (about 9 meters) wide and 45 feet (about 13.5 meters) high　　*e 3,16* That is, about 30 feet (about 9 meters)　　*f 3,23* That is, about 15 feet (about 4.5 meters)　　*g 6* That is, about 7 1/2 feet (about 2.3 meters); also in verses 10 and 24　　*h 6* That is, about 9 feet (about 2.7 meters)　　*i 6* That is, about 10 1/2 feet (about 3.1 meters)　　*j 8* Septuagint; Hebrew *middle*　　*k 17* That is, about 60 feet (about 18 meters)　　*l 20* That is, about 30 feet (about 9 meters) long, wide and high sured ten cubits, for the two cherubim were identical in size and shape. ²⁶The height of each cherub was ten cubits. ²⁷He placed the cherubim inside the innermost room of the temple, with their wings spread out. The wing of one cherub touched one wall, while the wing of the other touched the other wall, and their wings touched each other in the middle of the room. ²⁸He overlaid the cherubim with gold.

²⁹On the walls all around the temple, in both the inner and outer rooms, he carved cherubim, palm trees and open flowers. ³⁰He also covered the floors of both the inner and outer rooms of the temple with gold.

³¹For the entrance of the inner sanctuary he made doors of olive wood with five-sided jambs. ³²And on the two olive wood doors he carved cherubim, palm trees and open flowers, and overlaid the cherubim and palm trees with beaten gold. ³³In the same way he made four-sided jambs of olive wood for the entrance to the main hall. ³⁴He also made two pine doors, each having two leaves that turned in sockets. ³⁵He carved cherubim, palm trees and open flowers on them and overlaid them with gold hammered evenly over the carvings.

³⁶And he built the inner courtyard of three courses of dressed stone and one course of trimmed cedar beams.

³⁷The foundation of the temple of the LORD was laid in the fourth year, in the month of Ziv. ³⁸In the eleventh year in the month of Bul, the eighth month, the temple was finished in all its details according to its specifications. He had spent seven years building it.

Solomon Builds His Palace

7 It took Solomon thirteen years, however, to complete the construction of his palace. ²He built the Palace of the Forest of Lebanon a hundred cubits long, fifty wide and thirty high,ᵃ with four rows of cedar columns supporting trimmed cedar beams. ³It was roofed with cedar above the beams that rested on the columns—forty-five beams, fifteen to a row. ⁴Its windows were placed high in sets of three, facing each other. ⁵All the doorways had rectangular frames; they were in the front part in sets of three, facing each other.ᵇ

⁶He made a colonnade fifty cubits long and thirty wide.ᶜ In front of it was a

portico, and in front of that were pillars and an overhanging roof.

⁷He built the throne hall, the Hall of Justice, where he was to judge, and he covered it with cedar from floor to ceiling.ᵈ ⁸And the palace in which he was to live, set farther back, was similar in design. Solomon also made a palace like this hall for Pharaoh's daughter, whom he had married.

⁹All these structures, from the outside to the great courtyard and from foundation to eaves, were made of blocks of high-grade stone cut to size and trimmed with a saw on their inner and outer faces. ¹⁰The foundations were laid with large stones of good quality, some measuring ten cubitsᵉ and some eight.ᶠ ¹¹Above were high-grade stones, cut to size, and cedar beams. ¹²The great courtyard was surrounded by a wall of three courses of dressed stone and one course of trimmed cedar beams, as was the inner courtyard of the temple of the LORD with its portico.

The Temple's Furnishings

¹³King Solomon sent to Tyre and brought Huram,ᵍ ¹⁴whose mother was a widow from the tribe of Naphtali and whose father was a man of Tyre and a craftsman in bronze. Huram was highly skilled and experienced in all kinds of bronze work. He came to King Solomon and did all the work assigned to him.

ᵃ2 That is, about 150 feet (about 46 meters) long, 75 feet (about 23 meters) wide and 45 feet (about 13.5 meters) high　ᵇ5 The meaning of the Hebrew for this verse is uncertain.　ᶜ6 That is, about 75 feet (about 23 meters) long and 45 feet (about 13.5 meters) wide　ᵈ7 Vulgate and Syriac; Hebrew *floor*　ᵉ10 That is, about 15 feet (about 4.5 meters)　ᶠ10 That is, about 12 feet (about 3.6 meters)　ᵍ13 Hebrew *Hiram*, a variant of *Huram*; also in verses 40 and 45

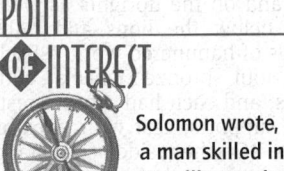

POINT OF INTEREST

1 Kings 7:13

Solomon wrote, "Do you see a man skilled in his work? He will serve before kings" (Proverbs 22:29). Huram was living proof for Solomon and for us that the path to notoriety is skill and diligence. Huram used his gifts in God's service. How might you go about doing the same?

¹⁵He cast two bronze pillars, each eighteen cubits high and twelve cubits around,ᵃ by line. ¹⁶He also made two capitals of cast bronze to set on the tops of the pillars; each capital was five cubitsᵇ high. ¹⁷A network of interwoven chains festooned the capitals on top of the pillars, seven for each capital. ¹⁸He made pomegranates in two rowsᶜ encircling each network to decorate the capitals on top of the pillars.ᵈ He did the same for each capital. ¹⁹The capitals on top of the pillars in the portico were in the shape of lilies, four cubitsᵉ high. ²⁰On the capitals of both pillars, above the bowl-shaped part next to the network, were the two hundred pomegranates in rows all around. ²¹He erected the pillars at the portico of the temple. The pillar to the south he named Jakinᶠ and the one to the north Boaz.ᵍ ²²The capitals on top were in the shape of lilies. And so the work on the pillars was completed.

²³He made the Sea of cast metal, circular in shape, measuring ten cubitsʰ from rim to rim and five cubits high. It took a line of thirty cubitsⁱ to measure around it. ²⁴Below the rim, gourds encircled it— ten to a cubit. The gourds were cast in two rows in one piece with the Sea.

²⁵The Sea stood on twelve bulls, three facing north, three facing west, three facing south and three facing east. The Sea rested on top of them, and their hindquarters were toward the center. ²⁶It was a handbreadthʲ in thickness, and its rim was like the rim of a cup, like a lily blossom. It held two thousand baths.ᵏ

²⁷He also made ten movable stands of bronze; each was four cubits long, four wide and three high.ˡ ²⁸This is how the stands were made: They had side panels attached to uprights. ²⁹On the panels between the uprights were lions, bulls and cherubim—and on the uprights as well. Above and below the lions and bulls were wreaths of hammered work. ³⁰Each stand had four bronze wheels with bronze axles, and each had a basin resting on four supports, cast with wreaths on each side. ³¹On the inside of the stand there was an opening that had a circular frame one cubitᵐ deep. This opening was round, and with its basework it measured a cubit and a half.ⁿ Around its opening there was engraving. The panels of the stands were square, not round. ³²The four wheels were under the panels,

and the axles of the wheels were attached to the stand. The diameter of each wheel was a cubit and a half. ³³The wheels were made like chariot wheels; the axles, rims, spokes and hubs were all of cast metal.

³⁴Each stand had four handles, one on each corner, projecting from the stand. ³⁵At the top of the stand there was a circular band half a cubitᵒ deep. The supports and panels were attached to the top of the stand. ³⁶He engraved cherubim, lions and palm trees on the surfaces of the supports and on the panels, in every available space, with wreaths all around. ³⁷This is the way he made the ten stands. They were all cast in the same molds and were identical in size and shape.

³⁸He then made ten bronze basins, each holding forty bathsᵖ and measuring four cubits across, one basin to go on each of the ten stands. ³⁹He placed five of the stands on the south side of the temple and five on the north. He placed the Sea on the south side, at the southeast corner of the temple. ⁴⁰He also made the basins and shovels and sprinkling bowls.

So Huram finished all the work he had undertaken for King Solomon in the temple of the Lord:

⁴¹the two pillars;
    the two bowl-shaped capitals on top of the pillars;
    the two sets of network decorating the two bowl-shaped capitals on top of the pillars;
⁴²the four hundred pomegranates for the two sets of network (two rows of pomegranates for each network, decorating the bowl-

---

ᵃ15 That is, about 27 feet (about 8.1 meters) high and 18 feet (about 5.4 meters) around   ᵇ16 That is, about 7 1/2 feet (about 2.3 meters); also in verse 23   ᶜ18 Two Hebrew manuscripts and Septuagint; most Hebrew manuscripts *made the pillars, and there were two rows*   ᵈ18 Many Hebrew manuscripts and Syriac; most Hebrew manuscripts *pomegranates*   ᵉ19 That is, about 6 feet (about 1.8 meters); also in verse 38   ᶠ21 *Jakin* probably means *he establishes.*   ᵍ21 *Boaz* probably means *in him is strength.*   ʰ23 That is, about 15 feet (about 4.5 meters)   ⁱ23 That is, about 45 feet (about 13.5 meters)   ʲ26 That is, about 3 inches (about 8 centimeters)   ᵏ26 That is, probably about 11,500 gallons (about 44 kiloliters); the Septuagint does not have this sentence.   ˡ27 That is, about 6 feet (about 1.8 meters) long and wide and about 4 1/2 feet (about 1.3 meters) high   ᵐ31 That is, about 1 1/2 feet (about 0.5 meter)   ⁿ31 That is, about 2 1/4 feet (about 0.7 meter); also in verse 32   ᵒ35 That is, about 3/4 foot (about 0.2 meter)   ᵖ38 That is, about 230 gallons (about 880 liters)

shaped capitals on top of the pillars);
43the ten stands with their ten basins;
44the Sea and the twelve bulls under it;
45the pots, shovels and sprinkling bowls.

All these objects that Huram made for King Solomon for the temple of the LORD were of burnished bronze. 46The king had them cast in clay molds in the plain of the Jordan between Succoth and Zarethan. 47Solomon left all these things unweighed, because there were so many; the weight of the bronze was not determined.

48Solomon also made all the furnishings that were in the LORD's temple:

the golden altar;
the golden table on which was the bread of the Presence;
49the lampstands of pure gold (five on the right and five on the left, in front of the inner sanctuary);
the gold floral work and lamps and tongs;
50the pure gold basins, wick trimmers, sprinkling bowls, dishes and censers;
and the gold sockets for the doors of the innermost room, the Most Holy Place, and also for the doors of the main hall of the temple.

51When all the work King Solomon had done for the temple of the LORD was finished, he brought in the things his father David had dedicated—the silver and gold and the furnishings—and he placed them in the treasuries of the LORD's temple.

The Ark Brought to the Temple

8 Then King Solomon summoned into his presence at Jerusalem the elders of Israel, all the heads of the tribes and the chiefs of the Israelite families, to bring up the ark of the LORD's covenant from Zion, the City of David. 2All the men of Israel came together to King Solomon at the time of the festival in the month of Ethanim, the seventh month.

3When all the elders of Israel had arrived, the priests took up the ark, 4and they brought up the ark of the LORD and the Tent of Meeting and all the sacred furnishings in it. The priests and Levites carried them up, 5and King Solomon and the entire assembly of Israel that had gathered about him were before the ark, sacrificing so many sheep and cattle that they could not be recorded or counted.

6The priests then brought the ark of the LORD's covenant to its place in the inner sanctuary of the temple, the Most Holy Place, and put it beneath the wings of the cherubim. 7The cherubim spread their wings over the place of the ark and overshadowed the ark and its carrying poles. 8These poles were so long that their ends could be seen from the Holy Place in front of the inner sanctuary, but not from outside the Holy Place; and they are still there today. 9There was nothing in the ark except the two stone tablets that Moses had placed in it at Horeb, where the LORD made a covenant with the Israelites after they came out of Egypt.

10When the priests withdrew from the Holy Place, the cloud filled the temple of the LORD. 11And the priests could not perform their service because of the cloud, for the glory of the LORD filled his temple.

12Then Solomon said, "The LORD has said that he would dwell in a dark cloud; 13I have indeed built a magnificent temple for you, a place for you to dwell forever."

14While the whole assembly of Israel was standing there, the king turned around and blessed them. 15Then he said:

"Praise be to the LORD, the God of Israel, who with his own hand has fulfilled what he promised with his own mouth to my father David. For he said, 16'Since the day I brought my people Israel out of Egypt, I have not chosen a city in any tribe of Israel to have a temple built for my Name to be there, but I have chosen David to rule my people Israel.'

17"My father David had it in his heart to build a temple for the Name of the LORD, the God of Israel. 18But the LORD said to my father David, 'Because it was in your heart to build a temple for my Name, you did well to have this in your heart. 19Nevertheless, you are not the one to build the temple, but your son, who is your own flesh and blood— he is the one who will build the temple for my Name.'

²⁰"The LORD has kept the promise he made: I have succeeded David my father and now I sit on the throne of Israel, just as the LORD promised, and I have built the temple for the Name of the LORD, the God of Israel. ²¹I have provided a place there for the ark, in which is the covenant of the LORD that he made with our fathers when he brought them out of Egypt."

Solomon's Prayer of Dedication

²²Then Solomon stood before the altar of the LORD in front of the whole assembly of Israel, spread out his hands toward heaven ²³and said:

"O LORD, God of Israel, there is no God like you in heaven above or on earth below—you who keep your covenant of love with your servants who continue wholeheartedly in your way. ²⁴You have kept your promise to your servant David my father; with your mouth you have promised and with your hand you have fulfilled it—as it is today.

²⁵"Now LORD, God of Israel, keep for your servant David my father the promises you made to him when you said, 'You shall never fail to have a man to sit before me on the throne of Israel, if only your sons are careful in all they do to walk before me as you have done.' ²⁶And now, O God of Israel, let your word that you promised your servant David my father come true.

²⁷"But will God really dwell on earth? The heavens, even the highest heaven, cannot contain you. How much less this temple I have built! ²⁸Yet give attention to your servant's prayer and his plea for mercy, O LORD my God. Hear the cry and the prayer that your servant is praying in your presence this day. ²⁹May your eyes be open toward this temple night and day, this place of which you said, 'My Name shall be there,' so that you will hear the prayer your servant prays toward this place. ³⁰Hear the supplication of your servant and of your people Israel when they pray toward this place. Hear from heaven, your dwelling place, and when you hear, forgive.

³¹"When a man wrongs his neighbor and is required to take an oath and he comes and swears the oath before your altar in this temple, ³²then hear from heaven and act. Judge between your servants, condemning the guilty and bringing down on his own head what he has done. Declare the innocent not guilty, and so establish his innocence.

³³"When your people Israel have been defeated by an enemy because they have sinned against you, and when they turn back to you and confess your name, praying and making supplication to you in this temple, ³⁴then hear from heaven and forgive the sin of your people Israel and bring them back to the land you gave to their fathers.

³⁵"When the heavens are shut up and there is no rain because your people have sinned against you, and when they pray toward this place and confess your name and turn from their sin because you have afflicted them, ³⁶then hear from heaven and forgive the sin of your servants, your people Israel. Teach them the right way to live, and send rain on the land you gave your people for an inheritance.

³⁷"When famine or plague comes to the land, or blight or mildew, locusts or grasshoppers, or when an enemy besieges them in any of their cities, whatever disaster or disease may come, ³⁸and when a prayer or plea is made by any of your people Israel—each one aware of the afflictions of his own heart, and spreading out his hands toward this temple— ³⁹then hear from heaven, your dwelling place. Forgive and act; deal with each man according to all he does, since you know his heart (for you alone know the hearts of all men), ⁴⁰so that they will fear you all the time they live in the land you gave our fathers.

⁴¹"As for the foreigner who does not belong to your people Israel but has come from a distant land because of your name— ⁴²for men will hear of your great name and your mighty hand and your outstretched arm—when he comes and

prays toward this temple, 43then hear from heaven, your dwelling place, and do whatever the foreigner asks of you, so that all the peoples of the earth may know your name and fear you, as do your own people Israel, and may know that this house I have built bears your Name.

44"When your people go to war against their enemies, wherever you send them, and when they pray to the LORD toward the city you have chosen and the temple I have built for your Name, 45then hear from heaven their prayer and their plea, and uphold their cause.

46"When they sin against you— for there is no one who does not sin—and you become angry with them and give them over to the enemy, who takes them captive to his own land, far away or near; 47and if they have a change of heart in the land where they are held captive, and repent and plead with you in the land of their conquerors and say, 'We have sinned, we have done wrong, we have acted wickedly'; 48and if they turn back to you

---

TUESDAY

Read 1 Kings 8:1–66
Key Verse 1 Kings 8:27

How Big Is Your God? —Eileen Anderson

A popular singer swaggered onto the stage to accept his award. He thanked a few people who had helped him in his musical career. Then, as though tossing a bone to a neglected puppy, he added, ". . . and thanks to 'The Big Man Upstairs.' "

That man's attitude is indicative of the terrible casualness that has permeated our culture's perception of God. It is true that God is kind, gentle and merciful, full of love and compassion. He is like a shepherd who "gathers the lambs in his arms and carries them close to his heart" (Isaiah 40:11). And he is as accessible as our "daddy," our "*Abba*, Father" (see Romans 8:15).

But God is also righteous and holy, and according to Psalm 33:8 we are to "Let all the earth fear the LORD; let all the people of the world revere him."

At times we mentally shrink God down to our size so that he seems more "user-friendly"—more understandable to our finite minds. But in trying to bring him down to our level, we can lose a rightful sense of awe in his presence. God is not, as the musician would have us believe, our "bud."

King Solomon had a healthy understanding of who God is. His words show that he grasped a sense of how big, how majestic and almighty God is, and that knowledge filled him with reverence and awe. Even so, he had a relationship with God that was personal and intimate enough to ask God to hear his prayers: "But will God really dwell on earth? The heavens, even the highest heaven, cannot contain you. How much less this temple I have built! Yet give attention to your servant's prayer and his plea for mercy, O LORD my God. Hear the cry and the prayer that your servant is praying in your presence this day" (1 Kings 8:27–28).

A Deeper Look
Job 38; Psalm 139:8; Isaiah 44:6–7

Go to page 384 for your next devotional reading.

with all their heart and soul in the land of their enemies who took them captive, and pray to you toward the land you gave their fathers, toward the city you have chosen and the temple I have built for your Name; ⁴⁹then from heaven, your dwelling place, hear their prayer and their plea, and uphold their cause. ⁵⁰And forgive your people, who have sinned against you; forgive all the offenses they have committed against you, and cause their conquerors to show them mercy; ⁵¹for they are your people and your inheritance, whom you brought out of Egypt, out of that iron-smelting furnace.

⁵²"May your eyes be open to your servant's plea and to the plea of your people Israel, and may you listen to them whenever they cry out to you. ⁵³For you singled them out from all the nations of the world to be your own inheritance, just as you declared through your servant Moses when you, O Sovereign Lord, brought our fathers out of Egypt."

⁵⁴When Solomon had finished all these prayers and supplications to the Lord, he rose from before the altar of the Lord, where he had been kneeling with his hands spread out toward heaven. ⁵⁵He stood and blessed the whole assembly of Israel in a loud voice, saying:

⁵⁶"Praise be to the Lord, who has given rest to his people Israel just as he promised. Not one word has failed of all the good promises he gave through his servant Moses. ⁵⁷May the Lord our God be with us as he was with our fathers; may he never leave us nor forsake us. ⁵⁸May he turn our hearts to him, to walk in all his ways and to keep the commands, decrees and regulations he gave our fathers. ⁵⁹And may these words of mine, which I have prayed before the Lord, be near to the Lord our God day and night, that he may uphold the cause of his servant and the cause of his people Israel according to each day's need, ⁶⁰so that all the peoples of the earth may know that the Lord is God and that there is no other. ⁶¹But your hearts must be fully committed to the Lord our God, to live by his de-

crees and obey his commands, as at this time."

The Dedication of the Temple

⁶²Then the king and all Israel with him offered sacrifices before the Lord. ⁶³Solomon offered a sacrifice of fellowship offerings[a] to the Lord: twenty-two thousand cattle and a hundred and twenty thousand sheep and goats. So the king and all the Israelites dedicated the temple of the Lord.

⁶⁴On that same day the king consecrated the middle part of the courtyard in front of the temple of the Lord, and there he offered burnt offerings, grain offerings and the fat of the fellowship offerings, because the bronze altar before the Lord was too small to hold the burnt offerings, the grain offerings and the fat of the fellowship offerings.

⁶⁵So Solomon observed the festival at that time, and all Israel with him—a vast assembly, people from Lebo[b] Hamath to the Wadi of Egypt. They celebrated it before the Lord our God for seven days and seven days more, fourteen days in all. ⁶⁶On the following day he sent the people away. They blessed the king and then went home, joyful and glad in heart for all the good things the Lord had done for his servant David and his people Israel.

The Lord Appears to Solomon

9 When Solomon had finished building the temple of the Lord and the royal palace, and had achieved all he had desired to do, ²the Lord appeared to him a second time, as he had appeared to him at Gibeon. ³The Lord said to him:

"I have heard the prayer and plea you have made before me; I have consecrated this temple, which you have built, by putting my Name there forever. My eyes and my heart will always be there.

⁴"As for you, if you walk before me in integrity of heart and uprightness, as David your father did, and do all I command and observe my decrees and laws, ⁵I will establish your royal throne over Israel forever, as I promised David your father when I said, 'You shall never fail to have a man on the throne of Israel.'

---

a63 Traditionally *peace offerings*; also in verse 64
b65 Or *from the entrance to*

6"But if you[a] or your sons turn away from me and do not observe the commands and decrees I have given you[a] and go off to serve other gods and worship them, 7then I will cut off Israel from the land I have given them and will reject this temple I have consecrated for my Name. Israel will then become a byword and an object of ridicule among all peoples. 8And though this temple is now imposing, all who pass by will be appalled and will scoff and say, 'Why has the LORD done such a thing to this land and to this temple?' 9People will answer, 'Because they have forsaken the LORD their God, who brought their fathers out of Egypt, and have embraced other gods, worshiping and serving them—that is why the LORD brought all this disaster on them.' "

Solomon's Other Activities

10At the end of twenty years, during which Solomon built these two buildings—the temple of the LORD and the royal palace— 11King Solomon gave twenty towns in Galilee to Hiram king of Tyre, because Hiram had supplied him with all the cedar and pine and gold he wanted. 12But when Hiram went from Tyre to see the towns that Solomon had given him, he was not pleased with them. 13"What kind of towns are these you have given me, my brother?" he asked. And he called them the Land of Cabul,[b] a name they have to this day. 14Now Hiram had sent to the king 120 talents[c] of gold.

15Here is the account of the forced labor King Solomon conscripted to build the LORD's temple, his own palace, the supporting terraces,[d] the wall of Jerusalem, and Hazor, Megiddo and Gezer. 16(Pharaoh king of Egypt had attacked and captured Gezer. He had set it on fire. He killed its Canaanite inhabitants and then gave it as a wedding gift to his daughter, Solomon's wife. 17And Solomon rebuilt Gezer.) He built up Lower Beth Horon, 18Baalath, and Tadmor[e] in the desert, within his land, 19as well as all his store cities and the towns for his chariots and for his horses[f]—whatever he desired to build in Jerusalem, in Lebanon and throughout all the territory he ruled. 20All the people left from the Amorites, Hittites, Perizzites, Hivites and Jebusites (these peoples were not Israelites), 21that is, their descendants remaining in the land, whom the Israelites could not exterminate[g]—these Solomon conscripted for his slave labor force, as it is to this day. 22But Solomon did not make slaves of any of the Israelites; they were his fighting men, his government officials, his officers, his captains, and the commanders of his chariots and charioteers. 23They were also the chief officials in charge of Solomon's projects—550 officials supervising the men who did the work.

24After Pharaoh's daughter had come up from the City of David to the palace Solomon had built for her, he constructed the supporting terraces.

25Three times a year Solomon sacrificed burnt offerings and fellowship offerings[h] on the altar he had built for the LORD, burning incense before the LORD along with them, and so fulfilled the temple obligations.

26King Solomon also built ships at Ezion Geber, which is near Elath in Edom, on the shore of the Red Sea.[i] 27And Hiram sent his men—sailors who knew the sea—to serve in the fleet with Solomon's men. 28They sailed to Ophir and brought back 420 talents[j] of gold, which they delivered to King Solomon.

[a]6 The Hebrew is plural.   [b]13 Cabul sounds like the Hebrew for good-for-nothing.   [c]14 That is, about 4 1/2 tons (about 4 metric tons)   [d]15 Or the Millo; also in verse 24   [e]18 The Hebrew may also be read Tamar.   [f]19 Or charioteers   [g]21 The Hebrew term refers to the irrevocable giving over of things or persons to the LORD, often by totally destroying them.   [h]25 Traditionally peace offerings   [i]26 Hebrew Yam Suph; that is, Sea of Reeds   [j]28 That is, about 16 tons (about 14.5 metric tons)

POINT OF INTEREST

1 Kings 9:2

How did God appear to Solomon? Go back to 1 Kings 3:5, where God appeared in a dream. God revealed himself differently to different people. Abraham saw God as an angel in Genesis 18, Saul of Tarsus had a vision in Acts 9, and Elijah heard a gentle whisper in 1 Kings 19:12. How might God reveal himself to you today?

The Queen of Sheba Visits Solomon

10 When the queen of Sheba heard about the fame of Solomon and his relation to the name of the Lord, she came to test him with hard questions. ²Arriving at Jerusalem with a very great caravan—with camels carrying spices, large quantities of gold, and precious stones—she came to Solomon and talked with him about all that she had on her mind. ³Solomon answered all her questions; nothing was too hard for the king to explain to her. ⁴When the queen of Sheba saw all the wisdom of Solomon and the palace he had built, ⁵the food on his table, the seating of his officials, the attending servants in their robes, his cup-bearers, and the burnt offerings he made at*ᵃ* the temple of the Lord, she was overwhelmed.

⁶She said to the king, "The report I heard in my own country about your achievements and your wisdom is true. ⁷But I did not believe these things until I came and saw with my own eyes. Indeed, not even half was told me; in wisdom and wealth you have far exceeded the report I heard. ⁸How happy your men must be! How happy your officials, who continually stand before you and hear your wisdom! ⁹Praise be to the Lord your God, who has delighted in you and placed you on the throne of Israel. Because of the Lord's eternal love for Israel, he has made you king, to maintain justice and righteousness."

¹⁰And she gave the king 120 talents*ᵇ* of gold, large quantities of spices, and precious stones. Never again were so many spices brought in as those the queen of Sheba gave to King Solomon.

¹¹(Hiram's ships brought gold from Ophir; and from there they brought great cargoes of almugwood*ᶜ* and precious stones. ¹²The king used the almugwood to make supports for the temple of the Lord and for the royal palace, and to make harps and lyres for the musicians. So much almugwood has never been imported or seen since that day.)

¹³King Solomon gave the queen of Sheba all she desired and asked for, besides what he had given her out of his royal bounty. Then she left and returned with her retinue to her own country.

Solomon's Splendor

¹⁴The weight of the gold that Solomon received yearly was 666 talents,*ᵈ* ¹⁵not including the revenues from merchants and traders and from all the Arabian kings and the governors of the land.

¹⁶King Solomon made two hundred large shields of hammered gold; six hundred bekas*ᵉ* of gold went into each shield. ¹⁷He also made three hundred small shields of hammered gold, with three minas*ᶠ* of gold in each shield. The king put them in the Palace of the Forest of Lebanon.

¹⁸Then the king made a great throne inlaid with ivory and overlaid with fine gold. ¹⁹The throne had six steps, and its back had a rounded top. On both sides of the seat were armrests, with a lion standing beside each of them. ²⁰Twelve lions stood on the six steps, one at either end of each step. Nothing like it had ever been made for any other kingdom. ²¹All King Solomon's goblets were gold, and all the household articles in the Palace of the Forest of Lebanon were pure gold. Nothing was made of silver, because silver was considered of little value in Solomon's days. ²²The king had a fleet of trading ships*ᵍ* at sea along with the ships of Hiram. Once every three years it returned, carrying gold, silver and ivory, and apes and baboons.

²³King Solomon was greater in riches and wisdom than all the other kings of the earth. ²⁴The whole world sought audience with Solomon to hear the wisdom God had put in his heart. ²⁵Year after year, everyone who came brought a gift—articles of silver and gold, robes, weapons and spices, and horses and mules.

²⁶Solomon accumulated chariots and horses; he had fourteen hundred chariots and twelve thousand horses,*ʰ* which he kept in the chariot cities and also with him in Jerusalem. ²⁷The king made silver as common in Jerusalem as stones, and cedar as plentiful as sycamore-fig trees in the foothills. ²⁸Solomon's horses were imported from Egypt*ⁱ* and from Kue*ʲ*—the royal merchants purchased

---

ᵃ5 Or *the ascent by which he went up to*
ᵇ10 That is, about 4 1/2 tons (about 4 metric tons)
ᶜ11 Probably a variant of *algumwood*; also in verse 12 *ᵈ14* That is, about 25 tons (about 23 metric tons) *ᵉ16* That is, about 7 1/2 pounds (about 3.5 kilograms) *ᶠ17* That is, about 3 3/4 pounds (about 1.7 kilograms) *ᵍ22* Hebrew *of ships of Tarshish* *ʰ26* Or *charioteers* *ⁱ28* Or possibly *Muzur*, a region in Cilicia; also in verse 29 *ʲ28* Probably *Cilicia*

them from Kue. ²⁹They imported a chariot from Egypt for six hundred shekels*a* of silver, and a horse for a hundred and fifty.*b* They also exported them to all the kings of the Hittites and of the Arameans.

Solomon's Wives

11 King Solomon, however, loved many foreign women besides Pharaoh's daughter—Moabites, Ammonites, Edomites, Sidonians and Hittites. ²They were from nations about which the LORD had told the Israelites, "You must not intermarry with them, because they will surely turn your hearts after their gods." Nevertheless, Solomon held fast to them in love. ³He had seven hundred wives of royal birth and three hundred concubines, and his wives led him astray. ⁴As Solomon grew old, his wives turned his heart after other gods, and his heart was not fully devoted to the LORD his God, as the heart of David his father had been. ⁵He followed Ashtoreth the goddess of the Sidonians, and Molech*c* the detestable god of the Ammonites. ⁶So Solomon did evil in the eyes of the LORD; he did not follow the LORD completely, as David his father had done.

⁷On a hill east of Jerusalem, Solomon built a high place for Chemosh the detestable god of Moab, and for Molech the detestable god of the Ammonites. ⁸He did the same for all his foreign wives, who burned incense and offered sacrifices to their gods.

⁹The LORD became angry with Solomon because his heart had turned away from the LORD, the God of Israel, who had appeared to him twice. ¹⁰Although he had forbidden Solomon to follow other gods, Solomon did not keep the LORD's command. ¹¹So the LORD said to Solomon, "Since this is your attitude and you have not kept my covenant and my decrees, which I commanded you, I will most certainly tear the kingdom away from you and give it to one of your subordinates. ¹²Nevertheless, for the sake of David your father, I will not do it during your lifetime. I will tear it out of the hand of your son. ¹³Yet I will not tear the whole kingdom from him, but will give him one tribe for the sake of David my servant and for the sake of Jerusalem, which I have chosen."

Solomon's Adversaries

¹⁴Then the LORD raised up against Solo-mon an adversary, Hadad the Edomite, from the royal line of Edom. ¹⁵Earlier when David was fighting with Edom, Joab the commander of the army, who had gone up to bury the dead, had struck down all the men in Edom. ¹⁶Joab and all the Israelites stayed there for six months, until they had destroyed all the men in Edom. ¹⁷But Hadad, still only a boy, fled to Egypt with some Edomite officials who had served his father. ¹⁸They set out from Midian and went to Paran. Then taking men from Paran with them, they went to Egypt, to Pharaoh king of Egypt, who gave Hadad a house and land and provided him with food.

¹⁹Pharaoh was so pleased with Hadad that he gave him a sister of his own wife, Queen Tahpenes, in marriage. ²⁰The sister of Tahpenes bore him a son named Genubath, whom Tahpenes brought up in the royal palace. There Genubath lived with Pharaoh's own children.

²¹While he was in Egypt, Hadad heard that David rested with his fathers and that Joab the commander of the army was also dead. Then Hadad said to Pharaoh, "Let me go, that I may return to my own country."

²²"What have you lacked here that you want to go back to your own country?" Pharaoh asked.

"Nothing," Hadad replied, "but do let me go!"

²³And God raised up against Solomon another adversary, Rezon son of Eliada, who had fled from his master, Hadadezer king of Zobah. ²⁴He gathered men around

a29 That is, about 15 pounds (about 7 kilograms) b29 That is, about 3 3/4 pounds (about 1.7 kilograms) c5 Hebrew Milcom; also in verse 33

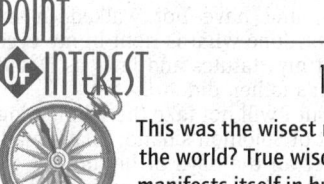

POINT OF INTEREST   1 Kings 11:1

This was the wisest man in the world? True wisdom manifests itself in humble obedience to the Lord. But Solomon ignored God's edict (see verse 2) and foolishly attached himself to an idol-worshiping crowd of foreign wives. Eventually he drifted away from the One who had endowed him with wisdom in the first place.

him and became the leader of a band of
rebels when David destroyed the forces*a*
⌐of Zobah⌐; the rebels went to Damascus,
where they settled and took control. 25Re-
zon was Israel's adversary as long as Solomon lived, adding to the trouble caused
by Hadad. So Rezon ruled in Aram and
was hostile toward Israel.

Jeroboam Rebels Against Solomon

26Also, Jeroboam son of Nebat rebelled against the king. He was one of
Solomon's officials, an Ephraimite from
Zeredah, and his mother was a widow
named Zeruah.

27Here is the account of how he rebelled against the king: Solomon had
built the supporting terraces*b* and had
filled in the gap in the wall of the city of
David his father. 28Now Jeroboam was a
man of standing, and when Solomon saw
how well the young man did his work,
he put him in charge of the whole labor
force of the house of Joseph.

29About that time Jeroboam was going
out of Jerusalem, and Ahijah the prophet
of Shiloh met him on the way, wearing a
new cloak. The two of them were alone
out in the country, 30and Ahijah took
hold of the new cloak he was wearing
and tore it into twelve pieces. 31Then he
said to Jeroboam, "Take ten pieces for
yourself, for this is what the LORD, the
God of Israel, says: 'See, I am going to
tear the kingdom out of Solomon's hand
and give you ten tribes. 32But for the sake
of my servant David and the city of Jerusalem, which I have chosen out of all the
tribes of Israel, he will have one tribe. 33I
will do this because they have*c* forsaken
me and worshiped Ashtoreth the goddess
of the Sidonians, Chemosh the god of the
Moabites, and Molech the god of the Ammonites, and have not walked in my
ways, nor done what is right in my eyes,
nor kept my statutes and laws as David,
Solomon's father, did.

34" 'But I will not take the whole kingdom out of Solomon's hand; I have made
him ruler all the days of his life for the
sake of David my servant, whom I chose
and who observed my commands and
statutes. 35I will take the kingdom from
his son's hands and give you ten tribes.
36I will give one tribe to his son so that
David my servant may always have a
lamp before me in Jerusalem, the city
where I chose to put my Name. 37Howev-
er, as for you, I will take you, and you

will rule over all that your heart desires;
you will be king over Israel. 38If you do
whatever I command you and walk in my
ways and do what is right in my eyes by
keeping my statutes and commands, as
David my servant did, I will be with you.
I will build you a dynasty as enduring as
the one I built for David and will give
Israel to you. 39I will humble David's
descendants because of this, but not forever.' "

40Solomon tried to kill Jeroboam, but
Jeroboam fled to Egypt, to Shishak the
king, and stayed there until Solomon's
death.

Solomon's Death

41As for the other events of Solomon's
reign—all he did and the wisdom he displayed—are they not written in the book
of the annals of Solomon? 42Solomon
reigned in Jerusalem over all Israel forty
years. 43Then he rested with his fathers
and was buried in the city of David his
father. And Rehoboam his son succeeded
him as king.

Israel Rebels Against Rehoboam

12 Rehoboam went to Shechem, for all
the Israelites had gone there to make
him king. 2When Jeroboam son of Nebat
heard this (he was still in Egypt, where
he had fled from King Solomon), he returned from*d* Egypt. 3So they sent for
Jeroboam, and he and the whole assembly of Israel went to Rehoboam and said
to him: 4"Your father put a heavy yoke
on us, but now lighten the harsh labor
and the heavy yoke he put on us, and we
will serve you."

5Rehoboam answered, "Go away for
three days and then come back to me."
So the people went away.

6Then King Rehoboam consulted the
elders who had served his father Solomon during his lifetime. "How would
you advise me to answer these people?"
he asked.

7They replied, "If today you will be a
servant to these people and serve them
and give them a favorable answer, they
will always be your servants."

8But Rehoboam rejected the advice the
elders gave him and consulted the young
men who had grown up with him and
were serving him. 9He asked them,

---

a24 Hebrew *destroyed them*   *b27* Or *the Millo*
c33 Hebrew; Septuagint, Vulgate and Syriac *because*
he has   *d2* Or *he remained in*

"What is your advice? How should we answer these people who say to me, 'Lighten the yoke your father put on us'?"

¹⁰The young men who had grown up with him replied, "Tell these people who have said to you, 'Your father put a heavy yoke on us, but make our yoke lighter'—tell them, 'My little finger is thicker than my father's waist. ¹¹My father laid on you a heavy yoke; I will make it even heavier. My father scourged you with whips; I will scourge you with scorpions.' "

¹²Three days later Jeroboam and all the people returned to Rehoboam, as the king had said, "Come back to me in three days." ¹³The king answered the people harshly. Rejecting the advice given him by the elders, ¹⁴he followed the advice of the young men and said, "My father made your yoke heavy; I will make it even heavier. My father scourged you with whips; I will scourge you with scorpions." ¹⁵So the king did not listen to the people, for this turn of events was from the LORD, to fulfill the word the LORD had spoken to Jeroboam son of Nebat through Ahijah the Shilonite.

¹⁶When all Israel saw that the king refused to listen to them, they answered the king:

"What share do we have in David,
    what part in Jesse's son?
To your tents, O Israel!
Look after your own house,
    O David!"

So the Israelites went home. ¹⁷But as for the Israelites who were living in the towns of Judah, Rehoboam still ruled over them.

¹⁸King Rehoboam sent out Adoniram,ᵃ who was in charge of forced labor, but all Israel stoned him to death. King Rehoboam, however, managed to get into his chariot and escape to Jerusalem. ¹⁹So Israel has been in rebellion against the house of David to this day.

²⁰When all the Israelites heard that Jeroboam had returned, they sent and called him to the assembly and made him king over all Israel. Only the tribe of Judah remained loyal to the house of David.

²¹When Rehoboam arrived in Jerusalem, he mustered the whole house of Judah and the tribe of Benjamin—a hundred and eighty thousand fighting men—to make war against the house of Israel and to regain the kingdom for Rehoboam son of Solomon.

²²But this word of God came to Shemaiah the man of God: ²³"Say to Rehoboam son of Solomon king of Judah, to the whole house of Judah and Benjamin, and to the rest of the people, ²⁴'This is what the LORD says: Do not go up to fight against your brothers, the Israelites. Go home, every one of you, for this is my doing.' " So they obeyed the word of the LORD and went home again, as the LORD had ordered.

Golden Calves at Bethel and Dan

²⁵Then Jeroboam fortified Shechem in the hill country of Ephraim and lived there. From there he went out and built up Peniel.ᵇ

²⁶Jeroboam thought to himself, "The kingdom will now likely revert to the house of David. ²⁷If these people go up to offer sacrifices at the temple of the LORD in Jerusalem, they will again give their allegiance to their lord, Rehoboam king of Judah. They will kill me and return to King Rehoboam."

²⁸After seeking advice, the king made two golden calves. He said to the people, "It is too much for you to go up to Jerusalem. Here are your gods, O Israel, who brought you up out of Egypt." ²⁹One he set up in Bethel, and the other in Dan. ³⁰And this thing became a sin; the people went even as far as Dan to worship the one there.

ᵃ18 Some Septuagint manuscripts and Syriac (see also 1 Kings 4:6 and 5:14); Hebrew *Adoram*
ᵇ25 Hebrew *Penuel*, a variant of *Peniel*

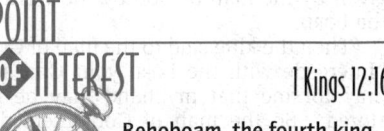

POINT OF INTEREST   1 Kings 12:16

Rehoboam, the fourth king of Israel, lacked his father Solomon's wisdom. It cost him the support of ten of Israel's twelve tribes. From then on Israel was divided into two kingdoms. The southern kingdom of Judah included Jerusalem, the temple, the priests and the tribe of Benjamin (see verse 21). The remaining ten tribes formed the northern kingdom of Israel.

³¹Jeroboam built shrines on high places and appointed priests from all sorts of people, even though they were not Levites. ³²He instituted a festival on the fifteenth day of the eighth month, like the festival held in Judah, and offered sacrifices on the altar. This he did in Bethel, sacrificing to the calves he had made. And at Bethel he also installed priests at the high places he had made. ³³On the fifteenth day of the eighth month, a month of his own choosing, he offered sacrifices on the altar he had built at Bethel. So he instituted the festival for the Israelites and went up to the altar to make offerings.

The Man of God From Judah

By the word of the LORD a man of God came from Judah to Bethel, as Jeroboam was standing by the altar to make an offering. ²He cried out against the altar by the word of the LORD: "O altar, altar! This is what the LORD says: 'A son named Josiah will be born to the house of David. On you he will sacrifice the priests of the high places who now make offerings here, and human bones will be burned on you.' " ³That same day the man of God gave a sign: "This is the sign the LORD has declared: The altar will be split apart and the ashes on it will be poured out."

⁴When King Jeroboam heard what the man of God cried out against the altar at Bethel, he stretched out his hand from the altar and said, "Seize him!" But the hand he stretched out toward the man shriveled up, so that he could not pull it back. ⁵Also, the altar was split apart and its ashes poured out according to the sign given by the man of God by the word of the LORD.

⁶Then the king said to the man of God, "Intercede with the LORD your God and pray for me that my hand may be restored." So the man of God interceded with the LORD, and the king's hand was restored and became as it was before.

⁷The king said to the man of God, "Come home with me and have something to eat, and I will give you a gift."

⁸But the man of God answered the king, "Even if you were to give me half your possessions, I would not go with you, nor would I eat bread or drink water here. ⁹For I was commanded by the word of the LORD: 'You must not eat bread or drink water or return by the way you

came.' " ¹⁰So he took another road and did not return by the way he had come to Bethel.

¹¹Now there was a certain old prophet living in Bethel, whose sons came and told him all that the man of God had done there that day. They also told their father what he had said to the king. ¹²Their father asked them, "Which way did he go?" And his sons showed him which road the man of God from Judah had taken. ¹³So he said to his sons, "Saddle the donkey for me." And when they had saddled the donkey for him, he mounted it ¹⁴and rode after the man of God. He found him sitting under an oak tree and asked, "Are you the man of God who came from Judah?"

"I am," he replied.

¹⁵So the prophet said to him, "Come home with me and eat."

¹⁶The man of God said, "I cannot turn back and go with you, nor can I eat bread or drink water with you in this place. ¹⁷I have been told by the word of the LORD: 'You must not eat bread or drink water there or return by the way you came.' "

¹⁸The old prophet answered, "I too am a prophet, as you are. And an angel said to me by the word of the LORD: 'Bring him back with you to your house so that he may eat bread and drink water.' " (But he was lying to him.) ¹⁹So the man of God returned with him and ate and drank in his house.

²⁰While they were sitting at the table, the word of the LORD came to the old prophet who had brought him back. ²¹He cried out to the man of God who had come from Judah, "This is what the LORD says: 'You have defied the word of the LORD and have not kept the command the LORD your God gave you. ²²You came back and ate bread and drank water in the place where he told you not to eat or drink. Therefore your body will not be buried in the tomb of your fathers.' "

²³When the man of God had finished eating and drinking, the prophet who had brought him back saddled his donkey for him. ²⁴As he went on his way, a lion met him on the road and killed him, and his body was thrown down on the road, with both the donkey and the lion standing beside it. ²⁵Some people who passed by saw the body thrown down there, with the lion standing beside the body, and they went and reported it in the city where the old prophet lived.

²⁶When the prophet who had brought him back from his journey heard of it, he said, "It is the man of God who defied the word of the LORD. The LORD has given him over to the lion, which has mauled him and killed him, as the word of the LORD had warned him."

²⁷The prophet said to his sons, "Saddle the donkey for me," and they did so. ²⁸Then he went out and found the body thrown down on the road, with the donkey and the lion standing beside it. The lion had neither eaten the body nor mauled the donkey. ²⁹So the prophet picked up the body of the man of God, laid it on the donkey, and brought it back to his own city to mourn for him and bury him. ³⁰Then he laid the body in his own tomb, and they mourned over him and said, "Oh, my brother!"

³¹After burying him, he said to his sons, "When I die, bury me in the grave where the man of God is buried; lay my bones beside his bones. ³²For the message he declared by the word of the LORD against the altar in Bethel and against all the shrines on the high places in the towns of Samaria will certainly come true."

³³Even after this, Jeroboam did not change his evil ways, but once more appointed priests for the high places from all sorts of people. Anyone who wanted to become a priest he consecrated for the high places. ³⁴This was the sin of the house of Jeroboam that led to its downfall and to its destruction from the face of the earth.

Ahijah's Prophecy Against Jeroboam

14 At that time Abijah son of Jeroboam became ill, ²and Jeroboam said to his wife, "Go, disguise yourself, so you won't be recognized as the wife of Jeroboam. Then go to Shiloh. Ahijah the prophet is there—the one who told me I would be king over this people. ³Take ten loaves of bread with you, some cakes and a jar of honey, and go to him. He will tell you what will happen to the boy." ⁴So Jeroboam's wife did what he said and went to Ahijah's house in Shiloh.

Now Ahijah could not see; his sight was gone because of his age. ⁵But the LORD had told Ahijah, "Jeroboam's wife is coming to ask you about her son, for he is ill, and you are to give her such and such an answer. When she arrives, she will pretend to be someone else."

⁶So when Ahijah heard the sound of her footsteps at the door, he said, "Come in, wife of Jeroboam. Why this pretense? I have been sent to you with bad news. ⁷Go, tell Jeroboam that this is what the LORD, the God of Israel, says: 'I raised you up from among the people and made you a leader over my people Israel. ⁸I tore the kingdom away from the house of David and gave it to you, but you have not been like my servant David, who kept my commands and followed me with all his heart, doing only what was right in my eyes. ⁹You have done more evil than all who lived before you. You have made for yourself other gods, idols made of metal; you have provoked me to anger and thrust me behind your back.

¹⁰" 'Because of this, I am going to bring disaster on the house of Jeroboam. I will cut off from Jeroboam every last male in Israel—slave or free. I will burn up the house of Jeroboam as one burns dung, until it is all gone. ¹¹Dogs will eat those belonging to Jeroboam who die in the city, and the birds of the air will feed on those who die in the country. The LORD has spoken!'

¹²"As for you, go back home. When you set foot in your city, the boy will die. ¹³All Israel will mourn for him and bury him. He is the only one belonging to Jeroboam who will be buried, because he is the only one in the house of Jeroboam in whom the LORD, the God of Israel, has found anything good.

¹⁴"The LORD will raise up for himself a king over Israel who will cut off the family of Jeroboam. This is the day! What? Yes, even now.ᵃ ¹⁵And the LORD will strike Israel, so that it will be like a reed swaying in the water. He will uproot Israel from this good land that he gave to their forefathers and scatter them beyond the River,ᵇ because they provoked the LORD to anger by making Asherah poles.ᶜ ¹⁶And he will give Israel up because of the sins Jeroboam has committed and has caused Israel to commit."

¹⁷Then Jeroboam's wife got up and left and went to Tirzah. As soon as she stepped over the threshold of the house, the boy died. ¹⁸They buried him, and all Israel mourned for him, as the LORD had

---

ᵃ14 The meaning of the Hebrew for this sentence is uncertain.   ᵇ15 That is, the Euphrates
ᶜ15 That is, symbols of the goddess Asherah; here and elsewhere in 1 Kings

said through his servant the prophet Ahijah.

¹⁹The other events of Jeroboam's reign, his wars and how he ruled, are written in the book of the annals of the kings of Israel. ²⁰He reigned for twenty-two years and then rested with his fathers. And Nadab his son succeeded him as king.

Rehoboam King of Judah

²¹Rehoboam son of Solomon was king in Judah. He was forty-one years old when he became king, and he reigned seventeen years in Jerusalem, the city the LORD had chosen out of all the tribes of Israel in which to put his Name. His mother's name was Naamah; she was an Ammonite.

²²Judah did evil in the eyes of the LORD. By the sins they committed they stirred up his jealous anger more than their fathers had done. ²³They also set up for themselves high places, sacred stones and Asherah poles on every high hill and under every spreading tree. ²⁴There were even male shrine prostitutes in the land; the people engaged in all the detestable practices of the nations the LORD had driven out before the Israelites.

²⁵In the fifth year of King Rehoboam, Shishak king of Egypt attacked Jerusalem. ²⁶He carried off the treasures of the temple of the LORD and the treasures of the royal palace. He took everything, including all the gold shields Solomon had made. ²⁷So King Rehoboam made bronze shields to replace them and assigned these to the commanders of the guard on duty at the entrance to the royal palace. ²⁸Whenever the king went to the LORD's temple, the guards bore the shields, and afterward they returned them to the guardroom.

²⁹As for the other events of Rehoboam's reign, and all he did, are they not written in the book of the annals of the kings of Judah? ³⁰There was continual warfare between Rehoboam and Jeroboam. ³¹And Rehoboam rested with his fathers and was buried with them in the City of David. His mother's name was Naamah; she was an Ammonite. And Abijah[a] his son succeeded him as king.

Abijah King of Judah

15 In the eighteenth year of the reign of Jeroboam son of Nebat, Abijah[b] became king of Judah, ²and he reigned in Jerusalem three years. His mother's name was Maacah daughter of Abishalom.[c]

³He committed all the sins his father had done before him; his heart was not fully devoted to the LORD his God, as the heart of David his forefather had been. ⁴Nevertheless, for David's sake the LORD his God gave him a lamp in Jerusalem by raising up a son to succeed him and by making Jerusalem strong. ⁵For David had done what was right in the eyes of the LORD and had not failed to keep any of the LORD's commands all the days of his life—except in the case of Uriah the Hittite.

⁶There was war between Rehoboam[d] and Jeroboam throughout ₍Abijah's₎ lifetime. ⁷As for the other events of Abijah's reign, and all he did, are they not written in the book of the annals of the kings of Judah? There was war between Abijah and Jeroboam. ⁸And Abijah rested with his fathers and was buried in the City of David. And Asa his son succeeded him as king.

Asa King of Judah

⁹In the twentieth year of Jeroboam king of Israel, Asa became king of Judah, ¹⁰and he reigned in Jerusalem forty-one years. His grandmother's name was Maacah daughter of Abishalom.

¹¹Asa did what was right in the eyes of the LORD, as his father David had done. ¹²He expelled the male shrine prostitutes

---

a31 Some Hebrew manuscripts and Septuagint (see also 2 Chron. 12:16); most Hebrew manuscripts *Abijam*   *b1* Some Hebrew manuscripts and Septuagint (see also 2 Chron. 12:16); most Hebrew manuscripts *Abijam*; also in verses 7 and 8   *c2* A variant of *Absalom*; also in verse 10   *d6* Most Hebrew manuscripts; some Hebrew manuscripts and Syriac *Abijam* (that is, Abijah)

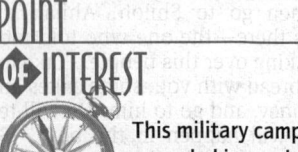

POINT OF INTEREST

1 Kings 14:25

This military campaign is recorded in carvings on the south wall of the Egyptian temple at Karnak (ancient Thebes). Many familiar Biblical places such as Megiddo, Aijalon, Shechem and Socoh are listed in these carvings as being captured by King Shishak. These records date from around 926 B.C.

from the land and got rid of all the idols his fathers had made. ¹³He even deposed his grandmother Maacah from her position as queen mother, because she had made a repulsive Asherah pole. Asa cut the pole down and burned it in the Kidron Valley. ¹⁴Although he did not remove the high places, Asa's heart was fully committed to the LORD all his life. ¹⁵He brought into the temple of the LORD the silver and gold and the articles that he and his father had dedicated.

¹⁶There was war between Asa and Baasha king of Israel throughout their reigns. ¹⁷Baasha king of Israel went up against Judah and fortified Ramah to prevent anyone from leaving or entering the territory of Asa king of Judah.

¹⁸Asa then took all the silver and gold that was left in the treasuries of the LORD's temple and of his own palace. He entrusted it to his officials and sent them to Ben-Hadad son of Tabrimmon, the son of Hezion, the king of Aram, who was ruling in Damascus. ¹⁹"Let there be a treaty between me and you," he said, "as there was between my father and your father. See, I am sending you a gift of silver and gold. Now break your treaty with Baasha king of Israel so he will withdraw from me."

²⁰Ben-Hadad agreed with King Asa and sent the commanders of his forces against the towns of Israel. He conquered Ijon, Dan, Abel Beth Maacah and all Kinnereth in addition to Naphtali. ²¹When Baasha heard this, he stopped building Ramah and withdrew to Tirzah. ²²Then King Asa issued an order to all Judah— no one was exempt—and they carried away from Ramah the stones and timber Baasha had been using there. With them King Asa built up Geba in Benjamin, and also Mizpah.

²³As for all the other events of Asa's reign, all his achievements, all he did and the cities he built, are they not written in the book of the annals of the kings of Judah? In his old age, however, his feet became diseased. ²⁴Then Asa rested with his fathers and was buried with them in the city of his father David. And Jehoshaphat his son succeeded him as king.

Nadab King of Israel

²⁵Nadab son of Jeroboam became king of Israel in the second year of Asa king of Judah, and he reigned over Israel two years. ²⁶He did evil in the eyes of the LORD, walking in the ways of his father and in his sin, which he had caused Israel to commit.

²⁷Baasha son of Ahijah of the house of Issachar plotted against him, and he struck him down at Gibbethon, a Philistine town, while Nadab and all Israel were besieging it. ²⁸Baasha killed Nadab in the third year of Asa king of Judah and succeeded him as king.

²⁹As soon as he began to reign, he killed Jeroboam's whole family. He did not leave Jeroboam anyone that breathed, but destroyed them all, according to the word of the LORD given through his servant Ahijah the Shilonite— ³⁰because of the sins Jeroboam had committed and had caused Israel to commit, and because he provoked the LORD, the God of Israel, to anger.

³¹As for the other events of Nadab's reign, and all he did, are they not written in the book of the annals of the kings of Israel? ³²There was war between Asa and Baasha king of Israel throughout their reigns.

Baasha King of Israel

³³In the third year of Asa king of Judah, Baasha son of Ahijah became king of all Israel in Tirzah, and he reigned twenty-four years. ³⁴He did evil in the eyes of the LORD, walking in the ways of Jeroboam and in his sin, which he had caused Israel to commit.

16 Then the word of the LORD came to Jehu son of Hanani against Baasha: ²"I lifted you up from the dust and made you leader of my people Israel, but you walked in the ways of Jeroboam and caused my people Israel to sin and to provoke me to anger by their sins. ³So I am about to consume Baasha and his house, and I will make your house like that of Jeroboam son of Nebat. ⁴Dogs will eat those belonging to Baasha who die in the city, and the birds of the air will feed on those who die in the country."

⁵As for the other events of Baasha's reign, what he did and his achievements, are they not written in the book of the annals of the kings of Israel? ⁶Baasha rested with his fathers and was buried in Tirzah. And Elah his son succeeded him as king.

⁷Moreover, the word of the LORD came through the prophet Jehu son of Hanani to Baasha and his house, because of all the evil he had done in the eyes of the

LORD, provoking him to anger by the things he did, and becoming like the house of Jeroboam—and also because he destroyed it.

Elah King of Israel

8In the twenty-sixth year of Asa king of Judah, Elah son of Baasha became king of Israel, and he reigned in Tirzah two years.

9Zimri, one of his officials, who had command of half his chariots, plotted against him. Elah was in Tirzah at the time, getting drunk in the home of Arza, the man in charge of the palace at Tirzah. 10Zimri came in, struck him down and killed him in the twenty-seventh year of Asa king of Judah. Then he succeeded him as king.

11As soon as he began to reign and was seated on the throne, he killed off Baasha's whole family. He did not spare a single male, whether relative or friend. 12So Zimri destroyed the whole family of Baasha, in accordance with the word of the LORD spoken against Baasha through the prophet Jehu— 13because of all the sins Baasha and his son Elah had committed and had caused Israel to commit, so that they provoked the LORD, the God of Israel, to anger by their worthless idols.

14As for the other events of Elah's reign, and all he did, are they not written in the book of the annals of the kings of Israel?

Zimri King of Israel

15In the twenty-seventh year of Asa king of Judah, Zimri reigned in Tirzah seven days. The army was encamped near Gibbethon, a Philistine town. 16When the Israelites in the camp heard that Zimri had plotted against the king and murdered him, they proclaimed Omri, the commander of the army, king over Israel that very day there in the camp. 17Then Omri and all the Israelites with him withdrew from Gibbethon and laid siege to Tirzah. 18When Zimri saw that the city was taken, he went into the citadel of the royal palace and set the palace on fire around him. So he died, 19because of the sins he had committed, doing evil in the eyes of the LORD and walking in the ways of Jeroboam and in the sin he had committed and had caused Israel to commit.

20As for the other events of Zimri's reign, and the rebellion he carried out, are they not written in the book of the annals of the kings of Israel?

Omri King of Israel

21Then the people of Israel were split into two factions; half supported Tibni son of Ginath for king, and the other half supported Omri. 22But Omri's followers proved stronger than those of Tibni son of Ginath. So Tibni died and Omri became king.

23In the thirty-first year of Asa king of Judah, Omri became king of Israel, and he reigned twelve years, six of them in Tirzah. 24He bought the hill of Samaria from Shemer for two talents*a* of silver and built a city on the hill, calling it Samaria, after Shemer, the name of the former owner of the hill.

25But Omri did evil in the eyes of the LORD and sinned more than all those before him. 26He walked in all the ways of Jeroboam son of Nebat and in his sin, which he had caused Israel to commit, so that they provoked the LORD, the God of Israel, to anger by their worthless idols.

27As for the other events of Omri's reign, what he did and the things he achieved, are they not written in the book of the annals of the kings of Israel? 28Omri rested with his fathers and was buried in Samaria. And Ahab his son succeeded him as king.

Ahab Becomes King of Israel

29In the thirty-eighth year of Asa king of Judah, Ahab son of Omri became king of Israel, and he reigned in Samaria over

a24 That is, about 150 pounds (about 70 kilograms)

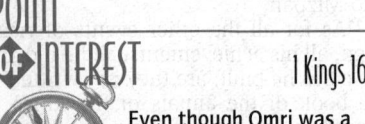

POINT OF INTEREST

1 Kings 16:23

Even though Omri was a powerful political leader in Israel's northern kingdom, the author only states that he was a wicked king who "sinned more than all of those before him" (verse 25). Omri was well known in international politics. He is mentioned on the Moabite Stone—a carved stone discovered in Moab in 1868 and dating from the ninth century B.C.

Israel twenty-two years. ³⁰Ahab son of Omri did more evil in the eyes of the Lord than any of those before him. ³¹He not only considered it trivial to commit the sins of Jeroboam son of Nebat, but he also married Jezebel daughter of Ethbaal king of the Sidonians, and began to serve Baal and worship him. ³²He set up an altar for Baal in the temple of Baal that he built in Samaria. ³³Ahab also made an Asherah pole and did more to provoke the Lord, the God of Israel, to anger than did all the kings of Israel before him. ³⁴In Ahab's time, Hiel of Bethel rebuilt Jericho. He laid its foundations at the cost of his firstborn son Abiram, and he set up its gates at the cost of his youngest son Segub, in accordance with the word of the Lord spoken by Joshua son of Nun.

Elijah Fed by Ravens

17 Now Elijah the Tishbite, from Tishbe*ᵃ* in Gilead, said to Ahab, "As the Lord, the God of Israel, lives, whom I serve, there will be neither dew nor rain in the next few years except at my word."

²Then the word of the Lord came to Elijah: ³"Leave here, turn eastward and hide in the Kerith Ravine, east of the Jordan. ⁴You will drink from the brook, and I have ordered the ravens to feed you there."

⁵So he did what the Lord had told him. He went to the Kerith Ravine, east of the Jordan, and stayed there. ⁶The ravens brought him bread and meat in the morning and bread and meat in the evening, and he drank from the brook.

The Widow at Zarephath

⁷Some time later the brook dried up because there had been no rain in the land. ⁸Then the word of the Lord came to him: ⁹"Go at once to Zarephath of Sidon and stay there. I have commanded a widow in that place to supply you with food." ¹⁰So he went to Zarephath. When he came to the town gate, a widow was there gathering sticks. He called to her and asked, "Would you bring me a little water in a jar so I may have a drink?" ¹¹As she was going to get it, he called, "And bring me, please, a piece of bread."

¹²"As surely as the Lord your God lives," she replied, "I don't have any bread—only a handful of flour in a jar and a little oil in a jug. I am gathering a few sticks to take home and make a meal for myself and my son, that we may eat it—and die."

¹³Elijah said to her, "Don't be afraid. Go home and do as you have said. But first make a small cake of bread for me from what you have and bring it to me, and then make something for yourself and your son. ¹⁴For this is what the Lord, the God of Israel, says: 'The jar of flour will not be used up and the jug of oil will not run dry until the day the Lord gives rain on the land.' "

¹⁵She went away and did as Elijah had told her. So there was food every day for Elijah and for the woman and her family. ¹⁶For the jar of flour was not used up and the jug of oil did not run dry, in keeping with the word of the Lord spoken by Elijah.

¹⁷Some time later the son of the woman who owned the house became ill. He grew worse and worse, and finally stopped breathing. ¹⁸She said to Elijah, "What do you have against me, man of God? Did you come to remind me of my sin and kill my son?"

¹⁹"Give me your son," Elijah replied. He took him from her arms, carried him to the upper room where he was staying, and laid him on his bed. ²⁰Then he cried out to the Lord, "O Lord my God, have you brought tragedy also upon this widow I am staying with, by causing her son to die?" ²¹Then he stretched himself out on the boy three times and cried to the Lord, "O Lord my God, let this boy's life return to him!"

²²The Lord heard Elijah's cry, and the boy's life returned to him, and he lived. ²³Elijah picked up the child and carried him down from the room into the house. He gave him to his mother and said, "Look, your son is alive!"

²⁴Then the woman said to Elijah, "Now I know that you are a man of God and that the word of the Lord from your mouth is the truth."

Elijah and Obadiah

18 After a long time, in the third year, the word of the Lord came to Elijah: "Go and present yourself to Ahab, and I will send rain on the land." ²So Elijah went to present himself to Ahab.

Now the famine was severe in Samaria, ³and Ahab had summoned Obadiah, who was in charge of his palace. (Obadi-

ᵃ1 Or Tishbite, of the settlers

ah was a devout believer in the LORD.
4While Jezebel was killing off the LORD's
prophets, Obadiah had taken a hundred
prophets and hidden them in two caves,
fifty in each, and had supplied them with
food and water.) 5Ahab had said to Obadiah, "Go through the land to all the
springs and valleys. Maybe we can find
some grass to keep the horses and mules
alive so we will not have to kill any of our
animals." 6So they divided the land they

were to cover, Ahab going in one direction and Obadiah in another.
    7As Obadiah was walking along, Elijah
met him. Obadiah recognized him,
bowed down to the ground, and said, "Is
it really you, my lord Elijah?"
    8"Yes," he replied. "Go tell your mas-
ter, 'Elijah is here.' "
    9"What have I done wrong," asked
Obadiah, "that you are handing your servant over to Ahab to be put to death? 10As

---

WEDNESDAY

Read 1 Kings 17:1–24
Key Verses 1 Kings 17:1–16

No Mistaking a Miracle – Julie Bundt

I had prayed about where to go to school in the fall; God had confirmed in several ways that I should go to the University of Kansas.
The only problem was that I had one thousand dollars saved, and
tuition was four thousand per semester, not including living expenses. I needed help!

I worked at a camp all that summer and earned only a small
amount of money toward my fall expenses. The camp staff was
praying with me, asking God to provide the funds for school. As the
summer ended, I still had very little money for classes. Two days
before I needed to move, I was in turmoil. Where was God? Was the
line disconnected? Had he been listening to my prayers? He owned
the cattle on a thousand hills (Psalm 50:10). Couldn't he just sell a
couple for me?

But I was reminded that he provides for our *daily* needs. I didn't
need the money until school officially started. So I moved with no
money to buy books, pay tuition, have my phone connected or even
buy groceries.

As I left one of my first classes, the professor handed me a note
that had been taped to the door during our lecture. The note told
me to meet a certain professor about a research assistantship—a
position I'd interviewed for in May. I had already received a rejection letter while at camp, but the professor had yet to fill the position, so he offered me the job. It paid my living expenses and provided a tuition waiver!

God had worked it out! There was no mistaking that he had
worked a miracle for me. That experience convinced me that God is
my provider in the small *and* big things: "The LORD is good to
all . . . The LORD is faithful to all his promises and loving toward all
he has made . . . The eyes of all look to you, and you give them their
food at the proper time. You open your hand and satisfy the desires
of every living thing" (Psalm 145:9,13,15–16).

A Deeper Look
Matthew 7:9–11; Philippians 4:19

Go to page 389 for your next devotional reading.

surely as the LORD your God lives, there is not a nation or kingdom where my master has not sent someone to look for you. And whenever a nation or kingdom claimed you were not there, he made them swear they could not find you. ¹¹But now you tell me to go to my master and say, 'Elijah is here.' ¹²I don't know where the Spirit of the LORD may carry you when I leave you. If I go and tell Ahab and he doesn't find you, he will kill me. Yet I your servant have worshiped the LORD since my youth. ¹³Haven't you heard, my lord, what I did while Jezebel was killing the prophets of the LORD? I hid a hundred of the LORD's prophets in two caves, fifty in each, and supplied them with food and water. ¹⁴And now you tell me to go to my master and say, 'Elijah is here.' He will kill me!"

¹⁵Elijah said, "As the LORD Almighty lives, whom I serve, I will surely present myself to Ahab today."

Elijah on Mount Carmel

¹⁶So Obadiah went to meet Ahab and told him, and Ahab went to meet Elijah. ¹⁷When he saw Elijah, he said to him, "Is that you, you troubler of Israel?"

¹⁸"I have not made trouble for Israel," Elijah replied. "But you and your father's family have. You have abandoned the LORD's commands and have followed the Baals. ¹⁹Now summon the people from all over Israel to meet me on Mount Carmel. And bring the four hundred and fifty prophets of Baal and the four hundred prophets of Asherah, who eat at Jezebel's table."

²⁰So Ahab sent word throughout all Israel and assembled the prophets on Mount Carmel. ²¹Elijah went before the people and said, "How long will you waver between two opinions? If the LORD is God, follow him; but if Baal is God, follow him."

But the people said nothing.

²²Then Elijah said to them, "I am the only one of the LORD's prophets left, but Baal has four hundred and fifty prophets. ²³Get two bulls for us. Let them choose one for themselves, and let them cut it into pieces and put it on the wood but not set fire to it. I will prepare the other bull and put it on the wood but not set fire to it. ²⁴Then you call on the name of your god, and I will call on the name of the LORD. The god who answers by fire—he is God."

Then all the people said, "What you say is good."

²⁵Elijah said to the prophets of Baal, "Choose one of the bulls and prepare it first, since there are so many of you. Call on the name of your god, but do not light the fire." ²⁶So they took the bull given them and prepared it.

Then they called on the name of Baal from morning till noon. "O Baal, answer us!" they shouted. But there was no response; no one answered. And they danced around the altar they had made.

²⁷At noon Elijah began to taunt them. "Shout louder!" he said. "Surely he is a god! Perhaps he is deep in thought, or busy, or traveling. Maybe he is sleeping and must be awakened." ²⁸So they shouted louder and slashed themselves with swords and spears, as was their custom, until their blood flowed. ²⁹Midday passed, and they continued their frantic prophesying until the time for the evening sacrifice. But there was no response, no one answered, no one paid attention.

³⁰Then Elijah said to all the people, "Come here to me." They came to him, and he repaired the altar of the LORD, which was in ruins. ³¹Elijah took twelve stones, one for each of the tribes descended from Jacob, to whom the word of the LORD had come, saying, "Your name shall be Israel." ³²With the stones he built an altar in the name of the LORD, and he dug a trench around it large enough to hold two seahs*a* of seed. ³³He arranged the wood, cut the bull into pieces and laid it on the wood. Then he said to them, "Fill four large jars with water and pour it on the offering and on the wood."

³⁴"Do it again," he said, and they did it again.

"Do it a third time," he ordered, and they did it the third time. ³⁵The water ran down around the altar and even filled the trench.

³⁶At the time of sacrifice, the prophet Elijah stepped forward and prayed: "O LORD, God of Abraham, Isaac and Israel, let it be known today that you are God in Israel and that I am your servant and have done all these things at your command. ³⁷Answer me, O LORD, answer me, so these people will know that you,

a32 That is, probably about 13 quarts (about 15 liters)

O Lord, are God, and that you are turning their hearts back again."

38Then the fire of the Lord fell and burned up the sacrifice, the wood, the stones and the soil, and also licked up the water in the trench.

39When all the people saw this, they fell prostrate and cried, "The Lord—he is God! The Lord—he is God!"

40Then Elijah commanded them, "Seize the prophets of Baal. Don't let anyone get away!" They seized them, and Elijah had them brought down to the Kishon Valley and slaughtered there.

41And Elijah said to Ahab, "Go, eat and drink, for there is the sound of a heavy rain." **42**So Ahab went off to eat and drink, but Elijah climbed to the top of Carmel, bent down to the ground and put his face between his knees.

43"Go and look toward the sea," he told his servant. And he went up and looked.

"There is nothing there," he said.

Seven times Elijah said, "Go back."

44The seventh time the servant reported, "A cloud as small as a man's hand is rising from the sea."

So Elijah said, "Go and tell Ahab, 'Hitch up your chariot and go down before the rain stops you.' "

45Meanwhile, the sky grew black with clouds, the wind rose, a heavy rain came on and Ahab rode off to Jezreel. **46**The power of the Lord came upon Elijah and, tucking his cloak into his belt, he ran ahead of Ahab all the way to Jezreel.

Elijah Flees to Horeb

19 Now Ahab told Jezebel everything Elijah had done and how he had killed all the prophets with the sword. **2**So Jezebel sent a messenger to Elijah to say, "May the gods deal with me, be it ever so severely, if by this time tomorrow I do not make your life like that of one of them."

3Elijah was afraid*a* and ran for his life. When he came to Beersheba in Judah, he left his servant there, **4**while he himself went a day's journey into the desert. He came to a broom tree, sat down under it and prayed that he might die. "I have had enough, Lord," he said. "Take my life; I am no better than my ancestors." **5**Then he lay down under the tree and fell asleep.

All at once an angel touched him and said, "Get up and eat." **6**He looked around, and there by his head was a cake of bread baked over hot coals, and a jar of water. He ate and drank and then lay down again.

7The angel of the Lord came back a second time and touched him and said, "Get up and eat, for the journey is too much for you." **8**So he got up and ate and drank. Strengthened by that food, he traveled forty days and forty nights until he reached Horeb, the mountain of God. **9**There he went into a cave and spent the night.

The Lord Appears to Elijah

And the word of the Lord came to him: "What are you doing here, Elijah?"

10He replied, "I have been very zealous for the Lord God Almighty. The Israelites have rejected your covenant, broken down your altars, and put your prophets to death with the sword. I am the only one left, and now they are trying to kill me too."

11The Lord said, "Go out and stand on the mountain in the presence of the Lord, for the Lord is about to pass by."

Then a great and powerful wind tore the mountains apart and shattered the rocks before the Lord, but the Lord was not in the wind. After the wind there was an earthquake, but the Lord was not in the earthquake. **12**After the earthquake came a fire, but the Lord was not in the fire. And after the fire came a gentle whisper. **13**When Elijah heard it, he pulled his cloak over his face and went out and stood at the mouth of the cave.

a3 Or *Elijah saw*

POINT OF INTEREST

1 Kings 19:3

Elijah had faced and defeated four hundred prophets on Mount Carmel. But even a hero can experience times of anxiety, fear and depression. God didn't abandon Elijah when he "ran for his life." Instead God met Elijah's physical and emotional needs with the refreshment of his mercy. If you ever feel the same way Elijah did, realize that God is there with you to help during those times.

Then a voice said to him, "What are you doing here, Elijah?"

¹⁴He replied, "I have been very zealous for the LORD God Almighty. The Israelites have rejected your covenant, broken down your altars, and put your prophets to death with the sword. I am the only one left, and now they are trying to kill me too."

¹⁵The LORD said to him, "Go back the way you came, and go to the Desert of Damascus. When you get there, anoint Hazael king over Aram. ¹⁶Also, anoint Jehu son of Nimshi king over Israel, and anoint Elisha son of Shaphat from Abel Meholah to succeed you as prophet. ¹⁷Jehu will put to death any who escape the sword of Hazael, and Elisha will put to death any who escape the sword of Jehu. ¹⁸Yet I reserve seven thousand in Israel—all whose knees have not bowed down to Baal and all whose mouths have not kissed him."

The Call of Elisha

¹⁹So Elijah went from there and found Elisha son of Shaphat. He was plowing with twelve yoke of oxen, and he himself was driving the twelfth pair. Elijah went up to him and threw his cloak around him. ²⁰Elisha then left his oxen and ran after Elijah. "Let me kiss my father and mother good-by," he said, "and then I will come with you."

"Go back," Elijah replied. "What have I done to you?"

²¹So Elisha left him and went back. He took his yoke of oxen and slaughtered them. He burned the plowing equipment to cook the meat and gave it to the people, and they ate. Then he set out to follow Elijah and became his attendant.

Ben-Hadad Attacks Samaria

20 Now Ben-Hadad king of Aram mustered his entire army. Accompanied by thirty-two kings with their horses and chariots, he went up and besieged Samaria and attacked it. ²He sent messengers into the city to Ahab king of Israel, saying, "This is what Ben-Hadad says: ³'Your silver and gold are mine, and the best of your wives and children are mine.' "

⁴The king of Israel answered, "Just as you say, my lord the king. I and all I have are yours."

⁵The messengers came again and said, "This is what Ben-Hadad says: 'I sent to demand your silver and gold, your wives and your children. ⁶But about this time tomorrow I am going to send my officials to search your palace and the houses of your officials. They will seize everything you value and carry it away.' "

⁷The king of Israel summoned all the elders of the land and said to them, "See how this man is looking for trouble! When he sent for my wives and my children, my silver and my gold, I did not refuse him."

⁸The elders and the people all answered, "Don't listen to him or agree to his demands."

⁹So he replied to Ben-Hadad's messengers, "Tell my lord the king, 'Your servant will do all you demanded the first time, but this demand I cannot meet.' " They left and took the answer back to Ben-Hadad.

¹⁰Then Ben-Hadad sent another message to Ahab: "May the gods deal with me, be it ever so severely, if enough dust remains in Samaria to give each of my men a handful."

¹¹The king of Israel answered, "Tell him: 'One who puts on his armor should not boast like one who takes it off.' "

¹²Ben-Hadad heard this message while he and the kings were drinking in their tents,ᵃ and he ordered his men: "Prepare to attack." So they prepared to attack the city.

Ahab Defeats Ben-Hadad

¹³Meanwhile a prophet came to Ahab king of Israel and announced, "This is what the LORD says: 'Do you see this vast army? I will give it into your hand today, and then you will know that I am the LORD.' "

¹⁴"But who will do this?" asked Ahab.

The prophet replied, "This is what the LORD says: 'The young officers of the provincial commanders will do it.' "

"And who will start the battle?" he asked.

The prophet answered, "You will."

¹⁵So Ahab summoned the young officers of the provincial commanders, 232 men. Then he assembled the rest of the Israelites, 7,000 in all. ¹⁶They set out at noon while Ben-Hadad and the 32 kings allied with him were in their tents getting drunk. ¹⁷The young officers of the provincial commanders went out first.

ᵃ12 Or *in Succoth*; also in verse 16

Now Ben-Hadad had dispatched scouts, who reported, "Men are advancing from Samaria."

18He said, "If they have come out for peace, take them alive; if they have come out for war, take them alive."

19The young officers of the provincial commanders marched out of the city with the army behind them 20and each one struck down his opponent. At that, the Arameans fled, with the Israelites in pursuit. But Ben-Hadad king of Aram escaped on horseback with some of his horsemen. 21The king of Israel advanced and overpowered the horses and chariots and inflicted heavy losses on the Arameans.

22Afterward, the prophet came to the king of Israel and said, "Strengthen your position and see what must be done, because next spring the king of Aram will attack you again."

23Meanwhile, the officials of the king of Aram advised him, "Their gods are gods of the hills. That is why they were too strong for us. But if we fight them on the plains, surely we will be stronger than they. 24Do this: Remove all the kings from their commands and replace them with other officers. 25You must also raise an army like the one you lost—horse for horse and chariot for chariot—so we can fight Israel on the plains. Then surely we will be stronger than they." He agreed with them and acted accordingly.

26The next spring Ben-Hadad mustered the Arameans and went up to Aphek to fight against Israel. 27When the Israelites were also mustered and given provisions, they marched out to meet them. The Israelites camped opposite them like two small flocks of goats, while the Arameans covered the countryside.

28The man of God came up and told the king of Israel, "This is what the LORD says: 'Because the Arameans think the LORD is a god of the hills and not a god of the valleys, I will deliver this vast army into your hands, and you will know that I am the LORD.'"

29For seven days they camped opposite each other, and on the seventh day the battle was joined. The Israelites inflicted a hundred thousand casualties on the Aramean foot soldiers in one day. 30The rest of them escaped to the city of Aphek, where the wall collapsed on twenty-seven thousand of them. And Ben-Hadad fled to the city and hid in an inner room.

31His officials said to him, "Look, we have heard that the kings of the house of Israel are merciful. Let us go to the king of Israel with sackcloth around our waists and ropes around our heads. Perhaps he will spare your life."

32Wearing sackcloth around their waists and ropes around their heads, they went to the king of Israel and said, "Your servant Ben-Hadad says: 'Please let me live.'"

The king answered, "Is he still alive? He is my brother."

33The men took this as a good sign and were quick to pick up his word. "Yes, your brother Ben-Hadad!" they said.

"Go and get him," the king said. When Ben-Hadad came out, Ahab had him come up into his chariot.

34"I will return the cities my father took from your father," Ben-Hadad offered. "You may set up your own market areas in Damascus, as my father did in Samaria."

⌐Ahab said,⌐ "On the basis of a treaty I will set you free." So he made a treaty with him, and let him go.

A Prophet Condemns Ahab

35By the word of the LORD one of the sons of the prophets said to his companion, "Strike me with your weapon," but the man refused.

36So the prophet said, "Because you have not obeyed the LORD, as soon as you leave me a lion will kill you." And after the man went away, a lion found him and killed him.

37The prophet found another man and said, "Strike me, please." So the man struck him and wounded him. 38Then the prophet went and stood by the road waiting for the king. He disguised himself with his headband down over his eyes. 39As the king passed by, the prophet called out to him, "Your servant went into the thick of the battle, and someone came to me with a captive and said, 'Guard this man. If he is missing, it will be your life for his life, or you must pay a talent[a] of silver.' 40While your servant was busy here and there, the man disappeared."

"That is your sentence," the king of

---

[a]39 That is, about 75 pounds (about 34 kilograms)

Israel said. "You have pronounced it yourself."

⁴¹Then the prophet quickly removed the headband from his eyes, and the king of Israel recognized him as one of the prophets. ⁴²He said to the king, "This is what the LORD says: 'You have set free a man I had determined should die.ᵃ Therefore it is your life for his life, your people for his people.' " ⁴³Sullen and angry, the king of Israel went to his palace in Samaria.

Naboth's Vineyard

21 Some time later there was an incident involving a vineyard belonging to Naboth the Jezreelite. The vineyard was in Jezreel, close to the palace of Ahab king of Samaria. ²Ahab said to Naboth, "Let me have your vineyard to use for a vegetable garden, since it is close to my palace. In exchange I will give you a better vineyard or, if you prefer, I will pay you whatever it is worth."

³But Naboth replied, "The LORD forbid that I should give you the inheritance of my fathers."

⁴So Ahab went home, sullen and angry because Naboth the Jezreelite had said, "I will not give you the inheritance of my fathers." He lay on his bed sulking and refused to eat.

⁵His wife Jezebel came in and asked him, "Why are you so sullen? Why won't you eat?"

⁶He answered her, "Because I said to Naboth the Jezreelite, 'Sell me your vine-

ᵃ42 The Hebrew term refers to the irrevocable giving over of things or persons to the LORD, often by totally destroying them.

THURSDAY

Read 1 Kings 20:13–43
Key Verse 1 Kings 20:40

Busyness and God's Kingdom – Chad Jeffreys

A tulip bulb growing out of a cinder block is an amazing sight. It starts simply, with a single bulb planted in good soil in a four-by-four inch hole in the middle of the concrete block. The following spring a beautiful flower emerges. The flower's fragrance is arresting. Its colors are captivating, especially for the bees that are drawn by its shades of bright pink and yellow. Its leaves gracefully sway in the breeze. The fruit of a year of preparation is a marvel to behold.

But underground, an amazing and troubling thing begins to take place; the bulb splits to produce more. When spring returns there are three or four flowers instead of one, but they don't seem as healthy. The following spring, many of the bulbs have split off, but only a few are producing flowers. Soon the splintered bulbs have filled the four-inch space, but hardly a flower can be found.

That tulip bulb shows me something about my own life. I realize God has allotted me limits of strength and ability like that four-inch square in the concrete block. Many times I have allowed myself to be "busy here and there," splitting my time and energy and spreading myself so thin that I can no longer produce God's desired fruit.

The lesson of the tulip teaches me to focus my efforts in a few areas and work at them with excellence in mind. Occasionally I need to clean out the splintered bulbs of busyness and set my sights on God's purposes so that he can produce much fruit in and through me.

A Deeper Look
Luke 10:38–42; John 15:1–2; Ephesians 2:10

Go to page 399 for your next devotional reading.

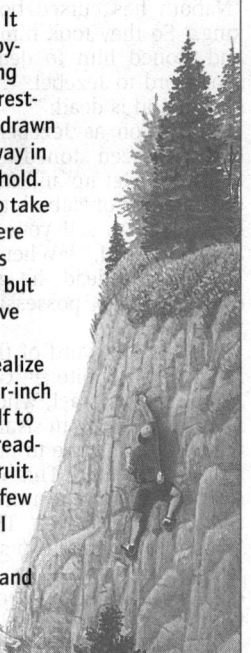

yard; or if you prefer, I will give you another vineyard in its place.' But he said, 'I will not give you my vineyard.' "

⁷Jezebel his wife said, "Is this how you act as king over Israel? Get up and eat! Cheer up. I'll get you the vineyard of Naboth the Jezreelite."

⁸So she wrote letters in Ahab's name, placed his seal on them, and sent them to the elders and nobles who lived in Naboth's city with him. ⁹In those letters she wrote:

"Proclaim a day of fasting and seat Naboth in a prominent place among the people. ¹⁰But seat two scoundrels opposite him and have them testify that he has cursed both God and the king. Then take him out and stone him to death."

¹¹So the elders and nobles who lived in Naboth's city did as Jezebel directed in the letters she had written to them. ¹²They proclaimed a fast and seated Naboth in a prominent place among the people. ¹³Then two scoundrels came and sat opposite him and brought charges against Naboth before the people, saying, "Naboth has cursed both God and the king." So they took him outside the city and stoned him to death. ¹⁴Then they sent word to Jezebel: "Naboth has been stoned and is dead."

¹⁵As soon as Jezebel heard that Naboth had been stoned to death, she said to Ahab, "Get up and take possession of the vineyard of Naboth the Jezreelite that he refused to sell you. He is no longer alive, but dead." ¹⁶When Ahab heard that Naboth was dead, he got up and went down to take possession of Naboth's vineyard.

¹⁷Then the word of the Lord came to Elijah the Tishbite: ¹⁸"Go down to meet Ahab king of Israel, who rules in Samaria. He is now in Naboth's vineyard, where he has gone to take possession of it. ¹⁹Say to him, 'This is what the Lord says: Have you not murdered a man and seized his property?' Then say to him, 'This is what the Lord says: In the place where dogs licked up Naboth's blood, dogs will lick up your blood—yes, yours!' "

²⁰Ahab said to Elijah, "So you have found me, my enemy!"

"I have found you," he answered, "because you have sold yourself to do evil in the eyes of the Lord. ²¹'I am going to

bring disaster on you. I will consume your descendants and cut off from Ahab every last male in Israel—slave or free. ²²I will make your house like that of Jeroboam son of Nebat and that of Baasha son of Ahijah, because you have provoked me to anger and have caused Israel to sin.'

²³"And also concerning Jezebel the Lord says: 'Dogs will devour Jezebel by the wall ofᵃ Jezreel.'

²⁴"Dogs will eat those belonging to Ahab who die in the city, and the birds of the air will feed on those who die in the country."

²⁵(There was never a man like Ahab, who sold himself to do evil in the eyes of the Lord, urged on by Jezebel his wife. ²⁶He behaved in the vilest manner by going after idols, like the Amorites the Lord drove out before Israel.)

²⁷When Ahab heard these words, he tore his clothes, put on sackcloth and fasted. He lay in sackcloth and went around meekly.

²⁸Then the word of the Lord came to Elijah the Tishbite: ²⁹"Have you noticed how Ahab has humbled himself before me? Because he has humbled himself, I will not bring this disaster in his day, but I will bring it on his house in the days of his son."

Micaiah Prophesies Against Ahab

22 For three years there was no war between Aram and Israel. ²But in the third year Jehoshaphat king of Judah went down to see the king of Israel. ³The king of Israel had said to his officials, "Don't you know that Ramoth Gilead belongs to us and yet we are doing nothing to retake it from the king of Aram?"

⁴So he asked Jehoshaphat, "Will you go with me to fight against Ramoth Gilead?"

Jehoshaphat replied to the king of Israel, "I am as you are, my people as your people, my horses as your horses." ⁵But Jehoshaphat also said to the king of Israel, "First seek the counsel of the Lord."

⁶So the king of Israel brought together the prophets—about four hundred men—and asked them, "Shall I go to war against Ramoth Gilead, or shall I refrain?"

ᵃ23 Most Hebrew manuscripts; a few Hebrew manuscripts, Vulgate and Syriac (see also 2 Kings 9:26) *the plot of ground at*

"Go," they answered, "for the Lord will give it into the king's hand."

⁷But Jehoshaphat asked, "Is there not a prophet of the LORD here whom we can inquire of?"

⁸The king of Israel answered Jehoshaphat, "There is still one man through whom we can inquire of the LORD, but I hate him because he never prophesies anything good about me, but always bad. He is Micaiah son of Imlah."

"The king should not say that," Jehoshaphat replied.

⁹So the king of Israel called one of his officials and said, "Bring Micaiah son of Imlah at once."

¹⁰Dressed in their royal robes, the king of Israel and Jehoshaphat king of Judah were sitting on their thrones at the threshing floor by the entrance of the gate of Samaria, with all the prophets prophesying before them. ¹¹Now Zedekiah son of Kenaanah had made iron horns and he declared, "This is what the LORD says: 'With these you will gore the Arameans until they are destroyed.'"

¹²All the other prophets were prophesying the same thing. "Attack Ramoth Gilead and be victorious," they said, "for the LORD will give it into the king's hand."

¹³The messenger who had gone to summon Micaiah said to him, "Look, as one man the other prophets are predicting success for the king. Let your word agree with theirs, and speak favorably."

¹⁴But Micaiah said, "As surely as the LORD lives, I can tell him only what the LORD tells me."

¹⁵When he arrived, the king asked him, "Micaiah, shall we go to war against Ramoth Gilead, or shall I refrain?"

"Attack and be victorious," he answered, "for the LORD will give it into the king's hand."

¹⁶The king said to him, "How many times must I make you swear to tell me nothing but the truth in the name of the LORD?"

¹⁷Then Micaiah answered, "I saw all Israel scattered on the hills like sheep without a shepherd, and the LORD said, 'These people have no master. Let each one go home in peace.'"

¹⁸The king of Israel said to Jehoshaphat, "Didn't I tell you that he never prophesies anything good about me, but only bad?"

¹⁹Micaiah continued, "Therefore hear the word of the LORD: I saw the LORD sitting on his throne with all the host of heaven standing around him on his right and on his left. ²⁰And the LORD said, 'Who will entice Ahab into attacking Ramoth Gilead and going to his death there?'

"One suggested this, and another that. ²¹Finally, a spirit came forward, stood before the LORD and said, 'I will entice him.'

²²"'By what means?' the LORD asked.

"'I will go out and be a lying spirit in the mouths of all his prophets,' he said.

"'You will succeed in enticing him,' said the LORD. 'Go and do it.'

²³"So now the LORD has put a lying spirit in the mouths of all these prophets of yours. The LORD has decreed disaster for you."

²⁴Then Zedekiah son of Kenaanah went up and slapped Micaiah in the face. "Which way did the spirit from*ᵃ* the LORD go when he went from me to speak to you?" he asked.

²⁵Micaiah replied, "You will find out on the day you go to hide in an inner room."

²⁶The king of Israel then ordered, "Take Micaiah and send him back to Amon the ruler of the city and to Joash the king's son ²⁷and say, 'This is what the king says: Put this fellow in prison and give him nothing but bread and water until I return safely.'"

²⁸Micaiah declared, "If you ever return safely, the LORD has not spoken through me." Then he added, "Mark my words, all you people!"

Ahab Killed at Ramoth Gilead

²⁹So the king of Israel and Jehoshaphat king of Judah went up to Ramoth Gilead.

ᵃ24 Or *Spirit of*

1 Kings 22:28

How could the Israelites discern whether a prophet was from God? First, they had to see whether God fulfilled the prophet's words (see Deuteronomy 18:21–22). Second, the prophet's words had to agree with what God had revealed earlier (see Isaiah 8:20). God would never contradict himself.

30The king of Israel said to Jehoshaphat, "I will enter the battle in disguise, but you wear your royal robes." So the king of Israel disguised himself and went into battle.

31Now the king of Aram had ordered his thirty-two chariot commanders, "Do not fight with anyone, small or great, except the king of Israel." **32**When the chariot commanders saw Jehoshaphat, they thought, "Surely this is the king of Israel." So they turned to attack him, but when Jehoshaphat cried out, **33**the chariot commanders saw that he was not the king of Israel and stopped pursuing him.

34But someone drew his bow at random and hit the king of Israel between the sections of his armor. The king told his chariot driver, "Wheel around and get me out of the fighting. I've been wounded." **35**All day long the battle raged, and the king was propped up in his chariot facing the Arameans. The blood from his wound ran onto the floor of the chariot, and that evening he died. **36**As the sun was setting, a cry spread through the army: "Every man to his town; everyone to his land!"

37So the king died and was brought to Samaria, and they buried him there. **38**They washed the chariot at a pool in Samaria (where the prostitutes bathed),^a and the dogs licked up his blood, as the word of the LORD had declared.

39As for the other events of Ahab's reign, including all he did, the palace he built and inlaid with ivory, and the cities he fortified, are they not written in the book of the annals of the kings of Israel? **40**Ahab rested with his fathers. And Ahaziah his son succeeded him as king.

Jehoshaphat King of Judah

41Jehoshaphat son of Asa became king of Judah in the fourth year of Ahab king of Israel. **42**Jehoshaphat was thirty-five years old when he became king, and he reigned in Jerusalem twenty-five years. His mother's name was Azubah daughter of Shilhi. **43**In everything he walked in the ways of his father Asa and did not stray from them; he did what was right in the eyes of the LORD. The high places, however, were not removed, and the people continued to offer sacrifices and burn incense there. **44**Jehoshaphat was also at peace with the king of Israel.

45As for the other events of Jehoshaphat's reign, the things he achieved and his military exploits, are they not written in the book of the annals of the kings of Judah? **46**He rid the land of the rest of the male shrine prostitutes who remained there even after the reign of his father Asa. **47**There was then no king in Edom; a deputy ruled.

48Now Jehoshaphat built a fleet of trading ships^b to go to Ophir for gold, but they never set sail—they were wrecked at Ezion Geber. **49**At that time Ahaziah son of Ahab said to Jehoshaphat, "Let my men sail with your men," but Jehoshaphat refused.

50Then Jehoshaphat rested with his fathers and was buried with them in the city of David his father. And Jehoram his son succeeded him.

Ahaziah King of Israel

51Ahaziah son of Ahab became king of Israel in Samaria in the seventeenth year of Jehoshaphat king of Judah, and he reigned over Israel two years. **52**He did evil in the eyes of the LORD, because he walked in the ways of his father and mother and in the ways of Jeroboam son of Nebat, who caused Israel to sin. **53**He served and worshiped Baal and provoked the LORD, the God of Israel, to anger, just as his father had done.

^a38 Or *Samaria and cleaned the weapons*
^b48 Hebrew *of ships of Tarshish*

Sometimes a nation's downfall is due more to inner corruption than outside domination. Second Kings shows how the Israelites' stubborn refusal to listen to the warnings from God's chosen prophets leads to their destruction. While most of the book details this downward slide, there are some bright spots. Though many bad rulers lead their people into lawlessness and ruin, a few kings and prophets—lights shining in the dark ages of Israel and Judah—are still "zealous for the LORD God Almighty" (1 Kings 19:10). Elijah, the amazing champion of God's law, is succeeded by Elisha, whose radical ministry shows how God communicates his power in often surprising ways.

2 KINGS

The LORD's Judgment on Ahaziah

1 After Ahab's death, Moab rebelled against Israel. ²Now Ahaziah had fallen through the lattice of his upper room in Samaria and injured himself. So he sent messengers, saying to them, "Go and consult Baal-Zebub, the god of Ekron, to see if I will recover from this injury."

³But the angel of the LORD said to Elijah the Tishbite, "Go up and meet the messengers of the king of Samaria and ask them, 'Is it because there is no God in Israel that you are going off to consult Baal-Zebub, the god of Ekron?' ⁴There-fore this is what the LORD says: 'You will not leave the bed you are lying on. You will certainly die!' " So Elijah went.

⁵When the messengers returned to the king, he asked them, "Why have you come back?"

⁶"A man came to meet us," they replied. "And he said to us, 'Go back to the king who sent you and tell him, "This is what the LORD says: Is it because there is no God in Israel that you are sending men to consult Baal-Zebub, the god of Ekron?

Therefore you will not leave the bed you are lying on. You will certainly die!" ' "

⁷The king asked them, "What kind of man was it who came to meet you and told you this?"

⁸They replied, "He was a man with a garment of hair and with a leather belt around his waist."

The king said, "That was Elijah the Tishbite."

⁹Then he sent to Elijah a captain with his company of fifty men. The captain went up to Elijah, who was sitting on the top of a hill, and said to him, "Man of God, the king says, 'Come down!' "

¹⁰Elijah answered the captain, "If I am a man of God, may fire come down from heaven and consume you and your fifty men!" Then fire fell from heaven and consumed the captain and his men.

¹¹At this the king sent to Elijah another captain with his fifty men. The captain said to him, "Man of God, this is what the king says, 'Come down at once!' "

¹²"If I am a man of God," Elijah replied, "may fire come down from heaven and consume you and your fifty men!" Then the fire of God fell from heaven and consumed him and his fifty men.

¹³So the king sent a third captain with his fifty men. This third captain went up and fell on his knees before Elijah. "Man of God," he begged, "please have respect for my life and the lives of these fifty men, your servants! ¹⁴See, fire has fallen from heaven and consumed the first two captains and all their men. But now have respect for my life!"

¹⁵The angel of the LORD said to Elijah, "Go down with him; do not be afraid of him." So Elijah got up and went down with him to the king.

¹⁶He told the king, "This is what the LORD says: Is it because there is no God in Israel for you to consult that you have sent messengers to consult Baal-Zebub, the god of Ekron? Because you have done this, you will never leave the bed you are lying on. You will certainly die!" ¹⁷So he died, according to the word of the LORD that Elijah had spoken.

Because Ahaziah had no son, Joram*a* succeeded him as king in the second year of Jehoram son of Jehoshaphat king of Judah. ¹⁸As for all the other events of Ahaziah's reign, and what he did, are they not written in the book of the annals of the kings of Israel?

Elijah Taken Up to Heaven

2 When the LORD was about to take Elijah up to heaven in a whirlwind, Elijah and Elisha were on their way from Gilgal. ²Elijah said to Elisha, "Stay here; the LORD has sent me to Bethel."

But Elisha said, "As surely as the LORD lives and as you live, I will not leave you." So they went down to Bethel.

³The company of the prophets at Bethel came out to Elisha and asked, "Do you know that the LORD is going to take your master from you today?"

"Yes, I know," Elisha replied, "but do not speak of it."

⁴Then Elijah said to him, "Stay here, Elisha; the LORD has sent me to Jericho."

And he replied, "As surely as the LORD lives and as you live, I will not leave you." So they went to Jericho.

⁵The company of the prophets at Jericho went up to Elisha and asked him, "Do you know that the LORD is going to take your master from you today?"

"Yes, I know," he replied, "but do not speak of it."

⁶Then Elijah said to him, "Stay here; the LORD has sent me to the Jordan."

And he replied, "As surely as the LORD lives and as you live, I will not leave you." So the two of them walked on.

⁷Fifty men of the company of the prophets went and stood at a distance, facing the place where Elijah and Elisha had stopped at the Jordan. ⁸Elijah took his cloak, rolled it up and struck the water with it. The water divided to the right and to the left, and the two of them crossed over on dry ground.

⁹When they had crossed, Elijah said to Elisha, "Tell me, what can I do for you before I am taken from you?"

"Let me inherit a double portion of your spirit," Elisha replied.

¹⁰"You have asked a difficult thing," Elijah said, "yet if you see me when I am taken from you, it will be yours—otherwise not."

¹¹As they were walking along and talking together, suddenly a chariot of fire and horses of fire appeared and separated the two of them, and Elijah went up to heaven in a whirlwind. ¹²Elisha saw this and cried out, "My father! My father! The chariots and horsemen of Israel!" And Elisha saw him no more. Then he took

a17 Hebrew *Jehoram*, a variant of *Joram*

hold of his own clothes and tore them apart.

¹³He picked up the cloak that had fallen from Elijah and went back and stood on the bank of the Jordan. ¹⁴Then he took the cloak that had fallen from him and struck the water with it. "Where now is the LORD, the God of Elijah?" he asked. When he struck the water, it divided to the right and to the left, and he crossed over.

¹⁵The company of the prophets from Jericho, who were watching, said, "The spirit of Elijah is resting on Elisha." And they went to meet him and bowed to the ground before him. ¹⁶"Look," they said, "we your servants have fifty able men. Let them go and look for your master. Perhaps the Spirit of the LORD has picked him up and set him down on some mountain or in some valley."

"No," Elisha replied, "do not send them."

¹⁷But they persisted until he was too ashamed to refuse. So he said, "Send them." And they sent fifty men, who searched for three days but did not find him. ¹⁸When they returned to Elisha, who was staying in Jericho, he said to them, "Didn't I tell you not to go?"

Healing of the Water

¹⁹The men of the city said to Elisha, "Look, our lord, this town is well situated, as you can see, but the water is bad and the land is unproductive."

²⁰"Bring me a new bowl," he said, "and put salt in it." So they brought it to him.

²¹Then he went out to the spring and threw the salt into it, saying, "This is what the LORD says: 'I have healed this water. Never again will it cause death or make the land unproductive.' " ²²And the water has remained wholesome to this day, according to the word Elisha had spoken.

Elisha Is Jeered

²³From there Elisha went up to Bethel. As he was walking along the road, some youths came out of the town and jeered at him. "Go on up, you baldhead!" they said. "Go on up, you baldhead!" ²⁴He turned around, looked at them and called down a curse on them in the name of the LORD. Then two bears came out of the woods and mauled forty-two of the youths. ²⁵And he went on to Mount

Carmel and from there returned to Samaria.

Moab Revolts

3 Joram[a] son of Ahab became king of Israel in Samaria in the eighteenth year of Jehoshaphat king of Judah, and he reigned twelve years. ²He did evil in the eyes of the LORD, but not as his father and mother had done. He got rid of the sacred stone of Baal that his father had made. ³Nevertheless he clung to the sins of Jeroboam son of Nebat, which he had caused Israel to commit; he did not turn away from them.

⁴Now Mesha king of Moab raised sheep, and he had to supply the king of Israel with a hundred thousand lambs and with the wool of a hundred thousand rams. ⁵But after Ahab died, the king of Moab rebelled against the king of Israel. ⁶So at that time King Joram set out from Samaria and mobilized all Israel. ⁷He also sent this message to Jehoshaphat king of Judah: "The king of Moab has rebelled against me. Will you go with me to fight against Moab?"

"I will go with you," he replied. "I am as you are, my people as your people, my horses as your horses."

⁸"By what route shall we attack?" he asked.

"Through the Desert of Edom," he answered.

⁹So the king of Israel set out with the king of Judah and the king of Edom. After a roundabout march of seven days, the army had no more water for themselves or for the animals with them.

¹⁰"What!" exclaimed the king of Israel. "Has the LORD called us three kings together only to hand us over to Moab?"

¹¹But Jehoshaphat asked, "Is there no

---

a 1 Hebrew *Jehoram,* a variant of *Joram*; also in verse 6

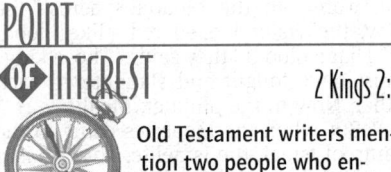

POINT OF INTEREST

2 Kings 2:11

Old Testament writers mention two people who entered heaven without dying. Elijah was one of them. Who was the other? (See Genesis 5:24. Hint: His name started with an "E" too.)

prophet of the LORD here, that we may inquire of the LORD through him?"

An officer of the king of Israel answered, "Elisha son of Shaphat is here. He used to pour water on the hands of Elijah.ᵃ"

¹²Jehoshaphat said, "The word of the LORD is with him." So the king of Israel and Jehoshaphat and the king of Edom went down to him.

¹³Elisha said to the king of Israel, "What do we have to do with each other? Go to the prophets of your father and the prophets of your mother."

"No," the king of Israel answered, "because it was the LORD who called us three kings together to hand us over to Moab."

¹⁴Elisha said, "As surely as the LORD Almighty lives, whom I serve, if I did not have respect for the presence of Jehoshaphat king of Judah, I would not look at you or even notice you. ¹⁵But now bring me a harpist."

While the harpist was playing, the hand of the LORD came upon Elisha ¹⁶and he said, "This is what the LORD says: Make this valley full of ditches. ¹⁷For this is what the LORD says: You will see neither wind nor rain, yet this valley will be filled with water, and you, your cattle and your other animals will drink. ¹⁸This is an easy thing in the eyes of the LORD; he will also hand Moab over to you. ¹⁹You will overthrow every fortified city and every major town. You will cut down every good tree, stop up all the springs, and ruin every good field with stones."

²⁰The next morning, about the time for offering the sacrifice, there it was—water flowing from the direction of Edom! And the land was filled with water.

²¹Now all the Moabites had heard that the kings had come to fight against them; so every man, young and old, who could bear arms was called up and stationed on the border. ²²When they got up early in the morning, the sun was shining on the water. To the Moabites across the way, the water looked red—like blood. ²³"That's blood!" they said. "Those kings must have fought and slaughtered each other. Now to the plunder, Moab!"

²⁴But when the Moabites came to the camp of Israel, the Israelites rose up and fought them until they fled. And the Israelites invaded the land and slaughtered the Moabites. ²⁵They destroyed the towns, and each man threw a stone on every good field until it was covered.

They stopped up all the springs and cut down every good tree. Only Kir Hareseth was left with its stones in place, but men armed with slings surrounded it and attacked it as well.

²⁶When the king of Moab saw that the battle had gone against him, he took with him seven hundred swordsmen to break through to the king of Edom, but they failed. ²⁷Then he took his firstborn son, who was to succeed him as king, and offered him as a sacrifice on the city wall. The fury against Israel was great; they withdrew and returned to their own land.

The Widow's Oil

4 The wife of a man from the company of the prophets cried out to Elisha, "Your servant my husband is dead, and you know that he revered the LORD. But now his creditor is coming to take my two boys as his slaves."

²Elisha replied to her, "How can I help you? Tell me, what do you have in your house?"

"Your servant has nothing there at all," she said, "except a little oil."

³Elisha said, "Go around and ask all your neighbors for empty jars. Don't ask for just a few. ⁴Then go inside and shut the door behind you and your sons. Pour oil into all the jars, and as each is filled, put it to one side."

⁵She left him and afterward shut the door behind her and her sons. They brought the jars to her and she kept pouring. ⁶When all the jars were full, she said to her son, "Bring me another one."

ᵃ 11 That is, he was Elijah's personal servant.

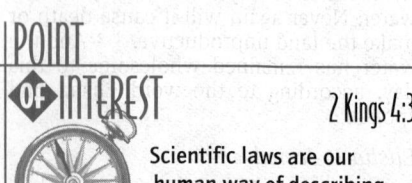

POINT OF INTEREST

2 Kings 4:3

Scientific laws are our human way of describing the "natural" order that we can observe. The definition of miracles is that they *seem* to violate scientific laws, but that definition doesn't make them contrary to the laws of the universe. The God who does miracles is the same sovereign and all-powerful God who created the universe.

But he replied, "There is not a jar left." Then the oil stopped flowing.

⁷She went and told the man of God, and he said, "Go, sell the oil and pay your debts. You and your sons can live on what is left."

The Shunammite's Son Restored to Life

⁸One day Elisha went to Shunem. And a well-to-do woman was there, who urged him to stay for a meal. So whenever he came by, he stopped there to eat. ⁹She said to her husband, "I know that this man who often comes our way is a holy man of God. ¹⁰Let's make a small room on the roof and put in it a bed and a table, a chair and a lamp for him. Then he can stay there whenever he comes to us."

¹¹One day when Elisha came, he went up to his room and lay down there. ¹²He said to his servant Gehazi, "Call the Shunammite." So he called her, and she stood before him. ¹³Elisha said to him, "Tell her, 'You have gone to all this trouble for us. Now what can be done for you? Can we speak on your behalf to the king or the commander of the army?' "

She replied, "I have a home among my own people."

¹⁴"What can be done for her?" Elisha asked.

Gehazi said, "Well, she has no son and her husband is old."

¹⁵Then Elisha said, "Call her." So he called her, and she stood in the doorway. ¹⁶"About this time next year," Elisha said, "you will hold a son in your arms."

"No, my lord," she objected. "Don't mislead your servant, O man of God!"

¹⁷But the woman became pregnant, and the next year about that same time she gave birth to a son, just as Elisha had told her.

¹⁸The child grew, and one day he went out to his father, who was with the reapers. ¹⁹"My head! My head!" he said to his father.

His father told a servant, "Carry him to his mother." ²⁰After the servant had lifted him up and carried him to his mother, the boy sat on her lap until noon, and then he died. ²¹She went up and laid him on the bed of the man of God, then shut the door and went out.

²²She called her husband and said, "Please send me one of the servants and a donkey so I can go to the man of God quickly and return."

²³"Why go to him today?" he asked. "It's not the New Moon or the Sabbath."

"It's all right," she said.

²⁴She saddled the donkey and said to her servant, "Lead on; don't slow down for me unless I tell you." ²⁵So she set out and came to the man of God at Mount Carmel.

When he saw her in the distance, the man of God said to his servant Gehazi, "Look! There's the Shunammite! ²⁶Run to meet her and ask her, 'Are you all right? Is your husband all right? Is your child all right?' "

"Everything is all right," she said.

²⁷When she reached the man of God at the mountain, she took hold of his feet. Gehazi came over to push her away, but the man of God said, "Leave her alone! She is in bitter distress, but the LORD has hidden it from me and has not told me why."

²⁸"Did I ask you for a son, my lord?" she said. "Didn't I tell you, 'Don't raise my hopes'?"

²⁹Elisha said to Gehazi, "Tuck your cloak into your belt, take my staff in your hand and run. If you meet anyone, do not greet him, and if anyone greets you, do not answer. Lay my staff on the boy's face."

³⁰But the child's mother said, "As surely as the LORD lives and as you live, I will not leave you." So he got up and followed her.

³¹Gehazi went on ahead and laid the staff on the boy's face, but there was no sound or response. So Gehazi went back to meet Elisha and told him, "The boy has not awakened."

³²When Elisha reached the house, there was the boy lying dead on his couch. ³³He went in, shut the door on the two of them and prayed to the LORD. ³⁴Then he got on the bed and lay upon the boy, mouth to mouth, eyes to eyes, hands to hands. As he stretched himself out upon him, the boy's body grew warm. ³⁵Elisha turned away and walked back and forth in the room and then got on the bed and stretched out upon him once more. The boy sneezed seven times and opened his eyes.

³⁶Elisha summoned Gehazi and said, "Call the Shunammite." And he did. When she came, he said, "Take your son." ³⁷She came in, fell at his feet and

bowed to the ground. Then she took her son and went out.

Death in the Pot

38Elisha returned to Gilgal and there was a famine in that region. While the company of the prophets was meeting with him, he said to his servant, "Put on the large pot and cook some stew for these men."

39One of them went out into the fields to gather herbs and found a wild vine. He gathered some of its gourds and filled the fold of his cloak. When he returned, he cut them up into the pot of stew, though no one knew what they were. **40**The stew was poured out for the men, but as they began to eat it, they cried out, "O man of God, there is death in the pot!" And they could not eat it.

41Elisha said, "Get some flour." He put it into the pot and said, "Serve it to the people to eat." And there was nothing harmful in the pot.

Feeding of a Hundred

42A man came from Baal Shalishah, bringing the man of God twenty loaves of barley bread baked from the first ripe grain, along with some heads of new grain. "Give it to the people to eat," Elisha said.

43"How can I set this before a hundred men?" his servant asked.

But Elisha answered, "Give it to the people to eat. For this is what the LORD says: 'They will eat and have some left over.' " **44**Then he set it before them, and they ate and had some left over, according to the word of the LORD.

Naaman Healed of Leprosy

5 Now Naaman was commander of the army of the king of Aram. He was a great man in the sight of his master and highly regarded, because through him the LORD had given victory to Aram. He was a valiant soldier, but he had leprosy.[a]

2Now bands from Aram had gone out and had taken captive a young girl from Israel, and she served Naaman's wife. **3**She said to her mistress, "If only my master would see the prophet who is in Samaria! He would cure him of his leprosy."

4Naaman went to his master and told him what the girl from Israel had said. **5**"By all means, go," the king of Aram replied. "I will send a letter to the king of Israel." So Naaman left, taking with him ten talents[b] of silver, six thousand shekels[c] of gold and ten sets of clothing. **6**The letter that he took to the king of Israel read: "With this letter I am sending my servant Naaman to you so that you may cure him of his leprosy."

7As soon as the king of Israel read the letter, he tore his robes and said, "Am I God? Can I kill and bring back to life? Why does this fellow send someone to me to be cured of his leprosy? See how he is trying to pick a quarrel with me!"

8When Elisha the man of God heard that the king of Israel had torn his robes, he sent him this message: "Why have you torn your robes? Have the man come to me and he will know that there is a prophet in Israel." **9**So Naaman went with his horses and chariots and stopped at the door of Elisha's house. **10**Elisha sent a messenger to say to him, "Go, wash yourself seven times in the Jordan, and your flesh will be restored and you will be cleansed."

11But Naaman went away angry and said, "I thought that he would surely come out to me and stand and call on the name of the LORD his God, wave his hand over the spot and cure me of my leprosy. **12**Are not Abana and Pharpar, the rivers of Damascus, better than any of the waters of Israel? Couldn't I wash in them and be cleansed?" So he turned and went off in a rage.

13Naaman's servants went to him and said, "My father, if the prophet had told you to do some great thing, would you not have done it? How much more, then, when he tells you, 'Wash and be cleansed'!" **14**So he went down and dipped himself in the Jordan seven times, as the man of God had told him, and his flesh was restored and became clean like that of a young boy.

15Then Naaman and all his attendants went back to the man of God. He stood before him and said, "Now I know that there is no God in all the world except in Israel. Please accept now a gift from your servant."

16The prophet answered, "As surely as the LORD lives, whom I serve, I will not

---

a1 The Hebrew word was used for various diseases affecting the skin—not necessarily leprosy; also in verses 3, 6, 7, 11 and 27.   *b5* That is, about 750 pounds (about 340 kilograms)   *c5* That is, about 150 pounds (about 70 kilograms) accept a thing." And even though Naaman urged him, he refused.

¹⁷"If you will not," said Naaman, "please let me, your servant, be given as much earth as a pair of mules can carry, for your servant will never again make burnt offerings and sacrifices to any other god but the LORD. ¹⁸But may the LORD forgive your servant for this one thing: When my master enters the temple of Rimmon to bow down and he is leaning on my arm and I bow there also—when I bow down in the temple of Rimmon, may the LORD forgive your servant for this."

¹⁹"Go in peace," Elisha said.

After Naaman had traveled some distance, ²⁰Gehazi, the servant of Elisha the man of God, said to himself, "My master was too easy on Naaman, this Aramean, by not accepting from him what he brought. As surely as the LORD lives, I will run after him and get something from him."

²¹So Gehazi hurried after Naaman. When Naaman saw him running toward him, he got down from the chariot to meet him. "Is everything all right?" he asked.

²²"Everything is all right," Gehazi answered. "My master sent me to say, 'Two young men from the company of the prophets have just come to me from the hill country of Ephraim. Please give them

---

FRIDAY

Read 2 Kings 5:1–27
Key Verses 2 Kings 5:2–3

The One God Uses – Dale Magnusson

She was just a young girl. She had been taken from her country, wrenched from the familiarity of her home and the comfort of her family, and forced to be a slave in a foreign land among foreign people.

How could one for whom life had been so cruel so quickly think of the well-being of someone else? "If only my master would see the prophet who is in Samaria! He would cure him of his leprosy" (2 Kings 5:3). Most in her position would wish their masters dead, but she wished hers to be cured. Her wish became reality, and her master (Naaman) became a true follower of the one true God: "Your servant will never again make burnt offerings and sacrifices to any other god but the LORD" (2 Kings 5:17).

This girl became a missionary, not by vocation but by attitude and action. The Lord had found her ready to be used. Her part in this incredible story has been recorded for eternity in God's Word—a significant achievement.

Obviously it wasn't the slave girl's ability to do something great that made her useful. It was her availability. Her life was available because her heart wasn't full of bitterness, anger, selfishness or self-pity.

Do you ever wonder if you are or ever will be "great enough" for God to use you? Do you ever think, "If only I knew this or understood that or was . . ." You fill in the rest. The next time you wonder whether or not God can use you, remember the young slave girl. Remember that God isn't looking for someone great—just someone who's willing.

A Deeper Look
1 Corinthians 2:1–5; 2 Corinthians 3:5; Philippians 2:4–5

Go to page 401 for your next devotional reading.

a talent*a* of silver and two sets of clothing.' "

²³"By all means, take two talents," said Naaman. He urged Gehazi to accept them, and then tied up the two talents of silver in two bags, with two sets of clothing. He gave them to two of his servants, and they carried them ahead of Gehazi. ²⁴When Gehazi came to the hill, he took the things from the servants and put them away in the house. He sent the men away and they left. ²⁵Then he went in and stood before his master Elisha.

"Where have you been, Gehazi?" Elisha asked.

"Your servant didn't go anywhere," Gehazi answered.

²⁶But Elisha said to him, "Was not my spirit with you when the man got down from his chariot to meet you? Is this the time to take money, or to accept clothes, olive groves, vineyards, flocks, herds, or menservants and maidservants? ²⁷Naaman's leprosy will cling to you and to your descendants forever." Then Gehazi went from Elisha's presence and he was leprous, as white as snow.

An Axhead Floats

6 The company of the prophets said to Elisha, "Look, the place where we meet with you is too small for us. ²Let us go to the Jordan, where each of us can get a pole; and let us build a place there for us to live."

And he said, "Go."

³Then one of them said, "Won't you please come with your servants?"

"I will," Elisha replied. ⁴And he went with them.

They went to the Jordan and began to cut down trees. ⁵As one of them was cutting down a tree, the iron axhead fell into the water. "Oh, my lord," he cried out, "it was borrowed!"

⁶The man of God asked, "Where did it fall?" When he showed him the place, Elisha cut a stick and threw it there, and made the iron float. ⁷"Lift it out," he said. Then the man reached out his hand and took it.

Elisha Traps Blinded Arameans

⁸Now the king of Aram was at war with Israel. After conferring with his officers, he said, "I will set up my camp in such and such a place."

⁹The man of God sent word to the king of Israel: "Beware of passing that place, because the Arameans are going down there." ¹⁰So the king of Israel checked on the place indicated by the man of God. Time and again Elisha warned the king, so that he was on his guard in such places.

¹¹This enraged the king of Aram. He summoned his officers and demanded of them, "Will you not tell me which of us is on the side of the king of Israel?"

¹²"None of us, my lord the king," said one of his officers, "but Elisha, the prophet who is in Israel, tells the king of Israel the very words you speak in your bedroom."

¹³"Go, find out where he is," the king ordered, "so I can send men and capture him." The report came back: "He is in Dothan." ¹⁴Then he sent horses and chariots and a strong force there. They went by night and surrounded the city.

¹⁵When the servant of the man of God got up and went out early the next morning, an army with horses and chariots had surrounded the city. "Oh, my lord, what shall we do?" the servant asked.

¹⁶"Don't be afraid," the prophet answered. "Those who are with us are more than those who are with them."

¹⁷And Elisha prayed, "O LORD, open his eyes so he may see." Then the LORD opened the servant's eyes, and he looked and saw the hills full of horses and chariots of fire all around Elisha.

¹⁸As the enemy came down toward him, Elisha prayed to the LORD, "Strike these people with blindness." So he struck them with blindness, as Elisha had asked.

¹⁹Elisha told them, "This is not the road and this is not the city. Follow me, and I will lead you to the man you are looking for." And he led them to Samaria.

a22 That is, about 75 pounds (about 34 kilograms)

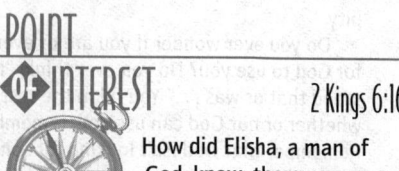

POINT OF INTEREST

2 Kings 6:16

How did Elisha, a man of God, know there was an angelic army protecting him? What, if anything, was wrong with his servant's faith and perception? What might this story say about the presence of angelic support around us today?

Read 2 Kings 6:1–23
Key Verse 2 Kings 6:16

God's Unlimited Resources

There are over 100 billion stars in the Milky Way galaxy. If you could travel at the speed of light, it would take more than one hundred thousand years to cross our galaxy. Yet God spoke the word—and the heavens and earth came into existence. From nothing he created everything, and he holds it all in the palm of his hand. You want to talk about resources—all of creation is God's and he can use it for any purpose.

When we are thrust into situations in which we need to rely on God's resources, we might respond like Elisha's servant. We can become fearful as we look at our own limited resources. Our needs can seem so big and our abilities so small. But when our eyes finally turn away from ourselves to our Creator—to God's power and resources—we realize he is sufficient to meet any and every need.

Digging Into the Word
1. What do these passages teach you about God and creation?—
   Psalm 24:1–2; Psalm 50:10–12
2. How do these passages help you trust God and his resources?—
   Psalm 23:1–4; Matthew 6:25–34

Discussion Starter
Fire up a conversation with friends by asking: What makes it difficult for you to trust in God's resources? How have you seen God provide his resources in your life this past year?

One Step Deeper
Psalm 46:1–3; Romans 8:31

Go to page 415 for your next devotional reading.

²⁰After they entered the city, Elisha said, "Lord, open the eyes of these men so they can see." Then the Lord opened their eyes and they looked, and there they were, inside Samaria.

²¹When the king of Israel saw them, he asked Elisha, "Shall I kill them, my father? Shall I kill them?"

²²"Do not kill them," he answered. "Would you kill men you have captured with your own sword or bow? Set food and water before them so that they may eat and drink and then go back to their master." ²³So he prepared a great feast for them, and after they had finished eating and drinking, he sent them away, and they returned to their master. So the bands from Aram stopped raiding Israel's territory.

Famine in Besieged Samaria

²⁴Some time later, Ben-Hadad king of Aram mobilized his entire army and marched up and laid siege to Samaria. ²⁵There was a great famine in the city; the siege lasted so long that a donkey's head sold for eighty shekels*a* of silver, and a quarter of a cab*b* of seed pods*c* for five shekels.*d*

²⁶As the king of Israel was passing by on the wall, a woman cried to him, "Help me, my lord the king!"

²⁷The king replied, "If the Lord does not help you, where can I get help for you? From the threshing floor? From the winepress?" ²⁸Then he asked her, "What's the matter?"

She answered, "This woman said to me, 'Give up your son so we may eat him today, and tomorrow we'll eat my son.' ²⁹So we cooked my son and ate him. The next day I said to her, 'Give up your son so we may eat him,' but she had hidden him."

³⁰When the king heard the woman's words, he tore his robes. As he went along the wall, the people looked, and there, underneath, he had sackcloth on his body. ³¹He said, "May God deal with me, be it ever so severely, if the head of Elisha son of Shaphat remains on his shoulders today!"

³²Now Elisha was sitting in his house, and the elders were sitting with him. The king sent a messenger ahead, but before he arrived, Elisha said to the elders, "Don't you see how this murderer is sending someone to cut off my head? Look, when the messenger comes, shut the door and hold it shut against him. Is not the sound of his master's footsteps behind him?"

³³While he was still talking to them, the messenger came down to him. And ⌊the king⌋ said, "This disaster is from the Lord. Why should I wait for the Lord any longer?"

7 Elisha said, "Hear the word of the Lord. This is what the Lord says: About this time tomorrow, a seah*e* of flour will sell for a shekel*f* and two seahs*g* of barley for a shekel at the gate of Samaria."

²The officer on whose arm the king was leaning said to the man of God, "Look, even if the Lord should open the floodgates of the heavens, could this happen?"

"You will see it with your own eyes," answered Elisha, "but you will not eat any of it!"

The Siege Lifted

³Now there were four men with leprosy*h* at the entrance of the city gate. They said to each other, "Why stay here until we die? ⁴If we say, 'We'll go into the city'—the famine is there, and we will die. And if we stay here, we will die. So let's go over to the camp of the Arameans and surrender. If they spare us, we live; if they kill us, then we die."

⁵At dusk they got up and went to the camp of the Arameans. When they reached the edge of the camp, not a man was there, ⁶for the Lord had caused the Arameans to hear the sound of chariots and horses and a great army, so that they said to one another, "Look, the king of Israel has hired the Hittite and Egyptian kings to attack us!" ⁷So they got up and fled in the dusk and abandoned their tents and their horses and donkeys. They left the camp as it was and ran for their lives.

⁸The men who had leprosy reached the edge of the camp and entered one of the tents. They ate and drank, and carried away silver, gold and clothes, and

a25 That is, about 2 pounds (about 1 kilogram)   *b25* That is, probably about 1/2 pint (about 0.3 liter)   *c25* Or of dove's dung   *d25* That is, about 2 ounces (about 55 grams)   *e1* That is, probably about 7 quarts (about 7.3 liters); also in verses 16 and 18   *f1* That is, about 2/5 ounce (about 11 grams); also in verses 16 and 18   *g1* That is, probably about 13 quarts (about 15 liters); also in verses 16 and 18   *h3* The Hebrew word is used for various diseases affecting the skin—not necessarily leprosy; also in verse 8.

went off and hid them. They returned and entered another tent and took some things from it and hid them also. ⁹Then they said to each other, "We're not doing right. This is a day of good news and we are keeping it to ourselves. If we wait until daylight, punishment will overtake us. Let's go at once and report this to the royal palace."

¹⁰So they went and called out to the city gatekeepers and told them, "We went into the Aramean camp and not a man was there—not a sound of anyone—only tethered horses and donkeys, and the tents left just as they were." ¹¹The gatekeepers shouted the news, and it was reported within the palace.

¹²The king got up in the night and said to his officers, "I will tell you what the Arameans have done to us. They know we are starving; so they have left the camp to hide in the countryside, thinking, 'They will surely come out, and then we will take them alive and get into the city.'"

¹³One of his officers answered, "Have some men take five of the horses that are left in the city. Their plight will be like that of all the Israelites left here—yes, they will only be like all these Israelites who are doomed. So let us send them to find out what happened."

¹⁴So they selected two chariots with their horses, and the king sent them after the Aramean army. He commanded the drivers, "Go and find out what has happened." ¹⁵They followed them as far as the Jordan, and they found the whole road strewn with the clothing and equipment the Arameans had thrown away in their headlong flight. So the messengers returned and reported to the king. ¹⁶Then the people went out and plundered the camp of the Arameans. So a seah of flour sold for a shekel, and two seahs of barley sold for a shekel, as the LORD had said.

¹⁷Now the king had put the officer on whose arm he leaned in charge of the gate, and the people trampled him in the gateway, and he died, just as the man of God had foretold when the king came down to his house. ¹⁸It happened as the man of God had said to the king: "About this time tomorrow, a seah of flour will sell for a shekel and two seahs of barley for a shekel at the gate of Samaria."

¹⁹The officer had said to the man of God, "Look, even if the LORD should open the floodgates of the heavens, could this happen?" The man of God had replied, "You will see it with your own eyes, but you will not eat any of it!" ²⁰And that is exactly what happened to him, for the people trampled him in the gateway, and he died.

The Shunammite's Land Restored

8 Now Elisha had said to the woman whose son he had restored to life, "Go away with your family and stay for a while wherever you can, because the LORD has decreed a famine in the land that will last seven years." ²The woman proceeded to do as the man of God said. She and her family went away and stayed in the land of the Philistines seven years.

³At the end of the seven years she came back from the land of the Philistines and went to the king to beg for her house and land. ⁴The king was talking to Gehazi, the servant of the man of God, and had said, "Tell me about all the great things Elisha has done." ⁵Just as Gehazi was telling the king how Elisha had restored the dead to life, the woman whose son Elisha had brought back to life came to beg the king for her house and land.

Gehazi said, "This is the woman, my lord the king, and this is her son whom Elisha restored to life." ⁶The king asked the woman about it, and she told him.

Then he assigned an official to her case and said to him, "Give back everything that belonged to her, including all the income from her land from the day she left the country until now."

Hazael Murders Ben-Hadad

⁷Elisha went to Damascus, and Ben-Hadad king of Aram was ill. When the king was told, "The man of God has come all the way up here," ⁸he said to Hazael, "Take a gift with you and go to meet the man of God. Consult the LORD through him; ask him, 'Will I recover from this illness?'"

⁹Hazael went to meet Elisha, taking with him as a gift forty camel-loads of all the finest wares of Damascus. He went in and stood before him, and said, "Your son Ben-Hadad king of Aram has sent me to ask, 'Will I recover from this illness?'"

¹⁰Elisha answered, "Go and say to him, 'You will certainly recover'; but*ᵃ* the LORD has revealed to me that he will in

---

ᵃ 10 The Hebrew may also be read Go and say, 'You will certainly not recover,' for.

fact die." ¹¹He stared at him with a fixed gaze until Hazael felt ashamed. Then the man of God began to weep.

¹²"Why is my lord weeping?" asked Hazael.

"Because I know the harm you will do to the Israelites," he answered. "You will set fire to their fortified places, kill their young men with the sword, dash their little children to the ground, and rip open their pregnant women."

¹³Hazael said, "How could your servant, a mere dog, accomplish such a feat?"

"The LORD has shown me that you will become king of Aram," answered Elisha.

¹⁴Then Hazael left Elisha and returned to his master. When Ben-Hadad asked, "What did Elisha say to you?" Hazael replied, "He told me that you would certainly recover." ¹⁵But the next day he took a thick cloth, soaked it in water and spread it over the king's face, so that he died. Then Hazael succeeded him as king.

Jehoram King of Judah

¹⁶In the fifth year of Joram son of Ahab king of Israel, when Jehoshaphat was king of Judah, Jehoram son of Jehoshaphat began his reign as king of Judah. ¹⁷He was thirty-two years old when he became king, and he reigned in Jerusalem eight years. ¹⁸He walked in the ways of the kings of Israel, as the house of Ahab had done, for he married a daughter of Ahab. He did evil in the eyes of the LORD. ¹⁹Nevertheless, for the sake of his servant David, the LORD was not willing to destroy Judah. He had promised to maintain a lamp for David and his descendants forever.

²⁰In the time of Jehoram, Edom rebelled against Judah and set up its own king. ²¹So Jehoram[a] went to Zair with all his chariots. The Edomites surrounded him and his chariot commanders, but he rose up and broke through by night; his army, however, fled back home. ²²To this day Edom has been in rebellion against Judah. Libnah revolted at the same time.

²³As for the other events of Jehoram's reign, and all he did, are they not written in the book of the annals of the kings of Judah? ²⁴Jehoram rested with his fathers and was buried with them in the City of David. And Ahaziah his son succeeded him as king.

Ahaziah King of Judah

²⁵In the twelfth year of Joram son of Ahab king of Israel, Ahaziah son of Jehoram king of Judah began to reign. ²⁶Ahaziah was twenty-two years old when he became king, and he reigned in Jerusalem one year. His mother's name was Athaliah, a granddaughter of Omri king of Israel. ²⁷He walked in the ways of the house of Ahab and did evil in the eyes of the LORD, as the house of Ahab had done, for he was related by marriage to Ahab's family.

²⁸Ahaziah went with Joram son of Ahab to war against Hazael king of Aram at Ramoth Gilead. The Arameans wounded Joram; ²⁹so King Joram returned to Jezreel to recover from the wounds the Arameans had inflicted on him at Ramoth[b] in his battle with Hazael king of Aram.

Then Ahaziah son of Jehoram king of Judah went down to Jezreel to see Joram son of Ahab, because he had been wounded.

Jehu Anointed King of Israel

9 The prophet Elisha summoned a man from the company of the prophets and said to him, "Tuck your cloak into your belt, take this flask of oil with you and go to Ramoth Gilead. ²When you get there, look for Jehu son of Jehoshaphat, the son of Nimshi. Go to him, get him away from his companions and take him into an inner room. ³Then take the flask and pour the oil on his head and declare, 'This is

---

[a]21 Hebrew *Joram*, a variant of *Jehoram*; also in verses 23 and 24   [b]29 Hebrew *Ramah*, a variant of *Ramoth*

POINT OF INTEREST

2 Kings 8:16

Jehoram, as king of Judah, was expected to be faithful to the true God. But Jehoram chose to imitate Israel's King Ahab, a wicked king who was controlled by an idol-worshiping wife. Considering that Jehoram married Ahab's daughter (see verse 18), what conclusions can you draw about Jehoram's character, conscience and commitment?

what the LORD says: I anoint you king over Israel.' Then open the door and run; don't delay!"

⁴So the young man, the prophet, went to Ramoth Gilead. ⁵When he arrived, he found the army officers sitting together. "I have a message for you, commander," he said.

"For which of us?" asked Jehu.

"For you, commander," he replied.

⁶Jehu got up and went into the house. Then the prophet poured the oil on Jehu's head and declared, "This is what the LORD, the God of Israel, says: 'I anoint you king over the LORD's people Israel. ⁷You are to destroy the house of Ahab your master, and I will avenge the blood of my servants the prophets and the blood of all the LORD's servants shed by Jezebel. ⁸The whole house of Ahab will perish. I will cut off from Ahab every last male in Israel—slave or free. ⁹I will make the house of Ahab like the house of Jeroboam son of Nebat and like the house of Baasha son of Ahijah. ¹⁰As for Jezebel, dogs will devour her on the plot of ground at Jezreel, and no one will bury her.' " Then he opened the door and ran.

¹¹When Jehu went out to his fellow officers, one of them asked him, "Is everything all right? Why did this madman come to you?"

"You know the man and the sort of things he says," Jehu replied.

¹²"That's not true!" they said. "Tell us."

Jehu said, "Here is what he told me: 'This is what the LORD says: I anoint you king over Israel.' "

¹³They hurried and took their cloaks and spread them under him on the bare steps. Then they blew the trumpet and shouted, "Jehu is king!"

Jehu Kills Joram and Ahaziah

¹⁴So Jehu son of Jehoshaphat, the son of Nimshi, conspired against Joram. (Now Joram and all Israel had been defending Ramoth Gilead against Hazael king of Aram, ¹⁵but King Joram*a* had returned to Jezreel to recover from the wounds the Arameans had inflicted on him in the battle with Hazael king of Aram.) Jehu said, "If this is the way you feel, don't let anyone slip out of the city to go and tell the news in Jezreel." ¹⁶Then he got into his chariot and rode to Jezreel, because Joram was resting there

and Ahaziah king of Judah had gone down to see him.

¹⁷When the lookout standing on the tower in Jezreel saw Jehu's troops approaching, he called out, "I see some troops coming."

"Get a horseman," Joram ordered. "Send him to meet them and ask, 'Do you come in peace?' "

¹⁸The horseman rode off to meet Jehu and said, "This is what the king says: 'Do you come in peace?' "

"What do you have to do with peace?" Jehu replied. "Fall in behind me."

The lookout reported, "The messenger has reached them, but he isn't coming back."

¹⁹So the king sent out a second horseman. When he came to them he said, "This is what the king says: 'Do you come in peace?' "

Jehu replied, "What do you have to do with peace? Fall in behind me."

²⁰The lookout reported, "He has reached them, but he isn't coming back either. The driving is like that of Jehu son of Nimshi—he drives like a madman."

²¹"Hitch up my chariot," Joram ordered. And when it was hitched up, Joram king of Israel and Ahaziah king of Judah rode out, each in his own chariot, to meet Jehu. They met him at the plot of ground that had belonged to Naboth the Jezreelite. ²²When Joram saw Jehu he asked, "Have you come in peace, Jehu?"

"How can there be peace," Jehu replied, "as long as all the idolatry and witchcraft of your mother Jezebel abound?"

²³Joram turned about and fled, calling out to Ahaziah, "Treachery, Ahaziah!"

²⁴Then Jehu drew his bow and shot Joram between the shoulders. The arrow pierced his heart and he slumped down in his chariot. ²⁵Jehu said to Bidkar, his chariot officer, "Pick him up and throw him on the field that belonged to Naboth the Jezreelite. Remember how you and I were riding together in chariots behind Ahab his father when the LORD made this prophecy about him: ²⁶'Yesterday I saw the blood of Naboth and the blood of his sons, declares the LORD, and I will surely make you pay for it on this plot of ground, declares the LORD.'*b* Now then, pick him up and throw him on that plot,

---

a15 Hebrew *Jehoram*, a variant of *Joram*; also in verses 17 and 21-24　　*b26* See 1 Kings 21:19.

in accordance with the word of the LORD." ²⁷When Ahaziah king of Judah saw what had happened, he fled up the road to Beth Haggan.ᵃ Jehu chased him, shouting, "Kill him too!" They wounded him in his chariot on the way up to Gur near Ibleam, but he escaped to Megiddo and died there. ²⁸His servants took him by chariot to Jerusalem and buried him with his fathers in his tomb in the City of David. ²⁹(In the eleventh year of Joram son of Ahab, Ahaziah had become king of Judah.)

Jezebel Killed

³⁰Then Jehu went to Jezreel. When Jezebel heard about it, she painted her eyes, arranged her hair and looked out of a window. ³¹As Jehu entered the gate, she asked, "Have you come in peace, Zimri, you murderer of your master?"ᵇ ³²He looked up at the window and called out, "Who is on my side? Who?" Two or three eunuchs looked down at him. ³³"Throw her down!" Jehu said. So they threw her down, and some of her blood spattered the wall and the horses as they trampled her underfoot.

³⁴Jehu went in and ate and drank. "Take care of that cursed woman," he said, "and bury her, for she was a king's daughter." ³⁵But when they went out to bury her, they found nothing except her skull, her feet and her hands. ³⁶They went back and told Jehu, who said, "This is the word of the LORD that he spoke through his servant Elijah the Tishbite: On the plot of ground at Jezreel dogs will devour Jezebel's flesh.ᶜ ³⁷Jezebel's body will be like refuse on the ground in the plot at Jezreel, so that no one will be able to say, 'This is Jezebel.'"

Ahab's Family Killed

10 Now there were in Samaria seventy sons of the house of Ahab. So Jehu wrote letters and sent them to Samaria: to the officials of Jezreel,ᵈ to the elders and to the guardians of Ahab's children. He said, ²"As soon as this letter reaches you, since your master's sons are with you and you have chariots and horses, a fortified city and weapons, ³choose the best and most worthy of your master's sons and set him on his father's throne. Then fight for your master's house."

⁴But they were terrified and said, "If two kings could not resist him, how can we?"

⁵So the palace administrator, the city governor, the elders and the guardians sent this message to Jehu: "We are your servants and we will do anything you say. We will not appoint anyone as king; you do whatever you think best."

⁶Then Jehu wrote them a second letter, saying, "If you are on my side and will obey me, take the heads of your master's sons and come to me in Jezreel by this time tomorrow."

Now the royal princes, seventy of them, were with the leading men of the city, who were rearing them. ⁷When the letter arrived, these men took the princes and slaughtered all seventy of them. They put their heads in baskets and sent them to Jehu in Jezreel. ⁸When the messenger arrived, he told Jehu, "They have brought the heads of the princes."

Then Jehu ordered, "Put them in two piles at the entrance of the city gate until morning."

⁹The next morning Jehu went out. He stood before all the people and said, "You are innocent. It was I who conspired against my master and killed him, but who killed all these? ¹⁰Know then, that not a word the LORD has spoken against the house of Ahab will fail. The LORD has done what he promised through his servant Elijah." ¹¹So Jehu killed everyone in Jezreel who remained of the house of Ahab, as well as all his chief men, his close friends and his priests, leaving him no survivor.

¹²Jehu then set out and went toward Samaria. At Beth Eked of the Shepherds, ¹³he met some relatives of Ahaziah king of Judah and asked, "Who are you?"

They said, "We are relatives of Ahaziah, and we have come down to greet the families of the king and of the queen mother."

¹⁴"Take them alive!" he ordered. So they took them alive and slaughtered them by the well of Beth Eked—forty-two men. He left no survivor.

¹⁵After he left there, he came upon Jehonadab son of Recab, who was on his way to meet him. Jehu greeted him and said, "Are you in accord with me, as I am with you?"

"I am," Jehonadab answered.

"If so," said Jehu, "give your

ᵃ27 Or *fled by way of the garden house*　ᵇ31 Or *"Did Zimri have peace, who murdered his master?"*　ᶜ36 See 1 Kings 21:23.　ᵈ1 Hebrew; some Septuagint manuscripts and Vulgate *of the city* hand." So he did, and Jehu helped him up into the chariot. ¹⁶Jehu said, "Come with me and see my zeal for the LORD." Then he had him ride along in his chariot.

¹⁷When Jehu came to Samaria, he killed all who were left there of Ahab's family; he destroyed them, according to the word of the LORD spoken to Elijah.

Ministers of Baal Killed

¹⁸Then Jehu brought all the people together and said to them, "Ahab served Baal a little; Jehu will serve him much. ¹⁹Now summon all the prophets of Baal, all his ministers and all his priests. See that no one is missing, because I am going to hold a great sacrifice for Baal. Anyone who fails to come will no longer live." But Jehu was acting deceptively in order to destroy the ministers of Baal.

²⁰Jehu said, "Call an assembly in honor of Baal." So they proclaimed it. ²¹Then he sent word throughout Israel, and all the ministers of Baal came; not one stayed away. They crowded into the temple of Baal until it was full from one end to the other. ²²And Jehu said to the keeper of the wardrobe, "Bring robes for all the ministers of Baal." So he brought out robes for them.

²³Then Jehu and Jehonadab son of Recab went into the temple of Baal. Jehu said to the ministers of Baal, "Look around and see that no servants of the LORD are here with you—only ministers of Baal." ²⁴So they went in to make sacrifices and burnt offerings. Now Jehu had posted eighty men outside with this warning: "If one of you lets any of the men I am placing in your hands escape, it will be your life for his life." ²⁵As soon as Jehu had finished making the burnt offering, he ordered the guards and officers: "Go in and kill them; let no one escape." So they cut them down with the sword. The guards and officers threw the bodies out and then entered the inner shrine of the temple of Baal. ²⁶They brought the sacred stone out of the temple of Baal and burned it. ²⁷They demolished the sacred stone of Baal and tore down the temple of Baal, and people have used it for a latrine to this day.

²⁸So Jehu destroyed Baal worship in Israel. ²⁹However, he did not turn away from the sins of Jeroboam son of Nebat, which he had caused Israel to commit—the worship of the golden calves at Bethel and Dan.

³⁰The LORD said to Jehu, "Because you have done well in accomplishing what is right in my eyes and have done to the house of Ahab all I had in mind to do, your descendants will sit on the throne of Israel to the fourth generation." ³¹Yet Jehu was not careful to keep the law of the LORD, the God of Israel, with all his heart. He did not turn away from the sins of Jeroboam, which he had caused Israel to commit.

³²In those days the LORD began to reduce the size of Israel. Hazael overpowered the Israelites throughout their territory ³³east of the Jordan in all the land of Gilead (the region of Gad, Reuben and Manasseh), from Aroer by the Arnon Gorge through Gilead to Bashan.

³⁴As for the other events of Jehu's reign, all he did, and all his achievements, are they not written in the book of the annals of the kings of Israel?

³⁵Jehu rested with his fathers and was buried in Samaria. And Jehoahaz his son succeeded him as king. ³⁶The time that Jehu reigned over Israel in Samaria was twenty-eight years.

Athaliah and Joash

11 When Athaliah the mother of Ahaziah saw that her son was dead, she proceeded to destroy the whole royal family. ²But Jehosheba, the daughter of King Jehoram*a* and sister of Ahaziah, took Joash son of Ahaziah and stole him away from among the royal princes, who were about to be murdered. She put him and his nurse in a bedroom to hide him from Athaliah; so he was not killed. ³He remained hidden with his nurse at the tem-

*a*2 Hebrew *Joram*, a variant of *Jehoram*

POINT OF INTEREST   2 Kings 10:17

As king of Israel, Ahab set an example of idolatry and wickedness for his people. God's punishment on Ahab's family also set an example for Ahab's subjects—an example of the fearful justice of a holy God.

ple of the LORD for six years while Athaliah ruled the land.

⁴In the seventh year Jehoiada sent for the commanders of units of a hundred, the Carites and the guards and had them brought to him at the temple of the LORD. He made a covenant with them and put them under oath at the temple of the LORD. Then he showed them the king's son. ⁵He commanded them, saying, "This is what you are to do: You who are in the three companies that are going on duty on the Sabbath—a third of you guarding the royal palace, ⁶a third at the Sur Gate, and a third at the gate behind the guard, who take turns guarding the temple— ⁷and you who are in the other two companies that normally go off Sabbath duty are all to guard the temple for the king. ⁸Station yourselves around the king, each man with his weapon in his hand. Anyone who approaches your ranksᵃ must be put to death. Stay close to the king wherever he goes."

⁹The commanders of units of a hundred did just as Jehoiada the priest ordered. Each one took his men—those who were going on duty on the Sabbath and those who were going off duty—and came to Jehoiada the priest. ¹⁰Then he gave the commanders the spears and shields that had belonged to King David and that were in the temple of the LORD. ¹¹The guards, each with his weapon in his hand, stationed themselves around the king—near the altar and the temple, from the south side to the north side of the temple.

¹²Jehoiada brought out the king's son and put the crown on him; he presented him with a copy of the covenant and proclaimed him king. They anointed him, and the people clapped their hands and shouted, "Long live the king!"

¹³When Athaliah heard the noise made by the guards and the people, she went to the people at the temple of the LORD. ¹⁴She looked and there was the king, standing by the pillar, as the custom was. The officers and the trumpeters were beside the king, and all the people of the land were rejoicing and blowing trumpets. Then Athaliah tore her robes and called out, "Treason! Treason!"

¹⁵Jehoiada the priest ordered the commanders of units of a hundred, who were in charge of the troops: "Bring her out between the ranksᵇ and put to the sword anyone who follows her." For the priest had said, "She must not be put to death in the temple of the LORD." ¹⁶So they seized her as she reached the place where the horses enter the palace grounds, and there she was put to death.

¹⁷Jehoiada then made a covenant between the LORD and the king and people that they would be the LORD's people. He also made a covenant between the king and the people. ¹⁸All the people of the land went to the temple of Baal and tore it down. They smashed the altars and idols to pieces and killed Mattan the priest of Baal in front of the altars.

Then Jehoiada the priest posted guards at the temple of the LORD. ¹⁹He took with him the commanders of hundreds, the Carites, the guards and all the people of the land, and together they brought the king down from the temple of the LORD and went into the palace, entering by way of the gate of the guards. The king then took his place on the royal throne, ²⁰and all the people of the land rejoiced. And the city was quiet, because Athaliah had been slain with the sword at the palace.

²¹Joashᶜ was seven years old when he began to reign.

Joash Repairs the Temple

12 In the seventh year of Jehu, Joashᵈ became king, and he reigned in Jerusalem forty years. His mother's name was Zibiah; she was from Beersheba. ²Joash did what was right in the eyes of the LORD all the years Jehoiada the priest instructed him. ³The high places, however, were not removed; the people continued to offer sacrifices and burn incense there.

⁴Joash said to the priests, "Collect all the money that is brought as sacred offerings to the temple of the LORD—the money collected from the census, the money received from personal vows and the money brought voluntarily to the temple. ⁵Let every priest receive the money from one of the treasurers, and let it be used to repair whatever damage is found in the temple."

⁶But by the twenty-third year of King Joash the priests still had not repaired the temple. ⁷Therefore King Joash summoned Jehoiada the priest and the other priests and asked them, "Why aren't you

---

ᵃ8 Or approaches the precincts ᵇ15 Or out from the precincts ᶜ21 Hebrew Jehoash, a variant of Joash ᵈ1 Hebrew Jehoash, a variant of Joash; also in verses 2, 4, 6, 7 and 18 repairing the damage done to the temple? Take no more money from your treasurers, but hand it over for repairing the temple." ⁸The priests agreed that they would not collect any more money from the people and that they would not repair the temple themselves.

⁹Jehoiada the priest took a chest and bored a hole in its lid. He placed it beside the altar, on the right side as one enters the temple of the LORD. The priests who guarded the entrance put into the chest all the money that was brought to the temple of the LORD. ¹⁰Whenever they saw that there was a large amount of money in the chest, the royal secretary and the high priest came, counted the money that had been brought into the temple of the LORD and put it into bags. ¹¹When the amount had been determined, they gave the money to the men appointed to supervise the work on the temple. With it they paid those who worked on the temple of the LORD—the carpenters and builders, ¹²the masons and stonecutters. They purchased timber and dressed stone for the repair of the temple of the LORD, and met all the other expenses of restoring the temple.

¹³The money brought into the temple was not spent for making silver basins, wick trimmers, sprinkling bowls, trumpets or any other articles of gold or silver for the temple of the LORD; ¹⁴it was paid to the workmen, who used it to repair the temple. ¹⁵They did not require an accounting from those to whom they gave the money to pay the workers, because they acted with complete honesty. ¹⁶The money from the guilt offerings and sin offerings was not brought into the temple of the LORD; it belonged to the priests.

¹⁷About this time Hazael king of Aram went up and attacked Gath and captured it. Then he turned to attack Jerusalem. ¹⁸But Joash king of Judah took all the sacred objects dedicated by his fathers—Jehoshaphat, Jehoram and Ahaziah, the kings of Judah—and the gifts he himself had dedicated and all the gold found in the treasuries of the temple of the LORD and of the royal palace, and he sent them to Hazael king of Aram, who then withdrew from Jerusalem.

¹⁹As for the other events of the reign of Joash, and all he did, are they not written in the book of the annals of the kings of Judah? ²⁰His officials conspired against him and assassinated him at Beth Millo,

on the road down to Silla. ²¹The officials who murdered him were Jozabad son of Shimeath and Jehozabad son of Shomer. He died and was buried with his fathers in the City of David. And Amaziah his son succeeded him as king.

Jehoahaz King of Israel

13 In the twenty-third year of Joash son of Ahaziah king of Judah, Jehoahaz son of Jehu became king of Israel in Samaria, and he reigned seventeen years. ²He did evil in the eyes of the LORD by following the sins of Jeroboam son of Nebat, which he had caused Israel to commit, and he did not turn away from them. ³So the LORD's anger burned against Israel, and for a long time he kept them under the power of Hazael king of Aram and Ben-Hadad his son.

⁴Then Jehoahaz sought the LORD's favor, and the LORD listened to him, for he saw how severely the king of Aram was oppressing Israel. ⁵The LORD provided a deliverer for Israel, and they escaped from the power of Aram. So the Israelites lived in their own homes as they had before. ⁶But they did not turn away from the sins of the house of Jeroboam, which he had caused Israel to commit; they continued in them. Also, the Asherah pole*ᵃ* remained standing in Samaria.

⁷Nothing had been left of the army of Jehoahaz except fifty horsemen, ten chariots and ten thousand foot soldiers, for the king of Aram had destroyed the rest and made them like the dust at threshing time.

⁸As for the other events of the reign of Jehoahaz, all he did and his achievements, are they not written in the book of the annals of the kings of Israel? ⁹Jehoahaz rested with his fathers and was buried in Samaria. And Jehoash*ᵇ* his son succeeded him as king.

Jehoash King of Israel

¹⁰In the thirty-seventh year of Joash king of Judah, Jehoash son of Jehoahaz became king of Israel in Samaria, and he reigned sixteen years. ¹¹He did evil in the eyes of the LORD and did not turn away from any of the sins of Jeroboam son of Nebat, which he had caused Israel to commit; he continued in them.

¹²As for the other events of the reign of

ᵃ6 That is, a symbol of the goddess Asherah; here and elsewhere in 2 Kings   *ᵇ9* Hebrew *Joash,* a variant of *Jehoash*; also in verses 12-14 and 25

Jehoash, all he did and his achievements, including his war against Amaziah king of Judah, are they not written in the book of the annals of the kings of Israel? ¹³Jehoash rested with his fathers, and Jeroboam succeeded him on the throne. Jehoash was buried in Samaria with the kings of Israel.

¹⁴Now Elisha was suffering from the illness from which he died. Jehoash king of Israel went down to see him and wept over him. "My father! My father!" he cried. "The chariots and horsemen of Israel!"

¹⁵Elisha said, "Get a bow and some arrows," and he did so. ¹⁶"Take the bow in your hands," he said to the king of Israel. When he had taken it, Elisha put his hands on the king's hands.

¹⁷"Open the east window," he said, and he opened it. "Shoot!" Elisha said, and he shot. "The LORD's arrow of victory, the arrow of victory over Aram!" Elisha declared. "You will completely destroy the Arameans at Aphek." ¹⁸Then he said, "Take the arrows," and the king took them. Elisha told him, "Strike the ground." He struck it three times and stopped. ¹⁹The man of God was angry with him and said, "You should have struck the ground five or six times; then you would have defeated Aram and completely destroyed it. But now you will defeat it only three times."

²⁰Elisha died and was buried.

Now Moabite raiders used to enter the country every spring. ²¹Once while some Israelites were burying a man, suddenly they saw a band of raiders; so they threw the man's body into Elisha's tomb. When the body touched Elisha's bones, the man came to life and stood up on his feet.

²²Hazael king of Aram oppressed Israel throughout the reign of Jehoahaz. ²³But the LORD was gracious to them and had compassion and showed concern for them because of his covenant with Abraham, Isaac and Jacob. To this day he has been unwilling to destroy them or banish them from his presence.

²⁴Hazael king of Aram died, and Ben-Hadad his son succeeded him as king. ²⁵Then Jehoash son of Jehoahaz recaptured from Ben-Hadad son of Hazael the towns he had taken in battle from his father Jehoahaz. Three times Jehoash defeated him, and so he recovered the Israelite towns.

Amaziah King of Judah

14 In the second year of Jehoash[a] son of Jehoahaz king of Israel, Amaziah son of Joash king of Judah began to reign. ²He was twenty-five years old when he became king, and he reigned in Jerusalem twenty-nine years. His mother's name was Jehoaddin; she was from Jerusalem. ³He did what was right in the eyes of the LORD, but not as his father David had done. In everything he followed the example of his father Joash. ⁴The high places, however, were not removed; the people continued to offer sacrifices and burn incense there.

⁵After the kingdom was firmly in his grasp, he executed the officials who had murdered his father the king. ⁶Yet he did not put the sons of the assassins to death, in accordance with what is written in the Book of the Law of Moses where the LORD commanded: "Fathers shall not be put to death for their children, nor children put to death for their fathers; each is to die for his own sins."[b]

⁷He was the one who defeated ten thousand Edomites in the Valley of Salt and captured Sela in battle, calling it Joktheel, the name it has to this day.

⁸Then Amaziah sent messengers to Jehoash son of Jehoahaz, the son of Jehu, king of Israel, with the challenge: "Come, meet me face to face."

⁹But Jehoash king of Israel replied to Amaziah king of Judah: "A thistle in Lebanon sent a message to a cedar in Lebanon, 'Give your daughter to my son in marriage.' Then a wild beast in Lebanon came along and trampled the thistle underfoot. ¹⁰You have indeed defeated Edom and now you are arrogant. Glory in

---

a1 Hebrew *Joash,* a variant of *Jehoash*; also in verses 13, 23 and 27   *b6* Deut. 24:16

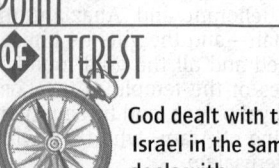

2 Kings 13:23

God dealt with the nation of Israel in the same way he deals with us as individuals. He is always righteous and gracious. When God makes a promise, he always keeps it. And when God gives a warning, we had better listen!

your victory, but stay at home! Why ask for trouble and cause your own downfall and that of Judah also?"

¹¹Amaziah, however, would not listen, so Jehoash king of Israel attacked. He and Amaziah king of Judah faced each other at Beth Shemesh in Judah. ¹²Judah was routed by Israel, and every man fled to his home. ¹³Jehoash king of Israel captured Amaziah king of Judah, the son of Joash, the son of Ahaziah, at Beth Shemesh. Then Jehoash went to Jerusalem and broke down the wall of Jerusalem from the Ephraim Gate to the Corner Gate—a section about six hundred feet long.ᵃ ¹⁴He took all the gold and silver and all the articles found in the temple of the LORD and in the treasuries of the royal palace. He also took hostages and returned to Samaria.

¹⁵As for the other events of the reign of Jehoash, what he did and his achievements, including his war against Amaziah king of Judah, are they not written in the book of the annals of the kings of Israel? ¹⁶Jehoash rested with his fathers and was buried in Samaria with the kings of Israel. And Jeroboam his son succeeded him as king.

¹⁷Amaziah son of Joash king of Judah lived for fifteen years after the death of Jehoash son of Jehoahaz king of Israel. ¹⁸As for the other events of Amaziah's reign, are they not written in the book of the annals of the kings of Judah?

¹⁹They conspired against him in Jerusalem, and he fled to Lachish, but they sent men after him to Lachish and killed him there. ²⁰He was brought back by horse and was buried in Jerusalem with his fathers, in the City of David.

²¹Then all the people of Judah took Azariah,ᵇ who was sixteen years old, and made him king in place of his father Amaziah. ²²He was the one who rebuilt Elath and restored it to Judah after Amaziah rested with his fathers.

Jeroboam II King of Israel

²³In the fifteenth year of Amaziah son of Joash king of Judah, Jeroboam son of Jehoash king of Israel became king in Samaria, and he reigned forty-one years. ²⁴He did evil in the eyes of the LORD and did not turn away from any of the sins of Jeroboam son of Nebat, which he had caused Israel to commit. ²⁵He was the one who restored the boundaries of Israel from Leboᶜ Hamath to the Sea of the

Arabah,ᵈ in accordance with the word of the LORD, the God of Israel, spoken through his servant Jonah son of Amittai, the prophet from Gath Hepher.

²⁶The LORD had seen how bitterly everyone in Israel, whether slave or free, was suffering; there was no one to help them. ²⁷And since the LORD had not said he would blot out the name of Israel from under heaven, he saved them by the hand of Jeroboam son of Jehoash.

²⁸As for the other events of Jeroboam's reign, all he did, and his military achievements, including how he recovered for Israel both Damascus and Hamath, which had belonged to Yaudi,ᵉ are they not written in the book of the annals of the kings of Israel? ²⁹Jeroboam rested with his fathers, the kings of Israel. And Zechariah his son succeeded him as king.

Azariah King of Judah

15 In the twenty-seventh year of Jeroboam king of Israel, Azariah son of Amaziah king of Judah began to reign. ²He was sixteen years old when he became king, and he reigned in Jerusalem fifty-two years. His mother's name was Jecoliah; she was from Jerusalem. ³He did what was right in the eyes of the LORD, just as his father Amaziah had done. ⁴The high places, however, were not removed; the people continued to offer sacrifices and burn incense there.

⁵The LORD afflicted the king with leprosyᶠ until the day he died, and he lived in a separate house.ᵍ Jotham the king's son had charge of the palace and governed the people of the land.

⁶As for the other events of Azariah's reign, and all he did, are they not written in the book of the annals of the kings of Judah? ⁷Azariah rested with his fathers and was buried near them in the City of David. And Jotham his son succeeded him as king.

Zechariah King of Israel

⁸In the thirty-eighth year of Azariah king of Judah, Zechariah son of Jeroboam became king of Israel in Samaria, and he reigned six months. ⁹He did evil in the eyes of the LORD, as his fathers had done.

ᵃ13 Hebrew *four hundred cubits* (about 180 meters)   ᵇ21 Also called *Uzziah*   ᶜ25 Or *from the entrance to*   ᵈ25 That is, the Dead Sea   ᵉ28 Or *Judah*   ᶠ5 The Hebrew word was used for various diseases affecting the skin—not necessarily leprosy.   ᵍ5 Or *in a house where he was relieved of responsibility*

He did not turn away from the sins of Jeroboam son of Nebat, which he had caused Israel to commit. ¹⁰Shallum son of Jabesh conspired against Zechariah. He attacked him in front of the people,ᵃ assassinated him and succeeded him as king. ¹¹The other events of Zechariah's reign are written in the book of the annals of the kings of Israel. ¹²So the word of the LORD spoken to Jehu was fulfilled: "Your descendants will sit on the throne of Israel to the fourth generation."ᵇ

Shallum King of Israel

¹³Shallum son of Jabesh became king in the thirty-ninth year of Uzziah king of Judah, and he reigned in Samaria one month. ¹⁴Then Menahem son of Gadi went from Tirzah up to Samaria. He attacked Shallum son of Jabesh in Samaria, assassinated him and succeeded him as king.

¹⁵The other events of Shallum's reign, and the conspiracy he led, are written in the book of the annals of the kings of Israel.

¹⁶At that time Menahem, starting out from Tirzah, attacked Tiphsah and everyone in the city and its vicinity, because they refused to open their gates. He sacked Tiphsah and ripped open all the pregnant women.

Menahem King of Israel

¹⁷In the thirty-ninth year of Azariah king of Judah, Menahem son of Gadi became king of Israel, and he reigned in Samaria ten years. ¹⁸He did evil in the eyes of the LORD. During his entire reign he did not turn away from the sins of Jeroboam son of Nebat, which he had caused Israel to commit. ¹⁹Then Pulᶜ king of Assyria invaded the land, and Menahem gave him a thousand talentsᵈ of silver to gain his support and strengthen his own hold on the kingdom. ²⁰Menahem exacted this money from Israel. Every wealthy man had to contribute fifty shekelsᵉ of silver to be given to the king of Assyria. So the king of Assyria withdrew and stayed in the land no longer.

²¹As for the other events of Menahem's reign, and all he did, are they not written in the book of the annals of the kings of Israel? ²²Menahem rested with his fathers. And Pekahiah his son succeeded him as king.

Pekahiah King of Israel

²³In the fiftieth year of Azariah king of Judah, Pekahiah son of Menahem became king of Israel in Samaria, and he reigned two years. ²⁴Pekahiah did evil in the eyes of the LORD. He did not turn away from the sins of Jeroboam son of Nebat, which he had caused Israel to commit. ²⁵One of his chief officers, Pekah son of Remaliah, conspired against him. Taking fifty men of Gilead with him, he assassinated Pekahiah, along with Argob and Arieh, in the citadel of the royal palace at Samaria. So Pekah killed Pekahiah and succeeded him as king.

²⁶The other events of Pekahiah's reign, and all he did, are written in the book of the annals of the kings of Israel.

Pekah King of Israel

²⁷In the fifty-second year of Azariah king of Judah, Pekah son of Remaliah became king of Israel in Samaria, and he reigned twenty years. ²⁸He did evil in the eyes of the LORD. He did not turn away from the sins of Jeroboam son of Nebat, which he had caused Israel to commit.

²⁹In the time of Pekah king of Israel, Tiglath-Pileser king of Assyria came and took Ijon, Abel Beth Maacah, Janoah, Kedesh and Hazor. He took Gilead and Galilee, including all the land of Naphtali, and deported the people to Assyria. ³⁰Then Hoshea son of Elah conspired against Pekah son of Remaliah. He attacked and assassinated him, and then succeeded him as king in the twentieth year of Jotham son of Uzziah.

³¹As for the other events of Pekah's reign, and all he did, are they not written

ᵃ10 Hebrew; some Septuagint manuscripts *in Ibleam*　　ᵇ12 2 Kings 10:30　　ᶜ19 Also called *Tiglath-Pileser*　　ᵈ19 That is, about 37 tons (about 34 metric tons)　　ᵉ20 That is, about 1 1/4 pounds (about 0.6 kilogram)

POINT OF INTEREST

2 Kings 15:19

Pul was the Babylonian name for the Assyrian ruler Tiglath-Pileser who ruled from 745–727 B.C. Assyrian annals mention this sizable tribute from Menahem—over *37 tons* of silver.

in the book of the annals of the kings of Israel?

Jotham King of Judah

³²In the second year of Pekah son of Remaliah king of Israel, Jotham son of Uzziah king of Judah began to reign. ³³He was twenty-five years old when he became king, and he reigned in Jerusalem sixteen years. His mother's name was Jerusha daughter of Zadok. ³⁴He did what was right in the eyes of the LORD, just as his father Uzziah had done. ³⁵The high places, however, were not removed; the people continued to offer sacrifices and burn incense there. Jotham rebuilt the Upper Gate of the temple of the LORD.

³⁶As for the other events of Jotham's reign, and what he did, are they not written in the book of the annals of the kings of Judah? ³⁷(In those days the LORD began to send Rezin king of Aram and Pekah son of Remaliah against Judah.) ³⁸Jotham rested with his fathers and was buried with them in the City of David, the city of his father. And Ahaz his son succeeded him as king.

Ahaz King of Judah

16 In the seventeenth year of Pekah son of Remaliah, Ahaz son of Jotham king of Judah began to reign. ²Ahaz was twenty years old when he became king, and he reigned in Jerusalem sixteen years. Unlike David his father, he did not do what was right in the eyes of the LORD his God. ³He walked in the ways of the kings of Israel and even sacrificed his son inª the fire, following the detestable ways of the nations the LORD had driven out before the Israelites. ⁴He offered sacrifices and burned incense at the high places, on the hilltops and under every spreading tree.

⁵Then Rezin king of Aram and Pekah son of Remaliah king of Israel marched up to fight against Jerusalem and besieged Ahaz, but they could not overpower him. ⁶At that time, Rezin king of Aram recovered Elath for Aram by driving out the men of Judah. Edomites then moved into Elath and have lived there to this day.

⁷Ahaz sent messengers to say to Tiglath-Pileser king of Assyria, "I am your servant and vassal. Come up and save me out of the hand of the king of Aram and of the king of Israel, who are attacking me." ⁸And Ahaz took the silver

and gold found in the temple of the LORD and in the treasuries of the royal palace and sent it as a gift to the king of Assyria. ⁹The king of Assyria complied by attacking Damascus and capturing it. He deported its inhabitants to Kir and put Rezin to death.

¹⁰Then King Ahaz went to Damascus to meet Tiglath-Pileser king of Assyria. He saw an altar in Damascus and sent to Uriah the priest a sketch of the altar, with detailed plans for its construction. ¹¹So Uriah the priest built an altar in accordance with all the plans that King Ahaz had sent from Damascus and finished it before King Ahaz returned. ¹²When the king came back from Damascus and saw the altar, he approached it and presented offeringsᵇ on it. ¹³He offered up his burnt offering and grain offering, poured out his drink offering, and sprinkled the blood of his fellowship offeringsᶜ on the altar. ¹⁴The bronze altar that stood before the LORD he brought from the front of the temple—from between the new altar and the temple of the LORD—and put it on the north side of the new altar.

¹⁵King Ahaz then gave these orders to Uriah the priest: "On the large new altar, offer the morning burnt offering and the evening grain offering, the king's burnt offering and his grain offering, and the burnt offering of all the people of the land, and their grain offering and their drink offering. Sprinkle on the altar all the blood of the burnt offerings and sacrifices. But I will use the bronze altar for seeking guidance." ¹⁶And Uriah the priest did just as King Ahaz had ordered.

¹⁷King Ahaz took away the side panels and removed the basins from the movable stands. He removed the Sea from the bronze bulls that supported it and set it on a stone base. ¹⁸He took away the Sabbath canopyᵈ that had been built at the temple and removed the royal entryway outside the temple of the LORD, in deference to the king of Assyria. ¹⁹As for the other events of the reign of Ahaz, and what he did, are they not written in the book of the annals of the kings of Judah? ²⁰Ahaz rested with his fathers and was buried with them in the City of David. And Hezekiah his son succeeded him as king.

ª3 Or *even made his son pass through*   ᵇ12 Or *and went up*   ᶜ13 Traditionally *peace offerings*   ᵈ18 Or *the dais of his throne* (see Septuagint)

Hoshea Last King of Israel

17 In the twelfth year of Ahaz king of Judah, Hoshea son of Elah became king of Israel in Samaria, and he reigned nine years. ²He did evil in the eyes of the LORD, but not like the kings of Israel who preceded him.

³Shalmaneser king of Assyria came up to attack Hoshea, who had been Shalmaneser's vassal and had paid him tribute. ⁴But the king of Assyria discovered that Hoshea was a traitor, for he had sent envoys to So*ᵃ* king of Egypt, and he no longer paid tribute to the king of Assyria, as he had done year by year. Therefore Shalmaneser seized him and put him in prison. ⁵The king of Assyria invaded the entire land, marched against Samaria and laid siege to it for three years. ⁶In the ninth year of Hoshea, the king of Assyria captured Samaria and deported the Israelites to Assyria. He settled them in Halah, in Gozan on the Habor River and in the towns of the Medes.

Israel Exiled Because of Sin

⁷All this took place because the Israelites had sinned against the LORD their God, who had brought them up out of Egypt from under the power of Pharaoh king of Egypt. They worshiped other gods ⁸and followed the practices of the nations the LORD had driven out before them, as well as the practices that the kings of Israel had introduced. ⁹The Israelites secretly did things against the LORD their God that were not right. From watchtower to fortified city they built themselves high places in all their towns. ¹⁰They set up sacred stones and Asherah poles on every high hill and under every spreading tree. ¹¹At every high place they burned incense, as the nations whom the LORD had driven out before them had done. They did wicked things that provoked the LORD to anger. ¹²They worshiped idols, though the LORD had said, "You shall not do this."*ᵇ* ¹³The LORD warned Israel and Judah through all his prophets and seers: "Turn from your evil ways. Observe my commands and decrees, in accordance with the entire Law that I commanded your fathers to obey and that I delivered to you through my servants the prophets."

¹⁴But they would not listen and were as stiff-necked as their fathers, who did not trust in the LORD their God. ¹⁵They rejected his decrees and the covenant he had made with their fathers and the warnings he had given them. They followed worthless idols and themselves became worthless. They imitated the nations around them although the LORD had ordered them, "Do not do as they do," and they did the things the LORD had forbidden them to do.

¹⁶They forsook all the commands of the LORD their God and made for themselves two idols cast in the shape of calves, and an Asherah pole. They bowed down to all the starry hosts, and they worshiped Baal. ¹⁷They sacrificed their sons and daughters in*ᶜ* the fire. They practiced divination and sorcery and sold themselves to do evil in the eyes of the LORD, provoking him to anger.

¹⁸So the LORD was very angry with Israel and removed them from his presence. Only the tribe of Judah was left, ¹⁹and even Judah did not keep the commands of the LORD their God. They followed the practices Israel had introduced. ²⁰Therefore the LORD rejected all the people of Israel; he afflicted them and gave them into the hands of plunderers, until he thrust them from his presence.

²¹When he tore Israel away from the house of David, they made Jeroboam son of Nebat their king. Jeroboam enticed Israel away from following the LORD and caused them to commit a great sin. ²²The Israelites persisted in all the sins of Jeroboam and did not turn away from them ²³until the LORD removed them from his presence, as he had warned through all his servants the prophets. So the people of Israel were taken from their homeland into exile in Assyria, and they are still there.

Samaria Resettled

²⁴The king of Assyria brought people from Babylon, Cuthah, Avva, Hamath and Sepharvaim and settled them in the towns of Samaria to replace the Israelites. They took over Samaria and lived in its towns. ²⁵When they first lived there, they did not worship the LORD; so he sent lions among them and they killed some of the people. ²⁶It was reported to the king of Assyria: "The people you deported and resettled in the towns of Samaria do not know what the god of that country re-

---

ᵃ4 Or *to Sais, to the*; *So* is possibly an abbreviation for *Osorkon.*　　*ᵇ12* Exodus 20:4, 5　　*ᶜ17* Or *They made their sons and daughters pass through* quires. He has sent lions among them, which are killing them off, because the people do not know what he requires."

²⁷Then the king of Assyria gave this order: "Have one of the priests you took captive from Samaria go back to live there and teach the people what the god of the land requires." ²⁸So one of the priests who had been exiled from Samaria came to live in Bethel and taught them how to worship the LORD.

²⁹Nevertheless, each national group made its own gods in the several towns where they settled, and set them up in the shrines the people of Samaria had made at the high places. ³⁰The men from Babylon made Succoth Benoth, the men from Cuthah made Nergal, and the men from Hamath made Ashima; ³¹the Avites made Nibhaz and Tartak, and the Sepharvites burned their children in the fire as sacrifices to Adrammelech and Anammelech, the gods of Sepharvaim. ³²They worshiped the LORD, but they also appointed all sorts of their own people to officiate for them as priests in the shrines at the high places. ³³They worshiped the LORD, but they also served their own gods in accordance with the customs of the nations from which they had been brought.

³⁴To this day they persist in their former practices. They neither worship the LORD nor adhere to the decrees and ordinances, the laws and commands that the LORD gave the descendants of Jacob, whom he named Israel. ³⁵When the LORD made a covenant with the Israelites, he commanded them: "Do not worship any other gods or bow down to them, serve them or sacrifice to them. ³⁶But the LORD, who brought you up out of Egypt with mighty power and outstretched arm, is the one you must worship. To him you

---

MONDAY

Read 2 Kings 17:1–41
Key Verses 2 Kings 17:14–15

Make Your Life Worthwhile — Steve Rugg

In college, I often reflected on my future. I had good grades and was set up for a great career in engineering. But I couldn't get rid of nagging doubts. What was so great about earning top grades when they just led to a job I'd have to work at until I was 65? Was that all there was to life? Depression started to eat at me. I was afraid that at the end of my life I'd have nothing to show for it.

Second Kings 17:15 tells us that following worthless idols actually does make us worthless. This is indeed what I was doing—making a worthless idol out of a potentially successful engineering career and staking my whole life on it. It wasn't that a job in engineering was bad or wrong; it just didn't have any lasting or eternal significance!

Fortunately, I had a good friend who introduced me to Jesus Christ. I discovered that God had created me and that Jesus had redeemed me. Because God had given me significance, following him was the most worthwhile thing I could do with my life. His love and direction could bring the meaning to my life that I'd never have otherwise. Because I had a relationship with Jesus Christ, I could have a confidence about my future that I'd never had before.

I still went on to be an engineer, but there has never been any doubt that it is Jesus, and not my career, that makes my life worthwhile.

A Deeper Look
Psalm 127:1; Ecclesiastes 2:20–23

Go to page 421 for your next devotional reading.

shall bow down and to him offer sacrifices. [37]You must always be careful to keep the decrees and ordinances, the laws and commands he wrote for you. Do not worship other gods. [38]Do not forget the covenant I have made with you, and do not worship other gods. [39]Rather, worship the LORD your God; it is he who will deliver you from the hand of all your enemies."

[40]They would not listen, however, but persisted in their former practices. [41]Even while these people were worshiping the LORD, they were serving their idols. To this day their children and grandchildren continue to do as their fathers did.

Hezekiah King of Judah

18 In the third year of Hoshea son of Elah king of Israel, Hezekiah son of Ahaz king of Judah began to reign. [2]He was twenty-five years old when he became king, and he reigned in Jerusalem twenty-nine years. His mother's name was Abijah[a] daughter of Zechariah. [3]He did what was right in the eyes of the LORD, just as his father David had done. [4]He removed the high places, smashed the sacred stones and cut down the Asherah poles. He broke into pieces the bronze snake Moses had made, for up to that time the Israelites had been burning incense to it. (It was called[b] Nehushtan.[c])

[5]Hezekiah trusted in the LORD, the God of Israel. There was no one like him among all the kings of Judah, either before him or after him. [6]He held fast to the LORD and did not cease to follow him; he kept the commands the LORD had given Moses. [7]And the LORD was with him; he was successful in whatever he undertook. He rebelled against the king of Assyria and did not serve him. [8]From watchtower to fortified city, he defeated the Philistines, as far as Gaza and its territory.

[9]In King Hezekiah's fourth year, which was the seventh year of Hoshea son of Elah king of Israel, Shalmaneser king of Assyria marched against Samaria and laid siege to it. [10]At the end of three years the Assyrians took it. So Samaria was captured in Hezekiah's sixth year, which was the ninth year of Hoshea king of Israel. [11]The king of Assyria deported Israel to Assyria and settled them in Halah, in Gozan on the Habor River and in towns of the Medes. [12]This happened because

they had not obeyed the LORD their God, but had violated his covenant—all that Moses the servant of the LORD commanded. They neither listened to the commands nor carried them out.

[13]In the fourteenth year of King Hezekiah's reign, Sennacherib king of Assyria attacked all the fortified cities of Judah and captured them. [14]So Hezekiah king of Judah sent this message to the king of Assyria at Lachish: "I have done wrong. Withdraw from me, and I will pay whatever you demand of me." The king of Assyria exacted from Hezekiah king of Judah three hundred talents[d] of silver and thirty talents[e] of gold. [15]So Hezekiah gave him all the silver that was found in the temple of the LORD and in the treasuries of the royal palace.

[16]At this time Hezekiah king of Judah stripped off the gold with which he had covered the doors and doorposts of the temple of the LORD, and gave it to the king of Assyria.

Sennacherib Threatens Jerusalem

[17]The king of Assyria sent his supreme commander, his chief officer and his field commander with a large army, from Lachish to King Hezekiah at Jerusalem. They came up to Jerusalem and stopped at the aqueduct of the Upper Pool, on the road to the Washerman's Field. [18]They called for the king; and Eliakim son of Hilkiah the palace administrator, Shebna the secretary, and Joah son of Asaph the recorder went out to them.

[19]The field commander said to them, "Tell Hezekiah:

" 'This is what the great king, the king of Assyria, says: On what are you basing this confidence of yours? [20]You say you have strategy and military strength—but you speak only empty words. On whom are you depending, that you rebel against me? [21]Look now, you are depending on Egypt, that splintered reed of a staff, which pierces a man's hand and wounds him if he leans on it! Such is Pharaoh king of Egypt to all who depend on him. [22]And if you say to me, "We are de-

---

[a]2 Hebrew *Abi*, a variant of *Abijah*   [b]4 Or *He called it*   [c]4 *Nehushtan* sounds like the Hebrew for *bronze* and *snake* and *unclean thing*.
[d]14 That is, about 11 tons (about 10 metric tons)
[e]14 That is, about 1 ton (about 1 metric ton)

pending on the LORD our God"—
isn't he the one whose high places
and altars Hezekiah removed, saying to Judah and Jerusalem, "You
must worship before this altar in Jerusalem"?

²³" 'Come now, make a bargain
with my master, the king of Assyria:
I will give you two thousand
horses—if you can put riders on
them! ²⁴How can you repulse one
officer of the least of my master's
officials, even though you are depending on Egypt for chariots and
horsemen*a*? ²⁵Furthermore, have I
come to attack and destroy this
place without word from the LORD?
The LORD himself told me to march
against this country and destroy it.' "

²⁶Then Eliakim son of Hilkiah, and
Shebna and Joah said to the field commander, "Please speak to your servants
in Aramaic, since we understand it. Don't
speak to us in Hebrew in the hearing of
the people on the wall."

²⁷But the commander replied, "Was it
only to your master and you that my
master sent me to say these things, and
not to the men sitting on the wall—who,
like you, will have to eat their own filth
and drink their own urine?"

²⁸Then the commander stood and
called out in Hebrew: "Hear the word of
the great king, the king of Assyria! ²⁹This
is what the king says: Do not let Hezekiah deceive you. He cannot deliver you
from my hand. ³⁰Do not let Hezekiah persuade you to trust in the LORD when he
says, 'The LORD will surely deliver us; this
city will not be given into the hand of the
king of Assyria.'

³¹"Do not listen to Hezekiah. This is
what the king of Assyria says: Make
peace with me and come out to me. Then
every one of you will eat from his own
vine and fig tree and drink water from his
own cistern, ³²until I come and take you
to a land like your own, a land of grain
and new wine, a land of bread and vineyards, a land of olive trees and honey.
Choose life and not death!

"Do not listen to Hezekiah, for he is
misleading you when he says, 'The LORD
will deliver us.' ³³Has the god of any nation ever delivered his land from the
hand of the king of Assyria? ³⁴Where are
the gods of Hamath and Arpad? Where

are the gods of Sepharvaim, Hena and
Ivvah? Have they rescued Samaria from
my hand? ³⁵Who of all the gods of these
countries has been able to save his land
from me? How then can the LORD deliver
Jerusalem from my hand?"

³⁶But the people remained silent and
said nothing in reply, because the king
had commanded, "Do not answer him."

³⁷Then Eliakim son of Hilkiah the palace administrator, Shebna the secretary
and Joah son of Asaph the recorder went
to Hezekiah, with their clothes torn, and
told him what the field commander had
said.

Jerusalem's Deliverance Foretold

19 When King Hezekiah heard this, he
tore his clothes and put on sackcloth
and went into the temple of the LORD. ²He
sent Eliakim the palace administrator,
Shebna the secretary and the leading
priests, all wearing sackcloth, to the
prophet Isaiah son of Amoz. ³They told
him, "This is what Hezekiah says: This
day is a day of distress and rebuke and
disgrace, as when children come to the
point of birth and there is no strength to
deliver them. ⁴It may be that the LORD
your God will hear all the words of the
field commander, whom his master, the
king of Assyria, has sent to ridicule
the living God, and that he will rebuke
him for the words the LORD your God has
heard. Therefore pray for the remnant
that still survives."

⁵When King Hezekiah's officials came
to Isaiah, ⁶Isaiah said to them, "Tell your
master, 'This is what the LORD says: Do
not be afraid of what you have heard—
those words with which the underlings of
the king of Assyria have blasphemed me.
⁷Listen! I am going to put such a spirit in
him that when he hears a certain report,
he will return to his own country, and
there I will have him cut down with the
sword.' "

⁸When the field commander heard
that the king of Assyria had left Lachish,
he withdrew and found the king fighting
against Libnah.

⁹Now Sennacherib received a report
that Tirhakah, the Cushite*b* king ˪of
Egypt˩, was marching out to fight against
him. So he again sent messengers to Hezekiah with this word: ¹⁰"Say to Hezekiah

---

*a*24 Or *charioteers*   *b*9 That is, from the upper
Nile region

king of Judah: Do not let the god you depend on deceive you when he says, 'Jerusalem will not be handed over to the king of Assyria.' ¹¹Surely you have heard what the kings of Assyria have done to all the countries, destroying them completely. And will you be delivered? ¹²Did the gods of the nations that were destroyed by my forefathers deliver them: the gods of Gozan, Haran, Rezeph and the people of Eden who were in Tel Assar? ¹³Where is the king of Hamath, the king of Arpad, the king of the city of Sepharvaim, or of Hena or Ivvah?"

Hezekiah's Prayer

¹⁴Hezekiah received the letter from the messengers and read it. Then he went up to the temple of the LORD and spread it out before the LORD. ¹⁵And Hezekiah prayed to the LORD: "O LORD, God of Israel, enthroned between the cherubim, you alone are God over all the kingdoms of the earth. You have made heaven and earth. ¹⁶Give ear, O LORD, and hear; open your eyes, O LORD, and see; listen to the words Sennacherib has sent to insult the living God.

¹⁷"It is true, O LORD, that the Assyrian kings have laid waste these nations and their lands. ¹⁸They have thrown their gods into the fire and destroyed them, for they were not gods but only wood and stone, fashioned by men's hands. ¹⁹Now, O LORD our God, deliver us from his hand, so that all kingdoms on earth may know that you alone, O LORD, are God."

Isaiah Prophesies Sennacherib's Fall

²⁰Then Isaiah son of Amoz sent a message to Hezekiah: "This is what the LORD, the God of Israel, says: I have heard your prayer concerning Sennacherib king of Assyria. ²¹This is the word that the LORD has spoken against him:

" 'The Virgin Daughter of Zion
    despises you and mocks you.
The Daughter of Jerusalem
    tosses her head as you flee.
²²Who is it you have insulted and
        blasphemed?
Against whom have you raised
        your voice
and lifted your eyes in pride?
Against the Holy One of Israel!
²³By your messengers
    you have heaped insults on the
        Lord.

And you have said,
"With my many chariots
I have ascended the heights of the
        mountains,
    the utmost heights of Lebanon.
I have cut down its tallest cedars,
    the choicest of its pines.
I have reached its remotest parts,
    the finest of its forests.
²⁴I have dug wells in foreign lands
    and drunk the water there.
With the soles of my feet
    I have dried up all the streams of
        Egypt."

²⁵" 'Have you not heard?
    Long ago I ordained it.
In days of old I planned it;
    now I have brought it to pass,
that you have turned fortified cities
    into piles of stone.
²⁶Their people, drained of power,
    are dismayed and put to shame.
They are like plants in the field,
    like tender green shoots,
like grass sprouting on the roof,
    scorched before it grows up.

²⁷" 'But I know where you stay
    and when you come and go
    and how you rage against me.
²⁸Because you rage against me
    and your insolence has reached my
        ears,
I will put my hook in your nose
    and my bit in your mouth,
and I will make you return
    by the way you came.'

²⁹"This will be the sign for you,
O Hezekiah:

"This year you will eat what grows
        by itself,

POINT OF INTEREST   2 Kings 19:25

Why would God "ordain" Assyria to devastate other nations? God is sovereign; he can use whatever means he wishes to accomplish his purposes. Sometimes he used natural events to judge nations. Other times he allowed one nation to punish another. All nations can be held to account and judged by God— and used by him as he chooses.

and the second year what springs
from that.
But in the third year sow and reap,
plant vineyards and eat their fruit.
³⁰Once more a remnant of the house of
Judah
will take root below and bear fruit
above.
³¹For out of Jerusalem will come a
remnant,
and out of Mount Zion a band of
survivors.

The zeal of the LORD Almighty will accomplish this.

³²"Therefore this is what the LORD says
concerning the king of Assyria:

"He will not enter this city
or shoot an arrow here.
He will not come before it with shield
or build a siege ramp against it.
³³By the way that he came he will
return;
he will not enter this city,
declares the LORD.
³⁴I will defend this city and save it,
for my sake and for the sake of
David my servant."

³⁵That night the angel of the LORD went
out and put to death a hundred and
eighty-five thousand men in the Assyrian
camp. When the people got up the next
morning—there were all the dead bodies! ³⁶So Sennacherib king of Assyria
broke camp and withdrew. He returned
to Nineveh and stayed there.

³⁷One day, while he was worshiping in
the temple of his god Nisroch, his sons
Adrammelech and Sharezer cut him
down with the sword, and they escaped
to the land of Ararat. And Esarhaddon his
son succeeded him as king.

Hezekiah's Illness

20 In those days Hezekiah became ill
and was at the point of death. The
prophet Isaiah son of Amoz went to him
and said, "This is what the LORD says: Put
your house in order, because you are going to die; you will not recover."

²Hezekiah turned his face to the wall
and prayed to the LORD, ³"Remember,
O LORD, how I have walked before you
faithfully and with wholehearted devotion and have done what is good in your
eyes." And Hezekiah wept bitterly.

⁴Before Isaiah had left the middle
court, the word of the LORD came to him:

⁵"Go back and tell Hezekiah, the leader
of my people, 'This is what the LORD, the
God of your father David, says: I have
heard your prayer and seen your tears; I
will heal you. On the third day from now
you will go up to the temple of the LORD.
⁶I will add fifteen years to your life. And
I will deliver you and this city from the
hand of the king of Assyria. I will defend
this city for my sake and for the sake of
my servant David.' "

⁷Then Isaiah said, "Prepare a poultice
of figs." They did so and applied it to the
boil, and he recovered.

⁸Hezekiah had asked Isaiah, "What
will be the sign that the LORD will heal me
and that I will go up to the temple of the
LORD on the third day from now?"

⁹Isaiah answered, "This is the LORD's
sign to you that the LORD will do what he
has promised: Shall the shadow go forward ten steps, or shall it go back ten
steps?"

¹⁰"It is a simple matter for the shadow
to go forward ten steps," said Hezekiah.
"Rather, have it go back ten steps."

¹¹Then the prophet Isaiah called upon
the LORD, and the LORD made the shadow
go back the ten steps it had gone down
on the stairway of Ahaz.

Envoys From Babylon

¹²At that time Merodach-Baladan son
of Baladan king of Babylon sent Hezekiah
letters and a gift, because he had heard of
Hezekiah's illness. ¹³Hezekiah received
the messengers and showed them all that
was in his storehouses—the silver, the
gold, the spices and the fine oil—his armory and everything found among his
treasures. There was nothing in his palace or in all his kingdom that Hezekiah
did not show them.

¹⁴Then Isaiah the prophet went to King
Hezekiah and asked, "What did those
men say, and where did they come
from?"

"From a distant land," Hezekiah replied. "They came from Babylon."

¹⁵The prophet asked, "What did they
see in your palace?"

"They saw everything in my palace,"
Hezekiah said. "There is nothing among
my treasures that I did not show them."

¹⁶Then Isaiah said to Hezekiah, "Hear
the word of the LORD: ¹⁷The time will
surely come when everything in your palace, and all that your fathers have stored
up until this day, will be carried off to

Babylon. Nothing will be left, says the Lord. ¹⁸And some of your descendants, your own flesh and blood, that will be born to you, will be taken away, and they will become eunuchs in the palace of the king of Babylon."

¹⁹"The word of the Lord you have spoken is good," Hezekiah replied. For he thought, "Will there not be peace and security in my lifetime?"

²⁰As for the other events of Hezekiah's reign, all his achievements and how he made the pool and the tunnel by which he brought water into the city, are they not written in the book of the annals of the kings of Judah? ²¹Hezekiah rested with his fathers. And Manasseh his son succeeded him as king.

Manasseh King of Judah

21 Manasseh was twelve years old when he became king, and he reigned in Jerusalem fifty-five years. His mother's name was Hephzibah. ²He did evil in the eyes of the Lord, following the detestable practices of the nations the Lord had driven out before the Israelites. ³He rebuilt the high places his father Hezekiah had destroyed; he also erected altars to Baal and made an Asherah pole, as Ahab king of Israel had done. He bowed down to all the starry hosts and worshiped them. ⁴He built altars in the temple of the Lord, of which the Lord had said, "In Jerusalem I will put my Name." ⁵In both courts of the temple of the Lord, he built altars to all the starry hosts. ⁶He sacrificed his own son in*a* the fire, practiced sorcery and divination, and consulted mediums and spiritists. He did much evil in the eyes of the Lord, provoking him to anger.

⁷He took the carved Asherah pole he had made and put it in the temple, of which the Lord had said to David and to his son Solomon, "In this temple and in Jerusalem, which I have chosen out of all the tribes of Israel, I will put my Name forever. ⁸I will not again make the feet of the Israelites wander from the land I gave their forefathers, if only they will be careful to do everything I commanded them and will keep the whole Law that my servant Moses gave them." ⁹But the people did not listen. Manasseh led them astray, so that they did more evil than the nations the Lord had destroyed before the Israelites.

¹⁰The Lord said through his servants the prophets: ¹¹"Manasseh king of Judah has committed these detestable sins. He has done more evil than the Amorites who preceded him and has led Judah into sin with his idols. ¹²Therefore this is what the Lord, the God of Israel, says: I am going to bring such disaster on Jerusalem and Judah that the ears of everyone who hears of it will tingle. ¹³I will stretch out over Jerusalem the measuring line used against Samaria and the plumb line used against the house of Ahab. I will wipe out Jerusalem as one wipes a dish, wiping it and turning it upside down. ¹⁴I will forsake the remnant of my inheritance and hand them over to their enemies. They will be looted and plundered by all their foes, ¹⁵because they have done evil in my eyes and have provoked me to anger from the day their forefathers came out of Egypt until this day."

¹⁶Moreover, Manasseh also shed so much innocent blood that he filled Jerusalem from end to end—besides the sin that he had caused Judah to commit, so that they did evil in the eyes of the Lord.

¹⁷As for the other events of Manasseh's reign, and all he did, including the sin he committed, are they not written in the book of the annals of the kings of Judah? ¹⁸Manasseh rested with his fathers and was buried in his palace garden, the garden of Uzza. And Amon his son succeeded him as king.

Amon King of Judah

¹⁹Amon was twenty-two years old when he became king, and he reigned in Jerusalem two years. His mother's name was Meshullemeth daughter of Haruz; she was from Jotbah. ²⁰He did evil in the eyes of the Lord, as his father Manasseh had done. ²¹He walked in all the ways of his father; he worshiped the idols his father had worshiped, and bowed down to them. ²²He forsook the Lord, the God of his fathers, and did not walk in the way of the Lord.

²³Amon's officials conspired against him and assassinated the king in his palace. ²⁴Then the people of the land killed all who had plotted against King Amon, and they made Josiah his son king in his place.

²⁵As for the other events of Amon's reign, and what he did, are they not written in the book of the annals of the kings of Judah? ²⁶He was buried in his grave in

a 6 Or He made his own son pass through

the garden of Uzza. And Josiah his son succeeded him as king.

The Book of the Law Found

22 Josiah was eight years old when he became king, and he reigned in Jerusalem thirty-one years. His mother's name was Jedidah daughter of Adaiah; she was from Bozkath. ²He did what was right in the eyes of the LORD and walked in all the ways of his father David, not turning aside to the right or to the left.

³In the eighteenth year of his reign, King Josiah sent the secretary, Shaphan son of Azaliah, the son of Meshullam, to the temple of the LORD. He said: ⁴"Go up to Hilkiah the high priest and have him get ready the money that has been brought into the temple of the LORD, which the doorkeepers have collected from the people. ⁵Have them entrust it to the men appointed to supervise the work on the temple. And have these men pay the workers who repair the temple of the LORD— ⁶the carpenters, the builders and the masons. Also have them purchase

timber and dressed stone to repair the temple. ⁷But they need not account for the money entrusted to them, because they are acting faithfully."

⁸Hilkiah the high priest said to Shaphan the secretary, "I have found the Book of the Law in the temple of the LORD." He gave it to Shaphan, who read it. ⁹Then Shaphan the secretary went to the king and reported to him: "Your officials have paid out the money that was in the temple of the LORD and have entrusted it to the workers and supervisors at the temple." ¹⁰Then Shaphan the secretary informed the king, "Hilkiah the priest has given me a book." And Shaphan read from it in the presence of the king.

¹¹When the king heard the words of the Book of the Law, he tore his robes. ¹²He gave these orders to Hilkiah the priest, Ahikam son of Shaphan, Acbor son of Micaiah, Shaphan the secretary and Asaiah the king's attendant: ¹³"Go and inquire of the LORD for me and for the people and for all Judah about what is written in this book that has been found.

TUESDAY

Read 2 Kings 22:1–20
Key Verses 2 Kings 22:1–2

Like a Child, Like a King – Eric Resler

When working with college students and young professionals, I often hear negative comments like, "I'm not old enough to do that for God" and "they aren't old enough to handle the responsibility." So it was great to hear a student share her excitement over Matthew 18:4, where Jesus says, "Therefore, whoever humbles himself like this child is the greatest in the kingdom of heaven." She understood that Jesus doesn't value age or experience as much as a childlike attitude of humility and a willing spirit.

God held King Josiah, who was crowned at the age of eight and went on to become a successful king, in the same esteem. Why? Because Josiah was willing to do "what was right in the eyes of the LORD . . . not turning aside to the right or to the left" (2 Kings 22:2). Josiah recognized that he was just a servant and that God was in charge. For his humble attitude, Josiah was given the privilege of turning the entire nation of Israel back to God and his Word.

Age is not an issue in serving God. Attitude is. Are you eager, teachable, motivated, excited and responsible? If you are a willing servant, God will use you no matter what your age!

A Deeper Look
Isaiah 1:19; Luke 18:17

Go to page 433 for your next devotional reading.

Great is the LORD's anger that burns against us because our fathers have not obeyed the words of this book; they have not acted in accordance with all that is written there concerning us."

[14]Hilkiah the priest, Ahikam, Acbor, Shaphan and Asaiah went to speak to the prophetess Huldah, who was the wife of Shallum son of Tikvah, the son of Harhas, keeper of the wardrobe. She lived in Jerusalem, in the Second District.

[15]She said to them, "This is what the LORD, the God of Israel, says: Tell the man who sent you to me, [16]'This is what the LORD says: I am going to bring disaster on this place and its people, according to everything written in the book the king of Judah has read. [17]Because they have forsaken me and burned incense to other gods and provoked me to anger by all the idols their hands have made,[a] my anger will burn against this place and will not be quenched.' [18]Tell the king of Judah, who sent you to inquire of the LORD, 'This is what the LORD, the God of Israel, says concerning the words you heard: [19]Because your heart was responsive and you humbled yourself before the LORD when you heard what I have spoken against this place and its people, that they would become accursed and laid waste, and because you tore your robes and wept in my presence, I have heard you, declares the LORD. [20]Therefore I will gather you to your fathers, and you will be buried in peace. Your eyes will not see all the disaster I am going to bring on this place.' "

So they took her answer back to the king.

Josiah Renews the Covenant

23 Then the king called together all the elders of Judah and Jerusalem. [2]He went up to the temple of the LORD with the men of Judah, the people of Jerusalem, the priests and the prophets—all the people from the least to the greatest. He read in their hearing all the words of the Book of the Covenant, which had been found in the temple of the LORD. [3]The king stood by the pillar and renewed the covenant in the presence of the LORD—to follow the LORD and keep his commands, regulations and decrees with all his heart and all his soul, thus confirming the words of the covenant written in this book. Then all the people pledged themselves to the covenant.

[4]The king ordered Hilkiah the high priest, the priests next in rank and the doorkeepers to remove from the temple of the LORD all the articles made for Baal and Asherah and all the starry hosts. He burned them outside Jerusalem in the fields of the Kidron Valley and took the ashes to Bethel. [5]He did away with the pagan priests appointed by the kings of Judah to burn incense on the high places of the towns of Judah and on those around Jerusalem—those who burned incense to Baal, to the sun and moon, to the constellations and to all the starry hosts. [6]He took the Asherah pole from the temple of the LORD to the Kidron Valley outside Jerusalem and burned it there. He ground it to powder and scattered the dust over the graves of the common people. [7]He also tore down the quarters of the male shrine prostitutes, which were in the temple of the LORD and where women did weaving for Asherah.

[8]Josiah brought all the priests from the towns of Judah and desecrated the high places, from Geba to Beersheba, where the priests had burned incense. He broke down the shrines[b] at the gates—at the entrance to the Gate of Joshua, the city governor, which is on the left of the city gate. [9]Although the priests of the high places did not serve at the altar of the LORD in Jerusalem, they ate unleavened bread with their fellow priests.

[10]He desecrated Topheth, which was in the Valley of Ben Hinnom, so no one could use it to sacrifice his son or daughter in[c] the fire to Molech. [11]He removed from the entrance to the temple of the LORD the horses that the kings of Judah

---

[a]17 Or *by everything they have done*   [b]8 Or *high places*   [c]10 Or *to make his son or daughter pass through*

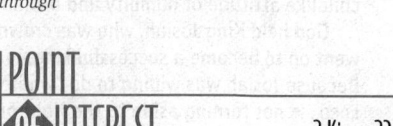

POINT OF INTEREST   2 Kings 23:2

Deuteronomy 17:18 records God's instruction that Israel's kings make personal copies of God's law, keep the copies with them and reread them often. Over the centuries this practice had been forgotten. Note the power for good that could have been at each king's disposal had he remained obedient to God's law.

had dedicated to the sun. They were in the court near the room of an official named Nathan-Melech. Josiah then burned the chariots dedicated to the sun.

¹²He pulled down the altars the kings of Judah had erected on the roof near the upper room of Ahaz, and the altars Manasseh had built in the two courts of the temple of the LORD. He removed them from there, smashed them to pieces and threw the rubble into the Kidron Valley. ¹³The king also desecrated the high places that were east of Jerusalem on the south of the Hill of Corruption—the ones Solomon king of Israel had built for Ashtoreth the vile goddess of the Sidonians, for Chemosh the vile god of Moab, and for Molech*ᵃ* the detestable god of the people of Ammon. ¹⁴Josiah smashed the sacred stones and cut down the Asherah poles and covered the sites with human bones.

¹⁵Even the altar at Bethel, the high place made by Jeroboam son of Nebat, who had caused Israel to sin—even that altar and high place he demolished. He burned the high place and ground it to powder, and burned the Asherah pole also. ¹⁶Then Josiah looked around, and when he saw the tombs that were there on the hillside, he had the bones removed from them and burned on the altar to defile it, in accordance with the word of the LORD proclaimed by the man of God who foretold these things.

¹⁷The king asked, "What is that tombstone I see?"

The men of the city said, "It marks the tomb of the man of God who came from Judah and pronounced against the altar of Bethel the very things you have done to it."

¹⁸"Leave it alone," he said. "Don't let anyone disturb his bones." So they spared his bones and those of the prophet who had come from Samaria.

¹⁹Just as he had done at Bethel, Josiah removed and defiled all the shrines at the high places that the kings of Israel had built in the towns of Samaria that had provoked the LORD to anger. ²⁰Josiah slaughtered all the priests of those high places on the altars and burned human bones on them. Then he went back to Jerusalem.

²¹The king gave this order to all the people: "Celebrate the Passover to the LORD your God, as it is written in this Book of the Covenant." ²²Not since the days of the judges who led Israel, nor throughout the days of the kings of Israel and the kings of Judah, had any such Passover been observed. ²³But in the eighteenth year of King Josiah, this Passover was celebrated to the LORD in Jerusalem.

²⁴Furthermore, Josiah got rid of the mediums and spiritists, the household gods, the idols and all the other detestable things seen in Judah and Jerusalem. This he did to fulfill the requirements of the law written in the book that Hilkiah the priest had discovered in the temple of the LORD. ²⁵Neither before nor after Josiah was there a king like him who turned to the LORD as he did—with all his heart and with all his soul and with all his strength, in accordance with all the Law of Moses.

²⁶Nevertheless, the LORD did not turn away from the heat of his fierce anger, which burned against Judah because of all that Manasseh had done to provoke him to anger. ²⁷So the LORD said, "I will remove Judah also from my presence as I removed Israel, and I will reject Jerusalem, the city I chose, and this temple, about which I said, 'There shall my Name be.'*ᵇ*"

²⁸As for the other events of Josiah's reign, and all he did, are they not written in the book of the annals of the kings of Judah?

²⁹While Josiah was king, Pharaoh Neco king of Egypt went up to the Euphrates River to help the king of Assyria. King Josiah marched out to meet him in battle, but Neco faced him and killed him at Megiddo. ³⁰Josiah's servants brought his body in a chariot from Megiddo to Jerusalem and buried him in his own tomb. And the people of the land took Jehoahaz son of Josiah and anointed him and made him king in place of his father.

Jehoahaz King of Judah

³¹Jehoahaz was twenty-three years old when he became king, and he reigned in Jerusalem three months. His mother's name was Hamutal daughter of Jeremiah; she was from Libnah. ³²He did evil in the eyes of the LORD, just as his fathers had done. ³³Pharaoh Neco put him in chains at Riblah in the land of Hamath*ᶜ*

ᵃ13 Hebrew *Milcom*   *ᵇ27* 1 Kings 8:29
ᶜ33 Hebrew; Septuagint (see also 2 Chron. 36:3)
Neco at Riblah in Hamath removed him

so that he might not reign in Jerusalem, and he imposed on Judah a levy of a hundred talents[a] of silver and a talent[b] of gold. 34Pharaoh Neco made Eliakim son of Josiah king in place of his father Josiah and changed Eliakim's name to Jehoiakim. But he took Jehoahaz and carried him off to Egypt, and there he died. 35Jehoiakim paid Pharaoh Neco the silver and gold he demanded. In order to do so, he taxed the land and exacted the silver and gold from the people of the land according to their assessments.

Jehoiakim King of Judah

36Jehoiakim was twenty-five years old when he became king, and he reigned in Jerusalem eleven years. His mother's name was Zebidah daughter of Pedaiah; she was from Rumah. 37And he did evil in the eyes of the LORD, just as his fathers had done.

24 During Jehoiakim's reign, Nebuchadnezzar king of Babylon invaded the land, and Jehoiakim became his vassal for three years. But then he changed his mind and rebelled against Nebuchadnezzar. 2The LORD sent Babylonian,[c] Aramean, Moabite and Ammonite raiders against him. He sent them to destroy Judah, in accordance with the word of the LORD proclaimed by his servants the prophets. 3Surely these things happened to Judah according to the LORD's command, in order to remove them from his presence because of the sins of Manasseh and all he had done, 4including the shedding of innocent blood. For he had filled Jerusalem with innocent blood, and the LORD was not willing to forgive.

5As for the other events of Jehoiakim's reign, and all he did, are they not written in the book of the annals of the kings of Judah? 6Jehoiakim rested with his fathers. And Jehoiachin his son succeeded him as king.

7The king of Egypt did not march out from his own country again, because the king of Babylon had taken all his territory, from the Wadi of Egypt to the Euphrates River.

Jehoiachin King of Judah

8Jehoiachin was eighteen years old when he became king, and he reigned in Jerusalem three months. His mother's name was Nehushta daughter of Elnathan; she was from Jerusalem. 9He did

evil in the eyes of the LORD, just as his father had done.

10At that time the officers of Nebuchadnezzar king of Babylon advanced on Jerusalem and laid siege to it, 11and Nebuchadnezzar himself came up to the city while his officers were besieging it. 12Jehoiachin king of Judah, his mother, his attendants, his nobles and his officials all surrendered to him.

In the eighth year of the reign of the king of Babylon, he took Jehoiachin prisoner. 13As the LORD had declared, Nebuchadnezzar removed all the treasures from the temple of the LORD and from the royal palace, and took away all the gold articles that Solomon king of Israel had made for the temple of the LORD. 14He carried into exile all Jerusalem: all the officers and fighting men, and all the craftsmen and artisans—a total of ten thousand. Only the poorest people of the land were left.

15Nebuchadnezzar took Jehoiachin captive to Babylon. He also took from Jerusalem to Babylon the king's mother, his wives, his officials and the leading men of the land. 16The king of Babylon also deported to Babylon the entire force of seven thousand fighting men, strong and fit for war, and a thousand craftsmen and artisans. 17He made Mattaniah, Jehoiachin's uncle, king in his place and changed his name to Zedekiah.

Zedekiah King of Judah

18Zedekiah was twenty-one years old when he became king, and he reigned in Jerusalem eleven years. His mother's name was Hamutal daughter of Jeremiah; she was from Libnah. 19He did evil in the eyes of the LORD, just as Jehoiakim had done. 20It was because of the LORD's anger that all this happened to Jerusalem and Judah, and in the end he thrust them from his presence.

The Fall of Jerusalem

Now Zedekiah rebelled against the king of Babylon.

25 So in the ninth year of Zedekiah's reign, on the tenth day of the tenth month, Nebuchadnezzar king of Babylon marched against Jerusalem with his whole army. He encamped outside the

---

a33 That is, about 3 3/4 tons (about 3.4 metric tons)   b33 That is, about 75 pounds (about 34 kilograms)   c2 Or Chaldean city and built siege works all around it. ²The city was kept under siege until the eleventh year of King Zedekiah. ³By the ninth day of the ⌊fourth⌋ᵃ month the famine in the city had become so severe that there was no food for the people to eat. ⁴Then the city wall was broken through, and the whole army fled at night through the gate between the two walls near the king's garden, though the Babylonians ᵇ were surrounding the city. They fled toward the Arabah,ᶜ ⁵but the Babylonian ᵈ army pursued the king and overtook him in the plains of Jericho. All his soldiers were separated from him and scattered, ⁶and he was captured. He was taken to the king of Babylon at Riblah, where sentence was pronounced on him. ⁷They killed the sons of Zedekiah before his eyes. Then they put out his eyes, bound him with bronze shackles and took him to Babylon.

⁸On the seventh day of the fifth month, in the nineteenth year of Nebuchadnezzar king of Babylon, Nebuzaradan commander of the imperial guard, an official of the king of Babylon, came to Jerusalem. ⁹He set fire to the temple of the LORD, the royal palace and all the houses of Jerusalem. Every important building he burned down. ¹⁰The whole Babylonian army, under the commander of the imperial guard, broke down the walls around Jerusalem. ¹¹Nebuzaradan the commander of the guard carried into exile the people who remained in the city, along with the rest of the populace and those who had gone over to the king of Babylon. ¹²But the commander left behind some of the poorest people of the land to work the vineyards and fields.

¹³The Babylonians broke up the bronze pillars, the movable stands and the bronze Sea that were at the temple of the LORD and they carried the bronze to Babylon. ¹⁴They also took away the pots, shovels, wick trimmers, dishes and all the bronze articles used in the temple service. ¹⁵The commander of the imperial guard took away the censers and sprinkling bowls—all that were made of pure gold or silver.

¹⁶The bronze from the two pillars, the Sea and the movable stands, which Solomon had made for the temple of the LORD, was more than could be weighed. ¹⁷Each pillar was twenty-seven feetᵉ high. The bronze capital on top of one pillar was four and a half feetᶠ high and was decorated with a network and pomegranates of bronze all around. The other pillar, with its network, was similar.

¹⁸The commander of the guard took as prisoners Seraiah the chief priest, Zephaniah the priest next in rank and the three doorkeepers. ¹⁹Of those still in the city, he took the officer in charge of the fighting men and five royal advisers. He also took the secretary who was chief officer in charge of conscripting the people of the land and sixty of his men who were found in the city. ²⁰Nebuzaradan the commander took them all and brought them to the king of Babylon at Riblah. ²¹There at Riblah, in the land of Hamath, the king had them executed.

So Judah went into captivity, away from her land.

²²Nebuchadnezzar king of Babylon appointed Gedaliah son of Ahikam, the son of Shaphan, to be over the people he had left behind in Judah. ²³When all the army officers and their men heard that the king of Babylon had appointed Gedaliah as governor, they came to Gedaliah at Mizpah—Ishmael son of Nethaniah, Johanan son of Kareah, Seraiah son of Tanhumeth the Netophathite, Jaazaniah the son of the Maacathite, and their men. ²⁴Gedaliah took an oath to reassure them and their men. "Do not be afraid of the Babylonian officials," he said. "Settle down in the land and serve the king of Babylon, and it will go well with you."

²⁵In the seventh month, however, Ishmael son of Nethaniah, the son of Elishama, who was of royal blood, came with ten men and assassinated Gedaliah and also the men of Judah and the Babylonians who were with him at Mizpah. ²⁶At this, all the people from the least to the greatest, together with the army officers, fled to Egypt for fear of the Babylonians.

Jehoiachin Released

²⁷In the thirty-seventh year of the exile of Jehoiachin king of Judah, in the year Evil-Merodach ᵍ became king of Babylon, he released Jehoiachin from prison on the twenty-seventh day of the twelfth

ᵃ3 See Jer. 52:6.   ᵇ4 Or *Chaldeans*; also in verses 13, 25 and 26   ᶜ4 Or *the Jordan Valley*   ᵈ5 Or *Chaldean*; also in verses 10 and 24   ᵉ17 Hebrew *eighteen cubits* (about 8.1 meters)   ᶠ17 Hebrew *three cubits* (about 1.3 meters)   ᵍ27 Also called *Amel-Marduk* month. ²⁸He spoke kindly to him and gave him a seat of honor higher than those of the other kings who were with him in Babylon. ²⁹So Jehoiachin put aside his prison clothes and for the rest of his life ate regularly at the king's table. ³⁰Day by day the king gave Jehoiachin a regular allowance as long as he lived.

When we get discouraged

with ourselves because of our sin, it's easy to lose sight of

God's love for us. Sometimes we need to be reminded that

God is always with us and that he wants to show us he is

faithful. The books of Chronicles were written to recon-

nect the Babylonian exiles with their history as a people

beloved and chosen by God. There may be a point in your

life when you ask the same question the exiles might have:

Is God still interested in me? Be open

to hearing God's answer as you

read 1 and 2 Chronicles.

1 CHRONICLES

Historical Records From Adam to Abraham

To Noah's Sons

Adam, Seth, Enosh, ²Kenan, Mahalalel, Jared, ³Enoch, Methuselah, Lamech, Noah.

⁴The sons of Noah:ᵃ
Shem, Ham and Japheth.

The Japhethites

⁵The sonsᵇ of Japheth:
Gomer, Magog, Madai, Javan, Tubal, Meshech and Tiras.
⁶The sons of Gomer:
Ashkenaz, Riphathᶜ and Togarmah.
⁷The sons of Javan:
Elishah, Tarshish, the Kittim and the Rodanim.

The Hamites

⁸The sons of Ham:
Cush, Mizraim,ᵈ Put and Canaan.
⁹The sons of Cush:
Seba, Havilah, Sabta, Raamah and Sabteca.
The sons of Raamah:
Sheba and Dedan.
¹⁰Cush was the fatherᵉ of
Nimrod, who grew to be a mighty warrior on earth.
¹¹Mizraim was the father of

ᵃ4 Septuagint; Hebrew does not have *The sons of Noah:*   ᵇ5 *Sons* may mean *descendants* or *successors* or *nations*; also in verses 6-10, 17 and 20.   ᶜ6 Many Hebrew manuscripts and Vulgate (see also Septuagint and Gen. 10:3); most Hebrew manuscripts *Diphath*   ᵈ8 That is, Egypt; also in verse 11   ᵉ10 *Father* may mean *ancestor* or *predecessor* or *founder*; also in verses 11, 13, 18 and 20.

the Ludites, Anamites, Leha-
bites, Naphtuhites, ¹²Pathru-
sites, Casluhites (from whom
the Philistines came) and Caph-
torites.
¹³Canaan was the father of
Sidon his firstborn,ᵃ and of the
Hittites, ¹⁴Jebusites, Amorites,
Girgashites, ¹⁵Hivites, Arkites,
Sinites, ¹⁶Arvadites, Zemarites
and Hamathites.

The Semites

¹⁷The sons of Shem:
Elam, Asshur, Arphaxad, Lud
and Aram.
The sons of Aramᵇ:
Uz, Hul, Gether and Meshech.
¹⁸Arphaxad was the father of Shelah,
and Shelah the father of Eber.
¹⁹Two sons were born to Eber:
One was named Peleg,ᶜ be-
cause in his time the earth was
divided; his brother was named
Joktan.
²⁰Joktan was the father of
Almodad, Sheleph, Hazarma-
veth, Jerah, ²¹Hadoram, Uzal,
Diklah, ²²Obal,ᵈ Abimael, Sheba, ²³Ophir, Havilah and Jobab.
All these were sons of Joktan.

²⁴Shem, Arphaxad,ᵉ Shelah,
²⁵Eber, Peleg, Reu,
²⁶Serug, Nahor, Terah
²⁷and Abram (that is, Abraham).

The Family of Abraham

²⁸The sons of Abraham:
Isaac and Ishmael.

Descendants of Hagar

²⁹These were their descendants:
Nebaioth the firstborn of Ishmael, Kedar, Adbeel, Mibsam,
³⁰Mishma, Dumah, Massa, Hadad, Tema, ³¹Jetur, Naphish and
Kedemah. These were the sons
of Ishmael.

Descendants of Keturah

³²The sons born to Keturah, Abraham's concubine:
Zimran, Jokshan, Medan, Midian, Ishbak and Shuah.
The sons of Jokshan:
Sheba and Dedan.
³³The sons of Midian:

Ephah, Epher, Hanoch, Abida
and Eldaah.
All these were descendants of Keturah.

Descendants of Sarah

³⁴Abraham was the father of Isaac.
The sons of Isaac:
Esau and Israel.

Esau's Sons

³⁵The sons of Esau:
Eliphaz, Reuel, Jeush, Jalam
and Korah.
³⁶The sons of Eliphaz:
Teman, Omar, Zepho,ᶠ Gatam
and Kenaz;
by Timna: Amalek.ᵍ
³⁷The sons of Reuel:
Nahath, Zerah, Shammah and
Mizzah.

The People of Seir in Edom

³⁸The sons of Seir:
Lotan, Shobal, Zibeon, Anah,
Dishon, Ezer and Dishan.
³⁹The sons of Lotan:
Hori and Homam. Timna was
Lotan's sister.
⁴⁰The sons of Shobal:
Alvan,ʰ Manahath, Ebal, She-
pho and Onam.
The sons of Zibeon:
Aiah and Anah.
⁴¹The son of Anah:
Dishon.
The sons of Dishon:
Hemdan,ⁱ Eshban, Ithran and
Keran.
⁴²The sons of Ezer:
Bilhan, Zaavan and Akan.ʲ

ᵃ13 Or of the Sidonians, the foremost   ᵇ17 One
Hebrew manuscript and some Septuagint
manuscripts (see also Gen. 10:23); most Hebrew
manuscripts do not have this line.   ᶜ19 Peleg
means division.   ᵈ22 Some Hebrew manuscripts
and Syriac (see also Gen. 10:28); most Hebrew
manuscripts Ebal   ᵉ24 Hebrew; some Septuagint
manuscripts Arphaxad, Cainan (see also note at
Gen. 11:10)   ᶠ36 Many Hebrew manuscripts,
some Septuagint manuscripts and Syriac (see also
Gen. 36:11); most Hebrew manuscripts Zephi
ᵍ36 Some Septuagint manuscripts (see also Gen.
36:12); Hebrew Gatam, Kenaz, Timna and Amalek
ʰ40 Many Hebrew manuscripts and some
Septuagint manuscripts (see also Gen. 36:23); most
Hebrew manuscripts Alian   ⁱ41 Many Hebrew
manuscripts and some Septuagint manuscripts (see
also Gen. 36:26); most Hebrew manuscripts
Hamran   ʲ42 Many Hebrew and Septuagint
manuscripts (see also Gen. 36:27); most Hebrew
manuscripts Zaavan, Jaakan

The sons of Dishan*a*:
Uz and Aran.

The Rulers of Edom

⁴³These were the kings who reigned
in Edom before any Israelite king
reigned*b*:
Bela son of Beor, whose city was
named Dinhabah.
⁴⁴When Bela died, Jobab son of Zerah from Bozrah succeeded him
as king.
⁴⁵When Jobab died, Husham from
the land of the Temanites succeeded him as king.
⁴⁶When Husham died, Hadad son of
Bedad, who defeated Midian in
the country of Moab, succeeded
him as king. His city was named
Avith.
⁴⁷When Hadad died, Samlah from
Masrekah succeeded him as
king.
⁴⁸When Samlah died, Shaul from Rehoboth on the river*c* succeeded
him as king.
⁴⁹When Shaul died, Baal-Hanan son
of Acbor succeeded him as king.
⁵⁰When Baal-Hanan died, Hadad
succeeded him as king. His city
was named Pau,*d* and his
wife's name was Mehetabel
daughter of Matred, the daughter of Me-Zahab. ⁵¹Hadad also
died.

The chiefs of Edom were:
Timna, Alvah, Jetheth, ⁵²Oholi-
bamah, Elah, Pinon, ⁵³Kenaz,
Teman, Mibzar, ⁵⁴Magdiel and
Iram. These were the chiefs of
Edom.

Israel's Sons

2 These were the sons of Israel:
Reuben, Simeon, Levi, Judah,
Issachar, Zebulun, ²Dan, Joseph, Benjamin, Naphtali, Gad
and Asher.

Judah

To Hezron's Sons

³The sons of Judah:
Er, Onan and Shelah. These
three were born to him by a Canaanite woman, the daughter of
Shua. Er, Judah's firstborn, was
wicked in the LORD's sight; so the
LORD put him to death. ⁴Tamar,
Judah's daughter-in-law, bore
him Perez and Zerah. Judah had
five sons in all.

⁵The sons of Perez:
Hezron and Hamul.
⁶The sons of Zerah:
Zimri, Ethan, Heman, Calcol
and Darda*e*—five in all.
⁷The son of Carmi:
Achar,*f* who brought trouble
on Israel by violating the ban on
taking devoted things.*g*
⁸The son of Ethan:
Azariah.
⁹The sons born to Hezron were:
Jerahmeel, Ram and Caleb.*h*

From Ram Son of Hezron

¹⁰Ram was the father of
Amminadab, and Amminadab
the father of Nahshon, the leader of the people of Judah. ¹¹Nah-
shon was the father of Salmon,*i* Salmon the father of
Boaz, ¹²Boaz the father of Obed
and Obed the father of Jesse.
¹³Jesse was the father of
Eliab his firstborn; the second
son was Abinadab, the third
Shimea, ¹⁴the fourth Nethanel,
the fifth Raddai, ¹⁵the sixth
Ozem and the seventh David.
¹⁶Their sisters were Zeruiah and
Abigail. Zeruiah's three sons
were Abishai, Joab and Asahel.
¹⁷Abigail was the mother of Amasa, whose father was Jether the
Ishmaelite.

Caleb Son of Hezron

¹⁸Caleb son of Hezron had children
by his wife Azubah (and by
Jerioth). These were her sons:
Jesher, Shobab and Ardon.
¹⁹When Azubah died, Caleb
married Ephrath, who bore him

---

*a*42 Hebrew *Dishon*, a variant of *Dishan*
*b*43 Or *before an Israelite king reigned over them*
*c*48 Possibly the Euphrates   *d*50 Many Hebrew
manuscripts, some Septuagint manuscripts, Vulgate
and Syriac (see also Gen. 36:39); most Hebrew
manuscripts *Pai*   *e*6 Many Hebrew manuscripts,
some Septuagint manuscripts and Syriac (see also
1 Kings 4:31); most Hebrew manuscripts *Dara*
*f*7 *Achar* means *trouble*; *Achar* is called *Achan* in
Joshua.   *g*7 The Hebrew term refers to the
irrevocable giving over of things or persons to the
LORD, often by totally destroying them.
*h*9 Hebrew *Kelubai*, a variant of *Caleb*
*i*11 Septuagint (see also Ruth 4:21); Hebrew *Salma*

Hur. ²⁰Hur was the father of Uri, and Uri the father of Bezalel.

²¹Later, Hezron lay with the daughter of Makir the father of Gilead (he had married her when he was sixty years old), and she bore him Segub. ²²Segub was the father of Jair, who controlled twenty-three towns in Gilead. ²³(But Geshur and Aram captured Havvoth Jair,ᵃ as well as Kenath with its surrounding settlements—sixty towns.) All these were descendants of Makir the father of Gilead.

²⁴After Hezron died in Caleb Ephrathah, Abijah the wife of Hezron bore him Ashhur the fatherᵇ of Tekoa.

Jerahmeel Son of Hezron

²⁵The sons of Jerahmeel the firstborn of Hezron:
Ram his firstborn, Bunah, Oren, Ozem andᶜ Ahijah. ²⁶Jerahmeel had another wife, whose name was Atarah; she was the mother of Onam.

²⁷The sons of Ram the firstborn of Jerahmeel:
Maaz, Jamin and Eker.

²⁸The sons of Onam:
Shammai and Jada.
The sons of Shammai:
Nadab and Abishur.

²⁹Abishur's wife was named Abihail, who bore him Ahban and Molid.

³⁰The sons of Nadab:
Seled and Appaim. Seled died without children.

³¹The son of Appaim:
Ishi, who was the father of Sheshan.
Sheshan was the father of Ahlai.

³²The sons of Jada, Shammai's brother:
Jether and Jonathan. Jether died without children.

³³The sons of Jonathan:
Peleth and Zaza.
These were the descendants of Jerahmeel.

³⁴Sheshan had no sons—only daughters.
He had an Egyptian servant named Jarha. ³⁵Sheshan gave his daughter in marriage to his servant Jarha, and she bore him Attai.

³⁶Attai was the father of Nathan, Nathan the father of Zabad, ³⁷Zabad the father of Ephlal, Ephlal the father of Obed, ³⁸Obed the father of Jehu, Jehu the father of Azariah, ³⁹Azariah the father of Helez, Helez the father of Eleasah, ⁴⁰Eleasah the father of Sismai, Sismai the father of Shallum, ⁴¹Shallum the father of Jekamiah, and Jekamiah the father of Elishama.

The Clans of Caleb

⁴²The sons of Caleb the brother of Jerahmeel:
Mesha his firstborn, who was the father of Ziph, and his son Mareshah,ᵈ who was the father of Hebron.

⁴³The sons of Hebron:
Korah, Tappuah, Rekem and Shema. ⁴⁴Shema was the father of Raham, and Raham the father of Jorkeam. Rekem was the father of Shammai. ⁴⁵The son of Shammai was Maon, and Maon was the father of Beth Zur.

⁴⁶Caleb's concubine Ephah was the mother of Haran, Moza and Gazez. Haran was the father of Gazez.

⁴⁷The sons of Jahdai:
Regem, Jotham, Geshan, Pelet, Ephah and Shaaph.

⁴⁸Caleb's concubine Maacah was the mother of Sheber and Tirhanah. ⁴⁹She also gave birth to Shaaph the father of Madmannah and to Sheva the father of Macbenah and Gibea. Caleb's daughter was Acsah. ⁵⁰These were the descendants of Caleb.

The sons of Hur the firstborn of Ephrathah:
Shobal the father of Kiriath Jearim, ⁵¹Salma the father of Bethlehem, and Hareph the father of Beth Gader.

ᵃ23 Or captured the settlements of Jair
ᵇ24 Father may mean civic leader or military leader; also in verses 42, 45, 49-52 and possibly elsewhere.
ᶜ25 Or Oren and Ozem, by   ᵈ42 The meaning of the Hebrew for this phrase is uncertain.

⁵²The descendants of Shobal the father of Kiriath Jearim were:
Haroeh, half the Manahathites, ⁵³and the clans of Kiriath Jearim: the Ithrites, Puthites, Shumathites and Mishraites. From these descended the Zorathites and Eshtaolites.

⁵⁴The descendants of Salma:
Bethlehem, the Netophathites, Atroth Beth Joab, half the Manahathites, the Zorites, ⁵⁵and the clans of scribes*a* who lived at Jabez: the Tirathites, Shimeathites and Sucathites. These are the Kenites who came from Hammath, the father of the house of Recab.*b*

The Sons of David

3 These were the sons of David born to him in Hebron:
The firstborn was Amnon the son of Ahinoam of Jezreel;
the second, Daniel the son of Abigail of Carmel;
²the third, Absalom the son of Maacah daughter of Talmai king of Geshur;
the fourth, Adonijah the son of Haggith;
³the fifth, Shephatiah the son of Abital;
and the sixth, Ithream, by his wife Eglah.

⁴These six were born to David in Hebron, where he reigned seven years and six months.
David reigned in Jerusalem thirty-three years, ⁵and these were the children born to him there:
Shammua,*c* Shobab, Nathan and Solomon. These four were by Bathsheba*d* daughter of Ammiel. ⁶There were also Ibhar, Elishua,*e* Eliphelet, ⁷Nogah, Nepheg, Japhia, ⁸Elishama, Eliada and Eliphelet—nine in all. ⁹All these were the sons of David, besides his sons by his concubines. And Tamar was their sister.

The Kings of Judah

¹⁰Solomon's son was Rehoboam,
Abijah his son,
Asa his son,
Jehoshaphat his son,
¹¹Jehoram*f* his son,

Ahaziah his son,
Joash his son,
¹²Amaziah his son,
Azariah his son,
Jotham his son,
¹³Ahaz his son,
Hezekiah his son,
Manasseh his son,
¹⁴Amon his son,
Josiah his son.
¹⁵The sons of Josiah:
Johanan the firstborn,
Jehoiakim the second son,
Zedekiah the third,
Shallum the fourth.
¹⁶The successors of Jehoiakim:
Jehoiachin*g* his son,
and Zedekiah.

The Royal Line After the Exile

¹⁷The descendants of Jehoiachin the captive:
Shealtiel his son, ¹⁸Malkiram, Pedaiah, Shenazzar, Jekamiah, Hoshama and Nedabiah.
¹⁹The sons of Pedaiah:
Zerubbabel and Shimei.
The sons of Zerubbabel:
Meshullam and Hananiah. Shelomith was their sister.
²⁰There were also five others:
Hashubah, Ohel, Berekiah, Hasadiah and Jushab-Hesed.
²¹The descendants of Hananiah:
Pelatiah and Jeshaiah, and the

---

a55 Or *of the Sopherites*   *b55* Or *father of Beth Recab*   *c5* Hebrew *Shimea*, a variant of *Shammua*   *d5* One Hebrew manuscript and Vulgate (see also Septuagint and 2 Samuel 11:3); most Hebrew manuscripts *Bathshua*   *e6* Two Hebrew manuscripts (see also 2 Samuel 5:15 and 1 Chron. 14:5); most Hebrew manuscripts *Elishama*   *f11* Hebrew *Joram*, a variant of *Jehoram*   *g16* Hebrew *Jeconiah*, a variant of *Jehoiachin*; also in verse 17

POINT OF INTEREST

1 Chronicles 3:5

Since Solomon was the youngest son of one of David's later wives, Solomon would not have been first in the normal line of royal succession. What might have motivated David to choose Solomon as his successor? Read 2 Samuel 12:15–24 for some extra insight.

sons of Rephaiah, of Arnan, of Obadiah and of Shecaniah.

²²The descendants of Shecaniah:
Shemaiah and his sons:
Hattush, Igal, Bariah, Neariah and Shaphat—six in all.

²³The sons of Neariah:
Elioenai, Hizkiah and Azrikam—three in all.

²⁴The sons of Elioenai:
Hodaviah, Eliashib, Pelaiah, Akkub, Johanan, Delaiah and Anani—seven in all.

Other Clans of Judah

4 The descendants of Judah:
Perez, Hezron, Carmi, Hur and Shobal.

²Reaiah son of Shobal was the father of Jahath, and Jahath the father of Ahumai and Lahad. These were the clans of the Zorathites.

³These were the sons*a* of Etam:
Jezreel, Ishma and Idbash. Their sister was named Hazzelelponi. ⁴Penuel was the father of Gedor, and Ezer the father of Hushah.

These were the descendants of Hur, the firstborn of Ephrathah and father*b* of Bethlehem.

⁵Ashhur the father of Tekoa had two wives, Helah and Naarah.

⁶Naarah bore him Ahuzzam, Hepher, Temeni and Haahashtari. These were the descendants of Naarah.

⁷The sons of Helah:
Zereth, Zohar, Ethnan, ⁸and Koz, who was the father of Anub and Hazzobebah and of the clans of Aharhel son of Harum.

⁹Jabez was more honorable than his brothers. His mother had named him Jabez,*c* saying, "I gave birth to him in pain." ¹⁰Jabez cried out to the God of Israel, "Oh, that you would bless me and enlarge my territory! Let your hand be with me, and keep me from harm so that I will be free from pain." And God granted his request.

¹¹Kelub, Shuhah's brother, was the father of Mehir, who was the father of Eshton. ¹²Eshton was the father of Beth Rapha, Paseah and Tehinnah the father of Ir

Nahash.*d* These were the men of Recah.

¹³The sons of Kenaz:
Othniel and Seraiah.
The sons of Othniel:
Hathath and Meonothai.*e* ¹⁴Meonothai was the father of Ophrah.

Seraiah was the father of Joab, the father of Ge Harashim.*f* It was called this because its people were craftsmen.

¹⁵The sons of Caleb son of Jephunneh:
Iru, Elah and Naam.
The son of Elah:
Kenaz.

¹⁶The sons of Jehallelel:
Ziph, Ziphah, Tiria and Asarel.

¹⁷The sons of Ezrah:
Jether, Mered, Epher and Jalon. One of Mered's wives gave birth to Miriam, Shammai and Ishbah the father of Eshtemoa. ¹⁸(His Judean wife gave birth to Jered the father of Gedor, Heber the father of Soco, and Jekuthiel the father of Zanoah.) These were the children of Pharaoh's daughter Bithiah, whom Mered had married.

¹⁹The sons of Hodiah's wife, the sister of Naham:
the father of Keilah the Garmite, and Eshtemoa the Maacathite.

²⁰The sons of Shimon:
Amnon, Rinnah, Ben-Hanan and Tilon.
The descendants of Ishi:
Zoheth and Ben-Zoheth.

²¹The sons of Shelah son of Judah:
Er the father of Lecah, Laadah the father of Mareshah and the clans of the linen workers at Beth Ashbea, ²²Jokim, the men of Cozeba, and Joash and Saraph, who ruled in Moab and Jashubi Lehem. (These records are from ancient times.) ²³They were the potters who lived at Netaim and Gederah; they

---

a3 Some Septuagint manuscripts (see also Vulgate); Hebrew *father*   *b4* Father may mean *civic leader* or *military leader*; also in verses 12, 14, 17, 18 and possibly elsewhere.   *c9* Jabez sounds like the Hebrew for *pain.*   *d12* Or *of the city of Nahash*   *e13* Some Septuagint manuscripts and Vulgate; Hebrew does not have *and Meonothai.*   *f14* Ge Harashim means *valley of craftsmen.*

stayed there and worked for the king.

Simeon

²⁴The descendants of Simeon:
Nemuel, Jamin, Jarib, Zerah and Shaul;
²⁵Shallum was Shaul's son, Mibsam his son and Mishma his son.
²⁶The descendants of Mishma:
Hammuel his son, Zaccur his son and Shimei his son.

²⁷Shimei had sixteen sons and six daughters, but his brothers did not have many children; so their entire clan did not become as numerous as the people of Judah. ²⁸They lived in Beersheba, Moladah, Hazar Shual, ²⁹Bilhah, Ezem, Tolad, ³⁰Bethuel, Hormah, Ziklag, ³¹Beth Marcaboth, Hazar Susim, Beth Biri and Shaaraim. These were their towns until the reign of David. ³²Their surrounding villages were Etam, Ain, Rimmon, Token and Ashan—five towns— ³³and all the villages around these towns as far as Ba-

---

WEDNESDAY

Read 1 Chronicles 4:1–21
Key Verses 1 Chronicles 4:9–10

Jabez's Prayer of Faith – Jim Lett

With a name meaning "Pain," Jabez must have foreseen a troubled life from a relatively early age. How would you handle a future destined for hardship? Where would you find hope? I had an opportunity to make Jabez's prayer my own. I was 24, just out of college (where I had become a follower of Jesus Christ), and I was beginning a career.

The doctor's voice on the phone was businesslike: "The tests indicate you have diabetes. We'll hospitalize you for a week or so, run more tests and regulate you on insulin." As I hung up, emotions of fear, confusion and bewilderment competed for my attention.

During my hospital stay I went through examinations, learned to give myself insulin injections and acquired a new diet. My life would become radically different, and, like Jabez, I wondered if my future would be filled with pain.

Following Jabez's pattern, I prayed, "God, you designed me and love me; bless me so that I will know you well. Use my circumstances to increase my influence for Jesus Christ. Let me experience your protection and provision so that even in troubled times I won't be a slave to pain."

It's been over 20 years since that prayer. I'm still a diabetic, but I know God so much better now. My disease has increased my capacity to share with others about God's faithfulness. My freedom from pain hasn't meant freedom from difficulty, but it has resulted in peace, joy and inner strength. God granted my request, just as he did for Jabez!

Would you pray like Jabez? Your prayer may set you apart as "more honorable" than those who are afraid or unwilling to commit their futures to a faithful Creator. Record your prayer of faith and watch to see him grant your request!

A Deeper Look
Psalm 9:10; Psalm 25:1–2

Go to page 447 for your next devotional reading.

alath.*a* These were their settlements. And they kept a genealogical record.

³⁴Meshobab, Jamlech, Joshah son of Amaziah, ³⁵Joel, Jehu son of Joshibiah, the son of Seraiah, the son of Asiel, ³⁶also Elioenai, Jaakobah, Jeshohaiah, Asaiah, Adiel, Jesimiel, Benaiah, ³⁷and Ziza son of Shiphi, the son of Allon, the son of Jedaiah, the son of Shimri, the son of Shemaiah.

³⁸The men listed above by name were leaders of their clans. Their families increased greatly, ³⁹and they went to the outskirts of Gedor to the east of the valley in search of pasture for their flocks. ⁴⁰They found rich, good pasture, and the land was spacious, peaceful and quiet. Some Hamites had lived there formerly. ⁴¹The men whose names were listed came in the days of Hezekiah king of Judah. They attacked the Hamites in their dwellings and also the Meunites who were there and completely destroyed*b* them, as is evident to this day. Then they settled in their place, because there was pasture for their flocks. ⁴²And five hundred of these Simeonites, led by Pelatiah, Neariah, Rephaiah and Uzziel, the sons of Ishi, invaded the hill country of Seir. ⁴³They killed the remaining Amalekites who had escaped, and they have lived there to this day.

Reuben

5 The sons of Reuben the firstborn of Israel (he was the firstborn, but when he defiled his father's marriage bed, his rights as firstborn were given to the sons of Joseph son of Israel; so he could not be listed in the genealogical record in accordance with his birthright, ²and though Judah was the strongest of his brothers and a ruler came from him, the rights of the firstborn belonged to Joseph)— ³the sons of Reuben the firstborn of Israel:

Hanoch, Pallu, Hezron and Carmi.

⁴The descendants of Joel:

Shemaiah his son, Gog his son, Shimei his son, ⁵Micah his son, Reaiah his son, Baal his son, ⁶and Beerah his son, whom Tiglath-Pileser*c* king of Assyria took into exile. Beerah was a leader of the Reubenites.

⁷Their relatives by clans, listed according to their genealogical records:

Jeiel the chief, Zechariah, ⁸and Bela son of Azaz, the son of Shema, the son of Joel. They settled in the area from Aroer to Nebo and Baal Meon. ⁹To the east they occupied the land up to the edge of the desert that extends to the Euphrates River, because their livestock had increased in Gilead.

¹⁰During Saul's reign they waged war against the Hagrites, who were defeated at their hands; they occupied the dwellings of the Hagrites throughout the entire region east of Gilead.

Gad

¹¹The Gadites lived next to them in Bashan, as far as Salecah:

¹²Joel was the chief, Shapham the second, then Janai and Shaphat, in Bashan.

¹³Their relatives, by families, were:

Michael, Meshullam, Sheba, Jorai, Jacan, Zia and Eber—seven in all.

¹⁴These were the sons of Abihail son of Huri, the son of Jaroah, the son of Gilead, the son of Michael, the son of Jeshishai, the son of Jahdo, the son of Buz.

¹⁵Ahi son of Abdiel, the son of Guni, was head of their family.

¹⁶The Gadites lived in Gilead, in Bashan and its outlying villages, and on all the pasturelands of Sharon as far as they extended.

¹⁷All these were entered in the genealogical records during the reigns of Jotham king of Judah and Jeroboam king of Israel.

¹⁸The Reubenites, the Gadites and the half-tribe of Manasseh had 44,760 men ready for military service—able-bodied men who could handle shield and sword, who could use a bow, and who were trained for battle. ¹⁹They waged war against the Hagrites, Jetur, Naphish and Nodab. ²⁰They were helped in fighting them, and God handed the Hagrites and all their allies over to them, because they cried out to him during the battle. He an-

---

*a*33 Some Septuagint manuscripts (see also Joshua 19:8); Hebrew *Baal*   *b*41 The Hebrew term refers to the irrevocable giving over of things or persons to the Lord, often by totally destroying them.   *c*6 Hebrew *Tilgath-Pilneser,* a variant of *Tiglath-Pileser;* also in verse 26 swered their prayers, because they trusted in him. ²¹They seized the livestock of the Hagrites—fifty thousand camels, two hundred fifty thousand sheep and two thousand donkeys. They also took one hundred thousand people captive, ²²and many others fell slain, because the battle was God's. And they occupied the land until the exile.

The Half-Tribe of Manasseh

²³The people of the half-tribe of Manasseh were numerous; they settled in the land from Bashan to Baal Hermon, that is, to Senir (Mount Hermon).

²⁴These were the heads of their families: Epher, Ishi, Eliel, Azriel, Jeremiah, Hodaviah and Jahdiel. They were brave warriors, famous men, and heads of their families. ²⁵But they were unfaithful to the God of their fathers and prostituted themselves to the gods of the peoples of the land, whom God had destroyed before them. ²⁶So the God of Israel stirred up the spirit of Pul king of Assyria (that is, Tiglath-Pileser king of Assyria), who took the Reubenites, the Gadites and the half-tribe of Manasseh into exile. He took them to Halah, Habor, Hara and the river of Gozan, where they are to this day.

Levi

6 The sons of Levi:
Gershon, Kohath and Merari.
²The sons of Kohath:
Amram, Izhar, Hebron and Uzziel.
³The children of Amram:
Aaron, Moses and Miriam.
The sons of Aaron:
Nadab, Abihu, Eleazar and Ithamar.
⁴Eleazar was the father of Phinehas,
Phinehas the father of Abishua,
⁵Abishua the father of Bukki,
Bukki the father of Uzzi,
⁶Uzzi the father of Zerahiah,
Zerahiah the father of Meraioth,
⁷Meraioth the father of Amariah,
Amariah the father of Ahitub,
⁸Ahitub the father of Zadok,
Zadok the father of Ahimaaz,
⁹Ahimaaz the father of Azariah,
Azariah the father of Johanan,
¹⁰Johanan the father of Azariah (it was he who served as priest in the temple Solomon built in Jerusalem),

¹¹Azariah the father of Amariah,
Amariah the father of Ahitub,
¹²Ahitub the father of Zadok,
Zadok the father of Shallum,
¹³Shallum the father of Hilkiah,
Hilkiah the father of Azariah,
¹⁴Azariah the father of Seraiah,
and Seraiah the father of Jehozadak.

¹⁵Jehozadak was deported when the LORD sent Judah and Jerusalem into exile by the hand of Nebuchadnezzar.

¹⁶The sons of Levi:
Gershon,ᵃ Kohath and Merari.
¹⁷These are the names of the sons of Gershon:
Libni and Shimei.
¹⁸The sons of Kohath:
Amram, Izhar, Hebron and Uzziel.
¹⁹The sons of Merari:
Mahli and Mushi.
These are the clans of the Levites listed according to their fathers:
²⁰Of Gershon:
Libni his son, Jehath his son,
Zimmah his son, ²¹Joah his son,
Iddo his son, Zerah his son
and Jeatherai his son.
²²The descendants of Kohath:
Amminadab his son, Korah his son,
Assir his son, ²³Elkanah his son,
Ebiasaph his son, Assir his son,
²⁴Tahath his son, Uriel his son,
Uzziah his son and Shaul his son.
²⁵The descendants of Elkanah:
Amasai, Ahimoth,
²⁶Elkanah his son,ᵇ Zophai his son,
Nahath his son, ²⁷Eliab his son,
Jeroham his son, Elkanah his son
and Samuel his son.ᶜ
²⁸The sons of Samuel:
Joelᵈ the firstborn
and Abijah the second son.
²⁹The descendants of Merari:

ᵃ16 Hebrew *Gershom*, a variant of *Gershon*; also in verses 17, 20, 43, 62 and 71   ᵇ26 Some Hebrew manuscripts, Septuagint and Syriac; most Hebrew manuscripts *Ahimoth* ²⁶*and Elkanah. The sons of Elkanah:*   ᶜ27 Some Septuagint manuscripts (see also 1 Samuel 1:19,20 and 1 Chron. 6:33,34); Hebrew does not have *and Samuel his son.*   ᵈ28 Some Septuagint manuscripts and Syriac (see also 1 Samuel 8:2 and 1 Chron. 6:33); Hebrew does not have *Joel.*

Mahli, Libni his son,
Shimei his son, Uzzah his son,
30Shimea his son, Haggiah his son
and Asaiah his son.

The Temple Musicians

31These are the men David put in
charge of the music in the house of the
LORD after the ark came to rest there.
32They ministered with music before the
tabernacle, the Tent of Meeting, until Solomon built the temple of the LORD in Jerusalem. They performed their duties according to the regulations laid down for
them.

33Here are the men who served, together with their sons:
From the Kohathites:
Heman, the musician,
the son of Joel, the son of Samuel,
34the son of Elkanah, the son of
Jeroham,
the son of Eliel, the son of Toah,
35the son of Zuph, the son of Elkanah,
the son of Mahath, the son of
Amasai,
36the son of Elkanah, the son of
Joel,
the son of Azariah, the son
of Zephaniah,
37the son of Tahath, the son of Assir,
the son of Ebiasaph, the son of
Korah,
38the son of Izhar, the son of Kohath,
the son of Levi, the son of Israel;
39and Heman's associate Asaph,
who served at his right hand:
Asaph son of Berekiah, the son
of Shimea,
40the son of Michael, the son of
Baaseiah,*a*
the son of Malkijah, 41the son of
Ethni,
the son of Zerah, the son of Adaiah,
42the son of Ethan, the son of Zimmah,
the son of Shimei, 43the son of
Jahath,
the son of Gershon, the son of
Levi;
44and from their associates, the Merarites, at his left hand:
Ethan son of Kishi, the son of
Abdi,

the son of Malluch, 45the son of
Hashabiah,
the son of Amaziah, the son of
Hilkiah,
46the son of Amzi, the son of Bani,
the son of Shemer, 47the son of
Mahli,
the son of Mushi, the son of Merari,
the son of Levi.

48Their fellow Levites were assigned to
all the other duties of the tabernacle, the
house of God. 49But Aaron and his
descendants were the ones who presented offerings on the altar of burnt offering
and on the altar of incense in connection
with all that was done in the Most Holy
Place, making atonement for Israel, in accordance with all that Moses the servant
of God had commanded.

50These were the descendants of
Aaron:
Eleazar his son, Phinehas his
son,
Abishua his son, 51Bukki his
son,
Uzzi his son, Zerahiah his son,
52Meraioth his son, Amariah his
son,
Ahitub his son, 53Zadok his son
and Ahimaaz his son.

54These were the locations of their settlements allotted as their territory (they
were assigned to the descendants of Aaron who were from the Kohathite clan,
because the first lot was for them):
55They were given Hebron in Judah with its surrounding pasturelands. 56But the fields and villages
around the city were given to Caleb
son of Jephunneh.
57So the descendants of Aaron
were given Hebron (a city of refuge), and Libnah,*b* Jattir, Eshtemoa, 58Hilen, Debir, 59Ashan, Juttah*c* and Beth Shemesh, together
with their pasturelands. 60And from
the tribe of Benjamin they were giv-
en Gibeon,*d* Geba, Alemeth and
Anathoth, together with their pasturelands.

a40 Most Hebrew manuscripts; some Hebrew
manuscripts, one Septuagint manuscript and Syriac
Maaseiah   *b57* See Joshua 21:13; Hebrew *given
the cities of refuge: Hebron, Libnah.*   *c59* Syriac
(see also Septuagint and Joshua 21:16); Hebrew
does not have *Juttah.*   *d60* See Joshua 21:17;
Hebrew does not have *Gibeon.*

These towns, which were distributed among the Kohathite clans, were thirteen in all.
⁶¹The rest of Kohath's descendants were allotted ten towns from the clans of half the tribe of Manasseh.

⁶²The descendants of Gershon, clan by clan, were allotted thirteen towns from the tribes of Issachar, Asher and Naphtali, and from the part of the tribe of Manasseh that is in Bashan.

⁶³The descendants of Merari, clan by clan, were allotted twelve towns from the tribes of Reuben, Gad and Zebulun.

⁶⁴So the Israelites gave the Levites these towns and their pasturelands. ⁶⁵From the tribes of Judah, Simeon and Benjamin they allotted the previously named towns.

⁶⁶Some of the Kohathite clans were given as their territory towns from the tribe of Ephraim.

⁶⁷In the hill country of Ephraim they were given Shechem (a city of refuge), and Gezer,ᵃ ⁶⁸Jokmeam, Beth Horon, ⁶⁹Aijalon and Gath Rimmon, together with their pasturelands.

⁷⁰And from half the tribe of Manasseh the Israelites gave Aner and Bileam, together with their pasturelands, to the rest of the Kohathite clans.

⁷¹The Gershonites received the following:
From the clan of the half-tribe of Manasseh
they received Golan in Bashan and also Ashtaroth, together with their pasturelands;
⁷²from the tribe of Issachar
they received Kedesh, Daberath, ⁷³Ramoth and Anem, together with their pasturelands;
⁷⁴from the tribe of Asher
they received Mashal, Abdon, ⁷⁵Hukok and Rehob, together with their pasturelands;
⁷⁶and from the tribe of Naphtali
they received Kedesh in Galilee, Hammon and Kiriathaim, together with their pasturelands.

⁷⁷The Merarites (the rest of the Levites) received the following:
From the tribe of Zebulun
they received Jokneam, Kartah,ᵇ Rimmono and Tabor, together with their pasturelands;

⁷⁸from the tribe of Reuben across the Jordan east of Jericho
they received Bezer in the desert, Jahzah, ⁷⁹Kedemoth and Mephaath, together with their pasturelands;
⁸⁰and from the tribe of Gad
they received Ramoth in Gilead, Mahanaim, ⁸¹Heshbon and Jazer, together with their pasturelands.

Issachar

7 The sons of Issachar:
Tola, Puah, Jashub and Shimron—four in all.
²The sons of Tola:
Uzzi, Rephaiah, Jeriel, Jahmai, Ibsam and Samuel—heads of their families. During the reign of David, the descendants of Tola listed as fighting men in their genealogy numbered 22,600.
³The son of Uzzi:
Izrahiah.
The sons of Izrahiah:
Michael, Obadiah, Joel and Isshiah. All five of them were chiefs. ⁴According to their family genealogy, they had 36,000 men ready for battle, for they had many wives and children.
⁵The relatives who were fighting men belonging to all the clans of Issachar, as listed in their genealogy, were 87,000 in all.

Benjamin

⁶Three sons of Benjamin:
Bela, Beker and Jediael.
⁷The sons of Bela:
Ezbon, Uzzi, Uzziel, Jerimoth and Iri, heads of families—five in all. Their genealogical record listed 22,034 fighting men.
⁸The sons of Beker:
Zemirah, Joash, Eliezer, Elioenai, Omri, Jeremoth, Abijah, Anathoth and Alemeth. All these were the sons of Beker. ⁹Their genealogical record listed the heads of families and 20,200 fighting men.

ᵃ67 See Joshua 21:21; Hebrew *given the cities of refuge: Shechem, Gezer.*   ᵇ77 See Septuagint and Joshua 21:34; Hebrew does not have *Jokneam, Kartah.*

¹⁰The son of Jediael:
Bilhan.
The sons of Bilhan:
Jeush, Benjamin, Ehud, Kenaa-
nah, Zethan, Tarshish and
Ahishahar. ¹¹All these sons of
Jediael were heads of families.
There were 17,200 fighting men
ready to go out to war.
¹²The Shuppites and Huppites were
the descendants of Ir, and the
Hushites the descendants of
Aher.

Naphtali

¹³The sons of Naphtali:
Jahziel, Guni, Jezer and Shillem*a*—the descendants of Bilhah.

Manasseh

¹⁴The descendants of Manasseh:
Asriel was his descendant
through his Aramean concubine.
She gave birth to Makir the father
of Gilead. ¹⁵Makir took a wife from
among the Huppites and Shuppites. His sister's name was Maacah.
Another descendant was named
Zelophehad, who had only daughters.
¹⁶Makir's wife Maacah gave
birth to a son and named him Pe-
resh. His brother was named She-
resh, and his sons were Ulam and
Rakem.
¹⁷The son of Ulam:
Bedan.
These were the sons of Gilead son
of Makir, the son of Manasseh.
¹⁸His sister Hammoleketh gave
birth to Ishhod, Abiezer and
Mahlah.
¹⁹The sons of Shemida were:
Ahian, Shechem, Likhi and
Aniam.

Ephraim

²⁰The descendants of Ephraim:
Shuthelah, Bered his son,
Tahath his son, Eleadah his son,
Tahath his son, ²¹Zabad his son
and Shuthelah his son.
Ezer and Elead were killed by
the native-born men of Gath, when
they went down to seize their livestock. ²²Their father Ephraim
mourned for them many days, and

his relatives came to comfort him.
²³Then he lay with his wife again,
and she became pregnant and gave
birth to a son. He named him Beriah,*b* because there had been misfortune in his family. ²⁴His daughter was Sheerah, who built Lower
and Upper Beth Horon as well as
Uzzen Sheerah.
²⁵Rephah was his son, Resheph his
son,*c*
Telah his son, Tahan his son,
²⁶Ladan his son, Ammihud his
son,
Elishama his son, ²⁷Nun his son
and Joshua his son.
²⁸Their lands and settlements included
Bethel and its surrounding villages, Naa-
ran to the east, Gezer and its villages to
the west, and Shechem and its villages
all the way to Ayyah and its villages.
²⁹Along the borders of Manasseh were
Beth Shan, Taanach, Megiddo and Dor,
together with their villages. The descendants of Joseph son of Israel lived in
these towns.

Asher

³⁰The sons of Asher:
Imnah, Ishvah, Ishvi and Beri-
ah. Their sister was Serah.
³¹The sons of Beriah:
Heber and Malkiel, who was the
father of Birzaith.
³²Heber was the father of Japhlet,
Shomer and Hotham and of
their sister Shua.
³³The sons of Japhlet:
Pasach, Bimhal and Ashvath.
These were Japhlet's sons.
³⁴The sons of Shomer:
Ahi, Rohgah,*d* Hubbah and
Aram.
³⁵The sons of his brother Helem:
Zophah, Imna, Shelesh and
Amal.
³⁶The sons of Zophah:
Suah, Harnepher, Shual, Beri,
Imrah, ³⁷Bezer, Hod, Shamma,
Shilshah, Ithran*e* and Beera.
³⁸The sons of Jether:
Jephunneh, Pispah and Ara.

a 13 Some Hebrew and Septuagint manuscripts (see
also Gen. 46:24 and Num. 26:49); most Hebrew
manuscripts *Shallum*   *b 23* *Beriah* sounds like
the Hebrew for *misfortune.*   *c 25* Some
Septuagint manuscripts; Hebrew does not have *his
son.*   *d 34* Or *of his brother Shomer: Rohgah*
e 37 Possibly a variant of *Jether*

³⁹The sons of Ulla:

Arah, Hanniel and Rizia.

⁴⁰All these were descendants of Asher—heads of families, choice men, brave warriors and outstanding leaders. The number of men ready for battle, as listed in their genealogy, was 26,000.

The Genealogy of Saul the Benjamite

8 Benjamin was the father of Bela his firstborn,

Ashbel the second son, Aharah the third,

²Nohah the fourth and Rapha the fifth.

³The sons of Bela were:

Addar, Gera, Abihud,ᵃ ⁴Abishua, Naaman, Ahoah, ⁵Gera, Shephuphan and Huram.

⁶These were the descendants of Ehud, who were heads of families of those living in Geba and were deported to Manahath:

⁷Naaman, Ahijah, and Gera, who deported them and who was the father of Uzza and Ahihud.

⁸Sons were born to Shaharaim in Moab after he had divorced his wives Hushim and Baara. ⁹By his wife Hodesh he had Jobab, Zibia, Mesha, Malcam, ¹⁰Jeuz, Sakia and Mirmah. These were his sons, heads of families. ¹¹By Hushim he had Abitub and Elpaal.

¹²The sons of Elpaal:

Eber, Misham, Shemed (who built Ono and Lod with its surrounding villages), ¹³and Beriah and Shema, who were heads of families of those living in Aijalon and who drove out the inhabitants of Gath.

¹⁴Ahio, Shashak, Jeremoth, ¹⁵Zebadiah, Arad, Eder, ¹⁶Michael, Ishpah and Joha were the sons of Beriah.

¹⁷Zebadiah, Meshullam, Hizki, Heber, ¹⁸Ishmerai, Izliah and Jobab were the sons of Elpaal.

¹⁹Jakim, Zicri, Zabdi, ²⁰Elienai, Zillethai, Eliel, ²¹Adaiah, Beraiah and Shimrath were the sons of Shimei.

²²Ishpan, Eber, Eliel, ²³Abdon, Zicri, Hanan, ²⁴Hananiah, Elam, Anthothijah, ²⁵Iphdeiah and Penuel were the sons of Shashak.

²⁶Shamsherai, Shehariah, Athaliah, ²⁷Jaareshiah, Elijah and Zicri were the sons of Jeroham.

²⁸All these were heads of families, chiefs as listed in their genealogy, and they lived in Jerusalem.

²⁹Jeielᵇ the fatherᶜ of Gibeon lived in Gibeon.

His wife's name was Maacah, ³⁰and his firstborn son was Abdon, followed by Zur, Kish, Baal, Ner,ᵈ Nadab, ³¹Gedor, Ahio, Zeker ³²and Mikloth, who was the father of Shimeah. They too lived near their relatives in Jerusalem.

³³Ner was the father of Kish, Kish the father of Saul, and Saul the father of Jonathan, Malki-Shua, Abinadab and Esh-Baal.ᵉ

³⁴The son of Jonathan:

Merib-Baal,ᶠ who was the father of Micah.

³⁵The sons of Micah:

Pithon, Melech, Tarea and Ahaz.

³⁶Ahaz was the father of Jehoaddah, Jehoaddah was the father of Alemeth, Azmaveth and Zimri, and Zimri was the father of Moza. ³⁷Moza was the father of Binea; Raphah was his son, Eleasah his son and Azel his son.

³⁸Azel had six sons, and these were their names:

Azrikam, Bokeru, Ishmael, Sheariah, Obadiah and Hanan. All these were the sons of Azel.

³⁹The sons of his brother Eshek:

Ulam his firstborn, Jeush the second son and Eliphelet the third. ⁴⁰The sons of Ulam were brave warriors who could handle the bow. They had many sons and grandsons—150 in all.

All these were the descendants of Benjamin.

9 All Israel was listed in the genealogies recorded in the book of the kings of Israel.

ᵃ3 Or *Gera the father of Ehud*   ᵇ29 Some Septuagint manuscripts (see also 1 Chron. 9:35); Hebrew does not have *Jeiel*.   ᶜ29 *Father* may mean *civic leader* or *military leader.*   ᵈ30 Some Septuagint manuscripts (see also 1 Chron. 9:36); Hebrew does not have *Ner.*   ᵉ33 Also known as *Ish-Bosheth*   ᶠ34 Also known as *Mephibosheth*

The People in Jerusalem

The people of Judah were taken captive to Babylon because of their unfaithfulness. ²Now the first to resettle on their own property in their own towns were some Israelites, priests, Levites and temple servants.

³Those from Judah, from Benjamin, and from Ephraim and Manasseh who lived in Jerusalem were:

⁴Uthai son of Ammihud, the son of Omri, the son of Imri, the son of Bani, a descendant of Perez son of Judah.

⁵Of the Shilonites:
Asaiah the firstborn and his sons.

⁶Of the Zerahites:
Jeuel.
The people from Judah numbered 690.

⁷Of the Benjamites:
Sallu son of Meshullam, the son of Hodaviah, the son of Hassenuah;

⁸Ibneiah son of Jeroham; Elah son of Uzzi, the son of Micri; and Meshullam son of Shephatiah, the son of Reuel, the son of Ibnijah.

⁹The people from Benjamin, as listed in their genealogy, numbered 956. All these men were heads of their families.

¹⁰Of the priests:
Jedaiah; Jehoiarib; Jakin;

¹¹Azariah son of Hilkiah, the son of Meshullam, the son of Zadok, the son of Meraioth, the son of Ahitub, the official in charge of the house of God;

¹²Adaiah son of Jeroham, the son of Pashhur, the son of Malkijah; and Maasai son of Adiel, the son of Jahzerah, the son of Meshullam, the son of Meshillemith, the son of Immer.

¹³The priests, who were heads of families, numbered 1,760. They were able men, responsible for ministering in the house of God.

¹⁴Of the Levites:
Shemaiah son of Hasshub, the son of Azrikam, the son of Hashabiah, a Merarite; ¹⁵Bakbakkar, Heresh, Galal and Mattaniah son of Mica, the son of Zicri, the son of Asaph; ¹⁶Obadiah son of Shemaiah, the son of Galal, the son of Jeduthun; and Berekiah son of Asa, the son of Elkanah, who lived in the villages of the Netophathites.

¹⁷The gatekeepers:
Shallum, Akkub, Talmon, Ahiman and their brothers, Shallum their chief ¹⁸being stationed at the King's Gate on the east, up to the present time. These were the gatekeepers belonging to the camp of the Levites. ¹⁹Shallum son of Kore, the son of Ebiasaph, the son of Korah, and his fellow gatekeepers from his family (the Korahites) were responsible for guarding the thresholds of the Tentᵃ just as their fathers had been responsible for guarding the entrance to the dwelling of the LORD. ²⁰In earlier times Phinehas son of Eleazar was in charge of the gatekeepers, and the LORD was with him. ²¹Zechariah son of Meshelemiah was the gatekeeper at the entrance to the Tent of Meeting.

²²Altogether, those chosen to be gatekeepers at the thresholds numbered 212. They were registered by genealogy in their villages. The gatekeepers had been assigned to their positions of trust by David and Samuel the seer. ²³They and their descendants were in charge of guarding the gates of the house of the LORD—the house called the Tent. ²⁴The gatekeepers were on the four sides: east, west, north and south. ²⁵Their brothers in their villages had to come from time to time and share their duties for seven-day periods. ²⁶But the four principal gatekeepers, who

ᵃ19 That is, the temple; also in verses 21 and 23

POINT OF INTEREST

1 Chronicles 9:1

The mention of Judah's captivity in this verse reminds us that the remainder of 1 Chronicles is a retelling of Israelite history. This retelling was intended for a later generation of Israelites, perhaps even those who lived during this exile.

were Levites, were entrusted with the responsibility for the rooms and treasuries in the house of God. **27**They would spend the night stationed around the house of God, because they had to guard it; and they had charge of the key for opening it each morning.

28Some of them were in charge of the articles used in the temple service; they counted them when they were brought in and when they were taken out. **29**Others were assigned to take care of the furnishings and all the other articles of the sanctuary, as well as the flour and wine, and the oil, incense and spices. **30**But some of the priests took care of mixing the spices. **31**A Levite named Mattithiah, the firstborn son of Shallum the Korahite, was entrusted with the responsibility for baking the offering bread. **32**Some of their Kohathite brothers were in charge of preparing for every Sabbath the bread set out on the table.

33Those who were musicians, heads of Levite families, stayed in the rooms of the temple and were exempt from other duties because they were responsible for the work day and night.

34All these were heads of Levite families, chiefs as listed in their genealogy, and they lived in Jerusalem.

The Genealogy of Saul

35Jeiel the father*a* of Gibeon lived in Gibeon.

His wife's name was Maacah, **36**and his firstborn son was Abdon, followed by Zur, Kish, Baal, Ner, Nadab, **37**Gedor, Ahio, Zechariah and Mikloth. **38**Mikloth was the father of Shimeam. They too lived near their relatives in Jerusalem.

39Ner was the father of Kish, Kish the father of Saul, and Saul the father of Jonathan, Malki-Shua, Abinadab and Esh-Baal.*b*

40The son of Jonathan:
Merib-Baal,*c* who was the father of Micah.

41The sons of Micah:
Pithon, Melech, Tahrea and Ahaz.*d*

42Ahaz was the father of Jadah, Jadah*e* was the father of Alemeth, Azmaveth and Zimri, and Zimri was the father of Moza.

43Moza was the father of Binea;

Rephaiah was his son, Eleasah his son and Azel his son.

44Azel had six sons, and these were their names:
Azrikam, Bokeru, Ishmael, Sheariah, Obadiah and Hanan. These were the sons of Azel.

Saul Takes His Life

10 Now the Philistines fought against Israel; the Israelites fled before them, and many fell slain on Mount Gilboa. **2**The Philistines pressed hard after Saul and his sons, and they killed his sons Jonathan, Abinadab and Malki-Shua. **3**The fighting grew fierce around Saul, and when the archers overtook him, they wounded him.

4Saul said to his armor-bearer, "Draw your sword and run me through, or these uncircumcised fellows will come and abuse me."

But his armor-bearer was terrified and would not do it; so Saul took his own sword and fell on it. **5**When the armor-bearer saw that Saul was dead, he too fell on his sword and died. **6**So Saul and his three sons died, and all his house died together.

7When all the Israelites in the valley saw that the army had fled and that Saul and his sons had died, they abandoned their towns and fled. And the Philistines came and occupied them.

8The next day, when the Philistines came to strip the dead, they found Saul and his sons fallen on Mount Gilboa.

---

a35 Father may mean *civic leader* or *military leader.*
b39 Also known as *Ish-Bosheth*　　*c40* Also known as *Mephibosheth*　　*d41* Vulgate and Syriac (see also Septuagint and 1 Chron. 8:35); Hebrew does not have *and Ahaz.*　　*e42* Some Hebrew manuscripts and Septuagint (see also 1 Chron. 8:36); most Hebrew manuscripts *Jarah, Jarah*

POINT OF INTEREST　　1 Chronicles 10:4

Saul had begun to rule with God's support and blessing, but his reign ended in defeat and suicide. What do you think might have happened if Saul had repented and asked God for help? Jesus said it is never too late to ask for aid (see Luke 8:49–50).

9They stripped him and took his head and his armor, and sent messengers throughout the land of the Philistines to proclaim the news among their idols and their people. 10They put his armor in the temple of their gods and hung up his head in the temple of Dagon.

11When all the inhabitants of Jabesh Gilead heard of everything the Philistines had done to Saul, 12all their valiant men went and took the bodies of Saul and his sons and brought them to Jabesh. Then they buried their bones under the great tree in Jabesh, and they fasted seven days.

13Saul died because he was unfaithful to the LORD; he did not keep the word of the LORD and even consulted a medium for guidance, 14and did not inquire of the LORD. So the LORD put him to death and turned the kingdom over to David son of Jesse.

David Becomes King Over Israel

All Israel came together to David at Hebron and said, "We are your own flesh and blood. 2In the past, even while Saul was king, you were the one who led Israel on their military campaigns. And the LORD your God said to you, 'You will shepherd my people Israel, and you will become their ruler.'"

3When all the elders of Israel had come to King David at Hebron, he made a compact with them at Hebron before the LORD, and they anointed David king over Israel, as the LORD had promised through Samuel.

David Conquers Jerusalem

4David and all the Israelites marched to Jerusalem (that is, Jebus). The Jebusites who lived there 5said to David, "You will not get in here." Nevertheless, David captured the fortress of Zion, the City of David.

6David had said, "Whoever leads the attack on the Jebusites will become commander-in-chief." Joab son of Zeruiah went up first, and so he received the command.

7David then took up residence in the fortress, and so it was called the City of David. 8He built up the city around it, from the supporting terracesa to the surrounding wall, while Joab restored the rest of the city. 9And David became more and more powerful, because the LORD Almighty was with him.

David's Mighty Men

10These were the chiefs of David's mighty men—they, together with all Israel, gave his kingship strong support to extend it over the whole land, as the LORD had promised— 11this is the list of David's mighty men:

Jashobeam,b a Hacmonite, was chief of the officersc; he raised his spear against three hundred men, whom he killed in one encounter.

12Next to him was Eleazar son of Dodai the Ahohite, one of the three mighty men. 13He was with David at Pas Dammim when the Philistines gathered there for battle. At a place where there was a field full of barley, the troops fled from the Philistines. 14But they took their stand in the middle of the field. They defended it and struck the Philistines down, and the LORD brought about a great victory.

15Three of the thirty chiefs came down to David to the rock at the cave of Adullam, while a band of Philistines was encamped in the Valley of Rephaim. 16At that time David was in the stronghold, and the Philistine garrison was at Bethlehem. 17David longed for water and said, "Oh, that someone would get me a drink of water from the well near the gate of Bethlehem!" 18So the Three broke through the Philistine lines, drew water from the well near the gate of Bethlehem and carried it back to David. But he refused to drink it; instead, he poured it out before the LORD. 19"God forbid that I should do this!" he said. "Should I drink the blood of these men who went at the risk of their lives?" Because they risked their lives to bring it back, David would not drink it.

Such were the exploits of the three mighty men.

20Abishai the brother of Joab was chief of the Three. He raised his spear against three hundred men, whom he killed, and so he became as famous as the Three. 21He was doubly honored above the Three and became their commander, even though he was not included among them.

22Benaiah son of Jehoiada was a valiant fighter from Kabzeel, who performed great exploits. He struck down two of

---

a8 Or the Millo   b11 Possibly a variant of Jashob-Baal   c11 Or Thirty; some Septuagint manuscripts Three (see also 2 Samuel 23:8)

Moab's best men. He also went down into a pit on a snowy day and killed a lion. 23And he struck down an Egyptian who was seven and a half feet*a* tall. Although the Egyptian had a spear like a weaver's rod in his hand, Benaiah went against him with a club. He snatched the spear from the Egyptian's hand and killed him with his own spear. 24Such were the exploits of Benaiah son of Jehoiada; he too was as famous as the three mighty men. 25He was held in greater honor than any of the Thirty, but he was not included among the Three. And David put him in charge of his bodyguard.

26The mighty men were:
Asahel the brother of Joab,
Elhanan son of Dodo from Bethlehem,
27Shammoth the Harorite,
Helez the Pelonite,
28Ira son of Ikkesh from Tekoa,
Abiezer from Anathoth,
29Sibbecai the Hushathite,
Ilai the Ahohite,
30Maharai the Netophathite,
Heled son of Baanah the Netophathite,
31Ithai son of Ribai from Gibeah in Benjamin,
Benaiah the Pirathonite,
32Hurai from the ravines of Gaash,
Abiel the Arbathite,
33Azmaveth the Baharumite,
Eliahba the Shaalbonite,
34the sons of Hashem the Gizonite,
Jonathan son of Shagee the Hararite,
35Ahiam son of Sacar the Hararite,
Eliphal son of Ur,
36Hepher the Mekerathite,
Ahijah the Pelonite,
37Hezro the Carmelite,
Naarai son of Ezbai,
38Joel the brother of Nathan,
Mibhar son of Hagri,
39Zelek the Ammonite,
Naharai the Berothite, the armor-bearer of Joab son of Zeruiah,
40Ira the Ithrite,
Gareb the Ithrite,
41Uriah the Hittite,
Zabad son of Ahlai,
42Adina son of Shiza the Reubenite, who was chief of the Reubenites, and the thirty with him,

43Hanan son of Maacah,
Joshaphat the Mithnite,
44Uzzia the Ashterathite,
Shama and Jeiel the sons of Hotham the Aroerite,
45Jediael son of Shimri,
his brother Joha the Tizite,
46Eliel the Mahavite,
Jeribai and Joshaviah the sons of Elnaam,
Ithmah the Moabite,
47Eliel, Obed and Jaasiel the Mezobaite.

Warriors Join David

12 These were the men who came to David at Ziklag, while he was banished from the presence of Saul son of Kish (they were among the warriors who helped him in battle; 2they were armed with bows and were able to shoot arrows or to sling stones right-handed or left-handed; they were kinsmen of Saul from the tribe of Benjamin):

3Ahiezer their chief and Joash the sons of Shemaah the Gibeathite; Jeziel and Pelet the sons of Azmaveth; Beracah, Jehu the Anathothite, 4and Ishmaiah the Gibeonite, a mighty man among the Thirty, who was a leader of the Thirty; Jeremiah, Jahaziel, Johanan, Jozabad the Gederathite, 5Eluzai, Jerimoth, Bealiah, Shemariah and Shephatiah the Haruphite; 6Elkanah, Isshiah, Azarel, Joezer and Jashobeam the Korahites; 7and Joelah and Zebadiah the sons of Jeroham from Gedor.

8Some Gadites defected to David at his stronghold in the desert. They were brave warriors, ready for battle and able to handle the shield and spear. Their faces were the faces of lions, and they were as swift as gazelles in the mountains.
9Ezer was the chief,
Obadiah the second in command,
Eliab the third,
10Mishmannah the fourth, Jeremiah the fifth,
11Attai the sixth, Eliel the seventh,
12Johanan the eighth, Elzabad the ninth,
13Jeremiah the tenth and Macbannai the eleventh.
14These Gadites were army command-

a23 Hebrew *five cubits* (about 2.3 meters)

ers; the least was a match for a hundred, and the greatest for a thousand. ¹⁵It was they who crossed the Jordan in the first month when it was overflowing all its banks, and they put to flight everyone living in the valleys, to the east and to the west.

¹⁶Other Benjamites and some men from Judah also came to David in his stronghold. ¹⁷David went out to meet them and said to them, "If you have come to me in peace, to help me, I am ready to have you unite with me. But if you have come to betray me to my enemies when my hands are free from violence, may the God of our fathers see it and judge you."

¹⁸Then the Spirit came upon Amasai, chief of the Thirty, and he said:

"We are yours, O David!
    We are with you, O son of Jesse!
Success, success to you,
    and success to those who help
        you,
    for your God will help you."

So David received them and made them leaders of his raiding bands.

¹⁹Some of the men of Manasseh defected to David when he went with the Philistines to fight against Saul. (He and his men did not help the Philistines because, after consultation, their rulers sent him away. They said, "It will cost us our heads if he deserts to his master Saul.") ²⁰When David went to Ziklag, these were the men of Manasseh who defected to him: Adnah, Jozabad, Jediael, Michael, Jozabad, Elihu and Zillethai, leaders of units of a thousand in Manasseh. ²¹They helped David against raiding bands, for all of them were brave warriors, and they were commanders in his army. ²²Day after day men came to help David, until he had a great army, like the army of God.ᵃ

Others Join David at Hebron

²³These are the numbers of the men armed for battle who came to David at Hebron to turn Saul's kingdom over to him, as the LORD had said:

²⁴men of Judah, carrying shield and spear—6,800 armed for battle;
²⁵men of Simeon, warriors ready for battle—7,100;
²⁶men of Levi—4,600, ²⁷including Jehoiada, leader of the family of Aaron, with 3,700 men, ²⁸and Zadok, a brave young warrior,

with 22 officers from his family;
²⁹men of Benjamin, Saul's kinsmen—3,000, most of whom had remained loyal to Saul's house until then;
³⁰men of Ephraim, brave warriors, famous in their own clans—20,800;
³¹men of half the tribe of Manasseh, designated by name to come and make David king—18,000;
³²men of Issachar, who understood the times and knew what Israel should do—200 chiefs, with all their relatives under their command;
³³men of Zebulun, experienced soldiers prepared for battle with every type of weapon, to help David with undivided loyalty—50,000;
³⁴men of Naphtali—1,000 officers, together with 37,000 men carrying shields and spears;
³⁵men of Dan, ready for battle—28,600;
³⁶men of Asher, experienced soldiers prepared for battle—40,000;
³⁷and from east of the Jordan, men of Reuben, Gad and the half-tribe of Manasseh, armed with every type of weapon—120,000.

³⁸All these were fighting men who volunteered to serve in the ranks. They came to Hebron fully determined to make David king over all Israel. All the rest of the Israelites were also of one mind to make David king. ³⁹The men spent three days there with David, eating and drinking, for their families had supplied provisions for them. ⁴⁰Also, their neighbors from as far away as Issachar, Zebulun and Naphtali came bringing food on don-

---

ᵃ22 Or *a great and mighty army*

POINT OF INTEREST

1 Chronicles 12:8

Note the metaphors used to describe the attributes of the men who followed David. Lions are fearless and feared by all. Gazelles are quick and sure-footed. These Gadites were not "weekend warriors"; they were skilled soldiers.

keys, camels, mules and oxen. There were plentiful supplies of flour, fig cakes, raisin cakes, wine, oil, cattle and sheep, for there was joy in Israel.

Bringing Back the Ark

13 David conferred with each of his officers, the commanders of thousands and commanders of hundreds. ²He then said to the whole assembly of Israel, "If it seems good to you and if it is the will of the LORD our God, let us send word far and wide to the rest of our brothers throughout the territories of Israel, and also to the priests and Levites who are with them in their towns and pasturelands, to come and join us. ³Let us bring the ark of our God back to us, for we did not inquire of*a* it*b* during the reign of Saul." ⁴The whole assembly agreed to do this, because it seemed right to all the people.

⁵So David assembled all the Israelites, from the Shihor River in Egypt to Lebo*c* Hamath, to bring the ark of God from Kiriath Jearim. ⁶David and all the Israelites with him went to Baalah of Judah (Kiriath Jearim) to bring up from there the ark of God the LORD, who is enthroned between the cherubim—the ark that is called by the Name.

⁷They moved the ark of God from Abinadab's house on a new cart, with Uzzah and Ahio guiding it. ⁸David and all the Israelites were celebrating with all their might before God, with songs and with harps, lyres, tambourines, cymbals and trumpets.

⁹When they came to the threshing floor of Kidon, Uzzah reached out his hand to steady the ark, because the oxen stumbled. ¹⁰The LORD's anger burned against Uzzah, and he struck him down because he had put his hand on the ark. So he died there before God.

¹¹Then David was angry because the LORD's wrath had broken out against Uzzah, and to this day that place is called Perez Uzzah.*d*

¹²David was afraid of God that day and asked, "How can I ever bring the ark of God to me?" ¹³He did not take the ark to be with him in the City of David. Instead, he took it aside to the house of Obed-Edom the Gittite. ¹⁴The ark of God remained with the family of Obed-Edom in his house for three months, and the LORD blessed his household and everything he had.

David's House and Family

14 Now Hiram king of Tyre sent messengers to David, along with cedar logs, stonemasons and carpenters to build a palace for him. ²And David knew that the LORD had established him as king over Israel and that his kingdom had been highly exalted for the sake of his people Israel.

³In Jerusalem David took more wives and became the father of more sons and daughters. ⁴These are the names of the children born to him there: Shammua, Shobab, Nathan, Solomon, ⁵Ibhar, Elishua, Elpelet, ⁶Nogah, Nepheg, Japhia, ⁷Elishama, Beeliada*e* and Eliphelet.

David Defeats the Philistines

⁸When the Philistines heard that David had been anointed king over all Israel, they went up in full force to search for him, but David heard about it and went out to meet them. ⁹Now the Philistines had come and raided the Valley of Rephaim; ¹⁰so David inquired of God: "Shall I go and attack the Philistines? Will you hand them over to me?"

The LORD answered him, "Go, I will hand them over to you."

¹¹So David and his men went up to Baal Perazim, and there he defeated them. He said, "As waters break out, God has broken out against my enemies by my hand." So that place was called Baal Perazim.*f* ¹²The Philistines had abandoned their gods there, and David gave orders to burn them in the fire.

¹³Once more the Philistines raided the

---

*a*3 Or we neglected   *b*3 Or him   *c*5 Or to the entrance to   *d*11 Perez Uzzah means outbreak against Uzzah.   *e*7 A variant of Eliada   *f*11 Baal Perazim means the lord who breaks out.

POINT OF INTEREST   1 Chronicles 13:9

Though Uzzah had good intentions in trying to steady the ark, his motives could not make up for disobeying God's law (see Exodus 25:10–22). The ark symbolized God's holiness, a holiness that would not accept sin in any form. Through Jesus Christ, we have access to God that Uzzah never had (see Ephesians 3:12).

valley; ¹⁴so David inquired of God again, and God answered him, "Do not go straight up, but circle around them and attack them in front of the balsam trees. ¹⁵As soon as you hear the sound of marching in the tops of the balsam trees, move out to battle, because that will mean God has gone out in front of you to strike the Philistine army." ¹⁶So David did as God commanded him, and they struck down the Philistine army, all the way from Gibeon to Gezer.

¹⁷So David's fame spread throughout every land, and the LORD made all the nations fear him.

The Ark Brought to Jerusalem

15 After David had constructed buildings for himself in the City of David, he prepared a place for the ark of God and pitched a tent for it. ²Then David said, "No one but the Levites may carry the ark of God, because the LORD chose them to carry the ark of the LORD and to minister before him forever."

³David assembled all Israel in Jerusalem to bring up the ark of the LORD to the place he had prepared for it. ⁴He called together the descendants of Aaron and the Levites:

⁵From the descendants of Kohath,
Uriel the leader and 120 relatives;
⁶from the descendants of Merari,
Asaiah the leader and 220 relatives;
⁷from the descendants of Gershon,ᵃ
Joel the leader and 130 relatives;
⁸from the descendants of Elizaphan,
Shemaiah the leader and 200 relatives;
⁹from the descendants of Hebron,
Eliel the leader and 80 relatives;
¹⁰from the descendants of Uzziel,
Amminadab the leader and 112 relatives.

¹¹Then David summoned Zadok and Abiathar the priests, and Uriel, Asaiah, Joel, Shemaiah, Eliel and Amminadab the Levites. ¹²He said to them, "You are the heads of the Levitical families; you and your fellow Levites are to consecrate yourselves and bring up the ark of the LORD, the God of Israel, to the place I have prepared for it. ¹³It was because you, the Levites, did not bring it up the first time that the LORD our God broke out in anger against us. We did not inquire of him

about how to do it in the prescribed way." ¹⁴So the priests and Levites consecrated themselves in order to bring up the ark of the LORD, the God of Israel. ¹⁵And the Levites carried the ark of God with the poles on their shoulders, as Moses had commanded in accordance with the word of the LORD.

¹⁶David told the leaders of the Levites to appoint their brothers as singers to sing joyful songs, accompanied by musical instruments: lyres, harps and cymbals.

¹⁷So the Levites appointed Heman son of Joel; from his brothers, Asaph son of Berekiah; and from their brothers the Merarites, Ethan son of Kushaiah; ¹⁸and with them their brothers next in rank: Zechariah,ᵇ Jaaziel, Shemiramoth, Jehiel, Unni, Eliab, Benaiah, Maaseiah, Mattithiah, Eliphelehu, Mikneiah, Obed-Edom and Jeiel,ᶜ the gatekeepers. ¹⁹The musicians Heman, Asaph and Ethan were to sound the bronze cymbals; ²⁰Zechariah, Aziel, Shemiramoth, Jehiel, Unni, Eliab, Maaseiah and Benaiah were to play the lyres according to *alamoth,*ᵈ ²¹and Mattithiah, Eliphelehu, Mikneiah, Obed-Edom, Jeiel and Azaziah were to play the harps, directing according to *sheminith.*ᵈ ²²Kenaniah the head Levite was in charge of the singing; that was his responsibility because he was skillful at it.

²³Berekiah and Elkanah were to be doorkeepers for the ark. ²⁴Shebaniah, Joshaphat, Nethanel, Amasai, Zechariah, Benaiah and Eliezer the priests were to blow trumpets before the ark of God. Obed-Edom and Jehiah were also to be doorkeepers for the ark.

²⁵So David and the elders of Israel and the commanders of units of a thousand went to bring up the ark of the covenant of the LORD from the house of Obed-Edom, with rejoicing. ²⁶Because God had helped the Levites who were carrying the ark of the covenant of the LORD, seven bulls and seven rams were sacrificed. ²⁷Now David was clothed in a robe of fine linen, as were all the Levites who were carrying the ark, and as were the singers,

ᵃ7 Hebrew *Gershom,* a variant of *Gershon*
ᵇ18 Three Hebrew manuscripts and most Septuagint manuscripts (see also verse 20 and 1 Chron. 16:5); most Hebrew manuscripts *Zechariah son and* or *Zechariah, Ben and*   ᶜ18 Hebrew; Septuagint (see also verse 21) *Jeiel and Azaziah*   ᵈ20,21 Probably a musical term

and Kenaniah, who was in charge of the singing of the choirs. David also wore a linen ephod. 28So all Israel brought up the ark of the covenant of the LORD with shouts, with the sounding of rams' horns and trumpets, and of cymbals, and the playing of lyres and harps.

29As the ark of the covenant of the LORD was entering the City of David, Michal daughter of Saul watched from a window. And when she saw King David dancing and celebrating, she despised him in her heart.

16 They brought the ark of God and set it inside the tent that David had pitched for it, and they presented burnt offerings and fellowship offerings*a* before God. 2After David had finished sacrificing the burnt offerings and fellowship offerings, he blessed the people in the name of the LORD. 3Then he gave a loaf of bread, a cake of dates and a cake of raisins to each Israelite man and woman.

4He appointed some of the Levites to minister before the ark of the LORD, to make petition, to give thanks, and to praise the LORD, the God of Israel: 5Asaph was the chief, Zechariah second, then Jeiel, Shemiramoth, Jehiel, Mattithiah, Eliab, Benaiah, Obed-Edom and Jeiel. They were to play the lyres and harps, Asaph was to sound the cymbals, 6and Benaiah and Jahaziel the priests were to blow the trumpets regularly before the ark of the covenant of God.

David's Psalm of Thanks

7That day David first committed to Asaph and his associates this psalm of thanks to the LORD:

a 1 Traditionally peace offerings; also in verse 2

THURSDAY

Read 1 Chronicles 15:11–29
Key Verses 1 Chronicles 15:22–23

Lessons From a Doorkeeper – Bill Mowry

"Where's Jim? We can't get started without him!"

Who was Jim? Was he the main speaker? The person in charge of the event? No, Jim was the behind-the-scenes guy. He was the person who knew the ins and outs of the sound system, the individual who knew where to find everything needed to successfully run a student conference, the one who could be counted on to set up the meeting rooms. No one really saw Jim because he was never in front of the audience, but the leaders knew how important he was.

God has recorded for all eternity the service of two men, Berekiah and Elkanah. Did they lead nations, preach stirring sermons, convert empires? Not exactly. They were doorkeepers. Doorkeeping may seem like a menial task to us, but it was a very important job in God's eyes.

There are lessons to learn from Berekiah and Elkanah—and from my friend Jim. Everyone who serves God is important. Fortunately, God shows us that our worth is found in doing the work he has chosen especially for us, not in the glamour of public popularity. It's important to do what God gives us the skill to do (see 1 Chronicles 15:22). If a doorkeeper can make it onto the pages of the Bible, we can be sure that no service for God will go unnoticed or unappreciated.

A Deeper Look
1 Corinthians 1:27–29; 1 Corinthians 12:14–27

Go to page 448 for your next devotional reading.

⁸Give thanks to the LORD, call on his
  name;
  make known among the nations
  what he has done.
⁹Sing to him, sing praise to him;
  tell of all his wonderful acts.
¹⁰Glory in his holy name;
  let the hearts of those who seek
  the LORD rejoice.
¹¹Look to the LORD and his strength;
  seek his face always.
¹²Remember the wonders he has done,
  his miracles, and the judgments he
  pronounced,
¹³O descendants of Israel his servant,
  O sons of Jacob, his chosen ones.

¹⁴He is the LORD our God;
  his judgments are in all the earth.
¹⁵He remembers*ᵃ* his covenant
  forever,
  the word he commanded, for a
  thousand generations,
¹⁶the covenant he made with Abraham,

the oath he swore to Isaac.
¹⁷He confirmed it to Jacob as a decree,
  to Israel as an everlasting
  covenant:
¹⁸"To you I will give the land of
  Canaan
  as the portion you will inherit."

¹⁹When they were but few in number,
  few indeed, and strangers in it,
²⁰theyᵇ wandered from nation to
  nation,
  from one kingdom to another.
²¹He allowed no man to oppress them;
  for their sake he rebuked kings:
²²"Do not touch my anointed ones;
  do my prophets no harm."

²³Sing to the LORD, all the earth;

ᵃ15 Some Septuagint manuscripts (see also Psalm
105:8); Hebrew *Remember*   *ᵇ18-20* One Hebrew
manuscript, Septuagint and Vulgate (see also Psalm
105:12); most Hebrew manuscripts *inherit,* /
¹⁹though you are but few in number, / *few indeed, and*
strangers in it." / *²⁰They*

FRIDAY

Read *1 Chronicles 16:1–43*
Key Verses *1 Chronicles 16:11–12*

Remember! —Inger Rudolph

I've had a hard day, struggling for answers about my future. My
emotions are raw. I still don't know where God wants me. He tells
me to seek him, his strength and his face, but how? As I read
1 Chronicles 16:11, I realize that God wants me to remember what
he's already done for me.

God provided for the Shunammite woman through Elisha (see
2 Kings 4:8–37). He gave her what she desired most, and when it
was taken away, he restored it to her again. God has often done
that very thing for me. As I remember those times, I am refreshed by
his love and goodness, by what he's given me, often even beyond
what I've asked for. I am reminded by Almighty God that his
strength is great enough, and so is his love.

God knows what I need, just as he knew what the Shunammite
woman needed. He's proved it before. As my immediate need for
answers melts into confidence and peace, I understand why he says
"seek" and "remember."

Have you had a hard day? Are you seeking the face of the One
who knows all about you and knows what you're going through?
Have your eyes connected with his? Have they in the past? If so,
don't forget. Remember!

A Deeper Look
Psalm 63; Isaiah 55:6–12; Jeremiah 29:12–13

Go to page 462 for your next devotional reading.

proclaim his salvation day after
  day.
²⁴Declare his glory among the nations,
  his marvelous deeds among all
    peoples.
²⁵For great is the Lord and most worthy
    of praise;
  he is to be feared above all gods.
²⁶For all the gods of the nations are
    idols,
  but the Lord made the heavens.
²⁷Splendor and majesty are before him;
  strength and joy in his dwelling
    place.
²⁸Ascribe to the Lord, O families of
    nations,
  ascribe to the Lord glory and
    strength,
²⁹ ascribe to the Lord the glory due
    his name.
  Bring an offering and come before
    him;
  worship the Lord in the splendor of
    his*ᵃ* holiness.
³⁰Tremble before him, all the earth!
  The world is firmly established; it
    cannot be moved.
³¹Let the heavens rejoice, let the earth
    be glad;
  let them say among the nations,
    "The Lord reigns!"
³²Let the sea resound, and all that is in
    it;
  let the fields be jubilant, and
    everything in them!
³³Then the trees of the forest will sing,
  they will sing for joy before the
    Lord,
  for he comes to judge the earth.

³⁴Give thanks to the Lord, for he is
    good;
  his love endures forever.
³⁵Cry out, "Save us, O God our Savior;
  gather us and deliver us from the
    nations,
  that we may give thanks to your holy
    name,
  that we may glory in your praise."
³⁶Praise be to the Lord, the God of
    Israel,
  from everlasting to everlasting.

Then all the people said "Amen" and
"Praise the Lord."

³⁷David left Asaph and his associates
before the ark of the covenant of the Lord
to minister there regularly, according to
each day's requirements. ³⁸He also left

Obed-Edom and his sixty-eight associates to minister with them. Obed-Edom
son of Jeduthun, and also Hosah, were
gatekeepers.

³⁹David left Zadok the priest and his
fellow priests before the tabernacle of the
Lord at the high place in Gibeon ⁴⁰to
present burnt offerings to the Lord on the
altar of burnt offering regularly, morning
and evening, in accordance with everything written in the Law of the Lord,
which he had given Israel. ⁴¹With them
were Heman and Jeduthun and the rest
of those chosen and designated by name
to give thanks to the Lord, "for his love
endures forever." ⁴²Heman and Jeduthun
were responsible for the sounding of the
trumpets and cymbals and for the playing
of the other instruments for sacred song.
The sons of Jeduthun were stationed at
the gate.

⁴³Then all the people left, each for his
own home, and David returned home to
bless his family.

God's Promise to David

17 After David was settled in his palace,
he said to Nathan the prophet, "Here
I am, living in a palace of cedar, while the
ark of the covenant of the Lord is under
a tent."

²Nathan replied to David, "Whatever
you have in mind, do it, for God is with
you."

³That night the word of God came to
Nathan, saying:

⁴"Go and tell my servant David,
'This is what the Lord says: You are
not the one to build me a house to
dwell in. ⁵I have not dwelt in a
house from the day I brought Israel
up out of Egypt to this day. I have
moved from one tent site to another, from one dwelling place to another. ⁶Wherever I have moved
with all the Israelites, did I ever say
to any of their leaders*ᵇ* whom I
commanded to shepherd my people, "Why have you not built me a
house of cedar?" '

⁷"Now then, tell my servant David, 'This is what the Lord Almighty
says: I took you from the pasture
and from following the flock, to be
ruler over my people Israel. ⁸I have
been with you wherever you have

---

*ᵃ*29 Or Lord *with the splendor of*
*ᵇ*6 Traditionally *judges*; also in verse 10

gone, and I have cut off all your enemies from before you. Now I will make your name like the names of the greatest men of the earth. ⁹And I will provide a place for my people Israel and will plant them so that they can have a home of their own and no longer be disturbed. Wicked people will not oppress them anymore, as they did at the beginning ¹⁰and have done ever since the time I appointed leaders over my people Israel. I will also subdue all your enemies.

" 'I declare to you that the LORD will build a house for you: ¹¹When your days are over and you go to be with your fathers, I will raise up your offspring to succeed you, one of your own sons, and I will establish his kingdom. ¹²He is the one who will build a house for me, and I will establish his throne forever. ¹³I will be his father, and he will be my son. I will never take my love away from him, as I took it away from your predecessor. ¹⁴I will set him over my house and my kingdom forever; his throne will be established forever.' "

¹⁵Nathan reported to David all the words of this entire revelation.

David's Prayer

¹⁶Then King David went in and sat before the LORD, and he said:

"Who am I, O LORD God, and what is my family, that you have brought me this far? ¹⁷And as if this were not enough in your sight, O God, you have spoken about the future of the house of your servant. You have looked on me as though I were the most exalted of men, O LORD God.

¹⁸"What more can David say to you for honoring your servant? For you know your servant, ¹⁹O LORD. For the sake of your servant and according to your will, you have done this great thing and made known all these great promises.

²⁰"There is no one like you, O LORD, and there is no God but you, as we have heard with our own ears. ²¹And who is like your people Israel—the one nation on earth whose God went out to re-deem a people for himself, and to make a name for yourself, and to perform great and awesome wonders by driving out nations from before your people, whom you redeemed from Egypt? ²²You made your people Israel your very own forever, and you, O LORD, have become their God.

²³"And now, LORD, let the promise you have made concerning your servant and his house be established forever. Do as you promised, ²⁴so that it will be established and that your name will be great forever. Then men will say, 'The LORD Almighty, the God over Israel, is Israel's God!' And the house of your servant David will be established before you.

²⁵"You, my God, have revealed to your servant that you will build a house for him. So your servant has found courage to pray to you. ²⁶O LORD, you are God! You have promised these good things to your servant. ²⁷Now you have been pleased to bless the house of your servant, that it may continue forever in your sight; for you, O LORD, have blessed it, and it will be blessed forever."

David's Victories

18 In the course of time, David defeated the Philistines and subdued them, and he took Gath and its surrounding villages from the control of the Philistines.

²David also defeated the Moabites, and they became subject to him and brought tribute.

³Moreover, David fought Hadadezer

POINT OF INTEREST

1 Chronicles 17:13

These verses refer to the Messianic King who would come from David's line. The concept of a father/son relationship between God and a person was revolutionary in Bible times. In fact, Jesus' claim of this intimate relationship prompted the people's incensed reaction in John 10:29–33.

king of Zobah, as far as Hamath, when he went to establish his control along the Euphrates River. [4]David captured a thousand of his chariots, seven thousand charioteers and twenty thousand foot soldiers. He hamstrung all but a hundred of the chariot horses.

[5]When the Arameans of Damascus came to help Hadadezer king of Zobah, David struck down twenty-two thousand of them. [6]He put garrisons in the Aramean kingdom of Damascus, and the Arameans became subject to him and brought tribute. The LORD gave David victory everywhere he went.

[7]David took the gold shields carried by the officers of Hadadezer and brought them to Jerusalem. [8]From Tebah[a] and Cun, towns that belonged to Hadadezer, David took a great quantity of bronze, which Solomon used to make the bronze Sea, the pillars and various bronze articles.

[9]When Tou king of Hamath heard that David had defeated the entire army of Hadadezer king of Zobah, [10]he sent his son Hadoram to King David to greet him and congratulate him on his victory in battle over Hadadezer, who had been at war with Tou. Hadoram brought all kinds of articles of gold and silver and bronze.

[11]King David dedicated these articles to the LORD, as he had done with the silver and gold he had taken from all these nations: Edom and Moab, the Ammonites and the Philistines, and Amalek.

[12]Abishai son of Zeruiah struck down eighteen thousand Edomites in the Valley of Salt. [13]He put garrisons in Edom, and all the Edomites became subject to David. The LORD gave David victory everywhere he went.

David's Officials

[14]David reigned over all Israel, doing what was just and right for all his people. [15]Joab son of Zeruiah was over the army; Jehoshaphat son of Ahilud was recorder; [16]Zadok son of Ahitub and Ahimelech[b] son of Abiathar were priests; Shavsha was secretary; [17]Benaiah son of Jehoiada was over the Kerethites and Pelethites; and David's sons were chief officials at the king's side.

The Battle Against the Ammonites

19 In the course of time, Nahash king of the Ammonites died, and his son succeeded him as king. [2]David thought, "I will show kindness to Hanun son of Nahash, because his father showed kindness to me." So David sent a delegation to express his sympathy to Hanun concerning his father.

When David's men came to Hanun in the land of the Ammonites to express sympathy to him, [3]the Ammonite nobles said to Hanun, "Do you think David is honoring your father by sending men to you to express sympathy? Haven't his men come to you to explore and spy out the country and overthrow it?" [4]So Hanun seized David's men, shaved them, cut off their garments in the middle at the buttocks, and sent them away.

[5]When someone came and told David about the men, he sent messengers to meet them, for they were greatly humiliated. The king said, "Stay at Jericho till your beards have grown, and then come back."

[6]When the Ammonites realized that they had become a stench in David's nostrils, Hanun and the Ammonites sent a thousand talents[c] of silver to hire chariots and charioteers from Aram Naharaim,[d] Aram Maacah and Zobah. [7]They hired thirty-two thousand chariots and charioteers, as well as the king of Maacah with his troops, who came and camped near Medeba, while the Ammonites were mustered from their towns and moved out for battle.

[8]On hearing this, David sent Joab out with the entire army of fighting men. [9]The Ammonites came out and drew up in battle formation at the entrance to their city, while the kings who had come were by themselves in the open country.

[10]Joab saw that there were battle lines in front of him and behind him; so he selected some of the best troops in Israel and deployed them against the Arameans. [11]He put the rest of the men under the command of Abishai his brother, and they were deployed against the Ammonites. [12]Joab said, "If the Arameans are too strong for me, then you are to rescue me; but if the Ammonites are too strong for you, then I will rescue you. [13]Be strong and let us fight bravely for our people

---

[a]8 Hebrew *Tibhath*, a variant of *Tebah*
[b]16 Some Hebrew manuscripts, Vulgate and Syriac (see also 2 Samuel 8:17); most Hebrew manuscripts *Abimelech*   [c]6 That is, about 37 tons (about 34 metric tons)   [d]6 That is, Northwest Mesopotamia

and the cities of our God. The LORD will do what is good in his sight."

¹⁴Then Joab and the troops with him advanced to fight the Arameans, and they fled before him. ¹⁵When the Ammonites saw that the Arameans were fleeing, they too fled before his brother Abishai and went inside the city. So Joab went back to Jerusalem.

¹⁶After the Arameans saw that they had been routed by Israel, they sent messengers and had Arameans brought from beyond the River,ᵃ with Shophach the commander of Hadadezer's army leading them.

¹⁷When David was told of this, he gathered all Israel and crossed the Jordan; he advanced against them and formed his battle lines opposite them. David formed his lines to meet the Arameans in battle, and they fought against him. ¹⁸But they fled before Israel, and David killed seven thousand of their charioteers and forty thousand of their foot soldiers. He also killed Shophach the commander of their army.

¹⁹When the vassals of Hadadezer saw that they had been defeated by Israel, they made peace with David and became subject to him.

So the Arameans were not willing to help the Ammonites anymore.

The Capture of Rabbah

20 In the spring, at the time when kings go off to war, Joab led out the armed forces. He laid waste the land of the Ammonites and went to Rabbah and besieged it, but David remained in Jerusalem. Joab attacked Rabbah and left it in ruins. ²David took the crown from the head of their kingᵇ—its weight was found to be a talentᶜ of gold, and it was set with precious stones—and it was placed on David's head. He took a great quantity of plunder from the city ³and brought out the people who were there, consigning them to labor with saws and with iron picks and axes. David did this to all the Ammonite towns. Then David and his entire army returned to Jerusalem.

War With the Philistines

⁴In the course of time, war broke out with the Philistines, at Gezer. At that time Sibbecai the Hushathite killed Sippai, one of the descendants of the Reph-

aites, and the Philistines were subjugated.

⁵In another battle with the Philistines, Elhanan son of Jair killed Lahmi the brother of Goliath the Gittite, who had a spear with a shaft like a weaver's rod.

⁶In still another battle, which took place at Gath, there was a huge man with six fingers on each hand and six toes on each foot—twenty-four in all. He also was descended from Rapha. ⁷When he taunted Israel, Jonathan son of Shimea, David's brother, killed him.

⁸These were descendants of Rapha in Gath, and they fell at the hands of David and his men.

David Numbers the Fighting Men

21 Satan rose up against Israel and incited David to take a census of Israel. ²So David said to Joab and the commanders of the troops, "Go and count the Israelites from Beersheba to Dan. Then report back to me so that I may know how many there are."

³But Joab replied, "May the LORD multiply his troops a hundred times over. My lord the king, are they not all my lord's subjects? Why does my lord want to do this? Why should he bring guilt on Israel?"

⁴The king's word, however, overruled Joab; so Joab left and went throughout Israel and then came back to Jerusalem. ⁵Joab reported the number of the fighting men to David: In all Israel there were one million one hundred thousand men who could handle a sword, including four hundred and seventy thousand in Judah. ⁶But Joab did not include Levi and Benjamin in the numbering, because the king's command was repulsive to him. ⁷This command was also evil in the sight of God; so he punished Israel.

⁸Then David said to God, "I have sinned greatly by doing this. Now, I beg you, take away the guilt of your servant. I have done a very foolish thing."

⁹The LORD said to Gad, David's seer, ¹⁰"Go and tell David, 'This is what the LORD says: I am giving you three options. Choose one of them for me to carry out against you.' "

¹¹So Gad went to David and said to him, "This is what the LORD says: 'Take your choice: ¹²three years of famine,

---

ᵃ16 That is, the Euphrates   ᵇ2 Or of Milcom, that is, Molech   ᶜ2 That is, about 75 pounds (about 34 kilograms) three months of being swept away[a] before your enemies, with their swords overtaking you, or three days of the sword of the LORD—days of plague in the land, with the angel of the LORD ravaging every part of Israel.' Now then, decide how I should answer the one who sent me."

¹³David said to Gad, "I am in deep distress. Let me fall into the hands of the LORD, for his mercy is very great; but do not let me fall into the hands of men."

¹⁴So the LORD sent a plague on Israel, and seventy thousand men of Israel fell dead. ¹⁵And God sent an angel to destroy Jerusalem. But as the angel was doing so, the LORD saw it and was grieved because of the calamity and said to the angel who was destroying the people, "Enough! Withdraw your hand." The angel of the LORD was then standing at the threshing floor of Araunah[b] the Jebusite.

¹⁶David looked up and saw the angel of the LORD standing between heaven and earth, with a drawn sword in his hand extended over Jerusalem. Then David and the elders, clothed in sackcloth, fell facedown.

¹⁷David said to God, "Was it not I who ordered the fighting men to be counted? I am the one who has sinned and done wrong. These are but sheep. What have they done? O LORD my God, let your hand fall upon me and my family, but do not let this plague remain on your people."

¹⁸Then the angel of the LORD ordered Gad to tell David to go up and build an altar to the LORD on the threshing floor of Araunah the Jebusite. ¹⁹So David went up in obedience to the word that Gad had spoken in the name of the LORD.

²⁰While Araunah was threshing wheat, he turned and saw the angel; his four sons who were with him hid themselves. ²¹Then David approached, and when Araunah looked and saw him, he left the threshing floor and bowed down before David with his face to the ground. ²²David said to him, "Let me have the site of your threshing floor so I can build an altar to the LORD, that the plague on the people may be stopped. Sell it to me at the full price."

²³Araunah said to David, "Take it! Let my lord the king do whatever pleases him. Look, I will give the oxen for the burnt offerings, the threshing sledges for the wood, and the wheat for the grain offering. I will give all this."

²⁴But King David replied to Araunah, "No, I insist on paying the full price. I will not take for the LORD what is yours, or sacrifice a burnt offering that costs me nothing."

²⁵So David paid Araunah six hundred shekels[c] of gold for the site. ²⁶David built an altar to the LORD there and sacrificed burnt offerings and fellowship offerings.[d] He called on the LORD, and the LORD answered him with fire from heaven on the altar of burnt offering.

²⁷Then the LORD spoke to the angel, and he put his sword back into its sheath. ²⁸At that time, when David saw that the LORD had answered him on the threshing floor of Araunah the Jebusite, he offered sacrifices there. ²⁹The tabernacle of the LORD, which Moses had made in the desert, and the altar of burnt offering were at that time on the high place at Gibeon. ³⁰But David could not go before it to inquire of God, because he was afraid of the sword of the angel of the LORD.

22 Then David said, "The house of the LORD God is to be here, and also the altar of burnt offering for Israel."

Preparations for the Temple

²So David gave orders to assemble the aliens living in Israel, and from among them he appointed stonecutters to prepare dressed stone for building the house of God. ³He provided a large amount of iron to make nails for the doors of the gateways and for the fittings, and more

---

[a]12 Hebrew; Septuagint and Vulgate (see also 2 Samuel 24:13) *of fleeing*   [b]15 Hebrew *Ornan*, a variant of *Araunah*; also in verses 18-28   [c]25 That is, about 15 pounds (about 7 kilograms)   [d]26 Traditionally *peace offerings*

POINT OF INTEREST

1 Chronicles 21:13

Why was David unafraid of God's punishment? Certainly God was capable of a retribution more terrible than anything that could be meted out by humans. But David realized that God's fundamental goodness and mercy made him an infinitely better disciplinarian than human beings ever could be.

bronze than could be weighed. ⁴He also provided more cedar logs than could be counted, for the Sidonians and Tyrians had brought large numbers of them to David.

⁵David said, "My son Solomon is young and inexperienced, and the house to be built for the LORD should be of great magnificence and fame and splendor in the sight of all the nations. Therefore I will make preparations for it." So David made extensive preparations before his death.

⁶Then he called for his son Solomon and charged him to build a house for the LORD, the God of Israel. ⁷David said to Solomon: "My son, I had it in my heart to build a house for the Name of the LORD my God. ⁸But this word of the LORD came to me: 'You have shed much blood and have fought many wars. You are not to build a house for my Name, because you have shed much blood on the earth in my sight. ⁹But you will have a son who will be a man of peace and rest, and I will give him rest from all his enemies on every side. His name will be Solomon,ᵃ and I will grant Israel peace and quiet during his reign. ¹⁰He is the one who will build a house for my Name. He will be my son, and I will be his father. And I will establish the throne of his kingdom over Israel forever.'

¹¹"Now, my son, the LORD be with you, and may you have success and build the house of the LORD your God, as he said you would. ¹²May the LORD give you discretion and understanding when he puts you in command over Israel, so that you may keep the law of the LORD your God. ¹³Then you will have success if you are careful to observe the decrees and laws that the LORD gave Moses for Israel. Be strong and courageous. Do not be afraid or discouraged.

¹⁴"I have taken great pains to provide for the temple of the LORD a hundred thousand talentsᵇ of gold, a million talentsᶜ of silver, quantities of bronze and iron too great to be weighed, and wood and stone. And you may add to them. ¹⁵You have many workmen: stonecutters, masons and carpenters, as well as men skilled in every kind of work ¹⁶in gold and silver, bronze and iron—craftsmen beyond number. Now begin the work, and the LORD be with you."

¹⁷Then David ordered all the leaders of Israel to help his son Solomon. ¹⁸He said to them, "Is not the LORD your God with you? And has he not granted you rest on every side? For he has handed the inhabitants of the land over to me, and the land is subject to the LORD and to his people. ¹⁹Now devote your heart and soul to seeking the LORD your God. Begin to build the sanctuary of the LORD God, so that you may bring the ark of the covenant of the LORD and the sacred articles belonging to God into the temple that will be built for the Name of the LORD."

The Levites

23 When David was old and full of years, he made his son Solomon king over Israel.

²He also gathered together all the leaders of Israel, as well as the priests and Levites. ³The Levites thirty years old or more were counted, and the total number of men was thirty-eight thousand. ⁴David said, "Of these, twenty-four thousand are to supervise the work of the temple of the LORD and six thousand are to be officials and judges. ⁵Four thousand are to be gatekeepers and four thousand are to praise the LORD with the musical instruments I have provided for that purpose."

⁶David divided the Levites into groups corresponding to the sons of Levi: Gershon, Kohath and Merari.

Gershonites

⁷Belonging to the Gershonites:
　　Ladan and Shimei.
⁸The sons of Ladan:
　　Jehiel the first, Zetham and Joel—three in all.
⁹The sons of Shimei:
　　Shelomoth, Haziel and Haran—three in all.
　　These were the heads of the families of Ladan.
¹⁰And the sons of Shimei:
　　Jahath, Ziza,ᵈ Jeush and Beriah.
　　These were the sons of Shimei—four in all.
¹¹Jahath was the first and Ziza the second, but Jeush and Beriah did not have many sons; so they

---

ᵃ9 *Solomon* sounds like and may be derived from the Hebrew for *peace*.   ᵇ14 That is, about 3,750 tons (about 3,450 metric tons)   ᶜ14 That is, about 37,500 tons (about 34,500 metric tons)   ᵈ10 One Hebrew manuscript, Septuagint and Vulgate (see also verse 11); most Hebrew manuscripts *Zina* were counted as one family with one assignment.

Kohathites

¹²The sons of Kohath:

Amram, Izhar, Hebron and Uzziel—four in all.

¹³The sons of Amram:

Aaron and Moses.

Aaron was set apart, he and his descendants forever, to consecrate the most holy things, to offer sacrifices before the LORD, to minister before him and to pronounce blessings in his name forever. ¹⁴The sons of Moses the man of God were counted as part of the tribe of Levi.

¹⁵The sons of Moses:

Gershom and Eliezer.

¹⁶The descendants of Gershom:

Shubael was the first.

¹⁷The descendants of Eliezer:

Rehabiah was the first.

Eliezer had no other sons, but the sons of Rehabiah were very numerous.

¹⁸The sons of Izhar:

Shelomith was the first.

¹⁹The sons of Hebron:

Jeriah the first, Amariah the second, Jahaziel the third and Jekameam the fourth.

²⁰The sons of Uzziel:

Micah the first and Isshiah the second.

Merarites

²¹The sons of Merari:

Mahli and Mushi.

The sons of Mahli:

Eleazar and Kish.

²²Eleazar died without having sons: he had only daughters. Their cousins, the sons of Kish, married them.

²³The sons of Mushi:

Mahli, Eder and Jerimoth—three in all.

²⁴These were the descendants of Levi by their families—the heads of families as they were registered under their names and counted individually, that is, the workers twenty years old or more who served in the temple of the LORD. ²⁵For David had said, "Since the LORD, the God of Israel, has granted rest to his people and has come to dwell in Jerusalem forever, ²⁶the Levites no longer need to carry the tabernacle or any of the articles used in its service." ²⁷According to the last instructions of David, the Levites were counted from those twenty years old or more.

²⁸The duty of the Levites was to help Aaron's descendants in the service of the temple of the LORD: to be in charge of the courtyards, the side rooms, the purification of all sacred things and the performance of other duties at the house of God. ²⁹They were in charge of the bread set out on the table, the flour for the grain offerings, the unleavened wafers, the baking and the mixing, and all measurements of quantity and size. ³⁰They were also to stand every morning to thank and praise the LORD. They were to do the same in the evening ³¹and whenever burnt offerings were presented to the LORD on Sabbaths and at New Moon festivals and at appointed feasts. They were to serve before the LORD regularly in the proper number and in the way prescribed for them.

³²And so the Levites carried out their responsibilities for the Tent of Meeting, for the Holy Place and, under their brothers the descendants of Aaron, for the service of the temple of the LORD.

The Divisions of Priests

24 These were the divisions of the sons of Aaron:

The sons of Aaron were Nadab, Abihu, Eleazar and Ithamar. ²But Nadab and Abihu died before their father did, and they had no sons; so Eleazar and Ithamar served as the priests. ³With the help of Zadok a descendant of Eleazar and Ahimelech a descendant of Ithamar, David separated them into divisions for their

POINT OF INTEREST   1 Chronicles 23:24

When are people considered adults—when they're old enough to drive, to vote, to get married? Maturity enough for various adult responsibilities comes at different ages. For a Levite, twenty years of age marked the entrance into adult responsibility and temple service.

appointed order of ministering. ⁴A larger number of leaders were found among Eleazar's descendants than among Ithamar's, and they were divided accordingly: sixteen heads of families from Eleazar's descendants and eight heads of families from Ithamar's descendants. ⁵They divided them impartially by drawing lots, for there were officials of the sanctuary and officials of God among the descendants of both Eleazar and Ithamar.

⁶The scribe Shemaiah son of Nethanel, a Levite, recorded their names in the presence of the king and of the officials: Zadok the priest, Ahimelech son of Abiathar and the heads of families of the priests and of the Levites—one family being taken from Eleazar and then one from Ithamar.

⁷The first lot fell to Jehoiarib,
  the second to Jedaiah,
⁸the third to Harim,
  the fourth to Seorim,
⁹the fifth to Malkijah,
  the sixth to Mijamin,
¹⁰the seventh to Hakkoz,
  the eighth to Abijah,
¹¹the ninth to Jeshua,
  the tenth to Shecaniah,
¹²the eleventh to Eliashib,
  the twelfth to Jakim,
¹³the thirteenth to Huppah,
  the fourteenth to Jeshebeab,
¹⁴the fifteenth to Bilgah,
  the sixteenth to Immer,
¹⁵the seventeenth to Hezir,
  the eighteenth to Happizzez,
¹⁶the nineteenth to Pethahiah,
  the twentieth to Jehezkel,
¹⁷the twenty-first to Jakin,
  the twenty-second to Gamul,
¹⁸the twenty-third to Delaiah
  and the twenty-fourth to Maaziah.

¹⁹This was their appointed order of ministering when they entered the temple of the Lord, according to the regulations prescribed for them by their forefather Aaron, as the Lord, the God of Israel, had commanded him.

The Rest of the Levites

²⁰As for the rest of the descendants of Levi:
  from the sons of Amram: Shubael;
  from the sons of Shubael: Jehdeiah.
  ²¹As for Rehabiah, from his sons:
  Isshiah was the first.

²²From the Izharites: Shelomoth;
  from the sons of Shelomoth: Jahath.
²³The sons of Hebron: Jeriah the first,ᵃ Amariah the second, Jahaziel the third and Jekameam the fourth.
²⁴The son of Uzziel: Micah;
  from the sons of Micah: Shamir.
  ²⁵The brother of Micah: Isshiah;
  from the sons of Isshiah: Zechariah.
²⁶The sons of Merari: Mahli and Mushi.
  The son of Jaaziah: Beno.
²⁷The sons of Merari:
  from Jaaziah: Beno, Shoham, Zaccur and Ibri.
²⁸From Mahli: Eleazar, who had no sons.
²⁹From Kish: the son of Kish: Jerahmeel.
³⁰And the sons of Mushi: Mahli, Eder and Jerimoth.

These were the Levites, according to their families. ³¹They also cast lots, just as their brothers the descendants of Aaron did, in the presence of King David and of Zadok, Ahimelech, and the heads of families of the priests and of the Levites. The families of the oldest brother were treated the same as those of the youngest.

The Singers

25 David, together with the commanders of the army, set apart some of the sons of Asaph, Heman and Jeduthun for the ministry of prophesying, accompanied by harps, lyres and cymbals. Here is the list of the men who performed this service:

²From the sons of Asaph:
  Zaccur, Joseph, Nethaniah and Asarelah. The sons of Asaph were under the supervision of Asaph, who prophesied under the king's supervision.
³As for Jeduthun, from his sons:
  Gedaliah, Zeri, Jeshaiah, Shimei,ᵇ Hashabiah and Mattithiah, six in all, under the supervision of their

ᵃ23 Two Hebrew manuscripts and some Septuagint manuscripts (see also 1 Chron. 23:19); most Hebrew manuscripts The sons of Jeriah: ᵇ3 One Hebrew manuscript and some Septuagint manuscripts (see also verse 17); most Hebrew manuscripts do not have Shimei.

father Jeduthun, who prophesied, using the harp in thanking and praising the LORD. [4]As for Heman, from his sons: Bukkiah, Mattaniah, Uzziel, Shubael and Jerimoth; Hananiah, Hanani, Eliathah, Giddalti and Romamti-Ezer; Joshbekashah, Mallothi, Hothir and Mahazioth. [5]All these were sons of Heman the king's seer. They were given him through the promises of God to exalt him.[a] God gave Heman fourteen sons and three daughters.

[6]All these men were under the supervision of their fathers for the music of the temple of the LORD, with cymbals, lyres and harps, for the ministry at the house of God. Asaph, Jeduthun and Heman were under the supervision of the king. [7]Along with their relatives—all of them trained and skilled in music for the LORD—they numbered 288. [8]Young and old alike, teacher as well as student, cast lots for their duties.

[9]The first lot, which was for Asaph, fell to Joseph,
his sons and relatives,[b]   12[c]
the second to Gedaliah,
he and his relatives and sons,   12
[10]the third to Zaccur,
his sons and relatives,   12
[11]the fourth to Izri,[d]
his sons and relatives,   12
[12]the fifth to Nethaniah,
his sons and relatives,   12
[13]the sixth to Bukkiah,
his sons and relatives,   12
[14]the seventh to Jesarelah,[e]
his sons and relatives,   12
[15]the eighth to Jeshaiah,
his sons and relatives,   12
[16]the ninth to Mattaniah,
his sons and relatives,   12
[17]the tenth to Shimei,
his sons and relatives,   12
[18]the eleventh to Azarel,[f]
his sons and relatives,   12
[19]the twelfth to Hashabiah,
his sons and relatives,   12
[20]the thirteenth to Shubael,
his sons and relatives,   12
[21]the fourteenth to Mattithiah,
his sons and relatives,   12
[22]the fifteenth to Jerimoth,
his sons and relatives,   12

[23]the sixteenth to Hananiah,
his sons and relatives,   12
[24]the seventeenth to Joshbekashah,
his sons and relatives,   12
[25]the eighteenth to Hanani,
his sons and relatives,   12
[26]the nineteenth to Mallothi,
his sons and relatives,   12
[27]the twentieth to Eliathah,
his sons and relatives,   12
[28]the twenty-first to Hothir,
his sons and relatives,   12
[29]the twenty-second to Giddalti,
his sons and relatives,   12
[30]the twenty-third to Mahazioth,
his sons and relatives,   12
[31]the twenty-fourth to Romamti-Ezer,
his sons and relatives,   12

The Gatekeepers

26 The divisions of the gatekeepers:

From the Korahites: Meshelemiah son of Kore, one of the sons of Asaph.
[2]Meshelemiah had sons:
Zechariah the firstborn,
Jediael the second,
Zebadiah the third,
Jathniel the fourth,
[3]Elam the fifth,
Jehohanan the sixth

[a]5 Hebrew *exalt the horn*   [b]9 See Septuagint; Hebrew does not have *his sons and relatives*.
[c]9 See the total in verse 7; Hebrew does not have *twelve.*   [d]11 A variant of *Zeri*   [e]14 A variant of *Asarelah*   [f]18 A variant of *Uzziel*

POINT OF INTEREST   1 Chronicles 25:1

If David had placed an ad for worship leaders in a newspaper, it might have read as follows: Levites wanted for temple ministry position. Must be able to prophesy, play several instruments and be able to praise God without ceasing. Apply in person to the king or to your local army commander.

and Eliehoenai the seventh.
⁴Obed-Edom also had sons:

Shemaiah the firstborn,
Jehozabad the second,
Joah the third,
Sacar the fourth,
Nethanel the fifth,
⁵Ammiel the sixth,
Issachar the seventh
and Peullethai the eighth.

(For God had blessed Obed-Edom.)

⁶His son Shemaiah also had sons, who were leaders in their father's family because they were very capable men. ⁷The sons of Shemaiah: Othni, Rephael, Obed and Elzabad; his relatives Elihu and Semakiah were also able men. ⁸All these were descendants of Obed-Edom; they and their sons and their relatives were capable men with the strength to do the work—descendants of Obed-Edom, 62 in all.

⁹Meshelemiah had sons and relatives, who were able men—18 in all.

¹⁰Hosah the Merarite had sons: Shimri the first (although he was not the firstborn, his father had appointed him the first), ¹¹Hilkiah the second, Tabaliah the third and Zechariah the fourth. The sons and relatives of Hosah were 13 in all.

¹²These divisions of the gatekeepers, through their chief men, had duties for ministering in the temple of the Lord, just as their relatives had. ¹³Lots were cast for each gate, according to their families, young and old alike.

¹⁴The lot for the East Gate fell to Shelemiah.[a] Then lots were cast for his son Zechariah, a wise counselor, and the lot for the North Gate fell to him. ¹⁵The lot for the South Gate fell to Obed-Edom, and the lot for the storehouse fell to his sons. ¹⁶The lots for the West Gate and the Shalleketh Gate on the upper road fell to Shuppim and Hosah.

Guard was alongside of guard: ¹⁷There were six Levites a day on the east, four a day on the north, four a day on the south and two at a time at the storehouse. ¹⁸As for the court to the west, there were four at the road and two at the court itself.

¹⁹These were the divisions of the gatekeepers who were descendants of Korah and Merari.

The Treasurers and Other Officials

²⁰Their fellow Levites were[b] in charge of the treasuries of the house of God and the treasuries for the dedicated things. ²¹The descendants of Ladan, who were Gershonites through Ladan and who were heads of families belonging to Ladan the Gershonite, were Jehieli, ²²the sons of Jehieli, Zetham and his brother Joel. They were in charge of the treasuries of the temple of the Lord.

²³From the Amramites, the Izharites, the Hebronites and the Uzzielites:

²⁴Shubael, a descendant of Gershom son of Moses, was the officer in charge of the treasuries. ²⁵His relatives through Eliezer: Rehabiah his son, Jeshaiah his son, Joram his son, Zicri his son and Shelomith his son. ²⁶Shelomith and his relatives were in charge of all the treasuries for the things dedicated by King David, by the heads of families who were the commanders of thousands and commanders of hundreds, and by the other army commanders. ²⁷Some of the plunder taken in battle they dedicated for the repair of the temple of the Lord. ²⁸And everything dedicated by Samuel the seer and by Saul son of Kish, Abner son of Ner and Joab son of Zeruiah, and all the other dedicated things were in the care of Shelomith and his relatives.

²⁹From the Izharites: Kenaniah and his sons were assigned duties away from the temple, as officials and judges over Israel.

³⁰From the Hebronites: Hashabiah and his relatives—seventeen hundred able men—were responsible in Israel west of the Jordan for all the work of the Lord and for the king's service.

³¹As for the Hebronites, Jeriah was their chief according to the genealogical records of their families. In the fortieth year of David's reign a search was made

---

[a] 14 A variant of *Meshelemiah*　[b] 20 Septuagint; Hebrew *As for the Levites, Ahijah was*

in the records, and capable men among the Hebronites were found at Jazer in Gilead. ³²Jeriah had twenty-seven hundred relatives, who were able men and heads of families, and King David put them in charge of the Reubenites, the Gadites and the half-tribe of Manasseh for every matter pertaining to God and for the affairs of the king.

Army Divisions

27 This is the list of the Israelites— heads of families, commanders of thousands and commanders of hundreds, and their officers, who served the king in all that concerned the army divisions that were on duty month by month throughout the year. Each division consisted of 24,000 men.

²In charge of the first division, for the first month, was Jashobeam son of Zabdiel. There were 24,000 men in his division. ³He was a descendant of Perez and chief of all the army officers for the first month. ⁴In charge of the division for the second month was Dodai the Ahohite; Mikloth was the leader of his division. There were 24,000 men in his division. ⁵The third army commander, for the third month, was Benaiah son of Jehoiada the priest. He was chief and there were 24,000 men in his division. ⁶This was the Benaiah who was a mighty man among the Thirty and was over the Thirty. His son Ammizabad was in charge of his division. ⁷The fourth, for the fourth month, was Asahel the brother of Joab; his son Zebadiah was his successor. There were 24,000 men in his division. ⁸The fifth, for the fifth month, was the commander Shamhuth the Izrahite. There were 24,000 men in his division. ⁹The sixth, for the sixth month, was Ira the son of Ikkesh the Tekoite. There were 24,000 men in his division. ¹⁰The seventh, for the seventh month, was Helez the Pelonite, an Ephraimite. There were 24,000 men in his division. ¹¹The eighth, for the eighth month, was Sibbecai the Hushathite, a Zerahite.

There were 24,000 men in his division. ¹²The ninth, for the ninth month, was Abiezer the Anathothite, a Benjamite. There were 24,000 men in his division. ¹³The tenth, for the tenth month, was Maharai the Netophathite, a Zerahite. There were 24,000 men in his division. ¹⁴The eleventh, for the eleventh month, was Benaiah the Pirathonite, an Ephraimite. There were 24,000 men in his division. ¹⁵The twelfth, for the twelfth month, was Heldai the Netophathite, from the family of Othniel. There were 24,000 men in his division.

Officers of the Tribes

¹⁶The officers over the tribes of Israel:

over the Reubenites: Eliezer son of Zicri;
over the Simeonites: Shephatiah son of Maacah;
¹⁷over Levi: Hashabiah son of Kemuel;
over Aaron: Zadok;
¹⁸over Judah: Elihu, a brother of David;
over Issachar: Omri son of Michael;
¹⁹over Zebulun: Ishmaiah son of Obadiah;
over Naphtali: Jerimoth son of Azriel;
²⁰over the Ephraimites: Hoshea son of Azaziah;
over half the tribe of Manasseh: Joel son of Pedaiah;
²¹over the half-tribe of Manasseh in Gilead: Iddo son of Zechariah;
over Benjamin: Jaasiel son of Abner;
²²over Dan: Azarel son of Jeroham.
These were the officers over the tribes of Israel.

²³David did not take the number of the men twenty years old or less, because the Lord had promised to make Israel as numerous as the stars in the sky. ²⁴Joab son of Zeruiah began to count the men but did not finish. Wrath came on Israel on account of this numbering, and the num-

ber was not entered in the book[a] of the annals of King David.

The King's Overseers

25Azmaveth son of Adiel was in charge of the royal storehouses.

Jonathan son of Uzziah was in charge of the storehouses in the outlying districts, in the towns, the villages and the watchtowers.

26Ezri son of Kelub was in charge of the field workers who farmed the land.

27Shimei the Ramathite was in charge of the vineyards.

Zabdi the Shiphmite was in charge of the produce of the vineyards for the wine vats.

28Baal-Hanan the Gederite was in charge of the olive and sycamore-fig trees in the western foothills.

Joash was in charge of the supplies of olive oil.

29Shitrai the Sharonite was in charge of the herds grazing in Sharon.

Shaphat son of Adlai was in charge of the herds in the valleys.

30Obil the Ishmaelite was in charge of the camels.

Jehdeiah the Meronothite was in charge of the donkeys.

31Jaziz the Hagrite was in charge of the flocks.

All these were the officials in charge of King David's property.

32Jonathan, David's uncle, was a counselor, a man of insight and a scribe. Jehiel son of Hacmoni took care of the king's sons.

33Ahithophel was the king's counselor. Hushai the Arkite was the king's friend. 34Ahithophel was succeeded by Jehoiada son of Benaiah and by Abiathar.

Joab was the commander of the royal army.

David's Plans for the Temple

28 David summoned all the officials of Israel to assemble at Jerusalem: the officers over the tribes, the commanders of the divisions in the service of the king, the commanders of thousands and commanders of hundreds, and the officials in charge of all the property and livestock belonging to the king and his sons, together with the palace officials, the mighty men and all the brave warriors.

2King David rose to his feet and said: "Listen to me, my brothers and my people. I had it in my heart to build a house as a place of rest for the ark of the covenant of the LORD, for the footstool of our God, and I made plans to build it. 3But God said to me, 'You are not to build a house for my Name, because you are a warrior and have shed blood.'

4"Yet the LORD, the God of Israel, chose me from my whole family to be king over Israel forever. He chose Judah as leader, and from the house of Judah he chose my family, and from my father's sons he was pleased to make me king over all Israel. 5Of all my sons—and the LORD has given me many—he has chosen my son Solomon to sit on the throne of the kingdom of the LORD over Israel. 6He said to me: 'Solomon your son is the one who will build my house and my courts, for I have chosen him to be my son, and I will be his father. 7I will establish his kingdom forever if he is unswerving in carrying out my commands and laws, as is being done at this time.'

8"So now I charge you in the sight of all Israel and of the assembly of the LORD, and in the hearing of our God: Be careful to follow all the commands of the LORD your God, that you may possess this good land and pass it on as an inheritance to your descendants forever.

9"And you, my son Solomon, acknowledge the God of your father, and serve him with wholehearted devotion and with a willing mind, for the LORD searches every heart and understands every motive behind the thoughts. If you seek him, he will be found by you; but if you forsake him, he will reject you forever. 10Consider now, for the LORD has chosen you to build a temple as a sanctuary. Be strong and do the work."

11Then David gave his son Solomon the plans for the portico of the temple, its buildings, its storerooms, its upper parts, its inner rooms and the place of atone-

a24 Septuagint; Hebrew *number*

POINT OF INTEREST

1 Chronicles 28:9

Can you keep a secret? Maybe from a friend or from a parent. But never from God!

ment. ¹²He gave him the plans of all that the Spirit had put in his mind for the courts of the temple of the LORD and all the surrounding rooms, for the treasuries of the temple of God and for the treasuries for the dedicated things. ¹³He gave him instructions for the divisions of the priests and Levites, and for all the work of serving in the temple of the LORD, as well as for all the articles to be used in its service. ¹⁴He designated the weight of gold for all the gold articles to be used in various kinds of service, and the weight of silver for all the silver articles to be used in various kinds of service: ¹⁵the weight of gold for the gold lampstands and their lamps, with the weight for each lampstand and its lamps; and the weight of silver for each silver lampstand and its lamps, according to the use of each lampstand; ¹⁶the weight of gold for each table for consecrated bread; the weight of silver for the silver tables; ¹⁷the weight of pure gold for the forks, sprinkling bowls and pitchers; the weight of gold for each gold dish; the weight of silver for each silver dish; ¹⁸and the weight of the refined gold for the altar of incense. He also gave him the plan for the chariot, that is, the cherubim of gold that spread their wings and shelter the ark of the covenant of the LORD.

¹⁹"All this," David said, "I have in writing from the hand of the LORD upon me, and he gave me understanding in all the details of the plan."

²⁰David also said to Solomon his son, "Be strong and courageous, and do the work. Do not be afraid or discouraged, for the LORD God, my God, is with you. He will not fail you or forsake you until all the work for the service of the temple of the LORD is finished. ²¹The divisions of the priests and Levites are ready for all the work on the temple of God, and every willing man skilled in any craft will help you in all the work. The officials and all the people will obey your every command."

Gifts for Building the Temple

29 Then King David said to the whole assembly: "My son Solomon, the one whom God has chosen, is young and inexperienced. The task is great, because this palatial structure is not for man but for the LORD God. ²With all my resources I have provided for the temple of my God—gold for the gold work, silver for

the silver, bronze for the bronze, iron for the iron and wood for the wood, as well as onyx for the settings, turquoise,ᵃ stones of various colors, and all kinds of fine stone and marble—all of these in large quantities. ³Besides, in my devotion to the temple of my God I now give my personal treasures of gold and silver for the temple of my God, over and above everything I have provided for this holy temple: ⁴three thousand talentsᵇ of gold (gold of Ophir) and seven thousand talentsᶜ of refined silver, for the overlaying of the walls of the buildings, ⁵for the gold work and the silver work, and for all the work to be done by the craftsmen. Now, who is willing to consecrate himself today to the LORD?"

⁶Then the leaders of families, the officers of the tribes of Israel, the commanders of thousands and commanders of hundreds, and the officials in charge of the king's work gave willingly. ⁷They gave toward the work on the temple of God five thousand talentsᵈ and ten thousand daricsᵉ of gold, ten thousand talentsᶠ of silver, eighteen thousand talentsᵍ of bronze and a hundred thousand talentsʰ of iron. ⁸Any who had precious stones gave them to the treasury of the temple of the LORD in the custody of Jehiel the Gershonite. ⁹The people rejoiced at the willing response of their leaders, for they had given freely and wholeheartedly to the LORD. David the king also rejoiced greatly.

David's Prayer

¹⁰David praised the LORD in the presence of the whole assembly, saying,

"Praise be to you, O LORD,
　　God of our father Israel,
　　from everlasting to everlasting.
¹¹Yours, O LORD, is the greatness and
　　the power
　　and the glory and the majesty and
　　the splendor,
　for everything in heaven and earth
　　is yours.
Yours, O LORD, is the kingdom;

ᵃ2 The meaning of the Hebrew for this word is uncertain.　ᵇ4 That is, about 110 tons (about 100 metric tons)　ᶜ4 That is, about 260 tons (about 240 metric tons)　ᵈ7 That is, about 190 tons (about 170 metric tons)　ᵉ7 That is, about 185 pounds (about 84 kilograms)　ᶠ7 That is, about 375 tons (about 345 metric tons)　ᵍ7 That is, about 675 tons (about 610 metric tons)　ʰ7 That is, about 3,750 tons (about 3,450 metric tons)

Read 1 Chronicles 29:1–30
Key Verse 1 Chronicles 29:17

A Matter of Integrity

David knew that when God takes the measure of a person, he holds the tape measure around the heart. God is more concerned about who we are than what we do, because he knows that if our heart is honest and upright, our actions will be right as well—the more integrity we develop, the more our inner beliefs and outward behavior will become "integrated."

Integrity begins with a commitment to honor and follow God's commands and his will for our lives (see 1 Kings 9:4–5). The fruit of integrity is living honestly and authentically. Our integrity—or our lack of it—can't be kept secret; others can see when we are truthful in the little things as well as the big things. People of integrity can be counted on; they are true to their word even when it hurts!

Digging Into the Word

1. What do you learn about integrity from these passages?— *Numbers 23:19; Proverbs 11:3; Mark 12:14*
2. What do these passages say about the type of person God works through?—*2 Timothy 2:20–21; Titus 1:6–8*

Action Challenge

Can you think of one area in your life in which you have lacked integrity? What will it take to make things right in this situation? How will you become a person of integrity? Commit yourself to take at least one action step toward this goal.

One Step Deeper

Psalm 1; Luke 16:10

Go to page 466 for your next devotional reading.

you are exalted as head over all.
¹²Wealth and honor come from you;
you are the ruler of all things.
In your hands are strength and power
to exalt and give strength to all.
¹³Now, our God, we give you thanks,
and praise your glorious name.

¹⁴"But who am I, and who are my people, that we should be able to give as generously as this? Everything comes from you, and we have given you only what comes from your hand. ¹⁵We are aliens and strangers in your sight, as were all our forefathers. Our days on earth are like a shadow, without hope. ¹⁶O LORD our God, as for all this abundance that we have provided for building you a temple for your Holy Name, it comes from your hand, and all of it belongs to you. ¹⁷I know, my God, that you test the heart and are pleased with integrity. All these things have I given willingly and with honest intent. And now I have seen with joy how willingly your people who are here have given to you. ¹⁸O LORD, God of our fathers Abraham, Isaac and Israel, keep this desire in the hearts of your people forever, and keep their hearts loyal to you. ¹⁹And give my son Solomon the wholehearted devotion to keep your commands, requirements and decrees and to do everything to build the palatial structure for which I have provided."

²⁰Then David said to the whole assembly, "Praise the LORD your God." So they all praised the LORD, the God of their fathers; they bowed low and fell prostrate before the LORD and the king.

Solomon Acknowledged as King

²¹The next day they made sacrifices to the LORD and presented burnt offerings to him: a thousand bulls, a thousand rams and a thousand male lambs, together with their drink offerings, and other sacrifices in abundance for all Israel. ²²They ate and drank with great joy in the presence of the LORD that day.

Then they acknowledged Solomon son of David as king a second time, anointing him before the LORD to be ruler and Zadok to be priest. ²³So Solomon sat on the throne of the LORD as king in place of his father David. He prospered and all Israel obeyed him. ²⁴All the officers and mighty men, as well as all of King David's sons, pledged their submission to King Solomon.

²⁵The LORD highly exalted Solomon in the sight of all Israel and bestowed on him royal splendor such as no king over Israel ever had before.

The Death of David

²⁶David son of Jesse was king over all Israel. ²⁷He ruled over Israel forty-seven years—seven in Hebron and thirty-three in Jerusalem. ²⁸He died at a good old age, having enjoyed long life, wealth and honor. His son Solomon succeeded him as king.

²⁹As for the events of King David's reign, from beginning to end, they are written in the records of Samuel the seer, the records of Nathan the prophet and the records of Gad the seer, ³⁰together with the details of his reign and power, and the circumstances that surrounded him and Israel and the kingdoms of all the other lands.

Jesus said in Matthew 6:21

that "where your treasure is, there your heart will be also."

In other words, our priorities—where we spend our time,

attention and energy—reveal where our minds and hearts

are focused. While 2 Chronicles repeats many of the his-

torical facts of 1 and 2 Kings, this chronicle is much more

than history. It's a critique of the careers of Judah's kings.

Notice that each king's merit is assessed not on his diplo-

matic abilities, military accomplishments or wealth, but

on whether or not his heart is focused on God. As you

read 2 Chronicles, think about

your priorities from this

perspective.

2 CHRONICLES

Solomon Asks for Wisdom

1 Solomon son of David established him-self firmly over his kingdom, for the LORD his God was with him and made him exceedingly great.

²Then Solomon spoke to all Israel—to the commanders of thousands and com-manders of hundreds, to the judges and to all the leaders in Israel, the heads of families— ³and Solomon and the whole assembly went to the high place at Gibe-on, for God's Tent of Meeting was there, which Moses the LORD's servant had made in the desert. ⁴Now David had brought up the ark of God from Kiriath Jearim to the place he had prepared for it,

because he had pitched a tent for it in Jerusalem. ⁵But the bronze altar that Bez-alel son of Uri, the son of Hur, had made was in Gibeon in front of the tabernacle of the LORD; so Solomon and the assembly inquired of him there. ⁶Solomon went up to the bronze altar before the LORD in the Tent of Meeting and offered a thousand burnt offerings on it.

⁷That night God appeared to Solomon and said to him, "Ask for whatever you want me to give you."

⁸Solomon answered God, "You have shown great kindness to David my father and have made me king in his place. ⁹Now, LORD God, let your promise to my

father David be confirmed, for you have made me king over a people who are as numerous as the dust of the earth. ¹⁰Give me wisdom and knowledge, that I may lead this people, for who is able to govern this great people of yours?"

¹¹God said to Solomon, "Since this is your heart's desire and you have not asked for wealth, riches or honor, nor for the death of your enemies, and since you have not asked for a long life but for wisdom and knowledge to govern my people over whom I have made you king, ¹²therefore wisdom and knowledge will be given you. And I will also give you wealth, riches and honor, such as no king who was before you ever had and none after you will have."

¹³Then Solomon went to Jerusalem from the high place at Gibeon, from before the Tent of Meeting. And he reigned over Israel.

¹⁴Solomon accumulated chariots and horses; he had fourteen hundred chariots and twelve thousand horses,ᵃ which he kept in the chariot cities and also with him in Jerusalem. ¹⁵The king made silver and gold as common in Jerusalem as stones, and cedar as plentiful as sycamore-fig trees in the foothills. ¹⁶Solomon's horses were imported from Egyptᵇ and from Kueᶜ—the royal merchants purchased them from Kue. ¹⁷They imported a chariot from Egypt for six hundred shekelsᵈ of silver, and a horse for a hundred and fifty.ᵉ They also exported them to all the kings of the Hittites and of the Arameans.

Preparations for Building the Temple

2 Solomon gave orders to build a temple for the Name of the LORD and a royal palace for himself. ²He conscripted seventy thousand men as carriers and eighty thousand as stonecutters in the hills and thirty-six hundred as foremen over them. ³Solomon sent this message to Hiramᶠ king of Tyre:

"Send me cedar logs as you did for my father David when you sent him cedar to build a palace to live in. ⁴Now I am about to build a temple for the Name of the LORD my God and to dedicate it to him for burning fragrant incense before him, for setting out the consecrated bread regularly, and for making burnt offerings every morning and evening

and on Sabbaths and New Moons and at the appointed feasts of the LORD our God. This is a lasting ordinance for Israel.

⁵"The temple I am going to build will be great, because our God is greater than all other gods. ⁶But who is able to build a temple for him, since the heavens, even the highest heavens, cannot contain him? Who then am I to build a temple for him, except as a place to burn sacrifices before him?

⁷"Send me, therefore, a man skilled to work in gold and silver, bronze and iron, and in purple, crimson and blue yarn, and experienced in the art of engraving, to work in Judah and Jerusalem with my skilled craftsmen, whom my father David provided.

⁸"Send me also cedar, pine and algumᵍ logs from Lebanon, for I know that your men are skilled in cutting timber there. My men will work with yours ⁹to provide me with plenty of lumber, because the temple I build must be large and magnificent. ¹⁰I will give your servants, the woodsmen who cut the timber, twenty thousand corsʰ of ground wheat, twenty thousand cors of barley, twenty thousand bathsⁱ of wine and twenty thousand baths of olive oil."

¹¹Hiram king of Tyre replied by letter to Solomon:

"Because the LORD loves his people, he has made you their king."

¹²And Hiram added:

"Praise be to the LORD, the God of Israel, who made heaven and earth! He has given King David a wise son, endowed with intelligence and discernment, who will build a temple for the LORD and a palace for himself.

¹³"I am sending you Huram-Abi,

ᵃ14 Or charioteers   ᵇ16 Or possibly Muzur, a region in Cilicia; also in verse 17   ᶜ16 Probably Cilicia   ᵈ17 That is, about 15 pounds (about 7 kilograms)   ᵉ17 That is, about 3 3/4 pounds (about 1.7 kilograms)   ᶠ3 Hebrew Huram, a variant of Hiram; also in verses 11 and 12   ᵍ8 Probably a variant of almug; possibly juniper   ʰ10 That is, probably about 125,000 bushels (about 4,400 kiloliters)   ⁱ10 That is, probably about 115,000 gallons (about 440 kiloliters) a man of great skill, ¹⁴whose mother was from Dan and whose father was from Tyre. He is trained to work in gold and silver, bronze and iron, stone and wood, and with purple and blue and crimson yarn and fine linen. He is experienced in all kinds of engraving and can execute any design given to him. He will work with your craftsmen and with those of my lord, David your father.

¹⁵"Now let my lord send his servants the wheat and barley and the olive oil and wine he promised, ¹⁶and we will cut all the logs from Lebanon that you need and will float them in rafts by sea down to Joppa. You can then take them up to Jerusalem."

¹⁷Solomon took a census of all the aliens who were in Israel, after the census his father David had taken; and they were found to be 153,600. ¹⁸He assigned 70,000 of them to be carriers and 80,000 to be stonecutters in the hills, with 3,600

MONDAY

Read 2 Chronicles 2:1–18
Key Verses 2 Chronicles 2:5–6

An Attitude of Humility — Kyle Kelley

Solomon discovered what it meant to undertake a big project when he began to build the temple. Becoming the general contractor was part of the job description when he became king. What a challenge! It was a monumental task, one that would occupy the first twenty years of his reign as king. Solomon's father, David, had wanted to build the temple, but God had clearly designated Solomon as the builder. David made sure that the plans, the advisers and the substantial resources were in place, then turned the project over to Solomon. What an honor!

That kind of power might have given Solomon an attitude problem, but out of humility Solomon had asked God for wisdom. When God gave him wisdom, he responded in humility (see 2 Chronicles 1:10). Solomon envisioned, as had his father David before him, a place where God's people could worship the Lord for his greatness and majesty. Solomon was aware that whatever temple he built could never "house" God; he was humbled by an awareness of the frailty of his efforts compared with God's infinite power and grace: "Who then am I to build a temple for him?" (2 Chronicles 2:6). Even though he had fervent desire, great wisdom and extensive resources, Solomon's humility and awe only added fuel to his desire to do something great for God.

When God gives us the opportunities, the talents and the resources to do something for him, how are we to respond? What should our attitude be? James's letter tells us that wisdom and humility go hand in hand in serving God: "Who is wise and understanding among you? Let him show it by his good life, by deeds done in the humility that comes from wisdom . . . the wisdom that comes from heaven is first of all pure; then peace-loving, considerate, submissive, full of mercy and good fruit, impartial and sincere" (James 3:13,17).

A Deeper Look
Mark 10:45; 2 Corinthians 4:5

Go to page 476 for your next devotional reading.

foremen over them to keep the people working.

Solomon Builds the Temple

3 Then Solomon began to build the temple of the LORD in Jerusalem on Mount Moriah, where the LORD had appeared to his father David. It was on the threshing floor of Araunah*a* the Jebusite, the place provided by David. ²He began building on the second day of the second month in the fourth year of his reign.

³The foundation Solomon laid for building the temple of God was sixty cubits long and twenty cubits wide*b* (using the cubit of the old standard). ⁴The portico at the front of the temple was twenty cubits*c* long across the width of the building and twenty cubits*d* high.

He overlaid the inside with pure gold. ⁵He paneled the main hall with pine and covered it with fine gold and decorated it with palm tree and chain designs. ⁶He adorned the temple with precious stones. And the gold he used was gold of Parvaim. ⁷He overlaid the ceiling beams, doorframes, walls and doors of the temple with gold, and he carved cherubim on the walls.

⁸He built the Most Holy Place, its length corresponding to the width of the temple—twenty cubits long and twenty cubits wide. He overlaid the inside with six hundred talents*e* of fine gold. ⁹The gold nails weighed fifty shekels.*f* He also overlaid the upper parts with gold.

¹⁰In the Most Holy Place he made a pair of sculptured cherubim and overlaid them with gold. ¹¹The total wingspan of the cherubim was twenty cubits. One wing of the first cherub was five cubits*g* long and touched the temple wall, while its other wing, also five cubits long, touched the wing of the other cherub. ¹²Similarly one wing of the second cherub was five cubits long and touched the other temple wall, and its other wing, also five cubits long, touched the wing of the first cherub. ¹³The wings of these cherubim extended twenty cubits. They stood on their feet, facing the main hall.*h*

¹⁴He made the curtain of blue, purple and crimson yarn and fine linen, with cherubim worked into it.

¹⁵In the front of the temple he made two pillars, which ˌtogetherˌ were thirty-five cubits*i* long, each with a capital on top measuring five cubits. ¹⁶He made interwoven chains*j* and put them on top of the pillars. He also made a hundred pomegranates and attached them to the chains. ¹⁷He erected the pillars in the front of the temple, one to the south and one to the north. The one to the south he named Jakin*k* and the one to the north Boaz.*l*

The Temple's Furnishings

4 He made a bronze altar twenty cubits long, twenty cubits wide and ten cubits high.*m* ²He made the Sea of cast metal, circular in shape, measuring ten cubits from rim to rim and five cubits*n* high. It took a line of thirty cubits*o* to measure around it. ³Below the rim, figures of bulls encircled it—ten to a cubit.*p* The bulls were cast in two rows in one piece with the Sea.

⁴The Sea stood on twelve bulls, three facing north, three facing west, three facing south and three facing east. The Sea rested on top of them, and their hindquarters were toward the center. ⁵It was

---

a1 Hebrew *Ornan*, a variant of *Araunah*   *b3* That is, about 90 feet (about 27 meters) long and 30 feet (about 9 meters) wide   *c4* That is, about 30 feet (about 9 meters); also in verses 8, 11 and 13   *d4* Some Septuagint and Syriac manuscripts; Hebrew *and a hundred and twenty*   *e8* That is, about 23 tons (about 21 metric tons)   *f9* That is, about 1 1/4 pounds (about 0.6 kilogram)   *g11* That is, about 7 1/2 feet (about 2.3 meters); also in verse 15   *h13* Or *facing inward*   *i15* That is, about 52 feet (about 16 meters)   *j16* Or possibly *made chains in the inner sanctuary*; the meaning of the Hebrew for this phrase is uncertain.   *k17* *Jakin* probably means *he establishes.*   *l17* *Boaz* probably means *in him is strength.*   *m1* That is, about 30 feet (about 9 meters) long and wide, and about 15 feet (about 4.5 meters) high   *n2* That is, about 7 1/2 feet (about 2.3 meters)   *o2* That is, about 45 feet (about 13.5 meters)   *p3* That is, about 1 1/2 feet (about 0.5 meter)

POINT OF INTEREST

2 Chronicles 3:10

Cherubim are angelic beings who serve God. After Adam and Eve sinned, cherubim were placed at the entrance to the Garden of Eden to keep anyone from entering it (see Genesis 3:24). The sculptures here served to remind God's people that they were denied entry into the Most Holy Place.

a handbreadth[a] in thickness, and its rim was like the rim of a cup, like a lily blossom. It held three thousand baths.[b]

6He then made ten basins for washing and placed five on the south side and five on the north. In them the things to be used for the burnt offerings were rinsed, but the Sea was to be used by the priests for washing.

7He made ten gold lampstands according to the specifications for them and placed them in the temple, five on the south side and five on the north.

8He made ten tables and placed them in the temple, five on the south side and five on the north. He also made a hundred gold sprinkling bowls.

9He made the courtyard of the priests, and the large court and the doors for the court, and overlaid the doors with bronze. 10He placed the Sea on the south side, at the southeast corner.

11He also made the pots and shovels and sprinkling bowls.

So Huram finished the work he had undertaken for King Solomon in the temple of God:

12the two pillars;

the two bowl-shaped capitals on top of the pillars;

the two sets of network decorating the two bowl-shaped capitals on top of the pillars;

13the four hundred pomegranates for the two sets of network (two rows of pomegranates for each network, decorating the bowl-shaped capitals on top of the pillars);

14the stands with their basins;

15the Sea and the twelve bulls under it;

16the pots, shovels, meat forks and all related articles.

All the objects that Huram-Abi made for King Solomon for the temple of the LORD were of polished bronze. 17The king had them cast in clay molds in the plain of the Jordan between Succoth and Zarethan.[c] 18All these things that Solomon made amounted to so much that the weight of the bronze was not determined.

19Solomon also made all the furnishings that were in God's temple:

the golden altar;

the tables on which was the bread of the Presence;

20the lampstands of pure gold with their lamps, to burn in front of the inner sanctuary as prescribed;

21the gold floral work and lamps and tongs (they were solid gold);

22the pure gold wick trimmers, sprinkling bowls, dishes and censers; and the gold doors of the temple: the inner doors to the Most Holy Place and the doors of the main hall.

5 When all the work Solomon had done for the temple of the LORD was finished, he brought in the things his father David had dedicated—the silver and gold and all the furnishings—and he placed them in the treasuries of God's temple.

The Ark Brought to the Temple

2Then Solomon summoned to Jerusalem the elders of Israel, all the heads of the tribes and the chiefs of the Israelite families, to bring up the ark of the LORD's covenant from Zion, the City of David. 3And all the men of Israel came together to the king at the time of the festival in the seventh month.

4When all the elders of Israel had arrived, the Levites took up the ark, 5and they brought up the ark and the Tent of Meeting and all the sacred furnishings in it. The priests, who were Levites, carried them up; 6and King Solomon and the entire assembly of Israel that had gathered about him were before the ark, sacrificing so many sheep and cattle that they could not be recorded or counted.

7The priests then brought the ark of the LORD's covenant to its place in the inner sanctuary of the temple, the Most Holy Place, and put it beneath the wings of the cherubim. 8The cherubim spread their wings over the place of the ark and covered the ark and its carrying poles. 9These poles were so long that their ends, extending from the ark, could be seen from in front of the inner sanctuary, but not from outside the Holy Place; and they are still there today. 10There was nothing in the ark except the two tablets that Moses had placed in it at Horeb, where the

---

a5 That is, about 3 inches (about 8 centimeters)   b5 That is, about 17,500 gallons (about 66 kiloliters)   c17 Hebrew *Zeredatha*, a variant of *Zarethan*

LORD made a covenant with the Israelites after they came out of Egypt.

[11]The priests then withdrew from the Holy Place. All the priests who were there had consecrated themselves, regardless of their divisions. [12]All the Levites who were musicians—Asaph, Heman, Jeduthun and their sons and relatives—stood on the east side of the altar, dressed in fine linen and playing cymbals, harps and lyres. They were accompanied by 120 priests sounding trumpets. [13]The trumpeters and singers joined in unison, as with one voice, to give praise and thanks to the LORD. Accompanied by trumpets, cymbals and other instruments, they raised their voices in praise to the LORD and sang:

"He is good;
   his love endures forever."

Then the temple of the LORD was filled with a cloud, [14]and the priests could not perform their service because of the cloud, for the glory of the LORD filled the temple of God.

6 Then Solomon said, "The LORD has said that he would dwell in a dark cloud; [2]I have built a magnificent temple for you, a place for you to dwell forever."

[3]While the whole assembly of Israel was standing there, the king turned around and blessed them. [4]Then he said:

"Praise be to the LORD, the God of Israel, who with his hands has fulfilled what he promised with his mouth to my father David. For he said, [5]'Since the day I brought my people out of Egypt, I have not chosen a city in any tribe of Israel to have a temple built for my Name to be there, nor have I chosen anyone to be the leader over my people Israel. [6]But now I have chosen Jerusalem for my Name to be there, and I have chosen David to rule my people Israel.'

[7]"My father David had it in his heart to build a temple for the Name of the LORD, the God of Israel. [8]But the LORD said to my father David, 'Because it was in your heart to build a temple for my Name, you did well to have this in your heart. [9]Nevertheless, you are not the one to build the temple, but your son, who is your own flesh and blood—

he is the one who will build the temple for my Name.'

[10]"The LORD has kept the promise he made. I have succeeded David my father and now I sit on the throne of Israel, just as the LORD promised, and I have built the temple for the Name of the LORD, the God of Israel. [11]There I have placed the ark, in which is the covenant of the LORD that he made with the people of Israel."

Solomon's Prayer of Dedication

[12]Then Solomon stood before the altar of the LORD in front of the whole assembly of Israel and spread out his hands. [13]Now he had made a bronze platform, five cubits[a] long, five cubits wide and three cubits[b] high, and had placed it in the center of the outer court. He stood on the platform and then knelt down before the whole assembly of Israel and spread out his hands toward heaven. [14]He said:

"O LORD, God of Israel, there is no God like you in heaven or on earth—you who keep your covenant of love with your servants who continue wholeheartedly in your way. [15]You have kept your promise to your servant David my father; with your mouth you have promised and with your hand you have fulfilled it—as it is today.

[16]"Now LORD, God of Israel, keep for your servant David my father the promises you made to him

---

[a]13 That is, about 7 1/2 feet (about 2.3 meters)
[b]13 That is, about 4 1/2 feet (about 1.3 meters)

POINT OF INTEREST

2 Chronicles 5:13

How big was the band? Old Testament musical instruments included horns, reeds, flutes, strings, cymbals and vocalists. In fact, we'd probably recognize most of those ancient instruments as ancestors of those we use today. Do you play an instrument? Whether you play in a classical quartet or an alternative rock band, see Psalm 150 for an exhortation to celebration.

when you said, 'You shall never fail to have a man to sit before me on the throne of Israel, if only your sons are careful in all they do to walk before me according to my law, as you have done.' ¹⁷And now, O LORD, God of Israel, let your word that you promised your servant David come true.

¹⁸"But will God really dwell on earth with men? The heavens, even the highest heavens, cannot contain you. How much less this temple I have built! ¹⁹Yet give attention to your servant's prayer and his plea for mercy, O LORD my God. Hear the cry and the prayer that your servant is praying in your presence. ²⁰May your eyes be open toward this temple day and night, this place of which you said you would put your Name there. May you hear the prayer your servant prays toward this place. ²¹Hear the supplications of your servant and of your people Israel when they pray toward this place. Hear from heaven, your dwelling place; and when you hear, forgive.

²²"When a man wrongs his neighbor and is required to take an oath and he comes and swears the oath before your altar in this temple, ²³then hear from heaven and act. Judge between your servants, repaying the guilty by bringing down on his own head what he has done. Declare the innocent not guilty and so establish his innocence.

²⁴"When your people Israel have been defeated by an enemy because they have sinned against you and when they turn back and confess your name, praying and making supplication before you in this temple, ²⁵then hear from heaven and forgive the sin of your people Israel and bring them back to the land you gave to them and their fathers.

²⁶"When the heavens are shut up and there is no rain because your people have sinned against you, and when they pray toward this place and confess your name and turn from their sin because you have afflicted them, ²⁷then hear from heaven and forgive the sin of your servants, your people Israel.

Teach them the right way to live, and send rain on the land you gave your people for an inheritance.

²⁸"When famine or plague comes to the land, or blight or mildew, locusts or grasshoppers, or when enemies besiege them in any of their cities, whatever disaster or disease may come, ²⁹and when a prayer or plea is made by any of your people Israel—each one aware of his afflictions and pains, and spreading out his hands toward this temple— ³⁰then hear from heaven, your dwelling place. Forgive, and deal with each man according to all he does, since you know his heart (for you alone know the hearts of men), ³¹so that they will fear you and walk in your ways all the time they live in the land you gave our fathers.

³²"As for the foreigner who does not belong to your people Israel but has come from a distant land because of your great name and your mighty hand and your outstretched arm—when he comes and prays toward this temple, ³³then hear from heaven, your dwelling place, and do whatever the foreigner asks of you, so that all the peoples of the earth may know your name and fear you, as do your own people Israel, and may know that this house I have built bears your Name.

³⁴"When your people go to war against their enemies, wherever you send them, and when they pray to you toward this city you have chosen and the temple I have built for your Name, ³⁵then hear from heaven their prayer and their plea, and uphold their cause.

³⁶"When they sin against you— for there is no one who does not sin—and you become angry with them and give them over to the enemy, who takes them captive to a land far away or near; ³⁷and if they have a change of heart in the land where they are held captive, and repent and plead with you in the land of their captivity and say, 'We have sinned, we have done wrong and acted wickedly'; ³⁸and if they turn back to you with all their heart and soul in the land of their captivity where they were taken, and pray toward the land you gave their fa-

thers, toward the city you have chosen and toward the temple I have built for your Name; ³⁹then from heaven, your dwelling place, hear their prayer and their pleas, and uphold their cause. And forgive your people, who have sinned against you.

⁴⁰"Now, my God, may your eyes be open and your ears attentive to the prayers offered in this place.

⁴¹"Now arise, O Lord God, and
　　come to your resting
　　place,
　　you and the ark of your
　　might.
May your priests, O Lord God,
　　be clothed with
　　salvation,
　　may your saints rejoice in
　　your goodness.
⁴²O Lord God, do not reject your
　　anointed one.
　　Remember the great love
　　promised to David your
　　servant."

The Dedication of the Temple

7 When Solomon finished praying, fire came down from heaven and consumed the burnt offering and the sacrifices, and the glory of the Lord filled the temple. ²The priests could not enter the temple of the Lord because the glory of the Lord filled it. ³When all the Israelites saw the fire coming down and the glory of the Lord above the temple, they knelt on the pavement with their faces to the ground, and they worshiped and gave thanks to the Lord, saying,

"He is good;
　　his love endures forever."

⁴Then the king and all the people offered sacrifices before the Lord. ⁵And King Solomon offered a sacrifice of twenty-two thousand head of cattle and a hundred and twenty thousand sheep and goats. So the king and all the people dedicated the temple of God. ⁶The priests took their positions, as did the Levites with the Lord's musical instruments, which King David had made for praising the Lord and which were used when he gave thanks, saying, "His love endures forever." Opposite the Levites, the priests blew their trumpets, and all the Israelites were standing.

⁷Solomon consecrated the middle part of the courtyard in front of the temple of the Lord, and there he offered burnt offerings and the fat of the fellowship offerings,ᵃ because the bronze altar he had made could not hold the burnt offerings, the grain offerings and the fat portions.

⁸So Solomon observed the festival at that time for seven days, and all Israel with him—a vast assembly, people from Leboᵇ Hamath to the Wadi of Egypt. ⁹On the eighth day they held an assembly, for they had celebrated the dedication of the altar for seven days and the festival for seven days more. ¹⁰On the twenty-third day of the seventh month he sent the people to their homes, joyful and glad in heart for the good things the Lord had done for David and Solomon and for his people Israel.

The Lord Appears to Solomon

¹¹When Solomon had finished the temple of the Lord and the royal palace, and had succeeded in carrying out all he had in mind to do in the temple of the Lord and in his own palace, ¹²the Lord appeared to him at night and said:

"I have heard your prayer and have chosen this place for myself as a temple for sacrifices.

¹³"When I shut up the heavens so that there is no rain, or command locusts to devour the land or send a plague among my people, ¹⁴if my people, who are called by my name, will humble themselves and pray and seek my face and turn from their wicked ways, then will I hear from heaven and will forgive their sin and will heal their land. ¹⁵Now my eyes will be open and my ears

---

ᵃ7 Traditionally *peace offerings*　　ᵇ8 Or *from the entrance to*

POINT OF INTEREST

2 Chronicles 6:36

Sometimes a single word can unlock a doorway to deeper Biblical understanding. Look closely at the beginning of this verse. Sin, along with the need for forgiveness and salvation, is not a matter of *if*, but of *when!*

attentive to the prayers offered in this place. [16]I have chosen and consecrated this temple so that my Name may be there forever. My eyes and my heart will always be there.

[17]"As for you, if you walk before me as David your father did, and do all I command, and observe my decrees and laws, [18]I will establish your royal throne, as I covenanted with David your father when I said, 'You shall never fail to have a man to rule over Israel.'

[19]"But if you[a] turn away and forsake the decrees and commands I have given you[a] and go off to serve other gods and worship them, [20]then I will uproot Israel from my land, which I have given them, and will reject this temple I have consecrated for my Name. I will make it a byword and an object of ridicule among all peoples. [21]And though this temple is now so imposing, all who pass by will be appalled and say, 'Why has the LORD done such a thing to this land and to this temple?' [22]People will answer, 'Because they have forsaken the LORD, the God of their fathers, who brought them out of Egypt, and have embraced other gods, worshiping and serving them—that is why he brought all this disaster on them.' "

Solomon's Other Activities

8 At the end of twenty years, during which Solomon built the temple of the LORD and his own palace, [2]Solomon rebuilt the villages that Hiram[b] had given him, and settled Israelites in them. [3]Solomon then went to Hamath Zobah and captured it. [4]He also built up Tadmor in the desert and all the store cities he had built in Hamath. [5]He rebuilt Upper Beth Horon and Lower Beth Horon as fortified cities, with walls and with gates and bars, [6]as well as Baalath and all his store cities, and all the cities for his chariots and for his horses[c]—whatever he desired to build in Jerusalem, in Lebanon and throughout all the territory he ruled.

[7]All the people left from the Hittites, Amorites, Perizzites, Hivites and Jebusites (these peoples were not Israelites), [8]that is, their descendants remaining in the land, whom the Israelites had not destroyed—these Solomon conscripted for his slave labor force, as it is to this day. [9]But Solomon did not make slaves of the Israelites for his work; they were his fighting men, commanders of his captains, and commanders of his chariots and charioteers. [10]They were also King Solomon's chief officials—two hundred and fifty officials supervising the men.

[11]Solomon brought Pharaoh's daughter up from the City of David to the palace he had built for her, for he said, "My wife must not live in the palace of David king of Israel, because the places the ark of the LORD has entered are holy."

[12]On the altar of the LORD that he had built in front of the portico, Solomon sacrificed burnt offerings to the LORD, [13]according to the daily requirement for offerings commanded by Moses for Sabbaths, New Moons and the three annual feasts—the Feast of Unleavened Bread, the Feast of Weeks and the Feast of Tabernacles. [14]In keeping with the ordinance of his father David, he appointed the divisions of the priests for their duties, and the Levites to lead the praise and to assist the priests according to each day's requirement. He also appointed the gatekeepers by divisions for the various gates, because this was what David the man of God had ordered. [15]They did not deviate from the king's commands to the priests or to the Levites in any matter, including that of the treasuries.

[16]All Solomon's work was carried out, from the day the foundation of the temple of the LORD was laid until its completion. So the temple of the LORD was finished.

[17]Then Solomon went to Ezion Geber and Elath on the coast of Edom. [18]And Hiram sent him ships commanded by his own officers, men who knew the sea. These, with Solomon's men, sailed to Ophir and brought back four hundred and fifty talents[d] of gold, which they delivered to King Solomon.

The Queen of Sheba Visits Solomon

9 When the queen of Sheba heard of Solomon's fame, she came to Jerusalem to test him with hard questions. Arriving with a very great caravan—with camels carrying spices, large quantities of gold, and precious stones—she came to Solomon and talked with him about all she

---

[a]19 The Hebrew is plural.   [b]2 Hebrew *Huram*, a variant of *Hiram*; also in verse 18   [c]6 Or *charioteers*   [d]18 That is, about 17 tons (about 16 metric tons)

had on her mind. ²Solomon answered all her questions; nothing was too hard for him to explain to her. ³When the queen of Sheba saw the wisdom of Solomon, as well as the palace he had built, ⁴the food on his table, the seating of his officials, the attending servants in their robes, the cupbearers in their robes and the burnt offerings he made at*ᵃ* the temple of the LORD, she was overwhelmed.

⁵She said to the king, "The report I heard in my own country about your achievements and your wisdom is true. ⁶But I did not believe what they said until I came and saw with my own eyes. Indeed, not even half the greatness of your wisdom was told me; you have far exceeded the report I heard. ⁷How happy your men must be! How happy your officials, who continually stand before you and hear your wisdom! ⁸Praise be to the LORD your God, who has delighted in you and placed you on his throne as king to rule for the LORD your God. Because of the love of your God for Israel and his desire to uphold them forever, he has made you king over them, to maintain justice and righteousness."

⁹Then she gave the king 120 talents*ᵇ* of gold, large quantities of spices, and precious stones. There had never been such spices as those the queen of Sheba gave to King Solomon.

¹⁰(The men of Hiram and the men of Solomon brought gold from Ophir; they also brought algumwood*ᶜ* and precious stones. ¹¹The king used the algumwood to make steps for the temple of the LORD and for the royal palace, and to make harps and lyres for the musicians. Nothing like them had ever been seen in Judah.)

¹²King Solomon gave the queen of Sheba all she desired and asked for; he gave her more than she had brought to him. Then she left and returned with her retinue to her own country.

Solomon's Splendor

¹³The weight of the gold that Solomon received yearly was 666 talents,*ᵈ* ¹⁴not including the revenues brought in by merchants and traders. Also all the kings of Arabia and the governors of the land brought gold and silver to Solomon.

¹⁵King Solomon made two hundred large shields of hammered gold; six hundred bekas*ᵉ* of hammered gold went into each shield. ¹⁶He also made three

hundred small shields of hammered gold, with three hundred bekas*ᶠ* of gold in each shield. The king put them in the Palace of the Forest of Lebanon.

¹⁷Then the king made a great throne inlaid with ivory and overlaid with pure gold. ¹⁸The throne had six steps, and a footstool of gold was attached to it. On both sides of the seat were armrests, with a lion standing beside each of them. ¹⁹Twelve lions stood on the six steps, one at either end of each step. Nothing like it had ever been made for any other kingdom. ²⁰All King Solomon's goblets were gold, and all the household articles in the Palace of the Forest of Lebanon were pure gold. Nothing was made of silver, because silver was considered of little value in Solomon's day. ²¹The king had a fleet of trading ships*ᵍ* manned by Hiram's*ʰ* men. Once every three years it returned, carrying gold, silver and ivory, and apes and baboons.

²²King Solomon was greater in riches and wisdom than all the other kings of the earth. ²³All the kings of the earth sought audience with Solomon to hear the wisdom God had put in his heart. ²⁴Year after year, everyone who came brought a gift—articles of silver and gold, and robes, weapons and spices, and horses and mules.

²⁵Solomon had four thousand stalls for horses and chariots, and twelve thousand

---

ᵃ4 Or *the ascent by which he went up to*
ᵇ9 That is, about 4 1/2 tons (about 4 metric tons)
ᶜ10 Probably a variant of *almugwood*   *ᵈ13* That is, about 25 tons (about 23 metric tons)
ᵉ15 That is, about 7 1/2 pounds (about 3.5 kilograms)   *ᶠ16* That is, about 3 3/4 pounds (about 1.7 kilograms)   *ᵍ21* Hebrew *of ships that could go to Tarshish*   *ʰ21* Hebrew *Huram,* a variant of *Hiram*

POINT OF INTEREST

2 Chronicles 9:1

The kingdom of Sheba was located in the area of what is now Yemen. The queen's camel caravan must have taken weeks to travel the nearly fifteen hundred miles of desert between Sheba and Jerusalem. This was no casual "drop-over-for-coffee" visit; rather, it was a quest to meet and interview a royal superstar.

horses,*a* which he kept in the chariot cities and also with him in Jerusalem. 26He ruled over all the kings from the River*b* to the land of the Philistines, as far as the border of Egypt. 27The king made silver as common in Jerusalem as stones, and cedar as plentiful as sycamore-fig trees in the foothills. 28Solomon's horses were imported from Egypt*c* and from all other countries.

Solomon's Death

29As for the other events of Solomon's reign, from beginning to end, are they not written in the records of Nathan the prophet, in the prophecy of Ahijah the Shilonite and in the visions of Iddo the seer concerning Jeroboam son of Nebat? 30Solomon reigned in Jerusalem over all Israel forty years. 31Then he rested with his fathers and was buried in the city of David his father. And Rehoboam his son succeeded him as king.

Israel Rebels Against Rehoboam

10 Rehoboam went to Shechem, for all the Israelites had gone there to make him king. 2When Jeroboam son of Nebat heard this (he was in Egypt, where he had fled from King Solomon), he returned from Egypt. 3So they sent for Jeroboam, and he and all Israel went to Rehoboam and said to him: 4"Your father put a heavy yoke on us, but now lighten the harsh labor and the heavy yoke he put on us, and we will serve you."

5Rehoboam answered, "Come back to me in three days." So the people went away.

6Then King Rehoboam consulted the elders who had served his father Solomon during his lifetime. "How would you advise me to answer these people?" he asked.

7They replied, "If you will be kind to these people and please them and give them a favorable answer, they will always be your servants."

8But Rehoboam rejected the advice the elders gave him and consulted the young men who had grown up with him and were serving him. 9He asked them, "What is your advice? How should we answer these people who say to me, 'Lighten the yoke your father put on us'?"

10The young men who had grown up with him replied, "Tell the people who have said to you, 'Your father put a heavy yoke on us, but make our yoke lighter'—tell them, 'My little finger is thicker than my father's waist. 11My father laid on you a heavy yoke; I will make it even heavier. My father scourged you with whips; I will scourge you with scorpions.' "

12Three days later Jeroboam and all the people returned to Rehoboam, as the king had said, "Come back to me in three days." 13The king answered them harshly. Rejecting the advice of the elders, 14he followed the advice of the young men and said, "My father made your yoke heavy; I will make it even heavier. My father scourged you with whips; I will scourge you with scorpions." 15So the king did not listen to the people, for this turn of events was from God, to fulfill the word the LORD had spoken to Jeroboam son of Nebat through Ahijah the Shilonite.

16When all Israel saw that the king refused to listen to them, they answered the king:

"What share do we have in David,
    what part in Jesse's son?
To your tents, O Israel!
    Look after your own house,
        O David!"

So all the Israelites went home. 17But as for the Israelites who were living in the towns of Judah, Rehoboam still ruled over them.

18King Rehoboam sent out Adoniram,*d* who was in charge of forced labor, but the Israelites stoned him to death. King Rehoboam, however, managed to get into his chariot and escape to Jerusalem. 19So Israel has been in rebellion against the house of David to this day.

11 When Rehoboam arrived in Jerusalem, he mustered the house of Judah and Benjamin—a hundred and eighty thousand fighting men—to make war against Israel and to regain the kingdom for Rehoboam.

2But this word of the LORD came to Shemaiah the man of God: 3"Say to Rehoboam son of Solomon king of Judah and to all the Israelites in Judah and Benjamin, 4'This is what the LORD says: Do not go up to fight against your brothers. Go home,

---

a25 Or *charioteers*   *b26* That is, the Euphrates
c28 Or possibly *Muzur*, a region in Cilicia
d18 Hebrew *Hadoram*, a variant of *Adoniram*

every one of you, for this is my doing.' "
So they obeyed the words of the LORD and
turned back from marching against Jeroboam.

Rehoboam Fortifies Judah

⁵Rehoboam lived in Jerusalem and
built up towns for defense in Judah:
⁶Bethlehem, Etam, Tekoa, ⁷Beth Zur,
Soco, Adullam, ⁸Gath, Mareshah, Ziph,
⁹Adoraim, Lachish, Azekah, ¹⁰Zorah, Aijalon and Hebron. These were fortified
cities in Judah and Benjamin. ¹¹He
strengthened their defenses and put commanders in them, with supplies of food,
olive oil and wine. ¹²He put shields and
spears in all the cities, and made them
very strong. So Judah and Benjamin were
his.

¹³The priests and Levites from all their
districts throughout Israel sided with
him. ¹⁴The Levites even abandoned their
pasturelands and property, and came to
Judah and Jerusalem because Jeroboam
and his sons had rejected them as priests
of the LORD. ¹⁵And he appointed his own
priests for the high places and for the
goat and calf idols he had made. ¹⁶Those
from every tribe of Israel who set their
hearts on seeking the LORD, the God of
Israel, followed the Levites to Jerusalem
to offer sacrifices to the LORD, the God
of their fathers. ¹⁷They strengthened the
kingdom of Judah and supported Rehoboam son of Solomon three years, walking in the ways of David and Solomon
during this time.

Rehoboam's Family

¹⁸Rehoboam married Mahalath, who
was the daughter of David's son Jerimoth
and of Abihail, the daughter of Jesse's
son Eliab. ¹⁹She bore him sons: Jeush,
Shemariah and Zaham. ²⁰Then he married Maacah daughter of Absalom, who
bore him Abijah, Attai, Ziza and Shelomith. ²¹Rehoboam loved Maacah daughter of Absalom more than any of his other
wives and concubines. In all, he had
eighteen wives and sixty concubines,
twenty-eight sons and sixty daughters.
²²Rehoboam appointed Abijah son of
Maacah to be the chief prince among his
brothers, in order to make him king. ²³He
acted wisely, dispersing some of his sons
throughout the districts of Judah and
Benjamin, and to all the fortified cities.
He gave them abundant provisions and
took many wives for them.

Shishak Attacks Jerusalem

12 After Rehoboam's position as king
was established and he had become
strong, he and all Israel*ᵃ* with him abandoned the law of the LORD. ²Because they
had been unfaithful to the LORD, Shishak
king of Egypt attacked Jerusalem in the
fifth year of King Rehoboam. ³With
twelve hundred chariots and sixty thousand horsemen and the innumerable
troops of Libyans, Sukkites and Cushites*ᵇ* that came with him from Egypt,
⁴he captured the fortified cities of Judah
and came as far as Jerusalem.

⁵Then the prophet Shemaiah came to
Rehoboam and to the leaders of Judah
who had assembled in Jerusalem for fear
of Shishak, and he said to them, "This
is what the LORD says, 'You have abandoned me; therefore, I now abandon you
to Shishak.' "

⁶The leaders of Israel and the king
humbled themselves and said, "The LORD
is just."

⁷When the LORD saw that they humbled themselves, this word of the LORD
came to Shemaiah: "Since they have
humbled themselves, I will not destroy
them but will soon give them deliverance. My wrath will not be poured out on
Jerusalem through Shishak. ⁸They will,
however, become subject to him, so that
they may learn the difference between
serving me and serving the kings of other
lands."

⁹When Shishak king of Egypt attacked
Jerusalem, he carried off the treasures of
the temple of the LORD and the treasures
of the royal palace. He took everything,
including the gold shields Solomon had
made. ¹⁰So King Rehoboam made bronze
shields to replace them and assigned
these to the commanders of the guard on
duty at the entrance to the royal palace.
¹¹Whenever the king went to the LORD's
temple, the guards went with him, bearing the shields, and afterward they returned them to the guardroom.

¹²Because Rehoboam humbled himself, the LORD's anger turned from him,
and he was not totally destroyed. Indeed,
there was some good in Judah.

¹³King Rehoboam established himself
firmly in Jerusalem and continued as
king. He was forty-one years old when he

ᵃ1 That is, Judah, as frequently in 2 Chronicles
ᵇ3 That is, people from the upper Nile region

became king, and he reigned seventeen years in Jerusalem, the city the LORD had chosen out of all the tribes of Israel in which to put his Name. His mother's name was Naamah; she was an Ammonite. ¹⁴He did evil because he had not set his heart on seeking the LORD.

¹⁵As for the events of Rehoboam's reign, from beginning to end, are they not written in the records of Shemaiah the prophet and of Iddo the seer that deal with genealogies? There was continual warfare between Rehoboam and Jeroboam. ¹⁶Rehoboam rested with his fathers and was buried in the City of David. And Abijah his son succeeded him as king.

Abijah King of Judah

13 In the eighteenth year of the reign of Jeroboam, Abijah became king of Judah, ²and he reigned in Jerusalem three years. His mother's name was Maacah,ᵃ a daughterᵇ of Uriel of Gibeah.

There was war between Abijah and Jeroboam. ³Abijah went into battle with a force of four hundred thousand able fighting men, and Jeroboam drew up a battle line against him with eight hundred thousand able troops.

⁴Abijah stood on Mount Zemaraim, in

ᵃ2 Most Septuagint manuscripts and Syriac (see also 2 Chron. 11:20 and 1 Kings 15:2); Hebrew *Micaiah*   ᵇ2 Or *granddaughter*

Read 2 Chronicles 12:1–16
Key Verse 2 Chronicles 12:14

The Right Place to Get Advice — Joe Bernardy

Solomon was the wisest, wealthiest king on earth, and he was popular in many ways. But he left behind a staggering national debt! When Rehoboam, his son and heir, succeeded him to the throne of Israel, the people came before him with a request: "Your father put a heavy yoke on us, but now lighten the harsh labor and the heavy yoke he put on us, and we will serve you" (2 Chronicles 10:4).

Rehoboam sought advice from each of two groups—the elders of Israel and his friends. The elders of Israel advised him that he would win the loyalty of the people by granting their request for mercy and generosity. But his friends advised him to make the people's load heavier and their treatment more harsh—to show them who was king!

The young king took the advice of his friends—with a terrible outcome. His kingdom was torn in two; only two of Israel's twelve tribes remained loyal to him. In Rehoboam's case, listening to the right advice would not only have been a good idea, but it would have averted centuries of suffering.

Rehoboam's actions are described as evil, but he was not so different from most of us. He listened to his friends. He followed the wisdom of the world, which says, "Assert yourself! Use your power." This was the sad conclusion reached after Rehoboam's 17-year reign: "He did evil because he had not set his heart on seeking the LORD" (2 Chronicles 12:14).

If we are to make wise choices and resist evil, we must set our hearts on seeking the LORD—making it a regular practice to read the Bible, pray and obey God.

A Deeper Look
2 Chronicles 7:14; Proverbs 1:20–33; Proverbs 18:15

Go to page 479 for your next devotional reading.

the hill country of Ephraim, and said, "Jeroboam and all Israel, listen to me! ⁵Don't you know that the Lord, the God of Israel, has given the kingship of Israel to David and his descendants forever by a covenant of salt? ⁶Yet Jeroboam son of Nebat, an official of Solomon son of David, rebelled against his master. ⁷Some worthless scoundrels gathered around him and opposed Rehoboam son of Solomon when he was young and indecisive and not strong enough to resist them.

⁸"And now you plan to resist the kingdom of the Lord, which is in the hands of David's descendants. You are indeed a vast army and have with you the golden calves that Jeroboam made to be your gods. ⁹But didn't you drive out the priests of the Lord, the sons of Aaron, and the Levites, and make priests of your own as the peoples of other lands do? Whoever comes to consecrate himself with a young bull and seven rams may become a priest of what are not gods.

¹⁰"As for us, the Lord is our God, and we have not forsaken him. The priests who serve the Lord are sons of Aaron, and the Levites assist them. ¹¹Every morning and evening they present burnt offerings and fragrant incense to the Lord. They set out the bread on the ceremonially clean table and light the lamps on the gold lampstand every evening. We are observing the requirements of the Lord our God. But you have forsaken him. ¹²God is with us; he is our leader. His priests with their trumpets will sound the battle cry against you. Men of Israel, do not fight against the Lord, the God of your fathers, for you will not succeed."

¹³Now Jeroboam had sent troops around to the rear, so that while he was in front of Judah the ambush was behind them. ¹⁴Judah turned and saw that they were being attacked at both front and rear. Then they cried out to the Lord. The priests blew their trumpets ¹⁵and the men of Judah raised the battle cry. At the sound of their battle cry, God routed Jeroboam and all Israel before Abijah and Judah. ¹⁶The Israelites fled before Judah, and God delivered them into their hands. ¹⁷Abijah and his men inflicted heavy losses on them, so that there were five hundred thousand casualties among Israel's able men. ¹⁸The men of Israel were subdued on that occasion, and the men of Judah were victorious because they relied on the Lord, the God of their fathers.

¹⁹Abijah pursued Jeroboam and took from him the towns of Bethel, Jeshanah and Ephron, with their surrounding villages. ²⁰Jeroboam did not regain power during the time of Abijah. And the Lord struck him down and he died.

²¹But Abijah grew in strength. He married fourteen wives and had twenty-two sons and sixteen daughters.

²²The other events of Abijah's reign, what he did and what he said, are written in the annotations of the prophet Iddo.

14 And Abijah rested with his fathers and was buried in the City of David. Asa his son succeeded him as king, and in his days the country was at peace for ten years.

Asa King of Judah

²Asa did what was good and right in the eyes of the Lord his God. ³He removed the foreign altars and the high places, smashed the sacred stones and cut down the Asherah poles.ᵃ ⁴He commanded Judah to seek the Lord, the God of their fathers, and to obey his laws and commands. ⁵He removed the high places and incense altars in every town in Judah, and the kingdom was at peace under him. ⁶He built up the fortified cities of Judah, since the land was at peace. No one was at war with him during those years, for the Lord gave him rest.

⁷"Let us build up these towns," he said to Judah, "and put walls around them, with towers, gates and bars. The land is still ours, because we have sought the Lord our God; we sought him and he has given us rest on every side." So they built and prospered.

⁸Asa had an army of three hundred thousand men from Judah, equipped with large shields and with spears, and two hundred and eighty thousand from Benjamin, armed with small shields and with bows. All these were brave fighting men.

⁹Zerah the Cushite marched out against them with a vast armyᵇ and three hundred chariots, and came as far as Mareshah. ¹⁰Asa went out to meet him, and they took up battle positions in the Valley of Zephathah near Mareshah. ¹¹Then Asa called to the Lord his God and said, "Lord, there is no one like you

ᵃ3 That is, symbols of the goddess Asherah; here and elsewhere in 2 Chronicles   ᵇ9 Hebrew *with an army of a thousand thousands* or *with an army of thousands upon thousands* to help the powerless against the mighty. Help us, O Lord our God, for we rely on you, and in your name we have come against this vast army. O Lord, you are our God; do not let man prevail against you."

¹²The Lord struck down the Cushites before Asa and Judah. The Cushites fled, ¹³and Asa and his army pursued them as far as Gerar. Such a great number of Cushites fell that they could not recover; they were crushed before the Lord and his forces. The men of Judah carried off a large amount of plunder. ¹⁴They destroyed all the villages around Gerar, for the terror of the Lord had fallen upon them. They plundered all these villages, since there was much booty there. ¹⁵They also attacked the camps of the herdsmen and carried off droves of sheep and goats and camels. Then they returned to Jerusalem.

Asa's Reform

15 The Spirit of God came upon Azariah son of Oded. ²He went out to meet Asa and said to him, "Listen to me, Asa and all Judah and Benjamin. The Lord is with you when you are with him. If you seek him, he will be found by you, but if you forsake him, he will forsake you. ³For a long time Israel was without the true God, without a priest to teach and without the law. ⁴But in their distress they turned to the Lord, the God of Israel, and sought him, and he was found by them. ⁵In those days it was not safe to travel about, for all the inhabitants of the lands were in great turmoil. ⁶One nation was being crushed by another and one city by another, because God was troubling them with every kind of distress. ⁷But as for you, be strong and do not give up, for your work will be rewarded."

⁸When Asa heard these words and the prophecy of Azariah son of[a] Oded the prophet, he took courage. He removed the detestable idols from the whole land of Judah and Benjamin and from the towns he had captured in the hills of Ephraim. He repaired the altar of the Lord that was in front of the portico of the Lord's temple.

⁹Then he assembled all Judah and Benjamin and the people from Ephraim, Manasseh and Simeon who had settled among them, for large numbers had come over to him from Israel when they saw that the Lord his God was with him.

¹⁰They assembled at Jerusalem in the third month of the fifteenth year of Asa's reign. ¹¹At that time they sacrificed to the Lord seven hundred head of cattle and seven thousand sheep and goats from the plunder they had brought back. ¹²They entered into a covenant to seek the Lord, the God of their fathers, with all their heart and soul. ¹³All who would not seek the Lord, the God of Israel, were to be put to death, whether small or great, man or woman. ¹⁴They took an oath to the Lord with loud acclamation, with shouting and with trumpets and horns. ¹⁵All Judah rejoiced about the oath because they had sworn it wholeheartedly. They sought God eagerly, and he was found by them. So the Lord gave them rest on every side.

¹⁶King Asa also deposed his grandmother Maacah from her position as queen mother, because she had made a repulsive Asherah pole. Asa cut the pole down, broke it up and burned it in the Kidron Valley. ¹⁷Although he did not remove the high places from Israel, Asa's heart was fully committed ⌊to the Lord⌋ all his life. ¹⁸He brought into the temple of God the silver and gold and the articles that he and his father had dedicated.

¹⁹There was no more war until the thirty-fifth year of Asa's reign.

Asa's Last Years

16 In the thirty-sixth year of Asa's reign Baasha king of Israel went up against Judah and fortified Ramah to prevent anyone from leaving or entering the territory of Asa king of Judah.

²Asa then took the silver and gold out of the treasuries of the Lord's temple and of his own palace and sent it to Ben-

---

a8 Vulgate and Syriac (see also Septuagint and verse 1); Hebrew does not have *Azariah son of.*

POINT OF INTEREST

2 Chronicles 15:2

God has bridged the chasm between himself and human beings with his gift of grace and forgiveness through Jesus Christ. But human beings have a responsibility too. God's grace is extended to us all—we must reach out, take it and rejoice in it.

Hadad king of Aram, who was ruling in Damascus. ³"Let there be a treaty between me and you," he said, "as there was between my father and your father. See, I am sending you silver and gold. Now break your treaty with Baasha king of Israel so he will withdraw from me."

⁴Ben-Hadad agreed with King Asa and sent the commanders of his forces against the towns of Israel. They conquered Ijon, Dan, Abel Maim*ᵃ* and all the store cities of Naphtali. ⁵When Baasha heard this, he stopped building Ramah and abandoned his work. ⁶Then King Asa brought all the men of Judah, and they carried away from Ramah the stones and timber Baasha had been using. With them he built up Geba and Mizpah.

⁷At that time Hanani the seer came to Asa king of Judah and said to him: "Because you relied on the king of Aram and not on the Lᴏʀᴅ your God, the army of the king of Aram has escaped from your hand. ⁸Were not the Cushites*ᵇ* and Libyans a mighty army with great numbers of chariots and horsemen*ᶜ*? Yet when you relied on the Lᴏʀᴅ, he delivered them into your hand. ⁹For the eyes of the Lᴏʀᴅ

ᵃ4 Also known as *Abel Beth Maacah*   *ᵇ8* That is, people from the upper Nile region   *ᶜ8* Or *charioteers*

Read 2 Chronicles 16:1–14
Key Verse 2 Chronicles 16:9

Wholehearted – Jan Rodgers

Sometimes, on warm summer nights when the sky is clear and the moon is bright, I like to escape to my backyard to stargaze. Clad in my favorite oversized sweatshirt, I sink into a patio chair and drink in the panoramic view. The beauty of the star-studded sky is breathtaking, forcing the troubles of the day off my shoulders and into the night air.

I wonder, as I stare into the infinite vastness of the sky, whether the eyes of the Lord are staring back at me. What do they see? Does God see a heart that belongs to him? Does he see a life yielded to him?

In the night's silence, when my heart is quiet, I am forced to admit that all too often I can be like that satellite blending in with the stars. To the Christians around me, I appear to have a whole heart, engaged in many good activities. But whether I'm in a Bible study, at church, in prayer or having a quiet time, God can see the ugly faces of the anger, jealously, discontent and pride I work so hard to disguise. All these attitudes keep my heart from being completely his.

I often ask God to renew my commitment and create a whole heart within me. I don't want to become like the Pharisees whom Jesus criticized: "You hypocrites! You clean the outside of the cup and dish, but inside they are full of greed and self-indulgence" (Matthew 23:25). But I pray that when God searches for whole hearts, his eyes will rest on me, "For God, who said, 'Let light shine out of darkness,' made his light shine in our hearts to give us the light of the knowledge of the glory of God in the face of Christ" (2 Corinthians 4:6).

A Deeper Look
Psalm 51; 1 John 1:9; 3:19–20

Go to page 483 for your next devotional reading.

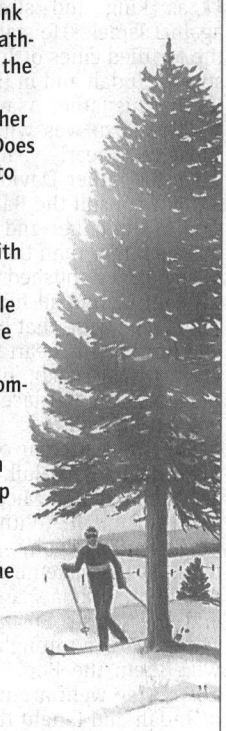

range throughout the earth to strengthen those whose hearts are fully committed to him. You have done a foolish thing, and from now on you will be at war."

¹⁰Asa was angry with the seer because of this; he was so enraged that he put him in prison. At the same time Asa brutally oppressed some of the people.

¹¹The events of Asa's reign, from beginning to end, are written in the book of the kings of Judah and Israel. ¹²In the thirty-ninth year of his reign Asa was afflicted with a disease in his feet. Though his disease was severe, even in his illness he did not seek help from the LORD, but only from the physicians. ¹³Then in the forty-first year of his reign Asa died and rested with his fathers. ¹⁴They buried him in the tomb that he had cut out for himself in the City of David. They laid him on a bier covered with spices and various blended perfumes, and they made a huge fire in his honor.

Jehoshaphat King of Judah

17 Jehoshaphat his son succeeded him as king and strengthened himself against Israel. ²He stationed troops in all the fortified cities of Judah and put garrisons in Judah and in the towns of Ephraim that his father Asa had captured.

³The LORD was with Jehoshaphat because in his early years he walked in the ways his father David had followed. He did not consult the Baals ⁴but sought the God of his father and followed his commands rather than the practices of Israel. ⁵The LORD established the kingdom under his control; and all Judah brought gifts to Jehoshaphat, so that he had great wealth and honor. ⁶His heart was devoted to the ways of the LORD; furthermore, he removed the high places and the Asherah poles from Judah.

⁷In the third year of his reign he sent his officials Ben-Hail, Obadiah, Zechariah, Nethanel and Micaiah to teach in the towns of Judah. ⁸With them were certain Levites—Shemaiah, Nethaniah, Zebadiah, Asahel, Shemiramoth, Jehonathan, Adonijah, Tobijah and Tob-Adonijah— and the priests Elishama and Jehoram. ⁹They taught throughout Judah, taking with them the Book of the Law of the LORD; they went around to all the towns of Judah and taught the people.

¹⁰The fear of the LORD fell on all the kingdoms of the lands surrounding Judah, so that they did not make war with

Jehoshaphat. ¹¹Some Philistines brought Jehoshaphat gifts and silver as tribute, and the Arabs brought him flocks: seven thousand seven hundred rams and seven thousand seven hundred goats.

¹²Jehoshaphat became more and more powerful; he built forts and store cities in Judah ¹³and had large supplies in the towns of Judah. He also kept experienced fighting men in Jerusalem. ¹⁴Their enrollment by families was as follows:

From Judah, commanders of units of 1,000:
  Adnah the commander, with 300,000 fighting men;
¹⁵next, Jehohanan the commander, with 280,000;
¹⁶next, Amasiah son of Zicri, who volunteered himself for the service of the LORD, with 200,000.
¹⁷From Benjamin:
  Eliada, a valiant soldier, with 200,000 men armed with bows and shields;
¹⁸next, Jehozabad, with 180,000 men armed for battle.

¹⁹These were the men who served the king, besides those he stationed in the fortified cities throughout Judah.

Micaiah Prophesies Against Ahab

18 Now Jehoshaphat had great wealth and honor, and he allied himself with Ahab by marriage. ²Some years later he went down to visit Ahab in Samaria. Ahab slaughtered many sheep and cattle for him and the people with him and urged him to attack Ramoth Gilead. ³Ahab king of Israel asked Jehoshaphat king of Judah, "Will you go with me against Ramoth Gilead?"

Jehoshaphat replied, "I am as you are, and my people as your people; we will join you in the war." ⁴But Jehoshaphat also said to the king of Israel, "First seek the counsel of the LORD."

⁵So the king of Israel brought together the prophets—four hundred men—and asked them, "Shall we go to war against Ramoth Gilead, or shall I refrain?"

"Go," they answered, "for God will give it into the king's hand."

⁶But Jehoshaphat asked, "Is there not a prophet of the LORD here whom we can inquire of?"

⁷The king of Israel answered Jehoshaphat, "There is still one man through

whom we can inquire of the Lord, but I hate him because he never prophesies anything good about me, but always bad. He is Micaiah son of Imlah."

"The king should not say that," Jehoshaphat replied.

⁸So the king of Israel called one of his officials and said, "Bring Micaiah son of Imlah at once."

⁹Dressed in their royal robes, the king of Israel and Jehoshaphat king of Judah were sitting on their thrones at the threshing floor by the entrance to the gate of Samaria, with all the prophets prophesying before them. ¹⁰Now Zedekiah son of Kenaanah had made iron horns, and he declared, "This is what the Lord says: 'With these you will gore the Arameans until they are destroyed.' "

¹¹All the other prophets were prophesying the same thing. "Attack Ramoth Gilead and be victorious," they said, "for the Lord will give it into the king's hand."

¹²The messenger who had gone to summon Micaiah said to him, "Look, as one man the other prophets are predicting success for the king. Let your word agree with theirs, and speak favorably."

¹³But Micaiah said, "As surely as the Lord lives, I can tell him only what my God says."

¹⁴When he arrived, the king asked him, "Micaiah, shall we go to war against Ramoth Gilead, or shall I refrain?"

"Attack and be victorious," he answered, "for they will be given into your hand."

¹⁵The king said to him, "How many times must I make you swear to tell me nothing but the truth in the name of the Lord?"

¹⁶Then Micaiah answered, "I saw all Israel scattered on the hills like sheep without a shepherd, and the Lord said, 'These people have no master. Let each one go home in peace.' "

¹⁷The king of Israel said to Jehoshaphat, "Didn't I tell you that he never prophesies anything good about me, but only bad?"

¹⁸Micaiah continued, "Therefore hear the word of the Lord: I saw the Lord sitting on his throne with all the host of heaven standing on his right and on his left. ¹⁹And the Lord said, 'Who will entice Ahab king of Israel into attacking Ramoth Gilead and going to his death there?'

"One suggested this, and another that. ²⁰Finally, a spirit came forward, stood before the Lord and said, 'I will entice him.'

" 'By what means?' the Lord asked.

²¹" 'I will go and be a lying spirit in the mouths of all his prophets,' he said.

" 'You will succeed in enticing him,' said the Lord. 'Go and do it.'

²²"So now the Lord has put a lying spirit in the mouths of these prophets of yours. The Lord has decreed disaster for you."

²³Then Zedekiah son of Kenaanah went up and slapped Micaiah in the face. "Which way did the spirit from*ᵃ* the Lord go when he went from me to speak to you?" he asked.

²⁴Micaiah replied, "You will find out on the day you go to hide in an inner room."

²⁵The king of Israel then ordered, "Take Micaiah and send him back to Amon the ruler of the city and to Joash the king's son, ²⁶and say, 'This is what the king says: Put this fellow in prison and give him nothing but bread and water until I return safely.' "

²⁷Micaiah declared, "If you ever return safely, the Lord has not spoken through me." Then he added, "Mark my words, all you people!"

Ahab Killed at Ramoth Gilead

²⁸So the king of Israel and Jehoshaphat king of Judah went up to Ramoth Gilead. ²⁹The king of Israel said to Jehoshaphat, "I will enter the battle in disguise, but you wear your royal robes." So the king of Israel disguised himself and went into battle.

³⁰Now the king of Aram had ordered his chariot commanders, "Do not fight with anyone, small or great, except the king of Israel." ³¹When the chariot commanders saw Jehoshaphat, they thought, "This is the king of Israel." So they turned to attack him, but Jehoshaphat cried out, and the Lord helped him. God drew them away from him, ³²for when the chariot commanders saw that he was not the king of Israel, they stopped pursuing him.

³³But someone drew his bow at random and hit the king of Israel between the sections of his armor. The king told the chariot driver, "Wheel around and get me out of the fighting. I've been wounded." ³⁴All day long the battle raged, and the king of Israel propped

ᵃ23 Or Spirit of

himself up in his chariot facing the Arameans until evening. Then at sunset he died.

19 When Jehoshaphat king of Judah returned safely to his palace in Jerusalem, ²Jehu the seer, the son of Hanani, went out to meet him and said to the king, "Should you help the wicked and love*a* those who hate the LORD? Because of this, the wrath of the LORD is upon you. ³There is, however, some good in you, for you have rid the land of the Asherah poles and have set your heart on seeking God."

Jehoshaphat Appoints Judges

⁴Jehoshaphat lived in Jerusalem, and he went out again among the people from Beersheba to the hill country of Ephraim and turned them back to the LORD, the God of their fathers. ⁵He appointed judges in the land, in each of the fortified cities of Judah. ⁶He told them, "Consider carefully what you do, because you are not judging for man but for the LORD, who is with you whenever you give a verdict. ⁷Now let the fear of the LORD be upon you. Judge carefully, for with the LORD our God there is no injustice or partiality or bribery."

⁸In Jerusalem also, Jehoshaphat appointed some of the Levites, priests and heads of Israelite families to administer the law of the LORD and to settle disputes. And they lived in Jerusalem. ⁹He gave them these orders: "You must serve faithfully and wholeheartedly in the fear of the LORD. ¹⁰In every case that comes before you from your fellow countrymen who live in the cities—whether bloodshed or other concerns of the law, commands, decrees or ordinances—you are to warn them not to sin against the LORD; otherwise his wrath will come on you and your brothers. Do this, and you will not sin.

¹¹"Amariah the chief priest will be over you in any matter concerning the LORD, and Zebadiah son of Ishmael, the leader of the tribe of Judah, will be over you in any matter concerning the king, and the Levites will serve as officials before you. Act with courage, and may the LORD be with those who do well."

Jehoshaphat Defeats Moab and Ammon

20 After this, the Moabites and Ammonites with some of the Meu-

nites*b* came to make war on Jehoshaphat.

²Some men came and told Jehoshaphat, "A vast army is coming against you from Edom,*c* from the other side of the Sea.*d* It is already in Hazazon Tamar" (that is, En Gedi). ³Alarmed, Jehoshaphat resolved to inquire of the LORD, and he proclaimed a fast for all Judah. ⁴The people of Judah came together to seek help from the LORD; indeed, they came from every town in Judah to seek him.

⁵Then Jehoshaphat stood up in the assembly of Judah and Jerusalem at the temple of the LORD in the front of the new courtyard ⁶and said:

"O LORD, God of our fathers, are you not the God who is in heaven? You rule over all the kingdoms of the nations. Power and might are in your hand, and no one can withstand you. ⁷O our God, did you not drive out the inhabitants of this land before your people Israel and give it forever to the descendants of Abraham your friend? ⁸They have lived in it and have built in it a sanctuary for your Name, saying, ⁹'If calamity comes upon us, whether the sword of judgment, or plague or famine, we will stand in your presence before this temple that bears your Name and will cry out to you in our distress, and you will hear us and save us.'

¹⁰"But now here are men from Ammon, Moab and Mount Seir, whose territory you would not allow Israel to invade when they came from Egypt; so they turned away from them and did not destroy them. ¹¹See how they are repaying us by coming to drive us out of the possession you gave us as an inheritance. ¹²O our God, will you not judge them? For we have no power to face this vast army that is attacking us. We do not know what to do, but our eyes are upon you."

¹³All the men of Judah, with their wives and children and little ones, stood there before the LORD.

---

*a*2 Or *and make alliances with*   *b*1 Some Septuagint manuscripts; Hebrew *Ammonites*   *c*2 One Hebrew manuscript; most Hebrew manuscripts, Septuagint and Vulgate *Aram*   *d*2 That is, the Dead Sea

¹⁴Then the Spirit of the LORD came upon Jahaziel son of Zechariah, the son of Benaiah, the son of Jeiel, the son of Mattaniah, a Levite and descendant of Asaph, as he stood in the assembly.

¹⁵He said: "Listen, King Jehoshaphat and all who live in Judah and Jerusalem! This is what the LORD says to you: 'Do not be afraid or discouraged because of this vast army. For the battle is not yours, but God's. ¹⁶Tomorrow march down against them. They will be climbing up by the Pass of Ziz, and you will find them at the end of the gorge in the Desert of Jeruel. ¹⁷You will not have to fight this battle. Take up your positions; stand firm and see the deliverance the LORD will give you, O Judah and Jerusalem. Do not be afraid; do not be discouraged. Go out to face them tomorrow, and the LORD will be with you.' "

¹⁸Jehoshaphat bowed with his face to the ground, and all the people of Judah and Jerusalem fell down in worship before the LORD. ¹⁹Then some Levites from the Kohathites and Korahites stood up

---

Read *2 Chronicles 20:1–30*
Key Verse *2 Chronicles 20:15*

The Battle Belongs to the Lord — Ward Ballard

How do you react when you're overwhelmed? Do you freak out? Do you run and hide? Do you start looking for someone to blame in case you fail? Do you take control and make demands? Where do you turn?

Jehoshaphat, the king of Judah, found himself in an overwhelming situation. One night he went to bed—his life and kingdom seemingly under control—but the next morning he was informed that enemies from neighboring regions were on their way to wipe him out.

How did he respond? First, he "resolved to inquire of the LORD" (2 Chronicles 20:3). Jehoshaphat *chose* to include God in his thinking. He turned to God in prayer and reminded God of his promise to save them. Jehoshaphat was realistic when he prayed, "We have no power to face this vast army that is attacking us. We do not know what to do, but our eyes are upon you" (2 Chronicles 20:12). He acknowledged his complete dependence upon God.

God sent his answer through the prophet Jahaziel: "Do not be afraid or discouraged because of this vast army. For the battle is not yours, but God's" (2 Chronicles 20:15).

He instructed the people to take their positions and stand firm. Jehoshaphat then called Judah to use these resources: "Have faith in the LORD your God and you will be upheld; have faith in his prophets and you will be successful" (2 Chronicles 20:20). As Judah followed Jehoshaphat's example of faith and began to sing and praise God, the Lord set ambushes, and Judah's enemies destroyed each other.

As believers, our lives are no longer our own; they are God's. So our conflicts are really God's, and they can be fought in his Spirit: " 'Not by might nor by power, but by my Spirit,' says the LORD Almighty" (Zechariah 4:6).

A Deeper Look
Psalm 20:7; Romans 8:35–37; Ephesians 6:10–17

Go to page 489 for your next devotional reading.

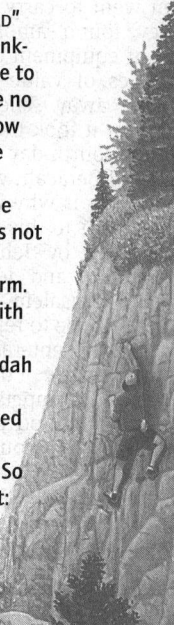

and praised the LORD, the God of Israel, with very loud voice.

²⁰Early in the morning they left for the Desert of Tekoa. As they set out, Jehoshaphat stood and said, "Listen to me, Judah and people of Jerusalem! Have faith in the LORD your God and you will be upheld; have faith in his prophets and you will be successful." ²¹After consulting the people, Jehoshaphat appointed men to sing to the LORD and to praise him for the splendor of his*a* holiness as they went out at the head of the army, saying:

"Give thanks to the LORD,
for his love endures forever."

²²As they began to sing and praise, the LORD set ambushes against the men of Ammon and Moab and Mount Seir who were invading Judah, and they were defeated. ²³The men of Ammon and Moab rose up against the men from Mount Seir to destroy and annihilate them. After they finished slaughtering the men from Seir, they helped to destroy one another.

²⁴When the men of Judah came to the place that overlooks the desert and looked toward the vast army, they saw only dead bodies lying on the ground; no one had escaped. ²⁵So Jehoshaphat and his men went to carry off their plunder, and they found among them a great amount of equipment and clothing*b* and also articles of value—more than they could take away. There was so much plunder that it took three days to collect it. ²⁶On the fourth day they assembled in the Valley of Beracah, where they praised the LORD. This is why it is called the Valley of Beracah*c* to this day.

²⁷Then, led by Jehoshaphat, all the men of Judah and Jerusalem returned joyfully to Jerusalem, for the LORD had given them cause to rejoice over their enemies. ²⁸They entered Jerusalem and went to the temple of the LORD with harps and lutes and trumpets.

²⁹The fear of God came upon all the kingdoms of the countries when they heard how the LORD had fought against the enemies of Israel. ³⁰And the kingdom of Jehoshaphat was at peace, for his God had given him rest on every side.

The End of Jehoshaphat's Reign

³¹So Jehoshaphat reigned over Judah. He was thirty-five years old when he became king of Judah, and he reigned in Jerusalem twenty-five years. His mother's name was Azubah daughter of Shilhi. ³²He walked in the ways of his father Asa and did not stray from them; he did what was right in the eyes of the LORD. ³³The high places, however, were not removed, and the people still had not set their hearts on the God of their fathers.

³⁴The other events of Jehoshaphat's reign, from beginning to end, are written in the annals of Jehu son of Hanani, which are recorded in the book of the kings of Israel.

³⁵Later, Jehoshaphat king of Judah made an alliance with Ahaziah king of Israel, who was guilty of wickedness. ³⁶He agreed with him to construct a fleet of trading ships.*d* After these were built at Ezion Geber, ³⁷Eliezer son of Dodavahu of Mareshah prophesied against Jehoshaphat, saying, "Because you have made an alliance with Ahaziah, the LORD will destroy what you have made." The ships were wrecked and were not able to set sail to trade.*e*

21 Then Jehoshaphat rested with his fathers and was buried with them in the City of David. And Jehoram his son succeeded him as king. ²Jehoram's brothers, the sons of Jehoshaphat, were Azariah, Jehiel, Zechariah, Azariahu, Michael and Shephatiah. All these were sons of Jehoshaphat king of Israel.*f* ³Their father had given them many gifts of silver and gold and articles of value, as well as fortified cities in Judah, but he had given the kingdom to Jehoram because he was his firstborn son.

Jehoram King of Judah

⁴When Jehoram established himself firmly over his father's kingdom, he put all his brothers to the sword along with some of the princes of Israel. ⁵Jehoram was thirty-two years old when he became king, and he reigned in Jerusalem eight years. ⁶He walked in the ways of the kings of Israel, as the house of Ahab had done, for he married a daughter of Ahab. He did evil in the eyes of the LORD. ⁷Nevertheless, because of the covenant the LORD had made with David, the LORD was not willing to destroy the house of David. He had promised to maintain a

---

a21 Or *him with the splendor of*   *b25* Some Hebrew manuscripts and Vulgate; most Hebrew manuscripts *corpses*   *c26* Beracah means *praise.*   *d36* Hebrew *of ships that could go to Tarshish*   *e37* Hebrew *sail for Tarshish*   *f2* That is, Judah, as frequently in 2 Chronicles lamp for him and his descendants forever.

⁸In the time of Jehoram, Edom rebelled against Judah and set up its own king. ⁹So Jehoram went there with his officers and all his chariots. The Edomites surrounded him and his chariot commanders, but he rose up and broke through by night. ¹⁰To this day Edom has been in rebellion against Judah.

Libnah revolted at the same time, because Jehoram had forsaken the LORD, the God of his fathers. ¹¹He had also built high places on the hills of Judah and had caused the people of Jerusalem to prostitute themselves and had led Judah astray.

¹²Jehoram received a letter from Elijah the prophet, which said:

"This is what the LORD, the God of your father David, says: 'You have not walked in the ways of your father Jehoshaphat or of Asa king of Judah. ¹³But you have walked in the ways of the kings of Israel, and you have led Judah and the people of Jerusalem to prostitute themselves, just as the house of Ahab did. You have also murdered your own brothers, members of your father's house, men who were better than you. ¹⁴So now the LORD is about to strike your people, your sons, your wives and everything that is yours, with a heavy blow. ¹⁵You yourself will be very ill with a lingering disease of the bowels, until the disease causes your bowels to come out.' "

¹⁶The LORD aroused against Jehoram the hostility of the Philistines and of the Arabs who lived near the Cushites. ¹⁷They attacked Judah, invaded it and carried off all the goods found in the king's palace, together with his sons and wives. Not a son was left to him except Ahaziah,ᵃ the youngest.

¹⁸After all this, the LORD afflicted Jehoram with an incurable disease of the bowels. ¹⁹In the course of time, at the end of the second year, his bowels came out because of the disease, and he died in great pain. His people made no fire in his honor, as they had for his fathers.

²⁰Jehoram was thirty-two years old when he became king, and he reigned in Jerusalem eight years. He passed away, to no one's regret, and was buried in the City of David, but not in the tombs of the kings.

Ahaziah King of Judah

22 The people of Jerusalem made Ahaziah, Jehoram's youngest son, king in his place, since the raiders, who came with the Arabs into the camp, had killed all the older sons. So Ahaziah son of Jehoram king of Judah began to reign.

²Ahaziah was twenty-twoᵇ years old when he became king, and he reigned in Jerusalem one year. His mother's name was Athaliah, a granddaughter of Omri.

³He too walked in the ways of the house of Ahab, for his mother encouraged him in doing wrong. ⁴He did evil in the eyes of the LORD, as the house of Ahab had done, for after his father's death they became his advisers, to his undoing. ⁵He also followed their counsel when he went with Joramᶜ son of Ahab king of Israel to war against Hazael king of Aram at Ramoth Gilead. The Arameans wounded Joram; ⁶so he returned to Jezreel to recover from the wounds they had inflicted on him at Ramothᵈ in his battle with Hazael king of Aram.

Then Ahaziahᵉ son of Jehoram king of Judah went down to Jezreel to see Joram son of Ahab because he had been wounded.

⁷Through Ahaziah's visit to Joram, God brought about Ahaziah's downfall. When Ahaziah arrived, he went out with Joram to meet Jehu son of Nimshi, whom the LORD had anointed to destroy the house of Ahab. ⁸While Jehu was executing judgment on the house of Ahab, he found the princes of Judah and the sons of Ahaziah's relatives, who had been attending Ahaziah, and he killed them. ⁹He then went in search of Ahaziah, and his men captured him while he was hiding in Samaria. He was brought to Jehu and put to death. They buried him, for they said, "He was a son of Jehoshaphat, who sought the LORD with all his heart." So there was no one in the house of Ahaziah powerful enough to retain the kingdom.

ᵃ17 Hebrew *Jehoahaz*, a variant of *Ahaziah*   ᵇ2 Some Septuagint manuscripts and Syriac (see also 2 Kings 8:26); Hebrew *forty-two*   ᶜ5 Hebrew *Jehoram*, a variant of *Joram*; also in verses 6 and 7   ᵈ6 Hebrew *Ramah*, a variant of *Ramoth*   ᵉ6 Some Hebrew manuscripts, Septuagint, Vulgate and Syriac (see also 2 Kings 8:29); most Hebrew manuscripts *Azariah*

Athaliah and Joash

¹⁰When Athaliah the mother of Ahaziah saw that her son was dead, she proceeded to destroy the whole royal family of the house of Judah. ¹¹But Jehosheba,ᵃ the daughter of King Jehoram, took Joash son of Ahaziah and stole him away from among the royal princes who were about to be murdered and put him and his nurse in a bedroom. Because Jehosheba,ᵃ the daughter of King Jehoram and wife of the priest Jehoiada, was Ahaziah's sister, she hid the child from Athaliah so she could not kill him. ¹²He remained hidden with them at the temple of God for six years while Athaliah ruled the land.

23 In the seventh year Jehoiada showed his strength. He made a covenant with the commanders of units of a hundred: Azariah son of Jeroham, Ishmael son of Jehohanan, Azariah son of Obed, Maaseiah son of Adaiah, and Elishaphat son of Zicri. ²They went throughout Judah and gathered the Levites and the heads of Israelite families from all the towns. When they came to Jerusalem, ³the whole assembly made a covenant with the king at the temple of God.

Jehoiada said to them, "The king's son shall reign, as the LORD promised concerning the descendants of David. ⁴Now this is what you are to do: A third of you priests and Levites who are going on duty on the Sabbath are to keep watch at the doors, ⁵a third of you at the royal palace and a third at the Foundation Gate, and all the other men are to be in the courtyards of the temple of the LORD. ⁶No one is to enter the temple of the LORD except the priests and Levites on duty; they may enter because they are consecrated, but all the other men are to guard what the LORD has assigned to them.ᵇ ⁷The Levites are to station themselves around the king, each man with his weapons in his hand. Anyone who enters the temple must be put to death. Stay close to the king wherever he goes."

⁸The Levites and all the men of Judah did just as Jehoiada the priest ordered. Each one took his men—those who were going on duty on the Sabbath and those who were going off duty—for Jehoiada the priest had not released any of the divisions. ⁹Then he gave the commanders of units of a hundred the spears and the large and small shields that had belonged to King David and that were in the temple of God. ¹⁰He stationed all the men, each with his weapon in his hand, around the king—near the altar and the temple, from the south side to the north side of the temple.

¹¹Jehoiada and his sons brought out the king's son and put the crown on him; they presented him with a copy of the covenant and proclaimed him king. They anointed him and shouted, "Long live the king!"

¹²When Athaliah heard the noise of the people running and cheering the king, she went to them at the temple of the LORD. ¹³She looked, and there was the king, standing by his pillar at the entrance. The officers and the trumpeters were beside the king, and all the people of the land were rejoicing and blowing trumpets, and singers with musical instruments were leading the praises. Then Athaliah tore her robes and shouted, "Treason! Treason!"

¹⁴Jehoiada the priest sent out the commanders of units of a hundred, who were in charge of the troops, and said to them: "Bring her out between the ranksᶜ and put to the sword anyone who follows her." For the priest had said, "Do not put her to death at the temple of the LORD." ¹⁵So they seized her as she reached the entrance of the Horse Gate on the palace grounds, and there they put her to death.

¹⁶Jehoiada then made a covenant that he and the people and the kingᵈ would

---

ᵃ *11* Hebrew *Jehoshabeath,* a variant of *Jehosheba*
ᵇ *6* Or *to observe the LORD's command ⌞not to enter⌟*
ᶜ *14* Or *out from the precincts*   ᵈ *16* Or *covenant between ⌞the LORD⌟ and the people and the king that they* (see 2 Kings 11:17)

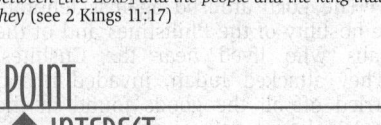

POINT OF INTEREST

2 Chronicles 22:11

For cultural reasons, women were not often highlighted in Old Testament stories. But here we are given a glimpse of one woman's bravery in the midst of a murderous conspiracy. Imagine the urgent whispers and quick footsteps as Jehosheba orchestrated the daring rescue of this young prince. What a true heroine!

be the LORD's people. ¹⁷All the people went to the temple of Baal and tore it down. They smashed the altars and idols and killed Mattan the priest of Baal in front of the altars.

¹⁸Then Jehoiada placed the oversight of the temple of the LORD in the hands of the priests, who were Levites, to whom David had made assignments in the temple, to present the burnt offerings of the LORD as written in the Law of Moses, with rejoicing and singing, as David had ordered. ¹⁹He also stationed doorkeepers at the gates of the LORD's temple so that no one who was in any way unclean might enter.

²⁰He took with him the commanders of hundreds, the nobles, the rulers of the people and all the people of the land and brought the king down from the temple of the LORD. They went into the palace through the Upper Gate and seated the king on the royal throne, ²¹and all the people of the land rejoiced. And the city was quiet, because Athaliah had been slain with the sword.

Joash Repairs the Temple

24 Joash was seven years old when he became king, and he reigned in Jerusalem forty years. His mother's name was Zibiah; she was from Beersheba. ²Joash did what was right in the eyes of the LORD all the years of Jehoiada the priest. ³Jehoiada chose two wives for him, and he had sons and daughters.

⁴Some time later Joash decided to restore the temple of the LORD. ⁵He called together the priests and Levites and said to them, "Go to the towns of Judah and collect the money due annually from all Israel, to repair the temple of your God. Do it now." But the Levites did not act at once.

⁶Therefore the king summoned Jehoiada the chief priest and said to him, "Why haven't you required the Levites to bring in from Judah and Jerusalem the tax imposed by Moses the servant of the LORD and by the assembly of Israel for the Tent of the Testimony?"

⁷Now the sons of that wicked woman Athaliah had broken into the temple of God and had used even its sacred objects for the Baals.

⁸At the king's command, a chest was made and placed outside, at the gate of the temple of the LORD. ⁹A proclamation was then issued in Judah and Jerusalem that they should bring to the LORD the tax that Moses the servant of God had required of Israel in the desert. ¹⁰All the officials and all the people brought their contributions gladly, dropping them into the chest until it was full. ¹¹Whenever the chest was brought in by the Levites to the king's officials and they saw that there was a large amount of money, the royal secretary and the officer of the chief priest would come and empty the chest and carry it back to its place. They did this regularly and collected a great amount of money. ¹²The king and Jehoiada gave it to the men who carried out the work required for the temple of the LORD. They hired masons and carpenters to restore the LORD's temple, and also workers in iron and bronze to repair the temple.

¹³The men in charge of the work were diligent, and the repairs progressed under them. They rebuilt the temple of God according to its original design and reinforced it. ¹⁴When they had finished, they brought the rest of the money to the king and Jehoiada, and with it were made articles for the LORD's temple: articles for the service and for the burnt offerings, and also dishes and other objects of gold and silver. As long as Jehoiada lived, burnt offerings were presented continually in the temple of the LORD.

¹⁵Now Jehoiada was old and full of years, and he died at the age of a hundred and thirty. ¹⁶He was buried with the kings in the City of David, because of the good he had done in Israel for God and his temple.

The Wickedness of Joash

¹⁷After the death of Jehoiada, the officials of Judah came and paid homage to the king, and he listened to them. ¹⁸They abandoned the temple of the LORD, the God of their fathers, and worshiped Asherah poles and idols. Because of their guilt, God's anger came upon Judah and Jerusalem. ¹⁹Although the LORD sent prophets to the people to bring them back to him, and though they testified against them, they would not listen.

²⁰Then the Spirit of God came upon Zechariah son of Jehoiada the priest. He stood before the people and said, "This is what God says: 'Why do you disobey the LORD's commands? You will not prosper. Because you have forsaken the LORD, he has forsaken you.'"

²¹But they plotted against him, and by

order of the king they stoned him to death in the courtyard of the LORD's temple. 22King Joash did not remember the kindness Zechariah's father Jehoiada had shown him but killed his son, who said as he lay dying, "May the LORD see this and call you to account."

23At the turn of the year,a the army of Aram marched against Joash; it invaded Judah and Jerusalem and killed all the leaders of the people. They sent all the plunder to their king in Damascus. 24Although the Aramean army had come with only a few men, the LORD delivered into their hands a much larger army. Because Judah had forsaken the LORD, the God of their fathers, judgment was executed on Joash. 25When the Arameans withdrew, they left Joash severely wounded. His officials conspired against him for murdering the son of Jehoiada the priest, and they killed him in his bed. So he died and was buried in the City of David, but not in the tombs of the kings. 26Those who conspired against him were Zabad,b son of Shimeath an Ammonite woman, and Jehozabad, son of Shimrithc a Moabite woman. 27The account of his sons, the many prophecies about him, and the record of the restoration of the temple of God are written in the annotations on the book of the kings. And Amaziah his son succeeded him as king.

Amaziah King of Judah

25 Amaziah was twenty-five years old when he became king, and he reigned in Jerusalem twenty-nine years. His mother's name was Jehoaddind; she was from Jerusalem. 2He did what was right in the eyes of the LORD, but not wholeheartedly. 3After the kingdom was firmly in his control, he executed the officials who had murdered his father the king. 4Yet he did not put their sons to death, but acted in accordance with what is written in the Law, in the Book of Moses, where the LORD commanded: "Fathers shall not be put to death for their children, nor children put to death for their fathers; each is to die for his own sins."e

5Amaziah called the people of Judah together and assigned them according to their families to commanders of thousands and commanders of hundreds for all Judah and Benjamin. He then mustered those twenty years old or more and found that there were three hundred thousand men ready for military service, able to handle the spear and shield. 6He also hired a hundred thousand fighting men from Israel for a hundred talentsf of silver.

7But a man of God came to him and said, "O king, these troops from Israel must not march with you, for the LORD is not with Israel—not with any of the people of Ephraim. 8Even if you go and fight courageously in battle, God will overthrow you before the enemy, for God has the power to help or to overthrow."

9Amaziah asked the man of God, "But what about the hundred talents I paid for these Israelite troops?"

The man of God replied, "The LORD can give you much more than that."

10So Amaziah dismissed the troops who had come to him from Ephraim and sent them home. They were furious with Judah and left for home in a great rage.

11Amaziah then marshaled his strength and led his army to the Valley of Salt, where he killed ten thousand men of Seir. 12The army of Judah also captured ten thousand men alive, took them to the top of a cliff and threw them down so that all were dashed to pieces.

13Meanwhile the troops that Amaziah had sent back and had not allowed to take part in the war raided Judean towns from Samaria to Beth Horon. They killed three thousand people and carried off great quantities of plunder.

14When Amaziah returned from slaughtering the Edomites, he brought back the gods of the people of Seir. He set them up as his own gods, bowed down to them and burned sacrifices to them. 15The anger of the LORD burned against Amaziah, and he sent a prophet to him, who said, "Why do you consult this people's gods, which could not save their own people from your hand?"

16While he was still speaking, the king said to him, "Have we appointed you an adviser to the king? Stop! Why be struck down?"

So the prophet stopped but said, "I know that God has determined to destroy you, because you have done this and have not listened to my counsel."

a23 Probably in the spring   b26 A variant of Jozabad   c26 A variant of Shomer   d1 Hebrew Jehoaddan, a variant of Jehoaddin   e4 Deut. 24:16   f6 That is, about 3 3/4 tons (about 3.4 metric tons); also in verse 9

¹⁷After Amaziah king of Judah consulted his advisers, he sent this challenge to Jehoash*a* son of Jehoahaz, the son of Jehu, king of Israel: "Come, meet me face to face."

¹⁸But Jehoash king of Israel replied to Amaziah king of Judah: "A thistle in Lebanon sent a message to a cedar in Lebanon, 'Give your daughter to my son in marriage.' Then a wild beast in Lebanon came along and trampled the thistle underfoot. ¹⁹You say to yourself that you have defeated Edom, and now you are arrogant and proud. But stay at home! Why ask for trouble and cause your own downfall and that of Judah also?"

²⁰Amaziah, however, would not listen, for God so worked that he might hand them over to ⌞Jehoash⌟, because they sought the gods of Edom. ²¹So Jehoash king of Israel attacked. He and Amaziah king of Judah faced each other at Beth Shemesh in Judah. ²²Judah was routed by Israel, and every man fled to his home. ²³Jehoash king of Israel captured Amaziah king of Judah, the son of Joash, the son of Ahaziah,*b* at Beth Shemesh. Then Jehoash brought him to Jerusalem and broke down the wall of Jerusalem from the Ephraim Gate to the Corner Gate—a section about six hundred feet*c* long. ²⁴He took all the gold and silver and all the articles found in the temple of God that had been in the care of Obed-Edom, together with the palace treasures and the hostages, and returned to Samaria.

a17 Hebrew *Joash,* a variant of *Jehoash*; also in verses 18, 21, 23 and 25   *b23* Hebrew *Jehoahaz,* a variant of *Ahaziah*   *c23* Hebrew *four hundred cubits* (about 180 meters)

FRIDAY

Read *2 Chronicles 25:1–28*
Key Verse *2 Chronicles 25:2*

With a Whole Heart — Megan Dunham

My job at the summer youth camp included caring for the camp director's four children and helping his wife with various household tasks. I specifically remember carrying a load of laundry to the washroom late one morning and thinking, "This must be my three hundredth load today, and who here notices or cares?" I continued on, of course, but my disposition remained sour, and I made a mental decision not to like what I was doing.

Three days later, while preparing for my Bible study group, I was drawn to 2 Chronicles 25:2. I recognized myself instantly. The verse might have read, "Megan did what was right in the eyes of the Lord, but not wholeheartedly." I was doing the job—everything I thought was necessary to serve the Lord by serving this family—but my heart was far from being whole in my service. I, like Amaziah, did not know what wholehearted service meant.

Deuteronomy 10:12 says, "And now, O Israel, what does the LORD your God ask of you but to fear the LORD your God, to walk in all his ways, to love him, to serve the LORD your God with all your heart and with all your soul." Serving has a lot more to do with me and my relationship with God than with the people who benefit from my work. God isn't as concerned with my output as he is with my heart. My labor done with half a heart might as well not have been done at all. I am thankful that in the midst of my halfheartedness, God continues to make my heart more wholly his.

A Deeper Look
1 Samuel 16:7; Psalm 51:10–12; Romans 12:11

Go to page 491 for your next devotional reading.

²⁵Amaziah son of Joash king of Judah lived for fifteen years after the death of Jehoash son of Jehoahaz king of Israel. ²⁶As for the other events of Amaziah's reign, from beginning to end, are they not written in the book of the kings of Judah and Israel? ²⁷From the time that Amaziah turned away from following the LORD, they conspired against him in Jerusalem and he fled to Lachish, but they sent men after him to Lachish and killed him there. ²⁸He was brought back by horse and was buried with his fathers in the City of Judah.

Uzziah King of Judah

26 Then all the people of Judah took Uzziah,ᵃ who was sixteen years old, and made him king in place of his father Amaziah. ²He was the one who rebuilt Elath and restored it to Judah after Amaziah rested with his fathers.

³Uzziah was sixteen years old when he became king, and he reigned in Jerusalem fifty-two years. His mother's name was Jecoliah; she was from Jerusalem. ⁴He did what was right in the eyes of the LORD, just as his father Amaziah had done. ⁵He sought God during the days of Zechariah, who instructed him in the fearᵇ of God. As long as he sought the LORD, God gave him success.

⁶He went to war against the Philistines and broke down the walls of Gath, Jabneh and Ashdod. He then rebuilt towns near Ashdod and elsewhere among the Philistines. ⁷God helped him against the Philistines and against the Arabs who lived in Gur Baal and against the Meunites. ⁸The Ammonites brought tribute to Uzziah, and his fame spread as far as the border of Egypt, because he had become very powerful.

⁹Uzziah built towers in Jerusalem at the Corner Gate, at the Valley Gate and at the angle of the wall, and he fortified them. ¹⁰He also built towers in the desert and dug many cisterns, because he had much livestock in the foothills and in the plain. He had people working his fields and vineyards in the hills and in the fertile lands, for he loved the soil.

¹¹Uzziah had a well-trained army, ready to go out by divisions according to their numbers as mustered by Jeiel the secretary and Maaseiah the officer under the direction of Hananiah, one of the royal officials. ¹²The total number of family leaders over the fighting men was 2,600. ¹³Under their command was an army of 307,500 men trained for war, a powerful force to support the king against his enemies. ¹⁴Uzziah provided shields, spears, helmets, coats of armor, bows and slingstones for the entire army. ¹⁵In Jerusalem he made machines designed by skillful men for use on the towers and on the corner defenses to shoot arrows and hurl large stones. His fame spread far and wide, for he was greatly helped until he became powerful.

¹⁶But after Uzziah became powerful, his pride led to his downfall. He was unfaithful to the LORD his God, and entered the temple of the LORD to burn incense on the altar of incense. ¹⁷Azariah the priest with eighty other courageous priests of the LORD followed him in. ¹⁸They confronted him and said, "It is not right for you, Uzziah, to burn incense to the LORD. That is for the priests, the descendants of Aaron, who have been consecrated to burn incense. Leave the sanctuary, for you have been unfaithful; and you will not be honored by the LORD God."

¹⁹Uzziah, who had a censer in his hand ready to burn incense, became angry. While he was raging at the priests in their presence before the incense altar in the LORD's temple, leprosyᶜ broke out on his forehead. ²⁰When Azariah the chief priest and all the other priests looked at him, they saw that he had leprosy on his forehead, so they hurried him out. Indeed, he himself was eager to leave, because the LORD had afflicted him.

²¹King Uzziah had leprosy until the day he died. He lived in a separate houseᵈ—leprous, and excluded from the temple of the LORD. Jotham his son had charge of the palace and governed the people of the land.

²²The other events of Uzziah's reign, from beginning to end, are recorded by the prophet Isaiah son of Amoz. ²³Uzziah rested with his fathers and was buried near them in a field for burial that belonged to the kings, for people said, "He had leprosy." And Jotham his son succeeded him as king.

ᵃ1 Also called *Azariah*   ᵇ5 Many Hebrew manuscripts, Septuagint and Syriac; other Hebrew manuscripts *vision*   ᶜ19 The Hebrew word was used for various diseases affecting the skin—not necessarily leprosy; also in verses 20, 21 and 23.   ᵈ21 Or *in a house where he was relieved of responsibilities*

Read 2 Chronicles 26:1–23
Key Verse 2 Chronicles 26:16

Got an Attitude?

Uzziah started well in his walk with God, but as his power swelled, so did his head. His pride led him to do things his way instead of God's, and God brought him down. Pride usually does not blast its way into our life; typically it creeps in with small steps. Pride feeds on itself—little by little, like Uzziah, we edge God off the throne of our lives and try to sit there instead. If we hold tightly to our pride, God will actively work to humble us. So we have two choices; we can humble ourselves, or we can hold on until God steps in and humbles us.

As frightening as it may be to contemplate being humbled in such a way, it's not the end of the story. For the God who humbles us is also the One who can lift us up again: "I live in a high and holy place, but also with him who is contrite and lowly in spirit, to revive the spirit of the lowly and to revive the heart of the contrite" (Isaiah 57:15).

Digging Into the Word

1. According to these passages, what are some consequences of pride?—*Proverbs 11:2; Proverbs 13:10; James 4:4–6*
2. What do you learn about humility from these passages?—*Proverbs 15:33; Proverbs 22:4; James 3:13*

Action Challenge

This action challenge is only for the courageous! Sit down with a friend and give him or her permission to tell you about one area of pride they see in your life. Ask them to be honest and promise to listen without becoming defensive. If they identify an area of pride in your life, ask them to let you know how they think you can be more humble in this area.

One Step Deeper

Isaiah 25:11; 1 Peter 5:5–6

Go to page 498 for your next devotional reading.

Jotham King of Judah

27 Jotham was twenty-five years old when he became king, and he reigned in Jerusalem sixteen years. His mother's name was Jerusha daughter of Zadok. ²He did what was right in the eyes of the LORD, just as his father Uzziah had done, but unlike him he did not enter the temple of the LORD. The people, however, continued their corrupt practices. ³Jotham rebuilt the Upper Gate of the temple of the LORD and did extensive work on the wall at the hill of Ophel. ⁴He built towns in the Judean hills and forts and towers in the wooded areas.

⁵Jotham made war on the king of the Ammonites and conquered them. That year the Ammonites paid him a hundred talents*a* of silver, ten thousand cors*b* of wheat and ten thousand cors of barley. The Ammonites brought him the same amount also in the second and third years.

⁶Jotham grew powerful because he walked steadfastly before the LORD his God.

⁷The other events in Jotham's reign, including all his wars and the other things he did, are written in the book of the kings of Israel and Judah. ⁸He was twenty-five years old when he became king, and he reigned in Jerusalem sixteen years. ⁹Jotham rested with his fathers and was buried in the City of David. And Ahaz his son succeeded him as king.

Ahaz King of Judah

28 Ahaz was twenty years old when he became king, and he reigned in Jerusalem sixteen years. Unlike David his father, he did not do what was right in the eyes of the LORD. ²He walked in the ways of the kings of Israel and also made cast idols for worshiping the Baals. ³He burned sacrifices in the Valley of Ben Hinnom and sacrificed his sons in the fire, following the detestable ways of the nations the LORD had driven out before the Israelites. ⁴He offered sacrifices and burned incense at the high places, on the hilltops and under every spreading tree.

⁵Therefore the LORD his God handed him over to the king of Aram. The Arameans defeated him and took many of his people as prisoners and brought them to Damascus.

He was also given into the hands of the king of Israel, who inflicted heavy ca-

sualties on him. ⁶In one day Pekah son of Remaliah killed a hundred and twenty thousand soldiers in Judah—because Judah had forsaken the LORD, the God of their fathers. ⁷Zicri, an Ephraimite warrior, killed Maaseiah the king's son, Azrikam the officer in charge of the palace, and Elkanah, second to the king. ⁸The Israelites took captive from their kinsmen two hundred thousand wives, sons and daughters. They also took a great deal of plunder, which they carried back to Samaria.

⁹But a prophet of the LORD named Oded was there, and he went out to meet the army when it returned to Samaria. He said to them, "Because the LORD, the God of your fathers, was angry with Judah, he gave them into your hand. But you have slaughtered them in a rage that reaches to heaven. ¹⁰And now you intend to make the men and women of Judah and Jerusalem your slaves. But aren't you also guilty of sins against the LORD your God? ¹¹Now listen to me! Send back your fellow countrymen you have taken as prisoners, for the LORD's fierce anger rests on you."

¹²Then some of the leaders in Ephraim—Azariah son of Jehohanan, Berekiah son of Meshillemoth, Jehizkiah son of Shallum, and Amasa son of Hadlai—confronted those who were arriving from the war. ¹³"You must not bring those prisoners here," they said, "or we will be guilty before the LORD. Do you intend to add to our sin and guilt? For our guilt is already great, and his fierce anger rests on Israel."

¹⁴So the soldiers gave up the prisoners and plunder in the presence of the officials and all the assembly. ¹⁵The men designated by name took the prisoners, and from the plunder they clothed all who were naked. They provided them with clothes and sandals, food and drink, and healing balm. All those who were weak they put on donkeys. So they took them back to their fellow countrymen at Jericho, the City of Palms, and returned to Samaria.

¹⁶At that time King Ahaz sent to the king*c* of Assyria for help. ¹⁷The Edomites had again come and attacked Judah

a5 That is, about 3 3/4 tons (about 3.4 metric tons)
b5 That is, probably about 62,000 bushels (about 2,200 kiloliters)   *c16* One Hebrew manuscript, Septuagint and Vulgate (see also 2 Kings 16:7); most Hebrew manuscripts *kings*

and carried away prisoners, ¹⁸while the Philistines had raided towns in the foothills and in the Negev of Judah. They captured and occupied Beth Shemesh, Aijalon and Gederoth, as well as Soco, Timnah and Gimzo, with their surrounding villages. ¹⁹The LORD had humbled Judah because of Ahaz king of Israel,ᵃ for he had promoted wickedness in Judah and had been most unfaithful to the LORD. ²⁰Tiglath-Pileserᵇ king of Assyria came to him, but he gave him trouble instead of help. ²¹Ahaz took some of the things from the temple of the LORD and from the royal palace and from the princes and presented them to the king of Assyria, but that did not help him.

²²In his time of trouble King Ahaz became even more unfaithful to the LORD. ²³He offered sacrifices to the gods of Damascus, who had defeated him; for he thought, "Since the gods of the kings of Aram have helped them, I will sacrifice to them so they will help me." But they were his downfall and the downfall of all Israel.

²⁴Ahaz gathered together the furnishings from the temple of God and took them away.ᶜ He shut the doors of the LORD's temple and set up altars at every street corner in Jerusalem. ²⁵In every town in Judah he built high places to burn sacrifices to other gods and provoked the LORD, the God of his fathers, to anger.

²⁶The other events of his reign and all his ways, from beginning to end, are written in the book of the kings of Judah and Israel. ²⁷Ahaz rested with his fathers and was buried in the city of Jerusalem, but he was not placed in the tombs of the kings of Israel. And Hezekiah his son succeeded him as king.

Hezekiah Purifies the Temple

29 Hezekiah was twenty-five years old when he became king, and he reigned in Jerusalem twenty-nine years. His mother's name was Abijah daughter of Zechariah. ²He did what was right in the eyes of the LORD, just as his father David had done.

³In the first month of the first year of his reign, he opened the doors of the temple of the LORD and repaired them. ⁴He brought in the priests and the Levites, assembled them in the square on the east side ⁵and said: "Listen to me, Levites! Consecrate yourselves now and conse-

crate the temple of the LORD, the God of your fathers. Remove all defilement from the sanctuary. ⁶Our fathers were unfaithful; they did evil in the eyes of the LORD our God and forsook him. They turned their faces away from the LORD's dwelling place and turned their backs on him. ⁷They also shut the doors of the portico and put out the lamps. They did not burn incense or present any burnt offerings at the sanctuary to the God of Israel. ⁸Therefore, the anger of the LORD has fallen on Judah and Jerusalem; he has made them an object of dread and horror and scorn, as you can see with your own eyes. ⁹This is why our fathers have fallen by the sword and why our sons and daughters and our wives are in captivity. ¹⁰Now I intend to make a covenant with the LORD, the God of Israel, so that his fierce anger will turn away from us. ¹¹My sons, do not be negligent now, for the LORD has chosen you to stand before him and serve him, to minister before him and to burn incense."

¹²Then these Levites set to work:
from the Kohathites,
Mahath son of Amasai and Joel son of Azariah;
from the Merarites,
Kish son of Abdi and Azariah son of Jehallelel;
from the Gershonites,
Joah son of Zimmah and Eden son of Joah;
¹³from the descendants of Elizaphan, Shimri and Jeiel;
from the descendants of Asaph, Zechariah and Mattaniah;

ᵃ19 That is, Judah, as frequently in 2 Chronicles
ᵇ20 Hebrew *Tilgath-Pilneser*, a variant of
Tiglath-Pileser   ᶜ24 Or *and cut them up*

POINT OF INTEREST

2 Chronicles 29:3

First things first! Hezekiah faced the same tasks as any new ruler, but he revealed his priorities early in his reign. The people's welfare depended on their relationship with God. Opening the temple doors was a first step toward restoring that relationship and therefore became King Hezekiah's first step as king.

¹⁴from the descendants of Heman,
  Jehiel and Shimei;
from the descendants of Jeduthun,
  Shemaiah and Uzziel.

¹⁵When they had assembled their brothers and consecrated themselves, they went in to purify the temple of the LORD, as the king had ordered, following the word of the LORD. ¹⁶The priests went into the sanctuary of the LORD to purify it. They brought out to the courtyard of the LORD's temple everything unclean that they found in the temple of the LORD. The Levites took it and carried it out to the Kidron Valley. ¹⁷They began the consecration on the first day of the first month, and by the eighth day of the month they reached the portico of the LORD. For eight more days they consecrated the temple of the LORD itself, finishing on the sixteenth day of the first month.

¹⁸Then they went in to King Hezekiah and reported: "We have purified the entire temple of the LORD, the altar of burnt offering with all its utensils, and the table for setting out the consecrated bread, with all its articles. ¹⁹We have prepared and consecrated all the articles that King Ahaz removed in his unfaithfulness while he was king. They are now in front of the LORD's altar."

²⁰Early the next morning King Hezekiah gathered the city officials together and went up to the temple of the LORD. ²¹They brought seven bulls, seven rams, seven male lambs and seven male goats as a sin offering for the kingdom, for the sanctuary and for Judah. The king commanded the priests, the descendants of Aaron, to offer these on the altar of the LORD. ²²So they slaughtered the bulls, and the priests took the blood and sprinkled it on the altar; next they slaughtered the rams and sprinkled their blood on the altar; then they slaughtered the lambs and sprinkled their blood on the altar. ²³The goats for the sin offering were brought before the king and the assembly, and they laid their hands on them. ²⁴The priests then slaughtered the goats and presented their blood on the altar for a sin offering to atone for all Israel, because the king had ordered the burnt offering and the sin offering for all Israel.

²⁵He stationed the Levites in the temple of the LORD with cymbals, harps and lyres in the way prescribed by David and Gad the king's seer and Nathan the prophet; this was commanded by the LORD through his prophets. ²⁶So the Levites stood ready with David's instruments, and the priests with their trumpets.

²⁷Hezekiah gave the order to sacrifice the burnt offering on the altar. As the offering began, singing to the LORD began also, accompanied by trumpets and the instruments of David king of Israel. ²⁸The whole assembly bowed in worship, while the singers sang and the trumpeters played. All this continued until the sacrifice of the burnt offering was completed.

²⁹When the offerings were finished, the king and everyone present with him knelt down and worshiped. ³⁰King Hezekiah and his officials ordered the Levites to praise the LORD with the words of David and of Asaph the seer. So they sang praises with gladness and bowed their heads and worshiped.

³¹Then Hezekiah said, "You have now dedicated yourselves to the LORD. Come and bring sacrifices and thank offerings to the temple of the LORD." So the assembly brought sacrifices and thank offerings, and all whose hearts were willing brought burnt offerings.

³²The number of burnt offerings the assembly brought was seventy bulls, a hundred rams and two hundred male lambs—all of them for burnt offerings to the LORD. ³³The animals consecrated as sacrifices amounted to six hundred bulls and three thousand sheep and goats. ³⁴The priests, however, were too few to skin all the burnt offerings; so their kinsmen the Levites helped them until the task was finished and until other priests had been consecrated, for the Levites had been more conscientious in consecrating themselves than the priests had been. ³⁵There were burnt offerings in abundance, together with the fat of the fellowship offerings[a] and the drink offerings that accompanied the burnt offerings.

So the service of the temple of the LORD was reestablished. ³⁶Hezekiah and all the people rejoiced at what God had brought about for his people, because it was done so quickly.

Hezekiah Celebrates the Passover

30 Hezekiah sent word to all Israel and Judah and also wrote letters to Ephraim and Manasseh, inviting them to come to the temple of the LORD in Jerusa-

---

a 35 Traditionally *peace offerings*

lem and celebrate the Passover to the LORD, the God of Israel. ²The king and his officials and the whole assembly in Jerusalem decided to celebrate the Passover in the second month. ³They had not been able to celebrate it at the regular time because not enough priests had consecrated themselves and the people had not assembled in Jerusalem. ⁴The plan seemed right both to the king and to the whole assembly. ⁵They decided to send a proclamation throughout Israel, from Beersheba to Dan, calling the people to come to Jerusalem and celebrate the Passover to the LORD, the God of Israel. It had not been celebrated in large numbers according to what was written.

⁶At the king's command, couriers went throughout Israel and Judah with letters from the king and from his officials, which read:

"People of Israel, return to the LORD, the God of Abraham, Isaac and Israel, that he may return to you who are left, who have escaped from the hand of the kings of Assyria. ⁷Do not be like your fathers and brothers, who were unfaithful to the LORD, the God of their fathers, so that he made them an object of horror, as you see. ⁸Do not be stiffnecked, as your fathers were; submit to the LORD. Come to the sanctuary, which he has consecrated forever. Serve the LORD your God, so that his fierce anger will turn away from you. ⁹If you return to the LORD, then your brothers and your children will be shown compassion by their captors and will come back to this land, for the LORD your God is gracious and compassionate. He will not turn his face from you if you return to him."

¹⁰The couriers went from town to town in Ephraim and Manasseh, as far as Zebulun, but the people scorned and ridiculed them. ¹¹Nevertheless, some men of Asher, Manasseh and Zebulun humbled themselves and went to Jerusalem. ¹²Also in Judah the hand of God was on the people to give them unity of mind to carry out what the king and his officials had ordered, following the word of the LORD.

¹³A very large crowd of people assembled in Jerusalem to celebrate the Feast of Unleavened Bread in the second month.

¹⁴They removed the altars in Jerusalem and cleared away the incense altars and threw them into the Kidron Valley.

¹⁵They slaughtered the Passover lamb on the fourteenth day of the second month. The priests and the Levites were ashamed and consecrated themselves and brought burnt offerings to the temple of the LORD. ¹⁶Then they took up their regular positions as prescribed in the Law of Moses the man of God. The priests sprinkled the blood handed to them by the Levites. ¹⁷Since many in the crowd had not consecrated themselves, the Levites had to kill the Passover lambs for all those who were not ceremonially clean and could not consecrate ⌊their lambs⌋ to the LORD. ¹⁸Although most of the many people who came from Ephraim, Manasseh, Issachar and Zebulun had not purified themselves, yet they ate the Passover, contrary to what was written. But Hezekiah prayed for them, saying, "May the LORD, who is good, pardon everyone ¹⁹who sets his heart on seeking God—the LORD, the God of his fathers—even if he is not clean according to the rules of the sanctuary." ²⁰And the LORD heard Hezekiah and healed the people.

²¹The Israelites who were present in Jerusalem celebrated the Feast of Unleavened Bread for seven days with great rejoicing, while the Levites and priests sang to the LORD every day, accompanied by the LORD's instruments of praise. ᵃ

²²Hezekiah spoke encouragingly to all the Levites, who showed good understanding of the service of the LORD. For the seven days they ate their assigned portion and offered fellowship offerings ᵇ and praised the LORD, the God of their fathers.

²³The whole assembly then agreed to celebrate the festival seven more days; so for another seven days they celebrated joyfully. ²⁴Hezekiah king of Judah provided a thousand bulls and seven thousand sheep and goats for the assembly, and the officials provided them with a thousand bulls and ten thousand sheep and goats. A great number of priests consecrated themselves. ²⁵The entire assembly of Judah rejoiced, along with the priests and Levites and all who had assembled from Israel, including the aliens

ᵃ21 Or *priests praised the LORD every day with resounding instruments belonging to the LORD*
ᵇ22 Traditionally *peace offerings*

who had come from Israel and those who lived in Judah. 26There was great joy in Jerusalem, for since the days of Solomon son of David king of Israel there had been nothing like this in Jerusalem. 27The priests and the Levites stood to bless the people, and God heard them, for their prayer reached heaven, his holy dwelling place.

31 When all this had ended, the Israelites who were there went out to the towns of Judah, smashed the sacred stones and cut down the Asherah poles. They destroyed the high places and the altars throughout Judah and Benjamin and in Ephraim and Manasseh. After they had destroyed all of them, the Israelites returned to their own towns and to their own property.

Contributions for Worship

2Hezekiah assigned the priests and Levites to divisions—each of them according to their duties as priests or Levites—to offer burnt offerings and fellowship offerings,a to minister, to give thanks and to sing praises at the gates of the LORD's dwelling. 3The king contributed from his own possessions for the morning and evening burnt offerings and for the burnt offerings on the Sabbaths, New Moons and appointed feasts as written in the Law of the LORD. 4He ordered the people living in Jerusalem to give the portion due the priests and Levites so they could devote themselves to the Law of the LORD. 5As soon as the order went out, the Israelites generously gave the firstfruits of their grain, new wine, oil and honey and all that the fields produced. They brought a great amount, a tithe of everything. 6The men of Israel and Judah who lived in the towns of Judah also brought a tithe of their herds and flocks and a tithe of the holy things dedicated to the LORD their God, and they piled them in heaps. 7They began doing this in the third month and finished in the seventh month. 8When Hezekiah and his officials came and saw the heaps, they praised the LORD and blessed his people Israel.

9Hezekiah asked the priests and Levites about the heaps; 10and Azariah the chief priest, from the family of Zadok, answered, "Since the people began to bring their contributions to the temple of the LORD, we have had enough to eat and plenty to spare, because the LORD has blessed his people, and this great amount is left over."

11Hezekiah gave orders to prepare storerooms in the temple of the LORD, and this was done. 12Then they faithfully brought in the contributions, tithes and dedicated gifts. Conaniah, a Levite, was in charge of these things, and his brother Shimei was next in rank. 13Jehiel, Azaziah, Nahath, Asahel, Jerimoth, Jozabad, Eliel, Ismakiah, Mahath and Benaiah were supervisors under Conaniah and Shimei his brother, by appointment of King Hezekiah and Azariah the official in charge of the temple of God.

14Kore son of Imnah the Levite, keeper of the East Gate, was in charge of the freewill offerings given to God, distributing the contributions made to the LORD and also the consecrated gifts. 15Eden, Miniamin, Jeshua, Shemaiah, Amariah and Shecaniah assisted him faithfully in the towns of the priests, distributing to their fellow priests according to their divisions, old and young alike.

16In addition, they distributed to the males three years old or more whose names were in the genealogical records—all who would enter the temple of the LORD to perform the daily duties of their various tasks, according to their responsibilities and their divisions. 17And they distributed to the priests enrolled by their families in the genealogical records and likewise to the Levites twenty years old or more, according to their responsibilities and their divisions. 18They included all the little ones, the wives, and the sons and daughters of the whole community listed in these genealogical records. For they were faithful in consecrating themselves.

19As for the priests, the descendants of Aaron, who lived on the farm lands around their towns or in any other towns, men were designated by name to distribute portions to every male among them and to all who were recorded in the genealogies of the Levites.

20This is what Hezekiah did throughout Judah, doing what was good and right and faithful before the LORD his God. 21In everything that he undertook in the service of God's temple and in obedience to the law and the commands, he sought his God and worked wholeheartedly. And so he prospered.

a2 Traditionally peace offerings

Sennacherib Threatens Jerusalem

32 After all that Hezekiah had so faithfully done, Sennacherib king of Assyria came and invaded Judah. He laid siege to the fortified cities, thinking to conquer them for himself. ²When Hezekiah saw that Sennacherib had come and that he intended to make war on Jerusalem, ³he consulted with his officials and military staff about blocking off the water from the springs outside the city, and they helped him. ⁴A large force of men assembled, and they blocked all the springs and the stream that flowed through the land. "Why should the kings*a* of Assyria come and find plenty of water?" they said. ⁵Then he worked hard repairing all the broken sections of the wall and building towers on it. He built another wall outside that one and reinforced the supporting terraces*b* of the City of David. He also made large numbers of weapons and shields.

⁶He appointed military officers over the people and assembled them before him in the square at the city gate and encouraged them with these words: ⁷"Be strong and courageous. Do not be afraid or discouraged because of the king of Assyria and the vast army with him, for there is a greater power with us than with him. ⁸With him is only the arm of flesh, but with us is the LORD our God to help us and to fight our battles." And the people gained confidence from what Hezekiah the king of Judah said.

⁹Later, when Sennacherib king of Assyria and all his forces were laying siege to Lachish, he sent his officers to Jerusalem with this message for Hezekiah king of Judah and for all the people of Judah who were there:

¹⁰"This is what Sennacherib king of Assyria says: On what are you basing your confidence, that you remain in Jerusalem under siege? ¹¹When Hezekiah says, 'The LORD our God will save us from the hand of the king of Assyria,' he is misleading you, to let you die of hunger and thirst. ¹²Did not Hezekiah himself remove this god's high places and altars, saying to Judah and Jerusalem, 'You must worship before one altar and burn sacrifices on it'? ¹³"Do you not know what I and my fathers have done to all the peoples of the other lands? Were the gods of those nations ever able to deliver their land from my hand? ¹⁴Who of all the gods of these nations that my fathers destroyed has been able to save his people from me? How then can your god deliver you from my hand? ¹⁵Now do not let Hezekiah deceive you and mislead you like this. Do not believe him, for no god of any nation or kingdom has been able to deliver his people from my hand or the hand of my fathers. How much less will your god deliver you from my hand!"

¹⁶Sennacherib's officers spoke further against the LORD God and against his servant Hezekiah. ¹⁷The king also wrote letters insulting the LORD, the God of Israel, and saying this against him: "Just as the gods of the peoples of the other lands did not rescue their people from my hand, so the god of Hezekiah will not rescue his people from my hand." ¹⁸Then they called out in Hebrew to the people of Jerusalem who were on the wall, to terrify them and make them afraid, in order to capture the city. ¹⁹They spoke about the God of Jerusalem as they did about the gods of the other peoples of the world—the work of men's hands.

²⁰King Hezekiah and the prophet Isaiah son of Amoz cried out in prayer to heaven about this. ²¹And the LORD sent an angel, who annihilated all the fighting men and the leaders and officers in the camp of the Assyrian king. So he withdrew to his own land in disgrace. And when he went into the temple of his god, some of his sons cut him down with the sword.

²²So the LORD saved Hezekiah and the people of Jerusalem from the hand of Sennacherib king of Assyria and from the hand of all others. He took care of them*c* on every side. ²³Many brought offerings to Jerusalem for the LORD and valuable gifts for Hezekiah king of Judah. From then on he was highly regarded by all the nations.

Hezekiah's Pride, Success and Death

²⁴In those days Hezekiah became ill and was at the point of death. He prayed to the LORD, who answered him and gave

---

a4 Hebrew; Septuagint and Syriac *king*   *b5* Or *the Millo*   *c22* Hebrew; Septuagint and Vulgate *He gave them rest* him a miraculous sign. ²⁵But Hezekiah's heart was proud and he did not respond to the kindness shown him; therefore the LORD's wrath was on him and on Judah and Jerusalem. ²⁶Then Hezekiah repented of the pride of his heart, as did the people of Jerusalem; therefore the LORD's wrath did not come upon them during the days of Hezekiah.

²⁷Hezekiah had very great riches and honor, and he made treasuries for his silver and gold and for his precious stones, spices, shields and all kinds of valuables. ²⁸He also made buildings to store the har-vest of grain, new wine and oil; and he made stalls for various kinds of cattle, and pens for the flocks. ²⁹He built villages and acquired great numbers of flocks and herds, for God had given him very great riches.

³⁰It was Hezekiah who blocked the upper outlet of the Gihon spring and chan-neled the water down to the west side of the City of David. He succeeded in every-thing he undertook. ³¹But when envoys were sent by the rulers of Babylon to ask him about the miraculous sign that had occurred in the land, God left him to test

MONDAY

Read 2 Chronicles 32:1–33
Key Verses 2 Chronicles 32:7–8

Strong and Courageous – Joey Fiorino

When I was a child, the thought of making the walk down the long, dark hallway to my bedroom each night was terrifying. I would make it only a short way and then run back to my parents and ask them to walk with me. With one of them beside me, holding my hand, the trip down that hallway was easier to make.

So many times we face difficulties and feel we'll never make it beyond them. The future looks like a long, dark hallway. We can't see a way out of our situation. We want to run away in defeat, feel-ing discouraged and alone.

Where do we find the courage to "keep on keeping on"? We could try to muster up enough courage from within ourselves. Or we could look to God. In the middle of trouble or hardship or conflict is the time when we most need to look for him and ask him to go with us as Hezekiah did. When he and his people were facing the vast Assyrian army, he rallied them with this encouragement: "Be strong and courageous. Do not be afraid or discouraged because of the king of Assyria and the vast army with him, for there is a greater power with us than with him. With him is only the arm of flesh, but with us is the LORD our God to help us and to fight our battles" (2 Chronicles 32:7–8).

Are you facing a tough situation? You are not alone. Be strong and courageous, not because you think you can handle the problem but because God himself will be with there with you. Read these words aloud to help you believe it: "The LORD is with me; I will not be afraid . . . he is my helper. I will look in triumph on my enemies . . . They surrounded me on every side, but in the name of the LORD I cut them off . . . the LORD helped me. The LORD is my strength and my song; he has become my salvation . . . The LORD's right hand has done mighty things!" (Psalm 118:6–7,11,13–15)

A Deeper Look
Deuteronomy 31:8; Matthew 28:20

Go to page 507 for your next devotional reading.

him and to know everything that was in his heart.

³²The other events of Hezekiah's reign and his acts of devotion are written in the vision of the prophet Isaiah son of Amoz in the book of the kings of Judah and Israel. ³³Hezekiah rested with his fathers and was buried on the hill where the tombs of David's descendants are. All Judah and the people of Jerusalem honored him when he died. And Manasseh his son succeeded him as king.

Manasseh King of Judah

33 Manasseh was twelve years old when he became king, and he reigned in Jerusalem fifty-five years. ²He did evil in the eyes of the LORD, following the detestable practices of the nations the LORD had driven out before the Israelites. ³He rebuilt the high places his father Hezekiah had demolished; he also erected altars to the Baals and made Asherah poles. He bowed down to all the starry hosts and worshiped them. ⁴He built altars in the temple of the LORD, of which the LORD had said, "My Name will remain in Jerusalem forever." ⁵In both courts of the temple of the LORD, he built altars to all the starry hosts. ⁶He sacrificed his sons in*a* the fire in the Valley of Ben Hinnom, practiced sorcery, divination and witchcraft, and consulted mediums and spiritists. He did much evil in the eyes of the LORD, provoking him to anger.

⁷He took the carved image he had made and put it in God's temple, of which God had said to David and to his son Solomon, "In this temple and in Jerusalem, which I have chosen out of all the tribes of Israel, I will put my Name forever. ⁸I will not again make the feet of the Israelites leave the land I assigned to your forefathers, if only they will be careful to do everything I commanded them concerning all the laws, decrees and ordinances given through Moses." ⁹But Manasseh led Judah and the people of Jerusalem astray, so that they did more evil than the nations the LORD had destroyed before the Israelites.

¹⁰The LORD spoke to Manasseh and his people, but they paid no attention. ¹¹So the LORD brought against them the army commanders of the king of Assyria, who took Manasseh prisoner, put a hook in his nose, bound him with bronze shackles and took him to Babylon. ¹²In his distress he sought the favor of the LORD his God and humbled himself greatly before the God of his fathers. ¹³And when he prayed to him, the LORD was moved by his entreaty and listened to his plea; so he brought him back to Jerusalem and to his kingdom. Then Manasseh knew that the LORD is God.

¹⁴Afterward he rebuilt the outer wall of the City of David, west of the Gihon spring in the valley, as far as the entrance of the Fish Gate and encircling the hill of Ophel; he also made it much higher. He stationed military commanders in all the fortified cities in Judah.

¹⁵He got rid of the foreign gods and removed the image from the temple of the LORD, as well as all the altars he had built on the temple hill and in Jerusalem; and he threw them out of the city. ¹⁶Then he restored the altar of the LORD and sacrificed fellowship offerings*b* and thank offerings on it, and told Judah to serve the LORD, the God of Israel. ¹⁷The people, however, continued to sacrifice at the high places, but only to the LORD their God.

¹⁸The other events of Manasseh's reign, including his prayer to his God and the words the seers spoke to him in the name of the LORD, the God of Israel, are written in the annals of the kings of Israel.*c* ¹⁹His prayer and how God was moved by his entreaty, as well as all his sins and unfaithfulness, and the sites where he built high places and set up Asherah poles and idols before he humbled himself—all are written in the

---

*a*6 Or *He made his sons pass through*
*b*16 Traditionally *peace offerings*   *c*18 That is, Judah, as frequently in 2 Chronicles

POINT OF INTEREST

2 Chronicles 33:12

"Many begin well, but few end well." That adage was true of the majority of kings listed in Chronicles. Manasseh is a notable exception. Though Manasseh began as one of the worst kings ever, his reign ended well. If a turn around like that could happen for Manasseh, it can happen for us too!

records of the seers.*a* 20Manasseh rested
with his fathers and was buried in his
palace. And Amon his son succeeded him
as king.

Amon King of Judah

21Amon was twenty-two years old
when he became king, and he reigned in
Jerusalem two years. 22He did evil in the
eyes of the LORD, as his father Manasseh
had done. Amon worshiped and offered
sacrifices to all the idols Manasseh had
made. 23But unlike his father Manasseh,
he did not humble himself before the
LORD; Amon increased his guilt.
24Amon's officials conspired against
him and assassinated him in his palace.
25Then the people of the land killed all
who had plotted against King Amon, and
they made Josiah his son king in his
place.

Josiah's Reforms

34 Josiah was eight years old when he
became king, and he reigned in Jerusalem thirty-one years. 2He did what was
right in the eyes of the LORD and walked
in the ways of his father David, not turning aside to the right or to the left.

3In the eighth year of his reign, while
he was still young, he began to seek the
God of his father David. In his twelfth
year he began to purge Judah and Jerusalem of high places, Asherah poles, carved
idols and cast images. 4Under his direction the altars of the Baals were torn
down; he cut to pieces the incense altars
that were above them, and smashed the
Asherah poles, the idols and the images.
These he broke to pieces and scattered
over the graves of those who had sacrificed to them. 5He burned the bones of
the priests on their altars, and so he
purged Judah and Jerusalem. 6In the
towns of Manasseh, Ephraim and Simeon, as far as Naphtali, and in the ruins
around them, 7he tore down the altars
and the Asherah poles and crushed the
idols to powder and cut to pieces all the
incense altars throughout Israel. Then he
went back to Jerusalem.

8In the eighteenth year of Josiah's
reign, to purify the land and the temple,
he sent Shaphan son of Azaliah and Maaseiah the ruler of the city, with Joah son
of Joahaz, the recorder, to repair the temple of the LORD his God.
9They went to Hilkiah the high priest
and gave him the money that had been

brought into the temple of God, which
the Levites who were the doorkeepers
had collected from the people of Manasseh, Ephraim and the entire remnant of
Israel and from all the people of Judah
and Benjamin and the inhabitants of Jerusalem. 10Then they entrusted it to the
men appointed to supervise the work on
the LORD's temple. These men paid the
workers who repaired and restored the
temple. 11They also gave money to
the carpenters and builders to purchase
dressed stone, and timber for joists and
beams for the buildings that the kings of
Judah had allowed to fall into ruin.
12The men did the work faithfully.
Over them to direct them were Jahath
and Obadiah, Levites descended from
Merari, and Zechariah and Meshullam,
descended from Kohath. The Levites—all
who were skilled in playing musical instruments— 13had charge of the laborers
and supervised all the workers from job
to job. Some of the Levites were secretaries, scribes and doorkeepers.

The Book of the Law Found

14While they were bringing out the
money that had been taken into the temple of the LORD, Hilkiah the priest found
the Book of the Law of the LORD that had
been given through Moses. 15Hilkiah said
to Shaphan the secretary, "I have found
the Book of the Law in the temple of the
LORD." He gave it to Shaphan.
16Then Shaphan took the book to the
king and reported to him: "Your officials
are doing everything that has been committed to them. 17They have paid out the
money that was in the temple of the LORD
and have entrusted it to the supervisors
and workers." 18Then Shaphan the secretary informed the king, "Hilkiah the
priest has given me a book." And Shaphan read from it in the presence of the
king.
19When the king heard the words of
the Law, he tore his robes. 20He gave
these orders to Hilkiah, Ahikam son of
Shaphan, Abdon son of Micah,*b* Shaphan the secretary and Asaiah the king's
attendant: 21"Go and inquire of the LORD
for me and for the remnant in Israel and
Judah about what is written in this book
that has been found. Great is the LORD's
anger that is poured out on us because

a19 One Hebrew manuscript and Septuagint; most
Hebrew manuscripts *of Hozai*   *b20* Also called
Acbor son of Micaiah

THE WHEEL ILLUSTRATION

The Wheel Illustration demonstrates six vitally important areas of a dynamic Christian life. All four spokes must be kept in balance. The Wheel is a good means for evaluating growth and balance in your spiritual life.

THE HUB: Christ the center
The daily decision to make Christ central in your life

THE RIM: Obedience to Christ
Actively following Christ's leading internally in your thoughts and attitudes and externally in your actions

THE SPOKES
• THE WORD
God speaks to us through his Word, the Bible

• FELLOWSHIP
Believers gather to stimulate and encourage one another

• WITNESSING
Sharing Christ with others

• PRAYER
We speak back to God

HOW TO MAKE DECISIONS IN GOD'S WILL

■ **The first step in making a decision within God's will is deciding to surrender to his will.**

God is all-knowing and all-powerful, and he has no trouble communicating what he wants us to do. Our problem is not so much in knowing God's will, but in doing it. Often we must be willing to do whatever he desires for us before he will let us know what that is. This attitude of letting go can be frightening as we contemplate an unknown future, but if we really know God and understand that he loves us and wants the best for us, we will also trust him. —John 7:17; Romans 12:1–2

■ **The second step is to discern how God is leading us. God uses five means to reveal his will to us:**

1. The Word of God—Psalm 119:105; Proverbs 6:22–23

Obviously, if something is contrary to a direct teaching in Scripture, it is not the will of God. God also reveals clear teaching from the Bible concerning our specific situations.

2. The confirmation of personal peace when we pray—Psalm 143:8,10; Isaiah 30:21; Philippians 4:6–7

When we pray for God's leading, we often experience a deep peace, a heart that is at rest in the knowledge that God is leading us. Though we may not have answers to all our questions, the Holy Spirit confirms that our decision is in God's will.

3. Counsel from mature believers—Proverbs 13:20; 15:22; 19:20

God often uses objective counsel from mature believers to give us perspective and direction. Finding counselors who know us and want God's best for us is a challenge. It is important to pray that God will send such counselors into our lives.

CONTINUED ON NEXT PAGE

4. Wisdom and careful thinking—1 Peter 1:13

Ask God for wisdom and knowledge. God gave us intelligence in order to use it for his glory.

Compare the positives and negatives when thinking through the decision. The Scriptures teach us not to lean on our own understanding (see Proverbs 3:5–6), but they don't say to stop using it!

5. Providential circumstances—Acts 16:6–9; Revelation 3:7–8

God will open doors to guide us and he will close doors in order to lead us toward open ones. He will provide opportunities that lead to even greater opportunities.

■ *The more that these five means point in the same direction, the more certain we can be that God is leading us. If one or two agree, but the others don't, we have two possibilities. Our decision may be in God's will, but the timing for it is wrong. Or it may not be God's leading. In either case, it's best to wait; immaturity will press ahead when things are not clear and pay a big price! (See Proverbs 19:2.) God will use time to clarify our choices.*

■ *When we make a decision with this method it's important to put our confidence in God's sovereignty: "You will keep in perfect peace him whose mind is steadfast, because he trusts in you. Trust in the LORD forever, for the LORD, the LORD, is the Rock eternal" (Isaiah 26:3–4). Trusting him and his leading is key to confidence and peace. On our own we can deceive ourselves; we can find verses to justify about anything. We can "have peace" about a lot of things but that peace is not necessarily from God. Satan can open doors of opportunity that may seem right to us at first. God knows this. He knows we can be confused, but he will not let us wander from his will, if we truly want to know it. So we can relax knowing that he will keep us and guide us.*

THE NAVIGATORS' TOPICAL MEMORY SYSTEM

Series A:
Live the New Life

Christ the Center
2 Corinthians 5:17
Galatians 2:20

Obedience to Christ
Romans 12:1
John 14:21

God's Word
2 Timothy 3:16
Joshua 1:8

Prayer
John 15:7
Philippians 4:6-7

Fellowship
Matthew 18:20
Hebrews 10:24-25

Witnessing
Matthew 4:19
Romans 1:16

Series B:
Proclaim Christ

All Have Sinned
Romans 3:23
Isaiah 53:6

Sin's Penalty
Romans 6:23
Hebrews 9:27

Christ Paid the Penalty
Romans 5:8
1 Peter 3:18

Salvation Not by Works
Ephesians 2:8-9
Titus 3:5

Must Receive Christ
John 1:12
Revelation 3:20

Assurance of Salvation
1 John 5:13
John 5:24

Series C:
Rely on God's Resources

His Spirit
1 Corinthians 3:16
1 Corinthians 2:12

His Strength
Isaiah 41:10
Philippians 4:13

His Faithfulness
Lamentations 3:22-23
Numbers 23:19

His Peace
Isaiah 26:3
1 Peter 5:7

His Provision
Romans 8:32
Philippians 4:19

His Help in Temptation
Hebrews 2:18
Psalm 119:9,11

Series D:
Be Christ's Disciple

Put Christ First
Matthew 6:33
Luke 9:23

Separate from the World
1 John 2:15-16
Romans 12:2

Be Steadfast
1 Corinthians 15:58
Hebrews 12:3

Serve Others
Mark 10:45
2 Corinthians 4:5

Give Generously
Proverbs 3:9-10
2 Corinthians 9:6-7

Develop World Vision
Acts 1:8
Matthew 28:19-20

Series E:
Grow in Christlikeness

Love
John 13:34-35
1 John 3:18

Humility
Philippians 2:3-4
1 Peter 5:5-6

Purity
Ephesians 5:3
1 Peter 2:11

Honesty
Leviticus 19:11
Acts 24:16

Faith
Hebrews 11:6
Romans 4:20-21

Good Works
Galatians 6:9-10
Matthew 5:16

our fathers have not kept the word of the LORD; they have not acted in accordance with all that is written in this book."

²²Hilkiah and those the king had sent with him*a* went to speak to the prophetess Huldah, who was the wife of Shallum son of Tokhath,*b* the son of Hasrah,*c* keeper of the wardrobe. She lived in Jerusalem, in the Second District.

²³She said to them, "This is what the LORD, the God of Israel, says: Tell the man who sent you to me, ²⁴'This is what the LORD says: I am going to bring disaster on this place and its people—all the curses written in the book that has been read in the presence of the king of Judah. ²⁵Because they have forsaken me and burned incense to other gods and provoked me to anger by all that their hands have made,*d* my anger will be poured out on this place and will not be quenched.' ²⁶Tell the king of Judah, who sent you to inquire of the LORD, 'This is what the LORD, the God of Israel, says concerning the words you heard: ²⁷Because your heart was responsive and you humbled yourself before God when you heard what he spoke against this place and its people, and because you humbled yourself before me and tore your robes and wept in my presence, I have heard you, declares the LORD. ²⁸Now I will gather you to your fathers, and you will be buried in peace. Your eyes will not see all the disaster I am going to bring on this place and on those who live here.' "

So they took her answer back to the king.

²⁹Then the king called together all the elders of Judah and Jerusalem. ³⁰He went up to the temple of the LORD with the men of Judah, the people of Jerusalem, the priests and the Levites—all the people from the least to the greatest. He read in their hearing all the words of the Book of the Covenant, which had been found in the temple of the LORD. ³¹The king stood by his pillar and renewed the covenant in the presence of the LORD—to follow the LORD and keep his commands, regulations and decrees with all his heart and all his soul, and to obey the words of the covenant written in this book.

³²Then he had everyone in Jerusalem and Benjamin pledge themselves to it; the people of Jerusalem did this in accordance with the covenant of God, the God of their fathers.

³³Josiah removed all the detestable idols from all the territory belonging to the Israelites, and he had all who were present in Israel serve the LORD their God. As long as he lived, they did not fail to follow the LORD, the God of their fathers.

Josiah Celebrates the Passover

35 Josiah celebrated the Passover to the LORD in Jerusalem, and the Passover lamb was slaughtered on the fourteenth day of the first month. ²He appointed the priests to their duties and encouraged them in the service of the LORD's temple. ³He said to the Levites, who instructed all Israel and who had been consecrated to the LORD: "Put the sacred ark in the temple that Solomon son of David king of Israel built. It is not to be carried about on your shoulders. Now serve the LORD your God and his people Israel. ⁴Prepare yourselves by families in your divisions, according to the directions written by David king of Israel and by his son Solomon.

⁵"Stand in the holy place with a group of Levites for each subdivision of the families of your fellow countrymen, the lay people. ⁶Slaughter the Passover lambs, consecrate yourselves and prepare ⌊the lambs⌋ for your fellow countrymen, doing what the LORD commanded through Moses."

⁷Josiah provided for all the lay people who were there a total of thirty thousand sheep and goats for the Passover offerings, and also three thousand cattle—all from the king's own possessions.

⁸His officials also contributed voluntarily to the people and the priests and Levites. Hilkiah, Zechariah and Jehiel, the administrators of God's temple, gave the priests twenty-six hundred Passover offerings and three hundred cattle. ⁹Also Conaniah along with Shemaiah and Nethanel, his brothers, and Hashabiah, Jeiel and Jozabad, the leaders of the Levites, provided five thousand Passover offerings and five hundred head of cattle for the Levites.

¹⁰The service was arranged and the priests stood in their places with the Levites in their divisions as the king had ordered. ¹¹The Passover lambs were slaughtered, and the priests sprinkled the

---

a22 One Hebrew manuscript, Vulgate and Syriac; most Hebrew manuscripts do not have *had sent with him.*   *b22* Also called *Tikvah*   *c22* Also called *Harhas*   *d25* Or *by everything they have done* blood handed to them, while the Levites skinned the animals. ¹²They set aside the burnt offerings to give them to the subdivisions of the families of the people to offer to the LORD, as is written in the Book of Moses. They did the same with the cattle. ¹³They roasted the Passover animals over the fire as prescribed, and boiled the holy offerings in pots, caldrons and pans and served them quickly to all the people. ¹⁴After this, they made preparations for themselves and for the priests, because the priests, the descendants of Aaron, were sacrificing the burnt offerings and the fat portions until nightfall. So the Levites made preparations for themselves and for the Aaronic priests.

¹⁵The musicians, the descendants of Asaph, were in the places prescribed by David, Asaph, Heman and Jeduthun the king's seer. The gatekeepers at each gate did not need to leave their posts, because their fellow Levites made the preparations for them.

¹⁶So at that time the entire service of the LORD was carried out for the celebration of the Passover and the offering of burnt offerings on the altar of the LORD, as King Josiah had ordered. ¹⁷The Israelites who were present celebrated the Passover at that time and observed the Feast of Unleavened Bread for seven days. ¹⁸The Passover had not been observed like this in Israel since the days of the prophet Samuel; and none of the kings of Israel had ever celebrated such a Passover as did Josiah, with the priests, the Levites and all Judah and Israel who were there with the people of Jerusalem. ¹⁹This Passover was celebrated in the eighteenth year of Josiah's reign.

The Death of Josiah

²⁰After all this, when Josiah had set the temple in order, Neco king of Egypt went up to fight at Carchemish on the Euphrates, and Josiah marched out to meet him in battle. ²¹But Neco sent messengers to him, saying, "What quarrel is there between you and me, O king of Judah? It is not you I am attacking at this time, but the house with which I am at war. God has told me to hurry; so stop opposing God, who is with me, or he will destroy you."

²²Josiah, however, would not turn away from him, but disguised himself to engage him in battle. He would not listen to what Neco had said at God's command

but went to fight him on the plain of Megiddo.

²³Archers shot King Josiah, and he told his officers, "Take me away; I am badly wounded." ²⁴So they took him out of his chariot, put him in the other chariot he had and brought him to Jerusalem, where he died. He was buried in the tombs of his fathers, and all Judah and Jerusalem mourned for him.

²⁵Jeremiah composed laments for Josiah, and to this day all the men and women singers commemorate Josiah in the laments. These became a tradition in Israel and are written in the Laments.

²⁶The other events of Josiah's reign and his acts of devotion, according to what is written in the Law of the LORD— ²⁷all the events, from beginning to end, are written in the book of the kings of Israel and Judah. **36** ¹And the people of the land took Jehoahaz son of Josiah and made him king in Jerusalem in place of his father.

Jehoahaz King of Judah

²Jehoahaz*ᵃ* was twenty-three years old when he became king, and he reigned in Jerusalem three months. ³The king of Egypt dethroned him in Jerusalem and imposed on Judah a levy of a hundred talents*ᵇ* of silver and a talent*ᶜ* of gold. ⁴The king of Egypt made Eliakim, a brother of Jehoahaz, king over Judah and Jerusalem and changed Eliakim's name to Jehoiakim. But Neco took Eliakim's brother Jehoahaz and carried him off to Egypt.

ᵃ2 Hebrew *Joahaz*, a variant of *Jehoahaz*; also in verse 4   *ᵇ3* That is, about 3 3/4 tons (about 3.4 metric tons)   *ᶜ3* That is, about 75 pounds (about 34 kilograms)

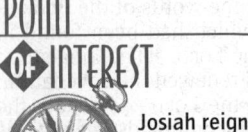

POINT OF INTEREST   2 Chronicles 35:12

Josiah reigned 300 years after King David and 700 years after Moses wrote the first five books of the Bible. Some people question the validity of the Bible because of its age. But Josiah knew that God's Word hadn't gone out-of-date even though it was 700 years old. It never will!

Jehoiakim King of Judah

⁵Jehoiakim was twenty-five years old when he became king, and he reigned in Jerusalem eleven years. He did evil in the eyes of the LORD his God. ⁶Nebuchadnezzar king of Babylon attacked him and bound him with bronze shackles to take him to Babylon. ⁷Nebuchadnezzar also took to Babylon articles from the temple of the LORD and put them in his temple*a* there.

⁸The other events of Jehoiakim's reign, the detestable things he did and all that was found against him, are written in the book of the kings of Israel and Judah. And Jehoiachin his son succeeded him as king.

Jehoiachin King of Judah

⁹Jehoiachin was eighteen*b* years old when he became king, and he reigned in Jerusalem three months and ten days. He did evil in the eyes of the LORD. ¹⁰In the spring, King Nebuchadnezzar sent for him and brought him to Babylon, together with articles of value from the temple of the LORD, and he made Jehoiachin's uncle,*c* Zedekiah, king over Judah and Jerusalem.

Zedekiah King of Judah

¹¹Zedekiah was twenty-one years old when he became king, and he reigned in Jerusalem eleven years. ¹²He did evil in the eyes of the LORD his God and did not humble himself before Jeremiah the prophet, who spoke the word of the LORD. ¹³He also rebelled against King Nebuchadnezzar, who had made him take an oath in God's name. He became stiff-necked and hardened his heart and would not turn to the LORD, the God of Israel. ¹⁴Furthermore, all the leaders of the priests and the people became more and more unfaithful, following all the detestable practices of the nations and defiling the temple of the LORD, which he had consecrated in Jerusalem.

The Fall of Jerusalem

¹⁵The LORD, the God of their fathers, sent word to them through his messengers again and again, because he had pity on his people and on his dwelling place. ¹⁶But they mocked God's messengers, despised his words and scoffed at his prophets until the wrath of the LORD was aroused against his people and there was no remedy. ¹⁷He brought up against them the king of the Babylonians,*d* who killed their young men with the sword in the sanctuary, and spared neither young man nor young woman, old man or aged. God handed all of them over to Nebuchadnezzar. ¹⁸He carried to Babylon all the articles from the temple of God, both large and small, and the treasures of the LORD's temple and the treasures of the king and his officials. ¹⁹They set fire to God's temple and broke down the wall of Jerusalem; they burned all the palaces and destroyed everything of value there.

²⁰He carried into exile to Babylon the remnant, who escaped from the sword, and they became servants to him and his sons until the kingdom of Persia came to power. ²¹The land enjoyed its sabbath rests; all the time of its desolation it rested, until the seventy years were completed in fulfillment of the word of the LORD spoken by Jeremiah.

²²In the first year of Cyrus king of Persia, in order to fulfill the word of the LORD spoken by Jeremiah, the LORD moved the heart of Cyrus king of Persia to make a proclamation throughout his realm and to put it in writing:

²³"This is what Cyrus king of Persia says:

" 'The LORD, the God of heaven, has given me all the kingdoms of the earth and he has appointed me to build a temple for him at Jerusalem in Judah. Anyone of his people among you—may the LORD his God be with him, and let him go up.' "

---

a 7 Or *palace*   *b 9* One Hebrew manuscript, some Septuagint manuscripts and Syriac (see also 2 Kings 24:8); most Hebrew manuscripts *eight*   *c 10* Hebrew *brother,* that is, relative (see 2 Kings 24:17)   *d 17* Or *Chaldeans*

In the book of Ezra, the Israelites' situation takes an upward swing. After a long exile in Babylon, they are allowed to return to Judah and rebuild the temple. What's more, God raises up a new leader in Ezra, a man devoted to studying and teaching the Law. While under Ezra's dynamic leadership, the temple is rebuilt and dedicated, and the people celebrate and renew their commitment to faithfulness and purity. The Israelites rejoice in the God who always gives his people a second chance to trust and follow him. So can we!

EZRA

Cyrus Helps the Exiles to Return

1 In the first year of Cyrus king of Persia, in order to fulfill the word of the LORD spoken by Jeremiah, the LORD moved the heart of Cyrus king of Persia to make a proclamation throughout his realm and to put it in writing:

2 "This is what Cyrus king of Persia says:

" 'The LORD, the God of heaven, has given me all the kingdoms of the earth and he has appointed me to build a temple for him at Jerusalem in Judah. 3 Anyone of his people among you—may his God be with him, and let him go up to Jerusalem in Judah and build the temple of the LORD, the God of Israel, the God who is in Jerusalem. 4 And the people of any place where survivors may now be living are to provide him with silver and gold, with goods and livestock, and with freewill offerings for the temple of God in Jerusalem.' "

5 Then the family heads of Judah and Benjamin, and the priests and Levites—everyone whose heart God had moved—prepared to go up and build the house of the LORD in Jerusalem. 6 All their neighbors assisted them with articles of silver and gold, with goods and livestock, and with valuable gifts, in addition to all the freewill offerings. 7 Moreover, King Cyrus brought out the articles belonging to the temple of the LORD, which Nebuchadnez-

zar had carried away from Jerusalem and had placed in the temple of his god.[a] [8]Cyrus king of Persia had them brought by Mithredath the treasurer, who counted them out to Sheshbazzar the prince of Judah.

[9]This was the inventory:

gold dishes	30
silver dishes	1,000
silver pans[b]	29
[10]gold bowls	30
matching silver bowls	410
other articles	1,000

[11]In all, there were 5,400 articles of gold and of silver. Sheshbazzar brought all these along when the exiles came up from Babylon to Jerusalem.

The List of the Exiles Who Returned

2 Now these are the people of the province who came up from the captivity of the exiles, whom Nebuchadnezzar king of Babylon had taken captive to Babylon (they returned to Jerusalem and Judah, each to his own town, [2]in company with Zerubbabel, Jeshua, Nehemiah, Seraiah, Reelaiah, Mordecai, Bilshan, Mispar, Bigvai, Rehum and Baanah):

The list of the men of the people of Israel:

[3]the descendants of Parosh	2,172
[4]of Shephatiah	372
[5]of Arah	775
[6]of Pahath-Moab (through the line of Jeshua and Joab)	2,812
[7]of Elam	1,254
[8]of Zattu	945
[9]of Zaccai	760
[10]of Bani	642
[11]of Bebai	623
[12]of Azgad	1,222
[13]of Adonikam	666
[14]of Bigvai	2,056
[15]of Adin	454
[16]of Ater (through Hezekiah)	98
[17]of Bezai	323
[18]of Jorah	112
[19]of Hashum	223
[20]of Gibbar	95
[21]the men of Bethlehem	123
[22]of Netophah	56
[23]of Anathoth	128
[24]of Azmaveth	42
[25]of Kiriath Jearim,[c] Kephirah and Beeroth	743
[26]of Ramah and Geba	621
[27]of Micmash	122
[28]of Bethel and Ai	223
[29]of Nebo	52
[30]of Magbish	156
[31]of the other Elam	1,254
[32]of Harim	320
[33]of Lod, Hadid and Ono	725
[34]of Jericho	345
[35]of Senaah	3,630

[36]The priests:

the descendants of Jedaiah (through the family of Jeshua)	973
[37]of Immer	1,052
[38]of Pashhur	1,247
[39]of Harim	1,017

[40]The Levites:

the descendants of Jeshua and Kadmiel (through the line of Hodaviah)	74

[41]The singers:

the descendants of Asaph	128

[42]The gatekeepers of the temple:

the descendants of Shallum, Ater, Talmon, Akkub, Hatita and Shobai	139

[43]The temple servants:

the descendants of
Ziha, Hasupha, Tabbaoth,
[44]Keros, Siaha, Padon,
[45]Lebanah, Hagabah, Akkub,
[46]Hagab, Shalmai, Hanan,
[47]Giddel, Gahar, Reaiah,

[a]7 Or *gods*   [b]9 The meaning of the Hebrew for this word is uncertain.   [c]25 See Septuagint (see also Neh. 7:29); Hebrew *Kiriath Arim.*

POINT OF INTEREST   Ezra 1:2

Was Cyrus a believer? We don't know for sure, but probably not. Cyrus seemed to use religious tolerance to win favor with conquered nations and to placate any deities he might have inadvertently offended.

48Rezin, Nekoda, Gazzam,
49Uzza, Paseah, Besai,
50Asnah, Meunim, Nephussim,
51Bakbuk, Hakupha, Harhur,
52Bazluth, Mehida, Harsha,
53Barkos, Sisera, Temah,
54Neziah and Hatipha

55The descendants of the servants of Solomon:

the descendants of
    Sotai, Hassophereth, Peruda,
56Jaala, Darkon, Giddel,
57Shephatiah, Hattil,
    Pokereth-Hazzebaim and Ami

58The temple servants and the
    descendants of the servants
    of Solomon   392

59The following came up from the towns of Tel Melah, Tel Harsha, Kerub, Addon and Immer, but they could not show that their families were descended from Israel:

60The descendants of
    Delaiah, Tobiah and
    Nekoda   652

61And from among the priests:

The descendants of
    Hobaiah, Hakkoz and Barzillai
    (a man who had married a
    daughter of Barzillai the
    Gileadite and was called by
    that name).

62These searched for their family records, but they could not find them and so were excluded from the priesthood as unclean. 63The governor ordered them not to eat any of the most sacred food until there was a priest ministering with the Urim and Thummim.

64The whole company numbered 42,360, 65besides their 7,337 menservants and maidservants; and they also had 200 men and women singers. 66They had 736 horses, 245 mules, 67435 camels and 6,720 donkeys.

68When they arrived at the house of the LORD in Jerusalem, some of the heads of the families gave freewill offerings toward the rebuilding of the house of God on its site. 69According to their ability they gave to the treasury for this work 61,000 drachmas*a* of gold, 5,000 mi-

nas*b* of silver and 100 priestly garments.

70The priests, the Levites, the singers, the gatekeepers and the temple servants settled in their own towns, along with some of the other people, and the rest of the Israelites settled in their towns.

Rebuilding the Altar

3 When the seventh month came and the Israelites had settled in their towns, the people assembled as one man in Jerusalem. 2Then Jeshua son of Jozadak and his fellow priests and Zerubbabel son of Shealtiel and his associates began to build the altar of the God of Israel to sacrifice burnt offerings on it, in accordance with what is written in the Law of Moses the man of God. 3Despite their fear of the peoples around them, they built the altar on its foundation and sacrificed burnt offerings on it to the LORD, both the morning and evening sacrifices. 4Then in accordance with what is written, they celebrated the Feast of Tabernacles with the required number of burnt offerings prescribed for each day. 5After that, they presented the regular burnt offerings, the New Moon sacrifices and the sacrifices for all the appointed sacred feasts of the LORD, as well as those brought as freewill offerings to the LORD. 6On the first day of the seventh month they began to offer burnt offerings to the LORD, though the foundation of the LORD's temple had not yet been laid.

Rebuilding the Temple

7Then they gave money to the masons and carpenters, and gave food and drink and oil to the people of Sidon and Tyre, so that they would bring cedar logs by sea from Lebanon to Joppa, as authorized by Cyrus king of Persia.

8In the second month of the second year after their arrival at the house of God in Jerusalem, Zerubbabel son of Shealtiel, Jeshua son of Jozadak and the rest of their brothers (the priests and the Levites and all who had returned from the captivity to Jerusalem) began the work, appointing Levites twenty years of age and older to supervise the building of the house of the LORD. 9Jeshua and his sons and brothers and Kadmiel and his sons (descendants of Hodaviah*c*) and the

a69 That is, about 1,100 pounds (about 500 kilograms)   b69 That is, about 3 tons (about 2.9 metric tons)   c9 Hebrew Yehudah, probably a variant of Hodaviah sons of Henadad and their sons and brothers—all Levites—joined together in supervising those working on the house of God.

¹⁰When the builders laid the foundation of the temple of the LORD, the priests in their vestments and with trumpets, and the Levites (the sons of Asaph) with cymbals, took their places to praise the LORD, as prescribed by David king of Israel. ¹¹With praise and thanksgiving they sang to the LORD:

"He is good;
   his love to Israel endures forever."

And all the people gave a great shout of praise to the LORD, because the foundation of the house of the LORD was laid. ¹²But many of the older priests and Levites and family heads, who had seen the former temple, wept aloud when they saw the foundation of this temple being laid, while many others shouted for joy. ¹³No one could distinguish the sound of

---

TUESDAY

Read *Ezra 3:1–13*
Key Verse *Ezra 3:3*

Freedom from Fear – Mistie Hutchison

When I was in graduate school I often encountered people who were indifferent or even hostile toward Christianity. A fellow graduate assistant had a small sign above his desk that read, "Jesus who?" This person delighted in making fun of Jesus and his followers. Needless to say, I felt intimidated. I wish I could say that I fearlessly shared Jesus Christ with him, but that wouldn't be true. Most of my interaction with him was marked by a sense of fear and nervousness.

I don't look back on that situation as a personal success story. However, God still uses it to teach me about fear, specifically the fear of people. Fear is one of the strongest emotions we can experience. Like other emotions it can be either a positive or a negative motivating factor in our lives. We typically respond to our fears in one of two ways: we withdraw, allowing our fears to control us, or one by one we face our fears and move toward God in deeper trust.

We see both of these responses in Scripture. When Moses sent the twelve spies into Canaan, ten returned afraid of the giants in the land, swaying an entire nation to fear (Numbers 13–14). However, in Ezra 3:3 the Israelites courageously worshiped God and began rebuilding the temple even though they were frightened by those around them. The difference between these situations isn't that fear was present in one and absent in the other. The difference lies in the people's response to their fears.

To experience fear isn't a sin, but it is a sin to allow fear to control us. God can help; his "perfect love drives out fear" (1 John 4:18). If we let him, he will chip away at our fears and teach us to overcome them. He releases us from fear's control so that we are able to work for him even in intimidating situations: "For God did not give us a spirit of timidity, but a spirit of power, of love and of self-discipline" (2 Timothy 1:7).

A Deeper Look
Psalm 27; Psalm 46; Philippians 4:6–7

Go to page 512 for your next devotional reading.

the shouts of joy from the sound of weeping, because the people made so much noise. And the sound was heard far away.

Opposition to the Rebuilding

4 When the enemies of Judah and Benjamin heard that the exiles were building a temple for the LORD, the God of Israel, ²they came to Zerubbabel and to the heads of the families and said, "Let us help you build because, like you, we seek your God and have been sacrificing to him since the time of Esarhaddon king of Assyria, who brought us here."

³But Zerubbabel, Jeshua and the rest of the heads of the families of Israel answered, "You have no part with us in building a temple to our God. We alone will build it for the LORD, the God of Israel, as King Cyrus, the king of Persia, commanded us."

⁴Then the peoples around them set out to discourage the people of Judah and make them afraid to go on building.ᵃ ⁵They hired counselors to work against them and frustrate their plans during the entire reign of Cyrus king of Persia and down to the reign of Darius king of Persia.

Later Opposition Under Xerxes and Artaxerxes

⁶At the beginning of the reign of Xerxes,ᵇ they lodged an accusation against the people of Judah and Jerusalem.

⁷And in the days of Artaxerxes king of Persia, Bishlam, Mithredath, Tabeel and the rest of his associates wrote a letter to Artaxerxes. The letter was written in Aramaic script and in the Aramaic language.ᶜ·ᵈ

⁸Rehum the commanding officer and Shimshai the secretary wrote a letter against Jerusalem to Artaxerxes the king as follows:

⁹Rehum the commanding officer and Shimshai the secretary, together with the rest of their associates— the judges and officials over the men from Tripolis, Persia,ᵉ Erech and Babylon, the Elamites of Susa, ¹⁰and the other people whom the great and honorable Ashurbanipalᶠ deported and settled in the city of Samaria and elsewhere in Trans-Euphrates.

¹¹(This is a copy of the letter they sent him.)

To King Artaxerxes,

From your servants, the men of Trans-Euphrates:

¹²The king should know that the Jews who came up to us from you have gone to Jerusalem and are rebuilding that rebellious and wicked city. They are restoring the walls and repairing the foundations.

¹³Furthermore, the king should know that if this city is built and its walls are restored, no more taxes, tribute or duty will be paid, and the royal revenues will suffer. ¹⁴Now since we are under obligation to the palace and it is not proper for us to see the king dishonored, we are sending this message to inform the king, ¹⁵so that a search may be made in the archives of your predecessors. In these records you will find that this city is a rebellious city, troublesome to kings and provinces, a place of rebellion from ancient times. That is why this city was destroyed. ¹⁶We inform the king that if this city is built and its walls are restored, you will be left with nothing in Trans-Euphrates.

¹⁷The king sent this reply:

To Rehum the commanding officer, Shimshai the secretary and the rest of their associates living in Samaria and elsewhere in Trans-Euphrates:

Greetings.

¹⁸The letter you sent us has been read and translated in my presence. ¹⁹I issued an order and a search was made, and it was found that this city has a long history of revolt against kings and has been a place of rebellion and sedition. ²⁰Jerusalem has had powerful kings ruling over the whole of Trans-Euphrates, and taxes, tribute and duty were paid to them. ²¹Now issue an order to these men to stop work, so that this city will not be rebuilt until I so order. ²²Be careful not to neglect

ᵃ4 Or and troubled them as they built
ᵇ6 Hebrew Ahasuerus, a variant of Xerxes' Persian name   ᶜ7 Or written in Aramaic and translated
ᵈ7 The text of Ezra 4:8—6:18 is in Aramaic.
ᵉ9 Or officials, magistrates and governors over the men from   ᶠ10 Aramaic Osnappar, a variant of Ashurbanipal

this matter. Why let this threat grow, to the detriment of the royal interests?

²³As soon as the copy of the letter of King Artaxerxes was read to Rehum and Shimshai the secretary and their associates, they went immediately to the Jews in Jerusalem and compelled them by force to stop.

²⁴Thus the work on the house of God in Jerusalem came to a standstill until the second year of the reign of Darius king of Persia.

Tattenai's Letter to Darius

5 Now Haggai the prophet and Zechariah the prophet, a descendant of Iddo, prophesied to the Jews in Judah and Jerusalem in the name of the God of Israel, who was over them. ²Then Zerubbabel son of Shealtiel and Jeshua son of Jozadak set to work to rebuild the house of God in Jerusalem. And the prophets of God were with them, helping them.

³At that time Tattenai, governor of Trans-Euphrates, and Shethar-Bozenai and their associates went to them and asked, "Who authorized you to rebuild this temple and restore this structure?" ⁴They also asked, "What are the names of the men constructing this building?"ᵃ ⁵But the eye of their God was watching over the elders of the Jews, and they were not stopped until a report could go to Darius and his written reply be received.

⁶This is a copy of the letter that Tattenai, governor of Trans-Euphrates, and Shethar-Bozenai and their associates, the officials of Trans-Euphrates, sent to King Darius. ⁷The report they sent him read as follows:

To King Darius:

Cordial greetings.

⁸The king should know that we went to the district of Judah, to the temple of the great God. The people are building it with large stones and placing the timbers in the walls. The work is being carried on with diligence and is making rapid progress under their direction.

⁹We questioned the elders and asked them, "Who authorized you to rebuild this temple and restore this structure?" ¹⁰We also asked them their names, so that we could write down the names of their leaders for your information.

¹¹This is the answer they gave us:

"We are the servants of the God of heaven and earth, and we are rebuilding the temple that was built many years ago, one that a great king of Israel built and finished. ¹²But because our fathers angered the God of heaven, he handed them over to Nebuchadnezzar the Chaldean, king of Babylon, who destroyed this temple and deported the people to Babylon.

¹³"However, in the first year of Cyrus king of Babylon, King Cyrus issued a decree to rebuild this house of God. ¹⁴He even removed from the templeᵇ of Babylon the gold and silver articles of the house of God, which Nebuchadnezzar had taken from the temple in Jerusalem and brought to the templeᵇ in Babylon.

"Then King Cyrus gave them to a man named Sheshbazzar, whom he had appointed governor, ¹⁵and told him, 'Take these articles and go and deposit them in the temple in Jerusalem. And rebuild the house of God on its site.' ¹⁶So this Sheshbazzar came and laid the foundations of the house of God in Jerusalem. From that day to the present it has been under construction but is not yet finished."

¹⁷Now if it pleases the king, let a search be made in the royal archives of Babylon to see if King Cyrus did in fact issue a decree to rebuild this house of God in Jerusalem. Then let the king send us his decision in this matter.

The Decree of Darius

6 King Darius then issued an order, and they searched in the archives stored in the treasury at Babylon. ²A scroll was found in the citadel of Ecbatana in the province of Media, and this was written on it:

Memorandum:

ᵃ4 See Septuagint; Aramaic *We told them the names of the men constructing this building.*
ᵇ14 Or *palace*

³In the first year of King Cyrus, the king issued a decree concerning the temple of God in Jerusalem:

Let the temple be rebuilt as a place to present sacrifices, and let its foundations be laid. It is to be ninety feet*a* high and ninety feet wide, ⁴with three courses of large stones and one of timbers. The costs are to be paid by the royal treasury. ⁵Also, the gold and silver articles of the house of God, which Nebuchadnezzar took from the temple in Jerusalem and brought to Babylon, are to be returned to their places in the temple in Jerusalem; they are to be deposited in the house of God.

⁶Now then, Tattenai, governor of Trans-Euphrates, and Shethar-Bozenai and you, their fellow officials of that province, stay away from there. ⁷Do not interfere with the work on this temple of God. Let the governor of the Jews and the Jewish elders rebuild this house of God on its site.

⁸Moreover, I hereby decree what you are to do for these elders of the Jews in the construction of this house of God:

The expenses of these men are to be fully paid out of the royal treasury, from the revenues of Trans-Euphrates, so that the work will not stop. ⁹Whatever is needed—young bulls, rams, male lambs for burnt offerings to the God of heaven, and wheat, salt, wine and oil, as requested by the priests in Jerusalem—must be given them daily without fail, ¹⁰so that they may offer sacrifices pleasing to the God of heaven and pray for the well-being of the king and his sons.

¹¹Furthermore, I decree that if anyone changes this edict, a beam is to be pulled from his house and he is to be lifted up and impaled on it. And for this crime his house is to be made a pile of rubble. ¹²May God, who has caused his Name to dwell there, overthrow any king or people who lifts a hand to change this decree or to destroy this temple in Jerusalem.

I Darius have decreed it. Let it be carried out with diligence.

Completion and Dedication of the Temple

¹³Then, because of the decree King Darius had sent, Tattenai, governor of Trans-Euphrates, and Shethar-Bozenai and their associates carried it out with diligence. ¹⁴So the elders of the Jews continued to build and prosper under the preaching of Haggai the prophet and Zechariah, a descendant of Iddo. They finished building the temple according to the command of the God of Israel and the decrees of Cyrus, Darius and Artaxerxes, kings of Persia. ¹⁵The temple was completed on the third day of the month Adar, in the sixth year of the reign of King Darius.

¹⁶Then the people of Israel—the priests, the Levites and the rest of the exiles—celebrated the dedication of the house of God with joy. ¹⁷For the dedication of this house of God they offered a hundred bulls, two hundred rams, four hundred male lambs and, as a sin offering for all Israel, twelve male goats, one for each of the tribes of Israel. ¹⁸And they installed the priests in their divisions and the Levites in their groups for the service of God at Jerusalem, according to what is written in the Book of Moses.

The Passover

¹⁹On the fourteenth day of the first month, the exiles celebrated the Passover. ²⁰The priests and Levites had purified themselves and were all ceremonially clean. The Levites slaughtered the Passover lamb for all the exiles, for their brothers the priests and for themselves. ²¹So the Israelites who had returned from the exile ate it, together with all who had

---

*a*3 Aramaic *sixty cubits* (about 27 meters)

POINT OF INTEREST

Ezra 6:1

The Bible is not the only extant document from ancient days. Inscriptions in stone and clay tablets, multiple papyri and skin parchments all indicate that ancient peoples maintained records of everything from child adoptions to legal transactions to governmental decrees.

separated themselves from the unclean practices of their Gentile neighbors in order to seek the LORD, the God of Israel. ²²For seven days they celebrated with joy the Feast of Unleavened Bread, because the LORD had filled them with joy by changing the attitude of the king of Assyria, so that he assisted them in the work on the house of God, the God of Israel.

Ezra Comes to Jerusalem

7 After these things, during the reign of Artaxerxes king of Persia, Ezra son of Seraiah, the son of Azariah, the son of Hilkiah, ²the son of Shallum, the son of Zadok, the son of Ahitub, ³the son of Amariah, the son of Azariah, the son of Meraioth, ⁴the son of Zerahiah, the son of Uzzi, the son of Bukki, ⁵the son of Abishua, the son of Phinehas, the son of Eleazar, the son of Aaron the chief priest— ⁶this Ezra came up from Babylon. He was a teacher well versed in the Law of Moses, which the LORD, the God of Israel, had given. The king had granted him everything he asked, for the hand of the LORD his God was on him. ⁷Some of the Israelites, including priests, Levites, singers, gatekeepers and temple servants, also came up to Jerusalem in the seventh year of King Artaxerxes.

⁸Ezra arrived in Jerusalem in the fifth month of the seventh year of the king. ⁹He had begun his journey from Babylon on the first day of the first month, and he arrived in Jerusalem on the first day of the fifth month, for the gracious hand of his God was on him. ¹⁰For Ezra had devoted himself to the study and observance of the Law of the LORD, and to teaching its decrees and laws in Israel.

King Artaxerxes' Letter to Ezra

¹¹This is a copy of the letter King Artaxerxes had given to Ezra the priest and teacher, a man learned in matters concerning the commands and decrees of the LORD for Israel:

¹²ᵃArtaxerxes, king of kings,

To Ezra the priest, a teacher of the Law of the God of heaven:

Greetings.

¹³Now I decree that any of the Israelites in my kingdom, including priests and Levites, who wish to go to Jerusalem with you, may go.

¹⁴You are sent by the king and his seven advisers to inquire about Judah and Jerusalem with regard to the Law of your God, which is in your hand. ¹⁵Moreover, you are to take with you the silver and gold that the king and his advisers have freely given to the God of Israel, whose dwelling is in Jerusalem, ¹⁶together with all the silver and gold you may obtain from the province of Babylon, as well as the freewill offerings of the people and priests for the temple of their God in Jerusalem. ¹⁷With this money be sure to buy bulls, rams and male lambs, together with their grain offerings and drink offerings, and sacrifice them on the altar of the temple of your God in Jerusalem.

¹⁸You and your brother Jews may then do whatever seems best with the rest of the silver and gold, in accordance with the will of your God. ¹⁹Deliver to the God of Jerusalem all the articles entrusted to you for worship in the temple of your God. ²⁰And anything else needed for the temple of your God that you may have occasion to supply, you may provide from the royal treasury.

²¹Now I, King Artaxerxes, order all the treasurers of Trans-Euphrates to provide with diligence whatever Ezra the priest, a teacher of the Law of the God of heaven, may ask of you— ²²up to a hundred talentsᵇ of silver, a hundred corsᶜ of wheat, a hundred bathsᵈ of wine, a hundred bathsᵈ of olive oil, and salt without limit. ²³Whatever the God of heaven has prescribed, let it be done with diligence for the temple of the God of heaven. Why should there be wrath against the realm of the king and of his sons? ²⁴You are also to know that you have no authority to impose taxes, tribute or duty on any of the priests, Levites, singers, gatekeepers, temple servants or other workers at this house of God.

²⁵And you, Ezra, in accordance

ᵃ12 The text of Ezra 7:12-26 is in Aramaic.
ᵇ22 That is, about 3 3/4 tons (about 3.4 metric tons)   ᶜ22 That is, probably about 600 bushels (about 22 kiloliters)   ᵈ22 That is, probably about 600 gallons (about 2.2 kiloliters)

with the wisdom of your God, which you possess, appoint magistrates and judges to administer justice to all the people of Trans-Euphrates—all who know the laws of your God. And you are to teach any who do not know them. 26Whoever does not obey the law of your God and the law of the king must surely be punished by death, banishment, confiscation of property, or imprisonment.

27Praise be to the LORD, the God of our fathers, who has put it into the king's heart to bring honor to the house of the LORD in Jerusalem in this way 28and who has extended his good favor to me before the king and his advisers and all the king's powerful officials. Because the hand of the LORD my God was on me, I took courage and gathered leading men from Israel to go up with me.

List of the Family Heads Returning With Ezra

8 These are the family heads and those registered with them who came up with me from Babylon during the reign of King Artaxerxes:

2of the descendants of Phinehas, Gershom;

of the descendants of Ithamar, Daniel;

of the descendants of David, Hattush 3of the descendants of Shecaniah;

of the descendants of Parosh,

WEDNESDAY

Read Ezra 7:1–28
Key Verse Ezra 7:10

The Hand of God – Glen Hougen

Think about what it means when someone you like places a hand on you. Sometimes it's the comforting hand of a warm embrace or a motivating pat from your coach as you go onto the court. It might be the firm, correcting hand of a father or a giving, helping hand from a friend. Have you ever felt God's hand like that? How big are his hands? What do you think it feels like to have his hand on your life? Do you wish you could know?

One man who knew how God's hand felt was Ezra. In the book of Ezra, chapters seven and eight, the writer notes that God's gracious hand rests on Ezra. Because God's hand was on Ezra, the king granted all of his requests, and God provided Ezra with everything he needed during his four-month journey from Babylon to Jerusalem. It sounds simple, doesn't it?

How did Ezra do it? How do we do it? Ezra 7:10 tells us that Ezra devoted himself to God's Word in three ways: by studying, observing and teaching. Ezra was "well versed" in the Scriptures—he knew what God's Word said. Then, he obeyed it and showed others how to know and follow the Word. Because of Ezra, the people turned back to God.

Do you want to feel God's hand like that? How well do you follow Ezra's example? How well do you know the Bible? Are you digging daily? Make sure you apply what you learn. Are you sharing the Word with someone else? Whom can you help? Try it—study, obey and share.

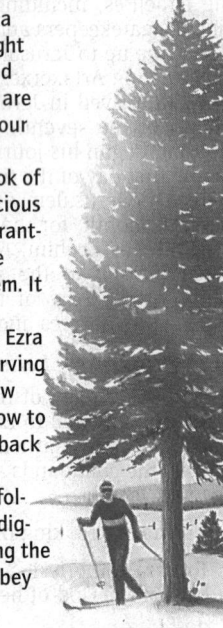

A Deeper Look
Deuteronomy 4:5–9; Nehemiah 8:18; Acts 17:11

Go to page 518 for your next devotional reading.

Zechariah, and with him were registered 150 men;

⁴of the descendants of Pahath-Moab, Eliehoenai son of Zerahiah, and with him 200 men;

⁵of the descendants of Zattu,ᵃ Shecaniah son of Jahaziel, and with him 300 men;

⁶of the descendants of Adin, Ebed son of Jonathan, and with him 50 men;

⁷of the descendants of Elam, Jeshaiah son of Athaliah, and with him 70 men;

⁸of the descendants of Shephatiah, Zebadiah son of Michael, and with him 80 men;

⁹of the descendants of Joab, Obadiah son of Jehiel, and with him 218 men;

¹⁰of the descendants of Bani,ᵇ Shelomith son of Josiphiah, and with him 160 men;

¹¹of the descendants of Bebai, Zechariah son of Bebai, and with him 28 men;

¹²of the descendants of Azgad, Johanan son of Hakkatan, and with him 110 men;

¹³of the descendants of Adonikam, the last ones, whose names were Eliphelet, Jeuel and Shemaiah, and with them 60 men;

¹⁴of the descendants of Bigvai, Uthai and Zaccur, and with them 70 men.

The Return to Jerusalem

¹⁵I assembled them at the canal that flows toward Ahava, and we camped there three days. When I checked among the people and the priests, I found no Levites there. ¹⁶So I summoned Eliezer, Ariel, Shemaiah, Elnathan, Jarib, Elnathan, Nathan, Zechariah and Meshullam, who were leaders, and Joiarib and Elnathan, who were men of learning, ¹⁷and I sent them to Iddo, the leader in Casiphia. I told them what to say to Iddo and his kinsmen, the temple servants in Casiphia, so that they might bring attendants to us for the house of our God. ¹⁸Because the gracious hand of our God was on us, they brought us Sherebiah, a capable man, from the descendants of Mahli son of Levi, the son of Israel, and Sherebiah's sons and brothers, 18 men; ¹⁹and Hashabiah, together with Jeshaiah from the descendants of Merari, and his brothers and nephews, 20 men. ²⁰They also brought 220 of the temple servants—a body that David and the officials had established to assist the Levites. All were registered by name.

²¹There, by the Ahava Canal, I proclaimed a fast, so that we might humble ourselves before our God and ask him for a safe journey for us and our children, with all our possessions. ²²I was ashamed to ask the king for soldiers and horsemen to protect us from enemies on the road, because we had told the king, "The gracious hand of our God is on everyone who looks to him, but his great anger is against all who forsake him." ²³So we fasted and petitioned our God about this, and he answered our prayer.

²⁴Then I set apart twelve of the leading priests, together with Sherebiah, Hashabiah and ten of their brothers, ²⁵and I weighed out to them the offering of silver and gold and the articles that the king, his advisers, his officials and all Israel present there had donated for the house of our God. ²⁶I weighed out to them 650 talentsᶜ of silver, silver articles weighing 100 talents,ᵈ 100 talentsᵈ of gold, ²⁷20 bowls of gold valued at 1,000 darics,ᵉ and two fine articles of polished bronze, as precious as gold.

²⁸I said to them, "You as well as these articles are consecrated to the LORD. The silver and gold are a freewill offering to the LORD, the God of your fathers. ²⁹Guard them carefully until you weigh them out in the chambers of the house of the LORD in Jerusalem before the leading priests and the Levites and the family heads of Israel." ³⁰Then the priests and Levites received the silver and gold and sacred articles that had been weighed out to be taken to the house of our God in Jerusalem.

³¹On the twelfth day of the first month we set out from the Ahava Canal to go to Jerusalem. The hand of our God was on us, and he protected us from enemies and bandits along the way. ³²So we arrived in Jerusalem, where we rested three days.

³³On the fourth day, in the house of our God, we weighed out the silver and gold and the sacred articles into the

---

ᵃ5 Some Septuagint manuscripts (also 1 Esdras 8:32); Hebrew does not have *Zattu.*   ᵇ10 Some Septuagint manuscripts (also 1 Esdras 8:36); Hebrew does not have *Bani.*   ᶜ26 That is, about 25 tons (about 22 metric tons)   ᵈ26 That is, about 3 3/4 tons (about 3.4 metric tons)   ᵉ27 That is, about 19 pounds (about 8.5 kilograms) hands of Meremoth son of Uriah, the priest. Eleazar son of Phinehas was with him, and so were the Levites Jozabad son of Jeshua and Noadiah son of Binnui. ³⁴Everything was accounted for by number and weight, and the entire weight was recorded at that time.

³⁵Then the exiles who had returned from captivity sacrificed burnt offerings to the God of Israel: twelve bulls for all Israel, ninety-six rams, seventy-seven male lambs and, as a sin offering, twelve male goats. All this was a burnt offering to the LORD. ³⁶They also delivered the king's orders to the royal satraps and to the governors of Trans-Euphrates, who then gave assistance to the people and to the house of God.

Ezra's Prayer About Intermarriage

9 After these things had been done, the leaders came to me and said, "The people of Israel, including the priests and the Levites, have not kept themselves separate from the neighboring peoples with their detestable practices, like those of the Canaanites, Hittites, Perizzites, Jebusites, Ammonites, Moabites, Egyptians and Amorites. ²They have taken some of their daughters as wives for themselves and their sons, and have mingled the holy race with the peoples around them. And the leaders and officials have led the way in this unfaithfulness."

³When I heard this, I tore my tunic and cloak, pulled hair from my head and beard and sat down appalled. ⁴Then everyone who trembled at the words of the God of Israel gathered around me because of this unfaithfulness of the exiles. And I sat there appalled until the evening sacrifice.

⁵Then, at the evening sacrifice, I rose from my self-abasement, with my tunic and cloak torn, and fell on my knees with my hands spread out to the LORD my God ⁶and prayed:

"O my God, I am too ashamed and disgraced to lift up my face to you, my God, because our sins are higher than our heads and our guilt has reached to the heavens. ⁷From the days of our forefathers until now, our guilt has been great. Because of our sins, we and our kings and our priests have been subjected to the sword and captivity, to pil-

lage and humiliation at the hand of foreign kings, as it is today.

⁸"But now, for a brief moment, the LORD our God has been gracious in leaving us a remnant and giving us a firm place in his sanctuary, and so our God gives light to our eyes and a little relief in our bondage. ⁹Though we are slaves, our God has not deserted us in our bondage. He has shown us kindness in the sight of the kings of Persia: He has granted us new life to rebuild the house of our God and repair its ruins, and he has given us a wall of protection in Judah and Jerusalem.

¹⁰"But now, O our God, what can we say after this? For we have disregarded the commands ¹¹you gave through your servants the prophets when you said: 'The land you are entering to possess is a land polluted by the corruption of its peoples. By their detestable practices they have filled it with their impurity from one end to the other. ¹²Therefore, do not give your daughters in marriage to their sons or take their daughters for your sons. Do not seek a treaty of friendship with them at any time, that you may be strong and eat the good things of the land and leave it to your children as an everlasting inheritance.'

¹³"What has happened to us is a result of our evil deeds and our great guilt, and yet, our God, you have punished us less than our sins have deserved and have given us a remnant like this. ¹⁴Shall we again

POINT OF INTEREST

Ezra 9:2

Does God condone racism? Some people have used Bible passages to justify their bigotry. But God accepts all races, as Galatians 3:28 and Colossians 3:11 attest. The issue addressed here was purity of *worship*, not race. The Israelites' worship was to remain pure, and was safeguarded by a ban on intermarriage with idolatrous people.

break your commands and intermarry with the peoples who commit such detestable practices?
Would you not be angry enough
with us to destroy us, leaving us no
remnant or survivor? ¹⁵O LORD, God
of Israel, you are righteous! We are
left this day as a remnant. Here we
are before you in our guilt, though
because of it not one of us can stand
in your presence."

The People's Confession of Sin

10 While Ezra was praying and confessing, weeping and throwing himself
down before the house of God, a large
crowd of Israelites—men, women and
children—gathered around him. They
too wept bitterly. ²Then Shecaniah son of
Jehiel, one of the descendants of Elam,
said to Ezra, "We have been unfaithful
to our God by marrying foreign women
from the peoples around us. But in spite
of this, there is still hope for Israel. ³Now
let us make a covenant before our God
to send away all these women and their
children, in accordance with the counsel
of my lord and of those who fear the commands of our God. Let it be done according to the Law. ⁴Rise up; this matter is in
your hands. We will support you, so take
courage and do it."

⁵So Ezra rose up and put the leading
priests and Levites and all Israel under
oath to do what had been suggested. And
they took the oath. ⁶Then Ezra withdrew
from before the house of God and went to
the room of Jehohanan son of Eliashib.
While he was there, he ate no food and
drank no water, because he continued to
mourn over the unfaithfulness of the exiles.

⁷A proclamation was then issued
throughout Judah and Jerusalem for all
the exiles to assemble in Jerusalem.
⁸Anyone who failed to appear within
three days would forfeit all his property,
in accordance with the decision of the
officials and elders, and would himself be
expelled from the assembly of the exiles.

⁹Within the three days, all the men of
Judah and Benjamin had gathered in Jerusalem. And on the twentieth day of the
ninth month, all the people were sitting
in the square before the house of God,
greatly distressed by the occasion and because of the rain. ¹⁰Then Ezra the priest
stood up and said to them, "You have

been unfaithful; you have married foreign women, adding to Israel's guilt.
¹¹Now make confession to the LORD, the
God of your fathers, and do his will. Separate yourselves from the peoples around
you and from your foreign wives."

¹²The whole assembly responded with
a loud voice: "You are right! We must do
as you say. ¹³But there are many people
here and it is the rainy season; so we
cannot stand outside. Besides, this matter
cannot be taken care of in a day or two,
because we have sinned greatly in this
thing. ¹⁴Let our officials act for the whole
assembly. Then let everyone in our
towns who has married a foreign woman
come at a set time, along with the elders
and judges of each town, until the fierce
anger of our God in this matter is turned
away from us." ¹⁵Only Jonathan son of
Asahel and Jahzeiah son of Tikvah, supported by Meshullam and Shabbethai the
Levite, opposed this.

¹⁶So the exiles did as was proposed.
Ezra the priest selected men who were
family heads, one from each family division, and all of them designated by name.
On the first day of the tenth month they
sat down to investigate the cases, ¹⁷and
by the first day of the first month they
finished dealing with all the men who
had married foreign women.

Those Guilty of Intermarriage

¹⁸Among the descendants of the
priests, the following had married foreign women:

From the descendants of Jeshua
son of Jozadak, and his brothers: Maaseiah, Eliezer, Jarib and
Gedaliah. ¹⁹(They all gave their
hands in pledge to put away
their wives, and for their guilt
they each presented a ram from
the flock as a guilt offering.)
²⁰From the descendants of Immer:
Hanani and Zebadiah.
²¹From the descendants of Harim:
Maaseiah, Elijah, Shemaiah, Jehiel and Uzziah.
²²From the descendants of Pashhur:
Elioenai, Maaseiah, Ishmael, Nethanel, Jozabad and Elasah.

²³Among the Levites:

Jozabad, Shimei, Kelaiah (that
is, Kelita), Pethahiah, Judah and
Eliezer.

24From the singers:
Eliashib.
From the gatekeepers:
Shallum, Telem and Uri.

25And among the other Israelites:

From the descendants of Parosh:
Ramiah, Izziah, Malkijah, Mija-
min, Eleazar, Malkijah and Be-
naiah.
26From the descendants of Elam:
Mattaniah, Zechariah, Jehiel,
Abdi, Jeremoth and Elijah.
27From the descendants of Zattu:
Elioenai, Eliashib, Mattaniah,
Jeremoth, Zabad and Aziza.
28From the descendants of Bebai:
Jehohanan, Hananiah, Zabbai
and Athlai.
29From the descendants of Bani:
Meshullam, Malluch, Adaiah,
Jashub, Sheal and Jeremoth.
30From the descendants of Pahath-
Moab:
Adna, Kelal, Benaiah, Maaseiah,
Mattaniah, Bezalel, Binnui and
Manasseh.
31From the descendants of Harim:

Eliezer, Ishijah, Malkijah, She-
maiah, Shimeon, 32Benjamin,
Malluch and Shemariah.
33From the descendants of Hashum:
Mattenai, Mattattah, Zabad,
Eliphelet, Jeremai, Manasseh
and Shimei.
34From the descendants of Bani:
Maadai, Amram, Uel, 35Benaiah,
Bedeiah, Keluhi, 36Vaniah, Mer-
emoth, Eliashib, 37Mattaniah,
Mattenai and Jaasu.
38From the descendants of Binnui:ᵃ
Shimei, 39Shelemiah, Nathan,
Adaiah, 40Macnadebai, Shashai,
Sharai, 41Azarel, Shelemiah,
Shemariah, 42Shallum, Amariah
and Joseph.
43From the descendants of Nebo:
Jeiel, Mattithiah, Zabad, Zebina,
Jaddai, Joel and Benaiah.

44All these had married foreign wom-
en, and some of them had children by
these wives.ᵇ

ᵃ37,38 See Septuagint (also 1 Esdras 9:34); Hebrew
Jaasu 38and Bani and Binnui,   ᵇ44 Or and they
sent them away with their children

In very simple terms, the second law of thermodynamics essentially states that things are in a steady state of decline. Unless an outside force is applied, things will break down and generally become useless. That's what had happened to the walls surrounding Jerusalem. Enter Nehemiah; he arrives in Jerusalem in 445 B.C. and leads the people in rebuilding Jerusalem's walls. In this book, we see the power behind Nehemiah's leadership: prayer. We can learn a lot from Nehemiah's example—he balances spirituality with down-to-earth action, a forceful combination that halts all kinds of destruction!

NEHEMIAH

Nehemiah's Prayer

1 The words of Nehemiah son of Hacaliah:

In the month of Kislev in the twentieth year, while I was in the citadel of Susa, ²Hanani, one of my brothers, came from Judah with some other men, and I questioned them about the Jewish remnant that survived the exile, and also about Jerusalem.

³They said to me, "Those who survived the exile and are back in the province are in great trouble and disgrace. The wall of Jerusalem is broken down, and its gates have been burned with fire."

⁴When I heard these things, I sat down and wept. For some days I mourned and fasted and prayed before the God of heaven. ⁵Then I said:

"O LORD, God of heaven, the great and awesome God, who keeps his covenant of love with those who love him and obey his commands, ⁶let your ear be attentive and your eyes open to hear the prayer your servant is praying before you day and night for your servants, the people of Israel. I confess the sins we Israelites, including myself and my father's house, have committed against you. ⁷We have acted very wickedly toward you. We have not obeyed the commands, decrees and laws you gave your servant Moses.

8"Remember the instruction you gave your servant Moses, saying, 'If you are unfaithful, I will scatter you among the nations, 9but if you return to me and obey my commands, then even if your exiled people are at the farthest horizon, I will gather them from there and bring them to the place I have chosen as a dwelling for my Name.'

10"They are your servants and your people, whom you redeemed by your great strength and your mighty hand. 11O Lord, let your ear be attentive to the prayer of this your servant and to the prayer of your servants who delight in revering your name. Give your servant success today by granting him favor in the presence of this man."

I was cupbearer to the king.

Artaxerxes Sends Nehemiah to Jerusalem

2 In the month of Nisan in the twentieth year of King Artaxerxes, when wine was brought for him, I took the wine and gave it to the king. I had not been sad in his presence before; 2so the king asked me, "Why does your face look so sad when you are not ill? This can be nothing but sadness of heart."

THURSDAY

Read Nehemiah 1:1–11
Key Verse Nehemiah 1:4

The Power of Prayer – Sharla Walstrom

She was an example I would never forget!

A girl a few doors down kept a large, dry-erase board on the far wall of her dorm room. She called this board her "prayer list." The list had two columns: one for specific prayer requests and the other for dates and answers to those requests. I was always curious what she had written on the board. I would often ask her if I could peek at the list, especially to see if my name was on it anywhere!

Not only did she pray specifically for herself, but she would pray for the special needs of her friends. One time her list included a pair of much-needed shoes for a girl on our floor. It wasn't long before I noticed this girl wearing new shoes. Boy, did my faith grow as I watched God answer her prayers!

Another time I noticed the names of five women on the list. These women lived on our floor and were not believers in Jesus Christ. My friend told me she was asking God to speak to them and to use her in their lives. She would often spend extended periods of time talking to God about them. I was amazed. During the rest of the school year, I would observe her eating in the cafeteria with one of those women, brushing her teeth by one in the bathroom, or walking to class with another. And on it went.

Nehemiah was clearly a man of prayer, and God used him to do incredible things. My friend, like Nehemiah, believed in the power of prayer, and God used her to make a difference. I was grateful to watch and learn from her life as the Lord etched her example on my life forever.

A Deeper Look
Matthew 6:5–8; 1 Thessalonians 5:17; 2 Thessalonians 1:11

Go to page 523 for your next devotional reading.

I was very much afraid, [3]but I said to the king, "May the king live forever! Why should my face not look sad when the city where my fathers are buried lies in ruins, and its gates have been destroyed by fire?"

[4]The king said to me, "What is it you want?"

Then I prayed to the God of heaven, [5]and I answered the king, "If it pleases the king and if your servant has found favor in his sight, let him send me to the city in Judah where my fathers are buried so that I can rebuild it."

[6]Then the king, with the queen sitting beside him, asked me, "How long will your journey take, and when will you get back?" It pleased the king to send me; so I set a time.

[7]I also said to him, "If it pleases the king, may I have letters to the governors of Trans-Euphrates, so that they will provide me safe-conduct until I arrive in Judah? [8]And may I have a letter to Asaph, keeper of the king's forest, so he will give me timber to make beams for the gates of the citadel by the temple and for the city wall and for the residence I will occupy?" And because the gracious hand of my God was upon me, the king granted my requests. [9]So I went to the governors of Trans-Euphrates and gave them the king's letters. The king had also sent army officers and cavalry with me.

[10]When Sanballat the Horonite and Tobiah the Ammonite official heard about this, they were very much disturbed that someone had come to promote the welfare of the Israelites.

Nehemiah Inspects Jerusalem's Walls

[11]I went to Jerusalem, and after staying there three days [12]I set out during the night with a few men. I had not told anyone what my God had put in my heart to do for Jerusalem. There were no mounts with me except the one I was riding on. [13]By night I went out through the Valley Gate toward the Jackal[a] Well and the Dung Gate, examining the walls of Jerusalem, which had been broken down, and its gates, which had been destroyed by fire. [14]Then I moved on toward the Fountain Gate and the King's Pool, but there was not enough room for my mount to get through; [15]so I went up the valley by night, examining the wall. Finally, I turned back and reentered through the Valley Gate. [16]The officials did not know where I had gone or what I was doing, because as yet I had said nothing to the Jews or the priests or nobles or officials or any others who would be doing the work.

[17]Then I said to them, "You see the trouble we are in: Jerusalem lies in ruins, and its gates have been burned with fire. Come, let us rebuild the wall of Jerusalem, and we will no longer be in disgrace." [18]I also told them about the gracious hand of my God upon me and what the king had said to me.

They replied, "Let us start rebuilding." So they began this good work.

[19]But when Sanballat the Horonite, Tobiah the Ammonite official and Geshem the Arab heard about it, they mocked and ridiculed us. "What is this you are doing?" they asked. "Are you rebelling against the king?"

[20]I answered them by saying, "The God of heaven will give us success. We his servants will start rebuilding, but as for you, you have no share in Jerusalem or any claim or historic right to it."

Builders of the Wall

3 Eliashib the high priest and his fellow priests went to work and rebuilt the Sheep Gate. They dedicated it and set its doors in place, building as far as the Tower of the Hundred, which they dedicated, and as far as the Tower of Hananel. [2]The men of Jericho built the adjoining section, and Zaccur son of Imri built next to them.

[3]The Fish Gate was rebuilt by the sons of Hassenaah. They laid its beams and put its doors and bolts and bars in place. [4]Meremoth son of Uriah, the son of Hakkoz, repaired the next section. Next to him Meshullam son of Berekiah, the son of Meshezabel, made repairs, and next to him Zadok son of Baana also made repairs. [5]The next section was repaired by the men of Tekoa, but their nobles would not put their shoulders to the work under their supervisors.[b]

[6]The Jeshanah[c] Gate was repaired by Joiada son of Paseah and Meshullam son of Besodeiah. They laid its beams and put its doors and bolts and bars in place.

---

[a]13 Or *Serpent* or *Fig*   [b]5 Or *their Lord* or *the governor*   [c]6 Or *Old*

7Next to them, repairs were made by men from Gibeon and Mizpah—Melatiah of Gibeon and Jadon of Meronoth—places under the authority of the governor of Trans-Euphrates. 8Uzziel son of Harhaiah, one of the goldsmiths, repaired the next section; and Hananiah, one of the perfume-makers, made repairs next to that. They restored*a* Jerusalem as far as the Broad Wall. 9Rephaiah son of Hur, ruler of a half-district of Jerusalem, repaired the next section. 10Adjoining this, Jedaiah son of Harumaph made repairs opposite his house, and Hattush son of Hashabneiah made repairs next to him. 11Malkijah son of Harim and Hasshub son of Pahath-Moab repaired another section and the Tower of the Ovens. 12Shallum son of Hallohesh, ruler of a half-district of Jerusalem, repaired the next section with the help of his daughters.

13The Valley Gate was repaired by Hanun and the residents of Zanoah. They rebuilt it and put its doors and bolts and bars in place. They also repaired five hundred yards*b* of the wall as far as the Dung Gate.

14The Dung Gate was repaired by Malkijah son of Recab, ruler of the district of Beth Hakkerem. He rebuilt it and put its doors and bolts and bars in place.

15The Fountain Gate was repaired by Shallun son of Col-Hozeh, ruler of the district of Mizpah. He rebuilt it, roofing it over and putting its doors and bolts and bars in place. He also repaired the wall of the Pool of Siloam,*c* by the King's Garden, as far as the steps going down from the City of David. 16Beyond him, Nehemiah son of Azbuk, ruler of a half-district of Beth Zur, made repairs up to a point opposite the tombs*d* of David, as far as the artificial pool and the House of the Heroes.

17Next to him, the repairs were made by the Levites under Rehum son of Bani. Beside him, Hashabiah, ruler of half the district of Keilah, carried out repairs for his district. 18Next to him, the repairs were made by their countrymen under Binnui*e* son of Henadad, ruler of the other half-district of Keilah. 19Next to him, Ezer son of Jeshua, ruler of Mizpah, repaired another section, from a point facing the ascent to the armory as far as the angle. 20Next to him, Baruch son of Zabbai zealously repaired another section, from the angle to the entrance of the house of Eliashib the high priest. 21Next to him, Meremoth son of Uriah, the son of Hakkoz, repaired another section, from the entrance of Eliashib's house to the end of it.

22The repairs next to him were made by the priests from the surrounding region. 23Beyond them, Benjamin and Hasshub made repairs in front of their house; and next to them, Azariah son of Maaseiah, the son of Ananiah, made repairs beside his house. 24Next to him, Binnui son of Henadad repaired another section, from Azariah's house to the angle and the corner, 25and Palal son of Uzai worked opposite the angle and the tower projecting from the upper palace near the court of the guard. Next to him, Pedaiah son of Parosh 26and the temple servants living on the hill of Ophel made repairs up to a point opposite the Water Gate toward the east and the projecting tower. 27Next to them, the men of Tekoa repaired another section, from the great projecting tower to the wall of Ophel.

28Above the Horse Gate, the priests made repairs, each in front of his own house. 29Next to them, Zadok son of Immer made repairs opposite his house. Next to him, Shemaiah son of Shecaniah, the guard at the East Gate, made repairs. 30Next to him, Hananiah son of Shelemiah, and Hanun, the sixth son of Zalaph, repaired another section. Next to them, Meshullam son of Berekiah made repairs opposite his living quarters. 31Next to him, Malkijah, one of the goldsmiths, made repairs as far as the house of the temple servants and the merchants, opposite the Inspection Gate, and as far as the room above the corner; 32and between the room above the corner and the Sheep Gate the goldsmiths and merchants made repairs.

Opposition to the Rebuilding

4 When Sanballat heard that we were rebuilding the wall, he became angry and was greatly incensed. He ridiculed the Jews, 2and in the presence of his as-

---

a8 Or *They left out part of*   *b13* Hebrew *a thousand cubits* (about 450 meters)   *c15* Hebrew *Shelah*, a variant of *Shiloah*, that is, Siloam   *d16* Hebrew; Septuagint, some Vulgate manuscripts and Syriac *tomb*   *e18* Two Hebrew manuscripts and Syriac (see also Septuagint and verse 24); most Hebrew manuscripts *Bavvai* sociates and the army of Samaria, he said, "What are those feeble Jews doing? Will they restore their wall? Will they offer sacrifices? Will they finish in a day? Can they bring the stones back to life from those heaps of rubble—burned as they are?"

³Tobiah the Ammonite, who was at his side, said, "What they are building—if even a fox climbed up on it, he would break down their wall of stones!"

⁴Hear us, O our God, for we are despised. Turn their insults back on their own heads. Give them over as plunder in a land of captivity. ⁵Do not cover up their guilt or blot out their sins from your sight, for they have thrown insults in the face of^a the builders.

⁶So we rebuilt the wall till all of it reached half its height, for the people worked with all their heart.

⁷But when Sanballat, Tobiah, the Arabs, the Ammonites and the men of Ashdod heard that the repairs to Jerusalem's walls had gone ahead and that the gaps were being closed, they were very angry. ⁸They all plotted together to come and fight against Jerusalem and stir up trouble against it. ⁹But we prayed to our God and posted a guard day and night to meet this threat.

¹⁰Meanwhile, the people in Judah said, "The strength of the laborers is giving out, and there is so much rubble that we cannot rebuild the wall."

¹¹Also our enemies said, "Before they know it or see us, we will be right there among them and will kill them and put an end to the work."

¹²Then the Jews who lived near them came and told us ten times over, "Wherever you turn, they will attack us."

¹³Therefore I stationed some of the people behind the lowest points of the wall at the exposed places, posting them by families, with their swords, spears and bows. ¹⁴After I looked things over, I stood up and said to the nobles, the officials and the rest of the people, "Don't be afraid of them. Remember the Lord, who is great and awesome, and fight for your brothers, your sons and your daughters, your wives and your homes."

¹⁵When our enemies heard that we were aware of their plot and that God had frustrated it, we all returned to the wall, each to his own work.

¹⁶From that day on, half of my men did the work, while the other half were equipped with spears, shields, bows and armor. The officers posted themselves behind all the people of Judah ¹⁷who were building the wall. Those who carried materials did their work with one hand and held a weapon in the other, ¹⁸and each of the builders wore his sword at his side as he worked. But the man who sounded the trumpet stayed with me.

¹⁹Then I said to the nobles, the officials and the rest of the people, "The work is extensive and spread out, and we are widely separated from each other along the wall. ²⁰Wherever you hear the sound of the trumpet, join us there. Our God will fight for us!"

²¹So we continued the work with half the men holding spears, from the first light of dawn till the stars came out. ²²At that time I also said to the people, "Have every man and his helper stay inside Jerusalem at night, so they can serve us as guards by night and workmen by day." ²³Neither I nor my brothers nor my men nor the guards with me took off our clothes; each had his weapon, even when he went for water.^b

Nehemiah Helps the Poor

5 Now the men and their wives raised a great outcry against their Jewish brothers. ²Some were saying, "We and our sons and daughters are numerous; in order for us to eat and stay alive, we must get grain."

³Others were saying, "We are mortgaging our fields, our vineyards and our homes to get grain during the famine."

⁴Still others were saying, "We have

a5 Or *have provoked you to anger before*
b23 The meaning of the Hebrew for this clause is uncertain.

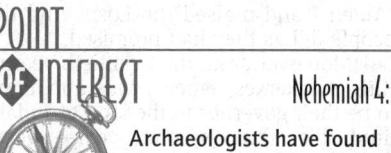

POINT OF INTEREST

Nehemiah 4:1

Archaeologists have found Sanballat's name in an ancient letter, written on papyrus, that was preserved in the dry heat of desert sands. It confirms Sanballat's position as the governor of Samaria.

had to borrow money to pay the king's tax on our fields and vineyards. ⁵Although we are of the same flesh and blood as our countrymen and though our sons are as good as theirs, yet we have to subject our sons and daughters to slavery. Some of our daughters have already been enslaved, but we are powerless, because our fields and our vineyards belong to others."

⁶When I heard their outcry and these charges, I was very angry. ⁷I pondered them in my mind and then accused the nobles and officials. I told them, "You are exacting usury from your own countrymen!" So I called together a large meeting to deal with them ⁸and said: "As far as possible, we have bought back our Jewish brothers who were sold to the Gentiles. Now you are selling your brothers, only for them to be sold back to us!" They kept quiet, because they could find nothing to say.

⁹So I continued, "What you are doing is not right. Shouldn't you walk in the fear of our God to avoid the reproach of our Gentile enemies? ¹⁰I and my brothers and my men are also lending the people money and grain. But let the exacting of usury stop! ¹¹Give back to them immediately their fields, vineyards, olive groves and houses, and also the usury you are charging them—the hundredth part of the money, grain, new wine and oil."

¹²"We will give it back," they said. "And we will not demand anything more from them. We will do as you say."

Then I summoned the priests and made the nobles and officials take an oath to do what they had promised. ¹³I also shook out the folds of my robe and said, "In this way may God shake out of his house and possessions every man who does not keep this promise. So may such a man be shaken out and emptied!"

At this the whole assembly said, "Amen," and praised the LORD. And the people did as they had promised.

¹⁴Moreover, from the twentieth year of King Artaxerxes, when I was appointed to be their governor in the land of Judah, until his thirty-second year—twelve years—neither I nor my brothers ate the food allotted to the governor. ¹⁵But the earlier governors—those preceding me—placed a heavy burden on the people and took forty shekels^a of silver from them in addition to food and wine. Their assistants also lorded it over the people. But

out of reverence for God I did not act like that. ¹⁶Instead, I devoted myself to the work on this wall. All my men were assembled there for the work; we^b did not acquire any land.

¹⁷Furthermore, a hundred and fifty Jews and officials ate at my table, as well as those who came to us from the surrounding nations. ¹⁸Each day one ox, six choice sheep and some poultry were prepared for me, and every ten days an abundant supply of wine of all kinds. In spite of all this, I never demanded the food allotted to the governor, because the demands were heavy on these people.

¹⁹Remember me with favor, O my God, for all I have done for these people.

Further Opposition to the Rebuilding

6 When word came to Sanballat, Tobiah, Geshem the Arab and the rest of our enemies that I had rebuilt the wall and not a gap was left in it — though up to that time I had not set the doors in the gates— ²Sanballat and Geshem sent me this message: "Come, let us meet together in one of the villages^c on the plain of Ono."

But they were scheming to harm me; ³so I sent messengers to them with this reply: "I am carrying on a great project and cannot go down. Why should the work stop while I leave it and go down to you?" ⁴Four times they sent me the same message, and each time I gave them the same answer.

⁵Then, the fifth time, Sanballat sent his aide to me with the same message, and in his hand was an unsealed letter ⁶in which was written:

"It is reported among the nations—and Geshem^d says it is true—that you and the Jews are plotting to revolt, and therefore you are building the wall. Moreover, according to these reports you are about to become their king ⁷and have even appointed prophets to make this proclamation about you in Jerusalem: 'There is a king in Judah!' Now this report will get back to the king; so come, let us confer together."

---

^{a}15 That is, about 1 pound (about 0.5 kilogram) ^{b}16 Most Hebrew manuscripts; some Hebrew manuscripts, Septuagint, Vulgate and Syriac I ^{c}2 Or in Kephirim ^{d}6 Hebrew Gashmu, a variant of Geshem

8I sent him this reply: "Nothing like what you are saying is happening; you are just making it up out of your head."

9They were all trying to frighten us, thinking, "Their hands will get too weak for the work, and it will not be completed."

⌐But I prayed,⌐ "Now strengthen my hands."

10One day I went to the house of Shemaiah son of Delaiah, the son of Mehetabel, who was shut in at his home. He said, "Let us meet in the house of God, inside the temple, and let us close the temple doors, because men are coming to kill you—by night they are coming to kill you."

11But I said, "Should a man like me run away? Or should one like me go into the temple to save his life? I will not go!" 12I realized that God had not sent him, but that he had prophesied against me because Tobiah and Sanballat had hired him. 13He had been hired to intimidate me so that I would commit a sin by doing this, and then they would give me a bad name to discredit me.

14Remember Tobiah and Sanballat, O my God, because of what they have done; remember also the prophetess Noadiah and the rest of the prophets who have been trying to intimidate me.

The Completion of the Wall

15So the wall was completed on the twenty-fifth of Elul, in fifty-two days.

FRIDAY

Read Nehemiah 6:1–19
Key Verse Nehemiah 6:3

The Perfect Job – Joe Bernardy

Are you stressed, frazzled, burned out? College life can be overwhelming with its demands and pressures. There are so many things competing for our time and attention that sometimes it's hard to focus on our most important tasks. But Nehemiah had a clear picture of what God had called him to do; he was to rebuild the wall around Jerusalem. He was opposed. He was criticized. He was threatened and mocked. Yet he stood his ground and focused on the task God had given him. When messengers tried to distract him, he said, "I am carrying on a great project and cannot go down" (Nehemiah 6:3).

Nehemiah was able to stay focused because he talked often with God. He used prayer as his weapon against his enemies and to bolster his confidence (Nehemiah 1:4; 2:4; 4:9; 6:9).

Like Nehemiah, we are "created in Christ Jesus to do good works, which God prepared in advance for us to do" (Ephesians 2:10). God has allowed events in our lives to prepare us for that work, and he promises to help us succeed. But like Nehemiah, we also have an enemy—the evil one—who will use all kinds of distractions to deter us. Ask God to show you his purpose for you—the reason he made you the way he did. Then, "Whatever you do, work at it with all your heart, as working for the Lord" (Colossians 3:23). When you feel overwhelmed, prioritize the things in your life according to this purpose and cut out the less important things. Then you will be free to work wholeheartedly and you won't be distracted from the plan God has for you.

A Deeper Look
Psalm 33:11; Proverbs 3:5–6; 2 Timothy 2:20–21

Go to page 527 for your next devotional reading.

16When all our enemies heard about this, all the surrounding nations were afraid and lost their self-confidence, because they realized that this work had been done with the help of our God.

17Also, in those days the nobles of Judah were sending many letters to Tobiah, and replies from Tobiah kept coming to them. 18For many in Judah were under oath to him, since he was son-in-law to Shecaniah son of Arah, and his son Jehohanan had married the daughter of Meshullam son of Berekiah. 19Moreover, they kept reporting to me his good deeds and then telling him what I said. And Tobiah sent letters to intimidate me.

7 After the wall had been rebuilt and I had set the doors in place, the gatekeepers and the singers and the Levites were appointed. 2I put in charge of Jerusalem my brother Hanani, along with*a* Hananiah the commander of the citadel, because he was a man of integrity and feared God more than most men do. 3I said to them, "The gates of Jerusalem are not to be opened until the sun is hot. While the gatekeepers are still on duty, have them shut the doors and bar them. Also appoint residents of Jerusalem as guards, some at their posts and some near their own houses."

The List of the Exiles Who Returned

4Now the city was large and spacious, but there were few people in it, and the houses had not yet been rebuilt. 5So my God put it into my heart to assemble the nobles, the officials and the common people for registration by families. I found the genealogical record of those who had been the first to return. This is what I found written there:

6These are the people of the province who came up from the captivity of the exiles whom Nebuchadnezzar king of Babylon had taken captive (they returned to Jerusalem and Judah, each to his own town, 7in company with Zerubbabel, Jeshua, Nehemiah, Azariah, Raamiah, Nahamani, Mordecai, Bilshan, Mispereth, Bigvai, Nehum and Baanah):

The list of the men of Israel:

8the descendants of Parosh	2,172
9of Shephatiah	372
10of Arah	652
11of Pahath-Moab (through the line of Jeshua and Joab)	2,818
12of Elam	1,254
13of Zattu	845
14of Zaccai	760
15of Binnui	648
16of Bebai	628
17of Azgad	2,322
18of Adonikam	667
19of Bigvai	2,067
20of Adin	655
21of Ater (through Hezekiah)	98
22of Hashum	328
23of Bezai	324
24of Hariph	112
25of Gibeon	95
26the men of Bethlehem and Netophah	188
27of Anathoth	128
28of Beth Azmaveth	42
29of Kiriath Jearim, Kephirah and Beeroth	743
30of Ramah and Geba	621
31of Micmash	122
32of Bethel and Ai	123
33of the other Nebo	52
34of the other Elam	1,254
35of Harim	320
36of Jericho	345
37of Lod, Hadid and Ono	721
38of Senaah	3,930

39The priests:

the descendants of Jedaiah (through the family of Jeshua)	973
40of Immer	1,052
41of Pashhur	1,247
42of Harim	1,017

43The Levites:

the descendants of Jeshua (through Kadmiel through the line of Hodaviah)	74

44The singers:

the descendants of Asaph	148

45The gatekeepers:

the descendants of Shallum, Ater, Talmon, Akkub, Hatita and Shobai	138

46The temple servants:

a2 Or Hanani, that is,

the descendants of
Ziha, Hasupha, Tabbaoth,
47Keros, Sia, Padon,
48Lebana, Hagaba, Shalmai,
49Hanan, Giddel, Gahar,
50Reaiah, Rezin, Nekoda,
51Gazzam, Uzza, Paseah,
52Besai, Meunim, Nephussim,
53Bakbuk, Hakupha, Harhur,
54Bazluth, Mehida, Harsha,
55Barkos, Sisera, Temah,
56Neziah and Hatipha

57The descendants of the servants of Solomon:

the descendants of
Sotai, Sophereth, Perida,
58Jaala, Darkon, Giddel,
59Shephatiah, Hattil,
Pokereth-Hazzebaim and
Amon

60The temple servants and
the descendants of the
servants of Solomon   392

61The following came up from the towns of Tel Melah, Tel Harsha, Kerub, Addon and Immer, but they could not show that their families were descended from Israel:

62the descendants of
Delaiah, Tobiah and
Nekoda   642

63And from among the priests:

the descendants of
Hobaiah, Hakkoz and Barzillai (a man who had married a daughter of Barzillai the Gileadite and was called by that name).

64These searched for their family records, but they could not find them and so were excluded from the priesthood as unclean. 65The governor, therefore, ordered them not to eat any of the most sacred food until there should be a priest ministering with the Urim and Thummim.

66The whole company numbered 42,360, 67besides their 7,337 menservants and maidservants; and they also had 245 men and women singers. 68There were 736 horses, 245 mules,a 69435 camels and 6,720 donkeys.

70Some of the heads of the families contributed to the work. The governor gave to the treasury 1,000 drachmasb of gold, 50 bowls and 530 garments for priests. 71Some of the heads of the families gave to the treasury for the work 20,000 drachmasc of gold and 2,200 minasd of silver. 72The total given by the rest of the people was 20,000 drachmas of gold, 2,000 minase of silver and 67 garments for priests. 73The priests, the Levites, the gatekeepers, the singers and the temple servants, along with certain of the people and the rest of the Israelites, settled in their own towns.

Ezra Reads the Law

When the seventh month came and the Israelites had settled in their towns, 8 1all the people assembled as one man in the square before the Water Gate. They told Ezra the scribe to bring out the Book of the Law of Moses, which the LORD had commanded for Israel.

2So on the first day of the seventh month Ezra the priest brought the Law before the assembly, which was made up of men and women and all who were able to understand. 3He read it aloud from daybreak till noon as he faced the square before the Water Gate in the presence of the men, women and others who could understand. And all the people listened attentively to the Book of the Law.

4Ezra the scribe stood on a high wooden platform built for the occasion. Beside him on his right stood Mattithiah, Shema, Anaiah, Uriah, Hilkiah and Maaseiah; and on his left were Pedaiah, Mishael, Malkijah, Hashum, Hashbaddanah, Zechariah and Meshullam.

5Ezra opened the book. All the people could see him because he was standing above them; and as he opened it, the people all stood up. 6Ezra praised the LORD, the great God; and all the people lifted their hands and responded, "Amen! Amen!" Then they bowed down and worshiped the LORD with their faces to the ground.

a68 Some Hebrew manuscripts (see also Ezra 2:66); most Hebrew manuscripts do not have this verse.   b70 That is, about 19 pounds (about 8.5 kilograms)   c71 That is, about 375 pounds (about 170 kilograms); also in verse 72   d71 That is, about 1 1/3 tons (about 1.2 metric tons)   e72 That is, about 1 1/4 tons (about 1.1 metric tons)

⁷The Levites—Jeshua, Bani, Sherebiah, Jamin, Akkub, Shabbethai, Hodiah, Maaseiah, Kelita, Azariah, Jozabad, Hanan and Pelaiah—instructed the people in the Law while the people were standing there. ⁸They read from the Book of the Law of God, making it clear*ᵃ* and giving the meaning so that the people could understand what was being read.

⁹Then Nehemiah the governor, Ezra the priest and scribe, and the Levites who were instructing the people said to them all, "This day is sacred to the Lᴏʀᴅ your God. Do not mourn or weep." For all the people had been weeping as they listened to the words of the Law.

¹⁰Nehemiah said, "Go and enjoy choice food and sweet drinks, and send some to those who have nothing prepared. This day is sacred to our Lord. Do not grieve, for the joy of the Lᴏʀᴅ is your strength."

¹¹The Levites calmed all the people, saying, "Be still, for this is a sacred day. Do not grieve."

¹²Then all the people went away to eat and drink, to send portions of food and to celebrate with great joy, because they now understood the words that had been made known to them.

¹³On the second day of the month, the heads of all the families, along with the priests and the Levites, gathered around Ezra the scribe to give attention to the words of the Law. ¹⁴They found written in the Law, which the Lᴏʀᴅ had commanded through Moses, that the Israelites were to live in booths during the feast of the seventh month ¹⁵and that they should proclaim this word and spread it throughout their towns and in Jerusalem: "Go out into the hill country and bring back branches from olive and wild olive trees, and from myrtles, palms and shade trees, to make booths"—as it is written.*ᵇ*

¹⁶So the people went out and brought back branches and built themselves booths on their own roofs, in their courtyards, in the courts of the house of God and in the square by the Water Gate and the one by the Gate of Ephraim. ¹⁷The whole company that had returned from exile built booths and lived in them. From the days of Joshua son of Nun until that day, the Israelites had not celebrated it like this. And their joy was very great.

¹⁸Day after day, from the first day to the last, Ezra read from the Book of the Law of God. They celebrated the feast for seven days, and on the eighth day, in accordance with the regulation, there was an assembly.

The Israelites Confess Their Sins

9 On the twenty-fourth day of the same month, the Israelites gathered together, fasting and wearing sackcloth and having dust on their heads. ²Those of Israelite descent had separated themselves from all foreigners. They stood in their places and confessed their sins and the wickedness of their fathers. ³They stood where they were and read from the Book of the Law of the Lᴏʀᴅ their God for a quarter of the day, and spent another quarter in confession and in worshiping the Lᴏʀᴅ their God. ⁴Standing on the stairs were the Levites—Jeshua, Bani, Kadmiel, Shebaniah, Bunni, Sherebiah, Bani and Kenani—who called with loud voices to the Lᴏʀᴅ their God. ⁵And the Levites—Jeshua, Kadmiel, Bani, Hashabneiah, Sherebiah, Hodiah, Shebaniah and Pethahiah—said: "Stand up and praise the Lᴏʀᴅ your God, who is from everlasting to everlasting.*ᶜ*"

"Blessed be your glorious name, and may it be exalted above all blessing and praise. ⁶You alone are the Lᴏʀᴅ. You made the heavens, even the highest heavens, and all their starry host, the earth and all that is on it, the seas and all that is in them. You give life to everything, and the multitudes of heaven worship you.

⁷"You are the Lᴏʀᴅ God, who

ᵃ8 Or *God, translating it*   *ᵇ15* See Lev. 23:37-40.
ᶜ5 Or *God for ever and ever*

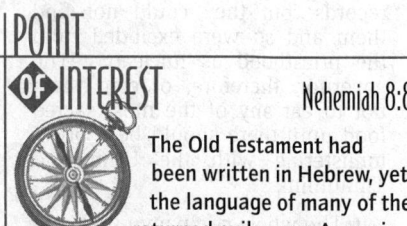

POINT OF INTEREST

Nehemiah 8:8

The Old Testament had been written in Hebrew, yet the language of many of the returned exiles was Aramaic. The Levites who read the law to these returned exiles acted as translators and Bible teachers, thus setting a pattern and precedent for modern Bible teachers and preachers.

Read Nehemiah 8:1–18
Key Verse Nehemiah 8:12

Celebrate!

Did you know that God loves a good party? He wants his people to enjoy him, to celebrate his goodness, to rejoice in his great power. The Bible account is teeming with celebrations, feasts and joyous festivals—God's gift to his people. They were to commemorate significant events in their history with him. The feasts in the Bible brought joy to the hearts of God's people as they remembered all he had done for them.

Even the Lord's Supper was intended to bring us joy. Jesus instituted the Lord's Supper as a way of helping us remember his sacrifice for us. And although it reminds us of the suffering he endured for us, it also causes us to celebrate our freedom from sin and judgment. If that's not worth celebrating, I don't know what is!

Digging Into the Word
1. Christians and non-Christians celebrate in different ways. What contrast in "celebration styles" do you see in the following passages?—*Nehemiah 8:1–12; Daniel 5:1–6*
2. What do you learn about celebrating the Lord's Supper from these passages?—*Luke 22:7–20; 1 Corinthians 11:17–34*

Action Challenge
The people of God have always celebrated great days from their religious history. Commit yourself to throw a spiritual birthday party for a Christian friend. Ask them when they became a Christian and plan a celebration to remember the goodness of God in bringing this person to faith in Jesus Christ.

One Step Deeper
Leviticus 23:1–44; Mark 14:22–26

Go to page 539 for your next devotional reading.

chose Abram and brought him out of Ur of the Chaldeans and named him Abraham. [8]You found his heart faithful to you, and you made a covenant with him to give to his descendants the land of the Canaanites, Hittites, Amorites, Perizzites, Jebusites and Girgashites. You have kept your promise because you are righteous.

[9]"You saw the suffering of our forefathers in Egypt; you heard their cry at the Red Sea.[a] [10]You sent miraculous signs and wonders against Pharaoh, against all his officials and all the people of his land, for you knew how arrogantly the Egyptians treated them. You made a name for yourself, which remains to this day. [11]You divided the sea before them, so that they passed through it on dry ground, but you hurled their pursuers into the depths, like a stone into mighty waters. [12]By day you led them with a pillar of cloud, and by night with a pillar of fire to give them light on the way they were to take.

[13]"You came down on Mount Sinai; you spoke to them from heaven. You gave them regulations and laws that are just and right, and decrees and commands that are good. [14]You made known to them your holy Sabbath and gave them commands, decrees and laws through your servant Moses. [15]In their hunger you gave them bread from heaven and in their thirst you brought them water from the rock; you told them to go in and take possession of the land you had sworn with uplifted hand to give them.

[16]"But they, our forefathers, became arrogant and stiff-necked, and did not obey your commands. [17]They refused to listen and failed to remember the miracles you performed among them. They became stiff-necked and in their rebellion appointed a leader in order to return to their slavery. But you are a forgiving God, gracious and compassionate, slow to anger and abounding in love. Therefore you did not desert them, [18]even when they cast for themselves an image of a calf and said, 'This is your god, who brought you up out of Egypt,' or

when they committed awful blasphemies.

[19]"Because of your great compassion you did not abandon them in the desert. By day the pillar of cloud did not cease to guide them on their path, nor the pillar of fire by night to shine on the way they were to take. [20]You gave your good Spirit to instruct them. You did not withhold your manna from their mouths, and you gave them water for their thirst. [21]For forty years you sustained them in the desert; they lacked nothing, their clothes did not wear out nor did their feet become swollen.

[22]"You gave them kingdoms and nations, allotting to them even the remotest frontiers. They took over the country of Sihon[b] king of Heshbon and the country of Og king of Bashan. [23]You made their sons as numerous as the stars in the sky, and you brought them into the land that you told their fathers to enter and possess. [24]Their sons went in and took possession of the land. You subdued before them the Canaanites, who lived in the land; you handed the Canaanites over to them, along with their kings and the peoples of the land, to deal with them as they pleased. [25]They captured fortified cities and fertile land; they took possession of houses filled with all kinds of good things, wells already dug, vineyards, olive groves and fruit trees in abundance. They ate to the full and were well-nourished; they reveled in your great goodness.

[26]"But they were disobedient and rebelled against you; they put your law behind their backs. They killed your prophets, who had admonished them in order to turn them back to you; they committed awful blasphemies. [27]So you handed them over to their enemies, who oppressed them. But when they were oppressed they cried out to you. From heaven you heard them, and in your great compassion you gave

---

[a]9 Hebrew *Yam Suph*; that is, Sea of Reeds
[b]22 One Hebrew manuscript and Septuagint; most Hebrew manuscripts *Sihon, that is, the country of the*

them deliverers, who rescued them from the hand of their enemies. ²⁸"But as soon as they were at rest, they again did what was evil in your sight. Then you abandoned them to the hand of their enemies so that they ruled over them. And when they cried out to you again, you heard from heaven, and in your compassion you delivered them time after time. ²⁹"You warned them to return to your law, but they became arrogant and disobeyed your commands. They sinned against your ordinances, by which a man will live if he obeys them. Stubbornly they turned their backs on you, became stiff-necked and refused to listen. ³⁰For many years you were patient with them. By your Spirit you admonished them through your prophets. Yet they paid no attention, so you handed them over to the neighboring peoples. ³¹But in your great mercy you did not put an end to them or abandon them, for you are a gracious and merciful God.

³²"Now therefore, O our God, the great, mighty and awesome God, who keeps his covenant of love, do not let all this hardship seem trifling in your eyes—the hardship that has come upon us, upon our kings and leaders, upon our priests and prophets, upon our fathers and all your people, from the days of the kings of Assyria until today. ³³In all that has happened to us, you have been just; you have acted faithfully, while we did wrong. ³⁴Our kings, our leaders, our priests and our fathers did not follow your law; they did not pay attention to your commands or the warnings you gave them. ³⁵Even while they were in their kingdom, enjoying your great goodness to them in the spacious and fertile land you gave them, they did not serve you or turn from their evil ways.

³⁶"But see, we are slaves today, slaves in the land you gave our forefathers so they could eat its fruit and the other good things it produces. ³⁷Because of our sins, its abundant harvest goes to the kings

you have placed over us. They rule over our bodies and our cattle as they please. We are in great distress.

The Agreement of the People

³⁸"In view of all this, we are making a binding agreement, putting it in writing, and our leaders, our Levites and our priests are affixing their seals to it."

10 Those who sealed it were:

Nehemiah the governor, the son of Hacaliah.

Zedekiah, ²Seraiah, Azariah, Jeremiah,
³Pashhur, Amariah, Malkijah,
⁴Hattush, Shebaniah, Malluch,
⁵Harim, Meremoth, Obadiah,
⁶Daniel, Ginnethon, Baruch,
⁷Meshullam, Abijah, Mijamin,
⁸Maaziah, Bilgai and Shemaiah.
These were the priests.

⁹The Levites:

Jeshua son of Azaniah, Binnui of the sons of Henadad, Kadmiel, ¹⁰and their associates: Shebaniah, Hodiah, Kelita, Pelaiah, Hanan, ¹¹Mica, Rehob, Hashabiah, ¹²Zaccur, Sherebiah, Shebaniah, ¹³Hodiah, Bani and Beninu.

¹⁴The leaders of the people:

Parosh, Pahath-Moab, Elam, Zattu, Bani,
¹⁵Bunni, Azgad, Bebai,
¹⁶Adonijah, Bigvai, Adin,
¹⁷Ater, Hezekiah, Azzur,
¹⁸Hodiah, Hashum, Bezai,
¹⁹Hariph, Anathoth, Nebai,
²⁰Magpiash, Meshullam, Hezir,
²¹Meshezabel, Zadok, Jaddua,
²²Pelatiah, Hanan, Anaiah,
²³Hoshea, Hananiah, Hasshub,
²⁴Hallohesh, Pilha, Shobek,
²⁵Rehum, Hashabnah, Maaseiah,
²⁶Ahiah, Hanan, Anan,
²⁷Malluch, Harim and Baanah.

²⁸"The rest of the people—priests, Levites, gatekeepers, singers, temple servants and all who separated themselves from the neighboring peoples for the sake of the Law of God, together with their wives and all their sons and daughters who are able to understand—

²⁹all these now join their brothers the nobles, and bind themselves with a curse and an oath to follow the Law of God given through Moses the servant of God and to obey carefully all the commands, regulations and decrees of the LORD our Lord.

³⁰"We promise not to give our daughters in marriage to the peoples around us or take their daughters for our sons.

³¹"When the neighboring peoples bring merchandise or grain to sell on the Sabbath, we will not buy from them on the Sabbath or on any holy day. Every seventh year we will forgo working the land and will cancel all debts.

³²"We assume the responsibility for carrying out the commands to give a third of a shekel[a] each year for the service of the house of our God: ³³for the bread set out on the table; for the regular grain offerings and burnt offerings; for the offerings on the Sabbaths, New Moon festivals and appointed feasts; for the holy offerings; for sin offerings to make atonement for Israel; and for all the duties of the house of our God.

³⁴"We—the priests, the Levites and the people—have cast lots to determine when each of our families is to bring to the house of our God at set times each year a contribution of wood to burn on the altar of the LORD our God, as it is written in the Law.

³⁵"We also assume responsibility for bringing to the house of the LORD each year the firstfruits of our crops and of every fruit tree.

³⁶"As it is also written in the Law, we will bring the firstborn of our sons and of our cattle, of our herds and of our flocks to the house of our God, to the priests ministering there.

³⁷"Moreover, we will bring to the storerooms of the house of our God, to the priests, the first of our ground meal, of our ∟grain⌟ offerings, of the fruit of all our trees and of our new wine and oil. And we will bring a tithe of our crops to the Levites, for it is the Levites who collect the tithes in all the towns where we work. ³⁸A priest descended from Aaron is to accompany the Levites when they receive the tithes, and the Levites are to bring a tenth of the tithes up to the house of our God, to the storerooms of the treasury. ³⁹The people of Israel, including the Levites, are to bring their contributions of grain, new wine and oil to the storerooms where the articles for the sanctuary are kept and where the ministering priests, the gatekeepers and the singers stay.

"We will not neglect the house of our God."

The New Residents of Jerusalem

11 Now the leaders of the people settled in Jerusalem, and the rest of the people cast lots to bring one out of every ten to live in Jerusalem, the holy city, while the remaining nine were to stay in their own towns. ²The people commended all the men who volunteered to live in Jerusalem.

³These are the provincial leaders who settled in Jerusalem (now some Israelites, priests, Levites, temple servants and descendants of Solomon's servants lived in the towns of Judah, each on his own property in the various towns, ⁴while other people from both Judah and Benjamin lived in Jerusalem):

From the descendants of Judah:

Athaiah son of Uzziah, the son of Zechariah, the son of Amariah, the son of Shephatiah, the son of Mahalalel, a descendant of Perez; ⁵and

a32 That is, about 1/8 ounce (about 4 grams)

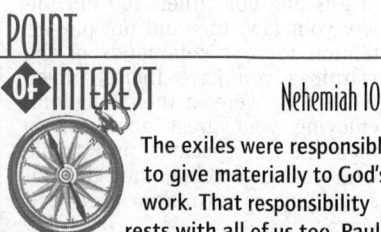

POINT OF INTEREST

Nehemiah 10:35

The exiles were responsible to give materially to God's work. That responsibility rests with all of us too. Paul White, a noted missionary doctor to Africa, said, "The sincerity of one's faith is tested when one's pocket is challenged." The exiles' gifts came willingly because their faith was sincere.

Maaseiah son of Baruch, the son of Col-Hozeh, the son of Hazaiah, the son of Adaiah, the son of Joiarib, the son of Zechariah, a descendant of Shelah. ⁶The descendants of Perez who lived in Jerusalem totaled 468 able men.

⁷From the descendants of Benjamin:

Sallu son of Meshullam, the son of Joed, the son of Pedaiah, the son of Kolaiah, the son of Maaseiah, the son of Ithiel, the son of Jeshaiah, ⁸and his followers, Gabbai and Sallai—928 men. ⁹Joel son of Zicri was their chief officer, and Judah son of Hassenuah was over the Second District of the city.

¹⁰From the priests:

Jedaiah; the son of Joiarib; Jakin; ¹¹Seraiah son of Hilkiah, the son of Meshullam, the son of Zadok, the son of Meraioth, the son of Ahitub, supervisor in the house of God, ¹²and their associates, who carried on work for the temple—822 men; Adaiah son of Jeroham, the son of Pelaliah, the son of Amzi, the son of Zechariah, the son of Pashhur, the son of Malkijah, ¹³and his associates, who were heads of families— 242 men; Amashsai son of Azarel, the son of Ahzai, the son of Meshillemoth, the son of Immer, ¹⁴and his*a* associates, who were able men—128. Their chief officer was Zabdiel son of Haggedolim.

¹⁵From the Levites:

Shemaiah son of Hasshub, the son of Azrikam, the son of Hashabiah, the son of Bunni; ¹⁶Shabbethai and Jozabad, two of the heads of the Levites, who had charge of the outside work of the house of God; ¹⁷Mattaniah son of Mica, the son of Zabdi, the son of Asaph, the director who led in thanksgiving and prayer; Bakbukiah, second among his associates; and Abda son of Shammua, the son of Galal, the son of Jeduthun. ¹⁸The Levites in the holy city totaled 284.

¹⁹The gatekeepers:

Akkub, Talmon and their associates, who kept watch at the gates— 172 men.

²⁰The rest of the Israelites, with the priests and Levites, were in all the towns of Judah, each on his ancestral property.

²¹The temple servants lived on the hill of Ophel, and Ziha and Gishpa were in charge of them.

²²The chief officer of the Levites in Jerusalem was Uzzi son of Bani, the son of Hashabiah, the son of Mattaniah, the son of Mica. Uzzi was one of Asaph's descendants, who were the singers responsible for the service of the house of God. ²³The singers were under the king's orders, which regulated their daily activity.

²⁴Pethahiah son of Meshezabel, one of the descendants of Zerah son of Judah, was the king's agent in all affairs relating to the people.

²⁵As for the villages with their fields, some of the people of Judah lived in Kiriath Arba and its surrounding settlements, in Dibon and its settlements, in Jekabzeel and its villages, ²⁶in Jeshua, in Moladah, in Beth Pelet, ²⁷in Hazar Shual, in Beersheba and its settlements, ²⁸in Ziklag, in Meconah and its settlements, ²⁹in En Rimmon, in Zorah, in Jarmuth, ³⁰Zanoah, Adullam and their villages, in Lachish and its fields, and in Azekah and its settlements. So they were living all the way from Beersheba to the Valley of Hinnom.

³¹The descendants of the Benjamites from Geba lived in Micmash, Aija, Bethel and its settlements, ³²in Anathoth, Nob and Ananiah, ³³in Hazor, Ramah and Gittaim, ³⁴in Hadid, Zeboim and Neballat, ³⁵in Lod and Ono, and in the Valley of the Craftsmen.

³⁶Some of the divisions of the Levites of Judah settled in Benjamin.

Priests and Levites

12 These were the priests and Levites who returned with Zerubbabel son of Shealtiel and with Jeshua:

Seraiah, Jeremiah, Ezra,
²Amariah, Malluch, Hattush,
³Shecaniah, Rehum, Meremoth,
⁴Iddo, Ginnethon,*b* Abijah,
⁵Mijamin,*c* Moadiah, Bilgah,
⁶Shemaiah, Joiarib, Jedaiah,
⁷Sallu, Amok, Hilkiah and Jedaiah.
These were the leaders of the priests and their associates in the days of Jeshua.
⁸The Levites were Jeshua, Binnui,

---

a14 Most Septuagint manuscripts; Hebrew *their*
b4 Many Hebrew manuscripts and Vulgate (see also Neh. 12:16); most Hebrew manuscripts *Ginnethoi*
c5 A variant of *Miniamin*

Kadmiel, Sherebiah, Judah, and also Mattaniah, who, together with his associates, was in charge of the songs of thanksgiving. ⁹Bakbukiah and Unni, their associates, stood opposite them in the services.

¹⁰Jeshua was the father of Joiakim, Joiakim the father of Eliashib, Eliashib the father of Joiada, ¹¹Joiada the father of Jonathan, and Jonathan the father of Jaddua.

¹²In the days of Joiakim, these were the heads of the priestly families:

of Seraiah's family, Meraiah;
of Jeremiah's, Hananiah;
¹³of Ezra's, Meshullam;
of Amariah's, Jehohanan;
¹⁴of Malluch's, Jonathan;
of Shecaniah's,ª Joseph;
¹⁵of Harim's, Adna;
of Meremoth's,ᵇ Helkai;
¹⁶of Iddo's, Zechariah;
of Ginnethon's, Meshullam;
¹⁷of Abijah's, Zicri;
of Miniamin's and of Moadiah's, Piltai;
¹⁸of Bilgah's, Shammua;
of Shemaiah's, Jehonathan;
¹⁹of Joiarib's, Mattenai;
of Jedaiah's, Uzzi;
²⁰of Sallu's, Kallai;
of Amok's, Eber;
²¹of Hilkiah's, Hashabiah;
of Jedaiah's, Nethanel.

²²The family heads of the Levites in the days of Eliashib, Joiada, Johanan and Jaddua, as well as those of the priests, were recorded in the reign of Darius the Persian. ²³The family heads among the descendants of Levi up to the time of Johanan son of Eliashib were recorded in the book of the annals. ²⁴And the leaders of the Levites were Hashabiah, Sherebiah, Jeshua son of Kadmiel, and their associates, who stood opposite them to give praise and thanksgiving, one section responding to the other, as prescribed by David the man of God.

²⁵Mattaniah, Bakbukiah, Obadiah, Meshullam, Talmon and Akkub were gatekeepers who guarded the storerooms at the gates. ²⁶They served in the days of Joiakim son of Jeshua, the son of Jozadak, and in the days of Nehemiah the governor and of Ezra the priest and scribe.

Dedication of the Wall of Jerusalem

²⁷At the dedication of the wall of Jerusalem, the Levites were sought out from where they lived and were brought to Jerusalem to celebrate joyfully the dedication with songs of thanksgiving and with the music of cymbals, harps and lyres. ²⁸The singers also were brought together from the region around Jerusalem—from the villages of the Netophathites, ²⁹from Beth Gilgal, and from the area of Geba and Azmaveth, for the singers had built villages for themselves around Jerusalem. ³⁰When the priests and Levites had purified themselves ceremonially, they purified the people, the gates and the wall.

³¹I had the leaders of Judah go up on topᶜ of the wall. I also assigned two large choirs to give thanks. One was to proceed on topᵈ of the wall to the right, toward the Dung Gate. ³²Hoshaiah and half the leaders of Judah followed them, ³³along with Azariah, Ezra, Meshullam, ³⁴Judah, Benjamin, Shemaiah, Jeremiah, ³⁵as well as some priests with trumpets, and also Zechariah son of Jonathan, the son of Shemaiah, the son of Mattaniah, the son of Micaiah, the son of Zaccur, the son of Asaph, ³⁶and his associates—Shemaiah, Azarel, Milalai, Gilalai, Maai, Nethanel, Judah and Hanani—with musical instruments ⌐prescribed by¬ David the man of God. Ezra the scribe led the procession. ³⁷At the Fountain Gate they continued directly up the steps of the City of David on the ascent to the wall and passed above the house of David to the Water Gate on the east.

³⁸The second choir proceeded in the opposite direction. I followed them on topᵉ of the wall, together with half the people—past the Tower of the Ovens to the Broad Wall, ³⁹over the Gate of Ephraim, the Jeshanahᶠ Gate, the Fish Gate, the Tower of Hananel and the Tower of the Hundred, as far as the Sheep Gate. At the Gate of the Guard they stopped.

⁴⁰The two choirs that gave thanks then took their places in the house of God; so did I, together with half the officials, ⁴¹as well as the priests—Eliakim, Maaseiah, Miniamin, Micaiah, Elioenai, Zechariah and Hananiah with their trumpets—

ª14 Very many Hebrew manuscripts, some Septuagint manuscripts and Syriac (see also Neh. 12:3); most Hebrew manuscripts *Shebaniah's*   ᵇ15 Some Septuagint manuscripts (see also Neh. 12:3); Hebrew *Meraioth's*   ᶜ31 Or *go alongside*   ᵈ31 Or *proceed alongside*   ᵉ38 Or *them alongside*   ᶠ39 Or *Old*

⁴²and also Maaseiah, Shemaiah, Eleazar, Uzzi, Jehohanan, Malkijah, Elam and Ezer. The choirs sang under the direction of Jezrahiah. ⁴³And on that day they offered great sacrifices, rejoicing because God had given them great joy. The women and children also rejoiced. The sound of rejoicing in Jerusalem could be heard far away.

⁴⁴At that time men were appointed to be in charge of the storerooms for the contributions, firstfruits and tithes. From the fields around the towns they were to bring into the storerooms the portions required by the Law for the priests and the Levites, for Judah was pleased with the ministering priests and Levites. ⁴⁵They performed the service of their God and the service of purification, as did also the singers and gatekeepers, according to the commands of David and his son Solomon. ⁴⁶For long ago, in the days of David and Asaph, there had been directors for the singers and for the songs of praise and thanksgiving to God. ⁴⁷So in the days of Zerubbabel and of Nehemiah, all Israel contributed the daily portions for the singers and gatekeepers. They also set aside the portion for the other Levites, and the Levites set aside the portion for the descendants of Aaron.

Nehemiah's Final Reforms

13 On that day the Book of Moses was read aloud in the hearing of the people and there it was found written that no Ammonite or Moabite should ever be admitted into the assembly of God, ²because they had not met the Israelites with food and water but had hired Balaam to call a curse down on them. (Our God, however, turned the curse into a blessing.) ³When the people heard this law, they excluded from Israel all who were of foreign descent.

⁴Before this, Eliashib the priest had been put in charge of the storerooms of the house of our God. He was closely associated with Tobiah, ⁵and he had provided him with a large room formerly used to store the grain offerings and incense and temple articles, and also the tithes of grain, new wine and oil prescribed for the Levites, singers and gatekeepers, as well as the contributions for the priests. ⁶But while all this was going on, I was not in Jerusalem, for in the thirty-second year of Artaxerxes king of Babylon I had returned to the king. Some time later I asked his permission ⁷and came back to Jerusalem. Here I learned about the evil thing Eliashib had done in providing Tobiah a room in the courts of the house of God. ⁸I was greatly displeased and threw all Tobiah's household goods out of the room. ⁹I gave orders to purify the rooms, and then I put back into them the equipment of the house of God, with the grain offerings and the incense.

¹⁰I also learned that the portions assigned to the Levites had not been given to them, and that all the Levites and singers responsible for the service had gone back to their own fields. ¹¹So I rebuked the officials and asked them, "Why is the house of God neglected?" Then I called them together and stationed them at their posts.

¹²All Judah brought the tithes of grain, new wine and oil into the storerooms. ¹³I put Shelemiah the priest, Zadok the scribe, and a Levite named Pedaiah in charge of the storerooms and made Hanan son of Zaccur, the son of Mattaniah, their assistant, because these men were considered trustworthy. They were made responsible for distributing the supplies to their brothers.

¹⁴Remember me for this, O my God, and do not blot out what I have so faithfully done for the house of my God and its services.

¹⁵In those days I saw men in Judah treading winepresses on the Sabbath and bringing in grain and loading it on donkeys, together with wine, grapes, figs and all other kinds of loads. And they were bringing all this into Jerusalem on the Sabbath. Therefore I warned them against selling food on that day. ¹⁶Men

POINT OF INTEREST

Nehemiah 13:10

Nehemiah had uncovered a serious problem. The people were not giving what they should. That meant the Levites had to neglect their temple responsibilities in order to feed their families. Read verses 11–12. What did Nehemiah do about this problem?

from Tyre who lived in Jerusalem were bringing in fish and all kinds of merchandise and selling them in Jerusalem on the Sabbath to the people of Judah. ¹⁷I rebuked the nobles of Judah and said to them, "What is this wicked thing you are doing—desecrating the Sabbath day? ¹⁸Didn't your forefathers do the same things, so that our God brought all this calamity upon us and upon this city? Now you are stirring up more wrath against Israel by desecrating the Sabbath."

¹⁹When evening shadows fell on the gates of Jerusalem before the Sabbath, I ordered the doors to be shut and not opened until the Sabbath was over. I stationed some of my own men at the gates so that no load could be brought in on the Sabbath day. ²⁰Once or twice the merchants and sellers of all kinds of goods spent the night outside Jerusalem. ²¹But I warned them and said, "Why do you spend the night by the wall? If you do this again, I will lay hands on you." From that time on they no longer came on the Sabbath. ²²Then I commanded the Levites to purify themselves and go and guard the gates in order to keep the Sabbath day holy.

Remember me for this also, O my God, and show mercy to me according to your great love.

²³Moreover, in those days I saw men of Judah who had married women from Ashdod, Ammon and Moab. ²⁴Half of their children spoke the language of Ashdod or the language of one of the other peoples, and did not know how to speak the language of Judah. ²⁵I rebuked them and called curses down on them. I beat some of the men and pulled out their hair. I made them take an oath in God's name and said: "You are not to give your daughters in marriage to their sons, nor are you to take their daughters in marriage for your sons or for yourselves. ²⁶Was it not because of marriages like these that Solomon king of Israel sinned? Among the many nations there was no king like him. He was loved by his God, and God made him king over all Israel, but even he was led into sin by foreign women. ²⁷Must we hear now that you too are doing all this terrible wickedness and are being unfaithful to our God by marrying foreign women?"

²⁸One of the sons of Joiada son of Eliashib the high priest was son-in-law to Sanballat the Horonite. And I drove him away from me.

²⁹Remember them, O my God, because they defiled the priestly office and the covenant of the priesthood and of the Levites.

³⁰So I purified the priests and the Levites of everything foreign, and assigned them duties, each to his own task. ³¹I also made provision for contributions of wood at designated times, and for the firstfruits.

Remember me with favor, O my God.

Intrigue. Deception. Romance.

Power struggles. All these can be found in the book of

Esther. Esther is a beautiful Jewish girl chosen by King

Xerxes of Persia to be his queen. The book of Esther vivid-

ly recounts the deliverance of the Jewish people after they

are sentenced to annihilation. It highlights the courage

and effectiveness of the intrepid queen and her steadfast

uncle, Mordecai, as the two of them take a stand against

the forces of hatred and bigotry. Although God's name

isn't specifically mentioned in the book, the events of this

fascinating story clearly reveal his

power and his care for his

people.

ESTHER

Queen Vashti Deposed

1 This is what happened during the time of Xerxes,[a] the Xerxes who ruled over 127 provinces stretching from India to Cush[b]: ²At that time King Xerxes reigned from his royal throne in the citadel of Susa, ³and in the third year of his reign he gave a banquet for all his nobles and officials. The military leaders of Persia and Media, the princes, and the nobles of the provinces were present.

⁴For a full 180 days he displayed the vast wealth of his kingdom and the splendor and glory of his majesty. ⁵When these days were over, the king gave a banquet, lasting seven days, in the en-

closed garden of the king's palace, for all the people from the least to the greatest, who were in the citadel of Susa. ⁶The garden had hangings of white and blue linen, fastened with cords of white linen and purple material to silver rings on marble pillars. There were couches of gold and silver on a mosaic pavement of porphyry, marble, mother-of-pearl and other costly stones. ⁷Wine was served in goblets of gold, each one different from the other, and the royal wine was abundant, in keeping with the king's liberali-

---

*a*1 Hebrew *Ahasuerus*, a variant of Xerxes' Persian name; here and throughout Esther   *b*1 That is, the upper Nile region ty. **8**By the king's command each guest was allowed to drink in his own way, for the king instructed all the wine stewards to serve each man what he wished.

9Queen Vashti also gave a banquet for the women in the royal palace of King Xerxes.

10On the seventh day, when King Xerxes was in high spirits from wine, he commanded the seven eunuchs who served him—Mehuman, Biztha, Harbona, Bigtha, Abagtha, Zethar and Carcas—**11**to bring before him Queen Vashti, wearing her royal crown, in order to display her beauty to the people and nobles, for she was lovely to look at. **12**But when the attendants delivered the king's command, Queen Vashti refused to come. Then the king became furious and burned with anger.

13Since it was customary for the king to consult experts in matters of law and justice, he spoke with the wise men who understood the times **14**and were closest to the king—Carshena, Shethar, Admatha, Tarshish, Meres, Marsena and Memucan, the seven nobles of Persia and Media who had special access to the king and were highest in the kingdom.

15"According to law, what must be done to Queen Vashti?" he asked. "She has not obeyed the command of King Xerxes that the eunuchs have taken to her."

16Then Memucan replied in the presence of the king and the nobles, "Queen Vashti has done wrong, not only against the king but also against all the nobles and the peoples of all the provinces of King Xerxes. **17**For the queen's conduct will become known to all the women, and so they will despise their husbands and say, 'King Xerxes commanded Queen Vashti to be brought before him, but she would not come.' **18**This very day the Persian and Median women of the nobility who have heard about the queen's conduct will respond to all the king's nobles in the same way. There will be no end of disrespect and discord.

19"Therefore, if it pleases the king, let him issue a royal decree and let it be written in the laws of Persia and Media, which cannot be repealed, that Vashti is never again to enter the presence of King Xerxes. Also let the king give her royal position to someone else who is better than she. **20**Then when the king's edict is proclaimed throughout all his vast realm, all the women will respect their husbands, from the least to the greatest."

21The king and his nobles were pleased with this advice, so the king did as Memucan proposed. **22**He sent dispatches to all parts of the kingdom, to each province in its own script and to each people in its own language, proclaiming in each people's tongue that every man should be ruler over his own household.

Esther Made Queen

2 Later when the anger of King Xerxes had subsided, he remembered Vashti and what she had done and what he had decreed about her. **2**Then the king's personal attendants proposed, "Let a search be made for beautiful young virgins for the king. **3**Let the king appoint commissioners in every province of his realm to bring all these beautiful girls into the harem at the citadel of Susa. Let them be placed under the care of Hegai, the king's eunuch, who is in charge of the women; and let beauty treatments be given to them. **4**Then let the girl who pleases the king be queen instead of Vashti." This advice appealed to the king, and he followed it.

5Now there was in the citadel of Susa a Jew of the tribe of Benjamin, named Mordecai son of Jair, the son of Shimei, the son of Kish, **6**who had been carried into exile from Jerusalem by Nebuchadnezzar king of Babylon, among those taken captive with Jehoiachin*a* king of Judah. **7**Mordecai had a cousin named Hadassah, whom he had brought up because she had neither father nor mother. This girl, who was also known as Esther, was lovely in form and features, and Mordecai had taken her as his own daughter when her father and mother died.

8When the king's order and edict had been proclaimed, many girls were brought to the citadel of Susa and put under the care of Hegai. Esther also was taken to the king's palace and entrusted to Hegai, who had charge of the harem. **9**The girl pleased him and won his favor. Immediately he provided her with her beauty treatments and special food. He assigned to her seven maids selected from the king's palace and moved her

---

*a*6 Hebrew *Jeconiah*, a variant of *Jehoiachin*

and her maids into the best place in the harem.

[10]Esther had not revealed her nationality and family background, because Mordecai had forbidden her to do so. [11]Every day he walked back and forth near the courtyard of the harem to find out how Esther was and what was happening to her.

[12]Before a girl's turn came to go in to King Xerxes, she had to complete twelve months of beauty treatments prescribed for the women, six months with oil of myrrh and six with perfumes and cosmetics. [13]And this is how she would go to the king: Anything she wanted was given her to take with her from the harem to the king's palace. [14]In the evening she would go there and in the morning return to another part of the harem to the care of Shaashgaz, the king's eunuch who was in charge of the concubines. She would not return to the king unless he was pleased with her and summoned her by name.

[15]When the turn came for Esther (the girl Mordecai had adopted, the daughter of his uncle Abihail) to go to the king, she asked for nothing other than what Hegai, the king's eunuch who was in charge of the harem, suggested. And Esther won the favor of everyone who saw her. [16]She was taken to King Xerxes in the royal residence in the tenth month, the month of Tebeth, in the seventh year of his reign.

[17]Now the king was attracted to Esther more than to any of the other women, and she won his favor and approval more than any of the other virgins. So he set a royal crown on her head and made her queen instead of Vashti. [18]And the king gave a great banquet, Esther's banquet, for all his nobles and officials. He proclaimed a holiday throughout the provinces and distributed gifts with royal liberality.

Mordecai Uncovers a Conspiracy

[19]When the virgins were assembled a second time, Mordecai was sitting at the king's gate. [20]But Esther had kept secret her family background and nationality just as Mordecai had told her to do, for she continued to follow Mordecai's instructions as she had done when he was bringing her up.

[21]During the time Mordecai was sitting at the king's gate, Bigthana[a] and Teresh, two of the king's officers who guarded the doorway, became angry and conspired to assassinate King Xerxes. [22]But Mordecai found out about the plot and told Queen Esther, who in turn reported it to the king, giving credit to Mordecai. [23]And when the report was investigated and found to be true, the two officials were hanged on a gallows.[b] All this was recorded in the book of the annals in the presence of the king.

Haman's Plot to Destroy the Jews

3 After these events, King Xerxes honored Haman son of Hammedatha, the Agagite, elevating him and giving him a seat of honor higher than that of all the other nobles. [2]All the royal officials at the king's gate knelt down and paid honor to Haman, for the king had commanded this concerning him. But Mordecai would not kneel down or pay him honor.

[3]Then the royal officials at the king's gate asked Mordecai, "Why do you disobey the king's command?" [4]Day after day they spoke to him but he refused to comply. Therefore they told Haman about it to see whether Mordecai's behavior would be tolerated, for he had told them he was a Jew.

[5]When Haman saw that Mordecai would not kneel down or pay him honor, he was enraged. [6]Yet having learned who Mordecai's people were, he scorned the idea of killing only Mordecai. Instead Haman looked for a way to destroy all Mordecai's people, the Jews, throughout the whole kingdom of Xerxes.

[7]In the twelfth year of King Xerxes, in the first month, the month of Nisan, they

---

[a]21 Hebrew *Bigthan*, a variant of *Bigthana*
[b]23 Or *were hung* (or *impaled*) *on poles*; similarly elsewhere in Esther

POINT OF INTEREST

Esther 2:10

The Jews' loyalty to God and refusal to bow to other gods or royal officials made them the target of scorn and hatred. Esther's silence about her background was a life-saving necessity in the hostile palace environment. Though she was silent, Esther did not forsake her beliefs or her people (see Esther 4:14–16).

cast the *pur* (that is, the lot) in the presence of Haman to select a day and month. And the lot fell on*a* the twelfth month, the month of Adar.

⁸Then Haman said to King Xerxes, "There is a certain people dispersed and scattered among the peoples in all the provinces of your kingdom whose customs are different from those of all other people and who do not obey the king's laws; it is not in the king's best interest to tolerate them. ⁹If it pleases the king, let a decree be issued to destroy them, and I will put ten thousand talents*b* of silver into the royal treasury for the men who carry out this business."

¹⁰So the king took his signet ring from his finger and gave it to Haman son of Hammedatha, the Agagite, the enemy of the Jews. ¹¹"Keep the money," the king said to Haman, "and do with the people as you please."

¹²Then on the thirteenth day of the first month the royal secretaries were summoned. They wrote out in the script of each province and in the language of each people all Haman's orders to the king's satraps, the governors of the various provinces and the nobles of the various peoples. These were written in the name of King Xerxes himself and sealed with his own ring. ¹³Dispatches were sent by couriers to all the king's provinces with the order to destroy, kill and annihilate all the Jews—young and old, women and little children—on a single day, the thirteenth day of the twelfth month, the month of Adar, and to plunder their goods. ¹⁴A copy of the text of the edict was to be issued as law in every province and made known to the people of every nationality so they would be ready for that day.

¹⁵Spurred on by the king's command, the couriers went out, and the edict was issued in the citadel of Susa. The king and Haman sat down to drink, but the city of Susa was bewildered.

Mordecai Persuades Esther to Help

4 When Mordecai learned of all that had been done, he tore his clothes, put on sackcloth and ashes, and went out into the city, wailing loudly and bitterly. ²But he went only as far as the king's gate, because no one clothed in sackcloth was allowed to enter it. ³In every province to which the edict and order of the king came, there was great mourning among the Jews, with fasting, weeping and wailing. Many lay in sackcloth and ashes.

⁴When Esther's maids and eunuchs came and told her about Mordecai, she was in great distress. She sent clothes for him to put on instead of his sackcloth, but he would not accept them. ⁵Then Esther summoned Hathach, one of the king's eunuchs assigned to attend her, and ordered him to find out what was troubling Mordecai and why.

⁶So Hathach went out to Mordecai in the open square of the city in front of the king's gate. ⁷Mordecai told him everything that had happened to him, including the exact amount of money Haman had promised to pay into the royal treasury for the destruction of the Jews. ⁸He also gave him a copy of the text of the edict for their annihilation, which had been published in Susa, to show to Esther and explain it to her, and he told him to urge her to go into the king's presence to beg for mercy and plead with him for her people.

⁹Hathach went back and reported to Esther what Mordecai had said. ¹⁰Then she instructed him to say to Mordecai, ¹¹"All the king's officials and the people of the royal provinces know that for any man or woman who approaches the king in the inner court without being summoned the king has but one law: that he be put to death. The only exception to this is for the king to extend the gold scepter to him and spare his life. But thirty days have passed since I was called to go to the king."

¹²When Esther's words were reported to Mordecai, ¹³he sent back this answer: "Do not think that because you are in the king's house you alone of all the Jews will escape. ¹⁴For if you remain silent at this time, relief and deliverance for the Jews will arise from another place, but you and your father's family will perish. And who knows but that you have come to royal position for such a time as this?"

¹⁵Then Esther sent this reply to Mordecai: ¹⁶"Go, gather together all the Jews who are in Susa, and fast for me. Do not eat or drink for three days, night or day. I and my maids will fast as you do. When this is done, I will go to the king, even

---

*a*7 Septuagint; Hebrew does not have *And the lot fell on.*   *b*9 That is, about 375 tons (about 345 metric tons) though it is against the law. And if I perish, I perish."

¹⁷So Mordecai went away and carried out all of Esther's instructions.

Esther's Request to the King

5 On the third day Esther put on her royal robes and stood in the inner court of the palace, in front of the king's hall. The king was sitting on his royal throne in the hall, facing the entrance. ²When he saw Queen Esther standing in the court, he was pleased with her and held out to her the gold scepter that was in his hand. So Esther approached and touched the tip of the scepter.

³Then the king asked, "What is it, Queen Esther? What is your request? Even up to half the kingdom, it will be given you."

⁴"If it pleases the king," replied Esther, "let the king, together with Haman, come today to a banquet I have prepared for him."

⁵"Bring Haman at once," the king said, "so that we may do what Esther asks."

So the king and Haman went to the banquet Esther had prepared. ⁶As they were drinking wine, the king again asked Esther, "Now what is your petition? It will be given you. And what is your request? Even up to half the kingdom, it will be granted."

⁷Esther replied, "My petition and my request is this: ⁸If the king regards me with favor and if it pleases the king to grant my petition and fulfill my request, let the king and Haman come tomorrow to the banquet I will prepare for them. Then I will answer the king's question."

MONDAY

Read Esther 4:1–17
Key Verses Esther 4:14–16

Divine Opportunity — Charla Vogelaar

After finishing graduate school, I realized I had many opportunities to go anywhere for my first "real" job. "Of course," I told God, "it would be nice to stay close to my family and my boyfriend." God then provided me with a wonderful opportunity. Unfortunately, it was about ten hours' travel from my family's home and twenty hours from where my boyfriend lived!

My dad and my boyfriend moved me into my apartment. I had no furniture, so they left me sitting on a pillow in my small living room and eating hot dogs—all I could afford at the time.

"God," I prayed, "what is my purpose here? I don't know anyone and all I have is my car and this pitiful, little, unfurnished apartment." It wasn't long until he showed me why he had brought me to the middle of nowhere. One day, after I had been working for a couple of months, a lady I was training asked what I believed. I told her about Jesus Christ. Later that same day, a coworker asked if I attended church and how I thought God fit into life today. A few hours later my boss told me over lunch that he was the son of a pastor and had become disillusioned with God and with the church. Three times in one day I had obvious opportunities to talk about God with people I would be seeing daily.

God's purpose was clear. He had brought me to "the middle of nowhere" because people were there who needed to know about him.

A Deeper Look
Proverbs 11:30; 1 Peter 3:15

Go to page 546 for your next devotional reading.

Haman's Rage Against Mordecai

⁹Haman went out that day happy and in high spirits. But when he saw Mordecai at the king's gate and observed that he neither rose nor showed fear in his presence, he was filled with rage against Mordecai. ¹⁰Nevertheless, Haman restrained himself and went home.

Calling together his friends and Zeresh, his wife, ¹¹Haman boasted to them about his vast wealth, his many sons, and all the ways the king had honored him and how he had elevated him above the other nobles and officials. ¹²"And that's not all," Haman added. "I'm the only person Queen Esther invited to accompany the king to the banquet she gave. And she has invited me along with the king tomorrow. ¹³But all this gives me no satisfaction as long as I see that Jew Mordecai sitting at the king's gate."

¹⁴His wife Zeresh and all his friends said to him, "Have a gallows built, seventy-five feetᵃ high, and ask the king in the morning to have Mordecai hanged on it. Then go with the king to the dinner and be happy." This suggestion delighted Haman, and he had the gallows built.

Mordecai Honored

6 That night the king could not sleep; so he ordered the book of the chronicles, the record of his reign, to be brought in and read to him. ²It was found recorded there that Mordecai had exposed Bigthana and Teresh, two of the king's officers who guarded the doorway, who had conspired to assassinate King Xerxes.

³"What honor and recognition has Mordecai received for this?" the king asked.

"Nothing has been done for him," his attendants answered.

⁴The king said, "Who is in the court?" Now Haman had just entered the outer court of the palace to speak to the king about hanging Mordecai on the gallows he had erected for him.

⁵His attendants answered, "Haman is standing in the court."

"Bring him in," the king ordered.

⁶When Haman entered, the king asked him, "What should be done for the man the king delights to honor?"

Now Haman thought to himself, "Who is there that the king would rather honor than me?" ⁷So he answered the king,

"For the man the king delights to honor, ⁸have them bring a royal robe the king has worn and a horse the king has ridden, one with a royal crest placed on its head. ⁹Then let the robe and horse be entrusted to one of the king's most noble princes. Let them robe the man the king delights to honor, and lead him on the horse through the city streets, proclaiming before him, 'This is what is done for the man the king delights to honor!' "

¹⁰"Go at once," the king commanded Haman. "Get the robe and the horse and do just as you have suggested for Mordecai the Jew, who sits at the king's gate. Do not neglect anything you have recommended."

¹¹So Haman got the robe and the horse. He robed Mordecai, and led him on horseback through the city streets, proclaiming before him, "This is what is done for the man the king delights to honor!"

¹²Afterward Mordecai returned to the king's gate. But Haman rushed home, with his head covered in grief, ¹³and told Zeresh his wife and all his friends everything that had happened to him.

His advisers and his wife Zeresh said to him, "Since Mordecai, before whom your downfall has started, is of Jewish origin, you cannot stand against him— you will surely come to ruin!" ¹⁴While they were still talking with him, the king's eunuchs arrived and hurried Haman away to the banquet Esther had prepared.

Haman Hanged

7 So the king and Haman went to dine with Queen Esther, ²and as they were drinking wine on that second day, the king again asked, "Queen Esther, what is your petition? It will be given you. What is your request? Even up to half the kingdom, it will be granted."

³Then Queen Esther answered, "If I have found favor with you, O king, and if it pleases your majesty, grant me my life—this is my petition. And spare my people—this is my request. ⁴For I and my people have been sold for destruction and slaughter and annihilation. If we had merely been sold as male and female slaves, I would have kept quiet, because

ᵃ 14 Hebrew *fifty cubits* (about 23 meters)

no such distress would justify disturbing the king. *a* "

5King Xerxes asked Queen Esther, "Who is he? Where is the man who has dared to do such a thing?"

6Esther said, "The adversary and enemy is this vile Haman."

Then Haman was terrified before the king and queen. 7The king got up in a rage, left his wine and went out into the palace garden. But Haman, realizing that the king had already decided his fate, stayed behind to beg Queen Esther for his life.

8Just as the king returned from the palace garden to the banquet hall, Haman was falling on the couch where Esther was reclining.

The king exclaimed, "Will he even molest the queen while she is with me in the house?"

As soon as the word left the king's mouth, they covered Haman's face. 9Then Harbona, one of the eunuchs attending the king, said, "A gallows seventy-five feet*b* high stands by Haman's house. He had it made for Mordecai, who spoke up to help the king."

The king said, "Hang him on it!" 10So they hanged Haman on the gallows he had prepared for Mordecai. Then the king's fury subsided.

The King's Edict in Behalf of the Jews

8 That same day King Xerxes gave Queen Esther the estate of Haman, the enemy of the Jews. And Mordecai came into the presence of the king, for Esther had told how he was related to her. 2The king took off his signet ring, which he had reclaimed from Haman, and presented it to Mordecai. And Esther appointed him over Haman's estate.

3Esther again pleaded with the king, falling at his feet and weeping. She begged him to put an end to the evil plan of Haman the Agagite, which he had devised against the Jews. 4Then the king extended the gold scepter to Esther and she arose and stood before him.

5"If it pleases the king," she said, "and if he regards me with favor and thinks it the right thing to do, and if he is pleased with me, let an order be written overruling the dispatches that Haman son of Hammedatha, the Agagite, devised and wrote to destroy the Jews in all the king's provinces. 6For how can I bear to see disaster fall on my people? How can I bear to see the destruction of my family?"

7King Xerxes replied to Queen Esther and to Mordecai the Jew, "Because Haman attacked the Jews, I have given his estate to Esther, and they have hanged him on the gallows. 8Now write another decree in the king's name in behalf of the Jews as seems best to you, and seal it with the king's signet ring—for no document written in the king's name and sealed with his ring can be revoked."

9At once the royal secretaries were summoned—on the twenty-third day of the third month, the month of Sivan. They wrote out all Mordecai's orders to the Jews, and to the satraps, governors and nobles of the 127 provinces stretching from India to Cush.*c* These orders were written in the script of each province and the language of each people and also to the Jews in their own script and language. 10Mordecai wrote in the name of King Xerxes, sealed the dispatches with the king's signet ring, and sent them by mounted couriers, who rode fast horses especially bred for the king.

11The king's edict granted the Jews in every city the right to assemble and protect themselves; to destroy, kill and annihilate any armed force of any nationality or province that might attack them and their women and children; and to plunder the property of their enemies. 12The day appointed for the Jews to do this in all the provinces of King Xerxes was the thirteenth day of the twelfth month, the month of Adar. 13A copy of the text of the edict was to be issued as law in every province and made known to the people of every nationality so that the Jews would be ready on that day to avenge themselves on their enemies.

14The couriers, riding the royal horses, raced out, spurred on by the king's command. And the edict was also issued in the citadel of Susa.

15Mordecai left the king's presence wearing royal garments of blue and white, a large crown of gold and a purple robe of fine linen. And the city of Susa held a joyous celebration. 16For the Jews it was a time of happiness and joy, gladness and honor. 17In every province and in every city, wherever the edict of the

a4 Or *quiet, but the compensation our adversary offers cannot be compared with the loss the king would suffer*   *b9* Hebrew *fifty cubits* (about 23 meters)   *c9* That is, the upper Nile region king went, there was joy and gladness among the Jews, with feasting and celebrating. And many people of other nationalities became Jews because fear of the Jews had seized them.

Triumph of the Jews

9 On the thirteenth day of the twelfth month, the month of Adar, the edict commanded by the king was to be carried out. On this day the enemies of the Jews had hoped to overpower them, but now the tables were turned and the Jews got the upper hand over those who hated them. ²The Jews assembled in their cities in all the provinces of King Xerxes to attack those seeking their destruction. No one could stand against them, because the people of all the other nationalities were afraid of them. ³And all the nobles of the provinces, the satraps, the governors and the king's administrators helped the Jews, because fear of Mordecai had seized them. ⁴Mordecai was prominent in the palace; his reputation spread throughout the provinces, and he became more and more powerful.

⁵The Jews struck down all their enemies with the sword, killing and destroying them, and they did what they pleased to those who hated them. ⁶In the citadel of Susa, the Jews killed and destroyed five hundred men. ⁷They also killed Parshandatha, Dalphon, Aspatha, ⁸Poratha, Adalia, Aridatha, ⁹Parmashta, Arisai, Aridai and Vaizatha, ¹⁰the ten sons of Haman son of Hammedatha, the enemy of the Jews. But they did not lay their hands on the plunder.

¹¹The number of those slain in the citadel of Susa was reported to the king that same day. ¹²The king said to Queen Esther, "The Jews have killed and destroyed five hundred men and the ten sons of Haman in the citadel of Susa. What have they done in the rest of the king's provinces? Now what is your petition? It will be given you. What is your request? It will also be granted."

¹³"If it pleases the king," Esther answered, "give the Jews in Susa permission to carry out this day's edict tomorrow also, and let Haman's ten sons be hanged on gallows."

¹⁴So the king commanded that this be done. An edict was issued in Susa, and they hanged the ten sons of Haman. ¹⁵The Jews in Susa came together on the fourteenth day of the month of Adar, and

they put to death in Susa three hundred men, but they did not lay their hands on the plunder.

¹⁶Meanwhile, the remainder of the Jews who were in the king's provinces also assembled to protect themselves and get relief from their enemies. They killed seventy-five thousand of them but did not lay their hands on the plunder. ¹⁷This happened on the thirteenth day of the month of Adar, and on the fourteenth they rested and made it a day of feasting and joy.

Purim Celebrated

¹⁸The Jews in Susa, however, had assembled on the thirteenth and fourteenth, and then on the fifteenth they rested and made it a day of feasting and joy.

¹⁹That is why rural Jews—those living in villages—observe the fourteenth of the month of Adar as a day of joy and feasting, a day for giving presents to each other.

²⁰Mordecai recorded these events, and he sent letters to all the Jews throughout the provinces of King Xerxes, near and far, ²¹to have them celebrate annually the fourteenth and fifteenth days of the month of Adar ²²as the time when the Jews got relief from their enemies, and as the month when their sorrow was turned into joy and their mourning into a day of celebration. He wrote them to observe the days as days of feasting and joy and giving presents of food to one another and gifts to the poor.

²³So the Jews agreed to continue the celebration they had begun, doing what Mordecai had written to them. ²⁴For Ha-

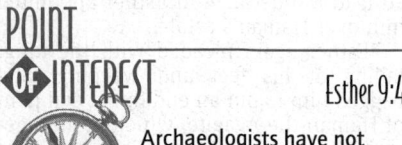

POINT OF INTEREST

Esther 9:4

Archaeologists have not found the name of the original Mordecai on any ancient inscriptions or government documents written during the reign of Xerxes. But the name Mordecai commonly appears in business records during the reign of the *next* king. Why do you think the number of men named Mordecai increased so suddenly?

man son of Hammedatha, the Agagite, the enemy of all the Jews, had plotted against the Jews to destroy them and had cast the *pur* (that is, the lot) for their ruin and destruction. ²⁵But when the plot came to the king's attention,ª he issued written orders that the evil scheme Haman had devised against the Jews should come back onto his own head, and that he and his sons should be hanged on the gallows. ²⁶(Therefore these days were called Purim, from the word *pur*.) Because of everything written in this letter and because of what they had seen and what had happened to them, ²⁷the Jews took it upon themselves to establish the custom that they and their descendants and all who join them should without fail observe these two days every year, in the way prescribed and at the time appointed. ²⁸These days should be remembered and observed in every generation by every family, and in every province and in every city. And these days of Purim should never cease to be celebrated by the Jews, nor should the memory of them die out among their descendants.

²⁹So Queen Esther, daughter of Abihail, along with Mordecai the Jew, wrote with full authority to confirm this second letter concerning Purim. ³⁰And Mordecai sent letters to all the Jews in the 127 provinces of the kingdom of Xerxes— words of goodwill and assurance— ³¹to establish these days of Purim at their designated times, as Mordecai the Jew and Queen Esther had decreed for them, and as they had established for themselves and their descendants in regard to their times of fasting and lamentation. ³²Esther's decree confirmed these regulations about Purim, and it was written down in the records.

The Greatness of Mordecai

10 King Xerxes imposed tribute throughout the empire, to its distant shores. ²And all his acts of power and might, together with a full account of the greatness of Mordecai to which the king had raised him, are they not written in the book of the annals of the kings of Media and Persia? ³Mordecai the Jew was second in rank to King Xerxes, preeminent among the Jews, and held in high esteem by his many fellow Jews, because he worked for the good of his people and spoke up for the welfare of all the Jews.

ª25 Or *when Esther came before the king*

Where is God when we hurt?

Why would a wise, just, loving God allow suffering to

stalk a man who seemed to do all the right things?

Because Job lost everything—wealth, family and health—

he wondered about these same questions, struggling to

make sense of his own misery in the light of God's justice.

But after the crying, the reasoning and the questioning,

he still trusted God. Although we may never fully under-

stand Job's suffering or our own, God is always in control.

And God restored to Job his health,

blessed him materially and

gave him a new family.

JOB

Prologue

1 In the land of Uz there lived a man whose name was Job. This man was blameless and upright; he feared God and shunned evil. ²He had seven sons and three daughters, ³and he owned seven thousand sheep, three thousand camels, five hundred yoke of oxen and five hundred donkeys, and had a large number of servants. He was the greatest man among all the people of the East.

⁴His sons used to take turns holding feasts in their homes, and they would invite their three sisters to eat and drink with them. ⁵When a period of feasting had run its course, Job would send and have them purified. Early in the morning he would sacrifice a burnt offering for each of them, thinking, "Perhaps my children have sinned and cursed God in their hearts." This was Job's regular custom.

Job's First Test

⁶One day the angels*a* came to present themselves before the LORD, and Satan*b* also came with them. ⁷The LORD said to Satan, "Where have you come from?"

Satan answered the LORD, "From roaming through the earth and going back and forth in it."

⁸Then the LORD said to Satan, "Have you considered my servant Job? There is

a6 Hebrew the sons of God   b6 Satan means accuser.

no one on earth like him; he is blameless and upright, a man who fears God and shuns evil."

⁹"Does Job fear God for nothing?" Satan replied. ¹⁰"Have you not put a hedge around him and his household and everything he has? You have blessed the work of his hands, so that his flocks and herds are spread throughout the land. ¹¹But stretch out your hand and strike everything he has, and he will surely curse you to your face."

¹²The LORD said to Satan, "Very well, then, everything he has is in your hands, but on the man himself do not lay a finger."

Then Satan went out from the presence of the LORD.

¹³One day when Job's sons and daughters were feasting and drinking wine at the oldest brother's house, ¹⁴a messenger came to Job and said, "The oxen were plowing and the donkeys were grazing nearby, ¹⁵and the Sabeans attacked and carried them off. They put the servants to the sword, and I am the only one who has escaped to tell you!"

¹⁶While he was still speaking, another messenger came and said, "The fire of God fell from the sky and burned up the sheep and the servants, and I am the only one who has escaped to tell you!"

¹⁷While he was still speaking, another messenger came and said, "The Chaldeans formed three raiding parties and swept down on your camels and carried them off. They put the servants to the sword, and I am the only one who has escaped to tell you!"

¹⁸While he was still speaking, yet another messenger came and said, "Your sons and daughters were feasting and drinking wine at the oldest brother's house, ¹⁹when suddenly a mighty wind swept in from the desert and struck the four corners of the house. It collapsed on them and they are dead, and I am the only one who has escaped to tell you!"

²⁰At this, Job got up and tore his robe and shaved his head. Then he fell to the ground in worship ²¹and said:

> "Naked I came from my mother's
>   womb,
>   and naked I will depart.ᵃ
> The LORD gave and the LORD has taken
>   away;

may the name of the LORD be
    praised."

²²In all this, Job did not sin by charging God with wrongdoing.

Job's Second Test

2 On another day the angelsᵇ came to present themselves before the LORD, and Satan also came with them to present himself before him. ²And the LORD said to Satan, "Where have you come from?"

Satan answered the LORD, "From roaming through the earth and going back and forth in it."

³Then the LORD said to Satan, "Have you considered my servant Job? There is no one on earth like him; he is blameless and upright, a man who fears God and shuns evil. And he still maintains his integrity, though you incited me against him to ruin him without any reason."

⁴"Skin for skin!" Satan replied. "A man will give all he has for his own life. ⁵But stretch out your hand and strike his flesh and bones, and he will surely curse you to your face."

⁶The LORD said to Satan, "Very well, then, he is in your hands; but you must spare his life."

⁷So Satan went out from the presence of the LORD and afflicted Job with painful sores from the soles of his feet to the top of his head. ⁸Then Job took a piece of broken pottery and scraped himself with it as he sat among the ashes.

⁹His wife said to him, "Are you still

ᵃ21 Or *will return there*   ᵇ1 Hebrew *the sons of God*

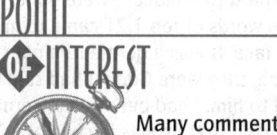

POINT OF INTEREST   Job 2:9

Many commentators over the years have harshly criticized Job's wife for her outburst in this verse. Indeed, Satan may have been using her to further test Job's resolve. But consider the context of this outburst before you blame her too harshly: Job's wife was suffering the same kind of soul-crushing grief and loss as her husband.

holding on to your integrity? Curse God and die!"

¹⁰He replied, "You are talking like a foolishᵃ woman. Shall we accept good from God, and not trouble?"

In all this, Job did not sin in what he said.

Job's Three Friends

¹¹When Job's three friends, Eliphaz the Temanite, Bildad the Shuhite and Zophar the Naamathite, heard about all the troubles that had come upon him, they set out from their homes and met together by agreement to go and sympathize with him and comfort him. ¹²When they saw him from a distance, they could hardly recognize him; they began to weep aloud, and they tore their robes and sprinkled dust on their heads. ¹³Then they sat on the ground with him for seven days and seven nights. No one said a word to him, because they saw how great his suffering was.

Job Speaks

3 After this, Job opened his mouth and cursed the day of his birth. ²He said:

³"May the day of my birth perish,
  and the night it was said, 'A boy is born!'
⁴That day—may it turn to darkness;
  may God above not care about it;
  may no light shine upon it.
⁵May darkness and deep shadowᵇ
  claim it once more;
  may a cloud settle over it;
  may blackness overwhelm its light.
⁶That night—may thick darkness seize it;
  may it not be included among the days of the year
  nor be entered in any of the months.

ᵃ 10 The Hebrew word rendered *foolish* denotes moral deficiency.   ᵇ 5 Or *and the shadow of death*

TUESDAY

***Read** Job 1:1–22*
***Key Verse** Job 1:21*

Who Owns Your Stuff? – Stefani Rae Carter

While taking a summer course at Oxford University, I lived in a wonderful dorm room. It was on the top floor with dormer windows looking out on the spires and steeples of Oxford. The view was incredible and the sunsets breathtaking. I thoroughly loved that room . . . until one rainy afternoon when I returned and found a window broken open, the chair overturned and many of my things stolen.

I was devastated. How dare someone invade my privacy and take my stuff? All the coins I had carefully collected, the clock and money converter, which were gifts from my friends, my hairdryer, some books—all were gone. I felt violated. *My* things—some that would be hard to replace—were gone. I fumed for an hour.

As the words of Job 1:21 came to mind, tears began to stream down my face. It was a gentle reminder that those things weren't really mine; they were God's. I had told him long ago that all I had belonged to him. I had been so concerned with those things that I had forgotten that he was in control.

God does expect us to take good care of the things we have, but he never wants us to cling to them. It's still his stuff, not ours. Whatever happens to it, we have to remember he knows what's happening and has a purpose, even though we may not see it.

A Deeper Look
Psalm 50:9–12; 1 Timothy 6:6–8

Go to page 549 for your next devotional reading.

7May that night be barren;
  may no shout of joy be heard in it.
8May those who curse days*a* curse
    that day,
  those who are ready to rouse
    Leviathan.
9May its morning stars become dark;
  may it wait for daylight in vain
  and not see the first rays of dawn,
10for it did not shut the doors of the
    womb on me
  to hide trouble from my eyes.

11"Why did I not perish at birth,
  and die as I came from the womb?
12Why were there knees to receive me
  and breasts that I might be nursed?
13For now I would be lying down in
    peace;
  I would be asleep and at rest
14with kings and counselors of the
    earth,
  who built for themselves places
    now lying in ruins,
15with rulers who had gold,
  who filled their houses with silver.
16Or why was I not hidden in the
    ground like a stillborn child,
  like an infant who never saw the
    light of day?
17There the wicked cease from turmoil,
  and there the weary are at rest.
18Captives also enjoy their ease;
  they no longer hear the slave
    driver's shout.
19The small and the great are there,
  and the slave is freed from his
    master.

20"Why is light given to those in
    misery,
  and life to the bitter of soul,
21to those who long for death that does
    not come,
  who search for it more than for
    hidden treasure,
22who are filled with gladness
  and rejoice when they reach the
    grave?
23Why is life given to a man
  whose way is hidden,
  whom God has hedged in?
24For sighing comes to me instead of
    food;
  my groans pour out like water.
25What I feared has come upon me;
  what I dreaded has happened to
    me.
26I have no peace, no quietness;
  I have no rest, but only turmoil."

Eliphaz

4 Then Eliphaz the Temanite replied:

2"If someone ventures a word with
    you, will you be impatient?
  But who can keep from speaking?
3Think how you have instructed
    many,
  how you have strengthened feeble
    hands.
4Your words have supported those
    who stumbled;
  you have strengthened faltering
    knees.
5But now trouble comes to you, and
    you are discouraged;
  it strikes you, and you are
    dismayed.
6Should not your piety be your
    confidence
  and your blameless ways your
    hope?

7"Consider now: Who, being innocent,
    has ever perished?
  Where were the upright ever
    destroyed?
8As I have observed, those who plow
    evil
  and those who sow trouble reap it.
9At the breath of God they are
    destroyed;
  at the blast of his anger they
    perish.
10The lions may roar and growl,
  yet the teeth of the great lions are
    broken.
11The lion perishes for lack of prey,
  and the cubs of the lioness are
    scattered.

12"A word was secretly brought to me,
  my ears caught a whisper of it.
13Amid disquieting dreams in the night,
  when deep sleep falls on men,
14fear and trembling seized me
  and made all my bones shake.
15A spirit glided past my face,
  and the hair on my body stood on
    end.
16It stopped,
  but I could not tell what it was.
  A form stood before my eyes,
  and I heard a hushed voice:
17'Can a mortal be more righteous than
    God?
  Can a man be more pure than his
    Maker?

a8 Or the sea

¹⁸If God places no trust in his servants,
　if he charges his angels with error,
¹⁹how much more those who live in
　　houses of clay,
　whose foundations are in the dust,
　who are crushed more readily than
　　a moth!
²⁰Between dawn and dusk they are
　　broken to pieces;
　unnoticed, they perish forever.
²¹Are not the cords of their tent pulled
　　up,
　so that they die without
　　wisdom?' *a*

5 "Call if you will, but who will
　　answer you?
　To which of the holy ones will you
　　turn?
²Resentment kills a fool,
　and envy slays the simple.
³I myself have seen a fool taking root,
　but suddenly his house was
　　cursed.
⁴His children are far from safety,
　crushed in court without a
　　defender.
⁵The hungry consume his harvest,
　taking it even from among thorns,
　and the thirsty pant after his
　　wealth.
⁶For hardship does not spring from the
　　soil,
　nor does trouble sprout from the
　　ground.
⁷Yet man is born to trouble
　as surely as sparks fly upward.

⁸"But if it were I, I would appeal to
　　God;
　I would lay my cause before him.
⁹He performs wonders that cannot be
　　fathomed,
　miracles that cannot be counted.
¹⁰He bestows rain on the earth;
　he sends water upon the
　　countryside.
¹¹The lowly he sets on high,
　and those who mourn are lifted to
　　safety.
¹²He thwarts the plans of the crafty,
　so that their hands achieve no
　　success.
¹³He catches the wise in their
　　craftiness,
　and the schemes of the wily are
　　swept away.
¹⁴Darkness comes upon them in the
　　daytime;
　at noon they grope as in the night.

¹⁵He saves the needy from the sword in
　　their mouth;
　he saves them from the clutches of
　　the powerful.
¹⁶So the poor have hope,
　and injustice shuts its mouth.

¹⁷"Blessed is the man whom God
　　corrects;
　so do not despise the discipline of
　　the Almighty. *b*
¹⁸For he wounds, but he also binds up;
　he injures, but his hands also heal.
¹⁹From six calamities he will rescue
　　you;
　in seven no harm will befall you.
²⁰In famine he will ransom you from
　　death,
　and in battle from the stroke of the
　　sword.
²¹You will be protected from the lash of
　　the tongue,
　and need not fear when
　　destruction comes.
²²You will laugh at destruction and
　　famine,
　and need not fear the beasts of the
　　earth.
²³For you will have a covenant with
　　the stones of the field,
　and the wild animals will be at
　　peace with you.
²⁴You will know that your tent is
　　secure;
　you will take stock of your
　　property and find nothing
　　missing.
²⁵You will know that your children will
　　be many,
　and your descendants like the
　　grass of the earth.
²⁶You will come to the grave in full
　　vigor,
　like sheaves gathered in season.

²⁷"We have examined this, and it is
　　true.
　So hear it and apply it to yourself."

Job

6 Then Job replied:

²"If only my anguish could be
　　weighed
　and all my misery be placed on the
　　scales!

<hr>

a21 Some interpreters end the quotation after
verse 17.　　*b17* Hebrew *Shaddai*; here and
throughout Job

³It would surely outweigh the sand of
the seas—
no wonder my words have been
impetuous.
⁴The arrows of the Almighty are in
me,
my spirit drinks in their poison;
God's terrors are marshaled against
me.
⁵Does a wild donkey bray when it has
grass,
or an ox bellow when it has
fodder?

⁶Is tasteless food eaten without salt,
or is there flavor in the white of an
egg*?
⁷I refuse to touch it;
such food makes me ill.

⁸"Oh, that I might have my request,
that God would grant what I hope
for,
⁹that God would be willing to crush
me,

*6 The meaning of the Hebrew for this phrase is
uncertain.

WEDNESDAY

Read Job 5:1–27
Key Verses Job 5:17–18

God's Training Program — Jim Lett

A coach barks out, "Some of you are doggin' it! Looks like we need
an extra set of wind sprints." You know his philosophy: *No pain, no
gain.*

A doctor x-rays a week-old arm injury: "Your arm is healing with
the bone out of alignment. It will be disfigured unless we break and
reset it," she offers calmly. Ouch!

Both of these scenarios show that pain and suffering can be beneficial even though, in our humanity, we try to avoid them at all
cost. Job experienced pain and loss that seemed unbearable. The
questions foremost in his mind were, "Why me?" and "Why this?"
But Eliphaz reminded Job of a truth about God and suffering—a
truth that invites hope and causes our faith to be stretched to a
new level: "Blessed is the man whom God corrects; so do not despise
the discipline of the Almighty. For he wounds, but he also binds up;
he injures, but his hands also heal" (Job 5:17).

God allowed tragedy to come into Job's life. As unfair as it all
seemed at first, Job discovered through his experiences that God is
perfect as well as Almighty. He is a loving parent who "disciplines
us for our good, that we may share in his holiness. No discipline
seems pleasant at the time, but painful. Later on, however, it produces a harvest of righteousness and peace for those who have
been trained by it" (Hebrews 12:10–11). And Job's ultimate hope
was that the God who disciplined him would also heal him (see Job
5:18).

We are easily tempted to resent God's discipline. We tend to
complain and grow bitter toward God or toward people who have
hurt us. But to know God intimately, we have to embrace all his
intentions for our life, even when they bring great pain. What a concept! It's one we can learn from Job, who has set us an example of
welcoming, rather than despising, God's discipline in his life.

A Deeper Look
Genesis 50:19–20; John 15:1–2; James 5:10–11

Go to page 556 for your next devotional reading.

to let loose his hand and cut me
off!
10Then I would still have this
consolation—
my joy in unrelenting pain—
that I had not denied the words of
the Holy One.

11"What strength do I have, that I
should still hope?
What prospects, that I should be
patient?
12Do I have the strength of stone?
Is my flesh bronze?
13Do I have any power to help myself,
now that success has been driven
from me?

14"A despairing man should have the
devotion of his friends,
even though he forsakes the fear of
the Almighty.
15But my brothers are as undependable
as intermittent streams,
as the streams that overflow
16when darkened by thawing ice
and swollen with melting snow,
17but that cease to flow in the dry
season,
and in the heat vanish from their
channels.
18Caravans turn aside from their routes;
they go up into the wasteland and
perish.
19The caravans of Tema look for water,
the traveling merchants of Sheba
look in hope.
20They are distressed, because they had
been confident;
they arrive there, only to be
disappointed.
21Now you too have proved to be of no
help;
you see something dreadful and
are afraid.
22Have I ever said, 'Give something on
my behalf,
pay a ransom for me from your
wealth,
23deliver me from the hand of the
enemy,
ransom me from the clutches of
the ruthless'?

24"Teach me, and I will be quiet;
show me where I have been
wrong.
25How painful are honest words!
But what do your arguments
prove?

26Do you mean to correct what I say,
and treat the words of a despairing
man as wind?
27You would even cast lots for the
fatherless
and barter away your friend.

28"But now be so kind as to look at
me.
Would I lie to your face?
29Relent, do not be unjust;
reconsider, for my integrity is at
stake.*a*
30Is there any wickedness on my lips?
Can my mouth not discern malice?

7 "Does not man have hard service on
earth?
Are not his days like those of a
hired man?
2Like a slave longing for the evening
shadows,
or a hired man waiting eagerly for
his wages,
3so I have been allotted months of
futility,
and nights of misery have been
assigned to me.
4When I lie down I think, 'How long
before I get up?'
The night drags on, and I toss till
dawn.
5My body is clothed with worms and
scabs,
my skin is broken and festering.

6"My days are swifter than a weaver's
shuttle,
and they come to an end without
hope.
7Remember, O God, that my life is but
a breath;
my eyes will never see happiness
again.
8The eye that now sees me will see
me no longer;
you will look for me, but I will be
no more.
9As a cloud vanishes and is gone,
so he who goes down to the
grave*b* does not return.
10He will never come to his house
again;
his place will know him no more.

11"Therefore I will not keep silent;
I will speak out in the anguish of
my spirit,

---

*a*29 Or *my righteousness still stands* *b*9 Hebrew
Sheol

I will complain in the bitterness of
    my soul.
¹²Am I the sea, or the monster of the
    deep,
    that you put me under guard?
¹³When I think my bed will comfort me
    and my couch will ease my
        complaint,
¹⁴even then you frighten me with
        dreams
    and terrify me with visions,
¹⁵so that I prefer strangling and death,
    rather than this body of mine.
¹⁶I despise my life; I would not live
        forever.
    Let me alone; my days have no
        meaning.

¹⁷"What is man that you make so
        much of him,
    that you give him so much
        attention,
¹⁸that you examine him every morning
    and test him every moment?
¹⁹Will you never look away from me,
    or let me alone even for an
        instant?
²⁰If I have sinned, what have I done to
        you,
    O watcher of men?
    Why have you made me your target?
    Have I become a burden to you?ᵃ
²¹Why do you not pardon my offenses
    and forgive my sins?
    For I will soon lie down in the dust;
    you will search for me, but I will
        be no more."

Bildad

8 Then Bildad the Shuhite replied:

²"How long will you say such things?
    Your words are a blustering wind.
³Does God pervert justice?
    Does the Almighty pervert what is
        right?
⁴When your children sinned against
        him,
    he gave them over to the penalty
        of their sin.
⁵But if you will look to God
    and plead with the Almighty,
⁶if you are pure and upright,
    even now he will rouse himself on
        your behalf
    and restore you to your rightful
        place.
⁷Your beginnings will seem humble,
    so prosperous will your future be.

⁸"Ask the former generations
    and find out what their fathers
        learned,
⁹for we were born only yesterday and
        know nothing,
    and our days on earth are but a
        shadow.
¹⁰Will they not instruct you and tell
        you?
    Will they not bring forth words
        from their understanding?
¹¹Can papyrus grow tall where there is
        no marsh?
    Can reeds thrive without water?
¹²While still growing and uncut,
    they wither more quickly than
        grass.
¹³Such is the destiny of all who forget
        God;
    so perishes the hope of the
        godless.
¹⁴What he trusts in is fragileᵇ;
    what he relies on is a spider's web.
¹⁵He leans on his web, but it gives
        way;
    he clings to it, but it does not hold.
¹⁶He is like a well-watered plant in the
        sunshine,
    spreading its shoots over the
        garden;
¹⁷it entwines its roots around a pile of
        rocks

ᵃ20 A few manuscripts of the Masoretic Text, an
ancient Hebrew scribal tradition and Septuagint;
most manuscripts of the Masoretic Text *I have
become a burden to myself.*   *ᵇ14* The meaning of
the Hebrew for this word is uncertain.

POINT OF INTEREST

Job 8:3

So often people respond in
anger and disbelief when
God allows things to happen
that they don't understand.
Others, like Job, use times of struggle and
questioning to analyze who God is and
where humans stand in relation to such a
perfect, all-knowing Being. Honest questioning is good; the book of Psalms is full
of such questions. But questioning God's
motives and doubting his goodness can
submerge us in our struggles when we
could be floating by faith.

and looks for a place among the
stones.
18But when it is torn from its spot,
that place disowns it and says, 'I
never saw you.'
19Surely its life withers away,
and*a* from the soil other plants
grow.

20"Surely God does not reject a
blameless man
or strengthen the hands of
evildoers.
21He will yet fill your mouth with
laughter
and your lips with shouts of joy.
22Your enemies will be clothed in
shame,
and the tents of the wicked will be
no more."

Job

9 Then Job replied:

2"Indeed, I know that this is true.
But how can a mortal be righteous
before God?
3Though one wished to dispute with
him,
he could not answer him one time
out of a thousand.
4His wisdom is profound, his power is
vast.
Who has resisted him and come
out unscathed?
5He moves mountains without their
knowing it
and overturns them in his anger.
6He shakes the earth from its place
and makes its pillars tremble.
7He speaks to the sun and it does not
shine;
he seals off the light of the stars.
8He alone stretches out the heavens
and treads on the waves of the
sea.
9He is the Maker of the Bear and
Orion,
the Pleiades and the constellations
of the south.
10He performs wonders that cannot be
fathomed,
miracles that cannot be counted.
11When he passes me, I cannot see
him;
when he goes by, I cannot perceive
him.
12If he snatches away, who can stop
him?

Who can say to him, 'What are
you doing?'
13God does not restrain his anger;
even the cohorts of Rahab cowered
at his feet.

14"How then can I dispute with him?
How can I find words to argue
with him?
15Though I were innocent, I could not
answer him;
I could only plead with my Judge
for mercy.
16Even if I summoned him and he
responded,
I do not believe he would give me
a hearing.
17He would crush me with a storm
and multiply my wounds for no
reason.
18He would not let me regain my
breath
but would overwhelm me with
misery.
19If it is a matter of strength, he is
mighty!
And if it is a matter of justice, who
will summon him*b*?
20Even if I were innocent, my mouth
would condemn me;
if I were blameless, it would
pronounce me guilty.

21"Although I am blameless,
I have no concern for myself;
I despise my own life.
22It is all the same; that is why I say,
'He destroys both the blameless
and the wicked.'
23When a scourge brings sudden death,
he mocks the despair of the
innocent.
24When a land falls into the hands of
the wicked,
he blindfolds its judges.
If it is not he, then who is it?

25"My days are swifter than a runner;
they fly away without a glimpse of
joy.
26They skim past like boats of papyrus,
like eagles swooping down on their
prey.
27If I say, 'I will forget my complaint,
I will change my expression, and
smile,'
28I still dread all my sufferings,

*a19 Or Surely all the joy it has / is that
b19 See Septuagint; Hebrew me.*

for I know you will not hold me
innocent.
²⁹Since I am already found guilty,
why should I struggle in vain?
³⁰Even if I washed myself with soapᵃ
and my hands with washing soda,
³¹you would plunge me into a slime pit
so that even my clothes would
detest me.

³²"He is not a man like me that I might
answer him,
that we might confront each other
in court.
³³If only there were someone to
arbitrate between us,
to lay his hand upon us both,
³⁴someone to remove God's rod from
me,
so that his terror would frighten
me no more.
³⁵Then I would speak up without fear
of him,
but as it now stands with me, I
cannot.

10 "I loathe my very life;
therefore I will give free rein to my
complaint
and speak out in the bitterness of
my soul.
²I will say to God: Do not condemn
me,
but tell me what charges you have
against me.
³Does it please you to oppress me,
to spurn the work of your hands,
while you smile on the schemes of
the wicked?
⁴Do you have eyes of flesh?
Do you see as a mortal sees?
⁵Are your days like those of a mortal
or your years like those of a man,
⁶that you must search out my faults
and probe after my sin—
⁷though you know that I am not guilty
and that no one can rescue me
from your hand?

⁸"Your hands shaped me and made
me.
Will you now turn and destroy me?
⁹Remember that you molded me like
clay.
Will you now turn me to dust
again?
¹⁰Did you not pour me out like milk
and curdle me like cheese,
¹¹clothe me with skin and flesh

and knit me together with bones
and sinews?
¹²You gave me life and showed me
kindness,
and in your providence watched
over my spirit.

¹³"But this is what you concealed in
your heart,
and I know that this was in your
mind:
¹⁴If I sinned, you would be watching
me
and would not let my offense go
unpunished.
¹⁵If I am guilty—woe to me!
Even if I am innocent, I cannot lift
my head,
for I am full of shame
and drowned inᵇ my affliction.
¹⁶If I hold my head high, you stalk me
like a lion
and again display your awesome
power against me.
¹⁷You bring new witnesses against me
and increase your anger toward
me;
your forces come against me wave
upon wave.

¹⁸"Why then did you bring me out of
the womb?
I wish I had died before any eye
saw me.
¹⁹If only I had never come into being,
or had been carried straight from
the womb to the grave!
²⁰Are not my few days almost over?
Turn away from me so I can have
a moment's joy
²¹before I go to the place of no return,
to the land of gloom and deep
shadow,ᶜ
²²to the land of deepest night,
of deep shadow and disorder,
where even the light is like
darkness."

Zophar

11 Then Zophar the Naamathite replied:

²"Are all these words to go
unanswered?
Is this talker to be vindicated?
³Will your idle talk reduce men to
silence?

ᵃ30 Or *snow*   ᵇ15 Or *and aware of*   ᶜ21 Or
and the shadow of death; also in verse 22

Will no one rebuke you when you
   mock?
⁴You say to God, 'My beliefs are
   flawless
and I am pure in your sight.'
⁵Oh, how I wish that God would
   speak,
that he would open his lips against
   you
⁶and disclose to you the secrets of
   wisdom,
for true wisdom has two sides.
Know this: God has even forgotten
   some of your sin.

⁷"Can you fathom the mysteries of
   God?
Can you probe the limits of the
   Almighty?
⁸They are higher than the heavens—
   what can you do?
They are deeper than the depths of
   the grave*—what can you
   know?
⁹Their measure is longer than the
   earth
and wider than the sea.

¹⁰"If he comes along and confines you
   in prison
and convenes a court, who can
   oppose him?
¹¹Surely he recognizes deceitful men;
and when he sees evil, does he not
   take note?
¹²But a witless man can no more
   become wise
than a wild donkey's colt can be
   born a man.*

¹³"Yet if you devote your heart to him
and stretch out your hands to him,
¹⁴if you put away the sin that is in
   your hand
and allow no evil to dwell in your
   tent,
¹⁵then you will lift up your face
   without shame;
you will stand firm and without
   fear.
¹⁶You will surely forget your trouble,
recalling it only as waters gone by.
¹⁷Life will be brighter than noonday,
and darkness will become like
   morning.
¹⁸You will be secure, because there is
   hope;
you will look about you and take
   your rest in safety.

¹⁹You will lie down, with no one to
   make you afraid,
and many will court your favor.
²⁰But the eyes of the wicked will fail,
and escape will elude them;
   their hope will become a dying
   gasp."

Job

12 Then Job replied:

²"Doubtless you are the people,
and wisdom will die with you!
³But I have a mind as well as you;
I am not inferior to you.
Who does not know all these
   things?

⁴"I have become a laughingstock to
   my friends,
though I called upon God and he
   answered—
a mere laughingstock, though
   righteous and blameless!
⁵Men at ease have contempt for
   misfortune
as the fate of those whose feet are
   slipping.
⁶The tents of marauders are
   undisturbed,
and those who provoke God are
   secure—
those who carry their god in their
   hands.*

⁷"But ask the animals, and they will
   teach you,
or the birds of the air, and they
   will tell you;

a8 Hebrew *than Sheol*   *b12* Or *wild donkey can
be born tame*   *c6* Or *secure / in what God's
hand brings them*

POINT OF INTEREST

Job 11:7

How much do you know
about God? God has re-
vealed a lot about himself
throughout the Bible and cre-
ation, but these revelations barely scratch
the surface of God's magnificence. We can
know something about God, but we will
never comprehend all there is to know
about the Creator of the universe.

⁸or speak to the earth, and it will
    teach you,
  or let the fish of the sea inform
    you.
⁹Which of all these does not know
  that the hand of the Lord has done
    this?
¹⁰In his hand is the life of every
    creature
  and the breath of all mankind.
¹¹Does not the ear test words
  as the tongue tastes food?
¹²Is not wisdom found among the aged?
  Does not long life bring
    understanding?

¹³"To God belong wisdom and power;
  counsel and understanding are his.
¹⁴What he tears down cannot be
    rebuilt;
  the man he imprisons cannot be
    released.
¹⁵If he holds back the waters, there is
    drought;
  if he lets them loose, they
    devastate the land.
¹⁶To him belong strength and victory;
  both deceived and deceiver are his.
¹⁷He leads counselors away stripped
  and makes fools of judges.
¹⁸He takes off the shackles put on by
    kings
  and ties a loincloth*a* around their
    waist.
¹⁹He leads priests away stripped
  and overthrows men long
    established.
²⁰He silences the lips of trusted
    advisers
  and takes away the discernment of
    elders.
²¹He pours contempt on nobles
  and disarms the mighty.
²²He reveals the deep things of
    darkness
  and brings deep shadows into the
    light.
²³He makes nations great, and destroys
    them;
  he enlarges nations, and disperses
    them.
²⁴He deprives the leaders of the earth
    of their reason;
  he sends them wandering through
    a trackless waste.
²⁵They grope in darkness with no light;
  he makes them stagger like
    drunkards.

13 "My eyes have seen all this,
  my ears have heard and
    understood it.
²What you know, I also know;
  I am not inferior to you.
³But I desire to speak to the Almighty
  and to argue my case with God.
⁴You, however, smear me with lies;
  you are worthless physicians, all of
    you!
⁵If only you would be altogether
    silent!
  For you, that would be wisdom.
⁶Hear now my argument;
  listen to the plea of my lips.
⁷Will you speak wickedly on God's
    behalf?
  Will you speak deceitfully for him?
⁸Will you show him partiality?
  Will you argue the case for God?
⁹Would it turn out well if he examined
    you?
  Could you deceive him as you
    might deceive men?
¹⁰He would surely rebuke you
  if you secretly showed partiality.
¹¹Would not his splendor terrify you?
  Would not the dread of him fall on
    you?
¹²Your maxims are proverbs of ashes;
  your defenses are defenses of clay.

¹³"Keep silent and let me speak;
  then let come to me what may.
¹⁴Why do I put myself in jeopardy
  and take my life in my hands?
¹⁵Though he slay me, yet will I hope in
    him;
  I will surely*b* defend my ways to
    his face.
¹⁶Indeed, this will turn out for my
    deliverance,
  for no godless man would dare
    come before him!
¹⁷Listen carefully to my words;
  let your ears take in what I say.
¹⁸Now that I have prepared my case,
  I know I will be vindicated.
¹⁹Can anyone bring charges against
    me?
  If so, I will be silent and die.

²⁰"Only grant me these two things,
    O God,
  and then I will not hide from you:
²¹Withdraw your hand far from me,

*a*18 Or *shackles of kings / and ties a belt*
*b*15 Or *He will surely slay me; I have no hope — /*
yet I will

and stop frightening me with your
  terrors.
²²Then summon me and I will answer,
  or let me speak, and you reply.
²³How many wrongs and sins have I
    committed?
  Show me my offense and my sin.
²⁴Why do you hide your face
  and consider me your enemy?
²⁵Will you torment a windblown leaf?
  Will you chase after dry chaff?
²⁶For you write down bitter things
    against me
  and make me inherit the sins of
    my youth.
²⁷You fasten my feet in shackles;
  you keep close watch on all my
    paths
  by putting marks on the soles of
    my feet.

²⁸"So man wastes away like something
    rotten,
  like a garment eaten by moths.

14 "Man born of woman
  is of few days and full of trouble.
²He springs up like a flower and
    withers away;
  like a fleeting shadow, he does not
    endure.
³Do you fix your eye on such a one?
  Will you bring him*ᵃ* before you
    for judgment?
⁴Who can bring what is pure from the
    impure?
  No one!
⁵Man's days are determined;
  you have decreed the number of
    his months

ᵃ3 Septuagint, Vulgate and Syriac; Hebrew *me*

THURSDAY

Read *Job 13:1–28*
Key Verse *Job 13:15*

The Perfect Plan – Jay Getz

I was only twenty-eight, but it seemed that I had waited decades for
a girl like Dawn. She was pretty, bright and determined to live life
completely for God. I felt sure she was the wife God had chosen for
me. So why had she chosen someone else?

I had tried for months to win Dawn. I wrote her long letters,
gave her wildflowers, even arranged a special trip to see her in
Boston. But when I got there she told me that she had someone
else in mind. I was devastated. I felt I had lost the only perfect girl
for me.

It was all over but the sighing. Then I read the story of Job and
how God allowed Satan to take many precious things from Job: his
possessions, his livelihood, his health, even his children. Job had reason to wonder if God was intent on killing him. Yet Job's response
was, "Though he slay me, yet will I hope in him" (Job 13:15).

After a time I began to hope in what God had planned for me
rather than in marriage to Dawn. I realized that I had to trust that
God works in all things for my good—even when my circumstances
or my emotions try to tell me otherwise (see Romans 8:28).

Within a couple of months Dawn called back and invited me to
Boston again. We exchanged dozens of letters, visits and a wedding
ring. Now the words of Job 13:15 hang on the wall of our bedroom,
and we "hope in God" together.

A Deeper Look
Psalm 25:4–5; Hebrews 10:23

Go to page 565 for your next devotional reading.

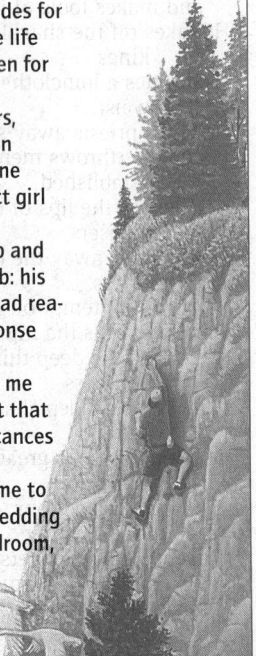

and have set limits he cannot
  exceed.
⁶So look away from him and let him
  alone,
  till he has put in his time like a
  hired man.

⁷"At least there is hope for a tree:
  If it is cut down, it will sprout
  again,
  and its new shoots will not fail.
⁸Its roots may grow old in the ground
  and its stump die in the soil,
⁹yet at the scent of water it will bud
  and put forth shoots like a plant.
¹⁰But man dies and is laid low;
  he breathes his last and is no
  more.
¹¹As water disappears from the sea
  or a riverbed becomes parched and
  dry,
¹²so man lies down and does not rise;
  till the heavens are no more, men
  will not awake
  or be roused from their sleep.

¹³"If only you would hide me in the
  grave*a*
  and conceal me till your anger has
  passed!
  If only you would set me a time
  and then remember me!
¹⁴If a man dies, will he live again?
  All the days of my hard service
  I will wait for my renewal*b* to
  come.
¹⁵You will call and I will answer you;
  you will long for the creature your
  hands have made.
¹⁶Surely then you will count my steps
  but not keep track of my sin.
¹⁷My offenses will be sealed up in a
  bag;
  you will cover over my sin.

¹⁸"But as a mountain erodes and
  crumbles
  and as a rock is moved from its
  place,
¹⁹as water wears away stones
  and torrents wash away the soil,
  so you destroy man's hope.
²⁰You overpower him once for all, and
  he is gone;
  you change his countenance and
  send him away.
²¹If his sons are honored, he does not
  know it;
  if they are brought low, he does
  not see it.

²²He feels but the pain of his own body
  and mourns only for himself."

Eliphaz

15 Then Eliphaz the Temanite replied:

²"Would a wise man answer with
  empty notions
  or fill his belly with the hot east
  wind?
³Would he argue with useless words,
  with speeches that have no value?
⁴But you even undermine piety
  and hinder devotion to God.
⁵Your sin prompts your mouth;
  you adopt the tongue of the crafty.
⁶Your own mouth condemns you, not
  mine;
  your own lips testify against you.

⁷"Are you the first man ever born?
  Were you brought forth before the
  hills?
⁸Do you listen in on God's council?
  Do you limit wisdom to yourself?
⁹What do you know that we do not
  know?
  What insights do you have that we
  do not have?
¹⁰The gray-haired and the aged are on
  our side,
  men even older than your father.
¹¹Are God's consolations not enough
  for you,
  words spoken gently to you?
¹²Why has your heart carried you
  away,
  and why do your eyes flash,
¹³so that you vent your rage against
  God
  and pour out such words from
  your mouth?

¹⁴"What is man, that he could be pure,
  or one born of woman, that he
  could be righteous?
¹⁵If God places no trust in his holy
  ones,
  if even the heavens are not pure in
  his eyes,
¹⁶how much less man, who is vile and
  corrupt,
  who drinks up evil like water!

¹⁷"Listen to me and I will explain to
  you;
  let me tell you what I have seen,

a13 Hebrew *Sheol*   *b14* Or *release*

¹⁸what wise men have declared,
hiding nothing received from their
fathers
¹⁹(to whom alone the land was given
when no alien passed among
them):
²⁰All his days the wicked man suffers
torment,
the ruthless through all the years
stored up for him.
²¹Terrifying sounds fill his ears;
when all seems well, marauders
attack him.
²²He despairs of escaping the darkness;
he is marked for the sword.
²³He wanders about—food for
vultures*ᵃ*;
he knows the day of darkness is at
hand.
²⁴Distress and anguish fill him with
terror;
they overwhelm him, like a king
poised to attack,
²⁵because he shakes his fist at God
and vaunts himself against the
Almighty,
²⁶defiantly charging against him
with a thick, strong shield.

²⁷"Though his face is covered with fat
and his waist bulges with flesh,
²⁸he will inhabit ruined towns
and houses where no one lives,
houses crumbling to rubble.
²⁹He will no longer be rich and his
wealth will not endure,
nor will his possessions spread
over the land.
³⁰He will not escape the darkness;
a flame will wither his shoots,
and the breath of God's mouth will
carry him away.
³¹Let him not deceive himself by
trusting what is worthless,
for he will get nothing in return.
³²Before his time he will be paid in
full,
and his branches will not flourish.
³³He will be like a vine stripped of its
unripe grapes,
like an olive tree shedding its
blossoms.
³⁴For the company of the godless will
be barren,
and fire will consume the tents of
those who love bribes.
³⁵They conceive trouble and give birth
to evil;
their womb fashions deceit."

Job

16 Then Job replied:

²"I have heard many things like these;
miserable comforters are you all!
³Will your long-winded speeches
never end?
What ails you that you keep on
arguing?
⁴I also could speak like you,
if you were in my place;
I could make fine speeches against
you
and shake my head at you.
⁵But my mouth would encourage you;
comfort from my lips would bring
you relief.

⁶"Yet if I speak, my pain is not
relieved;
and if I refrain, it does not go
away.
⁷Surely, O God, you have worn me
out;
you have devastated my entire
household.
⁸You have bound me—and it has
become a witness;
my gauntness rises up and testifies
against me.
⁹God assails me and tears me in his
anger
and gnashes his teeth at me;
my opponent fastens on me his
piercing eyes.
¹⁰Men open their mouths to jeer at me;
they strike my cheek in scorn
and unite together against me.
¹¹God has turned me over to evil men

ᵃ23 Or about, looking for food

POINT OF INTEREST

Job 16:2

What does a broken heart
need? Often we want to
offer advice or try to fix the
hurt. Job's friends began well,
sitting by him in silence for seven days in a
gesture of deep sorrow and solidarity (see
Job 2:13). When they tried to explain Job's
predicament and give advice, however, the
trouble began.

and thrown me into the clutches of
the wicked.
¹²All was well with me, but he
shattered me;
he seized me by the neck and
crushed me.
He has made me his target;
¹³   his archers surround me.
Without pity, he pierces my kidneys
and spills my gall on the ground.
¹⁴Again and again he bursts upon me;
he rushes at me like a warrior.

¹⁵"I have sewed sackcloth over my skin
and buried my brow in the dust.
¹⁶My face is red with weeping,
deep shadows ring my eyes;
¹⁷yet my hands have been free of
violence
and my prayer is pure.

¹⁸"O earth, do not cover my blood;
may my cry never be laid to rest!
¹⁹Even now my witness is in heaven;
my advocate is on high.
²⁰My intercessor is my friend*ª*
as my eyes pour out tears to God;
²¹on behalf of a man he pleads with
God
as a man pleads for his friend.

²²"Only a few years will pass
before I go on the journey of no
return.

17 ¹My spirit is broken,
my days are cut short,
the grave awaits me.
²Surely mockers surround me;
my eyes must dwell on their
hostility.

³"Give me, O God, the pledge you
demand.
Who else will put up security for
me?
⁴You have closed their minds to
understanding;
therefore you will not let them
triumph.
⁵If a man denounces his friends for
reward,
the eyes of his children will fail.

⁶"God has made me a byword to
everyone,
a man in whose face people spit.
⁷My eyes have grown dim with grief;
my whole frame is but a shadow.
⁸Upright men are appalled at this;
the innocent are aroused against
the ungodly.

⁹Nevertheless, the righteous will hold
to their ways,
and those with clean hands will
grow stronger.

¹⁰"But come on, all of you, try again!
I will not find a wise man among
you.
¹¹My days have passed, my plans are
shattered,
and so are the desires of my heart.
¹²These men turn night into day;
in the face of darkness they say,
'Light is near.'
¹³If the only home I hope for is the
grave,*ᵇ*
if I spread out my bed in darkness,
¹⁴if I say to corruption, 'You are my
father,'
and to the worm, 'My mother' or
'My sister,'
¹⁵where then is my hope?
Who can see any hope for me?
¹⁶Will it go down to the gates of
death*ᵇ*?
Will we descend together into the
dust?"

Bildad

18 Then Bildad the Shuhite replied:

²"When will you end these speeches?
Be sensible, and then we can talk.
³Why are we regarded as cattle
and considered stupid in your
sight?
⁴You who tear yourself to pieces in
your anger,
is the earth to be abandoned for
your sake?
Or must the rocks be moved from
their place?

⁵"The lamp of the wicked is snuffed
out;
the flame of his fire stops burning.
⁶The light in his tent becomes dark;
the lamp beside him goes out.
⁷The vigor of his step is weakened;
his own schemes throw him down.
⁸His feet thrust him into a net
and he wanders into its mesh.
⁹A trap seizes him by the heel;
a snare holds him fast.
¹⁰A noose is hidden for him on the
ground;
a trap lies in his path.

ª20 Or *My friends treat me with scorn*
ᵇ13,16 Hebrew *Sheol*

¹¹Terrors startle him on every side
and dog his every step.
¹²Calamity is hungry for him;
disaster is ready for him when he
falls.
¹³It eats away parts of his skin;
death's firstborn devours his limbs.
¹⁴He is torn from the security of his
tent
and marched off to the king of
terrors.
¹⁵Fire resides ᵃ in his tent;
burning sulfur is scattered over his
dwelling.
¹⁶His roots dry up below
and his branches wither above.
¹⁷The memory of him perishes from the
earth;
he has no name in the land.
¹⁸He is driven from light into darkness
and is banished from the world.
¹⁹He has no offspring or descendants
among his people,
no survivor where once he lived.
²⁰Men of the west are appalled at his
fate;
men of the east are seized with
horror.
²¹Surely such is the dwelling of an evil
man;
such is the place of one who
knows not God."

Job

19 Then Job replied:

²"How long will you torment me
and crush me with words?
³Ten times now you have reproached
me;
shamelessly you attack me.
⁴If it is true that I have gone astray,
my error remains my concern
alone.
⁵If indeed you would exalt yourselves
above me
and use my humiliation against
me,
⁶then know that God has wronged me
and drawn his net around me.

⁷"Though I cry, 'I've been wronged!' I
get no response;
though I call for help, there is no
justice.
⁸He has blocked my way so I cannot
pass;
he has shrouded my paths in
darkness.

⁹He has stripped me of my honor
and removed the crown from my
head.
¹⁰He tears me down on every side till I
am gone;
he uproots my hope like a tree.
¹¹His anger burns against me;
he counts me among his enemies.
¹²His troops advance in force;
they build a siege ramp against me
and encamp around my tent.

¹³"He has alienated my brothers from
me;
my acquaintances are completely
estranged from me.
¹⁴My kinsmen have gone away;
my friends have forgotten me.
¹⁵My guests and my maidservants
count me a stranger;
they look upon me as an alien.
¹⁶I summon my servant, but he does
not answer,
though I beg him with my own
mouth.
¹⁷My breath is offensive to my wife;
I am loathsome to my own
brothers.
¹⁸Even the little boys scorn me;
when I appear, they ridicule me.
¹⁹All my intimate friends detest me;
those I love have turned against
me.
²⁰I am nothing but skin and bones;
I have escaped with only the skin
of my teeth. ᵇ

²¹"Have pity on me, my friends, have
pity,
for the hand of God has struck me.
²²Why do you pursue me as God does?
Will you never get enough of my
flesh?

²³"Oh, that my words were recorded,
that they were written on a scroll,
²⁴that they were inscribed with an iron
tool on ᶜ lead,
or engraved in rock forever!
²⁵I know that my Redeemer ᵈ lives,
and that in the end he will stand
upon the earth. ᵉ
²⁶And after my skin has been
destroyed,
yet ᶠ in ᵍ my flesh I will see God;

ᵃ15 Or *Nothing he had remains*   ᵇ20 Or *only my*
gums   ᶜ24 Or *and*   ᵈ25 Or *defender*
ᵉ25 Or *upon my grave*   ᶠ26 Or *And after I*
awake, / though this ⸤body⸥ has been destroyed, /
then   ᵍ26 Or */ apart from*

²⁷I myself will see him
  with my own eyes—I, and not
    another.
  How my heart yearns within me!

²⁸"If you say, 'How we will hound
    him,
  since the root of the trouble lies in
    him,ᵃ'
²⁹you should fear the sword yourselves;
  for wrath will bring punishment by
    the sword,
  and then you will know that there
    is judgment.ᵇ"

Zophar

20 Then Zophar the Naamathite replied:

²"My troubled thoughts prompt me to
    answer
  because I am greatly disturbed.
³I hear a rebuke that dishonors me,
  and my understanding inspires me
    to reply.

⁴"Surely you know how it has been
    from of old,
  ever since manᶜ was placed on
    the earth,
⁵that the mirth of the wicked is brief,
  the joy of the godless lasts but a
    moment.
⁶Though his pride reaches to the
    heavens
  and his head touches the clouds,
⁷he will perish forever, like his own
    dung;
  those who have seen him will say,
    'Where is he?'
⁸Like a dream he flies away, no more
    to be found,
  banished like a vision of the night.
⁹The eye that saw him will not see
    him again;
  his place will look on him no
    more.
¹⁰His children must make amends to
    the poor;
  his own hands must give back his
    wealth.
¹¹The youthful vigor that fills his bones
  will lie with him in the dust.

¹²"Though evil is sweet in his mouth
  and he hides it under his tongue,
¹³though he cannot bear to let it go
  and keeps it in his mouth,
¹⁴yet his food will turn sour in his
    stomach;

it will become the venom of
    serpents within him.
¹⁵He will spit out the riches he
    swallowed;
  God will make his stomach vomit
    them up.
¹⁶He will suck the poison of serpents;
  the fangs of an adder will kill him.
¹⁷He will not enjoy the streams,
  the rivers flowing with honey and
    cream.
¹⁸What he toiled for he must give back
    uneaten;
  he will not enjoy the profit from
    his trading.
¹⁹For he has oppressed the poor and
    left them destitute;
  he has seized houses he did not
    build.

²⁰"Surely he will have no respite from
    his craving;
  he cannot save himself by his
    treasure.
²¹Nothing is left for him to devour;
  his prosperity will not endure.
²²In the midst of his plenty, distress
    will overtake him;
  the full force of misery will come
    upon him.
²³When he has filled his belly,
  God will vent his burning anger
    against him
  and rain down his blows upon
    him.
²⁴Though he flees from an iron
    weapon,
  a bronze-tipped arrow pierces him.
²⁵He pulls it out of his back,
  the gleaming point out of his liver.
  Terrors will come over him;

ᵃ28 Many Hebrew manuscripts, Septuagint and
Vulgate; most Hebrew manuscripts *me*   ᵇ29 Or /
that you may come to know the Almighty   ᶜ4 Or
Adam

POINT OF INTEREST

Job 19:25

When Job called God his
"Redeemer," he was using
the same word used of a
family member who would
bring justice for the innocent. In spite of
what happened to him, Job still had confidence in God's justice and goodness.

26 total darkness lies in wait for his
treasures.
A fire unfanned will consume him
and devour what is left in his tent.
27The heavens will expose his guilt;
the earth will rise up against him.
28A flood will carry off his house,
rushing waters*a* on the day of
God's wrath.
29Such is the fate God allots the
wicked,
the heritage appointed for them by
God.' "

Job

21 Then Job replied:

2"Listen carefully to my words;
let this be the consolation you give
me.
3Bear with me while I speak,
and after I have spoken, mock on.

4"Is my complaint directed to man?
Why should I not be impatient?
5Look at me and be astonished;
clap your hand over your mouth.
6When I think about this, I am
terrified;
trembling seizes my body.
7Why do the wicked live on,
growing old and increasing in
power?
8They see their children established
around them,
their offspring before their eyes.
9Their homes are safe and free from
fear;
the rod of God is not upon them.
10Their bulls never fail to breed;
their cows calve and do not
miscarry.
11They send forth their children as a
flock;
their little ones dance about.
12They sing to the music of tambourine
and harp;
they make merry to the sound of
the flute.
13They spend their years in prosperity
and go down to the grave*b* in
peace.*c*
14Yet they say to God, 'Leave us alone!
We have no desire to know your
ways.
15Who is the Almighty, that we should
serve him?
What would we gain by praying to
him?'

16But their prosperity is not in their
own hands,
so I stand aloof from the counsel
of the wicked.

17"Yet how often is the lamp of the
wicked snuffed out?
How often does calamity come
upon them,
the fate God allots in his anger?
18How often are they like straw before
the wind,
like chaff swept away by a gale?
19It is said, ₁ 'God stores up a man's
punishment for his sons.'
Let him repay the man himself, so
that he will know it!
20Let his own eyes see his destruction;
let him drink of the wrath of the
Almighty.*d*
21For what does he care about the
family he leaves behind
when his allotted months come to
an end?

22"Can anyone teach knowledge to
God,
since he judges even the highest?
23One man dies in full vigor,
completely secure and at ease,
24his body*e* well nourished,
his bones rich with marrow.
25Another man dies in bitterness of
soul,
never having enjoyed anything
good.
26Side by side they lie in the dust,
and worms cover them both.

27"I know full well what you are
thinking,
the schemes by which you would
wrong me.
28You say, 'Where now is the great
man's house,
the tents where wicked men lived?'
29Have you never questioned those
who travel?
Have you paid no regard to their
accounts—
30that the evil man is spared from the
day of calamity,

a28 Or *The possessions in his house will be carried
off, / washed away*   *b13* Hebrew *Sheol*
c13 Or *in an instant*   *d17-20* Verses 17 and 18
may be taken as exclamations and 19 and 20 as
declarations.   *e24* The meaning of the Hebrew
for this word is uncertain.

that he is delivered from*ᵃ* the day
of wrath?
³¹Who denounces his conduct to his
face?
Who repays him for what he has
done?
³²He is carried to the grave,
and watch is kept over his tomb.
³³The soil in the valley is sweet to him;
all men follow after him,
and a countless throng goesᵇ
before him.

³⁴"So how can you console me with
your nonsense?
Nothing is left of your answers but
falsehood!"

Eliphaz

22 Then Eliphaz the Temanite replied:

²"Can a man be of benefit to God?
Can even a wise man benefit him?
³What pleasure would it give the
Almighty if you were
righteous?
What would he gain if your ways
were blameless?

⁴"Is it for your piety that he rebukes
you
and brings charges against you?
⁵Is not your wickedness great?
Are not your sins endless?
⁶You demanded security from your
brothers for no reason;
you stripped men of their clothing,
leaving them naked.
⁷You gave no water to the weary
and you withheld food from the
hungry,
⁸though you were a powerful man,
owning land—
an honored man, living on it.
⁹And you sent widows away
empty-handed
and broke the strength of the
fatherless.
¹⁰That is why snares are all around
you,
why sudden peril terrifies you,
¹¹why it is so dark you cannot see,
and why a flood of water covers
you.

¹²"Is not God in the heights of heaven?
And see how lofty are the highest
stars!
¹³Yet you say, 'What does God know?

Does he judge through such
darkness?
¹⁴Thick clouds veil him, so he does not
see us
as he goes about in the vaulted
heavens.'
¹⁵Will you keep to the old path
that evil men have trod?
¹⁶They were carried off before their
time,
their foundations washed away by
a flood.
¹⁷They said to God, 'Leave us alone!
What can the Almighty do to us?'
¹⁸Yet it was he who filled their houses
with good things,
so I stand aloof from the counsel
of the wicked.

¹⁹"The righteous see their ruin and
rejoice;
the innocent mock them, saying,
²⁰'Surely our foes are destroyed,
and fire devours their wealth.'

²¹"Submit to God and be at peace with
him;
in this way prosperity will come to
you.
²²Accept instruction from his mouth
and lay up his words in your heart.
²³If you return to the Almighty, you
will be restored:
If you remove wickedness far from
your tent
²⁴and assign your nuggets to the dust,
your gold of Ophir to the rocks in
the ravines,
²⁵then the Almighty will be your gold,
the choicest silver for you.

---

*ᵃ30 Or man is reserved for the day of calamity, /
that he is brought forth to　ᵇ33 Or / as a
countless throng went*

POINT OF INTEREST

Job 22:6

In ancient business transactions, an article of clothing could be claimed as security for a loan. Yet this verse reminds us that shrewd but compassionless business practices are unrighteous in God's eyes. Both sides should be treated fairly in a business deal, for all individuals are precious in God's sight.

26Surely then you will find delight in
    the Almighty
  and will lift up your face to God.
27You will pray to him, and he will
    hear you,
  and you will fulfill your vows.
28What you decide on will be done,
  and light will shine on your ways.
29When men are brought low and you
    say, 'Lift them up!'
  then he will save the downcast.
30He will deliver even one who is not
    innocent,
  who will be delivered through the
    cleanness of your hands."

Job

23 Then Job replied:

2"Even today my complaint is bitter;
  his hand*a* is heavy in spite of*b*
    my groaning.
3If only I knew where to find him;
  if only I could go to his dwelling!
4I would state my case before him
  and fill my mouth with arguments.
5I would find out what he would
    answer me,
  and consider what he would say.
6Would he oppose me with great
    power?
  No, he would not press charges
    against me.
7There an upright man could present
    his case before him,
  and I would be delivered forever
    from my judge.

8"But if I go to the east, he is not
    there;
  if I go to the west, I do not find
    him.
9When he is at work in the north, I do
    not see him;
  when he turns to the south, I catch
    no glimpse of him.
10But he knows the way that I take;
  when he has tested me, I will
    come forth as gold.
11My feet have closely followed his
    steps;
  I have kept to his way without
    turning aside.
12I have not departed from the
    commands of his lips;
  I have treasured the words of his
    mouth more than my daily
    bread.

13"But he stands alone, and who can
    oppose him?
  He does whatever he pleases.
14He carries out his decree against me,
  and many such plans he still has
    in store.
15That is why I am terrified before him;
  when I think of all this, I fear him.
16God has made my heart faint;
  the Almighty has terrified me.
17Yet I am not silenced by the
    darkness,
  by the thick darkness that covers
    my face.

24 "Why does the Almighty not set
    times for judgment?
  Why must those who know him
    look in vain for such days?
2Men move boundary stones;
  they pasture flocks they have
    stolen.
3They drive away the orphan's donkey
  and take the widow's ox in pledge.
4They thrust the needy from the path
  and force all the poor of the land
    into hiding.
5Like wild donkeys in the desert,
  the poor go about their labor of
    foraging food;
  the wasteland provides food for
    their children.
6They gather fodder in the fields
  and glean in the vineyards of the
    wicked.
7Lacking clothes, they spend the night
    naked;
  they have nothing to cover
    themselves in the cold.
8They are drenched by mountain rains
  and hug the rocks for lack of
    shelter.
9The fatherless child is snatched from
    the breast;
  the infant of the poor is seized for
    a debt.
10Lacking clothes, they go about naked;
  they carry the sheaves, but still go
    hungry.
11They crush olives among the
    terraces*c*;
  they tread the winepresses, yet
    suffer thirst.
12The groans of the dying rise from the
    city,

a2 Septuagint and Syriac; Hebrew / *the hand on me*
b2 Or *heavy on me in*   *c11* Or *olives between the
millstones;* the meaning of the Hebrew for this word
is uncertain.

and the souls of the wounded cry
out for help.
But God charges no one with
wrongdoing.

13"There are those who rebel against
the light,
who do not know its ways
or stay in its paths.
14When daylight is gone, the murderer
rises up
and kills the poor and needy;
in the night he steals forth like a
thief.
15The eye of the adulterer watches for
dusk;
he thinks, 'No eye will see me,'
and he keeps his face concealed.
16In the dark, men break into houses,
but by day they shut themselves
in;

they want nothing to do with the
light.
17For all of them, deep darkness is their
morning*a*;
they make friends with the terrors
of darkness.*b*

18"Yet they are foam on the surface of
the water;
their portion of the land is cursed,
so that no one goes to the
vineyards.
19As heat and drought snatch away the
melted snow,
so the grave*c* snatches away those
who have sinned.
20The womb forgets them,
the worm feasts on them;

*a*17 Or *them, their morning is like the shadow of
death*   *b*17 Or *of the shadow of death*
*c*19 Hebrew *Sheol*

FRIDAY

Read Job 23:1–17
Key Verse Job 23:10

To Come Forth as Gold — Dawn Getz

I cried as I looked at myself in the mirror. As I focused on the bright
red lumps on my forehead and cheeks, I wondered, "How many more
years will I have this terrible acne? How many thousands of dollars
will my parents and I have to spend trying to clear it up?" I couldn't
stand the scary scene I saw above the bathroom sink anymore.
Yuck!

People told me, "Oh, it doesn't matter, Dawn. You have such an
outgoing personality that nobody even notices." Well, I noticed, and
I was sure guys did too. I hadn't been diagnosed with terminal cancer, but to me the acne was intensely devastating.

It was only by God's grace that, even in the midst of that really
bad time, I didn't doubt his goodness. I knew he had created me and
fashioned me, complexion problems and all: "For you created my
inmost being; you knit me together in my mother's womb. I praise
you because I am fearfully and wonderfully made; your works are
wonderful, I know that full well"(Psalm 139:13–14).

As I look back now, I'm truly thankful for those hard years. God
used my struggles to help me seek him instead of popularity. I
wasn't voted homecoming queen, but I did think deeply about
who he wanted me to become on the inside. I had to choose to
believe that God is faithful; he "knows the way that I take" and he
used that bad time to help me "come forth as gold" (Job 23:10).

A Deeper Look
James 1:12; 5:11; 1 Peter 4:12–14

Go to page 571 for your next devotional reading.

evil men are no longer remembered
but are broken like a tree.
²¹They prey on the barren and childless
woman,
and to the widow show no
kindness.
²²But God drags away the mighty by
his power;
though they become established,
they have no assurance of
life.
²³He may let them rest in a feeling of
security,
but his eyes are on their ways.
²⁴For a little while they are exalted, and
then they are gone;
they are brought low and gathered
up like all others;
they are cut off like heads of grain.

²⁵"If this is not so, who can prove me
false
and reduce my words to nothing?"

Bildad

25 Then Bildad the Shuhite replied:

²"Dominion and awe belong to God;
he establishes order in the heights
of heaven.
³Can his forces be numbered?
Upon whom does his light not rise?
⁴How then can a man be righteous
before God?
How can one born of woman be
pure?
⁵If even the moon is not bright
and the stars are not pure in his
eyes,
⁶how much less man, who is but a
maggot—
a son of man, who is only a
worm!"

Job

26 Then Job replied:

²"How you have helped the
powerless!
How you have saved the arm that
is feeble!
³What advice you have offered to one
without wisdom!
And what great insight you have
displayed!
⁴Who has helped you utter these
words?
And whose spirit spoke from your
mouth?

⁵"The dead are in deep anguish,
those beneath the waters and all
that live in them.
⁶Deathᵃ is naked before God;
Destructionᵇ lies uncovered.
⁷He spreads out the northern ⌞skies⌟
over empty space;
he suspends the earth over
nothing.
⁸He wraps up the waters in his clouds,
yet the clouds do not burst under
their weight.
⁹He covers the face of the full moon,
spreading his clouds over it.
¹⁰He marks out the horizon on the face
of the waters
for a boundary between light and
darkness.
¹¹The pillars of the heavens quake,
aghast at his rebuke.
¹²By his power he churned up the sea;
by his wisdom he cut Rahab to
pieces.
¹³By his breath the skies became fair;
his hand pierced the gliding
serpent.
¹⁴And these are but the outer fringe of
his works;
how faint the whisper we hear of
him!
Who then can understand the
thunder of his power?"

27 And Job continued his discourse:

²"As surely as God lives, who has
denied me justice,
the Almighty, who has made me
taste bitterness of soul,
³as long as I have life within me,
the breath of God in my nostrils,

ᵃ6 Hebrew *Sheol*   ᵇ6 Hebrew *Abaddon*

POINT OF INTEREST

Job 25:2

The systematic approach of
the scientific method de-
pends on the orderliness of
the universe. Yet most scientists insist that such order emerged from
the chaos of random chance. Why is it less
reasonable to attribute the incredibly
complex and orderly interactions of the
universe to a Creator?

⁴my lips will not speak wickedness,
and my tongue will utter no deceit.
⁵I will never admit you are in the
right;
till I die, I will not deny my
integrity.
⁶I will maintain my righteousness and
never let go of it;
my conscience will not reproach
me as long as I live.

⁷"May my enemies be like the wicked,
my adversaries like the unjust!
⁸For what hope has the godless when
he is cut off,
when God takes away his life?
⁹Does God listen to his cry
when distress comes upon him?
¹⁰Will he find delight in the Almighty?
Will he call upon God at all times?

¹¹"I will teach you about the power of
God;
the ways of the Almighty I will not
conceal.
¹²You have all seen this yourselves.
Why then this meaningless talk?

¹³"Here is the fate God allots to the
wicked,
the heritage a ruthless man
receives from the Almighty:
¹⁴However many his children, their fate
is the sword;
his offspring will never have
enough to eat.
¹⁵The plague will bury those who
survive him,
and their widows will not weep for
them.
¹⁶Though he heaps up silver like dust
and clothes like piles of clay,
¹⁷what he lays up the righteous will
wear,
and the innocent will divide his
silver.
¹⁸The house he builds is like a moth's
cocoon,
like a hut made by a watchman.
¹⁹He lies down wealthy, but will do so
no more;
when he opens his eyes, all is
gone.
²⁰Terrors overtake him like a flood;
a tempest snatches him away in
the night.
²¹The east wind carries him off, and he
is gone;
it sweeps him out of his place.

²²It hurls itself against him without
mercy
as he flees headlong from its
power.
²³It claps its hands in derision
and hisses him out of his place.

28 "There is a mine for silver
and a place where gold is refined.
²Iron is taken from the earth,
and copper is smelted from ore.
³Man puts an end to the darkness;
he searches the farthest recesses
for ore in the blackest darkness.
⁴Far from where people dwell he cuts
a shaft,
in places forgotten by the foot of
man;
far from men he dangles and
sways.
⁵The earth, from which food comes,
is transformed below as by fire;
⁶sapphires*a* come from its rocks,
and its dust contains nuggets of
gold.
⁷No bird of prey knows that hidden
path,
no falcon's eye has seen it.
⁸Proud beasts do not set foot on it,
and no lion prowls there.
⁹Man's hand assaults the flinty rock
and lays bare the roots of the
mountains.
¹⁰He tunnels through the rock;
his eyes see all its treasures.
¹¹He searches*b* the sources of the
rivers
and brings hidden things to light.

¹²"But where can wisdom be found?
Where does understanding dwell?
¹³Man does not comprehend its worth;
it cannot be found in the land of
the living.
¹⁴The deep says, 'It is not in me';
the sea says, 'It is not with me.'
¹⁵It cannot be bought with the finest
gold,
nor can its price be weighed in
silver.
¹⁶It cannot be bought with the gold of
Ophir,
with precious onyx or sapphires.
¹⁷Neither gold nor crystal can compare
with it,

a6 Or lapis lazuli; also in verse 16
*b11 Septuagint, Aquila and Vulgate; Hebrew He
dams up*

nor can it be had for jewels of
  gold.
¹⁸Coral and jasper are not worthy of
  mention;
  the price of wisdom is beyond
  rubies.
¹⁹The topaz of Cush cannot compare
  with it;
  it cannot be bought with pure gold.

²⁰"Where then does wisdom come
  from?
  Where does understanding dwell?
²¹It is hidden from the eyes of every
  living thing,
  concealed even from the birds of
  the air.
²²Destruction*a* and Death say,
  'Only a rumor of it has reached
  our ears.'
²³God understands the way to it
  and he alone knows where it
  dwells,
²⁴for he views the ends of the earth
  and sees everything under the
  heavens.
²⁵When he established the force of the
  wind
  and measured out the waters,
²⁶when he made a decree for the rain
  and a path for the thunderstorm,
²⁷then he looked at wisdom and
  appraised it;
  he confirmed it and tested it.
²⁸And he said to man,
  'The fear of the Lord—that is
  wisdom,
  and to shun evil is
  understanding.' "

29 Job continued his discourse:

²"How I long for the months gone by,
  for the days when God watched
  over me,
³when his lamp shone upon my head
  and by his light I walked through
  darkness!
⁴Oh, for the days when I was in my
  prime,
  when God's intimate friendship
  blessed my house,
⁵when the Almighty was still with me
  and my children were around me,
⁶when my path was drenched with
  cream
  and the rock poured out for me
  streams of olive oil.
⁷"When I went to the gate of the city

and took my seat in the public
  square,
⁸the young men saw me and stepped
  aside
  and the old men rose to their feet;
⁹the chief men refrained from speaking
  and covered their mouths with
  their hands;
¹⁰the voices of the nobles were hushed,
  and their tongues stuck to the roof
  of their mouths.
¹¹Whoever heard me spoke well of me,
  and those who saw me
  commended me,
¹²because I rescued the poor who cried
  for help,
  and the fatherless who had none to
  assist him.
¹³The man who was dying blessed me;
  I made the widow's heart sing.
¹⁴I put on righteousness as my
  clothing;
  justice was my robe and my
  turban.
¹⁵I was eyes to the blind
  and feet to the lame.
¹⁶I was a father to the needy;
  I took up the case of the stranger.
¹⁷I broke the fangs of the wicked
  and snatched the victims from
  their teeth.

¹⁸"I thought, 'I will die in my own
  house,
  my days as numerous as the grains
  of sand.
¹⁹My roots will reach to the water,
  and the dew will lie all night on
  my branches.
²⁰My glory will remain fresh in me,
  the bow ever new in my hand.'

²¹"Men listened to me expectantly,
  waiting in silence for my counsel.

a22 Hebrew *Abaddon*

POINT OF INTEREST

Job 28:23

In a world that worships
knowledge but desperately
needs wisdom, where do we
go to find it? We begin with
the One who knows everything—God.
Jump ahead to Proverbs 1:7 and James 1:5
for additional insights.

²²After I had spoken, they spoke no
more;
my words fell gently on their ears.
²³They waited for me as for showers
and drank in my words as the
spring rain.
²⁴When I smiled at them, they scarcely
believed it;
the light of my face was precious
to them.ᵃ
²⁵I chose the way for them and sat as
their chief;
I dwelt as a king among his troops;
I was like one who comforts
mourners.

30 "But now they mock me,
men younger than I,
whose fathers I would have disdained
to put with my sheep dogs.
²Of what use was the strength of their
hands to me,
since their vigor had gone from
them?
³Haggard from want and hunger,
they roamedᵇ the parched land
in desolate wastelands at night.
⁴In the brush they gathered salt herbs,
and their foodᶜ was the root of
the broom tree.
⁵They were banished from their fellow
men,
shouted at as if they were thieves.
⁶They were forced to live in the dry
stream beds,
among the rocks and in holes in
the ground.
⁷They brayed among the bushes
and huddled in the undergrowth.
⁸A base and nameless brood,
they were driven out of the land.

⁹"And now their sons mock me in
song;
I have become a byword among
them.
¹⁰They detest me and keep their
distance;
they do not hesitate to spit in my
face.
¹¹Now that God has unstrung my bow
and afflicted me,
they throw off restraint in my
presence.
¹²On my right the tribeᵈ attacks;
they lay snares for my feet,
they build their siege ramps against
me.
¹³They break up my road;
they succeed in destroying me—

without anyone's helping them.ᵉ
¹⁴They advance as through a gaping
breach;
amid the ruins they come rolling
in.
¹⁵Terrors overwhelm me;
my dignity is driven away as by
the wind,
my safety vanishes like a cloud.

¹⁶"And now my life ebbs away;
days of suffering grip me.
¹⁷Night pierces my bones;
my gnawing pains never rest.
¹⁸In his great power ⌊God⌋ becomes like
clothing to meᶠ;
he binds me like the neck of my
garment.
¹⁹He throws me into the mud,
and I am reduced to dust and
ashes.

²⁰"I cry out to you, O God, but you do
not answer;
I stand up, but you merely look at
me.
²¹You turn on me ruthlessly;
with the might of your hand you
attack me.
²²You snatch me up and drive me
before the wind;
you toss me about in the storm.
²³I know you will bring me down to
death,
to the place appointed for all the
living.

²⁴"Surely no one lays a hand on a
broken man
when he cries for help in his
distress.
²⁵Have I not wept for those in trouble?
Has not my soul grieved for the
poor?
²⁶Yet when I hoped for good, evil
came;
when I looked for light, then came
darkness.
²⁷The churning inside me never stops;
days of suffering confront me.
²⁸I go about blackened, but not by the
sun;
I stand up in the assembly and cry
for help.
²⁹I have become a brother of jackals,

ᵃ24 The meaning of the Hebrew for this clause is
uncertain.   ᵇ3 Or gnawed   ᶜ4 Or fuel
ᵈ12 The meaning of the Hebrew for this word is
uncertain.   ᵉ13 Or me. / 'No one can help him,'
⌊they say⌋.   ᶠ18 Hebrew; Septuagint ⌊God⌋ grasps
my clothing

a companion of owls.
30My skin grows black and peels;
   my body burns with fever.
31My harp is tuned to mourning,
   and my flute to the sound of
      wailing.

31 "I made a covenant with my eyes
   not to look lustfully at a girl.
2For what is man's lot from God
   above,
   his heritage from the Almighty on
      high?
3Is it not ruin for the wicked,
   disaster for those who do wrong?
4Does he not see my ways
   and count my every step?

5"If I have walked in falsehood
   or my foot has hurried after
      deceit—
6let God weigh me in honest scales
   and he will know that I am
      blameless—
7if my steps have turned from the
      path,
   if my heart has been led by my
      eyes,
   or if my hands have been defiled,
8then may others eat what I have
      sown,
   and may my crops be uprooted.

9"If my heart has been enticed by a
      woman,
   or if I have lurked at my
      neighbor's door,
10then may my wife grind another
      man's grain,
   and may other men sleep with her.
11For that would have been shameful,
   a sin to be judged.
12It is a fire that burns to
      Destruction*a*;
   it would have uprooted my
      harvest.

13"If I have denied justice to my
      menservants and
      maidservants
   when they had a grievance against
      me,
14what will I do when God confronts
      me?
   What will I answer when called to
      account?
15Did not he who made me in the
      womb make them?
   Did not the same one form us both
      within our mothers?

16"If I have denied the desires of the
      poor
   or let the eyes of the widow grow
      weary,
17if I have kept my bread to myself,
   not sharing it with the fatherless—
18but from my youth I reared him as
      would a father,
   and from my birth I guided the
      widow—
19if I have seen anyone perishing for
      lack of clothing,
   or a needy man without a garment,
20and his heart did not bless me
   for warming him with the fleece
      from my sheep,
21if I have raised my hand against the
      fatherless,
   knowing that I had influence in
      court,
22then let my arm fall from the
      shoulder,
   let it be broken off at the joint.
23For I dreaded destruction from God,
   and for fear of his splendor I could
      not do such things.

24"If I have put my trust in gold
   or said to pure gold, 'You are my
      security,'
25if I have rejoiced over my great
      wealth,
   the fortune my hands had gained,
26if I have regarded the sun in its
      radiance
   or the moon moving in splendor,
27so that my heart was secretly enticed
   and my hand offered them a kiss
      of homage,
28then these also would be sins to be
      judged,

a12 Hebrew *Abaddon*

POINT OF INTEREST

Job 31:1

What's wrong with just looking? Looking isn't the problem; lust is. Rather than
giving temptation a foothold,
Job chose not to look at all. Jesus indicated that Job's decision was a wise one.
Lustful looking, Jesus said, violates one of
the Ten Commandments (see Matthew
5:28).

Read Job 31:1–40
Key Verse Job 31:1

A Holy War

Our minds are battlefields. On one side of the fields are countless images bombarding us, countless messages that can twist and contort our thinking. Let's face it, what we see and hear has a powerful influence on our thinking. Advertisers on Madison Avenue bank on it, spending hundreds of millions of dollars convincing us to buy one product or another.

Against all those negative influences, one voice—God's holy voice—calls us to "be holy, because I am holy" (1 Peter 1:16). Job was a great example of personal holiness. He made a conscious decision to limit what he looked at, committing himself to moral purity.

In reality, the war is already won. When we trust in Jesus Christ as Savior, we are made clean and perfectly holy. God no longer sees us as sinful. And yet we need to work at growing in personal holiness by following the leading of the Holy Spirit, in whom we bear the fruit of self-control.

Digging Into the Word

1. What do the following passages teach you about God's holiness?—*Leviticus 11:44–45; Leviticus 20:7,26*
2. How are you challenged to live in holiness as you read the following passages?—*2 Corinthians 7:1; 1 Peter 1:14–15*

Action Challenge

Too often we get casual about what we let enter our minds through the window of our eyes. Take time to honestly evaluate what you are looking at. What books and magazines do you read? What movies do you see? Where do you wander on the Internet? Is it time to turn off the tube, change the channel, cancel the subscription? Ask yourself if you need to make a change today!

One Step Deeper

1 Corinthians 6:12–20; Ephesians 4:20–24

Go to page 583 for your next devotional reading.

for I would have been unfaithful to
God on high.

29"If I have rejoiced at my enemy's
        misfortune
    or gloated over the trouble that
        came to him—
30I have not allowed my mouth to sin
    by invoking a curse against his
        life—
31if the men of my household have
        never said,
    'Who has not had his fill of Job's
        meat?'—
32but no stranger had to spend the
        night in the street,
    for my door was always open to
        the traveler—
33if I have concealed my sin as men
        do,*a*
    by hiding my guilt in my heart
34because I so feared the crowd
    and so dreaded the contempt of
        the clans
    that I kept silent and would not go
        outside

35("Oh, that I had someone to hear me!
    I sign now my defense—let the
        Almighty answer me;
    let my accuser put his indictment
        in writing.
36Surely I would wear it on my
        shoulder,
    I would put it on like a crown.
37I would give him an account of my
        every step;
    like a prince I would approach
        him.)—

38"if my land cries out against me
    and all its furrows are wet with
        tears,
39if I have devoured its yield without
        payment
    or broken the spirit of its tenants,
40then let briers come up instead of
        wheat
    and weeds instead of barley."

The words of Job are ended.

Elihu

32 So these three men stopped answering Job, because he was righteous in
his own eyes. 2But Elihu son of Barakel
the Buzite, of the family of Ram, became
very angry with Job for justifying himself
rather than God. 3He was also angry with
the three friends, because they had found
no way to refute Job, and yet had condemned him.*b* 4Now Elihu had waited
before speaking to Job because they were
older than he. 5But when he saw that the
three men had nothing more to say, his
anger was aroused.

6So Elihu son of Barakel the Buzite
said:

"I am young in years,
    and you are old;
that is why I was fearful,
    not daring to tell you what I know.
7I thought, 'Age should speak;
    advanced years should teach
        wisdom.'
8But it is the spirit*c* in a man,
    the breath of the Almighty, that
        gives him understanding.
9It is not only the old*d* who are wise,
    not only the aged who understand
        what is right.

10"Therefore I say: Listen to me;
    I too will tell you what I know.
11I waited while you spoke,
    I listened to your reasoning;
    while you were searching for words,
12   I gave you my full attention.
    But not one of you has proved Job
        wrong;
    none of you has answered his
        arguments.
13Do not say, 'We have found wisdom;
    let God refute him, not man.'
14But Job has not marshaled his words
        against me,
    and I will not answer him with
        your arguments.

15"They are dismayed and have no
        more to say;
    words have failed them.
16Must I wait, now that they are silent,
    now that they stand there with no
        reply?
17I too will have my say;
    I too will tell what I know.
18For I am full of words,
    and the spirit within me compels
        me;
19inside I am like bottled-up wine,
    like new wineskins ready to burst.
20I must speak and find relief;
    I must open my lips and reply.
21I will show partiality to no one,
    nor will I flatter any man;

---

*a*33 Or as Adam did   *b*3 Masoretic Text; an
ancient Hebrew scribal tradition *Job, and so had
condemned God*   *c*8 Or *Spirit*; also in verse 18
*d*9 Or *many*; or *great*

²²for if I were skilled in flattery,
my Maker would soon take me
away.

33 "But now, Job, listen to my words;
pay attention to everything I say.
²I am about to open my mouth;
my words are on the tip of my
tongue.
³My words come from an upright
heart;
my lips sincerely speak what I
know.
⁴The Spirit of God has made me;
the breath of the Almighty gives
me life.
⁵Answer me then, if you can;
prepare yourself and confront me.
⁶I am just like you before God;
I too have been taken from clay.
⁷No fear of me should alarm you,
nor should my hand be heavy
upon you.

⁸"But you have said in my hearing—
I heard the very words—
⁹'I am pure and without sin;
I am clean and free from guilt.
¹⁰Yet God has found fault with me;
he considers me his enemy.
¹¹He fastens my feet in shackles;
he keeps close watch on all my
paths.'

¹²"But I tell you, in this you are not
right,
for God is greater than man.
¹³Why do you complain to him
that he answers none of man's
words*ᵃ*?
¹⁴For God does speak—now one way,
now another—
though man may not perceive it.
¹⁵In a dream, in a vision of the night,
when deep sleep falls on men
as they slumber in their beds,
¹⁶he may speak in their ears
and terrify them with warnings,
¹⁷to turn man from wrongdoing
and keep him from pride,
¹⁸to preserve his soul from the pit,ᵇ
his life from perishing by the
sword.ᶜ
¹⁹Or a man may be chastened on a bed
of pain
with constant distress in his bones,
²⁰so that his very being finds food
repulsive
and his soul loathes the choicest
meal.

²¹His flesh wastes away to nothing,
and his bones, once hidden, now
stick out.
²²His soul draws near to the pit,ᵈ
and his life to the messengers of
death.ᵉ

²³"Yet if there is an angel on his side
as a mediator, one out of a
thousand,
to tell a man what is right for him,
²⁴to be gracious to him and say,
'Spare him from going down to the
pitᶠ;
I have found a ransom for him'—
²⁵then his flesh is renewed like a
child's;
it is restored as in the days of his
youth.
²⁶He prays to God and finds favor with
him,
he sees God's face and shouts for
joy;
he is restored by God to his
righteous state.
²⁷Then he comes to men and says,
'I sinned, and perverted what was
right,
but I did not get what I deserved.
²⁸He redeemed my soul from going
down to the pit,ᵍ
and I will live to enjoy the light.'

²⁹"God does all these things to a
man—
twice, even three times—
³⁰to turn back his soul from the pit,ʰ

ᵃ13 Or *that he does not answer for any of his
actions*   ᵇ18 Or *preserve him from the grave*
ᶜ18 Or *from crossing the River*   ᵈ22 Or *He draws
near to the grave*   ᵉ22 Or *to the dead*   ᶠ24 Or
grave   ᵍ28 Or *redeemed me from going down to
the grave*   ʰ30 Or *turn him back from the grave*

POINT OF INTEREST

Job 33:28

Is the God of the Old
Testament different from
the God of the New Testa-
ment? The Old Testament
shows us a God of judgment, while the
New Testament reveals a God of grace. Yet
here, in one of the oldest books of the
Bible, God's grace shines clearly. God has
always been gracious, and he always will be.

that the light of life may shine on
    him.

31"Pay attention, Job, and listen to me;
    be silent, and I will speak.
32If you have anything to say, answer
    me;
    speak up, for I want you to be
      cleared.
33But if not, then listen to me;
    be silent, and I will teach you
      wisdom."

34 Then Elihu said:

2"Hear my words, you wise men;
    listen to me, you men of learning.
3For the ear tests words
    as the tongue tastes food.
4Let us discern for ourselves what is
    right;
    let us learn together what is good.

5"Job says, 'I am innocent,
    but God denies me justice.
6Although I am right,
    I am considered a liar;
  although I am guiltless,
    his arrow inflicts an incurable
      wound.'
7What man is like Job,
    who drinks scorn like water?
8He keeps company with evildoers;
    he associates with wicked men.
9For he says, 'It profits a man nothing
    when he tries to please God.'

10"So listen to me, you men of
    understanding.
    Far be it from God to do evil,
    from the Almighty to do wrong.
11He repays a man for what he has
    done;
    he brings upon him what his
      conduct deserves.
12It is unthinkable that God would do
    wrong,
    that the Almighty would pervert
      justice.
13Who appointed him over the earth?
    Who put him in charge of the
      whole world?
14If it were his intention
    and he withdrew his spirit*a* and
      breath,
15all mankind would perish together
    and man would return to the dust.

16"If you have understanding, hear this;
    listen to what I say.
17Can he who hates justice govern?

Will you condemn the just and
    mighty One?
18Is he not the One who says to kings,
    'You are worthless,'
    and to nobles, 'You are wicked,'
19who shows no partiality to princes
    and does not favor the rich over
      the poor,
    for they are all the work of his
      hands?
20They die in an instant, in the middle
    of the night;
    the people are shaken and they
      pass away;
    the mighty are removed without
      human hand.

21"His eyes are on the ways of men;
    he sees their every step.
22There is no dark place, no deep
    shadow,
    where evildoers can hide.
23God has no need to examine men
    further,
    that they should come before him
      for judgment.
24Without inquiry he shatters the
    mighty
    and sets up others in their place.
25Because he takes note of their deeds,
    he overthrows them in the night
    and they are crushed.
26He punishes them for their
    wickedness
    where everyone can see them,
27because they turned from following
    him
    and had no regard for any of his
      ways.
28They caused the cry of the poor to
    come before him,
    so that he heard the cry of the
      needy.
29But if he remains silent, who can
    condemn him?
    If he hides his face, who can see
      him?
    Yet he is over man and nation alike,
30   to keep a godless man from ruling,
    from laying snares for the people.

31"Suppose a man says to God,
    'I am guilty but will offend no
      more.
32Teach me what I cannot see;
    if I have done wrong, I will not do
      so again.'

a 14 Or *Spirit*

³³Should God then reward you on your
terms,
when you refuse to repent?
You must decide, not I;
so tell me what you know.

³⁴"Men of understanding declare,
wise men who hear me say to me,
³⁵'Job speaks without knowledge;
his words lack insight.'
³⁶Oh, that Job might be tested to the
utmost
for answering like a wicked man!
³⁷To his sin he adds rebellion;
scornfully he claps his hands
among us
and multiplies his words against
God."

35 Then Elihu said:

²"Do you think this is just?
You say, 'I will be cleared by
God.ᵃ'
³Yet you ask him, 'What profit is it to
me,ᵇ
and what do I gain by not
sinning?'

⁴"I would like to reply to you
and to your friends with you.
⁵Look up at the heavens and see;
gaze at the clouds so high above
you.
⁶If you sin, how does that affect him?
If your sins are many, what does
that do to him?
⁷If you are righteous, what do you
give to him,
or what does he receive from your
hand?
⁸Your wickedness affects only a man
like yourself,
and your righteousness only the
sons of men.

⁹"Men cry out under a load of
oppression;
they plead for relief from the arm
of the powerful.
¹⁰But no one says, 'Where is God my
Maker,
who gives songs in the night,
¹¹who teaches more to us than toᶜ the
beasts of the earth
and makes us wiser thanᵈ the
birds of the air?'
¹²He does not answer when men cry
out

because of the arrogance of the
wicked.
¹³Indeed, God does not listen to their
empty plea;
the Almighty pays no attention to
it.
¹⁴How much less, then, will he listen
when you say that you do not see
him,
that your case is before him
and you must wait for him,
¹⁵and further, that his anger never
punishes
and he does not take the least
notice of wickedness.ᵉ
¹⁶So Job opens his mouth with empty
talk;
without knowledge he multiplies
words."

36 Elihu continued:

²"Bear with me a little longer and I
will show you
that there is more to be said in
God's behalf.
³I get my knowledge from afar;
I will ascribe justice to my Maker.
⁴Be assured that my words are not
false;
one perfect in knowledge is with
you.

⁵"God is mighty, but does not despise
men;
he is mighty, and firm in his
purpose.
⁶He does not keep the wicked alive

ᵃ2 Or *My righteousness is more than God's*
ᵇ3 Or *you*   ᶜ11 Or *teaches us by*   ᵈ11 Or *us
wise by*   ᵉ15 Symmachus, Theodotion and
Vulgate; the meaning of the Hebrew for this word is
uncertain.

POINT OF INTEREST

Job 34:33

Children often complain,
"That's not fair!" A child's
estimation of fairness depends on his or her own rules
manipulating the outcome. Often we are
like whining children, approaching God on
terms we have designed to manipulate a
positive result. The Bible says we cannot
come to God on *our* terms, but only on *his*.

but gives the afflicted their rights.
⁷He does not take his eyes off the
righteous;
he enthrones them with kings
and exalts them forever.
⁸But if men are bound in chains,
held fast by cords of affliction,
⁹he tells them what they have done—
that they have sinned arrogantly.
¹⁰He makes them listen to correction
and commands them to repent of
their evil.
¹¹If they obey and serve him,
they will spend the rest of their
days in prosperity
and their years in contentment.
¹²But if they do not listen,
they will perish by the sword*ᵃ*
and die without knowledge.

¹³"The godless in heart harbor
resentment;
even when he fetters them, they do
not cry for help.
¹⁴They die in their youth,
among male prostitutes of the
shrines.
¹⁵But those who suffer he delivers in
their suffering;
he speaks to them in their
affliction.

¹⁶"He is wooing you from the jaws of
distress
to a spacious place free from
restriction,
to the comfort of your table laden
with choice food.
¹⁷But now you are laden with the
judgment due the wicked;
judgment and justice have taken
hold of you.
¹⁸Be careful that no one entices you by
riches;
do not let a large bribe turn you
aside.
¹⁹Would your wealth
or even all your mighty efforts
sustain you so you would not be in
distress?
²⁰Do not long for the night,
to drag people away from their
homes.*ᵇ*
²¹Beware of turning to evil,
which you seem to prefer to
affliction.

²²"God is exalted in his power.
Who is a teacher like him?
²³Who has prescribed his ways for him,
or said to him, 'You have done
wrong'?
²⁴Remember to extol his work,
which men have praised in song.
²⁵All mankind has seen it;
men gaze on it from afar.
²⁶How great is God—beyond our
understanding!
The number of his years is past
finding out.

²⁷"He draws up the drops of water,
which distill as rain to the
streams*ᶜ*;
²⁸the clouds pour down their moisture
and abundant showers fall on
mankind.
²⁹Who can understand how he spreads
out the clouds,
how he thunders from his pavilion?
³⁰See how he scatters his lightning
about him,
bathing the depths of the sea.
³¹This is the way he governs*ᵈ* the
nations
and provides food in abundance.
³²He fills his hands with lightning
and commands it to strike its
mark.
³³His thunder announces the coming
storm;
even the cattle make known its
approach.*ᵉ*

37 "At this my heart pounds
and leaps from its place.
²Listen! Listen to the roar of his voice,
to the rumbling that comes from
his mouth.
³He unleashes his lightning beneath
the whole heaven
and sends it to the ends of the
earth.
⁴After that comes the sound of his
roar;
he thunders with his majestic
voice.
When his voice resounds,
he holds nothing back.
⁵God's voice thunders in marvelous
ways;
he does great things beyond our
understanding.
⁶He says to the snow, 'Fall on the
earth,'

ᵃ12 Or *will cross the River*   *ᵇ20* The meaning of
the Hebrew for verses 18-20 is uncertain.
ᶜ27 Or *distill from the mist as rain*   *ᵈ31* Or
nourishes   *ᵉ33* Or *announces his coming— / the
One zealous against evil*

and to the rain shower, 'Be a
    mighty downpour.'
[7]So that all men he has made may
    know his work,
    he stops every man from his
      labor.[a]
[8]The animals take cover;
    they remain in their dens.
[9]The tempest comes out from its
    chamber,
    the cold from the driving winds.
[10]The breath of God produces ice,
    and the broad waters become
      frozen.
[11]He loads the clouds with moisture;
    he scatters his lightning through
      them.
[12]At his direction they swirl around
    over the face of the whole earth
    to do whatever he commands
      them.
[13]He brings the clouds to punish men,
    or to water his earth[b] and show
      his love.

[14]"Listen to this, Job;
    stop and consider God's wonders.
[15]Do you know how God controls the
    clouds
    and makes his lightning flash?
[16]Do you know how the clouds hang
    poised,
    those wonders of him who is
      perfect in knowledge?
[17]You who swelter in your clothes
    when the land lies hushed under
      the south wind,
[18]can you join him in spreading out the
    skies,
    hard as a mirror of cast bronze?

[19]"Tell us what we should say to him;
    we cannot draw up our case
      because of our darkness.
[20]Should he be told that I want to
    speak?
    Would any man ask to be
      swallowed up?
[21]Now no one can look at the sun,
    bright as it is in the skies
    after the wind has swept them
      clean.
[22]Out of the north he comes in golden
    splendor;
    God comes in awesome majesty.
[23]The Almighty is beyond our reach
    and exalted in power;
    in his justice and great
      righteousness, he does not
      oppress.

[24]Therefore, men revere him,
    for does he not have regard for all
      the wise in heart?[c] "

The LORD Speaks

38 Then the LORD answered Job out of
    the storm. He said:

[2]"Who is this that darkens my counsel
    with words without knowledge?
[3]Brace yourself like a man;
    I will question you,
    and you shall answer me.

[4]"Where were you when I laid the
    earth's foundation?
    Tell me, if you understand.
[5]Who marked off its dimensions?
    Surely you know!
    Who stretched a measuring line
      across it?
[6]On what were its footings set,
    or who laid its cornerstone—
[7]while the morning stars sang together
    and all the angels[d] shouted for
      joy?

[8]"Who shut up the sea behind doors
    when it burst forth from the
      womb,
[9]when I made the clouds its garment
    and wrapped it in thick darkness,
[10]when I fixed limits for it
    and set its doors and bars in place,
[11]when I said, 'This far you may come
    and no farther;
    here is where your proud waves
      halt'?

[12]"Have you ever given orders to the
    morning,
    or shown the dawn its place,

---

[a]7 Or / he fills all men with fear by his power
[b]13 Or to favor them   [c]24 Or for he does not
have regard for any who think they are wise.
[d]7 Hebrew the sons of God

POINT OF INTEREST

Job 38:4

In legal matters, an eyewitness account bears a lot of
weight. Scientists' attempts
to explain the origins of the
universe lack this key element. They
weren't there at the beginning! But God
was. He's our eyewitness.

¹³that it might take the earth by the
   edges
and shake the wicked out of it?
¹⁴The earth takes shape like clay under
   a seal;
   its features stand out like those of
     a garment.
¹⁵The wicked are denied their light,
   and their upraised arm is broken.

¹⁶"Have you journeyed to the springs
   of the sea
   or walked in the recesses of the
     deep?
¹⁷Have the gates of death been shown
   to you?
   Have you seen the gates of the
     shadow of death*ᵃ*?
¹⁸Have you comprehended the vast
   expanses of the earth?
   Tell me, if you know all this.

¹⁹"What is the way to the abode of
   light?
   And where does darkness reside?
²⁰Can you take them to their places?
   Do you know the paths to their
     dwellings?
²¹Surely you know, for you were
   already born!
   You have lived so many years!

²²"Have you entered the storehouses of
   the snow
   or seen the storehouses of the hail,
²³which I reserve for times of trouble,
   for days of war and battle?
²⁴What is the way to the place where
   the lightning is dispersed,
   or the place where the east winds
     are scattered over the earth?
²⁵Who cuts a channel for the torrents
   of rain,
   and a path for the thunderstorm,
²⁶to water a land where no man lives,
   a desert with no one in it,
²⁷to satisfy a desolate wasteland
   and make it sprout with grass?
²⁸Does the rain have a father?
   Who fathers the drops of dew?
²⁹From whose womb comes the ice?
   Who gives birth to the frost from
     the heavens
³⁰when the waters become hard as
   stone,
   when the surface of the deep is
     frozen?

³¹"Can you bind the beautifulᵇ
   Pleiades?
   Can you loose the cords of Orion?

³²Can you bring forth the constellations
   in their seasonsᶜ
   or lead out the Bearᵈ with its
     cubs?
³³Do you know the laws of the
   heavens?
   Can you set up ⌐God'sᵉ⌐ dominion
     over the earth?

³⁴"Can you raise your voice to the
   clouds
   and cover yourself with a flood of
     water?
³⁵Do you send the lightning bolts on
   their way?
   Do they report to you, 'Here we
     are'?
³⁶Who endowed the heartᶠ with
   wisdom
   or gave understanding to the
     mindᶠ?
³⁷Who has the wisdom to count the
   clouds?
   Who can tip over the water jars of
     the heavens
³⁸when the dust becomes hard
   and the clods of earth stick
     together?

³⁹"Do you hunt the prey for the lioness
   and satisfy the hunger of the lions
⁴⁰when they crouch in their dens
   or lie in wait in a thicket?
⁴¹Who provides food for the raven
   when its young cry out to God
   and wander about for lack of food?

39 "Do you know when the mountain
   goats give birth?
   Do you watch when the doe bears
     her fawn?
²Do you count the months till they
   bear?
   Do you know the time they give
     birth?
³They crouch down and bring forth
   their young;
   their labor pains are ended.
⁴Their young thrive and grow strong
   in the wilds;
   they leave and do not return.

⁵"Who let the wild donkey go free?
   Who untied his ropes?
⁶I gave him the wasteland as his
   home,

ᵃ17 Or *gates of deep shadows*   ᵇ31 Or *the
twinkling;* or *the chains of the*   ᶜ32 Or *the
morning star in its season*   ᵈ32 Or *out Leo*
ᵉ33 Or *his;* or *their*   ᶠ36 The meaning of the
Hebrew for this word is uncertain.

the salt flats as his habitat.
⁷He laughs at the commotion in the
town;
he does not hear a driver's shout.
⁸He ranges the hills for his pasture
and searches for any green thing.

⁹"Will the wild ox consent to serve
you?
Will he stay by your manger at
night?
¹⁰Can you hold him to the furrow with
a harness?
Will he till the valleys behind you?
¹¹Will you rely on him for his great
strength?
Will you leave your heavy work to
him?
¹²Can you trust him to bring in your
grain
and gather it to your threshing
floor?

¹³"The wings of the ostrich flap
joyfully,
but they cannot compare with the
pinions and feathers of the
stork.
¹⁴She lays her eggs on the ground
and lets them warm in the sand,
¹⁵unmindful that a foot may crush
them,
that some wild animal may trample
them.
¹⁶She treats her young harshly, as if
they were not hers;
she cares not that her labor was in
vain,
¹⁷for God did not endow her with
wisdom
or give her a share of good sense.
¹⁸Yet when she spreads her feathers to
run,
she laughs at horse and rider.

¹⁹"Do you give the horse his strength
or clothe his neck with a flowing
mane?
²⁰Do you make him leap like a locust,
striking terror with his proud
snorting?
²¹He paws fiercely, rejoicing in his
strength,
and charges into the fray.
²²He laughs at fear, afraid of nothing;
he does not shy away from the
sword.
²³The quiver rattles against his side,
along with the flashing spear and
lance.
²⁴In frenzied excitement he eats up the
ground;
he cannot stand still when the
trumpet sounds.
²⁵At the blast of the trumpet he snorts,
'Aha!'
He catches the scent of battle from
afar,
the shout of commanders and the
battle cry.

²⁶"Does the hawk take flight by your
wisdom
and spread his wings toward the
south?
²⁷Does the eagle soar at your command
and build his nest on high?
²⁸He dwells on a cliff and stays there at
night;
a rocky crag is his stronghold.
²⁹From there he seeks out his food;
his eyes detect it from afar.
³⁰His young ones feast on blood,
and where the slain are, there is
he."

40 The LORD said to Job:

²"Will the one who contends with the
Almighty correct him?
Let him who accuses God answer
him!"

³Then Job answered the LORD:

⁴"I am unworthy—how can I reply to
you?
I put my hand over my mouth.
⁵I spoke once, but I have no answer—
twice, but I will say no more."

⁶Then the LORD spoke to Job out of the
storm:

⁷"Brace yourself like a man;

POINT OF INTEREST

Job 40:2

This verse makes us stop and think for a minute: God designed everything from DNA to thermodynamics. Do we really think we know more about our own lives than he does? He knows what he's doing and he is never late. He won't fail us.

I will question you,
and you shall answer me.
8"Would you discredit my justice?
Would you condemn me to justify
yourself?
9Do you have an arm like God's,
and can your voice thunder like
his?
10Then adorn yourself with glory and
splendor,
and clothe yourself in honor and
majesty.
11Unleash the fury of your wrath,
look at every proud man and bring
him low,
12look at every proud man and humble
him,
crush the wicked where they
stand.
13Bury them all in the dust together;
shroud their faces in the grave.
14Then I myself will admit to you
that your own right hand can save
you.

15"Look at the behemoth,*a*
which I made along with you
and which feeds on grass like an
ox.
16What strength he has in his loins,
what power in the muscles of his
belly!
17His tail*b* sways like a cedar;
the sinews of his thighs are
close-knit.
18His bones are tubes of bronze,
his limbs like rods of iron.
19He ranks first among the works of
God,
yet his Maker can approach him
with his sword.
20The hills bring him their produce,
and all the wild animals play
nearby.
21Under the lotus plants he lies,
hidden among the reeds in the
marsh.
22The lotuses conceal him in their
shadow;
the poplars by the stream surround
him.
23When the river rages, he is not
alarmed;
he is secure, though the Jordan
should surge against his
mouth.
24Can anyone capture him by the
eyes,*c*
or trap him and pierce his nose?

41 "Can you pull in the leviathan*d*
with a fishhook
or tie down his tongue with a
rope?
2Can you put a cord through his nose
or pierce his jaw with a hook?
3Will he keep begging you for mercy?
Will he speak to you with gentle
words?
4Will he make an agreement with you
for you to take him as your slave
for life?
5Can you make a pet of him like a
bird
or put him on a leash for your
girls?
6Will traders barter for him?
Will they divide him up among the
merchants?
7Can you fill his hide with harpoons
or his head with fishing spears?
8If you lay a hand on him,
you will remember the struggle
and never do it again!
9Any hope of subduing him is false;
the mere sight of him is
overpowering.
10No one is fierce enough to rouse him.
Who then is able to stand against
me?
11Who has a claim against me that I
must pay?
Everything under heaven belongs
to me.

12"I will not fail to speak of his limbs,
his strength and his graceful form.
13Who can strip off his outer coat?
Who would approach him with a
bridle?
14Who dares open the doors of his
mouth,
ringed about with his fearsome
teeth?
15His back has*e* rows of shields
tightly sealed together;
16each is so close to the next
that no air can pass between.
17They are joined fast to one another;
they cling together and cannot be
parted.
18His snorting throws out flashes of
light;
his eyes are like the rays of dawn.
19Firebrands stream from his mouth;

*a*15 Possibly the hippopotamus or the elephant
*b*17 Possibly trunk   *c*24 Or *by a water hole*
*d*1 Possibly the crocodile   *e*15 Or *His pride
is his*

sparks of fire shoot out.
²⁰Smoke pours from his nostrils
  as from a boiling pot over a fire of
    reeds.
²¹His breath sets coals ablaze,
  and flames dart from his mouth.
²²Strength resides in his neck;
  dismay goes before him.
²³The folds of his flesh are tightly
    joined;
  they are firm and immovable.
²⁴His chest is hard as rock,
  hard as a lower millstone.
²⁵When he rises up, the mighty are
    terrified;
  they retreat before his thrashing.
²⁶The sword that reaches him has no
    effect,
  nor does the spear or the dart or
    the javelin.
²⁷Iron he treats like straw
  and bronze like rotten wood.
²⁸Arrows do not make him flee;
  slingstones are like chaff to him.
²⁹A club seems to him but a piece of
    straw;
  he laughs at the rattling of the
    lance.
³⁰His undersides are jagged potsherds,
  leaving a trail in the mud like a
    threshing sledge.
³¹He makes the depths churn like a
    boiling caldron
  and stirs up the sea like a pot of
    ointment.
³²Behind him he leaves a glistening
    wake;
  one would think the deep had
    white hair.
³³Nothing on earth is his equal—
  a creature without fear.
³⁴He looks down on all that are
    haughty;
  he is king over all that are proud."

Job

42 Then Job replied to the LORD:

²"I know that you can do all things;
  no plan of yours can be thwarted.
³⌞You asked,⌟ 'Who is this that
    obscures my counsel without
    knowledge?'
  Surely I spoke of things I did not
    understand,
  things too wonderful for me to
    know.

⁴⌞"You said,⌟ 'Listen now, and I will
    speak;
  I will question you,
    and you shall answer me.'
⁵My ears had heard of you
  but now my eyes have seen you.
⁶Therefore I despise myself
  and repent in dust and ashes."

Epilogue

⁷After the LORD had said these things to Job, he said to Eliphaz the Temanite, "I am angry with you and your two friends, because you have not spoken of me what is right, as my servant Job has. ⁸So now take seven bulls and seven rams and go to my servant Job and sacrifice a burnt offering for yourselves. My servant Job will pray for you, and I will accept his prayer and not deal with you according to your folly. You have not spoken of me what is right, as my servant Job has." ⁹So Eliphaz the Temanite, Bildad the Shuhite and Zophar the Naamathite did what the LORD told them; and the LORD accepted Job's prayer.

¹⁰After Job had prayed for his friends, the LORD made him prosperous again and gave him twice as much as he had before. ¹¹All his brothers and sisters and everyone who had known him before came and ate with him in his house. They comforted and consoled him over all the trouble the LORD had brought upon him, and each one gave him a piece of silver[a] and a gold ring.

¹²The LORD blessed the latter part of Job's life more than the first. He had fourteen thousand sheep, six thousand camels, a thousand yoke of oxen and a thousand donkeys. ¹³And he also had seven sons and three daughters. ¹⁴The first daughter he named Jemimah, the second Keziah and the third Keren-Happuch. ¹⁵Nowhere in all the land were there found women as beautiful as Job's daughters, and their father granted them an inheritance along with their brothers.

¹⁶After this, Job lived a hundred and forty years; he saw his children and their children to the fourth generation. ¹⁷And so he died, old and full of years.

---

[a]11 Hebrew *him a kesitah*; a kesitah was a unit of money of unknown weight and value.

God deserves our most honest and sincere worship. Perhaps nothing reflects who we are as much as the way in which we express our most intimate thoughts about him. Psalms is a collection of prayers and songs written by a variety of authors who voice their praises, fears and questions. The psalms help us discover what it means to be "real" with God, for we often hear our own emotions reflected in these timeless songs. Through the psalms we discover what it means to "worship [him] in spirit and in truth" (John 4:24).

PSALMS

BOOK I
Psalms 1–41

Psalm 1

¹Blessed is the man
   who does not walk in the counsel
     of the wicked
or stand in the way of sinners
   or sit in the seat of mockers.
²But his delight is in the law of the
   LORD,
   and on his law he meditates day
     and night.
³He is like a tree planted by streams of
   water,
   which yields its fruit in season
and whose leaf does not wither.
   Whatever he does prospers.

⁴Not so the wicked!

They are like chaff
   that the wind blows away.
⁵Therefore the wicked will not stand
   in the judgment,
   nor sinners in the assembly of the
     righteous.

⁶For the LORD watches over the way of
   the righteous,
   but the way of the wicked will
     perish.

Psalm 2

¹Why do the nations conspire[a]
   and the peoples plot in vain?
²The kings of the earth take their
   stand
   and the rulers gather together
against the LORD

[a]1 Hebrew; Septuagint *rage*

and against his Anointed One. *a*

³"Let us break their chains," they say,
"and throw off their fetters."

⁴The One enthroned in heaven laughs;
the Lord scoffs at them.
⁵Then he rebukes them in his anger
and terrifies them in his wrath,
saying,
⁶"I have installed my King *b*
on Zion, my holy hill."

⁷I will proclaim the decree of the LORD:

He said to me, "You are my Son *c*;
today I have become your
Father. *d*
⁸Ask of me,
and I will make the nations your
inheritance,
the ends of the earth your
possession.
⁹You will rule them with an iron
scepter *e*;
you will dash them to pieces like
pottery."

¹⁰Therefore, you kings, be wise;
be warned, you rulers of the earth.
¹¹Serve the LORD with fear
and rejoice with trembling.
¹²Kiss the Son, lest he be angry
and you be destroyed in your way,
for his wrath can flare up in a
moment.
Blessed are all who take refuge in
him.

Psalm 3

A psalm of David. When he fled from
his son Absalom.

¹O LORD, how many are my foes!
How many rise up against me!
²Many are saying of me,
"God will not deliver him."   *Selah f*

---

a2 Or *anointed one*   *b6* Or *king*   *c7* Or *son*;
also in verse 12   *d7* Or *have begotten you*
e9 Or *will break them with a rod of iron*
f2 A word of uncertain meaning, occurring
frequently in the Psalms; possibly a musical term

MONDAY

Read Psalms 1:1—2:12
Key Verses Psalm 1:1–3

Putting Down Roots – Sharla Walstrom

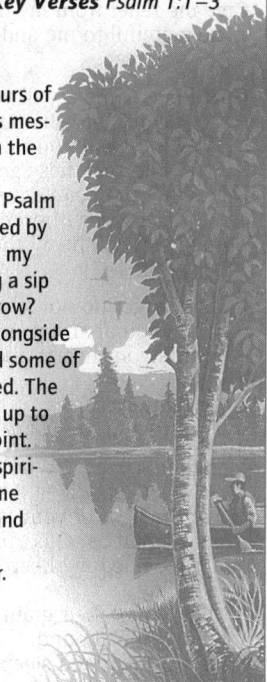

I dragged myself to church one morning after only a few hours of
sleep. The fog inside my head obscured most of the pastor's message. But one of his questions burned into my mind through the
haze: "How are your roots?"

The pastor was talking about my relationship with God. Psalm
1:3 says that one who loves God's Word is "like a tree planted by
streams of water." Was I spending time in the Word, sinking my
roots deep enough to get nourishment? Or was I just taking a sip
now and then, absorbing too little for our relationship to grow?

When I got back to my dorm, I noticed the large trees alongside
the street. A recent storm had passed through the area and some of
the smaller trees had been knocked over, their roots exposed. The
larger trees had stayed strong and upright. They had stood up to
the storm. They were a vivid picture of the pastor's main point.

What "storms" will I encounter in my life? Will I still be spiritually standing afterward? My prayer is that God will help me
"delight . . . in the law of the LORD," to meditate on it "day and
night" (Psalm 1:2), so I don't have to be afraid of the high
winds and rain—or any of the difficulties I might encounter.

A Deeper Look
Psalm 119:72; John 15:5–8; Colossians 2:6–7

Go to page 585 for your next devotional reading.

³But you are a shield around me,
> O LORD;
> you bestow glory on me and lift^a
> up my head.

⁴To the LORD I cry aloud,
> and he answers me from his holy
> hill.   *Selah*

⁵I lie down and sleep;
> I wake again, because the LORD
> sustains me.

⁶I will not fear the tens of thousands
> drawn up against me on every
> side.

⁷Arise, O LORD!
> Deliver me, O my God!
> Strike all my enemies on the jaw;
> break the teeth of the wicked.

⁸From the LORD comes deliverance.
> May your blessing be on your
> people.   *Selah*

Psalm 4

For the director of music. With stringed
instruments. A psalm of David.

¹Answer me when I call to you,
> O my righteous God.
> Give me relief from my distress;
> be merciful to me and hear my
> prayer.

²How long, O men, will you turn my
> glory into shame^b?
> How long will you love delusions
> and seek false gods^c?   *Selah*

³Know that the LORD has set apart the
> godly for himself;
> the LORD will hear when I call to
> him.

⁴In your anger do not sin;
> when you are on your beds,
> search your hearts and be silent.
>   *Selah*

⁵Offer right sacrifices
> and trust in the LORD.

⁶Many are asking, "Who can show us
> any good?"
> Let the light of your face shine
> upon us, O LORD.

⁷You have filled my heart with greater
> joy
> than when their grain and new
> wine abound.

⁸I will lie down and sleep in peace,
> for you alone, O LORD,
> make me dwell in safety.

Psalm 5

For the director of music. For flutes.
A psalm of David.

¹Give ear to my words, O LORD,
> consider my sighing.

²Listen to my cry for help,
> my King and my God,
> for to you I pray.

³In the morning, O LORD, you hear my
> voice;
> in the morning I lay my requests
> before you
> and wait in expectation.

⁴You are not a God who takes
> pleasure in evil;
> with you the wicked cannot dwell.

⁵The arrogant cannot stand in your
> presence;
> you hate all who do wrong.

⁶You destroy those who tell lies;
> bloodthirsty and deceitful men
> the LORD abhors.

⁷But I, by your great mercy,
> will come into your house;
> in reverence will I bow down
> toward your holy temple.

⁸Lead me, O LORD, in your
> righteousness
> because of my enemies—
> make straight your way before me.

⁹Not a word from their mouth can be
> trusted;
> their heart is filled with
> destruction.
> Their throat is an open grave;
> with their tongue they speak
> deceit.

¹⁰Declare them guilty, O God!
> Let their intrigues be their
> downfall.
> Banish them for their many sins,
> for they have rebelled against you.

¹¹But let all who take refuge in you be
> glad;
> let them ever sing for joy.
> Spread your protection over them,
> that those who love your name
> may rejoice in you.

¹²For surely, O LORD, you bless the
> righteous;

---

^a3 Or LORD, / my Glorious One, who lifts   ^b2 Or
you dishonor my Glorious One   ^c2 Or seek lies

you surround them with your favor
  as with a shield.

Psalm 6

For the director of music. With stringed
instruments. According to *sheminith.* [a]
A psalm of David.

[1] O LORD, do not rebuke me in your
    anger
  or discipline me in your wrath.
[2] Be merciful to me, LORD, for I am
    faint;
  O LORD, heal me, for my bones are
    in agony.
[3] My soul is in anguish.
  How long, O LORD, how long?

[4] Turn, O LORD, and deliver me;
  save me because of your unfailing
    love.

[5] No one remembers you when he is
    dead.
  Who praises you from the grave [b]?

[6] I am worn out from groaning;
  all night long I flood my bed with
    weeping
  and drench my couch with tears.
[7] My eyes grow weak with sorrow;
  they fail because of all my foes.

[8] Away from me, all you who do evil,
  for the LORD has heard my
    weeping.
[9] The LORD has heard my cry for mercy;
  the LORD accepts my prayer.
[10] All my enemies will be ashamed and
    dismayed;

[a] Title: Probably a musical term   [b] 5 Hebrew
Sheol

TUESDAY

Read *Psalm 5:1–12*
Key Verse *Psalm 5:3*

The Only One Who Can Help – Don Lenze

The second my alarm went off that morning, I knew I had to get up.
I wanted to be first in line. I *needed* to be first in line.

Perhaps you've been where I was on that day. Spring semester.
Senior year. Late registration for classes. If I didn't get this one specific class, I wouldn't graduate. I had to talk to someone in the Reg-
istrar's office who was willing and had the authority to help me. This
request was so important, I just had to hear a yes! I needed to find
that person—the only one who could help.

As I reflect on that morning, I wonder if I feel that same urgency
about finding God. I know I need him before anything else. While
there is no bad time to talk to God, King David seemed to opt for
the morning (see Psalm 5:3). By beginning his day with God, David
was saying, "God, I need to talk to you. Only you can deal with my
requests. Talking to you is the first item on the list of all I have to
do today. You are the author of my day, and I look forward to what
you are going to do."

God has both the willingness to listen to us and the authority to
meet all of our needs. Like David, a master of prayer, we can pray, "I
call on you, O God, for you will answer me; give ear to me and hear
my prayer. Show the wonder of your great love . . . And I—in righteousness I will see your face; when I awake, I will be satisfied with
seeing your likeness" (Psalm 17:6–7,15).

(Oh, by the way, I got the class!)

A Deeper Look
Isaiah 50:4; Mark 1:35

Go to page 590 for your next devotional reading.

they will turn back in sudden
disgrace.

Psalm 7

A *shiggaion*[a] of David, which he sang
to the Lord concerning Cush,
a Benjamite.

¹O Lord my God, I take refuge in you;
save and deliver me from all who
pursue me,
²or they will tear me like a lion
and rip me to pieces with no one
to rescue me.

³O Lord my God, if I have done this
and there is guilt on my hands—
⁴if I have done evil to him who is at
peace with me
or without cause have robbed my
foe—
⁵then let my enemy pursue and
overtake me;
let him trample my life to the
ground
and make me sleep in the dust.
                                        Selah

⁶Arise, O Lord, in your anger;
rise up against the rage of my
enemies.
Awake, my God; decree justice.
⁷Let the assembled peoples gather
around you.
Rule over them from on high;
8   let the Lord judge the peoples.
Judge me, O Lord, according to my
righteousness,
according to my integrity, O Most
High.
⁹O righteous God,
who searches minds and hearts,
bring to an end the violence of the
wicked
and make the righteous secure.

¹⁰My shield[b] is God Most High,
who saves the upright in heart.
¹¹God is a righteous judge,
a God who expresses his wrath
every day.
¹²If he does not relent,
he[c] will sharpen his sword;
he will bend and string his bow.
¹³He has prepared his deadly weapons;
he makes ready his flaming
arrows.

¹⁴He who is pregnant with evil

and conceives trouble gives birth
to disillusionment.
¹⁵He who digs a hole and scoops it out
falls into the pit he has made.
¹⁶The trouble he causes recoils on
himself;
his violence comes down on his
own head.

¹⁷I will give thanks to the Lord because
of his righteousness
and will sing praise to the name of
the Lord Most High.

Psalm 8

For the director of music. According to
gittith.[d] A psalm of David.

¹O Lord, our Lord,
how majestic is your name in all
the earth!

You have set your glory
above the heavens.
²From the lips of children and infants
you have ordained praise[e]
because of your enemies,
to silence the foe and the avenger.

³When I consider your heavens,
the work of your fingers,
the moon and the stars,
which you have set in place,
⁴what is man that you are mindful of
him,
the son of man that you care for
him?
⁵You made him a little lower than the
heavenly beings[f]
and crowned him with glory and
honor.

[a]Title: Probably a literary or musical term
[b]10 Or *sovereign*   [c]12 Or *If a man does not
repent, / God*   [d]Title: Probably a musical term
[e]2 Or *strength*   [f]5 Or *than God*

POINT OF INTEREST

Psalm 8:2

You're never too young to
know God and praise him.
Read Matthew 21:15–16 to
see how Jesus used this passage when he was rebuked by the chief
priests and teachers of the law.

6You made him ruler over the works
of your hands;
you put everything under his feet:
7all flocks and herds,
and the beasts of the field,
8the birds of the air,
and the fish of the sea,
all that swim the paths of the seas.

9O LORD, our Lord,
how majestic is your name in all
the earth!

Psalm 9[a]

For the director of music. To ⌐the tune
of⌐ "The Death of the Son." A psalm
of David.

1I will praise you, O LORD, with all my
heart;
I will tell of all your wonders.
2I will be glad and rejoice in you;
I will sing praise to your name,
O Most High.

3My enemies turn back;
they stumble and perish before
you.
4For you have upheld my right and
my cause;
you have sat on your throne,
judging righteously.
5You have rebuked the nations and
destroyed the wicked;
you have blotted out their name
for ever and ever.
6Endless ruin has overtaken the
enemy,
you have uprooted their cities;
even the memory of them has
perished.

7The LORD reigns forever;
he has established his throne for
judgment.
8He will judge the world in
righteousness;
he will govern the peoples with
justice.
9The LORD is a refuge for the
oppressed,
a stronghold in times of trouble.
10Those who know your name will
trust in you,
for you, LORD, have never forsaken
those who seek you.

11Sing praises to the LORD, enthroned in
Zion;
proclaim among the nations what
he has done.
12For he who avenges blood
remembers;
he does not ignore the cry of the
afflicted.

13O LORD, see how my enemies
persecute me!
Have mercy and lift me up from
the gates of death,
14that I may declare your praises
in the gates of the Daughter of
Zion
and there rejoice in your salvation.
15The nations have fallen into the pit
they have dug;
their feet are caught in the net they
have hidden.
16The LORD is known by his justice;
the wicked are ensnared by the
work of their hands.
Higgaion. [b] *Selah*
17The wicked return to the grave,[c]
all the nations that forget God.
18But the needy will not always be
forgotten,
nor the hope of the afflicted ever
perish.

19Arise, O LORD, let not man triumph;
let the nations be judged in your
presence.
20Strike them with terror, O LORD;
let the nations know they are but
men.   *Selah*

Psalm 10[a]

1Why, O LORD, do you stand far off?
Why do you hide yourself in times
of trouble?

2In his arrogance the wicked man
hunts down the weak,
who are caught in the schemes he
devises.
3He boasts of the cravings of his heart;
he blesses the greedy and reviles
the LORD.
4In his pride the wicked does not seek
him;

---

aPsalms 9 and 10 may have been originally a single
acrostic poem, the stanzas of which begin with the
successive letters of the Hebrew alphabet. In the
Septuagint they constitute one psalm.   b16 Or
Meditation; possibly a musical notation
c17 Hebrew *Sheol*

in all his thoughts there is no room
for God.
[5]His ways are always prosperous;
he is haughty and your laws are
far from him;
he sneers at all his enemies.
[6]He says to himself, "Nothing will
shake me;
I'll always be happy and never
have trouble."
[7]His mouth is full of curses and lies
and threats;
trouble and evil are under his
tongue.
[8]He lies in wait near the villages;
from ambush he murders the
innocent,
watching in secret for his victims.
[9]He lies in wait like a lion in cover;
he lies in wait to catch the
helpless;
he catches the helpless and drags
them off in his net.
[10]His victims are crushed, they
collapse;
they fall under his strength.
[11]He says to himself, "God has
forgotten;
he covers his face and never sees."

[12]Arise, LORD! Lift up your hand,
O God.
Do not forget the helpless.
[13]Why does the wicked man revile
God?
Why does he say to himself,
"He won't call me to account"?
[14]But you, O God, do see trouble and
grief;
you consider it to take it in hand.
The victim commits himself to you;
you are the helper of the
fatherless.
[15]Break the arm of the wicked and evil
man;
call him to account for his
wickedness
that would not be found out.

[16]The LORD is King for ever and ever;
the nations will perish from his
land.
[17]You hear, O LORD, the desire of the
afflicted;
you encourage them, and you
listen to their cry,
[18]defending the fatherless and the
oppressed,
in order that man, who is of the
earth, may terrify no more.

Psalm 11

For the director of music. Of David.

[1]In the LORD I take refuge.
How then can you say to me:
"Flee like a bird to your mountain.
[2]For look, the wicked bend their bows;
they set their arrows against the
strings
to shoot from the shadows
at the upright in heart.
[3]When the foundations are being
destroyed,
what can the righteous do[a]?"

[4]The LORD is in his holy temple;
the LORD is on his heavenly throne.
He observes the sons of men;
his eyes examine them.
[5]The LORD examines the righteous,
but the wicked[b] and those who
love violence
his soul hates.
[6]On the wicked he will rain
fiery coals and burning sulfur;
a scorching wind will be their lot.

[7]For the LORD is righteous,
he loves justice;
upright men will see his face.

Psalm 12

For the director of music. According to
sheminith.[c] A psalm of David.

[1]Help, LORD, for the godly are no more;
the faithful have vanished from
among men.
[2]Everyone lies to his neighbor;
their flattering lips speak with
deception.

[3]May the LORD cut off all flattering lips
and every boastful tongue
[4]that says, "We will triumph with our
tongues;
we own our lips[d]—who is our
master?"

[5]"Because of the oppression of the
weak
and the groaning of the needy,
I will now arise," says the LORD.
"I will protect them from those
who malign them."

---

[a]3 Or *what is the Righteous One doing*　　[b]5 Or
The LORD, the Righteous One, examines the wicked, /
[c]Title: Probably a musical term　　[d]4 Or / *our
lips are our plowshares*

⁶And the words of the LORD are
flawless,
like silver refined in a furnace of
clay,
purified seven times.
⁷O LORD, you will keep us safe
and protect us from such people
forever.
⁸The wicked freely strut about
when what is vile is honored
among men.

Psalm 13

*For the director of music. A psalm
of David.*

¹How long, O LORD? Will you forget me
forever?
How long will you hide your face
from me?
²How long must I wrestle with my
thoughts
and every day have sorrow in my
heart?
How long will my enemy triumph
over me?

³Look on me and answer, O LORD my
God.
Give light to my eyes, or I will
sleep in death;
⁴my enemy will say, "I have overcome
him,"
and my foes will rejoice when I
fall.

⁵But I trust in your unfailing love;
my heart rejoices in your salvation.
⁶I will sing to the LORD,
for he has been good to me.

Psalm 14

For the director of music. Of David.

¹The fool*a* says in his heart,
"There is no God."
They are corrupt, their deeds are vile;
there is no one who does good.

²The LORD looks down from heaven
on the sons of men
to see if there are any who
understand,
any who seek God.
³All have turned aside,
they have together become corrupt;
there is no one who does good,
not even one.

⁴Will evildoers never learn—
those who devour my people as
men eat bread
and who do not call on the LORD?
⁵There they are, overwhelmed with
dread,
for God is present in the company
of the righteous.
⁶You evildoers frustrate the plans of
the poor,
but the LORD is their refuge.

⁷Oh, that salvation for Israel would
come out of Zion!
When the LORD restores the
fortunes of his people,
let Jacob rejoice and Israel be
glad!

Psalm 15

A psalm of David.

¹LORD, who may dwell in your
sanctuary?
Who may live on your holy hill?

²He whose walk is blameless
and who does what is righteous,
who speaks the truth from his heart
³ and has no slander on his tongue,
who does his neighbor no wrong
and casts no slur on his
fellowman,
⁴who despises a vile man
but honors those who fear the
LORD,
who keeps his oath
even when it hurts,
⁵who lends his money without usury
and does not accept a bribe against
the innocent.

He who does these things
will never be shaken.

Psalm 16

*A miktam*b *of David.*

¹Keep me safe, O God,
for in you I take refuge.

²I said to the LORD, "You are my
Lord;

a1 The Hebrew words rendered *fool* in Psalms
denote one who is morally deficient.   *b*Title:
Probably a literary or musical term

apart from you I have no good
thing."
³As for the saints who are in the land,
they are the glorious ones in whom
is all my delight.ᵃ
⁴The sorrows of those will increase
who run after other gods.
I will not pour out their libations of
blood
or take up their names on my lips.

⁵Lᴏʀᴅ, you have assigned me my
portion and my cup;
you have made my lot secure.
⁶The boundary lines have fallen for
me in pleasant places;
surely I have a delightful
inheritance.

ᵃ3 Or *As for the pagan priests who are in the land /
and the nobles in whom all delight, I said:*

WEDNESDAY

Read *Psalm 14:1–7*
Key Verses *Psalm 14:1–2*

Leaving God Out — Jim Lett

Albert Einstein theorized that science perceives only three percent
of all that can be known. And even though he possessed one of the
most brilliant intellects of the twentieth century, he estimated that
he perceived only one percent of that small amount. Compared to
Einstein, most of us carry far less knowledge around in our heads. If
what Einstein said is true, and over ninety-nine percent of what can
be known is unknown to us, how can a person say with any conviction that God doesn't exist?

In light of such odds, the argument that atheism is an intellectual choice is absurd—it's totally illogical. An atheist's argument
against the existence of God, therefore, has to be primarily moral,
not intellectual. As the psalmist said, "The fool says in his heart,"
not his mind, that "'there is no God'" (Psalm 14:1).

Atheists often say "there is no God," not by their arguments, but
by the way they conduct their lives. Many make a decision about
God's existence based on their observations and not on principles.
They invent standards of morality and ethics based on the consequences of what they do. Good and evil are relative terms; no
absolutes exist. Atheism is essentially a religion of pride; another
psalm declares that "in his pride the wicked does not seek [the
Lord]; in all his thoughts there is no room for God" (Psalm 10:4)

Christians can fall into this same trap. Without realizing it, we
can become practical atheists when we don't acknowledge God and
his standards in our lives, when we don't pray about decisions or
compare our values to those in the Bible or evaluate our actions
using God's guidelines, when we do not seek him or make room in
our hearts for him. What we *do* speaks much more loudly about our
belief in God than what we *say.*

Are you acting like an atheist? Are you leaving God out of your
life? Ask him to show you his will. Ask him to reveal it to you day by
day. And live in the joy of knowing that God is real and that he is at
work in you to draw you closer to him.

A Deeper Look
Psalm 10:3–4; Romans 1:18–20

Go to page 591 for your next devotional reading.

⁷I will praise the LORD, who counsels me;
even at night my heart instructs me.
⁸I have set the LORD always before me.
Because he is at my right hand,
I will not be shaken.

⁹Therefore my heart is glad and my tongue rejoices;
my body also will rest secure,

¹⁰because you will not abandon me to the grave,ᵃ
nor will you let your Holy Oneᵇ see decay.
¹¹You have madeᶜ known to me the path of life;
you will fill me with joy in your presence,

---

a 10 Hebrew *Sheol* *b 10* Or *your faithful one*
c 11 Or *You will make*

Read *Psalm 16:1–11*
Key Verse *Psalm 16:11*

Experiencing God – Rich Jarvi

This psalm is a song of praise to God for his promise of eternal life. But this psalm also holds the promise—one that fills the psalmist with joy—of experiencing eternity right now. He speaks in the present tense when he declares, "Surely I have a delightful inheritance. I will praise the LORD, who counsels me . . . Because he is at my right hand, I will not be shaken" (Psalm 16:6–8). Eternal life is not just a future dimension but an upward one that we experience when we know God—the living God who counsels and instructs us and makes us secure.

How do we seek God? There are many ways to do so: attending discipleship seminars and church services; listening to sermons; engaging in Bible study, Scripture memory, daily devotions and so on. Yet if we get so caught up in the mechanics of all these valuable activities, or become too intent on our performance of them, we might miss communicating with God himself.

For the sake of illustration, remember the last time you spoke on the telephone with a close friend? What did the phone look like? What did the phone smell like? Did you get emotionally involved with this phone? Did you find yourself wanting to use this specific phone again and again?

Of course, these questions are ludicrous! Though we use phones all the time, we rarely pay attention to their distinct characteristics. It's not the phone but *the person on the other end of the phone* that we're getting to know. Our relationship with God is much the same. All the activities we do to get to know God are like using the telephone. They are tools of communication that help us to know God and his work in the world; they're not an end in themselves.

No matter what activity we use to get to know God, we need to key in on *him* through that activity. Our focus needs to be not on the *means* to get to know him, but on *him*. Then he will fill us with joy in his presence (see Psalm 16:11).

A Deeper Look
Hosea 6:3; John 10:3–4

Go to page 596 for your next devotional reading.

with eternal pleasures at your right
hand.

Psalm 17

A prayer of David.

¹Hear, O LORD, my righteous plea;
    listen to my cry.
Give ear to my prayer—
    it does not rise from deceitful lips.
²May my vindication come from you;
    may your eyes see what is right.

³Though you probe my heart and
    examine me at night,
though you test me, you will find
    nothing;
I have resolved that my mouth will
    not sin.
⁴As for the deeds of men—
    by the word of your lips
I have kept myself
    from the ways of the violent.
⁵My steps have held to your paths;
    my feet have not slipped.

⁶I call on you, O God, for you will
    answer me;
give ear to me and hear my prayer.
⁷Show the wonder of your great love,
    you who save by your right hand
those who take refuge in you from
    their foes.
⁸Keep me as the apple of your eye;
    hide me in the shadow of your
    wings
⁹from the wicked who assail me,
    from my mortal enemies who
    surround me.

¹⁰They close up their callous hearts,
    and their mouths speak with
    arrogance.
¹¹They have tracked me down, they
    now surround me,
with eyes alert, to throw me to the
    ground.
¹²They are like a lion hungry for prey,
    like a great lion crouching in
    cover.

¹³Rise up, O LORD, confront them, bring
    them down;
rescue me from the wicked by your
    sword.
¹⁴O LORD, by your hand save me from
    such men,
from men of this world whose
    reward is in this life.

You still the hunger of those you
    cherish;
their sons have plenty,
    and they store up wealth for their
    children.
¹⁵And I—in righteousness I will see
    your face;
when I awake, I will be satisfied
    with seeing your likeness.

Psalm 18

For the director of music. Of David the
servant of the LORD. He sang to the LORD
the words of this song when the LORD
delivered him from the hand of all
his enemies and from the hand
of Saul. He said:

¹I love you, O LORD, my strength.

²The LORD is my rock, my fortress and
    my deliverer;
my God is my rock, in whom I
    take refuge.
He is my shield and the horn*ᵃ* of
    my salvation, my stronghold.
³I call to the LORD, who is worthy of
    praise,
and I am saved from my enemies.

⁴The cords of death entangled me;
    the torrents of destruction
    overwhelmed me.
⁵The cords of the grave*ᵇ* coiled
    around me;
the snares of death confronted me.
⁶In my distress I called to the LORD;
    I cried to my God for help.
From his temple he heard my voice;
    my cry came before him, into his
    ears.

⁷The earth trembled and quaked,
    and the foundations of the
    mountains shook;
they trembled because he was
    angry.
⁸Smoke rose from his nostrils;
    consuming fire came from his
    mouth,
burning coals blazed out of it.
⁹He parted the heavens and came
    down;
dark clouds were under his feet.
¹⁰He mounted the cherubim and flew;
    he soared on the wings of the
    wind.

ᵃ2 Horn here symbolizes strength.   *ᵇ5 Hebrew*
Sheol

¹¹He made darkness his covering, his
  canopy around him—
  the dark rain clouds of the sky.
¹²Out of the brightness of his presence
  clouds advanced,
  with hailstones and bolts of
  lightning.
¹³The LORD thundered from heaven;
  the voice of the Most High
  resounded.ᵃ
¹⁴He shot his arrows and scattered ˌthe
  enemiesˌ,
  great bolts of lightning and routed
  them.
¹⁵The valleys of the sea were exposed
  and the foundations of the earth
  laid bare
at your rebuke, O LORD,
  at the blast of breath from your
  nostrils.

¹⁶He reached down from on high and
  took hold of me;
  he drew me out of deep waters.
¹⁷He rescued me from my powerful
  enemy,
  from my foes, who were too strong
  for me.
¹⁸They confronted me in the day of my
  disaster,
  but the LORD was my support.
¹⁹He brought me out into a spacious
  place;
  he rescued me because he
  delighted in me.

²⁰The LORD has dealt with me according
  to my righteousness;
  according to the cleanness of my
  hands he has rewarded me.
²¹For I have kept the ways of the LORD;
  I have not done evil by turning
  from my God.
²²All his laws are before me;
  I have not turned away from his
  decrees.
²³I have been blameless before him
  and have kept myself from sin.
²⁴The LORD has rewarded me according
  to my righteousness,
  according to the cleanness of my
  hands in his sight.

²⁵To the faithful you show yourself
  faithful,
  to the blameless you show yourself
  blameless,
²⁶to the pure you show yourself pure,
  but to the crooked you show
  yourself shrewd.

²⁷You save the humble
  but bring low those whose eyes are
  haughty.
²⁸You, O LORD, keep my lamp burning;
  my God turns my darkness into
  light.
²⁹With your help I can advance against
  a troopᵇ;
  with my God I can scale a wall.

³⁰As for God, his way is perfect;
  the word of the LORD is flawless.
He is a shield
  for all who take refuge in him.
³¹For who is God besides the LORD?
  And who is the Rock except our
  God?
³²It is God who arms me with strength
  and makes my way perfect.
³³He makes my feet like the feet of a
  deer;
  he enables me to stand on the
  heights.
³⁴He trains my hands for battle;
  my arms can bend a bow of
  bronze.
³⁵You give me your shield of victory,
  and your right hand sustains me;
  you stoop down to make me great.
³⁶You broaden the path beneath me,
  so that my ankles do not turn.

³⁷I pursued my enemies and overtook
  them;
  I did not turn back till they were
  destroyed.
³⁸I crushed them so that they could not
  rise;
  they fell beneath my feet.

ᵃ13 Some Hebrew manuscripts and Septuagint (see
also 2 Samuel 22:14); most Hebrew manuscripts
resounded, / amid hailstones and bolts of lightning
ᵇ29 Or *can run through a barricade*

POINT OF INTEREST   Psalm 18:31

To better understand the
psalms we need to under-
stand their use of simile and
metaphor. When the psalmists
refer to God as a "Rock," they mean that
God is as enduring as a solid foundation—
strong enough to care for us and completely trustworthy. This metaphor is used
23 times in 150 psalms.

³⁹You armed me with strength for
　　battle;
　　you made my adversaries bow at
　　　my feet.
⁴⁰You made my enemies turn their
　　backs in flight,
　　and I destroyed my foes.
⁴¹They cried for help, but there was no
　　one to save them—
　　to the LORD, but he did not answer.
⁴²I beat them as fine as dust borne on
　　the wind;
　　I poured them out like mud in the
　　streets.

⁴³You have delivered me from the
　　attacks of the people;
　　you have made me the head of
　　nations;
　　people I did not know are subject
　　　to me.
⁴⁴As soon as they hear me, they obey
　　me;
　　foreigners cringe before me.
⁴⁵They all lose heart;
　　they come trembling from their
　　strongholds.

⁴⁶The LORD lives! Praise be to my Rock!
　　Exalted be God my Savior!
⁴⁷He is the God who avenges me,
　　who subdues nations under me,
⁴⁸　who saves me from my enemies.
　You exalted me above my foes;
　　from violent men you rescued me.
⁴⁹Therefore I will praise you among the
　　nations, O LORD;
　　I will sing praises to your name.

⁵⁰He gives his king great victories;
　　he shows unfailing kindness to his
　　anointed,
　　to David and his descendants
　　forever.

Psalm 19

For the director of music. A psalm
of David.

¹The heavens declare the glory of God;
　　the skies proclaim the work of his
　　hands.
²Day after day they pour forth speech;
　　night after night they display
　　knowledge.
³There is no speech or language
　　where their voice is not heard.ᵃ
⁴Their voiceᵇ goes out into all the
　　earth,

their words to the ends of the
　　world.

In the heavens he has pitched a tent
　　for the sun,
⁵　which is like a bridegroom coming
　　forth from his pavilion,
　　like a champion rejoicing to run
　　his course.
⁶It rises at one end of the heavens
　　and makes its circuit to the other;
　　nothing is hidden from its heat.

⁷The law of the LORD is perfect,
　　reviving the soul.
　The statutes of the LORD are
　　trustworthy,
　　making wise the simple.
⁸The precepts of the LORD are right,
　　giving joy to the heart.
　The commands of the LORD are
　　radiant,
　　giving light to the eyes.
⁹The fear of the LORD is pure,
　　enduring forever.
　The ordinances of the LORD are sure
　　and altogether righteous.
¹⁰They are more precious than gold,
　　than much pure gold;
　they are sweeter than honey,
　　than honey from the comb.
¹¹By them is your servant warned;
　　in keeping them there is great
　　reward.

¹²Who can discern his errors?
　　Forgive my hidden faults.
¹³Keep your servant also from willful
　　sins;
　　may they not rule over me.

ᵃ3 Or *They have no speech, there are no words; / no
sound is heard from them*　　ᵇ4 Septuagint,
Jerome and Syriac; Hebrew *line*

POINT OF INTEREST

Psalm 19:1

Imagine the young shepherd
David lying on a hillside
night after night, looking at
the heavens and praising their
Creator. Get in touch with God David's
way. Grab a blanket and take a "field trip"
away from the city lights. Lie down on
your back and look at the night sky. "Listen" to it declare God's glory and majesty.

Then will I be blameless,
  innocent of great transgression.

14May the words of my mouth and the
    meditation of my heart
  be pleasing in your sight,
  O Lord, my Rock and my
    Redeemer.

Psalm 20

For the director of music. A psalm
of David.

1May the Lord answer you when you
    are in distress;
  may the name of the God of Jacob
    protect you.
2May he send you help from the
    sanctuary
  and grant you support from Zion.
3May he remember all your sacrifices
  and accept your burnt offerings.
                                    Selah
4May he give you the desire of your
    heart
  and make all your plans succeed.
5We will shout for joy when you are
    victorious
  and will lift up our banners in the
    name of our God.
  May the Lord grant all your requests.

6Now I know that the Lord saves his
    anointed;
  he answers him from his holy
    heaven
  with the saving power of his right
    hand.
7Some trust in chariots and some in
    horses,
  but we trust in the name of the
    Lord our God.
8They are brought to their knees and
    fall,
  but we rise up and stand firm.

9O Lord, save the king!
  Answer*a* us when we call!

Psalm 21

For the director of music. A psalm
of David.

1O Lord, the king rejoices in your
    strength.
  How great is his joy in the
    victories you give!
2You have granted him the desire of
    his heart

and have not withheld the request
    of his lips.   *Selah*
3You welcomed him with rich
    blessings
  and placed a crown of pure gold
    on his head.
4He asked you for life, and you gave it
    to him—
  length of days, for ever and ever.
5Through the victories you gave, his
    glory is great;
  you have bestowed on him
    splendor and majesty.
6Surely you have granted him eternal
    blessings
  and made him glad with the joy of
    your presence.
7For the king trusts in the Lord;
  through the unfailing love of the
    Most High
  he will not be shaken.

8Your hand will lay hold on all your
    enemies;
  your right hand will seize your
    foes.
9At the time of your appearing
  you will make them like a fiery
    furnace.
  In his wrath the Lord will swallow
    them up,
  and his fire will consume them.
10You will destroy their descendants
    from the earth,
  their posterity from mankind.
11Though they plot evil against you
  and devise wicked schemes, they
    cannot succeed;
12for you will make them turn their
    backs
  when you aim at them with drawn
    bow.

13Be exalted, O Lord, in your strength;
  we will sing and praise your might.

Psalm 22

For the director of music. To ˻the tune
of˼ "The Doe of the Morning." A psalm
of David.

1My God, my God, why have you
    forsaken me?
  Why are you so far from saving
    me,
  so far from the words of my
    groaning?

*a*9 Or *save! / O King, answer*

²O my God, I cry out by day, but you
  do not answer,
by night, and am not silent.

³Yet you are enthroned as the Holy
  One;
you are the praise of Israel. *a*
⁴In you our fathers put their trust;
  they trusted and you delivered
  them.
⁵They cried to you and were saved;
  in you they trusted and were not
  disappointed.

⁶But I am a worm and not a man,
scorned by men and despised by
  the people.
⁷All who see me mock me;
  they hurl insults, shaking their
  heads:
⁸"He trusts in the LORD;
  let the LORD rescue him.
Let him deliver him,
  since he delights in him."

⁹Yet you brought me out of the womb;
  you made me trust in you
  even at my mother's breast.

a 3 Or Yet you are holy, / enthroned on the praises of Israel

---

FRIDAY

Read Psalm 20:1–9
Key Verse Psalm 20:7

Driving over Potholes —Liesl Oberly

As a child, I put my trust in my family, the most real and loving thing I knew. My mom and dad were everything to me, and I loved them very much, as I still do. They invested innumerable hours in my life—playing with me, encouraging me and teaching me countless valuable lessons.

My best friend's parents were divorced. She lived with her mother, and I remember feeling frustrated that every other weekend she would have to be away visiting her father. I can vividly remember lying in bed at night, telling myself that my family would always be together. Little did I know I was putting my trust in what this psalmist calls a "chariot." Like an ancient warrior, I trusted this vehicle, my family, to carry me down the road of life.

Not many years later, my chariot crashed—my parents' marriage dissolved. Soon *I* was living the frustration of switching houses each weekend. Life had turned upside down. My chariot, which at one time had looked so strong, so unbreakable, had hit an enormous pothole and had shattered into a thousand pieces.

At the time it seemed that nothing good could come from the situation. Now as I look back on those times of great confusion and heartache, I can see that during that period of life I learned to put my trust in God, who is unchanging and permanent. I learned the reality of Psalm 22:5: "They cried to you and were saved; in you they trusted and were not disappointed."

Even now I sometimes find myself trusting in rickety old chariots—relationships, a job, an education. And again and again God reminds me that only he is eternal and trustworthy. All other things are just temporary; no matter how strong they might appear, they'll never hold up against the deep potholes of life.

A Deeper Look
Psalm 22:4–5; 33:16–22; Hebrews 13:8

Go to page 598 for your next devotional reading.

¹⁰From birth I was cast upon you;
    from my mother's womb you have
        been my God.
¹¹Do not be far from me,
    for trouble is near
    and there is no one to help.

¹²Many bulls surround me;
    strong bulls of Bashan encircle me.
¹³Roaring lions tearing their prey
    open their mouths wide against
        me.
¹⁴I am poured out like water,
    and all my bones are out of joint.
  My heart has turned to wax;
    it has melted away within me.
¹⁵My strength is dried up like a
        potsherd,
    and my tongue sticks to the roof of
        my mouth;
    you lay me*ᵃ* in the dust of death.
¹⁶Dogs have surrounded me;
    a band of evil men has encircled
        me,
    they have pierced*ᵇ* my hands and
        my feet.
¹⁷I can count all my bones;
    people stare and gloat over me.
¹⁸They divide my garments among
        them
    and cast lots for my clothing.

¹⁹But you, O Lord, be not far off;
    O my Strength, come quickly to
        help me.
²⁰Deliver my life from the sword,
    my precious life from the power of
        the dogs.
²¹Rescue me from the mouth of the
        lions;
    save*ᶜ* me from the horns of the
        wild oxen.

²²I will declare your name to my
        brothers;
    in the congregation I will praise
        you.
²³You who fear the Lord, praise him!
    All you descendants of Jacob,
        honor him!
    Revere him, all you descendants of
        Israel!
²⁴For he has not despised or disdained
    the suffering of the afflicted one;
  he has not hidden his face from him
    but has listened to his cry for help.

²⁵From you comes the theme of my
        praise in the great assembly;
    before those who fear you*ᵈ* will I
        fulfill my vows.

²⁶The poor will eat and be satisfied;
    they who seek the Lord will praise
        him—
    may your hearts live forever!
²⁷All the ends of the earth
    will remember and turn to the
        Lord,
  and all the families of the nations
    will bow down before him,
²⁸for dominion belongs to the Lord
    and he rules over the nations.

²⁹All the rich of the earth will feast and
        worship;
    all who go down to the dust will
        kneel before him—
    those who cannot keep themselves
        alive.
³⁰Posterity will serve him;
    future generations will be told
        about the Lord.
³¹They will proclaim his righteousness
    to a people yet unborn—
    for he has done it.

Psalm 23

A psalm of David.

¹The Lord is my shepherd, I shall not
        be in want.
²   He makes me lie down in green
        pastures,
  he leads me beside quiet waters,
³   he restores my soul.
  He guides me in paths of
        righteousness
    for his name's sake.
⁴Even though I walk

ᵃ15 Or */ I am laid*   *ᵇ16* Some Hebrew
manuscripts, Septuagint and Syriac; most Hebrew
manuscripts */ like the lion,*   *ᶜ21* Or */ you have
heard*   *ᵈ25* Hebrew *him*

POINT OF INTEREST

Psalm 22:14-18

Psalm 22 was written hundreds of years before Jesus was born, yet it accurately prefigures some of the details of Jesus' crucifixion: His hands and feet would be pierced, he would endure public ridicule, and men would divide his garments and gamble for them.

Read *Psalm 23:1–6*
Key Verse *Psalm 23:1*

The Care and Feeding of Sheep

Sheep *need* a shepherd. They are essentially clueless. They don't have the know-how to find water or good pasture or shelter in a storm. They can't defend themselves. When a flock of sheep is frightened, they scatter and get lost. Wandering alone, a sheep without a shepherd is likely to become a snack for a hungry predator.

We are a lot like those helpless sheep. Without God's protection, we are easy prey for another kind of predator, the devil. As a matter of fact, the devil is called a prowling lion who is looking for someone to devour (see 1 Peter 5:8). God is a trustworthy and reliable shepherd, and we can count on him to provide us with what we need, to give us guidance and to keep his watchful eye on us. He's our own Good Shepherd!

Digging Into the Word
1. How do you feel when you read these passages about how God protects and provides for you?—*2 Corinthians 9:6–11; Philippians 4:19*
2. What do you realize about God's protection in the following passages?—*Psalm 91:1–8; Isaiah 41:10*

Personal Reflection
Make a list of the fears, challenges and decisions you are facing, leaving space between the lines. Then, with a brighter ink color, write the words of Psalm 23 between the lines of your list, appropriating David's song of faith as your own.

One Step Deeper
Psalm 5:10–12; 34:4–10

Go to page 601 for your next devotional reading.

through the valley of the shadow
of death,^a
I will fear no evil,
for you are with me;
your rod and your staff,
they comfort me.

⁵You prepare a table before me
in the presence of my enemies.
You anoint my head with oil;
my cup overflows.
⁶Surely goodness and love will follow
me
all the days of my life,
and I will dwell in the house of the
LORD
forever.

Psalm 24

Of David. A psalm.

¹The earth is the LORD's, and
everything in it,
the world, and all who live in it;
²for he founded it upon the seas
and established it upon the waters.

³Who may ascend the hill of the LORD?
Who may stand in his holy place?
⁴He who has clean hands and a pure
heart,
who does not lift up his soul to an
idol
or swear by what is false.^b
⁵He will receive blessing from the
LORD
and vindication from God his
Savior.
⁶Such is the generation of those who
seek him,
who seek your face, O God of
Jacob.^c   Selah

⁷Lift up your heads, O you gates;
be lifted up, you ancient doors,
that the King of glory may come
in.
⁸Who is this King of glory?
The LORD strong and mighty,
the LORD mighty in battle.
⁹Lift up your heads, O you gates;
lift them up, you ancient doors,
that the King of glory may come
in.
¹⁰Who is he, this King of glory?

The LORD Almighty—
he is the King of glory.   Selah

Psalm 25^d

Of David.

¹To you, O LORD, I lift up my soul;
² in you I trust, O my God.
Do not let me be put to shame,
nor let my enemies triumph over
me.
³No one whose hope is in you
will ever be put to shame,
but they will be put to shame
who are treacherous without
excuse.

⁴Show me your ways, O LORD,
teach me your paths;
⁵guide me in your truth and teach me,
for you are God my Savior,
and my hope is in you all day
long.
⁶Remember, O LORD, your great mercy
and love,
for they are from of old.
⁷Remember not the sins of my youth
and my rebellious ways;
according to your love remember me,
for you are good, O LORD.

⁸Good and upright is the LORD;
therefore he instructs sinners in his
ways.
⁹He guides the humble in what is right
and teaches them his way.
¹⁰All the ways of the LORD are loving
and faithful
for those who keep the demands of
his covenant.
¹¹For the sake of your name, O LORD,
forgive my iniquity, though it is
great.
¹²Who, then, is the man that fears the
LORD?
He will instruct him in the way
chosen for him.
¹³He will spend his days in prosperity,
and his descendants will inherit
the land.
¹⁴The LORD confides in those who fear
him;

^a4 Or *through the darkest valley*   ^b4 Or *swear
falsely*   ^c6 Two Hebrew manuscripts and Syriac
(see also Septuagint); most Hebrew manuscripts
face, Jacob   ^dThis psalm is an acrostic poem, the
verses of which begin with the successive letters of
the Hebrew alphabet.

he makes his covenant known to
    them.
[15]My eyes are ever on the LORD,
    for only he will release my feet
    from the snare.

[16]Turn to me and be gracious to me,
    for I am lonely and afflicted.
[17]The troubles of my heart have
    multiplied;
    free me from my anguish.
[18]Look upon my affliction and my
    distress
    and take away all my sins.
[19]See how my enemies have increased
    and how fiercely they hate me!
[20]Guard my life and rescue me;
    let me not be put to shame,
    for I take refuge in you.
[21]May integrity and uprightness protect
    me,
    because my hope is in you.

[22]Redeem Israel, O God,
    from all their troubles!

Psalm 26

Of David.

[1]Vindicate me, O LORD,
    for I have led a blameless life;
I have trusted in the LORD
    without wavering.
[2]Test me, O LORD, and try me,
    examine my heart and my mind;
[3]for your love is ever before me,
    and I walk continually in your
    truth.
[4]I do not sit with deceitful men,
    nor do I consort with hypocrites;
[5]I abhor the assembly of evildoers
    and refuse to sit with the wicked.
[6]I wash my hands in innocence,
    and go about your altar, O LORD,
[7]proclaiming aloud your praise
    and telling of all your wonderful
    deeds.
[8]I love the house where you live,
    O LORD,
    the place where your glory dwells.

[9]Do not take away my soul along with
    sinners,
    my life with bloodthirsty men,
[10]in whose hands are wicked schemes,
    whose right hands are full of
    bribes.
[11]But I lead a blameless life;
    redeem me and be merciful to me.

[12]My feet stand on level ground;
    in the great assembly I will praise
    the LORD.

Psalm 27

Of David.

[1]The LORD is my light and my
    salvation—
    whom shall I fear?
The LORD is the stronghold of my
    life—
    of whom shall I be afraid?
[2]When evil men advance against me
    to devour my flesh,[a]
when my enemies and my foes attack
    me,
    they will stumble and fall.
[3]Though an army besiege me,
    my heart will not fear;
though war break out against me,
    even then will I be confident.

[4]One thing I ask of the LORD,
    this is what I seek:
that I may dwell in the house of the
    LORD
    all the days of my life,
to gaze upon the beauty of the LORD
    and to seek him in his temple.
[5]For in the day of trouble
    he will keep me safe in his
    dwelling;
he will hide me in the shelter of his
    tabernacle
    and set me high upon a rock.
[6]Then my head will be exalted
    above the enemies who surround
    me;
at his tabernacle will I sacrifice with
    shouts of joy;
    I will sing and make music to the
    LORD.

[7]Hear my voice when I call, O LORD;
    be merciful to me and answer me.
[8]My heart says of you, "Seek his[b]
    face!"
    Your face, LORD, I will seek.
[9]Do not hide your face from me,
    do not turn your servant away in
    anger;
    you have been my helper.
Do not reject me or forsake me,
    O God my Savior.

[a]2 Or *to slander me*   [b]8 Or *To you, O my heart,*
he has said, "Seek my

¹⁰Though my father and mother forsake
me,
the Lᴏʀᴅ will receive me.
¹¹Teach me your way, O Lᴏʀᴅ;
lead me in a straight path
because of my oppressors.
¹²Do not turn me over to the desire of
my foes,
for false witnesses rise up against
me,
breathing out violence.

¹³I am still confident of this:
I will see the goodness of the Lᴏʀᴅ
in the land of the living.
¹⁴Wait for the Lᴏʀᴅ;
be strong and take heart
and wait for the Lᴏʀᴅ.

Psalm 28

Of David.

¹To you I call, O Lᴏʀᴅ my Rock;
do not turn a deaf ear to me.
For if you remain silent,
I will be like those who have gone
down to the pit.
²Hear my cry for mercy
as I call to you for help,
as I lift up my hands
toward your Most Holy Place.

³Do not drag me away with the
wicked,
with those who do evil,
who speak cordially with their
neighbors

MONDAY

Read Psalm 27:1–14
Key Verse Psalm 27:3

Always Secure – Bill Gensky

Security—almost everyone craves it. Job security. Security in relationships. Protection from getting hurt—or being hurt again. Deep
inside, we want to protect ourselves and make ourselves secure.
Unfortunately, this never seems to work on a long-term basis. Even
if things go well for a while, sooner or later our efforts to keep ourselves safe end in failure and disappointment.

Why is security so difficult to achieve? Perhaps it's because we
follow the human tendency to look for security in people and circumstances. And the trouble is, hard as we may try, we can't control
either one. In our efforts to do so, we set ourselves up for pain. But
life doesn't have to be totally unstable.

David found security in God. He called God "my light and my salvation . . . the stronghold of my life" (Psalm 27:1). Even though men
were trying to kill him, David refused to live in fear. How did he
come by this sense of security? He focused on God: "This is what I
seek: that I may dwell in the house of the Lᴏʀᴅ all the days of my
life, to gaze upon the beauty of the Lᴏʀᴅ and to seek him in his temple" (Psalm 27:4).

David aspired to dwell in God's presence. Actively. Persistently.
Being in God's presence gave him perspective and assured him that
God's power and peace were much bigger than his own immediate
circumstances (see Psalm 27:5–6). And he knew, by experience,
that God's love and commitment to him exceeded those of even the
closest of human relationships (see Psalm 27:10). Now that's security. Real, unwavering security.

A Deeper Look
Isaiah 42:6; 43:1–4; Jeremiah 29:11–13

Go to page 605 for your next devotional reading.

but harbor malice in their hearts.
⁴Repay them for their deeds
  and for their evil work;
repay them for what their hands have
    done
  and bring back upon them what
    they deserve.
⁵Since they show no regard for the
    works of the LORD
  and what his hands have done,
he will tear them down
  and never build them up again.

⁶Praise be to the LORD,
  for he has heard my cry for mercy.
⁷The LORD is my strength and my
    shield;
  my heart trusts in him, and I am
    helped.
My heart leaps for joy
  and I will give thanks to him in
    song.

⁸The LORD is the strength of his people,
  a fortress of salvation for his
    anointed one.
⁹Save your people and bless your
    inheritance;
  be their shepherd and carry them
    forever.

Psalm 29

A psalm of David.

¹Ascribe to the LORD, O mighty ones,
  ascribe to the LORD glory and
    strength.
²Ascribe to the LORD the glory due his
    name;
  worship the LORD in the splendor of
    his*ᵃ holiness.

³The voice of the LORD is over the
    waters;
  the God of glory thunders,
  the LORD thunders over the mighty
    waters.
⁴The voice of the LORD is powerful;
  the voice of the LORD is majestic.
⁵The voice of the LORD breaks the
    cedars;
  the LORD breaks in pieces the
    cedars of Lebanon.
⁶He makes Lebanon skip like a calf,
  Sirionᵇ like a young wild ox.
⁷The voice of the LORD strikes
  with flashes of lightning.

⁸The voice of the LORD shakes the
    desert;
  the LORD shakes the Desert of
    Kadesh.
⁹The voice of the LORD twists the
    oaksᶜ
  and strips the forests bare.
And in his temple all cry, "Glory!"

¹⁰The LORD sitsᵈ enthroned over the
    flood;
  the LORD is enthroned as King
    forever.
¹¹The LORD gives strength to his people;
  the LORD blesses his people with
    peace.

Psalm 30

A psalm. A song. For the dedication of
  the temple.ᵉ Of David.

¹I will exalt you, O LORD,
  for you lifted me out of the depths
  and did not let my enemies gloat
    over me.
²O LORD my God, I called to you for
    help
  and you healed me.
³O LORD, you brought me up from the
    graveᶠ;
  you spared me from going down
    into the pit.

⁴Sing to the LORD, you saints of his;
  praise his holy name.
⁵For his anger lasts only a moment,
  but his favor lasts a lifetime;
weeping may remain for a night,
  but rejoicing comes in the
    morning.

⁶When I felt secure, I said,
  "I will never be shaken."
⁷O LORD, when you favored me,
  you made my mountainᵍ stand
    firm;
but when you hid your face,
  I was dismayed.

⁸To you, O LORD, I called;
  to the Lord I cried for mercy:
⁹"What gain is there in my
    destruction,ʰ
  in my going down into the pit?

ᵃ2 Or LORD with the splendor of   ᵇ6 That is,
Mount Hermon   ᶜ9 Or LORD makes the deer give
birth   ᵈ10 Or sat   ᵉTitle: Or palace
ᶠ3 Hebrew Sheol   ᵍ7 Or hill country   ʰ9 Or
there if I am silenced

Will the dust praise you?
Will it proclaim your faithfulness?
¹⁰Hear, O LORD, and be merciful to me;
O LORD, be my help."

¹¹You turned my wailing into dancing;
you removed my sackcloth and
clothed me with joy,
¹²that my heart may sing to you and
not be silent.
O LORD my God, I will give you
thanks forever.

Psalm 31

For the director of music. A psalm
of David.

¹In you, O LORD, I have taken refuge;
let me never be put to shame;
deliver me in your righteousness.
²Turn your ear to me,
come quickly to my rescue;
be my rock of refuge,
a strong fortress to save me.
³Since you are my rock and my
fortress,
for the sake of your name lead and
guide me.
⁴Free me from the trap that is set for
me,
for you are my refuge.
⁵Into your hands I commit my spirit;
redeem me, O LORD, the God of
truth.

⁶I hate those who cling to worthless
idols;
I trust in the LORD.
⁷I will be glad and rejoice in your
love,
for you saw my affliction
and knew the anguish of my soul.
⁸You have not handed me over to the
enemy
but have set my feet in a spacious
place.

⁹Be merciful to me, O LORD, for I am in
distress;
my eyes grow weak with sorrow,
my soul and my body with grief.
¹⁰My life is consumed by anguish
and my years by groaning;
my strength fails because of my
affliction,ᵃ
and my bones grow weak.
¹¹Because of all my enemies,
I am the utter contempt of my
neighbors;
I am a dread to my friends—

those who see me on the street flee
from me.
¹²I am forgotten by them as though I
were dead;
I have become like broken pottery.
¹³For I hear the slander of many;
there is terror on every side;
they conspire against me
and plot to take my life.

¹⁴But I trust in you, O LORD;
I say, "You are my God."
¹⁵My times are in your hands;
deliver me from my enemies
and from those who pursue me.
¹⁶Let your face shine on your servant;
save me in your unfailing love.
¹⁷Let me not be put to shame, O LORD,
for I have cried out to you;
but let the wicked be put to shame
and lie silent in the grave.ᵇ
¹⁸Let their lying lips be silenced,
for with pride and contempt
they speak arrogantly against the
righteous.

¹⁹How great is your goodness,
which you have stored up for
those who fear you,
which you bestow in the sight of men
on those who take refuge in you.
²⁰In the shelter of your presence you
hide them
from the intrigues of men;
in your dwelling you keep them safe
from accusing tongues.

²¹Praise be to the LORD,
for he showed his wonderful love
to me

ᵃ10 Or guilt   ᵇ17 Hebrew Sheol

POINT OF INTEREST

Psalm 31:14

When it seems that you
can't trust anyone, when
your enemies are breathing
down your neck, or when your
friends can't remember your name, where
do you turn? David faced such situations
many times. In this verse he tells us that
the key to his survival was an unwavering
trust in God.

when I was in a besieged city.
²²In my alarm I said,
"I am cut off from your sight!"
Yet you heard my cry for mercy
when I called to you for help.

²³Love the LORD, all his saints!
The LORD preserves the faithful,
but the proud he pays back in full.
²⁴Be strong and take heart,
all you who hope in the LORD.

Psalm 32

Of David. A *maskil.* ᵃ

¹Blessed is he
whose transgressions are forgiven,
whose sins are covered.
²Blessed is the man
whose sin the LORD does not count
against him
and in whose spirit is no deceit.

³When I kept silent,
my bones wasted away
through my groaning all day long.
⁴For day and night
your hand was heavy upon me;
my strength was sapped
as in the heat of summer.   *Selah*
⁵Then I acknowledged my sin to you
and did not cover up my iniquity.
I said, "I will confess
my transgressions to the LORD"—
and you forgave
the guilt of my sin.   *Selah*

⁶Therefore let everyone who is godly
pray to you
while you may be found;
surely when the mighty waters rise,
they will not reach him.
⁷You are my hiding place;
you will protect me from trouble
and surround me with songs of
deliverance.   *Selah*

⁸I will instruct you and teach you in
the way you should go;
I will counsel you and watch over
you.
⁹Do not be like the horse or the mule,
which have no understanding
but must be controlled by bit and
bridle
or they will not come to you.
¹⁰Many are the woes of the wicked,
but the LORD's unfailing love

surrounds the man who trusts in
him.
¹¹Rejoice in the LORD and be glad, you
righteous;
sing, all you who are upright in
heart!

Psalm 33

¹Sing joyfully to the LORD, you
righteous;
it is fitting for the upright to praise
him.
²Praise the LORD with the harp;
make music to him on the
ten-stringed lyre.
³Sing to him a new song;
play skillfully, and shout for joy.

⁴For the word of the LORD is right and
true;
he is faithful in all he does.
⁵The LORD loves righteousness and
justice;
the earth is full of his unfailing
love.

⁶By the word of the LORD were the
heavens made,
their starry host by the breath of
his mouth.
⁷He gathers the waters of the sea into
jarsᵇ;
he puts the deep into storehouses.
⁸Let all the earth fear the LORD;
let all the people of the world
revere him.
⁹For he spoke, and it came to be;
he commanded, and it stood firm.
¹⁰The LORD foils the plans of the
nations;
he thwarts the purposes of the
peoples.
¹¹But the plans of the LORD stand firm
forever,
the purposes of his heart through
all generations.

¹²Blessed is the nation whose God is
the LORD,
the people he chose for his
inheritance.
¹³From heaven the LORD looks down
and sees all mankind;
¹⁴from his dwelling place he watches
all who live on earth—
¹⁵he who forms the hearts of all,

ᵃTitle: Probably a literary or musical term
ᵇ7 Or *sea as into a heap*

who considers everything they do.
¹⁶No king is saved by the size of his
   army;
   no warrior escapes by his great
      strength.
¹⁷A horse is a vain hope for
      deliverance;
   despite all its great strength it
      cannot save.
¹⁸But the eyes of the LORD are on those
      who fear him,
   on those whose hope is in his
      unfailing love,
¹⁹to deliver them from death
   and keep them alive in famine.

²⁰We wait in hope for the LORD;
   he is our help and our shield.
²¹In him our hearts rejoice,
   for we trust in his holy name.
²²May your unfailing love rest upon us,
      O LORD,
   even as we put our hope in you.

Psalm 34 ᵃ

Of David. When he pretended to be
insane before Abimelech, who drove
   him away, and he left.

¹I will extol the LORD at all times;
   his praise will always be on my
      lips.
²My soul will boast in the LORD;
   let the afflicted hear and rejoice.
³Glorify the LORD with me;
   let us exalt his name together.

⁴I sought the LORD, and he answered
      me;
   he delivered me from all my fears.
⁵Those who look to him are radiant;
   their faces are never covered with
      shame.

ᵃThis psalm is an acrostic poem, the verses of
which begin with the successive letters of the
Hebrew alphabet.

TUESDAY

Read Psalm 32:1–11
Key Verse Psalm 32:8

Following God's Lead – Richard Gregg

As you trek through life each day, do you ever feel confused about
what direction to take? Decision making can be overwhelming at
times, especially if we think we have to carry the burden of our decisions alone. Thankfully, Psalm 32 gives us a different perspective.

Verse eight tells us two things. First, that God takes responsibility to show us which way to go. Second, he promises to be with us
and watch over us. He doesn't make us hunt for his will as if we're
on a scavenger hunt; nor does God just set us on a course and wave
good-bye as we walk out of sight.

God's commitment to helping us relieves us of the full weight of
decision making. When we're living by the description of the "godly"
in verses six and seven, we will be able to discern more clearly what
God's will is. Our responsibility in making decisions is to learn to see
his will and to wholeheartedly follow his leading. God doesn't want
to mechanically direct us, like the horses and mules in verse nine, in
order to get us to pay attention. He wants to lead us, not drag us.
He wants us to be like sheep who hear his voice and choose to follow him (see John 10:27). He wants to be our "hiding place" (Psalm
32:7).

On the path of life, God is our trail guide, navigator and companion; we just have to take the hike.

A Deeper Look
Jeremiah 29:11–13; Hosea 14:9; Romans 12:1–2

Go to page 608 for your next devotional reading.

⁶This poor man called, and the LORD
heard him;
he saved him out of all his
troubles.
⁷The angel of the LORD encamps
around those who fear him,
and he delivers them.

⁸Taste and see that the LORD is good;
blessed is the man who takes
refuge in him.
⁹Fear the LORD, you his saints,
for those who fear him lack
nothing.
¹⁰The lions may grow weak and
hungry,
but those who seek the LORD lack
no good thing.

¹¹Come, my children, listen to me;
I will teach you the fear of the
LORD.
¹²Whoever of you loves life
and desires to see many good days,
¹³keep your tongue from evil
and your lips from speaking lies.
¹⁴Turn from evil and do good;
seek peace and pursue it.

¹⁵The eyes of the LORD are on the
righteous
and his ears are attentive to their
cry;
¹⁶the face of the LORD is against those
who do evil,
to cut off the memory of them
from the earth.

¹⁷The righteous cry out, and the LORD
hears them;
he delivers them from all their
troubles.
¹⁸The LORD is close to the
brokenhearted
and saves those who are crushed
in spirit.

¹⁹A righteous man may have many
troubles,
but the LORD delivers him from
them all;
²⁰he protects all his bones,
not one of them will be broken.

²¹Evil will slay the wicked;
the foes of the righteous will be
condemned.
²²The LORD redeems his servants;
no one will be condemned who
takes refuge in him.

Psalm 35

Of David.

¹Contend, O LORD, with those who
contend with me;
fight against those who fight
against me.
²Take up shield and buckler;
arise and come to my aid.
³Brandish spear and javelin*ᵃ*
against those who pursue me.
Say to my soul,
"I am your salvation."

⁴May those who seek my life
be disgraced and put to shame;
may those who plot my ruin
be turned back in dismay.
⁵May they be like chaff before the
wind,
with the angel of the LORD driving
them away;
⁶may their path be dark and slippery,
with the angel of the LORD pursuing
them.
⁷Since they hid their net for me
without cause
and without cause dug a pit for
me,
⁸may ruin overtake them by
surprise—
may the net they hid entangle
them,
may they fall into the pit, to their
ruin.
⁹Then my soul will rejoice in the LORD
and delight in his salvation.
¹⁰My whole being will exclaim,
"Who is like you, O LORD?

ᵃ3 Or and block the way

POINT OF INTEREST

Psalm 34:18

Have you ever felt you
should be "up" but you were
just too "down" to pull it
off? You may have felt like a
spiritual failure for experiencing "the
blues." Perhaps the resulting guilt left you
even more depressed. Whenever you find
yourself "crushed in spirit," take heart—
God is right there beside you.

You rescue the poor from those too
strong for them,
the poor and needy from those
who rob them."

11Ruthless witnesses come forward;
they question me on things I know
nothing about.
12They repay me evil for good
and leave my soul forlorn.
13Yet when they were ill, I put on
sackcloth
and humbled myself with fasting.
When my prayers returned to me
unanswered,
14 I went about mourning
as though for my friend or brother.
I bowed my head in grief
as though weeping for my mother.
15But when I stumbled, they gathered
in glee;
attackers gathered against me
when I was unaware.
They slandered me without
ceasing.
16Like the ungodly they maliciously
mocked*a*;
they gnashed their teeth at me.
17O Lord, how long will you look on?
Rescue my life from their ravages,
my precious life from these lions.
18I will give you thanks in the great
assembly;
among throngs of people I will
praise you.

19Let not those gloat over me
who are my enemies without
cause;
let not those who hate me without
reason
maliciously wink the eye.
20They do not speak peaceably,
but devise false accusations
against those who live quietly in
the land.
21They gape at me and say, "Aha! Aha!
With our own eyes we have seen
it."

22O Lord, you have seen this; be not
silent.
Do not be far from me, O Lord.
23Awake, and rise to my defense!
Contend for me, my God and
Lord.
24Vindicate me in your righteousness,
O Lord my God;
do not let them gloat over me.
25Do not let them think, "Aha, just
what we wanted!"

or say, "We have swallowed him
up."

26May all who gloat over my distress
be put to shame and confusion;
may all who exalt themselves over
me
be clothed with shame and
disgrace.
27May those who delight in my
vindication
shout for joy and gladness;
may they always say, "The Lord be
exalted,
who delights in the well-being of
his servant."
28My tongue will speak of your
righteousness
and of your praises all day long.

Psalm 36

For the director of music. Of David the
servant of the Lord.

1An oracle is within my heart
concerning the sinfulness of the
wicked:*b*
There is no fear of God
before his eyes.
2For in his own eyes he flatters
himself
too much to detect or hate his sin.
3The words of his mouth are wicked
and deceitful;
he has ceased to be wise and to do
good.
4Even on his bed he plots evil;
he commits himself to a sinful
course
and does not reject what is wrong.

5Your love, O Lord, reaches to the
heavens,
your faithfulness to the skies.
6Your righteousness is like the mighty
mountains,
your justice like the great deep.
O Lord, you preserve both man and
beast.
7 How priceless is your unfailing
love!
Both high and low among men
find*c* refuge in the shadow of
your wings.

*a16 Septuagint; Hebrew may mean ungodly circle of
mockers.   b1 Or heart: / Sin proceeds from the
wicked.   c7 Or love, O God! / Men find; or love!
/ Both heavenly beings and men / find*

⁸They feast on the abundance of your
house;
you give them drink from your
river of delights.
⁹For with you is the fountain of
life;
in your light we see light.

¹⁰Continue your love to those who
know you,
your righteousness to the upright
in heart.
¹¹May the foot of the proud not come
against me,
nor the hand of the wicked drive
me away.
¹²See how the evildoers lie fallen—
thrown down, not able to rise!

Psalm 37 ᵃ

Of David.

¹Do not fret because of evil men
or be envious of those who do
wrong;
²for like the grass they will soon wither,
like green plants they will soon die
away.

³Trust in the LORD and do good;
dwell in the land and enjoy safe
pasture.
⁴Delight yourself in the LORD

ᵃThis psalm is an acrostic poem, the stanzas of
which begin with the successive letters of the
Hebrew alphabet.

WEDNESDAY

Read Psalm 37:1–40
Key Verse Psalm 37:4

Father Knows Best —Dean Storelli

Picture it—a 1960-something AMC Rambler, dented and rusting, spray painted various shades of blue. I just had to have it. My friends and I all thought it was the perfect car. "Hey," they joked, "if you run into a tree with it, who cares? Back it up and drive home."

It could have been mine for just fifty bucks. And that's why I couldn't understand my father. I had the money, but he kept telling me to wait. What was his problem? I really did need a car to get to school, to help with family chores and the like. This car would fit the bill. Why did he want me to wait?

I discovered the logic behind my dad's reasoning the night he drove home with a different answer to my transportation needs: a car ten years newer, one color, undented (so far) and rust-free! He wanted to give me something better than the one I had picked out. When I saw it, I realized this car was what I had really wanted all along. Dad knew best after all!

Is there something in your life that you're waiting for? Perhaps there's a job, a special relationship or some other thing you want, but you seem to be getting no help from God. Are you trying to find the answer on your own—settling for something that will get you by, like that fifty-dollar Rambler? Believe me, your heavenly Father doesn't want you to settle for something mediocre. He wants to give you his best, but you have to be willing to trust him and wait. While you may feel disappointed, confused and even angry at first, yield your heart to him and God will do just what my dad did for me— delight your socks off!

A Deeper Look
Matthew 7:7–11; 1 John 3:22–24

Go to page 613 for your next devotional reading.

and he will give you the desires of
your heart.

⁵Commit your way to the Lord;
    trust in him and he will do this:
⁶He will make your righteousness
    shine like the dawn,
    the justice of your cause like the
        noonday sun.

⁷Be still before the Lord and wait
    patiently for him;
    do not fret when men succeed in
        their ways,
    when they carry out their wicked
        schemes.

⁸Refrain from anger and turn from
        wrath;
    do not fret—it leads only to evil.
⁹For evil men will be cut off,
    but those who hope in the Lord
        will inherit the land.

¹⁰A little while, and the wicked will be
        no more;
    though you look for them, they
        will not be found.
¹¹But the meek will inherit the land
    and enjoy great peace.

¹²The wicked plot against the righteous
    and gnash their teeth at them;
¹³but the Lord laughs at the wicked,
    for he knows their day is coming.

¹⁴The wicked draw the sword
    and bend the bow
    to bring down the poor and needy,
    to slay those whose ways are
        upright.
¹⁵But their swords will pierce their own
        hearts,
    and their bows will be broken.

¹⁶Better the little that the righteous
        have
    than the wealth of many wicked;
¹⁷for the power of the wicked will be
        broken,
    but the Lord upholds the righteous.

¹⁸The days of the blameless are known
        to the Lord,
    and their inheritance will endure
        forever.
¹⁹In times of disaster they will not
        wither;
    in days of famine they will enjoy
        plenty.
²⁰But the wicked will perish:

The Lord's enemies will be like the
        beauty of the fields,
    they will vanish—vanish like
        smoke.

²¹The wicked borrow and do not repay,
    but the righteous give generously;
²²those the Lord blesses will inherit the
        land,
    but those he curses will be cut off.

²³If the Lord delights in a man's way,
    he makes his steps firm;
²⁴though he stumble, he will not fall,
    for the Lord upholds him with his
        hand.

²⁵I was young and now I am old,
    yet I have never seen the righteous
        forsaken
    or their children begging bread.
²⁶They are always generous and lend
        freely;
    their children will be blessed.

²⁷Turn from evil and do good;
    then you will dwell in the land
        forever.
²⁸For the Lord loves the just
    and will not forsake his faithful
        ones.

They will be protected forever,
    but the offspring of the wicked will
        be cut off;
²⁹the righteous will inherit the land
    and dwell in it forever.

³⁰The mouth of the righteous man
        utters wisdom,
    and his tongue speaks what is just.
³¹The law of his God is in his heart;
    his feet do not slip.

³²The wicked lie in wait for the
        righteous,
    seeking their very lives;
³³but the Lord will not leave them in
        their power
    or let them be condemned when
        brought to trial.

³⁴Wait for the Lord
    and keep his way.
    He will exalt you to inherit the land;
    when the wicked are cut off, you
        will see it.

³⁵I have seen a wicked and ruthless
        man
    flourishing like a green tree in its
        native soil,

³⁶but he soon passed away and was no
more;
though I looked for him, he could
not be found.

³⁷Consider the blameless, observe the
upright;
there is a future*ᵃ* for the man of
peace.
³⁸But all sinners will be destroyed;
the future*ᵇ* of the wicked will be
cut off.

³⁹The salvation of the righteous comes
from the LORD;
he is their stronghold in time of
trouble.
⁴⁰The LORD helps them and delivers
them;
he delivers them from the wicked
and saves them,
because they take refuge in him.

Psalm 38

A psalm of David. A petition.

¹O LORD, do not rebuke me in your
anger
or discipline me in your wrath.
²For your arrows have pierced me,
and your hand has come down
upon me.
³Because of your wrath there is no
health in my body;
my bones have no soundness
because of my sin.
⁴My guilt has overwhelmed me
like a burden too heavy to bear.

⁵My wounds fester and are loathsome
because of my sinful folly.
⁶I am bowed down and brought very
low;
all day long I go about mourning.
⁷My back is filled with searing pain;
there is no health in my body.
⁸I am feeble and utterly crushed;
I groan in anguish of heart.

⁹All my longings lie open before you,
O Lord;
my sighing is not hidden from you.
¹⁰My heart pounds, my strength fails
me;
even the light has gone from my
eyes.
¹¹My friends and companions avoid me
because of my wounds;
my neighbors stay far away.

¹²Those who seek my life set their
traps,
those who would harm me talk of
my ruin;
all day long they plot deception.

¹³I am like a deaf man, who cannot
hear,
like a mute, who cannot open his
mouth;
¹⁴I have become like a man who does
not hear,
whose mouth can offer no reply.
¹⁵I wait for you, O LORD;
you will answer, O Lord my God.
¹⁶For I said, "Do not let them gloat
or exalt themselves over me when
my foot slips."

¹⁷For I am about to fall,
and my pain is ever with me.
¹⁸I confess my iniquity;
I am troubled by my sin.
¹⁹Many are those who are my vigorous
enemies;
those who hate me without reason
are numerous.
²⁰Those who repay my good with evil
slander me when I pursue what is
good.

²¹O LORD, do not forsake me;
be not far from me, O my God.
²²Come quickly to help me,
O Lord my Savior.

Psalm 39

*For the director of music. For Jeduthun.
A psalm of David.*

¹I said, "I will watch my ways
and keep my tongue from sin;
I will put a muzzle on my mouth
as long as the wicked are in my
presence."
²But when I was silent and still,
not even saying anything good,
my anguish increased.
³My heart grew hot within me,
and as I meditated, the fire burned;
then I spoke with my tongue:

⁴"Show me, O LORD, my life's end
and the number of my days;
let me know how fleeting is my
life.
⁵You have made my days a mere
handbreadth;

ᵃ37 Or *there will be posterity*   *ᵇ38* Or *posterity*

the span of my years is as nothing
  before you.
  Each man's life is but a breath.
                                        Selah
[6]Man is a mere phantom as he goes to
    and fro:
  He bustles about, but only in vain;
  he heaps up wealth, not knowing
    who will get it.

[7]"But now, Lord, what do I look for?
  My hope is in you.
[8]Save me from all my transgressions;
  do not make me the scorn of fools.
[9]I was silent; I would not open my
    mouth,
  for you are the one who has done
    this.
[10]Remove your scourge from me;
  I am overcome by the blow of your
    hand.
[11]You rebuke and discipline men for
    their sin;
  you consume their wealth like a
    moth—
  each man is but a breath.   *Selah*

[12]"Hear my prayer, O LORD,
  listen to my cry for help;
  be not deaf to my weeping.
  For I dwell with you as an alien,
  a stranger, as all my fathers were.
[13]Look away from me, that I may
    rejoice again
  before I depart and am no more."

Psalm 40

For the director of music. Of David.
A psalm.

[1]I waited patiently for the LORD;
  he turned to me and heard my cry.
[2]He lifted me out of the slimy pit,
  out of the mud and mire;
  he set my feet on a rock
  and gave me a firm place to stand.
[3]He put a new song in my mouth,
  a hymn of praise to our God.
  Many will see and fear
  and put their trust in the LORD.

[4]Blessed is the man
  who makes the LORD his trust,
  who does not look to the proud,
  to those who turn aside to false
    gods.[a]
[5]Many, O LORD my God,
  are the wonders you have done.
  The things you planned for us
  no one can recount to you;

were I to speak and tell of them,
  they would be too many to
    declare.

[6]Sacrifice and offering you did not
    desire,
  but my ears you have pierced[b,c];
  burnt offerings and sin offerings
    you did not require.
[7]Then I said, "Here I am, I have
    come—
  it is written about me in the
    scroll.[d]
[8]I desire to do your will, O my God;
  your law is within my heart."

[9]I proclaim righteousness in the great
    assembly;
  I do not seal my lips,
  as you know, O LORD.
[10]I do not hide your righteousness in
    my heart;
  I speak of your faithfulness and
    salvation.
  I do not conceal your love and your
    truth
  from the great assembly.

[11]Do not withhold your mercy from
    me, O LORD;
  may your love and your truth
    always protect me.
[12]For troubles without number
    surround me;
  my sins have overtaken me, and I
    cannot see.
  They are more than the hairs of my
    head,
  and my heart fails within me.

[13]Be pleased, O LORD, to save me;
  O LORD, come quickly to help me.
[14]May all who seek to take my life

---

[a]4 Or *to falsehood*   [b]6 Hebrew; Septuagint *but a
body you have prepared for me* (see also
Symmachus and Theodotion)   [c]6 Or *opened*
[d]7 Or *come / with the scroll written for me*

POINT OF INTEREST   Psalm 40:9-10

Abraham Lincoln often
quoted the proverb, "Never
miss an opportunity to keep
your mouth shut." This is good
advice most of the time. When it comes to
the Good News about God, however, speak
up whenever you get the chance!

be put to shame and confusion;
may all who desire my ruin
be turned back in disgrace.
15May those who say to me, "Aha!
Aha!"
be appalled at their own shame.
16But may all who seek you
rejoice and be glad in you;
may those who love your salvation
always say,
"The LORD be exalted!"

17Yet I am poor and needy;
may the Lord think of me.
You are my help and my deliverer;
O my God, do not delay.

Psalm 41

For the director of music. A psalm
of David.

1Blessed is he who has regard for the
weak;
the LORD delivers him in times of
trouble.
2The LORD will protect him and
preserve his life;
he will bless him in the land
and not surrender him to the
desire of his foes.
3The LORD will sustain him on his
sickbed
and restore him from his bed of
illness.

4I said, "O LORD, have mercy on me;
heal me, for I have sinned against
you."
5My enemies say of me in malice,
"When will he die and his name
perish?"
6Whenever one comes to see me,
he speaks falsely, while his heart
gathers slander;
then he goes out and spreads it
abroad.

7All my enemies whisper together
against me;
they imagine the worst for me,
saying,
8"A vile disease has beset him;
he will never get up from the place
where he lies."
9Even my close friend, whom I
trusted,
he who shared my bread,
has lifted up his heel against me.

10But you, O LORD, have mercy on me;

raise me up, that I may repay
them.
11I know that you are pleased with me,
for my enemy does not triumph
over me.
12In my integrity you uphold me
and set me in your presence
forever.

13Praise be to the LORD, the God of
Israel,
from everlasting to everlasting.
Amen and Amen.

BOOK II

Psalms 42–72

Psalm 42 *a*

For the director of music. A *maskil* *b* of
the Sons of Korah.

1As the deer pants for streams of
water,
so my soul pants for you, O God.
2My soul thirsts for God, for the living
God.
When can I go and meet with God?
3My tears have been my food
day and night,
while men say to me all day long,
"Where is your God?"
4These things I remember
as I pour out my soul:
how I used to go with the multitude,
leading the procession to the house
of God,
with shouts of joy and thanksgiving
among the festive throng.

5Why are you downcast, O my soul?
Why so disturbed within me?
Put your hope in God,
for I will yet praise him,
my Savior and 6my God.

My *c* soul is downcast within me;
therefore I will remember you
from the land of the Jordan,
the heights of Hermon—from
Mount Mizar.
7Deep calls to deep
in the roar of your waterfalls;

*a*In many Hebrew manuscripts Psalms 42 and 43
constitute one psalm.   *b*Title: Probably a literary
or musical term   *c*5,6 A few Hebrew
manuscripts, Septuagint and Syriac; most Hebrew
manuscripts *praise him for his saving help.* / *6O my
God, my*

all your waves and breakers
  have swept over me.

⁸By day the LORD directs his love,
  at night his song is with me—
  a prayer to the God of my life.

⁹I say to God my Rock,
  "Why have you forgotten me?
Why must I go about mourning,
  oppressed by the enemy?"
¹⁰My bones suffer mortal agony
  as my foes taunt me,
saying to me all day long,
  "Where is your God?"

¹¹Why are you downcast, O my soul?
  Why so disturbed within me?
Put your hope in God,
  for I will yet praise him,
  my Savior and my God.

Psalm 43ᵃ

¹Vindicate me, O God,
  and plead my cause against an
    ungodly nation;
  rescue me from deceitful and
    wicked men.

ᵃIn many Hebrew manuscripts Psalms 42 and 43
constitute one psalm.

THURSDAY

Read *Psalms 42:1—43:5*
Key Verse *Psalm 43:5*

Faith Encouraging Faith — Mark Lewis

Ever talk to yourself? I do—all the time. But when you talk to yourself, are your discussions based on positive truth or on negative emotions? One easy way to check is to step back and "listen" to the conversations you have in your head.

In Psalms 42 and 43 we eavesdrop on the thoughts of a man who was overwhelmed with sorrow. These are two sad but beautiful poems written by a temple singer who was in exile far from his home, family and place of worship (see Psalm 42:6). He was being treated unjustly, and he had every reason to sit down and throw himself a pity party.

But he didn't. Despite his feelings and circumstances, he insisted on remembering God's faithfulness. Three times in the two psalms he asked himself, "Why are you downcast, O my soul? Why so disturbed within me?" He reminded himself where that source of help could be found—in God. By ending his mental "conversation" with expressions of truth and positive assurance, he was able to stop a downward spiral of despair. Just as despair leads to more despair, faith encourages faith; his faith answered the questions his doubts asked (see Psalm 42:5).

This psalmist wasn't living in denial. Both psalms are filled with honest pleas and cries for deliverance from his trials. But he didn't stop there. He laid those thoughts before God and chose to praise the One who was able to help him.

So what do you say when you talk to yourself? Are you engaging in right thinking or wallowing in self-pity? We can be honest with God about our sorrows and challenges, as the psalmist was. Nevertheless, we must still remember that, regardless of our circumstances, our help and hope come from God.

A Deeper Look
Romans 8:24–26; 2 Thessalonians 2:16–17

Go to page 617 for your next devotional reading.

²You are God my stronghold.
    Why have you rejected me?
Why must I go about mourning,
    oppressed by the enemy?
³Send forth your light and your truth,
    let them guide me;
let them bring me to your holy
        mountain,
    to the place where you dwell.
⁴Then will I go to the altar of God,
    to God, my joy and my delight.
I will praise you with the harp,
    O God, my God.

⁵Why are you downcast, O my soul?
    Why so disturbed within me?
Put your hope in God,
    for I will yet praise him,
    my Savior and my God.

Psalm 44

For the director of music. Of the Sons
    of Korah. A *maskil.* ᵃ

¹We have heard with our ears, O God;
    our fathers have told us
what you did in their days,
    in days long ago.
²With your hand you drove out the
        nations
    and planted our fathers;
you crushed the peoples
    and made our fathers flourish.
³It was not by their sword that they
        won the land,
    nor did their arm bring them
        victory;
it was your right hand, your arm,
    and the light of your face, for you
        loved them.

⁴You are my King and my God,
    who decrees ᵇ victories for Jacob.
⁵Through you we push back our
        enemies;
    through your name we trample our
        foes.
⁶I do not trust in my bow,
    my sword does not bring me
        victory;
⁷but you give us victory over our
        enemies,
    you put our adversaries to shame.
⁸In God we make our boast all day
        long,
    and we will praise your name
        forever.   *Selah*

⁹But now you have rejected and
        humbled us;

you no longer go out with our
        armies.
¹⁰You made us retreat before the
        enemy,
    and our adversaries have
        plundered us.
¹¹You gave us up to be devoured like
        sheep
    and have scattered us among the
        nations.
¹²You sold your people for a pittance,
    gaining nothing from their sale.

¹³You have made us a reproach to our
        neighbors,
    the scorn and derision of those
        around us.
¹⁴You have made us a byword among
        the nations;
    the peoples shake their heads at
        us.
¹⁵My disgrace is before me all day long,
    and my face is covered with shame
¹⁶at the taunts of those who reproach
        and revile me,
    because of the enemy, who is bent
        on revenge.

¹⁷All this happened to us,
    though we had not forgotten you
    or been false to your covenant.
¹⁸Our hearts had not turned back;
    our feet had not strayed from your
        path.
¹⁹But you crushed us and made us a
        haunt for jackals
    and covered us over with deep
        darkness.

²⁰If we had forgotten the name of our
        God
    or spread out our hands to a
        foreign god,
²¹would not God have discovered it,
    since he knows the secrets of the
        heart?
²²Yet for your sake we face death all
        day long;
    we are considered as sheep to be
        slaughtered.

²³Awake, O Lord! Why do you sleep?
    Rouse yourself! Do not reject us
        forever.
²⁴Why do you hide your face
    and forget our misery and
        oppression?

ᵃTitle: Probably a literary or musical term
ᵇ4 Septuagint, Aquila and Syriac; Hebrew *King,
O God; / command*

²⁵We are brought down to the dust;
  our bodies cling to the ground.
²⁶Rise up and help us;
  redeem us because of your
    unfailing love.

Psalm 45

For the director of music. To ⌊the tune
of⌋ "Lilies." Of the Sons of Korah. A
*maskil.*ᵃ A wedding song.

¹My heart is stirred by a noble theme
  as I recite my verses for the king;
  my tongue is the pen of a skillful
    writer.

²You are the most excellent of men
  and your lips have been anointed
    with grace,
  since God has blessed you forever.
³Gird your sword upon your side,
    O mighty one;
  clothe yourself with splendor and
    majesty.
⁴In your majesty ride forth victoriously
  in behalf of truth, humility and
    righteousness;
  let your right hand display
    awesome deeds.
⁵Let your sharp arrows pierce the
    hearts of the king's enemies;
  let the nations fall beneath your
    feet.
⁶Your throne, O God, will last for ever
    and ever;
  a scepter of justice will be the
    scepter of your kingdom.
⁷You love righteousness and hate
    wickedness;
  therefore God, your God, has set
    you above your companions
  by anointing you with the oil of
    joy.
⁸All your robes are fragrant with
    myrrh and aloes and cassia;
  from palaces adorned with ivory
    the music of the strings makes you
    glad.
⁹Daughters of kings are among your
    honored women;
  at your right hand is the royal
    bride in gold of Ophir.

¹⁰Listen, O daughter, consider and give
    ear:
  Forget your people and your
    father's house.
¹¹The king is enthralled by your
    beauty;

honor him, for he is your lord.
¹²The Daughter of Tyre will come with
    a gift,ᵇ
  men of wealth will seek your
    favor.
¹³All glorious is the princess within ⌊her
    chamber⌋;
  her gown is interwoven with gold.
¹⁴In embroidered garments she is led to
    the king;
  her virgin companions follow her
    and are brought to you.
¹⁵They are led in with joy and
    gladness;
  they enter the palace of the king.

¹⁶Your sons will take the place of your
    fathers;
  you will make them princes
    throughout the land.
¹⁷I will perpetuate your memory
    through all generations;
  therefore the nations will praise
    you for ever and ever.

Psalm 46

For the director of music. Of the Sons
of Korah. According to *alamoth.*ᶜ
A song.

¹God is our refuge and strength,
  an ever-present help in trouble.
²Therefore we will not fear, though
    the earth give way
  and the mountains fall into the
    heart of the sea,
³though its waters roar and foam
  and the mountains quake with
    their surging.   *Selah*

⁴There is a river whose streams make
    glad the city of God,
  the holy place where the Most
    High dwells.
⁵God is within her, she will not fall;
  God will help her at break of day.
⁶Nations are in uproar, kingdoms fall;
  he lifts his voice, the earth melts.

⁷The LORD Almighty is with us;
  the God of Jacob is our fortress.
                              Selah

⁸Come and see the works of the LORD,
  the desolations he has brought on
    the earth.

ᵃTitle: Probably a literary or musical term
ᵇ12 Or *A Tyrian robe is among the gifts*
ᶜTitle: Probably a musical term

⁹He makes wars cease to the ends of
the earth;
he breaks the bow and shatters the
spear,
he burns the shields*ᵃ* with fire.
¹⁰"Be still, and know that I am God;
I will be exalted among the
nations,
I will be exalted in the earth."

¹¹The Lᴏʀᴅ Almighty is with us;
the God of Jacob is our fortress.
Selah

Psalm 47

For the director of music. Of the Sons
of Korah. A psalm.

¹Clap your hands, all you nations;
shout to God with cries of joy.
²How awesome is the Lᴏʀᴅ Most High,
the great King over all the earth!
³He subdued nations under us,
peoples under our feet.
⁴He chose our inheritance for us,
the pride of Jacob, whom he loved.
Selah

⁵God has ascended amid shouts of joy,
the Lᴏʀᴅ amid the sounding of
trumpets.
⁶Sing praises to God, sing praises;
sing praises to our King, sing
praises.

⁷For God is the King of all the earth;
sing to him a psalm*ᵇ* of praise.
⁸God reigns over the nations;
God is seated on his holy throne.
⁹The nobles of the nations assemble
as the people of the God of
Abraham,
for the kings*ᶜ* of the earth belong to
God;
he is greatly exalted.

Psalm 48

A song. A psalm of the Sons of Korah.

¹Great is the Lᴏʀᴅ, and most worthy of
praise,
in the city of our God, his holy
mountain.
²It is beautiful in its loftiness,
the joy of the whole earth.
Like the utmost heights of Zaphon*ᵈ*
is Mount Zion,
the*ᵉ* city of the Great King.
³God is in her citadels;

he has shown himself to be her
fortress.

⁴When the kings joined forces,
when they advanced together,
⁵they saw ⌊her⌋ and were astounded;
they fled in terror.
⁶Trembling seized them there,
pain like that of a woman in labor.
⁷You destroyed them like ships of
Tarshish
shattered by an east wind.

⁸As we have heard,
so have we seen
in the city of the Lᴏʀᴅ Almighty,
in the city of our God:
God makes her secure forever.
Selah

⁹Within your temple, O God,
we meditate on your unfailing
love.
¹⁰Like your name, O God,
your praise reaches to the ends of
the earth;
your right hand is filled with
righteousness.
¹¹Mount Zion rejoices,
the villages of Judah are glad
because of your judgments.

¹²Walk about Zion, go around her,
count her towers,
¹³consider well her ramparts,
view her citadels,
that you may tell of them to the
next generation.
¹⁴For this God is our God for ever and
ever;
he will be our guide even to the
end.

Psalm 49

For the director of music. Of the Sons
of Korah. A psalm.

¹Hear this, all you peoples;
listen, all who live in this world,
²both low and high,
rich and poor alike:
³My mouth will speak words of
wisdom;
the utterance from my heart will
give understanding.

ᵃ9 Or chariots   *ᵇ7 Or a maskil (probably a
literary or musical term)*   *ᶜ9 Or shields*
*ᵈ2 Zaphon can refer to a sacred mountain or the
direction north.*   *ᵉ2 Or earth, / Mount Zion, on
the northern side / of the*

⁴I will turn my ear to a proverb;
  with the harp I will expound my
    riddle:

⁵Why should I fear when evil days
    come,
  when wicked deceivers surround
    me—
⁶those who trust in their wealth
  and boast of their great riches?
⁷No man can redeem the life of
    another
  or give to God a ransom for him—
⁸the ransom for a life is costly,
  no payment is ever enough—

⁹that he should live on forever
  and not see decay.

¹⁰For all can see that wise men die;
  the foolish and the senseless alike
    perish
  and leave their wealth to others.
¹¹Their tombs will remain their
    houses*a* forever,
  their dwellings for endless
    generations,
  though they had*b* named lands
    after themselves.

a 11 Septuagint and Syriac; Hebrew *In their thoughts
their houses will remain*   *b 11* Or / *for they have*

FRIDAY

Read *Psalm 48:1–14*
Key Verses *Psalm 48:12–14*

Out of the Desert — Ellen B. Susman

At last, instead of wandering around in a desert, the Israelites could
stand and look around at their walled city. But how, after picking
sand out of their teeth for forty years, could they now feel secure in
God's guidance and protection? This psalm is a tribute to how far
God had taken them—and to Israel's trust in his strength.

The Israelites remembered where they had come from. They had
been a captive people, slaves in Egypt. But God had brought them
through the desert, established them in the land he had promised to
their ancestors, and made them into a whole nation. He'd given
them a beautiful capital city—safe and well-protected—complete
with towers and walls. It was a grand representation of the future
city of God in heaven.

Today, too, we have our times of isolation and wandering. A
friend of mine described her college and post-college years as a
desert like experience similar to that of the Israelites. I felt overwhelmed when I finished college and saw my whole life stretched
out ahead of me. "What career should I pursue?" "Where should I
live?" "Should I get married now?"

The Israelites very likely asked a lot of questions of God as the
desert sands swirled around them and the sun beat down. But this
psalm of Israel celebrates God's guidance, direction and protection
(see Psalm 48:14).

If you find yourself "in the desert," realize that though God may
let you wander for a while, he doesn't want you to wander forever.
He may be preparing you to enter a land full of milk and honey (see
Numbers 13:27). God will call you to a place and give you the
power to "conquer" it. Then one day you'll be able to look around at
the strength—the "citadels" and "ramparts"—he's built into you.

A Deeper Look
Job 23:10; Hebrews 12:1–11

Go to page 620 for your next devotional reading.

12But man, despite his riches, does not
endure;
he is*a* like the beasts that perish.

13This is the fate of those who trust in
themselves,
and of their followers, who
approve their sayings.　*Selah*
14Like sheep they are destined for the
grave,*b*
and death will feed on them.
The upright will rule over them in the
morning;
their forms will decay in the
grave,*b*
far from their princely mansions.
15But God will redeem my life*c* from
the grave;
he will surely take me to himself.
Selah

16Do not be overawed when a man
grows rich,
when the splendor of his house
increases;
17for he will take nothing with him
when he dies,
his splendor will not descend with
him.
18Though while he lived he counted
himself blessed—
and men praise you when you
prosper—
19he will join the generation of his
fathers,
who will never see the light ⌐of
life⌐.

20A man who has riches without
understanding
is like the beasts that perish.

Psalm 50

A psalm of Asaph.

1The Mighty One, God, the Lord,
speaks and summons the earth
from the rising of the sun to the
place where it sets.
2From Zion, perfect in beauty,
God shines forth.
3Our God comes and will not be silent;
a fire devours before him,
and around him a tempest rages.
4He summons the heavens above,
and the earth, that he may judge
his people:
5"Gather to me my consecrated ones,

who made a covenant with me by
sacrifice."
6And the heavens proclaim his
righteousness,
for God himself is judge.　*Selah*

7"Hear, O my people, and I will speak,
O Israel, and I will testify against
you:
I am God, your God.
8I do not rebuke you for your
sacrifices
or your burnt offerings, which are
ever before me.
9I have no need of a bull from your
stall
or of goats from your pens,
10for every animal of the forest is mine,
and the cattle on a thousand hills.
11I know every bird in the mountains,
and the creatures of the field are
mine.
12If I were hungry I would not tell you,
for the world is mine, and all that
is in it.
13Do I eat the flesh of bulls
or drink the blood of goats?
14Sacrifice thank offerings to God,
fulfill your vows to the Most High,
15and call upon me in the day of
trouble;
I will deliver you, and you will
honor me."

16But to the wicked, God says:

"What right have you to recite my
laws
or take my covenant on your lips?
17You hate my instruction
and cast my words behind you.
18When you see a thief, you join with
him;
you throw in your lot with
adulterers.
19You use your mouth for evil
and harness your tongue to deceit.
20You speak continually against your
brother
and slander your own mother's
son.
21These things you have done and I
kept silent;
you thought I was altogether*d* like
you.

---

a12 Hebrew; Septuagint and Syriac read verse 12
the same as verse 20.　　*b14* Hebrew *Sheol*; also
in verse 15　　*c15* Or *soul*　　*d21* Or *thought the
'I AM' was*

But I will rebuke you
and accuse you to your face.

22"Consider this, you who forget God,
or I will tear you to pieces, with
none to rescue:
23He who sacrifices thank offerings
honors me,
and he prepares the way
so that I may show him*a* the
salvation of God."

Psalm 51

For the director of music. A psalm of
David. When the prophet Nathan came
to him after David had committed
adultery with Bathsheba.

1Have mercy on me, O God,
according to your unfailing love;
according to your great compassion
blot out my transgressions.
2Wash away all my iniquity
and cleanse me from my sin.

3For I know my transgressions,
and my sin is always before me.
4Against you, you only, have I sinned
and done what is evil in your
sight,
so that you are proved right when
you speak
and justified when you judge.
5Surely I was sinful at birth,
sinful from the time my mother
conceived me.
6Surely you desire truth in the inner
parts*b*;
you teach*c* me wisdom in the
inmost place.

7Cleanse me with hyssop, and I will
be clean;
wash me, and I will be whiter than
snow.
8Let me hear joy and gladness;
let the bones you have crushed
rejoice.
9Hide your face from my sins
and blot out all my iniquity.

10Create in me a pure heart, O God,
and renew a steadfast spirit within
me.
11Do not cast me from your presence
or take your Holy Spirit from me.
12Restore to me the joy of your
salvation
and grant me a willing spirit, to
sustain me.

13Then I will teach transgressors your
ways,
and sinners will turn back to you.
14Save me from bloodguilt, O God,
the God who saves me,
and my tongue will sing of your
righteousness.
15O Lord, open my lips,
and my mouth will declare your
praise.
16You do not delight in sacrifice, or I
would bring it;
you do not take pleasure in burnt
offerings.
17The sacrifices of God are*d* a broken
spirit;
a broken and contrite heart,
O God, you will not despise.

18In your good pleasure make Zion
prosper;
build up the walls of Jerusalem.
19Then there will be righteous
sacrifices,
whole burnt offerings to delight
you;
then bulls will be offered on your
altar.

Psalm 52

For the director of music. A *maskil*e
of David. When Doeg the Edomite had
gone to Saul and told him: "David has
gone to the house of Ahimelech."

1Why do you boast of evil, you mighty
man?
Why do you boast all day long,
you who are a disgrace in the eyes
of God?
2Your tongue plots destruction;
it is like a sharpened razor,
you who practice deceit.
3You love evil rather than good,
falsehood rather than speaking the
truth.   *Selah*
4You love every harmful word,
O you deceitful tongue!

5Surely God will bring you down to
everlasting ruin:
He will snatch you up and tear you
from your tent;

a23 Or *and to him who considers his way / I will
show*   *b6* The meaning of the Hebrew for this
phrase is uncertain.   *c6* Or *you desired . . . ; /
you taught*   *d17* Or *My sacrifice, O God, is*
*e*Title: Probably a literary or musical term

Read Psalm 51:1–19
Key Verse Psalm 51:7

God's Forgiveness

David wrote this psalm after he had committed adultery with
Bathsheba, murdered her husband and lied to cover his tracks.
Though he was clearly guilty, he thought he had gotten away with
murder. But God had sent the prophet Nathan to tell David his sin
hadn't gone without notice. Aware of both the seriousness of his sin
and the standard of God's holiness, David asked God to cleanse him
and bring him back into God's presence.

Like David, we need God's forgiveness. It does not take a
prophet like Nathan to tell us; the Holy Spirit prods our awareness,
sometimes in unexpected ways, when we sin against God. When
that happens, we, like David, can go straight to God, counting on
his mercy, love and forgiveness. When we cry out, "Create in me a
pure heart, O God" (Psalm 51:10), our sins are forgiven . . . all of
them. Remember this psalm as a model for a lifetime of honest confession.

Digging Into the Word
1. How do these passages confirm the need for confession?—*Psalm
   32:1–5; 1 John 1:5–10*
2. What do these passages say about God's love and forgiveness?—
   Psalm 130:1–6; Ephesians 1:3–10

Action Challenge
Personalize Psalm 51 by sitting down and rewriting each verse in
your own words. What is David asking God for in each stanza? Then
pray through the psalm using your own words. Keep your personal
version of Psalm 51 in your Bible and use it the next time you've
"blown it" before God.

One Step Deeper
Acts 13:38–39; Ephesians 4:32

Go to page 623 for your next devotional reading.

he will uproot you from the land of
the living.   *Selah*
6The righteous will see and fear;
they will laugh at him, saying,
7"Here now is the man
who did not make God his
stronghold
but trusted in his great wealth
and grew strong by destroying
others!"

8But I am like an olive tree
flourishing in the house of God;
I trust in God's unfailing love
for ever and ever.
9I will praise you forever for what you
have done;
in your name I will hope, for your
name is good.
I will praise you in the presence of
your saints.

Psalm 53

For the director of music. According to
mahalath. *a* A *maskil* *b* of David.

1The fool says in his heart,
"There is no God."
They are corrupt, and their ways are
vile;
there is no one who does good.

2God looks down from heaven
on the sons of men
to see if there are any who
understand,
any who seek God.
3Everyone has turned away,
they have together become corrupt;
there is no one who does good,
not even one.

4Will the evildoers never learn—
those who devour my people as
men eat bread
and who do not call on God?
5There they were, overwhelmed with
dread,
where there was nothing to dread.
God scattered the bones of those who
attacked you;
you put them to shame, for God
despised them.

6Oh, that salvation for Israel would
come out of Zion!
When God restores the fortunes
of his people,
let Jacob rejoice and Israel be
glad!

Psalm 54

For the director of music. With stringed
instruments. A *maskil* *b* of David.
When the Ziphites had gone
to Saul and said, "Is not David
hiding among us?"

1Save me, O God, by your name;
vindicate me by your might.
2Hear my prayer, O God;
listen to the words of my mouth.

3Strangers are attacking me;
ruthless men seek my life—
men without regard for God.   *Selah*

4Surely God is my help;
the Lord is the one who sustains
me.

5Let evil recoil on those who slander
me;
in your faithfulness destroy them.

6I will sacrifice a freewill offering to
you;
I will praise your name, O Lord,
for it is good.
7For he has delivered me from all my
troubles,
and my eyes have looked in
triumph on my foes.

*a*Title: Probably a musical term   *b*Title: Probably
a literary or musical term

POINT OF INTEREST

Psalm 52:6-8

Many people think if they
just work hard enough, they
will be prosperous; they will
find security in material
goods, ease and comfort. But the world
doesn't always automatically reward hardworking and upright people. Instead, it
often seems as if the arrogant and manipulative are the same people who can pay
for lives of ease, security and luxury. But in
God's scheme of things the righteous will
ultimately be rewarded. Compare Isaiah
65:16–24 with Jeremiah 9:10–23 to see
how God defines prosperity, and how he
will ultimately distribute it.

Psalm 55

For the director of music. With stringed instruments. A *maskil*[a] of David.

[1] Listen to my prayer, O God,
do not ignore my plea;
[2]   hear me and answer me.
My thoughts trouble me and I am
distraught
[3]   at the voice of the enemy,
at the stares of the wicked;
for they bring down suffering upon
me
and revile me in their anger.

[4] My heart is in anguish within me;
the terrors of death assail me.
[5] Fear and trembling have beset me;
horror has overwhelmed me.
[6] I said, "Oh, that I had the wings of a
dove!
I would fly away and be at rest—
[7] I would flee far away
and stay in the desert;   *Selah*
[8] I would hurry to my place of shelter,
far from the tempest and storm."

[9] Confuse the wicked, O Lord,
confound their speech,
for I see violence and strife in the
city.
[10] Day and night they prowl about on
its walls;
malice and abuse are within it.
[11] Destructive forces are at work in the
city;
threats and lies never leave its
streets.

[12] If an enemy were insulting me,
I could endure it;
if a foe were raising himself against
me,
I could hide from him.
[13] But it is you, a man like myself,
my companion, my close friend,
[14] with whom I once enjoyed sweet
fellowship
as we walked with the throng at
the house of God.

[15] Let death take my enemies by
surprise;
let them go down alive to the
grave,[b]
for evil finds lodging among them.

[16] But I call to God,
and the LORD saves me.

[17] Evening, morning and noon
I cry out in distress,
and he hears my voice.
[18] He ransoms me unharmed
from the battle waged against me,
even though many oppose me.
[19] God, who is enthroned forever,
will hear them and afflict them—
Selah
men who never change their ways
and have no fear of God.

[20] My companion attacks his friends;
he violates his covenant.
[21] His speech is smooth as butter,
yet war is in his heart;
his words are more soothing than oil,
yet they are drawn swords.

[22] Cast your cares on the LORD
and he will sustain you;
he will never let the righteous fall.
[23] But you, O God, will bring down the
wicked
into the pit of corruption;
bloodthirsty and deceitful men
will not live out half their days.

But as for me, I trust in you.

Psalm 56

For the director of music. To ˻the tune
of˼ "A Dove on Distant Oaks." Of
David. A *miktam*.[a] When the
Philistines had seized him in Gath.

[1] Be merciful to me, O God, for men
hotly pursue me;
all day long they press their attack.
[2] My slanderers pursue me all day
long;
many are attacking me in their
pride.

[3] When I am afraid,
I will trust in you.
[4] In God, whose word I praise,
in God I trust; I will not be afraid.
What can mortal man do to me?

[5] All day long they twist my words;
they are always plotting to harm
me.
[6] They conspire, they lurk,
they watch my steps,
eager to take my life.

[a] Title: Probably a literary or musical term
[b] 15 Hebrew *Sheol*

⁷On no account let them escape;
  in your anger, O God, bring down
    the nations.
⁸Record my lament;
  list my tears on your scroll*a*—
  are they not in your record?

⁹Then my enemies will turn back
  when I call for help.
  By this I will know that God is for
    me.
¹⁰In God, whose word I praise,
  in the LORD, whose word I
    praise—
¹¹in God I trust; I will not be afraid.
  What can man do to me?

¹²I am under vows to you, O God;
  I will present my thank offerings to
    you.
¹³For you have delivered me*b* from
    death
  and my feet from stumbling,
that I may walk before God
  in the light of life.*c*

Psalm 57

For the director of music. ⌊To the tune
of⌋ "Do Not Destroy." Of David. A
miktam. *d* When he had fled
  from Saul into the cave.

¹Have mercy on me, O God, have
    mercy on me,
  for in you my soul takes refuge.
I will take refuge in the shadow of
    your wings
  until the disaster has passed.

²I cry out to God Most High,
  to God, who fulfills ⌊his purpose⌋
    for me.
³He sends from heaven and saves me,
  rebuking those who hotly pursue
    me;   *Selah*
  God sends his love and his
    faithfulness.

a8 Or / *put my tears in your wineskin*   *b13* Or
my soul   *c13* Or *the land of the living*   *d*Title:
Probably a literary or musical term

MONDAY

Read *Psalm 56:1–13*
Key Verses *Psalm 56:3–4*

When I'm Afraid – Linda Llewelyn

I've found that keeping a daily journal is helpful for me. It shows me
what I'm learning and helps me identify areas where I need to grow
spiritually.

As I look back at my journals, they reveal that the biggest area
of struggle for me over the years has been fear. Since the time I
wrote that I was afraid of getting lost in junior high, fear has sur-
faced time and again. Sometimes the fears have legitimate causes;
often they don't. Themes that keep showing up are fear of what others think, fear of failure and fear of loneliness.

I'm grateful that God chose to address our fears in the Bible. He
knows that we have them—it's no surprise to him. But sometimes
the answer he gives, "Just trust me," seems too simple. David, however, perceived the awesome depth and security in that statement.
He wrote, "When I am afraid, I will trust in you" (Psalm 56:3).

Most of the things I'm afraid of never happen. But fear is a
strong emotion. The things I'm afraid of can seem so real that the
fear can be paralyzing. God is helping me, however, to make the
choice to focus on him and not on my situation, and to say in my
heart, "I *will* trust in you."

A Deeper Look
Psalm 34:4; 91:2

Go to page 627 for your next devotional reading.

⁴I am in the midst of lions;
    I lie among ravenous beasts—
men whose teeth are spears and
        arrows,
    whose tongues are sharp swords.

⁵Be exalted, O God, above the
        heavens;
    let your glory be over all the earth.

⁶They spread a net for my feet—
    I was bowed down in distress.
They dug a pit in my path—
    but they have fallen into it
        themselves.   *Selah*

⁷My heart is steadfast, O God,
    my heart is steadfast;
    I will sing and make music.
⁸Awake, my soul!
    Awake, harp and lyre!
    I will awaken the dawn.

⁹I will praise you, O Lord, among the
        nations;
    I will sing of you among the
        peoples.
¹⁰For great is your love, reaching to the
        heavens;
    your faithfulness reaches to the
        skies.

¹¹Be exalted, O God, above the
        heavens;
    let your glory be over all the earth.

Psalm 58

For the director of music. ⌊To the tune
of⌋ "Do Not Destroy." Of David.
A *miktam.* ª

¹Do you rulers indeed speak justly?
    Do you judge uprightly among
        men?
²No, in your heart you devise
        injustice,
    and your hands mete out violence
        on the earth.
³Even from birth the wicked go astray;
    from the womb they are wayward
        and speak lies.
⁴Their venom is like the venom of a
        snake,
    like that of a cobra that has
        stopped its ears,
⁵that will not heed the tune of the
        charmer,
    however skillful the enchanter may
        be.

⁶Break the teeth in their mouths,
        O God;
    tear out, O LORD, the fangs of the
        lions!
⁷Let them vanish like water that flows
        away;
    when they draw the bow, let their
        arrows be blunted.
⁸Like a slug melting away as it moves
        along,
    like a stillborn child, may they not
        see the sun.
⁹Before your pots can feel ⌊the heat of⌋
        the thorns—
    whether they be green or dry—the
        wicked will be swept away. ᵇ
¹⁰The righteous will be glad when they
        are avenged,
    when they bathe their feet in the
        blood of the wicked.
¹¹Then men will say,
    "Surely the righteous still are
        rewarded;
    surely there is a God who judges
        the earth."

Psalm 59

For the director of music. ⌊To the tune
of⌋ "Do Not Destroy." Of David. A
miktam. ª When Saul had sent men
to watch David's house in order to
kill him.

¹Deliver me from my enemies, O God;
    protect me from those who rise up
        against me.
²Deliver me from evildoers
    and save me from bloodthirsty
        men.

³See how they lie in wait for me!
    Fierce men conspire against me
    for no offense or sin of mine,
        O LORD.
⁴I have done no wrong, yet they are
        ready to attack me.
    Arise to help me; look on my
        plight!
⁵O LORD God Almighty, the God of
        Israel,
    rouse yourself to punish all the
        nations;
    show no mercy to wicked traitors.
                                    Selah

⁶They return at evening,

ªTitle: Probably a literary or musical term
ᵇ9 The meaning of the Hebrew for this verse is
uncertain.

snarling like dogs,
and prowl about the city.
⁷See what they spew from their
mouths—
they spew out swords from their
lips,
and they say, "Who can hear us?"
⁸But you, O LORD, laugh at them;
you scoff at all those nations.

⁹O my Strength, I watch for you;
you, O God, are my fortress, ¹⁰my
loving God.

God will go before me
and will let me gloat over those
who slander me.
¹¹But do not kill them, O Lord our
shield,ᵃ
or my people will forget.
In your might make them wander
about,
and bring them down.
¹²For the sins of their mouths,
for the words of their lips,
let them be caught in their pride.
For the curses and lies they utter,
13   consume them in wrath,
consume them till they are no
more.
Then it will be known to the ends of
the earth
that God rules over Jacob.   *Selah*

¹⁴They return at evening,
snarling like dogs,
and prowl about the city.
¹⁵They wander about for food
and howl if not satisfied.
¹⁶But I will sing of your strength,
in the morning I will sing of your
love;
for you are my fortress,
my refuge in times of trouble.

¹⁷O my Strength, I sing praise to you;
you, O God, are my fortress, my
loving God.

Psalm 60

For the director of music. To ˻the tune
of˼ "The Lily of the Covenant." A
*miktam*ᵇ of David. For teaching. When
he fought Aram Naharaimᶜ and Aram
Zobah,ᵈ and when Joab returned and
struck down twelve thousand Edomites
in the Valley of Salt.

¹You have rejected us, O God, and
burst forth upon us;

you have been angry—now restore
us!
²You have shaken the land and torn it
open;
mend its fractures, for it is
quaking.
³You have shown your people
desperate times;
you have given us wine that makes
us stagger.

⁴But for those who fear you, you have
raised a banner
to be unfurled against the bow.
                                    Selah

⁵Save us and help us with your right
hand,
that those you love may be
delivered.
⁶God has spoken from his sanctuary:
"In triumph I will parcel out
Shechem
and measure off the Valley of
Succoth.
⁷Gilead is mine, and Manasseh is
mine;
Ephraim is my helmet,
Judah my scepter.
⁸Moab is my washbasin,
upon Edom I toss my sandal;
over Philistia I shout in triumph."

⁹Who will bring me to the fortified
city?
Who will lead me to Edom?
¹⁰Is it not you, O God, you who have
rejected us
and no longer go out with our
armies?
¹¹Give us aid against the enemy,
for the help of man is worthless.
¹²With God we will gain the victory,
and he will trample down our
enemies.

Psalm 61

For the director of music. With stringed
instruments. Of David.

¹Hear my cry, O God;
listen to my prayer.

²From the ends of the earth I call to
you,
I call as my heart grows faint;

ᵃ11 Or *sovereign*   ᵇTitle: Probably a literary or
musical term   ᶜTitle: That is, Arameans of
Northwest Mesopotamia   ᵈTitle: That is,
Arameans of central Syria

lead me to the rock that is higher
than I.
3For you have been my refuge,
a strong tower against the foe.

4I long to dwell in your tent forever
and take refuge in the shelter of
your wings.   *Selah*
5For you have heard my vows, O God;
you have given me the heritage of
those who fear your name.

6Increase the days of the king's life,
his years for many generations.
7May he be enthroned in God's
presence forever;
appoint your love and faithfulness
to protect him.

8Then will I ever sing praise to your
name
and fulfill my vows day after day.

Psalm 62

For the director of music. For Jeduthun.
A psalm of David.

1My soul finds rest in God alone;
my salvation comes from him.
2He alone is my rock and my
salvation;
he is my fortress, I will never be
shaken.

3How long will you assault a man?
Would all of you throw him
down—
this leaning wall, this tottering
fence?
4They fully intend to topple him
from his lofty place;
they take delight in lies.
With their mouths they bless,
but in their hearts they curse.
Selah

5Find rest, O my soul, in God alone;
my hope comes from him.
6He alone is my rock and my
salvation;
he is my fortress, I will not be
shaken.
7My salvation and my honor depend
on God*a*;
he is my mighty rock, my refuge.
8Trust in him at all times, O people;
pour out your hearts to him,
for God is our refuge.   *Selah*

9Lowborn men are but a breath,
the highborn are but a lie;

if weighed on a balance, they are
nothing;
together they are only a breath.
10Do not trust in extortion
or take pride in stolen goods;
though your riches increase,
do not set your heart on them.

11One thing God has spoken,
two things have I heard:
that you, O God, are strong,
12   and that you, O Lord, are loving.
Surely you will reward each person
according to what he has done.

Psalm 63

A psalm of David. When he was in the
Desert of Judah.

1O God, you are my God,
earnestly I seek you;
my soul thirsts for you,
my body longs for you,
in a dry and weary land
where there is no water.

2I have seen you in the sanctuary
and beheld your power and your
glory.
3Because your love is better than life,
my lips will glorify you.
4I will praise you as long as I live,
and in your name I will lift up my
hands.
5My soul will be satisfied as with the
richest of foods;
with singing lips my mouth will
praise you.

a7 Or / God Most High is my salvation and my honor

POINT OF INTEREST

Psalm 62:11-12

There is much we don't
know about God. But as we
climb the cliff of life, the
things we do know about God
constitute the ringbolts and pitons we
drive into the rock. Our life depends on
them. We gain confidence in God's hand-
holds when we read these words: "One
thing God has spoken, two things have I
heard: that you, O God, are strong, and
that you, O Lord, are loving."

⁶On my bed I remember you;
   I think of you through the watches
     of the night.
⁷Because you are my help,
   I sing in the shadow of your
     wings.
⁸My soul clings to you;
   your right hand upholds me.

⁹They who seek my life will be
   destroyed;
   they will go down to the depths of
     the earth.
¹⁰They will be given over to the sword
   and become food for jackals.

¹¹But the king will rejoice in God;
   all who swear by God's name will
     praise him,
   while the mouths of liars will be
     silenced.

Psalm 64

For the director of music. A psalm
    of David.

¹Hear me, O God, as I voice my
    complaint;
   protect my life from the threat of
    the enemy.
²Hide me from the conspiracy of the
    wicked,
   from that noisy crowd of evildoers.

³They sharpen their tongues like
    swords
   and aim their words like deadly
    arrows.
⁴They shoot from ambush at the
    innocent man;
   they shoot at him suddenly,
    without fear.

TUESDAY

Read *Psalm 62:1–12*
Key Verse *Psalm 62:5*

My Never-Failing Hope — Jenny Forsberg

I was lonely, and I desperately wanted to believe that God would bring that special person into my life soon. It seemed that all my good friends were in serious dating relationships. What was wrong with me? Why wasn't God giving me what I so longed for? How many more years would I have to wait?

That's how I used to feel. But now God is teaching me to hope in him instead of the dream of finding just the right person. Though it's still not easy to be single, he is teaching me to rest in him when I'm lonely and to talk to him when I'm fearful. He invites me to share with him the sad things and the humorous things that happen to me and to share my dreams and my desires. He wants to be at the center of my life, regardless of whether I'm single or married. Although he has gifted me with family and friends, he wants me to depend on him alone, because he won't fail me.

I realize that whatever God has in store for me, he is going to be with me. He wants to fill my deepest needs with his love.

My lifetime desire to get married and share my life with someone is still important to me. Like many desires I have in my life, that's totally legitimate. But should it be my ultimate hope? No. God desires good things for me, too, but he never wants those things to take his place. He wants to be first in my life—to be my perfect and never-failing hope.

A Deeper Look
Acts 2:25–28; Romans 5:5, Hebrews 6:19

Go to page 630 for your next devotional reading.

⁵They encourage each other in evil
plans,
they talk about hiding their snares;
they say, "Who will see them*a*?"
⁶They plot injustice and say,
"We have devised a perfect plan!"
Surely the mind and heart of man
are cunning.

⁷But God will shoot them with arrows;
suddenly they will be struck down.
⁸He will turn their own tongues
against them
and bring them to ruin;
all who see them will shake their
heads in scorn.

⁹All mankind will fear;
they will proclaim the works of
God
and ponder what he has done.
¹⁰Let the righteous rejoice in the LORD
and take refuge in him;
let all the upright in heart praise
him!

Psalm 65

For the director of music. A psalm
of David. A song.

¹Praise awaits*b* you, O God, in Zion;
to you our vows will be fulfilled.
²O you who hear prayer,
to you all men will come.
³When we were overwhelmed by sins,
you forgave*c* our transgressions.
⁴Blessed are those you choose
and bring near to live in your
courts!
We are filled with the good things of
your house,
of your holy temple.

⁵You answer us with awesome deeds
of righteousness,
O God our Savior,
the hope of all the ends of the earth
and of the farthest seas,
⁶who formed the mountains by your
power,
having armed yourself with
strength,
⁷who stilled the roaring of the seas,
the roaring of their waves,
and the turmoil of the nations.
⁸Those living far away fear your
wonders;
where morning dawns and evening
fades
you call forth songs of joy.

⁹You care for the land and water it;
you enrich it abundantly.
The streams of God are filled with
water
to provide the people with grain,
for so you have ordained it.*d*
¹⁰You drench its furrows
and level its ridges;
you soften it with showers
and bless its crops.
¹¹You crown the year with your
bounty,
and your carts overflow with
abundance.
¹²The grasslands of the desert overflow;
the hills are clothed with gladness.
¹³The meadows are covered with flocks
and the valleys are mantled with
grain;
they shout for joy and sing.

Psalm 66

For the director of music. A song.
A psalm.

¹Shout with joy to God, all the earth!
²   Sing the glory of his name;
make his praise glorious!
³Say to God, "How awesome are your
deeds!
So great is your power
that your enemies cringe before
you.
⁴All the earth bows down to you;
they sing praise to you,
they sing praise to your name."
                                    Selah

⁵Come and see what God has done,
how awesome his works in man's
behalf!
⁶He turned the sea into dry land,
they passed through the waters on
foot—
come, let us rejoice in him.
⁷He rules forever by his power,
his eyes watch the nations—
let not the rebellious rise up
against him.   *Selah*

⁸Praise our God, O peoples,
let the sound of his praise be
heard;
⁹he has preserved our lives
and kept our feet from slipping.

a5 Or *us*   *b1* Or *befits*; the meaning of the
Hebrew for this word is uncertain.   *c3* Or *made
atonement for*   *d9* Or *for that is how you prepare
the land*

¹⁰For you, O God, tested us;
  you refined us like silver.
¹¹You brought us into prison
  and laid burdens on our backs.
¹²You let men ride over our heads;
  we went through fire and water,
  but you brought us to a place of
    abundance.

¹³I will come to your temple with burnt
    offerings
  and fulfill my vows to you—
¹⁴vows my lips promised and my
    mouth spoke
  when I was in trouble.
¹⁵I will sacrifice fat animals to you
  and an offering of rams;
  I will offer bulls and goats.   *Selah*

¹⁶Come and listen, all you who fear
    God;
  let me tell you what he has done
    for me.
¹⁷I cried out to him with my mouth;
  his praise was on my tongue.
¹⁸If I had cherished sin in my heart,
  the Lord would not have listened;
¹⁹but God has surely listened
  and heard my voice in prayer.
²⁰Praise be to God,
  who has not rejected my prayer
  or withheld his love from me!

Psalm 67

For the director of music. With stringed
  instruments. A psalm. A song.

¹May God be gracious to us and bless
    us
  and make his face shine upon us,
                                    Selah
²that your ways may be known on
    earth,
  your salvation among all nations.

³May the peoples praise you, O God;
  may all the peoples praise you.
⁴May the nations be glad and sing for
    joy,
  for you rule the peoples justly
  and guide the nations of the earth.
                                    Selah
⁵May the peoples praise you, O God;
  may all the peoples praise you.

⁶Then the land will yield its harvest,
  and God, our God, will bless us.
⁷God will bless us,
  and all the ends of the earth will
    fear him.

Psalm 68

For the director of music. Of David.
    A psalm. A song.

¹May God arise, may his enemies be
    scattered;
  may his foes flee before him.
²As smoke is blown away by the
    wind,
  may you blow them away;
  as wax melts before the fire,
  may the wicked perish before God.
³But may the righteous be glad
  and rejoice before God;
  may they be happy and joyful.

⁴Sing to God, sing praise to his name,
  extol him who rides on the
    clouds*ᵃ*—
  his name is the LORD—
  and rejoice before him.
⁵A father to the fatherless, a defender
    of widows,
  is God in his holy dwelling.
⁶God sets the lonely in families,*ᵇ*
  he leads forth the prisoners with
    singing;
  but the rebellious live in a
    sun-scorched land.

⁷When you went out before your
    people, O God,
  when you marched through the
    wasteland,   *Selah*
⁸the earth shook,
  the heavens poured down rain,
  before God, the One of Sinai,
  before God, the God of Israel.
⁹You gave abundant showers, O God;
  you refreshed your weary
    inheritance.
¹⁰Your people settled in it,
  and from your bounty, O God, you
    provided for the poor.

¹¹The Lord announced the word,
  and great was the company of
    those who proclaimed it:
¹²"Kings and armies flee in haste;
  in the camps men divide the
    plunder.
¹³Even while you sleep among the
    campfires,*ᶜ*
  the wings of ⌊my⌋ dove are
    sheathed with silver,
  its feathers with shining gold."

ᵃ4 Or / *prepare the way for him who rides through
the deserts   *ᵇ6* Or *the desolate in a homeland*
ᶜ13 Or *saddlebags*

¹⁴When the Almighty*a* scattered the
    kings in the land,
  it was like snow fallen on Zalmon.

¹⁵The mountains of Bashan are majestic
    mountains;
  rugged are the mountains of
    Bashan.
¹⁶Why gaze in envy, O rugged
    mountains,
  at the mountain where God
    chooses to reign,

where the LORD himself will dwell
    forever?
¹⁷The chariots of God are tens of
    thousands
  and thousands of thousands;
  the Lord ⌊has come⌋ from Sinai into
    his sanctuary.
¹⁸When you ascended on high,
  you led captives in your train;
  you received gifts from men,

a 14 Hebrew *Shaddai*

Read *Psalm 66:1–20*
Key Verses *Psalm 66:18–19*

Back in Touch – Sharla Walstrom

My roommate was sound asleep as I got ready for my eight o'clock
class. What time did she get in last night? She and her other friends
stayed up late almost every night.

I slammed my dresser drawers in frustration. I was trying to get
ready by as little light as possible in our tiny dorm room. Why did
she have to sleep all morning? Why couldn't she live by *my* schedule,
like a normal person?

She stirred in her bed and I said some things that I knew would
hurt her. Then I slammed the door as I left for the day. But the incident left me feeling empty. Later that afternoon I began to pray
about my relationship with my roommate. I asked God about the situation I was in. God's questions began to ring in my heart: "Do you
think that your schedule is more important than hers? Can you love
her just as she is, as I do?" I knew then that I needed God's forgiveness for my bad attitude. I also knew that I needed to ask my roommate to forgive me.

God can work in us only if we are willing to swallow our pride
and confess our sinful actions and attitudes. The psalmist knew
that; if he had not been willing to confess his sin, "the Lord would
not have listened" (Psalm 66:18). It isn't that God doesn't already
know about our sin, but that acknowledgment of sinful attitudes
and actions is an act of humility—humility that breaks down the
wall of deceit we have built between God and ourselves. Confession
prepares us to accept his ready forgiveness and the joy and the
strength he renews in us (see Psalm 32:1–5).

The humility and openness of confession also break down the
walls between ourselves and others. When I asked my roommate to
forgive me, the Lord restored our relationship. The next day we
worked out a compromise in our schedules. That act of confession
not only drew my roommate and me closer in friendship, it also put
me back in touch with God.

A Deeper Look
Matthew 6:14; Mark 11:25

Go to page 635 for your next devotional reading.

even from*a* the rebellious—
  that you,*b* O LORD God, might
    dwell there.
¹⁹Praise be to the Lord, to God our
    Savior,
  who daily bears our burdens.   *Selah*
²⁰Our God is a God who saves;
  from the Sovereign LORD comes
    escape from death.

²¹Surely God will crush the heads of
    his enemies,
  the hairy crowns of those who go
    on in their sins.
²²The Lord says, "I will bring them
    from Bashan;
  I will bring them from the depths
    of the sea,
²³that you may plunge your feet in the
    blood of your foes,
  while the tongues of your dogs
    have their share."

²⁴Your procession has come into view,
    O God,
  the procession of my God and King
    into the sanctuary.
²⁵In front are the singers, after them
    the musicians;
  with them are the maidens playing
    tambourines.
²⁶Praise God in the great congregation;
  praise the LORD in the assembly of
    Israel.
²⁷There is the little tribe of Benjamin,
    leading them,
  there the great throng of Judah's
    princes,
  and there the princes of Zebulun
    and of Naphtali.

²⁸Summon your power, O God*c*;
  show us your strength, O God, as
    you have done before.
²⁹Because of your temple at Jerusalem
  kings will bring you gifts.
³⁰Rebuke the beast among the reeds,
  the herd of bulls among the calves
    of the nations.
  Humbled, may it bring bars of silver.
  Scatter the nations who delight in
    war.
³¹Envoys will come from Egypt;
  Cush*d* will submit herself to God.

³²Sing to God, O kingdoms of the earth,
  sing praise to the Lord,   *Selah*
³³to him who rides the ancient skies
    above,
  who thunders with mighty voice.

³⁴Proclaim the power of God,
  whose majesty is over Israel,
  whose power is in the skies.
³⁵You are awesome, O God, in your
    sanctuary;
  the God of Israel gives power and
    strength to his people.

Praise be to God!

Psalm 69

For the director of music. To ⌊the tune
of⌋ "Lilies." Of David.

¹Save me, O God,
  for the waters have come up to my
    neck.
²I sink in the miry depths,
  where there is no foothold.
  I have come into the deep waters;
  the floods engulf me.
³I am worn out calling for help;
  my throat is parched.
  My eyes fail,
    looking for my God.
⁴Those who hate me without reason
  outnumber the hairs of my head;
  many are my enemies without cause,
    those who seek to destroy me.
  I am forced to restore
    what I did not steal.

⁵You know my folly, O God;
  my guilt is not hidden from you.

⁶May those who hope in you
  not be disgraced because of me,
    O Lord, the LORD Almighty;
  may those who seek you
  not be put to shame because of
    me,
    O God of Israel.
⁷For I endure scorn for your sake,
  and shame covers my face.
⁸I am a stranger to my brothers,
  an alien to my own mother's sons;
⁹for zeal for your house consumes me,
  and the insults of those who insult
    you fall on me.
¹⁰When I weep and fast,
  I must endure scorn;
¹¹when I put on sackcloth,
  people make sport of me.
¹²Those who sit at the gate mock me,

a18 Or *gifts for men, / even*   *b18* Or *they*
c28 Many Hebrew manuscripts, Septuagint and
Syriac; most Hebrew manuscripts *Your God has
summoned power for you*   *d31* That is, the
upper Nile region

and I am the song of the
    drunkards.
13But I pray to you, O LORD,
    in the time of your favor;
in your great love, O God,
    answer me with your sure
      salvation.
14Rescue me from the mire,
    do not let me sink;
deliver me from those who hate me,
    from the deep waters.
15Do not let the floodwaters engulf me
    or the depths swallow me up
    or the pit close its mouth over me.
16Answer me, O LORD, out of the
      goodness of your love;
in your great mercy turn to me.
17Do not hide your face from your
      servant;
answer me quickly, for I am in
      trouble.
18Come near and rescue me;
    redeem me because of my foes.

19You know how I am scorned,
    disgraced and shamed;
all my enemies are before you.
20Scorn has broken my heart
    and has left me helpless;
I looked for sympathy, but there was
      none,
for comforters, but I found none.
21They put gall in my food
    and gave me vinegar for my thirst.

22May the table set before them
    become a snare;
may it become retribution and*a* a
    trap.
23May their eyes be darkened so they
    cannot see,
and their backs be bent forever.
24Pour out your wrath on them;
    let your fierce anger overtake
      them.
25May their place be deserted;
    let there be no one to dwell in
      their tents.
26For they persecute those you wound
    and talk about the pain of those
      you hurt.
27Charge them with crime upon crime;
    do not let them share in your
      salvation.
28May they be blotted out of the book
    of life
and not be listed with the
      righteous.

29I am in pain and distress;

may your salvation, O God, protect
    me.

30I will praise God's name in song
    and glorify him with thanksgiving.
31This will please the LORD more than
    an ox,
more than a bull with its horns
    and hoofs.
32The poor will see and be glad—
    you who seek God, may your
      hearts live!
33The LORD hears the needy
    and does not despise his captive
      people.

34Let heaven and earth praise him,
    the seas and all that move in them,
35for God will save Zion
    and rebuild the cities of Judah.
Then people will settle there and
      possess it;
36   the children of his servants will
      inherit it,
and those who love his name will
      dwell there.

Psalm 70

For the director of music. Of David.
A petition.

1Hasten, O God, to save me;
    O LORD, come quickly to help me.
2May those who seek my life
    be put to shame and confusion;
may all who desire my ruin
    be turned back in disgrace.
3May those who say to me, "Aha!
    Aha!"
turn back because of their shame.
4But may all who seek you
    rejoice and be glad in you;

a22 Or snare / and their fellowship become

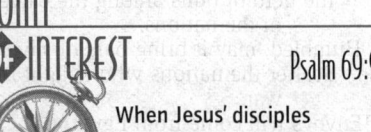

POINT OF INTEREST   Psalm 69:9

When Jesus' disciples
observed his reaction to the
merchants' desecration of
the temple courts, they
remembered this verse (see John 2:13–
17). When people see your actions, do
they see you defending God's interests?

may those who love your salvation
always say,
"Let God be exalted!"
⁵Yet I am poor and needy;
come quickly to me, O God.
You are my help and my deliverer;
O LORD, do not delay.

Psalm 71

¹In you, O LORD, I have taken refuge;
let me never be put to shame.
²Rescue me and deliver me in your
righteousness;
turn your ear to me and save me.
³Be my rock of refuge,
to which I can always go;
give the command to save me,
for you are my rock and my
fortress.
⁴Deliver me, O my God, from the hand
of the wicked,
from the grasp of evil and cruel
men.

⁵For you have been my hope,
O Sovereign LORD,
my confidence since my youth.
⁶From birth I have relied on you;
you brought me forth from my
mother's womb.
I will ever praise you.
⁷I have become like a portent to
many,
but you are my strong refuge.
⁸My mouth is filled with your praise,
declaring your splendor all day
long.

⁹Do not cast me away when I am old;
do not forsake me when my
strength is gone.
¹⁰For my enemies speak against me;
those who wait to kill me conspire
together.
¹¹They say, "God has forsaken him;
pursue him and seize him,
for no one will rescue him."
¹²Be not far from me, O God;
come quickly, O my God, to help
me.
¹³May my accusers perish in shame;
may those who want to harm me
be covered with scorn and
disgrace.

¹⁴But as for me, I will always have
hope;
I will praise you more and more.

¹⁵My mouth will tell of your
righteousness,
of your salvation all day long,
though I know not its measure.
¹⁶I will come and proclaim your mighty
acts, O Sovereign LORD;
I will proclaim your righteousness,
yours alone.
¹⁷Since my youth, O God, you have
taught me,
and to this day I declare your
marvelous deeds.
¹⁸Even when I am old and gray,
do not forsake me, O God,
till I declare your power to the next
generation,
your might to all who are to come.

¹⁹Your righteousness reaches to the
skies, O God,
you who have done great things.
Who, O God, is like you?
²⁰Though you have made me see
troubles, many and bitter,
you will restore my life again;
from the depths of the earth
you will again bring me up.
²¹You will increase my honor
and comfort me once again.

²²I will praise you with the harp
for your faithfulness, O my God;
I will sing praise to you with the lyre,
O Holy One of Israel.
²³My lips will shout for joy
when I sing praise to you—
I, whom you have redeemed.
²⁴My tongue will tell of your righteous
acts
all day long,
for those who wanted to harm me
have been put to shame and
confusion.

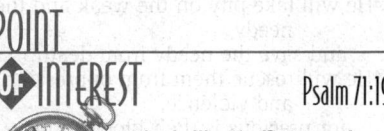

POINT OF INTEREST

Psalm 71:19

Who is like God? No one!
God is not just one choice
from a menu of possible
deities. God is unique, the only
power in the universe worthy of our worship and awe. Read Job 40:7—42:6 to see
how God sees himself. Then read John 14:6
to see how Jesus Christ defines himself.

Psalm 72

Of Solomon.

¹Endow the king with your justice,
   O God,
   the royal son with your
      righteousness.
²He will*ᵃ* judge your people in
      righteousness,
   your afflicted ones with justice.
³The mountains will bring prosperity
      to the people,
   the hills the fruit of righteousness.
⁴He will defend the afflicted among
      the people
   and save the children of the needy;
   he will crush the oppressor.

⁵He will endure*ᵇ* as long as the sun,
   as long as the moon, through all
      generations.
⁶He will be like rain falling on a
      mown field,
   like showers watering the earth.
⁷In his days the righteous will flourish;
   prosperity will abound till the
      moon is no more.

⁸He will rule from sea to sea
   and from the River*ᶜ* to the ends of
      the earth.*ᵈ*
⁹The desert tribes will bow before him
   and his enemies will lick the dust.
¹⁰The kings of Tarshish and of distant
      shores
   will bring tribute to him;
   the kings of Sheba and Seba
   will present him gifts.
¹¹All kings will bow down to him
   and all nations will serve him.

¹²For he will deliver the needy who cry
      out,
   the afflicted who have no one to
      help.
¹³He will take pity on the weak and the
      needy
   and save the needy from death.
¹⁴He will rescue them from oppression
      and violence,
   for precious is their blood in his
      sight.
¹⁵Long may he live!
   May gold from Sheba be given
      him.
   May people ever pray for him
   and bless him all day long.
¹⁶Let grain abound throughout the
      land;

on the tops of the hills may it
      sway.
   Let its fruit flourish like Lebanon;
   let it thrive like the grass of the
      field.
¹⁷May his name endure forever;
   may it continue as long as the sun.

   All nations will be blessed through
      him,
   and they will call him blessed.

¹⁸Praise be to the Lᴏʀᴅ God, the God of
      Israel,
   who alone does marvelous deeds.
¹⁹Praise be to his glorious name
      forever;
   may the whole earth be filled with
      his glory.
         Amen and Amen.

²⁰This concludes the prayers of David
      son of Jesse.

BOOK III

Psalms 73–89

Psalm 73

A psalm of Asaph.

¹Surely God is good to Israel,
   to those who are pure in heart.

²But as for me, my feet had almost
      slipped;
   I had nearly lost my foothold.
³For I envied the arrogant
   when I saw the prosperity of the
      wicked.

⁴They have no struggles;
   their bodies are healthy and
      strong.*ᵉ*
⁵They are free from the burdens
      common to man;
   they are not plagued by human
      ills.
⁶Therefore pride is their necklace;
   they clothe themselves with
      violence.
⁷From their callous hearts comes
      iniquity*ᶠ*;

---

*ᵃ*2 Or *May he*; similarly in verses 3-11 and 17
*ᵇ*5 Septuagint; Hebrew *You will be feared*
*ᶜ*8 That is, the Euphrates   *ᵈ*8 Or *the end of the
land*   *ᵉ*4 With a different word division of the
Hebrew; Masoretic Text *struggles at their death; /
their bodies are healthy*   *ᶠ*7 Syriac (see also
Septuagint); Hebrew *Their eyes bulge with fat*

the evil conceits of their minds
     know no limits.
[8]They scoff, and speak with malice;
     in their arrogance they threaten
     oppression.
[9]Their mouths lay claim to heaven,
     and their tongues take possession
     of the earth.
[10]Therefore their people turn to them
     and drink up waters in
     abundance.[a]
[11]They say, "How can God know?
     Does the Most High have
     knowledge?"

[12]This is what the wicked are like—
     always carefree, they increase in
     wealth.

[13]Surely in vain have I kept my heart
     pure;
     in vain have I washed my hands in
     innocence.
[14]All day long I have been plagued;
     I have been punished every
     morning.

[15]If I had said, "I will speak thus,"
     I would have betrayed your
     children.
[16]When I tried to understand all this,
     it was oppressive to me
[17]till I entered the sanctuary of God;
     then I understood their final
     destiny.

[a] 10 The meaning of the Hebrew for this verse is
uncertain.

THURSDAY

Read *Psalm 73:1–28*
Key Verses *Psalm 73:16–17*

Perspective Is Everything — Carol Rugg

Imagine yourself sitting outside on a clear summer night. A full
moon is shining brilliantly in the sky. You know that the moon is
2,160 miles in diameter, but if you position your thumb in just the
right spot between your eye and the moon, you can completely
cover that bright sphere. Your less-than-one-inch-wide thumb looks
bigger than the moon. The lesson in this? *Perspective is everything.*

To Asaph, the author of Psalm 73, that statement was certainly
true. He was envious—barely able to keep his foothold when he
saw God allowing evil people to enjoy good things and to prosper
(see Psalm 73:2–3). But when Asaph "entered the sanctuary of
God," his perspective changed. In the midst of immediate confusion
and injustice he understood the "final destiny" of the wicked (see
Psalm 73:17). He was able to see and understand his position in life,
and that of others, from God's perspective.

God is all-powerful, all-knowing and all-loving. His wisdom is so
vast compared to our problems. Yet so often we let our "thumbs"
get in the way. When our problems seem insurmountable, when situations don't seem just or fair, we lose sight of God—we lose our
perspective.

When we measure our problems against God's greatness instead
of our weakness, taking care to focus on who God is, we can move
through life with an *eternal* perspective rather than with our *limited*
perspective. Like Asaph, we must stop and spend time with God in
order to maintain his perspective on life.

A Deeper Look
Jeremiah 12:1–5; 2 Corinthians 4:18; Colossians 3:2

Go to page 644 for your next devotional reading.

¹⁸Surely you place them on slippery
     ground;
   you cast them down to ruin.
¹⁹How suddenly are they destroyed,
   completely swept away by terrors!
²⁰As a dream when one awakes,
   so when you arise, O Lord,
   you will despise them as fantasies.

²¹When my heart was grieved
   and my spirit embittered,
²²I was senseless and ignorant;
   I was a brute beast before you.

²³Yet I am always with you;
   you hold me by my right hand.
²⁴You guide me with your counsel,
   and afterward you will take me
     into glory.
²⁵Whom have I in heaven but you?
   And earth has nothing I desire
     besides you.
²⁶My flesh and my heart may fail,
   but God is the strength of my heart
   and my portion forever.

²⁷Those who are far from you will
     perish;
   you destroy all who are unfaithful
     to you.
²⁸But as for me, it is good to be near
     God.
   I have made the Sovereign LORD my
     refuge;
   I will tell of all your deeds.

Psalm 74

A *maskil*[a] of Asaph.

¹Why have you rejected us forever,
   O God?
   Why does your anger smolder
   against the sheep of your
     pasture?
²Remember the people you purchased
   of old,
   the tribe of your inheritance,
   whom you redeemed—
   Mount Zion, where you dwelt.
³Turn your steps toward these
     everlasting ruins,
   all this destruction the enemy has
   brought on the sanctuary.

⁴Your foes roared in the place where
     you met with us;
   they set up their standards as
     signs.
⁵They behaved like men wielding axes
   to cut through a thicket of trees.

⁶They smashed all the carved paneling
   with their axes and hatchets.
⁷They burned your sanctuary to the
     ground;
   they defiled the dwelling place of
     your Name.
⁸They said in their hearts, "We will
   crush them completely!"
   They burned every place where
   God was worshiped in the
     land.
⁹We are given no miraculous signs;
   no prophets are left,
   and none of us knows how long
     this will be.

¹⁰How long will the enemy mock you,
   O God?
   Will the foe revile your name
     forever?
¹¹Why do you hold back your hand,
     your right hand?
   Take it from the folds of your
   garment and destroy them!

¹²But you, O God, are my king from of
     old;
   you bring salvation upon the earth.
¹³It was you who split open the sea by
     your power;
   you broke the heads of the
     monster in the waters.
¹⁴It was you who crushed the heads of
     Leviathan
   and gave him as food to the
     creatures of the desert.
¹⁵It was you who opened up springs
     and streams;
   you dried up the ever flowing
     rivers.
¹⁶The day is yours, and yours also the
     night;
   you established the sun and moon.
¹⁷It was you who set all the boundaries
     of the earth;
   you made both summer and
     winter.

¹⁸Remember how the enemy has
     mocked you, O LORD,
   how foolish people have reviled
     your name.
¹⁹Do not hand over the life of your
     dove to wild beasts;
   do not forget the lives of your
     afflicted people forever.
²⁰Have regard for your covenant,

---

a Title: Probably a literary or musical term

because haunts of violence fill the
dark places of the land.
²¹Do not let the oppressed retreat in
disgrace;
may the poor and needy praise
your name.

²²Rise up, O God, and defend your
cause;
remember how fools mock you all
day long.
²³Do not ignore the clamor of your
adversaries,
the uproar of your enemies, which
rises continually.

Psalm 75

For the director of music. ⌊To the tune
of⌋ "Do Not Destroy." A psalm of
Asaph. A song.

¹We give thanks to you, O God,
we give thanks, for your Name is
near;
men tell of your wonderful deeds.

²You say, "I choose the appointed
time;
it is I who judge uprightly.
³When the earth and all its people
quake,
it is I who hold its pillars firm.
                                        Selah
⁴To the arrogant I say, 'Boast no
more,'
and to the wicked, 'Do not lift up
your horns.
⁵Do not lift your horns against heaven;
do not speak with outstretched
neck.' "

⁶No one from the east or the west
or from the desert can exalt a man.
⁷But it is God who judges:
He brings one down, he exalts
another.
⁸In the hand of the LORD is a cup
full of foaming wine mixed with
spices;
he pours it out, and all the wicked of
the earth
drink it down to its very dregs.

⁹As for me, I will declare this forever;
I will sing praise to the God of
Jacob.
¹⁰I will cut off the horns of all the
wicked,
but the horns of the righteous will
be lifted up.

Psalm 76

For the director of music. With stringed
instruments. A psalm of Asaph. A song.

¹In Judah God is known;
his name is great in Israel.
²His tent is in Salem,
his dwelling place in Zion.
³There he broke the flashing arrows,
the shields and the swords, the
weapons of war.   *Selah*

⁴You are resplendent with light,
more majestic than mountains rich
with game.
⁵Valiant men lie plundered,
they sleep their last sleep;
not one of the warriors
can lift his hands.
⁶At your rebuke, O God of Jacob,
both horse and chariot lie still.
⁷You alone are to be feared.
Who can stand before you when
you are angry?
⁸From heaven you pronounced
judgment,
and the land feared and was
quiet—
⁹when you, O God, rose up to judge,
to save all the afflicted of the land.
                                        Selah
¹⁰Surely your wrath against men brings
you praise,
and the survivors of your wrath
are restrained.*ᵃ*

¹¹Make vows to the LORD your God and
fulfill them;
let all the neighboring lands
bring gifts to the One to be feared.
¹²He breaks the spirit of rulers;
he is feared by the kings of the
earth.

Psalm 77

For the director of music. For Jeduthun.
Of Asaph. A psalm.

¹I cried out to God for help;
I cried out to God to hear me.
²When I was in distress, I sought the
Lord;
at night I stretched out untiring
hands
and my soul refused to be
comforted.

*ᵃ 10 Or Surely the wrath of men brings you praise, /
and with the remainder of wrath you arm yourself*

³I remembered you, O God, and I
    groaned;
  I mused, and my spirit grew faint.
                       Selah
⁴You kept my eyes from closing;
  I was too troubled to speak.
⁵I thought about the former days,
  the years of long ago;
⁶I remembered my songs in the night.
  My heart mused and my spirit
    inquired:

⁷"Will the Lord reject forever?
  Will he never show his favor
    again?
⁸Has his unfailing love vanished
    forever?
  Has his promise failed for all time?
⁹Has God forgotten to be merciful?
  Has he in anger withheld his
    compassion?"   *Selah*

¹⁰Then I thought, "To this I will
    appeal:
  the years of the right hand of the
    Most High."
¹¹I will remember the deeds of the
    Lord;
  yes, I will remember your miracles
    of long ago.
¹²I will meditate on all your works
  and consider all your mighty
    deeds.

¹³Your ways, O God, are holy.
  What god is so great as our God?
¹⁴You are the God who performs
    miracles;
  you display your power among the
    peoples.
¹⁵With your mighty arm you redeemed
    your people,
  the descendants of Jacob and
    Joseph.   *Selah*

¹⁶The waters saw you, O God,
  the waters saw you and writhed;
  the very depths were convulsed.
¹⁷The clouds poured down water,
  the skies resounded with thunder;
  your arrows flashed back and
    forth.
¹⁸Your thunder was heard in the
    whirlwind,
  your lightning lit up the world;
  the earth trembled and quaked.
¹⁹Your path led through the sea,
  your way through the mighty
    waters,
  though your footprints were not
    seen.

²⁰You led your people like a flock
  by the hand of Moses and Aaron.

Psalm 78

A *maskil*[a] of Asaph.

¹O my people, hear my teaching;
  listen to the words of my mouth.
²I will open my mouth in parables,
  I will utter hidden things, things
    from of old—
³what we have heard and known,
  what our fathers have told us.
⁴We will not hide them from their
    children;
  we will tell the next generation
  the praiseworthy deeds of the Lord,
  his power, and the wonders he has
    done.
⁵He decreed statutes for Jacob
  and established the law in Israel,
  which he commanded our forefathers
  to teach their children,
⁶so the next generation would know
    them,
  even the children yet to be born,
  and they in turn would tell their
    children.
⁷Then they would put their trust in
    God
  and would not forget his deeds
  but would keep his commands.

*a*Title: Probably a literary or musical term

POINT OF INTEREST

Psalm 77:12

Asaph here meditates on God's mighty deeds and then sings out in God's praise. The practice of meditation is as old as the Judeo-Christian tradition itself. But because many other religions practice meditation, some Christians are suspicious of it. Used properly, however, meditation is a valuable tool. Meditation is concentrated, repetitive thinking about something—and it is as good as what it is focused upon. If we meditate on God, his Word and his truth, that's the best. Check it out with Asaph.

8They would not be like their
forefathers—
a stubborn and rebellious
generation,
whose hearts were not loyal to God,
whose spirits were not faithful to
him.

9The men of Ephraim, though armed
with bows,
turned back on the day of battle;
10they did not keep God's covenant
and refused to live by his law.
11They forgot what he had done,
the wonders he had shown them.
12He did miracles in the sight of their
fathers
in the land of Egypt, in the region
of Zoan.
13He divided the sea and led them
through;
he made the water stand firm like
a wall.
14He guided them with the cloud by
day
and with light from the fire all
night.
15He split the rocks in the desert
and gave them water as abundant
as the seas;
16he brought streams out of a rocky
crag
and made water flow down like
rivers.

17But they continued to sin against
him,
rebelling in the desert against the
Most High.
18They willfully put God to the test
by demanding the food they
craved.
19They spoke against God, saying,
"Can God spread a table in the
desert?
20When he struck the rock, water
gushed out,
and streams flowed abundantly.
But can he also give us food?
Can he supply meat for his
people?"
21When the LORD heard them, he was
very angry;
his fire broke out against Jacob,
and his wrath rose against Israel,
22for they did not believe in God
or trust in his deliverance.
23Yet he gave a command to the skies
above

and opened the doors of the
heavens;
24he rained down manna for the people
to eat,
he gave them the grain of heaven.
25Men ate the bread of angels;
he sent them all the food they
could eat.
26He let loose the east wind from the
heavens
and led forth the south wind by his
power.
27He rained meat down on them like
dust,
flying birds like sand on the
seashore.
28He made them come down inside
their camp,
all around their tents.
29They ate till they had more than
enough,
for he had given them what they
craved.
30But before they turned from the food
they craved,
even while it was still in their
mouths,
31God's anger rose against them;
he put to death the sturdiest
among them,
cutting down the young men of
Israel.

32In spite of all this, they kept on
sinning;
in spite of his wonders, they did
not believe.
33So he ended their days in futility
and their years in terror.
34Whenever God slew them, they
would seek him;
they eagerly turned to him again.
35They remembered that God was their
Rock,
that God Most High was their
Redeemer.
36But then they would flatter him with
their mouths,
lying to him with their tongues;
37their hearts were not loyal to him,
they were not faithful to his
covenant.
38Yet he was merciful;
he forgave their iniquities
and did not destroy them.
Time after time he restrained his
anger
and did not stir up his full wrath.

³⁹He remembered that they were but
flesh,
a passing breeze that does not
return.

⁴⁰How often they rebelled against him
in the desert
and grieved him in the wasteland!
⁴¹Again and again they put God to the
test;
they vexed the Holy One of Israel.
⁴²They did not remember his power—
the day he redeemed them from
the oppressor,
⁴³the day he displayed his miraculous
signs in Egypt,
his wonders in the region of Zoan.
⁴⁴He turned their rivers to blood;
they could not drink from their
streams.
⁴⁵He sent swarms of flies that devoured
them,
and frogs that devastated them.
⁴⁶He gave their crops to the
grasshopper,
their produce to the locust.
⁴⁷He destroyed their vines with hail
and their sycamore-figs with sleet.
⁴⁸He gave over their cattle to the hail,
their livestock to bolts of lightning.
⁴⁹He unleashed against them his hot
anger,
his wrath, indignation and
hostility—
a band of destroying angels.
⁵⁰He prepared a path for his anger;
he did not spare them from death
but gave them over to the plague.
⁵¹He struck down all the firstborn of
Egypt,
the firstfruits of manhood in the
tents of Ham.
⁵²But he brought his people out like a
flock;
he led them like sheep through the
desert.
⁵³He guided them safely, so they were
unafraid;
but the sea engulfed their enemies.
⁵⁴Thus he brought them to the border
of his holy land,
to the hill country his right hand
had taken.
⁵⁵He drove out nations before them
and allotted their lands to them as
an inheritance;
he settled the tribes of Israel in
their homes.

⁵⁶But they put God to the test

and rebelled against the Most High;
they did not keep his statutes.
⁵⁷Like their fathers they were disloyal
and faithless,
as unreliable as a faulty bow.
⁵⁸They angered him with their high
places;
they aroused his jealousy with
their idols.
⁵⁹When God heard them, he was very
angry;
he rejected Israel completely.
⁶⁰He abandoned the tabernacle of
Shiloh,
the tent he had set up among men.
⁶¹He sent ˌthe ark ofˌ his might into
captivity,
his splendor into the hands of the
enemy.
⁶²He gave his people over to the sword;
he was very angry with his
inheritance.
⁶³Fire consumed their young men,
and their maidens had no wedding
songs;
⁶⁴their priests were put to the sword,
and their widows could not weep.

⁶⁵Then the Lord awoke as from sleep,
as a man wakes from the stupor of
wine.
⁶⁶He beat back his enemies;
he put them to everlasting shame.
⁶⁷Then he rejected the tents of Joseph,
he did not choose the tribe of
Ephraim;
⁶⁸but he chose the tribe of Judah,
Mount Zion, which he loved.
⁶⁹He built his sanctuary like the
heights,
like the earth that he established
forever.
⁷⁰He chose David his servant
and took him from the sheep pens;
⁷¹from tending the sheep he brought
him
to be the shepherd of his people
Jacob,
of Israel his inheritance.
⁷²And David shepherded them with
integrity of heart;
with skillful hands he led them.

Psalm 79

A psalm of Asaph.

¹O God, the nations have invaded your
inheritance;

they have defiled your holy temple,
they have reduced Jerusalem to
rubble.
²They have given the dead bodies of
your servants
as food to the birds of the air,
the flesh of your saints to the
beasts of the earth.
³They have poured out blood like
water
all around Jerusalem,
and there is no one to bury the
dead.
⁴We are objects of reproach to our
neighbors,
of scorn and derision to those
around us.

⁵How long, O Lᴏʀᴅ? Will you be angry
forever?
How long will your jealousy burn
like fire?
⁶Pour out your wrath on the nations
that do not acknowledge you,
on the kingdoms
that do not call on your name;
⁷for they have devoured Jacob
and destroyed his homeland.
⁸Do not hold against us the sins of the
fathers;
may your mercy come quickly to
meet us,
for we are in desperate need.

⁹Help us, O God our Savior,
for the glory of your name;
deliver us and forgive our sins
for your name's sake.
¹⁰Why should the nations say,
"Where is their God?"
Before our eyes, make known among
the nations
that you avenge the outpoured
blood of your servants.
¹¹May the groans of the prisoners come
before you;
by the strength of your arm
preserve those condemned to
die.
¹²Pay back into the laps of our
neighbors seven times
the reproach they have hurled at
you, O Lord.
¹³Then we your people, the sheep of
your pasture,
will praise you forever;
from generation to generation
we will recount your praise.

Psalm 80

For the director of music. To ⌜the tune
of⌝ "The Lilies of the Covenant."
Of Asaph. A psalm.

¹Hear us, O Shepherd of Israel,
you who lead Joseph like a flock;
you who sit enthroned between the
cherubim, shine forth
²   before Ephraim, Benjamin and
Manasseh.
Awaken your might;
come and save us.

³Restore us, O God;
make your face shine upon us,
that we may be saved.

⁴O Lᴏʀᴅ God Almighty,
how long will your anger smolder
against the prayers of your people?
⁵You have fed them with the bread of
tears;
you have made them drink tears
by the bowlful.
⁶You have made us a source of
contention to our neighbors,
and our enemies mock us.

⁷Restore us, O God Almighty;
make your face shine upon us,
that we may be saved.

⁸You brought a vine out of Egypt;
you drove out the nations and
planted it.
⁹You cleared the ground for it,
and it took root and filled the land.
¹⁰The mountains were covered with its
shade,
the mighty cedars with its
branches.

POINT OF INTEREST

Psalm 78:72

David spent many of his youthful years working as a shepherd. While this job was far from glamorous, God used this time to give David the skills he needed to shepherd Israel. God is working in your life too. Your waiting time is not wasted time. Patiently trust God to prepare you for the life he has waiting for you.

¹¹It sent out its boughs to the Sea,ᵃ
  its shoots as far as the River.ᵇ

¹²Why have you broken down its walls
  so that all who pass by pick its
    grapes?
¹³Boars from the forest ravage it
  and the creatures of the field feed
    on it.
¹⁴Return to us, O God Almighty!
  Look down from heaven and see!
  Watch over this vine,
¹⁵ the root your right hand has
    planted,
  the sonᶜ you have raised up for
    yourself.

¹⁶Your vine is cut down, it is burned
    with fire;
  at your rebuke your people perish.
¹⁷Let your hand rest on the man at
    your right hand,
  the son of man you have raised up
    for yourself.
¹⁸Then we will not turn away from
    you;
  revive us, and we will call on your
    name.

¹⁹Restore us, O Lord God Almighty;
  make your face shine upon us,
  that we may be saved.

Psalm 81

For the director of music. According to
  gittith.ᵈ Of Asaph.

¹Sing for joy to God our strength;
  shout aloud to the God of Jacob!
²Begin the music, strike the
    tambourine,
  play the melodious harp and lyre.

³Sound the ram's horn at the New
    Moon,
  and when the moon is full, on the
    day of our Feast;
⁴this is a decree for Israel,
  an ordinance of the God of Jacob.
⁵He established it as a statute for
    Joseph
  when he went out against Egypt,
  where we heard a language we did
    not understand.ᵉ

⁶He says, "I removed the burden from
    their shoulders;
  their hands were set free from the
    basket.
⁷In your distress you called and I
    rescued you,

I answered you out of a
    thundercloud;
  I tested you at the waters of
    Meribah.   *Selah*

⁸"Hear, O my people, and I will warn
    you—
  if you would but listen to me,
    O Israel!
⁹You shall have no foreign god among
    you;
  you shall not bow down to an
    alien god.
¹⁰I am the Lord your God,
  who brought you up out of Egypt.
  Open wide your mouth and I will
    fill it.

¹¹"But my people would not listen to
    me;
  Israel would not submit to me.
¹²So I gave them over to their stubborn
    hearts
  to follow their own devices.

¹³"If my people would but listen to me,
  if Israel would follow my ways,
¹⁴how quickly would I subdue their
    enemies
  and turn my hand against their
    foes!
¹⁵Those who hate the Lord would
    cringe before him,
  and their punishment would last
    forever.
¹⁶But you would be fed with the finest
    of wheat;

ᵃ11 Probably the Mediterranean   ᵇ11 That is,
the Euphrates   ᶜ15 Or *branch*   ᵈTitle:
Probably a musical term   ᵉ5 Or / *and we heard
a voice we had not known*

POINT OF INTEREST   Psalm 81:10

Imagine a nest filled with
hungry baby birds. When
the mother bird flies in with
insects or seeds, every mouth
pops open. Little chirps chorus, "Me, me!
Feed me!" as the mother places food in
each eager mouth. God invites us to be
like baby birds, hungry for his Word and
eager to always receive more. He cares for
us just as he did the people of Israel in the
desert.

with honey from the rock I would
satisfy you."

Psalm 82

A psalm of Asaph.

¹God presides in the great assembly;
he gives judgment among the
"gods":

²"How long will you[a] defend the
unjust
and show partiality to the wicked?
Selah
³Defend the cause of the weak and
fatherless;
maintain the rights of the poor and
oppressed.
⁴Rescue the weak and needy;
deliver them from the hand of the
wicked.

⁵"They know nothing, they understand
nothing.
They walk about in darkness;
all the foundations of the earth are
shaken.

⁶"I said, 'You are "gods";
you are all sons of the Most High.'
⁷But you will die like mere men;
you will fall like every other ruler."

⁸Rise up, O God, judge the earth,
for all the nations are your
inheritance.

Psalm 83

A song. A psalm of Asaph.

¹O God, do not keep silent;
be not quiet, O God, be not still.
²See how your enemies are astir,
how your foes rear their heads.
³With cunning they conspire against
your people;
they plot against those you cherish.
⁴"Come," they say, "let us destroy
them as a nation,
that the name of Israel be
remembered no more."

⁵With one mind they plot together;
they form an alliance against
you—
⁶the tents of Edom and the
Ishmaelites,
of Moab and the Hagrites,
⁷Gebal,[b] Ammon and Amalek,
Philistia, with the people of Tyre.

⁸Even Assyria has joined them
to lend strength to the descendants
of Lot. *Selah*

⁹Do to them as you did to Midian,
as you did to Sisera and Jabin at
the river Kishon,
¹⁰who perished at Endor
and became like refuse on the
ground.
¹¹Make their nobles like Oreb and
Zeeb,
all their princes like Zebah and
Zalmunna,
¹²who said, "Let us take possession
of the pasturelands of God."

¹³Make them like tumbleweed, O my
God,
like chaff before the wind.
¹⁴As fire consumes the forest
or a flame sets the mountains
ablaze,
¹⁵so pursue them with your tempest
and terrify them with your storm.
¹⁶Cover their faces with shame
so that men will seek your name,
O LORD.

¹⁷May they ever be ashamed and
dismayed;
may they perish in disgrace.
¹⁸Let them know that you, whose name
is the LORD—
that you alone are the Most High
over all the earth.

Psalm 84

*For the director of music. According to
gittith.[c] Of the Sons of Korah.
A psalm.*

¹How lovely is your dwelling place,
O LORD Almighty!
²My soul yearns, even faints,
for the courts of the LORD;
my heart and my flesh cry out
for the living God.

³Even the sparrow has found a home,
and the swallow a nest for herself,
where she may have her young—
a place near your altar,
O LORD Almighty, my King and my
God.
⁴Blessed are those who dwell in your
house;
they are ever praising you. *Selah*

---

a2 The Hebrew is plural.   *b7* That is, Byblos
*c*Title: Probably a musical term

⁵Blessed are those whose strength is in
    you,
who have set their hearts on
    pilgrimage.
⁶As they pass through the Valley of
    Baca,
they make it a place of springs;
the autumn rains also cover it with
    pools.ᵃ
⁷They go from strength to strength,
till each appears before God in
    Zion.

⁸Hear my prayer, O LORD God
    Almighty;
listen to me, O God of Jacob.   *Selah*

⁹Look upon our shield,ᵇ O God;
    look with favor on your anointed
    one.
¹⁰Better is one day in your courts
    than a thousand elsewhere;
I would rather be a doorkeeper in the
    house of my God
than dwell in the tents of the
    wicked.
¹¹For the LORD God is a sun and shield;
    the LORD bestows favor and honor;
no good thing does he withhold
    from those whose walk is
    blameless.

ᵃ6 Or blessings   *ᵇ9 Or sovereign*

FRIDAY

Read Psalm 84:1–12
Key Verse Psalm 84:11

Under the Circumstances or Under God? – Phil Ward

"Dogpile!"

That was a dreaded word during my college days. You know the routine: One person is targeted by umpteen others to be buried beneath a pile of bodies. My recollections of being the guy on the bottom are still pretty vivid. For some reason, all 5'7" and 130 pounds of me were deemed prime "dogpile" fodder by my college buddies. Miraculously, I was never seriously hurt by the variety of larger guys who threw themselves on top of me and each other.

It wasn't until I saw photographs of one of these infamous "dog-piles" that I understood how I survived. Among those sprawled over my slight frame were a few stouthearted guys whose outstretched arms were supporting a good portion of the weight above me. So, while I bore part of the load, my true friends were shielding me from the brunt of the weight and discomfort.

Sometimes life "dogpiles" us like that too. So often our struggles make us feel as if we have little recourse but to give in and give up. But when we find ourselves under those heavy circumstances, it is comforting to know that God, even more than my strong college friends, shields us in times when trouble is piled on trouble. He promises we won't get squashed. No worldly weight is any match for God's protective arms.

What pile do you find yourself under today—bills you can't imagine being able to pay, course work that seems to surpass your abilities, a relationship that seems beyond repair? Whatever circumstances you're under, remember who is bearing the load. Look up to the One who is able to shield you from harm and pull you out of the heap.

A Deeper Look
2 Samuel 22:3,31; Psalm 18:2; 1 John 5:18

Go to page 650 for your next devotional reading.

¹²O Lᴏʀᴅ Almighty,
　　blessed is the man who trusts in
　　　you.

Psalm 85

For the director of music. Of the Sons
of Korah. A psalm.

¹You showed favor to your land,
　　O Lᴏʀᴅ;
　　you restored the fortunes of Jacob.
²You forgave the iniquity of your
　　people
　　and covered all their sins.　　*Selah*
³You set aside all your wrath
　　and turned from your fierce anger.

⁴Restore us again, O God our Savior,
　　and put away your displeasure
　　　toward us.
⁵Will you be angry with us forever?
　　Will you prolong your anger
　　　through all generations?
⁶Will you not revive us again,
　　that your people may rejoice in
　　　you?
⁷Show us your unfailing love, O Lᴏʀᴅ,
　　and grant us your salvation.

⁸I will listen to what God the Lᴏʀᴅ will
　　say;
　　he promises peace to his people,
　　　his saints—
　　but let them not return to folly.
⁹Surely his salvation is near those who
　　fear him,
　　that his glory may dwell in our
　　　land.

¹⁰Love and faithfulness meet together;
　　righteousness and peace kiss each
　　　other.
¹¹Faithfulness springs forth from the
　　earth,
　　and righteousness looks down from
　　　heaven.
¹²The Lᴏʀᴅ will indeed give what is
　　good,
　　and our land will yield its harvest.
¹³Righteousness goes before him
　　and prepares the way for his steps.

Psalm 86

A prayer of David.

¹Hear, O Lᴏʀᴅ, and answer me,
　　for I am poor and needy.
²Guard my life, for I am devoted to
　　you.
You are my God; save your servant
　　who trusts in you.
³Have mercy on me, O Lord,
　　for I call to you all day long.
⁴Bring joy to your servant,
　　for to you, O Lord,
　　I lift up my soul.

⁵You are forgiving and good, O Lord,
　　abounding in love to all who call
　　　to you.
⁶Hear my prayer, O Lᴏʀᴅ;
　　listen to my cry for mercy.
⁷In the day of my trouble I will call to
　　you,
　　for you will answer me.

⁸Among the gods there is none like
　　you, O Lord;
　　no deeds can compare with yours.
⁹All the nations you have made
　　will come and worship before you,
　　　O Lord;
　　they will bring glory to your name.
¹⁰For you are great and do marvelous
　　deeds;
　　you alone are God.

¹¹Teach me your way, O Lᴏʀᴅ,
　　and I will walk in your truth;
give me an undivided heart,
　　that I may fear your name.
¹²I will praise you, O Lord my God,
　　with all my heart;
　　I will glorify your name forever.
¹³For great is your love toward me;
　　you have delivered me from the
　　　depths of the grave.[a]

¹⁴The arrogant are attacking me,
　　O God;
　　a band of ruthless men seeks my
　　　life—
　　men without regard for you.
¹⁵But you, O Lord, are a compassionate
　　and gracious God,
　　slow to anger, abounding in love
　　　and faithfulness.
¹⁶Turn to me and have mercy on me;
　　grant your strength to your servant
　　and save the son of your
　　　maidservant.[b]
¹⁷Give me a sign of your goodness,
　　that my enemies may see it and be
　　　put to shame,
　　for you, O Lᴏʀᴅ, have helped me
　　　and comforted me.

---

[a] 13 Hebrew *Sheol*　　[b] 16 Or *save your faithful son*

Psalm 87

Of the Sons of Korah. A psalm. A song.

¹He has set his foundation on the holy
mountain;
² the LORD loves the gates of Zion
more than all the dwellings of
Jacob.
³Glorious things are said of you,
O city of God: Selah
⁴"I will record Rahab[a] and Babylon
among those who acknowledge
me—
Philistia too, and Tyre, along with
Cush[b]—
and will say, 'This[c] one was born
in Zion.' "

⁵Indeed, of Zion it will be said,
"This one and that one were born
in her,
and the Most High himself will
establish her."
⁶The LORD will write in the register of
the peoples:
"This one was born in Zion." Selah
⁷As they make music they will sing,
"All my fountains are in you."

Psalm 88

A song. A psalm of the Sons of Korah.
For the director of music. According to
mahalath leannoth.[d] A *maskil*[e] of
Heman the Ezrahite.

¹O LORD, the God who saves me,
day and night I cry out before you.
²May my prayer come before you;
turn your ear to my cry.

³For my soul is full of trouble
and my life draws near the
grave.[f]
⁴I am counted among those who go
down to the pit;
I am like a man without strength.
⁵I am set apart with the dead,
like the slain who lie in the grave,
whom you remember no more,
who are cut off from your care.

⁶You have put me in the lowest pit,
in the darkest depths.
⁷Your wrath lies heavily upon me;
you have overwhelmed me with all
your waves.   Selah
⁸You have taken from me my closest
friends

and have made me repulsive to
them.
I am confined and cannot escape;
⁹ my eyes are dim with grief.

I call to you, O LORD, every day;
I spread out my hands to you.
¹⁰Do you show your wonders to the
dead?
Do those who are dead rise up and
praise you?   Selah
¹¹Is your love declared in the grave,
your faithfulness in Destruction[g]?
¹²Are your wonders known in the place
of darkness,
or your righteous deeds in the land
of oblivion?

¹³But I cry to you for help, O LORD;
in the morning my prayer comes
before you.
¹⁴Why, O LORD, do you reject me
and hide your face from me?

¹⁵From my youth I have been afflicted
and close to death;
I have suffered your terrors and
am in despair.
¹⁶Your wrath has swept over me;
your terrors have destroyed me.
¹⁷All day long they surround me like a
flood;
they have completely engulfed me.
¹⁸You have taken my companions and
loved ones from me;
the darkness is my closest friend.

Psalm 89

A *maskil*[e] of Ethan the Ezrahite.

¹I will sing of the LORD's great love
forever;
with my mouth I will make your
faithfulness known through
all generations.
²I will declare that your love stands
firm forever,
that you established your
faithfulness in heaven itself.

³You said, "I have made a covenant
with my chosen one,
I have sworn to David my servant,
⁴'I will establish your line forever

---

a4 A poetic name for Egypt   *b4* That is, the
upper Nile region   *c4* Or *"O Rahab and Babylon,
/ Philistia, Tyre and Cush, / I will record concerning
those who acknowledge me: / 'This*   *d*Title:
Possibly a tune, "The Suffering of Affliction"
*e*Title: Probably a literary or musical term
f3 Hebrew *Sheol*   *g11* Hebrew *Abaddon*

and make your throne firm through
all generations.' " *Selah*

⁵The heavens praise your wonders,
O LORD,
your faithfulness too, in the
assembly of the holy ones.
⁶For who in the skies above can
compare with the LORD?
Who is like the LORD among the
heavenly beings?
⁷In the council of the holy ones God is
greatly feared;
he is more awesome than all who
surround him.
⁸O LORD God Almighty, who is like
you?
You are mighty, O LORD, and your
faithfulness surrounds you.

⁹You rule over the surging sea;
when its waves mount up, you still
them.
¹⁰You crushed Rahab like one of the
slain;
with your strong arm you scattered
your enemies.
¹¹The heavens are yours, and yours
also the earth;
you founded the world and all that
is in it.
¹²You created the north and the south;
Tabor and Hermon sing for joy at
your name.
¹³Your arm is endued with power;
your hand is strong, your right
hand exalted.

¹⁴Righteousness and justice are the
foundation of your throne;
love and faithfulness go before
you.
¹⁵Blessed are those who have learned
to acclaim you,
who walk in the light of your
presence, O LORD.
¹⁶They rejoice in your name all day
long;
they exult in your righteousness.
¹⁷For you are their glory and strength,
and by your favor you exalt our
horn.ᵃ
¹⁸Indeed, our shieldᵇ belongs to the
LORD,
our king to the Holy One of Israel.

¹⁹Once you spoke in a vision,
to your faithful people you said:
"I have bestowed strength on a
warrior;

I have exalted a young man from
among the people.
²⁰I have found David my servant;
with my sacred oil I have anointed
him.
²¹My hand will sustain him;
surely my arm will strengthen him.
²²No enemy will subject him to tribute;
no wicked man will oppress him.
²³I will crush his foes before him
and strike down his adversaries.
²⁴My faithful love will be with him,
and through my name his hornᶜ
will be exalted.
²⁵I will set his hand over the sea,
his right hand over the rivers.
²⁶He will call out to me, 'You are my
Father,
my God, the Rock my Savior.'
²⁷I will also appoint him my firstborn,
the most exalted of the kings of the
earth.
²⁸I will maintain my love to him
forever,
and my covenant with him will
never fail.
²⁹I will establish his line forever,
his throne as long as the heavens
endure.

³⁰"If his sons forsake my law
and do not follow my statutes,
³¹if they violate my decrees
and fail to keep my commands,
³²I will punish their sin with the rod,
their iniquity with flogging;
³³but I will not take my love from him,
nor will I ever betray my
faithfulness.
³⁴I will not violate my covenant

ᵃ*17* Horn here symbolizes strong one.   ᵇ*18* Or
sovereign   ᶜ*24* Horn here symbolizes strength.

POINT OF INTEREST

Psalm 89:1-4

God made a promise to David that carried eternal implications. Matthew 1:1–17 identifies Jesus as the fulfillment of this promise. By human standards God may take some time to fulfill his promises, but he will always do so according to his perfect time line, which "begins" and "ends" in eternity.

or alter what my lips have uttered.
³⁵Once for all, I have sworn by my
holiness—
and I will not lie to David—
³⁶that his line will continue forever
and his throne endure before me
like the sun;
³⁷it will be established forever like the
moon,
the faithful witness in the sky."
Selah

³⁸But you have rejected, you have
spurned,
you have been very angry with
your anointed one.
³⁹You have renounced the covenant
with your servant
and have defiled his crown in the
dust.
⁴⁰You have broken through all his
walls
and reduced his strongholds to
ruins.
⁴¹All who pass by have plundered him;
he has become the scorn of his
neighbors.
⁴²You have exalted the right hand of
his foes;
you have made all his enemies
rejoice.
⁴³You have turned back the edge of his
sword
and have not supported him in
battle.
⁴⁴You have put an end to his splendor
and cast his throne to the ground.
⁴⁵You have cut short the days of his
youth;
you have covered him with a
mantle of shame. *Selah*

⁴⁶How long, O Lord? Will you hide
yourself forever?
How long will your wrath burn
like fire?
⁴⁷Remember how fleeting is my life.
For what futility you have created
all men!
⁴⁸What man can live and not see death,
or save himself from the power of
the grave*ᵃ*? *Selah*
⁴⁹O Lord, where is your former great
love,
which in your faithfulness you
swore to David?
⁵⁰Remember, Lord, how your servant
has*ᵇ* been mocked,
how I bear in my heart the taunts
of all the nations,

⁵¹the taunts with which your enemies
have mocked, O Lord,
with which they have mocked
every step of your anointed
one.

⁵²Praise be to the Lord forever!
Amen and Amen.

BOOK IV
Psalms 90–106

Psalm 90

A prayer of Moses the man of God.

¹Lord, you have been our dwelling
place
throughout all generations.
²Before the mountains were born
or you brought forth the earth and
the world,
from everlasting to everlasting you
are God.

³You turn men back to dust,
saying, "Return to dust, O sons of
men."
⁴For a thousand years in your sight
are like a day that has just gone
by,
or like a watch in the night.
⁵You sweep men away in the sleep of
death;
they are like the new grass of the
morning—
⁶though in the morning it springs up
new,
by evening it is dry and withered.

⁷We are consumed by your anger
and terrified by your indignation.
⁸You have set our iniquities before
you,
our secret sins in the light of your
presence.
⁹All our days pass away under your
wrath;
we finish our years with a moan.
¹⁰The length of our days is seventy
years—
or eighty, if we have the strength;
yet their span*ᶜ* is but trouble and
sorrow,
for they quickly pass, and we fly
away.

¹¹Who knows the power of your anger?

ᵃ48 Hebrew *Sheol*   *ᵇ50* Or *your servants have*
ᶜ10 Or *yet the best of them*

For your wrath is as great as the
fear that is due you.
¹²Teach us to number our days aright,
that we may gain a heart of
wisdom.

¹³Relent, O LORD! How long will it be?
Have compassion on your servants.
¹⁴Satisfy us in the morning with your
unfailing love,
that we may sing for joy and be
glad all our days.
¹⁵Make us glad for as many days as
you have afflicted us,
for as many years as we have seen
trouble.
¹⁶May your deeds be shown to your
servants,
your splendor to their children.

¹⁷May the favor*a* of the Lord our God
rest upon us;
establish the work of our hands for
us—
yes, establish the work of our
hands.

Psalm 91

¹He who dwells in the shelter of the
Most High
will rest in the shadow of the
Almighty.*b*
²I will say*c* of the LORD, "He is my
refuge and my fortress,
my God, in whom I trust."

³Surely he will save you from the
fowler's snare
and from the deadly pestilence.
⁴He will cover you with his feathers,
and under his wings you will find
refuge;
his faithfulness will be your shield
and rampart.
⁵You will not fear the terror of night,
nor the arrow that flies by day,
⁶nor the pestilence that stalks in the
darkness,
nor the plague that destroys at
midday.
⁷A thousand may fall at your side,
ten thousand at your right hand,
but it will not come near you.
⁸You will only observe with your eyes
and see the punishment of the
wicked.

⁹If you make the Most High your
dwelling—
even the LORD, who is my refuge—
¹⁰then no harm will befall you,
no disaster will come near your
tent.
¹¹For he will command his angels
concerning you
to guard you in all your ways;
¹²they will lift you up in their hands,
so that you will not strike your
foot against a stone.
¹³You will tread upon the lion and the
cobra;
you will trample the great lion and
the serpent.

¹⁴"Because he loves me," says the LORD,
"I will rescue him;
I will protect him, for he
acknowledges my name.
¹⁵He will call upon me, and I will
answer him;
I will be with him in trouble,
I will deliver him and honor him.
¹⁶With long life will I satisfy him
and show him my salvation."

Psalm 92

A psalm. A song. For the Sabbath day.

¹It is good to praise the LORD
and make music to your name,
O Most High,
²to proclaim your love in the morning
and your faithfulness at night,
³to the music of the ten-stringed lyre
and the melody of the harp.

⁴For you make me glad by your deeds,
O LORD;
I sing for joy at the works of your
hands.
⁵How great are your works, O LORD,
how profound your thoughts!
⁶The senseless man does not know,
fools do not understand,
⁷that though the wicked spring up like
grass
and all evildoers flourish,
they will be forever destroyed.

⁸But you, O LORD, are exalted forever.

⁹For surely your enemies, O LORD,
surely your enemies will perish;
all evildoers will be scattered.
¹⁰You have exalted my horn*d* like that
of a wild ox;

---

a17 Or *beauty*   *b1* Hebrew *Shaddai*   *c2* Or
He says   *d10* Horn here symbolizes strength.

Read Psalm 91:1–16
Key Verses Psalm 91:5–8

Under His Wings

Dangerous and difficult times occur in everyone's life. We tend to ask, "Why?" Unfortunately, we can't answer this difficult question completely because we don't have God's boundless perspective. The psalmist *does* tell us that our security as God's children is not in the absence of danger but—in the presence of the Lord.

In Psalm 91 David paints lavish images of God as his protector and ours. God is a shelter, a refuge, a shield, a rampart, a dwelling, a tent—a place to run to and to hide in. And symbolically, David catalogs almost every possible situation—disease, snipers, war, dangerous animals, traps, trouble and "the terror of the night" (or sports injuries, family break-ups, car accidents and muggers). It's not that we won't ever experience such disasters but that God will be there with us, like a mighty eagle, shadowing us under his wings—using all his resources, even angels, to protect us. And when God does allow painful things to happen, he promises "that neither death nor life, neither angels nor demons, neither the present nor the future, nor any powers, neither height nor depth, nor anything else in all creation, will be able to separate us from the love of God that is in Christ Jesus our Lord" (Romans 8:38–39).

Digging Into the Word
1. Much of God's protection goes unseen and unnoticed. What do you learn about God's protection in the following passages?—*Psalm 34:7; 2 Thessalonians 3:3*
2. How might these passages help you deal with even the most serious of life's hardships—facing death?—*Philippians 1:20–21; 2 Timothy 1:8–10*

Personal Reflection
Can you think of some situation in which you sensed that God was protecting you from harm? Write it down in your journal or the margin of your Bible next to Psalm 91. Take time to thank him for his loving protection over you.

One Step Deeper
Psalm 50:15; 2 Corinthians 1:8–11

Go to page 655 for your next devotional reading.

fine oils have been poured upon
   me.
¹¹My eyes have seen the defeat of my
   adversaries;
   my ears have heard the rout of my
      wicked foes.

¹²The righteous will flourish like a
   palm tree,
   they will grow like a cedar of
      Lebanon;
¹³planted in the house of the LORD,
   they will flourish in the courts of
      our God.
¹⁴They will still bear fruit in old age,
   they will stay fresh and green,
¹⁵proclaiming, "The LORD is upright;
   he is my Rock, and there is no
      wickedness in him."

Psalm 93

¹The LORD reigns, he is robed in
   majesty;
   the LORD is robed in majesty
   and is armed with strength.
The world is firmly established;
   it cannot be moved.
²Your throne was established long ago;
   you are from all eternity.

³The seas have lifted up, O LORD,
   the seas have lifted up their voice;
   the seas have lifted up their
      pounding waves.
⁴Mightier than the thunder of the great
   waters,
   mightier than the breakers of the
      sea—
   the LORD on high is mighty.

⁵Your statutes stand firm;
   holiness adorns your house
   for endless days, O LORD.

Psalm 94

¹O LORD, the God who avenges,
   O God who avenges, shine forth.
²Rise up, O Judge of the earth;
   pay back to the proud what they
      deserve.
³How long will the wicked, O LORD,
   how long will the wicked be
      jubilant?

⁴They pour out arrogant words;
   all the evildoers are full of
      boasting.
⁵They crush your people, O LORD;
   they oppress your inheritance.

⁶They slay the widow and the alien;
   they murder the fatherless.
⁷They say, "The LORD does not see;
   the God of Jacob pays no heed."

⁸Take heed, you senseless ones among
   the people;
   you fools, when will you become
      wise?
⁹Does he who implanted the ear not
   hear?
   Does he who formed the eye not
      see?
¹⁰Does he who disciplines nations not
   punish?
   Does he who teaches man lack
      knowledge?
¹¹The LORD knows the thoughts of man;
   he knows that they are futile.

¹²Blessed is the man you discipline,
   O LORD,
   the man you teach from your law;
¹³you grant him relief from days of
   trouble,
   till a pit is dug for the wicked.
¹⁴For the LORD will not reject his
   people;
   he will never forsake his
      inheritance.
¹⁵Judgment will again be founded on
   righteousness,
   and all the upright in heart will
      follow it.

¹⁶Who will rise up for me against the
   wicked?
   Who will take a stand for me
      against evildoers?
¹⁷Unless the LORD had given me help,

POINT OF INTEREST

Psalm 92:12-14

One of the great characteristics of youth is an openness to new ideas and to
new ventures. Because they
are often ready for anything, young people
can be very useful to God! Living and
remaining in him, the Source of life,
ensures that even as we age, we will stay
green and growing and as fruitful (see
John 15:1–8). That's a lot more appealing
than becoming a petrified old stump!

I would soon have dwelt in the
   silence of death.
18When I said, "My foot is slipping,"
   your love, O LORD, supported me.
19When anxiety was great within me,
   your consolation brought joy to my
      soul.

20Can a corrupt throne be allied with
      you—
   one that brings on misery by its
      decrees?
21They band together against the
      righteous
   and condemn the innocent to
      death.
22But the LORD has become my fortress,
   and my God the rock in whom I
      take refuge.
23He will repay them for their sins
   and destroy them for their
      wickedness;
   the LORD our God will destroy
      them.

Psalm 95

1Come, let us sing for joy to the LORD;
   let us shout aloud to the Rock of
      our salvation.
2Let us come before him with
      thanksgiving
   and extol him with music and
      song.

3For the LORD is the great God,
   the great King above all gods.
4In his hand are the depths of the
      earth,
   and the mountain peaks belong to
      him.
5The sea is his, for he made it,
   and his hands formed the dry land.

6Come, let us bow down in worship,
   let us kneel before the LORD our
      Maker;
7for he is our God
   and we are the people of his
      pasture,
   the flock under his care.

Today, if you hear his voice,
8   do not harden your hearts as you
         did at Meribah,*a*
   as you did that day at Massah*b* in
      the desert,
9where your fathers tested and tried
      me,
   though they had seen what I did.

10For forty years I was angry with that
      generation;
   I said, "They are a people whose
      hearts go astray,
   and they have not known my
      ways."
11So I declared on oath in my anger,
   "They shall never enter my rest."

Psalm 96

1Sing to the LORD a new song;
   sing to the LORD, all the earth.
2Sing to the LORD, praise his name;
   proclaim his salvation day after
      day.
3Declare his glory among the nations,
   his marvelous deeds among all
      peoples.

4For great is the LORD and most worthy
      of praise;
   he is to be feared above all gods.
5For all the gods of the nations are
      idols,
   but the LORD made the heavens.
6Splendor and majesty are before him;
   strength and glory are in his
      sanctuary.

7Ascribe to the LORD, O families of
      nations,
   ascribe to the LORD glory and
      strength.
8Ascribe to the LORD the glory due his
      name;
   bring an offering and come into his
      courts.
9Worship the LORD in the splendor of
      his*c* holiness;
   tremble before him, all the earth.

a8 Meribah means *quarreling.*   *b8 Massah*
means *testing.*   *c9* Or *LORD with the splendor of*

POINT OF INTEREST

Psalm 96:4-6

Is God merely the highest
god in a pantheon of gods?
Is he only an idea conjured
up by humans to explain life's
mysteries? No! There is only one true God,
and "By faith we understand that the universe was formed at God's command, so
that what is seen was not made out of
what was visible" (Hebrews 11:3).

¹⁰Say among the nations, "The LORD
     reigns."
The world is firmly established, it
     cannot be moved;
he will judge the peoples with
     equity.
¹¹Let the heavens rejoice, let the earth
     be glad;
let the sea resound, and all that is
     in it;
12   let the fields be jubilant, and
     everything in them.
Then all the trees of the forest will
     sing for joy;
13   they will sing before the LORD, for
     he comes,
he comes to judge the earth.
He will judge the world in
     righteousness
and the peoples in his truth.

Psalm 97

¹The LORD reigns, let the earth be glad;
let the distant shores rejoice.

²Clouds and thick darkness surround
     him;
righteousness and justice are the
     foundation of his throne.
³Fire goes before him
     and consumes his foes on every
     side.
⁴His lightning lights up the world;
     the earth sees and trembles.
⁵The mountains melt like wax before
     the LORD,
before the Lord of all the earth.
⁶The heavens proclaim his
     righteousness,
and all the peoples see his glory.

⁷All who worship images are put to
     shame,
     those who boast in idols—
worship him, all you gods!

⁸Zion hears and rejoices
     and the villages of Judah are glad
     because of your judgments, O LORD.
⁹For you, O LORD, are the Most High
     over all the earth;
     you are exalted far above all gods.

¹⁰Let those who love the LORD hate evil,
     for he guards the lives of his
          faithful ones
     and delivers them from the hand of
          the wicked.
¹¹Light is shed upon the righteous
     and joy on the upright in heart.

¹²Rejoice in the LORD, you who are
     righteous,
and praise his holy name.

Psalm 98

A psalm.

¹Sing to the LORD a new song,
     for he has done marvelous things;
his right hand and his holy arm
     have worked salvation for him.
²The LORD has made his salvation
     known
and revealed his righteousness to
     the nations.
³He has remembered his love
     and his faithfulness to the house of
     Israel;
all the ends of the earth have seen
     the salvation of our God.

⁴Shout for joy to the LORD, all the
     earth,
     burst into jubilant song with
          music;
⁵make music to the LORD with the
     harp,
     with the harp and the sound of
          singing,
⁶with trumpets and the blast of the
     ram's horn—
     shout for joy before the LORD, the
          King.

⁷Let the sea resound, and everything
     in it,
     the world, and all who live in it.
⁸Let the rivers clap their hands,
     let the mountains sing together for
          joy;
⁹let them sing before the LORD,
     for he comes to judge the earth.
He will judge the world in
     righteousness
and the peoples with equity.

Psalm 99

¹The LORD reigns,
     let the nations tremble;
he sits enthroned between the
     cherubim,
     let the earth shake.
²Great is the LORD in Zion;
     he is exalted over all the nations.
³Let them praise your great and
          awesome name—
     he is holy.

⁴The King is mighty, he loves justice—

you have established equity;
in Jacob you have done
 what is just and right.
⁵Exalt the LORD our God
 and worship at his footstool;
 he is holy.

⁶Moses and Aaron were among his
  priests,
 Samuel was among those who
  called on his name;
they called on the LORD
 and he answered them.
⁷He spoke to them from the pillar of
  cloud;
 they kept his statutes and the
  decrees he gave them.

⁸O LORD our God,
 you answered them;
you were to Israel*a* a forgiving God,
 though you punished their
  misdeeds.*b*
⁹Exalt the LORD our God
 and worship at his holy mountain,
 for the LORD our God is holy.

Psalm 100

A psalm. For giving thanks.

¹Shout for joy to the LORD, all the
  earth.
2 Worship the LORD with gladness;
 come before him with joyful songs.
³Know that the LORD is God.
 It is he who made us, and we are
  his*c*;
 we are his people, the sheep of his
  pasture.

⁴Enter his gates with thanksgiving
 and his courts with praise;
 give thanks to him and praise his
  name.
⁵For the LORD is good and his love
  endures forever;
 his faithfulness continues through
  all generations.

Psalm 101

Of David. A psalm.

¹I will sing of your love and justice;
 to you, O LORD, I will sing praise.
²I will be careful to lead a blameless
  life—
 when will you come to me?

I will walk in my house
 with blameless heart.
³I will set before my eyes
 no vile thing.

The deeds of faithless men I hate;
 they will not cling to me.
⁴Men of perverse heart shall be far
  from me;
 I will have nothing to do with evil.

⁵Whoever slanders his neighbor in
  secret,
 him will I put to silence;
whoever has haughty eyes and a
  proud heart,
 him will I not endure.

⁶My eyes will be on the faithful in the
  land,
 that they may dwell with me;
he whose walk is blameless
 will minister to me.

⁷No one who practices deceit
 will dwell in my house;
no one who speaks falsely
 will stand in my presence.

⁸Every morning I will put to silence
 all the wicked in the land;
I will cut off every evildoer
 from the city of the LORD.

Psalm 102

*A prayer of an afflicted man. When he
is faint and pours out his lament
before the LORD.*

¹Hear my prayer, O LORD;
 let my cry for help come to you.
²Do not hide your face from me
 when I am in distress.
Turn your ear to me;
 when I call, answer me quickly.

³For my days vanish like smoke;
 my bones burn like glowing
  embers.
⁴My heart is blighted and withered like
  grass;
 I forget to eat my food.
⁵Because of my loud groaning
 I am reduced to skin and bones.
⁶I am like a desert owl,
 like an owl among the ruins.
⁷I lie awake; I have become
 like a bird alone on a roof.

---

*a*8 Hebrew *them* *b*8 Or / *an avenger of the
wrongs done to them* *c*3 Or *and not we
ourselves*

⁸All day long my enemies taunt me;
  those who rail against me use my
    name as a curse.
⁹For I eat ashes as my food
  and mingle my drink with tears
¹⁰because of your great wrath,
  for you have taken me up and
    thrown me aside.
¹¹My days are like the evening shadow;
  I wither away like grass.

¹²But you, O LORD, sit enthroned
    forever;
  your renown endures through all
    generations.

¹³You will arise and have compassion
    on Zion,
  for it is time to show favor to
    her;
  the appointed time has come.
¹⁴For her stones are dear to your
    servants;
  her very dust moves them to pity.
¹⁵The nations will fear the name of the
    LORD,
  all the kings of the earth will
    revere your glory.
¹⁶For the LORD will rebuild Zion
  and appear in his glory.

MONDAY

Read *Psalm 101:1–8*
Key Verses *Psalm 101:2–3*

What's the Standard? — Doug Serven

I sat with my friend in his dorm room. We pushed aside some of the dirty clothes and piles of homework and settled into a discussion about walking with God. I shared openly with him that, at times, I have a thief's heart—one that wants things that aren't mine. He looked shocked (like I was about to burgle some of his CD's) and dismissed me with, "Well, *I* don't have any problems with stealing . . ."

I felt a bit rebuffed by his words, even more so when I noticed that on the wall behind him were fifteen or twenty menus that he'd lifted from restaurants. As he sat there, he was literally framed by the evidence that he was guilty of the very sin he'd just denied.

To my friend, taking menus wasn't really stealing because they weren't of much value. As many people in our culture do, he thought that some dishonesty was okay as long as it was above some arbitrary median level.

We constantly try to redefine what's right and wrong, as if personal holiness is based on a curved grading scale. We examine our lives and think, "Hey, I'm better than the average person." But God's standard is one hundred percent perfection.

God calls us to "be holy as he is holy" (1 Peter 1:15–16). He takes even our "smallest" sins seriously, and we should too. When we agree with God that what we've done is wrong, he forgives us through Jesus Christ. We are called to rely on the Spirit who lives within us and helps us change our sinful behaviors. We are to live as God's holy people, so that our lives can serve as an example and a witness to others (see Philippians 3:17–21).

What are some habits you need to change in order to live closer to God's standard? Find a friend to help you be accountable for cleaning up your life and cling to God for true holiness.

A Deeper Look
Psalm 51:1–13; Ephesians 5:3–4; 1 Peter 2:11–12

Go to page 657 for your next devotional reading.

¹⁷He will respond to the prayer of the
destitute;
he will not despise their plea.

¹⁸Let this be written for a future
generation,
that a people not yet created may
praise the LORD:
¹⁹"The LORD looked down from his
sanctuary on high,
from heaven he viewed the earth,
²⁰to hear the groans of the prisoners
and release those condemned to
death."
²¹So the name of the LORD will be
declared in Zion
and his praise in Jerusalem
²²when the peoples and the kingdoms
assemble to worship the LORD.

²³In the course of my life*a* he broke
my strength;
he cut short my days.
²⁴So I said:
"Do not take me away, O my God,
in the midst of my days;
your years go on through all
generations.
²⁵In the beginning you laid the
foundations of the earth,
and the heavens are the work of
your hands.
²⁶They will perish, but you remain;
they will all wear out like a
garment.
Like clothing you will change them
and they will be discarded.
²⁷But you remain the same,
and your years will never end.
²⁸The children of your servants will live
in your presence;
their descendants will be
established before you."

Psalm 103

Of David.

¹Praise the LORD, O my soul;
all my inmost being, praise his
holy name.
²Praise the LORD, O my soul,
and forget not all his benefits—
³who forgives all your sins
and heals all your diseases,
⁴who redeems your life from the pit
and crowns you with love and
compassion,
⁵who satisfies your desires with good
things

so that your youth is renewed like
the eagle's.

⁶The LORD works righteousness
and justice for all the oppressed.

⁷He made known his ways to Moses,
his deeds to the people of Israel:
⁸The LORD is compassionate and
gracious,
slow to anger, abounding in love.
⁹He will not always accuse,
nor will he harbor his anger
forever;
¹⁰he does not treat us as our sins
deserve
or repay us according to our
iniquities.
¹¹For as high as the heavens are above
the earth,
so great is his love for those who
fear him;
¹²as far as the east is from the west,
so far has he removed our
transgressions from us.
¹³As a father has compassion on his
children,
so the LORD has compassion on
those who fear him;
¹⁴for he knows how we are formed,
he remembers that we are dust.
¹⁵As for man, his days are like grass,
he flourishes like a flower of the
field;
¹⁶the wind blows over it and it is gone,
and its place remembers it no
more.
¹⁷But from everlasting to everlasting
the LORD's love is with those who
fear him,
and his righteousness with their
children's children—
¹⁸with those who keep his covenant
and remember to obey his
precepts.

¹⁹The LORD has established his throne in
heaven,
and his kingdom rules over all.

²⁰Praise the LORD, you his angels,
you mighty ones who do his
bidding,
who obey his word.
²¹Praise the LORD, all his heavenly
hosts,
you his servants who do his will.

a23 Or *By his power*

²²Praise the LORD, all his works
everywhere in his dominion.

Praise the LORD, O my soul.

Psalm 104

¹Praise the LORD, O my soul.

O LORD my God, you are very great;
you are clothed with splendor and
majesty.
²He wraps himself in light as with a
garment;

he stretches out the heavens like a
tent
³   and lays the beams of his upper
chambers on their waters.
He makes the clouds his chariot
and rides on the wings of the
wind.
⁴He makes winds his messengers,ᵃ
flames of fire his servants.

⁵He set the earth on its foundations;
it can never be moved.

ᵃ4 Or angels

TUESDAY

Read *Psalm 103:1–22*
Key Verses *Psalm 103:8–13*

As Far As the East Is from the West — Ellen B. Susman

"I want my freedom. I just need to be on my own for now. I'm sorry."
With those words, a three-year relationship was over. All of my
hopes and dreams had been shattered with a single phone call. I
cried for several hours. I didn't know if I could go on living.

A few days later it hit me: "I'm not going to marry this guy." I
thought about what our physical relationship had been like, and
how I had justified it by thinking that we'd get married soon anyway. So I was left facing my sin. No excuses now—I had to deal with
it before God.

Forgiveness seemed to come in stages. I had to forgive my former boyfriend; I had to forgive myself. The hardest part, though,
was accepting God's forgiveness. I kept thinking I needed to make it
up to God in some way—run extra laps, study all night, eat my broc-
coli without whining. But Psalm 103:12 gave me great comfort: "As
far as the east is from the west, so far has he removed our transgressions from us."

I realized that God doesn't sit up in heaven with a big book of
sins, refusing to cross them off until I confess them. Even though I
still needed to ask for forgiveness, God had forgiven me even before
I recognized my sin. Why? Because Jesus' sacrifice already paid the
penalty for my sin: "But God demonstrates his own love for us in
this: While we were still sinners, Christ died for us" (Romans 5:8).
Jesus' sacrifice made me "as white as snow" (Isaiah 1:18). I just
needed to accept his forgiveness. And this passage promises that
God won't keep track of my sin. He will never bring it up again.
Knowing that God forgives me allows me to forgive myself, to forgive others and to get on with my life. His forgiveness gave me the
freedom to turn from my mistakes, accept his mercy and discover
the joy of his grace.

A Deeper Look
Micah 7:18–20; 1 John 1:9

Go to page 666 for your next devotional reading.

⁶You covered it with the deep as with
    a garment;
  the waters stood above the
    mountains.
⁷But at your rebuke the waters fled,
  at the sound of your thunder they
    took to flight;
⁸they flowed over the mountains,
  they went down into the valleys,
  to the place you assigned for them.
⁹You set a boundary they cannot
    cross;
  never again will they cover the
    earth.

¹⁰He makes springs pour water into the
    ravines;
  it flows between the mountains.
¹¹They give water to all the beasts of
    the field;
  the wild donkeys quench their
    thirst.
¹²The birds of the air nest by the
    waters;
  they sing among the branches.
¹³He waters the mountains from his
    upper chambers;
  the earth is satisfied by the fruit of
    his work.
¹⁴He makes grass grow for the cattle,
  and plants for man to cultivate—
  bringing forth food from the earth:
¹⁵wine that gladdens the heart of man,
  oil to make his face shine,
  and bread that sustains his heart.
¹⁶The trees of the LORD are well
    watered,
  the cedars of Lebanon that he
    planted.
¹⁷There the birds make their nests;
  the stork has its home in the pine
    trees.
¹⁸The high mountains belong to the
    wild goats;
  the crags are a refuge for the
    coneys.ᵃ

¹⁹The moon marks off the seasons,
  and the sun knows when to go
    down.
²⁰You bring darkness, it becomes night,
  and all the beasts of the forest
    prowl.
²¹The lions roar for their prey
  and seek their food from God.
²²The sun rises, and they steal away;
  they return and lie down in their
    dens.
²³Then man goes out to his work,
  to his labor until evening.

²⁴How many are your works, O LORD!
  In wisdom you made them all;
  the earth is full of your creatures.
²⁵There is the sea, vast and spacious,
  teeming with creatures beyond
    number—
  living things both large and small.
²⁶There the ships go to and fro,
  and the leviathan, which you
    formed to frolic there.

²⁷These all look to you
  to give them their food at the
    proper time.
²⁸When you give it to them,
  they gather it up;
  when you open your hand,
  they are satisfied with good things.
²⁹When you hide your face,
  they are terrified;
  when you take away their breath,
  they die and return to the dust.
³⁰When you send your Spirit,
  they are created,
  and you renew the face of the
    earth.

³¹May the glory of the LORD endure
    forever;
  may the LORD rejoice in his
    works—
³²he who looks at the earth, and it
    trembles,
  who touches the mountains, and
    they smoke.

³³I will sing to the LORD all my life;
  I will sing praise to my God as
    long as I live.
³⁴May my meditation be pleasing to
    him,
  as I rejoice in the LORD.
³⁵But may sinners vanish from the
    earth
  and the wicked be no more.

  Praise the LORD, O my soul.

  Praise the LORD.ᵇ

Psalm 105

¹Give thanks to the LORD, call on his
    name;
  make known among the nations
    what he has done.
²Sing to him, sing praise to him;
  tell of all his wonderful acts.

ᵃ18 That is, the hyrax or rock badger
ᵇ35 Hebrew *Hallelu Yah*; in the Septuagint this line
stands at the beginning of Psalm 105.

³Glory in his holy name;
  let the hearts of those who seek
    the LORD rejoice.
⁴Look to the LORD and his strength;
  seek his face always.

⁵Remember the wonders he has done,
  his miracles, and the judgments he
    pronounced,
⁶O descendants of Abraham his
    servant,
  O sons of Jacob, his chosen ones.
⁷He is the LORD our God;
  his judgments are in all the earth.

⁸He remembers his covenant forever,
  the word he commanded, for a
    thousand generations,
⁹the covenant he made with Abraham,
  the oath he swore to Isaac.
¹⁰He confirmed it to Jacob as a decree,
  to Israel as an everlasting
    covenant:
¹¹"To you I will give the land of
    Canaan
  as the portion you will inherit."

¹²When they were but few in number,
  few indeed, and strangers in it,
¹³they wandered from nation to nation,
  from one kingdom to another.
¹⁴He allowed no one to oppress them;
  for their sake he rebuked kings:
¹⁵"Do not touch my anointed ones;
  do my prophets no harm."

¹⁶He called down famine on the land
  and destroyed all their supplies of
    food;
¹⁷and he sent a man before them—
  Joseph, sold as a slave.
¹⁸They bruised his feet with shackles,
  his neck was put in irons,
¹⁹till what he foretold came to pass,
  till the word of the LORD proved
    him true.
²⁰The king sent and released him,
  the ruler of peoples set him free.
²¹He made him master of his
    household,
  ruler over all he possessed,
²²to instruct his princes as he pleased
  and teach his elders wisdom.

²³Then Israel entered Egypt;
  Jacob lived as an alien in the land
    of Ham.
²⁴The LORD made his people very
    fruitful;
  he made them too numerous for
    their foes,

²⁵whose hearts he turned to hate his
    people,
  to conspire against his servants.
²⁶He sent Moses his servant,
  and Aaron, whom he had chosen.
²⁷They performed his miraculous signs
    among them,
  his wonders in the land of Ham.
²⁸He sent darkness and made the land
    dark—
  for had they not rebelled against
    his words?
²⁹He turned their waters into blood,
  causing their fish to die.
³⁰Their land teemed with frogs,
  which went up into the bedrooms
    of their rulers.
³¹He spoke, and there came swarms of
    flies,
  and gnats throughout their
    country.
³²He turned their rain into hail,
  with lightning throughout their
    land;
³³he struck down their vines and fig
    trees
  and shattered the trees of their
    country.
³⁴He spoke, and the locusts came,
  grasshoppers without number;
³⁵they ate up every green thing in their
    land,
  ate up the produce of their soil.
³⁶Then he struck down all the firstborn
    in their land,
  the firstfruits of all their manhood.

³⁷He brought out Israel, laden with
    silver and gold,

POINT OF INTEREST

Psalm 105:5-8

God made many covenants with his Old Testament people and never forgot one of them. God's covenant agreement with one person (such as Abram in Genesis 15:18) didn't constitute a free ride for subsequent generations. God confirmed the initial covenant with others (such as Isaac in Genesis 17:19). Similarly, in the New Testament covenant of salvation, God has no grandchildren. Each of us must respond to him individually.

and from among their tribes no
one faltered.
38Egypt was glad when they left,
because dread of Israel had fallen
on them.
39He spread out a cloud as a covering,
and a fire to give light at night.
40They asked, and he brought them
quail
and satisfied them with the bread
of heaven.
41He opened the rock, and water
gushed out;
like a river it flowed in the desert.

42For he remembered his holy promise
given to his servant Abraham.
43He brought out his people with
rejoicing,
his chosen ones with shouts of joy;
44he gave them the lands of the
nations,
and they fell heir to what others
had toiled for—
45that they might keep his precepts
and observe his laws.

Praise the LORD.*a*

Psalm 106

1Praise the LORD.*b*

Give thanks to the LORD, for he is
good;
his love endures forever.
2Who can proclaim the mighty acts of
the LORD
or fully declare his praise?
3Blessed are they who maintain
justice,
who constantly do what is right.
4Remember me, O LORD, when you
show favor to your people,
come to my aid when you save
them,
5that I may enjoy the prosperity of
your chosen ones,
that I may share in the joy of your
nation
and join your inheritance in giving
praise.

6We have sinned, even as our fathers
did;
we have done wrong and acted
wickedly.
7When our fathers were in Egypt,
they gave no thought to your
miracles;

they did not remember your many
kindnesses,
and they rebelled by the sea, the
Red Sea.*c*
8Yet he saved them for his name's
sake,
to make his mighty power known.
9He rebuked the Red Sea, and it dried
up;
he led them through the depths as
through a desert.
10He saved them from the hand of the
foe;
from the hand of the enemy he
redeemed them.
11The waters covered their adversaries;
not one of them survived.
12Then they believed his promises
and sang his praise.

13But they soon forgot what he had
done
and did not wait for his counsel.
14In the desert they gave in to their
craving;
in the wasteland they put God to
the test.
15So he gave them what they asked for,
but sent a wasting disease upon
them.

16In the camp they grew envious of
Moses
and of Aaron, who was
consecrated to the LORD.
17The earth opened up and swallowed
Dathan;
it buried the company of Abiram.
18Fire blazed among their followers;
a flame consumed the wicked.

19At Horeb they made a calf
and worshiped an idol cast from
metal.
20They exchanged their Glory
for an image of a bull, which eats
grass.
21They forgot the God who saved them,
who had done great things in
Egypt,
22miracles in the land of Ham
and awesome deeds by the Red
Sea.
23So he said he would destroy them—
had not Moses, his chosen one,
stood in the breach before him

*a*45 Hebrew *Hallelu Yah*   *b*1 Hebrew *Hallelu
Yah*; also in verse 48   *c*7 Hebrew *Yam Suph*;
that is, Sea of Reeds; also in verses 9 and 22

to keep his wrath from destroying
them.

²⁴Then they despised the pleasant land;
they did not believe his promise.
²⁵They grumbled in their tents
and did not obey the LORD.
²⁶So he swore to them with uplifted
hand
that he would make them fall in
the desert,
²⁷make their descendants fall among
the nations
and scatter them throughout the
lands.

²⁸They yoked themselves to the Baal of
Peor
and ate sacrifices offered to lifeless
gods;
²⁹they provoked the LORD to anger by
their wicked deeds,
and a plague broke out among
them.
³⁰But Phinehas stood up and
intervened,
and the plague was checked.
³¹This was credited to him as
righteousness
for endless generations to come.

³²By the waters of Meribah they
angered the LORD,
and trouble came to Moses because
of them;
³³for they rebelled against the Spirit of
God,
and rash words came from Moses'
lips.ᵃ

³⁴They did not destroy the peoples
as the LORD had commanded them,
³⁵but they mingled with the nations
and adopted their customs.
³⁶They worshiped their idols,
which became a snare to them.
³⁷They sacrificed their sons
and their daughters to demons.
³⁸They shed innocent blood,
the blood of their sons and
daughters,
whom they sacrificed to the idols of
Canaan,
and the land was desecrated by
their blood.
³⁹They defiled themselves by what they
did;
by their deeds they prostituted
themselves.

⁴⁰Therefore the LORD was angry with his
people
and abhorred his inheritance.
⁴¹He handed them over to the nations,
and their foes ruled over them.
⁴²Their enemies oppressed them
and subjected them to their power.
⁴³Many times he delivered them,
but they were bent on rebellion
and they wasted away in their sin.

⁴⁴But he took note of their distress
when he heard their cry;
⁴⁵for their sake he remembered his
covenant
and out of his great love he
relented.
⁴⁶He caused them to be pitied
by all who held them captive.

⁴⁷Save us, O LORD our God,
and gather us from the nations,
that we may give thanks to your holy
name
and glory in your praise.

⁴⁸Praise be to the LORD, the God of
Israel,
from everlasting to everlasting.
Let all the people say, "Amen!"

Praise the LORD.

BOOK V

Psalms 107–150

Psalm 107

¹Give thanks to the LORD, for he is
good;
his love endures forever.
²Let the redeemed of the LORD say
this—
those he redeemed from the hand
of the foe,
³those he gathered from the lands,
from east and west, from north
and south.ᵇ

⁴Some wandered in desert wastelands,
finding no way to a city where
they could settle.
⁵They were hungry and thirsty,
and their lives ebbed away.
⁶Then they cried out to the LORD in
their trouble,
and he delivered them from their
distress.
⁷He led them by a straight way

ᵃ33 Or *against his spirit,* / *and rash words came
from his lips*   ᵇ3 Hebrew *north and the sea*

to a city where they could settle.
⁸Let them give thanks to the LORD for
   his unfailing love
   and his wonderful deeds for men,
⁹for he satisfies the thirsty
   and fills the hungry with good
      things.

¹⁰Some sat in darkness and the deepest
      gloom,
   prisoners suffering in iron chains,
¹¹for they had rebelled against the
      words of God
   and despised the counsel of the
      Most High.
¹²So he subjected them to bitter labor;
   they stumbled, and there was no
      one to help.
¹³Then they cried to the LORD in their
      trouble,
   and he saved them from their
      distress.
¹⁴He brought them out of darkness and
      the deepest gloom
   and broke away their chains.
¹⁵Let them give thanks to the LORD for
   his unfailing love
   and his wonderful deeds for men,
¹⁶for he breaks down gates of bronze
   and cuts through bars of iron.

¹⁷Some became fools through their
      rebellious ways
   and suffered affliction because of
      their iniquities.
¹⁸They loathed all food
   and drew near the gates of death.
¹⁹Then they cried to the LORD in their
      trouble,
   and he saved them from their
      distress.
²⁰He sent forth his word and healed
      them;
   he rescued them from the grave.
²¹Let them give thanks to the LORD for
   his unfailing love
   and his wonderful deeds for men.
²²Let them sacrifice thank offerings
   and tell of his works with songs of
      joy.

²³Others went out on the sea in ships;
   they were merchants on the mighty
      waters.
²⁴They saw the works of the LORD,
   his wonderful deeds in the deep.
²⁵For he spoke and stirred up a tempest
   that lifted high the waves.
²⁶They mounted up to the heavens and
   went down to the depths;

in their peril their courage melted
   away.
²⁷They reeled and staggered like
      drunken men;
   they were at their wits' end.
²⁸Then they cried out to the LORD in
      their trouble,
   and he brought them out of their
      distress.
²⁹He stilled the storm to a whisper;
   the waves of the sea were hushed.
³⁰They were glad when it grew calm,
   and he guided them to their
      desired haven.
³¹Let them give thanks to the LORD for
   his unfailing love
   and his wonderful deeds for men.
³²Let them exalt him in the assembly of
      the people
   and praise him in the council of
      the elders.

³³He turned rivers into a desert,
   flowing springs into thirsty ground,
³⁴and fruitful land into a salt waste,
   because of the wickedness of those
      who lived there.
³⁵He turned the desert into pools of
      water
   and the parched ground into
      flowing springs;
³⁶there he brought the hungry to live,
   and they founded a city where
      they could settle.
³⁷They sowed fields and planted
      vineyards
   that yielded a fruitful harvest;
³⁸he blessed them, and their numbers
      greatly increased,
   and he did not let their herds
      diminish.

³⁹Then their numbers decreased, and
      they were humbled
   by oppression, calamity and
      sorrow;

POINT OF INTEREST

Psalm 107:33–34

All too often, greed, ignorance and disregard for the
beauty and grandeur of
God's creation result in the
abuse of fertile land and beautiful natural
settings. Sin wrecks the earth as well as
the people who live on it!

⁴⁰he who pours contempt on nobles
made them wander in a trackless
waste.
⁴¹But he lifted the needy out of their
affliction
and increased their families like
flocks.
⁴²The upright see and rejoice,
but all the wicked shut their
mouths.

⁴³Whoever is wise, let him heed these
things
and consider the great love of the
LORD.

Psalm 108

A song. A psalm of David.

¹My heart is steadfast, O God;
I will sing and make music with all
my soul.
²Awake, harp and lyre!
I will awaken the dawn.
³I will praise you, O LORD, among the
nations;
I will sing of you among the
peoples.
⁴For great is your love, higher than the
heavens;
your faithfulness reaches to the
skies.
⁵Be exalted, O God, above the
heavens,
and let your glory be over all the
earth.

⁶Save us and help us with your right
hand,
that those you love may be
delivered.
⁷God has spoken from his sanctuary:
"In triumph I will parcel out
Shechem
and measure off the Valley of
Succoth.
⁸Gilead is mine, Manasseh is mine;
Ephraim is my helmet,
Judah my scepter.
⁹Moab is my washbasin,
upon Edom I toss my sandal;
over Philistia I shout in triumph."

¹⁰Who will bring me to the fortified
city?
Who will lead me to Edom?
¹¹Is it not you, O God, you who have
rejected us
and no longer go out with our
armies?

¹²Give us aid against the enemy,
for the help of man is worthless.
¹³With God we will gain the victory,
and he will trample down our
enemies.

Psalm 109

For the director of music. Of David.
A psalm.

¹O God, whom I praise,
do not remain silent,
²for wicked and deceitful men
have opened their mouths against
me;
they have spoken against me with
lying tongues.
³With words of hatred they surround
me;
they attack me without cause.
⁴In return for my friendship they
accuse me,
but I am a man of prayer.
⁵They repay me evil for good,
and hatred for my friendship.

⁶Appointᵃ an evil manᵇ to oppose
him;
let an accuserᶜ stand at his right
hand.
⁷When he is tried, let him be found
guilty,
and may his prayers condemn him.
⁸May his days be few;
may another take his place of
leadership.
⁹May his children be fatherless
and his wife a widow.
¹⁰May his children be wandering
beggars;
may they be drivenᵈ from their
ruined homes.
¹¹May a creditor seize all he has;
may strangers plunder the fruits of
his labor.
¹²May no one extend kindness to him
or take pity on his fatherless
children.
¹³May his descendants be cut off,
their names blotted out from the
next generation.
¹⁴May the iniquity of his fathers be
remembered before the LORD;
may the sin of his mother never be
blotted out.

ᵃ6 Or ⌞They say:⌟ "Appoint (with quotation marks
at the end of verse 19)   ᵇ6 Or the Evil One
ᶜ6 Or let Satan   ᵈ10 Septuagint; Hebrew sought

¹⁵May their sins always remain before
the Lord,
that he may cut off the memory of
them from the earth.

¹⁶For he never thought of doing a
kindness,
but hounded to death the poor
and the needy and the
brokenhearted.
¹⁷He loved to pronounce a curse—
may it*ᵃ* come on him;
he found no pleasure in blessing—
may it be*ᵇ* far from him.
¹⁸He wore cursing as his garment;
it entered into his body like water,
into his bones like oil.
¹⁹May it be like a cloak wrapped about
him,
like a belt tied forever around him.
²⁰May this be the Lord's payment to my
accusers,
to those who speak evil of me.

²¹But you, O Sovereign Lord,
deal well with me for your name's
sake;
out of the goodness of your love,
deliver me.
²²For I am poor and needy,
and my heart is wounded within
me.
²³I fade away like an evening shadow;
I am shaken off like a locust.
²⁴My knees give way from fasting;
my body is thin and gaunt.
²⁵I am an object of scorn to my
accusers;
when they see me, they shake their
heads.

²⁶Help me, O Lord my God;
save me in accordance with your
love.
²⁷Let them know that it is your hand,
that you, O Lord, have done it.
²⁸They may curse, but you will bless;
when they attack they will be put
to shame,
but your servant will rejoice.
²⁹My accusers will be clothed with
disgrace
and wrapped in shame as in a
cloak.

³⁰With my mouth I will greatly extol
the Lord;
in the great throng I will praise
him.

³¹For he stands at the right hand of the
needy one,
to save his life from those who
condemn him.

Psalm 110

Of David. A psalm.

¹The Lord says to my Lord:
"Sit at my right hand
until I make your enemies
a footstool for your feet."

²The Lord will extend your mighty
scepter from Zion;
you will rule in the midst of your
enemies.
³Your troops will be willing
on your day of battle.
Arrayed in holy majesty,
from the womb of the dawn
you will receive the dew of your
youth.*ᶜ*

⁴The Lord has sworn
and will not change his mind:
"You are a priest forever,
in the order of Melchizedek."

⁵The Lord is at your right hand;
he will crush kings on the day of
his wrath.
⁶He will judge the nations, heaping up
the dead
and crushing the rulers of the
whole earth.
⁷He will drink from a brook beside the
way*ᵈ*;
therefore he will lift up his head.

Psalm 111 *ᵉ*

¹Praise the Lord.*ᶠ*

I will extol the Lord with all my heart
in the council of the upright and in
the assembly.

²Great are the works of the Lord;
they are pondered by all who
delight in them.
³Glorious and majestic are his deeds,
and his righteousness endures
forever.

---

a17 Or *curse, / and it has*   *b17* Or *blessing, /
and it is*   *c3* Or / *your young men will come to
you like the dew*   *d7* Or / *The One who grants
succession will set him in authority*   *e*This psalm
is an acrostic poem, the lines of which begin with
the successive letters of the Hebrew alphabet.
f1 Hebrew *Hallelu Yah*

⁴He has caused his wonders to be
remembered;
the Lord is gracious and
compassionate.
⁵He provides food for those who fear
him;
he remembers his covenant
forever.
⁶He has shown his people the power
of his works,
giving them the lands of other
nations.
⁷The works of his hands are faithful
and just;
all his precepts are trustworthy.
⁸They are steadfast for ever and ever,
done in faithfulness and
uprightness.
⁹He provided redemption for his
people;
he ordained his covenant forever—
holy and awesome is his name.
¹⁰The fear of the Lord is the beginning
of wisdom;
all who follow his precepts have
good understanding.
To him belongs eternal praise.

Psalm 112ᵃ

¹Praise the Lord.ᵇ

Blessed is the man who fears the
Lord,
who finds great delight in his
commands.
²His children will be mighty in the
land;
the generation of the upright will
be blessed.
³Wealth and riches are in his house,
and his righteousness endures
forever.
⁴Even in darkness light dawns for the
upright,
for the gracious and compassionate
and righteous man.ᶜ
⁵Good will come to him who is
generous and lends freely,
who conducts his affairs with
justice.
⁶Surely he will never be shaken;
a righteous man will be
remembered forever.
⁷He will have no fear of bad news;
his heart is steadfast, trusting in
the Lord.
⁸His heart is secure, he will have no
fear;

in the end he will look in triumph
on his foes.
⁹He has scattered abroad his gifts to
the poor,
his righteousness endures forever;
his hornᵈ will be lifted high in
honor.

¹⁰The wicked man will see and be
vexed,
he will gnash his teeth and waste
away;
the longings of the wicked will
come to nothing.

Psalm 113

¹Praise the Lord.ᵉ

Praise, O servants of the Lord,
praise the name of the Lord.
²Let the name of the Lord be praised,
both now and forevermore.
³From the rising of the sun to the
place where it sets,
the name of the Lord is to be
praised.

⁴The Lord is exalted over all the
nations,
his glory above the heavens.
⁵Who is like the Lord our God,
the One who sits enthroned on
high,
⁶who stoops down to look
on the heavens and the earth?

⁷He raises the poor from the dust
and lifts the needy from the ash
heap;
⁸he seats them with princes,
with the princes of their people.
⁹He settles the barren woman in her
home
as a happy mother of children.

Praise the Lord.

Psalm 114

¹When Israel came out of Egypt,
the house of Jacob from a people
of foreign tongue,

ᵃThis psalm is an acrostic poem, the lines of which
begin with the successive letters of the Hebrew
alphabet.   ᵇ1 Hebrew *Hallelu Yah*   ᶜ4 Or /
*for ˌthe Lordˌ is gracious and compassionate and
righteous*   ᵈ9 *Horn* here symbolizes dignity.
ᵉ1 Hebrew *Hallelu Yah*; also in verse 9

²Judah became God's sanctuary,
  Israel his dominion.

³The sea looked and fled,
  the Jordan turned back;
⁴the mountains skipped like rams,
  the hills like lambs.

⁵Why was it, O sea, that you fled,
  O Jordan, that you turned back,
⁶you mountains, that you skipped like
    rams,
  you hills, like lambs?

⁷Tremble, O earth, at the presence of
    the Lord,
  at the presence of the God of
    Jacob,
⁸who turned the rock into a pool,
  the hard rock into springs of water.

Psalm 115

¹Not to us, O Lord, not to us
  but to your name be the glory,
  because of your love and
    faithfulness.

²Why do the nations say,
  "Where is their God?"
³Our God is in heaven;
  he does whatever pleases him.
⁴But their idols are silver and gold,
  made by the hands of men.
⁵They have mouths, but cannot speak,
  eyes, but they cannot see;
⁶they have ears, but cannot hear,
  noses, but they cannot smell;
⁷they have hands, but cannot feel,
  feet, but they cannot walk;

WEDNESDAY

Read *Psalm 112:1–10*
Key Verses *Psalm 112:7–8*

"No Fear" Living – Dana Yeakley

When I first went with my family to the mission field, I believed that because we were so totally committed to God, he wouldn't let anything bad happen to me, my family or my friends. That belief was soon thoroughly challenged.

During the first six months we witnessed difficulty after difficulty. A friend's son was hit by a car and suffered severe brain damage. Another friend developed appendicitis; while she was still recovering from surgery, she received word that her mother had died of cancer. She was not able to attend the funeral. Another friend's daughter was hit by a car and nearly lost her life. A fourth friend became sick with typhoid fever and was in bed for a month. All of these friends were committed missionaries.

By then I was truly ready to return to the good ol' USA, but Jesus spoke to me from John 6:67: "You do not want to leave too, do you?" My heart was breaking because, yes, I did want to leave. I began to realize God had never guaranteed that he would keep tragedy away from me or from those I loved, but he had promised to be with me in the midst of it.

Peter's words in John 6:68–69 became my prayer: "Lord, to whom shall we go? You have the words of eternal life. We believe and know that you are the Holy One of God." This was the response that God wanted me to learn. He taught me that in this life there will always be "bad news," no matter where we live. But in those bad-news situations, he promised to take care of me and help me live a "no fear" life.

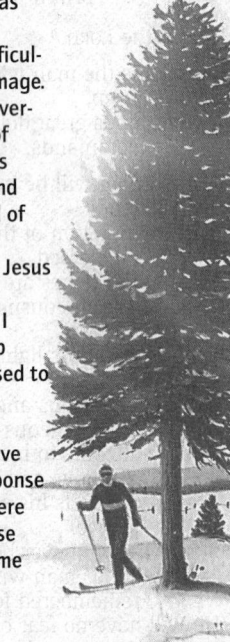

A Deeper Look
Job 13:15; Psalm 91:1–8; Habakkuk 3:17–18

Go to page 669 for your next devotional reading.

nor can they utter a sound with
their throats.
⁸Those who make them will be like
them,
and so will all who trust in them.

⁹O house of Israel, trust in the LORD—
he is their help and shield.
¹⁰O house of Aaron, trust in the LORD—
he is their help and shield.
¹¹You who fear him, trust in the LORD—
he is their help and shield.

¹²The LORD remembers us and will bless
us:
He will bless the house of Israel,
he will bless the house of Aaron,
¹³he will bless those who fear the
LORD—
small and great alike.

¹⁴May the LORD make you increase,
both you and your children.
¹⁵May you be blessed by the LORD,
the Maker of heaven and earth.

¹⁶The highest heavens belong to the
LORD,
but the earth he has given to man.
¹⁷It is not the dead who praise the
LORD,
those who go down to silence;
¹⁸it is we who extol the LORD,
both now and forevermore.

Praise the LORD.ᵃ

Psalm 116

¹I love the LORD, for he heard my
voice;
he heard my cry for mercy.
²Because he turned his ear to me,
I will call on him as long as I live.

³The cords of death entangled me,
the anguish of the graveᵇ came
upon me;
I was overcome by trouble and
sorrow.
⁴Then I called on the name of the
LORD:
"O LORD, save me!"

⁵The LORD is gracious and righteous;
our God is full of compassion.
⁶The LORD protects the simplehearted;
when I was in great need, he
saved me.

⁷Be at rest once more, O my soul,
for the LORD has been good to you.

⁸For you, O LORD, have delivered my
soul from death,
my eyes from tears,
my feet from stumbling,
⁹that I may walk before the LORD
in the land of the living.
¹⁰I believed; thereforeᶜ I said,
"I am greatly afflicted."
¹¹And in my dismay I said,
"All men are liars."

¹²How can I repay the LORD
for all his goodness to me?
¹³I will lift up the cup of salvation
and call on the name of the LORD.
¹⁴I will fulfill my vows to the LORD
in the presence of all his people.

¹⁵Precious in the sight of the LORD
is the death of his saints.
¹⁶O LORD, truly I am your servant;
I am your servant, the son of your
maidservantᵈ;
you have freed me from my
chains.

¹⁷I will sacrifice a thank offering to you
and call on the name of the LORD.
¹⁸I will fulfill my vows to the LORD
in the presence of all his people,
¹⁹in the courts of the house of the
LORD—
in your midst, O Jerusalem.

Praise the LORD.ᵃ

Psalm 117

¹Praise the LORD, all you nations;
extol him, all you peoples.
²For great is his love toward us,
and the faithfulness of the LORD
endures forever.

Praise the LORD.ᵃ

Psalm 118

¹Give thanks to the LORD, for he is
good;
his love endures forever.

²Let Israel say:
"His love endures forever."
³Let the house of Aaron say:
"His love endures forever."
⁴Let those who fear the LORD say:
"His love endures forever."

⁵In my anguish I cried to the LORD,

ᵃ18,19,2 Hebrew Hallelu Yah   ᵇ3 Hebrew Sheol
ᶜ10 Or believed even when   ᵈ16 Or servant, your
faithful son

and he answered by setting me
free.
⁶The LORD is with me; I will not be
afraid.
What can man do to me?
⁷The LORD is with me; he is my helper.
I will look in triumph on my
enemies.

⁸It is better to take refuge in the LORD
than to trust in man.
⁹It is better to take refuge in the LORD
than to trust in princes.

¹⁰All the nations surrounded me,
but in the name of the LORD I cut
them off.
¹¹They surrounded me on every side,
but in the name of the LORD I cut
them off.
¹²They swarmed around me like bees,
but they died out as quickly as
burning thorns;
in the name of the LORD I cut them
off.

¹³I was pushed back and about to fall,
but the LORD helped me.
¹⁴The LORD is my strength and my song;
he has become my salvation.

¹⁵Shouts of joy and victory
resound in the tents of the
righteous:
"The LORD's right hand has done
mighty things!
¹⁶   The LORD's right hand is lifted high;
the LORD's right hand has done
mighty things!"

¹⁷I will not die but live,
and will proclaim what the LORD
has done.
¹⁸The LORD has chastened me severely,
but he has not given me over to
death.

¹⁹Open for me the gates of
righteousness;
I will enter and give thanks to the
LORD.
²⁰This is the gate of the LORD
through which the righteous may
enter.
²¹I will give you thanks, for you
answered me;
you have become my salvation.

²²The stone the builders rejected
has become the capstone;
²³the LORD has done this,
and it is marvelous in our eyes.

²⁴This is the day the LORD has made;
let us rejoice and be glad in it.

²⁵O LORD, save us;
O LORD, grant us success.
²⁶Blessed is he who comes in the name
of the LORD.
From the house of the LORD we
bless you.ᵃ
²⁷The LORD is God,
and he has made his light shine
upon us.
With boughs in hand, join in the
festal procession
upᵇ to the horns of the altar.

²⁸You are my God, and I will give you
thanks;
you are my God, and I will exalt
you.

²⁹Give thanks to the LORD, for he is
good;
his love endures forever.

Psalm 119ᶜ

א Aleph

¹Blessed are they whose ways are
blameless,
who walk according to the law of
the LORD.
²Blessed are they who keep his
statutes
and seek him with all their heart.
³They do nothing wrong;
they walk in his ways.
⁴You have laid down precepts
that are to be fully obeyed.
⁵Oh, that my ways were steadfast
in obeying your decrees!
⁶Then I would not be put to shame
when I consider all your
commands.
⁷I will praise you with an upright
heart
as I learn your righteous laws.
⁸I will obey your decrees;
do not utterly forsake me.

ב Beth

⁹How can a young man keep his way
pure?
By living according to your word.
¹⁰I seek you with all my heart;

ᵃ26 The Hebrew is plural.   ᵇ27 Or *Bind the
festal sacrifice with ropes / and take it*   ᶜThis
psalm is an acrostic poem; the verses of each stanza
begin with the same letter of the Hebrew alphabet.

do not let me stray from your
      commands.
[11]I have hidden your word in my heart
      that I might not sin against you.
[12]Praise be to you, O LORD;
      teach me your decrees.
[13]With my lips I recount
      all the laws that come from your
      mouth.
[14]I rejoice in following your statutes
      as one rejoices in great riches.
[15]I meditate on your precepts
      and consider your ways.
[16]I delight in your decrees;
      I will not neglect your word.

ג   Gimel

[17]Do good to your servant, and I will
      live;
      I will obey your word.
[18]Open my eyes that I may see
      wonderful things in your law.
[19]I am a stranger on earth;
      do not hide your commands from
      me.
[20]My soul is consumed with longing
      for your laws at all times.

[21]You rebuke the arrogant, who are
      cursed
      and who stray from your
      commands.
[22]Remove from me scorn and
      contempt,
      for I keep your statutes.
[23]Though rulers sit together and slander
      me,
      your servant will meditate on your
      decrees.
[24]Your statutes are my delight;
      they are my counselors.

ד   Daleth

[25]I am laid low in the dust;
      preserve my life according to your
      word.
[26]I recounted my ways and you
      answered me;
      teach me your decrees.
[27]Let me understand the teaching of
      your precepts;
      then I will meditate on your
      wonders.
[28]My soul is weary with sorrow;
      strengthen me according to your
      word.

THURSDAY

Read *Psalm 119:1–24*
Key Verses *Psalm 119:9,11*

By Heart – Rich Jarvi

As a young Christian I knew that memorizing three verses a day
would be tough. But I also knew that I wanted to memorize Scripture so I'd stay focused on Jesus Christ as I worked on the railroad
during the summer. I decided to leave for work with my memory
verses written on cards in a pocket-sized pack.

I was afraid to let anyone see my pack of verses, but I had told
the Lord that I wouldn't be ashamed of it. It took only ten seconds
for one of my coworkers to ask me what it was. I was dubbed "The
Rev" for the rest of the summer.

To my surprise, the guys started asking me for the verses of the
day and checking to see if I'd gotten all the words right! Soon I
started picking memory verses that focused on the gospel, and what
had begun as a personal discipline became a great witnessing tool.

I had already known that hiding the Word in my heart would
help me "keep [my] way pure" (Psalm 119:9). That summer I
learned that it could also equip me for sharing my faith.

A Deeper Look
Acts 1:8; 2 Timothy 3:16

Go to page 672 for your next devotional reading.

²⁹Keep me from deceitful ways;
  be gracious to me through your
    law.
³⁰I have chosen the way of truth;
  I have set my heart on your laws.
³¹I hold fast to your statutes, O Lord;
  do not let me be put to shame.
³²I run in the path of your commands,
  for you have set my heart free.

ה   He

³³Teach me, O Lord, to follow your
    decrees;
  then I will keep them to the end.
³⁴Give me understanding, and I will
    keep your law
  and obey it with all my heart.
³⁵Direct me in the path of your
    commands,
  for there I find delight.
³⁶Turn my heart toward your statutes
  and not toward selfish gain.
³⁷Turn my eyes away from worthless
    things;
  preserve my life according to your
    word.ᵃ
³⁸Fulfill your promise to your servant,
  so that you may be feared.
³⁹Take away the disgrace I dread,
  for your laws are good.
⁴⁰How I long for your precepts!
  Preserve my life in your
    righteousness.

ו   Waw

⁴¹May your unfailing love come to me,
    O Lord,
  your salvation according to your
    promise;
⁴²then I will answer the one who
    taunts me,
  for I trust in your word.
⁴³Do not snatch the word of truth from
    my mouth,
  for I have put my hope in your
    laws.
⁴⁴I will always obey your law,
  for ever and ever.
⁴⁵I will walk about in freedom,
  for I have sought out your
    precepts.
⁴⁶I will speak of your statutes before
    kings
  and will not be put to shame,
⁴⁷for I delight in your commands
  because I love them.
⁴⁸I lift up my hands toᵇ your
    commands, which I love,
  and I meditate on your decrees.

ז   Zayin

⁴⁹Remember your word to your
    servant,
  for you have given me hope.
⁵⁰My comfort in my suffering is this:
  Your promise preserves my life.
⁵¹The arrogant mock me without
    restraint,
  but I do not turn from your law.
⁵²I remember your ancient laws,
    O Lord,
  and I find comfort in them.
⁵³Indignation grips me because of the
    wicked,
  who have forsaken your law.
⁵⁴Your decrees are the theme of my
    song
  wherever I lodge.
⁵⁵In the night I remember your name,
    O Lord,
  and I will keep your law.
⁵⁶This has been my practice:
  I obey your precepts.

ח   Heth

⁵⁷You are my portion, O Lord;
  I have promised to obey your
    words.
⁵⁸I have sought your face with all my
    heart;
  be gracious to me according to
    your promise.
⁵⁹I have considered my ways
  and have turned my steps to your
    statutes.
⁶⁰I will hasten and not delay
  to obey your commands.
⁶¹Though the wicked bind me with
    ropes,
  I will not forget your law.
⁶²At midnight I rise to give you thanks
  for your righteous laws.
⁶³I am a friend to all who fear you,
  to all who follow your precepts.
⁶⁴The earth is filled with your love,
    O Lord;
  teach me your decrees.

ט   Teth

⁶⁵Do good to your servant
  according to your word, O Lord.
⁶⁶Teach me knowledge and good
    judgment,
  for I believe in your commands.

ᵃ37 Two manuscripts of the Masoretic Text and
Dead Sea Scrolls; most manuscripts of the Masoretic
Text *life in your way*   ᵇ48 Or *for*

⁶⁷Before I was afflicted I went astray,
　　but now I obey your word.
⁶⁸You are good, and what you do is
　　good;
　　teach me your decrees.
⁶⁹Though the arrogant have smeared
　　me with lies,
　　I keep your precepts with all my
　　heart.
⁷⁰Their hearts are callous and
　　unfeeling,
　　but I delight in your law.
⁷¹It was good for me to be afflicted
　　so that I might learn your decrees.
⁷²The law from your mouth is more
　　precious to me
　　than thousands of pieces of silver
　　and gold.

י　Yodh

⁷³Your hands made me and formed me;
　　give me understanding to learn
　　your commands.
⁷⁴May those who fear you rejoice when
　　they see me,
　　for I have put my hope in your
　　word.
⁷⁵I know, O LORD, that your laws are
　　righteous,
　　and in faithfulness you have
　　afflicted me.
⁷⁶May your unfailing love be my
　　comfort,
　　according to your promise to your
　　servant.
⁷⁷Let your compassion come to me that
　　I may live,
　　for your law is my delight.
⁷⁸May the arrogant be put to shame for
　　wronging me without cause;
　　but I will meditate on your
　　precepts.
⁷⁹May those who fear you turn to me,
　　those who understand your
　　statutes.
⁸⁰May my heart be blameless toward
　　your decrees,
　　that I may not be put to shame.

כ　Kaph

⁸¹My soul faints with longing for your
　　salvation,
　　but I have put my hope in your
　　word.
⁸²My eyes fail, looking for your
　　promise;
　　I say, "When will you comfort
　　me?"

⁸³Though I am like a wineskin in the
　　smoke,
　　I do not forget your decrees.
⁸⁴How long must your servant wait?
　　When will you punish my
　　persecutors?
⁸⁵The arrogant dig pitfalls for me,
　　contrary to your law.
⁸⁶All your commands are trustworthy;
　　help me, for men persecute me
　　without cause.
⁸⁷They almost wiped me from the
　　earth,
　　but I have not forsaken your
　　precepts.
⁸⁸Preserve my life according to your
　　love,
　　and I will obey the statutes of your
　　mouth.

ל　Lamedh

⁸⁹Your word, O LORD, is eternal;
　　it stands firm in the heavens.
⁹⁰Your faithfulness continues through
　　all generations;
　　you established the earth, and it
　　endures.
⁹¹Your laws endure to this day,
　　for all things serve you.
⁹²If your law had not been my delight,
　　I would have perished in my
　　affliction.
⁹³I will never forget your precepts,
　　for by them you have preserved
　　my life.
⁹⁴Save me, for I am yours;
　　I have sought out your precepts.
⁹⁵The wicked are waiting to destroy
　　me,
　　but I will ponder your statutes.
⁹⁶To all perfection I see a limit;
　　but your commands are boundless.

מ　Mem

⁹⁷Oh, how I love your law!
　　I meditate on it all day long.
⁹⁸Your commands make me wiser than
　　my enemies,
　　for they are ever with me.
⁹⁹I have more insight than all my
　　teachers,
　　for I meditate on your statutes.
¹⁰⁰I have more understanding than the
　　elders,
　　for I obey your precepts.
¹⁰¹I have kept my feet from every evil
　　path
　　so that I might obey your word.

102I have not departed from your laws,
  for you yourself have taught me.
103How sweet are your words to my
    taste,
  sweeter than honey to my mouth!
104I gain understanding from your
    precepts;
  therefore I hate every wrong path.

נ Nun

105Your word is a lamp to my feet
  and a light for my path.
106I have taken an oath and
    confirmed it,
  that I will follow your righteous
    laws.
107I have suffered much;

preserve my life, O LORD, according
    to your word.
108Accept, O LORD, the willing praise of
    my mouth,
  and teach me your laws.
109Though I constantly take my life in
    my hands,
  I will not forget your law.
110The wicked have set a snare for me,
  but I have not strayed from your
    precepts.
111Your statutes are my heritage
    forever;
  they are the joy of my heart.
112My heart is set on keeping your
    decrees
  to the very end.

FRIDAY

Read Psalm 119:89–112
Key Verse Psalm 119:97

The Wisdom of the Word – Eric Resler

Several years ago a friend and I were discussing some Scriptures we had read and he mentioned a verse that I had been trying to find. I asked where he had found the verse. When he told me it was in the book of Hezekiah, I began to page frantically through the Minor Prophets. As he started to chuckle, I realized that I was on a wild verse chase. There's no such book as Hezekiah in the Bible!

Some time later, however, that scenario started to bother me. If it was that easy for my friend to trick me, how much easier would it be for Satan to do the same? I decided my Bible knowledge needed work.

Later I found verses such as Psalm 119:97–99 that promised that meditating on God's law could make me wiser than my "enemies," who trust in human arrogance; more insightful than "teachers," who teach human knowledge; and more understanding than "elders," who can share only human experience. So I began to pour over God's Word several times a day. That practice eventually turned into a consistent three times a day—sometimes more. I began to see the Bible's deep wisdom, just as the psalmist had promised. In a university atmosphere where truth seemed to be up for grabs, I found my time in the Word each day refreshing. In fact it became my main source of strength and encouragement.

When God began to bring people into my life who were in pain or struggling and needed a listening ear, I found that I knew exactly where to help them find God's wisdom for their situations. Not only had God taught me how to be "wiser than my enemies"; he also allowed me to share that wisdom with others in need.

A Deeper Look
Joshua 1:8; Psalm 1:1–3; Colossians 3:16

Go to page 675 for your next devotional reading.

ס   Samekh

113I hate double-minded men,
    but I love your law.
114You are my refuge and my shield;
    I have put my hope in your word.
115Away from me, you evildoers,
    that I may keep the commands of
        my God!
116Sustain me according to your
        promise, and I will live;
    do not let my hopes be dashed.
117Uphold me, and I will be delivered;
    I will always have regard for your
        decrees.
118You reject all who stray from your
        decrees,
    for their deceitfulness is in vain.
119All the wicked of the earth you
        discard like dross;
    therefore I love your statutes.
120My flesh trembles in fear of you;
    I stand in awe of your laws.

ע   Ayin

121I have done what is righteous and
        just;
    do not leave me to my oppressors.
122Ensure your servant's well-being;
    let not the arrogant oppress me.
123My eyes fail, looking for your
        salvation,
    looking for your righteous promise.
124Deal with your servant according to
        your love
    and teach me your decrees.
125I am your servant; give me
        discernment
    that I may understand your
        statutes.
126It is time for you to act, O LORD;
    your law is being broken.
127Because I love your commands
    more than gold, more than pure
        gold,
128and because I consider all your
        precepts right,
    I hate every wrong path.

פ   Pe

129Your statutes are wonderful;
    therefore I obey them.
130The unfolding of your words gives
        light;
    it gives understanding to the
        simple.
131I open my mouth and pant,
    longing for your commands.
132Turn to me and have mercy on me,

as you always do to those who
        love your name.
133Direct my footsteps according to
        your word;
    let no sin rule over me.
134Redeem me from the oppression of
        men,
    that I may obey your precepts.
135Make your face shine upon your
        servant
    and teach me your decrees.
136Streams of tears flow from my eyes,
    for your law is not obeyed.

צ   Tsadhe

137Righteous are you, O LORD,
    and your laws are right.
138The statutes you have laid down are
        righteous;
    they are fully trustworthy.
139My zeal wears me out,
    for my enemies ignore your words.
140Your promises have been thoroughly
        tested,
    and your servant loves them.
141Though I am lowly and despised,
    I do not forget your precepts.
142Your righteousness is everlasting
    and your law is true.
143Trouble and distress have come
        upon me,
    but your commands are my
        delight.
144Your statutes are forever right;
    give me understanding that I may
        live.

ק   Qoph

145I call with all my heart; answer me,
        O LORD,
    and I will obey your decrees.
146I call out to you; save me
    and I will keep your statutes.
147I rise before dawn and cry for help;
    I have put my hope in your word.
148My eyes stay open through the
        watches of the night,
    that I may meditate on your
        promises.
149Hear my voice in accordance with
        your love;
    preserve my life, O LORD, according
        to your laws.
150Those who devise wicked schemes
        are near,
    but they are far from your law.
151Yet you are near, O LORD,
    and all your commands are true.

152Long ago I learned from your
        statutes
    that you established them to last
        forever.

ר   Resh

153Look upon my suffering and
        deliver me,
    for I have not forgotten your law.
154Defend my cause and redeem me;
    preserve my life according to your
        promise.
155Salvation is far from the wicked,
    for they do not seek out your
        decrees.
156Your compassion is great, O Lord;
    preserve my life according to your
        laws.
157Many are the foes who
        persecute me,
    but I have not turned from your
        statutes.
158I look on the faithless with loathing,
    for they do not obey your word.
159See how I love your precepts;
    preserve my life, O Lord, according
        to your love.
160All your words are true;
    all your righteous laws are eternal.

ש   Sin and Shin

161Rulers persecute me without cause,
    but my heart trembles at your
        word.
162I rejoice in your promise
    like one who finds great spoil.
163I hate and abhor falsehood
    but I love your law.
164Seven times a day I praise you
    for your righteous laws.
165Great peace have they who love
        your law,
    and nothing can make them
        stumble.
166I wait for your salvation, O Lord,
    and I follow your commands.
167I obey your statutes,
    for I love them greatly.
168I obey your precepts and your
        statutes,
    for all my ways are known to you.

ת   Taw

169May my cry come before you,
        O Lord;
    give me understanding according
        to your word.
170May my supplication come before
        you;

deliver me according to your
        promise.
171May my lips overflow with praise,
    for you teach me your decrees.
172May my tongue sing of your word,
    for all your commands are
        righteous.
173May your hand be ready to help me,
    for I have chosen your precepts.
174I long for your salvation, O Lord,
    and your law is my delight.
175Let me live that I may praise you,
    and may your laws sustain me.
176I have strayed like a lost sheep.
    Seek your servant,
    for I have not forgotten your
        commands.

Psalm 120

A song of ascents.

1I call on the Lord in my distress,
    and he answers me.
2Save me, O Lord, from lying lips
    and from deceitful tongues.

3What will he do to you,
    and what more besides, O deceitful
        tongue?
4He will punish you with a warrior's
        sharp arrows,
    with burning coals of the broom
        tree.

5Woe to me that I dwell in Meshech,
    that I live among the tents of
        Kedar!
6Too long have I lived
    among those who hate peace.
7I am a man of peace;
    but when I speak, they are for war.

POINT OF INTEREST   Psalm 119:147

When do you read your
Bible? Many people rise
early in the morning and
spend the first moments of
the day with God. One trick to acquiring
this self-discipline is to feed your soul
before you feed your body. Your growling
stomach will become a reminder of your
hungry soul.

Read Psalm 119:129–176
Key Verse Psalm 119:160

Facing the Truth

Does the world sometimes spin so fast it makes you feel dizzy? We encounter so much information, so many opinions and options—and many of them based on relativism and shifting moral standards. It can be a great relief to anchor ourselves to something solid and unchanging —the Bible. It is eternal, everlasting, forever. While the Bible remains the always trustworthy and true Word of God, it is forever vital and up-to-date.

Sometimes we slip into thinking that the Word of God is a list of static rules. But when the psalmist looks at the Word, he is looking at the face of God in a living relationship. He uses phrases such as "I call out to you; save me and I will keep your statutes" (Psalm 119:146), and "you are near, O LORD, and all your commands are true" (Psalm 119:151). These thoughts are as real and alive today as they were when they were written. That's the mystery of the eternal, yet always relevant, Word of God.

Digging Into the Word
1. God's Word is the measuring rod for truth. What new perspective do you gain about the Word of God from these passages?— Psalm 119:142,151,160; John 17:17
2. Jesus is the living Word of God. What do you learn about him from these passages?—John 1:1–5,14; John 18:33–37

Discussion Starter
Fire up a conversation with some Christian friends by asking: "When was a time you read something in the Bible that contradicted your own belief system or lifestyle? What did you do about it?" Or ask each friend to look for one Scripture passage or verse that is real and alive to them and then talk about them.

One Step Deeper
John 5:24; Hebrews 6:13–20

Go to page 677 for your next devotional reading.

Psalm 121

A song of ascents.

1I lift up my eyes to the hills—
  where does my help come from?
2My help comes from the LORD,
  the Maker of heaven and earth.

3He will not let your foot slip—
  he who watches over you will not
    slumber;
4indeed, he who watches over Israel
  will neither slumber nor sleep.

5The LORD watches over you—
  the LORD is your shade at your right
    hand;
6the sun will not harm you by day,
  nor the moon by night.

7The LORD will keep you from all
    harm—
  he will watch over your life;
8the LORD will watch over your coming
    and going
  both now and forevermore.

Psalm 122

A song of ascents. Of David.

1I rejoiced with those who said to me,
  "Let us go to the house of the
    LORD."
2Our feet are standing
  in your gates, O Jerusalem.

3Jerusalem is built like a city
  that is closely compacted together.
4That is where the tribes go up,
  the tribes of the LORD,
  to praise the name of the LORD
  according to the statute given to
    Israel.
5There the thrones for judgment stand,
  the thrones of the house of David.

6Pray for the peace of Jerusalem:
  "May those who love you be
    secure.
7May there be peace within your walls
  and security within your citadels."
8For the sake of my brothers and
    friends,
  I will say, "Peace be within you."
9For the sake of the house of the LORD
    our God,
  I will seek your prosperity.

Psalm 123

A song of ascents.

1I lift up my eyes to you,
  to you whose throne is in heaven.
2As the eyes of slaves look to the hand
    of their master,
  as the eyes of a maid look to the
    hand of her mistress,
  so our eyes look to the LORD our God,
    till he shows us his mercy.

3Have mercy on us, O LORD, have
    mercy on us,
  for we have endured much
    contempt.
4We have endured much ridicule from
    the proud,
  much contempt from the arrogant.

Psalm 124

A song of ascents. Of David.

1If the LORD had not been on our
    side—
  let Israel say—
2if the LORD had not been on our side
  when men attacked us,
3when their anger flared against us,
  they would have swallowed us
    alive;
4the flood would have engulfed us,
  the torrent would have swept over
    us,
5the raging waters
  would have swept us away.

6Praise be to the LORD,
  who has not let us be torn by their
    teeth.
7We have escaped like a bird
  out of the fowler's snare;
  the snare has been broken,
  and we have escaped.
8Our help is in the name of the LORD,
  the Maker of heaven and earth.

Psalm 125

A song of ascents.

1Those who trust in the LORD are like
    Mount Zion,
  which cannot be shaken but
    endures forever.
2As the mountains surround
    Jerusalem,
  so the LORD surrounds his people
  both now and forevermore.

³The scepter of the wicked will not
      remain
   over the land allotted to the
      righteous,
for then the righteous might use
   their hands to do evil.

⁴Do good, O Lord, to those who are
      good,
   to those who are upright in heart.
⁵But those who turn to crooked ways
   the Lord will banish with the
      evildoers.

Peace be upon Israel.

Psalm 126

A song of ascents.

¹When the Lord brought back the
      captives to*ᵃ* Zion,
   we were like men who dreamed.*ᵇ*
²Our mouths were filled with laughter,
   our tongues with songs of joy.

Then it was said among the nations,
   "The Lord has done great things
      for them."
³The Lord has done great things for us,
   and we are filled with joy.

⁴Restore our fortunes,*ᶜ* O Lord,
   like streams in the Negev.
⁵Those who sow in tears
   will reap with songs of joy.
⁶He who goes out weeping,
   carrying seed to sow,
will return with songs of joy,
   carrying sheaves with him.

Psalm 127

A song of ascents. Of Solomon.

¹Unless the Lord builds the house,
   its builders labor in vain.
Unless the Lord watches over the city,

*ᵃ1 Or Lord restored the fortunes of   ᵇ1 Or men
restored to health   ᶜ4 Or Bring back our captives*

MONDAY

Read Psalms 125:1—128:6
Key Verse Psalm 127:1

Who's Building Your House? – Sharla Walstrom

I sat across the table from the guy I had been dating for six months.
He was a nice Christian guy; any girl would feel comfortable taking
him home to meet her parents. He made me laugh, and we had a lot
of fun together. So why did I feel so uneasy about our relationship
today?

That morning I had read Psalm 127:1: "Unless the Lord builds
the house, its builders labor in vain." Both of us wondered whether
the Lord was building this relationship, or if we were building it in
our own strength. If God was not first in both of our lives, this relationship was doomed to fail. Had God been in our relationship as it
grew? I wasn't sure anymore.

After a lot of discussion and prayer, we decided to end our relationship. We knew that if God wanted us to be together sometime in
the future, he would lead us in that direction. Then he would really
be the builder of our house.

Are you trying to build your life on your own? Nothing is worse
than wasting countless hours of time and energy on something that
doesn't follow God's way. Discover God's blueprint for your life
through his Word and through prayer so that your labor is not in
vain.

A Deeper Look
Proverbs 3:5–6; Luke 6:46–49

Go to page 680 for your next devotional reading.

the watchmen stand guard in vain.
²In vain you rise early
and stay up late,
toiling for food to eat—
for he grants sleep to*ᵃ* those he
loves.

³Sons are a heritage from the LORD,
children a reward from him.
⁴Like arrows in the hands of a warrior
are sons born in one's youth.
⁵Blessed is the man
whose quiver is full of them.
They will not be put to shame
when they contend with their
enemies in the gate.

Psalm 128

A song of ascents.

¹Blessed are all who fear the LORD,
who walk in his ways.
²You will eat the fruit of your labor;
blessings and prosperity will be
yours.
³Your wife will be like a fruitful vine
within your house;
your sons will be like olive shoots
around your table.
⁴Thus is the man blessed
who fears the LORD.

⁵May the LORD bless you from Zion
all the days of your life;
may you see the prosperity of
Jerusalem,
⁶ and may you live to see your
children's children.

Peace be upon Israel.

Psalm 129

A song of ascents.

¹They have greatly oppressed me from
my youth—
let Israel say—
²they have greatly oppressed me from
my youth,
but they have not gained the
victory over me.
³Plowmen have plowed my back
and made their furrows long.
⁴But the LORD is righteous;
he has cut me free from the cords
of the wicked.
⁵May all who hate Zion
be turned back in shame.

⁶May they be like grass on the roof,
which withers before it can grow;
⁷with it the reaper cannot fill his
hands,
nor the one who gathers fill his
arms.
⁸May those who pass by not say,
"The blessing of the LORD be upon
you;
we bless you in the name of the
LORD."

Psalm 130

A song of ascents.

¹Out of the depths I cry to you,
O LORD;
² O Lord, hear my voice.
Let your ears be attentive
to my cry for mercy.

³If you, O LORD, kept a record of sins,
O Lord, who could stand?
⁴But with you there is forgiveness;
therefore you are feared.

⁵I wait for the LORD, my soul waits,
and in his word I put my hope.
⁶My soul waits for the Lord
more than watchmen wait for the
morning,
more than watchmen wait for the
morning.

⁷O Israel, put your hope in the LORD,
for with the LORD is unfailing love
and with him is full redemption.
⁸He himself will redeem Israel
from all their sins.

Psalm 131

A song of ascents. Of David.

¹My heart is not proud, O LORD,
my eyes are not haughty;
I do not concern myself with great
matters
or things too wonderful for me.
²But I have stilled and quieted my
soul;
like a weaned child with its
mother,
like a weaned child is my soul
within me.

³O Israel, put your hope in the LORD
both now and forevermore.

ᵃ2 Or eat— / for while they sleep he provides for

Psalm 132

A song of ascents.

¹O LORD, remember David
and all the hardships he endured.

²He swore an oath to the LORD
and made a vow to the Mighty
One of Jacob:
³"I will not enter my house
or go to my bed—
⁴I will allow no sleep to my eyes,
no slumber to my eyelids,
⁵till I find a place for the LORD,
a dwelling for the Mighty One of
Jacob."

⁶We heard it in Ephrathah,
we came upon it in the fields of
Jaar*a;b*
⁷"Let us go to his dwelling place;
let us worship at his footstool—
⁸arise, O LORD, and come to your
resting place,
you and the ark of your might.
⁹May your priests be clothed with
righteousness;
may your saints sing for joy."

¹⁰For the sake of David your servant,
do not reject your anointed one.

¹¹The LORD swore an oath to David,
a sure oath that he will not revoke:
"One of your own descendants
I will place on your throne—
¹²if your sons keep my covenant
and the statutes I teach them,
then their sons will sit
on your throne for ever and ever."

¹³For the LORD has chosen Zion,
he has desired it for his dwelling:
¹⁴"This is my resting place for ever and
ever;
here I will sit enthroned, for I have
desired it—
¹⁵I will bless her with abundant
provisions;
her poor will I satisfy with food.
¹⁶I will clothe her priests with
salvation,
and her saints will ever sing for
joy.

¹⁷"Here I will make a horn*c* grow for
David
and set up a lamp for my anointed
one.
¹⁸I will clothe his enemies with shame,

but the crown on his head will be
resplendent."

Psalm 133

A song of ascents. Of David.

¹How good and pleasant it is
when brothers live together in
unity!
²It is like precious oil poured on the
head,
running down on the beard,
running down on Aaron's beard,
down upon the collar of his robes.
³It is as if the dew of Hermon
were falling on Mount Zion.
For there the LORD bestows his
blessing,
even life forevermore.

Psalm 134

A song of ascents.

¹Praise the LORD, all you servants of
the LORD
who minister by night in the house
of the LORD.
²Lift up your hands in the sanctuary
and praise the LORD.

³May the LORD, the Maker of heaven
and earth,
bless you from Zion.

Psalm 135

¹Praise the LORD.*d*

Praise the name of the LORD;
praise him, you servants of the
LORD,
²you who minister in the house of the
LORD,
in the courts of the house of our
God.

³Praise the LORD, for the LORD is good;
sing praise to his name, for that is
pleasant.
⁴For the LORD has chosen Jacob to be
his own,
Israel to be his treasured
possession.

⁵I know that the LORD is great,

---

a6 That is, Kiriath Jearim   *b6* Or *heard of it in
Ephrathah, / we found it in the fields of Jaar.* (And
no quotes around verses 7-9)   *c17 Horn* here
symbolizes strong one, that is, king.   *d1* Hebrew
Hallelu Yah; also in verses 3 and 21

that our Lord is greater than all
    gods.
⁶The Lord does whatever pleases him,
    in the heavens and on the earth,
    in the seas and all their depths.
⁷He makes clouds rise from the ends
    of the earth;
he sends lightning with the rain
and brings out the wind from his
    storehouses.

⁸He struck down the firstborn of
    Egypt,
    the firstborn of men and animals.
⁹He sent his signs and wonders into
    your midst, O Egypt,
    against Pharaoh and all his
    servants.
¹⁰He struck down many nations
    and killed mighty kings—
¹¹Sihon king of the Amorites,

TUESDAY

Read Psalm 133:1–3
Key Verse Psalm 133:1

Value Unity — Bill Gensky

"Can't we all just get along?" . . . "Visualize world peace." What do
these sayings have in common? They indicate our desire to live
together in peace—a noble idea. However, history has proven that,
in general, we humans don't do a very good job of living out that
ideal. In spite of our best efforts, we always seem to find something
to fight about—even those of us in the Christian community.

So what do we do about it? What does unity look like? Ephesians
4:3–6 tells us we should "make every effort to keep the unity of the
Spirit through the bond of peace. There is one body and one Spirit—
just as you were called to one hope when you were called—one
Lord, one faith, one baptism; one God and Father of all, who is over
all and through all and in all." Unity starts with a common confession of "one Lord," a commitment to each other as God's children,
and a willingness to be alert to issues and situations that can tear
at the fabric of the unity already given to us by God.

Unity is strengthened when we focus on our common confession
rather than on issues that may be a matter of preference or tradition (see Romans 14:5–23). Rather than judging and disapproving
of others' weaknesses, we are to encourage and support them (see
Romans 15:1). We are to use our spiritual gifts to build up the body
(see Ephesians 4:11). We are not to compare ourselves with one
another (see Galatians 6:4–5.) We are to clothe ourselves "with
compassion, kindness, humility, gentleness and patience. Bear with
each other and forgive whatever grievances you may have against
one another. Forgive as the Lord forgave you. And over all these
virtues put on love, which binds them all together in perfect unity"
(Colossians 3:12–14).

Finally, we are to value and protect unity as a gift from God:
"May the God who gives endurance and encouragement give you a
spirit of unity among yourselves as you follow Christ Jesus, so that
with one heart and mouth you may glorify the God and Father of
our Lord Jesus Christ" (Romans 15:5).

A Deeper Look
John 17:20–23; 1 Corinthians 12:21–27

Go to page 683 for your next devotional reading.

Og king of Bashan
and all the kings of Canaan—
¹²and he gave their land as an
inheritance,
an inheritance to his people Israel.

¹³Your name, O LORD, endures forever,
your renown, O LORD, through all
generations.
¹⁴For the LORD will vindicate his people
and have compassion on his
servants.

¹⁵The idols of the nations are silver and
gold,
made by the hands of men.
¹⁶They have mouths, but cannot speak,
eyes, but they cannot see;
¹⁷they have ears, but cannot hear,
nor is there breath in their mouths.
¹⁸Those who make them will be like
them,
and so will all who trust in them.

¹⁹O house of Israel, praise the LORD;
O house of Aaron, praise the LORD;
²⁰O house of Levi, praise the LORD;
you who fear him, praise the LORD.
²¹Praise be to the LORD from Zion,
to him who dwells in Jerusalem.

Praise the LORD.

Psalm 136

¹Give thanks to the LORD, for he is
good.
His love endures forever.
²Give thanks to the God of gods.
His love endures forever.
³Give thanks to the Lord of lords:
His love endures forever.

⁴to him who alone does great
wonders,
His love endures forever.
⁵who by his understanding made the
heavens,
His love endures forever.
⁶who spread out the earth upon the
waters,
His love endures forever.
⁷who made the great lights—
His love endures forever.
⁸the sun to govern the day,
His love endures forever.
⁹the moon and stars to govern the
night;
His love endures forever.

¹⁰to him who struck down the firstborn
of Egypt
His love endures forever.
¹¹and brought Israel out from among
them
His love endures forever.
¹²with a mighty hand and outstretched
arm;
His love endures forever.
¹³to him who divided the Red Sea*ᵃ*
asunder
His love endures forever.
¹⁴and brought Israel through the midst
of it,
His love endures forever.
¹⁵but swept Pharaoh and his army into
the Red Sea;
His love endures forever.
¹⁶to him who led his people through
the desert,
His love endures forever.
¹⁷who struck down great kings,
His love endures forever.
¹⁸and killed mighty kings—
His love endures forever.
¹⁹Sihon king of the Amorites
His love endures forever.
²⁰and Og king of Bashan—
His love endures forever.
²¹and gave their land as an inheritance,
His love endures forever.
²²an inheritance to his servant Israel;
His love endures forever.

²³to the One who remembered us in
our low estate
His love endures forever.
²⁴and freed us from our enemies,
His love endures forever.
²⁵and who gives food to every creature.
His love endures forever.

²⁶Give thanks to the God of heaven.
His love endures forever.

Psalm 137

¹By the rivers of Babylon we sat and
wept
when we remembered Zion.
²There on the poplars
we hung our harps,
³for there our captors asked us for
songs,
our tormentors demanded songs of
joy;

ᵃ13 Hebrew *Yam Suph*; that is, Sea of Reeds; also
in verse 15

they said, "Sing us one of the
songs of Zion!"

⁴How can we sing the songs of the
LORD
   while in a foreign land?
⁵If I forget you, O Jerusalem,
   may my right hand forget ⌐its skill⌐.
⁶May my tongue cling to the roof of
      my mouth
   if I do not remember you,
if I do not consider Jerusalem
   my highest joy.

⁷Remember, O LORD, what the
      Edomites did
   on the day Jerusalem fell.
"Tear it down," they cried,
   "tear it down to its foundations!"

⁸O Daughter of Babylon, doomed to
      destruction,
   happy is he who repays you
   for what you have done to us—
⁹he who seizes your infants
   and dashes them against the rocks.

Psalm 138

Of David.

¹I will praise you, O LORD, with all my
      heart;
   before the "gods" I will sing your
      praise.
²I will bow down toward your holy
      temple
   and will praise your name
for your love and your faithfulness,
   for you have exalted above all things
   your name and your word.
³When I called, you answered me;
   you made me bold and
      stouthearted.

⁴May all the kings of the earth praise
      you, O LORD,
   when they hear the words of your
      mouth.
⁵May they sing of the ways of the
      LORD,
   for the glory of the LORD is great.
⁶Though the LORD is on high, he looks
      upon the lowly,
   but the proud he knows from afar.
⁷Though I walk in the midst of
      trouble,
   you preserve my life;
you stretch out your hand against the
      anger of my foes,
   with your right hand you save me.

⁸The LORD will fulfill ⌐his purpose⌐ for
      me;
   your love, O LORD, endures
      forever—
   do not abandon the works of your
      hands.

Psalm 139

*For the director of music. Of David.
A psalm.*

¹O LORD, you have searched me
   and you know me.
²You know when I sit and when I rise;
   you perceive my thoughts from
      afar.
³You discern my going out and my
      lying down;
   you are familiar with all my ways.
⁴Before a word is on my tongue
   you know it completely, O LORD.

⁵You hem me in—behind and before;
   you have laid your hand upon me.
⁶Such knowledge is too wonderful for
      me,
   too lofty for me to attain.

⁷Where can I go from your Spirit?
   Where can I flee from your
      presence?
⁸If I go up to the heavens, you are
      there;
   if I make my bed in the depths,ᵃ
      you are there.
⁹If I rise on the wings of the dawn,
   if I settle on the far side of the sea,
¹⁰even there your hand will guide me,
   your right hand will hold me fast.

¹¹If I say, "Surely the darkness will
      hide me
   and the light become night around
      me,"
¹²even the darkness will not be dark to
      you;
   the night will shine like the day,
   for darkness is as light to you.

¹³For you created my inmost being;
   you knit me together in my
      mother's womb.
¹⁴I praise you because I am fearfully
      and wonderfully made;
   your works are wonderful,
   I know that full well.
¹⁵My frame was not hidden from you

ᵃ8 Hebrew *Sheol*

when I was made in the secret
place.
When I was woven together in the
depths of the earth,
16 your eyes saw my unformed body.
All the days ordained for me
were written in your book
before one of them came to be.

17How precious to*a* me are your
thoughts, O God!
How vast is the sum of them!
18Were I to count them,

they would outnumber the grains
of sand.
When I awake,
I am still with you.

19If only you would slay the wicked,
O God!
Away from me, you bloodthirsty
men!
20They speak of you with evil intent;
your adversaries misuse your
name.

a 17 Or *concerning*

WEDNESDAY

Read *Psalm 139:1–24*
Key Verses *Psalm 139:13–16*

In the Eyes of the Beholder — Mistie Hutchison

"You know, no one has ever told me that I'm pretty or beautiful or special," said the young college woman seated across from me. Tears welled in her eyes as she added, "I sometimes wonder if there is anything important or valuable about me."

While I longed for my friend to embrace God's view of her, I was reminded of my own struggles in this area. Having been born with a physical disability, there have been times when I haven't felt pretty or special or significant. There have been times when I've questioned God's goodness and love in choosing to create me the way he did.

When we don't feel accepted by others, we begin to question God's goodness, love and wisdom in how he created us. We think, "If only I could be this way . . . or if only I could look like that," and those thoughts proliferate, crowding out God's perspective and sovereignty.

That's why we need to be reminded of the truths David embraced in Psalm 139. From our inmost being (our thoughts, feelings and values) to our outside appearance (our height, weight and shape), God knows and values us. From our past ("your eyes saw my unformed body") to our future ("all the days ordained for me were written in your book"), God is there (Psalm 139:16). We know that David accepted God as his creator because of his outburst of praise: "Your works are wonderful" (Psalm 139:14).

There aren't any easy formulas for accepting ourselves or the ways of the One who made us. But there is something that changes in us when we come to God and ask him to search our hearts and thoughts. Instead of being inclined to question and criticize, we become inclined to worship and love. When we adopt a correct view of God, we find a correct view of ourselves.

A Deeper Look
Psalm 23:1–6; Isaiah 46:3–4; Jeremiah 31:3

Go to page 687 for your next devotional reading.

²¹Do I not hate those who hate you,
O Lᴏʀᴅ,
   and abhor those who rise up
against you?
²²I have nothing but hatred for them;
   I count them my enemies.

²³Search me, O God, and know my
heart;
   test me and know my anxious
thoughts.
²⁴See if there is any offensive way in
me,
   and lead me in the way
everlasting.

Psalm 140

For the director of music. A psalm
of David.

¹Rescue me, O Lᴏʀᴅ, from evil men;
   protect me from men of violence,
²who devise evil plans in their hearts
   and stir up war every day.
³They make their tongues as sharp as
a serpent's;
   the poison of vipers is on their
lips.   *Selah*

⁴Keep me, O Lᴏʀᴅ, from the hands of
the wicked;
   protect me from men of violence
   who plan to trip my feet.
⁵Proud men have hidden a snare for
me;
   they have spread out the cords of
their net
   and have set traps for me along
my path.   *Selah*

⁶O Lᴏʀᴅ, I say to you, "You are my
God."
   Hear, O Lᴏʀᴅ, my cry for mercy.
⁷O Sovereign Lᴏʀᴅ, my strong
deliverer,
   who shields my head in the day of
battle—
⁸do not grant the wicked their desires,
O Lᴏʀᴅ;
   do not let their plans succeed,
   or they will become proud.   *Selah*

⁹Let the heads of those who surround
me
   be covered with the trouble their
lips have caused.
¹⁰Let burning coals fall upon them;

   may they be thrown into the fire,
   into miry pits, never to rise.
¹¹Let slanderers not be established in
the land;
   may disaster hunt down men of
violence.

¹²I know that the Lᴏʀᴅ secures justice
for the poor
   and upholds the cause of the
needy.
¹³Surely the righteous will praise your
name
   and the upright will live before
you.

Psalm 141

A psalm of David.

¹O Lᴏʀᴅ, I call to you; come quickly to
me.
   Hear my voice when I call to you.
²May my prayer be set before you like
incense;
   may the lifting up of my hands be
like the evening sacrifice.

³Set a guard over my mouth, O Lᴏʀᴅ;
   keep watch over the door of my
lips.
⁴Let not my heart be drawn to what is
evil,
   to take part in wicked deeds
with men who are evildoers;
   let me not eat of their delicacies.

⁵Let a righteous man*ᵃ* strike me—it is
a kindness;

ᵃ5 Or Let the Righteous One

POINT OF INTEREST

Psalm 139:13-16

If you have low self-esteem,
memorize and recite this
psalm to yourself regularly.
In these few short verses, the
psalmist captures the wonder of God's all-
knowing presence. God knew you completely even before he formed you in your
mother's womb. His hand was on you then;
he knows every detail of your past, your
present and your future. Amazing!

let him rebuke me—it is oil on my
    head.
My head will not refuse it.

Yet my prayer is ever against the
    deeds of evildoers;
6   their rulers will be thrown down
        from the cliffs,
    and the wicked will learn that my
        words were well spoken.
7⌊They will say,⌋ "As one plows and
        breaks up the earth,
    so our bones have been scattered
        at the mouth of the grave.ᵃ"

⁸But my eyes are fixed on you,
        O Sovereign LORD;
    in you I take refuge—do not give
        me over to death.
⁹Keep me from the snares they have
        laid for me,
    from the traps set by evildoers.
¹⁰Let the wicked fall into their own
        nets,
    while I pass by in safety.

Psalm 142

A *maskil*ᵇ of David. When he was in
the cave. A prayer.

¹I cry aloud to the LORD;
    I lift up my voice to the LORD for
        mercy.
²I pour out my complaint before him;
    before him I tell my trouble.

³When my spirit grows faint within
        me,
    it is you who know my way.
In the path where I walk
    men have hidden a snare for me.
⁴Look to my right and see;
    no one is concerned for me.
I have no refuge;
    no one cares for my life.

⁵I cry to you, O LORD;
    I say, "You are my refuge,
    my portion in the land of the
        living."
⁶Listen to my cry,
    for I am in desperate need;
rescue me from those who pursue
        me,
    for they are too strong for me.
⁷Set me free from my prison,
    that I may praise your name.

Then the righteous will gather about
        me
    because of your goodness to me.

Psalm 143

A psalm of David.

¹O LORD, hear my prayer,
    listen to my cry for mercy;
in your faithfulness and righteousness
    come to my relief.
²Do not bring your servant into
        judgment,
    for no one living is righteous
        before you.

³The enemy pursues me,
    he crushes me to the ground;
he makes me dwell in darkness
    like those long dead.
⁴So my spirit grows faint within me;
    my heart within me is dismayed.

⁵I remember the days of long ago;
    I meditate on all your works
    and consider what your hands
        have done.
⁶I spread out my hands to you;
    my soul thirsts for you like a
        parched land.   *Selah*

⁷Answer me quickly, O LORD;
    my spirit fails.
Do not hide your face from me
    or I will be like those who go
        down to the pit.
⁸Let the morning bring me word of
        your unfailing love,
    for I have put my trust in you.
Show me the way I should go,
    for to you I lift up my soul.
⁹Rescue me from my enemies, O LORD,
    for I hide myself in you.
¹⁰Teach me to do your will,
    for you are my God;
may your good Spirit
    lead me on level ground.

¹¹For your name's sake, O LORD,
        preserve my life;
    in your righteousness, bring me
        out of trouble.
¹²In your unfailing love, silence my
        enemies;
    destroy all my foes,
    for I am your servant.

ᵃ7 Hebrew *Sheol*   ᵇTitle: Probably a literary or
musical term

Psalm 144

Of David.

¹Praise be to the LORD my Rock,
  who trains my hands for war,
  my fingers for battle.
²He is my loving God and my fortress,
  my stronghold and my deliverer,
my shield, in whom I take refuge,
  who subdues peoples*a* under me.

³O LORD, what is man that you care for
  him,
  the son of man that you think of
  him?
⁴Man is like a breath;
  his days are like a fleeting shadow.

⁵Part your heavens, O LORD, and come
  down;
  touch the mountains, so that they
  smoke.
⁶Send forth lightning and scatter ⌊the
  enemies⌋;
  shoot your arrows and rout them.
⁷Reach down your hand from on high;
  deliver me and rescue me
from the mighty waters,
  from the hands of foreigners
⁸whose mouths are full of lies,
  whose right hands are deceitful.

⁹I will sing a new song to you, O God;
  on the ten-stringed lyre I will make
  music to you,
¹⁰to the One who gives victory to
  kings,
  who delivers his servant David
  from the deadly sword.

¹¹Deliver me and rescue me
  from the hands of foreigners
whose mouths are full of lies,
  whose right hands are deceitful.

¹²Then our sons in their youth
  will be like well-nurtured plants,
and our daughters will be like pillars
  carved to adorn a palace.
¹³Our barns will be filled
  with every kind of provision.
Our sheep will increase by thousands,
  by tens of thousands in our fields;
¹⁴ our oxen will draw heavy loads.*b*
There will be no breaching of walls,
  no going into captivity,
  no cry of distress in our streets.

¹⁵Blessed are the people of whom this
  is true;

blessed are the people whose God
  is the LORD.

Psalm 145*c*

A psalm of praise. Of David.

¹I will exalt you, my God the King;
  I will praise your name for ever
  and ever.
²Every day I will praise you
  and extol your name for ever and
  ever.
³Great is the LORD and most worthy of
  praise;
  his greatness no one can fathom.
⁴One generation will commend your
  works to another;
  they will tell of your mighty acts.
⁵They will speak of the glorious
  splendor of your majesty,
  and I will meditate on your
  wonderful works.*d*
⁶They will tell of the power of your
  awesome works,
  and I will proclaim your great
  deeds.
⁷They will celebrate your abundant
  goodness
  and joyfully sing of your
  righteousness.

⁸The LORD is gracious and
  compassionate,
  slow to anger and rich in love.
⁹The LORD is good to all;
  he has compassion on all he has
  made.
¹⁰All you have made will praise you,
  O LORD;
  your saints will extol you.
¹¹They will tell of the glory of your
  kingdom
  and speak of your might,
¹²so that all men may know of your
  mighty acts
  and the glorious splendor of your
  kingdom.
¹³Your kingdom is an everlasting
  kingdom,

a2 Many manuscripts of the Masoretic Text, Dead
Sea Scrolls, Aquila, Jerome and Syriac; most
manuscripts of the Masoretic Text *subdues my
people*   *b14* Or *our chieftains will be firmly
established*   *c*This psalm is an acrostic poem, the
verses of which (including verse 13b) begin with
the successive letters of the Hebrew alphabet.
d5 Dead Sea Scrolls and Syriac (see also
Septuagint); Masoretic Text *On the glorious splendor
of your majesty / and on your wonderful works I
will meditate*

and your dominion endures
through all generations.

The LORD is faithful to all his promises
and loving toward all he has
made.*a*
¹⁴The LORD upholds all those who fall
and lifts up all who are bowed
down.
¹⁵The eyes of all look to you,
and you give them their food at
the proper time.
¹⁶You open your hand
and satisfy the desires of every
living thing.

¹⁷The LORD is righteous in all his ways
and loving toward all he has made.
¹⁸The LORD is near to all who call on
him,
to all who call on him in truth.
¹⁹He fulfills the desires of those who
fear him;
he hears their cry and saves them.
²⁰The LORD watches over all who love
him,
but all the wicked he will destroy.

a 13 One manuscript of the Masoretic Text, Dead
Sea Scrolls and Syriac (see also Septuagint); most
manuscripts of the Masoretic Text do not have the
last two lines of verse 13.

THURSDAY

Read *Psalm 145:1–21*
Key Verses *Psalm 145:3–7*

Pass It On – Margery Van Zante

During the first semester of my freshman year in college, I eagerly
joined a Bible study group. We focused on ways to study God's Word;
we memorized Scripture and shared our faith with others. It was an
incredible time of learning.

As my sophomore year approached, I looked forward to doing
the same thing—more study, more learning. But to my surprise, my
leader approached me at the end of my freshman year with a
request: "Would you consider leading your own small group next
year?" *Me? What could I offer?* I wondered. I still had so much to
learn.

As we talked through the idea, my leader told me that her vision
for me was to start passing on what I had already learned. Yes, I still
had much to learn myself, but there were ways I could help others
grow. I had learned about prayer, so I could help others do the same.
I had learned how to study the Bible, so I could teach others what I
knew.

My group leader was trying to impress on me the need for spiritual multiplication. As the psalmist says, we are to tell the next
generation about God and all that we have learned about him (see
Psalm 145:3–6). For me, the "next generation" was the following
year's freshman class.

Perhaps you feel, as I did, that you don't have much to offer the
"next generation." Sometimes it's hard to be objective enough to
see how far you've come—how much you've learned. But if you look
a little closer, you'll probably find more than a few things you've
learned that you can pass on to someone else. Prayerfully consider
your options, and ask God to open the doors of opportunity to share
what you've learned with others.

A Deeper Look
Matthew 28:18–20; 2 Timothy 2:2

Go to page 688 for your next devotional reading.

²¹My mouth will speak in praise of the
  LORD.
Let every creature praise his holy
  name
for ever and ever.

Psalm 146

¹Praise the LORD.ᵃ

Praise the LORD, O my soul.
² I will praise the LORD all my life;
  I will sing praise to my God as
  long as I live.

³Do not put your trust in princes,
  in mortal men, who cannot save.
⁴When their spirit departs, they return
  to the ground;
  on that very day their plans come
  to nothing.

⁵Blessed is he whose help is the God
  of Jacob,
  whose hope is in the LORD his God,
⁶the Maker of heaven and earth,
  the sea, and everything in them—

ᵃ1 Hebrew *Hallelu Yah*; also in verse 10

FRIDAY

Read *Psalm 146:1–10*
Key Verses *Psalm 146:3–6*

Don't Trust in Princes, Cinderella — Michael Vander Klipp

Are you trusting in princes? Or princesses? Not literally, of course, but are you still looking for that special person who will come along and transform you into your most perfect self? The one who will love you so much that you will be perfectly fulfilled and happy? Are you looking for the person who will adore you so completely that he or she will totally miss that mean streak you try to gloss over? One who won't notice when you're being arrogant or manipulative or selfish?

When taken to the extreme, the idea sounds rather silly. Deep inside, though, many of us dabble in this kind of fantasy life. Our culture tends to perpetuate the Cinderella myth that there exists one person who will complement us so perfectly that we will finally feel whole—in fact, we'll *be* whole. The problem with such a fantasy is that it raises our expectations to impossible standards, and that puts quite a strain on a dating or marriage relationship. It pushes God from the center of our lives and substitutes a fallible and mortal human being for an eternal and sovereign Savior.

Psalm 146 tells us that if our sense of personal worth depends on others, we will be continually disappointed. No one but God can save us from ourselves and our own weaknesses. Only God can truly make us complete or give us a sense of who we are, or give us a sense of purpose and calling.

Marriage is a gift from God, and a good marriage relationship can be fulfilling in many ways. But two people who rely on Jesus Christ as their Savior give each other the gift of a realistic, interdependent relationship—a relationship of mutual accountability and growth. They build a relationship in which their ultimate hope is not in each other, but in "the Maker of heaven and earth, the sea, and everything in them—the LORD, who remains faithful forever" (Psalm 146:6).

A Deeper Look
Psalm 33:18; John 14:1; 1 Timothy 5:5

Go to page 694 for your next devotional reading.

the LORD, who remains faithful
    forever.
⁷He upholds the cause of the
    oppressed
    and gives food to the hungry.
The LORD sets prisoners free,
⁸   the LORD gives sight to the blind,
    the LORD lifts up those who are bowed
      down,
    the LORD loves the righteous.
⁹The LORD watches over the alien
    and sustains the fatherless and the
      widow,
    but he frustrates the ways of the
      wicked.
¹⁰The LORD reigns forever,
    your God, O Zion, for all
      generations.

Praise the LORD.

Psalm 147

¹Praise the LORD.ᵃ

How good it is to sing praises to our
    God,
    how pleasant and fitting to praise
      him!

²The LORD builds up Jerusalem;
    he gathers the exiles of Israel.
³He heals the brokenhearted
    and binds up their wounds.
⁴He determines the number of the
      stars
    and calls them each by name.
⁵Great is our Lord and mighty in
      power;
    his understanding has no limit.
⁶The LORD sustains the humble
    but casts the wicked to the ground.

⁷Sing to the LORD with thanksgiving;
    make music to our God on the
      harp.
⁸He covers the sky with clouds;
    he supplies the earth with rain
    and makes grass grow on the hills.
⁹He provides food for the cattle
    and for the young ravens when
      they call.

¹⁰His pleasure is not in the strength of
      the horse,
    nor his delight in the legs of a
      man;
¹¹the LORD delights in those who fear
      him,
    who put their hope in his unfailing
      love.

¹²Extol the LORD, O Jerusalem;
    praise your God, O Zion,
¹³for he strengthens the bars of your
      gates
    and blesses your people within
      you.
¹⁴He grants peace to your borders
    and satisfies you with the finest of
      wheat.

¹⁵He sends his command to the earth;
    his word runs swiftly.
¹⁶He spreads the snow like wool
    and scatters the frost like ashes.
¹⁷He hurls down his hail like pebbles.
    Who can withstand his icy blast?
¹⁸He sends his word and melts them;
    he stirs up his breezes, and the
      waters flow.

¹⁹He has revealed his word to Jacob,
    his laws and decrees to Israel.
²⁰He has done this for no other nation;
    they do not know his laws.

Praise the LORD.

Psalm 148

¹Praise the LORD.ᵇ

Praise the LORD from the heavens,
    praise him in the heights above.
²Praise him, all his angels,
    praise him, all his heavenly hosts.
³Praise him, sun and moon,
    praise him, all you shining stars.
⁴Praise him, you highest heavens
    and you waters above the skies.
⁵Let them praise the name of the LORD,
    for he commanded and they were
      created.

ᵃ1 Hebrew *Hallelu Yah*; also in verse 20
ᵇ1 Hebrew *Hallelu Yah*; also in verse 14

POINT OF INTEREST

Psalm 147:10-11

We may be impressed by rippling muscles on a well-toned body, or dazzled by the newest gadgets and technology, or delighted by an unexpected windfall of wealth. But none of these things impresses God. God is delighted with people "who fear him, who put their hope in his unfailing love."

⁶He set them in place for ever and
  ever;
  he gave a decree that will never
  pass away.

⁷Praise the Lord from the earth,
  you great sea creatures and all
  ocean depths,
⁸lightning and hail, snow and clouds,
  stormy winds that do his bidding,
⁹you mountains and all hills,
  fruit trees and all cedars,
¹⁰wild animals and all cattle,
  small creatures and flying birds,
¹¹kings of the earth and all nations,
  you princes and all rulers on earth,
¹²young men and maidens,
  old men and children.

¹³Let them praise the name of the Lord,
  for his name alone is exalted;
  his splendor is above the earth and
  the heavens.
¹⁴He has raised up for his people a
  horn,ᵃ
  the praise of all his saints,
  of Israel, the people close to his
  heart.

  Praise the Lord.

Psalm 149

¹Praise the Lord.ᵇ

Sing to the Lord a new song,
  his praise in the assembly of the
  saints.
²Let Israel rejoice in their Maker;
  let the people of Zion be glad in
  their King.
³Let them praise his name with
  dancing
  and make music to him with
  tambourine and harp.
⁴For the Lord takes delight in his
  people;

he crowns the humble with
  salvation.
⁵Let the saints rejoice in this honor
  and sing for joy on their beds.

⁶May the praise of God be in their
  mouths
  and a double-edged sword in their
  hands,
⁷to inflict vengeance on the nations
  and punishment on the peoples,
⁸to bind their kings with fetters,
  their nobles with shackles of iron,
⁹to carry out the sentence written
  against them.
  This is the glory of all his saints.

  Praise the Lord.

Psalm 150

¹Praise the Lord.ᶜ

Praise God in his sanctuary;
  praise him in his mighty heavens.
²Praise him for his acts of power;
  praise him for his surpassing
  greatness.
³Praise him with the sounding of the
  trumpet,
  praise him with the harp and lyre,
⁴praise him with tambourine and
  dancing,
  praise him with the strings and
  flute,
⁵praise him with the clash of cymbals,
  praise him with resounding
  cymbals.

⁶Let everything that has breath praise
  the Lord.

  Praise the Lord.

ᵃ14 *Horn* here symbolizes strong one, that is, king.
ᵇ1 Hebrew *Hallelu Yah*; also in verse 9
ᶜ1 Hebrew *Hallelu Yah*; also in verse 6

Sometimes the deepest truths

are contained in simple sayings. The book of Proverbs

is like that—simple sentences, yet full of wisdom and

truth. Proverbs was written so that its readers might gain

wisdom for avoiding some of the most common pitfalls of

life. Do you need guidance in making decisions? Are you

trying to shape a balanced and fulfilling life? Would you

like to understand what it means to "fear the Lord"? Read-

ing Proverbs offers a wealth of practical advice on the art

of living—wisdom that works

and insights that won't

wear out.

PROVERBS

Prologue: Purpose and Theme

1 The proverbs of Solomon son of David,
king of Israel:

2for attaining wisdom and discipline;
   for understanding words of insight;
3for acquiring a disciplined and
      prudent life,
   doing what is right and just and
      fair;
4for giving prudence to the simple,
   knowledge and discretion to the
      young—
5let the wise listen and add to their
      learning,
   and let the discerning get
      guidance—

6for understanding proverbs and
      parables,
   the sayings and riddles of the wise.

7The fear of the LORD is the beginning
      of knowledge,
   but fools*a* despise wisdom and
      discipline.

Exhortations to Embrace Wisdom

Warning Against Enticement

8Listen, my son, to your father's
      instruction

---

*a*7 The Hebrew words rendered *fool* in Proverbs,
and often elsewhere in the Old Testament, denote
one who is morally deficient.

and do not forsake your mother's
teaching.
⁹They will be a garland to grace your
head
and a chain to adorn your neck.

¹⁰My son, if sinners entice you,
do not give in to them.
¹¹If they say, "Come along with us;
let's lie in wait for someone's
blood,
let's waylay some harmless soul;
¹²let's swallow them alive, like the
grave,ᵃ
and whole, like those who go
down to the pit;
¹³we will get all sorts of valuable things
and fill our houses with plunder;
¹⁴throw in your lot with us,
and we will share a common
purse"—
¹⁵my son, do not go along with them,
do not set foot on their paths;
¹⁶for their feet rush into sin,
they are swift to shed blood.
¹⁷How useless to spread a net
in full view of all the birds!
¹⁸These men lie in wait for their own
blood;
they waylay only themselves!
¹⁹Such is the end of all who go after
ill-gotten gain;
it takes away the lives of those
who get it.

Warning Against Rejecting Wisdom

²⁰Wisdom calls aloud in the street,
she raises her voice in the public
squares;
²¹at the head of the noisy streetsᵇ she
cries out,
in the gateways of the city she
makes her speech:

²²"How long will you simple onesᶜ
love your simple ways?
How long will mockers delight in
mockery
and fools hate knowledge?
²³If you had responded to my rebuke,
I would have poured out my heart
to you
and made my thoughts known to you.
²⁴But since you rejected me when I
called
and no one gave heed when I
stretched out my hand,
²⁵since you ignored all my advice
and would not accept my rebuke,

²⁶I in turn will laugh at your disaster;
I will mock when calamity
overtakes you—
²⁷when calamity overtakes you like a
storm,
when disaster sweeps over you like
a whirlwind,
when distress and trouble
overwhelm you.

²⁸"Then they will call to me but I will
not answer;
they will look for me but will not
find me.
²⁹Since they hated knowledge
and did not choose to fear the Lord,
³⁰since they would not accept my
advice
and spurned my rebuke,
³¹they will eat the fruit of their ways
and be filled with the fruit of their
schemes.
³²For the waywardness of the simple
will kill them,
and the complacency of fools will
destroy them;
³³but whoever listens to me will live in
safety
and be at ease, without fear of
harm."

Moral Benefits of Wisdom

2 My son, if you accept my words
and store up my commands within
you,
²turning your ear to wisdom
and applying your heart to
understanding,

ᵃ12 Hebrew *Sheol*   ᵇ21 Hebrew; Septuagint / *on
the tops of the walls*   ᶜ22 The Hebrew word
rendered *simple* in Proverbs generally denotes one
without moral direction and inclined to evil.

POINT OF INTEREST

Proverbs 1:7

What does "the fear of the
Lord" mean? It does *not*
mean that we live in dread
of an unpredictable and capri-
cious despot. "The fear of the Lord" *is* a
healthy respect and reverence for the holy
and powerful Creator of the universe.
Fearing God by honoring and obeying his
Word in everything will ensure that we
have nothing in this world to fear.

³and if you call out for insight
    and cry aloud for understanding,
⁴and if you look for it as for silver
    and search for it as for hidden
        treasure,
⁵then you will understand the fear of
        the LORD
    and find the knowledge of God.
⁶For the LORD gives wisdom,
    and from his mouth come
        knowledge and
        understanding.
⁷He holds victory in store for the
        upright,
    he is a shield to those whose walk
        is blameless,
⁸for he guards the course of the just
    and protects the way of his faithful
        ones.

⁹Then you will understand what is
        right and just
    and fair—every good path.
¹⁰For wisdom will enter your heart,
    and knowledge will be pleasant to
        your soul.
¹¹Discretion will protect you,
    and understanding will guard you.

¹²Wisdom will save you from the ways
        of wicked men,
    from men whose words are
        perverse,
¹³who leave the straight paths
    to walk in dark ways,
¹⁴who delight in doing wrong
    and rejoice in the perverseness of
        evil,
¹⁵whose paths are crooked
    and who are devious in their ways.

¹⁶It will save you also from the
        adulteress,
    from the wayward wife with her
        seductive words,
¹⁷who has left the partner of her youth
    and ignored the covenant she
        made before God.ᵃ
¹⁸For her house leads down to death
    and her paths to the spirits of the
        dead.
¹⁹None who go to her return
    or attain the paths of life.

²⁰Thus you will walk in the ways of
        good men
    and keep to the paths of the
        righteous.
²¹For the upright will live in the land,
    and the blameless will remain in it;

²²but the wicked will be cut off from
        the land,
    and the unfaithful will be torn
        from it.

Further Benefits of Wisdom

3 My son, do not forget my teaching,
    but keep my commands in your
        heart,
²for they will prolong your life many
        years
    and bring you prosperity.

³Let love and faithfulness never leave
        you;
    bind them around your neck,
    write them on the tablet of your
        heart.
⁴Then you will win favor and a good
        name
    in the sight of God and man.

⁵Trust in the LORD with all your heart
    and lean not on your own
        understanding;
⁶in all your ways acknowledge him,
    and he will make your paths
        straight.ᵇ

⁷Do not be wise in your own eyes;
    fear the LORD and shun evil.
⁸This will bring health to your body
    and nourishment to your bones.

⁹Honor the LORD with your wealth,
    with the firstfruits of all your
        crops;

ᵃ17 Or *covenant of her God*   ᵇ6 Or *will direct
your paths*

POINT OF INTEREST

Proverbs 3:5

The proverbs writer isn't telling you to ignore the common sense God has given you. God is concerned with where you put your final trust. Do you tend to rely on your best judgment, or do you, "by prayer and petition, with thanksgiving, present your requests to God" (Philippians 4:6)? God's power and wisdom is exceedingly trustworthy; rely on him to guide you in the decisions you make.

Read Proverbs 3:1–35
Key Verses Proverbs 3:9–10

Giving Back to God

When the first settlers stepped out onto the North American conti-
nent, they found riches beyond their wildest dreams. Tall stands of
timber, mountains full of minerals, rivers flowing with clean, fresh
water and soil so rich it has grown food for millions of people for
almost four hundred years. All of it was a gift from God. Each time
we go through the dining hall line or shop at the corner store or
pick up a paycheck, God is still giving to us out of his immense treasure.

God entrusts part of his great wealth to each of us. He wants us
to manage his resources responsibly but never to forget who owns
them (see Matthew 25:14–30). Out of all he has given us, he asks
us to give some of it back to him and to his kingdom—and to give
it enthusiastically! Some believers have the gift of giving (see
Romans 12:6–8). They seem to give naturally, and with surprising
generosity. Those who give and give and give some more find that
giving is *not* a burden or a frustrating duty but a source of great
joy!

Digging Into the Word
1. In the Old Testament, believers were instructed to give specific
   amounts to God. But in the New Testament we are free to determine the amount we give. What do you learn about giving in the
   following passages? — *2 Corinthians 8:1 – 15; 2 Corinthians 9:6 –15*
2. What do the following passages teach you about the object of
   your giving?—*Galatians 6:6; James 2:15–16; 1 John 3:16–18*

Action Challenge
Sometimes giving is really tough, especially when we have more
outgo than income. However, it is an important way to express that
we know that all we have comes from God. Challenge yourself to do
two things in the coming month. First, evaluate your attitude
toward giving. Pray for it to be joyous and generous. Second, challenge yourself to increase your giving, whether monetarily or in service to others, as a sign of your growing faith.

One Step Deeper
Proverbs 21:26; 1 Corinthians 16:2

Go to page 699 for your next devotional reading.

¹⁰then your barns will be filled to
overflowing,
and your vats will brim over with
new wine.

¹¹My son, do not despise the LORD's
discipline
and do not resent his rebuke,
¹²because the LORD disciplines those he
loves,
as a father*a* the son he delights
in.

¹³Blessed is the man who finds
wisdom,
the man who gains understanding,
¹⁴for she is more profitable than silver
and yields better returns than gold.
¹⁵She is more precious than rubies;
nothing you desire can compare
with her.
¹⁶Long life is in her right hand;
in her left hand are riches and
honor.
¹⁷Her ways are pleasant ways,
and all her paths are peace.
¹⁸She is a tree of life to those who
embrace her;
those who lay hold of her will be
blessed.

¹⁹By wisdom the LORD laid the earth's
foundations,
by understanding he set the
heavens in place;
²⁰by his knowledge the deeps were
divided,
and the clouds let drop the dew.

²¹My son, preserve sound judgment
and discernment,
do not let them out of your sight;
²²they will be life for you,
an ornament to grace your neck.
²³Then you will go on your way in
safety,
and your foot will not stumble;
²⁴when you lie down, you will not be
afraid;
when you lie down, your sleep will
be sweet.
²⁵Have no fear of sudden disaster
or of the ruin that overtakes the
wicked,
²⁶for the LORD will be your confidence
and will keep your foot from being
snared.

²⁷Do not withhold good from those
who deserve it,
when it is in your power to act.

²⁸Do not say to your neighbor,
"Come back later; I'll give it
tomorrow"—
when you now have it with you.
²⁹Do not plot harm against your
neighbor,
who lives trustfully near you.
³⁰Do not accuse a man for no reason—
when he has done you no harm.
³¹Do not envy a violent man
or choose any of his ways,
³²for the LORD detests a perverse man
but takes the upright into his
confidence.

³³The LORD's curse is on the house of
the wicked,
but he blesses the home of the
righteous.
³⁴He mocks proud mockers
but gives grace to the humble.
³⁵The wise inherit honor,
but fools he holds up to shame.

Wisdom Is Supreme

4 Listen, my sons, to a father's
instruction;
pay attention and gain
understanding.
²I give you sound learning,
so do not forsake my teaching.
³When I was a boy in my father's
house,
still tender, and an only child of
my mother,
⁴he taught me and said,
"Lay hold of my words with all
your heart;
keep my commands and you will
live.
⁵Get wisdom, get understanding;
do not forget my words or swerve
from them.
⁶Do not forsake wisdom, and she will
protect you;
love her, and she will watch over
you.
⁷Wisdom is supreme; therefore get
wisdom.
Though it cost all you have,*b* get
understanding.
⁸Esteem her, and she will exalt you;
embrace her, and she will honor
you.
⁹She will set a garland of grace on
your head

a 12 Hebrew; Septuagint / *and he punishes*
b 7 Or *Whatever else you get*

and present you with a crown of
     splendor."

¹⁰Listen, my son, accept what I say,
     and the years of your life will be
          many.
¹¹I guide you in the way of wisdom
     and lead you along straight paths.
¹²When you walk, your steps will not
          be hampered;
     when you run, you will not
          stumble.
¹³Hold on to instruction, do not let it
          go;
     guard it well, for it is your life.
¹⁴Do not set foot on the path of the
          wicked
     or walk in the way of evil men.
¹⁵Avoid it, do not travel on it;
     turn from it and go on your way.
¹⁶For they cannot sleep till they do evil;
     they are robbed of slumber till they
          make someone fall.
¹⁷They eat the bread of wickedness
     and drink the wine of violence.

¹⁸The path of the righteous is like the
          first gleam of dawn,
     shining ever brighter till the full
          light of day.
¹⁹But the way of the wicked is like
          deep darkness;
     they do not know what makes
          them stumble.

²⁰My son, pay attention to what I say;
     listen closely to my words.
²¹Do not let them out of your sight,
     keep them within your heart;
²²for they are life to those who find
          them
     and health to a man's whole body.
²³Above all else, guard your heart,
     for it is the wellspring of life.
²⁴Put away perversity from your
          mouth;
     keep corrupt talk far from your
          lips.
²⁵Let your eyes look straight ahead,
     fix your gaze directly before you.
²⁶Make level*ᵃ* paths for your feet
     and take only ways that are firm.
²⁷Do not swerve to the right or the left;
     keep your foot from evil.

Warning Against Adultery

5 My son, pay attention to my wisdom,
     listen well to my words of insight,
²that you may maintain discretion

and your lips may preserve
     knowledge.
³For the lips of an adulteress drip
          honey,
     and her speech is smoother than
          oil;
⁴but in the end she is bitter as gall,
     sharp as a double-edged sword.
⁵Her feet go down to death;
     her steps lead straight to the
          grave.*ᵇ*
⁶She gives no thought to the way of
          life;
     her paths are crooked, but she
          knows it not.

⁷Now then, my sons, listen to me;
     do not turn aside from what I say.
⁸Keep to a path far from her,
     do not go near the door of her
          house,
⁹lest you give your best strength to
          others
     and your years to one who is
          cruel,
¹⁰lest strangers feast on your wealth
     and your toil enrich another man's
          house.
¹¹At the end of your life you will groan,
     when your flesh and body are
          spent.
¹²You will say, "How I hated
          discipline!
     How my heart spurned correction!
¹³I would not obey my teachers
     or listen to my instructors.
¹⁴I have come to the brink of utter ruin
     in the midst of the whole
          assembly."

¹⁵Drink water from your own cistern,
     running water from your own well.
¹⁶Should your springs overflow in the
          streets,

ᵃ26 Or *Consider the*   *ᵇ5* Hebrew *Sheol*

POINT OF INTEREST   Proverbs 5:3–5

**Things aren't always what
they seem, and you can't
always trust everything you
hear. Deceptive speech can be
quite believable and attractive. Sin can
also sound like a good idea at the time—
but, oh, the consequences!**

your streams of water in the public
squares?
¹⁷Let them be yours alone,
never to be shared with strangers.
¹⁸May your fountain be blessed,
and may you rejoice in the wife of
your youth.
¹⁹A loving doe, a graceful deer—
may her breasts satisfy you always,
may you ever be captivated by her
love.
²⁰Why be captivated, my son, by an
adulteress?
Why embrace the bosom of
another man's wife?
²¹For a man's ways are in full view of
the LORD,
and he examines all his paths.
²²The evil deeds of a wicked man
ensnare him;
the cords of his sin hold him fast.
²³He will die for lack of discipline,
led astray by his own great folly.

Warnings Against Folly

6 My son, if you have put up security
for your neighbor,
if you have struck hands in pledge
for another,
²if you have been trapped by what
you said,
ensnared by the words of your
mouth,
³then do this, my son, to free yourself,
since you have fallen into your
neighbor's hands:
Go and humble yourself;
press your plea with your
neighbor!
⁴Allow no sleep to your eyes,
no slumber to your eyelids.
⁵Free yourself, like a gazelle from the
hand of the hunter,
like a bird from the snare of the
fowler.

⁶Go to the ant, you sluggard;
consider its ways and be wise!
⁷It has no commander,
no overseer or ruler,
⁸yet it stores its provisions in summer
and gathers its food at harvest.
⁹How long will you lie there, you
sluggard?
When will you get up from your
sleep?
¹⁰A little sleep, a little slumber,

a little folding of the hands to
rest—
¹¹and poverty will come on you like a
bandit
and scarcity like an armed man.ᵃ

¹²A scoundrel and villain,
who goes about with a corrupt
mouth,
13 who winks with his eye,
signals with his feet
and motions with his fingers,
14 who plots evil with deceit in his
heart—
he always stirs up dissension.
¹⁵Therefore disaster will overtake him
in an instant;
he will suddenly be destroyed—
without remedy.

¹⁶There are six things the LORD hates,
seven that are detestable to him:
17 haughty eyes,
a lying tongue,
hands that shed innocent blood,
18 a heart that devises wicked
schemes,
feet that are quick to rush into
evil,
19 a false witness who pours out
lies
and a man who stirs up
dissension among brothers.

Warning Against Adultery

²⁰My son, keep your father's
commands
and do not forsake your mother's
teaching.
²¹Bind them upon your heart forever;
fasten them around your neck.
²²When you walk, they will guide you;
when you sleep, they will watch
over you;
when you awake, they will speak
to you.
²³For these commands are a lamp,
this teaching is a light,
and the corrections of discipline
are the way to life,
²⁴keeping you from the immoral
woman,
from the smooth tongue of the
wayward wife.
²⁵Do not lust in your heart after her
beauty
or let her captivate you with her
eyes,

ᵃ11 Or *like a vagrant / and scarcity like a beggar*

26for the prostitute reduces you to a
 loaf of bread,
  and the adulteress preys upon your
   very life.
27Can a man scoop fire into his lap
  without his clothes being burned?
28Can a man walk on hot coals
  without his feet being scorched?
29So is he who sleeps with another
   man's wife;
  no one who touches her will go
   unpunished.

30Men do not despise a thief if he steals
  to satisfy his hunger when he is
   starving.
31Yet if he is caught, he must pay
   sevenfold,
  though it costs him all the wealth
   of his house.
32But a man who commits adultery
   lacks judgment;
  whoever does so destroys himself.
33Blows and disgrace are his lot,
  and his shame will never be wiped
   away;
34for jealousy arouses a husband's fury,
  and he will show no mercy when
   he takes revenge.
35He will not accept any compensation;
  he will refuse the bribe, however
   great it is.

Warning Against the Adulteress

7 My son, keep my words
  and store up my commands within
   you.
2Keep my commands and you will
   live;
  guard my teachings as the apple of
   your eye.
3Bind them on your fingers;
  write them on the tablet of your
   heart.
4Say to wisdom, "You are my sister,"
  and call understanding your
   kinsman;
5they will keep you from the
   adulteress,
  from the wayward wife with her
   seductive words.

6At the window of my house
  I looked out through the lattice.
7I saw among the simple,
  I noticed among the young men,
  a youth who lacked judgment.
8He was going down the street near
   her corner,

walking along in the direction of
  her house
9at twilight, as the day was fading,
  as the dark of night set in.

10Then out came a woman to meet
  him,
  dressed like a prostitute and with
   crafty intent.
11(She is loud and defiant,
  her feet never stay at home;
12now in the street, now in the squares,
  at every corner she lurks.)
13She took hold of him and kissed him
  and with a brazen face she said:

14"I have fellowship offerings[a] at
   home;
  today I fulfilled my vows.
15So I came out to meet you;
  I looked for you and have found
   you!
16I have covered my bed
  with colored linens from Egypt.
17I have perfumed my bed
  with myrrh, aloes and cinnamon.
18Come, let's drink deep of love till
   morning;
  let's enjoy ourselves with love!
19My husband is not at home;
  he has gone on a long journey.
20He took his purse filled with money
  and will not be home till full
   moon."

21With persuasive words she led him
   astray;
  she seduced him with her smooth
   talk.
22All at once he followed her
  like an ox going to the slaughter,
  like a deer[b] stepping into a noose[c]
23 till an arrow pierces his liver,
  like a bird darting into a snare,
   little knowing it will cost him his
    life.

24Now then, my sons, listen to me;
  pay attention to what I say.
25Do not let your heart turn to her
   ways
  or stray into her paths.
26Many are the victims she has brought
   down;
  her slain are a mighty throng.
27Her house is a highway to the
   grave,[d]

a14 Traditionally *peace offerings*   b22 Syriac
(see also Septuagint); Hebrew *fool*
c22 The meaning of the Hebrew for this line is
uncertain.   d27 Hebrew *Sheol*

leading down to the chambers of
death.

Wisdom's Call

8 Does not wisdom call out?
Does not understanding raise her
voice?
²On the heights along the way,
where the paths meet, she takes
her stand;
³beside the gates leading into the city,
at the entrances, she cries aloud:
⁴"To you, O men, I call out;
I raise my voice to all mankind.
⁵You who are simple, gain prudence;
you who are foolish, gain
understanding.
⁶Listen, for I have worthy things to
say;
I open my lips to speak what is
right.

⁷My mouth speaks what is true,
for my lips detest wickedness.
⁸All the words of my mouth are
just;
none of them is crooked or
perverse.
⁹To the discerning all of them are
right;
they are faultless to those who
have knowledge.
¹⁰Choose my instruction instead of
silver,
knowledge rather than choice
gold,
¹¹for wisdom is more precious than
rubies,
and nothing you desire can
compare with her.

¹²"I, wisdom, dwell together with
prudence;

MONDAY

Read Proverbs 7:1–27
Key Verses Proverbs 7:8–9,22

Fatal Attraction – Jay Getz

A friend of mine once told me that before he became a Christian he
was so promiscuous that when he looked at any woman, he would
undress her in his mind within seconds. He wasn't proud of it. He
was explaining that although God had healed him from his sin, he
still had emotional and mental scars from it.

In seeking help and forgiveness, my friend acted more responsibly than the young man in Proverbs 7. This guy chose a sexual liai-
son over purity, and in doing so chose death over life. Proverbs 7:22
pictures the young man as "an ox going to the slaughter." He certainly didn't set out to tighten a noose around his own neck; he
probably just believed one too many lies about so-called "sexual
freedom" and stepped into the trap.

The young man in this proverb chose to be in the wrong place,
"walking along in the direction of her house," at the wrong time,
when "the dark of night set in" (Proverbs 7:8–9). He said "yes" to
sexual immorality because his previous decisions made it easy for
him. He had started down the path to sin long before he ever saw or
heard the adulterous woman.

Sexual immorality can leave physical, emotional and spiritual
scars. While God's grace can heal those scars, disobeying his directives can still cost in terms of physical and emotional health. It can
cost in terms of relationships and opportunity. This passage shows
that it cost at least one young man his life.

A Deeper Look
2 Corinthians 7:1; 1 Thessalonians 4:3–8

Go to page 701 for your next devotional reading.

I possess knowledge and
    discretion.
¹³To fear the LORD is to hate evil;
    I hate pride and arrogance,
    evil behavior and perverse speech.
¹⁴Counsel and sound judgment are
    mine;
    I have understanding and power.
¹⁵By me kings reign
    and rulers make laws that are just;
¹⁶by me princes govern,
    and all nobles who rule on earth.ᵃ
¹⁷I love those who love me,
    and those who seek me find me.
¹⁸With me are riches and honor,
    enduring wealth and prosperity.
¹⁹My fruit is better than fine gold;
    what I yield surpasses choice
    silver.
²⁰I walk in the way of righteousness,
    along the paths of justice,
²¹bestowing wealth on those who love
    me
    and making their treasuries full.

²²"The LORD brought me forth as the
    first of his works,ᵇ,ᶜ
    before his deeds of old;
²³I was appointedᵈ from eternity,
    from the beginning, before the
    world began.
²⁴When there were no oceans, I was
    given birth,
    when there were no springs
    abounding with water;
²⁵before the mountains were settled in
    place,
    before the hills, I was given birth,
²⁶before he made the earth or its fields
    or any of the dust of the world.
²⁷I was there when he set the heavens
    in place,
    when he marked out the horizon
    on the face of the deep,
²⁸when he established the clouds above
    and fixed securely the fountains of
    the deep,
²⁹when he gave the sea its boundary
    so the waters would not overstep
    his command,
    and when he marked out the
    foundations of the earth.
³⁰   Then I was the craftsman at his
    side.
    I was filled with delight day after
    day,
    rejoicing always in his presence,
³¹rejoicing in his whole world
    and delighting in mankind.

³²"Now then, my sons, listen to me;
    blessed are those who keep my
    ways.
³³Listen to my instruction and be wise;
    do not ignore it.
³⁴Blessed is the man who listens to me,
    watching daily at my doors,
    waiting at my doorway.
³⁵For whoever finds me finds life
    and receives favor from the LORD.
³⁶But whoever fails to find me harms
    himself;
    all who hate me love death."

Invitations of Wisdom and of Folly

9 Wisdom has built her house;
    she has hewn out its seven pillars.
²She has prepared her meat and mixed
    her wine;
    she has also set her table.
³She has sent out her maids, and she
    calls
    from the highest point of the city.
⁴"Let all who are simple come in
    here!"
    she says to those who lack
    judgment.
⁵"Come, eat my food
    and drink the wine I have mixed.
⁶Leave your simple ways and you will
    live;
    walk in the way of understanding.

⁷"Whoever corrects a mocker invites
    insult;
    whoever rebukes a wicked man
    incurs abuse.
⁸Do not rebuke a mocker or he will
    hate you;
    rebuke a wise man and he will
    love you.
⁹Instruct a wise man and he will be
    wiser still;
    teach a righteous man and he will
    add to his learning.

¹⁰"The fear of the LORD is the beginning
    of wisdom,
    and knowledge of the Holy One is
    understanding.
¹¹For through me your days will be
    many,
    and years will be added to your
    life.

ᵃ16 Many Hebrew manuscripts and Septuagint;
most Hebrew manuscripts *and nobles—all righteous
rulers*   ᵇ22 Or *way;* or *dominion*   ᶜ22 Or *The
LORD possessed me at the beginning of his work;* or
*The LORD brought me forth at the beginning of his
work*   ᵈ23 Or *fashioned*

¹²If you are wise, your wisdom will
    reward you;
  if you are a mocker, you alone will
    suffer."

¹³The woman Folly is loud;
  she is undisciplined and without
    knowledge.
¹⁴She sits at the door of her house,
  on a seat at the highest point of
    the city,
¹⁵calling out to those who pass by,
  who go straight on their way.
¹⁶"Let all who are simple come in
    here!"
  she says to those who lack
    judgment.
¹⁷"Stolen water is sweet;
  food eaten in secret is delicious!"
¹⁸But little do they know that the dead
  are there,

that her guests are in the depths of
    the grave.ᵃ

Proverbs of Solomon

10 The proverbs of Solomon:

A wise son brings joy to his father,
  but a foolish son grief to his
    mother.

²Ill-gotten treasures are of no value,
  but righteousness delivers from
    death.

³The LORD does not let the righteous go
    hungry
  but he thwarts the craving of the
    wicked.

ᵃ18 Hebrew *Sheol*

TUESDAY

Read *Proverbs 8:1–36*
Key Verses *Proverbs 8:32–36*

Wisdom's Source — Greg Bryan

Imagine yourself in this telephone conversation from campus to home: "Hi Dad. Fine, fine. I'm doing great in all my classes except one—I'm failing my computer class. I just can't seem to learn this stuff. No, I don't need a tutor. I should be able to pick this up myself. My buddy Bill across the hall is pretty good with computers; maybe I should . . . Yeah, you're right, Dad, I should go talk with him, but . . ."

Suppose your buddy Bill was actually a young Bill Gates, the founder of Microsoft Corporation. You knew him, he was friendly toward you, he always kept his door open, and he was always there to talk when you walked by. But despite his accessibility, you never asked him to help you with your computer homework. Wouldn't you be foolish for not asking him?

Yet we often do much the same with God! We don't go ask him, or go and consult with him, even though he is the Creator of this universe and knows everything about it. He can help us with any situation in life, and he's instantly accessible.

A friend of mine once said, "Before you seek the faces of people, seek the face of God." That's good advice. We usually forget to ask God for help simply because we're not in the habit of communicating with him every day. If we can just get used to seeking him all the time, we will begin to integrate his wisdom and his perspectives into our everyday lives. He's the expert—the source of all wisdom!

A Deeper Look
Isaiah 33:6; Romans 11:33; Colossians 2:3

Go to page 702 for your next devotional reading.

⁴Lazy hands make a man poor,
   but diligent hands bring wealth.

⁵He who gathers crops in summer is a
      wise son,
   but he who sleeps during harvest
      is a disgraceful son.

⁶Blessings crown the head of the
      righteous,
   but violence overwhelms the
      mouth of the wicked. *a*

⁷The memory of the righteous will be
      a blessing,
   but the name of the wicked will
      rot.

⁸The wise in heart accept commands,
   but a chattering fool comes to ruin.

⁹The man of integrity walks securely,
   but he who takes crooked paths
      will be found out.

¹⁰He who winks maliciously causes
      grief,
   and a chattering fool comes to
      ruin.

¹¹The mouth of the righteous is a
      fountain of life,
   but violence overwhelms the
      mouth of the wicked.

*a6 Or but the mouth of the wicked conceals violence;
also in verse 11*

WEDNESDAY

Read *Proverbs 10:1–32*
Key Verses *Proverbs 10:4–5*

Destination: Diligence – Darren Lindblom

During the last semester of my senior year, I had a certain form that
I needed to fill out and take to the business office before I would be
allowed to graduate. I picked up the form two months before graduation, but it took me one month and twenty-nine days to turn it in.
Was it important to me? Yes! Did I want to graduate? Absolutely!
Was I being diligent? No! At the time I probably developed a few
good reasons for not turning in the form before the final hour, but in
my heart I know it was because I was lazy. I procrastinated and
almost "slept during the harvest" (see Proverbs 10:5). I came close
to not graduating.

Many students struggle with laziness, as I did. Yet I have never
met a student who said his or her life's goal was to be poor, nor
have I ever met a student who wanted to be seen as disgraceful.
God's Word gives us a sentence that should become the slogan for
all students who make it their goal to succeed: "Lazy hands make a
man poor, but diligent hands bring wealth" (Proverbs 10:4).

Diligence is a habit that can—and should—be cultivated. God
can use a diligent person more readily than someone who never
seems to "get around to it." When we begin by being faithful in little things, such as turning in a paper on time, we will then learn to
be faithful in more important matters (see Luke 16:10).

Is God speaking to you about being diligent in a particular matter? Do you have important projects that you have started but that
remain unfinished? Is there a friend you need to talk to about salvation in Jesus Christ? Don't delay—start today. Work hard at bringing in the harvest, no matter what crop you've planted.

A Deeper Look
Proverbs 6:6–11; Romans 12:11; Hebrews 6:10–12

Go to page 707 for your next devotional reading.

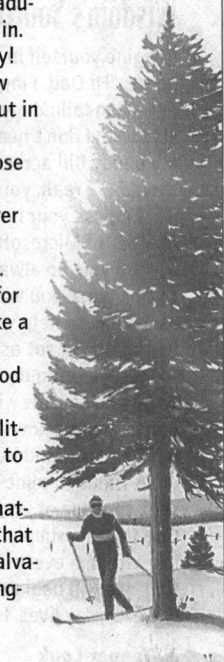

12Hatred stirs up dissension,
  but love covers over all wrongs.

13Wisdom is found on the lips of the
    discerning,
  but a rod is for the back of him
    who lacks judgment.

14Wise men store up knowledge,
  but the mouth of a fool invites
    ruin.

15The wealth of the rich is their
    fortified city,
  but poverty is the ruin of the poor.

16The wages of the righteous bring
    them life,
  but the income of the wicked
    brings them punishment.

17He who heeds discipline shows the
    way to life,
  but whoever ignores correction
    leads others astray.

18He who conceals his hatred has lying
    lips,
  and whoever spreads slander is a
    fool.

19When words are many, sin is not
    absent,
  but he who holds his tongue is
    wise.

20The tongue of the righteous is choice
    silver,
  but the heart of the wicked is of
    little value.

21The lips of the righteous nourish
    many,
  but fools die for lack of judgment.

22The blessing of the LORD brings
    wealth,
  and he adds no trouble to it.

23A fool finds pleasure in evil conduct,
  but a man of understanding
    delights in wisdom.

24What the wicked dreads will overtake
    him;
  what the righteous desire will be
    granted.

25When the storm has swept by, the
    wicked are gone,
  but the righteous stand firm
    forever.

26As vinegar to the teeth and smoke to
    the eyes,

so is a sluggard to those who send
    him.

27The fear of the LORD adds length to
    life,
  but the years of the wicked are cut
    short.

28The prospect of the righteous is joy,
  but the hopes of the wicked come
    to nothing.

29The way of the LORD is a refuge for
    the righteous,
  but it is the ruin of those who do
    evil.

30The righteous will never be uprooted,
  but the wicked will not remain in
    the land.

31The mouth of the righteous brings
    forth wisdom,
  but a perverse tongue will be cut
    out.

32The lips of the righteous know what
    is fitting,
  but the mouth of the wicked only
    what is perverse.

11 The LORD abhors dishonest scales,
  but accurate weights are his
    delight.

2When pride comes, then comes
    disgrace,
  but with humility comes wisdom.

3The integrity of the upright guides
    them,
  but the unfaithful are destroyed by
    their duplicity.

4Wealth is worthless in the day of
    wrath,
  but righteousness delivers from
    death.

5The righteousness of the blameless
    makes a straight way for
    them,
  but the wicked are brought down
    by their own wickedness.

6The righteousness of the upright
    delivers them,
  but the unfaithful are trapped by
    evil desires.

7When a wicked man dies, his hope
    perishes;
  all he expected from his power
    comes to nothing.

⁸The righteous man is rescued from
     trouble,
   and it comes on the wicked
     instead.

⁹With his mouth the godless destroys
     his neighbor,
   but through knowledge the
     righteous escape.

¹⁰When the righteous prosper, the city
     rejoices;
   when the wicked perish, there are
     shouts of joy.

¹¹Through the blessing of the upright a
     city is exalted,
   but by the mouth of the wicked it
     is destroyed.

¹²A man who lacks judgment derides
     his neighbor,
   but a man of understanding holds
     his tongue.

¹³A gossip betrays a confidence,
   but a trustworthy man keeps a
     secret.

¹⁴For lack of guidance a nation falls,
   but many advisers make victory
     sure.

¹⁵He who puts up security for another
     will surely suffer,
   but whoever refuses to strike
     hands in pledge is safe.

¹⁶A kindhearted woman gains respect,
   but ruthless men gain only wealth.

¹⁷A kind man benefits himself,
   but a cruel man brings trouble on
     himself.

¹⁸The wicked man earns deceptive
     wages,
   but he who sows righteousness
     reaps a sure reward.

¹⁹The truly righteous man attains life,
   but he who pursues evil goes to
     his death.

²⁰The LORD detests men of perverse
     heart
   but he delights in those whose
     ways are blameless.

²¹Be sure of this: The wicked will not
     go unpunished,
   but those who are righteous will go
     free.

²²Like a gold ring in a pig's snout

is a beautiful woman who shows
   no discretion.

²³The desire of the righteous ends only
     in good,
   but the hope of the wicked only in
     wrath.

²⁴One man gives freely, yet gains even
     more;
   another withholds unduly, but
     comes to poverty.

²⁵A generous man will prosper;
   he who refreshes others will
     himself be refreshed.

²⁶People curse the man who hoards
     grain,
   but blessing crowns him who is
     willing to sell.

²⁷He who seeks good finds goodwill,
   but evil comes to him who
     searches for it.

²⁸Whoever trusts in his riches will fall,
   but the righteous will thrive like a
     green leaf.

²⁹He who brings trouble on his family
     will inherit only wind,
   and the fool will be servant to the
     wise.

³⁰The fruit of the righteous is a tree of
     life,
   and he who wins souls is wise.

³¹If the righteous receive their due on
     earth,
   how much more the ungodly and
     the sinner!

12 Whoever loves discipline loves
     knowledge,
   but he who hates correction is
     stupid.

²A good man obtains favor from the
     LORD,
   but the LORD condemns a crafty
     man.

³A man cannot be established through
     wickedness,
   but the righteous cannot be
     uprooted.

⁴A wife of noble character is her
     husband's crown,
   but a disgraceful wife is like decay
     in his bones.

⁵The plans of the righteous are just,

but the advice of the wicked is deceitful.

⁶The words of the wicked lie in wait for blood,
but the speech of the upright rescues them.

⁷Wicked men are overthrown and are no more,
but the house of the righteous stands firm.

⁸A man is praised according to his wisdom,
but men with warped minds are despised.

⁹Better to be a nobody and yet have a servant
than pretend to be somebody and have no food.

¹⁰A righteous man cares for the needs of his animal,
but the kindest acts of the wicked are cruel.

¹¹He who works his land will have abundant food,
but he who chases fantasies lacks judgment.

¹²The wicked desire the plunder of evil men,
but the root of the righteous flourishes.

¹³An evil man is trapped by his sinful talk,
but a righteous man escapes trouble.

¹⁴From the fruit of his lips a man is filled with good things
as surely as the work of his hands rewards him.

¹⁵The way of a fool seems right to him,
but a wise man listens to advice.

¹⁶A fool shows his annoyance at once,
but a prudent man overlooks an insult.

¹⁷A truthful witness gives honest testimony,
but a false witness tells lies.

¹⁸Reckless words pierce like a sword,
but the tongue of the wise brings healing.

¹⁹Truthful lips endure forever,
but a lying tongue lasts only a moment.

²⁰There is deceit in the hearts of those who plot evil,
but joy for those who promote peace.

²¹No harm befalls the righteous,
but the wicked have their fill of trouble.

²²The LORD detests lying lips,
but he delights in men who are truthful.

²³A prudent man keeps his knowledge to himself,
but the heart of fools blurts out folly.

²⁴Diligent hands will rule,
but laziness ends in slave labor.

²⁵An anxious heart weighs a man down,
but a kind word cheers him up.

²⁶A righteous man is cautious in friendship,ᵃ
but the way of the wicked leads them astray.

²⁷The lazy man does not roastᵇ his game,
but the diligent man prizes his possessions.

²⁸In the way of righteousness there is life;
along that path is immortality.

13 A wise son heeds his father's instruction,
but a mocker does not listen to rebuke.

ᵃ26 Or *man is a guide to his neighbor*
ᵇ27 The meaning of the Hebrew for this word is uncertain.

POINT OF INTEREST

Proverbs 12:13–23

The book of Proverbs makes many references to the quality and quantity of our words. Words can cut like a knife, but they can also heal. Words can start a fight, but they can also cool a temper (see Proverbs 15:1). Make no mistake about it: What we say *does* matter (see James 3:9–10).

²From the fruit of his lips a man
    enjoys good things,
  but the unfaithful have a craving
    for violence.

³He who guards his lips guards his
    life,
  but he who speaks rashly will
    come to ruin.

⁴The sluggard craves and gets nothing,
  but the desires of the diligent are
    fully satisfied.

⁵The righteous hate what is false,
  but the wicked bring shame and
    disgrace.

⁶Righteousness guards the man of
    integrity,
  but wickedness overthrows the
    sinner.

⁷One man pretends to be rich, yet has
    nothing;
  another pretends to be poor, yet
    has great wealth.

⁸A man's riches may ransom his life,
  but a poor man hears no threat.

⁹The light of the righteous shines
    brightly,
  but the lamp of the wicked is
    snuffed out.

¹⁰Pride only breeds quarrels,
  but wisdom is found in those who
    take advice.

¹¹Dishonest money dwindles away,
  but he who gathers money little by
    little makes it grow.

¹²Hope deferred makes the heart sick,
  but a longing fulfilled is a tree of
    life.

¹³He who scorns instruction will pay
    for it,
  but he who respects a command is
    rewarded.

¹⁴The teaching of the wise is a fountain
    of life,
  turning a man from the snares of
    death.

¹⁵Good understanding wins favor,
  but the way of the unfaithful is
    hard.ᵃ

¹⁶Every prudent man acts out of
    knowledge,
  but a fool exposes his folly.

¹⁷A wicked messenger falls into
    trouble,
  but a trustworthy envoy brings
    healing.

¹⁸He who ignores discipline comes to
    poverty and shame,
  but whoever heeds correction is
    honored.

¹⁹A longing fulfilled is sweet to the
    soul,
  but fools detest turning from evil.

²⁰He who walks with the wise grows
    wise,
  but a companion of fools suffers
    harm.

²¹Misfortune pursues the sinner,
  but prosperity is the reward of the
    righteous.

²²A good man leaves an inheritance for
    his children's children,
  but a sinner's wealth is stored up
    for the righteous.

²³A poor man's field may produce
    abundant food,
  but injustice sweeps it away.

²⁴He who spares the rod hates his son,
  but he who loves him is careful to
    discipline him.

²⁵The righteous eat to their hearts'
    content,
  but the stomach of the wicked goes
    hungry.

14 The wise woman builds her house,
  but with her own hands the foolish
    one tears hers down.

²He whose walk is upright fears the
    LORD,
  but he whose ways are devious
    despises him.

³A fool's talk brings a rod to his back,
  but the lips of the wise protect
    them.

⁴Where there are no oxen, the manger
    is empty,
  but from the strength of an ox
    comes an abundant harvest.

⁵A truthful witness does not deceive,
  but a false witness pours out lies.

⁶The mocker seeks wisdom and finds
    none,

ᵃ15 Or unfaithful does not endure

but knowledge comes easily to the
discerning.

⁷Stay away from a foolish man,
for you will not find knowledge on
his lips.

⁸The wisdom of the prudent is to give
thought to their ways,
but the folly of fools is deception.

⁹Fools mock at making amends for
sin,
but goodwill is found among the
upright.

¹⁰Each heart knows its own bitterness,
and no one else can share its joy.

¹¹The house of the wicked will be
destroyed,
but the tent of the upright will
flourish.

¹²There is a way that seems right to a
man,
but in the end it leads to death.

¹³Even in laughter the heart may ache,
and joy may end in grief.

¹⁴The faithless will be fully repaid for
their ways,
and the good man rewarded for
his.

¹⁵A simple man believes anything,

THURSDAY

Read Proverbs 13:1–25
Key Verse Proverbs 13:20

Walking with the Wise – Carol Rugg

During the course of a conversation with my friend Jennifer, she picked up on one of my feelings. She said to me, "You're mad at Andy."

"No, I'm not," I replied. Our conversation changed for a moment but seemed to find its way back to Andy again. Jennifer once again mentioned, "You're angry with Andy." Irritated, I retorted, "I am not!"

I changed the subject a second time, but within minutes we had circled back around to this same topic. This time my response was somewhat different. "I don't think I'm angry, but I can tell I'm being defensive. So, maybe you're right. Perhaps I am mad at Andy." Jennifer then encouraged me to be honest about my anger and helped me work on my relationship with Andy. Because I walked alongside a wise woman that day, God began to work deep within me. When he changed my attitude about Andy, he also began to change my attitudes toward men in general.

Who are the wise people in your life? If wise friends show you your blind spots or point out issues you need to deal with, do you bristle and become defensive, or do you think about their words carefully? Do you ever wonder whether God might be speaking through them?

Don't be surprised when others see the imperfections in your life, and don't waste energy being defensive and trying to justify yourself. If you trust your friends and value their honest opinions, simply ask them for examples and helpful hints on how to become more Christlike. You'll be surprised at how it will change your relationships . . . and you!

A Deeper Look
Proverbs 8:11; 9:8–9; Ephesians 5:15–16

Go to page 709 for your next devotional reading.

but a prudent man gives thought to
　　his steps.

16A wise man fears the LORD and shuns
　　evil,
　　but a fool is hotheaded and
　　　reckless.

17A quick-tempered man does foolish
　　things,
　　and a crafty man is hated.

18The simple inherit folly,
　　but the prudent are crowned with
　　　knowledge.

19Evil men will bow down in the
　　presence of the good,
　　and the wicked at the gates of the
　　　righteous.

20The poor are shunned even by their
　　neighbors,
　　but the rich have many friends.

21He who despises his neighbor sins,
　　but blessed is he who is kind to
　　　the needy.

22Do not those who plot evil go astray?
　　But those who plan what is good
　　　find*a* love and faithfulness.

23All hard work brings a profit,
　　but mere talk leads only to
　　　poverty.

24The wealth of the wise is their crown,
　　but the folly of fools yields folly.

25A truthful witness saves lives,
　　but a false witness is deceitful.

26He who fears the LORD has a secure
　　fortress,
　　and for his children it will be a
　　　refuge.

27The fear of the LORD is a fountain of
　　life,
　　turning a man from the snares of
　　　death.

28A large population is a king's glory,
　　but without subjects a prince is
　　　ruined.

29A patient man has great
　　understanding,
　　but a quick-tempered man displays
　　　folly.

30A heart at peace gives life to the
　　body,
　　but envy rots the bones.

31He who oppresses the poor shows
　　contempt for their Maker,
　　but whoever is kind to the needy
　　　honors God.

32When calamity comes, the wicked are
　　brought down,
　　but even in death the righteous
　　　have a refuge.

33Wisdom reposes in the heart of the
　　discerning
　　and even among fools she lets
　　　herself be known.*b*

34Righteousness exalts a nation,
　　but sin is a disgrace to any people.

35A king delights in a wise servant,
　　but a shameful servant incurs his
　　　wrath.

15 A gentle answer turns away wrath,
　　but a harsh word stirs up anger.

2The tongue of the wise commends
　　knowledge,
　　but the mouth of the fool gushes
　　　folly.

3The eyes of the LORD are everywhere,
　　keeping watch on the wicked and
　　　the good.

4The tongue that brings healing is a
　　tree of life,
　　but a deceitful tongue crushes the
　　　spirit.

5A fool spurns his father's discipline,
　　but whoever heeds correction
　　　shows prudence.

6The house of the righteous contains
　　great treasure,
　　but the income of the wicked
　　　brings them trouble.

7The lips of the wise spread
　　knowledge;
　　not so the hearts of fools.

8The LORD detests the sacrifice of the
　　wicked,
　　but the prayer of the upright
　　　pleases him.

9The LORD detests the way of the
　　wicked
　　but he loves those who pursue
　　　righteousness.

*a*22 Or *show*　　*b*33 Hebrew; Septuagint and
Syriac / *but in the heart of fools she is not known*

¹⁰Stern discipline awaits him who
    leaves the path;
  he who hates correction will die.

¹¹Death and Destruction*a* lie open
    before the LORD—
  how much more the hearts of men!

¹²A mocker resents correction;
  he will not consult the wise.

¹³A happy heart makes the face
    cheerful,
  but heartache crushes the spirit.

¹⁴The discerning heart seeks
    knowledge,
  but the mouth of a fool feeds on
    folly.

¹⁵All the days of the oppressed are
    wretched,
  but the cheerful heart has a
    continual feast.

¹⁶Better a little with the fear of the LORD
    than great wealth with turmoil.

¹⁷Better a meal of vegetables where
    there is love
  than a fattened calf with hatred.

¹⁸A hot-tempered man stirs up
    dissension,
  but a patient man calms a quarrel.

¹⁹The way of the sluggard is blocked
    with thorns,

a 11 Hebrew *Sheol and Abaddon*

FRIDAY

Read Proverbs 15:1–33
Key Verse Proverbs 15:3

The Eyes of the Lord – Doug Serven

I borrowed my dad's prized possession—his red sports car. It was such a thrill to drive! But on the way home, as I searched for my wallet, I took my eyes off the road for a moment and drove into a ditch. Thankfully, I was unharmed, and the car came out of the ditch with only a few scratches and weeds hanging from the bumpers and the wheel wells—oh, and a missing front license plate. As I pulled back on the road, I wondered, "How am I ever going to explain this to Dad?"

I hatched a plan before I pulled into the driveway. Because Dad hadn't seen the wreck happen, I figured I could tell him some story about swerving to miss a box in the middle of the road, going into the ditch and losing the plate. After all, seeing is believing, right? And, if he didn't see it, he'd have to take my word for it. The story might have worked, except that in reality the plate had been missing from the car for a while already, which made the lie obvious.

How often don't we try the same thing with God? We try to cover up our sins, thinking he won't see them. But this verse tells us that God, as spirit (see John 4:24), sees everything. He's not limited, as my dad was, by eyes that can only be in one place at a time. God sees and knows about everything we do.

That notion tends to make our hearts sink into our stomachs. We think it means we can't get away with anything, which is true. But it also means that God is never out of reach. No corner of the universe lies beyond God's vision or reach. And God is not only there watching us; he's also there to help us when we falter.

A Deeper Look
2 Chronicles 16:9; Psalm 11:4–5; Hebrews 4:11–14

Go to page 712 for your next devotional reading.

but the path of the upright is a
highway.

²⁰A wise son brings joy to his father,
but a foolish man despises his
mother.

²¹Folly delights a man who lacks
judgment,
but a man of understanding keeps
a straight course.

²²Plans fail for lack of counsel,
but with many advisers they
succeed.

²³A man finds joy in giving an apt
reply—
and how good is a timely word!

²⁴The path of life leads upward for the
wise
to keep him from going down to
the grave.^a

²⁵The LORD tears down the proud man's
house
but he keeps the widow's
boundaries intact.

²⁶The LORD detests the thoughts of the
wicked,
but those of the pure are pleasing
to him.

²⁷A greedy man brings trouble to his
family,
but he who hates bribes will live.

²⁸The heart of the righteous weighs its
answers,
but the mouth of the wicked
gushes evil.

²⁹The LORD is far from the wicked
but he hears the prayer of the
righteous.

³⁰A cheerful look brings joy to the
heart,
and good news gives health to the
bones.

³¹He who listens to a life-giving rebuke
will be at home among the wise.

³²He who ignores discipline despises
himself,
but whoever heeds correction gains
understanding.

³³The fear of the LORD teaches a man
wisdom,^b
and humility comes before honor.

16

¹To man belong the plans of the
heart,
but from the LORD comes the reply
of the tongue.

²All a man's ways seem innocent to
him,
but motives are weighed by the
LORD.

³Commit to the LORD whatever you do,
and your plans will succeed.

⁴The LORD works out everything for his
own ends—
even the wicked for a day of
disaster.

⁵The LORD detests all the proud of
heart.
Be sure of this: They will not go
unpunished.

⁶Through love and faithfulness sin is
atoned for;
through the fear of the LORD a man
avoids evil.

⁷When a man's ways are pleasing to
the LORD,
he makes even his enemies live at
peace with him.

⁸Better a little with righteousness
than much gain with injustice.

⁹In his heart a man plans his course,
but the LORD determines his steps.

¹⁰The lips of a king speak as an oracle,
and his mouth should not betray
justice.

¹¹Honest scales and balances are from
the LORD;
all the weights in the bag are of his
making.

¹²Kings detest wrongdoing,
for a throne is established through
righteousness.

¹³Kings take pleasure in honest lips;
they value a man who speaks the
truth.

¹⁴A king's wrath is a messenger of
death,
but a wise man will appease it.

¹⁵When a king's face brightens, it
means life;

---

^a24 Hebrew *Sheol*   ^b33 Or *Wisdom teaches the
fear of the* LORD

his favor is like a rain cloud in
    spring.

¹⁶How much better to get wisdom than
    gold,
  to choose understanding rather
    than silver!

¹⁷The highway of the upright avoids
    evil;
  he who guards his way guards his
    life.

¹⁸Pride goes before destruction,
  a haughty spirit before a fall.

¹⁹Better to be lowly in spirit and among
    the oppressed
  than to share plunder with the
    proud.

²⁰Whoever gives heed to instruction
    prospers,
  and blessed is he who trusts in the
    LORD.

²¹The wise in heart are called
    discerning,
  and pleasant words promote
    instruction.ᵃ

²²Understanding is a fountain of life to
    those who have it,
  but folly brings punishment to
    fools.

²³A wise man's heart guides his mouth,
  and his lips promote instruction.ᵇ

²⁴Pleasant words are a honeycomb,
  sweet to the soul and healing to
    the bones.

²⁵There is a way that seems right to a
    man,
  but in the end it leads to death.

²⁶The laborer's appetite works for him;
  his hunger drives him on.

²⁷A scoundrel plots evil,
  and his speech is like a scorching
    fire.

²⁸A perverse man stirs up dissension,
  and a gossip separates close
    friends.

²⁹A violent man entices his neighbor
  and leads him down a path that is
    not good.

³⁰He who winks with his eye is plotting
    perversity;
  he who purses his lips is bent on
    evil.

³¹Gray hair is a crown of splendor;
  it is attained by a righteous life.

³²Better a patient man than a warrior,
  a man who controls his temper
    than one who takes a city.

³³The lot is cast into the lap,
  but its every decision is from the
    LORD.

17 Better a dry crust with peace and
    quiet
  than a house full of feasting,ᶜ
    with strife.

²A wise servant will rule over a
    disgraceful son,
  and will share the inheritance as
    one of the brothers.

³The crucible for silver and the
    furnace for gold,
  but the LORD tests the heart.

⁴A wicked man listens to evil lips;
  a liar pays attention to a malicious
    tongue.

⁵He who mocks the poor shows
    contempt for their Maker;
  whoever gloats over disaster will
    not go unpunished.

⁶Children's children are a crown to the
    aged,
  and parents are the pride of their
    children.

⁷Arrogantᵈ lips are unsuited to a
    fool—
  how much worse lying lips to a
    ruler!

⁸A bribe is a charm to the one who
    gives it;
  wherever he turns, he succeeds.

⁹He who covers over an offense
    promotes love,
  but whoever repeats the matter
    separates close friends.

¹⁰A rebuke impresses a man of
    discernment
  more than a hundred lashes a fool.

¹¹An evil man is bent only on rebellion;
  a merciless official will be sent
    against him.

ᵃ21 Or *words make a man persuasive*   ᵇ23 Or
mouth / and makes his lips persuasive
ᶜ1 Hebrew *sacrifices*   ᵈ7 Or *Eloquent*

Read Proverbs 16:1–33
Key Verse Proverbs 16:24

Got Honey?

People are like bees; they are attracted to sweetness. And like bees that go back to the hive, people migrate toward those whose words are sweet—kind, encouraging, affirming, fair, knowledgeable, true and authentic. Proverbs tells us that positive words are a honeycomb, "sweet to the soul and healing to the bones." That's energy food for the spirit! Those around us are listening to see whether Jesus really makes a difference in how we live—whether his presence in our lives turns our speech into honey!

Because we are Jesus' ambassadors, we are called to be diplomatic—to use our words to encourage, comfort and build up others. We are to avoid slander and judgmental remarks, because once someone has been hurt by our words it is difficult to repair the damage (see Proverbs 18:19). Instead we are to speak the truth with sensitivity and grace (see Colossians 4:6).

Digging Into the Word
1. Controlling our tongue is a struggle. What do the following passages have to say about this topic?—*Ephesians 5:3–4; 1 Timothy 4:12; James 3:1–12*
2. What do you observe about positive speech in the following passages?— *1 Thessalonians 5:11; Hebrews 10:24–25*

Move Into Service
One of the greatest acts of service we can offer to others is to encourage, affirm and build them up with our words. In the coming week, serve three people by: (1) writing a letter of encouragement to someone; (2) making a phone call to someone you have not seen for a while and letting them know you miss and appreciate them; (3) meeting with someone face to face and telling them how much they mean to you.

One Step Deeper
2 Corinthians 1:3–5; 1 Peter 4:11

Go to page 713 for your next devotional reading.

¹²Better to meet a bear robbed of her
        cubs
    than a fool in his folly.

¹³If a man pays back evil for good,
    evil will never leave his house.

¹⁴Starting a quarrel is like breaching a
        dam;
    so drop the matter before a dispute
        breaks out.

¹⁵Acquitting the guilty and condemning
        the innocent—
    the LORD detests them both.

¹⁶Of what use is money in the hand of
        a fool,
    since he has no desire to get
        wisdom?

¹⁷A friend loves at all times,
    and a brother is born for adversity.

¹⁸A man lacking in judgment strikes
        hands in pledge

and puts up security for his
        neighbor.

¹⁹He who loves a quarrel loves sin;
    he who builds a high gate invites
        destruction.

²⁰A man of perverse heart does not
        prosper;
    he whose tongue is deceitful falls
        into trouble.

²¹To have a fool for a son brings grief;
    there is no joy for the father of a
        fool.

²²A cheerful heart is good medicine,
    but a crushed spirit dries up the
        bones.

²³A wicked man accepts a bribe in
        secret
    to pervert the course of justice.

²⁴A discerning man keeps wisdom in
        view,

MONDAY

Read *Proverbs 17:1–28*
Key Verse *Proverbs 17:22*

Choosing Joy – Betsy Reinheimer

My friend Heidi has a radiance that draws people to her. Her shining
smile, dancing eyes and encouraging words cause both strangers
and friends to seek her out. Heidi is one of the most loving, cheerful
people I know.

Her joy does not come from her circumstances, however. In the
world's eyes, Heidi has no earthly reason to be happy. Every day she
battles the pain and frustration of having a terrible, debilitating disease—lupus. Some days she cannot get out of bed. Often she cannot even read or write. Although lupus has invaded Heidi's body, she
has not allowed it to control her spirit. Heidi chooses to have joy in
her life. Her joy comes from keeping her eyes focused on Jesus
Christ, the only One who can provide peace in spite of all her pain.
Her faithful "spirit sustains [her] in sickness" (Proverbs 18:14).
According to the proverb, Heidi's cheerful heart is "good medicine"
for her soul and her body.

The key to a cheerful and joyful heart is choosing to keep our
eyes on God when life is hard and circumstances look bleak. Job, an
expert on pain, learned that it was in the midst of his suffering that
he truly found God: "My ears had heard of you but now my eyes
have seen you" (Job 42:5).

A Deeper Look
John 15:9–11; Philippians 4:10–13; 1 Peter 4:12–19

Go to page 716 for your next devotional reading.

but a fool's eyes wander to the
ends of the earth.

25A foolish son brings grief to his father
and bitterness to the one who bore
him.

26It is not good to punish an innocent
man,
or to flog officials for their
integrity.

27A man of knowledge uses words with
restraint,
and a man of understanding is
even-tempered.

28Even a fool is thought wise if he
keeps silent,
and discerning if he holds his
tongue.

18 An unfriendly man pursues selfish
ends;
he defies all sound judgment.

2A fool finds no pleasure in
understanding
but delights in airing his own
opinions.

3When wickedness comes, so does
contempt,
and with shame comes disgrace.

4The words of a man's mouth are
deep waters,
but the fountain of wisdom is a
bubbling brook.

5It is not good to be partial to the
wicked
or to deprive the innocent of
justice.

6A fool's lips bring him strife,
and his mouth invites a beating.

7A fool's mouth is his undoing,
and his lips are a snare to his soul.

8The words of a gossip are like choice
morsels;
they go down to a man's inmost
parts.

9One who is slack in his work
is brother to one who destroys.

10The name of the LORD is a strong
tower;
the righteous run to it and are safe.

11The wealth of the rich is their
fortified city;
they imagine it an unscalable wall.

12Before his downfall a man's heart is
proud,
but humility comes before honor.

13He who answers before listening—
that is his folly and his shame.

14A man's spirit sustains him in
sickness,
but a crushed spirit who can bear?

15The heart of the discerning acquires
knowledge;
the ears of the wise seek it out.

16A gift opens the way for the giver
and ushers him into the presence
of the great.

17The first to present his case seems
right,
till another comes forward and
questions him.

18Casting the lot settles disputes
and keeps strong opponents apart.

19An offended brother is more
unyielding than a fortified
city,
and disputes are like the barred
gates of a citadel.

20From the fruit of his mouth a man's
stomach is filled;
with the harvest from his lips he is
satisfied.

21The tongue has the power of life and
death,
and those who love it will eat its
fruit.

22He who finds a wife finds what is
good
and receives favor from the LORD.

23A poor man pleads for mercy,
but a rich man answers harshly.

24A man of many companions may
come to ruin,
but there is a friend who sticks
closer than a brother.

19 Better a poor man whose walk is
blameless
than a fool whose lips are
perverse.

2It is not good to have zeal without
knowledge,
nor to be hasty and miss the way.

3A man's own folly ruins his life,

yet his heart rages against the
LORD.

4Wealth brings many friends,
  but a poor man's friend deserts
    him.

5A false witness will not go
    unpunished,
  and he who pours out lies will not
    go free.

6Many curry favor with a ruler,
  and everyone is the friend of a
    man who gives gifts.

7A poor man is shunned by all his
    relatives—
  how much more do his friends
    avoid him!
Though he pursues them with
    pleading,
  they are nowhere to be found.ᵃ

8He who gets wisdom loves his own
    soul;
  he who cherishes understanding
    prospers.

9A false witness will not go
    unpunished,
  and he who pours out lies will
    perish.

10It is not fitting for a fool to live in
    luxury—
  how much worse for a slave to
    rule over princes!

11A man's wisdom gives him patience;
  it is to his glory to overlook an
    offense.

12A king's rage is like the roar of a
    lion,
  but his favor is like dew on the
    grass.

13A foolish son is his father's ruin,
  and a quarrelsome wife is like a
    constant dripping.

14Houses and wealth are inherited from
    parents,
  but a prudent wife is from the
    LORD.

15Laziness brings on deep sleep,
  and the shiftless man goes hungry.

16He who obeys instructions guards his
    life,
  but he who is contemptuous of his
    ways will die.

17He who is kind to the poor lends to
    the LORD,
  and he will reward him for what
    he has done.

18Discipline your son, for in that there
    is hope;
  do not be a willing party to his
    death.

19A hot-tempered man must pay the
    penalty;
  if you rescue him, you will have to
    do it again.

20Listen to advice and accept
    instruction,
  and in the end you will be wise.

21Many are the plans in a man's heart,
  but it is the LORD's purpose that
    prevails.

22What a man desires is unfailing
    loveᵇ;
  better to be poor than a liar.

23The fear of the LORD leads to life:
  Then one rests content, untouched
    by trouble.

24The sluggard buries his hand in the
    dish;
  he will not even bring it back to
    his mouth!

25Flog a mocker, and the simple will
    learn prudence;
  rebuke a discerning man, and he
    will gain knowledge.

26He who robs his father and drives out
    his mother
  is a son who brings shame and
    disgrace.

27Stop listening to instruction, my son,
  and you will stray from the words
    of knowledge.

28A corrupt witness mocks at justice,
  and the mouth of the wicked gulps
    down evil.

29Penalties are prepared for mockers,
  and beatings for the backs of fools.

20 Wine is a mocker and beer a
    brawler;
  whoever is led astray by them is
    not wise.

ᵃ7 The meaning of the Hebrew for this sentence is
uncertain.   ᵇ22 Or A man's greed is his shame

²A king's wrath is like the roar of a
        lion;
he who angers him forfeits his life.

³It is to a man's honor to avoid strife,
        but every fool is quick to quarrel.

⁴A sluggard does not plow in season;
        so at harvest time he looks but
        finds nothing.

⁵The purposes of a man's heart are
        deep waters,

but a man of understanding draws
        them out.

⁶Many a man claims to have unfailing
        love,
but a faithful man who can find?

⁷The righteous man leads a blameless
        life;
blessed are his children after him.

⁸When a king sits on his throne to
        judge,

TUESDAY

Read *Proverbs 20:1–30*
Key Verse *Proverbs 20:1*

Servant or Master? — Sjanna W. Hargrove

Many Christians conclude that there is no place for alcohol in a
believer's life. Others believe that, as with many things created for
our use such as food, material possessions and pain-killing medi-
cines, there is no innate sin in drinking alcoholic beverages. In many
passages the Bible doesn't seem to condemn the use of alcohol; in
Bible times wine was a common and acceptable choice and was
often used as medicine (see 1 Timothy 5:23). Scripture does, however, speak of the potential for alcohol to "lead us astray"—into
overindulgence and even to addiction. When the use of alcohol
becomes abuse of alcohol, a substance God intended as a gift (see
Psalm 104:14–15) becomes destructive.

  This passage in Proverbs and others like it cause the thoughtful
reader to ask some hard questions. What do I believe about the use
of alcohol? If I drink, why do I? How often? How much? Do I drink
alcohol as a means to an end? Giving simple and honest answers to
these questions helps us detect faulty reasoning and improper ratio-
nalization. Checking out our beliefs and motives helps us assess
how the use of alcohol fits into our Christian lifestyle—whether it
has become an easy "high" or a shortcut to the "joy" we might otherwise look for in God (see Ephesians 5:18). Or we may decide that
God is calling us to abstain from alcohol altogether. Measuring our
attitudes toward alcohol may also help us decide if drinking is personally dangerous in terms of addiction and if we need to seek the
help of Christian professionals in dealing with it.

  As with our use of so many things, we may believe that we are
completely in control of alcohol. But if we consistently overindulge
in alcohol (or anything else for that matter), it becomes a
"mocker"—it controls us and keeps us wanting more, spending our
extra cash and time on "living the high life." If we allow ourselves to
be "led astray," we can become slaves to a substance that God gives
us for our responsible use.

A Deeper Look
Psalm 104:14–15; Proverbs 23:29–35; John 2:10

Go to page 719 for your next devotional reading.

he winnows out all evil with his
eyes.

⁹Who can say, "I have kept my heart
pure;
I am clean and without sin"?

¹⁰Differing weights and differing
measures—
the LORD detests them both.

¹¹Even a child is known by his actions,
by whether his conduct is pure and
right.

¹²Ears that hear and eyes that see—
the LORD has made them both.

¹³Do not love sleep or you will grow
poor;
stay awake and you will have food
to spare.

¹⁴"It's no good, it's no good!" says the
buyer;
then off he goes and boasts about
his purchase.

¹⁵Gold there is, and rubies in
abundance,
but lips that speak knowledge are
a rare jewel.

¹⁶Take the garment of one who puts up
security for a stranger;
hold it in pledge if he does it for a
wayward woman.

¹⁷Food gained by fraud tastes sweet to
a man,
but he ends up with a mouth full
of gravel.

¹⁸Make plans by seeking advice;
if you wage war, obtain guidance.

¹⁹A gossip betrays a confidence;
so avoid a man who talks too
much.

²⁰If a man curses his father or mother,
his lamp will be snuffed out in
pitch darkness.

²¹An inheritance quickly gained at the
beginning
will not be blessed at the end.

²²Do not say, "I'll pay you back for this
wrong!"
Wait for the LORD, and he will
deliver you.

²³The LORD detests differing weights,
and dishonest scales do not please
him.

²⁴A man's steps are directed by the
LORD.
How then can anyone understand
his own way?

²⁵It is a trap for a man to dedicate
something rashly
and only later to consider his
vows.

²⁶A wise king winnows out the wicked;
he drives the threshing wheel over
them.

²⁷The lamp of the LORD searches the
spirit of a man*ª*;
it searches out his inmost being.

²⁸Love and faithfulness keep a king
safe;
through love his throne is made
secure.

²⁹The glory of young men is their
strength,
gray hair the splendor of the old.

³⁰Blows and wounds cleanse away evil,
and beatings purge the inmost
being.

21 The king's heart is in the hand of
the LORD;
he directs it like a watercourse
wherever he pleases.

²All a man's ways seem right to him,
but the LORD weighs the heart.

³To do what is right and just
is more acceptable to the LORD than
sacrifice.

⁴Haughty eyes and a proud heart,
the lamp of the wicked, are sin!

⁵The plans of the diligent lead to profit
as surely as haste leads to poverty.

⁶A fortune made by a lying tongue
is a fleeting vapor and a deadly
snare.*ᵇ*

⁷The violence of the wicked will drag
them away,
for they refuse to do what is right.

⁸The way of the guilty is devious,
but the conduct of the innocent is
upright.

⁹Better to live on a corner of the roof

ª27 Or *The spirit of man is the* LORD's *lamp*
ᵇ6 Some Hebrew manuscripts, Septuagint and
Vulgate; most Hebrew manuscripts *vapor for those
who seek death*

than share a house with a
quarrelsome wife.

¹⁰The wicked man craves evil;
his neighbor gets no mercy from
him.

¹¹When a mocker is punished, the
simple gain wisdom;
when a wise man is instructed, he
gets knowledge.

¹²The Righteous One*a* takes note of
the house of the wicked
and brings the wicked to ruin.

¹³If a man shuts his ears to the cry of
the poor,
he too will cry out and not be
answered.

¹⁴A gift given in secret soothes anger,
and a bribe concealed in the cloak
pacifies great wrath.

¹⁵When justice is done, it brings joy to
the righteous
but terror to evildoers.

¹⁶A man who strays from the path of
understanding
comes to rest in the company of
the dead.

¹⁷He who loves pleasure will become
poor;
whoever loves wine and oil will
never be rich.

¹⁸The wicked become a ransom for the
righteous,
and the unfaithful for the upright.

¹⁹Better to live in a desert
than with a quarrelsome and
ill-tempered wife.

²⁰In the house of the wise are stores of
choice food and oil,
but a foolish man devours all he
has.

²¹He who pursues righteousness and
love
finds life, prosperity*b* and honor.

²²A wise man attacks the city of the
mighty
and pulls down the stronghold in
which they trust.

²³He who guards his mouth and his
tongue

keeps himself from calamity.

²⁴The proud and arrogant man—
"Mocker" is his name;
he behaves with overweening
pride.

²⁵The sluggard's craving will be the
death of him,
because his hands refuse to work.
²⁶All day long he craves for more,
but the righteous give without
sparing.

²⁷The sacrifice of the wicked is
detestable—
how much more so when brought
with evil intent!

²⁸A false witness will perish,
and whoever listens to him will be
destroyed forever.*c*

²⁹A wicked man puts up a bold front,
but an upright man gives thought
to his ways.

³⁰There is no wisdom, no insight, no
plan
that can succeed against the LORD.

³¹The horse is made ready for the day
of battle,
but victory rests with the LORD.

22 A good name is more desirable
than great riches;
to be esteemed is better than silver
or gold.

²Rich and poor have this in common:
The LORD is the Maker of them all.

³A prudent man sees danger and takes
refuge,
but the simple keep going and
suffer for it.

⁴Humility and the fear of the LORD
bring wealth and honor and life.

⁵In the paths of the wicked lie thorns
and snares,
but he who guards his soul stays
far from them.

⁶Train*d* a child in the way he should
go,
and when he is old he will not
turn from it.

⁷The rich rule over the poor,

---

a 12 Or *The righteous man*   *b 21* Or *righteousness*
c 28 Or / *but the words of an obedient man will live
on*   *d 6* Or *Start*

and the borrower is servant to the
    lender.

⁸He who sows wickedness reaps
    trouble,
and the rod of his fury will be
    destroyed.

⁹A generous man will himself be
    blessed,
for he shares his food with the
    poor.

¹⁰Drive out the mocker, and out goes
    strife;
quarrels and insults are ended.

¹¹He who loves a pure heart and whose
    speech is gracious
will have the king for his friend.

¹²The eyes of the LORD keep watch over
    knowledge,
but he frustrates the words of the
    unfaithful.

¹³The sluggard says, "There is a lion
    outside!"
or, "I will be murdered in the
    streets!"

¹⁴The mouth of an adulteress is a deep
    pit;

WEDNESDAY

Read *Proverbs 22:1–29*
Key Verse *Proverbs 22:7*

Bailing Out of Debt — Scott L. Moore

Credit cards are so easy for students to get these days—flashy
applications are handed out right along with class schedules. They
shout, "Pre-approved! $3,500 credit line! You deserve it!" I had
nearly $10,000 in credit card debt alone by the time I graduated
from college. When I got married a year later, my wife and I together had $20,000 in credit card and student loan debt. We'll be dig-
ging ourselves out of this hole for years to come.

The burden of debt can make us feel as if God doesn't care. We
can confess the sin of poor stewardship and be forgiven by God. But
the monetary debt still has to be paid, and when debt looms large,
joy slips away. Everyday expenses seem to become monumental pur-
chases. Even going out to a restaurant with friends is an occasion
for guilt, knowing that the next costly surprise, such as car repairs
or medical bills will make the hole even deeper.

That's the way debt works: "The borrower is servant to the
lender" (Proverbs 22:7). To be sure, we need lending institutions in
our society—they help us purchase large items that are truly
investments, such as a home or a college education. But credit isn't
just an issue of finding the lowest interest rates. Unjustified debt is
an indication that we are not content to live within our means. And
if we don't keep debt under control, our dependence on bank loans
and credit can become a matter of spiritual warfare. Debt is one of
the many effective weapons Satan uses to discourage us.

Are you sinking into debt? God wants you to be free of the
tyranny of debt and will give you help as you work to dig yourself
out. If you are tempted by those enticing offers of credit, think
twice. Make sure that you are in control of your credit line before it
controls you.

A Deeper Look
Matthew 6:24–34; Romans 13:8; 1 Corinthians 7:23

Go to page 724 for your next devotional reading.

he who is under the LORD's wrath
will fall into it.

15Folly is bound up in the heart of a
child,
but the rod of discipline will drive
it far from him.

16He who oppresses the poor to
increase his wealth
and he who gives gifts to the
rich—both come to poverty.

Sayings of the Wise

17Pay attention and listen to the sayings
of the wise;
apply your heart to what I teach,
18for it is pleasing when you keep them
in your heart
and have all of them ready on your
lips.
19So that your trust may be in the LORD,
I teach you today, even you.
20Have I not written thirty*a* sayings for
you,
sayings of counsel and knowledge,
21teaching you true and reliable words,
so that you can give sound
answers
to him who sent you?

22Do not exploit the poor because they
are poor
and do not crush the needy in
court,
23for the LORD will take up their case
and will plunder those who
plunder them.

24Do not make friends with a
hot-tempered man,
do not associate with one easily
angered,
25or you may learn his ways
and get yourself ensnared.

26Do not be a man who strikes hands
in pledge
or puts up security for debts;
27if you lack the means to pay,
your very bed will be snatched
from under you.

28Do not move an ancient boundary
stone
set up by your forefathers.

29Do you see a man skilled in his
work?
He will serve before kings;
he will not serve before obscure
men.

23 When you sit to dine with a ruler,
note well what*b* is before you,
2and put a knife to your throat
if you are given to gluttony.
3Do not crave his delicacies,
for that food is deceptive.

4Do not wear yourself out to get rich;
have the wisdom to show restraint.
5Cast but a glance at riches, and they
are gone,
for they will surely sprout wings
and fly off to the sky like an eagle.

6Do not eat the food of a stingy man,
do not crave his delicacies;
7for he is the kind of man
who is always thinking about the
cost.*c*
"Eat and drink," he says to you,
but his heart is not with you.
8You will vomit up the little you have
eaten
and will have wasted your
compliments.

9Do not speak to a fool,
for he will scorn the wisdom of
your words.

10Do not move an ancient boundary
stone
or encroach on the fields of the
fatherless,
11for their Defender is strong;
he will take up their case against
you.

12Apply your heart to instruction
and your ears to words of
knowledge.

13Do not withhold discipline from a
child;
if you punish him with the rod, he
will not die.
14Punish him with the rod
and save his soul from death.*d*

15My son, if your heart is wise,
then my heart will be glad;
16my inmost being will rejoice
when your lips speak what is right.

17Do not let your heart envy sinners,
but always be zealous for the fear
of the LORD.
18There is surely a future hope for you,
and your hope will not be cut off.

a20 Or *not formerly written; or not written excellent*
b1 Or *who*   *c7* Or *for as he thinks within
himself, / so he is; or for as he puts on a feast, / so
he is*   *d14* Hebrew *Sheol*

¹⁹Listen, my son, and be wise,
and keep your heart on the right
path.
²⁰Do not join those who drink too
much wine
or gorge themselves on meat,
²¹for drunkards and gluttons become
poor,
and drowsiness clothes them in
rags.

²²Listen to your father, who gave you
life,
and do not despise your mother
when she is old.
²³Buy the truth and do not sell it;
get wisdom, discipline and
understanding.
²⁴The father of a righteous man has
great joy;
he who has a wise son delights in
him.
²⁵May your father and mother be glad;
may she who gave you birth
rejoice!

²⁶My son, give me your heart
and let your eyes keep to my
ways,
²⁷for a prostitute is a deep pit
and a wayward wife is a narrow
well.
²⁸Like a bandit she lies in wait,
and multiplies the unfaithful
among men.

²⁹Who has woe? Who has sorrow?
Who has strife? Who has
complaints?
Who has needless bruises? Who
has bloodshot eyes?
³⁰Those who linger over wine,
who go to sample bowls of mixed
wine.
³¹Do not gaze at wine when it is red,
when it sparkles in the cup,
when it goes down smoothly!
³²In the end it bites like a snake
and poisons like a viper.
³³Your eyes will see strange sights
and your mind imagine confusing
things.
³⁴You will be like one sleeping on the
high seas,
lying on top of the rigging.
³⁵"They hit me," you will say, "but I'm
not hurt!
They beat me, but I don't feel it!
When will I wake up
so I can find another drink?"

24 Do not envy wicked men,
do not desire their company;
²for their hearts plot violence,
and their lips talk about making
trouble.

³By wisdom a house is built,
and through understanding it is
established;
⁴through knowledge its rooms are
filled
with rare and beautiful treasures.

⁵A wise man has great power,
and a man of knowledge increases
strength;
⁶for waging war you need guidance,
and for victory many advisers.

⁷Wisdom is too high for a fool;
in the assembly at the gate he has
nothing to say.

⁸He who plots evil
will be known as a schemer.
⁹The schemes of folly are sin,
and men detest a mocker.

¹⁰If you falter in times of trouble,
how small is your strength!

¹¹Rescue those being led away to
death;
hold back those staggering toward
slaughter.
¹²If you say, "But we knew nothing
about this,"
does not he who weighs the heart
perceive it?

POINT OF INTEREST

Proverbs 24:11–12

As Christians, we are held
accountable to help the
helpless, find the lost and
rescue the perishing. We have
heard about babies being aborted, people
who are hungry and kids who need love
and attention. We know about drug and
alcohol abusers and those who are strick-
en with disease. Most of us have the
resources to help in one way or another.
We have a responsibility to help that just
can't be rationalized away with protesta-
tions of ignorance or inadequacy.

Does not he who guards your life
    know it?
Will he not repay each person
    according to what he has
    done?

13Eat honey, my son, for it is good;
    honey from the comb is sweet to
    your taste.
14Know also that wisdom is sweet to
    your soul;
    if you find it, there is a future hope
    for you,
    and your hope will not be cut off.

15Do not lie in wait like an outlaw
    against a righteous man's
    house,
    do not raid his dwelling place;
16for though a righteous man falls
    seven times, he rises again,
    but the wicked are brought down
    by calamity.

17Do not gloat when your enemy falls;
    when he stumbles, do not let your
    heart rejoice,
18or the LORD will see and disapprove
    and turn his wrath away from him.

19Do not fret because of evil men
    or be envious of the wicked,
20for the evil man has no future hope,
    and the lamp of the wicked will be
    snuffed out.

21Fear the LORD and the king, my son,
    and do not join with the rebellious,
22for those two will send sudden
    destruction upon them,
    and who knows what calamities
    they can bring?

Further Sayings of the Wise

23These also are sayings of the wise:

To show partiality in judging is not
    good:
24Whoever says to the guilty, "You are
    innocent"—
    peoples will curse him and nations
    denounce him.
25But it will go well with those who
    convict the guilty,
    and rich blessing will come upon
    them.

26An honest answer
    is like a kiss on the lips.

27Finish your outdoor work

and get your fields ready;
    after that, build your house.

28Do not testify against your neighbor
    without cause,
    or use your lips to deceive.
29Do not say, "I'll do to him as he has
    done to me;
    I'll pay that man back for what he
    did."

30I went past the field of the sluggard,
    past the vineyard of the man who
    lacks judgment;
31thorns had come up everywhere,
    the ground was covered with
    weeds,
    and the stone wall was in ruins.
32I applied my heart to what I observed
    and learned a lesson from what I
    saw:
33A little sleep, a little slumber,
    a little folding of the hands to
    rest—
34and poverty will come on you like a
    bandit
    and scarcity like an armed man.a

More Proverbs of Solomon

25 These are more proverbs of Solomon,
    copied by the men of Hezekiah king
of Judah:

2It is the glory of God to conceal a
    matter;
    to search out a matter is the glory
    of kings.

3As the heavens are high and the earth
    is deep,
    so the hearts of kings are
    unsearchable.

4Remove the dross from the silver,
    and out comes material forb the
    silversmith;
5remove the wicked from the king's
    presence,
    and his throne will be established
    through righteousness.

6Do not exalt yourself in the king's
    presence,
    and do not claim a place among
    great men;
7it is better for him to say to you,
    "Come up here,"
    than for him to humiliate you
    before a nobleman.

a34 Or like a vagrant / and scarcity like a beggar
b4 Or comes a vessel from

What you have seen with your eyes
8   do not bring*a* hastily to court,
for what will you do in the end
    if your neighbor puts you to
        shame?

9If you argue your case with a
        neighbor,
do not betray another man's
        confidence,
10or he who hears it may shame you
and you will never lose your bad
        reputation.

11A word aptly spoken
is like apples of gold in settings of
        silver.

12Like an earring of gold or an
        ornament of fine gold
is a wise man's rebuke to a
        listening ear.

13Like the coolness of snow at harvest
        time
is a trustworthy messenger to those
        who send him;
he refreshes the spirit of his
        masters.

14Like clouds and wind without rain
is a man who boasts of gifts he
        does not give.

15Through patience a ruler can be
        persuaded,
and a gentle tongue can break a
        bone.

16If you find honey, eat just enough—
too much of it, and you will vomit.

17Seldom set foot in your neighbor's
        house—
too much of you, and he will hate
        you.

18Like a club or a sword or a sharp
        arrow
is the man who gives false
        testimony against his
        neighbor.

19Like a bad tooth or a lame foot
is reliance on the unfaithful in
        times of trouble.

20Like one who takes away a garment
        on a cold day,
or like vinegar poured on soda,
is one who sings songs to a heavy
        heart.

21If your enemy is hungry, give him
        food to eat;
if he is thirsty, give him water to
        drink.
22In doing this, you will heap burning
        coals on his head,
and the LORD will reward you.

23As a north wind brings rain,
so a sly tongue brings angry looks.

24Better to live on a corner of the roof
than share a house with a
        quarrelsome wife.

25Like cold water to a weary soul
is good news from a distant land.

26Like a muddied spring or a polluted
        well
is a righteous man who gives way
        to the wicked.

27It is not good to eat too much honey,
nor is it honorable to seek one's
        own honor.

28Like a city whose walls are broken
        down
is a man who lacks self-control.

26 Like snow in summer or rain in
        harvest,
honor is not fitting for a fool.

2Like a fluttering sparrow or a darting
        swallow,
an undeserved curse does not
        come to rest.

3A whip for the horse, a halter for the
        donkey,
and a rod for the backs of fools!

4Do not answer a fool according to his
        folly,
or you will be like him yourself.

5Answer a fool according to his folly,
or he will be wise in his own eyes.

6Like cutting off one's feet or drinking
        violence
is the sending of a message by the
        hand of a fool.

7Like a lame man's legs that hang
        limp
is a proverb in the mouth of a fool.

8Like tying a stone in a sling
is the giving of honor to a fool.

*a7,8 Or nobleman / on whom you had set your
eyes. / 8Do not go*

⁹Like a thornbush in a drunkard's hand
 is a proverb in the mouth of a fool.

¹⁰Like an archer who wounds at
   random
 is he who hires a fool or any
   passer-by.

¹¹As a dog returns to its vomit,
 so a fool repeats his folly.

¹²Do you see a man wise in his own
   eyes?
 There is more hope for a fool than
   for him.

¹³The sluggard says, "There is a lion in
   the road,
 a fierce lion roaming the streets!"

¹⁴As a door turns on its hinges,
 so a sluggard turns on his bed.

¹⁵The sluggard buries his hand in the
   dish;
 he is too lazy to bring it back to
   his mouth.

¹⁶The sluggard is wiser in his own eyes
 than seven men who answer
   discreetly.

THURSDAY

Read *Proverbs 25:1–28*
Key Verse *Proverbs 25:28*

Growing Deeper in Personal Discipline – Bob Boardman

Dawson Trotman, the founder of The Navigators, was known for the discipline with which he trained young men. I was one of those young men. And while the teaching, correction and chastisement from Daws could be hard to take, it molded and strengthened me. Most important, his discipline trained me in self-control.

No matter where we learn discipline, whether from a background in athletics, academics or the armed forces, we must learn to make it personal. Daws disciplined me out of love and concern for my spiritual growth. Now that he's gone, those lessons are still working in my life because they taught me how to discipline myself.

For me, there are at least three basic sources of personal discipline. First, I keep my eyes constantly on the Lord Jesus Christ and on the cross he willingly embraced for me. He was the most disciplined man of all time, and his example motivates me to take up my cross daily and follow him. My self-control is motivated first and foremost by his sacrifice.

I also find discipline by keeping a focus on my own faults, sins, weaknesses and needs and by trying to keep my eyes off others' faults. What I do with my failures and weaknesses shows who I really am. To truly succeed, I must be willing to fail and to learn from my failures.

Finally, self-control comes from an intense and eager expectation of Jesus Christ's return. His coming is my greatest hope, not only for the future, but also for this very moment. This hope affects my conduct and makes me pursue personal discipline today.

I find it so much easier to control my will and submit it to God's will when I remember what Jesus did for me, what my shortcomings really are, and what I want to be like when I see Jesus face to face. Give some thought to these issues in your own life.

A Deeper Look
Luke 9:23–25; 2 Timothy 1:7; Hebrews 12:8–11

Go to page 726 for your next devotional reading.

¹⁷Like one who seizes a dog by the
  ears
  is a passer-by who meddles in a
  quarrel not his own.

¹⁸Like a madman shooting
  firebrands or deadly arrows
¹⁹is a man who deceives his neighbor
  and says, "I was only joking!"

²⁰Without wood a fire goes out;
  without gossip a quarrel dies
  down.

²¹As charcoal to embers and as wood
  to fire,
  so is a quarrelsome man for
  kindling strife.

²²The words of a gossip are like choice
  morsels;
  they go down to a man's inmost
  parts.

²³Like a coating of glaze*ᵃ* over
  earthenware
  are fervent lips with an evil heart.

²⁴A malicious man disguises himself
  with his lips,
  but in his heart he harbors deceit.
²⁵Though his speech is charming, do
  not believe him,
  for seven abominations fill his
  heart.
²⁶His malice may be concealed by
  deception,
  but his wickedness will be exposed
  in the assembly.

²⁷If a man digs a pit, he will fall into it;
  if a man rolls a stone, it will roll
  back on him.

²⁸A lying tongue hates those it hurts,
  and a flattering mouth works ruin.

27 Do not boast about tomorrow,
  for you do not know what a day
  may bring forth.

²Let another praise you, and not your
  own mouth;
  someone else, and not your own
  lips.

³Stone is heavy and sand a burden,
  but provocation by a fool is
  heavier than both.

⁴Anger is cruel and fury
  overwhelming,
  but who can stand before jealousy?

⁵Better is open rebuke
  than hidden love.

⁶Wounds from a friend can be trusted,
  but an enemy multiplies kisses.

⁷He who is full loathes honey,
  but to the hungry even what is
  bitter tastes sweet.

⁸Like a bird that strays from its nest
  is a man who strays from his
  home.

⁹Perfume and incense bring joy to the
  heart,
  and the pleasantness of one's
  friend springs from his
  earnest counsel.

¹⁰Do not forsake your friend and the
  friend of your father,
  and do not go to your brother's
  house when disaster strikes
  you—
  better a neighbor nearby than a
  brother far away.

¹¹Be wise, my son, and bring joy to my
  heart;
  then I can answer anyone who
  treats me with contempt.

¹²The prudent see danger and take
  refuge,
  but the simple keep going and
  suffer for it.

¹³Take the garment of one who puts up
  security for a stranger;
  hold it in pledge if he does it for a
  wayward woman.

¹⁴If a man loudly blesses his neighbor
  early in the morning,
  it will be taken as a curse.

¹⁵A quarrelsome wife is like
  a constant dripping on a rainy day;
¹⁶restraining her is like restraining the
  wind
  or grasping oil with the hand.

¹⁷As iron sharpens iron,
  so one man sharpens another.

¹⁸He who tends a fig tree will eat its
  fruit,
  and he who looks after his master
  will be honored.

¹⁹As water reflects a face,

*ᵃ23 With a different word division of the Hebrew;
Masoretic Text of silver dross*

so a man's heart reflects the man.

²⁰Death and Destruction*a* are never
  satisfied,
and neither are the eyes of man.

²¹The crucible for silver and the
  furnace for gold,
but man is tested by the praise he
  receives.

²²Though you grind a fool in a mortar,
  grinding him like grain with a
  pestle,
you will not remove his folly from
  him.

²³Be sure you know the condition of
  your flocks,
give careful attention to your
  herds;
²⁴for riches do not endure forever,
  and a crown is not secure for all
  generations.
²⁵When the hay is removed and new
  growth appears
and the grass from the hills is
  gathered in,
²⁶the lambs will provide you with
  clothing,

a20 Hebrew *Sheol and Abaddon*

FRIDAY

Read Proverbs 27:1–27
Key Verse Proverbs 27:17

The Cutting Edge – Doug Serven

I was in college when I first heard about one-to-one discipleship. It was really pretty simple. My friend Brad asked if I'd be willing to meet with him to talk about the Bible. I said I would.

And that was it. Brad began to teach me what he knew about living life as a Christian. He opened my eyes to the disciplines of reading the Bible every day, memorizing Scripture, praying effectively and applying God's Word to my life. There was no fanfare or big to-do—just Brad and I meeting in the student union to read the Bible together. And wow, did he help me grow!

The principle of discipleship that Brad shared with me during that time is the same one found in Proverbs 27:17. God uses his Word and his people to "sharpen" his children. We, like swords, need a hot fire, a strong hand and some banging hammers in our lives to mold and shape us so that our spiritual life stays on the cutting edge. We need people like Brad who are willing to show us what they've learned about being a Christian, challenge us and help us to become spiritually mature. Then we can pass on to others what we've learned.

Wood does not sharpen iron. Plastic doesn't do the trick either. But iron sharpens iron to make tools that are useful to the Father. The discipline of being sharpened by another or by long experience is what qualifies you for the task of sharpening another person.

Are you feeling dull? Do you want to be on the cutting edge? Let yourself be sharpened by someone who is willing to teach you. Are you already being sharpened? Have you learned something about being a Christian? Ask someone with less experience as a Christian to meet with you. Share the basic principles you've learned and "sharpen another." Give it a try.

A Deeper Look
2 Timothy 2:2; Hebrews 10:23–25

Go to page 731 for your next devotional reading.

and the goats with the price of a
field.
²⁷You will have plenty of goats' milk
to feed you and your family
and to nourish your servant girls.

28 The wicked man flees though no
one pursues,
but the righteous are as bold as a
lion.

²When a country is rebellious, it has
many rulers,
but a man of understanding and
knowledge maintains order.

³A ruler*ᵃ* who oppresses the poor
is like a driving rain that leaves no
crops.

⁴Those who forsake the law praise the
wicked,
but those who keep the law resist
them.

⁵Evil men do not understand justice,
but those who seek the LORD
understand it fully.

⁶Better a poor man whose walk is
blameless
than a rich man whose ways are
perverse.

⁷He who keeps the law is a discerning
son,
but a companion of gluttons
disgraces his father.

⁸He who increases his wealth by
exorbitant interest
amasses it for another, who will be
kind to the poor.

⁹If anyone turns a deaf ear to the law,
even his prayers are detestable.

¹⁰He who leads the upright along an
evil path
will fall into his own trap,
but the blameless will receive a
good inheritance.

¹¹A rich man may be wise in his own
eyes,
but a poor man who has
discernment sees through
him.

¹²When the righteous triumph, there is
great elation;
but when the wicked rise to
power, men go into hiding.

¹³He who conceals his sins does not
prosper,
but whoever confesses and
renounces them finds mercy.

¹⁴Blessed is the man who always fears
the LORD,
but he who hardens his heart falls
into trouble.

¹⁵Like a roaring lion or a charging bear
is a wicked man ruling over a
helpless people.

¹⁶A tyrannical ruler lacks judgment,
but he who hates ill-gotten gain
will enjoy a long life.

¹⁷A man tormented by the guilt of
murder
will be a fugitive till death;
let no one support him.

¹⁸He whose walk is blameless is kept
safe,
but he whose ways are perverse
will suddenly fall.

¹⁹He who works his land will have
abundant food,
but the one who chases fantasies
will have his fill of poverty.

²⁰A faithful man will be richly blessed,
but one eager to get rich will not
go unpunished.

²¹To show partiality is not good—
yet a man will do wrong for a
piece of bread.

²²A stingy man is eager to get rich
and is unaware that poverty awaits
him.

²³He who rebukes a man will in the
end gain more favor
than he who has a flattering
tongue.

²⁴He who robs his father or mother
and says, "It's not wrong"—
he is partner to him who destroys.

²⁵A greedy man stirs up dissension,
but he who trusts in the LORD will
prosper.

²⁶He who trusts in himself is a fool,
but he who walks in wisdom is
kept safe.

²⁷He who gives to the poor will lack
nothing,

ᵃ3 Or *A poor man*

but he who closes his eyes to them
  receives many curses.

²⁸When the wicked rise to power,
  people go into hiding;
  but when the wicked perish, the
  righteous thrive.

29 A man who remains stiff-necked
  after many rebukes
  will suddenly be destroyed—
  without remedy.

²When the righteous thrive, the people
  rejoice;
  when the wicked rule, the people
  groan.

³A man who loves wisdom brings joy
  to his father,
  but a companion of prostitutes
  squanders his wealth.

⁴By justice a king gives a country
  stability,
  but one who is greedy for bribes
  tears it down.

⁵Whoever flatters his neighbor
  is spreading a net for his feet.

⁶An evil man is snared by his own sin,
  but a righteous one can sing and
  be glad.

⁷The righteous care about justice for
  the poor,
  but the wicked have no such
  concern.

⁸Mockers stir up a city,
  but wise men turn away anger.

⁹If a wise man goes to court with a
  fool,
  the fool rages and scoffs, and there
  is no peace.

¹⁰Bloodthirsty men hate a man of
  integrity
  and seek to kill the upright.

¹¹A fool gives full vent to his anger,
  but a wise man keeps himself
  under control.

¹²If a ruler listens to lies,
  all his officials become wicked.

¹³The poor man and the oppressor
  have this in common:
  The Lord gives sight to the eyes of
  both.

¹⁴If a king judges the poor with
  fairness,
  his throne will always be secure.

¹⁵The rod of correction imparts
  wisdom,
  but a child left to himself disgraces
  his mother.

¹⁶When the wicked thrive, so does sin,
  but the righteous will see their
  downfall.

¹⁷Discipline your son, and he will give
  you peace;
  he will bring delight to your soul.

¹⁸Where there is no revelation, the
  people cast off restraint;
  but blessed is he who keeps the
  law.

¹⁹A servant cannot be corrected by
  mere words;
  though he understands, he will not
  respond.

²⁰Do you see a man who speaks in
  haste?
  There is more hope for a fool than
  for him.

²¹If a man pampers his servant from
  youth,
  he will bring grief*a* in the end.

²²An angry man stirs up dissension,
  and a hot-tempered one commits
  many sins.

²³A man's pride brings him low,
  but a man of lowly spirit gains
  honor.

²⁴The accomplice of a thief is his own
  enemy;
  he is put under oath and dare not
  testify.

²⁵Fear of man will prove to be a snare,
  but whoever trusts in the Lord is
  kept safe.

²⁶Many seek an audience with a ruler,
  but it is from the Lord that man
  gets justice.

²⁷The righteous detest the dishonest;
  the wicked detest the upright.

a21 The meaning of the Hebrew for this word is
uncertain.

Sayings of Agur

30 The sayings of Agur son of Jakeh—
an oracle[a]:

This man declared to Ithiel,
to Ithiel and to Ucal:[b]

2"I am the most ignorant of men;
  I do not have a man's
    understanding.
3I have not learned wisdom,
  nor have I knowledge of the Holy
    One.
4Who has gone up to heaven and
    come down?
  Who has gathered up the wind in
    the hollow of his hands?
  Who has wrapped up the waters in
    his cloak?
  Who has established all the ends
    of the earth?
  What is his name, and the name of
    his son?
  Tell me if you know!

5"Every word of God is flawless;
  he is a shield to those who take
    refuge in him.
6Do not add to his words,
  or he will rebuke you and prove
    you a liar.

7"Two things I ask of you, O LORD;
  do not refuse me before I die:
8Keep falsehood and lies far from me;
  give me neither poverty nor riches,
  but give me only my daily bread.
9Otherwise, I may have too much and
    disown you
  and say, 'Who is the LORD?'
  Or I may become poor and steal,
  and so dishonor the name of my
    God.

10"Do not slander a servant to his
    master,
  or he will curse you, and you will
    pay for it.

11"There are those who curse their
    fathers
  and do not bless their mothers;
12those who are pure in their own eyes
  and yet are not cleansed of their
    filth;
13those whose eyes are ever so
    haughty,
  whose glances are so disdainful;
14those whose teeth are swords
  and whose jaws are set with
    knives

to devour the poor from the earth,
  the needy from among mankind.

15"The leech has two daughters.
  'Give! Give!' they cry.

"There are three things that are never
    satisfied,
  four that never say, 'Enough!':
16the grave,[c] the barren womb,
  land, which is never satisfied with
    water,
  and fire, which never says,
    'Enough!'

17"The eye that mocks a father,
  that scorns obedience to a mother,
  will be pecked out by the ravens of
    the valley,
  will be eaten by the vultures.

18"There are three things that are too
    amazing for me,
  four that I do not understand:
19the way of an eagle in the sky,
  the way of a snake on a rock,
  the way of a ship on the high seas,
  and the way of a man with a
    maiden.

20"This is the way of an adulteress:
  She eats and wipes her mouth
  and says, 'I've done nothing
    wrong.'

21"Under three things the earth
    trembles,
  under four it cannot bear up:
22a servant who becomes king,
  a fool who is full of food,
23an unloved woman who is married,
  and a maidservant who displaces
    her mistress.

24"Four things on earth are small,
  yet they are extremely wise:
25Ants are creatures of little strength,
  yet they store up their food in the
    summer;
26coneys[d] are creatures of little power,
  yet they make their home in the
    crags;
27locusts have no king,
  yet they advance together in ranks;
28a lizard can be caught with the hand,
  yet it is found in kings' palaces.

---

a1 Or *Jakeh of Massa*   *b1* Masoretic Text; with
a different word division of the Hebrew *declared, "I
am weary, O God; / I am weary, O God, and faint.*
c16 Hebrew *Sheol*   *d26* That is, the hyrax or
rock badger

²⁹"There are three things that are
     stately in their stride,
  four that move with stately
     bearing:
³⁰a lion, mighty among beasts,
  who retreats before nothing;
³¹a strutting rooster, a he-goat,
  and a king with his army around
     him.ᵃ

³²"If you have played the fool and
     exalted yourself,
  or if you have planned evil,
  clap your hand over your mouth!
³³For as churning the milk produces
     butter,
  and as twisting the nose produces
     blood,
  so stirring up anger produces
     strife."

Sayings of King Lemuel

31 The sayings of King Lemuel—an ora-
     cleᵇ his mother taught him:

²"O my son, O son of my womb,
  O son of my vows,ᶜ
³do not spend your strength on
     women,
  your vigor on those who ruin
     kings.

⁴"It is not for kings, O Lemuel—
  not for kings to drink wine,
  not for rulers to crave beer,
⁵lest they drink and forget what the
     law decrees,
  and deprive all the oppressed of
     their rights.
⁶Give beer to those who are perishing,
  wine to those who are in anguish;
⁷let them drink and forget their
     poverty
  and remember their misery no
     more.

⁸"Speak up for those who cannot
     speak for themselves,
  for the rights of all who are
     destitute.
⁹Speak up and judge fairly;
  defend the rights of the poor and
     needy."

Epilogue: The Wife of Noble Character

¹⁰ᵈA wife of noble character who can
     find?
  She is worth far more than rubies.

¹¹Her husband has full confidence in
     her
  and lacks nothing of value.
¹²She brings him good, not harm,
  all the days of her life.
¹³She selects wool and flax
  and works with eager hands.
¹⁴She is like the merchant ships,
  bringing her food from afar.
¹⁵She gets up while it is still dark;
  she provides food for her family
  and portions for her servant girls.
¹⁶She considers a field and buys it;
  out of her earnings she plants a
     vineyard.
¹⁷She sets about her work vigorously;
  her arms are strong for her tasks.
¹⁸She sees that her trading is profitable,
  and her lamp does not go out at
     night.
¹⁹In her hand she holds the distaff
  and grasps the spindle with her
     fingers.
²⁰She opens her arms to the poor
  and extends her hands to the
     needy.
²¹When it snows, she has no fear for
     her household;
  for all of them are clothed in
     scarlet.
²²She makes coverings for her bed;
  she is clothed in fine linen and
     purple.
²³Her husband is respected at the city
     gate,

ᵃ31 Or *king secure against revolt*   ᵇ1 Or *of Lemuel king of Massa, which*   ᶜ2 Or / *the answer to my prayers*   ᵈ10 Verses 10-31 are an acrostic, each verse beginning with a successive letter of the Hebrew alphabet.

POINT OF INTEREST

Proverbs 30:24-28

A prisoner once found hope by watching a spider's tireless and repeated efforts to scale a seemingly insurmountable obstacle. The Bible urges us to observe the simple, the weak and the seemingly insignificant to gain inspiration and understanding for our own lives. God speaks to us and teaches us through surprising means. What are you watching today?

Read Proverbs 31:1–31
Key Verse Proverbs 31:10

Mining for Rubies

What do most of us notice first when we're looking for someone to date? Let's be honest—it's likely that we focus on the face, the figure, the physique or the clothes.

But when we're seeking our spouse, we'd better look farther than skin-deep. What characteristics should a godly man look for in a woman? And what kind of man should a godly women seek? In this passage we gain insight on this topic from King Lemuel's mom, a very wise woman, who says that a woman of noble character is "worth far more than rubies." And perhaps we can say that a man of noble character is just as rare and beautiful! Generations have passed since the king wrote this proverb, but the Queen Mother's good advice is still worth listening to today.

Digging Into the Word
1. Beauty is a wonderful gift, but it doesn't last. It's just not enough to carry a relationship for a lifetime. What do you learn from these passages regarding beauty and character?—*Proverbs 6:20–26; 1 Peter 3:3–4*
2. How many qualities of a godly woman can you find in Proverbs 31:10–31? How can you affirm and praise these qualities in the women you know?

Discussion Starter
Fire up a conversation with friends with these questions: What do most men look for in a woman? What should godly men be looking for in a woman? What should godly women be looking for in a man?

One Step Deeper
Proverbs 11:22; 12:4

Go to page 735 for your next devotional reading.

where he takes his seat among the
    elders of the land.
²⁴She makes linen garments and sells
    them,
    and supplies the merchants with
      sashes.
²⁵She is clothed with strength and
    dignity;
    she can laugh at the days to
      come.
²⁶She speaks with wisdom,
    and faithful instruction is on her
      tongue.
²⁷She watches over the affairs of her
    household

and does not eat the bread of
    idleness.
²⁸Her children arise and call her
    blessed;
    her husband also, and he praises
      her:
²⁹"Many women do noble things,
    but you surpass them all."
³⁰Charm is deceptive, and beauty is
    fleeting;
    but a woman who fears the LORD is
      to be praised.
³¹Give her the reward she has earned,
    and let her works bring her praise
      at the city gate.

Imagine what it would be like to look back over your life and discover that everything you had done had been meaningless. The writer of Ecclesiastes, most likely Solomon, faced this very situation. Though he enjoyed more knowledge, accomplishments, opulence and pleasure than many of us could even dream of, he concludes that a life without God at its very center is futile. He honestly confesses his struggles with doubt and disillusionment. As you read this book, think about your own sense of purpose and how you can cultivate a God-centered life.

ECCLESIASTES

Everything Is Meaningless

1 The words of the Teacher,[a] son of David, king in Jerusalem:

2 "Meaningless! Meaningless!"
    says the Teacher.
  "Utterly meaningless!
    Everything is meaningless."

3 What does man gain from all his
      labor
    at which he toils under the sun?
4 Generations come and generations go,
    but the earth remains forever.
5 The sun rises and the sun sets,
    and hurries back to where it rises.
6 The wind blows to the south
    and turns to the north;
  round and round it goes,
    ever returning on its course.
7 All streams flow into the sea,
    yet the sea is never full.
  To the place the streams come from,
    there they return again.
8 All things are wearisome,
    more than one can say.
  The eye never has enough of seeing,
    nor the ear its fill of hearing.
9 What has been will be again,
    what has been done will be done
      again;
    there is nothing new under the
      sun.
10 Is there anything of which one can
      say,

---

[a]1 Or *leader of the assembly*; also in verses 2 and 12

"Look! This is something new"?
It was here already, long ago;
    it was here before our time.
¹¹There is no remembrance of men of
    old,
    and even those who are yet to
      come
will not be remembered
    by those who follow.

Wisdom Is Meaningless

¹²I, the Teacher, was king over Israel in Jerusalem. ¹³I devoted myself to study and to explore by wisdom all that is done under heaven. What a heavy burden God has laid on men! ¹⁴I have seen all the things that are done under the sun; all of them are meaningless, a chasing after the wind.

¹⁵What is twisted cannot be
    straightened;
    what is lacking cannot be counted.

¹⁶I thought to myself, "Look, I have grown and increased in wisdom more than anyone who has ruled over Jerusalem before me; I have experienced much of wisdom and knowledge." ¹⁷Then I applied myself to the understanding of wisdom, and also of madness and folly, but I learned that this, too, is a chasing after the wind.

¹⁸For with much wisdom comes much
    sorrow;
    the more knowledge, the more
      grief.

Pleasures Are Meaningless

2 I thought in my heart, "Come now, I will test you with pleasure to find out what is good." But that also proved to be meaningless. ²"Laughter," I said, "is foolish. And what does pleasure accomplish?" ³I tried cheering myself with wine, and embracing folly—my mind still guiding me with wisdom. I wanted to see what was worthwhile for men to do under heaven during the few days of their lives.

⁴I undertook great projects: I built houses for myself and planted vineyards. ⁵I made gardens and parks and planted all kinds of fruit trees in them. ⁶I made reservoirs to water groves of flourishing trees. ⁷I bought male and female slaves and had other slaves who were born in my house. I also owned more herds and flocks than anyone in Jerusalem before

me. ⁸I amassed silver and gold for myself, and the treasure of kings and provinces. I acquired men and women singers, and a harem*a* as well—the delights of the heart of man. ⁹I became greater by far than anyone in Jerusalem before me. In all this my wisdom stayed with me.

¹⁰I denied myself nothing my eyes
    desired;
    I refused my heart no pleasure.
My heart took delight in all my work,
    and this was the reward for all my
      labor.
¹¹Yet when I surveyed all that my
    hands had done
    and what I had toiled to achieve,
everything was meaningless, a
    chasing after the wind;
    nothing was gained under the sun.

Wisdom and Folly Are Meaningless

¹²Then I turned my thoughts to
    consider wisdom,
    and also madness and folly.
What more can the king's successor
    do
    than what has already been done?
¹³I saw that wisdom is better than
    folly,
    just as light is better than
      darkness.
¹⁴The wise man has eyes in his head,
    while the fool walks in the
      darkness;
but I came to realize

---

*a*8 The meaning of the Hebrew for this phrase is uncertain.

POINT OF INTEREST

Ecclesiastes 1:2–11

How often don't we get exhausted by the pace of life and wonder, "Why am I doing this? Will this have any lasting value?" The message of Ecclesiastes is that while we live on this earth ("under the sun") with no knowledge of our Creator, all our efforts to find fulfillment are in vain. God has "set eternity" in our hearts, and he is the only One who can permanently fill our longing for permanence (see Ecclesiastes 3:11–14).

that the same fate overtakes them both.

15Then I thought in my heart,

"The fate of the fool will overtake me
    also.
What then do I gain by being
    wise?"
I said in my heart,
    "This too is meaningless."
16For the wise man, like the fool, will
    not be long remembered;
in days to come both will be
    forgotten.
Like the fool, the wise man too must
    die!

Toil Is Meaningless

17So I hated life, because the work that is done under the sun was grievous to me. All of it is meaningless, a chasing after the wind. 18I hated all the things I had toiled for under the sun, because I must leave them to the one who comes after me. 19And who knows whether he will be a wise man or a fool? Yet he will have control over all the work into which I have poured my effort and skill under the sun. This too is meaningless. 20So my heart began to despair over all my toilsome labor under the sun. 21For a man may do his work with wisdom, knowledge and skill, and then he must leave all

---

MONDAY

Read Ecclesiastes 2:1–26
Key Verses Ecclesiastes 2:10–11

Filling the Human Void – Robert M. Bertrand

"If I only had a car (house, job, etc.) like that, life would be spectacular!" We have all made statements such as this at one time or another. Still, when we reach our goal, we are inevitably disappointed that life's pleasures and perks don't bring the kind of fulfillment we expect.

Ecclesiastes is a report on Solomon's great experiment on the meaning of life. After trying to find meaning in grand-scale building and gardening projects, and in agriculture, wealth, art, sex, power and knowledge, he was able to say, "I denied myself nothing my eyes desired; I refused my heart no pleasure" (Ecclesiastes 2:10). Yet his conclusion was, "everything was meaningless . . . nothing was gained under the sun" (Ecclesiastes 2:11).

Not many people have the opportunity to attempt to fill this emptiness on the scale that King Solomon did. But if we can learn from Solomon's experience, we may be able to avoid treading along the same pathway and eventually arriving at the same conclusion (see Ecclesiastes 3:11–14). God has placed within us a void that so often we attempt to fill with pleasure, knowledge, power and material possessions. But the message of Ecclesiastes is that only God can fill that emptiness in our lives. The meaning of life can only be seen from a point beyond the sun. Only God can give us that vantage point.

Fortunately, the message of Ecclesiastes is not without hope. More than once the author encourages us to "find satisfaction" in this life (Ecclesiastes 2:24; 5:18). This life has meaning when we recognize that new cars and such things can be truly enjoyed only when God, the giver of all things, comes first in our lives.

A Deeper Look
Matthew 6:33; Luke 8:5–15

Go to page 737 for your next devotional reading.

he owns to someone who has not worked for it. This too is meaningless and a great misfortune. 22What does a man get for all the toil and anxious striving with which he labors under the sun? 23All his days his work is pain and grief; even at night his mind does not rest. This too is meaningless.

24A man can do nothing better than to eat and drink and find satisfaction in his work. This too, I see, is from the hand of God, 25for without him, who can eat or find enjoyment? 26To the man who pleases him, God gives wisdom, knowledge and happiness, but to the sinner he gives the task of gathering and storing up wealth to hand it over to the one who pleases God. This too is meaningless, a chasing after the wind.

A Time for Everything

3 There is a time for everything,
　　and a season for every activity
　　　under heaven:

2　a time to be born and a time to
　　　die,
　　a time to plant and a time to
　　　uproot,
3　a time to kill and a time to heal,
　　a time to tear down and a time to
　　　build,
4　a time to weep and a time to
　　　laugh,
　　a time to mourn and a time to
　　　dance,
5　a time to scatter stones and a time
　　　to gather them,
　　a time to embrace and a time to
　　　refrain,
6　a time to search and a time to give
　　　up,
　　a time to keep and a time to throw
　　　away,
7　a time to tear and a time to mend,
　　a time to be silent and a time to
　　　speak,
8　a time to love and a time to hate,
　　a time for war and a time for
　　　peace.

9What does the worker gain from his toil? 10I have seen the burden God has laid on men. 11He has made everything beautiful in its time. He has also set eternity in the hearts of men; yet they cannot fathom what God has done from beginning to end. 12I know that there is nothing better for men than to be happy and do good while they live. 13That everyone may eat and drink, and find satisfaction in all his toil—this is the gift of God. 14I know that everything God does will endure forever; nothing can be added to it and nothing taken from it. God does it so that men will revere him.

15Whatever is has already been,
　　and what will be has been before;
　　and God will call the past to
　　　account.a

16And I saw something else under the sun:

In the place of judgment—wickedness
　　　was there,
　　in the place of justice—wickedness
　　　was there.

17I thought in my heart,

"God will bring to judgment
　　both the righteous and the wicked,
　for there will be a time for every
　　　activity,
　　a time for every deed."

18I also thought, "As for men, God tests them so that they may see that they are like the animals. 19Man's fate is like that of the animals; the same fate awaits them both: As one dies, so dies the other. All have the same breathb; man has no advantage over the animal. Everything is meaningless. 20All go to the same place; all come from dust, and to dust all return. 21Who knows if the spirit of man rises upward and if the spirit of the animalc goes down into the earth?"

22So I saw that there is nothing better for a man than to enjoy his work, because that is his lot. For who can bring him to see what will happen after him?

Oppression, Toil, Friendlessness

4 Again I looked and saw all the oppression that was taking place under the sun:

I saw the tears of the oppressed—
　　and they have no comforter;
　power was on the side of their
　　　oppressors—
　　and they have no comforter.
2And I declared that the dead,
　　who had already died,

a15 Or God calls back the past　b19 Or spirit
c21 Or Who knows the spirit of man, which rises upward, or the spirit of the animal, which

are happier than the living,
who are still alive.
³But better than both
is he who has not yet been,
who has not seen the evil
that is done under the sun.

⁴And I saw that all labor and all achievement spring from man's envy of his neighbor. This too is meaningless, a chasing after the wind.

⁵The fool folds his hands
and ruins himself.
⁶Better one handful with tranquillity
than two handfuls with toil
and chasing after the wind.

⁷Again I saw something meaningless under the sun:

⁸There was a man all alone;
he had neither son nor brother.
There was no end to his toil,
yet his eyes were not content with
his wealth.
"For whom am I toiling," he asked,
"and why am I depriving myself of
enjoyment?"
This too is meaningless—
a miserable business!

⁹Two are better than one,
because they have a good return
for their work:

TUESDAY

Read Ecclesiastes 4:1–12
Key Verses Ecclesiastes 4:9–12

The Power of Friendship – Joe Bernardy

"I need to confess something to you," Sam, my roommate, said as we sat in our room one day. He proceeded to tell me about some doubts he had been struggling with. As he opened up about his life and asked me to pray for him, I was surprised to learn that he was experiencing the same kind of struggle I had been dealing with in my life. But until that night, I thought I was probably the only Christian who had that kind of problem with doubt.

As I related my own story to Sam and we prayed together, I felt as if a heavy weight had been lifted. Sharing was liberating! We promised to pray for each other and to encourage each other in this area. In the succeeding weeks and months, we continued to share our struggles and our successes and to pray together. I began to experience freedom in a way I had never before thought possible.

Why the difference? Because "two are better than one." God, in his infinite wisdom, has designed his children to be interdependent—neither independent "lone rangers" with no need for anyone else; nor codependent in an unhealthy way. Because we are interdependent, we can draw from each other's strengths to help us in our areas of weakness. When two or more believers come together to pray with, encourage or challenge each other, that gathering results in a sum that is greater than its parts, and we honor God by our unity.

"Two are better than one . . . A chord of three strands is not quickly broken" (Ecclesiastes 4:9,12). Jesus, the third strand, ties our spirits together and empowers us. Are you alone in the battle today? Ask God for a friend with whom you can team up for mutual help and encouragement.

A Deeper Look
1 Samuel 18:1; James 5:16

Go to page 739 for your next devotional reading.

¹⁰If one falls down,
   his friend can help him up.
But pity the man who falls
   and has no one to help him up!
¹¹Also, if two lie down together, they
     will keep warm.
But how can one keep warm
     alone?
¹²Though one may be overpowered,
   two can defend themselves.
A cord of three strands is not quickly
     broken.

Advancement Is Meaningless

¹³Better a poor but wise youth than an old but foolish king who no longer knows how to take warning. ¹⁴The youth may have come from prison to the kingship, or he may have been born in poverty within his kingdom. ¹⁵I saw that all who lived and walked under the sun followed the youth, the king's successor. ¹⁶There was no end to all the people who were before them. But those who came later were not pleased with the successor. This too is meaningless, a chasing after the wind.

Stand in Awe of God

5 Guard your steps when you go to the house of God. Go near to listen rather than to offer the sacrifice of fools, who do not know that they do wrong.

²Do not be quick with your mouth,
   do not be hasty in your heart
   to utter anything before God.
God is in heaven
   and you are on earth,
   so let your words be few.
³As a dream comes when there are
     many cares,
so the speech of a fool when there
     are many words.

⁴When you make a vow to God, do not delay in fulfilling it. He has no pleasure in fools; fulfill your vow. ⁵It is better not to vow than to make a vow and not fulfill it. ⁶Do not let your mouth lead you into sin. And do not protest to the ₍temple₎ messenger, "My vow was a mistake." Why should God be angry at what you say and destroy the work of your hands? ⁷Much dreaming and many words are meaningless. Therefore stand in awe of God.

Riches Are Meaningless

⁸If you see the poor oppressed in a district, and justice and rights denied, do not be surprised at such things; for one official is eyed by a higher one, and over them both are others higher still. ⁹The increase from the land is taken by all; the king himself profits from the fields.

¹⁰Whoever loves money never has
     money enough;
whoever loves wealth is never
     satisfied with his income.
This too is meaningless.

¹¹As goods increase,
   so do those who consume them.
And what benefit are they to the
     owner
   except to feast his eyes on them?

¹²The sleep of a laborer is sweet,
   whether he eats little or much,
but the abundance of a rich man
   permits him no sleep.

¹³I have seen a grievous evil under the sun:

wealth hoarded to the harm of its
     owner,
¹⁴ or wealth lost through some
     misfortune,
so that when he has a son
   there is nothing left for him.
¹⁵Naked a man comes from his
     mother's womb,
and as he comes, so he departs.
He takes nothing from his labor
   that he can carry in his hand.

¹⁶This too is a grievous evil:

As a man comes, so he departs,
   and what does he gain,

POINT OF INTEREST

Ecclesiastes 5:10

This verse comes to us from one who knew the dissatisfaction and gnawing hunger for more that riches produce. Greed was just as vicious in ancient times as it is today. Even so, in our age of street corner ATM access and universally accepted credit cards, we have to be that much more diligent to live within our means and be satisfied with our best efforts at producing income.

since he toils for the wind?
17All his days he eats in darkness,
with great frustration, affliction
and anger.

18Then I realized that it is good and proper for a man to eat and drink, and to find satisfaction in his toilsome labor under the sun during the few days of life God has given him—for this is his lot. 19Moreover, when God gives any man wealth and possessions, and enables him to enjoy them, to accept his lot and be happy in his work—this is a gift of God. 20He seldom reflects on the days of his life, because God keeps him occupied with gladness of heart.

6 I have seen another evil under the sun, and it weighs heavily on men: 2God gives a man wealth, possessions and honor, so that he lacks nothing his heart desires, but God does not enable him to enjoy them, and a stranger enjoys them instead. This is meaningless, a grievous evil.

3A man may have a hundred children and live many years; yet no matter how long he lives, if he cannot enjoy his prosperity and does not receive proper burial, I say that a stillborn child is better off

---

Read *Ecclesiastes 5:1–20*
Key Verses *Ecclesiastes 5:10–11*

Never Enough – Jay Getz

NOW'S YOUR CHANCE to take advantage of our Platinum Spend-O-Rama Card! You can use it NOW to gratify your every desire for things that will never satisfy! The Platinum Spend-O-Rama Card will enable you to spend much more than you earn. Just think—you'll be spending money you don't have on important items such as:
- CDs you'll soon grow tired of
- shoes that will be out of fashion next spring
- groceries that will be gone in a day, or fast food that will be gone in minutes!

Yes, ALL THIS CAN BE YOURS, along with so much more that you never dreamed you could afford (because you can't). Our $10-a-month payment plan will enable you to amass a huge debt. And with our high interest rate, you'll be able to watch that debt grow every year until it will be virtually impossible to pay it off! SIGN UP NOW and start buying the things that will soon control your life—so you won't have to.

Wouldn't it be nice if every credit card offer was this honest? But it's hard enough to be honest with ourselves. It's so easy to fall into the trap of gathering things around us. Ecclesiastes 5:10 says, "Whoever loves money never has money enough." And this was spoken thousands of years ago by one of the richest people who ever lived! In fact, Solomon said of his possessions, "What benefit are they to the owner except to feast his eyes on them?" (Ecclesiastes 5:11).

Only Jesus can guarantee an abundant life. He says, "I have come that they may have life, *and have it to the full*" (John 10:10, italics added). Next time you're in a store and feasting your eyes on something, choose to take advantage of God's offer to live life to the full—without having to fill your life with stuff!

A Deeper Look
Luke 12:15; Hebrews 13:5

Go to page 744 for your next devotional reading.

than he. ⁴It comes without meaning, it departs in darkness, and in darkness its name is shrouded. ⁵Though it never saw the sun or knew anything, it has more rest than does that man— ⁶even if he lives a thousand years twice over but fails to enjoy his prosperity. Do not all go to the same place?

⁷All man's efforts are for his mouth,
  yet his appetite is never satisfied.
⁸What advantage has a wise man
    over a fool?
  What does a poor man gain
    by knowing how to conduct
      himself before others?
⁹Better what the eye sees
    than the roving of the appetite.
  This too is meaningless,
    a chasing after the wind.

¹⁰Whatever exists has already been
      named,
  and what man is has been known;
  no man can contend
    with one who is stronger than he.
¹¹The more the words,
    the less the meaning,
    and how does that profit anyone?

¹²For who knows what is good for a man in life, during the few and meaningless days he passes through like a shadow? Who can tell him what will happen under the sun after he is gone?

Wisdom

7 A good name is better than fine
      perfume,
  and the day of death better than
      the day of birth.
²It is better to go to a house of
      mourning
  than to go to a house of feasting,
  for death is the destiny of every man;
    the living should take this to heart.
³Sorrow is better than laughter,
    because a sad face is good for the
      heart.
⁴The heart of the wise is in the house
      of mourning,
  but the heart of fools is in the
      house of pleasure.
⁵It is better to heed a wise man's
      rebuke
  than to listen to the song of fools.
⁶Like the crackling of thorns under the
      pot,
  so is the laughter of fools.
  This too is meaningless.

⁷Extortion turns a wise man into a
      fool,
  and a bribe corrupts the heart.
⁸The end of a matter is better than its
      beginning,
  and patience is better than pride.
⁹Do not be quickly provoked in your
      spirit,
  for anger resides in the lap of
      fools.

¹⁰Do not say, "Why were the old days
      better than these?"
  For it is not wise to ask such
      questions.

¹¹Wisdom, like an inheritance, is a
      good thing
  and benefits those who see the
      sun.
¹²Wisdom is a shelter
    as money is a shelter,
  but the advantage of knowledge is
      this:
    that wisdom preserves the life of
      its possessor.

¹³Consider what God has done:

  Who can straighten
    what he has made crooked?
¹⁴When times are good, be happy;
    but when times are bad, consider:
  God has made the one
    as well as the other.
  Therefore, a man cannot discover
    anything about his future.

¹⁵In this meaningless life of mine I have seen both of these:

  a righteous man perishing in his
      righteousness,
  and a wicked man living long in
      his wickedness.
¹⁶Do not be overrighteous,
    neither be overwise—
    why destroy yourself?
¹⁷Do not be overwicked,
    and do not be a fool—
    why die before your time?
¹⁸It is good to grasp the one
    and not let go of the other.
  The man who fears God will avoid
    all ⌊extremes⌋.ᵃ

¹⁹Wisdom makes one wise man more
      powerful
  than ten rulers in a city.

ᵃ18 Or *will follow them both*

²⁰There is not a righteous man on earth
who does what is right and never
sins.

²¹Do not pay attention to every word
people say,
or you may hear your servant
cursing you—
²²for you know in your heart
that many times you yourself have
cursed others.

²³All this I tested by wisdom and I
said,

"I am determined to be wise"—
but this was beyond me.
²⁴Whatever wisdom may be,
it is far off and most profound—
who can discover it?
²⁵So I turned my mind to understand,
to investigate and to search out
wisdom and the scheme of
things
and to understand the stupidity of
wickedness
and the madness of folly.

²⁶I find more bitter than death
the woman who is a snare,
whose heart is a trap
and whose hands are chains.
The man who pleases God will
escape her,
but the sinner she will ensnare.

²⁷"Look," says the Teacher,^a "this is
what I have discovered:

"Adding one thing to another to
discover the scheme of
things—
²⁸   while I was still searching
but not finding—
I found one ⌐upright⌐ man among a
thousand,
but not one ⌐upright⌐ woman
among them all.
²⁹This only have I found:
God made mankind upright,
but men have gone in search of
many schemes."

8 Who is like the wise man?
Who knows the explanation of
things?
Wisdom brightens a man's face
and changes its hard appearance.

Obey the King

²Obey the king's command, I say, be-
cause you took an oath before God. ³Do
not be in a hurry to leave the king's presence. Do not stand up for a bad cause, for
he will do whatever he pleases. ⁴Since a
king's word is supreme, who can say to
him, "What are you doing?"

⁵Whoever obeys his command will
come to no harm,
and the wise heart will know the
proper time and procedure.
⁶For there is a proper time and
procedure for every matter,
though a man's misery weighs
heavily upon him.

⁷Since no man knows the future,
who can tell him what is to come?
⁸No man has power over the wind to
contain it^b;
so no one has power over the day
of his death.
As no one is discharged in time of
war,
so wickedness will not release
those who practice it.

⁹All this I saw, as I applied my mind to
everything done under the sun. There is
a time when a man lords it over others to
his own^c hurt. ¹⁰Then too, I saw the
wicked buried—those who used to come
and go from the holy place and receive
praise^d in the city where they did this.
This too is meaningless. ¹¹When the sentence for a crime is not
quickly carried out, the hearts of the peo-
ple are filled with schemes to do wrong.
¹²Although a wicked man commits a
hundred crimes and still lives a long
time, I know that it will go better with
God-fearing men, who are reverent before God. ¹³Yet because the wicked do
not fear God, it will not go well with
them, and their days will not lengthen
like a shadow. ¹⁴There is something else meaningless
that occurs on earth: righteous men who
get what the wicked deserve, and wicked
men who get what the righteous deserve.
This too, I say, is meaningless. ¹⁵So I
commend the enjoyment of life, because
nothing is better for a man under the sun
than to eat and drink and be glad. Then
joy will accompany him in his work all
the days of the life God has given him
under the sun.

^a27 Or *leader of the assembly*   ^b8 Or *over his
spirit to retain it*   ^c9 Or *to their*   ^d10 Some
Hebrew manuscripts and Septuagint (Aquila); most
Hebrew manuscripts *and are forgotten*

16When I applied my mind to know wisdom and to observe man's labor on earth—his eyes not seeing sleep day or night— 17then I saw all that God has done. No one can comprehend what goes on under the sun. Despite all his efforts to search it out, man cannot discover its meaning. Even if a wise man claims he knows, he cannot really comprehend it.

A Common Destiny for All

9 So I reflected on all this and concluded that the righteous and the wise and what they do are in God's hands, but no man knows whether love or hate awaits him. 2All share a common destiny—the righteous and the wicked, the good and the bad,*a* the clean and the unclean, those who offer sacrifices and those who do not.

As it is with the good man,
    so with the sinner;
as it is with those who take oaths,
    so with those who are afraid to
        take them.

3This is the evil in everything that happens under the sun: The same destiny overtakes all. The hearts of men, moreover, are full of evil and there is madness in their hearts while they live, and afterward they join the dead. 4Anyone who is among the living has hope*b*—even a live dog is better off than a dead lion!

5For the living know that they will die,
    but the dead know nothing;
they have no further reward,
    and even the memory of them is
        forgotten.
6Their love, their hate
    and their jealousy have long since
        vanished;
never again will they have a part
    in anything that happens under the
        sun.

7Go, eat your food with gladness, and drink your wine with a joyful heart, for it is now that God favors what you do. 8Always be clothed in white, and always anoint your head with oil. 9Enjoy life with your wife, whom you love, all the days of this meaningless life that God has given you under the sun—all your meaningless days. For this is your lot in life and in your toilsome labor under the sun. 10Whatever your hand finds to do, do it with all your might, for in the grave,*c* where you are going, there is neither working nor planning nor knowledge nor wisdom.

11I have seen something else under the sun:

The race is not to the swift
    or the battle to the strong,
nor does food come to the wise
    or wealth to the brilliant
    or favor to the learned;
but time and chance happen to them
    all.

12Moreover, no man knows when his hour will come:

As fish are caught in a cruel net,
    or birds are taken in a snare,
so men are trapped by evil times
    that fall unexpectedly upon them.

Wisdom Better Than Folly

13I also saw under the sun this example of wisdom that greatly impressed me: 14There was once a small city with only a few people in it. And a powerful king came against it, surrounded it and built huge siegeworks against it. 15Now there lived in that city a man poor but wise, and he saved the city by his wisdom. But nobody remembered that poor man. 16So I said, "Wisdom is better than strength." But the poor man's wisdom is despised, and his words are no longer heeded.

17The quiet words of the wise are more
        to be heeded
    than the shouts of a ruler of fools.
18Wisdom is better than weapons of
        war,
    but one sinner destroys much good.

10 As dead flies give perfume a bad
        smell,
    so a little folly outweighs wisdom
        and honor.
2The heart of the wise inclines to the
        right,
    but the heart of the fool to the left.
3Even as he walks along the road,
    the fool lacks sense
    and shows everyone how stupid he
        is.
4If a ruler's anger rises against you,
    do not leave your post;

---

*a*2 Septuagint (Aquila), Vulgate and Syriac; Hebrew does not have *and the bad.*   *b*4 Or *What then is to be chosen? With all who live, there is hope*   *c*10 Hebrew *Sheol*

calmness can lay great errors to
rest.

⁵There is an evil I have seen under the
sun,
the sort of error that arises from a
ruler:
⁶Fools are put in many high positions,
while the rich occupy the low
ones.
⁷I have seen slaves on horseback,
while princes go on foot like
slaves.

⁸Whoever digs a pit may fall into it;
whoever breaks through a wall
may be bitten by a snake.
⁹Whoever quarries stones may be
injured by them;
whoever splits logs may be
endangered by them.

¹⁰If the ax is dull
and its edge unsharpened,
more strength is needed
but skill will bring success.

¹¹If a snake bites before it is charmed,
there is no profit for the charmer.

¹²Words from a wise man's mouth are
gracious,
but a fool is consumed by his own
lips.
¹³At the beginning his words are folly;
at the end they are wicked
madness—
¹⁴   and the fool multiplies words.

No one knows what is coming—
who can tell him what will happen
after him?

¹⁵A fool's work wearies him;
he does not know the way to
town.

¹⁶Woe to you, O land whose king was
a servant*a*
and whose princes feast in the
morning.
¹⁷Blessed are you, O land whose king is
of noble birth
and whose princes eat at a proper
time—
for strength and not for
drunkenness.

¹⁸If a man is lazy, the rafters sag;
if his hands are idle, the house
leaks.

¹⁹A feast is made for laughter,
and wine makes life merry,

but money is the answer for
everything.

²⁰Do not revile the king even in your
thoughts,
or curse the rich in your bedroom,
because a bird of the air may carry
your words,
and a bird on the wing may report
what you say.

Bread Upon the Waters

11 Cast your bread upon the waters,
for after many days you will find it
again.
²Give portions to seven, yes to eight,
for you do not know what disaster
may come upon the land.

³If clouds are full of water,
they pour rain upon the earth.
Whether a tree falls to the south or to
the north,
in the place where it falls, there
will it lie.
⁴Whoever watches the wind will not
plant;
whoever looks at the clouds will
not reap.

⁵As you do not know the path of the
wind,
or how the body is formed*b* in a
mother's womb,
so you cannot understand the work
of God,
the Maker of all things.

⁶Sow your seed in the morning,
and at evening let not your hands
be idle,
for you do not know which will
succeed,
whether this or that,
or whether both will do equally
well.

Remember Your Creator While Young

⁷Light is sweet,
and it pleases the eyes to see the
sun.
⁸However many years a man may live,
let him enjoy them all.
But let him remember the days of
darkness,
for they will be many.
Everything to come is meaningless.

---

a 16 Or *king is a child*   *b 5* Or *know how life* (or
the spirit) / *enters the body being formed*

⁹Be happy, young man, while you are
    young,
and let your heart give you joy in
    the days of your youth.
Follow the ways of your heart
    and whatever your eyes see,
but know that for all these things
    God will bring you to judgment.
¹⁰So then, banish anxiety from your
    heart
and cast off the troubles of your
    body,
for youth and vigor are
    meaningless.

12 Remember your Creator
    in the days of your youth,
before the days of trouble come
    and the years approach when you
    will say,

"I find no pleasure in them"—
²before the sun and the light
    and the moon and the stars grow
    dark,
and the clouds return after the
    rain;
³when the keepers of the house
    tremble,
and the strong men stoop,
when the grinders cease because they
    are few,
and those looking through the
    windows grow dim;
⁴when the doors to the street are
    closed
and the sound of grinding fades;
when men rise up at the sound of
    birds,
but all their songs grow faint;

THURSDAY

Read Ecclesiastes 10:1–11:10
Key Verse Ecclesiastes 11:6

The Rewards of Diligence — Joe Bernardy

As a student and new believer, I was fascinated by stories friends told me about amazing answers to prayer that they had experienced. I was especially impressed with stories of good grades some of them had received in answer to prayer! So I devised a new strategy for schoolwork: study my Bible, enjoy the fellowship of my friends, share the gospel . . . and pray for my classes. After a few weeks of greatly enjoying this new strategy, I was dismayed to find that my grades were going downhill—fast! The strategy wasn't working. What was wrong?

Later in my college career, I registered for a chemistry class. I studied hard and did the assignments, but still felt completely lost. When the time came for the final exam, I asked my friends to pray for a miracle—for me to pass this test! The professor apologized for the way he had taught his class and told us that if we were happy with our current grade, we could skip the final. I had an "A"!

What was the difference? In the first case I had been irresponsible and had expected God to bail me out. In the second case I had been diligent in my responsibilities, and God had honored that. Having faith that God will work things out in your life is not an excuse to be lazy or irresponsible. God honors diligence and faithfulness. As you "sow your seed in the morning, and at evening let not your hands be idle," your work will bring God's blessing.

A Deeper Look
Proverbs 24:33–34; Colossians 3:23–24

Go to page 745 for your next devotional reading.

⁵when men are afraid of heights
and of dangers in the streets;
when the almond tree blossoms
and the grasshopper drags himself
along
and desire no longer is stirred.
Then man goes to his eternal home
and mourners go about the streets.

⁶Remember him—before the silver
cord is severed,
or the golden bowl is broken;
before the pitcher is shattered at the
spring,
or the wheel broken at the well,
⁷and the dust returns to the ground it
came from,
and the spirit returns to God who
gave it.

⁸"Meaningless! Meaningless!" says the
Teacher. ᵃ
"Everything is meaningless!"

The Conclusion of the Matter

⁹Not only was the Teacher wise, but
also he imparted knowledge to the people. He pondered and searched out and
set in order many proverbs. ¹⁰The Teacher searched to find just the right words,
and what he wrote was upright and
true.

¹¹The words of the wise are like goads,
their collected sayings like firmly embed-
ded nails—given by one Shepherd. ¹²Be

ᵃ8 Or the leader of the assembly; also in verses 9
and 10

FRIDAY

Read *Ecclesiastes 12:1–14*
Key Verses *Ecclesiastes 11:9; 12:1*

Solid Foundations – Erica Searl

When hard times come your way, do you ever catch yourself saying,
"Why is this happening? Why me, God?" I often ask those kinds of
questions. But there's a different way, a better way to look at hardship.

While I cannot see what my future holds for me, I can be certain
that the choices I make today will affect my future. Choosing wisely
among my options for career, marriage and lifestyle will have long-
term, even eternal, consequences. And if I seek God and come to
know him while I am still young and pliable, he is able to change
and mold me according to his will; I will be building patterns of spiritual growth into a lifetime of walking with him. That's especially
true in terms of how I handle stress and hardship.

Jesus told a story in Matthew 7:24–27 about a wise man and a
foolish man. The rain fell on them both and the storms beat against
both of their houses, yet one house stood firm while the other collapsed. The difference was not in the degree of the hardships, but in
the ability of the one man's house to weather the storm. The wise
man built his house on a solid foundation. Knowing God is the spiritual foundation we need to build into our lives so that we can out-
last any storm.

Instead of asking, "Why me?" I need to ask myself if I'm ready for
the future. Am I remembering "[my] Creator in the days of [my]
youth"? Am I building my life on the wisdom to be found in his
Word? If I do, I'll be able to stand firm under the hard times to come.
The good choices I make today will prepare me for tomorrow.

A Deeper Look
Matthew 7:24–27; James 1:2–5

Go to page 753 for your next devotional reading.

warned, my son, of anything in addition to them.

Of making many books there is no end, and much study wearies the body.

13Now all has been heard;
here is the conclusion of the
matter:

Fear God and keep his
commandments,
for this is the whole ⌊duty⌋ of
man.
14For God will bring every deed into
judgment,
including every hidden thing,
whether it is good or evil.

Turn on the television or radio, walk into any bookstore or even down a city street and you'll be inundated with songs and images about romantic love. Often it seems as though nothing consumes us so much as the desire to experience intimacy with another person. So it stands to reason that the God who created us with these desires has something to say about love, intimacy and marriage. Song of Songs acclaims the passion, delight and allure of married love. Song of Songs is a celebration of the love between a man and a woman— one of God's choicest gifts.

SONG OF SONGS

1 Solomon's Song of Songs.

Beloved[a]

2Let him kiss me with the kisses of his
mouth—
for your love is more delightful
than wine.
3Pleasing is the fragrance of your
perfumes;
your name is like perfume poured
out.
No wonder the maidens love you!
4Take me away with you—let us
hurry!
Let the king bring me into his
chambers.

Friends

We rejoice and delight in you[b];

we will praise your love more than
wine.

Beloved

How right they are to adore you!

5Dark am I, yet lovely,
O daughters of Jerusalem,
dark like the tents of Kedar,
like the tent curtains of Solomon.[c]
6Do not stare at me because I am
dark,

---

[a]Primarily on the basis of the gender of the Hebrew
pronouns used, male and female speakers are
indicated in the margins by the captions *Lover* and
Beloved respectively. The words of others are
marked *Friends*. In some instances the divisions and
their captions are debatable.   [b]4 The Hebrew is
masculine singular.   [c]5 Or *Salma*

because I am darkened by the sun.
My mother's sons were angry with
　　me
and made me take care of the
　　vineyards;
my own vineyard I have neglected.
⁷Tell me, you whom I love, where you
　　graze your flock
and where you rest your sheep at
　　midday.
Why should I be like a veiled woman
beside the flocks of your friends?

Friends

⁸If you do not know, most beautiful of
　　women,
follow the tracks of the sheep
and graze your young goats
　　by the tents of the shepherds.

Lover

⁹I liken you, my darling, to a mare
harnessed to one of the chariots of
　　Pharaoh.
¹⁰Your cheeks are beautiful with
　　earrings,
your neck with strings of jewels.
¹¹We will make you earrings of gold,
studded with silver.

Beloved

¹²While the king was at his table,
my perfume spread its fragrance.
¹³My lover is to me a sachet of myrrh
resting between my breasts.
¹⁴My lover is to me a cluster of henna
　　blossoms
from the vineyards of En Gedi.

Lover

¹⁵How beautiful you are, my darling!
Oh, how beautiful!
Your eyes are doves.

Beloved

¹⁶How handsome you are, my lover!
Oh, how charming!
And our bed is verdant.

Lover

¹⁷The beams of our house are cedars;
our rafters are firs.

Beloved[a]

2 I am a rose[b] of Sharon,
　　a lily of the valleys.

Lover

²Like a lily among thorns
is my darling among the maidens.

Beloved

³Like an apple tree among the trees of
　　the forest
is my lover among the young men.
I delight to sit in his shade,
and his fruit is sweet to my taste.
⁴He has taken me to the banquet hall,
and his banner over me is love.
⁵Strengthen me with raisins,
refresh me with apples,
for I am faint with love.
⁶His left arm is under my head,
and his right arm embraces me.
⁷Daughters of Jerusalem, I charge you
by the gazelles and by the does of
　　the field:
Do not arouse or awaken love
until it so desires.

⁸Listen! My lover!
Look! Here he comes,
leaping across the mountains,
bounding over the hills.
⁹My lover is like a gazelle or a young
　　stag.
Look! There he stands behind our
　　wall,
gazing through the windows,
peering through the lattice.
¹⁰My lover spoke and said to me,
"Arise, my darling,
my beautiful one, and come with
　　me.
¹¹See! The winter is past;

ᵃ1 Or Lover　　ᵇ1 Possibly a member of the
crocus family

POINT OF INTEREST

Song of Songs 2:2-4

Song of Songs is a passionate love song. Some understand this book as an
illustration of God's love for
his people. Others view it as a celebration
of the kind of romance and sexuality that
God intended for us in marriage. However
you interpret this book of poetry, one
thing is obvious: The relationship it celebrates is exclusive, intensely personal and
dramatically exciting for both parties.

the rains are over and gone.
¹²Flowers appear on the earth;
  the season of singing has come,
  the cooing of doves
  is heard in our land.
¹³The fig tree forms its early fruit;
  the blossoming vines spread their
    fragrance.
Arise, come, my darling;
  my beautiful one, come with me.ʺ

Lover

¹⁴My dove in the clefts of the rock,
  in the hiding places on the
    mountainside,
show me your face,
  let me hear your voice;
for your voice is sweet,
  and your face is lovely.
¹⁵Catch for us the foxes,
  the little foxes
that ruin the vineyards,
  our vineyards that are in bloom.

Beloved

¹⁶My lover is mine and I am his;
  he browses among the lilies.
¹⁷Until the day breaks
  and the shadows flee,
turn, my lover,
  and be like a gazelle
or like a young stag
  on the rugged hills.ᵃ

3 All night long on my bed
  I looked for the one my heart
    loves;
  I looked for him but did not find
    him.
²I will get up now and go about the
    city,
  through its streets and squares;
I will search for the one my heart
    loves.
So I looked for him but did not
    find him.
³The watchmen found me
  as they made their rounds in the
    city.
  ʺHave you seen the one my heart
    loves?ʺ
⁴Scarcely had I passed them
  when I found the one my heart
    loves.
I held him and would not let him go
  till I had brought him to my
    mother's house,
  to the room of the one who
    conceived me.

⁵Daughters of Jerusalem, I charge you
  by the gazelles and by the does of
    the field:
Do not arouse or awaken love
  until it so desires.

⁶Who is this coming up from the
    desert
  like a column of smoke,
perfumed with myrrh and incense
  made from all the spices of the
    merchant?
⁷Look! It is Solomon's carriage,
  escorted by sixty warriors,
  the noblest of Israel,
⁸all of them wearing the sword,
  all experienced in battle,
each with his sword at his side,
  prepared for the terrors of the
    night.
⁹King Solomon made for himself the
    carriage;
  he made it of wood from Lebanon.
¹⁰Its posts he made of silver,
  its base of gold.
Its seat was upholstered with purple,
  its interior lovingly inlaid
  byᵇ the daughters of Jerusalem.
¹¹Come out, you daughters of Zion,
  and look at King Solomon wearing
    the crown,
  the crown with which his mother
    crowned him
on the day of his wedding,
  the day his heart rejoiced.

Lover

4 How beautiful you are, my darling!
  Oh, how beautiful!
  Your eyes behind your veil are
    doves.
Your hair is like a flock of goats
  descending from Mount Gilead.
²Your teeth are like a flock of sheep
  just shorn,
  coming up from the washing.
Each has its twin;
  not one of them is alone.
³Your lips are like a scarlet ribbon;
  your mouth is lovely.
Your temples behind your veil
  are like the halves of a
    pomegranate.
⁴Your neck is like the tower of David,
  built with eleganceᶜ;
on it hang a thousand shields,

ᵃ17 Or *the hills of Bether*   *ᵇ10* Or *its inlaid
interior a gift of love / from*   *ᶜ4* The meaning of
the Hebrew for this word is uncertain.

all of them shields of warriors.
⁵Your two breasts are like two fawns,
   like twin fawns of a gazelle
   that browse among the lilies.
⁶Until the day breaks
   and the shadows flee,
 I will go to the mountain of myrrh
   and to the hill of incense.
⁷All beautiful you are, my darling;
   there is no flaw in you.

⁸Come with me from Lebanon, my
      bride,
   come with me from Lebanon.
Descend from the crest of Amana,
   from the top of Senir, the summit
      of Hermon,
 from the lions' dens
   and the mountain haunts of the
      leopards.
⁹You have stolen my heart, my sister,
      my bride;
   you have stolen my heart
 with one glance of your eyes,
   with one jewel of your necklace.
¹⁰How delightful is your love, my
      sister, my bride!
   How much more pleasing is your
      love than wine,
   and the fragrance of your perfume
      than any spice!
¹¹Your lips drop sweetness as the
      honeycomb, my bride;
   milk and honey are under your
      tongue.
   The fragrance of your garments is
      like that of Lebanon.
¹²You are a garden locked up, my
      sister, my bride;
   you are a spring enclosed, a sealed
      fountain.
¹³Your plants are an orchard of
      pomegranates
   with choice fruits,
   with henna and nard,
14   nard and saffron,
   calamus and cinnamon,
   with every kind of incense tree,
   with myrrh and aloes
   and all the finest spices.
¹⁵You are*ᵃ* a garden fountain,
   a well of flowing water
   streaming down from Lebanon.

Beloved

¹⁶Awake, north wind,
   and come, south wind!
Blow on my garden,

that its fragrance may spread
   abroad.
Let my lover come into his garden
   and taste its choice fruits.

Lover

5 I have come into my garden, my
      sister, my bride;
   I have gathered my myrrh with my
      spice.
 I have eaten my honeycomb and my
      honey;
   I have drunk my wine and my
      milk.

Friends

Eat, O friends, and drink;
   drink your fill, O lovers.

Beloved

²I slept but my heart was awake.
   Listen! My lover is knocking:
"Open to me, my sister, my darling,
   my dove, my flawless one.
My head is drenched with dew,
   my hair with the dampness of the
      night."
³I have taken off my robe—
   must I put it on again?
I have washed my feet—
   must I soil them again?
⁴My lover thrust his hand through the
      latch-opening;
   my heart began to pound for him.
⁵I arose to open for my lover,
   and my hands dripped with myrrh,
 my fingers with flowing myrrh,
   on the handles of the lock.
⁶I opened for my lover,
   but my lover had left; he was
      gone.
   My heart sank at his departure.*ᵇ*
I looked for him but did not find him.

*ᵃ15 Or I am (spoken by the Beloved)   ᵇ6 Or
heart had gone out to him when he spoke*

POINT OF INTEREST

Song of Songs 4:2

Was this a compliment?
Though these images don't
necessarily appeal to our
modern imaginations, ancient
civilizations would have readily recognized
them as attractive.

I called him but he did not answer.
⁷The watchmen found me
    as they made their rounds in the
        city.
They beat me, they bruised me;
    they took away my cloak,
    those watchmen of the walls!
⁸O daughters of Jerusalem, I charge
      you—
    if you find my lover,
what will you tell him?
    Tell him I am faint with love.

Friends

⁹How is your beloved better than
      others,
    most beautiful of women?
How is your beloved better than
      others,
    that you charge us so?

Beloved

¹⁰My lover is radiant and ruddy,
    outstanding among ten thousand.
¹¹His head is purest gold;
    his hair is wavy
    and black as a raven.
¹²His eyes are like doves
    by the water streams,
washed in milk,
    mounted like jewels.
¹³His cheeks are like beds of spice
    yielding perfume.
His lips are like lilies
    dripping with myrrh.
¹⁴His arms are rods of gold
    set with chrysolite.
His body is like polished ivory
    decorated with sapphires.ᵃ
¹⁵His legs are pillars of marble
    set on bases of pure gold.
His appearance is like Lebanon,
    choice as its cedars.
¹⁶His mouth is sweetness itself;
    he is altogether lovely.
This is my lover, this my friend,
    O daughters of Jerusalem.

Friends

6 Where has your lover gone,
    most beautiful of women?
Which way did your lover turn,
    that we may look for him with
      you?

Beloved

²My lover has gone down to his
      garden,
    to the beds of spices,

to browse in the gardens
    and to gather lilies.
³I am my lover's and my lover is
      mine;
    he browses among the lilies.

Lover

⁴You are beautiful, my darling, as
      Tirzah,
    lovely as Jerusalem,
    majestic as troops with banners.
⁵Turn your eyes from me;
    they overwhelm me.
Your hair is like a flock of goats
    descending from Gilead.
⁶Your teeth are like a flock of sheep
    coming up from the washing.
Each has its twin,
    not one of them is alone.
⁷Your temples behind your veil
    are like the halves of a
      pomegranate.
⁸Sixty queens there may be,
    and eighty concubines,
    and virgins beyond number;
⁹but my dove, my perfect one, is
      unique,
    the only daughter of her mother,
    the favorite of the one who bore
      her.
The maidens saw her and called her
      blessed;
    the queens and concubines praised
      her.

Friends

¹⁰Who is this that appears like the
      dawn,
    fair as the moon, bright as the sun,
    majestic as the stars in procession?

Lover

¹¹I went down to the grove of nut trees
    to look at the new growth in the
      valley,
    to see if the vines had budded
    or the pomegranates were in
      bloom.
¹²Before I realized it,
    my desire set me among the royal
      chariots of my people.ᵇ

Friends

¹³Come back, come back,
    O Shulammite;

---

a 14 Or *lapis lazuli*   *b 12* Or *among the chariots
of Amminadab;* or *among the chariots of the people
of the prince*

come back, come back, that we
    may gaze on you!

Lover

Why would you gaze on the
    Shulammite
as on the dance of Mahanaim?

7 How beautiful your sandaled feet,
    O prince's daughter!
Your graceful legs are like jewels,
    the work of a craftsman's hands.
2Your navel is a rounded goblet
    that never lacks blended wine.
Your waist is a mound of wheat
    encircled by lilies.
3Your breasts are like two fawns,
    twins of a gazelle.
4Your neck is like an ivory tower.
Your eyes are the pools of Heshbon
    by the gate of Bath Rabbim.
Your nose is like the tower of
    Lebanon
    looking toward Damascus.
5Your head crowns you like Mount
    Carmel.
    Your hair is like royal tapestry;
    the king is held captive by its
    tresses.
6How beautiful you are and how
    pleasing,
    O love, with your delights!
7Your stature is like that of the palm,
    and your breasts like clusters of
    fruit.
8I said, "I will climb the palm tree;
    I will take hold of its fruit."
May your breasts be like the clusters
    of the vine,
    the fragrance of your breath like
    apples,
9   and your mouth like the best wine.

Beloved

May the wine go straight to my lover,
    flowing gently over lips and
    teeth. *a*
10I belong to my lover,
    and his desire is for me.
11Come, my lover, let us go to the
    countryside,
    let us spend the night in the
    villages. *b*
12Let us go early to the vineyards
    to see if the vines have budded,
    if their blossoms have opened,
    and if the pomegranates are in
    bloom—
    there I will give you my love.

13The mandrakes send out their
    fragrance,
    and at our door is every delicacy,
both new and old,
    that I have stored up for you, my
    lover.

8 If only you were to me like a
    brother,
    who was nursed at my mother's
    breasts!
Then, if I found you outside,
    I would kiss you,
    and no one would despise me.
2I would lead you
    and bring you to my mother's
    house—
    she who has taught me.
I would give you spiced wine to
    drink,
    the nectar of my pomegranates.
3His left arm is under my head
    and his right arm embraces me.
4Daughters of Jerusalem, I charge you:
    Do not arouse or awaken love
    until it so desires.

Friends

5Who is this coming up from the
    desert
    leaning on her lover?

Beloved

Under the apple tree I roused you;
    there your mother conceived you,
    there she who was in labor gave
    you birth.
6Place me like a seal over your heart,
    like a seal on your arm;
for love is as strong as death,
    its jealousy*c* unyielding as the
    grave.*d*
It burns like blazing fire,
    like a mighty flame.*e*
7Many waters cannot quench love;
    rivers cannot wash it away.
If one were to give
    all the wealth of his house for
    love,
    it*f* would be utterly scorned.

Friends

8We have a young sister,
    and her breasts are not yet grown.
What shall we do for our sister

*a9 Septuagint, Aquila, Vulgate and Syriac; Hebrew
lips of sleepers   b11 Or henna bushes   c6 Or
ardor   d6 Hebrew Sheol   e6 Or / like the very
flame of the LORD   f7 Or he*

Read Song of Songs 6:1—8:7
Key Verse Song of Songs 8:6

Tending the Fire

Song of Songs is a poem of passionate, sensual, true love that praises the gift of sexuality God has given us. It is the expression of the
intimate relationship God had in mind when he created man and
woman at the beginning of time and declared, "this was very good."
Song of Songs 8:6 suggests that this is no merely dutiful relationship; this kind of love no more gives up the lover than the grave
gives up the dead! The writer likens it to a blazing fire, a mighty
flame. Sounds like the movies! But this kind of love doesn't die
when the credits roll; the writer uses an expression suggesting that
this kind of love is kindled by God. It reflects the same enduring
and self-giving love that God has shown to us.

Even so, a fire needs careful tending. It has to be fed, the logs
rearranged, and the embers stirred up. With such care, the passion
of the initial intense attraction matures into a passionate commitment to love and serve each other sacrificially and tenaciously.
Tending a marriage, like tending a fire, is hard work but well worth
it. This kind of love is meant to keep two people warm for a lifetime!

Digging Into the Word
1. What do the following passages say about God's love?—*John
   15:12–13; Romans 5:8; 1 John 3:16*
2. God wants us to know the difference between true love and
   infatuation. Read 1 Corinthians 13:4–7 and list as many characteristics of real love as you can find.

Action Challenge
Choose two of the characteristics of love listed in 1 Corinthians 13
and commit yourself to seek to develop these in your life. What
needs to happen for you to develop these characteristics in the
relationships you have with those you love?

One Step Deeper
Genesis 29:16–20; Song of Songs 8:7

Go to page 757 for your next devotional reading.

for the day she is spoken for?
⁹If she is a wall,
  we will build towers of silver on
    her.
 If she is a door,
  we will enclose her with panels of
    cedar.

Beloved

¹⁰I am a wall,
  and my breasts are like towers.
Thus I have become in his eyes
  like one bringing contentment.
¹¹Solomon had a vineyard in Baal
    Hamon;
  he let out his vineyard to tenants.
Each was to bring for its fruit
  a thousand shekels*a* of silver.
¹²But my own vineyard is mine to give;

the thousand shekels are for you,
    O Solomon,
and two hundred*b* are for those
  who tend its fruit.

Lover

¹³You who dwell in the gardens
  with friends in attendance,
  let me hear your voice!

Beloved

¹⁴Come away, my lover,
  and be like a gazelle
 or like a young stag
  on the spice-laden mountains.

a 11 That is, about 25 pounds (about 11.5 kilograms); also in verse 12   *b 12* That is, about 5 pounds (about 2.3 kilograms) *hrough the visions God gave him, Isaiah unveils the full dimensions of God's judgment against sin in images of destruction and death that are difficult to read and even more difficult to think about. But the prophet also paints a picture of comfort, redemption and restoration for those who put their hope in God. Many of Isaiah's most stirring prophecies are those that predict the coming of the Messiah, the One who is to restore and redeem the earth—and his people—to the divine ideal so that the God of Israel will be praised and glorified.*

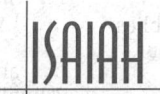

ISAIAH

1

The vision concerning Judah and Jerusalem that Isaiah son of Amoz saw during the reigns of Uzziah, Jotham, Ahaz and Hezekiah, kings of Judah.

A Rebellious Nation

²Hear, O heavens! Listen, O earth!
    For the LORD has spoken:
"I reared children and brought them up,
    but they have rebelled against me.
³The ox knows his master,
    the donkey his owner's manger,
but Israel does not know,
    my people do not understand."

⁴Ah, sinful nation,
    a people loaded with guilt,
a brood of evildoers,
    children given to corruption!
They have forsaken the LORD;
    they have spurned the Holy One of
        Israel
    and turned their backs on him.

⁵Why should you be beaten anymore?
    Why do you persist in rebellion?
Your whole head is injured,
    your whole heart afflicted.
⁶From the sole of your foot to the top
        of your head
    there is no soundness—
only wounds and welts
    and open sores,
not cleansed or bandaged
    or soothed with oil.

⁷Your country is desolate,
    your cities burned with fire;

your fields are being stripped by
  foreigners
right before you,
laid waste as when overthrown by
  strangers.
⁸The Daughter of Zion is left
  like a shelter in a vineyard,
like a hut in a field of melons,
like a city under siege.
⁹Unless the LORD Almighty
  had left us some survivors,
we would have become like Sodom,
we would have been like
  Gomorrah.

¹⁰Hear the word of the LORD,
  you rulers of Sodom;
listen to the law of our God,
  you people of Gomorrah!
¹¹"The multitude of your sacrifices—
  what are they to me?" says the
    LORD.
"I have more than enough of burnt
  offerings,
of rams and the fat of fattened
  animals;
I have no pleasure
  in the blood of bulls and lambs
    and goats.
¹²When you come to appear before me,
  who has asked this of you,
this trampling of my courts?
¹³Stop bringing meaningless offerings!
  Your incense is detestable to me.
New Moons, Sabbaths and
  convocations—
I cannot bear your evil assemblies.
¹⁴Your New Moon festivals and your
  appointed feasts
my soul hates.
They have become a burden to me;
  I am weary of bearing them.
¹⁵When you spread out your hands in
  prayer,
I will hide my eyes from you;
even if you offer many prayers,
  I will not listen.
Your hands are full of blood;
¹⁶ wash and make yourselves clean.
Take your evil deeds
  out of my sight!
Stop doing wrong,
¹⁷ learn to do right!
Seek justice,
  encourage the oppressed.ᵃ
Defend the cause of the fatherless,
  plead the case of the widow.

¹⁸"Come now, let us reason together,"
  says the LORD.

"Though your sins are like scarlet,
  they shall be as white as snow;
though they are red as crimson,
  they shall be like wool.
¹⁹If you are willing and obedient,
  you will eat the best from the land;
²⁰but if you resist and rebel,
  you will be devoured by the
    sword."
      For the mouth of the LORD
        has spoken.

²¹See how the faithful city
  has become a harlot!
She once was full of justice;
  righteousness used to dwell in
    her—
but now murderers!
²²Your silver has become dross,
  your choice wine is diluted with
    water.
²³Your rulers are rebels,
  companions of thieves;
they all love bribes
  and chase after gifts.
They do not defend the cause of the
  fatherless;
the widow's case does not come
  before them.
²⁴Therefore the Lord, the LORD
  Almighty,
  the Mighty One of Israel, declares:
"Ah, I will get relief from my foes
  and avenge myself on my enemies.
²⁵I will turn my hand against you;
  I will thoroughly purge away your
    dross
and remove all your impurities.
²⁶I will restore your judges as in days
  of old,
  your counselors as at the
    beginning.
Afterward you will be called
  the City of Righteousness,
  the Faithful City."

²⁷Zion will be redeemed with justice,
  her penitent ones with
    righteousness.
²⁸But rebels and sinners will both be
  broken,
  and those who forsake the LORD
    will perish.

²⁹"You will be ashamed because of the
  sacred oaks
  in which you have delighted;

ᵃ17 Or / rebuke the oppressor

PERSPECTIVES FROM THE BIBLE

What to Read When:

The Future Seems Hopeless—Isaiah 54:1–7; Lamentations 3:19–24; 1 Corinthians 15:20–28; 1 Peter 1:1–9; 1 Peter 5:10–11;Revelation 11:15–19

You Are Seeking God's Direction—1 Kings 3:1–14; Proverbs 2:1–6; Romans 12:1–3; Ephesians 5:15–17; Colossians 1:9–14; James 1:5–8

You Need Comfort—Isaiah 12; Isaiah 40:1–11; Jeremiah 31:10–13; 2 Corinthians 1:3–7; 2 Corinthians 7:6–13

Others Disagree with You—Matthew 7:1–5; Romans 12:9–21; Romans 14:1–15:7; 2 Corinthians 5:11–21

The World Seems Enticing—Genesis 3:1–7; Ecclesiastes 2:1–11; 2 Corinthians 6:14–7:1; James 1:26–27; James 4:4–10; 1 John 2:15–17

You Need Assurance of Salvation—Psalm 91:14–16; Micah 7:18–20; John 3:14–21; John 11:25–26; Acts 16:31–34; 1 John 5:9–13

Others Have Offended You—Genesis 33:1–4; Genesis 50:15–20; Matthew 6:14–15; Matthew 18:21–35; Colossians 3:12–14; James 2:12–13

You Are Tempted to Be Bitter—Psalm 4; Psalm 73; Proverbs 16:32; 1 Corinthians 13; Ephesians 4:29–5:2; Hebrews 12:14–15

You Are Tempted to Neglect Corporate Worship—Exodus 20:8–11; Psalm 95:1–7; Acts 2:42–47; Hebrews 10:19–25

Your Faith Needs Strengthening—Genesis 15:1–6; Proverbs 3:5–9; Romans 5:1–11; 1 Corinthians 9:24–27; Hebrews 10:19–25, 35–39; Hebrews 11:1–12:13

You Need to Control Your Tongue—Psalm 39:1; Proverbs 10:18–20; Matthew 15:1–20; James 3:1–12

You Are Prone to Judge Others—Matthew 7:1–5; 1 Corinthians 4:1–5; James 2:1–13; James 4:11–12

You Have Been Cheated—Genesis 33:1–4; Matthew 18:15–17; 1 Corinthians 6:1–8; James 5:1–8

Things Are Going Well—Job 31:24–28; Proverbs 15:27; Luke 12:13–21; 1 Timothy 6:3–19; Hebrews 13:5; James 2:1–17

You Wonder About Your Spiritual Gifts—Romans 12:3–8; 1 Corinthians 1:4–9; 1 Corinthians 12:1–14:25; 1 Peter 4:7–11

You Are Starting a New Job—1 Kings 3:1–14; Proverbs 10:4–5; Matthew 5:13–16; Romans 12:1–2; Galatians 5:13–26; Ephesians 1:3–14

You Are in a Position of Responsibility—1 Kings 3:1–14; Proverbs 3:21–27; Mark 10:35–45; Luke 7:1–10; 1 Corinthians 16:13–14; Galatians 6:9–10

You Are Establishing a New Home—Genesis 2:19–25; Ecclesiastes 9:7–10; Ephesians 5:22–33; 1 Peter 3:1–7

CONTINUED ON NEXT PAGE

What to Read When:

You Are Involved in Conflict—Genesis
13:5–11; Psalm 133; 1 Corinthians 3; Ephesians
4:1–6, 4:15–5:2; 2 Timothy 2:14–26; James
4:1–12

You Are Challenged by Dark Forces—
Joshua 1:6–9; Psalm 56:1–4; Romans 8:38–39;
2 Corinthians 4:7–18; Ephesians 6:10–18;
2 Timothy 4:3–7

You Are Jealous—Numbers 12:1–15;
Numbers 16:1–35; Galatians 5:13–15, 19–21;
James 3:13–18;

You Struggle with Laziness—Proverbs
6:6–11; Proverbs 10:4–5; Ephesians 5:15–16;
Philippians 2:12–13; 1 Thessalonians 4:11–12;
2 Thessalonians 3:6–15

You Struggle with Lust—Deuteronomy
22:22–24; 2 Samuel 11:1–12:14; Matthew
5:27–30; Romans 13:8–14; James 1:13–18

You Are Angry—Genesis 4:1–12; Psalm 4:4;
Matthew 5:21–22; Matthew 18:21–35;
Ephesians 4:25–5:2; James 1:19–21

You Desire Revenge—Deuteronomy
32:34–35; Psalm 94:1; Proverbs 25:21–22;
Matthew 5:38–42; Romans 12:17–21;
1 Thessalonians 5:12–15; 1 Peter 3:8–14

You Are Proud—Proverbs 8:12–14; Matthew
25:34–40; Mark 10:35–45; Romans 12:3;
Philippians 2:1–11

You Struggle with Addiction—Psalm
18:28–36; Proverbs 23:29–35; Romans
6:1–23; Romans 12:1–2; 1 Corinthians
6:12–20; Philippians 3:17–4:1

You Are Greedy—Psalm 62:1–2,10;
Ecclesiastes 2:1–11; Luke 12:13–21;
2 Corinthians 9:6–15; Ephesians 5:3–7; 1 John
3:16–18

You Want to Learn How to Pray—
2 Chronicles 6:13–42; 2 Chronicles 20:5–12;
Matthew 6:5–15; Mark 11:22–25; Luke
18:9–14; Philippians 4:4–7

You Struggle with Apathy—Numbers
25:10–13; Ecclesiastes 9:10; Matthew 25:1–13;
Luke 12:35–48; 1 Thessalonians 5:1–11;
Revelation 3:1–6,14–22

PERSPECTIVES FROM THE BIBLE

What the Bible Says About:

Adultery—Exodus 20:14; Leviticus 20:10; Deuteronomy 22:22–24; Matthew 5:27–32; Galatians 5:13–26; Ephesians 4:17–5:3

Ambition—1 Kings 3:5–12; Haggai 1:2–8; Matthew 16:21–27; Mark 9:33–37; Mark 10:35–45; Philippians 2:1–4

Anger—Genesis 4:1–12; Psalm 4:4; Psalm 38:7–9; Proverbs 16:32; Matthew 5:21–26; Ephesians 4:25–5:2; James 1:19–27

Anxiety—Psalm 94:17–19; Ecclesiastes 2:22–25; Luke 12:22–34; Philippians 4:4–9; Hebrews 13:5–6

Baptism—Matthew 3:1–12; Matthew 28:16–20; Romans 6:1–5

Bible Reading—Nehemiah 8:1–6; Psalm 1; 2 Timothy 3:14–17; Hebrews 4:12; James 1:19–27

Christ's Body and Blood—Matthew 26:27–29; Hebrews 9:11–28

Body of Christ—1 Corinthians 12:12–31; Ephesians 5:23; Colossians 1:24

Celibacy—Matthew 19:4–12; 1 Corinthians 7:32–40; 1 Timothy 4:1–5

Children—Psalm 78:1–7; Psalm 127; Psalm 128; Matthew 18:1–9; Mark 10:13–16; Ephesians 6:1–4

Compassion—Psalm 103:8–12; Psalm 116:5–6; Micah 6:8; John 11:17–44; 2 Corinthians 1:3–7; 1 John 3:11–24

Conversion—Deuteronomy 4:30–31; 2 Chronicles 7:14; Ezekiel 18:30–32; John 3:1–21; 2 Corinthians 5:17–19; Ephesians 2:1–10

Creation—Genesis 1–2; Psalm 8; Psalm 19; Psalm 104; Romans 1:18–23; Romans 8:18–27; Colossians 1:15–17

Cross—Mark 8:31–9:1; Luke 23:26–49

Death—Psalm 116:15–16; Isaiah 57:1–2; John 12:23–26; Romans 6:1–23; 1 Corinthians 15

Discipleship—Luke 14:25–33; John 15:1–17; John 21:15–19

Discipline—Proverbs 3:11–12; Proverbs 13:24; 1 Corinthians 11:27–32;Hebrews 12:1–13; Revelation 3:19

Divorce—Deuteronomy 24:1–4; Malachi 2:13–16; Matthew 19:1–12; Mark 10:2–12; 1 Corinthians 7:10–16

Eternal Life—Job 19:25–27; Psalm 23; Matthew 19:16–30; John 3:1–21; Romans 6:15–23

Faith—Genesis 15:1–6; Psalm 119:65–72; Proverbs 3:5–6; Matthew 6:25–34; Romans 3:21–5:11; Hebrews 11

Freedom—John 8:31–42; Romans 8:1–17; Galatians 4:21–5:26

Friendship—Proverbs 17:17; Proverbs 27:6; Ecclesiastes 4:9–12; John 14:23–15:17; Colossians 3:12–17; 1 John 1:1–7

Giving—Deuteronomy 15:7–11; Proverbs 3:9; Malachi 3:10–12; Matthew 6:1–4; 2 Corinthians 8—9

Grace—Psalm 86; Psalm 103; Micah 7:18–20; Luke 15:11–31; Romans 5; Ephesians 2

Greed—1 Kings 21:1–22; Proverbs 15:27; Luke 12:13–21; 1 Timothy 6:3–10; James 5:1–6

Happiness—Psalm 33; Isaiah 12; Isaiah 52:7–10; Matthew 5:1–12; John 13:1–17; Philippians 4:4–9

Heaven—1 Kings 8:23–30; Isaiah 65:17–25; Matthew 6:19–24; Matthew 25:31–46; Philippians 3:12–4:1; Revelation 21

CONTINUED ON NEXT PAGE

What the Bible Says About:

Holy Spirit—Isaiah 61:1–3; Joel 2:28–32; John 14:15–31; John 16:5–16; Acts 2; Romans 8:1–17

Homosexuality—Leviticus 18:22; Leviticus 20;13; Romans 1:18–32; 1 Corinthians 6:9–11; 1 Timothy 1:9–11

Hope—Psalm 42; Psalm 130; Romans 5:1–11; Colossians 1:3–27; 1 Peter 1:3–9

Hospitality—Genesis 18:1–8; 2 Samuel 9:1–7; Luke 14:12–14; Romans 12:13; 1 Peter 4:9

Hypocrisy—1 Samuel 12:1–23; Isaiah 1:10–15; Zechariah 7:2–14; Matthew 6:1–24; Matthew 23; James 1:22–27

Joy—Isaiah 12; Isaiah 52:7–10; Luke 15; James 1:2–18; 1 Peter 4:12–19

Loneliness—1 Kings 19:1–18; Psalm 41; Matthew 26:36–46; 2 Timothy 4:16–18

Lord's Supper—Luke 22:7–23; John 13; 1 Corinthians 11:17–34

Love—Leviticus 19:18,34; Deuteronomy 6:1–5; Song of Songs 1–2; Mark 12:28–34; 1 Corinthians 13; 1 John 4:7–21

Marriage—Genesis 2:19–25; Ecclesiastes 9:7–10; Matthew 19:1–12; 1 Corinthians 7; Ephesians 5:22–33

Peace—Numbers 6:24–26; Psalm 122; Isaiah 9:2–7; John 14:25–27; Romans 5:1–11; Ephesians 2:14–18; Philippians 4:4–9

Poor—Deuteronomy 15:1–11; Isaiah 58:1–9; Amos 5:11–15; Matthew 25:31–46; Luke 1:39–56; James 2:1–13

Profanity—Exodus 20:7; Leviticus 24:10–16; Proverbs 30:10–14; Ephesians 4:29–32; James 3:1–12

Reconciliation—Genesis 33:1–4; Genesis 50:15–21; Matthew 5:23–26; 2 Corinthians 5:11–6:2; Ephesians 2:11–22

Repentance—Deuteronomy 4:30–31; 2 Chronicles 7:14; Ezekiel 18:30–32; Matthew 4:12–17; Luke 18:9–14; Acts 2:38–41

Resurrection—Job 19:23–27; Psalm 16; Daniel 12:1–4; Matthew 27:57–28:20; 1 Corinthians 15

Revenge—Deuteronomy 32:34–35; Psalm 94:1; Proverbs 25:21–22; Matthew 5:38–47; Romans 12:17–21

Reward—Leviticus 26:3–39; Psalm 19:1–11; Isaiah 61:8–11; Matthew 5:3–12; Mark 10:29–31; 1 Corinthians 3:10–15

Salvation—Exodus 15:1–18; Psalm 62; Isaiah 59:15–20; Luke 19:1–10; Acts 16:16–34; Ephesians 2:1–10

Sanctification—2 Corinthians 7:1; 1 Thessalonians 5:23; 2 Peter 1:3–11

Second Coming—Matthew 24; John 14:1–4; 1 Corinthians 15:12–28; 1 Thessalonians 4:13–5:11

Stewardship—1 Chronicles 29:1–9; Matthew 25:14–30; Luke 12:35–48

Suffering—Deuteronomy 8:1–5; Job 1–2; Psalm 77; Isaiah 53; Romans 8:12–17; 1 Peter 3:8–22; 1 Peter 4:12–19

Unity—Psalm 133; John 17; Ephesians 4:1–16

you will be disgraced because of the
         gardens
    that you have chosen.
30You will be like an oak with fading
         leaves,
    like a garden without water.
31The mighty man will become tinder
    and his work a spark;
both will burn together,
    with no one to quench the fire."

The Mountain of the LORD

2 This is what Isaiah son of Amoz saw
concerning Judah and Jerusalem:

   2In the last days

the mountain of the LORD's temple
         will be established
    as chief among the mountains;
it will be raised above the hills,
    and all nations will stream to it.

3Many peoples will come and say,

"Come, let us go up to the mountain
         of the LORD,
    to the house of the God of Jacob.
He will teach us his ways,
    so that we may walk in his paths."
The law will go out from Zion,
    the word of the LORD from
         Jerusalem.
4He will judge between the nations
    and will settle disputes for many
         peoples.
They will beat their swords into
         plowshares
    and their spears into pruning
         hooks.
Nation will not take up sword against
         nation,
    nor will they train for war
         anymore.

5Come, O house of Jacob,
    let us walk in the light of the LORD.

MONDAY

Read *Isaiah 1:1–31*
Key Verse *Isaiah 1:18*

Really Clean! —Eric Resler

One morning at a student retreat a friend pulled me aside to talk. He had recently come to know God after spending several fruitless years exploring Buddhism. After some personal Bible study, he was worried. He had read how God does not want us to pursue other gods, yet he had spent extended time "serving other gods," as he put it. This young man had asked the Lord to forgive his sins, but he wanted to know what he needed to do to make up for his disobedience. He felt that he had to earn forgiveness for this, his "biggest sin."

I shared with him many passages about God's forgiveness and unconditional love, but for him Isaiah 1:18 painted the best mental picture. Our sin is like a "scarlet" stain on our soul, but Jesus Christ's sacrifice on our behalf makes it "as white as snow." That is really clean! When we confess our sins and rely on God for forgiveness, he separates us from our sin and removes it from us completely.

God doesn't turn the stain of sin to a faded pink that we need to scrub until it passes for white. God does all the work and turns the stain of our sin a "blinding" white. This unconditional gift is one we simply receive. Though we may live with the consequences of our sin, or even with reminders of the past, we are totally forgiven, my friend included.

A Deeper Look
Psalm 103:12; John 15:3; Revelation 19:14

Go to page 762 for your next devotional reading.

The Day of the LORD

⁶You have abandoned your people,
　　the house of Jacob.
They are full of superstitions from the
　　East;
　　they practice divination like the
　　　　Philistines
and clasp hands with pagans.
⁷Their land is full of silver and gold;
　　there is no end to their treasures.
Their land is full of horses;
　　there is no end to their chariots.
⁸Their land is full of idols;
　　they bow down to the work of
　　　　their hands,
　　to what their fingers have made.
⁹So man will be brought low
　　and mankind humbled—
　　do not forgive them.ᵃ

¹⁰Go into the rocks,
　　hide in the ground
from dread of the LORD
　　and the splendor of his majesty!
¹¹The eyes of the arrogant man will be
　　humbled
　　and the pride of men brought low;
the LORD alone will be exalted in that
　　day.

¹²The LORD Almighty has a day in store
　　for all the proud and lofty,
　　for all that is exalted
　　　(and they will be humbled),
¹³for all the cedars of Lebanon, tall and
　　lofty,
　　and all the oaks of Bashan,
¹⁴for all the towering mountains
　　and all the high hills,
¹⁵for every lofty tower
　　and every fortified wall,
¹⁶for every trading shipᵇ
　　and every stately vessel.
¹⁷The arrogance of man will be brought
　　low
　　and the pride of men humbled;
the LORD alone will be exalted in that
　　day,
¹⁸　and the idols will totally disappear.

¹⁹Men will flee to caves in the rocks
　　and to holes in the ground
from dread of the LORD
　　and the splendor of his majesty,
　　when he rises to shake the earth.
²⁰In that day men will throw away
　　to the rodents and bats
their idols of silver and idols of gold,
　　which they made to worship.
²¹They will flee to caverns in the rocks

and to the overhanging crags
from dread of the LORD
　　and the splendor of his majesty,
　　when he rises to shake the earth.

²²Stop trusting in man,
　　who has but a breath in his
　　　　nostrils.
Of what account is he?

Judgment on Jerusalem and Judah

3 See now, the Lord,
　　the LORD Almighty,
is about to take from Jerusalem and
　　Judah
　　both supply and support:
all supplies of food and all supplies of
　　water,
² 　the hero and warrior,
　　the judge and prophet,
　　the soothsayer and elder,
³the captain of fifty and man of rank,
　　the counselor, skilled craftsman
　　and clever enchanter.

⁴I will make boys their officials;
　　mere children will govern them.
⁵People will oppress each other—
　　man against man, neighbor against
　　　　neighbor.
The young will rise up against the
　　old,
　　the base against the honorable.

⁶A man will seize one of his brothers
　　at his father's home, and say,
"You have a cloak, you be our leader;
　　take charge of this heap of ruins!"
⁷But in that day he will cry out,
　　"I have no remedy.
I have no food or clothing in my
　　house;
　　do not make me the leader of the
　　　　people."

⁸Jerusalem staggers,
　　Judah is falling;
their words and deeds are against the
　　LORD,
　　defying his glorious presence.
⁹The look on their faces testifies
　　against them;
　　they parade their sin like Sodom;
　　they do not hide it.
Woe to them!
　　They have brought disaster upon
　　　　themselves.

ᵃ9 Or *not raise them up*　　ᵇ16 Hebrew *every ship
of Tarshish*

¹⁰Tell the righteous it will be well with
them,
for they will enjoy the fruit of their
deeds.
¹¹Woe to the wicked! Disaster is upon
them!
They will be paid back for what their
hands have done.

¹²Youths oppress my people,
women rule over them.
O my people, your guides lead you
astray;
they turn you from the path.

¹³The LORD takes his place in court;
he rises to judge the people.
¹⁴The LORD enters into judgment
against the elders and leaders of
his people:
"It is you who have ruined my
vineyard;
the plunder from the poor is in
your houses.
¹⁵What do you mean by crushing my
people
and grinding the faces of the
poor?"
declares the Lord,
the LORD Almighty.

¹⁶The LORD says,
"The women of Zion are haughty,
walking along with outstretched
necks,
flirting with their eyes,
tripping along with mincing steps,
with ornaments jingling on their
ankles.
¹⁷Therefore the Lord will bring sores on
the heads of the women of
Zion;
the LORD will make their scalps
bald."

¹⁸In that day the Lord will snatch away
their finery: the bangles and headbands
and crescent necklaces, ¹⁹the earrings
and bracelets and veils, ²⁰the head-
dresses and ankle chains and sashes, the
perfume bottles and charms, ²¹the signet
rings and nose rings, ²²the fine robes and
the capes and cloaks, the purses ²³and
mirrors, and the linen garments and ti-
aras and shawls.

²⁴Instead of fragrance there will be a
stench;
instead of a sash, a rope;
instead of well-dressed hair,
baldness;

instead of fine clothing, sackcloth;
instead of beauty, branding.
²⁵Your men will fall by the sword,
your warriors in battle.
²⁶The gates of Zion will lament and
mourn;
destitute, she will sit on the
ground.

4 In that day seven women
will take hold of one man
and say, "We will eat our own food
and provide our own clothes;
only let us be called by your name.
Take away our disgrace!"

The Branch of the LORD

²In that day the Branch of the LORD will
be beautiful and glorious, and the fruit of
the land will be the pride and glory of the
survivors in Israel. ³Those who are left in
Zion, who remain in Jerusalem, will be
called holy, all who are recorded among
the living in Jerusalem. ⁴The Lord will
wash away the filth of the women of
Zion; he will cleanse the bloodstains
from Jerusalem by a spirit[a] of judgment
and a spirit[a] of fire. ⁵Then the LORD will
create over all of Mount Zion and over
those who assemble there a cloud of
smoke by day and a glow of flaming fire
by night; over all the glory will be a canopy. ⁶It will be a shelter and shade from
the heat of the day, and a refuge and hiding place from the storm and rain.

The Song of the Vineyard

5 I will sing for the one I love
a song about his vineyard:
My loved one had a vineyard
on a fertile hillside.
²He dug it up and cleared it of stones
and planted it with the choicest
vines.
He built a watchtower in it
and cut out a winepress as well.
Then he looked for a crop of good
grapes,
but it yielded only bad fruit.

³"Now you dwellers in Jerusalem and
men of Judah,
judge between me and my
vineyard.
⁴What more could have been done for
my vineyard
than I have done for it?
When I looked for good grapes,
why did it yield only bad?

a4 Or the Spirit

⁵Now I will tell you
  what I am going to do to my
    vineyard:
I will take away its hedge,
  and it will be destroyed;
I will break down its wall,
  and it will be trampled.
⁶I will make it a wasteland,
  neither pruned nor cultivated,
  and briers and thorns will grow
    there.
I will command the clouds
  not to rain on it."

⁷The vineyard of the LORD Almighty
  is the house of Israel,
and the men of Judah
  are the garden of his delight.
And he looked for justice, but saw
    bloodshed;
  for righteousness, but heard cries
    of distress.

Woes and Judgments

⁸Woe to you who add house to house
  and join field to field
till no space is left
  and you live alone in the land.

⁹The LORD Almighty has declared in my
hearing:

"Surely the great houses will become
    desolate,
  the fine mansions left without
    occupants.
¹⁰A ten-acreᵃ vineyard will produce
    only a bathᵇ of wine,
  a homerᶜ of seed only an ephahᵈ
    of grain."

¹¹Woe to those who rise early in the
    morning
  to run after their drinks,
who stay up late at night
  till they are inflamed with wine.
¹²They have harps and lyres at their
    banquets,
  tambourines and flutes and wine,
but they have no regard for the deeds
    of the LORD,
  no respect for the work of his
    hands.
¹³Therefore my people will go into exile
  for lack of understanding;
their men of rank will die of hunger
  and their masses will be parched
    with thirst.
¹⁴Therefore the graveᵉ enlarges its
    appetite
  and opens its mouth without limit;

into it will descend their nobles and
    masses
  with all their brawlers and
    revelers.
¹⁵So man will be brought low
  and mankind humbled,
  the eyes of the arrogant humbled.
¹⁶But the LORD Almighty will be exalted
    by his justice,
  and the holy God will show
    himself holy by his
    righteousness.
¹⁷Then sheep will graze as in their own
    pasture;
  lambs will feedᶠ among the ruins
    of the rich.

¹⁸Woe to those who draw sin along
    with cords of deceit,
  and wickedness as with cart ropes,
¹⁹to those who say, "Let God hurry,
  let him hasten his work
  so we may see it.
Let it approach,
  let the plan of the Holy One of
    Israel come,
  so we may know it."

²⁰Woe to those who call evil good
    and good evil,
who put darkness for light
    and light for darkness,
who put bitter for sweet
    and sweet for bitter.

ᵃ10 Hebrew *ten-yoke*, that is, the land plowed by
10 yoke of oxen in one day   ᵇ10 That is,
probably about 6 gallons (about 22 liters)
ᶜ10 That is, probably about 6 bushels (about 220
liters)   ᵈ10 That is, probably about 3/5 bushel
(about 22 liters)   ᵉ14 Hebrew *Sheol*
ᶠ17 Septuagint; Hebrew / *strangers will eat*

POINT OF INTEREST   Isaiah 5:11

History has recorded the
night life of many "party
animals," and the conse-
quences of their actions have
always been painful, destructive and
unavoidable. When you see the Bible begin
a sentence with the word "Woe," think
"Whoa!" Be prepared to consider your own
actions in light of what the Bible says
about questionable behaviors.

²¹Woe to those who are wise in their
  own eyes
  and clever in their own sight.

²²Woe to those who are heroes at
  drinking wine
  and champions at mixing drinks,
²³who acquit the guilty for a bribe,
  but deny justice to the innocent.
²⁴Therefore, as tongues of fire lick up
  straw
  and as dry grass sinks down in the
  flames,
so their roots will decay
  and their flowers blow away like
  dust;
for they have rejected the law of the
  Lord Almighty
  and spurned the word of the Holy
  One of Israel.
²⁵Therefore the Lord's anger burns
  against his people;
  his hand is raised and he strikes
  them down.
The mountains shake,
  and the dead bodies are like refuse
  in the streets.

Yet for all this, his anger is not
  turned away,
  his hand is still upraised.

²⁶He lifts up a banner for the distant
  nations,
  he whistles for those at the ends of
  the earth.
Here they come,
  swiftly and speedily!
²⁷Not one of them grows tired or
  stumbles,
  not one slumbers or sleeps;
not a belt is loosened at the waist,
  not a sandal thong is broken.
²⁸Their arrows are sharp,
  all their bows are strung;
their horses' hoofs seem like flint,
  their chariot wheels like a
  whirlwind.
²⁹Their roar is like that of the lion,
  they roar like young lions;
they growl as they seize their prey
  and carry it off with no one to
  rescue.
³⁰In that day they will roar over it
  like the roaring of the sea.
And if one looks at the land,
  he will see darkness and distress;
  even the light will be darkened by
  the clouds.

Isaiah's Commission

6 In the year that King Uzziah died, I
  saw the Lord seated on a throne, high
and exalted, and the train of his robe
filled the temple. ²Above him were seraphs, each with six wings: With two
wings they covered their faces, with two
they covered their feet, and with
two they were flying. ³And they were
calling to one another:

"Holy, holy, holy is the Lord
  Almighty;
  the whole earth is full of his
  glory."

⁴At the sound of their voices the door-
posts and thresholds shook and the temple was filled with smoke.
  ⁵"Woe to me!" I cried. "I am ruined!
For I am a man of unclean lips, and I live
among a people of unclean lips, and my
eyes have seen the King, the Lord Almighty."
  ⁶Then one of the seraphs flew to me
with a live coal in his hand, which he had
taken with tongs from the altar. ⁷With it
he touched my mouth and said, "See, this
has touched your lips; your guilt is taken
away and your sin atoned for."
  ⁸Then I heard the voice of the Lord
saying, "Whom shall I send? And who
will go for us?"
  And I said, "Here am I. Send me!"
  ⁹He said, "Go and tell this people:

" 'Be ever hearing, but never
  understanding;
  be ever seeing, but never
  perceiving.'
¹⁰Make the heart of this people
  calloused;
  make their ears dull
  and close their eyes.^a
Otherwise they might see with their
  eyes,
  hear with their ears,
  understand with their hearts,
and turn and be healed."

¹¹Then I said, "For how long, O Lord?"
  And he answered:

"Until the cities lie ruined
  and without inhabitant,

^a9,10 Hebrew; Septuagint 'You will be ever hearing,
but never understanding; / you will be ever seeing,
but never perceiving.' / ¹⁰This people's heart has
become calloused; / they hardly hear with their ears,
/ and they have closed their eyes

until the houses are left deserted
and the fields ruined and ravaged,
12until the LORD has sent everyone far
away
and the land is utterly forsaken.
13And though a tenth remains in the
land,
it will again be laid waste.
But as the terebinth and oak
leave stumps when they are cut
down,
so the holy seed will be the stump
in the land."

The Sign of Immanuel

7 When Ahaz son of Jotham, the son of
Uzziah, was king of Judah, King Rezin
of Aram and Pekah son of Remaliah king
of Israel marched up to fight against Jerusalem, but they could not overpower it.
²Now the house of David was told,
"Aram has allied itself with*a* Ephraim";
so the hearts of Ahaz and his people were
shaken, as the trees of the forest are shaken by the wind.

a2 Or *has set up camp in*

TUESDAY

Read *Isaiah 6:1–13*
Key Verse *Isaiah 6:8*

Always Available – Travis Stewart

When my mother used to ask me to do my part of the household
chores, my usual answer was, "At the commercial, Mom." Though I
knew the importance of contributing work around the house and
responding to my parents' efforts to teach me, my inclination was to
grudgingly do what I was asked, and then only when it was convenient. Isn't that typical? Absorbed in our own little worlds, we are
unwilling to move from where we are, unwilling to help meet the
needs of others.

Why, then, when God asked, "Whom shall I send? And who will
go for us?" did Isaiah respond, "Here am I. Send me!" (Isaiah 6:8).
What moved Isaiah to move for God?

Isaiah had seen God—his majesty, glory and holiness. And Isaiah's glimpse of a holy God revealed the depravity of his own condition, the depth of his own impurity. The principle behind Isaiah's
experience still holds true for us today: The more we see of God, the
more clearly we see the mind-boggling differences between God
and ourselves.

When we see ourselves as God sees us and call on him for forgiveness, our lives are transformed and we become motivated to
live for him. By his grace and love and through Jesus' life, death and
resurrection, our guilt is taken away and our sin atoned for. Isaiah's
experience of God's forgiveness moved him to say, "Here am I. Send
me!" I'm available. I'll go wherever you want. I'll do whatever you
ask. Just use me.

Do we need to grow in obedience? We need to experience his
grace. Do we need to develop an unselfish attitude? We need to
understand his forgiveness. Do we want to be increasingly available
to his work? We need to see more of God. When we understand the
great things God has done for us, we become available to God so
that he can do great things through us.

A Deeper Look
1 Samuel 3:2–10; Hebrews 11:8

Go to page 765 for your next devotional reading.

³Then the LORD said to Isaiah, "Go out, you and your son Shear-Jashub,ᵃ to meet Ahaz at the end of the aqueduct of the Upper Pool, on the road to the Washerman's Field. ⁴Say to him, 'Be careful, keep calm and don't be afraid. Do not lose heart because of these two smoldering stubs of firewood—because of the fierce anger of Rezin and Aram and of the son of Remaliah. ⁵Aram, Ephraim and Remaliah's son have plotted your ruin, saying, ⁶"Let us invade Judah; let us tear it apart and divide it among ourselves, and make the son of Tabeel king over it." ⁷Yet this is what the Sovereign LORD says:

" 'It will not take place,
   it will not happen,
⁸for the head of Aram is Damascus,
   and the head of Damascus is only
      Rezin.
Within sixty-five years
   Ephraim will be too shattered to be
      a people.
⁹The head of Ephraim is Samaria,
   and the head of Samaria is only
      Remaliah's son.
If you do not stand firm in your faith,
   you will not stand at all.' "

¹⁰Again the LORD spoke to Ahaz, ¹¹"Ask the LORD your God for a sign, whether in the deepest depths or in the highest heights."

¹²But Ahaz said, "I will not ask; I will not put the LORD to the test."

¹³Then Isaiah said, "Hear now, you house of David! Is it not enough to try the patience of men? Will you try the patience of my God also? ¹⁴Therefore the Lord himself will give youᵇ a sign: The virgin will be with child and will give birth to a son, andᶜ will call him Immanuel.ᵈ ¹⁵He will eat curds and honey when he knows enough to reject the wrong and choose the right. ¹⁶But before the boy knows enough to reject the wrong and choose the right, the land of the two kings you dread will be laid waste. ¹⁷The LORD will bring on you and on your people and on the house of your father a time unlike any since Ephraim broke away from Judah—he will bring the king of Assyria."

¹⁸In that day the LORD will whistle for flies from the distant streams of Egypt and for bees from the land of Assyria. ¹⁹They will all come and settle in the steep ravines and in the crevices in the rocks, on all the thornbushes and at all the water holes. ²⁰In that day the Lord will use a razor hired from beyond the Riverᵉ—the king of Assyria—to shave your head and the hair of your legs, and to take off your beards also. ²¹In that day, a man will keep alive a young cow and two goats. ²²And because of the abundance of the milk they give, he will have curds to eat. All who remain in the land will eat curds and honey. ²³In that day, in every place where there were a thousand vines worth a thousand silver shekels,ᶠ there will be only briers and thorns. ²⁴Men will go there with bow and arrow, for the land will be covered with briers and thorns. ²⁵As for all the hills once cultivated by the hoe, you will no longer go there for fear of the briers and thorns; they will become places where cattle are turned loose and where sheep run.

Assyria, the LORD's Instrument

8 The LORD said to me, "Take a large scroll and write on it with an ordinary pen: Maher-Shalal-Hash-Baz.ᵍ ²And I will call in Uriah the priest and Zechariah son of Jeberekiah as reliable witnesses for me."

³Then I went to the prophetess, and she conceived and gave birth to a son. And the LORD said to me, "Name him Maher-Shalal-Hash-Baz. ⁴Before the boy knows how to say 'My father' or 'My mother,' the wealth of Damascus and the plunder of Samaria will be carried off by the king of Assyria."

⁵The LORD spoke to me again:

⁶"Because this people has rejected
   the gently flowing waters of
      Shiloah
and rejoices over Rezin
   and the son of Remaliah,
⁷therefore the Lord is about to bring
      against them
   the mighty floodwaters of the
      Riverᵉ—
   the king of Assyria with all his
      pomp.
It will overflow all its channels,
   run over all its banks

ᵃ3 Shear-Jashub means a remnant will return.
ᵇ14 The Hebrew is plural.   ᶜ14 Masoretic Text; Dead Sea Scrolls and he or and they
ᵈ14 Immanuel means God with us.
ᵉ20,7 That is, the Euphrates   ᶠ23 That is, about 25 pounds (about 11.5 kilograms)
ᵍ1 Maher-Shalal-Hash-Baz means quick to the plunder, swift to the spoil; also in verse 3.

⁸and sweep on into Judah, swirling
    over it,
  passing through it and reaching up
    to the neck.
Its outspread wings will cover the
    breadth of your land,
  O Immanuel*ª*!"

⁹Raise the war cry,*ᵇ* you nations, and
    be shattered!
  Listen, all you distant lands.
Prepare for battle, and be shattered!
  Prepare for battle, and be
    shattered!
¹⁰Devise your strategy, but it will be
    thwarted;
  propose your plan, but it will not
    stand,
  for God is with us.*ᶜ*

Fear God

¹¹The LORD spoke to me with his strong
hand upon me, warning me not to follow
the way of this people. He said:

¹²"Do not call conspiracy
    everything that these people call
      conspiracy*ᵈ*;
  do not fear what they fear,
    and do not dread it.
¹³The LORD Almighty is the one you are
    to regard as holy,
  he is the one you are to fear,
  he is the one you are to dread,
¹⁴and he will be a sanctuary;
  but for both houses of Israel he
    will be
  a stone that causes men to stumble
    and a rock that makes them fall.
  And for the people of Jerusalem he
    will be
  a trap and a snare.
¹⁵Many of them will stumble;
  they will fall and be broken,
  they will be snared and captured."

¹⁶Bind up the testimony
  and seal up the law among my
    disciples.
¹⁷I will wait for the LORD,
  who is hiding his face from the
    house of Jacob.
  I will put my trust in him.

¹⁸Here am I, and the children the LORD
has given me. We are signs and symbols
in Israel from the LORD Almighty, who
dwells on Mount Zion.

¹⁹When men tell you to consult mediums and spiritists, who whisper and mutter, should not a people inquire of their

God? Why consult the dead on behalf of
the living? ²⁰To the law and to the testimony! If they do not speak according to
this word, they have no light of dawn.
²¹Distressed and hungry, they will roam
through the land; when they are famished, they will become enraged and,
looking upward, will curse their king and
their God. ²²Then they will look toward
the earth and see only distress and darkness and fearful gloom, and they will be
thrust into utter darkness.

To Us a Child Is Born

9 Nevertheless, there will be no more
  gloom for those who were in distress.
In the past he humbled the land of Zebulun and the land of Naphtali, but in the
future he will honor Galilee of the Gentiles, by the way of the sea, along the
Jordan—

²The people walking in darkness
  have seen a great light;
  on those living in the land of the
    shadow of death*ᵉ*
  a light has dawned.
³You have enlarged the nation
  and increased their joy;
  they rejoice before you
    as people rejoice at the harvest,
  as men rejoice
    when dividing the plunder.
⁴For as in the day of Midian's defeat,
  you have shattered
  the yoke that burdens them,
    the bar across their shoulders,
    the rod of their oppressor.
⁵Every warrior's boot used in battle
  and every garment rolled in blood
  will be destined for burning,
    will be fuel for the fire.
⁶For to us a child is born,
    to us a son is given,
  and the government will be on his
    shoulders.
And he will be called
  Wonderful Counselor,*ᶠ* Mighty
    God,
  Everlasting Father, Prince of Peace.
⁷Of the increase of his government
    and peace
  there will be no end.
  He will reign on David's throne

---

*ª*8 *Immanuel* means *God with us.*   *ᵇ*9 Or *Do
your worst*   *ᶜ*10 Hebrew *Immanuel*   *ᵈ*12 Or
*Do not call for a treaty / every time these people call
for a treaty*   *ᵉ*2 Or *land of darkness*   *ᶠ*6 Or
Wonderful, Counselor

and over his kingdom,
establishing and upholding it
   with justice and righteousness
from that time on and forever.
The zeal of the LORD Almighty
   will accomplish this.

The LORD's Anger Against Israel

⁸The Lord has sent a message against
   Jacob;
   it will fall on Israel.
⁹All the people will know it—
   Ephraim and the inhabitants of
      Samaria—
who say with pride
   and arrogance of heart,
¹⁰"The bricks have fallen down,
   but we will rebuild with dressed
      stone;
the fig trees have been felled,

but we will replace them with
   cedars."
¹¹But the LORD has strengthened Rezin's
   foes against them
   and has spurred their enemies on.
¹²Arameans from the east and
      Philistines from the west
have devoured Israel with open
   mouth.

Yet for all this, his anger is not
   turned away,
   his hand is still upraised.

¹³But the people have not returned to
   him who struck them,
nor have they sought the LORD
   Almighty.
¹⁴So the LORD will cut off from Israel
   both head and tail,
both palm branch and reed in a
   single day;

WEDNESDAY

Read *Isaiah 9:1–7*
Key Verse *Isaiah 9:6*

Who Is Jesus? —Greg Bryan

This verse from Isaiah is perhaps one of the most well-known prophecies in the entire Bible. It's a verse that George Frideric Handel memorialized in his famous oratorio, *Messiah*, and a verse that is read every year at countless Christmas worship services. With these words, Isaiah predicted the birth of the Messiah—God in human flesh—hundreds of years before Jesus was born. This passage and others that point to the life, death and resurrection of Jesus force us to consider who Jesus truly was and is.

Was Jesus just a great moral teacher? Few would argue that he was anything less than that. But was he God? Based on this and other passages, many will argue that he was. But to truly answer that question, we must investigate what Jesus taught about himself—that he was, and is, God (John 10:30).

Who do you think Jesus is? If you're not convinced that he's more than just a great moralist, investigate further. Read the Gospels of Matthew, Mark, Luke and John. Ask those who know him as their Savior. You'll discover that he's much more than simply an outstanding human teacher.

If you do believe Jesus is God, ask a classmate or a friend who they think Jesus is and see what kind of conversation begins. Share with your friend Isaiah's prophecy that Jesus will be called "Mighty God, Everlasting Father."

A Deeper Look
Luke 9:18–20; John 1:1–5,14; Colossians 2:9

Go to page 769 for your next devotional reading.

¹⁵the elders and prominent men are the
head,
    the prophets who teach lies are the
tail.
¹⁶Those who guide this people mislead
them,
    and those who are guided are led
astray.
¹⁷Therefore the Lord will take no
pleasure in the young men,
    nor will he pity the fatherless and
widows,
for everyone is ungodly and wicked,
    every mouth speaks vileness.

Yet for all this, his anger is not
turned away,
    his hand is still upraised.

¹⁸Surely wickedness burns like a fire;
    it consumes briers and thorns,
it sets the forest thickets ablaze,
    so that it rolls upward in a column
of smoke.
¹⁹By the wrath of the LORD Almighty
    the land will be scorched
and the people will be fuel for the
fire;
    no one will spare his brother.
²⁰On the right they will devour,
    but still be hungry;
on the left they will eat,
    but not be satisfied.
Each will feed on the flesh of his own
offspring*ª*:
²¹   Manasseh will feed on Ephraim,
    and Ephraim on Manasseh;
together they will turn against
Judah.

Yet for all this, his anger is not
turned away,
    his hand is still upraised.

10 Woe to those who make unjust
laws,
    to those who issue oppressive
decrees,
²to deprive the poor of their rights
    and withhold justice from the
oppressed of my people,
making widows their prey
    and robbing the fatherless.
³What will you do on the day of
reckoning,
    when disaster comes from afar?
To whom will you run for help?
    Where will you leave your riches?

⁴Nothing will remain but to cringe
among the captives
    or fall among the slain.

Yet for all this, his anger is not
turned away,
    his hand is still upraised.

God's Judgment on Assyria

⁵"Woe to the Assyrian, the rod of my
anger,
    in whose hand is the club of my
wrath!
⁶I send him against a godless nation,
    I dispatch him against a people
who anger me,
to seize loot and snatch plunder,
    and to trample them down like
mud in the streets.
⁷But this is not what he intends,
    this is not what he has in mind;
his purpose is to destroy,
    to put an end to many nations.
⁸'Are not my commanders all kings?'
    he says.
⁹   'Has not Calno fared like
Carchemish?
Is not Hamath like Arpad,
    and Samaria like Damascus?
¹⁰As my hand seized the kingdoms of
the idols,
    kingdoms whose images excelled
those of Jerusalem and
Samaria—
¹¹shall I not deal with Jerusalem and
her images
    as I dealt with Samaria and her
idols?' "

¹²When the Lord has finished all his
work against Mount Zion and Jerusalem,
he will say, "I will punish the king of
Assyria for the willful pride of his heart
and the haughty look in his eyes. ¹³For he
says:

" 'By the strength of my hand I have
done this,
    and by my wisdom, because I have
understanding.
I removed the boundaries of nations,
    I plundered their treasures;
    like a mighty one I subdued*ᵇ* their
kings.
¹⁴As one reaches into a nest,
    so my hand reached for the wealth
of the nations;
as men gather abandoned eggs,
    so I gathered all the countries;

a 20 Or *arm*   *b 13* Or / *I subdued the mighty,*

not one flapped a wing,
　　or opened its mouth to chirp.' "

15Does the ax raise itself above him
　　who swings it,
　　or the saw boast against him who
　　　uses it?
As if a rod were to wield him who
　　lifts it up,
　　or a club brandish him who is not
　　　wood!
16Therefore, the Lord, the LORD
　　Almighty,
　　will send a wasting disease upon
　　　his sturdy warriors;
under his pomp a fire will be kindled
　　like a blazing flame.
17The Light of Israel will become a fire,
　　their Holy One a flame;
in a single day it will burn and
　　consume
　　his thorns and his briers.
18The splendor of his forests and fertile
　　fields
　　it will completely destroy,
　　as when a sick man wastes away.
19And the remaining trees of his forests
　　will be so few
　　that a child could write them
　　　down.

The Remnant of Israel

20In that day the remnant of Israel,
　　the survivors of the house of
　　　Jacob,
will no longer rely on him
　　who struck them down
but will truly rely on the LORD,
　　the Holy One of Israel.
21A remnant will return,a a remnant of
　　Jacob
　　will return to the Mighty God.
22Though your people, O Israel, be like
　　the sand by the sea,
　　only a remnant will return.
Destruction has been decreed,
　　overwhelming and righteous.
23The Lord, the LORD Almighty, will
　　carry out
　　the destruction decreed upon the
　　　whole land.

24Therefore, this is what the Lord, the
LORD Almighty, says:

"O my people who live in Zion,
　　do not be afraid of the Assyrians,
who beat you with a rod
　　and lift up a club against you, as
　　　Egypt did.

25Very soon my anger against you will
　　end
and my wrath will be directed to
　　their destruction."

26The LORD Almighty will lash them
　　with a whip,
　　as when he struck down Midian at
　　　the rock of Oreb;
and he will raise his staff over the
　　waters,
　　as he did in Egypt.
27In that day their burden will be lifted
　　from your shoulders,
　　their yoke from your neck;
the yoke will be broken
　　because you have grown so fat.b

28They enter Aiath;
　　they pass through Migron;
　　they store supplies at Micmash.
29They go over the pass, and say,
　　"We will camp overnight at Geba."
Ramah trembles;
　　Gibeah of Saul flees.
30Cry out, O Daughter of Gallim!
　　Listen, O Laishah!
　　Poor Anathoth!
31Madmenah is in flight;
　　the people of Gebim take cover.
32This day they will halt at Nob;
　　they will shake their fist
at the mount of the Daughter of Zion,
　　at the hill of Jerusalem.

33See, the Lord, the LORD Almighty,
　　will lop off the boughs with great
　　　power.
The lofty trees will be felled,
　　the tall ones will be brought low.

a21 Hebrew shear-jashub; also in verse 22
b27 Hebrew; Septuagint broken / from your
shoulders

POINT OF INTEREST

Isaiah 10:12-19

God used Assyria, a foreign nation, to punish Israel. Rather than crediting God with the victory, the Assyrians boasted that they had won the battle in their own strength, assisted only by their false gods. Even though God used Assyria for his purposes, he ultimately punished this nation for its sinful arrogance.

34He will cut down the forest thickets
with an ax;
Lebanon will fall before the Mighty
One.

The Branch From Jesse

11 A shoot will come up from the
stump of Jesse;
from his roots a Branch will bear
fruit.
2The Spirit of the LORD will rest on
him—
the Spirit of wisdom and of
understanding,
the Spirit of counsel and of power,
the Spirit of knowledge and of the
fear of the LORD—
3and he will delight in the fear of the
LORD.

He will not judge by what he sees
with his eyes,
or decide by what he hears with
his ears;
4but with righteousness he will judge
the needy,
with justice he will give decisions
for the poor of the earth.
He will strike the earth with the rod
of his mouth;
with the breath of his lips he will
slay the wicked.
5Righteousness will be his belt
and faithfulness the sash around
his waist.

6The wolf will live with the lamb,
the leopard will lie down with the
goat,
the calf and the lion and the
yearlinga together;
and a little child will lead them.
7The cow will feed with the bear,
their young will lie down together,
and the lion will eat straw like the
ox.
8The infant will play near the hole of
the cobra,
and the young child put his hand
into the viper's nest.
9They will neither harm nor destroy
on all my holy mountain,
for the earth will be full of the
knowledge of the LORD
as the waters cover the sea.

10In that day the Root of Jesse will
stand as a banner for the peoples; the
nations will rally to him, and his place of
rest will be glorious. 11In that day the

Lord will reach out his hand a second
time to reclaim the remnant that is left
of his people from Assyria, from Lower
Egypt, from Upper Egypt,b from Cush,c
from Elam, from Babylonia,d from Hamath and from the islands of the sea.

12He will raise a banner for the nations
and gather the exiles of Israel;
he will assemble the scattered people
of Judah
from the four quarters of the earth.
13Ephraim's jealousy will vanish,
and Judah's enemiese will be cut
off;
Ephraim will not be jealous of Judah,
nor Judah hostile toward Ephraim.
14They will swoop down on the slopes
of Philistia to the west;
together they will plunder the
people to the east.
They will lay hands on Edom and
Moab,
and the Ammonites will be subject
to them.
15The LORD will dry up
the gulf of the Egyptian sea;
with a scorching wind he will sweep
his hand
over the Euphrates River.f
He will break it up into seven streams
so that men can cross over in
sandals.
16There will be a highway for the
remnant of his people
that is left from Assyria,
as there was for Israel
when they came up from Egypt.

Songs of Praise

12 In that day you will say:

"I will praise you, O LORD.
Although you were angry with me,
your anger has turned away
and you have comforted me.
2Surely God is my salvation;
I will trust and not be afraid.
The LORD, the LORD, is my strength
and my song;
he has become my salvation."
3With joy you will draw water
from the wells of salvation.

4In that day you will say:

a6 Hebrew; Septuagint lion will feed
b11 Hebrew from Pathros   c11 That is, the
upper Nile region   d11 Hebrew Shinar
e13 Or hostility   f15 Hebrew the River

"Give thanks to the LORD, call on his
name;
make known among the nations
what he has done,
and proclaim that his name is
exalted.
⁵Sing to the LORD, for he has done
glorious things;
let this be known to all the world.
⁶Shout aloud and sing for joy, people
of Zion,
for great is the Holy One of Israel
among you."

A Prophecy Against Babylon

13 An oracle concerning Babylon that
Isaiah son of Amoz saw:

²Raise a banner on a bare hilltop,
shout to them;
beckon to them
to enter the gates of the nobles.
³I have commanded my holy ones;
I have summoned my warriors to
carry out my wrath—
those who rejoice in my triumph.

⁴Listen, a noise on the mountains,

THURSDAY

Read Isaiah 12:1–6
Key Verses Isaiah 12:4–5

Hope for the Hopeless — John Littleton

Walking through the maze of Phnom Phen's dusty back streets, I
ducked into an old trinket shop to escape the blazing sun. As my
eyes adjusted to the dim light of the store, lit only by the red glow
of an idol box, they met those of the wrinkled woman behind the
counter.

She examined this foreigner who had happened upon her alcove.
Although she was only an arm's reach away, an intangible gulf separated us. I cannot forget the look she gave me or the hopelessness it
contained. I had witnessed the same hollow gaze in the eyes of the
young man who swept my street every morning and the Malay child
who practiced his English with me. Their eyes all asked the same
question: "Why am I here?"

As I reflected on their faces, I became aware of my callousness. I
found myself so wrapped up in my own spiritual condition that I
had little concern left for these people. By the world's standards
these individuals were insignificant, yet Jesus weeps and longs for
people such as these to come to him for hope and salvation. God
shares the same love and burden for that old woman as he has for
me. When I imagined myself in her place—living without purpose—
I realized how self-centered and stagnant I had become in my own
security.

Our God-given task to reach those around us demands an
unselfish attitude and a ready heart. By introducing the knowledge
of the living God to just one of those millions who exists without it,
we cause great joy in heaven. "Lost" people are not just a distant
cause in distant countries; they are the eyes without hope that surround us each and every day—in the workplace, in the classroom, in
our neighborhoods and even in our own families. Jesus is humanity's ultimate hope. To whom will we reveal that powerful truth?

A Deeper Look
Isaiah 49:6; Matthew 28:19–20; Luke 15:3–10

Go to page 780 for your next devotional reading.

like that of a great multitude!
Listen, an uproar among the
kingdoms,
like nations massing together!
The LORD Almighty is mustering
an army for war.
5They come from faraway lands,
from the ends of the heavens—
the LORD and the weapons of his
wrath—
to destroy the whole country.

6Wail, for the day of the LORD is near;
it will come like destruction from
the Almighty.*a*
7Because of this, all hands will go
limp,
every man's heart will melt.
8Terror will seize them,
pain and anguish will grip them;
they will writhe like a woman in
labor.
They will look aghast at each other,
their faces aflame.

9See, the day of the LORD is coming
—a cruel day, with wrath and
fierce anger—
to make the land desolate
and destroy the sinners within it.
10The stars of heaven and their
constellations
will not show their light.
The rising sun will be darkened
and the moon will not give its
light.
11I will punish the world for its evil,
the wicked for their sins.
I will put an end to the arrogance of
the haughty
and will humble the pride of the
ruthless.
12I will make man scarcer than pure
gold,
more rare than the gold of Ophir.
13Therefore I will make the heavens
tremble;
and the earth will shake from its
place
at the wrath of the LORD Almighty,
in the day of his burning anger.

14Like a hunted gazelle,
like sheep without a shepherd,
each will return to his own people,
each will flee to his native land.
15Whoever is captured will be thrust
through;
all who are caught will fall by the
sword.

16Their infants will be dashed to pieces
before their eyes;
their houses will be looted and
their wives ravished.

17See, I will stir up against them the
Medes,
who do not care for silver
and have no delight in gold.
18Their bows will strike down the
young men;
they will have no mercy on infants
nor will they look with compassion
on children.
19Babylon, the jewel of kingdoms,
the glory of the Babylonians'*b*
pride,
will be overthrown by God
like Sodom and Gomorrah.
20She will never be inhabited
or lived in through all generations;
no Arab will pitch his tent there,
no shepherd will rest his flocks
there.
21But desert creatures will lie there,
jackals will fill her houses;
there the owls will dwell,
and there the wild goats will leap
about.
22Hyenas will howl in her strongholds,
jackals in her luxurious palaces.
Her time is at hand,
and her days will not be
prolonged.

14 The LORD will have compassion on
Jacob;
once again he will choose Israel
and will settle them in their own
land.
Aliens will join them
and unite with the house of Jacob.
2Nations will take them
and bring them to their own place.
And the house of Israel will possess
the nations
as menservants and maidservants
in the LORD's land.
They will make captives of their
captors
and rule over their oppressors.

3On the day the LORD gives you relief
from suffering and turmoil and cruel
bondage, 4you will take up this taunt
against the king of Babylon:

*a*6 Hebrew *Shaddai*　　*b*19 Or *Chaldeans'*

How the oppressor has come to an
end!
How his fury[a] has ended!
⁵The Lord has broken the rod of the
wicked,
the scepter of the rulers,
⁶which in anger struck down peoples
with unceasing blows,
and in fury subdued nations
with relentless aggression.
⁷All the lands are at rest and at peace;
they break into singing.
⁸Even the pine trees and the cedars of
Lebanon
exult over you and say,
"Now that you have been laid low,
no woodsman comes to cut us
down."

⁹The grave[b] below is all astir
to meet you at your coming;
it rouses the spirits of the departed to
greet you—
all those who were leaders in the
world;
it makes them rise from their
thrones—
all those who were kings over the
nations.
¹⁰They will all respond,
they will say to you,
"You also have become weak, as we
are;
you have become like us."
¹¹All your pomp has been brought
down to the grave,
along with the noise of your harps;
maggots are spread out beneath you
and worms cover you.

¹²How you have fallen from heaven,
O morning star, son of the dawn!
You have been cast down to the
earth,
you who once laid low the nations!
¹³You said in your heart,
"I will ascend to heaven;
I will raise my throne
above the stars of God;
I will sit enthroned on the mount of
assembly,
on the utmost heights of the sacred
mountain.[c]
¹⁴I will ascend above the tops of the
clouds;
I will make myself like the Most
High."
¹⁵But you are brought down to the
grave,
to the depths of the pit.

¹⁶Those who see you stare at you,
they ponder your fate:
"Is this the man who shook the earth
and made kingdoms tremble,
¹⁷the man who made the world a
desert,
who overthrew its cities
and would not let his captives go
home?"

¹⁸All the kings of the nations lie in
state,
each in his own tomb.
¹⁹But you are cast out of your tomb
like a rejected branch;
you are covered with the slain,
with those pierced by the sword,
those who descend to the stones of
the pit.
Like a corpse trampled underfoot,
20   you will not join them in burial,
for you have destroyed your land
and killed your people.

The offspring of the wicked
will never be mentioned again.
²¹Prepare a place to slaughter his sons
for the sins of their forefathers;
they are not to rise to inherit the land
and cover the earth with their
cities.

²²"I will rise up against them,"
declares the Lord Almighty.
"I will cut off from Babylon her name
and survivors,
her offspring and descendants,"
declares the Lord.
²³"I will turn her into a place for owls
and into swampland;
I will sweep her with the broom of
destruction,"
declares the Lord Almighty.

A Prophecy Against Assyria

²⁴The Lord Almighty has sworn,

"Surely, as I have planned, so it will
be,
and as I have purposed, so it will
stand.
²⁵I will crush the Assyrian in my land;
on my mountains I will trample
him down.
His yoke will be taken from my
people,

---

a4 Dead Sea Scrolls, Septuagint and Syriac; the
meaning of the word in the Masoretic Text is
uncertain.   b9 Hebrew Sheol; also in verses 11
and 15   c13 Or the north; Hebrew Zaphon

and his burden removed from their
 shoulders."

²⁶This is the plan determined for the
 whole world;
this is the hand stretched out over
 all nations.
²⁷For the LORD Almighty has purposed,
 and who can thwart him?
His hand is stretched out, and who
 can turn it back?

A Prophecy Against the Philistines

²⁸This oracle came in the year King
Ahaz died:

²⁹Do not rejoice, all you Philistines,
 that the rod that struck you is
  broken;
from the root of that snake will
 spring up a viper,
its fruit will be a darting,
 venomous serpent.
³⁰The poorest of the poor will find
 pasture,
and the needy will lie down in
 safety.
But your root I will destroy by
 famine;
it will slay your survivors.

³¹Wail, O gate! Howl, O city!
 Melt away, all you Philistines!
A cloud of smoke comes from the
 north,
and there is not a straggler in its
 ranks.
³²What answer shall be given
 to the envoys of that nation?
"The LORD has established Zion,
 and in her his afflicted people will
 find refuge."

A Prophecy Against Moab

15 An oracle concerning Moab:

Ar in Moab is ruined,
 destroyed in a night!
Kir in Moab is ruined,
 destroyed in a night!
²Dibon goes up to its temple,
 to its high places to weep;
Moab wails over Nebo and
 Medeba.
Every head is shaved
 and every beard cut off.
³In the streets they wear sackcloth;
 on the roofs and in the public
  squares
they all wail,

prostrate with weeping.
⁴Heshbon and Elealeh cry out,
 their voices are heard all the way
  to Jahaz.
Therefore the armed men of Moab cry
 out,
 and their hearts are faint.

⁵My heart cries out over Moab;
 her fugitives flee as far as Zoar,
 as far as Eglath Shelishiyah.
They go up the way to Luhith,
 weeping as they go;
on the road to Horonaim
 they lament their destruction.
⁶The waters of Nimrim are dried up
 and the grass is withered;
the vegetation is gone
 and nothing green is left.
⁷So the wealth they have acquired and
 stored up
they carry away over the Ravine of
 the Poplars.
⁸Their outcry echoes along the border
 of Moab;
their wailing reaches as far as
 Eglaim,
their lamentation as far as Beer
 Elim.
⁹Dimon's*ᵃ* waters are full of blood,
 but I will bring still more upon
  Dimon*ᵃ*—
a lion upon the fugitives of Moab
 and upon those who remain in the
  land.

16 Send lambs as tribute
 to the ruler of the land,
from Sela, across the desert,
 to the mount of the Daughter of
  Zion.

ᵃ9 Masoretic Text; Dead Sea Scrolls, some
Septuagint manuscripts and Vulgate *Dibon*

POINT OF INTEREST

Isaiah 14:27

Nothing can prevent God
from doing what he intends
to do—not government officials or judges or legislators
or media or public opinion or anything
else. How does that knowledge make you
feel about the plans God has for you (see
Jeremiah 29:11)?

²Like fluttering birds
   pushed from the nest,
so are the women of Moab
   at the fords of the Arnon.
³"Give us counsel,
   render a decision.
Make your shadow like night—
   at high noon.
Hide the fugitives,
   do not betray the refugees.
⁴Let the Moabite fugitives stay with
      you;
   be their shelter from the
      destroyer."

The oppressor will come to an end,
   and destruction will cease;
   the aggressor will vanish from the
      land.
⁵In love a throne will be established;
   in faithfulness a man will sit on
      it—
   one from the house*a* of David—
one who in judging seeks justice
   and speeds the cause of
      righteousness.

⁶We have heard of Moab's pride—
   her overweening pride and conceit,
   her pride and her insolence—
   but her boasts are empty.
⁷Therefore the Moabites wail,
   they wail together for Moab.
Lament and grieve
   for the men*b* of Kir Hareseth.
⁸The fields of Heshbon wither,
   the vines of Sibmah also.
The rulers of the nations
   have trampled down the choicest
      vines,
which once reached Jazer
   and spread toward the desert.
Their shoots spread out
   and went as far as the sea.
⁹So I weep, as Jazer weeps,
   for the vines of Sibmah.
O Heshbon, O Elealeh,
   I drench you with tears!
The shouts of joy over your ripened
      fruit
   and over your harvests have been
      stilled.
¹⁰Joy and gladness are taken away
      from the orchards;
   no one sings or shouts in the
      vineyards;
no one treads out wine at the presses,
   for I have put an end to the
      shouting.

¹¹My heart laments for Moab like a
      harp,
   my inmost being for Kir Hareseth.
¹²When Moab appears at her high
      place,
   she only wears herself out;
when she goes to her shrine to pray,
   it is to no avail.

¹³This is the word the LORD has already
spoken concerning Moab. ¹⁴But now the
LORD says: "Within three years, as a servant bound by contract would count
them, Moab's splendor and all her many
people will be despised, and her survivors will be very few and feeble."

An Oracle Against Damascus

17 An oracle concerning Damascus:

"See, Damascus will no longer be a
      city
   but will become a heap of ruins.
²The cities of Aroer will be deserted
   and left to flocks, which will lie
      down,
   with no one to make them afraid.
³The fortified city will disappear from
      Ephraim,
   and royal power from Damascus;
the remnant of Aram will be
   like the glory of the Israelites,"
      declares the LORD Almighty.

⁴"In that day the glory of Jacob will
      fade;
   the fat of his body will waste
      away.
⁵It will be as when a reaper gathers
   the standing grain
   and harvests the grain with his
      arm—
as when a man gleans heads of grain
   in the Valley of Rephaim.
⁶Yet some gleanings will remain,
   as when an olive tree is beaten,
leaving two or three olives on the
   topmost branches,
   four or five on the fruitful boughs,"
      declares the LORD, the God
         of Israel.

⁷In that day men will look to their
      Maker
   and turn their eyes to the Holy
      One of Israel.
⁸They will not look to the altars,
   the work of their hands,

*a5 Hebrew tent   b7 Or "raisin cakes," a
wordplay*

and they will have no regard for the
Asherah poles[a]
and the incense altars their fingers
have made.

⁹In that day their strong cities, which
they left because of the Israelites, will be
like places abandoned to thickets and undergrowth. And all will be desolation.

¹⁰You have forgotten God your Savior;
you have not remembered the
Rock, your fortress.
Therefore, though you set out the
finest plants
and plant imported vines,
¹¹though on the day you set them out,
you make them grow,
and on the morning when you
plant them, you bring them to
bud,
yet the harvest will be as nothing
in the day of disease and incurable
pain.

¹²Oh, the raging of many nations—
they rage like the raging sea!
Oh, the uproar of the peoples—
they roar like the roaring of great
waters!
¹³Although the peoples roar like the
roar of surging waters,
when he rebukes them they flee far
away,
driven before the wind like chaff on
the hills,
like tumbleweed before a gale.
¹⁴In the evening, sudden terror!
Before the morning, they are gone!
This is the portion of those who loot
us,
the lot of those who plunder us.

A Prophecy Against Cush

18 Woe to the land of whirring
wings[b]
along the rivers of Cush,[c]
²which sends envoys by sea
in papyrus boats over the water.

Go, swift messengers,
to a people tall and smooth-skinned,
to a people feared far and wide,
an aggressive nation of strange
speech,
whose land is divided by rivers.

³All you people of the world,
you who live on the earth,
when a banner is raised on the
mountains,

you will see it,
and when a trumpet sounds,
you will hear it.
⁴This is what the LORD says to me:
"I will remain quiet and will look
on from my dwelling place,
like shimmering heat in the sunshine,
like a cloud of dew in the heat of
harvest."
⁵For, before the harvest, when the
blossom is gone
and the flower becomes a ripening
grape,
he will cut off the shoots with
pruning knives,
and cut down and take away the
spreading branches.
⁶They will all be left to the mountain
birds of prey
and to the wild animals;
the birds will feed on them all
summer,
the wild animals all winter.

⁷At that time gifts will be brought to
the LORD Almighty

from a people tall and
smooth-skinned,
from a people feared far and wide,
an aggressive nation of strange
speech,
whose land is divided by rivers—

the gifts will be brought to Mount Zion,
the place of the Name of the LORD Almighty.

A Prophecy About Egypt

19 An oracle concerning Egypt:

See, the LORD rides on a swift cloud
and is coming to Egypt.
The idols of Egypt tremble before
him,
and the hearts of the Egyptians
melt within them.

²"I will stir up Egyptian against
Egyptian—
brother will fight against brother,
neighbor against neighbor,
city against city,
kingdom against kingdom.
³The Egyptians will lose heart,
and I will bring their plans to
nothing;

---

a 8 That is, symbols of the goddess Asherah
b 1 Or *of locusts*   *c 1* That is, the upper Nile
region

they will consult the idols and the
   spirits of the dead,
the mediums and the spiritists.
⁴I will hand the Egyptians over
   to the power of a cruel master,
and a fierce king will rule over
   them,"
   declares the Lord, the LORD
      Almighty.

⁵The waters of the river will dry up,
   and the riverbed will be parched
      and dry.
⁶The canals will stink;
   the streams of Egypt will dwindle
      and dry up.
The reeds and rushes will wither,
⁷   also the plants along the Nile,
   at the mouth of the river.
Every sown field along the Nile
   will become parched, will blow
      away and be no more.
⁸The fishermen will groan and lament,
   all who cast hooks into the Nile;
those who throw nets on the water
   will pine away.
⁹Those who work with combed flax
   will despair,
   the weavers of fine linen will lose
      hope.
¹⁰The workers in cloth will be dejected,
   and all the wage earners will be
      sick at heart.

¹¹The officials of Zoan are nothing but
      fools;
   the wise counselors of Pharaoh
      give senseless advice.
How can you say to Pharaoh,
   "I am one of the wise men,
   a disciple of the ancient kings"?

¹²Where are your wise men now?
   Let them show you and make
      known
what the LORD Almighty
   has planned against Egypt.
¹³The officials of Zoan have become
      fools,
   the leaders of Memphis*a* are
      deceived;
the cornerstones of her peoples
   have led Egypt astray.
¹⁴The LORD has poured into them
   a spirit of dizziness;
they make Egypt stagger in all that
      she does,
   as a drunkard staggers around in
      his vomit.

¹⁵There is nothing Egypt can do—
   head or tail, palm branch or reed.

¹⁶In that day the Egyptians will be like
women. They will shudder with fear at
the uplifted hand that the LORD Almighty
raises against them. ¹⁷And the land of Judah will bring terror to the Egyptians; everyone to whom Judah is mentioned will
be terrified, because of what the LORD Almighty is planning against them.

¹⁸In that day five cities in Egypt will
speak the language of Canaan and swear
allegiance to the LORD Almighty. One of
them will be called the City of Destruction.*b* ¹⁹In that day there will be an altar to
the LORD in the heart of Egypt, and a monument to the LORD at its border. ²⁰It will
be a sign and witness to the LORD Almighty in the land of Egypt. When they
cry out to the LORD because of their oppressors, he will send them a savior and
defender, and he will rescue them. ²¹So
the LORD will make himself known to the
Egyptians, and in that day they will acknowledge the LORD. They will worship
with sacrifices and grain offerings; they
will make vows to the LORD and keep
them. ²²The LORD will strike Egypt with
a plague; he will strike them and heal
them. They will turn to the LORD, and he
will respond to their pleas and heal them.
²³In that day there will be a highway
from Egypt to Assyria. The Assyrians will
go to Egypt and the Egyptians to Assyria.
The Egyptians and Assyrians will worship together. ²⁴In that day Israel will be
the third, along with Egypt and Assyria,
a blessing on the earth. ²⁵The LORD Almighty will bless them, saying, "Blessed
be Egypt my people, Assyria my handiwork, and Israel my inheritance."

A Prophecy Against Egypt and Cush

20 In the year that the supreme commander, sent by Sargon king of Assyria, came to Ashdod and attacked and
captured it— ²at that time the LORD spoke
through Isaiah son of Amoz. He said to
him, "Take off the sackcloth from your
body and the sandals from your feet."
And he did so, going around stripped and
barefoot.
³Then the LORD said, "Just as my ser-

*a*13 Hebrew *Noph*   *b*18 Most manuscripts of the
Masoretic Text; some manuscripts of the Masoretic
Text, Dead Sea Scrolls and Vulgate *City of the Sun*
(that is, Heliopolis)

vant Isaiah has gone stripped and barefoot for three years, as a sign and portent against Egypt and Cush,ᵃ ⁴so the king of Assyria will lead away stripped and barefoot the Egyptian captives and Cushite exiles, young and old, with buttocks bared—to Egypt's shame. ⁵Those who trusted in Cush and boasted in Egypt will be afraid and put to shame. ⁶In that day the people who live on this coast will say, 'See what has happened to those we relied on, those we fled to for help and deliverance from the king of Assyria! How then can we escape?' "

A Prophecy Against Babylon

21 An oracle concerning the Desert by the Sea:

Like whirlwinds sweeping through
the southland,
an invader comes from the desert,
from a land of terror.

²A dire vision has been shown to me:
The traitor betrays, the looter takes
loot.
Elam, attack! Media, lay siege!
I will bring to an end all the
groaning she caused.

³At this my body is racked with pain,
pangs seize me, like those of a
woman in labor;
I am staggered by what I hear,
I am bewildered by what I see.
⁴My heart falters,
fear makes me tremble;
the twilight I longed for
has become a horror to me.

⁵They set the tables,
they spread the rugs,
they eat, they drink!
Get up, you officers,
oil the shields!

⁶This is what the Lord says to me:

"Go, post a lookout
and have him report what he sees.
⁷When he sees chariots
with teams of horses,
riders on donkeys
or riders on camels,
let him be alert,
fully alert."

⁸And the lookoutᵇ shouted,

"Day after day, my lord, I stand on
the watchtower;
every night I stay at my post.

⁹Look, here comes a man in a chariot
with a team of horses.
And he gives back the answer:
'Babylon has fallen, has fallen!
All the images of its gods
lie shattered on the ground!' "

¹⁰O my people, crushed on the
threshing floor,
I tell you what I have heard
from the LORD Almighty,
from the God of Israel.

A Prophecy Against Edom

¹¹An oracle concerning Dumahᶜ:

Someone calls to me from Seir,
"Watchman, what is left of the
night?
Watchman, what is left of the
night?"
¹²The watchman replies,
"Morning is coming, but also the
night.
If you would ask, then ask;
and come back yet again."

A Prophecy Against Arabia

¹³An oracle concerning Arabia:

You caravans of Dedanites,
who camp in the thickets of
Arabia,
¹⁴ bring water for the thirsty;
you who live in Tema,
bring food for the fugitives.
¹⁵They flee from the sword,
from the drawn sword,
from the bent bow
and from the heat of battle.

¹⁶This is what the Lord says to me: "Within one year, as a servant bound by contract would count it, all the pomp of Kedar will come to an end. ¹⁷The survivors of the bowmen, the warriors of Kedar, will be few." The LORD, the God of Israel, has spoken.

A Prophecy About Jerusalem

22 An oracle concerning the Valley of Vision:

What troubles you now,
that you have all gone up on the
roofs,
²O town full of commotion,

ᵃ3 That is, the upper Nile region; also in verse 5
ᵇ8 Dead Sea Scrolls and Syriac; Masoretic Text A lion   ᶜ11 Dumah means silence or stillness, a wordplay on Edom.

O city of tumult and revelry?
Your slain were not killed by the
     sword,
   nor did they die in battle.
³All your leaders have fled together;
   they have been captured without
     using the bow.
All you who were caught were taken
     prisoner together,
   having fled while the enemy was
     still far away.
⁴Therefore I said, "Turn away from
     me;
   let me weep bitterly.
Do not try to console me
   over the destruction of my people."

⁵The Lord, the Lᴏʀᴅ Almighty, has a
     day
   of tumult and trampling and terror
     in the Valley of Vision,
   a day of battering down walls
   and of crying out to the mountains.
⁶Elam takes up the quiver,
   with her charioteers and horses;
   Kir uncovers the shield.
⁷Your choicest valleys are full of
     chariots,
   and horsemen are posted at the
     city gates;
⁸   the defenses of Judah are stripped
     away.

And you looked in that day
   to the weapons in the Palace of the
     Forest;
⁹you saw that the City of David
   had many breaches in its defenses;
   you stored up water
     in the Lower Pool.
¹⁰You counted the buildings in
     Jerusalem
   and tore down houses to
     strengthen the wall.
¹¹You built a reservoir between the two
     walls
   for the water of the Old Pool,
   but you did not look to the One who
     made it,
   or have regard for the One who
     planned it long ago.

¹²The Lord, the Lᴏʀᴅ Almighty,
     called you on that day
   to weep and to wail,
   to tear out your hair and put on
     sackcloth.
¹³But see, there is joy and revelry,
   slaughtering of cattle and killing of
     sheep,

eating of meat and drinking of
     wine!
"Let us eat and drink," you say,
   "for tomorrow we die!"

¹⁴The Lᴏʀᴅ Almighty has revealed this
in my hearing: "Till your dying day this
sin will not be atoned for," says the Lord,
the Lᴏʀᴅ Almighty.

¹⁵This is what the Lord, the Lᴏʀᴅ Almighty, says:

"Go, say to this steward,
   to Shebna, who is in charge of the
     palace:
¹⁶What are you doing here and who
     gave you permission
   to cut out a grave for yourself
     here,
   hewing your grave on the height
   and chiseling your resting place in
     the rock?

¹⁷"Beware, the Lᴏʀᴅ is about to take
     firm hold of you
   and hurl you away, O you mighty
     man.
¹⁸He will roll you up tightly like a ball
   and throw you into a large
     country.
There you will die
   and there your splendid chariots
     will remain—
   you disgrace to your master's
     house!
¹⁹I will depose you from your office,
   and you will be ousted from your
     position.

²⁰"In that day I will summon my servant, Eliakim son of Hilkiah. ²¹I will
clothe him with your robe and fasten
your sash around him and hand your au-

POINT OF INTEREST   Isaiah 22:13

"Eat! Drink! Tomorrow we
die!" This fatalistic philosophy came from people who
believed that nothing they did
had eternal significance and that they had
no hope of eternal life. Both Jesus (see
Luke 12:18–20) and Paul (see 1 Corinthians 15:32) refer to this attitude that
smacks of stubborn despair.

thority over to him. He will be a father to those who live in Jerusalem and to the house of Judah. [22]I will place on his shoulder the key to the house of David; what he opens no one can shut, and what he shuts no one can open. [23]I will drive him like a peg into a firm place; he will be a seat[a] of honor for the house of his father. [24]All the glory of his family will hang on him: its offspring and offshoots—all its lesser vessels, from the bowls to all the jars.

[25]"In that day," declares the LORD Almighty, "the peg driven into the firm place will give way; it will be sheared off and will fall, and the load hanging on it will be cut down." The LORD has spoken.

A Prophecy About Tyre

23 An oracle concerning Tyre:

Wail, O ships of Tarshish!
   For Tyre is destroyed
   and left without house or harbor.
From the land of Cyprus[b]
   word has come to them.

[2]Be silent, you people of the island
   and you merchants of Sidon,
   whom the seafarers have enriched.
[3]On the great waters
   came the grain of the Shihor;
the harvest of the Nile[c] was the
      revenue of Tyre,
   and she became the marketplace of
      the nations.

[4]Be ashamed, O Sidon, and you,
   O fortress of the sea,
   for the sea has spoken:
"I have neither been in labor nor
      given birth;
   I have neither reared sons nor
      brought up daughters."
[5]When word comes to Egypt,
   they will be in anguish at the
      report from Tyre.

[6]Cross over to Tarshish;
   wail, you people of the island.
[7]Is this your city of revelry,
   the old, old city,
   whose feet have taken her
   to settle in far-off lands?
[8]Who planned this against Tyre,
   the bestower of crowns,
   whose merchants are princes,
      whose traders are renowned in the
         earth?
[9]The LORD Almighty planned it,

   to bring low the pride of all glory
   and to humble all who are
      renowned on the earth.

[10]Till[d] your land as along the Nile,
   O Daughter of Tarshish,
   for you no longer have a harbor.
[11]The LORD has stretched out his hand
      over the sea
   and made its kingdoms tremble.
He has given an order concerning
      Phoenicia[e]
   that her fortresses be destroyed.
[12]He said, "No more of your reveling,
   O Virgin Daughter of Sidon, now
      crushed!

"Up, cross over to Cyprus[b];
   even there you will find no rest."
[13]Look at the land of the
      Babylonians,[f]
   this people that is now of no
      account!
The Assyrians have made it
   a place for desert creatures;
they raised up their siege towers,
   they stripped its fortresses bare
   and turned it into a ruin.

[14]Wail, you ships of Tarshish;
   your fortress is destroyed!

[15]At that time Tyre will be forgotten for seventy years, the span of a king's life. But at the end of these seventy years, it will happen to Tyre as in the song of the prostitute:

[16]"Take up a harp, walk through the
      city,
   O prostitute forgotten;
play the harp well, sing many a song,
   so that you will be remembered."

[17]At the end of seventy years, the LORD will deal with Tyre. She will return to her hire as a prostitute and will ply her trade with all the kingdoms on the face of the earth. [18]Yet her profit and her earnings will be set apart for the LORD; they will not be stored up or hoarded. Her profits will go to those who live before the LORD, for abundant food and fine clothes.

---

[a]23 Or throne   [b]1,12 Hebrew Kittim
[c]2,3 Masoretic Text; one Dead Sea Scroll Sidon, / who cross over the sea; / your envoys [3]are on the great waters. / The grain of the Shihor, / the harvest of the Nile,   [d]10 Dead Sea Scrolls and some Septuagint manuscripts; Masoretic Text Go through   [e]11 Hebrew Canaan   [f]13 Or Chaldeans

The Lord's Devastation of the Earth

24 See, the Lord is going to lay waste
the earth
and devastate it;
he will ruin its face
and scatter its inhabitants—
²it will be the same
for priest as for people,
for master as for servant,
for mistress as for maid,
for seller as for buyer,
for borrower as for lender,
for debtor as for creditor.
³The earth will be completely laid
waste
and totally plundered.
    The Lord has spoken
        this word.

⁴The earth dries up and withers,
the world languishes and withers,
the exalted of the earth languish.
⁵The earth is defiled by its people;
they have disobeyed the laws,
violated the statutes
and broken the everlasting
covenant.
⁶Therefore a curse consumes the earth;
its people must bear their guilt.
Therefore earth's inhabitants are
burned up,
and very few are left.
⁷The new wine dries up and the vine
withers;
all the merrymakers groan.
⁸The gaiety of the tambourines is
stilled,
the noise of the revelers has
stopped,
the joyful harp is silent.
⁹No longer do they drink wine with a
song;
the beer is bitter to its drinkers.
¹⁰The ruined city lies desolate;
the entrance to every house is
barred.
¹¹In the streets they cry out for wine;
all joy turns to gloom,
all gaiety is banished from the
earth.
¹²The city is left in ruins,
its gate is battered to pieces.
¹³So will it be on the earth
and among the nations,
as when an olive tree is beaten,
or as when gleanings are left after
the grape harvest.

¹⁴They raise their voices, they shout for
joy;
from the west they acclaim the
Lord's majesty.
¹⁵Therefore in the east give glory to the
Lord;
exalt the name of the Lord, the
God of Israel,
in the islands of the sea.
¹⁶From the ends of the earth we hear
singing:
"Glory to the Righteous One."

But I said, "I waste away, I waste
away!
Woe to me!
The treacherous betray!
With treachery the treacherous
betray!"
¹⁷Terror and pit and snare await you,
O people of the earth.
¹⁸Whoever flees at the sound of terror
will fall into a pit;
whoever climbs out of the pit
will be caught in a snare.

The floodgates of the heavens are
opened,
the foundations of the earth shake.
¹⁹The earth is broken up,
the earth is split asunder,
the earth is thoroughly shaken.
²⁰The earth reels like a drunkard,
it sways like a hut in the wind;
so heavy upon it is the guilt of its
rebellion
that it falls—never to rise again.

²¹In that day the Lord will punish
the powers in the heavens above
and the kings on the earth below.
²²They will be herded together
like prisoners bound in a dungeon;
they will be shut up in prison
and be punished*a* after many
days.
²³The moon will be abashed, the sun
ashamed;
for the Lord Almighty will reign
on Mount Zion and in Jerusalem,
and before its elders, gloriously.

Praise to the Lord

25 O Lord, you are my God;
I will exalt you and praise your
name,
for in perfect faithfulness
you have done marvelous things,
things planned long ago.

a22 Or released

2 You have made the city a heap of
  rubble,
  the fortified town a ruin,
the foreigners' stronghold a city no
    more;
  it will never be rebuilt.
3 Therefore strong peoples will honor
    you;
  cities of ruthless nations will revere
    you.
4 You have been a refuge for the poor,
  a refuge for the needy in his
    distress,
a shelter from the storm
  and a shade from the heat.
For the breath of the ruthless
  is like a storm driving against a
    wall
5   and like the heat of the desert.

You silence the uproar of foreigners;
  as heat is reduced by the shadow
    of a cloud,
  so the song of the ruthless is
    stilled.

6 On this mountain the Lord Almighty
    will prepare
  a feast of rich food for all peoples,
a banquet of aged wine—
  the best of meats and the finest of
    wines.
7 On this mountain he will destroy
  the shroud that enfolds all peoples,
the sheet that covers all nations;
8   he will swallow up death forever.
The Sovereign Lord will wipe away
    the tears
  from all faces;

FRIDAY

Read Isaiah 25:1–12
Key Verse Isaiah 25:1

Perfect Faithfulness – Nancy Dorrell

A little boy sits on the front steps full of anticipation for the great day ahead. He squirms with joy and sings a little song as he thinks of what Dad said they'd do together today. As time goes on his singing eventually stops, but he stays on the steps, watching closely every car that comes into view. "Is it Dad? He promised he'd come, so I know he will," he reassures himself.

Hours later, the boy finally gives up hope and goes inside, dragging his feet. He hides his tears as he goes into his room and shuts the door on this, the first in a long line of disappointments.

This same scene plays over and over with boys and girls and men and women of all ages. Maybe you have been in the same position as that boy. We've all been let down by the lack of faithfulness of someone we love, and all of us have ourselves been unfaithful to others.

There is only One who is always faithful. He has planned everything in advance, and he will carry out his plans as he promises. God himself, says Isaiah, acts in perfect faithfulness (see Isaiah 25:1).

In the Bible God records for us many of his plans, as well as how he has been fulfilling his promises over the centuries. God's ultimate plan for us was sending Jesus to make a way for his people to come to him. Jesus did come, and he promises to return for his people. We can count on that return. We know he is coming, because God has proven his faithfulness time and again. When we wait on him, we won't be disappointed.

A Deeper Look
Psalm 27:13–14; 145:13; Jeremiah 29:11–13

Go to page 782 for your next devotional reading.

he will remove the disgrace of his
        people
from all the earth.
                The LORD has spoken.

⁹In that day they will say,

"Surely this is our God;
    we trusted in him, and he saved
        us.
This is the LORD, we trusted in him;
    let us rejoice and be glad in his
        salvation."

¹⁰The hand of the LORD will rest on this
        mountain;
    but Moab will be trampled under
        him
    as straw is trampled down in the
        manure.
¹¹They will spread out their hands in it,
    as a swimmer spreads out his
        hands to swim.
God will bring down their pride
    despite the cleverness*a* of their
        hands.
¹²He will bring down your high
        fortified walls
    and lay them low;
he will bring them down to the
        ground,
    to the very dust.

A Song of Praise

26 In that day this song will be sung in
the land of Judah:

We have a strong city;
    God makes salvation
        its walls and ramparts.
²Open the gates
    that the righteous nation may
        enter,
    the nation that keeps faith.
³You will keep in perfect peace
    him whose mind is steadfast,
    because he trusts in you.
⁴Trust in the LORD forever,
    for the LORD, the LORD, is the Rock
        eternal.
⁵He humbles those who dwell on high,
    he lays the lofty city low;
he levels it to the ground
    and casts it down to the dust.
⁶Feet trample it down—
    the feet of the oppressed,
    the footsteps of the poor.

⁷The path of the righteous is level;
    O upright One, you make the way
        of the righteous smooth.

⁸Yes, LORD, walking in the way of your
        laws,*b*
    we wait for you;
    your name and renown
        are the desire of our hearts.
⁹My soul yearns for you in the night;
    in the morning my spirit longs for
        you.
When your judgments come upon the
        earth,
    the people of the world learn
        righteousness.
¹⁰Though grace is shown to the wicked,
    they do not learn righteousness;
    even in a land of uprightness they go
        on doing evil
    and regard not the majesty of the
        LORD.
¹¹O LORD, your hand is lifted high,
    but they do not see it.
Let them see your zeal for your
        people and be put to shame;
    let the fire reserved for your
        enemies consume them.

¹²LORD, you establish peace for us;
    all that we have accomplished you
        have done for us.
¹³O LORD, our God, other lords besides
        you have ruled over us,
    but your name alone do we honor.
¹⁴They are now dead, they live no
        more;
    those departed spirits do not rise.
You punished them and brought them
        to ruin;
    you wiped out all memory of them.
¹⁵You have enlarged the nation, O LORD;
    you have enlarged the nation.
You have gained glory for yourself;
    you have extended all the borders
        of the land.

¹⁶LORD, they came to you in their
        distress;
    when you disciplined them,
    they could barely whisper a
        prayer.*c*
¹⁷As a woman with child and about to
        give birth
    writhes and cries out in her pain,
    so were we in your presence,
        O LORD.
¹⁸We were with child, we writhed in
        pain,
    but we gave birth to wind.

a 11 The meaning of the Hebrew for this word is
uncertain.   *b 8* Or *judgments*
c 16 The meaning of the Hebrew for this clause is
uncertain.

Read Isaiah 26:1–21
Key Verse Isaiah 26:3

Finding Peace

In a world filled with war, hunger, racial tension and environmental crises, we have many reasons to be anxious. And then there are the more personal sources of anxiety: difficult relationships, self-doubt, health concerns, academic and financial pressures. No wonder peace is so hard to find! God doesn't promise a life without conflict or struggle, but he does promise to be our source of peace.

That reality may not change the list of heartbreaking tragedies on the evening news, but it can change our response to them. It still hurts to see lives wasted or destroyed; it's frustrating to encounter social, economic and political dilemmas that seem too complicated to resolve. But personal peace is an inner calm that comes from trusting that our heavenly Father is in control of all circumstances. Ultimately, he is in charge. Nothing can happen to us unless God allows it. Knowing that God is in control and experiencing his love put personal peace within our grasp.

Digging Into the Word
1. God promises a peace that will overcome our fears. What do you learn about the peace of God from these passages?—*John 14:27; Philippians 4:6–7*
2. Trusting God develops peace, while despairing over our circumstances can lead to fear. What do you learn about fear from these passage?—*Psalm 55; Psalm 112:1–8; Luke 12:4–7*

Discussion Starter
Fire up a conversation with friends by asking: Think of one time you went through a troubling time but still experienced God's peace. How did his peace help to carry you through?

One Step Deeper
John 14:1; 16:33

Go to page 788 for your next devotional reading.

We have not brought salvation to the
earth;
we have not given birth to people
of the world.

¹⁹But your dead will live;
their bodies will rise.
You who dwell in the dust,
wake up and shout for joy.
Your dew is like the dew of the
morning;
the earth will give birth to her
dead.

²⁰Go, my people, enter your rooms
and shut the doors behind you;
hide yourselves for a little while
until his wrath has passed by.
²¹See, the Lord is coming out of his
dwelling
to punish the people of the earth
for their sins.
The earth will disclose the blood shed
upon her;
she will conceal her slain no
longer.

Deliverance of Israel

27 In that day,

the Lord will punish with his sword,
his fierce, great and powerful
sword,
Leviathan the gliding serpent,
Leviathan the coiling serpent;
he will slay the monster of the sea.

²In that day—

"Sing about a fruitful vineyard:
3   I, the Lord, watch over it;
I water it continually.
I guard it day and night
so that no one may harm it.
4   I am not angry.
If only there were briers and thorns
confronting me!
I would march against them in
battle;
I would set them all on fire.
⁵Or else let them come to me for
refuge;
let them make peace with me,
yes, let them make peace with
me."

⁶In days to come Jacob will take root,
Israel will bud and blossom
and fill all the world with fruit.

⁷Has ⌊the Lord⌋ struck her

as he struck down those who
struck her?
Has she been killed
as those were killed who killed
her?
⁸By warfare*ᵃ* and exile you contend
with her—
with his fierce blast he drives her
out,
as on a day the east wind blows.
⁹By this, then, will Jacob's guilt be
atoned for,
and this will be the full fruitage of
the removal of his sin:
When he makes all the altar stones
to be like chalk stones crushed to
pieces,
no Asherah poles*ᵇ* or incense altars
will be left standing.
¹⁰The fortified city stands desolate,
an abandoned settlement, forsaken
like the desert;
there the calves graze,
there they lie down;
they strip its branches bare.
¹¹When its twigs are dry, they are
broken off
and women come and make fires
with them.
For this is a people without
understanding;
so their Maker has no compassion
on them,
and their Creator shows them no
favor.

¹²In that day the Lord will thresh from
the flowing Euphrates*ᶜ* to the Wadi of
Egypt, and you, O Israelites, will be gathered up one by one. ¹³And in that day
a great trumpet will sound. Those who
were perishing in Assyria and those who
were exiled in Egypt will come and worship the Lord on the holy mountain in
Jerusalem.

Woe to Ephraim

28 Woe to that wreath, the pride of
Ephraim's drunkards,
to the fading flower, his glorious
beauty,
set on the head of a fertile valley—
to that city, the pride of those laid
low by wine!
²See, the Lord has one who is
powerful and strong.

ᵃ8 See Septuagint; the meaning of the Hebrew for
this word is uncertain.   *ᵇ9* That is, symbols of
the goddess Asherah   *ᶜ12* Hebrew *River*

Like a hailstorm and a destructive
wind,
like a driving rain and a flooding
downpour,
he will throw it forcefully to the
ground.
³That wreath, the pride of Ephraim's
drunkards,
will be trampled underfoot.
⁴That fading flower, his glorious
beauty,
set on the head of a fertile valley,
will be like a fig ripe before harvest—
as soon as someone sees it and
takes it in his hand,
he swallows it.

⁵In that day the Lord Almighty
will be a glorious crown,
a beautiful wreath
for the remnant of his people.
⁶He will be a spirit of justice
to him who sits in judgment,
a source of strength
to those who turn back the battle
at the gate.

⁷And these also stagger from wine
and reel from beer:
Priests and prophets stagger from
beer
and are befuddled with wine;
they reel from beer,
they stagger when seeing visions,
they stumble when rendering
decisions.
⁸All the tables are covered with vomit
and there is not a spot without
filth.

⁹"Who is it he is trying to teach?
To whom is he explaining his
message?
To children weaned from their milk,
to those just taken from the breast?
¹⁰For it is:
Do and do, do and do,
rule on rule, rule on rule ᵃ;
a little here, a little there."

¹¹Very well then, with foreign lips and
strange tongues
God will speak to this people,
¹²to whom he said,
"This is the resting place, let the
weary rest";
and, "This is the place of repose"—
but they would not listen.
¹³So then, the word of the Lord to them
will become:
Do and do, do and do,

rule on rule, rule on rule;
a little here, a little there—
so that they will go and fall
backward,
be injured and snared and
captured.

¹⁴Therefore hear the word of the Lord,
you scoffers
who rule this people in Jerusalem.
¹⁵You boast, "We have entered into a
covenant with death,
with the grave ᵇ we have made an
agreement.
When an overwhelming scourge
sweeps by,
it cannot touch us,
for we have made a lie our refuge
and falsehood ᶜ our hiding place."

¹⁶So this is what the Sovereign Lord
says:

"See, I lay a stone in Zion,
a tested stone,
a precious cornerstone for a sure
foundation;
the one who trusts will never be
dismayed.
¹⁷I will make justice the measuring line
and righteousness the plumb line;
hail will sweep away your refuge, the
lie,
and water will overflow your
hiding place.
¹⁸Your covenant with death will be
annulled;
your agreement with the grave will
not stand.

ᵃ10 Hebrew / sav lasav sav lasav / kav lakav kav
lakav (possibly meaningless sounds; perhaps a
mimicking of the prophet's words); also in verse 13
ᵇ15 Hebrew Sheol; also in verse 18　　ᶜ15 Or false
gods

POINT OF INTEREST

Isaiah 28:16

A cornerstone was tradi-
tionally the first block laid
in any building. The
strength and durability of the
entire structure depended on the cornerstone's alignment on the foundation. Peter
later applies this image to Jesus, the cornerstone and foundation of our faith (see
1 Peter 2:6–8).

When the overwhelming scourge
　　sweeps by,
　you will be beaten down by it.
¹⁹As often as it comes it will carry you
　　away;
　　morning after morning, by day and
　　　by night,
　it will sweep through."

The understanding of this message
　will bring sheer terror.
²⁰The bed is too short to stretch out on,
　the blanket too narrow to wrap
　　around you.
²¹The LORD will rise up as he did at
　　Mount Perazim,
　he will rouse himself as in the
　　Valley of Gibeon—
to do his work, his strange work,
　and perform his task, his alien
　　task.
²²Now stop your mocking,
　or your chains will become
　　heavier;
　the Lord, the LORD Almighty, has told
　　me
　of the destruction decreed against
　　the whole land.

²³Listen and hear my voice;
　pay attention and hear what I say.
²⁴When a farmer plows for planting,
　　does he plow continually?
　Does he keep on breaking up and
　　harrowing the soil?
²⁵When he has leveled the surface,
　　does he not sow caraway and
　　scatter cummin?
Does he not plant wheat in its
　　place,ᵃ
　barley in its plot,ᵃ
　and spelt in its field?
²⁶His God instructs him
　and teaches him the right way.

²⁷Caraway is not threshed with a
　　sledge,
　nor is a cartwheel rolled over
　　cummin;
　caraway is beaten out with a rod,
　　and cummin with a stick.
²⁸Grain must be ground to make bread;
　so one does not go on threshing it
　　forever.
Though he drives the wheels of his
　　threshing cart over it,
　his horses do not grind it.
²⁹All this also comes from the LORD
　　Almighty,

wonderful in counsel and
　magnificent in wisdom.

Woe to David's City

29 Woe to you, Ariel, Ariel,
　the city where David settled!
Add year to year
　and let your cycle of festivals go
　　on.
²Yet I will besiege Ariel;
　she will mourn and lament,
　she will be to me like an altar
　　hearth.ᵇ
³I will encamp against you all around;
　I will encircle you with towers
　and set up my siege works against
　　you.
⁴Brought low, you will speak from the
　　ground;
　your speech will mumble out of
　　the dust.
Your voice will come ghostlike from
　　the earth;
　out of the dust your speech will
　　whisper.

⁵But your many enemies will become
　　like fine dust,
　the ruthless hordes like blown
　　chaff.
Suddenly, in an instant,
⁶　the LORD Almighty will come
with thunder and earthquake and
　　great noise,
　with windstorm and tempest and
　　flames of a devouring fire.
⁷Then the hordes of all the nations
　　that fight against Ariel,
　that attack her and her fortress and
　　besiege her,
will be as it is with a dream,
　with a vision in the night—
⁸as when a hungry man dreams that
　　he is eating,
　but he awakens, and his hunger
　　remains;
as when a thirsty man dreams that he
　　is drinking,
　but he awakens faint, with his
　　thirst unquenched.
So will it be with the hordes of all the
　　nations
　that fight against Mount Zion.

⁹Be stunned and amazed,
　blind yourselves and be sightless;
　be drunk, but not from wine,

ᵃ25 The meaning of the Hebrew for this word is
uncertain.　　ᵇ2　The Hebrew for *altar hearth*
sounds like the Hebrew for *Ariel.*

stagger, but not from beer.
¹⁰The LORD has brought over you a
deep sleep:
He has sealed your eyes (the
prophets);
he has covered your heads (the
seers).

¹¹For you this whole vision is nothing
but words sealed in a scroll. And if you
give the scroll to someone who can read,
and say to him, "Read this, please," he
will answer, "I can't; it is sealed." ¹²Or if
you give the scroll to someone who cannot read, and say, "Read this, please," he
will answer, "I don't know how to read."

¹³The Lord says:

"These people come near to me with
their mouth
and honor me with their lips,
but their hearts are far from me.
Their worship of me
is made up only of rules taught by
men.ᵃ
¹⁴Therefore once more I will astound
these people
with wonder upon wonder;
the wisdom of the wise will perish,
the intelligence of the intelligent
will vanish."
¹⁵Woe to those who go to great depths
to hide their plans from the LORD,
who do their work in darkness and
think,
"Who sees us? Who will know?"
¹⁶You turn things upside down,
as if the potter were thought to be
like the clay!
Shall what is formed say to him who
formed it,
"He did not make me"?
Can the pot say of the potter,
"He knows nothing"?

¹⁷In a very short time, will not Lebanon
be turned into a fertile field
and the fertile field seem like a
forest?
¹⁸In that day the deaf will hear the
words of the scroll,
and out of gloom and darkness
the eyes of the blind will see.
¹⁹Once more the humble will rejoice in
the LORD;
the needy will rejoice in the Holy
One of Israel.
²⁰The ruthless will vanish,
the mockers will disappear,

and all who have an eye for evil
will be cut down—
²¹those who with a word make a man
out to be guilty,
who ensnare the defender in court
and with false testimony deprive
the innocent of justice.

²²Therefore this is what the LORD, who
redeemed Abraham, says to the house of
Jacob:

"No longer will Jacob be ashamed;
no longer will their faces grow
pale.
²³When they see among them their
children,
the work of my hands,
they will keep my name holy;
they will acknowledge the holiness
of the Holy One of Jacob,
and will stand in awe of the God
of Israel.
²⁴Those who are wayward in spirit will
gain understanding;
those who complain will accept
instruction."

Woe to the Obstinate Nation

30 "Woe to the obstinate children,"
declares the LORD,
"to those who carry out plans that
are not mine,
forming an alliance, but not by my
Spirit,
heaping sin upon sin;
²who go down to Egypt
without consulting me;
who look for help to Pharaoh's
protection,
to Egypt's shade for refuge.

ᵃ13 Hebrew; Septuagint *They worship me in vain; /
their teachings are but rules taught by men*

POINT OF INTEREST

Isaiah 30:1

"I did it my way." Are you
ever tempted to say that—
to do things *your* way; to go
it alone? Listen to this: God
declares that it's much better to ask him
to show you *his* plan. Remember that your
asking will always fall short of his ability
to give. Don't be like an obstinate child.
Be patient. He *will* lead you.

³But Pharaoh's protection will be to
   your shame,
   Egypt's shade will bring you
      disgrace.
⁴Though they have officials in Zoan
   and their envoys have arrived in
      Hanes,
⁵everyone will be put to shame
   because of a people useless to
      them,
who bring neither help nor
      advantage,
   but only shame and disgrace."

   ⁶An oracle concerning the animals of
the Negev:

Through a land of hardship and
      distress,
   of lions and lionesses,
   of adders and darting snakes,
the envoys carry their riches on
      donkeys' backs,
   their treasures on the humps of
      camels,
to that unprofitable nation,
⁷   to Egypt, whose help is utterly
      useless.
Therefore I call her
   Rahab the Do-Nothing.

⁸Go now, write it on a tablet for them,
   inscribe it on a scroll,
that for the days to come
   it may be an everlasting witness.
⁹These are rebellious people, deceitful
      children,
   children unwilling to listen to the
      LORD's instruction.
¹⁰They say to the seers,
   "See no more visions!"
and to the prophets,
   "Give us no more visions of what
      is right!
Tell us pleasant things,
   prophesy illusions.
¹¹Leave this way,
   get off this path,
and stop confronting us
   with the Holy One of Israel!"

¹²Therefore, this is what the Holy One
of Israel says:

"Because you have rejected this
      message,
   relied on oppression
   and depended on deceit,
¹³this sin will become for you
   like a high wall, cracked and
      bulging,

that collapses suddenly, in an
      instant.
¹⁴It will break in pieces like pottery,
   shattered so mercilessly
that among its pieces not a fragment
      will be found
   for taking coals from a hearth
   or scooping water out of a cistern."

¹⁵This is what the Sovereign LORD, the
Holy One of Israel, says:

"In repentance and rest is your
      salvation,
   in quietness and trust is your
      strength,
   but you would have none of it.
¹⁶You said, 'No, we will flee on
      horses.'
   Therefore you will flee!
You said, 'We will ride off on swift
      horses.'
   Therefore your pursuers will be
      swift!
¹⁷A thousand will flee
   at the threat of one;
at the threat of five
   you will all flee away,
till you are left
   like a flagstaff on a mountaintop,
   like a banner on a hill."

¹⁸Yet the LORD longs to be gracious to
      you;
   he rises to show you compassion.
For the LORD is a God of justice.
   Blessed are all who wait for him!

   ¹⁹O people of Zion, who live in Jerusalem, you will weep no more. How gra-
cious he will be when you cry for help!
As soon as he hears, he will answer you.
²⁰Although the Lord gives you the bread
of adversity and the water of affliction,
your teachers will be hidden no more;
with your own eyes you will see them.
²¹Whether you turn to the right or to the
left, your ears will hear a voice behind
you, saying, "This is the way; walk in it."
²²Then you will defile your idols overlaid
with silver and your images covered with
gold; you will throw them away like a
menstrual cloth and say to them, "Away
with you!"

   ²³He will also send you rain for the
seed you sow in the ground, and the food
that comes from the land will be rich and
plentiful. In that day your cattle will
graze in broad meadows. ²⁴The oxen and
donkeys that work the soil will eat fodder

and mash, spread out with fork and shovel. ²⁵In the day of great slaughter, when the towers fall, streams of water will flow on every high mountain and every lofty hill. ²⁶The moon will shine like the sun, and the sunlight will be seven times brighter, like the light of seven full days, when the LORD binds up the bruises of his people and heals the wounds he inflicted.

²⁷See, the Name of the LORD comes
    from afar,
  with burning anger and dense
    clouds of smoke;
his lips are full of wrath,
  and his tongue is a consuming fire.
²⁸His breath is like a rushing torrent,
  rising up to the neck.
He shakes the nations in the sieve of
    destruction;

he places in the jaws of the
    peoples
  a bit that leads them astray.
²⁹And you will sing
  as on the night you celebrate a
    holy festival;
your hearts will rejoice
  as when people go up with flutes
to the mountain of the LORD,
  to the Rock of Israel.
³⁰The LORD will cause men to hear his
    majestic voice
  and will make them see his arm
    coming down
with raging anger and consuming fire,
  with cloudburst, thunderstorm and
    hail.
³¹The voice of the LORD will shatter
    Assyria;

MONDAY

Read Isaiah 30:19–33
Key Verse Isaiah 30:21

When It's Time to Decide — Tina Larson

I was facing one of those momentous decision-making times. Having just finished my undergraduate degree, I needed to decide my next course of action. The number of options was staggering: Should I pursue graduate studies, or possibly get further spiritual and ministry training? Should I follow the "guy of my heart" and get married? Should I go overseas on a short-term mission project? Should I try to find a job? I felt that whatever choice I made would radically affect the rest of my life. I didn't know what to do.

Hoping to make the process easier, I tried to involve God. I prayed and read the Bible but still felt paralyzed with fear. As I tried to figure out why, I realized that in my heart I really didn't trust God to answer me. I'd always pictured him as a kind of "Big Brother," watching over me not with eyes of love but eyes of judgment, waiting for me to make mistakes or choose the wrong path.

Then I came across Isaiah 30:21: "Whether you turn to the right or to the left, your ears will hear a voice behind you, saying, ' This is the way; walk in it.' " I was amazed. God is not watching me from far away, waiting for me to mess up. No, he's right here *with* me as I make decisions! He is so concerned for me that he will correct me if I take a wrong turn or get off the path. But I have to know his Word, listen for his voice and have a heart to obey it—no matter what!

Do you have some important decisions to make? Do you need guidance? God wants you to make the right choice. And he'll help you find it. He certainly helped me.

A Deeper Look
Psalm 25:8–10; Proverbs 3:5–6

Go to page 790 for your next devotional reading.

with his scepter he will strike them
down.
³²Every stroke the LORD lays on them
with his punishing rod
will be to the music of tambourines
and harps,
as he fights them in battle with the
blows of his arm.
³³Topheth has long been prepared;
it has been made ready for the
king.
Its fire pit has been made deep and
wide,
with an abundance of fire and
wood;
the breath of the LORD,
like a stream of burning sulfur,
sets it ablaze.

Woe to Those Who Rely on Egypt

31 Woe to those who go down to Egypt
for help,
who rely on horses,
who trust in the multitude of their
chariots
and in the great strength of their
horsemen,
but do not look to the Holy One of
Israel,
or seek help from the LORD.
²Yet he too is wise and can bring
disaster;
he does not take back his words.
He will rise up against the house of
the wicked,
against those who help evildoers.
³But the Egyptians are men and not
God;
their horses are flesh and not
spirit.
When the LORD stretches out his
hand,
he who helps will stumble,
he who is helped will fall;
both will perish together.

⁴This is what the LORD says to me:

"As a lion growls,
a great lion over his prey—
and though a whole band of
shepherds
is called together against him,
he is not frightened by their shouts
or disturbed by their clamor—
so the LORD Almighty will come down
to do battle on Mount Zion and on
its heights.
⁵Like birds hovering overhead,

the LORD Almighty will shield
Jerusalem;
he will shield it and deliver it,
he will 'pass over' it and will
rescue it."

⁶Return to him you have so greatly revolted against, O Israelites. ⁷For in that
day every one of you will reject the idols
of silver and gold your sinful hands have
made.

⁸"Assyria will fall by a sword that is
not of man;
a sword, not of mortals, will
devour them.
They will flee before the sword
and their young men will be put to
forced labor.
⁹Their stronghold will fall because of
terror;
at sight of the battle standard their
commanders will panic,"
declares the LORD,
whose fire is in Zion,
whose furnace is in Jerusalem.

The Kingdom of Righteousness

32 See, a king will reign in
righteousness
and rulers will rule with justice.
²Each man will be like a shelter from
the wind
and a refuge from the storm,
like streams of water in the desert
and the shadow of a great rock in
a thirsty land.
³Then the eyes of those who see will
no longer be closed,
and the ears of those who hear
will listen.
⁴The mind of the rash will know and
understand,
and the stammering tongue will be
fluent and clear.
⁵No longer will the fool be called
noble
nor the scoundrel be highly
respected.
⁶For the fool speaks folly,
his mind is busy with evil:
He practices ungodliness
and spreads error concerning the
LORD;
the hungry he leaves empty
and from the thirsty he withholds
water.
⁷The scoundrel's methods are wicked,
he makes up evil schemes

to destroy the poor with lies,
  even when the plea of the needy is
    just.
8But the noble man makes noble
    plans,
  and by noble deeds he stands.

The Women of Jerusalem

9You women who are so complacent,
    rise up and listen to me;
  you daughters who feel secure,
    hear what I have to say!
10In little more than a year
    you who feel secure will tremble;
  the grape harvest will fail,
    and the harvest of fruit will not
      come.
11Tremble, you complacent women;
    shudder, you daughters who feel
      secure!
  Strip off your clothes,
    put sackcloth around your waists.
12Beat your breasts for the pleasant
    fields,
  for the fruitful vines
13and for the land of my people,

a land overgrown with thorns and
    briers—
  yes, mourn for all houses of
    merriment
  and for this city of revelry.
14The fortress will be abandoned,
    the noisy city deserted;
  citadel and watchtower will become a
    wasteland forever,
  the delight of donkeys, a pasture
    for flocks,
15till the Spirit is poured upon us from
    on high,
  and the desert becomes a fertile
    field,
  and the fertile field seems like a
    forest.
16Justice will dwell in the desert
  and righteousness live in the fertile
    field.
17The fruit of righteousness will be
    peace;
  the effect of righteousness will be
    quietness and confidence
      forever.
18My people will live in peaceful
    dwelling places,

***Read** Isaiah 32:1–20*
***Key Verse** Isaiah 32:17*

Finding Peace – Terry Cook

There was a sickening feeling in the pit of my stomach. The phone seemed glued to my ear. My dad spoke to me from a hospital emergency room, explaining that my mom had suffered a heart attack. My whole world seemed to stop in one big nightmare.

Questions flooded my mind: "How can this be happening? It can't be serious, can it? Will she make it through? Should I catch the next flight out?" All the while, that sickening feeling lingered like a shadow.

I hung up the phone and dropped to my knees in prayer. One of the verses I had memorized came to mind—Isaiah 26:3: "You will keep in perfect peace him whose mind is steadfast, because he trusts in you."

We need peace more than we need answers. The peace, quietness and confidence mentioned in Isaiah 32:17 are the outcomes, not of understanding the whys, but of experiencing the ways of a loving, righteous God. Focusing on God rather than on our own circumstances enables his peace to quiet our fears.

A Deeper Look
Isaiah 43:2; Philippians 4:6–7

Go to page 797 for your next devotional reading.

in secure homes,
in undisturbed places of rest.
¹⁹Though hail flattens the forest
and the city is leveled completely,
²⁰how blessed you will be,
sowing your seed by every stream,
and letting your cattle and donkeys
range free.

Distress and Help

33 Woe to you, O destroyer,
you who have not been destroyed!
Woe to you, O traitor,
you who have not been betrayed!
When you stop destroying,
you will be destroyed;
when you stop betraying,
you will be betrayed.

²O LORD, be gracious to us;
we long for you.
Be our strength every morning,
our salvation in time of distress.
³At the thunder of your voice, the
peoples flee;
when you rise up, the nations
scatter.
⁴Your plunder, O nations, is harvested
as by young locusts;
like a swarm of locusts men
pounce on it.

⁵The LORD is exalted, for he dwells on
high;
he will fill Zion with justice and
righteousness.
⁶He will be the sure foundation for
your times,
a rich store of salvation and
wisdom and knowledge;
the fear of the LORD is the key to
this treasure. ᵃ

⁷Look, their brave men cry aloud in
the streets;
the envoys of peace weep bitterly.
⁸The highways are deserted,
no travelers are on the roads.
The treaty is broken,
its witnessesᵇ are despised,
no one is respected.
⁹The land mournsᶜ and wastes away,
Lebanon is ashamed and withers;
Sharon is like the Arabah,
and Bashan and Carmel drop their
leaves.

¹⁰"Now will I arise," says the LORD.
"Now will I be exalted;
now will I be lifted up.
¹¹You conceive chaff,

you give birth to straw;
your breath is a fire that consumes
you.
¹²The peoples will be burned as if to
lime;
like cut thornbushes they will be
set ablaze."

¹³You who are far away, hear what I
have done;
you who are near, acknowledge
my power!
¹⁴The sinners in Zion are terrified;
trembling grips the godless:
"Who of us can dwell with the
consuming fire?
Who of us can dwell with
everlasting burning?"
¹⁵He who walks righteously
and speaks what is right,
who rejects gain from extortion
and keeps his hand from accepting
bribes,
who stops his ears against plots of
murder
and shuts his eyes against
contemplating evil—
¹⁶this is the man who will dwell on the
heights,
whose refuge will be the mountain
fortress.
His bread will be supplied,
and water will not fail him.

¹⁷Your eyes will see the king in his
beauty
and view a land that stretches afar.
¹⁸In your thoughts you will ponder the
former terror:
"Where is that chief officer?
Where is the one who took the
revenue?
Where is the officer in charge of
the towers?"
¹⁹You will see those arrogant people no
more,
those people of an obscure speech,
with their strange,
incomprehensible tongue.

²⁰Look upon Zion, the city of our
festivals;
your eyes will see Jerusalem,
a peaceful abode, a tent that will
not be moved;
its stakes will never be pulled up,
nor any of its ropes broken.

ᵃ6 Or *is a treasure from him*   ᵇ8 Dead Sea
Scrolls; Masoretic Text / *the cities*   ᶜ9 Or *dries
up*

²¹There the LORD will be our Mighty
One.
It will be like a place of broad
rivers and streams.
No galley with oars will ride them,
no mighty ship will sail them.
²²For the LORD is our judge,
the LORD is our lawgiver,
the LORD is our king;
it is he who will save us.

²³Your rigging hangs loose:
The mast is not held secure,
the sail is not spread.
Then an abundance of spoils will be
divided
and even the lame will carry off
plunder.
²⁴No one living in Zion will say, "I am
ill";
and the sins of those who dwell
there will be forgiven.

Judgment Against the Nations

34 Come near, you nations, and listen;
pay attention, you peoples!
Let the earth hear, and all that is in
it,
the world, and all that comes out
of it!
²The LORD is angry with all nations;
his wrath is upon all their armies.
He will totally destroy*a* them,
he will give them over to
slaughter.
³Their slain will be thrown out,
their dead bodies will send up a
stench;
the mountains will be soaked with
their blood.
⁴All the stars of the heavens will be
dissolved
and the sky rolled up like a scroll;
all the starry host will fall
like withered leaves from the vine,
like shriveled figs from the fig tree.

⁵My sword has drunk its fill in the
heavens;
see, it descends in judgment on
Edom,
the people I have totally destroyed.
⁶The sword of the LORD is bathed in
blood,
it is covered with fat—
the blood of lambs and goats,
fat from the kidneys of rams.
For the LORD has a sacrifice in Bozrah
and a great slaughter in Edom.

⁷And the wild oxen will fall with
them,
the bull calves and the great bulls.
Their land will be drenched with
blood,
and the dust will be soaked with
fat.

⁸For the LORD has a day of vengeance,
a year of retribution, to uphold
Zion's cause.
⁹Edom's streams will be turned into
pitch,
her dust into burning sulfur;
her land will become blazing pitch!
¹⁰It will not be quenched night and
day;
its smoke will rise forever.
From generation to generation it will
lie desolate;
no one will ever pass through it
again.
¹¹The desert owl*b* and screech owl*b*
will possess it;
the great owl*b* and the raven will
nest there.
God will stretch out over Edom
the measuring line of chaos
and the plumb line of desolation.
¹²Her nobles will have nothing there to
be called a kingdom,
all her princes will vanish away.
¹³Thorns will overrun her citadels,
nettles and brambles her
strongholds.
She will become a haunt for jackals,
a home for owls.
¹⁴Desert creatures will meet with
hyenas,
and wild goats will bleat to each
other;
there the night creatures will also
repose
and find for themselves places of
rest.
¹⁵The owl will nest there and lay eggs,
she will hatch them, and care for
her young under the shadow
of her wings;
there also the falcons will gather,
each with its mate.

¹⁶Look in the scroll of the LORD and
read:

a2 The Hebrew term refers to the irrevocable giving
over of things or persons to the LORD, often by
totally destroying them; also in verse 5.
b11 The precise identification of these birds is
uncertain.

None of these will be missing,
    not one will lack her mate.
For it is his mouth that has given the
        order,
    and his Spirit will gather them
        together.
¹⁷He allots their portions;
    his hand distributes them by
        measure.
They will possess it forever
    and dwell there from generation to
        generation.

Joy of the Redeemed

35 The desert and the parched land
        will be glad;
    the wilderness will rejoice and
        blossom.
Like the crocus, ²it will burst into
        bloom;
    it will rejoice greatly and shout for
        joy.
The glory of Lebanon will be given to
        it,
    the splendor of Carmel and Sharon;
    they will see the glory of the LORD,
        the splendor of our God.

³Strengthen the feeble hands,
    steady the knees that give way;
⁴say to those with fearful hearts,
    "Be strong, do not fear;
your God will come,
    he will come with vengeance;
with divine retribution
    he will come to save you."

⁵Then will the eyes of the blind be
        opened
    and the ears of the deaf unstopped.
⁶Then will the lame leap like a deer,
    and the mute tongue shout for joy.
Water will gush forth in the
        wilderness
    and streams in the desert.
⁷The burning sand will become a pool,
    the thirsty ground bubbling
        springs.
In the haunts where jackals once lay,
    grass and reeds and papyrus will
        grow.

⁸And a highway will be there;
    it will be called the Way of
        Holiness.
The unclean will not journey on it;
    it will be for those who walk in
        that Way;

wicked fools will not go about on
    it.*ᵃ*
⁹No lion will be there,
    nor will any ferocious beast get up
        on it;
    they will not be found there.
But only the redeemed will walk
        there,
¹⁰   and the ransomed of the LORD will
        return.
They will enter Zion with singing;
    everlasting joy will crown their
        heads.
Gladness and joy will overtake them,
    and sorrow and sighing will flee
        away.

Sennacherib Threatens Jerusalem

36 In the fourteenth year of King Hezekiah's reign, Sennacherib king of Assyria attacked all the fortified cities of Judah and captured them. ²Then the king of
Assyria sent his field commander with a
large army from Lachish to King Hezekiah at Jerusalem. When the commander
stopped at the aqueduct of the Upper
Pool, on the road to the Washerman's
Field, ³Eliakim son of Hilkiah the palace
administrator, Shebna the secretary, and
Joah son of Asaph the recorder went out
to him.

⁴The field commander said to them,
"Tell Hezekiah,

   " 'This is what the great king, the
   king of Assyria, says: On what are
   you basing this confidence of yours?
   ⁵You say you have strategy and military strength—but you speak only
   empty words. On whom are you depending, that you rebel against me?
   ⁶Look now, you are depending on
   Egypt, that splintered reed of a staff,
   which pierces a man's hand and
   wounds him if he leans on it! Such
   is Pharaoh king of Egypt to all who
   depend on him. ⁷And if you say to
   me, "We are depending on the LORD
   our God"—isn't he the one whose
   high places and altars Hezekiah removed, saying to Judah and Jerusalem, "You must worship before this
   altar"?
   ⁸" 'Come now, make a bargain
   with my master, the king of Assyria:
   I will give you two thousand
   horses—if you can put riders on
   them! ⁹How then can you repulse

ᵃ8 Or / the simple will not stray from it

one officer of the least of my master's officials, even though you are depending on Egypt for chariots and horsemen? ¹⁰Furthermore, have I come to attack and destroy this land without the LORD? The LORD himself told me to march against this country and destroy it.' "

¹¹Then Eliakim, Shebna and Joah said to the field commander, "Please speak to your servants in Aramaic, since we understand it. Don't speak to us in Hebrew in the hearing of the people on the wall."

¹²But the commander replied, "Was it only to your master and you that my master sent me to say these things, and not to the men sitting on the wall—who, like you, will have to eat their own filth and drink their own urine?"

¹³Then the commander stood and called out in Hebrew, "Hear the words of the great king, the king of Assyria! ¹⁴This is what the king says: Do not let Hezekiah deceive you. He cannot deliver you! ¹⁵Do not let Hezekiah persuade you to trust in the LORD when he says, 'The LORD will surely deliver us; this city will not be given into the hand of the king of Assyria.'

¹⁶"Do not listen to Hezekiah. This is what the king of Assyria says: Make peace with me and come out to me. Then every one of you will eat from his own vine and fig tree and drink water from his own cistern, ¹⁷until I come and take you to a land like your own—a land of grain and new wine, a land of bread and vineyards.

¹⁸"Do not let Hezekiah mislead you when he says, 'The LORD will deliver us.' Has the god of any nation ever delivered his land from the hand of the king of Assyria? ¹⁹Where are the gods of Hamath and Arpad? Where are the gods of Sepharvaim? Have they rescued Samaria from my hand? ²⁰Who of all the gods of these countries has been able to save his land from me? How then can the LORD deliver Jerusalem from my hand?"

²¹But the people remained silent and said nothing in reply, because the king had commanded, "Do not answer him."

²²Then Eliakim son of Hilkiah the palace administrator, Shebna the secretary, and Joah son of Asaph the recorder went to Hezekiah, with their clothes torn, and told him what the field commander had said.

Jerusalem's Deliverance Foretold

37 When King Hezekiah heard this, he tore his clothes and put on sackcloth and went into the temple of the LORD. ²He sent Eliakim the palace administrator, Shebna the secretary, and the leading priests, all wearing sackcloth, to the prophet Isaiah son of Amoz. ³They told him, "This is what Hezekiah says: This day is a day of distress and rebuke and disgrace, as when children come to the point of birth and there is no strength to deliver them. ⁴It may be that the LORD your God will hear the words of the field commander, whom his master, the king of Assyria, has sent to ridicule the living God, and that he will rebuke him for the words the LORD your God has heard. Therefore pray for the remnant that still survives."

⁵When King Hezekiah's officials came to Isaiah, ⁶Isaiah said to them, "Tell your master, 'This is what the LORD says: Do not be afraid of what you have heard—those words with which the underlings of the king of Assyria have blasphemed me. ⁷Listen! I am going to put a spirit in him so that when he hears a certain report, he will return to his own country, and there I will have him cut down with the sword.' "

⁸When the field commander heard that the king of Assyria had left Lachish, he withdrew and found the king fighting against Libnah.

⁹Now Sennacherib received a report that Tirhakah, the Cushite[a] king ⌐of Egypt⌐, was marching out to fight against him. When he heard it, he sent messengers to Hezekiah with this word: ¹⁰"Say

---

a9 That is, from the upper Nile region

POINT OF INTEREST

Isaiah 37:1

In ancient times, fine clothing was expensive because the cloth was handmade. Tearing one's clothes was an expression of a grief so severe that it didn't matter how expensive they were. Grieving people replaced their torn garments with clothes made from the rough cloth used for grain sacks.

to Hezekiah king of Judah: Do not let the god you depend on deceive you when he says, 'Jerusalem will not be handed over to the king of Assyria.' ¹¹Surely you have heard what the kings of Assyria have done to all the countries, destroying them completely. And will you be delivered? ¹²Did the gods of the nations that were destroyed by my forefathers deliver them—the gods of Gozan, Haran, Rezeph and the people of Eden who were in Tel Assar? ¹³Where is the king of Hamath, the king of Arpad, the king of the city of Sepharvaim, or of Hena or Ivvah?"

Hezekiah's Prayer

¹⁴Hezekiah received the letter from the messengers and read it. Then he went up to the temple of the LORD and spread it out before the LORD. ¹⁵And Hezekiah prayed to the LORD: ¹⁶"O LORD Almighty, God of Israel, enthroned between the cherubim, you alone are God over all the kingdoms of the earth. You have made heaven and earth. ¹⁷Give ear, O LORD, and hear; open your eyes, O LORD, and see; listen to all the words Sennacherib has sent to insult the living God.

¹⁸"It is true, O LORD, that the Assyrian kings have laid waste all these peoples and their lands. ¹⁹They have thrown their gods into the fire and destroyed them, for they were not gods but only wood and stone, fashioned by human hands. ²⁰Now, O LORD our God, deliver us from his hand, so that all kingdoms on earth may know that you alone, O LORD, are God.ᵃ"

Sennacherib's Fall

²¹Then Isaiah son of Amoz sent a message to Hezekiah: "This is what the LORD, the God of Israel, says: Because you have prayed to me concerning Sennacherib king of Assyria, ²²this is the word the LORD has spoken against him:

"The Virgin Daughter of Zion
    despises and mocks you.
The Daughter of Jerusalem
    tosses her head as you flee.
²³Who is it you have insulted and
    blasphemed?
Against whom have you raised
    your voice
and lifted your eyes in pride?
Against the Holy One of Israel!
²⁴By your messengers

you have heaped insults on the
    Lord.
And you have said,
    'With my many chariots
I have ascended the heights of the
    mountains,
    the utmost heights of Lebanon.
I have cut down its tallest cedars,
    the choicest of its pines.
I have reached its remotest heights,
    the finest of its forests.
²⁵I have dug wells in foreign landsᵇ
    and drunk the water there.
With the soles of my feet
    I have dried up all the streams of
    Egypt.'

²⁶"Have you not heard?
    Long ago I ordained it.
In days of old I planned it;
    now I have brought it to pass,
that you have turned fortified cities
    into piles of stone.
²⁷Their people, drained of power,
    are dismayed and put to shame.
They are like plants in the field,
    like tender green shoots,
like grass sprouting on the roof,
    scorchedᶜ before it grows up.

²⁸"But I know where you stay
    and when you come and go
    and how you rage against me.
²⁹Because you rage against me
    and because your insolence has
      reached my ears,
I will put my hook in your nose
    and my bit in your mouth,
and I will make you return
    by the way you came.

³⁰"This will be the sign for you,
O Hezekiah:

"This year you will eat what grows
    by itself,
    and the second year what springs
      from that.
But in the third year sow and reap,
    plant vineyards and eat their fruit.
³¹Once more a remnant of the house of
    Judah
    will take root below and bear fruit
    above.

ᵃ20 Dead Sea Scrolls (see also 2 Kings 19:19); Masoretic Text *alone are the* LORD   ᵇ25 Dead Sea Scrolls (see also 2 Kings 19:24); Masoretic Text does not have *in foreign lands.*   ᶜ27 Some manuscripts of the Masoretic Text, Dead Sea Scrolls and some Septuagint manuscripts (see also 2 Kings 19:26); most manuscripts of the Masoretic Text *roof / and terraced fields*

³²For out of Jerusalem will come a
    remnant,
  and out of Mount Zion a band of
    survivors.
The zeal of the LORD Almighty
  will accomplish this.

³³"Therefore this is what the LORD says
concerning the king of Assyria:

"He will not enter this city
  or shoot an arrow here.
He will not come before it with shield
  or build a siege ramp against it.
³⁴By the way that he came he will
    return;
  he will not enter this city,"
                    declares the LORD.
³⁵"I will defend this city and save it,
  for my sake and for the sake of
    David my servant!"

³⁶Then the angel of the LORD went out
and put to death a hundred and eighty-
five thousand men in the Assyrian camp.
When the people got up the next morning—there were all the dead bodies! ³⁷So
Sennacherib king of Assyria broke camp
and withdrew. He returned to Nineveh
and stayed there.

³⁸One day, while he was worshiping in
the temple of his god Nisroch, his sons
Adrammelech and Sharezer cut him
down with the sword, and they escaped
to the land of Ararat. And Esarhaddon his
son succeeded him as king.

Hezekiah's Illness

38 In those days Hezekiah became ill
and was at the point of death. The
prophet Isaiah son of Amoz went to him
and said, "This is what the LORD says: Put
your house in order, because you are going to die; you will not recover."

²Hezekiah turned his face to the wall
and prayed to the LORD, ³"Remember,
O LORD, how I have walked before you
faithfully and with wholehearted devotion and have done what is good in your
eyes." And Hezekiah wept bitterly.

⁴Then the word of the LORD came to
Isaiah: ⁵"Go and tell Hezekiah, 'This is
what the LORD, the God of your father David, says: I have heard your prayer and
seen your tears; I will add fifteen years to
your life. ⁶And I will deliver you and this
city from the hand of the king of Assyria.
I will defend this city.

⁷" 'This is the LORD's sign to you that
the LORD will do what he has promised: ⁸I

will make the shadow cast by the sun go
back the ten steps it has gone down on
the stairway of Ahaz.' " So the sunlight
went back the ten steps it had gone
down.

⁹A writing of Hezekiah king of Judah
after his illness and recovery:

¹⁰I said, "In the prime of my life
  must I go through the gates of
    death*a*
  and be robbed of the rest of my
    years?"
¹¹I said, "I will not again see the LORD,
  the LORD, in the land of the living;
no longer will I look on mankind,
  or be with those who now dwell in
    this world.*b*
¹²Like a shepherd's tent my house
  has been pulled down and taken
    from me.
Like a weaver I have rolled up my
    life,
  and he has cut me off from the
    loom;
  day and night you made an end of
    me.
¹³I waited patiently till dawn,
  but like a lion he broke all my
    bones;
  day and night you made an end of
    me.
¹⁴I cried like a swift or thrush,
  I moaned like a mourning dove.
My eyes grew weak as I looked to the
    heavens.
  I am troubled; O Lord, come to my
    aid!"

¹⁵But what can I say?
  He has spoken to me, and he
    himself has done this.
I will walk humbly all my years
  because of this anguish of my soul.
¹⁶Lord, by such things men live;
  and my spirit finds life in them
    too.
You restored me to health
  and let me live.
¹⁷Surely it was for my benefit
  that I suffered such anguish.
In your love you kept me
  from the pit of destruction;
you have put all my sins
  behind your back.
¹⁸For the grave*a* cannot praise you,

*a*10,18 Hebrew *Sheol*   *b*11 A few Hebrew
manuscripts; most Hebrew manuscripts *in the place
of cessation*

death cannot sing your praise;
those who go down to the pit
cannot hope for your faithfulness.
¹⁹The living, the living—they praise
you,
as I am doing today;
fathers tell their children
about your faithfulness.

²⁰The LORD will save me,
and we will sing with stringed
instruments
all the days of our lives
in the temple of the LORD.

²¹Isaiah had said, "Prepare a poultice of figs and apply it to the boil, and he will recover."

²²Hezekiah had asked, "What will be the sign that I will go up to the temple of the LORD?"

Envoys From Babylon

39 At that time Merodach-Baladan son of Baladan king of Babylon sent Hezekiah letters and a gift, because he had heard of his illness and recovery. ²Hezekiah received the envoys gladly and showed them what was in his storehouses—the silver, the gold, the spices, the fine oil, his entire armory and everything found among his treasures. There was nothing in his palace or in all his kingdom that Hezekiah did not show them.

³Then Isaiah the prophet went to King Hezekiah and asked, "What did those

---

WEDNESDAY

Read Isaiah 38:1–22
Key Verses Isaiah 38:1–2,17

God's Long-Term Care — Kyle Kelley

"Why me?" I asked God as I cried in the shower. I had recently experienced a cardiac arrest while playing soccer and had been in the hospital for more than a month. The next morning I was scheduled for yet another test on my heart to determine the best remedy. Even though the doctors seemed confident that they could find a solution, they hadn't yet discovered the best option for treatment. I was tired of being kept in the hospital, sick of being poked and prodded and analyzed, discouraged by my illness. Like Hezekiah, I couldn't do anything but pray.

God doesn't want us to be anxious. He wants us to come to him instead: "Do not be anxious about anything, but in everything, by prayer and petition, with thanksgiving, present your requests to God. And the peace of God, which transcends all understanding, will guard your hearts and your minds in Christ Jesus" (Philippians 4:6–7). When I thought about that verse, I felt better. Being reminded of God's understanding and faithfulness renewed my spirit, and I began to look at my situation differently. Instead of worrying, I was able to thank him for all that he had done for me, especially for sparing my life during and after the cardiac arrest. God sustained me through the surgery I needed and then through my recuperation time.

Our lives will never be totally free from confusion and pain. But, like Hezekiah, we can learn to pour out our frustration, hurt and despair to God, asking for his healing power and mercy and praising him for his faithfulness (see Isaiah 38:1–6).

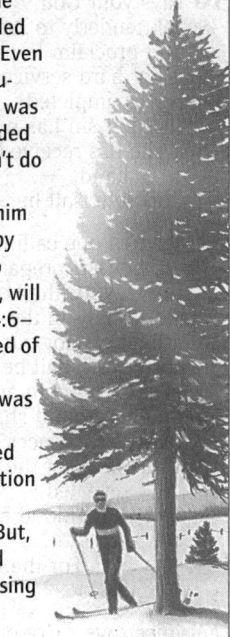

A Deeper Look
Romans 8:26–39; James 1:2–4; 1 Peter 4:12–19

Go to page 800 for your next devotional reading.

men say, and where did they come from?"

"From a distant land," Hezekiah replied. "They came to me from Babylon."

⁴The prophet asked, "What did they see in your palace?"

"They saw everything in my palace," Hezekiah said. "There is nothing among my treasures that I did not show them."

⁵Then Isaiah said to Hezekiah, "Hear the word of the Lord Almighty: ⁶The time will surely come when everything in your palace, and all that your fathers have stored up until this day, will be carried off to Babylon. Nothing will be left, says the Lord. ⁷And some of your descendants, your own flesh and blood who will be born to you, will be taken away, and they will become eunuchs in the palace of the king of Babylon."

⁸"The word of the Lord you have spoken is good," Hezekiah replied. For he thought, "There will be peace and security in my lifetime."

Comfort for God's People

40 Comfort, comfort my people,
    says your God.
²Speak tenderly to Jerusalem,
    and proclaim to her
that her hard service has been
    completed,
that her sin has been paid for,
that she has received from the Lord's
    hand
double for all her sins.

³A voice of one calling:
"In the desert prepare
    the way for the Lord*a*;
make straight in the wilderness
    a highway for our God.*b*
⁴Every valley shall be raised up,
    every mountain and hill made low;
the rough ground shall become level,
    the rugged places a plain.
⁵And the glory of the Lord will be
    revealed,
and all mankind together will see
    it.
      For the mouth of the Lord
        has spoken."

⁶A voice says, "Cry out."
    And I said, "What shall I cry?"

"All men are like grass,
    and all their glory is like the
      flowers of the field.

⁷The grass withers and the flowers
    fall,
because the breath of the Lord
    blows on them.
Surely the people are grass.
⁸The grass withers and the flowers
    fall,
but the word of our God stands
    forever."

⁹You who bring good tidings to Zion,
    go up on a high mountain.
You who bring good tidings to
      Jerusalem,*c*
lift up your voice with a shout,
lift it up, do not be afraid;
say to the towns of Judah,
    "Here is your God!"
¹⁰See, the Sovereign Lord comes with
    power,
    and his arm rules for him.
See, his reward is with him,
    and his recompense accompanies
      him.
¹¹He tends his flock like a shepherd:
    He gathers the lambs in his arms
and carries them close to his heart;
    he gently leads those that have
      young.

¹²Who has measured the waters in the
    hollow of his hand,
or with the breadth of his hand
    marked off the heavens?
Who has held the dust of the earth in
    a basket,
or weighed the mountains on the
    scales
and the hills in a balance?
¹³Who has understood the mind*d* of
    the Lord,
or instructed him as his counselor?
¹⁴Whom did the Lord consult to
    enlighten him,
and who taught him the right way?
Who was it that taught him
    knowledge
or showed him the path of
    understanding?

¹⁵Surely the nations are like a drop in a
    bucket;
they are regarded as dust on the
    scales;

---

a3 Or *A voice of one calling in the desert: / "Prepare the way for the Lord*   *b3* Hebrew; Septuagint *make straight the paths of our God*   *c9* Or *O Zion, bringer of good tidings, / go up on a high mountain. / O Jerusalem, bringer of good tidings*   *d13* Or *Spirit*; or *spirit*

he weighs the islands as though
they were fine dust.
¹⁶Lebanon is not sufficient for altar
fires,
nor its animals enough for burnt
offerings.
¹⁷Before him all the nations are as
nothing;
they are regarded by him as
worthless
and less than nothing.

¹⁸To whom, then, will you compare
God?
What image will you compare him
to?
¹⁹As for an idol, a craftsman casts it,
and a goldsmith overlays it with
gold
and fashions silver chains for it.
²⁰A man too poor to present such an
offering
selects wood that will not rot.
He looks for a skilled craftsman
to set up an idol that will not
topple.

²¹Do you not know?
Have you not heard?
Has it not been told you from the
beginning?
Have you not understood since the
earth was founded?
²²He sits enthroned above the circle of
the earth,
and its people are like
grasshoppers.
He stretches out the heavens like a
canopy,
and spreads them out like a tent to
live in.
²³He brings princes to naught
and reduces the rulers of this
world to nothing.
²⁴No sooner are they planted,
no sooner are they sown,
no sooner do they take root in the
ground,
than he blows on them and they
wither,
and a whirlwind sweeps them
away like chaff.

²⁵"To whom will you compare me?
Or who is my equal?" says the
Holy One.
²⁶Lift your eyes and look to the
heavens:
Who created all these?

He who brings out the starry host one
by one,
and calls them each by name.
Because of his great power and
mighty strength,
not one of them is missing.

²⁷Why do you say, O Jacob,
and complain, O Israel,
"My way is hidden from the LORD;
my cause is disregarded by my
God"?
²⁸Do you not know?
Have you not heard?
The LORD is the everlasting God,
the Creator of the ends of the
earth.
He will not grow tired or weary,
and his understanding no one can
fathom.
²⁹He gives strength to the weary
and increases the power of the
weak.
³⁰Even youths grow tired and weary,
and young men stumble and fall;
³¹but those who hope in the LORD
will renew their strength.
They will soar on wings like eagles;
they will run and not grow weary,
they will walk and not be faint.

The Helper of Israel

41 "Be silent before me, you islands!
Let the nations renew their
strength!
Let them come forward and speak;
let us meet together at the place of
judgment.

²"Who has stirred up one from the
east,
calling him in righteousness to his
service ᵃ?
He hands nations over to him
and subdues kings before him.
He turns them to dust with his
sword,
to windblown chaff with his bow.
³He pursues them and moves on
unscathed,
by a path his feet have not
traveled before.
⁴Who has done this and carried it
through,
calling forth the generations from
the beginning?
I, the LORD—with the first of them
and with the last—I am he."

ᵃ2 Or / whom victory meets at every step

5The islands have seen it and fear;
　　the ends of the earth tremble.
They approach and come forward;
6　each helps the other
　　and says to his brother, "Be
　　　strong!"
7The craftsman encourages the
　　goldsmith,
　and he who smooths with the
　　hammer
spurs on him who strikes the anvil.
He says of the welding, "It is good."
He nails down the idol so it will
　　not topple.

8"But you, O Israel, my servant,
　　Jacob, whom I have chosen,
　　you descendants of Abraham my
　　　friend,
9I took you from the ends of the earth,
　　from its farthest corners I called
　　　you.
I said, 'You are my servant';
　　I have chosen you and have not
　　　rejected you.
10So do not fear, for I am with you;
　　do not be dismayed, for I am your
　　　God.
I will strengthen you and help you;

THURSDAY

Read *Isaiah 40:1–31*
Key Verses *Isaiah 40:30–31*

God's Strength Is Ours —Dennis Stokes

"Help! I'm losing my grip! I have no more strength!" my friend Fouad cried as his body swung away from the zooming train. In the heat and frenzy of the Cairo rush hour, the crowd of commuters had surged, pushing Fouad out the open door and me in the other direction. I watched, horrified and helpless, as the crowd pressed in against me—I could barely breathe, let alone help my friend.

At the last second, another man saw Fouad's dilemma, reached out his hand and pulled him back inside the train. Later Fouad said, "It was like the hand of Jesus rescuing me when I had no strength left."

Fouad's plight that day is an accurate picture of modern life. Too often we feel as if we are barely holding on, and our strength is dwindling. What a tremendous toll our hectic lifestyles take! Anxieties often swallow us up. Too many classes, tests, and financial and relational pressures sap our strength. What to do? God's solution is simple: "Those who hope in the LORD will renew their strength" (Isaiah 40:31). When we are "tired and weary," God has more than enough strength.

We can bask in God's renewal any time we are weary—every day, hour, minute or second. When our strength and our hope are gone, God is still there. When we don't know how to keep on going, he is there. When we can't think straight, he is there. When we don't feel him there, even then he is still there.

Is physical, spiritual, emotional, relational or mental tiredness overcoming you? Are struggles with sin bringing you down? God's promises remain true when you feel like you are losing your grip, or when you do lose it. You are God's prized possession, his child. Let go long enough to focus your hope on him alone. He'll reach out and pull you close to his heart.

A Deeper Look
2 Samuel 22:32–34; Psalm 27:14

Go to page 801 for your next devotional reading.

I will uphold you with my
    righteous right hand.

11"All who rage against you
    will surely be ashamed and
      disgraced;
  those who oppose you
    will be as nothing and perish.
12Though you search for your enemies,
    you will not find them.
  Those who wage war against you
    will be as nothing at all.
13For I am the LORD, your God,
    who takes hold of your right hand
  and says to you, Do not fear;
    I will help you.
14Do not be afraid, O worm Jacob,
    O little Israel,

for I myself will help you," declares
    the LORD,
  your Redeemer, the Holy One of
    Israel.
15"See, I will make you into a threshing
    sledge,
  new and sharp, with many teeth.
  You will thresh the mountains and
    crush them,
  and reduce the hills to chaff.
16You will winnow them, the wind will
    pick them up,
  and a gale will blow them away.
  But you will rejoice in the LORD
    and glory in the Holy One of Israel.

17"The poor and needy search for
    water,
  but there is none;

FRIDAY

Read Isaiah 41:1–29
Key Verse Isaiah 41:10

Rely on His Strength — Larry Bauer

Picture yourself as a baby chick, ready to be hatched. You are surrounded by the white shell that has protected you to this point, but
as you've grown you've filled up all the space. It's cramped, hot and
you want out—now! Your prayer might be something like this:
"God, help me. Send someone to break this shell. Get me out of here,
now! Please!"

God's answer is clear, "Don't be afraid. I am with you. I will help
you and strengthen you. Just start pecking." "But God," you answer,
"just have someone come and crack the shell." Knowing the end
result of that request, God responds, "If I did that for you, my little
chick, you would die."

A baby chick's neck muscles will never develop enough to allow
it to eat unless it pecks its way out of its shell. In the same way, we
will never grow unless we experience times of trial. God does not
promise deliverance from our problems; he promises that he will be
with us in the midst of those problems, using them to develop us as
men and women of God.

Are you overwhelmed by life's pressures? Does a certain class
syllabus look like a huge mountain? Are finances or relationships
getting you down? Do you want to get out from under the pressure
right now? Your need for help is real, but how will God help you in
your time of need?

God has promised to be with you and see you through these
tests. Rely on him and his resources, and watch him work. Keep
"pecking" in his strength, and watch the breakthrough!

A Deeper Look
Psalm 28:7; Hebrews 13:6; James 1:2–4

Go to page 804 for your next devotional reading.

their tongues are parched with
thirst.
But I the LORD will answer them;
I, the God of Israel, will not
forsake them.
¹⁸I will make rivers flow on barren
heights,
and springs within the valleys.
I will turn the desert into pools of
water,
and the parched ground into
springs.
¹⁹I will put in the desert
the cedar and the acacia, the
myrtle and the olive.
I will set pines in the wasteland,
the fir and the cypress together,
²⁰so that people may see and know,
may consider and understand,
that the hand of the LORD has done
this,
that the Holy One of Israel has
created it.

²¹"Present your case," says the LORD.
"Set forth your arguments," says
Jacob's King.
²²"Bring in ∟ your idols⌐ to tell us
what is going to happen.
Tell us what the former things were,
so that we may consider them
and know their final outcome.
Or declare to us the things to come,
²³   tell us what the future holds,
so we may know that you are
gods.
Do something, whether good or bad,
so that we will be dismayed and
filled with fear.
²⁴But you are less than nothing
and your works are utterly
worthless;
he who chooses you is detestable.

²⁵"I have stirred up one from the north,
and he comes—
one from the rising sun who calls
on my name.
He treads on rulers as if they were
mortar,
as if he were a potter treading the
clay.
²⁶Who told of this from the beginning,
so we could know,
or beforehand, so we could say,
'He was right'?
No one told of this,
no one foretold it,
no one heard any words from you.

²⁷I was the first to tell Zion, 'Look,
here they are!'
I gave to Jerusalem a messenger of
good tidings.
²⁸I look but there is no one—
no one among them to give
counsel,
no one to give answer when I ask
them.
²⁹See, they are all false!
Their deeds amount to nothing;
their images are but wind and
confusion.

The Servant of the LORD

42 "Here is my servant, whom I
uphold,
my chosen one in whom I delight;
I will put my Spirit on him
and he will bring justice to the
nations.
²He will not shout or cry out,
or raise his voice in the streets.
³A bruised reed he will not break,
and a smoldering wick he will not
snuff out.
In faithfulness he will bring forth
justice;
⁴   he will not falter or be discouraged
till he establishes justice on earth.
In his law the islands will put their
hope."

⁵This is what God the LORD says—
he who created the heavens and
stretched them out,
who spread out the earth and all
that comes out of it,
who gives breath to its people,
and life to those who walk on it:
⁶"I, the LORD, have called you in
righteousness;
I will take hold of your hand.
I will keep you and will make you
to be a covenant for the people
and a light for the Gentiles,
⁷to open eyes that are blind,
to free captives from prison
and to release from the dungeon
those who sit in darkness.

⁸"I am the LORD; that is my name!
I will not give my glory to another
or my praise to idols.
⁹See, the former things have taken
place,
and new things I declare;
before they spring into being
I announce them to you."

Song of Praise to the LORD

¹⁰Sing to the LORD a new song,
　　his praise from the ends of the
　　　earth,
　　you who go down to the sea, and all
　　　that is in it,
　　you islands, and all who live in
　　　them.
¹¹Let the desert and its towns raise
　　their voices;
　　let the settlements where Kedar
　　　lives rejoice.
　　Let the people of Sela sing for joy;
　　let them shout from the
　　　mountaintops.
¹²Let them give glory to the LORD
　　and proclaim his praise in the
　　　islands.
¹³The LORD will march out like a mighty
　　man,
　　like a warrior he will stir up his
　　　zeal;
　　with a shout he will raise the battle
　　　cry
　　and will triumph over his enemies.

¹⁴"For a long time I have kept silent,
　　I have been quiet and held myself
　　　back.
　　But now, like a woman in childbirth,
　　I cry out, I gasp and pant.
¹⁵I will lay waste the mountains and
　　hills
　　and dry up all their vegetation;
　　I will turn rivers into islands
　　and dry up the pools.
¹⁶I will lead the blind by ways they
　　have not known,
　　along unfamiliar paths I will guide
　　　them;
　　I will turn the darkness into light
　　　before them
　　and make the rough places
　　　smooth.
　　These are the things I will do;
　　I will not forsake them.
¹⁷But those who trust in idols,
　　who say to images, 'You are our
　　　gods,'
　　will be turned back in utter shame.

Israel Blind and Deaf

¹⁸"Hear, you deaf;
　　look, you blind, and see!
¹⁹Who is blind but my servant,
　　and deaf like the messenger I send?
　　Who is blind like the one committed
　　　to me,
　　blind like the servant of the LORD?

²⁰You have seen many things, but have
　　paid no attention;
　　your ears are open, but you hear
　　　nothing."
²¹It pleased the LORD
　　for the sake of his righteousness
　　to make his law great and glorious.
²²But this is a people plundered and
　　looted,
　　all of them trapped in pits
　　or hidden away in prisons.
　　They have become plunder,
　　with no one to rescue them;
　　they have been made loot,
　　with no one to say, "Send them
　　　back."

²³Which of you will listen to this
　　or pay close attention in time to
　　　come?
²⁴Who handed Jacob over to become
　　loot,
　　and Israel to the plunderers?
　　Was it not the LORD,
　　against whom we have sinned?
　　For they would not follow his ways;
　　they did not obey his law.
²⁵So he poured out on them his
　　burning anger,
　　the violence of war.
　　It enveloped them in flames, yet they
　　　did not understand;
　　it consumed them, but they did not
　　　take it to heart.

Israel's Only Savior

43 But now, this is what the LORD
　　says—
　　he who created you, O Jacob,
　　he who formed you, O Israel:
　　"Fear not, for I have redeemed you;
　　I have summoned you by name;
　　　you are mine.
²When you pass through the waters,
　　I will be with you;
　　and when you pass through the
　　　rivers,
　　they will not sweep over you.
　　When you walk through the fire,
　　you will not be burned;
　　the flames will not set you ablaze.
³For I am the LORD, your God,
　　the Holy One of Israel, your Savior;
　　I give Egypt for your ransom,
　　Cush*ᵃ* and Seba in your stead.
⁴Since you are precious and honored
　　in my sight,
　　and because I love you,

ᵃ3 That is, the upper Nile region

Read Isaiah 43:1–28
Key Verses Isaiah 43:4–7

Identity and Purpose

God "formed and made" us and "created [us] for [his] glory," so why wouldn't he be proud of what he has made? In his wisdom, God designed each of us and made us unique; he determines our gender, race, temperament, intellect and physical characteristics. Sometimes we might look at ourselves and say, "This is not so good!" God looks at us and says, "Very good." Who are we going to believe?

God created the world—majestic mountains, surging oceans, a myriad of plants and animals. And he took special care to design and create *you* for a divine purpose. You are made in his image and for his glory. He takes a personal interest in your life. Believe it. You matter to God.

Digging Into the Word
1. What do the following passages say about the purpose of God's creation?—*Psalm 19:1–4; Colossians 1:16*
2. What is said in the following passages about how God has made and designed us?—*Job 33:4; Psalm 139:13–16; John 9:1–3*

Personal Reflection
What is one thing about yourself (appearance, temperament . . . and the like) that you would change if you could? Take time to thank God for this part of yourself every day for a week. Ask him to give you the eyes to see yourself the way he sees you.

One Step Deeper
Acts 17:24–28; Ephesians 2:10

Go to page 813 for your next devotional reading.

I will give men in exchange for you,
   and people in exchange for your
     life.
⁵Do not be afraid, for I am with you;
   I will bring your children from the
     east
   and gather you from the west.
⁶I will say to the north, 'Give them
     up!'
   and to the south, 'Do not hold
     them back.'
Bring my sons from afar
   and my daughters from the ends of
     the earth—
⁷everyone who is called by my name,
   whom I created for my glory,
   whom I formed and made."

⁸Lead out those who have eyes but are
     blind,
   who have ears but are deaf.
⁹All the nations gather together
   and the peoples assemble.
Which of them foretold this
   and proclaimed to us the former
     things?
Let them bring in their witnesses to
     prove they were right,
   so that others may hear and say,
     "It is true."
¹⁰"You are my witnesses," declares the
     LORD,
   "and my servant whom I have
     chosen,
so that you may know and believe
     me
   and understand that I am he.
Before me no god was formed,
   nor will there be one after me.
¹¹I, even I, am the LORD,
   and apart from me there is no
     savior.
¹²I have revealed and saved and
     proclaimed—
   I, and not some foreign god among
     you.
You are my witnesses," declares the
     LORD, "that I am God.
¹³ Yes, and from ancient days I am
     he.
No one can deliver out of my hand.
   When I act, who can reverse it?"

God's Mercy and Israel's Unfaithfulness

¹⁴This is what the LORD says—
   your Redeemer, the Holy One of
     Israel:
"For your sake I will send to Babylon
and bring down as fugitives all the
     Babylonians,ᵃ
in the ships in which they took
     pride.
¹⁵I am the LORD, your Holy One,
   Israel's Creator, your King."

¹⁶This is what the LORD says—
   he who made a way through the
     sea,
   a path through the mighty waters,
¹⁷who drew out the chariots and
     horses,
   the army and reinforcements
     together,
and they lay there, never to rise
     again,
   extinguished, snuffed out like a
     wick:
¹⁸"Forget the former things;
   do not dwell on the past.
¹⁹See, I am doing a new thing!
   Now it springs up; do you not
     perceive it?
I am making a way in the desert
   and streams in the wasteland.
²⁰The wild animals honor me,
   the jackals and the owls,
because I provide water in the desert
   and streams in the wasteland,
to give drink to my people, my
     chosen,
²¹ the people I formed for myself
   that they may proclaim my praise.

²²"Yet you have not called upon me,
     O Jacob,
   you have not wearied yourselves
     for me, O Israel.
²³You have not brought me sheep for
     burnt offerings,

ᵃ14 Or *Chaldeans*

POINT OF INTEREST

Isaiah 43:10-12

There is only one God. No matter how many idols we may create, they will never rival God. We will never be gods either, no matter how wealthy, prominent, powerful or "spiritual" we become. This is the message that God, through Isaiah, repeated over and over again: "I, even I, am the LORD."

nor honored me with your
sacrifices.
I have not burdened you with grain
offerings
nor wearied you with demands for
incense.
24You have not bought any fragrant
calamus for me,
or lavished on me the fat of your
sacrifices.
But you have burdened me with your
sins
and wearied me with your
offenses.

25"I, even I, am he who blots out
your transgressions, for my own
sake,
and remembers your sins no more.
26Review the past for me,
let us argue the matter together;
state the case for your innocence.
27Your first father sinned;
your spokesmen rebelled against
me.
28So I will disgrace the dignitaries of
your temple,
and I will consign Jacob to
destruction*a*
and Israel to scorn.

Israel the Chosen

44 "But now listen, O Jacob, my
servant,
Israel, whom I have chosen.
2This is what the LORD says—
he who made you, who formed
you in the womb,
and who will help you:
Do not be afraid, O Jacob, my
servant,
Jeshurun, whom I have chosen.
3For I will pour water on the thirsty
land,
and streams on the dry ground;
I will pour out my Spirit on your
offspring,
and my blessing on your
descendants.
4They will spring up like grass in a
meadow,
like poplar trees by flowing
streams.
5One will say, 'I belong to the LORD';
another will call himself by the
name of Jacob;
still another will write on his hand,
'The LORD's,'
and will take the name Israel.

The LORD, Not Idols

6"This is what the LORD says—
Israel's King and Redeemer, the
LORD Almighty:
I am the first and I am the last;
apart from me there is no God.
7Who then is like me? Let him
proclaim it.
Let him declare and lay out before
me
what has happened since I
established my ancient
people,
and what is yet to come—
yes, let him foretell what will
come.
8Do not tremble, do not be afraid.
Did I not proclaim this and foretell
it long ago?
You are my witnesses. Is there any
God besides me?
No, there is no other Rock; I know
not one."

9All who make idols are nothing,
and the things they treasure are
worthless.
Those who would speak up for them
are blind;
they are ignorant, to their own
shame.
10Who shapes a god and casts an idol,
which can profit him nothing?
11He and his kind will be put to shame;
craftsmen are nothing but men.
Let them all come together and take
their stand;
they will be brought down to terror
and infamy.

12The blacksmith takes a tool
and works with it in the coals;
he shapes an idol with hammers,
he forges it with the might of his
arm.
He gets hungry and loses his
strength;
he drinks no water and grows
faint.
13The carpenter measures with a line
and makes an outline with a
marker;
he roughs it out with chisels
and marks it with compasses.
He shapes it in the form of man,
of man in all his glory,

---

a28 The Hebrew term refers to the irrevocable
giving over of things or persons to the LORD, often
by totally destroying them.

that it may dwell in a shrine.
¹⁴He cut down cedars,
　or perhaps took a cypress or oak.
He let it grow among the trees of the
　　forest,
　or planted a pine, and the rain
　　made it grow.
¹⁵It is man's fuel for burning;
　some of it he takes and warms
　　himself,
　he kindles a fire and bakes bread.
But he also fashions a god and
　　worships it;
　he makes an idol and bows down
　　to it.
¹⁶Half of the wood he burns in the fire;
　over it he prepares his meal,
　he roasts his meat and eats his fill.
He also warms himself and says,
　"Ah! I am warm; I see the fire."
¹⁷From the rest he makes a god, his
　　idol;
　he bows down to it and worships.
He prays to it and says,
　"Save me; you are my god."
¹⁸They know nothing, they understand
　　nothing;
　their eyes are plastered over so
　　they cannot see,
　and their minds closed so they
　　cannot understand.
¹⁹No one stops to think,
　no one has the knowledge or
　　understanding to say,
"Half of it I used for fuel;
　I even baked bread over its coals,
　I roasted meat and I ate.
Shall I make a detestable thing from
　　what is left?
Shall I bow down to a block of
　　wood?"
²⁰He feeds on ashes, a deluded heart
　　misleads him;
　he cannot save himself, or say,
　"Is not this thing in my right hand
　　a lie?"

²¹"Remember these things, O Jacob,
　for you are my servant, O Israel.
I have made you, you are my servant;
　O Israel, I will not forget you.
²²I have swept away your offenses like
　　a cloud,
　your sins like the morning mist.
Return to me,
　for I have redeemed you."

²³Sing for joy, O heavens, for the LORD
　　has done this;
　shout aloud, O earth beneath.

Burst into song, you mountains,
　you forests and all your trees,
for the LORD has redeemed Jacob,
　he displays his glory in Israel.

Jerusalem to Be Inhabited

²⁴"This is what the LORD says—
　your Redeemer, who formed you
　　in the womb:

I am the LORD,
　who has made all things,
　who alone stretched out the heavens,
　who spread out the earth by myself,

²⁵who foils the signs of false prophets
　and makes fools of diviners,
who overthrows the learning of the
　　wise
　and turns it into nonsense,
²⁶who carries out the words of his
　　servants
　and fulfills the predictions of his
　　messengers,

who says of Jerusalem, 'It shall be
　　inhabited,'
of the towns of Judah, 'They shall
　　be built,'
　and of their ruins, 'I will restore
　　them,'
²⁷who says to the watery deep, 'Be dry,
　and I will dry up your streams,'
²⁸who says of Cyrus, 'He is my
　　shepherd
　and will accomplish all that I
　　please;
he will say of Jerusalem, "Let it be
　　rebuilt,"
　and of the temple, "Let its
　　foundations be laid." '

POINT OF INTEREST Isaiah 44:24

God rules the entire universe, yet he is also near to each one of us. This verse tells us that the Creator of millions of stars and planets is intimately concerned even with the development of a tiny baby in a mother's womb. How can we be satisfied with anything less than to worship him and devote our lives to him— each day, every moment?

45 "This is what the Lord says to his
anointed,
to Cyrus, whose right hand I take
hold of
to subdue nations before him
and to strip kings of their armor,
to open doors before him
so that gates will not be shut:
²I will go before you
and will level the mountains^a;
I will break down gates of bronze
and cut through bars of iron.
³I will give you the treasures of
darkness,
riches stored in secret places,
so that you may know that I am the
Lord,
the God of Israel, who summons
you by name.
⁴For the sake of Jacob my servant,
of Israel my chosen,
I summon you by name
and bestow on you a title of honor,
though you do not acknowledge
me.
⁵I am the Lord, and there is no other;
apart from me there is no God.
I will strengthen you,
though you have not
acknowledged me,
⁶so that from the rising of the sun
to the place of its setting
men may know there is none besides
me.
I am the Lord, and there is no
other.
⁷I form the light and create darkness,
I bring prosperity and create
disaster;
I, the Lord, do all these things.

⁸"You heavens above, rain down
righteousness;
let the clouds shower it down.
Let the earth open wide,
let salvation spring up,
let righteousness grow with it;
I, the Lord, have created it.

⁹"Woe to him who quarrels with his
Maker,
to him who is but a potsherd
among the potsherds on the
ground.
Does the clay say to the potter,
'What are you making?'
Does your work say,
'He has no hands'?
¹⁰Woe to him who says to his father,
'What have you begotten?'

or to his mother,
'What have you brought to birth?'

¹¹"This is what the Lord says—
the Holy One of Israel, and its
Maker:
Concerning things to come,
do you question me about my
children,
or give me orders about the work
of my hands?
¹²It is I who made the earth
and created mankind upon it.
My own hands stretched out the
heavens;
I marshaled their starry hosts.
¹³I will raise up Cyrus^b in my
righteousness:
I will make all his ways straight.
He will rebuild my city
and set my exiles free,
but not for a price or reward,
says the Lord Almighty."

¹⁴This is what the Lord says:

"The products of Egypt and the
merchandise of Cush,^c
and those tall Sabeans—
they will come over to you
and will be yours;
they will trudge behind you,
coming over to you in chains.
They will bow down before you
and plead with you, saying,
'Surely God is with you, and there is
no other;
there is no other god.' "

¹⁵Truly you are a God who hides
himself,
O God and Savior of Israel.
¹⁶All the makers of idols will be put to
shame and disgraced;
they will go off into disgrace
together.
¹⁷But Israel will be saved by the Lord
with an everlasting salvation;
you will never be put to shame or
disgraced,
to ages everlasting.

¹⁸For this is what the Lord says—
he who created the heavens,
he is God;
he who fashioned and made the
earth,

---

^a2 Dead Sea Scrolls and Septuagint; the meaning of
the word in the Masoretic Text is uncertain.
^b13 Hebrew *him*   ^c14 That is, the upper Nile
region

he founded it;
he did not create it to be empty,
but formed it to be inhabited—
he says:
"I am the LORD,
and there is no other.
¹⁹I have not spoken in secret,
from somewhere in a land of
darkness;
I have not said to Jacob's
descendants,
'Seek me in vain.'
I, the LORD, speak the truth;
I declare what is right.

²⁰"Gather together and come;
assemble, you fugitives from the
nations.
Ignorant are those who carry about
idols of wood,
who pray to gods that cannot save.
²¹Declare what is to be, present it—
let them take counsel together.
Who foretold this long ago,
who declared it from the distant
past?
Was it not I, the LORD?
And there is no God apart from
me,
a righteous God and a Savior;
there is none but me.

²²"Turn to me and be saved,
all you ends of the earth;
for I am God, and there is no
other.
²³By myself I have sworn,
my mouth has uttered in all
integrity
a word that will not be revoked:
Before me every knee will bow;
by me every tongue will swear.
²⁴They will say of me, 'In the LORD
alone
are righteousness and strength.' "
All who have raged against him
will come to him and be put to
shame.
²⁵But in the LORD all the descendants of
Israel
will be found righteous and will
exult.

Gods of Babylon

46 Bel bows down, Nebo stoops low;
their idols are borne by beasts of
burden.ᵃ
The images that are carried about are
burdensome,
a burden for the weary.

²They stoop and bow down together;
unable to rescue the burden,
they themselves go off into
captivity.

³"Listen to me, O house of Jacob,
all you who remain of the house of
Israel,
you whom I have upheld since you
were conceived,
and have carried since your birth.
⁴Even to your old age and gray hairs
I am he, I am he who will sustain
you.
I have made you and I will carry you;
I will sustain you and I will rescue
you.

⁵"To whom will you compare me or
count me equal?
To whom will you liken me that
we may be compared?
⁶Some pour out gold from their bags
and weigh out silver on the scales;
they hire a goldsmith to make it into
a god,
and they bow down and worship
it.
⁷They lift it to their shoulders and
carry it;
they set it up in its place, and
there it stands.
From that spot it cannot move.
Though one cries out to it, it does not
answer;
it cannot save him from his
troubles.

⁸"Remember this, fix it in mind,
take it to heart, you rebels.
⁹Remember the former things, those of
long ago;
I am God, and there is no other;

ᵃ1 Or *are but beasts and cattle*

POINT OF INTEREST

Isaiah 46:8-10

What has God done in your past? Though the Bible records God's actions throughout ancient history, he hasn't stopped working in individual lives. Take a moment to remember, perhaps even write down, what God has done for you.

I am God, and there is none like
me.
¹⁰I make known the end from the
beginning,
from ancient times, what is still to
come.
I say: My purpose will stand,
and I will do all that I please.
¹¹From the east I summon a bird of
prey;
from a far-off land, a man to fulfill
my purpose.
What I have said, that will I bring
about;
what I have planned, that will I
do.
¹²Listen to me, you stubborn-hearted,
you who are far from
righteousness.
¹³I am bringing my righteousness near,
it is not far away;
and my salvation will not be
delayed.
I will grant salvation to Zion,
my splendor to Israel.

The Fall of Babylon

47 "Go down, sit in the dust,
Virgin Daughter of Babylon;
sit on the ground without a throne,
Daughter of the Babylonians.ᵃ
No more will you be called
tender or delicate.
²Take millstones and grind flour;
take off your veil.
Lift up your skirts, bare your legs,
and wade through the streams.
³Your nakedness will be exposed
and your shame uncovered.
I will take vengeance;
I will spare no one."

⁴Our Redeemer—the LORD Almighty is
his name—
is the Holy One of Israel.

⁵"Sit in silence, go into darkness,
Daughter of the Babylonians;
no more will you be called
queen of kingdoms.
⁶I was angry with my people
and desecrated my inheritance;
I gave them into your hand,
and you showed them no mercy.
Even on the aged
you laid a very heavy yoke.
⁷You said, 'I will continue forever—
the eternal queen!'
But you did not consider these things
or reflect on what might happen.

⁸"Now then, listen, you wanton
creature,
lounging in your security
and saying to yourself,
'I am, and there is none besides
me.
I will never be a widow
or suffer the loss of children.'
⁹Both of these will overtake you
in a moment, on a single day:
loss of children and widowhood.
They will come upon you in full
measure,
in spite of your many sorceries
and all your potent spells.
¹⁰You have trusted in your wickedness
and have said, 'No one sees me.'
Your wisdom and knowledge mislead
you
when you say to yourself,
'I am, and there is none besides
me.'
¹¹Disaster will come upon you,
and you will not know how to
conjure it away.
A calamity will fall upon you
that you cannot ward off with a
ransom;
a catastrophe you cannot foresee
will suddenly come upon you.

¹²"Keep on, then, with your magic
spells
and with your many sorceries,
which you have labored at since
childhood.
Perhaps you will succeed,
perhaps you will cause terror.
¹³All the counsel you have received has
only worn you out!
Let your astrologers come forward,
those stargazers who make
predictions month by month,
let them save you from what is
coming upon you.
¹⁴Surely they are like stubble;
the fire will burn them up.
They cannot even save themselves
from the power of the flame.
Here are no coals to warm anyone;
here is no fire to sit by.
¹⁵That is all they can do for you—
these you have labored with
and trafficked with since
childhood.
Each of them goes on in his error;
there is not one that can save you.

ᵃ1 Or *Chaldeans*; also in verse 5

Stubborn Israel

48 "Listen to this, O house of Jacob,
you who are called by the name of
Israel
and come from the line of Judah,
you who take oaths in the name of
the LORD
and invoke the God of Israel—
but not in truth or righteousness—
²you who call yourselves citizens of
the holy city
and rely on the God of Israel—
the LORD Almighty is his name:
³I foretold the former things long ago,
my mouth announced them and I
made them known;
then suddenly I acted, and they
came to pass.
⁴For I knew how stubborn you were;
the sinews of your neck were iron,
your forehead was bronze.
⁵Therefore I told you these things long
ago;
before they happened I announced
them to you
so that you could not say,
'My idols did them;
my wooden image and metal god
ordained them.'
⁶You have heard these things; look at
them all.
Will you not admit them?

"From now on I will tell you of new
things,
of hidden things unknown to you.
⁷They are created now, and not long
ago;
you have not heard of them before
today.
So you cannot say,
'Yes, I knew of them.'
⁸You have neither heard nor
understood;
from of old your ear has not been
open.
Well do I know how treacherous you
are;
you were called a rebel from birth.
⁹For my own name's sake I delay my
wrath;
for the sake of my praise I hold it
back from you,
so as not to cut you off.
¹⁰See, I have refined you, though not
as silver;
I have tested you in the furnace of
affliction.

¹¹For my own sake, for my own sake, I
do this.
How can I let myself be defamed?
I will not yield my glory to
another.

Israel Freed

¹²"Listen to me, O Jacob,
Israel, whom I have called:
I am he;
I am the first and I am the last.
¹³My own hand laid the foundations of
the earth,
and my right hand spread out the
heavens;
when I summon them,
they all stand up together.

¹⁴"Come together, all of you, and
listen:
Which of ⌞the idols⌟ has foretold
these things?
The LORD's chosen ally
will carry out his purpose against
Babylon;
his arm will be against the
Babylonians. ᵃ
¹⁵I, even I, have spoken;
yes, I have called him.
I will bring him,
and he will succeed in his mission.

¹⁶"Come near me and listen to this:

"From the first announcement I have
not spoken in secret;
at the time it happens, I am there."

And now the Sovereign LORD has sent
me,
with his Spirit.

¹⁷This is what the LORD says—
your Redeemer, the Holy One of
Israel:
"I am the LORD your God,
who teaches you what is best for
you,
who directs you in the way you
should go.
¹⁸If only you had paid attention to my
commands,
your peace would have been like a
river,
your righteousness like the waves
of the sea.
¹⁹Your descendants would have been
like the sand,
your children like its numberless
grains;

ᵃ14 Or *Chaldeans*; also in verse 20

their name would never be cut off
     nor destroyed from before me."

²⁰Leave Babylon,
     flee from the Babylonians!
Announce this with shouts of joy
     and proclaim it.
Send it out to the ends of the earth;
     say, "The Lord has redeemed his
       servant Jacob."
²¹They did not thirst when he led them
       through the deserts;
     he made water flow for them from
       the rock;
he split the rock
     and water gushed out.

²²"There is no peace," says the Lord,
     "for the wicked."

The Servant of the Lord

49 Listen to me, you islands;
     hear this, you distant nations:
Before I was born the Lord called me;
     from my birth he has made
       mention of my name.
²He made my mouth like a sharpened
       sword,
     in the shadow of his hand he hid
       me;
he made me into a polished arrow
     and concealed me in his quiver.
³He said to me, "You are my servant,
     Israel, in whom I will display my
       splendor."
⁴But I said, "I have labored to no
       purpose;
     I have spent my strength in vain
       and for nothing.
Yet what is due me is in the Lord's
       hand,
     and my reward is with my God."

⁵And now the Lord says—
     he who formed me in the womb to
       be his servant
to bring Jacob back to him
     and gather Israel to himself,
for I am honored in the eyes of the
     Lord
     and my God has been my
       strength—
⁶he says:
"It is too small a thing for you to be
     my servant
to restore the tribes of Jacob
     and bring back those of Israel I
       have kept.

I will also make you a light for the
     Gentiles,
     that you may bring my salvation to
       the ends of the earth."

⁷This is what the Lord says—
     the Redeemer and Holy One of
       Israel—
to him who was despised and
       abhorred by the nation,
to the servant of rulers:
"Kings will see you and rise up,
     princes will see and bow down,
because of the Lord, who is faithful,
     the Holy One of Israel, who has
       chosen you."

Restoration of Israel

⁸This is what the Lord says:

"In the time of my favor I will
       answer you,
     and in the day of salvation I will
       help you;
I will keep you and will make you
     to be a covenant for the people,
to restore the land
     and to reassign its desolate
       inheritances,
⁹to say to the captives, 'Come out,'
     and to those in darkness, 'Be free!'

"They will feed beside the roads
     and find pasture on every barren
       hill.
¹⁰They will neither hunger nor thirst,
     nor will the desert heat or the sun
       beat upon them.
He who has compassion on them will
       guide them
     and lead them beside springs of
       water.
¹¹I will turn all my mountains into
       roads,
     and my highways will be raised
       up.
¹²See, they will come from afar—
     some from the north, some from
       the west,
some from the region of
     Aswan.ᵃ"

¹³Shout for joy, O heavens;
     rejoice, O earth;
     burst into song, O mountains!
For the Lord comforts his people
     and will have compassion on his
       afflicted ones.

ᵃ12 Dead Sea Scrolls; Masoretic Text *Sinim*

¹⁴But Zion said, "The LORD has forsaken me,
　the Lord has forgotten me."

¹⁵"Can a mother forget the baby at her breast
　and have no compassion on the child she has borne?
Though she may forget,
　I will not forget you!
¹⁶See, I have engraved you on the palms of my hands;
　your walls are ever before me.

¹⁷Your sons hasten back,
　and those who laid you waste depart from you.
¹⁸Lift up your eyes and look around;
　all your sons gather and come to you.
As surely as I live," declares the LORD,
　"you will wear them all as ornaments;
　you will put them on, like a bride.

¹⁹"Though you were ruined and made desolate

MONDAY

Read Isaiah 49:1–26
Key Verses Isaiah 49:5–6

Pass It On – Pete Dorrell

Often at Christmas Eve church services, the house lights are extinguished, leaving the sanctuary in darkness except for the light of one candle. From that one flame, a few other candles are lit, and then each of those are used to ignite a candle held by someone at the beginning of each row. Then each person in that row lights the candle of the person next to them. Within minutes the sanctuary is transformed—ablaze with the light of many candles. If one person had to go around and light all of the candles individually, the congregation would still be there on New Year's Day!

Jesus Christ was a light to the world, even though he never traveled more than two hundred miles from home and spent most of his time with the same twelve guys. He used the candle principle—he shared his life and his truths with his best friends, who in turn passed on what he had taught them, and then they passed it on to many others. Jesus knew that his disciples, and those who believed through them, would live for God and teach others about him (see John 17). He commissioned these men to go and make disciples, just as he had made them disciples (see Matthew 28:18–20). They were to be his light to the world.

And Jesus' light is still being passed on today. He has fulfilled the prophecy, "Arise, shine, for your light has come, and the glory of the LORD rises upon you" (Isaiah 60:1). Missionaries are trained and sent out to be beacons of that light. Evangelists certainly light a lot of fires under many people. But nothing beats one-to-one evangelism—just one person sharing the light of Jesus' love with another.

God tells us it is "too small a thing" for us to be his servants; he doesn't want us to hold our light cupped in our hands until there's nothing left but melted wax. Instead we are to pass it on, to light up our dorms, our schools, even our world.

A Deeper Look
Isaiah 52:7; Matthew 5:14; John 9:5

Go to page 818 for your next devotional reading.

and your land laid waste,
now you will be too small for your
   people,
and those who devoured you will
   be far away.
20The children born during your
   bereavement
will yet say in your hearing,
'This place is too small for us;
   give us more space to live in.'
21Then you will say in your heart,
'Who bore me these?
I was bereaved and barren;
   I was exiled and rejected.
Who brought these up?
I was left all alone,
   but these—where have they come
   from?' "

22This is what the Sovereign LORD says:

"See, I will beckon to the Gentiles,
   I will lift up my banner to the
   peoples;
they will bring your sons in their
   arms
   and carry your daughters on their
   shoulders.
23Kings will be your foster fathers,
   and their queens your nursing
   mothers.
They will bow down before you with
   their faces to the ground;
   they will lick the dust at your feet.
Then you will know that I am the
   LORD;
   those who hope in me will not be
   disappointed."

24Can plunder be taken from warriors,
   or captives rescued from the
   fierce*a*?

25But this is what the LORD says:

"Yes, captives will be taken from
   warriors,
   and plunder retrieved from the
   fierce;
I will contend with those who
   contend with you,
   and your children I will save.
26I will make your oppressors eat their
   own flesh;
   they will be drunk on their own
   blood, as with wine.
Then all mankind will know
   that I, the LORD, am your Savior,
   your Redeemer, the Mighty One of
   Jacob."

Israel's Sin and the Servant's Obedience

50 This is what the LORD says:

"Where is your mother's certificate of
   divorce
with which I sent her away?
Or to which of my creditors
   did I sell you?
Because of your sins you were sold;
   because of your transgressions
   your mother was sent away.
2When I came, why was there no one?
   When I called, why was there no
   one to answer?
Was my arm too short to ransom
   you?
Do I lack the strength to rescue
   you?
By a mere rebuke I dry up the sea,
   I turn rivers into a desert;
their fish rot for lack of water
   and die of thirst.
3I clothe the sky with darkness
   and make sackcloth its covering."

4The Sovereign LORD has given me an
   instructed tongue,
to know the word that sustains the
   weary.
He wakens me morning by morning,
   wakens my ear to listen like one
   being taught.
5The Sovereign LORD has opened my
   ears,
   and I have not been rebellious;
   I have not drawn back.
6I offered my back to those who beat
   me,
   my cheeks to those who pulled out
   my beard;
I did not hide my face
   from mocking and spitting.
7Because the Sovereign LORD helps me,
   I will not be disgraced.
Therefore have I set my face like
   flint,
   and I know I will not be put to
   shame.
8He who vindicates me is near.
   Who then will bring charges
   against me?
Let us face each other!
Who is my accuser?
   Let him confront me!

---

a24 Dead Sea Scrolls, Vulgate and Syriac (see also
Septuagint and verse 25); Masoretic Text *righteous*

⁹It is the Sovereign LORD who helps
me.
Who is he that will condemn me?
They will all wear out like a garment;
the moths will eat them up.

¹⁰Who among you fears the LORD
and obeys the word of his servant?
Let him who walks in the dark,
who has no light,
trust in the name of the LORD
and rely on his God.
¹¹But now, all you who light fires
and provide yourselves with
flaming torches,
go, walk in the light of your fires
and of the torches you have set
ablaze.
This is what you shall receive from
my hand:
You will lie down in torment.

Everlasting Salvation for Zion

51 "Listen to me, you who pursue
righteousness
and who seek the LORD:
Look to the rock from which you
were cut
and to the quarry from which you
were hewn;
²look to Abraham, your father,
and to Sarah, who gave you birth.
When I called him he was but one,
and I blessed him and made him
many.
³The LORD will surely comfort Zion
and will look with compassion on
all her ruins;
he will make her deserts like Eden,
her wastelands like the garden of
the LORD.
Joy and gladness will be found in
her,
thanksgiving and the sound of
singing.

⁴"Listen to me, my people;
hear me, my nation:
The law will go out from me;
my justice will become a light to
the nations.
⁵My righteousness draws near
speedily,
my salvation is on the way,
and my arm will bring justice to
the nations.
The islands will look to me
and wait in hope for my arm.
⁶Lift up your eyes to the heavens,
look at the earth beneath;

the heavens will vanish like smoke,
the earth will wear out like a
garment
and its inhabitants die like flies.
But my salvation will last forever,
my righteousness will never fail.

⁷"Hear me, you who know what is
right,
you people who have my law in
your hearts:
Do not fear the reproach of men
or be terrified by their insults.
⁸For the moth will eat them up like a
garment;
the worm will devour them like
wool.
But my righteousness will last
forever,
my salvation through all
generations."

⁹Awake, awake! Clothe yourself with
strength,
O arm of the LORD;
awake, as in days gone by,
as in generations of old.
Was it not you who cut Rahab to
pieces,
who pierced that monster through?
¹⁰Was it not you who dried up the sea,
the waters of the great deep,
who made a road in the depths of the
sea
so that the redeemed might cross
over?
¹¹The ransomed of the LORD will return.
They will enter Zion with singing;
everlasting joy will crown their
heads.
Gladness and joy will overtake them,
and sorrow and sighing will flee
away.

POINT OF INTEREST

Isaiah 51:2

Want to help your church
fellowship grow in atten-
dance? While the current
outlook may be discouraging,
look at the story of Abraham's life and
answer these questions: (1) How big was
his group when God called him? (2) How
did it grow? (3) How can you apply those
same principles to your church family?

¹²"I, even I, am he who comforts you.
Who are you that you fear mortal
men,
the sons of men, who are but
grass,
¹³that you forget the LORD your Maker,
who stretched out the heavens
and laid the foundations of the
earth,
that you live in constant terror every
day
because of the wrath of the
oppressor,
who is bent on destruction?
For where is the wrath of the
oppressor?
¹⁴   The cowering prisoners will soon
be set free;
they will not die in their dungeon,
nor will they lack bread.
¹⁵For I am the LORD your God,
who churns up the sea so that its
waves roar—
the LORD Almighty is his name.
¹⁶I have put my words in your mouth
and covered you with the shadow
of my hand—
I who set the heavens in place,
who laid the foundations of the
earth,
and who say to Zion, 'You are my
people.' "

The Cup of the LORD's Wrath

¹⁷Awake, awake!
Rise up, O Jerusalem,
you who have drunk from the hand
of the LORD
the cup of his wrath,
you who have drained to its dregs
the goblet that makes men stagger.
¹⁸Of all the sons she bore
there was none to guide her;
of all the sons she reared
there was none to take her by the
hand.
¹⁹These double calamities have come
upon you—
who can comfort you?—
ruin and destruction, famine and
sword—
who canᵃ console you?
²⁰Your sons have fainted;
they lie at the head of every street,
like antelope caught in a net.
They are filled with the wrath of the
LORD
and the rebuke of your God.

²¹Therefore hear this, you afflicted one,
made drunk, but not with wine.
²²This is what your Sovereign LORD
says,
your God, who defends his people:
"See, I have taken out of your hand
the cup that made you stagger;
from that cup, the goblet of my
wrath,
you will never drink again.
²³I will put it into the hands of your
tormentors,
who said to you,
'Fall prostrate that we may walk
over you.'
And you made your back like the
ground,
like a street to be walked over."

52 Awake, awake, O Zion,
clothe yourself with strength.
Put on your garments of splendor,
O Jerusalem, the holy city.
The uncircumcised and defiled
will not enter you again.
²Shake off your dust;
rise up, sit enthroned,
O Jerusalem.
Free yourself from the chains on your
neck,
O captive Daughter of Zion.

³For this is what the LORD says:

"You were sold for nothing,
and without money you will be
redeemed."

⁴For this is what the Sovereign LORD
says:

"At first my people went down to
Egypt to live;
lately, Assyria has oppressed them.

⁵"And now what do I have here?" declares the LORD.

"For my people have been taken
away for nothing,
and those who rule them mock,ᵇ"
declares the LORD.
"And all day long
my name is constantly
blasphemed.
⁶Therefore my people will know my
name;

ᵃ19 Dead Sea Scrolls, Septuagint, Vulgate and
Syriac; Masoretic Text / how can I   ᵇ5 Dead Sea
Scrolls and Vulgate; Masoretic Text wail

therefore in that day they will know
that it is I who foretold it.
Yes, it is I."

7How beautiful on the mountains
are the feet of those who bring
good news,
who proclaim peace,
who bring good tidings,
who proclaim salvation,
who say to Zion,
"Your God reigns!"
8Listen! Your watchmen lift up their
voices;
together they shout for joy.
When the LORD returns to Zion,
they will see it with their own
eyes.
9Burst into songs of joy together,
you ruins of Jerusalem,
for the LORD has comforted his people,
he has redeemed Jerusalem.
10The LORD will lay bare his holy arm
in the sight of all the nations,
and all the ends of the earth will see
the salvation of our God.

11Depart, depart, go out from there!
Touch no unclean thing!
Come out from it and be pure,
you who carry the vessels of the
LORD.
12But you will not leave in haste
or go in flight;
for the LORD will go before you,
the God of Israel will be your rear
guard.

The Suffering and Glory of the Servant

13See, my servant will act wisely[a];
he will be raised and lifted up and
highly exalted.
14Just as there were many who were
appalled at him[b]—
his appearance was so disfigured
beyond that of any man
and his form marred beyond
human likeness—
15so will he sprinkle many nations,[c]
and kings will shut their mouths
because of him.
For what they were not told, they will
see,
and what they have not heard,
they will understand.

53 Who has believed our message
and to whom has the arm of the
LORD been revealed?
2He grew up before him like a tender
shoot,
and like a root out of dry ground.
He had no beauty or majesty to
attract us to him,
nothing in his appearance that we
should desire him.
3He was despised and rejected by
men,
a man of sorrows, and familiar
with suffering.
Like one from whom men hide their
faces
he was despised, and we esteemed
him not.

4Surely he took up our infirmities
and carried our sorrows,
yet we considered him stricken by
God,
smitten by him, and afflicted.
5But he was pierced for our
transgressions,
he was crushed for our iniquities;
the punishment that brought us peace
was upon him,
and by his wounds we are healed.
6We all, like sheep, have gone astray,
each of us has turned to his own
way;
and the LORD has laid on him
the iniquity of us all.

7He was oppressed and afflicted,
yet he did not open his mouth;
he was led like a lamb to the
slaughter,
and as a sheep before her shearers
is silent,
so he did not open his mouth.
8By oppression[d] and judgment he
was taken away.
And who can speak of his
descendants?
For he was cut off from the land of
the living;
for the transgression of my people
he was stricken.[e]
9He was assigned a grave with the
wicked,

a13 Or will prosper   b14 Hebrew you
c15 Hebrew; Septuagint so will many nations
marvel at him   d8 Or From arrest   e8 Or
away. / Yet who of his generation considered / that
he was cut off from the land of the living / for the
transgression of my people, / to whom the blow was
due?

and with the rich in his death,
  though he had done no violence,
  nor was any deceit in his mouth.

¹⁰Yet it was the LORD's will to crush
    him and cause him to suffer,
  and though the LORD makes[a] his
    life a guilt offering,
he will see his offspring and prolong
    his days,
  and the will of the LORD will
    prosper in his hand.
¹¹After the suffering of his soul,

he will see the light ˌof lifeˌ[b] and
    be satisfied[c];
  by his knowledge[d] my righteous
    servant will justify many,
  and he will bear their iniquities.
¹²Therefore I will give him a portion
    among the great,[e]

Read Isaiah 53:1–12
Key Verse Isaiah 53:6

Wandering Sheep — John Frese

The front door burst open. "My sheep are gone!" my brother gasped.
A few days earlier, he had entered the sheep-herding world by
investing in two of the wooly creatures. Now Wendy and Cromwell
had found a breach in the fence surrounding their small pasture and
were on the loose.

The whole family dropped everything and went out to the barn
to investigate. Finding their escape route, we began to scour the
nearby creek and woods for them. We hoped they hadn't wandered
very far—beyond the creek was open pasture where predators
would love to make an easy meal out of the two defenseless sheep.
We spent the rest of the day searching fruitlessly for them. My
brother was so preoccupied with finding them that he hardly ate
and slept.

Wendy and Cromwell escaped because they didn't realize that
the fence was intended to protect them from harm. They just wanted to get to the appealing grass beyond it. They didn't recognize my
brother's barn as their home, or my brother as their shepherd.
Instead, they "turned to [their] own way" (Isaiah 53:6). The next
day we found the sheep at the far end of the open pasture, amazingly alive and unhurt, wandering by themselves without purpose or
direction.

We are a lot like Wendy and Cromwell. Left to our own devices
we go astray, looking for the greenest grass, the easiest route, the
path of least resistance to whatever pleasure we fancy at the
moment. Fortunately, our Good Shepherd goes looking for us. Jesus
"came to seek and to save what was lost" (Luke 19:10). And God
"laid on him the iniquity of us all" (Isaiah 53:6). In doing so, he
made us "smart sheep"; now we know the shepherd and can hear his
voice (see John 10:3–5). He calls us by name, and when we know
him, those greener pastures just don't look so green anymore!

A Deeper Look
Psalm 78:52–54; Ezekiel 34:11–16

Go to page 821 for your next devotional reading.

and he will divide the spoils with
    the strong,*a*
because he poured out his life unto
    death,
    and was numbered with the
        transgressors.
For he bore the sin of many,
    and made intercession for the
        transgressors.

The Future Glory of Zion

54 "Sing, O barren woman,
    you who never bore a child;
burst into song, shout for joy,
    you who were never in labor;
because more are the children of the
        desolate woman
    than of her who has a husband,"
                 says the LORD.
²"Enlarge the place of your tent,
    stretch your tent curtains wide,
    do not hold back;
lengthen your cords,
    strengthen your stakes.
³For you will spread out to the right
    and to the left;
    your descendants will dispossess
        nations
    and settle in their desolate cities.

⁴"Do not be afraid; you will not suffer
    shame.
    Do not fear disgrace; you will not
        be humiliated.
You will forget the shame of your
        youth
    and remember no more the
        reproach of your widowhood.
⁵For your Maker is your husband—
    the LORD Almighty is his name—
    the Holy One of Israel is your
        Redeemer;
he is called the God of all the
    earth.
⁶The LORD will call you back
    as if you were a wife deserted and
        distressed in spirit—
a wife who married young,
    only to be rejected," says your
        God.
⁷"For a brief moment I abandoned
    you,
    but with deep compassion I will
        bring you back.
⁸In a surge of anger
    I hid my face from you for a
        moment,
but with everlasting kindness

    I will have compassion on you,"
    says the LORD your Redeemer.

⁹"To me this is like the days of Noah,
    when I swore that the waters of
        Noah would never again
        cover the earth.
So now I have sworn not to be angry
    with you,
    never to rebuke you again.
¹⁰Though the mountains be shaken
    and the hills be removed,
yet my unfailing love for you will not
    be shaken
    nor my covenant of peace be
        removed,"
    says the LORD, who has compassion
    on you.

¹¹"O afflicted city, lashed by storms
    and not comforted,
I will build you with stones of
    turquoise,*b*
    your foundations with sapphires.*c*
¹²I will make your battlements of
    rubies,
    your gates of sparkling jewels,
    and all your walls of precious
        stones.
¹³All your sons will be taught by the
    LORD,
    and great will be your children's
        peace.
¹⁴In righteousness you will be
    established:
Tyranny will be far from you;
    you will have nothing to fear.
Terror will be far removed;
    it will not come near you.
¹⁵If anyone does attack you, it will not
    be my doing;
    whoever attacks you will surrender
    to you.

¹⁶"See, it is I who created the
    blacksmith
who fans the coals into flame
    and forges a weapon fit for its
        work.
And it is I who have created the
    destroyer to work havoc;
¹⁷ no weapon forged against you will
    prevail,
    and you will refute every tongue
    that accuses you.
This is the heritage of the servants of
    the LORD,

---

a 12 Or *numerous*   *b 11* The meaning of the
Hebrew for this word is uncertain.   *c 11* Or *lapis
lazuli*

and this is their vindication from
me,"
declares the LORD.

Invitation to the Thirsty

55 "Come, all you who are thirsty,
come to the waters;
and you who have no money,
come, buy and eat!
Come, buy wine and milk
without money and without cost.
²Why spend money on what is not
bread,
and your labor on what does not
satisfy?
Listen, listen to me, and eat what is
good,
and your soul will delight in the
richest of fare.
³Give ear and come to me;
hear me, that your soul may live.
I will make an everlasting covenant
with you,
my faithful love promised to
David.
⁴See, I have made him a witness to
the peoples,
a leader and commander of the
peoples.
⁵Surely you will summon nations you
know not,
and nations that do not know you
will hasten to you,
because of the LORD your God,
the Holy One of Israel,
for he has endowed you with
splendor."

⁶Seek the LORD while he may be found;
call on him while he is near.
⁷Let the wicked forsake his way
and the evil man his thoughts.
Let him turn to the LORD, and he will
have mercy on him,
and to our God, for he will freely
pardon.
⁸"For my thoughts are not your
thoughts,
neither are your ways my ways,"
declares the LORD.
⁹"As the heavens are higher than the
earth,
so are my ways higher than your
ways
and my thoughts than your
thoughts.
¹⁰As the rain and the snow
come down from heaven,
and do not return to it

without watering the earth
and making it bud and flourish,
so that it yields seed for the sower
and bread for the eater,
¹¹so is my word that goes out from my
mouth:
It will not return to me empty,
but will accomplish what I desire
and achieve the purpose for which
I sent it.
¹²You will go out in joy
and be led forth in peace;
the mountains and hills
will burst into song before you,
and all the trees of the field
will clap their hands.
¹³Instead of the thornbush will grow
the pine tree,
and instead of briers the myrtle
will grow.
This will be for the LORD's renown,
for an everlasting sign,
which will not be destroyed."

Salvation for Others

56 This is what the LORD says:

"Maintain justice
and do what is right,
for my salvation is close at hand
and my righteousness will soon be
revealed.
²Blessed is the man who does this,
the man who holds it fast,
who keeps the Sabbath without
desecrating it,
and keeps his hand from doing any
evil."

³Let no foreigner who has bound
himself to the LORD say,
"The LORD will surely exclude me
from his people."
And let not any eunuch complain,
"I am only a dry tree."

⁴For this is what the LORD says:

"To the eunuchs who keep my
Sabbaths,
who choose what pleases me
and hold fast to my covenant—
⁵to them I will give within my temple
and its walls
a memorial and a name
better than sons and daughters;
I will give them an everlasting name
that will not be cut off.
⁶And foreigners who bind themselves
to the LORD

to serve him,
to love the name of the LORD,
  and to worship him,
all who keep the Sabbath without
    desecrating it
  and who hold fast to my
    covenant—
⁷these I will bring to my holy
    mountain
  and give them joy in my house of
    prayer.
Their burnt offerings and sacrifices
  will be accepted on my altar;
for my house will be called
  a house of prayer for all nations."
⁸The Sovereign LORD declares—
  he who gathers the exiles of Israel:
"I will gather still others to them
  besides those already gathered."

God's Accusation Against the Wicked

⁹Come, all you beasts of the field,
  come and devour, all you beasts of
    the forest!
¹⁰Israel's watchmen are blind,
  they all lack knowledge;
they are all mute dogs,
  they cannot bark;
they lie around and dream,
  they love to sleep.
¹¹They are dogs with mighty appetites;
  they never have enough.
They are shepherds who lack
    understanding;
  they all turn to their own way,
  each seeks his own gain.
¹²"Come," each one cries, "let me get
    wine!
Let us drink our fill of beer!

WEDNESDAY

Read Isaiah 55:1–13
Key Verses Isaiah 55:8–11

God's Ways – Roger Hamilton

We'd had a great summer in Siberia, studying the Bible with Russian students who were eager to understand its wisdom and get to know God. But I didn't meet Maxim until the last day. In the midst of packing and saying good-bye to the others, he and I had only one short hour to discuss the gospel.

After our discussion I was left wondering why the Lord hadn't brought us together earlier. If we could have had the whole summer, Maxim might have accepted Jesus Christ. What I didn't know then was that Maxim *would* accept Christ—two years after I left Siberia.

I get uptight when things don't go as I planned. Through this experience, however, I learned that God's thoughts are not mine nor are his ways the same as mine. In fact, "As the heavens are higher than the earth, so are [God's] ways higher than [my] ways and [God's] thoughts than [my] thoughts" (Isaiah 55:9). His timing is never off and his methods are never short of perfect. I also experience firsthand the truth of Isaiah 55:11—that God's Word will always accomplish his purposes. When I shared God's Word with Maxim, God promised that it *would* make an impact, even if I wasn't there to see the results.

God is not bound by our sense of time and space. He works far beyond our limited perceptions of either one. He does use us to accomplish his purposes, but we don't have to bear the burden of timing and outcome. As surely as rain and snow produce growing plants on the earth, so will God do what he sets out to do.

A Deeper Look
Psalm 90:1–4; Proverbs 19:21; James 4:13–17

Go to page 824 for your next devotional reading.

And tomorrow will be like today,
or even far better.' "

57 The righteous perish,
and no one ponders it in his heart;
devout men are taken away,
and no one understands
that the righteous are taken away
to be spared from evil.
² Those who walk uprightly
enter into peace;
they find rest as they lie in death.

³ "But you—come here, you sons of a
sorceress,
you offspring of adulterers and
prostitutes!
⁴ Whom are you mocking?
At whom do you sneer
and stick out your tongue?
Are you not a brood of rebels,
the offspring of liars?
⁵ You burn with lust among the oaks
and under every spreading tree;
you sacrifice your children in the
ravines
and under the overhanging crags.
⁶ ⌊The idols⌋ among the smooth stones
of the ravines are your
portion;
they, they are your lot.
Yes, to them you have poured out
drink offerings
and offered grain offerings.
In the light of these things, should
I relent?
⁷ You have made your bed on a high
and lofty hill;
there you went up to offer your
sacrifices.
⁸ Behind your doors and your
doorposts
you have put your pagan symbols.
Forsaking me, you uncovered your
bed,
you climbed into it and opened it
wide;
you made a pact with those whose
beds you love,
and you looked on their
nakedness.
⁹ You went to Molech ᵃ with olive oil
and increased your perfumes.
You sent your ambassadors ᵇ far
away;
you descended to the grave ᶜ
itself!
¹⁰ You were wearied by all your ways,
but you would not say, 'It is
hopeless.'
You found renewal of your strength,
and so you did not faint.

¹¹ "Whom have you so dreaded and
feared
that you have been false to me,
and have neither remembered me
nor pondered this in your hearts?
Is it not because I have long been
silent
that you do not fear me?
¹² I will expose your righteousness and
your works,
and they will not benefit you.
¹³ When you cry out for help,
let your collection ⌊of idols⌋ save
you!
The wind will carry all of them off,
a mere breath will blow them
away.
But the man who makes me his
refuge
will inherit the land
and possess my holy mountain."

Comfort for the Contrite

¹⁴ And it will be said:

"Build up, build up, prepare the road!
Remove the obstacles out of the
way of my people."
¹⁵ For this is what the high and lofty
One says—
he who lives forever, whose name
is holy:
"I live in a high and holy place,
but also with him who is contrite
and lowly in spirit,
to revive the spirit of the lowly
and to revive the heart of the
contrite.
¹⁶ I will not accuse forever,
nor will I always be angry,
for then the spirit of man would grow
faint before me—
the breath of man that I have
created.
¹⁷ I was enraged by his sinful greed;
I punished him, and hid my face in
anger,
yet he kept on in his willful ways.
¹⁸ I have seen his ways, but I will heal
him;
I will guide him and restore
comfort to him,

ᵃ9 Or to the king   ᵇ9 Or idols   ᶜ9 Hebrew
Sheol

19 creating praise on the lips of the
        mourners in Israel.
Peace, peace, to those far and near,"
    says the LORD. "And I will heal
    them."
20But the wicked are like the tossing
        sea,
    which cannot rest,
    whose waves cast up mire and
        mud.
21"There is no peace," says my God,
    "for the wicked."

True Fasting

58 "Shout it aloud, do not hold back.
    Raise your voice like a trumpet.
Declare to my people their rebellion
    and to the house of Jacob their
        sins.
2For day after day they seek me out;
    they seem eager to know my ways,
as if they were a nation that does
        what is right
    and has not forsaken the
        commands of its God.
They ask me for just decisions
    and seem eager for God to come
        near them.
3'Why have we fasted,' they say,
    'and you have not seen it?
Why have we humbled ourselves,
    and you have not noticed?'

"Yet on the day of your fasting, you
        do as you please
    and exploit all your workers.
4Your fasting ends in quarreling and
        strife,
    and in striking each other with
        wicked fists.
You cannot fast as you do today
    and expect your voice to be heard
        on high.
5Is this the kind of fast I have chosen,
    only a day for a man to humble
        himself?
Is it only for bowing one's head like a
        reed
    and for lying on sackcloth and
        ashes?
Is that what you call a fast,
    a day acceptable to the LORD?

6"Is not this the kind of fasting I have
        chosen:
to loose the chains of injustice
    and untie the cords of the yoke,
to set the oppressed free
    and break every yoke?

7Is it not to share your food with the
        hungry
    and to provide the poor wanderer
        with shelter—
when you see the naked, to clothe
        him,
    and not to turn away from your
        own flesh and blood?
8Then your light will break forth like
        the dawn,
    and your healing will quickly
        appear;
then your righteousness*a* will go
        before you,
    and the glory of the LORD will be
        your rear guard.
9Then you will call, and the LORD will
        answer;
    you will cry for help, and he will
        say: Here am I.

"If you do away with the yoke of
        oppression,
    with the pointing finger and
        malicious talk,
10and if you spend yourselves in behalf
        of the hungry
    and satisfy the needs of the
        oppressed,
then your light will rise in the
        darkness,
    and your night will become like
        the noonday.
11The LORD will guide you always;
    he will satisfy your needs in a
        sun-scorched land
    and will strengthen your frame.
You will be like a well-watered
        garden,
    like a spring whose waters never
        fail.
12Your people will rebuild the ancient
        ruins
    and will raise up the age-old
        foundations;
you will be called Repairer of Broken
        Walls,
    Restorer of Streets with Dwellings.

13"If you keep your feet from breaking
        the Sabbath
    and from doing as you please on
        my holy day,
if you call the Sabbath a delight
    and the LORD's holy day honorable,
and if you honor it by not going your
        own way

a8 Or your righteous One

and not doing as you please or
    speaking idle words,
¹⁴then you will find your joy in the
    LORD,
and I will cause you to ride on the
    heights of the land
and to feast on the inheritance of
    your father Jacob."
                The mouth of the LORD
                    has spoken.

Sin, Confession and Redemption

59 Surely the arm of the LORD is not
    too short to save,
nor his ear too dull to hear.

²But your iniquities have separated
    you from your God;
your sins have hidden his face from
    you,
    so that he will not hear.
³For your hands are stained with
    blood,
    your fingers with guilt.
Your lips have spoken lies,
    and your tongue mutters wicked
        things.
⁴No one calls for justice;
    no one pleads his case with
        integrity.
They rely on empty arguments and
    speak lies;

THURSDAY

Read Isaiah 58:1–14
Key Verses Isaiah 58:10–12

Scorched or Spent? —Jeanne Hougen

Sometimes it seems as if the "sun-scorched land" that we live in is
determined to suck us dry. We're like plants in a desert that strive to
get enough water to survive. We send our roots out, hoping to find
water. In the process we take water away from another plant that is
also struggling to survive. We tend to fight bitterly for anything we
can get.

But Isaiah gives us a different perspective on this hopeless picture—a surprising one! What would happen if we generously
offered our resources to someone else—to spend ourselves in service to others? We may be afraid that doing so will leave us depleted, and we probably become drained if we are working on our own
strength, but that's not necessarily so. God promises that when we
do away with maliciousness and blame, when we spend ourselves
looking for justice and meeting the needs of those who cannot provide for themselves, that we'll actually flourish instead of burning
out like a scorched cactus. We will instead become like a beautiful,
lush garden in the middle of that desert.

How does this happen? When we live as God would have us live,
we tap into a supply of "living water." While our own needs are
legitimate, God loves us so deeply that he longs to meet those
needs himself. When we are fully supplied, we then have the
resources to help others, showing God's love in a concrete way to
those in need.

In our culture, we don't like to rely on anything or anyone to provide for us. It just goes against our natural inclinations. But if we
can learn to trust God to take care of us, we'll do much more than
survive—we'll thrive *and* help others along the way.

A Deeper Look
Jeremiah 2:13; John 4:13–14

Go to page 827 for your next devotional reading.

they conceive trouble and give
    birth to evil.
⁵They hatch the eggs of vipers
    and spin a spider's web.
Whoever eats their eggs will die,
    and when one is broken, an adder
    is hatched.
⁶Their cobwebs are useless for
    clothing;
    they cannot cover themselves with
    what they make.
Their deeds are evil deeds,
    and acts of violence are in their
    hands.
⁷Their feet rush into sin;
    they are swift to shed innocent
    blood.
Their thoughts are evil thoughts;
    ruin and destruction mark their
    ways.
⁸The way of peace they do not know;
    there is no justice in their paths.
They have turned them into crooked
    roads;
    no one who walks in them will
    know peace.

⁹So justice is far from us,
    and righteousness does not reach
    us.
We look for light, but all is darkness;
    for brightness, but we walk in
    deep shadows.
¹⁰Like the blind we grope along the
    wall,
    feeling our way like men without
    eyes.
At midday we stumble as if it were
    twilight;
    among the strong, we are like the
    dead.
¹¹We all growl like bears;
    we moan mournfully like doves.
We look for justice, but find none;
    for deliverance, but it is far away.
¹²For our offenses are many in your
    sight,
    and our sins testify against us.
Our offenses are ever with us,
    and we acknowledge our iniquities:
¹³rebellion and treachery against the
    Lord,
    turning our backs on our God,
fomenting oppression and revolt,
    uttering lies our hearts have
    conceived.
¹⁴So justice is driven back,
    and righteousness stands at a
    distance;

truth has stumbled in the streets,
    honesty cannot enter.
¹⁵Truth is nowhere to be found,
    and whoever shuns evil becomes a
    prey.

The Lord looked and was displeased
    that there was no justice.
¹⁶He saw that there was no one,
    he was appalled that there was no
    one to intervene;
so his own arm worked salvation for
    him,
    and his own righteousness
    sustained him.
¹⁷He put on righteousness as his
    breastplate,
    and the helmet of salvation on his
    head;
he put on the garments of vengeance
    and wrapped himself in zeal as in
    a cloak.
¹⁸According to what they have done,
    so will he repay
wrath to his enemies
    and retribution to his foes;
    he will repay the islands their due.
¹⁹From the west, men will fear the
    name of the Lord,
    and from the rising of the sun,
    they will revere his glory.
For he will come like a pent-up flood
    that the breath of the Lord drives
    along.ᵃ

²⁰"The Redeemer will come to Zion,
    to those in Jacob who repent of
    their sins,"

                    declares the Lord.

²¹"As for me, this is my covenant with
them," says the Lord. "My Spirit, who is
on you, and my words that I have put in
your mouth will not depart from your
mouth, or from the mouths of your children, or from the mouths of their descendants from this time on and forever,"
says the Lord.

The Glory of Zion

60 "Arise, shine, for your light has
    come,
    and the glory of the Lord rises
    upon you.
²See, darkness covers the earth
    and thick darkness is over the
    peoples,
but the Lord rises upon you

ᵃ19 Or *When the enemy comes in like a flood, / the
Spirit of the Lord will put him to flight*

and his glory appears over you.
³Nations will come to your light,
and kings to the brightness of your
dawn.

⁴"Lift up your eyes and look about
you:
All assemble and come to you;
your sons come from afar,
and your daughters are carried on
the arm.
⁵Then you will look and be radiant,
your heart will throb and swell
with joy;
the wealth on the seas will be
brought to you,
to you the riches of the nations
will come.
⁶Herds of camels will cover your land,
young camels of Midian and
Ephah.
And all from Sheba will come,
bearing gold and incense
and proclaiming the praise of the
LORD.
⁷All Kedar's flocks will be gathered to
you,
the rams of Nebaioth will serve
you;
they will be accepted as offerings on
my altar,
and I will adorn my glorious
temple.

⁸"Who are these that fly along like
clouds,
like doves to their nests?
⁹Surely the islands look to me;
in the lead are the ships of
Tarshish,ᵃ
bringing your sons from afar,
with their silver and gold,
to the honor of the LORD your God,
the Holy One of Israel,
for he has endowed you with
splendor.

¹⁰"Foreigners will rebuild your walls,
and their kings will serve you.
Though in anger I struck you,
in favor I will show you
compassion.
¹¹Your gates will always stand open,
they will never be shut, day or
night,
so that men may bring you the
wealth of the nations—
their kings led in triumphal
procession.

¹²For the nation or kingdom that will
not serve you will perish;
it will be utterly ruined.

¹³"The glory of Lebanon will come to
you,
the pine, the fir and the cypress
together,
to adorn the place of my sanctuary;
and I will glorify the place of my
feet.
¹⁴The sons of your oppressors will
come bowing before you;
all who despise you will bow
down at your feet
and will call you the City of the LORD,
Zion of the Holy One of Israel.

¹⁵"Although you have been forsaken
and hated,
with no one traveling through,
I will make you the everlasting pride
and the joy of all generations.
¹⁶You will drink the milk of nations
and be nursed at royal breasts.
Then you will know that I, the LORD,
am your Savior,
your Redeemer, the Mighty One of
Jacob.
¹⁷Instead of bronze I will bring you
gold,
and silver in place of iron.
Instead of wood I will bring you
bronze,
and iron in place of stones.
I will make peace your governor
and righteousness your ruler.
¹⁸No longer will violence be heard in
your land,
nor ruin or destruction within your
borders,
but you will call your walls Salvation
and your gates Praise.
¹⁹The sun will no more be your light
by day,
nor will the brightness of the moon
shine on you,
for the LORD will be your everlasting
light,
and your God will be your glory.
²⁰Your sun will never set again,
and your moon will wane no more;
the LORD will be your everlasting light,
and your days of sorrow will end.
²¹Then will all your people be righteous
and they will possess the land
forever.
They are the shoot I have planted,

ᵃ9 Or the trading ships

the work of my hands,
for the display of my splendor.
²²The least of you will become a
thousand,
the smallest a mighty nation.
I am the LORD;
in its time I will do this swiftly."

The Year of the LORD's Favor

61 The Spirit of the Sovereign LORD is
on me,
because the LORD has anointed me
to preach good news to the poor.

He has sent me to bind up the
brokenhearted,
to proclaim freedom for the
captives
and release from darkness for the
prisoners,ᵃ
²to proclaim the year of the LORD's
favor
and the day of vengeance of our
God,
to comfort all who mourn,

ᵃ1 Hebrew; Septuagint *the blind*

FRIDAY

Read Isaiah 60:1–22
Key Verse Isaiah 60:22

Feeling Small? – Rich Jarvi

We often hear about the importance of one life. Teachers endeavor
to touch the life of one child; politicians assure us that our one vote
counts. But many of us who are caught up in the daily grind often
find it hard to believe that our one life matters much. Our world
seems full of more problems than solutions, more criminals than
heroes. Can we *really* make a difference?

Enter God's perspective. Consider his promise to Isaiah and to
Israel in this prophetic passage. Consider his call to Abraham in the
book of Genesis: "I will surely bless you and make your descendants
as numerous as the stars in the sky and as the sand on the
seashore" (Genesis 22:17). It seems that God is in the business of
taking one seemingly insignificant life and multiplying it for his
glory.

God's work doesn't necessarily happen overnight, however. The
promise Isaiah heard thousands of years ago has yet to reach its
complete fulfillment. Many years and more than a few problems
passed before Abraham ever saw the child through whom this
promise was to be fulfilled. Then, though Abraham had been given a
grand promise, he held in his arms only one helpless little baby—a
very small start on building a nation. But he also had deep faith.
Despite what seemed like impossible odds, Abraham saw in Isaac
the potential for the nation God had promised.

What about us? Do we believe that God can work in us and
through us in the lives of those we know? Do we have, as Abraham
did, enough vision to see the potential for God's work in the everyday moments and actions of our lives? Do we believe that we are
really working to bring about the kingdom of God? Like Isaiah, do
we continually look for the Messianic kingdom that is to come and
remember that God has a vision for each of us to really make a difference?

A Deeper Look
Numbers 23:19; Romans 4:18–22; Ephesians 3:20–21

Go to page 833 for your next devotional reading.

³ and provide for those who grieve
    in Zion—
to bestow on them a crown of beauty
    instead of ashes,
the oil of gladness
    instead of mourning,
and a garment of praise
    instead of a spirit of despair.
They will be called oaks of
    righteousness,
a planting of the LORD
    for the display of his splendor.

⁴They will rebuild the ancient ruins
    and restore the places long
      devastated;
they will renew the ruined cities
    that have been devastated for
      generations.
⁵Aliens will shepherd your flocks;
    foreigners will work your fields
      and vineyards.
⁶And you will be called priests of the
    LORD,
you will be named ministers of our
    God.
You will feed on the wealth of
    nations,
and in their riches you will boast.

⁷Instead of their shame
    my people will receive a double
      portion,
and instead of disgrace
    they will rejoice in their
      inheritance;
and so they will inherit a double
    portion in their land,
    and everlasting joy will be theirs.

⁸"For I, the LORD, love justice;
    I hate robbery and iniquity.
In my faithfulness I will reward them
    and make an everlasting covenant
      with them.
⁹Their descendants will be known
    among the nations
    and their offspring among the
      peoples.
All who see them will acknowledge
    that they are a people the LORD has
      blessed."

¹⁰I delight greatly in the LORD;
    my soul rejoices in my God.
For he has clothed me with garments
    of salvation
and arrayed me in a robe of
    righteousness,
as a bridegroom adorns his head like
    a priest,

and as a bride adorns herself with
    her jewels.
¹¹For as the soil makes the sprout come
    up
and a garden causes seeds to grow,
so the Sovereign LORD will make
    righteousness and praise
    spring up before all nations.

Zion's New Name

62 For Zion's sake I will not keep
    silent,
    for Jerusalem's sake I will not
      remain quiet,
till her righteousness shines out like
    the dawn,
    her salvation like a blazing torch.
²The nations will see your
    righteousness,
    and all kings your glory;
you will be called by a new name
    that the mouth of the LORD will
      bestow.
³You will be a crown of splendor in
    the LORD's hand,
    a royal diadem in the hand of your
      God.
⁴No longer will they call you Deserted,
    or name your land Desolate.
But you will be called Hephzibah,[a]
    and your land Beulah[b];
for the LORD will take delight in you,
    and your land will be married.
⁵As a young man marries a maiden,
    so will your sons[c] marry you;
as a bridegroom rejoices over his
    bride,
    so will your God rejoice over you.

⁶I have posted watchmen on your
    walls, O Jerusalem;
they will never be silent day or
    night.
You who call on the LORD,
    give yourselves no rest,
⁷and give him no rest till he
    establishes Jerusalem
and makes her the praise of the
    earth.

⁸The LORD has sworn by his right hand
    and by his mighty arm:
"Never again will I give your grain
    as food for your enemies,
and never again will foreigners drink
    the new wine
    for which you have toiled;

---

a4 *Hephzibah* means *my delight is in her.*
b4 *Beulah* means *married.*   *c5* Or *Builder*

⁹but those who harvest it will eat it
  and praise the LORD,
and those who gather the grapes will
    drink it
  in the courts of my sanctuary."

¹⁰Pass through, pass through the gates!
  Prepare the way for the people.
Build up, build up the highway!
  Remove the stones.
Raise a banner for the nations.

¹¹The LORD has made proclamation
  to the ends of the earth:
"Say to the Daughter of Zion,
  'See, your Savior comes!
See, his reward is with him,
  and his recompense accompanies
    him.' "
¹²They will be called the Holy People,
  the Redeemed of the LORD;
and you will be called Sought After,
  the City No Longer Deserted.

God's Day of Vengeance
and Redemption

63 Who is this coming from Edom,
     from Bozrah, with his garments
       stained crimson?
Who is this, robed in splendor,
  striding forward in the greatness of
    his strength?

"It is I, speaking in righteousness,
  mighty to save."

²Why are your garments red,
  like those of one treading the
    winepress?

³"I have trodden the winepress alone;
  from the nations no one was with
    me.
I trampled them in my anger
  and trod them down in my wrath;
their blood spattered my garments,
  and I stained all my clothing.
⁴For the day of vengeance was in my
    heart,
  and the year of my redemption has
    come.
⁵I looked, but there was no one to
    help,
  I was appalled that no one gave
    support;
so my own arm worked salvation for
    me,
  and my own wrath sustained me.
⁶I trampled the nations in my anger;

in my wrath I made them drunk
  and poured their blood on the
    ground."

Praise and Prayer
⁷I will tell of the kindnesses of the
    LORD,
  the deeds for which he is to be
    praised,
according to all the LORD has done
    for us—
yes, the many good things he has
    done
  for the house of Israel,
according to his compassion and
    many kindnesses.
⁸He said, "Surely they are my people,
  sons who will not be false to me";
and so he became their Savior.
⁹In all their distress he too was
    distressed,
  and the angel of his presence
    saved them.
In his love and mercy he redeemed
    them;
  he lifted them up and carried them
    all the days of old.
¹⁰Yet they rebelled
  and grieved his Holy Spirit.
So he turned and became their enemy
  and he himself fought against
    them.

¹¹Then his people recalled*a* the days
    of old,
  the days of Moses and his
    people—
where is he who brought them
    through the sea,
  with the shepherd of his flock?
Where is he who set
  his Holy Spirit among them,
¹²who sent his glorious arm of power
  to be at Moses' right hand,
who divided the waters before them,
  to gain for himself everlasting
    renown,
¹³who led them through the depths?
Like a horse in open country,
  they did not stumble;
¹⁴like cattle that go down to the plain,
  they were given rest by the Spirit
    of the LORD.
This is how you guided your people
  to make for yourself a glorious
    name.

---

a 11 Or *But may he recall*

¹⁵Look down from heaven and see
　　from your lofty throne, holy and
　　glorious.
Where are your zeal and your might?
　　Your tenderness and compassion
　　are withheld from us.
¹⁶But you are our Father,
　　though Abraham does not know us
　　or Israel acknowledge us;
you, O LORD, are our Father,
　　our Redeemer from of old is your
　　name.
¹⁷Why, O LORD, do you make us
　　wander from your ways
　　and harden our hearts so we do
　　not revere you?
Return for the sake of your servants,
　　the tribes that are your inheritance.
¹⁸For a little while your people
　　possessed your holy place,
　　but now our enemies have
　　trampled down your
　　sanctuary.
¹⁹We are yours from of old;
　　but you have not ruled over them,
　　they have not been called by your
　　name.ᵃ

64 Oh, that you would rend the
　　heavens and come down,
　　that the mountains would tremble
　　before you!
²As when fire sets twigs ablaze
　　and causes water to boil,
come down to make your name
　　known to your enemies
　　and cause the nations to quake
　　before you!
³For when you did awesome things
　　that we did not expect,
　　you came down, and the
　　mountains trembled before
　　you.
⁴Since ancient times no one has heard,
　　no ear has perceived,
no eye has seen any God besides
　　you,
　　who acts on behalf of those who
　　wait for him.
⁵You come to the help of those who
　　gladly do right,
　　who remember your ways.
But when we continued to sin against
　　them,
　　you were angry.
　　How then can we be saved?
⁶All of us have become like one who
　　is unclean,

and all our righteous acts are like
　　filthy rags;
we all shrivel up like a leaf,
　　and like the wind our sins sweep
　　us away.
⁷No one calls on your name
　　or strives to lay hold of you;
for you have hidden your face from
　　us
　　and made us waste away because
　　of our sins.

⁸Yet, O LORD, you are our Father.
　　We are the clay, you are the
　　potter;
　　we are all the work of your hand.
⁹Do not be angry beyond measure,
　　O LORD;
　　do not remember our sins forever.
Oh, look upon us, we pray,
　　for we are all your people.
¹⁰Your sacred cities have become a
　　desert;
　　even Zion is a desert, Jerusalem a
　　desolation.
¹¹Our holy and glorious temple, where
　　our fathers praised you,
has been burned with fire,
　　and all that we treasured lies in
　　ruins.
¹²After all this, O LORD, will you hold
　　yourself back?
　　Will you keep silent and punish us
　　beyond measure?

ᵃ19 Or *We are like those you have never ruled, /
like those never called by your name*

POINT OF INTEREST

Isaiah 64:8

This image of the potter working in clay occurs several times in Scripture. It illustrates that we are as helpless as lumps of clay to make anything valuable of ourselves. God has the sovereignty to shape us as he sees fit, much as a potter has the power and the right to mold the clay. How pliable and moldable are we going to be? Will we question God about his motives (see Isaiah 45:9), or will we let God shape us and make us ready for his use? (See 2 Timothy 2:20.)

Judgment and Salvation

65 "I revealed myself to those who did
  not ask for me;
  I was found by those who did not
    seek me.
To a nation that did not call on my
    name,
  I said, 'Here am I, here am I.'
²All day long I have held out my
    hands
  to an obstinate people,
who walk in ways not good,
  pursuing their own imaginations—
³a people who continually provoke me
    to my very face,
offering sacrifices in gardens
  and burning incense on altars of
    brick;
⁴who sit among the graves
  and spend their nights keeping
    secret vigil;
who eat the flesh of pigs,
  and whose pots hold broth of
    unclean meat;
⁵who say, 'Keep away; don't come
    near me,
  for I am too sacred for you!'
Such people are smoke in my nostrils,
  a fire that keeps burning all day.

⁶"See, it stands written before me:
  I will not keep silent but will pay
    back in full;
  I will pay it back into their laps—
⁷both your sins and the sins of your
    fathers,"
  says the LORD.
"Because they burned sacrifices on
    the mountains
  and defied me on the hills,
I will measure into their laps
  the full payment for their former
    deeds."

⁸This is what the LORD says:

"As when juice is still found in a
    cluster of grapes
  and men say, 'Don't destroy it,
    there is yet some good in it,'
so will I do in behalf of my servants;
  I will not destroy them all.
⁹I will bring forth descendants from
    Jacob,
  and from Judah those who will
    possess my mountains;
my chosen people will inherit them,
  and there will my servants live.
¹⁰Sharon will become a pasture for
    flocks,

and the Valley of Achor a resting
    place for herds,
  for my people who seek me.

¹¹"But as for you who forsake the LORD
  and forget my holy mountain,
who spread a table for Fortune
  and fill bowls of mixed wine for
    Destiny,
¹²I will destine you for the sword,
  and you will all bend down for the
    slaughter;
for I called but you did not answer,
  I spoke but you did not listen.
You did evil in my sight
  and chose what displeases me."

¹³Therefore this is what the Sovereign
LORD says:

"My servants will eat,
  but you will go hungry;
my servants will drink,
  but you will go thirsty;
my servants will rejoice,
  but you will be put to shame.
¹⁴My servants will sing
  out of the joy of their hearts,
but you will cry out
  from anguish of heart
  and wail in brokenness of spirit.
¹⁵You will leave your name
  to my chosen ones as a curse;
the Sovereign LORD will put you to
    death,
  but to his servants he will give
    another name.
¹⁶Whoever invokes a blessing in the
    land
  will do so by the God of truth;
he who takes an oath in the land
  will swear by the God of truth.
For the past troubles will be forgotten
  and hidden from my eyes.

New Heavens and a New Earth

¹⁷"Behold, I will create
  new heavens and a new earth.
The former things will not be
    remembered,
  nor will they come to mind.
¹⁸But be glad and rejoice forever
  in what I will create,
for I will create Jerusalem to be a
    delight
  and its people a joy.
¹⁹I will rejoice over Jerusalem
  and take delight in my people;
the sound of weeping and of crying
  will be heard in it no more.

20"Never again will there be in it
    an infant who lives but a few days,
    or an old man who does not live
        out his years;
he who dies at a hundred
    will be thought a mere youth;
he who fails to reach*a* a hundred
    will be considered accursed.
21They will build houses and dwell in
        them;
    they will plant vineyards and eat
        their fruit.
22No longer will they build houses and
        others live in them,
    or plant and others eat.
For as the days of a tree,
    so will be the days of my people;
my chosen ones will long enjoy
    the works of their hands.
23They will not toil in vain
    or bear children doomed to
        misfortune;
for they will be a people blessed by
        the LORD,
    they and their descendants with
        them.
24Before they call I will answer;
    while they are still speaking I will
        hear.
25The wolf and the lamb will feed
        together,
    and the lion will eat straw like the
        ox,
    but dust will be the serpent's food.
They will neither harm nor destroy
    on all my holy mountain,"
                says the LORD.

Judgment and Hope

66 This is what the LORD says:

"Heaven is my throne,
    and the earth is my footstool.
Where is the house you will build for
        me?
Where will my resting place be?
2Has not my hand made all these
        things,
    and so they came into being?"
             declares the LORD.

"This is the one I esteem:
    he who is humble and contrite in
        spirit,
    and trembles at my word.
3But whoever sacrifices a bull
    is like one who kills a man,
and whoever offers a lamb,
    like one who breaks a dog's neck;

whoever makes a grain offering
    is like one who presents pig's
        blood,
and whoever burns memorial incense,
    like one who worships an idol.
They have chosen their own ways,
    and their souls delight in their
        abominations;
4so I also will choose harsh treatment
        for them
    and will bring upon them what
        they dread.
For when I called, no one answered,
    when I spoke, no one listened.
They did evil in my sight
    and chose what displeases me."

5Hear the word of the LORD,
    you who tremble at his word:
"Your brothers who hate you,
    and exclude you because of my
        name, have said,
'Let the LORD be glorified,
    that we may see your joy!'
Yet they will be put to shame.
6Hear that uproar from the city,
    hear that noise from the temple!
It is the sound of the LORD
    repaying his enemies all they
        deserve.

7"Before she goes into labor,
    she gives birth;
before the pains come upon her,
    she delivers a son.
8Who has ever heard of such a thing?
    Who has ever seen such things?
Can a country be born in a day
    or a nation be brought forth in a
        moment?
Yet no sooner is Zion in labor
    than she gives birth to her
        children.
9Do I bring to the moment of birth
    and not give delivery?" says the
        LORD.
"Do I close up the womb
    when I bring to delivery?" says
        your God.
10"Rejoice with Jerusalem and be glad
        for her,
    all you who love her;
rejoice greatly with her,
    all you who mourn over her.
11For you will nurse and be satisfied
    at her comforting breasts;
    you will drink deeply

a20 Or / *the sinner who reaches*

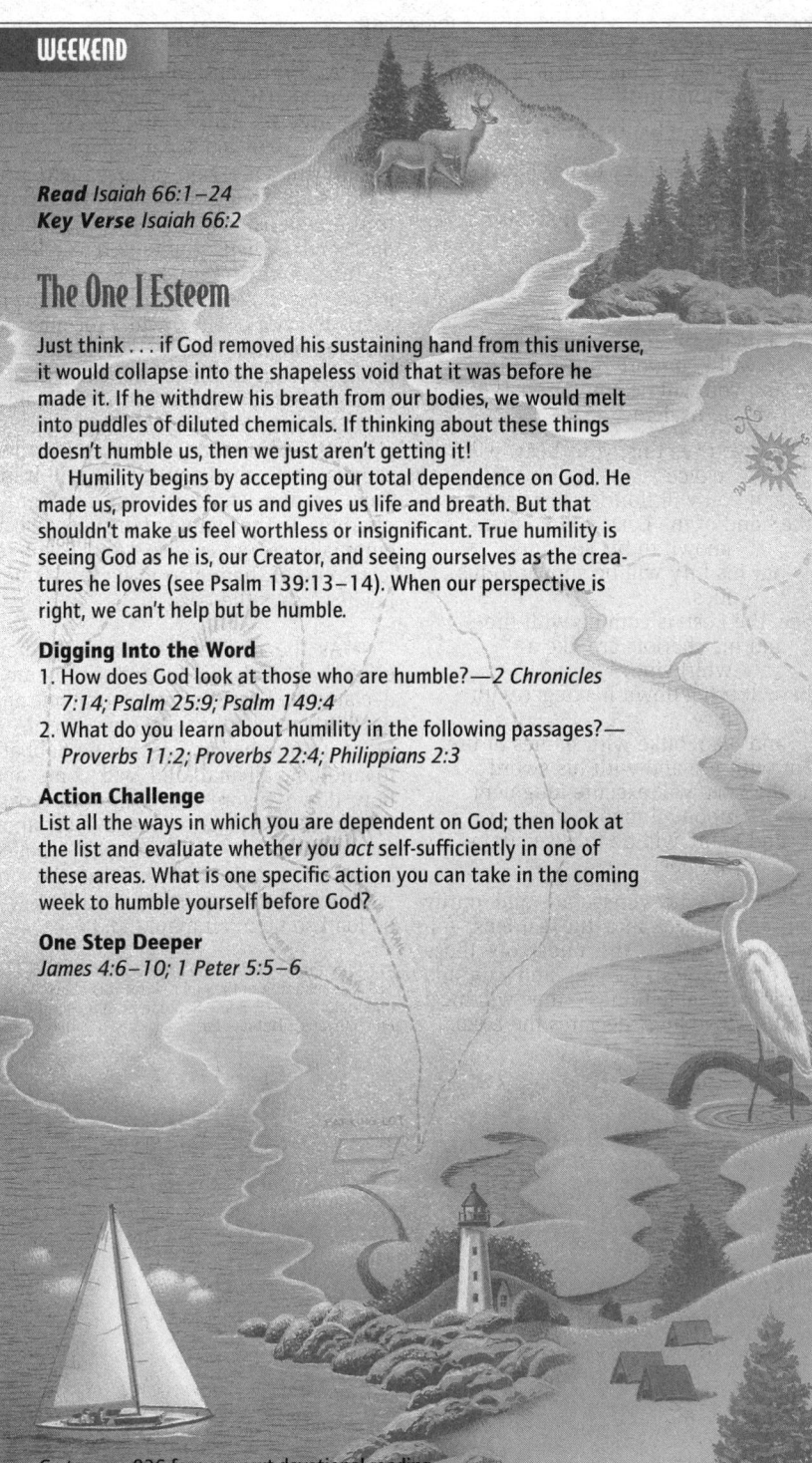

Read Isaiah 66:1–24
Key Verse Isaiah 66:2

The One I Esteem

Just think . . . if God removed his sustaining hand from this universe, it would collapse into the shapeless void that it was before he made it. If he withdrew his breath from our bodies, we would melt into puddles of diluted chemicals. If thinking about these things doesn't humble us, then we just aren't getting it!

Humility begins by accepting our total dependence on God. He made us, provides for us and gives us life and breath. But that shouldn't make us feel worthless or insignificant. True humility is seeing God as he is, our Creator, and seeing ourselves as the creatures he loves (see Psalm 139:13–14). When our perspective is right, we can't help but be humble.

Digging Into the Word
1. How does God look at those who are humble?—*2 Chronicles 7:14; Psalm 25:9; Psalm 149:4*
2. What do you learn about humility in the following passages?—*Proverbs 11:2; Proverbs 22:4; Philippians 2:3*

Action Challenge
List all the ways in which you are dependent on God; then look at the list and evaluate whether you *act* self-sufficiently in one of these areas. What is one specific action you can take in the coming week to humble yourself before God?

One Step Deeper
James 4:6–10; 1 Peter 5:5–6

Go to page 836 for your next devotional reading.

and delight in her overflowing abundance."

12For this is what the LORD says:

"I will extend peace to her like a
river,
and the wealth of nations like a
flooding stream;
you will nurse and be carried on her
arm
and dandled on her knees.
13As a mother comforts her child,
so will I comfort you;
and you will be comforted over
Jerusalem."

14When you see this, your heart will
rejoice
and you will flourish like grass;
the hand of the LORD will be made
known to his servants,
but his fury will be shown to his
foes.
15See, the LORD is coming with fire,
and his chariots are like a
whirlwind;
he will bring down his anger with
fury,
and his rebuke with flames of fire.
16For with fire and with his sword
the LORD will execute judgment
upon all men,
and many will be those slain by
the LORD.

17"Those who consecrate and purify themselves to go into the gardens, following the one in the midst of[a] those who eat the flesh of pigs and rats and other abominable things—they will meet their end together," declares the LORD.

18"And I, because of their actions and their imaginations, am about to come[b] and gather all nations and tongues, and they will come and see my glory.

19"I will set a sign among them, and I will send some of those who survive to the nations—to Tarshish, to the Libyans[c] and Lydians (famous as archers), to Tubal and Greece, and to the distant islands that have not heard of my fame or seen my glory. They will proclaim my glory among the nations. 20And they will bring all your brothers, from all the nations, to my holy mountain in Jerusalem as an offering to the LORD—on horses, in chariots and wagons, and on mules and camels," says the LORD. "They will bring them, as the Israelites bring their grain offerings, to the temple of the LORD in ceremonially clean vessels. 21And I will select some of them also to be priests and Levites," says the LORD.

22"As the new heavens and the new earth that I make will endure before me," declares the LORD, "so will your name and descendants endure. 23From one New Moon to another and from one Sabbath to another, all mankind will come and bow down before me," says the LORD. 24"And they will go out and look upon the dead bodies of those who rebelled against me; their worm will not die, nor will their fire be quenched, and they will be loathsome to all mankind."

[a]17 Or gardens behind one of your temples, and
[b]18 The meaning of the Hebrew for this clause is uncertain. [c]19 Some Septuagint manuscripts Put (Libyans); Hebrew Pul

Jeremiah had the grim job of prophesying to people who were indifferent, rebellious and even hostile. Perhaps they characterized him, as we might even today, as a "gloom and doom" prophet because he emphasized sin and judgment. But the book of Jeremiah is not all dark prophecies; the prophet also offers God's people the hope that their sincere repentance will postpone the inevitable, and even that their punishment will end with restoration. Jeremiah pictures God as an incomprehensibly powerful Creator and Judge; at the same time, he reaffirms God's deep concern for each and every one of his people.

JEREMIAH

1 The words of Jeremiah son of Hilkiah, one of the priests at Anathoth in the territory of Benjamin. ²The word of the LORD came to him in the thirteenth year of the reign of Josiah son of Amon king of Judah, ³and through the reign of Jehoiakim son of Josiah king of Judah, down to the fifth month of the eleventh year of Zedekiah son of Josiah king of Judah, when the people of Jerusalem went into exile.

The Call of Jeremiah

⁴The word of the LORD came to me, saying,

⁵"Before I formed you in the womb I
    knew*a* you,
  before you were born I set you apart;
  I appointed you as a prophet to the
    nations."

⁶"Ah, Sovereign LORD," I said, "I do not know how to speak; I am only a child."

⁷But the LORD said to me, "Do not say, 'I am only a child.' You must go to everyone I send you to and say whatever I command you. ⁸Do not be afraid of them, for I am with you and will rescue you," declares the LORD.

---

a 5 Or chose

⁹Then the LORD reached out his hand and touched my mouth and said to me, "Now, I have put my words in your mouth. ¹⁰See, today I appoint you over nations and kingdoms to uproot and tear down, to destroy and overthrow, to build and to plant."

¹¹The word of the LORD came to me: "What do you see, Jeremiah?"

"I see the branch of an almond tree," I replied.

¹²The LORD said to me, "You have seen correctly, for I am watching*ᵃ* to see that my word is fulfilled."

¹³The word of the LORD came to me again: "What do you see?"

"I see a boiling pot, tilting away from the north," I answered.

¹⁴The LORD said to me, "From the north disaster will be poured out on all who live in the land. ¹⁵I am about to summon all the peoples of the northern kingdoms," declares the LORD.

"Their kings will come and set up their thrones
  in the entrance of the gates of Jerusalem;
they will come against all her surrounding walls
  and against all the towns of Judah.
¹⁶I will pronounce my judgments on my people
  because of their wickedness in forsaking me,
in burning incense to other gods

ᵃ12 The Hebrew for *watching* sounds like the Hebrew for *almond tree.*

MONDAY

Read Jeremiah 1:1–19
Key Verses Jeremiah 1:5–8

God's Unique Purpose for You — Sjanna W. Hargrove

You are unique. There never has been, nor will there ever be, another you. God conceived and orchestrated the score of your life long before he formed you in your mother's womb (see Psalm 139). Every physical trait, talent, ability and capacity you possess is part of his gift of life for you. God desires that you use this uniqueness in his service.

Jeremiah heard his unique call firsthand. But, like Jeremiah, we don't always respond in obedience even when confronted by God himself. Instead of believing his promises and "just doing it," we often focus on the limits rather than on the potential of our abilities. We spend much of our time watching others and wishing that we looked like them, acted like them and had what they have. We envy the life God has given to someone else, thinking it more exciting or meaningful than the life given us. But this mentality denies the unique nature God has built into each one of us. It boxes us into a negative "me too" spiral that only distracts us rather than directing us toward more positive, God-honoring goals.

Whether your life is private and quiet or spent mainly in the spotlight, it possesses great purpose and destiny. Your life is God's unique and precious masterpiece. How can you believe that and make it real? By spending time in God's Word and finding out what kind of person he intends you to be, and by praying for God's direction in your life. As you wait patiently and look for answers to those prayers, make a conscious effort to use your unique talents in his service.

A Deeper Look
Genesis 12:1–3; John 15:16; Acts 9:11–19

Go to page 845 for your next devotional reading.

and in worshiping what their
hands have made.

[17]"Get yourself ready! Stand up and say to them whatever I command you. Do not be terrified by them, or I will terrify you before them. [18]Today I have made you a fortified city, an iron pillar and a bronze wall to stand against the whole land—against the kings of Judah, its officials, its priests and the people of the land. [19]They will fight against you but will not overcome you, for I am with you and will rescue you," declares the LORD.

Israel Forsakes God

2 The word of the LORD came to me: [2]"Go and proclaim in the hearing of Jerusalem:

" 'I remember the devotion of your
youth,
how as a bride you loved me
and followed me through the desert,
through a land not sown.
[3]Israel was holy to the LORD,
the firstfruits of his harvest;
all who devoured her were held
guilty,
and disaster overtook them,' "
declares the LORD.

[4]Hear the word of the LORD, O house
of Jacob,
all you clans of the house of Israel.

[5]This is what the LORD says:

"What fault did your fathers find in
me,
that they strayed so far from me?
They followed worthless idols
and became worthless themselves.
[6]They did not ask, 'Where is the LORD,
who brought us up out of Egypt
and led us through the barren
wilderness,
through a land of deserts and rifts,
a land of drought and darkness,[a]
a land where no one travels and
no one lives?'
[7]I brought you into a fertile land
to eat its fruit and rich produce.
But you came and defiled my land
and made my inheritance
detestable.
[8]The priests did not ask,
'Where is the LORD?'
Those who deal with the law did not
know me;
the leaders rebelled against me.

The prophets prophesied by Baal,
following worthless idols.

[9]"Therefore I bring charges against
you again,"
declares the LORD.
"And I will bring charges against
your children's children.
[10]Cross over to the coasts of Kittim[b]
and look,
send to Kedar[c] and observe
closely;
see if there has ever been anything
like this:
[11]Has a nation ever changed its gods?
(Yet they are not gods at all.)
But my people have exchanged
their[d] Glory
for worthless idols.
[12]Be appalled at this, O heavens,
and shudder with great horror,"
declares the LORD.
[13]"My people have committed two sins:
They have forsaken me,
the spring of living water,
and have dug their own cisterns,
broken cisterns that cannot hold
water.
[14]Is Israel a servant, a slave by birth?
Why then has he become plunder?
[15]Lions have roared;
they have growled at him.
They have laid waste his land;
his towns are burned and deserted.

[a]6 Or *and the shadow of death*   [b]10 That is,
Cyprus and western coastlands   [c]10 The home
of Bedouin tribes in the Syro-Arabian desert
[d]11 Masoretic Text; an ancient Hebrew scribal
tradition *my*

POINT OF INTEREST   Jeremiah 2:5

Our characters tend to reflect the nature of the things we worship. If we worship our "toys," we may become entertaining but essentially useless. Worshiping money makes a person greedy and cold. Worshiping lust leads a person to be a "user." But a person who worships the God who is good beyond measure will begin to emulate him—and become more compassionate, just, merciful and loving.

¹⁶Also, the men of Memphis*ᵃ* and
    Tahpanhes
  have shaved the crown of your
    head.*ᵇ*
¹⁷Have you not brought this on
    yourselves
  by forsaking the LORD your God
  when he led you in the way?
¹⁸Now why go to Egypt
  to drink water from the Shihor*ᶜ*?
  And why go to Assyria
  to drink water from the River*ᵈ*?
¹⁹Your wickedness will punish you;
  your backsliding will rebuke you.
  Consider then and realize
  how evil and bitter it is for you
  when you forsake the LORD your God
  and have no awe of me,"
                    declares the Lord,
                    the LORD Almighty.

²⁰"Long ago you broke off your yoke
  and tore off your bonds;
  you said, 'I will not serve you!'
  Indeed, on every high hill
  and under every spreading tree
  you lay down as a prostitute.
²¹I had planted you like a choice vine
  of sound and reliable stock.
  How then did you turn against me
  into a corrupt, wild vine?
²²Although you wash yourself with
    soda
  and use an abundance of soap,
  the stain of your guilt is still before
    me,"
                    declares the Sovereign LORD.
²³"How can you say, 'I am not defiled;
  I have not run after the Baals'?
  See how you behaved in the valley;
  consider what you have done.
  You are a swift she-camel
  running here and there,
²⁴a wild donkey accustomed to the
    desert,
  sniffing the wind in her craving—
  in her heat who can restrain her?
  Any males that pursue her need not
    tire themselves;
  at mating time they will find her.
²⁵Do not run until your feet are bare
  and your throat is dry.
  But you said, 'It's no use!
  I love foreign gods,
  and I must go after them.'

²⁶"As a thief is disgraced when he is
    caught,
  so the house of Israel is
    disgraced—

they, their kings and their officials,
  their priests and their prophets.
²⁷They say to wood, 'You are my
    father,'
  and to stone, 'You gave me birth.'
  They have turned their backs to me
  and not their faces;
  yet when they are in trouble, they
    say,
  'Come and save us!'
²⁸Where then are the gods you made
    for yourselves?
  Let them come if they can save
    you
  when you are in trouble!
  For you have as many gods
  as you have towns, O Judah.

²⁹"Why do you bring charges against
    me?
  You have all rebelled against me,"
                    declares the LORD.
³⁰"In vain I punished your people;
  they did not respond to correction.
  Your sword has devoured your
    prophets
  like a ravening lion.

³¹"You of this generation, consider the
word of the LORD:

"Have I been a desert to Israel
  or a land of great darkness?
  Why do my people say, 'We are free
    to roam;
  we will come to you no more'?
³²Does a maiden forget her jewelry,
  a bride her wedding ornaments?
  Yet my people have forgotten me,
  days without number.
³³How skilled you are at pursuing love!
  Even the worst of women can
    learn from your ways.
³⁴On your clothes men find
  the lifeblood of the innocent poor,
  though you did not catch them
    breaking in.
  Yet in spite of all this
³⁵ you say, 'I am innocent;
  he is not angry with me.'
  But I will pass judgment on you
  because you say, 'I have not
    sinned.'
³⁶Why do you go about so much,
  changing your ways?
  You will be disappointed by Egypt
  as you were by Assyria.

---

*ᵃ*16 Hebrew *Noph*   *ᵇ*16 Or *have cracked your*
skull   *ᶜ*18 That is, a branch of the Nile
*ᵈ*18 That is, the Euphrates

37You will also leave that place
    with your hands on your head,
for the LORD has rejected those you
    trust;
    you will not be helped by them.

3 "If a man divorces his wife
    and she leaves him and marries
      another man,
should he return to her again?
    Would not the land be completely
      defiled?
But you have lived as a prostitute
    with many lovers—
    would you now return to me?"
               declares the LORD.
2"Look up to the barren heights and
      see.
Is there any place where you have
    not been ravished?
By the roadside you sat waiting for
    lovers,
    sat like a nomad*a* in the desert.
You have defiled the land
    with your prostitution and
      wickedness.
3Therefore the showers have been
    withheld,
    and no spring rains have fallen.
Yet you have the brazen look of a
    prostitute;
    you refuse to blush with shame.
4Have you not just called to me:
    'My Father, my friend from my
      youth,
5will you always be angry?
    Will your wrath continue forever?'
This is how you talk,
    but you do all the evil you can."

Unfaithful Israel

6During the reign of King Josiah, the
LORD said to me, "Have you seen what
faithless Israel has done? She has gone
up on every high hill and under every
spreading tree and has committed adultery there. **7**I thought that after she had
done all this she would return to me but
she did not, and her unfaithful sister Judah saw it. **8**I gave faithless Israel her certificate of divorce and sent her away because of all her adulteries. Yet I saw that
her unfaithful sister Judah had no fear;
she also went out and committed adultery. **9**Because Israel's immorality mat-
tered so little to her, she defiled the land
and committed adultery with stone and
wood. **10**In spite of all this, her unfaithful
sister Judah did not return to me with all
her heart, but only in pretense," declares
the LORD.

11The LORD said to me, "Faithless Israel
is more righteous than unfaithful Judah.
12Go, proclaim this message toward the
north:

" 'Return, faithless Israel,' declares
    the LORD,
'I will frown on you no longer,
for I am merciful,' declares the LORD,
'I will not be angry forever.
13Only acknowledge your guilt—
    you have rebelled against the LORD
      your God,
you have scattered your favors to
    foreign gods
under every spreading tree,
    and have not obeyed me,' "
               declares the LORD.

14"Return, faithless people," declares
the LORD, "for I am your husband. I will
choose you—one from a town and two
from a clan—and bring you to Zion.
15Then I will give you shepherds after my
own heart, who will lead you with
knowledge and understanding. **16**In those
days, when your numbers have increased
greatly in the land," declares the LORD,
"men will no longer say, 'The ark of the
covenant of the LORD.' It will never enter
their minds or be remembered; it will not
be missed, nor will another one be made.
17At that time they will call Jerusalem
The Throne of the LORD, and all nations
will gather in Jerusalem to honor the
name of the LORD. No longer will they follow the stubbornness of their evil hearts.

a2 Or *an Arab*

POINT OF INTEREST

Jeremiah 3:12-13

The Old Testament replays
again and again the same
theme—Israel sinned
against God, God inevitably
punished Israel and Israel repented and
was restored. Each time the cycle repeated, God willingly forgave his people. How
many times have you or I failed God?
Don't despair! No matter how often we
fail, God forgives us too—we just have to
ask.

¹⁸In those days the house of Judah will join the house of Israel, and together they will come from a northern land to the land I gave your forefathers as an inheritance.

¹⁹"I myself said,

" 'How gladly would I treat you like
sons
and give you a desirable land,
the most beautiful inheritance of
any nation.'
I thought you would call me 'Father'
and not turn away from following
me.
²⁰But like a woman unfaithful to her
husband,
so you have been unfaithful to me,
O house of Israel,"
declares the LORD.

²¹A cry is heard on the barren heights,
the weeping and pleading of the
people of Israel,
because they have perverted their
ways
and have forgotten the LORD their
God.

²²"Return, faithless people;
I will cure you of backsliding."

"Yes, we will come to you,
for you are the LORD our God.
²³Surely the ⌊idolatrous⌋ commotion on
the hills
and mountains is a deception;
surely in the LORD our God
is the salvation of Israel.
²⁴From our youth shameful gods have
consumed
the fruits of our fathers' labor—
their flocks and herds,
their sons and daughters.
²⁵Let us lie down in our shame,
and let our disgrace cover us.
We have sinned against the LORD our
God,
both we and our fathers;
from our youth till this day
we have not obeyed the LORD our
God."

4 "If you will return, O Israel,
return to me,"
declares the LORD.
"If you put your detestable idols out
of my sight
and no longer go astray,
²and if in a truthful, just and righteous
way

you swear, 'As surely as the LORD
lives,'
then the nations will be blessed by
him
and in him they will glory."

³This is what the LORD says to the men of Judah and to Jerusalem:

"Break up your unplowed ground
and do not sow among thorns.
⁴Circumcise yourselves to the LORD,
circumcise your hearts,
you men of Judah and people of
Jerusalem,
or my wrath will break out and burn
like fire
because of the evil you have
done—
burn with no one to quench it.

Disaster From the North

⁵"Announce in Judah and proclaim in
Jerusalem and say:
'Sound the trumpet throughout the
land!'
Cry aloud and say:
'Gather together!
Let us flee to the fortified cities!'
⁶Raise the signal to go to Zion!
Flee for safety without delay!
For I am bringing disaster from the
north,
even terrible destruction."

⁷A lion has come out of his lair;
a destroyer of nations has set out.
He has left his place
to lay waste your land.
Your towns will lie in ruins
without inhabitant.
⁸So put on sackcloth,
lament and wail,
for the fierce anger of the LORD
has not turned away from us.

⁹"In that day," declares the LORD,
"the king and the officials will lose
heart,
the priests will be horrified,
and the prophets will be appalled."

¹⁰Then I said, "Ah, Sovereign LORD, how completely you have deceived this people and Jerusalem by saying, 'You will have peace,' when the sword is at our throats."

¹¹At that time this people and Jerusalem will be told, "A scorching wind from the barren heights in the desert blows toward my people, but not to winnow or

cleanse; ¹²a wind too strong for that comes from me.ᵃ Now I pronounce my judgments against them."

¹³Look! He advances like the clouds,
    his chariots come like a whirlwind,
  his horses are swifter than eagles.
    Woe to us! We are ruined!
¹⁴O Jerusalem, wash the evil from your
    heart and be saved.
  How long will you harbor wicked
    thoughts?
¹⁵A voice is announcing from Dan,
    proclaiming disaster from the hills
    of Ephraim.
¹⁶"Tell this to the nations,
    proclaim it to Jerusalem:
  'A besieging army is coming from a
    distant land,
  raising a war cry against the cities
    of Judah.
¹⁷They surround her like men guarding
    a field,
  because she has rebelled against
    me,' "
                  declares the LORD.
¹⁸"Your own conduct and actions
    have brought this upon you.
  This is your punishment.
    How bitter it is!
    How it pierces to the heart!"

¹⁹Oh, my anguish, my anguish!
    I writhe in pain.
  Oh, the agony of my heart!
    My heart pounds within me,
    I cannot keep silent.
  For I have heard the sound of the
    trumpet;
    I have heard the battle cry.
²⁰Disaster follows disaster;
    the whole land lies in ruins.
  In an instant my tents are destroyed,
    my shelter in a moment.
²¹How long must I see the battle
    standard
  and hear the sound of the trumpet?

²²"My people are fools;
    they do not know me.
  They are senseless children;
    they have no understanding.
  They are skilled in doing evil;
    they know not how to do good."

²³I looked at the earth,
    and it was formless and empty;
  and at the heavens,
    and their light was gone.
²⁴I looked at the mountains,
    and they were quaking;
  all the hills were swaying.
²⁵I looked, and there were no people;
    every bird in the sky had flown
    away.
²⁶I looked, and the fruitful land was a
    desert;
  all its towns lay in ruins
  before the LORD, before his fierce
    anger.

²⁷This is what the LORD says:

"The whole land will be ruined,
    though I will not destroy it
    completely.
²⁸Therefore the earth will mourn
    and the heavens above grow dark,
  because I have spoken and will not
    relent,
  I have decided and will not turn
    back."

²⁹At the sound of horsemen and
    archers
    every town takes to flight.
  Some go into the thickets;
    some climb up among the rocks.
  All the towns are deserted;
    no one lives in them.

³⁰What are you doing, O devastated
    one?
  Why dress yourself in scarlet
    and put on jewels of gold?
  Why shade your eyes with paint?
    You adorn yourself in vain.
  Your lovers despise you;
    they seek your life.

³¹I hear a cry as of a woman in labor,
    a groan as of one bearing her first
    child—

ᵃ12 Or *comes at my command*

POINT OF INTEREST

Jeremiah 4:14

Who among us hasn't had wicked thoughts? God's warnings to the people of the Old Testament can often be applied to us today. Check out these verses: Jeremiah 4:22; 5:3–4, 12, 27–28. Do these people sound like anyone you know? How about the person in the mirror?

the cry of the Daughter of Zion
 gasping for breath,
stretching out her hands and
 saying,
"Alas! I am fainting;
 my life is given over to
  murderers."

Not One Is Upright

5 "Go up and down the streets of
 Jerusalem,
look around and consider,
 search through her squares.
If you can find but one person
 who deals honestly and seeks the
  truth,
 I will forgive this city.
²Although they say, 'As surely as the
 LORD lives,'
 still they are swearing falsely."

³O LORD, do not your eyes look for
 truth?
You struck them, but they felt no
 pain;
 you crushed them, but they
  refused correction.
They made their faces harder than
 stone
 and refused to repent.
⁴I thought, "These are only the poor;
 they are foolish,
for they do not know the way of the
 LORD,
 the requirements of their God.
⁵So I will go to the leaders
 and speak to them;
surely they know the way of the
 LORD,
 the requirements of their God."
But with one accord they too had
 broken off the yoke
 and torn off the bonds.
⁶Therefore a lion from the forest will
 attack them,
 a wolf from the desert will ravage
  them,
a leopard will lie in wait near their
 towns
 to tear to pieces any who venture
  out,
for their rebellion is great
 and their backslidings many.

⁷"Why should I forgive you?
 Your children have forsaken me
 and sworn by gods that are not
  gods.
I supplied all their needs,
 yet they committed adultery

and thronged to the houses of
 prostitutes.
⁸They are well-fed, lusty stallions,
 each neighing for another man's
  wife.
⁹Should I not punish them for this?"
 declares the LORD.
"Should I not avenge myself
 on such a nation as this?

¹⁰"Go through her vineyards and
 ravage them,
but do not destroy them
 completely.
Strip off her branches,
 for these people do not belong to
  the LORD.
¹¹The house of Israel and the house of
 Judah
have been utterly unfaithful to
 me,"

      declares the LORD.

¹²They have lied about the LORD;
 they said, "He will do nothing!
No harm will come to us;
 we will never see sword or famine.
¹³The prophets are but wind
 and the word is not in them;
 so let what they say be done to
  them."

 ¹⁴Therefore this is what the LORD God
Almighty says:

"Because the people have spoken
 these words,
 I will make my words in your
  mouth a fire
and these people the wood it
 consumes.
¹⁵O house of Israel," declares the LORD,

POINT OF INTEREST

Jeremiah 5:12

These people must have had
short memories! Israel's history is full of rebellion and
disobedience—marked with
periodic pleas for God's intervention on
their behalf (see Psalm 107:11–14). They
had said God wouldn't do anything! Read
in verses 14 through 17 about their rude
awakening. Are our memories any better
today?

"I am bringing a distant nation
against you—
an ancient and enduring nation,
a people whose language you do
not know,
whose speech you do not
understand.
16Their quivers are like an open grave;
all of them are mighty warriors.
17They will devour your harvests and
food,
devour your sons and daughters;
they will devour your flocks and
herds,
devour your vines and fig trees.
With the sword they will destroy
the fortified cities in which you
trust.

18"Yet even in those days," declares
the LORD, "I will not destroy you completely. 19And when the people ask,
'Why has the LORD our God done all this
to us?' you will tell them, 'As you have
forsaken me and served foreign gods in
your own land, so now you will serve
foreigners in a land not your own.'

20"Announce this to the house of Jacob
and proclaim it in Judah:
21Hear this, you foolish and senseless
people,
who have eyes but do not see,
who have ears but do not hear:
22Should you not fear me?" declares the
LORD.
"Should you not tremble in my
presence?
I made the sand a boundary for the
sea,
an everlasting barrier it cannot
cross.
The waves may roll, but they cannot
prevail;
they may roar, but they cannot
cross it.
23But these people have stubborn and
rebellious hearts;
they have turned aside and gone
away.
24They do not say to themselves,
'Let us fear the LORD our God,
who gives autumn and spring rains in
season,
who assures us of the regular
weeks of harvest.'
25Your wrongdoings have kept these
away;
your sins have deprived you of
good.

26"Among my people are wicked men
who lie in wait like men who
snare birds
and like those who set traps to
catch men.
27Like cages full of birds,
their houses are full of deceit;
they have become rich and powerful
28 and have grown fat and sleek.
Their evil deeds have no limit;
they do not plead the case of the
fatherless to win it,
they do not defend the rights of
the poor.
29Should I not punish them for this?"
declares the LORD.
"Should I not avenge myself
on such a nation as this?

30"A horrible and shocking thing
has happened in the land:
31The prophets prophesy lies,
the priests rule by their own
authority,
and my people love it this way.
But what will you do in the end?

Jerusalem Under Siege

6 "Flee for safety, people of Benjamin!
Flee from Jerusalem!
Sound the trumpet in Tekoa!
Raise the signal over Beth
Hakkerem!
For disaster looms out of the north,
even terrible destruction.
2I will destroy the Daughter of Zion,
so beautiful and delicate.
3Shepherds with their flocks will come
against her;
they will pitch their tents around
her,
each tending his own portion."

4"Prepare for battle against her!
Arise, let us attack at noon!
But, alas, the daylight is fading,
and the shadows of evening grow
long.
5So arise, let us attack at night
and destroy her fortresses!"

6This is what the LORD Almighty says:

"Cut down the trees
and build siege ramps against
Jerusalem.
This city must be punished;
it is filled with oppression.
7As a well pours out its water,
so she pours out her wickedness.

Violence and destruction resound in
her;
her sickness and wounds are ever
before me.
⁸Take warning, O Jerusalem,
or I will turn away from you
and make your land desolate
so no one can live in it."

⁹This is what the LORD Almighty says:

"Let them glean the remnant of Israel
as thoroughly as a vine;
pass your hand over the branches
again,
like one gathering grapes."

¹⁰To whom can I speak and give
warning?
Who will listen to me?
Their ears are closed*a*
so they cannot hear.
The word of the LORD is offensive to
them;
they find no pleasure in it.
¹¹But I am full of the wrath of the LORD,
and I cannot hold it in.

"Pour it out on the children in the
street
and on the young men gathered
together;
both husband and wife will be caught
in it,
and the old, those weighed down
with years.
¹²Their houses will be turned over to
others,
together with their fields and their
wives,
when I stretch out my hand
against those who live in the
land,"
declares the LORD.
¹³"From the least to the greatest,
all are greedy for gain;
prophets and priests alike,
all practice deceit.
¹⁴They dress the wound of my people
as though it were not serious.
'Peace, peace,' they say,
when there is no peace.
¹⁵Are they ashamed of their loathsome
conduct?
No, they have no shame at all;
they do not even know how to
blush.
So they will fall among the fallen;
they will be brought down when I
punish them,"
says the LORD.

¹⁶This is what the LORD says:

"Stand at the crossroads and look;
ask for the ancient paths,
ask where the good way is, and walk
in it,
and you will find rest for your
souls.
But you said, 'We will not walk in
it.'
¹⁷I appointed watchmen over you and
said,
'Listen to the sound of the
trumpet!'
But you said, 'We will not listen.'
¹⁸Therefore hear, O nations;
observe, O witnesses,
what will happen to them.
¹⁹Hear, O earth:
I am bringing disaster on this people,
the fruit of their schemes,
because they have not listened to my
words
and have rejected my law.
²⁰What do I care about incense from
Sheba
or sweet calamus from a distant
land?
Your burnt offerings are not
acceptable;
your sacrifices do not please me."

²¹Therefore this is what the LORD says:

"I will put obstacles before this
people.
Fathers and sons alike will stumble
over them;
neighbors and friends will perish."

²²This is what the LORD says:

"Look, an army is coming
from the land of the north;
a great nation is being stirred up
from the ends of the earth.
²³They are armed with bow and spear;
they are cruel and show no mercy.
They sound like the roaring sea
as they ride on their horses;
they come like men in battle
formation
to attack you, O Daughter of Zion."

²⁴We have heard reports about them,
and our hands hang limp.
Anguish has gripped us,
pain like that of a woman in labor.
²⁵Do not go out to the fields
or walk on the roads,

a 10 Hebrew *uncircumcised*

for the enemy has a sword,
and there is terror on every side.
²⁶O my people, put on sackcloth
and roll in ashes;
mourn with bitter wailing
as for an only son,
for suddenly the destroyer
will come upon us.

²⁷"I have made you a tester of metals
and my people the ore,
that you may observe
and test their ways.
²⁸They are all hardened rebels,
going about to slander.
They are bronze and iron;
they all act corruptly.
²⁹The bellows blow fiercely
to burn away the lead with fire,
but the refining goes on in vain;
the wicked are not purged out.

³⁰They are called rejected silver,
because the LORD has rejected
them."

False Religion Worthless

7 This is the word that came to Jeremiah from the LORD: ²"Stand at the gate of the LORD's house and there proclaim this message:

" 'Hear the word of the LORD, all you people of Judah who come through these gates to worship the LORD. ³This is what the LORD Almighty, the God of Israel, says: Reform your ways and your actions, and I will let you live in this place. ⁴Do not trust in deceptive words and say, "This is the temple of the LORD, the temple of the LORD, the temple of the LORD!" ⁵If you really change your ways and your actions and deal with each other justly,

---

TUESDAY

Read *Jeremiah 6:1–30*
Key Verse *Jeremiah 6:15*

Ashamed of Sin – Dawn Getz

I had lied to her and in my head I kept going over what I had said and done, trying to rationalize my actions. I didn't initially intend to lie; it just came out of my mouth when the situation arose. She's probably already forgotten it. But what will she think of me if she finds out the truth? Finally I talked myself into ignoring my conscience.

A few days later I sat down to study the Bible. I read Genesis 27, which relates the account of Jacob tricking his father to steal his brother's blessing. I was amazed at Jacob's audacity in deceiving his father. But then I sensed the Holy Spirit telling me, "Dawn, you just lied too, remember? Don't be so shocked at Jacob."

I felt disgusted and miserable when I finally came to grips with my own sin. "Okay, Lord," I said, "I'll call her." My hand shook as I dialed her number. As we talked, I admitted what I'd done and asked her to forgive me. Thankfully, she did.

In Jeremiah 6:15 God says that he considers deceit to be "loathsome conduct" and that he expects us to be ashamed of our sin. But God doesn't want that shame to push us away from him; he doesn't want us to be overwhelmed with guilt. Rather, God's motive is always to draw us to repentance and to a deeper dependence on him. He wants us to take that first step of confession and restore our relationships, both with him and with others whom we've wronged.

A Deeper Look
Job 11:13–20; Proverbs 6:16–19; 1 John 1:8–9

Go to page 849 for your next devotional reading.

⁶if you do not oppress the alien, the fatherless or the widow and do not shed innocent blood in this place, and if you do not follow other gods to your own harm, ⁷then I will let you live in this place, in the land I gave your forefathers for ever and ever. ⁸But look, you are trusting in deceptive words that are worthless.

⁹" 'Will you steal and murder, commit adultery and perjury,ᵃ burn incense to Baal and follow other gods you have not known, ¹⁰and then come and stand before me in this house, which bears my Name, and say, "We are safe"—safe to do all these detestable things? ¹¹Has this house, which bears my Name, become a den of robbers to you? But I have been watching! declares the LORD.

¹²" 'Go now to the place in Shiloh where I first made a dwelling for my Name, and see what I did to it because of the wickedness of my people Israel. ¹³While you were doing all these things, declares the LORD, I spoke to you again and again, but you did not listen; I called you, but you did not answer. ¹⁴Therefore, what I did to Shiloh I will now do to the house that bears my Name, the temple you trust in, the place I gave to you and your fathers. ¹⁵I will thrust you from my presence, just as I did all your brothers, the people of Ephraim.'

¹⁶"So do not pray for this people nor offer any plea or petition for them; do not plead with me, for I will not listen to you. ¹⁷Do you not see what they are doing in the towns of Judah and in the streets of Jerusalem? ¹⁸The children gather wood, the fathers light the fire, and the women knead the dough and make cakes of bread for the Queen of Heaven. They pour out drink offerings to other gods to provoke me to anger. ¹⁹But am I the one they are provoking? declares the LORD. Are they not rather harming themselves, to their own shame?

²⁰" 'Therefore this is what the Sovereign LORD says: My anger and my wrath will be poured out on this place, on man and beast, on the trees of the field and on the fruit of the ground, and it will burn and not be quenched.

²¹" 'This is what the LORD Almighty, the God of Israel, says: Go ahead, add your burnt offerings to your other sacrifices and eat the meat yourselves! ²²For when I brought your forefathers out of Egypt and spoke to them, I did not just give them commands about burnt offerings and sacrifices, ²³but I gave them this command: Obey me, and I will be your God and you will be my people. Walk in all the ways I command you, that it may go well with you. ²⁴But they did not listen or pay attention; instead, they followed the stubborn inclinations of their evil hearts. They went backward and not forward. ²⁵From the time your forefathers left Egypt until now, day after day, again and again I sent you my servants the prophets. ²⁶But they did not listen to me or pay attention. They were stiff-necked and did more evil than their forefathers.'

²⁷"When you tell them all this, they will not listen to you; when you call to them, they will not answer. ²⁸Therefore say to them, 'This is the nation that has not obeyed the LORD its God or responded to correction. Truth has perished; it has vanished from their lips. ²⁹Cut off your hair and throw it away; take up a lament on the barren heights, for the LORD has rejected and abandoned this generation that is under his wrath.

The Valley of Slaughter

³⁰" 'The people of Judah have done evil in my eyes, declares the LORD. They have set up their detestable idols in the house that bears my Name and have defiled it. ³¹They have built the high places of Topheth in the Valley of Ben Hinnom to burn their sons and daughters in the fire—something I did not command, nor did it enter my mind. ³²So beware, the days are coming, declares the LORD, when people will no longer call it Topheth or the Valley of Ben Hinnom, but the Valley of Slaughter, for they will bury the dead

ᵃ9 Or and swear by false gods

POINT OF INTEREST   Jeremiah 7:9–12

The presence of God has never been a safe place for unrepentant hypocrites. God pulled them up short, called them on the carpet and gave them a stinging rebuke for their deceptive assumptions. Jesus wasn't easy on hypocrites either (see Matthew 23:23–29; Luke 13:5).

in Topheth until there is no more room. ³³Then the carcasses of this people will become food for the birds of the air and the beasts of the earth, and there will be no one to frighten them away. ³⁴I will bring an end to the sounds of joy and gladness and to the voices of bride and bridegroom in the towns of Judah and the streets of Jerusalem, for the land will become desolate.

8 " 'At that time, declares the LORD, the bones of the kings and officials of Judah, the bones of the priests and prophets, and the bones of the people of Jerusalem will be removed from their graves. ²They will be exposed to the sun and the moon and all the stars of the heavens, which they have loved and served and which they have followed and consulted and worshiped. They will not be gathered up or buried, but will be like refuse lying on the ground. ³Wherever I banish them, all the survivors of this evil nation will prefer death to life, declares the LORD Almighty.'

Sin and Punishment

⁴"Say to them, 'This is what the LORD says:

" 'When men fall down, do they not
get up?
When a man turns away, does he
not return?
⁵Why then have these people turned
away?
Why does Jerusalem always turn
away?
They cling to deceit;
they refuse to return.
⁶I have listened attentively,
but they do not say what is right.
No one repents of his wickedness,
saying, "What have I done?"
Each pursues his own course
like a horse charging into battle.
⁷Even the stork in the sky
knows her appointed seasons,
and the dove, the swift and the
thrush
observe the time of their migration.
But my people do not know
the requirements of the LORD.

⁸" 'How can you say, "We are wise,
for we have the law of the LORD,"
when actually the lying pen of the
scribes
has handled it falsely?
⁹The wise will be put to shame;

they will be dismayed and trapped.
Since they have rejected the word of
the LORD,
what kind of wisdom do they
have?
¹⁰Therefore I will give their wives to
other men
and their fields to new owners.
From the least to the greatest,
all are greedy for gain;
prophets and priests alike,
all practice deceit.
¹¹They dress the wound of my people
as though it were not serious.
"Peace, peace," they say,
when there is no peace.
¹²Are they ashamed of their loathsome
conduct?
No, they have no shame at all;
they do not even know how to
blush.
So they will fall among the fallen;
they will be brought down when
they are punished,
says the LORD.

¹³" 'I will take away their harvest,
declares the LORD.
There will be no grapes on the
vine.
There will be no figs on the tree,
and their leaves will wither.
What I have given them
will be taken from them.ᵃ' "

¹⁴"Why are we sitting here?
Gather together!
Let us flee to the fortified cities
and perish there!
For the LORD our God has doomed us
to perish
and given us poisoned water to
drink,
because we have sinned against
him.
¹⁵We hoped for peace
but no good has come,
for a time of healing
but there was only terror.
¹⁶The snorting of the enemy's horses
is heard from Dan;
at the neighing of their stallions
the whole land trembles.
They have come to devour
the land and everything in it,
the city and all who live there."

ᵃ13 The meaning of the Hebrew for this sentence is uncertain.

¹⁷"See, I will send venomous snakes
        among you,
    vipers that cannot be charmed,
    and they will bite you,"
                declares the LORD.

¹⁸O my Comforter*a* in sorrow,
    my heart is faint within me.
¹⁹Listen to the cry of my people
    from a land far away:
"Is the LORD not in Zion?
    Is her King no longer there?"

"Why have they provoked me to
        anger with their images,
    with their worthless foreign idols?"

²⁰"The harvest is past,
    the summer has ended,
    and we are not saved."

²¹Since my people are crushed, I am
        crushed;
    I mourn, and horror grips me.
²²Is there no balm in Gilead?
    Is there no physician there?
Why then is there no healing
    for the wound of my people?

9 ¹Oh, that my head were a spring of
        water
    and my eyes a fountain of tears!
I would weep day and night
    for the slain of my people.
²Oh, that I had in the desert
    a lodging place for travelers,
so that I might leave my people
    and go away from them;
for they are all adulterers,
    a crowd of unfaithful people.

³"They make ready their tongue
    like a bow, to shoot lies;
it is not by truth
    that they triumph*b* in the land.
They go from one sin to another;
    they do not acknowledge me,"
                declares the LORD.
⁴"Beware of your friends;
    do not trust your brothers.
For every brother is a deceiver,*c*
    and every friend a slanderer.
⁵Friend deceives friend,
    and no one speaks the truth.
They have taught their tongues to lie;
    they weary themselves with
        sinning.
⁶You*d* live in the midst of deception;
    in their deceit they refuse to
        acknowledge me,"
                declares the LORD.

⁷Therefore this is what the LORD Almighty says:

"See, I will refine and test them,
    for what else can I do
    because of the sin of my people?
⁸Their tongue is a deadly arrow;
    it speaks with deceit.
With his mouth each speaks cordially
        to his neighbor,
    but in his heart he sets a trap for
        him.
⁹Should I not punish them for this?"
    declares the LORD.
"Should I not avenge myself
    on such a nation as this?"

¹⁰I will weep and wail for the
        mountains
    and take up a lament concerning
        the desert pastures.
They are desolate and untraveled,
    and the lowing of cattle is not
        heard.
The birds of the air have fled
    and the animals are gone.

¹¹"I will make Jerusalem a heap of
        ruins,
    a haunt of jackals;
and I will lay waste the towns of
        Judah
    so no one can live there."

¹²What man is wise enough to understand this? Who has been instructed by the LORD and can explain it? Why has the land been ruined and laid waste like a desert that no one can cross?

¹³The LORD said, "It is because they have forsaken my law, which I set before them; they have not obeyed me or followed my law. ¹⁴Instead, they have followed the stubbornness of their hearts; they have followed the Baals, as their fathers taught them." ¹⁵Therefore, this is what the LORD Almighty, the God of Israel, says: "See, I will make this people eat bitter food and drink poisoned water. ¹⁶I will scatter them among nations that neither they nor their fathers have known, and I will pursue them with the sword until I have destroyed them."

¹⁷This is what the LORD Almighty says:

"Consider now! Call for the wailing
        women to come;

a 18 The meaning of the Hebrew for this word is uncertain.   *b 3* Or *lies; / they are not valiant for truth*   *c 4* Or *a deceiving Jacob*   *d 6* That is, Jeremiah (the Hebrew is singular)

send for the most skillful of them.
¹⁸Let them come quickly
    and wail over us
till our eyes overflow with tears
    and water streams from our
        eyelids.
¹⁹The sound of wailing is heard from
        Zion:
'How ruined we are!
    How great is our shame!
We must leave our land
    because our houses are in ruins.' "

²⁰Now, O women, hear the word of the
        LORD;
    open your ears to the words of his
        mouth.
Teach your daughters how to wail;
    teach one another a lament.
²¹Death has climbed in through our
        windows

and has entered our fortresses;
    it has cut off the children from the
        streets
    and the young men from the public
        squares.

²²Say, "This is what the LORD declares:

" 'The dead bodies of men will lie
    like refuse on the open field,
like cut grain behind the reaper,
    with no one to gather them.' "

²³This is what the LORD says:

"Let not the wise man boast of his
        wisdom
    or the strong man boast of his
        strength
    or the rich man boast of his riches,
²⁴but let him who boasts boast about
        this:

WEDNESDAY

Read *Jeremiah 9:1–26*
Key Verses *Jeremiah 9:23–24*

In These I Delight – Margo Balsis

What matters most? Ask Ellen, your classmate, who routinely gives
up sleep and friendships to ensure top-ranking grades. Or ask Ed,
who works out every day at the gym, running and lifting and toning.
Or ask Todd and Amy who live across the hall in your apartment
building; their fast-track careers provide them with plenty of possessions.

  Ask your friends what brings them the most pleasure and pride.
Then ask yourself, "Does my greatest security lie in how much I
know, in how powerful and capable I am, or in my influence and possessions? What matters most to me?"

  We may work hard pursuing wisdom, strength or riches, and God
may give us all these things. But these things are not what matter
most to him. God delights most of all in his relationship with us (see
Jeremiah 9:24). His eyes roam our classrooms and the places where
we live, work and play. He longs to find people whose greatest passion is knowing him. At the end of each day, no matter what activities we have pursued, God would like each of us to be able to say, "I
know God! And this is what I know about God: that kindness and
justice characterize all he is and does" (see Jeremiah 9:24).

  As you build up your mind, body or career, be alert for ways in
which God shows you his love and righteousness. Then in the classroom, at the gym and on the job, delight him with acts of love and
justice that demonstrate that you know and follow him.

  That, after all, is what matters most.

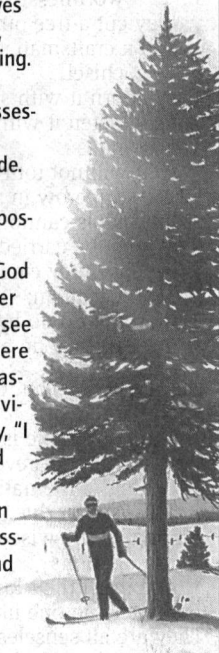

A Deeper Look
Ecclesiastes 2:24–26; 1 Corinthians 3:18–20; James 3:13–16

Go to page 857 for your next devotional reading.

that he understands and knows
  me,
that I am the LORD, who exercises
  kindness,
  justice and righteousness on earth,
  for in these I delight,"
                    declares the LORD.

²⁵"The days are coming," declares the
LORD, "when I will punish all who are circumcised only in the flesh— ²⁶Egypt, Judah, Edom, Ammon, Moab and all who
live in the desert in distant places.ᵃ For
all these nations are really uncircumcised, and even the whole house of Israel
is uncircumcised in heart."

God and Idols

10 Hear what the LORD says to you,
O house of Israel. ²This is what the
LORD says:

"Do not learn the ways of the nations
  or be terrified by signs in the sky,
  though the nations are terrified by
    them.
³For the customs of the peoples are
    worthless;
  they cut a tree out of the forest,
  and a craftsman shapes it with his
    chisel.
⁴They adorn it with silver and gold;
  they fasten it with hammer and
    nails
  so it will not totter.
⁵Like a scarecrow in a melon patch,
  their idols cannot speak;
they must be carried
  because they cannot walk.
Do not fear them;
  they can do no harm
  nor can they do any good."

⁶No one is like you, O LORD;
  you are great,
  and your name is mighty in power.
⁷Who should not revere you,
  O King of the nations?
  This is your due.
Among all the wise men of the
    nations
  and in all their kingdoms,
  there is no one like you.
⁸They are all senseless and foolish;
  they are taught by worthless
    wooden idols.
⁹Hammered silver is brought from
    Tarshish
  and gold from Uphaz.

What the craftsman and goldsmith
  have made
is then dressed in blue and
  purple—
all made by skilled workers.
¹⁰But the LORD is the true God;
  he is the living God, the eternal
    King.
When he is angry, the earth trembles;
  the nations cannot endure his
    wrath.

¹¹"Tell them this: 'These gods, who
did not make the heavens and the earth,
will perish from the earth and from under
the heavens.' "ᵇ

¹²But God made the earth by his
    power;
  he founded the world by his
    wisdom
  and stretched out the heavens by
    his understanding.
¹³When he thunders, the waters in the
    heavens roar;
  he makes clouds rise from the ends
    of the earth.
He sends lightning with the rain
  and brings out the wind from his
    storehouses.

¹⁴Everyone is senseless and without
    knowledge;
  every goldsmith is shamed by his
    idols.
His images are a fraud;
  they have no breath in them.
¹⁵They are worthless, the objects of
    mockery;
  when their judgment comes, they
    will perish.
¹⁶He who is the Portion of Jacob is not
    like these,
  for he is the Maker of all things,
including Israel, the tribe of his
    inheritance—
  the LORD Almighty is his name.

Coming Destruction

¹⁷Gather up your belongings to leave
    the land,
  you who live under siege.
¹⁸For this is what the LORD says:
"At this time I will hurl out
    those who live in this land;
  I will bring distress on them
    so that they may be captured."

ᵃ26 Or desert and who clip the hair by their
foreheads   ᵇ11 The text of this verse is in
Aramaic.

19Woe to me because of my injury!
  My wound is incurable!
Yet I said to myself,
  "This is my sickness, and I must
    endure it."
20My tent is destroyed;
  all its ropes are snapped.
My sons are gone from me and are
    no more;
  no one is left now to pitch my tent
    or to set up my shelter.
21The shepherds are senseless
  and do not inquire of the LORD;
so they do not prosper
  and all their flock is scattered.
22Listen! The report is coming—
  a great commotion from the land
    of the north!
It will make the towns of Judah
    desolate,
  a haunt of jackals.

Jeremiah's Prayer

23I know, O LORD, that a man's life is
    not his own;
  it is not for man to direct his steps.
24Correct me, LORD, but only with
    justice—
  not in your anger,
    lest you reduce me to nothing.
25Pour out your wrath on the nations
  that do not acknowledge you,
    on the peoples who do not call on
      your name.
For they have devoured Jacob;
  they have devoured him
    completely
  and destroyed his homeland.

The Covenant Is Broken

11 This is the word that came to Jeremiah from the LORD: 2"Listen to the terms of this covenant and tell them to the people of Judah and to those who live in Jerusalem. 3Tell them that this is what the LORD, the God of Israel, says: 'Cursed is the man who does not obey the terms of this covenant— 4the terms I commanded your forefathers when I brought them out of Egypt, out of the iron-smelting furnace.' I said, 'Obey me and do everything I command you, and you will be my people, and I will be your God. 5Then I will fulfill the oath I swore to your forefathers, to give them a land flowing with milk and honey'—the land you possess today."

I answered, "Amen, LORD."

6The LORD said to me, "Proclaim all these words in the towns of Judah and in the streets of Jerusalem: 'Listen to the terms of this covenant and follow them. 7From the time I brought your forefathers up from Egypt until today, I warned them again and again, saying, "Obey me." 8But they did not listen or pay attention; instead, they followed the stubbornness of their evil hearts. So I brought on them all the curses of the covenant I had commanded them to follow but that they did not keep.' "

9Then the LORD said to me, "There is a conspiracy among the people of Judah and those who live in Jerusalem. 10They have returned to the sins of their forefathers, who refused to listen to my words. They have followed other gods to serve them. Both the house of Israel and the house of Judah have broken the covenant I made with their forefathers. 11Therefore this is what the LORD says: 'I will bring on them a disaster they cannot escape. Although they cry out to me, I will not listen to them. 12The towns of Judah and the people of Jerusalem will go and cry out to the gods to whom they burn incense, but they will not help them at all when disaster strikes. 13You have as many gods as you have towns, O Judah; and the altars you have set up to burn incense to that shameful god Baal are as many as the streets of Jerusalem.'

14"Do not pray for this people nor offer any plea or petition for them, because I will not listen when they call to me in the time of their distress.

15"What is my beloved doing in my
    temple
  as she works out her evil schemes
    with many?
  Can consecrated meat avert L your
    punishment_?
When you engage in your
    wickedness,
  then you rejoice.ª "

16The LORD called you a thriving olive
    tree
  with fruit beautiful in form.
But with the roar of a mighty storm
  he will set it on fire,
    and its branches will be broken.

17The LORD Almighty, who planted you,
has decreed disaster for you, because the house of Israel and the house of Judah

ª15 Or *Could consecrated meat avert your
punishment? / Then you would rejoice*

have done evil and provoked me to anger
by burning incense to Baal.

Plot Against Jeremiah

¹⁸Because the LORD revealed their plot
to me, I knew it, for at that time he
showed me what they were doing. ¹⁹I had
been like a gentle lamb led to the slaughter; I did not realize that they had plotted
against me, saying,

"Let us destroy the tree and its fruit;
let us cut him off from the land of
the living,
that his name be remembered no
more."
²⁰But, O LORD Almighty, you who judge
righteously
and test the heart and mind,
let me see your vengeance upon
them,
for to you I have committed my
cause.

²¹"Therefore this is what the LORD says
about the men of Anathoth who are seeking your life and saying, 'Do not prophesy in the name of the LORD or you will die
by our hands'— ²²therefore this is what
the LORD Almighty says: 'I will punish
them. Their young men will die by the
sword, their sons and daughters by famine. ²³Not even a remnant will be left to
them, because I will bring disaster on the
men of Anathoth in the year of their punishment.' "

Jeremiah's Complaint

12 You are always righteous, O LORD,
when I bring a case before you.
Yet I would speak with you about
your justice:
Why does the way of the wicked
prosper?
Why do all the faithless live at
ease?
²You have planted them, and they
have taken root;
they grow and bear fruit.
You are always on their lips
but far from their hearts.
³Yet you know me, O LORD;
you see me and test my thoughts
about you.
Drag them off like sheep to be
butchered!
Set them apart for the day of
slaughter!
⁴How long will the land lie parched*a*

and the grass in every field be
withered?
Because those who live in it are
wicked,
the animals and birds have
perished.
Moreover, the people are saying,
"He will not see what happens to
us."

God's Answer

⁵"If you have raced with men on foot
and they have worn you out,
how can you compete with horses?
If you stumble in safe country,*b*
how will you manage in the
thickets by*c* the Jordan?
⁶Your brothers, your own family—
even they have betrayed you;
they have raised a loud cry against
you.
Do not trust them,
though they speak well of you.

⁷"I will forsake my house,
abandon my inheritance;
I will give the one I love
into the hands of her enemies.
⁸My inheritance has become to me
like a lion in the forest.
She roars at me;
therefore I hate her.
⁹Has not my inheritance become to me
like a speckled bird of prey
that other birds of prey surround
and attack?
Go and gather all the wild beasts;
bring them to devour.

---

*a*4 Or *land mourn*
in a land of safety   *b*5 Or *If you put your trust*
                            *c*5 Or *the flooding of*

POINT OF INTEREST

Jeremiah 12:1-4

Are there any questions we
can't ask God? Can we complain when God seems
unfair? This passage demonstrates that God will permit such complaints and questions as long as our
attitude is right. Questions asked to gain
understanding are always appropriate;
questions that challenge his character and
sovereignty are not.

¹⁰Many shepherds will ruin my
          vineyard
    and trample down my field;
    they will turn my pleasant field
          into a desolate wasteland.
¹¹It will be made a wasteland,
          parched and desolate before me;
    the whole land will be laid waste
          because there is no one who cares.
¹²Over all the barren heights in the
          desert
    destroyers will swarm,
    for the sword of the LORD will devour
          from one end of the land to the
          other;
    no one will be safe.
¹³They will sow wheat but reap thorns;
    they will wear themselves out but
          gain nothing.
    So bear the shame of your harvest
          because of the LORD's fierce anger."

¹⁴This is what the LORD says: "As for all
my wicked neighbors who seize the inheritance I gave my people Israel, I will
uproot them from their lands and I will
uproot the house of Judah from among
them. ¹⁵But after I uproot them, I will
again have compassion and will bring
each of them back to his own inheritance
and his own country. ¹⁶And if they learn
well the ways of my people and swear by
my name, saying, 'As surely as the LORD
lives'—even as they once taught my people to swear by Baal—then they will be
established among my people. ¹⁷But if
any nation does not listen, I will completely uproot and destroy it," declares
the LORD.

A Linen Belt

13 This is what the LORD said to me: "Go
and buy a linen belt and put it around
your waist, but do not let it touch water."
²So I bought a belt, as the LORD directed,
and put it around my waist.

³Then the word of the LORD came to
me a second time: ⁴"Take the belt you
bought and are wearing around your
waist, and go now to Perath[a] and hide it
there in a crevice in the rocks." ⁵So I went
and hid it at Perath, as the LORD told me.

⁶Many days later the LORD said to me,
"Go now to Perath and get the belt I told
you to hide there." ⁷So I went to Perath
and dug up the belt and took it from the
place where I had hidden it, but now it
was ruined and completely useless.

⁸Then the word of the LORD came to

me: ⁹"This is what the LORD says: 'In the
same way I will ruin the pride of Judah
and the great pride of Jerusalem. ¹⁰These
wicked people, who refuse to listen to my
words, who follow the stubbornness of
their hearts and go after other gods to
serve and worship them, will be like this
belt—completely useless! ¹¹For as a belt
is bound around a man's waist, so I
bound the whole house of Israel and the
whole house of Judah to me,' declares
the LORD, 'to be my people for my renown
and praise and honor. But they have not
listened.'

Wineskins

¹²"Say to them: 'This is what the LORD,
the God of Israel, says: Every wineskin
should be filled with wine.' And if they
say to you, 'Don't we know that every
wineskin should be filled with wine?'
¹³then tell them, 'This is what the LORD
says: I am going to fill with drunkenness
all who live in this land, including the
kings who sit on David's throne, the
priests, the prophets and all those living
in Jerusalem. ¹⁴I will smash them one
against the other, fathers and sons alike,
declares the LORD. I will allow no pity or
mercy or compassion to keep me from
destroying them.' "

Threat of Captivity

¹⁵Hear and pay attention,
    do not be arrogant,
    for the LORD has spoken.
¹⁶Give glory to the LORD your God
    before he brings the darkness,
    before your feet stumble
          on the darkening hills.
    You hope for light,
    but he will turn it to thick
          darkness
    and change it to deep gloom.
¹⁷But if you do not listen,
    I will weep in secret
    because of your pride;
    my eyes will weep bitterly,
          overflowing with tears,
    because the LORD's flock will be
          taken captive.

¹⁸Say to the king and to the queen
          mother,
    "Come down from your thrones,
    for your glorious crowns
          will fall from your heads."

---

[a]4 Or possibly *the Euphrates*; also in verses 5-7

¹⁹The cities in the Negev will be shut
    up,
and there will be no one to open
    them.
All Judah will be carried into exile,
    carried completely away.

²⁰Lift up your eyes and see
    those who are coming from the
       north.
Where is the flock that was entrusted
    to you,
    the sheep of which you boasted?
²¹What will you say when ⌊the LORD⌋
    sets over you
those you cultivated as your
    special allies?
Will not pain grip you
    like that of a woman in labor?
²²And if you ask yourself,
    "Why has this happened to me?"—
it is because of your many sins
    that your skirts have been torn off
    and your body mistreated.
²³Can the Ethiopian*a* change his skin
    or the leopard its spots?
Neither can you do good
    who are accustomed to doing evil.

²⁴"I will scatter you like chaff
    driven by the desert wind.
²⁵This is your lot,
    the portion I have decreed for
       you,"

                    declares the LORD,
"because you have forgotten me
    and trusted in false gods.
²⁶I will pull up your skirts over your
    face
    that your shame may be seen—
²⁷your adulteries and lustful neighings,
    your shameless prostitution!
I have seen your detestable acts
    on the hills and in the fields.
Woe to you, O Jerusalem!
    How long will you be unclean?"

Drought, Famine, Sword

14 This is the word of the LORD to Jeremiah concerning the drought:

²"Judah mourns,
    her cities languish;
they wail for the land,
    and a cry goes up from Jerusalem.
³The nobles send their servants for
    water;
they go to the cisterns
    but find no water.
They return with their jars unfilled;

dismayed and despairing,
    they cover their heads.
⁴The ground is cracked
    because there is no rain in the
       land;
the farmers are dismayed
    and cover their heads.
⁵Even the doe in the field
    deserts her newborn fawn
    because there is no grass.
⁶Wild donkeys stand on the barren
       heights
    and pant like jackals;
their eyesight fails
    for lack of pasture."

⁷Although our sins testify against us,
    O LORD, do something for the sake
       of your name.
For our backsliding is great;
    we have sinned against you.
⁸O Hope of Israel,
    its Savior in times of distress,
why are you like a stranger in the
       land,
    like a traveler who stays only a
       night?
⁹Why are you like a man taken by
       surprise,
    like a warrior powerless to save?
You are among us, O LORD,
    and we bear your name;
    do not forsake us!

¹⁰This is what the LORD says about this
people:

"They greatly love to wander;
    they do not restrain their feet.
So the LORD does not accept them;
    he will now remember their
       wickedness
    and punish them for their sins."

¹¹Then the LORD said to me, "Do not pray for the well-being of this people. ¹²Although they fast, I will not listen to their cry; though they offer burnt offerings and grain offerings, I will not accept them. Instead, I will destroy them with the sword, famine and plague."

¹³But I said, "Ah, Sovereign LORD, the prophets keep telling them, 'You will not see the sword or suffer famine. Indeed, I will give you lasting peace in this place.' "

¹⁴Then the LORD said to me, "The prophets are prophesying lies in my

---

a23 Hebrew *Cushite* (probably a person from the upper Nile region) name. I have not sent them or appointed them or spoken to them. They are prophesying to you false visions, divinations, idolatries*a* and the delusions of their own minds. 15Therefore, this is what the LORD says about the prophets who are prophesying in my name: I did not send them, yet they are saying, 'No sword or famine will touch this land.' Those same prophets will perish by sword and famine. 16And the people they are prophesying to will be thrown out into the streets of Jerusalem because of the famine and sword. There will be no one to bury them or their wives, their sons or their daughters. I will pour out on them the calamity they deserve.

17"Speak this word to them:

" 'Let my eyes overflow with tears
    night and day without ceasing;
for my virgin daughter—my people—
    has suffered a grievous wound,
    a crushing blow.
18If I go into the country,
    I see those slain by the sword;
if I go into the city,
    I see the ravages of famine.
Both prophet and priest
    have gone to a land they know
        not.' "

19Have you rejected Judah completely?
    Do you despise Zion?
Why have you afflicted us
    so that we cannot be healed?
We hoped for peace
    but no good has come,
for a time of healing
    but there is only terror.
20O LORD, we acknowledge our
        wickedness
    and the guilt of our fathers;
    we have indeed sinned against
        you.
21For the sake of your name do not
        despise us;
    do not dishonor your glorious
        throne.
Remember your covenant with us
    and do not break it.
22Do any of the worthless idols of the
        nations bring rain?
    Do the skies themselves send down
        showers?
No, it is you, O LORD our God.
    Therefore our hope is in you,
    for you are the one who does all
        this.

15 Then the LORD said to me: "Even if Moses and Samuel were to stand before me, my heart would not go out to this people. Send them away from my presence! Let them go! 2And if they ask you, 'Where shall we go?' tell them, 'This is what the LORD says:

" 'Those destined for death, to death;
those for the sword, to the sword;
those for starvation, to starvation;
those for captivity, to captivity.'

3"I will send four kinds of destroyers against them," declares the LORD, "the sword to kill and the dogs to drag away and the birds of the air and the beasts of the earth to devour and destroy. 4I will make them abhorrent to all the kingdoms of the earth because of what Manasseh son of Hezekiah king of Judah did in Jerusalem.

5"Who will have pity on you,
        O Jerusalem?
Who will mourn for you?
Who will stop to ask how you are?
6You have rejected me," declares the
        LORD.
"You keep on backsliding.
So I will lay hands on you and
        destroy you;
    I can no longer show compassion.
7I will winnow them with a
        winnowing fork
    at the city gates of the land.
I will bring bereavement and
        destruction on my people,
    for they have not changed their
        ways.
8I will make their widows more
        numerous
    than the sand of the sea.
At midday I will bring a destroyer
    against the mothers of their young
        men;
suddenly I will bring down on them
    anguish and terror.
9The mother of seven will grow faint
    and breathe her last.
Her sun will set while it is still day;
    she will be disgraced and
        humiliated.
I will put the survivors to the sword
    before their enemies,"
                    declares the LORD.

10Alas, my mother, that you gave me
        birth,

a 14 Or *visions, worthless divinations*

a man with whom the whole land
    strives and contends!
I have neither lent nor borrowed,
    yet everyone curses me.

11The LORD said,

"Surely I will deliver you for a good
    purpose;
surely I will make your enemies
    plead with you
in times of disaster and times of
    distress.

12"Can a man break iron—
    iron from the north—or bronze?
13Your wealth and your treasures
    I will give as plunder, without
        charge,
because of all your sins
    throughout your country.
14I will enslave you to your enemies
    in*a* a land you do not know,
for my anger will kindle a fire
    that will burn against you."

15You understand, O LORD;
    remember me and care for me.
Avenge me on my persecutors.
You are long-suffering—do not take
    me away;
think of how I suffer reproach for
    your sake.
16When your words came, I ate them;
    they were my joy and my heart's
        delight,
for I bear your name,
    O LORD God Almighty.
17I never sat in the company of
    revelers,
    never made merry with them;
I sat alone because your hand was on
    me
    and you had filled me with
        indignation.
18Why is my pain unending
    and my wound grievous and
        incurable?
Will you be to me like a deceptive
    brook,
    like a spring that fails?

19Therefore this is what the LORD says:

"If you repent, I will restore you
    that you may serve me;
if you utter worthy, not worthless,
    words,
    you will be my spokesman.
Let this people turn to you,
    but you must not turn to them.

20I will make you a wall to this people,
    a fortified wall of bronze;
they will fight against you
    but will not overcome you,
for I am with you
    to rescue and save you,"
                    declares the LORD.
21"I will save you from the hands of
    the wicked
    and redeem you from the grasp of
        the cruel."

Day of Disaster

16 Then the word of the LORD came to
    me: 2"You must not marry and have
sons or daughters in this place." 3For this
is what the LORD says about the sons and
daughters born in this land and about the
women who are their mothers and the
men who are their fathers: 4"They will
die of deadly diseases. They will not be
mourned or buried but will be like refuse
lying on the ground. They will perish by
sword and famine, and their dead bodies
will become food for the birds of the air
and the beasts of the earth."

5For this is what the LORD says: "Do not
enter a house where there is a funeral
meal; do not go to mourn or show sympathy, because I have withdrawn my
blessing, my love and my pity from this
people," declares the LORD. 6"Both high
and low will die in this land. They will
not be buried or mourned, and no one
will cut himself or shave his head for
them. 7No one will offer food to comfort
those who mourn for the dead—not even
for a father or a mother—nor will anyone
give them a drink to console them.

8"And do not enter a house where
there is feasting and sit down to eat and
drink. 9For this is what the LORD Almighty, the God of Israel, says: Before
your eyes and in your days I will bring an
end to the sounds of joy and gladness and
to the voices of bride and bridegroom in
this place.

10"When you tell these people all this
and they ask you, 'Why has the LORD decreed such a great disaster against us?
What wrong have we done? What sin
have we committed against the LORD our
God?' 11then say to them, 'It is because
your fathers forsook me,' declares the
LORD, 'and followed other gods and

---

a 14 Some Hebrew manuscripts, Septuagint and
Syriac (see also Jer. 17:4); most Hebrew
manuscripts *I will cause your enemies to bring you /
into*

served and worshiped them. They forsook me and did not keep my law. ¹²But you have behaved more wickedly than your fathers. See how each of you is following the stubbornness of his evil heart instead of obeying me. ¹³So I will throw you out of this land into a land neither you nor your fathers have known, and there you will serve other gods day and night, for I will show you no favor.'

¹⁴"However, the days are coming," declares the LORD, "when men will no longer say, 'As surely as the LORD lives, who brought the Israelites up out of Egypt,' ¹⁵but they will say, 'As surely as the LORD lives, who brought the Israelites up out of

the land of the north and out of all the countries where he had banished them.' For I will restore them to the land I gave their forefathers.

¹⁶"But now I will send for many fishermen," declares the LORD, "and they will catch them. After that I will send for many hunters, and they will hunt them down on every mountain and hill and from the crevices of the rocks. ¹⁷My eyes are on all their ways; they are not hidden from me, nor is their sin concealed from my eyes. ¹⁸I will repay them double for their wickedness and their sin, because they have defiled my land with the lifeless forms of their vile images and have

---

THURSDAY

Read Jeremiah 15:1–21
Key Verse Jeremiah 15:16

Food for the Soul – Dr. Stephen Hayner

To Jeremiah, God's Word was like deep-dish pizza. He devoured it and loved how it fed his soul. God's Word changed Jeremiah's life. It gave him perspective and assured him that he was loved and had a purpose.

But knowing God's Word and obeying it can have a downside. For Jeremiah, it meant persecution, apparent failure in his assigned work, huge misunderstandings with his family and deep agony in his spirit over what he saw in the world. Knowing God's Word was a joy, but it also brought pain. At times Jeremiah even felt as though God had abandoned him. He assumed that if he were obedient, everything would work out well in his life.

Isn't that the way life is supposed to work? You obey God, then God makes you successful. It doesn't always happen quite that way. When this formula doesn't work in our lives, we sometimes become bitter and resentful. But let's take a lesson from the prophet. When Jeremiah didn't feel very successful, he wondered where God was. But Jeremiah didn't quit believing in God and walk away. Instead he consistently turned toward God, even with his complaints. He poured out his hurt, anger and disillusionment honestly. God's assurance was, "Just do what is right, Jeremiah. Be faithful, be consistent, be obedient. I love you. I will protect you. And I will use you for my glory" (see Jeremiah 1:4–10).

Even when God's words go down more like bitter herbs than deep-dish pizza, he promises that it will truly nourish us: "Listen, listen to me, and eat what is good, and your soul will delight in the richest of fare. Give ear and come to me; hear me, that your soul may live" (Isaiah 55:2–3).

A Deeper Look
Psalm 1:1–3; Jeremiah 17:7–8; 1 Peter 2:2

Go to page 866 for your next devotional reading.

filled my inheritance with their detestable idols."

¹⁹O Lord, my strength and my fortress,
　　my refuge in time of distress,
to you the nations will come
　　from the ends of the earth and say,
"Our fathers possessed nothing but
　　false gods,
　　worthless idols that did them no
　　good.
²⁰Do men make their own gods?
　　Yes, but they are not gods!"

²¹"Therefore I will teach them—
　　this time I will teach them
　　my power and might.
Then they will know
　　that my name is the Lord.

17 "Judah's sin is engraved with an
　　iron tool,
　　inscribed with a flint point,
on the tablets of their hearts
　　and on the horns of their altars.
²Even their children remember
　　their altars and Asherah poles*ᵃ*
beside the spreading trees
　　and on the high hills.
³My mountain in the land
　　and your*ᵇ* wealth and all your
　　treasures
I will give away as plunder,
　　together with your high places,
　　because of sin throughout your
　　country.
⁴Through your own fault you will lose
　　the inheritance I gave you.
I will enslave you to your enemies
　　in a land you do not know,
for you have kindled my anger,
　　and it will burn forever."

⁵This is what the Lord says:

"Cursed is the one who trusts in
　　man,
　　who depends on flesh for his
　　strength
　　and whose heart turns away from
　　the Lord.
⁶He will be like a bush in the
　　wastelands;
　　he will not see prosperity when it
　　comes.
He will dwell in the parched places of
　　the desert,
　　in a salt land where no one lives.

⁷"But blessed is the man who trusts in
　　the Lord,
　　whose confidence is in him.
⁸He will be like a tree planted by the
　　water
　　that sends out its roots by the
　　stream.
It does not fear when heat comes;
　　its leaves are always green.
It has no worries in a year of drought
　　and never fails to bear fruit."

⁹The heart is deceitful above all things
　　and beyond cure.
　　Who can understand it?

¹⁰"I the Lord search the heart
　　and examine the mind,
to reward a man according to his
　　conduct,
　　according to what his deeds
　　deserve."

¹¹Like a partridge that hatches eggs it
　　did not lay
　　is the man who gains riches by
　　unjust means.
When his life is half gone, they will
　　desert him,
　　and in the end he will prove to be
　　a fool.

¹²A glorious throne, exalted from the
　　beginning,
　　is the place of our sanctuary.
¹³O Lord, the hope of Israel,
　　all who forsake you will be put to
　　shame.
Those who turn away from you will
　　be written in the dust

ᵃ2 That is, symbols of the goddess Asherah
ᵇ2,3 Or hills / ³and the mountains of the land. /
Your

POINT OF INTEREST

Jeremiah 16:20

We often manufacture our false gods gradually, almost without realizing it. Our dependence on another person, a job, a financial portfolio or a growing fan club can creep up on us slowly and deceptively. We tend to think that these things will always be there and hold us up when we run out of options. Such gods, however, are powerless to deliver anything—or anyone.

because they have forsaken the
    LORD,
  the spring of living water.

¹⁴Heal me, O LORD, and I will be
    healed;
  save me and I will be saved,
  for you are the one I praise.
¹⁵They keep saying to me,
  "Where is the word of the LORD?
    Let it now be fulfilled!"
¹⁶I have not run away from being your
    shepherd;
  you know I have not desired the
    day of despair.
  What passes my lips is open before
    you.
¹⁷Do not be a terror to me;
  you are my refuge in the day of
    disaster.
¹⁸Let my persecutors be put to shame,
  but keep me from shame;
  let them be terrified,
  but keep me from terror.
  Bring on them the day of disaster;
    destroy them with double
    destruction.

Keeping the Sabbath Holy

¹⁹This is what the LORD said to me: "Go and stand at the gate of the people, through which the kings of Judah go in and out; stand also at all the other gates of Jerusalem. ²⁰Say to them, 'Hear the word of the LORD, O kings of Judah and all people of Judah and everyone living in Jerusalem who come through these gates. ²¹This is what the LORD says: Be careful not to carry a load on the Sabbath day or bring it through the gates of Jerusalem. ²²Do not bring a load out of your houses or do any work on the Sabbath, but keep the Sabbath day holy, as I commanded your forefathers. ²³Yet they did not listen or pay attention; they were stiff-necked and would not listen or respond to discipline. ²⁴But if you are careful to obey me, declares the LORD, and bring no load through the gates of this city on the Sabbath, but keep the Sabbath day holy by not doing any work on it, ²⁵then kings who sit on David's throne will come through the gates of this city with their officials. They and their officials will come riding in chariots and on horses, accompanied by the men of Judah and those living in Jerusalem, and this city will be inhabited forever. ²⁶People will come from the towns of Judah and the villages around Jerusalem, from the territory of Benjamin and the western foothills, from the hill country and the Negev, bringing burnt offerings and sacrifices, grain offerings, incense and thank offerings to the house of the LORD. ²⁷But if you do not obey me to keep the Sabbath day holy by not carrying any load as you come through the gates of Jerusalem on the Sabbath day, then I will kindle an unquenchable fire in the gates of Jerusalem that will consume her fortresses.' "

At the Potter's House

18 This is the word that came to Jeremiah from the LORD: ²"Go down to the potter's house, and there I will give you my message." ³So I went down to the potter's house, and I saw him working at the wheel. ⁴But the pot he was shaping from the clay was marred in his hands; so the potter formed it into another pot, shaping it as seemed best to him.

⁵Then the word of the LORD came to me: ⁶"O house of Israel, can I not do with you as this potter does?" declares the LORD. "Like clay in the hand of the potter, so are you in my hand, O house of Israel. ⁷If at any time I announce that a nation or kingdom is to be uprooted, torn down and destroyed, ⁸and if that nation I warned repents of its evil, then I will relent and not inflict on it the disaster I had planned. ⁹And if at another time I announce that a nation or kingdom is to be built up and planted, ¹⁰and if it does evil in my sight and does not obey me, then I will reconsider the good I had intended to do for it.

¹¹"Now therefore say to the people of Judah and those living in Jerusalem, 'This is what the LORD says: Look! I am preparing a disaster for you and devising a plan against you. So turn from your evil ways, each one of you, and reform your ways and your actions.' ¹²But they will reply, 'It's no use. We will continue with our own plans; each of us will follow the stubbornness of his evil heart.' "

¹³Therefore this is what the LORD says:

  "Inquire among the nations:
    Who has ever heard anything like
      this?
  A most horrible thing has been done
    by Virgin Israel.
¹⁴Does the snow of Lebanon
    ever vanish from its rocky slopes?

Do its cool waters from distant
    sources
  ever cease to flow?*a*
15Yet my people have forgotten me;
  they burn incense to worthless
    idols,
which made them stumble in their
    ways
  and in the ancient paths.
They made them walk in bypaths
  and on roads not built up.
16Their land will be laid waste,
  an object of lasting scorn;
all who pass by will be appalled
  and will shake their heads.
17Like a wind from the east,
  I will scatter them before their
    enemies;
I will show them my back and not
    my face
  in the day of their disaster."

18They said, "Come, let's make plans
against Jeremiah; for the teaching of the
law by the priest will not be lost, nor will
counsel from the wise, nor the word from
the prophets. So come, let's attack him
with our tongues and pay no attention to
anything he says."

19Listen to me, O LORD;
  hear what my accusers are saying!
20Should good be repaid with evil?
  Yet they have dug a pit for me.
Remember that I stood before you
  and spoke in their behalf
  to turn your wrath away from
    them.
21So give their children over to famine;
  hand them over to the power of
    the sword.
Let their wives be made childless and
    widows;
  let their men be put to death,
  their young men slain by the
    sword in battle.
22Let a cry be heard from their houses
  when you suddenly bring invaders
    against them,
for they have dug a pit to capture me
  and have hidden snares for my
    feet.
23But you know, O LORD,
  all their plots to kill me.
Do not forgive their crimes
  or blot out their sins from your
    sight.
Let them be overthrown before you;
  deal with them in the time of your
    anger.

19 This is what the LORD says: "Go and
buy a clay jar from a potter. Take
along some of the elders of the people
and of the priests 2and go out to the Valley of Ben Hinnom, near the entrance of
the Potsherd Gate. There proclaim the
words I tell you, 3and say, 'Hear the word
of the LORD, O kings of Judah and people
of Jerusalem. This is what the LORD Almighty, the God of Israel, says: Listen! I
am going to bring a disaster on this place
that will make the ears of everyone who
hears of it tingle. 4For they have forsaken
me and made this a place of foreign gods;
they have burned sacrifices in it to gods
that neither they nor their fathers nor the
kings of Judah ever knew, and they have
filled this place with the blood of the innocent. 5They have built the high places
of Baal to burn their sons in the fire as
offerings to Baal—something I did not
command or mention, nor did it enter my
mind. 6So beware, the days are coming,
declares the LORD, when people will no
longer call this place Topheth or the Valley of Ben Hinnom, but the Valley of
Slaughter.

7" 'In this place I will ruin*b* the plans
of Judah and Jerusalem. I will make them
fall by the sword before their enemies, at
the hands of those who seek their lives,
and I will give their carcasses as food to
the birds of the air and the beasts of the
earth. 8I will devastate this city and make
it an object of scorn; all who pass by will
be appalled and will scoff because of all
its wounds. 9I will make them eat the
flesh of their sons and daughters, and
they will eat one another's flesh during
the stress of the siege imposed on them
by the enemies who seek their lives.'

10"Then break the jar while those who
go with you are watching, 11and say to
them, 'This is what the LORD Almighty
says: I will smash this nation and this city
just as this potter's jar is smashed and
cannot be repaired. They will bury the
dead in Topheth until there is no more
room. 12This is what I will do to this place
and to those who live here, declares the
LORD. I will make this city like Topheth.
13The houses in Jerusalem and those of
the kings of Judah will be defiled like this
place, Topheth—all the houses where
they burned incense on the roofs to all

*a14 The meaning of the Hebrew for this sentence is
uncertain.   *b7 The Hebrew for *ruin* sounds like
the Hebrew for *jar* (see verses 1 and 10).

the starry hosts and poured out drink offerings to other gods.' "

¹⁴Jeremiah then returned from Topheth, where the Lᴏʀᴅ had sent him to
prophesy, and stood in the court of the
Lᴏʀᴅ's temple and said to all the people,
¹⁵"This is what the Lᴏʀᴅ Almighty, the
God of Israel, says: 'Listen! I am going to
bring on this city and the villages around
it every disaster I pronounced against
them, because they were stiff-necked
and would not listen to my words.' "

Jeremiah and Pashhur

20 When the priest Pashhur son of Immer, the chief officer in the temple of
the Lᴏʀᴅ, heard Jeremiah prophesying
these things, ²he had Jeremiah the prophet beaten and put in the stocks at the
Upper Gate of Benjamin at the Lᴏʀᴅ's
temple. ³The next day, when Pashhur
released him from the stocks, Jeremiah
said to him, "The Lᴏʀᴅ's name for you is
not Pashhur, but Magor-Missabib.ᵃ ⁴For
this is what the Lᴏʀᴅ says: 'I will make
you a terror to yourself and to all your
friends; with your own eyes you will see
them fall by the sword of their enemies.
I will hand all Judah over to the king of
Babylon, who will carry them away to
Babylon or put them to the sword. ⁵I will
hand over to their enemies all the wealth
of this city—all its products, all its valuables and all the treasures of the kings of
Judah. They will take it away as plunder
and carry it off to Babylon. ⁶And you,
Pashhur, and all who live in your house
will go into exile to Babylon. There you
will die and be buried, you and all your
friends to whom you have prophesied
lies.' "

Jeremiah's Complaint

⁷O Lᴏʀᴅ, you deceivedᵇ me, and I
    was deceivedᵇ;
  you overpowered me and
    prevailed.
I am ridiculed all day long;
  everyone mocks me.
⁸Whenever I speak, I cry out
  proclaiming violence and
    destruction.
So the word of the Lᴏʀᴅ has brought
    me
  insult and reproach all day long.
⁹But if I say, "I will not mention him
  or speak any more in his name,"
his word is in my heart like a fire,
  a fire shut up in my bones.

I am weary of holding it in;
  indeed, I cannot.
¹⁰I hear many whispering,
  "Terror on every side!
  Report him! Let's report him!"
All my friends
  are waiting for me to slip, saying,
"Perhaps he will be deceived;
  then we will prevail over him
  and take our revenge on him."

¹¹But the Lᴏʀᴅ is with me like a mighty
    warrior;
  so my persecutors will stumble and
    not prevail.
They will fail and be thoroughly
    disgraced;
  their dishonor will never be
    forgotten.
¹²O Lᴏʀᴅ Almighty, you who examine
    the righteous
  and probe the heart and mind,
let me see your vengeance upon
    them,
  for to you I have committed my
    cause.

¹³Sing to the Lᴏʀᴅ!
  Give praise to the Lᴏʀᴅ!
He rescues the life of the needy
  from the hands of the wicked.

¹⁴Cursed be the day I was born!
  May the day my mother bore me
    not be blessed!
¹⁵Cursed be the man who brought my
    father the news,
  who made him very glad, saying,
  "A child is born to you—a son!"
¹⁶May that man be like the towns

ᵃ3 *Magor-Missabib* means *terror on every side.*
ᵇ7 Or *persuaded*

POINT OF INTEREST

Jeremiah 20:7-8

Have you ever stood up for
God and then felt like a fool
because you did? Maybe,
like Jeremiah, you felt that
God had deceived you somehow. God is
incapable of deceit, but he does sometimes allow us to face difficult situations
when we think we deserve to be bailed
out. How did Jeremiah resolve these negative feelings?

the LORD overthrew without pity.
May he hear wailing in the morning,
    a battle cry at noon.
17For he did not kill me in the womb,
    with my mother as my grave,
    her womb enlarged forever.
18Why did I ever come out of the
    womb
to see trouble and sorrow
and to end my days in shame?

God Rejects Zedekiah's Request

21 The word came to Jeremiah from the LORD when King Zedekiah sent to him Pashhur son of Malkijah and the priest Zephaniah son of Maaseiah. They said: 2"Inquire now of the LORD for us because Nebuchadnezzar*a* king of Babylon is attacking us. Perhaps the LORD will perform wonders for us as in times past so that he will withdraw from us."

3But Jeremiah answered them, "Tell Zedekiah, 4'This is what the LORD, the God of Israel, says: I am about to turn against you the weapons of war that are in your hands, which you are using to fight the king of Babylon and the Babylonians*b* who are outside the wall besieging you. And I will gather them inside this city. 5I myself will fight against you with an outstretched hand and a mighty arm in anger and fury and great wrath. 6I will strike down those who live in this city—both men and animals—and they will die of a terrible plague. 7After that, declares the LORD, I will hand over Zedekiah king of Judah, his officials and the people in this city who survive the plague, sword and famine, to Nebuchadnezzar king of Babylon and to their enemies who seek their lives. He will put them to the sword; he will show them no mercy or pity or compassion.'

8"Furthermore, tell the people, 'This is what the LORD says: See, I am setting before you the way of life and the way of death. 9Whoever stays in this city will die by the sword, famine or plague. But whoever goes out and surrenders to the Babylonians who are besieging you will live; he will escape with his life. 10I have determined to do this city harm and not good, declares the LORD. It will be given into the hands of the king of Babylon, and he will destroy it with fire.'

11"Moreover, say to the royal house of Judah, 'Hear the word of the LORD; 12O house of David, this is what the LORD says:

" 'Administer justice every morning;
rescue from the hand of his
    oppressor
the one who has been robbed,
or my wrath will break out and burn
    like fire
because of the evil you have
    done—
burn with no one to quench it.
13I am against you, ⌊Jerusalem,⌋
    you who live above this valley
    on the rocky plateau,
                declares the LORD—
you who say, "Who can come against
    us?
Who can enter our refuge?"
14I will punish you as your deeds
    deserve,
                declares the LORD.
I will kindle a fire in your forests
that will consume everything
    around you.' "

Judgment Against Evil Kings

22 This is what the LORD says: "Go down to the palace of the king of Judah and proclaim this message there: 2'Hear the word of the LORD, O king of Judah, you who sit on David's throne—you, your officials and your people who come through these gates. 3This is what the LORD says: Do what is just and right. Rescue from the hand of his oppressor the one who has been robbed. Do no wrong or violence to the alien, the fatherless or the widow, and do not shed innocent blood in this place. 4For if you are careful to carry out these commands, then kings who sit on David's throne will come through the gates of this palace, riding in chariots and on horses, accompanied by their officials and their people. 5But if you do not obey these commands, declares the LORD, I swear by myself that this palace will become a ruin.' "

6For this is what the LORD says about the palace of the king of Judah:

"Though you are like Gilead to me,
    like the summit of Lebanon,
I will surely make you like a desert,
    like towns not inhabited.
7I will send destroyers against you,
    each man with his weapons,

---

*a*2 Hebrew *Nebuchadrezzar*, of which *Nebuchadnezzar* is a variant; here and often in Jeremiah and Ezekiel   *b*4 Or *Chaldeans*; also in verse 9

and they will cut up your fine cedar
    beams
and throw them into the fire.

8"People from many nations will pass
by this city and will ask one another,
'Why has the LORD done such a thing to
this great city?' 9And the answer will be:
'Because they have forsaken the covenant of the LORD their God and have worshiped and served other gods.' "

10Do not weep for the dead ⌊king⌋ or
    mourn his loss;
rather, weep bitterly for him who
    is exiled,
because he will never return
    nor see his native land again.

11For this is what the LORD says about
Shallum*a* son of Josiah, who succeeded
his father as king of Judah but has gone
from this place: "He will never return.
12He will die in the place where they have
led him captive; he will not see this land
again."

13"Woe to him who builds his palace
    by unrighteousness,
    his upper rooms by injustice,
making his countrymen work for
    nothing,
    not paying them for their labor.
14He says, 'I will build myself a great
    palace
    with spacious upper rooms.'
So he makes large windows in it,
    panels it with cedar
    and decorates it in red.

15"Does it make you a king
    to have more and more cedar?
Did not your father have food and
    drink?
He did what was right and just,
    so all went well with him.
16He defended the cause of the poor
    and needy,
    and so all went well.
Is that not what it means to know
    me?"
    declares the LORD.
17"But your eyes and your heart
    are set only on dishonest gain,
on shedding innocent blood
    and on oppression and extortion."

18Therefore this is what the LORD says
about Jehoiakim son of Josiah king of Judah:

"They will not mourn for him:

'Alas, my brother! Alas, my sister!'
They will not mourn for him:
    'Alas, my master! Alas, his
        splendor!'
19He will have the burial of a donkey—
    dragged away and thrown
    outside the gates of Jerusalem."

20"Go up to Lebanon and cry out,
    let your voice be heard in Bashan,
cry out from Abarim,
    for all your allies are crushed.
21I warned you when you felt secure,
    but you said, 'I will not listen!'
This has been your way from your
    youth;
    you have not obeyed me.
22The wind will drive all your
    shepherds away,
    and your allies will go into exile.
Then you will be ashamed and
    disgraced
    because of all your wickedness.
23You who live in 'Lebanon,*b*'
    who are nestled in cedar buildings,
how you will groan when pangs
    come upon you,
    pain like that of a woman in labor!

24"As surely as I live," declares the
LORD, "even if you, Jehoiachin*c* son of
Jehoiakim king of Judah, were a signet
ring on my right hand, I would still pull
you off. 25I will hand you over to those
who seek your life, those you fear—to
Nebuchadnezzar king of Babylon and to
the Babylonians.*d* 26I will hurl you and
the mother who gave you birth into another country, where neither of you was
born, and there you both will die. 27You
will never come back to the land you long
to return to."

28Is this man Jehoiachin a despised,
        broken pot,
    an object no one wants?
Why will he and his children be
        hurled out,
    cast into a land they do not know?
29O land, land, land,
    hear the word of the LORD!
30This is what the LORD says:
"Record this man as if childless,
    a man who will not prosper in his
        lifetime,
for none of his offspring will prosper,

---

a 11 Also called *Jehoahaz*   *b 23* That is, the
palace in Jerusalem (see 1 Kings 7:2)
c 24 Hebrew *Coniah*, a variant of *Jehoiachin*; also in
verse 28   *d 25* Or *Chaldeans*

none will sit on the throne of
David
or rule anymore in Judah."

The Righteous Branch

23 "Woe to the shepherds who are destroying and scattering the sheep of my pasture!" declares the LORD. ²Therefore this is what the LORD, the God of Israel, says to the shepherds who tend my people: "Because you have scattered my flock and driven them away and have not bestowed care on them, I will bestow punishment on you for the evil you have done," declares the LORD. ³"I myself will gather the remnant of my flock out of all the countries where I have driven them and will bring them back to their pasture, where they will be fruitful and increase in number. ⁴I will place shepherds over them who will tend them, and they will no longer be afraid or terrified, nor will any be missing," declares the LORD.

⁵"The days are coming," declares the
LORD,
"when I will raise up to David*a* a
righteous Branch,
a King who will reign wisely
and do what is just and right in
the land.
⁶In his days Judah will be saved
and Israel will live in safety.
This is the name by which he will be
called:
The LORD Our Righteousness.

⁷"So then, the days are coming," declares the LORD, "when people will no longer say, 'As surely as the LORD lives, who brought the Israelites up out of Egypt,' ⁸but they will say, 'As surely as the LORD lives, who brought the descendants of Israel up out of the land of the north and out of all the countries where he had banished them.' Then they will live in their own land."

Lying Prophets

⁹Concerning the prophets:

My heart is broken within me;
all my bones tremble.
I am like a drunken man,
like a man overcome by wine,
because of the LORD
and his holy words.
¹⁰The land is full of adulterers;
because of the curse*b* the land lies
parched*c*

and the pastures in the desert are
withered.
The ∟prophets⌐ follow an evil course
and use their power unjustly.

¹¹"Both prophet and priest are godless;
even in my temple I find their
wickedness,"
declares the LORD.
¹²"Therefore their path will become
slippery;
they will be banished to darkness
and there they will fall.
I will bring disaster on them
in the year they are punished,"
declares the LORD.

¹³"Among the prophets of Samaria
I saw this repulsive thing:
They prophesied by Baal
and led my people Israel astray.
¹⁴And among the prophets of Jerusalem
I have seen something horrible:
They commit adultery and live a
lie.
They strengthen the hands of
evildoers,
so that no one turns from his
wickedness.
They are all like Sodom to me;
the people of Jerusalem are like
Gomorrah."

¹⁵Therefore, this is what the LORD Almighty says concerning the prophets:

"I will make them eat bitter food
and drink poisoned water,
because from the prophets of
Jerusalem
ungodliness has spread throughout
the land."

¹⁶This is what the LORD Almighty says:

---

a5 Or *up from David's line*   *b10* Or *because of
these things*   *c10* Or *land mourns*

Jeremiah 23:5-6

The "righteous Branch" Jeremiah refers to is Jesus. John 15 uses a similar metaphor in comparing Jesus to the vine and his followers to the branches. Compare and contrast the two passages.

"Do not listen to what the prophets
are prophesying to you;
they fill you with false hopes.
They speak visions from their own
minds,
not from the mouth of the LORD.
¹⁷They keep saying to those who
despise me,
'The LORD says: You will have
peace.'
And to all who follow the
stubbornness of their hearts
they say, 'No harm will come to
you.'
¹⁸But which of them has stood in the
council of the LORD
to see or to hear his word?
Who has listened and heard his
word?
¹⁹See, the storm of the LORD
will burst out in wrath,
a whirlwind swirling down
on the heads of the wicked.
²⁰The anger of the LORD will not turn
back
until he fully accomplishes
the purposes of his heart.
In days to come
you will understand it clearly.
²¹I did not send these prophets,
yet they have run with their
message;
I did not speak to them,
yet they have prophesied.
²²But if they had stood in my council,
they would have proclaimed my
words to my people
and would have turned them from
their evil ways
and from their evil deeds.

²³"Am I only a God nearby,"
declares the LORD,
"and not a God far away?
²⁴Can anyone hide in secret places
so that I cannot see him?"
declares the LORD.
"Do not I fill heaven and earth?"
declares the LORD.

²⁵"I have heard what the prophets say
who prophesy lies in my name. They say,
'I had a dream! I had a dream!' ²⁶How
long will this continue in the hearts of
these lying prophets, who prophesy the
delusions of their own minds? ²⁷They
think the dreams they tell one another
will make my people forget my name,
just as their fathers forgot my name
through Baal worship. ²⁸Let the prophet
who has a dream tell his dream, but let
the one who has my word speak it faithfully. For what has straw to do with
grain?" declares the LORD. ²⁹"Is not my
word like fire," declares the LORD, "and
like a hammer that breaks a rock in
pieces?

³⁰"Therefore," declares the LORD, "I am
against the prophets who steal from one
another words supposedly from me.
³¹Yes," declares the LORD, "I am against
the prophets who wag their own tongues
and yet declare, 'The LORD declares.' ³²Indeed, I am against those who prophesy
false dreams," declares the LORD. "They
tell them and lead my people astray with
their reckless lies, yet I did not send or
appoint them. They do not benefit these
people in the least," declares the LORD.

False Oracles and False Prophets

³³"When these people, or a prophet or
a priest, ask you, 'What is the oracle[a] of
the LORD?' say to them, 'What oracle?[b] I
will forsake you, declares the LORD.' ³⁴If a
prophet or a priest or anyone else claims,
'This is the oracle of the LORD,' I will punish that man and his household. ³⁵This is
what each of you keeps on saying to his
friend or relative: 'What is the LORD's answer?' or 'What has the LORD spoken?'
³⁶But you must not mention 'the oracle
of the LORD' again, because every man's
own word becomes his oracle and so you
distort the words of the living God, the
LORD Almighty, our God. ³⁷This is what
you keep saying to a prophet: 'What is
the LORD's answer to you?' or 'What has
the LORD spoken?' ³⁸Although you claim,
'This is the oracle of the LORD,' this is
what the LORD says: You used the words,
'This is the oracle of the LORD,' even
though I told you that you must not
claim, 'This is the oracle of the LORD.'
³⁹Therefore, I will surely forget you and
cast you out of my presence along with
the city I gave to you and your fathers. ⁴⁰I
will bring upon you everlasting disgrace—everlasting shame that will not be
forgotten."

Two Baskets of Figs

24 After Jehoiachin[c] son of Jehoiakim
king of Judah and the officials, the

---
a33 Or *burden* (see Septuagint and Vulgate)
b33 Hebrew; Septuagint and Vulgate '*You are the
burden.* (The Hebrew for *oracle* and *burden* is the
same.)   c1 Hebrew *Jeconiah*, a variant of
Jehoiachin

craftsmen and the artisans of Judah were carried into exile from Jerusalem to Babylon by Nebuchadnezzar king of Babylon, the LORD showed me two baskets of figs placed in front of the temple of the LORD. ²One basket had very good figs, like those that ripen early; the other basket had very poor figs, so bad they could not be eaten.

³Then the LORD asked me, "What do you see, Jeremiah?"

"Figs," I answered. "The good ones are very good, but the poor ones are so bad they cannot be eaten."

⁴Then the word of the LORD came to me: ⁵"This is what the LORD, the God of Israel, says: 'Like these good figs, I regard as good the exiles from Judah, whom I sent away from this place to the land of the Babylonians.ᵃ ⁶My eyes will watch over them for their good, and I will bring them back to this land. I will build them up and not tear them down; I will plant them and not uproot them. ⁷I will give

them a heart to know me, that I am the LORD. They will be my people, and I will be their God, for they will return to me with all their heart.

⁸"'But like the poor figs, which are so bad they cannot be eaten,' says the LORD, 'so will I deal with Zedekiah king of Judah, his officials and the survivors from Jerusalem, whether they remain in this land or live in Egypt. ⁹I will make them abhorrent and an offense to all the kingdoms of the earth, a reproach and a byword, an object of ridicule and cursing, wherever I banish them. ¹⁰I will send the sword, famine and plague against them until they are destroyed from the land I gave to them and their fathers.'"

Seventy Years of Captivity

25 The word came to Jeremiah concerning all the people of Judah in the fourth year of Jehoiakim son of Josiah

ᵃ5 Or Chaldeans

FRIDAY

Read Jeremiah 23:1–32
Key Verse Jeremiah 23:29

Sudden Impact: God's Word — Kent Walstrom

Cruisin' across campus, thinkin' I've got the world by the tail. Just smoked an exam right on the heels of debugging a computer program until it worked to perfection. I think to myself, *I'm able to do things with a computer that others can't. I'm able to solve difficult problems where others fail.* Cruisin' across campus, thinkin' I've got the world by the tail.

Then a still but persistent voice inside my head brings back a Bible verse memorized long ago: "Your attitude should be the same as that of Christ Jesus: Who, being in very nature God . . . made himself nothing . . . he humbled himself" (Philippians 2:5–8). As the prophet Jeremiah predicted, God's fiery Word consumes my arrogance.

I stop cruisin'. My heart hurts, and I have to stop right there and make the sacrifice of a "broken and contrite heart" (Psalm 51:17). I thank God for giving me my talents and abilities, for I know that everything I have is a gift from his hand. I ask God to forgive me for taking the credit. I thank him that his Word *is* like fire and like a hammer that breaks my rocky heart with his truth. Were it not for God's Word, I would be like one of these false prophets, deluded by my own mind.

A Deeper Look
Romans 12:3–8; 2 Timothy 3:16–17; Hebrews 4:12–13

Go to page 872 for your next devotional reading.

king of Judah, which was the first year of Nebuchadnezzar king of Babylon. ²So Jeremiah the prophet said to all the people of Judah and to all those living in Jerusalem: ³For twenty-three years— from the thirteenth year of Josiah son of Amon king of Judah until this very day— the word of the LORD has come to me and I have spoken to you again and again, but you have not listened.

⁴And though the LORD has sent all his servants the prophets to you again and again, you have not listened or paid any attention. ⁵They said, "Turn now, each of you, from your evil ways and your evil practices, and you can stay in the land the LORD gave to you and your fathers for ever and ever. ⁶Do not follow other gods to serve and worship them; do not provoke me to anger with what your hands have made. Then I will not harm you."

⁷"But you did not listen to me," declares the LORD, "and you have provoked me with what your hands have made, and you have brought harm to yourselves."

⁸Therefore the LORD Almighty says this: "Because you have not listened to my words, ⁹I will summon all the peoples of the north and my servant Nebuchadnezzar king of Babylon," declares the LORD, "and I will bring them against this land and its inhabitants and against all the surrounding nations. I will completely destroy*a* them and make them an object of horror and scorn, and an everlasting ruin. ¹⁰I will banish from them the sounds of joy and gladness, the voices of bride and bridegroom, the sound of millstones and the light of the lamp. ¹¹This whole country will become a desolate wasteland, and these nations will serve the king of Babylon seventy years.

¹²"But when the seventy years are fulfilled, I will punish the king of Babylon and his nation, the land of the Babylonians,*b* for their guilt," declares the LORD, "and will make it desolate forever. ¹³I will bring upon that land all the things I have spoken against it, all that are written in this book and prophesied by Jeremiah against all the nations. ¹⁴They themselves will be enslaved by many nations and great kings; I will repay them according to their deeds and the work of their hands."

The Cup of God's Wrath

¹⁵This is what the LORD, the God of Is-

rael, said to me: "Take from my hand this cup filled with the wine of my wrath and make all the nations to whom I send you drink it. ¹⁶When they drink it, they will stagger and go mad because of the sword I will send among them."

¹⁷So I took the cup from the LORD's hand and made all the nations to whom he sent me drink it: ¹⁸Jerusalem and the towns of Judah, its kings and officials, to make them a ruin and an object of horror and scorn and cursing, as they are today; ¹⁹Pharaoh king of Egypt, his attendants, his officials and all his people, ²⁰and all the foreign people there; all the kings of Uz; all the kings of the Philistines (those of Ashkelon, Gaza, Ekron, and the people left at Ashdod); ²¹Edom, Moab and Ammon; ²²all the kings of Tyre and Sidon; the kings of the coastlands across the sea; ²³Dedan, Tema, Buz and all who are in distant places*c*; ²⁴all the kings of Arabia and all the kings of the foreign people who live in the desert; ²⁵all the kings of Zimri, Elam and Media; ²⁶and all the kings of the north, near and far, one after the other—all the kingdoms on the face of the earth. And after all of them, the king of Sheshach*d* will drink it too.

²⁷"Then tell them, 'This is what the LORD Almighty, the God of Israel, says: Drink, get drunk and vomit, and fall to rise no more because of the sword I will send among you.' ²⁸But if they refuse to take the cup from your hand and drink, tell them, 'This is what the LORD Almighty says: You must drink it! ²⁹See, I am beginning to bring disaster on the city that bears my Name, and will you indeed go

---

a9 The Hebrew term refers to the irrevocable giving over of things or persons to the LORD, often by totally destroying them.   *b12* Or *Chaldeans*
c23 Or *who clip the hair by their foreheads*
d26 Sheshach is a cryptogram for Babylon.

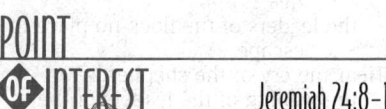

POINT OF INTEREST

Jeremiah 24:8-10

How would you like your life to be an object lesson entitled *What Happens to Those Who Turn Away From God?* The prospect of the pain and shame that Zedekiah faced should stimulate a fresh commitment to obedience. That was Jeremiah's intention here.

unpunished? You will not go unpunished, for I am calling down a sword upon all who live on the earth, declares the LORD Almighty.'

³⁰"Now prophesy all these words against them and say to them:

" 'The LORD will roar from on high;
    he will thunder from his holy
        dwelling
and roar mightily against his land.
He will shout like those who tread
        the grapes,
    shout against all who live on the
        earth.
³¹The tumult will resound to the ends
        of the earth,
    for the LORD will bring charges
        against the nations;
he will bring judgment on all
        mankind
    and put the wicked to the
        sword,' "
                    declares the LORD.

³²This is what the LORD Almighty says:

"Look! Disaster is spreading
    from nation to nation;
a mighty storm is rising
    from the ends of the earth."

³³At that time those slain by the LORD will be everywhere—from one end of the earth to the other. They will not be mourned or gathered up or buried, but will be like refuse lying on the ground.

³⁴Weep and wail, you shepherds;
    roll in the dust, you leaders of the
        flock.
For your time to be slaughtered has
        come;
    you will fall and be shattered like
        fine pottery.
³⁵The shepherds will have nowhere to
        flee,
    the leaders of the flock no place to
        escape.
³⁶Hear the cry of the shepherds,
    the wailing of the leaders of the
        flock,
for the LORD is destroying their
        pasture.
³⁷The peaceful meadows will be laid
        waste
    because of the fierce anger of the
        LORD.
³⁸Like a lion he will leave his lair,
    and their land will become
        desolate

because of the sword[a] of the
        oppressor
    and because of the LORD's fierce
        anger.

Jeremiah Threatened With Death

26 Early in the reign of Jehoiakim son of Josiah king of Judah, this word came from the LORD: ²"This is what the LORD says: Stand in the courtyard of the LORD's house and speak to all the people of the towns of Judah who come to worship in the house of the LORD. Tell them everything I command you; do not omit a word. ³Perhaps they will listen and each will turn from his evil way. Then I will relent and not bring on them the disaster I was planning because of the evil they have done. ⁴Say to them, 'This is what the LORD says: If you do not listen to me and follow my law, which I have set before you, ⁵and if you do not listen to the words of my servants the prophets, whom I have sent to you again and again (though you have not listened), ⁶then I will make this house like Shiloh and this city an object of cursing among all the nations of the earth.' "

⁷The priests, the prophets and all the people heard Jeremiah speak these words in the house of the LORD. ⁸But as soon as Jeremiah finished telling all the people everything the LORD had commanded him to say, the priests, the prophets and all the people seized him and said, "You must die! ⁹Why do you prophesy in the LORD's name that this house will be like Shiloh and this city will be desolate and deserted?" And all the people crowded

---

[a]38 Some Hebrew manuscripts and Septuagint (see also Jer. 46:16 and 50:16); most Hebrew manuscripts *anger*

POINT OF INTEREST

Jeremiah 25:11-14

Israel was sentenced to seventy years in exile—no time off for good behavior and no chance for parole. The sentence was not endless, however; it carried hope for a future restoration. The Hebrews exiled to Babylon clung to this hope as a written promise from God (see Daniel 9:2).

around Jeremiah in the house of the LORD. ¹⁰When the officials of Judah heard about these things, they went up from the royal palace to the house of the LORD and took their places at the entrance of the New Gate of the LORD's house. ¹¹Then the priests and the prophets said to the officials and all the people, "This man should be sentenced to death because he has prophesied against this city. You have heard it with your own ears!"

¹²Then Jeremiah said to all the officials and all the people: "The LORD sent me to prophesy against this house and this city all the things you have heard. ¹³Now reform your ways and your actions and obey the LORD your God. Then the LORD will relent and not bring the disaster he has pronounced against you. ¹⁴As for me, I am in your hands; do with me whatever you think is good and right. ¹⁵Be assured, however, that if you put me to death, you will bring the guilt of innocent blood on yourselves and on this city and on those who live in it, for in truth the LORD has sent me to you to speak all these words in your hearing."

¹⁶Then the officials and all the people said to the priests and the prophets, "This man should not be sentenced to death! He has spoken to us in the name of the LORD our God."

¹⁷Some of the elders of the land stepped forward and said to the entire assembly of people, ¹⁸"Micah of Moresheth prophesied in the days of Hezekiah king of Judah. He told all the people of Judah, 'This is what the LORD Almighty says:

" 'Zion will be plowed like a field,
    Jerusalem will become a heap of
        rubble,
    the temple hill a mound overgrown
        with thickets.'ᵃ

¹⁹"Did Hezekiah king of Judah or anyone else in Judah put him to death? Did not Hezekiah fear the LORD and seek his favor? And did not the LORD relent, so that he did not bring the disaster he pronounced against them? We are about to bring a terrible disaster on ourselves!"

²⁰(Now Uriah son of Shemaiah from Kiriath Jearim was another man who prophesied in the name of the LORD; he prophesied the same things against this city and this land as Jeremiah did. ²¹When King Jehoiakim and all his officers and officials heard his words, the king sought to put him to death. But Uriah heard of it and fled in fear to Egypt. ²²King Jehoiakim, however, sent Elnathan son of Acbor to Egypt, along with some other men. ²³They brought Uriah out of Egypt and took him to King Jehoiakim, who had him struck down with a sword and his body thrown into the burial place of the common people.) ²⁴Furthermore, Ahikam son of Shaphan supported Jeremiah, and so he was not handed over to the people to be put to death.

Judah to Serve Nebuchadnezzar

27 Early in the reign of Zedekiahᵇ son of Josiah king of Judah, this word came to Jeremiah from the LORD: ²This is what the LORD said to me: "Make a yoke out of straps and crossbars and put it on your neck. ³Then send word to the kings of Edom, Moab, Ammon, Tyre and Sidon through the envoys who have come to Jerusalem to Zedekiah king of Judah. ⁴Give them a message for their masters and say, 'This is what the LORD Almighty, the God of Israel, says: "Tell this to your masters: ⁵With my great power and outstretched arm I made the earth and its people and the animals that are on it, and I give it to anyone I please. ⁶Now I will hand all your countries over to my servant Nebuchadnezzar king of Babylon; I will make even the wild animals subject to him. ⁷All nations will serve him and his son and his grandson until the time for his land comes; then many nations and great kings will subjugate him.

⁸" "If, however, any nation or kingdom will not serve Nebuchadnezzar king of Babylon or bow its neck under his yoke, I will punish that nation with the sword, famine and plague, declares the LORD, until I destroy it by his hand. ⁹So do not listen to your prophets, your diviners, your interpreters of dreams, your mediums or your sorcerers who tell you, 'You will not serve the king of Babylon.' ¹⁰They prophesy lies to you that will only serve to remove you far from your lands; I will banish you and you will perish. ¹¹But if any nation will bow its neck under the yoke of the king of Babylon and serve him, I will let that nation remain in

---

ᵃ 18 Micah 3:12   ᵇ 1 A few Hebrew manuscripts and Syriac (see also Jer. 27:3, 12 and 28:1); most Hebrew manuscripts *Jehoiakim* (Most Septuagint manuscripts do not have this verse.)

its own land to till it and to live there, declares the LORD." ' "

¹²I gave the same message to Zedekiah king of Judah. I said, "Bow your neck under the yoke of the king of Babylon; serve him and his people, and you will live. ¹³Why will you and your people die by the sword, famine and plague with which the LORD has threatened any nation that will not serve the king of Babylon? ¹⁴Do not listen to the words of the prophets who say to you, 'You will not serve the king of Babylon,' for they are prophesying lies to you. ¹⁵'I have not sent them,' declares the LORD. 'They are prophesying lies in my name. Therefore, I will banish you and you will perish, both you and the prophets who prophesy to you.' "

¹⁶Then I said to the priests and all these people, "This is what the LORD says: Do not listen to the prophets who say, 'Very soon now the articles from the LORD's house will be brought back from Babylon.' They are prophesying lies to you. ¹⁷Do not listen to them. Serve the king of Babylon, and you will live. Why should this city become a ruin? ¹⁸If they are prophets and have the word of the LORD, let them plead with the LORD Almighty that the furnishings remaining in the house of the LORD and in the palace of the king of Judah and in Jerusalem not be taken to Babylon. ¹⁹For this is what the LORD Almighty says about the pillars, the Sea, the movable stands and the other furnishings that are left in this city, ²⁰which Nebuchadnezzar king of Babylon did not take away when he carried Jehoiachinᵃ son of Jehoiakim king of Judah into exile from Jerusalem to Babylon, along with all the nobles of Judah and Jerusalem— ²¹yes, this is what the LORD Almighty, the God of Israel, says about the things that are left in the house of the LORD and in the palace of the king of Judah and in Jerusalem: ²²'They will be taken to Babylon and there they will remain until the day I come for them,' declares the LORD. 'Then I will bring them back and restore them to this place.' "

The False Prophet Hananiah

28 In the fifth month of that same year, the fourth year, early in the reign of Zedekiah king of Judah, the prophet Hananiah son of Azzur, who was from Gibeon, said to me in the house of the LORD in the presence of the priests and all the people: ²"This is what the LORD Almighty,

the God of Israel, says: 'I will break the yoke of the king of Babylon. ³Within two years I will bring back to this place all the articles of the LORD's house that Nebuchadnezzar king of Babylon removed from here and took to Babylon. ⁴I will also bring back to this place Jehoiachinᵃ son of Jehoiakim king of Judah and all the other exiles from Judah who went to Babylon,' declares the LORD, 'for I will break the yoke of the king of Babylon.' "

⁵Then the prophet Jeremiah replied to the prophet Hananiah before the priests and all the people who were standing in the house of the LORD. ⁶He said, "Amen! May the LORD do so! May the LORD fulfill the words you have prophesied by bringing the articles of the LORD's house and all the exiles back to this place from Babylon. ⁷Nevertheless, listen to what I have to say in your hearing and in the hearing of all the people: ⁸From early times the prophets who preceded you and me have prophesied war, disaster and plague against many countries and great kingdoms. ⁹But the prophet who prophesies peace will be recognized as one truly sent by the LORD only if his prediction comes true."

¹⁰Then the prophet Hananiah took the yoke off the neck of the prophet Jeremiah and broke it, ¹¹and he said before all the people, "This is what the LORD says: 'In the same way will I break the yoke of Nebuchadnezzar king of Babylon off the neck of all the nations within two years.' " At this, the prophet Jeremiah went on his way.

¹²Shortly after the prophet Hananiah had broken the yoke off the neck of the prophet Jeremiah, the word of the LORD came to Jeremiah: ¹³"Go and tell Hananiah, 'This is what the LORD says: You have broken a wooden yoke, but in its place you will get a yoke of iron. ¹⁴This is what the LORD Almighty, the God of Israel, says: I will put an iron yoke on the necks of all these nations to make them serve Nebuchadnezzar king of Babylon, and they will serve him. I will even give him control over the wild animals.' "

¹⁵Then the prophet Jeremiah said to Hananiah the prophet, "Listen, Hananiah! The LORD has not sent you, yet you have persuaded this nation to trust in lies. ¹⁶Therefore, this is what the LORD says: 'I am about to remove you from the

---

ᵃ20,4 Hebrew *Jeconiah*, a variant of *Jehoiachin*

face of the earth. This very year you are going to die, because you have preached rebellion against the LORD.' "

¹⁷In the seventh month of that same year, Hananiah the prophet died.

A Letter to the Exiles

29 This is the text of the letter that the prophet Jeremiah sent from Jerusalem to the surviving elders among the exiles and to the priests, the prophets and all the other people Nebuchadnezzar had carried into exile from Jerusalem to Babylon. ²(This was after King Jehoiachin*ᵃ* and the queen mother, the court officials and the leaders of Judah and Jerusalem, the craftsmen and the artisans had gone into exile from Jerusalem.) ³He entrusted the letter to Elasah son of Shaphan and to Gemariah son of Hilkiah, whom Zedekiah king of Judah sent to King Nebuchadnezzar in Babylon. It said:

⁴This is what the LORD Almighty, the God of Israel, says to all those I carried into exile from Jerusalem to Babylon: ⁵"Build houses and settle down; plant gardens and eat what they produce. ⁶Marry and have sons and daughters; find wives for your sons and give your daughters in marriage, so that they too may have sons and daughters. Increase in number there; do not decrease. ⁷Also, seek the peace and prosperity of the city to which I have carried you into exile. Pray to the LORD for it, because if it prospers, you too will prosper." ⁸Yes, this is what the LORD Almighty, the God of Israel, says: "Do not let the prophets and diviners among you deceive you. Do not listen to the dreams they encourage them to have. ⁹They are prophesying lies to you in my name. I have not sent them," declares the LORD.

¹⁰This is what the LORD says: "When seventy years are completed for Babylon, I will come to you and fulfill my gracious promise to bring you back to this place. ¹¹For I know the plans I have for you," declares the LORD, "plans to prosper you and not to harm you, plans to give you hope and a future. ¹²Then you will call upon me and come and pray to me, and I will listen to you. ¹³You will seek me and find me when you seek me with all your heart. ¹⁴I will be found by you," declares the LORD, "and will bring you back from captivity.*ᵇ* I will gather you from all the nations and places where I have banished you," declares the LORD, "and will bring you back to the place from which I carried you into exile."

¹⁵You may say, "The LORD has raised up prophets for us in Babylon," ¹⁶but this is what the LORD says about the king who sits on David's throne and all the people who remain in this city, your countrymen who did not go with you into exile— ¹⁷yes, this is what the LORD Almighty says: "I will send the sword, famine and plague against them and I will make them like poor figs that are so bad they cannot be eaten. ¹⁸I will pursue them with the sword, famine and plague and will make them abhorrent to all the kingdoms of the earth and an object of cursing and horror, of scorn and reproach, among all the nations where I drive them. ¹⁹For they have not listened to my words," declares the LORD, "words that I sent to them again and again by my servants the prophets. And you exiles have not listened either," declares the LORD.

²⁰Therefore, hear the word of the LORD, all you exiles whom I have sent away from Jerusalem to Babylon. ²¹This is what the LORD Almighty, the God of Israel, says about Ahab son of Kolaiah and Zedekiah son of Maaseiah, who are prophesying lies to you in my name: "I will hand them over to Nebuchadnezzar king of Babylon, and he will put them to death before your very eyes. ²²Because of them, all the exiles from Judah who are in Babylon will use this curse: 'The LORD treat you like Zedekiah and Ahab, whom the king of Babylon burned in the fire.' ²³For they have done outrageous things in Israel; they have committed adultery with their neighbors' wives and in my name have spoken lies, which I did not tell them to do. I know it and

---

*ᵃ*2 Hebrew *Jeconiah*, a variant of *Jehoiachin*
*ᵇ*14 Or *will restore your fortunes*

Read *Jeremiah 29:1–23*
Key Verses *Jeremiah 29:11–13*

A Plan to Give You Hope

Within Jeremiah's letter to the exiles from Jerusalem we find this gem of a promise: " ' For I know the plans I have for you,' declares the LORD, ' plans to prosper you and not to harm you, plans to give you hope and a future.' " When our future looms so vast and uncertain before us, what a relief to know that God our Father is thinking and planning ahead for each of us. And from his vantage point he can see all the events and obstacles we will encounter as the future unfolds.

When we seek God with all our heart, he will not leave us wondering about his plan. God gives us his guidance as well as the power we need to follow him. Yet he rarely shows his entire plan up front; if we focus on listening to God's voice and follow him, we discover that God often reveals his will one step at a time.

Digging Into the Word
1. What do these passages highlight about God's guidance?—
   Psalm 119:105; 2 Timothy 3:16–17
2. God speaks to us through the wisdom of counselors. How do these passages challenge you to seek counsel from others?—
   Proverbs 13:20; Proverbs 15:22; Proverbs 19:20

Personal Reflection
Write a mission statement for your life. A mission statement is a guiding principle that shapes and focuses your life. As you work on it, consider the following: What has God already taught you about his direction for your life? What characteristics, abilities and interests has God given you? What are your spiritual gifts? List some words that describe your values and do a search through an on-line Bible to see what it has to say about them. Search for a life verse or verses to incorporate into your mission statement. After you write your mission statement, tape it in the front of your Bible and check back regularly to see if you're on course.

One Step Deeper
Proverbs 3:5–6; Romans 12:1–2

Go to page 879 for your next devotional reading.

am a witness to it," declares the LORD.

Message to Shemaiah

24Tell Shemaiah the Nehelamite, 25"This is what the LORD Almighty, the God of Israel, says: You sent letters in your own name to all the people in Jerusalem, to Zephaniah son of Maaseiah the priest, and to all the other priests. You said to Zephaniah, 26'The LORD has appointed you priest in place of Jehoiada to be in charge of the house of the LORD; you should put any madman who acts like a prophet into the stocks and neck-irons. 27So why have you not reprimanded Jeremiah from Anathoth, who poses as a prophet among you? 28He has sent this message to us in Babylon: It will be a long time. Therefore build houses and settle down; plant gardens and eat what they produce.' "

29Zephaniah the priest, however, read the letter to Jeremiah the prophet. 30Then the word of the LORD came to Jeremiah: 31"Send this message to all the exiles: 'This is what the LORD says about Shemaiah the Nehelamite: Because Shemaiah has prophesied to you, even though I did not send him, and has led you to believe a lie, 32this is what the LORD says: I will surely punish Shemaiah the Nehelamite and his descendants. He will have no one left among this people, nor will he see the good things I will do for my people, declares the LORD, because he has preached rebellion against me.' "

Restoration of Israel

30 This is the word that came to Jeremiah from the LORD: 2"This is what the LORD, the God of Israel, says: 'Write in a book all the words I have spoken to you. 3The days are coming,' declares the LORD, 'when I will bring my people Israel and Judah back from captivity*a* and restore them to the land I gave their forefathers to possess,' says the LORD."

4These are the words the LORD spoke concerning Israel and Judah: 5"This is what the LORD says:

" 'Cries of fear are heard—
    terror, not peace.
6Ask and see:
    Can a man bear children?
Then why do I see every strong man
    with his hands on his stomach like
    a woman in labor,

every face turned deathly pale?
7How awful that day will be!
    None will be like it.
It will be a time of trouble for Jacob,
    but he will be saved out of it.

8" 'In that day,' declares the LORD
        Almighty,
    'I will break the yoke off their
        necks
and will tear off their bonds;
    no longer will foreigners enslave
        them.
9Instead, they will serve the LORD their
        God
    and David their king,
    whom I will raise up for them.

10" 'So do not fear, O Jacob my
        servant;
    do not be dismayed, O Israel,'
                    declares the LORD.
'I will surely save you out of a distant
        place,
    your descendants from the land of
        their exile.
Jacob will again have peace and
        security,
    and no one will make him afraid.
11I am with you and will save you,'
    declares the LORD.
'Though I completely destroy all the
        nations
    among which I scatter you,
    I will not completely destroy you.
I will discipline you but only with
        justice;
    I will not let you go entirely
        unpunished.'

12"This is what the LORD says:

" 'Your wound is incurable,
    your injury beyond healing.
13There is no one to plead your cause,
    no remedy for your sore,
    no healing for you.
14All your allies have forgotten you;
    they care nothing for you.
I have struck you as an enemy would
    and punished you as would the
        cruel,
because your guilt is so great
    and your sins so many.
15Why do you cry out over your
        wound,
    your pain that has no cure?

---

a3 Or will restore the fortunes of my people Israel and Judah

Because of your great guilt and many
    sins
  I have done these things to you.

16" 'But all who devour you will be
        devoured;
  all your enemies will go into exile.
  Those who plunder you will be
        plundered;
  all who make spoil of you I will
        despoil.
17But I will restore you to health
  and heal your wounds,'
                    declares the LORD,
  'because you are called an outcast,
    Zion for whom no one cares.'

18"This is what the LORD says:

  " 'I will restore the fortunes of
        Jacob's tents
  and have compassion on his
        dwellings;
  the city will be rebuilt on her ruins,
    and the palace will stand in its
        proper place.
19From them will come songs of
        thanksgiving
  and the sound of rejoicing.
  I will add to their numbers,
    and they will not be decreased;
  I will bring them honor,
    and they will not be disdained.
20Their children will be as in days of
        old,
  and their community will be
        established before me;
  I will punish all who oppress them.
21Their leader will be one of their own;
    their ruler will arise from among
        them.
  I will bring him near and he will
        come close to me,
  for who is he who will devote
        himself
    to be close to me?'
                    declares the LORD.
22" 'So you will be my people,
    and I will be your God.' "

23See, the storm of the LORD
  will burst out in wrath,
  a driving wind swirling down
    on the heads of the wicked.
24The fierce anger of the LORD will not
        turn back
  until he fully accomplishes
    the purposes of his heart.
  In days to come
    you will understand this.

31 "At that time," declares the LORD, "I
    will be the God of all the clans of Isra-
el, and they will be my people."

2This is what the LORD says:

  "The people who survive the sword
    will find favor in the desert;
  I will come to give rest to Israel."

3The LORD appeared to us in the past,[a]
saying:

  "I have loved you with an everlasting
        love;
  I have drawn you with
        loving-kindness.
4I will build you up again
    and you will be rebuilt, O Virgin
        Israel.
  Again you will take up your
        tambourines
    and go out to dance with the
        joyful.
5Again you will plant vineyards
    on the hills of Samaria;
  the farmers will plant them
    and enjoy their fruit.
6There will be a day when watchmen
        cry out
    on the hills of Ephraim,
  'Come, let us go up to Zion,
    to the LORD our God.' "

7This is what the LORD says:

  "Sing with joy for Jacob;
    shout for the foremost of the
        nations.
  Make your praises heard, and say,
    'O LORD, save your people,
    the remnant of Israel.'
8See, I will bring them from the land
        of the north
    and gather them from the ends of
        the earth.
  Among them will be the blind and
        the lame,
    expectant mothers and women in
        labor;
  a great throng will return.
9They will come with weeping;
    they will pray as I bring them
        back.
  I will lead them beside streams of
        water
    on a level path where they will not
        stumble,
  because I am Israel's father,
    and Ephraim is my firstborn son.

a3 Or LORD has appeared to us from afar

¹⁰"Hear the word of the LORD,
    O nations;
proclaim it in distant coastlands:
'He who scattered Israel will gather
    them
and will watch over his flock like a
    shepherd.'
¹¹For the LORD will ransom Jacob
    and redeem them from the hand of
    those stronger than they.
¹²They will come and shout for joy on
    the heights of Zion;
they will rejoice in the bounty of
    the LORD—
the grain, the new wine and the oil,
    the young of the flocks and herds.
They will be like a well-watered
    garden,
and they will sorrow no more.
¹³Then maidens will dance and be glad,
    young men and old as well.
I will turn their mourning into
    gladness;
I will give them comfort and joy
    instead of sorrow.
¹⁴I will satisfy the priests with
    abundance,
and my people will be filled with
    my bounty,"
                  declares the LORD.

¹⁵This is what the LORD says:

"A voice is heard in Ramah,
    mourning and great weeping,
Rachel weeping for her children
    and refusing to be comforted,
    because her children are no more."

¹⁶This is what the LORD says:

"Restrain your voice from weeping
    and your eyes from tears,
for your work will be rewarded,"
                  declares the LORD.
"They will return from the land of
    the enemy.
¹⁷So there is hope for your future,"
                  declares the LORD.
"Your children will return to their
    own land.

¹⁸"I have surely heard Ephraim's
    moaning:
'You disciplined me like an unruly
    calf,
and I have been disciplined.
Restore me, and I will return,
    because you are the LORD my God.
¹⁹After I strayed,
    I repented;

after I came to understand,
    I beat my breast.
I was ashamed and humiliated
    because I bore the disgrace of my
    youth.'
²⁰Is not Ephraim my dear son,
    the child in whom I delight?
Though I often speak against him,
    I still remember him.
Therefore my heart yearns for him;
    I have great compassion for him,"
                  declares the LORD.

²¹"Set up road signs;
    put up guideposts.
Take note of the highway,
    the road that you take.
Return, O Virgin Israel,
    return to your towns.
²²How long will you wander,
    O unfaithful daughter?
The LORD will create a new thing on
    earth—
a woman will surround*ᵃ* a man."

²³This is what the LORD Almighty, the God of Israel, says: "When I bring them back from captivity,*ᵇ* the people in the land of Judah and in its towns will once again use these words: 'The LORD bless you, O righteous dwelling, O sacred mountain.' ²⁴People will live together in Judah and all its towns—farmers and those who move about with their flocks. ²⁵I will refresh the weary and satisfy the faint."

²⁶At this I awoke and looked around. My sleep had been pleasant to me.

²⁷"The days are coming," declares the LORD, "when I will plant the house of Israel and the house of Judah with the offspring of men and of animals. ²⁸Just as I watched over them to uproot and tear down, and to overthrow, destroy and bring disaster, so I will watch over them to build and to plant," declares the LORD. ²⁹"In those days people will no longer say,

'The fathers have eaten sour grapes,
    and the children's teeth are set on
      edge.'

³⁰Instead, everyone will die for his own sin; whoever eats sour grapes—his own teeth will be set on edge.

³¹"The time is coming," declares the
    LORD,

ᵃ22 Or *will go about ⌊seeking⌋;* or *will protect*
ᵇ23 Or *I restore their fortunes*

"when I will make a new covenant
with the house of Israel
   and with the house of Judah.
³²It will not be like the covenant
   I made with their forefathers
when I took them by the hand
   to lead them out of Egypt,
because they broke my covenant,
   though I was a husband to*ª*
    them,*ᵇ*"
              declares the LORD.
³³"This is the covenant I will make
   with the house of Israel
   after that time," declares the LORD.
"I will put my law in their minds
   and write it on their hearts.
I will be their God,
   and they will be my people.
³⁴No longer will a man teach his
    neighbor,
   or a man his brother, saying,
    'Know the LORD,'
because they will all know me,
   from the least of them to the
    greatest,"
              declares the LORD.
"For I will forgive their wickedness
   and will remember their sins no
    more."

³⁵This is what the LORD says,

he who appoints the sun
   to shine by day,
who decrees the moon and stars
   to shine by night,
who stirs up the sea
   so that its waves roar—
   the LORD Almighty is his name:
³⁶"Only if these decrees vanish from
    my sight,"
   declares the LORD,
"will the descendants of Israel ever
    cease
   to be a nation before me."

³⁷This is what the LORD says:

"Only if the heavens above can be
    measured
   and the foundations of the earth
    below be searched out
will I reject all the descendants of
    Israel
because of all they have done,"
             declares the LORD.

³⁸"The days are coming," declares the
LORD, "when this city will be rebuilt for
me from the Tower of Hananel to the
Corner Gate. ³⁹The measuring line will

stretch from there straight to the hill of
Gareb and then turn to Goah. ⁴⁰The
whole valley where dead bodies and
ashes are thrown, and all the terraces out
to the Kidron Valley on the east as far as
the corner of the Horse Gate, will be holy
to the LORD. The city will never again be
uprooted or demolished."

Jeremiah Buys a Field

32 This is the word that came to Jeremiah from the LORD in the tenth year of Zedekiah king of Judah, which was the eighteenth year of Nebuchadnezzar. ²The army of the king of Babylon was then besieging Jerusalem, and Jeremiah the prophet was confined in the courtyard of the guard in the royal palace of Judah.

³Now Zedekiah king of Judah had imprisoned him there, saying, "Why do you prophesy as you do? You say, 'This is what the LORD says: I am about to hand this city over to the king of Babylon, and he will capture it. ⁴Zedekiah king of Judah will not escape out of the hands of the Babylonians*ᶜ* but will certainly be handed over to the king of Babylon, and will speak with him face to face and see him with his own eyes. ⁵He will take Zedekiah to Babylon, where he will remain until I deal with him, declares the LORD. If you fight against the Babylonians, you will not succeed.' "

⁶Jeremiah said, "The word of the LORD

ª32 Hebrew; Septuagint and Syriac / *and I turned
away from*   *ᵇ32* Or *was their master*   *ᶜ4* Or
Chaldeans; also in verses 5, 24, 25, 28, 29 and 43

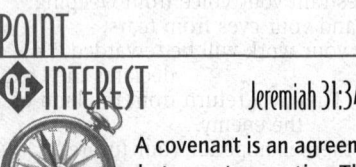

POINT OF INTEREST

Jeremiah 31:34-40

A covenant is an agreement between two parties. This verse foreshadows the covenant God would make with those who would believe in Jesus Christ. Two striking aspects of this new contract were the finality of Jesus' atonement and the totality of God's forgiveness through him. To an Old Testament person living under the restrictions of the law, the promise of such substitutionary forgiveness was wonderful news.

came to me: [7]Hanamel son of Shallum your uncle is going to come to you and say, 'Buy my field at Anathoth, because as nearest relative it is your right and duty to buy it.'

[8]"Then, just as the LORD had said, my cousin Hanamel came to me in the courtyard of the guard and said, 'Buy my field at Anathoth in the territory of Benjamin. Since it is your right to redeem it and possess it, buy it for yourself.'

"I knew that this was the word of the LORD; [9]so I bought the field at Anathoth from my cousin Hanamel and weighed out for him seventeen shekels[a] of silver. [10]I signed and sealed the deed, had it witnessed, and weighed out the silver on the scales. [11]I took the deed of purchase—the sealed copy containing the terms and conditions, as well as the unsealed copy— [12]and I gave this deed to Baruch son of Neriah, the son of Mahseiah, in the presence of my cousin Hanamel and of the witnesses who had signed the deed and of all the Jews sitting in the courtyard of the guard.

[13]"In their presence I gave Baruch these instructions: [14]'This is what the LORD Almighty, the God of Israel, says: Take these documents, both the sealed and unsealed copies of the deed of purchase, and put them in a clay jar so they will last a long time. [15]For this is what the LORD Almighty, the God of Israel, says: Houses, fields and vineyards will again be bought in this land.'

[16]"After I had given the deed of purchase to Baruch son of Neriah, I prayed to the LORD:

[17]"Ah, Sovereign LORD, you have made the heavens and the earth by your great power and outstretched arm. Nothing is too hard for you. [18]You show love to thousands but bring the punishment for the fathers' sins into the laps of their children after them. O great and powerful God, whose name is the LORD Almighty, [19]great are your purposes and mighty are your deeds. Your eyes are open to all the ways of men; you reward everyone according to his conduct and as his deeds deserve. [20]You performed miraculous signs and wonders in Egypt and have continued them to this day, both in Israel and among all mankind, and have gained the re-

nown that is still yours. [21]You brought your people Israel out of Egypt with signs and wonders, by a mighty hand and an outstretched arm and with great terror. [22]You gave them this land you had sworn to give their forefathers, a land flowing with milk and honey. [23]They came in and took possession of it, but they did not obey you or follow your law; they did not do what you commanded them to do. So you brought all this disaster upon them.

[24]"See how the siege ramps are built up to take the city. Because of the sword, famine and plague, the city will be handed over to the Babylonians who are attacking it. What you said has happened, as you now see. [25]And though the city will be handed over to the Babylonians, you, O Sovereign LORD, say to me, 'Buy the field with silver and have the transaction witnessed.' "

[26]Then the word of the LORD came to Jeremiah: [27]"I am the LORD, the God of all mankind. Is anything too hard for me? [28]Therefore, this is what the LORD says: I am about to hand this city over to the Babylonians and to Nebuchadnezzar king of Babylon, who will capture it. [29]The Babylonians who are attacking this city will come in and set it on fire; they will burn it down, along with the houses where the people provoked me to anger by burning incense on the roofs to Baal and by pouring out drink offerings to other gods.

[30]"The people of Israel and Judah have done nothing but evil in my sight from their youth; indeed, the people of Israel have done nothing but provoke me with what their hands have made, declares the LORD. [31]From the day it was built until now, this city has so aroused my anger and wrath that I must remove it from my sight. [32]The people of Israel and Judah have provoked me by all the evil they have done—they, their kings and officials, their priests and prophets, the men of Judah and the people of Jerusalem. [33]They turned their backs to me and not their faces; though I taught them again and again, they would not listen or respond to discipline. [34]They set up their

a9 That is, about 7 ounces (about 200 grams)

abominable idols in the house that bears my Name and defiled it. ³⁵They built high places for Baal in the Valley of Ben Hinnom to sacrifice their sons and daughters*a* to Molech, though I never commanded, nor did it enter my mind, that they should do such a detestable thing and so make Judah sin.

³⁶"You are saying about this city, 'By the sword, famine and plague it will be handed over to the king of Babylon'; but this is what the Lord, the God of Israel, says: ³⁷I will surely gather them from all the lands where I banish them in my furious anger and great wrath; I will bring them back to this place and let them live in safety. ³⁸They will be my people, and I will be their God. ³⁹I will give them singleness of heart and action, so that they will always fear me for their own good and the good of their children after them. ⁴⁰I will make an everlasting covenant with them: I will never stop doing good to them, and I will inspire them to fear me, so that they will never turn away from me. ⁴¹I will rejoice in doing them good and will assuredly plant them in this land with all my heart and soul.

⁴²"This is what the Lord says: As I have brought all this great calamity on this people, so I will give them all the prosperity I have promised them. ⁴³Once more fields will be bought in this land of which you say, 'It is a desolate waste, without men or animals, for it has been handed over to the Babylonians.' ⁴⁴Fields will be bought for silver, and deeds will be signed, sealed and witnessed in the territory of Benjamin, in the villages around Jerusalem, in the towns of Judah and in the towns of the hill country, of the western foothills and of the Negev, because I will restore their fortunes,*b* declares the Lord."

Promise of Restoration

33 While Jeremiah was still confined in the courtyard of the guard, the word of the Lord came to him a second time: ²"This is what the Lord says, he who made the earth, the Lord who formed it and established it—the Lord is his name: ³'Call to me and I will answer you and tell you great and unsearchable things you do not know.' ⁴For this is what the Lord, the God of Israel, says about the houses in this city and the royal palaces of Judah that have been torn down to be used against the siege ramps and the sword ⁵in

the fight with the Babylonians*c*: 'They will be filled with the dead bodies of the men I will slay in my anger and wrath. I will hide my face from this city because of all its wickedness.

⁶" 'Nevertheless, I will bring health and healing to it; I will heal my people and will let them enjoy abundant peace and security. ⁷I will bring Judah and Israel back from captivity*d* and will rebuild them as they were before. ⁸I will cleanse them from all the sin they have committed against me and will forgive all their sins of rebellion against me. ⁹Then this city will bring me renown, joy, praise and honor before all nations on earth that hear of all the good things I do for it; and they will be in awe and will tremble at the abundant prosperity and peace I provide for it.'

¹⁰"This is what the Lord says: 'You say about this place, "It is a desolate waste, without men or animals." Yet in the towns of Judah and the streets of Jerusalem that are deserted, inhabited by neither men nor animals, there will be heard once more ¹¹the sounds of joy and gladness, the voices of bride and bridegroom, and the voices of those who bring thank offerings to the house of the Lord, saying,

"Give thanks to the Lord Almighty,
    for the Lord is good;
    his love endures forever."

For I will restore the fortunes of the land as they were before,' says the Lord.

¹²"This is what the Lord Almighty says: 'In this place, desolate and without men or animals—in all its towns there will again be pastures for shepherds to rest their flocks. ¹³In the towns of the hill country, of the western foothills and of the Negev, in the territory of Benjamin, in the villages around Jerusalem and in the towns of Judah, flocks will again pass under the hand of the one who counts them,' says the Lord.

¹⁴" 'The days are coming,' declares the Lord, 'when I will fulfill the gracious promise I made to the house of Israel and to the house of Judah.

¹⁵" 'In those days and at that time
    I will make a righteous Branch
        sprout from David's line;

---

a35 Or to make their sons and daughters pass through ⌐the fire⌐   b44 Or will bring them back from captivity   c5 Or Chaldeans   d7 Or will restore the fortunes of Judah and Israel

he will do what is just and right in
    the land.
¹⁶In those days Judah will be saved
    and Jerusalem will live in safety.
This is the name by which it*ᵃ* will
    be called:
    The Lᴏʀᴅ Our Righteousness.'

¹⁷For this is what the Lᴏʀᴅ says: 'David
will never fail to have a man to sit on the
throne of the house of Israel, ¹⁸nor will
the priests, who are Levites, ever fail to
have a man to stand before me continually to offer burnt offerings, to burn grain
offerings and to present sacrifices.' "

¹⁹The word of the Lᴏʀᴅ came to Jeremiah: ²⁰"This is what the Lᴏʀᴅ says: 'If you
can break my covenant with the day and
my covenant with the night, so that day
and night no longer come at their appointed time, ²¹then my covenant with
David my servant—and my covenant

with the Levites who are priests ministering before me—can be broken and David
will no longer have a descendant to
reign on his throne. ²²I will make the descendants of David my servant and
the Levites who minister before me as
countless as the stars of the sky and
as measureless as the sand on the seashore.' "

²³The word of the Lᴏʀᴅ came to Jeremiah: ²⁴"Have you not noticed that these
people are saying, 'The Lᴏʀᴅ has rejected
the two kingdomsᵇ he chose'? So they
despise my people and no longer regard
them as a nation. ²⁵This is what the Lᴏʀᴅ
says: 'If I have not established my covenant with day and night and the fixed
laws of heaven and earth, ²⁶then I will
reject the descendants of Jacob and David my servant and will not choose one of

ᵃ16 Or he   ᵇ24 Or families

MONDAY

Read *Jeremiah 33:1–26*
Key Verse *Jeremiah 33:3*

The Need to Pray – Roger Hamilton

As long as professors continue to give exams, there will continue to
be prayer in school. Many students can recall at least one time
when they've begged God to tell them "great and unsearchable
things" (Jeremiah 33:3) to help them survive a particularly brutal
exam. But certainly there is more to this verse than a "bailout" from
God when our minds fail us!

In prayer we are invited to bring our questions to a limitless and
loving God. Isaiah 30:18 tells us that "the Lᴏʀᴅ longs to be gracious
to you; he rises to show you compassion." God wants the opportunity to answer our doubts and questions, to teach us what he wants
us to know about himself and about his universe. Even though he
might not answer in the way we anticipate, he will answer in some
way.

My struggles come when I forget that I *need* to pray. I'm inclined
to feel that I can do everything on my own, and I think I have all the
answers. Like the people of Judah in Jeremiah's day, I tend to ignore
God until circumstances get desperate. But when I call on him, God
promises to tell me "great and unsearchable things" that I don't
know. Every day I encounter things that I don't know about God, his
Word and his world. How awesome to be able to ask anything, at
any time, in any place, through Jesus Christ, "in whom are hidden all
the treasures of wisdom and knowledge" (Colossians 2:3).

A Deeper Look
Isaiah 58:9; Luke 11:5–13; Philippians 4:6–7

Go to page 890 for your next devotional reading.

his sons to rule over the descendants of Abraham, Isaac and Jacob. For I will restore their fortunes*a* and have compassion on them.' "

Warning to Zedekiah

34 While Nebuchadnezzar king of Babylon and all his army and all the kingdoms and peoples in the empire he ruled were fighting against Jerusalem and all its surrounding towns, this word came to Jeremiah from the LORD: ²"This is what the LORD, the God of Israel, says: Go to Zedekiah king of Judah and tell him, 'This is what the LORD says: I am about to hand this city over to the king of Babylon, and he will burn it down. ³You will not escape from his grasp but will surely be captured and handed over to him. You will see the king of Babylon with your own eyes, and he will speak with you face to face. And you will go to Babylon.

⁴" 'Yet hear the promise of the LORD, O Zedekiah king of Judah. This is what the LORD says concerning you: You will not die by the sword; ⁵you will die peacefully. As people made a funeral fire in honor of your fathers, the former kings who preceded you, so they will make a fire in your honor and lament, "Alas, O master!" I myself make this promise, declares the LORD.' "

⁶Then Jeremiah the prophet told all this to Zedekiah king of Judah, in Jerusalem, ⁷while the army of the king of Babylon was fighting against Jerusalem and the other cities of Judah that were still holding out—Lachish and Azekah. These were the only fortified cities left in Judah.

Freedom for Slaves

⁸The word came to Jeremiah from the LORD after King Zedekiah had made a covenant with all the people in Jerusalem to proclaim freedom for the slaves. ⁹Everyone was to free his Hebrew slaves, both male and female; no one was to hold a fellow Jew in bondage. ¹⁰So all the officials and people who entered into this covenant agreed that they would free their male and female slaves and no longer hold them in bondage. They agreed, and set them free. ¹¹But afterward they changed their minds and took back the slaves they had freed and enslaved them again.

¹²Then the word of the LORD came to Jeremiah: ¹³"This is what the LORD, the God of Israel, says: I made a covenant with your forefathers when I brought them out of Egypt, out of the land of slavery. I said, ¹⁴'Every seventh year each of you must free any fellow Hebrew who has sold himself to you. After he has served you six years, you must let him go free.'*b* Your fathers, however, did not listen to me or pay attention to me. ¹⁵Recently you repented and did what is right in my sight: Each of you proclaimed freedom to his countrymen. You even made a covenant before me in the house that bears my Name. ¹⁶But now you have turned around and profaned my name; each of you has taken back the male and female slaves you had set free to go where they wished. You have forced them to become your slaves again.

¹⁷"Therefore, this is what the LORD says: You have not obeyed me; you have not proclaimed freedom for your fellow countrymen. So I now proclaim 'freedom' for you, declares the LORD—'freedom' to fall by the sword, plague and famine. I will make you abhorrent to all the kingdoms of the earth. ¹⁸The men who have violated my covenant and have not fulfilled the terms of the covenant they made before me, I will treat like the calf they cut in two and then walked between its pieces. ¹⁹The leaders of Judah and Jerusalem, the court officials, the priests and all the people of the land who walked between the pieces of the calf, ²⁰I will hand over to their enemies who seek their lives. Their dead bodies will become food for the birds of the air and the beasts of the earth.

²¹"I will hand Zedekiah king of Judah and his officials over to their enemies who seek their lives, to the army of the king of Babylon, which has withdrawn from you. ²²I am going to give the order, declares the LORD, and I will bring them back to this city. They will fight against it, take it and burn it down. And I will lay waste the towns of Judah so no one can live there."

The Recabites

35 This is the word that came to Jeremiah from the LORD during the reign of Jehoiakim son of Josiah king of Judah: ²"Go to the Recabite family and invite them to come to one of the side rooms of

---

a26 Or *will bring them back from captivity*
b14 Deut. 15:12

the house of the LORD and give them wine to drink."

³So I went to get Jaazaniah son of Jeremiah, the son of Habazziniah, and his brothers and all his sons—the whole family of the Recabites. ⁴I brought them into the house of the LORD, into the room of the sons of Hanan son of Igdaliah the man of God. It was next to the room of the officials, which was over that of Maaseiah son of Shallum the doorkeeper. ⁵Then I set bowls full of wine and some cups before the men of the Recabite family and said to them, "Drink some wine."

⁶But they replied, "We do not drink wine, because our forefather Jonadab son of Recab gave us this command: 'Neither you nor your descendants must ever drink wine. ⁷Also you must never build houses, sow seed or plant vineyards; you must never have any of these things, but must always live in tents. Then you will live a long time in the land where you are nomads.' ⁸We have obeyed everything our forefather Jonadab son of Recab commanded us. Neither we nor our wives nor our sons and daughters have ever drunk wine ⁹or built houses to live in or had vineyards, fields or crops. ¹⁰We have lived in tents and have fully obeyed everything our forefather Jonadab commanded us. ¹¹But when Nebuchadnezzar king of Babylon invaded this land, we said, 'Come, we must go to Jerusalem to escape the Babylonianᵃ and Aramean armies.' So we have remained in Jerusalem."

¹²Then the word of the LORD came to Jeremiah, saying: ¹³"This is what the LORD Almighty, the God of Israel, says: Go and tell the men of Judah and the people of Jerusalem, 'Will you not learn a lesson and obey my words?' declares the LORD. ¹⁴'Jonadab son of Recab ordered his sons not to drink wine and this command has been kept. To this day they do not drink wine, because they obey their forefather's command. But I have spoken to you again and again, yet you have not obeyed me. ¹⁵Again and again I sent all my servants the prophets to you. They said, "Each of you must turn from your wicked ways and reform your actions; do not follow other gods to serve them. Then you will live in the land I have given to you and your fathers." But you have not paid attention or listened to me. ¹⁶The descendants of Jonadab son of Recab have carried out the command their forefather gave them, but these people have not obeyed me.'

¹⁷"Therefore, this is what the LORD God Almighty, the God of Israel, says: 'Listen! I am going to bring on Judah and on everyone living in Jerusalem every disaster I pronounced against them. I spoke to them, but they did not listen; I called to them, but they did not answer.' "

¹⁸Then Jeremiah said to the family of the Recabites, "This is what the LORD Almighty, the God of Israel, says: 'You have obeyed the command of your forefather Jonadab and have followed all his instructions and have done everything he ordered.' ¹⁹Therefore, this is what the LORD Almighty, the God of Israel, says: 'Jonadab son of Recab will never fail to have a man to serve me.' "

Jehoiakim Burns Jeremiah's Scroll

36 In the fourth year of Jehoiakim son of Josiah king of Judah, this word came to Jeremiah from the LORD: ²"Take a scroll and write on it all the words I have spoken to you concerning Israel, Judah and all the other nations from the time I began speaking to you in the reign of Josiah till now. ³Perhaps when the people of Judah hear about every disaster I plan to inflict on them, each of them will turn from his wicked way; then I will forgive their wickedness and their sin."

⁴So Jeremiah called Baruch son of Neriah, and while Jeremiah dictated all the words the LORD had spoken to him, Baruch wrote them on the scroll. ⁵Then Jeremiah told Baruch, "I am restricted; I can-

ᵃ11 Or Chaldean

POINT OF INTEREST

Jeremiah 35:2-16

Even though most Israelites drank wine, the Recabites did not. What was okay for others was not permissible for the Recabites, because one of their ancestors had made a vow several centuries before. The Recabites had more respect for the tradition of their ancestors than the Israelites had for God's written law, and God holds them up as an example to Israel.

not go to the LORD's temple. ⁶So you go to the house of the LORD on a day of fasting and read to the people from the scroll the words of the LORD that you wrote as I dictated. Read them to all the people of Judah who come in from their towns. ⁷Perhaps they will bring their petition before the LORD, and each will turn from his wicked ways, for the anger and wrath pronounced against this people by the LORD are great."

⁸Baruch son of Neriah did everything Jeremiah the prophet told him to do; at the LORD's temple he read the words of the LORD from the scroll. ⁹In the ninth month of the fifth year of Jehoiakim son of Josiah king of Judah, a time of fasting before the LORD was proclaimed for all the people in Jerusalem and those who had come from the towns of Judah. ¹⁰From the room of Gemariah son of Shaphan the secretary, which was in the upper courtyard at the entrance of the New Gate of the temple, Baruch read to all the people at the LORD's temple the words of Jeremiah from the scroll.

¹¹When Micaiah son of Gemariah, the son of Shaphan, heard all the words of the LORD from the scroll, ¹²he went down to the secretary's room in the royal palace, where all the officials were sitting: Elishama the secretary, Delaiah son of Shemaiah, Elnathan son of Acbor, Gemariah son of Shaphan, Zedekiah son of Hananiah, and all the other officials. ¹³After Micaiah told them everything he had heard Baruch read to the people from the scroll, ¹⁴all the officials sent Jehudi son of Nethaniah, the son of Shelemiah, the son of Cushi, to say to Baruch, "Bring the scroll from which you have read to the people and come." So Baruch son of Neriah went to them with the scroll in his hand. ¹⁵They said to him, "Sit down, please, and read it to us."

So Baruch read it to them. ¹⁶When they heard all these words, they looked at each other in fear and said to Baruch, "We must report all these words to the king." ¹⁷Then they asked Baruch, "Tell us, how did you come to write all this? Did Jeremiah dictate it?"

¹⁸"Yes," Baruch replied, "he dictated all these words to me, and I wrote them in ink on the scroll."

¹⁹Then the officials said to Baruch, "You and Jeremiah, go and hide. Don't let anyone know where you are."

²⁰After they put the scroll in the room of Elishama the secretary, they went to the king in the courtyard and reported everything to him. ²¹The king sent Jehudi to get the scroll, and Jehudi brought it from the room of Elishama the secretary and read it to the king and all the officials standing beside him. ²²It was the ninth month and the king was sitting in the winter apartment, with a fire burning in the firepot in front of him. ²³Whenever Jehudi had read three or four columns of the scroll, the king cut them off with a scribe's knife and threw them into the firepot, until the entire scroll was burned in the fire. ²⁴The king and all his attendants who heard all these words showed no fear, nor did they tear their clothes. ²⁵Even though Elnathan, Delaiah and Gemariah urged the king not to burn the scroll, he would not listen to them. ²⁶Instead, the king commanded Jerahmeel, a son of the king, Seraiah son of Azriel and Shelemiah son of Abdeel to arrest Baruch the scribe and Jeremiah the prophet. But the LORD had hidden them.

²⁷After the king burned the scroll containing the words that Baruch had written at Jeremiah's dictation, the word of the LORD came to Jeremiah: ²⁸"Take another scroll and write on it all the words that were on the first scroll, which Jehoiakim king of Judah burned up. ²⁹Also tell Jehoiakim king of Judah, 'This is what the LORD says: You burned that scroll and said, "Why did you write on it that the king of Babylon would certainly come and destroy this land and cut off both men and animals from it?" ³⁰Therefore, this is what the LORD says about Jehoiakim king of Judah: He will have no one to sit on the throne of David; his body will be thrown out and exposed to the heat by day and the frost by night. ³¹I will punish him and his children and his attendants for their wickedness; I will bring on them and those living in Jerusalem and the people of Judah every disaster I pronounced against them, because they have not listened.' "

³²So Jeremiah took another scroll and gave it to the scribe Baruch son of Neriah, and as Jeremiah dictated, Baruch wrote on it all the words of the scroll that Jehoiakim king of Judah had burned in the fire. And many similar words were added to them.

Jeremiah in Prison

37 Zedekiah son of Josiah was made king of Judah by Nebuchadnezzar king of Babylon; he reigned in place of Jehoiachin[a] son of Jehoiakim. ²Neither he nor his attendants nor the people of the land paid any attention to the words the LORD had spoken through Jeremiah the prophet.

³King Zedekiah, however, sent Jehucal son of Shelemiah with the priest Zephaniah son of Maaseiah to Jeremiah the prophet with this message: "Please pray to the LORD our God for us."

⁴Now Jeremiah was free to come and go among the people, for he had not yet been put in prison. ⁵Pharaoh's army had marched out of Egypt, and when the Babylonians[b] who were besieging Jerusalem heard the report about them, they withdrew from Jerusalem.

⁶Then the word of the LORD came to Jeremiah the prophet: ⁷"This is what the LORD, the God of Israel, says: Tell the king of Judah, who sent you to inquire of me, 'Pharaoh's army, which has marched out to support you, will go back to its own land, to Egypt. ⁸Then the Babylonians will return and attack this city; they will capture it and burn it down.'

⁹"This is what the LORD says: Do not deceive yourselves, thinking, 'The Babylonians will surely leave us.' They will not! ¹⁰Even if you were to defeat the entire Babylonian[c] army that is attacking you and only wounded men were left in their tents, they would come out and burn this city down."

¹¹After the Babylonian army had withdrawn from Jerusalem because of Pharaoh's army, ¹²Jeremiah started to leave the city to go to the territory of Benjamin to get his share of the property among the people there. ¹³But when he reached the Benjamin Gate, the captain of the guard, whose name was Irijah son of Shelemiah, the son of Hananiah, arrested him and said, "You are deserting to the Babylonians!"

¹⁴"That's not true!" Jeremiah said. "I am not deserting to the Babylonians." But Irijah would not listen to him; instead, he arrested Jeremiah and brought him to the officials. ¹⁵They were angry with Jeremiah and had him beaten and imprisoned in the house of Jonathan the secretary, which they had made into a prison.

¹⁶Jeremiah was put into a vaulted cell in a dungeon, where he remained a long time. ¹⁷Then King Zedekiah sent for him and had him brought to the palace, where he asked him privately, "Is there any word from the LORD?"

"Yes," Jeremiah replied, "you will be handed over to the king of Babylon."

¹⁸Then Jeremiah said to King Zedekiah, "What crime have I committed against you or your officials or this people, that you have put me in prison? ¹⁹Where are your prophets who prophesied to you, 'The king of Babylon will not attack you or this land'? ²⁰But now, my lord the king, please listen. Let me bring my petition before you: Do not send me back to the house of Jonathan the secretary, or I will die there."

²¹King Zedekiah then gave orders for Jeremiah to be placed in the courtyard of the guard and given bread from the street of the bakers each day until all the bread in the city was gone. So Jeremiah remained in the courtyard of the guard.

Jeremiah Thrown Into a Cistern

38 Shephatiah son of Mattan, Gedaliah son of Pashhur, Jehucal[d] son of Shelemiah, and Pashhur son of Malkijah heard what Jeremiah was telling all the people when he said, ²"This is what the LORD says: 'Whoever stays in this city will die by the sword, famine or plague, but whoever goes over to the Babylonians[e] will live. He will escape with his life; he will live.' ³And this is what the LORD says: 'This city will certainly be handed over to the army of the king of Babylon, who will capture it.' "

---

a 1 Hebrew *Coniah,* a variant of *Jehoiachin*
b 5 Or *Chaldeans*; also in verses 8, 9, 13 and 14
c 10 Or *Chaldean*; also in verse 11　　*d* 1 Hebrew *Jucal,* a variant of *Jehucal*　　*e* 2 Or *Chaldeans*; also in verses 18, 19 and 23

POINT OF INTEREST

Jeremiah 37:5

History records this battle as the campaign of Pharaoh Hophra in 588 B.C. The respite provided by the Egyptian's intervention was short-lived, however. The Babylonians returned within a year to finally destroy Jerusalem.

⁴Then the officials said to the king, "This man should be put to death. He is discouraging the soldiers who are left in this city, as well as all the people, by the things he is saying to them. This man is not seeking the good of these people but their ruin."

⁵"He is in your hands," King Zedekiah answered. "The king can do nothing to oppose you."

⁶So they took Jeremiah and put him into the cistern of Malkijah, the king's son, which was in the courtyard of the guard. They lowered Jeremiah by ropes into the cistern; it had no water in it, only mud, and Jeremiah sank down into the mud.

⁷But Ebed-Melech, a Cushite,ᵃ an official ᵇ in the royal palace, heard that they had put Jeremiah into the cistern. While the king was sitting in the Benjamin Gate, ⁸Ebed-Melech went out of the palace and said to him, ⁹"My lord the king, these men have acted wickedly in all they have done to Jeremiah the prophet. They have thrown him into a cistern, where he will starve to death when there is no longer any bread in the city."

¹⁰Then the king commanded Ebed-Melech the Cushite, "Take thirty men from here with you and lift Jeremiah the prophet out of the cistern before he dies."

¹¹So Ebed-Melech took the men with him and went to a room under the treasury in the palace. He took some old rags and worn-out clothes from there and let them down with ropes to Jeremiah in the cistern. ¹²Ebed-Melech the Cushite said to Jeremiah, "Put these old rags and worn-out clothes under your arms to pad the ropes." Jeremiah did so, ¹³and they pulled him up with the ropes and lifted him out of the cistern. And Jeremiah remained in the courtyard of the guard.

Zedekiah Questions Jeremiah Again

¹⁴Then King Zedekiah sent for Jeremiah the prophet and had him brought to the third entrance to the temple of the LORD. "I am going to ask you something," the king said to Jeremiah. "Do not hide anything from me."

¹⁵Jeremiah said to Zedekiah, "If I give you an answer, will you not kill me? Even if I did give you counsel, you would not listen to me."

¹⁶But King Zedekiah swore this oath secretly to Jeremiah: "As surely as the LORD lives, who has given us breath, I will neither kill you nor hand you over to those who are seeking your life."

¹⁷Then Jeremiah said to Zedekiah, "This is what the LORD God Almighty, the God of Israel, says: 'If you surrender to the officers of the king of Babylon, your life will be spared and this city will not be burned down; you and your family will live. ¹⁸But if you will not surrender to the officers of the king of Babylon, this city will be handed over to the Babylonians and they will burn it down; you yourself will not escape from their hands.' "

¹⁹King Zedekiah said to Jeremiah, "I am afraid of the Jews who have gone over to the Babylonians, for the Babylonians may hand me over to them and they will mistreat me."

²⁰"They will not hand you over," Jeremiah replied. "Obey the LORD by doing what I tell you. Then it will go well with you, and your life will be spared. ²¹But if you refuse to surrender, this is what the LORD has revealed to me: ²²All the women left in the palace of the king of Judah will be brought out to the officials of the king of Babylon. Those women will say to you:

" 'They misled you and overcame
      you—
   those trusted friends of yours.
Your feet are sunk in the mud;
   your friends have deserted you.'

²³"All your wives and children will be brought out to the Babylonians. You yourself will not escape from their hands but will be captured by the king of Babylon; and this city willᶜ be burned down."

²⁴Then Zedekiah said to Jeremiah, "Do not let anyone know about this conversation, or you may die. ²⁵If the officials hear that I talked with you, and they come to you and say, 'Tell us what you said to the king and what the king said to you; do not hide it from us or we will kill you,' ²⁶then tell them, 'I was pleading with the king not to send me back to Jonathan's house to die there.' "

²⁷All the officials did come to Jeremiah and question him, and he told them everything the king had ordered him to say. So they said no more to him, for no one had heard his conversation with the king.

²⁸And Jeremiah remained in the court-

ᵃ7 Probably from the upper Nile region　　ᵇ7 Or
a eunuch　　ᶜ23 Or and you will cause this city to

yard of the guard until the day Jerusalem was captured.

The Fall of Jerusalem

39 This is how Jerusalem was taken: ¹In the ninth year of Zedekiah king of Judah, in the tenth month, Nebuchadnezzar king of Babylon marched against Jerusalem with his whole army and laid siege to it. ²And on the ninth day of the fourth month of Zedekiah's eleventh year, the city wall was broken through. ³Then all the officials of the king of Babylon came and took seats in the Middle Gate: Nergal-Sharezer of Samgar, Nebo-Sarsekim*a* a chief officer, Nergal-Sharezer a high official and all the other officials of the king of Babylon. ⁴When Zedekiah king of Judah and all the soldiers saw them, they fled; they left the city at night by way of the king's garden, through the gate between the two walls, and headed toward the Arabah.*b*

⁵But the Babylonian*c* army pursued them and overtook Zedekiah in the plains of Jericho. They captured him and took him to Nebuchadnezzar king of Babylon at Riblah in the land of Hamath, where he pronounced sentence on him. ⁶There at Riblah the king of Babylon slaughtered the sons of Zedekiah before his eyes and also killed all the nobles of Judah. ⁷Then he put out Zedekiah's eyes and bound him with bronze shackles to take him to Babylon.

⁸The Babylonians*d* set fire to the royal palace and the houses of the people and broke down the walls of Jerusalem. ⁹Nebuzaradan commander of the imperial guard carried into exile to Babylon the people who remained in the city, along with those who had gone over to him, and the rest of the people. ¹⁰But Nebuzaradan the commander of the guard left behind in the land of Judah some of the poor people, who owned nothing; and at that time he gave them vineyards and fields.

¹¹Now Nebuchadnezzar king of Babylon had given these orders about Jeremiah through Nebuzaradan commander of the imperial guard: ¹²"Take him and look after him; don't harm him but do for him whatever he asks." ¹³So Nebuzaradan the commander of the guard, Nebushazban a chief officer, Nergal-Sharezer a high official and all the other officers of the king of Babylon ¹⁴sent and had Jeremiah taken out of the courtyard of the guard. They turned him over to Gedaliah son of Ahikam, the son of Shaphan, to take him back to his home. So he remained among his own people.

¹⁵While Jeremiah had been confined in the courtyard of the guard, the word of the LORD came to him: ¹⁶"Go and tell Ebed-Melech the Cushite, 'This is what the LORD Almighty, the God of Israel, says: I am about to fulfill my words against this city through disaster, not prosperity. At that time they will be fulfilled before your eyes. ¹⁷But I will rescue you on that day, declares the LORD; you will not be handed over to those you fear. ¹⁸I will save you; you will not fall by the sword but will escape with your life, because you trust in me, declares the LORD.'"

Jeremiah Freed

40 The word came to Jeremiah from the LORD after Nebuzaradan commander of the imperial guard had released him at Ramah. He had found Jeremiah bound in chains among all the captives from Jerusalem and Judah who were being carried into exile to Babylon. ²When the commander of the guard found Jeremiah, he said to him, "The LORD your God decreed this disaster for this place. ³And now the LORD has brought it about; he has done just as he said he would. All this happened because you people sinned against the LORD and did not obey him. ⁴But today I am freeing you from the chains on your wrists. Come with me to Babylon, if you like, and I will look after you; but if you do not want to, then don't come. Look, the whole country lies before you; go wherever you please." ⁵However, before Jeremiah turned to go,*e* Nebuzaradan added, "Go back to Gedaliah son of Ahi-

a3 Or *Nergal-Sharezer, Samgar-Nebo, Sarsekim*
b4 Or *the Jordan Valley*   *c5* Or *Chaldean*
d8 Or *Chaldeans*   *e5* Or *Jeremiah answered*

kam, the son of Shaphan, whom the king of Babylon has appointed over the towns of Judah, and live with him among the people, or go anywhere else you please."

Then the commander gave him provisions and a present and let him go. **6**So Jeremiah went to Gedaliah son of Ahikam at Mizpah and stayed with him among the people who were left behind in the land.

Gedaliah Assassinated

7When all the army officers and their men who were still in the open country heard that the king of Babylon had appointed Gedaliah son of Ahikam as governor over the land and had put him in charge of the men, women and children who were the poorest in the land and who had not been carried into exile to Babylon, **8**they came to Gedaliah at Mizpah—Ishmael son of Nethaniah, Johanan and Jonathan the sons of Kareah, Seraiah son of Tanhumeth, the sons of Ephai the Netophathite, and Jaazaniah*a* the son of the Maacathite, and their men. **9**Gedaliah son of Ahikam, the son of Shaphan, took an oath to reassure them and their men. "Do not be afraid to serve the Babylonians,*b*" he said. "Settle down in the land and serve the king of Babylon, and it will go well with you. **10**I myself will stay at Mizpah to represent you before the Babylonians who come to us, but you are to harvest the wine, summer fruit and oil, and put them in your storage jars, and live in the towns you have taken over."

11When all the Jews in Moab, Ammon, Edom and all the other countries heard that the king of Babylon had left a remnant in Judah and had appointed Gedaliah son of Ahikam, the son of Shaphan, as governor over them, **12**they all came back to the land of Judah, to Gedaliah at Mizpah, from all the countries where they had been scattered. And they harvested an abundance of wine and summer fruit.

13Johanan son of Kareah and all the army officers still in the open country came to Gedaliah at Mizpah **14**and said to him, "Don't you know that Baalis king of the Ammonites has sent Ishmael son of Nethaniah to take your life?" But Gedaliah son of Ahikam did not believe them.

15Then Johanan son of Kareah said privately to Gedaliah in Mizpah, "Let me go and kill Ishmael son of Nethaniah, and no one will know it. Why should he take your life and cause all the Jews who are gathered around you to be scattered and the remnant of Judah to perish?"

16But Gedaliah son of Ahikam said to Johanan son of Kareah, "Don't do such a thing! What you are saying about Ishmael is not true."

41 In the seventh month Ishmael son of Nethaniah, the son of Elishama, who was of royal blood and had been one of the king's officers, came with ten men to Gedaliah son of Ahikam at Mizpah. While they were eating together there, **2**Ishmael son of Nethaniah and the ten men who were with him got up and struck down Gedaliah son of Ahikam, the son of Shaphan, with the sword, killing the one whom the king of Babylon had appointed as governor over the land. **3**Ishmael also killed all the Jews who were with Gedaliah at Mizpah, as well as the Babylonian*c* soldiers who were there.

4The day after Gedaliah's assassination, before anyone knew about it, **5**eighty men who had shaved off their beards, torn their clothes and cut themselves came from Shechem, Shiloh and Samaria, bringing grain offerings and incense with them to the house of the LORD. **6**Ishmael son of Nethaniah went out from Mizpah to meet them, weeping as he went. When he met them, he said, "Come to Gedaliah son of Ahikam." **7**When they went into the city, Ishmael son of Nethaniah and the men who were with him slaughtered them and threw them into a cistern. **8**But ten of them said to Ishmael, "Don't kill us! We have wheat and barley, oil and honey, hidden in a field." So he let them alone and did not kill them with the others. **9**Now the cistern where he threw all the bodies of the men he had killed along with Gedaliah was the one King Asa had made as part of his defense against Baasha king of Israel. Ishmael son of Nethaniah filled it with the dead.

10Ishmael made captives of all the rest of the people who were in Mizpah—the king's daughters along with all the others who were left there, over whom Nebuzaradan commander of the imperial guard had appointed Gedaliah son of Ahikam. Ishmael son of Nethaniah took

a8 Hebrew *Jezaniah,* a variant of *Jaazaniah*   *b9* Or *Chaldeans*; also in verse 10   *c3* Or *Chaldean* them captive and set out to cross over to the Ammonites.

[11] When Johanan son of Kareah and all the army officers who were with him heard about all the crimes Ishmael son of Nethaniah had committed, [12] they took all their men and went to fight Ishmael son of Nethaniah. They caught up with him near the great pool in Gibeon. [13] When all the people Ishmael had with him saw Johanan son of Kareah and the army officers who were with him, they were glad. [14] All the people Ishmael had taken captive at Mizpah turned and went over to Johanan son of Kareah. [15] But Ishmael son of Nethaniah and eight of his men escaped from Johanan and fled to the Ammonites.

Flight to Egypt

[16] Then Johanan son of Kareah and all the army officers who were with him led away all the survivors from Mizpah whom he had recovered from Ishmael son of Nethaniah after he had assassinated Gedaliah son of Ahikam: the soldiers, women, children and court officials he had brought from Gibeon. [17] And they went on, stopping at Geruth Kimham near Bethlehem on their way to Egypt [18] to escape the Babylonians.[a] They were afraid of them because Ishmael son of Nethaniah had killed Gedaliah son of Ahikam, whom the king of Babylon had appointed as governor over the land.

42 Then all the army officers, including Johanan son of Kareah and Jezaniah[b] son of Hoshaiah, and all the people from the least to the greatest approached [2] Jeremiah the prophet and said to him, "Please hear our petition and pray to the LORD your God for this entire remnant. For as you now see, though we were once many, now only a few are left. [3] Pray that the LORD your God will tell us where we should go and what we should do."

[4] "I have heard you," replied Jeremiah the prophet. "I will certainly pray to the LORD your God as you have requested; I will tell you everything the LORD says and will keep nothing back from you."

[5] Then they said to Jeremiah, "May the LORD be a true and faithful witness against us if we do not act in accordance with everything the LORD your God sends you to tell us. [6] Whether it is favorable or unfavorable, we will obey the LORD our God, to whom we are sending you, so that it will go well with us, for we will obey the LORD our God."

[7] Ten days later the word of the LORD came to Jeremiah. [8] So he called together Johanan son of Kareah and all the army officers who were with him and all the people from the least to the greatest. [9] He said to them, "This is what the LORD, the God of Israel, to whom you sent me to present your petition, says: [10] 'If you stay in this land, I will build you up and not tear you down; I will plant you and not uproot you, for I am grieved over the disaster I have inflicted on you. [11] Do not be afraid of the king of Babylon, whom you now fear. Do not be afraid of him, declares the LORD, for I am with you and will save you and deliver you from his hands. [12] I will show you compassion so that he will have compassion on you and restore you to your land.'

[13] "However, if you say, 'We will not stay in this land,' and so disobey the LORD your God, [14] and if you say, 'No, we will go and live in Egypt, where we will not see war or hear the trumpet or be hungry for bread,' [15] then hear the word of the LORD, O remnant of Judah. This is what the LORD Almighty, the God of Israel, says: 'If you are determined to go to Egypt and you do go to settle there, [16] then the sword you fear will overtake you there, and the famine you dread will follow you into Egypt, and there you will die. [17] Indeed, all who are determined to go to Egypt to settle there will die by the sword, famine and plague; not one of them will survive or escape the disaster I will bring on them.' [18] This is what the LORD Almighty, the God of Israel, says: 'As my anger and wrath have been poured out on those who lived in Jerusalem, so will my wrath be poured out on you when you go to Egypt. You will be an object of cursing and horror, of condemnation and reproach; you will never see this place again.'

[19] "O remnant of Judah, the LORD has told you, 'Do not go to Egypt.' Be sure of this: I warn you today [20] that you made a fatal mistake[c] when you sent me to the LORD your God and said, 'Pray to the LORD our God for us; tell us everything he says and we will do it.' [21] I have told you today, but you still have not obeyed the

---

a18 Or *Chaldeans*
(also 43:2)
b1 Hebrew; Septuagint (see
also 43:2) *Azariah*
c20 Or *you erred in your*
hearts

LORD your God in all he sent me to tell you. ²²So now, be sure of this: You will die by the sword, famine and plague in the place where you want to go to settle."

43 When Jeremiah finished telling the people all the words of the LORD their God—everything the LORD had sent him to tell them— ²Azariah son of Hoshaiah and Johanan son of Kareah and all the arrogant men said to Jeremiah, "You are lying! The LORD our God has not sent you to say, 'You must not go to Egypt to settle there.' ³But Baruch son of Neriah is inciting you against us to hand us over to the Babylonians,ᵃ so they may kill us or carry us into exile to Babylon."

⁴So Johanan son of Kareah and all the army officers and all the people disobeyed the LORD's command to stay in the land of Judah. ⁵Instead, Johanan son of Kareah and all the army officers led away all the remnant of Judah who had come back to live in the land of Judah from all the nations where they had been scattered. ⁶They also led away all the men, women and children and the king's daughters whom Nebuzaradan commander of the imperial guard had left with Gedaliah son of Ahikam, the son of Shaphan, and Jeremiah the prophet and Baruch son of Neriah. ⁷So they entered Egypt in disobedience to the LORD and went as far as Tahpanhes.

⁸In Tahpanhes the word of the LORD came to Jeremiah: ⁹"While the Jews are watching, take some large stones with you and bury them in clay in the brick pavement at the entrance to Pharaoh's palace in Tahpanhes. ¹⁰Then say to them, 'This is what the LORD Almighty, the God of Israel, says: I will send for my servant Nebuchadnezzar king of Babylon, and I will set his throne over these stones I have buried here; he will spread his royal canopy above them. ¹¹He will come and attack Egypt, bringing death to those destined for death, captivity to those destined for captivity, and the sword to those destined for the sword. ¹²Heᵇ will set fire to the temples of the gods of Egypt; he will burn their temples and take their gods captive. As a shepherd wraps his garment around him, so will he wrap Egypt around himself and depart from there unscathed. ¹³There in the temple of the sunᶜ in Egypt he will demolish the sacred pillars and will burn down the temples of the gods of Egypt.' "

Disaster Because of Idolatry

44 This word came to Jeremiah concerning all the Jews living in Lower Egypt—in Migdol, Tahpanhes and Memphisᵈ—and in Upper Egyptᵉ: ²"This is what the LORD Almighty, the God of Israel, says: You saw the great disaster I brought on Jerusalem and on all the towns of Judah. Today they lie deserted and in ruins ³because of the evil they have done. They provoked me to anger by burning incense and by worshiping other gods that neither they nor you nor your fathers ever knew. ⁴Again and again I sent my servants the prophets, who said, 'Do not do this detestable thing that I hate!' ⁵But they did not listen or pay attention; they did not turn from their wickedness or stop burning incense to other gods. ⁶Therefore, my fierce anger was poured out; it raged against the towns of Judah and the streets of Jerusalem and made them the desolate ruins they are today.

⁷"Now this is what the LORD God Almighty, the God of Israel, says: Why bring such great disaster on yourselves by cutting off from Judah the men and women, the children and infants, and so leave yourselves without a remnant? ⁸Why provoke me to anger with what your hands have made, burning incense to other gods in Egypt, where you have come to live? You will destroy yourselves and make yourselves an object of cursing and reproach among all the nations on earth. ⁹Have you forgotten the wickedness committed by your fathers and by the kings and queens of Judah and the wickedness committed by you and your

---

ᵃ3 Or *Chaldeans*   ᵇ12 Or *I*   ᶜ13 Or *in Heliopolis*   ᵈ1 Hebrew *Noph*   ᵉ1 Hebrew *in Pathros*

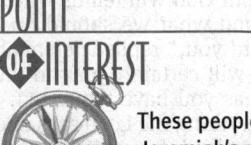

POINT OF INTEREST   Jeremiah 43:2-3

These people didn't want Jeremiah's advice. Their minds were made up ahead of time, and they merely wanted God to rubber-stamp their plans with a big "OK!" Read on for the warning given to those who ask for God's opinion but don't really want it.

wives in the land of Judah and the streets of Jerusalem? ¹⁰To this day they have not humbled themselves or shown reverence, nor have they followed my law and the decrees I set before you and your fathers.

¹¹"Therefore, this is what the LORD Almighty, the God of Israel, says: I am determined to bring disaster on you and to destroy all Judah. ¹²I will take away the remnant of Judah who were determined to go to Egypt to settle there. They will all perish in Egypt; they will fall by the sword or die from famine. From the least to the greatest, they will die by sword or famine. They will become an object of cursing and horror, of condemnation and reproach. ¹³I will punish those who live in Egypt with the sword, famine and plague, as I punished Jerusalem. ¹⁴None of the remnant of Judah who have gone to live in Egypt will escape or survive to return to the land of Judah, to which they long to return and live; none will return except a few fugitives."

¹⁵Then all the men who knew that their wives were burning incense to other gods, along with all the women who were present—a large assembly—and all the people living in Lower and Upper Egypt,ᵃ said to Jeremiah, ¹⁶"We will not listen to the message you have spoken to us in the name of the LORD! ¹⁷We will certainly do everything we said we would: We will burn incense to the Queen of Heaven and will pour out drink offerings to her just as we and our fathers, our kings and our officials did in the towns of Judah and in the streets of Jerusalem. At that time we had plenty of food and were well off and suffered no harm. ¹⁸But ever since we stopped burning incense to the Queen of Heaven and pouring out drink offerings to her, we have had nothing and have been perishing by sword and famine."

¹⁹The women added, "When we burned incense to the Queen of Heaven and poured out drink offerings to her, did not our husbands know that we were making cakes like her image and pouring out drink offerings to her?"

²⁰Then Jeremiah said to all the people, both men and women, who were answering him, ²¹"Did not the LORD remember and think about the incense burned in the towns of Judah and the streets of Jerusalem by you and your fathers, your kings and your officials and the people of the land? ²²When the LORD could no longer endure your wicked actions and the detestable things you did, your land became an object of cursing and a desolate waste without inhabitants, as it is today. ²³Because you have burned incense and have sinned against the LORD and have not obeyed him or followed his law or his decrees or his stipulations, this disaster has come upon you, as you now see."

²⁴Then Jeremiah said to all the people, including the women, "Hear the word of the LORD, all you people of Judah in Egypt. ²⁵This is what the LORD Almighty, the God of Israel, says: You and your wives have shown by your actions what you promised when you said, 'We will certainly carry out the vows we made to burn incense and pour out drink offerings to the Queen of Heaven.'

"Go ahead then, do what you promised! Keep your vows! ²⁶But hear the word of the LORD, all Jews living in Egypt: 'I swear by my great name,' says the LORD, 'that no one from Judah living anywhere in Egypt will ever again invoke my name or swear, "As surely as the Sovereign LORD lives." ²⁷For I am watching over them for harm, not for good; the Jews in Egypt will perish by sword and famine until they are all destroyed. ²⁸Those who escape the sword and return to the land of Judah from Egypt will be very few. Then the whole remnant of Judah who came to live in Egypt will know whose word will stand—mine or theirs.

²⁹" 'This will be the sign to you that I will punish you in this place,' declares the LORD, 'so that you will know that my threats of harm against you will surely stand.' ³⁰This is what the LORD says: 'I am going to hand Pharaoh Hophra king of Egypt over to his enemies who seek his life, just as I handed Zedekiah king of Judah over to Nebuchadnezzar king of Babylon, the enemy who was seeking his life.' "

A Message to Baruch

45 This is what Jeremiah the prophet told Baruch son of Neriah in the fourth year of Jehoiakim son of Josiah king of Judah, after Baruch had written on a scroll the words Jeremiah was then dictating: ²"This is what the LORD, the God of Israel, says to you, Baruch: ³You said, 'Woe to me! The LORD has added

---

ᵃ15 Hebrew *in Egypt and Pathros*

sorrow to my pain; I am worn out with groaning and find no rest.' "

4 The LORD said, "Say this to him: 'This is what the LORD says: I will overthrow what I have built and uproot what I have planted, throughout the land. 5 Should you then seek great things for yourself? Seek them not. For I will bring disaster on all people, declares the LORD, but wherever you go I will let you escape with your life.' "

A Message About Egypt

46 This is the word of the LORD that came to Jeremiah the prophet concerning the nations:

Read Jeremiah 44:1—45:5
Key Verse Jeremiah 45:5

Seeking Greatness in Humility – Larry Bauer

Have you ever envisioned yourself as the next Tiger Woods or Bill Gates? Do you dream about what it would be like to be famous, have all the cash you need and have people waiting in line to get your autograph? A culture steeped in human ambition encourages us to seek personal greatness, to build our identity around our own accomplishments and to position ourselves somewhere higher on the greatness scale.

Think it through. Being ambitious and seeking greatness may work in the human scheme of things, but in God's kingdom, humility is the key that opens the door to greatness. Jesus Christ himself illustrated this principle like no one else—the God of the universe became a man, humbling himself and coming as a servant to die on the cross (see Philippians 2:6–8).

Embracing humility doesn't mean we slink around moaning about our low position like Uriah Heep did in the novel *David Copperfield*. Nor does it mean hiding our gifts and talents and never striving for excellence. But developing our God-given gifts and talents will only lead to greatness in God's kingdom if we put Jesus at the center of our lives and not our own pride and ambition. Eric Liddell, for example, used his gifts for God's glory and not his own, and God chose to exalt him. Martin Luther King, Jr., found greatness in serving God and proclaiming justice. Mother Teresa found greatness in serving the poor. Even the apostle Paul, the greatest evangelist who ever lived, humbled himself and made himself a servant. And all of them were doing what God had gifted them to do, and all of them loved what they did.

Becoming God's servant is the only greatness we should aspire to, and in the end it will be the most fulfilling and enriching "success story" we can imagine: "And God raised us up with Christ and seated us with him in the heavenly realms in Christ Jesus, in order that in the coming ages he might show the incomparable riches of his grace, expressed in his kindness to us in Christ Jesus. For it is by grace you have been saved, through faith—and this not from yourselves, it is the gift of God" (Ephesians 2:6–9).

A Deeper Look
Proverbs 27:2; Jeremiah 9:23–24; Matthew 23:12

Go to page 910 for your next devotional reading.

²Concerning Egypt:

This is the message against the army of Pharaoh Neco king of Egypt, which was defeated at Carchemish on the Euphrates River by Nebuchadnezzar king of Babylon in the fourth year of Jehoiakim son of Josiah king of Judah:

³"Prepare your shields, both large and
    small,
  and march out for battle!
⁴Harness the horses,
  mount the steeds!
Take your positions
  with helmets on!
Polish your spears,
  put on your armor!
⁵What do I see?
  They are terrified,
they are retreating,
  their warriors are defeated.
They flee in haste
  without looking back,
  and there is terror on every side,"
              declares the LORD.
⁶"The swift cannot flee
  nor the strong escape.
In the north by the River Euphrates
  they stumble and fall.

⁷"Who is this that rises like the Nile,
  like rivers of surging waters?
⁸Egypt rises like the Nile,
  like rivers of surging waters.
She says, 'I will rise and cover the
    earth;
I will destroy cities and their
    people.'
⁹Charge, O horses!
  Drive furiously, O charioteers!
March on, O warriors—
  men of Cush*ᵃ* and Put who carry
    shields,
  men of Lydia who draw the bow.
¹⁰But that day belongs to the Lord, the
    LORD Almighty—
a day of vengeance, for vengeance
  on his foes.
The sword will devour till it is
    satisfied,
  till it has quenched its thirst with
    blood.
For the Lord, the LORD Almighty, will
  offer sacrifice
in the land of the north by the
  River Euphrates.

¹¹"Go up to Gilead and get balm,
  O Virgin Daughter of Egypt.
But you multiply remedies in vain;

there is no healing for you.
¹²The nations will hear of your shame;
  your cries will fill the earth.
One warrior will stumble over
    another;
  both will fall down together."

¹³This is the message the LORD spoke to Jeremiah the prophet about the coming of Nebuchadnezzar king of Babylon to attack Egypt:

¹⁴"Announce this in Egypt, and
    proclaim it in Migdol;
  proclaim it also in Memphisᵇ and
    Tahpanhes:
'Take your positions and get ready,
  for the sword devours those
    around you.'
¹⁵Why will your warriors be laid low?
  They cannot stand, for the LORD
    will push them down.
¹⁶They will stumble repeatedly;
  they will fall over each other.
They will say, 'Get up, let us go back
  to our own people and our native
    lands,
away from the sword of the
    oppressor.'
¹⁷There they will exclaim,
  'Pharaoh king of Egypt is only a
    loud noise;
  he has missed his opportunity.'

¹⁸"As surely as I live," declares the
    King,
  whose name is the LORD Almighty,
"one will come who is like Tabor
    among the mountains,
like Carmel by the sea.
¹⁹Pack your belongings for exile,
  you who live in Egypt,
for Memphis will be laid waste
  and lie in ruins without inhabitant.

²⁰"Egypt is a beautiful heifer,
  but a gadfly is coming
  against her from the north.
²¹The mercenaries in her ranks
  are like fattened calves.
They too will turn and flee together,
  they will not stand their ground,
for the day of disaster is coming upon
    them,
  the time for them to be punished.
²²Egypt will hiss like a fleeing serpent
  as the enemy advances in force;
  they will come against her with axes,

ᵃ9 That is, the upper Nile region   ᵇ14 Hebrew
Noph; also in verse 19

like men who cut down trees.
²³They will chop down her forest,"
          declares the Lord,
"dense though it be.
They are more numerous than
          locusts,
     they cannot be counted.
²⁴The Daughter of Egypt will be put to
          shame,
     handed over to the people of the
          north."

²⁵The Lord Almighty, the God of Israel,
says: "I am about to bring punishment on
Amon god of Thebes,ᵃ on Pharaoh, on
Egypt and her gods and her kings, and
on those who rely on Pharaoh. ²⁶I will
hand them over to those who seek their
lives, to Nebuchadnezzar king of Babylon and his officers. Later, however,
Egypt will be inhabited as in times past,"
declares the Lord.

²⁷"Do not fear, O Jacob my servant;
     do not be dismayed, O Israel.
I will surely save you out of a distant
          place,
     your descendants from the land of
          their exile.
Jacob will again have peace and
          security,
     and no one will make him afraid.
²⁸Do not fear, O Jacob my servant,
     for I am with you," declares the
          Lord.
"Though I completely destroy all the
          nations
     among which I scatter you,
I will not completely destroy you.
I will discipline you but only with
          justice;
     I will not let you go entirely
          unpunished."

A Message About the Philistines

47 This is the word of the Lord that
     came to Jeremiah the prophet con-
cerning the Philistines before Pharaoh attacked Gaza:

²This is what the Lord says:

"See how the waters are rising in the
          north;
     they will become an overflowing
          torrent.
They will overflow the land and
          everything in it,
     the towns and those who live in
          them.
The people will cry out;

all who dwell in the land will wail
³at the sound of the hoofs of galloping
          steeds,
     at the noise of enemy chariots
     and the rumble of their wheels.
Fathers will not turn to help their
          children;
     their hands will hang limp.
⁴For the day has come
     to destroy all the Philistines
and to cut off all survivors
     who could help Tyre and Sidon.
The Lord is about to destroy the
          Philistines,
     the remnant from the coasts of
          Caphtor.ᵇ
⁵Gaza will shave her head in
          mourning;
     Ashkelon will be silenced.
O remnant on the plain,
     how long will you cut yourselves?

⁶" 'Ah, sword of the Lord,' ⌐ you cry,⌐
     'how long till you rest?
Return to your scabbard;
     cease and be still.'
⁷But how can it rest
     when the Lord has commanded it,
when he has ordered it
     to attack Ashkelon and the coast?"

A Message About Moab

48 Concerning Moab:

  This is what the Lord Almighty, the
God of Israel, says:

"Woe to Nebo, for it will be ruined.
     Kiriathaim will be disgraced and
          captured;
     the strongholdᶜ will be disgraced
          and shattered.
²Moab will be praised no more;
     in Heshbonᵈ men will plot her
          downfall:
     'Come, let us put an end to that
          nation.'
You too, O Madmen,ᵉ will be
          silenced;
     the sword will pursue you.
³Listen to the cries from Horonaim,
     cries of great havoc and
          destruction.
⁴Moab will be broken;

ᵃ25 Hebrew *No*   ᵇ4 That is, Crete   ᶜ1 Or
/ *Misgab*   ᵈ2 The Hebrew for *Heshbon* sounds
like the Hebrew for *plot*.   ᵉ2 The name of the
Moabite town Madmen sounds like the Hebrew for
be silenced.

her little ones will cry out.*a*
⁵They go up the way to Luhith,
   weeping bitterly as they go;
on the road down to Horonaim
   anguished cries over the
      destruction are heard.
⁶Flee! Run for your lives;
   become like a bush*b* in the desert.
⁷Since you trust in your deeds and
      riches,
   you too will be taken captive,
and Chemosh will go into exile,
   together with his priests and
      officials.
⁸The destroyer will come against every
      town,
   and not a town will escape.
The valley will be ruined
   and the plateau destroyed,
because the LORD has spoken.
⁹Put salt on Moab,
   for she will be laid waste*c*;
her towns will become desolate,
   with no one to live in them.

¹⁰"A curse on him who is lax in doing
      the LORD's work!
   A curse on him who keeps his
      sword from bloodshed!

¹¹"Moab has been at rest from youth,
   like wine left on its dregs,
not poured from one jar to another—
   she has not gone into exile.
So she tastes as she did,
   and her aroma is unchanged.
¹²But days are coming,"
   declares the LORD,
"when I will send men who pour
      from jars,
   and they will pour her out;
they will empty her jars
   and smash her jugs.
¹³Then Moab will be ashamed of
      Chemosh,
   as the house of Israel was ashamed
      when they trusted in Bethel.

¹⁴"How can you say, 'We are warriors,
   men valiant in battle'?
¹⁵Moab will be destroyed and her
      towns invaded;
   her finest young men will go down
      in the slaughter,"
declares the King, whose name is
   the LORD Almighty.
¹⁶"The fall of Moab is at hand;
   her calamity will come quickly.
¹⁷Mourn for her, all who live around
      her,

all who know her fame;
   say, 'How broken is the mighty
      scepter,
   how broken the glorious staff!'

¹⁸"Come down from your glory
   and sit on the parched ground,
O inhabitants of the Daughter of
      Dibon,
for he who destroys Moab
   will come up against you
   and ruin your fortified cities.
¹⁹Stand by the road and watch,
   you who live in Aroer.
Ask the man fleeing and the woman
      escaping,
   ask them, 'What has happened?'
²⁰Moab is disgraced, for she is
      shattered.
   Wail and cry out!
Announce by the Arnon
   that Moab is destroyed.
²¹Judgment has come to the plateau—
   to Holon, Jahzah and Mephaath,
²²   to Dibon, Nebo and Beth
      Diblathaim,
²³   to Kiriathaim, Beth Gamul and
      Beth Meon,
²⁴   to Kerioth and Bozrah—
   to all the towns of Moab, far and
      near.
²⁵Moab's horn*d* is cut off;
   her arm is broken,"
                  declares the LORD.

²⁶"Make her drunk,
   for she has defied the LORD.
Let Moab wallow in her vomit;
   let her be an object of ridicule.
²⁷Was not Israel the object of your
      ridicule?
   Was she caught among thieves,
that you shake your head in scorn
   whenever you speak of her?
²⁸Abandon your towns and dwell
      among the rocks,
   you who live in Moab.
Be like a dove that makes its nest
   at the mouth of a cave.

²⁹"We have heard of Moab's pride—
   her overweening pride and conceit,
her pride and arrogance
   and the haughtiness of her heart.
³⁰I know her insolence but it is futile,"
                  declares the LORD,

---

*a*4 Hebrew; Septuagint / *proclaim it to Zoar*
*b*6 Or *like Aroer*   *c*9 Or *Give wings to Moab, /
for she will fly away*   *d*25 *Horn* here symbolizes
strength.

"and her boasts accomplish
  nothing.
³¹Therefore I wail over Moab,
  for all Moab I cry out,
  I moan for the men of Kir
    Hareseth.
³²I weep for you, as Jazer weeps,
  O vines of Sibmah.
Your branches spread as far as the
    sea;
  they reached as far as the sea of
    Jazer.
The destroyer has fallen
  on your ripened fruit and grapes.
³³Joy and gladness are gone
  from the orchards and fields of
    Moab.
I have stopped the flow of wine from
    the presses;
  no one treads them with shouts of
    joy.
Although there are shouts,
  they are not shouts of joy.

³⁴"The sound of their cry rises
  from Heshbon to Elealeh and
    Jahaz,
  from Zoar as far as Horonaim and
    Eglath Shelishiyah,
  for even the waters of Nimrim are
    dried up.
³⁵In Moab I will put an end
  to those who make offerings on the
    high places
  and burn incense to their gods,"
    declares the LORD.
³⁶"So my heart laments for Moab like a
    flute;
  it laments like a flute for the men
    of Kir Hareseth.
The wealth they acquired is gone.
³⁷Every head is shaved
  and every beard cut off;
  every hand is slashed
  and every waist is covered with
    sackcloth.
³⁸On all the roofs in Moab
  and in the public squares
  there is nothing but mourning,
  for I have broken Moab
  like a jar that no one wants,"
    declares the LORD.
³⁹"How shattered she is! How they
    wail!
How Moab turns her back in
    shame!
Moab has become an object of
    ridicule,

an object of horror to all those
  around her."

⁴⁰This is what the LORD says:

"Look! An eagle is swooping down,
  spreading its wings over Moab.
⁴¹Kerioth*a* will be captured
  and the strongholds taken.
In that day the hearts of Moab's
    warriors
  will be like the heart of a woman
    in labor.
⁴²Moab will be destroyed as a nation
  because she defied the LORD.
⁴³Terror and pit and snare await you,
  O people of Moab,"
    declares the LORD.
⁴⁴"Whoever flees from the terror
  will fall into a pit,
  whoever climbs out of the pit
  will be caught in a snare;
  for I will bring upon Moab
  the year of her punishment,"
    declares the LORD.

⁴⁵"In the shadow of Heshbon
  the fugitives stand helpless,
  for a fire has gone out from Heshbon,
  a blaze from the midst of Sihon;
  it burns the foreheads of Moab,
  the skulls of the noisy boasters.
⁴⁶Woe to you, O Moab!
  The people of Chemosh are
    destroyed;
  your sons are taken into exile
  and your daughters into captivity.

⁴⁷"Yet I will restore the fortunes of
    Moab

a41 Or *The cities*

POINT OF INTEREST

Jeremiah 48:46

Jeremiah described Israel's enemies as the offspring of their gods. His implication is that the worshipers acted like the gods they worshiped. Worship of Chemosh, the Moabite god, required human sacrifice. Jeremiah's words indicate that these gods were not only false, they were also deadly.

in days to come,"
                        declares the LORD.
Here ends the judgment on Moab.

A Message About Ammon

49 Concerning the Ammonites:

This is what the LORD says:

"Has Israel no sons?
    Has she no heirs?
Why then has Molech*a* taken
        possession of Gad?
    Why do his people live in its
        towns?
²But the days are coming,"
    declares the LORD,
"when I will sound the battle cry
    against Rabbah of the Ammonites;
it will become a mound of ruins,
    and its surrounding villages will be
        set on fire.
Then Israel will drive out
    those who drove her out,"
                        says the LORD.
³"Wail, O Heshbon, for Ai is
        destroyed!
    Cry out, O inhabitants of Rabbah!
Put on sackcloth and mourn;
    rush here and there inside the
        walls,
for Molech will go into exile,
    together with his priests and
        officials.
⁴Why do you boast of your valleys,
    boast of your valleys so fruitful?
O unfaithful daughter,
    you trust in your riches and say,
    'Who will attack me?'
⁵I will bring terror on you
    from all those around you,"
                    declares the Lord,
                    the LORD Almighty.
"Every one of you will be driven
        away,
    and no one will gather the
        fugitives.
⁶"Yet afterward, I will restore the
        fortunes of the Ammonites,"
                        declares the LORD.

A Message About Edom

⁷Concerning Edom:

This is what the LORD Almighty says:

"Is there no longer wisdom in
        Teman?

Has counsel perished from the
        prudent?
    Has their wisdom decayed?
⁸Turn and flee, hide in deep caves,
    you who live in Dedan,
for I will bring disaster on Esau
    at the time I punish him.
⁹If grape pickers came to you,
    would they not leave a few grapes?
If thieves came during the night,
    would they not steal only as much
        as they wanted?
¹⁰But I will strip Esau bare;
    I will uncover his hiding places,
    so that he cannot conceal himself.
His children, relatives and neighbors
        will perish,
    and he will be no more.
¹¹Leave your orphans; I will protect
        their lives.
    Your widows too can trust in me."

¹²This is what the LORD says: "If those
who do not deserve to drink the cup must
drink it, why should you go unpunished?
You will not go unpunished, but must
drink it. ¹³I swear by myself," declares
the LORD, "that Bozrah will become a ruin
and an object of horror, of reproach and
of cursing; and all its towns will be in
ruins forever."

¹⁴I have heard a message from the
        LORD:
    An envoy was sent to the nations
        to say,
"Assemble yourselves to attack it!
    Rise up for battle!"

¹⁵"Now I will make you small among
        the nations,
    despised among men.
¹⁶The terror you inspire
    and the pride of your heart have
        deceived you,
you who live in the clefts of the
        rocks,
    who occupy the heights of the hill.
Though you build your nest as high
        as the eagle's,
    from there I will bring you down,"
                        declares the LORD.
¹⁷"Edom will become an object of
        horror;
    all who pass by will be appalled
        and will scoff
    because of all its wounds.

a 1 Or *their king*; Hebrew *malcam*; also in verse 3

18As Sodom and Gomorrah were
 overthrown,
 along with their neighboring
 towns,"
    says the Lord,
 "so no one will live there;
 no man will dwell in it.

19"Like a lion coming up from Jordan's
 thickets
 to a rich pastureland,
I will chase Edom from its land in an
 instant.
 Who is the chosen one I will
 appoint for this?
 Who is like me and who can
 challenge me?
 And what shepherd can stand
 against me?"
20Therefore, hear what the Lord has
 planned against Edom,
 what he has purposed against
 those who live in Teman:
 The young of the flock will be
 dragged away;
 he will completely destroy their
 pasture because of them.
21At the sound of their fall the earth
 will tremble;
 their cry will resound to the Red
 Sea.*a*
22Look! An eagle will soar and swoop
 down,
 spreading its wings over Bozrah.
 In that day the hearts of Edom's
 warriors
 will be like the heart of a woman
 in labor.

A Message About Damascus

23Concerning Damascus:

"Hamath and Arpad are dismayed,
 for they have heard bad news.
They are disheartened,
 troubled like*b* the restless sea.
24Damascus has become feeble,
 she has turned to flee
 and panic has gripped her;
anguish and pain have seized her,
 pain like that of a woman in labor.
25Why has the city of renown not been
 abandoned,
 the town in which I delight?
26Surely, her young men will fall in the
 streets;
 all her soldiers will be silenced in
 that day,"
    declares the Lord Almighty.

27"I will set fire to the walls of
 Damascus;
 it will consume the fortresses of
 Ben-Hadad."

A Message About Kedar and Hazor

28Concerning Kedar and the kingdoms
of Hazor, which Nebuchadnezzar king of
Babylon attacked:

This is what the Lord says:

"Arise, and attack Kedar
 and destroy the people of the East.
29Their tents and their flocks will be
 taken;
 their shelters will be carried off
 with all their goods and camels.
Men will shout to them,
 'Terror on every side!'

30"Flee quickly away!
 Stay in deep caves, you who live
 in Hazor,"
    declares the Lord.
 "Nebuchadnezzar king of Babylon
 has plotted against you;
 he has devised a plan against you.

31"Arise and attack a nation at ease,
 which lives in confidence,"
    declares the Lord,
 "a nation that has neither gates nor
 bars;
 its people live alone.
32Their camels will become plunder,
 and their large herds will be booty.
I will scatter to the winds those who
 are in distant places*c*
 and will bring disaster on them
 from every side,"
    declares the Lord.
33"Hazor will become a haunt of
 jackals,
 a desolate place forever.
No one will live there;
 no man will dwell in it."

A Message About Elam

34This is the word of the Lord that
came to Jeremiah the prophet concerning
Elam, early in the reign of Zedekiah king
of Judah:

35This is what the Lord Almighty says:

"See, I will break the bow of Elam,
 the mainstay of their might.

---

a21 Hebrew *Yam Suph*; that is, Sea of Reeds
b23 Hebrew *on* or *by*   *c32* Or *who clip the hair
by their foreheads*

³⁶I will bring against Elam the four
winds
from the four quarters of the
heavens;
I will scatter them to the four winds,
and there will not be a nation
where Elam's exiles do not go.
³⁷I will shatter Elam before their foes,
before those who seek their lives;
I will bring disaster upon them,
even my fierce anger,"
declares the LORD.
"I will pursue them with the sword
until I have made an end of them.
³⁸I will set my throne in Elam
and destroy her king and officials,"
declares the LORD.
³⁹"Yet I will restore the fortunes of
Elam
in days to come,"
declares the LORD.

A Message About Babylon

50 This is the word the LORD spoke
through Jeremiah the prophet concerning Babylon and the land of the Bab-
ylonians^a:

²"Announce and proclaim among the
nations,
lift up a banner and proclaim it;
keep nothing back, but say,
'Babylon will be captured;
Bel will be put to shame,
Marduk filled with terror.
Her images will be put to shame
and her idols filled with terror.'
³A nation from the north will attack
her
and lay waste her land.
No one will live in it;
both men and animals will flee
away.

⁴"In those days, at that time,"
declares the LORD,
"the people of Israel and the people
of Judah together
will go in tears to seek the LORD
their God.
⁵They will ask the way to Zion
and turn their faces toward it.
They will come and bind themselves
to the LORD
in an everlasting covenant
that will not be forgotten.

⁶"My people have been lost sheep;
their shepherds have led them
astray

and caused them to roam on the
mountains.
They wandered over mountain and
hill
and forgot their own resting place.
⁷Whoever found them devoured them;
their enemies said, 'We are not
guilty,
for they sinned against the LORD, their
true pasture,
the LORD, the hope of their fathers.'

⁸"Flee out of Babylon;
leave the land of the Babylonians,
and be like the goats that lead the
flock.
⁹For I will stir up and bring against
Babylon
an alliance of great nations from
the land of the north.
They will take up their positions
against her,
and from the north she will be
captured.
Their arrows will be like skilled
warriors
who do not return empty-handed.
¹⁰So Babylonia^b will be plundered;
all who plunder her will have their
fill,"
declares the LORD.

¹¹"Because you rejoice and are glad,
you who pillage my inheritance,
because you frolic like a heifer
threshing grain
and neigh like stallions,
¹²your mother will be greatly ashamed;
she who gave you birth will be
disgraced.
She will be the least of the nations—
a wilderness, a dry land, a desert.
¹³Because of the LORD's anger she will
not be inhabited
but will be completely desolate.
All who pass Babylon will be
horrified and scoff
because of all her wounds.

¹⁴"Take up your positions around
Babylon,
all you who draw the bow.
Shoot at her! Spare no arrows,
for she has sinned against the LORD.
¹⁵Shout against her on every side!
She surrenders, her towers fall,
her walls are torn down.

---

^a1 Or *Chaldeans*; also in verses 8, 25, 35 and 45
^b10 Or *Chaldea*

Since this is the vengeance of the
LORD,
take vengeance on her;
do to her as she has done to
others.
¹⁶Cut off from Babylon the sower,
and the reaper with his sickle at
harvest.
Because of the sword of the oppressor
let everyone return to his own
people,
let everyone flee to his own land.

¹⁷"Israel is a scattered flock
that lions have chased away.
The first to devour him
was the king of Assyria;
the last to crush his bones
was Nebuchadnezzar king of
Babylon."

¹⁸Therefore this is what the LORD Almighty, the God of Israel, says:

"I will punish the king of Babylon
and his land
as I punished the king of Assyria.
¹⁹But I will bring Israel back to his own
pasture
and he will graze on Carmel and
Bashan;
his appetite will be satisfied
on the hills of Ephraim and Gilead.
²⁰In those days, at that time,"
declares the LORD,
"search will be made for Israel's guilt,
but there will be none,
and for the sins of Judah,
but none will be found,
for I will forgive the remnant I
spare.

²¹"Attack the land of Merathaim
and those who live in Pekod.
Pursue, kill and completely destroy*
them,"
declares the LORD.
"Do everything I have commanded
you.
²²The noise of battle is in the land,
the noise of great destruction!
²³How broken and shattered
is the hammer of the whole earth!
How desolate is Babylon
among the nations!
²⁴I set a trap for you, O Babylon,
and you were caught before you
knew it;
you were found and captured
because you opposed the LORD.
²⁵The LORD has opened his arsenal

and brought out the weapons of
his wrath,
for the Sovereign LORD Almighty has
work to do
in the land of the Babylonians.
²⁶Come against her from afar.
Break open her granaries;
pile her up like heaps of grain.
Completely destroy her
and leave her no remnant.
²⁷Kill all her young bulls;
let them go down to the slaughter!
Woe to them! For their day has
come,
the time for them to be punished.
²⁸Listen to the fugitives and refugees
from Babylon
declaring in Zion
how the LORD our God has taken
vengeance,
vengeance for his temple.

²⁹"Summon archers against Babylon,
all those who draw the bow.
Encamp all around her;
let no one escape.
Repay her for her deeds;
do to her as she has done.
For she has defied the LORD,
the Holy One of Israel.
³⁰Therefore, her young men will fall in
the streets;
all her soldiers will be silenced in
that day,"
declares the LORD.
³¹"See, I am against you, O arrogant
one,"
declares the Lord, the LORD
Almighty,
"for your day has come,
the time for you to be punished.
³²The arrogant one will stumble and
fall
and no one will help her up;
I will kindle a fire in her towns
that will consume all who are
around her."

³³This is what the LORD Almighty says:

"The people of Israel are oppressed,
and the people of Judah as well.
All their captors hold them fast,
refusing to let them go.
³⁴Yet their Redeemer is strong;
the LORD Almighty is his name.
He will vigorously defend their cause

---

*21 The Hebrew term refers to the irrevocable
giving over of things or persons to the LORD, often
by totally destroying them; also in verse 26.

so that he may bring rest to their
land,
but unrest to those who live in
Babylon.

35"A sword against the Babylonians!"
declares the LORD—
"against those who live in Babylon
and against her officials and wise
men!
36A sword against her false prophets!
They will become fools.
A sword against her warriors!
They will be filled with terror.
37A sword against her horses and
chariots
and all the foreigners in her ranks!
They will become women.
A sword against her treasures!
They will be plundered.
38A drought on*a* her waters!
They will dry up.
For it is a land of idols,
idols that will go mad with terror.

39"So desert creatures and hyenas will
live there,
and there the owl will dwell.
It will never again be inhabited
or lived in from generation to
generation.
40As God overthrew Sodom and
Gomorrah
along with their neighboring
towns,"
declares the LORD,
"so no one will live there;
no man will dwell in it.

41"Look! An army is coming from the
north;
a great nation and many kings
are being stirred up from the ends
of the earth.
42They are armed with bows and
spears;
they are cruel and without mercy.
They sound like the roaring sea
as they ride on their horses;
they come like men in battle
formation
to attack you, O Daughter of
Babylon.
43The king of Babylon has heard
reports about them,
and his hands hang limp.
Anguish has gripped him,
pain like that of a woman in labor.
44Like a lion coming up from Jordan's
thickets

to a rich pastureland,
I will chase Babylon from its land in
an instant.
Who is the chosen one I will
appoint for this?
Who is like me and who can
challenge me?
And what shepherd can stand
against me?"
45Therefore, hear what the LORD has
planned against Babylon,
what he has purposed against the
land of the Babylonians:
The young of the flock will be
dragged away;
he will completely destroy their
pasture because of them.
46At the sound of Babylon's capture the
earth will tremble;
its cry will resound among the
nations.

51 This is what the LORD says:

"See, I will stir up the spirit of a
destroyer
against Babylon and the people of
Leb Kamai.*b*
2I will send foreigners to Babylon
to winnow her and to devastate
her land;
they will oppose her on every side
in the day of her disaster.
3Let not the archer string his bow,
nor let him put on his armor.
Do not spare her young men;

---

*a*38 Or *A sword against*   *b*1 *Leb Kamai* is a
cryptogram for Chaldea, that is, Babylonia.

POINT OF INTEREST   Jeremiah 50:38-40

Imagine someone today
using these terms to predict
the obliteration of Los
Angeles. Due to the prolifera-
tion of nuclear weapons, such a thing
would be feasible in our day. Isaiah, however, made this prediction about Babylon
2,500 years ago. Within 50 years Isaiah's
prophecy against Babylon had become a
reality. The once-impressive city of Babylon remains a ruin to this day.

completely destroy[a] her army.
⁴They will fall down slain in
Babylon,[b]
fatally wounded in her streets.
⁵For Israel and Judah have not been
forsaken
by their God, the Lord Almighty,
though their land[c] is full of guilt
before the Holy One of Israel.

⁶"Flee from Babylon!
Run for your lives!
Do not be destroyed because of her
sins.
It is time for the Lord's vengeance;
he will pay her what she deserves.
⁷Babylon was a gold cup in the Lord's
hand;
she made the whole earth drunk.
The nations drank her wine;
therefore they have now gone mad.
⁸Babylon will suddenly fall and be
broken.
Wail over her!
Get balm for her pain;
perhaps she can be healed.

⁹" 'We would have healed Babylon,
but she cannot be healed;
let us leave her and each go to his
own land,
for her judgment reaches to the
skies,
it rises as high as the clouds.'

¹⁰" 'The Lord has vindicated us;
come, let us tell in Zion
what the Lord our God has done.'

¹¹"Sharpen the arrows,
take up the shields!
The Lord has stirred up the kings of
the Medes,
because his purpose is to destroy
Babylon.
The Lord will take vengeance,
vengeance for his temple.
¹²Lift up a banner against the walls of
Babylon!
Reinforce the guard,
station the watchmen,
prepare an ambush!
The Lord will carry out his purpose,
his decree against the people of
Babylon.
¹³You who live by many waters
and are rich in treasures,
your end has come,
the time for you to be cut off.
¹⁴The Lord Almighty has sworn by
himself:

I will surely fill you with men, as
with a swarm of locusts,
and they will shout in triumph
over you.

¹⁵"He made the earth by his power;
he founded the world by his
wisdom
and stretched out the heavens by
his understanding.
¹⁶When he thunders, the waters in the
heavens roar;
he makes clouds rise from the ends
of the earth.
He sends lightning with the rain
and brings out the wind from his
storehouses.

¹⁷"Every man is senseless and without
knowledge;
every goldsmith is shamed by his
idols.
His images are a fraud;
they have no breath in them.
¹⁸They are worthless, the objects of
mockery;
when their judgment comes, they
will perish.
¹⁹He who is the Portion of Jacob is not
like these,
for he is the Maker of all things,
including the tribe of his
inheritance—
the Lord Almighty is his name.

²⁰"You are my war club,
my weapon for battle—
with you I shatter nations,
with you I destroy kingdoms,
²¹with you I shatter horse and rider,
with you I shatter chariot and
driver,
²²with you I shatter man and woman,
with you I shatter old man and
youth,
with you I shatter young man and
maiden,
²³with you I shatter shepherd and
flock,
with you I shatter farmer and
oxen,
with you I shatter governors and
officials.

²⁴"Before your eyes I will repay Babylon and all who live in Babylonia[d] for

---

[a]3 The Hebrew term refers to the irrevocable giving over of things or persons to the Lord, often by totally destroying them.   [b]4 Or *Chaldea*
[c]5 Or */ and the land ⌊of the Babylonians⌋*
[d]24 Or *Chaldea*; also in verse 35

all the wrong they have done in Zion,"
declares the LORD.

25"I am against you, O destroying
    mountain,
you who destroy the whole earth,"
    declares the LORD.
"I will stretch out my hand against
    you,
roll you off the cliffs,
and make you a burned-out
    mountain.
26No rock will be taken from you for a
    cornerstone,
nor any stone for a foundation,
for you will be desolate forever,"
    declares the LORD.

27"Lift up a banner in the land!
Blow the trumpet among the
    nations!
Prepare the nations for battle against
    her;
summon against her these
    kingdoms:
Ararat, Minni and Ashkenaz.
Appoint a commander against her;
send up horses like a swarm of
    locusts.
28Prepare the nations for battle against
    her—
the kings of the Medes,
their governors and all their officials,
and all the countries they rule.
29The land trembles and writhes,
for the LORD's purposes against
    Babylon stand—
to lay waste the land of Babylon
so that no one will live there.
30Babylon's warriors have stopped
    fighting;
they remain in their strongholds.
Their strength is exhausted;
they have become like women.
Her dwellings are set on fire;
the bars of her gates are broken.
31One courier follows another
and messenger follows messenger
to announce to the king of Babylon
that his entire city is captured,
32the river crossings seized,
the marshes set on fire,
and the soldiers terrified."

33This is what the LORD Almighty, the
God of Israel, says:

"The Daughter of Babylon is like a
    threshing floor
at the time it is trampled;

the time to harvest her will soon
    come."

34"Nebuchadnezzar king of Babylon
    has devoured us,
he has thrown us into confusion,
he has made us an empty jar.
Like a serpent he has swallowed us
and filled his stomach with our
    delicacies,
and then has spewed us out.
35May the violence done to our flesh*a*
    be upon Babylon,"
say the inhabitants of Zion.
"May our blood be on those who live
    in Babylonia,"
says Jerusalem.

36Therefore, this is what the LORD says:

"See, I will defend your cause
and avenge you;
I will dry up her sea
and make her springs dry.
37Babylon will be a heap of ruins,
a haunt of jackals,
an object of horror and scorn,
a place where no one lives.
38Her people all roar like young lions,
they growl like lion cubs.
39But while they are aroused,
I will set out a feast for them
and make them drunk,
so that they shout with laughter—
then sleep forever and not awake,"
    declares the LORD.
40"I will bring them down
like lambs to the slaughter,
like rams and goats.

41"How Sheshach*b* will be captured,
the boast of the whole earth
    seized!
What a horror Babylon will be
among the nations!
42The sea will rise over Babylon;
its roaring waves will cover her.
43Her towns will be desolate,
a dry and desert land,
a land where no one lives,
through which no man travels.
44I will punish Bel in Babylon
and make him spew out what he
    has swallowed.
The nations will no longer stream to
    him.
And the wall of Babylon will fall.

45"Come out of her, my people!

a35 Or *done to us and to our children*
b41 *Sheshach* is a cryptogram for Babylon.

Run for your lives!
Run from the fierce anger of the
LORD.
⁴⁶Do not lose heart or be afraid
when rumors are heard in the
land;
one rumor comes this year, another
the next,
rumors of violence in the land
and of ruler against ruler.
⁴⁷For the time will surely come
when I will punish the idols of
Babylon;
her whole land will be disgraced
and her slain will all lie fallen
within her.
⁴⁸Then heaven and earth and all that is
in them
will shout for joy over Babylon,
for out of the north
destroyers will attack her,"
declares the LORD.

⁴⁹"Babylon must fall because of Israel's
slain,
just as the slain in all the earth
have fallen because of Babylon.
⁵⁰You who have escaped the sword,
leave and do not linger!
Remember the LORD in a distant land,
and think on Jerusalem."

⁵¹"We are disgraced,
for we have been insulted
and shame covers our faces,
because foreigners have entered
the holy places of the LORD's
house."

⁵²"But days are coming," declares the
LORD,
"when I will punish her idols,
and throughout her land
the wounded will groan.
⁵³Even if Babylon reaches the sky
and fortifies her lofty stronghold,
I will send destroyers against her,"
declares the LORD.

⁵⁴"The sound of a cry comes from
Babylon,
the sound of great destruction
from the land of the
Babylonians.ᵃ
⁵⁵The LORD will destroy Babylon;
he will silence her noisy din.
Waves ⌊of enemies⌋ will rage like
great waters;
the roar of their voices will
resound.

⁵⁶A destroyer will come against
Babylon;
her warriors will be captured,
and their bows will be broken.
For the LORD is a God of retribution;
he will repay in full.
⁵⁷I will make her officials and wise
men drunk,
her governors, officers and
warriors as well;
they will sleep forever and not
awake,"
declares the King, whose name is
the LORD Almighty.

⁵⁸This is what the LORD Almighty says:

"Babylon's thick wall will be leveled
and her high gates set on fire;
the peoples exhaust themselves for
nothing,
the nations' labor is only fuel for
the flames."

⁵⁹This is the message Jeremiah gave to
the staff officer Seraiah son of Neriah, the
son of Mahseiah, when he went to Babylon with Zedekiah king of Judah in the
fourth year of his reign. ⁶⁰Jeremiah had
written on a scroll about all the disasters
that would come upon Babylon—all that
had been recorded concerning Babylon.
⁶¹He said to Seraiah, "When you get to
Babylon, see that you read all these
words aloud. ⁶²Then say, 'O LORD, you
have said you will destroy this place, so
that neither man nor animal will live in it;
it will be desolate forever.' ⁶³When you
finish reading this scroll, tie a stone to it
and throw it into the Euphrates. ⁶⁴Then
say, 'So will Babylon sink to rise no more
because of the disaster I will bring upon
her. And her people will fall.' "

The words of Jeremiah end here.

The Fall of Jerusalem

52 Zedekiah was twenty-one years old
when he became king, and he
reigned in Jerusalem eleven years. His
mother's name was Hamutal daughter of
Jeremiah; she was from Libnah. ²He did
evil in the eyes of the LORD, just as Jehoiakim had done. ³It was because of the
LORD's anger that all this happened to Jerusalem and Judah, and in the end he
thrust them from his presence.

Now Zedekiah rebelled against the
king of Babylon.

ᵃ54 Or Chaldeans

⁴So in the ninth year of Zedekiah's reign, on the tenth day of the tenth month, Nebuchadnezzar king of Babylon marched against Jerusalem with his whole army. They camped outside the city and built siege works all around it. ⁵The city was kept under siege until the eleventh year of King Zedekiah.

⁶By the ninth day of the fourth month the famine in the city had become so severe that there was no food for the people to eat. ⁷Then the city wall was broken through, and the whole army fled. They left the city at night through the gate between the two walls near the king's garden, though the Babylonians*a* were surrounding the city. They fled toward the Arabah,*b* ⁸but the Babylonian*c* army pursued King Zedekiah and overtook him in the plains of Jericho. All his soldiers were separated from him and scattered, ⁹and he was captured.

He was taken to the king of Babylon at Riblah in the land of Hamath, where he pronounced sentence on him. ¹⁰There at Riblah the king of Babylon slaughtered the sons of Zedekiah before his eyes; he also killed all the officials of Judah. ¹¹Then he put out Zedekiah's eyes, bound him with bronze shackles and took him to Babylon, where he put him in prison till the day of his death.

¹²On the tenth day of the fifth month, in the nineteenth year of Nebuchadnezzar king of Babylon, Nebuzaradan commander of the imperial guard, who served the king of Babylon, came to Jerusalem. ¹³He set fire to the temple of the LORD, the royal palace and all the houses of Jerusalem. Every important building he burned down. ¹⁴The whole Babylonian army under the commander of the imperial guard broke down all the walls around Jerusalem. ¹⁵Nebuzaradan the commander of the guard carried into exile some of the poorest people and those who remained in the city, along with the rest of the craftsmen*d* and those who had gone over to the king of Babylon. ¹⁶But Nebuzaradan left behind the rest of the poorest people of the land to work the vineyards and fields.

¹⁷The Babylonians broke up the bronze pillars, the movable stands and the bronze Sea that were at the temple of the LORD and they carried all the bronze to Babylon. ¹⁸They also took away the pots, shovels, wick trimmers, sprinkling bowls, dishes and all the bronze articles used in the temple service. ¹⁹The commander of the imperial guard took away the basins, censers, sprinkling bowls, pots, lampstands, dishes and bowls used for drink offerings—all that were made of pure gold or silver.

²⁰The bronze from the two pillars, the Sea and the twelve bronze bulls under it, and the movable stands, which King Solomon had made for the temple of the LORD, was more than could be weighed. ²¹Each of the pillars was eighteen cubits high and twelve cubits in circumference*e*; each was four fingers thick, and hollow. ²²The bronze capital on top of the one pillar was five cubits*f* high and was decorated with a network and pomegranates of bronze all around. The other pillar, with its pomegranates, was similar. ²³There were ninety-six pomegranates on the sides; the total number of pomegranates above the surrounding network was a hundred.

²⁴The commander of the guard took as prisoners Seraiah the chief priest, Zephaniah the priest next in rank and the three doorkeepers. ²⁵Of those still in the city, he took the officer in charge of the fighting men, and seven royal advisers. He also took the secretary who was chief officer in charge of conscripting the people of the land and sixty of his men who were found in the city. ²⁶Nebuzaradan the commander took them all and brought them to the king of Babylon at Riblah. ²⁷There at Riblah, in the land of Hamath, the king had them executed.

So Judah went into captivity, away from her land. ²⁸This is the number of the people Nebuchadnezzar carried into exile:

in the seventh year, 3,023 Jews;
²⁹in Nebuchadnezzar's eighteenth year,
832 people from Jerusalem;
³⁰in his twenty-third year,
745 Jews taken into exile by Nebuzaradan the commander of the imperial guard.
There were 4,600 people in all.

Jehoiachin Released

³¹In the thirty-seventh year of the exile

---

a 7 Or *Chaldeans*; also in verse 17   *b 7* Or *the Jordan Valley*   *c 8* Or *Chaldean*; also in verse 14   *d 15* Or *populace*   *e 21* That is, about 27 feet (about 8.1 meters) high and 18 feet (about 5.4 meters) in circumference   *f 22* That is, about 7 1/2 feet (about 2.3 meters) of Jehoiachin king of Judah, in the year Evil-Merodach[a] became king of Babylon, he released Jehoiachin king of Judah and freed him from prison on the twenty-fifth day of the twelfth month. [32]He spoke kindly to him and gave him a seat of honor higher than those of the other kings who were with him in Babylon. [33]So Jehoiachin put aside his prison clothes and for the rest of his life ate regularly at the king's table. [34]Day by day the king of Babylon gave Jehoiachin a regular allowance as long as he lived, till the day of his death.

[a]31 Also called *Amel-Marduk*

A *lament is a song or poem articulating intense grief, a genre more in vogue in ancient Jewish tradition than today. The book of Lamentations was most likely written by Jeremiah; the tangible agony in the words of the poem suggests that the writer was an eyewitness who wandered among the ruins of Jerusalem and its temple. Lamentations expresses the pain of the conquered people while it acknowledges the judgment of a righteous God. Despite his deep sadness over the plight of his people, Jeremiah rejoices in God's goodness and mercy, "for his compassions never fail" (3:22).*

LAMENTATIONS

1 *a* How deserted lies the city,
   once so full of people!
How like a widow is she,
   who once was great among the
      nations!
She who was queen among the
      provinces
   has now become a slave.

²Bitterly she weeps at night,
   tears are upon her cheeks.
Among all her lovers
   there is none to comfort her.
All her friends have betrayed her;
   they have become her enemies.

³After affliction and harsh labor,
   Judah has gone into exile.
She dwells among the nations;
   she finds no resting place.
All who pursue her have overtaken
      her
   in the midst of her distress.

⁴The roads to Zion mourn,
   for no one comes to her appointed
      feasts.
All her gateways are desolate,
   her priests groan,
her maidens grieve,
   and she is in bitter anguish.

*a*This chapter is an acrostic poem, the verses of which begin with the successive letters of the Hebrew alphabet.

⁵Her foes have become her masters;
  her enemies are at ease.
The Lord has brought her grief
  because of her many sins.
Her children have gone into exile,
  captive before the foe.

⁶All the splendor has departed
  from the Daughter of Zion.
Her princes are like deer
  that find no pasture;
in weakness they have fled
  before the pursuer.

⁷In the days of her affliction and
    wandering
  Jerusalem remembers all the
    treasures
  that were hers in days of old.
When her people fell into enemy
    hands,
  there was no one to help her.
Her enemies looked at her
  and laughed at her destruction.

⁸Jerusalem has sinned greatly
  and so has become unclean.
All who honored her despise her,
  for they have seen her nakedness;
she herself groans
  and turns away.

⁹Her filthiness clung to her skirts;
  she did not consider her future.
Her fall was astounding;
  there was none to comfort her.
"Look, O Lord, on my affliction,
  for the enemy has triumphed."

¹⁰The enemy laid hands
  on all her treasures;
she saw pagan nations
  enter her sanctuary—
those you had forbidden
  to enter your assembly.

¹¹All her people groan
  as they search for bread;
they barter their treasures for food
  to keep themselves alive.
"Look, O Lord, and consider,
  for I am despised."

¹²"Is it nothing to you, all you who
    pass by?
  Look around and see.
Is any suffering like my suffering
  that was inflicted on me,
that the Lord brought on me
  in the day of his fierce anger?

¹³"From on high he sent fire,
  sent it down into my bones.

He spread a net for my feet
  and turned me back.
He made me desolate,
  faint all the day long.

¹⁴"My sins have been bound into a
    yoke*ᵃ*;
  by his hands they were woven
    together.
They have come upon my neck
  and the Lord has sapped my
    strength.
He has handed me over
  to those I cannot withstand.

¹⁵"The Lord has rejected
  all the warriors in my midst;
he has summoned an army against
    me
  toᵇ crush my young men.
In his winepress the Lord has
    trampled
  the Virgin Daughter of Judah.

¹⁶"This is why I weep
  and my eyes overflow with tears.
No one is near to comfort me,
  no one to restore my spirit.
My children are destitute
  because the enemy has prevailed."

¹⁷Zion stretches out her hands,
  but there is no one to comfort her.
The Lord has decreed for Jacob
  that his neighbors become his foes;
Jerusalem has become
  an unclean thing among them.

¹⁸"The Lord is righteous,
  yet I rebelled against his command.
Listen, all you peoples;
  look upon my suffering.

ᵃ14 Most Hebrew manuscripts; Septuagint *He kept
watch over my sins*   ᵇ15 Or *has set a time for
me / when he will*

POINT OF INTEREST

Lamentations 1:1

The book of Lamentations
reveals Jeremiah's deep sorrow. Read the first four
verses of Lamentations 1
aloud, slowly. The words drip with grief.
God has given us every human emotion for
a purpose, and these words from Jeremiah's broken heart demonstrate that godly
sorrow is appropriate.

My young men and maidens
  have gone into exile.

¹⁹"I called to my allies
  but they betrayed me.
My priests and my elders
  perished in the city
while they searched for food
  to keep themselves alive.

²⁰"See, O Lord, how distressed I am!
  I am in torment within,
and in my heart I am disturbed,
  for I have been most rebellious.
Outside, the sword bereaves;
  inside, there is only death.

²¹"People have heard my groaning,
  but there is no one to comfort me.
All my enemies have heard of my
    distress;
  they rejoice at what you have
    done.
May you bring the day you have
    announced
  so they may become like me.

²²"Let all their wickedness come before
    you;
  deal with them
as you have dealt with me
  because of all my sins.
My groans are many
  and my heart is faint."

2 ^{*a*} How the Lord has covered the
    Daughter of Zion
  with the cloud of his anger^{*b*}!
He has hurled down the splendor of
    Israel
  from heaven to earth;
he has not remembered his footstool
  in the day of his anger.

²Without pity the Lord has swallowed
    up
  all the dwellings of Jacob;
in his wrath he has torn down
  the strongholds of the Daughter of
    Judah.
He has brought her kingdom and its
    princes
  down to the ground in dishonor.

³In fierce anger he has cut off
  every horn^{*c*} of Israel.
He has withdrawn his right hand
  at the approach of the enemy.
He has burned in Jacob like a flaming
    fire
  that consumes everything around
    it.

⁴Like an enemy he has strung his
    bow;
  his right hand is ready.
Like a foe he has slain
  all who were pleasing to the eye;
he has poured out his wrath like fire
  on the tent of the Daughter of
    Zion.

⁵The Lord is like an enemy;
  he has swallowed up Israel.
He has swallowed up all her palaces
  and destroyed her strongholds.
He has multiplied mourning and
    lamentation
  for the Daughter of Judah.

⁶He has laid waste his dwelling like a
    garden;
  he has destroyed his place of
    meeting.
The Lord has made Zion forget
  her appointed feasts and her
    Sabbaths;
in his fierce anger he has spurned
  both king and priest.

⁷The Lord has rejected his altar
  and abandoned his sanctuary.
He has handed over to the enemy
  the walls of her palaces;
they have raised a shout in the house
    of the Lord
  as on the day of an appointed
    feast.

⁸The Lord determined to tear down
  the wall around the Daughter of
    Zion.
He stretched out a measuring line
  and did not withhold his hand
    from destroying.
He made ramparts and walls lament;
  together they wasted away.

⁹Her gates have sunk into the ground;
  their bars he has broken and
    destroyed.
Her king and her princes are exiled
    among the nations,
  the law is no more,
and her prophets no longer find
  visions from the Lord.

¹⁰The elders of the Daughter of Zion
  sit on the ground in silence;

---

^{*a*}This chapter is an acrostic poem, the verses of
which begin with the successive letters of the
Hebrew alphabet.   ^{*b*}1 Or *How the Lord in his
anger / has treated the Daughter of Zion with
contempt*   ^{*c*}3 Or / *all the strength*; or *every king*;
horn here symbolizes strength.

they have sprinkled dust on their
heads
and put on sackcloth.
The young women of Jerusalem
have bowed their heads to the
ground.

¹¹My eyes fail from weeping,
I am in torment within,
my heart is poured out on the ground
because my people are destroyed,
because children and infants faint
in the streets of the city.

¹²They say to their mothers,
"Where is bread and wine?"
as they faint like wounded men
in the streets of the city,
as their lives ebb away
in their mothers' arms.

¹³What can I say for you?
With what can I compare you,
O Daughter of Jerusalem?
To what can I liken you,
that I may comfort you,
O Virgin Daughter of Zion?
Your wound is as deep as the sea.
Who can heal you?

¹⁴The visions of your prophets
were false and worthless;
they did not expose your sin
to ward off your captivity.
The oracles they gave you
were false and misleading.

¹⁵All who pass your way
clap their hands at you;
they scoff and shake their heads
at the Daughter of Jerusalem:
"Is this the city that was called
the perfection of beauty,
the joy of the whole earth?"

¹⁶All your enemies open their mouths
wide against you;
they scoff and gnash their teeth
and say, "We have swallowed her
up.
This is the day we have waited for;
we have lived to see it."

¹⁷The LORD has done what he planned;
he has fulfilled his word,
which he decreed long ago.
He has overthrown you without pity,
he has let the enemy gloat over
you,
he has exalted the horn*a* of your
foes.

¹⁸The hearts of the people

cry out to the Lord.
O wall of the Daughter of Zion,
let your tears flow like a river
day and night;
give yourself no relief,
your eyes no rest.

¹⁹Arise, cry out in the night,
as the watches of the night begin;
pour out your heart like water
in the presence of the Lord.
Lift up your hands to him
for the lives of your children,
who faint from hunger
at the head of every street.

²⁰"Look, O LORD, and consider:
Whom have you ever treated like
this?
Should women eat their offspring,
the children they have cared for?
Should priest and prophet be killed
in the sanctuary of the Lord?

²¹"Young and old lie together
in the dust of the streets;
my young men and maidens
have fallen by the sword.
You have slain them in the day of
your anger;
you have slaughtered them without
pity.

²²"As you summon to a feast day,
so you summoned against me
terrors on every side.
In the day of the LORD's anger
no one escaped or survived;
those I cared for and reared,
my enemy has destroyed."

3 *b*I am the man who has seen
affliction
by the rod of his wrath.
²He has driven me away and made me
walk
in darkness rather than light;
³indeed, he has turned his hand
against me
again and again, all day long.

⁴He has made my skin and my flesh
grow old
and has broken my bones.
⁵He has besieged me and surrounded
me

---

a17 Horn here symbolizes strength.   *b*This
chapter is an acrostic poem; the verses of each
stanza begin with the successive letters of the
Hebrew alphabet, and the verses within each stanza
begin with the same letter.

with bitterness and hardship.
⁶He has made me dwell in darkness
    like those long dead.

⁷He has walled me in so I cannot
        escape;
    he has weighed me down with
        chains.
⁸Even when I call out or cry for help,
    he shuts out my prayer.
⁹He has barred my way with blocks of
        stone;
    he has made my paths crooked.

¹⁰Like a bear lying in wait,
    like a lion in hiding,
¹¹he dragged me from the path and
        mangled me
    and left me without help.
¹²He drew his bow
    and made me the target for his
        arrows.

¹³He pierced my heart
    with arrows from his quiver.
¹⁴I became the laughingstock of all my
        people;
    they mock me in song all day long.
¹⁵He has filled me with bitter herbs
    and sated me with gall.

¹⁶He has broken my teeth with gravel;
    he has trampled me in the dust.
¹⁷I have been deprived of peace;
    I have forgotten what prosperity is.
¹⁸So I say, "My splendor is gone
    and all that I had hoped from the
        LORD."

¹⁹I remember my affliction and my
        wandering,
    the bitterness and the gall.
²⁰I well remember them,
    and my soul is downcast within
        me.
²¹Yet this I call to mind
    and therefore I have hope:

²²Because of the LORD's great love we
        are not consumed,
    for his compassions never fail.
²³They are new every morning;
    great is your faithfulness.
²⁴I say to myself, "The LORD is my
        portion;
    therefore I will wait for him."

²⁵The LORD is good to those whose hope
        is in him,
    to the one who seeks him;
²⁶it is good to wait quietly
    for the salvation of the LORD.

²⁷It is good for a man to bear the yoke
    while he is young.

²⁸Let him sit alone in silence,
    for the LORD has laid it on him.
²⁹Let him bury his face in the dust—
    there may yet be hope.
³⁰Let him offer his cheek to one who
        would strike him,
    and let him be filled with disgrace.

³¹For men are not cast off
    by the Lord forever.
³²Though he brings grief, he will show
        compassion,
    so great is his unfailing love.
³³For he does not willingly bring
        affliction
    or grief to the children of men.

³⁴To crush underfoot
    all prisoners in the land,
³⁵to deny a man his rights
    before the Most High,
³⁶to deprive a man of justice—
    would not the Lord see such
        things?

³⁷Who can speak and have it happen
    if the Lord has not decreed it?
³⁸Is it not from the mouth of the Most
        High
    that both calamities and good
        things come?
³⁹Why should any living man complain
    when punished for his sins?

⁴⁰Let us examine our ways and test
        them,
    and let us return to the LORD.
⁴¹Let us lift up our hearts and our
        hands
    to God in heaven, and say:
⁴²"We have sinned and rebelled
    and you have not forgiven.

⁴³"You have covered yourself with
        anger and pursued us;
    you have slain without pity.
⁴⁴You have covered yourself with a
        cloud
    so that no prayer can get through.
⁴⁵You have made us scum and refuse
    among the nations.

⁴⁶"All our enemies have opened their
        mouths
    wide against us.
⁴⁷We have suffered terror and pitfalls,
    ruin and destruction."
⁴⁸Streams of tears flow from my eyes
    because my people are destroyed.

⁴⁹My eyes will flow unceasingly,
     without relief,
⁵⁰until the LORD looks down
     from heaven and sees.
⁵¹What I see brings grief to my soul
     because of all the women of my
         city.

⁵²Those who were my enemies without
         cause
     hunted me like a bird.
⁵³They tried to end my life in a pit
     and threw stones at me;
⁵⁴the waters closed over my head,
     and I thought I was about to be
         cut off.

⁵⁵I called on your name, O LORD,
     from the depths of the pit.
⁵⁶You heard my plea: "Do not close
         your ears
     to my cry for relief."
⁵⁷You came near when I called you,
     and you said, "Do not fear."

⁵⁸O Lord, you took up my case;
     you redeemed my life.
⁵⁹You have seen, O LORD, the wrong
         done to me.
     Uphold my cause!
⁶⁰You have seen the depth of their
         vengeance,
     all their plots against me.

⁶¹O LORD, you have heard their insults,
     all their plots against me—

WEDNESDAY

Read *Lamentations 3:1–27*
Key Verses *Lamentations 3:21–24*

God's Unfailing Compassion —Michelle Murray

I began my sophomore year in college with "one of those days." As soon as I woke up on the first day of registration, I just knew I was facing some cliff-hanging challenges. Thinking back on that day, I'm reminded of the children's classic, *Alexander and the Terrible, Horrible, No Good, Very Bad Day.*

I encountered obstacles everywhere I turned. First, my roommate locked me out of our room when she left for class; then the required courses I had planned to take were packed; finally, the financial aid office had no record of my student loan check. And this all occurred before lunch! I was at the end of my rope.

That same day God reminded me of Lamentations 3:22: "Because of the LORD's great love we are not consumed, for his compassions never fail." Just when my world seemed to be crumbling around me, God's words gave me hope. His compassion, his love, will *never* fail!

If those words could be true for Jeremiah, they can be true for us. We often struggle with myriad annoyances that erode our peace of mind bit by bit. Sometimes we face great floods of tragedy and crisis. But God comforts us with the promise that those troubles won't consume us, he won't let us drown in them.

Whatever your struggles, whether they are large or small, let go of them for a moment. Make a point of turning them over to him. Think about how compassionate and faithful God has been in the past. He will restore you again and give you the strength to face each new morning. He will. Trust me. Better yet, trust him.

A Deeper Look
Psalm 103:1–22; Ephesians 3:16–21

Go to page 921 for your next devotional reading.

⁶²what my enemies whisper and mutter
  against me all day long.
⁶³Look at them! Sitting or standing,
  they mock me in their songs.

⁶⁴Pay them back what they deserve,
    O LORD,
  for what their hands have done.
⁶⁵Put a veil over their hearts,
  and may your curse be on them!
⁶⁶Pursue them in anger and destroy
    them
  from under the heavens of the
    LORD.

4 ᵃ How the gold has lost its luster,
    the fine gold become dull!
  The sacred gems are scattered
    at the head of every street.

²How the precious sons of Zion,
  once worth their weight in gold,
  are now considered as pots of clay,
    the work of a potter's hands!

³Even jackals offer their breasts
    to nurse their young,
  but my people have become heartless
    like ostriches in the desert.

⁴Because of thirst the infant's tongue
    sticks to the roof of its mouth;
  the children beg for bread,
    but no one gives it to them.

⁵Those who once ate delicacies
    are destitute in the streets.
  Those nurtured in purple
    now lie on ash heaps.

⁶The punishment of my people
    is greater than that of Sodom,
  which was overthrown in a moment
    without a hand turned to help her.

⁷Their princes were brighter than
    snow
    and whiter than milk,
  their bodies more ruddy than rubies,
    their appearance like sapphires.ᵇ

⁸But now they are blacker than soot;
  they are not recognized in the
    streets.
  Their skin has shriveled on their
    bones;
    it has become as dry as a stick.

⁹Those killed by the sword are better
    off
    than those who die of famine;
  racked with hunger, they waste away
    for lack of food from the field.

¹⁰With their own hands compassionate
    women
  have cooked their own children,
  who became their food
    when my people were destroyed.

¹¹The LORD has given full vent to his
    wrath;
  he has poured out his fierce anger.
  He kindled a fire in Zion
    that consumed her foundations.

¹²The kings of the earth did not
    believe,
    nor did any of the world's people,
  that enemies and foes could enter
    the gates of Jerusalem.

¹³But it happened because of the sins
    of her prophets
    and the iniquities of her priests,
  who shed within her
    the blood of the righteous.

¹⁴Now they grope through the streets
    like men who are blind.
  They are so defiled with blood
    that no one dares to touch their
      garments.

¹⁵"Go away! You are unclean!" men
    cry to them.
  "Away! Away! Don't touch us!"
  When they flee and wander about,
    people among the nations say,
  "They can stay here no longer."

¹⁶The LORD himself has scattered them;
    he no longer watches over them.
  The priests are shown no honor,
    the elders no favor.

¹⁷Moreover, our eyes failed,
    looking in vain for help;
  from our towers we watched
    for a nation that could not save us.

¹⁸Men stalked us at every step,
    so we could not walk in our
      streets.
  Our end was near, our days were
    numbered,
    for our end had come.

¹⁹Our pursuers were swifter
    than eagles in the sky;
  they chased us over the mountains
    and lay in wait for us in the desert.

ᵃThis chapter is an acrostic poem, the verses of
which begin with the successive letters of the
Hebrew alphabet.   ᵇ7 Or *lapis lazuli*

²⁰The LORD's anointed, our very life
    breath,
    was caught in their traps.
  We thought that under his shadow
    we would live among the nations.

²¹Rejoice and be glad, O Daughter of
    Edom,
    you who live in the land of Uz.
  But to you also the cup will be
    passed;
    you will be drunk and stripped
    naked.

²²O Daughter of Zion, your punishment
    will end;
    he will not prolong your exile.
  But, O Daughter of Edom, he will
    punish your sin
    and expose your wickedness.

5 Remember, O LORD, what has
    happened to us;
    look, and see our disgrace.
²Our inheritance has been turned over
    to aliens,
    our homes to foreigners.
³We have become orphans and
    fatherless,
    our mothers like widows.
⁴We must buy the water we drink;
    our wood can be had only at a
    price.
⁵Those who pursue us are at our
    heels;
    we are weary and find no rest.
⁶We submitted to Egypt and Assyria
    to get enough bread.
⁷Our fathers sinned and are no more,
    and we bear their punishment.
⁸Slaves rule over us,

and there is none to free us from
    their hands.
⁹We get our bread at the risk of our
    lives
    because of the sword in the desert.
¹⁰Our skin is hot as an oven,
    feverish from hunger.
¹¹Women have been ravished in Zion,
    and virgins in the towns of Judah.
¹²Princes have been hung up by their
    hands;
    elders are shown no respect.
¹³Young men toil at the millstones;
    boys stagger under loads of wood.
¹⁴The elders are gone from the city
    gate;
    the young men have stopped their
    music.
¹⁵Joy is gone from our hearts;
    our dancing has turned to
    mourning.
¹⁶The crown has fallen from our head.
    Woe to us, for we have sinned!
¹⁷Because of this our hearts are faint,
    because of these things our eyes
    grow dim
¹⁸for Mount Zion, which lies desolate,
    with jackals prowling over it.

¹⁹You, O LORD, reign forever;
    your throne endures from
    generation to generation.
²⁰Why do you always forget us?
    Why do you forsake us so long?
²¹Restore us to yourself, O LORD, that
    we may return;
    renew our days as of old
²²unless you have utterly rejected us
    and are angry with us beyond
    measure.

Ezekiel, in exile among his people, uses words, visions and "mini-dramas" as he communicates God's messages to his people. Even though the book was written when more than 3,000 Jews were in oppressive exile in Babylon, the main theme is hope. Although God has righteously judged his people, he hasn't forsaken them but promises to remain with them in exile and return with them someday to their home. Through Ezekiel, God told the Jews to "know that I am the LORD" (6:14). God promises to be with us even in the remotest and most unlikely places.

EZEKIEL

The Living Creatures and the Glory of the LORD

1 In the^a thirtieth year, in the fourth month on the fifth day, while I was among the exiles by the Kebar River, the heavens were opened and I saw visions of God.

2On the fifth of the month—it was the fifth year of the exile of King Jehoiachin— 3the word of the LORD came to Ezekiel the priest, the son of Buzi,^b by the Kebar River in the land of the Babylonians.^c There the hand of the LORD was upon him.

4I looked, and I saw a windstorm coming out of the north—an immense cloud with flashing lightning and surrounded by brilliant light. The center of the fire looked like glowing metal, 5and in the fire was what looked like four living creatures. In appearance their form was that of a man, 6but each of them had four faces and four wings. 7Their legs were straight; their feet were like those of a calf and gleamed like burnished bronze. 8Under their wings on their four sides they had the hands of a man. All four of them had faces and wings, 9and their wings touched one another. Each one went straight ahead; they did not turn as they moved.

10Their faces looked like this: Each of the four had the face of a man, and on the

<hr>

a1 Or my   b3 Or Ezekiel son of Buzi the priest
c3 Or Chaldeans

right side each had the face of a lion, and on the left the face of an ox; each also had the face of an eagle. ¹¹Such were their faces. Their wings were spread out upward; each had two wings, one touching the wing of another creature on either side, and two wings covering its body. ¹²Each one went straight ahead. Wherever the spirit would go, they would go, without turning as they went. ¹³The appearance of the living creatures was like burning coals of fire or like torches. Fire moved back and forth among the creatures; it was bright, and lightning flashed out of it. ¹⁴The creatures sped back and forth like flashes of lightning.

¹⁵As I looked at the living creatures, I saw a wheel on the ground beside each creature with its four faces. ¹⁶This was the appearance and structure of the wheels: They sparkled like chrysolite, and all four looked alike. Each appeared to be made like a wheel intersecting a wheel. ¹⁷As they moved, they would go in any one of the four directions the creatures faced; the wheels did not turn about*ᵃ* as the creatures went. ¹⁸Their rims were high and awesome, and all four rims were full of eyes all around.

¹⁹When the living creatures moved, the wheels beside them moved; and when the living creatures rose from the ground, the wheels also rose. ²⁰Wherever the spirit would go, they would go, and the wheels would rise along with them, because the spirit of the living creatures was in the wheels. ²¹When the creatures moved, they also moved; when the creatures stood still, they also stood still; and when the creatures rose from the ground, the wheels rose along with them, because the spirit of the living creatures was in the wheels.

²²Spread out above the heads of the living creatures was what looked like an expanse, sparkling like ice, and awesome. ²³Under the expanse their wings were stretched out one toward the other, and each had two wings covering its body. ²⁴When the creatures moved, I heard the sound of their wings, like the roar of rushing waters, like the voice of the Almighty,*ᵇ* like the tumult of an army. When they stood still, they lowered their wings.

²⁵Then there came a voice from above the expanse over their heads as they stood with lowered wings. ²⁶Above the expanse over their heads was what

looked like a throne of sapphire,*ᶜ* and high above on the throne was a figure like that of a man. ²⁷I saw that from what appeared to be his waist up he looked like glowing metal, as if full of fire, and that from there down he looked like fire; and brilliant light surrounded him. ²⁸Like the appearance of a rainbow in the clouds on a rainy day, so was the radiance around him.

This was the appearance of the likeness of the glory of the LORD. When I saw it, I fell facedown, and I heard the voice of one speaking.

Ezekiel's Call

2 He said to me, "Son of man, stand up on your feet and I will speak to you." ²As he spoke, the Spirit came into me and raised me to my feet, and I heard him speaking to me.

³He said: "Son of man, I am sending you to the Israelites, to a rebellious nation that has rebelled against me; they and their fathers have been in revolt against me to this very day. ⁴The people to whom I am sending you are obstinate and stubborn. Say to them, 'This is what the Sovereign LORD says.' ⁵And whether they listen or fail to listen—for they are a rebellious house—they will know that a prophet has been among them. ⁶And you, son of man, do not be afraid of them or their words. Do not be afraid, though briers and thorns are all around you and you live among scorpions. Do not be afraid of what they say or terrified by them, though they are a rebellious house. ⁷You must speak my words to them, whether they listen or fail to listen, for they are rebellious. ⁸But you, son of man, listen to what I say to you. Do not rebel like that rebellious house; open your mouth and eat what I give you."

⁹Then I looked, and I saw a hand stretched out to me. In it was a scroll, ¹⁰which he unrolled before me. On both sides of it were written words of lament and mourning and woe.

3 And he said to me, "Son of man, eat what is before you, eat this scroll; then go and speak to the house of Israel." ²So I opened my mouth, and he gave me the scroll to eat.

³Then he said to me, "Son of man, eat this scroll I am giving you and fill your

ᵃ17 Or *aside*   ᵇ24 Hebrew *Shaddai*   ᶜ26 Or *lapis lazuli* stomach with it." So I ate it, and it tasted as sweet as honey in my mouth.

⁴He then said to me: "Son of man, go now to the house of Israel and speak my words to them. ⁵You are not being sent to a people of obscure speech and difficult language, but to the house of Israel— ⁶not to many peoples of obscure speech and difficult language, whose words you cannot understand. Surely if I had sent you to them, they would have listened to you. ⁷But the house of Israel is not willing to listen to you because they are not willing to listen to me, for the whole house of Israel is hardened and obstinate. ⁸But I will make you as unyielding and hardened as they are. ⁹I will make your forehead like the hardest stone, harder than flint. Do not be afraid of them or terrified by them, though they are a rebellious house."

¹⁰And he said to me, "Son of man, listen carefully and take to heart all the words I speak to you. ¹¹Go now to your countrymen in exile and speak to them. Say to them, 'This is what the Sovereign LORD says,' whether they listen or fail to listen."

¹²Then the Spirit lifted me up, and I heard behind me a loud rumbling sound—May the glory of the LORD be praised in his dwelling place!— ¹³the sound of the wings of the living creatures brushing against each other and the sound of the wheels beside them, a loud rumbling sound. ¹⁴The Spirit then lifted me up and took me away, and I went in bitterness and in the anger of my spirit, with the strong hand of the LORD upon me. ¹⁵I came to the exiles who lived at Tel Abib near the Kebar River. And there, where they were living, I sat among them for seven days—overwhelmed.

Warning to Israel

¹⁶At the end of seven days the word of the LORD came to me: ¹⁷"Son of man, I have made you a watchman for the house of Israel; so hear the word I speak and give them warning from me. ¹⁸When I say to a wicked man, 'You will surely die,' and you do not warn him or speak out to dissuade him from his evil ways in order to save his life, that wicked man will die for*a* his sin, and I will hold you accountable for his blood. ¹⁹But if you do warn the wicked man and he does not turn from his wickedness or from his evil

ways, he will die for his sin; but you will have saved yourself.

²⁰"Again, when a righteous man turns from his righteousness and does evil, and I put a stumbling block before him, he will die. Since you did not warn him, he will die for his sin. The righteous things he did will not be remembered, and I will hold you accountable for his blood. ²¹But if you do warn the righteous man not to sin and he does not sin, he will surely live because he took warning, and you will have saved yourself."

²²The hand of the LORD was upon me there, and he said to me, "Get up and go out to the plain, and there I will speak to you." ²³So I got up and went out to the plain. And the glory of the LORD was standing there, like the glory I had seen by the Kebar River, and I fell facedown. ²⁴Then the Spirit came into me and raised me to my feet. He spoke to me and said: "Go, shut yourself inside your house. ²⁵And you, son of man, they will tie with ropes; you will be bound so that you cannot go out among the people. ²⁶I will make your tongue stick to the roof of your mouth so that you will be silent and unable to rebuke them, though they are a rebellious house. ²⁷But when I speak to you, I will open your mouth and you shall say to them, 'This is what the Sovereign LORD says.' Whoever will listen let him listen, and whoever will refuse let him refuse; for they are a rebellious house.

Siege of Jerusalem Symbolized

4 "Now, son of man, take a clay tablet, put it in front of you and draw the city of Jerusalem on it. ²Then lay siege to it: Erect siege works against it, build a ramp up to it, set up camps against it and put battering rams around it. ³Then take an

---

a 18 Or *in*; also in verses 19 and 20

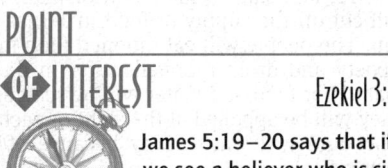

Ezekiel 3:18

James 5:19–20 says that if we see a believer who is sinning and work to help turn that person away from sin, we have done a good thing. How is this passage in Ezekiel similar? How is it different?

iron pan, place it as an iron wall between you and the city and turn your face toward it. It will be under siege, and you shall besiege it. This will be a sign to the house of Israel.

⁴"Then lie on your left side and put the sin of the house of Israel upon yourself.ᵃ You are to bear their sin for the number of days you lie on your side. ⁵I have assigned you the same number of days as the years of their sin. So for 390 days you will bear the sin of the house of Israel.

⁶"After you have finished this, lie down again, this time on your right side, and bear the sin of the house of Judah. I have assigned you 40 days, a day for each year. ⁷Turn your face toward the siege of Jerusalem and with bared arm prophesy against her. ⁸I will tie you up with ropes so that you cannot turn from one side to the other until you have finished the days of your siege.

⁹"Take wheat and barley, beans and lentils, millet and spelt; put them in a storage jar and use them to make bread for yourself. You are to eat it during the 390 days you lie on your side. ¹⁰Weigh out twenty shekelsᵇ of food to eat each day and eat it at set times. ¹¹Also measure out a sixth of a hinᶜ of water and drink it at set times. ¹²Eat the food as you would a barley cake; bake it in the sight of the people, using human excrement for fuel." ¹³The Lᴏʀᴅ said, "In this way the people of Israel will eat defiled food among the nations where I will drive them."

¹⁴Then I said, "Not so, Sovereign Lᴏʀᴅ! I have never defiled myself. From my youth until now I have never eaten anything found dead or torn by wild animals. No unclean meat has ever entered my mouth."

¹⁵"Very well," he said, "I will let you bake your bread over cow manure instead of human excrement."

¹⁶He then said to me: "Son of man, I will cut off the supply of food in Jerusalem. The people will eat rationed food in anxiety and drink rationed water in despair, ¹⁷for food and water will be scarce. They will be appalled at the sight of each other and will waste away because ofᵈ their sin.

5 "Now, son of man, take a sharp sword and use it as a barber's razor to shave your head and your beard. Then take a set of scales and divide up the hair. ²When the days of your siege come to an end, burn a third of the hair with fire inside the city. Take a third and strike it with the sword all around the city. And scatter a third to the wind. For I will pursue them with drawn sword. ³But take a few strands of hair and tuck them away in the folds of your garment. ⁴Again, take a few of these and throw them into the fire and burn them up. A fire will spread from there to the whole house of Israel.

⁵"This is what the Sovereign Lᴏʀᴅ says: This is Jerusalem, which I have set in the center of the nations, with countries all around her. ⁶Yet in her wickedness she has rebelled against my laws and decrees more than the nations and countries around her. She has rejected my laws and has not followed my decrees.

⁷"Therefore this is what the Sovereign Lᴏʀᴅ says: You have been more unruly than the nations around you and have not followed my decrees or kept my laws. You have not evenᵉ conformed to the standards of the nations around you.

⁸"Therefore this is what the Sovereign Lᴏʀᴅ says: I myself am against you, Jerusalem, and I will inflict punishment on you in the sight of the nations. ⁹Because of all your detestable idols, I will do to you what I have never done before and will never do again. ¹⁰Therefore in your midst fathers will eat their children, and children will eat their fathers. I will inflict punishment on you and will scatter all your survivors to the winds. ¹¹Therefore as surely as I live, declares the Sovereign Lᴏʀᴅ, because you have defiled my sanctuary with all your vile images and detestable practices, I myself will withdraw my favor; I will not look on you with pity or spare you. ¹²A third of your people will die of the plague or perish by famine inside you; a third will fall by the sword outside your walls; and a third I will scatter to the winds and pursue with drawn sword.

¹³"Then my anger will cease and my wrath against them will subside, and I will be avenged. And when I have spent my wrath upon them, they will know that I the Lᴏʀᴅ have spoken in my zeal.

¹⁴"I will make you a ruin and a reproach among the nations around you, in

ᵃ4 Or your side   ᵇ10 That is, about 8 ounces (about 0.2 kilogram)   ᶜ11 That is, about 2/3 quart (about 0.6 liter)   ᵈ17 Or away in   ᵉ7 Most Hebrew manuscripts; some Hebrew manuscripts and Syriac You have the sight of all who pass by. ¹⁵You will be a reproach and a taunt, a warning and an object of horror to the nations around you when I inflict punishment on you in anger and in wrath and with stinging rebuke. I the LORD have spoken. ¹⁶When I shoot at you with my deadly and destructive arrows of famine, I will shoot to destroy you. I will bring more and more famine upon you and cut off your supply of food. ¹⁷I will send famine and wild beasts against you, and they will leave you childless. Plague and bloodshed will sweep through you, and I will bring the sword against you. I the LORD have spoken."

A Prophecy Against the Mountains of Israel

6 The word of the LORD came to me: ²"Son of man, set your face against the mountains of Israel; prophesy against them ³and say: 'O mountains of Israel, hear the word of the Sovereign LORD. This is what the Sovereign LORD says to the mountains and hills, to the ravines and valleys: I am about to bring a sword against you, and I will destroy your high places. ⁴Your altars will be demolished and your incense altars will be smashed; and I will slay your people in front of your idols. ⁵I will lay the dead bodies of the Israelites in front of their idols, and I will scatter your bones around your altars. ⁶Wherever you live, the towns will be laid waste and the high places demolished, so that your altars will be laid waste and devastated, your idols smashed and ruined, your incense altars broken down, and what you have made wiped out. ⁷Your people will fall slain among you, and you will know that I am the LORD.

⁸" 'But I will spare some, for some of you will escape the sword when you are scattered among the lands and nations. ⁹Then in the nations where they have been carried captive, those who escape will remember me—how I have been grieved by their adulterous hearts, which have turned away from me, and by their eyes, which have lusted after their idols. They will loathe themselves for the evil they have done and for all their detestable practices. ¹⁰And they will know that I am the LORD; I did not threaten in vain to bring this calamity on them.

¹¹" 'This is what the Sovereign LORD says: Strike your hands together and stamp your feet and cry out "Alas!" because of all the wicked and detestable practices of the house of Israel, for they will fall by the sword, famine and plague. ¹²He that is far away will die of the plague, and he that is near will fall by the sword, and he that survives and is spared will die of famine. So will I spend my wrath upon them. ¹³And they will know that I am the LORD, when their people lie slain among their idols around their altars, on every high hill and on all the mountaintops, under every spreading tree and every leafy oak—places where they offered fragrant incense to all their idols. ¹⁴And I will stretch out my hand against them and make the land a desolate waste from the desert to Diblah*ᵃ*— wherever they live. Then they will know that I am the LORD.' "

The End Has Come

7 The word of the LORD came to me: ²"Son of man, this is what the Sovereign LORD says to the land of Israel: The end! The end has come upon the four corners of the land. ³The end is now upon you and I will unleash my anger against you. I will judge you according to your conduct and repay you for all your detestable practices. ⁴I will not look on you with pity or spare you; I will surely repay you for your conduct and the detestable practices among you. Then you will know that I am the LORD.

⁵"This is what the Sovereign LORD says: Disaster! An unheard-ofᵇ disaster is coming. ⁶The end has come! The end has come! It has roused itself against you. It has come! ⁷Doom has come upon you—you who dwell in the land. The time has come, the day is near; there is panic, not joy, upon the mountains. ⁸I am about to pour out my wrath on you and spend my anger against you; I will judge you according to your conduct and repay you for all your detestable practices. ⁹I will not look on you with pity or spare you; I will repay you in accordance with your conduct and the detestable practices among you. Then you will know that it is I the LORD who strikes the blow.

¹⁰"The day is here! It has come! Doom has burst forth, the rod has budded, arrogance has blossomed! ¹¹Violence has

ᵃ14 Most Hebrew manuscripts; a few Hebrew manuscripts *Riblah*   ᵇ5 Most Hebrew manuscripts; some Hebrew manuscripts and Syriac *Disaster after* grown into*a* a rod to punish wickedness; none of the people will be left, none of that crowd—no wealth, nothing of value. ¹²The time has come, the day has arrived. Let not the buyer rejoice nor the seller grieve, for wrath is upon the whole crowd. ¹³The seller will not recover the land he has sold as long as both of them live, for the vision concerning the whole crowd will not be reversed. Because of their sins, not one of them will preserve his life. ¹⁴Though they blow the trumpet and get everything ready, no one will go into battle, for my wrath is upon the whole crowd.

¹⁵"Outside is the sword, inside are plague and famine; those in the country will die by the sword, and those in the city will be devoured by famine and plague. ¹⁶All who survive and escape will be in the mountains, moaning like doves of the valleys, each because of his sins. ¹⁷Every hand will go limp, and every knee will become as weak as water. ¹⁸They will put on sackcloth and be clothed with terror. Their faces will be covered with shame and their heads will be shaved. ¹⁹They will throw their silver into the streets, and their gold will be an unclean thing. Their silver and gold will not be able to save them in the day of the LORD's wrath. They will not satisfy their hunger or fill their stomachs with it, for it has made them stumble into sin. ²⁰They were proud of their beautiful jewelry and used it to make their detestable idols and vile images. Therefore I will turn these into an unclean thing for them. ²¹I will hand it all over as plunder to foreigners and as loot to the wicked of the earth, and they will defile it. ²²I will turn my face away from them, and they will desecrate my treasured place; robbers will enter it and desecrate it.

²³"Prepare chains, because the land is full of bloodshed and the city is full of violence. ²⁴I will bring the most wicked of the nations to take possession of their houses; I will put an end to the pride of the mighty, and their sanctuaries will be desecrated. ²⁵When terror comes, they will seek peace, but there will be none. ²⁶Calamity upon calamity will come, and rumor upon rumor. They will try to get a vision from the prophet; the teaching of the law by the priest will be lost, as will the counsel of the elders. ²⁷The king will mourn, the prince will be clothed with despair, and the hands of the people of the land will tremble. I will deal with them according to their conduct, and by their own standards I will judge them. Then they will know that I am the LORD."

Idolatry in the Temple

8 In the sixth year, in the sixth month on the fifth day, while I was sitting in my house and the elders of Judah were sitting before me, the hand of the Sovereign LORD came upon me there. ²I looked, and I saw a figure like that of a man.*b* From what appeared to be his waist down he was like fire, and from there up his appearance was as bright as glowing metal. ³He stretched out what looked like a hand and took me by the hair of my head. The Spirit lifted me up between earth and heaven and in visions of God he took me to Jerusalem, to the entrance to the north gate of the inner court, where the idol that provokes to jealousy stood. ⁴And there before me was the glory of the God of Israel, as in the vision I had seen in the plain.

⁵Then he said to me, "Son of man, look toward the north." So I looked, and in the entrance north of the gate of the altar I saw this idol of jealousy.

⁶And he said to me, "Son of man, do you see what they are doing—the utterly detestable things the house of Israel is doing here, things that will drive me far from my sanctuary? But you will see things that are even more detestable."

⁷Then he brought me to the entrance to the court. I looked, and I saw a hole in the wall. ⁸He said to me, "Son of man, now dig into the wall." So I dug into the wall and saw a doorway there.

⁹And he said to me, "Go in and see the wicked and detestable things they are doing here." ¹⁰So I went in and looked, and

---

*a*11 Or *The violent one has become*   *b*2 Or *saw a fiery figure*

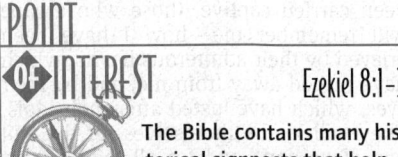

POINT OF INTEREST

Ezekiel 8:1-3

The Bible contains many historical signposts that help us tie it to the time in which it was written. This event took place in Ezekiel's home in Babylon near the Kebar River in 592 B.C.

I saw portrayed all over the walls all kinds of crawling things and detestable animals and all the idols of the house of Israel. ¹¹In front of them stood seventy elders of the house of Israel, and Jaazaniah son of Shaphan was standing among them. Each had a censer in his hand, and a fragrant cloud of incense was rising.

¹²He said to me, "Son of man, have you seen what the elders of the house of Israel are doing in the darkness, each at the shrine of his own idol? They say, 'The LORD does not see us; the LORD has forsaken the land.' " ¹³Again, he said, "You will see them doing things that are even more detestable."

¹⁴Then he brought me to the entrance to the north gate of the house of the LORD, and I saw women sitting there, mourning for Tammuz. ¹⁵He said to me, "Do you see this, son of man? You will see things that are even more detestable than this."

¹⁶He then brought me into the inner court of the house of the LORD, and there at the entrance to the temple, between the portico and the altar, were about twenty-five men. With their backs toward the temple of the LORD and their faces toward the east, they were bowing down to the sun in the east.

¹⁷He said to me, "Have you seen this, son of man? Is it a trivial matter for the house of Judah to do the detestable things they are doing here? Must they also fill the land with violence and continually provoke me to anger? Look at them putting the branch to their nose! ¹⁸Therefore I will deal with them in anger; I will not look on them with pity or spare them. Although they shout in my ears, I will not listen to them."

Idolaters Killed

9 Then I heard him call out in a loud voice, "Bring the guards of the city here, each with a weapon in his hand." ²And I saw six men coming from the direction of the upper gate, which faces north, each with a deadly weapon in his hand. With them was a man clothed in linen who had a writing kit at his side. They came in and stood beside the bronze altar.

³Now the glory of the God of Israel went up from above the cherubim, where it had been, and moved to the threshold of the temple. Then the LORD called to the man clothed in linen who had the writing kit at his side ⁴and said to him, "Go

throughout the city of Jerusalem and put a mark on the foreheads of those who grieve and lament over all the detestable things that are done in it."

⁵As I listened, he said to the others, "Follow him through the city and kill, without showing pity or compassion. ⁶Slaughter old men, young men and maidens, women and children, but do not touch anyone who has the mark. Begin at my sanctuary." So they began with the elders who were in front of the temple.

⁷Then he said to them, "Defile the temple and fill the courts with the slain. Go!" So they went out and began killing throughout the city. ⁸While they were killing and I was left alone, I fell facedown, crying out, "Ah, Sovereign LORD! Are you going to destroy the entire remnant of Israel in this outpouring of your wrath on Jerusalem?"

⁹He answered me, "The sin of the house of Israel and Judah is exceedingly great; the land is full of bloodshed and the city is full of injustice. They say, 'The LORD has forsaken the land; the LORD does not see.' ¹⁰So I will not look on them with pity or spare them, but I will bring down on their own heads what they have done."

¹¹Then the man in linen with the writing kit at his side brought back word, saying, "I have done as you commanded."

The Glory Departs From the Temple

10 I looked, and I saw the likeness of a throne of sapphire^a above the expanse that was over the heads of the cherubim. ²The LORD said to the man clothed in linen, "Go in among the wheels beneath the cherubim. Fill your hands with burning coals from among the cherubim and scatter them over the city." And as I watched, he went in.

³Now the cherubim were standing on the south side of the temple when the man went in, and a cloud filled the inner court. ⁴Then the glory of the LORD rose from above the cherubim and moved to the threshold of the temple. The cloud filled the temple, and the court was full of the radiance of the glory of the LORD. ⁵The sound of the wings of the cherubim could be heard as far away as the outer court, like the voice of God Almighty^b when he speaks.

a1 Or *lapis lazuli*   *b5* Hebrew *El-Shaddai*

⁶When the Lord commanded the man in linen, "Take fire from among the wheels, from among the cherubim," the man went in and stood beside a wheel. ⁷Then one of the cherubim reached out his hand to the fire that was among them. He took up some of it and put it into the hands of the man in linen, who took it and went out. ⁸(Under the wings of the cherubim could be seen what looked like the hands of a man.)

⁹I looked, and I saw beside the cherubim four wheels, one beside each of the cherubim; the wheels sparkled like chrysolite. ¹⁰As for their appearance, the four of them looked alike; each was like a wheel intersecting a wheel. ¹¹As they moved, they would go in any one of the four directions the cherubim faced; the wheels did not turn about[a] as the cherubim went. The cherubim went in whatever direction the head faced, without turning as they went. ¹²Their entire bodies, including their backs, their hands and their wings, were completely full of eyes, as were their four wheels. ¹³I heard the wheels being called "the whirling wheels." ¹⁴Each of the cherubim had four faces: One face was that of a cherub, the second the face of a man, the third the face of a lion, and the fourth the face of an eagle.

¹⁵Then the cherubim rose upward. These were the living creatures I had seen by the Kebar River. ¹⁶When the cherubim moved, the wheels beside them moved; and when the cherubim spread their wings to rise from the ground, the wheels did not leave their side. ¹⁷When the cherubim stood still, they also stood still; and when the cherubim rose, they rose with them, because the spirit of the living creatures was in them.

¹⁸Then the glory of the Lord departed from over the threshold of the temple and stopped above the cherubim. ¹⁹While I watched, the cherubim spread their wings and rose from the ground, and as they went, the wheels went with them. They stopped at the entrance to the east gate of the Lord's house, and the glory of the God of Israel was above them.

²⁰These were the living creatures I had seen beneath the God of Israel by the Kebar River, and I realized that they were cherubim. ²¹Each had four faces and four wings, and under their wings was what looked like the hands of a man. ²²Their faces had the same appearance as those I had seen by the Kebar River. Each one went straight ahead.

Judgment on Israel's Leaders

11 Then the Spirit lifted me up and brought me to the gate of the house of the Lord that faces east. There at the entrance to the gate were twenty-five men, and I saw among them Jaazaniah son of Azzur and Pelatiah son of Benaiah, leaders of the people. ²The Lord said to me, "Son of man, these are the men who are plotting evil and giving wicked advice in this city. ³They say, 'Will it not soon be time to build houses?[b] This city is a cooking pot, and we are the meat.' ⁴Therefore prophesy against them; prophesy, son of man."

⁵Then the Spirit of the Lord came upon me, and he told me to say: "This is what the Lord says: That is what you are saying, O house of Israel, but I know what is going through your mind. ⁶You have killed many people in this city and filled its streets with the dead.

⁷"Therefore this is what the Sovereign Lord says: The bodies you have thrown there are the meat and this city is the pot, but I will drive you out of it. ⁸You fear the sword, and the sword is what I will bring against you, declares the Sovereign Lord. ⁹I will drive you out of the city and hand you over to foreigners and inflict punishment on you. ¹⁰You will fall by the sword, and I will execute judgment on you at the borders of Israel. Then you will know that I am the Lord. ¹¹This city will not be a pot for you, nor will you be the meat in it; I will execute judgment on you at the borders of Israel. ¹²And you will know that I am the Lord, for you have not followed my decrees or kept my laws but have conformed to the standards of the nations around you."

¹³Now as I was prophesying, Pelatiah son of Benaiah died. Then I fell facedown and cried out in a loud voice, "Ah, Sovereign Lord! Will you completely destroy the remnant of Israel?"

¹⁴The word of the Lord came to me: ¹⁵"Son of man, your brothers—your brothers who are your blood relatives[c] and the whole house of Israel—are those of whom the people of Jerusalem have

---

a 11 Or *aside*   *b 3* Or *This is not the time to build houses.*   *c 15* Or *are in exile with you* (see Septuagint and Syriac) said, 'They are[a] far away from the LORD; this land was given to us as our possession.'

Promised Return of Israel

16"Therefore say: 'This is what the Sovereign LORD says: Although I sent them far away among the nations and scattered them among the countries, yet for a little while I have been a sanctuary for them in the countries where they have gone.'

17"Therefore say: 'This is what the Sovereign LORD says: I will gather you

from the nations and bring you back from the countries where you have been scattered, and I will give you back the land of Israel again.'

18"They will return to it and remove all its vile images and detestable idols. 19I will give them an undivided heart and put a new spirit in them; I will remove from them their heart of stone and give them a heart of flesh. 20Then they will follow my decrees and be careful to keep

[a] 15 Or those to whom the people of Jerusalem have said, 'Stay

---

Read Ezekiel 11:1–25
Key Verse Ezekiel 11:12

Salamander Faith – Steve Draper

When I was a kid, visiting my grandmother's home in New Hampshire, summer rain showers always signaled the beginning of the hunt. Armed only with glass jars with holey lids, we would search the sides of Grandma's meandering driveway for salamanders. They were hard to find because they blended so well with their environment.

I don't know about you, but I sometimes exhibit that trait too. At times I feel like I have "salamander faith"—I tend to adapt what I believe to fit the people around me; I hate to be different. Standing up for my convictions when it seems everyone else is sitting down takes courage!

That's exactly what God asked Ezekiel to do in this passage. He had to stand in front of twenty-five influential leaders and prophesy God's judgment on them (see Ezekiel 11:1–5). In the New Testament, Peter learned through failure about speaking up courageously for Jesus Christ. Because he was afraid to admit knowing Jesus, he disowned Jesus three times and found that the pain of disowning Jesus was worse than that fear. Jesus later confronted him about his behavior and asked Peter to recommit himself three times, a strategy that allowed him to regain a confidence grounded in Jesus himself and not just in his own weak will (see John 21). Peter became a strong and unwavering spokesman for the early church, as he faced opposition from both Roman and Jewish leadership.

These men, along with other Biblical and contemporary figures, inspire me to turn from my "salamander faith," and instead to "stand firm and hold to the teachings . . . passed on to [me]" (2 Thessalonians 2:15). My hope is in this: that Jesus Christ himself will encourage my heart and strengthen me in every good deed and word (see 2 Thessalonians 2:16–17).

A Deeper Look
Romans 12:2; 1 Peter 1:13–16

Go to page 935 for your next devotional reading.

my laws. They will be my people, and I will be their God. ²¹But as for those whose hearts are devoted to their vile images and detestable idols, I will bring down on their own heads what they have done, declares the Sovereign LORD."

²²Then the cherubim, with the wheels beside them, spread their wings, and the glory of the God of Israel was above them. ²³The glory of the LORD went up from within the city and stopped above the mountain east of it. ²⁴The Spirit lifted me up and brought me to the exiles in Babylonia*a* in the vision given by the Spirit of God.

Then the vision I had seen went up from me, ²⁵and I told the exiles everything the LORD had shown me.

The Exile Symbolized

12 The word of the LORD came to me: ²"Son of man, you are living among a rebellious people. They have eyes to see but do not see and ears to hear but do not hear, for they are a rebellious people.

³"Therefore, son of man, pack your belongings for exile and in the daytime, as they watch, set out and go from where you are to another place. Perhaps they will understand, though they are a rebellious house. ⁴During the daytime, while they watch, bring out your belongings packed for exile. Then in the evening, while they are watching, go out like those who go into exile. ⁵While they watch, dig through the wall and take your belongings out through it. ⁶Put them on your shoulder as they are watching and carry them out at dusk. Cover your face so that you cannot see the land, for I have made you a sign to the house of Israel."

⁷So I did as I was commanded. During the day I brought out my things packed for exile. Then in the evening I dug through the wall with my hands. I took my belongings out at dusk, carrying them on my shoulders while they watched.

⁸In the morning the word of the LORD came to me: ⁹"Son of man, did not that rebellious house of Israel ask you, 'What are you doing?'

¹⁰"Say to them, 'This is what the Sovereign LORD says: This oracle concerns the prince in Jerusalem and the whole house of Israel who are there.' ¹¹Say to them, 'I am a sign to you.'

"As I have done, so it will be done to them. They will go into exile as captives.

¹²"The prince among them will put his things on his shoulder at dusk and leave, and a hole will be dug in the wall for him to go through. He will cover his face so that he cannot see the land. ¹³I will spread my net for him, and he will be caught in my snare; I will bring him to Babylonia, the land of the Chaldeans, but he will not see it, and there he will die. ¹⁴I will scatter to the winds all those around him—his staff and all his troops—and I will pursue them with drawn sword.

¹⁵"They will know that I am the LORD, when I disperse them among the nations and scatter them through the countries. ¹⁶But I will spare a few of them from the sword, famine and plague, so that in the nations where they go they may acknowledge all their detestable practices. Then they will know that I am the LORD."

¹⁷The word of the LORD came to me: ¹⁸"Son of man, tremble as you eat your food, and shudder in fear as you drink your water. ¹⁹Say to the people of the land: 'This is what the Sovereign LORD says about those living in Jerusalem and in the land of Israel: They will eat their food in anxiety and drink their water in despair, for their land will be stripped of everything in it because of the violence of all who live there. ²⁰The inhabited towns will be laid waste and the land will be desolate. Then you will know that I am the LORD.' "

²¹The word of the LORD came to me: ²²"Son of man, what is this proverb you have in the land of Israel: 'The days go by and every vision comes to nothing'? ²³Say to them, 'This is what the Sovereign LORD says: I am going to put an end to this proverb, and they will no longer quote it in Israel.' Say to them, 'The days are near when every vision will be fulfilled. ²⁴For there will be no more false visions or flattering divinations among the people of Israel. ²⁵But I the LORD will speak what I will, and it shall be fulfilled without delay. For in your days, you rebellious house, I will fulfill whatever I say, declares the Sovereign LORD.' "

²⁶The word of the LORD came to me: ²⁷"Son of man, the house of Israel is saying, 'The vision he sees is for many years from now, and he prophesies about the distant future.'

²⁸"Therefore say to them, 'This is what the Sovereign LORD says: None of my words will be delayed any longer;

a24 Or *Chaldea*

whatever I say will be fulfilled, declares the Sovereign LORD.' "

False Prophets Condemned

13 The word of the LORD came to me: ²"Son of man, prophesy against the prophets of Israel who are now prophesying. Say to those who prophesy out of their own imagination: 'Hear the word of the LORD! ³This is what the Sovereign LORD says: Woe to the foolish*a* prophets who follow their own spirit and have seen nothing! ⁴Your prophets, O Israel, are like jackals among ruins. ⁵You have not gone up to the breaks in the wall to repair it for the house of Israel so that it will stand firm in the battle on the day of the LORD. ⁶Their visions are false and their divinations a lie. They say, "The LORD declares," when the LORD has not sent them; yet they expect their words to be fulfilled. ⁷Have you not seen false visions and uttered lying divinations when you say, "The LORD declares," though I have not spoken?

⁸" 'Therefore this is what the Sovereign LORD says: Because of your false words and lying visions, I am against you, declares the Sovereign LORD. ⁹My hand will be against the prophets who see false visions and utter lying divinations. They will not belong to the council of my people or be listed in the records of the house of Israel, nor will they enter the land of Israel. Then you will know that I am the Sovereign LORD.

¹⁰" 'Because they lead my people astray, saying, "Peace," when there is no peace, and because, when a flimsy wall is built, they cover it with whitewash, ¹¹therefore tell those who cover it with whitewash that it is going to fall. Rain will come in torrents, and I will send hailstones hurtling down, and violent winds will burst forth. ¹²When the wall collapses, will people not ask you, "Where is the whitewash you covered it with?"

¹³" 'Therefore this is what the Sovereign LORD says: In my wrath I will unleash a violent wind, and in my anger hailstones and torrents of rain will fall with destructive fury. ¹⁴I will tear down the wall you have covered with whitewash and will level it to the ground so that its foundation will be laid bare. When it*b* falls, you will be destroyed in it; and you will know that I am the LORD. ¹⁵So I will spend my wrath against the wall and against those who covered it with white-

wash. I will say to you, "The wall is gone and so are those who whitewashed it, ¹⁶those prophets of Israel who prophesied to Jerusalem and saw visions of peace for her when there was no peace, declares the Sovereign LORD." '

¹⁷"Now, son of man, set your face against the daughters of your people who prophesy out of their own imagination. Prophesy against them ¹⁸and say, 'This is what the Sovereign LORD says: Woe to the women who sew magic charms on all their wrists and make veils of various lengths for their heads in order to ensnare people. Will you ensnare the lives of my people but preserve your own? ¹⁹You have profaned me among my people for a few handfuls of barley and scraps of bread. By lying to my people, who listen to lies, you have killed those who should not have died and have spared those who should not live.

²⁰" 'Therefore this is what the Sovereign LORD says: I am against your magic charms with which you ensnare people like birds and I will tear them from your arms; I will set free the people that you ensnare like birds. ²¹I will tear off your veils and save my people from your hands, and they will no longer fall prey to your power. Then you will know that I am the LORD. ²²Because you disheartened the righteous with your lies, when I had brought them no grief, and because you encouraged the wicked not to turn from their evil ways and so save their lives, ²³therefore you will no longer see false visions or practice divination. I will save my people from your hands. And then you will know that I am the LORD.' "

Idolaters Condemned

14 Some of the elders of Israel came to me and sat down in front of me. ²Then the word of the LORD came to me: ³"Son of man, these men have set up idols in their hearts and put wicked stumbling blocks before their faces. Should I let them inquire of me at all? ⁴Therefore speak to them and tell them, 'This is what the Sovereign LORD says: When any Israelite sets up idols in his heart and puts a wicked stumbling block before his face and then goes to a prophet, I the LORD will answer him myself in keeping with his great idolatry. ⁵I will do this to recapture the hearts of the people of Isra-

*a*3 Or *wicked*   *b*14 Or *the city*

el, who have all deserted me for their idols.'

6"Therefore say to the house of Israel, 'This is what the Sovereign LORD says: Repent! Turn from your idols and renounce all your detestable practices!

7" 'When any Israelite or any alien living in Israel separates himself from me and sets up idols in his heart and puts a wicked stumbling block before his face and then goes to a prophet to inquire of me, I the LORD will answer him myself. 8I will set my face against that man and make him an example and a byword. I will cut him off from my people. Then you will know that I am the LORD.

9" 'And if the prophet is enticed to utter a prophecy, I the LORD have enticed that prophet, and I will stretch out my hand against him and destroy him from among my people Israel. 10They will bear their guilt—the prophet will be as guilty as the one who consults him. 11Then the people of Israel will no longer stray from me, nor will they defile themselves anymore with all their sins. They will be my people, and I will be their God, declares the Sovereign LORD.' "

Judgment Inescapable

12The word of the LORD came to me: 13"Son of man, if a country sins against me by being unfaithful and I stretch out my hand against it to cut off its food supply and send famine upon it and kill its men and their animals, 14even if these three men—Noah, Daniel[a] and Job—were in it, they could save only themselves by their righteousness, declares the Sovereign LORD.

15"Or if I send wild beasts through that country and they leave it childless and it becomes desolate so that no one can pass through it because of the beasts, 16as surely as I live, declares the Sovereign LORD, even if these three men were in it, they could not save their own sons or daughters. They alone would be saved, but the land would be desolate.

17"Or if I bring a sword against that country and say, 'Let the sword pass throughout the land,' and I kill its men and their animals, 18as surely as I live, declares the Sovereign LORD, even if these three men were in it, they could not save their own sons or daughters. They alone would be saved.

19"Or if I send a plague into that land and pour out my wrath upon it through bloodshed, killing its men and their animals, 20as surely as I live, declares the Sovereign LORD, even if Noah, Daniel and Job were in it, they could save neither son nor daughter. They would save only themselves by their righteousness.

21"For this is what the Sovereign LORD says: How much worse will it be when I send against Jerusalem my four dreadful judgments—sword and famine and wild beasts and plague—to kill its men and their animals! 22Yet there will be some survivors—sons and daughters who will be brought out of it. They will come to you, and when you see their conduct and their actions, you will be consoled regarding the disaster I have brought upon Jerusalem—every disaster I have brought upon it. 23You will be consoled when you see their conduct and their actions, for you will know that I have done nothing in it without cause, declares the Sovereign LORD."

Jerusalem, A Useless Vine

15 The word of the LORD came to me: 2"Son of man, how is the wood of a vine better than that of a branch on any of the trees in the forest? 3Is wood ever taken from it to make anything useful? Do they make pegs from it to hang things on? 4And after it is thrown on the fire as fuel and the fire burns both ends and chars the middle, is it then useful for anything? 5If it was not useful for anything when it was whole, how much less can it be made into something useful when the fire has burned it and it is charred?

a14 Or *Danel*; the Hebrew spelling may suggest a person other than the prophet Daniel; also in verse 20.

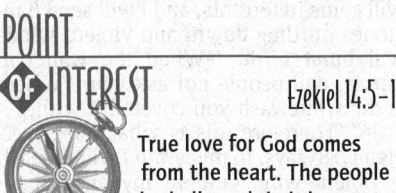

POINT OF INTEREST   Ezekiel 14:5–11

True love for God comes from the heart. The people had allowed their hearts to be captured by Babylonian idolatry. God declared in this passage that if they loved him wholeheartedly there would be no room in their hearts for idols. God wanted from them what he wants from us: hearts that turn away from sin and toward him in repentance and love.

6"Therefore this is what the Sovereign LORD says: As I have given the wood of the vine among the trees of the forest as fuel for the fire, so will I treat the people living in Jerusalem. 7I will set my face against them. Although they have come out of the fire, the fire will yet consume them. And when I set my face against them, you will know that I am the LORD. 8I will make the land desolate because they have been unfaithful, declares the Sovereign LORD."

An Allegory of Unfaithful Jerusalem

16 The word of the LORD came to me: 2"Son of man, confront Jerusalem with her detestable practices 3and say, 'This is what the Sovereign LORD says to Jerusalem: Your ancestry and birth were in the land of the Canaanites; your father was an Amorite and your mother a Hittite. 4On the day you were born your cord was not cut, nor were you washed with water to make you clean, nor were you rubbed with salt or wrapped in cloths. 5No one looked on you with pity or had compassion enough to do any of these things for you. Rather, you were thrown out into the open field, for on the day you were born you were despised.

6" 'Then I passed by and saw you kicking about in your blood, and as you lay there in your blood I said to you, "Live!"a 7I made you grow like a plant of the field. You grew up and developed and became the most beautiful of jewels.b Your breasts were formed and your hair grew, you who were naked and bare.

8" 'Later I passed by, and when I looked at you and saw that you were old enough for love, I spread the corner of my garment over you and covered your nakedness. I gave you my solemn oath and entered into a covenant with you, declares the Sovereign LORD, and you became mine.

9" 'I bathedc you with water and washed the blood from you and put ointments on you. 10I clothed you with an embroidered dress and put leather sandals on you. I dressed you in fine linen and covered you with costly garments. 11I adorned you with jewelry: I put bracelets on your arms and a necklace around your neck, 12and I put a ring on your nose, earrings on your ears and a beautiful crown on your head. 13So you were adorned with gold and silver; your clothes were of fine linen and costly fab-

ric and embroidered cloth. Your food was fine flour, honey and olive oil. You became very beautiful and rose to be a queen. 14And your fame spread among the nations on account of your beauty, because the splendor I had given you made your beauty perfect, declares the Sovereign LORD.

15" 'But you trusted in your beauty and used your fame to become a prostitute. You lavished your favors on anyone who passed by and your beauty became his.d 16You took some of your garments to make gaudy high places, where you carried on your prostitution. Such things should not happen, nor should they ever occur. 17You also took the fine jewelry I gave you, the jewelry made of my gold and silver, and you made for yourself male idols and engaged in prostitution with them. 18And you took your embroidered clothes to put on them, and you offered my oil and incense before them. 19Also the food I provided for you—the fine flour, olive oil and honey I gave you to eat—you offered as fragrant incense before them. That is what happened, declares the Sovereign LORD.

20" 'And you took your sons and daughters whom you bore to me and sacrificed them as food to the idols. Was your prostitution not enough? 21You slaughtered my children and sacrificed theme to the idols. 22In all your detestable practices and your prostitution you did not remember the days of your youth, when you were naked and bare, kicking about in your blood.

23" 'Woe! Woe to you, declares the Sovereign LORD. In addition to all your other wickedness, 24you built a mound for yourself and made a lofty shrine in every public square. 25At the head of every street you built your lofty shrines and degraded your beauty, offering your body with increasing promiscuity to anyone who passed by. 26You engaged in prostitution with the Egyptians, your lustful neighbors, and provoked me to anger with your increasing promiscuity. 27So I stretched out my hand against you and reduced your territory; I gave you over to

---

a6 A few Hebrew manuscripts, Septuagint and Syriac; most Hebrew manuscripts "Live!" And as you lay there in your blood I said to you, "Live!"
b7 Or became mature　c9 Or I had bathed
d15 Most Hebrew manuscripts; one Hebrew manuscript (see some Septuagint manuscripts) by. Such a thing should not happen　e21 Or and made them pass through ˌthe fireˌ

the greed of your enemies, the daughters of the Philistines, who were shocked by your lewd conduct. ²⁸You engaged in prostitution with the Assyrians too, because you were insatiable; and even after that, you still were not satisfied. ²⁹Then you increased your promiscuity to include Babylonia,*a* a land of merchants, but even with this you were not satisfied.

³⁰" 'How weak-willed you are, declares the Sovereign Lord, when you do all these things, acting like a brazen prostitute! ³¹When you built your mounds at the head of every street and made your lofty shrines in every public square, you were unlike a prostitute, because you scorned payment.

³²" 'You adulterous wife! You prefer strangers to your own husband! ³³Every prostitute receives a fee, but you give gifts to all your lovers, bribing them to come to you from everywhere for your illicit favors. ³⁴So in your prostitution you are the opposite of others; no one runs after you for your favors. You are the very opposite, for you give payment and none is given to you.

³⁵" 'Therefore, you prostitute, hear the word of the Lord! ³⁶This is what the Sovereign Lord says: Because you poured out your wealth*b* and exposed your nakedness in your promiscuity with your lovers, and because of all your detestable idols, and because you gave them your children's blood, ³⁷therefore I am going to gather all your lovers, with whom you found pleasure, those you loved as well as those you hated. I will gather them against you from all around and will strip you in front of them, and they will see all your nakedness. ³⁸I will sentence you to the punishment of women who commit adultery and who shed blood; I will bring upon you the blood vengeance of my wrath and jealous anger. ³⁹Then I will hand you over to your lovers, and they will tear down your mounds and destroy your lofty shrines. They will strip you of your clothes and take your fine jewelry and leave you naked and bare. ⁴⁰They will bring a mob against you, who will stone you and hack you to pieces with their swords. ⁴¹They will burn down your houses and inflict punishment on you in the sight of many women. I will put a stop to your prostitution, and you will no longer pay your lovers. ⁴²Then my wrath against you will subside and my jealous

anger will turn away from you; I will be calm and no longer angry.

⁴³" 'Because you did not remember the days of your youth but enraged me with all these things, I will surely bring down on your head what you have done, declares the Sovereign Lord. Did you not add lewdness to all your other detestable practices?

⁴⁴" 'Everyone who quotes proverbs will quote this proverb about you: "Like mother, like daughter." ⁴⁵You are a true daughter of your mother, who despised her husband and her children; and you are a true sister of your sisters, who despised their husbands and their children. Your mother was a Hittite and your father an Amorite. ⁴⁶Your older sister was Samaria, who lived to the north of you with her daughters; and your younger sister, who lived to the south of you with her daughters, was Sodom. ⁴⁷You not only walked in their ways and copied their detestable practices, but in all your ways you soon became more depraved than they. ⁴⁸As surely as I live, declares the Sovereign Lord, your sister Sodom and her daughters never did what you and your daughters have done.

⁴⁹" 'Now this was the sin of your sister Sodom: She and her daughters were arrogant, overfed and unconcerned; they did not help the poor and needy. ⁵⁰They were haughty and did detestable things before me. Therefore I did away with them as you have seen. ⁵¹Samaria did not commit half the sins you did. You have done more detestable things than they, and have made your sisters seem righteous by all these things you have done. ⁵²Bear your disgrace, for you have furnished some justification for your sisters. Because your sins were more vile than theirs, they appear more righteous than you. So then, be ashamed and bear your disgrace, for you have made your sisters appear righteous.

⁵³" 'However, I will restore the fortunes of Sodom and her daughters and of Samaria and her daughters, and your fortunes along with them, ⁵⁴so that you may bear your disgrace and be ashamed of all you have done in giving them comfort. ⁵⁵And your sisters, Sodom with her daughters and Samaria with her daughters, will return to what they were before; and you and your daughters will return

a29 Or *Chaldea*   *b36* Or *lust*

to what you were before. ⁵⁶You would not even mention your sister Sodom in the day of your pride, ⁵⁷before your wickedness was uncovered. Even so, you are now scorned by the daughters of Edom*ᵃ* and all her neighbors and the daughters of the Philistines—all those around you who despise you. ⁵⁸You will bear the consequences of your lewdness and your detestable practices, declares the LORD.

⁵⁹" 'This is what the Sovereign LORD says: I will deal with you as you deserve, because you have despised my oath by breaking the covenant. ⁶⁰Yet I will remember the covenant I made with you in the days of your youth, and I will establish an everlasting covenant with you. ⁶¹Then you will remember your ways and be ashamed when you receive your sisters, both those who are older than you and those who are younger. I will give them to you as daughters, but not on the basis of my covenant with you. ⁶²So I will establish my covenant with you, and you will know that I am the LORD. ⁶³Then, when I make atonement for you for all you have done, you will remember and be ashamed and never again open your mouth because of your humiliation, declares the Sovereign LORD.' "

Two Eagles and a Vine

17 The word of the LORD came to me: ²"Son of man, set forth an allegory and tell the house of Israel a parable. ³Say to them, 'This is what the Sovereign LORD says: A great eagle with powerful wings, long feathers and full plumage of varied colors came to Lebanon. Taking hold of the top of a cedar, ⁴he broke off its topmost shoot and carried it away to a land of merchants, where he planted it in a city of traders.

⁵" 'He took some of the seed of your land and put it in fertile soil. He planted it like a willow by abundant water, ⁶and it sprouted and became a low, spreading vine. Its branches turned toward him, but its roots remained under it. So it became a vine and produced branches and put out leafy boughs.

⁷" 'But there was another great eagle with powerful wings and full plumage. The vine now sent out its roots toward him from the plot where it was planted and stretched out its branches to him for water. ⁸It had been planted in good soil by abundant water so that it would pro-

duce branches, bear fruit and become a splendid vine.'

⁹"Say to them, 'This is what the Sovereign LORD says: Will it thrive? Will it not be uprooted and stripped of its fruit so that it withers? All its new growth will wither. It will not take a strong arm or many people to pull it up by the roots. ¹⁰Even if it is transplanted, will it thrive? Will it not wither completely when the east wind strikes it—wither away in the plot where it grew?' "

¹¹Then the word of the LORD came to me: ¹²"Say to this rebellious house, 'Do you not know what these things mean?' Say to them: 'The king of Babylon went to Jerusalem and carried off her king and her nobles, bringing them back with him to Babylon. ¹³Then he took a member of the royal family and made a treaty with him, putting him under oath. He also carried away the leading men of the land, ¹⁴so that the kingdom would be brought low, unable to rise again, surviving only by keeping his treaty. ¹⁵But the king rebelled against him by sending his envoys to Egypt to get horses and a large army. Will he succeed? Will he who does such things escape? Will he break the treaty and yet escape?

¹⁶" 'As surely as I live, declares the Sovereign LORD, he shall die in Babylon, in the land of the king who put him on the throne, whose oath he despised and whose treaty he broke. ¹⁷Pharaoh with his mighty army and great horde will be of no help to him in war, when ramps are built and siege works erected to destroy many lives. ¹⁸He despised the oath by breaking the covenant. Because he had given his hand in pledge and yet did all these things, he shall not escape.

¹⁹" 'Therefore this is what the Sovereign LORD says: As surely as I live, I will bring down on his head my oath that he despised and my covenant that he broke. ²⁰I will spread my net for him, and he will be caught in my snare. I will bring him to Babylon and execute judgment upon him there because he was unfaithful to me. ²¹All his fleeing troops will fall by the sword, and the survivors will be scattered to the winds. Then you will know that I the LORD have spoken.

²²" 'This is what the Sovereign LORD says: I myself will take a shoot from the

---

ᵃ57 Many Hebrew manuscripts and Syriac; most Hebrew manuscripts, Septuagint and Vulgate *Aram* very top of a cedar and plant it; I will break off a tender sprig from its topmost shoots and plant it on a high and lofty mountain. ²³On the mountain heights of Israel I will plant it; it will produce branches and bear fruit and become a splendid cedar. Birds of every kind will nest in it; they will find shelter in the shade of its branches. ²⁴All the trees of the field will know that I the LORD bring down the tall tree and make the low tree grow tall. I dry up the green tree and make the dry tree flourish.

" 'I the LORD have spoken, and I will do it.' "

The Soul Who Sins Will Die

18 The word of the LORD came to me: ²"What do you people mean by quoting this proverb about the land of Israel:

" 'The fathers eat sour grapes,
    and the children's teeth are set on
      edge'?

³"As surely as I live, declares the Sovereign LORD, you will no longer quote this proverb in Israel. ⁴For every living soul belongs to me, the father as well as the son—both alike belong to me. The soul who sins is the one who will die.

⁵"Suppose there is a righteous man
    who does what is just and right.
⁶He does not eat at the mountain
    shrines
    or look to the idols of the house of
      Israel.
He does not defile his neighbor's wife
    or lie with a woman during her
      period.
⁷He does not oppress anyone,
    but returns what he took in pledge
      for a loan.
He does not commit robbery
    but gives his food to the hungry
    and provides clothing for the
      naked.
⁸He does not lend at usury
    or take excessive interest.^a
He withholds his hand from doing
    wrong
    and judges fairly between man and
      man.
⁹He follows my decrees
    and faithfully keeps my laws.
That man is righteous;
    he will surely live,
        declares the Sovereign LORD.

¹⁰"Suppose he has a violent son, who

sheds blood or does any of these other things^b ¹¹(though the father has done none of them):

"He eats at the mountain shrines.
He defiles his neighbor's wife.
¹²He oppresses the poor and needy.
He commits robbery.
He does not return what he took in
    pledge.
He looks to the idols.
He does detestable things.
¹³He lends at usury and takes excessive
    interest.

Will such a man live? He will not! Because he has done all these detestable things, he will surely be put to death and his blood will be on his own head.

¹⁴"But suppose this son has a son who sees all the sins his father commits, and though he sees them, he does not do such things:

¹⁵"He does not eat at the mountain
    shrines
    or look to the idols of the house of
      Israel.
He does not defile his neighbor's
    wife.
¹⁶He does not oppress anyone
    or require a pledge for a loan.
He does not commit robbery
    but gives his food to the hungry
    and provides clothing for the
      naked.
¹⁷He withholds his hand from sin^c
    and takes no usury or excessive
      interest.
He keeps my laws and follows my
    decrees.

He will not die for his father's sin; he will surely live. ¹⁸But his father will die for his own sin, because he practiced extortion, robbed his brother and did what was wrong among his people.

¹⁹"Yet you ask, 'Why does the son not share the guilt of his father?' Since the son has done what is just and right and has been careful to keep all my decrees, he will surely live. ²⁰The soul who sins is the one who will die. The son will not share the guilt of the father, nor will the father share the guilt of the son. The righteousness of the righteous man will be credited to him, and the wickedness of

^a8 Or take interest; similarly in verses 13 and 17
^b10 Or things to a brother   ^c17 Septuagint (see also verse 8); Hebrew from the poor

the wicked will be charged against him.

²¹"But if a wicked man turns away from all the sins he has committed and keeps all my decrees and does what is just and right, he will surely live; he will not die. ²²None of the offenses he has committed will be remembered against him. Because of the righteous things he has done, he will live. ²³Do I take any pleasure in the death of the wicked? declares the Sovereign LORD. Rather, am I not pleased when they turn from their ways and live?

²⁴"But if a righteous man turns from his righteousness and commits sin and does the same detestable things the wicked man does, will he live? None of the righteous things he has done will be remembered. Because of the unfaithfulness he is guilty of and because of the sins he has committed, he will die.

²⁵"Yet you say, 'The way of the Lord is not just.' Hear, O house of Israel: Is my way unjust? Is it not your ways that are unjust? ²⁶If a righteous man turns from his righteousness and commits sin, he will die for it; because of the sin he has committed he will die. ²⁷But if a wicked man turns away from the wickedness he has committed and does what is just and right, he will save his life. ²⁸Because he considers all the offenses he has committed and turns away from them, he will surely live; he will not die. ²⁹Yet the house of Israel says, 'The way of the Lord is not just.' Are my ways unjust, O house of Israel? Is it not your ways that are unjust?

³⁰"Therefore, O house of Israel, I will judge you, each one according to his ways, declares the Sovereign LORD. Repent! Turn away from all your offenses; then sin will not be your downfall. ³¹Rid yourselves of all the offenses you have committed, and get a new heart and a new spirit. Why will you die, O house of Israel? ³²For I take no pleasure in the death of anyone, declares the Sovereign LORD. Repent and live!

A Lament for Israel's Princes

19 "Take up a lament concerning the princes of Israel ²and say:

" 'What a lioness was your mother
    among the lions!
She lay down among the young lions
    and reared her cubs.
³She brought up one of her cubs,

and he became a strong lion.
He learned to tear the prey
    and he devoured men.
⁴The nations heard about him,
    and he was trapped in their pit.
They led him with hooks
    to the land of Egypt.

⁵" 'When she saw her hope
        unfulfilled,
    her expectation gone,
she took another of her cubs
    and made him a strong lion.
⁶He prowled among the lions,
    for he was now a strong lion.
He learned to tear the prey
    and he devoured men.
⁷He broke down[a] their strongholds
    and devastated their towns.
The land and all who were in it
    were terrified by his roaring.
⁸Then the nations came against him,
    those from regions round about.
They spread their net for him,
    and he was trapped in their pit.
⁹With hooks they pulled him into a
        cage
    and brought him to the king of
        Babylon.
They put him in prison,
    so his roar was heard no longer
    on the mountains of Israel.

¹⁰" 'Your mother was like a vine in
        your vineyard[b]
    planted by the water;
it was fruitful and full of branches
    because of abundant water.
¹¹Its branches were strong,

---

[a]7 Targum (see Septuagint); Hebrew *He knew*
[b]10 Two Hebrew manuscripts; most Hebrew manuscripts *your blood*

POINT OF INTEREST

Ezekiel 18:31-32

When we read through the Old Testament, we may get the impression that God is judging, stern and exacting. These verses show the softer side of God's heart: He is gracious and loving, and he offers life and love to everyone who comes to him. He offered a new heart and a new spirit to Israel, and he offers the same to us in Christ Jesus today! (See Acts 15:8.)

fit for a ruler's scepter.
It towered high
   above the thick foliage,
conspicuous for its height
   and for its many branches.
¹²But it was uprooted in fury
   and thrown to the ground.
The east wind made it shrivel,
   it was stripped of its fruit;
its strong branches withered
   and fire consumed them.
¹³Now it is planted in the desert,
   in a dry and thirsty land.
¹⁴Fire spread from one of its main*a*
      branches
   and consumed its fruit.
No strong branch is left on it
   fit for a ruler's scepter.'

This is a lament and is to be used as a
lament."

Rebellious Israel

20 In the seventh year, in the fifth
month on the tenth day, some of the
elders of Israel came to inquire of the
LORD, and they sat down in front of me.

²Then the word of the LORD came to
me: ³"Son of man, speak to the elders of
Israel and say to them, 'This is what the
Sovereign LORD says: Have you come to
inquire of me? As surely as I live, I will
not let you inquire of me, declares the
Sovereign LORD.'

⁴"Will you judge them? Will you judge
them, son of man? Then confront them
with the detestable practices of their fathers ⁵and say to them: 'This is what the
Sovereign LORD says: On the day I chose
Israel, I swore with uplifted hand to the
descendants of the house of Jacob and
revealed myself to them in Egypt. With
uplifted hand I said to them, "I am the
LORD your God." ⁶On that day I swore to
them that I would bring them out of
Egypt into a land I had searched out for
them, a land flowing with milk and honey, the most beautiful of all lands. ⁷And I
said to them, "Each of you, get rid of the
vile images you have set your eyes on,
and do not defile yourselves with the
idols of Egypt. I am the LORD your God."

⁸" 'But they rebelled against me and
would not listen to me; they did not get
rid of the vile images they had set their
eyes on, nor did they forsake the idols
of Egypt. So I said I would pour out my
wrath on them and spend my anger
against them in Egypt. ⁹But for the sake

of my name I did what would keep it
from being profaned in the eyes of the
nations they lived among and in whose
sight I had revealed myself to the Israelites by bringing them out of Egypt.
¹⁰Therefore I led them out of Egypt and
brought them into the desert. ¹¹I gave
them my decrees and made known
to them my laws, for the man who obeys
them will live by them. ¹²Also I gave
them my Sabbaths as a sign between us,
so they would know that I the LORD made
them holy.

¹³" 'Yet the people of Israel rebelled
against me in the desert. They did not
follow my decrees but rejected my
laws—although the man who obeys
them will live by them—and they utterly
desecrated my Sabbaths. So I said I
would pour out my wrath on them and
destroy them in the desert. ¹⁴But for the
sake of my name I did what would keep
it from being profaned in the eyes of the
nations in whose sight I had brought
them out. ¹⁵Also with uplifted hand I
swore to them in the desert that I would
not bring them into the land I had given
them—a land flowing with milk and honey, most beautiful of all lands— ¹⁶because they rejected my laws and did not
follow my decrees and desecrated my
Sabbaths. For their hearts were devoted
to their idols. ¹⁷Yet I looked on them with
pity and did not destroy them or put an
end to them in the desert. ¹⁸I said to their
children in the desert, "Do not follow the
statutes of your fathers or keep their laws
or defile yourselves with their idols. ¹⁹I
am the LORD your God; follow my decrees
and be careful to keep my laws. ²⁰Keep
my Sabbaths holy, that they may be a
sign between us. Then you will know
that I am the LORD your God."

²¹" 'But the children rebelled against
me: They did not follow my decrees, they
were not careful to keep my laws—
although the man who obeys them will
live by them—and they desecrated my
Sabbaths. So I said I would pour out
my wrath on them and spend my anger
against them in the desert. ²²But I withheld my hand, and for the sake of my
name I did what would keep it from being profaned in the eyes of the nations
in whose sight I had brought them out.
²³Also with uplifted hand I swore to them
in the desert that I would disperse them

a14 Or from under its

among the nations and scatter them through the countries, 24because they had not obeyed my laws but had rejected my decrees and desecrated my Sabbaths, and their eyes ⌊lusted⌋ after their fathers' idols. 25I also gave them over to statutes that were not good and laws they could not live by; 26I let them become defiled through their gifts—the sacrifice of every firstborn*a*—that I might fill them with horror so they would know that I am the LORD.'

27"Therefore, son of man, speak to the people of Israel and say to them, 'This is what the Sovereign LORD says: In this also your fathers blasphemed me by forsaking me: 28When I brought them into the land I had sworn to give them and they saw any high hill or any leafy tree, there they offered their sacrifices, made offerings that provoked me to anger, presented their fragrant incense and poured out their drink offerings. 29Then I said to them: What is this high place you go to?' " (It is called Bamah*b* to this day.)

Judgment and Restoration

30"Therefore say to the house of Israel: 'This is what the Sovereign LORD says: Will you defile yourselves the way your fathers did and lust after their vile images? 31When you offer your gifts—the sacrifice of your sons in*c* the fire—you continue to defile yourselves with all your idols to this day. Am I to let you inquire of me, O house of Israel? As surely as I live, declares the Sovereign LORD, I will not let you inquire of me.

32" 'You say, "We want to be like the nations, like the peoples of the world, who serve wood and stone." But what you have in mind will never happen. 33As surely as I live, declares the Sovereign LORD, I will rule over you with a mighty hand and an outstretched arm and with outpoured wrath. 34I will bring you from the nations and gather you from the countries where you have been scattered—with a mighty hand and an outstretched arm and with outpoured wrath. 35I will bring you into the desert of the nations and there, face to face, I will execute judgment upon you. 36As I judged your fathers in the desert of the land of Egypt, so I will judge you, declares the Sovereign LORD. 37I will take note of you as you pass under my rod, and I will bring you into the bond of the covenant. 38I will purge you of those who revolt and

rebel against me. Although I will bring them out of the land where they are living, yet they will not enter the land of Israel. Then you will know that I am the LORD.

39" 'As for you, O house of Israel, this is what the Sovereign LORD says: Go and serve your idols, every one of you! But afterward you will surely listen to me and no longer profane my holy name with your gifts and idols. 40For on my holy mountain, the high mountain of Israel, declares the Sovereign LORD, there in the land the entire house of Israel will serve me, and there I will accept them. There I will require your offerings and your choice gifts,*d* along with all your holy sacrifices. 41I will accept you as fragrant incense when I bring you out from the nations and gather you from the countries where you have been scattered, and I will show myself holy among you in the sight of the nations. 42Then you will know that I am the LORD, when I bring you into the land of Israel, the land I had sworn with uplifted hand to give to your fathers. 43There you will remember your conduct and all the actions by which you have defiled yourselves, and you will loathe yourselves for all the evil you have done. 44You will know that I am the LORD, when I deal with you for my name's sake and not according to your evil ways and your corrupt practices, O house of Israel, declares the Sovereign LORD.' "

Prophecy Against the South

45The word of the LORD came to me:

---

*a*26 Or —making every firstborn pass through ⌊the fire⌋   *b*29 Bamah means high place.   *c*31 Or —making your sons pass through   *d*40 Or and the gifts of your firstfruits

POINT OF INTEREST

Ezekiel 20:32

The people's desire to fit in and be like everyone else who worshiped idols sounds somewhat like their ancestors' cry for a king (see 1 Samuel 8:5). God wants his children to be different from people in the world. Romans 12:2 shows us how we should handle our desire to be like the people of the world.

⁴⁶"Son of man, set your face toward the south; preach against the south and prophesy against the forest of the southland. ⁴⁷Say to the southern forest: 'Hear the word of the LORD. This is what the Sovereign LORD says: I am about to set fire to you, and it will consume all your trees, both green and dry. The blazing flame will not be quenched, and every face from south to north will be scorched by it. ⁴⁸Everyone will see that I the LORD have kindled it; it will not be quenched.' "

⁴⁹Then I said, "Ah, Sovereign LORD! They are saying of me, 'Isn't he just telling parables?' "

Babylon, God's Sword of Judgment

21 The word of the LORD came to me: ²"Son of man, set your face against Jerusalem and preach against the sanctuary. Prophesy against the land of Israel ³and say to her: 'This is what the LORD says: I am against you. I will draw my sword from its scabbard and cut off from you both the righteous and the wicked. ⁴Because I am going to cut off the righteous and the wicked, my sword will be unsheathed against everyone from south to north. ⁵Then all people will know that I the LORD have drawn my sword from its scabbard; it will not return again.'

⁶"Therefore groan, son of man! Groan before them with broken heart and bitter grief. ⁷And when they ask you, 'Why are you groaning?' you shall say, 'Because of the news that is coming. Every heart will melt and every hand go limp; every spirit will become faint and every knee become as weak as water.' It is coming! It will surely take place, declares the Sovereign LORD."

⁸The word of the LORD came to me: ⁹"Son of man, prophesy and say, 'This is what the Lord says:

" 'A sword, a sword,
    sharpened and polished—
¹⁰sharpened for the slaughter,
    polished to flash like lightning!

" 'Shall we rejoice in the scepter of my son ⌐Judah⌐? The sword despises every such stick.

¹¹" 'The sword is appointed to be polished,
    to be grasped with the hand;
it is sharpened and polished,
    made ready for the hand of the slayer.

¹²Cry out and wail, son of man,
    for it is against my people;
    it is against all the princes of
        Israel.
They are thrown to the sword
    along with my people.
Therefore beat your breast.

¹³" 'Testing will surely come. And what if the scepter ⌐of Judah⌐, which the sword despises, does not continue? declares the Sovereign LORD.'

¹⁴"So then, son of man, prophesy
    and strike your hands together.
Let the sword strike twice,
    even three times.
It is a sword for slaughter—
    a sword for great slaughter,
    closing in on them from every side.
¹⁵So that hearts may melt
    and the fallen be many,
I have stationed the sword for
    slaughter[a]
    at all their gates.
Oh! It is made to flash like lightning,
    it is grasped for slaughter.
¹⁶O sword, slash to the right,
    then to the left,
    wherever your blade is turned.
¹⁷I too will strike my hands together,
    and my wrath will subside.
I the LORD have spoken."

¹⁸The word of the LORD came to me: ¹⁹"Son of man, mark out two roads for the sword of the king of Babylon to take, both starting from the same country. Make a signpost where the road branches off to the city. ²⁰Mark out one road for the sword to come against Rabbah of the Ammonites and another against Judah and fortified Jerusalem. ²¹For the king of Babylon will stop at the fork in the road, at the junction of the two roads, to seek an omen: He will cast lots with arrows, he will consult his idols, he will examine the liver. ²²Into his right hand will come the lot for Jerusalem, where he is to set up battering rams, to give the command to slaughter, to sound the battle cry, to set battering rams against the gates, to build a ramp and to erect siege works. ²³It will seem like a false omen to those who have sworn allegiance to him, but he will remind them of their guilt and take them captive.

²⁴"Therefore this is what the Sover-

---

a15 Septuagint; the meaning of the Hebrew for this word is uncertain.

eign Lord says: 'Because you people have brought to mind your guilt by your open rebellion, revealing your sins in all that you do—because you have done this, you will be taken captive.

25" 'O profane and wicked prince of Israel, whose day has come, whose time of punishment has reached its climax, 26this is what the Sovereign Lord says: Take off the turban, remove the crown. It will not be as it was: The lowly will be exalted and the exalted will be brought low. 27A ruin! A ruin! I will make it a ruin! It will not be restored until he comes to whom it rightfully belongs; to him I will give it.'

28"And you, son of man, prophesy and say, 'This is what the Sovereign Lord says about the Ammonites and their insults:

" 'A sword, a sword,
     drawn for the slaughter,
  polished to consume
     and to flash like lightning!
29Despite false visions concerning you
     and lying divinations about you,
  it will be laid on the necks
     of the wicked who are to be slain,
  whose day has come,
     whose time of punishment has
        reached its climax.
30Return the sword to its scabbard.
     In the place where you were
        created,
  in the land of your ancestry,
     I will judge you.
31I will pour out my wrath upon you
     and breathe out my fiery anger
        against you;
  I will hand you over to brutal men,
     men skilled in destruction.
32You will be fuel for the fire,
     your blood will be shed in your
        land,
  you will be remembered no more;
     for I the Lord have spoken.' "

Jerusalem's Sins

22 The word of the Lord came to me: 2"Son of man, will you judge her? Will you judge this city of bloodshed? Then confront her with all her detestable practices 3and say: 'This is what the Sovereign Lord says: O city that brings on herself doom by shedding blood in her midst and defiles herself by making idols, 4you have become guilty because of the blood you have shed and have become defiled by the idols you have made. You have brought your days to a close, and

the end of your years has come. Therefore I will make you an object of scorn to the nations and a laughingstock to all the countries. 5Those who are near and those who are far away will mock you, O infamous city, full of turmoil.

6" 'See how each of the princes of Israel who are in you uses his power to shed blood. 7In you they have treated father and mother with contempt; in you they have oppressed the alien and mistreated the fatherless and the widow. 8You have despised my holy things and desecrated my Sabbaths. 9In you are slanderous men bent on shedding blood; in you are those who eat at the mountain shrines and commit lewd acts. 10In you are those who dishonor their fathers' bed; in you are those who violate women during their period, when they are ceremonially unclean. 11In you one man commits a detestable offense with his neighbor's wife, another shamefully defiles his daughter-in-law, and another violates his sister, his own father's daughter. 12In you men accept bribes to shed blood; you take usury and excessive interest[a] and make unjust gain from your neighbors by extortion. And you have forgotten me, declares the Sovereign Lord.

13" 'I will surely strike my hands together at the unjust gain you have made and at the blood you have shed in your midst. 14Will your courage endure or your hands be strong in the day I deal with you? I the Lord have spoken, and I will do it. 15I will disperse you among the nations and scatter you through the countries; and I will put an end to your uncleanness. 16When you have been defiled[b] in the eyes of the nations, you will know that I am the Lord.' "

17Then the word of the Lord came to me: 18"Son of man, the house of Israel has become dross to me; all of them are the copper, tin, iron and lead left inside a furnace. They are but the dross of silver. 19Therefore this is what the Sovereign Lord says: 'Because you have all become dross, I will gather you into Jerusalem. 20As men gather silver, copper, iron, lead and tin into a furnace to melt it with a fiery blast, so will I gather you in my anger and my wrath and put you inside the city and melt you. 21I will gather you and I will blow on you with my fiery wrath,

---

a12 Or *usury and interest*   *b16* Or *When I have allotted you your inheritance* and you will be melted inside her. ²²As silver is melted in a furnace, so you will be melted inside her, and you will know that I the Lord have poured out my wrath upon you.' "

²³Again the word of the Lord came to me: ²⁴"Son of man, say to the land, 'You are a land that has had no rain or showers[a] in the day of wrath.' ²⁵There is a conspiracy of her princes[b] within her like a roaring lion tearing its prey; they devour people, take treasures and precious things and make many widows within her. ²⁶Her priests do violence to my law and profane my holy things; they do not distinguish between the holy and the common; they teach that there is no difference between the unclean and the clean; and they shut their eyes to the keeping of my Sabbaths, so that I am profaned among them. ²⁷Her officials within her are like wolves tearing their prey; they shed blood and kill people to make unjust gain. ²⁸Her prophets whitewash these deeds for them by false visions and lying divinations. They say, 'This is what the Sovereign Lord says'—when the Lord has not spoken. ²⁹The people of the land practice extortion and commit robbery; they oppress the poor and needy and mistreat the alien, denying them justice.

³⁰"I looked for a man among them who would build up the wall and stand before me in the gap on behalf of the land so I would not have to destroy it, but I found none. ³¹So I will pour out my wrath on them and consume them with my fiery anger, bringing down on their own heads all they have done, declares the Sovereign Lord."

Two Adulterous Sisters

23 The word of the Lord came to me: ²"Son of man, there were two women, daughters of the same mother. ³They became prostitutes in Egypt, engaging in prostitution from their youth. In that land their breasts were fondled and their virgin bosoms caressed. ⁴The older was named Oholah, and her sister was Oholibah. They were mine and gave birth to sons and daughters. Oholah is Samaria, and Oholibah is Jerusalem.

⁵"Oholah engaged in prostitution while she was still mine; and she lusted after her lovers, the Assyrians—warriors ⁶clothed in blue, governors and commanders, all of them handsome young men, and mounted horsemen. ⁷She gave herself as a prostitute to all the elite of the Assyrians and defiled herself with all the idols of everyone she lusted after. ⁸She did not give up the prostitution she began in Egypt, when during her youth men slept with her, caressed her virgin bosom and poured out their lust upon her.

⁹"Therefore I handed her over to her lovers, the Assyrians, for whom she lusted. ¹⁰They stripped her naked, took away her sons and daughters and killed her with the sword. She became a byword among women, and punishment was inflicted on her.

¹¹"Her sister Oholibah saw this, yet in her lust and prostitution she was more depraved than her sister. ¹²She too lusted after the Assyrians—governors and commanders, warriors in full dress, mounted horsemen, all handsome young men. ¹³I saw that she too defiled herself; both of them went the same way.

¹⁴"But she carried her prostitution still further. She saw men portrayed on a wall, figures of Chaldeans[c] portrayed in red, ¹⁵with belts around their waists and flowing turbans on their heads; all of them looked like Babylonian chariot officers, natives of Chaldea.[d] ¹⁶As soon as she saw them, she lusted after them and sent messengers to them in Chaldea. ¹⁷Then the Babylonians came to her, to the bed of love, and in their lust they defiled her. After she had been defiled by them, she turned away from them in disgust. ¹⁸When she carried on her prostitution openly and exposed her nakedness, I turned away from her in disgust, just as I had turned away from her sister. ¹⁹Yet she became more and more promiscuous as she recalled the days of her youth, when she was a prostitute in Egypt. ²⁰There she lusted after her lovers, whose genitals were like those of donkeys and whose emission was like that of horses. ²¹So you longed for the lewdness of your youth, when in Egypt your bosom was caressed and your young breasts fondled.[e]

²²"Therefore, Oholibah, this is what the Sovereign Lord says: I will stir up your lovers against you, those you turned away from in disgust, and I will bring them against you from every side— ²³the

---

a24 Septuagint; Hebrew *has not been cleansed or rained on*   b25 Septuagint; Hebrew *prophets*   c14 Or *Babylonians*   d15 Or *Babylonia*; also in verse 16   e21 Syriac (see also verse 3); Hebrew *caressed because of your young breasts*

Babylonians and all the Chaldeans, the men of Pekod and Shoa and Koa, and all the Assyrians with them, handsome young men, all of them governors and commanders, chariot officers and men of high rank, all mounted on horses. ²⁴They will come against you with weapons,ᵃ chariots and wagons and with a throng of people; they will take up positions against you on every side with large and small shields and with helmets. I will turn you over to them for punishment, and they will punish you according to

their standards. ²⁵I will direct my jealous anger against you, and they will deal with you in fury. They will cut off your noses and your ears, and those of you who are left will fall by the sword. They will take away your sons and daughters, and those of you who are left will be consumed by fire. ²⁶They will also strip you of your clothes and take your fine jewelry. ²⁷So I will put a stop to the lewdness

ᵃ24 The meaning of the Hebrew for this word is uncertain.

Read Ezekiel 22:1–31
Key Verse Ezekiel 22:30

Standing in the Gap —Thomas Betts

Throughout the book of Ezekiel, the prophet tells us how Jerusalem and Israel have been rebellious and unfaithful and have sinned against God. The people are immersing themselves in immorality, taking bribes, murdering, worshiping idols, prophesying falsely, and generally breaking every one of God's laws. Sound familiar? That same kind of behavior isn't uncommon today. And as surely as God pronounced judgment on Israel, God will judge those who indulge in sin (see Ezekiel 22:13–16, 31).

However, when we look at verse 30, the tone of God's message changes from anger to sad regret. God is looking for someone to "stand in the gap" on behalf of Israel so he will not have to destroy it. Stop . . . listen. God is saying, "I love my people, I don't want any to be lost." He wants to find someone to "stand in the gap." He is looking for someone to intervene on his behalf and bring his people back to him as Moses, Joshua, Deborah, Samuel, Elijah, Ezra, Nehemiah, Isaiah and countless others did. Of all those who have heard God and obeyed, Jesus Christ remains the ultimate example of someone who "stands in the gap" on our behalf; by his death and resurrection he restores us to communion with the living God.

Although the work of Jesus Christ in making us righteous is complete and all-sufficient, I can't escape the idea that God still looks for people to "stand in the gap." "Standing in the gap" today means telling others that Jesus wants to give them eternal and abundant life. God is calling us to help bring his people back to him through evangelism, prayer and the example of a daily life lived in his name. God is asking all of us the same question he asked the prophet Isaiah: "Whom shall I send? And who will go for us?" (Isaiah 6:8–9). Will we give the same response as Isaiah? "Here am I. Send me!"

A Deeper Look
Isaiah 52:7; Acts 16:9

Go to page 951 for your next devotional reading.

and prostitution you began in Egypt. You will not look on these things with longing or remember Egypt anymore.

28"For this is what the Sovereign LORD says: I am about to hand you over to those you hate, to those you turned away from in disgust. 29They will deal with you in hatred and take away everything you have worked for. They will leave you naked and bare, and the shame of your prostitution will be exposed. Your lewdness and promiscuity 30have brought this upon you, because you lusted after the nations and defiled yourself with their idols. 31You have gone the way of your sister; so I will put her cup into your hand.

32"This is what the Sovereign LORD says:

"You will drink your sister's cup,
    a cup large and deep;
it will bring scorn and derision,
    for it holds so much.
33You will be filled with drunkenness
        and sorrow,
    the cup of ruin and desolation,
    the cup of your sister Samaria.
34You will drink it and drain it dry;
    you will dash it to pieces
    and tear your breasts.

I have spoken, declares the Sovereign LORD.

35"Therefore this is what the Sovereign LORD says: Since you have forgotten me and thrust me behind your back, you must bear the consequences of your lewdness and prostitution."

36The LORD said to me: "Son of man, will you judge Oholah and Oholibah? Then confront them with their detestable practices, 37for they have committed adultery and blood is on their hands. They committed adultery with their idols; they even sacrificed their children, whom they bore to me,a as food for them. 38They have also done this to me: At that same time they defiled my sanctuary and desecrated my Sabbaths. 39On the very day they sacrificed their children to their idols, they entered my sanctuary and desecrated it. That is what they did in my house.

40"They even sent messengers for men who came from far away, and when they arrived you bathed yourself for them, painted your eyes and put on your jewelry. 41You sat on an elegant couch, with a table spread before it on which you had placed the incense and oil that belonged to me.

42"The noise of a carefree crowd was around her; Sabeansb were brought from the desert along with men from the rabble, and they put bracelets on the arms of the woman and her sister and beautiful crowns on their heads. 43Then I said about the one worn out by adultery, 'Now let them use her as a prostitute, for that is all she is.' 44And they slept with her. As men sleep with a prostitute, so they slept with those lewd women, Oholah and Oholibah. 45But righteous men will sentence them to the punishment of women who commit adultery and shed blood, because they are adulterous and blood is on their hands.

46"This is what the Sovereign LORD says: Bring a mob against them and give them over to terror and plunder. 47The mob will stone them and cut them down with their swords; they will kill their sons and daughters and burn down their houses.

48"So I will put an end to lewdness in the land, that all women may take warning and not imitate you. 49You will suffer the penalty for your lewdness and bear the consequences of your sins of idolatry. Then you will know that I am the Sovereign LORD."

The Cooking Pot

24 In the ninth year, in the tenth month on the tenth day, the word of the LORD came to me: 2"Son of man, record this date, this very date, because the king of Babylon has laid siege to Jerusalem this very day. 3Tell this rebellious house a parable and say to them: 'This is what the Sovereign LORD says:

" 'Put on the cooking pot; put it on
    and pour water into it.
4Put into it the pieces of meat,
    all the choice pieces—the leg and
        the shoulder.
Fill it with the best of these bones;
5   take the pick of the flock.
Pile wood beneath it for the bones;
    bring it to a boil
    and cook the bones in it.

6" 'For this is what the Sovereign LORD says:

a37 Or even made the children they bore to me pass through ⌊the fire⌋   b42 Or drunkards

" 'Woe to the city of bloodshed,
    to the pot now encrusted,
    whose deposit will not go away!
Empty it piece by piece
    without casting lots for them.

⁷" 'For the blood she shed is in her
        midst:
    She poured it on the bare rock;
she did not pour it on the ground,
    where the dust would cover it.
⁸To stir up wrath and take revenge
    I put her blood on the bare rock,
    so that it would not be covered.

⁹" 'Therefore this is what the Sovereign
Lᴏʀᴅ says:

" 'Woe to the city of bloodshed!
    I, too, will pile the wood high.
¹⁰So heap on the wood
    and kindle the fire.
Cook the meat well,
    mixing in the spices;
    and let the bones be charred.
¹¹Then set the empty pot on the coals
    till it becomes hot and its copper
        glows
so its impurities may be melted
    and its deposit burned away.
¹²It has frustrated all efforts;
    its heavy deposit has not been
        removed,
    not even by fire.

¹³" 'Now your impurity is lewdness.
Because I tried to cleanse you but you
would not be cleansed from your impurity, you will not be clean again until my
wrath against you has subsided.

¹⁴" 'I the Lᴏʀᴅ have spoken. The time
has come for me to act. I will not hold
back; I will not have pity, nor will I relent. You will be judged according to
your conduct and your actions, declares
the Sovereign Lᴏʀᴅ.' "

Ezekiel's Wife Dies

¹⁵The word of the Lᴏʀᴅ came to me:
¹⁶"Son of man, with one blow I am about
to take away from you the delight of your
eyes. Yet do not lament or weep or shed
any tears. ¹⁷Groan quietly; do not mourn
for the dead. Keep your turban fastened
and your sandals on your feet; do not
cover the lower part of your face or eat
the customary food ⌊of mourners⌋."
¹⁸So I spoke to the people in the morning, and in the evening my wife died. The

next morning I did as I had been commanded.
¹⁹Then the people asked me, "Won't
you tell us what these things have to do
with us?"
²⁰So I said to them, "The word of the
Lᴏʀᴅ came to me: ²¹Say to the house of
Israel, 'This is what the Sovereign Lᴏʀᴅ
says: I am about to desecrate my sanctuary—the stronghold in which you take
pride, the delight of your eyes, the object
of your affection. The sons and daughters
you left behind will fall by the sword.
²²And you will do as I have done. You
will not cover the lower part of your face
or eat the customary food ⌊of mourners⌋.
²³You will keep your turbans on your
heads and your sandals on your feet. You
will not mourn or weep but will waste
away because of*a* your sins and groan
among yourselves. ²⁴Ezekiel will be a
sign to you; you will do just as he has
done. When this happens, you will know
that I am the Sovereign Lᴏʀᴅ.'
²⁵"And you, son of man, on the day I
take away their stronghold, their joy and
glory, the delight of their eyes, their
heart's desire, and their sons and daughters as well— ²⁶on that day a fugitive will
come to tell you the news. ²⁷At that time
your mouth will be opened; you will
speak with him and will no longer be silent. So you will be a sign to them, and
they will know that I am the Lᴏʀᴅ."

A Prophecy Against Ammon

25 The word of the Lᴏʀᴅ came to me:
²"Son of man, set your face against
the Ammonites and prophesy against

---

a23 Or *away in*

POINT OF INTEREST

Ezekiel 24:16

God never does anything
capriciously, but he sometimes does allow his people
to suffer in order to bring
about a greater good. Though Ezekiel was
stricken by his wife's death, he obeyed
God. His strange method of mourning
became a symbolic warning to the
Israelites, forcing them to confront their
sinfulness.

them. ³Say to them, 'Hear the word of the Sovereign LORD. This is what the Sovereign LORD says: Because you said "Aha!" over my sanctuary when it was desecrated and over the land of Israel when it was laid waste and over the people of Judah when they went into exile, ⁴therefore I am going to give you to the people of the East as a possession. They will set up their camps and pitch their tents among you; they will eat your fruit and drink your milk. ⁵I will turn Rabbah into a pasture for camels and Ammon into a resting place for sheep. Then you will know that I am the LORD. ⁶For this is what the Sovereign LORD says: Because you have clapped your hands and stamped your feet, rejoicing with all the malice of your heart against the land of Israel, ⁷therefore I will stretch out my hand against you and give you as plunder to the nations. I will cut you off from the nations and exterminate you from the countries. I will destroy you, and you will know that I am the LORD.' "

A Prophecy Against Moab

⁸"This is what the Sovereign LORD says: 'Because Moab and Seir said, "Look, the house of Judah has become like all the other nations," ⁹therefore I will expose the flank of Moab, beginning at its frontier towns—Beth Jeshimoth, Baal Meon and Kiriathaim—the glory of that land. ¹⁰I will give Moab along with the Ammonites to the people of the East as a possession, so that the Ammonites will not be remembered among the nations; ¹¹and I will inflict punishment on Moab. Then they will know that I am the LORD.' "

A Prophecy Against Edom

¹²"This is what the Sovereign LORD says: 'Because Edom took revenge on the house of Judah and became very guilty by doing so, ¹³therefore this is what the Sovereign LORD says: I will stretch out my hand against Edom and kill its men and their animals. I will lay it waste, and from Teman to Dedan they will fall by the sword. ¹⁴I will take vengeance on Edom by the hand of my people Israel, and they will deal with Edom in accordance with my anger and my wrath; they will know my vengeance, declares the Sovereign LORD.' "

A Prophecy Against Philistia

¹⁵"This is what the Sovereign LORD says: 'Because the Philistines acted in vengeance and took revenge with malice in their hearts, and with ancient hostility sought to destroy Judah, ¹⁶therefore this is what the Sovereign LORD says: I am about to stretch out my hand against the Philistines, and I will cut off the Kerethites and destroy those remaining along the coast. ¹⁷I will carry out great vengeance on them and punish them in my wrath. Then they will know that I am the LORD, when I take vengeance on them.' "

A Prophecy Against Tyre

26 In the eleventh year, on the first day of the month, the word of the LORD came to me: ²"Son of man, because Tyre has said of Jerusalem, 'Aha! The gate to the nations is broken, and its doors have swung open to me; now that she lies in ruins I will prosper,' ³therefore this is what the Sovereign LORD says: I am against you, O Tyre, and I will bring many nations against you, like the sea casting up its waves. ⁴They will destroy the walls of Tyre and pull down her towers; I will scrape away her rubble and make her a bare rock. ⁵Out in the sea she will become a place to spread fishnets, for I have spoken, declares the Sovereign LORD. She will become plunder for the nations, ⁶and her settlements on the mainland will be ravaged by the sword. Then they will know that I am the LORD.

⁷"For this is what the Sovereign LORD says: From the north I am going to bring against Tyre Nebuchadnezzar*a* king of Babylon, king of kings, with horses and chariots, with horsemen and a great army. ⁸He will ravage your settlements on the mainland with the sword; he will set up siege works against you, build a ramp up to your walls and raise his shields against you. ⁹He will direct the blows of his battering rams against your walls and demolish your towers with his weapons. ¹⁰His horses will be so many that they will cover you with dust. Your walls will tremble at the noise of the war horses, wagons and chariots when he enters your gates as men enter a city whose walls have been broken through. ¹¹The hoofs of his horses will trample all your

---

a7 Hebrew *Nebuchadrezzar,* of which *Nebuchadnezzar* is a variant; here and often in Ezekiel and Jeremiah streets; he will kill your people with the sword, and your strong pillars will fall to the ground. ¹²They will plunder your wealth and loot your merchandise; they will break down your walls and demolish your fine houses and throw your stones, timber and rubble into the sea. ¹³I will put an end to your noisy songs, and the music of your harps will be heard no more. ¹⁴I will make you a bare rock, and you will become a place to spread fishnets. You will never be rebuilt, for I the Lord have spoken, declares the Sovereign Lord.

¹⁵"This is what the Sovereign Lord says to Tyre: Will not the coastlands tremble at the sound of your fall, when the wounded groan and the slaughter takes place in you? ¹⁶Then all the princes of the coast will step down from their thrones and lay aside their robes and take off their embroidered garments. Clothed with terror, they will sit on the ground, trembling every moment, appalled at you. ¹⁷Then they will take up a lament concerning you and say to you:

" 'How you are destroyed, O city of
        renown,
    peopled by men of the sea!
You were a power on the seas,
    you and your citizens;
you put your terror
    on all who lived there.
¹⁸Now the coastlands tremble
    on the day of your fall;
the islands in the sea
    are terrified at your collapse.'

¹⁹"This is what the Sovereign Lord says: When I make you a desolate city, like cities no longer inhabited, and when I bring the ocean depths over you and its vast waters cover you, ²⁰then I will bring you down with those who go down to the pit, to the people of long ago. I will make you dwell in the earth below, as in ancient ruins, with those who go down to the pit, and you will not return or take your place*a* in the land of the living. ²¹I will bring you to a horrible end and you will be no more. You will be sought, but you will never again be found, declares the Sovereign Lord."

A Lament for Tyre

27 The word of the Lord came to me: ²"Son of man, take up a lament concerning Tyre. ³Say to Tyre, situated at the gateway to the sea, merchant of peoples on many coasts, 'This is what the Sovereign Lord says:

" 'You say, O Tyre,
    "I am perfect in beauty."
⁴Your domain was on the high seas;
    your builders brought your beauty
        to perfection.
⁵They made all your timbers
    of pine trees from Senir*b*;
they took a cedar from Lebanon
    to make a mast for you.
⁶Of oaks from Bashan
    they made your oars;
of cypress wood*c* from the coasts of
        Cyprus*d*
    they made your deck, inlaid with
        ivory.
⁷Fine embroidered linen from Egypt
        was your sail
    and served as your banner;
your awnings were of blue and
        purple
    from the coasts of Elishah.
⁸Men of Sidon and Arvad were your
        oarsmen;
    your skilled men, O Tyre, were
        aboard as your seamen.
⁹Veteran craftsmen of Gebal*e* were on
        board
    as shipwrights to caulk your
        seams.
All the ships of the sea and their
        sailors
    came alongside to trade for your
        wares.

¹⁰" 'Men of Persia, Lydia and Put
    served as soldiers in your army.
They hung their shields and helmets
        on your walls,
    bringing you splendor.
¹¹Men of Arvad and Helech
    manned your walls on every side;
men of Gammad
    were in your towers.
They hung their shields around your
        walls;
    they brought your beauty to
        perfection.

¹²" 'Tarshish did business with you because of your great wealth of goods; they exchanged silver, iron, tin and lead for your merchandise.

¹³" 'Greece, Tubal and Meshech trad-

---

a20 Septuagint; Hebrew *return, and I will give glory*
b5 That is, Hermon   *c6* Targum; the Masoretic
Text has a different division of the consonants.
d6 Hebrew *Kittim*   *e9* That is, Byblos

ed with you; they exchanged slaves and articles of bronze for your wares.

¹⁴" 'Men of Beth Togarmah exchanged work horses, war horses and mules for your merchandise.

¹⁵" 'The men of Rhodes*a* traded with you, and many coastlands were your customers; they paid you with ivory tusks and ebony.

¹⁶" 'Aram*b* did business with you because of your many products; they exchanged turquoise, purple fabric, embroidered work, fine linen, coral and rubies for your merchandise.

¹⁷" 'Judah and Israel traded with you; they exchanged wheat from Minnith and confections,*c* honey, oil and balm for your wares.

¹⁸" 'Damascus, because of your many products and great wealth of goods, did business with you in wine from Helbon and wool from Zahar.

¹⁹" 'Danites and Greeks from Uzal bought your merchandise; they exchanged wrought iron, cassia and calamus for your wares.

²⁰" 'Dedan traded in saddle blankets with you.

²¹" 'Arabia and all the princes of Kedar were your customers; they did business with you in lambs, rams and goats.

²²" 'The merchants of Sheba and Raamah traded with you; for your merchandise they exchanged the finest of all kinds of spices and precious stones, and gold.

²³" 'Haran, Canneh and Eden and merchants of Sheba, Asshur and Kilmad traded with you. ²⁴In your marketplace they traded with you beautiful garments, blue fabric, embroidered work and multicolored rugs with cords twisted and tightly knotted.

²⁵" 'The ships of Tarshish serve
as carriers for your wares.
You are filled with heavy cargo
in the heart of the sea.
²⁶Your oarsmen take you
out to the high seas.
But the east wind will break you to
pieces
in the heart of the sea.
²⁷Your wealth, merchandise and wares,
your mariners, seamen and
shipwrights,
your merchants and all your soldiers,
and everyone else on board
will sink into the heart of the sea
on the day of your shipwreck.

²⁸The shorelands will quake
when your seamen cry out.
²⁹All who handle the oars
will abandon their ships;
the mariners and all the seamen
will stand on the shore.
³⁰They will raise their voice
and cry bitterly over you;
they will sprinkle dust on their heads
and roll in ashes.
³¹They will shave their heads because
of you
and will put on sackcloth.
They will weep over you with
anguish of soul
and with bitter mourning.
³²As they wail and mourn over you,
they will take up a lament
concerning you:
"Who was ever silenced like Tyre,
surrounded by the sea?"
³³When your merchandise went out on
the seas,
you satisfied many nations;
with your great wealth and your
wares
you enriched the kings of the
earth.
³⁴Now you are shattered by the sea
in the depths of the waters;
your wares and all your company
have gone down with you.
³⁵All who live in the coastlands
are appalled at you;
their kings shudder with horror
and their faces are distorted with
fear.
³⁶The merchants among the nations
hiss at you;
you have come to a horrible end
and will be no more.' "

A Prophecy Against the King of Tyre

28 The word of the LORD came to me: ²"Son of man, say to the ruler of Tyre, 'This is what the Sovereign LORD says:

" 'In the pride of your heart
you say, "I am a god;
I sit on the throne of a god
in the heart of the seas."
But you are a man and not a god,
though you think you are as wise
as a god.

a15 Septuagint; Hebrew *Dedan*   *b16* Most Hebrew manuscripts; some Hebrew manuscripts and Syriac *Edom*   *c17* The meaning of the Hebrew for this word is uncertain.

³Are you wiser than Daniel*ᵃ*?
  Is no secret hidden from you?
⁴By your wisdom and understanding
  you have gained wealth for
    yourself
and amassed gold and silver
  in your treasuries.
⁵By your great skill in trading
  you have increased your wealth,
and because of your wealth
  your heart has grown proud.

⁶" 'Therefore this is what the Sovereign LORD says:

" 'Because you think you are wise,
  as wise as a god,
⁷I am going to bring foreigners against
    you,
  the most ruthless of nations;
they will draw their swords against
    your beauty and wisdom
  and pierce your shining splendor.
⁸They will bring you down to the pit,
  and you will die a violent death
  in the heart of the seas.
⁹Will you then say, "I am a god,"
  in the presence of those who kill
    you?
You will be but a man, not a god,
  in the hands of those who slay
    you.
¹⁰You will die the death of the
    uncircumcised
  at the hands of foreigners.

I have spoken, declares the Sovereign
LORD.' "

¹¹The word of the LORD came to me:
¹²"Son of man, take up a lament concerning the king of Tyre and say to him: 'This is what the Sovereign LORD says:

" 'You were the model of perfection,
  full of wisdom and perfect in
    beauty.
¹³You were in Eden,
  the garden of God;
every precious stone adorned you:
  ruby, topaz and emerald,
  chrysolite, onyx and jasper,
  sapphire,*ᵇ* turquoise and beryl.*ᶜ*
Your settings and mountings*ᵈ* were
    made of gold;
  on the day you were created they
    were prepared.
¹⁴You were anointed as a guardian
    cherub,
  for so I ordained you.
You were on the holy mount of God;

you walked among the fiery
    stones.
¹⁵You were blameless in your ways
  from the day you were created
  till wickedness was found in you.
¹⁶Through your widespread trade
  you were filled with violence,
  and you sinned.
So I drove you in disgrace from the
    mount of God,
  and I expelled you, O guardian
    cherub,
  from among the fiery stones.
¹⁷Your heart became proud
  on account of your beauty,
and you corrupted your wisdom
  because of your splendor.
So I threw you to the earth;
  I made a spectacle of you before
    kings.
¹⁸By your many sins and dishonest
    trade
  you have desecrated your
    sanctuaries.
So I made a fire come out from you,
  and it consumed you,
and I reduced you to ashes on the
    ground
  in the sight of all who were
    watching.
¹⁹All the nations who knew you
  are appalled at you;
you have come to a horrible end
  and will be no more.' "

ᵃ3 Or *Danel*; the Hebrew spelling may suggest a person other than the prophet Daniel.   *ᵇ13* Or *lapis lazuli*   *ᶜ13* The precise identification of some of these precious stones is uncertain.   *ᵈ13* The meaning of the Hebrew for this phrase is uncertain.

POINT OF INTEREST

Ezekiel 28:6

At one time or another, each one of us has thought we were smarter than someone else, saying, "I would never do something as foolish as *that*." Ultimately our self-important attitude proves our own foolishness (see Romans 1:22). We possess true wisdom when we mirror Jesus' attitude and consider others better (and wiser) than ourselves (see Philippians 2:3–5).

A Prophecy Against Sidon

²⁰The word of the LORD came to me: ²¹"Son of man, set your face against Sidon; prophesy against her ²²and say: 'This is what the Sovereign LORD says:

" 'I am against you, O Sidon,
  and I will gain glory within you.
They will know that I am the LORD,
  when I inflict punishment on her
  and show myself holy within her.
²³I will send a plague upon her
  and make blood flow in her
    streets.
The slain will fall within her,
  with the sword against her on
    every side.
Then they will know that I am the
  LORD.

²⁴" 'No longer will the people of Israel have malicious neighbors who are painful briers and sharp thorns. Then they will know that I am the Sovereign LORD.

²⁵" 'This is what the Sovereign LORD says: When I gather the people of Israel from the nations where they have been scattered, I will show myself holy among them in the sight of the nations. Then they will live in their own land, which I gave to my servant Jacob. ²⁶They will live there in safety and will build houses and plant vineyards; they will live in safety when I inflict punishment on all their neighbors who maligned them. Then they will know that I am the LORD their God.' "

A Prophecy Against Egypt

29 In the tenth year, in the tenth month on the twelfth day, the word of the LORD came to me: ²"Son of man, set your face against Pharaoh king of Egypt and prophesy against him and against all Egypt. ³Speak to him and say: 'This is what the Sovereign LORD says:

" 'I am against you, Pharaoh king of
    Egypt,
  you great monster lying among
    your streams.
You say, "The Nile is mine;
  I made it for myself."
⁴But I will put hooks in your jaws
  and make the fish of your streams
    stick to your scales.
I will pull you out from among your
    streams,
  with all the fish sticking to your
    scales.

⁵I will leave you in the desert,
  you and all the fish of your
    streams.
You will fall on the open field
  and not be gathered or picked up.
I will give you as food
  to the beasts of the earth and the
    birds of the air.

⁶Then all who live in Egypt will know that I am the LORD.

" 'You have been a staff of reed for the house of Israel. ⁷When they grasped you with their hands, you splintered and you tore open their shoulders; when they leaned on you, you broke and their backs were wrenched.ᵃ

⁸" 'Therefore this is what the Sovereign LORD says: I will bring a sword against you and kill your men and their animals. ⁹Egypt will become a desolate wasteland. Then they will know that I am the LORD.

" 'Because you said, "The Nile is mine; I made it," ¹⁰therefore I am against you and against your streams, and I will make the land of Egypt a ruin and a desolate waste from Migdol to Aswan, as far as the border of Cush.ᵇ ¹¹No foot of man or animal will pass through it; no one will live there for forty years. ¹²I will make the land of Egypt desolate among devastated lands, and her cities will lie desolate forty years among ruined cities. And I will disperse the Egyptians among the nations and scatter them through the countries.

¹³" 'Yet this is what the Sovereign LORD says: At the end of forty years I will gather the Egyptians from the nations where they were scattered. ¹⁴I will bring them back from captivity and return them to Upper Egypt,ᶜ the land of their ancestry. There they will be a lowly kingdom. ¹⁵It will be the lowliest of kingdoms and will never again exalt itself above the other nations. I will make it so weak that it will never again rule over the nations. ¹⁶Egypt will no longer be a source of confidence for the people of Israel but will be a reminder of their sin in turning to her for help. Then they will know that I am the Sovereign LORD.' "

¹⁷In the twenty-seventh year, in the first month on the first day, the word of

---

ᵃ7 Syriac (see also Septuagint and Vulgate); Hebrew *and you caused their backs to stand*   ᵇ10 That is, the upper Nile region   ᶜ14 Hebrew *to Pathros* the LORD came to me: ¹⁸"Son of man, Nebuchadnezzar king of Babylon drove his army in a hard campaign against Tyre; every head was rubbed bare and every shoulder made raw. Yet he and his army got no reward from the campaign he led against Tyre. ¹⁹Therefore this is what the Sovereign LORD says: I am going to give Egypt to Nebuchadnezzar king of Babylon, and he will carry off its wealth. He will loot and plunder the land as pay for his army. ²⁰I have given him Egypt as a reward for his efforts because he and his army did it for me, declares the Sovereign LORD.

²¹"On that day I will make a horn*a* grow for the house of Israel, and I will open your mouth among them. Then they will know that I am the LORD."

A Lament for Egypt

30 The word of the LORD came to me: ²"Son of man, prophesy and say: 'This is what the Sovereign LORD says:

> " 'Wail and say,
>> "Alas for that day!"
> ³For the day is near,
>> the day of the LORD is near—
> a day of clouds,
>> a time of doom for the nations.
> ⁴A sword will come against Egypt,
>> and anguish will come upon
>>> Cush.*b*
> When the slain fall in Egypt,
>> her wealth will be carried away
>> and her foundations torn down.

⁵Cush and Put, Lydia and all Arabia, Libya*c* and the people of the covenant land will fall by the sword along with Egypt.

⁶" 'This is what the LORD says:

> " 'The allies of Egypt will fall
>> and her proud strength will fail.
> From Migdol to Aswan
>> they will fall by the sword within
>>> her,
>>>> declares the Sovereign LORD.
> ⁷" 'They will be desolate
>> among desolate lands,
> and their cities will lie
>> among ruined cities.
> ⁸Then they will know that I am the
>> LORD,
> when I set fire to Egypt
>> and all her helpers are crushed.

⁹" 'On that day messengers will go out from me in ships to frighten Cush out of her complacency. Anguish will take hold

of them on the day of Egypt's doom, for it is sure to come.

¹⁰" 'This is what the Sovereign LORD says:

> " 'I will put an end to the hordes of
>> Egypt
> by the hand of Nebuchadnezzar
>> king of Babylon.
> ¹¹He and his army—the most ruthless
>> of nations—
> will be brought in to destroy the
>> land.
> They will draw their swords against
>> Egypt
> and fill the land with the slain.
> ¹²I will dry up the streams of the Nile
>> and sell the land to evil men;
> by the hand of foreigners
>> I will lay waste the land and
>> everything in it.

I the LORD have spoken.

¹³" 'This is what the Sovereign LORD says:

> " 'I will destroy the idols
>> and put an end to the images in
>>> Memphis.*d*
> No longer will there be a prince in
>> Egypt,
> and I will spread fear throughout
>> the land.
> ¹⁴I will lay waste Upper Egypt,*e*
>> set fire to Zoan
> and inflict punishment on
>> Thebes.*f*
> ¹⁵I will pour out my wrath on
>> Pelusium,*g*
> the stronghold of Egypt,
>> and cut off the hordes of Thebes.
> ¹⁶I will set fire to Egypt;
>> Pelusium will writhe in agony.
> Thebes will be taken by storm;
>> Memphis will be in constant
>>> distress.
> ¹⁷The young men of Heliopolis*h* and
>> Bubastis*i*
> will fall by the sword,
>> and the cities themselves will go
>> into captivity.
> ¹⁸Dark will be the day at Tahpanhes
>> when I break the yoke of Egypt;

---

a21 Horn here symbolizes strength.   *b4* That is, the upper Nile region; also in verses 5 and 9   *c5* Hebrew *Cub*   *d13* Hebrew *Noph*; also in verse 16   *e14* Hebrew *waste Pathros*   *f14* Hebrew *No*; also in verses 15 and 16   *g15* Hebrew *Sin*; also in verse 16   *h17* Hebrew *Awen* (or *On*)   *i17* Hebrew *Pi Beseth*

there her proud strength will come
    to an end.
She will be covered with clouds,
    and her villages will go into
      captivity.
¹⁹So I will inflict punishment on Egypt,
    and they will know that I am the
    Lord.' "

²⁰In the eleventh year, in the first month on the seventh day, the word of the Lord came to me: ²¹"Son of man, I have broken the arm of Pharaoh king of Egypt. It has not been bound up for healing or put in a splint so as to become strong enough to hold a sword. ²²Therefore this is what the Sovereign Lord says: I am against Pharaoh king of Egypt. I will break both his arms, the good arm as well as the broken one, and make the sword fall from his hand. ²³I will disperse the Egyptians among the nations and scatter them through the countries. ²⁴I will strengthen the arms of the king of Babylon and put my sword in his hand, but I will break the arms of Pharaoh, and he will groan before him like a mortally wounded man. ²⁵I will strengthen the arms of the king of Babylon, but the arms of Pharaoh will fall limp. Then they will know that I am the Lord, when I put my sword into the hand of the king of Babylon and he brandishes it against Egypt. ²⁶I will disperse the Egyptians among the nations and scatter them through the countries. Then they will know that I am the Lord."

A Cedar in Lebanon

31 In the eleventh year, in the third month on the first day, the word of the Lord came to me: ²"Son of man, say to Pharaoh king of Egypt and to his hordes:

" 'Who can be compared with you in
    majesty?
³Consider Assyria, once a cedar in
    Lebanon,
    with beautiful branches
      overshadowing the forest;
    it towered on high,
      its top above the thick foliage.
⁴The waters nourished it,
    deep springs made it grow tall;
    their streams flowed
      all around its base
    and sent their channels
      to all the trees of the field.
⁵So it towered higher

than all the trees of the field;
    its boughs increased
    and its branches grew long,
    spreading because of abundant
      waters.
⁶All the birds of the air
    nested in its boughs,
    all the beasts of the field
      gave birth under its branches;
    all the great nations
      lived in its shade.
⁷It was majestic in beauty,
    with its spreading boughs,
    for its roots went down
      to abundant waters.
⁸The cedars in the garden of God
    could not rival it,
    nor could the pine trees
      equal its boughs,
    nor could the plane trees
      compare with its branches—
    no tree in the garden of God
      could match its beauty.
⁹I made it beautiful
    with abundant branches,
    the envy of all the trees of Eden
      in the garden of God.

¹⁰" 'Therefore this is what the Sovereign Lord says: Because it towered on high, lifting its top above the thick foliage, and because it was proud of its height, ¹¹I handed it over to the ruler of the nations, for him to deal with according to its wickedness. I cast it aside, ¹²and the most ruthless of foreign nations cut it down and left it. Its boughs fell on the mountains and in all the valleys; its branches lay broken in all the ravines of the land. All the nations of the earth came out from under its shade and left it. ¹³All the birds of the air settled on the fallen tree, and all the beasts of the field were among its branches. ¹⁴Therefore no other trees by the waters are ever to tower proudly on high, lifting their tops above the thick foliage. No other trees so well-watered are ever to reach such a height; they are all destined for death, for the earth below, among mortal men, with those who go down to the pit.

¹⁵" 'This is what the Sovereign Lord says: On the day it was brought down to the grave^a I covered the deep springs with mourning for it; I held back its streams, and its abundant waters were restrained. Because of it I clothed Leba-

---

^a15 Hebrew *Sheol*; also in verses 16 and 17

non with gloom, and all the trees of the field withered away. ¹⁶I made the nations tremble at the sound of its fall when I brought it down to the grave with those who go down to the pit. Then all the trees of Eden, the choicest and best of Lebanon, all the trees that were well-watered, were consoled in the earth below. ¹⁷Those who lived in its shade, its allies among the nations, had also gone down to the grave with it, joining those killed by the sword.

¹⁸ 'Which of the trees of Eden can be compared with you in splendor and majesty? Yet you, too, will be brought down with the trees of Eden to the earth below; you will lie among the uncircumcised, with those killed by the sword.

" 'This is Pharaoh and all his hordes, declares the Sovereign LORD.' "

A Lament for Pharaoh

32 In the twelfth year, in the twelfth month on the first day, the word of the LORD came to me: ²"Son of man, take up a lament concerning Pharaoh king of Egypt and say to him:

" 'You are like a lion among the
            nations;
    you are like a monster in the seas
thrashing about in your streams,
    churning the water with your feet
    and muddying the streams.

³ 'This is what the Sovereign LORD says:

" 'With a great throng of people
    I will cast my net over you,
    and they will haul you up in my
            net.
⁴I will throw you on the land
    and hurl you on the open field.
I will let all the birds of the air settle
            on you
    and all the beasts of the earth
    gorge themselves on you.
⁵I will spread your flesh on the
            mountains
    and fill the valleys with your
            remains.
⁶I will drench the land with your
            flowing blood
    all the way to the mountains,
    and the ravines will be filled with
            your flesh.
⁷When I snuff you out, I will cover the
            heavens
    and darken their stars;

I will cover the sun with a cloud,
    and the moon will not give its
            light.
⁸All the shining lights in the heavens
    I will darken over you;
    I will bring darkness over your
            land,
            declares the Sovereign LORD.
⁹I will trouble the hearts of many
            peoples
    when I bring about your
            destruction among the
            nations,
    amongᵃ lands you have not
            known.
¹⁰I will cause many peoples to be
            appalled at you,
    and their kings will shudder with
            horror because of you
    when I brandish my sword before
            them.
On the day of your downfall
    each of them will tremble
    every moment for his life.

¹¹ " 'For this is what the Sovereign LORD says:

" 'The sword of the king of Babylon
    will come against you.
¹²I will cause your hordes to fall
    by the swords of mighty men—
    the most ruthless of all nations.
They will shatter the pride of Egypt,
    and all her hordes will be
            overthrown.
¹³I will destroy all her cattle
    from beside abundant waters
no longer to be stirred by the foot of
            man
    or muddied by the hoofs of cattle.
¹⁴Then I will let her waters settle
    and make her streams flow like oil,
            declares the Sovereign LORD.
¹⁵When I make Egypt desolate
    and strip the land of everything in
            it,
    when I strike down all who live
            there,
    then they will know that I am the
            LORD.'

¹⁶"This is the lament they will chant for her. The daughters of the nations will chant it; for Egypt and all her hordes they will chant it, declares the Sovereign LORD."

ᵃ9 Hebrew; Septuagint *bring you into captivity among the nations, /* to

¹⁷In the twelfth year, on the fifteenth day of the month, the word of the LORD came to me: ¹⁸"Son of man, wail for the hordes of Egypt and consign to the earth below both her and the daughters of mighty nations, with those who go down to the pit. ¹⁹Say to them, 'Are you more favored than others? Go down and be laid among the uncircumcised.' ²⁰They will fall among those killed by the sword. The sword is drawn; let her be dragged off with all her hordes. ²¹From within the grave*a* the mighty leaders will say of Egypt and her allies, 'They have come down and they lie with the uncircumcised, with those killed by the sword.'

²²"Assyria is there with her whole army; she is surrounded by the graves of all her slain, all who have fallen by the sword. ²³Their graves are in the depths of the pit and her army lies around her grave. All who had spread terror in the land of the living are slain, fallen by the sword.

²⁴"Elam is there, with all her hordes around her grave. All of them are slain, fallen by the sword. All who had spread terror in the land of the living went down uncircumcised to the earth below. They bear their shame with those who go down to the pit. ²⁵A bed is made for her among the slain, with all her hordes around her grave. All of them are uncircumcised, killed by the sword. Because their terror had spread in the land of the living, they bear their shame with those who go down to the pit; they are laid among the slain.

²⁶"Meshech and Tubal are there, with all their hordes around their graves. All of them are uncircumcised, killed by the sword because they spread their terror in the land of the living. ²⁷Do they not lie with the other uncircumcised warriors who have fallen, who went down to the grave with their weapons of war, whose swords were placed under their heads? The punishment for their sins rested on their bones, though the terror of these warriors had stalked through the land of the living.

²⁸"You too, O Pharaoh, will be broken and will lie among the uncircumcised, with those killed by the sword.

²⁹"Edom is there, her kings and all her princes; despite their power, they are laid with those killed by the sword. They lie with the uncircumcised, with those who go down to the pit.

³⁰"All the princes of the north and all the Sidonians are there; they went down with the slain in disgrace despite the terror caused by their power. They lie uncircumcised with those killed by the sword and bear their shame with those who go down to the pit.

³¹"Pharaoh—he and all his army—will see them and he will be consoled for all his hordes that were killed by the sword, declares the Sovereign LORD. ³²Although I had him spread terror in the land of the living, Pharaoh and all his hordes will be laid among the uncircumcised, with those killed by the sword, declares the Sovereign LORD."

Ezekiel a Watchman

33 The word of the LORD came to me: ²"Son of man, speak to your countrymen and say to them: 'When I bring the sword against a land, and the people of the land choose one of their men and make him their watchman, ³and he sees the sword coming against the land and blows the trumpet to warn the people, ⁴then if anyone hears the trumpet but does not take warning and the sword comes and takes his life, his blood will be on his own head. ⁵Since he heard the sound of the trumpet but did not take warning, his blood will be on his own head. If he had taken warning, he would have saved himself. ⁶But if the watchman sees the sword coming and does not blow the trumpet to warn the people and the sword comes and takes the life of one of them, that man will be taken away because of his sin, but I will hold the watchman accountable for his blood.'

⁷"Son of man, I have made you a watchman for the house of Israel; so hear the word I speak and give them warning from me. ⁸When I say to the wicked, 'O wicked man, you will surely die,' and you do not speak out to dissuade him from his ways, that wicked man will die for*b* his sin, and I will hold you accountable for his blood. ⁹But if you do warn the wicked man to turn from his ways and he does not do so, he will die for his sin, but you will have saved yourself.

¹⁰"Son of man, say to the house of Israel, 'This is what you are saying: "Our offenses and sins weigh us down, and we are wasting away because of*c* them.

---

a21 Hebrew *Sheol*; also in verse 27   *b8* Or *in*; also in verse 9   *c10* Or *away in*

How then can we live?" ' ¹¹Say to them, 'As surely as I live, declares the Sovereign LORD, I take no pleasure in the death of the wicked, but rather that they turn from their ways and live. Turn! Turn from your evil ways! Why will you die, O house of Israel?'

¹²"Therefore, son of man, say to your countrymen, 'The righteousness of the righteous man will not save him when he disobeys, and the wickedness of the wicked man will not cause him to fall when he turns from it. The righteous man, if he sins, will not be allowed to live because of his former righteousness.' ¹³If I tell the righteous man that he will surely live, but then he trusts in his righteousness and does evil, none of the righteous things he has done will be remembered; he will die for the evil he has done. ¹⁴And if I say to the wicked man, 'You will surely die,' but he then turns away from his sin and does what is just and right— ¹⁵if he gives back what he took in pledge for a loan, returns what he has stolen, follows the decrees that give life, and does no evil, he will surely live; he will not die. ¹⁶None of the sins he has committed will be remembered against him. He has done what is just and right; he will surely live.

¹⁷"Yet your countrymen say, 'The way of the Lord is not just.' But it is their way that is not just. ¹⁸If a righteous man turns from his righteousness and does evil, he will die for it. ¹⁹And if a wicked man turns away from his wickedness and does what is just and right, he will live by doing so. ²⁰Yet, O house of Israel, you say, 'The way of the Lord is not just.' But I will judge each of you according to his own ways."

Jerusalem's Fall Explained

²¹In the twelfth year of our exile, in the tenth month on the fifth day, a man who had escaped from Jerusalem came to me and said, "The city has fallen!" ²²Now the evening before the man arrived, the hand of the LORD was upon me, and he opened my mouth before the man came to me in the morning. So my mouth was opened and I was no longer silent.

²³Then the word of the LORD came to me: ²⁴"Son of man, the people living in those ruins in the land of Israel are saying, 'Abraham was only one man, yet he possessed the land. But we are many; surely the land has been given to us as our possession.' ²⁵Therefore say to them, 'This is what the Sovereign LORD says: Since you eat meat with the blood still in it and look to your idols and shed blood, should you then possess the land? ²⁶You rely on your sword, you do detestable things, and each of you defiles his neighbor's wife. Should you then possess the land?'

²⁷"Say this to them: 'This is what the Sovereign LORD says: As surely as I live, those who are left in the ruins will fall by the sword, those out in the country I will give to the wild animals to be devoured, and those in strongholds and caves will die of a plague. ²⁸I will make the land a desolate waste, and her proud strength will come to an end, and the mountains of Israel will become desolate so that no one will cross them. ²⁹Then they will know that I am the LORD, when I have made the land a desolate waste because of all the detestable things they have done.'

³⁰"As for you, son of man, your countrymen are talking together about you by the walls and at the doors of the houses, saying to each other, 'Come and hear the message that has come from the LORD.' ³¹My people come to you, as they usually do, and sit before you to listen to your words, but they do not put them into practice. With their mouths they express devotion, but their hearts are greedy for unjust gain. ³²Indeed, to them you are nothing more than one who sings love songs with a beautiful voice and plays an instrument well, for they hear your words but do not put them into practice.

³³"When all this comes true—and it surely will—then they will know that a prophet has been among them."

POINT OF INTEREST

Ezekiel 33:32

This literary picture of ancient Israel could easily depict a group of Christians today. We can be excited about getting together for worship and fellowship. We love the singing and are quick to enthuse, "Wasn't the sermon moving!" But even in the middle of the celebration, our hearts may be far from God.

Shepherds and Sheep

34 The word of the LORD came to me: 2"Son of man, prophesy against the shepherds of Israel; prophesy and say to them: 'This is what the Sovereign LORD says: Woe to the shepherds of Israel who only take care of themselves! Should not shepherds take care of the flock? 3You eat the curds, clothe yourselves with the wool and slaughter the choice animals, but you do not take care of the flock. 4You have not strengthened the weak or healed the sick or bound up the injured. You have not brought back the strays or searched for the lost. You have ruled them harshly and brutally. 5So they were scattered because there was no shepherd, and when they were scattered they became food for all the wild animals. 6My sheep wandered over all the mountains and on every high hill. They were scattered over the whole earth, and no one searched or looked for them.

7" 'Therefore, you shepherds, hear the word of the LORD: 8As surely as I live, declares the Sovereign LORD, because my flock lacks a shepherd and so has been plundered and has become food for all the wild animals, and because my shepherds did not search for my flock but cared for themselves rather than for my flock, 9therefore, O shepherds, hear the word of the LORD: 10This is what the Sovereign LORD says: I am against the shepherds and will hold them accountable for my flock. I will remove them from tending the flock so that the shepherds can no longer feed themselves. I will rescue my flock from their mouths, and it will no longer be food for them.

11" 'For this is what the Sovereign LORD says: I myself will search for my sheep and look after them. 12As a shepherd looks after his scattered flock when he is with them, so will I look after my sheep. I will rescue them from all the places where they were scattered on a day of clouds and darkness. 13I will bring them out from the nations and gather them from the countries, and I will bring them into their own land. I will pasture them on the mountains of Israel, in the ravines and in all the settlements in the land. 14I will tend them in a good pasture, and the mountain heights of Israel will be their grazing land. There they will lie down in good grazing land, and there they will feed in a rich pasture on the mountains of Israel. 15I myself will tend my sheep and have them lie down, declares the Sovereign LORD. 16I will search for the lost and bring back the strays. I will bind up the injured and strengthen the weak, but the sleek and the strong I will destroy. I will shepherd the flock with justice.

17" 'As for you, my flock, this is what the Sovereign LORD says: I will judge between one sheep and another, and between rams and goats. 18Is it not enough for you to feed on the good pasture? Must you also trample the rest of your pasture with your feet? Is it not enough for you to drink clear water? Must you also muddy the rest with your feet? 19Must my flock feed on what you have trampled and drink what you have muddied with your feet?

20" 'Therefore this is what the Sovereign LORD says to them: See, I myself will judge between the fat sheep and the lean sheep. 21Because you shove with flank and shoulder, butting all the weak sheep with your horns until you have driven them away, 22I will save my flock, and they will no longer be plundered. I will judge between one sheep and another. 23I will place over them one shepherd, my servant David, and he will tend them; he will tend them and be their shepherd. 24I the LORD will be their God, and my servant David will be prince among them. I the LORD have spoken.

25" 'I will make a covenant of peace with them and rid the land of wild beasts so that they may live in the desert and sleep in the forests in safety. 26I will bless them and the places surrounding my hill.ᵃ I will send down showers in season; there will be showers of blessing. 27The trees of the field will yield their fruit and the ground will yield its crops; the people will be secure in their land. They will know that I am the LORD, when I break the bars of their yoke and rescue them from the hands of those who enslaved them. 28They will no longer be plundered by the nations, nor will wild animals devour them. They will live in safety, and no one will make them afraid. 29I will provide for them a land renowned for its crops, and they will no longer be victims of famine in the land or bear the scorn of the nations. 30Then they will

---

ᵃ26 Or I will make them and the places surrounding my hill a blessing know that I, the LORD their God, am with them and that they, the house of Israel, are my people, declares the Sovereign LORD. ³¹You my sheep, the sheep of my pasture, are people, and I am your God, declares the Sovereign LORD.' "

A Prophecy Against Edom

35 The word of the LORD came to me: ²"Son of man, set your face against Mount Seir; prophesy against it ³and say: 'This is what the Sovereign LORD says: I am against you, Mount Seir, and I will stretch out my hand against you and make you a desolate waste. ⁴I will turn your towns into ruins and you will be desolate. Then you will know that I am the LORD.

⁵" 'Because you harbored an ancient hostility and delivered the Israelites over to the sword at the time of their calamity, the time their punishment reached its climax, ⁶therefore as surely as I live, declares the Sovereign LORD, I will give you over to bloodshed and it will pursue you. Since you did not hate bloodshed, bloodshed will pursue you. ⁷I will make Mount Seir a desolate waste and cut off from it all who come and go. ⁸I will fill your mountains with the slain; those killed by the sword will fall on your hills and in your valleys and in all your ravines. ⁹I will make you desolate forever; your towns will not be inhabited. Then you will know that I am the LORD.

¹⁰" 'Because you have said, "These two nations and countries will be ours and we will take possession of them," even though I the LORD was there, ¹¹therefore as surely as I live, declares the Sovereign LORD, I will treat you in accordance with the anger and jealousy you showed in your hatred of them and I will make myself known among them when I judge you. ¹²Then you will know that I the LORD have heard all the contemptible things you have said against the mountains of Israel. You said, "They have been laid waste and have been given over to us to devour." ¹³You boasted against me and spoke against me without restraint, and I heard it. ¹⁴This is what the Sovereign LORD says: While the whole earth rejoices, I will make you desolate. ¹⁵Because you rejoiced when the inheritance of the house of Israel became desolate, that is how I will treat you. You will be desolate, O Mount Seir, you and all of Edom. Then they will know that I am the LORD.' "

A Prophecy to the Mountains of Israel

36 "Son of man, prophesy to the mountains of Israel and say, 'O mountains of Israel, hear the word of the LORD. ²This is what the Sovereign LORD says: The enemy said of you, "Aha! The ancient heights have become our possession." ' ³Therefore prophesy and say, 'This is what the Sovereign LORD says: Because they ravaged and hounded you from every side so that you became the possession of the rest of the nations and the object of people's malicious talk and slander, ⁴therefore, O mountains of Israel, hear the word of the Sovereign LORD: This is what the Sovereign LORD says to the mountains and hills, to the ravines and valleys, to the desolate ruins and the deserted towns that have been plundered and ridiculed by the rest of the nations around you— ⁵this is what the Sovereign LORD says: In my burning zeal I have spoken against the rest of the nations, and against all Edom, for with glee and with malice in their hearts they made my land their own possession so that they might plunder its pastureland.' ⁶Therefore prophesy concerning the land of Israel and say to the mountains and hills, to the ravines and valleys: 'This is what the Sovereign LORD says: I speak in my jealous wrath because you have suffered the scorn of the nations. ⁷Therefore this is what the Sovereign LORD says: I swear with uplifted hand that the nations around you will also suffer scorn.

⁸" 'But you, O mountains of Israel, will produce branches and fruit for my people Israel, for they will soon come home. ⁹I am concerned for you and will look on you with favor; you will be plowed and sown, ¹⁰and I will multiply the number of people upon you, even the whole house of Israel. The towns will be inhabited and the ruins rebuilt. ¹¹I will increase the number of men and animals upon you, and they will be fruitful and become numerous. I will settle people on you as in the past and will make you prosper more than before. Then you will know that I am the LORD. ¹²I will cause people, my people Israel, to walk upon you. They will possess you, and you will be their inheritance; you will never again deprive them of their children.

¹³" 'This is what the Sovereign LORD says: Because people say to you, "You

devour men and deprive your nation of its children," ¹⁴therefore you will no longer devour men or make your nation childless, declares the Sovereign LORD. ¹⁵No longer will I make you hear the taunts of the nations, and no longer will you suffer the scorn of the peoples or cause your nation to fall, declares the Sovereign LORD.' "

¹⁶Again the word of the LORD came to me: ¹⁷"Son of man, when the people of Israel were living in their own land, they defiled it by their conduct and their actions. Their conduct was like a woman's monthly uncleanness in my sight. ¹⁸So I poured out my wrath on them because they had shed blood in the land and because they had defiled it with their idols. ¹⁹I dispersed them among the nations, and they were scattered through the countries; I judged them according to their conduct and their actions. ²⁰And wherever they went among the nations they profaned my holy name, for it was said of them, 'These are the LORD's people, and yet they had to leave his land.' ²¹I had concern for my holy name, which the house of Israel profaned among the nations where they had gone.

²²"Therefore say to the house of Israel, 'This is what the Sovereign LORD says: It is not for your sake, O house of Israel, that I am going to do these things, but for the sake of my holy name, which you have profaned among the nations where you have gone. ²³I will show the holiness of my great name, which has been profaned among the nations, the name you have profaned among them. Then the nations will know that I am the LORD, declares the Sovereign LORD, when I show myself holy through you before their eyes.

²⁴"'For I will take you out of the nations; I will gather you from all the countries and bring you back into your own land. ²⁵I will sprinkle clean water on you, and you will be clean; I will cleanse you from all your impurities and from all your idols. ²⁶I will give you a new heart and put a new spirit in you; I will remove from you your heart of stone and give you a heart of flesh. ²⁷And I will put my Spirit in you and move you to follow my decrees and be careful to keep my laws. ²⁸You will live in the land I gave your forefathers; you will be my people, and I will be your God. ²⁹I will save you from all your uncleanness. I will call for the

grain and make it plentiful and will not bring famine upon you. ³⁰I will increase the fruit of the trees and the crops of the field, so that you will no longer suffer disgrace among the nations because of famine. ³¹Then you will remember your evil ways and wicked deeds, and you will loathe yourselves for your sins and detestable practices. ³²I want you to know that I am not doing this for your sake, declares the Sovereign LORD. Be ashamed and disgraced for your conduct, O house of Israel!

³³"'This is what the Sovereign LORD says: On the day I cleanse you from all your sins, I will resettle your towns, and the ruins will be rebuilt. ³⁴The desolate land will be cultivated instead of lying desolate in the sight of all who pass through it. ³⁵They will say, "This land that was laid waste has become like the garden of Eden; the cities that were lying in ruins, desolate and destroyed, are now fortified and inhabited." ³⁶Then the nations around you that remain will know that I the LORD have rebuilt what was destroyed and have replanted what was desolate. I the LORD have spoken, and I will do it.'

³⁷"This is what the Sovereign LORD says: Once again I will yield to the plea of the house of Israel and do this for them: I will make their people as numerous as sheep, ³⁸as numerous as the flocks for offerings at Jerusalem during her appointed feasts. So will the ruined cities be filled with flocks of people. Then they will know that I am the LORD."

The Valley of Dry Bones

37 The hand of the LORD was upon me, and he brought me out by the Spirit of the LORD and set me in the middle of a valley; it was full of bones. ²He led me

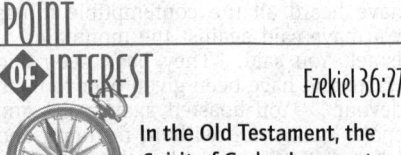

POINT OF INTEREST

Ezekiel 36:27

In the Old Testament, the Spirit of God only came to people at a specific time and for a specific purpose. It was not until some six hundred years after Ezekiel's prophetic career that God's indwelling Spirit became available at all times for all believers (see Acts 2:1–21).

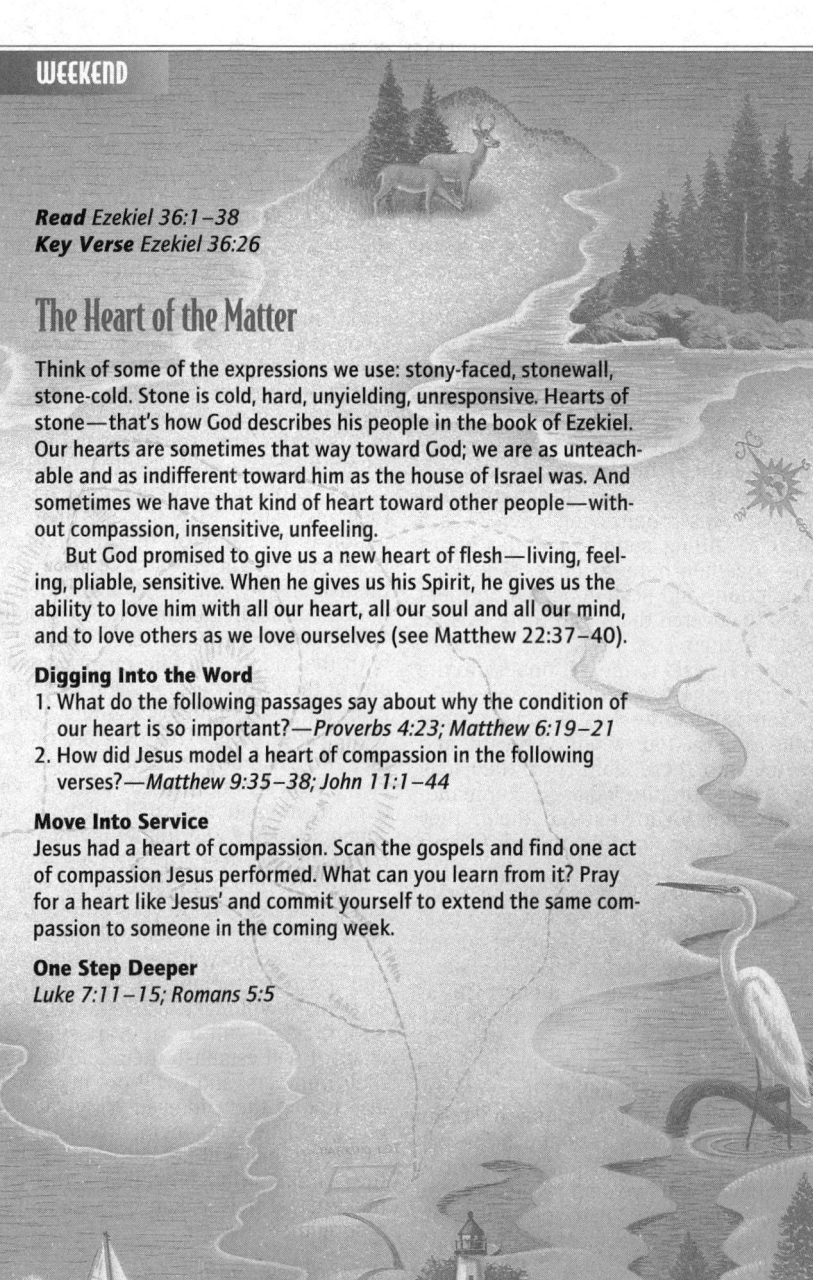

Read Ezekiel 36:1–38
Key Verse Ezekiel 36:26

The Heart of the Matter

Think of some of the expressions we use: stony-faced, stonewall, stone-cold. Stone is cold, hard, unyielding, unresponsive. Hearts of stone—that's how God describes his people in the book of Ezekiel. Our hearts are sometimes that way toward God; we are as unteachable and as indifferent toward him as the house of Israel was. And sometimes we have that kind of heart toward other people—without compassion, insensitive, unfeeling.

But God promised to give us a new heart of flesh—living, feeling, pliable, sensitive. When he gives us his Spirit, he gives us the ability to love him with all our heart, all our soul and all our mind, and to love others as we love ourselves (see Matthew 22:37–40).

Digging Into the Word
1. What do the following passages say about why the condition of our heart is so important?—*Proverbs 4:23; Matthew 6:19–21*
2. How did Jesus model a heart of compassion in the following verses?—*Matthew 9:35–38; John 11:1–44*

Move Into Service
Jesus had a heart of compassion. Scan the gospels and find one act of compassion Jesus performed. What can you learn from it? Pray for a heart like Jesus' and commit yourself to extend the same compassion to someone in the coming week.

One Step Deeper
Luke 7:11–15; Romans 5:5

Go to page 967 for your next devotional reading.

back and forth among them, and I saw a great many bones on the floor of the valley, bones that were very dry. ³He asked me, "Son of man, can these bones live?"

I said, "O Sovereign LORD, you alone know."

⁴Then he said to me, "Prophesy to these bones and say to them, 'Dry bones, hear the word of the LORD! ⁵This is what the Sovereign LORD says to these bones: I will make breath*a* enter you, and you will come to life. ⁶I will attach tendons to you and make flesh come upon you and cover you with skin; I will put breath in you, and you will come to life. Then you will know that I am the LORD.' "

⁷So I prophesied as I was commanded. And as I was prophesying, there was a noise, a rattling sound, and the bones came together, bone to bone. ⁸I looked, and tendons and flesh appeared on them and skin covered them, but there was no breath in them.

⁹Then he said to me, "Prophesy to the breath; prophesy, son of man, and say to it, 'This is what the Sovereign LORD says: Come from the four winds, O breath, and breathe into these slain, that they may live.' " ¹⁰So I prophesied as he commanded me, and breath entered them; they came to life and stood up on their feet—a vast army.

¹¹Then he said to me: "Son of man, these bones are the whole house of Israel. They say, 'Our bones are dried up and our hope is gone; we are cut off.' ¹²Therefore prophesy and say to them: 'This is what the Sovereign LORD says: O my people, I am going to open your graves and bring you up from them; I will bring you back to the land of Israel. ¹³Then you, my people, will know that I am the LORD, when I open your graves and bring you up from them. ¹⁴I will put my Spirit in you and you will live, and I will settle you in your own land. Then you will know that I the LORD have spoken, and I have done it, declares the LORD.' "

One Nation Under One King

¹⁵The word of the LORD came to me: ¹⁶"Son of man, take a stick of wood and write on it, 'Belonging to Judah and the Israelites associated with him.' Then take another stick of wood, and write on it, 'Ephraim's stick, belonging to Joseph and all the house of Israel associated with him.' ¹⁷Join them together into one stick so that they will become one in your hand.

¹⁸"When your countrymen ask you, 'Won't you tell us what you mean by this?' ¹⁹say to them, 'This is what the Sovereign LORD says: I am going to take the stick of Joseph—which is in Ephraim's hand—and of the Israelite tribes associated with him, and join it to Judah's stick, making them a single stick of wood, and they will become one in my hand.' ²⁰Hold before their eyes the sticks you have written on ²¹and say to them, 'This is what the Sovereign LORD says: I will take the Israelites out of the nations where they have gone. I will gather them from all around and bring them back into their own land. ²²I will make them one nation in the land, on the mountains of Israel. There will be one king over all of them and they will never again be two nations or be divided into two kingdoms. ²³They will no longer defile themselves with their idols and vile images or with any of their offenses, for I will save them from all their sinful backsliding,*b* and I will cleanse them. They will be my people, and I will be their God.

²⁴" 'My servant David will be king over them, and they will all have one shepherd. They will follow my laws and be careful to keep my decrees. ²⁵They will live in the land I gave to my servant Jacob, the land where your fathers lived. They and their children and their children's children will live there forever, and David my servant will be their prince forever. ²⁶I will make a covenant of peace with them; it will be an everlasting covenant. I will establish them and increase their numbers, and I will put my sanctuary among them forever. ²⁷My dwelling place will be with them; I will be their God, and they will be my people. ²⁸Then the nations will know that I the LORD make Israel holy, when my sanctuary is among them forever.' "

A Prophecy Against Gog

38 The word of the LORD came to me: ²"Son of man, set your face against Gog, of the land of Magog, the chief prince of*c* Meshech and Tubal; prophesy against him ³and say: 'This is what the

---

a5 The Hebrew for this word can also mean *wind* or *spirit* (see verses 6-14).   *b23* Many Hebrew manuscripts (see also Septuagint); most Hebrew manuscripts *all their dwelling places where they sinned*   *c2* Or *the prince of Rosh,*

Sovereign LORD says: I am against you, O Gog, chief prince of*a* Meshech and Tubal. **4**I will turn you around, put hooks in your jaws and bring you out with your whole army—your horses, your horsemen fully armed, and a great horde with large and small shields, all of them brandishing their swords. **5**Persia, Cush*b* and Put will be with them, all with shields and helmets, **6**also Gomer with all its troops, and Beth Togarmah from the far north with all its troops—the many nations with you.

7" 'Get ready; be prepared, you and all the hordes gathered about you, and take command of them. **8**After many days you will be called to arms. In future years you will invade a land that has recovered from war, whose people were gathered from many nations to the mountains of Israel, which had long been desolate. They had been brought out from the nations, and now all of them live in safety. **9**You and all your troops and the many nations with you will go up, advancing like a storm; you will be like a cloud covering the land.

10" 'This is what the Sovereign LORD says: On that day thoughts will come into your mind and you will devise an evil scheme. **11**You will say, "I will invade a land of unwalled villages; I will attack a peaceful and unsuspecting people—all of them living without walls and without gates and bars. **12**I will plunder and loot and turn my hand against the resettled ruins and the people gathered from the nations, rich in livestock and goods, living at the center of the land." **13**Sheba and Dedan and the merchants of Tarshish and all her villages*c* will say to you, "Have you come to plunder? Have you gathered your hordes to loot, to carry off silver and gold, to take away livestock and goods and to seize much plunder?" '

14"Therefore, son of man, prophesy and say to Gog: 'This is what the Sovereign LORD says: In that day, when my people Israel are living in safety, will you not take notice of it? **15**You will come from your place in the far north, you and many nations with you, all of them riding on horses, a great horde, a mighty army. **16**You will advance against my people Israel like a cloud that covers the land. In days to come, O Gog, I will bring you against my land, so that the nations may know me when I show myself holy through you before their eyes.

17" 'This is what the Sovereign LORD says: Are you not the one I spoke of in former days by my servants the prophets of Israel? At that time they prophesied for years that I would bring you against them. **18**This is what will happen in that day: When Gog attacks the land of Israel, my hot anger will be aroused, declares the Sovereign LORD. **19**In my zeal and fiery wrath I declare that at that time there shall be a great earthquake in the land of Israel. **20**The fish of the sea, the birds of the air, the beasts of the field, every creature that moves along the ground, and all the people on the face of the earth will tremble at my presence. The mountains will be overturned, the cliffs will crumble and every wall will fall to the ground. **21**I will summon a sword against Gog on all my mountains, declares the Sovereign LORD. Every man's sword will be against his brother. **22**I will execute judgment upon him with plague and bloodshed; I will pour down torrents of rain, hailstones and burning sulfur on him and on his troops and on the many nations with him. **23**And so I will show my greatness and my holiness, and I will make myself known in the sight of many nations. Then they will know that I am the LORD.'

39 "Son of man, prophesy against Gog and say: 'This is what the Sovereign LORD says: I am against you, O Gog, chief prince of*a* Meshech and Tubal. **2**I will turn you around and drag you along. I will bring you from the far north and

---

a3,1 Or Gog, prince of Rosh,   *b5 That is, the upper Nile region*   *c13 Or her strong lions*

POINT OF INTEREST

Ezekiel 38:10-12

When Ezekiel gave this prophecy, the idea of a single village living without protective walls, much less an entire population living on an exposed plain, was preposterous. To put this in modern terms, it would be like a bank without a vault. Travel to Israel today, however, and you will see the scenario envisioned by Ezekiel 2,500 years ago. A lucky guess? A prophecy from God? You decide!

send you against the mountains of Israel. ³Then I will strike your bow from your left hand and make your arrows drop from your right hand. ⁴On the mountains of Israel you will fall, you and all your troops and the nations with you. I will give you as food to all kinds of carrion birds and to the wild animals. ⁵You will fall in the open field, for I have spoken, declares the Sovereign LORD. ⁶I will send fire on Magog and on those who live in safety in the coastlands, and they will know that I am the LORD.

⁷" 'I will make known my holy name among my people Israel. I will no longer let my holy name be profaned, and the nations will know that I the LORD am the Holy One in Israel. ⁸It is coming! It will surely take place, declares the Sovereign LORD. This is the day I have spoken of.

⁹" 'Then those who live in the towns of Israel will go out and use the weapons for fuel and burn them up—the small and large shields, the bows and arrows, the war clubs and spears. For seven years they will use them for fuel. ¹⁰They will not need to gather wood from the fields or cut it from the forests, because they will use the weapons for fuel. And they will plunder those who plundered them and loot those who looted them, declares the Sovereign LORD.

¹¹" 'On that day I will give Gog a burial place in Israel, in the valley of those who travel east toward*a* the Sea.*b* It will block the way of travelers, because Gog and all his hordes will be buried there. So it will be called the Valley of Hamon Gog.*c*

¹²" 'For seven months the house of Israel will be burying them in order to cleanse the land. ¹³All the people of the land will bury them, and the day I am glorified will be a memorable day for them, declares the Sovereign LORD.

¹⁴" 'Men will be regularly employed to cleanse the land. Some will go throughout the land and, in addition to them, others will bury those that remain on the ground. At the end of the seven months they will begin their search. ¹⁵As they go through the land and one of them sees a human bone, he will set up a marker beside it until the gravediggers have buried it in the Valley of Hamon Gog. ¹⁶(Also a town called Hamonah*d* will be there.) And so they will cleanse the land.'

¹⁷"Son of man, this is what the Sovereign LORD says: Call out to every kind of bird and all the wild animals: 'Assemble and come together from all around to the sacrifice I am preparing for you, the great sacrifice on the mountains of Israel. There you will eat flesh and drink blood. ¹⁸You will eat the flesh of mighty men and drink the blood of the princes of the earth as if they were rams and lambs, goats and bulls—all of them fattened animals from Bashan. ¹⁹At the sacrifice I am preparing for you, you will eat fat till you are glutted and drink blood till you are drunk. ²⁰At my table you will eat your fill of horses and riders, mighty men and soldiers of every kind,' declares the Sovereign LORD.

²¹"I will display my glory among the nations, and all the nations will see the punishment I inflict and the hand I lay upon them. ²²From that day forward the house of Israel will know that I am the LORD their God. ²³And the nations will know that the people of Israel went into exile for their sin, because they were unfaithful to me. So I hid my face from them and handed them over to their enemies, and they all fell by the sword. ²⁴I dealt with them according to their uncleanness and their offenses, and I hid my face from them.

²⁵"Therefore this is what the Sovereign LORD says: I will now bring Jacob back from captivity*e* and will have compassion on all the people of Israel, and I will be zealous for my holy name. ²⁶They will forget their shame and all the unfaithfulness they showed toward me when they lived in safety in their land with no one to make them afraid. ²⁷When I have brought them back from the nations and have gathered them from the countries of their enemies, I will show myself holy through them in the sight of many nations. ²⁸Then they will know that I am the LORD their God, for though I sent them into exile among the nations, I will gather them to their own land, not leaving any behind. ²⁹I will no longer hide my face from them, for I will pour out my Spirit on the house of Israel, declares the Sovereign LORD."

The New Temple Area

40 In the twenty-fifth year of our exile, at the beginning of the year, on the

---

a 11 Or *of*   *b 11* That is, the Dead Sea
c 11 Hamon Gog means *hordes of Gog.*
d 16 Hamonah means *horde.*   *e 25* Or *now restore the fortunes of Jacob*

tenth of the month, in the fourteenth year after the fall of the city—on that very day the hand of the LORD was upon me and he took me there. ²In visions of God he took me to the land of Israel and set me on a very high mountain, on whose south side were some buildings that looked like a city. ³He took me there, and I saw a man whose appearance was like bronze; he was standing in the gateway with a linen cord and a measuring rod in his hand. ⁴The man said to me, "Son of man, look with your eyes and hear with your ears and pay attention to everything I am going to show you, for that is why you have been brought here. Tell the house of Israel everything you see."

The East Gate to the Outer Court

⁵I saw a wall completely surrounding the temple area. The length of the measuring rod in the man's hand was six long cubits, each of which was a cubit*a* and a handbreadth.*b* He measured the wall; it was one measuring rod thick and one rod high.

⁶Then he went to the gate facing east. He climbed its steps and measured the threshold of the gate; it was one rod deep.*c* ⁷The alcoves for the guards were one rod long and one rod wide, and the projecting walls between the alcoves were five cubits thick. And the threshold of the gate next to the portico facing the temple was one rod deep.

⁸Then he measured the portico of the gateway; ⁹it*d* was eight cubits deep and its jambs were two cubits thick. The portico of the gateway faced the temple.

¹⁰Inside the east gate were three alcoves on each side; the three had the same measurements, and the faces of the projecting walls on each side had the same measurements. ¹¹Then he measured the width of the entrance to the gateway; it was ten cubits and its length was thirteen cubits. ¹²In front of each alcove was a wall one cubit high, and the alcoves were six cubits square. ¹³Then he measured the gateway from the top of the rear wall of one alcove to the top of the opposite one; the distance was twenty-five cubits from one parapet opening to the opposite one. ¹⁴He measured along the faces of the projecting walls all around the inside of the gateway—sixty cubits. The measurement was up to the portico*e* facing the courtyard.*f* ¹⁵The distance from the entrance of the gate-

way to the far end of its portico was fifty cubits. ¹⁶The alcoves and the projecting walls inside the gateway were surmounted by narrow parapet openings all around, as was the portico; the openings all around faced inward. The faces of the projecting walls were decorated with palm trees.

The Outer Court

¹⁷Then he brought me into the outer court. There I saw some rooms and a pavement that had been constructed all around the court; there were thirty rooms along the pavement. ¹⁸It abutted the sides of the gateways and was as wide as they were long; this was the lower pavement. ¹⁹Then he measured the distance from the inside of the lower gateway to the outside of the inner court; it was a hundred cubits on the east side as well as on the north.

The North Gate

²⁰Then he measured the length and width of the gate facing north, leading into the outer court. ²¹Its alcoves—three on each side—its projecting walls and its portico had the same measurements as those of the first gateway. It was fifty cubits long and twenty-five cubits wide. ²²Its openings, its portico and its palm tree decorations had the same measurements as those of the gate facing east. Seven steps led up to it, with its portico opposite them. ²³There was a gate to the inner court facing the north gate, just as there was on the east. He measured from one gate to the opposite one; it was a hundred cubits.

The South Gate

²⁴Then he led me to the south side and I saw a gate facing south. He measured its jambs and its portico, and they had the same measurements as the others. ²⁵The gateway and its portico had narrow openings all around, like the openings of the others. It was fifty cubits long and twenty-five cubits wide. ²⁶Seven steps

a5 The common cubit was about 1 1/2 feet (about 0.5 meter). *b5* That is, about 3 inches (about 8 centimeters) *c6* Septuagint; Hebrew *deep, the first threshold, one rod deep* *d8,9* Many Hebrew manuscripts, Septuagint, Vulgate and Syriac; most Hebrew manuscripts *gateway facing the temple; it was one rod deep; it* *9Then he measured the portico of the gateway; it* *e14* Septuagint; Hebrew *projecting wall* *f14* The meaning of the Hebrew for this verse is uncertain.

led up to it, with its portico opposite them; it had palm tree decorations on the faces of the projecting walls on each side. ²⁷The inner court also had a gate facing south, and he measured from this gate to the outer gate on the south side; it was a hundred cubits.

Gates to the Inner Court

²⁸Then he brought me into the inner court through the south gate, and he measured the south gate; it had the same measurements as the others. ²⁹Its alcoves, its projecting walls and its portico had the same measurements as the others. The gateway and its portico had openings all around. It was fifty cubits long and twenty-five cubits wide. ³⁰(The porticoes of the gateways around the inner court were twenty-five cubits wide and five cubits deep.) ³¹Its portico faced the outer court; palm trees decorated its jambs, and eight steps led up to it.

³²Then he brought me to the inner court on the east side, and he measured the gateway; it had the same measurements as the others. ³³Its alcoves, its projecting walls and its portico had the same measurements as the others. The gateway and its portico had openings all around. It was fifty cubits long and twenty-five cubits wide. ³⁴Its portico faced the outer court; palm trees decorated the jambs on either side, and eight steps led up to it.

³⁵Then he brought me to the north gate and measured it. It had the same measurements as the others, ³⁶as did its alcoves, its projecting walls and its portico, and it had openings all around. It was fifty cubits long and twenty-five cubits wide. ³⁷Its portico*a* faced the outer court; palm trees decorated the jambs on either side, and eight steps led up to it.

The Rooms for Preparing Sacrifices

³⁸A room with a doorway was by the portico in each of the inner gateways, where the burnt offerings were washed. ³⁹In the portico of the gateway were two tables on each side, on which the burnt offerings, sin offerings and guilt offerings were slaughtered. ⁴⁰By the outside wall of the portico of the gateway, near the steps at the entrance to the north gateway were two tables, and on the other side of the steps were two tables. ⁴¹So there were four tables on one side of the gateway and four on the other—eight ta-

bles in all—on which the sacrifices were slaughtered. ⁴²There were also four tables of dressed stone for the burnt offerings, each a cubit and a half long, a cubit and a half wide and a cubit high. On them were placed the utensils for slaughtering the burnt offerings and the other sacrifices. ⁴³And double-pronged hooks, each a handbreadth long, were attached to the wall all around. The tables were for the flesh of the offerings.

Rooms for the Priests

⁴⁴Outside the inner gate, within the inner court, were two rooms, one*b* at the side of the north gate and facing south, and another at the side of the south*c* gate and facing north. ⁴⁵He said to me, "The room facing south is for the priests who have charge of the temple, ⁴⁶and the room facing north is for the priests who have charge of the altar. These are the sons of Zadok, who are the only Levites who may draw near to the LORD to minister before him."

⁴⁷Then he measured the court: It was square—a hundred cubits long and a hundred cubits wide. And the altar was in front of the temple.

The Temple

⁴⁸He brought me to the portico of the temple and measured the jambs of the portico; they were five cubits wide on either side. The width of the entrance was fourteen cubits and its projecting walls were*d* three cubits wide on either side. ⁴⁹The portico was twenty cubits wide, and twelve*e* cubits from front to back. It was reached by a flight of stairs,*f* and there were pillars on each side of the jambs.

41 Then the man brought me to the outer sanctuary and measured the jambs; the width of the jambs was six cubits*g* on each side.*h* ²The entrance was ten cubits wide, and the projecting walls on each side of it were five cubits wide. He also measured the outer sanctu-

---

a37 Septuagint (see also verses 31 and 34); Hebrew *jambs*　*b44* Septuagint; Hebrew *were rooms for singers, which were*　*c44* Septuagint; Hebrew *east*　*d48* Septuagint; Hebrew *entrance was*　*e49* Septuagint; Hebrew *eleven*　*f49* Hebrew; Septuagint *Ten steps led up to it*　*g1* The common cubit was about 1 1/2 feet (about 0.5 meter).　*h1* One Hebrew manuscript and Septuagint; most Hebrew manuscripts *side, the width of the tent* ary; it was forty cubits long and twenty cubits wide.

³Then he went into the inner sanctuary and measured the jambs of the entrance; each was two cubits wide. The entrance was six cubits wide, and the projecting walls on each side of it were seven cubits wide. ⁴And he measured the length of the inner sanctuary; it was twenty cubits, and its width was twenty cubits across the end of the outer sanctuary. He said to me, "This is the Most Holy Place."

⁵Then he measured the wall of the temple; it was six cubits thick, and each side room around the temple was four cubits wide. ⁶The side rooms were on three levels, one above another, thirty on each level. There were ledges all around the wall of the temple to serve as supports for the side rooms, so that the supports were not inserted into the wall of the temple. ⁷The side rooms all around the temple were wider at each successive level. The structure surrounding the temple was built in ascending stages, so that the rooms widened as one went upward. A stairway went up from the lowest floor to the top floor through the middle floor.

⁸I saw that the temple had a raised base all around it, forming the foundation of the side rooms. It was the length of the rod, six long cubits. ⁹The outer wall of the side rooms was five cubits thick. The open area between the side rooms of the temple ¹⁰and the ⌐priests'⌐ rooms was twenty cubits wide all around the temple. ¹¹There were entrances to the side rooms from the open area, one on the north and another on the south; and the base adjoining the open area was five cubits wide all around.

¹²The building facing the temple courtyard on the west side was seventy cubits wide. The wall of the building was five cubits thick all around, and its length was ninety cubits.

¹³Then he measured the temple; it was a hundred cubits long, and the temple courtyard and the building with its walls were also a hundred cubits long. ¹⁴The width of the temple courtyard on the east, including the front of the temple, was a hundred cubits.

¹⁵Then he measured the length of the building facing the courtyard at the rear of the temple, including its galleries on each side; it was a hundred cubits.

The outer sanctuary, the inner sanctu-

ary and the portico facing the court, ¹⁶as well as the thresholds and the narrow windows and galleries around the three of them—everything beyond and including the threshold was covered with wood. The floor, the wall up to the windows, and the windows were covered. ¹⁷In the space above the outside of the entrance to the inner sanctuary and on the walls at regular intervals all around the inner and outer sanctuary ¹⁸were carved cherubim and palm trees. Palm trees alternated with cherubim. Each cherub had two faces: ¹⁹the face of a man toward the palm tree on one side and the face of a lion toward the palm tree on the other. They were carved all around the whole temple. ²⁰From the floor to the area above the entrance, cherubim and palm trees were carved on the wall of the outer sanctuary.

²¹The outer sanctuary had a rectangular doorframe, and the one at the front of the Most Holy Place was similar. ²²There was a wooden altar three cubits high and two cubits square^a; its corners, its base^b and its sides were of wood. The man said to me, "This is the table that is before the LORD." ²³Both the outer sanctuary and the Most Holy Place had double doors. ²⁴Each door had two leaves—two hinged leaves for each door. ²⁵And on the doors of the outer sanctuary were carved cherubim and palm trees like those carved on the walls, and there was a wooden overhang on the front of the portico. ²⁶On the sidewalls of the portico were narrow windows with palm trees carved on each side. The side rooms of the temple also had overhangs.

Rooms for the Priests

42 Then the man led me northward into the outer court and brought me to the rooms opposite the temple courtyard and opposite the outer wall on the north side. ²The building whose door faced north was a hundred cubits^c long and fifty cubits wide. ³Both in the section twenty cubits from the inner court and in the section opposite the pavement of the outer court, gallery faced gallery at the three levels. ⁴In front of the rooms was an inner passageway ten cubits wide and a hundred cubits^d long. Their doors were

^{a}22 Septuagint; Hebrew *long* ^{b}22 Septuagint; Hebrew *length* ^{c}2 The common cubit was about 1 1/2 feet (about 0.5 meter). ^{d}4 Septuagint and Syriac; Hebrew *and one cubit* on the north. ⁵Now the upper rooms were narrower, for the galleries took more space from them than from the rooms on the lower and middle floors of the building. ⁶The rooms on the third floor had no pillars, as the courts had; so they were smaller in floor space than those on the lower and middle floors. ⁷There was an outer wall parallel to the rooms and the outer court; it extended in front of the rooms for fifty cubits. ⁸While the row of rooms on the side next to the outer court was fifty cubits long, the row on the side nearest the sanctuary was a hundred cubits long. ⁹The lower rooms had an entrance on the east side as one enters them from the outer court.

¹⁰On the south side*a* along the length of the wall of the outer court, adjoining the temple courtyard and opposite the outer wall, were rooms ¹¹with a passageway in front of them. These were like the rooms on the north; they had the same length and width, with similar exits and dimensions. Similar to the doorways on the north ¹²were the doorways of the rooms on the south. There was a doorway at the beginning of the passageway that was parallel to the corresponding wall extending eastward, by which one enters the rooms.

¹³Then he said to me, "The north and south rooms facing the temple courtyard are the priests' rooms, where the priests who approach the LORD will eat the most holy offerings. There they will put the most holy offerings—the grain offerings, the sin offerings and the guilt offerings—for the place is holy. ¹⁴Once the priests enter the holy precincts, they are not to go into the outer court until they leave behind the garments in which they minister, for these are holy. They are to put on other clothes before they go near the places that are for the people."

¹⁵When he had finished measuring what was inside the temple area, he led me out by the east gate and measured the area all around: ¹⁶He measured the east side with the measuring rod; it was five hundred cubits.*b* ¹⁷He measured the north side; it was five hundred cubits*c* by the measuring rod. ¹⁸He measured the south side; it was five hundred cubits by the measuring rod. ¹⁹Then he turned to the west side and measured; it was five hundred cubits by the measuring rod. ²⁰So he measured the area on all four sides. It had a wall around it, five hun-

dred cubits long and five hundred cubits wide, to separate the holy from the common.

The Glory Returns to the Temple

43 Then the man brought me to the gate facing east, ²and I saw the glory of the God of Israel coming from the east. His voice was like the roar of rushing waters, and the land was radiant with his glory. ³The vision I saw was like the vision I had seen when he*d* came to destroy the city and like the visions I had seen by the Kebar River, and I fell facedown. ⁴The glory of the LORD entered the temple through the gate facing east. ⁵Then the Spirit lifted me up and brought me into the inner court, and the glory of the LORD filled the temple.

⁶While the man was standing beside me, I heard someone speaking to me from inside the temple. ⁷He said: "Son of man, this is the place of my throne and the place for the soles of my feet. This is where I will live among the Israelites forever. The house of Israel will never again defile my holy name—neither they nor their kings—by their prostitution*e* and the lifeless idols*f* of their kings at their high places. ⁸When they placed their threshold next to my threshold and their doorposts beside my doorposts, with only a wall between me and them, they defiled my holy name by their detestable practices. So I destroyed them in my anger. ⁹Now let them put away from me their prostitution and the lifeless idols of their kings, and I will live among them forever.

¹⁰"Son of man, describe the temple to the people of Israel, that they may be ashamed of their sins. Let them consider the plan, ¹¹and if they are ashamed of all they have done, make known to them the design of the temple—its arrangement, its exits and entrances—its whole design and all its regulations*g* and laws. Write these down before them so that they may be faithful to its design and follow all its regulations.

¹²"This is the law of the temple: All the

---

a 10 Septuagint; Hebrew *Eastward*
b 16 See Septuagint of verse 17; Hebrew *rods*; also in verses 18 and 19.　　*c 17* Septuagint; Hebrew *rods*　　*d 3* Some Hebrew manuscripts and Vulgate; most Hebrew manuscripts *I*　　*e 7* Or *their spiritual adultery*; also in verse 9　　*f 7* Or *the corpses*; also in verse 9　　*g 11* Some Hebrew manuscripts and Septuagint; most Hebrew manuscripts *regulations and its whole design*

surrounding area on top of the mountain will be most holy. Such is the law of the temple.

The Altar

¹³"These are the measurements of the altar in long cubits, that cubit being a cubit*a* and a handbreadth*b*: Its gutter is a cubit deep and a cubit wide, with a rim of one span*c* around the edge. And this is the height of the altar: ¹⁴From the gutter on the ground up to the lower ledge it is two cubits high and a cubit wide, and from the smaller ledge up to the larger ledge it is four cubits high and a cubit wide. ¹⁵The altar hearth is four cubits high, and four horns project upward from the hearth. ¹⁶The altar hearth is square, twelve cubits long and twelve cubits wide. ¹⁷The upper ledge also is square, fourteen cubits long and fourteen cubits wide, with a rim of half a cubit and a gutter of a cubit all around. The steps of the altar face east."

¹⁸Then he said to me, "Son of man, this is what the Sovereign Lord says: These will be the regulations for sacrificing burnt offerings and sprinkling blood upon the altar when it is built: ¹⁹You are to give a young bull as a sin offering to the priests, who are Levites, of the family of Zadok, who come near to minister before me, declares the Sovereign Lord. ²⁰You are to take some of its blood and put it on the four horns of the altar and on the four corners of the upper ledge and all around the rim, and so purify the altar and make atonement for it. ²¹You are to take the bull for the sin offering and burn it in the designated part of the temple area outside the sanctuary.

²²"On the second day you are to offer a male goat without defect for a sin offering, and the altar is to be purified as it was purified with the bull. ²³When you have finished purifying it, you are to offer a young bull and a ram from the flock, both without defect. ²⁴You are to offer them before the Lord, and the priests are to sprinkle salt on them and sacrifice them as a burnt offering to the Lord.

²⁵"For seven days you are to provide a male goat daily for a sin offering; you are also to provide a young bull and a ram from the flock, both without defect. ²⁶For seven days they are to make atonement for the altar and cleanse it; thus they will dedicate it. ²⁷At the end of these days, from the eighth day on, the priests are to present your burnt offerings and fellowship offerings*d* on the altar. Then I will accept you, declares the Sovereign Lord."

The Prince, the Levites, the Priests

44 Then the man brought me back to the outer gate of the sanctuary, the one facing east, and it was shut. ²The Lord said to me, "This gate is to remain shut. It must not be opened; no one may enter through it. It is to remain shut because the Lord, the God of Israel, has entered through it. ³The prince himself is the only one who may sit inside the gateway to eat in the presence of the Lord. He is to enter by way of the portico of the gateway and go out the same way."

⁴Then the man brought me by way of the north gate to the front of the temple. I looked and saw the glory of the Lord filling the temple of the Lord, and I fell facedown.

⁵The Lord said to me, "Son of man, look carefully, listen closely and give attention to everything I tell you concerning all the regulations regarding the temple of the Lord. Give attention to the entrance of the temple and all the exits of the sanctuary. ⁶Say to the rebellious house of Israel, 'This is what the Sovereign Lord says: Enough of your detestable practices, O house of Israel! ⁷In addition to all your other detestable practices, you brought foreigners uncircumcised in heart and flesh into my sanctuary, desecrating my temple while you offered me food, fat and blood, and you broke my covenant. ⁸Instead of carrying out your duty in regard to my holy things, you put others in charge of my sanctuary. ⁹This is what the Sovereign Lord says: No foreigner uncircumcised in heart and flesh is to enter my sanctuary, not even the foreigners who live among the Israelites.

¹⁰" 'The Levites who went far from me when Israel went astray and who wandered from me after their idols must bear the consequences of their sin. ¹¹They may serve in my sanctuary, having charge of the gates of the temple and serving in it; they may slaughter the burnt offerings and sacrifices for the people and stand before the people and serve them. ¹²But because they served them in

---

a13 The common cubit was about 1 1/2 feet (about 0.5 meter).　　*b13* That is, about 3 inches (about 8 centimeters)　　*c13* That is, about 9 inches (about 22 centimeters)　　*d27* Traditionally *peace offerings* the presence of their idols and made the house of Israel fall into sin, therefore I have sworn with uplifted hand that they must bear the consequences of their sin, declares the Sovereign LORD. 13They are not to come near to serve me as priests or come near any of my holy things or my most holy offerings; they must bear the shame of their detestable practices. 14Yet I will put them in charge of the duties of the temple and all the work that is to be done in it.

15" 'But the priests, who are Levites and descendants of Zadok and who faithfully carried out the duties of my sanctuary when the Israelites went astray from me, are to come near to minister before me; they are to stand before me to offer sacrifices of fat and blood, declares the Sovereign LORD. 16They alone are to enter my sanctuary; they alone are to come near my table to minister before me and perform my service.

17" 'When they enter the gates of the inner court, they are to wear linen clothes; they must not wear any woolen garment while ministering at the gates of the inner court or inside the temple. 18They are to wear linen turbans on their heads and linen undergarments around their waists. They must not wear anything that makes them perspire. 19When they go out into the outer court where the people are, they are to take off the clothes they have been ministering in and are to leave them in the sacred rooms, and put on other clothes, so that they do not consecrate the people by means of their garments.

20" 'They must not shave their heads or let their hair grow long, but they are to keep the hair of their heads trimmed. 21No priest is to drink wine when he enters the inner court. 22They must not marry widows or divorced women; they may marry only virgins of Israelite descent or widows of priests. 23They are to teach my people the difference between the holy and the common and show them how to distinguish between the unclean and the clean.

24" 'In any dispute, the priests are to serve as judges and decide it according to my ordinances. They are to keep my laws and my decrees for all my appointed feasts, and they are to keep my Sabbaths holy.

25" 'A priest must not defile himself by going near a dead person; however, if the dead person was his father or mother, son or daughter, brother or unmarried sister, then he may defile himself. 26After he is cleansed, he must wait seven days. 27On the day he goes into the inner court of the sanctuary to minister in the sanctuary, he is to offer a sin offering for himself, declares the Sovereign LORD.

28" 'I am to be the only inheritance the priests have. You are to give them no possession in Israel; I will be their possession. 29They will eat the grain offerings, the sin offerings and the guilt offerings; and everything in Israel devoteda to the LORD will belong to them. 30The best of all the firstfruits and of all your special gifts will belong to the priests. You are to give them the first portion of your ground meal so that a blessing may rest on your household. 31The priests must not eat anything, bird or animal, found dead or torn by wild animals.

Division of the Land

45 " 'When you allot the land as an inheritance, you are to present to the LORD a portion of the land as a sacred district, 25,000 cubits long and 20,000b cubits wide; the entire area will be holy. 2Of this, a section 500 cubits square is to be for the sanctuary, with 50 cubits around it for open land. 3In the sacred district, measure off a section 25,000 cubitsc long and 10,000 cubitsd wide. In it will be the sanctuary, the Most Holy Place. 4It will be the sacred portion of the land for the priests, who minister in the sanctuary and who draw near to minister before the LORD. It will be a place for their houses as well as a holy place for the sanctuary. 5An area 25,000 cubits long and 10,000 cubits wide will belong to the Levites, who serve in the temple, as their possession for towns to live in.e

6" 'You are to give the city as its property an area 5,000 cubits wide and 25,000 cubits long, adjoining the sacred portion; it will belong to the whole house of Israel.

7" 'The prince will have the land bordering each side of the area formed by the sacred district and the property of the

---

a29 The Hebrew term refers to the irrevocable giving over of things or persons to the LORD.
b1 Septuagint (see also verses 3 and 5 and 48:9); Hebrew 10,000   c3 That is, about 7 miles (about 12 kilometers)   d3 That is, about 3 miles (about 5 kilometers)   e5 Septuagint; Hebrew temple; they will have as their possession 20 rooms

city. It will extend westward from the west side and eastward from the east side, running lengthwise from the western to the eastern border parallel to one of the tribal portions. ⁸This land will be his possession in Israel. And my princes will no longer oppress my people but will allow the house of Israel to possess the land according to their tribes.

⁹" 'This is what the Sovereign LORD says: You have gone far enough, O princes of Israel! Give up your violence and oppression and do what is just and right. Stop dispossessing my people, declares the Sovereign LORD. ¹⁰You are to use accurate scales, an accurate ephah*ᵃ* and an accurate bath.*ᵇ* ¹¹The ephah and the bath are to be the same size, the bath containing a tenth of a homer*ᶜ* and the ephah a tenth of a homer; the homer is to be the standard measure for both. ¹²The shekel*ᵈ* is to consist of twenty gerahs. Twenty shekels plus twenty-five shekels plus fifteen shekels equal one mina.*ᵉ*

Offerings and Holy Days

¹³" 'This is the special gift you are to offer: a sixth of an ephah from each homer of wheat and a sixth of an ephah from each homer of barley. ¹⁴The prescribed portion of oil, measured by the bath, is a tenth of a bath from each cor (which consists of ten baths or one homer, for ten baths are equivalent to a homer). ¹⁵Also one sheep is to be taken from every flock of two hundred from the well-watered pastures of Israel. These will be used for the grain offerings, burnt offerings and fellowship offerings*ᶠ* to make atonement for the people, declares the Sovereign LORD. ¹⁶All the people of the land will participate in this special gift for the use of the prince in Israel. ¹⁷It will be the duty of the prince to provide the burnt offerings, grain offerings and drink offerings at the festivals, the New Moons and the Sabbaths—at all the appointed feasts of the house of Israel. He will provide the sin offerings, grain offerings, burnt offerings and fellowship offerings to make atonement for the house of Israel.

¹⁸" 'This is what the Sovereign LORD says: In the first month on the first day you are to take a young bull without defect and purify the sanctuary. ¹⁹The priest is to take some of the blood of the sin offering and put it on the doorposts of the temple, on the four corners of the upper ledge of the altar and on the gateposts of the inner court. ²⁰You are to do the same on the seventh day of the month for anyone who sins unintentionally or through ignorance; so you are to make atonement for the temple.

²¹" 'In the first month on the fourteenth day you are to observe the Passover, a feast lasting seven days, during which you shall eat bread made without yeast. ²²On that day the prince is to provide a bull as a sin offering for himself and for all the people of the land. ²³Every day during the seven days of the Feast he is to provide seven bulls and seven rams without defect as a burnt offering to the LORD, and a male goat for a sin offering. ²⁴He is to provide as a grain offering an ephah for each bull and an ephah for each ram, along with a hin*ᵍ* of oil for each ephah.

²⁵" 'During the seven days of the Feast, which begins in the seventh month on the fifteenth day, he is to make the same provision for sin offerings, burnt offerings, grain offerings and oil.

46 " 'This is what the Sovereign LORD says: The gate of the inner court facing east is to be shut on the six working days, but on the Sabbath day and on the day of the New Moon it is to be opened. ²The prince is to enter from the outside

---

ᵃ10 An ephah was a dry measure.   *ᵇ10* A bath was a liquid measure.   *ᶜ11* A homer was a dry measure.   *ᵈ12* A shekel weighed about 2/5 ounce (about 11.5 grams).   *ᵉ12* That is, 60 shekels; the common mina was 50 shekels.
ᶠ15 Traditionally *peace offerings*; also in verse 17
ᵍ24 That is, probably about 4 quarts (about 4 liters)

POINT OF INTEREST

Ezekiel 45:9-12

Perhaps more people have compromised their integrity by cheating in academics or in business than by cheating on their spouses. It's so easy to "share" someone else's homework, dip a little from the till, or get even with an unkind worker or boss. But cheating is cheating, whether it's on a test, in a relationship or at work. Ezekiel's message from God is as unchanging as God himself: Treat others with fairness and justice.

through the portico of the gateway and stand by the gatepost. The priests are to sacrifice his burnt offering and his fellowship offerings.*a* He is to worship at the threshold of the gateway and then go out, but the gate will not be shut until evening. ³On the Sabbaths and New Moons the people of the land are to worship in the presence of the LORD at the entrance to that gateway. ⁴The burnt offering the prince brings to the LORD on the Sabbath day is to be six male lambs and a ram, all without defect. ⁵The grain offering given with the ram is to be an ephah,*b* and the grain offering with the lambs is to be as much as he pleases, along with a hin*c* of oil for each ephah. ⁶On the day of the New Moon he is to offer a young bull, six lambs and a ram, all without defect. ⁷He is to provide as a grain offering one ephah with the bull, one ephah with the ram, and with the lambs as much as he wants to give, along with a hin of oil with each ephah. ⁸When the prince enters, he is to go in through the portico of the gateway, and he is to come out the same way.

⁹" 'When the people of the land come before the LORD at the appointed feasts, whoever enters by the north gate to worship is to go out the south gate; and whoever enters by the south gate is to go out the north gate. No one is to return through the gate by which he entered, but each is to go out the opposite gate. ¹⁰The prince is to be among them, going in when they go in and going out when they go out.

¹¹" 'At the festivals and the appointed feasts, the grain offering is to be an ephah with a bull, an ephah with a ram, and with the lambs as much as one pleases, along with a hin of oil for each ephah. ¹²When the prince provides a freewill offering to the LORD—whether a burnt offering or fellowship offerings—the gate facing east is to be opened for him. He shall offer his burnt offering or his fellowship offerings as he does on the Sabbath day. Then he shall go out, and after he has gone out, the gate will be shut.

¹³" 'Every day you are to provide a year-old lamb without defect for a burnt offering to the LORD; morning by morning you shall provide it. ¹⁴You are also to provide with it morning by morning a grain offering, consisting of a sixth of an ephah with a third of a hin of oil to moisten the flour. The presenting of this grain offering to the LORD is a lasting ordinance. ¹⁵So

the lamb and the grain offering and the oil shall be provided morning by morning for a regular burnt offering.

¹⁶" 'This is what the Sovereign LORD says: If the prince makes a gift from his inheritance to one of his sons, it will also belong to his descendants; it is to be their property by inheritance. ¹⁷If, however, he makes a gift from his inheritance to one of his servants, the servant may keep it until the year of freedom; then it will revert to the prince. His inheritance belongs to his sons only; it is theirs. ¹⁸The prince must not take any of the inheritance of the people, driving them off their property. He is to give his sons their inheritance out of his own property, so that none of my people will be separated from his property.' "

¹⁹Then the man brought me through the entrance at the side of the gate to the sacred rooms facing north, which belonged to the priests, and showed me a place at the western end. ²⁰He said to me, "This is the place where the priests will cook the guilt offering and the sin offering and bake the grain offering, to avoid bringing them into the outer court and consecrating the people."

²¹He then brought me to the outer court and led me around to its four corners, and I saw in each corner another court. ²²In the four corners of the outer court were enclosed*d* courts, forty cubits long and thirty cubits wide; each of the courts in the four corners was the same size. ²³Around the inside of each of the four courts was a ledge of stone, with places for fire built all around under the ledge. ²⁴He said to me, "These are the kitchens where those who minister at the temple will cook the sacrifices of the people."

The River From the Temple

47 The man brought me back to the entrance of the temple, and I saw water coming out from under the threshold of the temple toward the east (for the temple faced east). The water was coming down from under the south side of the temple, south of the altar. ²He then brought me out through the north gate and led me around the outside to the out-

---

a2 Traditionally *peace offerings*; also in verse 12
b5 That is, probably about 3/5 bushel (about 22 liters)　　*c5* That is, probably about 4 quarts (about 4 liters)　　*d22* The meaning of the Hebrew for this word is uncertain.

er gate facing east, and the water was flowing from the south side.

³As the man went eastward with a measuring line in his hand, he measured off a thousand cubits[a] and then led me through water that was ankle-deep. ⁴He measured off another thousand cubits and led me through water that was knee-deep. He measured off another thousand and led me through water that was up to the waist. ⁵He measured off another thousand, but now it was a river that I could not cross, because the water had risen and was deep enough to swim in— a river that no one could cross. ⁶He asked me, "Son of man, do you see this?"

Then he led me back to the bank of the river. ⁷When I arrived there, I saw a great number of trees on each side of the river. ⁸He said to me, "This water flows toward the eastern region and goes down into the Arabah,[b] where it enters the Sea.[c] When it empties into the Sea,[c] the water there becomes fresh. ⁹Swarms of living creatures will live wherever the river flows. There will be large numbers of fish, because this water flows there and makes the salt water fresh; so where the river flows everything will live. ¹⁰Fishermen will stand along the shore; from En Gedi to En Eglaim there will be places for spreading nets. The fish will be of many kinds—like the fish of the Great Sea.[d] ¹¹But the swamps and marshes will not become fresh; they will be left for salt. ¹²Fruit trees of all kinds will grow on both banks of the river. Their leaves will not wither, nor will their fruit fail. Every month they will bear, because the water from the sanctuary flows to them. Their fruit will serve for food and their leaves for healing."

The Boundaries of the Land

¹³This is what the Sovereign LORD says: "These are the boundaries by which you are to divide the land for an inheritance among the twelve tribes of Israel, with two portions for Joseph. ¹⁴You are to divide it equally among them. Because I swore with uplifted hand to give it to your forefathers, this land will become your inheritance.

¹⁵"This is to be the boundary of the land:

"On the north side it will run from the Great Sea by the Hethlon road past Lebo[e] Hamath to Zedad, ¹⁶Bero-

thah[f] and Sibraim (which lies on the border between Damascus and Hamath), as far as Hazer Hatticon, which is on the border of Hauran. ¹⁷The boundary will extend from the sea to Hazar Enan,[g] along the northern border of Damascus, with the border of Hamath to the north. This will be the north boundary.

¹⁸"On the east side the boundary will run between Hauran and Damascus, along the Jordan between Gilead and the land of Israel, to the eastern sea and as far as Tamar.[h] This will be the east boundary.

¹⁹"On the south side it will run from Tamar as far as the waters of Meribah Kadesh, then along the Wadi [i]of Egypt[j] to the Great Sea. This will be the south boundary.

²⁰"On the west side, the Great Sea will be the boundary to a point opposite Lebo[i] Hamath. This will be the west boundary.

²¹"You are to distribute this land among yourselves according to the tribes of Israel. ²²You are to allot it as an inheritance for yourselves and for the aliens who have settled among you and who have children. You are to consider them as native-born Israelites; along with you they are to be allotted an inheritance among the tribes of Israel. ²³In whatever tribe the alien settles, there you are to give him his inheritance," declares the Sovereign LORD.

The Division of the Land

48 "These are the tribes, listed by name: At the northern frontier, Dan will have one portion; it will follow the Hethlon road to Lebo[j] Hamath; Hazar Enan and the northern border of Damascus next to Hamath will be part of its border from the east side to the west side.

²"Asher will have one portion; it will border the territory of Dan from east to west.

³"Naphtali will have one portion; it

---

a3 That is, about 1,500 feet (about 450 meters)
b8 Or the Jordan Valley   c8 That is, the Dead Sea   d10 That is, the Mediterranean; also in verses 15, 19 and 20   e15 Or past the entrance to   f15,16 See Septuagint and Ezekiel 48:1; Hebrew road to go into Zedad, 16Hamath, Berothah   g17 Hebrew Enon, a variant of Enan   h18 Septuagint and Syriac; Hebrew Israel. You will measure to the eastern sea   i20 Or opposite the entrance to   j1 Or to the entrance to

will border the territory of Asher from east to west.

⁴"Manasseh will have one portion; it will border the territory of Naphtali from east to west.

⁵"Ephraim will have one portion; it will border the territory of Manasseh from east to west.

⁶"Reuben will have one portion; it will border the territory of Ephraim from east to west.

⁷"Judah will have one portion; it will border the territory of Reuben from east to west.

⁸"Bordering the territory of Judah from east to west will be the portion you are to present as a special gift. It will be 25,000 cubits*a* wide, and its length from east to west will equal one of the tribal portions; the sanctuary will be in the center of it.

⁹"The special portion you are to offer to the LORD will be 25,000 cubits long and 10,000 cubits*b* wide. ¹⁰This will be the sacred portion for the priests. It will be 25,000 cubits long on the north side, 10,000 cubits wide on the west side, 10,000 cubits wide on the east side and 25,000 cubits long on the south side. In the center of it will be the sanctuary of the LORD. ¹¹This will be for the consecrated priests, the Zadokites, who were faithful in serving me and did not go astray as the Levites did when the Israelites went astray. ¹²It will be a special gift to them from the sacred portion of the land, a most holy portion, bordering the territory of the Levites.

¹³"Alongside the territory of the priests, the Levites will have an allotment 25,000 cubits long and 10,000 cubits wide. Its total length will be 25,000 cubits and its width 10,000 cubits. ¹⁴They must not sell or exchange any of it. This is the best of the land and must not pass into other hands, because it is holy to the LORD.

¹⁵"The remaining area, 5,000 cubits wide and 25,000 cubits long, will be for the common use of the city, for houses and for pastureland. The city will be in the center of it ¹⁶and will have these measurements: the north side 4,500 cubits, the south side 4,500 cubits, the east side 4,500 cubits, and the west side 4,500 cubits. ¹⁷The pastureland for the city will be 250 cubits on the north, 250 cubits on the south, 250 cubits on the east, and 250

cubits on the west. ¹⁸What remains of the area, bordering on the sacred portion and running the length of it, will be 10,000 cubits on the east side and 10,000 cubits on the west side. Its produce will supply food for the workers of the city. ¹⁹The workers from the city who farm it will come from all the tribes of Israel. ²⁰The entire portion will be a square, 25,000 cubits on each side. As a special gift you will set aside the sacred portion, along with the property of the city.

²¹"What remains on both sides of the area formed by the sacred portion and the city property will belong to the prince. It will extend eastward from the 25,000 cubits of the sacred portion to the eastern border, and westward from the 25,000 cubits to the western border. Both these areas running the length of the tribal portions will belong to the prince, and the sacred portion with the temple sanctuary will be in the center of them. ²²So the property of the Levites and the property of the city will lie in the center of the area that belongs to the prince. The area belonging to the prince will lie between the border of Judah and the border of Benjamin.

²³"As for the rest of the tribes: Benjamin will have one portion; it will extend from the east side to the west side.

²⁴"Simeon will have one portion; it will border the territory of Benjamin from east to west.

²⁵"Issachar will have one portion; it will border the territory of Simeon from east to west.

²⁶"Zebulun will have one portion; it will border the territory of Issachar from east to west.

²⁷"Gad will have one portion; it will border the territory of Zebulun from east to west.

²⁸"The southern boundary of Gad will run south from Tamar to the waters of Meribah Kadesh, then along the Wadi ⌐of Egypt⌐ to the Great Sea.*c*

²⁹"This is the land you are to allot as an inheritance to the tribes of Israel, and these will be their portions," declares the Sovereign LORD.

The Gates of the City

³⁰"These will be the exits of the city:

a8 That is, about 7 miles (about 12 kilometers)
b9 That is, about 3 miles (about 5 kilometers)
c28 That is, the Mediterranean

Beginning on the north side, which is 4,500 cubits long, [31]the gates of the city will be named after the tribes of Israel. The three gates on the north side will be the gate of Reuben, the gate of Judah and the gate of Levi.

[32]"On the east side, which is 4,500 cubits long, will be three gates: the gate of Joseph, the gate of Benjamin and the gate of Dan.

[33]"On the south side, which measures 4,500 cubits, will be three gates: the gate of Simeon, the gate of Issachar and the gate of Zebulun.

[34]"On the west side, which is 4,500 cubits long, will be three gates: the gate of Gad, the gate of Asher and the gate of Naphtali.

[35]"The distance all around will be 18,000 cubits.

"And the name of the city from that time on will be:

THE LORD IS THERE."

fiery furnaces and lions' dens,
dreams and visions—these are the larger-than-life experiences recounted by Daniel. Yet even greater than these
events is the God who controlled them. One of the most
compelling realities in these stories is that God works
through Daniel and his three friends—Shadrach,
Meshach and Abednego—even though they are young.
These four live out their faith in amazing ways that reveal
God's power and his ability to save them (and us). As you
read this book, try imagining your-
self in their place. How might
you respond?

DANIEL

Daniel's Training in Babylon

1 In the third year of the reign of Jehoiakim king of Judah, Nebuchadnezzar
king of Babylon came to Jerusalem and
besieged it. ²And the Lord delivered Jehoiakim king of Judah into his hand,
along with some of the articles from the
temple of God. These he carried off to the
temple of his god in Babylonia*a* and put
in the treasure house of his god.

³Then the king ordered Ashpenaz,
chief of his court officials, to bring in
some of the Israelites from the royal family and the nobility— ⁴young men without any physical defect, handsome,
showing aptitude for every kind of learning, well informed, quick to understand,
and qualified to serve in the king's pal-

ace. He was to teach them the language
and literature of the Babylonians.*b* ⁵The
king assigned them a daily amount of
food and wine from the king's table.
They were to be trained for three years,
and after that they were to enter the
king's service.

⁶Among these were some from Judah:
Daniel, Hananiah, Mishael and Azariah.
⁷The chief official gave them new names:
to Daniel, the name Belteshazzar; to Hananiah, Shadrach; to Mishael, Meshach;
and to Azariah, Abednego.

⁸But Daniel resolved not to defile himself with the royal food and wine, and he
asked the chief official for permission not

*a*2 Hebrew *Shinar*   *b*4 Or *Chaldeans*

to defile himself this way. ⁹Now God had caused the official to show favor and sympathy to Daniel, ¹⁰but the official told Daniel, "I am afraid of my lord the king, who has assigned your*a* food and drink. Why should he see you looking worse than the other young men your age? The king would then have my head because of you."

¹¹Daniel then said to the guard whom the chief official had appointed over Daniel, Hananiah, Mishael and Azariah,

¹²"Please test your servants for ten days: Give us nothing but vegetables to eat and water to drink. ¹³Then compare our appearance with that of the young men who eat the royal food, and treat your servants in accordance with what you see." ¹⁴So he agreed to this and tested them for ten days.

¹⁵At the end of the ten days they

a 10 The Hebrew for *your* and *you* in this verse is plural.

MONDAY

Read *Daniel 1:1–21*
Key Verse *Daniel 1:8*

Personal Resolve – Don Allen

In many Christian circles we hear exhortations to be pure and to "go against the grain" of our culture. But most people find it easy to be confused about what that means in real life. The life of Daniel offers insight into the dilemmas, choices and convictions of one godly man.

Daniel was a young man in a strange land, yet he made up his mind he wouldn't defile himself with the royal food and wine—even though refusing it meant risking the wrath of his captors. What prompted Daniel to live this way? He lived by his convictions. At some point he had resolved to obey God no matter what.

While I don't live in a "strange land," living in Southern California and ministering to college students has its challenges. The culture here places a strong emphasis on physical attractiveness. And because we don't have long, cold winters, we are constantly barraged with visual sexual images such as bikinis on the beach year-round. It's a challenge for me to keep my thoughts pure.

The Holy Spirit has reminded me of Daniel's example more than once when I faced sexual temptation. The battle begins in my mind each time I'm confronted with temptation. I can resist, but only in God's strength and protection: "No temptation has seized you except what is common to man. And God is faithful; he will not let you be tempted beyond what you can bear. But when you are tempted, he will also provide a way out so that you can stand up under it" (1 Corinthians 10:13).

Whatever our circumstances and whatever temptations we face, we can memorize Daniel 1:8 and ask God to give us the same kind of conviction and determination Daniel had. Those qualities will enable us to live fully committed to God's standards rather than those of the culture we find ourselves living in. Then, by the power of the Holy Spirit, we can be like Daniel, who "resolved not to defile himself" (Daniel 1:8).

A Deeper Look
Ephesians 4:22–24; Colossians 3:1–6; James 1:13–15

Go to page 971 for your next devotional reading.

looked healthier and better nourished than any of the young men who ate the royal food. ¹⁶So the guard took away their choice food and the wine they were to drink and gave them vegetables instead.

¹⁷To these four young men God gave knowledge and understanding of all kinds of literature and learning. And Daniel could understand visions and dreams of all kinds.

¹⁸At the end of the time set by the king to bring them in, the chief official presented them to Nebuchadnezzar. ¹⁹The king talked with them, and he found none equal to Daniel, Hananiah, Mishael and Azariah; so they entered the king's service. ²⁰In every matter of wisdom and understanding about which the king questioned them, he found them ten times better than all the magicians and enchanters in his whole kingdom.

²¹And Daniel remained there until the first year of King Cyrus.

Nebuchadnezzar's Dream

2 In the second year of his reign, Nebuchadnezzar had dreams; his mind was troubled and he could not sleep. ²So the king summoned the magicians, enchanters, sorcerers and astrologers*a* to tell him what he had dreamed. When they came in and stood before the king, ³he said to them, "I have had a dream that troubles me and I want to know what it means.*b*"

⁴Then the astrologers answered the king in Aramaic,*c* "O king, live forever! Tell your servants the dream, and we will interpret it."

⁵The king replied to the astrologers, "This is what I have firmly decided: If you do not tell me what my dream was and interpret it, I will have you cut into pieces and your houses turned into piles of rubble. ⁶But if you tell me the dream and explain it, you will receive from me gifts and rewards and great honor. So tell me the dream and interpret it for me."

⁷Once more they replied, "Let the king tell his servants the dream, and we will interpret it."

⁸Then the king answered, "I am certain that you are trying to gain time, because you realize that this is what I have firmly decided: ⁹If you do not tell me the dream, there is just one penalty for you. You have conspired to tell me misleading

and wicked things, hoping the situation will change. So then, tell me the dream, and I will know that you can interpret it for me."

¹⁰The astrologers answered the king, "There is not a man on earth who can do what the king asks! No king, however great and mighty, has ever asked such a thing of any magician or enchanter or astrologer. ¹¹What the king asks is too difficult. No one can reveal it to the king except the gods, and they do not live among men."

¹²This made the king so angry and furious that he ordered the execution of all the wise men of Babylon. ¹³So the decree was issued to put the wise men to death, and men were sent to look for Daniel and his friends to put them to death.

¹⁴When Arioch, the commander of the king's guard, had gone out to put to death the wise men of Babylon, Daniel spoke to him with wisdom and tact. ¹⁵He asked the king's officer, "Why did the king issue such a harsh decree?" Arioch then explained the matter to Daniel. ¹⁶At this, Daniel went in to the king and asked for time, so that he might interpret the dream for him.

¹⁷Then Daniel returned to his house and explained the matter to his friends Hananiah, Mishael and Azariah. ¹⁸He urged them to plead for mercy from the God of heaven concerning this mystery, so that he and his friends might not be executed with the rest of the wise men of Babylon. ¹⁹During the night the mystery was revealed to Daniel in a vision. Then Daniel praised the God of heaven ²⁰and said:

"Praise be to the name of God for
    ever and ever;
    wisdom and power are his.
²¹He changes times and seasons;
    he sets up kings and deposes them.
He gives wisdom to the wise
    and knowledge to the discerning.
²²He reveals deep and hidden things;
    he knows what lies in darkness,
    and light dwells with him.
²³I thank and praise you, O God of my
    fathers:
    You have given me wisdom and
        power,

a2 Or *Chaldeans*; also in verses 4, 5 and 10
b3 Or *was*   *c4* The text from here through chapter 7 is in Aramaic.

you have made known to me what
we asked of you,
you have made known to us the
dream of the king."

Daniel Interprets the Dream

24Then Daniel went to Arioch, whom
the king had appointed to execute the
wise men of Babylon, and said to him,
"Do not execute the wise men of Babylon. Take me to the king, and I will interpret his dream for him."

25Arioch took Daniel to the king at
once and said, "I have found a man
among the exiles from Judah who can tell
the king what his dream means."

26The king asked Daniel (also called
Belteshazzar), "Are you able to tell me
what I saw in my dream and interpret it?"

27Daniel replied, "No wise man, enchanter, magician or diviner can explain
to the king the mystery he has asked
about, 28but there is a God in heaven who
reveals mysteries. He has shown King
Nebuchadnezzar what will happen in
days to come. Your dream and the visions that passed through your mind as
you lay on your bed are these:

29"As you were lying there, O king,
your mind turned to things to come, and
the revealer of mysteries showed you
what is going to happen. 30As for me, this
mystery has been revealed to me, not because I have greater wisdom than other
living men, but so that you, O king, may
know the interpretation and that you
may understand what went through your
mind.

31"You looked, O king, and there before you stood a large statue—an enormous, dazzling statue, awesome in appearance. 32The head of the statue was
made of pure gold, its chest and arms of
silver, its belly and thighs of bronze, 33its
legs of iron, its feet partly of iron and
partly of baked clay. 34While you were
watching, a rock was cut out, but not by
human hands. It struck the statue on its
feet of iron and clay and smashed them.
35Then the iron, the clay, the bronze, the
silver and the gold were broken to pieces
at the same time and became like chaff
on a threshing floor in the summer. The
wind swept them away without leaving a
trace. But the rock that struck the statue
became a huge mountain and filled the
whole earth.

36"This was the dream, and now we
will interpret it to the king. 37You,
O king, are the king of kings. The God
of heaven has given you dominion and
power and might and glory; 38in your
hands he has placed mankind and the
beasts of the field and the birds of the air.
Wherever they live, he has made you ruler over them all. You are that head of
gold.

39"After you, another kingdom will
rise, inferior to yours. Next, a third kingdom, one of bronze, will rule over the
whole earth. 40Finally, there will be a
fourth kingdom, strong as iron—for iron
breaks and smashes everything—and as
iron breaks things to pieces, so it will
crush and break all the others. 41Just as
you saw that the feet and toes were partly
of baked clay and partly of iron, so this
will be a divided kingdom; yet it will
have some of the strength of iron in it,
even as you saw iron mixed with clay.
42As the toes were partly iron and partly
clay, so this kingdom will be partly
strong and partly brittle. 43And just as
you saw the iron mixed with baked clay,
so the people will be a mixture and will
not remain united, any more than iron
mixes with clay.

44"In the time of those kings, the God
of heaven will set up a kingdom that will
never be destroyed, nor will it be left to
another people. It will crush all those
kingdoms and bring them to an end, but
it will itself endure forever. 45This is the
meaning of the vision of the rock cut
out of a mountain, but not by human
hands—a rock that broke the iron, the
bronze, the clay, the silver and the gold
to pieces.

"The great God has shown the king
what will take place in the future. The
dream is true and the interpretation is
trustworthy."

46Then King Nebuchadnezzar fell
prostrate before Daniel and paid him
honor and ordered that an offering and
incense be presented to him. 47The king
said to Daniel, "Surely your God is the
God of gods and the Lord of kings and a
revealer of mysteries, for you were able
to reveal this mystery."

48Then the king placed Daniel in a high
position and lavished many gifts on him.
He made him ruler over the entire province of Babylon and placed him in charge
of all its wise men. 49Moreover, at Dan-

iel's request the king appointed Shadrach, Meshach and Abednego administrators over the province of Babylon, while Daniel himself remained at the royal court.

The Image of Gold and the Fiery Furnace

3 King Nebuchadnezzar made an image of gold, ninety feet high and nine feet*a* wide, and set it up on the plain of Dura in the province of Babylon. ²He then summoned the satraps, prefects, governors, advisers, treasurers, judges, magistrates and all the other provincial officials to come to the dedication of the image he had set up. ³So the satraps, prefects, governors, advisers, treasurers, judges, magistrates and all the other provincial officials assembled for the dedication of the image that King Nebuchadnezzar had set up, and they stood before it.

⁴Then the herald loudly proclaimed, "This is what you are commanded to do, O peoples, nations and men of every language: ⁵As soon as you hear the sound of the horn, flute, zither, lyre, harp, pipes and all kinds of music, you must fall down and worship the image of gold that King Nebuchadnezzar has set up. ⁶Whoever does not fall down and worship will immediately be thrown into a blazing furnace."

⁷Therefore, as soon as they heard the sound of the horn, flute, zither, lyre, harp and all kinds of music, all the peoples, nations and men of every language fell down and worshiped the image of gold that King Nebuchadnezzar had set up.

⁸At this time some astrologers*b* came forward and denounced the Jews. ⁹They said to King Nebuchadnezzar, "O king, live forever! ¹⁰You have issued a decree, O king, that everyone who hears the sound of the horn, flute, zither, lyre, harp, pipes and all kinds of music must fall down and worship the image of gold, ¹¹and that whoever does not fall down and worship will be thrown into a blazing furnace. ¹²But there are some Jews whom you have set over the affairs of the province of Babylon—Shadrach, Meshach and Abednego—who pay no attention to you, O king. They neither serve your gods nor worship the image of gold you have set up."

¹³Furious with rage, Nebuchadnezzar summoned Shadrach, Meshach and Abednego. So these men were brought before the king, ¹⁴and Nebuchadnezzar said to them, "Is it true, Shadrach, Meshach and Abednego, that you do not serve my gods or worship the image of gold I have set up? ¹⁵Now when you hear the sound of the horn, flute, zither, lyre, harp, pipes and all kinds of music, if you are ready to fall down and worship the image I made, very good. But if you do not worship it, you will be thrown immediately into a blazing furnace. Then what god will be able to rescue you from my hand?"

¹⁶Shadrach, Meshach and Abednego replied to the king, "O Nebuchadnezzar, we do not need to defend ourselves before you in this matter. ¹⁷If we are thrown into the blazing furnace, the God we serve is able to save us from it, and he will rescue us from your hand, O king. ¹⁸But even if he does not, we want you to know, O king, that we will not serve your gods or worship the image of gold you have set up."

¹⁹Then Nebuchadnezzar was furious with Shadrach, Meshach and Abednego, and his attitude toward them changed. He ordered the furnace heated seven times hotter than usual ²⁰and commanded some of the strongest soldiers in his army to tie up Shadrach, Meshach and Abednego and throw them into the blazing furnace. ²¹So these men, wearing their robes, trousers, turbans and other clothes, were bound and thrown into the blazing furnace. ²²The king's command was so urgent and the furnace so hot that the flames of the fire killed the soldiers

a1 Aramaic *sixty cubits high and six cubits wide* (about 27 meters high and 2.7 meters wide) *b8* Or *Chaldeans*

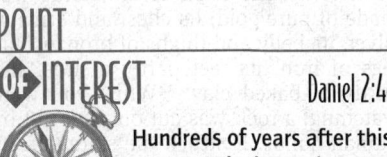

POINT OF INTEREST   Daniel 2:48

Hundreds of years after this scene took place, wise men came from "the east" (probably from this very area) to look for a promised Messiah (see Matthew 2:1). Could Daniel, their former leader, have left a legacy among them that prompted their journey? What do you think?

who took up Shadrach, Meshach and Abednego, 23and these three men, firmly tied, fell into the blazing furnace.

24Then King Nebuchadnezzar leaped to his feet in amazement and asked his advisers, "Weren't there three men that we tied up and threw into the fire?"

They replied, "Certainly, O king."

25He said, "Look! I see four men walking around in the fire, unbound and unharmed, and the fourth looks like a son of the gods."

26Nebuchadnezzar then approached the opening of the blazing furnace and shouted, "Shadrach, Meshach and Abednego, servants of the Most High God, come out! Come here!"

So Shadrach, Meshach and Abednego came out of the fire, 27and the satraps, prefects, governors and royal advisers crowded around them. They saw that the fire had not harmed their bodies, nor was a hair of their heads singed; their robes were not scorched, and there was no smell of fire on them.

28Then Nebuchadnezzar said, "Praise be to the God of Shadrach, Meshach and Abednego, who has sent his angel and rescued his servants! They trusted in him and defied the king's command and were willing to give up their lives rather than serve or worship any god except their own God. 29Therefore I decree that the people of any nation or language who say anything against the God of Shadrach, Meshach and Abednego be cut into pieces and their houses be turned into piles of rubble, for no other god can save in this way."

30Then the king promoted Shadrach, Meshach and Abednego in the province of Babylon.

TUESDAY

Read Daniel 3:1–30
Key Verses Daniel 3:17–18

No Box Big Enough – Terry Cook

I was angry at God. But even more than angry, I was hurt. God had not come through as I expected. I had been praying Philippians 4:19, "And my God will meet all your needs according to his glorious riches in Christ Jesus." He promised to meet my needs, yet we found ourselves with our savings depleted. My faith was really shaken.

As I was fuming to myself over this unfairness, three verses I had previously memorized came to mind. The first was Isaiah 55:8: "'For my thoughts are not your thoughts, neither are your ways my ways,' declares the LORD." I realized God is not obligated to perform according to my pattern of thinking; his "knowledge is too wonderful for me, too lofty for me to attain" (Psalm 139:6).

Another passage I recalled was Daniel 3:17–18. Shadrach, Meshach and Abednego were confident that God would deliver them from the fiery furnace. They declared, "But even if he does not, we want you to know, O king, that we will not serve your gods." If God didn't come through with deliverance, they would be dead. But these three brave men resolved to obey God regardless of the outcome.

I discovered that my anger stemmed from trying to fit God into my own box. But God will not be boxed in by my personal definitions. My faith in or obedience to God can't be determined by my expectations of him. Rather, they must be based on who he is.

A Deeper Look
Isaiah 55:8–9; Romans 11:33–36

Go to page 976 for your next devotional reading.

Nebuchadnezzar's Dream of a Tree

4 King Nebuchadnezzar,

To the peoples, nations and men of every language, who live in all the world:

May you prosper greatly!

²It is my pleasure to tell you about the miraculous signs and wonders that the Most High God has performed for me.

³How great are his signs,
    how mighty his wonders!
His kingdom is an eternal
        kingdom;
    his dominion endures from
        generation to generation.

⁴I, Nebuchadnezzar, was at home in my palace, contented and prosperous. ⁵I had a dream that made me afraid. As I was lying in my bed, the images and visions that passed through my mind terrified me. ⁶So I commanded that all the wise men of Babylon be brought before me to interpret the dream for me. ⁷When the magicians, enchanters, astrologers*a* and diviners came, I told them the dream, but they could not interpret it for me. ⁸Finally, Daniel came into my presence and I told him the dream. (He is called Belteshazzar, after the name of my god, and the spirit of the holy gods is in him.)

⁹I said, "Belteshazzar, chief of the magicians, I know that the spirit of the holy gods is in you, and no mystery is too difficult for you. Here is my dream; interpret it for me. ¹⁰These are the visions I saw while lying in my bed: I looked, and there before me stood a tree in the middle of the land. Its height was enormous. ¹¹The tree grew large and strong and its top touched the sky; it was visible to the ends of the earth. ¹²Its leaves were beautiful, its fruit abundant, and on it was food for all. Under it the beasts of the field found shelter, and the birds of the air lived in its branches; from it every creature was fed.

¹³"In the visions I saw while lying in my bed, I looked, and there before me was a messenger,*b* a holy one, coming down from heaven. ¹⁴He called in a loud voice: 'Cut down the tree and trim off its branches; strip off its leaves and scatter its fruit. Let the animals flee from under it and the birds from its branches. ¹⁵But let the stump and its roots, bound with iron and bronze, remain in the ground, in the grass of the field.

" 'Let him be drenched with the dew of heaven, and let him live with the animals among the plants of the earth. ¹⁶Let his mind be changed from that of a man and let him be given the mind of an animal, till seven times*c* pass by for him.

¹⁷" 'The decision is announced by messengers, the holy ones declare the verdict, so that the living may know that the Most High is sovereign over the kingdoms of men and gives them to anyone he wishes and sets over them the lowliest of men.'

¹⁸"This is the dream that I, King Nebuchadnezzar, had. Now, Belteshazzar, tell me what it means, for none of the wise men in my kingdom can interpret it for me. But you can, because the spirit of the holy gods is in you."

Daniel Interprets the Dream

¹⁹Then Daniel (also called Belteshazzar) was greatly perplexed for a time, and his thoughts terrified him. So the king said, "Belteshazzar, do not let the dream or its meaning alarm you."

Belteshazzar answered, "My lord, if only the dream applied to your enemies and its meaning to your adversaries! ²⁰The tree you saw, which grew large and strong, with its top touching the sky, visible to the whole earth, ²¹with beautiful leaves and abundant fruit, providing food for all, giving shelter to the beasts of the field, and having nesting places in its branches for the birds of the air— ²²you, O king, are that tree! You have become great and strong; your greatness has grown until it reaches the sky, and

a7 Or *Chaldeans*
verses 17 and 23
b13 Or *watchman*; also in
verses 17 and 23
c16 Or *years*; also in verses
23, 25 and 32

your dominion extends to distant parts of the earth.

²³"You, O king, saw a messenger, a holy one, coming down from heaven and saying, 'Cut down the tree and destroy it, but leave the stump, bound with iron and bronze, in the grass of the field, while its roots remain in the ground. Let him be drenched with the dew of heaven; let him live like the wild animals, until seven times pass by for him.'

²⁴"This is the interpretation, O king, and this is the decree the Most High has issued against my lord the king: ²⁵You will be driven away from people and will live with the wild animals; you will eat grass like cattle and be drenched with the dew of heaven. Seven times will pass by for you until you acknowledge that the Most High is sovereign over the kingdoms of men and gives them to anyone he wishes. ²⁶The command to leave the stump of the tree with its roots means that your kingdom will be restored to you when you acknowledge that Heaven rules. ²⁷Therefore, O king, be pleased to accept my advice: Renounce your sins by doing what is right, and your wickedness by being kind to the oppressed. It may be that then your prosperity will continue."

The Dream Is Fulfilled

²⁸All this happened to King Nebuchadnezzar. ²⁹Twelve months later, as the king was walking on the roof of the royal palace of Babylon, ³⁰he said, "Is not this the great Babylon I have built as the royal residence, by my mighty power and for the glory of my majesty?"

³¹The words were still on his lips when a voice came from heaven, "This is what is decreed for you, King Nebuchadnezzar: Your royal authority has been taken from you. ³²You will be driven away from people and will live with the wild animals; you will eat grass like cattle. Seven times will pass by for you until you acknowledge that the Most High is sovereign over the kingdoms of men and gives them to anyone he wishes."

³³Immediately what had been said about Nebuchadnezzar was fulfilled. He was driven away from people and ate grass like cattle. His body was drenched with the dew of heaven until his hair grew like the feathers of an eagle and his nails like the claws of a bird.

³⁴At the end of that time, I, Nebuchadnezzar, raised my eyes toward heaven, and my sanity was restored. Then I praised the Most High; I honored and glorified him who lives forever.

His dominion is an eternal dominion;
  his kingdom endures from
    generation to generation.
³⁵All the peoples of the earth
  are regarded as nothing.
He does as he pleases
  with the powers of heaven
  and the peoples of the earth.
No one can hold back his hand
  or say to him: "What have you
    done?"

³⁶At the same time that my sanity was restored, my honor and splendor were returned to me for the glory of my kingdom. My advisers and nobles sought me out, and I was restored to my throne and became even greater than before. ³⁷Now I, Nebuchadnezzar, praise and exalt and glorify the King of heaven, because everything he does is right and all his ways are just. And those who walk in pride he is able to humble.

POINT OF INTEREST

Daniel 4:37

Nebuchadnezzar is one of the best known of Israel's ancient conquerors. His capital city of Babylon has been extensively excavated and his histories translated. In this verse, King Nebuchadnezzar acknowledged the one, true God. Did this lead to a lasting commitment or a saving faith? Will we see Nebuchadnezzar in heaven? Intriguing questions, but only God knows for sure.

The Writing on the Wall

5 King Belshazzar gave a great banquet for a thousand of his nobles and drank wine with them. [2]While Belshazzar was drinking his wine, he gave orders to bring in the gold and silver goblets that Nebuchadnezzar his father[a] had taken from the temple in Jerusalem, so that the king and his nobles, his wives and his concubines might drink from them. [3]So they brought in the gold goblets that had been taken from the temple of God in Jerusalem, and the king and his nobles, his wives and his concubines drank from them. [4]As they drank the wine, they praised the gods of gold and silver, of bronze, iron, wood and stone.

[5]Suddenly the fingers of a human hand appeared and wrote on the plaster of the wall, near the lampstand in the royal palace. The king watched the hand as it wrote. [6]His face turned pale and he was so frightened that his knees knocked together and his legs gave way.

[7]The king called out for the enchanters, astrologers[b] and diviners to be brought and said to these wise men of Babylon, "Whoever reads this writing and tells me what it means will be clothed in purple and have a gold chain placed around his neck, and he will be made the third highest ruler in the kingdom."

[8]Then all the king's wise men came in, but they could not read the writing or tell the king what it meant. [9]So King Belshazzar became even more terrified and his face grew more pale. His nobles were baffled.

[10]The queen,[c] hearing the voices of the king and his nobles, came into the banquet hall. "O king, live forever!" she said. "Don't be alarmed! Don't look so pale! [11]There is a man in your kingdom who has the spirit of the holy gods in him. In the time of your father he was found to have insight and intelligence and wisdom like that of the gods. King Nebuchadnezzar your father—your father the king, I say—appointed him chief of the magicians, enchanters, astrologers and diviners. [12]This man Daniel, whom the king called Belteshazzar, was found to have a keen mind and knowledge and understanding, and also the ability to interpret dreams, explain riddles and solve difficult problems. Call for Daniel, and he will tell you what the writing means."

[13]So Daniel was brought before the king, and the king said to him, "Are you Daniel, one of the exiles my father the king brought from Judah? [14]I have heard that the spirit of the gods is in you and that you have insight, intelligence and outstanding wisdom. [15]The wise men and enchanters were brought before me to read this writing and tell me what it means, but they could not explain it. [16]Now I have heard that you are able to give interpretations and to solve difficult problems. If you can read this writing and tell me what it means, you will be clothed in purple and have a gold chain placed around your neck, and you will be made the third highest ruler in the kingdom."

[17]Then Daniel answered the king, "You may keep your gifts for yourself and give your rewards to someone else. Nevertheless, I will read the writing for the king and tell him what it means.

[18]"O king, the Most High God gave your father Nebuchadnezzar sovereignty and greatness and glory and splendor. [19]Because of the high position he gave him, all the peoples and nations and men of every language dreaded and feared him. Those the king wanted to put to death, he put to death; those he wanted to spare, he spared; those he wanted to promote, he promoted; and those he wanted to humble, he humbled. [20]But when his heart became arrogant and hardened with pride, he was deposed from his royal throne and stripped of his glory. [21]He was driven away from people and given the mind of an animal; he lived with the wild donkeys and ate grass like cattle; and his body was drenched with the dew of heaven, until he acknowledged that the Most High God is sovereign over the kingdoms of men and sets over them anyone he wishes.

[22]"But you his son,[d] O Belshazzar, have not humbled yourself, though you knew all this. [23]Instead, you have set yourself up against the Lord of heaven. You had the goblets from his temple brought to you, and you and your nobles, your wives and your concubines drank wine from them. You praised the gods of silver and gold, of bronze, iron, wood and stone, which cannot see or hear or

---

[a]2 Or *ancestor*; or *predecessor*; also in verses 11, 13 and 18   [b]7 Or *Chaldeans*; also in verse 11
[c]10 Or *queen mother*   [d]22 Or *descendant*; or *successor*

understand. But you did not honor the God who holds in his hand your life and all your ways. ²⁴Therefore he sent the hand that wrote the inscription.

²⁵"This is the inscription that was written:

MENE, MENE, TEKEL, PARSIN*ᵃ*

²⁶"This is what these words mean:

*Mene*ᵇ: God has numbered the days of your reign and brought it to an end.

²⁷*Tekel*ᶜ: You have been weighed on the scales and found wanting.

²⁸*Peres*ᵈ: Your kingdom is divided and given to the Medes and Persians."

²⁹Then at Belshazzar's command, Daniel was clothed in purple, a gold chain was placed around his neck, and he was proclaimed the third highest ruler in the kingdom.

³⁰That very night Belshazzar, king of the Babylonians,ᵉ was slain, ³¹and Darius the Mede took over the kingdom, at the age of sixty-two.

Daniel in the Den of Lions

6 It pleased Darius to appoint 120 satraps to rule throughout the kingdom, ²with three administrators over them, one of whom was Daniel. The satraps were made accountable to them so that the king might not suffer loss. ³Now Daniel so distinguished himself among the administrators and the satraps by his exceptional qualities that the king planned to set him over the whole kingdom. ⁴At this, the administrators and the satraps tried to find grounds for charges against Daniel in his conduct of government affairs, but they were unable to do so. They could find no corruption in him, because he was trustworthy and neither corrupt nor negligent. ⁵Finally these men said, "We will never find any basis for charges against this man Daniel unless it has something to do with the law of his God."

⁶So the administrators and the satraps went as a group to the king and said: "O King Darius, live forever! ⁷The royal administrators, prefects, satraps, advisers and governors have all agreed that the king should issue an edict and enforce the decree that anyone who prays to any god or man during the next thirty days, except to you, O king, shall be thrown into the lions' den. ⁸Now, O king, issue the decree and put it in writing so that it cannot be altered—in accordance with the laws of the Medes and Persians, which cannot be repealed." ⁹So King Darius put the decree in writing.

¹⁰Now when Daniel learned that the decree had been published, he went home to his upstairs room where the windows opened toward Jerusalem. Three times a day he got down on his knees and prayed, giving thanks to his God, just as he had done before. ¹¹Then these men went as a group and found Daniel praying and asking God for help. ¹²So they went to the king and spoke to him about his royal decree: "Did you not publish a decree that during the next thirty days anyone who prays to any god or man except to you, O king, would be thrown into the lions' den?"

The king answered, "The decree stands—in accordance with the laws of the Medes and Persians, which cannot be repealed."

¹³Then they said to the king, "Daniel, who is one of the exiles from Judah, pays no attention to you, O king, or to the decree you put in writing. He still prays three times a day." ¹⁴When the king heard this, he was greatly distressed; he was determined to rescue Daniel and made every effort until sundown to save him.

¹⁵Then the men went as a group to the king and said to him, "Remember, O king, that according to the law of the Medes and Persians no decree or edict that the king issues can be changed."

¹⁶So the king gave the order, and they brought Daniel and threw him into the lions' den. The king said to Daniel, "May your God, whom you serve continually, rescue you!"

¹⁷A stone was brought and placed over the mouth of the den, and the king sealed it with his own signet ring and with the rings of his nobles, so that Daniel's situation might not be changed. ¹⁸Then the king returned to his palace and spent the night without eating and without any entertainment being brought to him. And he could not sleep.

ᵃ25 Aramaic *UPARSIN* (that is, *AND PARSIN*)
ᵇ26 Mene can mean *numbered* or *mina* (a unit of money).   *ᶜ27 Tekel* can mean *weighed* or *shekel*.
ᵈ28 Peres (the singular of *Parsin*) can mean *divided* or *Persia* or *a half mina* or *a half shekel*.
ᵉ30 Or *Chaldeans*

¹⁹At the first light of dawn, the king got up and hurried to the lions' den. ²⁰When he came near the den, he called to Daniel in an anguished voice, "Daniel, servant of the living God, has your God, whom you serve continually, been able to rescue you from the lions?"

²¹Daniel answered, "O king, live forever! ²²My God sent his angel, and he shut the mouths of the lions. They have not hurt me, because I was found innocent in his sight. Nor have I ever done any wrong before you, O king."

²³The king was overjoyed and gave orders to lift Daniel out of the den. And when Daniel was lifted from the den, no wound was found on him, because he had trusted in his God.

²⁴At the king's command, the men who had falsely accused Daniel were brought in and thrown into the lions' den, along with their wives and children. And before they reached the floor of the den, the lions overpowered them and crushed all their bones.

²⁵Then King Darius wrote to all the peoples, nations and men of every language throughout the land:

"May you prosper greatly!

²⁶"I issue a decree that in every part of my kingdom people must

Read Daniel 6:1–28
Key Verse Daniel 6:4

Gotta Be Creative – Doug Serven

On a whim, I enrolled in a drawing class; I figured I could use something fun and easy in my schedule. After I bought supplies and spent the first few weeks shading fruits and chairs, the instructor dropped a bomb: Next week we would begin drawing live, nude models.

Yikes! This kind of intense study of anatomy may be necessary for a serious art student, but it wasn't for me. The idea of staring at a nude woman for three hours wasn't exactly my idea of purity. In struggling through the dilemma, I happened to run across this story of Daniel. He, too, had a problem—to pray and honor God, or not to pray according to the king's decree. I used Daniel as a model, and I prayed for cooperation from my instructor.

Nervously, I approached my professor the day before the first nude model was to be present. I gulped and asked him what would happen if I didn't draw in class for the next few weeks. He balked, but I already had an idea worked up. I suggested that when a nude model was to pose, I'd go to the museum on campus and draw statues. If my work was satisfactory, then I could continue. If not, I'd return. He agreed.

Check out the parallels between Daniel 1 and Daniel 6. Daniel committed himself to purity; God honored him—and that set a pattern of personal integrity for the rest of his life. Likewise, God honored my desire to be pure, and he gave me success. I finished with an A in the class and no nudes in my portfolio.

There is always a way out. Ask God to help you be like Daniel—committed to purity, creative in difficult situations and trusting God for the outcome.

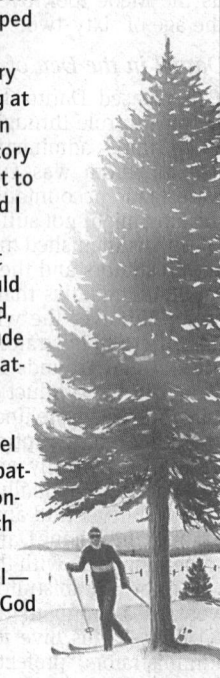

A Deeper Look
Romans 15:13; 1 Corinthians 10:13; Hebrews 4:14–16

Go to page 984 for your next devotional reading.

fear and reverence the God of Daniel.

"For he is the living God
and he endures forever;
his kingdom will not be destroyed,
his dominion will never end.
²⁷He rescues and he saves;
he performs signs and wonders
in the heavens and on the earth.
He has rescued Daniel
from the power of the lions."

²⁸So Daniel prospered during the reign of Darius and the reign of Cyrus*a* the Persian.

Daniel's Dream of Four Beasts

7 In the first year of Belshazzar king of Babylon, Daniel had a dream, and visions passed through his mind as he was lying on his bed. He wrote down the substance of his dream.

²Daniel said: "In my vision at night I looked, and there before me were the four winds of heaven churning up the great sea. ³Four great beasts, each different from the others, came up out of the sea.

⁴"The first was like a lion, and it had the wings of an eagle. I watched until its wings were torn off and it was lifted from the ground so that it stood on two feet like a man, and the heart of a man was given to it.

⁵"And there before me was a second beast, which looked like a bear. It was raised up on one of its sides, and it had three ribs in its mouth between its teeth. It was told, 'Get up and eat your fill of flesh!'

⁶"After that, I looked, and there before me was another beast, one that looked like a leopard. And on its back it had four wings like those of a bird. This beast had four heads, and it was given authority to rule.

⁷"After that, in my vision at night I looked, and there before me was a fourth beast—terrifying and frightening and very powerful. It had large iron teeth; it crushed and devoured its victims and trampled underfoot whatever was left. It was different from all the former beasts, and it had ten horns.

⁸"While I was thinking about the horns, there before me was another horn, a little one, which came up among them; and three of the first horns were uprooted before it. This horn had eyes like the eyes

of a man and a mouth that spoke boastfully.

⁹"As I looked,

"thrones were set in place,
and the Ancient of Days took his
seat.
His clothing was as white as snow;
the hair of his head was white like
wool.
His throne was flaming with fire,
and its wheels were all ablaze.
¹⁰A river of fire was flowing,
coming out from before him.
Thousands upon thousands attended
him;
ten thousand times ten thousand
stood before him.
The court was seated,
and the books were opened.

¹¹"Then I continued to watch because of the boastful words the horn was speaking. I kept looking until the beast was slain and its body destroyed and thrown into the blazing fire. ¹²(The other beasts had been stripped of their authority, but were allowed to live for a period of time.)

¹³"In my vision at night I looked, and there before me was one like a son of man, coming with the clouds of heaven. He approached the Ancient of Days and was led into his presence. ¹⁴He was given authority, glory and sovereign power; all peoples, nations and men of every language worshiped him. His dominion is an everlasting dominion that will not pass away, and his kingdom is one that will never be destroyed.

The Interpretation of the Dream

¹⁵"I, Daniel, was troubled in spirit, and the visions that passed through my mind disturbed me. ¹⁶I approached one of those standing there and asked him the true meaning of all this.

"So he told me and gave me the interpretation of these things: ¹⁷'The four great beasts are four kingdoms that will rise from the earth. ¹⁸But the saints of the Most High will receive the kingdom and will possess it forever—yes, for ever and ever.'

¹⁹"Then I wanted to know the true meaning of the fourth beast, which was different from all the others and most terrifying, with its iron teeth and bronze

a28 Or Darius, that is, the reign of Cyrus

claws—the beast that crushed and devoured its victims and trampled underfoot whatever was left. ²⁰I also wanted to know about the ten horns on its head and about the other horn that came up, before which three of them fell—the horn that looked more imposing than the others and that had eyes and a mouth that spoke boastfully. ²¹As I watched, this horn was waging war against the saints and defeating them, ²²until the Ancient of Days came and pronounced judgment in favor of the saints of the Most High, and the time came when they possessed the kingdom.

²³"He gave me this explanation: 'The fourth beast is a fourth kingdom that will appear on earth. It will be different from all the other kingdoms and will devour the whole earth, trampling it down and crushing it. ²⁴The ten horns are ten kings who will come from this kingdom. After them another king will arise, different from the earlier ones; he will subdue three kings. ²⁵He will speak against the Most High and oppress his saints and try to change the set times and the laws. The saints will be handed over to him for a time, times and half a time.ᵃ

²⁶" 'But the court will sit, and his power will be taken away and completely destroyed forever. ²⁷Then the sovereignty, power and greatness of the kingdoms under the whole heaven will be handed over to the saints, the people of the Most High. His kingdom will be an everlasting kingdom, and all rulers will worship and obey him.'

²⁸"This is the end of the matter. I, Daniel, was deeply troubled by my thoughts, and my face turned pale, but I kept the matter to myself."

Daniel's Vision of a Ram and a Goat

8 In the third year of King Belshazzar's reign, I, Daniel, had a vision, after the one that had already appeared to me. ²In my vision I saw myself in the citadel of Susa in the province of Elam; in the vision I was beside the Ulai Canal. ³I looked up, and there before me was a ram with two horns, standing beside the canal, and the horns were long. One of the horns was longer than the other but grew up later. ⁴I watched the ram as he charged toward the west and the north and the south. No animal could stand against him, and none could rescue from

his power. He did as he pleased and became great.

⁵As I was thinking about this, suddenly a goat with a prominent horn between his eyes came from the west, crossing the whole earth without touching the ground. ⁶He came toward the two-horned ram I had seen standing beside the canal and charged at him in great rage. ⁷I saw him attack the ram furiously, striking the ram and shattering his two horns. The ram was powerless to stand against him; the goat knocked him to the ground and trampled on him, and none could rescue the ram from his power. ⁸The goat became very great, but at the height of his power his large horn was broken off, and in its place four prominent horns grew up toward the four winds of heaven.

⁹Out of one of them came another horn, which started small but grew in power to the south and to the east and toward the Beautiful Land. ¹⁰It grew until it reached the host of the heavens, and it threw some of the starry host down to the earth and trampled on them. ¹¹It set itself up to be as great as the Prince of the host; it took away the daily sacrifice from him, and the place of his sanctuary was brought low. ¹²Because of rebellion, the host ⌊of the saints⌋ᵇ and the daily sacrifice were given over to it. It prospered in everything it did, and truth was thrown to the ground.

¹³Then I heard a holy one speaking, and another holy one said to him, "How long will it take for the vision to be fulfilled—the vision concerning the daily sacrifice, the rebellion that causes desolation, and the surrender of the sanctuary and of the host that will be trampled underfoot?"

¹⁴He said to me, "It will take 2,300 evenings and mornings; then the sanctuary will be reconsecrated."

The Interpretation of the Vision

¹⁵While I, Daniel, was watching the vision and trying to understand it, there before me stood one who looked like a man. ¹⁶And I heard a man's voice from the Ulai calling, "Gabriel, tell this man the meaning of the vision."

¹⁷As he came near the place where I was standing, I was terrified and fell

─────────────

ᵃ25 Or for a year, two years and half a year
ᵇ12 Or rebellion, the armies

prostrate. "Son of man," he said to me, "understand that the vision concerns the time of the end."

¹⁸While he was speaking to me, I was in a deep sleep, with my face to the ground. Then he touched me and raised me to my feet.

¹⁹He said: "I am going to tell you what will happen later in the time of wrath, because the vision concerns the appointed time of the end.ᵃ ²⁰The two-horned ram that you saw represents the kings of Media and Persia. ²¹The shaggy goat is the king of Greece, and the large horn between his eyes is the first king. ²²The four horns that replaced the one that was broken off represent four kingdoms that will emerge from his nation but will not have the same power.

²³"In the latter part of their reign, when rebels have become completely wicked, a stern-faced king, a master of intrigue, will arise. ²⁴He will become very strong, but not by his own power. He will cause astounding devastation and will succeed in whatever he does. He will destroy the mighty men and the holy people. ²⁵He will cause deceit to prosper, and he will consider himself superior. When they feel secure, he will destroy many and take his stand against the Prince of princes. Yet he will be destroyed, but not by human power.

²⁶"The vision of the evenings and mornings that has been given you is true, but seal up the vision, for it concerns the distant future."

²⁷I, Daniel, was exhausted and lay ill for several days. Then I got up and went about the king's business. I was appalled by the vision; it was beyond understanding.

Daniel's Prayer

9 In the first year of Darius son of Xerxesᵇ (a Mede by descent), who was made ruler over the Babylonianᶜ kingdom— ²in the first year of his reign, I, Daniel, understood from the Scriptures, according to the word of the LORD given to Jeremiah the prophet, that the desolation of Jerusalem would last seventy years. ³So I turned to the Lord God and pleaded with him in prayer and petition, in fasting, and in sackcloth and ashes.

⁴I prayed to the LORD my God and confessed:

"O Lord, the great and awesome God, who keeps his covenant of love with all who love him and obey his commands, ⁵we have sinned and done wrong. We have been wicked and have rebelled; we have turned away from your commands and laws. ⁶We have not listened to your servants the prophets, who spoke in your name to our kings, our princes and our fathers, and to all the people of the land.

⁷"Lord, you are righteous, but this day we are covered with shame—the men of Judah and people of Jerusalem and all Israel, both near and far, in all the countries where you have scattered us because of our unfaithfulness to you. ⁸O LORD, we and our kings, our princes and our fathers are covered with shame because we have sinned against you. ⁹The Lord our God is merciful and forgiving, even though we have rebelled against him; ¹⁰we have not obeyed the LORD our God or kept the laws he gave us through his servants the prophets. ¹¹All Israel has transgressed your law and turned away, refusing to obey you.

"Therefore the curses and sworn judgments written in the Law of Moses, the servant of God, have been poured out on us, because we have sinned against you. ¹²You have fulfilled the words spoken against us and against our rulers by

---

ᵃ19 Or *because the end will be at the appointed time*   ᵇ1 Hebrew *Ahasuerus*   ᶜ1 Or *Chaldean*

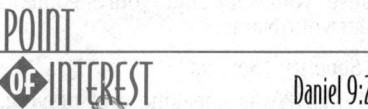

POINT OF INTEREST

Daniel 9:2-19

In Daniel's time, Jeremiah's writings and the rest of the existing Old Testament were recognized as holy writings from God to be trusted and studied. Daniel took Jeremiah's prophecy literally and never doubted it. He only needed to understand his role in the prophecy, and he began in the right place—by asking God to restore the people to their homeland as promised.

bringing upon us great disaster. Under the whole heaven nothing has ever been done like what has been done to Jerusalem. [13]Just as it is written in the Law of Moses, all this disaster has come upon us, yet we have not sought the favor of the LORD our God by turning from our sins and giving attention to your truth. [14]The LORD did not hesitate to bring the disaster upon us, for the LORD our God is righteous in everything he does; yet we have not obeyed him.

[15]"Now, O Lord our God, who brought your people out of Egypt with a mighty hand and who made for yourself a name that endures to this day, we have sinned, we have done wrong. [16]O Lord, in keeping with all your righteous acts, turn away your anger and your wrath from Jerusalem, your city, your holy hill. Our sins and the iniquities of our fathers have made Jerusalem and your people an object of scorn to all those around us.

[17]"Now, our God, hear the prayers and petitions of your servant. For your sake, O Lord, look with favor on your desolate sanctuary. [18]Give ear, O God, and hear; open your eyes and see the desolation of the city that bears your Name. We do not make requests of you because we are righteous, but because of your great mercy. [19]O Lord, listen! O Lord, forgive! O Lord, hear and act! For your sake, O my God, do not delay, because your city and your people bear your Name."

The Seventy "Sevens"

[20]While I was speaking and praying, confessing my sin and the sin of my people Israel and making my request to the LORD my God for his holy hill— [21]while I was still in prayer, Gabriel, the man I had seen in the earlier vision, came to me in swift flight about the time of the evening sacrifice. [22]He instructed me and said to me, "Daniel, I have now come to give you insight and understanding. [23]As soon as you began to pray, an answer was given, which I have come to tell you, for you are highly esteemed. Therefore, consider the message and understand the vision:

[24]"Seventy 'sevens'[a] are decreed for your people and your holy city to finish[b] transgression, to put an end to sin, to atone for wickedness, to bring in everlasting righteousness, to seal up vision and prophecy and to anoint the most holy.[c]

[25]"Know and understand this: From the issuing of the decree[d] to restore and rebuild Jerusalem until the Anointed One,[e] the ruler, comes, there will be seven 'sevens,' and sixty-two 'sevens.' It will be rebuilt with streets and a trench, but in times of trouble. [26]After the sixty-two 'sevens,' the Anointed One will be cut off and will have nothing.[f] The people of the ruler who will come will destroy the city and the sanctuary. The end will come like a flood: War will continue until the end, and desolations have been decreed. [27]He will confirm a covenant with many for one 'seven.'[g] In the middle of the 'seven'[g] he will put an end to sacrifice and offering. And on a wing ⌊of the temple⌋ he will set up an abomination that causes desolation, until the end that is decreed is poured out on him.[h]"[i]

Daniel's Vision of a Man

10 In the third year of Cyrus king of Persia, a revelation was given to Daniel (who was called Belteshazzar). Its message was true and it concerned a great war.[j] The understanding of the message came to him in a vision.

[2]At that time I, Daniel, mourned for three weeks. [3]I ate no choice food; no meat or wine touched my lips; and I used no lotions at all until the three weeks were over.

[4]On the twenty-fourth day of the first month, as I was standing on the bank of the great river, the Tigris, [5]I looked up and there before me was a man dressed in linen, with a belt of the finest gold around his waist. [6]His body was like chrysolite, his face like lightning, his eyes like flaming torches, his arms and legs

a24 Or 'weeks'; also in verses 25 and 26   b24 Or restrain   c24 Or Most Holy Place; or most holy One   d25 Or word   e25 Or an anointed one; also in verse 26   f26 Or off and will have no one; or off, but not for himself   g27 Or 'week'   h27 Or it   i27 Or And one who causes desolation will come upon the pinnacle of the abominable ⌊temple⌋, until the end that is decreed is poured out on the desolated ⌊city⌋   j1 Or true and burdensome like the gleam of burnished bronze, and his voice like the sound of a multitude. ⁷I, Daniel, was the only one who saw the vision; the men with me did not see it, but such terror overwhelmed them that they fled and hid themselves. ⁸So I was left alone, gazing at this great vision; I had no strength left, my face turned deathly pale and I was helpless. ⁹Then I heard him speaking, and as I listened to him, I fell into a deep sleep, my face to the ground.

¹⁰A hand touched me and set me trembling on my hands and knees. ¹¹He said, "Daniel, you who are highly esteemed, consider carefully the words I am about to speak to you, and stand up, for I have now been sent to you." And when he said this to me, I stood up trembling.

¹²Then he continued, "Do not be afraid, Daniel. Since the first day that you set your mind to gain understanding and to humble yourself before your God, your words were heard, and I have come in response to them. ¹³But the prince of the Persian kingdom resisted me twenty-one days. Then Michael, one of the chief princes, came to help me, because I was detained there with the king of Persia. ¹⁴Now I have come to explain to you what will happen to your people in the future, for the vision concerns a time yet to come."

¹⁵While he was saying this to me, I bowed with my face toward the ground and was speechless. ¹⁶Then one who looked like a manᵃ touched my lips, and I opened my mouth and began to speak. I said to the one standing before me, "I am overcome with anguish because of the vision, my lord, and I am helpless. ¹⁷How can I, your servant, talk with you, my lord? My strength is gone and I can hardly breathe."

¹⁸Again the one who looked like a man touched me and gave me strength. ¹⁹"Do not be afraid, O man highly esteemed," he said. "Peace! Be strong now; be strong."

When he spoke to me, I was strengthened and said, "Speak, my lord, since you have given me strength."

²⁰So he said, "Do you know why I have come to you? Soon I will return to fight against the prince of Persia, and when I go, the prince of Greece will come; ²¹but first I will tell you what is written in the Book of Truth. (No one

supports me against them except Micha-
11 el, your prince. ¹And in the first year of Darius the Mede, I took my stand to support and protect him.)

The Kings of the South and the North

²"Now then, I tell you the truth: Three more kings will appear in Persia, and then a fourth, who will be far richer than all the others. When he has gained power by his wealth, he will stir up everyone against the kingdom of Greece. ³Then a mighty king will appear, who will rule with great power and do as he pleases. ⁴After he has appeared, his empire will be broken up and parceled out toward the four winds of heaven. It will not go to his descendants, nor will it have the power he exercised, because his empire will be uprooted and given to others.

⁵"The king of the South will become strong, but one of his commanders will become even stronger than he and will rule his own kingdom with great power. ⁶After some years, they will become allies. The daughter of the king of the South will go to the king of the North to make an alliance, but she will not retain her power, and he and his powerᵇ will not last. In those days she will be handed over, together with her royal escort and her fatherᶜ and the one who supported her.

⁷"One from her family line will arise to

ᵃ16 Most manuscripts of the Masoretic Text; one manuscript of the Masoretic Text, Dead Sea Scrolls and Septuagint *Then something that looked like a man's hand*   ᵇ6 Or *offspring*   ᶜ6 Or *child* (see Vulgate and Syriac)

POINT OF INTEREST

Daniel 10:12–14

"There are more things in heaven and earth, Horatio, than are dreamt of in your philosophy," Hamlet tells his friend (*Hamlet* 1.5.123). What happened when Daniel prayed? These verses tell us that an angel was immediately dispatched to answer his prayer but was detained by spiritual conflict. There is more going on in the spiritual realm than we, like Horatio, could dream of.

take her place. He will attack the forces of the king of the North and enter his fortress; he will fight against them and be victorious. ⁸He will also seize their gods, their metal images and their valuable articles of silver and gold and carry them off to Egypt. For some years he will leave the king of the North alone. ⁹Then the king of the North will invade the realm of the king of the South but will retreat to his own country. ¹⁰His sons will prepare for war and assemble a great army, which will sweep on like an irresistible flood and carry the battle as far as his fortress.

¹¹"Then the king of the South will march out in a rage and fight against the king of the North, who will raise a large army, but it will be defeated. ¹²When the army is carried off, the king of the South will be filled with pride and will slaughter many thousands, yet he will not remain triumphant. ¹³For the king of the North will muster another army, larger than the first; and after several years, he will advance with a huge army fully equipped.

¹⁴"In those times many will rise against the king of the South. The violent men among your own people will rebel in fulfillment of the vision, but without success. ¹⁵Then the king of the North will come and build up siege ramps and will capture a fortified city. The forces of the South will be powerless to resist; even their best troops will not have the strength to stand. ¹⁶The invader will do as he pleases; no one will be able to stand against him. He will establish himself in the Beautiful Land and will have the power to destroy it. ¹⁷He will determine to come with the might of his entire kingdom and will make an alliance with the king of the South. And he will give him a daughter in marriage in order to overthrow the kingdom, but his plans*a* will not succeed or help him. ¹⁸Then he will turn his attention to the coastlands and will take many of them, but a commander will put an end to his insolence and will turn his insolence back upon him. ¹⁹After this, he will turn back toward the fortresses of his own country but will stumble and fall, to be seen no more.

²⁰"His successor will send out a tax collector to maintain the royal splendor. In a few years, however, he will be destroyed, yet not in anger or in battle.

²¹"He will be succeeded by a contemptible person who has not been given the honor of royalty. He will invade the kingdom when its people feel secure, and he will seize it through intrigue. ²²Then an overwhelming army will be swept away before him; both it and a prince of the covenant will be destroyed. ²³After coming to an agreement with him, he will act deceitfully, and with only a few people he will rise to power. ²⁴When the richest provinces feel secure, he will invade them and will achieve what neither his fathers nor his forefathers did. He will distribute plunder, loot and wealth among his followers. He will plot the overthrow of fortresses—but only for a time.

²⁵"With a large army he will stir up his strength and courage against the king of the South. The king of the South will wage war with a large and very powerful army, but he will not be able to stand because of the plots devised against him. ²⁶Those who eat from the king's provisions will try to destroy him; his army will be swept away, and many will fall in battle. ²⁷The two kings, with their hearts bent on evil, will sit at the same table and lie to each other, but to no avail, because an end will still come at the appointed time. ²⁸The king of the North will return to his own country with great wealth, but his heart will be set against the holy covenant. He will take action against it and then return to his own country.

²⁹"At the appointed time he will invade the South again, but this time the outcome will be different from what it was before. ³⁰Ships of the western coastlands*b* will oppose him, and he will lose heart. Then he will turn back and vent his fury against the holy covenant. He will return and show favor to those who forsake the holy covenant.

³¹"His armed forces will rise up to desecrate the temple fortress and will abolish the daily sacrifice. Then they will set up the abomination that causes desolation. ³²With flattery he will corrupt those who have violated the covenant, but the people who know their God will firmly resist him.

³³"Those who are wise will instruct many, though for a time they will fall by the sword or be burned or captured or plundered. ³⁴When they fall, they will re-

---

a 17 Or *but she*　　*b 30* Hebrew *of Kittim*

ceive a little help, and many who are not sincere will join them. ³⁵Some of the wise will stumble, so that they may be refined, purified and made spotless until the time of the end, for it will still come at the appointed time.

The King Who Exalts Himself

³⁶"The king will do as he pleases. He will exalt and magnify himself above every god and will say unheard-of things against the God of gods. He will be successful until the time of wrath is completed, for what has been determined must take place. ³⁷He will show no regard for the gods of his fathers or for the one desired by women, nor will he regard any god, but will exalt himself above them all. ³⁸Instead of them, he will honor a god of fortresses; a god unknown to his fathers he will honor with gold and silver, with precious stones and costly gifts. ³⁹He will attack the mightiest fortresses with the help of a foreign god and will greatly honor those who acknowledge him. He will make them rulers over many people and will distribute the land at a price.^a

⁴⁰"At the time of the end the king of the South will engage him in battle, and the king of the North will storm out against him with chariots and cavalry and a great fleet of ships. He will invade many countries and sweep through them like a flood. ⁴¹He will also invade the Beautiful Land. Many countries will fall, but Edom, Moab and the leaders of Ammon will be delivered from his hand. ⁴²He will extend his power over many countries; Egypt will not escape. ⁴³He will gain control of the treasures of gold and silver and all the riches of Egypt, with the Libyans and Nubians in submission. ⁴⁴But reports from the east and the north will alarm him, and he will set out in a great rage to destroy and annihilate many. ⁴⁵He will pitch his royal tents between the seas at^b the beautiful holy mountain. Yet he will come to his end, and no one will help him.

The End Times

12 "At that time Michael, the great prince who protects your people, will arise. There will be a time of distress such as has not happened from the beginning of nations until then. But at that time your people—everyone whose name is found written in the book—will be delivered. ²Multitudes who sleep in the dust of the earth will awake: some to everlasting life, others to shame and everlasting contempt. ³Those who are wise^c will shine like the brightness of the heavens, and those who lead many to righteousness, like the stars for ever and ever. ⁴But you, Daniel, close up and seal the words of the scroll until the time of the end. Many will go here and there to increase knowledge."

⁵Then I, Daniel, looked, and there before me stood two others, one on this bank of the river and one on the opposite bank. ⁶One of them said to the man clothed in linen, who was above the waters of the river, "How long will it be before these astonishing things are fulfilled?"

⁷The man clothed in linen, who was above the waters of the river, lifted his right hand and his left hand toward heaven, and I heard him swear by him who lives forever, saying, "It will be for a time, times and half a time.^d When the power of the holy people has been finally broken, all these things will be completed."

⁸I heard, but I did not understand. So I asked, "My lord, what will the outcome of all this be?"

⁹He replied, "Go your way, Daniel, because the words are closed up and sealed until the time of the end. ¹⁰Many will be purified, made spotless and refined, but the wicked will continue to be wicked.

---

^a39 Or *land for a reward*   ^b45 Or *the sea and*
^c3 Or *who impart wisdom*   ^d7 Or *a year, two years and half a year*

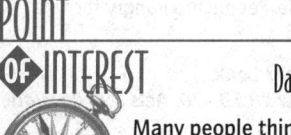

POINT OF INTEREST

Daniel 11:36-39

Many people think this prophecy refers to the antichrist who will appear in the end times. The antichrist will be a world leader who seems to bring peace but then turns to exalt himself and attempts to destroy God's people in the process. See Revelation 20 for the rest of the story.

None of the wicked will understand, but those who are wise will understand.

¹¹"From the time that the daily sacrifice is abolished and the abomination that causes desolation is set up, there will be 1,290 days. ¹²Blessed is the one who waits for and reaches the end of the 1,335 days.

¹³"As for you, go your way till the end. You will rest, and then at the end of the days you will rise to receive your allotted inheritance."

Read *Daniel 12:1–13*
Key Verse *Daniel 12:3*

On Cheeses and Other Conversation Starters – Craig Parker

One afternoon I was finishing a long conversation with a student named Louis. Christa, whom I had never met before, stopped by our table to meet Louis for dinner. She said, "Hi Louis, I'm ready for dinner whenever you are."

Louis replied, "Great, Christa, I'm ready. By the way, this is my friend, Craig."

"Hi. Are you a professor here?"

As a Navigator staff member ministering among students at Dartmouth College, I never really know what to say when I'm asked this question by a student. "No," I replied, "I'm a campus minister."

"Oh, that's nice," she said. After a few minutes of talking with Louis, she suddenly turned to me and asked, "What is it you do again?"

Now I was stumped, so I thought I'd try another approach. "Well, I love Jesus, and I try to help students follow him." Once again, she politely replied, "Oh, that's nice."

We finished our conversation, and Louis and Christa left for their dinner appointment. As they walked away, she asked Louis, "What does that guy do again? He loves cheeses?"

"Not cheeses," Louis replied, "Jesus—he loves Jesus."

"Oh, Jesus! I thought he said cheeses," she laughed. "Well, that's really cool." With that they began a two-hour conversation about Jesus. Seven months later, after investigating Christianity with her friends, she received Jesus Christ into her life. She's been talking about him ever since.

Are you open to discussing Jesus with your friends or family? Sometimes all it takes to start the conversation is the mention of his name. People are hungry for what God offers. That's Jesus, not cheeses.

A Deeper Look
Matthew 28:19–20; Acts 1:8; Revelation 12:11

Go to page 989 for your next devotional reading.

*S*ometimes God uses unexpected methods to teach us about himself; the prophet Hosea was a case in point. God told Hosea to marry a prostitute and then to forgive her unfaithfulness—more than once! Why? Because God wanted to create a vivid, living picture of his love for the people of Israel. The book of Hosea is a vignette of God as a lover who's been repeatedly abandoned, letting us see God's hurt and anger as well as his unrelenting devotion to his people and his willingness to forgive them time and again.

HOSEA

1 The word of the LORD that came to Hosea son of Beeri during the reigns of Uzziah, Jotham, Ahaz and Hezekiah, kings of Judah, and during the reign of Jeroboam son of Jehoash*a* king of Israel:

Hosea's Wife and Children

2When the LORD began to speak through Hosea, the LORD said to him, "Go, take to yourself an adulterous wife and children of unfaithfulness, because the land is guilty of the vilest adultery in departing from the LORD." 3So he married Gomer daughter of Diblaim, and she conceived and bore him a son.

4Then the LORD said to Hosea, "Call him Jezreel, because I will soon punish the house of Jehu for the massacre at Jezreel, and I will put an end to the kingdom of Israel. 5In that day I will break Israel's bow in the Valley of Jezreel."

6Gomer conceived again and gave birth to a daughter. Then the LORD said to Hosea, "Call her Lo-Ruhamah,*b* for I will no longer show love to the house of Israel, that I should at all forgive them. 7Yet I will show love to the house of Judah; and I will save them—not by bow, sword or battle, or by horses and horsemen, but by the LORD their God."

8After she had weaned Lo-Ruhamah, Gomer had another son. 9Then the LORD said, "Call him Lo-Ammi,*c* for you are not my people, and I am not your God.

10"Yet the Israelites will be like the sand on the seashore, which cannot be measured or counted. In the place where it was said to them, 'You are not my people,' they will be called 'sons of the living

*a*1 Hebrew *Joash,* a variant of *Jehoash*
*b*6 *Lo-Ruhamah* means *not loved.* *c*9 *Lo-Ammi* means *not my people.*

God.' ¹¹The people of Judah and the people of Israel will be reunited, and they will appoint one leader and will come up out of the land, for great will be the day of Jezreel.

2 "Say of your brothers, 'My people,' and of your sisters, 'My loved one.'

Israel Punished and Restored

²"Rebuke your mother, rebuke her,
  for she is not my wife,
  and I am not her husband.
Let her remove the adulterous look
    from her face
  and the unfaithfulness from
    between her breasts.
³Otherwise I will strip her naked
  and make her as bare as on the
    day she was born;
I will make her like a desert,
  turn her into a parched land,
  and slay her with thirst.
⁴I will not show my love to her
    children,
  because they are the children of
    adultery.
⁵Their mother has been unfaithful
  and has conceived them in
    disgrace.
She said, 'I will go after my lovers,
  who give me my food and my
    water,
  my wool and my linen, my oil and
    my drink.'
⁶Therefore I will block her path with
    thornbushes;
  I will wall her in so that she
    cannot find her way.
⁷She will chase after her lovers but not
    catch them;
  she will look for them but not find
    them.
Then she will say,
  'I will go back to my husband as
    at first,
  for then I was better off than now.'
⁸She has not acknowledged that I was
    the one
  who gave her the grain, the new
    wine and oil,
  who lavished on her the silver and
    gold—
  which they used for Baal.

⁹"Therefore I will take away my grain
    when it ripens,
  and my new wine when it is
    ready.

I will take back my wool and my
    linen,
  intended to cover her nakedness.
¹⁰So now I will expose her lewdness
    before the eyes of her lovers;
  no one will take her out of my
    hands.
¹¹I will stop all her celebrations:
  her yearly festivals, her New
    Moons,
  her Sabbath days—all her
    appointed feasts.
¹²I will ruin her vines and her fig trees,
  which she said were her pay from
    her lovers;
I will make them a thicket,
  and wild animals will devour
    them.
¹³I will punish her for the days
  she burned incense to the Baals;
she decked herself with rings and
    jewelry,
  and went after her lovers,
  but me she forgot,"
                    declares the LORD.

¹⁴"Therefore I am now going to allure
    her;
  I will lead her into the desert
  and speak tenderly to her.
¹⁵There I will give her back her
    vineyards,
  and will make the Valley of
    Achorᵃ a door of hope.
There she will singᵇ as in the days
    of her youth,
  as in the day she came up out of
    Egypt.

¹⁶"In that day," declares the LORD,
  "you will call me 'my husband';
  you will no longer call me 'my
    master.ᶜ'
¹⁷I will remove the names of the Baals
    from her lips;
  no longer will their names be
    invoked.
¹⁸In that day I will make a covenant for
    them
  with the beasts of the field and the
    birds of the air
  and the creatures that move along
    the ground.
Bow and sword and battle
  I will abolish from the land,
  so that all may lie down in safety.
¹⁹I will betroth you to me forever;

ᵃ15 Achor means trouble.　　ᵇ15 Or respond
ᶜ16 Hebrew baal

I will betroth you in[a]
   righteousness and justice,
   in[b] love and compassion.
20I will betroth you in faithfulness,
   and you will acknowledge the
   Lord.

21"In that day I will respond,"
   declares the Lord—
"I will respond to the skies,
   and they will respond to the earth;
22and the earth will respond to the
      grain,
   the new wine and oil,
   and they will respond to Jezreel.[c]
23I will plant her for myself in the land;
   I will show my love to the one I
      called 'Not my loved one.[d]'
I will say to those called 'Not my
      people,[e]' 'You are my
      people';
   and they will say, 'You are my
      God.' "

Hosea's Reconciliation With His Wife

3 The Lord said to me, "Go, show your love to your wife again, though she is loved by another and is an adulteress. Love her as the Lord loves the Israelites, though they turn to other gods and love the sacred raisin cakes." **2**So I bought her for fifteen shekels[f] of silver and about a homer and a lethek[g] of barley. **3**Then I told her, "You are to live with[h] me many days; you must not be a prostitute or be intimate with any man, and I will live with[h] you."

4For the Israelites will live many days without king or prince, without sacrifice or sacred stones, without ephod or idol. **5**Afterward the Israelites will return and seek the Lord their God and David their king. They will come trembling to the Lord and to his blessings in the last days.

The Charge Against Israel

4 Hear the word of the Lord, you
      Israelites,
   because the Lord has a charge to
      bring
   against you who live in the land:
"There is no faithfulness, no love,
   no acknowledgment of God in the
      land.
2There is only cursing,[i] lying and
      murder,
   stealing and adultery;
   they break all bounds,

and bloodshed follows bloodshed.
3Because of this the land mourns,[j]
   and all who live in it waste away;
   the beasts of the field and the birds
      of the air
   and the fish of the sea are dying.

4"But let no man bring a charge,
   let no man accuse another,
   for your people are like those
      who bring charges against a priest.
5You stumble day and night,
   and the prophets stumble with
      you.
So I will destroy your mother—
6 my people are destroyed from lack
      of knowledge.

"Because you have rejected
      knowledge,
   I also reject you as my priests;
because you have ignored the law of
      your God,
   I also will ignore your children.
7The more the priests increased,
   the more they sinned against me;
   they exchanged[k] their[l] Glory for
      something disgraceful.
8They feed on the sins of my people
   and relish their wickedness.
9And it will be: Like people, like
      priests.

[a]*19 Or with*; also in verse 20   [b]*19 Or with*
[c]*22 Jezreel means God plants.*   [d]*23 Hebrew
Lo-Ruhamah*   [e]*23 Hebrew Lo-Ammi*   [f]*2 That
is, about 6 ounces (about 170 grams)*   [g]*2 That
is, probably about 10 bushels (about 330 liters)*
[h]*3 Or wait for*   [i]*2 That is, to pronounce a curse
upon*   [j]*3 Or dries up*   [k]*7 Syriac and an
ancient Hebrew scribal tradition; Masoretic Text I
will exchange*   [l]*7 Masoretic Text; an ancient
Hebrew scribal tradition my*

POINT OF INTEREST   Hosea 4:3

Many experts agree that our ecosystem is deteriorating. Could sin, the source of death for human beings, have a detrimental influence on the biosphere? Could it be because human beings have produced mountains of garbage? Are internal combustion engines and industrial concerns releasing too many pollutants into the atmosphere? What do you think?

I will punish both of them for their
       ways
and repay them for their deeds.

¹⁰"They will eat but not have enough;
     they will engage in prostitution but
         not increase,
because they have deserted the LORD
     to give themselves ¹¹to prostitution,
to old wine and new,
     which take away the
         understanding ¹²of my people.
They consult a wooden idol
     and are answered by a stick of
         wood.
A spirit of prostitution leads them
     astray;
     they are unfaithful to their God.
¹³They sacrifice on the mountaintops
     and burn offerings on the hills,
under oak, poplar and terebinth,
     where the shade is pleasant.
Therefore your daughters turn to
         prostitution
     and your daughters-in-law to
         adultery.

¹⁴"I will not punish your daughters
     when they turn to prostitution,
nor your daughters-in-law
     when they commit adultery,
because the men themselves consort
         with harlots
     and sacrifice with shrine
         prostitutes—
a people without understanding
     will come to ruin!

¹⁵"Though you commit adultery,
         O Israel,
     let not Judah become guilty.

"Do not go to Gilgal;
     do not go up to Beth Aven.ᵃ
     And do not swear, 'As surely as
         the LORD lives!'
¹⁶The Israelites are stubborn,
     like a stubborn heifer.
How then can the LORD pasture them
     like lambs in a meadow?
¹⁷Ephraim is joined to idols;
     leave him alone!
¹⁸Even when their drinks are gone,
     they continue their prostitution;
     their rulers dearly love shameful
         ways.
¹⁹A whirlwind will sweep them away,
     and their sacrifices will bring them
         shame.

Judgment Against Israel

5 "Hear this, you priests!
     Pay attention, you Israelites!
Listen, O royal house!
     This judgment is against you:
You have been a snare at Mizpah,
     a net spread out on Tabor.
²The rebels are deep in slaughter.
     I will discipline all of them.
³I know all about Ephraim;
     Israel is not hidden from me.
Ephraim, you have now turned to
         prostitution;
     Israel is corrupt.

⁴"Their deeds do not permit them
     to return to their God.
A spirit of prostitution is in their
         heart;
     they do not acknowledge the
         LORD.
⁵Israel's arrogance testifies against
         them;
     the Israelites, even Ephraim,
         stumble in their sin;
     Judah also stumbles with them.
⁶When they go with their flocks and
         herds
     to seek the LORD,
they will not find him;
     he has withdrawn himself from
         them.
⁷They are unfaithful to the LORD;
     they give birth to illegitimate
         children.
Now their New Moon festivals
     will devour them and their fields.

⁸"Sound the trumpet in Gibeah,
     the horn in Ramah.
Raise the battle cry in Beth Avenᵃ;
     lead on, O Benjamin.
⁹Ephraim will be laid waste
     on the day of reckoning.
Among the tribes of Israel
     I proclaim what is certain.
¹⁰Judah's leaders are like those
     who move boundary stones.
I will pour out my wrath on them
     like a flood of water.
¹¹Ephraim is oppressed,
     trampled in judgment,
     intent on pursuing idols.ᵇ
¹²I am like a moth to Ephraim,
     like rot to the people of Judah.

ᵃ15,8 *Beth Aven* means *house of wickedness* (a
name for Bethel, which means *house of God*).
ᵇ11 The meaning of the Hebrew for this word is
uncertain.

13"When Ephraim saw his sickness,
  and Judah his sores,
then Ephraim turned to Assyria,
  and sent to the great king for help.
But he is not able to cure you,
  not able to heal your sores.
14For I will be like a lion to Ephraim,
  like a great lion to Judah.
I will tear them to pieces and go
    away;
  I will carry them off, with no one
    to rescue them.
15Then I will go back to my place
  until they admit their guilt.
And they will seek my face;
  in their misery they will earnestly
    seek me."

Israel Unrepentant

6 "Come, let us return to the LORD.
  He has torn us to pieces
    but he will heal us;
he has injured us
  but he will bind up our wounds.
2After two days he will revive us;

on the third day he will restore us,
  that we may live in his presence.
3Let us acknowledge the LORD;
  let us press on to acknowledge
    him.
As surely as the sun rises,
  he will appear;
he will come to us like the winter
    rains,
  like the spring rains that water the
    earth."

4"What can I do with you, Ephraim?
  What can I do with you, Judah?
Your love is like the morning mist,
  like the early dew that disappears.
5Therefore I cut you in pieces with my
    prophets,
  I killed you with the words of my
    mouth;
my judgments flashed like
    lightning upon you.
6For I desire mercy, not sacrifice,
  and acknowledgment of God rather
    than burnt offerings.

FRIDAY

Read *Hosea 6:1–11*
Key Verse *Hosea 6:3*

Pressing On to Know Him – Dawn Getz

Fresh out of college, I began my first nursing job. To put it bluntly, life was miserable. In school my professors had given me shining evaluations, the hospital staff had complimented me on my competency, and my friends had encouraged me in my walk with God.

How quickly things had changed. Now I was working late hours to pay school loans, and my college friends were far away. Worst of all, the nurse who was taking me through my probation time said that if I didn't catch on faster, she was going to fire me.

Fearful, humiliated and lonely, I searched my Bible for help. During those times God used Hosea 6:3 to motivate me to "press on to [know] him." God chipped away at my self-sufficient pride and called me to acknowledge him. He promised that he would come to me; he reminded me that I could count on him. As surely as "the spring rains that water the earth," he was certain to meet me in my frustration.

Soon the hospital wasn't such a scary place. I realized that God hadn't changed my circumstances, but he *had* changed my perspective. In doing so, God demonstrated his constant presence and care, leading me to a deeper understanding of his faithfulness.

A Deeper Look
Jeremiah 9:24; Philippians 3:10–14

Go to page 994 for your next devotional reading.

⁷Like Adam,ᵃ they have broken the
　　covenant—
they were unfaithful to me there.
⁸Gilead is a city of wicked men,
　　stained with footprints of blood.
⁹As marauders lie in ambush for a
　　man,
　　so do bands of priests;
they murder on the road to Shechem,
　　committing shameful crimes.
¹⁰I have seen a horrible thing
　　in the house of Israel.
There Ephraim is given to prostitution
　　and Israel is defiled.

¹¹"Also for you, Judah,
　　a harvest is appointed.

"Whenever I would restore the
　　fortunes of my people,
7 ¹ whenever I would heal Israel,
　　the sins of Ephraim are exposed
　　and the crimes of Samaria
　　　revealed.
They practice deceit,
　　thieves break into houses,
　　bandits rob in the streets;
²but they do not realize
　　that I remember all their evil
　　　deeds.
Their sins engulf them;
　　they are always before me.

³"They delight the king with their
　　wickedness,
　　the princes with their lies.
⁴They are all adulterers,
　　burning like an oven
whose fire the baker need not stir
　　from the kneading of the dough till
　　　it rises.
⁵On the day of the festival of our king
　　the princes become inflamed with
　　　wine,
　　and he joins hands with the
　　　mockers.
⁶Their hearts are like an oven;
　　they approach him with intrigue.
Their passion smolders all night;
　　in the morning it blazes like a
　　　flaming fire.
⁷All of them are hot as an oven;
　　they devour their rulers.
All their kings fall,
　　and none of them calls on me.

⁸"Ephraim mixes with the nations;
　　Ephraim is a flat cake not turned
　　　over.
⁹Foreigners sap his strength,

but he does not realize it.
His hair is sprinkled with gray,
　　but he does not notice.
¹⁰Israel's arrogance testifies against
　　him,
　　but despite all this
he does not return to the Lᴏʀᴅ his
　　God
　　or search for him.

¹¹"Ephraim is like a dove,
　　easily deceived and senseless—
now calling to Egypt,
　　now turning to Assyria.
¹²When they go, I will throw my net
　　over them;
　　I will pull them down like birds of
　　　the air.
When I hear them flocking together,
　　I will catch them.
¹³Woe to them,
　　because they have strayed from
　　　me!
Destruction to them,
　　because they have rebelled against
　　　me!
I long to redeem them
　　but they speak lies against me.
¹⁴They do not cry out to me from their
　　hearts
　　but wail upon their beds.
They gather togetherᵇ for grain and
　　new wine
　　but turn away from me.
¹⁵I trained them and strengthened
　　them,
　　but they plot evil against me.
¹⁶They do not turn to the Most High;
　　they are like a faulty bow.
Their leaders will fall by the sword
　　because of their insolent words.
For this they will be ridiculed
　　in the land of Egypt.

Israel to Reap the Whirlwind

8 "Put the trumpet to your lips!
　　An eagle is over the house of the
　　　Lᴏʀᴅ
because the people have broken my
　　covenant
　　and rebelled against my law.
²Israel cries out to me,
　　'O our God, we acknowledge you!'
³But Israel has rejected what is good;

ᵃ7 Or As at Adam; or Like men　　ᵇ14 Most
Hebrew manuscripts; some Hebrew manuscripts
and Septuagint They slash themselves

an enemy will pursue him.
⁴They set up kings without my
consent;
they choose princes without my
approval.
With their silver and gold
they make idols for themselves
to their own destruction.
⁵Throw out your calf-idol, O Samaria!
My anger burns against them.
How long will they be incapable of
purity?
⁶ They are from Israel!
This calf—a craftsman has made it;
it is not God.
It will be broken in pieces,
that calf of Samaria.

⁷"They sow the wind
and reap the whirlwind.
The stalk has no head;
it will produce no flour.
Were it to yield grain,
foreigners would swallow it up.
⁸Israel is swallowed up;
now she is among the nations
like a worthless thing.
⁹For they have gone up to Assyria
like a wild donkey wandering
alone.
Ephraim has sold herself to lovers.
¹⁰Although they have sold themselves
among the nations,
I will now gather them together.
They will begin to waste away
under the oppression of the mighty
king.

¹¹"Though Ephraim built many altars
for sin offerings,
these have become altars for
sinning.
¹²I wrote for them the many things of
my law,
but they regarded them as
something alien.
¹³They offer sacrifices given to me
and they eat the meat,
but the LORD is not pleased with
them.
Now he will remember their
wickedness
and punish their sins:
They will return to Egypt.
¹⁴Israel has forgotten his Maker
and built palaces;
Judah has fortified many towns.
But I will send fire upon their cities
that will consume their fortresses."

Punishment for Israel

9 Do not rejoice, O Israel;
do not be jubilant like the other
nations.
For you have been unfaithful to your
God;
you love the wages of a prostitute
at every threshing floor.
²Threshing floors and winepresses will
not feed the people;
the new wine will fail them.
³They will not remain in the LORD's
land;
Ephraim will return to Egypt
and eat unclean*ᵃ* food in Assyria.
⁴They will not pour out wine offerings
to the LORD,
nor will their sacrifices please him.
Such sacrifices will be to them like
the bread of mourners;
all who eat them will be unclean.
This food will be for themselves;
it will not come into the temple of
the LORD.

⁵What will you do on the day of your
appointed feasts,
on the festival days of the LORD?
⁶Even if they escape from destruction,
Egypt will gather them,
and Memphis will bury them.
Their treasures of silver will be taken
over by briers,
and thorns will overrun their tents.
⁷The days of punishment are coming,
the days of reckoning are at hand.
Let Israel know this.
Because your sins are so many
and your hostility so great,
the prophet is considered a fool,
the inspired man a maniac.
⁸The prophet, along with my God,
is the watchman over Ephraim,*ᵇ*
yet snares await him on all his paths,
and hostility in the house of his
God.
⁹They have sunk deep into corruption,
as in the days of Gibeah.
God will remember their wickedness
and punish them for their sins.

¹⁰"When I found Israel,
it was like finding grapes in the
desert;
when I saw your fathers,

ᵃ3 That is, ceremonially unclean   *ᵇ8* Or *The
prophet is the watchman over Ephraim, / the people
of my God*

it was like seeing the early fruit on
the fig tree.
But when they came to Baal Peor,
they consecrated themselves to that
shameful idol
and became as vile as the thing
they loved.
¹¹Ephraim's glory will fly away like a
bird—
no birth, no pregnancy, no
conception.
¹²Even if they rear children,
I will bereave them of every one.
Woe to them
when I turn away from them!
¹³I have seen Ephraim, like Tyre,
planted in a pleasant place.
But Ephraim will bring out
their children to the slayer."

¹⁴Give them, O Lord—
what will you give them?
Give them wombs that miscarry
and breasts that are dry.

¹⁵"Because of all their wickedness in
Gilgal,
I hated them there.
Because of their sinful deeds,
I will drive them out of my house.
I will no longer love them;
all their leaders are rebellious.
¹⁶Ephraim is blighted,
their root is withered,
they yield no fruit.
Even if they bear children,
I will slay their cherished
offspring."

¹⁷My God will reject them
because they have not obeyed him;
they will be wanderers among the
nations.

10 Israel was a spreading vine;
he brought forth fruit for himself.
As his fruit increased,
he built more altars;
as his land prospered,
he adorned his sacred stones.
²Their heart is deceitful,
and now they must bear their guilt.
The Lord will demolish their altars
and destroy their sacred stones.

³Then they will say, "We have no king
because we did not revere the
Lord.
But even if we had a king,
what could he do for us?"
⁴They make many promises,

take false oaths
and make agreements;
therefore lawsuits spring up
like poisonous weeds in a plowed
field.
⁵The people who live in Samaria fear
for the calf-idol of Beth Aven.^a
Its people will mourn over it,
and so will its idolatrous priests,
those who had rejoiced over its
splendor,
because it is taken from them into
exile.
⁶It will be carried to Assyria
as tribute for the great king.
Ephraim will be disgraced;
Israel will be ashamed of its
wooden idols.^b
⁷Samaria and its king will float away
like a twig on the surface of the
waters.
⁸The high places of wickedness^c will
be destroyed—
it is the sin of Israel.
Thorns and thistles will grow up
and cover their altars.
Then they will say to the mountains,
"Cover us!"
and to the hills, "Fall on us!"

⁹"Since the days of Gibeah, you have
sinned, O Israel,
and there you have remained.^d
Did not war overtake
the evildoers in Gibeah?
¹⁰When I please, I will punish them;
nations will be gathered against
them
to put them in bonds for their
double sin.
¹¹Ephraim is a trained heifer
that loves to thresh;
so I will put a yoke
on her fair neck.
I will drive Ephraim,
Judah must plow,
and Jacob must break up the
ground.
¹²Sow for yourselves righteousness,
reap the fruit of unfailing love,
and break up your unplowed ground;
for it is time to seek the Lord,
until he comes
and showers righteousness on you.

^a5 Beth Aven means house of wickedness (a name
for Bethel, which means house of God).   ^b6 Or
its counsel   ^c8 Hebrew aven, a reference to Beth
Aven (a derogatory name for Bethel)   ^d9 Or
there a stand was taken

13But you have planted wickedness,
  you have reaped evil,
  you have eaten the fruit of
    deception.
Because you have depended on your
    own strength
  and on your many warriors,
14the roar of battle will rise against
    your people,
  so that all your fortresses will be
    devastated—
as Shalman devastated Beth Arbel on
    the day of battle,
  when mothers were dashed to the
    ground with their children.
15Thus will it happen to you, O Bethel,
  because your wickedness is great.
When that day dawns,
  the king of Israel will be
    completely destroyed.

God's Love for Israel

11 "When Israel was a child, I loved
    him,
  and out of Egypt I called my son.
2But the more I *a* called Israel,
  the further they went from me. *b*
They sacrificed to the Baals
  and they burned incense to images.
3It was I who taught Ephraim to walk,
  taking them by the arms;
but they did not realize
  it was I who healed them.
4I led them with cords of human
    kindness,
  with ties of love;
I lifted the yoke from their neck
  and bent down to feed them.

5"Will they not return to Egypt
  and will not Assyria rule over them
  because they refuse to repent?
6Swords will flash in their cities,
  will destroy the bars of their gates
  and put an end to their plans.
7My people are determined to turn
    from me.
  Even if they call to the Most High,
  he will by no means exalt them.

8"How can I give you up, Ephraim?
  How can I hand you over, Israel?
How can I treat you like Admah?
  How can I make you like Zeboiim?
My heart is changed within me;
  all my compassion is aroused.
9I will not carry out my fierce anger,
  nor will I turn and devastate
    Ephraim.
For I am God, and not man—

the Holy One among you.
  I will not come in wrath. *c*
10They will follow the LORD;
  he will roar like a lion.
When he roars,
  his children will come trembling
    from the west.
11They will come trembling
  like birds from Egypt,
  like doves from Assyria.
I will settle them in their homes,"
  declares the LORD.

Israel's Sin

12Ephraim has surrounded me with lies,
  the house of Israel with deceit.
And Judah is unruly against God,
  even against the faithful Holy One.
12 1Ephraim feeds on the wind;
  he pursues the east wind all day
  and multiplies lies and violence.
He makes a treaty with Assyria
  and sends olive oil to Egypt.
2The LORD has a charge to bring
    against Judah;
  he will punish Jacob *d* according
    to his ways
  and repay him according to his
    deeds.
3In the womb he grasped his brother's
    heel;
  as a man he struggled with God.
4He struggled with the angel and
    overcame him;
  he wept and begged for his favor.
He found him at Bethel
  and talked with him there—
5the LORD God Almighty,
  the LORD is his name of renown!
6But you must return to your God;

a2 Some Septuagint manuscripts; Hebrew *they*
b2 Septuagint; Hebrew *them*   *c9* Or *come
against any city*   *d2* Jacob means *he grasps the
heel* (figuratively, *he deceives*).

POINT OF INTEREST   Hosea 11:9

One of God's characteristics
is that he is forgiving.
That's not always true of his
children. While we like to
imagine ourselves compassionate and
kind, compared with God we are cruel and
vindictive. God does not give us what we
deserve. And that's a really good thing!

Read Hosea 11:1–11
Key Verses Hosea 11:3–4

Amazing Love!

Everything seems to have a price tag. From the time we toddle into a toy store, we learn the hard lesson that if we want something, we better be ready to pay for it! Then God comes along and disrupts our neatly organized you-get-what-you-pay-for view of things. He offers his amazing love as a *free gift*. He calls us his children and pours out his love with boundless generosity.

God loved us and redeemed us even before we knew about it or asked for forgiveness (see Romans 5:6–8). He shows his love by caring for us, guiding us, healing us and changing us day by day. We are tempted to keep asking, "What do I need to do to be worthy of this amazing display of agape (divine love) from God?" The answer is, "Nothing!" He simply wants us to accept it.

Digging Into the Word
1. How do these passages touch your heart when you see God's ultimate demonstration of love for you?—*John 3:16; Romans 5:6–8*
2. How does God want you to demonstrate his love through your life?—*John 13:34–35; 1 John 4:7–12*

Personal Reflection
What is one specific way you can demonstrate the love of God to a member of your family in the coming week?

One Step Deeper
John 15:12–13; 1 John 4:13–21

Go to page 999 for your next devotional reading.

maintain love and justice,
and wait for your God always.

⁷The merchant uses dishonest scales;
he loves to defraud.
⁸Ephraim boasts,
"I am very rich; I have become
wealthy.
With all my wealth they will not find
in me
any iniquity or sin."

⁹"I am the LORD your God,
˪who brought you˩ out of*a* Egypt;
I will make you live in tents again,
as in the days of your appointed
feasts.
¹⁰I spoke to the prophets,
gave them many visions
and told parables through them."

¹¹Is Gilead wicked?
Its people are worthless!
Do they sacrifice bulls in Gilgal?
Their altars will be like piles of
stones
on a plowed field.
¹²Jacob fled to the country of Aram*b*;
Israel served to get a wife,
and to pay for her he tended
sheep.
¹³The LORD used a prophet to bring
Israel up from Egypt,
by a prophet he cared for him.
¹⁴But Ephraim has bitterly provoked
him to anger;
his Lord will leave upon him the
guilt of his bloodshed
and will repay him for his
contempt.

The LORD's Anger Against Israel

13 When Ephraim spoke, men
trembled;
he was exalted in Israel.
But he became guilty of Baal
worship and died.
²Now they sin more and more;
they make idols for themselves
from their silver,
cleverly fashioned images,
all of them the work of craftsmen.
It is said of these people,
"They offer human sacrifice
and kiss*c* the calf-idols."
³Therefore they will be like the
morning mist,
like the early dew that disappears,
like chaff swirling from a threshing
floor,

like smoke escaping through a
window.

⁴"But I am the LORD your God,
˪who brought you˩ out of*a* Egypt.
You shall acknowledge no God but
me,
no Savior except me.
⁵I cared for you in the desert,
in the land of burning heat.
⁶When I fed them, they were satisfied;
when they were satisfied, they
became proud;
then they forgot me.
⁷So I will come upon them like a lion,
like a leopard I will lurk by the
path.
⁸Like a bear robbed of her cubs,
I will attack them and rip them
open.
Like a lion I will devour them;
a wild animal will tear them apart.

⁹"You are destroyed, O Israel,
because you are against me,
against your helper.
¹⁰Where is your king, that he may save
you?
Where are your rulers in all your
towns,
of whom you said,
'Give me a king and princes'?
¹¹So in my anger I gave you a king,
and in my wrath I took him away.
¹²The guilt of Ephraim is stored up,
his sins are kept on record.
¹³Pains as of a woman in childbirth
come to him,
but he is a child without wisdom;
when the time arrives,
he does not come to the opening of
the womb.

¹⁴"I will ransom them from the power
of the grave*d*;
I will redeem them from death.
Where, O death, are your plagues?
Where, O grave,*d* is your
destruction?

"I will have no compassion,
15   even though he thrives among his
brothers.
An east wind from the LORD will
come,
blowing in from the desert;
his spring will fail

---

*a*9,4 Or *God / ever since you were in*   *b*12 That
is, Northwest Mesopotamia   *c*2 Or *"Men who
sacrifice / kiss*   *d*14 Hebrew *Sheol*

and his well dry up.
His storehouse will be plundered
 of all its treasures.
16The people of Samaria must bear
 their guilt,
because they have rebelled against
 their God.
They will fall by the sword;
 their little ones will be dashed to
 the ground,
 their pregnant women ripped
 open."

Repentance to Bring Blessing

14 Return, O Israel, to the LORD your
 God.
Your sins have been your
 downfall!
2Take words with you
 and return to the LORD.
Say to him:
 "Forgive all our sins
and receive us graciously,
 that we may offer the fruit of our
 lips.ᵃ
3Assyria cannot save us;
 we will not mount war-horses.
We will never again say 'Our gods'
 to what our own hands have
 made,
for in you the fatherless find
 compassion."

4"I will heal their waywardness
 and love them freely,
for my anger has turned away
 from them.
5I will be like the dew to Israel;
 he will blossom like a lily.
Like a cedar of Lebanon
 he will send down his roots;
6 his young shoots will grow.
His splendor will be like an olive tree,

his fragrance like a cedar of
 Lebanon.
7Men will dwell again in his shade.
 He will flourish like the grain.
He will blossom like a vine,
 and his fame will be like the wine
 from Lebanon.
8O Ephraim, what more have Iᵇ to do
 with idols?
I will answer him and care for
 him.
I am like a green pine tree;
 your fruitfulness comes from me."

9Who is wise? He will realize these
 things.
Who is discerning? He will
 understand them.
The ways of the LORD are right;
 the righteous walk in them,
 but the rebellious stumble in them.

ᵃ2 Or *offer our lips as sacrifices of bulls* ᵇ8 Or
What more has Ephraim

POINT OF INTEREST

Hosea 14:2

Words can be "full of sound and fury, signifying nothing" (*Macbeth* 5.5.17). Words can even convey the opposite of what they are intended to mean. Words can heal, but they can also hurt. Words can be used to deceive, to discourage and to equivocate. That's why we need to be careful as we relate to others. When we approach God with our words, we need to be doubly careful to speak in honest words that come from our hearts.

Have you ever wondered if there is spiritual significance in natural disasters such as floods, hurricanes and earthquakes? The book of Joel may give you a clue. Joel views the plague of locusts as a catastrophic foretaste of God's judgment on people who are cold and indifferent toward him. Joel warns of the coming judgment for all nations, including the Israelites. He calls the nation to repent and paints a picture of the restoration and healing that will follow if they do. Consider this as you read the book of Joel: In God's eyes, the worst disaster is a human heart that is closed to his love.

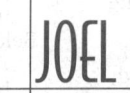

JOEL

1 The word of the LORD that came to Joel son of Pethuel.

An Invasion of Locusts

²Hear this, you elders;
  listen, all who live in the land.
Has anything like this ever happened
    in your days
  or in the days of your forefathers?
³Tell it to your children,
    and let your children tell it to their
      children,
    and their children to the next
      generation.
⁴What the locust swarm has left
  the great locusts have eaten;
what the great locusts have left
  the young locusts have eaten;
what the young locusts have left
  other locusts*a* have eaten.

⁵Wake up, you drunkards, and weep!
  Wail, all you drinkers of wine;
wail because of the new wine,
  for it has been snatched from your
    lips.
⁶A nation has invaded my land,
  powerful and without number;
it has the teeth of a lion,
  the fangs of a lioness.

---

*a4 The precise meaning of the four Hebrew words
used here for locusts is uncertain.*

⁷It has laid waste my vines
   and ruined my fig trees.
It has stripped off their bark
   and thrown it away,
   leaving their branches white.

⁸Mourn like a virgin*a* in sackcloth
   grieving for the husband*b* of her
      youth.
⁹Grain offerings and drink offerings
   are cut off from the house of the
      LORD.
The priests are in mourning,
   those who minister before the
      LORD.
¹⁰The fields are ruined,
   the ground is dried up*c*;
the grain is destroyed,
   the new wine is dried up,
   the oil fails.
¹¹Despair, you farmers,
   wail, you vine growers;
grieve for the wheat and the barley,
   because the harvest of the field is
      destroyed.
¹²The vine is dried up
   and the fig tree is withered;
the pomegranate, the palm and the
      apple tree—
   all the trees of the field—are dried
      up.
Surely the joy of mankind
   is withered away.

A Call to Repentance

¹³Put on sackcloth, O priests, and
      mourn;
   wail, you who minister before the
      altar.
Come, spend the night in sackcloth,
   you who minister before my God;
for the grain offerings and drink
      offerings
   are withheld from the house of
      your God.
¹⁴Declare a holy fast;
   call a sacred assembly.
Summon the elders
   and all who live in the land
to the house of the LORD your God,
   and cry out to the LORD.

¹⁵Alas for that day!
   For the day of the LORD is near;
   it will come like destruction from
      the Almighty.*d*

¹⁶Has not the food been cut off
   before our very eyes—
joy and gladness

from the house of our God?
¹⁷The seeds are shriveled
   beneath the clods.*e*
The storehouses are in ruins,
   the granaries have been broken
      down,
for the grain has dried up.
¹⁸How the cattle moan!
   The herds mill about
because they have no pasture;
   even the flocks of sheep are
      suffering.

¹⁹To you, O LORD, I call,
   for fire has devoured the open
      pastures
and flames have burned up all the
      trees of the field.
²⁰Even the wild animals pant for you;
   the streams of water have dried up
   and fire has devoured the open
      pastures.

An Army of Locusts

2 Blow the trumpet in Zion;
   sound the alarm on my holy hill.
Let all who live in the land tremble,
   for the day of the LORD is coming.
It is close at hand—
²   a day of darkness and gloom,
   a day of clouds and blackness.
Like dawn spreading across the
      mountains
   a large and mighty army comes,
such as never was of old
   nor ever will be in ages to come.

³Before them fire devours,
   behind them a flame blazes.
Before them the land is like the
      garden of Eden,
   behind them, a desert waste—
   nothing escapes them.
⁴They have the appearance of horses;
   they gallop along like cavalry.
⁵With a noise like that of chariots
   they leap over the mountaintops,
like a crackling fire consuming
      stubble,
   like a mighty army drawn up for
      battle.

⁶At the sight of them, nations are in
      anguish;
   every face turns pale.
⁷They charge like warriors;

---

*a*8 Or *young woman*   *b*8 Or *betrothed*
*c*10 Or *ground mourns*   *d*15 Hebrew *Shaddai*
*e*17 The meaning of the Hebrew for this word is
uncertain.

they scale walls like soldiers.
They all march in line,
  not swerving from their course.
8They do not jostle each other;
  each marches straight ahead.
They plunge through defenses
  without breaking ranks.
9They rush upon the city;
  they run along the wall.
They climb into the houses;
  like thieves they enter through the
    windows.

10Before them the earth shakes,
  the sky trembles,
the sun and moon are darkened,
  and the stars no longer shine.
11The LORD thunders
  at the head of his army;
his forces are beyond number,

and mighty are those who obey his
    command.
The day of the LORD is great;
  it is dreadful.
Who can endure it?

Rend Your Heart

12"Even now," declares the LORD,
  "return to me with all your heart,
  with fasting and weeping and
    mourning."

13Rend your heart
  and not your garments.
Return to the LORD your God,
  for he is gracious and
    compassionate,
slow to anger and abounding in love,
  and he relents from sending
    calamity.

MONDAY

Read Joel 2:1–27
Key Verses Joel 2:12–13

Gracious and Compassionate — Ellen B. Susman

Having your ideas shot down in front of others is no fun. I learned this firsthand one day when a professor unmercifully dissed my ideas in front of all my classmates. I was embarrassed, hurt and angry. *That's the last time I talk in her class,* I decided.

Later that same professor apologized to me and explained why she had been so critical. I had a choice. Would I make her pay by sulking, being uncooperative and slandering her and her class, or would I graciously accept her apology and forgive her?

Fortunately, God had deflated my anger enough so I could forgive her. The up side of this incident with my professor was that it prompted me to think about how much we hurt God, and yet his forgiveness flows to infinite depths.

In Joel 2 the prophet declares God's righteous judgment on Israel. They had abandoned him and his laws; they had stomped on God's gifts and walked away laughing; they had prostituted themselves to other gods. Yet even with that kind of affront, God offered to forgive them if they would return to him with all their hearts.

In some ways I reject God every day: I miss time with him. I refuse to respond to the Holy Spirit's nudging. I don't speak out on Jesus' behalf. When I pray, I list my requests without listening in return. But even though I hurt him, God continues to be "gracious and compassionate, slow to anger and abounding in love." I have offended God so much, and yet he forgives me. Can I do any less than forgive others?

A Deeper Look
Matthew 6:14; Ephesians 4:32; Colossians 3:13

Go to page 1006 for your next devotional reading.

14Who knows? He may turn and have
pity
and leave behind a blessing—
grain offerings and drink offerings
for the LORD your God.

15Blow the trumpet in Zion,
declare a holy fast,
call a sacred assembly.
16Gather the people,
consecrate the assembly;
bring together the elders,
gather the children,
those nursing at the breast.
Let the bridegroom leave his room
and the bride her chamber.
17Let the priests, who minister before
the LORD,
weep between the temple porch
and the altar.
Let them say, "Spare your people,
O LORD.
Do not make your inheritance an
object of scorn,
a byword among the nations.
Why should they say among the
peoples,
'Where is their God?' "

The LORD's Answer

18Then the LORD will be jealous for his
land
and take pity on his people.

19The LORD will reply*a* to them:

"I am sending you grain, new wine
and oil,
enough to satisfy you fully;
never again will I make you
an object of scorn to the nations.

20"I will drive the northern army far
from you,
pushing it into a parched and
barren land,
with its front columns going into the
eastern sea*b*
and those in the rear into the
western sea.*c*
And its stench will go up;
its smell will rise."

Surely he has done great things.*d*
21   Be not afraid, O land;
be glad and rejoice.
Surely the LORD has done great things.
22   Be not afraid, O wild animals,
for the open pastures are becoming
green.
The trees are bearing their fruit;

the fig tree and the vine yield their
riches.
23Be glad, O people of Zion,
rejoice in the LORD your God,
for he has given you
the autumn rains in
righteousness.*e*
He sends you abundant showers,
both autumn and spring rains, as
before.
24The threshing floors will be filled
with grain;
the vats will overflow with new
wine and oil.

25"I will repay you for the years the
locusts have eaten—
the great locust and the young
locust,
the other locusts and the locust
swarm*f*—
my great army that I sent among you.
26You will have plenty to eat, until you
are full,
and you will praise the name of
the LORD your God,
who has worked wonders for you;
never again will my people be
shamed.
27Then you will know that I am in
Israel,
that I am the LORD your God,
and that there is no other;
never again will my people be
shamed.

The Day of the LORD

28"And afterward,
I will pour out my Spirit on all
people.
Your sons and daughters will
prophesy,
your old men will dream dreams,
your young men will see visions.
29Even on my servants, both men and
women,
I will pour out my Spirit in those
days.
30I will show wonders in the heavens
and on the earth,
blood and fire and billows of
smoke.
31The sun will be turned to darkness

a18,19 Or LORD *was jealous* . . . / *and took pity* . . .
/ *19The* LORD *replied*   *b20* That is, the Dead Sea
c20 That is, the Mediterranean   *d20* Or *rise.* /
Surely it has done great things."   *e23* Or / *the
teacher for righteousness:*   *f25* The precise
meaning of the four Hebrew words used here for
locusts is uncertain.

and the moon to blood
before the coming of the great and
    dreadful day of the LORD.
32And everyone who calls
on the name of the LORD will be
    saved;
for on Mount Zion and in Jerusalem
there will be deliverance,
as the LORD has said,
among the survivors
whom the LORD calls.

The Nations Judged

3 "In those days and at that time,
    when I restore the fortunes of
      Judah and Jerusalem,
2I will gather all nations
    and bring them down to the Valley
      of Jehoshaphat.a
There I will enter into judgment
    against them
concerning my inheritance, my
    people Israel,
for they scattered my people among
    the nations
and divided up my land.
3They cast lots for my people
    and traded boys for prostitutes;
they sold girls for wine
    that they might drink.

4"Now what have you against me,
O Tyre and Sidon and all you regions of
Philistia? Are you repaying me for something
I have done? If you are paying me
back, I will swiftly and speedily return on
your own heads what you have done.
5For you took my silver and my gold and
carried off my finest treasures to your
temples. 6You sold the people of Judah
and Jerusalem to the Greeks, that you
might send them far from their homeland.

7"See, I am going to rouse them out of
the places to which you sold them, and I
will return on your own heads what you
have done. 8I will sell your sons and
daughters to the people of Judah, and
they will sell them to the Sabeans, a nation
far away." The LORD has spoken.

9Proclaim this among the nations:
    Prepare for war!
Rouse the warriors!
    Let all the fighting men draw near
      and attack.
10Beat your plowshares into swords
    and your pruning hooks into
      spears.
Let the weakling say,

    "I am strong!"
11Come quickly, all you nations from
    every side,
    and assemble there.

Bring down your warriors, O LORD!

12"Let the nations be roused;
    let them advance into the Valley of
      Jehoshaphat,
for there I will sit
    to judge all the nations on every
      side.
13Swing the sickle,
    for the harvest is ripe.
Come, trample the grapes,
    for the winepress is full
    and the vats overflow—
so great is their wickedness!"

14Multitudes, multitudes
    in the valley of decision!
For the day of the LORD is near
    in the valley of decision.
15The sun and moon will be darkened,
    and the stars no longer shine.
16The LORD will roar from Zion
    and thunder from Jerusalem;
    the earth and the sky will tremble.
But the LORD will be a refuge for his
    people,
    a stronghold for the people of
      Israel.

Blessings for God's People

17"Then you will know that I, the LORD
    your God,
    dwell in Zion, my holy hill.
Jerusalem will be holy;

a2 Jehoshaphat means the LORD judges; also in
verse 12.

POINT OF INTEREST

Joel 3:12-17

People often ask, "If God is
so good, why doesn't he just
stop evil?" The Bible
answers that question—God
will eventually stop evil. This verse prophesies
the final battle—the forces of an
entire planet will rebel against God and
will be defeated by angelic hosts. Take
heart, because "the day of the LORD is
near."

never again will foreigners invade
  her.
18"In that day the mountains will drip
    new wine,
  and the hills will flow with milk;
  all the ravines of Judah will run
    with water.
A fountain will flow out of the Lord's
    house
  and will water the valley of
    acacias. *a*
19But Egypt will be desolate,
  Edom a desert waste,

because of violence done to the
    people of Judah,
  in whose land they shed innocent
    blood.
20Judah will be inhabited forever
  and Jerusalem through all
    generations.
21Their bloodguilt, which I have not
    pardoned,
  I will pardon."

The Lord dwells in Zion!

a 18 Or *Valley of Shittim*

What is it about prosperity that seems to lead to corruption? Many great nations have accumulated riches and power only to crumble into vice, economic inequity and social injustice. The prophet Amos is living during such a time in the nation of Israel. He speaks out against those who made themselves powerful at the expense of the poor, and he urges the nation to return to justice. Amos delivers a timeless message of social justice we would do well to heed—and to respond to with compassionate hearts.

AMOS

1 The words of Amos, one of the shepherds of Tekoa—what he saw concerning Israel two years before the earthquake, when Uzziah was king of Judah and Jeroboam son of Jehoash*a* was king of Israel.

²He said:

"The LORD roars from Zion
    and thunders from Jerusalem;
the pastures of the shepherds dry
        up,*b*
    and the top of Carmel withers."

Judgment on Israel's Neighbors

³This is what the LORD says:

"For three sins of Damascus,
    even for four, I will not turn back
        ⌞my wrath⌟.
Because she threshed Gilead
    with sledges having iron teeth,

⁴I will send fire upon the house of
        Hazael
    that will consume the fortresses of
        Ben-Hadad.
⁵I will break down the gate of
        Damascus;
    I will destroy the king who is in*c*
        the Valley of Aven*d*
and the one who holds the scepter in
        Beth Eden.
    The people of Aram will go into
        exile to Kir,"
                        says the LORD.

⁶This is what the LORD says:

"For three sins of Gaza,
    even for four, I will not turn back
        ⌞my wrath⌟.

---

*a*1 Hebrew *Joash*, a variant of *Jehoash*   *b*2 Or
shepherds mourn   *c*5 Or *the inhabitants of*
*d*5 *Aven* means *wickedness*.

Because she took captive whole
communities
and sold them to Edom,
7I will send fire upon the walls of
Gaza
that will consume her fortresses.
8I will destroy the king*a* of Ashdod
and the one who holds the scepter
in Ashkelon.
I will turn my hand against Ekron,
till the last of the Philistines is
dead,"
　　　　　says the Sovereign LORD.

9This is what the LORD says:

"For three sins of Tyre,
even for four, I will not turn back
⌐my wrath⌐.
Because she sold whole communities
of captives to Edom,
disregarding a treaty of
brotherhood,
10I will send fire upon the walls of Tyre
that will consume her fortresses."

11This is what the LORD says:

"For three sins of Edom,
even for four, I will not turn back
⌐my wrath⌐.
Because he pursued his brother with
a sword,
stifling all compassion,*b*
because his anger raged continually
and his fury flamed unchecked,
12I will send fire upon Teman
that will consume the fortresses of
Bozrah."

13This is what the LORD says:

"For three sins of Ammon,
even for four, I will not turn back
⌐my wrath⌐.
Because he ripped open the pregnant
women of Gilead
in order to extend his borders,
14I will set fire to the walls of Rabbah
that will consume her fortresses
amid war cries on the day of battle,
amid violent winds on a stormy
day.
15Her king*c* will go into exile,
he and his officials together,"
　　　　　　　says the LORD.

2 This is what the LORD says:

"For three sins of Moab,
even for four, I will not turn back
⌐my wrath⌐.
Because he burned, as if to lime,
the bones of Edom's king,
2I will send fire upon Moab
that will consume the fortresses of
Kerioth.*d*
Moab will go down in great tumult
amid war cries and the blast of the
trumpet.
3I will destroy her ruler
and kill all her officials with him,"
　　　　　says the LORD.

4This is what the LORD says:

"For three sins of Judah,
even for four, I will not turn back
⌐my wrath⌐.
Because they have rejected the law of
the LORD
and have not kept his decrees,
because they have been led astray by
false gods,*e*
the gods*f* their ancestors
followed,
5I will send fire upon Judah
that will consume the fortresses of
Jerusalem."

Judgment on Israel

6This is what the LORD says:

"For three sins of Israel,
even for four, I will not turn back
⌐my wrath⌐.
They sell the righteous for silver,
and the needy for a pair of
sandals.
7They trample on the heads of the
poor
as upon the dust of the ground
and deny justice to the oppressed.
Father and son use the same girl
and so profane my holy name.
8They lie down beside every altar
on garments taken in pledge.
In the house of their god
they drink wine taken as fines.

9"I destroyed the Amorite before them,
though he was tall as the cedars
and strong as the oaks.
I destroyed his fruit above
and his roots below.
10"I brought you up out of Egypt,
and I led you forty years in the
desert

---

*a*8 Or *inhabitants*　　*b*11 Or *sword / and
destroyed his allies*　　*c*15 Or / Molech; Hebrew
malcam*　　*d*2 Or *of her cities*　　*e*4 Or *by lies
f*4 Or *lies*

to give you the land of the
Amorites.
¹¹I also raised up prophets from among
your sons
and Nazirites from among your
young men.
Is this not true, people of Israel?"
declares the LORD.
¹²"But you made the Nazirites drink
wine
and commanded the prophets not
to prophesy.

¹³"Now then, I will crush you
as a cart crushes when loaded with
grain.
¹⁴The swift will not escape,
the strong will not muster their
strength,
and the warrior will not save his
life.
¹⁵The archer will not stand his ground,
the fleet-footed soldier will not get
away,
and the horseman will not save his
life.
¹⁶Even the bravest warriors
will flee naked on that day,"
declares the LORD.

Witnesses Summoned Against Israel

3 Hear this word the LORD has spoken
against you, O people of Israel—
against the whole family I brought up out
of Egypt:

²"You only have I chosen
of all the families of the earth;
therefore I will punish you
for all your sins."

³Do two walk together
unless they have agreed to do so?
⁴Does a lion roar in the thicket
when he has no prey?
Does he growl in his den
when he has caught nothing?
⁵Does a bird fall into a trap on the
ground
where no snare has been set?
Does a trap spring up from the earth
when there is nothing to catch?
⁶When a trumpet sounds in a city,
do not the people tremble?
When disaster comes to a city,
has not the LORD caused it?

⁷Surely the Sovereign LORD does
nothing
without revealing his plan

to his servants the prophets.
⁸The lion has roared—
who will not fear?
The Sovereign LORD has spoken—
who can but prophesy?

⁹Proclaim to the fortresses of Ashdod
and to the fortresses of Egypt:
"Assemble yourselves on the
mountains of Samaria;
see the great unrest within her
and the oppression among her
people."

¹⁰"They do not know how to do right,"
declares the LORD,
"who hoard plunder and loot in
their fortresses."

¹¹Therefore this is what the Sovereign
LORD says:

"An enemy will overrun the land;
he will pull down your strongholds
and plunder your fortresses."

¹²This is what the LORD says:

"As a shepherd saves from the lion's
mouth
only two leg bones or a piece of an
ear,
so will the Israelites be saved,
those who sit in Samaria
on the edge of their beds
and in Damascus on their
couches.ᵃ"

¹³"Hear this and testify against the
house of Jacob," declares the Lord, the
LORD God Almighty.

¹⁴"On the day I punish Israel for her
sins,
I will destroy the altars of Bethel;
the horns of the altar will be cut off
and fall to the ground.
¹⁵I will tear down the winter house
along with the summer house;
the houses adorned with ivory will be
destroyed
and the mansions will be
demolished,"
declares the LORD.

Israel Has Not Returned to God

4 Hear this word, you cows of Bashan
on Mount Samaria,

ᵃ12 The meaning of the Hebrew for this line is
uncertain.

you women who oppress the poor
  and crush the needy
and say to your husbands, "Bring
  us some drinks!"
²The Sovereign LORD has sworn by his
  holiness:
"The time will surely come
when you will be taken away with
  hooks,
  the last of you with fishhooks.
³You will each go straight out
  through breaks in the wall,
and you will be cast out toward
  Harmon,ᵃ"
                    declares the LORD.
⁴"Go to Bethel and sin;
  go to Gilgal and sin yet more.
Bring your sacrifices every morning,

your tithes every three years.ᵇ
⁵Burn leavened bread as a thank
  offering
and brag about your freewill
  offerings—
boast about them, you Israelites,
  for this is what you love to do,"
            declares the Sovereign LORD.

⁶"I gave you empty stomachsᶜ in
  every city
and lack of bread in every town,
  yet you have not returned to me,"
                    declares the LORD.

ᵃ3 Masoretic Text; with a different word division of
the Hebrew (see Septuagint) *out, O mountain of
oppression*   ᵇ4 Or *tithes on the third day*
ᶜ6 Hebrew *you cleanness of teeth*

TUESDAY

Read Amos 3:1–15
Key Verse Amos 3:3

Walking Together – Stephanie Choat

You could have cut the tension in that dorm room with a knife. My
roommate Ann and I were not looking at each other, but we were
aware of each other's every move and breath. She wouldn't speak to
me, so I tried to force her to say something . . . anything. Ann shattered the silence by yelling something unrepeatable at me, and in a
warped way I felt triumphant because I had broken her will to
ignore me.

Ann and I didn't know what an adventure it would be to live with
someone we hardly knew while getting used to college life and the
academic workload. At times we loved each other's company, but at
other times each of us felt seething anger toward the other.

The day of that outburst came at the low end of a downhill slide
in our relationship. After that we spent less and less time together,
until one day we asked the question that was still hanging in the air
between us: "Do we want to continue working out this relationship?" What an odd concept! I had always believed that relationships just happened and that the best ones were those that didn't
take much effort to maintain.

The truth in Amos 3:3 is startling if one takes time to think
about it. People don't "walk together" unless they've made that
decision. Life presents too many obstacles—hurts, complications
and busyness—for relationships to "just happen."

Believe it or not, Ann and I eventually decided to "walk together." While our relationship has required work, we have found it very
rewarding to have a friendship we have chosen.

A Deeper Look
Proverbs 17:17; 27:6

Go to page 1013 for your next devotional reading.

7"I also withheld rain from you
   when the harvest was still three
     months away.
I sent rain on one town,
   but withheld it from another.
One field had rain;
   another had none and dried up.
8People staggered from town to town
   for water
   but did not get enough to drink,
   yet you have not returned to me,"
          declares the LORD.

9"Many times I struck your gardens
   and vineyards,
   I struck them with blight and
     mildew.
Locusts devoured your fig and olive
   trees,
   yet you have not returned to me,"
          declares the LORD.

10"I sent plagues among you
   as I did to Egypt.
I killed your young men with the
   sword,
   along with your captured horses.
I filled your nostrils with the stench
   of your camps,
   yet you have not returned to me,"
          declares the LORD.

11"I overthrew some of you
   as I*a* overthrew Sodom and
     Gomorrah.
You were like a burning stick
   snatched from the fire,
   yet you have not returned to me,"
          declares the LORD.

12"Therefore this is what I will do to
   you, Israel,
   and because I will do this to you,
   prepare to meet your God,
   O Israel."

13He who forms the mountains,
   creates the wind,
   and reveals his thoughts to man,
he who turns dawn to darkness,
   and treads the high places of the
     earth—
   the LORD God Almighty is his name.

A Lament and Call to Repentance

5 Hear this word, O house of Israel, this
  lament I take up concerning you:

2"Fallen is Virgin Israel,
   never to rise again,
deserted in her own land,
   with no one to lift her up."

3This is what the Sovereign LORD says:

"The city that marches out a
   thousand strong for Israel
will have only a hundred left;
the town that marches out a hundred
   strong
will have only ten left."

4This is what the LORD says to the
house of Israel:

"Seek me and live;
5   do not seek Bethel,
do not go to Gilgal,
   do not journey to Beersheba.
For Gilgal will surely go into exile,
   and Bethel will be reduced to
     nothing.*b*"
6Seek the LORD and live,
   or he will sweep through the house
     of Joseph like a fire;
it will devour,
   and Bethel will have no one to
     quench it.

7You who turn justice into bitterness
   and cast righteousness to the
     ground
8(he who made the Pleiades and
   Orion,
   who turns blackness into dawn
   and darkens day into night,
who calls for the waters of the sea
   and pours them out over the face
     of the land—

a 11 Hebrew *God*   *b 5* Or *grief*; or *wickedness*;
Hebrew *aven*, a reference to Beth Aven (a
derogatory name for Bethel)

POINT OF INTEREST

Amos 5:4-24

Franklin D. Roosevelt said
that "the test of our
progress is not whether we
add more to the abundance of
those who have much; it is whether we
provide enough for those who have too little." Here Amos cries out against people
who give God only lip service, who pile
religious practice on religious practice
without putting their beliefs *into* practice.
Amos's cry rings down the centuries to us
today as clearly as it did to the Israelites
of long ago.

the LORD is his name—
⁹he flashes destruction on the
stronghold
and brings the fortified city to
ruin),
¹⁰you hate the one who reproves in
court
and despise him who tells the
truth.

¹¹You trample on the poor
and force him to give you grain.
Therefore, though you have built
stone mansions,
you will not live in them;
though you have planted lush
vineyards,
you will not drink their wine.
¹²For I know how many are your
offenses
and how great your sins.

You oppress the righteous and take
bribes
and you deprive the poor of justice
in the courts.
¹³Therefore the prudent man keeps
quiet in such times,
for the times are evil.

¹⁴Seek good, not evil,
that you may live.
Then the LORD God Almighty will be
with you,
just as you say he is.
¹⁵Hate evil, love good;
maintain justice in the courts.
Perhaps the LORD God Almighty will
have mercy
on the remnant of Joseph.

¹⁶Therefore this is what the Lord, the
LORD God Almighty, says:

"There will be wailing in all the
streets
and cries of anguish in every
public square.
The farmers will be summoned to
weep
and the mourners to wail.
¹⁷There will be wailing in all the
vineyards,
for I will pass through your midst,"
says the LORD.

The Day of the LORD

¹⁸Woe to you who long
for the day of the LORD!
Why do you long for the day of the
LORD?

That day will be darkness, not
light.
¹⁹It will be as though a man fled from
a lion
only to meet a bear,
as though he entered his house
and rested his hand on the wall
only to have a snake bite him.
²⁰Will not the day of the LORD be
darkness, not light—
pitch-dark, without a ray of
brightness?

²¹"I hate, I despise your religious
feasts;
I cannot stand your assemblies.
²²Even though you bring me burnt
offerings and grain offerings,
I will not accept them.
Though you bring choice fellowship
offerings,ᵃ
I will have no regard for them.
²³Away with the noise of your songs!
I will not listen to the music of
your harps.
²⁴But let justice roll on like a river,
righteousness like a never-failing
stream!

²⁵"Did you bring me sacrifices and
offerings
forty years in the desert, O house
of Israel?
²⁶You have lifted up the shrine of your
king,
the pedestal of your idols,
the star of your godᵇ—
which you made for yourselves.
²⁷Therefore I will send you into exile
beyond Damascus,"
says the LORD, whose name is God
Almighty.

Woe to the Complacent

6 Woe to you who are complacent in
Zion,
and to you who feel secure on
Mount Samaria,
you notable men of the foremost
nation,
to whom the people of Israel
come!
²Go to Calneh and look at it;
go from there to great Hamath,

ᵃ22 Traditionally *peace offerings*   ᵇ26 Or *lifted
up Sakkuth your king / and Kaiwan your idols, /
your star-gods*; Septuagint *lifted up the shrine of
Molech / and the star of your god Rephan, / their
idols*

and then go down to Gath in
Philistia.
Are they better off than your two
kingdoms?
Is their land larger than yours?
³You put off the evil day
and bring near a reign of terror.
⁴You lie on beds inlaid with ivory
and lounge on your couches.
You dine on choice lambs
and fattened calves.
⁵You strum away on your harps like
David
and improvise on musical
instruments.
⁶You drink wine by the bowlful
and use the finest lotions,
but you do not grieve over the ruin
of Joseph.
⁷Therefore you will be among the first
to go into exile;
your feasting and lounging will
end.

The LORD Abhors the Pride of Israel

⁸The Sovereign LORD has sworn by
himself—the LORD God Almighty declares:

"I abhor the pride of Jacob
and detest his fortresses;
I will deliver up the city
and everything in it."

⁹If ten men are left in one house, they
too will die. ¹⁰And if a relative who is to
burn the bodies comes to carry them out
of the house and asks anyone still hiding
there, "Is anyone with you?" and he says,
"No," then he will say, "Hush! We must
not mention the name of the LORD."

¹¹For the LORD has given the command,
and he will smash the great house
into pieces
and the small house into bits.

¹²Do horses run on the rocky crags?
Does one plow there with oxen?
But you have turned justice into
poison
and the fruit of righteousness into
bitterness—
¹³you who rejoice in the conquest of Lo
Debar*a*
and say, "Did we not take
Karnaim*b* by our own
strength?"

¹⁴For the LORD God Almighty declares,

"I will stir up a nation against you,
O house of Israel,
that will oppress you all the way
from Lebo*c* Hamath to the valley
of the Arabah."

Locusts, Fire and a Plumb Line

7 This is what the Sovereign LORD
showed me: He was preparing swarms
of locusts after the king's share had been
harvested and just as the second crop
was coming up. ²When they had stripped
the land clean, I cried out, "Sovereign
LORD, forgive! How can Jacob survive? He
is so small!"

³So the LORD relented.
"This will not happen," the LORD said.

⁴This is what the Sovereign LORD
showed me: The Sovereign LORD was calling for judgment by fire; it dried up the
great deep and devoured the land. ⁵Then
I cried out, "Sovereign LORD, I beg you,
stop! How can Jacob survive? He is so
small!"

⁶So the LORD relented.
"This will not happen either," the Sovereign LORD said.

⁷This is what he showed me: The Lord
was standing by a wall that had been
built true to plumb, with a plumb line in
his hand. ⁸And the LORD asked me, "What
do you see, Amos?"
"A plumb line," I replied.
Then the Lord said, "Look, I am setting a plumb line among my people Israel; I will spare them no longer.

⁹"The high places of Isaac will be
destroyed
and the sanctuaries of Israel will
be ruined;
with my sword I will rise against
the house of Jeroboam."

Amos and Amaziah

¹⁰Then Amaziah the priest of Bethel
sent a message to Jeroboam king of Israel: "Amos is raising a conspiracy against
you in the very heart of Israel. The land
cannot bear all his words. ¹¹For this is
what Amos is saying:

" 'Jeroboam will die by the sword,
and Israel will surely go into exile,
away from their native land.' "

¹²Then Amaziah said to Amos, "Get

---

a 13 Lo Debar means nothing.   *b* 13 Karnaim
means horns; horn here symbolizes strength.
c 14 Or from the entrance to

out, you seer! Go back to the land of Judah. Earn your bread there and do your prophesying there. 13Don't prophesy anymore at Bethel, because this is the king's sanctuary and the temple of the kingdom."

14Amos answered Amaziah, "I was neither a prophet nor a prophet's son, but I was a shepherd, and I also took care of sycamore-fig trees. 15But the LORD took me from tending the flock and said to me, 'Go, prophesy to my people Israel.' 16Now then, hear the word of the LORD. You say,

" 'Do not prophesy against Israel,
    and stop preaching against the
        house of Isaac.'

17"Therefore this is what the LORD says:

" 'Your wife will become a prostitute
        in the city,
    and your sons and daughters will
        fall by the sword.
Your land will be measured and
        divided up,
    and you yourself will die in a
        pagan*a* country.
And Israel will certainly go into exile,
    away from their native land.' "

A Basket of Ripe Fruit

8 This is what the Sovereign LORD showed me: a basket of ripe fruit. 2"What do you see, Amos?" he asked.

"A basket of ripe fruit," I answered.

Then the LORD said to me, "The time is ripe for my people Israel; I will spare them no longer.

3"In that day," declares the Sovereign LORD, "the songs in the temple will turn to wailing.*b* Many, many bodies—flung everywhere! Silence!"

4Hear this, you who trample the needy
    and do away with the poor of the
        land,

5saying,

"When will the New Moon be over
        that we may sell grain,
    and the Sabbath be ended
        that we may market wheat?"—
skimping the measure,
        boosting the price
        and cheating with dishonest scales,
6buying the poor with silver
        and the needy for a pair of
            sandals,

selling even the sweepings with the wheat.

7The LORD has sworn by the Pride of Jacob: "I will never forget anything they have done.

8"Will not the land tremble for this,
    and all who live in it mourn?
The whole land will rise like the Nile;
    it will be stirred up and then sink
    like the river of Egypt.

9"In that day," declares the Sovereign LORD,

"I will make the sun go down at
        noon
    and darken the earth in broad
        daylight.
10I will turn your religious feasts into
        mourning
    and all your singing into weeping.
I will make all of you wear sackcloth
    and shave your heads.
I will make that time like mourning
        for an only son
    and the end of it like a bitter day.

11"The days are coming," declares the
        Sovereign LORD,
"when I will send a famine
        through the land—
not a famine of food or a thirst for
        water,
    but a famine of hearing the words
        of the LORD.
12Men will stagger from sea to sea
    and wander from north to east,
searching for the word of the LORD,
    but they will not find it.

13"In that day

"the lovely young women and strong
        young men
    will faint because of thirst.
14They who swear by the shame*c* of
        Samaria,
    or say, 'As surely as your god
        lives, O Dan,'
or, 'As surely as the god*d* of
        Beersheba lives'—
they will fall,
    never to rise again."

Israel to Be Destroyed

9 I saw the Lord standing by the altar, and he said:

---

*a*17 Hebrew *an unclean*   *b*3 Or *"the temple singers will wail*   *c*14 Or *by Ashima*; or *by the idol*   *d*14 Or *power*

"Strike the tops of the pillars
　　so that the thresholds shake.
Bring them down on the heads of all
　　　the people;
　　those who are left I will kill with
　　　the sword.
Not one will get away,
　　none will escape.
²Though they dig down to the depths
　　of the grave,ᵃ
　　from there my hand will take
　　　them.
Though they climb up to the heavens,
　　from there I will bring them down.
³Though they hide themselves on the
　　top of Carmel,
　　there I will hunt them down and
　　　seize them.
Though they hide from me at the
　　bottom of the sea,
　　there I will command the serpent
　　　to bite them.
⁴Though they are driven into exile by
　　their enemies,
　　there I will command the sword to
　　　slay them.
I will fix my eyes upon them
　　for evil and not for good."

⁵The Lord, the LORD Almighty,
　　he who touches the earth and it
　　　melts,
　　and all who live in it mourn—
the whole land rises like the Nile,
　　then sinks like the river of Egypt—
⁶he who builds his lofty palaceᵇ in
　　the heavens
　　and sets its foundationᶜ on the
　　　earth,
who calls for the waters of the sea
　　and pours them out over the face
　　　of the land—
　　the LORD is his name.

⁷"Are not you Israelites
　　the same to me as the Cushitesᵈ?"
　　　　　　　　　declares the LORD.
"Did I not bring Israel up from Egypt,
　　the Philistines from Caphtorᵉ
　　and the Arameans from Kir?

⁸"Surely the eyes of the Sovereign LORD
　　are on the sinful kingdom.
I will destroy it
　　from the face of the earth—
yet I will not totally destroy
　　the house of Jacob,"
　　　　　　　　　declares the LORD.

⁹"For I will give the command,
　　and I will shake the house of Israel
　　　among all the nations
as grain is shaken in a sieve,
　　and not a pebble will reach the
　　　ground.
¹⁰All the sinners among my people
　　will die by the sword,
all those who say,
　　'Disaster will not overtake or meet
　　　us.'

Israel's Restoration

¹¹"In that day I will restore
　　David's fallen tent.
I will repair its broken places,
　　restore its ruins,
　　and build it as it used to be,
¹²so that they may possess the remnant
　　of Edom
　　and all the nations that bear my
　　　name,ᶠ"
　　　　　　　　declares the LORD,
　　　　　　　　who will do these things.

¹³"The days are coming," declares the
LORD,

"when the reaper will be overtaken
　　by the plowman
　　and the planter by the one treading
　　　grapes.
New wine will drip from the
　　mountains
　　and flow from all the hills.
¹⁴I will bring back my exiledᵍ people
　　Israel;
　　they will rebuild the ruined cities
　　　and live in them.
They will plant vineyards and drink
　　their wine;
　　they will make gardens and eat
　　　their fruit.
¹⁵I will plant Israel in their own land,
　　never again to be uprooted
　　from the land I have given them,"

　　　　　　　　says the LORD your God.

ᵃ2 Hebrew *to Sheol*　　ᵇ6 The meaning of the
Hebrew for this phrase is uncertain.
ᶜ6 The meaning of the Hebrew for this word is
uncertain.　　ᵈ7 That is, people from the upper
Nile region　　ᵉ7 That is, Crete　　ᶠ12 Hebrew;
Septuagint *so that the remnant of men / and all the
nations that bear my name may seek* ⌊*the Lord*⌋
ᵍ14 Or *will restore the fortunes of my*

Remember Jacob and Esau from Genesis? The Edomites (descendants of Esau) still haven't forgiven Jacob for stealing Esau's birthright. So they gloat when the Israelites (descendants of Jacob) are devastated by foreign powers. Then Obadiah enters the picture, rebuking the Edomites for their pride and announcing that they will be destroyed for their attitude and actions. Obadiah further declares that God will deliver Israel and cause his kingdom to be victorious.

OBADIAH

¹The vision of Obadiah.

This is what the Sovereign LORD says about Edom—

We have heard a message from the
    LORD:
An envoy was sent to the nations
    to say,
"Rise, and let us go against her for
    battle"—

²"See, I will make you small among
    the nations;
    you will be utterly despised.
³The pride of your heart has deceived
    you,
    you who live in the clefts of the
        rocks*a*
and make your home on the
    heights,
you who say to yourself,
    'Who can bring me down to the
        ground?'

⁴Though you soar like the eagle
    and make your nest among the
        stars,
    from there I will bring you down,"
        declares the LORD.
⁵"If thieves came to you,
    if robbers in the night—
Oh, what a disaster awaits you—
    would they not steal only as much
        as they wanted?
If grape pickers came to you,
    would they not leave a few grapes?
⁶But how Esau will be ransacked,
    his hidden treasures pillaged!
⁷All your allies will force you to the
        border;
    your friends will deceive and
        overpower you;
those who eat your bread will set a
    trap for you,*b*
    but you will not detect it.

*a*3 Or *of Sela*   *b*7 The meaning of the Hebrew
for this clause is uncertain.

THE PROMISES OF GOD

The following is a list of Scriptural promises compiled by topic:

1. Salvation / Eternal Life
2. Assurance of Salvation
3. Forgiveness of Sin
4. God's Love and Care
5. Comfort from God
6. God's Protection
7. Power of God
8. Answers to Prayer
9. God's Provision
10. Guidance
11. Peace
12. Meditation
13. Obedience
14. Faith
15. Patience / Perseverance
16. Relationships
17. Giving
18. Resurrection
19. Rewards
20. Heaven

SALVATION and ETERNAL LIFE
John 1:12
John 3:16
John 5:24
John 6:47
John 20:31
Acts 16:31
Romans 6:22–23
Romans 10:9
Romans 10:13
Titus 1:3
Titus 3:4–7
1 John 2:25
Revelation 3:20

ASSURANCE of SALVATION
Isaiah 12:2
John 10:27–30
John 14:16–17
Romans 8:35–39
Ephesians 1:12–14
Ephesians 4:30
Philippians 1:6
1 Peter 1:5
1 John 5:11–13
2 John 1:2

FORGIVENESS of SIN
2 Chronicles 7:14
Psalm 32:5–6
Psalm 103:12
Isaiah 1:18
Isaiah 55:6–7
Matthew 6:14
Acts 10:43
2 Corinthians 5:17
Hebrews 8:12
1 John 1:9

CONTINUED ON NEXT PAGE

GOD'S LOVE and CARE
Job 23:10
Psalm 103:17
Nahum 1:7
Matthew 6:31–33
Matthew 10:29–31
John 14:21
John 15:9–10
Romans 5:8
Romans 8:32
1 Corinthians 10:13
Hebrews 12:11
1 Peter 5:7

COMFORT from GOD
Psalm 23:4
Psalm 27:10
Isaiah 40:31
Isaiah 42:3
Psalm 51:17
Psalm 55:22
Psalm 103:13–14
Isaiah 43:2
Isaiah 50:7
Matthew 5:4
Matthew 11:28–30
Matthew 28:20
Romans 8:28
2 Corinthians 1:3–4
1 Peter 5:6–7

GOD'S PROTECTION
2 Chronicles 16:9a
Psalm 5:11–12
Psalm 20:7
Psalm 27:1–3
Psalm 34:7
Psalm 46:1
Psalm 68:5
Psalm 73:23
Psalm 84:11
Psalm 91:5–8

Isaiah 41:10
Jeremiah 17:7–8
Romans 8:31
2 Thessalonians 3:3

POWER of GOD
1 Chronicles 29:11
Job 42:2
Psalm 50:9–12
Psalm 115:3
Psalm 147:5
Isaiah 40:25–26
Isaiah 45:2–3
Jeremiah 27:5
Jeremiah 32:17,27
Luke 1:37
Ephesians 3:20–21
1 John 4:4

ANSWERS to PRAYER
1 Kings 18:37
Psalm 34:4
Psalm 37:4
Psalm 50:15
Psalm 86:7
Jeremiah 33:3
Luke 11:9–10
John 16:24
Philippians 4:6–7
James 5:15–16
1 John 5:14–15

GOD'S PROVISION
Psalm 23:1
Psalm 34:9–10
Psalm 37:25
Psalm 69:33
Psalm 72:13
Psalm 95:6–7
Psalm 111:5
Proverbs 13:4
Matthew 6:33

CONTINUED ON NEXT PAGE

Mark 10:29–30
2 Corinthians 9:8
Philippians 4:19

GUIDANCE
Psalm 32:8
Proverbs 3:5–6
Proverbs 16:3
Proverbs 21:5
Isaiah 30:21
Isaiah 40:11
Isaiah 42:16
Isaiah 45:2–3
Jeremiah 29:11
John 16:13
Romans 12:1–2
James 1:5

PEACE
Exodus 33:14
Psalm 85:8
Psalm 119:165
Isaiah 26:3
Matthew 11:28–29
John 14:27
Romans 5:1
Romans 8:6
Colossians 3:15
1 Peter 3:9–11

MEDITATION
Joshua 1:8
Psalm 1:2–3
Psalm 19:14
Psalm 37:31
Psalm 63:6–8
Psalm 119:11
Psalm 119:97–99
Psalm 119:130
Psalm 119:147–149
Psalm 119:165

OBEDIENCE
Deuteronomy 4:39–40
Job 17:9
Psalm 119:57–58
Proverbs 1:32–33
Proverbs 16:7
Isaiah 1:19
Matthew 5:19
Luke 6:46–48
John 14:21,23
John 15:5
John 15:10–12
1 John 3:21–22

FAITH
Psalm 5:11
Psalm 32:10
Psalm 118:8–9
Proverbs 29:25
Matthew 21:21–22
Mark 5:36
Mark 9:23–24
Mark 11:22–24
Romans 8:31
Ephesians 2:8–9
Hebrews 6:12
Hebrews 11:6
Hebrews 13:6
1 John 5:4

PATIENCE and PERSEVERANCE
Psalm 27:14
Psalm 37:7
Isaiah 40:31
Romans 2:7
Romans 5:3–5
1 Corinthians 15:58
Galatians 6:9–10
Hebrews 10:35–36
James 1:2–4
James 5:7–8
2 Peter 3:8–9

CONTINUED ON NEXT PAGE

RELATIONSHIPS

Proverbs 16:7
Ecclesiastes 4:9–10
Luke 6:35–37
Romans 12:17–20
Romans 14:1–4
Romans 15:7
Ephesians 4:2–3
Ephesians 4:15
Ephesians 4:29–32
Ephesians 6:1–3
1 Peter 3:7
1 Peter 3:8–9

GIVING

Psalm 112:5
Proverbs 3:9–10
Proverbs 11:24–25
Proverbs 19:17
Proverbs 28:27
Malachi 3:10
Matthew 6:1–4
Luke 6:38
Luke 14:12–14
Luke 16:9
2 Corinthians 8:12
2 Corinthians 9:6
2 Corinthians 9:8–11
1 Timothy 6:17–19

RESURRECTION

Psalm 49:15
Isaiah 26:19
Daniel 12:2–3
Matthew 22:30
Matthew 25:31–34
Luke 14:14
John 5:25,28–29
John 11:25–26
John 14:19
1 Corinthians 15:42–44
2 Corinthians 4:14

REWARDS

Jeremiah 17:10
Matthew 6:4
Matthew 10:42
Mark 10:29–30
Luke 14:14
John 12:26
1 Corinthians 15:58
2 Corinthians 5:10
Ephesians 6:7
Colossians 3:23–24
2 Timothy 4:8
Hebrews 6:10

HEAVEN

Zechariah 2:10
Matthew 5:3
Matthew 5:10
John 6:51
John 14:2–3
Colossians 3:4
1 Thessalonians 4:16–17
Hebrews 9:28
Hebrews 10:37
1 John 3:2

8"In that day," declares the LORD,
  "will I not destroy the wise men of
    Edom,
  men of understanding in the
    mountains of Esau?
9Your warriors, O Teman, will be
    terrified,
  and everyone in Esau's mountains
  will be cut down in the slaughter.
10Because of the violence against your
    brother Jacob,
  you will be covered with shame;
  you will be destroyed forever.
11On the day you stood aloof
    while strangers carried off his
    wealth
  and foreigners entered his gates
    and cast lots for Jerusalem,
  you were like one of them.
12You should not look down on your
    brother
  in the day of his misfortune,
  nor rejoice over the people of Judah
    in the day of their destruction,
  nor boast so much
    in the day of their trouble.
13You should not march through the
    gates of my people

  in the day of their disaster,
  nor look down on them in their
    calamity
  in the day of their disaster,
  nor seize their wealth
    in the day of their disaster.
14You should not wait at the crossroads
    to cut down their fugitives,
  nor hand over their survivors
    in the day of their trouble.

15"The day of the LORD is near
    for all nations.
  As you have done, it will be done to
    you;
  your deeds will return upon your
    own head.
16Just as you drank on my holy hill,
  so all the nations will drink
    continually;
  they will drink and drink
    and be as if they had never been.
17But on Mount Zion will be
    deliverance;
  it will be holy,
  and the house of Jacob
    will possess its inheritance.
18The house of Jacob will be a fire
    and the house of Joseph a flame;

WEDNESDAY

Read Obadiah 1–21
Key Verses Obadiah 3–4

Who, Me? —Colette Magoon

In a world of cynics on every part,
Lord, take the pessimism from my heart —
The part of me that tends to say,
"You are wrong. That's not the way."
The part that chooses to distrust,
assuming they are filled with lust,
with egotism, greed and pride,
Lord, show me I too have that side —
the arrogance that hides within,
a subtle, sly and devious sin.
Replace it with humility
that serves and loves and dies to me.

A Deeper Look
Ecclesiastes 7:8; 1 Corinthians 13:4

Go to page 1017 for your next devotional reading.

the house of Esau will be stubble,
  and they will set it on fire and
    consume it.
There will be no survivors
  from the house of Esau."
                        The LORD has spoken.

19People from the Negev will occupy
    the mountains of Esau,
  and people from the foothills will
      possess
    the land of the Philistines.
They will occupy the fields of
      Ephraim and Samaria,
  and Benjamin will possess Gilead.

20This company of Israelite exiles who
      are in Canaan
  will possess ⌊the land⌋ as far as
      Zarephath;
the exiles from Jerusalem who are in
      Sepharad
  will possess the towns of the
      Negev.
21Deliverers will go up on*a* Mount
      Zion
  to govern the mountains of Esau.
  And the kingdom will be the
      LORD's.

a21 Or *from*

Have you ever been in a situation when you knew God wanted you to do something, but instead of obeying him, you tried to hide? If so, you and Jonah would connect. Jonah had tried to refuse God's call but later got angry when God didn't do what he expected. Despite Jonah's resistance, God used Jonah to demonstrate his mercy to Nineveh. Through Jonah's story we see that God goes to great lengths to pursue his people and that he responds with compassion and forgiveness when they return to him.

JONAH

Jonah Flees From the LORD

1 The word of the LORD came to Jonah son of Amittai: ²"Go to the great city of Nineveh and preach against it, because its wickedness has come up before me."

³But Jonah ran away from the LORD and headed for Tarshish. He went down to Joppa, where he found a ship bound for that port. After paying the fare, he went aboard and sailed for Tarshish to flee from the LORD.

⁴Then the LORD sent a great wind on the sea, and such a violent storm arose that the ship threatened to break up. ⁵All the sailors were afraid and each cried out to his own god. And they threw the cargo into the sea to lighten the ship.

But Jonah had gone below deck, where he lay down and fell into a deep sleep. ⁶The captain went to him and said, "How can you sleep? Get up and call on your god! Maybe he will take notice of us, and we will not perish."

⁷Then the sailors said to each other, "Come, let us cast lots to find out who is responsible for this calamity." They cast lots and the lot fell on Jonah.

⁸So they asked him, "Tell us, who is responsible for making all this trouble for us? What do you do? Where do you come from? What is your country? From what people are you?"

⁹He answered, "I am a Hebrew and I worship the LORD, the God of heaven, who made the sea and the land."

¹⁰This terrified them and they asked, "What have you done?" (They knew he was running away from the LORD, because he had already told them so.)

¹¹The sea was getting rougher and rougher. So they asked him, "What

should we do to you to make the sea calm down for us?"

12"Pick me up and throw me into the sea," he replied, "and it will become calm. I know that it is my fault that this great storm has come upon you."

13Instead, the men did their best to row back to land. But they could not, for the sea grew even wilder than before. 14Then they cried to the LORD, "O LORD, please do not let us die for taking this man's life. Do not hold us accountable for killing an innocent man, for you, O LORD, have done as you pleased." 15Then they took Jonah and threw him overboard, and the raging sea grew calm. 16At this the men greatly feared the LORD, and they offered a sacrifice to the LORD and made vows to him.

17But the LORD provided a great fish to swallow Jonah, and Jonah was inside the fish three days and three nights.

Jonah's Prayer

2 From inside the fish Jonah prayed to the LORD his God. 2He said:

"In my distress I called to the LORD,
　　and he answered me.
From the depths of the grave*a* I
　　　　called for help,
　　and you listened to my cry.
3You hurled me into the deep,
　　into the very heart of the seas,
　　and the currents swirled about me;
all your waves and breakers
　　swept over me.
4I said, 'I have been banished
　　from your sight;
yet I will look again
　　toward your holy temple.'
5The engulfing waters threatened
　　me,*b*
　　the deep surrounded me;
　　seaweed was wrapped around my
　　　　head.
6To the roots of the mountains I sank
　　　　down;
　　the earth beneath barred me in
　　　　forever.
But you brought my life up from the
　　　　pit,
　　O LORD my God.

7"When my life was ebbing away,
　　I remembered you, LORD,
and my prayer rose to you,
　　to your holy temple.

8"Those who cling to worthless idols

forfeit the grace that could be
　　theirs.
9But I, with a song of thanksgiving,
　　will sacrifice to you.
What I have vowed I will make good.
　　Salvation comes from the LORD."

10And the LORD commanded the fish, and it vomited Jonah onto dry land.

Jonah Goes to Nineveh

3 Then the word of the LORD came to Jonah a second time: 2"Go to the great city of Nineveh and proclaim to it the message I give you."

3Jonah obeyed the word of the LORD and went to Nineveh. Now Nineveh was a very important city—a visit required three days. 4On the first day, Jonah started into the city. He proclaimed: "Forty more days and Nineveh will be overturned." 5The Ninevites believed God. They declared a fast, and all of them, from the greatest to the least, put on sackcloth.

6When the news reached the king of Nineveh, he rose from his throne, took off his royal robes, covered himself with sackcloth and sat down in the dust. 7Then he issued a proclamation in Nineveh:

"By the decree of the king and his nobles:

Do not let any man or beast, herd or flock, taste anything; do not let them eat or drink. 8But let man and beast be covered with sackcloth. Let everyone call urgently on God. Let them give up their evil ways and their violence. 9Who knows? God may yet relent and with compassion turn from his fierce anger so that we will not perish."

10When God saw what they did and how they turned from their evil ways, he had compassion and did not bring upon them the destruction he had threatened.

Jonah's Anger at the LORD's Compassion

4 But Jonah was greatly displeased and became angry. 2He prayed to the LORD, "O LORD, is this not what I said when I was still at home? That is why I was so quick to flee to Tarshish. I knew that you

---

a2 Hebrew *Sheol*　　*b5* Or *waters were at my throat*

are a gracious and compassionate God, slow to anger and abounding in love, a God who relents from sending calamity. ³Now, O LORD, take away my life, for it is better for me to die than to live."

⁴But the LORD replied, "Have you any right to be angry?"

⁵Jonah went out and sat down at a place east of the city. There he made himself a shelter, sat in its shade and waited to see what would happen to the city. ⁶Then the LORD God provided a vine and made it grow up over Jonah to give shade for his head to ease his discomfort, and Jonah was very happy about the vine. ⁷But at dawn the next day God provided a worm, which chewed the vine so that it withered. ⁸When the sun rose, God pro-

vided a scorching east wind, and the sun blazed on Jonah's head so that he grew faint. He wanted to die, and said, "It would be better for me to die than to live."

⁹But God said to Jonah, "Do you have a right to be angry about the vine?"

"I do," he said. "I am angry enough to die."

¹⁰But the LORD said, "You have been concerned about this vine, though you did not tend it or make it grow. It sprang up overnight and died overnight. ¹¹But Nineveh has more than a hundred and twenty thousand people who cannot tell their right hand from their left, and many cattle as well. Should I not be concerned about that great city?"

THURSDAY

Read *Jonah 1:1—3:10*
Key Verses *Jonah 3:1—3*

The God of Second Chances – Stephanie Carter

When was the last time you really blew it—failed the final exam, fell asleep writing a paper, let the secret slip or drank too much? What was your response—begging the professor for mercy, asking for an extension, avoiding your friend, hiding yourself or running away? At such times the obstacles seem insurmountable, the relationships beyond repair, the extra semester unbearable, the shame overwhelming. Don't you sometimes think it would be easier to just throw away your old life and start over?

Jonah knew the despair of failure. The Lord commanded Jonah to speak, but Jonah hid. He withheld God's prophetic word from the Ninevites, endangered the lives of his shipmates and rejected the One who created and called him.

Where was God in all this? Was he angry, looking the other way, weeping, frustrated? God didn't give up on this reluctant prophet. God blessed him with three undisturbed days to think about what he had done. In the belly of a fish, Jonah's old life died; God gave him a second chance. The Lord again commanded him to go, and he went. Where? To the wicked city of Nineveh, to people whom God was also giving a second chance to repent.

Is God a God of second chances? Yes! And third, fourth and fifth chances as well. So no matter how bad things are, take hope, admit your failure and ask God to give you another chance. He's still there with you, and your failures will never outweigh his mercy.

A Deeper Look
Lamentations 3:21—23; John 8:2—11; Ephesians 2:1—5

Go to page 1023 for your next devotional reading.

Nothing eats away at the fabric of a nation like social injustice and empty spirituality. When the rich get richer at the expense of the less powerful, when political leaders habitually accept bribes and when spiritual leaders lead others astray, God takes notice—and he isn't pleased. The prophet Micah lived during a time when the Israelites experienced all these things, and his message to them resounds with judgment. Yet Micah also provides a message of hope—hope of deliverance, comfort and forgiveness through the coming Messiah.

MICAH

1 The word of the LORD that came to Micah of Moresheth during the reigns of Jotham, Ahaz and Hezekiah, kings of Judah—the vision he saw concerning Samaria and Jerusalem.

²Hear, O peoples, all of you,
   listen, O earth and all who are in
      it,
   that the Sovereign LORD may witness
      against you,
   the Lord from his holy temple.

Judgment Against Samaria and Jerusalem

³Look! The LORD is coming from his
      dwelling place;
   he comes down and treads the
      high places of the earth.

⁴The mountains melt beneath him
   and the valleys split apart,
like wax before the fire,
   like water rushing down a slope.
⁵All this is because of Jacob's
      transgression,
   because of the sins of the house of
      Israel.
What is Jacob's transgression?
   Is it not Samaria?
What is Judah's high place?
   Is it not Jerusalem?

⁶"Therefore I will make Samaria a
      heap of rubble,
   a place for planting vineyards.
I will pour her stones into the valley
   and lay bare her foundations.
⁷All her idols will be broken to pieces;

all her temple gifts will be burned
with fire;
I will destroy all her images.
Since she gathered her gifts from the
wages of prostitutes,
as the wages of prostitutes they
will again be used."

Weeping and Mourning

8Because of this I will weep and
wail;
I will go about barefoot and
naked.
I will howl like a jackal
and moan like an owl.
9For her wound is incurable;
it has come to Judah.
It*a* has reached the very gate of my
people,
even to Jerusalem itself.
10Tell it not in Gath*b*;
weep not at all.*c*
In Beth Ophrah*d*
roll in the dust.
11Pass on in nakedness and shame,
you who live in Shaphir.*e*
Those who live in Zaanan*f*
will not come out.
Beth Ezel is in mourning;
its protection is taken from you.
12Those who live in Maroth*g* writhe in
pain,
waiting for relief,
because disaster has come from the
LORD,
even to the gate of Jerusalem.
13You who live in Lachish,*h*
harness the team to the chariot.
You were the beginning of sin
to the Daughter of Zion,
for the transgressions of Israel
were found in you.
14Therefore you will give parting gifts
to Moresheth Gath.
The town of Aczib*i* will prove
deceptive
to the kings of Israel.
15I will bring a conqueror against
you
who live in Mareshah.*j*
He who is the glory of Israel
will come to Adullam.
16Shave your heads in mourning
for the children in whom you
delight;
make yourselves as bald as the
vulture,
for they will go from you into
exile.

Man's Plans and God's

2 Woe to those who plan iniquity,
to those who plot evil on their
beds!
At morning's light they carry it out
because it is in their power to do
it.
2They covet fields and seize them,
and houses, and take them.
They defraud a man of his home,
a fellowman of his inheritance.

3Therefore, the LORD says:

"I am planning disaster against this
people,
from which you cannot save
yourselves.
You will no longer walk proudly,
for it will be a time of calamity.
4In that day men will ridicule you;
they will taunt you with this
mournful song:
'We are utterly ruined;
my people's possession is divided
up.
He takes it from me!
He assigns our fields to traitors.' "

5Therefore you will have no one in the
assembly of the LORD
to divide the land by lot.

False Prophets

6"Do not prophesy," their prophets
say.
"Do not prophesy about these
things;
disgrace will not overtake us."
7Should it be said, O house of Jacob:
"Is the Spirit of the LORD angry?
Does he do such things?"

"Do not my words do good
to him whose ways are upright?
8Lately my people have risen up
like an enemy.
You strip off the rich robe
from those who pass by without a
care,
like men returning from battle.
9You drive the women of my people

*a*9 Or He   *b*10 *Gath* sounds like the Hebrew for
tell.   *c*10 Hebrew; Septuagint may suggest *not in
Acco.* The Hebrew for *in Acco* sounds like the
Hebrew for *weep.*   *d*10 *Beth Ophrah* means
house of dust.   *e*11 *Shaphir* means *pleasant.*
*f*11 *Zaanan* sounds like the Hebrew for *come out.*
*g*12 *Maroth* sounds like the Hebrew for *bitter.*
*h*13 *Lachish* sounds like the Hebrew for *team.*
*i*14 *Aczib* means *deception.*   *j*15 *Mareshah*
sounds like the Hebrew for *conqueror.*

from their pleasant homes.
You take away my blessing
　from their children forever.
¹⁰Get up, go away!
　For this is not your resting place,
because it is defiled,
　it is ruined, beyond all remedy.
¹¹If a liar and deceiver comes and says,
　'I will prophesy for you plenty of
　　wine and beer,'
　he would be just the prophet for
　　this people!

Deliverance Promised

¹²"I will surely gather all of you,
　　O Jacob;
　I will surely bring together the
　　remnant of Israel.
I will bring them together like sheep
　　in a pen,
　like a flock in its pasture;
　the place will throng with people.
¹³One who breaks open the way will go
　　up before them;
　they will break through the gate
　　and go out.
Their king will pass through before
　　them,
　the LORD at their head."

Leaders and Prophets Rebuked

3 Then I said,

"Listen, you leaders of Jacob,
　you rulers of the house of Israel.
Should you not know justice,
² 　you who hate good and love evil;
who tear the skin from my people
　and the flesh from their bones;
³who eat my people's flesh,
　strip off their skin
　and break their bones in pieces;
who chop them up like meat for the
　　pan,
　like flesh for the pot?"

⁴Then they will cry out to the LORD,
　but he will not answer them.
At that time he will hide his face
　　from them
　because of the evil they have done.

⁵This is what the LORD says:

"As for the prophets
　who lead my people astray,
if one feeds them,
　they proclaim 'peace';

if he does not,
　they prepare to wage war against
　　him.
⁶Therefore night will come over you,
　　without visions,
　and darkness, without divination.
The sun will set for the prophets,
　and the day will go dark for them.
⁷The seers will be ashamed
　and the diviners disgraced.
They will all cover their faces
　because there is no answer from
　　God."

⁸But as for me, I am filled with power,
　with the Spirit of the LORD,
　and with justice and might,
to declare to Jacob his transgression,
　to Israel his sin.
⁹Hear this, you leaders of the house of
　　Jacob,
　you rulers of the house of Israel,
who despise justice
　and distort all that is right;
¹⁰who build Zion with bloodshed,
　and Jerusalem with wickedness.
¹¹Her leaders judge for a bribe,
　her priests teach for a price,
　and her prophets tell fortunes for
　　money.
Yet they lean upon the LORD and say,
　"Is not the LORD among us?
　No disaster will come upon us."
¹²Therefore because of you,
　Zion will be plowed like a field,
Jerusalem will become a heap of
　　rubble,
　the temple hill a mound overgrown
　　with thickets.

The Mountain of the LORD

4 In the last days

the mountain of the LORD's temple
　will be established

POINT OF INTEREST

Micah 3:8

What does a prophet of God do? This verse is a compact self-definition. Note the power source and the job description. Would you want to interview for this position?

as chief among the mountains;
it will be raised above the hills,
and peoples will stream to it.

²Many nations will come and say,

"Come, let us go up to the mountain
of the LORD,
to the house of the God of Jacob.
He will teach us his ways,
so that we may walk in his paths."
The law will go out from Zion,
the word of the LORD from
Jerusalem.
³He will judge between many peoples
and will settle disputes for strong
nations far and wide.
They will beat their swords into
plowshares
and their spears into pruning
hooks.
Nation will not take up sword against
nation,
nor will they train for war
anymore.
⁴Every man will sit under his own
vine
and under his own fig tree,
and no one will make them afraid,
for the LORD Almighty has spoken.
⁵All the nations may walk
in the name of their gods;
we will walk in the name of the LORD
our God for ever and ever.

The LORD's Plan

⁶"In that day," declares the LORD,

"I will gather the lame;
I will assemble the exiles
and those I have brought to grief.
⁷I will make the lame a remnant,
those driven away a strong nation.
The LORD will rule over them in
Mount Zion
from that day and forever.
⁸As for you, O watchtower of the
flock,
O stronghold*a* of the Daughter of
Zion,
the former dominion will be restored
to you;
kingship will come to the Daughter
of Jerusalem."

⁹Why do you now cry aloud—
have you no king?
Has your counselor perished,
that pain seizes you like that of a
woman in labor?

¹⁰Writhe in agony, O Daughter of Zion,
like a woman in labor,
for now you must leave the city
to camp in the open field.
You will go to Babylon;
there you will be rescued.
There the LORD will redeem you
out of the hand of your enemies.

¹¹But now many nations
are gathered against you.
They say, "Let her be defiled,
let our eyes gloat over Zion!"
¹²But they do not know
the thoughts of the LORD;
they do not understand his plan,
he who gathers them like sheaves
to the threshing floor.

¹³"Rise and thresh, O Daughter of Zion,
for I will give you horns of iron;
I will give you hoofs of bronze
and you will break to pieces many
nations."

You will devote their ill-gotten gains
to the LORD,
their wealth to the Lord of all the
earth.

A Promised Ruler From Bethlehem

5 Marshal your troops, O city of
troops,*b*
for a siege is laid against us.
They will strike Israel's ruler
on the cheek with a rod.

²"But you, Bethlehem Ephrathah,
though you are small among the
clans*c* of Judah,
out of you will come for me
one who will be ruler over Israel,
whose origins*d* are from of old,
from ancient times.*e*"

³Therefore Israel will be abandoned
until the time when she who is in
labor gives birth
and the rest of his brothers return
to join the Israelites.

⁴He will stand and shepherd his flock
in the strength of the LORD,
in the majesty of the name of the
LORD his God.

---

*a*8 Or *hill*   *b*1 Or *Strengthen your walls, O walled
city*   *c*2 Or *rulers*   *d*2 Hebrew *goings
out*   *e*2 Or *from days of eternity*

And they will live securely, for then
his greatness
    will reach to the ends of the earth.
5   And he will be their peace.

Deliverance and Destruction

When the Assyrian invades our land
    and marches through our
      fortresses,
we will raise against him seven
    shepherds,
    even eight leaders of men.
⁶They will rule*a* the land of Assyria
    with the sword,
    the land of Nimrod with drawn
      sword.*b*
He will deliver us from the Assyrian
    when he invades our land
    and marches into our borders.

⁷The remnant of Jacob will be
    in the midst of many peoples
like dew from the LORD,
    like showers on the grass,
which do not wait for man
    or linger for mankind.
⁸The remnant of Jacob will be among
    the nations,
    in the midst of many peoples,
like a lion among the beasts of the
    forest,
like a young lion among flocks of
    sheep,
which mauls and mangles as it goes,
    and no one can rescue.
⁹Your hand will be lifted up in
      triumph over your enemies,
    and all your foes will be destroyed.

¹⁰"In that day," declares the LORD,

"I will destroy your horses from
      among you
    and demolish your chariots.
¹¹I will destroy the cities of your land
    and tear down all your
      strongholds.
¹²I will destroy your witchcraft
    and you will no longer cast spells.
¹³I will destroy your carved images
    and your sacred stones from
      among you;
you will no longer bow down
    to the work of your hands.
¹⁴I will uproot from among you your
      Asherah poles*c*
    and demolish your cities.
¹⁵I will take vengeance in anger and
      wrath
    upon the nations that have not
      obeyed me."

The LORD's Case Against Israel

6 Listen to what the LORD says:

"Stand up, plead your case before the
    mountains;
    let the hills hear what you have to
      say.
²Hear, O mountains, the LORD's
    accusation;
    listen, you everlasting foundations
      of the earth.
For the LORD has a case against his
    people;
    he is lodging a charge against
      Israel.

³"My people, what have I done to
      you?
    How have I burdened you? Answer
      me.
⁴I brought you up out of Egypt
    and redeemed you from the land of
      slavery.
I sent Moses to lead you,
    also Aaron and Miriam.
⁵My people, remember
    what Balak king of Moab
      counseled
    and what Balaam son of Beor
      answered.
Remember ∟ your journey⌐ from
      Shittim to Gilgal,
    that you may know the righteous
      acts of the LORD."

⁶With what shall I come before the
      LORD
    and bow down before the exalted
      God?

a6 Or *crush*   *b6* Or *Nimrod in its gates*
c14 That is, symbols of the goddess Asherah

POINT OF INTEREST

Micah 5:2

Bethlehem wasn't a promi-
nent city in Judah. But God
chose this small town to
become the Messiah's birth-
place, as it did in fact become some seven
hundred years after this prophecy. When
King Herod asked the Bible scholars of his
day where the Messiah would be born,
they referred him to this passage (see
Matthew 2:4–5).

Shall I come before him with burnt
     offerings,
  with calves a year old?
⁷Will the LORD be pleased with
     thousands of rams,
  with ten thousand rivers of oil?

Shall I offer my firstborn for my
     transgression,
  the fruit of my body for the sin of
     my soul?
⁸He has showed you, O man, what is
  good.

Read Micah 6:1–16
Key Verse Micah 6:8

People Really *Are* Watching – Rich Jarvi

As a young Christian I was committed to "[walking] humbly with [my] God" and I wanted to be used by him. But one summer I wasn't too sure how obvious I wanted to be because I worked with a bunch of rough individuals. I decided to keep my focus on God by memorizing Scripture during breaks.

As I worked, ate and lived with the other guys on a construction crew, I felt as though I stuck out like a sore thumb. It wasn't easy to "act justly" in a tough bunch like that; at the first sign of uprightness they would be ragging on me unmercifully. There were times I didn't socialize with my coworkers because I didn't want to put myself in a compromising situation. Still, I was determined not to be ashamed of God. During that summer I grew in my faith, but I wondered if any of the guys would ever come to know God. Often they would ask me questions about God and I would share with them how personal he was and what a relationship with him was like. Late in the summer I found out that at least one of the guys had been listening.

It happened late one extremely hot afternoon when we were working outside. As the sun beat down, I watched storm clouds forming on the horizon and hoped they would come our way. They moved in slowly and brought relief from the intense heat. Suddenly the sky turned nasty—glancing up, I saw a funnel cloud dipping down from the clouds. I was wrenched from my machine and thrown into the ditch, but not by the tornado. The force that moved me was Hog, a six-foot, 300-pound foreman who could set a 200-pound keg of nails on one shoulder and, with a little help, another one on the other shoulder.

Later I discovered that Hog had run a quarter of a mile to jump into the ditch with me. While Hog's action didn't really represent a sudden conversion, it did show me that Hog had been listening. He thought he would be safe if he was as close as possible to someone who knew God.

Paul exhorts us to "make the most of every opportunity" (Colossians 4:5). Walking humbly with God wasn't always easy that summer. But the experience stands as a reminder that when I follow God, others notice him.

A Deeper Look
Daniel 12:3; Titus 2:6–8

Go to page 1027 for your next devotional reading.

And what does the LORD require of
you?
To act justly and to love mercy
and to walk humbly with your
God.

Israel's Guilt and Punishment

⁹Listen! The LORD is calling to the
city—
and to fear your name is
wisdom—
"Heed the rod and the One who
appointed it.ᵃ
¹⁰Am I still to forget, O wicked house,
your ill-gotten treasures
and the short ephah,ᵇ which is
accursed?
¹¹Shall I acquit a man with dishonest
scales,
with a bag of false weights?
¹²Her rich men are violent;
her people are liars
and their tongues speak deceitfully.
¹³Therefore, I have begun to destroy
you,
to ruin you because of your sins.
¹⁴You will eat but not be satisfied;
your stomach will still be empty.ᶜ
You will store up but save nothing,
because what you save I will give
to the sword.
¹⁵You will plant but not harvest;
you will press olives but not use
the oil on yourselves,
you will crush grapes but not drink
the wine.
¹⁶You have observed the statutes of
Omri
and all the practices of Ahab's
house,
and you have followed their
traditions.
Therefore I will give you over to ruin
and your people to derision;
you will bear the scorn of the
nations.ᵈ "

Israel's Misery

7 What misery is mine!
I am like one who gathers summer
fruit
at the gleaning of the vineyard;
there is no cluster of grapes to eat,
none of the early figs that I crave.
²The godly have been swept from the
land;
not one upright man remains.
All men lie in wait to shed blood;
each hunts his brother with a net.

³Both hands are skilled in doing evil;
the ruler demands gifts,
the judge accepts bribes,
the powerful dictate what they
desire—
they all conspire together.
⁴The best of them is like a brier,
the most upright worse than a
thorn hedge.
The day of your watchmen has come,
the day God visits you.
Now is the time of their confusion.
⁵Do not trust a neighbor;
put no confidence in a friend.
Even with her who lies in your
embrace
be careful of your words.
⁶For a son dishonors his father,
a daughter rises up against her
mother,
a daughter-in-law against her
mother-in-law—
a man's enemies are the members
of his own household.

⁷But as for me, I watch in hope for the
LORD,
I wait for God my Savior;
my God will hear me.

Israel Will Rise

⁸Do not gloat over me, my enemy!
Though I have fallen, I will rise.
Though I sit in darkness,
the LORD will be my light.
⁹Because I have sinned against him,
I will bear the LORD's wrath,
until he pleads my case
and establishes my right.
He will bring me out into the light;
I will see his righteousness.
¹⁰Then my enemy will see it
and will be covered with shame,
she who said to me,
"Where is the LORD your God?"
My eyes will see her downfall;
even now she will be trampled
underfoot
like mire in the streets.

¹¹The day for building your walls will
come,
the day for extending your
boundaries.
¹²In that day people will come to you

ᵃ9 The meaning of the Hebrew for this line is
uncertain.   ᵇ10 An ephah was a dry measure.
ᶜ14 The meaning of the Hebrew for this word is
uncertain.   ᵈ16 Septuagint; Hebrew *scorn due
my people*

from Assyria and the cities of
  Egypt,
even from Egypt to the Euphrates
and from sea to sea
and from mountain to mountain.
13The earth will become desolate
  because of its inhabitants,
as the result of their deeds.

Prayer and Praise

14Shepherd your people with your staff,
  the flock of your inheritance,
which lives by itself in a forest,
  in fertile pasturelands.*a*
Let them feed in Bashan and Gilead
  as in days long ago.

15"As in the days when you came out
  of Egypt,
I will show them my wonders."

16Nations will see and be ashamed,
  deprived of all their power.
They will lay their hands on their
  mouths
  and their ears will become deaf.

17They will lick dust like a snake,
  like creatures that crawl on the
  ground.
They will come trembling out of their
  dens;
  they will turn in fear to the LORD
  our God
  and will be afraid of you.
18Who is a God like you,
  who pardons sin and forgives the
  transgression
  of the remnant of his inheritance?
You do not stay angry forever
  but delight to show mercy.
19You will again have compassion on
  us;
  you will tread our sins underfoot
  and hurl all our iniquities into the
  depths of the sea.
20You will be true to Jacob,
  and show mercy to Abraham,
as you pledged on oath to our fathers
  in days long ago.

a 14 Or *in the middle of Carmel*

Nahum (meaning "comfort")

prophesies that the Assyrian city of Nineveh will fall,

which actually occurred in 612 B.C. Nahum prophesies

against the cruelty and wickedness of Assyria, and he high-

lights God's sovereignty, mercy and justice. Nahum com-

forts Judah with the assurance that God is in control of

the present as well as the future and will not allow evil to

triumph. We too can take comfort that

God is the Lord of world events

and that his kingdom will prevail.

NAHUM

1 An oracle concerning Nineveh. The book of the vision of Nahum the Elkoshite.

The LORD's Anger Against Nineveh

²The LORD is a jealous and avenging God;
   the LORD takes vengeance and is filled with wrath.
The LORD takes vengeance on his foes
   and maintains his wrath against his enemies.
³The LORD is slow to anger and great in power;
   the LORD will not leave the guilty unpunished.
His way is in the whirlwind and the storm,
   and clouds are the dust of his feet.
⁴He rebukes the sea and dries it up;
   he makes all the rivers run dry.
Bashan and Carmel wither
   and the blossoms of Lebanon fade.

⁵The mountains quake before him
   and the hills melt away.
The earth trembles at his presence,
   the world and all who live in it.
⁶Who can withstand his indignation?
   Who can endure his fierce anger?
His wrath is poured out like fire;
   the rocks are shattered before him.

⁷The LORD is good,
   a refuge in times of trouble.
He cares for those who trust in him,
⁸   but with an overwhelming flood
he will make an end of ⌊Nineveh⌋;
   he will pursue his foes into darkness.

⁹Whatever they plot against the LORD
   he^a will bring to an end;
   trouble will not come a second time.
¹⁰They will be entangled among thorns
   and drunk from their wine;

a9 Or What do you foes plot against the LORD? / He

Read Nahum 1:1–15
Key Verse Nahum 1:7

God *Is* Good

"Is God good? Is God just and fair?" People have been asking these questions from the dawn of time. We can grow cynical about the goodness and justice of God when we look at our world and see it degenerating. We might look at the human condition and wonder if there is hope for humankind and if so, where it can be found. The prophet Nahum answers our questions with an emphatic, "Yes!" "The LORD is good, a refuge in times of trouble. He cares for those who trust in him, but . . . he will pursue his foes into darkness" (Nahum 1:7–8).

Some of us have had authority figures such as parents, teachers or pastors who, although they should have been good and fair, failed or abused us instead. After that kind of experience, it can be hard to trust anyone, including God. But God is not like anyone else. He *is* always good. He *is* always fair. He *can* be trusted. He will *not* disappoint us.

Digging Into the Word
1. How does the Bible answer the question, "Is God good?"—*Psalm 34:8; Psalm 119:68*
2. How do the following passages answer the question, "Does God always do good?"—*Matthew 7:7–11; Romans 8:28*

Personal Reflection
Make a "Top Ten" list of ways God has been good to you. Put it where you will see it daily, especially whenever you begin to wonder if God is good.

One Step Deeper
Matthew 19:17; Romans 12:2

Go to page 1031 for your next devotional reading.

they will be consumed like dry
    stubble. *a*
11From you, ⌞O Nineveh,⌟ has one
    come forth
who plots evil against the LORD
    and counsels wickedness.

12This is what the LORD says:

"Although they have allies and are
    numerous,
    they will be cut off and pass away.
Although I have afflicted you,
    ⌞O Judah,⌟
I will afflict you no more.
13Now I will break their yoke from
    your neck
    and tear your shackles away."

14The LORD has given a command
    concerning you, ⌞Nineveh⌟:
    "You will have no descendants to
    bear your name.
I will destroy the carved images and
    cast idols
    that are in the temple of your gods.
I will prepare your grave,
    for you are vile."

15Look, there on the mountains,
    the feet of one who brings good
    news,
    who proclaims peace!
Celebrate your festivals, O Judah,
    and fulfill your vows.
No more will the wicked invade you;
    they will be completely destroyed.

Nineveh to Fall

2 An attacker advances against you,
    ⌞Nineveh⌟.
    Guard the fortress,
    watch the road,
    brace yourselves,
    marshal all your strength!

2The LORD will restore the splendor of
    Jacob
    like the splendor of Israel,
though destroyers have laid them
    waste
    and have ruined their vines.

3The shields of his soldiers are red;
    the warriors are clad in scarlet.
The metal on the chariots flashes
    on the day they are made ready;
    the spears of pine are
    brandished. *b*
4The chariots storm through the
    streets,

rushing back and forth through the
    squares.
They look like flaming torches;
    they dart about like lightning.

5He summons his picked troops,
    yet they stumble on their way.
They dash to the city wall;
    the protective shield is put in
    place.
6The river gates are thrown open
    and the palace collapses.
7It is decreed*c* that ⌞the city⌟
    be exiled and carried away.
Its slave girls moan like doves
    and beat upon their breasts.
8Nineveh is like a pool,
    and its water is draining away.
"Stop! Stop!" they cry,
    but no one turns back.
9Plunder the silver!
    Plunder the gold!
The supply is endless,
    the wealth from all its treasures!
10She is pillaged, plundered, stripped!
    Hearts melt, knees give way,
    bodies tremble, every face grows
    pale.

11Where now is the lions' den,
    the place where they fed their
    young,
where the lion and lioness went,
    and the cubs, with nothing to fear?
12The lion killed enough for his cubs
    and strangled the prey for his
    mate,
filling his lairs with the kill
    and his dens with the prey.

13"I am against you,"
    declares the LORD Almighty.
"I will burn up your chariots in
    smoke,
    and the sword will devour your
    young lions.
I will leave you no prey on the
    earth.
The voices of your messengers
    will no longer be heard."

Woe to Nineveh

3 Woe to the city of blood,
    full of lies,
full of plunder,
    never without victims!

---

a 10 The meaning of the Hebrew for this verse is
uncertain.   *b 3* Hebrew; Septuagint and Syriac /
the horsemen rush to and fro   *c 7* The meaning
of the Hebrew for this word is uncertain.

²The crack of whips,
the clatter of wheels,
galloping horses
and jolting chariots!
³Charging cavalry,
flashing swords
and glittering spears!
Many casualties,
piles of dead,
bodies without number,
people stumbling over the
corpses—
⁴all because of the wanton lust of a
harlot,
alluring, the mistress of sorceries,
who enslaved nations by her
prostitution
and peoples by her witchcraft.
⁵"I am against you," declares the LORD
Almighty.
"I will lift your skirts over your
face.
I will show the nations your
nakedness
and the kingdoms your shame.
⁶I will pelt you with filth,
I will treat you with contempt
and make you a spectacle.
⁷All who see you will flee from you
and say,
'Nineveh is in ruins—who will
mourn for her?'
Where can I find anyone to
comfort you?"

⁸Are you better than Thebes,ᵃ
situated on the Nile,
with water around her?
The river was her defense,
the waters her wall.
⁹Cushᵇ and Egypt were her boundless
strength;
Put and Libya were among her
allies.
¹⁰Yet she was taken captive
and went into exile.
Her infants were dashed to pieces
at the head of every street.
Lots were cast for her nobles,
and all her great men were put in
chains.
¹¹You too will become drunk;
you will go into hiding
and seek refuge from the enemy.

¹²All your fortresses are like fig trees
with their first ripe fruit;
when they are shaken,
the figs fall into the mouth of the
eater.
¹³Look at your troops—
they are all women!
The gates of your land
are wide open to your enemies;
fire has consumed their bars.

¹⁴Draw water for the siege,
strengthen your defenses!
Work the clay,
tread the mortar,
repair the brickwork!
¹⁵There the fire will devour you;
the sword will cut you down
and, like grasshoppers, consume
you.
Multiply like grasshoppers,
multiply like locusts!
¹⁶You have increased the number of
your merchants
till they are more than the stars of
the sky,
but like locusts they strip the land
and then fly away.
¹⁷Your guards are like locusts,
your officials like swarms of
locusts
that settle in the walls on a cold
day—
but when the sun appears they fly
away,
and no one knows where.

¹⁸O king of Assyria, your shepherdsᶜ
slumber;
your nobles lie down to rest.
Your people are scattered on the
mountains
with no one to gather them.
¹⁹Nothing can heal your wound;
your injury is fatal.
Everyone who hears the news about
you
claps his hands at your fall,
for who has not felt
your endless cruelty?

ᵃ8 Hebrew *No Amon*   ᵇ9 That is, the upper Nile
region   ᶜ18 Or *rulers*

If you could have a Q&A time with God, what would you ask? The prophet Habakkuk had such an opportunity. The book of Habakkuk is like a transcript of his conversation with God. Habakkuk poses two questions that we still wonder about today: (1) Why does God tolerate cruelty and injustice, and (2) why is God silent when wicked people seem to be in control? God answers, declaring that when the time is right, the wicked will be punished and the faithful rewarded. As you read this book, you might realize, as Habakkuk did, that God is willing enough and powerful enough to see justice done.

HABAKKUK

1 The oracle that Habakkuk the prophet received.

Habakkuk's Complaint

² How long, O LORD, must I call for
  help,
    but you do not listen?
  Or cry out to you, "Violence!"
    but you do not save?
³ Why do you make me look at
  injustice?
  Why do you tolerate wrong?
  Destruction and violence are before
    me;
    there is strife, and conflict
      abounds.

⁴ Therefore the law is paralyzed,
    and justice never prevails.
  The wicked hem in the righteous,
    so that justice is perverted.

The LORD's Answer

⁵ "Look at the nations and watch—
    and be utterly amazed.
  For I am going to do something in
    your days
  that you would not believe,
    even if you were told.
⁶ I am raising up the Babylonians,ᵃ
    that ruthless and impetuous
      people,

ᵃ6 Or *Chaldeans*

who sweep across the whole earth
  to seize dwelling places not their
    own.
⁷They are a feared and dreaded
    people;
  they are a law to themselves
  and promote their own honor.
⁸Their horses are swifter than
      leopards,
  fiercer than wolves at dusk.
Their cavalry gallops headlong;
  their horsemen come from afar.
They fly like a vulture swooping to
    devour;
⁹   they all come bent on violence.
Their hordes*ᵃ* advance like a desert
    wind
  and gather prisoners like sand.
¹⁰They deride kings

and scoff at rulers.
They laugh at all fortified cities;
  they build earthen ramps and
    capture them.
¹¹Then they sweep past like the wind
    and go on—
  guilty men, whose own strength is
    their god."

Habakkuk's Second Complaint

¹²O Lᴏʀᴅ, are you not from everlasting?
  My God, my Holy One, we will not
    die.
O Lᴏʀᴅ, you have appointed them to
    execute judgment;
  O Rock, you have ordained them
    to punish.

ᵃ9 The meaning of the Hebrew for this word is
uncertain.

Read Habakkuk 1:12—2:20
Key Verses Habakkuk 1:12–13

When Life Isn't Fair —Tom Toomer

"Where are you, Lord? This doesn't seem fair! I try to do what's
right, but people either take advantage of me or stomp on me as
they steal and lie to get their way."

Sound like a familiar prayer? Maybe you were ridiculed by your
professor because you defended God's Word. Maybe your family
rejected you when you tried to tell them how Jesus Christ has
changed your life. If you have ever felt this way, you aren't alone;
Habakkuk went through similar frustration, as have countless other
believers over the centuries.

Habakkuk watched corrupt, cruel people ridicule and abuse
those who followed God. Confused, he cried out in prayer, "God, why
do you allow this?" He knew that God was holy and hated evil, so it
just didn't make sense.

Habakkuk's circumstances did make sense to God, however. In
Habakkuk 2:2–20 God clearly promised a future punishment for
wickedness. But at the same time, God let Habakkuk know that
everything happens in his perfect timing and that the promised punishment wouldn't come right away. Habakkuk had to trust in God's
goodness and wait patiently for God's justice.

We serve the same God that Habakkuk did—One who is holy
and who will not tolerate evil. Sometimes, though, we have to wait
to see him intervene. God is always present; he doesn't forget us; he
does, however, give us opportunities to deepen our faith as we wait
for him.

A Deeper Look
Psalm 5:4–8; Jeremiah 20:7–18; Hebrews 10:32–39

Go to page 1033 for your next devotional reading.

¹³Your eyes are too pure to look on
    evil;
  you cannot tolerate wrong.
Why then do you tolerate the
    treacherous?
  Why are you silent while the
    wicked
  swallow up those more righteous
    than themselves?
¹⁴You have made men like fish in the
    sea,
  like sea creatures that have no
    ruler.
¹⁵The wicked foe pulls all of them up
    with hooks,
  he catches them in his net,
he gathers them up in his dragnet;
  and so he rejoices and is glad.
¹⁶Therefore he sacrifices to his net
  and burns incense to his dragnet,
for by his net he lives in luxury
  and enjoys the choicest food.
¹⁷Is he to keep on emptying his net,
  destroying nations without mercy?

2 I will stand at my watch
  and station myself on the ramparts;
I will look to see what he will say to
    me,
  and what answer I am to give to
    this complaint.^a

The Lord's Answer

  ²Then the Lord replied:

"Write down the revelation
  and make it plain on tablets
so that a herald^b may run with it.
³For the revelation awaits an
    appointed time;
  it speaks of the end
  and will not prove false.
Though it linger, wait for it;
  it^c will certainly come and will
    not delay.

⁴"See, he is puffed up;
  his desires are not upright—
  but the righteous will live by his
    faith^d—
⁵indeed, wine betrays him;
  he is arrogant and never at rest.
Because he is as greedy as the
    grave^e
  and like death is never satisfied,
he gathers to himself all the nations
  and takes captive all the peoples.

  ⁶"Will not all of them taunt him with
ridicule and scorn, saying,

" 'Woe to him who piles up stolen
    goods
  and makes himself wealthy by
    extortion!
  How long must this go on?'
⁷Will not your debtors^f suddenly
    arise?
  Will they not wake up and make
    you tremble?
  Then you will become their victim.
⁸Because you have plundered many
    nations,
  the peoples who are left will
    plunder you.
For you have shed man's blood;
  you have destroyed lands and
    cities and everyone in them.

⁹"Woe to him who builds his realm by
    unjust gain
  to set his nest on high,
  to escape the clutches of ruin!
¹⁰You have plotted the ruin of many
    peoples,
  shaming your own house and
    forfeiting your life.
¹¹The stones of the wall will cry out,
  and the beams of the woodwork
    will echo it.

¹²"Woe to him who builds a city with
    bloodshed
  and establishes a town by crime!
¹³Has not the Lord Almighty
    determined
  that the people's labor is only fuel
    for the fire,
  that the nations exhaust
    themselves for nothing?
¹⁴For the earth will be filled with the
    knowledge of the glory of the
    Lord,
  as the waters cover the sea.

¹⁵"Woe to him who gives drink to his
    neighbors,
  pouring it from the wineskin till
    they are drunk,
  so that he can gaze on their naked
    bodies.
¹⁶You will be filled with shame instead
    of glory.
  Now it is your turn! Drink and be
    exposed^g!

^a1 Or *and what to answer when I am rebuked*
^b2 Or *so that whoever reads it*   ^c3 Or *Though he
linger, wait for him; / he*   ^d4 Or *faithfulness*
^e5 Hebrew *Sheol*   ^f7 Or *creditors*
^g16 Masoretic Text; Dead Sea Scrolls, Aquila,
Vulgate and Syriac (see also Septuagint) *and stagger*

The cup from the LORD's right hand is
　　coming around to you,
　and disgrace will cover your glory.
[17]The violence you have done to
　　Lebanon will overwhelm
　　you,
　and your destruction of animals
　　will terrify you.
For you have shed man's blood;
　you have destroyed lands and
　　cities and everyone in them.

[18]"Of what value is an idol, since a
　　man has carved it?

Or an image that teaches lies?
For he who makes it trusts in his
　　own creation;
　he makes idols that cannot
　　speak.
[19]Woe to him who says to wood,
　　'Come to life!'
Or to lifeless stone, 'Wake up!'
Can it give guidance?
　It is covered with gold and silver;
　　there is no breath in it.
[20]But the LORD is in his holy temple;
　　let all the earth be silent before
　　him."

TUESDAY

Read Habakkuk 3:1–19
Key Verses Habakkuk 3:17–19

Surprising Joy – Don Allen

Most of us want joy and success, but how do we get them? What do they really mean? We're very familiar with our culture's definition of joy and success, but what is God's?

After I came to know Jesus Christ, God began to do amazing things—he provided great opportunities for spiritual growth and enabled me to succeed beyond my expectations in school. He also opened doors for great career development.

Shortly after I graduated from college, I read the book of Habakkuk for the first time. As I reflected on this book, these verses impressed me deeply: "Though the fig tree does not bud and there are no grapes on the vines, though the olive crop fails and the fields produce no food, though there are no sheep in the pen and no cattle in the stalls, yet I will rejoice in the LORD, I will be joyful in God my Savior. The Sovereign LORD is my strength; he makes my feet like the feet of a deer, he enables me to go on the heights" (Habakkuk 3:17–19).

This came as a great truth to me, but I wasn't aware of how much I would experience that passage in the following year. While the previous three years had been full of blessings, the year after graduation was full of failure and disappointment. The ministry team I was leading divided instead of multiplied. My job was dull and unchallenging. I was tired, and my spiritual eagerness waned.

That year was definitely a time of testing for me. Even now I'm not sure how well I passed the test. But God used that time to show me his desire for me—that I rejoice in him even when life isn't going great. He taught me that success can come and go and that I need to rejoice in him no matter what. Real joy—joy that is rooted in him—endures the ups and downs of life.

A Deeper Look
Job 23:8–10; Romans 12:12; James 5:7–8

Go to page 1038 for your next devotional reading.

Habakkuk's Prayer

3 A prayer of Habakkuk the prophet. On shigionoth.ᵃ

²Lᴏʀᴅ, I have heard of your fame;
  I stand in awe of your deeds,
    O Lᴏʀᴅ.
 Renew them in our day,
  in our time make them known;
  in wrath remember mercy.

³God came from Teman,
  the Holy One from Mount Paran. *Selah*ᵇ
 His glory covered the heavens
  and his praise filled the earth.
⁴His splendor was like the sunrise;
  rays flashed from his hand,
  where his power was hidden.
⁵Plague went before him;
  pestilence followed his steps.
⁶He stood, and shook the earth;
  he looked, and made the nations
    tremble.
 The ancient mountains crumbled
  and the age-old hills collapsed.
 His ways are eternal.
⁷I saw the tents of Cushan in distress,
  the dwellings of Midian in anguish.

⁸Were you angry with the rivers,
    O Lᴏʀᴅ?
 Was your wrath against the
    streams?
 Did you rage against the sea
  when you rode with your horses
  and your victorious chariots?
⁹You uncovered your bow,
  you called for many arrows. *Selah*
 You split the earth with rivers;
¹⁰   the mountains saw you and
    writhed.
 Torrents of water swept by;
  the deep roared
  and lifted its waves on high.

¹¹Sun and moon stood still in the
    heavens
  at the glint of your flying arrows,
 at the lightning of your flashing
    spear.
¹²In wrath you strode through the earth
  and in anger you threshed the
    nations.
¹³You came out to deliver your people,
  to save your anointed one.
 You crushed the leader of the land of
    wickedness,
  you stripped him from head to
    foot. *Selah*
¹⁴With his own spear you pierced his
    head
  when his warriors stormed out to
    scatter us,
 gloating as though about to devour
  the wretched who were in hiding.
¹⁵You trampled the sea with your
    horses,
  churning the great waters.

¹⁶I heard and my heart pounded,
  my lips quivered at the sound;
 decay crept into my bones,
  and my legs trembled.
 Yet I will wait patiently for the day of
    calamity
  to come on the nation invading us.
¹⁷Though the fig tree does not bud
  and there are no grapes on the
    vines,
 though the olive crop fails
  and the fields produce no food,
 though there are no sheep in the pen
  and no cattle in the stalls,
¹⁸yet I will rejoice in the Lᴏʀᴅ,
  I will be joyful in God my Savior.

¹⁹The Sovereign Lᴏʀᴅ is my strength;
  he makes my feet like the feet of a
    deer,
  he enables me to go on the
    heights.

For the director of music. On my
  stringed instruments.

ᵃ1 Probably a literary or musical term
ᵇ3 A word of uncertain meaning; possibly a musical term; also in verses 9 and 13

The day of the Lord. Sounds ominous. Although no one really knows what it will be like, it's a safe bet we won't want to experience it! Zephaniah's prophecy depicts the stark horror of that ordeal, the force of God's anger against sin. But Zephaniah doesn't stop there. While God does punish people for their flagrant and deliberate sin, he's always merciful to those who seek him with humility. As you read, look for the note of hope—that God's judgment will pave the way for a new day when all people will worship the Lord.

ZEPHANIAH

1 The word of the LORD that came to Zephaniah son of Cushi, the son of Gedaliah, the son of Amariah, the son of Hezekiah, during the reign of Josiah son of Amon king of Judah:

Warning of Coming Destruction

2"I will sweep away everything
   from the face of the earth,"
                    declares the LORD.
3"I will sweep away both men and
      animals;
   I will sweep away the birds of the
      air
   and the fish of the sea.
The wicked will have only heaps of
      rubble[a]
   when I cut off man from the face
      of the earth,"
                    declares the LORD.

Against Judah

4"I will stretch out my hand against
      Judah
   and against all who live in
      Jerusalem.
I will cut off from this place every
      remnant of Baal,
   the names of the pagan and the
      idolatrous priests—
5those who bow down on the roofs
   to worship the starry host,
those who bow down and swear by
      the LORD
   and who also swear by Molech,[b]
6those who turn back from following
      the LORD
   and neither seek the LORD nor
      inquire of him.

a3 The meaning of the Hebrew for this line is uncertain.   b5 Hebrew *Malcam*, that is, Milcom

7Be silent before the Sovereign Lord,
    for the day of the Lord is near.
The Lord has prepared a sacrifice;
    he has consecrated those he has
        invited.
8On the day of the Lord's sacrifice
    I will punish the princes
    and the king's sons
and all those clad
    in foreign clothes.
9On that day I will punish
    all who avoid stepping on the
        threshold,[a]
who fill the temple of their gods
    with violence and deceit.

10"On that day," declares the Lord,
    "a cry will go up from the Fish
        Gate,
    wailing from the New Quarter,
    and a loud crash from the hills.
11Wail, you who live in the market
        district[b];
    all your merchants will be wiped
        out,
    all who trade with[c] silver will be
        ruined.
12At that time I will search Jerusalem
        with lamps
    and punish those who are
        complacent,
    who are like wine left on its dregs,
who think, 'The Lord will do nothing,
    either good or bad.'
13Their wealth will be plundered,
    their houses demolished.
They will build houses
    but not live in them;
they will plant vineyards
    but not drink the wine.

The Great Day of the Lord

14"The great day of the Lord is near—
    near and coming quickly.
Listen! The cry on the day of the Lord
    will be bitter,
    the shouting of the warrior there.
15That day will be a day of wrath,
    a day of distress and anguish,
a day of trouble and ruin,
    a day of darkness and gloom,
    a day of clouds and blackness,
16a day of trumpet and battle cry
    against the fortified cities
    and against the corner towers.
17I will bring distress on the people
    and they will walk like blind men,
    because they have sinned against
        the Lord.

Their blood will be poured out like
        dust
    and their entrails like filth.
18Neither their silver nor their gold
    will be able to save them
    on the day of the Lord's wrath.
In the fire of his jealousy
    the whole world will be consumed,
for he will make a sudden end
    of all who live in the earth."

2 Gather together, gather together,
    O shameful nation,
2before the appointed time arrives
    and that day sweeps on like chaff,
before the fierce anger of the Lord
    comes upon you,
    before the day of the Lord's wrath
        comes upon you.
3Seek the Lord, all you humble of the
        land,
    you who do what he commands.
Seek righteousness, seek humility;
    perhaps you will be sheltered
    on the day of the Lord's anger.

Against Philistia

4Gaza will be abandoned
    and Ashkelon left in ruins.
At midday Ashdod will be emptied
    and Ekron uprooted.
5Woe to you who live by the sea,
    O Kerethite people;
the word of the Lord is against you,
    O Canaan, land of the Philistines.

"I will destroy you,
    and none will be left."

6The land by the sea, where the
        Kerethites[d] dwell,
    will be a place for shepherds and
        sheep pens.
7It will belong to the remnant of the
        house of Judah;
    there they will find pasture.
In the evening they will lie down
    in the houses of Ashkelon.
The Lord their God will care for them;
    he will restore their fortunes.[e]

Against Moab and Ammon

8"I have heard the insults of Moab
    and the taunts of the Ammonites,
who insulted my people

---

a9 See 1 Samuel 5:5.   b11 Or the Mortar
c11 Or in   d6 The meaning of the Hebrew for
this word is uncertain.   e7 Or will bring back
their captives

and made threats against their
  land.
⁹Therefore, as surely as I live,"
  declares the LORD Almighty, the
    God of Israel,
"surely Moab will become like
    Sodom,
  the Ammonites like Gomorrah—
a place of weeds and salt pits,
  a wasteland forever.
The remnant of my people will
    plunder them;
  the survivors of my nation will
    inherit their land."

¹⁰This is what they will get in return
    for their pride,
  for insulting and mocking the
    people of the LORD Almighty.
¹¹The LORD will be awesome to them
  when he destroys all the gods of
    the land.
The nations on every shore will
    worship him,
  every one in its own land.

Against Cush

¹²"You too, O Cushites,ᵃ
  will be slain by my sword."

Against Assyria

¹³He will stretch out his hand against
    the north
  and destroy Assyria,
leaving Nineveh utterly desolate
  and dry as the desert.
¹⁴Flocks and herds will lie down there,
  creatures of every kind.
The desert owl and the screech owl
  will roost on her columns.
Their calls will echo through the
    windows,
  rubble will be in the doorways,
  the beams of cedar will be
    exposed.
¹⁵This is the carefree city
  that lived in safety.
She said to herself,
  "I am, and there is none besides
    me."
What a ruin she has become,
  a lair for wild beasts!
All who pass by her scoff
  and shake their fists.

The Future of Jerusalem

3 Woe to the city of oppressors,
  rebellious and defiled!
²She obeys no one,

she accepts no correction.
She does not trust in the LORD,
  she does not draw near to her God.
³Her officials are roaring lions,
  her rulers are evening wolves,
  who leave nothing for the morning.
⁴Her prophets are arrogant;
  they are treacherous men.
Her priests profane the sanctuary
  and do violence to the law.
⁵The LORD within her is righteous;
  he does no wrong.
Morning by morning he dispenses his
    justice,
  and every new day he does not
    fail,
  yet the unrighteous know no
    shame.

⁶"I have cut off nations;
  their strongholds are demolished.
I have left their streets deserted,
  with no one passing through.
Their cities are destroyed;
  no one will be left—no one at all.
⁷I said to the city,
  'Surely you will fear me
  and accept correction!'
Then her dwelling would not be cut
    off,
  nor all my punishments come upon
    her.
But they were still eager
  to act corruptly in all they did.
⁸Therefore wait for me," declares the
    LORD,
  "for the day I will stand up to
    testify.ᵇ
I have decided to assemble the
    nations,
  to gather the kingdoms
and to pour out my wrath on them—
  all my fierce anger.
The whole world will be consumed
  by the fire of my jealous anger.

⁹"Then will I purify the lips of the
    peoples,
  that all of them may call on the
    name of the LORD
  and serve him shoulder to
    shoulder.
¹⁰From beyond the rivers of Cushᶜ
  my worshipers, my scattered
    people,
  will bring me offerings.

ᵃ12 That is, people from the upper Nile region
ᵇ8 Septuagint and Syriac; Hebrew *will rise up to
plunder*   ᶜ10 That is, the upper Nile region

¹¹On that day you will not be put to
        shame
    for all the wrongs you have done
        to me,
  because I will remove from this city
    those who rejoice in their pride.
  Never again will you be haughty
    on my holy hill.
¹²But I will leave within you
    the meek and humble,
  who trust in the name of the LORD.
¹³The remnant of Israel will do no
        wrong;
    they will speak no lies,
    nor will deceit be found in their
        mouths.
  They will eat and lie down
    and no one will make them
        afraid."

¹⁴Sing, O Daughter of Zion;
    shout aloud, O Israel!
  Be glad and rejoice with all your
        heart,
    O Daughter of Jerusalem!
¹⁵The LORD has taken away your
        punishment,
    he has turned back your enemy.
  The LORD, the King of Israel, is with
        you;
    never again will you fear any
        harm.
¹⁶On that day they will say to
        Jerusalem,
    "Do not fear, O Zion;
    do not let your hands hang limp.
¹⁷The LORD your God is with you,
    he is mighty to save.
  He will take great delight in you,

Read Zephaniah 3:1–20
Key Verse Zephaniah 3:17

God Delights in You — Jenny Forsberg

The dark Colorado sky was completely clear and sprinkled with brilliant stars as twenty-five other conferees and I sat by the campfire for our last evening together. The day had been physically grueling and emotions in the group were still running high. Even so, I surprised myself by crying when it was my turn to tell everyone what I'd learned that day.

The morning had started out great, but then my rappelling group left without me because they couldn't find me. I should have been relieved to miss the outing, because I'm actually terrified of rappelling. But I wasn't relieved; I was disappointed. I had a lot of time to wonder what everyone would think of me. Were they thinking I had wimped out and couldn't handle the fear? I also wondered what God thought of me. Was he disappointed that I had missed the group or that I was unable to prove my trust in him?

I don't know what the group thought. But I don't think God was disappointed. Zephaniah 3:17 tells me that my performance doesn't gain God's love. He isn't standing ready to throw me out of his family each time that I reveal a weakness—when I am afraid or need to grow in faith. He simply delights in loving me and in rejoicing over me as his child! I have never been, nor will I ever be, able to earn God's love. He wouldn't even accept the attempt.

That's why the tears came that night. I was simply overwhelmed when I realized that I don't have to prove anything before God who loves me just the way I am.

A Deeper Look
Isaiah 43:4; Jeremiah 31:3; Ephesians 3:16–19

Go to page 1041 for your next devotional reading.

he will quiet you with his love,
he will rejoice over you with
    singing."
18"The sorrows for the appointed
        feasts
I will remove from you;
they are a burden and a reproach
    to you.*a*
19At that time I will deal
    with all who oppressed you;
I will rescue the lame
    and gather those who have been
        scattered.

I will give them praise and honor
    in every land where they were put
        to shame.
20At that time I will gather you;
    at that time I will bring you home.
I will give you honor and praise
    among all the peoples of the earth
when I restore your fortunes*b*
    before your very eyes,"
                    says the LORD.

a18 Or *"I will gather you who mourn for the
appointed feasts; / your reproach is a burden to you*
b20 Or *I bring back your captives*

"Look, I'd love to help but I have to study." "I need time to grow and mature. When I feel more ready, then I'll help." "I know God's work is important, but I have to think about my career."

Haggai is a book about priorities. When God's people give priority to building his house, they are blessed. Haggai instructs them that although they may gain some things by putting their interests before God's, they will miss the very best of what God promises—the encouragement and strength of his Spirit. As you read, notice what God values and ask yourself if his priorities are also yours.

HAGGAI

A Call to Build the House of the LORD

1 In the second year of King Darius, on the first day of the sixth month, the word of the LORD came through the prophet Haggai to Zerubbabel son of Shealtiel, governor of Judah, and to Joshua*a* son of Jehozadak, the high priest:

²This is what the LORD Almighty says: "These people say, 'The time has not yet come for the LORD's house to be built.' "

³Then the word of the LORD came through the prophet Haggai: ⁴"Is it a time for you yourselves to be living in your paneled houses, while this house remains a ruin?"

⁵Now this is what the LORD Almighty says: "Give careful thought to your ways. ⁶You have planted much, but have harvested little. You eat, but never have enough. You drink, but never have your fill. You put on clothes, but are not warm. You earn wages, only to put them in a purse with holes in it."

⁷This is what the LORD Almighty says: "Give careful thought to your ways. ⁸Go up into the mountains and bring down timber and build the house, so that I may take pleasure in it and be honored," says the LORD. ⁹"You expected much, but see, it turned out to be little. What you brought home, I blew away. Why?" declares the LORD Almighty. "Because of my house, which remains a ruin, while each of you is busy with his own house.

a1 A variant of *Jeshua*; here and elsewhere in Haggai

[10]Therefore, because of you the heavens have withheld their dew and the earth its crops. [11]I called for a drought on the fields and the mountains, on the grain, the new wine, the oil and whatever the ground produces, on men and cattle, and on the labor of your hands."

[12]Then Zerubbabel son of Shealtiel, Joshua son of Jehozadak, the high priest, and the whole remnant of the people obeyed the voice of the LORD their God and the message of the prophet Haggai, because the LORD their God had sent him. And the people feared the LORD. [13]Then Haggai, the LORD's messenger, gave this message of the LORD to the people: "I am with you," declares the LORD. [14]So the LORD stirred up the spirit of Zerubbabel son of Shealtiel, governor of Judah, and the spirit of Joshua son of Je-

hozadak, the high priest, and the spirit of the whole remnant of the people. They came and began to work on the house of the LORD Almighty, their God, [15]on the twenty-fourth day of the sixth month in the second year of King Darius.

The Promised Glory of the New House

2 On the twenty-first day of the seventh month, the word of the LORD came through the prophet Haggai: [2]"Speak to Zerubbabel son of Shealtiel, governor of Judah, to Joshua son of Jehozadak, the high priest, and to the remnant of the people. Ask them, [3]'Who of you is left who saw this house in its former glory? How does it look to you now? Does it not seem to you like nothing? [4]But now be strong, O Zerubbabel,' declares the LORD. 'Be strong, O Joshua son of Jehozadak,

---

THURSDAY

Read Haggai 1:1–15
Key Verse Haggai 1:9

What Are You Building? —Phil Ward

Although we have almost made it an art form, busyness wasn't invented in the Western world. As early as 520 B.C., the Israelites were perfecting the practice of putting their own desires ahead of God's. While the temple lay in ruins, God's people busied themselves with their own agendas, saying, "The time has not yet come for the LORD's house to be built" (Haggai 1:2). The saying "A person makes time for what is most important" seems applicable in this situation. The Israelites made their choice—they decided to complete their own houses before building God's house.

Centuries later we find ourselves struggling with similar issues. While sometimes the way to serve God may be as clear as it was for Judah (house or temple?), often our choices are much more complicated. Through the prophet Haggai, God tells the people of Judah to "give careful thought to [their] ways" (Haggai 1:7). That's valid advice for today as well. It takes thought and commitment to lay a solid foundation of Biblical principles. It takes careful thought to decide on a career, choose a marriage partner and decide which ministries to participate in. It takes careful, thoughtful listening to hear what God is telling us about ourselves, our gifts, our passions and our limitations. We won't always choose the right ways. But with our eyes on the Master Planner, even our mistakes will take us closer to him.

A Deeper Look
Matthew 7:24–27; 11:28–30; 1 Corinthians 3:11–17

Go to page 1047 for your next devotional reading.

the high priest. Be strong, all you people of the land,' declares the LORD, 'and work. For I am with you,' declares the LORD Almighty. 5'This is what I covenanted with you when you came out of Egypt. And my Spirit remains among you. Do not fear.'

6"This is what the LORD Almighty says: 'In a little while I will once more shake the heavens and the earth, the sea and the dry land. 7I will shake all nations, and the desired of all nations will come, and I will fill this house with glory,' says the LORD Almighty. 8'The silver is mine and the gold is mine,' declares the LORD Almighty. 9'The glory of this present house will be greater than the glory of the former house,' says the LORD Almighty. 'And in this place I will grant peace,' declares the LORD Almighty."

Blessings for a Defiled People

10On the twenty-fourth day of the ninth month, in the second year of Darius, the word of the LORD came to the prophet Haggai: 11"This is what the LORD Almighty says: 'Ask the priests what the law says: 12If a person carries consecrated meat in the fold of his garment, and that fold touches some bread or stew, some wine, oil or other food, does it become consecrated?' "

The priests answered, "No."

13Then Haggai said, "If a person defiled by contact with a dead body touches one of these things, does it become defiled?"

"Yes," the priests replied, "it becomes defiled."

14Then Haggai said, " 'So it is with this people and this nation in my sight,' de-clares the LORD. 'Whatever they do and whatever they offer there is defiled.

15" 'Now give careful thought to this from this day on*a*—consider how things were before one stone was laid on another in the LORD's temple. 16When anyone came to a heap of twenty measures, there were only ten. When anyone went to a wine vat to draw fifty measures, there were only twenty. 17I struck all the work of your hands with blight, mildew and hail, yet you did not turn to me,' declares the LORD. 18'From this day on, from this twenty-fourth day of the ninth month, give careful thought to the day when the foundation of the LORD's temple was laid. Give careful thought: 19Is there yet any seed left in the barn? Until now, the vine and the fig tree, the pomegranate and the olive tree have not borne fruit.

" 'From this day on I will bless you.' "

Zerubbabel the LORD's Signet Ring

20The word of the LORD came to Haggai a second time on the twenty-fourth day of the month: 21"Tell Zerubbabel governor of Judah that I will shake the heavens and the earth. 22I will overturn royal thrones and shatter the power of the foreign kingdoms. I will overthrow chariots and their drivers; horses and their riders will fall, each by the sword of his brother.

23" 'On that day,' declares the LORD Almighty, 'I will take you, my servant Zerubbabel son of Shealtiel,' declares the LORD, 'and I will make you like my signet ring, for I have chosen you,' declares the LORD Almighty."

*a*15 Or to the days past

you may notice that the book of Zechariah conveys a sense of urgency and anticipation. Maybe it's because Zechariah is concerned about the rebuilding of the temple, or because he really wants people to experience spiritual renewal. Perhaps it's because God has given Zechariah so many prophecies concerning the coming Messiah. To a people discouraged about the gargantuan task of building a temple, Zechariah's prophecy encourages the Jews as they return to their homeland and restores to them a renewed vision of God's ultimate purposes.

ZECHARIAH

A Call to Return to the LORD

1 In the eighth month of the second year of Darius, the word of the LORD came to the prophet Zechariah son of Berekiah, the son of Iddo:

² "The LORD was very angry with your forefathers. ³Therefore tell the people: This is what the LORD Almighty says: 'Return to me,' declares the LORD Almighty, 'and I will return to you,' says the LORD Almighty. ⁴Do not be like your forefathers, to whom the earlier prophets proclaimed: This is what the LORD Almighty says: 'Turn from your evil ways and your evil practices.' But they would not listen or pay attention to me, declares the LORD. ⁵Where are your forefathers now? And the prophets, do they live forever? ⁶But did not my words and my decrees, which I commanded my servants the prophets, overtake your forefathers?

"Then they repented and said, 'The LORD Almighty has done to us what our ways and practices deserve, just as he determined to do.' "

The Man Among the Myrtle Trees

⁷On the twenty-fourth day of the eleventh month, the month of Shebat, in the second year of Darius, the word of the LORD came to the prophet Zechariah son of Berekiah, the son of Iddo.

⁸During the night I had a vision—and there before me was a man riding a red horse! He was standing among the myrtle trees in a ravine. Behind him were red, brown and white horses.

⁹I asked, "What are these, my lord?"

The angel who was talking with me answered, "I will show you what they are."

¹⁰Then the man standing among the myrtle trees explained, "They are the ones the LORD has sent to go throughout the earth."

¹¹And they reported to the angel of the LORD, who was standing among the myrtle trees, "We have gone throughout the earth and found the whole world at rest and in peace."

¹²Then the angel of the LORD said, "LORD Almighty, how long will you withhold mercy from Jerusalem and from the towns of Judah, which you have been angry with these seventy years?" ¹³So the LORD spoke kind and comforting words to the angel who talked with me.

¹⁴Then the angel who was speaking to me said, "Proclaim this word: This is what the LORD Almighty says: 'I am very jealous for Jerusalem and Zion, ¹⁵but I am very angry with the nations that feel secure. I was only a little angry, but they added to the calamity.'

¹⁶"Therefore, this is what the LORD says: 'I will return to Jerusalem with mercy, and there my house will be rebuilt. And the measuring line will be stretched out over Jerusalem,' declares the LORD Almighty.

¹⁷"Proclaim further: This is what the LORD Almighty says: 'My towns will again overflow with prosperity, and the LORD will again comfort Zion and choose Jerusalem.' "

Four Horns and Four Craftsmen

¹⁸Then I looked up—and there before me were four horns! ¹⁹I asked the angel who was speaking to me, "What are these?"

He answered me, "These are the horns that scattered Judah, Israel and Jerusalem."

²⁰Then the LORD showed me four craftsmen. ²¹I asked, "What are these coming to do?"

He answered, "These are the horns that scattered Judah so that no one could raise his head, but the craftsmen have come to terrify them and throw down these horns of the nations who lifted up their horns against the land of Judah to scatter its people."

A Man With a Measuring Line

2 Then I looked up—and there before me was a man with a measuring line in his hand! ²I asked, "Where are you going?"

He answered me, "To measure Jerusalem, to find out how wide and how long it is."

³Then the angel who was speaking to me left, and another angel came to meet him ⁴and said to him: "Run, tell that young man, 'Jerusalem will be a city without walls because of the great number of men and livestock in it. ⁵And I myself will be a wall of fire around it,' declares the LORD, 'and I will be its glory within.'

⁶"Come! Come! Flee from the land of the north," declares the LORD, "for I have scattered you to the four winds of heaven," declares the LORD.

⁷"Come, O Zion! Escape, you who live in the Daughter of Babylon!" ⁸For this is what the LORD Almighty says: "After he has honored me and has sent me against the nations that have plundered you—for whoever touches you touches the apple of his eye— ⁹I will surely raise my hand against them so that their slaves will plunder them.ᵃ Then you will know that the LORD Almighty has sent me.

¹⁰"Shout and be glad, O Daughter of Zion. For I am coming, and I will live among you," declares the LORD. ¹¹"Many nations will be joined with the LORD in that day and will become my people. I will live among you and you will know that the LORD Almighty has sent me to you. ¹²The LORD will inherit Judah as his portion in the holy land and will again choose Jerusalem. ¹³Be still before the LORD, all mankind, because he has roused himself from his holy dwelling."

Clean Garments for the High Priest

3 Then he showed me Joshuaᵇ the high priest standing before the angel of the LORD, and Satanᶜ standing at his right side to accuse him. ²The LORD said to Satan, "The LORD rebuke you, Satan! The LORD, who has chosen Jerusalem, rebuke you! Is not this man a burning stick snatched from the fire?"

³Now Joshua was dressed in filthy clothes as he stood before the angel. ⁴The

ᵃ8,9 Or says after . . . eye: 9"I . . . plunder them."
ᵇ1 A variant of Jeshua; here and elsewhere in Zechariah   ᶜ1 Satan means accuser.

angel said to those who were standing before him, "Take off his filthy clothes."

Then he said to Joshua, "See, I have taken away your sin, and I will put rich garments on you."

⁵Then I said, "Put a clean turban on his head." So they put a clean turban on his head and clothed him, while the angel of the LORD stood by.

⁶The angel of the LORD gave this charge to Joshua: ⁷"This is what the LORD Almighty says: 'If you will walk in my ways and keep my requirements, then you will govern my house and have charge of my courts, and I will give you a place among these standing here.

⁸" 'Listen, O high priest Joshua and your associates seated before you, who are men symbolic of things to come: I am going to bring my servant, the Branch. ⁹See, the stone I have set in front of Joshua! There are seven eyes*a* on that one stone, and I will engrave an inscription on it,' says the LORD Almighty, 'and I will remove the sin of this land in a single day.

¹⁰" 'In that day each of you will invite his neighbor to sit under his vine and fig tree,' declares the LORD Almighty."

The Gold Lampstand and the Two Olive Trees

4 Then the angel who talked with me returned and wakened me, as a man is wakened from his sleep. ²He asked me, "What do you see?"

I answered, "I see a solid gold lampstand with a bowl at the top and seven lights on it, with seven channels to the lights. ³Also there are two olive trees by it, one on the right of the bowl and the other on its left."

⁴I asked the angel who talked with me, "What are these, my lord?"

⁵He answered, "Do you not know what these are?"

"No, my lord," I replied.

⁶So he said to me, "This is the word of the LORD to Zerubbabel: 'Not by might nor by power, but by my Spirit,' says the LORD Almighty.

⁷"What*b* are you, O mighty mountain? Before Zerubbabel you will become level ground. Then he will bring out the capstone to shouts of 'God bless it! God bless it!' "

⁸Then the word of the LORD came to me: ⁹"The hands of Zerubbabel have laid the foundation of this temple; his hands

will also complete it. Then you will know that the LORD Almighty has sent me to you.

¹⁰"Who despises the day of small things? Men will rejoice when they see the plumb line in the hand of Zerubbabel.

"(These seven are the eyes of the LORD, which range throughout the earth.)"

¹¹Then I asked the angel, "What are these two olive trees on the right and the left of the lampstand?"

¹²Again I asked him, "What are these two olive branches beside the two gold pipes that pour out golden oil?"

¹³He replied, "Do you not know what these are?"

"No, my lord," I said.

¹⁴So he said, "These are the two who are anointed to*c* serve the Lord of all the earth."

The Flying Scroll

5 I looked again—and there before me was a flying scroll!

²He asked me, "What do you see?"

I answered, "I see a flying scroll, thirty feet long and fifteen feet wide.*d* "

³And he said to me, "This is the curse that is going out over the whole land; for according to what it says on one side, every thief will be banished, and according to what it says on the other, everyone

---

a9 Or *facets*   *b7* Or *Who*   *c14* Or *two who*
bring oil and   *d2* Hebrew *twenty cubits long and
ten cubits wide* (about 9 meters long and 4.5 meters wide)

POINT
OF INTEREST   Zechariah 3:9

If you heard that all of the world's evil would be destroyed in a single day— every murder averted, every child protected from abuse, every political corruption made right, every oppressed individual given freedom—and that all crime would stop forever, would you believe it? This prophecy would have been just as hard for an ancient Hebrew to believe. How could God remove the land's sin in a single day? Hint: That day will be called "Good . . ." (See also Zechariah 12:10—13:1.)

who swears falsely will be banished. ⁴The LORD Almighty declares, 'I will send it out, and it will enter the house of the thief and the house of him who swears falsely by my name. It will remain in his house and destroy it, both its timbers and its stones.' "

The Woman in a Basket

⁵Then the angel who was speaking to me came forward and said to me, "Look up and see what this is that is appearing."

⁶I asked, "What is it?"

He replied, "It is a measuring basket.ᵃ" And he added, "This is the iniquityᵇ of the people throughout the land."

⁷Then the cover of lead was raised, and there in the basket sat a woman! ⁸He said, "This is wickedness," and he pushed her back into the basket and pushed the lead cover down over its mouth.

⁹Then I looked up—and there before me were two women, with the wind in their wings! They had wings like those of a stork, and they lifted up the basket between heaven and earth.

¹⁰"Where are they taking the basket?" I asked the angel who was speaking to me.

¹¹He replied, "To the country of Babyloniaᶜ to build a house for it. When it is ready, the basket will be set there in its place."

Four Chariots

6 I looked up again—and there before me were four chariots coming out from between two mountains—mountains of bronze! ²The first chariot had red horses, the second black, ³the third white, and the fourth dappled—all of them powerful. ⁴I asked the angel who was speaking to me, "What are these, my lord?"

⁵The angel answered me, "These are the four spiritsᵈ of heaven, going out from standing in the presence of the Lord of the whole world. ⁶The one with the black horses is going toward the north country, the one with the white horses toward the west,ᵉ and the one with the dappled horses toward the south."

⁷When the powerful horses went out, they were straining to go throughout the earth. And he said, "Go throughout the earth!" So they went throughout the earth.

⁸Then he called to me, "Look, those going toward the north country have given my Spiritᶠ rest in the land of the north."

A Crown for Joshua

⁹The word of the LORD came to me: ¹⁰"Take ⌐silver and gold⌐ from the exiles Heldai, Tobijah and Jedaiah, who have arrived from Babylon. Go the same day to the house of Josiah son of Zephaniah. ¹¹Take the silver and gold and make a crown, and set it on the head of the high priest, Joshua son of Jehozadak. ¹²Tell him this is what the LORD Almighty says: 'Here is the man whose name is the Branch, and he will branch out from his place and build the temple of the LORD. ¹³It is he who will build the temple of the LORD, and he will be clothed with majesty and will sit and rule on his throne. And he will be a priest on his throne. And there will be harmony between the two.' ¹⁴The crown will be given to Heldai,ᵍ Tobijah, Jedaiah and Henʰ son of Zephaniah as a memorial in the temple of the LORD. ¹⁵Those who are far away will come and help to build the temple of the LORD, and you will know that the LORD Almighty has sent me to you. This will happen if you diligently obey the LORD your God."

Justice and Mercy, Not Fasting

7 In the fourth year of King Darius, the word of the LORD came to Zechariah on the fourth day of the ninth month, the month of Kislev. ²The people of Bethel had sent Sharezer and Regem-Melech, together with their men, to entreat the LORD ³by asking the priests of the house of the LORD Almighty and the prophets, "Should I mourn and fast in the fifth month, as I have done for so many years?"

⁴Then the word of the LORD Almighty came to me: ⁵"Ask all the people of the land and the priests, 'When you fasted and mourned in the fifth and seventh months for the past seventy years, was it really for me that you fasted? ⁶And when you were eating and drinking, were you not just feasting for yourselves? ⁷Are

ᵃ6 Hebrew *an ephah*; also in verses 7-11   ᵇ6 Or *appearance*   ᶜ11 Hebrew *Shinar*   ᵈ5 Or *winds*   ᵉ6 Or *horses after them*   ᶠ8 Or *spirit*   ᵍ14 Syriac; Hebrew *Helem*   ʰ14 Or *and the gracious one, the* these not the words the LORD proclaimed through the earlier prophets when Jerusalem and its surrounding towns were at rest and prosperous, and the Negev and the western foothills were settled?' "

⁸And the word of the LORD came again to Zechariah: ⁹"This is what the LORD Almighty says: 'Administer true justice; show mercy and compassion to one another. ¹⁰Do not oppress the widow or the fatherless, the alien or the poor. In your hearts do not think evil of each other.'

¹¹"But they refused to pay attention; stubbornly they turned their backs and stopped up their ears. ¹²They made their hearts as hard as flint and would not listen to the law or to the words that the LORD Almighty had sent by his Spirit through the earlier prophets. So the LORD Almighty was very angry.

¹³" 'When I called, they did not listen; so when they called, I would not listen,' says the LORD Almighty. ¹⁴'I scattered them with a whirlwind among all the nations, where they were strangers. The land was left so desolate behind them that no one could come or go. This is how they made the pleasant land desolate.' "

FRIDAY

Read Zechariah 7:1–14
Key Verses Zechariah 7:9–10

Perfect in His Eyes — Linda Llewelyn

The beach is covered with seashells—some glistening in the sun, others partially covered with sand as if trying to hide. They come in all sizes and shapes. Some have rough surfaces; others are satin-smooth. Some seem to echo the sounds of the sea, while others are silent. Each is created to be unique; no two are exactly alike.

As I walk along the beach, I scan the sand for shells to take home with me. I keep the most beautiful ones as my treasures and throw back ones that seem ordinary or are chipped. I don't even bother with shells that look dirty. Why take the time to wash them, when there are plenty of others to choose from that are nearly perfect?

As I reflect on my selectivity, I am struck by the fact that we tend to be selective with people too. We tend to look past those who make us feel uncomfortable. Maybe it's because they're rumpled and dirty. Maybe they're in need of a friend, but that longing look in their eyes spells "time" that we don't want to give. Or maybe there's just something about them that causes us to label them "hard to love."

Is it okay to walk past those who make us uncomfortable and instead associate only with people who come closer to our standard of perfection? Would Jesus do that? Did he walk past the man with leprosy, the prostitute or the demon-possessed man? (See Luke 5:12–14; 7:36–38; 8:26–38). Romans 15:7 says, "Accept one another, then, just as Christ accepted you."

In spite of the fact that none of us will ever be perfect on this earth, Jesus Christ accepts each one of us, chipped and dirty though we are. When he looks at us, he sees us as the whole and glorious people he has redeemed us to be. As we become more like him, that's how we'll see others too.

A Deeper Look
1 Samuel 16:7; Hebrews 10:14

Go to page 1055 for your next devotional reading.

The Lord Promises to Bless Jerusalem

8 Again the word of the Lord Almighty came to me. ²This is what the Lord Almighty says: "I am very jealous for Zion; I am burning with jealousy for her."

³This is what the Lord says: "I will return to Zion and dwell in Jerusalem. Then Jerusalem will be called the City of Truth, and the mountain of the Lord Almighty will be called the Holy Mountain."

⁴This is what the Lord Almighty says: "Once again men and women of ripe old age will sit in the streets of Jerusalem, each with cane in hand because of his age. ⁵The city streets will be filled with boys and girls playing there."

⁶This is what the Lord Almighty says: "It may seem marvelous to the remnant of this people at that time, but will it seem marvelous to me?" declares the Lord Almighty.

⁷This is what the Lord Almighty says: "I will save my people from the countries of the east and the west. ⁸I will bring them back to live in Jerusalem; they will be my people, and I will be faithful and righteous to them as their God."

⁹This is what the Lord Almighty says: "You who now hear these words spoken by the prophets who were there when the foundation was laid for the house of the Lord Almighty, let your hands be strong so that the temple may be built. ¹⁰Before that time there were no wages for man or beast. No one could go about his business safely because of his enemy, for I had turned every man against his neighbor. ¹¹But now I will not deal with the remnant of this people as I did in the past," declares the Lord Almighty.

¹²"The seed will grow well, the vine will yield its fruit, the ground will produce its crops, and the heavens will drop their dew. I will give all these things as an inheritance to the remnant of this people. ¹³As you have been an object of cursing among the nations, O Judah and Israel, so will I save you, and you will be a blessing. Do not be afraid, but let your hands be strong."

¹⁴This is what the Lord Almighty says: "Just as I had determined to bring disaster upon you and showed no pity when your fathers angered me," says the Lord Almighty, ¹⁵"so now I have determined to do good again to Jerusalem and Judah. Do not be afraid. ¹⁶These are the things you are to do: Speak the truth to each other, and render true and sound judgment in your courts; ¹⁷do not plot evil against your neighbor, and do not love to swear falsely. I hate all this," declares the Lord.

¹⁸Again the word of the Lord Almighty came to me. ¹⁹This is what the Lord Almighty says: "The fasts of the fourth, fifth, seventh and tenth months will become joyful and glad occasions and happy festivals for Judah. Therefore love truth and peace."

²⁰This is what the Lord Almighty says: "Many peoples and the inhabitants of many cities will yet come, ²¹and the inhabitants of one city will go to another and say, 'Let us go at once to entreat the Lord and seek the Lord Almighty. I myself am going.' ²²And many peoples and powerful nations will come to Jerusalem to seek the Lord Almighty and to entreat him."

²³This is what the Lord Almighty says: "In those days ten men from all languages and nations will take firm hold of one Jew by the hem of his robe and say, 'Let us go with you, because we have heard that God is with you.'"

Judgment on Israel's Enemies

An Oracle

9 The word of the Lord is against the
  land of Hadrach
    and will rest upon Damascus—
  for the eyes of men and all the tribes
    of Israel
    are on the Lord— *a*
²and upon Hamath too, which borders
    on it,
  and upon Tyre and Sidon, though
    they are very skillful.
³Tyre has built herself a stronghold;
  she has heaped up silver like dust,
    and gold like the dirt of the streets.
⁴But the Lord will take away her
    possessions
  and destroy her power on the sea,
    and she will be consumed by fire.
⁵Ashkelon will see it and fear;
  Gaza will writhe in agony,
    and Ekron too, for her hope will
      wither.
  Gaza will lose her king
    and Ashkelon will be deserted.
⁶Foreigners will occupy Ashdod,

*a 1 Or Damascus. / For the eye of the Lord is on all
mankind, / as well as on the tribes of Israel,*

and I will cut off the pride of the
Philistines.
⁷I will take the blood from their
mouths,
the forbidden food from between
their teeth.
Those who are left will belong to our
God
and become leaders in Judah,
and Ekron will be like the
Jebusites.
⁸But I will defend my house
against marauding forces.
Never again will an oppressor
overrun my people,
for now I am keeping watch.

The Coming of Zion's King

⁹Rejoice greatly, O Daughter of Zion!
Shout, Daughter of Jerusalem!
See, your king*ᵃ* comes to you,
righteous and having salvation,
gentle and riding on a donkey,
on a colt, the foal of a donkey.
¹⁰I will take away the chariots from
Ephraim
and the war-horses from
Jerusalem,
and the battle bow will be broken.
He will proclaim peace to the nations.
His rule will extend from sea to
sea
and from the River*ᵇ* to the ends of
the earth.*ᶜ*
¹¹As for you, because of the blood of
my covenant with you,
I will free your prisoners from the
waterless pit.
¹²Return to your fortress, O prisoners of
hope;
even now I announce that I will
restore twice as much to you.
¹³I will bend Judah as I bend my bow
and fill it with Ephraim.
I will rouse your sons, O Zion,
against your sons, O Greece,
and make you like a warrior's
sword.

The Lord Will Appear

¹⁴Then the Lord will appear over them;
his arrow will flash like lightning.
The Sovereign Lord will sound the
trumpet;
he will march in the storms of the
south,
¹⁵ and the Lord Almighty will shield
them.
They will destroy

and overcome with slingstones.
They will drink and roar as with
wine;
they will be full like a bowl
used for sprinkling*ᵈ* the corners of
the altar.
¹⁶The Lord their God will save them on
that day
as the flock of his people.
They will sparkle in his land
like jewels in a crown.
¹⁷How attractive and beautiful they will
be!
Grain will make the young men
thrive,
and new wine the young women.

The Lord Will Care for Judah

10 Ask the Lord for rain in the
springtime;
it is the Lord who makes the storm
clouds.
He gives showers of rain to men,
and plants of the field to everyone.
²The idols speak deceit,
diviners see visions that lie;
they tell dreams that are false,
they give comfort in vain.
Therefore the people wander like
sheep
oppressed for lack of a shepherd.

³"My anger burns against the
shepherds,
and I will punish the leaders;
for the Lord Almighty will care
for his flock, the house of Judah,
and make them like a proud horse
in battle.
⁴From Judah will come the
cornerstone,
from him the tent peg,
from him the battle bow,
from him every ruler.
⁵Together they*ᵉ* will be like mighty
men
trampling the muddy streets in
battle.
Because the Lord is with them,
they will fight and overthrow the
horsemen.

⁶"I will strengthen the house of Judah
and save the house of Joseph.
I will restore them
because I have compassion on
them.

*ᵃ9 Or King   ᵇ10 That is, the Euphrates
ᶜ10 Or the end of the land   ᵈ15 Or bowl, / like
ᵉ4,5 Or ruler, all of them together. / ⁵They*

They will be as though
    I had not rejected them,
for I am the LORD their God
    and I will answer them.
⁷The Ephraimites will become like
      mighty men,
    and their hearts will be glad as
      with wine.
Their children will see it and be
      joyful;
    their hearts will rejoice in the LORD.
⁸I will signal for them
    and gather them in.
Surely I will redeem them;
    they will be as numerous as
      before.
⁹Though I scatter them among the
      peoples,
    yet in distant lands they will
      remember me.
They and their children will survive,
    and they will return.
¹⁰I will bring them back from Egypt
    and gather them from Assyria.
I will bring them to Gilead and
      Lebanon,
    and there will not be room enough
      for them.
¹¹They will pass through the sea of
      trouble;
    the surging sea will be subdued
    and all the depths of the Nile will
      dry up.
Assyria's pride will be brought down
    and Egypt's scepter will pass away.
¹²I will strengthen them in the LORD
    and in his name they will walk,"
                declares the LORD.

11 Open your doors, O Lebanon,
    so that fire may devour your
      cedars!
²Wail, O pine tree, for the cedar has
      fallen;
    the stately trees are ruined!
Wail, oaks of Bashan;
    the dense forest has been cut
      down!
³Listen to the wail of the shepherds;
    their rich pastures are destroyed!
Listen to the roar of the lions;
    the lush thicket of the Jordan is
      ruined!

Two Shepherds

⁴This is what the LORD my God says:
"Pasture the flock marked for slaughter.
⁵Their buyers slaughter them and go unpunished. Those who sell them say,
'Praise the LORD, I am rich!' Their own shepherds do not spare them. ⁶For I will no longer have pity on the people of the land," declares the LORD. "I will hand everyone over to his neighbor and his king. They will oppress the land, and I will not rescue them from their hands."

⁷So I pastured the flock marked for slaughter, particularly the oppressed of the flock. Then I took two staffs and called one Favor and the other Union, and I pastured the flock. ⁸In one month I got rid of the three shepherds.

The flock detested me, and I grew weary of them ⁹and said, "I will not be your shepherd. Let the dying die, and the perishing perish. Let those who are left eat one another's flesh."

¹⁰Then I took my staff called Favor and broke it, revoking the covenant I had made with all the nations. ¹¹It was revoked on that day, and so the afflicted of the flock who were watching me knew it was the word of the LORD.

¹²I told them, "If you think it best, give me my pay; but if not, keep it." So they paid me thirty pieces of silver.

¹³And the LORD said to me, "Throw it to the potter"—the handsome price at which they priced me! So I took the thirty pieces of silver and threw them into the house of the LORD to the potter.

¹⁴Then I broke my second staff called Union, breaking the brotherhood between Judah and Israel.

¹⁵Then the LORD said to me, "Take again the equipment of a foolish shepherd. ¹⁶For I am going to raise up a shepherd over the land who will not care for the lost, or seek the young, or heal the injured, or feed the healthy, but will eat the meat of the choice sheep, tearing off their hoofs.

¹⁷"Woe to the worthless shepherd,
    who deserts the flock!
May the sword strike his arm and his
      right eye!
May his arm be completely
      withered,
    his right eye totally blinded!"

Jerusalem's Enemies to Be Destroyed

An Oracle

12 This is the word of the LORD concerning Israel. The LORD, who stretches out the heavens, who lays the foundation of the earth, and who forms the spirit of man within him, declares: ²"I am going to make Jerusalem a cup that sends all the surrounding peoples reeling. Judah will be besieged as well as Jerusalem. ³On that day, when all the nations of the earth are gathered against her, I will make Jerusalem an immovable rock for all the nations. All who try to move it will injure themselves. ⁴On that day I will strike every horse with panic and its rider with madness," declares the LORD. "I will keep a watchful eye over the house of Judah, but I will blind all the horses of the nations. ⁵Then the leaders of Judah will say in their hearts, 'The people of Jerusalem are strong, because the LORD Almighty is their God.'

⁶"On that day I will make the leaders of Judah like a firepot in a woodpile, like a flaming torch among sheaves. They will consume right and left all the surrounding peoples, but Jerusalem will remain intact in her place.

⁷"The LORD will save the dwellings of Judah first, so that the honor of the house of David and of Jerusalem's inhabitants may not be greater than that of Judah. ⁸On that day the LORD will shield those who live in Jerusalem, so that the feeblest among them will be like David, and the house of David will be like God, like the Angel of the LORD going before them. ⁹On that day I will set out to destroy all the nations that attack Jerusalem.

Mourning for the One They Pierced

¹⁰"And I will pour out on the house of David and the inhabitants of Jerusalem a spirit*a* of grace and supplication. They will look on*b* me, the one they have pierced, and they will mourn for him as one mourns for an only child, and grieve bitterly for him as one grieves for a first-born son. ¹¹On that day the weeping in Jerusalem will be great, like the weeping of Hadad Rimmon in the plain of Megiddo. ¹²The land will mourn, each clan by itself, with their wives by themselves: the clan of the house of David and their wives, the clan of the house of Nathan and their wives, ¹³the clan of the house of Levi and their wives, the clan of Shimei and their wives, ¹⁴and all the rest of the clans and their wives.

Cleansing From Sin

13 "On that day a fountain will be opened to the house of David and the inhabitants of Jerusalem, to cleanse them from sin and impurity.

²"On that day, I will banish the names of the idols from the land, and they will be remembered no more," declares the LORD Almighty. "I will remove both the prophets and the spirit of impurity from the land. ³And if anyone still prophesies, his father and mother, to whom he was born, will say to him, 'You must die, because you have told lies in the LORD's name.' When he prophesies, his own parents will stab him.

⁴"On that day every prophet will be ashamed of his prophetic vision. He will not put on a prophet's garment of hair in order to deceive. ⁵He will say, 'I am not a prophet. I am a farmer; the land has been my livelihood since my youth.*c*' ⁶If someone asks him, 'What are these wounds on your body*d*?' he will answer, 'The wounds I was given at the house of my friends.'

The Shepherd Struck, the Sheep Scattered

⁷"Awake, O sword, against my
        shepherd,
    against the man who is close to
        me!"
    declares the LORD Almighty.
  "Strike the shepherd,
    and the sheep will be scattered,
    and I will turn my hand against
        the little ones.
⁸In the whole land," declares the LORD,
    "two-thirds will be struck down
        and perish;
    yet one-third will be left in it.
⁹This third I will bring into the fire;
    I will refine them like silver
    and test them like gold.

---

*a*10 Or *the Spirit*   *b*10 Or *to*   *c*5 Or *farmer; a man sold me in my youth*   *d*6 Or *wounds between your hands*

Zechariah 12:10–13:1

God chose the Israelites as his holy people. Many scholars believe that at the end of the age there will come a time when Jews will recognize Jesus as the Messiah. Romans 11:25–27 gives us a preview of why and how this will come about. God has not abandoned his people!

They will call on my name
　　and I will answer them;
I will say, 'They are my people,'
　　and they will say, 'The LORD is our
　　　God.' "

The LORD Comes and Reigns

14 A day of the LORD is coming when
your plunder will be divided among
you.

²I will gather all the nations to Jerusalem to fight against it; the city will be
captured, the houses ransacked, and the
women raped. Half of the city will go into
exile, but the rest of the people will not
be taken from the city. ³Then the LORD will go out and fight
against those nations, as he fights in the
day of battle. ⁴On that day his feet will
stand on the Mount of Olives, east of Jerusalem, and the Mount of Olives will be
split in two from east to west, forming a
great valley, with half of the mountain
moving north and half moving south.
⁵You will flee by my mountain valley, for
it will extend to Azel. You will flee as you
fled from the earthquake[a] in the days of
Uzziah king of Judah. Then the LORD my
God will come, and all the holy ones with
him.

⁶On that day there will be no light, no
cold or frost. ⁷It will be a unique day,
without daytime or nighttime—a day
known to the LORD. When evening comes,
there will be light.

⁸On that day living water will flow out
from Jerusalem, half to the eastern sea[b]
and half to the western sea,[c] in summer
and in winter.

⁹The LORD will be king over the whole
earth. On that day there will be one LORD,
and his name the only name.

¹⁰The whole land, from Geba to Rimmon, south of Jerusalem, will become
like the Arabah. But Jerusalem will be
raised up and remain in its place, from
the Benjamin Gate to the site of the First
Gate, to the Corner Gate, and from the
Tower of Hananel to the royal winepresses. ¹¹It will be inhabited; never

again will it be destroyed. Jerusalem will
be secure.

¹²This is the plague with which the
LORD will strike all the nations that fought
against Jerusalem: Their flesh will rot
while they are still standing on their feet,
their eyes will rot in their sockets, and
their tongues will rot in their mouths.
¹³On that day men will be stricken by the
LORD with great panic. Each man will
seize the hand of another, and they will
attack each other. ¹⁴Judah too will fight
at Jerusalem. The wealth of all the surrounding nations will be collected—great
quantities of gold and silver and clothing.
¹⁵A similar plague will strike the horses
and mules, the camels and donkeys, and
all the animals in those camps.

¹⁶Then the survivors from all the nations that have attacked Jerusalem will
go up year after year to worship the King,
the LORD Almighty, and to celebrate the
Feast of Tabernacles. ¹⁷If any of the peoples of the earth do not go up to Jerusalem to worship the King, the LORD Almighty, they will have no rain. ¹⁸If the
Egyptian people do not go up and take
part, they will have no rain. The LORD[d]
will bring on them the plague he inflicts
on the nations that do not go up to celebrate the Feast of Tabernacles. ¹⁹This will
be the punishment of Egypt and the punishment of all the nations that do not go
up to celebrate the Feast of Tabernacles.

²⁰On that day HOLY TO THE LORD will be
inscribed on the bells of the horses, and
the cooking pots in the LORD's house will
be like the sacred bowls in front of the
altar. ²¹Every pot in Jerusalem and Judah
will be holy to the LORD Almighty, and all
who come to sacrifice will take some of
the pots and cook in them. And on that
day there will no longer be a Canaanite[e]
in the house of the LORD Almighty.

---

[a]5 Or ⁵My mountain valley will be blocked and will
extend to Azel. It will be blocked as it was blocked
because of the earthquake　　[b]8 That is, the Dead
Sea　　[c]8 That is, the Mediterranean　　[d]18 Or
part, then the LORD　　[e]21 Or merchant

How do you feel when some-
one "breaks faith" with you? Perhaps they lie to you or
just "go through the motions" of loving you. In the book of
Malachi we witness God's wrenching grief when his people
break faith with him, robbing him of the proper tithes,
breaking his laws for marriage and perpetuating injustice.
Malachi announces that the Lord will send his messenger
to refine and purify his people. He implores them to return
to God and remain faithful to
him, to be his "treasured
possession" (3:17).

MALACHI

1 An oracle: The word of the Lord to Israel through Malachi.*

Jacob Loved, Esau Hated

²"I have loved you," says the Lord.
"But you ask, 'How have you
loved us?'

"Was not Esau Jacob's brother?" the
Lord says. "Yet I have loved Jacob, ³but
Esau I have hated, and I have turned his
mountains into a wasteland and left his
inheritance to the desert jackals."

⁴Edom may say, "Though we have
been crushed, we will rebuild the ruins."
But this is what the Lord Almighty
says: "They may build, but I will demolish. They will be called the Wicked Land,
a people always under the wrath of the
Lord. ⁵You will see it with your own eyes
and say, 'Great is the Lord—even beyond
the borders of Israel!'

Blemished Sacrifices

⁶"A son honors his father, and a servant his master. If I am a father, where
is the honor due me? If I am a master,
where is the respect due me?" says the
Lord Almighty. "It is you, O priests, who
show contempt for my name.

"But you ask, 'How have we shown
contempt for your name?'

⁷"You place defiled food on my altar.

"But you ask, 'How have we defiled
you?'

"By saying that the Lord's table is contemptible. ⁸When you bring blind animals for sacrifice, is that not wrong?
When you sacrifice crippled or diseased
animals, is that not wrong? Try offering
them to your governor! Would he be

1 Malachi means my messenger.

pleased with you? Would he accept you?" says the LORD Almighty.

⁹"Now implore God to be gracious to us. With such offerings from your hands, will he accept you?"—says the LORD Almighty.

¹⁰"Oh, that one of you would shut the temple doors, so that you would not light useless fires on my altar! I am not pleased with you," says the LORD Almighty, "and I will accept no offering from your hands. ¹¹My name will be great among the nations, from the rising to the setting of the sun. In every place incense and pure offerings will be brought to my name, because my name will be great among the nations," says the LORD Almighty.

¹²"But you profane it by saying of the Lord's table, 'It is defiled,' and of its food, 'It is contemptible.' ¹³And you say, 'What a burden!' and you sniff at it contemptuously," says the LORD Almighty.

"When you bring injured, crippled or diseased animals and offer them as sacrifices, should I accept them from your hands?" says the LORD. ¹⁴"Cursed is the cheat who has an acceptable male in his flock and vows to give it, but then sacrifices a blemished animal to the Lord. For I am a great king," says the LORD Almighty, "and my name is to be feared among the nations.

Admonition for the Priests

2 "And now this admonition is for you, O priests. ²If you do not listen, and if you do not set your heart to honor my name," says the LORD Almighty, "I will send a curse upon you, and I will curse your blessings. Yes, I have already cursed them, because you have not set your heart to honor me.

³"Because of you I will rebuke*a* your descendants*b*; I will spread on your faces the offal from your festival sacrifices, and you will be carried off with it. ⁴And you will know that I have sent you this admonition so that my covenant with Levi may continue," says the LORD Almighty. ⁵"My covenant was with him, a covenant of life and peace, and I gave them to him; this called for reverence and he revered me and stood in awe of my name. ⁶True instruction was in his mouth and nothing false was found on his lips. He walked with me in peace and uprightness, and turned many from sin.

⁷"For the lips of a priest ought to preserve knowledge, and from his mouth men should seek instruction—because he is the messenger of the LORD Almighty. ⁸But you have turned from the way and by your teaching have caused many to stumble; you have violated the covenant with Levi," says the LORD Almighty. ⁹"So I have caused you to be despised and humiliated before all the people, because you have not followed my ways but have shown partiality in matters of the law."

Judah Unfaithful

¹⁰Have we not all one Father*c*? Did not one God create us? Why do we profane the covenant of our fathers by breaking faith with one another?

¹¹Judah has broken faith. A detestable thing has been committed in Israel and in Jerusalem: Judah has desecrated the sanctuary the LORD loves, by marrying the daughter of a foreign god. ¹²As for the man who does this, whoever he may be, may the LORD cut him off from the tents of Jacob*d*—even though he brings offerings to the LORD Almighty.

¹³Another thing you do: You flood the LORD's altar with tears. You weep and wail because he no longer pays attention to your offerings or accepts them with pleasure from your hands. ¹⁴You ask, "Why?" It is because the LORD is acting as the witness between you and the wife of your youth, because you have broken faith with her, though she is your partner, the wife of your marriage covenant.

¹⁵Has not ˻the LORD˼ made them one? In flesh and spirit they are his. And why one? Because he was seeking godly offspring.*e* So guard yourself in your spirit, and do not break faith with the wife of your youth.

¹⁶"I hate divorce," says the LORD God of Israel, "and I hate a man's covering himself*f* with violence as well as with his garment," says the LORD Almighty.

So guard yourself in your spirit, and do not break faith.

The Day of Judgment

¹⁷You have wearied the LORD with your words.

---

a3 Or *cut off* (see Septuagint)   *b3* Or *will blight your grain*   *c10* Or *father*   *d12* Or *12May the LORD cut off from the tents of Jacob anyone who gives testimony in behalf of the man who does this*   *e15* Or *15But the one ˻who is our father˼ did not do this, not as long as life remained in him. And what was he seeking? An offspring from God*   *f16* Or *his wife*

Read Malachi 2:10—3:18
Key Verse Malachi 2:16

Divorce – The Broken Promise

Marriage involves a lot of promises. In fact, it is the promise of a lifetime and for a lifetime. According to the Bible, keeping the promise of marriage is "keeping faith." Malachi 2:16 tells us that God hates divorce. He hates the pain and division it creates, because he makes two people one in body and spirit when they marry.

The marriage covenant mirrors God's covenant with his people. The prophet Malachi told the people of Judah that God wasn't listening to their prayers or accepting their offerings because they had "broken faith" (Malachi 2:14) with the wives of their youth. Breaking the promise of marriage that they had made before God was symptomatic of their hardened, unfaithful hearts, not only toward their spouses, but also toward God.

Making a lifetime commitment isn't easy. Marriage is like an equation with few constants and many variables. It takes work and faith to work out the equation and keep it in balance regardless of the difficulties, conflicts and fluctuating emotions that enter into it. But God's love, care and forgiveness are constants, and he wants us to be constant in keeping our promise and to stay devoted for a lifetime.

Digging Into the Word
1. What do the following verses say about God's design for marriage?—*Genesis 2:18–25; Ephesians 5:22–33; Colossians 3:18–20*
2. What is said in the following passages regarding God's attitude toward divorce?—*Matthew 5:31–32; Matthew 19:1–12; 1 Peter 3:1–7*

Discussion Starter
Fire up a conversation with friends by asking this question: What steps can we take to prepare ourselves for healthy, lifetime marriages?

One Step Deeper
Jeremiah 3:1; 1 Corinthians 7:10–16

Go to page 1061 for your next devotional reading.

"How have we wearied him?" you ask.

By saying, "All who do evil are good in the eyes of the LORD, and he is pleased with them" or "Where is the God of justice?"

3 "See, I will send my messenger, who will prepare the way before me. Then suddenly the Lord you are seeking will come to his temple; the messenger of the covenant, whom you desire, will come," says the LORD Almighty.

²But who can endure the day of his coming? Who can stand when he appears? For he will be like a refiner's fire or a launderer's soap. ³He will sit as a refiner and purifier of silver; he will purify the Levites and refine them like gold and silver. Then the LORD will have men who will bring offerings in righteousness, ⁴and the offerings of Judah and Jerusalem will be acceptable to the LORD, as in days gone by, as in former years.

⁵"So I will come near to you for judgment. I will be quick to testify against sorcerers, adulterers and perjurers, against those who defraud laborers of their wages, who oppress the widows and the fatherless, and deprive aliens of justice, but do not fear me," says the LORD Almighty.

Robbing God

⁶"I the LORD do not change. So you, O descendants of Jacob, are not destroyed. ⁷Ever since the time of your forefathers you have turned away from my decrees and have not kept them. Return to me, and I will return to you," says the LORD Almighty.

"But you ask, 'How are we to return?'

⁸"Will a man rob God? Yet you rob me.

"But you ask, 'How do we rob you?'

"In tithes and offerings. ⁹You are under a curse—the whole nation of you—because you are robbing me. ¹⁰Bring the whole tithe into the storehouse, that there may be food in my house. Test me in this," says the LORD Almighty, "and see if I will not throw open the floodgates of heaven and pour out so much blessing that you will not have room enough for it. ¹¹I will prevent pests from devouring your crops, and the vines in your fields will not cast their fruit," says the LORD Almighty. ¹²"Then all the nations will call you blessed, for yours will be a delightful land," says the LORD Almighty.

¹³"You have said harsh things against me," says the LORD.

"Yet you ask, 'What have we said against you?'

¹⁴"You have said, 'It is futile to serve God. What did we gain by carrying out his requirements and going about like mourners before the LORD Almighty? ¹⁵But now we call the arrogant blessed. Certainly the evildoers prosper, and even those who challenge God escape.' "

¹⁶Then those who feared the LORD talked with each other, and the LORD listened and heard. A scroll of remembrance was written in his presence concerning those who feared the LORD and honored his name.

¹⁷"They will be mine," says the LORD Almighty, "in the day when I make up my treasured possession.ᵃ I will spare them, just as in compassion a man spares his son who serves him. ¹⁸And you will again see the distinction between the righteous and the wicked, between those who serve God and those who do not.

The Day of the LORD

4 "Surely the day is coming; it will burn like a furnace. All the arrogant and every evildoer will be stubble, and that day that is coming will set them on fire," says the LORD Almighty. "Not a root or a branch will be left to them. ²But for you who revere my name, the sun of righteousness will rise with healing in its wings. And you will go out and leap like calves released from the stall. ³Then you will trample down the wicked; they will be ashes under the soles of your feet on the day when I do these things," says the LORD Almighty.

⁴"Remember the law of my servant Moses, the decrees and laws I gave him at Horeb for all Israel.

⁵"See, I will send you the prophet Elijah before that great and dreadful day of the LORD comes. ⁶He will turn the hearts of the fathers to their children, and the hearts of the children to their fathers; or else I will come and strike the land with a curse."

ᵃ17 Or Almighty, "my treasured possession, in the day when I act

NEW TESTAMENT

Have you ever read a sequel to a novel without having read the original story? The book of Matthew picks up the story line between the Old and New Testaments, helping us understand how the life and teachings of Jesus build upon what God had promised his people for centuries. The Jewish people in Jesus' day had been waiting for the promised Messiah to come to inaugurate God's kingdom on earth. Matthew draws heavily from Old Testament material, offering proof that Jesus is the One Israel has been waiting for.

MATTHEW

The Genealogy of Jesus

See Ruth 4:18–22; 1 Chronicles 3:10–17; Luke 3:23–38

A record of the genealogy of Jesus Christ the son of David, the son of Abraham:

²Abraham was the father of Isaac,
Isaac the father of Jacob,
Jacob the father of Judah and his brothers,
³Judah the father of Perez and Zerah, whose mother was Tamar,
Perez the father of Hezron,
Hezron the father of Ram,
⁴Ram the father of Amminadab,
Amminadab the father of Nahshon,
Nahshon the father of Salmon,
⁵Salmon the father of Boaz, whose mother was Rahab,
Boaz the father of Obed, whose mother was Ruth,
Obed the father of Jesse,
⁶and Jesse the father of King David.

David was the father of Solomon, whose mother had been Uriah's wife,
⁷Solomon the father of Rehoboam,
Rehoboam the father of Abijah,
Abijah the father of Asa,
⁸Asa the father of Jehoshaphat,
Jehoshaphat the father of Jehoram,

Jehoram the father of Uzziah,
9Uzziah the father of Jotham,
Jotham the father of Ahaz,
Ahaz the father of Hezekiah,
10Hezekiah the father of Manasseh,
Manasseh the father of Amon,
Amon the father of Josiah,
11and Josiah the father of Jeconiah[a] and his brothers at the time of the exile to Babylon.

12After the exile to Babylon:
Jeconiah was the father of Shealtiel,
Shealtiel the father of Zerubbabel,
13Zerubbabel the father of Abiud,
Abiud the father of Eliakim,
Eliakim the father of Azor,
14Azor the father of Zadok,
Zadok the father of Akim,
Akim the father of Eliud,
15Eliud the father of Eleazar,
Eleazar the father of Matthan,
Matthan the father of Jacob,
16and Jacob the father of Joseph, the husband of Mary, of whom was born Jesus, who is called Christ.

17Thus there were fourteen generations in all from Abraham to David, fourteen from David to the exile to Babylon, and fourteen from the exile to the Christ.[b]

The Birth of Jesus Christ

18This is how the birth of Jesus Christ came about: His mother Mary was pledged to be married to Joseph, but before they came together, she was found to be with child through the Holy Spirit. 19Because Joseph her husband was a righteous man and did not want to expose her to public disgrace, he had in mind to divorce her quietly.

20But after he had considered this, an angel of the Lord appeared to him in a dream and said, "Joseph son of David, do not be afraid to take Mary home as your wife, because what is conceived in her is from the Holy Spirit. 21She will give birth to a son, and you are to give him the name Jesus,[c] because he will save his people from their sins."

22All this took place to fulfill what the Lord had said through the prophet: 23"The virgin will be with child and will give birth to a son, and they will call

him Immanuel"[d]—which means, "God with us."

24When Joseph woke up, he did what the angel of the Lord had commanded him and took Mary home as his wife. 25But he had no union with her until she gave birth to a son. And he gave him the name Jesus.

The Visit of the Magi

2 After Jesus was born in Bethlehem in Judea, during the time of King Herod, Magi[e] from the east came to Jerusalem 2and asked, "Where is the one who has been born king of the Jews? We saw his star in the east[f] and have come to worship him."

3When King Herod heard this he was disturbed, and all Jerusalem with him. 4When he had called together all the people's chief priests and teachers of the law, he asked them where the Christ[g] was to be born. 5"In Bethlehem in Judea," they replied, "for this is what the prophet has written:

6" 'But you, Bethlehem, in the land of Judah,
are by no means least among the rulers of Judah;
for out of you will come a ruler
who will be the shepherd of my people Israel.'[h] "

7Then Herod called the Magi secretly and found out from them the exact time the star had appeared. 8He sent them to Bethlehem and said, "Go and make a careful search for the child. As soon as you find him, report to me, so that I too may go and worship him."

9After they had heard the king, they went on their way, and the star they had seen in the east[i] went ahead of them until it stopped over the place where the child was. 10When they saw the star, they were overjoyed. 11On coming to the house, they saw the child with his mother Mary, and they bowed down and worshiped him. Then they opened their treasures and presented him with gifts of gold and of incense and of myrrh. 12And

a11 That is, Jehoiachin; also in verse 12   b17 Or Messiah. "The Christ" (Greek) and "the Messiah" (Hebrew) both mean "the Anointed One."
c21 Jesus is the Greek form of Joshua, which means the LORD saves.   d23 Isaiah 7:14
e1 Traditionally Wise Men   f2 Or star when it rose   g4 Or Messiah   h6 Micah 5:2   i9 Or seen when it rose

having been warned in a dream not to go back to Herod, they returned to their country by another route.

The Escape to Egypt

13When they had gone, an angel of the Lord appeared to Joseph in a dream. "Get up," he said, "take the child and his mother and escape to Egypt. Stay there until I tell you, for Herod is going to search for the child to kill him."

14So he got up, took the child and his mother during the night and left for Egypt, 15where he stayed until the death of Herod. And so was fulfilled what the Lord had said through the prophet: "Out of Egypt I called my son."a

a15 Hosea 11:1

Read Matthew 1:1–25
Key Verse Matthew 1:23

God With Us – Dennis Stokes

Imagine a farmer feeling compassion for the ant colony facing destruction from his tractor's plow. Wanting to finish plowing before the approaching storm comes, the farmer goes over to the ant hill. "Ants, if you just move over here into the woods, you will be safe from the plow." No response. He writes a little note saying the same thing. No response. Finally, he realizes he can only communicate by becoming an ant!

God in Jesus Christ made a transformational leap that was even greater. He left the splendor and safety of heaven to live as a human being within his creation for thirty-three years. Just think, as a man, Jesus revealed truth, justice, wisdom, holiness and love as never before. He touched, healed, walked and talked with people to communicate what real life and the kingdom of God were all about! He was Immanuel, "God with us"!

Yet the miracle of Jesus Christ's incarnation met with seeming tragedy. The very people he came to redeem rejected and killed him. But the Father had a plan. Before his death, Jesus had trained disciples and given them his Word. After he rose from the dead, he sent his Spirit to empower and guide them to go out bearing his name and modeling his love.

I once met Fred, a Jewish man, on a plane trip, and we spent the next twelve days traveling through Israel together. We spent many hours discussing Biblical topics. On the day we parted, I took one last opportunity to share the gospel with him. "I am pondering all these things we have discussed," Fred responded, "but I will never forget how I have seen God in your life as we have traveled together."

God was with us in Jesus Christ; he is now with us in his body, the church. We are God's ambassadors to the world: "And he has committed to us the message of reconciliation. We are therefore Christ's ambassadors, as though God were making his appeal through us" (2 Corinthians 5:19–20). God was with us so that he can work through us!

A Deeper Look
Isaiah 7:14; Colossians 1:27

Go to page 1064 for your next devotional reading.

¹⁶When Herod realized that he had been outwitted by the Magi, he was furious, and he gave orders to kill all the boys in Bethlehem and its vicinity who were two years old and under, in accordance with the time he had learned from the Magi. ¹⁷Then what was said through the prophet Jeremiah was fulfilled:

¹⁸"A voice is heard in Ramah,
　　weeping and great mourning,
Rachel weeping for her children
　　and refusing to be comforted,
because they are no more."ᵃ

The Return to Nazareth

¹⁹After Herod died, an angel of the Lord appeared in a dream to Joseph in Egypt ²⁰and said, "Get up, take the child and his mother and go to the land of Israel, for those who were trying to take the child's life are dead."

²¹So he got up, took the child and his mother and went to the land of Israel. ²²But when he heard that Archelaus was reigning in Judea in place of his father Herod, he was afraid to go there. Having been warned in a dream, he withdrew to the district of Galilee, ²³and he went and lived in a town called Nazareth. So was fulfilled what was said through the prophets: "He will be called a Nazarene."

John the Baptist Prepares the Way

See Mark 1:3–8; Luke 3:2–17

3 In those days John the Baptist came, preaching in the Desert of Judea ²and saying, "Repent, for the kingdom of heaven is near." ³This is he who was spoken of through the prophet Isaiah:

"A voice of one calling in the desert,
'Prepare the way for the Lord,
　　make straight paths for him.' "ᵇ

⁴John's clothes were made of camel's hair, and he had a leather belt around his waist. His food was locusts and wild honey. ⁵People went out to him from Jerusalem and all Judea and the whole region of the Jordan. ⁶Confessing their sins, they were baptized by him in the Jordan River.

⁷But when he saw many of the Pharisees and Sadducees coming to where he was baptizing, he said to them: "You brood of vipers! Who warned you to flee from the coming wrath? ⁸Produce fruit in keeping with repentance. ⁹And do not think you can say to yourselves, 'We

have Abraham as our father.' I tell you that out of these stones God can raise up children for Abraham. ¹⁰The ax is already at the root of the trees, and every tree that does not produce good fruit will be cut down and thrown into the fire.

¹¹"I baptize you withᶜ water for repentance. But after me will come one who is more powerful than I, whose sandals I am not fit to carry. He will baptize you with the Holy Spirit and with fire. ¹²His winnowing fork is in his hand, and he will clear his threshing floor, gathering his wheat into the barn and burning up the chaff with unquenchable fire."

The Baptism of Jesus

See Mark 1:9–11; Luke 3:21–22; John 1:31–34

¹³Then Jesus came from Galilee to the Jordan to be baptized by John. ¹⁴But John tried to deter him, saying, "I need to be baptized by you, and do you come to me?"

¹⁵Jesus replied, "Let it be so now; it is proper for us to do this to fulfill all righteousness." Then John consented.

¹⁶As soon as Jesus was baptized, he went up out of the water. At that moment heaven was opened, and he saw the Spirit of God descending like a dove and lighting on him. ¹⁷And a voice from heaven said, "This is my Son, whom I love; with him I am well pleased."

The Temptation of Jesus

See Mark 1:12–13; Luke 4:1–13

4 Then Jesus was led by the Spirit into the desert to be tempted by the devil. ²After fasting forty days and forty nights, he was hungry. ³The tempter came to him and said, "If you are the Son of God, tell these stones to become bread."

⁴Jesus answered, "It is written: 'Man does not live on bread alone, but on every word that comes from the mouth of God.'ᵈ "

⁵Then the devil took him to the holy city and had him stand on the highest point of the temple. ⁶"If you are the Son of God," he said, "throw yourself down. For it is written:

" 'He will command his angels
　　concerning you,
　　and they will lift you up in their
　　　hands,

ᵃ18 Jer. 31:15　　ᵇ3 Isaiah 40:3　　ᶜ11 Or in
ᵈ4 Deut. 8:3

so that you will not strike your foot against a stone.'*a* "

7Jesus answered him, "It is also written: 'Do not put the Lord your God to the test.'*b* "

8Again, the devil took him to a very high mountain and showed him all the kingdoms of the world and their splendor. 9"All this I will give you," he said, "if you will bow down and worship me."

10Jesus said to him, "Away from me, Satan! For it is written: 'Worship the Lord your God, and serve him only.'*c* "

11Then the devil left him, and angels came and attended him.

Jesus Begins to Preach

12When Jesus heard that John had been put in prison, he returned to Galilee. 13Leaving Nazareth, he went and lived in Capernaum, which was by the lake in the area of Zebulun and Naphtali— 14to fulfill what was said through the prophet Isaiah:

15"Land of Zebulun and land of
      Naphtali,
   the way to the sea, along the
      Jordan,
   Galilee of the Gentiles—
16the people living in darkness
   have seen a great light;
on those living in the land of the
      shadow of death
   a light has dawned."*d*

17From that time on Jesus began to preach, "Repent, for the kingdom of heaven is near."

The Calling of the First Disciples

See Mark 1:16–20; Luke 5:2–11; John 1:35–42

18As Jesus was walking beside the Sea of Galilee, he saw two brothers, Simon called Peter and his brother Andrew. They were casting a net into the lake, for they were fishermen. 19"Come, follow me," Jesus said, "and I will make you fishers of men." 20At once they left their nets and followed him.

21Going on from there, he saw two other brothers, James son of Zebedee and his brother John. They were in a boat with their father Zebedee, preparing their nets. Jesus called them, 22and immediately they left the boat and their father and followed him.

Jesus Heals the Sick

23Jesus went throughout Galilee, teaching in their synagogues, preaching the good news of the kingdom, and healing every disease and sickness among the people. 24News about him spread all over Syria, and people brought to him all who were ill with various diseases, those suffering severe pain, the demon-possessed, those having seizures, and the paralyzed, and he healed them. 25Large crowds from Galilee, the Decapolis,*e* Jerusalem, Judea and the region across the Jordan followed him.

The Beatitudes

See Luke 6:20–23

5 Now when he saw the crowds, he went up on a mountainside and sat down. His disciples came to him, 2and he began to teach them, saying:

3"Blessed are the poor in spirit,
   for theirs is the kingdom of
      heaven.
4Blessed are those who mourn,
   for they will be comforted.
5Blessed are the meek,
   for they will inherit the earth.
6Blessed are those who hunger and
      thirst for righteousness,
   for they will be filled.
7Blessed are the merciful,
   for they will be shown mercy.
8Blessed are the pure in heart,
   for they will see God.
9Blessed are the peacemakers,
   for they will be called sons of God.
10Blessed are those who are persecuted
      because of righteousness,
   for theirs is the kingdom of
      heaven.

11"Blessed are you when people insult you, persecute you and falsely say all kinds of evil against you because of me. 12Rejoice and be glad, because great is your reward in heaven, for in the same way they persecuted the prophets who were before you.

Salt and Light

13"You are the salt of the earth. But if the salt loses its saltiness, how can it be made salty again? It is no longer good for

a6 Psalm 91:11,12   *b7* Deut. 6:16
c10 Deut. 6:13   *d16* Isaiah 9:1,2   *e25* That is, the Ten Cities

anything, except to be thrown out and trampled by men.

14"You are the light of the world. A city on a hill cannot be hidden. 15Neither do people light a lamp and put it under a bowl. Instead they put it on its stand, and it gives light to everyone in the house. 16In the same way, let your light shine before men, that they may see your good deeds and praise your Father in heaven.

The Fulfillment of the Law

17"Do not think that I have come to abolish the Law or the Prophets; I have not come to abolish them but to fulfill them. 18I tell you the truth, until heaven and earth disappear, not the smallest letter, not the least stroke of a pen, will by

any means disappear from the Law until everything is accomplished. 19Anyone who breaks one of the least of these commandments and teaches others to do the same will be called least in the kingdom of heaven, but whoever practices and teaches these commands will be called great in the kingdom of heaven. 20For I tell you that unless your righteousness surpasses that of the Pharisees and the teachers of the law, you will certainly not enter the kingdom of heaven.

Murder

21"You have heard that it was said to the people long ago, 'Do not murder,ᵃ

a21 Exodus 20:13

TUESDAY

Read *Matthew 4:1–25*
Key Verse *Matthew 4:19*

Fishers of Men – Kathy Brackman

I don't want to go, Lord. Surely you can't mean me. I'm not the type—even for a short-term "missionary experience." They don't even have hot showers over there! And Lord, it's so dirty. How could I live there?

" 'Come follow me,' Jesus said, 'and I will make you fishers of men' " (Matthew 4:19).

All right. I know you want me to follow you and learn from you how to love people and tell them about you. Maybe I'll go later when it's convenient and I have my life more together.

"At once they left their nets and followed him" (Matthew 4:20).

So maybe now *is* a good time. But I'll have to leave so many friends and family and everything familiar.

"Though [Jesus Christ] was rich, yet for your sakes he became poor, so that you through his poverty might become rich" (2 Corinthians 8:9).

You're right, Lord. You've given me your riches, and now I have the opportunity to become poor by leaving the things and relationships that I value. But do I really have the right personality or abilities? What about making it in another country? Can I learn a new language? Will I be able to relate to the people?

"Not that we are competent in ourselves to claim anything for ourselves, but our competence comes from God" (2 Corinthians 3:5).

I see. I don't have to do it on my own. *You* will enable me to reach people with your truth. And *you* will teach me to "fish for men" as I follow you. Help me, Lord!

A Deeper Look
Exodus 4:10–11; John 15:16

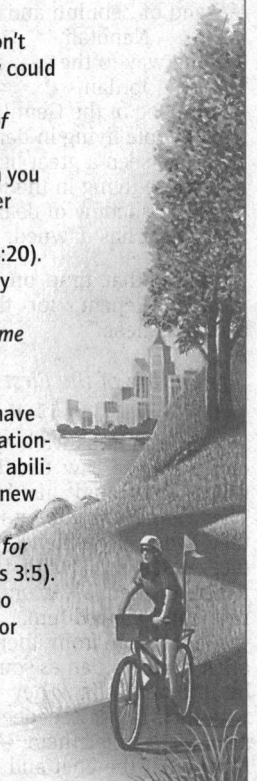

Go to page 1065 for your next devotional reading.

and anyone who murders will be subject to judgment.' ²²But I tell you that anyone who is angry with his brother*a* will be subject to judgment. Again, anyone who says to his brother, 'Raca,*b*' is answerable to the Sanhedrin. But anyone who says, 'You fool!' will be in danger of the fire of hell.

²³"Therefore, if you are offering your gift at the altar and there remember that your brother has something against you, ²⁴leave your gift there in front of the altar. First go and be reconciled to your brother; then come and offer your gift.

²⁵"Settle matters quickly with your adversary who is taking you to court. Do it while you are still with him on the way, or he may hand you over to the judge, and the judge may hand you over to the officer, and you may be thrown into prison. ²⁶I tell you the truth, you will not get out until you have paid the last penny.*c*

Adultery

²⁷"You have heard that it was said, 'Do not commit adultery.'*d* ²⁸But I tell you that anyone who looks at a woman lustfully has already committed adultery with her in his heart. ²⁹If your right eye causes you to sin, gouge it out and throw it away. It is better for you to lose one

---

a22 Some manuscripts *brother without cause*
b22 An Aramaic term of contempt   *c26* Greek *kodrantes*   *d27* Exodus 20:14

WEDNESDAY

Read Matthew 5:1–48
Key Verse Matthew 5:16

Shine Like Stars – Robert M. Bertrand

Several glow-in-the-dark stars adorn the ceiling of my son's bedroom. Each night when the light is turned off, the ceiling glows like the night sky. But if those stars have had limited exposure to light during the day, they're barely visible against the dark ceiling.

Jesus declares that as Christians we are the "light of the world" and that we are to "let [our] light shine before men, that they may see [our] good deeds and praise [our] Father in heaven" (Matthew 5:14,16).

But like the stars in my son's room, our light will be dim and barely noticeable if we are not continually exposed to the light of Jesus. Through prayer and studying the Word, we begin to glow with his light—"I am the light of the world. Whoever follows me will never walk in darkness, but will have the light of life" (John 8:12).

An interesting thing about those stars is that the more there are, the brighter the room will be. If there were only one star, it would still be noticeable, but not as awe-inspiring as a whole "sky" full. We shine brighter in the world when we live and work and witness shoulder to shoulder with other Christians in the body. Each of us is a part of the body; working together we reflect Jesus Christ more completely to others.

Consider letting your light shine more brightly by spending consistent time alone with God and serving him alongside other believers, "so that you may become blameless and pure, children of God without fault in a crooked and depraved generation, in which you shine like stars in the universe as you hold out the word of life" (Philippians 2:15–16).

A Deeper Look
Daniel 12:3; 1 Peter 2:12

Go to page 1068 for your next devotional reading.

part of your body than for your whole body to be thrown into hell. ³⁰And if your right hand causes you to sin, cut it off and throw it away. It is better for you to lose one part of your body than for your whole body to go into hell.

Divorce

³¹"It has been said, 'Anyone who divorces his wife must give her a certificate of divorce.'ᵃ ³²But I tell you that anyone who divorces his wife, except for marital unfaithfulness, causes her to become an adulteress, and anyone who marries the divorced woman commits adultery.

Oaths

³³"Again, you have heard that it was said to the people long ago, 'Do not break your oath, but keep the oaths you have made to the Lord.' ³⁴But I tell you, Do not swear at all: either by heaven, for it is God's throne; ³⁵or by the earth, for it is his footstool; or by Jerusalem, for it is the city of the Great King. ³⁶And do not swear by your head, for you cannot make even one hair white or black. ³⁷Simply let your 'Yes' be 'Yes,' and your 'No,' 'No'; anything beyond this comes from the evil one.

An Eye for an Eye

³⁸"You have heard that it was said, 'Eye for eye, and tooth for tooth.'ᵇ ³⁹But I tell you, Do not resist an evil person. If someone strikes you on the right cheek, turn to him the other also. ⁴⁰And if someone wants to sue you and take your tunic, let him have your cloak as well. ⁴¹If someone forces you to go one mile, go with him two miles. ⁴²Give to the one who asks you, and do not turn away from the one who wants to borrow from you.

Love for Enemies

⁴³"You have heard that it was said, 'Love your neighborᶜ and hate your enemy.' ⁴⁴But I tell you: Love your enemiesᵈ and pray for those who persecute you, ⁴⁵that you may be sons of your Father in heaven. He causes his sun to rise on the evil and the good, and sends rain on the righteous and the unrighteous. ⁴⁶If you love those who love you, what reward will you get? Are not even the tax collectors doing that? ⁴⁷And if you greet only your brothers, what are you doing more than others? Do not even pagans

do that? ⁴⁸Be perfect, therefore, as your heavenly Father is perfect.

Giving to the Needy

6 "Be careful not to do your 'acts of righteousness' before men, to be seen by them. If you do, you will have no reward from your Father in heaven.

²"So when you give to the needy, do not announce it with trumpets, as the hypocrites do in the synagogues and on the streets, to be honored by men. I tell you the truth, they have received their reward in full. ³But when you give to the needy, do not let your left hand know what your right hand is doing, ⁴so that your giving may be in secret. Then your Father, who sees what is done in secret, will reward you.

Prayer

See Luke 11:2–4

⁵"And when you pray, do not be like the hypocrites, for they love to pray standing in the synagogues and on the street corners to be seen by men. I tell you the truth, they have received their reward in full. ⁶But when you pray, go into your room, close the door and pray to your Father, who is unseen. Then your Father, who sees what is done in secret, will reward you. ⁷And when you pray, do not keep on babbling like pagans, for they think they will be heard because of their many words. ⁸Do not be like them, for your Father knows what you need before you ask him.

⁹"This, then, is how you should pray:

---

a31 Deut. 24:1   *b38* Exodus 21:24; Lev. 24:20; Deut. 19:21   *c43* Lev. 19:18   *d44* Some late manuscripts *enemies, bless those who curse you, do good to those who hate you*

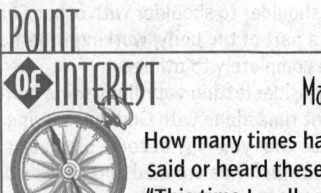

POINT OF INTEREST

Matthew 5:37

How many times have you said or heard these words: "This time I really mean it!" Oaths that attempt to prove our sincerity should be unnecessary if we have consistently kept our word. Jesus says that, whatever our reason, such oaths are unnecessary; there is no substitute for a simple, honest "yes" or "no."

" 'Our Father in heaven,
  hallowed be your name,
10your kingdom come,
  your will be done
    on earth as it is in heaven.
11Give us today our daily bread.
12Forgive us our debts,
    as we also have forgiven our
      debtors.
13And lead us not into temptation,
  but deliver us from the evil one.*a*'

14For if you forgive men when they sin against you, your heavenly Father will also forgive you. 15But if you do not forgive men their sins, your Father will not forgive your sins.

Fasting

16"When you fast, do not look somber as the hypocrites do, for they disfigure their faces to show men they are fasting. I tell you the truth, they have received their reward in full. 17But when you fast, put oil on your head and wash your face, 18so that it will not be obvious to men that you are fasting, but only to your Father, who is unseen; and your Father, who sees what is done in secret, will reward you.

Treasures in Heaven

19"Do not store up for yourselves treasures on earth, where moth and rust destroy, and where thieves break in and steal. 20But store up for yourselves treasures in heaven, where moth and rust do not destroy, and where thieves do not break in and steal. 21For where your treasure is, there your heart will be also.

22"The eye is the lamp of the body. If your eyes are good, your whole body will be full of light. 23But if your eyes are bad, your whole body will be full of darkness. If then the light within you is darkness, how great is that darkness!

24"No one can serve two masters. Either he will hate the one and love the other, or he will be devoted to the one and despise the other. You cannot serve both God and Money.

Do Not Worry

See Luke 12:22–31

25"Therefore I tell you, do not worry about your life, what you will eat or drink; or about your body, what you will wear. Is not life more important than food, and the body more important than

clothes? 26Look at the birds of the air; they do not sow or reap or store away in barns, and yet your heavenly Father feeds them. Are you not much more valuable than they? 27Who of you by worrying can add a single hour to his life*b*?

28"And why do you worry about clothes? See how the lilies of the field grow. They do not labor or spin. 29Yet I tell you that not even Solomon in all his splendor was dressed like one of these. 30If that is how God clothes the grass of the field, which is here today and tomorrow is thrown into the fire, will he not much more clothe you, O you of little faith? 31So do not worry, saying, 'What shall we eat?' or 'What shall we drink?' or 'What shall we wear?' 32For the pagans run after all these things, and your heavenly Father knows that you need them. 33But seek first his kingdom and his righteousness, and all these things will be given to you as well. 34Therefore do not worry about tomorrow, for tomorrow will worry about itself. Each day has enough trouble of its own.

Judging Others

See Luke 6:41–42

7 "Do not judge, or you too will be judged. 2For in the same way you judge others, you will be judged, and with the measure you use, it will be measured to you.

3"Why do you look at the speck of sawdust in your brother's eye and pay no attention to the plank in your own eye? 4How can you say to your brother, 'Let me take the speck out of your eye,' when all the time there is a plank in your own eye? 5You hypocrite, first take the plank out of your own eye, and then you will see clearly to remove the speck from your brother's eye.

6"Do not give dogs what is sacred; do not throw your pearls to pigs. If you do, they may trample them under their feet, and then turn and tear you to pieces.

Ask, Seek, Knock

See Luke 11:9–13

7"Ask and it will be given to you; seek and you will find; knock and the door will be opened to you. 8For everyone who asks receives; he who seeks finds; and

*a*13 Or *from evil*; some late manuscripts *one, / for yours is the kingdom and the power and the glory forever. Amen.*   *b*27 Or *single cubit to his height* to him who knocks, the door will be opened.

9"Which of you, if his son asks for bread, will give him a stone? 10Or if he asks for a fish, will give him a snake? 11If you, then, though you are evil, know how to give good gifts to your children, how much more will your Father in heaven give good gifts to those who ask him! 12So in everything, do to others what you would have them do to you, for this sums up the Law and the Prophets.

The Narrow and Wide Gates

13"Enter through the narrow gate. For wide is the gate and broad is the road that leads to destruction, and many enter through it. 14But small is the gate and narrow the road that leads to life, and only a few find it.

A Tree and Its Fruit

15"Watch out for false prophets. They come to you in sheep's clothing, but inwardly they are ferocious wolves. 16By their fruit you will recognize them. Do people pick grapes from thornbushes, or figs from thistles? 17Likewise every good tree bears good fruit, but a bad tree bears bad fruit. 18A good tree cannot bear bad fruit, and a bad tree cannot bear good fruit. 19Every tree that does not bear good fruit is cut down and thrown into the fire. 20Thus, by their fruit you will recognize them.

21"Not everyone who says to me, 'Lord, Lord,' will enter the kingdom of heaven, but only he who does the will of my Father who is in heaven. 22Many will say to me on that day, 'Lord, Lord, did we not prophesy in your name, and in

---

THURSDAY

Read Matthew 6:25–34
Key Verse Matthew 6:33

Seeking Christ First — Colette Magoon

How did you decide what to do last weekend? Did you consider what it would cost? What others would think of you? How fun and exciting it would be? How comfortable you would be? Who else would be going? How much time it would take?

We can usually tell what's most important to us by examining the values that control our decisions. If we consider money important, then how much something costs is what we consider first. If we're focused on getting a job, then we'll do what will look good on a résumé. And if we're most concerned about who we are with, then we'll go where there are people we like.

While we tend to worry about cost, impressions, relationships, comfort and time, Jesus seems to be telling us to hold all these things in an open hand and to travel lightly toward the kingdom. He tells us not to worry about making our way in the world but rather to "seek first his kingdom and his righteousness." How do we do that? If we're trying to follow Jesus, the questions we need to ask ourselves are: "Is this something that God really wants me to do? Does it fit within his priorities?"

Reviewing your decision-making process is a great way to discover whether anything in your life is coming ahead of Jesus Christ. This weekend, put God's kingdom and righteousness first in your decisions. You can't lose, because he also says, "and all these things will be given to you as well."

A Deeper Look
Joshua 24:15; Psalm 37:4–6; Luke 9:23–25

Go to page 1072 for your next devotional reading.

your name drive out demons and perform many miracles?' 23Then I will tell them plainly, 'I never knew you. Away from me, you evildoers!'

The Wise and Foolish Builders
See Luke 6:47–49

24"Therefore everyone who hears these words of mine and puts them into practice is like a wise man who built his house on the rock. 25The rain came down, the streams rose, and the winds blew and beat against that house; yet it did not fall, because it had its foundation on the rock. 26But everyone who hears these words of mine and does not put them into practice is like a foolish man who built his house on sand. 27The rain came down, the streams rose, and the winds blew and beat against that house, and it fell with a great crash."

28When Jesus had finished saying these things, the crowds were amazed at his teaching, 29because he taught as one who had authority, and not as their teachers of the law.

The Man With Leprosy
See Mark 1:40–44; Luke 5:12–14

8 When he came down from the mountainside, large crowds followed him. 2A man with leprosy*a* came and knelt before him and said, "Lord, if you are willing, you can make me clean."

3Jesus reached out his hand and touched the man. "I am willing," he said. "Be clean!" Immediately he was cured*b* of his leprosy. 4Then Jesus said to him, "See that you don't tell anyone. But go, show yourself to the priest and offer the gift Moses commanded, as a testimony to them."

The Faith of the Centurion
See Luke 7:1–10

5When Jesus had entered Capernaum, a centurion came to him, asking for help. 6"Lord," he said, "my servant lies at home paralyzed and in terrible suffering."

7Jesus said to him, "I will go and heal him."

8The centurion replied, "Lord, I do not deserve to have you come under my roof. But just say the word, and my servant will be healed. 9For I myself am a man under authority, with soldiers under me. I tell this one, 'Go,' and he goes; and that

one, 'Come,' and he comes. I say to my servant, 'Do this,' and he does it."

10When Jesus heard this, he was astonished and said to those following him, "I tell you the truth, I have not found anyone in Israel with such great faith. 11I say to you that many will come from the east and the west, and will take their places at the feast with Abraham, Isaac and Jacob in the kingdom of heaven. 12But the subjects of the kingdom will be thrown outside, into the darkness, where there will be weeping and gnashing of teeth."

13Then Jesus said to the centurion, "Go! It will be done just as you believed it would." And his servant was healed at that very hour.

Jesus Heals Many
See Mark 1:29–34; Luke 4:38–41

14When Jesus came into Peter's house, he saw Peter's mother-in-law lying in bed with a fever. 15He touched her hand and the fever left her, and she got up and began to wait on him.

16When evening came, many who were demon-possessed were brought to him, and he drove out the spirits with a word and healed all the sick. 17This was to fulfill what was spoken through the prophet Isaiah:

"He took up our infirmities
    and carried our diseases."*c*

The Cost of Following Jesus
See Luke 9:57–60

18When Jesus saw the crowd around him, he gave orders to cross to the other side of the lake. 19Then a teacher of the law came to him and said, "Teacher, I will follow you wherever you go."

20Jesus replied, "Foxes have holes and birds of the air have nests, but the Son of Man has no place to lay his head." 21Another disciple said to him, "Lord, first let me go and bury my father."

22But Jesus told him, "Follow me, and let the dead bury their own dead."

Jesus Calms the Storm
See Mark 4:36–41; Luke 8:22–25

23Then he got into the boat and his disciples followed him. 24Without warning, a furious storm came up on the lake,

a2 The Greek word was used for various diseases affecting the skin—not necessarily leprosy. *b3* Greek *made clean*   *c17* Isaiah 53:4

so that the waves swept over the boat. But Jesus was sleeping. 25The disciples went and woke him, saying, "Lord, save us! We're going to drown!"

26He replied, "You of little faith, why are you so afraid?" Then he got up and rebuked the winds and the waves, and it was completely calm.

27The men were amazed and asked, "What kind of man is this? Even the winds and the waves obey him!"

The Healing of Two Demon-possessed Men
See Mark 5:1–17; Luke 8:26–37

28When he arrived at the other side in the region of the Gadarenes,a two demon-possessed men coming from the tombs met him. They were so violent that no one could pass that way. 29"What do you want with us, Son of God?" they shouted. "Have you come here to torture us before the appointed time?"

30Some distance from them a large herd of pigs was feeding. 31The demons begged Jesus, "If you drive us out, send us into the herd of pigs."

32He said to them, "Go!" So they came out and went into the pigs, and the whole herd rushed down the steep bank into the lake and died in the water. 33Those tending the pigs ran off, went into the town and reported all this, including what had happened to the demon-possessed men. 34Then the whole town went out to meet Jesus. And when they saw him, they pleaded with him to leave their region.

Jesus Heals a Paralytic
See Mark 2:3–12; Luke 5:18–26

9 Jesus stepped into a boat, crossed over and came to his own town. 2Some men brought to him a paralytic, lying on a mat. When Jesus saw their faith, he said to the paralytic, "Take heart, son; your sins are forgiven."

3At this, some of the teachers of the law said to themselves, "This fellow is blaspheming!"

4Knowing their thoughts, Jesus said, "Why do you entertain evil thoughts in your hearts? 5Which is easier: to say, 'Your sins are forgiven,' or to say, 'Get up and walk'? 6But so that you may know that the Son of Man has authority on earth to forgive sins . . . ." Then he said to the paralytic, "Get up, take your mat and go home." 7And the man got up and went home. 8When the crowd saw this,

they were filled with awe; and they praised God, who had given such authority to men.

The Calling of Matthew
See Mark 2:14–17; Luke 5:27–32

9As Jesus went on from there, he saw a man named Matthew sitting at the tax collector's booth. "Follow me," he told him, and Matthew got up and followed him.

10While Jesus was having dinner at Matthew's house, many tax collectors and "sinners" came and ate with him and his disciples. 11When the Pharisees saw this, they asked his disciples, "Why does your teacher eat with tax collectors and 'sinners'?"

12On hearing this, Jesus said, "It is not the healthy who need a doctor, but the sick. 13But go and learn what this means: 'I desire mercy, not sacrifice.'b For I have not come to call the righteous, but sinners."

Jesus Questioned About Fasting
See Mark 2:18–22; Luke 5:33–39

14Then John's disciples came and asked him, "How is it that we and the Pharisees fast, but your disciples do not fast?"

15Jesus answered, "How can the guests of the bridegroom mourn while he is with them? The time will come when the bridegroom will be taken from them; then they will fast.

16"No one sews a patch of unshrunk cloth on an old garment, for the patch will pull away from the garment, making the tear worse. 17Neither do men pour new wine into old wineskins. If they do, the skins will burst, the wine will run out and the wineskins will be ruined. No, they pour new wine into new wineskins, and both are preserved."

A Dead Girl and a Sick Woman
See Mark 5:22–43; Luke 8:41–56

18While he was saying this, a ruler came and knelt before him and said, "My daughter has just died. But come and put your hand on her, and she will live." 19Jesus got up and went with him, and so did his disciples.

20Just then a woman who had been subject to bleeding for twelve years came

---

a28 Some manuscripts *Gergesenes*; others *Gerasenes*
b13 Hosea 6:6

up behind him and touched the edge of his cloak. ²¹She said to herself, "If I only touch his cloak, I will be healed."

²²Jesus turned and saw her. "Take heart, daughter," he said, "your faith has healed you." And the woman was healed from that moment.

²³When Jesus entered the ruler's house and saw the flute players and the noisy crowd, ²⁴he said, "Go away. The girl is not dead but asleep." But they laughed at him. ²⁵After the crowd had been put outside, he went in and took the girl by the hand, and she got up. ²⁶News of this spread through all that region.

Jesus Heals the Blind and Mute

²⁷As Jesus went on from there, two blind men followed him, calling out, "Have mercy on us, Son of David!"

²⁸When he had gone indoors, the blind men came to him, and he asked them, "Do you believe that I am able to do this?"

"Yes, Lord," they replied.

²⁹Then he touched their eyes and said, "According to your faith will it be done to you"; ³⁰and their sight was restored. Jesus warned them sternly, "See that no one knows about this." ³¹But they went out and spread the news about him all over that region.

³²While they were going out, a man who was demon-possessed and could not talk was brought to Jesus. ³³And when the demon was driven out, the man who had been mute spoke. The crowd was amazed and said, "Nothing like this has ever been seen in Israel."

³⁴But the Pharisees said, "It is by the prince of demons that he drives out demons."

The Workers Are Few

³⁵Jesus went through all the towns and villages, teaching in their synagogues, preaching the good news of the kingdom and healing every disease and sickness. ³⁶When he saw the crowds, he had compassion on them, because they were harassed and helpless, like sheep without a shepherd. ³⁷Then he said to his disciples, "The harvest is plentiful but the workers are few. ³⁸Ask the Lord of the harvest, therefore, to send out workers into his harvest field."

Jesus Sends Out the Twelve

See Mark 6:8–11; Luke 9:3–5; 10:4–12

10 He called his twelve disciples to him and gave them authority to drive out evil*a* spirits and to heal every disease and sickness.

²These are the names of the twelve apostles: first, Simon (who is called Peter) and his brother Andrew; James son of Zebedee, and his brother John; ³Philip and Bartholomew; Thomas and Matthew the tax collector; James son of Alphaeus, and Thaddaeus; ⁴Simon the Zealot and Judas Iscariot, who betrayed him.

⁵These twelve Jesus sent out with the following instructions: "Do not go among the Gentiles or enter any town of the Samaritans. ⁶Go rather to the lost sheep of Israel. ⁷As you go, preach this message: 'The kingdom of heaven is near.' ⁸Heal the sick, raise the dead, cleanse those who have leprosy,*b* drive out demons. Freely you have received, freely give. ⁹Do not take along any gold or silver or copper in your belts; ¹⁰take no bag for the journey, or extra tunic, or sandals or a staff; for the worker is worth his keep.

¹¹"Whatever town or village you enter, search for some worthy person there and stay at his house until you leave. ¹²As you enter the home, give it your greeting. ¹³If the home is deserving, let your peace rest on it; if it is not, let your peace return to you. ¹⁴If anyone will not welcome you or listen to your words, shake the dust off your feet when you leave that home or town. ¹⁵I tell you the truth, it will be more bearable for Sodom and Gomorrah on the day of judgment than for that town. ¹⁶I am sending you out like sheep among wolves. Therefore be as shrewd as snakes and as innocent as doves.

¹⁷"Be on your guard against men; they will hand you over to the local councils and flog you in their synagogues. ¹⁸On my account you will be brought before governors and kings as witnesses to them and to the Gentiles. ¹⁹But when they arrest you, do not worry about what to say or how to say it. At that time you will be given what to say, ²⁰for it will not be you speaking, but the Spirit of your Father speaking through you.

²¹"Brother will betray brother to death, and a father his child; children will

---

a1 Greek *unclean*   *b8* The Greek word was used for various diseases affecting the skin—not necessarily leprosy.

rebel against their parents and have them put to death. ²²All men will hate you because of me, but he who stands firm to the end will be saved. ²³When you are persecuted in one place, flee to another. I tell you the truth, you will not finish going through the cities of Israel before the Son of Man comes.

²⁴"A student is not above his teacher, nor a servant above his master. ²⁵It is enough for the student to be like his teacher, and the servant like his master. If the head of the house has been called Beelzebub,ᵃ how much more the members of his household!

²⁶"So do not be afraid of them. There is nothing concealed that will not be disclosed, or hidden that will not be made known. ²⁷What I tell you in the dark, speak in the daylight; what is whispered in your ear, proclaim from the roofs. ²⁸Do not be afraid of those who kill the body but cannot kill the soul. Rather, be afraid of the One who can destroy both soul and body in hell. ²⁹Are not two sparrows sold for a pennyᵇ? Yet not one of them will fall to the ground apart from the will of

ᵃ25 Greek *Beezeboul* or *Beelzeboul*　　ᵇ29 Greek *an assarion*

FRIDAY

Read Matthew 9:1–38
Key Verses Matthew 9:36–38

Simple Multiplication – Don Allen

As I watched hundreds of other students milling about on the floor below the balcony where I was studying, I wondered, "How can I possibly tell all these people about Jesus Christ?" When I took the whole job on my own shoulders, it seemed just too overwhelming; my time seemed too limited.

But then the Lord reminded me of Matthew 9:37–38: "The harvest is plentiful but the workers are few. Ask the Lord of the harvest, therefore, to send out workers into his harvest field." It occurred to me that I didn't need to reach all these students but to ask the Lord to raise up others who would reach them—and then trust him to do it. Over the years, this truth has shaped the way I view ministry.

Think of it this way. If alone I led ten people to Christ every day for the next thirty years, I would see 109,500 people come to Christ. However, if I led one person to Christ in a year, taught that one how to walk with him and tell others about him, the next year we could both lead someone else to Christ. Then those two could be discipled to the point of each leading someone to Christ. Soon two becomes four . . . four becomes eight . . . and so on. If this process continued for thirty years, the result would be 536,870,912 followers of Jesus Christ! All from one life multiplied by an extraordinary God.

Jesus has a great, compassionate heart for those who don't know him. Maybe some of them are your classmates, your family, the people you work with. Ask God to send out bold laborers among them, and ask him to show you where you fit in. Are you a "Paul" who could teach others or a "Timothy" who is willing to learn? By God's grace, *you* could have a sprawling spiritual "family tree."

A Deeper Look
Joel 1:3; 2 Corinthians 5:18–21

Go to page 1077 for your next devotional reading.

your Father. ³⁰And even the very hairs of your head are all numbered. ³¹So don't be afraid; you are worth more than many sparrows.

³²"Whoever acknowledges me before men, I will also acknowledge him before my Father in heaven. ³³But whoever disowns me before men, I will disown him before my Father in heaven.

³⁴"Do not suppose that I have come to bring peace to the earth. I did not come to bring peace, but a sword. ³⁵For I have come to turn

" 'a man against his father,
    a daughter against her mother,
    a daughter-in-law against her
        mother-in-law—
³⁶   a man's enemies will be the
      members of his own
      household.'ᵃ

³⁷"Anyone who loves his father or mother more than me is not worthy of me; anyone who loves his son or daughter more than me is not worthy of me; ³⁸and anyone who does not take his cross and follow me is not worthy of me. ³⁹Whoever finds his life will lose it, and whoever loses his life for my sake will find it.

⁴⁰"He who receives you receives me, and he who receives me receives the one who sent me. ⁴¹Anyone who receives a prophet because he is a prophet will receive a prophet's reward, and anyone who receives a righteous man because he is a righteous man will receive a righteous man's reward. ⁴²And if anyone gives even a cup of cold water to one of these little ones because he is my disciple, I tell you the truth, he will certainly not lose his reward."

Jesus and John the Baptist

See Luke 7:18–35

11 After Jesus had finished instructing his twelve disciples, he went on from there to teach and preach in the towns of Galilee.ᵇ

²When John heard in prison what Christ was doing, he sent his disciples ³to ask him, "Are you the one who was to come, or should we expect someone else?"

⁴Jesus replied, "Go back and report to John what you hear and see: ⁵The blind receive sight, the lame walk, those who have leprosyᶜ are cured, the deaf hear, the dead are raised, and the good news is preached to the poor. ⁶Blessed is the man who does not fall away on account of me."

⁷As John's disciples were leaving, Jesus began to speak to the crowd about John: "What did you go out into the desert to see? A reed swayed by the wind? ⁸If not, what did you go out to see? A man dressed in fine clothes? No, those who wear fine clothes are in kings' palaces. ⁹Then what did you go out to see? A prophet? Yes, I tell you, and more than a prophet. ¹⁰This is the one about whom it is written:

" 'I will send my messenger ahead of
    you,
   who will prepare your way before
    you.'ᵈ

¹¹I tell you the truth: Among those born of women there has not risen anyone greater than John the Baptist; yet he who is least in the kingdom of heaven is greater than he. ¹²From the days of John the Baptist until now, the kingdom of heaven has been forcefully advancing, and forceful men lay hold of it. ¹³For all the Prophets and the Law prophesied until John. ¹⁴And if you are willing to accept it, he is the Elijah who was to come. ¹⁵He who has ears, let him hear.

¹⁶"To what can I compare this generation? They are like children sitting in the marketplaces and calling out to others:

¹⁷" 'We played the flute for you,
    and you did not dance;
  we sang a dirge,
    and you did not mourn.'

¹⁸For John came neither eating nor drinking, and they say, 'He has a demon.' ¹⁹The Son of Man came eating and drinking, and they say, 'Here is a glutton and a drunkard, a friend of tax collectors and "sinners." ' But wisdom is proved right by her actions."

Woe on Unrepentant Cities

See Luke 10:13–15

²⁰Then Jesus began to denounce the cities in which most of his miracles had been performed, because they did not repent. ²¹"Woe to you, Korazin! Woe to you, Bethsaida! If the miracles that were performed in you had been performed in

---

ᵃ36 Micah 7:6   ᵇ1 Greek *in their towns*
ᶜ5 The Greek word was used for various diseases affecting the skin—not necessarily leprosy.
ᵈ10 Mal. 3:1

Tyre and Sidon, they would have repented long ago in sackcloth and ashes. ²²But I tell you, it will be more bearable for Tyre and Sidon on the day of judgment than for you. ²³And you, Capernaum, will you be lifted up to the skies? No, you will go down to the depths.*ᵃ* If the miracles that were performed in you had been performed in Sodom, it would have remained to this day. ²⁴But I tell you that it will be more bearable for Sodom on the day of judgment than for you."

Rest for the Weary

See Luke 10:21–22

²⁵At that time Jesus said, "I praise you, Father, Lord of heaven and earth, because you have hidden these things from the wise and learned, and revealed them to little children. ²⁶Yes, Father, for this was your good pleasure.

²⁷"All things have been committed to me by my Father. No one knows the Son except the Father, and no one knows the Father except the Son and those to whom the Son chooses to reveal him.

²⁸"Come to me, all you who are weary and burdened, and I will give you rest. ²⁹Take my yoke upon you and learn from me, for I am gentle and humble in heart, and you will find rest for your souls. ³⁰For my yoke is easy and my burden is light."

Lord of the Sabbath

See Mark 2:23 — 3:6; Luke 6:1–11

12 At that time Jesus went through the grainfields on the Sabbath. His disciples were hungry and began to pick some heads of grain and eat them. ²When the Pharisees saw this, they said to him, "Look! Your disciples are doing what is unlawful on the Sabbath."

³He answered, "Haven't you read what David did when he and his companions were hungry? ⁴He entered the house of God, and he and his companions ate the consecrated bread—which was not lawful for them to do, but only for the priests. ⁵Or haven't you read in the Law that on the Sabbath the priests in the temple desecrate the day and yet are innocent? ⁶I tell you that oneᵇ greater than the temple is here. ⁷If you had known what these words mean, 'I desire mercy, not sacrifice,'ᶜ you would not have condemned the innocent. ⁸For the Son of Man is Lord of the Sabbath."

⁹Going on from that place, he went into their synagogue, ¹⁰and a man with a shriveled hand was there. Looking for a reason to accuse Jesus, they asked him, "Is it lawful to heal on the Sabbath?"

¹¹He said to them, "If any of you has a sheep and it falls into a pit on the Sabbath, will you not take hold of it and lift it out? ¹²How much more valuable is a man than a sheep! Therefore it is lawful to do good on the Sabbath."

¹³Then he said to the man, "Stretch out your hand." So he stretched it out and it was completely restored, just as sound as the other. ¹⁴But the Pharisees went out and plotted how they might kill Jesus.

God's Chosen Servant

¹⁵Aware of this, Jesus withdrew from that place. Many followed him, and he healed all their sick, ¹⁶warning them not to tell who he was. ¹⁷This was to fulfill what was spoken through the prophet Isaiah:

¹⁸"Here is my servant whom I have
    chosen,
  the one I love, in whom I delight;
 I will put my Spirit on him,
    and he will proclaim justice to the
      nations.
¹⁹He will not quarrel or cry out;
  no one will hear his voice in the
    streets.
²⁰A bruised reed he will not break,
  and a smoldering wick he will not
    snuff out,
 till he leads justice to victory.
²¹   In his name the nations will put
    their hope."ᵈ

Jesus and Beelzebub

See Mark 3:23–27; Luke 11:17–22

²²Then they brought him a demon-possessed man who was blind and mute, and Jesus healed him, so that he could both talk and see. ²³All the people were astonished and said, "Could this be the Son of David?"

²⁴But when the Pharisees heard this, they said, "It is only by Beelzebub,ᵉ the prince of demons, that this fellow drives out demons."

²⁵Jesus knew their thoughts and said to them, "Every kingdom divided against

---

ᵃ23 Greek *Hades*   *ᵇ6* Or *something;*
also in verses 41 and 42   *ᶜ7* Hosea 6:6
ᵈ21 Isaiah 42:1-4   *ᵉ24* Greek *Beezeboul* or
Beelzeboul; also in verse 27

itself will be ruined, and every city or household divided against itself will not stand. 26If Satan drives out Satan, he is divided against himself. How then can his kingdom stand? 27And if I drive out demons by Beelzebub, by whom do your people drive them out? So then, they will be your judges. 28But if I drive out demons by the Spirit of God, then the kingdom of God has come upon you.

29"Or again, how can anyone enter a strong man's house and carry off his possessions unless he first ties up the strong man? Then he can rob his house.

30"He who is not with me is against me, and he who does not gather with me scatters. 31And so I tell you, every sin and blasphemy will be forgiven men, but the blasphemy against the Spirit will not be forgiven. 32Anyone who speaks a word against the Son of Man will be forgiven, but anyone who speaks against the Holy Spirit will not be forgiven, either in this age or in the age to come.

33"Make a tree good and its fruit will be good, or make a tree bad and its fruit will be bad, for a tree is recognized by its fruit. 34You brood of vipers, how can you who are evil say anything good? For out of the overflow of the heart the mouth speaks. 35The good man brings good things out of the good stored up in him, and the evil man brings evil things out of the evil stored up in him. 36But I tell you that men will have to give account on the day of judgment for every careless word they have spoken. 37For by your words you will be acquitted, and by your words you will be condemned."

The Sign of Jonah
See Luke 11:29–32

38Then some of the Pharisees and teachers of the law said to him, "Teacher, we want to see a miraculous sign from you."

39He answered, "A wicked and adulterous generation asks for a miraculous sign! But none will be given it except the sign of the prophet Jonah. 40For as Jonah was three days and three nights in the belly of a huge fish, so the Son of Man will be three days and three nights in the heart of the earth. 41The men of Nineveh will stand up at the judgment with this generation and condemn it; for they repented at the preaching of Jonah, and now one*a* greater than Jonah is here. 42The Queen of the South will rise at the

judgment with this generation and condemn it; for she came from the ends of the earth to listen to Solomon's wisdom, and now one greater than Solomon is here.

43"When an evil*b* spirit comes out of a man, it goes through arid places seeking rest and does not find it. 44Then it says, 'I will return to the house I left.' When it arrives, it finds the house unoccupied, swept clean and put in order. 45Then it goes and takes with it seven other spirits more wicked than itself, and they go in and live there. And the final condition of that man is worse than the first. That is how it will be with this wicked generation."

Jesus' Mother and Brothers
See Mark 3:31–35; Luke 8:19–21

46While Jesus was still talking to the crowd, his mother and brothers stood outside, wanting to speak to him. 47Someone told him, "Your mother and brothers are standing outside, wanting to speak to you."*c*

48He replied to him, "Who is my mother, and who are my brothers?" 49Pointing to his disciples, he said, "Here are my mother and my brothers. 50For whoever does the will of my Father in heaven is my brother and sister and mother."

The Parable of the Sower
See Mark 4:1–20; Luke 8:4–15

13 That same day Jesus went out of the house and sat by the lake. 2Such large crowds gathered around him that he got

---

a41 Or something; also in verse 42　　*b43* Greek *unclean*　　*c47* Some manuscripts do not have verse 47.

POINT OF INTEREST

Matthew 12:40-42

Here Jesus uses a well-known story to illustrate his own work on earth. The Pharisees who listened to him were well aware of Jonah's story, and Jesus' claims must have infuriated them. But, just as the Pharisees had believed the amazing story of Jonah by faith, so Jesus was challenging them (and us) to believe his story by faith.

into a boat and sat in it, while all the people stood on the shore. ³Then he told them many things in parables, saying: "A farmer went out to sow his seed. ⁴As he was scattering the seed, some fell along the path, and the birds came and ate it up. ⁵Some fell on rocky places, where it did not have much soil. It sprang up quickly, because the soil was shallow. ⁶But when the sun came up, the plants were scorched, and they withered because they had no root. ⁷Other seed fell among thorns, which grew up and choked the plants. ⁸Still other seed fell on good soil, where it produced a crop—a hundred, sixty or thirty times what was sown. ⁹He who has ears, let him hear."

¹⁰The disciples came to him and asked, "Why do you speak to the people in parables?"

¹¹He replied, "The knowledge of the secrets of the kingdom of heaven has been given to you, but not to them. ¹²Whoever has will be given more, and he will have an abundance. Whoever does not have, even what he has will be taken from him. ¹³This is why I speak to them in parables:

"Though seeing, they do not see;
  though hearing, they do not hear
    or understand.

¹⁴In them is fulfilled the prophecy of Isaiah:

" 'You will be ever hearing but never understanding;
  you will be ever seeing but never perceiving.
¹⁵For this people's heart has become calloused;
  they hardly hear with their ears,
  and they have closed their eyes.
Otherwise they might see with their eyes,
  hear with their ears,
  understand with their hearts
and turn, and I would heal them.'ᵃ

¹⁶But blessed are your eyes because they see, and your ears because they hear. ¹⁷For I tell you the truth, many prophets and righteous men longed to see what you see but did not see it, and to hear what you hear but did not hear it.

¹⁸"Listen then to what the parable of the sower means: ¹⁹When anyone hears the message about the kingdom and does not understand it, the evil one comes and snatches away what was sown in his

heart. This is the seed sown along the path. ²⁰The one who received the seed that fell on rocky places is the man who hears the word and at once receives it with joy. ²¹But since he has no root, he lasts only a short time. When trouble or persecution comes because of the word, he quickly falls away. ²²The one who received the seed that fell among the thorns is the man who hears the word, but the worries of this life and the deceitfulness of wealth choke it, making it unfruitful. ²³But the one who received the seed that fell on good soil is the man who hears the word and understands it. He produces a crop, yielding a hundred, sixty or thirty times what was sown."

The Parable of the Weeds

²⁴Jesus told them another parable: "The kingdom of heaven is like a man who sowed good seed in his field. ²⁵But while everyone was sleeping, his enemy came and sowed weeds among the wheat, and went away. ²⁶When the wheat sprouted and formed heads, then the weeds also appeared.

²⁷"The owner's servants came to him and said, 'Sir, didn't you sow good seed in your field? Where then did the weeds come from?'

²⁸" 'An enemy did this,' he replied.

"The servants asked him, 'Do you want us to go and pull them up?'

²⁹" 'No,' he answered, 'because while you are pulling the weeds, you may root up the wheat with them. ³⁰Let both grow together until the harvest. At that time I will tell the harvesters: First collect the weeds and tie them in bundles to be burned; then gather the wheat and bring it into my barn.' "

The Parables of the Mustard Seed and the Yeast

See Mark 4:30–32; Luke 13:18–21

³¹He told them another parable: "The kingdom of heaven is like a mustard seed, which a man took and planted in his field. ³²Though it is the smallest of all your seeds, yet when it grows, it is the largest of garden plants and becomes a tree, so that the birds of the air come and perch in its branches."

³³He told them still another parable: "The kingdom of heaven is like yeast that a woman took and mixed into a large

ᵃ15 Isaiah 6:9,10

Read *Matthew 13:1–52*
Key Verse *Matthew 13:23*

Are You Ready to Grow?

In the Parable of the Sower, Jesus mentions four different types of soil. Each is planted with seed but only the good soil produces a crop. The problem is not with the seed but with the soil. Some soil is soft and receptive, yielding a big harvest. Some is hard and weed infested, growing nothing. How can we be sure we are like the good soil? Ask any farmer—the secret of a good harvest is in the soil preparation. Soil does not produce a crop, but it does provide an environment for the seed to reach its full potential.

A good way to prepare the soil of our hearts is to read and reflect on the Scriptures regularly. Meditating on God's Word is like a plowing; it breaks up the clumps of ignorance and turns over our willful, weedy roots. It prepares our spirits to receive the seeds of truth that God plants. And God's Word is also like the rain that falls on the prepared soil, making the seeds sprout and yielding a crop (see Isaiah 55:10–11).

Digging Into the Word
1. What do you learn about the power of God's Word in the follow-ing verses?—*Jeremiah 23:29; Hebrews 4:12*
2. What kind of crop does God want in your life?—*Matthew 7:15–20; Galatians 5:19–26*

Action Challenge
Identify one action or behavior in your life that might be causing you to have a hard heart toward God. Challenge yourself to reverse this behavior or action for one month and see what begins to grow in your life.

One Step Deeper
Jeremiah 17:7–8; John 15:1–17

Go to page 1080 for your next devotional reading.

amount[a] of flour until it worked all through the dough."

34Jesus spoke all these things to the crowd in parables; he did not say anything to them without using a parable. 35So was fulfilled what was spoken through the prophet:

"I will open my mouth in parables,
   I will utter things hidden since the
      creation of the world."[b]

The Parable of the Weeds Explained

36Then he left the crowd and went into the house. His disciples came to him and said, "Explain to us the parable of the weeds in the field."

37He answered, "The one who sowed the good seed is the Son of Man. 38The field is the world, and the good seed stands for the sons of the kingdom. The weeds are the sons of the evil one, 39and the enemy who sows them is the devil. The harvest is the end of the age, and the harvesters are angels.

40"As the weeds are pulled up and burned in the fire, so it will be at the end of the age. 41The Son of Man will send out his angels, and they will weed out of his kingdom everything that causes sin and all who do evil. 42They will throw them into the fiery furnace, where there will be weeping and gnashing of teeth. 43Then the righteous will shine like the sun in the kingdom of their Father. He who has ears, let him hear.

The Parables of the Hidden Treasure and the Pearl

44"The kingdom of heaven is like treasure hidden in a field. When a man found it, he hid it again, and then in his joy went and sold all he had and bought that field.

45"Again, the kingdom of heaven is like a merchant looking for fine pearls. 46When he found one of great value, he went away and sold everything he had and bought it.

The Parable of the Net

47"Once again, the kingdom of heaven is like a net that was let down into the lake and caught all kinds of fish. 48When it was full, the fishermen pulled it up on the shore. Then they sat down and collected the good fish in baskets, but threw the bad away. 49This is how it will be at the end of the age. The angels will come

and separate the wicked from the righteous 50and throw them into the fiery furnace, where there will be weeping and gnashing of teeth.

51"Have you understood all these things?" Jesus asked.

"Yes," they replied.

52He said to them, "Therefore every teacher of the law who has been instructed about the kingdom of heaven is like the owner of a house who brings out of his storeroom new treasures as well as old."

A Prophet Without Honor

See Mark 6:1–6

53When Jesus had finished these parables, he moved on from there. 54Coming to his hometown, he began teaching the people in their synagogue, and they were amazed. "Where did this man get this wisdom and these miraculous powers?" they asked. 55"Isn't this the carpenter's son? Isn't his mother's name Mary, and aren't his brothers James, Joseph, Simon and Judas? 56Aren't all his sisters with us? Where then did this man get all these things?" 57And they took offense at him.

But Jesus said to them, "Only in his hometown and in his own house is a prophet without honor."

58And he did not do many miracles there because of their lack of faith.

John the Baptist Beheaded

See Mark 6:14–29

14 At that time Herod the tetrarch heard the reports about Jesus, 2and he said to his attendants, "This is John the Baptist; he has risen from the dead! That is

---

a33 Greek *three satas* (probably about 1/2 bushel or 22 liters)   *b35* Psalm 78:2

POINT OF INTEREST

Matthew 13:44

How valuable is the kingdom of God? What price would you be willing to pay to gain it? Jesus told a series of stories to explain the inestimable value of salvation. When we really understand these stories and the awesome reality of the gift of salvation, we realize how priceless a treasure it is.

why miraculous powers are at work in him."

³Now Herod had arrested John and bound him and put him in prison because of Herodias, his brother Philip's wife, ⁴for John had been saying to him: "It is not lawful for you to have her." ⁵Herod wanted to kill John, but he was afraid of the people, because they considered him a prophet.

⁶On Herod's birthday the daughter of Herodias danced for them and pleased Herod so much ⁷that he promised with an oath to give her whatever she asked. ⁸Prompted by her mother, she said, "Give me here on a platter the head of John the Baptist." ⁹The king was distressed, but because of his oaths and his dinner guests, he ordered that her request be granted ¹⁰and had John beheaded in the prison. ¹¹His head was brought in on a platter and given to the girl, who carried it to her mother. ¹²John's disciples came and took his body and buried it. Then they went and told Jesus.

Jesus Feeds the Five Thousand

See Mark 6:32–44; Luke 9:10–17; John 6:1–13

¹³When Jesus heard what had happened, he withdrew by boat privately to a solitary place. Hearing of this, the crowds followed him on foot from the towns. ¹⁴When Jesus landed and saw a large crowd, he had compassion on them and healed their sick.

¹⁵As evening approached, the disciples came to him and said, "This is a remote place, and it's already getting late. Send the crowds away, so they can go to the villages and buy themselves some food."

¹⁶Jesus replied, "They do not need to go away. You give them something to eat."

¹⁷"We have here only five loaves of bread and two fish," they answered.

¹⁸"Bring them here to me," he said. ¹⁹And he directed the people to sit down on the grass. Taking the five loaves and the two fish and looking up to heaven, he gave thanks and broke the loaves. Then he gave them to the disciples, and the disciples gave them to the people. ²⁰They all ate and were satisfied, and the disciples picked up twelve basketfuls of broken pieces that were left over. ²¹The number of those who ate was about five thousand men, besides women and children.

Jesus Walks on the Water

See Mark 6:45–51; John 6:15–21

²²Immediately Jesus made the disciples get into the boat and go on ahead of him to the other side, while he dismissed the crowd. ²³After he had dismissed them, he went up on a mountainside by himself to pray. When evening came, he was there alone, ²⁴but the boat was already a considerable distance*ᵃ* from land, buffeted by the waves because the wind was against it.

²⁵During the fourth watch of the night Jesus went out to them, walking on the lake. ²⁶When the disciples saw him walking on the lake, they were terrified. "It's a ghost," they said, and cried out in fear.

²⁷But Jesus immediately said to them: "Take courage! It is I. Don't be afraid."

²⁸"Lord, if it's you," Peter replied, "tell me to come to you on the water."

²⁹"Come," he said.

Then Peter got down out of the boat, walked on the water and came toward Jesus. ³⁰But when he saw the wind, he was afraid and, beginning to sink, cried out, "Lord, save me!"

³¹Immediately Jesus reached out his hand and caught him. "You of little faith," he said, "why did you doubt?"

³²And when they climbed into the boat, the wind died down. ³³Then those who were in the boat worshiped him, saying, "Truly you are the Son of God."

³⁴When they had crossed over, they landed at Gennesaret. ³⁵And when the men of that place recognized Jesus, they sent word to all the surrounding country. People brought all their sick to him ³⁶and begged him to let the sick just touch the edge of his cloak, and all who touched him were healed.

Clean and Unclean

See Mark 7:1–23

15 Then some Pharisees and teachers of the law came to Jesus from Jerusalem and asked, ²"Why do your disciples break the tradition of the elders? They don't wash their hands before they eat!"

³Jesus replied, "And why do you break the command of God for the sake of your tradition? ⁴For God said, 'Honor your father and mother'*ᵇ* and 'Anyone who curses his father or mother must be put to death.'*ᶜ* ⁵But you say that if a man says

---

ᵃ24 Greek *many stadia*   *ᵇ4* Exodus 20:12; Deut. 5:16   *ᶜ4* Exodus 21:17; Lev. 20:9

to his father or mother, 'Whatever help you might otherwise have received from me is a gift devoted to God,' ⁶he is not to 'honor his father*ᵃ*' with it. Thus you nullify the word of God for the sake of your tradition. ⁷You hypocrites! Isaiah was right when he prophesied about you:

⁸" 'These people honor me with their
      lips,
   but their hearts are far from me.
⁹They worship me in vain;
   their teachings are but rules taught
      by men.'*ᵇ*"

¹⁰Jesus called the crowd to him and said, "Listen and understand. ¹¹What goes into a man's mouth does not make him 'unclean,' but what comes out of his mouth, that is what makes him 'unclean.' "

¹²Then the disciples came to him and asked, "Do you know that the Pharisees were offended when they heard this?"

¹³He replied, "Every plant that my heavenly Father has not planted will be pulled up by the roots. ¹⁴Leave them; they are blind guides.*ᶜ* If a blind man leads a blind man, both will fall into a pit."

¹⁵Peter said, "Explain the parable to us."

¹⁶"Are you still so dull?" Jesus asked them. ¹⁷"Don't you see that whatever en-

ᵃ6 Some manuscripts *father or his mother*
ᵇ9 Isaiah 29:13   *ᶜ14* Some manuscripts *guides of the blind*

Read *Matthew 15:1–39*
Key Verses *Matthew 15:8–9*

The Genuine Thing — Kathleen Selje

You have likely heard someone say: "I would never become a Christian because Christians are a bunch of hypocrites." A friend of mine said that once, after I had spent many months listening to her bad-mouth God and religion in general. As a child she had been physically abused by a significant person in her church. It was no wonder that her experience soured her on Christians and, more importantly, on God. But was she right? Is the church really full of hypocrites?

Many people decide to say "yes" or "no" to Jesus Christ based on their perceptions of the Christians they know. If they see Jesus Christ mirrored in those who profess his name—if they see Christians living out their faith in gentleness, joy, kindness and goodness—they will probably decide they want what they see. But if they don't observe God in the very people who talk most about him, they won't see much point in believing in him. And unbelievers are most impressed when they are respected and regarded as friends rather than as "projects."

Hypocrisy doesn't only exist in extreme cases such as my friend's. Even the small gaps in our sincerity can turn people off. Maybe our talk doesn't ring true because we have let an unloving attitude creep in. Or maybe we hold on to one particle of ethical or moral compromise that just doesn't match up with what we profess.

I have to ask myself: How genuine am I? How often do my actions match the words that I say and what I profess to believe? Moreover, how does my authenticity or lack of it affect how others view Jesus Christ? I may be the only Christian they know!

A Deeper Look
John 17:20–23; 1 Timothy 4:12–16

Go to page 1084 for your next devotional reading.

ters the mouth goes into the stomach and then out of the body? ¹⁸But the things that come out of the mouth come from the heart, and these make a man 'unclean.' ¹⁹For out of the heart come evil thoughts, murder, adultery, sexual immorality, theft, false testimony, slander. ²⁰These are what make a man 'unclean'; but eating with unwashed hands does not make him 'unclean.' "

The Faith of the Canaanite Woman

See Mark 7:24–30

²¹Leaving that place, Jesus withdrew to the region of Tyre and Sidon. ²²A Canaanite woman from that vicinity came to him, crying out, "Lord, Son of David, have mercy on me! My daughter is suffering terribly from demon-possession."

²³Jesus did not answer a word. So his disciples came to him and urged him, "Send her away, for she keeps crying out after us."

²⁴He answered, "I was sent only to the lost sheep of Israel."

²⁵The woman came and knelt before him. "Lord, help me!" she said.

²⁶He replied, "It is not right to take the children's bread and toss it to their dogs."

²⁷"Yes, Lord," she said, "but even the dogs eat the crumbs that fall from their masters' table."

²⁸Then Jesus answered, "Woman, you have great faith! Your request is granted." And her daughter was healed from that very hour.

Jesus Feeds the Four Thousand

See Mark 8:1–10

²⁹Jesus left there and went along the Sea of Galilee. Then he went up on a mountainside and sat down. ³⁰Great crowds came to him, bringing the lame, the blind, the crippled, the mute and many others, and laid them at his feet; and he healed them. ³¹The people were amazed when they saw the mute speaking, the crippled made well, the lame walking and the blind seeing. And they praised the God of Israel.

³²Jesus called his disciples to him and said, "I have compassion for these people; they have already been with me three days and have nothing to eat. I do not want to send them away hungry, or they may collapse on the way."

³³His disciples answered, "Where could we get enough bread in this remote place to feed such a crowd?"

³⁴"How many loaves do you have?" Jesus asked.

"Seven," they replied, "and a few small fish."

³⁵He told the crowd to sit down on the ground. ³⁶Then he took the seven loaves and the fish, and when he had given thanks, he broke them and gave them to the disciples, and they in turn to the people. ³⁷They all ate and were satisfied. Afterward the disciples picked up seven basketfuls of broken pieces that were left over. ³⁸The number of those who ate was four thousand, besides women and children. ³⁹After Jesus had sent the crowd away, he got into the boat and went to the vicinity of Magadan.

The Demand for a Sign

See Mark 8:11–21

16 The Pharisees and Sadducees came to Jesus and tested him by asking him to show them a sign from heaven.

²He replied,ª "When evening comes, you say, 'It will be fair weather, for the sky is red,' ³and in the morning, 'Today it will be stormy, for the sky is red and overcast.' You know how to interpret the appearance of the sky, but you cannot interpret the signs of the times. ⁴A wicked and adulterous generation looks for a miraculous sign, but none will be given it except the sign of Jonah." Jesus then left them and went away.

The Yeast of the Pharisees and Sadducees

⁵When they went across the lake, the disciples forgot to take bread. ⁶"Be careful," Jesus said to them. "Be on your guard against the yeast of the Pharisees and Sadducees."

⁷They discussed this among themselves and said, "It is because we didn't bring any bread."

⁸Aware of their discussion, Jesus asked, "You of little faith, why are you talking among yourselves about having no bread? ⁹Do you still not understand? Don't you remember the five loaves for the five thousand, and how many basketfuls you gathered? ¹⁰Or the seven loaves for the four thousand, and how many basketfuls you gathered? ¹¹How is it you

---

ª2 Some early manuscripts do not have the rest of verse 2 and all of verse 3.

don't understand that I was not talking to you about bread? But be on your guard against the yeast of the Pharisees and Sadducees." 12Then they understood that he was not telling them to guard against the yeast used in bread, but against the teaching of the Pharisees and Sadducees.

Peter's Confession of Christ
See Mark 8:27–29; Luke 9:18–20

13When Jesus came to the region of Caesarea Philippi, he asked his disciples, "Who do people say the Son of Man is?" 14They replied, "Some say John the Baptist; others say Elijah; and still others, Jeremiah or one of the prophets." 15"But what about you?" he asked. "Who do you say I am?" 16Simon Peter answered, "You are the Christ,*a* the Son of the living God." 17Jesus replied, "Blessed are you, Simon son of Jonah, for this was not revealed to you by man, but by my Father in heaven. 18And I tell you that you are Peter,*b* and on this rock I will build my church, and the gates of Hades*c* will not overcome it.*d* 19I will give you the keys of the kingdom of heaven; whatever you bind on earth will be*e* bound in heaven, and whatever you loose on earth will be*e* loosed in heaven." 20Then he warned his disciples not to tell anyone that he was the Christ.

Jesus Predicts His Death
See Mark 8:31—9:1; Luke 9:22–27

21From that time on Jesus began to explain to his disciples that he must go to Jerusalem and suffer many things at the hands of the elders, chief priests and teachers of the law, and that he must be killed and on the third day be raised to life. 22Peter took him aside and began to rebuke him. "Never, Lord!" he said. "This shall never happen to you!" 23Jesus turned and said to Peter, "Get behind me, Satan! You are a stumbling block to me; you do not have in mind the things of God, but the things of men." 24Then Jesus said to his disciples, "If anyone would come after me, he must deny himself and take up his cross and follow me. 25For whoever wants to save his life*f* will lose it, but whoever loses his life for me will find it. 26What good will it be for a man if he gains the whole world, yet forfeits his soul? Or what can a man give in exchange for his soul? 27For

the Son of Man is going to come in his Father's glory with his angels, and then he will reward each person according to what he has done. 28I tell you the truth, some who are standing here will not taste death before they see the Son of Man coming in his kingdom."

The Transfiguration
See Mark 9:2–13; Luke 9:28–36

17 After six days Jesus took with him Peter, James and John the brother of James, and led them up a high mountain by themselves. 2There he was transfigured before them. His face shone like the sun, and his clothes became as white as the light. 3Just then there appeared before them Moses and Elijah, talking with Jesus.

4Peter said to Jesus, "Lord, it is good for us to be here. If you wish, I will put up three shelters—one for you, one for Moses and one for Elijah."

5While he was still speaking, a bright cloud enveloped them, and a voice from the cloud said, "This is my Son, whom I love; with him I am well pleased. Listen to him!"

*a*16 Or *Messiah*; also in verse 20   *b*18 *Peter* means *rock.*   *c*18 Or *hell*   *d*18 Or *not prove stronger than it*   *e*19 Or *have been*
*f*25 The Greek word means either *life* or *soul*; also in verse 26.

POINT OF INTEREST   Matthew 16:9

Bread, simple bread. In our day of supermarket variety and smorgasbord eating, we tend to think of bread as a handle for sandwich fillings. But in Jesus' day, it was indeed the "staff of life." Jesus never downgrades the importance of meeting people's physical needs for food; he had fed four thousand hungry people with five loaves just prior to this incident. Yet he didn't want the disciples to be so concerned with physical bread that they missed the spiritual truths he was teaching about the "yeast" of the Pharisees and the false spiritual sustenance they peddled. Jesus declares in John 6:35 that *he* is the "bread of life."

⁶When the disciples heard this, they fell facedown to the ground, terrified. ⁷But Jesus came and touched them. "Get up," he said. "Don't be afraid." ⁸When they looked up, they saw no one except Jesus.

⁹As they were coming down the mountain, Jesus instructed them, "Don't tell anyone what you have seen, until the Son of Man has been raised from the dead."

¹⁰The disciples asked him, "Why then do the teachers of the law say that Elijah must come first?"

¹¹Jesus replied, "To be sure, Elijah comes and will restore all things. ¹²But I tell you, Elijah has already come, and they did not recognize him, but have done to him everything they wished. In the same way the Son of Man is going to suffer at their hands." ¹³Then the disciples understood that he was talking to them about John the Baptist.

The Healing of a Boy With a Demon
See Mark 9:14–28; Luke 9:37–42

¹⁴When they came to the crowd, a man approached Jesus and knelt before him. ¹⁵"Lord, have mercy on my son," he said. "He has seizures and is suffering greatly. He often falls into the fire or into the water. ¹⁶I brought him to your disciples, but they could not heal him."

¹⁷"O unbelieving and perverse generation," Jesus replied, "how long shall I stay with you? How long shall I put up with you? Bring the boy here to me." ¹⁸Jesus rebuked the demon, and it came out of the boy, and he was healed from that moment.

¹⁹Then the disciples came to Jesus in private and asked, "Why couldn't we drive it out?"

²⁰He replied, "Because you have so little faith. I tell you the truth, if you have faith as small as a mustard seed, you can say to this mountain, 'Move from here to there' and it will move. Nothing will be impossible for you.ᵃ"

²²When they came together in Galilee, he said to them, "The Son of Man is going to be betrayed into the hands of men. ²³They will kill him, and on the third day he will be raised to life." And the disciples were filled with grief.

The Temple Tax

²⁴After Jesus and his disciples arrived in Capernaum, the collectors of the two-drachma tax came to Peter and asked, "Doesn't your teacher pay the temple taxᵇ?"

²⁵"Yes, he does," he replied.

When Peter came into the house, Jesus was the first to speak. "What do you think, Simon?" he asked. "From whom do the kings of the earth collect duty and taxes—from their own sons or from others?"

²⁶"From others," Peter answered.

"Then the sons are exempt," Jesus said to him. ²⁷"But so that we may not offend them, go to the lake and throw out your line. Take the first fish you catch; open its mouth and you will find a four-drachma coin. Take it and give it to them for my tax and yours."

The Greatest in the Kingdom of Heaven
See Mark 9:33–37; Luke 9:46–48

18 At that time the disciples came to Jesus and asked, "Who is the greatest in the kingdom of heaven?"

²He called a little child and had him stand among them. ³And he said: "I tell you the truth, unless you change and become like little children, you will never enter the kingdom of heaven. ⁴Therefore, whoever humbles himself like this child is the greatest in the kingdom of heaven.

⁵"And whoever welcomes a little child like this in my name welcomes me. ⁶But if anyone causes one of these little ones who believe in me to sin, it would be better for him to have a large millstone hung around his neck and to be drowned in the depths of the sea.

⁷"Woe to the world because of the things that cause people to sin! Such things must come, but woe to the man through whom they come! ⁸If your hand or your foot causes you to sin, cut it off and throw it away. It is better for you to enter life maimed or crippled than to have two hands or two feet and be thrown into eternal fire. ⁹And if your eye causes you to sin, gouge it out and throw it away. It is better for you to enter life

---

ᵃ20 Some manuscripts you. ²¹But this kind does not go out except by prayer and fasting.   ᵇ24 Greek the two drachmas with one eye than to have two eyes and be thrown into the fire of hell.

The Parable of the Lost Sheep

See Luke 15:4–7

¹⁰"See that you do not look down on one of these little ones. For I tell you that their angels in heaven always see the face of my Father in heaven.ᵃ

¹²"What do you think? If a man owns a hundred sheep, and one of them wanders away, will he not leave the ninety-nine on the hills and go to look for the one that wandered off? ¹³And if he finds it, I tell you the truth, he is happier about that one sheep than about the ninety-nine that did not wander off. ¹⁴In the

same way your Father in heaven is not willing that any of these little ones should be lost.

A Brother Who Sins Against You

¹⁵"If your brother sins against you,ᵇ go and show him his fault, just between the two of you. If he listens to you, you have won your brother over. ¹⁶But if he will not listen, take one or two others along, so that 'every matter may be established by the testimony of two or three witnesses.'ᶜ ¹⁷If he refuses to listen to

ᵃ 10 Some manuscripts *heaven.* 11 *The Son of Man came to save what was lost.*   ᵇ 15 Some manuscripts do not have *against you.*   ᶜ 16 Deut. 19:15

TUESDAY

Read Matthew 18:1–35
Key Verse Matthew 18:15

Built Up in Love – Lindy Black

She'd done it *again*! As the three of us chatted and walked our four-mile route, she had interrupted us repeatedly. She did that a lot, and it bugged me. I chose, however, to put up with her rudeness rather than have an uncomfortable conversation with her about it. I rationalized by assuming that someone else must have tried to help her and prayed that God would help her see the negative impact she had on conversations.

But on this occasion, I could not escape the issue. I thought about what Jesus would have said and done in this situation. As I drove home, my heart was sad for my friend. I wondered how many others she had hurt or unknowingly pushed away by interrupting them?

Jesus said that we are to approach people who have sinned against us. With love and concern we are to confront them about what has hurt or offended us in order to turn them away from sin. Four days passed before the timing seemed right. I picked up the phone, started to dial and put the receiver back down. I prayed and tried again. My voice shook as I told her I loved her. I pointed out the pattern I had observed, including the instances during our walk.

Later I found out that she had prayed for God to show her areas of sin in her life and that she was grateful I'd pointed out the problem. She's trying to be more sensitive in conversations, and the level of trust in our friendship is even stronger than before.

It isn't easy to go to the one who has offended you, but Jesus said to do it. Although it seems scary, helping each other grow in Jesus Christ is worth the risk.

A Deeper Look
Ephesians 4:14–16; James 5:16–20

Go to page 1088 for your next devotional reading.

them, tell it to the church; and if he refuses to listen even to the church, treat him as you would a pagan or a tax collector.

¹⁸"I tell you the truth, whatever you bind on earth will be*a* bound in heaven, and whatever you loose on earth will be*a* loosed in heaven.

¹⁹"Again, I tell you that if two of you on earth agree about anything you ask for, it will be done for you by my Father in heaven. ²⁰For where two or three come together in my name, there am I with them."

The Parable of the Unmerciful Servant

²¹Then Peter came to Jesus and asked, "Lord, how many times shall I forgive my brother when he sins against me? Up to seven times?"

²²Jesus answered, "I tell you, not seven times, but seventy-seven times.*b*

²³"Therefore, the kingdom of heaven is like a king who wanted to settle accounts with his servants. ²⁴As he began the settlement, a man who owed him ten thousand talents*c* was brought to him. ²⁵Since he was not able to pay, the master ordered that he and his wife and his children and all that he had be sold to repay the debt.

²⁶"The servant fell on his knees before him. 'Be patient with me,' he begged, 'and I will pay back everything.' ²⁷The servant's master took pity on him, canceled the debt and let him go.

²⁸"But when that servant went out, he found one of his fellow servants who owed him a hundred denarii.*d* He grabbed him and began to choke him. 'Pay back what you owe me!' he demanded.

²⁹"His fellow servant fell to his knees and begged him, 'Be patient with me, and I will pay you back.'

³⁰"But he refused. Instead, he went off and had the man thrown into prison until he could pay the debt. ³¹When the other servants saw what had happened, they were greatly distressed and went and told their master everything that had happened.

³²"Then the master called the servant in. 'You wicked servant,' he said, 'I canceled all that debt of yours because you begged me to. ³³Shouldn't you have had

mercy on your fellow servant just as I had on you?' ³⁴In anger his master turned him over to the jailers to be tortured, until he should pay back all he owed.

³⁵"This is how my heavenly Father will treat each of you unless you forgive your brother from your heart."

Divorce

See Mark 10:1–12

19 When Jesus had finished saying these things, he left Galilee and went into the region of Judea to the other side of the Jordan. ²Large crowds followed him, and he healed them there.

³Some Pharisees came to him to test him. They asked, "Is it lawful for a man to divorce his wife for any and every reason?"

⁴"Haven't you read," he replied, "that at the beginning the Creator 'made them male and female,'*e* ⁵and said, 'For this reason a man will leave his father and mother and be united to his wife, and the two will become one flesh'*f*? ⁶So they are no longer two, but one. Therefore what God has joined together, let man not separate."

⁷"Why then," they asked, "did Moses command that a man give his wife a certificate of divorce and send her away?"

⁸Jesus replied, "Moses permitted you to divorce your wives because your hearts were hard. But it was not this way from the beginning. ⁹I tell you that anyone who divorces his wife, except for marital unfaithfulness, and marries another woman commits adultery."

¹⁰The disciples said to him, "If this is the situation between a husband and wife, it is better not to marry."

¹¹Jesus replied, "Not everyone can accept this word, but only those to whom it has been given. ¹²For some are eunuchs because they were born that way; others were made that way by men; and others have renounced marriage*g* because of the kingdom of heaven. The one who can accept this should accept it."

The Little Children and Jesus

See Mark 10:13–16; Luke 18:15–17

¹³Then little children were brought to Jesus for him to place his hands on them

---

a18 Or *have been*   *b22* Or *seventy times seven*
c24 That is, millions of dollars   *d28* That is, a few dollars   *e4* Gen. 1:27   *f5* Gen. 2:24
g12 Or *have made themselves eunuchs*

and pray for them. But the disciples rebuked those who brought them.

¹⁴Jesus said, "Let the little children come to me, and do not hinder them, for the kingdom of heaven belongs to such as these." ¹⁵When he had placed his hands on them, he went on from there.

The Rich Young Man

See Mark 10:17–30; Luke 18:18–30

¹⁶Now a man came up to Jesus and asked, "Teacher, what good thing must I do to get eternal life?"

¹⁷"Why do you ask me about what is good?" Jesus replied. "There is only One who is good. If you want to enter life, obey the commandments."

¹⁸"Which ones?" the man inquired.

Jesus replied, " 'Do not murder, do not commit adultery, do not steal, do not give false testimony, ¹⁹honor your father and mother,'ᵃ and 'love your neighbor as yourself.'ᵇ "

²⁰"All these I have kept," the young man said. "What do I still lack?"

²¹Jesus answered, "If you want to be perfect, go, sell your possessions and give to the poor, and you will have treasure in heaven. Then come, follow me."

²²When the young man heard this, he went away sad, because he had great wealth.

²³Then Jesus said to his disciples, "I tell you the truth, it is hard for a rich man to enter the kingdom of heaven. ²⁴Again I tell you, it is easier for a camel to go through the eye of a needle than for a rich man to enter the kingdom of God."

²⁵When the disciples heard this, they were greatly astonished and asked, "Who then can be saved?"

²⁶Jesus looked at them and said, "With man this is impossible, but with God all things are possible."

²⁷Peter answered him, "We have left everything to follow you! What then will there be for us?"

²⁸Jesus said to them, "I tell you the truth, at the renewal of all things, when the Son of Man sits on his glorious throne, you who have followed me will also sit on twelve thrones, judging the twelve tribes of Israel. ²⁹And everyone who has left houses or brothers or sisters or father or motherᶜ or children or fields for my sake will receive a hundred times as much and will inherit eternal life. ³⁰But many who are first will be last, and many who are last will be first.

The Parable of the Workers in the Vineyard

20 "For the kingdom of heaven is like a landowner who went out early in the morning to hire men to work in his vineyard. ²He agreed to pay them a denarius for the day and sent them into his vineyard.

³"About the third hour he went out and saw others standing in the marketplace doing nothing. ⁴He told them, 'You also go and work in my vineyard, and I will pay you whatever is right.' ⁵So they went.

"He went out again about the sixth hour and the ninth hour and did the same thing. ⁶About the eleventh hour he went out and found still others standing around. He asked them, 'Why have you been standing here all day long doing nothing?'

⁷" 'Because no one has hired us,' they answered.

"He said to them, 'You also go and work in my vineyard.'

⁸"When evening came, the owner of the vineyard said to his foreman, 'Call the workers and pay them their wages, beginning with the last ones hired and going on to the first.'

⁹"The workers who were hired about the eleventh hour came and each received a denarius. ¹⁰So when those came who were hired first, they expected to receive more. But each one of them also

---

ᵃ19 Exodus 20:12-16; Deut. 5:16-20
ᵇ19 Lev. 19:18   ᶜ29 Some manuscripts *mother or wife*

POINT OF INTEREST

Matthew 19:23

Does God dislike rich people? No. In fact, one Gospel writer tells us how much Jesus loved this rich young man (see Mark 10:21). But the young man was not willing to give up his wealth and position to become Jesus' follower. What the young man did not realize was that Jesus had given up far more—the glory and riches of heaven—so that all people, including that rich young man, could have access to heaven.

received a denarius. ¹¹When they received it, they began to grumble against the landowner. ¹²'These men who were hired last worked only one hour,' they said, 'and you have made them equal to us who have borne the burden of the work and the heat of the day.'

¹³"But he answered one of them, 'Friend, I am not being unfair to you. Didn't you agree to work for a denarius? ¹⁴Take your pay and go. I want to give the man who was hired last the same as I gave you. ¹⁵Don't I have the right to do what I want with my own money? Or are you envious because I am generous?'

¹⁶"So the last will be first, and the first will be last."

Jesus Again Predicts His Death
See Mark 10:32–34; Luke 18:31–33

¹⁷Now as Jesus was going up to Jerusalem, he took the twelve disciples aside and said to them, ¹⁸"We are going up to Jerusalem, and the Son of Man will be betrayed to the chief priests and the teachers of the law. They will condemn him to death ¹⁹and will turn him over to the Gentiles to be mocked and flogged and crucified. On the third day he will be raised to life!"

A Mother's Request
See Mark 10:35–45

²⁰Then the mother of Zebedee's sons came to Jesus with her sons and, kneeling down, asked a favor of him.

²¹"What is it you want?" he asked.

She said, "Grant that one of these two sons of mine may sit at your right and the other at your left in your kingdom."

²²"You don't know what you are asking," Jesus said to them. "Can you drink the cup I am going to drink?"

"We can," they answered.

²³Jesus said to them, "You will indeed drink from my cup, but to sit at my right or left is not for me to grant. These places belong to those for whom they have been prepared by my Father."

²⁴When the ten heard about this, they were indignant with the two brothers. ²⁵Jesus called them together and said, "You know that the rulers of the Gentiles lord it over them, and their high officials exercise authority over them. ²⁶Not so with you. Instead, whoever wants to become great among you must be your servant, ²⁷and whoever wants to be first must be your slave— ²⁸just as the Son of Man did not come to be served, but to serve, and to give his life as a ransom for many."

Two Blind Men Receive Sight
See Mark 10:46–52; Luke 18:35–43

²⁹As Jesus and his disciples were leaving Jericho, a large crowd followed him. ³⁰Two blind men were sitting by the roadside, and when they heard that Jesus was going by, they shouted, "Lord, Son of David, have mercy on us!"

³¹The crowd rebuked them and told them to be quiet, but they shouted all the louder, "Lord, Son of David, have mercy on us!"

³²Jesus stopped and called them. "What do you want me to do for you?" he asked.

³³"Lord," they answered, "we want our sight."

³⁴Jesus had compassion on them and touched their eyes. Immediately they received their sight and followed him.

The Triumphal Entry
See Mark 11:1–10; Luke 19:29–38; John 12:12–15

21 As they approached Jerusalem and came to Bethphage on the Mount of Olives, Jesus sent two disciples, ²saying to them, "Go to the village ahead of you, and at once you will find a donkey tied there, with her colt by her. Untie them and bring them to me. ³If anyone says anything to you, tell him that the Lord needs them, and he will send them right away."

⁴This took place to fulfill what was spoken through the prophet:

⁵"Say to the Daughter of Zion,
  'See, your king comes to you,
 gentle and riding on a donkey,
  on a colt, the foal of a donkey.' "ᵃ

⁶The disciples went and did as Jesus had instructed them. ⁷They brought the donkey and the colt, placed their cloaks on them, and Jesus sat on them. ⁸A very large crowd spread their cloaks on the road, while others cut branches from the trees and spread them on the road. ⁹The crowds that went ahead of him and those that followed shouted,

 "Hosannaᵇ to the Son of David!"

ᵃ5 Zech. 9:9   ᵇ9 A Hebrew expression meaning "Save!" which became an exclamation of praise; also in verse 15

"Blessed is he who comes in the name of the Lord!"[a]

"Hosanna[b] in the highest!"

[10]When Jesus entered Jerusalem, the whole city was stirred and asked, "Who is this?"

[11]The crowds answered, "This is Jesus, the prophet from Nazareth in Galilee."

Jesus at the Temple

See Mark 11:15–18; Luke 19:45–47

[12]Jesus entered the temple area and drove out all who were buying and sell-ing there. He overturned the tables of the money changers and the benches of those selling doves. [13]"It is written," he said to them, " 'My house will be called a house of prayer,'[c] but you are making it a 'den of robbers.'[d] "

[14]The blind and the lame came to him at the temple, and he healed them. [15]But when the chief priests and the teachers of the law saw the wonderful things he did and the children shouting in the temple

a9 Psalm 118:26   b9 A Hebrew expression meaning "Save!" which became an exclamation of praise; also in verse 15   c13 Isaiah 56:7   d13 Jer. 7:11

Read Matthew 20:1–34
Key Verse Matthew 20:32

Great Expectations – Cheri Ruggles

When asked what he wanted for his birthday, Travis thought for a moment and then answered, "a new deck of cards." The 11-year-old boy had spent the last few months in Russia, and because a limited number of toys were available, he had set his sights fairly low. He would have been truly satisfied with a deck of cards, while his friends back in America would yearn for more sophisticated and expensive electronic toys!

Being content with a little might be admirable when we're talking about material goods, but God wants us to have great expectations when we ask for things from him. Like Travis, we get used to "making do" with limited resources. We ask for the equivalent of a "deck of cards" from the Creator of the universe rather than for the salvation of a roommate or the healing of a friend's marriage. We get used to the limitations of our finite world and forget that God is "able to do immeasurably more than all we ask or imagine, according to his power that is at work within us" (Ephesians 3:20).

Jesus Christ lived among us in the physical world as a lowly carpenter, but he also held the keys to the unlimited resources of heaven, power over the natural world and power over life and death. And although we often relegate the miracles he performed to the past, he "is the same yesterday and today and forever" (Hebrews 13:8).

Let's set our sights higher. When the God of creation asks us, "What do you want me to do for you?" we might think a little higher, ask a little bigger. We can ask for God-sized answers from a God-sized God. As J. Oswald Sanders said, "God encourages us to ask for the impossible as well as the possible. For to him all difficulties are the same—less than himself."

A Deeper Look
Jeremiah 32:17, 27; Matthew 7:9–11; Luke 1:37

Go to page 1091 for your next devotional reading.

area, "Hosanna to the Son of David," they were indignant.

¹⁶"Do you hear what these children are saying?" they asked him.

"Yes," replied Jesus, "have you never read,

" 'From the lips of children and
 infants
 you have ordained praise'ᵃ?"

¹⁷And he left them and went out of the city to Bethany, where he spent the night.

The Fig Tree Withers
See Mark 11:12–14,20–24

¹⁸Early in the morning, as he was on his way back to the city, he was hungry. ¹⁹Seeing a fig tree by the road, he went up to it but found nothing on it except leaves. Then he said to it, "May you never bear fruit again!" Immediately the tree withered.

²⁰When the disciples saw this, they were amazed. "How did the fig tree wither so quickly?" they asked.

²¹Jesus replied, "I tell you the truth, if you have faith and do not doubt, not only can you do what was done to the fig tree, but also you can say to this mountain, 'Go, throw yourself into the sea,' and it will be done. ²²If you believe, you will receive whatever you ask for in prayer."

The Authority of Jesus Questioned
See Mark 11:27–33; Luke 20:1–8

²³Jesus entered the temple courts, and, while he was teaching, the chief priests and the elders of the people came to him. "By what authority are you doing these things?" they asked. "And who gave you this authority?"

²⁴Jesus replied, "I will also ask you one question. If you answer me, I will tell you by what authority I am doing these things. ²⁵John's baptism—where did it come from? Was it from heaven, or from men?"

They discussed it among themselves and said, "If we say, 'From heaven,' he will ask, 'Then why didn't you believe him?' ²⁶But if we say, 'From men'—we are afraid of the people, for they all hold that John was a prophet."

²⁷So they answered Jesus, "We don't know."

Then he said, "Neither will I tell you by what authority I am doing these things.

The Parable of the Two Sons

²⁸"What do you think? There was a man who had two sons. He went to the first and said, 'Son, go and work today in the vineyard.'

²⁹" 'I will not,' he answered, but later he changed his mind and went.

³⁰"Then the father went to the other son and said the same thing. He answered, 'I will, sir,' but he did not go.

³¹"Which of the two did what his father wanted?"

"The first," they answered.

Jesus said to them, "I tell you the truth, the tax collectors and the prostitutes are entering the kingdom of God ahead of you. ³²For John came to you to show you the way of righteousness, and you did not believe him, but the tax collectors and the prostitutes did. And even after you saw this, you did not repent and believe him.

The Parable of the Tenants
See Mark 12:1–12; Luke 20:9–19

³³"Listen to another parable: There was a landowner who planted a vineyard. He put a wall around it, dug a winepress in it and built a watchtower. Then he rented the vineyard to some farmers and went away on a journey. ³⁴When the harvest time approached, he sent his servants to the tenants to collect his fruit.

³⁵"The tenants seized his servants; they beat one, killed another, and stoned a third. ³⁶Then he sent other servants to them, more than the first time, and the tenants treated them the same way. ³⁷Last of all, he sent his son to them. 'They will respect my son,' he said.

³⁸"But when the tenants saw the son, they said to each other, 'This is the heir. Come, let's kill him and take his inheritance.' ³⁹So they took him and threw him out of the vineyard and killed him.

⁴⁰"Therefore, when the owner of the vineyard comes, what will he do to those tenants?"

⁴¹"He will bring those wretches to a wretched end," they replied, "and he will rent the vineyard to other tenants, who will give him his share of the crop at harvest time."

⁴²Jesus said to them, "Have you never read in the Scriptures:

" 'The stone the builders rejected

ᵃ16 Psalm 8:2

has become the capstone[a];
the Lord has done this,
    and it is marvelous in our eyes'[b]?

43"Therefore I tell you that the kingdom of God will be taken away from you and given to a people who will produce its fruit. 44He who falls on this stone will be broken to pieces, but he on whom it falls will be crushed."[c]

45When the chief priests and the Pharisees heard Jesus' parables, they knew he was talking about them. 46They looked for a way to arrest him, but they were afraid of the crowd because the people held that he was a prophet.

The Parable of the Wedding Banquet

22 Jesus spoke to them again in parables, saying: 2"The kingdom of heaven is like a king who prepared a wedding banquet for his son. 3He sent his servants to those who had been invited to the banquet to tell them to come, but they refused to come.

4"Then he sent some more servants and said, 'Tell those who have been invited that I have prepared my dinner: My oxen and fattened cattle have been butchered, and everything is ready. Come to the wedding banquet.'

5"But they paid no attention and went off—one to his field, another to his business. 6The rest seized his servants, mistreated them and killed them. 7The king was enraged. He sent his army and destroyed those murderers and burned their city.

8"Then he said to his servants, 'The wedding banquet is ready, but those I invited did not deserve to come. 9Go to the street corners and invite to the banquet anyone you find.' 10So the servants went out into the streets and gathered all the people they could find, both good and bad, and the wedding hall was filled with guests.

11"But when the king came in to see the guests, he noticed a man there who was not wearing wedding clothes. 12'Friend,' he asked, 'how did you get in here without wedding clothes?' The man was speechless.

13"Then the king told the attendants, 'Tie him hand and foot, and throw him outside, into the darkness, where there will be weeping and gnashing of teeth.'

14"For many are invited, but few are chosen."

Paying Taxes to Caesar
See Mark 12:13–17; Luke 20:20–26

15Then the Pharisees went out and laid plans to trap him in his words. 16They sent their disciples to him along with the Herodians. "Teacher," they said, "we know you are a man of integrity and that you teach the way of God in accordance with the truth. You aren't swayed by men, because you pay no attention to who they are. 17Tell us then, what is your opinion? Is it right to pay taxes to Caesar or not?"

18But Jesus, knowing their evil intent, said, "You hypocrites, why are you trying to trap me? 19Show me the coin used for paying the tax." They brought him a denarius, 20and he asked them, "Whose portrait is this? And whose inscription?"

21"Caesar's," they replied.

Then he said to them, "Give to Caesar what is Caesar's, and to God what is God's."

22When they heard this, they were amazed. So they left him and went away.

Marriage at the Resurrection
See Mark 12:18–27; Luke 20:27–40

23That same day the Sadducees, who say there is no resurrection, came to him with a question. 24"Teacher," they said, "Moses told us that if a man dies without having children, his brother must marry the widow and have children for him. 25Now there were seven brothers among us. The first one married and died, and since he had no children, he left his wife to his brother. 26The same thing happened to the second and third brother, right on down to the seventh. 27Finally, the woman died. 28Now then, at the resurrection, whose wife will she be of the seven, since all of them were married to her?"

29Jesus replied, "You are in error because you do not know the Scriptures or the power of God. 30At the resurrection people will neither marry nor be given in marriage; they will be like the angels in heaven. 31But about the resurrection of the dead—have you not read what God said to you, 32'I am the God of Abraham, the God of Isaac, and the God of Jacob'[d]? He is not the God of the dead but of the living."

---

[a]42 Or cornerstone   [b]42 Psalm 118:22,23
[c]44 Some manuscripts do not have verse 44.
[d]32 Exodus 3:6

³³When the crowds heard this, they were astonished at his teaching.

The Greatest Commandment
See Mark 12:28–31

³⁴Hearing that Jesus had silenced the Sadducees, the Pharisees got together. ³⁵One of them, an expert in the law, tested him with this question: ³⁶"Teacher, which is the greatest commandment in the Law?"

³⁷Jesus replied: " 'Love the Lord your God with all your heart and with all your soul and with all your mind.'^a ³⁸This is the first and greatest commandment. ³⁹And the second is like it: 'Love your neighbor as yourself.'^b ⁴⁰All the Law and the Prophets hang on these two commandments."

Whose Son Is the Christ?
See Mark 12:35–37; Luke 20:41–44

⁴¹While the Pharisees were gathered together, Jesus asked them, ⁴²"What do you think about the Christ^c? Whose son is he?"

"The son of David," they replied.

⁴³He said to them, "How is it then that David, speaking by the Spirit, calls him 'Lord'? For he says,

⁴⁴" 'The Lord said to my Lord:

^a37 Deut. 6:5   ^b39 Lev. 19:18   ^c42 Or *Messiah*

THURSDAY

Read Matthew 22:1–46
Key Verse Matthew 22:37

Above All Else – Kyong A. Lee

As a single person, I struggle with questions about marriage. Will I ever marry? Whom will I marry? When? Will I get stuck with someone I'm not happy with? Is the person I'm currently interested in *the one*? I have so many questions and no answers!

In the midst of all these questions, I realize that my struggle is really with contentment. I find that I am always able to identify something I would like to change—my marital status, grade point average, living conditions and so forth. But if I base all my contentment and happiness on these things, am I truly loving the Lord my God with all my heart and with all my soul and with all my mind? Does my lack of contentment declare to him that he has not met my needs?

God is teaching me to operate on his truth and not on my feelings. When I feel insecure, God reminds me that, "It is only with perfect love that I love you. Trust my love." When I wonder, "What in the world are you doing with my life?" he says, "Remember that I am working out my perfect purposes in your life. I see the future, and in my perfect wisdom, this is where I need you to be. Trust my plan for your life." When I don't sense his goodness, he reassures me by saying, "I am at work in your life with perfect faithfulness. Trust my goodness."

Although I don't have answers to all my questions, I know that I am to give my heart, fears, longings and impatience to God's care . . . again and again. The answers will come at the right time. But *today* and each day hereafter I am seeking to love him with all that I have, leaving my future in his loving, perfect hands.

A Deeper Look
Proverbs 3:5–6; Jeremiah 29:11; Philippians 4:12–13

Go to page 1094 for your next devotional reading.

"Sit at my right hand
until I put your enemies
under your feet." ' *a*

⁴⁵If then David calls him 'Lord,' how can he be his son?" ⁴⁶No one could say a word in reply, and from that day on no one dared to ask him any more questions.

Seven Woes

See Mark 12:38–39; Luke 20:45–46

23 Then Jesus said to the crowds and to his disciples: ²"The teachers of the law and the Pharisees sit in Moses' seat. ³So you must obey them and do everything they tell you. But do not do what they do, for they do not practice what they preach. ⁴They tie up heavy loads and put them on men's shoulders, but they themselves are not willing to lift a finger to move them.

⁵"Everything they do is done for men to see: They make their phylacteries*b* wide and the tassels on their garments long; ⁶they love the place of honor at banquets and the most important seats in the synagogues; ⁷they love to be greeted in the marketplaces and to have men call them 'Rabbi.'

⁸"But you are not to be called 'Rabbi,' for you have only one Master and you are all brothers. ⁹And do not call anyone on earth 'father,' for you have one Father, and he is in heaven. ¹⁰Nor are you to be called 'teacher,' for you have one Teacher, the Christ.*c* ¹¹The greatest among you will be your servant. ¹²For whoever exalts himself will be humbled, and whoever humbles himself will be exalted.

¹³"Woe to you, teachers of the law and Pharisees, you hypocrites! You shut the kingdom of heaven in men's faces. You yourselves do not enter, nor will you let those enter who are trying to.*d*

¹⁵"Woe to you, teachers of the law and Pharisees, you hypocrites! You travel over land and sea to win a single convert, and when he becomes one, you make him twice as much a son of hell as you are.

¹⁶"Woe to you, blind guides! You say, 'If anyone swears by the temple, it means nothing; but if anyone swears by the gold of the temple, he is bound by his oath.' ¹⁷You blind fools! Which is greater: the gold, or the temple that makes the gold sacred? ¹⁸You also say, 'If anyone swears by the altar, it means nothing; but if any-

one swears by the gift on it, he is bound by his oath.' ¹⁹You blind men! Which is greater: the gift, or the altar that makes the gift sacred? ²⁰Therefore, he who swears by the altar swears by it and by everything on it. ²¹And he who swears by the temple swears by it and by the one who dwells in it. ²²And he who swears by heaven swears by God's throne and by the one who sits on it.

²³"Woe to you, teachers of the law and Pharisees, you hypocrites! You give a tenth of your spices—mint, dill and cummin. But you have neglected the more important matters of the law—justice, mercy and faithfulness. You should have practiced the latter, without neglecting the former. ²⁴You blind guides! You strain out a gnat but swallow a camel.

²⁵"Woe to you, teachers of the law and Pharisees, you hypocrites! You clean the outside of the cup and dish, but inside they are full of greed and self-indulgence. ²⁶Blind Pharisee! First clean the inside of the cup and dish, and then the outside also will be clean.

²⁷"Woe to you, teachers of the law and Pharisees, you hypocrites! You are like whitewashed tombs, which look beautiful on the outside but on the inside are full of dead men's bones and everything unclean. ²⁸In the same way, on the out-

---

*a*44 Psalm 110:1   *b*5 That is, boxes containing Scripture verses, worn on forehead and arm *c*10 Or *Messiah*   *d*13 Some manuscripts *to.* *14Woe to you, teachers of the law and Pharisees, you hypocrites! You devour widows' houses and for a show make lengthy prayers. Therefore you will be punished more severely.*

POINT OF INTEREST

Matthew 23:27–28

White is the color of purity and holiness, and those who walk with the Lamb are to be dressed in white robes (see Isaiah 1:18; Revelation 6:11; 7:9,14). Notice the irony with which Jesus characterizes the Pharisees as he turns their hypocrisy against them in the "Seven Woes." He says they are like tombs painted over with whitewash to look beautiful on the outside, but filled with decaying bodies and everything that is unclean.

side you appear to people as righteous but on the inside you are full of hypocrisy and wickedness.

²⁹"Woe to you, teachers of the law and Pharisees, you hypocrites! You build tombs for the prophets and decorate the graves of the righteous. ³⁰And you say, 'If we had lived in the days of our forefathers, we would not have taken part with them in shedding the blood of the prophets.' ³¹So you testify against yourselves that you are the descendants of those who murdered the prophets. ³²Fill up, then, the measure of the sin of your forefathers!

³³"You snakes! You brood of vipers! How will you escape being condemned to hell? ³⁴Therefore I am sending you prophets and wise men and teachers. Some of them you will kill and crucify; others you will flog in your synagogues and pursue from town to town. ³⁵And so upon you will come all the righteous blood that has been shed on earth, from the blood of righteous Abel to the blood of Zechariah son of Berekiah, whom you murdered between the temple and the altar. ³⁶I tell you the truth, all this will come upon this generation.

³⁷"O Jerusalem, Jerusalem, you who kill the prophets and stone those sent to you, how often I have longed to gather your children together, as a hen gathers her chicks under her wings, but you were not willing. ³⁸Look, your house is left to you desolate. ³⁹For I tell you, you will not see me again until you say, 'Blessed is he who comes in the name of the Lord.'ᵃ"

Signs of the End of the Age

See Mark 13:1–37; Luke 21:5–36

24 Jesus left the temple and was walking away when his disciples came up to him to call his attention to its buildings. ²"Do you see all these things?" he asked. "I tell you the truth, not one stone here will be left on another; every one will be thrown down."

³As Jesus was sitting on the Mount of Olives, the disciples came to him privately. "Tell us," they said, "when will this happen, and what will be the sign of your coming and of the end of the age?"

⁴Jesus answered: "Watch out that no one deceives you. ⁵For many will come in my name, claiming, 'I am the Christ,ᵇ' and will deceive many. ⁶You will hear of wars and rumors of wars, but see to it that you are not alarmed. Such things

must happen, but the end is still to come. ⁷Nation will rise against nation, and kingdom against kingdom. There will be famines and earthquakes in various places. ⁸All these are the beginning of birth pains.

⁹"Then you will be handed over to be persecuted and put to death, and you will be hated by all nations because of me. ¹⁰At that time many will turn away from the faith and will betray and hate each other, ¹¹and many false prophets will appear and deceive many people. ¹²Because of the increase of wickedness, the love of most will grow cold, ¹³but he who stands firm to the end will be saved. ¹⁴And this gospel of the kingdom will be preached in the whole world as a testimony to all nations, and then the end will come.

¹⁵"So when you see standing in the holy place 'the abomination that causes desolation,'ᶜ spoken of through the prophet Daniel—let the reader understand— ¹⁶then let those who are in Judea flee to the mountains. ¹⁷Let no one on the roof of his house go down to take anything out of the house. ¹⁸Let no one in the field go back to get his cloak. ¹⁹How dreadful it will be in those days for pregnant women and nursing mothers! ²⁰Pray that your flight will not take place in winter or on the Sabbath. ²¹For then there will be great distress, unequaled from the beginning of the world until now—and never to be equaled again. ²²If those days had not been cut short, no one would survive, but for the sake of the elect those days will be shortened. ²³At that time if anyone says to you, 'Look, here is the Christ!' or, 'There he is!' do not believe it. ²⁴For false Christs and false prophets will appear and perform great signs and miracles to deceive even the elect—if that were possible. ²⁵See, I have told you ahead of time.

²⁶"So if anyone tells you, 'There he is, out in the desert,' do not go out; or, 'Here he is, in the inner rooms,' do not believe it. ²⁷For as lightning that comes from the east is visible even in the west, so will be the coming of the Son of Man. ²⁸Wherever there is a carcass, there the vultures will gather.

²⁹"Immediately after the distress of those days

" 'the sun will be darkened,

ᵃ39 Psalm 118:26   ᵇ5 Or *Messiah*; also in verse 23   ᶜ15 Daniel 9:27; 11:31; 12:11

and the moon will not give its
   light;
the stars will fall from the sky,
   and the heavenly bodies will be
     shaken.'*a*

30"At that time the sign of the Son of
Man will appear in the sky, and all the
nations of the earth will mourn. They will
see the Son of Man coming on the clouds
of the sky, with power and great glory.
31And he will send his angels with a loud
trumpet call, and they will gather his
elect from the four winds, from one end
of the heavens to the other.
32"Now learn this lesson from the fig
tree: As soon as its twigs get tender and
its leaves come out, you know that summer is near. **33**Even so, when you see all
these things, you know that it*b* is near,
right at the door. **34**I tell you the truth,
this generation*c* will certainly not pass
away until all these things have happened. **35**Heaven and earth will pass

away, but my words will never pass
away.

The Day and Hour Unknown
See Luke 12:42–46; 17:26–27

36"No one knows about that day or
hour, not even the angels in heaven, nor
the Son,*d* but only the Father. **37**As it
was in the days of Noah, so it will be at
the coming of the Son of Man. **38**For in
the days before the flood, people were
eating and drinking, marrying and giving
in marriage, up to the day Noah entered
the ark; **39**and they knew nothing about
what would happen until the flood came
and took them all away. That is how it
will be at the coming of the Son of Man.
40Two men will be in the field; one will
be taken and the other left. **41**Two women
will be grinding with a hand mill; one
will be taken and the other left.

a29 Isaiah 13:10; 34:4   *b33* Or *he*   *c34* Or
race   *d36* Some manuscripts do not have *nor the*
Son.

FRIDAY

Read *Matthew 24:1–51*
Key Verse *Matthew 24:35*

God's Lasting Word – Dr. Jerry White

I remember my first new car. I cared for it as though it would last
forever. But it wasn't long before dents and scratches marred its surface. Parts began to break. After a few years, it was just another
used car needing to be replaced.

Something inside me longs for material satisfaction. Time after
time, I have bought things thinking that somehow they would last
and satisfy me. But they never do. Everything, even my own body,
will wear out one day. Even some of my greatest treasures will pass
away when I die.

But there is one thing that lasts—God's Word. It has outlasted
kings and pharaohs, wars and famines, empires and nations. It
outlasts traditions, trends, pleasure and pain. Jesus said that
though even the world will disappear, "[his] words will never pass
away."

God's Word will give us joy that no possession ever will. Unlike
my new cars, God's Word will never rust, lose power or be outdated.
And his Word makes a difference in my life when I read it because
he promises, "I am watching to see that my word is fulfilled" (Jeremiah 1:12).

A Deeper Look
Matthew 6:19–21; Luke 16:17

Go to page 1101 for your next devotional reading.

⁴²"Therefore keep watch, because you do not know on what day your Lord will come. ⁴³But understand this: If the owner of the house had known at what time of night the thief was coming, he would have kept watch and would not have let his house be broken into. ⁴⁴So you also must be ready, because the Son of Man will come at an hour when you do not expect him.

⁴⁵"Who then is the faithful and wise servant, whom the master has put in charge of the servants in his household to give them their food at the proper time? ⁴⁶It will be good for that servant whose master finds him doing so when he returns. ⁴⁷I tell you the truth, he will put him in charge of all his possessions. ⁴⁸But suppose that servant is wicked and says to himself, 'My master is staying away a long time,' ⁴⁹and he then begins to beat his fellow servants and to eat and drink with drunkards. ⁵⁰The master of that servant will come on a day when he does not expect him and at an hour he is not aware of. ⁵¹He will cut him to pieces and assign him a place with the hypocrites, where there will be weeping and gnashing of teeth.

The Parable of the Ten Virgins

25 "At that time the kingdom of heaven will be like ten virgins who took their lamps and went out to meet the bridegroom. ²Five of them were foolish and five were wise. ³The foolish ones took their lamps but did not take any oil with them. ⁴The wise, however, took oil in jars along with their lamps. ⁵The bridegroom was a long time in coming, and they all became drowsy and fell asleep.

⁶"At midnight the cry rang out: 'Here's the bridegroom! Come out to meet him!'

⁷"Then all the virgins woke up and trimmed their lamps. ⁸The foolish ones said to the wise, 'Give us some of your oil; our lamps are going out.'

⁹"'No,' they replied, 'there may not be enough for both us and you. Instead, go to those who sell oil and buy some for yourselves.'

¹⁰"But while they were on their way to buy the oil, the bridegroom arrived. The virgins who were ready went in with him to the wedding banquet. And the door was shut.

¹¹"Later the others also came. 'Sir! Sir!' they said. 'Open the door for us!'

¹²"But he replied, 'I tell you the truth, I don't know you.'

¹³"Therefore keep watch, because you do not know the day or the hour.

The Parable of the Talents

¹⁴"Again, it will be like a man going on a journey, who called his servants and entrusted his property to them. ¹⁵To one he gave five talents*a* of money, to another two talents, and to another one talent, each according to his ability. Then he went on his journey. ¹⁶The man who had received the five talents went at once and put his money to work and gained five more. ¹⁷So also, the one with the two talents gained two more. ¹⁸But the man who had received the one talent went off, dug a hole in the ground and hid his master's money.

¹⁹"After a long time the master of those servants returned and settled accounts with them. ²⁰The man who had received the five talents brought the other five. 'Master,' he said, 'you entrusted me with five talents. See, I have gained five more.'

²¹"His master replied, 'Well done, good and faithful servant! You have been faithful with a few things; I will put you in charge of many things. Come and share your master's happiness!'

²²"The man with the two talents also came. 'Master,' he said, 'you entrusted me with two talents; see, I have gained two more.'

²³"His master replied, 'Well done, good and faithful servant! You have been faithful with a few things; I will put you in charge of many things. Come and share your master's happiness!'

²⁴"Then the man who had received the one talent came. 'Master,' he said, 'I knew that you are a hard man, harvesting where you have not sown and gathering where you have not scattered seed. ²⁵So I was afraid and went out and hid your talent in the ground. See, here is what belongs to you.'

²⁶"His master replied, 'You wicked, lazy servant! So you knew that I harvest where I have not sown and gather where I have not scattered seed? ²⁷Well then, you should have put my money on deposit with the bankers, so that when I

---

a 15 A talent was worth more than a thousand dollars.

returned I would have received it back with interest.

²⁸" 'Take the talent from him and give it to the one who has the ten talents. ²⁹For everyone who has will be given more, and he will have an abundance. Whoever does not have, even what he has will be taken from him. ³⁰And throw that worthless servant outside, into the darkness, where there will be weeping and gnashing of teeth.'

The Sheep and the Goats

³¹"When the Son of Man comes in his glory, and all the angels with him, he will sit on his throne in heavenly glory. ³²All the nations will be gathered before him, and he will separate the people one from another as a shepherd separates the sheep from the goats. ³³He will put the sheep on his right and the goats on his left.

³⁴"Then the King will say to those on his right, 'Come, you who are blessed by my Father; take your inheritance, the kingdom prepared for you since the creation of the world. ³⁵For I was hungry and you gave me something to eat, I was thirsty and you gave me something to drink, I was a stranger and you invited me in, ³⁶I needed clothes and you clothed me, I was sick and you looked after me, I was in prison and you came to visit me.'

³⁷"Then the righteous will answer him, 'Lord, when did we see you hungry and feed you, or thirsty and give you something to drink? ³⁸When did we see you a stranger and invite you in, or needing clothes and clothe you? ³⁹When did we see you sick or in prison and go to visit you?'

⁴⁰"The King will reply, 'I tell you the truth, whatever you did for one of the least of these brothers of mine, you did for me.'

⁴¹"Then he will say to those on his left, 'Depart from me, you who are cursed, into the eternal fire prepared for the devil and his angels. ⁴²For I was hungry and you gave me nothing to eat, I was thirsty and you gave me nothing to drink, ⁴³I was a stranger and you did not invite me in, I needed clothes and you did not clothe me, I was sick and in prison and you did not look after me.'

⁴⁴"They also will answer, 'Lord, when did we see you hungry or thirsty or a stranger or needing clothes or sick or in prison, and did not help you?'

⁴⁵"He will reply, 'I tell you the truth, whatever you did not do for one of the least of these, you did not do for me.'

⁴⁶"Then they will go away to eternal punishment, but the righteous to eternal life."

The Plot Against Jesus

See Mark 14:1–2; Luke 22:1–2

26 When Jesus had finished saying all these things, he said to his disciples, ²"As you know, the Passover is two days away—and the Son of Man will be handed over to be crucified."

³Then the chief priests and the elders of the people assembled in the palace of the high priest, whose name was Caiaphas, ⁴and they plotted to arrest Jesus in some sly way and kill him. ⁵"But not during the Feast," they said, "or there may be a riot among the people."

Jesus Anointed at Bethany

See Mark 14:3–9

⁶While Jesus was in Bethany in the home of a man known as Simon the Leper, ⁷a woman came to him with an alabaster jar of very expensive perfume, which she poured on his head as he was reclining at the table.

⁸When the disciples saw this, they were indignant. "Why this waste?" they asked. ⁹"This perfume could have been sold at a high price and the money given to the poor."

¹⁰Aware of this, Jesus said to them, "Why are you bothering this woman? She has done a beautiful thing to me. ¹¹The poor you will always have with you, but you will not always have me. ¹²When she poured this perfume on my body, she did it to prepare me for burial. ¹³I tell you the truth, wherever this gospel

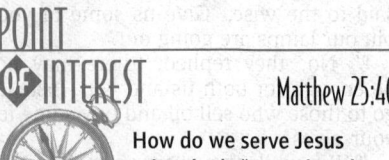

POINT OF INTEREST

Matthew 25:40

How do we serve Jesus when he is "seated at the right hand of God"? (Colossians 3:1). Jesus identifies so completely with those in need that when we serve them, we are serving Jesus himself.

is preached throughout the world, what she has done will also be told, in memory of her."

Judas Agrees to Betray Jesus
See Mark 14:10–11; Luke 22:3–6

14Then one of the Twelve—the one called Judas Iscariot—went to the chief priests **15**and asked, "What are you willing to give me if I hand him over to you?" So they counted out for him thirty silver coins. **16**From then on Judas watched for an opportunity to hand him over.

The Lord's Supper
See Mark 14:12–25; Luke 22:7–13

17On the first day of the Feast of Unleavened Bread, the disciples came to Jesus and asked, "Where do you want us to make preparations for you to eat the Passover?"

18He replied, "Go into the city to a certain man and tell him, 'The Teacher says: My appointed time is near. I am going to celebrate the Passover with my disciples at your house.' " **19**So the disciples did as Jesus had directed them and prepared the Passover.

20When evening came, Jesus was reclining at the table with the Twelve. **21**And while they were eating, he said, "I tell you the truth, one of you will betray me."

22They were very sad and began to say to him one after the other, "Surely not I, Lord?"

23Jesus replied, "The one who has dipped his hand into the bowl with me will betray me. **24**The Son of Man will go just as it is written about him. But woe to that man who betrays the Son of Man! It would be better for him if he had not been born."

25Then Judas, the one who would betray him, said, "Surely not I, Rabbi?"

Jesus answered, "Yes, it is you."*a*

26While they were eating, Jesus took bread, gave thanks and broke it, and gave it to his disciples, saying, "Take and eat; this is my body."

27Then he took the cup, gave thanks and offered it to them, saying, "Drink from it, all of you. **28**This is my blood of the*b* covenant, which is poured out for many for the forgiveness of sins. **29**I tell you, I will not drink of this fruit of the vine from now on until that day when I drink it anew with you in my Father's kingdom."

30When they had sung a hymn, they went out to the Mount of Olives.

Jesus Predicts Peter's Denial
See Mark 14:27–31; Luke 22:31–34

31Then Jesus told them, "This very night you will all fall away on account of me, for it is written:

" 'I will strike the shepherd,
    and the sheep of the flock will be
        scattered.'*c*

32But after I have risen, I will go ahead of you into Galilee."

33Peter replied, "Even if all fall away on account of you, I never will."

34"I tell you the truth," Jesus answered, "this very night, before the rooster crows, you will disown me three times."

35But Peter declared, "Even if I have to die with you, I will never disown you." And all the other disciples said the same.

Gethsemane
See Mark 14:32–42; Luke 22:40–46

36Then Jesus went with his disciples to a place called Gethsemane, and he said to them, "Sit here while I go over there and pray." **37**He took Peter and the two sons of Zebedee along with him, and he began to be sorrowful and troubled. **38**Then he said to them, "My soul is overwhelmed with sorrow to the point of death. Stay here and keep watch with me."

39Going a little farther, he fell with his face to the ground and prayed, "My Father, if it is possible, may this cup be taken from me. Yet not as I will, but as you will."

40Then he returned to his disciples and found them sleeping. "Could you men not keep watch with me for one hour?" he asked Peter. **41**"Watch and pray so that you will not fall into temptation. The spirit is willing, but the body is weak."

42He went away a second time and prayed, "My Father, if it is not possible for this cup to be taken away unless I drink it, may your will be done."

43When he came back, he again found them sleeping, because their eyes were heavy. **44**So he left them and went away once more and prayed the third time, saying the same thing.

45Then he returned to the disciples and

a25 Or *"You yourself have said it"*   *b28* Some manuscripts *the new*   *c31* Zech. 13:7

said to them, "Are you still sleeping and resting? Look, the hour is near, and the Son of Man is betrayed into the hands of sinners. ⁴⁶Rise, let us go! Here comes my betrayer!"

Jesus Arrested

See Mark 14:43–50; Luke 22:47–53

⁴⁷While he was still speaking, Judas, one of the Twelve, arrived. With him was a large crowd armed with swords and clubs, sent from the chief priests and the elders of the people. ⁴⁸Now the betrayer had arranged a signal with them: "The one I kiss is the man; arrest him." ⁴⁹Going at once to Jesus, Judas said, "Greetings, Rabbi!" and kissed him.

⁵⁰Jesus replied, "Friend, do what you came for."ᵃ

Then the men stepped forward, seized Jesus and arrested him. ⁵¹With that, one of Jesus' companions reached for his sword, drew it out and struck the servant of the high priest, cutting off his ear.

⁵²"Put your sword back in its place," Jesus said to him, "for all who draw the sword will die by the sword. ⁵³Do you think I cannot call on my Father, and he will at once put at my disposal more than twelve legions of angels? ⁵⁴But how then would the Scriptures be fulfilled that say it must happen in this way?"

⁵⁵At that time Jesus said to the crowd, "Am I leading a rebellion, that you have come out with swords and clubs to capture me? Every day I sat in the temple courts teaching, and you did not arrest me. ⁵⁶But this has all taken place that the writings of the prophets might be fulfilled." Then all the disciples deserted him and fled.

Before the Sanhedrin

See Mark 14:53–65; John 18:12–13,19–24

⁵⁷Those who had arrested Jesus took him to Caiaphas, the high priest, where the teachers of the law and the elders had assembled. ⁵⁸But Peter followed him at a distance, right up to the courtyard of the high priest. He entered and sat down with the guards to see the outcome.

⁵⁹The chief priests and the whole Sanhedrin were looking for false evidence against Jesus so that they could put him to death. ⁶⁰But they did not find any, though many false witnesses came forward.

Finally two came forward ⁶¹and declared, "This fellow said, 'I am able to destroy the temple of God and rebuild it in three days.' "

⁶²Then the high priest stood up and said to Jesus, "Are you not going to answer? What is this testimony that these men are bringing against you?" ⁶³But Jesus remained silent.

The high priest said to him, "I charge you under oath by the living God: Tell us if you are the Christ,ᵇ the Son of God."

⁶⁴"Yes, it is as you say," Jesus replied. "But I say to all of you: In the future you will see the Son of Man sitting at the right hand of the Mighty One and coming on the clouds of heaven."

⁶⁵Then the high priest tore his clothes and said, "He has spoken blasphemy! Why do we need any more witnesses? Look, now you have heard the blasphemy. ⁶⁶What do you think?"

"He is worthy of death," they answered.

⁶⁷Then they spit in his face and struck him with their fists. Others slapped him ⁶⁸and said, "Prophesy to us, Christ. Who hit you?"

Peter Disowns Jesus

See Mark 14:66–72; Luke 22:52–62; John 18:16–18,25–27

⁶⁹Now Peter was sitting out in the courtyard, and a servant girl came to him. "You also were with Jesus of Galilee," she said.

⁷⁰But he denied it before them all. "I don't know what you're talking about," he said.

⁷¹Then he went out to the gateway, where another girl saw him and said to the people there, "This fellow was with Jesus of Nazareth."

⁷²He denied it again, with an oath: "I don't know the man!"

⁷³After a little while, those standing there went up to Peter and said, "Surely you are one of them, for your accent gives you away."

⁷⁴Then he began to call down curses on himself and he swore to them, "I don't know the man!"

Immediately a rooster crowed. ⁷⁵Then Peter remembered the word Jesus had spoken: "Before the rooster crows, you will disown me three times." And he went outside and wept bitterly.

ᵃ50 Or "Friend, why have you come?"　ᵇ63 Or Messiah; also in verse 68

Judas Hangs Himself

27 Early in the morning, all the chief priests and the elders of the people came to the decision to put Jesus to death. ²They bound him, led him away and handed him over to Pilate, the governor.

³When Judas, who had betrayed him, saw that Jesus was condemned, he was seized with remorse and returned the thirty silver coins to the chief priests and the elders. ⁴"I have sinned," he said, "for I have betrayed innocent blood."

"What is that to us?" they replied. "That's your responsibility."

⁵So Judas threw the money into the temple and left. Then he went away and hanged himself.

⁶The chief priests picked up the coins and said, "It is against the law to put this into the treasury, since it is blood money." ⁷So they decided to use the money to buy the potter's field as a burial place for foreigners. ⁸That is why it has been called the Field of Blood to this day. ⁹Then what was spoken by Jeremiah the prophet was fulfilled: "They took the thirty silver coins, the price set on him by the people of Israel, ¹⁰and they used them to buy the potter's field, as the Lord commanded me."[a]

Jesus Before Pilate

See Mark 15:2–15; Luke 23:2–3,18–25; John 18:29—19:16

¹¹Meanwhile Jesus stood before the governor, and the governor asked him, "Are you the king of the Jews?"

"Yes, it is as you say," Jesus replied.

¹²When he was accused by the chief priests and the elders, he gave no answer. ¹³Then Pilate asked him, "Don't you hear the testimony they are bringing against you?" ¹⁴But Jesus made no reply, not even to a single charge—to the great amazement of the governor.

¹⁵Now it was the governor's custom at the Feast to release a prisoner chosen by the crowd. ¹⁶At that time they had a notorious prisoner, called Barabbas. ¹⁷So when the crowd had gathered, Pilate asked them, "Which one do you want me to release to you: Barabbas, or Jesus who is called Christ?" ¹⁸For he knew it was out of envy that they had handed Jesus over to him.

¹⁹While Pilate was sitting on the judge's seat, his wife sent him this message: "Don't have anything to do with that innocent man, for I have suffered a great deal today in a dream because of him."

²⁰But the chief priests and the elders persuaded the crowd to ask for Barabbas and to have Jesus executed.

²¹"Which of the two do you want me to release to you?" asked the governor.

"Barabbas," they answered.

²²"What shall I do, then, with Jesus who is called Christ?" Pilate asked.

They all answered, "Crucify him!"

²³"Why? What crime has he committed?" asked Pilate.

But they shouted all the louder, "Crucify him!"

²⁴When Pilate saw that he was getting nowhere, but that instead an uproar was starting, he took water and washed his hands in front of the crowd. "I am innocent of this man's blood," he said. "It is your responsibility!"

²⁵All the people answered, "Let his blood be on us and on our children!"

²⁶Then he released Barabbas to them. But he had Jesus flogged, and handed him over to be crucified.

The Soldiers Mock Jesus

See Mark 15:16–20

²⁷Then the governor's soldiers took Jesus into the Praetorium and gathered the whole company of soldiers around him. ²⁸They stripped him and put a scarlet robe on him, ²⁹and then twisted together a crown of thorns and set it on his head. They put a staff in his right hand and knelt in front of him and mocked him. "Hail, king of the Jews!" they said. ³⁰They spit on him, and took the staff and struck him on the head again and again. ³¹After they had mocked him, they took off the robe and put his own clothes on him. Then they led him away to crucify him.

The Crucifixion

See Mark 15:22–32; Luke 23:33–43; John 19:17–24

³²As they were going out, they met a man from Cyrene, named Simon, and they forced him to carry the cross. ³³They came to a place called Golgotha (which means The Place of the Skull). ³⁴There they offered Jesus wine to drink, mixed with gall; but after tasting it, he refused

a 10 See Zech. 11:12,13; Jer. 19:1-13; 32:6-9.

to drink it. ³⁵When they had crucified him, they divided up his clothes by casting lots.ᵃ ³⁶And sitting down, they kept watch over him there. ³⁷Above his head they placed the written charge against him: THIS IS JESUS, THE KING OF THE JEWS. ³⁸ Two robbers were crucified with him, one on his right and one on his left. ³⁹Those who passed by hurled insults at him, shaking their heads ⁴⁰and saying, "You who are going to destroy the temple and build it in three days, save yourself! Come down from the cross, if you are the Son of God!"

⁴¹In the same way the chief priests, the teachers of the law and the elders mocked him. ⁴²"He saved others," they said, "but he can't save himself! He's the King of Israel! Let him come down now from the cross, and we will believe in him. ⁴³He trusts in God. Let God rescue him now if he wants him, for he said, 'I am the Son of God.' " ⁴⁴In the same way the robbers who were crucified with him also heaped insults on him.

The Death of Jesus

See Mark 15:33–41; Luke 23:44–49; John 19:29–30

⁴⁵From the sixth hour until the ninth hour darkness came over all the land. ⁴⁶About the ninth hour Jesus cried out in a loud voice, *"Eloi, Eloi,ᵇ lama sabachthani?"*—which means, "My God, my God, why have you forsaken me?"ᶜ

⁴⁷When some of those standing there heard this, they said, "He's calling Elijah."

⁴⁸Immediately one of them ran and got a sponge. He filled it with wine vinegar, put it on a stick, and offered it to Jesus to drink. ⁴⁹The rest said, "Now leave him alone. Let's see if Elijah comes to save him."

⁵⁰And when Jesus had cried out again in a loud voice, he gave up his spirit.

⁵¹At that moment the curtain of the temple was torn in two from top to bottom. The earth shook and the rocks split. ⁵²The tombs broke open and the bodies of many holy people who had died were raised to life. ⁵³They came out of the tombs, and after Jesus' resurrection they went into the holy city and appeared to many people.

⁵⁴When the centurion and those with him who were guarding Jesus saw the earthquake and all that had happened,

they were terrified, and exclaimed, "Surely he was the Sonᵈ of God!"

⁵⁵Many women were there, watching from a distance. They had followed Jesus from Galilee to care for his needs. ⁵⁶Among them were Mary Magdalene, Mary the mother of James and Joses, and the mother of Zebedee's sons.

The Burial of Jesus

See Mark 15:42–47; Luke 23:50–56; John 19:38–42

⁵⁷As evening approached, there came a rich man from Arimathea, named Joseph, who had himself become a disciple of Jesus. ⁵⁸Going to Pilate, he asked for Jesus' body, and Pilate ordered that it be given to him. ⁵⁹Joseph took the body, wrapped it in a clean linen cloth, ⁶⁰and placed it in his own new tomb that he had cut out of the rock. He rolled a big stone in front of the entrance to the tomb and went away. ⁶¹Mary Magdalene and the other Mary were sitting there opposite the tomb.

The Guard at the Tomb

⁶²The next day, the one after Preparation Day, the chief priests and the Pharisees went to Pilate. ⁶³"Sir," they said, "we remember that while he was still alive that deceiver said, 'After three days I will rise again.' ⁶⁴So give the order for the tomb to be made secure until the third day. Otherwise, his disciples may come and steal the body and tell the people that he has been raised from the dead. This last deception will be worse than the first."

⁶⁵"Take a guard," Pilate answered. "Go, make the tomb as secure as you know how." ⁶⁶So they went and made the tomb secure by putting a seal on the stone and posting the guard.

The Resurrection

See Mark 16:1–8; Luke 24:1–10; John 20:1–8

28 After the Sabbath, at dawn on the first day of the week, Mary Magdalene and the other Mary went to look at the tomb.

²There was a violent earthquake, for an angel of the Lord came down from

---

ᵃ35 A few late manuscripts *lots that the word spoken by the prophet might be fulfilled: "They divided my garments among themselves and cast lots for my clothing"* (Psalm 22:18)   ᵇ46 Some manuscripts *Eli, Eli*   ᶜ46 Psalm 22:1   ᵈ54 Or *a son*

Read Matthew 28:1–20
Key Verses Matthew 28:18–20

The Great Commission

This passage is often called the "Great Commission." This short passage is like a time capsule of the hope and vision that God in Jesus Christ has for his church. Jesus sends his disciples out with a mission and the power and authority to carry it out.

Jesus' emphatic command is given to all who follow him. It's called "Great" because its scope is worldwide. God wants everyone to have the opportunity to hear his Good News—people from every nation and every race, from the noisy dorm mates next door to the tribe of strangers on the other side of the globe.

If we are followers of Jesus Christ, our instructions are clear. We are to make disciples—to reach out to those he puts in our life and then prepare them to do likewise. The Great Commission stands as a fresh challenge for each new generation of believers.

Digging Into the Word
1. What do the following passages say about God's heart for the world?—*Psalm 145:10–13; Isaiah 49:6; Romans 16:25–27*
2. How do these passages help you see the needs of the world through God's eyes?—*Isaiah 35:1–10; Isaiah 61:1; Matthew 9:36–38*

Personal Reflection
How are you personally involved in helping to fulfill the Great Commission? Who can you begin praying for today?

One Step Deeper
John 3:16–17; 1 Timothy 2:1–3

Go to page 1105 for your next devotional reading.

heaven and, going to the tomb, rolled back the stone and sat on it. [3]His appearance was like lightning, and his clothes were white as snow. [4]The guards were so afraid of him that they shook and became like dead men.

[5]The angel said to the women, "Do not be afraid, for I know that you are looking for Jesus, who was crucified. [6]He is not here; he has risen, just as he said. Come and see the place where he lay. [7]Then go quickly and tell his disciples: 'He has risen from the dead and is going ahead of you into Galilee. There you will see him.' Now I have told you."

[8]So the women hurried away from the tomb, afraid yet filled with joy, and ran to tell his disciples. [9]Suddenly Jesus met them. "Greetings," he said. They came to him, clasped his feet and worshiped him. [10]Then Jesus said to them, "Do not be afraid. Go and tell my brothers to go to Galilee; there they will see me."

The Guards' Report

[11]While the women were on their way, some of the guards went into the city and reported to the chief priests everything that had happened. [12]When the chief priests had met with the elders and devised a plan, they gave the soldiers a large sum of money, [13]telling them, "You are to say, 'His disciples came during the night and stole him away while we were asleep.' [14]If this report gets to the governor, we will satisfy him and keep you out of trouble." [15]So the soldiers took the money and did as they were instructed. And this story has been widely circulated among the Jews to this very day.

The Great Commission

[16]Then the eleven disciples went to Galilee, to the mountain where Jesus had told them to go. [17]When they saw him, they worshiped him; but some doubted. [18]Then Jesus came to them and said, "All authority in heaven and on earth has been given to me. [19]Therefore go and make disciples of all nations, baptizing them in[a] the name of the Father and of the Son and of the Holy Spirit, [20]and teaching them to obey everything I have commanded you. And surely I am with you always, to the very end of the age."

[a]19 Or *into*; see Acts 8:16; 19:5; Romans 6:3; 1 Cor. 1:13; 10:2 and Gal. 3:27.

"**J**ust the facts" is what Mark gives us in his fast-paced Gospel—the highlights of Jesus' life and ministry told in a "news flash" style. The shortest and probably the oldest of the four Gospels, the book of Mark is detailed but action-oriented. It explains Jewish customs for the benefit of non-Jewish readers, records the high points of Jesus' miracles and describes the weeks before his crucifixion. Mark's Gospel describes Jesus' ministry in action terms: Jesus calls people, heals them, prays to the Father, teaches the crowds, appoints disciples, drives out demons, serves others and gives his life for us (see 10:45).

MARK

John the Baptist Prepares the Way

See Matthew 3:1–11; Luke 3:2–16

1 The beginning of the gospel about Jesus Christ, the Son of God.[a]

2It is written in Isaiah the prophet:

"I will send my messenger ahead of
you,
who will prepare your way"[b]—
3"a voice of one calling in the desert,
'Prepare the way for the Lord,
make straight paths for him.' "[c]

4And so John came, baptizing in the desert region and preaching a baptism of repentance for the forgiveness of sins. 5The whole Judean countryside and all the people of Jerusalem went out to him. Confessing their sins, they were baptized by him in the Jordan River. 6John wore clothing made of camel's hair, with a leather belt around his waist, and he ate locusts and wild honey. 7And this was his message: "After me will come one more powerful than I, the thongs of whose sandals I am not worthy to stoop down and untie. 8I baptize you with[d] water, but he will baptize you with the Holy Spirit."

[a]1 Some manuscripts do not have *the Son of God.*
[b]2 Mal. 3:1   [c]3 Isaiah 40:3   [d]8 Or *in*

The Baptism and Temptation of Jesus

See Matthew 3:13–17; 4:1–11; Luke 3:21–22; 4:1–13

⁹At that time Jesus came from Nazareth in Galilee and was baptized by John in the Jordan. ¹⁰As Jesus was coming up out of the water, he saw heaven being torn open and the Spirit descending on him like a dove. ¹¹And a voice came from heaven: "You are my Son, whom I love; with you I am well pleased."

¹²At once the Spirit sent him out into the desert, ¹³and he was in the desert forty days, being tempted by Satan. He was with the wild animals, and angels attended him.

The Calling of the First Disciples

See Matthew 4:18–22; Luke 5:2–11; John 1:35–42

¹⁴After John was put in prison, Jesus went into Galilee, proclaiming the good news of God. ¹⁵"The time has come," he said. "The kingdom of God is near. Repent and believe the good news!"

¹⁶As Jesus walked beside the Sea of Galilee, he saw Simon and his brother Andrew casting a net into the lake, for they were fishermen. ¹⁷"Come, follow me," Jesus said, "and I will make you fishers of men." ¹⁸At once they left their nets and followed him.

¹⁹When he had gone a little farther, he saw James son of Zebedee and his brother John in a boat, preparing their nets. ²⁰Without delay he called them, and they left their father Zebedee in the boat with the hired men and followed him.

Jesus Drives Out an Evil Spirit

See Luke 4:31–37

²¹They went to Capernaum, and when the Sabbath came, Jesus went into the synagogue and began to teach. ²²The people were amazed at his teaching, because he taught them as one who had authority, not as the teachers of the law. ²³Just then a man in their synagogue who was possessed by an evil[a] spirit cried out, ²⁴"What do you want with us, Jesus of Nazareth? Have you come to destroy us? I know who you are—the Holy One of God!"

²⁵"Be quiet!" said Jesus sternly. "Come out of him!" ²⁶The evil spirit shook the man violently and came out of him with a shriek.

²⁷The people were all so amazed that they asked each other, "What is this? A new teaching—and with authority! He even gives orders to evil spirits and they obey him." ²⁸News about him spread quickly over the whole region of Galilee.

Jesus Heals Many

See Matthew 8:14–17; Luke 4:38–41

²⁹As soon as they left the synagogue, they went with James and John to the home of Simon and Andrew. ³⁰Simon's mother-in-law was in bed with a fever, and they told Jesus about her. ³¹So he went to her, took her hand and helped her up. The fever left her and she began to wait on them.

³²That evening after sunset the people brought to Jesus all the sick and demon-possessed. ³³The whole town gathered at the door, ³⁴and Jesus healed many who had various diseases. He also drove out many demons, but he would not let the demons speak because they knew who he was.

Jesus Prays in a Solitary Place

See Luke 4:42–43

³⁵Very early in the morning, while it was still dark, Jesus got up, left the house and went off to a solitary place, where he prayed. ³⁶Simon and his companions went to look for him, ³⁷and when they found him, they exclaimed: "Everyone is looking for you!"

³⁸Jesus replied, "Let us go somewhere else—to the nearby villages—so I can preach there also. That is why I have come." ³⁹So he traveled throughout Galilee, preaching in their synagogues and driving out demons.

A Man With Leprosy

See Matthew 8:2–4; Luke 5:12–14

⁴⁰A man with leprosy[b] came to him and begged him on his knees, "If you are willing, you can make me clean."

⁴¹Filled with compassion, Jesus reached out his hand and touched the man. "I am willing," he said. "Be clean!" ⁴²Immediately the leprosy left him and he was cured.

⁴³Jesus sent him away at once with a strong warning: ⁴⁴"See that you don't tell this to anyone. But go, show yourself to

a23 Greek unclean; also in verses 26 and 27
b40 The Greek word was used for various diseases affecting the skin—not necessarily leprosy.

the priest and offer the sacrifices that Moses commanded for your cleansing, as a testimony to them." ⁴⁵Instead he went out and began to talk freely, spreading the news. As a result, Jesus could no longer enter a town openly but stayed outside in lonely places. Yet the people still came to him from everywhere.

Jesus Heals a Paralytic
See Matthew 9:2–8; Luke 5:18–26

2 A few days later, when Jesus again entered Capernaum, the people heard that he had come home. ²So many gathered that there was no room left, not even outside the door, and he preached the word to them. ³Some men came, bringing to him a paralytic, carried by four of them. ⁴Since they could not get him to Jesus because of the crowd, they made an opening in the roof above Jesus and, after digging through it, lowered the mat the paralyzed man was lying on. ⁵When Jesus saw their faith, he said to the paralytic, "Son, your sins are forgiven."

⁶Now some teachers of the law were sitting there, thinking to themselves, ⁷"Why does this fellow talk like that? He's blaspheming! Who can forgive sins but God alone?"

⁸Immediately Jesus knew in his spirit that this was what they were thinking in their hearts, and he said to them, "Why are you thinking these things? ⁹Which is easier: to say to the paralytic, 'Your sins are forgiven,' or to say, 'Get up, take your mat and walk'? ¹⁰But that you may know that the Son of Man has authority on earth to forgive sins . . . ." He said to the paralytic, ¹¹"I tell you, get up, take your mat and go home." ¹²He got up, took his mat and walked out in full view of them all. This amazed everyone and they

---

MONDAY

Read Mark 1:1–39
Key Verse Mark 1:35

Time Alone – Joe Bernardy

It had been "one of those days." All day long Jesus had been pressed by people and their needs. He had been in the synagogue, teaching and driving out demons. Later he was at Peter and Andrew's house, healing one person after another. It seemed the whole city needed his help, keeping him up late into the night. Certainly he deserved to sleep late the next morning!

If anyone could get by without time with God, Jesus could. But he got up early the next morning for some time alone with his Father. Why? Because Jesus loved him and wanted intimate contact with him. Just as a couple in love will find ways to spend time together in spite of schedules and obstacles, so too Jesus found a way to be with the Father.

Jesus also knew that even he needed time with the Father to be prepared for the demands of his day. And there were demands! Even before he had finished praying, his disciples came with their plans: "Everyone is looking for you!" But he wasn't controlled by their program. He followed God's agenda for the day instead: "Let us go somewhere else (Mark 1:38)."

If Jesus Christ needed time with God to shape his day, how much more do we need to make our quiet time a daily priority! Today is a good day to start!

A Deeper Look
Psalm 5:3; Psalm 143:8; Isaiah 30:15

Go to page 1107 for your next devotional reading.

praised God, saying, "We have never seen anything like this!"

The Calling of Levi
See Matthew 9:9–13; Luke 5:27–32

¹³Once again Jesus went out beside the lake. A large crowd came to him, and he began to teach them. ¹⁴As he walked along, he saw Levi son of Alphaeus sitting at the tax collector's booth. "Follow me," Jesus told him, and Levi got up and followed him.

¹⁵While Jesus was having dinner at Levi's house, many tax collectors and "sinners" were eating with him and his disciples, for there were many who followed him. ¹⁶When the teachers of the law who were Pharisees saw him eating with the "sinners" and tax collectors, they asked his disciples: "Why does he eat with tax collectors and 'sinners'?"

¹⁷On hearing this, Jesus said to them, "It is not the healthy who need a doctor, but the sick. I have not come to call the righteous, but sinners."

Jesus Questioned About Fasting
See Matthew 9:14–17; Luke 5:33–38

¹⁸Now John's disciples and the Pharisees were fasting. Some people came and asked Jesus, "How is it that John's disciples and the disciples of the Pharisees are fasting, but yours are not?"

¹⁹Jesus answered, "How can the guests of the bridegroom fast while he is with them? They cannot, so long as they have him with them. ²⁰But the time will come when the bridegroom will be taken from them, and on that day they will fast.

²¹"No one sews a patch of unshrunk cloth on an old garment. If he does, the new piece will pull away from the old, making the tear worse. ²²And no one pours new wine into old wineskins. If he does, the wine will burst the skins, and both the wine and the wineskins will be ruined. No, he pours new wine into new wineskins."

Lord of the Sabbath
See Matthew 12:1–14; Luke 6:1–11

²³One Sabbath Jesus was going through the grainfields, and as his disciples walked along, they began to pick some heads of grain. ²⁴The Pharisees said to him, "Look, why are they doing what is unlawful on the Sabbath?"

²⁵He answered, "Have you never read what David did when he and his companions were hungry and in need? ²⁶In the days of Abiathar the high priest, he entered the house of God and ate the consecrated bread, which is lawful only for priests to eat. And he also gave some to his companions."

²⁷Then he said to them, "The Sabbath was made for man, not man for the Sabbath. ²⁸So the Son of Man is Lord even of the Sabbath."

3 Another time he went into the synagogue, and a man with a shriveled hand was there. ²Some of them were looking for a reason to accuse Jesus, so they watched him closely to see if he would heal him on the Sabbath. ³Jesus said to the man with the shriveled hand, "Stand up in front of everyone."

⁴Then Jesus asked them, "Which is lawful on the Sabbath: to do good or to do evil, to save life or to kill?" But they remained silent.

⁵He looked around at them in anger and, deeply distressed at their stubborn hearts, said to the man, "Stretch out your hand." He stretched it out, and his hand was completely restored. ⁶Then the Pharisees went out and began to plot with the Herodians how they might kill Jesus.

Crowds Follow Jesus
See Matthew 12:15–16; Luke 6:17–19

⁷Jesus withdrew with his disciples to the lake, and a large crowd from Galilee followed. ⁸When they heard all he was doing, many people came to him from

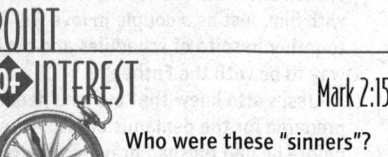

POINT OF INTEREST
Mark 2:15

Who were these "sinners"? Levi's dinner party may have included prostitutes, tax collectors and other "disreputable" persons. However, the Pharisees also considered "sinners" those who didn't follow all of their detailed rules and regulations. Jesus' self-righteous opponents used the word "sinner" as an insult and never would have applied the term to themselves. But look at Romans 3:23 for the Bible's inclusive definition of a sinner.

Judea, Jerusalem, Idumea, and the regions across the Jordan and around Tyre and Sidon. ⁹Because of the crowd he told his disciples to have a small boat ready for him, to keep the people from crowding him. ¹⁰For he had healed many, so that those with diseases were pushing forward to touch him. ¹¹Whenever the evil*a* spirits saw him, they fell down before him and cried out, "You are the Son of God." ¹²But he gave them strict orders not to tell who he was.

The Appointing of the Twelve Apostles

¹³Jesus went up on a mountainside and called to him those he wanted, and they came to him. ¹⁴He appointed twelve—designating them apostles*b*—that they might be with him and that he might send them out to preach ¹⁵and to have authority to drive out demons. ¹⁶These are the twelve he appointed: Simon (to whom he gave the name Peter); ¹⁷James son of Zebedee and his brother John (to them he gave the name Boanerges, which means Sons of Thunder); ¹⁸Andrew, Philip, Bartholomew, Matthew, Thomas, James son of Alphaeus, Thaddaeus, Simon the Zealot ¹⁹and Judas Iscariot, who betrayed him.

a 11 Greek *unclean*; also in verse 30   *b 14* Some manuscripts do not have *designating them apostles.*

TUESDAY

Read Mark 3:1–35
Key Verses Mark 3:14–15

Multiplying Your Life — Jim Rinella

Imagine a terrible disaster has just struck! You are the leader of the first rescue team to appear at the scene. Then you get word that you will be the only rescue team because the access road you used is now impassable. You realize that there are two approaches that you could use to direct your team as you face this crisis situation.

You could tell each member of your five-person team to help injured people as they discover them. No matter how severe the injury, each person has the same individual worth and needs help and attention (an additive approach).

Or you could walk around the disaster site calling, "Is anyone OK? Is anyone out there uninjured?" Then, after identifying the uninjured, you could quickly coach these people on some elementary rescue techniques, multiplying the size of your team (a multiplication approach). Which approach would show more compassion? Which approach will allow you to save the most people?

The second approach is likely to save more lives overall. And it was the approach that Jesus used to save souls as well. He spent months training his disciples for the spiritual battle they would encounter. They became the rescue team members looking for other disciples to help them reach the hurting and the lost—those who hadn't yet met the Great Physician.

The spiritual battle we face is not unlike a medical triage situation; we just don't see the blood and hear the moans. Are you maximizing the impact of your efforts? Are you teaching others who can in turn help? Become part of a multiplying team rather than an additive team in the spiritual battle around you.

A Deeper Look
Romans 12:3–8; 2 Timothy 2:2

Go to page 1110 for your next devotional reading.

Jesus and Beelzebub

See Matthew 12:25–29; Luke 11:17–22

²⁰Then Jesus entered a house, and again a crowd gathered, so that he and his disciples were not even able to eat. ²¹When his family heard about this, they went to take charge of him, for they said, "He is out of his mind."

²²And the teachers of the law who came down from Jerusalem said, "He is possessed by Beelzebub*ᵃ*! By the prince of demons he is driving out demons."

²³So Jesus called them and spoke to them in parables: "How can Satan drive out Satan? ²⁴If a kingdom is divided against itself, that kingdom cannot stand. ²⁵If a house is divided against itself, that house cannot stand. ²⁶And if Satan opposes himself and is divided, he cannot stand; his end has come. ²⁷In fact, no one can enter a strong man's house and carry off his possessions unless he first ties up the strong man. Then he can rob his house. ²⁸I tell you the truth, all the sins and blasphemies of men will be forgiven them. ²⁹But whoever blasphemes against the Holy Spirit will never be forgiven; he is guilty of an eternal sin."

³⁰He said this because they were saying, "He has an evil spirit."

Jesus' Mother and Brothers

See Matthew 12:46–50; Luke 8:19–21

³¹Then Jesus' mother and brothers arrived. Standing outside, they sent someone in to call him. ³²A crowd was sitting around him, and they told him, "Your mother and brothers are outside looking for you."

³³"Who are my mother and my brothers?" he asked.

³⁴Then he looked at those seated in a circle around him and said, "Here are my mother and my brothers! ³⁵Whoever does God's will is my brother and sister and mother."

The Parable of the Sower

See Matthew 13:1–15,18–23; Luke 8:4–15

4 Again Jesus began to teach by the lake. The crowd that gathered around him was so large that he got into a boat and sat in it out on the lake, while all the people were along the shore at the water's edge. ²He taught them many things by parables, and in his teaching said: ³"Listen! A farmer went out to sow his seed. ⁴As he was scattering the seed,

some fell along the path, and the birds came and ate it up. ⁵Some fell on rocky places, where it did not have much soil. It sprang up quickly, because the soil was shallow. ⁶But when the sun came up, the plants were scorched, and they withered because they had no root. ⁷Other seed fell among thorns, which grew up and choked the plants, so that they did not bear grain. ⁸Still other seed fell on good soil. It came up, grew and produced a crop, multiplying thirty, sixty, or even a hundred times."

⁹Then Jesus said, "He who has ears to hear, let him hear."

¹⁰When he was alone, the Twelve and the others around him asked him about the parables. ¹¹He told them, "The secret of the kingdom of God has been given to you. But to those on the outside everything is said in parables ¹²so that,

> " 'they may be ever seeing but never
>   perceiving,
>   and ever hearing but never
>   understanding;
> otherwise they might turn and be
>   forgiven!'*ᵇ*"

¹³Then Jesus said to them, "Don't you understand this parable? How then will you understand any parable? ¹⁴The farmer sows the word. ¹⁵Some people are like seed along the path, where the word is sown. As soon as they hear it, Satan comes and takes away the word that was sown in them. ¹⁶Others, like seed sown on rocky places, hear the word and at once receive it with joy. ¹⁷But since they have no root, they last only a short time. When trouble or persecution comes because of the word, they quickly fall away. ¹⁸Still others, like seed sown among thorns, hear the word; ¹⁹but the worries of this life, the deceitfulness of wealth and the desires for other things come in and choke the word, making it unfruitful. ²⁰Others, like seed sown on good soil, hear the word, accept it, and produce a crop—thirty, sixty or even a hundred times what was sown."

A Lamp on a Stand

²¹He said to them, "Do you bring in a lamp to put it under a bowl or a bed? Instead, don't you put it on its stand? ²²For whatever is hidden is meant to be

---

ᵃ22 Greek *Beezeboul* or *Beelzeboul*
ᵇ12 Isaiah 6:9,10

disclosed, and whatever is concealed is meant to be brought out into the open. 23If anyone has ears to hear, let him hear."

24"Consider carefully what you hear," he continued. "With the measure you use, it will be measured to you—and even more. 25Whoever has will be given more; whoever does not have, even what he has will be taken from him."

The Parable of the Growing Seed

26He also said, "This is what the kingdom of God is like. A man scatters seed on the ground. 27Night and day, whether he sleeps or gets up, the seed sprouts and grows, though he does not know how. 28All by itself the soil produces grain—first the stalk, then the head, then the full kernel in the head. 29As soon as the grain is ripe, he puts the sickle to it, because the harvest has come."

The Parable of the Mustard Seed

See Matthew 13:31–32; Luke 13:18–19

30Again he said, "What shall we say the kingdom of God is like, or what parable shall we use to describe it? 31It is like a mustard seed, which is the smallest seed you plant in the ground. 32Yet when planted, it grows and becomes the largest of all garden plants, with such big branches that the birds of the air can perch in its shade."

33With many similar parables Jesus spoke the word to them, as much as they could understand. 34He did not say anything to them without using a parable. But when he was alone with his own disciples, he explained everything.

Jesus Calms the Storm

See Matthew 8:18,23–27; Luke 8:22–25

35That day when evening came, he said to his disciples, "Let us go over to the other side." 36Leaving the crowd behind, they took him along, just as he was, in the boat. There were also other boats with him. 37A furious squall came up, and the waves broke over the boat, so that it was nearly swamped. 38Jesus was in the stern, sleeping on a cushion. The disciples woke him and said to him, "Teacher, don't you care if we drown?"

39He got up, rebuked the wind and said to the waves, "Quiet! Be still!" Then the wind died down and it was completely calm.

40He said to his disciples, "Why are you so afraid? Do you still have no faith?"

41They were terrified and asked each other, "Who is this? Even the wind and the waves obey him!"

The Healing of a Demon-possessed Man

See Matthew 8:28–34; Luke 8:26–39

5 They went across the lake to the region of the Gerasenes.ᵃ 2When Jesus got out of the boat, a man with an evilᵇ spirit came from the tombs to meet him. 3This man lived in the tombs, and no one could bind him any more, not even with a chain. 4For he had often been chained hand and foot, but he tore the chains apart and broke the irons on his feet. No one was strong enough to subdue him. 5Night and day among the tombs and in the hills he would cry out and cut himself with stones.

6When he saw Jesus from a distance, he ran and fell on his knees in front of him. 7He shouted at the top of his voice, "What do you want with me, Jesus, Son of the Most High God? Swear to God that you won't torture me!" 8For Jesus had said to him, "Come out of this man, you evil spirit!"

9Then Jesus asked him, "What is your name?"

"My name is Legion," he replied, "for we are many." 10And he begged Jesus again and again not to send them out of the area.

11A large herd of pigs was feeding on the nearby hillside. 12The demons begged Jesus, "Send us among the pigs; allow us to go into them." 13He gave them permission, and the evil spirits came out and went into the pigs. The herd, about two thousand in number, rushed down the steep bank into the lake and were drowned.

14Those tending the pigs ran off and reported this in the town and countryside, and the people went out to see what had happened. 15When they came to Jesus, they saw the man who had been possessed by the legion of demons, sitting there, dressed and in his right mind; and they were afraid. 16Those who had seen it told the people what had happened to the demon-possessed man—and told about the pigs as well. 17Then

ᵃ1 Some manuscripts *Gadarenes*; other manuscripts *Gergesenes*　　ᵇ2 Greek *unclean*; also in verses 8 and 13 the people began to plead with Jesus to leave their region.

¹⁸As Jesus was getting into the boat, the man who had been demon-possessed begged to go with him. ¹⁹Jesus did not let him, but said, "Go home to your family and tell them how much the Lord has done for you, and how he has had mercy on you." ²⁰So the man went away and began to tell in the Decapolis*ᵃ how much Jesus had done for him. And all the people were amazed.

A Dead Girl and a Sick Woman

See Matthew 9:18–26; Luke 8:41–56

²¹When Jesus had again crossed over by boat to the other side of the lake, a large crowd gathered around him while he was by the lake. ²²Then one of the

ᵃ20 That is, the Ten Cities

WEDNESDAY

Read Mark 4:1–41
Key Verse Mark 4:39

In the Middle of the Storm — Sue Grindheim

Have you ever visited the cockpit of a jetliner during a flight? You probably found the pilots chatting calmly, drinking coffee and seeming very relaxed and confident. Flying high over the ocean en route to Asia, Africa or some other far-off place, they set the controls to automatic pilot, trusting electronics to get them and their precious cargo to their destination.

As Jesus set out in the boat he said, "Let us go over to the other side" (Mark 4:35). Then he calmly lay down to rest from his busy schedule. The storm came up quickly and frightened even the most seasoned sailors among the disciples. They had to awaken Jesus from a deep sleep to ask his help, saying, "Don't you care if we drown?" (Mark 4:38).

When Jesus said, "Let us go over to the other side," it was as if he were putting the fishing boat on "automatic pilot." He had spoken; the boat *would* arrive safely on the other side. Consequently, he could sleep peacefully, confident of this outcome. His disciples, on the other hand, were terrified and bewildered that Jesus could sleep in the middle of such chaos. Jesus asked them, "Why are you so afraid?" (Mark 4:40). Jesus was using the situation to help their faith in him grow.

We will get caught in many storms as we go through life—conflict, family problems, school and job stress, accidents, sickness—but Jesus, the One who has the power to calm the wind and level the waves, is piloting our "boat." No matter what the wind velocity or the wave height, he really is in control and wants us to reach out in faith. Occasionally we will feel we're going to drown, but he is our life preserver. If you think you're going down, read Psalm 121: "My help comes from the LORD, the Maker of heaven and earth. He will not let your foot slip—he who watches over you will not slumber . . . The LORD will keep you from all harm—he will watch over your life; the LORD will watch over your coming and going both now and forevermore" (Psalm 121:2–3,7–8).

A Deeper Look
Isaiah 26:3; 43:1–2; John 14:27

Go to page 1119 for your next devotional reading.

synagogue rulers, named Jairus, came there. Seeing Jesus, he fell at his feet ²³and pleaded earnestly with him, "My little daughter is dying. Please come and put your hands on her so that she will be healed and live." ²⁴So Jesus went with him.

A large crowd followed and pressed around him. ²⁵And a woman was there who had been subject to bleeding for twelve years. ²⁶She had suffered a great deal under the care of many doctors and had spent all she had, yet instead of getting better she grew worse. ²⁷When she heard about Jesus, she came up behind him in the crowd and touched his cloak, ²⁸because she thought, "If I just touch his clothes, I will be healed." ²⁹Immediately her bleeding stopped and she felt in her body that she was freed from her suffering.

³⁰At once Jesus realized that power had gone out from him. He turned around in the crowd and asked, "Who touched my clothes?"

³¹"You see the people crowding against you," his disciples answered, "and yet you can ask, 'Who touched me?' "

³²But Jesus kept looking around to see who had done it. ³³Then the woman, knowing what had happened to her, came and fell at his feet and, trembling with fear, told him the whole truth. ³⁴He said to her, "Daughter, your faith has healed you. Go in peace and be freed from your suffering."

³⁵While Jesus was still speaking, some men came from the house of Jairus, the synagogue ruler. "Your daughter is dead," they said. "Why bother the teacher any more?"

³⁶Ignoring what they said, Jesus told the synagogue ruler, "Don't be afraid; just believe."

³⁷He did not let anyone follow him except Peter, James and John the brother of James. ³⁸When they came to the home of the synagogue ruler, Jesus saw a commotion, with people crying and wailing loudly. ³⁹He went in and said to them, "Why all this commotion and wailing? The child is not dead but asleep." ⁴⁰But they laughed at him.

After he put them all out, he took the child's father and mother and the disciples who were with him, and went in where the child was. ⁴¹He took her by the hand and said to her, "Talitha koum!"

(which means, "Little girl, I say to you, get up!"). ⁴²Immediately the girl stood up and walked around (she was twelve years old). At this they were completely astonished. ⁴³He gave strict orders not to let anyone know about this, and told them to give her something to eat.

A Prophet Without Honor
See Matthew 13:54–58

6 Jesus left there and went to his hometown, accompanied by his disciples. ²When the Sabbath came, he began to teach in the synagogue, and many who heard him were amazed.

"Where did this man get these things?" they asked. "What's this wisdom that has been given him, that he even does miracles! ³Isn't this the carpenter? Isn't this Mary's son and the brother of James, Joseph,ᵃ Judas and Simon? Aren't his sisters here with us?" And they took offense at him.

⁴Jesus said to them, "Only in his hometown, among his relatives and in his own house is a prophet without honor." ⁵He could not do any miracles there, except lay his hands on a few sick people and heal them. ⁶And he was amazed at their lack of faith.

Jesus Sends Out the Twelve
See Matthew 10:1,9–14; Luke 9:1,3–5

Then Jesus went around teaching from village to village. ⁷Calling the Twelve to him, he sent them out two by two and gave them authority over evilᵇ spirits.

⁸These were his instructions: "Take nothing for the journey except a staff—no bread, no bag, no money in your belts. ⁹Wear sandals but not an extra tunic. ¹⁰Whenever you enter a house, stay there until you leave that town. ¹¹And if any place will not welcome you or listen to

ᵃ3 Greek *Joses*, a variant of *Joseph*   ᵇ7 Greek *unclean*

POINT OF INTEREST

Mark 6:6

Imagine having so little faith that you would actually surprise Jesus! But what else amazes Jesus? Take a look at Luke 7:9 for the answer.

you, shake the dust off your feet when you leave, as a testimony against them."

¹²They went out and preached that people should repent. ¹³They drove out many demons and anointed many sick people with oil and healed them.

John the Baptist Beheaded

See Matthew 14:1–12

¹⁴King Herod heard about this, for Jesus' name had become well known. Some were saying,[a] "John the Baptist has been raised from the dead, and that is why miraculous powers are at work in him."

¹⁵Others said, "He is Elijah."

And still others claimed, "He is a prophet, like one of the prophets of long ago."

¹⁶But when Herod heard this, he said, "John, the man I beheaded, has been raised from the dead!"

¹⁷For Herod himself had given orders to have John arrested, and he had him bound and put in prison. He did this because of Herodias, his brother Philip's wife, whom he had married. ¹⁸For John had been saying to Herod, "It is not lawful for you to have your brother's wife." ¹⁹So Herodias nursed a grudge against John and wanted to kill him. But she was not able to, ²⁰because Herod feared John and protected him, knowing him to be a righteous and holy man. When Herod heard John, he was greatly puzzled[b]; yet he liked to listen to him.

²¹Finally the opportune time came. On his birthday Herod gave a banquet for his high officials and military commanders and the leading men of Galilee. ²²When the daughter of Herodias came in and danced, she pleased Herod and his dinner guests.

The king said to the girl, "Ask me for anything you want, and I'll give it to you." ²³And he promised her with an oath, "Whatever you ask I will give you, up to half my kingdom."

²⁴She went out and said to her mother, "What shall I ask for?"

"The head of John the Baptist," she answered.

²⁵At once the girl hurried in to the king with the request: "I want you to give me right now the head of John the Baptist on a platter."

²⁶The king was greatly distressed, but because of his oaths and his dinner guests, he did not want to refuse her. ²⁷So

he immediately sent an executioner with orders to bring John's head. The man went, beheaded John in the prison, ²⁸and brought back his head on a platter. He presented it to the girl, and she gave it to her mother. ²⁹On hearing of this, John's disciples came and took his body and laid it in a tomb.

Jesus Feeds the Five Thousand

See Matthew 14:13–21; Luke 9:10–17; John 6:5–13

³⁰The apostles gathered around Jesus and reported to him all they had done and taught. ³¹Then, because so many people were coming and going that they did not even have a chance to eat, he said to them, "Come with me by yourselves to a quiet place and get some rest."

³²So they went away by themselves in a boat to a solitary place. ³³But many who saw them leaving recognized them and ran on foot from all the towns and got there ahead of them. ³⁴When Jesus landed and saw a large crowd, he had compassion on them, because they were like sheep without a shepherd. So he began teaching them many things.

³⁵By this time it was late in the day, so his disciples came to him. "This is a remote place," they said, "and it's already very late. ³⁶Send the people away so they can go to the surrounding countryside and villages and buy themselves something to eat."

³⁷But he answered, "You give them something to eat."

They said to him, "That would take eight months of a man's wages[c]! Are we to go and spend that much on bread and give it to them to eat?"

³⁸"How many loaves do you have?" he asked. "Go and see."

When they found out, they said, "Five—and two fish."

³⁹Then Jesus directed them to have all the people sit down in groups on the green grass. ⁴⁰So they sat down in groups of hundreds and fifties. ⁴¹Taking the five loaves and the two fish and looking up to heaven, he gave thanks and broke the loaves. Then he gave them to his disciples to set before the people. He also divided the two fish among them all. ⁴²They all ate and were satisfied, ⁴³and the disciples picked up twelve basketfuls

a 14 Some early manuscripts He was saying
b 20 Some early manuscripts he did many things
c 37 Greek take two hundred denarii

of broken pieces of bread and fish. **44**The number of the men who had eaten was five thousand.

Jesus Walks on the Water
See Matthew 14:22–32; John 6:15–21

45Immediately Jesus made his disciples get into the boat and go on ahead of him to Bethsaida, while he dismissed the crowd. **46**After leaving them, he went up on a mountainside to pray.

47When evening came, the boat was in the middle of the lake, and he was alone on land. **48**He saw the disciples straining at the oars, because the wind was against them. About the fourth watch of the night he went out to them, walking on the lake. He was about to pass by them, **49**but when they saw him walking on the lake, they thought he was a ghost. They cried out, **50**because they all saw him and were terrified.

Immediately he spoke to them and said, "Take courage! It is I. Don't be afraid." **51**Then he climbed into the boat with them, and the wind died down. They were completely amazed, **52**for they had not understood about the loaves; their hearts were hardened.

53When they had crossed over, they landed at Gennesaret and anchored there. **54**As soon as they got out of the boat, people recognized Jesus. **55**They ran throughout that whole region and carried the sick on mats to wherever they heard he was. **56**And wherever he went— into villages, towns or countryside—they placed the sick in the marketplaces. They begged him to let them touch even the edge of his cloak, and all who touched him were healed.

Clean and Unclean
See Matthew 15:1–20

7 The Pharisees and some of the teachers of the law who had come from Jerusalem gathered around Jesus and **2**saw some of his disciples eating food with hands that were "unclean," that is, unwashed. **3**(The Pharisees and all the Jews do not eat unless they give their hands a ceremonial washing, holding to the tradition of the elders. **4**When they come from the marketplace they do not eat unless they wash. And they observe many other traditions, such as the washing of cups, pitchers and kettles.*a*)

5So the Pharisees and teachers of the law asked Jesus, "Why don't your disci-

ples live according to the tradition of the elders instead of eating their food with 'unclean' hands?"

6He replied, "Isaiah was right when he prophesied about you hypocrites; as it is written:

> " 'These people honor me with their
>   lips,
> but their hearts are far from me.
> **7**They worship me in vain;
>   their teachings are but rules taught
>   by men.'*b*

8You have let go of the commands of God and are holding on to the traditions of men."

9And he said to them: "You have a fine way of setting aside the commands of God in order to observe*c* your own traditions! **10**For Moses said, 'Honor your father and your mother,'*d* and, 'Anyone who curses his father or mother must be put to death.'*e* **11**But you say that if a man says to his father or mother: 'Whatever help you might otherwise have received from me is Corban' (that is, a gift devoted to God), **12**then you no longer let him do anything for his father or mother. **13**Thus you nullify the word of God by your tradition that you have handed

a4 Some early manuscripts *pitchers, kettles and dining couches*   *b6,7* Isaiah 29:13   *c9* Some manuscripts *set up*   *d10* Exodus 20:12; Deut. 5:16   *e10* Exodus 21:17; Lev. 20:9

POINT OF INTEREST
Mark 7:6

God had originally designed the Old Testament rituals of worship so as to demonstrate both his holiness and the need of his people to be made spiritually clean before him. The Pharisees had piled so many rules and regulations on top of God's law that the people, including the Pharisees themselves, weren't able to recognize their need of a Savior—or even the Savior himself. The Pharisees had actually twisted worship to demonstrate *their* holiness rather than God's, and the people's need of *their* blessing rather than God's saving grace.

down. And you do many things like that."

¹⁴Again Jesus called the crowd to him and said, "Listen to me, everyone, and understand this. ¹⁵Nothing outside a man can make him 'unclean' by going into him. Rather, it is what comes out of a man that makes him 'unclean.'ᵃ"

¹⁷After he had left the crowd and entered the house, his disciples asked him about this parable. ¹⁸"Are you so dull?" he asked. "Don't you see that nothing that enters a man from the outside can make him 'unclean'? ¹⁹For it doesn't go into his heart but into his stomach, and then out of his body." (In saying this, Jesus declared all foods "clean.")

²⁰He went on: "What comes out of a man is what makes him 'unclean.' ²¹For from within, out of men's hearts, come evil thoughts, sexual immorality, theft, murder, adultery, ²²greed, malice, deceit, lewdness, envy, slander, arrogance and folly. ²³All these evils come from inside and make a man 'unclean.' "

The Faith of a Syrophoenician Woman

See Matthew 15:21–28

²⁴Jesus left that place and went to the vicinity of Tyre.ᵇ He entered a house and did not want anyone to know it; yet he could not keep his presence secret. ²⁵In fact, as soon as she heard about him, a woman whose little daughter was possessed by an evilᶜ spirit came and fell at his feet. ²⁶The woman was a Greek, born in Syrian Phoenicia. She begged Jesus to drive the demon out of her daughter.

²⁷"First let the children eat all they want," he told her, "for it is not right to take the children's bread and toss it to their dogs."

²⁸"Yes, Lord," she replied, "but even the dogs under the table eat the children's crumbs."

²⁹Then he told her, "For such a reply, you may go; the demon has left your daughter."

³⁰She went home and found her child lying on the bed, and the demon gone.

The Healing of a Deaf and Mute Man

See Matthew 15:29–31

³¹Then Jesus left the vicinity of Tyre and went through Sidon, down to the Sea of Galilee and into the region of the De-

capolis.ᵈ ³²There some people brought to him a man who was deaf and could hardly talk, and they begged him to place his hand on the man.

³³After he took him aside, away from the crowd, Jesus put his fingers into the man's ears. Then he spit and touched the man's tongue. ³⁴He looked up to heaven and with a deep sigh said to him, *"Eph-phatha!"* (which means, "Be opened!"). ³⁵At this, the man's ears were opened, his tongue was loosened and he began to speak plainly.

³⁶Jesus commanded them not to tell anyone. But the more he did so, the more they kept talking about it. ³⁷People were overwhelmed with amazement. "He has done everything well," they said. "He even makes the deaf hear and the mute speak."

Jesus Feeds the Four Thousand

See Matthew 15:32–39

8 During those days another large crowd gathered. Since they had nothing to eat, Jesus called his disciples to him and said, ²"I have compassion for these people; they have already been with me three days and have nothing to eat. ³If I send them home hungry, they will collapse on the way, because some of them have come a long distance."

⁴His disciples answered, "But where in this remote place can anyone get enough bread to feed them?"

⁵"How many loaves do you have?" Jesus asked.

"Seven," they replied.

⁶He told the crowd to sit down on the ground. When he had taken the seven loaves and given thanks, he broke them and gave them to his disciples to set before the people, and they did so. ⁷They had a few small fish as well; he gave thanks for them also and told the disciples to distribute them. ⁸The people ate and were satisfied. Afterward the disciples picked up seven basketfuls of broken pieces that were left over. ⁹About four thousand men were present. And having sent them away, ¹⁰he got into the boat with his disciples and went to the region of Dalmanutha.

¹¹The Pharisees came and began to question Jesus. To test him, they asked

---

ᵃ15 Some early manuscripts *'unclean.' 16If anyone has ears to hear, let him hear.*   ᵇ24 Many early manuscripts *Tyre and Sidon*   ᶜ25 Greek *unclean*
ᵈ31 That is, the Ten Cities

him for a sign from heaven. [12]He sighed deeply and said, "Why does this generation ask for a miraculous sign? I tell you the truth, no sign will be given to it." [13]Then he left them, got back into the boat and crossed to the other side.

The Yeast of the Pharisees and Herod

[14]The disciples had forgotten to bring bread, except for one loaf they had with them in the boat. [15]"Be careful," Jesus warned them. "Watch out for the yeast of the Pharisees and that of Herod."

[16]They discussed this with one another and said, "It is because we have no bread."

[17]Aware of their discussion, Jesus asked them: "Why are you talking about having no bread? Do you still not see or understand? Are your hearts hardened? [18]Do you have eyes but fail to see, and ears but fail to hear? And don't you remember? [19]When I broke the five loaves for the five thousand, how many basketfuls of pieces did you pick up?"

"Twelve," they replied.

[20]"And when I broke the seven loaves for the four thousand, how many basketfuls of pieces did you pick up?"

They answered, "Seven."

[21]He said to them, "Do you still not understand?"

The Healing of a Blind Man at Bethsaida

[22]They came to Bethsaida, and some people brought a blind man and begged Jesus to touch him. [23]He took the blind man by the hand and led him outside the village. When he had spit on the man's eyes and put his hands on him, Jesus asked, "Do you see anything?"

[24]He looked up and said, "I see people; they look like trees walking around."

[25]Once more Jesus put his hands on the man's eyes. Then his eyes were opened, his sight was restored, and he saw everything clearly. [26]Jesus sent him home, saying, "Don't go into the village.[a]"

Peter's Confession of Christ

See Matthew 16:13–16; Luke 9:18–20

[27]Jesus and his disciples went on to the villages around Caesarea Philippi. On the way he asked them, "Who do people say I am?"

[28]They replied, "Some say John the Baptist; others say Elijah; and still others, one of the prophets."

[29]"But what about you?" he asked. "Who do you say I am?"

Peter answered, "You are the Christ.[b]"

[30]Jesus warned them not to tell anyone about him.

Jesus Predicts His Death

See Matthew 16:21–28; Luke 9:22–27

[31]He then began to teach them that the Son of Man must suffer many things and be rejected by the elders, chief priests and teachers of the law, and that he must be killed and after three days rise again. [32]He spoke plainly about this, and Peter took him aside and began to rebuke him.

[33]But when Jesus turned and looked at his disciples, he rebuked Peter. "Get behind me, Satan!" he said. "You do not have in mind the things of God, but the things of men."

[34]Then he called the crowd to him along with his disciples and said: "If anyone would come after me, he must deny himself and take up his cross and follow me. [35]For whoever wants to save his life[c] will lose it, but whoever loses his life for me and for the gospel will save it. [36]What good is it for a man to gain the whole world, yet forfeit his soul? [37]Or what can a man give in exchange for his soul? [38]If anyone is ashamed of me and my words in this adulterous and sinful generation, the Son of Man will be ashamed of him when he comes in his Father's glory with the holy angels."

9 And he said to them, "I tell you the truth, some who are standing here will not taste death before they see the kingdom of God come with power."

The Transfiguration

See Matthew 17:1–13; Luke 9:28–36

[2]After six days Jesus took Peter, James and John with him and led them up a high mountain, where they were all alone. There he was transfigured before them. [3]His clothes became dazzling white, whiter than anyone in the world could bleach them. [4]And there appeared before them Elijah and Moses, who were talking with Jesus.

---

[a]26 Some manuscripts *Don't go and tell anyone in the village*　[b]29 Or *Messiah*. "The Christ" (Greek) and "the Messiah" (Hebrew) both mean "the Anointed One."　[c]35 The Greek word means either *life* or *soul*; also in verse 36.

⁵Peter said to Jesus, "Rabbi, it is good for us to be here. Let us put up three shelters—one for you, one for Moses and one for Elijah." ⁶(He did not know what to say, they were so frightened.)

⁷Then a cloud appeared and enveloped them, and a voice came from the cloud: "This is my Son, whom I love. Listen to him!"

⁸Suddenly, when they looked around, they no longer saw anyone with them except Jesus.

⁹As they were coming down the mountain, Jesus gave them orders not to tell anyone what they had seen until the Son of Man had risen from the dead. ¹⁰They kept the matter to themselves, discussing what "rising from the dead" meant.

¹¹And they asked him, "Why do the teachers of the law say that Elijah must come first?"

¹²Jesus replied, "To be sure, Elijah does come first, and restores all things. Why then is it written that the Son of Man must suffer much and be rejected? ¹³But I tell you, Elijah has come, and they have done to him everything they wished, just as it is written about him."

The Healing of a Boy With an Evil Spirit

See Matthew 17:14–19,22–23; Luke 9:37–45

¹⁴When they came to the other disciples, they saw a large crowd around them and the teachers of the law arguing with them. ¹⁵As soon as all the people saw Jesus, they were overwhelmed with wonder and ran to greet him.

¹⁶"What are you arguing with them about?" he asked.

¹⁷A man in the crowd answered, "Teacher, I brought you my son, who is possessed by a spirit that has robbed him of speech. ¹⁸Whenever it seizes him, it throws him to the ground. He foams at the mouth, gnashes his teeth and becomes rigid. I asked your disciples to drive out the spirit, but they could not."

¹⁹"O unbelieving generation," Jesus replied, "how long shall I stay with you? How long shall I put up with you? Bring the boy to me."

²⁰So they brought him. When the spirit saw Jesus, it immediately threw the boy into a convulsion. He fell to the ground and rolled around, foaming at the mouth.

²¹Jesus asked the boy's father, "How long has he been like this?"

"From childhood," he answered. ²²"It has often thrown him into fire or water to kill him. But if you can do anything, take pity on us and help us."

²³" 'If you can'?" said Jesus. "Everything is possible for him who believes."

²⁴Immediately the boy's father exclaimed, "I do believe; help me overcome my unbelief!"

²⁵When Jesus saw that a crowd was running to the scene, he rebuked the evilᵃ spirit. "You deaf and mute spirit," he said, "I command you, come out of him and never enter him again."

²⁶The spirit shrieked, convulsed him violently and came out. The boy looked so much like a corpse that many said, "He's dead." ²⁷But Jesus took him by the hand and lifted him to his feet, and he stood up.

²⁸After Jesus had gone indoors, his disciples asked him privately, "Why couldn't we drive it out?"

²⁹He replied, "This kind can come out only by prayer.ᵇ"

³⁰They left that place and passed through Galilee. Jesus did not want anyone to know where they were, ³¹because he was teaching his disciples. He said to them, "The Son of Man is going to be betrayed into the hands of men. They will kill him, and after three days he will rise." ³²But they did not understand what he meant and were afraid to ask him about it.

ᵃ25 Greek *unclean*   ᵇ29 Some manuscripts *prayer and fasting*

POINT OF INTEREST

Mark 9:24

Most of us have been in the position of wanting to trust God completely but only being able to trust him partway. Some of us spend a lot of time in this "sort of" trusting mode. We can't bluff God; he knows how much we trust him. But he honors even a small faith presented to him honestly. Jesus' response to this man's admission was to drive the demon out of the boy, a miracle that ought to cause anyone's faith to grow from "sort of" to "totally!"

Who Is the Greatest?

See Matthew 18:1–5; Luke 9:46–48

33They came to Capernaum. When he was in the house, he asked them, "What were you arguing about on the road?" **34**But they kept quiet because on the way they had argued about who was the greatest.

35Sitting down, Jesus called the Twelve and said, "If anyone wants to be first, he must be the very last, and the servant of all."

36He took a little child and had him stand among them. Taking him in his arms, he said to them, **37**"Whoever welcomes one of these little children in my name welcomes me; and whoever welcomes me does not welcome me but the one who sent me."

Whoever Is Not Against Us Is for Us

See Luke 9:49–50

38"Teacher," said John, "we saw a man driving out demons in your name and we told him to stop, because he was not one of us."

39"Do not stop him," Jesus said. "No one who does a miracle in my name can in the next moment say anything bad about me, **40**for whoever is not against us is for us. **41**I tell you the truth, anyone who gives you a cup of water in my name because you belong to Christ will certainly not lose his reward.

Causing to Sin

42"And if anyone causes one of these little ones who believe in me to sin, it would be better for him to be thrown into the sea with a large millstone tied around his neck. **43**If your hand causes you to sin, cut it off. It is better for you to enter life maimed than with two hands to go into hell, where the fire never goes out.*a* **45**And if your foot causes you to sin, cut it off. It is better for you to enter life crippled than to have two feet and be thrown into hell.*b* **47**And if your eye causes you to sin, pluck it out. It is better for you to enter the kingdom of God with one eye than to have two eyes and be thrown into hell, **48**where

" 'their worm does not die,
and the fire is not quenched.'*c*

49Everyone will be salted with fire.

50"Salt is good, but if it loses its saltiness, how can you make it salty again?

Have salt in yourselves, and be at peace with each other."

Divorce

See Matthew 19:1–9

10 Jesus then left that place and went into the region of Judea and across the Jordan. Again crowds of people came to him, and as was his custom, he taught them.

2Some Pharisees came and tested him by asking, "Is it lawful for a man to divorce his wife?"

3"What did Moses command you?" he replied.

4They said, "Moses permitted a man to write a certificate of divorce and send her away."

5"It was because your hearts were hard that Moses wrote you this law," Jesus replied. **6**"But at the beginning of creation God 'made them male and female.'*d* **7**'For this reason a man will leave his father and mother and be united to his wife,*e* **8**and the two will become one flesh.'*f* So they are no longer two, but one. **9**Therefore what God has joined together, let man not separate."

10When they were in the house again, the disciples asked Jesus about this. **11**He answered, "Anyone who divorces his wife and marries another woman commits adultery against her. **12**And if she divorces her husband and marries another man, she commits adultery."

The Little Children and Jesus

See Matthew 19:13–15; Luke 18:15–17

13People were bringing little children to Jesus to have him touch them, but the disciples rebuked them. **14**When Jesus saw this, he was indignant. He said to them, "Let the little children come to me, and do not hinder them, for the kingdom of God belongs to such as these. **15**I tell you the truth, anyone who will not receive the kingdom of God like a little child will never enter it." **16**And he took the children in his arms, put his hands on them and blessed them.

a43 Some manuscripts *out, 44where / " 'their worm does not die, / and the fire is not quenched.'*
b45 Some manuscripts *hell, 46where / " 'their worm does not die, / and the fire is not quenched.'*
c48 Isaiah 66:24   *d6* Gen. 1:27   *e7* Some early manuscripts do not have *and be united to his wife.*   *f8* Gen. 2:24

The Rich Young Man

See Matthew 19:16–30; Luke 18:18–30

¹⁷As Jesus started on his way, a man ran up to him and fell on his knees before him. "Good teacher," he asked, "what must I do to inherit eternal life?"

¹⁸"Why do you call me good?" Jesus answered. "No one is good—except God alone. ¹⁹You know the commandments: 'Do not murder, do not commit adultery, do not steal, do not give false testimony, do not defraud, honor your father and mother.'ᵃ"

²⁰"Teacher," he declared, "all these I have kept since I was a boy."

²¹Jesus looked at him and loved him. "One thing you lack," he said. "Go, sell everything you have and give to the poor, and you will have treasure in heaven. Then come, follow me."

²²At this the man's face fell. He went away sad, because he had great wealth.

²³Jesus looked around and said to his disciples, "How hard it is for the rich to enter the kingdom of God!"

²⁴The disciples were amazed at his words. But Jesus said again, "Children, how hard it isᵇ to enter the kingdom of God! ²⁵It is easier for a camel to go through the eye of a needle than for a rich man to enter the kingdom of God."

²⁶The disciples were even more amazed, and said to each other, "Who then can be saved?"

²⁷Jesus looked at them and said, "With man this is impossible, but not with God; all things are possible with God."

²⁸Peter said to him, "We have left everything to follow you!"

²⁹"I tell you the truth," Jesus replied, "no one who has left home or brothers or sisters or mother or father or children or fields for me and the gospel ³⁰will fail to receive a hundred times as much in this present age (homes, brothers, sisters, mothers, children and fields—and with them, persecutions) and in the age to come, eternal life. ³¹But many who are first will be last, and the last first."

Jesus Again Predicts His Death

See Matthew 20:17–19; Luke 18:31–33

³²They were on their way up to Jerusalem, with Jesus leading the way, and the disciples were astonished, while those who followed were afraid. Again he took the Twelve aside and told them what was going to happen to him. ³³"We are going up to Jerusalem," he said, "and the Son of Man will be betrayed to the chief priests and teachers of the law. They will condemn him to death and will hand him over to the Gentiles, ³⁴who will mock him and spit on him, flog him and kill him. Three days later he will rise."

The Request of James and John

See Matthew 20:20–28

³⁵Then James and John, the sons of Zebedee, came to him. "Teacher," they said, "we want you to do for us whatever we ask."

³⁶"What do you want me to do for you?" he asked.

³⁷They replied, "Let one of us sit at your right and the other at your left in your glory."

³⁸"You don't know what you are asking," Jesus said. "Can you drink the cup I drink or be baptized with the baptism I am baptized with?"

³⁹"We can," they answered.

Jesus said to them, "You will drink the cup I drink and be baptized with the baptism I am baptized with, ⁴⁰but to sit at my right or left is not for me to grant. These places belong to those for whom they have been prepared."

⁴¹When the ten heard about this, they became indignant with James and John. ⁴²Jesus called them together and said, "You know that those who are regarded as rulers of the Gentiles lord it over them, and their high officials exercise authority over them. ⁴³Not so with you. Instead, whoever wants to become great among you must be your servant, ⁴⁴and whoever wants to be first must be slave of all. ⁴⁵For even the Son of Man did not come to be served, but to serve, and to give his life as a ransom for many."

Blind Bartimaeus Receives His Sight

See Matthew 20:29–34; Luke 18:35–43

⁴⁶Then they came to Jericho. As Jesus and his disciples, together with a large crowd, were leaving the city, a blind man, Bartimaeus (that is, the Son of Timaeus), was sitting by the roadside begging. ⁴⁷When he heard that it was Jesus of Nazareth, he began to shout, "Jesus, Son of David, have mercy on me!"

⁴⁸Many rebuked him and told him to

ᵃ19 Exodus 20:12-16; Deut. 5:16-20   ᵇ24 Some manuscripts *is for those who trust in riches* be quiet, but he shouted all the more, "Son of David, have mercy on me!"

⁴⁹Jesus stopped and said, "Call him."

So they called to the blind man, "Cheer up! On your feet! He's calling you." ⁵⁰Throwing his cloak aside, he jumped to his feet and came to Jesus.

⁵¹"What do you want me to do for you?" Jesus asked him.

The blind man said, "Rabbi, I want to see."

⁵²"Go," said Jesus, "your faith has healed you." Immediately he received his sight and followed Jesus along the road.

The Triumphal Entry

See Matthew 21:1–9; Luke 19:29–38; John 12:12–15

11 As they approached Jerusalem and came to Bethphage and Bethany at the Mount of Olives, Jesus sent two of his disciples, ²saying to them, "Go to the village ahead of you, and just as you enter it, you will find a colt tied there, which no one has ever ridden. Untie it and bring it here. ³If anyone asks you, 'Why are you doing this?' tell him, 'The Lord needs it and will send it back here shortly.' "

Read Mark 10:1–45
Key Verse Mark 10:45

A Servant Heart — Shaunda McQueeney

Today I'm scrubbing my parents' basement stairs. They live in a beautiful farmhouse that is full of my childhood memories. But these stairs . . . I remember loathing this job, half-heartedly swishing my rag over the grit and dead insects, glancing away as I stuck my hand into the dirty water before another swipe. I used to grumble and complain until my mother's ears were worn out.

But today I'm having a great time. I am shocked to discover that I *enjoy* cleaning these steps. Why is my attitude so much better now? It's because Mom and I share a similar vision—we both want this house to be immaculate for my sister's wedding.

I wonder whether my spiritual attitude has changed as well, causing me to be joyful when God has given me a distasteful job. I ask myself, "Have fourteen years of walking with God cultivated a heart that serves him as gladly as I now serve Mom?" Not really. As I think of recent times when my complaining has probably worn out God's ears, I have to admit that I have a ways to go in this area.

Jesus Christ knew God's vision for his life: "For even the Son of Man did not come to be served, but to serve, and to give his life as a ransom for many" (Mark 10:45). Jesus wasn't reluctant to roll up his sleeves and wash his disciples' dirty feet (see John 13). Even though he was God, he took on the nature of a servant and humbled himself so that eventually "every tongue [would] confess that Jesus Christ is Lord, to the glory of God the Father" (Philippians 2:11).

If I want to serve God gladly, then I need to share that vision, "for it is God who works in [me] to will and to act according to his good purpose" (Philippians 2:13). There are a lot of not-so-great jobs that need to be done in God's kingdom, my real "home," but if I focus on the end result, maybe I'll enjoy them as much as I do scrubbing steps!

A Deeper Look
John 12:26; Ephesians 6:7–8; 1 Peter 4:10

Go to page 1122 for your next devotional reading.

[4]They went and found a colt outside in the street, tied at a doorway. As they untied it, [5]some people standing there asked, "What are you doing, untying that colt?" [6]They answered as Jesus had told them to, and the people let them go. [7]When they brought the colt to Jesus and threw their cloaks over it, he sat on it. [8]Many people spread their cloaks on the road, while others spread branches they had cut in the fields. [9]Those who went ahead and those who followed shouted,

"Hosanna![a]"

"Blessed is he who comes in the
name of the Lord!"[b]

[10]"Blessed is the coming kingdom of
our father David!"

"Hosanna in the highest!"

[11]Jesus entered Jerusalem and went to the temple. He looked around at everything, but since it was already late, he went out to Bethany with the Twelve.

Jesus Clears the Temple
See Matthew 21:12–16; Luke 19:45–47;
John 2:13–16

[12]The next day as they were leaving Bethany, Jesus was hungry. [13]Seeing in the distance a fig tree in leaf, he went to find out if it had any fruit. When he reached it, he found nothing but leaves, because it was not the season for figs. [14]Then he said to the tree, "May no one ever eat fruit from you again." And his disciples heard him say it.

[15]On reaching Jerusalem, Jesus entered the temple area and began driving out those who were buying and selling there. He overturned the tables of the money changers and the benches of those selling doves, [16]and would not allow anyone to carry merchandise through the temple courts. [17]And as he taught them, he said, "Is it not written:

" 'My house will be called
a house of prayer for all
nations'[c]?

But you have made it 'a den of robbers.'[d] "

[18]The chief priests and the teachers of the law heard this and began looking for a way to kill him, for they feared him, because the whole crowd was amazed at his teaching.

[19]When evening came, they[e] went out of the city.

The Withered Fig Tree
See Matthew 21:19–22

[20]In the morning, as they went along, they saw the fig tree withered from the roots. [21]Peter remembered and said to Jesus, "Rabbi, look! The fig tree you cursed has withered!"

[22]"Have[f] faith in God," Jesus answered. [23]"I tell you the truth, if anyone says to this mountain, 'Go, throw yourself into the sea,' and does not doubt in his heart but believes that what he says will happen, it will be done for him. [24]Therefore I tell you, whatever you ask for in prayer, believe that you have received it, and it will be yours. [25]And when you stand praying, if you hold anything against anyone, forgive him, so that your Father in heaven may forgive you your sins.[g]"

The Authority of Jesus Questioned
See Matthew 21:23–27; Luke 20:1–8

[27]They arrived again in Jerusalem, and while Jesus was walking in the temple courts, the chief priests, the teachers of the law and the elders came to him. [28]"By what authority are you doing these things?" they asked. "And who gave you authority to do this?"

[29]Jesus replied, "I will ask you one question. Answer me, and I will tell you by what authority I am doing these things. [30]John's baptism—was it from heaven, or from men? Tell me!"

[31]They discussed it among themselves and said, "If we say, 'From heaven,' he will ask, 'Then why didn't you believe him?' [32]But if we say, 'From men' . . . ." (They feared the people, for everyone held that John really was a prophet.)

[33]So they answered Jesus, "We don't know."

Jesus said, "Neither will I tell you by what authority I am doing these things."

[a]9 A Hebrew expression meaning "Save!" which became an exclamation of praise; also in verse 10 [b]9 Psalm 118:25,26 [c]17 Isaiah 56:7 [d]17 Jer. 7:11 [e]19 Some early manuscripts he [f]22 Some early manuscripts If you have [g]25 Some manuscripts sins. 26But if you do not forgive, neither will your Father who is in heaven forgive your sins.

The Parable of the Tenants

See Matthew 21:33–46; Luke 20:9–19

12 He then began to speak to them in parables: "A man planted a vineyard. He put a wall around it, dug a pit for the winepress and built a watchtower. Then he rented the vineyard to some farmers and went away on a journey. ²At harvest time he sent a servant to the tenants to collect from them some of the fruit of the vineyard. ³But they seized him, beat him and sent him away empty-handed. ⁴Then he sent another servant to them; they struck this man on the head and treated him shamefully. ⁵He sent still another, and that one they killed. He sent many others; some of them they beat, others they killed.

⁶"He had one left to send, a son, whom he loved. He sent him last of all, saying, 'They will respect my son.'

⁷"But the tenants said to one another, 'This is the heir. Come, let's kill him, and the inheritance will be ours.' ⁸So they took him and killed him, and threw him out of the vineyard.

⁹"What then will the owner of the vineyard do? He will come and kill those tenants and give the vineyard to others. ¹⁰Haven't you read this scripture:

" 'The stone the builders rejected
    has become the capstone[a];
¹¹the Lord has done this,
    and it is marvelous in our
        eyes'[b]?"

¹²Then they looked for a way to arrest him because they knew he had spoken the parable against them. But they were afraid of the crowd; so they left him and went away.

Paying Taxes to Caesar

See Matthew 22:15–22; Luke 20:20–26

¹³Later they sent some of the Pharisees and Herodians to Jesus to catch him in his words. ¹⁴They came to him and said, "Teacher, we know you are a man of integrity. You aren't swayed by men, because you pay no attention to who they are; but you teach the way of God in accordance with the truth. Is it right to pay taxes to Caesar or not? ¹⁵Should we pay or shouldn't we?"

But Jesus knew their hypocrisy. "Why are you trying to trap me?" he asked. "Bring me a denarius and let me look at it." ¹⁶They brought the coin, and he asked them, "Whose portrait is this? And whose inscription?"

"Caesar's," they replied.

¹⁷Then Jesus said to them, "Give to Caesar what is Caesar's and to God what is God's."

And they were amazed at him.

Marriage at the Resurrection

See Matthew 22:23–33; Luke 20:27–38

¹⁸Then the Sadducees, who say there is no resurrection, came to him with a question. ¹⁹"Teacher," they said, "Moses wrote for us that if a man's brother dies and leaves a wife but no children, the man must marry the widow and have children for his brother. ²⁰Now there were seven brothers. The first one married and died without leaving any children. ²¹The second one married the widow, but he also died, leaving no child. It was the same with the third. ²²In fact, none of the seven left any children. Last of all, the woman died too. ²³At the resurrection[c] whose wife will she be, since the seven were married to her?"

²⁴Jesus replied, "Are you not in error because you do not know the Scriptures or the power of God? ²⁵When the dead rise, they will neither marry nor be given in marriage; they will be like the angels in heaven. ²⁶Now about the dead rising— have you not read in the book of Moses, in the account of the bush, how God said to him, 'I am the God of Abraham, the God of Isaac, and the God of Jacob'[d]? ²⁷He is not the God of the dead, but of the living. You are badly mistaken!"

The Greatest Commandment

See Matthew 22:34–40

²⁸One of the teachers of the law came and heard them debating. Noticing that Jesus had given them a good answer, he asked him, "Of all the commandments, which is the most important?"

²⁹"The most important one," answered Jesus, "is this: 'Hear, O Israel, the Lord our God, the Lord is one.[e] ³⁰Love the Lord your God with all your heart and with all your soul and with all your mind and with all your strength.'[f]

---

[a]10 Or cornerstone   [b]11 Psalm 118:22,23
[c]23 Some manuscripts resurrection, when men rise from the dead,   [d]26 Exodus 3:6   [e]29 Or the Lord our God is one Lord   [f]30 Deut. 6:4,5

³¹The second is this: 'Love your neighbor as yourself.'ᵃ There is no commandment greater than these."

³²"Well said, teacher," the man replied. "You are right in saying that God is one and there is no other but him. ³³To love him with all your heart, with all your understanding and with all your strength, and to love your neighbor as yourself is more important than all burnt offerings and sacrifices."

³⁴When Jesus saw that he had answered wisely, he said to him, "You are not far from the kingdom of God." And from then on no one dared ask him any more questions.

ᵃ31 Lev. 19:18

FRIDAY

Read Mark 12:1–40
Key Verse Mark 12:24

The Explosive Power of God – Roger Hamilton

The English word dynamite comes from the Greek word *dunamis*, which means "power." Dynamite is powerful stuff. In the hands of someone who knows how to use it, dynamite can be invaluable. Well-placed explosions have saved road builders thousands of hours of pick-and-shovel labor. And were it not for the energy stored in those little sticks, many more lives would be risked to unearth deep mineral deposits.

In Mark 12:24 Jesus rebuked the Sadducees because they didn't know "the Scriptures or the power of God." They did not know the power of God to reshape life after the resurrection. Nor did they acknowledge the power of God to raise people from the dead.

When Jesus speaks of the power of God, he is talking about power infinitely greater than any number of sticks of dynamite. It's the power of energy great enough to infuse a dead body with life: "That power is like the working of his mighty strength, which he exerted in Christ when he raised him from the dead and seated him at his right hand in the heavenly realms" (Ephesians 1:19–20; see also 2 Kings 4:32–35; John 11). It's a power that saves lives for eternity: "So will it be with the resurrection of the dead. The body that is sown is perishable . . . it is raised imperishable . . . it is sown in weakness, it is raised in power" (1 Corinthians 15:42–43).

Ironically, the Sadducees may have thought they "knew" the Scriptures when they tried to trip Jesus up, but they did not understand that Abraham, Isaac and Jacob were already partaking of eternal life ("I *am* the God of Abraham," not "I *was*") and that God would raise their bodies at the resurrection.

The stored energy of dynamite is tremendous. It's wonderful for blowing things up, but it has to destroy before it can do any good. How much greater is the energy of God, who created and made all living things—who breathed his own spirit into men and women. How much more awesome is the energy, the power of God, that renews, heals and restores our spirits and our bodies. How much more powerful is the power of God to raise us to new life in Jesus Christ!

A Deeper Look
Exodus 3:6; Romans 1:4; 1 Peter 1:3–5

Go to page 1126 for your next devotional reading.

Whose Son Is the Christ?

See Matthew 22:41–46; Luke 20:41–47

35While Jesus was teaching in the temple courts, he asked, "How is it that the teachers of the law say that the Christ[a] is the son of David? 36David himself, speaking by the Holy Spirit, declared:

" 'The Lord said to my Lord:
"Sit at my right hand
until I put your enemies
under your feet." '[b]

37David himself calls him 'Lord.' How then can he be his son?"

The large crowd listened to him with delight.

38As he taught, Jesus said, "Watch out for the teachers of the law. They like to walk around in flowing robes and be greeted in the marketplaces, 39and have the most important seats in the synagogues and the places of honor at banquets. 40They devour widows' houses and for a show make lengthy prayers. Such men will be punished most severely."

The Widow's Offering

See Luke 21:1–4

41Jesus sat down opposite the place where the offerings were put and watched the crowd putting their money into the temple treasury. Many rich people threw in large amounts. 42But a poor widow came and put in two very small copper coins,[c] worth only a fraction of a penny.[d]

43Calling his disciples to him, Jesus said, "I tell you the truth, this poor widow has put more into the treasury than all the others. 44They all gave out of their wealth; but she, out of her poverty, put in everything—all she had to live on."

Signs of the End of the Age

See Matthew 24:1–51; Luke 21:5–36

13 As he was leaving the temple, one of his disciples said to him, "Look, Teacher! What massive stones! What magnificent buildings!"

2"Do you see all these great buildings?" replied Jesus. "Not one stone here will be left on another; every one will be thrown down."

3As Jesus was sitting on the Mount of Olives opposite the temple, Peter, James, John and Andrew asked him privately,

4"Tell us, when will these things happen? And what will be the sign that they are all about to be fulfilled?"

5Jesus said to them: "Watch out that no one deceives you. 6Many will come in my name, claiming, 'I am he,' and will deceive many. 7When you hear of wars and rumors of wars, do not be alarmed. Such things must happen, but the end is still to come. 8Nation will rise against nation, and kingdom against kingdom. There will be earthquakes in various places, and famines. These are the beginning of birth pains.

9"You must be on your guard. You will be handed over to the local councils and flogged in the synagogues. On account of me you will stand before governors and kings as witnesses to them. 10And the gospel must first be preached to all nations. 11Whenever you are arrested and brought to trial, do not worry beforehand about what to say. Just say whatever is given you at the time, for it is not you speaking, but the Holy Spirit.

12"Brother will betray brother to death, and a father his child. Children will rebel against their parents and have them put to death. 13All men will hate you because of me, but he who stands firm to the end will be saved.

14"When you see 'the abomination that causes desolation'[e] standing where it[f] does not belong—let the reader understand—then let those who are in Judea flee to the mountains. 15Let no one on the roof of his house go down or enter the house to take anything out. 16Let no one in the field go back to get his cloak. 17How dreadful it will be in those days for pregnant women and nursing mothers! 18Pray that this will not take place in winter, 19because those will be days of distress unequaled from the beginning, when God created the world, until now—and never to be equaled again. 20If the Lord had not cut short those days, no one would survive. But for the sake of the elect, whom he has chosen, he has shortened them. 21At that time if anyone says to you, 'Look, here is the Christ[a]!' or, 'Look, there he is!' do not believe it. 22For false Christs and false prophets will appear and perform signs and miracles to

---

[a]35,21 Or *Messiah*   [b]36 Psalm 110:1
[c]42 Greek *two lepta*   [d]42 Greek *kodrantes*
[e]14 Daniel 9:27; 11:31; 12:11   [f]14 Or *he*; also in verse 29

deceive the elect—if that were possible. 23So be on your guard; I have told you everything ahead of time.

24"But in those days, following that distress,

" 'the sun will be darkened,
and the moon will not give its light;
25the stars will fall from the sky,
and the heavenly bodies will be shaken.'*a*

26"At that time men will see the Son of Man coming in clouds with great power and glory. 27And he will send his angels and gather his elect from the four winds, from the ends of the earth to the ends of the heavens.

28"Now learn this lesson from the fig tree: As soon as its twigs get tender and its leaves come out, you know that summer is near. 29Even so, when you see these things happening, you know that it is near, right at the door. 30I tell you the truth, this generation*b* will certainly not pass away until all these things have happened. 31Heaven and earth will pass away, but my words will never pass away.

The Day and Hour Unknown

32"No one knows about that day or hour, not even the angels in heaven, nor the Son, but only the Father. 33Be on guard! Be alert*c*! You do not know when that time will come. 34It's like a man going away: He leaves his house and puts his servants in charge, each with his assigned task, and tells the one at the door to keep watch.

35"Therefore keep watch because you do not know when the owner of the house will come back—whether in the evening, or at midnight, or when the rooster crows, or at dawn. 36If he comes suddenly, do not let him find you sleeping. 37What I say to you, I say to everyone: 'Watch!' "

Jesus Anointed at Bethany

See Matthew 26:2–16; Luke 22:1–6

14 Now the Passover and the Feast of Unleavened Bread were only two days away, and the chief priests and the teachers of the law were looking for some sly way to arrest Jesus and kill him. 2"But not during the Feast," they said, "or the people may riot."

3While he was in Bethany, reclining at the table in the home of a man known as Simon the Leper, a woman came with an alabaster jar of very expensive perfume, made of pure nard. She broke the jar and poured the perfume on his head.

4Some of those present were saying indignantly to one another, "Why this waste of perfume? 5It could have been sold for more than a year's wages*d* and the money given to the poor." And they rebuked her harshly.

6"Leave her alone," said Jesus. "Why are you bothering her? She has done a beautiful thing to me. 7The poor you will always have with you, and you can help them any time you want. But you will not always have me. 8She did what she could. She poured perfume on my body beforehand to prepare for my burial. 9I tell you the truth, wherever the gospel is preached throughout the world, what she has done will also be told, in memory of her."

10Then Judas Iscariot, one of the Twelve, went to the chief priests to betray Jesus to them. 11They were delighted to hear this and promised to give him money. So he watched for an opportunity to hand him over.

The Lord's Supper

See Matthew 26:17–30; Luke 22:7–23

12On the first day of the Feast of Un-

a25 Isaiah 13:10; 34:4   *b30* Or race   *c33* Some manuscripts *alert and pray*   *d5* Greek *than three hundred denarii*

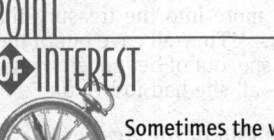

POINT OF INTEREST

Mark 13:35

Sometimes the world seems to be fast-forwarding toward its demise. Christians and non-Christians alike spend a lot of time wondering when that will happen and when Jesus will return. But if Jesus himself didn't know, how can we dare to speculate? Jesus said not to worry or spend time in guessing games, but instead to be spiritually alert and aware, ready at any moment to meet him face to face without regret or shame.

leavened Bread, when it was customary to sacrifice the Passover lamb, Jesus' disciples asked him, "Where do you want us to go and make preparations for you to eat the Passover?"

[13]So he sent two of his disciples, telling them, "Go into the city, and a man carrying a jar of water will meet you. Follow him. [14]Say to the owner of the house he enters, 'The Teacher asks: Where is my guest room, where I may eat the Passover with my disciples?' [15]He will show you a large upper room, furnished and ready. Make preparations for us there."

[16]The disciples left, went into the city and found things just as Jesus had told them. So they prepared the Passover.

[17]When evening came, Jesus arrived with the Twelve. [18]While they were reclining at the table eating, he said, "I tell you the truth, one of you will betray me—one who is eating with me."

[19]They were saddened, and one by one they said to him, "Surely not I?"

[20]"It is one of the Twelve," he replied, "one who dips bread into the bowl with me. [21]The Son of Man will go just as it is written about him. But woe to that man who betrays the Son of Man! It would be better for him if he had not been born."

[22]While they were eating, Jesus took bread, gave thanks and broke it, and gave it to his disciples, saying, "Take it; this is my body."

[23]Then he took the cup, gave thanks and offered it to them, and they all drank from it.

[24]"This is my blood of the[a] covenant, which is poured out for many," he said to them. [25]"I tell you the truth, I will not drink again of the fruit of the vine until that day when I drink it anew in the kingdom of God."

[26]When they had sung a hymn, they went out to the Mount of Olives.

Jesus Predicts Peter's Denial

See Matthew 26:31–35

[27]"You will all fall away," Jesus told them, "for it is written:

" 'I will strike the shepherd,
　　and the sheep will be scattered.'[b]

[28]But after I have risen, I will go ahead of you into Galilee."

[29]Peter declared, "Even if all fall away, I will not."

[30]"I tell you the truth," Jesus answered, "today—yes, tonight—before

the rooster crows twice[c] you yourself will disown me three times."

[31]But Peter insisted emphatically, "Even if I have to die with you, I will never disown you." And all the others said the same.

Gethsemane

See Matthew 26:36–46; Luke 22:40–46

[32]They went to a place called Gethsemane, and Jesus said to his disciples, "Sit here while I pray." [33]He took Peter, James and John along with him, and he began to be deeply distressed and troubled. [34]"My soul is overwhelmed with sorrow to the point of death," he said to them. "Stay here and keep watch."

[35]Going a little farther, he fell to the ground and prayed that if possible the hour might pass from him. [36]"Abba,[d] Father," he said, "everything is possible for you. Take this cup from me. Yet not what I will, but what you will."

[37]Then he returned to his disciples and found them sleeping. "Simon," he said to Peter, "are you asleep? Could you not keep watch for one hour? [38]Watch and pray so that you will not fall into temptation. The spirit is willing, but the body is weak."

[39]Once more he went away and prayed the same thing. [40]When he came back, he again found them sleeping, because their eyes were heavy. They did not know what to say to him.

[41]Returning the third time, he said to them, "Are you still sleeping and resting? Enough! The hour has come. Look, the Son of Man is betrayed into the hands of sinners. [42]Rise! Let us go! Here comes my betrayer!"

Jesus Arrested

See Matthew 26:47–56; Luke 22:47–50; John 18:3–11

[43]Just as he was speaking, Judas, one of the Twelve, appeared. With him was a crowd armed with swords and clubs, sent from the chief priests, the teachers of the law, and the elders. [44]Now the betrayer had arranged a signal with them: "The one I kiss is the man; arrest him and lead him away under guard." [45]Going at once to Jesus, Judas said, "Rabbi!" and kissed him. [46]The men seized Jesus and arrested him.

[a]24 Some manuscripts the new　　[b]27 Zech. 13:7
[c]30 Some early manuscripts do not have twice.
[d]36 Aramaic for Father

Read *Mark 14:1–42*
Key Verses *Mark 14:35–38*

Being Honest With God

When Jesus prayed in the Garden of Gethsemane, he prayed not to a remote or impersonal being, but to his beloved "Abba," (his "Daddy"). God wants us to pray like that, and he listens with the attention and openness of a loving dad. Whether our emotions overflow with praise or sorrow or even honest anger and doubt, God wants to hear it all! The heartbeat of prayer is being real, open and transparent with him. Even when our words can't express what we are feeling (see Romans 8:26-27), the Holy Spirit knows what we want to say and expresses it for us.

Does God always answer our prayers? Yes, though sometimes his answer is "No." Even Jesus was told no by his Father (Luke 22:41–44)! In God's eternal perspective there are times it's better that we don't receive what we ask for. Again, he is our loving Father; the "no" isn't a reflection of God's inability or unwillingness to give us what we want, but a reflection of his wisdom and love.

Digging Into the Word
1. What does God promise if you pray?—*Jeremiah 29:13; John 14:12–14; 1 John 5:14–15*
2. What are the conditions for answered prayer?—*Matthew 6:5–15; James 4:3*

Action Challenge
God is waiting for you to come to him with complete honesty. Make a list of ten joys, fears, needs and dreams. Take time daily this week to pray openly and expectantly about these four areas of your life.

One Step Deeper
Mark 11:22–24; Luke 18:1–8

Go to page 1132 for your next devotional reading.

⁴⁷Then one of those standing near drew his sword and struck the servant of the high priest, cutting off his ear.

⁴⁸"Am I leading a rebellion," said Jesus, "that you have come out with swords and clubs to capture me? ⁴⁹Every day I was with you, teaching in the temple courts, and you did not arrest me. But the Scriptures must be fulfilled." ⁵⁰Then everyone deserted him and fled.

⁵¹A young man, wearing nothing but a linen garment, was following Jesus. When they seized him, ⁵²he fled naked, leaving his garment behind.

Before the Sanhedrin

See Matthew 26:57–68; John 18:12–13,19–24

⁵³They took Jesus to the high priest, and all the chief priests, elders and teachers of the law came together. ⁵⁴Peter followed him at a distance, right into the courtyard of the high priest. There he sat with the guards and warmed himself at the fire.

⁵⁵The chief priests and the whole Sanhedrin were looking for evidence against Jesus so that they could put him to death, but they did not find any. ⁵⁶Many testified falsely against him, but their statements did not agree.

⁵⁷Then some stood up and gave this false testimony against him: ⁵⁸"We heard him say, 'I will destroy this man-made temple and in three days will build another, not made by man.' " ⁵⁹Yet even then their testimony did not agree.

⁶⁰Then the high priest stood up before them and asked Jesus, "Are you not going to answer? What is this testimony that these men are bringing against you?" ⁶¹But Jesus remained silent and gave no answer.

Again the high priest asked him, "Are you the Christ,[a] the Son of the Blessed One?"

⁶²"I am," said Jesus. "And you will see the Son of Man sitting at the right hand of the Mighty One and coming on the clouds of heaven."

⁶³The high priest tore his clothes. "Why do we need any more witnesses?" he asked. ⁶⁴"You have heard the blasphemy. What do you think?"

They all condemned him as worthy of death. ⁶⁵Then some began to spit at him; they blindfolded him, struck him with their fists, and said, "Prophesy!" And the guards took him and beat him.

Peter Disowns Jesus

See Matthew 26:69–75; Luke 22:56–62; John 18:16–18,25–27

⁶⁶While Peter was below in the courtyard, one of the servant girls of the high priest came by. ⁶⁷When she saw Peter warming himself, she looked closely at him.

"You also were with that Nazarene, Jesus," she said.

⁶⁸But he denied it. "I don't know or understand what you're talking about," he said, and went out into the entryway.[b]

⁶⁹When the servant girl saw him there, she said again to those standing around, "This fellow is one of them." ⁷⁰Again he denied it.

After a little while, those standing near said to Peter, "Surely you are one of them, for you are a Galilean."

⁷¹He began to call down curses on himself, and he swore to them, "I don't know this man you're talking about."

⁷²Immediately the rooster crowed the second time.[c] Then Peter remembered the word Jesus had spoken to him: "Before the rooster crows twice[d] you will disown me three times." And he broke down and wept.

Jesus Before Pilate

See Matthew 27:11–26; Luke 23:2–3,18–25; John 18:29—19:16

15 Very early in the morning, the chief priests, with the elders, the teachers of the law and the whole Sanhedrin, reached a decision. They bound Jesus, led him away and handed him over to Pilate.

²"Are you the king of the Jews?" asked Pilate.

"Yes, it is as you say," Jesus replied.

³The chief priests accused him of many things. ⁴So again Pilate asked him, "Aren't you going to answer? See how many things they are accusing you of."

⁵But Jesus still made no reply, and Pilate was amazed.

⁶Now it was the custom at the Feast to release a prisoner whom the people requested. ⁷A man called Barabbas was in prison with the insurrectionists who had committed murder in the uprising. ⁸The

---

*a*61 Or *Messiah*   *b*68 Some early manuscripts *entryway and the rooster crowed*   *c*72 Some early manuscripts do not have *the second time.*
*d*72 Some early manuscripts do not have *twice.*

crowd came up and asked Pilate to do for them what he usually did.

⁹"Do you want me to release to you the king of the Jews?" asked Pilate, ¹⁰knowing it was out of envy that the chief priests had handed Jesus over to him. ¹¹But the chief priests stirred up the crowd to have Pilate release Barabbas instead.

¹²"What shall I do, then, with the one you call the king of the Jews?" Pilate asked them.

¹³"Crucify him!" they shouted.

¹⁴"Why? What crime has he committed?" asked Pilate.

But they shouted all the louder, "Crucify him!"

¹⁵Wanting to satisfy the crowd, Pilate released Barabbas to them. He had Jesus flogged, and handed him over to be crucified.

The Soldiers Mock Jesus

See Matthew 27:27–31

¹⁶The soldiers led Jesus away into the palace (that is, the Praetorium) and called together the whole company of soldiers. ¹⁷They put a purple robe on him, then twisted together a crown of thorns and set it on him. ¹⁸And they began to call out to him, "Hail, king of the Jews!" ¹⁹Again and again they struck him on the head with a staff and spit on him. Falling on their knees, they paid homage to him. ²⁰And when they had mocked him, they took off the purple robe and put his own clothes on him. Then they led him out to crucify him.

The Crucifixion

See Matthew 27:33–44; Luke 23:33–43; John 19:17–24

²¹A certain man from Cyrene, Simon, the father of Alexander and Rufus, was passing by on his way in from the country, and they forced him to carry the cross. ²²They brought Jesus to the place called Golgotha (which means The Place of the Skull). ²³Then they offered him wine mixed with myrrh, but he did not take it. ²⁴And they crucified him. Dividing up his clothes, they cast lots to see what each would get.

²⁵It was the third hour when they crucified him. ²⁶The written notice of the charge against him read: THE KING OF THE JEWS. ²⁷They crucified two robbers with him, one on his right and one on his left.[a] ²⁹Those who passed by hurled insults at him, shaking their heads and saying, "So! You who are going to destroy the temple and build it in three days, ³⁰come down from the cross and save yourself!"

³¹In the same way the chief priests and the teachers of the law mocked him among themselves. "He saved others," they said, "but he can't save himself! ³²Let this Christ,[b] this King of Israel, come down now from the cross, that we may see and believe." Those crucified with him also heaped insults on him.

The Death of Jesus

See Matthew 27:45–56; Luke 23:44–49; John 19:29–30

³³At the sixth hour darkness came over the whole land until the ninth hour. ³⁴And at the ninth hour Jesus cried out in a loud voice, "Eloi, Eloi, lama sabachthani?"—which means, "My God, my God, why have you forsaken me?"[c]

³⁵When some of those standing near heard this, they said, "Listen, he's calling Elijah."

³⁶One man ran, filled a sponge with wine vinegar, put it on a stick, and offered it to Jesus to drink. "Now leave him alone. Let's see if Elijah comes to take him down," he said.

³⁷With a loud cry, Jesus breathed his last.

³⁸The curtain of the temple was torn in two from top to bottom. ³⁹And when the centurion, who stood there in front of Jesus, heard his cry and[d] saw how he died, he said, "Surely this man was the Son[e] of God!"

⁴⁰Some women were watching from a distance. Among them were Mary Magdalene, Mary the mother of James the younger and of Joses, and Salome. ⁴¹In Galilee these women had followed him and cared for his needs. Many other women who had come up with him to Jerusalem were also there.

The Burial of Jesus

See Matthew 27:57–61; Luke 23:50–56; John 19:38–42

⁴²It was Preparation Day (that is, the day before the Sabbath). So as evening approached, ⁴³Joseph of Arimathea, a

---

a27 Some manuscripts left, 28and the scripture was fulfilled which says, "He was counted with the lawless ones" (Isaiah 53:12)   b32 Or Messiah   c34 Psalm 22:1   d39 Some manuscripts do not have heard his cry and   e39 Or a son prominent member of the Council, who was himself waiting for the kingdom of God, went boldly to Pilate and asked for Jesus' body. [44]Pilate was surprised to hear that he was already dead. Summoning the centurion, he asked him if Jesus had already died. [45]When he learned from the centurion that it was so, he gave the body to Joseph. [46]So Joseph bought some linen cloth, took down the body, wrapped it in the linen, and placed it in a tomb cut out of rock. Then he rolled a stone against the entrance of the tomb. [47]Mary Magdalene and Mary the mother of Joses saw where he was laid.

The Resurrection

See Matthew 28:1–8; Luke 24:1–10

16 When the Sabbath was over, Mary Magdalene, Mary the mother of James, and Salome bought spices so that they might go to anoint Jesus' body. [2]Very early on the first day of the week, just after sunrise, they were on their way to the tomb [3]and they asked each other, "Who will roll the stone away from the entrance of the tomb?"

[4]But when they looked up, they saw that the stone, which was very large, had been rolled away. [5]As they entered the tomb, they saw a young man dressed in a white robe sitting on the right side, and they were alarmed.

[6]"Don't be alarmed," he said. "You are looking for Jesus the Nazarene, who was crucified. He has risen! He is not here. See the place where they laid him. [7]But go, tell his disciples and Peter, 'He is going ahead of you into Galilee. There you will see him, just as he told you.' "

[8]Trembling and bewildered, the women went out and fled from the tomb. They said nothing to anyone, because they were afraid.

[The earliest manuscripts and some other ancient witnesses do not have Mark 16:9–20.]

[9]When Jesus rose early on the first day of the week, he appeared first to Mary Magdalene, out of whom he had driven seven demons. [10]She went and told those who had been with him and who were mourning and weeping. [11]When they heard that Jesus was alive and that she had seen him, they did not believe it.

[12]Afterward Jesus appeared in a different form to two of them while they were walking in the country. [13]These returned and reported it to the rest; but they did not believe them either.

[14]Later Jesus appeared to the Eleven as they were eating; he rebuked them for their lack of faith and their stubborn refusal to believe those who had seen him after he had risen.

[15]He said to them, "Go into all the world and preach the good news to all creation. [16]Whoever believes and is baptized will be saved, but whoever does not believe will be condemned. [17]And these signs will accompany those who believe: In my name they will drive out demons; they will speak in new tongues; [18]they will pick up snakes with their hands; and when they drink deadly poison, it will not hurt them at all; they will place their hands on sick people, and they will get well."

[19]After the Lord Jesus had spoken to them, he was taken up into heaven and he sat at the right hand of God. [20]Then the disciples went out and preached everywhere, and the Lord worked with them and confirmed his word by the signs that accompanied it.

POINT OF INTEREST

Mark 15:44-45

Some of Jesus' detractors were suggesting that Jesus didn't really die on the cross but that he merely fainted and recovered in the cool air of the tomb (a theory that still circulates today). The centurion, an experienced executioner, testifies otherwise. Jesus did in fact die on that cross. And when he walked out of the tomb three days later, he had overcome the power of death for all time! Remember Paul's words from 1 Corinthians 15:17,20: "And if Christ has not been raised, your faith is futile; you are still in your sins . . . But Christ has indeed been raised from the dead."

The Gospel of Luke is like a richly textured portrait that captures the depth of who Jesus is. This Gospel gives the fullest account of Jesus' life. The physician Luke highlights Jesus' warmth and humanity, his love for all people—Jew and Gentile alike—as well as his power as God's Son. We glimpse Jesus' childhood, observe his gentleness toward the poor and oppressed, and we smile as he welcomes little children. But the power of his teaching and miracles proclaim that he also is God. More than any other Gospel, Luke demonstrates that Jesus is both God and man.

LUKE

Introduction

Many have undertaken to draw up an account of the things that have been fulfilled[a] among us, ²just as they were handed down to us by those who from the first were eyewitnesses and servants of the word. ³Therefore, since I myself have carefully investigated everything from the beginning, it seemed good also to me to write an orderly account for you, most excellent Theophilus, ⁴so that you may know the certainty of the things you have been taught.

The Birth of John the Baptist Foretold

⁵In the time of Herod king of Judea there was a priest named Zechariah, who belonged to the priestly division of Abijah; his wife Elizabeth was also a descendant of Aaron. ⁶Both of them were upright in the sight of God, observing all the Lord's commandments and regulations blamelessly. ⁷But they had no children, because Elizabeth was barren; and they were both well along in years.

⁸Once when Zechariah's division was on duty and he was serving as priest before God, ⁹he was chosen by lot, according to the custom of the priesthood, to go into the temple of the Lord and burn incense. ¹⁰And when the time for the burning of incense came, all the assembled worshipers were praying outside.

¹¹Then an angel of the Lord appeared

a 1 Or been surely believed

to him, standing at the right side of the altar of incense. [12]When Zechariah saw him, he was startled and was gripped with fear. [13]But the angel said to him: "Do not be afraid, Zechariah; your prayer has been heard. Your wife Elizabeth will bear you a son, and you are to give him the name John. [14]He will be a joy and delight to you, and many will rejoice because of his birth, [15]for he will be great in the sight of the Lord. He is never to take wine or other fermented drink, and he will be filled with the Holy Spirit even from birth.[a] [16]Many of the people of Israel will he bring back to the Lord their God. [17]And he will go on before the Lord, in the spirit and power of Elijah, to turn the hearts of the fathers to their children and the disobedient to the wisdom of the righteous—to make ready a people prepared for the Lord."

[18]Zechariah asked the angel, "How can I be sure of this? I am an old man and my wife is well along in years."

[19]The angel answered, "I am Gabriel. I stand in the presence of God, and I have been sent to speak to you and to tell you this good news. [20]And now you will be silent and not able to speak until the day this happens, because you did not believe my words, which will come true at their proper time."

[21]Meanwhile, the people were waiting for Zechariah and wondering why he stayed so long in the temple. [22]When he came out, he could not speak to them. They realized he had seen a vision in the temple, for he kept making signs to them but remained unable to speak.

[23]When his time of service was completed, he returned home. [24]After this his wife Elizabeth became pregnant and for five months remained in seclusion. [25]"The Lord has done this for me," she said. "In these days he has shown his favor and taken away my disgrace among the people."

The Birth of Jesus Foretold

[26]In the sixth month, God sent the angel Gabriel to Nazareth, a town in Galilee, [27]to a virgin pledged to be married to a man named Joseph, a descendant of David. The virgin's name was Mary. [28]The angel went to her and said, "Greetings, you who are highly favored! The Lord is with you."

[29]Mary was greatly troubled at his words and wondered what kind of greeting this might be. [30]But the angel said to her, "Do not be afraid, Mary, you have found favor with God. [31]You will be with child and give birth to a son, and you are to give him the name Jesus. [32]He will be great and will be called the Son of the Most High. The Lord God will give him the throne of his father David, [33]and he will reign over the house of Jacob forever; his kingdom will never end."

[34]"How will this be," Mary asked the angel, "since I am a virgin?"

[35]The angel answered, "The Holy Spirit will come upon you, and the power of the Most High will overshadow you. So the holy one to be born will be called[b] the Son of God. [36]Even Elizabeth your relative is going to have a child in her old age, and she who was said to be barren is in her sixth month. [37]For nothing is impossible with God."

[38]"I am the Lord's servant," Mary answered. "May it be to me as you have said." Then the angel left her.

Mary Visits Elizabeth

[39]At that time Mary got ready and hurried to a town in the hill country of Judea, [40]where she entered Zechariah's home and greeted Elizabeth. [41]When Elizabeth heard Mary's greeting, the baby leaped in her womb, and Elizabeth was filled with the Holy Spirit. [42]In a loud voice she exclaimed: "Blessed are you among women, and blessed is the child

[a]15 Or *from his mother's womb*   [b]35 Or *So the child to be born will be called holy,*

POINT OF INTEREST   Luke 1:3

Luke had not actually traveled with Jesus, but he was a careful researcher who based his Gospel on interviews with eyewitnesses to Jesus' ministry and miracles. Luke's Gospel is an authoritative, sequential record that all of his readers can trust. And the historical markers he placed within the text (see Luke 1:5; 2:1; 3:1 and other verses) have helped scholars place the events of Jesus' ministry within a documented historical time line.

you will bear! **43**But why am I so favored, that the mother of my Lord should come to me? **44**As soon as the sound of your greeting reached my ears, the baby in my womb leaped for joy. **45**Blessed is she who has believed that what the Lord has said to her will be accomplished!"

Mary's Song

See 1 Samuel 2:1–10

46And Mary said:

"My soul glorifies the Lord
47   and my spirit rejoices in God my
            Savior,
48for he has been mindful
        of the humble state of his servant.
From now on all generations will call
        me blessed,
49   for the Mighty One has done great
            things for me—
        holy is his name.
50His mercy extends to those who fear
        him,
        from generation to generation.

51He has performed mighty deeds with
        his arm;
    he has scattered those who are
        proud in their inmost
        thoughts.
52He has brought down rulers from
        their thrones
    but has lifted up the humble.
53He has filled the hungry with good
        things
    but has sent the rich away empty.
54He has helped his servant Israel,
        remembering to be merciful
55to Abraham and his descendants
        forever,
    even as he said to our fathers."

56Mary stayed with Elizabeth for about three months and then returned home.

The Birth of John the Baptist

57When it was time for Elizabeth to have her baby, she gave birth to a son. **58**Her neighbors and relatives heard that

---

MONDAY

Read Luke 1:1–45
Key Verse Luke 1:37

Nothing Is Impossible With God — Jessica Gengler

Before school began in the fall, I needed two things for my dorm room: a bookshelf and a couch. I prayed that God would provide them and that my roommate and I would each have to pay $10 or less. The time came to move in, and we had no couch or shelves!

The day after I moved, I helped a girl across the hall carry in her things. We made rapid progress until we discovered that the couch she had brought did not fit in her room. Funny! She decided to lend it to us.

Still, we had no shelves. We drove to the store and found a set for $25. Divided between us, the cost was $2.50 apiece more than we could afford, so we decided not to buy it. Disappointed, we finished our shopping. On the way to the check-out stand, we happened to pass by the shelf section again. The employees had put up a new display of shelves: CLEARANCE—$13. They were exactly what we had been looking for!

God taught us not to settle for less than his best—no matter how little the request seems! Wait for God to answer your prayers and don't accept easy-out alternatives. Nothing is impossible with God!

A Deeper Look
Ephesians 3:20–21; Philippians 4:6

Go to page 1135 for your next devotional reading.

the Lord had shown her great mercy, and they shared her joy.

⁵⁹On the eighth day they came to circumcise the child, and they were going to name him after his father Zechariah, ⁶⁰but his mother spoke up and said, "No! He is to be called John."

⁶¹They said to her, "There is no one among your relatives who has that name."

⁶²Then they made signs to his father, to find out what he would like to name the child. ⁶³He asked for a writing tablet, and to everyone's astonishment he wrote, "His name is John." ⁶⁴Immediately his mouth was opened and his tongue was loosed, and he began to speak, praising God. ⁶⁵The neighbors were all filled with awe, and throughout the hill country of Judea people were talking about all these things. ⁶⁶Everyone who heard this wondered about it, asking, "What then is this child going to be?" For the Lord's hand was with him.

Zechariah's Song

⁶⁷His father Zechariah was filled with the Holy Spirit and prophesied:

⁶⁸"Praise be to the Lord, the God of
    Israel,
    because he has come and has
        redeemed his people.
⁶⁹He has raised up a horn^a of
        salvation for us
    in the house of his servant David
⁷⁰(as he said through his holy prophets
        of long ago),
⁷¹salvation from our enemies
    and from the hand of all who hate
        us—
⁷²to show mercy to our fathers
    and to remember his holy
        covenant,
⁷³   the oath he swore to our father
        Abraham:
⁷⁴to rescue us from the hand of our
        enemies,
    and to enable us to serve him
        without fear
⁷⁵   in holiness and righteousness
        before him all our days.

⁷⁶And you, my child, will be called a
        prophet of the Most High;
    for you will go on before the Lord
        to prepare the way for him,
⁷⁷to give his people the knowledge of
        salvation

    through the forgiveness of their
        sins,
⁷⁸because of the tender mercy of our
        God,
    by which the rising sun will come
        to us from heaven
⁷⁹to shine on those living in darkness
    and in the shadow of death,
    to guide our feet into the path of
        peace."

⁸⁰And the child grew and became strong in spirit; and he lived in the desert until he appeared publicly to Israel.

The Birth of Jesus

2 In those days Caesar Augustus issued a decree that a census should be taken of the entire Roman world. ²(This was the first census that took place while Quirinius was governor of Syria.) ³And everyone went to his own town to register.

⁴So Joseph also went up from the town of Nazareth in Galilee to Judea, to Bethlehem the town of David, because he belonged to the house and line of David. ⁵He went there to register with Mary, who was pledged to be married to him and was expecting a child. ⁶While they were there, the time came for the baby to be born, ⁷and she gave birth to her firstborn, a son. She wrapped him in cloths and placed him in a manger, because there was no room for them in the inn.

The Shepherds and the Angels

⁸And there were shepherds living out in the fields nearby, keeping watch over their flocks at night. ⁹An angel of the Lord appeared to them, and the glory of the Lord shone around them, and they were terrified. ¹⁰But the angel said to them, "Do not be afraid. I bring you good news of great joy that will be for all the people. ¹¹Today in the town of David a Savior has been born to you; he is Christ^b the Lord. ¹²This will be a sign to you: You will find a baby wrapped in cloths and lying in a manger."

¹³Suddenly a great company of the heavenly host appeared with the angel, praising God and saying,

¹⁴"Glory to God in the highest,
    and on earth peace to men on
        whom his favor rests."

---

^a69 *Horn* here symbolizes strength.   ^b11 Or *Messiah.* "The Christ" (Greek) and "the Messiah" (Hebrew) both mean "the Anointed One"; also in verse 26.

15When the angels had left them and gone into heaven, the shepherds said to one another, "Let's go to Bethlehem and see this thing that has happened, which the Lord has told us about."

16So they hurried off and found Mary and Joseph, and the baby, who was lying in the manger. 17When they had seen him, they spread the word concerning what had been told them about this child, 18and all who heard it were amazed at what the shepherds said to them. 19But Mary treasured up all these things and pondered them in her heart. 20The shepherds returned, glorifying and praising God for all the things they had heard and seen, which were just as they had been told.

Jesus Presented in the Temple

21On the eighth day, when it was time to circumcise him, he was named Jesus, the name the angel had given him before he had been conceived.

22When the time of their purification according to the Law of Moses had been completed, Joseph and Mary took him to Jerusalem to present him to the Lord 23(as it is written in the Law of the Lord, "Every firstborn male is to be consecrated to the Lord"a), 24and to offer a sacrifice in keeping with what is said in the Law of the Lord: "a pair of doves or two young pigeons."b

25Now there was a man in Jerusalem called Simeon, who was righteous and devout. He was waiting for the consolation of Israel, and the Holy Spirit was upon him. 26It had been revealed to him by the Holy Spirit that he would not die before he had seen the Lord's Christ. 27Moved by the Spirit, he went into the temple courts. When the parents brought in the child Jesus to do for him what the custom of the Law required, 28Simeon took him in his arms and praised God, saying:

29"Sovereign Lord, as you have
        promised,
    you now dismissc your servant in
        peace.
30For my eyes have seen your
        salvation,
31   which you have prepared in the
        sight of all people,
32a light for revelation to the Gentiles
        and for glory to your people
        Israel."

33The child's father and mother marveled at what was said about him. 34Then Simeon blessed them and said to Mary, his mother: "This child is destined to cause the falling and rising of many in Israel, and to be a sign that will be spoken against, 35so that the thoughts of many hearts will be revealed. And a sword will pierce your own soul too."

36There was also a prophetess, Anna, the daughter of Phanuel, of the tribe of Asher. She was very old; she had lived with her husband seven years after her marriage, 37and then was a widow until she was eighty-four.d She never left the temple but worshiped night and day, fasting and praying. 38Coming up to them at that very moment, she gave thanks to God and spoke about the child to all who were looking forward to the redemption of Jerusalem.

39When Joseph and Mary had done everything required by the Law of the Lord, they returned to Galilee to their own town of Nazareth. 40And the child grew and became strong; he was filled with wisdom, and the grace of God was upon him.

The Boy Jesus at the Temple

41Every year his parents went to Jerusalem for the Feast of the Passover. 42When he was twelve years old, they went up to the Feast, according to the custom. 43After the Feast was over, while his parents were returning home, the boy Jesus stayed behind in Jerusalem, but they were unaware of it. 44Thinking he was in their company, they traveled on for a day. Then they began looking for him among their relatives and friends. 45When they did not find him, they went back to Jerusalem to look for him. 46After three days they found him in the temple courts, sitting among the teachers, listening to them and asking them questions. 47Everyone who heard him was amazed at his understanding and his answers. 48When his parents saw him, they were astonished. His mother said to him, "Son, why have you treated us like this? Your father and I have been anxiously searching for you."

49"Why were you searching for me?" he asked. "Didn't you know I had to be in my Father's house?" 50But they did not

a23 Exodus 13:2,12   b24 Lev. 12:8   c29 Or
promised, / now dismiss   d37 Or widow for
eighty-four years

understand what he was saying to them.

⁵¹Then he went down to Nazareth with them and was obedient to them. But his mother treasured all these things in her heart. ⁵²And Jesus grew in wisdom and stature, and in favor with God and men.

John the Baptist Prepares the Way

See Matthew 3:1–10; Mark 1:3–5

3 In the fifteenth year of the reign of Tiberius Caesar—when Pontius Pilate was governor of Judea, Herod tetrarch of Galilee, his brother Philip tetrarch of Iturea and Traconitis, and Lysanias tetrarch of Abilene— ²during the high priesthood of Annas and Caiaphas, the word of God came to John son of Zechariah in the desert. ³He went into all the country around the Jordan, preaching a baptism of repentance for the forgiveness of sins. ⁴As is written in the book of the words of Isaiah the prophet:

"A voice of one calling in the desert,

TUESDAY

Read *Luke 2:1–52*
Key Verse *Luke 2:52*

In Process – Jim Lett

"P.B.P.G.I.N.F.W.M.Y." What does that mean? "Please Be Patient. God Is Not Finished With Me Yet." As followers of Jesus, you and I are people in process, not finished products. Our lives are being sculpted and shaped by God according to his purpose and design. Just as Jesus had a mission and a plan, God also has one in mind for each of us—one that will maximize our strengths, talents and experiences so we can make the contributions he created us for.

Our growth is a cooperative effort. The apostle Paul tells us to "continue to work out your salvation with fear and trembling, for it is God who works in you to will and to act according to his good purpose" (Philippians 2:12–13). Like Jesus, we must grow! If we will give attention to the four dimensions of life described here, we will grow toward maturity in a balanced way.

- Jesus grew in "wisdom" (the intellectual dimension). He was educated according to Jewish custom, studying the Scriptures and learning practical living skills. He learned the carpentry trade under Joseph's watchful eye and embarked on a career.
- Jesus grew in "stature" (the physical dimension). He was a working man and a craftsman, strong and sturdy. He walked miles over the countryside, developing stamina and endurance.
- Jesus grew "in favor with God" (the spiritual dimension). He had an intimate relationship with his heavenly Father. He knew the Scriptures thoroughly and lived by them perfectly. He prayed about his concerns and the needs of others.
- Jesus grew "in favor with . . . men" (the social dimension). His love for the people he met was real, often startling and always life-changing. When he looked at them, he looked deeply. When he listened, he listened with his heart. When he prayed for them, they knew God had heard.

How is your progress in these four areas of life? Remember them as you assess your own growth.

A Deeper Look
Colossians 2:6–7; 2 Peter 1:5–8

Go to page 1137 for your next devotional reading.

'Prepare the way for the Lord,
  make straight paths for him.
⁵Every valley shall be filled in,
  every mountain and hill made low.
The crooked roads shall become
    straight,
  the rough ways smooth.
⁶And all mankind will see God's
    salvation.' "ᵃ

⁷John said to the crowds coming out to be baptized by him, "You brood of vipers! Who warned you to flee from the coming wrath? ⁸Produce fruit in keeping with repentance. And do not begin to say to yourselves, 'We have Abraham as our father.' For I tell you that out of these stones God can raise up children for Abraham. ⁹The ax is already at the root of the trees, and every tree that does not produce good fruit will be cut down and thrown into the fire."

¹⁰"What should we do then?" the crowd asked.

¹¹John answered, "The man with two tunics should share with him who has none, and the one who has food should do the same."

¹²Tax collectors also came to be baptized. "Teacher," they asked, "what should we do?"

¹³"Don't collect any more than you are required to," he told them.

¹⁴Then some soldiers asked him, "And what should we do?"

He replied, "Don't extort money and don't accuse people falsely—be content with your pay."

¹⁵The people were waiting expectantly and were all wondering in their hearts if John might possibly be the Christ.ᵇ ¹⁶John answered them all, "I baptize you withᶜ water. But one more powerful than I will come, the thongs of whose sandals I am not worthy to untie. He will baptize you with the Holy Spirit and with fire. ¹⁷His winnowing fork is in his hand to clear his threshing floor and to gather the wheat into his barn, but he will burn up the chaff with unquenchable fire." ¹⁸And with many other words John exhorted the people and preached the good news to them.

¹⁹But when John rebuked Herod the tetrarch because of Herodias, his brother's wife, and all the other evil things he had done, ²⁰Herod added this to them all: He locked John up in prison.

The Baptism and Genealogy of Jesus

See Matthew 1:1–17; 3:13–17; Mark 1:9–11

²¹When all the people were being baptized, Jesus was baptized too. And as he was praying, heaven was opened ²²and the Holy Spirit descended on him in bodily form like a dove. And a voice came from heaven: "You are my Son, whom I love; with you I am well pleased."

²³Now Jesus himself was about thirty years old when he began his ministry. He was the son, so it was thought, of Joseph,

the son of Heli, ²⁴the son of Matthat,
the son of Levi, the son of Melki,
the son of Jannai, the son of Joseph,
²⁵the son of Mattathias, the son of Amos,
the son of Nahum, the son of Esli,
the son of Naggai, ²⁶the son of Maath,
the son of Mattathias, the son of Semein,
the son of Josech, the son of Joda,
²⁷the son of Joanan, the son of Rhesa,
the son of Zerubbabel, the son of Shealtiel,
the son of Neri, ²⁸the son of Melki,
the son of Addi, the son of Cosam,
the son of Elmadam, the son of Er,
²⁹the son of Joshua, the son of Eliezer,
the son of Jorim, the son of Matthat,
the son of Levi, ³⁰the son of Simeon,
the son of Judah, the son of Joseph,
the son of Jonam, the son of Eliakim,
³¹the son of Melea, the son of Menna,
the son of Mattatha, the son of Nathan,
the son of David, ³²the son of Jesse,
the son of Obed, the son of Boaz,
the son of Salmon,ᵈ the son of Nahshon,
³³the son of Amminadab, the son of Ram,ᵉ

ᵃ6 Isaiah 40:3-5   ᵇ15 Or *Messiah*   ᶜ16 Or *in*
ᵈ32 Some early manuscripts *Sala*   ᵉ33 Some manuscripts *Amminadab, the son of Admin, the son of Arni*; other manuscripts vary widely.

the son of Hezron, the son of Perez,
the son of Judah, ³⁴the son of Jacob,
the son of Isaac, the son of Abraham,
the son of Terah, the son of Nahor,
³⁵the son of Serug, the son of Reu,
the son of Peleg, the son of Eber,
the son of Shelah, ³⁶the son of Cainan,
the son of Arphaxad, the son of
Shem,
the son of Noah, the son of Lamech,
³⁷the son of Methuselah, the son of
Enoch,
the son of Jared, the son of Mahalalel,
the son of Kenan, ³⁸the son of
Enosh,
the son of Seth, the son of Adam,
the son of God.

The Temptation of Jesus

See Matthew 4:1–11; Mark 1:12–13

4 Jesus, full of the Holy Spirit, returned from the Jordan and was led by the Spirit in the desert, ²where for forty days he was tempted by the devil. He ate nothing during those days, and at the end of them he was hungry.

³The devil said to him, "If you are the Son of God, tell this stone to become bread."

⁴Jesus answered, "It is written: 'Man does not live on bread alone.'ᵃ"

⁵The devil led him up to a high place and showed him in an instant all the kingdoms of the world. ⁶And he said to him, "I will give you all their authority and splendor, for it has been given to me, and I can give it to anyone I want to. ⁷So if you worship me, it will all be yours."

⁸Jesus answered, "It is written: 'Wor-

ᵃ4 Deut. 8:3

Read Luke 4:1–44
Key Verse Luke 4:4

Somewhere in the Bible – Deb Maschhoff

Two young men were standing on the street corner. One man was witnessing about Jesus Christ to his friend, a lawyer. The Christian repeatedly used the phrase, "somewhere in the Bible it says . . ." The lawyer looked perplexed at this young man and said, "Come to my office with me."

So the two went to his office. When they arrived the lawyer showed his friend the four walls of his office all lined with books. He looked at his friend and said, "If you came to me with a legal problem, I would know exactly which book deals with your situation. You, as a Christian, have one book to master, to learn, to memorize and to handle correctly, yet you do not know where anything is to be found. You tell me the central person of this book is the most important thing in your life. I find that hard to believe."

Jesus proved the importance of knowing God's Word when he confronted the devil with specific passages of Scripture. If the Son of God saw the necessity of knowing God's Word by heart, how much more should we? If God is to speak to me in everyday situations, I need to study, memorize and know how to apply his words. Then the insights that hit me where I live are the ones I can share with others. After all, I can't share what I don't know.

A Deeper Look
Deuteronomy 32:46–47; 2 Timothy 2:1–5; 3:14–17

Go to page 1140 for your next devotional reading.

ship the Lord your God and serve him only.'ᵃ"

⁹The devil led him to Jerusalem and had him stand on the highest point of the temple. "If you are the Son of God," he said, "throw yourself down from here. ¹⁰For it is written:

" 'He will command his angels
concerning you
to guard you carefully;
¹¹they will lift you up in their hands,
so that you will not strike your
foot against a stone.'ᵇ "

¹²Jesus answered, "It says: 'Do not put the Lord your God to the test.'ᶜ "

¹³When the devil had finished all this tempting, he left him until an opportune time.

Jesus Rejected at Nazareth

¹⁴Jesus returned to Galilee in the power of the Spirit, and news about him spread through the whole countryside. ¹⁵He taught in their synagogues, and everyone praised him.

¹⁶He went to Nazareth, where he had been brought up, and on the Sabbath day he went into the synagogue, as was his custom. And he stood up to read. ¹⁷The scroll of the prophet Isaiah was handed to him. Unrolling it, he found the place where it is written:

¹⁸"The Spirit of the Lord is on me,
because he has anointed me
to preach good news to the poor.
He has sent me to proclaim freedom
for the prisoners
and recovery of sight for the blind,
to release the oppressed,
¹⁹ to proclaim the year of the Lord's
favor."ᵈ

²⁰Then he rolled up the scroll, gave it back to the attendant and sat down. The eyes of everyone in the synagogue were fastened on him, ²¹and he began by saying to them, "Today this scripture is fulfilled in your hearing."

²²All spoke well of him and were amazed at the gracious words that came from his lips. "Isn't this Joseph's son?" they asked.

²³Jesus said to them, "Surely you will quote this proverb to me: 'Physician, heal yourself! Do here in your hometown what we have heard that you did in Capernaum.' "

²⁴"I tell you the truth," he continued,

"no prophet is accepted in his hometown. ²⁵I assure you that there were many widows in Israel in Elijah's time, when the sky was shut for three and a half years and there was a severe famine throughout the land. ²⁶Yet Elijah was not sent to any of them, but to a widow in Zarephath in the region of Sidon. ²⁷And there were many in Israel with leprosyᵉ in the time of Elisha the prophet, yet not one of them was cleansed—only Naaman the Syrian."

²⁸All the people in the synagogue were furious when they heard this. ²⁹They got up, drove him out of the town, and took him to the brow of the hill on which the town was built, in order to throw him down the cliff. ³⁰But he walked right through the crowd and went on his way.

Jesus Drives Out an Evil Spirit

³¹Then he went down to Capernaum, a town in Galilee, and on the Sabbath began to teach the people. ³²They were amazed at his teaching, because his message had authority.

³³In the synagogue there was a man possessed by a demon, an evilᶠ spirit. He cried out at the top of his voice, ³⁴"Ha! What do you want with us, Jesus of Nazareth? Have you come to destroy us? I know who you are—the Holy One of God!"

³⁵"Be quiet!" Jesus said sternly. "Come out of him!" Then the demon threw the man down before them all and came out without injuring him.

³⁶All the people were amazed and said to each other, "What is this teaching? With authority and power he gives orders to evil spirits and they come out!" ³⁷And the news about him spread throughout the surrounding area.

Jesus Heals Many

See Matthew 8:14–17; Mark 1:29–38

³⁸Jesus left the synagogue and went to the home of Simon. Now Simon's mother-in-law was suffering from a high fever, and they asked Jesus to help her. ³⁹So he bent over her and rebuked the fever, and it left her. She got up at once and began to wait on them.

⁴⁰When the sun was setting, the peo-

ᵃ8 Deut. 6:13   ᵇ11 Psalm 91:11,12
ᶜ12 Deut. 6:16   ᵈ19 Isaiah 61:1,2
ᵉ27 The Greek word was used for various diseases affecting the skin—not necessarily leprosy.
ᶠ33 Greek unclean; also in verse 36

ple brought to Jesus all who had various kinds of sickness, and laying his hands on each one, he healed them. ⁴¹Moreover, demons came out of many people, shouting, "You are the Son of God!" But he rebuked them and would not allow them to speak, because they knew he was the Christ.ᵃ

⁴²At daybreak Jesus went out to a solitary place. The people were looking for him and when they came to where he was, they tried to keep him from leaving them. ⁴³But he said, "I must preach the good news of the kingdom of God to the other towns also, because that is why I was sent." ⁴⁴And he kept on preaching in the synagogues of Judea.ᵇ

The Calling of the First Disciples

See Matthew 4:18–22; Mark 1:16–20; John 1:40–42

One day as Jesus was standing by the Lake of Gennesaret,ᶜ with the people crowding around him and listening to the word of God, ²he saw at the water's edge two boats, left there by the fishermen, who were washing their nets. ³He got into one of the boats, the one belonging to Simon, and asked him to put out a little from shore. Then he sat down and taught the people from the boat.

⁴When he had finished speaking, he said to Simon, "Put out into deep water, and let downᵈ the nets for a catch."

⁵Simon answered, "Master, we've worked hard all night and haven't caught anything. But because you say so, I will let down the nets."

⁶When they had done so, they caught such a large number of fish that their nets began to break. ⁷So they signaled their partners in the other boat to come and help them, and they came and filled both boats so full that they began to sink.

⁸When Simon Peter saw this, he fell at Jesus' knees and said, "Go away from me, Lord; I am a sinful man!" ⁹For he and all his companions were astonished at the catch of fish they had taken, ¹⁰and so were James and John, the sons of Zebedee, Simon's partners.

Then Jesus said to Simon, "Don't be afraid; from now on you will catch men." ¹¹So they pulled their boats up on shore, left everything and followed him.

The Man With Leprosy

See Matthew 8:2–4; Mark 1:40–44

¹²While Jesus was in one of the towns, a man came along who was covered with leprosy.ᵉ When he saw Jesus, he fell with his face to the ground and begged him, "Lord, if you are willing, you can make me clean."

¹³Jesus reached out his hand and touched the man. "I am willing," he said. "Be clean!" And immediately the leprosy left him.

¹⁴Then Jesus ordered him, "Don't tell anyone, but go, show yourself to the priest and offer the sacrifices that Moses commanded for your cleansing, as a testimony to them."

¹⁵Yet the news about him spread all the more, so that crowds of people came to hear him and to be healed of their sicknesses. ¹⁶But Jesus often withdrew to lonely places and prayed.

Jesus Heals a Paralytic

See Matthew 9:2–8; Mark 2:3–12

¹⁷One day as he was teaching, Pharisees and teachers of the law, who had come from every village of Galilee and from Judea and Jerusalem, were sitting there. And the power of the Lord was present for him to heal the sick. ¹⁸Some men came carrying a paralytic on a mat and tried to take him into the house to lay him before Jesus. ¹⁹When they could not find a way to do this because of the crowd, they went up on the roof and lowered him on his mat through the tiles into the middle of the crowd, right in front of Jesus.

²⁰When Jesus saw their faith, he said, "Friend, your sins are forgiven."

²¹The Pharisees and the teachers of the law began thinking to themselves, "Who is this fellow who speaks blasphemy? Who can forgive sins but God alone?"

²²Jesus knew what they were thinking and asked, "Why are you thinking these things in your hearts? ²³Which is easier: to say, 'Your sins are forgiven,' or to say, 'Get up and walk'? ²⁴But that you may know that the Son of Man has authority on earth to forgive sins . . . ." He said to the paralyzed man, "I tell you, get up, take your mat and go home." ²⁵Immediately he stood up in front of them, took what he had been lying on and went home praising God. ²⁶Everyone was

---

ᵃ41 Or *Messiah*   ᵇ44 Or *the land of the Jews;* some manuscripts *Galilee*   ᶜ1 That is, Sea of Galilee   ᵈ4 The Greek verb is plural.
ᵉ12 The Greek word was used for various diseases affecting the skin—not necessarily leprosy.

amazed and gave praise to God. They were filled with awe and said, "We have seen remarkable things today."

The Calling of Levi
See Matthew 9:9–13; Mark 2:14–17

27After this, Jesus went out and saw a tax collector by the name of Levi sitting at his tax booth. "Follow me," Jesus said to him, 28and Levi got up, left everything and followed him.

29Then Levi held a great banquet for Jesus at his house, and a large crowd of tax collectors and others were eating with them. 30But the Pharisees and the teachers of the law who belonged to their sect complained to his disciples, "Why do you eat and drink with tax collectors and 'sinners'?"

31Jesus answered them, "It is not the healthy who need a doctor, but the sick. 32I have not come to call the righteous, but sinners to repentance."

Jesus Questioned About Fasting
See Matthew 9:14–17; Mark 2:18–22

33They said to him, "John's disciples often fast and pray, and so do the disciples of the Pharisees, but yours go on eating and drinking."

34Jesus answered, "Can you make the guests of the bridegroom fast while he is with them? 35But the time will come when the bridegroom will be taken from them; in those days they will fast."

36He told them this parable: "No one tears a patch from a new garment and sews it on an old one. If he does, he will have torn the new garment, and the patch from the new will not match the old. 37And no one pours new wine into old wineskins. If he does, the new wine will burst the skins, the wine will run out and the wineskins will be ruined. 38No, new wine must be poured into new wineskins. 39And no one after drinking old wine wants the new, for he says, 'The old is better.' "

THURSDAY

Read Luke 5:1–32
Key Verses Luke 5:27–28

"Follow Me" – Sharla Walstrom

"Follow me," the Lord said to Levi. Levi got up and followed him—no questions asked. No whining, no rationalizing. What did he see in Jesus to make him follow? What was Jesus asking of him?

And what about when Jesus spoke those two short words to me? What would following mean to me? What would I give up? To follow Jesus means to be like him and to do what he did. But did I love him enough to live such a selfless, possibly difficult life? Did I love him enough to be willing to leave everything behind? Could I let him be my "first love" (see Revelation 2:4–5)?

I had to test that once; I was holding on tightly to a relationship with a special guy. I didn't want to give him up, but I realized that the relationship was coming before my relationship with Jesus Christ. Though it was very hard, I had to open my hand and surrender what seemed most desirable at the time—I decided to let Jesus Christ be the first love of my life.

Leaving everything and following Jesus has not been disappointing. Eventually I married a wonderful man; but more importantly, my first love, Jesus, continually delights my heart and shows me how much I gain by leaving everything to follow him.

A Deeper Look
Luke 9:23–25; Revelation 2:4–5

Go to page 1143 for your next devotional reading.

Lord of the Sabbath

See Matthew 12:1–14; Mark 2:23—3:6

6 One Sabbath Jesus was going through the grainfields, and his disciples began to pick some heads of grain, rub them in their hands and eat the kernels. ²Some of the Pharisees asked, "Why are you doing what is unlawful on the Sabbath?"

³Jesus answered them, "Have you never read what David did when he and his companions were hungry? ⁴He entered the house of God, and taking the consecrated bread, he ate what is lawful only for priests to eat. And he also gave some to his companions." ⁵Then Jesus said to them, "The Son of Man is Lord of the Sabbath."

⁶On another Sabbath he went into the synagogue and was teaching, and a man was there whose right hand was shriveled. ⁷The Pharisees and the teachers of the law were looking for a reason to accuse Jesus, so they watched him closely to see if he would heal on the Sabbath. ⁸But Jesus knew what they were thinking and said to the man with the shriveled hand, "Get up and stand in front of everyone." So he got up and stood there.

⁹Then Jesus said to them, "I ask you, which is lawful on the Sabbath: to do good or to do evil, to save life or to destroy it?"

¹⁰He looked around at them all, and then said to the man, "Stretch out your hand." He did so, and his hand was completely restored. ¹¹But they were furious and began to discuss with one another what they might do to Jesus.

The Twelve Apostles

See Matthew 10:2–4; Mark 3:16–19; Acts 1:13

¹²One of those days Jesus went out to a mountainside to pray, and spent the night praying to God. ¹³When morning came, he called his disciples to him and chose twelve of them, whom he also designated apostles: ¹⁴Simon (whom he named Peter), his brother Andrew, James, John, Philip, Bartholomew, ¹⁵Matthew, Thomas, James son of Alphaeus, Simon who was called the Zealot, ¹⁶Judas son of James, and Judas Iscariot, who became a traitor.

Blessings and Woes

See Matthew 5:3–12

¹⁷He went down with them and stood on a level place. A large crowd of his disciples was there and a great number of people from all over Judea, from Jerusalem, and from the coast of Tyre and Sidon, ¹⁸who had come to hear him and to be healed of their diseases. Those troubled by evil*a* spirits were cured, ¹⁹and the people all tried to touch him, because power was coming from him and healing them all.

²⁰Looking at his disciples, he said:

"Blessed are you who are poor,
for yours is the kingdom of God.
²¹Blessed are you who hunger now,
for you will be satisfied.
Blessed are you who weep now,
for you will laugh.
²²Blessed are you when men hate you,
when they exclude you and insult
you
and reject your name as evil,
because of the Son of Man.

²³"Rejoice in that day and leap for joy, because great is your reward in heaven. For that is how their fathers treated the prophets.

²⁴"But woe to you who are rich,
for you have already received your
comfort.
²⁵Woe to you who are well fed now,
for you will go hungry.
Woe to you who laugh now,
for you will mourn and weep.
²⁶Woe to you when all men speak well
of you,
for that is how their fathers treated
the false prophets.

Love for Enemies

²⁷"But I tell you who hear me: Love your enemies, do good to those who hate you, ²⁸bless those who curse you, pray for those who mistreat you. ²⁹If someone strikes you on one cheek, turn to him the other also. If someone takes your cloak, do not stop him from taking your tunic. ³⁰Give to everyone who asks you, and if anyone takes what belongs to you, do not demand it back. ³¹Do to others as you would have them do to you.

³²"If you love those who love you, what credit is that to you? Even 'sinners' love those who love them. ³³And if you do good to those who are good to you, what credit is that to you? Even 'sinners' do that. ³⁴And if you lend to those from whom you expect repayment, what cred-

a 18 Greek *unclean*

it is that to you? Even 'sinners' lend to 'sinners,' expecting to be repaid in full. ³⁵But love your enemies, do good to them, and lend to them without expecting to get anything back. Then your reward will be great, and you will be sons of the Most High, because he is kind to the ungrateful and wicked. ³⁶Be merciful, just as your Father is merciful.

Judging Others
See Matthew 7:1–5

³⁷"Do not judge, and you will not be judged. Do not condemn, and you will not be condemned. Forgive, and you will be forgiven. ³⁸Give, and it will be given to you. A good measure, pressed down, shaken together and running over, will be poured into your lap. For with the measure you use, it will be measured to you."

³⁹He also told them this parable: "Can a blind man lead a blind man? Will they not both fall into a pit? ⁴⁰A student is not above his teacher, but everyone who is fully trained will be like his teacher.

⁴¹"Why do you look at the speck of sawdust in your brother's eye and pay no attention to the plank in your own eye? ⁴²How can you say to your brother, 'Brother, let me take the speck out of your eye,' when you yourself fail to see the plank in your own eye? You hypocrite, first take the plank out of your eye, and then you will see clearly to remove the speck from your brother's eye.

A Tree and Its Fruit
See Matthew 7:16,18,20

⁴³"No good tree bears bad fruit, nor does a bad tree bear good fruit. ⁴⁴Each tree is recognized by its own fruit. People do not pick figs from thornbushes, or grapes from briers. ⁴⁵The good man brings good things out of the good stored up in his heart, and the evil man brings evil things out of the evil stored up in his heart. For out of the overflow of his heart his mouth speaks.

The Wise and Foolish Builders
See Matthew 7:24–27

⁴⁶"Why do you call me, 'Lord, Lord,' and do not do what I say? ⁴⁷I will show you what he is like who comes to me and hears my words and puts them into practice. ⁴⁸He is like a man building a house,

who dug down deep and laid the foundation on rock. When a flood came, the torrent struck that house but could not shake it, because it was well built. ⁴⁹But the one who hears my words and does not put them into practice is like a man who built a house on the ground without a foundation. The moment the torrent struck that house, it collapsed and its destruction was complete."

The Faith of the Centurion
See Matthew 8:5–13

7 When Jesus had finished saying all this in the hearing of the people, he entered Capernaum. ²There a centurion's servant, whom his master valued highly, was sick and about to die. ³The centurion heard of Jesus and sent some elders of the Jews to him, asking him to come and heal his servant. ⁴When they came to Jesus, they pleaded earnestly with him, "This man deserves to have you do this, ⁵because he loves our nation and has built our synagogue." ⁶So Jesus went with them.

He was not far from the house when the centurion sent friends to say to him: "Lord, don't trouble yourself, for I do not deserve to have you come under my roof. ⁷That is why I did not even consider myself worthy to come to you. But say the word, and my servant will be healed. ⁸For I myself am a man under authority, with soldiers under me. I tell this one, 'Go,' and he goes; and that one, 'Come,' and he comes. I say to my servant, 'Do this,' and he does it."

⁹When Jesus heard this, he was amazed at him, and turning to the crowd following him, he said, "I tell you, I have not found such great faith even in Israel." ¹⁰Then the men who had been sent returned to the house and found the servant well.

Jesus Raises a Widow's Son

¹¹Soon afterward, Jesus went to a town called Nain, and his disciples and a large crowd went along with him. ¹²As he approached the town gate, a dead person was being carried out—the only son of his mother, and she was a widow. And a large crowd from the town was with her. ¹³When the Lord saw her, his heart went out to her and he said, "Don't cry."

¹⁴Then he went up and touched the coffin, and those carrying it stood still.

He said, "Young man, I say to you, get up!" **15**The dead man sat up and began to talk, and Jesus gave him back to his mother.

16They were all filled with awe and praised God. "A great prophet has appeared among us," they said. "God has come to help his people." **17**This news about Jesus spread throughout Judea*a* and the surrounding country.

Jesus and John the Baptist
See Matthew 11:2–19

18John's disciples told him about all these things. Calling two of them, **19**he sent them to the Lord to ask, "Are you the one who was to come, or should we expect someone else?"

a17 Or the land of the Jews

FRIDAY

Read *Luke 6:1–49*
Key Verse *Luke 6:46*

Jesus Is Lord – Joe Bernardy

In our Western culture we have developed an extremely high regard for our individual rights; sometimes we seem to value them over all else. We value our right to privacy, to "life, liberty, and the pursuit of happiness." We jealously guard our right to make our own decisions and use our time at our discretion. The Bible, however, turns those values upside down.

When we call Jesus "Lord," we give up our rights in exchange for the privilege of living for him. We give him the right to lead us as he directs; we commit ourselves to following him wherever he leads. We surrender our exclusive ownership of our time, our finances and our choice of career and marriage partner to his leading and guidance.

It's something like registering for a class. We do it voluntarily, but once we begin classes, we submit ourselves to the professor and the college regulations. For example, we give up our right to decide where we're going to be on Mondays, Wednesdays and Fridays at 10 A.M. We willingly (but perhaps not cheerfully) sacrifice our free time on Saturdays to put in the required study time. We submit ourselves to the heavy labor of cranking out a fifteen-page term paper. Our submission isn't always fun or easy, but it has benefits: learning about something we're interested in, earning degrees and building a foundation for a future life and career.

But the benefits of submitting to the will of Jesus Christ are greater and more far-reaching. We experience the joy of coming to him and knowing him. And we know that when we obey him, we are laying a solid foundation on which to build our spiritual future. When we submit our will to Jesus Christ, our great teacher, we are following the One who loved us enough to lay down his life for us (see Romans 5:8). His teaching is dynamic. His syllabus, the Word of God, is always dependable. His grading scale is always fair.

Are there certain "rights" that the Lord Jesus is asking you to give up today? Experience the freedom, love and fulfillment of a life of submission to him!

A Deeper Look
John 15:14–15; James 1:22–25

Go to page 1148 for your next devotional reading.

20When the men came to Jesus, they said, "John the Baptist sent us to you to ask, 'Are you the one who was to come, or should we expect someone else?' "

21At that very time Jesus cured many who had diseases, sicknesses and evil spirits, and gave sight to many who were blind. 22So he replied to the messengers, "Go back and report to John what you have seen and heard: The blind receive sight, the lame walk, those who have leprosy*a* are cured, the deaf hear, the dead are raised, and the good news is preached to the poor. 23Blessed is the man who does not fall away on account of me."

24After John's messengers left, Jesus began to speak to the crowd about John: "What did you go out into the desert to see? A reed swayed by the wind? 25If not, what did you go out to see? A man dressed in fine clothes? No, those who wear expensive clothes and indulge in luxury are in palaces. 26But what did you go out to see? A prophet? Yes, I tell you, and more than a prophet. 27This is the one about whom it is written:

" 'I will send my messenger ahead of
    you,
  who will prepare your way before
    you.'*b*

28I tell you, among those born of women there is no one greater than John; yet the one who is least in the kingdom of God is greater than he."

29(All the people, even the tax collectors, when they heard Jesus' words, acknowledged that God's way was right, because they had been baptized by John. 30But the Pharisees and experts in the law rejected God's purpose for themselves, because they had not been baptized by John.)

31"To what, then, can I compare the people of this generation? What are they like? 32They are like children sitting in the marketplace and calling out to each other:

" 'We played the flute for you,
    and you did not dance;
  we sang a dirge,
    and you did not cry.'

33For John the Baptist came neither eating bread nor drinking wine, and you say, 'He has a demon.' 34The Son of Man came eating and drinking, and you say, 'Here is a glutton and a drunkard, a friend of tax collectors and "sinners." ' 35But wisdom is proved right by all her children."

Jesus Anointed by a Sinful Woman

36Now one of the Pharisees invited Jesus to have dinner with him, so he went to the Pharisee's house and reclined at the table. 37When a woman who had lived a sinful life in that town learned that Jesus was eating at the Pharisee's house, she brought an alabaster jar of perfume, 38and as she stood behind him at his feet weeping, she began to wet his feet with her tears. Then she wiped them with her hair, kissed them and poured perfume on them.

39When the Pharisee who had invited him saw this, he said to himself, "If this man were a prophet, he would know who is touching him and what kind of woman she is—that she is a sinner."

40Jesus answered him, "Simon, I have something to tell you."

"Tell me, teacher," he said.

41"Two men owed money to a certain moneylender. One owed him five hundred denarii,*c* and the other fifty. 42Neither of them had the money to pay him back, so he canceled the debts of both. Now which of them will love him more?"

43Simon replied, "I suppose the one who had the bigger debt canceled."

"You have judged correctly," Jesus said.

44Then he turned toward the woman and said to Simon, "Do you see this woman? I came into your house. You did not give me any water for my feet, but she wet my feet with her tears and wiped them with her hair. 45You did not give me a kiss, but this woman, from the time I entered, has not stopped kissing my feet. 46You did not put oil on my head, but she has poured perfume on my feet. 47Therefore, I tell you, her many sins have been forgiven—for she loved much. But he who has been forgiven little loves little."

48Then Jesus said to her, "Your sins are forgiven."

49The other guests began to say among themselves, "Who is this who even forgives sins?"

50Jesus said to the woman, "Your faith has saved you; go in peace."

---

a22 The Greek word was used for various diseases affecting the skin—not necessarily leprosy.
b27 Mal. 3:1   *c41* A denarius was a coin worth about a day's wages.

The Parable of the Sower

See Matthew 13:2–23; Mark 4:1–20

8 After this, Jesus traveled about from one town and village to another, proclaiming the good news of the kingdom of God. The Twelve were with him, ²and also some women who had been cured of evil spirits and diseases: Mary (called Magdalene) from whom seven demons had come out; ³Joanna the wife of Cuza, the manager of Herod's household; Susanna; and many others. These women were helping to support them out of their own means.

⁴While a large crowd was gathering and people were coming to Jesus from town after town, he told this parable: ⁵"A farmer went out to sow his seed. As he was scattering the seed, some fell along the path; it was trampled on, and the birds of the air ate it up. ⁶Some fell on rock, and when it came up, the plants withered because they had no moisture. ⁷Other seed fell among thorns, which grew up with it and choked the plants. ⁸Still other seed fell on good soil. It came up and yielded a crop, a hundred times more than was sown."

When he said this, he called out, "He who has ears to hear, let him hear."

⁹His disciples asked him what this parable meant. ¹⁰He said, "The knowledge of the secrets of the kingdom of God has been given to you, but to others I speak in parables, so that,

" 'though seeing, they may not see;
  though hearing, they may not
    understand.'ᵃ

¹¹"This is the meaning of the parable: The seed is the word of God. ¹²Those along the path are the ones who hear, and then the devil comes and takes away the word from their hearts, so that they may not believe and be saved. ¹³Those on the rock are the ones who receive the word with joy when they hear it, but they have no root. They believe for a while, but in the time of testing they fall away. ¹⁴The seed that fell among thorns stands for those who hear, but as they go on their way they are choked by life's worries, riches and pleasures, and they do not mature. ¹⁵But the seed on good soil stands for those with a noble and good heart, who hear the word, retain it, and by persevering produce a crop.

A Lamp on a Stand

¹⁶"No one lights a lamp and hides it in a jar or puts it under a bed. Instead, he puts it on a stand, so that those who come in can see the light. ¹⁷For there is nothing hidden that will not be disclosed, and nothing concealed that will not be known or brought out into the open. ¹⁸Therefore consider carefully how you listen. Whoever has will be given more; whoever does not have, even what he thinks he has will be taken from him."

Jesus' Mother and Brothers

See Matthew 12:46–50; Mark 3:31–35

¹⁹Now Jesus' mother and brothers came to see him, but they were not able to get near him because of the crowd. ²⁰Someone told him, "Your mother and brothers are standing outside, wanting to see you."

²¹He replied, "My mother and brothers are those who hear God's word and put it into practice."

Jesus Calms the Storm

See Matthew 8:23–27; Mark 4:36–41

²²One day Jesus said to his disciples, "Let's go over to the other side of the lake." So they got into a boat and set out. ²³As they sailed, he fell asleep. A squall came down on the lake, so that the boat was being swamped, and they were in great danger.

²⁴The disciples went and woke him,

ᵃ10 Isaiah 6:9

POINT OF INTEREST

Luke 8:11

This parable summarizes four types of soil: trampled-down soil, weed-filled soil, rocky soil and good soil. Each soil type illustrates a possible condition of the human heart toward God. It seems clear that a heart like the trampled soil is so hard that the devil can snatch away faith before it even takes root, and the "good and noble" heart sprouts faith in abundance, but what of the other two? What do you think? What's your heart's "soil type"?

saying, "Master, Master, we're going to drown!"

He got up and rebuked the wind and the raging waters; the storm subsided, and all was calm. ²⁵"Where is your faith?" he asked his disciples.

In fear and amazement they asked one another, "Who is this? He commands even the winds and the water, and they obey him."

The Healing of a Demon-possessed Man

See Matthew 8:28–34; Mark 5:1–20

²⁶They sailed to the region of the Gerasenes,ᵃ which is across the lake from Galilee. ²⁷When Jesus stepped ashore, he was met by a demon-possessed man from the town. For a long time this man had not worn clothes or lived in a house, but had lived in the tombs. ²⁸When he saw Jesus, he cried out and fell at his feet, shouting at the top of his voice, "What do you want with me, Jesus, Son of the Most High God? I beg you, don't torture me!" ²⁹For Jesus had commanded the evilᵇ spirit to come out of the man. Many times it had seized him, and though he was chained hand and foot and kept under guard, he had broken his chains and had been driven by the demon into solitary places.

³⁰Jesus asked him, "What is your name?"

"Legion," he replied, because many demons had gone into him. ³¹And they begged him repeatedly not to order them to go into the Abyss.

³²A large herd of pigs was feeding there on the hillside. The demons begged Jesus to let them go into them, and he gave them permission. ³³When the demons came out of the man, they went into the pigs, and the herd rushed down the steep bank into the lake and was drowned.

³⁴When those tending the pigs saw what had happened, they ran off and reported this in the town and countryside, ³⁵and the people went out to see what had happened. When they came to Jesus, they found the man from whom the demons had gone out, sitting at Jesus' feet, dressed and in his right mind; and they were afraid. ³⁶Those who had seen it told the people how the demon-possessed man had been cured. ³⁷Then all the people of the region of the Gerasenes asked Jesus to leave them, because they were overcome with fear. So he got into the boat and left.

³⁸The man from whom the demons had gone out begged to go with him, but Jesus sent him away, saying, ³⁹"Return home and tell how much God has done for you." So the man went away and told all over town how much Jesus had done for him.

A Dead Girl and a Sick Woman

See Matthew 9:18–26; Mark 5:22–43

⁴⁰Now when Jesus returned, a crowd welcomed him, for they were all expecting him. ⁴¹Then a man named Jairus, a ruler of the synagogue, came and fell at Jesus' feet, pleading with him to come to his house ⁴²because his only daughter, a girl of about twelve, was dying.

As Jesus was on his way, the crowds almost crushed him. ⁴³And a woman was there who had been subject to bleeding for twelve years,ᶜ but no one could heal her. ⁴⁴She came up behind him and touched the edge of his cloak, and immediately her bleeding stopped.

⁴⁵"Who touched me?" Jesus asked.

When they all denied it, Peter said, "Master, the people are crowding and pressing against you."

⁴⁶But Jesus said, "Someone touched me; I know that power has gone out from me."

⁴⁷Then the woman, seeing that she could not go unnoticed, came trembling and fell at his feet. In the presence of all the people, she told why she had touched him and how she had been instantly healed. ⁴⁸Then he said to her, "Daughter, your faith has healed you. Go in peace."

⁴⁹While Jesus was still speaking, someone came from the house of Jairus, the synagogue ruler. "Your daughter is dead," he said. "Don't bother the teacher any more."

⁵⁰Hearing this, Jesus said to Jairus, "Don't be afraid; just believe, and she will be healed."

⁵¹When he arrived at the house of Jairus, he did not let anyone go in with him except Peter, John and James, and the child's father and mother. ⁵²Meanwhile, all the people were wailing and mourning for her. "Stop wailing," Jesus said. "She is not dead but asleep."

ᵃ26 Some manuscripts *Gadarenes*; other manuscripts *Gergesenes*; also in verse 37
ᵇ29 Greek *unclean*   ᶜ43 Many manuscripts *years, and she had spent all she had on doctors*

⁵³They laughed at him, knowing that she was dead. ⁵⁴But he took her by the hand and said, "My child, get up!" ⁵⁵Her spirit returned, and at once she stood up. Then Jesus told them to give her something to eat. ⁵⁶Her parents were astonished, but he ordered them not to tell anyone what had happened.

Jesus Sends Out the Twelve

See Matthew 10:9–15; Mark 6:8–11

9 When Jesus had called the Twelve together, he gave them power and authority to drive out all demons and to cure diseases, ²and he sent them out to preach the kingdom of God and to heal the sick. ³He told them: "Take nothing for the journey—no staff, no bag, no bread, no money, no extra tunic. ⁴Whatever house you enter, stay there until you leave that town. ⁵If people do not welcome you, shake the dust off your feet when you leave their town, as a testimony against them." ⁶So they set out and went from village to village, preaching the gospel and healing people everywhere.

⁷Now Herod the tetrarch heard about all that was going on. And he was perplexed, because some were saying that John had been raised from the dead, ⁸others that Elijah had appeared, and still others that one of the prophets of long ago had come back to life. ⁹But Herod said, "I beheaded John. Who, then, is this I hear such things about?" And he tried to see him.

Jesus Feeds the Five Thousand

See Matthew 14:13–21; Mark 6:32–44; John 6:5–13

¹⁰When the apostles returned, they reported to Jesus what they had done. Then he took them with him and they withdrew by themselves to a town called Bethsaida, ¹¹but the crowds learned about it and followed him. He welcomed them and spoke to them about the kingdom of God, and healed those who needed healing.

¹²Late in the afternoon the Twelve came to him and said, "Send the crowd away so they can go to the surrounding villages and countryside and find food and lodging, because we are in a remote place here."

¹³He replied, "You give them something to eat."

They answered, "We have only five loaves of bread and two fish—unless we go and buy food for all this crowd." ¹⁴(About five thousand men were there.)

But he said to his disciples, "Have them sit down in groups of about fifty each." ¹⁵The disciples did so, and everybody sat down. ¹⁶Taking the five loaves and the two fish and looking up to heaven, he gave thanks and broke them. Then he gave them to the disciples to set before the people. ¹⁷They all ate and were satisfied, and the disciples picked up twelve basketfuls of broken pieces that were left over.

Peter's Confession of Christ

See Matthew 16:13–16; Mark 8:27–29

¹⁸Once when Jesus was praying in private and his disciples were with him, he asked them, "Who do the crowds say I am?"

¹⁹They replied, "Some say John the Baptist; others say Elijah; and still others, that one of the prophets of long ago has come back to life."

²⁰"But what about you?" he asked. "Who do you say I am?"

Peter answered, "The Christ[a] of God."

²¹Jesus strictly warned them not to tell this to anyone. ²²And he said, "The Son of Man must suffer many things and be rejected by the elders, chief priests and teachers of the law, and he must be killed and on the third day be raised to life."

²³Then he said to them all: "If anyone would come after me, he must deny himself and take up his cross daily and follow me. ²⁴For whoever wants to save his life will lose it, but whoever loses his life for me will save it. ²⁵What good is it for a man to gain the whole world, and yet lose or forfeit his very self? ²⁶If anyone is ashamed of me and my words, the Son of Man will be ashamed of him when he comes in his glory and in the glory of the Father and of the holy angels. ²⁷I tell you the truth, some who are standing here will not taste death before they see the kingdom of God."

The Transfiguration

See Matthew 17:1–8; Mark 9:2–8

²⁸About eight days after Jesus said this, he took Peter, John and James with him and went up onto a mountain to pray. ²⁹As he was praying, the appear-

a 20 Or *Messiah*

Read *Luke 9:1–36*
Key Verse *Luke 9:23*

The Cost of Discipleship

Salvation is a free gift . . . but following Jesus Christ will cost us everything! What? How can both statements be true? It's true that there is absolutely nothing we can do to earn God's favor or forgiveness and nothing we can do to make ourselves holy before him. Yet it is only by denying ourselves, emptying ourselves, that we are able to receive the gift of God, Christ Jesus himself. When we take up our cross, we identify with Jesus' sacrificial death by nailing the ownership of our desires, thoughts, feelings and plans to the cross with him. We die to ourselves daily—in fact, each moment—by making a decision to live for Jesus even when it hurts.

Our natural inclination is to cling to the idea that we are most ourselves when we are "free" to go our own way—that we can be "self-actualized." Paradoxically, it is only through denying self and letting Jesus live in us that we can really be free of the warping, limiting effects of sin and be free to be our true "God-actualized" selves.

Digging Into the Word
1. What will it cost to follow Jesus?—*Matthew 8:18–22; Luke 14:25–33*
2. What will it take for you to die to yourself?—*John 12:24–26; Romans 12:1–2*

Personal Reflection
What is one commitment you have been reluctant to make as you follow Jesus? What is it going to take for you to deny yourself and take up your cross in this area of your life?

One Step Deeper
Mark 10:28–31; Philippians 3:7–11

Go to page 1154 for your next devotional reading.

ance of his face changed, and his clothes became as bright as a flash of lightning. ³⁰Two men, Moses and Elijah, ³¹appeared in glorious splendor, talking with Jesus. They spoke about his departure, which he was about to bring to fulfillment at Jerusalem. ³²Peter and his companions were very sleepy, but when they became fully awake, they saw his glory and the two men standing with him. ³³As the men were leaving Jesus, Peter said to him, "Master, it is good for us to be here. Let us put up three shelters—one for you, one for Moses and one for Elijah." (He did not know what he was saying.)

³⁴While he was speaking, a cloud appeared and enveloped them, and they were afraid as they entered the cloud. ³⁵A voice came from the cloud, saying, "This is my Son, whom I have chosen; listen to him." ³⁶When the voice had spoken, they found that Jesus was alone. The disciples kept this to themselves, and told no one at that time what they had seen.

The Healing of a Boy With an Evil Spirit
See Matthew 17:14–18,22–23; Mark 9:14–27,30–32

³⁷The next day, when they came down from the mountain, a large crowd met him. ³⁸A man in the crowd called out, "Teacher, I beg you to look at my son, for he is my only child. ³⁹A spirit seizes him and he suddenly screams; it throws him into convulsions so that he foams at the mouth. It scarcely ever leaves him and is destroying him. ⁴⁰I begged your disciples to drive it out, but they could not."

⁴¹"O unbelieving and perverse generation," Jesus replied, "how long shall I stay with you and put up with you? Bring your son here."

⁴²Even while the boy was coming, the demon threw him to the ground in a convulsion. But Jesus rebuked the evilᵃ spirit, healed the boy and gave him back to his father. ⁴³And they were all amazed at the greatness of God.

While everyone was marveling at all that Jesus did, he said to his disciples, ⁴⁴"Listen carefully to what I am about to tell you: The Son of Man is going to be betrayed into the hands of men." ⁴⁵But they did not understand what this meant. It was hidden from them, so that they did not grasp it, and they were afraid to ask him about it.

Who Will Be the Greatest?
See Matthew 18:1–5; Mark 9:33–40

⁴⁶An argument started among the disciples as to which of them would be the greatest. ⁴⁷Jesus, knowing their thoughts, took a little child and had him stand beside him. ⁴⁸Then he said to them, "Whoever welcomes this little child in my name welcomes me; and whoever welcomes me welcomes the one who sent me. For he who is least among you all— he is the greatest."

⁴⁹"Master," said John, "we saw a man driving out demons in your name and we tried to stop him, because he is not one of us."

⁵⁰"Do not stop him," Jesus said, "for whoever is not against you is for you."

Samaritan Opposition

⁵¹As the time approached for him to be taken up to heaven, Jesus resolutely set out for Jerusalem. ⁵²And he sent messengers on ahead, who went into a Samaritan village to get things ready for him; ⁵³but the people there did not welcome him, because he was heading for Jerusalem. ⁵⁴When the disciples James and John saw this, they asked, "Lord, do you want us to call fire down from heaven to destroy themᵇ?" ⁵⁵But Jesus turned and rebuked them, ⁵⁶andᶜ they went to another village.

The Cost of Following Jesus
See Matthew 8:19–22

⁵⁷As they were walking along the road, a man said to him, "I will follow you wherever you go."

⁵⁸Jesus replied, "Foxes have holes and birds of the air have nests, but the Son of Man has no place to lay his head."

⁵⁹He said to another man, "Follow me."

But the man replied, "Lord, first let me go and bury my father."

⁶⁰Jesus said to him, "Let the dead bury their own dead, but you go and proclaim the kingdom of God."

⁶¹Still another said, "I will follow you, Lord; but first let me go back and say good-by to my family."

⁶²Jesus replied, "No one who puts his

ᵃ42 Greek *unclean*   ᵇ54 Some manuscripts *them, even as Elijah did*   ᶜ55,56 Some manuscripts *them. And he said, "You do not know what kind of spirit you are of, for the Son of Man did not come to destroy men's lives, but to save them."* ⁵⁶*And* hand to the plow and looks back is fit for service in the kingdom of God."

Jesus Sends Out the Seventy-two

See Luke 9:3–5

10 After this the Lord appointed seventy-two[a] others and sent them two by two ahead of him to every town and place where he was about to go. ²He told them, "The harvest is plentiful, but the workers are few. Ask the Lord of the harvest, therefore, to send out workers into his harvest field. ³Go! I am sending you out like lambs among wolves. ⁴Do not take a purse or bag or sandals; and do not greet anyone on the road.

⁵"When you enter a house, first say, 'Peace to this house.' ⁶If a man of peace is there, your peace will rest on him; if not, it will return to you. ⁷Stay in that house, eating and drinking whatever they give you, for the worker deserves his wages. Do not move around from house to house.

⁸"When you enter a town and are welcomed, eat what is set before you. ⁹Heal the sick who are there and tell them, 'The kingdom of God is near you.' ¹⁰But when you enter a town and are not welcomed, go into its streets and say, ¹¹'Even the dust of your town that sticks to our feet we wipe off against you. Yet be sure of this: The kingdom of God is near.' ¹²I tell you, it will be more bearable on that day for Sodom than for that town.

¹³"Woe to you, Korazin! Woe to you, Bethsaida! For if the miracles that were performed in you had been performed in Tyre and Sidon, they would have repented long ago, sitting in sackcloth and ashes. ¹⁴But it will be more bearable for Tyre and Sidon at the judgment than for you. ¹⁵And you, Capernaum, will you be lifted up to the skies? No, you will go down to the depths.[b]

¹⁶"He who listens to you listens to me; he who rejects you rejects me; but he who rejects me rejects him who sent me."

¹⁷The seventy-two returned with joy and said, "Lord, even the demons submit to us in your name."

¹⁸He replied, "I saw Satan fall like lightning from heaven. ¹⁹I have given you authority to trample on snakes and scorpions and to overcome all the power of the enemy; nothing will harm you. ²⁰However, do not rejoice that the spirits submit to you, but rejoice that your names are written in heaven."

²¹At that time Jesus, full of joy through the Holy Spirit, said, "I praise you, Father, Lord of heaven and earth, because you have hidden these things from the wise and learned, and revealed them to little children. Yes, Father, for this was your good pleasure.

²²"All things have been committed to me by my Father. No one knows who the Son is except the Father, and no one knows who the Father is except the Son and those to whom the Son chooses to reveal him."

²³Then he turned to his disciples and said privately, "Blessed are the eyes that see what you see. ²⁴For I tell you that many prophets and kings wanted to see what you see but did not see it, and to hear what you hear but did not hear it."

The Parable of the Good Samaritan

See Matthew 22:34–40; Mark 12:28–31

²⁵On one occasion an expert in the law stood up to test Jesus. "Teacher," he asked, "what must I do to inherit eternal life?"

²⁶"What is written in the Law?" he replied. "How do you read it?"

²⁷He answered: " 'Love the Lord your God with all your heart and with all your soul and with all your strength and with all your mind'[c]; and, 'Love your neighbor as yourself.'[d] "

²⁸"You have answered correctly," Jesus replied. "Do this and you will live."

²⁹But he wanted to justify himself, so he asked Jesus, "And who is my neighbor?"

³⁰In reply Jesus said: "A man was going down from Jerusalem to Jericho, when he fell into the hands of robbers. They stripped him of his clothes, beat him and went away, leaving him half dead. ³¹A priest happened to be going down the same road, and when he saw the man, he passed by on the other side. ³²So too, a Levite, when he came to the place and saw him, passed by on the other side. ³³But a Samaritan, as he traveled, came where the man was; and when he saw him, he took pity on him. ³⁴He went to him and bandaged his wounds, pouring on oil and wine. Then he put the man

---

a1 Some manuscripts *seventy*; also in verse 17   b15 Greek *Hades*   c27 Deut. 6:5   d27 Lev. 19:18

on his own donkey, took him to an inn and took care of him. [35]The next day he took out two silver coins[a] and gave them to the innkeeper. 'Look after him,' he said, 'and when I return, I will reimburse you for any extra expense you may have.'

[36]"Which of these three do you think was a neighbor to the man who fell into the hands of robbers?"

[37]The expert in the law replied, "The one who had mercy on him."

Jesus told him, "Go and do likewise."

At the Home of Martha and Mary

[38]As Jesus and his disciples were on their way, he came to a village where a woman named Martha opened her home to him. [39]She had a sister called Mary, who sat at the Lord's feet listening to what he said. [40]But Martha was distracted by all the preparations that had to be made. She came to him and asked, "Lord, don't you care that my sister has left me to do the work by myself? Tell her to help me!"

[41]"Martha, Martha," the Lord answered, "you are worried and upset about many things, [42]but only one thing is needed.[b] Mary has chosen what is better, and it will not be taken away from her."

Jesus' Teaching on Prayer

See Matthew 6:9–13; 7:7–11

11 One day Jesus was praying in a certain place. When he finished, one of his disciples said to him, "Lord, teach us to pray, just as John taught his disciples."

[2]He said to them, "When you pray, say:

" 'Father,[c]
hallowed be your name,
your kingdom come.[d]
[3]Give us each day our daily bread.
[4]Forgive us our sins,
   for we also forgive everyone who
      sins against us.[e]
And lead us not into temptation.[f] ' "

[5]Then he said to them, "Suppose one of you has a friend, and he goes to him at midnight and says, 'Friend, lend me three loaves of bread, [6]because a friend of mine on a journey has come to me, and I have nothing to set before him.'

[7]"Then the one inside answers, 'Don't bother me. The door is already locked, and my children are with me in bed. I can't get up and give you anything.' [8]I tell you, though he will not get up and give him the bread because he is his friend, yet because of the man's boldness[g] he will get up and give him as much as he needs.

[9]"So I say to you: Ask and it will be given to you; seek and you will find; knock and the door will be opened to you. [10]For everyone who asks receives; he who seeks finds; and to him who knocks, the door will be opened.

[11]"Which of you fathers, if your son asks for[h] a fish, will give him a snake instead? [12]Or if he asks for an egg, will give him a scorpion? [13]If you then, though you are evil, know how to give good gifts to your children, how much more will your Father in heaven give the Holy Spirit to those who ask him!"

Jesus and Beelzebub

See Matthew 12:22,24–29,43–45; Mark 3:23–27

[14]Jesus was driving out a demon that was mute. When the demon left, the man who had been mute spoke, and the crowd was amazed. [15]But some of them said, "By Beelzebub,[i] the prince of demons, he is driving out demons." [16]Others tested him by asking for a sign from heaven.

[17]Jesus knew their thoughts and said to them: "Any kingdom divided against

---

[a]35 Greek two denarii   [b]42 Some manuscripts but few things are needed—or only one   [c]2 Some manuscripts Our Father in heaven   [d]2 Some manuscripts come. May your will be done on earth as it is in heaven.   [e]4 Greek everyone who is indebted to us   [f]4 Some manuscripts temptation but deliver us from the evil one   [g]8 Or persistence   [h]11 Some manuscripts for bread, will give him a stone; or if he asks for   [i]15 Greek Beezeboul or Beelzeboul; also in verses 18 and 19

POINT OF INTEREST

Luke 10:42

What do you think about Mary's actions and Martha's response in this short account? In this verse Jesus is teaching Martha that being *with* God—listening and talking with him—is even more important than our service *for* God. Still, he never said that we weren't to help with the dishes!

itself will be ruined, and a house divided against itself will fall. [18]If Satan is divided against himself, how can his kingdom stand? I say this because you claim that I drive out demons by Beelzebub. [19]Now if I drive out demons by Beelzebub, by whom do your followers drive them out? So then, they will be your judges. [20]But if I drive out demons by the finger of God, then the kingdom of God has come to you.

[21]"When a strong man, fully armed, guards his own house, his possessions are safe. [22]But when someone stronger attacks and overpowers him, he takes away the armor in which the man trusted and divides up the spoils.

[23]"He who is not with me is against me, and he who does not gather with me, scatters.

[24]"When an evil[a] spirit comes out of a man, it goes through arid places seeking rest and does not find it. Then it says, 'I will return to the house I left.' [25]When it arrives, it finds the house swept clean and put in order. [26]Then it goes and takes seven other spirits more wicked than itself, and they go in and live there. And the final condition of that man is worse than the first."

[27]As Jesus was saying these things, a woman in the crowd called out, "Blessed is the mother who gave you birth and nursed you."

[28]He replied, "Blessed rather are those who hear the word of God and obey it."

The Sign of Jonah

See Matthew 12:39–42

[29]As the crowds increased, Jesus said, "This is a wicked generation. It asks for a miraculous sign, but none will be given it except the sign of Jonah. [30]For as Jonah was a sign to the Ninevites, so also will the Son of Man be to this generation. [31]The Queen of the South will rise at the judgment with the men of this generation and condemn them; for she came from the ends of the earth to listen to Solomon's wisdom, and now one[b] greater than Solomon is here. [32]The men of Nineveh will stand up at the judgment with this generation and condemn it; for they repented at the preaching of Jonah, and now one greater than Jonah is here.

The Lamp of the Body

See Matthew 6:22–23

[33]"No one lights a lamp and puts it in

a place where it will be hidden, or under a bowl. Instead he puts it on its stand, so that those who come in may see the light. [34]Your eye is the lamp of your body. When your eyes are good, your whole body also is full of light. But when they are bad, your body also is full of darkness. [35]See to it, then, that the light within you is not darkness. [36]Therefore, if your whole body is full of light, and no part of it dark, it will be completely lighted, as when the light of a lamp shines on you."

Six Woes

[37]When Jesus had finished speaking, a Pharisee invited him to eat with him; so he went in and reclined at the table. [38]But the Pharisee, noticing that Jesus did not first wash before the meal, was surprised.

[39]Then the Lord said to him, "Now then, you Pharisees clean the outside of the cup and dish, but inside you are full of greed and wickedness. [40]You foolish people! Did not the one who made the outside make the inside also? [41]But give what is inside ⌊the dish⌋[c] to the poor, and everything will be clean for you.

[42]"Woe to you Pharisees, because you give God a tenth of your mint, rue and all other kinds of garden herbs, but you neglect justice and the love of God. You should have practiced the latter without leaving the former undone.

[43]"Woe to you Pharisees, because you love the most important seats in the synagogues and greetings in the marketplaces.

[44]"Woe to you, because you are like unmarked graves, which men walk over without knowing it."

[45]One of the experts in the law answered him, "Teacher, when you say these things, you insult us also."

[46]Jesus replied, "And you experts in the law, woe to you, because you load people down with burdens they can hardly carry, and you yourselves will not lift one finger to help them.

[47]"Woe to you, because you build tombs for the prophets, and it was your forefathers who killed them. [48]So you testify that you approve of what your forefathers did; they killed the prophets, and you build their tombs. [49]Because of this,

---

a24 Greek unclean   b31 Or something; also in verse 32   c41 Or what you have

God in his wisdom said, 'I will send them prophets and apostles, some of whom they will kill and others they will persecute.' ⁵⁰Therefore this generation will be held responsible for the blood of all the prophets that has been shed since the beginning of the world, ⁵¹from the blood of Abel to the blood of Zechariah, who was killed between the altar and the sanctuary. Yes, I tell you, this generation will be held responsible for it all.

⁵²"Woe to you experts in the law, because you have taken away the key to knowledge. You yourselves have not entered, and you have hindered those who were entering."

⁵³When Jesus left there, the Pharisees and the teachers of the law began to oppose him fiercely and to besiege him with questions, ⁵⁴waiting to catch him in something he might say.

Warnings and Encouragements

See Matthew 10:26–33

12 Meanwhile, when a crowd of many thousands had gathered, so that they were trampling on one another, Jesus began to speak first to his disciples, saying: "Be on your guard against the yeast of the Pharisees, which is hypocrisy. ²There is nothing concealed that will not be disclosed, or hidden that will not be made known. ³What you have said in the dark will be heard in the daylight, and what you have whispered in the ear in the inner rooms will be proclaimed from the roofs.

⁴"I tell you, my friends, do not be afraid of those who kill the body and after that can do no more. ⁵But I will show you whom you should fear: Fear him who, after the killing of the body, has power to throw you into hell. Yes, I tell you, fear him. ⁶Are not five sparrows sold for two pennies*a*? Yet not one of them is forgotten by God. ⁷Indeed, the very hairs of your head are all numbered. Don't be afraid; you are worth more than many sparrows.

⁸"I tell you, whoever acknowledges me before men, the Son of Man will also acknowledge him before the angels of God. ⁹But he who disowns me before men will be disowned before the angels of God. ¹⁰And everyone who speaks a word against the Son of Man will be forgiven, but anyone who blasphemes against the Holy Spirit will not be forgiven.

¹¹"When you are brought before synagogues, rulers and authorities, do not worry about how you will defend yourselves or what you will say, ¹²for the Holy Spirit will teach you at that time what you should say."

The Parable of the Rich Fool

¹³Someone in the crowd said to him, "Teacher, tell my brother to divide the inheritance with me."

¹⁴Jesus replied, "Man, who appointed me a judge or an arbiter between you?" ¹⁵Then he said to them, "Watch out! Be on your guard against all kinds of greed; a man's life does not consist in the abundance of his possessions."

¹⁶And he told them this parable: "The ground of a certain rich man produced a good crop. ¹⁷He thought to himself, 'What shall I do? I have no place to store my crops.'

¹⁸"Then he said, 'This is what I'll do. I will tear down my barns and build bigger ones, and there I will store all my grain and my goods. ¹⁹And I'll say to myself, "You have plenty of good things laid up for many years. Take life easy; eat, drink and be merry." '

²⁰"But God said to him, 'You fool! This very night your life will be demanded from you. Then who will get what you have prepared for yourself?'

²¹"This is how it will be with anyone who stores up things for himself but is not rich toward God."

Do Not Worry

See Matthew 6:25–33

²²Then Jesus said to his disciples: "Therefore I tell you, do not worry about your life, what you will eat; or about your body, what you will wear. ²³Life is more than food, and the body more than clothes. ²⁴Consider the ravens: They do not sow or reap, they have no storeroom or barn; yet God feeds them. And how much more valuable you are than birds! ²⁵Who of you by worrying can add a single hour to his life*b*? ²⁶Since you cannot do this very little thing, why do you worry about the rest?

²⁷"Consider how the lilies grow. They do not labor or spin. Yet I tell you, not even Solomon in all his splendor was dressed like one of these. ²⁸If that is how

---

*a*6 Greek *two assaria*   *b*25 Or *single cubit to his height*

God clothes the grass of the field, which is here today, and tomorrow is thrown into the fire, how much more will he clothe you, O you of little faith! 29And do not set your heart on what you will eat or drink; do not worry about it. 30For the pagan world runs after all such things, and your Father knows that you need them. 31But seek his kingdom, and these things will be given to you as well.

Read Luke 12:1–34
Key Verses Luke 12:13–21

What Is "Real Life"? — Ken Larson

In 1923, a very important meeting was held at the Edgewater Beach Hotel in Chicago. Attending this meeting were nine of the world's most successful financiers. But where were the participants twenty-five years later?

- The president of the largest independent steel company had lived on borrowed money for five years before his death and died bankrupt.
- The president of the largest utility company had died penniless and a fugitive from justice in a foreign land.
- The president of the largest gas company had gone insane.
- The greatest wheat speculator had died abroad, insolvent.
- The president of the New York Stock Exchange had spent several years in prison.
- A cabinet member of the United States government had been pardoned from prison so he could die at home.
- The greatest "bear" on Wall Street had committed suicide.
- The head of the world's greatest monopoly had committed suicide.
- The president of the Bank of International Settlements had committed suicide.

All these men had learned the art of making money, but it doesn't appear that any of them had learned how to live. In Luke 12:15 Jesus was talking about the nature of "life." Greed chases after wealth and possessions. Putting hope and trust in things is not "living," but people often substitute this for "real life," which is found in seeking and loving God.

Sometimes we fall victim to the thought that somehow, if we only had money and position, we'd have more of a "life" and that things would go more smoothly, be more fun, more comfortable. But it just doesn't work that way, and God wants us to know and believe that life is found in him: "Do not love the world or anything in the world. If anyone loves the world, the love of the Father is not in him. For everything in the world—the cravings of sinful man, the lust of his eyes and the boasting of what he has and does—comes not from the Father but from the world. The world and its desires pass away, but the man who does the will of God lives forever" (1 John 2:15–17).

A Deeper Look
Isaiah 55:2; Matthew 6:19–21

Go to page 1158 for your next devotional reading.

32"Do not be afraid, little flock, for your Father has been pleased to give you the kingdom. 33Sell your possessions and give to the poor. Provide purses for yourselves that will not wear out, a treasure in heaven that will not be exhausted, where no thief comes near and no moth destroys. 34For where your treasure is, there your heart will be also.

Watchfulness
See Matthew 24:43–51; Mark 13:33–37

35"Be dressed ready for service and keep your lamps burning, 36like men waiting for their master to return from a wedding banquet, so that when he comes and knocks they can immediately open the door for him. 37It will be good for those servants whose master finds them watching when he comes. I tell you the truth, he will dress himself to serve, will have them recline at the table and will come and wait on them. 38It will be good for those servants whose master finds them ready, even if he comes in the second or third watch of the night. 39But understand this: If the owner of the house had known at what hour the thief was coming, he would not have let his house be broken into. 40You also must be ready, because the Son of Man will come at an hour when you do not expect him."

41Peter asked, "Lord, are you telling this parable to us, or to everyone?"

42The Lord answered, "Who then is the faithful and wise manager, whom the master puts in charge of his servants to give them their food allowance at the proper time? 43It will be good for that servant whom the master finds doing so when he returns. 44I tell you the truth, he will put him in charge of all his possessions. 45But suppose the servant says to himself, 'My master is taking a long time in coming,' and he then begins to beat the menservants and maidservants and to eat and drink and get drunk. 46The master of that servant will come on a day when he does not expect him and at an hour he is not aware of. He will cut him to pieces and assign him a place with the unbelievers.

47"That servant who knows his master's will and does not get ready or does not do what his master wants will be beaten with many blows. 48But the one who does not know and does things deserving punishment will be beaten with few blows. From everyone who has been given much, much will be demanded; and from the one who has been entrusted with much, much more will be asked.

Not Peace but Division
See Matthew 10:34–36

49"I have come to bring fire on the earth, and how I wish it were already kindled! 50But I have a baptism to undergo, and how distressed I am until it is completed! 51Do you think I came to bring peace on earth? No, I tell you, but division. 52From now on there will be five in one family divided against each other, three against two and two against three. 53They will be divided, father against son and son against father, mother against daughter and daughter against mother, mother-in-law against daughter-in-law and daughter-in-law against mother-in-law."

Interpreting the Times

54He said to the crowd: "When you see a cloud rising in the west, immediately you say, 'It's going to rain,' and it does. 55And when the south wind blows, you say, 'It's going to be hot,' and it is. 56Hypocrites! You know how to interpret the appearance of the earth and the sky. How is it that you don't know how to interpret this present time?

57"Why don't you judge for yourselves what is right? 58As you are going with your adversary to the magistrate, try hard to be reconciled to him on the way, or he may drag you off to the judge, and the judge turn you over to the officer, and the officer throw you into prison. 59I tell you, you will not get out until you have paid the last penny.ᵃ "

Repent or Perish

13 Now there were some present at that time who told Jesus about the Galileans whose blood Pilate had mixed with their sacrifices. 2Jesus answered, "Do you think that these Galileans were worse sinners than all the other Galileans because they suffered this way? 3I tell you, no! But unless you repent, you too will all perish. 4Or those eighteen who died when the tower in Siloam fell on them—do you think they were more guilty than all the others living in Jerusalem? 5I tell you, no! But unless you repent, you too will all perish."

ᵃ59 Greek lepton

6Then he told this parable: "A man had a fig tree, planted in his vineyard, and he went to look for fruit on it, but did not find any. 7So he said to the man who took care of the vineyard, 'For three years now I've been coming to look for fruit on this fig tree and haven't found any. Cut it down! Why should it use up the soil?'

8" 'Sir,' the man replied, 'leave it alone for one more year, and I'll dig around it and fertilize it. 9If it bears fruit next year, fine! If not, then cut it down.' "

A Crippled Woman Healed on the Sabbath

10On a Sabbath Jesus was teaching in one of the synagogues, 11and a woman was there who had been crippled by a spirit for eighteen years. She was bent over and could not straighten up at all. 12When Jesus saw her, he called her forward and said to her, "Woman, you are set free from your infirmity." 13Then he put his hands on her, and immediately she straightened up and praised God.

14Indignant because Jesus had healed on the Sabbath, the synagogue ruler said to the people, "There are six days for work. So come and be healed on those days, not on the Sabbath."

15The Lord answered him, "You hypocrites! Doesn't each of you on the Sabbath untie his ox or donkey from the stall and lead it out to give it water? 16Then should not this woman, a daughter of Abraham, whom Satan has kept bound for eighteen long years, be set free on the Sabbath day from what bound her?"

17When he said this, all his opponents were humiliated, but the people were delighted with all the wonderful things he was doing.

The Parables of the Mustard Seed and the Yeast

See Matthew 13:31–33; Mark 4:30–32

18Then Jesus asked, "What is the kingdom of God like? What shall I compare it to? 19It is like a mustard seed, which a man took and planted in his garden. It grew and became a tree, and the birds of the air perched in its branches."

20Again he asked, "What shall I compare the kingdom of God to? 21It is like yeast that a woman took and mixed into a large amount*a* of flour until it worked all through the dough."

The Narrow Door

22Then Jesus went through the towns and villages, teaching as he made his way to Jerusalem. 23Someone asked him, "Lord, are only a few people going to be saved?"

He said to them, 24"Make every effort to enter through the narrow door, because many, I tell you, will try to enter and will not be able to. 25Once the owner of the house gets up and closes the door, you will stand outside knocking and pleading, 'Sir, open the door for us.'

"But he will answer, 'I don't know you or where you come from.'

26"Then you will say, 'We ate and drank with you, and you taught in our streets.'

27"But he will reply, 'I don't know you or where you come from. Away from me, all you evildoers!'

28"There will be weeping there, and gnashing of teeth, when you see Abraham, Isaac and Jacob and all the prophets in the kingdom of God, but you yourselves thrown out. 29People will come from east and west and north and south, and will take their places at the feast in the kingdom of God. 30Indeed there are those who are last who will be first, and first who will be last."

Jesus' Sorrow for Jerusalem

See Matthew 23:37–39

31At that time some Pharisees came to Jesus and said to him, "Leave this place and go somewhere else. Herod wants to kill you."

32He replied, "Go tell that fox, 'I will drive out demons and heal people today and tomorrow, and on the third day I will reach my goal.' 33In any case, I must keep going today and tomorrow and the next day—for surely no prophet can die outside Jerusalem!

34"O Jerusalem, Jerusalem, you who kill the prophets and stone those sent to you, how often I have longed to gather your children together, as a hen gathers her chicks under her wings, but you were not willing! 35Look, your house is left to you desolate. I tell you, you will not see me again until you say, 'Blessed is he who comes in the name of the Lord.'*b* "

---

a21 Greek *three satas* (probably about 1/2 bushel or 22 liters)   *b35* Psalm 118:26

Jesus at a Pharisee's House

14 One Sabbath, when Jesus went to eat in the house of a prominent Pharisee, he was being carefully watched. ²There in front of him was a man suffering from dropsy. ³Jesus asked the Pharisees and experts in the law, "Is it lawful to heal on the Sabbath or not?" ⁴But they remained silent. So taking hold of the man, he healed him and sent him away.

⁵Then he asked them, "If one of you has a son*a* or an ox that falls into a well on the Sabbath day, will you not immediately pull him out?" ⁶And they had nothing to say.

⁷When he noticed how the guests picked the places of honor at the table, he told them this parable: ⁸"When someone invites you to a wedding feast, do not take the place of honor, for a person more distinguished than you may have been invited. ⁹If so, the host who invited both of you will come and say to you, 'Give this man your seat.' Then, humiliated, you will have to take the least important place. ¹⁰But when you are invited, take the lowest place, so that when your host comes, he will say to you, 'Friend, move up to a better place.' Then you will be honored in the presence of all your fellow guests. ¹¹For everyone who exalts himself will be humbled, and he who humbles himself will be exalted."

¹²Then Jesus said to his host, "When you give a luncheon or dinner, do not invite your friends, your brothers or relatives, or your rich neighbors; if you do, they may invite you back and so you will be repaid. ¹³But when you give a banquet, invite the poor, the crippled, the lame, the blind, ¹⁴and you will be blessed. Although they cannot repay you, you will be repaid at the resurrection of the righteous."

The Parable of the Great Banquet

¹⁵When one of those at the table with him heard this, he said to Jesus, "Blessed is the man who will eat at the feast in the kingdom of God."

¹⁶Jesus replied: "A certain man was preparing a great banquet and invited many guests. ¹⁷At the time of the banquet he sent his servant to tell those who had been invited, 'Come, for everything is now ready.'

¹⁸"But they all alike began to make excuses. The first said, 'I have just bought a field, and I must go and see it. Please excuse me.'

¹⁹"Another said, 'I have just bought five yoke of oxen, and I'm on my way to try them out. Please excuse me.'

²⁰"Still another said, 'I just got married, so I can't come.'

²¹"The servant came back and reported this to his master. Then the owner of the house became angry and ordered his servant, 'Go out quickly into the streets and alleys of the town and bring in the poor, the crippled, the blind and the lame.'

²²"'Sir,' the servant said, 'what you ordered has been done, but there is still room.'

²³"Then the master told his servant, 'Go out to the roads and country lanes and make them come in, so that my house will be full. ²⁴I tell you, not one of those men who were invited will get a taste of my banquet.'"

The Cost of Being a Disciple

²⁵Large crowds were traveling with Jesus, and turning to them he said: ²⁶"If anyone comes to me and does not hate his father and mother, his wife and children, his brothers and sisters—yes, even his own life—he cannot be my disciple. ²⁷And anyone who does not carry his cross and follow me cannot be my disciple.

²⁸"Suppose one of you wants to build a tower. Will he not first sit down and estimate the cost to see if he has enough money to complete it? ²⁹For if he lays the foundation and is not able to finish it, everyone who sees it will ridicule him, ³⁰saying, 'This fellow began to build and was not able to finish.'

³¹"Or suppose a king is about to go to war against another king. Will he not first sit down and consider whether he is able with ten thousand men to oppose the one coming against him with twenty thousand? ³²If he is not able, he will send a delegation while the other is still a long way off and will ask for terms of peace. ³³In the same way, any of you who does not give up everything he has cannot be my disciple.

³⁴"Salt is good, but if it loses its saltiness, how can it be made salty again? ³⁵It is fit neither for the soil nor for the manure pile; it is thrown out.

a 5 Some manuscripts donkey

"He who has ears to hear, let him hear."

The Parable of the Lost Sheep
See Matthew 18:12–14

15 Now the tax collectors and "sinners" were all gathering around to hear him. 2But the Pharisees and the teachers of the law muttered, "This man welcomes sinners and eats with them."

3Then Jesus told them this parable:

4"Suppose one of you has a hundred sheep and loses one of them. Does he not leave the ninety-nine in the open country and go after the lost sheep until he finds it? 5And when he finds it, he joyfully puts it on his shoulders 6and goes home. Then he calls his friends and neighbors together and says, 'Rejoice with me; I have found my lost sheep.' 7I tell you that in the same way there will be more rejoicing in heaven over one sinner who repents

---

TUESDAY

Read Luke 14:1–35
Key Verses Luke 14:26–28

What Does It Cost? — Lynn Feldner

When I decided to follow Jesus Christ in college, I knew that my life would change. I knew that some of my choices would not be popular with some of my peers. I knew the decision I made would cost me something.

When I decided to spend my last two college summers at Eagle Lake Camp, the cost was clear. It meant low pay and long hours. I would spend an extra semester at Illinois State because summer school wasn't an option. And as a music major, it would cost me the opportunity to practice and perform all summer. The cost of those two summers seems small now, yet I have learned it is through the small sacrifices that God prepares us for the bigger ones.

But sometimes I get complacent. I get wrapped up in my life, my friends and my possessions, and God takes the back seat. Then God impresses Luke 14:26 on my heart and confronts me with the question, "Do you love me more than everything else?"

Is God really asking me to forsake all things to follow him? I wish I could always say yes to him, but as I consider the cost of following him, everything else weighs heavily against it. God continues to tug at my heart as I read, "And anyone who does not carry his cross and follow me cannot be my disciple."

Jesus probably isn't saying we have to sell all our possessions and give everything away (although he may be) but that we are to hold on to "things" loosely, abandoning the right to ownership and the desire to cling to them. He wants us instead to hold on to *him* tightly, as Francis of Assisi did. When he was in his early twenties, Francis abandoned all his rights and all his possessions as a wealthy merchant's son, even his clothes. He took a vow of poverty and began healing the sick and rebuilding churches. And after he had done so, he exclaimed, "This is what I want! This is what I desire! This is what I long for with all my heart and soul!"

A Deeper Look
Mark 10:29–30; Romans 12:1

Go to page 1160 for your next devotional reading.

than over ninety-nine righteous persons who do not need to repent.

The Parable of the Lost Coin

8"Or suppose a woman has ten silver coins^a and loses one. Does she not light a lamp, sweep the house and search carefully until she finds it? 9And when she finds it, she calls her friends and neighbors together and says, 'Rejoice with me; I have found my lost coin.' 10In the same way, I tell you, there is rejoicing in the presence of the angels of God over one sinner who repents."

The Parable of the Lost Son

11Jesus continued: "There was a man who had two sons. 12The younger one said to his father, 'Father, give me my share of the estate.' So he divided his property between them.

13"Not long after that, the younger son got together all he had, set off for a distant country and there squandered his wealth in wild living. 14After he had spent everything, there was a severe famine in that whole country, and he began to be in need. 15So he went and hired himself out to a citizen of that country, who sent him to his fields to feed pigs. 16He longed to fill his stomach with the pods that the pigs were eating, but no one gave him anything.

17"When he came to his senses, he said, 'How many of my father's hired men have food to spare, and here I am starving to death! 18I will set out and go back to my father and say to him: Father, I have sinned against heaven and against you. 19I am no longer worthy to be called your son; make me like one of your hired men.' 20So he got up and went to his father.

"But while he was still a long way off, his father saw him and was filled with compassion for him; he ran to his son, threw his arms around him and kissed him.

21"The son said to him, 'Father, I have sinned against heaven and against you. I am no longer worthy to be called your son.^b'

22"But the father said to his servants, 'Quick! Bring the best robe and put it on him. Put a ring on his finger and sandals on his feet. 23Bring the fattened calf and kill it. Let's have a feast and celebrate.

24For this son of mine was dead and is alive again; he was lost and is found.' So they began to celebrate.

25"Meanwhile, the older son was in the field. When he came near the house, he heard music and dancing. 26So he called one of the servants and asked him what was going on. 27'Your brother has come,' he replied, 'and your father has killed the fattened calf because he has him back safe and sound.'

28"The older brother became angry and refused to go in. So his father went out and pleaded with him. 29But he answered his father, 'Look! All these years I've been slaving for you and never disobeyed your orders. Yet you never gave me even a young goat so I could celebrate with my friends. 30But when this son of yours who has squandered your property with prostitutes comes home, you kill the fattened calf for him!'

31"'My son,' the father said, 'you are always with me, and everything I have is yours. 32But we had to celebrate and be glad, because this brother of yours was dead and is alive again; he was lost and is found.'"

The Parable of the Shrewd Manager

16 Jesus told his disciples: "There was a rich man whose manager was accused of wasting his possessions. 2So he called him in and asked him, 'What is this I hear about you? Give an account of your management, because you cannot be manager any longer.'

3"The manager said to himself, 'What shall I do now? My master is taking away my job. I'm not strong enough to dig, and I'm ashamed to beg— 4I know what I'll do so that, when I lose my job here, people will welcome me into their houses.'

5"So he called in each one of his master's debtors. He asked the first, 'How much do you owe my master?'

6"'Eight hundred gallons^c of olive oil,' he replied.

"The manager told him, 'Take your bill, sit down quickly, and make it four hundred.'

7"Then he asked the second, 'And how much do you owe?'

---

^a8 Greek *ten drachmas,* each worth about a day's wages   ^b21 Some early manuscripts *son. Make me like one of your hired men.*   ^c6 Greek *one hundred batous* (probably about 3 kiloliters)

" 'A thousand bushels*a* of wheat,' he replied.

"He told him, 'Take your bill and make it eight hundred.'

⁸"The master commended the dishonest manager because he had acted shrewdly. For the people of this world are more shrewd in dealing with their own kind than are the people of the light. ⁹I tell you, use worldly wealth to gain friends for yourselves, so that when it is gone, you will be welcomed into eternal dwellings.

¹⁰"Whoever can be trusted with very little can also be trusted with much, and whoever is dishonest with very little will

---

a7 Greek *one hundred korous* (probably about 35 kiloliters)

Read Luke 15:1–32
Key Verses Luke 15:11–32

Will the Real Prodigal Please Stand Up? —Eileen Anderson

Once there was a young guy who was bored and tired of working hard. He wanted to go to parties, meet girls and have fun. He convinced his father to give him his share of the estate and then left for the city.

Meanwhile, his older brother continued to work hard on the farm. He listened to his dad and never asked for a thing. Late at night, his muscles sore from a long day of baling hay, feeding livestock and mending fences, he thought about his younger brother. He may have pictured him having a great time, dressed in stylish clothes, eating great food and dating beautiful women. Resentment began to eat at him.

As the months passed, the older brother continued to play the role of the devoted son. He began to calculate how his hard work was going to pay off eventually; his dad would be so grateful that his older son had stuck around and been the "good kid" that he would get all Dad's love *and* inherit the farm.

When his reprobate brother showed up—smelly, dirty and flat broke—their dad was so happy that he went all out and threw a big barbecue. Big brother blew up. He reminded his father of how he had faithfully slaved—he'd never been given so much as a party for his friends. The bitterness and jealousy he felt were more than he could handle.

In the light of God's great love there is no room for comparison, resentment or competition. We can't earn his love with our faithfulness or righteousness anyway. He loves us equally—as his children (see 1 John 3:1).

How do you handle it when someone you consider less deserving gets credit or glory? Do you worry about who deserves what? Galatians 6:4 tells us that "each one should test his own actions. Then he can take pride in himself, without comparing himself to somebody else." If we really believe that God loves us equally, we'll be free to be glad for others without feeling resentment or "keeping score." After all, we're all "prodigals."

A Deeper Look
Proverbs 4:23; 14:30

Go to page 1162 for your next devotional reading.

also be dishonest with much. ¹¹So if you have not been trustworthy in handling worldly wealth, who will trust you with true riches? ¹²And if you have not been trustworthy with someone else's property, who will give you property of your own?

¹³"No servant can serve two masters. Either he will hate the one and love the other, or he will be devoted to the one and despise the other. You cannot serve both God and Money."

¹⁴The Pharisees, who loved money, heard all this and were sneering at Jesus. ¹⁵He said to them, "You are the ones who justify yourselves in the eyes of men, but God knows your hearts. What is highly valued among men is detestable in God's sight.

Additional Teachings

¹⁶"The Law and the Prophets were proclaimed until John. Since that time, the good news of the kingdom of God is being preached, and everyone is forcing his way into it. ¹⁷It is easier for heaven and earth to disappear than for the least stroke of a pen to drop out of the Law.

¹⁸"Anyone who divorces his wife and marries another woman commits adultery, and the man who marries a divorced woman commits adultery.

The Rich Man and Lazarus

¹⁹"There was a rich man who was dressed in purple and fine linen and lived in luxury every day. ²⁰At his gate was laid a beggar named Lazarus, covered with sores ²¹and longing to eat what fell from the rich man's table. Even the dogs came and licked his sores.

²²"The time came when the beggar died and the angels carried him to Abraham's side. The rich man also died and was buried. ²³In hell,ᵃ where he was in torment, he looked up and saw Abraham far away, with Lazarus by his side. ²⁴So he called to him, 'Father Abraham, have pity on me and send Lazarus to dip the tip of his finger in water and cool my tongue, because I am in agony in this fire.'

²⁵"But Abraham replied, 'Son, remember that in your lifetime you received your good things, while Lazarus received bad things, but now he is comforted here and you are in agony. ²⁶And besides all this, between us and you a great chasm has been fixed, so that those who want to

go from here to you cannot, nor can anyone cross over from there to us.'

²⁷"He answered, 'Then I beg you, father, send Lazarus to my father's house, ²⁸for I have five brothers. Let him warn them, so that they will not also come to this place of torment.'

²⁹"Abraham replied, 'They have Moses and the Prophets; let them listen to them.'

³⁰"'No, father Abraham,' he said, 'but if someone from the dead goes to them, they will repent.'

³¹"He said to him, 'If they do not listen to Moses and the Prophets, they will not be convinced even if someone rises from the dead.'"

Sin, Faith, Duty

17 Jesus said to his disciples: "Things that cause people to sin are bound to come, but woe to that person through whom they come. ²It would be better for him to be thrown into the sea with a millstone tied around his neck than for him to cause one of these little ones to sin. ³So watch yourselves.

"If your brother sins, rebuke him, and if he repents, forgive him. ⁴If he sins against you seven times in a day, and seven times comes back to you and says, 'I repent,' forgive him."

⁵The apostles said to the Lord, "Increase our faith!"

⁶He replied, "If you have faith as small as a mustard seed, you can say to this mulberry tree, 'Be uprooted and planted in the sea,' and it will obey you.

⁷"Suppose one of you had a servant plowing or looking after the sheep. Would he say to the servant when he comes in from the field, 'Come along now and sit down to eat'? ⁸Would he not rather say, 'Prepare my supper, get yourself ready and wait on me while I eat and drink; after that you may eat and drink'? ⁹Would he thank the servant because he did what he was told to do? ¹⁰So you also, when you have done everything you were told to do, should say, 'We are unworthy servants; we have only done our duty.'"

Ten Healed of Leprosy

¹¹Now on his way to Jerusalem, Jesus traveled along the border between Samaria and Galilee. ¹²As he was going into

ᵃ23 Greek *Hades*

a village, ten men who had leprosy*a* met him. They stood at a distance ¹³and called out in a loud voice, "Jesus, Master, have pity on us!"

¹⁴When he saw them, he said, "Go, show yourselves to the priests." And as they went, they were cleansed.

¹⁵One of them, when he saw he was healed, came back, praising God in a loud voice. ¹⁶He threw himself at Jesus' feet and thanked him—and he was a Samaritan.

¹⁷Jesus asked, "Were not all ten cleansed? Where are the other nine? ¹⁸Was no one found to return and give praise to God except this foreigner?" ¹⁹Then he said to him, "Rise and go; your faith has made you well."

The Coming of the Kingdom of God

²⁰Once, having been asked by the Pharisees when the kingdom of God would come, Jesus replied, "The kingdom of God does not come with your careful observation, ²¹nor will people say, 'Here it is,' or 'There it is,' because the kingdom of God is within*b* you."

²²Then he said to his disciples, "The time is coming when you will long to see one of the days of the Son of Man, but you will not see it. ²³Men will tell you, 'There he is!' or 'Here he is!' Do not go running after them. ²⁴For the Son of Man in his day*c* will be like the lightning, which flashes and lights up the sky from one end to the other. ²⁵But first he must suffer many things and be rejected by this generation.

a12 The Greek word was used for various diseases affecting the skin—not necessarily leprosy.
b21 Or *among*   *c24* Some manuscripts do not have *in his day.*

THURSDAY

Read Luke 17:1–37
Key Verse Luke 17:10

God's Training Program – Doug Serven

I had signed up for a collegiate summer training program and moved to St. Louis to learn about God. Instead I found myself in a basement pit, filling chlorine buckets at 6 A.M. every morning. I was ticked off. Every day I'd show up at the swimming pool store grumbling about how little sleep I'd gotten, how my shoes and clothes were being eaten away and how inefficient the whole crazy system was. After all, I had a college education and shouldn't be the guy stomping down the trash in the dumpster every day.

But Jesus had something to say about my situation. In Luke 17:10 he told me that my response should be, "[I] have only done [my] duty." I am a servant. We like the *idea* of servanthood. It sounds noble and good. Obedient to the end. A hard and faithful worker. But when we're actually being treated like a servant, we can think of a thousand things we'd rather be doing. We feel as though our rights are being violated, that it's "un-American" for someone to treat us in such a way. Without rights. Without recognition.

I did learn about the Bible and prayer that summer. And I hung out with lots of cool people. But I'll always remember the hard work—perhaps the hardest of my life. After I overcame my bad attitude, God helped me see that working in the chlorine pit *was* the training program for me, because that was where he worked on my character and my heart.

A Deeper Look
Matthew 20:26–28; Philippians 2:1–8

Go to page 1164 for your next devotional reading.

26"Just as it was in the days of Noah, so also will it be in the days of the Son of Man. 27People were eating, drinking, marrying and being given in marriage up to the day Noah entered the ark. Then the flood came and destroyed them all. 28"It was the same in the days of Lot. People were eating and drinking, buying and selling, planting and building. 29But the day Lot left Sodom, fire and sulfur rained down from heaven and destroyed them all.

30"It will be just like this on the day the Son of Man is revealed. 31On that day no one who is on the roof of his house, with his goods inside, should go down to get them. Likewise, no one in the field should go back for anything. 32Remember Lot's wife! 33Whoever tries to keep his life will lose it, and whoever loses his life will preserve it. 34I tell you, on that night two people will be in one bed; one will be taken and the other left. 35Two women will be grinding grain together; one will be taken and the other left.ª" 37"Where, Lord?" they asked.

He replied, "Where there is a dead body, there the vultures will gather."

The Parable of the Persistent Widow

18 Then Jesus told his disciples a parable to show them that they should always pray and not give up. 2He said: "In a certain town there was a judge who neither feared God nor cared about men. 3And there was a widow in that town who kept coming to him with the plea, 'Grant me justice against my adversary.'

4"For some time he refused. But finally he said to himself, 'Even though I don't fear God or care about men, 5yet because this widow keeps bothering me, I will see that she gets justice, so that she won't eventually wear me out with her coming!' "

6And the Lord said, "Listen to what the unjust judge says. 7And will not God bring about justice for his chosen ones, who cry out to him day and night? Will he keep putting them off? 8I tell you, he will see that they get justice, and quickly. However, when the Son of Man comes, will he find faith on the earth?"

The Parable of the Pharisee and the Tax Collector

9To some who were confident of their own righteousness and looked down on

everybody else, Jesus told this parable: 10"Two men went up to the temple to pray, one a Pharisee and the other a tax collector. 11The Pharisee stood up and prayed aboutᵇ himself: 'God, I thank you that I am not like other men—robbers, evildoers, adulterers—or even like this tax collector. 12I fast twice a week and give a tenth of all I get.'

13"But the tax collector stood at a distance. He would not even look up to heaven, but beat his breast and said, 'God, have mercy on me, a sinner.'

14"I tell you that this man, rather than the other, went home justified before God. For everyone who exalts himself will be humbled, and he who humbles himself will be exalted."

The Little Children and Jesus
See Matthew 19:13–15; Mark 10:13–16

15People were also bringing babies to Jesus to have him touch them. When the disciples saw this, they rebuked them. 16But Jesus called the children to him and said, "Let the little children come to me, and do not hinder them, for the kingdom of God belongs to such as these. 17I tell you the truth, anyone who will not receive the kingdom of God like a little child will never enter it."

The Rich Ruler
See Matthew 19:16–29; Mark 10:17–30

18A certain ruler asked him, "Good teacher, what must I do to inherit eternal life?"

19"Why do you call me good?" Jesus answered. "No one is good—except God alone. 20You know the commandments:

ª35 Some manuscripts left. 36Two men will be in the field; one will be taken and the other left.
ᵇ11 Or to

POINT OF INTEREST   Luke 18:1

We should never stop praying. If God says "no" in answer to one prayer, it doesn't mean that he won't say "yes" in another situation. Think about this verse in light of what you learn from Matthew 21:22; Mark 14:32–42; James 4:2–7.

'Do not commit adultery, do not murder, do not steal, do not give false testimony, honor your father and mother.'*ᵃ*"

²¹"All these I have kept since I was a boy," he said.

²²When Jesus heard this, he said to him, "You still lack one thing. Sell everything you have and give to the poor, and you will have treasure in heaven. Then come, follow me."

²³When he heard this, he became very sad, because he was a man of great wealth. ²⁴Jesus looked at him and said, "How hard it is for the rich to enter the kingdom of God! ²⁵Indeed, it is easier for a camel to go through the eye of a needle than for a rich man to enter the kingdom of God."

²⁶Those who heard this asked, "Who then can be saved?"

²⁷Jesus replied, "What is impossible with men is possible with God."

²⁸Peter said to him, "We have left all we had to follow you!"

²⁹"I tell you the truth," Jesus said to them, "no one who has left home or wife or brothers or parents or children for the sake of the kingdom of God ³⁰will fail to receive many times as much in this age and, in the age to come, eternal life."

Jesus Again Predicts His Death
See Matthew 20:17–19; Mark 10:32–34

³¹Jesus took the Twelve aside and told them, "We are going up to Jerusalem, and everything that is written by the prophets about the Son of Man will be fulfilled. ³²He will be handed over to the

ᵃ20 Exodus 20:12-16; Deut. 5:16-20

FRIDAY

Read Luke 18:1–43
Key Verses Luke 18:29–30

So Much More – Dawn Getz

Night had fallen and the Ugandan mountain air was cool. I sat on a short three-legged stool and watched the beans boil over an open fire. The flames licked around the edge of the open pot. Our day's work in the clinic was finished, and the other women and I were talking and laughing together. Before I left the United States to work for three years as a nurse and Christian teacher in rural Africa, I could never have imagined that God would give me so much while I was there.

But long ago Jesus made it clear to a rich ruler that if he would give up what he had to follow Jesus Christ, he would receive much more in return—both in the "right now" and in eternity.

God proved the same principle to me in Uganda. I lived without electricity or running water. Yet amid military coups, bouts with malaria, triple-digit inflation and gasoline shortages, I was surprisingly content. I had everything I needed, including a big pickup truck for four-wheeling through the bush. In my letters home I tried to communicate that I was not suffering as a missionary. Most of the time, life was a blast!

My brief experience taught me that there are times when Jesus asks us to make hard choices in the course of following him. But I also learned that during those times we can experience the greatest measure of joy. The choice that comes disguised as a sacrifice becomes a pleasure!

A Deeper Look
John 15:9–11; Hebrews 11:6

Go to page 1166 for your next devotional reading.

Gentiles. They will mock him, insult him, spit on him, flog him and kill him. ³³On the third day he will rise again."

³⁴The disciples did not understand any of this. Its meaning was hidden from them, and they did not know what he was talking about.

A Blind Beggar Receives His Sight

See Matthew 20:29–34; Mark 10:46–52

³⁵As Jesus approached Jericho, a blind man was sitting by the roadside begging. ³⁶When he heard the crowd going by, he asked what was happening. ³⁷They told him, "Jesus of Nazareth is passing by."

³⁸He called out, "Jesus, Son of David, have mercy on me!"

³⁹Those who led the way rebuked him and told him to be quiet, but he shouted all the more, "Son of David, have mercy on me!"

⁴⁰Jesus stopped and ordered the man to be brought to him. When he came near, Jesus asked him, ⁴¹"What do you want me to do for you?"

"Lord, I want to see," he replied.

⁴²Jesus said to him, "Receive your sight; your faith has healed you." ⁴³Immediately he received his sight and followed Jesus, praising God. When all the people saw it, they also praised God.

Zacchaeus the Tax Collector

19 Jesus entered Jericho and was passing through. ²A man was there by the name of Zacchaeus; he was a chief tax collector and was wealthy. ³He wanted to see who Jesus was, but being a short man he could not, because of the crowd. ⁴So he ran ahead and climbed a sycamore-fig tree to see him, since Jesus was coming that way.

⁵When Jesus reached the spot, he looked up and said to him, "Zacchaeus, come down immediately. I must stay at your house today." ⁶So he came down at once and welcomed him gladly.

⁷All the people saw this and began to mutter, "He has gone to be the guest of a 'sinner.' "

⁸But Zacchaeus stood up and said to the Lord, "Look, Lord! Here and now I give half of my possessions to the poor, and if I have cheated anybody out of anything, I will pay back four times the amount."

⁹Jesus said to him, "Today salvation has come to this house, because this man, too, is a son of Abraham. ¹⁰For the

Son of Man came to seek and to save what was lost."

The Parable of the Ten Minas

¹¹While they were listening to this, he went on to tell them a parable, because he was near Jerusalem and the people thought that the kingdom of God was going to appear at once. ¹²He said: "A man of noble birth went to a distant country to have himself appointed king and then to return. ¹³So he called ten of his servants and gave them ten minas.ᵃ 'Put this money to work,' he said, 'until I come back.'

¹⁴"But his subjects hated him and sent a delegation after him to say, 'We don't want this man to be our king.'

¹⁵"He was made king, however, and returned home. Then he sent for the servants to whom he had given the money, in order to find out what they had gained with it.

¹⁶"The first one came and said, 'Sir, your mina has earned ten more.'

¹⁷" 'Well done, my good servant!' his master replied. 'Because you have been trustworthy in a very small matter, take charge of ten cities.'

¹⁸"The second came and said, 'Sir, your mina has earned five more.'

¹⁹"His master answered, 'You take charge of five cities.'

²⁰"Then another servant came and said, 'Sir, here is your mina; I have kept it laid away in a piece of cloth. ²¹I was afraid of you, because you are a hard man. You take out what you did not put in and reap what you did not sow.'

²²"His master replied, 'I will judge you by your own words, you wicked servant! You knew, did you, that I am a hard man, taking out what I did not put in, and reaping what I did not sow? ²³Why then didn't you put my money on deposit, so that when I came back, I could have collected it with interest?'

²⁴"Then he said to those standing by, 'Take his mina away from him and give it to the one who has ten minas.'

²⁵" 'Sir,' they said, 'he already has ten!'

²⁶"He replied, 'I tell you that to everyone who has, more will be given, but as for the one who has nothing, even what he has will be taken away. ²⁷But those enemies of mine who did not want me to

ᵃ13 A mina was about three months' wages.

Read *Luke 19:1–27*
Key Verse *Luke 19:10*

A Heart for People

For centuries people have asked, "Why did Jesus come to live on earth?" The best way to answer this question is to look at what Jesus did. Despite social taboos, Jesus reached out in genuine friendship to Zacchaeus, who was an outcast because he was a tax collector. Jesus said, "The Son of Man came to seek and to save what was lost," and he lived out this truth on a daily basis. He looked for the lost, talked with them and touched them. He was concerned for their physical, emotional, social and spiritual well-being.

God's heart breaks for people who don't know the depth of his love or his power to heal and forgive them. As Jesus' followers we must take on his passion for people—we are to proclaim him Lord and demonstrate his love, power and forgiveness in self-giving service.

Digging Into the Word
1. What do the parables in Luke 15 reveal about God's heart for the lost?—*Luke 15:1–7; Luke 15:8–10; Luke 15:11–32*
2. What do you learn from these passages about developing a heart for people?—*Ezekiel 36:26; 2 Peter 1:5–9*

Move Into Service
Identify one person in your life who does not yet know Jesus Christ. Consider doing the following things: (1) Pray daily for your heart to reflect God's heart toward that person. (2) Pray daily for his or her heart to open to God's love. (3) Find a way to serve or care for that person. (4) Look for an opportunity to tell that person about God's love and forgiveness.

One Step Deeper
Psalm 51:10; Romans 8:5–11

Go to page 1174 for your next devotional reading.

be king over them—bring them here and kill them in front of me.' "

The Triumphal Entry

See Matthew 21:1–9; Mark 11:1–10; John 12:12–15

28After Jesus had said this, he went on ahead, going up to Jerusalem. **29**As he approached Bethphage and Bethany at the hill called the Mount of Olives, he sent two of his disciples, saying to them, **30**"Go to the village ahead of you, and as you enter it, you will find a colt tied there, which no one has ever ridden. Untie it and bring it here. **31**If anyone asks you, 'Why are you untying it?' tell him, 'The Lord needs it.' "

32Those who were sent ahead went and found it just as he had told them. **33**As they were untying the colt, its owners asked them, "Why are you untying the colt?"

34They replied, "The Lord needs it."

35They brought it to Jesus, threw their cloaks on the colt and put Jesus on it. **36**As he went along, people spread their cloaks on the road.

37When he came near the place where the road goes down the Mount of Olives, the whole crowd of disciples began joyfully to praise God in loud voices for all the miracles they had seen:

38"Blessed is the king who comes in
    the name of the Lord!"*a*

"Peace in heaven and glory in the
    highest!"

39Some of the Pharisees in the crowd said to Jesus, "Teacher, rebuke your disciples!"

40"I tell you," he replied, "if they keep quiet, the stones will cry out."

41As he approached Jerusalem and saw the city, he wept over it **42**and said, "If you, even you, had only known on this day what would bring you peace—but now it is hidden from your eyes. **43**The days will come upon you when your enemies will build an embankment against you and encircle you and hem you in on every side. **44**They will dash you to the ground, you and the children within your walls. They will not leave one stone on another, because you did not recognize the time of God's coming to you."

Jesus at the Temple

See Matthew 21:12–16; Mark 11:15–18; John 2:13–16

45Then he entered the temple area and began driving out those who were selling. **46**"It is written," he said to them, " 'My house will be a house of prayer'*b*; but you have made it 'a den of robbers.'*c* "

47Every day he was teaching at the temple. But the chief priests, the teachers of the law and the leaders among the people were trying to kill him. **48**Yet they could not find any way to do it, because all the people hung on his words.

The Authority of Jesus Questioned

See Matthew 21:23–27; Mark 11:27–33

20 One day as he was teaching the people in the temple courts and preaching the gospel, the chief priests and the teachers of the law, together with the elders, came up to him. **2**"Tell us by what authority you are doing these things," they said. "Who gave you this authority?"

3He replied, "I will also ask you a question. Tell me, **4**John's baptism—was it from heaven, or from men?"

5They discussed it among themselves and said, "If we say, 'From heaven,' he will ask, 'Why didn't you believe him?' **6**But if we say, 'From men,' all the people will stone us, because they are persuaded that John was a prophet."

7So they answered, "We don't know where it was from."

8Jesus said, "Neither will I tell you by what authority I am doing these things."

The Parable of the Tenants

See Matthew 21:33–46; Mark 12:1–12

9He went on to tell the people this parable: "A man planted a vineyard, rented it to some farmers and went away for a long time. **10**At harvest time he sent a servant to the tenants so they would give him some of the fruit of the vineyard. But the tenants beat him and sent him away empty-handed. **11**He sent another servant, but that one also they beat and treated shamefully and sent away empty-handed. **12**He sent still a third, and they wounded him and threw him out.

13"Then the owner of the vineyard said, 'What shall I do? I will send my son,

a38 Psalm 118:26   *b46* Isaiah 56:7
c46 Jer. 7:11

whom I love; perhaps they will respect him.'

¹⁴"But when the tenants saw him, they talked the matter over. 'This is the heir,' they said. 'Let's kill him, and the inheritance will be ours.' ¹⁵So they threw him out of the vineyard and killed him.

"What then will the owner of the vineyard do to them? ¹⁶He will come and kill those tenants and give the vineyard to others."

When the people heard this, they said, "May this never be!"

¹⁷Jesus looked directly at them and asked, "Then what is the meaning of that which is written:

" 'The stone the builders rejected
    has become the capstone*ᵃ'ᵇ*?

¹⁸Everyone who falls on that stone will be broken to pieces, but he on whom it falls will be crushed."

¹⁹The teachers of the law and the chief priests looked for a way to arrest him immediately, because they knew he had spoken this parable against them. But they were afraid of the people.

Paying Taxes to Caesar

See Matthew 22:15–22; Mark 12:13–17

²⁰Keeping a close watch on him, they sent spies, who pretended to be honest. They hoped to catch Jesus in something he said so that they might hand him over to the power and authority of the governor. ²¹So the spies questioned him: "Teacher, we know that you speak and teach what is right, and that you do not show partiality but teach the way of God in accordance with the truth. ²²Is it right for us to pay taxes to Caesar or not?"

²³He saw through their duplicity and said to them, ²⁴"Show me a denarius. Whose portrait and inscription are on it?"

²⁵"Caesar's," they replied.

He said to them, "Then give to Caesar what is Caesar's, and to God what is God's."

²⁶They were unable to trap him in what he had said there in public. And astonished by his answer, they became silent.

The Resurrection and Marriage

See Matthew 22:23–33; Mark 12:18–27

²⁷Some of the Sadducees, who say there is no resurrection, came to Jesus with a question. ²⁸"Teacher," they said,

"Moses wrote for us that if a man's brother dies and leaves a wife but no children, the man must marry the widow and have children for his brother. ²⁹Now there were seven brothers. The first one married a woman and died childless. ³⁰The second ³¹and then the third married her, and in the same way the seven died, leaving no children. ³²Finally, the woman died too. ³³Now then, at the resurrection whose wife will she be, since the seven were married to her?"

³⁴Jesus replied, "The people of this age marry and are given in marriage. ³⁵But those who are considered worthy of taking part in that age and in the resurrection from the dead will neither marry nor be given in marriage, ³⁶and they can no longer die; for they are like the angels. They are God's children, since they are children of the resurrection. ³⁷But in the account of the bush, even Moses showed that the dead rise, for he calls the Lord 'the God of Abraham, and the God of Isaac, and the God of Jacob.'ᶜ ³⁸He is not the God of the dead, but of the living, for to him all are alive."

³⁹Some of the teachers of the law responded, "Well said, teacher!" ⁴⁰And no one dared to ask him any more questions.

ᵃ17 Or *cornerstone*   *ᵇ17* Psalm 118:22
ᶜ37 Exodus 3:6

POINT OF INTEREST

Luke 20:35

What will we be like in heaven? Jesus explains that we will be like the angels in that we will not be married and that we will never die. Some passages suggest that our bodies will be transformed (see Philippians 3:20–21); other passages give vivid and symbolic descriptions of heaven's glory (see Revelation 4 and 5). While we won't know much about heaven until we get there, we do know that "God himself will be with [us] . . . He will wipe every tear from [our] eyes. There will be no more death or mourning or crying or pain, for the old order of things has passed away" (Revelation 21:3–4).

Whose Son Is the Christ?

See Matthew 22:41—23:7; Mark 12:35–40

⁴¹Then Jesus said to them, "How is it that they say the Christ*a* is the Son of David? ⁴²David himself declares in the Book of Psalms:

" 'The Lord said to my Lord:
"Sit at my right hand
⁴³until I make your enemies
a footstool for your feet." ' *b*

⁴⁴David calls him 'Lord.' How then can he be his son?"

⁴⁵While all the people were listening, Jesus said to his disciples, ⁴⁶"Beware of the teachers of the law. They like to walk around in flowing robes and love to be greeted in the marketplaces and have the most important seats in the synagogues and the places of honor at banquets. ⁴⁷They devour widows' houses and for a show make lengthy prayers. Such men will be punished most severely."

The Widow's Offering

See Mark 12:41–44

21 As he looked up, Jesus saw the rich putting their gifts into the temple treasury. ²He also saw a poor widow put in two very small copper coins.*c* ³"I tell you the truth," he said, "this poor widow has put in more than all the others. ⁴All these people gave their gifts out of their wealth; but she out of her poverty put in all she had to live on."

Signs of the End of the Age

See Matthew 24; Mark 13

⁵Some of his disciples were remarking about how the temple was adorned with beautiful stones and with gifts dedicated to God. But Jesus said, ⁶"As for what you see here, the time will come when not one stone will be left on another; every one of them will be thrown down."

⁷"Teacher," they asked, "when will these things happen? And what will be the sign that they are about to take place?"

⁸He replied: "Watch out that you are not deceived. For many will come in my name, claiming, 'I am he,' and, 'The time is near.' Do not follow them. ⁹When you hear of wars and revolutions, do not be frightened. These things must happen first, but the end will not come right away."

¹⁰Then he said to them: "Nation will rise against nation, and kingdom against kingdom. ¹¹There will be great earthquakes, famines and pestilences in various places, and fearful events and great signs from heaven.

¹²"But before all this, they will lay hands on you and persecute you. They will deliver you to synagogues and prisons, and you will be brought before kings and governors, and all on account of my name. ¹³This will result in your being witnesses to them. ¹⁴But make up your mind not to worry beforehand how you will defend yourselves. ¹⁵For I will give you words and wisdom that none of your adversaries will be able to resist or contradict. ¹⁶You will be betrayed even by parents, brothers, relatives and friends, and they will put some of you to death. ¹⁷All men will hate you because of me. ¹⁸But not a hair of your head will perish. ¹⁹By standing firm you will gain life.

²⁰"When you see Jerusalem being surrounded by armies, you will know that its desolation is near. ²¹Then let those who are in Judea flee to the mountains, let those in the city get out, and let those in the country not enter the city. ²²For this is the time of punishment in fulfillment of all that has been written. ²³How dreadful it will be in those days for pregnant women and nursing mothers! There will be great distress in the land and wrath against this people. ²⁴They will fall by the sword and will be taken as prisoners to all the nations. Jerusalem will be trampled on by the Gentiles until the times of the Gentiles are fulfilled.

²⁵"There will be signs in the sun, moon and stars. On the earth, nations will be in anguish and perplexity at the roaring and tossing of the sea. ²⁶Men will faint from terror, apprehensive of what is coming on the world, for the heavenly bodies will be shaken. ²⁷At that time they will see the Son of Man coming in a cloud with power and great glory. ²⁸When these things begin to take place, stand up and lift up your heads, because your redemption is drawing near."

²⁹He told them this parable: "Look at the fig tree and all the trees. ³⁰When they sprout leaves, you can see for yourselves and know that summer is near. ³¹Even so, when you see these things happening,

---

a 41 Or *Messiah*   *b* 43 Psalm 110:1   *c* 2 Greek *two lepta* you know that the kingdom of God is near.

32"I tell you the truth, this generation[a] will certainly not pass away until all these things have happened. 33Heaven and earth will pass away, but my words will never pass away.

34"Be careful, or your hearts will be weighed down with dissipation, drunkenness and the anxieties of life, and that day will close on you unexpectedly like a trap. 35For it will come upon all those who live on the face of the whole earth. 36Be always on the watch, and pray that you may be able to escape all that is about to happen, and that you may be able to stand before the Son of Man."

37Each day Jesus was teaching at the temple, and each evening he went out to spend the night on the hill called the Mount of Olives, 38and all the people came early in the morning to hear him at the temple.

Judas Agrees to Betray Jesus
See Matthew 26:2–5; Mark 14:1–2,10–11

22 Now the Feast of Unleavened Bread, called the Passover, was approaching, 2and the chief priests and the teachers of the law were looking for some way to get rid of Jesus, for they were afraid of the people. 3Then Satan entered Judas, called Iscariot, one of the Twelve. 4And Judas went to the chief priests and the officers of the temple guard and discussed with them how he might betray Jesus. 5They were delighted and agreed to give him money. 6He consented, and watched for an opportunity to hand Jesus over to them when no crowd was present.

The Last Supper
See Matthew 26:17–19,26–29;
Mark 14:12–16,22–25

7Then came the day of Unleavened Bread on which the Passover lamb had to be sacrificed. 8Jesus sent Peter and John, saying, "Go and make preparations for us to eat the Passover."

9"Where do you want us to prepare for it?" they asked.

10He replied, "As you enter the city, a man carrying a jar of water will meet you. Follow him to the house that he enters, 11and say to the owner of the house, 'The Teacher asks: Where is the guest room, where I may eat the Passover with my disciples?' 12He will show you a large

upper room, all furnished. Make preparations there."

13They left and found things just as Jesus had told them. So they prepared the Passover.

14When the hour came, Jesus and his apostles reclined at the table. 15And he said to them, "I have eagerly desired to eat this Passover with you before I suffer. 16For I tell you, I will not eat it again until it finds fulfillment in the kingdom of God."

17After taking the cup, he gave thanks and said, "Take this and divide it among you. 18For I tell you I will not drink again of the fruit of the vine until the kingdom of God comes."

19And he took bread, gave thanks and broke it, and gave it to them, saying, "This is my body given for you; do this in remembrance of me."

20In the same way, after the supper he took the cup, saying, "This cup is the new covenant in my blood, which is poured out for you. 21But the hand of him who is going to betray me is with mine on the table. 22The Son of Man will go as it has been decreed, but woe to that man who betrays him." 23They began to question among themselves which of them it might be who would do this.

24Also a dispute arose among them as to which of them was considered to be greatest. 25Jesus said to them, "The kings of the Gentiles lord it over them; and those who exercise authority over them call themselves Benefactors. 26But you are not to be like that. Instead, the greatest among you should be like the youngest, and the one who rules like the one who serves. 27For who is greater, the one who is at the table or the one who serves? Is it not the one who is at the table? But I am among you as one who serves. 28You are those who have stood by me in my trials. 29And I confer on you a kingdom, just as my Father conferred one on me, 30so that you may eat and drink at my table in my kingdom and sit on thrones, judging the twelve tribes of Israel.

31"Simon, Simon, Satan has asked to sift you[b] as wheat. 32But I have prayed for you, Simon, that your faith may not fail. And when you have turned back, strengthen your brothers."

a32 Or race   b31 The Greek is plural.

³³But he replied, "Lord, I am ready to go with you to prison and to death."

³⁴Jesus answered, "I tell you, Peter, before the rooster crows today, you will deny three times that you know me."

³⁵Then Jesus asked them, "When I sent you without purse, bag or sandals, did you lack anything?"

"Nothing," they answered.

³⁶He said to them, "But now if you have a purse, take it, and also a bag; and if you don't have a sword, sell your cloak and buy one. ³⁷It is written: 'And he was numbered with the transgressors'ᵃ; and I tell you that this must be fulfilled in me. Yes, what is written about me is reaching its fulfillment."

³⁸The disciples said, "See, Lord, here are two swords."

"That is enough," he replied.

Jesus Prays on the Mount of Olives

See Matthew 26:36–46; Mark 14:32–42

³⁹Jesus went out as usual to the Mount of Olives, and his disciples followed him. ⁴⁰On reaching the place, he said to them, "Pray that you will not fall into temptation." ⁴¹He withdrew about a stone's throw beyond them, knelt down and prayed, ⁴²"Father, if you are willing, take this cup from me; yet not my will, but yours be done." ⁴³An angel from heaven appeared to him and strengthened him. ⁴⁴And being in anguish, he prayed more earnestly, and his sweat was like drops of blood falling to the ground.ᵇ

⁴⁵When he rose from prayer and went back to the disciples, he found them asleep, exhausted from sorrow. ⁴⁶"Why are you sleeping?" he asked them. "Get up and pray so that you will not fall into temptation."

Jesus Arrested

See Matthew 26:47–56; Mark 14:43–50; John 18:3–11

⁴⁷While he was still speaking a crowd came up, and the man who was called Judas, one of the Twelve, was leading them. He approached Jesus to kiss him, ⁴⁸but Jesus asked him, "Judas, are you betraying the Son of Man with a kiss?"

⁴⁹When Jesus' followers saw what was going to happen, they said, "Lord, should we strike with our swords?" ⁵⁰And one of them struck the servant of the high priest, cutting off his right ear.

⁵¹But Jesus answered, "No more of this!" And he touched the man's ear and healed him.

⁵²Then Jesus said to the chief priests, the officers of the temple guard, and the elders, who had come for him, "Am I leading a rebellion, that you have come with swords and clubs? ⁵³Every day I was with you in the temple courts, and you did not lay a hand on me. But this is your hour—when darkness reigns."

Peter Disowns Jesus

See Matthew 26:69–75; Mark 14:66–72; John 18:16–18,25–27

⁵⁴Then seizing him, they led him away and took him into the house of the high priest. Peter followed at a distance. ⁵⁵But when they had kindled a fire in the middle of the courtyard and had sat down together, Peter sat down with them. ⁵⁶A servant girl saw him seated there in the firelight. She looked closely at him and said, "This man was with him."

⁵⁷But he denied it. "Woman, I don't know him," he said.

⁵⁸A little later someone else saw him and said, "You also are one of them."

"Man, I am not!" Peter replied.

⁵⁹About an hour later another asserted, "Certainly this fellow was with him, for he is a Galilean."

⁶⁰Peter replied, "Man, I don't know what you're talking about!" Just as he was speaking, the rooster crowed. ⁶¹The Lord turned and looked straight at Peter. Then Peter remembered the word the Lord had spoken to him: "Before the rooster crows today, you will disown me

ᵃ37 Isaiah 53:12   ᵇ44 Some early manuscripts do not have verses 43 and 44.

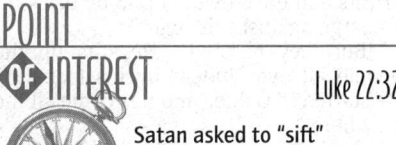

POINT OF INTEREST

Luke 22:32

Satan asked to "sift" Peter—to shake him up like wheat. Jesus, wanting to separate the kernel of Peter's faith from the chaff of his grandiose self-sufficiency, allowed it. This "sifting" was probably Peter's denial of Jesus. Jesus knew that Peter would eventually turn back to him. Jesus never gave up on Peter, and he will never give up on you.

three times." ⁶²And he went outside and wept bitterly.

The Guards Mock Jesus

See Matthew 26:67–68; Mark 14:65;
John 18:22–23

⁶³The men who were guarding Jesus began mocking and beating him. ⁶⁴They blindfolded him and demanded, "Prophesy! Who hit you?" ⁶⁵And they said many other insulting things to him.

Jesus Before Pilate and Herod

See Matthew 26:63–66; Mark 14:61–63;
John 18:19–21

⁶⁶At daybreak the council of the elders of the people, both the chief priests and teachers of the law, met together, and Jesus was led before them. ⁶⁷"If you are the Christ,ᵃ" they said, "tell us."

Jesus answered, "If I tell you, you will not believe me, ⁶⁸and if I asked you, you would not answer. ⁶⁹But from now on, the Son of Man will be seated at the right hand of the mighty God."

⁷⁰They all asked, "Are you then the Son of God?"

He replied, "You are right in saying I am."

⁷¹Then they said, "Why do we need any more testimony? We have heard it from his own lips."

23 Then the whole assembly rose and led him off to Pilate. ²And they began to accuse him, saying, "We have found this man subverting our nation. He opposes payment of taxes to Caesar and claims to be Christ,ᵇ a king."

³So Pilate asked Jesus, "Are you the king of the Jews?"

"Yes, it is as you say," Jesus replied.

⁴Then Pilate announced to the chief priests and the crowd, "I find no basis for a charge against this man."

⁵But they insisted, "He stirs up the people all over Judeaᶜ by his teaching. He started in Galilee and has come all the way here."

⁶On hearing this, Pilate asked if the man was a Galilean. ⁷When he learned that Jesus was under Herod's jurisdiction, he sent him to Herod, who was also in Jerusalem at that time.

⁸When Herod saw Jesus, he was greatly pleased, because for a long time he had been wanting to see him. From what he had heard about him, he hoped to see him perform some miracle. ⁹He plied him with many questions, but Jesus gave him no answer. ¹⁰The chief priests and the teachers of the law were standing there, vehemently accusing him. ¹¹Then Herod and his soldiers ridiculed and mocked him. Dressing him in an elegant robe, they sent him back to Pilate. ¹²That day Herod and Pilate became friends—before this they had been enemies.

¹³Pilate called together the chief priests, the rulers and the people, ¹⁴and said to them, "You brought me this man as one who was inciting the people to rebellion. I have examined him in your presence and have found no basis for your charges against him. ¹⁵Neither has Herod, for he sent him back to us; as you can see, he has done nothing to deserve death. ¹⁶Therefore, I will punish him and then release him.ᵈ"

¹⁸With one voice they cried out, "Away with this man! Release Barabbas to us!" ¹⁹(Barabbas had been thrown into prison for an insurrection in the city, and for murder.)

²⁰Wanting to release Jesus, Pilate appealed to them again. ²¹But they kept shouting, "Crucify him! Crucify him!"

²²For the third time he spoke to them: "Why? What crime has this man committed? I have found in him no grounds for the death penalty. Therefore I will have him punished and then release him."

²³But with loud shouts they insistently demanded that he be crucified, and their shouts prevailed. ²⁴So Pilate decided to grant their demand. ²⁵He released the man who had been thrown into prison for insurrection and murder, the one they asked for, and surrendered Jesus to their will.

The Crucifixion

See Matthew 27:33–44; Mark 15:22–32;
John 19:17–24

²⁶As they led him away, they seized Simon from Cyrene, who was on his way in from the country, and put the cross on him and made him carry it behind Jesus. ²⁷A large number of people followed him, including women who mourned and wailed for him. ²⁸Jesus turned and said to them, "Daughters of Jerusalem, do not weep for me; weep for yourselves and for your children. ²⁹For the time will come when you will say, 'Blessed are the bar-

ᵃ67 Or *Messiah*   ᵇ2 Or *Messiah*; also in verses 35 and 39   ᶜ5 Or *over the land of the Jews*   ᵈ16 Some manuscripts *him." ¹⁷Now he was obliged to release one man to them at the Feast.*

ren women, the wombs that never bore and the breasts that never nursed!' [30]Then

" 'they will say to the mountains,
"Fall on us!"
and to the hills, "Cover us!" ' [a]

[31]For if men do these things when the tree is green, what will happen when it is dry?"

[32]Two other men, both criminals, were also led out with him to be executed. [33]When they came to the place called the Skull, there they crucified him, along with the criminals—one on his right, the other on his left. [34]Jesus said, "Father, forgive them, for they do not know what they are doing." [b] And they divided up his clothes by casting lots.

[35]The people stood watching, and the rulers even sneered at him. They said, "He saved others; let him save himself if he is the Christ of God, the Chosen One."

[36]The soldiers also came up and mocked him. They offered him wine vinegar [37]and said, "If you are the king of the Jews, save yourself."

[38] There was a written notice above him, which read: THIS IS THE KING OF THE JEWS.

[39]One of the criminals who hung there hurled insults at him: "Aren't you the Christ? Save yourself and us!"

[40]But the other criminal rebuked him. "Don't you fear God," he said, "since you are under the same sentence? [41]We are punished justly, for we are getting what our deeds deserve. But this man has done nothing wrong."

[42]Then he said, "Jesus, remember me when you come into your kingdom. [c] "

[43]Jesus answered him, "I tell you the truth, today you will be with me in paradise."

Jesus' Death

See Matthew 27:45–56; Mark 15:33–41; John 19:29–30

[44]It was now about the sixth hour, and darkness came over the whole land until the ninth hour, [45]for the sun stopped shining. And the curtain of the temple was torn in two. [46]Jesus called out with a loud voice, "Father, into your hands I commit my spirit." When he had said this, he breathed his last.

[47]The centurion, seeing what had happened, praised God and said, "Surely this was a righteous man." [48]When all the people who had gathered to witness this

sight saw what took place, they beat their breasts and went away. [49]But all those who knew him, including the women who had followed him from Galilee, stood at a distance, watching these things.

Jesus' Burial

See Matthew 27:57–61; Mark 15:42–47; John 19:38–42

[50]Now there was a man named Joseph, a member of the Council, a good and upright man, [51]who had not consented to their decision and action. He came from the Judean town of Arimathea and he was waiting for the kingdom of God. [52]Going to Pilate, he asked for Jesus' body. [53]Then he took it down, wrapped it in linen cloth and placed it in a tomb cut in the rock, one in which no one had yet been laid. [54]It was Preparation Day, and the Sabbath was about to begin.

[55]The women who had come with Jesus from Galilee followed Joseph and saw the tomb and how his body was laid in it. [56]Then they went home and prepared spices and perfumes. But they rested on the Sabbath in obedience to the commandment.

The Resurrection

See Matthew 28:1–8; Mark 16:1–8; John 20:1–8

24 On the first day of the week, very early in the morning, the women took the spices they had prepared and went to the tomb. [2]They found the stone rolled away from the tomb, [3]but when they entered, they did not find the body of the Lord Jesus. [4]While they were wondering about this, suddenly two men in clothes that gleamed like lightning stood beside them. [5]In their fright the women bowed down with their faces to the ground, but the men said to them, "Why do you look for the living among the dead? [6]He is not here; he has risen! Remember how he told you, while he was still with you in Galilee: [7]'The Son of Man must be delivered into the hands of sinful men, be crucified and on the third day be raised again.' " [8]Then they remembered his words.

[9]When they came back from the tomb, they told all these things to the Eleven and to all the others. [10]It was Mary Magdalene, Joanna, Mary the mother of

[a]30 Hosea 10:8 [b]34 Some early manuscripts do not have this sentence. [c]42 Some manuscripts *come with your kingly power*

James, and the others with them who told this to the apostles. ¹¹But they did not believe the women, because their words seemed to them like nonsense. ¹²Peter, however, got up and ran to the tomb. Bending over, he saw the strips of linen lying by themselves, and he went away, wondering to himself what had happened.

On the Road to Emmaus

¹³Now that same day two of them were going to a village called Emmaus, about seven miles*ª* from Jerusalem. ¹⁴They were talking with each other about everything that had happened. ¹⁵As they talked and discussed these things with each other, Jesus himself came up and walked along with them;

¹⁶but they were kept from recognizing him.

¹⁷He asked them, "What are you discussing together as you walk along?"

They stood still, their faces downcast. ¹⁸One of them, named Cleopas, asked him, "Are you only a visitor to Jerusalem and do not know the things that have happened there in these days?"

¹⁹"What things?" he asked.

"About Jesus of Nazareth," they replied. "He was a prophet, powerful in word and deed before God and all the people. ²⁰The chief priests and our rulers handed him over to be sentenced to death, and they crucified him; ²¹but we had hoped that he was the one who was going to redeem Israel. And what is

ª13 Greek *sixty stadia* (about 11 kilometers)

Read Luke 24:1–53
Key Verses Luke 24:1–8

Trust in a Risen Lord — Jenny Forsberg

Rude and insensitive. That's what my behavior had been toward my teammates as we traveled through Israel. Why did I always feel the need to have things my way? I wanted to be agreeable as we made plans, but the words that came out of my mouth were anything but.

A good friend pulled me aside later and talked with me about my attitude. She explained that my actions stemmed from the beliefs I have about God. She asked me if I believed God would always take care of me. I had to answer no, even though I knew Jesus had proven his love for me and his power over *everything* by dying on the cross and rising from the grave. We prayed, asking God to forgive me and help me believe his Word.

The next morning we visited the garden and tomb where Jesus is said to have been buried. After leaving the noise of the surrounding city, the utter quietness of the garden was very peaceful. I stepped into the tomb and noticed a sign on the door that read: "He is not here, for he is risen."

That simple sentence melted me. I was struck by the peace, forgiveness and love Jesus offered in his resurrection and the love that I had recently seen in my friend and gracious teammates.

As it was to the women who first discovered it, that empty tomb was a powerful sight to me that morning. Jesus wasn't in there; he is with the Father. It reminded me that Jesus' resurrection really does give us power over sin and death. Alleluia!

A Deeper Look

Isaiah 26:3; Mark 16:1–8; 1 Corinthians 15:54–58

Go to page 1177 for your next devotional reading.

more, it is the third day since all this took place. **22**In addition, some of our women amazed us. They went to the tomb early this morning **23**but didn't find his body. They came and told us that they had seen a vision of angels, who said he was alive. **24**Then some of our companions went to the tomb and found it just as the women had said, but him they did not see."

25He said to them, "How foolish you are, and how slow of heart to believe all that the prophets have spoken! **26**Did not the Christ*ᵃ* have to suffer these things and then enter his glory?" **27**And beginning with Moses and all the Prophets, he explained to them what was said in all the Scriptures concerning himself.

28As they approached the village to which they were going, Jesus acted as if he were going farther. **29**But they urged him strongly, "Stay with us, for it is nearly evening; the day is almost over." So he went in to stay with them.

30When he was at the table with them, he took bread, gave thanks, broke it and began to give it to them. **31**Then their eyes were opened and they recognized him, and he disappeared from their sight. **32**They asked each other, "Were not our hearts burning within us while he talked with us on the road and opened the Scriptures to us?"

33They got up and returned at once to Jerusalem. There they found the Eleven and those with them, assembled together **34**and saying, "It is true! The Lord has risen and has appeared to Simon." **35**Then the two told what had happened on the way, and how Jesus was recognized by them when he broke the bread.

Jesus Appears to the Disciples

36While they were still talking about this, Jesus himself stood among them and said to them, "Peace be with you."

37They were startled and frightened, thinking they saw a ghost. **38**He said to them, "Why are you troubled, and why do doubts rise in your minds? **39**Look at my hands and my feet. It is I myself! Touch me and see; a ghost does not have flesh and bones, as you see I have."

40When he had said this, he showed them his hands and feet. **41**And while they still did not believe it because of joy and amazement, he asked them, "Do you have anything here to eat?" **42**They gave him a piece of broiled fish, **43**and he took it and ate it in their presence.

44He said to them, "This is what I told you while I was still with you: Everything must be fulfilled that is written about me in the Law of Moses, the Prophets and the Psalms."

45Then he opened their minds so they could understand the Scriptures. **46**He told them, "This is what is written: The Christ will suffer and rise from the dead on the third day, **47**and repentance and forgiveness of sins will be preached in his name to all nations, beginning at Jerusalem. **48**You are witnesses of these things. **49**I am going to send you what my Father has promised; but stay in the city until you have been clothed with power from on high."

The Ascension

50When he had led them out to the vicinity of Bethany, he lifted up his hands and blessed them. **51**While he was blessing them, he left them and was taken up into heaven. **52**Then they worshiped him and returned to Jerusalem with great joy. **53**And they stayed continually at the temple, praising God.

ᵃ26 Or *Messiah*; also in verse 46

Knowing about Jesus involves

acquiring information about him. But knowing Jesus also

means to embrace him with eager belief as the Son of

God. John writes this Gospel to encourage us to choose

this second response to Jesus. John's Gospel highlights the

rich symbolic language Jesus himself uses to show that he

is "the way and the truth and the life" (14:6), sent by the

Father. As you read this book, meditate on the many

facets of Jesus as the source of life: He is the Lamb of God

(1:29) and the living water (4:10), the bread of life

(6:35) and the light of the world

(8:12). He is also our good shep-

herd (10:14).

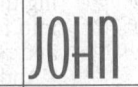

JOHN

The Word Became Flesh

1 In the beginning was the Word, and the Word was with God, and the Word was God. ²He was with God in the beginning.

³Through him all things were made; without him nothing was made that has been made. ⁴In him was life, and that life was the light of men. ⁵The light shines in the darkness, but the darkness has not understood*a* it.

⁶There came a man who was sent from God; his name was John. ⁷He came as a witness to testify concerning that light, so that through him all men might believe. ⁸He himself was not the light; he came only as a witness to the light. ⁹The true light that gives light to every man was coming into the world.*b*

¹⁰He was in the world, and though the world was made through him, the world did not recognize him. ¹¹He came to that which was his own, but his own did not receive him. ¹²Yet to all who received him, to those who believed in his name, he gave the right to become children of God— ¹³children born not of natural descent,*c* nor of human decision or a husband's will, but born of God.

*a*5 Or *darkness, and the darkness has not overcome*
*b*9 Or *This was the true light that gives light to every man who comes into the world*   *c*13 Greek *of bloods*

¹⁴The Word became flesh and made his dwelling among us. We have seen his glory, the glory of the One and Only,ᵃ who came from the Father, full of grace and truth.

¹⁵John testifies concerning him. He cries out, saying, "This was he of whom I said, 'He who comes after me has surpassed me because he was before me.' " ¹⁶From the fullness of his grace we have all received one blessing after another. ¹⁷For the law was given through Moses;

grace and truth came through Jesus Christ. ¹⁸No one has ever seen God, but God the One and Only,ᵃ,ᵇ who is at the Father's side, has made him known.

John the Baptist Denies Being the Christ

¹⁹Now this was John's testimony when the Jews of Jerusalem sent priests and

ᵃ*14,18* Or *the Only Begotten*   ᵇ*18* Some manuscripts *but the only* (or *only begotten*) *Son*

TUESDAY

Read *John 1:1–34*
Key Verse *John 1:12*

The One for You — Lindy Black

When I first met my husband, I thought he was a nice-looking guy. That was about it. I didn't want to marry him. I didn't really want to get to know him. I certainly didn't love him. But over a period of time, I not only wanted to get to know him better, but I knew I didn't want to live without him—ever. I eventually realized that God had a plan for our lives together, and I believed that this man was the one I wanted to marry. But it wasn't until we exchanged vows as husband and wife that we were married.

The same is true with becoming a child of God. Before the beginning of the world, God chose to reach out to people with truly amazing grace. Even though people sin and rebel against him, God offers salvation and a renewed relationship with himself through the work of Jesus Christ on our behalf. When we're first introduced to Jesus, few of us are ready to make a lifelong commitment to him. But as God enables us to understand who Jesus is and what he says about himself, we find ourselves drawn into a relationship with him.

However, there still must come a moment of believing and receiving, of reaching out to Jesus in repentance and faith. A wedding ceremony marks the end of questioning, "Is this the one for me?" So too, when we receive Jesus Christ, we are acknowledging that he is the one to whom we belong. It marks the beginning of a relationship of mutual commitment for all eternity.

My husband and I had one wedding, a day we will certainly never forget. Our relationship is dramatically different as a result. On that day we fulfilled part of God's plan for our lives together. I also received Jesus Christ once. This brought me into a renewed relationship with God in accordance with his original plan that I be his child. How about you? "Be all the more eager to make your calling and election sure. For if you do these things, you will never fall, and you will receive a rich welcome into the eternal kingdom of our Lord and Savior Jesus Christ" (2 Peter 1:10–11).

A Deeper Look
Deuteronomy 14:2; 2 Corinthians 6:18

Go to page 1181 for your next devotional reading.

Levites to ask him who he was. 20He did not fail to confess, but confessed freely, "I am not the Christ.*a*"

21They asked him, "Then who are you? Are you Elijah?"

He said, "I am not."

"Are you the Prophet?"

He answered, "No."

22Finally they said, "Who are you? Give us an answer to take back to those who sent us. What do you say about yourself?"

23John replied in the words of Isaiah the prophet, "I am the voice of one calling in the desert, 'Make straight the way for the Lord.' "*b*

24Now some Pharisees who had been sent 25questioned him, "Why then do you baptize if you are not the Christ, nor Elijah, nor the Prophet?"

26"I baptize with*c* water," John replied, "but among you stands one you do not know. 27He is the one who comes after me, the thongs of whose sandals I am not worthy to untie."

28This all happened at Bethany on the other side of the Jordan, where John was baptizing.

Jesus the Lamb of God

29The next day John saw Jesus coming toward him and said, "Look, the Lamb of God, who takes away the sin of the world! 30This is the one I meant when I said, 'A man who comes after me has surpassed me because he was before me.' 31I myself did not know him, but the reason I came baptizing with water was that he might be revealed to Israel."

32Then John gave this testimony: "I saw the Spirit come down from heaven as a dove and remain on him. 33I would not have known him, except that the one who sent me to baptize with water told me, 'The man on whom you see the Spirit come down and remain is he who will baptize with the Holy Spirit.' 34I have seen and I testify that this is the Son of God."

Jesus' First Disciples

35The next day John was there again with two of his disciples. 36When he saw Jesus passing by, he said, "Look, the Lamb of God!"

37When the two disciples heard him say this, they followed Jesus. 38Turning around, Jesus saw them following and asked, "What do you want?"

They said, "Rabbi" (which means Teacher), "where are you staying?"

39"Come," he replied, "and you will see."

So they went and saw where he was staying, and spent that day with him. It was about the tenth hour.

40Andrew, Simon Peter's brother, was one of the two who heard what John had said and who had followed Jesus. 41The first thing Andrew did was to find his brother Simon and tell him, "We have found the Messiah" (that is, the Christ). 42And he brought him to Jesus.

Jesus looked at him and said, "You are Simon son of John. You will be called Cephas" (which, when translated, is Peter*d*).

Jesus Calls Philip and Nathanael

43The next day Jesus decided to leave for Galilee. Finding Philip, he said to him, "Follow me."

44Philip, like Andrew and Peter, was from the town of Bethsaida. 45Philip found Nathanael and told him, "We have found the one Moses wrote about in the Law, and about whom the prophets also wrote—Jesus of Nazareth, the son of Joseph."

46"Nazareth! Can anything good come from there?" Nathanael asked.

"Come and see," said Philip.

47When Jesus saw Nathanael approaching, he said of him, "Here is a true Israelite, in whom there is nothing false."

48"How do you know me?" Nathanael asked.

Jesus answered, "I saw you while you were still under the fig tree before Philip called you."

49Then Nathanael declared, "Rabbi, you are the Son of God; you are the King of Israel."

50Jesus said, "You believe*e* because I told you I saw you under the fig tree. You shall see greater things than that." 51He then added, "I tell you*f* the truth, you*f* shall see heaven open, and the angels of God ascending and descending on the Son of Man."

---

a20 Or *Messiah.* "The Christ" (Greek) and "the Messiah" (Hebrew) both mean "the Anointed One"; also in verse 25.   *b23* Isaiah 40:3   *c26* Or *in;* also in verses 31 and 33   *d42* Both *Cephas* (Aramaic) and *Peter* (Greek) mean *rock.*   *e50* Or *Do you believe . . . ?*   *f51* The Greek is plural.

Jesus Changes Water to Wine

2 On the third day a wedding took place at Cana in Galilee. Jesus' mother was there, ²and Jesus and his disciples had also been invited to the wedding. ³When the wine was gone, Jesus' mother said to him, "They have no more wine."

⁴"Dear woman, why do you involve me?" Jesus replied. "My time has not yet come."

⁵His mother said to the servants, "Do whatever he tells you."

⁶Nearby stood six stone water jars, the kind used by the Jews for ceremonial washing, each holding from twenty to thirty gallons.ᵃ

⁷Jesus said to the servants, "Fill the jars with water"; so they filled them to the brim.

⁸Then he told them, "Now draw some out and take it to the master of the banquet."

They did so, ⁹and the master of the banquet tasted the water that had been turned into wine. He did not realize where it had come from, though the servants who had drawn the water knew. Then he called the bridegroom aside ¹⁰and said, "Everyone brings out the choice wine first and then the cheaper wine after the guests have had too much to drink; but you have saved the best till now."

¹¹This, the first of his miraculous signs, Jesus performed at Cana in Galilee. He thus revealed his glory, and his disciples put their faith in him.

Jesus Clears the Temple

See Matthew 21:12–13; Mark 11:15–17;
Luke 19:45–46

¹²After this he went down to Capernaum with his mother and brothers and his disciples. There they stayed for a few days.

¹³When it was almost time for the Jewish Passover, Jesus went up to Jerusalem. ¹⁴In the temple courts he found men selling cattle, sheep and doves, and others sitting at tables exchanging money. ¹⁵So he made a whip out of cords, and drove all from the temple area, both sheep and cattle; he scattered the coins of the money changers and overturned their tables. ¹⁶To those who sold doves he said, "Get these out of here! How dare you turn my Father's house into a market!"

¹⁷His disciples remembered that it is written: "Zeal for your house will consume me."ᵇ

¹⁸Then the Jews demanded of him, "What miraculous sign can you show us to prove your authority to do all this?"

¹⁹Jesus answered them, "Destroy this temple, and I will raise it again in three days."

²⁰The Jews replied, "It has taken forty-six years to build this temple, and you are going to raise it in three days?" ²¹But the temple he had spoken of was his body. ²²After he was raised from the dead, his disciples recalled what he had said. Then they believed the Scripture and the words that Jesus had spoken.

²³Now while he was in Jerusalem at the Passover Feast, many people saw the miraculous signs he was doing and believed in his name.ᶜ ²⁴But Jesus would not entrust himself to them, for he knew all men. ²⁵He did not need man's testimony about man, for he knew what was in a man.

Jesus Teaches Nicodemus

3 Now there was a man of the Pharisees named Nicodemus, a member of the Jewish ruling council. ²He came to Jesus at night and said, "Rabbi, we know you are a teacher who has come from God. For no one could perform the miraculous signs you are doing if God were not with him."

³In reply Jesus declared, "I tell you the

ᵃ6 Greek *two to three metretes* (probably about 75 to 115 liters)   ᵇ17 Psalm 69:9   ᶜ23 Or *and believed in him*

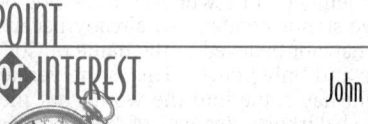

POINT OF INTEREST

John 2:5

Who is Mary talking about in this passage? She is speaking of the son she bore, washed, fed, and taught—Jesus, the Son of God, Creator of the universe, God incarnate; the flesh-bearing, sandal-wearing, living, breathing King who embodies total wisdom, power, righteousness, holiness, truth and love. Now read Mary's advice again and take it to heart!

truth, no one can see the kingdom of God unless he is born again.*a*"

4"How can a man be born when he is old?" Nicodemus asked. "Surely he cannot enter a second time into his mother's womb to be born!"

5Jesus answered, "I tell you the truth, no one can enter the kingdom of God unless he is born of water and the Spirit. 6Flesh gives birth to flesh, but the Spirit*b* gives birth to spirit. 7You should not be surprised at my saying, 'You*c* must be born again.' 8The wind blows wherever it pleases. You hear its sound, but you cannot tell where it comes from or where it is going. So it is with everyone born of the Spirit."

9"How can this be?" Nicodemus asked.

10"You are Israel's teacher," said Jesus, "and do you not understand these things? 11I tell you the truth, we speak of what we know, and we testify to what we have seen, but still you people do not accept our testimony. 12I have spoken to you of earthly things and you do not believe; how then will you believe if I speak of heavenly things? 13No one has ever gone into heaven except the one who came from heaven—the Son of Man.*d* 14Just as Moses lifted up the snake in the desert, so the Son of Man must be lifted up, 15that everyone who believes in him may have eternal life.*e*

16"For God so loved the world that he gave his one and only Son,*f* that whoever believes in him shall not perish but have eternal life. 17For God did not send his Son into the world to condemn the world, but to save the world through him. 18Whoever believes in him is not condemned, but whoever does not believe stands condemned already because he has not believed in the name of God's one and only Son.*g* 19This is the verdict: Light has come into the world, but men loved darkness instead of light because their deeds were evil. 20Everyone who does evil hates the light, and will not come into the light for fear that his deeds will be exposed. 21But whoever lives by the truth comes into the light, so that it may be seen plainly that what he has done has been done through God."*h*

John the Baptist's Testimony About Jesus

22After this, Jesus and his disciples went out into the Judean countryside, where he spent some time with them, and baptized. 23Now John also was baptizing at Aenon near Salim, because there was plenty of water, and people were constantly coming to be baptized. 24(This was before John was put in prison.) 25An argument developed between some of John's disciples and a certain Jew*i* over the matter of ceremonial washing. 26They came to John and said to him, "Rabbi, that man who was with you on the other side of the Jordan—the one you testified about—well, he is baptizing, and everyone is going to him."

27To this John replied, "A man can receive only what is given him from heaven. 28You yourselves can testify that I said, 'I am not the Christ*j* but am sent ahead of him.' 29The bride belongs to the bridegroom. The friend who attends the bridegroom waits and listens for him, and is full of joy when he hears the bridegroom's voice. That joy is mine, and it is now complete. 30He must become greater; I must become less.

31"The one who comes from above is above all; the one who is from the earth belongs to the earth, and speaks as one from the earth. The one who comes from heaven is above all. 32He testifies to what he has seen and heard, but no one accepts his testimony. 33The man who has accepted it has certified that God is truthful. 34For the one whom God has sent speaks the words of God, for God*k* gives

a3 Or *born from above*; also in verse 7   *b6* Or *but spirit*   *c7* The Greek is plural.   *d13* Some manuscripts *Man, who is in heaven*
e15 Or *believes may have eternal life in him*
f16 Or *his only begotten Son*   *g18* Or *God's only begotten Son*   *h21* Some interpreters end the quotation after verse 15.   *i25* Some manuscripts *and certain Jews*   *j28* Or *Messiah*   *k34* Greek *he*

POINT OF INTEREST

John 3:16

This is probably the best-known verse in the entire Bible. Children quote it for Sunday school prizes. Football fans display it on banners. It has become part of our cultural memory, capturing the essence of the Good News about Jesus. We've heard it so many times—but does it sink in?

the Spirit without limit. ³⁵The Father loves the Son and has placed everything in his hands. ³⁶Whoever believes in the Son has eternal life, but whoever rejects the Son will not see life, for God's wrath remains on him."ᵃ

Jesus Talks With a Samaritan Woman

4 The Pharisees heard that Jesus was gaining and baptizing more disciples than John, ²although in fact it was not Jesus who baptized, but his disciples. ³When the Lord learned of this, he left Judea and went back once more to Galilee.

⁴Now he had to go through Samaria. ⁵So he came to a town in Samaria called Sychar, near the plot of ground Jacob had given to his son Joseph. ⁶Jacob's well was there, and Jesus, tired as he was from the journey, sat down by the well. It was about the sixth hour.

⁷When a Samaritan woman came to draw water, Jesus said to her, "Will you give me a drink?" ⁸(His disciples had gone into the town to buy food.)

⁹The Samaritan woman said to him, "You are a Jew and I am a Samaritan woman. How can you ask me for a drink?" (For Jews do not associate with Samaritans.ᵇ)

¹⁰Jesus answered her, "If you knew

ᵃ36 Some interpreters end the quotation after verse 30.   ᵇ9 Or *do not use dishes Samaritans have used*

WEDNESDAY

Read *John 4:1–38*
Key Verse *John 4:10*

Living Water – Sue Grindheim

She was a jaded woman, used up in every way. Maybe she was "a woman of the night." Her only security appeared to be the ability to find men to hang on to—one more man, one more husband. Then she came to the well to draw water and met a man like none she had ever known. When Jesus asked, "Will you give me a drink?" (John 4:7), she probably assumed he was asking for more than that! After all, it wasn't culturally appropriate for a Jewish man to even speak to her—a Samaritan and a woman!

His next words confused her. He turned the tables and said, "If you knew the gift of God and who it is that asks you for a drink, you would have asked him and he would have given you living water" (John 4:10). It's as if Jesus were telling her, "If you only knew who you were talking to, you would ask me for so much more."

Her perspective was shallow, mortal and material. She talked of geography and politics. His perspective was deeper than the deepest well—he talked of eternal life. What were her deepest, unsatisfied needs? He offered her living water to satisfy her soul: "Whoever drinks the water I give him will never thirst. Indeed, the water I give him will become in him a spring of water welling up to eternal life" (John 4:14).

Imagine talking to the Savior of the world, the Creator of the universe, the King of kings. What would you ask him? Would you think to ask for *living* water—water that would satisfy your innermost needs? No matter who you are or how badly you've blown it, he's waiting for you at the well—the well of living water.

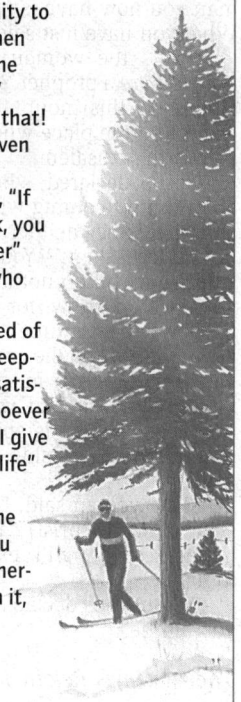

A Deeper Look
Matthew 7:7–11; Ephesians 3:20–21

Go to page 1184 for your next devotional reading.

the gift of God and who it is that asks you for a drink, you would have asked him and he would have given you living water."

¹¹"Sir," the woman said, "you have nothing to draw with and the well is deep. Where can you get this living water? ¹²Are you greater than our father Jacob, who gave us the well and drank from it himself, as did also his sons and his flocks and herds?"

¹³Jesus answered, "Everyone who drinks this water will be thirsty again, ¹⁴but whoever drinks the water I give him will never thirst. Indeed, the water I give him will become in him a spring of water welling up to eternal life."

¹⁵The woman said to him, "Sir, give me this water so that I won't get thirsty and have to keep coming here to draw water."

¹⁶He told her, "Go, call your husband and come back."

¹⁷"I have no husband," she replied.

Jesus said to her, "You are right when you say you have no husband. ¹⁸The fact is, you have had five husbands, and the man you now have is not your husband. What you have just said is quite true."

¹⁹"Sir," the woman said, "I can see that you are a prophet. ²⁰Our fathers worshiped on this mountain, but you Jews claim that the place where we must worship is in Jerusalem."

²¹Jesus declared, "Believe me, woman, a time is coming when you will worship the Father neither on this mountain nor in Jerusalem. ²²You Samaritans worship what you do not know; we worship what we do know, for salvation is from the Jews. ²³Yet a time is coming and has now come when the true worshipers will worship the Father in spirit and truth, for they are the kind of worshipers the Father seeks. ²⁴God is spirit, and his worshipers must worship in spirit and in truth."

²⁵The woman said, "I know that Messiah" (called Christ) "is coming. When he comes, he will explain everything to us."

²⁶Then Jesus declared, "I who speak to you am he."

The Disciples Rejoin Jesus

²⁷Just then his disciples returned and were surprised to find him talking with a woman. But no one asked, "What do you want?" or "Why are you talking with her?"

²⁸Then, leaving her water jar, the woman went back to the town and said to the people, ²⁹"Come, see a man who told me everything I ever did. Could this be the Christ^a?" ³⁰They came out of the town and made their way toward him.

³¹Meanwhile his disciples urged him, "Rabbi, eat something."

³²But he said to them, "I have food to eat that you know nothing about."

³³Then his disciples said to each other, "Could someone have brought him food?"

³⁴"My food," said Jesus, "is to do the will of him who sent me and to finish his work. ³⁵Do you not say, 'Four months more and then the harvest'? I tell you, open your eyes and look at the fields! They are ripe for harvest. ³⁶Even now the reaper draws his wages, even now he harvests the crop for eternal life, so that the sower and the reaper may be glad together. ³⁷Thus the saying 'One sows and another reaps' is true. ³⁸I sent you to reap what you have not worked for. Others have done the hard work, and you have reaped the benefits of their labor."

Many Samaritans Believe

³⁹Many of the Samaritans from that town believed in him because of the woman's testimony, "He told me everything I ever did." ⁴⁰So when the Samaritans came to him, they urged him to stay with them, and he stayed two days. ⁴¹And because of his words many more became believers.

⁴²They said to the woman, "We no longer believe just because of what you said; now we have heard for ourselves, and we know that this man really is the Savior of the world."

Jesus Heals the Official's Son

⁴³After the two days he left for Galilee. ⁴⁴(Now Jesus himself had pointed out that a prophet has no honor in his own country.) ⁴⁵When he arrived in Galilee, the Galileans welcomed him. They had seen all that he had done in Jerusalem at the Passover Feast, for they also had been there.

⁴⁶Once more he visited Cana in Galilee, where he had turned the water into wine. And there was a certain royal offi-

^{a}29 Or Messiah

cial whose son lay sick at Capernaum. ⁴⁷When this man heard that Jesus had arrived in Galilee from Judea, he went to him and begged him to come and heal his son, who was close to death.

⁴⁸"Unless you people see miraculous signs and wonders," Jesus told him, "you will never believe."

⁴⁹The royal official said, "Sir, come down before my child dies."

⁵⁰Jesus replied, "You may go. Your son will live."

The man took Jesus at his word and departed. ⁵¹While he was still on the way, his servants met him with the news that his boy was living. ⁵²When he inquired as to the time when his son got better, they said to him, "The fever left him yesterday at the seventh hour."

⁵³Then the father realized that this was the exact time at which Jesus had said to him, "Your son will live." So he and all his household believed.

⁵⁴This was the second miraculous sign that Jesus performed, having come from Judea to Galilee.

The Healing at the Pool

5 Some time later, Jesus went up to Jerusalem for a feast of the Jews. ²Now there is in Jerusalem near the Sheep Gate a pool, which in Aramaic is called Bethesdaᵃ and which is surrounded by five covered colonnades. ³Here a great number of disabled people used to lie—the blind, the lame, the paralyzed.ᵇ ⁵One who was there had been an invalid for thirty-eight years. ⁶When Jesus saw him lying there and learned that he had been in this condition for a long time, he asked him, "Do you want to get well?"

⁷"Sir," the invalid replied, "I have no one to help me into the pool when the water is stirred. While I am trying to get in, someone else goes down ahead of me."

⁸Then Jesus said to him, "Get up! Pick up your mat and walk." ⁹At once the man was cured; he picked up his mat and walked.

The day on which this took place was a Sabbath, ¹⁰and so the Jews said to the man who had been healed, "It is the Sabbath; the law forbids you to carry your mat."

¹¹But he replied, "The man who made me well said to me, 'Pick up your mat and walk.'"

¹²So they asked him, "Who is this fellow who told you to pick it up and walk?"

¹³The man who was healed had no idea who it was, for Jesus had slipped away into the crowd that was there.

¹⁴Later Jesus found him at the temple and said to him, "See, you are well again. Stop sinning or something worse may happen to you." ¹⁵The man went away and told the Jews that it was Jesus who had made him well.

Life Through the Son

¹⁶So, because Jesus was doing these things on the Sabbath, the Jews persecuted him. ¹⁷Jesus said to them, "My Father is always at his work to this very day, and I, too, am working." ¹⁸For this reason the Jews tried all the harder to kill him; not only was he breaking the Sabbath, but he was even calling God his own Father, making himself equal with God.

¹⁹Jesus gave them this answer: "I tell you the truth, the Son can do nothing by himself; he can do only what he sees his Father doing, because whatever the Father does the Son also does. ²⁰For the Father loves the Son and shows him all he does. Yes, to your amazement he will show him even greater things than these. ²¹For just as the Father raises the dead and gives them life, even so the Son gives life to whom he is pleased to give it. ²²Moreover, the Father judges no one, but has entrusted all judgment to the Son, ²³that all may honor the Son just as they honor the Father. He who does not honor the Son does not honor the Father, who sent him.

²⁴"I tell you the truth, whoever hears my word and believes him who sent me has eternal life and will not be condemned; he has crossed over from death to life. ²⁵I tell you the truth, a time is coming and has now come when the dead will hear the voice of the Son of God and those who hear will live. ²⁶For as the Father has life in himself, so he has granted the Son to have life in himself. ²⁷And he has given him authority to judge because he is the Son of Man.

²⁸"Do not be amazed at this, for a time is coming when all who are in their

---

ᵃ2 Some manuscripts Bethzatha; other manuscripts Bethsaida   ᵇ3 Some less important manuscripts paralyzed—and they waited for the moving of the waters. ⁴From time to time an angel of the Lord would come down and stir up the waters. The first one into the pool after each such disturbance would be cured of whatever disease he had.

graves will hear his voice ²⁹and come out—those who have done good will rise to live, and those who have done evil will rise to be condemned. ³⁰By myself I can do nothing; I judge only as I hear, and my judgment is just, for I seek not to please myself but him who sent me.

Testimonies About Jesus

³¹"If I testify about myself, my testimony is not valid. ³²There is another who testifies in my favor, and I know that his testimony about me is valid.

³³"You have sent to John and he has testified to the truth. ³⁴Not that I accept human testimony; but I mention it that you may be saved. ³⁵John was a lamp that burned and gave light, and you chose for a time to enjoy his light.

³⁶"I have testimony weightier than that of John. For the very work that the Father has given me to finish, and which I am doing, testifies that the Father has

---

THURSDAY

Read John 5:1–47
Key Verse John 5:24

Total Absolution – Paula Gibson

Suppose for a moment that you haven't believed in Jesus yet. Perhaps you really don't believe that you are a sinner, or at least you suspect that you aren't as bad as some other people. Perhaps you feel dissatisfied with your life and that you are searching for something meaningful for which to work and live, for someone to love you. Perhaps you are wondering if you will ever be forgiven for some of the things you've done—if you can ever forgive yourself.

One day you hear the Good News. You meet Jesus Christ, and you find out that he is the One who loves you, who gives your life meaning and offers you forgiveness. You say, "Yes, Lord," and accept his offer of forgiveness.

But what if you're a convicted child molester or an atheist who has militantly rejected God; what if you are lying in a cold, dirty gutter, about to die? Are Jesus' words still valid for you?

As far as Jesus is concerned, the answer to that question is an emphatic "Yes!" But sometimes we like to think one sin is worse than another. As a result, we begin to make subtle judgments about who is "savable" and who isn't. We want to share our faith only with those with whom we feel safe. We secretly believe God should only save "good" people.

But Jesus made no such distinctions when he proclaimed to the Jewish authorities that *anyone* who "hears my word and believes him who sent me has eternal life." God's awesome grace covers the sin of all those who are willing to hear and believe: "There is no difference, for all have sinned and fall short of the glory of God, and are justified freely by his grace through the redemption that came by Christ Jesus" (Romans 3:22–24).

It may not be easy for us to understand God's grace, but it is our duty to proclaim, just as boldly as Jesus did, that the gift of eternal life in Christ Jesus is available to anyone.

A Deeper Look
Jonah 1:1—4:11; Matthew 9:12–13; Luke 18:9–14

Go to page 1190 for your next devotional reading.

sent me. [37]And the Father who sent me has himself testified concerning me. You have never heard his voice nor seen his form, [38]nor does his word dwell in you, for you do not believe the one he sent. [39]You diligently study[a] the Scriptures because you think that by them you possess eternal life. These are the Scriptures that testify about me, [40]yet you refuse to come to me to have life.

[41]"I do not accept praise from men, [42]but I know you. I know that you do not have the love of God in your hearts. [43]I have come in my Father's name, and you do not accept me; but if someone else comes in his own name, you will accept him. [44]How can you believe if you accept praise from one another, yet make no effort to obtain the praise that comes from the only God[b]?

[45]"But do not think I will accuse you before the Father. Your accuser is Moses, on whom your hopes are set. [46]If you believed Moses, you would believe me, for he wrote about me. [47]But since you do not believe what he wrote, how are you going to believe what I say?"

Jesus Feeds the Five Thousand
See Matthew 14:13–21; Mark 6:32–44; Luke 9:10–17

6 Some time after this, Jesus crossed to the far shore of the Sea of Galilee (that is, the Sea of Tiberias), [2]and a great crowd of people followed him because they saw the miraculous signs he had performed on the sick. [3]Then Jesus went up on a mountainside and sat down with his disciples. [4]The Jewish Passover Feast was near.

[5]When Jesus looked up and saw a great crowd coming toward him, he said to Philip, "Where shall we buy bread for these people to eat?" [6]He asked this only to test him, for he already had in mind what he was going to do.

[7]Philip answered him, "Eight months' wages[c] would not buy enough bread for each one to have a bite!"

[8]Another of his disciples, Andrew, Simon Peter's brother, spoke up, [9]"Here is a boy with five small barley loaves and two small fish, but how far will they go among so many?"

[10]Jesus said, "Have the people sit down." There was plenty of grass in that place, and the men sat down, about five thousand of them. [11]Jesus then took the loaves, gave thanks, and distributed to those who were seated as much as they wanted. He did the same with the fish.

[12]When they had all had enough to eat, he said to his disciples, "Gather the pieces that are left over. Let nothing be wasted." [13]So they gathered them and filled twelve baskets with the pieces of the five barley loaves left over by those who had eaten.

[14]After the people saw the miraculous sign that Jesus did, they began to say, "Surely this is the Prophet who is to come into the world." [15]Jesus, knowing that they intended to come and make him king by force, withdrew again to a mountain by himself.

Jesus Walks on the Water
See Matthew 14:22–33; Mark 6:47–51

[16]When evening came, his disciples went down to the lake, [17]where they got into a boat and set off across the lake for Capernaum. By now it was dark, and Jesus had not yet joined them. [18]A strong wind was blowing and the waters grew rough. [19]When they had rowed three or three and a half miles,[d] they saw Jesus approaching the boat, walking on the water; and they were terrified. [20]But he said to them, "It is I; don't be afraid." [21]Then they were willing to take him into the boat, and immediately the boat reached the shore where they were heading.

[22]The next day the crowd that had stayed on the opposite shore of the lake realized that only one boat had been there, and that Jesus had not entered it with his disciples, but that they had gone away alone. [23]Then some boats from Tiberias landed near the place where the people had eaten the bread after the Lord had given thanks. [24]Once the crowd realized that neither Jesus nor his disciples were there, they got into the boats and went to Capernaum in search of Jesus.

Jesus the Bread of Life

[25]When they found him on the other side of the lake, they asked him, "Rabbi, when did you get here?"

[26]Jesus answered, "I tell you the truth, you are looking for me, not because you saw miraculous signs but because you ate the loaves and had your fill. [27]Do not work for food that spoils, but for food

[a]39 Or *Study diligently* (the imperative)
[b]44 Some early manuscripts *the Only One*
[c]7 Greek *two hundred denarii* [d]19 Greek *rowed twenty-five or thirty stadia* (about 5 or 6 kilometers)

that endures to eternal life, which the Son of Man will give you. On him God the Father has placed his seal of approval."

28Then they asked him, "What must we do to do the works God requires?"

29Jesus answered, "The work of God is this: to believe in the one he has sent."

30So they asked him, "What miraculous sign then will you give that we may see it and believe you? What will you do? 31Our forefathers ate the manna in the desert; as it is written: 'He gave them bread from heaven to eat.'*a*"

32Jesus said to them, "I tell you the truth, it is not Moses who has given you the bread from heaven, but it is my Father who gives you the true bread from heaven. 33For the bread of God is he who comes down from heaven and gives life to the world."

34"Sir," they said, "from now on give us this bread."

35Then Jesus declared, "I am the bread of life. He who comes to me will never go hungry, and he who believes in me will never be thirsty. 36But as I told you, you have seen me and still you do not believe. 37All that the Father gives me will come to me, and whoever comes to me I will never drive away. 38For I have come down from heaven not to do my will but to do the will of him who sent me. 39And this is the will of him who sent me, that I shall lose none of all that he has given me, but raise them up at the last day. 40For my Father's will is that everyone who looks to the Son and believes in him shall have eternal life, and I will raise him up at the last day."

41At this the Jews began to grumble about him because he said, "I am the bread that came down from heaven." 42They said, "Is this not Jesus, the son of Joseph, whose father and mother we know? How can he now say, 'I came down from heaven'?"

43"Stop grumbling among yourselves," Jesus answered. 44"No one can come to me unless the Father who sent me draws him, and I will raise him up at the last day. 45It is written in the Prophets: 'They will all be taught by God.'*b* Everyone who listens to the Father and learns from him comes to me. 46No one has seen the Father except the one who is from God; only he has seen the Father. 47I tell you the truth, he who believes has everlasting life. 48I am the bread of life. 49Your forefa-

thers ate the manna in the desert, yet they died. 50But here is the bread that comes down from heaven, which a man may eat and not die. 51I am the living bread that came down from heaven. If anyone eats of this bread, he will live forever. This bread is my flesh, which I will give for the life of the world."

52Then the Jews began to argue sharply among themselves, "How can this man give us his flesh to eat?"

53Jesus said to them, "I tell you the truth, unless you eat the flesh of the Son of Man and drink his blood, you have no life in you. 54Whoever eats my flesh and drinks my blood has eternal life, and I will raise him up at the last day. 55For my flesh is real food and my blood is real drink. 56Whoever eats my flesh and drinks my blood remains in me, and I in him. 57Just as the living Father sent me and I live because of the Father, so the one who feeds on me will live because of me. 58This is the bread that came down from heaven. Your forefathers ate manna and died, but he who feeds on this bread will live forever." 59He said this while teaching in the synagogue in Capernaum.

Many Disciples Desert Jesus

60On hearing it, many of his disciples said, "This is a hard teaching. Who can accept it?"

61Aware that his disciples were grumbling about this, Jesus said to them, "Does this offend you? 62What if you see the Son of Man ascend to where he was before! 63The Spirit gives life; the flesh counts for nothing. The words I have spoken to you are spirit*c* and they are life. 64Yet there are some of you who do not believe." For Jesus had known from the beginning which of them did not believe and who would betray him. 65He went on to say, "This is why I told you that no one can come to me unless the Father has enabled him."

66From this time many of his disciples turned back and no longer followed him.

67"You do not want to leave too, do you?" Jesus asked the Twelve.

68Simon Peter answered him, "Lord, to whom shall we go? You have the words of eternal life. 69We believe and know that you are the Holy One of God."

70Then Jesus replied, "Have I not cho-

a31 Exodus 16:4; Neh. 9:15; Psalm 78:24,25
b45 Isaiah 54:13   *c63* Or *Spirit*

sen you, the Twelve? Yet one of you is a devil!" ⁷¹(He meant Judas, the son of Simon Iscariot, who, though one of the Twelve, was later to betray him.)

Jesus Goes to the Feast of Tabernacles

7 After this, Jesus went around in Galilee, purposely staying away from Judea because the Jews there were waiting to take his life. ²But when the Jewish Feast of Tabernacles was near, ³Jesus' brothers said to him, "You ought to leave here and go to Judea, so that your disciples may see the miracles you do. ⁴No one who wants to become a public figure acts in secret. Since you are doing these things, show yourself to the world." ⁵For even his own brothers did not believe in him.

⁶Therefore Jesus told them, "The right time for me has not yet come; for you any time is right. ⁷The world cannot hate you, but it hates me because I testify that what it does is evil. ⁸You go to the Feast. I am not yet*ᵃ* going up to this Feast, because for me the right time has not yet come." ⁹Having said this, he stayed in Galilee.

¹⁰However, after his brothers had left for the Feast, he went also, not publicly, but in secret. ¹¹Now at the Feast the Jews were watching for him and asking, "Where is that man?"

¹²Among the crowds there was widespread whispering about him. Some said, "He is a good man."

Others replied, "No, he deceives the people." ¹³But no one would say anything publicly about him for fear of the Jews.

Jesus Teaches at the Feast

¹⁴Not until halfway through the Feast did Jesus go up to the temple courts and begin to teach. ¹⁵The Jews were amazed and asked, "How did this man get such learning without having studied?"

¹⁶Jesus answered, "My teaching is not my own. It comes from him who sent me. ¹⁷If anyone chooses to do God's will, he will find out whether my teaching comes from God or whether I speak on my own. ¹⁸He who speaks on his own does so to gain honor for himself, but he who works for the honor of the one who sent him is a man of truth; there is nothing false about him. ¹⁹Has not Moses given you the law? Yet not one of you keeps the law. Why are you trying to kill me?"

²⁰"You are demon-possessed," the crowd answered. "Who is trying to kill you?"

²¹Jesus said to them, "I did one miracle, and you are all astonished. ²²Yet, because Moses gave you circumcision (though actually it did not come from Moses, but from the patriarchs), you circumcise a child on the Sabbath. ²³Now if a child can be circumcised on the Sabbath so that the law of Moses may not be broken, why are you angry with me for healing the whole man on the Sabbath? ²⁴Stop judging by mere appearances, and make a right judgment."

Is Jesus the Christ?

²⁵At that point some of the people of Jerusalem began to ask, "Isn't this the man they are trying to kill? ²⁶Here he is, speaking publicly, and they are not saying a word to him. Have the authorities really concluded that he is the Christ*ᵇ*? ²⁷But we know where this man is from; when the Christ comes, no one will know where he is from."

²⁸Then Jesus, still teaching in the temple courts, cried out, "Yes, you know me, and you know where I am from. I am not here on my own, but he who sent me is true. You do not know him, ²⁹but I know him because I am from him and he sent me."

³⁰At this they tried to seize him, but no

ᵃ8 Some early manuscripts do not have *yet.*
ᵇ26 Or *Messiah*; also in verses 27, 31, 41 and 42

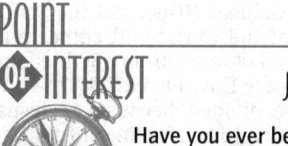

POINT OF INTEREST
John 6:66–69

Have you ever been tempted to give up trying to live a Christian life? How many people have heard Jesus' teaching and thought that he was asking too much of them, that his teachings were too difficult? How many slipped silently away? Still, Peter's answer to Jesus' question has been echoed by countless people over the centuries. Who could possibly love us more? Who could possibly save us more completely? Who is more worthy than Jesus of our allegiance, gratitude and love? Think about it.

one laid a hand on him, because his time had not yet come. ³¹Still, many in the crowd put their faith in him. They said, "When the Christ comes, will he do more miraculous signs than this man?"

³²The Pharisees heard the crowd whispering such things about him. Then the chief priests and the Pharisees sent temple guards to arrest him.

³³Jesus said, "I am with you for only a short time, and then I go to the one who sent me. ³⁴You will look for me, but you will not find me; and where I am, you cannot come."

³⁵The Jews said to one another, "Where does this man intend to go that we cannot find him? Will he go where our people live scattered among the Greeks, and teach the Greeks? ³⁶What did he mean when he said, 'You will look for me, but you will not find me,' and 'Where I am, you cannot come'?"

³⁷On the last and greatest day of the Feast, Jesus stood and said in a loud voice, "If anyone is thirsty, let him come to me and drink. ³⁸Whoever believes in me, as*a* the Scripture has said, streams of living water will flow from within him." ³⁹By this he meant the Spirit, whom those who believed in him were later to receive. Up to that time the Spirit had not been given, since Jesus had not yet been glorified.

⁴⁰On hearing his words, some of the people said, "Surely this man is the Prophet."

⁴¹Others said, "He is the Christ."

Still others asked, "How can the Christ come from Galilee? ⁴²Does not the Scripture say that the Christ will come from David's family*b* and from Bethlehem, the town where David lived?" ⁴³Thus the people were divided because of Jesus. ⁴⁴Some wanted to seize him, but no one laid a hand on him.

Unbelief of the Jewish Leaders

⁴⁵Finally the temple guards went back to the chief priests and Pharisees, who asked them, "Why didn't you bring him in?"

⁴⁶"No one ever spoke the way this man does," the guards declared.

⁴⁷"You mean he has deceived you also?" the Pharisees retorted. ⁴⁸"Has any of the rulers or of the Pharisees believed in him? ⁴⁹No! But this mob that knows nothing of the law—there is a curse on them."

⁵⁰Nicodemus, who had gone to Jesus earlier and who was one of their own number, asked, ⁵¹"Does our law condemn anyone without first hearing him to find out what he is doing?"

⁵²They replied, "Are you from Galilee, too? Look into it, and you will find that a prophet*c* does not come out of Galilee."

[The earliest manuscripts and many other ancient witnesses do not have John 7:53–8:11.]

⁵³Then each went to his own home. **8** But Jesus went to the Mount of Olives. ²At dawn he appeared again in the temple courts, where all the people gathered around him, and he sat down to teach them. ³The teachers of the law and the Pharisees brought in a woman caught in adultery. They made her stand before the group ⁴and said to Jesus, "Teacher, this woman was caught in the act of adultery. ⁵In the Law Moses commanded us to stone such women. Now what do you say?" ⁶They were using this question as a trap, in order to have a basis for accusing him.

But Jesus bent down and started to write on the ground with his finger. ⁷When they kept on questioning him, he straightened up and said to them, "If any one of you is without sin, let him be the first to throw a stone at her." ⁸Again he stooped down and wrote on the ground.

⁹At this, those who heard began to go away one at a time, the older ones first, until only Jesus was left, with the woman still standing there. ¹⁰Jesus straightened up and asked her, "Woman, where are they? Has no one condemned you?"

¹¹"No one, sir," she said.

"Then neither do I condemn you," Jesus declared. "Go now and leave your life of sin."

The Validity of Jesus' Testimony

¹²When Jesus spoke again to the people, he said, "I am the light of the world. Whoever follows me will never walk in

---

*a*37,38 Or / If anyone is thirsty, let him come to me. / And let him drink, *38who believes in me.* / As
*b*42 Greek seed   *c*52 Two early manuscripts the Prophet

darkness, but will have the light of life." 13The Pharisees challenged him, "Here you are, appearing as your own witness; your testimony is not valid."

14Jesus answered, "Even if I testify on my own behalf, my testimony is valid, for I know where I came from and where I am going. But you have no idea where I come from or where I am going. 15You judge by human standards; I pass judgment on no one. 16But if I do judge, my decisions are right, because I am not alone. I stand with the Father, who sent me. 17In your own Law it is written that the testimony of two men is valid. 18I am one who testifies for myself; my other witness is the Father, who sent me."

19Then they asked him, "Where is your father?"

"You do not know me or my Father," Jesus replied. "If you knew me, you would know my Father also." 20He spoke these words while teaching in the temple area near the place where the offerings were put. Yet no one seized him, because his time had not yet come.

21Once more Jesus said to them, "I am going away, and you will look for me, and you will die in your sin. Where I go, you cannot come."

22This made the Jews ask, "Will he kill himself? Is that why he says, 'Where I go, you cannot come'?"

23But he continued, "You are from below; I am from above. You are of this world; I am not of this world. 24I told you that you would die in your sins; if you do not believe that I am ⌊the one I claim to be⌋,ᵃ you will indeed die in your sins."

25"Who are you?" they asked.

"Just what I have been claiming all along," Jesus replied. 26"I have much to say in judgment of you. But he who sent me is reliable, and what I have heard from him I tell the world."

27They did not understand that he was telling them about his Father. 28So Jesus said, "When you have lifted up the Son of Man, then you will know that I am ⌊the one I claim to be⌋, and that I do nothing on my own but speak just what the Father has taught me. 29The one who sent me is with me; he has not left me alone, for I always do what pleases him." 30Even as he spoke, many put their faith in him.

The Children of Abraham

31To the Jews who had believed him, Jesus said, "If you hold to my teaching, you are really my disciples. 32Then you will know the truth, and the truth will set you free."

33They answered him, "We are Abraham's descendantsᵇ and have never been slaves of anyone. How can you say that we shall be set free?"

34Jesus replied, "I tell you the truth, everyone who sins is a slave to sin. 35Now a slave has no permanent place in the family, but a son belongs to it forever. 36So if the Son sets you free, you will be free indeed. 37I know you are Abraham's descendants. Yet you are ready to kill me, because you have no room for my word. 38I am telling you what I have seen in the Father's presence, and you do what you have heard from your father.ᶜ "

39"Abraham is our father," they answered.

"If you were Abraham's children," said Jesus, "then you wouldᵈ do the things Abraham did. 40As it is, you are determined to kill me, a man who has told you the truth that I heard from God. Abraham did not do such things. 41You are doing the things your own father does."

"We are not illegitimate children," they protested. "The only Father we have is God himself."

The Children of the Devil

42Jesus said to them, "If God were your Father, you would love me, for I came from God and now am here. I have not come on my own; but he sent me. 43Why is my language not clear to you? Because you are unable to hear what I say. 44You belong to your father, the devil, and you want to carry out your father's desire. He was a murderer from the beginning, not holding to the truth, for there is no truth in him. When he lies, he speaks his native language, for he is a liar and the father of lies. 45Yet because I tell the truth, you do not believe me! 46Can any of you prove me guilty of sin? If I am telling the truth, why don't you believe me? 47He who belongs to God hears what God says. The reason you do not hear is that you do not belong to God."

ᵃ24 Or I am he; also in verse 28   ᵇ33 Greek seed; also in verse 37   ᶜ38 Or presence. Therefore do what you have heard from the Father. ᵈ39 Some early manuscripts "If you are Abraham's children," said Jesus, "then

The Claims of Jesus About Himself

⁴⁸The Jews answered him, "Aren't we right in saying that you are a Samaritan and demon-possessed?"

⁴⁹"I am not possessed by a demon," said Jesus, "but I honor my Father and you dishonor me. ⁵⁰I am not seeking glory for myself; but there is one who seeks it, and he is the judge. ⁵¹I tell you the truth, if anyone keeps my word, he will never see death."

⁵²At this the Jews exclaimed, "Now we know that you are demon-possessed! Abraham died and so did the prophets, yet you say that if anyone keeps your word, he will never taste death. ⁵³Are you greater than our father Abraham? He died, and so did the prophets. Who do you think you are?"

⁵⁴Jesus replied, "If I glorify myself, my glory means nothing. My Father, whom you claim as your God, is the one who glorifies me. ⁵⁵Though you do not know him, I know him. If I said I did not, I would be a liar like you, but I do know him and keep his word. ⁵⁶Your father Abraham rejoiced at the thought of seeing my day; he saw it and was glad."

⁵⁷"You are not yet fifty years old," the Jews said to him, "and you have seen Abraham!"

⁵⁸"I tell you the truth," Jesus answered, "before Abraham was born, I am!" ⁵⁹At this, they picked up stones to stone him, but Jesus hid himself, slipping away from the temple grounds.

Jesus Heals a Man Born Blind

9 As he went along, he saw a man blind from birth. ²His disciples asked him,

---

FRIDAY

Read John 8:1–41
Key Verses John 8:31–36

Freedom in Christ — Helene Ashker

Billy Graham, famous preacher and evangelist, once said of our modern mindset, "We have confused liberty with license—and we are paying the awful price. We are a society poised on the brink of self-destruction."

One professional I met typified the confusion Graham described. Carol enjoyed living on the edge. She even flew on a stunt flying team until one day a teammate crashed and burned before her eyes. Moving across the country to avoid her parent's disapproval, she lived fast and loose. She was looking for freedom, but her "freedom" only tightened the chains of conscience around her. Eventually she crashed in a severe depression.

Jesus says in John 8:34, "I tell you the truth, everyone who sins is a slave to sin." Satan's deception is to confuse us with appealing habits that may be fun for the moment but get us hooked until we can't break free. Like the Pharisees, we want to protest and say we've never been a slave to anything. But we might be a slave to an addiction, a bad habit, negative attitudes that are deeply ingrained in us, or the effects of child abuse.

But the story doesn't end there. Jesus says in John 8:36, "So if the Son sets you free, you will be free indeed." He sets us free by giving us the power to say no when we face temptation. He gives us freedom from guilt. Through his forgiveness we become free to grow into all that God designed us to be.

A Deeper Look
Romans 8:2; Galatians 5:1

Go to page 1193 for your next devotional reading.

"Rabbi, who sinned, this man or his parents, that he was born blind?"

³"Neither this man nor his parents sinned," said Jesus, "but this happened so that the work of God might be displayed in his life. ⁴As long as it is day, we must do the work of him who sent me. Night is coming, when no one can work. ⁵While I am in the world, I am the light of the world."

⁶Having said this, he spit on the ground, made some mud with the saliva, and put it on the man's eyes. ⁷"Go," he told him, "wash in the Pool of Siloam" (this word means Sent). So the man went and washed, and came home seeing.

⁸His neighbors and those who had formerly seen him begging asked, "Isn't this the same man who used to sit and beg?" ⁹Some claimed that he was.

Others said, "No, he only looks like him."

But he himself insisted, "I am the man."

¹⁰"How then were your eyes opened?" they demanded.

¹¹He replied, "The man they call Jesus made some mud and put it on my eyes. He told me to go to Siloam and wash. So I went and washed, and then I could see."

¹²"Where is this man?" they asked him.

"I don't know," he said.

The Pharisees Investigate the Healing

¹³They brought to the Pharisees the man who had been blind. ¹⁴Now the day on which Jesus had made the mud and opened the man's eyes was a Sabbath. ¹⁵Therefore the Pharisees also asked him how he had received his sight. "He put mud on my eyes," the man replied, "and I washed, and now I see."

¹⁶Some of the Pharisees said, "This man is not from God, for he does not keep the Sabbath."

But others asked, "How can a sinner do such miraculous signs?" So they were divided.

¹⁷Finally they turned again to the blind man, "What have you to say about him? It was your eyes he opened."

The man replied, "He is a prophet."

¹⁸The Jews still did not believe that he had been blind and had received his sight until they sent for the man's parents. ¹⁹"Is this your son?" they asked. "Is this

the one you say was born blind? How is it that now he can see?"

²⁰"We know he is our son," the parents answered, "and we know he was born blind. ²¹But how he can see now, or who opened his eyes, we don't know. Ask him. He is of age; he will speak for himself." ²²His parents said this because they were afraid of the Jews, for already the Jews had decided that anyone who acknowledged that Jesus was the Christ*ᵃ* would be put out of the synagogue. ²³That was why his parents said, "He is of age; ask him."

²⁴A second time they summoned the man who had been blind. "Give glory to God,ᵇ" they said. "We know this man is a sinner."

²⁵He replied, "Whether he is a sinner or not, I don't know. One thing I do know. I was blind but now I see!"

²⁶Then they asked him, "What did he do to you? How did he open your eyes?"

²⁷He answered, "I have told you already and you did not listen. Why do you want to hear it again? Do you want to become his disciples, too?"

²⁸Then they hurled insults at him and said, "You are this fellow's disciple! We are disciples of Moses! ²⁹We know that God spoke to Moses, but as for this fellow, we don't even know where he comes from."

³⁰The man answered, "Now that is remarkable! You don't know where he comes from, yet he opened my eyes. ³¹We know that God does not listen to sinners. He listens to the godly man who does his will. ³²Nobody has ever heard of opening the eyes of a man born blind. ³³If this man were not from God, he could do nothing."

³⁴To this they replied, "You were steeped in sin at birth; how dare you lecture us!" And they threw him out.

Spiritual Blindness

³⁵Jesus heard that they had thrown him out, and when he found him, he said, "Do you believe in the Son of Man?"

³⁶"Who is he, sir?" the man asked. "Tell me so that I may believe in him."

³⁷Jesus said, "You have now seen him; in fact, he is the one speaking with you."

³⁸Then the man said, "Lord, I believe," and he worshiped him.

ᵃ22 Or *Messiah*   *ᵇ24* A solemn charge to tell the truth (see Joshua 7:19)

³⁹Jesus said, "For judgment I have come into this world, so that the blind will see and those who see will become blind."

⁴⁰Some Pharisees who were with him heard him say this and asked, "What? Are we blind too?"

⁴¹Jesus said, "If you were blind, you would not be guilty of sin; but now that you claim you can see, your guilt remains.

The Shepherd and His Flock

10 "I tell you the truth, the man who does not enter the sheep pen by the gate, but climbs in by some other way, is a thief and a robber. ²The man who enters by the gate is the shepherd of his sheep. ³The watchman opens the gate for him, and the sheep listen to his voice. He calls his own sheep by name and leads them out. ⁴When he has brought out all his own, he goes on ahead of them, and his sheep follow him because they know his voice. ⁵But they will never follow a stranger; in fact, they will run away from him because they do not recognize a stranger's voice." ⁶Jesus used this figure of speech, but they did not understand what he was telling them.

⁷Therefore Jesus said again, "I tell you the truth, I am the gate for the sheep. ⁸All who ever came before me were thieves and robbers, but the sheep did not listen to them. ⁹I am the gate; whoever enters through me will be saved.ᵃ He will come in and go out, and find pasture. ¹⁰The thief comes only to steal and kill and destroy; I have come that they may have life, and have it to the full.

¹¹"I am the good shepherd. The good shepherd lays down his life for the sheep. ¹²The hired hand is not the shepherd who owns the sheep. So when he sees the wolf coming, he abandons the sheep and runs away. Then the wolf attacks the flock and scatters it. ¹³The man runs away because he is a hired hand and cares nothing for the sheep.

¹⁴"I am the good shepherd; I know my sheep and my sheep know me— ¹⁵just as the Father knows me and I know the Father—and I lay down my life for the sheep. ¹⁶I have other sheep that are not of this sheep pen. I must bring them also. They too will listen to my voice, and there shall be one flock and one shepherd. ¹⁷The reason my Father loves me is that I lay down my life—only to take it

up again. ¹⁸No one takes it from me, but I lay it down of my own accord. I have authority to lay it down and authority to take it up again. This command I received from my Father."

¹⁹At these words the Jews were again divided. ²⁰Many of them said, "He is demon-possessed and raving mad. Why listen to him?"

²¹But others said, "These are not the sayings of a man possessed by a demon. Can a demon open the eyes of the blind?"

The Unbelief of the Jews

²²Then came the Feast of Dedicationᵇ at Jerusalem. It was winter, ²³and Jesus was in the temple area walking in Solomon's Colonnade. ²⁴The Jews gathered around him, saying, "How long will you keep us in suspense? If you are the Christ,ᶜ tell us plainly."

²⁵Jesus answered, "I did tell you, but you do not believe. The miracles I do in my Father's name speak for me, ²⁶but you do not believe because you are not my sheep. ²⁷My sheep listen to my voice; I know them, and they follow me. ²⁸I give them eternal life, and they shall never perish; no one can snatch them out of my hand. ²⁹My Father, who has given them to me, is greater than allᵈ; no one can snatch them out of my Father's hand. ³⁰I and the Father are one."

³¹Again the Jews picked up stones to stone him, ³²but Jesus said to them, "I have shown you many great miracles from the Father. For which of these do you stone me?"

³³"We are not stoning you for any of

ᵃ9 Or *kept safe*　　ᵇ22 That is, Hanukkah
ᶜ24 Or *Messiah*　　ᵈ29 Many early manuscripts
What my Father has given me is greater than all

POINT OF INTEREST

John 10:10

Some people view God as some kind of cosmic killjoy who is out to punish anyone who tries to have fun. But the God of the Bible wants to *give* us joy. God is the One who gives us a vibrant and meaningful life. Satan is the real thief who steals our hearts, kills our hope and destroys our joy with sin (see 1 Peter 5:8–9).

Read *John 10:1–21*
Key Verse *John 10:11*

His Life on the Line

What would you be willing to die for? When would you say, "Okay, this is it; it's time to take a stand even if they kill me." Or maybe the question is *whom* would you die for? Your family? Your friends? If it came down to you or them, would you put your life on the line?

Jesus did lay his life on the line when he said, "I am the good shepherd. The good shepherd lays down his life for the sheep." Jesus wasn't talking in allegories or abstract concepts only. Even though he knew exactly what would happen to him, Jesus said he would die for the ones his Father gave him—his friends. He said it even as he saw many of them standing around him—John, Peter, Andrew, Martha, Mary Magdalene.

Jesus was speaking about other friends as well. He was referring to those of us he calls his sheep. He knows us intimately and individually and calls us each by name. Jesus laid his life on the line for all of us who know his voice and follow him (see John 10:27–28).

Digging Into the Word
1. What do the following passages say about following Jesus?— *John 15:1–8,12–14*
2. Jesus cares for sheep that are lost. He searches for them that they may be brought back to the flock. What is stated in the following passages about Jesus' searching for lost sheep?—*Ezekiel 34:11–16; Matthew 18:10–14; Luke 15:1–7*

Personal Reflection
Draw a time line of your spiritual life. What did Jesus do to find you when you were lost and bring you into his flock? Think back and map on it some of the times when Jesus found you, called you and asked you to let him shepherd you. What are some of the significant milestones of your walk with him? When did you decide to follow him? Keep your time line in your Bible at John 10:11.

One Step Deeper
Matthew 10:29–31; 1 John 4:7–11

Go to page 1197 for your next devotional reading.

these," replied the Jews, "but for blasphemy, because you, a mere man, claim to be God."

³⁴Jesus answered them, "Is it not written in your Law, 'I have said you are gods'ᵃ? ³⁵If he called them 'gods,' to whom the word of God came—and the Scripture cannot be broken— ³⁶what about the one whom the Father set apart as his very own and sent into the world? Why then do you accuse me of blasphemy because I said, 'I am God's Son'? ³⁷Do not believe me unless I do what my Father does. ³⁸But if I do it, even though you do not believe me, believe the miracles, that you may know and understand that the Father is in me, and I in the Father." ³⁹Again they tried to seize him, but he escaped their grasp.

⁴⁰Then Jesus went back across the Jordan to the place where John had been baptizing in the early days. Here he stayed ⁴¹and many people came to him. They said, "Though John never performed a miraculous sign, all that John said about this man was true." ⁴²And in that place many believed in Jesus.

The Death of Lazarus

Now a man named Lazarus was sick. He was from Bethany, the village of Mary and her sister Martha. ²This Mary, whose brother Lazarus now lay sick, was the same one who poured perfume on the Lord and wiped his feet with her hair. ³So the sisters sent word to Jesus, "Lord, the one you love is sick."

⁴When he heard this, Jesus said, "This sickness will not end in death. No, it is for God's glory so that God's Son may be glorified through it." ⁵Jesus loved Martha and her sister and Lazarus. ⁶Yet when he heard that Lazarus was sick, he stayed where he was two more days.

⁷Then he said to his disciples, "Let us go back to Judea."

⁸"But Rabbi," they said, "a short while ago the Jews tried to stone you, and yet you are going back there?"

⁹Jesus answered, "Are there not twelve hours of daylight? A man who walks by day will not stumble, for he sees by this world's light. ¹⁰It is when he walks by night that he stumbles, for he has no light."

¹¹After he had said this, he went on to tell them, "Our friend Lazarus has fallen asleep; but I am going there to wake him up."

¹²His disciples replied, "Lord, if he sleeps, he will get better." ¹³Jesus had been speaking of his death, but his disciples thought he meant natural sleep.

¹⁴So then he told them plainly, "Lazarus is dead, ¹⁵and for your sake I am glad I was not there, so that you may believe. But let us go to him."

¹⁶Then Thomas (called Didymus) said to the rest of the disciples, "Let us also go, that we may die with him."

Jesus Comforts the Sisters

¹⁷On his arrival, Jesus found that Lazarus had already been in the tomb for four days. ¹⁸Bethany was less than two milesᵇ from Jerusalem, ¹⁹and many Jews had come to Martha and Mary to comfort them in the loss of their brother. ²⁰When Martha heard that Jesus was coming, she went out to meet him, but Mary stayed at home.

²¹"Lord," Martha said to Jesus, "if you had been here, my brother would not have died. ²²But I know that even now God will give you whatever you ask."

²³Jesus said to her, "Your brother will rise again."

²⁴Martha answered, "I know he will rise again in the resurrection at the last day."

²⁵Jesus said to her, "I am the resurrection and the life. He who believes in me will live, even though he dies; ²⁶and whoever lives and believes in me will never die. Do you believe this?"

²⁷"Yes, Lord," she told him, "I believe that you are the Christ,ᶜ the Son of God, who was to come into the world."

ᵃ34 Psalm 82:6   ᵇ18 Greek *fifteen stadia* (about 3 kilometers)   ᶜ27 Or *Messiah*

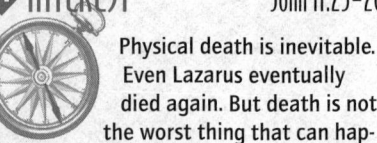

POINT OF INTEREST

John 11:25-26

Physical death is inevitable. Even Lazarus eventually died again. But death is not the worst thing that can happen to us—what counts is what happens to us after death. Jesus asks the most important question we will ever answer: "Do you believe this?" Martha's answer demonstrates her faith. How might you answer?

28And after she had said this, she went back and called her sister Mary aside. "The Teacher is here," she said, "and is asking for you." 29When Mary heard this, she got up quickly and went to him. 30Now Jesus had not yet entered the village, but was still at the place where Martha had met him. 31When the Jews who had been with Mary in the house, comforting her, noticed how quickly she got up and went out, they followed her, supposing she was going to the tomb to mourn there.

32When Mary reached the place where Jesus was and saw him, she fell at his feet and said, "Lord, if you had been here, my brother would not have died."

33When Jesus saw her weeping, and the Jews who had come along with her also weeping, he was deeply moved in spirit and troubled. 34"Where have you laid him?" he asked.

"Come and see, Lord," they replied.

35Jesus wept.

36Then the Jews said, "See how he loved him!"

37But some of them said, "Could not he who opened the eyes of the blind man have kept this man from dying?"

Jesus Raises Lazarus From the Dead

38Jesus, once more deeply moved, came to the tomb. It was a cave with a stone laid across the entrance. 39"Take away the stone," he said.

"But, Lord," said Martha, the sister of the dead man, "by this time there is a bad odor, for he has been there four days."

40Then Jesus said, "Did I not tell you that if you believed, you would see the glory of God?"

41So they took away the stone. Then Jesus looked up and said, "Father, I thank you that you have heard me. 42I knew that you always hear me, but I said this for the benefit of the people standing here, that they may believe that you sent me."

43When he had said this, Jesus called in a loud voice, "Lazarus, come out!" 44The dead man came out, his hands and feet wrapped with strips of linen, and a cloth around his face.

Jesus said to them, "Take off the grave clothes and let him go."

The Plot to Kill Jesus

45Therefore many of the Jews who had come to visit Mary, and had seen what Jesus did, put their faith in him. 46But some of them went to the Pharisees and told them what Jesus had done. 47Then the chief priests and the Pharisees called a meeting of the Sanhedrin.

"What are we accomplishing?" they asked. "Here is this man performing many miraculous signs. 48If we let him go on like this, everyone will believe in him, and then the Romans will come and take away both our place*a* and our nation."

49Then one of them, named Caiaphas, who was high priest that year, spoke up, "You know nothing at all! 50You do not realize that it is better for you that one man die for the people than that the whole nation perish."

51He did not say this on his own, but as high priest that year he prophesied that Jesus would die for the Jewish nation, 52and not only for that nation but also for the scattered children of God, to bring them together and make them one. 53So from that day on they plotted to take his life.

54Therefore Jesus no longer moved about publicly among the Jews. Instead he withdrew to a region near the desert, to a village called Ephraim, where he stayed with his disciples.

55When it was almost time for the Jewish Passover, many went up from the country to Jerusalem for their ceremonial cleansing before the Passover. 56They kept looking for Jesus, and as they stood in the temple area they asked one another, "What do you think? Isn't he coming to the Feast at all?" 57But the chief priests and Pharisees had given orders that if anyone found out where Jesus was, he should report it so that they might arrest him.

Jesus Anointed at Bethany

12 Six days before the Passover, Jesus arrived at Bethany, where Lazarus lived, whom Jesus had raised from the dead. 2Here a dinner was given in Jesus' honor. Martha served, while Lazarus was among those reclining at the table with him. 3Then Mary took about a pint*b* of pure nard, an expensive perfume; she poured it on Jesus' feet and wiped his feet with her hair. And the house was filled with the fragrance of the perfume.

4But one of his disciples, Judas Iscari-

---

*a*48 Or *temple*   *b*3 Greek *a litra* (probably about 0.5 liter) ot, who was later to betray him, objected, 5"Why wasn't this perfume sold and the money given to the poor? It was worth a year's wages.*a*" 6He did not say this because he cared about the poor but because he was a thief; as keeper of the money bag, he used to help himself to what was put into it.

7"Leave her alone," Jesus replied. "⌐It was intended⌐ that she should save this perfume for the day of my burial. 8You will always have the poor among you, but you will not always have me."

9Meanwhile a large crowd of Jews found out that Jesus was there and came, not only because of him but also to see Lazarus, whom he had raised from the dead. 10So the chief priests made plans to kill Lazarus as well, 11for on account of him many of the Jews were going over to Jesus and putting their faith in him.

The Triumphal Entry

See Matthew 21:4–9; Mark 11:7–10; Luke 19:35–38

12The next day the great crowd that had come for the Feast heard that Jesus was on his way to Jerusalem. 13They took palm branches and went out to meet him, shouting,

"Hosanna!*b*"

"Blessed is he who comes in the name of the Lord!"*c*

"Blessed is the King of Israel!"

14Jesus found a young donkey and sat upon it, as it is written,

15"Do not be afraid, O Daughter of Zion;
see, your king is coming,
seated on a donkey's colt."*d*

16At first his disciples did not understand all this. Only after Jesus was glorified did they realize that these things had been written about him and that they had done these things to him.

17Now the crowd that was with him when he called Lazarus from the tomb and raised him from the dead continued to spread the word. 18Many people, because they had heard that he had given this miraculous sign, went out to meet him. 19So the Pharisees said to one another, "See, this is getting us nowhere. Look how the whole world has gone after him!"

Jesus Predicts His Death

20Now there were some Greeks among those who went up to worship at the Feast. 21They came to Philip, who was from Bethsaida in Galilee, with a request. "Sir," they said, "we would like to see Jesus." 22Philip went to tell Andrew; Andrew and Philip in turn told Jesus.

23Jesus replied, "The hour has come for the Son of Man to be glorified. 24I tell you the truth, unless a kernel of wheat falls to the ground and dies, it remains only a single seed. But if it dies, it produces many seeds. 25The man who loves his life will lose it, while the man who hates his life in this world will keep it for eternal life. 26Whoever serves me must follow me; and where I am, my servant also will be. My Father will honor the one who serves me.

27"Now my heart is troubled, and what shall I say? 'Father, save me from this hour'? No, it was for this very reason I came to this hour. 28Father, glorify your name!"

Then a voice came from heaven, "I have glorified it, and will glorify it again." 29The crowd that was there and heard it said it had thundered; others said an angel had spoken to him.

30Jesus said, "This voice was for your benefit, not mine. 31Now is the time for judgment on this world; now the prince of this world will be driven out. 32But I, when I am lifted up from the earth, will draw all men to myself." 33He said this to show the kind of death he was going to die.

34The crowd spoke up, "We have heard from the Law that the Christ*e* will remain forever, so how can you say, 'The Son of Man must be lifted up'? Who is this 'Son of Man'?"

35Then Jesus told them, "You are going to have the light just a little while longer. Walk while you have the light, before darkness overtakes you. The man who walks in the dark does not know where he is going. 36Put your trust in the light while you have it, so that you may become sons of light." When he had finished speaking, Jesus left and hid himself from them.

*a*5 Greek *three hundred denarii*   *b*13 A Hebrew expression meaning "Save!" which became an exclamation of praise   *c*13 Psalm 118:25, 26   *d*15 Zech. 9:9   *e*34 Or *Messiah*

The Jews Continue in Their Unbelief

³⁷Even after Jesus had done all these miraculous signs in their presence, they still would not believe in him. ³⁸This was to fulfill the word of Isaiah the prophet:

"Lord, who has believed our message
    and to whom has the arm of the
        Lord been revealed?"ᵃ

³⁹For this reason they could not believe, because, as Isaiah says elsewhere:

⁴⁰"He has blinded their eyes
    and deadened their hearts,
so they can neither see with their
        eyes,
    nor understand with their hearts,
    nor turn—and I would heal
        them."ᵇ

⁴¹Isaiah said this because he saw Jesus' glory and spoke about him.

⁴²Yet at the same time many even among the leaders believed in him. But because of the Pharisees they would not confess their faith for fear they would be put out of the synagogue; ⁴³for they loved praise from men more than praise from God.

⁴⁴Then Jesus cried out, "When a man believes in me, he does not believe in me only, but in the one who sent me. ⁴⁵When he looks at me, he sees the one who sent me. ⁴⁶I have come into the world as a light, so that no one who believes in me should stay in darkness.

⁴⁷"As for the person who hears my words but does not keep them, I do not judge him. For I did not come to judge the world, but to save it. ⁴⁸There is a judge for the one who rejects me and does not accept my words; that very word which I spoke will condemn him at the last day. ⁴⁹For I did not speak of my own accord, but the Father who sent me commanded me what to say and how to say it. ⁵⁰I know that his command leads to eternal life. So whatever I say is just what the Father has told me to say."

ᵃ38 Isaiah 53:1   ᵇ40 Isaiah 6:10

MONDAY

Read John 12:20–36
Key Verses John 12:24–25

The Struggle — Jennifer Colquitt

In the garden—suspended between time and eternity—
Jesus sweat beads of blood
as humanity mingled with deity.
Anguish overwhelming, he prayed more earnestly.
Though twice he asked to be released, he was
twice denied. He must die for all to live.

In my garden—battling between flesh and spirit—
I die to self-sufficiency
as my will crumbles into his,
like a kernel of wheat consumed in earth.
Confident of his empathy, I rest;
I submit. I must die so he can live in me.

A Deeper Look
Romans 6:1–14; Hebrews 12:4–7

Go to page 1199 for your next devotional reading.

Jesus Washes His Disciples' Feet

13 It was just before the Passover Feast. Jesus knew that the time had come for him to leave this world and go to the Father. Having loved his own who were in the world, he now showed them the full extent of his love. *a*

2The evening meal was being served, and the devil had already prompted Judas Iscariot, son of Simon, to betray Jesus. 3Jesus knew that the Father had put all things under his power, and that he had come from God and was returning to God; 4so he got up from the meal, took off his outer clothing, and wrapped a towel around his waist. 5After that, he poured water into a basin and began to wash his disciples' feet, drying them with the towel that was wrapped around him.

6He came to Simon Peter, who said to him, "Lord, are you going to wash my feet?"

7Jesus replied, "You do not realize now what I am doing, but later you will understand."

8"No," said Peter, "you shall never wash my feet."

Jesus answered, "Unless I wash you, you have no part with me."

9"Then, Lord," Simon Peter replied, "not just my feet but my hands and my head as well!"

10Jesus answered, "A person who has had a bath needs only to wash his feet; his whole body is clean. And you are clean, though not every one of you." 11For he knew who was going to betray him, and that was why he said not every one was clean.

12When he had finished washing their feet, he put on his clothes and returned to his place. "Do you understand what I have done for you?" he asked them. 13"You call me 'Teacher' and 'Lord,' and rightly so, for that is what I am. 14Now that I, your Lord and Teacher, have washed your feet, you also should wash one another's feet. 15I have set you an example that you should do as I have done for you. 16I tell you the truth, no servant is greater than his master, nor is a messenger greater than the one who sent him. 17Now that you know these things, you will be blessed if you do them.

Jesus Predicts His Betrayal

18"I am not referring to all of you; I know those I have chosen. But this is to fulfill the scripture: 'He who shares my bread has lifted up his heel against me.' *b*

19"I am telling you now before it happens, so that when it does happen you will believe that I am He. 20I tell you the truth, whoever accepts anyone I send accepts me; and whoever accepts me accepts the one who sent me."

21After he had said this, Jesus was troubled in spirit and testified, "I tell you the truth, one of you is going to betray me."

22His disciples stared at one another, at a loss to know which of them he meant. 23One of them, the disciple whom Jesus loved, was reclining next to him. 24Simon Peter motioned to this disciple and said, "Ask him which one he means."

25Leaning back against Jesus, he asked him, "Lord, who is it?"

26Jesus answered, "It is the one to whom I will give this piece of bread when I have dipped it in the dish." Then, dipping the piece of bread, he gave it to Judas Iscariot, son of Simon. 27As soon as Judas took the bread, Satan entered into him.

"What you are about to do, do quickly," Jesus told him, 28but no one at the meal understood why Jesus said this to him. 29Since Judas had charge of the money, some thought Jesus was telling him to buy what was needed for the Feast, or to give something to the poor. 30As soon as Judas had taken the bread, he went out. And it was night.

Jesus Predicts Peter's Denial

See Matthew 26:33–35; Mark 14:29–31; Luke 22:33–34

31When he was gone, Jesus said, "Now is the Son of Man glorified and God is glorified in him. 32If God is glorified in him, *c* God will glorify the Son in himself, and will glorify him at once.

33"My children, I will be with you only a little longer. You will look for me, and just as I told the Jews, so I tell you now: Where I am going, you cannot come.

34"A new command I give you: Love

---

*a*1 Or *he loved them to the last*   *b*18 Psalm 41:9
*c*32 Many early manuscripts do not have *If God is glorified in him.*

one another. As I have loved you, so you must love one another. ³⁵By this all men will know that you are my disciples, if you love one another."

³⁶Simon Peter asked him, "Lord, where are you going?"

Jesus replied, "Where I am going, you cannot follow now, but you will follow later."

³⁷Peter asked, "Lord, why can't I follow you now? I will lay down my life for you."

³⁸Then Jesus answered, "Will you really lay down your life for me? I tell you the truth, before the rooster crows, you will disown me three times!

Jesus Comforts His Disciples

14 "Do not let your hearts be troubled. Trust in God*ᵃ*; trust also in me. ²In my Father's house are many rooms; if it were not so, I would have told you. I am going there to prepare a place for you. ³And if I go and prepare a place for you, I will come back and take you to be with me that you also may be where I am. ⁴You know the way to the place where I am going."

Jesus the Way to the Father

⁵Thomas said to him, "Lord, we don't

*ᵃ*1 Or *You trust in God*

TUESDAY

Read *John 13:1–38*
Key Verses *John 13:34–35*

Love One Another — Lindy Black

Six of us girls were living in a small, two-bedroom townhouse for the summer. Tom, the guy next door, was intrigued as he encountered us coming and going. He'd never seen two girls rooming together in peace, much less six! Tom saw us go to work, eat dinner together and go out to exercise in the evenings. As he saw other friends come over for fun and fellowship, he wondered what went on within the walls of our small house.

After two weeks, Tom couldn't stand it any longer. He showed up at the door—six-pack in hand—to join our "party." Our party happened to include a discussion of a New Testament passage, singing and prayer. Over the next few weeks he asked many questions concerning Jesus, whom we spoke of as if he were a personal friend. He came to understand that becoming a child of God requires putting our trust in him. Soon Tom chose to believe and become a disciple of Jesus Christ!

The love we shared for one another was radically different from anything Tom had ever known, and it was also inviting to him. He longed to be with friends who genuinely cared about him. Eventually he chose to follow Jesus Christ. Later, when asked how he became a Christian, Tom would explain, saying, "There were these six girls who moved in next door for the summer . . ."

Jesus told us to "love one another." His command is the heart of the gospel. And this command should be at the heart of all our relationships, because people are always watching and evaluating to see how real our faith is. It's one way people will recognize that we belong to Jesus Christ. And perhaps they will want to know him as well.

A Deeper Look
Matthew 22:39; 1 Peter 1:22

Go to page 1201 for your next devotional reading.

know where you are going, so how can we know the way?"

⁶Jesus answered, "I am the way and the truth and the life. No one comes to the Father except through me. ⁷If you really knew me, you would know*a* my Father as well. From now on, you do know him and have seen him."

⁸Philip said, "Lord, show us the Father and that will be enough for us."

⁹Jesus answered: "Don't you know me, Philip, even after I have been among you such a long time? Anyone who has seen me has seen the Father. How can you say, 'Show us the Father'? ¹⁰Don't you believe that I am in the Father, and that the Father is in me? The words I say to you are not just my own. Rather, it is the Father, living in me, who is doing his work. ¹¹Believe me when I say that I am in the Father and the Father is in me; or at least believe on the evidence of the miracles themselves. ¹²I tell you the truth, anyone who has faith in me will do what I have been doing. He will do even greater things than these, because I am going to the Father. ¹³And I will do whatever you ask in my name, so that the Son may bring glory to the Father. ¹⁴You may ask me for anything in my name, and I will do it.

Jesus Promises the Holy Spirit

¹⁵"If you love me, you will obey what I command. ¹⁶And I will ask the Father, and he will give you another Counselor to be with you forever— ¹⁷the Spirit of truth. The world cannot accept him, because it neither sees him nor knows him. But you know him, for he lives with you and will be*b* in you. ¹⁸I will not leave you as orphans; I will come to you. ¹⁹Before long, the world will not see me anymore, but you will see me. Because I live, you also will live. ²⁰On that day you will realize that I am in my Father, and you are in me, and I am in you. ²¹Whoever has my commands and obeys them, he is the one who loves me. He who loves me will be loved by my Father, and I too will love him and show myself to him."

²²Then Judas (not Judas Iscariot) said, "But, Lord, why do you intend to show yourself to us and not to the world?"

²³Jesus replied, "If anyone loves me, he will obey my teaching. My Father will love him, and we will come to him and make our home with him. ²⁴He who does not love me will not obey my teaching.

These words you hear are not my own; they belong to the Father who sent me.

²⁵"All this I have spoken while still with you. ²⁶But the Counselor, the Holy Spirit, whom the Father will send in my name, will teach you all things and will remind you of everything I have said to you. ²⁷Peace I leave with you; my peace I give you. I do not give to you as the world gives. Do not let your hearts be troubled and do not be afraid.

²⁸"You heard me say, 'I am going away and I am coming back to you.' If you loved me, you would be glad that I am going to the Father, for the Father is greater than I. ²⁹I have told you now before it happens, so that when it does happen you will believe. ³⁰I will not speak with you much longer, for the prince of this world is coming. He has no hold on me, ³¹but the world must learn that I love the Father and that I do exactly what my Father has commanded me.

"Come now; let us leave.

The Vine and the Branches

15 "I am the true vine, and my Father is the gardener. ²He cuts off every branch in me that bears no fruit, while every branch that does bear fruit he prunes*c* so that it will be even more fruitful. ³You are already clean because of the word I have spoken to you. ⁴Remain in me, and I will remain in you. No branch can bear fruit by itself; it must remain in the vine. Neither can you bear fruit unless you remain in me.

⁵"I am the vine; you are the branches. If a man remains in me and I in him, he will bear much fruit; apart from me you can do nothing. ⁶If anyone does not remain in me, he is like a branch that is thrown away and withers; such branches are picked up, thrown into the fire and burned. ⁷If you remain in me and my words remain in you, ask whatever you wish, and it will be given you. ⁸This is to my Father's glory, that you bear much fruit, showing yourselves to be my disciples.

⁹"As the Father has loved me, so have I loved you. Now remain in my love. ¹⁰If you obey my commands, you will remain in my love, just as I have obeyed my Father's commands and remain in his love.

a 7 Some early manuscripts *If you really have known me, you will know   b 17* Some early manuscripts *and is   c 2* The Greek for *prunes* also means *cleans.*

[11]I have told you this so that my joy may be in you and that your joy may be complete. [12]My command is this: Love each other as I have loved you. [13]Greater love has no one than this, that he lay down his life for his friends. [14]You are my friends if you do what I command. [15]I no longer call you servants, because a servant does not know his master's business. Instead, I have called you friends, for everything that I learned from my Father I have made known to you. [16]You did not choose me, but I chose you and appointed you to go and bear fruit—fruit that will last. Then the Father will give you whatever you ask in my name. [17]This is my command: Love each other.

The World Hates the Disciples

[18]"If the world hates you, keep in mind that it hated me first. [19]If you belonged to the world, it would love you as its own. As it is, you do not belong to the world, but I have chosen you out of the world. That is why the world hates you. [20]Remember the words I spoke to you: 'No servant is greater than his master.'[a] If they persecuted me, they will persecute you also. If they obeyed my teaching,

[a]20 John 13:16

WEDNESDAY

Read *John 14:1–31*
Key Verse *John 14:21*

Falling Out of Step — Larry Bauer

Picture yourself sitting in the stands of the football stadium, waiting for your chance to take the field with the rest of the marching band. But you're preoccupied, thinking about the tailgate party that you had to miss because of an early-morning rehearsal. Half-time comes and you're on the field, but you simply can't get that party out of your head. Although the music is right in front of you and you can see the director, your mind wanders and you fall out of step. The band turns east, but you turn west and find yourself alone in the end zone. Yikes! Because of your preoccupation, the music and the director's instruction quickly became irrelevant.

Now picture entering a room and opening your Bible. As you read his Word, God speaks to you about a particular area of your life. You know it's important to listen to his direction, but rather than immediately obeying, you ignore his voice in your heart. You close your Bible and allow your mind to wander. As you begin to think about the day's activities, God's voice in your heart fades, drowned out by the other voices of your day.

God's message to us may be loud and clear. But if we don't promptly act on it, the Spirit's voice easily becomes mental background noise as we go about the day's events. We soon find out, sometimes too late, that we've taken a wrong turn.

Don't allow God's Word and the Spirit's voice to become irrelevant. Study his Word and listen to his commands as they ring in your heart and mind. Then promptly obey what you hear. You'll soon find the music of God's love playing loudly in your heart and following you into the classroom, out onto the athletic field and into the dormitory.

A Deeper Look
Luke 6:46; James 1:22

Go to page 1203 for your next devotional reading.

they will obey yours also. ²¹They will treat you this way because of my name, for they do not know the One who sent me. ²²If I had not come and spoken to them, they would not be guilty of sin. Now, however, they have no excuse for their sin. ²³He who hates me hates my Father as well. ²⁴If I had not done among them what no one else did, they would not be guilty of sin. But now they have seen these miracles, and yet they have hated both me and my Father. ²⁵But this is to fulfill what is written in their Law: 'They hated me without reason.'ᵃ

²⁶"When the Counselor comes, whom I will send to you from the Father, the Spirit of truth who goes out from the Father, he will testify about me. ²⁷And you also must testify, for you have been with me from the beginning.

16 "All this I have told you so that you will not go astray. ²They will put you out of the synagogue; in fact, a time is coming when anyone who kills you will think he is offering a service to God. ³They will do such things because they have not known the Father or me. ⁴I have told you this, so that when the time comes you will remember that I warned you. I did not tell you this at first because I was with you.

The Work of the Holy Spirit

⁵"Now I am going to him who sent me, yet none of you asks me, 'Where are you going?' ⁶Because I have said these things, you are filled with grief. ⁷But I tell you the truth: It is for your good that I am going away. Unless I go away, the Counselor will not come to you; but if I go, I will send him to you. ⁸When he comes, he will convict the world of guiltᵇ in regard to sin and righteousness and judgment: ⁹in regard to sin, because men do not believe in me; ¹⁰in regard to righteousness, because I am going to the Father, where you can see me no longer; ¹¹and in regard to judgment, because the prince of this world now stands condemned.

¹²"I have much more to say to you, more than you can now bear. ¹³But when he, the Spirit of truth, comes, he will guide you into all truth. He will not speak on his own; he will speak only what he hears, and he will tell you what is yet to come. ¹⁴He will bring glory to me by taking from what is mine and making it known to you. ¹⁵All that belongs to the Father is mine. That is why I said the Spirit will take from what is mine and make it known to you.

¹⁶"In a little while you will see me no more, and then after a little while you will see me."

The Disciples' Grief Will Turn to Joy

¹⁷Some of his disciples said to one another, "What does he mean by saying, 'In a little while you will see me no more, and then after a little while you will see me,' and 'Because I am going to the Father'?" ¹⁸They kept asking, "What does he mean by 'a little while'? We don't understand what he is saying."

¹⁹Jesus saw that they wanted to ask him about this, so he said to them, "Are you asking one another what I meant when I said, 'In a little while you will see me no more, and then after a little while you will see me'? ²⁰I tell you the truth, you will weep and mourn while the world rejoices. You will grieve, but your grief will turn to joy. ²¹A woman giving birth to a child has pain because her time has come; but when her baby is born she forgets the anguish because of her joy that a child is born into the world. ²²So with you: Now is your time of grief, but I will see you again and you will rejoice, and no one will take away your joy. ²³In that day you will no longer ask me anything. I tell you the truth, my Father will give you whatever you ask in my name. ²⁴Until now you have not asked for anything in my name. Ask and you will receive, and your joy will be complete.

²⁵"Though I have been speaking figuratively, a time is coming when I will no longer use this kind of language but will tell you plainly about my Father. ²⁶In that day you will ask in my name. I am not saying that I will ask the Father on your behalf. ²⁷No, the Father himself loves you because you have loved me and have believed that I came from God. ²⁸I came from the Father and entered the world; now I am leaving the world and going back to the Father."

²⁹Then Jesus' disciples said, "Now you are speaking clearly and without figures of speech. ³⁰Now we can see that you know all things and that you do not even need to have anyone ask you questions.

ᵃ25 Psalms 35:19; 69:4   ᵇ8 Or *will expose the guilt of the world*

This makes us believe that you came from God."

31 "You believe at last!" *a* Jesus answered. **32** "But a time is coming, and has come, when you will be scattered, each to his own home. You will leave me all alone. Yet I am not alone, for my Father is with me.

33 "I have told you these things, so that in me you may have peace. In this world you will have trouble. But take heart! I have overcome the world."

Jesus Prays for Himself

17 After Jesus said this, he looked toward heaven and prayed:

"Father, the time has come. Glorify your Son, that your Son may glorify you. **2** For you granted him authority over all people that he might give eternal life to all those you have given him. **3** Now this is eternal life: that they may know you, the only true God, and Jesus Christ, whom you have sent. **4** I have brought you glory on earth by completing the work you gave me to do. **5** And now, Father, glorify me in your presence with the glory I had with you before the world began.

Jesus Prays for His Disciples

6 "I have revealed you *b* to those whom you gave me out of the world. They were yours; you gave

a31 Or *"Do you now believe?"*　　*b6* Greek *your name*; also in verse 26

Read *John 16:1–33*
Key Verses *John 16:13–14*

What Will I Say? – Jenny Forsberg

I turned over for what seemed like the twentieth time and looked at the clock. It was late. I was tired and needed sleep, but I couldn't stop thinking about the next day. In ten hours I would meet with two people to discuss a school project. As the facilitator and leader for the group, it was my role to help us evaluate how we were progressing on the project. Not only did I have to swallow my pride and admit I'd made some mistakes in our work, but I also needed to point out areas in which the other two could improve.

As I tossed and turned, the Holy Spirit reminded me of Philippians 4:6: "Do not be anxious about anything, but in everything, by prayer and petition, with thanksgiving, present your requests to God." After I prayed about my anxiety and about the peace God promises in those verses, I felt at peace and was able to sleep.

When morning came, though, I began wrestling with not knowing what to say or how to say it. But as I listened and prayed for the Holy Spirit to counsel me, I was able to come up with agenda ideas for our meeting time—ideas about what to say and some insight into how God was working in my group members' lives.

The next day I evaluated how our meeting had gone and thought about comments from the other two people in my group. I was overwhelmed with thankfulness. The meeting that might have been negative and maybe even hurtful proved to be positive and encouraging. I learned that I could "cast all [my] anxiety on [God] because he cares for [me]" (1 Peter 5:7).

A Deeper Look
Psalm 32:8; Colossians 4:5–6

Go to page 1205 for your next devotional reading.

them to me and they have obeyed your word. ⁷Now they know that everything you have given me comes from you. ⁸For I gave them the words you gave me and they accepted them. They knew with certainty that I came from you, and they believed that you sent me. ⁹I pray for them. I am not praying for the world, but for those you have given me, for they are yours. ¹⁰All I have is yours, and all you have is mine. And glory has come to me through them. ¹¹I will remain in the world no longer, but they are still in the world, and I am coming to you. Holy Father, protect them by the power of your name—the name you gave me—so that they may be one as we are one. ¹²While I was with them, I protected them and kept them safe by that name you gave me. None has been lost except the one doomed to destruction so that Scripture would be fulfilled.

¹³"I am coming to you now, but I say these things while I am still in the world, so that they may have the full measure of my joy within them. ¹⁴I have given them your word and the world has hated them, for they are not of the world any more than I am of the world. ¹⁵My prayer is not that you take them out of the world but that you protect them from the evil one. ¹⁶They are not of the world, even as I am not of it. ¹⁷Sanctify*a* them by the truth; your word is truth. ¹⁸As you sent me into the world, I have sent them into the world. ¹⁹For them I sanctify myself, that they too may be truly sanctified.

Jesus Prays for All Believers

²⁰"My prayer is not for them alone. I pray also for those who will believe in me through their message, ²¹that all of them may be one, Father, just as you are in me and I am in you. May they also be in us so that the world may believe that you have sent me. ²²I have given them the glory that you gave me, that they may be one as we are one: ²³I in them and you in me. May they be brought to complete unity to let the world know that you sent me and have loved them even as you have loved me.

²⁴"Father, I want those you have given me to be with me where I am, and to see my glory, the glory you have given me because you loved me before the creation of the world.

²⁵"Righteous Father, though the world does not know you, I know you, and they know that you have sent me. ²⁶I have made you known to them, and will continue to make you known in order that the love you have for me may be in them and that I myself may be in them."

Jesus Arrested

See Matthew 26:47–56; Mark 14:43–50; Luke 22:47–53

18 When he had finished praying, Jesus left with his disciples and crossed the Kidron Valley. On the other side there was an olive grove, and he and his disciples went into it.

²Now Judas, who betrayed him, knew the place, because Jesus had often met there with his disciples. ³So Judas came to the grove, guiding a detachment of soldiers and some officials from the chief priests and Pharisees. They were carrying torches, lanterns and weapons.

⁴Jesus, knowing all that was going to happen to him, went out and asked them, "Who is it you want?"

⁵"Jesus of Nazareth," they replied.

"I am he," Jesus said. (And Judas the traitor was standing there with them.) ⁶When Jesus said, "I am he," they drew back and fell to the ground.

⁷Again he asked them, "Who is it you want?"

And they said, "Jesus of Nazareth."

⁸"I told you that I am he," Jesus answered. "If you are looking for me, then let these men go." ⁹This happened so that the words he had spoken would be fulfilled: "I have not lost one of those you gave me."*b*

¹⁰Then Simon Peter, who had a sword, drew it and struck the high priest's servant, cutting off his right ear. (The servant's name was Malchus.)

¹¹Jesus commanded Peter, "Put your

---

a17 Greek *hagiazo (set apart for sacred use* or *make holy); also in verse 19*   *b9* John 6:39

sword away! Shall I not drink the cup the Father has given me?"

Jesus Taken to Annas
See Matthew 26:57

¹²Then the detachment of soldiers with its commander and the Jewish officials arrested Jesus. They bound him ¹³and brought him first to Annas, who was the father-in-law of Caiaphas, the high priest that year. ¹⁴Caiaphas was the one who had advised the Jews that it would be good if one man died for the people.

Peter's First Denial
See Matthew 26:69–70; Mark 14:66–68; Luke 22:55–57

¹⁵Simon Peter and another disciple were following Jesus. Because this disciple was known to the high priest, he went with Jesus into the high priest's courtyard, ¹⁶but Peter had to wait outside at the door. The other disciple, who was known to the high priest, came back, spoke to the girl on duty there and brought Peter in.

¹⁷"You are not one of his disciples, are you?" the girl at the door asked Peter.

FRIDAY

Read John 17:1–26
Key Verse John 17:18

For Jesus Christ – Dr. Bill Bright

Jesus sent his disciples into the world to tell others the Good News. Likewise, he sends all who believe in him into the world with the message of forgiveness. History has shown that college men and women can be very effective witnesses for Jesus Christ. But why should we get personally involved in this process? Let me suggest three reasons.

First, we get involved because the Lord said to do it. He commanded his disciples, and that includes college students who are his followers, to make disciples of all nations, teaching them to obey all that he commanded (see Matthew 28:18–20).

Second, the love that God demonstrated through his Son is so great and so magnificent that it simply must be communicated to all the earth! This begins with reaching those on your campus! God has purposefully and strategically placed you on your campus in order to reach other students, faculty members and staff for Jesus Christ.

Third, the proclamation of God's truths is the only way spiritual light will come to the world, replacing the darkness that exists in many souls and also in whole nations. Millions of people live without hope for the future. They live in constant fear of the demonic idols and false gods that they worship. They are slaves in Satan's kingdom, and only Jesus Christ can set them free. We must tell them of God's great love for them!

The secret to knowing God in an intimate, personal way is to demonstrate our love for him by obeying him (see John 14:21,23). Because Jesus came to seek and save lost people, we bring great pleasure to God when we seek to introduce people to Jesus Christ. Whom has God placed in your life that he wants you to tell about his Son? Why not tell them today?

A Deeper Look
Luke 24:46–48; Romans 1:14,16

Go to page 1209 for your next devotional reading.

He replied, "I am not."

¹⁸It was cold, and the servants and officials stood around a fire they had made to keep warm. Peter also was standing with them, warming himself.

The High Priest Questions Jesus

See Matthew 26:59–68; Mark 14:55–65; Luke 22:63–71

¹⁹Meanwhile, the high priest questioned Jesus about his disciples and his teaching.

²⁰"I have spoken openly to the world," Jesus replied. "I always taught in synagogues or at the temple, where all the Jews come together. I said nothing in secret. ²¹Why question me? Ask those who heard me. Surely they know what I said."

²²When Jesus said this, one of the officials nearby struck him in the face. "Is this the way you answer the high priest?" he demanded.

²³"If I said something wrong," Jesus replied, "testify as to what is wrong. But if I spoke the truth, why did you strike me?" ²⁴Then Annas sent him, still bound, to Caiaphas the high priest.*a*

Peter's Second and Third Denials

See Matthew 26:71–75; Mark 14:69–72; Luke 22:58–62

²⁵As Simon Peter stood warming himself, he was asked, "You are not one of his disciples, are you?"

He denied it, saying, "I am not."

²⁶One of the high priest's servants, a relative of the man whose ear Peter had cut off, challenged him, "Didn't I see you with him in the olive grove?" ²⁷Again Peter denied it, and at that moment a rooster began to crow.

Jesus Before Pilate

See Matthew 27:11–18,20–23; Mark 15:2–15; Luke 23:2–3,18–25

²⁸Then the Jews led Jesus from Caiaphas to the palace of the Roman governor. By now it was early morning, and to avoid ceremonial uncleanness the Jews did not enter the palace; they wanted to be able to eat the Passover. ²⁹So Pilate came out to them and asked, "What charges are you bringing against this man?"

³⁰"If he were not a criminal," they replied, "we would not have handed him over to you."

³¹Pilate said, "Take him yourselves and judge him by your own law."

"But we have no right to execute anyone," the Jews objected. ³²This happened so that the words Jesus had spoken indicating the kind of death he was going to die would be fulfilled.

³³Pilate then went back inside the palace, summoned Jesus and asked him, "Are you the king of the Jews?"

³⁴"Is that your own idea," Jesus asked, "or did others talk to you about me?"

³⁵"Am I a Jew?" Pilate replied. "It was your people and your chief priests who handed you over to me. What is it you have done?"

³⁶Jesus said, "My kingdom is not of this world. If it were, my servants would fight to prevent my arrest by the Jews. But now my kingdom is from another place."

³⁷"You are a king, then!" said Pilate.

Jesus answered, "You are right in saying I am a king. In fact, for this reason I was born, and for this I came into the world, to testify to the truth. Everyone on the side of truth listens to me."

³⁸"What is truth?" Pilate asked. With this he went out again to the Jews and said, "I find no basis for a charge against him. ³⁹But it is your custom for me to release to you one prisoner at the time of the Passover. Do you want me to release 'the king of the Jews'?"

⁴⁰They shouted back, "No, not him! Give us Barabbas!" Now Barabbas had taken part in a rebellion.

a24 Or *(Now Annas had sent him, still bound, to Caiaphas the high priest.)*

POINT OF INTEREST

John 18:38

In one of his last concerts, the late hard-rock musician Jimi Hendrix asked his audience this very same question. No one could answer him. People of the twentieth century are engulfed in a philosophical vacuum resulting from a world without absolutes. Now many of us are more like Pontius Pilate than we care to admit.

Jesus Sentenced to Be Crucified

See Matthew 27:27–31; Mark 15:16–20

19 Then Pilate took Jesus and had him flogged. ²The soldiers twisted together a crown of thorns and put it on his head. They clothed him in a purple robe ³and went up to him again and again, saying, "Hail, king of the Jews!" And they struck him in the face.

⁴Once more Pilate came out and said to the Jews, "Look, I am bringing him out to you to let you know that I find no basis for a charge against him." ⁵When Jesus came out wearing the crown of thorns and the purple robe, Pilate said to them, "Here is the man!"

⁶As soon as the chief priests and their officials saw him, they shouted, "Crucify! Crucify!"

But Pilate answered, "You take him and crucify him. As for me, I find no basis for a charge against him."

⁷The Jews insisted, "We have a law, and according to that law he must die, because he claimed to be the Son of God."

⁸When Pilate heard this, he was even more afraid, ⁹and he went back inside the palace. "Where do you come from?" he asked Jesus, but Jesus gave him no answer. ¹⁰"Do you refuse to speak to me?" Pilate said. "Don't you realize I have power either to free you or to crucify you?"

¹¹Jesus answered, "You would have no power over me if it were not given to you from above. Therefore the one who handed me over to you is guilty of a greater sin."

¹²From then on, Pilate tried to set Jesus free, but the Jews kept shouting, "If you let this man go, you are no friend of Caesar. Anyone who claims to be a king opposes Caesar."

¹³When Pilate heard this, he brought Jesus out and sat down on the judge's seat at a place known as the Stone Pavement (which in Aramaic is Gabbatha). ¹⁴It was the day of Preparation of Passover Week, about the sixth hour.

"Here is your king," Pilate said to the Jews.

¹⁵But they shouted, "Take him away! Take him away! Crucify him!"

"Shall I crucify your king?" Pilate asked.

"We have no king but Caesar," the chief priests answered.

¹⁶Finally Pilate handed him over to them to be crucified.

The Crucifixion

See Matthew 27:33–44; Mark 15:22–32; Luke 23:33–43

So the soldiers took charge of Jesus. ¹⁷Carrying his own cross, he went out to the place of the Skull (which in Aramaic is called Golgotha). ¹⁸Here they crucified him, and with him two others—one on each side and Jesus in the middle.

¹⁹Pilate had a notice prepared and fastened to the cross. It read: JESUS OF NAZARETH, THE KING OF THE JEWS. ²⁰Many of the Jews read this sign, for the place where Jesus was crucified was near the city, and the sign was written in Aramaic, Latin and Greek. ²¹The chief priests of the Jews protested to Pilate, "Do not write 'The King of the Jews,' but that this man claimed to be king of the Jews."

²²Pilate answered, "What I have written, I have written."

²³When the soldiers crucified Jesus, they took his clothes, dividing them into four shares, one for each of them, with the undergarment remaining. This garment was seamless, woven in one piece from top to bottom.

²⁴"Let's not tear it," they said to one another. "Let's decide by lot who will get it."

This happened that the scripture might be fulfilled which said,

"They divided my garments among
them
and cast lots for my clothing." *a*

So this is what the soldiers did.

a24 Psalm 22:18

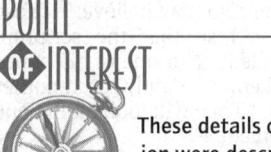

POINT OF INTEREST

John 19:23

These details of the crucifixion were described hundreds of years before the event occurred (see Psalm 22:18). Imagine one of your ancestors describing your death a thousand years before you were even born. The chance of all these circumstances occurring together by accident is absurdly minuscule. Only God could have inspired such prophecy about the life and death of his own Son.

²⁵Near the cross of Jesus stood his mother, his mother's sister, Mary the wife of Clopas, and Mary Magdalene. ²⁶When Jesus saw his mother there, and the disciple whom he loved standing nearby, he said to his mother, "Dear woman, here is your son," ²⁷and to the disciple, "Here is your mother." From that time on, this disciple took her into his home.

The Death of Jesus

See Matthew 27:48,50; Mark 15:36–37; Luke 23:36

²⁸Later, knowing that all was now completed, and so that the Scripture would be fulfilled, Jesus said, "I am thirsty." ²⁹A jar of wine vinegar was there, so they soaked a sponge in it, put the sponge on a stalk of the hyssop plant, and lifted it to Jesus' lips. ³⁰When he had received the drink, Jesus said, "It is finished." With that, he bowed his head and gave up his spirit.

³¹Now it was the day of Preparation, and the next day was to be a special Sabbath. Because the Jews did not want the bodies left on the crosses during the Sabbath, they asked Pilate to have the legs broken and the bodies taken down. ³²The soldiers therefore came and broke the legs of the first man who had been crucified with Jesus, and then those of the other. ³³But when they came to Jesus and found that he was already dead, they did not break his legs. ³⁴Instead, one of the soldiers pierced Jesus' side with a spear, bringing a sudden flow of blood and water. ³⁵The man who saw it has given testimony, and his testimony is true. He knows that he tells the truth, and he testifies so that you also may believe. ³⁶These things happened so that the scripture would be fulfilled: "Not one of his bones will be broken,"ᵃ ³⁷and, as another scripture says, "They will look on the one they have pierced."ᵇ

The Burial of Jesus

See Matthew 27:57–61; Mark 15:42–47; Luke 23:50–56

³⁸Later, Joseph of Arimathea asked Pilate for the body of Jesus. Now Joseph was a disciple of Jesus, but secretly because he feared the Jews. With Pilate's permission, he came and took the body away. ³⁹He was accompanied by Nicodemus, the man who earlier had visited Jesus at night. Nicodemus brought a mixture of myrrh and aloes, about seventy-five pounds.ᶜ ⁴⁰Taking Jesus' body, the two of them wrapped it, with the spices, in strips of linen. This was in accordance with Jewish burial customs. ⁴¹At the place where Jesus was crucified, there was a garden, and in the garden a new tomb, in which no one had ever been laid. ⁴²Because it was the Jewish day of Preparation and since the tomb was nearby, they laid Jesus there.

The Empty Tomb

See Matthew 28:1–8; Mark 16:1–8; Luke 24:1–10

20 Early on the first day of the week, while it was still dark, Mary Magdalene went to the tomb and saw that the stone had been removed from the entrance. ²So she came running to Simon Peter and the other disciple, the one Jesus loved, and said, "They have taken the Lord out of the tomb, and we don't know where they have put him!"

³So Peter and the other disciple started for the tomb. ⁴Both were running, but the other disciple outran Peter and reached the tomb first. ⁵He bent over and looked in at the strips of linen lying there but did not go in. ⁶Then Simon Peter, who was behind him, arrived and went into the tomb. He saw the strips of linen lying there, ⁷as well as the burial cloth that had been around Jesus' head. The cloth was folded up by itself, separate from the linen. ⁸Finally the other disciple, who had reached the tomb first, also went inside. He saw and believed. ⁹(They still did not understand from Scripture that Jesus had to rise from the dead.)

Jesus Appears to Mary Magdalene

¹⁰Then the disciples went back to their homes, ¹¹but Mary stood outside the tomb crying. As she wept, she bent over to look into the tomb ¹²and saw two angels in white, seated where Jesus' body had been, one at the head and the other at the foot.

¹³They asked her, "Woman, why are you crying?"

"They have taken my Lord away," she said, "and I don't know where they have put him." ¹⁴At this, she turned around

---

ᵃ36 Exodus 12:46; Num. 9:12; Psalm 34:20
ᵇ37 Zech. 12:10   ᶜ39 Greek *a hundred litrai* (about 34 kilograms)

Read John 19:1–37
Key Verse John 19:30

Only the Beginning

Jesus' last words from the cross were, "It is finished." What was finished? Certainly it seemed that his life was finished. But what about his ministry? In three years he had only preached the Good News to a few thousand, fed a few thousand, healed a handful. Wasn't there more to be done? He had only traveled a few miles, touched a mere corner of civilization, scratched the surface of human need. How could he say his job was complete?

But Jesus' task *was* complete. With his death, he had finished the work of redeeming humankind. He paid for all the guilt, hostility and alienation that the human race could heap on his shoulders. "For Christ died for sins once for all, the righteous for the unrighteous, to bring you to God" (1 Peter 3:18). With his death, he took away the finality of ours. *It was finished!* In human history there had never been a truer statement.

Digging Into the Word
1. What do the following passages say about the gospel?—
   Matthew 24:14; Mark 1:14–15; 2 Thessalonians 1:5–10
2. What is said in the following passages about Jesus' death?—
   Romans 5:12–19; Hebrews 10:5–14

Personal Reflection
How do you feel when you read each of these statements? (1) Jesus died in your place. You deserve the punishment he suffered. (2) When Jesus was on the cross, he knew you by name. It was love for you that kept him on the cross.

One Step Deeper
John 12:23–28; Titus 2:11–14

Go to page 1211 for your next devotional reading.

and saw Jesus standing there, but she did not realize that it was Jesus.

15"Woman," he said, "why are you crying? Who is it you are looking for?"

Thinking he was the gardener, she said, "Sir, if you have carried him away, tell me where you have put him, and I will get him."

16Jesus said to her, "Mary."

She turned toward him and cried out in Aramaic, "Rabboni!" (which means Teacher).

17Jesus said, "Do not hold on to me, for I have not yet returned to the Father. Go instead to my brothers and tell them, 'I am returning to my Father and your Father, to my God and your God.'"

18Mary Magdalene went to the disciples with the news: "I have seen the Lord!" And she told them that he had said these things to her.

Jesus Appears to His Disciples

19On the evening of that first day of the week, when the disciples were together, with the doors locked for fear of the Jews, Jesus came and stood among them and said, "Peace be with you!" 20After he said this, he showed them his hands and side. The disciples were overjoyed when they saw the Lord.

21Again Jesus said, "Peace be with you! As the Father has sent me, I am sending you." 22And with that he breathed on them and said, "Receive the Holy Spirit. 23If you forgive anyone his sins, they are forgiven; if you do not forgive them, they are not forgiven."

Jesus Appears to Thomas

24Now Thomas (called Didymus), one of the Twelve, was not with the disciples when Jesus came. 25So the other disciples told him, "We have seen the Lord!"

But he said to them, "Unless I see the nail marks in his hands and put my finger where the nails were, and put my hand into his side, I will not believe it."

26A week later his disciples were in the house again, and Thomas was with them. Though the doors were locked, Jesus came and stood among them and said, "Peace be with you!" 27Then he said to Thomas, "Put your finger here; see my hands. Reach out your hand and put it into my side. Stop doubting and believe."

28Thomas said to him, "My Lord and my God!"

29Then Jesus told him, "Because you have seen me, you have believed; blessed are those who have not seen and yet have believed."

30Jesus did many other miraculous signs in the presence of his disciples, which are not recorded in this book. 31But these are written that you maya believe that Jesus is the Christ, the Son of God, and that by believing you may have life in his name.

Jesus and the Miraculous Catch of Fish

21 Afterward Jesus appeared again to his disciples, by the Sea of Tiberias.b It happened this way: 2Simon Peter, Thomas (called Didymus), Nathanael from Cana in Galilee, the sons of Zebedee, and two other disciples were together. 3"I'm going out to fish," Simon Peter told them, and they said, "We'll go with you." So they went out and got into the boat, but that night they caught nothing.

4Early in the morning, Jesus stood on the shore, but the disciples did not realize that it was Jesus.

5He called out to them, "Friends, haven't you any fish?"

"No," they answered.

6He said, "Throw your net on the right side of the boat and you will find some." When they did, they were unable to haul the net in because of the large number of fish.

7Then the disciple whom Jesus loved said to Peter, "It is the Lord!" As soon as Simon Peter heard him say, "It is the Lord," he wrapped his outer garment around him (for he had taken it off) and jumped into the water. 8The other disciples followed in the boat, towing the net full of fish, for they were not far from shore, about a hundred yards.c 9When they landed, they saw a fire of burning coals there with fish on it, and some bread.

10Jesus said to them, "Bring some of the fish you have just caught."

11Simon Peter climbed aboard and dragged the net ashore. It was full of large fish, 153, but even with so many the net was not torn. 12Jesus said to them, "Come and have breakfast." None

---

of the disciples dared ask him, "Who are you?" They knew it was the Lord. [13]Jesus came, took the bread and gave it to them, and did the same with the fish. [14]This was now the third time Jesus appeared to his disciples after he was raised from the dead.

Jesus Reinstates Peter

[15]When they had finished eating, Jesus said to Simon Peter, "Simon son of John, do you truly love me more than these?"

"Yes, Lord," he said, "you know that I love you."

Jesus said, "Feed my lambs."

[16]Again Jesus said, "Simon son of John, do you truly love me?"

He answered, "Yes, Lord, you know that I love you."

Jesus said, "Take care of my sheep."

[17]The third time he said to him, "Simon son of John, do you love me?"

Peter was hurt because Jesus asked him the third time, "Do you love me?" He said, "Lord, you know all things; you know that I love you."

Jesus said, "Feed my sheep. [18]I tell you the truth, when you were younger you dressed yourself and went where you wanted; but when you are old you will stretch out your hands, and someone else will dress you and lead you where you do not want to go." [19]Jesus said this to indicate the kind of death by which Peter would glorify God. Then he said to him, "Follow me!"

[20]Peter turned and saw that the disciple whom Jesus loved was following them. (This was the one who had leaned

---

MONDAY

Read *John 21:1–25*
Key Verses *John 21:15–17*

Free To Meet His Eyes – Lynn Feldner

I've done it again. All it takes is a slip of the tongue or a little burst of pride. When I find myself face to face with an old, familiar sin, I'd rather just ignore it than go to God and ask him to forgive me. I'd rather run away from him.

I often think of Peter and how he must have felt the moment he disowned Jesus for the third time and his eyes met Jesus' eyes across the courtyard. Luke says that "he went outside and wept bitterly" (Luke 22:62). Peter was crushed by his own total lack of loyalty and probably never wanted to look Jesus in the eye again—ever. He must have spent days walking around with his head low and his shoulders slumped.

At the same time, though, I imagine Jesus' eyes were filled with compassion when they met Peter's. Even though Peter's betrayal must have hurt him terribly, he was willing to forgive Peter and give him another chance at friendship and leadership. Jesus led Peter through a process that took away the sting of guilt and let him express his dedication to Jesus once again. Just as Peter had denied Jesus three times, Jesus asked Peter three times if he loved him. Each time Peter responded, "Yes, Lord, you know that I love you."

Jesus' response to Peter was, "Feed my sheep." As far as Jesus was concerned, Peter was healed, forgiven and ready to do God's work. And he was ready to meet Jesus' eyes again.

A Deeper Look
Psalm 103:11–13; Romans 7:21—8:2; 1 John 1:9

Go to page 1214 for your next devotional reading.

back against Jesus at the supper and had said, "Lord, who is going to betray you?") 21When Peter saw him, he asked, "Lord, what about him?"

22Jesus answered, "If I want him to remain alive until I return, what is that to you? You must follow me." 23Because of this, the rumor spread among the brothers that this disciple would not die. But Jesus did not say that he would not die;

he only said, "If I want him to remain alive until I return, what is that to you?"

24This is the disciple who testifies to these things and who wrote them down. We know that his testimony is true.

25Jesus did many other things as well. If every one of them were written down, I suppose that even the whole world would not have room for the books that would be written.

The book of Acts picks up the story of the embryonic church where the Gospel of Luke ends—with Jesus' ascension. In this book the physician Luke compresses a broad range of information about the development of the church after Jesus' ascension. He begins with the centerpiece event: the awe-inspiring descent of the Holy Spirit on the believers assembled at Jerusalem. Luke goes on to narrate the ministries of Peter and Paul and the outreach of the early Christian community. The book of Acts is much more than an historical account—each chapter is illuminated with the power and grace of the Holy Spirit.

ACTS

Jesus Taken Up Into Heaven

1 In my former book, Theophilus, I wrote about all that Jesus began to do and to teach ²until the day he was taken up to heaven, after giving instructions through the Holy Spirit to the apostles he had chosen. ³After his suffering, he showed himself to these men and gave many convincing proofs that he was alive. He appeared to them over a period of forty days and spoke about the kingdom of God. ⁴On one occasion, while he was eating with them, he gave them this command: "Do not leave Jerusalem, but wait for the gift my Father promised, which you have heard me speak about. ⁵For John baptized with*a* water, but in a few days you will be baptized with the Holy Spirit."

⁶So when they met together, they asked him, "Lord, are you at this time going to restore the kingdom to Israel?"

⁷He said to them: "It is not for you to know the times or dates the Father has set by his own authority. ⁸But you will receive power when the Holy Spirit comes on you; and you will be my witnesses in Jerusalem, and in all Judea and Samaria, and to the ends of the earth."

⁹After he said this, he was taken up

a5 Or in

before their very eyes, and a cloud hid him from their sight.

10They were looking intently up into the sky as he was going, when suddenly two men dressed in white stood beside them. 11"Men of Galilee," they said, "why do you stand here looking into the sky? This same Jesus, who has been taken from you into heaven, will come back in the same way you have seen him go into heaven."

Matthias Chosen to Replace Judas

12Then they returned to Jerusalem from the hill called the Mount of Olives, a Sabbath day's walk*a* from the city. 13When they arrived, they went upstairs to the room where they were staying. Those present were Peter, John, James and Andrew; Philip and Thomas, Bartholomew and Matthew; James son of Al-

phaeus and Simon the Zealot, and Judas son of James. 14They all joined together constantly in prayer, along with the women and Mary the mother of Jesus, and with his brothers.

15In those days Peter stood up among the believers*b* (a group numbering about a hundred and twenty) 16and said, "Brothers, the Scripture had to be fulfilled which the Holy Spirit spoke long ago through the mouth of David concerning Judas, who served as guide for those who arrested Jesus— 17he was one of our number and shared in this ministry."

18(With the reward he got for his wickedness, Judas bought a field; there he fell headlong, his body burst open and all his intestines spilled out. 19Everyone in Jerusalem heard about this, so they called

*a*12 That is, about 3/4 mile (about 1,100 meters)
*b*15 Greek *brothers*

Read Acts 1:1–26
Key Verse Acts 1:8

To the Ends of the Earth – Jay Getz

I squeezed out of the old bus and stepped into the cool evening air of the market in Taiwan. Vendors shouted in a language I couldn't understand. Aromas from strange foods hovered around me. It seemed that with each step I bumped into someone bustling by me. I lifted my eyes and looked out over a sea of faces very different from my own.

As my senses were assaulted that night, God drove a clear image into my mind. For the first time, I realized there are people all over the world who have never had the opportunity to hear about him.

God opens our eyes like that. Jesus did it for the disciples with his last words, telling them of the task that awaited them. He said they would be his witnesses "in Jerusalem, and in all Judea and Samaria, and to the ends of the earth." That eye-opener must have seemed overwhelming for the small band of fishermen, tax collectors and tradesmen who had never traveled more than a few miles outside their hometowns.

Today God asks us to look beyond our own comfortable environment, our "Jerusalem"—beyond even our own nation. There are still many who need Jesus Christ. Ask God to open your eyes to those in your own "Jerusalem" who need him and to expand your vision to the "ends of the earth" as well.

A Deeper Look
Isaiah 49:6; Luke 24:45–49

Go to page 1217 for your next devotional reading.

that field in their language Akeldama, that is, Field of Blood.)

²⁰"For," said Peter, "it is written in the book of Psalms,

" 'May his place be deserted;
 let there be no one to dwell in
 it,' ᵃ

and,

" 'May another take his place of
 leadership.' ᵇ

²¹Therefore it is necessary to choose one of the men who have been with us the whole time the Lord Jesus went in and out among us, ²²beginning from John's baptism to the time when Jesus was taken up from us. For one of these must become a witness with us of his resurrection."

²³So they proposed two men: Joseph called Barsabbas (also known as Justus) and Matthias. ²⁴Then they prayed, "Lord, you know everyone's heart. Show us which of these two you have chosen ²⁵to take over this apostolic ministry, which Judas left to go where he belongs." ²⁶Then they cast lots, and the lot fell to Matthias; so he was added to the eleven apostles.

The Holy Spirit Comes at Pentecost

2 When the day of Pentecost came, they were all together in one place. ²Suddenly a sound like the blowing of a violent wind came from heaven and filled the whole house where they were sitting. ³They saw what seemed to be tongues of fire that separated and came to rest on each of them. ⁴All of them were filled with the Holy Spirit and began to speak in other tonguesᶜ as the Spirit enabled them.

⁵Now there were staying in Jerusalem God-fearing Jews from every nation under heaven. ⁶When they heard this sound, a crowd came together in bewilderment, because each one heard them speaking in his own language. ⁷Utterly amazed, they asked: "Are not all these men who are speaking Galileans? ⁸Then how is it that each of us hears them in his own native language? ⁹Parthians, Medes and Elamites; residents of Mesopotamia, Judea and Cappadocia, Pontus and Asia, ¹⁰Phrygia and Pamphylia, Egypt and the parts of Libya near Cyrene; visitors from Rome ¹¹(both Jews and converts to Judaism); Cretans and Arabs—we hear them

declaring the wonders of God in our own tongues!" ¹²Amazed and perplexed, they asked one another, "What does this mean?"

¹³Some, however, made fun of them and said, "They have had too much wine.ᵈ"

Peter Addresses the Crowd

¹⁴Then Peter stood up with the Eleven, raised his voice and addressed the crowd: "Fellow Jews and all of you who live in Jerusalem, let me explain this to you; listen carefully to what I say. ¹⁵These men are not drunk, as you suppose. It's only nine in the morning! ¹⁶No, this is what was spoken by the prophet Joel:

¹⁷" 'In the last days, God says,
 I will pour out my Spirit on all
 people.
Your sons and daughters will
 prophesy,
 your young men will see visions,
 your old men will dream dreams.
¹⁸Even on my servants, both men and
 women,
 I will pour out my Spirit in those
 days,
 and they will prophesy.
¹⁹I will show wonders in the heaven
 above
 and signs on the earth below,
 blood and fire and billows of
 smoke.
²⁰The sun will be turned to darkness
 and the moon to blood
 before the coming of the great and
 glorious day of the Lord.
²¹And everyone who calls

ᵃ20 Psalm 69:25   ᵇ20 Psalm 109:8   ᶜ4 Or
languages; also in verse 11   ᵈ13 Or sweet wine

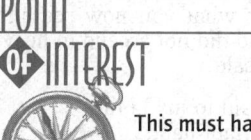

POINT OF INTEREST

Acts 2:4

This must have sounded like the noon rush in the cafeteria at the United Nations building! The "tongues" here were actual languages, supernaturally bestowed on the apostles and recognizable by the people from those individual language groups.

on the name of the Lord will be saved.'*a*

22"Men of Israel, listen to this: Jesus of Nazareth was a man accredited by God to you by miracles, wonders and signs, which God did among you through him, as you yourselves know. 23This man was handed over to you by God's set purpose and foreknowledge; and you, with the help of wicked men,*b* put him to death by nailing him to the cross. 24But God raised him from the dead, freeing him from the agony of death, because it was impossible for death to keep its hold on him. 25David said about him:

" 'I saw the Lord always before me.
    Because he is at my right hand,
    I will not be shaken.
26Therefore my heart is glad and my
        tongue rejoices;
    my body also will live in hope,
27because you will not abandon me to
        the grave,
    nor will you let your Holy One see
        decay.
28You have made known to me the
        paths of life;
    you will fill me with joy in your
        presence.'*c*

29"Brothers, I can tell you confidently that the patriarch David died and was buried, and his tomb is here to this day. 30But he was a prophet and knew that God had promised him on oath that he would place one of his descendants on his throne. 31Seeing what was ahead, he spoke of the resurrection of the Christ,*d* that he was not abandoned to the grave, nor did his body see decay. 32God has raised this Jesus to life, and we are all witnesses of the fact. 33Exalted to the right hand of God, he has received from the Father the promised Holy Spirit and has poured out what you now see and hear. 34For David did not ascend to heaven, and yet he said,

" 'The Lord said to my Lord:
    "Sit at my right hand
35until I make your enemies
    a footstool for your feet." '*e*

36"Therefore let all Israel be assured of this: God has made this Jesus, whom you crucified, both Lord and Christ."

37When the people heard this, they were cut to the heart and said to Peter

and the other apostles, "Brothers, what shall we do?"

38Peter replied, "Repent and be baptized, every one of you, in the name of Jesus Christ for the forgiveness of your sins. And you will receive the gift of the Holy Spirit. 39The promise is for you and your children and for all who are far off—for all whom the Lord our God will call."

40With many other words he warned them; and he pleaded with them, "Save yourselves from this corrupt generation." 41Those who accepted his message were baptized, and about three thousand were added to their number that day.

The Fellowship of the Believers

42They devoted themselves to the apostles' teaching and to the fellowship, to the breaking of bread and to prayer. 43Everyone was filled with awe, and many wonders and miraculous signs were done by the apostles. 44All the believers were together and had everything in common. 45Selling their possessions and goods, they gave to anyone as he had need. 46Every day they continued to meet together in the temple courts. They broke bread in their homes and ate together with glad and sincere hearts, 47praising God and enjoying the favor of all the people. And the Lord added to their number daily those who were being saved.

Peter Heals the Crippled Beggar

3 One day Peter and John were going up to the temple at the time of prayer—at three in the afternoon. 2Now a man crippled from birth was being carried to the temple gate called Beautiful, where he was put every day to beg from those going into the temple courts. 3When he saw Peter and John about to enter, he asked them for money. 4Peter looked straight at him, as did John. Then Peter said, "Look at us!" 5So the man gave them his attention, expecting to get something from them.

6Then Peter said, "Silver or gold I do not have, but what I have I give you. In the name of Jesus Christ of Nazareth, walk." 7Taking him by the right hand, he helped him up, and instantly the man's

---

a21 Joel 2:28-32   *b23* Or *of those not having the law* (that is, Gentiles)   *c28* Psalm 16:8-11
d31 Or *Messiah.* "The Christ" (Greek) and "the Messiah" (Hebrew) both mean "the Anointed One"; also in verse 36.   *e35* Psalm 110:1

feet and ankles became strong. ⁸He jumped to his feet and began to walk. Then he went with them into the temple courts, walking and jumping, and praising God. ⁹When all the people saw him walking and praising God, ¹⁰they recognized him as the same man who used to sit begging at the temple gate called Beautiful, and they were filled with wonder and amazement at what had happened to him.

Peter Speaks to the Onlookers

¹¹While the beggar held on to Peter and John, all the people were astonished and came running to them in the place called Solomon's Colonnade. ¹²When Pe-

ter saw this, he said to them: "Men of Israel, why does this surprise you? Why do you stare at us as if by our own power or godliness we had made this man walk? ¹³The God of Abraham, Isaac and Jacob, the God of our fathers, has glorified his servant Jesus. You handed him over to be killed, and you disowned him before Pilate, though he had decided to let him go. ¹⁴You disowned the Holy and Righteous One and asked that a murderer be released to you. ¹⁵You killed the author of life, but God raised him from the dead. We are witnesses of this. ¹⁶By faith in the name of Jesus, this man whom you see and know was made strong. It is Jesus' name and the faith that comes through

WEDNESDAY

Read Acts 2:1–47
Key Verse Acts 2:42

Friends Forever – Jay Getz

I sat in a circle of close friends, some of whom I hadn't seen for years. We talked and laughed and looked at old photographs, flooded with memories. At Illinois State University, we'd depended on each other as we learned to follow God and share Jesus with others. Now our informal reunion brought us back to the Midwest from states as distant as Arizona and California.

Greg and I had lived in the same dorm. We had eaten and laughed together, sometimes talking for hours. We had studied the Bible and prayed together. Margaret had lived nearby. Her laughter was infectious, and so was her commitment to helping young believers grow in Jesus Christ. Tim and I had been roommates for a year. Between games of backgammon, we prayed for the men on our dorm floor, and God helped us share the Good News of Jesus Christ with most of them. John had been as enthusiastic about encouraging other believers as we both were about Illinois State basketball. Mike had encouraged our friend Chet to grow spiritually as Chet wrestled with difficult family, work and school demands.

God cemented these relationships through the kind of fellowship described in Acts 2:42. Like the early Christian church, we learned, talked, ate and prayed—together. Like the early believers, our love for one another spilled over to the world around us.

Throughout my life, my most meaningful relationships have been with friends like Greg, Margaret, Tim and the rest—believers who have lived out Acts 2:42 with me. There's no substitute for intimate fellowship with a group of believers; and there's no way we can get by without this divine gift—our "forever" friends.

A Deeper Look
Proverbs 27:17; Ecclesiastes 4:7–12

Go to page 1220 for your next devotional reading.

him that has given this complete healing to him, as you can all see.

17"Now, brothers, I know that you acted in ignorance, as did your leaders. 18But this is how God fulfilled what he had foretold through all the prophets, saying that his Christ*a* would suffer. 19Repent, then, and turn to God, so that your sins may be wiped out, that times of refreshing may come from the Lord, 20and that he may send the Christ, who has been appointed for you—even Jesus. 21He must remain in heaven until the time comes for God to restore everything, as he promised long ago through his holy prophets. 22For Moses said, 'The Lord your God will raise up for you a prophet like me from among your own people; you must listen to everything he tells you. 23Anyone who does not listen to him will be completely cut off from among his people.'*b* 24"Indeed, all the prophets from Samuel on, as many as have spoken, have foretold these days. 25And you are heirs of the prophets and of the covenant God made with your fathers. He said to Abraham, 'Through your offspring all peoples on earth will be blessed.'*c* 26When God raised up his servant, he sent him first to you to bless you by turning each of you from your wicked ways."

Peter and John Before the Sanhedrin

4 The priests and the captain of the temple guard and the Sadducees came up to Peter and John while they were speaking to the people. 2They were greatly disturbed because the apostles were teaching the people and proclaiming in Jesus the resurrection of the dead. 3They seized Peter and John, and because it was evening, they put them in jail until the next day. 4But many who heard the message believed, and the number of men grew to about five thousand.

5The next day the rulers, elders and teachers of the law met in Jerusalem. 6Annas the high priest was there, and so were Caiaphas, John, Alexander and the other men of the high priest's family. 7They had Peter and John brought before them and began to question them: "By what power or what name did you do this?"

8Then Peter, filled with the Holy Spirit, said to them: "Rulers and elders of the people! 9If we are being called to account today for an act of kindness shown to a cripple and are asked how he was healed, 10then know this, you and all the people of Israel: It is by the name of Jesus Christ of Nazareth, whom you crucified but whom God raised from the dead, that this man stands before you healed. 11He is

" 'the stone you builders rejected,
    which has become the
    capstone.*d'e*

12Salvation is found in no one else, for there is no other name under heaven given to men by which we must be saved."

13When they saw the courage of Peter and John and realized that they were unschooled, ordinary men, they were astonished and they took note that these men had been with Jesus. 14But since they could see the man who had been healed standing there with them, there was nothing they could say. 15So they ordered them to withdraw from the Sanhedrin and then conferred together. 16"What are we going to do with these men?" they asked. "Everybody living in Jerusalem knows they have done an outstanding miracle, and we cannot deny it. 17But to stop this thing from spreading any further among the people, we must warn these men to speak no longer to anyone in this name."

18Then they called them in again and commanded them not to speak or teach at all in the name of Jesus. 19But Peter and John replied, "Judge for yourselves whether it is right in God's sight to obey you rather than God. 20For we cannot help speaking about what we have seen and heard."

21After further threats they let them go. They could not decide how to punish them, because all the people were praising God for what had happened. 22For the man who was miraculously healed was over forty years old.

The Believers' Prayer

23On their release, Peter and John went back to their own people and reported all that the chief priests and elders had said to them. 24When they heard this, they raised their voices together in prayer to God. "Sovereign Lord," they said, "you made the heaven and the earth and the sea, and everything in them. 25You spoke by the Holy Spirit through

---

*a*18 Or *Messiah*; also in verse 20
*b*23 Deut. 18:15,18,19　　*c*25 Gen. 22:18; 26:4
*d*11 Or *cornerstone*　　*e*11 Psalm 118:22

the mouth of your servant, our father David:

" 'Why do the nations rage
and the peoples plot in vain?
26The kings of the earth take their
stand
and the rulers gather together
against the Lord
and against his Anointed One.*a'b*

27Indeed Herod and Pontius Pilate met together with the Gentiles and the people*c* of Israel in this city to conspire against your holy servant Jesus, whom you anointed. 28They did what your power and will had decided beforehand should happen. 29Now, Lord, consider their threats and enable your servants to speak your word with great boldness. 30Stretch out your hand to heal and perform miraculous signs and wonders through the name of your holy servant Jesus." 31After they prayed, the place where they were meeting was shaken. And they were all filled with the Holy Spirit and spoke the word of God boldly.

The Believers Share Their Possessions

32All the believers were one in heart and mind. No one claimed that any of his possessions was his own, but they shared everything they had. 33With great power the apostles continued to testify to the resurrection of the Lord Jesus, and much grace was upon them all. 34There were no needy persons among them. For from time to time those who owned lands or houses sold them, brought the money from the sales 35and put it at the apostles' feet, and it was distributed to anyone as he had need.

36Joseph, a Levite from Cyprus, whom the apostles called Barnabas (which means Son of Encouragement), 37sold a field he owned and brought the money and put it at the apostles' feet.

Ananias and Sapphira

5 Now a man named Ananias, together with his wife Sapphira, also sold a piece of property. 2With his wife's full knowledge he kept back part of the money for himself, but brought the rest and put it at the apostles' feet.

3Then Peter said, "Ananias, how is it that Satan has so filled your heart that you have lied to the Holy Spirit and have kept for yourself some of the money you received for the land? 4Didn't it belong to you before it was sold? And after it was sold, wasn't the money at your disposal? What made you think of doing such a thing? You have not lied to men but to God."

5When Ananias heard this, he fell down and died. And great fear seized all who heard what had happened. 6Then the young men came forward, wrapped up his body, and carried him out and buried him.

7About three hours later his wife came in, not knowing what had happened. 8Peter asked her, "Tell me, is this the price you and Ananias got for the land?"

"Yes," she said, "that is the price."

9Peter said to her, "How could you agree to test the Spirit of the Lord? Look! The feet of the men who buried your husband are at the door, and they will carry you out also."

10At that moment she fell down at his feet and died. Then the young men came in and, finding her dead, carried her out and buried her beside her husband. 11Great fear seized the whole church and all who heard about these events.

The Apostles Heal Many

12The apostles performed many miraculous signs and wonders among the people. And all the believers used to meet together in Solomon's Colonnade. 13No one else dared join them, even though they were highly regarded by the people. 14Nevertheless, more and more men and women believed in the Lord and were added to their number. 15As a result, people brought the sick into the streets and laid them on beds and mats so that at least Peter's shadow might fall on some of them as he passed by. 16Crowds gathered also from the towns around Jerusalem, bringing their sick and those tormented by evil*d* spirits, and all of them were healed.

The Apostles Persecuted

17Then the high priest and all his associates, who were members of the party of the Sadducees, were filled with jealousy. 18They arrested the apostles and put them in the public jail. 19But during the night an angel of the Lord opened the doors of the jail and brought them out. 20"Go, stand in the temple courts," he

---

a26 That is, Christ or Messiah   *b26* Psalm 2:1,2
c27 The Greek is plural.   *d16* Greek *unclean*

said, "and tell the people the full message of this new life."

21At daybreak they entered the temple courts, as they had been told, and began to teach the people.

When the high priest and his associates arrived, they called together the Sanhedrin—the full assembly of the elders of Israel—and sent to the jail for the apostles. 22But on arriving at the jail, the officers did not find them there. So they went back and reported, 23"We found the jail securely locked, with the guards standing at the doors; but when we opened them, we found no one inside." 24On hearing this report, the captain of the temple guard and the chief priests were puzzled, wondering what would come of this.

25Then someone came and said, "Look! The men you put in jail are standing in the temple courts teaching the people." 26At that, the captain went with his officers and brought the apostles. They did not use force, because they feared that the people would stone them.

27Having brought the apostles, they made them appear before the Sanhedrin to be questioned by the high priest. 28"We gave you strict orders not to teach in this name," he said. "Yet you have filled Jerusalem with your teaching and are determined to make us guilty of this man's blood."

THURSDAY

Read Acts 5:1–42
Key Verse Acts 5:4

Integrity — Julie Bundt

While I was in college I had a part-time job as a student assistant. We had a sheet next to each phone, copy machine and laser printer in our office to record personal calls or copies. Occasionally when I needed to make calls for our campus ministry, I'd use the office phone. I was terrible about recording my calls, often because I just didn't take the time to write them down. Sometimes I'd overestimate a printing job to try to account for my mistakes, but these were halfhearted efforts.

Several times as I was reading the Word in my quiet time, God would remind me that I was shortchanging the office. I kept trying to justify my actions in my mind—you know, "they don't really pay me a fair wage," and "I often use my own pens and paper for office work." In fact, no one else felt guilty about these little things, so I figured my conscience was probably too tender. But finally, the burden of my conscience became too heavy. I gave up my mental gymnastics and agreed with God that I was stealing from the office.

The story of Ananias and Sapphira is a piercing reminder of how seriously God takes this type of sin. When I justified my actions in my mind, I was lying to God. Even if my boss told me it was no big deal, God said it was sin and I needed to repent. So, I followed the Zacchaeus model (see Luke 19:8) and paid back what I thought I owed the office—plus a little more, just in case I was deceiving myself.

After I had made peace with God and made it right with the office, I felt like a load had been lifted off my shoulders—the guilt was gone! I had won this battle for integrity.

A Deeper Look
Luke 16:10–12; Luke 19:1–10; Titus 2:9–10

Go to page 1226 for your next devotional reading.

²⁹Peter and the other apostles replied: "We must obey God rather than men! ³⁰The God of our fathers raised Jesus from the dead—whom you had killed by hanging him on a tree. ³¹God exalted him to his own right hand as Prince and Savior that he might give repentance and forgiveness of sins to Israel. ³²We are witnesses of these things, and so is the Holy Spirit, whom God has given to those who obey him."

³³When they heard this, they were furious and wanted to put them to death. ³⁴But a Pharisee named Gamaliel, a teacher of the law, who was honored by all the people, stood up in the Sanhedrin and ordered that the men be put outside for a little while. ³⁵Then he addressed them: "Men of Israel, consider carefully what you intend to do to these men. ³⁶Some time ago Theudas appeared, claiming to be somebody, and about four hundred men rallied to him. He was killed, all his followers were dispersed, and it all came to nothing. ³⁷After him, Judas the Galilean appeared in the days of the census and led a band of people in revolt. He too was killed, and all his followers were scattered. ³⁸Therefore, in the present case I advise you: Leave these men alone! Let them go! For if their purpose or activity is of human origin, it will fail. ³⁹But if it is from God, you will not be able to stop these men; you will only find yourselves fighting against God."

⁴⁰His speech persuaded them. They called the apostles in and had them flogged. Then they ordered them not to speak in the name of Jesus, and let them go.

⁴¹The apostles left the Sanhedrin, rejoicing because they had been counted worthy of suffering disgrace for the Name. ⁴²Day after day, in the temple courts and from house to house, they never stopped teaching and proclaiming the good news that Jesus is the Christ.*

The Choosing of the Seven

6 In those days when the number of disciples was increasing, the Grecian Jews among them complained against the Hebraic Jews because their widows were being overlooked in the daily distribution of food. ²So the Twelve gathered all the disciples together and said, "It would not be right for us to neglect the ministry of the word of God in order to wait on tables. ³Brothers, choose seven men from among you who are known to be full of the Spirit and wisdom. We will turn this responsibility over to them ⁴and will give our attention to prayer and the ministry of the word."

⁵This proposal pleased the whole group. They chose Stephen, a man full of faith and of the Holy Spirit; also Philip, Procorus, Nicanor, Timon, Parmenas, and Nicolas from Antioch, a convert to Judaism. ⁶They presented these men to the apostles, who prayed and laid their hands on them.

⁷So the word of God spread. The number of disciples in Jerusalem increased rapidly, and a large number of priests became obedient to the faith.

Stephen Seized

⁸Now Stephen, a man full of God's grace and power, did great wonders and miraculous signs among the people. ⁹Opposition arose, however, from members of the Synagogue of the Freedmen (as it was called)—Jews of Cyrene and Alexandria as well as the provinces of Cilicia and Asia. These men began to argue with Stephen, ¹⁰but they could not stand up against his wisdom or the Spirit by whom he spoke.

¹¹Then they secretly persuaded some men to say, "We have heard Stephen speak words of blasphemy against Moses and against God."

¹²So they stirred up the people and the elders and the teachers of the law. They seized Stephen and brought him before the Sanhedrin. ¹³They produced false witnesses, who testified, "This fellow never stops speaking against this holy place and against the law. ¹⁴For we have heard him say that this Jesus of Nazareth will destroy this place and change the customs Moses handed down to us."

¹⁵All who were sitting in the Sanhedrin looked intently at Stephen, and they saw that his face was like the face of an angel.

Stephen's Speech to the Sanhedrin

7 Then the high priest asked him, "Are these charges true?"

²To this he replied: "Brothers and fathers, listen to me! The God of glory appeared to our father Abraham while he was still in Mesopotamia, before he lived in Haran. ³'Leave your country and your

*42 Or Messiah

people,' God said, 'and go to the land I will show you.'a

4"So he left the land of the Chaldeans and settled in Haran. After the death of his father, God sent him to this land where you are now living. 5He gave him no inheritance here, not even a foot of ground. But God promised him that he and his descendants after him would possess the land, even though at that time Abraham had no child. 6God spoke to him in this way: 'Your descendants will be strangers in a country not their own, and they will be enslaved and mistreated four hundred years. 7But I will punish the nation they serve as slaves,' God said, 'and afterward they will come out of that country and worship me in this place.'b 8Then he gave Abraham the covenant of circumcision. And Abraham became the father of Isaac and circumcised him eight days after his birth. Later Isaac became the father of Jacob, and Jacob became the father of the twelve patriarchs.

9"Because the patriarchs were jealous of Joseph, they sold him as a slave into Egypt. But God was with him 10and rescued him from all his troubles. He gave Joseph wisdom and enabled him to gain the goodwill of Pharaoh king of Egypt; so he made him ruler over Egypt and all his palace.

11"Then a famine struck all Egypt and Canaan, bringing great suffering, and our fathers could not find food. 12When Jacob heard that there was grain in Egypt, he sent our fathers on their first visit. 13On their second visit, Joseph told his brothers who he was, and Pharaoh learned about Joseph's family. 14After this, Joseph sent for his father Jacob and his whole family, seventy-five in all. 15Then Jacob went down to Egypt, where he and our fathers died. 16Their bodies were brought back to Shechem and placed in the tomb that Abraham had bought from the sons of Hamor at Shechem for a certain sum of money.

17"As the time drew near for God to fulfill his promise to Abraham, the number of our people in Egypt greatly increased. 18Then another king, who knew nothing about Joseph, became ruler of Egypt. 19He dealt treacherously with our people and oppressed our forefathers by forcing them to throw out their newborn babies so that they would die.

20"At that time Moses was born, and he was no ordinary child.c For three months he was cared for in his father's house. 21When he was placed outside, Pharaoh's daughter took him and brought him up as her own son. 22Moses was educated in all the wisdom of the Egyptians and was powerful in speech and action.

23"When Moses was forty years old, he decided to visit his fellow Israelites. 24He saw one of them being mistreated by an Egyptian, so he went to his defense and avenged him by killing the Egyptian. 25Moses thought that his own people would realize that God was using him to rescue them, but they did not. 26The next day Moses came upon two Israelites who were fighting. He tried to reconcile them by saying, 'Men, you are brothers; why do you want to hurt each other?'

27"But the man who was mistreating the other pushed Moses aside and said, 'Who made you ruler and judge over us? 28Do you want to kill me as you killed the Egyptian yesterday?'d 29When Moses heard this, he fled to Midian, where he settled as a foreigner and had two sons.

30"After forty years had passed, an angel appeared to Moses in the flames of a burning bush in the desert near Mount Sinai. 31When he saw this, he was amazed at the sight. As he went over to look more closely, he heard the Lord's voice: 32'I am the God of your fathers, the God of Abraham, Isaac and Jacob.'e Moses trembled with fear and did not dare to look.

33"Then the Lord said to him, 'Take off your sandals; the place where you are standing is holy ground. 34I have indeed seen the oppression of my people in Egypt. I have heard their groaning and have come down to set them free. Now come, I will send you back to Egypt.'f 35"This is the same Moses whom they had rejected with the words, 'Who made you ruler and judge?' He was sent to be their ruler and deliverer by God himself, through the angel who appeared to him in the bush. 36He led them out of Egypt and did wonders and miraculous signs in Egypt, at the Red Seag and for forty years in the desert.

37"This is that Moses who told the Israelites, 'God will send you a prophet like me from your own people.'h 38He was in

a3 Gen. 12:1   b7 Gen. 15:13,14   c20 Or was fair in the sight of God   d28 Exodus 2:14 e32 Exodus 3:6   f34 Exodus 3:5,7,8,10 g36 That is, Sea of Reeds   h37 Deut. 18:15

the assembly in the desert, with the angel who spoke to him on Mount Sinai, and with our fathers; and he received living words to pass on to us. [39]"But our fathers refused to obey him. Instead, they rejected him and in their hearts turned back to Egypt. [40]They told Aaron, 'Make us gods who will go before us. As for this fellow Moses who led us out of Egypt—we don't know what has happened to him!'[a] [41]That was the time they made an idol in the form of a calf. They brought sacrifices to it and held a celebration in honor of what their hands had made. [42]But God turned away and gave them over to the worship of the heavenly bodies. This agrees with what is written in the book of the prophets:

" 'Did you bring me sacrifices and offerings
    forty years in the desert, O house of Israel?
[43]You have lifted up the shrine of Molech
    and the star of your god Rephan,
    the idols you made to worship.
Therefore I will send you into exile'[b]
    beyond Babylon.

[44]"Our forefathers had the tabernacle of the Testimony with them in the desert. It had been made as God directed Moses, according to the pattern he had seen. [45]Having received the tabernacle, our fathers under Joshua brought it with them when they took the land from the nations God drove out before them. It remained in the land until the time of David, [46]who enjoyed God's favor and asked that he might provide a dwelling place for the God of Jacob.[c] [47]But it was Solomon who built the house for him.

[48]"However, the Most High does not live in houses made by men. As the prophet says:

[49]" 'Heaven is my throne,
    and the earth is my footstool.
What kind of house will you build for me?
    says the Lord.
Or where will my resting place be?
[50]Has not my hand made all these things?'[d]

[51]"You stiff-necked people, with un-circumcised hearts and ears! You are just like your fathers: You always resist the Holy Spirit! [52]Was there ever a prophet your fathers did not persecute? They even killed those who predicted the coming of the Righteous One. And now you have betrayed and murdered him—[53]you who have received the law that was put into effect through angels but have not obeyed it."

The Stoning of Stephen

[54]When they heard this, they were furious and gnashed their teeth at him. [55]But Stephen, full of the Holy Spirit, looked up to heaven and saw the glory of God, and Jesus standing at the right hand of God. [56]"Look," he said, "I see heaven open and the Son of Man standing at the right hand of God."

[57]At this they covered their ears and, yelling at the top of their voices, they all rushed at him, [58]dragged him out of the city and began to stone him. Meanwhile, the witnesses laid their clothes at the feet of a young man named Saul.

[59]While they were stoning him, Stephen prayed, "Lord Jesus, receive my spirit." [60]Then he fell on his knees and cried out, "Lord, do not hold this sin against them." When he had said this, he fell asleep.

8 And Saul was there, giving approval to his death.

[a]40 Exodus 32:1   [b]43 Amos 5:25-27
[c]46 Some early manuscripts *the house of Jacob*
[d]50 Isaiah 66:1,2

POINT OF INTEREST   Acts 7:54-60

In order to hurl stones the size of bricks or cobblestones with enough force to injure, the mob had to stand close enough for Stephen to recognize them and look them in the eyes. How would you have felt if you had been one of the stone throwers, standing close enough to hear Stephen's final words? Saul, later called Paul, was there, "giving approval" to this brutal business. He later expressed his remorse over his persecution of the early church (1 Corinthians 15:9). Surely this was one regrettable episode that must have stood out in his memory.

The Church Persecuted and Scattered

On that day a great persecution broke out against the church at Jerusalem, and all except the apostles were scattered throughout Judea and Samaria. ²Godly men buried Stephen and mourned deeply for him. ³But Saul began to destroy the church. Going from house to house, he dragged off men and women and put them in prison.

Philip in Samaria

⁴Those who had been scattered preached the word wherever they went. ⁵Philip went down to a city in Samaria and proclaimed the Christ*a* there. ⁶When the crowds heard Philip and saw the miraculous signs he did, they all paid close attention to what he said. ⁷With shrieks, evil*b* spirits came out of many, and many paralytics and cripples were healed. ⁸So there was great joy in that city.

Simon the Sorcerer

⁹Now for some time a man named Simon had practiced sorcery in the city and amazed all the people of Samaria. He boasted that he was someone great, ¹⁰and all the people, both high and low, gave him their attention and exclaimed, "This man is the divine power known as the Great Power." ¹¹They followed him because he had amazed them for a long time with his magic. ¹²But when they believed Philip as he preached the good news of the kingdom of God and the name of Jesus Christ, they were baptized, both men and women. ¹³Simon himself believed and was baptized. And he followed Philip everywhere, astonished by the great signs and miracles he saw.

¹⁴When the apostles in Jerusalem heard that Samaria had accepted the word of God, they sent Peter and John to them. ¹⁵When they arrived, they prayed for them that they might receive the Holy Spirit, ¹⁶because the Holy Spirit had not yet come upon any of them; they had simply been baptized into*c* the name of the Lord Jesus. ¹⁷Then Peter and John placed their hands on them, and they received the Holy Spirit.

¹⁸When Simon saw that the Spirit was given at the laying on of the apostles' hands, he offered them money ¹⁹and said, "Give me also this ability so that everyone on whom I lay my hands may receive the Holy Spirit."

²⁰Peter answered: "May your money perish with you, because you thought you could buy the gift of God with money! ²¹You have no part or share in this ministry, because your heart is not right before God. ²²Repent of this wickedness and pray to the Lord. Perhaps he will forgive you for having such a thought in your heart. ²³For I see that you are full of bitterness and captive to sin."

²⁴Then Simon answered, "Pray to the Lord for me so that nothing you have said may happen to me."

²⁵When they had testified and proclaimed the word of the Lord, Peter and John returned to Jerusalem, preaching the gospel in many Samaritan villages.

Philip and the Ethiopian

²⁶Now an angel of the Lord said to Philip, "Go south to the road—the desert road—that goes down from Jerusalem to Gaza." ²⁷So he started out, and on his way he met an Ethiopian*d* eunuch, an important official in charge of all the treasury of Candace, queen of the Ethiopians. This man had gone to Jerusalem to worship, ²⁸and on his way home was sitting in his chariot reading the book of Isaiah the prophet. ²⁹The Spirit told Philip, "Go to that chariot and stay near it."

³⁰Then Philip ran up to the chariot and heard the man reading Isaiah the prophet. "Do you understand what you are reading?" Philip asked.

³¹"How can I," he said, "unless someone explains it to me?" So he invited Philip to come up and sit with him.

³²The eunuch was reading this passage of Scripture:

"He was led like a sheep to the
      slaughter,
   and as a lamb before the shearer is
      silent,
   so he did not open his mouth.
³³In his humiliation he was deprived of
      justice.
   Who can speak of his descendants?
   For his life was taken from the
      earth."*e*

³⁴The eunuch asked Philip, "Tell me, please, who is the prophet talking about, himself or someone else?" ³⁵Then Philip

a5 Or *Messiah*   *b7* Greek *unclean*   *c16* Or *in*
d27 That is, from the upper Nile region
e33 Isaiah 53:7,8

began with that very passage of Scripture and told him the good news about Jesus.

³⁶As they traveled along the road, they came to some water and the eunuch said, "Look, here is water. Why shouldn't I be baptized?"ᵃ ³⁸And he gave orders to stop the chariot. Then both Philip and the eunuch went down into the water and Philip baptized him. ³⁹When they came up out of the water, the Spirit of the Lord suddenly took Philip away, and the eunuch did not see him again, but went on his way rejoicing. ⁴⁰Philip, however, appeared at Azotus and traveled about, preaching the gospel in all the towns until he reached Caesarea.

Saul's Conversion

9 Meanwhile, Saul was still breathing out murderous threats against the Lord's disciples. He went to the high priest ²and asked him for letters to the synagogues in Damascus, so that if he found any there who belonged to the Way, whether men or women, he might take them as prisoners to Jerusalem. ³As he neared Damascus on his journey, suddenly a light from heaven flashed around him. ⁴He fell to the ground and heard a voice say to him, "Saul, Saul, why do you persecute me?"

⁵"Who are you, Lord?" Saul asked.

"I am Jesus, whom you are persecuting," he replied. ⁶"Now get up and go into the city, and you will be told what you must do."

⁷The men traveling with Saul stood there speechless; they heard the sound but did not see anyone. ⁸Saul got up from the ground, but when he opened his eyes he could see nothing. So they led him by the hand into Damascus. ⁹For three days he was blind, and did not eat or drink anything.

¹⁰In Damascus there was a disciple named Ananias. The Lord called to him in a vision, "Ananias!"

"Yes, Lord," he answered.

¹¹The Lord told him, "Go to the house of Judas on Straight Street and ask for a man from Tarsus named Saul, for he is praying. ¹²In a vision he has seen a man named Ananias come and place his hands on him to restore his sight."

¹³"Lord," Ananias answered, "I have heard many reports about this man and all the harm he has done to your saints in Jerusalem. ¹⁴And he has come here with

authority from the chief priests to arrest all who call on your name."

¹⁵But the Lord said to Ananias, "Go! This man is my chosen instrument to carry my name before the Gentiles and their kings and before the people of Israel. ¹⁶I will show him how much he must suffer for my name."

¹⁷Then Ananias went to the house and entered it. Placing his hands on Saul, he said, "Brother Saul, the Lord—Jesus, who appeared to you on the road as you were coming here—has sent me so that you may see again and be filled with the Holy Spirit." ¹⁸Immediately, something like scales fell from Saul's eyes, and he could see again. He got up and was baptized, ¹⁹and after taking some food, he regained his strength.

Saul in Damascus and Jerusalem

Saul spent several days with the disciples in Damascus. ²⁰At once he began to preach in the synagogues that Jesus is the Son of God. ²¹All those who heard him were astonished and asked, "Isn't he the man who raised havoc in Jerusalem among those who call on this name? And hasn't he come here to take them as prisoners to the chief priests?" ²²Yet Saul grew more and more powerful and baffled the Jews living in Damascus by proving that Jesus is the Christ.ᵇ

²³After many days had gone by, the Jews conspired to kill him, ²⁴but Saul learned of their plan. Day and night they kept close watch on the city gates in order to kill him. ²⁵But his followers took him by night and lowered him in a basket through an opening in the wall.

²⁶When he came to Jerusalem, he tried to join the disciples, but they were all afraid of him, not believing that he really was a disciple. ²⁷But Barnabas took him and brought him to the apostles. He told them how Saul on his journey had seen the Lord and that the Lord had spoken to him, and how in Damascus he had preached fearlessly in the name of Jesus. ²⁸So Saul stayed with them and moved about freely in Jerusalem, speaking boldly in the name of the Lord. ²⁹He talked and debated with the Grecian Jews, but they tried to kill him. ³⁰When the broth-

---

ᵃ36 Some late manuscripts *baptized?" ³⁷Philip said, "If you believe with all your heart, you may." The eunuch answered, "I believe that Jesus Christ is the Son of God."* ᵇ22 Or *Messiah* ers learned of this, they took him down to Caesarea and sent him off to Tarsus.

[31] Then the church throughout Judea, Galilee and Samaria enjoyed a time of peace. It was strengthened; and encouraged by the Holy Spirit, it grew in numbers, living in the fear of the Lord.

Aeneas and Dorcas

[32] As Peter traveled about the country, he went to visit the saints in Lydda. [33] There he found a man named Aeneas, a paralytic who had been bedridden for eight years. [34] "Aeneas," Peter said to him, "Jesus Christ heals you. Get up and take care of your mat." Immediately Ae-

neas got up. [35] All those who lived in Lydda and Sharon saw him and turned to the Lord.

[36] In Joppa there was a disciple named Tabitha (which, when translated, is Dorcas[a]), who was always doing good and helping the poor. [37] About that time she became sick and died, and her body was washed and placed in an upstairs room. [38] Lydda was near Joppa; so when the disciples heard that Peter was in Lydda, they sent two men to him and urged him, "Please come at once!"

[a] 36 Both Tabitha (Aramaic) and Dorcas (Greek) mean gazelle.

FRIDAY

Read Acts 9:1–31
Key Verses Acts 9:10–17

Even When It Doesn't Make Sense — Roger Hamilton

I've often wondered where Ananias placed his hands on Saul of Tarsus when he visited the brand-new believer. Surely he had good reason to grab him by the throat and squeeze. After all, Saul had been responsible for much of the persecution of the believers in Jerusalem and had been intent on continuing his destructive work in Damascus.

Ananias was not at all excited about the task God had given him. He even tried to help God get his facts straight by telling him who this Saul of Tarsus really was. Even though it didn't make sense to him, he obeyed God and went to meet Saul. Even though it was the last thing on earth he wanted to do, he carried out his assignment with a beautiful expression of Jesus Christ's love (see Acts 9:17; see also Luke 4:40).

I have a hunch that the words "Brother Saul" were accompanied by a pair of gentle, compassionate hands, one on Saul's head and perhaps the other on his shoulder. Rather than venting his anger on this enemy of the faith, Ananias welcomed a blind and confused man into the family of believers, affirmed him in his new faith and opened his blind eyes.

When God calls me to do something that doesn't make sense, I find it more natural to rationalize it away and do my own thing, or else to obey him on my own terms. I'm glad that Ananias had the courage to obey God, even when he had his doubts. As a result, he played a crucial role in the transformation of Saul of Tarsus, the man who had tried to destroy the church, into the apostle Paul, the man who would turn the world upside down by boldly proclaiming the gospel of Jesus Christ.

A Deeper Look
Genesis 22:2–3; Jonah 3:1–3,10; 2 John 6

Go to page 1229 for your next devotional reading.

39Peter went with them, and when he arrived he was taken upstairs to the room. All the widows stood around him, crying and showing him the robes and other clothing that Dorcas had made while she was still with them.

40Peter sent them all out of the room; then he got down on his knees and prayed. Turning toward the dead woman, he said, "Tabitha, get up." She opened her eyes, and seeing Peter she sat up. **41**He took her by the hand and helped her to her feet. Then he called the believers and the widows and presented her to them alive. **42**This became known all over Joppa, and many people believed in the Lord. **43**Peter stayed in Joppa for some time with a tanner named Simon.

Cornelius Calls for Peter

10 At Caesarea there was a man named Cornelius, a centurion in what was known as the Italian Regiment. **2**He and all his family were devout and God-fearing; he gave generously to those in need and prayed to God regularly. **3**One day at about three in the afternoon he had a vision. He distinctly saw an angel of God, who came to him and said, "Cornelius!"

4Cornelius stared at him in fear. "What is it, Lord?" he asked.

The angel answered, "Your prayers and gifts to the poor have come up as a memorial offering before God. **5**Now send men to Joppa to bring back a man named Simon who is called Peter. **6**He is staying with Simon the tanner, whose house is by the sea."

7When the angel who spoke to him had gone, Cornelius called two of his servants and a devout soldier who was one of his attendants. **8**He told them everything that had happened and sent them to Joppa.

Peter's Vision

9About noon the following day as they were on their journey and approaching the city, Peter went up on the roof to pray. **10**He became hungry and wanted something to eat, and while the meal was being prepared, he fell into a trance. **11**He saw heaven opened and something like a large sheet being let down to earth by its four corners. **12**It contained all kinds of four-footed animals, as well as reptiles of the earth and birds of the air. **13**Then a voice told him, "Get up, Peter. Kill and eat."

14"Surely not, Lord!" Peter replied. "I have never eaten anything impure or unclean."

15The voice spoke to him a second time, "Do not call anything impure that God has made clean."

16This happened three times, and immediately the sheet was taken back to heaven.

17While Peter was wondering about the meaning of the vision, the men sent by Cornelius found out where Simon's house was and stopped at the gate. **18**They called out, asking if Simon who was known as Peter was staying there.

19While Peter was still thinking about the vision, the Spirit said to him, "Simon, three*a* men are looking for you. **20**So get up and go downstairs. Do not hesitate to go with them, for I have sent them."

21Peter went down and said to the men, "I'm the one you're looking for. Why have you come?"

22The men replied, "We have come from Cornelius the centurion. He is a righteous and God-fearing man, who is respected by all the Jewish people. A holy angel told him to have you come to his house so that he could hear what you have to say." **23**Then Peter invited the men into the house to be his guests.

Peter at Cornelius' House

The next day Peter started out with them, and some of the brothers from Joppa went along. **24**The following day he arrived in Caesarea. Cornelius was expecting them and had called together his relatives and close friends. **25**As Peter entered the house, Cornelius met him and fell at his feet in reverence. **26**But Peter made him get up. "Stand up," he said, "I am only a man myself."

27Talking with him, Peter went inside and found a large gathering of people. **28**He said to them: "You are well aware that it is against our law for a Jew to associate with a Gentile or visit him. But God has shown me that I should not call any man impure or unclean. **29**So when I was sent for, I came without raising any objection. May I ask why you sent for me?"

a19 One early manuscript *two;* other manuscripts do not have the number.

30Cornelius answered: "Four days ago I was in my house praying at this hour, at three in the afternoon. Suddenly a man in shining clothes stood before me 31and said, 'Cornelius, God has heard your prayer and remembered your gifts to the poor. 32Send to Joppa for Simon who is called Peter. He is a guest in the home of Simon the tanner, who lives by the sea.' 33So I sent for you immediately, and it was good of you to come. Now we are all here in the presence of God to listen to everything the Lord has commanded you to tell us."

34Then Peter began to speak: "I now realize how true it is that God does not show favoritism 35but accepts men from every nation who fear him and do what is right. 36You know the message God sent to the people of Israel, telling the good news of peace through Jesus Christ, who is Lord of all. 37You know what has happened throughout Judea, beginning in Galilee after the baptism that John preached— 38how God anointed Jesus of Nazareth with the Holy Spirit and power, and how he went around doing good and healing all who were under the power of the devil, because God was with him.

39"We are witnesses of everything he did in the country of the Jews and in Jerusalem. They killed him by hanging him on a tree, 40but God raised him from the dead on the third day and caused him to be seen. 41He was not seen by all the people, but by witnesses whom God had already chosen—by us who ate and drank with him after he rose from the dead. 42He commanded us to preach to the people and to testify that he is the one whom God appointed as judge of the living and the dead. 43All the prophets testify about him that everyone who believes in him receives forgiveness of sins through his name."

44While Peter was still speaking these words, the Holy Spirit came on all who heard the message. 45The circumcised believers who had come with Peter were astonished that the gift of the Holy Spirit had been poured out even on the Gentiles. 46For they heard them speaking in tongues[a] and praising God.

Then Peter said, 47"Can anyone keep these people from being baptized with water? They have received the Holy Spirit just as we have." 48So he ordered that they be baptized in the name of Jesus Christ. Then they asked Peter to stay with them for a few days.

Peter Explains His Actions

11 The apostles and the brothers throughout Judea heard that the Gentiles also had received the word of God. 2So when Peter went up to Jerusalem, the circumcised believers criticized him 3and said, "You went into the house of uncircumcised men and ate with them."

4Peter began and explained everything to them precisely as it had happened: 5"I was in the city of Joppa praying, and in a trance I saw a vision. I saw something like a large sheet being let down from heaven by its four corners, and it came down to where I was. 6I looked into it and saw four-footed animals of the earth, wild beasts, reptiles, and birds of the air. 7Then I heard a voice telling me, 'Get up, Peter. Kill and eat.'

8"I replied, 'Surely not, Lord! Nothing impure or unclean has ever entered my mouth.'

9"The voice spoke from heaven a second time, 'Do not call anything impure that God has made clean.' 10This happened three times, and then it was all pulled up to heaven again.

11"Right then three men who had been sent to me from Caesarea stopped at the house where I was staying. 12The Spirit told me to have no hesitation about going with them. These six brothers also went with me, and we entered the man's house. 13He told us how he had seen an

a46 Or other languages

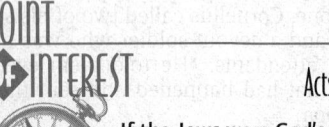

POINT OF INTEREST

Acts 10:28

If the Jews were God's chosen people, why would he be concerned with the Gentiles? The early Christians held this attitude for quite some time before they understood that the Good News was for everyone, Jew and Gentile alike. But it would have been as difficult for them to picture this reality as it is for us to imagine a toddler writing a thesis on quantum theory. Earth-shattering news, wouldn't you say?

Read Acts 10:1–48
Key Verses Acts 10:34–35

No More Playing Favorites

Peter's Jewish background had taught him that Gentiles (non-Jewish people) were unclean. In his mind, all Gentiles were unacceptable to God and should be avoided scrupulously. Cornelius was a Gentile who wanted to follow Jesus, but Peter was skeptical. God had to persuade Peter with visions and heavenly voices before he finally got the point—no more playing favorites!

In the same way that Jesus Christ broke down the barriers between Jews and Gentiles, he supersedes human barriers among nations, races, classes and genders (see Galatians 3:28). God loves and accepts equally everyone who comes to him. As his ambassadors we are called to model that same love and acceptance . . . no more playing favorites!

Digging Into the Word
1. How does God's love for the world challenge you to love others?—*John 3:16; Titus 2:11; 1 John 2:2*
2. How does God call us to love and accept others?—*1 Timothy 5:21; James 2:1,9*

Action Challenge
We all tend to build walls of prejudice. Identify one prejudice you hold in your heart and commit yourself to reach out to a person in this particular group. How can you reach across the barriers you have in your heart and seek to show the love of Jesus to that person?

One Step Deeper
Leviticus 19:15; 1 John 4:13–21

Go to page 1231 for your next devotional reading.

angel appear in his house and say, 'Send to Joppa for Simon who is called Peter. ¹⁴He will bring you a message through which you and all your household will be saved.'

¹⁵"As I began to speak, the Holy Spirit came on them as he had come on us at the beginning. ¹⁶Then I remembered what the Lord had said: 'John baptized with*ᵃ* water, but you will be baptized with the Holy Spirit.' ¹⁷So if God gave them the same gift as he gave us, who believed in the Lord Jesus Christ, who was I to think that I could oppose God?"

¹⁸When they heard this, they had no further objections and praised God, saying, "So then, God has granted even the Gentiles repentance unto life."

The Church in Antioch

¹⁹Now those who had been scattered by the persecution in connection with Stephen traveled as far as Phoenicia, Cyprus and Antioch, telling the message only to Jews. ²⁰Some of them, however, men from Cyprus and Cyrene, went to Antioch and began to speak to Greeks also, telling them the good news about the Lord Jesus. ²¹The Lord's hand was with them, and a great number of people believed and turned to the Lord.

²²News of this reached the ears of the church at Jerusalem, and they sent Barnabas to Antioch. ²³When he arrived and saw the evidence of the grace of God, he was glad and encouraged them all to remain true to the Lord with all their hearts. ²⁴He was a good man, full of the Holy Spirit and faith, and a great number of people were brought to the Lord.

²⁵Then Barnabas went to Tarsus to look for Saul, ²⁶and when he found him, he brought him to Antioch. So for a whole year Barnabas and Saul met with the church and taught great numbers of people. The disciples were called Christians first at Antioch.

²⁷During this time some prophets came down from Jerusalem to Antioch. ²⁸One of them, named Agabus, stood up and through the Spirit predicted that a severe famine would spread over the entire Roman world. (This happened during the reign of Claudius.) ²⁹The disciples, each according to his ability, decided to provide help for the brothers living in Judea. ³⁰This they did, sending their gift to the elders by Barnabas and Saul.

Peter's Miraculous Escape From Prison

12 It was about this time that King Herod arrested some who belonged to the church, intending to persecute them. ²He had James, the brother of John, put to death with the sword. ³When he saw that this pleased the Jews, he proceeded to seize Peter also. This happened during the Feast of Unleavened Bread. ⁴After arresting him, he put him in prison, handing him over to be guarded by four squads of four soldiers each. Herod intended to bring him out for public trial after the Passover.

⁵So Peter was kept in prison, but the church was earnestly praying to God for him.

⁶The night before Herod was to bring him to trial, Peter was sleeping between two soldiers, bound with two chains, and sentries stood guard at the entrance. ⁷Suddenly an angel of the Lord appeared and a light shone in the cell. He struck Peter on the side and woke him up. "Quick, get up!" he said, and the chains fell off Peter's wrists.

⁸Then the angel said to him, "Put on your clothes and sandals." And Peter did so. "Wrap your cloak around you and follow me," the angel told him. ⁹Peter followed him out of the prison, but he had no idea that what the angel was doing was really happening; he thought he was seeing a vision. ¹⁰They passed the first and second guards and came to the iron gate leading to the city. It opened for them by itself, and they went through it. When they had walked the length of one street, suddenly the angel left him.

¹¹Then Peter came to himself and said, "Now I know without a doubt that the Lord sent his angel and rescued me from Herod's clutches and from everything the Jewish people were anticipating."

¹²When this had dawned on him, he went to the house of Mary the mother of John, also called Mark, where many people had gathered and were praying. ¹³Peter knocked at the outer entrance, and a servant girl named Rhoda came to answer the door. ¹⁴When she recognized Peter's voice, she was so overjoyed she ran back without opening it and exclaimed, "Peter is at the door!"

¹⁵"You're out of your mind," they told

ᵃ16 Or in

her. When she kept insisting that it was so, they said, "It must be his angel."

16But Peter kept on knocking, and when they opened the door and saw him, they were astonished. 17Peter motioned with his hand for them to be quiet and described how the Lord had brought him out of prison. "Tell James and the brothers about this," he said, and then he left for another place.

18In the morning, there was no small commotion among the soldiers as to what had become of Peter. 19After Herod had a thorough search made for him and did not find him, he cross-examined the guards and ordered that they be executed.

Herod's Death

Then Herod went from Judea to Caesarea and stayed there a while. 20He had been quarreling with the people of Tyre and Sidon; they now joined together and sought an audience with him. Having secured the support of Blastus, a trusted personal servant of the king, they asked for peace, because they depended on the king's country for their food supply.

MONDAY

Read *Acts 11:1–30*
Key Verses *Acts 11:22–26*

Wanted: Spiritual Parents — Kirt Conroy

Cindy became a Christian her sophomore year of college and experienced radical changes in her values and lifestyle. She bubbled with excitement as she told her friends and suitemates about what Jesus had done in her life, and what he could do in theirs. By the end of her senior year, however, Cindy had slipped back into her old lifestyle and was no longer following Jesus.

Why is it that so many people who eagerly and enthusiastically accept Jesus don't "make it" over the long stretch? Perhaps there are some who, though they seem eager, never possess a sincere faith, while others just fail to thrive.

First Peter 2:2 gives some insight into why this happens. Peter compares young Christians to "newborn babies" who need to be fed with "pure spiritual milk." Think about it. New Christians are like babies—spiritually speaking. They need someone to feed, nurture and love them. No one gives birth to a baby and then leaves her to feed and care for herself. Yet so often Christians help someone begin a relationship with Jesus Christ but fail to follow up with that person, seeing that they get the proper nourishment from the Word, that they become part of a vital Christian "family," spending time with them and giving them guidance and attention.

Paul and Barnabas understood this principle. When Barnabas got to Antioch, he encouraged the Christians to continue following the Lord, and then he went and found Paul. Together they went back to Antioch and stayed there for an entire year to teach and encourage these "baby" Christians.

We are often called to be someone's Paul or Barnabas. It's a big responsibility to help someone to mature in Jesus Christ. It involves teaching not only with words but also with our lives. It's an investment that pays eternal dividends.

A Deeper Look
1 Thessalonians 2:7–13; 1 Timothy 4:11–16

Go to page 1232 for your next devotional reading.

²¹On the appointed day Herod, wearing his royal robes, sat on his throne and delivered a public address to the people. ²²They shouted, "This is the voice of a god, not of a man." ²³Immediately, because Herod did not give praise to God, an angel of the Lord struck him down, and he was eaten by worms and died.

²⁴But the word of God continued to increase and spread.

²⁵When Barnabas and Saul had finished their mission, they returned from*ᵃ* Jerusalem, taking with them John, also called Mark.

Barnabas and Saul Sent Off

13 In the church at Antioch there were prophets and teachers: Barnabas, Simeon called Niger, Lucius of Cyrene, Manaen (who had been brought up with Herod the tetrarch) and Saul. ²While they were worshiping the Lord and fasting, the Holy Spirit said, "Set apart for me Barnabas and Saul for the work to which I have called them." ³So after they had fasted and prayed, they placed their hands on them and sent them off.

ᵃ25 Some manuscripts *to*

Read *Acts 13:1–52*
Key Verses *Acts 13:1–3*

No Reserves, No Retreats, No Regrets – Dr. Tom Yeakley

William Borden came from a family whose success in the dairy business was well known. As a high-school graduation gift, William's parents sent him and a chaperone on an around-the-world trip to help prepare him for college at Yale. They gave him a Bible to read on the journey. Somewhere in Asia he was struck by the enormity of the task of reaching the world for Jesus Christ. He realized that he had to give up everything to do it. He penned two words in the first page of his Bible: "No Reserves."

Borden entered Yale to study business, where he became friends with a zealous missionary named Samuel Zwemmer. William was soon caught up in Zwemmer's passion for reaching Muslims with the gospel. He sensed God calling him to bring the Good News to the Muslim people of western China. Explaining to his parents that he would not take over the family dairy business after graduation, he wrote two more words in the front of his Bible: "No Retreats."

Borden pursued Biblical studies at Princeton, then sailed for Egypt to study Arabic before moving on to China. After only six months of language study, he contracted cerebral meningitis and died. His mother sailed from New York to Cairo to collect his personal belongings, including his Bible. Opening it, she read two more words that William had added to the front page: "No Regrets."

Borden's total commitment to Jesus Christ compelled him to give his life for world evangelism. Borden's story does not suggest that we should all become missionaries; his story does teach us that God's highest good for us is to discover his will and then to do it with this kind of total commitment: "No Reserves!" "No Retreats!" "No Regrets!"

A Deeper Look
Luke 14:33; Romans 12:1–2

Go to page 1238 for your next devotional reading.

On Cyprus

[4]The two of them, sent on their way by the Holy Spirit, went down to Seleucia and sailed from there to Cyprus. [5]When they arrived at Salamis, they proclaimed the word of God in the Jewish synagogues. John was with them as their helper.

[6]They traveled through the whole island until they came to Paphos. There they met a Jewish sorcerer and false prophet named Bar-Jesus, [7]who was an attendant of the proconsul, Sergius Paulus. The proconsul, an intelligent man, sent for Barnabas and Saul because he wanted to hear the word of God. [8]But Elymas the sorcerer (for that is what his name means) opposed them and tried to turn the proconsul from the faith. [9]Then Saul, who was also called Paul, filled with the Holy Spirit, looked straight at Elymas and said, [10]"You are a child of the devil and an enemy of everything that is right! You are full of all kinds of deceit and trickery. Will you never stop perverting the right ways of the Lord? [11]Now the hand of the Lord is against you. You are going to be blind, and for a time you will be unable to see the light of the sun."

Immediately mist and darkness came over him, and he groped about, seeking someone to lead him by the hand. [12]When the proconsul saw what had happened, he believed, for he was amazed at the teaching about the Lord.

In Pisidian Antioch

[13]From Paphos, Paul and his companions sailed to Perga in Pamphylia, where John left them to return to Jerusalem. [14]From Perga they went on to Pisidian Antioch. On the Sabbath they entered the synagogue and sat down. [15]After the reading from the Law and the Prophets, the synagogue rulers sent word to them, saying, "Brothers, if you have a message of encouragement for the people, please speak."

[16]Standing up, Paul motioned with his hand and said: "Men of Israel and you Gentiles who worship God, listen to me! [17]The God of the people of Israel chose our fathers; he made the people prosper during their stay in Egypt, with mighty power he led them out of that country, [18]he endured their conduct[a] for about forty years in the desert, [19]he overthrew seven nations in Canaan and gave their land to his people as their inheritance. [20]All this took about 450 years.

"After this, God gave them judges until the time of Samuel the prophet. [21]Then the people asked for a king, and he gave them Saul son of Kish, of the tribe of Benjamin, who ruled forty years. [22]After removing Saul, he made David their king. He testified concerning him: 'I have found David son of Jesse a man after my own heart; he will do everything I want him to do.'

[23]"From this man's descendants God has brought to Israel the Savior Jesus, as he promised. [24]Before the coming of Jesus, John preached repentance and baptism to all the people of Israel. [25]As John was completing his work, he said: 'Who do you think I am? I am not that one. No, but he is coming after me, whose sandals I am not worthy to untie.'

[26]"Brothers, children of Abraham, and you God-fearing Gentiles, it is to us that this message of salvation has been sent. [27]The people of Jerusalem and their rulers did not recognize Jesus, yet in condemning him they fulfilled the words of the prophets that are read every Sabbath. [28]Though they found no proper ground for a death sentence, they asked Pilate to have him executed. [29]When they had carried out all that was written about him, they took him down from the tree and laid him in a tomb. [30]But God raised him from the dead, [31]and for many days he was seen by those who had traveled with him from Galilee to Jerusalem. They are now his witnesses to our people.

[32]"We tell you the good news: What God promised our fathers [33]he has fulfilled for us, their children, by raising up Jesus. As it is written in the second Psalm:

" 'You are my Son;
   today I have become your
     Father.[b][c]

[34]The fact that God raised him from the dead, never to decay, is stated in these words:

" 'I will give you the holy and sure
     blessings promised to
     David.'[d]

[35]So it is stated elsewhere:

---

[a]18 Some manuscripts *and cared for them*
[b]33 Or *have begotten you*   [c]33 Psalm 2:7
[d]34 Isaiah 55:3

" 'You will not let your Holy One see decay.'*a*

36"For when David had served God's purpose in his own generation, he fell asleep; he was buried with his fathers and his body decayed. 37But the one whom God raised from the dead did not see decay.

38"Therefore, my brothers, I want you to know that through Jesus the forgiveness of sins is proclaimed to you. 39Through him everyone who believes is justified from everything you could not be justified from by the law of Moses. 40Take care that what the prophets have said does not happen to you:

41" 'Look, you scoffers,
    wonder and perish,
  for I am going to do something in
      your days
    that you would never believe,
    even if someone told you.'*b* "

42As Paul and Barnabas were leaving the synagogue, the people invited them to speak further about these things on the next Sabbath. 43When the congregation was dismissed, many of the Jews and devout converts to Judaism followed Paul and Barnabas, who talked with them and urged them to continue in the grace of God.

44On the next Sabbath almost the whole city gathered to hear the word of the Lord. 45When the Jews saw the crowds, they were filled with jealousy and talked abusively against what Paul was saying.

46Then Paul and Barnabas answered them boldly: "We had to speak the word of God to you first. Since you reject it and do not consider yourselves worthy of eternal life, we now turn to the Gentiles. 47For this is what the Lord has commanded us:

" 'I have made you*c* a light for the
      Gentiles,
  that you*c* may bring salvation to
      the ends of the earth.'*d* "

48When the Gentiles heard this, they were glad and honored the word of the Lord; and all who were appointed for eternal life believed.

49The word of the Lord spread through the whole region. 50But the Jews incited the God-fearing women of high standing and the leading men of the city. They stirred up persecution against Paul and Barnabas, and expelled them from their region. 51So they shook the dust from their feet in protest against them and went to Iconium. 52And the disciples were filled with joy and with the Holy Spirit.

In Iconium

14 At Iconium Paul and Barnabas went as usual into the Jewish synagogue. There they spoke so effectively that a great number of Jews and Gentiles believed. 2But the Jews who refused to believe stirred up the Gentiles and poisoned their minds against the brothers. 3So Paul and Barnabas spent considerable time there, speaking boldly for the Lord, who confirmed the message of his grace by enabling them to do miraculous signs and wonders. 4The people of the city were divided; some sided with the Jews, others with the apostles. 5There was a plot afoot among the Gentiles and Jews, together with their leaders, to mistreat them and stone them. 6But they found out about it and fled to the Lycaonian cities of Lystra and Derbe and to the surrounding country, 7where they continued to preach the good news.

In Lystra and Derbe

8In Lystra there sat a man crippled in his feet, who was lame from birth and had never walked. 9He listened to Paul as he was speaking. Paul looked directly at him, saw that he had faith to be healed 10and called out, "Stand up on your feet!" At that, the man jumped up and began to walk.

11When the crowd saw what Paul had done, they shouted in the Lycaonian language, "The gods have come down to us in human form!" 12Barnabas they called Zeus, and Paul they called Hermes because he was the chief speaker. 13The priest of Zeus, whose temple was just outside the city, brought bulls and wreaths to the city gates because he and the crowd wanted to offer sacrifices to them.

14But when the apostles Barnabas and Paul heard of this, they tore their clothes and rushed out into the crowd, shouting:

a35 Psalm 16:10   *b41* Hab. 1:5
c47 The Greek is singular.   *d47* Isaiah 49:6

15"Men, why are you doing this? We too are only men, human like you. We are bringing you good news, telling you to turn from these worthless things to the living God, who made heaven and earth and sea and everything in them. 16In the past, he let all nations go their own way. 17Yet he has not left himself without testimony: He has shown kindness by giving you rain from heaven and crops in their seasons; he provides you with plenty of food and fills your hearts with joy." 18Even with these words, they had difficulty keeping the crowd from sacrificing to them.

19Then some Jews came from Antioch and Iconium and won the crowd over. They stoned Paul and dragged him outside the city, thinking he was dead. 20But after the disciples had gathered around him, he got up and went back into the city. The next day he and Barnabas left for Derbe.

The Return to Antioch in Syria

21They preached the good news in that city and won a large number of disciples. Then they returned to Lystra, Iconium and Antioch, 22strengthening the disciples and encouraging them to remain true to the faith. "We must go through many hardships to enter the kingdom of God," they said. 23Paul and Barnabas appointed elders*a* for them in each church and, with prayer and fasting, committed them to the Lord, in whom they had put their trust. 24After going through Pisidia, they came into Pamphylia, 25and when they had preached the word in Perga, they went down to Attalia.

26From Attalia they sailed back to Antioch, where they had been committed to the grace of God for the work they had now completed. 27On arriving there, they gathered the church together and reported all that God had done through them and how he had opened the door of faith to the Gentiles. 28And they stayed there a long time with the disciples.

The Council at Jerusalem

15 Some men came down from Judea to Antioch and were teaching the brothers: "Unless you are circumcised, according to the custom taught by Moses, you cannot be saved." 2This brought Paul and Barnabas into sharp dispute and debate with them. So Paul and Barnabas were appointed, along with some other believers, to go up to Jerusalem to see the apostles and elders about this question. 3The church sent them on their way, and as they traveled through Phoenicia and Samaria, they told how the Gentiles had been converted. This news made all the brothers very glad. 4When they came to Jerusalem, they were welcomed by the church and the apostles and elders, to whom they reported everything God had done through them.

5Then some of the believers who belonged to the party of the Pharisees stood up and said, "The Gentiles must be circumcised and required to obey the law of Moses."

6The apostles and elders met to consider this question. 7After much discussion, Peter got up and addressed them: "Brothers, you know that some time ago God made a choice among you that the Gentiles might hear from my lips the message of the gospel and believe. 8God, who knows the heart, showed that he accepted them by giving the Holy Spirit to them, just as he did to us. 9He made no distinction between us and them, for he purified their hearts by faith. 10Now then, why do you try to test God by putting on the necks of the disciples a yoke that neither we nor our fathers have been able to bear? 11No! We believe it is through the grace of our Lord Jesus that we are saved, just as they are."

12The whole assembly became silent as they listened to Barnabas and Paul telling about the miraculous signs and wonders God had done among the Gentiles through them. 13When they finished, James spoke up: "Brothers, listen to me. 14Simon*b* has described to us how God at first showed his concern by taking from the Gentiles a people for himself. 15The words of the prophets are in agreement with this, as it is written:

16" 'After this I will return
    and rebuild David's fallen tent.
  Its ruins I will rebuild,
    and I will restore it,
17that the remnant of men may seek
      the Lord,
    and all the Gentiles who bear my
      name,

---

a23 Or *Barnabas ordained elders*; or *Barnabas had elders elected*   *b14* Greek *Simeon,* a variant of *Simon*; that is, Peter says the Lord, who does these things'[a]

18   that have been known for ages.[b]

19"It is my judgment, therefore, that we should not make it difficult for the Gentiles who are turning to God. 20Instead we should write to them, telling them to abstain from food polluted by idols, from sexual immorality, from the meat of strangled animals and from blood. 21For Moses has been preached in every city from the earliest times and is read in the synagogues on every Sabbath."

The Council's Letter to Gentile Believers

22Then the apostles and elders, with the whole church, decided to choose some of their own men and send them to Antioch with Paul and Barnabas. They chose Judas (called Barsabbas) and Silas, two men who were leaders among the brothers. 23With them they sent the following letter:

The apostles and elders, your brothers,

To the Gentile believers in Antioch, Syria and Cilicia:

Greetings.

24We have heard that some went out from us without our authorization and disturbed you, troubling your minds by what they said. 25So we all agreed to choose some men and send them to you with our dear friends Barnabas and Paul— 26men who have risked their lives for the name of our Lord Jesus Christ. 27Therefore we are sending Judas and Silas to confirm by word of mouth what we are writing. 28It seemed good to the Holy Spirit and to us not to burden you with anything beyond the following requirements: 29You are to abstain from food sacrificed to idols, from blood, from the meat of strangled animals and from sexual immorality. You will do well to avoid these things.

Farewell.

30The men were sent off and went down to Antioch, where they gathered the church together and delivered the let-ter. 31The people read it and were glad for its encouraging message. 32Judas and Silas, who themselves were prophets, said much to encourage and strengthen the brothers. 33After spending some time there, they were sent off by the brothers with the blessing of peace to return to those who had sent them.[c] 35But Paul and Barnabas remained in Antioch, where they and many others taught and preached the word of the Lord.

Disagreement Between Paul and Barnabas

36Some time later Paul said to Barnabas, "Let us go back and visit the brothers in all the towns where we preached the word of the Lord and see how they are doing." 37Barnabas wanted to take John, also called Mark, with them, 38but Paul did not think it wise to take him, because he had deserted them in Pamphylia and had not continued with them in the work. 39They had such a sharp disagreement that they parted company. Barnabas took Mark and sailed for Cyprus, 40but Paul chose Silas and left, commended by the brothers to the grace of the Lord. 41He went through Syria and Cilicia, strengthening the churches.

a17 Amos 9:11,12   b17,18 Some manuscripts things'— / 18known to the Lord for ages is his work c33 Some manuscripts them, 34but Silas decided to remain there

POINT OF INTEREST   Acts 15:19

Our music, their music; our church, their church; our way of worship, their way of worship. Such differences have often divided groups of believers. Getting along with other Christians has been a difficult issue from even the earliest days of the church. This verse gives wise advice: Do not sin in dealing with these differences, and try your best not to offend other believers. See Paul's advice to the Corinthians regarding church unity in 1 Corinthians 1:10–12 and chapters 11 through 14.

Timothy Joins Paul and Silas

16 He came to Derbe and then to Lystra, where a disciple named Timothy lived, whose mother was a Jewess and a believer, but whose father was a Greek. ²The brothers at Lystra and Iconium spoke well of him. ³Paul wanted to take him along on the journey, so he circumcised him because of the Jews who lived in that area, for they all knew that his father was a Greek. ⁴As they traveled from town to town, they delivered the decisions reached by the apostles and elders in Jerusalem for the people to obey. ⁵So the churches were strengthened in the faith and grew daily in numbers.

Paul's Vision of the Man of Macedonia

⁶Paul and his companions traveled throughout the region of Phrygia and Galatia, having been kept by the Holy Spirit from preaching the word in the province of Asia. ⁷When they came to the border of Mysia, they tried to enter Bithynia, but the Spirit of Jesus would not allow them to. ⁸So they passed by Mysia and went down to Troas. ⁹During the night Paul had a vision of a man of Macedonia standing and begging him, "Come over to Macedonia and help us." ¹⁰After Paul had seen the vision, we got ready at once to leave for Macedonia, concluding that God had called us to preach the gospel to them.

Lydia's Conversion in Philippi

¹¹From Troas we put out to sea and sailed straight for Samothrace, and the next day on to Neapolis. ¹²From there we traveled to Philippi, a Roman colony and the leading city of that district of Macedonia. And we stayed there several days.

¹³On the Sabbath we went outside the city gate to the river, where we expected to find a place of prayer. We sat down and began to speak to the women who had gathered there. ¹⁴One of those listening was a woman named Lydia, a dealer in purple cloth from the city of Thyatira, who was a worshiper of God. The Lord opened her heart to respond to Paul's message. ¹⁵When she and the members of her household were baptized, she invited us to her home. "If you consider me a believer in the Lord," she said, "come and stay at my house." And she persuaded us.

Paul and Silas in Prison

¹⁶Once when we were going to the place of prayer, we were met by a slave girl who had a spirit by which she predicted the future. She earned a great deal of money for her owners by fortune-telling. ¹⁷This girl followed Paul and the rest of us, shouting, "These men are servants of the Most High God, who are telling you the way to be saved." ¹⁸She kept this up for many days. Finally Paul became so troubled that he turned around and said to the spirit, "In the name of Jesus Christ I command you to come out of her!" At that moment the spirit left her.

¹⁹When the owners of the slave girl realized that their hope of making money was gone, they seized Paul and Silas and dragged them into the marketplace to face the authorities. ²⁰They brought them before the magistrates and said, "These men are Jews, and are throwing our city into an uproar ²¹by advocating customs unlawful for us Romans to accept or practice."

²²The crowd joined in the attack against Paul and Silas, and the magistrates ordered them to be stripped and beaten. ²³After they had been severely flogged, they were thrown into prison, and the jailer was commanded to guard them carefully. ²⁴Upon receiving such orders, he put them in the inner cell and fastened their feet in the stocks.

²⁵About midnight Paul and Silas were praying and singing hymns to God, and the other prisoners were listening to them. ²⁶Suddenly there was such a violent earthquake that the foundations of the prison were shaken. At once all the prison doors flew open, and everybody's chains came loose. ²⁷The jailer woke up, and when he saw the prison doors open, he drew his sword and was about to kill himself because he thought the prisoners had escaped. ²⁸But Paul shouted, "Don't harm yourself! We are all here!"

²⁹The jailer called for lights, rushed in and fell trembling before Paul and Silas. ³⁰He then brought them out and asked, "Sirs, what must I do to be saved?"

³¹They replied, "Believe in the Lord Jesus, and you will be saved—you and your household." ³²Then they spoke the word of the Lord to him and to all the others in his house. ³³At that hour of

the night the jailer took them and washed their wounds; then immediately he and all his family were baptized. 34The jailer brought them into his house and set a meal before them; he was filled with joy because he had come to believe in God— he and his whole family.

35When it was daylight, the magistrates sent their officers to the jailer with the order: "Release those men." 36The jailer told Paul, "The magistrates have ordered that you and Silas be released. Now you can leave. Go in peace."

37But Paul said to the officers: "They beat us publicly without a trial, even though we are Roman citizens, and threw us into prison. And now do they want to get rid of us quietly? No! Let them come themselves and escort us out."

38The officers reported this to the magistrates, and when they heard that Paul and Silas were Roman citizens, they were alarmed. 39They came to appease them and escorted them from the prison, requesting them to leave the city. 40After Paul and Silas came out of the prison, they went to Lydia's house, where they met with the brothers and encouraged them. Then they left.

WEDNESDAY

Read Acts 16:1–40
Key Verse Acts 16:31

Doesn't God Grade on the Curve? — Dr. Tom Yeakley

I was in my third year at college, sitting in a dorm lobby, when I noticed another student—an old friend that I hadn't seen since the seventh grade. I hadn't even known he attended Florida State. We had a few minutes to chat before his date arrived and we began to get caught up on what had been going on in our lives. As we parted, he handed me a small booklet, saying, "I'm sorry I haven't got time to explain this to you. Please read it; the message in here changed my life!"

I accepted the booklet and stuffed it into my pocket as my date arrived. We went to the theater and sat down, and I retrieved the booklet and began to read before the movie began. As I read, for the first time in my life I began to understand that I personally had done things that were displeasing to God and that I would be punished because of my wrongs. Until that night I had thought that God would grade my life on the curve and that I would fall somewhere in the upper percentiles. That night I understood that life is "pass–fail"—and that I had failed.

As I read on I understood that God loved me so much that he had sent his Son to pay the price for my failure. Jesus accepted punishment on my behalf. There in the theater I prayed, asking God to forgive me and accepting Jesus Christ as my Savior. There in the theater I was saved from my eternal punishment. Like the Philippian jailer, I too had become a member of God's family.

I have not seen the student who was kind enough to share Christ with me since that evening. He appeared in my life for a moment and made an impact for an eternity. All I had needed was the clear explanation contained in that booklet. Whom in your life has God prepared for you to share Christ with? Why not share with that person today?

A Deeper Look
John 1:12; Romans 5:18–21; Romans 10:9–15

Go to page 1240 for your next devotional reading.

In Thessalonica

17 When they had passed through Amphipolis and Apollonia, they came to Thessalonica, where there was a Jewish synagogue. ²As his custom was, Paul went into the synagogue, and on three Sabbath days he reasoned with them from the Scriptures, ³explaining and proving that the Christ*ᵃ* had to suffer and rise from the dead. "This Jesus I am proclaiming to you is the Christ,*ᵃ*" he said. ⁴Some of the Jews were persuaded and joined Paul and Silas, as did a large number of God-fearing Greeks and not a few prominent women.

⁵But the Jews were jealous; so they rounded up some bad characters from the marketplace, formed a mob and started a riot in the city. They rushed to Jason's house in search of Paul and Silas in order to bring them out to the crowd.*ᵇ* ⁶But when they did not find them, they dragged Jason and some other brothers before the city officials, shouting: "These men who have caused trouble all over the world have now come here, ⁷and Jason has welcomed them into his house. They are all defying Caesar's decrees, saying that there is another king, one called Jesus." ⁸When they heard this, the crowd and the city officials were thrown into turmoil. ⁹Then they made Jason and the others post bond and let them go.

In Berea

¹⁰As soon as it was night, the brothers sent Paul and Silas away to Berea. On arriving there, they went to the Jewish synagogue. ¹¹Now the Bereans were of more noble character than the Thessalonians, for they received the message with great eagerness and examined the Scriptures every day to see if what Paul said was true. ¹²Many of the Jews believed, as did also a number of prominent Greek women and many Greek men.

¹³When the Jews in Thessalonica learned that Paul was preaching the word of God at Berea, they went there too, agitating the crowds and stirring them up. ¹⁴The brothers immediately sent Paul to the coast, but Silas and Timothy stayed at Berea. ¹⁵The men who escorted Paul brought him to Athens and then left with instructions for Silas and Timothy to join him as soon as possible.

In Athens

¹⁶While Paul was waiting for them in Athens, he was greatly distressed to see that the city was full of idols. ¹⁷So he reasoned in the synagogue with the Jews and the God-fearing Greeks, as well as in the marketplace day by day with those who happened to be there. ¹⁸A group of Epicurean and Stoic philosophers began to dispute with him. Some of them asked, "What is this babbler trying to say?" Others remarked, "He seems to be advocating foreign gods." They said this because Paul was preaching the good news about Jesus and the resurrection. ¹⁹Then they took him and brought him to a meeting of the Areopagus, where they said to him, "May we know what this new teaching is that you are presenting? ²⁰You are bringing some strange ideas to our ears, and we want to know what they mean." ²¹(All the Athenians and the foreigners who lived there spent their time doing nothing but talking about and listening to the latest ideas.)

²²Paul then stood up in the meeting of the Areopagus and said: "Men of Athens! I see that in every way you are very religious. ²³For as I walked around and looked carefully at your objects of worship, I even found an altar with this inscription: TO AN UNKNOWN GOD. Now what you worship as something unknown I am going to proclaim to you.

²⁴"The God who made the world and everything in it is the Lord of heaven and earth and does not live in temples built by hands. ²⁵And he is not served by human hands, as if he needed anything, because he himself gives all men life and breath and everything else. ²⁶From one man he made every nation of men, that they should inhabit the whole earth; and he determined the times set for them and the exact places where they should live. ²⁷God did this so that men would seek him and perhaps reach out for him and find him, though he is not far from each one of us. ²⁸'For in him we live and move and have our being.' As some of your own poets have said, 'We are his offspring.'

²⁹"Therefore since we are God's offspring, we should not think that the divine being is like gold or silver or stone—an image made by man's design and skill. ³⁰In the past God overlooked such ignorance, but now he commands all people

ᵃ3 Or *Messiah*   *ᵇ5* Or *the assembly of the people*

everywhere to repent. ³¹For he has set a day when he will judge the world with justice by the man he has appointed. He has given proof of this to all men by raising him from the dead."

³²When they heard about the resurrection of the dead, some of them sneered, but others said, "We want to hear you again on this subject." ³³At that, Paul left the Council. ³⁴A few men became followers of Paul and believed. Among them was Dionysius, a member of the Areopagus, also a woman named Damaris, and a number of others.

In Corinth

18 After this, Paul left Athens and went to Corinth. ²There he met a Jew named Aquila, a native of Pontus, who had recently come from Italy with his

---

THURSDAY

Read Acts 17:1–34
Key Verse Acts 17:11

Noble Characters – Jay Getz

Anyone walking by the dorm room might have done a double take at our study group. There was Phil, forever starting a beard, who drawled out one sentence every five minutes. Nick had a buzz haircut, but the bulging veins in his neck were the best signal that he was a Marine. Stu was shaped like a pear and wore the same set of green hospital scrubs every day. Jason was the smallest person in the room, yet he wore a black eye from Saturday night when his "beer muscles" had gotten him into another fight.

Most of the guys were better at burning lounge couches than attending all their classes. They were "characters" all right. But if you looked closely you would see something "noble" in them; they were not afraid to talk about the Bible. They asked good questions and pushed for meaningful answers. Some, like Phil, often asked questions long past midnight. After I went to bed, he and my roommate would talk in the dark dorm hallway well into the night. And at some point in his question asking, Phil became convinced that Jesus Christ was the answer.

The apostle Paul dealt with a similar group in Berea (see Acts 17:11). They were eager to study the Word, not content to take Paul's comments at face value. They "examined the Scriptures" to see whether Paul was making it all up, and they were considered "of noble character."

Searching the Scriptures does increase our knowledge, guide us and develop our character, but it does even more: God's Word has the power to work in us to make us holy (see Ephesians 5:26) and to heal us (see Psalm 107:20). Like a living and active sword, it has the ability to cut through all the rubbish we accumulate in our souls (see Hebrews 4:12). And best of all, Jesus himself said that it is through the Word that we know his Father and belong to him: "For I gave them the words you gave me and they accepted them. They knew with certainty that I came from you, and they believed that you sent me. I pray for them . . . for they are yours" (John 17:8–9).

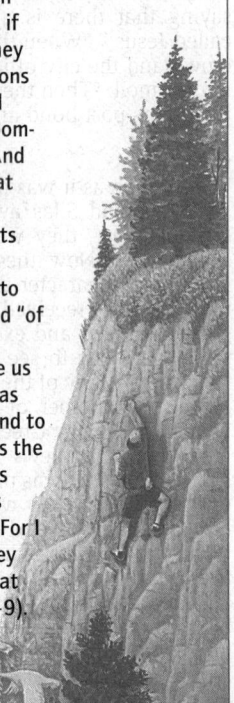

A Deeper Look
Ezra 7:10; 2 Timothy 3:16–17

Go to page 1244 for your next devotional reading.

wife Priscilla, because Claudius had ordered all the Jews to leave Rome. Paul went to see them, ³and because he was a tentmaker as they were, he stayed and worked with them. ⁴Every Sabbath he reasoned in the synagogue, trying to persuade Jews and Greeks.

⁵When Silas and Timothy came from Macedonia, Paul devoted himself exclusively to preaching, testifying to the Jews that Jesus was the Christ.ᵃ ⁶But when the Jews opposed Paul and became abusive, he shook out his clothes in protest and said to them, "Your blood be on your own heads! I am clear of my responsibility. From now on I will go to the Gentiles."

⁷Then Paul left the synagogue and went next door to the house of Titius Justus, a worshiper of God. ⁸Crispus, the synagogue ruler, and his entire household believed in the Lord; and many of the Corinthians who heard him believed and were baptized.

⁹One night the Lord spoke to Paul in a vision: "Do not be afraid; keep on speaking, do not be silent. ¹⁰For I am with you, and no one is going to attack and harm you, because I have many people in this city." ¹¹So Paul stayed for a year and a half, teaching them the word of God.

¹²While Gallio was proconsul of Achaia, the Jews made a united attack on Paul and brought him into court. ¹³"This man," they charged, "is persuading the people to worship God in ways contrary to the law."

¹⁴Just as Paul was about to speak, Gallio said to the Jews, "If you Jews were making a complaint about some misdemeanor or serious crime, it would be reasonable for me to listen to you. ¹⁵But since it involves questions about words and names and your own law—settle the matter yourselves. I will not be a judge of such things." ¹⁶So he had them ejected from the court. ¹⁷Then they all turned on Sosthenes the synagogue ruler and beat him in front of the court. But Gallio showed no concern whatever.

Priscilla, Aquila and Apollos

¹⁸Paul stayed on in Corinth for some time. Then he left the brothers and sailed for Syria, accompanied by Priscilla and Aquila. Before he sailed, he had his hair cut off at Cenchrea because of a vow he had taken. ¹⁹They arrived at Ephesus, where Paul left Priscilla and Aquila. He himself went into the synagogue and reasoned with the Jews. ²⁰When they asked him to spend more time with them, he declined. ²¹But as he left, he promised, "I will come back if it is God's will." Then he set sail from Ephesus. ²²When he landed at Caesarea, he went up and greeted the church and then went down to Antioch.

²³After spending some time in Antioch, Paul set out from there and traveled from place to place throughout the region of Galatia and Phrygia, strengthening all the disciples.

²⁴Meanwhile a Jew named Apollos, a native of Alexandria, came to Ephesus. He was a learned man, with a thorough knowledge of the Scriptures. ²⁵He had been instructed in the way of the Lord, and he spoke with great fervorᵇ and taught about Jesus accurately, though he knew only the baptism of John. ²⁶He began to speak boldly in the synagogue. When Priscilla and Aquila heard him, they invited him to their home and explained to him the way of God more adequately.

²⁷When Apollos wanted to go to Achaia, the brothers encouraged him and wrote to the disciples there to welcome him. On arriving, he was a great help to those who by grace had believed. ²⁸For he vigorously refuted the Jews in public debate, proving from the Scriptures that Jesus was the Christ.

ᵃ5 Or *Messiah;* also in verse 28   ᵇ25 Or *with fervor in the Spirit*

POINT OF INTEREST

Acts 18:18

Priscilla and Aquila were partners in marriage and ministry. The Bible's writers placed Priscilla's name first in five of the seven instances in which this couple is mentioned. Many scholars have interpreted this as an indication that Priscilla actively participated in the gospel outreach during a time when women did not necessarily hold a prominent role in either ministry or marriage.

Paul in Ephesus

19 While Apollos was at Corinth, Paul took the road through the interior and arrived at Ephesus. There he found some disciples ²and asked them, "Did you receive the Holy Spirit when*a* you believed?"

They answered, "No, we have not even heard that there is a Holy Spirit."

³So Paul asked, "Then what baptism did you receive?"

"John's baptism," they replied.

⁴Paul said, "John's baptism was a baptism of repentance. He told the people to believe in the one coming after him, that is, in Jesus." ⁵On hearing this, they were baptized into*b* the name of the Lord Jesus. ⁶When Paul placed his hands on them, the Holy Spirit came on them, and they spoke in tongues*c* and prophesied. ⁷There were about twelve men in all.

⁸Paul entered the synagogue and spoke boldly there for three months, arguing persuasively about the kingdom of God. ⁹But some of them became obstinate; they refused to believe and publicly maligned the Way. So Paul left them. He took the disciples with him and had discussions daily in the lecture hall of Tyrannus. ¹⁰This went on for two years, so that all the Jews and Greeks who lived in the province of Asia heard the word of the Lord.

¹¹God did extraordinary miracles through Paul, ¹²so that even handkerchiefs and aprons that had touched him were taken to the sick, and their illnesses were cured and the evil spirits left them.

¹³Some Jews who went around driving out evil spirits tried to invoke the name of the Lord Jesus over those who were demon-possessed. They would say, "In the name of Jesus, whom Paul preaches, I command you to come out." ¹⁴Seven sons of Sceva, a Jewish chief priest, were doing this. ¹⁵⌞One day⌟ the evil spirit answered them, "Jesus I know, and I know about Paul, but who are you?" ¹⁶Then the man who had the evil spirit jumped on them and overpowered them all. He gave them such a beating that they ran out of the house naked and bleeding.

¹⁷When this became known to the Jews and Greeks living in Ephesus, they were all seized with fear, and the name of the Lord Jesus was held in high honor. ¹⁸Many of those who believed now came and openly confessed their evil deeds.

¹⁹A number who had practiced sorcery brought their scrolls together and burned them publicly. When they calculated the value of the scrolls, the total came to fifty thousand drachmas.*d* ²⁰In this way the word of the Lord spread widely and grew in power.

²¹After all this had happened, Paul decided to go to Jerusalem, passing through Macedonia and Achaia. "After I have been there," he said, "I must visit Rome also." ²²He sent two of his helpers, Timothy and Erastus, to Macedonia, while he stayed in the province of Asia a little longer.

The Riot in Ephesus

²³About that time there arose a great disturbance about the Way. ²⁴A silversmith named Demetrius, who made silver shrines of Artemis, brought in no little business for the craftsmen. ²⁵He called them together, along with the workmen in related trades, and said: "Men, you know we receive a good income from this business. ²⁶And you see and hear how this fellow Paul has convinced and led astray large numbers of people here in Ephesus and in practically the whole province of Asia. He says that man-made gods are no gods at all. ²⁷There is danger not only that our trade will lose its good name, but also that the temple of the great goddess Artemis will be discredited, and the goddess herself, who is worshiped throughout the province of Asia and the world, will be robbed of her divine majesty."

²⁸When they heard this, they were furious and began shouting: "Great is Artemis of the Ephesians!" ²⁹Soon the whole city was in an uproar. The people seized Gaius and Aristarchus, Paul's traveling companions from Macedonia, and rushed as one man into the theater. ³⁰Paul wanted to appear before the crowd, but the disciples would not let him. ³¹Even some of the officials of the province, friends of Paul, sent him a message begging him not to venture into the theater.

³²The assembly was in confusion: Some were shouting one thing, some another. Most of the people did not even know why they were there. ³³The Jews pushed Alexander to the front, and some

a2 Or *after*   *b5* Or *in*   *c6* Or *other languages*
d19 A drachma was a silver coin worth about a day's wages.

of the crowd shouted instructions to him. He motioned for silence in order to make a defense before the people. [34]But when they realized he was a Jew, they all shouted in unison for about two hours: "Great is Artemis of the Ephesians!"

[35]The city clerk quieted the crowd and said: "Men of Ephesus, doesn't all the world know that the city of Ephesus is the guardian of the temple of the great Artemis and of her image, which fell from heaven? [36]Therefore, since these facts are undeniable, you ought to be quiet and not do anything rash. [37]You have brought these men here, though they have neither robbed temples nor blasphemed our goddess. [38]If, then, Demetrius and his fellow craftsmen have a grievance against anybody, the courts are open and there are proconsuls. They can press charges. [39]If there is anything further you want to bring up, it must be settled in a legal assembly. [40]As it is, we are in danger of being charged with rioting because of today's events. In that case we would not be able to account for this commotion, since there is no reason for it." [41]After he had said this, he dismissed the assembly.

Through Macedonia and Greece

20 When the uproar had ended, Paul sent for the disciples and, after encouraging them, said good-by and set out for Macedonia. [2]He traveled through that area, speaking many words of encouragement to the people, and finally arrived in Greece, [3]where he stayed three months. Because the Jews made a plot against him just as he was about to sail for Syria, he decided to go back through Macedonia. [4]He was accompanied by Sopater son of Pyrrhus from Berea, Aristarchus and Secundus from Thessalonica, Gaius from Derbe, Timothy also, and Tychicus and Trophimus from the province of Asia. [5]These men went on ahead and waited for us at Troas. [6]But we sailed from Philippi after the Feast of Unleavened Bread, and five days later joined the others at Troas, where we stayed seven days.

Eutychus Raised From the Dead at Troas

[7]On the first day of the week we came together to break bread. Paul spoke to the people and, because he intended to leave the next day, kept on talking until midnight. [8]There were many lamps in the upstairs room where we were meeting. [9]Seated in a window was a young man named Eutychus, who was sinking into a deep sleep as Paul talked on and on. When he was sound asleep, he fell to the ground from the third story and was picked up dead. [10]Paul went down, threw himself on the young man and put his arms around him. "Don't be alarmed," he said. "He's alive!" [11]Then he went upstairs again and broke bread and ate. After talking until daylight, he left. [12]The people took the young man home alive and were greatly comforted.

Paul's Farewell to the Ephesian Elders

[13]We went on ahead to the ship and sailed for Assos, where we were going to take Paul aboard. He had made this arrangement because he was going there on foot. [14]When he met us at Assos, we took him aboard and went on to Mitylene. [15]The next day we set sail from there and arrived off Kios. The day after that we crossed over to Samos, and on the following day arrived at Miletus. [16]Paul had decided to sail past Ephesus to avoid spending time in the province of Asia, for he was in a hurry to reach Jerusalem, if possible, by the day of Pentecost.

[17]From Miletus, Paul sent to Ephesus for the elders of the church. [18]When they arrived, he said to them: "You know how I lived the whole time I was with you, from the first day I came into the province of Asia. [19]I served the Lord with great humility and with tears, although I was severely tested by the plots of the Jews. [20]You know that I have not hesitated to preach anything that would be helpful to you but have taught you publicly and from house to house. [21]I have declared to both Jews and Greeks that they must turn to God in repentance and have faith in our Lord Jesus.

[22]"And now, compelled by the Spirit, I am going to Jerusalem, not knowing what will happen to me there. [23]I only know that in every city the Holy Spirit warns me that prison and hardships are facing me. [24]However, I consider my life worth nothing to me, if only I may finish the race and complete the task the Lord Jesus has given me—the task of testifying to the gospel of God's grace.

[25]"Now I know that none of you among whom I have gone about preaching the kingdom will ever see me again.

26Therefore, I declare to you today that I am innocent of the blood of all men. 27For I have not hesitated to proclaim to you the whole will of God. 28Keep watch over yourselves and all the flock of which the Holy Spirit has made you overseers.*a* Be shepherds of the church of God,*b* which he bought with his own blood. 29I know that after I leave, savage wolves will come in among you and will not spare the flock. 30Even from your own number men will arise and distort the truth in order to draw away disciples after them. 31So be on your guard! Remember that for three years I never stopped warning each of you night and day with tears.

32"Now I commit you to God and to the word of his grace, which can build you up and give you an inheritance among all those who are sanctified. 33I have not coveted anyone's silver or gold

or clothing. 34You yourselves know that these hands of mine have supplied my own needs and the needs of my companions. 35In everything I did, I showed you that by this kind of hard work we must help the weak, remembering the words the Lord Jesus himself said: 'It is more blessed to give than to receive.' "

36When he had said this, he knelt down with all of them and prayed. 37They all wept as they embraced him and kissed him. 38What grieved them most was his statement that they would never see his face again. Then they accompanied him to the ship.

On to Jerusalem

21 After we had torn ourselves away from them, we put out to sea and sailed straight to Cos. The next day we

a28 Traditionally *bishops*   *b28* Many manuscripts *of the Lord*

FRIDAY

Read Acts 20:1–38
Key Verse Acts 20:24

What's Your Purpose? — Joe Bernardy

In the movie *Braveheart*, actor Mel Gibson portrayed William Wallace, a rebel and freedom fighter in medieval Scotland. Wallace willingly faced torture and death in pursuit of freedom for his country. He refused the queen's secret offer of poison as a means of avoiding his execution. He also refused to beg for mercy in exchange for an end to the torture. On the executioner's block he summoned his last bit of strength to shout his final word, "Freedom!" His dream of freedom would not allow him to compromise his purpose in life. Because of his commitment, others took up the cause and won freedom for Scotland.

As followers of Jesus Christ, we have been entrusted with an even greater purpose. Paul said, "I consider my life worth nothing to me, if only I may finish the race and complete the task the Lord Jesus has given me—the task of testifying to the gospel of God's grace."

Everyone gives his or her life to something. We all make choices about how we will spend the moments, hours and days. Our years will pass quickly, and we'll spend them in pursuit of something. How are we going to spend them? On making ourselves comfortable, looking for status or accumulating possessions? Or will we invest our lives in changing the world with the gospel of Jesus Christ?

A Deeper Look
John 6:27; John 12:24–26; Philippians 1:20–21

Go to page 1249 for your next devotional reading.

went to Rhodes and from there to Patara. ²We found a ship crossing over to Phoenicia, went on board and set sail. ³After sighting Cyprus and passing to the south of it, we sailed on to Syria. We landed at Tyre, where our ship was to unload its cargo. ⁴Finding the disciples there, we stayed with them seven days. Through the Spirit they urged Paul not to go on to Jerusalem. ⁵But when our time was up, we left and continued on our way. All the disciples and their wives and children accompanied us out of the city, and there on the beach we knelt to pray. ⁶After saying good-by to each other, we went aboard the ship, and they returned home.

⁷We continued our voyage from Tyre and landed at Ptolemais, where we greeted the brothers and stayed with them for a day. ⁸Leaving the next day, we reached Caesarea and stayed at the house of Philip the evangelist, one of the Seven. ⁹He had four unmarried daughters who prophesied.

¹⁰After we had been there a number of days, a prophet named Agabus came down from Judea. ¹¹Coming over to us, he took Paul's belt, tied his own hands and feet with it and said, "The Holy Spirit says, 'In this way the Jews of Jerusalem will bind the owner of this belt and will hand him over to the Gentiles.' "

¹²When we heard this, we and the people there pleaded with Paul not to go up to Jerusalem. ¹³Then Paul answered, "Why are you weeping and breaking my heart? I am ready not only to be bound, but also to die in Jerusalem for the name of the Lord Jesus." ¹⁴When he would not be dissuaded, we gave up and said, "The Lord's will be done."

¹⁵After this, we got ready and went up to Jerusalem. ¹⁶Some of the disciples from Caesarea accompanied us and brought us to the home of Mnason, where we were to stay. He was a man from Cyprus and one of the early disciples.

Paul's Arrival at Jerusalem

¹⁷When we arrived at Jerusalem, the brothers received us warmly. ¹⁸The next day Paul and the rest of us went to see James, and all the elders were present. ¹⁹Paul greeted them and reported in detail what God had done among the Gentiles through his ministry.

²⁰When they heard this, they praised God. Then they said to Paul: "You see, brother, how many thousands of Jews have believed, and all of them are zealous for the law. ²¹They have been informed that you teach all the Jews who live among the Gentiles to turn away from Moses, telling them not to circumcise their children or live according to our customs. ²²What shall we do? They will certainly hear that you have come, ²³so do what we tell you. There are four men with us who have made a vow. ²⁴Take these men, join in their purification rites and pay their expenses, so that they can have their heads shaved. Then everybody will know there is no truth in these reports about you, but that you yourself are living in obedience to the law. ²⁵As for the Gentile believers, we have written to them our decision that they should abstain from food sacrificed to idols, from blood, from the meat of strangled animals and from sexual immorality."

²⁶The next day Paul took the men and purified himself along with them. Then he went to the temple to give notice of the date when the days of purification would end and the offering would be made for each of them.

Paul Arrested

²⁷When the seven days were nearly over, some Jews from the province of Asia saw Paul at the temple. They stirred up the whole crowd and seized him, ²⁸shouting, "Men of Israel, help us! This is the man who teaches all men everywhere against our people and our law and this place. And besides, he has brought Greeks into the temple area and defiled this holy place." ²⁹(They had previously seen Trophimus the Ephesian in the city with Paul and assumed that Paul had brought him into the temple area.)

³⁰The whole city was aroused, and the people came running from all directions. Seizing Paul, they dragged him from the temple, and immediately the gates were shut. ³¹While they were trying to kill him, news reached the commander of the Roman troops that the whole city of Jerusalem was in an uproar. ³²He at once took some officers and soldiers and ran down to the crowd. When the rioters saw the commander and his soldiers, they stopped beating Paul.

³³The commander came up and arrested him and ordered him to be bound with two chains. Then he asked who he was and what he had done. ³⁴Some in the

crowd shouted one thing and some another, and since the commander could not get at the truth because of the uproar, he ordered that Paul be taken into the barracks. ³⁵When Paul reached the steps, the violence of the mob was so great he had to be carried by the soldiers. ³⁶The crowd that followed kept shouting, "Away with him!"

Paul Speaks to the Crowd

³⁷As the soldiers were about to take Paul into the barracks, he asked the commander, "May I say something to you?"

"Do you speak Greek?" he replied. ³⁸"Aren't you the Egyptian who started a revolt and led four thousand terrorists out into the desert some time ago?"

³⁹Paul answered, "I am a Jew, from Tarsus in Cilicia, a citizen of no ordinary city. Please let me speak to the people."

⁴⁰Having received the commander's permission, Paul stood on the steps and motioned to the crowd. When they were all silent, he said to them in Aramaic*ª*:

22 ¹"Brothers and fathers, listen now to my defense."

²When they heard him speak to them in Aramaic, they became very quiet.

Then Paul said: ³"I am a Jew, born in Tarsus of Cilicia, but brought up in this city. Under Gamaliel I was thoroughly trained in the law of our fathers and was just as zealous for God as any of you are today. ⁴I persecuted the followers of this Way to their death, arresting both men and women and throwing them into prison, ⁵as also the high priest and all the Council can testify. I even obtained letters from them to their brothers in Damascus, and went there to bring these people as prisoners to Jerusalem to be punished.

⁶"About noon as I came near Damascus, suddenly a bright light from heaven flashed around me. ⁷I fell to the ground and heard a voice say to me, 'Saul! Saul! Why do you persecute me?'

⁸" 'Who are you, Lord?' I asked.

" 'I am Jesus of Nazareth, whom you are persecuting,' he replied. ⁹My companions saw the light, but they did not understand the voice of him who was speaking to me.

¹⁰" 'What shall I do, Lord?' I asked.

" 'Get up,' the Lord said, 'and go into Damascus. There you will be told all that you have been assigned to do.' ¹¹My companions led me by the hand into Da-

mascus, because the brilliance of the light had blinded me.

¹²"A man named Ananias came to see me. He was a devout observer of the law and highly respected by all the Jews living there. ¹³He stood beside me and said, 'Brother Saul, receive your sight!' And at that very moment I was able to see him.

¹⁴"Then he said: 'The God of our fathers has chosen you to know his will and to see the Righteous One and to hear words from his mouth. ¹⁵You will be his witness to all men of what you have seen and heard. ¹⁶And now what are you waiting for? Get up, be baptized and wash your sins away, calling on his name.'

¹⁷"When I returned to Jerusalem and was praying at the temple, I fell into a trance ¹⁸and saw the Lord speaking. 'Quick!' he said to me. 'Leave Jerusalem immediately, because they will not accept your testimony about me.'

¹⁹" 'Lord,' I replied, 'these men know that I went from one synagogue to another to imprison and beat those who believe in you. ²⁰And when the blood of your martyr*ᵇ* Stephen was shed, I stood there giving my approval and guarding the clothes of those who were killing him.'

²¹"Then the Lord said to me, 'Go; I will send you far away to the Gentiles.' "

Paul the Roman Citizen

²²The crowd listened to Paul until he said this. Then they raised their voices and shouted, "Rid the earth of him! He's not fit to live!"

²³As they were shouting and throwing off their cloaks and flinging dust into the air, ²⁴the commander ordered Paul to be taken into the barracks. He directed that he be flogged and questioned in order to find out why the people were shouting at him like this. ²⁵As they stretched him out to flog him, Paul said to the centurion standing there, "Is it legal for you to flog a Roman citizen who hasn't even been found guilty?"

²⁶When the centurion heard this, he went to the commander and reported it. "What are you going to do?" he asked. "This man is a Roman citizen."

²⁷The commander went to Paul and asked, "Tell me, are you a Roman citizen?"

ª40 Or possibly *Hebrew*; also in 22:2   *ᵇ20* Or *witness*

"Yes, I am," he answered.

28Then the commander said, "I had to pay a big price for my citizenship."

"But I was born a citizen," Paul replied.

29Those who were about to question him withdrew immediately. The commander himself was alarmed when he realized that he had put Paul, a Roman citizen, in chains.

Before the Sanhedrin

30The next day, since the commander wanted to find out exactly why Paul was being accused by the Jews, he released him and ordered the chief priests and all the Sanhedrin to assemble. Then he brought Paul and had him stand before them.

23 Paul looked straight at the Sanhedrin and said, "My brothers, I have fulfilled my duty to God in all good conscience to this day." 2At this the high priest Ananias ordered those standing near Paul to strike him on the mouth. 3Then Paul said to him, "God will strike you, you whitewashed wall! You sit there to judge me according to the law, yet you yourself violate the law by commanding that I be struck!"

4Those who were standing near Paul said, "You dare to insult God's high priest?"

5Paul replied, "Brothers, I did not realize that he was the high priest; for it is written: 'Do not speak evil about the ruler of your people.'a"

6Then Paul, knowing that some of them were Sadducees and the others Pharisees, called out in the Sanhedrin, "My brothers, I am a Pharisee, the son of a Pharisee. I stand on trial because of my hope in the resurrection of the dead." 7When he said this, a dispute broke out between the Pharisees and the Sadducees, and the assembly was divided. 8(The Sadducees say that there is no resurrection, and that there are neither angels nor spirits, but the Pharisees acknowledge them all.)

9There was a great uproar, and some of the teachers of the law who were Pharisees stood up and argued vigorously. "We find nothing wrong with this man," they said. "What if a spirit or an angel has spoken to him?" 10The dispute became so violent that the commander was afraid Paul would be torn to pieces by them. He ordered the troops to go down and take him away from them by force and bring him into the barracks.

11The following night the Lord stood near Paul and said, "Take courage! As you have testified about me in Jerusalem, so you must also testify in Rome."

The Plot to Kill Paul

12The next morning the Jews formed a conspiracy and bound themselves with an oath not to eat or drink until they had killed Paul. 13More than forty men were involved in this plot. 14They went to the chief priests and elders and said, "We have taken a solemn oath not to eat anything until we have killed Paul. 15Now then, you and the Sanhedrin petition the commander to bring him before you on the pretext of wanting more accurate information about his case. We are ready to kill him before he gets here."

16But when the son of Paul's sister heard of this plot, he went into the barracks and told Paul.

17Then Paul called one of the centurions and said, "Take this young man to the commander; he has something to tell him." 18So he took him to the commander.

The centurion said, "Paul, the prisoner, sent for me and asked me to bring this young man to you because he has something to tell you."

19The commander took the young man by the hand, drew him aside and asked, "What is it you want to tell me?"

20He said: "The Jews have agreed to ask you to bring Paul before the Sanhedrin tomorrow on the pretext of wanting

a5 Exodus 22:28

POINT OF INTEREST   Acts 22:29

Roman citizenship carried powerful rights and privileges, including protection against unlawful punishment and the right to appeal to Caesar (see Acts 25:11). Paul claimed these rights for himself in order to further the spread of the gospel. Contrast this passage with Paul's attitude and discussion about rights in 1 Corinthians 9:11–15.

more accurate information about him. ²¹Don't give in to them, because more than forty of them are waiting in ambush for him. They have taken an oath not to eat or drink until they have killed him. They are ready now, waiting for your consent to their request."

²²The commander dismissed the young man and cautioned him, "Don't tell anyone that you have reported this to me."

Paul Transferred to Caesarea

²³Then he called two of his centurions and ordered them, "Get ready a detachment of two hundred soldiers, seventy horsemen and two hundred spearmen*ᵃ* to go to Caesarea at nine tonight. ²⁴Provide mounts for Paul so that he may be taken safely to Governor Felix."

²⁵He wrote a letter as follows:

²⁶Claudius Lysias,

To His Excellency, Governor Felix:

Greetings.

²⁷This man was seized by the Jews and they were about to kill him, but I came with my troops and rescued him, for I had learned that he is a Roman citizen. ²⁸I wanted to know why they were accusing him, so I brought him to their Sanhedrin. ²⁹I found that the accusation had to do with questions about their law, but there was no charge against him that deserved death or imprisonment. ³⁰When I was informed of a plot to be carried out against the man, I sent him to you at once. I also ordered his accusers to present to you their case against him.

³¹So the soldiers, carrying out their orders, took Paul with them during the night and brought him as far as Antipatris. ³²The next day they let the cavalry go on with him, while they returned to the barracks. ³³When the cavalry arrived in Caesarea, they delivered the letter to the governor and handed Paul over to him. ³⁴The governor read the letter and asked what province he was from. Learning that he was from Cilicia, ³⁵he said, "I will hear your case when your accusers get here." Then he ordered that Paul be kept under guard in Herod's palace.

The Trial Before Felix

24 Five days later the high priest Ananias went down to Caesarea with some of the elders and a lawyer named Tertullus, and they brought their charges against Paul before the governor. ²When Paul was called in, Tertullus presented his case before Felix: "We have enjoyed a long period of peace under you, and your foresight has brought about reforms in this nation. ³Everywhere and in every way, most excellent Felix, we acknowledge this with profound gratitude. ⁴But in order not to weary you further, I would request that you be kind enough to hear us briefly.

⁵"We have found this man to be a troublemaker, stirring up riots among the Jews all over the world. He is a ringleader of the Nazarene sect ⁶and even tried to desecrate the temple; so we seized him. ⁸By*ᵇ* examining him yourself you will be able to learn the truth about all these charges we are bringing against him."

⁹The Jews joined in the accusation, asserting that these things were true.

¹⁰When the governor motioned for him to speak, Paul replied: "I know that for a number of years you have been a judge over this nation; so I gladly make my defense. ¹¹You can easily verify that no more than twelve days ago I went up to Jerusalem to worship. ¹²My accusers did not find me arguing with anyone at the temple, or stirring up a crowd in the synagogues or anywhere else in the city. ¹³And they cannot prove to you the charges they are now making against me. ¹⁴However, I admit that I worship the God of our fathers as a follower of the Way, which they call a sect. I believe everything that agrees with the Law and that is written in the Prophets, ¹⁵and I have the same hope in God as these men, that there will be a resurrection of both the righteous and the wicked. ¹⁶So I strive always to keep my conscience clear before God and man.

¹⁷"After an absence of several years, I came to Jerusalem to bring my people gifts for the poor and to present offerings. ¹⁸I was ceremonially clean when they found me in the temple courts doing this.

ᵃ23 The meaning of the Greek for this word is uncertain. *ᵇ6-8* Some manuscripts *him and wanted to judge him according to our law. ⁷But the commander, Lysias, came and with the use of much force snatched him from our hands ⁸and ordered his accusers to come before you. By*

Read Acts 24:1–27
Key Verse Acts 24:16

A Clear Conscience

God has put an alarm system inside of us. No one else can hear it, but we sure can. Sometimes a voice whispers, *"Come back to me."* Sometimes the alarm is a loud and clear, *"You just blew it!"* or even a deafening, *"Stop, don't do it!"* The problem is that our conscience can get dull from sin and the alarm can be muffled. The solution is to ask the Holy Spirit to clean off the alarm and create in us a divine restlessness until we recognize our need to confess a bad attitude or questionable activity or whatever is standing between us and God.

God wants us to keep a clean slate with him. When we confess our sins, the restlessness gets wiped away, along with the cloud of guilt and fear. A squeaky-clean conscience allows us to have a brand new sense of joy and peace.

Digging Into the Word
1. How do these passages motivate you to hunger for a clear conscience?—*2 Corinthians 1:12; 1 Timothy 1:5,18–19*
2. What are some possible effects of a guilty conscience?—*Romans 2:12–16; Romans 13:3–5*

Action Challenge
If you have done something wrong and your conscience is sounding an alarm, identify one specific action you can take to make things right. Commit to do this within the next few weeks.

One Step Deeper
1 Corinthians 10:23–33; Hebrews 9:14

Go to page 1257 for your next devotional reading.

There was no crowd with me, nor was I involved in any disturbance. [19]But there are some Jews from the province of Asia, who ought to be here before you and bring charges if they have anything against me. [20]Or these who are here should state what crime they found in me when I stood before the Sanhedrin— [21]unless it was this one thing I shouted as I stood in their presence: 'It is concerning the resurrection of the dead that I am on trial before you today.' "

[22]Then Felix, who was well acquainted with the Way, adjourned the proceedings. "When Lysias the commander comes," he said, "I will decide your case." [23]He ordered the centurion to keep Paul under guard but to give him some freedom and permit his friends to take care of his needs.

[24]Several days later Felix came with his wife Drusilla, who was a Jewess. He sent for Paul and listened to him as he spoke about faith in Christ Jesus. [25]As Paul discoursed on righteousness, self-control and the judgment to come, Felix was afraid and said, "That's enough for now! You may leave. When I find it convenient, I will send for you." [26]At the same time he was hoping that Paul would offer him a bribe, so he sent for him frequently and talked with him.

[27]When two years had passed, Felix was succeeded by Porcius Festus, but because Felix wanted to grant a favor to the Jews, he left Paul in prison.

The Trial Before Festus

25 Three days after arriving in the province, Festus went up from Caesarea to Jerusalem, [2]where the chief priests and Jewish leaders appeared before him and presented the charges against Paul. [3]They urgently requested Festus, as a favor to them, to have Paul transferred to Jerusalem, for they were preparing an ambush to kill him along the way. [4]Festus answered, "Paul is being held at Caesarea, and I myself am going there soon. [5]Let some of your leaders come with me and press charges against the man there, if he has done anything wrong."

[6]After spending eight or ten days with them, he went down to Caesarea, and the next day he convened the court and ordered that Paul be brought before him. [7]When Paul appeared, the Jews who had come down from Jerusalem stood around him, bringing many serious charges against him, which they could not prove.

[8]Then Paul made his defense: "I have done nothing wrong against the law of the Jews or against the temple or against Caesar."

[9]Festus, wishing to do the Jews a favor, said to Paul, "Are you willing to go up to Jerusalem and stand trial before me there on these charges?"

[10]Paul answered: "I am now standing before Caesar's court, where I ought to be tried. I have not done any wrong to the Jews, as you yourself know very well. [11]If, however, I am guilty of doing anything deserving death, I do not refuse to die. But if the charges brought against me by these Jews are not true, no one has the right to hand me over to them. I appeal to Caesar!"

[12]After Festus had conferred with his council, he declared: "You have appealed to Caesar. To Caesar you will go!"

Festus Consults King Agrippa

[13]A few days later King Agrippa and Bernice arrived at Caesarea to pay their respects to Festus. [14]Since they were spending many days there, Festus discussed Paul's case with the king. He said: "There is a man here whom Felix left as a prisoner. [15]When I went to Jerusalem, the chief priests and elders of the Jews brought charges against him and asked that he be condemned.

POINT OF INTEREST

Acts 24:26-27

The Roman historian Tacitus describes Felix as a cruel, greedy and immoral ruler. Consistent with his reputation, Felix kept Paul, an innocent man, in jail for two years, all the while hoping for a bribe. Little is known of Festus, but his sense of justice in Paul's case is a vast improvement over that of his predecessor (see Acts 25:1–12). Both rulers, however, unwittingly played key parts in God's plan; Paul was to bring the Good News to people in Rome, which was in that time the world's most powerful city (see Acts 28:11–31).

[16] "I told them that it is not the Roman custom to hand over any man before he has faced his accusers and has had an opportunity to defend himself against their charges. [17] When they came here with me, I did not delay the case, but convened the court the next day and ordered the man to be brought in. [18] When his accusers got up to speak, they did not charge him with any of the crimes I had expected. [19] Instead, they had some points of dispute with him about their own religion and about a dead man named Jesus who Paul claimed was alive. [20] I was at a loss how to investigate such matters; so I asked if he would be willing to go to Jerusalem and stand trial there on these charges. [21] When Paul made his appeal to be held over for the Emperor's decision, I ordered him held until I could send him to Caesar."

[22] Then Agrippa said to Festus, "I would like to hear this man myself."

He replied, "Tomorrow you will hear him."

Paul Before Agrippa

[23] The next day Agrippa and Bernice came with great pomp and entered the audience room with the high ranking officers and the leading men of the city. At the command of Festus, Paul was brought in. [24] Festus said: "King Agrippa, and all who are present with us, you see this man! The whole Jewish community has petitioned me about him in Jerusalem and here in Caesarea, shouting that he ought not to live any longer. [25] I found he had done nothing deserving of death, but because he made his appeal to the Emperor I decided to send him to Rome. [26] But I have nothing definite to write to His Majesty about him. Therefore I have brought him before all of you, and especially before you, King Agrippa, so that as a result of this investigation I may have something to write. [27] For I think it is unreasonable to send on a prisoner without specifying the charges against him."

26 Then Agrippa said to Paul, "You have permission to speak for yourself."

So Paul motioned with his hand and began his defense: [2] "King Agrippa, I consider myself fortunate to stand before you today as I make my defense against all the accusations of the Jews, [3] and especially so because you are well acquainted with all the Jewish customs and contro-

versies. Therefore, I beg you to listen to me patiently.

[4] "The Jews all know the way I have lived ever since I was a child, from the beginning of my life in my own country, and also in Jerusalem. [5] They have known me for a long time and can testify, if they are willing, that according to the strictest sect of our religion, I lived as a Pharisee. [6] And now it is because of my hope in what God has promised our fathers that I am on trial today. [7] This is the promise our twelve tribes are hoping to see fulfilled as they earnestly serve God day and night. O king, it is because of this hope that the Jews are accusing me. [8] Why should any of you consider it incredible that God raises the dead?

[9] "I too was convinced that I ought to do all that was possible to oppose the name of Jesus of Nazareth. [10] And that is just what I did in Jerusalem. On the authority of the chief priests I put many of the saints in prison, and when they were put to death, I cast my vote against them. [11] Many a time I went from one synagogue to another to have them punished, and I tried to force them to blaspheme. In my obsession against them, I even went to foreign cities to persecute them.

[12] "On one of these journeys I was going to Damascus with the authority and commission of the chief priests. [13] About noon, O king, as I was on the road, I saw a light from heaven, brighter than the sun, blazing around me and my companions. [14] We all fell to the ground, and I heard a voice saying to me in Aramaic,[a] 'Saul, Saul, why do you persecute me? It is hard for you to kick against the goads.' [15] "Then I asked, 'Who are you, Lord?'

" 'I am Jesus, whom you are persecuting,' the Lord replied. [16] 'Now get up and stand on your feet. I have appeared to you to appoint you as a servant and as a witness of what you have seen of me and what I will show you. [17] I will rescue you from your own people and from the Gentiles. I am sending you to them [18] to open their eyes and turn them from darkness to light, and from the power of Satan to God, so that they may receive forgiveness of sins and a place among those who are sanctified by faith in me.'

[19] "So then, King Agrippa, I was not disobedient to the vision from heaven. [20] First to those in Damascus, then to

_____

a 14 Or Hebrew

those in Jerusalem and in all Judea, and to the Gentiles also, I preached that they should repent and turn to God and prove their repentance by their deeds. ²¹That is why the Jews seized me in the temple courts and tried to kill me. ²²But I have had God's help to this very day, and so I stand here and testify to small and great alike. I am saying nothing beyond what the prophets and Moses said would happen— ²³that the Christ*a* would suffer and, as the first to rise from the dead, would proclaim light to his own people and to the Gentiles."

²⁴At this point Festus interrupted Paul's defense. "You are out of your mind, Paul!" he shouted. "Your great learning is driving you insane."

²⁵"I am not insane, most excellent Festus," Paul replied. "What I am saying is true and reasonable. ²⁶The king is familiar with these things, and I can speak freely to him. I am convinced that none of this has escaped his notice, because it was not done in a corner. ²⁷King Agrippa, do you believe the prophets? I know you do."

²⁸Then Agrippa said to Paul, "Do you think that in such a short time you can persuade me to be a Christian?"

²⁹Paul replied, "Short time or long—I pray God that not only you but all who are listening to me today may become what I am, except for these chains."

³⁰The king rose, and with him the governor and Bernice and those sitting with them. ³¹They left the room, and while talking with one another, they said, "This man is not doing anything that deserves death or imprisonment."

³²Agrippa said to Festus, "This man could have been set free if he had not appealed to Caesar."

Paul Sails for Rome

27 When it was decided that we would sail for Italy, Paul and some other prisoners were handed over to a centurion named Julius, who belonged to the Imperial Regiment. ²We boarded a ship from Adramyttium about to sail for ports along the coast of the province of Asia, and we put out to sea. Aristarchus, a Macedonian from Thessalonica, was with us.

³The next day we landed at Sidon; and Julius, in kindness to Paul, allowed him to go to his friends so they might provide for his needs. ⁴From there we put out to sea again and passed to the lee of Cyprus because the winds were against us. ⁵When we had sailed across the open sea off the coast of Cilicia and Pamphylia, we landed at Myra in Lycia. ⁶There the centurion found an Alexandrian ship sailing for Italy and put us on board. ⁷We made slow headway for many days and had difficulty arriving off Cnidus. When the wind did not allow us to hold our course, we sailed to the lee of Crete, opposite Salmone. ⁸We moved along the coast with difficulty and came to a place called Fair Havens, near the town of Lasea.

⁹Much time had been lost, and sailing had already become dangerous because by now it was after the Fast.*b* So Paul warned them, ¹⁰"Men, I can see that our voyage is going to be disastrous and bring great loss to ship and cargo, and to our own lives also." ¹¹But the centurion, instead of listening to what Paul said, followed the advice of the pilot and of the owner of the ship. ¹²Since the harbor was unsuitable to winter in, the majority decided that we should sail on, hoping to reach Phoenix and winter there. This was a harbor in Crete, facing both southwest and northwest.

The Storm

¹³When a gentle south wind began to blow, they thought they had obtained what they wanted; so they weighed anchor and sailed along the shore of Crete. ¹⁴Before very long, a wind of hurricane force, called the "northeaster," swept down from the island. ¹⁵The ship was caught by the storm and could not head into the wind; so we gave way to it and were driven along. ¹⁶As we passed to the

---

a23 Or *Messiah*   *b9* That is, the Day of Atonement (Yom Kippur)

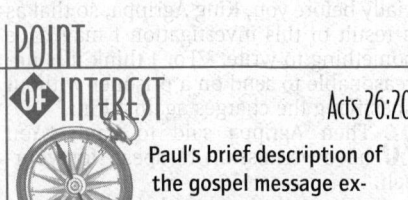

POINT OF INTEREST   Acts 26:20

Paul's brief description of the gospel message explains the link between faith and good deeds. Good deeds won't save us, but they are evidence that we have put our faith in Jesus Christ (see James 2:18). The faith that saves us, changes us!

lee of a small island called Cauda, we were hardly able to make the lifeboat secure. ¹⁷When the men had hoisted it aboard, they passed ropes under the ship itself to hold it together. Fearing that they would run aground on the sandbars of Syrtis, they lowered the sea anchor and let the ship be driven along. ¹⁸We took such a violent battering from the storm that the next day they began to throw the cargo overboard. ¹⁹On the third day, they threw the ship's tackle overboard with their own hands. ²⁰When neither sun nor stars appeared for many days and the storm continued raging, we finally gave up all hope of being saved.

²¹After the men had gone a long time without food, Paul stood up before them and said: "Men, you should have taken my advice not to sail from Crete; then you would have spared yourselves this damage and loss. ²²But now I urge you to keep up your courage, because not one of you will be lost; only the ship will be destroyed. ²³Last night an angel of the God whose I am and whom I serve stood beside me ²⁴and said, 'Do not be afraid, Paul. You must stand trial before Caesar; and God has graciously given you the lives of all who sail with you.' ²⁵So keep up your courage, men, for I have faith in God that it will happen just as he told me. ²⁶Nevertheless, we must run aground on some island."

The Shipwreck

²⁷On the fourteenth night we were still being driven across the Adriatic[a] Sea, when about midnight the sailors sensed they were approaching land. ²⁸They took soundings and found that the water was a hundred and twenty feet[b] deep. A short time later they took soundings again and found it was ninety feet[c] deep. ²⁹Fearing that we would be dashed against the rocks, they dropped four anchors from the stern and prayed for daylight. ³⁰In an attempt to escape from the ship, the sailors let the lifeboat down into the sea, pretending they were going to lower some anchors from the bow. ³¹Then Paul said to the centurion and the soldiers, "Unless these men stay with the ship, you cannot be saved." ³²So the soldiers cut the ropes that held the lifeboat and let it fall away.

³³Just before dawn Paul urged them all to eat. "For the last fourteen days," he said, "you have been in constant suspense and have gone without food—you haven't eaten anything. ³⁴Now I urge you to take some food. You need it to survive. Not one of you will lose a single hair from his head." ³⁵After he said this, he took some bread and gave thanks to God in front of them all. Then he broke it and began to eat. ³⁶They were all encouraged and ate some food themselves. ³⁷Altogether there were 276 of us on board. ³⁸When they had eaten as much as they wanted, they lightened the ship by throwing the grain into the sea.

³⁹When daylight came, they did not recognize the land, but they saw a bay with a sandy beach, where they decided to run the ship aground if they could. ⁴⁰Cutting loose the anchors, they left them in the sea and at the same time untied the ropes that held the rudders. Then they hoisted the foresail to the wind and made for the beach. ⁴¹But the ship struck a sandbar and ran aground. The bow stuck fast and would not move, and the stern was broken to pieces by the pounding of the surf.

⁴²The soldiers planned to kill the prisoners to prevent any of them from swimming away and escaping. ⁴³But the centurion wanted to spare Paul's life and kept them from carrying out their plan. He ordered those who could swim to jump overboard first and get to land. ⁴⁴The rest were to get there on planks or on pieces

---

[a]27 In ancient times the name referred to an area extending well south of Italy.   [b]28 Greek *twenty orguias* (about 37 meters)   [c]28 Greek *fifteen orguias* (about 27 meters)

POINT OF INTEREST

Acts 27:23-25

Of the many faithful people listed in the Bible, only a handful experienced a personal vision such as Paul records here. Yet all of them, like Paul, believed the promises that God had spoken long before. We, too, have God's promises—promises recorded for us in the pages of Scripture. Through these words we can still "hear" God's voice. And though God's promises were recorded long ago, he keeps them still today.

of the ship. In this way everyone reached land in safety.

Ashore on Malta

28 Once safely on shore, we found out that the island was called Malta. ²The islanders showed us unusual kindness. They built a fire and welcomed us all because it was raining and cold. ³Paul gathered a pile of brushwood and, as he put it on the fire, a viper, driven out by the heat, fastened itself on his hand. ⁴When the islanders saw the snake hanging from his hand, they said to each other, "This man must be a murderer; for though he escaped from the sea, Justice has not allowed him to live." ⁵But Paul shook the snake off into the fire and suffered no ill effects. ⁶The people expected him to swell up or suddenly fall dead, but after waiting a long time and seeing nothing unusual happen to him, they changed their minds and said he was a god.

⁷There was an estate nearby that belonged to Publius, the chief official of the island. He welcomed us to his home and for three days entertained us hospitably. ⁸His father was sick in bed, suffering from fever and dysentery. Paul went in to see him and, after prayer, placed his hands on him and healed him. ⁹When this had happened, the rest of the sick on the island came and were cured. ¹⁰They honored us in many ways and when we were ready to sail, they furnished us with the supplies we needed.

Arrival at Rome

¹¹After three months we put out to sea in a ship that had wintered in the island. It was an Alexandrian ship with the figurehead of the twin gods Castor and Pollux. ¹²We put in at Syracuse and stayed there three days. ¹³From there we set sail and arrived at Rhegium. The next day the south wind came up, and on the following day we reached Puteoli. ¹⁴There we found some brothers who invited us to spend a week with them. And so we came to Rome. ¹⁵The brothers there had heard that we were coming, and they traveled as far as the Forum of Appius and the Three Taverns to meet us. At the sight of these men Paul thanked God and was encouraged. ¹⁶When we got to Rome, Paul was allowed to live by himself, with a soldier to guard him.

Paul Preaches at Rome Under Guard

¹⁷Three days later he called together the leaders of the Jews. When they had assembled, Paul said to them: "My brothers, although I have done nothing against our people or against the customs of our ancestors, I was arrested in Jerusalem and handed over to the Romans. ¹⁸They examined me and wanted to release me, because I was not guilty of any crime deserving death. ¹⁹But when the Jews objected, I was compelled to appeal to Caesar—not that I had any charge to bring against my own people. ²⁰For this reason I have asked to see you and talk with you. It is because of the hope of Israel that I am bound with this chain."

²¹They replied, "We have not received any letters from Judea concerning you, and none of the brothers who have come from there has reported or said anything bad about you. ²²But we want to hear what your views are, for we know that people everywhere are talking against this sect."

²³They arranged to meet Paul on a certain day, and came in even larger numbers to the place where he was staying. From morning till evening he explained and declared to them the kingdom of God and tried to convince them about Jesus from the Law of Moses and from the Prophets. ²⁴Some were convinced by what he said, but others would not believe. ²⁵They disagreed among themselves and began to leave after Paul had made this final statement: "The Holy

POINT OF INTEREST

Acts 28:30-31

Paul's first imprisonment was similar to a house arrest. Ironically, his limited freedom afforded a fine ministry opportunity, for he was able to preach "boldly and without hindrance." When Paul got his day in court around A.D. 63, he was released, and he resumed his traveling ministry. After his second arrest he was confined under much harsher circumstances in a Roman dungeon. According to early historians, Paul was beheaded outside of Rome around A.D. 67.

Spirit spoke the truth to your forefathers when he said through Isaiah the prophet:

²⁶" 'Go to this people and say,
"You will be ever hearing but never understanding;
you will be ever seeing but never perceiving."
²⁷For this people's heart has become calloused;
they hardly hear with their ears,
and they have closed their eyes.
Otherwise they might see with their eyes,
hear with their ears,

understand with their hearts
and turn, and I would heal them.'[a]

²⁸"Therefore I want you to know that God's salvation has been sent to the Gentiles, and they will listen!"[b]

³⁰For two whole years Paul stayed there in his own rented house and welcomed all who came to see him. ³¹Boldly and without hindrance he preached the kingdom of God and taught about the Lord Jesus Christ.

[a]27 Isaiah 6:9,10   [b]28 Some manuscripts
listen!" ²⁹After he said this, the Jews left, arguing vigorously among themselves.

*W*hy do some people accept Jesus as Savior and Lord but others don't? Why do I struggle with sin even though I'm a Christian? How can a gracious and loving God judge and punish people? If you've ever wanted answers for questions like these, you'll find a clear expression of Christian belief in lively, practical terms in the book of Romans. But be prepared! Reading this book has been a turning point for many, including Martin Luther and John Wesley. If you're hungry for spiritual renewal, read Romans—it's a great place to begin.

ROMANS

1 Paul, a servant of Christ Jesus, called to be an apostle and set apart for the gospel of God— ²the gospel he promised beforehand through his prophets in the Holy Scriptures ³regarding his Son, who as to his human nature was a descendant of David, ⁴and who through the Spirit*a* of holiness was declared with power to be the Son of God*b* by his resurrection from the dead: Jesus Christ our Lord. ⁵Through him and for his name's sake, we received grace and apostleship to call people from among all the Gentiles to the obedience that comes from faith. ⁶And you also are among those who are called to belong to Jesus Christ.

⁷To all in Rome who are loved by God and called to be saints:

Grace and peace to you from God our Father and from the Lord Jesus Christ.

Paul's Longing to Visit Rome

⁸First, I thank my God through Jesus Christ for all of you, because your faith is being reported all over the world. ⁹God, whom I serve with my whole heart in preaching the gospel of his Son, is my witness how constantly I remember you ¹⁰in my prayers at all times; and I pray that now at last by God's will the way may be opened for me to come to you.

¹¹I long to see you so that I may impart to you some spiritual gift to make you

---

a4 Or *who as to his spirit*   *b4* Or *was appointed to be the Son of God with power* strong— [12]that is, that you and I may be mutually encouraged by each other's faith. [13]I do not want you to be unaware, brothers, that I planned many times to come to you (but have been prevented from doing so until now) in order that I might have a harvest among you, just as I have had among the other Gentiles. [14]I am obligated both to Greeks and non-Greeks, both to the wise and the foolish. [15]That is why I am so eager to preach the gospel also to you who are at Rome.

[16]I am not ashamed of the gospel, because it is the power of God for the salvation of everyone who believes: first for the Jew, then for the Gentile. [17]For in the gospel a righteousness from God is revealed, a righteousness that is by faith from first to last,[a] just as it is written: "The righteous will live by faith."[b]

God's Wrath Against Mankind

[18]The wrath of God is being revealed from heaven against all the godlessness and wickedness of men who suppress the truth by their wickedness, [19]since what may be known about God is plain to them, because God has made it plain to them. [20]For since the creation of the world God's invisible qualities—his eternal power and divine nature—have been clearly seen, being understood from what has been made, so that men are without excuse.

[21]For although they knew God, they neither glorified him as God nor gave thanks to him, but their thinking became futile and their foolish hearts were darkened. [22]Although they claimed to be wise, they became fools [23]and exchanged the glory of the immortal God for images

[a]17 Or *is from faith to faith*   [b]17 Hab. 2:4

MONDAY

Read *Romans 1:1–32*
Key Verse *Romans 1:16*

The Power of the Gospel — Margery Van Zante

As a friend and I walked dorm room to dorm room inviting people to join a Bible discussion, I didn't know what kinds of reactions to expect. While I knew that "the gospel . . . is the power of God for the salvation of everyone who believes," powerful was the last thing I was feeling. I felt fear, insecurity and doubt, but certainly not power. My hope was that people would be interested in a Bible study on the life of Jesus Christ.

When the night of the first meeting rolled around, my friend and I waited and prayed anxiously. Although neither of us said it, deep inside we wondered whether anyone would come. But soon, to our great delight, five young women filed into the small dorm room. What a great beginning!

As the weeks turned into months, we saw their lives transformed as the girls explored God's Word. We began praying for four students in particular, and by the end of the semester all four had come to trust Christ as their personal Savior.

Throughout those months my friend and I saw the power of the gospel in a very real way. We didn't do any coercing or convincing; we merely let the Word of God go to work. Through that process we saw firsthand how the gospel is relevant for every person and powerful enough to change lives.

A Deeper Look
Jonah 3:1–5; Hebrews 4:12

Go to page 1260 for your next devotional reading.

made to look like mortal man and birds and animals and reptiles.

24Therefore God gave them over in the sinful desires of their hearts to sexual impurity for the degrading of their bodies with one another. 25They exchanged the truth of God for a lie, and worshiped and served created things rather than the Creator—who is forever praised. Amen.

26Because of this, God gave them over to shameful lusts. Even their women exchanged natural relations for unnatural ones. 27In the same way the men also abandoned natural relations with women and were inflamed with lust for one another. Men committed indecent acts with other men, and received in themselves the due penalty for their perversion.

28Furthermore, since they did not think it worthwhile to retain the knowledge of God, he gave them over to a depraved mind, to do what ought not to be done. 29They have become filled with every kind of wickedness, evil, greed and depravity. They are full of envy, murder, strife, deceit and malice. They are gossips, 30slanderers, God-haters, insolent, arrogant and boastful; they invent ways of doing evil; they disobey their parents; 31they are senseless, faithless, heartless, ruthless. 32Although they know God's righteous decree that those who do such things deserve death, they not only continue to do these very things but also approve of those who practice them.

God's Righteous Judgment

2 You, therefore, have no excuse, you who pass judgment on someone else, for at whatever point you judge the other, you are condemning yourself, because you who pass judgment do the same things. 2Now we know that God's judgment against those who do such things is based on truth. 3So when you, a mere man, pass judgment on them and yet do the same things, do you think you will escape God's judgment? 4Or do you show contempt for the riches of his kindness, tolerance and patience, not realizing that God's kindness leads you toward repentance?

5But because of your stubbornness and your unrepentant heart, you are storing up wrath against yourself for the day of God's wrath, when his righteous judgment will be revealed. 6God "will give to each person according to what he has done."a 7To those who by persistence in doing good seek glory, honor and immortality, he will give eternal life. 8But for those who are self-seeking and who reject the truth and follow evil, there will be wrath and anger. 9There will be trouble and distress for every human being who does evil: first for the Jew, then for the Gentile; 10but glory, honor and peace for everyone who does good: first for the Jew, then for the Gentile. 11For God does not show favoritism.

12All who sin apart from the law will also perish apart from the law, and all who sin under the law will be judged by the law. 13For it is not those who hear the law who are righteous in God's sight, but it is those who obey the law who will be declared righteous. 14(Indeed, when Gentiles, who do not have the law, do by nature things required by the law, they are a law for themselves, even though they do not have the law, 15since they show that the requirements of the law are written on their hearts, their consciences also bearing witness, and their thoughts now accusing, now even defending them.) 16This will take place on the day when God will judge men's secrets through Jesus Christ, as my gospel declares.

The Jews and the Law

17Now you, if you call yourself a Jew; if you rely on the law and brag about your relationship to God; 18if you know

a6 Psalm 62:12; Prov. 24:12

POINT OF INTEREST

Romans 1:12

Paul, perhaps the greatest evangelist who ever lived, didn't begin building churches by hiring an architect or an engineer or going to the bank for financing. He began by telling others the Good News; by fostering loving, trusting personal relationships; and by holding his friends accountable when they strayed from the truth. As you read through his letters, look for other clues that show how Paul maintained these relationships. His model of relational evangelism is one worth emulating today.

his will and approve of what is superior because you are instructed by the law; [19]if you are convinced that you are a guide for the blind, a light for those who are in the dark, [20]an instructor of the foolish, a teacher of infants, because you have in the law the embodiment of knowledge and truth— [21]you, then, who teach others, do you not teach yourself? You who preach against stealing, do you steal? [22]You who say that people should not commit adultery, do you commit adultery? You who abhor idols, do you rob temples? [23]You who brag about the law, do you dishonor God by breaking the law? [24]As it is written: "God's name is blasphemed among the Gentiles because of you."[a]

[25]Circumcision has value if you observe the law, but if you break the law, you have become as though you had not been circumcised. [26]If those who are not circumcised keep the law's requirements, will they not be regarded as though they were circumcised? [27]The one who is not circumcised physically and yet obeys the law will condemn you who, even though you have the[b] written code and circumcision, are a lawbreaker.

[28]A man is not a Jew if he is only one outwardly, nor is circumcision merely outward and physical. [29]No, a man is a Jew if he is one inwardly; and circumcision is circumcision of the heart, by the Spirit, not by the written code. Such a man's praise is not from men, but from God.

God's Faithfulness

3 What advantage, then, is there in being a Jew, or what value is there in circumcision? [2]Much in every way! First of all, they have been entrusted with the very words of God.

[3]What if some did not have faith? Will their lack of faith nullify God's faithfulness? [4]Not at all! Let God be true, and every man a liar. As it is written:

"So that you may be proved right
    when you speak
and prevail when you judge."[c]

[5]But if our unrighteousness brings out God's righteousness more clearly, what shall we say? That God is unjust in bringing his wrath on us? (I am using a human argument.) [6]Certainly not! If that were so, how could God judge the world? [7]Someone might argue, "If my falsehood

enhances God's truthfulness and so increases his glory, why am I still condemned as a sinner?" [8]Why not say—as we are being slanderously reported as saying and as some claim that we say— "Let us do evil that good may result"? Their condemnation is deserved.

No One Is Righteous

[9]What shall we conclude then? Are we any better[d]? Not at all! We have already made the charge that Jews and Gentiles alike are all under sin. [10]As it is written:

"There is no one righteous, not even
        one;
[11]   there is no one who understands,
        no one who seeks God.
[12]All have turned away,
        they have together become
            worthless;
    there is no one who does good,
        not even one."[e]
[13]"Their throats are open graves;
        their tongues practice deceit."[f]
"The poison of vipers is on their
        lips."[g]
[14]   "Their mouths are full of cursing
            and bitterness."[h]
[15]"Their feet are swift to shed blood;
[16]   ruin and misery mark their ways,
[17]and the way of peace they do not
            know."[i]
[18]   "There is no fear of God before
            their eyes."[j]

[19]Now we know that whatever the law says, it says to those who are under the law, so that every mouth may be silenced and the whole world held accountable to God. [20]Therefore no one will be declared righteous in his sight by observing the law; rather, through the law we become conscious of sin.

Righteousness Through Faith

[21]But now a righteousness from God, apart from law, has been made known, to which the Law and the Prophets testify. [22]This righteousness from God comes through faith in Jesus Christ to all who believe. There is no difference, [23]for all have sinned and fall short of the glory of God, [24]and are justified freely by his

[a]24 Isaiah 52:5; Ezek. 36:22   [b]27 Or who, by means of a   [c]4 Psalm 51:4   [d]9 Or worse   [e]12 Psalms 14:1-3; 53:1-3; Eccles. 7:20   [f]13 Psalm 5:9   [g]13 Psalm 140:3   [h]14 Psalm 10:7   [i]17 Isaiah 59:7,8   [j]18 Psalm 36:1

grace through the redemption that came by Christ Jesus. ²⁵God presented him as a sacrifice of atonement,ᵃ through faith in his blood. He did this to demonstrate his justice, because in his forbearance he had left the sins committed beforehand unpunished— ²⁶he did it to demonstrate his justice at the present time, so as to be just and the one who justifies those who have faith in Jesus.

²⁷Where, then, is boasting? It is excluded. On what principle? On that of observing the law? No, but on that of faith. ²⁸For we maintain that a man is justified by faith apart from observing the law.

²⁹Is God the God of Jews only? Is he not the God of Gentiles too? Yes, of Gentiles too, ³⁰since there is only one God, who will justify the circumcised by faith and the uncircumcised through that same faith. ³¹Do we, then, nullify the law by this faith? Not at all! Rather, we uphold the law.

Abraham Justified by Faith

4 What then shall we say that Abraham, our forefather, discovered in this mat-

ᵃ25 Or *as the one who would turn aside his wrath, taking away sin*

TUESDAY

Read *Romans 3:9–31*
Key Verse *Romans 3:23*

A New Fragrance — Shannon Gayk

My father is a veterinarian with one particularly unusual client— the Catman. The Catman is a homeless man with a soft spot in his heart for felines. Nicknamed by my dad's office staff, the Catman regularly appears in the lobby of the animal hospital with a new friend he has found in the street and brought in for medical treatment.

Though he is very attentive to the needs of his animal friends, the Catman is not nearly as concerned about his own personal hygiene. In fact, his body odor often remains in the lobby long after he has left with his cats. When they spot the Catman coming, my father's staff have often taken to the back rooms to avoid the smell.

When my dad first related this situation to me, I realized how much we are like the Catman when we stand before God. We reek of sin with a stench so strong it's surprising that he doesn't just drop us into the garbage can. But just as the Catman doesn't realize how bad he smells to others, we don't appreciate how horrendous our own sin is before God.

Yet God does not react like my father's staff—somehow he does the opposite. Rather than hiding from us, he embraces us and rids us of our stinking sin. What we have to do is confess our sin and ask him, as the psalmist David did, to wash us clean: "Cleanse me with hyssop, and I will be clean; wash me, and I will be whiter than snow" (Psalm 51:7). Through Jesus Christ, God gives a thorough washing, and he gives us a priceless perfume to put on, a new fragrance that is meant to attract others to Jesus: "But thanks be to God, who always leads us in triumphal procession in Christ and through us spreads everywhere the fragrance of the knowledge of him" (2 Corinthians 2:14).

A Deeper Look
Isaiah 1:18; 1 John 1:9

Go to page 1262 for your next devotional reading.

ter? [2]If, in fact, Abraham was justified by works, he had something to boast about—but not before God. [3]What does the Scripture say? "Abraham believed God, and it was credited to him as righteousness."[a]

[4]Now when a man works, his wages are not credited to him as a gift, but as an obligation. [5]However, to the man who does not work but trusts God who justifies the wicked, his faith is credited as righteousness. [6]David says the same thing when he speaks of the blessedness of the man to whom God credits righteousness apart from works:

[7]"Blessed are they
   whose transgressions are forgiven,
   whose sins are covered.
[8]Blessed is the man
   whose sin the Lord will never
      count against him."[b]

[9]Is this blessedness only for the circumcised, or also for the uncircumcised? We have been saying that Abraham's faith was credited to him as righteousness. [10]Under what circumstances was it credited? Was it after he was circumcised, or before? It was not after, but before! [11]And he received the sign of circumcision, a seal of the righteousness that he had by faith while he was still uncircumcised. So then, he is the father of all who believe but have not been circumcised, in order that righteousness might be credited to them. [12]And he is also the father of the circumcised who not only are circumcised but who also walk in the footsteps of the faith that our father Abraham had before he was circumcised.

[13]It was not through law that Abraham and his offspring received the promise that he would be heir of the world, but through the righteousness that comes by faith. [14]For if those who live by law are heirs, faith has no value and the promise is worthless, [15]because law brings wrath. And where there is no law there is no transgression.

[16]Therefore, the promise comes by faith, so that it may be by grace and may be guaranteed to all Abraham's offspring—not only to those who are of the law but also to those who are of the faith of Abraham. He is the father of us all. [17]As it is written: "I have made you a father of many nations."[c] He is our father in the sight of God, in whom he be-

lieved—the God who gives life to the dead and calls things that are not as though they were.

[18]Against all hope, Abraham in hope believed and so became the father of many nations, just as it had been said to him, "So shall your offspring be."[d] [19]Without weakening in his faith, he faced the fact that his body was as good as dead—since he was about a hundred years old—and that Sarah's womb was also dead. [20]Yet he did not waver through unbelief regarding the promise of God, but was strengthened in his faith and gave glory to God, [21]being fully persuaded that God had power to do what he had promised. [22]This is why "it was credited to him as righteousness." [23]The words "it was credited to him" were written not for him alone, [24]but also for us, to whom God will credit righteousness—for us who believe in him who raised Jesus our Lord from the dead. [25]He was delivered over to death for our sins and was raised to life for our justification.

Peace and Joy

5 Therefore, since we have been justified through faith, we[e] have peace with God through our Lord Jesus Christ, [2]through whom we have gained access by faith into this grace in which we now stand. And we[e] rejoice in the hope of the glory of God. [3]Not only so, but we[e] also rejoice in our sufferings, because we know that suffering produces perseverance; [4]perseverance, character; and character, hope. [5]And hope does not disappoint us, because God has poured out his

[a]3 Gen. 15:6; also in verse 22   [b]8 Psalm 32:1,2
[c]17 Gen. 17:5   [d]18 Gen. 15:5   [e]1,2,3 Or
let us

POINT OF INTEREST

Romans 3:19-22

As a former Pharisee, Paul knew the Hebrew Scriptures very well. After his conversion, his vast and detailed knowledge of Old Testament law gave him extraordinary insight into the theology of salvation. Here he speaks with authority on both the Mosaic code and the new covenant in Jesus Christ.

love into our hearts by the Holy Spirit, whom he has given us.

⁶You see, at just the right time, when we were still powerless, Christ died for the ungodly. ⁷Very rarely will anyone die for a righteous man, though for a good man someone might possibly dare to die. ⁸But God demonstrates his own love for us in this: While we were still sinners, Christ died for us.

⁹Since we have now been justified by his blood, how much more shall we be saved from God's wrath through him!

¹⁰For if, when we were God's enemies, we were reconciled to him through the death of his Son, how much more, having been reconciled, shall we be saved through his life! ¹¹Not only is this so, but we also rejoice in God through our Lord Jesus Christ, through whom we have now received reconciliation.

Death Through Adam, Life Through Christ

¹²Therefore, just as sin entered the world through one man, and death

---

WEDNESDAY

Read *Romans 4:1–25*
Key Verses *Romans 4:20–21*

Don't Waver! – Dr. Jerry White

A grizzled sergeant yelled, "Stand up!" We did. "Hook up!" We each snapped our lanyard to the wire running the length of the airplane. "Stand in the door!" We moved. Because I was the ranking officer, the sergeant had me leaning out of the open door of the airplane. The ground was rushing by below us. Then, "Go!" In rapid succession, each of us jumped into nothingness. There was the moment of faith when I stepped off into air, waiting for the promised safety of an unfurled chute. The lanyard was pulled by the static line, followed by the upward snap and jerk of the parachute. Once again, everything had worked.

Did I waver? Some. Did I fear? Yes. Did I believe I would be safe? Not 100 percent. I knew there was always a chance of failure, yet I jumped.

Parachutes sometimes fail, but the assurance of God's dependability and reliability is complete. Time after time throughout the history of God's people, there is evidence that God always fulfills his promises. Even without all the history we have today, Abraham believed the impossible would happen—he fathered a child from an ancient body. And because of his faith, God considered his account fully paid.

We have so much more evidence than Abraham. Jesus was promised—and he came. His death and resurrection were prophesied, and we live because of it. "Not one word has failed of all the good promises he gave through his servant Moses" (1 Kings 8:56). "We tell you the good news: What God promised our fathers he has fulfilled for us, their children, by raising up Jesus" (Acts 13:32–33).

Daily we have far greater assurance with God than with a human-packed parachute: "The one who calls you is faithful and he will do it" (1 Thessalonians 5:24). God promises that he is our parachute, and he always works!

A Deeper Look
Joshua 21:45; Psalm 57:10; 119:140

Go to page 1264 for your next devotional reading.

through sin, and in this way death came to all men, because all sinned— ¹³for before the law was given, sin was in the world. But sin is not taken into account when there is no law. ¹⁴Nevertheless, death reigned from the time of Adam to the time of Moses, even over those who did not sin by breaking a command, as did Adam, who was a pattern of the one to come.

¹⁵But the gift is not like the trespass. For if the many died by the trespass of the one man, how much more did God's grace and the gift that came by the grace of the one man, Jesus Christ, overflow to the many! ¹⁶Again, the gift of God is not like the result of the one man's sin: The judgment followed one sin and brought condemnation, but the gift followed many trespasses and brought justification. ¹⁷For if, by the trespass of the one man, death reigned through that one man, how much more will those who receive God's abundant provision of grace and of the gift of righteousness reign in life through the one man, Jesus Christ.

¹⁸Consequently, just as the result of one trespass was condemnation for all men, so also the result of one act of righteousness was justification that brings life for all men. ¹⁹For just as through the disobedience of the one man the many were made sinners, so also through the obedience of the one man the many will be made righteous.

²⁰The law was added so that the trespass might increase. But where sin increased, grace increased all the more, ²¹so that, just as sin reigned in death, so also grace might reign through righteousness to bring eternal life through Jesus Christ our Lord.

Dead to Sin, Alive in Christ

6 What shall we say, then? Shall we go on sinning so that grace may increase? ²By no means! We died to sin; how can we live in it any longer? ³Or don't you know that all of us who were baptized into Christ Jesus were baptized into his death? ⁴We were therefore buried with him through baptism into death in order that, just as Christ was raised from the dead through the glory of the Father, we too may live a new life.

⁵If we have been united with him like this in his death, we will certainly also be united with him in his resurrection. ⁶For we know that our old self was crucified with him so that the body of sin might be done away with,ᵃ that we should no longer be slaves to sin— ⁷because anyone who has died has been freed from sin.

⁸Now if we died with Christ, we believe that we will also live with him. ⁹For we know that since Christ was raised from the dead, he cannot die again; death no longer has mastery over him. ¹⁰The death he died, he died to sin once for all; but the life he lives, he lives to God.

¹¹In the same way, count yourselves dead to sin but alive to God in Christ Jesus. ¹²Therefore do not let sin reign in your mortal body so that you obey its evil desires. ¹³Do not offer the parts of your body to sin, as instruments of wickedness, but rather offer yourselves to God, as those who have been brought from death to life; and offer the parts of your body to him as instruments of righteousness. ¹⁴For sin shall not be your master, because you are not under law, but under grace.

Slaves to Righteousness

¹⁵What then? Shall we sin because we are not under law but under grace? By no means! ¹⁶Don't you know that when you offer yourselves to someone to obey him as slaves, you are slaves to the one whom you obey—whether you are slaves to sin, which leads to death, or to obedience, which leads to righteousness? ¹⁷But

ᵃ6 Or *be rendered powerless*

POINT OF INTEREST

Romans 5:1

How we long for peace and hope! All around us we see abuse, crime and broken families. We experience work overload, intense pressure to succeed and countless other stresses. But Paul speaks of the hope that is accessible to us in Jesus Christ, our Savior. Certainly we have to cope in the here-and-now, get an education and work to make our way in the world. But with the hope of eternal peace as the background for our behavior, we can have a heavenly perspective on our earthly lives.

thanks be to God that, though you used to be slaves to sin, you wholeheartedly obeyed the form of teaching to which you were entrusted. [18]You have been set free from sin and have become slaves to righteousness.

[19]I put this in human terms because you are weak in your natural selves. Just as you used to offer the parts of your body in slavery to impurity and to ever-increasing wickedness, so now offer them in slavery to righteousness leading to holiness. [20]When you were slaves to sin, you were free from the control of righteousness. [21]What benefit did you reap at that time from the things you are now ashamed of? Those things result in death! [22]But now that you have been set free from sin and have become slaves to God, the benefit you reap leads to holiness, and the result is eternal life. [23]For the wages of sin is death, but the gift of God is eternal life in[a] Christ Jesus our Lord.

An Illustration From Marriage

7 Do you not know, brothers—for I am speaking to men who know the law—that the law has authority over a man only as long as he lives? [2]For example, by law a married woman is bound to her husband as long as he is alive, but if her husband dies, she is released from the law of marriage. [3]So then, if she marries another man while her husband is still alive, she is called an adulteress. But if her husband dies, she is released from

[a]23 Or *through*

THURSDAY

Read *Romans 6:1–23*
Key Verse *Romans 6:23*

Penalty – Scott L. Moore

Soccer fans understand the saying, "There's no such thing as a free kick—it's just a matter of who pays." Just ask any soccer player who has stood in the middle of a wall of defenders after a penalty and taken an opponent's "free kick" in the face. The same principle applies in life. Nothing is free—someone's got to pay. But a big problem turns up when we don't have the means to pay off a debt we've already incurred.

We're not talking about school loans or credit cards here. In this verse Paul tells us that each one of us is indebted to God because of our sin. Every day we live on this earth, we earn the "wages" of our sinful way of life.

Our situation is comparable to the dilemma faced by the servant in a story Jesus once told (see Matthew 18:23–35). This servant owed his king a huge debt, one the servant could never repay. All this man could do was plead that his debt be forgiven. Taking pity on him, the king canceled the debt. When the king forgave the servant's debt, the king didn't get his money back. It cost him.

And that's exactly what God has done for us. Jesus' death paid the penalty that sin demands so that we won't have to pay it. But this act wasn't "free" for him. He had to stand firm and take the opponent's "free kick." We could never have paid off all that we owe God. Never in a million years. Instead, because of Jesus, we've been forgiven. We have life because he paid the price.

A Deeper Look
Isaiah 52:14; Hebrews 9:26–28

Go to page 1266 for your next devotional reading.

that law and is not an adulteress, even though she marries another man.

[4]So, my brothers, you also died to the law through the body of Christ, that you might belong to another, to him who was raised from the dead, in order that we might bear fruit to God. [5]For when we were controlled by the sinful nature,[a] the sinful passions aroused by the law were at work in our bodies, so that we bore fruit for death. [6]But now, by dying to what once bound us, we have been released from the law so that we serve in the new way of the Spirit, and not in the old way of the written code.

Struggling With Sin

[7]What shall we say, then? Is the law sin? Certainly not! Indeed I would not have known what sin was except through the law. For I would not have known what coveting really was if the law had not said, "Do not covet."[b] [8]But sin, seizing the opportunity afforded by the commandment, produced in me every kind of covetous desire. For apart from law, sin is dead. [9]Once I was alive apart from law; but when the commandment came, sin sprang to life and I died. [10]I found that the very commandment that was intended to bring life actually brought death. [11]For sin, seizing the opportunity afforded by the commandment, deceived me, and through the commandment put me to death. [12]So then, the law is holy, and the commandment is holy, righteous and good.

[13]Did that which is good, then, become death to me? By no means! But in order that sin might be recognized as sin, it produced death in me through what was good, so that through the commandment sin might become utterly sinful. [14]We know that the law is spiritual; but I am unspiritual, sold as a slave to sin. [15]I do not understand what I do. For what I want to do I do not do, but what I hate I do. [16]And if I do what I do not want to do, I agree that the law is good. [17]As it is, it is no longer I myself who do it, but it is sin living in me. [18]I know that nothing good lives in me, that is, in my sinful nature.[c] For I have the desire to do what is good, but I cannot carry it out. [19]For what I do is not the good I want to do; no, the evil I do not want to do—this I keep on doing. [20]Now if I do what I do not want to do, it is no longer I who do it, but it is sin living in me that does it.

[21]So I find this law at work: When I want to do good, evil is right there with me. [22]For in my inner being I delight in God's law; [23]but I see another law at work in the members of my body, waging war against the law of my mind and making me a prisoner of the law of sin at work within my members. [24]What a wretched man I am! Who will rescue me from this body of death? [25]Thanks be to God—through Jesus Christ our Lord!

So then, I myself in my mind am a slave to God's law, but in the sinful nature a slave to the law of sin.

Life Through the Spirit

8 Therefore, there is now no condemnation for those who are in Christ Jesus,[d] [2]because through Christ Jesus the law of the Spirit of life set me free from the law of sin and death. [3]For what the law was powerless to do in that it was weakened by the sinful nature,[e] God did by sending his own Son in the likeness of sinful man to be a sin offering.[f] And so he condemned sin in sinful man,[g] [4]in order that the righteous requirements of the law might be fully met in us, who do not live according to the sinful nature but according to the Spirit.

[5]Those who live according to the sinful nature have their minds set on what that nature desires; but those who live in accordance with the Spirit have their minds set on what the Spirit desires. [6]The mind of sinful man[h] is death, but the mind

[a]5 Or *the flesh*; also in verse 25
[b]7 Exodus 20:17; Deut. 5:21   [c]18 Or *my flesh*
[d]1 Some later manuscripts *Jesus, who do not live according to the sinful nature but according to the Spirit,*   [e]3 Or *the flesh*; also in verses 4, 5, 8, 9, 12 and 13   [f]3 Or *man, for sin*   [g]3 Or *in the flesh*   [h]6 Or *mind set on the flesh*

POINT OF INTEREST

Romans 6:6-11

"Our old self was crucified with him." Have you ever considered personally the ramifications of that statement? Our old, sinful selves are just as dead as Jesus was on that cross. We must therefore "count [our]selves dead to sin but alive to God in Christ Jesus." What does that mean to you today?

controlled by the Spirit is life and peace; [7]the sinful mind[a] is hostile to God. It does not submit to God's law, nor can it do so. [8]Those controlled by the sinful nature cannot please God.

[9]You, however, are controlled not by the sinful nature but by the Spirit, if the Spirit of God lives in you. And if anyone does not have the Spirit of Christ, he does not belong to Christ. [10]But if Christ is in you, your body is dead because of sin, yet your spirit is alive because of righteousness. [11]And if the Spirit of him who raised Jesus from the dead is living in you, he who raised Christ from the dead will also give life to your mortal bodies through his Spirit, who lives in you.

[12]Therefore, brothers, we have an obligation—but it is not to the sinful nature, to live according to it. [13]For if you live according to the sinful nature, you will die; but if by the Spirit you put to death the misdeeds of the body, you will live, [14]because those who are led by the Spirit of God are sons of God. [15]For you did not receive a spirit that makes you a slave again to fear, but you received the

[a]7 Or *the mind set on the flesh*

FRIDAY

Read Romans 7:1—8:17
Key Verses Romans 7:21—23

Why Did I Do That? — Randy C. Johnson

Why did I do that? Why did I speak unkindly, act thoughtlessly or neglect my responsibility? Why do I still fail God and hurt others and myself in the process?

Sometimes I feel like the cartoon character who has the devil on one shoulder and an angel on the other, each doling out free advice. The angel keeps urging me to consider the spiritual and moral consequences while the devil says, "Go for it; let your hair down."

In reality, a struggle goes on within the soul of every Christian. The apostle Paul says it is the tension between the "law of God" and the "law of the body" (see Romans 7:21–23), between the "flesh" and the "Spirit" (see Romans 8).

The "flesh" is who we are from birth. Since the time of Adam we humans have been born with a nature to sin that creates in us a craving to satisfy our appetites, grab at whatever we can get and glory in what we have done (see 1 John 2:16). These cravings whisper to us, "If it feels good, do it!"

The spiritual person is who we become at rebirth, at the moment of our salvation. This is when the Holy Spirit comes to reside in the life of the believer (see 1 Corinthians 3:16). Now there is a new voice whispering in our ear—the still, small voice that asks, "Are you pleasing God?"

What do I do to quiet my flesh? Two things help me keep my spiritual ears attuned to God's voice: being consistent in my daily quiet time and seeking out fellowship with other Christians. The voice of the flesh fades because of the grace of a Holy God. "Thanks be to God—through Jesus Christ our Lord!" (Romans 7:25).

A Deeper Look
Romans 6:4—7; 1 John 5:4—5

Go to page 1268 for your next devotional reading.

Spirit of sonship.*a* And by him we cry, *"Abba,*b *Father."* 16The Spirit himself testifies with our spirit that we are God's children. 17Now if we are children, then we are heirs—heirs of God and co-heirs with Christ, if indeed we share in his sufferings in order that we may also share in his glory.

Future Glory

18I consider that our present sufferings are not worth comparing with the glory that will be revealed in us. 19The creation waits in eager expectation for the sons of God to be revealed. 20For the creation was subjected to frustration, not by its own choice, but by the will of the one who subjected it, in hope 21that*c* the creation itself will be liberated from its bondage to decay and brought into the glorious freedom of the children of God.

22We know that the whole creation has been groaning as in the pains of childbirth right up to the present time. 23Not only so, but we ourselves, who have the firstfruits of the Spirit, groan inwardly as we wait eagerly for our adoption as sons, the redemption of our bodies. 24For in this hope we were saved. But hope that is seen is no hope at all. Who hopes for what he already has? 25But if we hope for what we do not yet have, we wait for it patiently.

26In the same way, the Spirit helps us in our weakness. We do not know what we ought to pray for, but the Spirit himself intercedes for us with groans that words cannot express. 27And he who searches our hearts knows the mind of the Spirit, because the Spirit intercedes for the saints in accordance with God's will.

More Than Conquerors

28And we know that in all things God works for the good of those who love him,*d* who*e* have been called according to his purpose. 29For those God foreknew he also predestined to be conformed to the likeness of his Son, that he might be the firstborn among many brothers. 30And those he predestined, he also called; those he called, he also justified; those he justified, he also glorified.

31What, then, shall we say in response to this? If God is for us, who can be against us? 32He who did not spare his own Son, but gave him up for us all—how will he not also, along with him,

graciously give us all things? 33Who will bring any charge against those whom God has chosen? It is God who justifies. 34Who is he that condemns? Christ Jesus, who died—more than that, who was raised to life—is at the right hand of God and is also interceding for us. 35Who shall separate us from the love of Christ? Shall trouble or hardship or persecution or famine or nakedness or danger or sword? 36As it is written:

> "For your sake we face death all day long;
> we are considered as sheep to be slaughtered."*f*

37No, in all these things we are more than conquerors through him who loved us. 38For I am convinced that neither death nor life, neither angels nor demons,*g* neither the present nor the future, nor any powers, 39neither height nor depth, nor anything else in all creation, will be able to separate us from the love of God that is in Christ Jesus our Lord.

God's Sovereign Choice

9 I speak the truth in Christ—I am not lying, my conscience confirms it in the Holy Spirit— 2I have great sorrow and unceasing anguish in my heart. 3For I could wish that I myself were cursed and cut off from Christ for the sake of my brothers, those of my own race, 4the people of Israel. Theirs is the adoption as

*a*15 Or *adoption*   *b*15 Aramaic for *Father*
*c*20,21 Or *subjected it in hope. 21For*   *d*28 Some manuscripts *And we know that all things work together for good to those who love God*   *e*28 Or *works together with those who love him to bring about what is good—with those who*
*f*36 Psalm 44:22   *g*38 Or *nor heavenly rulers*

POINT OF INTEREST

Romans 7:14-25

Here Paul speaks to the human condition, for all of us have "unspiritual" hearts. Paul goes on to describe the battle raging within all Christians. How can we win this battle? We win by trusting in our amazing God, who has shown us grace through his Son to help us in our struggles with sin. Jesus Christ has won the war for us (see 1 Corinthians 15:57).

Read Romans 8:1–39
Key Verses Romans 8:35–39

Safe and Secure

Losing things—a dorm key, a debit card, a term's worth of biology notes—is frustrating and sometimes expensive. Losing something more significant—a special relationship, a dream, a loved one—carries an even deeper sense of, well, loss! And getting our personal stuff ripped off—a favorite CD, a backpack or even a bike—leaves us feeling violated and angry. But these things happen to all of us at one time or another. Wouldn't you love to possess one thing that is absolutely safe and secure? Something that could never be lost or taken away?

When Jesus has called us into a relationship with him, we belong to him and he to us. Jesus promises to be with us forever. When we enter a relationship with him, nothing can destroy the bonds that are built . . . nothing "in all creation" will be able to "separate us from the love of God that is in Christ Jesus our Lord"! Even though we might lose everything else, his love is tenacious and durable, even when we feel far from him. What amazing love! What security!

Digging Into the Word
1. How is God committed to you? — *Matthew 28:20; John 10:27–30*
2. How does God provide security for you?—*Romans 8:31; Hebrews 13:5–6*

Discussion Starter
Jesus is always with us. This can bring a sense of security, but it is also a wake-up call. Start up a conversation among your friends with these questions: If you knew Jesus was going to appear in bodily form and walk with you through the coming week, what would you change in your schedule? What would you decide not to do? What would you make a point of doing?

One Step Deeper
Proverbs 3:23–26; 2 Timothy 2:11–13

Go to page 1272 for your next devotional reading.

THE BRIDGE ILLUSTRATION

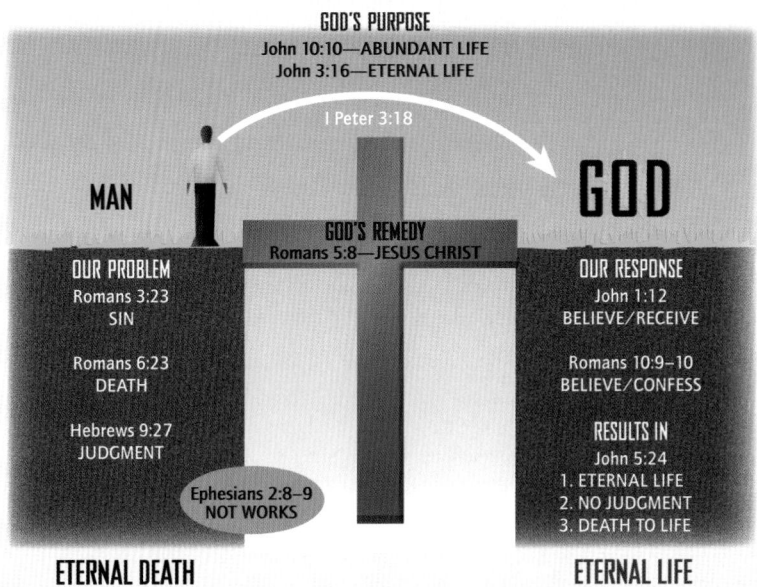

The Bridge Illustration is a tool that can be used to present the gospel. There are four concepts that you will want to communicate using this method.

1. GOD'S PURPOSE	Abundant Life	John 10:10
	Eternal Life	John 3:16
2. OUR PROBLEM	All Have Sinned	Romans 3:23
	Sin's Penalty	Romans 6:23; Hebrews 9:27
3. GOD'S REMEDY	Christ Paid the Penalty	Romans 5:8; I Peter 3:18
	Salvation Not by Works	Ephesians 2:8–9
4. OUR RESPONSE	Must Receive Christ	John 1:12; Romans 10:9–10
	Assurance of Salvation	John 5:24 (I John 5:13)

TEN TIPS FOR PREPARING A PERSONAL TESTIMONY

One of the most powerful means of sharing our faith is telling the story of how we trusted Jesus Christ and how he has affected our lives. The Scriptures show how God uses personal testimonies to touch others. Because of the Samaritan woman's testimony, "many of the Samaritans from that town believed in him" (John 4:39). Paul shared his personal testimony when standing before King Agrippa (see Acts 26). John testified about his relationship with Jesus when he wrote, "we proclaim to you what we have seen and heard" (1 John 1:3). God can use our stories of faith to bring others to him; it's our job to be prepared to share them. Here's how:

■ Follow Paul's model in Acts 26 using the outline "before, how, and after." Share briefly what your life was like before salvation, how you decided to accept Christ as your personal Savior and what your life has been like since that decision.

■ Keep it short. Cover the essential points of your story in three to five minutes.

■ Keep it simple. Mention only a few people, places and events that were instrumental in your conversion.

■ In the "before" section, share some positive and negative aspects of your life as well as some interesting non-spiritual details.

■ In the "how" section, share a few key Bible verses to help explain the gospel. Be sure to include the four elements of the gospel—that all people have fallen short of God's standard, that our punishment for this disobedience is death, that Jesus was punished in our place, and that we each must personally accept Jesus Christ.

■ In the "after" section, summarize with a statement that includes the "bottom line," perhaps something like, "And now I know for sure that if I were to die tonight I would go to heaven." Listeners often will comment on your last statement and this will open a door for further discussion.

■ Share your story but don't preach! Use words such as "I" and "me," not "you."

■ Use your own words. Avoid religious phrases or jargon that someone from a non-Christian background will not easily understand.

■ Write out your testimony in outline form and practice sharing it with a Christian friend.

■ Ask the Lord to give you an opportunity to share your testimony with a non-Christian, and then do so with sensitivity, "Always be prepared to give an answer to everyone who asks you to give the reason for the hope that you have. But do this with gentleness and respect" (1 Peter 3:15).

BECOMING A SKILLED SMALL GROUP LEADER

Leading a small group Bible study is a learned skill that must be developed through training and experience. Even though you might already possess the spiritual gifts to lead this kind of group, the task requires an investment in time and preparation in order to be successful. Here are a few basic guidelines for leading a small group study.

Before the Group Arrives

■ Pray that your group members will be teachable. Pray for wisdom and discernment for yourself and each of the members. Ask God to stop the devil from disturbing the study or hindering members from coming. Pray that the Holy Spirit will use God's Word to renew and transform those who attend.

■ Prepare yourself well. Prepare an outline of the material. Break it into sections and decide approximately how much time to spend on each section. Decide which sections you will want to emphasize during your discussion. Prepare interesting, open-ended discussion questions that will stimulate thinking and discussion among group members. Know the material thoroughly.

■ The members of your Bible study groups will likely come from a variety of backgrounds and have various levels of commitment. Be aware that the task of leading will vary in difficulty, depending on the group and that you may need to adjust your methods and expectations accordingly.

■ When recruiting group members, remind them that there are three requirements: (1) regular attendance, (2) coming with the materials completed, (3) participating in the discussion.

CONTINUED ON NEXT PAGE

CONTINUED FROM PREVIOUS PAGE

During the Bible Study

■ Begin on time. Establishing structure and sticking to it will set a tone of discipline for the group in other, more important areas.

■ Begin by giving the group an overview of the meeting. Ask a group member (in advance) to pray for the study.

■ Remind the group of the small group philosophy—that we gather together to encourage, stimulate and strengthen each other, as well as to answer any questions or difficulties. Encourage the group members to study the material on their own, in addition to coming to the study.

■ Get into the Bible! Remind the group to look up the verses being discussed and ask a group member to read them aloud.

■ Be sensitive to the leading of the Holy Spirit as the discussion progresses. Be sensitive to members' confusion or questions. Be careful to draw the answers from the group rather than delivering them yourself.

■ Summarize each main point of discussion before launching a new topic. You may ask for someone from the group to summarize for the others.

■ End on time.

■ Close with prayer.

sons; theirs the divine glory, the covenants, the receiving of the law, the temple worship and the promises. ⁵Theirs are the patriarchs, and from them is traced the human ancestry of Christ, who is God over all, forever praised!ᵃ Amen.

⁶It is not as though God's word had failed. For not all who are descended from Israel are Israel. ⁷Nor because they are his descendants are they all Abraham's children. On the contrary, "It is through Isaac that your offspring will be reckoned."ᵇ ⁸In other words, it is not the natural children who are God's children, but it is the children of the promise who are regarded as Abraham's offspring. ⁹For this was how the promise was stated: "At the appointed time I will return, and Sarah will have a son."ᶜ

¹⁰Not only that, but Rebekah's children had one and the same father, our father Isaac. ¹¹Yet, before the twins were born or had done anything good or bad—in order that God's purpose in election might stand: ¹²not by works but by him who calls—she was told, "The older will serve the younger."ᵈ ¹³Just as it is written: "Jacob I loved, but Esau I hated."ᵉ

¹⁴What then shall we say? Is God unjust? Not at all! ¹⁵For he says to Moses,

"I will have mercy on whom I have
    mercy,
and I will have compassion on
    whom I have compassion."ᶠ

¹⁶It does not, therefore, depend on man's desire or effort, but on God's mercy. ¹⁷For the Scripture says to Pharaoh: "I raised you up for this very purpose, that I might display my power in you and that my name might be proclaimed in all the earth."ᵍ ¹⁸Therefore God has mercy on whom he wants to have mercy, and he hardens whom he wants to harden.

¹⁹One of you will say to me: "Then why does God still blame us? For who resists his will?" ²⁰But who are you, O man, to talk back to God? "Shall what is formed say to him who formed it, 'Why did you make me like this?' "ʰ ²¹Does not the potter have the right to make out of the same lump of clay some pottery for noble purposes and some for common use?

²²What if God, choosing to show his wrath and make his power known, bore with great patience the objects of his wrath—prepared for destruction? ²³What if he did this to make the riches of his

glory known to the objects of his mercy, whom he prepared in advance for glory— ²⁴even us, whom he also called, not only from the Jews but also from the Gentiles? ²⁵As he says in Hosea:

"I will call them 'my people' who are
    not my people;
and I will call her 'my loved one'
    who is not my loved one,"ⁱ

²⁶and,

"It will happen that in the very place
    where it was said to them,
'You are not my people,'
they will be called 'sons of the living
    God.' "ʲ

²⁷Isaiah cries out concerning Israel:

"Though the number of the Israelites
    be like the sand by the sea,
only the remnant will be saved.
²⁸For the Lord will carry out
    his sentence on earth with speed
    and finality."ᵏ

²⁹It is just as Isaiah said previously:

"Unless the Lord Almighty
    had left us descendants,
we would have become like Sodom,
    we would have been like
      Gomorrah."ˡ

Israel's Unbelief

³⁰What then shall we say? That the Gentiles, who did not pursue righteous-

ᵃ5 Or *Christ, who is over all. God be forever praised!* Or *Christ. God who is over all be forever praised!* ᵇ7 Gen. 21:12 ᶜ9 Gen. 18:10,14 ᵈ12 Gen. 25:23 ᵉ13 Mal. 1:2,3 ᶠ15 Exodus 33:19 ᵍ17 Exodus 9:16 ʰ20 Isaiah 29:16; 45:9 ⁱ25 Hosea 2:23 ʲ26 Hosea 1:10 ᵏ28 Isaiah 10:22,23 ˡ29 Isaiah 1:9

POINT OF INTEREST

Romans 8:31-39

"If God is for us, who can be against us?" That's a powerfully liberating question.

God is not bound by the constraints of time, space, life or death, and he rules supreme over all spiritual powers. Confident of God's unchanging character, Paul testifies about these great promises to us, his readers.

ness, have obtained it, a righteousness that is by faith; **31**but Israel, who pursued a law of righteousness, has not attained it. **32**Why not? Because they pursued it not by faith but as if it were by works. They stumbled over the "stumbling stone." **33**As it is written:

> "See, I lay in Zion a stone that causes
>   men to stumble
> and a rock that makes them fall,
> and the one who trusts in him will
>   never be put to shame."*a*

10 Brothers, my heart's desire and prayer to God for the Israelites is that they may be saved. **2**For I can testify about them that they are zealous for God, but their zeal is not based on knowledge. **3**Since they did not know the righteousness that comes from God and sought to establish their own, they did not submit to God's righteousness. **4**Christ is the end of the law so that there may be righteousness for everyone who believes.

5Moses describes in this way the righteousness that is by the law: "The man who does these things will live by them."*b* **6**But the righteousness that is by faith says: "Do not say in your heart, 'Who will ascend into heaven?'*c*" (that is, to bring Christ down) **7**"or 'Who will descend into the deep?'*d*" (that is, to bring Christ up from the dead). **8**But what does it say? "The word is near you; it is in your mouth and in your heart,"*e* that is, the word of faith we are proclaiming: **9**That if you confess with your mouth, "Jesus is Lord," and believe in your heart that God raised him from the dead, you will be saved. **10**For it is with your heart that you believe and are justified, and it is with your mouth that you confess and are saved. **11**As the Scripture says, "Anyone who trusts in him will never be put to shame."*f* **12**For there is no difference between Jew and Gentile—the same Lord is Lord of all and richly blesses all who call on him, **13**for, "Everyone who calls on the name of the Lord will be saved."*g*

14How, then, can they call on the one they have not believed in? And how can they believe in the one of whom they have not heard? And how can they hear without someone preaching to them? **15**And how can they preach unless they are sent? As it is written, "How beautiful are the feet of those who bring good news!"*h*

16But not all the Israelites accepted the good news. For Isaiah says, "Lord, who has believed our message?"*i* **17**Consequently, faith comes from hearing the message, and the message is heard through the word of Christ. **18**But I ask: Did they not hear? Of course they did:

> "Their voice has gone out into all the
>   earth,
>   their words to the ends of the
>   world."*j*

19Again I ask: Did Israel not understand? First, Moses says,

> "I will make you envious by those
>   who are not a nation;
> I will make you angry by a nation
>   that has no understanding."*k*

20And Isaiah boldly says,

> "I was found by those who did not
>   seek me;
> I revealed myself to those who did
>   not ask for me."*l*

21But concerning Israel he says,

> "All day long I have held out my
>   hands
> to a disobedient and obstinate
>   people."*m*

The Remnant of Israel

11 I ask then: Did God reject his people? By no means! I am an Israelite myself, a descendant of Abraham, from the tribe

---

a 33 Isaiah 8:14; 28:16   *b 5* Lev. 18:5
c 6 Deut. 30:12   *d 7* Deut. 30:13
e 8 Deut. 30:14   *f 11* Isaiah 28:16
g 13 Joel 2:32   *h 15* Isaiah 52:7
i 16 Isaiah 53:1   *j 18* Psalm 19:4
k 19 Deut. 32:21   *l 20* Isaiah 65:1
m 21 Isaiah 65:2

POINT OF INTEREST

Romans 10:14

Paul hammers at his readers with logic and reason, insisting that everyone will have the opportunity for salvation if only disciples of Jesus will go and share it with them. But many people, though they have the opportunity to hear and believe the message of God, don't. Go back and read chapter nine to find out why.

of Benjamin. ²God did not reject his people, whom he foreknew. Don't you know what the Scripture says in the passage about Elijah—how he appealed to God against Israel: ³"Lord, they have killed your prophets and torn down your altars; I am the only one left, and they are trying to kill me"*ᵃ*? ⁴And what was God's answer to him? "I have reserved for myself seven thousand who have not bowed the knee to Baal."*ᵇ* ⁵So too, at the present time there is a remnant chosen by grace. ⁶And if by grace, then it is no longer by works; if it were, grace would no longer be grace.*ᶜ*

⁷What then? What Israel sought so earnestly it did not obtain, but the elect did. The others were hardened, ⁸as it is written:

"God gave them a spirit of stupor,
    eyes so that they could not see
    and ears so that they could not
      hear,
to this very day."*ᵈ*

⁹And David says:

"May their table become a snare and
    a trap,
    a stumbling block and a retribution
    for them.
¹⁰May their eyes be darkened so they
    cannot see,
    and their backs be bent forever."*ᵉ*

Ingrafted Branches

¹¹Again I ask: Did they stumble so as to fall beyond recovery? Not at all! Rather, because of their transgression, salvation has come to the Gentiles to make Israel envious. ¹²But if their transgression means riches for the world, and their loss means riches for the Gentiles, how much greater riches will their fullness bring!

¹³I am talking to you Gentiles. Inasmuch as I am the apostle to the Gentiles, I make much of my ministry ¹⁴in the hope that I may somehow arouse my own people to envy and save some of them. ¹⁵For if their rejection is the reconciliation of the world, what will their acceptance be but life from the dead? ¹⁶If the part of the dough offered as firstfruits is holy, then the whole batch is holy; if the root is holy, so are the branches.

¹⁷If some of the branches have been broken off, and you, though a wild olive shoot, have been grafted in among the others and now share in the nourishing sap from the olive root, ¹⁸do not boast over those branches. If you do, consider this: You do not support the root, but the root supports you. ¹⁹You will say then, "Branches were broken off so that I could be grafted in." ²⁰Granted. But they were broken off because of unbelief, and you stand by faith. Do not be arrogant, but be afraid. ²¹For if God did not spare the natural branches, he will not spare you either.

²²Consider therefore the kindness and sternness of God: sternness to those who fell, but kindness to you, provided that you continue in his kindness. Otherwise, you also will be cut off. ²³And if they do not persist in unbelief, they will be grafted in, for God is able to graft them in again. ²⁴After all, if you were cut out of an olive tree that is wild by nature, and contrary to nature were grafted into a cultivated olive tree, how much more readily will these, the natural branches, be grafted into their own olive tree!

All Israel Will Be Saved

²⁵I do not want you to be ignorant of this mystery, brothers, so that you may not be conceited: Israel has experienced a hardening in part until the full number of the Gentiles has come in. ²⁶And so all Israel will be saved, as it is written:

"The deliverer will come from Zion;
    he will turn godlessness away from
      Jacob.
²⁷And this is*ᶠ* my covenant with them
    when I take away their sins."*ᵍ*

²⁸As far as the gospel is concerned, they are enemies on your account; but as far as election is concerned, they are loved on account of the patriarchs, ²⁹for God's gifts and his call are irrevocable. ³⁰Just as you who were at one time disobedient to God have now received mercy as a result of their disobedience, ³¹so they too have now become disobedient in order that they too may now*ʰ* receive mercy as a result of God's mercy to you. ³²For God has bound all men over to dis-

---

ᵃ3 1 Kings 19:10,14   *ᵇ4* 1 Kings 19:18
ᶜ6 Some manuscripts *by grace. But if by works,
then it is no longer grace; if it were, work would no
longer be work.*   *ᵈ8* Deut. 29:4; Isaiah 29:10
ᵉ10 Psalm 69:22,23   *ᶠ27* Or *will be*
ᵍ27 Isaiah 59:20,21; 27:9; Jer. 31:33,34
ʰ31 Some manuscripts do not have *now.*

obedience so that he may have mercy on them all.

Doxology

33Oh, the depth of the riches of the
    wisdom and*a* knowledge of
    God!
How unsearchable his judgments,
    and his paths beyond tracing out!
34"Who has known the mind of the
    Lord?
Or who has been his counselor?"*b*
35"Who has ever given to God,
    that God should repay him?"*c*
36For from him and through him and to
    him are all things.
To him be the glory forever!
    Amen.

Living Sacrifices

12 Therefore, I urge you, brothers, in
view of God's mercy, to offer your
bodies as living sacrifices, holy and
pleasing to God—this is your spiritual*d*
act of worship. 2Do not conform any
longer to the pattern of this world, but
be transformed by the renewing of your
mind. Then you will be able to test and
approve what God's will is—his good,
pleasing and perfect will.

3For by the grace given me I say to
every one of you: Do not think of yourself
more highly than you ought, but rather

a33 Or *riches and the wisdom and the*
b34 Isaiah 40:13   *c35* Job 41:11   *d1* Or
reasonable

Read *Romans 12:1–21*
Key Verses *Romans 12:1–2*

A Living Sacrifice – Shaunda McQueeney

Have you ever pictured what a "living sacrifice" might have looked
like? It probably wasn't still and unconscious, but wriggling and
squirming around on the altar. How much easier it would have been
if the priests could have offered something dead, something without
active nerve endings and with no inclination to fight back!

I've heard people say that the problem with being "living sacrifices" is that we keep jumping off the altar. How true this is of me!
Sometimes I leap down, shocked that God has really ignited that
painful fire. I stand before him, stiff and rebellious, demanding to
know why this sacrifice is required of me. Other times I quietly and
unconsciously slip from my place on the altar, away from the purifying flames.

I'm more comfortable when I'm off the altar, but it sure gets cold.
It's not as painful, but I miss out on joy, because it's only through
self-sacrifice that I can experience the joy of a growing faith, maturity and wisdom (see James 1:2).

All God asks of me is to give myself, the most intimate of gifts.
My plans, my wants, my self-imposed "rights" melt down in the
flames of his consuming love, and with clearer vision I look my Savior in the eye. The pride, the self-absorption, the "stuff" I foolishly
cling to just doesn't mean anything "compared to the surpassing
greatness of knowing Christ Jesus my Lord" (Philippians 3:8).

Are you really hungry to know God intimately? Climb onto the
altar and give him the sacrifice of self. You won't get burned, but
you *will* find life with the One who loves you most.

A Deeper Look
Psalm 56:13; Romans 6:13–19; Hebrews 13:15–16

Go to page 1275 for your next devotional reading.

think of yourself with sober judgment, in accordance with the measure of faith God has given you. ⁴Just as each of us has one body with many members, and these members do not all have the same function, ⁵so in Christ we who are many form one body, and each member belongs to all the others. ⁶We have different gifts, according to the grace given us. If a man's gift is prophesying, let him use it in proportion to his*ᵃ* faith. ⁷If it is serving, let him serve; if it is teaching, let him teach; ⁸if it is encouraging, let him encourage; if it is contributing to the needs of others, let him give generously; if it is leadership, let him govern diligently; if it is showing mercy, let him do it cheerfully.

Love

⁹Love must be sincere. Hate what is evil; cling to what is good. ¹⁰Be devoted to one another in brotherly love. Honor one another above yourselves. ¹¹Never be lacking in zeal, but keep your spiritual fervor, serving the Lord. ¹²Be joyful in hope, patient in affliction, faithful in prayer. ¹³Share with God's people who are in need. Practice hospitality.

¹⁴Bless those who persecute you; bless and do not curse. ¹⁵Rejoice with those who rejoice; mourn with those who mourn. ¹⁶Live in harmony with one another. Do not be proud, but be willing to associate with people of low position.*ᵇ* Do not be conceited.

¹⁷Do not repay anyone evil for evil. Be careful to do what is right in the eyes of everybody. ¹⁸If it is possible, as far as it depends on you, live at peace with everyone. ¹⁹Do not take revenge, my friends, but leave room for God's wrath, for it is written: "It is mine to avenge; I will repay,"*ᶜ* says the Lord. ²⁰On the contrary:

"If your enemy is hungry, feed him;
   if he is thirsty, give him something
     to drink.
In doing this, you will heap burning
     coals on his head."*ᵈ*

²¹Do not be overcome by evil, but overcome evil with good.

Submission to the Authorities

13 Everyone must submit himself to the governing authorities, for there is no authority except that which God has established. The authorities that exist have been established by God. ²Consequently, he who rebels against the authority is rebelling against what God has instituted, and those who do so will bring judgment on themselves. ³For rulers hold no terror for those who do right, but for those who do wrong. Do you want to be free from fear of the one in authority? Then do what is right and he will commend you. ⁴For he is God's servant to do you good. But if you do wrong, be afraid, for he does not bear the sword for nothing. He is God's servant, an agent of wrath to bring punishment on the wrongdoer. ⁵Therefore, it is necessary to submit to the authorities, not only because of possible punishment but also because of conscience.

⁶This is also why you pay taxes, for the authorities are God's servants, who give their full time to governing. ⁷Give everyone what you owe him: If you owe taxes, pay taxes; if revenue, then revenue; if respect, then respect; if honor, then honor.

Love, for the Day Is Near

⁸Let no debt remain outstanding, except the continuing debt to love one another, for he who loves his fellowman has fulfilled the law. ⁹The commandments, "Do not commit adultery," "Do not murder," "Do not steal," "Do not covet,"*ᵉ* and whatever other commandment there may be, are summed up in this one rule: "Love your neighbor as yourself."*ᶠ* ¹⁰Love does no harm to its

---

*ᵃ*6 Or *in agreement with the*   *ᵇ*16 Or *willing to do menial work*   *ᶜ*19 Deut. 32:35
*ᵈ*20 Prov. 25:21,22   *ᵉ*9 Exodus 20:13-15,17; Deut. 5:17-19,21   *ᶠ*9 Lev. 19:18

POINT OF INTEREST

Romans 12:13

Is hospitality really one of Paul's directives to the Romans? Could fellowship and evangelism be as easy as inviting friends over for dinner or caring for their needs? Paul thought so, and so did John as he wrote a brief letter to a man named Gaius (see 3 John; Acts 19:29; 20:4). Take up Paul's challenge—find creative ways to show hospitality to your believing and nonbelieving friends alike.

neighbor. Therefore love is the fulfillment of the law.

¹¹And do this, understanding the present time. The hour has come for you to wake up from your slumber, because our salvation is nearer now than when we first believed. ¹²The night is nearly over; the day is almost here. So let us put aside the deeds of darkness and put on the armor of light. ¹³Let us behave decently, as in the daytime, not in orgies and drunkenness, not in sexual immorality and debauchery, not in dissension and jealousy. ¹⁴Rather, clothe yourselves with the Lord Jesus Christ, and do not think about how to gratify the desires of the sinful nature.ᵃ

The Weak and the Strong

14 Accept him whose faith is weak, without passing judgment on disputable matters. ²One man's faith allows him to eat everything, but another man, whose faith is weak, eats only vegetables. ³The man who eats everything must not look down on him who does not, and the man who does not eat everything must not condemn the man who does, for God has accepted him. ⁴Who are you to judge someone else's servant? To his own master he stands or falls. And he will stand, for the Lord is able to make him stand.

⁵One man considers one day more sacred than another; another man considers every day alike. Each one should be fully convinced in his own mind. ⁶He who regards one day as special, does so to the Lord. He who eats meat, eats to the Lord, for he gives thanks to God; and he who abstains, does so to the Lord and gives thanks to God. ⁷For none of us lives to himself alone and none of us dies to himself alone. ⁸If we live, we live to the Lord; and if we die, we die to the Lord. So, whether we live or die, we belong to the Lord.

⁹For this very reason, Christ died and returned to life so that he might be the Lord of both the dead and the living. ¹⁰You, then, why do you judge your brother? Or why do you look down on your brother? For we will all stand before God's judgment seat. ¹¹It is written:

" 'As surely as I live,' says the Lord,
'every knee will bow before me;
    every tongue will confess to
        God.' "ᵇ

¹²So then, each of us will give an account of himself to God.

¹³Therefore let us stop passing judgment on one another. Instead, make up your mind not to put any stumbling block or obstacle in your brother's way. ¹⁴As one who is in the Lord Jesus, I am fully convinced that no foodᶜ is unclean in itself. But if anyone regards something as unclean, then for him it is unclean. ¹⁵If your brother is distressed because of what you eat, you are no longer acting in love. Do not by your eating destroy your brother for whom Christ died. ¹⁶Do not allow what you consider good to be spoken of as evil. ¹⁷For the kingdom of God is not a matter of eating and drinking, but of righteousness, peace and joy in the Holy Spirit, ¹⁸because anyone who serves Christ in this way is pleasing to God and approved by men.

¹⁹Let us therefore make every effort to do what leads to peace and to mutual edification. ²⁰Do not destroy the work of God for the sake of food. All food is clean, but it is wrong for a man to eat anything that causes someone else to stumble. ²¹It is better not to eat meat or drink wine or to do anything else that will cause your brother to fall.

²²So whatever you believe about these things keep between yourself and God. Blessed is the man who does not condemn himself by what he approves. ²³But the man who has doubts is condemned if he eats, because his eating is not from faith; and everything that does not come from faith is sin.

15 We who are strong ought to bear with the failings of the weak and not to please ourselves. ²Each of us should please his neighbor for his good, to build him up. ³For even Christ did not please himself but, as it is written: "The insults of those who insult you have fallen on me."ᵈ ⁴For everything that was written in the past was written to teach us, so that through endurance and the encouragement of the Scriptures we might have hope.

⁵May the God who gives endurance and encouragement give you a spirit of unity among yourselves as you follow Christ Jesus, ⁶so that with one heart and mouth you may glorify the God and Father of our Lord Jesus Christ.

ᵃ14 Or the flesh   ᵇ11 Isaiah 45:23   ᶜ14 Or
that nothing   ᵈ3 Psalm 69:9

⁷Accept one another, then, just as Christ accepted you, in order to bring praise to God. ⁸For I tell you that Christ has become a servant of the Jews*a* on behalf of God's truth, to confirm the promises made to the patriarchs ⁹so that the Gentiles may glorify God for his mercy, as it is written:

"Therefore I will praise you among
     the Gentiles;
I will sing hymns to your name."*b*

¹⁰Again, it says,

"Rejoice, O Gentiles, with his
     people."*c*

¹¹And again,

"Praise the Lord, all you Gentiles,
     and sing praises to him, all you
     peoples."*d*

¹²And again, Isaiah says,

"The Root of Jesse will spring up,
     one who will arise to rule over the
        nations;
the Gentiles will hope in him."*e*

¹³May the God of hope fill you with all joy and peace as you trust in him, so that

a8 Greek *circumcision*   *b9* 2 Samuel 22:50;
Psalm 18:49   *c10* Deut. 32:43
d11 Psalm 117:1   *e12* Isaiah 11:10

TUESDAY

Read *Romans 14:1–23*
Key Verses *Romans 14:19–21*

Shades of Gray – Dennis Stokes

Ever been around someone who takes any issue and tries to make the answer black or white—wrong or right—for everyone in every situation? This person knows what *you* should and should not watch, eat, drink, wear, believe, spend your time on, listen to, and so forth. They seem to think that there is one solution—theirs—to every problem. Now don't get me wrong: Clear absolutes and limits from God's Word do exist. Yet there are areas—gray areas—where God just doesn't give us a clear word, situations that require us to be wise and discerning.

The key is to focus on the kingdom of God, which is "righteousness, peace and joy in the Holy Spirit." It's building each other up and not creating dissension over nonessential issues. It means not going beyond what Scripture says, imposing our own standards on others or making following Jesus more difficult than necessary (see Romans 14:22).

Does Scripture speak clearly on an issue? If not, then it is a matter of freedom, discernment and application of principles from God's Word. Have you cultivated your own convictions on such flexible issues? Then don't use them as a club to harm others. And don't be too quick to pass judgment on others who live out their Christian lives differently from you. Instead, "speak and act as those who are going to be judged by the law that gives freedom, because judgment without mercy will be shown to anyone who has not been merciful. Mercy triumphs over judgment!" (James 2:12–13).

O Lord, please help me be solid on truth but compassionate and sensitive to my brothers and sisters on matters of opinion.

A Deeper Look
Matthew 7:1–5; James 4:11–12

Go to page 1277 for your next devotional reading.

you may overflow with hope by the power of the Holy Spirit.

Paul the Minister to the Gentiles

¹⁴I myself am convinced, my brothers, that you yourselves are full of goodness, complete in knowledge and competent to instruct one another. ¹⁵I have written you quite boldly on some points, as if to remind you of them again, because of the grace God gave me ¹⁶to be a minister of Christ Jesus to the Gentiles with the priestly duty of proclaiming the gospel of God, so that the Gentiles might become an offering acceptable to God, sanctified by the Holy Spirit.

¹⁷Therefore I glory in Christ Jesus in my service to God. ¹⁸I will not venture to speak of anything except what Christ has accomplished through me in leading the Gentiles to obey God by what I have said and done— ¹⁹by the power of signs and miracles, through the power of the Spirit. So from Jerusalem all the way around to Illyricum, I have fully proclaimed the gospel of Christ. ²⁰It has always been my ambition to preach the gospel where Christ was not known, so that I would not be building on someone else's foundation. ²¹Rather, as it is written:

"Those who were not told about him
    will see,
and those who have not heard will
    understand."ᵃ

²²This is why I have often been hindered from coming to you.

Paul's Plan to Visit Rome

²³But now that there is no more place for me to work in these regions, and since I have been longing for many years to see you, ²⁴I plan to do so when I go to Spain. I hope to visit you while passing through and to have you assist me on my journey there, after I have enjoyed your company for a while. ²⁵Now, however, I am on my way to Jerusalem in the service of the saints there. ²⁶For Macedonia and Achaia were pleased to make a contribution for the poor among the saints in Jerusalem. ²⁷They were pleased to do it, and indeed they owe it to them. For if the Gentiles have shared in the Jews' spiritual blessings, they owe it to the Jews to share with them their material blessings. ²⁸So after I have completed this task and have made sure that they have received this fruit, I will go to Spain and visit you on the way. ²⁹I know that when I come to you, I will come in the full measure of the blessing of Christ.

³⁰I urge you, brothers, by our Lord Jesus Christ and by the love of the Spirit, to join me in my struggle by praying to God for me. ³¹Pray that I may be rescued from the unbelievers in Judea and that my service in Jerusalem may be acceptable to the saints there, ³²so that by God's will I may come to you with joy and together with you be refreshed. ³³The God of peace be with you all. Amen.

Personal Greetings

16 I commend to you our sister Phoebe, a servantᵇ of the church in Cenchrea. ²I ask you to receive her in the Lord in a way worthy of the saints and to give her any help she may need from you, for she has been a great help to many people, including me.

³Greet Priscillaᶜ and Aquila, my fellow workers in Christ Jesus. ⁴They risked their lives for me. Not only I but all the churches of the Gentiles are grateful to them.

⁵Greet also the church that meets at their house.

Greet my dear friend Epenetus, who was the first convert to Christ in the province of Asia.

⁶Greet Mary, who worked very hard for you.

⁷Greet Andronicus and Junias, my relatives who have been in prison with me. They are outstanding among the apostles, and they were in Christ before I was.

⁸Greet Ampliatus, whom I love in the Lord.

⁹Greet Urbanus, our fellow worker in Christ, and my dear friend Stachys.

¹⁰Greet Apelles, tested and approved in Christ.

Greet those who belong to the household of Aristobulus.

¹¹Greet Herodion, my relative.

Greet those in the household of Narcissus who are in the Lord.

¹²Greet Tryphena and Tryphosa, those women who work hard in the Lord.

Greet my dear friend Persis, another

ᵃ21 Isaiah 52:15   ᵇ1 Or *deaconess*   ᶜ3 Greek *Prisca*, a variant of *Priscilla* woman who has worked very hard in the Lord.

¹³Greet Rufus, chosen in the Lord, and his mother, who has been a mother to me, too. ¹⁴Greet Asyncritus, Phlegon, Hermes, Patrobas, Hermas and the brothers with them. ¹⁵Greet Philologus, Julia, Nereus and his sister, and Olympas and all the saints with them.

¹⁶Greet one another with a holy kiss.

All the churches of Christ send greetings.

¹⁷I urge you, brothers, to watch out for those who cause divisions and put obstacles in your way that are contrary to the teaching you have learned. Keep away from them. ¹⁸For such people are not serving our Lord Christ, but their own appetites. By smooth talk and flattery they deceive the minds of naive people.

¹⁹Everyone has heard about your obedience, so I am full of joy over you; but I want you to be wise about what is good, and innocent about what is evil. ²⁰The God of peace will soon crush Satan under your feet.

The grace of our Lord Jesus be with you.

²¹Timothy, my fellow worker, sends his greetings to you, as do Lucius, Jason and Sosipater, my relatives.

²²I, Tertius, who wrote down this letter, greet you in the Lord.

²³Gaius, whose hospitality I and the whole church here enjoy, sends you his greetings.

Erastus, who is the city's director of public works, and our brother Quartus send you their greetings.ᵃ

ᵃ23 Some manuscripts *their greetings.* ²⁴*May the grace of our Lord Jesus Christ be with all of you. Amen.*

Read *Romans 16:1–27*
Key Verse *Romans 16:19*

Wise About What is Good – Dawn Getz

The monstrous warehouse smelled like diesel fumes, but because of the excellent wage package, I was thrilled to have been hired to work there. That summer after my sophomore year in college, I was the only female among fifty loading-dock workers. Often as I descended the stairs to the dock, I noticed the men would stop talking. Later I found out the guys didn't want to embarrass me with their conversations about sex.

As I recall that job I can see how God protected my mind through men I hardly even knew. It makes me ask myself what I'm doing now to be "wise about what is good, and innocent about what is evil."

My choices affect all aspects of my life—social, physical, mental or spiritual—when I'm choosing what movies to see, what foods to feed my body or what kind of reading I do. And when I'm hurt and tempted to think negative things about the people I love, I can meditate on God's Word instead and believe the best.

God has given us the ability to make sound decisions about what is good. Other people usually won't shield us from things that could harm us. But by God's grace we can take active steps to be wise and innocent.

A Deeper Look
Matthew 10:16; Luke 2:52; 1 Corinthians 14:20

Go to page 1280 for your next devotional reading.

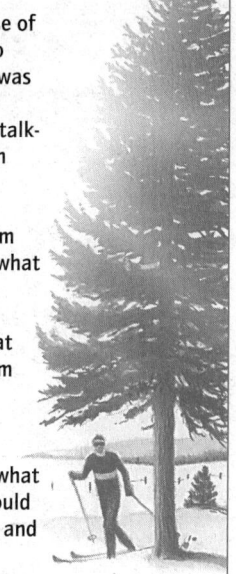

25Now to him who is able to establish you by my gospel and the proclamation of Jesus Christ, according to the revelation of the mystery hidden for long ages past, 26but now revealed and made known through the prophetic writings by the command of the eternal God, so that all nations might believe and obey him— 27to the only wise God be glory forever through Jesus Christ! Amen.

There's a good chance that Corinth might have ranked first on the "Top 10" list for "The Ancient World's Most Wicked Cities." The Corinthian Christians faced the difficulty of following Jesus Christ in the midst of a contaminated culture. The church had to deal with problems such as sexual immorality, dissension among various groups, Christians suing Christians and misuse of spiritual gifts. Paul's letter addresses these issues, but it also tackles some underlying spiritual issues—inspiring readers with a few words on love (chapter 13) and on the resurrection (chapter 15). Let this book inspire you to renew your efforts to follow Jesus while living in a worldly culture.

1 CORINTHIANS

1 Paul, called to be an apostle of Christ Jesus by the will of God, and our brother Sosthenes,

²To the church of God in Corinth, to those sanctified in Christ Jesus and called to be holy, together with all those everywhere who call on the name of our Lord Jesus Christ—their Lord and ours:

³Grace and peace to you from God our Father and the Lord Jesus Christ.

Thanksgiving

⁴I always thank God for you because of his grace given you in Christ Jesus. ⁵For in him you have been enriched in every way—in all your speaking and in all your knowledge— ⁶because our testimony about Christ was confirmed in you. ⁷Therefore you do not lack any spiritual gift as you eagerly wait for our Lord Jesus Christ to be revealed. ⁸He will keep you strong to the end, so that you will be blameless on the day of our Lord Jesus Christ. ⁹God, who has called you into fellowship with his Son Jesus Christ our Lord, is faithful.

Divisions in the Church

¹⁰I appeal to you, brothers, in the

name of our Lord Jesus Christ, that all of you agree with one another so that there may be no divisions among you and that you may be perfectly united in mind and thought. ¹¹My brothers, some from Chloe's household have informed me that there are quarrels among you. ¹²What I mean is this: One of you says, "I follow Paul"; another, "I follow Apollos"; another, "I follow Cephas*a*"; still another, "I follow Christ."

¹³Is Christ divided? Was Paul crucified for you? Were you baptized into*b* the name of Paul? ¹⁴I am thankful that I did not baptize any of you except Crispus and Gaius, ¹⁵so no one can say that you were baptized into my name. ¹⁶(Yes, I also baptized the household of Stephanas; beyond that, I don't remember if I baptized anyone else.) ¹⁷For Christ did not send me to baptize, but to preach the gospel—not with words of human wisdom, lest the cross of Christ be emptied of its power.

Christ the Wisdom and Power of God

¹⁸For the message of the cross is foolishness to those who are perishing, but to us who are being saved it is the power of God. ¹⁹For it is written:

"I will destroy the wisdom of the
    wise;
    the intelligence of the intelligent I
    will frustrate."*c*

²⁰Where is the wise man? Where is the scholar? Where is the philosopher of this

a12 That is, Peter   *b13* Or *in*; also in verse 15
c19 Isaiah 29:14

THURSDAY

Read *1 Corinthians 1:1–31*
Key Verses *1 Corinthians 1:4–9*

Living by Grace – Doug Serven

Many people seem to live out their faith in one of two ways: (1) a lackadaisical lifestyle with little fruit or discipline, or (2) a performance lifestyle with guilt and frustration. As a new Christian I chose Option #2. The pressure to have seven quiet times per week, memorize two verses weekly, have daily prayer, and the like, *did* bring me closer to God, but it also buried me in obligations. I so much wanted to be a proven disciple that I worked, worked, worked.

It was as if I wanted to get to the second floor of a building every day by vaulting up through a second-story window instead of walking through the front door and climbing the stairs one at a time. I *looked* like I was making a good effort, but I was going about it all wrong. My vault would fall short repeatedly as I collapsed in a pile on the sidewalk. After a few days (or weeks), I'd regroup and try again.

That was no way to live. As Paul said, "Are you so foolish? After beginning with the Spirit, are you now trying to attain your goal by human effort?" (Galatians 3:3). I was. Just as I needed God's grace when I accepted Jesus Christ, I need his grace *today*. Because of the grace of his gospel, I don't have to try to vault to a higher spiritual level on my own. With gratitude rooted in grace, I can grow as Jesus' disciple through spiritual disciplines (prayer, reading God's Word), and I can eventually help someone else find him. It is *God* who is faithful, and it is *God* who keeps me strong and growing.

A Deeper Look
Colossians 2:6–7; 1 Timothy 1:15–16

Go to page 1282 for your next devotional reading.

age? Has not God made foolish the wisdom of the world? ²¹For since in the wisdom of God the world through its wisdom did not know him, God was pleased through the foolishness of what was preached to save those who believe. ²²Jews demand miraculous signs and Greeks look for wisdom, ²³but we preach Christ crucified: a stumbling block to Jews and foolishness to Gentiles, ²⁴but to those whom God has called, both Jews and Greeks, Christ the power of God and the wisdom of God. ²⁵For the foolishness of God is wiser than man's wisdom, and the weakness of God is stronger than man's strength.

²⁶Brothers, think of what you were when you were called. Not many of you were wise by human standards; not many were influential; not many were of noble birth. ²⁷But God chose the foolish things of the world to shame the wise; God chose the weak things of the world to shame the strong. ²⁸He chose the lowly things of this world and the despised things—and the things that are not—to nullify the things that are, ²⁹so that no one may boast before him. ³⁰It is because of him that you are in Christ Jesus, who has become for us wisdom from God—that is, our righteousness, holiness and redemption. ³¹Therefore, as it is written: "Let him who boasts boast in the Lord."ᵃ

2 When I came to you, brothers, I did not come with eloquence or superior wisdom as I proclaimed to you the testimony about God.ᵇ ²For I resolved to know nothing while I was with you except Jesus Christ and him crucified. ³I came to you in weakness and fear, and with much trembling. ⁴My message and my preaching were not with wise and persuasive words, but with a demonstration of the Spirit's power, ⁵so that your faith might not rest on men's wisdom, but on God's power.

Wisdom From the Spirit

⁶We do, however, speak a message of wisdom among the mature, but not the wisdom of this age or of the rulers of this age, who are coming to nothing. ⁷No, we speak of God's secret wisdom, a wisdom that has been hidden and that God destined for our glory before time began. ⁸None of the rulers of this age understood it, for if they had, they would not have crucified the Lord of glory. ⁹However, as it is written:

"No eye has seen,
    no ear has heard,
no mind has conceived
    what God has prepared for those
        who love him"ᶜ—

¹⁰but God has revealed it to us by his Spirit.

The Spirit searches all things, even the deep things of God. ¹¹For who among men knows the thoughts of a man except the man's spirit within him? In the same way no one knows the thoughts of God except the Spirit of God. ¹²We have not received the spirit of the world but the Spirit who is from God, that we may understand what God has freely given us. ¹³This is what we speak, not in words taught us by human wisdom but in words taught by the Spirit, expressing spiritual truths in spiritual words.ᵈ ¹⁴The man without the Spirit does not accept the things that come from the Spirit of God, for they are foolishness to him, and he cannot understand them, because they are spiritually discerned. ¹⁵The spiritual man makes judgments about all things, but he himself is not subject to any man's judgment:

¹⁶"For who has known the mind of the Lord
    that he may instruct him?"ᵉ

But we have the mind of Christ.

ᵃ31 Jer. 9:24   ᵇ1 Some manuscripts as I proclaimed to you God's mystery   ᶜ9 Isaiah 64:4   ᵈ13 Or Spirit, interpreting spiritual truths to spiritual men   ᵉ16 Isaiah 40:13

POINT OF INTEREST

1 Corinthians 2:13

In the first two chapters of 1 Corinthians, Paul leads his readers through an in-depth study of the differences between the "wisdom of the world" and the "wisdom of God" (see 1 Corinthians 1:20–21). Take a few moments to read through these chapters. Which is your source of wisdom?

On Divisions in the Church

3 Brothers, I could not address you as spiritual but as worldly—mere infants in Christ. ²I gave you milk, not solid food, for you were not yet ready for it. Indeed, you are still not ready. ³You are still worldly. For since there is jealousy and quarreling among you, are you not worldly? Are you not acting like mere men? ⁴For when one says, "I follow Paul," and another, "I follow Apollos," are you not mere men?

⁵What, after all, is Apollos? And what is Paul? Only servants, through whom you came to believe—as the Lord has assigned to each his task. ⁶I planted the seed, Apollos watered it, but God made it grow. ⁷So neither he who plants nor he who waters is anything, but only God, who makes things grow. ⁸The man who plants and the man who waters have one purpose, and each will be rewarded according to his own labor. ⁹For we are God's fellow workers; you are God's field, God's building.

¹⁰By the grace God has given me, I laid a foundation as an expert builder, and someone else is building on it. But each one should be careful how he builds. ¹¹For no one can lay any foundation other than the one already laid, which is Jesus Christ. ¹²If any man builds on this foundation using gold, silver, costly stones, wood, hay or straw, ¹³his work will be shown for what it is, because the Day will bring it to light. It will be revealed with fire, and the fire will test the quality of each man's work. ¹⁴If what he

---

FRIDAY

Read 1 Corinthians 3:1–23
Key Verses 1 Corinthians 3:9–15

Building Another Life – Dave Bowman

I sensed that my friend Brian was struggling. What I understood from his words and actions was that he had been reversing the priority of the Great Commandment (see Matthew 22:34–40) and the Great Commission (see Matthew 28:18–20). "Doing" for God had become more important than loving him and being his disciple. He thought living as a Christian meant he had to work harder and harder at it, and he couldn't keep up. I sensed his frustration and prayed about how I could help.

I began to realize that Brian was building the wrong things onto his spiritual foundation. And, as his "fellow builder," I wanted to help Brian build his life with gold, silver and costly stones (see 1 Corinthians 3:12). I think of these as the values of faith—knowing that salvation is through grace alone (see Ephesians 2:8–9); hope—turning one's eyes from the pressures of this world to the promise of being in Jesus' presence forever (see John 3:16,36); and love—learning to live in love for others out of gratitude for the salvation that Jesus Christ has accomplished (see Colossians 3:16–17).

Our values often determine our actions, but sometimes the motivation comes after we begin doing something. We can't ignore the vital disciplines of Bible reading, praying and sharing our faith, but when discipline exceeds desire, the result is drudgery. Realizing this, I know I also need to ask God to build these values deeper into my life, so that I can demonstrate to Brian and to others what it means to live by these key values.

A Deeper Look
John 8:31–32; 1 Corinthians 13:1–5; Colossians 2:1–3

Go to page 1285 for your next devotional reading.

has built survives, he will receive his reward. ¹⁵If it is burned up, he will suffer loss; he himself will be saved, but only as one escaping through the flames.

¹⁶Don't you know that you yourselves are God's temple and that God's Spirit lives in you? ¹⁷If anyone destroys God's temple, God will destroy him; for God's temple is sacred, and you are that temple.

¹⁸Do not deceive yourselves. If any one of you thinks he is wise by the standards of this age, he should become a "fool" so that he may become wise. ¹⁹For the wisdom of this world is foolishness in God's sight. As it is written: "He catches the wise in their craftiness"ᵃ; ²⁰and again, "The Lord knows that the thoughts of the wise are futile."ᵇ ²¹So then, no more boasting about men! All things are yours, ²²whether Paul or Apollos or Cephasᶜ or the world or life or death or the present or the future—all are yours, ²³and you are of Christ, and Christ is of God.

Apostles of Christ

4 So then, men ought to regard us as servants of Christ and as those entrusted with the secret things of God. ²Now it is required that those who have been given a trust must prove faithful. ³I care very little if I am judged by you or by any human court; indeed, I do not even judge myself. ⁴My conscience is clear, but that does not make me innocent. It is the Lord who judges me. ⁵Therefore judge nothing before the appointed time; wait till the Lord comes. He will bring to light what is hidden in darkness and will expose the motives of men's hearts. At that time each will receive his praise from God.

⁶Now, brothers, I have applied these things to myself and Apollos for your benefit, so that you may learn from us the meaning of the saying, "Do not go beyond what is written." Then you will not take pride in one man over against another. ⁷For who makes you different from anyone else? What do you have that you did not receive? And if you did receive it, why do you boast as though you did not?

⁸Already you have all you want! Already you have become rich! You have become kings—and that without us! How I wish that you really had become kings so that we might be kings with you! ⁹For it seems to me that God has put us apostles on display at the end of the procession, like men condemned to die in the arena. We have been made a spectacle to the whole universe, to angels as well as to men. ¹⁰We are fools for Christ, but you are so wise in Christ! We are weak, but you are strong! You are honored, we are dishonored! ¹¹To this very hour we go hungry and thirsty, we are in rags, we are brutally treated, we are homeless. ¹²We work hard with our own hands. When we are cursed, we bless; when we are persecuted, we endure it; ¹³when we are slandered, we answer kindly. Up to this moment we have become the scum of the earth, the refuse of the world.

¹⁴I am not writing this to shame you, but to warn you, as my dear children. ¹⁵Even though you have ten thousand guardians in Christ, you do not have many fathers, for in Christ Jesus I became your father through the gospel. ¹⁶Therefore I urge you to imitate me. ¹⁷For this reason I am sending to you Timothy, my son whom I love, who is faithful in the Lord. He will remind you of my way of life in Christ Jesus, which agrees with what I teach everywhere in every church.

¹⁸Some of you have become arrogant, as if I were not coming to you. ¹⁹But I will come to you very soon, if the Lord is willing, and then I will find out not only how these arrogant people are talking, but what power they have. ²⁰For the kingdom of God is not a matter of talk but of power. ²¹What do you prefer? Shall I come to you with a whip, or in love and with a gentle spirit?

ᵃ19 Job 5:13   ᵇ20 Psalm 94:11   ᶜ22 That is, Peter

POINT OF INTEREST

1 Corinthians 4:4

In this verse Paul gives us insight into the fallibility of the human conscience. People can justify all kinds of dishonorable and downright sinful behavior by saying that "It just feels right" or "I feel at peace with this decision." However, Paul reminds us that God will eventually turn our hearts inside out in the "light" to see what's there.

Expel the Immoral Brother!

5 It is actually reported that there is sexual immorality among you, and of a kind that does not occur even among pagans: A man has his father's wife. [2]And you are proud! Shouldn't you rather have been filled with grief and have put out of your fellowship the man who did this? [3]Even though I am not physically present, I am with you in spirit. And I have already passed judgment on the one who did this, just as if I were present. [4]When you are assembled in the name of our Lord Jesus and I am with you in spirit, and the power of our Lord Jesus is present, [5]hand this man over to Satan, so that the sinful nature[a] may be destroyed and his spirit saved on the day of the Lord.

[6]Your boasting is not good. Don't you know that a little yeast works through the whole batch of dough? [7]Get rid of the old yeast that you may be a new batch without yeast—as you really are. For Christ, our Passover lamb, has been sacrificed. [8]Therefore let us keep the Festival, not with the old yeast, the yeast of malice and wickedness, but with bread without yeast, the bread of sincerity and truth.

[9]I have written you in my letter not to associate with sexually immoral people— [10]not at all meaning the people of this world who are immoral, or the greedy and swindlers, or idolaters. In that case you would have to leave this world. [11]But now I am writing you that you must not associate with anyone who calls himself a brother but is sexually immoral or greedy, an idolater or a slanderer, a drunkard or a swindler. With such a man do not even eat.

[12]What business is it of mine to judge those outside the church? Are you not to judge those inside? [13]God will judge those outside. "Expel the wicked man from among you."[b]

Lawsuits Among Believers

6 If any of you has a dispute with another, dare he take it before the ungodly for judgment instead of before the saints? [2]Do you not know that the saints will judge the world? And if you are to judge the world, are you not competent to judge trivial cases? [3]Do you not know that we will judge angels? How much more the things of this life! [4]Therefore, if you have disputes about such matters, appoint as judges even men of little account in the church![c] [5]I say this to shame you. Is it possible that there is nobody among you wise enough to judge a dispute between believers? [6]But instead, one brother goes to law against another—and this in front of unbelievers!

[7]The very fact that you have lawsuits among you means you have been completely defeated already. Why not rather be wronged? Why not rather be cheated? [8]Instead, you yourselves cheat and do wrong, and you do this to your brothers.

[9]Do you not know that the wicked will not inherit the kingdom of God? Do not be deceived: Neither the sexually immoral nor idolaters nor adulterers nor male prostitutes nor homosexual offenders [10]nor thieves nor the greedy nor drunkards nor slanderers nor swindlers will inherit the kingdom of God. [11]And that is what some of you were. But you were washed, you were sanctified, you were justified in the name of the Lord Jesus Christ and by the Spirit of our God.

Sexual Immorality

[12]"Everything is permissible for me"—but not everything is beneficial. "Everything is permissible for me"—but I will not be mastered by anything. [13]"Food for the stomach and the stomach for food"—but God will destroy them both. The body is not meant for sexual immorality, but for the Lord, and the Lord for the body. [14]By his power God raised the Lord from the dead, and he will raise us also. [15]Do you not know that your bodies are members of Christ himself? Shall I then take the members of Christ and unite them with a prostitute? Never! [16]Do you not know that he who unites himself with a prostitute is one with her in body? For it is said, "The two will become one flesh."[d] [17]But he who unites himself with the Lord is one with him in spirit.

[18]Flee from sexual immorality. All other sins a man commits are outside his body, but he who sins sexually sins against his own body. [19]Do you not know that your body is a temple of the Holy Spirit, who is in you, whom you have received from God? You are not your own; [20]you were bought at a price. Therefore honor God with your body.

[a]5 Or *that his body;* or *that the flesh*
[b]13 Deut. 17:7; 19:19; 21:21; 22:21,24; 24:7
[c]4 Or *matters, do you appoint as judges men of little account in the church?*   [d]16 Gen. 2:24

Read 1 Corinthians 6:12–7:16
Key Verse 1 Corinthians 6:18

A Gift from God

Sexual intercourse is a wonderful gift from God, so why not accept it? Right? Not always! God has set a clear limit on the expression of this gift—it's reserved for marriage. The desire to seek love and sexual intimacy is God-given, but God wants us to save it for the sanctity, the safety and the commitment of the marriage relationship. God's plan is not to spoil our fun but to help us experience sexual intimacy to the fullest. Paul says that our bodies are temples of the Holy Spirit and as such we are not to defile them; avoiding inappropriate sexual behavior protects them from exposure to disease or other harm.

In his love for us, God also gives another clear boundary for our sexual desires. He warns us to guard against lust in our minds. When we unite ourselves with the Lord, we are one with him in spirit, and that gives us the motivation and the power to keep our minds and spirits clean for him!

Digging Into the Word
1. How does God's view of lust compare with many of the attitudes of our culture?—*Matthew 5:27–30; 1 John 2:15–17*
2. How does God tell us to deal with sexual immorality?—*Ephesians 5:3; 1 Thessalonians 4:3–8*

Action Challenge
Much of the sexual pressure we experience comes from the media. Consider taking a thirty-day break from any forms of entertainment that have "lust appeal." At the end of this experiment, evaluate how your thoughts have been influenced by this decision.

One Step Deeper
Galatians 5:16–21; Colossians 3:5

Go to page 1288 for your next devotional reading.

Marriage

7 Now for the matters you wrote about: It is good for a man not to marry.[a] ²But since there is so much immorality, each man should have his own wife, and each woman her own husband. ³The husband should fulfill his marital duty to his wife, and likewise the wife to her husband. ⁴The wife's body does not belong to her alone but also to her husband. In the same way, the husband's body does not belong to him alone but also to his wife. ⁵Do not deprive each other except by mutual consent and for a time, so that you may devote yourselves to prayer. Then come together again so that Satan will not tempt you because of your lack of self-control. ⁶I say this as a concession, not as a command. ⁷I wish that all men were as I am. But each man has his own gift from God; one has this gift, another has that.

⁸Now to the unmarried and the widows I say: It is good for them to stay unmarried, as I am. ⁹But if they cannot control themselves, they should marry, for it is better to marry than to burn with passion.

¹⁰To the married I give this command (not I, but the Lord): A wife must not separate from her husband. ¹¹But if she does, she must remain unmarried or else be reconciled to her husband. And a husband must not divorce his wife.

¹²To the rest I say this (I, not the Lord): If any brother has a wife who is not a believer and she is willing to live with him, he must not divorce her. ¹³And if a woman has a husband who is not a believer and he is willing to live with her, she must not divorce him. ¹⁴For the unbelieving husband has been sanctified through his wife, and the unbelieving wife has been sanctified through her believing husband. Otherwise your children would be unclean, but as it is, they are holy.

¹⁵But if the unbeliever leaves, let him do so. A believing man or woman is not bound in such circumstances; God has called us to live in peace. ¹⁶How do you know, wife, whether you will save your husband? Or, how do you know, husband, whether you will save your wife?

¹⁷Nevertheless, each one should retain the place in life that the Lord assigned to him and to which God has called him. This is the rule I lay down in all the churches. ¹⁸Was a man already circumcised when he was called? He should not become uncircumcised. Was a man uncircumcised when he was called? He should not be circumcised. ¹⁹Circumcision is nothing and uncircumcision is nothing. Keeping God's commands is what counts. ²⁰Each one should remain in the situation which he was in when God called him. ²¹Were you a slave when you were called? Don't let it trouble you—although if you can gain your freedom, do so. ²²For he who was a slave when he was called by the Lord is the Lord's freedman; similarly, he who was a free man when he was called is Christ's slave. ²³You were bought at a price; do not become slaves of men. ²⁴Brothers, each man, as responsible to God, should remain in the situation God called him to.

²⁵Now about virgins: I have no command from the Lord, but I give a judgment as one who by the Lord's mercy is trustworthy. ²⁶Because of the present crisis, I think that it is good for you to remain as you are. ²⁷Are you married? Do not seek a divorce. Are you unmarried? Do not look for a wife. ²⁸But if you do marry, you have not sinned; and if a virgin marries, she has not sinned. But those who marry will face many troubles in this life, and I want to spare you this.

²⁹What I mean, brothers, is that the time is short. From now on those who have wives should live as if they had none; ³⁰those who mourn, as if they did not; those who are happy, as if they were not; those who buy something, as if it were not theirs to keep; ³¹those who use the things of the world, as if not engrossed in them. For this world in its present form is passing away.

³²I would like you to be free from concern. An unmarried man is concerned about the Lord's affairs—how he can please the Lord. ³³But a married man is concerned about the affairs of this world—how he can please his wife— ³⁴and his interests are divided. An unmarried woman or virgin is concerned about the Lord's affairs: Her aim is to be devoted to the Lord in both body and spirit. But a married woman is concerned about the affairs of this world—how she can please her husband. ³⁵I am saying

---

a 1 Or "It is good for a man not to have sexual relations with a woman."

this for your own good, not to restrict you, but that you may live in a right way in undivided devotion to the Lord.

³⁶If anyone thinks he is acting improperly toward the virgin he is engaged to, and if she is getting along in years and he feels he ought to marry, he should do as he wants. He is not sinning. They should get married. ³⁷But the man who has settled the matter in his own mind, who is under no compulsion but has control over his own will, and who has made up his mind not to marry the virgin—this man also does the right thing. ³⁸So then, he who marries the virgin does right, but he who does not marry her does even better. *a*

³⁹A woman is bound to her husband as long as he lives. But if her husband dies, she is free to marry anyone she wishes, but he must belong to the Lord. ⁴⁰In my judgment, she is happier if she stays as she is—and I think that I too have the Spirit of God.

Food Sacrificed to Idols

8 Now about food sacrificed to idols: We know that we all possess knowledge. *b* Knowledge puffs up, but love builds up. ²The man who thinks he knows something does not yet know as he ought to know. ³But the man who loves God is known by God.

⁴So then, about eating food sacrificed to idols: We know that an idol is nothing at all in the world and that there is no God but one. ⁵For even if there are so-called gods, whether in heaven or on earth (as indeed there are many "gods" and many "lords"), ⁶yet for us there is but one God, the Father, from whom all things came and for whom we live; and there is but one Lord, Jesus Christ, through whom all things came and through whom we live.

⁷But not everyone knows this. Some people are still so accustomed to idols that when they eat such food they think of it as having been sacrificed to an idol, and since their conscience is weak, it is defiled. ⁸But food does not bring us near to God; we are no worse if we do not eat, and no better if we do.

⁹Be careful, however, that the exercise of your freedom does not become a stumbling block to the weak. ¹⁰For if anyone with a weak conscience sees you who have this knowledge eating in an idol's temple, won't he be emboldened to eat

what has been sacrificed to idols? ¹¹So this weak brother, for whom Christ died, is destroyed by your knowledge. ¹²When you sin against your brothers in this way and wound their weak conscience, you sin against Christ. ¹³Therefore, if what I eat causes my brother to fall into sin, I will never eat meat again, so that I will not cause him to fall.

The Rights of an Apostle

9 Am I not free? Am I not an apostle? Have I not seen Jesus our Lord? Are you not the result of my work in the Lord? ²Even though I may not be an apostle to others, surely I am to you! For you are the seal of my apostleship in the Lord.

³This is my defense to those who sit in judgment on me. ⁴Don't we have the right to food and drink? ⁵Don't we have the right to take a believing wife along with us, as do the other apostles and the Lord's brothers and Cephas *c*? ⁶Or is it only I and Barnabas who must work for a living?

⁷Who serves as a soldier at his own expense? Who plants a vineyard and does not eat of its grapes? Who tends a flock and does not drink of the milk? ⁸Do I say this merely from a human point of view? Doesn't the Law say the same thing? ⁹For it is written in the Law of Moses: "Do not muzzle an ox while it is treading out the grain." *d* Is it about oxen that God is concerned? ¹⁰Surely he says this for us, doesn't he? Yes, this was written for us, because when the plowman plows and the thresher threshes, they ought to do so in the hope of sharing in the harvest. ¹¹If we have sown spiritual seed among you, is it too much if we reap a material harvest from you? ¹²If others have this right of support from you, shouldn't we have it all the more?

But we did not use this right. On the contrary, we put up with anything rather than hinder the gospel of Christ. ¹³Don't

---

a 36-38 Or *36If anyone thinks he is not treating his daughter properly, and if she is getting along in years, and he feels she ought to marry, he should do as he wants. He is not sinning. He should let her get married. 37But the man who has settled the matter in his own mind, who is under no compulsion but has control over his own will, and who has made up his mind to keep the virgin unmarried—this man also does the right thing. 38So then, he who gives his virgin in marriage does right, but he who does not give her in marriage does even better.*   *b 1* Or *"We all possess knowledge," as you say*   *c 5* That is, Peter   *d 9* Deut. 25:4

you know that those who work in the temple get their food from the temple, and those who serve at the altar share in what is offered on the altar? ¹⁴In the same way, the Lord has commanded that those who preach the gospel should receive their living from the gospel.

¹⁵But I have not used any of these rights. And I am not writing this in the hope that you will do such things for me.

I would rather die than have anyone deprive me of this boast. ¹⁶Yet when I preach the gospel, I cannot boast, for I am compelled to preach. Woe to me if I do not preach the gospel! ¹⁷If I preach voluntarily, I have a reward; if not voluntarily, I am simply discharging the trust committed to me. ¹⁸What then is my reward? Just this: that in preaching the gospel I may offer it free of charge, and so

---

MONDAY

Read 1 Corinthians 8:1–13
Key Verses 1 Corinthians 8:1–3

Puffed Up – Paula Gibson

I was about forty miles from home, traveling on the freeway on a busy Friday. The engine of my car was billowing smoke, but I hoped to make it to the next exit. Instead, the car stopped. I was alone, and it was nightfall. With emergency flashers blinking, I opened the hood, then sat behind the wheel, praying that I'd get out of this situation safely.

No one was stopping to help. Then my heart jumped with fear when a rusty old car pulled up behind me. But God had sent an older married couple to my rescue. They helped and comforted me— drove me to a gas station, called a reputable towing company and kept their car running so I could warm up. They stayed with me while the tow-truck driver hooked up my car. They made sure that I was taken care of before they left.

That couple personified the type of people my friends and I would have made fun of if we had seen them on the the street. They were overweight, wore cheap tacky clothing and sounded as though they didn't have much education. But I was "puffed up" with my college education, my sense of style and my knowledge of the world. I could claim to love others, knowing the command of Jesus Christ, but here were a husband and wife setting an example of Christlike behavior for me. Fortunately they had no sense of smugness or indifference that prevented them from helping me that night.

Jesus loved us with a love so strong that he died for us. And he asks us to love in that same way: "Be imitators of God, therefore, as dearly loved children and live a life of love, just as Christ loved us and gave himself up for us as a fragrant offering and sacrifice to God" (Ephesians 5:1–2). As we become more Christlike and loving, stumbling blocks to our humility such as education, social status and cultural differences diminish. Loving others and being there to support and help them—family, friends and even those we meet along the freeway—are the ways we offer ourselves as a "fragrant offering" to God.

A Deeper Look
Mark 10:42–45; Philippians 2:3–4; James 3:13–16

Go to page 1289 for your next devotional reading.

not make use of my rights in preaching it.

¹⁹Though I am free and belong to no man, I make myself a slave to everyone, to win as many as possible. ²⁰To the Jews I became like a Jew, to win the Jews. To those under the law I became like one under the law (though I myself am not under the law), so as to win those under the law. ²¹To those not having the law I became like one not having the law (though I am not free from God's law but am under Christ's law), so as to win those not having the law. ²²To the weak I became weak, to win the weak. I have become all things to all men so that by all possible means I might save some. ²³I do all this for the sake of the gospel, that I may share in its blessings.

²⁴Do you not know that in a race all the runners run, but only one gets the prize? Run in such a way as to get the prize. ²⁵Everyone who competes in the games goes into strict training. They do it to get a crown that will not last; but we do it to get a crown that will last forever. ²⁶Therefore I do not run like a man running aimlessly; I do not fight like a man beating the air. ²⁷No, I beat my body and make it my slave so that after I have preached to others, I myself will not be disqualified for the prize.

TUESDAY

Read 1 Corinthians 9:1–27
Key Verses 1 Corinthians 9:24–27

Go for the Gold – Roger Hamilton

The apostle Paul was familiar with the concept of Olympic Games. The word he used for crown was also used for the laurel wreath placed on the heads of the winners in the early Olympic Games. He knew that athletes are often driven people. They arrive at practice early and stay late. They sacrifice time and pleasure, endure injuries and pain; they eat, breathe and sleep their sport in order to win the prize.

Paul makes it clear that God offers a prize as well—a prize we will cherish for eternity—a prize for those who finish well in the Christian life. But instead of a medal or a laurel that can be enjoyed only for a while, the Christian receives "a crown that will last forever."

The crown Paul mentions may be the "crown of righteousness" that he refers to in 2 Timothy 4:8 or the "crown of life" mentioned in James 1:12 and Revelation 2:10. But though Paul does not specify the "what" here, he does emphasize the "how." Paul declares that the training for this race is just as strict and rigorous as it is for the Olympics. He knew what it meant to expend every ounce of physical, mental and emotional energy in order to run the race to which God had called him. He ran with focus, not "like a man running aimlessly." He knew his competition; he did not "fight like a man beating the air." The writer of Hebrews adds that we are to "run with perseverance the race marked out for us" (Hebrews 12:1).

God wants us to run like Olympians; his desire is not merely that we run, but that we run for the prize. Nothing less is worth our time and energy—and nothing else is more rewarding.

A Deeper Look
Philippians 3:14; Hebrews 12:1–13

Go to page 1290 for your next devotional reading.

Warnings From Israel's History

10 For I do not want you to be ignorant of the fact, brothers, that our forefathers were all under the cloud and that they all passed through the sea. ²They were all baptized into Moses in the cloud and in the sea. ³They all ate the same spiritual food ⁴and drank the same spiritual drink; for they drank from the spiritual rock that accompanied them, and that rock was Christ. ⁵Nevertheless, God was not pleased with most of them; their bodies were scattered over the desert.

⁶Now these things occurred as examples[a] to keep us from setting our hearts on evil things as they did. ⁷Do not be idolaters, as some of them were; as it is written: "The people sat down to eat and drink and got up to indulge in pagan revelry."[b] ⁸We should not commit sexual immorality, as some of them did—and in one day twenty-three thousand of them died. ⁹We should not test the Lord, as some of them did—and were killed by snakes. ¹⁰And do not grumble, as some of them did—and were killed by the destroying angel.

¹¹These things happened to them as examples and were written down as warnings for us, on whom the fulfillment of the ages has come. ¹²So, if you think you are standing firm, be careful that you don't fall! ¹³No temptation has seized you except what is common to man. And God is faithful; he will not let you be tempted beyond what you can bear. But when you are tempted, he will also provide a way out so that you can stand up under it.

Idol Feasts and the Lord's Supper

¹⁴Therefore, my dear friends, flee from idolatry. ¹⁵I speak to sensible people;

a6 Or types; also in verse 11   b7 Exodus 32:6

WEDNESDAY

Read 1 Corinthians 10:1–13
Key Verse 1 Corinthians 10:13

Facing Down Temptation — LeRoy Eims

What do you do when you face temptation? None of us can claim immunity to thoughts and desires that lure us away from undivided devotion to Jesus Christ. But by looking at the example of Jesus in Luke 4:1–13, we can learn how to face down our own temptations.

Jesus faced three temptations, each of which challenged his identity and required him to choose whom he would worship. Each temptation appealed to a common human desire—to satisfy physical needs, to attain power and prestige, and to see God do something spectacular. Each time Jesus faced these temptations by quoting God's Word.

Why? Certainly Jesus knew the Word of God was alive and more powerful than Satan. The power of God's Word helped him escape from the devil's seductive offers. But I think he also quoted Scripture to provide an example for us, because that same power is available to us when we need it today.

Like Jesus, we may be challenged to take a stand on who we are and whose we are. However, we can count on the knowledge that God knows and understands what we are facing. Because Jesus was "tempted in every way, just as we are—yet was without sin" (Hebrews 4:15), we can freely come to him with our struggles. And, in his mercy and grace, he will point us to the way out.

A Deeper Look
Matthew 6:13; Hebrews 4:14–16; James 1:13–15

Go to page 1293 for your next devotional reading.

judge for yourselves what I say. ¹⁶Is not the cup of thanksgiving for which we give thanks a participation in the blood of Christ? And is not the bread that we break a participation in the body of Christ? ¹⁷Because there is one loaf, we, who are many, are one body, for we all partake of the one loaf.

¹⁸Consider the people of Israel: Do not those who eat the sacrifices participate in the altar? ¹⁹Do I mean that a sacrifice offered to an idol is anything, or that an idol is anything? ²⁰No, but the sacrifices of pagans are offered to demons, not to God, and I do not want you to be participants with demons. ²¹You cannot drink the cup of the Lord and the cup of demons too; you cannot have a part in both the Lord's table and the table of demons. ²²Are we trying to arouse the Lord's jealousy? Are we stronger than he?

The Believer's Freedom

²³"Everything is permissible"—but not everything is beneficial. "Everything is permissible"—but not everything is constructive. ²⁴Nobody should seek his own good, but the good of others.

²⁵Eat anything sold in the meat market without raising questions of conscience, ²⁶for, "The earth is the Lord's, and everything in it."ᵃ

²⁷If some unbeliever invites you to a meal and you want to go, eat whatever is put before you without raising questions of conscience. ²⁸But if anyone says to you, "This has been offered in sacrifice," then do not eat it, both for the sake of the man who told you and for conscience' sakeᵇ— ²⁹the other man's conscience, I mean, not yours. For why should my freedom be judged by another's conscience? ³⁰If I take part in the meal with thankfulness, why am I denounced because of something I thank God for?

³¹So whether you eat or drink or whatever you do, do it all for the glory of God. ³²Do not cause anyone to stumble, whether Jews, Greeks or the church of God— ³³even as I try to please everybody in every way. For I am not seeking my own good but the good of many, so that they may be saved. ¹Follow my example, as I follow the example of Christ.

Propriety in Worship

²I praise you for remembering me in everything and for holding to the teachings,ᶜ just as I passed them on to you.

³Now I want you to realize that the head of every man is Christ, and the head of the woman is man, and the head of Christ is God. ⁴Every man who prays or prophesies with his head covered dishonors his head. ⁵And every woman who prays or prophesies with her head uncovered dishonors her head—it is just as though her head were shaved. ⁶If a woman does not cover her head, she should have her hair cut off; and if it is a disgrace for a woman to have her hair cut or shaved off, she should cover her head. ⁷A man ought not to cover his head,ᵈ since he is the image and glory of God; but the woman is the glory of man. ⁸For man did not come from woman, but woman from man; ⁹neither was man created for woman, but woman for man. ¹⁰For this reason, and because of the angels, the woman ought to have a sign of authority on her head.

¹¹In the Lord, however, woman is not independent of man, nor is man independent of woman. ¹²For as woman came

---

ᵃ26 Psalm 24:1   ᵇ28 Some manuscripts conscience' sake, for "the earth is the Lord's and everything in it"   ᶜ2 Or traditions   ᵈ4-7 Or ⁴Every man who prays or prophesies with long hair dishonors his head. ⁵And every woman who prays or prophesies with no covering ⌊of hair⌋ on her head dishonors her head—she is just like one of the "shorn women." ⁶If a woman has no covering, let her be for now with short hair, ̕but since it is a disgrace for a woman to have her hair shorn or shaved, she should grow it again. ⁷A man ought not to have long hair

---

POINT OF INTEREST

1 Corinthians 11:1

Paul encouraged the Corinthians to follow his example, not because of any special skill or righteousness that he had, but because he was following the example of Jesus Christ (see 2:1–5). That's what discipleship is all about— following in the footsteps of others who demonstrate humility and who honor God in their relationship with Jesus. For the Corinthians, Paul's life "put skin" on Jesus' teachings. You can do the same in the lives of others as you set a godly example in your own life.

from man, so also man is born of woman. But everything comes from God. ¹³Judge for yourselves: Is it proper for a woman to pray to God with her head uncovered? ¹⁴Does not the very nature of things teach you that if a man has long hair, it is a disgrace to him, ¹⁵but that if a woman has long hair, it is her glory? For long hair is given to her as a covering. ¹⁶If anyone wants to be contentious about this, we have no other practice—nor do the churches of God.

The Lord's Supper

¹⁷In the following directives I have no praise for you, for your meetings do more harm than good. ¹⁸In the first place, I hear that when you come together as a church, there are divisions among you, and to some extent I believe it. ¹⁹No doubt there have to be differences among you to show which of you have God's approval. ²⁰When you come together, it is not the Lord's Supper you eat, ²¹for as you eat, each of you goes ahead without waiting for anybody else. One remains hungry, another gets drunk. ²²Don't you have homes to eat and drink in? Or do you despise the church of God and humiliate those who have nothing? What shall I say to you? Shall I praise you for this? Certainly not!

²³For I received from the Lord what I also passed on to you: The Lord Jesus, on the night he was betrayed, took bread, ²⁴and when he had given thanks, he broke it and said, "This is my body, which is for you; do this in remembrance of me." ²⁵In the same way, after supper he took the cup, saying, "This cup is the new covenant in my blood; do this, whenever you drink it, in remembrance of me." ²⁶For whenever you eat this bread and drink this cup, you proclaim the Lord's death until he comes.

²⁷Therefore, whoever eats the bread or drinks the cup of the Lord in an unworthy manner will be guilty of sinning against the body and blood of the Lord. ²⁸A man ought to examine himself before he eats of the bread and drinks of the cup. ²⁹For anyone who eats and drinks without recognizing the body of the Lord eats and drinks judgment on himself. ³⁰That is why many among you are weak and sick, and a number of you have fallen asleep. ³¹But if we judged ourselves, we would not come under judgment. ³²When we are judged by the Lord, we are being disciplined so that we will not be condemned with the world.

³³So then, my brothers, when you come together to eat, wait for each other. ³⁴If anyone is hungry, he should eat at home, so that when you meet together it may not result in judgment.

And when I come I will give further directions.

Spiritual Gifts

12 Now about spiritual gifts, brothers, I do not want you to be ignorant. ²You know that when you were pagans, somehow or other you were influenced and led astray to mute idols. ³Therefore I tell you that no one who is speaking by the Spirit of God says, "Jesus be cursed," and no one can say, "Jesus is Lord," except by the Holy Spirit.

⁴There are different kinds of gifts, but the same Spirit. ⁵There are different kinds of service, but the same Lord. ⁶There are different kinds of working, but the same God works all of them in all men.

⁷Now to each one the manifestation of the Spirit is given for the common good. ⁸To one there is given through the Spirit the message of wisdom, to another the message of knowledge by means of the same Spirit, ⁹to another faith by the same Spirit, to another gifts of healing by that one Spirit, ¹⁰to another miraculous powers, to another prophecy, to another distinguishing between spirits, to another speaking in different kinds of tongues,ᵃ and to still another the interpretation of tongues.ᵃ ¹¹All these are the work of one and the same Spirit, and he gives them to each one, just as he determines.

One Body, Many Parts

¹²The body is a unit, though it is made up of many parts; and though all its parts are many, they form one body. So it is with Christ. ¹³For we were all baptized byᵇ one Spirit into one body—whether Jews or Greeks, slave or free—and we were all given the one Spirit to drink.

¹⁴Now the body is not made up of one part but of many. ¹⁵If the foot should say, "Because I am not a hand, I do not belong to the body," it would not for that reason cease to be part of the body. ¹⁶And if the ear should say, "Because I am not an eye, I do not belong to the body," it

ᵃ10 Or languages; also in verse 28   ᵇ13 Or with; or in

would not for that reason cease to be part of the body. ¹⁷If the whole body were an eye, where would the sense of hearing be? If the whole body were an ear, where would the sense of smell be? ¹⁸But in fact God has arranged the parts in the body, every one of them, just as he wanted them to be. ¹⁹If they were all one part, where would the body be? ²⁰As it is, there are many parts, but one body.

²¹The eye cannot say to the hand, "I don't need you!" And the head cannot say to the feet, "I don't need you!" ²²On the contrary, those parts of the body that seem to be weaker are indispensable, ²³and the parts that we think are less honorable we treat with special honor. And the parts that are unpresentable are treated with special modesty, ²⁴while our presentable parts need no special treatment. But God has combined the members of the body and has given greater honor to the parts that lacked it, ²⁵so that there should be no division in the body, but that its parts should have equal concern for each other. ²⁶If one part suffers, every part suffers with it; if one part is honored, every part rejoices with it.

²⁷Now you are the body of Christ, and each one of you is a part of it. ²⁸And in the church God has appointed first of all apostles, second prophets, third teachers, then workers of miracles, also those having gifts of healing, those able to help others, those with gifts of administration, and those speaking in different kinds of tongues. ²⁹Are all apostles? Are all prophets? Are all teachers? Do all work mira-

---

THURSDAY

Read *1 Corinthians 12:1−31*
Key Verses *1 Corinthians 12:4−11*

Play Your Part – Lynn M. Hamilton

As I listened to the speaker at a conference, I frantically tried to write down every word she said. She seemed so wise, so experienced, so "together."

I admired her. I admired her gifts, but soon I started to compare my gifts with hers. I didn't have the same gift of faith that she had; her stories of faith stretched my imagination. And she seemed to speak so effortlessly and communicate so clearly. God was using her to touch many of us.

I looked at my life and thought, "Surely God couldn't use me in the same way he uses her! I'm not gifted like her, and I'm too young. Nobody would take me seriously. Maybe God can use me when I'm older and more experienced."

But eventually God taught me that he has made me with a unique combination of personality traits and spiritual gifts, and he wants me to use them for his glory. As part of the body of Christ, I have a distinct function—one that no one else can fulfill.

God used that experience to show me that he wants to work through me. Maybe not in the same way as the speaker but in my own special way—a way that will accomplish what he has in mind for me.

Now when I catch myself looking at others' gifts and abilities or thinking I don't have anything to offer, I try to remember that whatever part of the body I am, whether I'm an eye or an elbow, my role is unique and valuable to God and to others.

A Deeper Look
Romans 12:3−5; 1 Peter 4:10−11

Go to page 1294 for your next devotional reading.

cles? ³⁰Do all have gifts of healing? Do all speak in tongues*ᵃ*? Do all interpret? ³¹But eagerly desire*ᵇ* the greater gifts.

Love

And now I will show you the most excellent way.

13 If I speak in the tongues*ᶜ* of men and of angels, but have not love, I am only a resounding gong or a clanging cymbal. ²If I have the gift of prophecy and can fathom all mysteries and all knowledge, and if I have a faith that can move mountains, but have not love, I am nothing. ³If I give all I possess to the poor and surrender my body to the flames,*ᵈ* but have not love, I gain nothing.

⁴Love is patient, love is kind. It does not envy, it does not boast, it is not

proud. ⁵It is not rude, it is not self-seeking, it is not easily angered, it keeps no record of wrongs. ⁶Love does not delight in evil but rejoices with the truth. ⁷It always protects, always trusts, always hopes, always perseveres.

⁸Love never fails. But where there are prophecies, they will cease; where there are tongues, they will be stilled; where there is knowledge, it will pass away. ⁹For we know in part and we prophesy in part, ¹⁰but when perfection comes, the imperfect disappears. ¹¹When I was a child, I talked like a child, I thought like a child, I reasoned like a child. When I became a man, I put childish ways be-

ᵃ30 Or other languages   ᵇ31 Or But you are eagerly desiring   ᶜ1 Or languages   ᵈ3 Some early manuscripts body that I may boast

---

FRIDAY

Read *1 Corinthians 13:1–13*
Key Verse *1 Corinthians 13:5*

Lessons in Loving – Cheri Ruggles

The tears started to well up in my eyes and roll down my cheeks. I was tired, so tired of the cold silence that seemed to echo against the concrete walls of our apartment.

My roommate and I were as different as we could be. When I wanted the door open, she wanted it closed. When I wanted friends over, she wanted privacy. The differences led to grudges, which turned into resentment and bitterness. We developed the habit of heading straight for our own rooms when we came home, closing the doors as tightly as we had closed ourselves off from each other; at least we were making it impossible to be hurt again.

My tears were nothing new, but this time, instead of feeling sorry for myself and defending my own actions, I decided to take responsibility for my own shortcomings. I realized how much the word "I" had been in my mind and vocabulary lately. I had been trying to protect myself and make sure my needs were met, but God says that love "is not self-seeking." Did I ever stop and think, "What does she need?" The answer to that question was humbling.

None of the descriptions of love in 1 Corinthians 13 is a natural response, because we are selfish by nature. Showing others we love them is much harder than telling them. But if we honestly want to learn how to love, God will show us how. We may make mistakes in the process, but he will put us back on the right track if we are willing to try.

A Deeper Look
John 13:34–35; 1 John 4:19

Go to page 1298 for your next devotional reading.

hind me. [12]Now we see but a poor reflection as in a mirror; then we shall see face to face. Now I know in part; then I shall know fully, even as I am fully known.

[13]And now these three remain: faith, hope and love. But the greatest of these is love.

Gifts of Prophecy and Tongues

14 Follow the way of love and eagerly desire spiritual gifts, especially the gift of prophecy. [2]For anyone who speaks in a tongue[a] does not speak to men but to God. Indeed, no one understands him; he utters mysteries with his spirit.[b] [3]But everyone who prophesies speaks to men for their strengthening, encouragement and comfort. [4]He who speaks in a tongue edifies himself, but he who prophesies edifies the church. [5]I would like every one of you to speak in tongues,[c] but I would rather have you prophesy. He who prophesies is greater than one who speaks in tongues,[c] unless he interprets, so that the church may be edified.

[6]Now, brothers, if I come to you and speak in tongues, what good will I be to you, unless I bring you some revelation or knowledge or prophecy or word of instruction? [7]Even in the case of lifeless things that make sounds, such as the flute or harp, how will anyone know what tune is being played unless there is a distinction in the notes? [8]Again, if the trumpet does not sound a clear call, who will get ready for battle? [9]So it is with you. Unless you speak intelligible words with your tongue, how will anyone know what you are saying? You will just be speaking into the air. [10]Undoubtedly there are all sorts of languages in the world, yet none of them is without meaning. [11]If then I do not grasp the meaning of what someone is saying, I am a foreigner to the speaker, and he is a foreigner to me. [12]So it is with you. Since you are eager to have spiritual gifts, try to excel in gifts that build up the church.

[13]For this reason anyone who speaks in a tongue should pray that he may interpret what he says. [14]For if I pray in a tongue, my spirit prays, but my mind is unfruitful. [15]So what shall I do? I will pray with my spirit, but I will also pray with my mind; I will sing with my spirit, but I will also sing with my mind. [16]If you are praising God with your spirit, how can one who finds himself among those who do not understand[d] say "Amen" to your thanksgiving, since he does not know what you are saying? [17]You may be giving thanks well enough, but the other man is not edified.

[18]I thank God that I speak in tongues more than all of you. [19]But in the church I would rather speak five intelligible words to instruct others than ten thousand words in a tongue.

[20]Brothers, stop thinking like children. In regard to evil be infants, but in your thinking be adults. [21]In the Law it is written:

"Through men of strange tongues
    and through the lips of foreigners
I will speak to this people,
    but even then they will not listen
        to me,"[e]
says the Lord.

[22]Tongues, then, are a sign, not for believers but for unbelievers; prophecy, however, is for believers, not for unbelievers. [23]So if the whole church comes together and everyone speaks in tongues, and some who do not understand[f] or some unbelievers come in, will they not say that you are out of your mind? [24]But if an unbeliever or someone who does not understand[g] comes in while everybody is prophesying, he will be convinced by all that he is a sinner and will be judged by all, [25]and the secrets of his heart will be laid bare. So he will fall down and worship God, exclaiming, "God is really among you!"

Orderly Worship

[26]What then shall we say, brothers? When you come together, everyone has a hymn, or a word of instruction, a revelation, a tongue or an interpretation. All of these must be done for the strengthening of the church. [27]If anyone speaks in a tongue, two—or at the most three—should speak, one at a time, and someone must interpret. [28]If there is no interpreter, the speaker should keep quiet in the church and speak to himself and God.

[29]Two or three prophets should speak, and the others should weigh carefully what is said. [30]And if a revelation comes to someone who is sitting down, the first speaker should stop. [31]For you can all

---

[a]2 Or another language; also in verses 4, 13, 14, 19, 26 and 27   [b]2 Or by the Spirit   [c]5 Or other languages; also in verses 6, 18, 22, 23 and 39   [d]16 Or among the inquirers   [e]21 Isaiah 28:11,12   [f]23 Or some inquirers   [g]24 Or or some inquirer

prophesy in turn so that everyone may be instructed and encouraged. ³²The spirits of prophets are subject to the control of prophets. ³³For God is not a God of disorder but of peace.

As in all the congregations of the saints, ³⁴women should remain silent in the churches. They are not allowed to speak, but must be in submission, as the Law says. ³⁵If they want to inquire about something, they should ask their own husbands at home; for it is disgraceful for a woman to speak in the church.

³⁶Did the word of God originate with you? Or are you the only people it has reached? ³⁷If anybody thinks he is a prophet or spiritually gifted, let him acknowledge that what I am writing to you is the Lord's command. ³⁸If he ignores this, he himself will be ignored.ᵃ

³⁹Therefore, my brothers, be eager to prophesy, and do not forbid speaking in tongues. ⁴⁰But everything should be done in a fitting and orderly way.

The Resurrection of Christ

15 Now, brothers, I want to remind you of the gospel I preached to you, which you received and on which you have taken your stand. ²By this gospel you are saved, if you hold firmly to the word I preached to you. Otherwise, you have believed in vain.

³For what I received I passed on to you as of first importanceᵇ: that Christ died for our sins according to the Scriptures, ⁴that he was buried, that he was raised on the third day according to the Scriptures, ⁵and that he appeared to Peter,ᶜ and then to the Twelve. ⁶After that, he appeared to more than five hundred of the brothers at the same time, most of whom are still living, though some have fallen asleep. ⁷Then he appeared to James, then to all the apostles, ⁸and last of all he appeared to me also, as to one abnormally born.

⁹For I am the least of the apostles and do not even deserve to be called an apostle, because I persecuted the church of God. ¹⁰But by the grace of God I am what I am, and his grace to me was not without effect. No, I worked harder than all of them—yet not I, but the grace of God that was with me. ¹¹Whether, then, it was I or they, this is what we preach, and this is what you believed.

The Resurrection of the Dead

¹²But if it is preached that Christ has been raised from the dead, how can some of you say that there is no resurrection of the dead? ¹³If there is no resurrection of the dead, then not even Christ has been raised. ¹⁴And if Christ has not been raised, our preaching is useless and so is your faith. ¹⁵More than that, we are then found to be false witnesses about God, for we have testified about God that he raised Christ from the dead. But he did not raise him if in fact the dead are not raised. ¹⁶For if the dead are not raised, then Christ has not been raised either. ¹⁷And if Christ has not been raised, your faith is futile; you are still in your sins. ¹⁸Then those also who have fallen asleep in Christ are lost. ¹⁹If only for this life we have hope in Christ, we are to be pitied more than all men.

²⁰But Christ has indeed been raised from the dead, the firstfruits of those who have fallen asleep. ²¹For since death came through a man, the resurrection of the dead comes also through a man. ²²For as in Adam all die, so in Christ all will be made alive. ²³But each in his own turn: Christ, the firstfruits; then, when he comes, those who belong to him. ²⁴Then the end will come, when he hands over the kingdom to God the Father after he has destroyed all dominion, authority and power. ²⁵For he must reign until he has put all his enemies under his feet. ²⁶The last enemy to be destroyed is death. ²⁷For he "has put everything under his feet."ᵈ Now when it says that "everything" has been put under him, it is clear that this does not include God

---

ᵃ38 Some manuscripts *If he is ignorant of this, let him be ignorant*   ᵇ3 Or *you at the first*   ᶜ5 Greek *Cephas*   ᵈ27 Psalm 8:6

POINT OF INTEREST

1 Corinthians 15:14

Paul says that if Jesus did not literally rise from the dead at a specific time in an actual place, then all of Christianity is a fraud. If you aren't sure about the veracity of Christianity, go back and review the facts. God's truth can and will stand up to any human scrutiny.

himself, who put everything under Christ. ²⁸When he has done this, then the Son himself will be made subject to him who put everything under him, so that God may be all in all.

²⁹Now if there is no resurrection, what will those do who are baptized for the dead? If the dead are not raised at all, why are people baptized for them? ³⁰And as for us, why do we endanger ourselves every hour? ³¹I die every day—I mean that, brothers—just as surely as I glory over you in Christ Jesus our Lord. ³²If I fought wild beasts in Ephesus for merely human reasons, what have I gained? If the dead are not raised,

"Let us eat and drink,
    for tomorrow we die."ᵃ

³³Do not be misled: "Bad company corrupts good character." ³⁴Come back to your senses as you ought, and stop sinning; for there are some who are ignorant of God—I say this to your shame.

The Resurrection Body

³⁵But someone may ask, "How are the dead raised? With what kind of body will they come?" ³⁶How foolish! What you sow does not come to life unless it dies. ³⁷When you sow, you do not plant the body that will be, but just a seed, perhaps of wheat or of something else. ³⁸But God gives it a body as he has determined, and to each kind of seed he gives its own body. ³⁹All flesh is not the same: Men have one kind of flesh, animals have another, birds another and fish another. ⁴⁰There are also heavenly bodies and there are earthly bodies; but the splendor of the heavenly bodies is one kind, and the splendor of the earthly bodies is another. ⁴¹The sun has one kind of splendor, the moon another and the stars another; and star differs from star in splendor.

⁴²So will it be with the resurrection of the dead. The body that is sown is perishable, it is raised imperishable; ⁴³it is sown in dishonor, it is raised in glory; it is sown in weakness, it is raised in power; ⁴⁴it is sown a natural body, it is raised a spiritual body.

If there is a natural body, there is also a spiritual body. ⁴⁵So it is written: "The first man Adam became a living being"ᵇ; the last Adam, a life-giving spirit. ⁴⁶The spiritual did not come first, but the natural, and after that the spiritual. ⁴⁷The first man was of the dust of the earth, the second man from heaven. ⁴⁸As was the earthly man, so are those who are of the earth; and as is the man from heaven, so also are those who are of heaven. ⁴⁹And just as we have borne the likeness of the earthly man, so shall weᶜ bear the likeness of the man from heaven.

⁵⁰I declare to you, brothers, that flesh and blood cannot inherit the kingdom of God, nor does the perishable inherit the imperishable. ⁵¹Listen, I tell you a mystery: We will not all sleep, but we will all be changed— ⁵²in a flash, in the twinkling of an eye, at the last trumpet. For the trumpet will sound, the dead will be raised imperishable, and we will be changed. ⁵³For the perishable must clothe itself with the imperishable, and the mortal with immortality. ⁵⁴When the perishable has been clothed with the imperishable, and the mortal with immortality, then the saying that is written will come true: "Death has been swallowed up in victory."ᵈ

⁵⁵"Where, O death, is your victory?
    Where, O death, is your sting?"ᵉ

⁵⁶The sting of death is sin, and the power of sin is the law. ⁵⁷But thanks be to God! He gives us the victory through our Lord Jesus Christ.

⁵⁸Therefore, my dear brothers, stand firm. Let nothing move you. Always give yourselves fully to the work of the Lord, because you know that your labor in the Lord is not in vain.

The Collection for God's People

16 Now about the collection for God's people: Do what I told the Galatian churches to do. ²On the first day of every week, each one of you should set aside a sum of money in keeping with his income, saving it up, so that when I come no collections will have to be made. ³Then, when I arrive, I will give letters of introduction to the men you approve and send them with your gift to Jerusalem. ⁴If it seems advisable for me to go also, they will accompany me.

Personal Requests

⁵After I go through Macedonia, I will come to you—for I will be going through Macedonia. ⁶Perhaps I will stay with you

---

ᵃ32 Isaiah 22:13   ᵇ45 Gen. 2:7   ᶜ49 Some early manuscripts *so let us*   ᵈ54 Isaiah 25:8
ᵉ55 Hosea 13:14

Read 1 Corinthians 15:12–58
Key Verses 1 Corinthians 15:54–55

The Other Side of the Door

The newspaper headlines or the evening news underscore the tragedy when a life is cut short. A promising young student is killed in an accident or dies from cancer. Statistically, it doesn't happen often, but to the victim and the victim's family and friends, statistics are meaningless. When death comes to the young, it seems an especially cruel and relentless enemy.

There's no denying the pain and loss of death. But those who share in the resurrection of Jesus Christ have the hope that their perishable natural bodies will be clothed with the imperishable—with immortality. Jesus' resurrection was the visible demonstration that God has won the victory over death. Even for the young and promising, death is the doorway to a new life. We can only imagine the full and joyful life that is waiting on the other side of the door!

Digging Into the Word
1. What do the following passages teach you about Jesus' resurrection?—*John 20:24–31; 1 Corinthians 15:3–8, 20–22*
2. What do you learn from the following passages about the hope of *your* resurrection?—*John 11:25–26; 1 Corinthians 15:35–44; 2 Corinthians 4:13–18*

Personal Reflection
If your life ended today, are you confident that Jesus would open the door of heaven and welcome you in? If so, take time to thank God for opening the way through his Son. If not, invite Jesus to come into your heart so that you can face life *and* death with the confidence of the imperishable and the immortal.

One Step Deeper
John 5:24–26; 6:38–40

Go to page 1301 for your next devotional reading.

awhile, or even spend the winter, so that you can help me on my journey, wherever I go. ⁷I do not want to see you now and make only a passing visit; I hope to spend some time with you, if the Lord permits. ⁸But I will stay on at Ephesus until Pentecost, ⁹because a great door for effective work has opened to me, and there are many who oppose me.

¹⁰If Timothy comes, see to it that he has nothing to fear while he is with you, for he is carrying on the work of the Lord, just as I am. ¹¹No one, then, should refuse to accept him. Send him on his way in peace so that he may return to me. I am expecting him along with the brothers.

¹²Now about our brother Apollos: I strongly urged him to go to you with the brothers. He was quite unwilling to go now, but he will go when he has the opportunity.

¹³Be on your guard; stand firm in the faith; be men of courage; be strong. ¹⁴Do everything in love.

¹⁵You know that the household of Stephanas were the first converts in Achaia, and they have devoted themselves to the service of the saints. I urge you, brothers, ¹⁶to submit to such as these and to everyone who joins in the work, and labors at it. ¹⁷I was glad when Stephanas, Fortunatus and Achaicus arrived, because they have supplied what was lacking from you. ¹⁸For they refreshed my spirit and yours also. Such men deserve recognition.

Final Greetings

¹⁹The churches in the province of Asia send you greetings. Aquila and Priscilla*a* greet you warmly in the Lord, and so does the church that meets at their house. ²⁰All the brothers here send you greetings. Greet one another with a holy kiss.

²¹I, Paul, write this greeting in my own hand.

²²If anyone does not love the Lord—a curse be on him. Come, O Lord*b*!

²³The grace of the Lord Jesus be with you.

²⁴My love to all of you in Christ Jesus. Amen.*c*

---

a19 Greek *Prisca*, a variant of *Priscilla*
b22 In Aramaic the expression *Come, O Lord* is *Marana tha.*   *c24* Some manuscripts do not have *Amen.*

"Wait a minute! That's not what I said—and that's not who I am." Thoughts like these must have raced through Paul's mind after his character and ministry were attacked in Corinth. Among other things, false teachers were challenging Paul's authority as an apostle and accusing him of stealing church collection money. So it's not surprising that Paul gets emotional and seesaws between despair and joy as he writes. Yet even as he defends himself, he challenges the Corinthians—and his contemporary readers—to let themselves be controlled by Jesus' love when they face conflict and to rely on his grace when they're weak.

2 CORINTHIANS

1 Paul, an apostle of Christ Jesus by the will of God, and Timothy our brother,

To the church of God in Corinth, together with all the saints throughout Achaia:

2Grace and peace to you from God our Father and the Lord Jesus Christ.

The God of All Comfort

3Praise be to the God and Father of our Lord Jesus Christ, the Father of compassion and the God of all comfort, 4who comforts us in all our troubles, so that we can comfort those in any trouble with the comfort we ourselves have received from God. 5For just as the sufferings of Christ flow over into our lives, so also through Christ our comfort overflows. 6If we are distressed, it is for your comfort and salvation; if we are comforted, it is for your comfort, which produces in you patient endurance of the same sufferings we suffer. 7And our hope for you is firm, because we know that just as you share in our sufferings, so also you share in our comfort.

8We do not want you to be uninformed, brothers, about the hardships we suffered in the province of Asia. We were under great pressure, far beyond our ability to endure, so that we despaired even of life. ⁹Indeed, in our hearts we felt the sentence of death. But this happened that we might not rely on ourselves but on God, who raises the dead. ¹⁰He has delivered us from such a deadly peril, and he will deliver us. On him we have set our hope that he will continue to deliver us, ¹¹as you help us by your prayers. Then many will give thanks on our*ᵃ* behalf for the gracious favor granted us in answer to the prayers of many.

Paul's Change of Plans

¹²Now this is our boast: Our conscience testifies that we have conducted ourselves in the world, and especially in our relations with you, in the holiness and sincerity that are from God. We have done so not according to worldly wisdom but according to God's grace. ¹³For we do not write you anything you cannot read or understand. And I hope that, ¹⁴as you

ᵃ 11 Many manuscripts *your*

---

monday

Read *2 Corinthians 1:1–24*
Key Verses *2 Corinthians 1:3–4*

Two Sides of Suffering – Inger Rudolph

Recently a friend and I were discussing our gratitude to God for allowing us to suffer, because our suffering has actually helped us to be closer to him. Does that sound strange? Not many people subscribe to this philosophy, especially in our culture; we value health, happiness and the pursuit of pleasure so much that suffering usually comes as an unpleasant surprise.

While the "pain is gain" idea isn't one that our culture promotes or even acknowledges, it is one that occurs many times in Scripture. Suffering produces growth in our faith and our character; it allows us to identify with Christ's sufferings and commends us to God; it will be recognized and blessed in God's time.

Like most people, my friend and I have experienced our share of pain and suffering. As we talked that day about our hurts, I was reminded of 2 Corinthians 1:4, which explains why we experience the pain and suffering of life. It is "so that we can comfort those in any trouble with the comfort we ourselves have received from God."

God allows us to experience disappointment, rejection, loneliness, abuse, violation—the list can go on and on—"so that" we can empathize with someone else, "so that" we can give comfort. Our difficulties don't need to end with our private pain. Instead, they may be the very thing God uses to minister to another person in need.

Look over your own life and identify times when God has comforted you. Have you experienced a death in the family? You can comfort a friend who has too. Have you struggled with a learning disability? Be a "support group" for someone with similar experiences. Have you worked through painful family problems? You can provide a listening ear. Have you struggled with homesickness, financial worries, depression? Look for opportunities to share the things he has taught you and the comfort he has given you.

A Deeper Look
Psalm 86:15–17; John 16:33; Hebrews 4:16

Go to page 1304 for your next devotional reading.

have understood us in part, you will come to understand fully that you can boast of us just as we will boast of you in the day of the Lord Jesus.

¹⁵Because I was confident of this, I planned to visit you first so that you might benefit twice. ¹⁶I planned to visit you on my way to Macedonia and to come back to you from Macedonia, and then to have you send me on my way to Judea. ¹⁷When I planned this, did I do it lightly? Or do I make my plans in a worldly manner so that in the same breath I say, "Yes, yes" and "No, no"?

¹⁸But as surely as God is faithful, our message to you is not "Yes" and "No." ¹⁹For the Son of God, Jesus Christ, who was preached among you by me and Silas*ᵃ* and Timothy, was not "Yes" and "No," but in him it has always been "Yes." ²⁰For no matter how many promises God has made, they are "Yes" in Christ. And so through him the "Amen" is spoken by us to the glory of God. ²¹Now it is God who makes both us and you stand firm in Christ. He anointed us, ²²set his seal of ownership on us, and put his Spirit in our hearts as a deposit, guaranteeing what is to come.

²³I call God as my witness that it was in order to spare you that I did not return to Corinth. ²⁴Not that we lord it over your faith, but we work with you for your joy, because it is by faith you stand firm. **2** ¹So I made up my mind that I would not make another painful visit to you. ²For if I grieve you, who is left to make me glad but you whom I have grieved? ³I wrote as I did so that when I came I should not be distressed by those who ought to make me rejoice. I had confidence in all of you, that you would all share my joy. ⁴For I wrote you out of great distress and anguish of heart and with many tears, not to grieve you but to let you know the depth of my love for you.

Forgiveness for the Sinner

⁵If anyone has caused grief, he has not so much grieved me as he has grieved all of you, to some extent—not to put it too severely. ⁶The punishment inflicted on him by the majority is sufficient for him. ⁷Now instead, you ought to forgive and comfort him, so that he will not be overwhelmed by excessive sorrow. ⁸I urge you, therefore, to reaffirm your love for him. ⁹The reason I wrote you was to see

if you would stand the test and be obedient in everything. ¹⁰If you forgive anyone, I also forgive him. And what I have forgiven—if there was anything to forgive—I have forgiven in the sight of Christ for your sake, ¹¹in order that Satan might not outwit us. For we are not unaware of his schemes.

Ministers of the New Covenant

¹²Now when I went to Troas to preach the gospel of Christ and found that the Lord had opened a door for me, ¹³I still had no peace of mind, because I did not find my brother Titus there. So I said good-by to them and went on to Macedonia.

¹⁴But thanks be to God, who always leads us in triumphal procession in Christ and through us spreads everywhere the fragrance of the knowledge of him. ¹⁵For we are to God the aroma of Christ among those who are being saved and those who are perishing. ¹⁶To the one we are the smell of death; to the other, the fragrance of life. And who is equal to such a task? ¹⁷Unlike so many, we do not peddle the word of God for profit. On the contrary, in Christ we speak before God with sincerity, like men sent from God.

3 Are we beginning to commend ourselves again? Or do we need, like some people, letters of recommendation to you or from you? ²You yourselves are our letter, written on our hearts, known and read by everybody. ³You show that you are a letter from Christ, the result of our ministry, written not with ink but with the Spirit of the living God, not on tablets

---

*ᵃ*19 Greek *Silvanus*, a variant of *Silas*

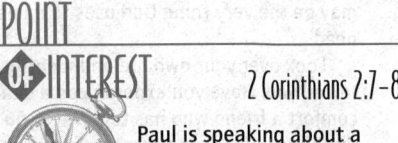

POINT OF INTEREST

2 Corinthians 2:7-8

Paul is speaking about a difficult situation in the Corinthian congregation. One particular individual had sinned and had hurt many people. When that person repented and asked to be restored, Paul counseled the congregation to do so, demonstrating God's forgiveness. Read Matthew 18:21–35 to find out what Jesus taught about forgiveness.

of stone but on tablets of human hearts. [4]Such confidence as this is ours through Christ before God. [5]Not that we are competent in ourselves to claim anything for ourselves, but our competence comes from God. [6]He has made us competent as ministers of a new covenant—not of the letter but of the Spirit; for the letter kills, but the Spirit gives life.

The Glory of the New Covenant

[7]Now if the ministry that brought death, which was engraved in letters on stone, came with glory, so that the Israelites could not look steadily at the face of Moses because of its glory, fading though it was, [8]will not the ministry of the Spirit be even more glorious? [9]If the ministry that condemns men is glorious, how much more glorious is the ministry that brings righteousness! [10]For what was glorious has no glory now in comparison with the surpassing glory. [11]And if what was fading away came with glory, how much greater is the glory of that which lasts!

[12]Therefore, since we have such a hope, we are very bold. [13]We are not like Moses, who would put a veil over his face to keep the Israelites from gazing at it while the radiance was fading away. [14]But their minds were made dull, for to this day the same veil remains when the old covenant is read. It has not been removed, because only in Christ is it taken away. [15]Even to this day when Moses is read, a veil covers their hearts. [16]But whenever anyone turns to the Lord, the veil is taken away. [17]Now the Lord is the Spirit, and where the Spirit of the Lord is, there is freedom. [18]And we, who with unveiled faces all reflect[a] the Lord's glory, are being transformed into his likeness with ever-increasing glory, which comes from the Lord, who is the Spirit.

Treasures in Jars of Clay

4 Therefore, since through God's mercy we have this ministry, we do not lose heart. [2]Rather, we have renounced secret and shameful ways; we do not use deception, nor do we distort the word of God. On the contrary, by setting forth the truth plainly we commend ourselves to every man's conscience in the sight of God. [3]And even if our gospel is veiled, it is veiled to those who are perishing. [4]The god of this age has blinded the minds of unbelievers, so that they cannot see the light of the gospel of the glory of Christ, who is the image of God. [5]For we do not preach ourselves, but Jesus Christ as Lord, and ourselves as your servants for Jesus' sake. [6]For God, who said, "Let light shine out of darkness,"[b] made his light shine in our hearts to give us the light of the knowledge of the glory of God in the face of Christ.

[7]But we have this treasure in jars of clay to show that this all-surpassing power is from God and not from us. [8]We are hard pressed on every side, but not crushed; perplexed, but not in despair; [9]persecuted, but not abandoned; struck down, but not destroyed. [10]We always carry around in our body the death of Jesus, so that the life of Jesus may also be revealed in our body. [11]For we who are alive are always being given over to death for Jesus' sake, so that his life may be revealed in our mortal body. [12]So then, death is at work in us, but life is at work in you.

[13]It is written: "I believed; therefore I have spoken."[c] With that same spirit of faith we also believe and therefore speak, [14]because we know that the one who raised the Lord Jesus from the dead will also raise us with Jesus and present us with you in his presence. [15]All this is for your benefit, so that the grace that is reaching more and more people may cause thanksgiving to overflow to the glory of God.

[16]Therefore we do not lose heart. Though outwardly we are wasting away, yet inwardly we are being renewed day by day. [17]For our light and momentary troubles are achieving for us an eternal glory that far outweighs them all. [18]So we fix our eyes not on what is seen, but on what is unseen. For what is seen is temporary, but what is unseen is eternal.

Our Heavenly Dwelling

5 Now we know that if the earthly tent we live in is destroyed, we have a building from God, an eternal house in heaven, not built by human hands. [2]Meanwhile we groan, longing to be clothed with our heavenly dwelling, [3]because when we are clothed, we will not be found naked. [4]For while we are in this tent, we groan and are burdened, because we do not wish to be unclothed but

a[18] Or contemplate   b[6] Gen. 1:3
c[13] Psalm 116:10

to be clothed with our heavenly dwelling, so that what is mortal may be swallowed up by life. ⁵Now it is God who has made us for this very purpose and has given us the Spirit as a deposit, guaranteeing what is to come.

⁶Therefore we are always confident and know that as long as we are at home in the body we are away from the Lord. ⁷We live by faith, not by sight. ⁸We are confident, I say, and would prefer to be away from the body and at home with the Lord. ⁹So we make it our goal to please him, whether we are at home in the body or away from it. ¹⁰For we must all appear before the judgment seat of Christ, that each one may receive what is

due him for the things done while in the body, whether good or bad.

The Ministry of Reconciliation

¹¹Since, then, we know what it is to fear the Lord, we try to persuade men. What we are is plain to God, and I hope it is also plain to your conscience. ¹²We are not trying to commend ourselves to you again, but are giving you an opportunity to take pride in us, so that you can answer those who take pride in what is seen rather than in what is in the heart. ¹³If we are out of our mind, it is for the sake of God; if we are in our right mind, it is for you. ¹⁴For Christ's love compels us, because we are convinced that one

---

TUESDAY

Read 2 Corinthians 4:1–18
Key Verses 2 Corinthians 4:5–6

Spotlight on Serving – Roger Hamilton

A spotlight is meant to draw attention to the object it illuminates. How ridiculous it would be for someone to point to a bright, colorful billboard and exclaim, "What an awesome spotlight that is!"

Paul knew the danger of being like a spotlight. Though God had given him an incredible mixture of gifts and abilities, Paul was keenly aware that he was to illuminate Jesus Christ and not to shine for himself. He also knew *how* to be a spotlight—by serving others for the sake of Jesus. Paul knew the words of Jesus well, that "the greatest among you will be your servant" (Matthew 23:11).

While the Corinthians struggled with arrogance and envy and challenged his authority, Paul described his apostleship in the language of slavery. Of the five Greek words that can be translated "servant," it is no accident that Paul chose the word for "slave" or "bondservant." His ministry was characterized by service to others so that Jesus Christ would be glorified.

Perhaps most important of all, Paul knew *where* his light was coming from. It was not his effort that determined the brightness of his light but rather how freely he allowed Jesus to shine through him.

Many of us struggle to be effective spotlights. We are too eager to shine out like "grand-opening" spotlights, calling attention to ourselves. Or we attempt to generate our own power source, to shine independently of the power of God. If we really want to let our light shine, we will do well to follow Paul's example and to echo the prayer of Psalm 115:1: "Not to us, O LORD, not to us but to your name be the glory, because of your love and faithfulness."

A Deeper Look
Mark 10:45; John 13:1–17; 1 Corinthians 4:1–2

Go to page 1305 for your next devotional reading.

died for all, and therefore all died. ¹⁵And he died for all, that those who live should no longer live for themselves but for him who died for them and was raised again.

¹⁶So from now on we regard no one from a worldly point of view. Though we once regarded Christ in this way, we do so no longer. ¹⁷Therefore, if anyone is in Christ, he is a new creation; the old has gone, the new has come! ¹⁸All this is from God, who reconciled us to himself through Christ and gave us the ministry of reconciliation: ¹⁹that God was reconciling the world to himself in Christ, not counting men's sins against them. And he has committed to us the message of reconciliation. ²⁰We are therefore Christ's ambassadors, as though God were making his appeal through us. We

implore you on Christ's behalf: Be reconciled to God. ²¹God made him who had no sin to be sin[a] for us, so that in him we might become the righteousness of God.

6 As God's fellow workers we urge you not to receive God's grace in vain. ²For he says,

"In the time of my favor I heard you,
    and in the day of salvation I
        helped you."[b]

I tell you, now is the time of God's favor, now is the day of salvation.

Paul's Hardships

³We put no stumbling block in any-

[a]21 Or *be a sin offering*   [b]2 Isaiah 49:8

WEDNESDAY

Read *2 Corinthians 5:1–21*
Key Verse *2 Corinthians 5:17*

A New Creation – Catherine DeVries

The timer rings. What seems like eons has only been three minutes. She walks into the bathroom, reads the results—and slumps down onto the floor. Positive.

What seemed impossible has suddenly become a heavy reality. Thoughts begin to churn . . . *What am I going to do? Should I call my boyfriend? Should I call my girlfriend? How far along am I? Should I end it now before anyone knows?* She wanted to have children someday, but now? Unmarried and right in the middle of her college education?

It's in times like these that we need Jesus the most. Oh, do we ever need him! If we are open to him, he comes to us with his comforting presence and his acceptance. He won't take away what has happened, but he can give us forgiveness and hope and help us to make the best choices.

Yes, he sees our mistakes, even our sin. But he also sees our potential to be "new creations." He has the power to renew us. As he showed time and again when talking with people while he was on this earth, Jesus is compassionate to all who seek him, and he gently asks them to repent and follow him.

If you've made some wrong decisions in the past or just recently—whatever they might have been—know that Jesus' invitation goes out to you as well. It's up to you whether or not you will answer his call and accept his forgiveness . . . and his love that will last forever.

A Deeper Look
John 4:7–26; Colossians 1:22–23

Go to page 1306 for your next devotional reading.

one's path, so that our ministry will not be discredited. ⁴Rather, as servants of God we commend ourselves in every way: in great endurance; in troubles, hardships and distresses; ⁵in beatings, imprisonments and riots; in hard work, sleepless nights and hunger; ⁶in purity, understanding, patience and kindness; in the Holy Spirit and in sincere love; ⁷in truthful speech and in the power of God; with weapons of righteousness in the right hand and in the left; ⁸through glory and dishonor, bad report and good report; genuine, yet regarded as impostors; ⁹known, yet regarded as unknown; dy-

ing, and yet we live on; beaten, and yet not killed; ¹⁰sorrowful, yet always rejoicing; poor, yet making many rich; having nothing, and yet possessing everything.

¹¹We have spoken freely to you, Corinthians, and opened wide our hearts to you. ¹²We are not withholding our affection from you, but you are withholding yours from us. ¹³As a fair exchange—I speak as to my children—open wide your hearts also.

Do Not Be Yoked With Unbelievers

¹⁴Do not be yoked together with unbelievers. For what do righteousness and

---

THURSDAY

Read 2 Corinthians 6:3—7:1
Key Verse 2 Corinthians 6:14

Hard Choices – Dawn Getz

Let's face it. There are some passages in Scripture that can be hard to accept, not only because they define what's right and wrong in God's eyes, but also because they deal with highly emotional issues. This verse in 2 Corinthians does both. It sets clear boundaries for the intimacy that God allows between believers and unbelievers, and it also addresses something very "close to home" for many of us—dating and marriage relationships.

This passage first became real to me when I was participating in a summer program for college students. Before I left home I talked about Jesus Christ with my boyfriend, an unbeliever, and told him how he could have a personal relationship with God. But he wasn't really interested. He was interested in me—so interested that he traveled five hundred miles to pay me a surprise visit that summer.

When I saw him my jaw dropped. My stomach started churning, because I knew we needed to talk about our relationships with God and with each other. As we talked I sensed that we were moving in opposite directions. I had read about the difficulties of being united with an unbeliever. I had hoped he would come to faith in Jesus Christ, but he hadn't.

Though it was painful, we broke up. If we didn't both have a relationship with God, how could we have one with each other? We would always have seen the world in such different ways that it would have affected every aspect of our life together.

At times God's call clashes with what we want and demands that we make hard choices. But his call is matched with the promise of 2 Corinthians 6:16: "For we are the temple of the living God. As God has said, 'I will live with them and walk among them, and I will be their God, and they will be my people.' "

A Deeper Look
Ezra 9:1–15; Psalm 84:11; 1 Corinthians 7:1–9

Go to page 1309 for your next devotional reading.

wickedness have in common? Or what fellowship can light have with darkness? [15]What harmony is there between Christ and Belial[a]? What does a believer have in common with an unbeliever? [16]What agreement is there between the temple of God and idols? For we are the temple of the living God. As God has said: "I will live with them and walk among them, and I will be their God, and they will be my people."[b]

[17]"Therefore come out from them
    and be separate,
                    says the Lord.
Touch no unclean thing,
    and I will receive you."[c]
[18]"I will be a Father to you,
    and you will be my sons and
        daughters,
            says the Lord Almighty."[d]

7 Since we have these promises, dear friends, let us purify ourselves from everything that contaminates body and spirit, perfecting holiness out of reverence for God.

Paul's Joy

[2]Make room for us in your hearts. We have wronged no one, we have corrupted no one, we have exploited no one. [3]I do not say this to condemn you; I have said before that you have such a place in our hearts that we would live or die with you. [4]I have great confidence in you; I take great pride in you. I am greatly encouraged; in all our troubles my joy knows no bounds.

[5]For when we came into Macedonia, this body of ours had no rest, but we were harassed at every turn—conflicts on the outside, fears within. [6]But God, who comforts the downcast, comforted us by the coming of Titus, [7]and not only by his coming but also by the comfort you had given him. He told us about your longing for me, your deep sorrow, your ardent concern for me, so that my joy was greater than ever.

[8]Even if I caused you sorrow by my letter, I do not regret it. Though I did regret it—I see that my letter hurt you, but only for a little while— [9]yet now I am happy, not because you were made sorry, but because your sorrow led you to repentance. For you became sorrowful as God intended and so were not harmed in any way by us. [10]Godly sorrow brings repentance that leads to salvation and leaves no regret, but worldly sorrow brings death. [11]See what this godly sorrow has produced in you: what earnestness, what eagerness to clear yourselves, what indignation, what alarm, what longing, what concern, what readiness to see justice done. At every point you have proved yourselves to be innocent in this matter. [12]So even though I wrote to you, it was not on account of the one who did the wrong or of the injured party, but rather that before God you could see for yourselves how devoted to us you are. [13]By all this we are encouraged.

In addition to our own encouragement, we were especially delighted to see how happy Titus was, because his spirit has been refreshed by all of you. [14]I had boasted to him about you, and you have not embarrassed me. But just as everything we said to you was true, so our boasting about you to Titus has proved to be true as well. [15]And his affection for you is all the greater when he remembers that you were all obedient, receiving him with fear and trembling. [16]I am glad I can have complete confidence in you.

Generosity Encouraged

8 And now, brothers, we want you to know about the grace that God has given the Macedonian churches. [2]Out of the most severe trial, their overflowing joy and their extreme poverty welled up in rich generosity. [3]For I testify that they gave as much as they were able, and even beyond their ability. Entirely on their own, [4]they urgently pleaded with us for the privilege of sharing in this service to the saints. [5]And they did not do as we expected, but they gave themselves first to the Lord and then to us in keeping with God's will. [6]So we urged Titus, since he had earlier made a beginning, to bring also to completion this act of grace on your part. [7]But just as you excel in everything—in faith, in speech, in knowledge, in complete earnestness and in your love for us[e]—see that you also excel in this grace of giving.

[8]I am not commanding you, but I want to test the sincerity of your love by com-

---

[a]15 Greek *Beliar*, a variant of *Belial*
[b]16 Lev. 26:12; Jer. 32:38; Ezek. 37:27
[c]17 Isaiah 52:11; Ezek. 20:34,41
[d]18 2 Samuel 7:14; 7:8   [e]7 Some manuscripts *in our love for you*

paring it with the earnestness of others. [9]For you know the grace of our Lord Jesus Christ, that though he was rich, yet for your sakes he became poor, so that you through his poverty might become rich.

[10]And here is my advice about what is best for you in this matter: Last year you were the first not only to give but also to have the desire to do so. [11]Now finish the work, so that your eager willingness to do it may be matched by your completion of it, according to your means. [12]For if the willingness is there, the gift is acceptable according to what one has, not according to what he does not have.

[13]Our desire is not that others might be relieved while you are hard pressed, but that there might be equality. [14]At the present time your plenty will supply what they need, so that in turn their plenty will supply what you need. Then there will be equality, [15]as it is written: "He who gathered much did not have too much, and he who gathered little did not have too little."[a]

Titus Sent to Corinth

[16]I thank God, who put into the heart of Titus the same concern I have for you. [17]For Titus not only welcomed our appeal, but he is coming to you with much enthusiasm and on his own initiative. [18]And we are sending along with him the brother who is praised by all the churches for his service to the gospel. [19]What is more, he was chosen by the churches to accompany us as we carry the offering, which we administer in order to honor the Lord himself and to show our eagerness to help. [20]We want to avoid any criticism of the way we administer this liberal gift. [21]For we are taking pains to do what is right, not only in the eyes of the Lord but also in the eyes of men.

[22]In addition, we are sending with them our brother who has often proved to us in many ways that he is zealous, and now even more so because of his great confidence in you. [23]As for Titus, he is my partner and fellow worker among you; as for our brothers, they are representatives of the churches and an honor to Christ. [24]Therefore show these men the proof of your love and the reason for our pride in you, so that the churches can see it.

[9]There is no need for me to write to you about this service to the saints. [2]For I know your eagerness to help, and I have been boasting about it to the Macedonians, telling them that since last year you in Achaia were ready to give; and your enthusiasm has stirred most of them to action. [3]But I am sending the brothers in order that our boasting about you in this matter should not prove hollow, but that you may be ready, as I said you would be. [4]For if any Macedonians come with me and find you unprepared, we—not to say anything about you—would be ashamed of having been so confident. [5]So I thought it necessary to urge the brothers to visit you in advance and finish the arrangements for the generous gift you had promised. Then it will be ready as a generous gift, not as one grudgingly given.

Sowing Generously

[6]Remember this: Whoever sows sparingly will also reap sparingly, and whoever sows generously will also reap generously. [7]Each man should give what he has decided in his heart to give, not reluctantly or under compulsion, for God loves a cheerful giver. [8]And God is able to make all grace abound to you, so that in all things at all times, having all that you need, you will abound in every good work. [9]As it is written:

"He has scattered abroad his gifts to
        the poor;
    his righteousness endures
        forever."[b]

[a]15 Exodus 16:18   [b]9 Psalm 112:9

POINT
OF INTEREST

2 Corinthians 8:7

Paul tells the Corinthians that their Christian lives are not complete without the gift of generosity, like a puzzle that is incomplete without that final piece. And as it was with the Corinthians, so it is with us. A quick glance through the checkbook ledger is usually all it takes to see whether or not that piece of the puzzle is missing.

¹⁰Now he who supplies seed to the sower and bread for food will also supply and increase your store of seed and will enlarge the harvest of your righteousness. ¹¹You will be made rich in every way so that you can be generous on every occasion, and through us your generosity will result in thanksgiving to God.

¹²This service that you perform is not only supplying the needs of God's people but is also overflowing in many expressions of thanks to God. ¹³Because of the service by which you have proved yourselves, men will praise God for the obedience that accompanies your confession of the gospel of Christ, and for your generosity in sharing with them and with everyone else. ¹⁴And in their prayers for you their hearts will go out to you, because of the surpassing grace God has given you. ¹⁵Thanks be to God for his indescribable gift!

Paul's Defense of His Ministry

10 By the meekness and gentleness of Christ, I appeal to you—I, Paul, who

---

FRIDAY

Read *2 Corinthians 9:1–15*
Key Verses *2 Corinthians 9:6–8*

Sowing Generously – Cathy Bowman

My friend Mark was very discouraged. After calculating his finances, he found that he had much less than he needed to pay for his next semester at school.

He went to his friend to discuss the issue. One of the questions this individual asked him was, "How have you been doing on giving?" Mark gulped. Because he had been so short on cash, he had let his giving slide for a few months. He planned to catch up when he could. His friend suggested that he pray about what to do.

After praying, Mark decided to figure out what his giving should have been. Then he took out his checkbook and wrote a check to cover it. It nearly emptied his account, but it felt right. But now the amount of money he had left couldn't even come close to meeting his needs for the next semester. He realized he was totally dependent on God to bring the money in; he also realized that it might be God's will that he temporarily drop out of school to work for a time. He was willing to do that if God wanted him to; he wanted to do whatever it took to obey God.

A few days later, Mark received a letter in the mail telling him that he had been awarded a scholarship that would cover all his needs for the next semester. Mark, and all of us who heard his story, were amazed and excited about how God chose to provide for Mark's needs.

Now, God is not some sort of celestial cash machine. He is under no obligation to provide for everyone in the way he did for Mark. The Bible makes it clear that those who believe in him will experience times of testing and hardship (see 1 Thessalonians 3:2–4; James 1:2–4; 1 Peter 1:3–7). In fact, the hardships we experience can serve to build up our faith. But Mark's case is an example of how God can provide for those who, through the prompting of the Spirit, choose to be obedient to his will and his Word.

A Deeper Look
Matthew 6:33; Philippians 4:19

Go to page 1312 for your next devotional reading.

am "timid" when face to face with you, but "bold" when away! [2]I beg you that when I come I may not have to be as bold as I expect to be toward some people who think that we live by the standards of this world. [3]For though we live in the world, we do not wage war as the world does. [4]The weapons we fight with are not the weapons of the world. On the contrary, they have divine power to demolish strongholds. [5]We demolish arguments and every pretension that sets itself up against the knowledge of God, and we take captive every thought to make it obedient to Christ. [6]And we will be ready to punish every act of disobedience, once your obedience is complete.

[7]You are looking only on the surface of things.[a] If anyone is confident that he belongs to Christ, he should consider again that we belong to Christ just as much as he. [8]For even if I boast somewhat freely about the authority the Lord gave us for building you up rather than pulling you down, I will not be ashamed of it. [9]I do not want to seem to be trying to frighten you with my letters. [10]For some say, "His letters are weighty and forceful, but in person he is unimpressive and his speaking amounts to nothing." [11]Such people should realize that what we are in our letters when we are absent, we will be in our actions when we are present.

[12]We do not dare to classify or compare ourselves with some who commend themselves. When they measure themselves by themselves and compare themselves with themselves, they are not wise. [13]We, however, will not boast beyond proper limits, but will confine our boasting to the field God has assigned to us, a field that reaches even to you. [14]We are not going too far in our boasting, as would be the case if we had not come to you, for we did get as far as you with the gospel of Christ. [15]Neither do we go beyond our limits by boasting of work done by others.[b] Our hope is that, as your faith continues to grow, our area of activity among you will greatly expand, [16]so that we can preach the gospel in the regions beyond you. For we do not want to boast about work already done in another man's territory. [17]But, "Let him who boasts boast in the Lord."[c] [18]For it is not the one who commends himself who is approved, but the one whom the Lord commends.

Paul and the False Apostles

11 I hope you will put up with a little of my foolishness; but you are already doing that. [2]I am jealous for you with a godly jealousy. I promised you to one husband, to Christ, so that I might present you as a pure virgin to him. [3]But I am afraid that just as Eve was deceived by the serpent's cunning, your minds may somehow be led astray from your sincere and pure devotion to Christ. [4]For if someone comes to you and preaches a Jesus other than the Jesus we preached, or if you receive a different spirit from the one you received, or a different gospel from the one you accepted, you put up with it easily enough. [5]But I do not think I am in the least inferior to those "super-apostles." [6]I may not be a trained speaker, but I do have knowledge. We have made this perfectly clear to you in every way.

[7]Was it a sin for me to lower myself in order to elevate you by preaching the gospel of God to you free of charge? [8]I robbed other churches by receiving support from them so as to serve you. [9]And when I was with you and needed something, I was not a burden to anyone, for the brothers who came from Macedonia supplied what I needed. I have kept myself from being a burden to you in any

[a]7 Or *Look at the obvious facts*　　[b]13-15 Or *13We, however, will not boast about things that cannot be measured, but we will boast according to the standard of measurement that the God of measure has assigned us—a measurement that relates even to you.* 14 . . . . *15Neither do we boast about things that cannot be measured in regard to the work done by others.*　　[c]17 Jer. 9:24

POINT OF INTEREST

2 Corinthians 11:3-4

False teachers were adding to the gospel message by attaching legalistic rules (from the old Jewish law) as conditions for salvation. Things haven't changed. Today, many *still* try to add to the gospel, saying that we have to do or say certain things to be saved. Paul speaks against legalism in all forms and encourages his readers to live in the freedom of "sincere and pure devotion to Christ."

way, and will continue to do so. ¹⁰As surely as the truth of Christ is in me, nobody in the regions of Achaia will stop this boasting of mine. ¹¹Why? Because I do not love you? God knows I do! ¹²And I will keep on doing what I am doing in order to cut the ground from under those who want an opportunity to be considered equal with us in the things they boast about.

¹³For such men are false apostles, deceitful workmen, masquerading as apostles of Christ. ¹⁴And no wonder, for Satan himself masquerades as an angel of light. ¹⁵It is not surprising, then, if his servants masquerade as servants of righteousness. Their end will be what their actions deserve.

Paul Boasts About His Sufferings

¹⁶I repeat: Let no one take me for a fool. But if you do, then receive me just as you would a fool, so that I may do a little boasting. ¹⁷In this self-confident boasting I am not talking as the Lord would, but as a fool. ¹⁸Since many are boasting in the way the world does, I too will boast. ¹⁹You gladly put up with fools since you are so wise! ²⁰In fact, you even put up with anyone who enslaves you or exploits you or takes advantage of you or pushes himself forward or slaps you in the face. ²¹To my shame I admit that we were too weak for that!

What anyone else dares to boast about—I am speaking as a fool—I also dare to boast about. ²²Are they Hebrews? So am I. Are they Israelites? So am I. Are they Abraham's descendants? So am I. ²³Are they servants of Christ? (I am out of my mind to talk like this.) I am more. I have worked much harder, been in prison more frequently, been flogged more severely, and been exposed to death again and again. ²⁴Five times I received from the Jews the forty lashes minus one. ²⁵Three times I was beaten with rods, once I was stoned, three times I was shipwrecked, I spent a night and a day in the open sea, ²⁶I have been constantly on the move. I have been in danger from rivers, in danger from bandits, in danger from my own countrymen, in danger from Gentiles; in danger in the city, in danger in the country, in danger at sea; and in danger from false brothers. ²⁷I have labored and toiled and have often gone without sleep; I have known hunger and thirst and have often gone without food;

I have been cold and naked. ²⁸Besides everything else, I face daily the pressure of my concern for all the churches. ²⁹Who is weak, and I do not feel weak? Who is led into sin, and I do not inwardly burn?

³⁰If I must boast, I will boast of the things that show my weakness. ³¹The God and Father of the Lord Jesus, who is to be praised forever, knows that I am not lying. ³²In Damascus the governor under King Aretas had the city of the Damascenes guarded in order to arrest me. ³³But I was lowered in a basket from a window in the wall and slipped through his hands.

Paul's Vision and His Thorn

12 I must go on boasting. Although there is nothing to be gained, I will go on to visions and revelations from the Lord. ²I know a man in Christ who fourteen years ago was caught up to the third heaven. Whether it was in the body or out of the body I do not know—God knows. ³And I know that this man—whether in the body or apart from the body I do not know, but God knows— ⁴was caught up to paradise. He heard inexpressible things, things that man is not permitted to tell. ⁵I will boast about a man like that, but I will not boast about myself, except about my weaknesses. ⁶Even if I should choose to boast, I would not be a fool, because I would be speaking the truth. But I refrain, so no one will think more of me than is warranted by what I do or say.

⁷To keep me from becoming conceited because of these surpassingly great revelations, there was given me a thorn in my flesh, a messenger of Satan, to torment me. ⁸Three times I pleaded with the Lord to take it away from me. ⁹But he said to me, "My grace is sufficient for you, for my power is made perfect in weakness." Therefore I will boast all the more gladly about my weaknesses, so that Christ's power may rest on me. ¹⁰That is why, for Christ's sake, I delight in weaknesses, in insults, in hardships, in persecutions, in difficulties. For when I am weak, then I am strong.

Paul's Concern for the Corinthians

¹¹I have made a fool of myself, but you drove me to it. I ought to have been commended by you, for I am not in the least inferior to the "super-apostles," even though I am nothing. ¹²The things that

Read 2 Corinthians 12:1–21
Key Verse 2 Corinthians 12:9

The Grace of God

Admitting a weakness is not something most of us like to do. We'd rather not let anyone know that we have a chink in the armor we put on before we go out to face the world each morning. So when Paul boasts of his weakness, it may seem very strange to us. What does he mean when he says the Lord told him "My grace is sufficient for you, for my power is made perfect in weakness"? That's the paradox: Human weakness is like an empty bottle into which God pours his enabling grace. Through the clear glass, people see not our strength, intellect or charisma but the sparkling beauty of God's grace.

God's gift of grace to this humble apostle was not a one-time deal; God gave it to him over and over, and he does the same for us each day "from strength to strength" (Psalm 84:7). God gives grace to meet the very weaknesses that make us most vulnerable. Instead of trying to cover the chinks in our armor, we let God be our "sun and shield," because "no good thing does he withhold from those whose walk is blameless" (Psalm 84:11).

Digging Into the Word
1. Why do we need God's grace?—*Romans 3:21–26; Ephesians 2:1–10*
2. How should our lives be changed because of the grace God gives us?—*Galatians 5:13–18; Titus 2:11–14*

Personal Reflection
Can you name one area in your life where you need God's power right now? Pray for his grace to fill your heart and life so that you overflow with the power to handle the situation.

One Step Deeper
Acts 15:6–11; Romans 5:15–17

Go to page 1315 for your next devotional reading.

mark an apostle—signs, wonders and miracles—were done among you with great perseverance. [13]How were you inferior to the other churches, except that I was never a burden to you? Forgive me this wrong!

[14]Now I am ready to visit you for the third time, and I will not be a burden to you, because what I want is not your possessions but you. After all, children should not have to save up for their parents, but parents for their children. [15]So I will very gladly spend for you everything I have and expend myself as well. If I love you more, will you love me less? [16]Be that as it may, I have not been a burden to you. Yet, crafty fellow that I am, I caught you by trickery! [17]Did I exploit you through any of the men I sent you? [18]I urged Titus to go to you and I sent our brother with him. Titus did not exploit you, did he? Did we not act in the same spirit and follow the same course?

[19]Have you been thinking all along that we have been defending ourselves to you? We have been speaking in the sight of God as those in Christ; and everything we do, dear friends, is for your strengthening. [20]For I am afraid that when I come I may not find you as I want you to be, and you may not find me as you want me to be. I fear that there may be quarreling, jealousy, outbursts of anger, factions, slander, gossip, arrogance and disorder. [21]I am afraid that when I come again my God will humble me before you, and I will be grieved over many who have sinned earlier and have not repented of the impurity, sexual sin and debauchery in which they have indulged.

Final Warnings

13 This will be my third visit to you. "Every matter must be established by the testimony of two or three witnesses."[a] [2]I already gave you a warning when I was with you the second time. I now repeat it while absent: On my return I will not spare those who sinned earlier or any of the others, [3]since you are demanding proof that Christ is speaking through me. He is not weak in dealing with you, but is powerful among you. [4]For to be sure, he was crucified in weakness, yet he lives by God's power. Likewise, we are weak in him, yet by God's power we will live with him to serve you.

[5]Examine yourselves to see whether you are in the faith; test yourselves. Do you not realize that Christ Jesus is in you—unless, of course, you fail the test? [6]And I trust that you will discover that we have not failed the test. [7]Now we pray to God that you will not do anything wrong. Not that people will see that we have stood the test but that you will do what is right even though we may seem to have failed. [8]For we cannot do anything against the truth, but only for the truth. [9]We are glad whenever we are weak but you are strong; and our prayer is for your perfection. [10]This is why I write these things when I am absent, that when I come I may not have to be harsh in my use of authority—the authority the Lord gave me for building you up, not for tearing you down.

Final Greetings

[11]Finally, brothers, good-by. Aim for perfection, listen to my appeal, be of one mind, live in peace. And the God of love and peace will be with you.

[12]Greet one another with a holy kiss. [13]All the saints send their greetings.

[14]May the grace of the Lord Jesus Christ, and the love of God, and the fellowship of the Holy Spirit be with you all.

a 1 Deut. 19:15

POINT OF INTEREST   2 Corinthians 12:10

How can being weak make us strong? We are by nature spiritual weaklings; Satan bullies us a little, and we fall down bleeding. Perhaps it is not until we quit relying on our own strength, and let God fight for us that we send the devil running. (See also James 4:7.)

What is salvation?

Select one:

A. Faith + listening to the right kind of music = salvation

B. Faith + having daily quiet times = salvation

C. Faith in Jesus Christ alone = salvation

D. Faith + attending every church service = salvation

C is correct, but we often live as if A, B and D

are the right responses. Paul wrote the Galatians to

remind them of the right answer because false teachers

were adding their own require-

ments to the gospel. Galatians

is a clear explanation of what it

means to be saved by faith.

GALATIANS

Paul, an apostle—sent not from men nor by man, but by Jesus Christ and God the Father, who raised him from the dead— ²and all the brothers with me,

To the churches in Galatia:

³Grace and peace to you from God our Father and the Lord Jesus Christ, ⁴who gave himself for our sins to rescue us from the present evil age, according to the will of our God and Father, ⁵to whom be glory for ever and ever. Amen.

No Other Gospel

⁶I am astonished that you are so quickly deserting the one who called you by the grace of Christ and are turning to a different gospel— ⁷which is really no gospel at all. Evidently some people are throwing you into confusion and are trying to pervert the gospel of Christ. ⁸But even if we or an angel from heaven should preach a gospel other than the one we preached to you, let him be eternally condemned! ⁹As we have already said, so now I say again: If anybody is preaching to you a gospel other than what you accepted, let him be eternally condemned!

¹⁰Am I now trying to win the approval of men, or of God? Or am I trying to please men? If I were still trying to please men, I would not be a servant of Christ.

Paul Called by God

¹¹I want you to know, brothers, that the gospel I preached is not something that man made up. ¹²I did not receive it

from any man, nor was I taught it; rather, I received it by revelation from Jesus Christ.

[13]For you have heard of my previous way of life in Judaism, how intensely I persecuted the church of God and tried to destroy it. [14]I was advancing in Judaism beyond many Jews of my own age and was extremely zealous for the traditions of my fathers. [15]But when God, who set me apart from birth[a] and called me by his grace, was pleased [16]to reveal his Son in me so that I might preach him among the Gentiles, I did not consult any man, [17]nor did I go up to Jerusalem to see those who were apostles before I was, but I went immediately into Arabia and later returned to Damascus.

[18]Then after three years, I went up to Jerusalem to get acquainted with Peter[b] and stayed with him fifteen days. [19]I saw none of the other apostles—only James, the Lord's brother. [20]I assure you before God that what I am writing you is no lie. [21]Later I went to Syria and Cilicia. [22]I was personally unknown to the churches of Judea that are in Christ. [23]They only heard the report: "The man who formerly persecuted us is now preaching the faith he once tried to destroy." [24]And they praised God because of me.

Paul Accepted by the Apostles

2 Fourteen years later I went up again to Jerusalem, this time with Barnabas. I took Titus along also. [2]I went in response to a revelation and set before them the gospel that I preach among the Gentiles.

[a]15 Or *from my mother's womb*   [b]18 Greek *Cephas*

MONDAY

***Read** Galatians 1:1–24*
***Key Verse** Galatians 1:10*

Who Am I Trying to Please? —Colette Magoon

It happens all the time. We get excited about a project, an idea, or a relationship and can't stop thinking about it for days. But in time the excitement dies and we forget all about it. What once seemed soooo good eventually seems ho-hum.

That's what happened to the Galatians and their relationship with Christ. The love and excitement they once had for Christ had crumbled, causing Paul to ask, "What has happened to all your joy?" (Galatians 4:15).

Just like the Galatians, we often allow our thinking about God and life to be influenced by trends, popular thinking and temporary fads. We swing between excitement and discouragement, depending on which "influence of the day" we are listening to.

Paul tried to stop this cycle by delving into the deeper issues. Who are we trying to please? Are we basing our hope on what people say or on what God says? Is our focus on what seems right at the time or on what will last for eternity?

Being God's servant demands a life based on solid, eternal principles, not on ever-changing opinions and fluctuating circumstances. By asking ourselves, "Who am I trying to please?" we can sift through those temporary ideas and keep our energies focused on eternal goals. Instead of acting out our lives to please anyone and everyone, we can study the role of a lifetime and play to an audience of One!

A Deeper Look
Ephesians 4:14–15; 1 Thessalonians 2:4

Go to page 1316 for your next devotional reading.

But I did this privately to those who seemed to be leaders, for fear that I was running or had run my race in vain. ³Yet not even Titus, who was with me, was compelled to be circumcised, even though he was a Greek. ⁴ˌThis matter aroseˌ because some false brothers had

infiltrated our ranks to spy on the freedom we have in Christ Jesus and to make us slaves. ⁵We did not give in to them for a moment, so that the truth of the gospel might remain with you.

⁶As for those who seemed to be important—whatever they were makes no dif-

---

TUESDAY

Read *Galatians 2:1–21*
Key Verse *Galatians 2:20*

Alive in Christ! — Randy C. Johnson

During the American Civil War, wealthy young men who had been drafted into the military would often pay other men to serve in their places. These hired soldiers marched, fought and often died for their "employers." Even though these wealthy individuals never saw any front-line action or experienced the horror and suffering of war, the draft board considered their obligation filled as if they had actually served their own time. Many young men survived that war simply because others were willing to go and fight in their places.

In a similar manner, each one of us has received notice from God through his Word. He calls us to account for the sinful actions and attitudes that result from our sinful natures. But we have no wealth of our own, no spiritual coinage with which we can pay another to work off our debts for us. Thankfully, Jesus offered to take our place. Jesus, the Son of God, came into this world to free us from the deadly wages of sin (see Romans 6:23). He has said, in effect, "I have stood in your place. I went to the front lines and fought the battle to the point of death on your behalf. You can be free from your debt if only you will believe and trust in me."

Jesus went to war for us. He served our time and went to battle against the forces of death and evil. He left his home in heaven and suffered total separation from God as he hung on a rough-hewn cross. Even though none of us has actually experienced the humiliation and suffering Jesus went through, his sacrifice on our behalf counts the same in God's eyes as if we had been nailed there with him. This is why the apostle Paul could write, "I have been crucified with Christ."

Today we live and have the hope of eternal life because Jesus was willing to die in our place. Can we ever repay him for the work he's done for us? No way. But the good news is that we don't have to. Jesus Christ's sacrifice is a free gift of grace. He did it simply because he loves us (see Romans 5:8). Does this mean we owe God nothing? Not at all. We owe him our undying gratitude, love and faithful allegiance.

A Deeper Look
John 3:1–21; Ephesians 2:8–9; Colossians 2:9–12

Go to page 1320 for your next devotional reading.

ference to me; God does not judge by external appearance—those men added nothing to my message. [7]On the contrary, they saw that I had been entrusted with the task of preaching the gospel to the Gentiles,[a] just as Peter had been to the Jews.[b] [8]For God, who was at work in the ministry of Peter as an apostle to the Jews, was also at work in my ministry as an apostle to the Gentiles. [9]James, Peter[c] and John, those reputed to be pillars, gave me and Barnabas the right hand of fellowship when they recognized the grace given to me. They agreed that we should go to the Gentiles, and they to the Jews. [10]All they asked was that we should continue to remember the poor, the very thing I was eager to do.

Paul Opposes Peter

[11]When Peter came to Antioch, I opposed him to his face, because he was clearly in the wrong. [12]Before certain men came from James, he used to eat with the Gentiles. But when they arrived, he began to draw back and separate himself from the Gentiles because he was afraid of those who belonged to the circumcision group. [13]The other Jews joined him in his hypocrisy, so that by their hypocrisy even Barnabas was led astray.

[14]When I saw that they were not acting in line with the truth of the gospel, I said to Peter in front of them all, "You are a Jew, yet you live like a Gentile and not like a Jew. How is it, then, that you force Gentiles to follow Jewish customs?

[15]"We who are Jews by birth and not 'Gentile sinners' [16]know that a man is not justified by observing the law, but by faith in Jesus Christ. So we, too, have put our faith in Christ Jesus that we may be justified by faith in Christ and not by observing the law, because by observing the law no one will be justified.

[17]"If, while we seek to be justified in Christ, it becomes evident that we ourselves are sinners, does that mean that Christ promotes sin? Absolutely not! [18]If I rebuild what I destroyed, I prove that I am a lawbreaker. [19]For through the law I died to the law so that I might live for God. [20]I have been crucified with Christ and I no longer live, but Christ lives in me. The life I live in the body, I live by faith in the Son of God, who loved me and gave himself for me. [21]I do not set aside the grace of God, for if righteous-

ness could be gained through the law, Christ died for nothing!"[d]

Faith or Observance of the Law

3 You foolish Galatians! Who has bewitched you? Before your very eyes Jesus Christ was clearly portrayed as crucified. [2]I would like to learn just one thing from you: Did you receive the Spirit by observing the law, or by believing what you heard? [3]Are you so foolish? After beginning with the Spirit, are you now trying to attain your goal by human effort? [4]Have you suffered so much for nothing—if it really was for nothing? [5]Does God give you his Spirit and work miracles among you because you observe the law, or because you believe what you heard?

[6]Consider Abraham: "He believed God, and it was credited to him as righteousness."[e] [7]Understand, then, that those who believe are children of Abraham. [8]The Scripture foresaw that God would justify the Gentiles by faith, and announced the gospel in advance to Abraham: "All nations will be blessed through you."[f] [9]So those who have faith are blessed along with Abraham, the man of faith.

[10]All who rely on observing the law are under a curse, for it is written: "Cursed is everyone who does not continue to do everything written in the Book of the Law."[g] [11]Clearly no one is justified before God by the law, because,

[a]7 Greek uncircumcised   [b]7 Greek circumcised; also in verses 8 and 9   [c]9 Greek Cephas; also in verses 11 and 14   [d]21 Some interpreters end the quotation after verse 14.   [e]6 Gen. 15:6 [f]8 Gen. 12:3; 18:18; 22:18   [g]10 Deut. 27:26

POINT OF INTEREST

Galatians 3:3

Wow—what an earful! Paul minced no words when dealing with people who believed they somehow had to earn salvation. The bad news is that no matter how hard we try, we'll never be able to save ourselves. The good news is—we don't have to! All we need is to believe and accept Jesus Christ's forgiveness. Praise God!

"The righteous will live by faith."[a] [12]The law is not based on faith; on the contrary, "The man who does these things will live by them."[b] [13]Christ redeemed us from the curse of the law by becoming a curse for us, for it is written: "Cursed is everyone who is hung on a tree."[c] [14]He redeemed us in order that the blessing given to Abraham might come to the Gentiles through Christ Jesus, so that by faith we might receive the promise of the Spirit.

The Law and the Promise

[15]Brothers, let me take an example from everyday life. Just as no one can set aside or add to a human covenant that has been duly established, so it is in this case. [16]The promises were spoken to Abraham and to his seed. The Scripture does not say "and to seeds," meaning many people, but "and to your seed,"[d] meaning one person, who is Christ. [17]What I mean is this: The law, introduced 430 years later, does not set aside the covenant previously established by God and thus do away with the promise. [18]For if the inheritance depends on the law, then it no longer depends on a promise; but God in his grace gave it to Abraham through a promise.

[19]What, then, was the purpose of the law? It was added because of transgressions until the Seed to whom the promise referred had come. The law was put into effect through angels by a mediator. [20]A mediator, however, does not represent just one party; but God is one.

[21]Is the law, therefore, opposed to the promises of God? Absolutely not! For if a law had been given that could impart life, then righteousness would certainly have come by the law. [22]But the Scripture declares that the whole world is a prisoner of sin, so that what was promised, being given through faith in Jesus Christ, might be given to those who believe.

[23]Before this faith came, we were held prisoners by the law, locked up until faith should be revealed. [24]So the law was put in charge to lead us to Christ[e] that we might be justified by faith. [25]Now that faith has come, we are no longer under the supervision of the law.

Sons of God

[26]You are all sons of God through faith in Christ Jesus, [27]for all of you who were baptized into Christ have clothed yourselves with Christ. [28]There is neither Jew nor Greek, slave nor free, male nor female, for you are all one in Christ Jesus. [29]If you belong to Christ, then you are Abraham's seed, and heirs according to the promise.

4 What I am saying is that as long as the heir is a child, he is no different from a slave, although he owns the whole estate. [2]He is subject to guardians and trustees until the time set by his father. [3]So also, when we were children, we were in slavery under the basic principles of the world. [4]But when the time had fully come, God sent his Son, born of a woman, born under law, [5]to redeem those under law, that we might receive the full rights of sons. [6]Because you are sons, God sent the Spirit of his Son into our hearts, the Spirit who calls out, "Abba,[f] Father." [7]So you are no longer a slave, but a son; and since you are a son, God has made you also an heir.

Paul's Concern for the Galatians

[8]Formerly, when you did not know God, you were slaves to those who by nature are not gods. [9]But now that you know God—or rather are known by God—how is it that you are turning back to those weak and miserable principles? Do you wish to be enslaved by them all over again? [10]You are observing special days and months and seasons and years!

[a]11 Hab. 2:4   [b]12 Lev. 18:5   [c]13 Deut. 21:23
[d]16 Gen. 12:7; 13:15; 24:7   [e]24 Or charge until Christ came   [f]6 Aramaic for Father

POINT OF INTEREST

Galatians 4:9

When we first come to Jesus Christ, our joy is fresh and our enthusiasm is high. Our relationship with God seems unclouded and uncomplicated. However, over time we may find ourselves drifting back into old habits and ways of thinking that obscure that clarity. The word "enslaved" describes the monumental consequences of this backward momentum. You have been set free. How can you live on in freedom? Look back at verses 6 and 7.

[11]I fear for you, that somehow I have wasted my efforts on you.

[12]I plead with you, brothers, become like me, for I became like you. You have done me no wrong. [13]As you know, it was because of an illness that I first preached the gospel to you. [14]Even though my illness was a trial to you, you did not treat me with contempt or scorn. Instead, you welcomed me as if I were an angel of God, as if I were Christ Jesus himself. [15]What has happened to all your joy? I can testify that, if you could have done so, you would have torn out your eyes and given them to me. [16]Have I now become your enemy by telling you the truth?

[17]Those people are zealous to win you over, but for no good. What they want is to alienate you ˌfrom usˌ, so that you may be zealous for them. [18]It is fine to be zealous, provided the purpose is good, and to be so always and not just when I am with you. [19]My dear children, for whom I am again in the pains of childbirth until Christ is formed in you, [20]how I wish I could be with you now and change my tone, because I am perplexed about you!

Hagar and Sarah

[21]Tell me, you who want to be under the law, are you not aware of what the law says? [22]For it is written that Abraham had two sons, one by the slave woman and the other by the free woman. [23]His son by the slave woman was born in the ordinary way; but his son by the free woman was born as the result of a promise.

[24]These things may be taken figuratively, for the women represent two covenants. One covenant is from Mount Sinai and bears children who are to be slaves: This is Hagar. [25]Now Hagar stands for Mount Sinai in Arabia and corresponds to the present city of Jerusalem, because she is in slavery with her children. [26]But the Jerusalem that is above is free, and she is our mother. [27]For it is written:

"Be glad, O barren woman,
    who bears no children;
break forth and cry aloud,
    you who have no labor pains;
because more are the children of the
        desolate woman
    than of her who has a husband."[a]

[28]Now you, brothers, like Isaac, are children of promise. [29]At that time the son born in the ordinary way persecuted the son born by the power of the Spirit. It is the same now. [30]But what does the Scripture say? "Get rid of the slave woman and her son, for the slave woman's son will never share in the inheritance with the free woman's son."[b] [31]Therefore, brothers, we are not children of the slave woman, but of the free woman.

Freedom in Christ

It is for freedom that Christ has set us free. Stand firm, then, and do not let yourselves be burdened again by a yoke of slavery.

[2]Mark my words! I, Paul, tell you that if you let yourselves be circumcised, Christ will be of no value to you at all. [3]Again I declare to every man who lets himself be circumcised that he is obligated to obey the whole law. [4]You who are trying to be justified by law have been alienated from Christ; you have fallen away from grace. [5]But by faith we eagerly await through the Spirit the righteousness for which we hope. [6]For in Christ Jesus neither circumcision nor uncircumcision has any value. The only thing that counts is faith expressing itself through love.

[7]You were running a good race. Who cut in on you and kept you from obeying the truth? [8]That kind of persuasion does not come from the one who calls you. [9]"A little yeast works through the whole batch of dough." [10]I am confident in the Lord that you will take no other view. The one who is throwing you into confusion will pay the penalty, whoever he may be. [11]Brothers, if I am still preaching circumcision, why am I still being persecuted? In that case the offense of the cross has been abolished. [12]As for those agitators, I wish they would go the whole way and emasculate themselves!

[13]You, my brothers, were called to be free. But do not use your freedom to indulge the sinful nature[c]; rather, serve one another in love. [14]The entire law is summed up in a single command: "Love your neighbor as yourself."[d] [15]If you keep on biting and devouring each other, watch out or you will be destroyed by each other.

a27 Isaiah 54:1   b30 Gen. 21:10   c13 Or the flesh; also in verses 16, 17, 19 and 24
d14 Lev. 19:18

Life by the Spirit

16So I say, live by the Spirit, and you will not gratify the desires of the sinful nature. 17For the sinful nature desires what is contrary to the Spirit, and the Spirit what is contrary to the sinful nature. They are in conflict with each other, so that you do not do what you want. 18But if you are led by the Spirit, you are not under law.

19The acts of the sinful nature are obvious: sexual immorality, impurity and debauchery; 20idolatry and witchcraft; hatred, discord, jealousy, fits of rage, selfish ambition, dissensions, factions 21and envy; drunkenness, orgies, and the like. I warn you, as I did before, that those who live like this will not inherit the kingdom of God.

22But the fruit of the Spirit is love, joy, peace, patience, kindness, goodness, faithfulness, 23gentleness and self-control. Against such things there is no law. 24Those who belong to Christ Jesus have crucified the sinful nature with its passions and desires. 25Since we live by the Spirit, let us keep in step with the Spirit. 26Let us not become conceited, provoking and envying each other.

Doing Good to All

6 Brothers, if someone is caught in a sin, you who are spiritual should restore him gently. But watch yourself, or you also may be tempted. 2Carry each other's burdens, and in this way you will fulfill the law of Christ. 3If anyone thinks he is something when he is nothing, he de-

---

Read *Galatians 5:1–26*
Key Verses *Galatians 5:22–23*

Hungry for Fruit —Don Allen

A favorite activity of many of my peers at college was to drive the eight miles from Pullman, Washington, to Moscow, Idaho, to cross the border into a state where the drinking age was 19 rather than 21. One night, when the guy next door returned from a night at the clubs in Moscow, I asked him how his evening had been. He said reflectively, "People are over there looking for something, but they're not going to find it."

That guy was right. So many students made this mass exodus on a frequent basis. I don't know whether they were in search of happiness, but I'm pretty sure they found no lasting fulfillment in their "night on the town." Whether we realize it or not, most of us deeply yearn for true love, lasting joy and a settled peace in our lives. But these things aren't found at the bottom of a beer bottle, or even in meeting "Mr./Ms. Right" on a Saturday night.

If I held the patents for love, joy, peace, patience, kindness, goodness, faithfulness, gentleness and self-control and could sell them in a drugstore, I would be a very wealthy man. Many people are in desperate need of this "fruit," but they don't know where to find it. Even though it can't be bought or sold, it is available in the Holy Spirit. As we abide in the "Vine," Jesus Christ, the fruit of the Spirit will grow and become evident in our lives. Then we'll demonstrate the difference that Jesus makes, and hungry people will see God and glorify him: "This is to my Father's glory, that you bear much fruit, showing yourselves to be my disciples" (John 15:8).

A Deeper Look
John 15:4–5; Ephesians 5:18–20

Go to page 1321 for your next devotional reading.

ceives himself. ⁴Each one should test his own actions. Then he can take pride in himself, without comparing himself to somebody else, ⁵for each one should carry his own load.

⁶Anyone who receives instruction in the word must share all good things with his instructor.

⁷Do not be deceived: God cannot be mocked. A man reaps what he sows. ⁸The one who sows to please his sinful nature, from that nature*a* will reap destruction; the one who sows to please the Spirit, from the Spirit will reap eternal life. ⁹Let us not become weary in doing good, for at the proper time we will reap a harvest if we do not give up. ¹⁰Therefore, as we have opportunity, let us do good to all people, especially to those who belong to the family of believers.

Not Circumcision but a New Creation

¹¹See what large letters I use as I write to you with my own hand! ¹²Those who want to make a good impression outwardly are trying to compel you to be circumcised. The only reason they do this is to avoid being persecuted for the cross of Christ. ¹³Not even those who are circumcised obey the law, yet

a8 Or his flesh, from the flesh

THURSDAY

Read Galatians 6:1–18
Key Verses Galatians 6:9–10

Doing Good! – Kisa Kampfer

My relationships at work were not going well. For the past several months I had been developing friendships with two campus coworkers. Now it seemed as though neither of them wanted to have anything to do with me! One coworker, Sarah, discovered that she had multiple sclerosis. I did not know how to respond and made mistakes in relating to her. I worried too much about her health and pushed her to talk when she wasn't ready.

My second friend, Melissa, had recently lost her grandfather. As we talked about her grief, I felt as though we had taken a step forward in our friendship. Later, however, she distanced herself from me. I was confused. I wondered if I had said something wrong, so I asked God to teach me how to show her his love. I also asked him to heal the relationship.

I didn't want to give up on these friendships, so I decided to talk to Melissa. It turned out that we had totally misunderstood our actions and intentions toward each other. My relationship with Sarah was harder. I tried to work things out, but she wasn't interested. It was only after I gave her the room she needed that she started talking to me again.

Friendships take a lot of work and patience, persistence and sensitivity. We can get "weary in doing good," especially if we make mistakes, which we are bound to do because we are human, or if our communication skills need improvement. But we have the Spirit with us to guide and teach us, even in the most difficult relationships. When we persist in doing "good to all people," the harvest will show itself at the proper time—a harvest of forgiveness, good will, maturity and great friendships.

A Deeper Look
Hebrews 13:16; 1 Peter 4:8; 1 John 4:18–21

Go to page 1324 for your next devotional reading.

they want you to be circumcised that they may boast about your flesh. ¹⁴May I never boast except in the cross of our Lord Jesus Christ, through which*a* the world has been crucified to me, and I to the world. ¹⁵Neither circumcision nor uncircumcision means anything; what counts is a new creation. ¹⁶Peace and mercy to all who follow this rule, even to the Israel of God.

¹⁷Finally, let no one cause me trouble, for I bear on my body the marks of Jesus.

¹⁸The grace of our Lord Jesus Christ be with your spirit, brothers. Amen.

a 14 Or *whom*

*S*ometimes the hardest thing

to do is to love other Christians and live in unity with

them. At times the only thing we have in common with

another believer is that we're both followers of Jesus! But

a key message of Ephesians is that the love and grace

we've received in Jesus are the means by which we live in

unity with each other as well as the reason we do so.

Notice that Paul emphasizes God's grace before encourag-

ing the Ephesians to "live a life of love" (5:2); it is only

by mirroring God's grace that we

can really live in peace with

each other.

EPHESIANS

Paul, an apostle of Christ Jesus by the will of God,

To the saints in Ephesus,*a* the faithful*b* in Christ Jesus:

²Grace and peace to you from God our Father and the Lord Jesus Christ.

Spiritual Blessings in Christ

³Praise be to the God and Father of our Lord Jesus Christ, who has blessed us in the heavenly realms with every spiritual blessing in Christ. ⁴For he chose us in him before the creation of the world to be holy and blameless in his sight. In love ⁵he*c* predestined us to be adopted as his sons through Jesus Christ, in accordance with his pleasure and will— ⁶to the praise of his glorious grace, which he has freely given us in the One he loves. ⁷In him we have redemption through his blood, the forgiveness of sins, in accordance with the riches of God's grace ⁸that he lavished on us with all wisdom and understanding. ⁹And he*d* made known to us the mystery of his will according to his good pleasure, which he purposed in Christ, ¹⁰to be put into effect when the times will have reached their fulfillment—to bring all things in heaven and on earth together under one head, even Christ.

¹¹In him we were also chosen,*e* having been predestined according to the

---

*a*1 Some early manuscripts do not have *in Ephesus.*
*b*1 Or *believers who are*   *c*4,5 Or *sight in love.* ⁵*He*   *d*8,9 Or *us. With all wisdom and understanding,* ⁹*he*   *e*11 Or *were made heirs*

plan of him who works out everything in conformity with the purpose of his will, 12in order that we, who were the first to hope in Christ, might be for the praise of his glory. 13And you also were included in Christ when you heard the word of truth, the gospel of your salvation. Having believed, you were marked in him with a seal, the promised Holy Spirit, 14who is a deposit guaranteeing our inheritance until the redemption of those who are God's possession—to the praise of his glory.

Thanksgiving and Prayer

15For this reason, ever since I heard

Read Ephesians 1:1–23
Key Verses Ephesians 1:13–14

Blessed Assurance — Karen Allen

"How do I know I'm really a Christian? What if I didn't pray the right prayer? Why don't I feel forgiven?" Do these questions sound familiar?

Have you ever wondered whether or not you are really saved? Many new believers doubt that they are really saved because they don't *feel* any different from the way they did before. The good news is that we don't have to *feel* something in order for it to be true. Our emotions aren't always reliable—but God is. He has promised that if we receive Jesus as our Savior, he will make us his children (see John 1:12).

God has filled the Bible with promises to reassure us that Jesus' work on the cross has saved us once and for all. Even though we're tempted daily, we are saved from both sin's penalty and its power because "he is faithful and just and will forgive us our sins and purify us from all unrighteousness" (1 John 1:9). Growing in righteousness is a lifelong process that God is committed to helping us complete (see Philippians 1:6).

We gain assurance by knowing and believing what God has promised. God tells us that he will never leave us (see Hebrews 13:5), that he will never drive away those who come to him (see John 6:37) and that nothing will be able to snatch us away from him (see John 10:27–28). Nothing can ever separate us from God and his love (see Romans 8:39). We can believe God because not only does God speak the truth—he *is* truth.

The next time you begin to doubt your salvation, remember that if you have put your trust in Jesus, your sins are forgiven. If you've asked him into your life, he's there. He will make himself known to you. Watch. Keep a journal to help you remember what he's done already in your life. When your emotions cause you to doubt, the written evidence will be there in black and white.

If you're not sure whether you've ever trusted Jesus, why not do that now? You can then be sure from this day forward that you are his and your sins are forgiven. It doesn't matter how you feel—the fact is that you're forgiven! Count on it!

A Deeper Look
Ephesians 4:30; Jude 24

Go to page 1326 for your next devotional reading.

about your faith in the Lord Jesus and your love for all the saints, [16]I have not stopped giving thanks for you, remembering you in my prayers. [17]I keep asking that the God of our Lord Jesus Christ, the glorious Father, may give you the Spirit[a] of wisdom and revelation, so that you may know him better. [18]I pray also that the eyes of your heart may be enlightened in order that you may know the hope to which he has called you, the riches of his glorious inheritance in the saints, [19]and his incomparably great power for us who believe. That power is like the working of his mighty strength, [20]which he exerted in Christ when he raised him from the dead and seated him at his right hand in the heavenly realms, [21]far above all rule and authority, power and dominion, and every title that can be given, not only in the present age but also in the one to come. [22]And God placed all things under his feet and appointed him to be head over everything for the church, [23]which is his body, the fullness of him who fills everything in every way.

Made Alive in Christ

2 As for you, you were dead in your transgressions and sins, [2]in which you used to live when you followed the ways of this world and of the ruler of the kingdom of the air, the spirit who is now at work in those who are disobedient. [3]All of us also lived among them at one time, gratifying the cravings of our sinful nature[b] and following its desires and thoughts. Like the rest, we were by nature objects of wrath. [4]But because of his great love for us, God, who is rich in mercy, [5]made us alive with Christ even when we were dead in transgressions—it is by grace you have been saved. [6]And God raised us up with Christ and seated us with him in the heavenly realms in Christ Jesus, [7]in order that in the coming ages he might show the incomparable riches of his grace, expressed in his kindness to us in Christ Jesus. [8]For it is by grace you have been saved, through faith—and this not from yourselves, it is the gift of God— [9]not by works, so that no one can boast. [10]For we are God's workmanship, created in Christ Jesus to do good works, which God prepared in advance for us to do.

One in Christ

[11]Therefore, remember that formerly you who are Gentiles by birth and called "uncircumcised" by those who call themselves "the circumcision" (that done in the body by the hands of men)— [12]remember that at that time you were separate from Christ, excluded from citizenship in Israel and foreigners to the covenants of the promise, without hope and without God in the world. [13]But now in Christ Jesus you who once were far away have been brought near through the blood of Christ.

[14]For he himself is our peace, who has made the two one and has destroyed the barrier, the dividing wall of hostility, [15]by abolishing in his flesh the law with its commandments and regulations. His purpose was to create in himself one new man out of the two, thus making peace, [16]and in this one body to reconcile both of them to God through the cross, by which he put to death their hostility. [17]He came and preached peace to you who were far away and peace to those who were near. [18]For through him we both have access to the Father by one Spirit.

[19]Consequently, you are no longer foreigners and aliens, but fellow citizens with God's people and members of God's household, [20]built on the foundation of the apostles and prophets, with Christ Jesus himself as the chief cornerstone. [21]In him the whole building is joined together and rises to become a holy temple in the Lord. [22]And in him you too are

[a]17 Or *a spirit*　　[b]3 Or *our flesh*

POINT OF INTEREST

Ephesians 2:14-20

We hear a lot these days about breaking down barriers among people in the church. These barriers take the form of such differences as race, ethnicity, socioeconomic status and denominational affiliation. But Paul gives us insight into the unity *we already have* in Jesus Christ. Reconciliation between people groups will occur when all sides acknowledge and claim his one-time work of breaking down the barrier between sinful humans and our holy God.

Read Ephesians 2:1–22
Key Verses Ephesians 2:8–10

Passing the Test

When we get to the end of the course called Life 101, we will discover that God does not grade on a curve but on a pass-fail basis. Bad news! God has written "fail" across the top of our tests, because all of us have sinned. Even when we try to do our best and study hard, it is impossible. Sounds pretty discouraging and depressing, doesn't it? Why even try when there is no way to make the grade?

What if you were told that someone already took the test and got an A+ and that you could have their grade? Good news! Consider it done. This is much like what Jesus has done. He knew we could never pass life's test on our own, so he came to this earth and "aced" the test for us. He has already earned the grade; now he offers it to all who will believe in him.

Digging Into the Word
1. What do you learn about salvation and good deeds in these verses?—*Galatians 2:15–16; Ephesians 2:8–10*
2. What is the difference between being saved by good deeds and doing good deeds?—*Matthew 5:16; Hebrews 13:16; 1 Peter 2:12*

Move Into Service
If you have accepted Jesus' offer of salvation and know his forgiveness, you are called to do good deeds. What is one act of service you can perform in your church or community to show that your faith is real? Commit yourself to begin within the next week.

One Step Deeper
Acts 10:37–38; James 2:17–18

Go to page 1328 for your next devotional reading.

being built together to become a dwelling in which God lives by his Spirit.

Paul the Preacher to the Gentiles

3 For this reason I, Paul, the prisoner of Christ Jesus for the sake of you Gentiles—

2Surely you have heard about the administration of God's grace that was given to me for you, 3that is, the mystery made known to me by revelation, as I have already written briefly. 4In reading this, then, you will be able to understand my insight into the mystery of Christ, 5which was not made known to men in other generations as it has now been revealed by the Spirit to God's holy apostles and prophets. 6This mystery is that through the gospel the Gentiles are heirs together with Israel, members together of one body, and sharers together in the promise in Christ Jesus.

7I became a servant of this gospel by the gift of God's grace given me through the working of his power. 8Although I am less than the least of all God's people, this grace was given me: to preach to the Gentiles the unsearchable riches of Christ, 9and to make plain to everyone the administration of this mystery, which for ages past was kept hidden in God, who created all things. 10His intent was that now, through the church, the manifold wisdom of God should be made known to the rulers and authorities in the heavenly realms, 11according to his eternal purpose which he accomplished in Christ Jesus our Lord. 12In him and through faith in him we may approach God with freedom and confidence. 13I ask you, therefore, not to be discouraged because of my sufferings for you, which are your glory.

A Prayer for the Ephesians

14For this reason I kneel before the Father, 15from whom his whole family[a] in heaven and on earth derives its name. 16I pray that out of his glorious riches he may strengthen you with power through his Spirit in your inner being, 17so that Christ may dwell in your hearts through faith. And I pray that you, being rooted and established in love, 18may have power, together with all the saints, to grasp how wide and long and high and deep is the love of Christ, 19and to know this love that surpasses knowledge—that you may

be filled to the measure of all the fullness of God.

20Now to him who is able to do immeasurably more than all we ask or imagine, according to his power that is at work within us, 21to him be glory in the church and in Christ Jesus throughout all generations, for ever and ever! Amen.

Unity in the Body of Christ

4 As a prisoner for the Lord, then, I urge you to live a life worthy of the calling you have received. 2Be completely humble and gentle; be patient, bearing with one another in love. 3Make every effort to keep the unity of the Spirit through the bond of peace. 4There is one body and one Spirit—just as you were called to one hope when you were called— 5one Lord, one faith, one baptism; 6one God and Father of all, who is over all and through all and in all.

7But to each one of us grace has been given as Christ apportioned it. 8This is why it[b] says:

"When he ascended on high,
    he led captives in his train
    and gave gifts to men."[c]

9(What does "he ascended" mean except that he also descended to the lower, earthly regions[d]? 10He who descended is the very one who ascended higher than all the heavens, in order to fill the whole universe.) 11It was he who gave some to be apostles, some to be prophets, some to be evangelists, and some to be pastors and teachers, 12to prepare God's people for works of service, so that the body of Christ may be built up 13until we all reach unity in the faith and in the knowledge of the Son of God and become mature, attaining to the whole measure of the fullness of Christ.

14Then we will no longer be infants, tossed back and forth by the waves, and blown here and there by every wind of teaching and by the cunning and craftiness of men in their deceitful scheming. 15Instead, speaking the truth in love, we will in all things grow up into him who is the Head, that is, Christ. 16From him the whole body, joined and held together by every supporting ligament, grows and builds itself up in love, as each part does its work.

a15 Or *whom all fatherhood*   b8 Or *God*
c8 Psalm 68:18   d9 Or *the depths of the earth*

Living as Children of Light

17So I tell you this, and insist on it in the Lord, that you must no longer live as the Gentiles do, in the futility of their thinking. 18They are darkened in their understanding and separated from the life of God because of the ignorance that is in them due to the hardening of their hearts. 19Having lost all sensitivity, they have given themselves over to sensuality so as to indulge in every kind of impurity, with a continual lust for more.

20You, however, did not come to know Christ that way. 21Surely you heard of him and were taught in him in accordance with the truth that is in Jesus. 22You were taught, with regard to your former way of life, to put off your old self, which is being corrupted by its deceitful desires; 23to be made new in the attitude of your minds; 24and to put on the new self, created to be like God in true righteousness and holiness.

25Therefore each of you must put off falsehood and speak truthfully to his neighbor, for we are all members of one body. 26"In your anger do not sin"*a*: Do not let the sun go down while you are still angry, 27and do not give the devil a foothold. 28He who has been stealing must steal no longer, but must work, doing something useful with his own hands, that he may have something to share with those in need.

29Do not let any unwholesome talk come out of your mouths, but only what

a26 Psalm 4:4

Read Ephesians 3:1–21
Key Verse Ephesians 3:20

What Can You Imagine? — Sharla Walstrom

Ever found yourself between a rock and a hard place? Well, I have. Like the time I was ready to begin my student-teaching assignment in the fall. I was all set to go, but I faced a major obstacle: I didn't have a car. A car was essential to get to my assigned school for student teaching, but I simply didn't have the resources to buy one. My parents wanted to help out, but they were unable to at the time. I thought about dropping out of school, but I was so close to graduation. I had been through too much to quit now!

I decided to ask God and began to ask specifically that he would provide me with reliable transportation. I prayed daily for a car. I asked God to make a way if it was his will for me to continue on with my schooling. I also told him that I was willing to do what he wanted; maybe sit out for awhile and earn some money at McDonald's or wherever, if that was his desire for me.

A month later when I came home for the summer, I noticed an older Buick LeSabre sitting in my parents' driveway. My mother hugged me and said, "Your grandparents gave us their car. They wanted to get a newer model, and we would like you to use this one for awhile."

I realized then and there that God cared so much more for me and my future than I could ever care for myself. I know that, while God doesn't always answer prayers in the way we want him to, he does answer. He proved to me that he truly is able to do more than we can ask or imagine.

A Deeper Look
Luke 1:37; 1 Timothy 6:17

Go to page 1329 for your next devotional reading.

is helpful for building others up according to their needs, that it may benefit those who listen. ³⁰And do not grieve the Holy Spirit of God, with whom you were sealed for the day of redemption. ³¹Get rid of all bitterness, rage and anger, brawling and slander, along with every form of malice. ³²Be kind and compassionate to one another, forgiving each other, just as in Christ God forgave you.

5 Be imitators of God, therefore, as dearly loved children ²and live a life of love, just as Christ loved us and gave himself up for us as a fragrant offering and sacrifice to God.

³But among you there must not be even a hint of sexual immorality, or of any kind of impurity, or of greed, because these are improper for God's holy people. ⁴Nor should there be obscenity, foolish talk or coarse joking, which are out of place, but rather thanksgiving. ⁵For of this you can be sure: No immoral, impure or greedy person—such a man is

---

TUESDAY

Read Ephesians 4:17—5:20
Key Verses Ephesians 4:29; 5:4

Words From the Heart – Colette Magoon

It had happened again. As I walked away from a conversation with a friend, I couldn't believe I had said the things I had. Even as the words had formed, a warning light had gone off in my mind, but I had ignored it and let the words come out.

Ironically, one of the topics our Bible study group had been discussing was our speech and the struggle not to gossip and criticize. We had made a group resolution to be positive and to be careful in speaking about others. But I had done it again.

Why is it so easy to say mean things? Probably because putting others down makes us feel superior on our own arbitrary scales of judgment. We sometimes join in with others making negative comments just to feel as though we're part of the group—it makes us feel as though we have something in common with them. And we do—we all have a mean spirit! Our thoughts and feelings about others often *are* negative and mean.

Negative and mean—that hits home for me. My words reveal what is in my heart. Jesus declared, "For out of the overflow of the heart the mouth speaks" (Matthew 12:34). Words come out so easily because they're lodged not far from our mouths—in our sinful hearts. Our hearts must change before our words can. If we want to speak kind and compassionate words, we have to ask God to give us "kind and compassionate" hearts (Ephesians 4:32).

To purposely intercept negative, cutting or inappropriate thoughts *before* they become words requires that we stay aware of and listen to God's prompting; he knows what we are going to say before we say it (see Psalm 139:4). Well-seasoned speech takes practice and courage, but it can be a powerful influence on what others think, feel and say. Paul, as Timothy's mentor, told him, "Don't let anyone look down on you because you are young, but set an example for the believers in speech, in life, in love, in faith and in purity" (1 Timothy 4:12).

A Deeper Look
Romans 14:9–13; James 3:1–12

Go to page 1330 for your next devotional reading.

an idolater—has any inheritance in the kingdom of Christ and of God.*a* ⁶Let no one deceive you with empty words, for because of such things God's wrath comes on those who are disobedient. ⁷Therefore do not be partners with them.

⁸For you were once darkness, but now you are light in the Lord. Live as children of light ⁹(for the fruit of the light consists in all goodness, righteousness and truth) ¹⁰and find out what pleases the Lord. ¹¹Have nothing to do with the fruitless deeds of darkness, but rather expose them. ¹²For it is shameful even to mention what the disobedient do in secret. ¹³But everything exposed by the light be-

comes visible, ¹⁴for it is light that makes everything visible. This is why it is said:

"Wake up, O sleeper,
    rise from the dead,
and Christ will shine on you."

¹⁵Be very careful, then, how you live—not as unwise but as wise, ¹⁶making the most of every opportunity, because the days are evil. ¹⁷Therefore do not be foolish, but understand what the Lord's will is. ¹⁸Do not get drunk on wine, which leads to debauchery. Instead, be filled with the Spirit. ¹⁹Speak

a5 Or kingdom of the Christ and God

Read Ephesians 5:22–33
Key Verses Ephesians 5:24–25

As He Loves Us —Megan Dunham

During my four years of college, I'd been around many students who had their sights set on marriage. For some this is just the next step after college, something they are expected to do. For others it is a monumental step; they think that "the one" will finally meet all their needs. For just about everyone, though, their picture of marriage is marred by misconceptions or delusions.

I was no exception. I just assumed that once I met my "special guy," all my struggles, frustrations and relational problems would go away. I was wrong. Now that I'm engaged, I'm beginning to develop a more realistic view of marriage. My fiancé, Craig, is incredible. He loves God and desires to serve him faithfully. But he also has human frailties that lead me to depend on God more than ever before.

Marriage has a way of forcing two sinful people to draw on their greatest resources. It's no wonder that Paul tells both husbands and wives to use the relationship between Jesus Christ and the church as a model for their marriage. Wives are not told merely to submit to their husbands but to submit to them "as the church submits to Christ" (Ephesians 5:24). Likewise, husbands are told to "love [their] wives, just as Christ loved the church and gave himself up for her" (Ephesians 5:25). What a challenge! As important as they are to each other, a holy relationship between a husband and wife requires both of them to first have a dynamic relationship with Jesus Christ!

However our marriage grows and changes, I pray that Craig and I will always look first to Jesus Christ as the foundation of our marriage, that we will look to him as the source of our love: "A new command I give you: Love one another. As I have loved you, so you must love one another" (John 13:34).

A Deeper Look
Psalm 73:25; Colossians 3:18–21; 1 John 4:7

Go to page 1335 for your next devotional reading.

to one another with psalms, hymns and spiritual songs. Sing and make music in your heart to the Lord, [20]always giving thanks to God the Father for everything, in the name of our Lord Jesus Christ.

[21]Submit to one another out of reverence for Christ.

Wives and Husbands

[22]Wives, submit to your husbands as to the Lord. [23]For the husband is the head of the wife as Christ is the head of the church, his body, of which he is the Savior. [24]Now as the church submits to Christ, so also wives should submit to their husbands in everything.

[25]Husbands, love your wives, just as Christ loved the church and gave himself up for her [26]to make her holy, cleansing[a] her by the washing with water through the word, [27]and to present her to himself as a radiant church, without stain or wrinkle or any other blemish, but holy and blameless. [28]In this same way, husbands ought to love their wives as their own bodies. He who loves his wife loves himself. [29]After all, no one ever hated his own body, but he feeds and cares for it, just as Christ does the church— [30]for we are members of his body. [31]"For this reason a man will leave his father and mother and be united to his wife, and the two will become one flesh."[b] [32]This is a profound mystery—but I am talking about Christ and the church. [33]However, each one of you also must love his wife as he loves himself, and the wife must respect her husband.

Children and Parents

6 Children, obey your parents in the Lord, for this is right. [2]"Honor your father and mother"—which is the first commandment with a promise— [3]"that it may go well with you and that you may enjoy long life on the earth."[c]

[4]Fathers, do not exasperate your children; instead, bring them up in the training and instruction of the Lord.

Slaves and Masters

[5]Slaves, obey your earthly masters with respect and fear, and with sincerity of heart, just as you would obey Christ. [6]Obey them not only to win their favor when their eye is on you, but like slaves of Christ, doing the will of God from your heart. [7]Serve wholeheartedly, as if you were serving the Lord, not men, [8]because you know that the Lord will reward everyone for whatever good he does, whether he is slave or free.

[9]And masters, treat your slaves in the same way. Do not threaten them, since you know that he who is both their Master and yours is in heaven, and there is no favoritism with him.

The Armor of God

[10]Finally, be strong in the Lord and in his mighty power. [11]Put on the full armor of God so that you can take your stand against the devil's schemes. [12]For our struggle is not against flesh and blood, but against the rulers, against the authorities, against the powers of this dark world and against the spiritual forces of evil in the heavenly realms. [13]Therefore put on the full armor of God, so that when the day of evil comes, you may be able to stand your ground, and after you have done everything, to stand. [14]Stand firm then, with the belt of truth buckled around your waist, with the breastplate of righteousness in place, [15]and with your feet fitted with the readiness that comes from the gospel of peace. [16]In addition to all this, take up the shield of faith, with which you can extinguish all the flaming arrows of the evil one. [17]Take the helmet of salvation and the sword of the Spirit, which is the word of God. [18]And pray in the Spirit on all occasions with all kinds of prayers and requests. With this in mind, be alert and always keep on praying for all the saints.

[19]Pray also for me, that whenever I open my mouth, words may be given me so that I will fearlessly make known the

[a]26 Or having cleansed   [b]31 Gen. 2:24
[c]3 Deut. 5:16

POINT OF INTEREST

Ephesians 6:12

This is the enemy against whom we struggle while we live in this world. This enemy is crafty, deceptive and opportunistic. Verses 13–18 tell us where to get the weapons to defeat the enemy— they're waiting for us in God's armory.

mystery of the gospel, **20**for which I am an ambassador in chains. Pray that I may declare it fearlessly, as I should.

Final Greetings

21Tychicus, the dear brother and faithful servant in the Lord, will tell you everything, so that you also may know how I am and what I am doing. **22**I am sending him to you for this very purpose, that you may know how we are, and that he may encourage you.

23Peace to the brothers, and love with faith from God the Father and the Lord Jesus Christ. **24**Grace to all who love our Lord Jesus Christ with an undying love.

*"**W**ARNING: Taking on the attitude of Jesus Christ leads to radical behavior. A relationship with Jesus produces symptoms such as humility, peace and generosity. The patient may exhibit the tendency to 'shine like [a star] in the universe' (2:15), and to 'stand firm in the Lord' (4:1). Prognosis: eventual citizenship in heaven with the Lord Jesus Christ."*

Even though Paul wasn't a doctor, he could have included this warning label on his letter to the Philippians. The heart of this book is joy, true joy that comes from knowing Jesus Christ and living in him. Joy is powerful—and contagious.

PHILIPPIANS

1 Paul and Timothy, servants of Christ Jesus,

To all the saints in Christ Jesus at Philippi, together with the overseers*a* and deacons:

²Grace and peace to you from God our Father and the Lord Jesus Christ.

Thanksgiving and Prayer

³I thank my God every time I remember you. ⁴In all my prayers for all of you, I always pray with joy ⁵because of your partnership in the gospel from the first day until now, ⁶being confident of this, that he who began a good work in you will carry it on to completion until the day of Christ Jesus.

⁷It is right for me to feel this way about all of you, since I have you in my heart; for whether I am in chains or defending and confirming the gospel, all of you share in God's grace with me. ⁸God can testify how I long for all of you with the affection of Christ Jesus.

⁹And this is my prayer: that your love may abound more and more in knowledge and depth of insight, ¹⁰so that you may be able to discern what is best and may be pure and blameless until the day

a 1 Traditionally *bishops*

of Christ, [11]filled with the fruit of righteousness that comes through Jesus Christ—to the glory and praise of God.

Paul's Chains Advance the Gospel

[12]Now I want you to know, brothers, that what has happened to me has really served to advance the gospel. [13]As a result, it has become clear throughout the whole palace guard[a] and to everyone else that I am in chains for Christ. [14]Because of my chains, most of the brothers in the Lord have been encouraged to speak the word of God more courageously and fearlessly.

[15]It is true that some preach Christ out of envy and rivalry, but others out of goodwill. [16]The latter do so in love, knowing that I am put here for the defense of the gospel. [17]The former preach Christ out of selfish ambition, not sincerely, supposing that they can stir up trouble for me while I am in chains.[b] [18]But what does it matter? The important thing is that in every way, whether from false motives or true, Christ is preached. And because of this I rejoice.

Yes, and I will continue to rejoice, [19]for I know that through your prayers and the help given by the Spirit of Jesus Christ, what has happened to me will turn out for my deliverance.[c] [20]I eagerly expect and hope that I will in no way be ashamed, but will have sufficient courage so that now as always Christ will be exalted in my body, whether by life or by death. [21]For to me, to live is Christ and to die is gain. [22]If I am to go on living in the body, this will mean fruitful labor for me. Yet what shall I choose? I do not know! [23]I am torn between the two: I desire to depart and be with Christ, which is better by far; [24]but it is more necessary for you that I remain in the body. [25]Convinced of this, I know that I will remain, and I will continue with all of you for your progress and joy in the faith, [26]so that through my being with you again your joy in Christ Jesus will overflow on account of me.

[27]Whatever happens, conduct yourselves in a manner worthy of the gospel of Christ. Then, whether I come and see you or only hear about you in my absence, I will know that you stand firm in one spirit, contending as one man for the faith of the gospel [28]without being frightened in any way by those who oppose you. This is a sign to them that they

will be destroyed, but that you will be saved—and that by God. [29]For it has been granted to you on behalf of Christ not only to believe on him, but also to suffer for him, [30]since you are going through the same struggle you saw I had, and now hear that I still have.

Imitating Christ's Humility

2 If you have any encouragement from being united with Christ, if any comfort from his love, if any fellowship with the Spirit, if any tenderness and compassion, [2]then make my joy complete by being like-minded, having the same love, being one in spirit and purpose. [3]Do nothing out of selfish ambition or vain conceit, but in humility consider others better than yourselves. [4]Each of you should look not only to your own interests, but also to the interests of others.

[5]Your attitude should be the same as that of Christ Jesus:

[6]Who, being in very nature[d] God,
did not consider equality with God
something to be grasped,
[7]but made himself nothing,
taking the very nature[e] of a
servant,
being made in human likeness.
[8]And being found in appearance as a
man,
he humbled himself
and became obedient to death—
even death on a cross!
[9]Therefore God exalted him to the
highest place
and gave him the name that is
above every name,

---

[a]13 Or *whole palace*   [b]16,17 Some late manuscripts have verses 16 and 17 in reverse order.   [c]19 Or *salvation*   [d]6 Or *in the form of*   [e]7 Or *the form*

POINT OF INTEREST

Philippians 1:21

Christians, these words echo the hope that we hold on to for dear life. Death for us is not an end, but the very beginning of a new and exciting reality. Paul couldn't contain his desire to be with Jesus Christ; that's where he is now.

¹⁰that at the name of Jesus every knee
should bow,
in heaven and on earth and under
the earth,
¹¹and every tongue confess that Jesus
Christ is Lord,
to the glory of God the Father.

Shining as Stars

¹²Therefore, my dear friends, as you
have always obeyed—not only in my
presence, but now much more in my absence—continue to work out your salva-
tion with fear and trembling, ¹³for it is
God who works in you to will and to act
according to his good purpose.

¹⁴Do everything without complaining
or arguing, ¹⁵so that you may become
blameless and pure, children of God
without fault in a crooked and depraved
generation, in which you shine like stars
in the universe ¹⁶as you hold out^a the
word of life—in order that I may boast on
the day of Christ that I did not run or
labor for nothing. ¹⁷But even if I am being
poured out like a drink offering on the
sacrifice and service coming from your
faith, I am glad and rejoice with all of
you. ¹⁸So you too should be glad and rejoice with me.

Timothy and Epaphroditus

¹⁹I hope in the Lord Jesus to send Tim-
othy to you soon, that I also may be

^a16 Or *hold on to*

Read *Philippians 1:12–30*
Key Verse *Philippians 1:27*

Worthy of the Gospel – Mike Jordahl

Why did I do that? I knew the rest of the answers. But that last
question left me clueless. Just a small twist of my head had given
me a view of the test in front of me—and the right answer. I quickly
scribbled it down—instant gratification! Then that first pang of
guilt hit me. A little voice inside asked, "Is it right for a follower of
Jesus Christ to cheat on a test?" I tried to convince myself that it
really didn't matter, that it wouldn't change my grade anyway.

But deep inside, I knew what I had done was wrong. A verse I
had recently memorized began repeating itself in my head: "So I
strive always to keep my conscience clear before God and man"
(Acts 24:16). I asked God what I should do next.

Handing in my test, I quietly told my professor, "Please mark
that last question wrong." He responded, "That's the right answer. I
don't need to mark it wrong." I persisted. "Actually, it would be best
if you could just mark it wrong." "But why?" he asked. "Well," I hesitated, "I cheated on that question. I saw the answer on another test
and copied it."

Other students looked on, mouths hanging open in surprise. My
professor shrugged and placed that familiar stroke of red ink across
my last answer. It was my turn to shrug.

Leaving the room, I breathed a prayer of renewed commitment:
"Thank you for helping me to be honest. Please help me to live a life
worthy of your gospel. Use me in the lives of my professor and fellow students—even though I blew it today. Thank you for your forgiveness."

A Deeper Look
Deuteronomy 18:13; Luke 16:10

Go to page 1336 for your next devotional reading.

cheered when I receive news about you. 20I have no one else like him, who takes a genuine interest in your welfare. 21For everyone looks out for his own interests, not those of Jesus Christ. 22But you know that Timothy has proved himself, because as a son with his father he has served with me in the work of the gospel. 23I hope, therefore, to send him as soon as I see how things go with me. 24And I am confident in the Lord that I myself will come soon.

25But I think it is necessary to send back to you Epaphroditus, my brother, fellow worker and fellow soldier, who is also your messenger, whom you sent to take care of my needs. 26For he longs for all of you and is distressed because you heard he was ill. 27Indeed he was ill, and almost died. But God had mercy on him, and not on him only but also on me, to spare me sorrow upon sorrow. 28Therefore I am all the more eager to send him, so that when you see him again you may be glad and I may have less anxiety. 29Welcome him in the Lord with great joy, and honor men like him, 30because he almost died for the work of Christ, risking his life to make up for the help you could not give me.

FRIDAY

Read Philippians 2:1–18
Key Verses Philippians 2:14–15

In All Things — Lynn M. Hamilton

There was a hot dog stuck to the window with ketchup and a full glass of soda pop overturned on the table, ready to pour over everything when I lifted it up.

"I quit!" I said aloud, but to no one in particular. "I've had enough! Why should I have to clean up other people's messes!"

I had no reason to complain. I hadn't made the mess, but because I worked for the dorm food service, it was part of my job to clean it up. For several minutes I grumbled out loud. Then the Lord quietly brought Philippians 2:14–15 to mind. "Lord, you don't mean *everything*, do you?" I asked. The answer was obvious. God was calling me to clean up the mess without complaining.

It was very difficult to work without complaining that night, but I made it through. Shortly after that experience, God showed me another passage about grumbling and complaining. Numbers 11:1 says, "Now the people complained about their hardships in the hearing of the Lord, and when he heard them his anger was aroused. Then fire from the Lord burned among them and consumed some of the outskirts of the camp." I hadn't realized how wrong complaining is and how complaining about my circumstances is really grumbling against God himself.

Now I also realize that when I complain, not only do I negatively affect my own attitude and actions, but I also affect those of the people around me. Likewise, when I choose *not* to complain, I affect others in a positive way.

It isn't easy to choose not to complain. But in responding to the Lord's gentle reminders, we give testimony to our faith in Jesus Christ and show ourselves to be like "stars [shining] in the universe" (Philippians 2:15).

A Deeper Look
Colossians 3:23–24; 2 Timothy 2:3; Hebrews 12:7–12

Go to page 1337 for your next devotional reading.

Read Philippians 3:1–21
Key Verse Philippians 3:8

The Greatness of Knowing Jesus

God could have created the human race, started the world spinning and left us to figure things out on our own. He could have planted a little human colony on the third rock from the sun and left us floating aimlessly among the billions of stars in the universe. But he didn't. In the Bible he says over and over, "I will be with you," to Abraham, Moses, Joshua, Gideon and Solomon—and to us.

God the Father desires a father/child relationship with us. He came to earth in the form of a human baby, Jesus, whom Isaiah called "Immanuel" or "God with us." As a man he could touch a person with leprosy, embrace a friend, hold a baby in his arms. Like us, he experienced hunger and thirst. He came to earth to be like us in every way, even experiencing the pain, loneliness and suffering of dying. There is no way God could have made himself any more personal or accessible.

That's why Paul considered "everything a loss compared to the surpassing greatness of knowing Christ Jesus my Lord" (Philippians 3:8). Jesus gives us the greatest privilege of all—knowing the living God.

Digging Into the Word
1. What do you learn from these passages about who Jesus is?
   —John 14:1–11; Hebrews 1:1–3
2. How can you enter into and grow in a relationship with God?
   —John 15:14–17; Romans 8:12–17

Personal Reflection
Do a Bible search with a concordance or an on-line Bible. What references to God the Father can you find? Make a list of his characteristics. Keep it in your Bible at 1 John 3:1.

One Step Deeper
John 12:44–46; 16:12–15

Go to page 1338 for your next devotional reading.

No Confidence in the Flesh

3 Finally, my brothers, rejoice in the Lord! It is no trouble for me to write the same things to you again, and it is a safeguard for you.

²Watch out for those dogs, those men who do evil, those mutilators of the flesh. ³For it is we who are the circumcision, we who worship by the Spirit of God, who glory in Christ Jesus, and who put no confidence in the flesh— ⁴though I myself have reasons for such confidence.

If anyone else thinks he has reasons to put confidence in the flesh, I have more:

⁵circumcised on the eighth day, of the people of Israel, of the tribe of Benjamin, a Hebrew of Hebrews; in regard to the law, a Pharisee; ⁶as for zeal, persecuting the church; as for legalistic righteousness, faultless.

⁷But whatever was to my profit I now consider loss for the sake of Christ. ⁸What is more, I consider everything a loss compared to the surpassing greatness of knowing Christ Jesus my Lord, for whose sake I have lost all things. I consider them rubbish, that I may gain Christ ⁹and be found in him, not having a righteousness of my own that comes

---

MONDAY

Read Philippians 4:1–20
Key Verses Philippians 4:6–7

Conversing with God – Carol Rugg

Picture yourself on your honeymoon with your new spouse. You wake up the first morning and look at each other but don't speak. As you sit down to breakfast, you simply say, "Thanks for being with me. Thanks, too, for providing this food for me!" No further conversation ensues during breakfast; in fact, you don't even talk again until you sit down at a lovely, romantic restaurant for lunch. Once again you mention how much you appreciate your spouse's love and presence with you. You also comment on how nice it is to have such a lovely place to eat.

You can see how ridiculous this would be—barely speaking to the one you love so much. But in actuality, isn't this what our prayer life is often like? We only take time for a few short bursts of communication with the Creator of the universe, although "apart from [him we] can do nothing" (John 15:5). What a missed opportunity on our part!

Prayer is meant to be a two-way conversation between us and our Creator. Prayer can be like the vision-expanding conversation of Abraham with the righteous Lord (see Genesis 18:16–33); Hannah's cry for fulfillment to the Source of Life (see 1 Samuel 1:1–20); the intimacy and fellowship David shared with his Comforter and Protector (see Psalm 27); the honest complaint Jeremiah filed with the Holy Judge; the heartrending plea for deliverance that Jesus himself uttered to the Father (see Matthew 26:36–42).

God is all of these things and more. And "the Lord is near" (Philippians 4:5). So how can we stand *not* to talk with him? Why do we put up with anxiety when we could ask our Savior for help? Why go without when we can ask him for anything? Why be restless and confused when he is the God of peace?

A Deeper Look
Acts 1:14; Ephesians 6:18; Colossians 4:2

Go to page 1342 for your next devotional reading.

from the law, but that which is through faith in Christ—the righteousness that comes from God and is by faith. [10]I want to know Christ and the power of his resurrection and the fellowship of sharing in his sufferings, becoming like him in his death, [11]and so, somehow, to attain to the resurrection from the dead.

Pressing on Toward the Goal

[12]Not that I have already obtained all this, or have already been made perfect, but I press on to take hold of that for which Christ Jesus took hold of me. [13]Brothers, I do not consider myself yet to have taken hold of it. But one thing I do: Forgetting what is behind and straining toward what is ahead, [14]I press on toward the goal to win the prize for which God has called me heavenward in Christ Jesus.

[15]All of us who are mature should take such a view of things. And if on some point you think differently, that too God will make clear to you. [16]Only let us live up to what we have already attained.

[17]Join with others in following my example, brothers, and take note of those who live according to the pattern we gave you. [18]For, as I have often told you before and now say again even with tears, many live as enemies of the cross of Christ. [19]Their destiny is destruction, their god is their stomach, and their glory is in their shame. Their mind is on earthly things. [20]But our citizenship is in heaven. And we eagerly await a Savior from there, the Lord Jesus Christ, [21]who, by the power that enables him to bring everything under his control, will transform our lowly bodies so that they will be like his glorious body.

4 Therefore, my brothers, you whom I love and long for, my joy and crown, that is how you should stand firm in the Lord, dear friends!

Exhortations

[2]I plead with Euodia and I plead with Syntyche to agree with each other in the Lord. [3]Yes, and I ask you, loyal yokefellow,[a] help these women who have contended at my side in the cause of the gospel, along with Clement and the rest of my fellow workers, whose names are in the book of life.

[4]Rejoice in the Lord always. I will say it again: Rejoice! [5]Let your gentleness be evident to all. The Lord is near. [6]Do not be anxious about anything, but in everything, by prayer and petition, with thanksgiving, present your requests to God. [7]And the peace of God, which transcends all understanding, will guard your hearts and your minds in Christ Jesus.

[8]Finally, brothers, whatever is true, whatever is noble, whatever is right, whatever is pure, whatever is lovely, whatever is admirable—if anything is excellent or praiseworthy—think about such things. [9]Whatever you have learned or received or heard from me, or seen in me—put it into practice. And the God of peace will be with you.

Thanks for Their Gifts

[10]I rejoice greatly in the Lord that at last you have renewed your concern for me. Indeed, you have been concerned, but you had no opportunity to show it. [11]I am not saying this because I am in need, for I have learned to be content whatever the circumstances. [12]I know what it is to be in need, and I know what it is to have plenty. I have learned the secret of being content in any and every situation, whether well fed or hungry, whether living in plenty or in want. [13]I can do everything through him who gives me strength.

[14]Yet it was good of you to share in my troubles. [15]Moreover, as you Philippians know, in the early days of your acquaintance with the gospel, when I set out from Macedonia, not one church shared with me in the matter of giving and receiving, except you only; [16]for even when I was in Thessalonica, you sent me aid again and again when I was in need. [17]Not that I am looking for a gift, but I am looking for what may be credited to your

[a]3 Or loyal Syzygus

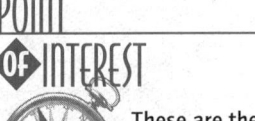

Philippians 4:12

These are the words of a man whose priorities are set squarely on the things of God and not on earthly stuff. Check out the book of Ecclesiastes for an in-depth analysis of the "benefits" of looking for significance here on earth.

account. [18]I have received full payment and even more; I am amply supplied, now that I have received from Epaphroditus the gifts you sent. They are a fragrant offering, an acceptable sacrifice, pleasing to God. [19]And my God will meet all your needs according to his glorious riches in Christ Jesus.

[20]To our God and Father be glory for ever and ever. Amen.

Final Greetings

[21]Greet all the saints in Christ Jesus. The brothers who are with me send greetings. [22]All the saints send you greetings, especially those who belong to Caesar's household.

[23]The grace of the Lord Jesus Christ be with your spirit. Amen.[a]

[a]23 Some manuscripts do not have *Amen*.

Jesus means different things to different people. Some regard him as a "good man" or a prophet. Some think him a magician or a fraud. The book of Colossians addresses the questions of who Jesus is and how he should affect us. Paul writes to the Colossians to refute teachings that relied on human philosophy and knowledge; he argued that only Jesus Christ is necessary for salvation. To this end, Paul asserts that Jesus is supreme over creation, sin, the church and even our relationships. As you read Colossians, ask yourself what difference it would make in your life if you lived in light of Jesus' supremacy.

COLOSSIANS

1 Paul, an apostle of Christ Jesus by the will of God, and Timothy our brother,

²To the holy and faithful*a* brothers in Christ at Colosse:

Grace and peace to you from God our Father.*b*

Thanksgiving and Prayer

³We always thank God, the Father of our Lord Jesus Christ, when we pray for you, ⁴because we have heard of your faith in Christ Jesus and of the love you have for all the saints— ⁵the faith and love that spring from the hope that is stored up for you in heaven and that you have already heard about in the word of truth, the gospel ⁶that has come to you. All over the world this gospel is bearing fruit and growing, just as it has been doing among you since the day you heard it and understood God's grace in all its truth. ⁷You learned it from Epaphras, our dear fellow servant, who is a faithful minister of Christ on our*c* behalf, ⁸and who also told us of your love in the Spirit.

⁹For this reason, since the day we

a2 Or *believing*   *b2* Some manuscripts *Father and the Lord Jesus Christ*   *c7* Some manuscripts *your* heard about you, we have not stopped praying for you and asking God to fill you with the knowledge of his will through all spiritual wisdom and understanding. ¹⁰And we pray this in order that you may live a life worthy of the Lord and may please him in every way: bearing fruit in every good work, growing in the knowledge of God, ¹¹being strengthened with all power according to his glorious might so that you may have great endurance and patience, and joyfully ¹²giving thanks to the Father, who has qualified you*a* to share in the inheritance of the saints in the kingdom of light. ¹³For he has rescued us from the dominion of darkness and brought us into the kingdom of the Son he loves, ¹⁴in whom we have redemption,*b* the forgiveness of sins.

The Supremacy of Christ

¹⁵He is the image of the invisible God, the firstborn over all creation. ¹⁶For by him all things were created: things in heaven and on earth, visible and invisible, whether thrones or powers or rulers or authorities; all things were created by him and for him. ¹⁷He is before all things, and in him all things hold together. ¹⁸And he is the head of the body, the church; he is the beginning and the firstborn from among the dead, so that in everything he

a12 Some manuscripts *us*   *b14* A few late manuscripts *redemption through his blood*

TUESDAY

Read *Colossians 1:1–29*
Key Verses *Colossians 1:15–20*

Who *Is* This Jesus? — Roger Hamilton

As a discussion turned to the deity of Jesus Christ, a conversation I'd had with a cult member on our campus several months earlier came back to me. His words began to gnaw at me, and seeds of doubt began to germinate in my brain. In desperation I left the meeting to be alone with God and his Word.

Paul warned the Colossians to put their faith in Jesus and not to follow the philosophies of the heretical teachers in Colosse, who taught that the Colossians had to follow a collection of rules along with believing in Jesus Christ. He reminded them that their society was trying to sell them a "hollow and deceptive philosophy, [based] on human tradition . . . rather than on Christ" (Colossians 2:8).

Then Paul painted a marvelous picture of Jesus to impress upon the Colossians that he alone is sufficient to save them, because he is supreme in everything. Supreme over creation, because "all things were created by him and for him" (Colossians 1:16). Supreme as the One who holds everything together. Supreme as the head of the church, which he bought with his own blood shed on the cross. Most important, however, Jesus is supreme as God himself, for we're told in Colossians 1:19, and again in Colossians 2:9, that all of God's fullness lives in Jesus Christ.

I'm thankful that God used this passage to help me solidify my conviction that Jesus Christ is indeed God. With a vast array of hollow and deceptive philosophies constantly bombarding us, it's critical to know who Jesus is as revealed in God's Word—the One supreme in everything, who is always with us to lead, guide and protect.

A Deeper Look
John 1:1–14; Philippians 2:6–11; Hebrews 1:1–14

Go to page 1344 for your next devotional reading.

might have the supremacy. ¹⁹For God was pleased to have all his fullness dwell in him, ²⁰and through him to reconcile to himself all things, whether things on earth or things in heaven, by making peace through his blood, shed on the cross.

²¹Once you were alienated from God and were enemies in your minds because of*a* your evil behavior. ²²But now he has reconciled you by Christ's physical body through death to present you holy in his sight, without blemish and free from accusation— ²³if you continue in your faith, established and firm, not moved from the hope held out in the gospel. This is the gospel that you heard and that has been proclaimed to every creature under heaven, and of which I, Paul, have become a servant.

Paul's Labor for the Church

²⁴Now I rejoice in what was suffered for you, and I fill up in my flesh what is still lacking in regard to Christ's afflictions, for the sake of his body, which is the church. ²⁵I have become its servant by the commission God gave me to present to you the word of God in its fullness— ²⁶the mystery that has been kept hidden for ages and generations, but is now disclosed to the saints. ²⁷To them God has chosen to make known among the Gentiles the glorious riches of this mystery, which is Christ in you, the hope of glory.

²⁸We proclaim him, admonishing and teaching everyone with all wisdom, so that we may present everyone perfect in Christ. ²⁹To this end I labor, struggling with all his energy, which so powerfully works in me.

2 I want you to know how much I am struggling for you and for those at Laodicea, and for all who have not met me personally. ²My purpose is that they may be encouraged in heart and united in love, so that they may have the full riches of complete understanding, in order that they may know the mystery of God, namely, Christ, ³in whom are hidden all the treasures of wisdom and knowledge. ⁴I tell you this so that no one may deceive you by fine-sounding arguments. ⁵For though I am absent from you in body, I am present with you in spirit and delight to see how orderly you are and how firm your faith in Christ is.

Freedom From Human Regulations Through Life With Christ

⁶So then, just as you received Christ Jesus as Lord, continue to live in him, ⁷rooted and built up in him, strengthened in the faith as you were taught, and overflowing with thankfulness.

⁸See to it that no one takes you captive through hollow and deceptive philosophy, which depends on human tradition and the basic principles of this world rather than on Christ.

⁹For in Christ all the fullness of the Deity lives in bodily form, ¹⁰and you have been given fullness in Christ, who is the head over every power and authority. ¹¹In him you were also circumcised, in the putting off of the sinful nature,*b* not with a circumcision done by the hands of men but with the circumcision done by Christ, ¹²having been buried with him in baptism and raised with him through your faith in the power of God, who raised him from the dead.

¹³When you were dead in your sins and in the uncircumcision of your sinful nature,*c* God made you*d* alive with Christ. He forgave us all our sins, ¹⁴having canceled the written code, with its regulations, that was against us and that stood opposed to us; he took it away, nailing it to the cross. ¹⁵And having disarmed the powers and authorities, he made a public spectacle of them, triumphing over them by the cross.*e*

*a*21 Or *minds, as shown by*   *b*11 Or *the flesh*
*c*13 Or *your flesh*   *d*13 Some manuscripts *us*
*e*15 Or *them in him*

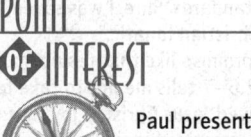

POINT OF INTEREST   Colossians 2:13

Paul presents an interesting word picture of us—before and after we know Jesus Christ. Before, we were as good as dead, just a collection of body parts—unable to lift a finger to help ourselves. But God breathes new life into us by sending his Spirit—just as surely as Adam was dust before God breathed life into him (see Genesis 2:7). See Ezekiel 37:4–6 for another "life from death" miracle.

¹⁶Therefore do not let anyone judge you by what you eat or drink, or with regard to a religious festival, a New Moon celebration or a Sabbath day. ¹⁷These are a shadow of the things that were to come; the reality, however, is found in Christ. ¹⁸Do not let anyone who delights in false humility and the worship of angels disqualify you for the prize. Such a person goes into great detail about what he has seen, and his unspiritual mind puffs him up with idle notions. ¹⁹He has lost connection with the Head, from whom the whole body, supported and held together by its ligaments and sinews, grows as God causes it to grow.

²⁰Since you died with Christ to the basic principles of this world, why, as though you still belonged to it, do you submit to its rules: ²¹"Do not handle! Do

---

WEDNESDAY

Read *Colossians 2:1–23*
Key Verses *Colossians 2:6–7*

This Is Just the Beginning – Paula Gibson

When I read these two verses, my first thought is: Why wouldn't any Christian be overflowing with thankfulness and become rooted with Bible study and prayer after receiving the Lord's saving and healing power?

On second thought, though, I wonder. In John 5:1–15 Jesus healed the lame man at the pool of Bethesda. This man hadn't walked for thirty-eight years. Jesus asked him, "Do you want to get well?" (John 5:6). But the man, rather than just saying yes, came up with excuses why he couldn't go or hadn't gone into the pool. Didn't he want to be healed?

That's the very same question Jesus asked me at one point in my life! Did I want to separate myself from the gossiping, lying, self-pitying and self-centered life I'd been living? Like the lame man, I had excuses why I couldn't be healed, but finally I did say yes. Unlike the man at the pool, I did thank God! I was praising Jesus, diligent with prayer times, digging into Scripture and living a new and exhilarating life.

But after some time had passed, I became more like the lame man. I wasn't amazed by my healing anymore. And just as the lame man failed to share his story of the power of Jesus with the Jewish officials, so I failed by trying to blend in and be accepted according to worldly standards. Sure, I was saved, but I didn't want to be labeled a "Christian fanatic."

But compromise like that results in an anemic, spindly faith. So Colossians 2:6–7 tells me not to take for granted the joy I had when I received Jesus Christ, a joy that will always be mine—if I nourish it by meeting him in Scripture and prayer. Being rooted and built up in him is a slow process, a daily process, an ongoing process. But I'm discovering that the real joy comes in the way my life has been blessed and enriched by Jesus' love since I accepted his healing. Jesus is more than just my healer; he is my Savior and my friend.

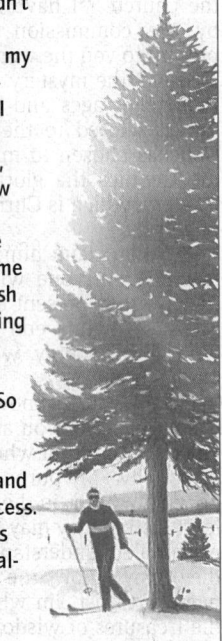

A Deeper Look
1 Corinthians 1:7–9; Philippians 1:6

Go to page 1345 for your next devotional reading.

not taste! Do not touch!"? ²²These are all destined to perish with use, because they are based on human commands and teachings. ²³Such regulations indeed have an appearance of wisdom, with their self-imposed worship, their false humility and their harsh treatment of the body, but they lack any value in restraining sensual indulgence.

Rules for Holy Living

3 Since, then, you have been raised with Christ, set your hearts on things above,

---

THURSDAY

Read *Colossians 3:1–17*
Key Verses *Colossians 3:1–4*

Set Your Mind on Jesus Christ – Bruce Knutson

The mind is a powerful tool. With it we create our opinions, develop our values and make our decisions. This passage speaks to the way followers of Jesus Christ are to use their minds: We are to "set [our] minds on things above." When through the Spirit's power we retain a godly mind-set, our responses to events and our actions will be godly. Yet how are we supposed to continually maintain such a mind-set? Such a thing doesn't seem possible. Here's where the Set-Let-Put principle can help.

First, we must *set* our minds on godly values at the start of each day, focusing on what is eternal and valuable to God. Much as football players get into a particular stance before each play, so we must take a mental position that prepares us to live and act according to God's will. That way we can remind ourselves often during the day to focus on these godly principles.

Second, after setting our minds on Jesus Christ, we are to *let* his Word live in us. Think of it as a spring rain. As the spring rain falls, some of it hits frozen ground and drains off, but some falls in thawed areas where it can soak in. In the same way we should "*let* the word of Christ dwell in [us] richly" (Colossians 3:16, italics added), soaking it up to help us learn and grow.

Having set our minds on Jesus Christ and having let his Word live in us, we now *put* on Christ's likeness. Do you enjoy putting on nice, new clothes? Do you like it when others notice? "As God's chosen people," we are to *put* on or "clothe [ourselves] with compassion, kindness, humility, gentleness and patience" (Colossians 3:12), and the rest of the fruits of the Spirit (see Galatians 5:22–23). Keeping our minds on him will help us put on God's best garments.

Prayerfully seek to apply the Set-Let-Put concept to your life. *Set* your mind on things that are "excellent [and] praiseworthy" (Philippians 4:8), *let* the Scriptures soak into your heart and *put* on the character qualities of Christ. As the Spirit enables you to conform to his likeness, you will find that your actions and reactions become more godly.

A Deeper Look
Romans 8:5–17; Philippians 4:8–9

Go to page 1347 for your next devotional reading.

where Christ is seated at the right hand of God. ²Set your minds on things above, not on earthly things. ³For you died, and your life is now hidden with Christ in God. ⁴When Christ, who is your*a* life, appears, then you also will appear with him in glory.

⁵Put to death, therefore, whatever belongs to your earthly nature: sexual immorality, impurity, lust, evil desires and greed, which is idolatry. ⁶Because of these, the wrath of God is coming.*b* ⁷You used to walk in these ways, in the life you once lived. ⁸But now you must rid yourselves of all such things as these: anger, rage, malice, slander, and filthy language from your lips. ⁹Do not lie to each other, since you have taken off your old self with its practices ¹⁰and have put on the new self, which is being renewed in knowledge in the image of its Creator. ¹¹Here there is no Greek or Jew, circumcised or uncircumcised, barbarian, Scythian, slave or free, but Christ is all, and is in all.

¹²Therefore, as God's chosen people, holy and dearly loved, clothe yourselves with compassion, kindness, humility, gentleness and patience. ¹³Bear with each other and forgive whatever grievances you may have against one another. Forgive as the Lord forgave you. ¹⁴And over all these virtues put on love, which binds them all together in perfect unity.

¹⁵Let the peace of Christ rule in your hearts, since as members of one body you were called to peace. And be thankful. ¹⁶Let the word of Christ dwell in you richly as you teach and admonish one another with all wisdom, and as you sing psalms, hymns and spiritual songs with gratitude in your hearts to God. ¹⁷And whatever you do, whether in word or deed, do it all in the name of the Lord Jesus, giving thanks to God the Father through him.

Rules for Christian Households

¹⁸Wives, submit to your husbands, as is fitting in the Lord.

¹⁹Husbands, love your wives and do not be harsh with them.

²⁰Children, obey your parents in everything, for this pleases the Lord.

²¹Fathers, do not embitter your children, or they will become discouraged.

²²Slaves, obey your earthly masters in everything; and do it, not only when their eye is on you and to win their favor, but

with sincerity of heart and reverence for the Lord. ²³Whatever you do, work at it with all your heart, as working for the Lord, not for men, ²⁴since you know that you will receive an inheritance from the Lord as a reward. It is the Lord Christ you are serving. ²⁵Anyone who does wrong will be repaid for his wrong, and there is no favoritism.

4 Masters, provide your slaves with what is right and fair, because you know that you also have a Master in heaven.

Further Instructions

²Devote yourselves to prayer, being watchful and thankful. ³And pray for us, too, that God may open a door for our message, so that we may proclaim the mystery of Christ, for which I am in chains. ⁴Pray that I may proclaim it clearly, as I should. ⁵Be wise in the way you act toward outsiders; make the most of every opportunity. ⁶Let your conversation be always full of grace, seasoned with salt, so that you may know how to answer everyone.

Final Greetings

⁷Tychicus will tell you all the news about me. He is a dear brother, a faithful minister and fellow servant in the Lord. ⁸I am sending him to you for the express purpose that you may know about our*c* circumstances and that he may encourage your hearts. ⁹He is coming with Onesimus, our faithful and dear brother, who is one of you. They will tell you everything that is happening here.

¹⁰My fellow prisoner Aristarchus sends you his greetings, as does Mark,

a4 Some manuscripts *our*   *b6* Some early manuscripts *coming on those who are disobedient*   *c8* Some manuscripts *that he may know about your*

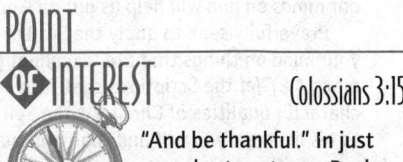

POINT OF INTEREST   Colossians 3:15

"And be thankful." In just one short sentence, Paul called his original readers to a life lived in gratitude. These three words describe an attitude of gratitude that should pervade the life of anyone who has even an inkling of what Jesus has done.

the cousin of Barnabas. (You have received instructions about him; if he comes to you, welcome him.) ¹¹Jesus, who is called Justus, also sends greetings. These are the only Jews among my fellow workers for the kingdom of God, and they have proved a comfort to me. ¹²Epaphras, who is one of you and a servant of Christ Jesus, sends greetings. He is always wrestling in prayer for you, that you may stand firm in all the will of God, mature and fully assured. ¹³I vouch for him that he is working hard for you and for those at Laodicea and Hierapolis.

¹⁴Our dear friend Luke, the doctor, and Demas send greetings. ¹⁵Give my greetings to the brothers at Laodicea, and to Nympha and the church in her house.

¹⁶After this letter has been read to you, see that it is also read in the church of the Laodiceans and that you in turn read the letter from Laodicea.

¹⁷Tell Archippus: "See to it that you complete the work you have received in the Lord."

¹⁸I, Paul, write this greeting in my own hand. Remember my chains. Grace be with you.

FRIDAY

Read *Colossians 4:1–18*
Key Verses *Colossians 4:5–6*

Make the Most of Opportunities – Charla Vogelaar

During my freshman year in college, I was anxious about the first round of exams. I couldn't wait to finish the semester and go home to be with my family. The mountain of schoolwork seemed impossible to climb over, but when I prayed before studying, I found it possible to keep working at it.

I noticed that my roommate, a professed atheist, was watching my study methods. One afternoon she asked, "You have twice as much to do as I do, but you're half as stressed. Why?" I hesitated. "Do you really want to know?" I asked. I was reluctant to find out how she would react. "Yes," she persisted, so I decided to make the most of the opportunity. "Well," I said, "I've been asking God to help me through my finals and he's given me peace and confidence as I take them."

Although my roommate had no immediate response, I later saw the risk pay off. After I openly told her that God was my source of confidence, she seemed more friendly about discussing spiritual things with me. By the end of the year, my roommate—who had often challenged my beliefs—was asking for my prayers.

A Deeper Look
Romans 1:16–17; 2 Corinthians 4:13–15

Go to page 1350 for your next devotional reading.

Though centuries old,

1 Thessalonians was written for times like ours. It speaks

to a culture filled with seductive images and sexual pres-

sures. It brings eternal perspective to discussions of mater-

ial things. It questions the secular values that undermine

God's ways. As you read, watch for practical ways that

Christians can live holy lives in a hostile culture.

Overshadowing all this is a perspective on life that is

shaped by eternity. And you'll find

exciting clues about the end

times and Jesus' second coming.

1 THESSALONIANS

Paul, Silas*ᵃ* and Timothy,

To the church of the Thessalonians in God the Father and the Lord Jesus Christ:

Grace and peace to you.*ᵇ*

Thanksgiving for the Thessalonians' Faith

²We always thank God for all of you, mentioning you in our prayers. ³We continually remember before our God and Father your work produced by faith, your labor prompted by love, and your endurance inspired by hope in our Lord Jesus Christ.

⁴For we know, brothers loved by God, that he has chosen you, ⁵because our gospel came to you not simply with words, but also with power, with the Holy Spirit and with deep conviction. You know how we lived among you for your sake. ⁶You became imitators of us and of the Lord; in spite of severe suffering, you welcomed the message with the joy given by the Holy Spirit. ⁷And so you became a model to all the believers in Macedonia and Achaia. ⁸The Lord's message rang out from you not only in Macedonia and Achaia—your faith in God has become known everywhere. Therefore we do not need to say anything about it, ⁹for they themselves report what kind of reception you gave us. They tell how you turned to God from idols to serve the living and true God, ¹⁰and to wait for his Son from heaven, whom he raised from the dead—Jesus, who rescues us from the coming wrath.

*ᵃ*1 Greek *Silvanus*, a variant of *Silas*   *ᵇ*1 Some early manuscripts *you from God our Father and the Lord Jesus Christ*

Paul's Ministry in Thessalonica

2 You know, brothers, that our visit to you was not a failure. ²We had previously suffered and been insulted in Philippi, as you know, but with the help of our God we dared to tell you his gospel in spite of strong opposition. ³For the appeal we make does not spring from error or impure motives, nor are we trying to trick you. ⁴On the contrary, we speak as men approved by God to be entrusted with the gospel. We are not trying to please men but God, who tests our hearts. ⁵You know we never used flattery, nor did we put on a mask to cover up greed—God is our witness. ⁶We were not looking for praise from men, not from you or anyone else.

As apostles of Christ we could have been a burden to you, ⁷but we were gentle among you, like a mother caring for her little children. ⁸We loved you so much that we were delighted to share with you not only the gospel of God but our lives as well, because you had become so dear to us. ⁹Surely you remember, brothers, our toil and hardship; we worked night and day in order not to be a burden to anyone while we preached the gospel of God to you.

¹⁰You are witnesses, and so is God, of how holy, righteous and blameless we were among you who believed. ¹¹For you know that we dealt with each of you as a father deals with his own children, ¹²encouraging, comforting and urging you to live lives worthy of God, who calls you into his kingdom and glory.

¹³And we also thank God continually because, when you received the word of God, which you heard from us, you accepted it not as the word of men, but as it actually is, the word of God, which is at work in you who believe. ¹⁴For you, brothers, became imitators of God's churches in Judea, which are in Christ Jesus: You suffered from your own countrymen the same things those churches suffered from the Jews, ¹⁵who killed the Lord Jesus and the prophets and also drove us out. They displease God and are hostile to all men ¹⁶in their effort to keep us from speaking to the Gentiles so that they may be saved. In this way they always heap up their sins to the limit. The wrath of God has come upon them at last.ᵃ

Paul's Longing to See the Thessalonians

¹⁷But, brothers, when we were torn away from you for a short time (in person, not in thought), out of our intense longing we made every effort to see you. ¹⁸For we wanted to come to you—certainly I, Paul, did, again and again—but Satan stopped us. ¹⁹For what is our hope, our joy, or the crown in which we will glory in the presence of our Lord Jesus when he comes? Is it not you? ²⁰Indeed, you are our glory and joy.

3 So when we could stand it no longer, we thought it best to be left by ourselves in Athens. ²We sent Timothy, who is our brother and God's fellow workerᵇ in spreading the gospel of Christ, to strengthen and encourage you in your faith, ³so that no one would be unsettled by these trials. You know quite well that we were destined for them. ⁴In fact, when we were with you, we kept telling you that we would be persecuted. And it turned out that way, as you well know. ⁵For this reason, when I could stand it no longer, I sent to find out about your faith. I was afraid that in some way the tempter might have tempted you and our efforts might have been useless.

Timothy's Encouraging Report

⁶But Timothy has just now come to us from you and has brought good news about your faith and love. He has told us that you always have pleasant memories of us and that you long to see us, just as we also long to see you. ⁷Therefore, brothers, in all our distress and persecution we were encouraged about you because of your faith. ⁸For now we really live, since you are standing firm in the Lord. ⁹How can we thank God enough for you in return for all the joy we have in the presence of our God because of you? ¹⁰Night and day we pray most earnestly that we may see you again and supply what is lacking in your faith.

¹¹Now may our God and Father himself and our Lord Jesus clear the way for us to come to you. ¹²May the Lord make your love increase and overflow for each other and for everyone else, just as ours does for you. ¹³May he strengthen your hearts so that you will be blameless and

ᵃ16 Or them fully   ᵇ2 Some manuscripts brother and fellow worker; other manuscripts brother and God's servant

Read 1 Thessalonians 1:1—2:20
Key Verses 1 Thessalonians 2:7–13

Spiritual Pediatrics

Research has found that babies who aren't held and loved may die from "failure to thrive" syndrome even if their basic physical needs are met. They need to be held and rocked and talked to. Similarly, if new Christians are going to thrive, grow and be healthy, they need special care, attention and love in the early years of their Christian life. They must be loved and nurtured to ensure their spiritual growth.

Dawson Trotman, founder of The Navigators, called the care of new believers "spiritual pediatrics." It is helping others grow in the basic foundations of their walk with God. It means teaching them Biblical truth, sharing our lives with them and loving them. It involves addressing their questions and challenging and encouraging them.

Digging Into the Word
1. What do the following passages say about our need to grow in Christ?—*Philippians 3:12–14; Colossians 2:6–7; 2 Peter 1:5–9*
2. How does God want to use us to help others grow in their relationship with Christ?—*1 Corinthians 3:5–15; 2 Peter 1:12–15*

Move Into Service
Name one or two new believers you know. What can you do over the coming month to consistently encourage, affirm and support them in their faith? Contact them soon and let them know you are committed to being there for them as they grow in their love for Jesus.

One Step Deeper
1 Corinthians 3:1–2; Colossians 1:28–29

Go to page 1351 for your next devotional reading.

holy in the presence of our God and Father when our Lord Jesus comes with all his holy ones.

Living to Please God

4 Finally, brothers, we instructed you how to live in order to please God, as in fact you are living. Now we ask you and urge you in the Lord Jesus to do this more and more. ²For you know what instructions we gave you by the authority of the Lord Jesus.

³It is God's will that you should be sanctified: that you should avoid sexual immorality; ⁴that each of you should learn to control his own body*a* in a way that is holy and honorable, ⁵not in passionate lust like the heathen, who do not know God; ⁶and that in this matter no one should wrong his brother or take advantage of him. The Lord will punish men for all such sins, as we have already told you and warned you. ⁷For God did not call us to be impure, but to live a holy life. ⁸Therefore, he who rejects this instruction does not reject man but God, who gives you his Holy Spirit.

⁹Now about brotherly love we do not need to write to you, for you yourselves

a4 Or learn to live with his own wife; or learn to acquire a wife

---

MONDAY

Read *1 Thessalonians 4:1–18*
Key Verses *1 Thessalonians 4:3–8*

Our Best Interests – Stephanie Carter

A conversation between two young men in a coffee shop went as follows: "Yeah, I slept with her again, but so what? I mean, she definitely wanted to."

"What do you mean, 'so what'? Don't you feel like you've done something wrong? The two of you aren't married, and you don't plan on marrying her. How does that square with your conscience?"

"You know, I thought about that before I asked her out again. But then I figured, 'God made sex, right? So how can it be bad?' And how can he possibly expect me to wait until I'm married?"

Believing that God wants to withhold good things from us can be the first step toward sin. That's what happened when Satan convinced Eve to disobey God by distorting the truth and casting doubt in her mind about God's goodness (see Genesis 3:1–6). Once she doubted God's love and the seriousness of his command, she willingly committed a sinful act.

Sex within the boundaries of marriage can be great! It's there that people find the true gift of sex—not just physical intimacy, but emotional intimacy as well. Both lead to the deepening of the relationship within the God-ordained institution of marriage. But outside of marriage, sex can produce guilt, shame, rejection, or, in the end, an even deeper sense of loneliness and isolation. If we choose personal pleasure over purity, we could cause a break in our relationship with God, and probably with other people as well.

Many people see God's commands about sex as joy killers, rules that God put in their way to rob them of a good time. God has our best interests in mind, and he establishes these guidelines because he wants us to experience sex in joyful holiness.

A Deeper Look
Ephesians 5:3; 1 John 2:15–17

Go to page 1352 for your next devotional reading.

have been taught by God to love each other. ¹⁰And in fact, you do love all the brothers throughout Macedonia. Yet we urge you, brothers, to do so more and more.

¹¹Make it your ambition to lead a quiet life, to mind your own business and to work with your hands, just as we told you, ¹²so that your daily life may win the respect of outsiders and so that you will not be dependent on anybody.

The Coming of the Lord

¹³Brothers, we do not want you to be ignorant about those who fall asleep, or to grieve like the rest of men, who have no hope. ¹⁴We believe that Jesus died and rose again and so we believe that God will bring with Jesus those who have fallen asleep in him. ¹⁵According to the Lord's own word, we tell you that we who are still alive, who are left till the coming of the Lord, will certainly not precede those who have fallen asleep. ¹⁶For the Lord himself will come down from heaven, with a loud command, with the voice of the archangel and with the trumpet call of God, and the dead in Christ will rise first. ¹⁷After that, we who are still alive and are left will be caught up together with them in the clouds to meet the Lord in the air. And so we will be with the Lord forever. ¹⁸Therefore encourage each other with these words.

5 Now, brothers, about times and dates we do not need to write to you, ²for you know very well that the day of the Lord will come like a thief in the night. ³While people are saying, "Peace and safety," destruction will come on them suddenly, as labor pains on a pregnant woman, and they will not escape.

⁴But you, brothers, are not in darkness so that this day should surprise you like

---

Read 1 Thessalonians 5:1–28
Key Verses 1 Thessalonians 5:12–13

Respect — Carol Rugg

One evening I was talking with a friend of mine, an older, godly woman. She knew I was seriously dating someone that I was ready to marry if asked. She also knew I had a history of struggling to respect men. After several minutes she asked, "What do you base your respect for your boyfriend on?" Immediately my face began turning red because I knew I based my respect on the wrong thing: competence. No person can be perfectly competent at all times. Thus, my respect for anyone would never last. At that point, I realized that I didn't know what to use as my foundation for respecting others.

Webster defines respect as holding in esteem or honor. What I needed to know was how someone gets to that place of honor. First Thessalonians 5:12–13 says *you* should respect them, and *you* should hold them in the highest regard. In other words, I learned I must freely give respect to others, instead of expecting them to earn it. They are human beings made in God's image, so I need to honor them as such.

Let me challenge you to think through all your relationships. On what do you base your respect for others: their performance or on grace you freely extend? Thanks be to God that he bases our individual worth not on our performance, but rather on his grace!

A Deeper Look
Romans 12:3,10; 1 Peter 2:17–20

Go to page 1355 for your next devotional reading.

a thief. 5You are all sons of the light and sons of the day. We do not belong to the night or to the darkness. 6So then, let us not be like others, who are asleep, but let us be alert and self-controlled. 7For those who sleep, sleep at night, and those who get drunk, get drunk at night. 8But since we belong to the day, let us be self-controlled, putting on faith and love as a breastplate, and the hope of salvation as a helmet. 9For God did not appoint us to suffer wrath but to receive salvation through our Lord Jesus Christ. 10He died for us so that, whether we are awake or asleep, we may live together with him. 11Therefore encourage one another and build each other up, just as in fact you are doing.

Final Instructions

12Now we ask you, brothers, to respect those who work hard among you, who are over you in the Lord and who admonish you. 13Hold them in the highest regard in love because of their work. Live in peace with each other. 14And we urge you, brothers, warn those who are idle, encourage the timid, help the weak, be patient with everyone. 15Make sure that nobody pays back wrong for wrong, but always try to be kind to each other and to everyone else.

16Be joyful always; 17pray continually; 18give thanks in all circumstances, for this is God's will for you in Christ Jesus.

19Do not put out the Spirit's fire; 20do not treat prophecies with contempt. 21Test everything. Hold on to the good. 22Avoid every kind of evil.

23May God himself, the God of peace, sanctify you through and through. May your whole spirit, soul and body be kept blameless at the coming of our Lord Jesus Christ. 24The one who calls you is faithful and he will do it.

25Brothers, pray for us. 26Greet all the brothers with a holy kiss. 27I charge you before the Lord to have this letter read to all the brothers.

28The grace of our Lord Jesus Christ be with you.

Have you ever been puzzled by what's going on in the world around you? This letter provides something stable—an eternal perspective—with which to evaluate society's shifting views. It reminds us that this world is terminal—careening toward its conclusion. But it also reminds us that Christians have a hope for eternity that enables them to live day-to-day in an anti-Christian environment. This letter, along with 1 Thessalonians, tells us much of what we know about the end times.

2 THESSALONIANS

Paul, Silas[a] and Timothy,

To the church of the Thessalonians in God our Father and the Lord Jesus Christ:

²Grace and peace to you from God the Father and the Lord Jesus Christ.

Thanksgiving and Prayer

³We ought always to thank God for you, brothers, and rightly so, because your faith is growing more and more, and the love every one of you has for each other is increasing. ⁴Therefore, among God's churches we boast about your perseverance and faith in all the persecutions and trials you are enduring.

⁵All this is evidence that God's judgment is right, and as a result you will be counted worthy of the kingdom of God, for which you are suffering. ⁶God is just: He will pay back trouble to those who trouble you ⁷and give relief to you who are troubled, and to us as well. This will happen when the Lord Jesus is revealed from heaven in blazing fire with his powerful angels. ⁸He will punish those who do not know God and do not obey the gospel of our Lord Jesus. ⁹They will be punished with everlasting destruction and shut out from the presence of the Lord and from the majesty of his power ¹⁰on the day he comes to be glorified in his holy people and to be marveled at among all those who have believed. This includes you, because you believed our testimony to you.

¹¹With this in mind, we constantly pray for you, that our God may count you worthy of his calling, and that by his power he may fulfill every good purpose

a1 Greek *Silvanus*, a variant of *Silas*

of yours and every act prompted by your faith. ¹²We pray this so that the name of our Lord Jesus may be glorified in you, and you in him, according to the grace of our God and the Lord Jesus Christ.*ᵃ*

The Man of Lawlessness

2 Concerning the coming of our Lord Jesus Christ and our being gathered to him, we ask you, brothers, ²not to become easily unsettled or alarmed by some prophecy, report or letter supposed to have come from us, saying that the day of the Lord has already come. ³Don't let anyone deceive you in any way, for ⌊that day will not come⌋ until the rebellion oc-

curs and the man of lawlessness*ᵇ* is revealed, the man doomed to destruction. ⁴He will oppose and will exalt himself over everything that is called God or is worshiped, so that he sets himself up in God's temple, proclaiming himself to be God.

⁵Don't you remember that when I was with you I used to tell you these things? ⁶And now you know what is holding him back, so that he may be revealed at the proper time. ⁷For the secret power of lawlessness is already at work; but the one

ᵃ12 Or *God and Lord, Jesus Christ*　　*ᵇ3* Some manuscripts *sin*

Read *2 Thessalonians 1:1–12*
Key Verses *2 Thessalonians 1:8–9*

Forever Is a Long Time – Mark Lewis

One night while I was channel surfing on television, my attention was arrested by an interview with inmates in a New Mexico prison. Frustration, poor food, overcrowding and gray monotony had boiled over into several hours of destructive chaos. The report put a human face on the story. One inmate described the experience of being locked in a cubicle day after day. I could almost feel the claustrophobia. Another talked about being shut away from his family. His need for human touch and comfort was tangible.

After several others had unburdened themselves about their experiences, the reporter finally came to a fellow whose face was lined and hardened. The inmate pointed to his friend and said, "Let me tell you the worst part. You see him—he's got two more years and he's out of here. And that guy over there—he's got ten years." Then looking into the camera he said, "But me, I've got two life sentences. I'm never getting out of here."

I thought about that—two life sentences was a long time. Then with a jolt I thought about how long eternity is—a long, long time. Surely eternity is one of the great horrors of hell. The Bible says of those in hell that "they will be punished with *everlasting* destruction" (2 Thessalonians 1:9, italics added). When that cell door closes, its captives are cut off from God. Forever.

I turned off the TV. The incandescent blue faded, but the image of that man's hardened face remained in my mind. Then and there I prayed for that guy—that his eternal sentence would be so much better than his earthly one. Then I thanked Jesus Christ for enduring the cross so that the cell door would never close on those who believe in him (see John 14:6).

A Deeper Look
Luke 16:19–31; Ephesians 1:1–10; Revelation 20:11–15

Go to page 1356 for your next devotional reading.

who now holds it back will continue to do so till he is taken out of the way. **8**And then the lawless one will be revealed, whom the Lord Jesus will overthrow with the breath of his mouth and destroy by the splendor of his coming. **9**The coming of the lawless one will be in accordance with the work of Satan displayed in all kinds of counterfeit miracles, signs and wonders, **10**and in every sort of evil that deceives those who are perishing. They perish because they refused to love the truth and so be saved. **11**For this reason God sends them a powerful delusion so that they will believe the lie **12**and so that all will be condemned who have not believed the truth but have delighted in wickedness.

Stand Firm

13But we ought always to thank God for you, brothers loved by the Lord, because from the beginning God chose

---

Read 2 Thessalonians 2:1–17
Key Verse 2 Thessalonians 2:15

Stand Firm on the Word – Jay Getz

An "evangelical atheist"—that was how one friend described my Ancient Western Civilization professor. My friend had warned me of the professor's penchant for discrediting Biblical authors, and I was now experiencing it firsthand.

Students generally don't flock to elective courses in ancient history. Only a handful of us took the course. We met in the professor's tiny office, where we wedged ourselves into chairs amid walls of books and papers. During the semester he analyzed, and often discredited, the claims of ancient Greek and Roman authors.

When we came to a section of the Bible, he clearly questioned both its accuracy and the integrity of its authors. He asked how two writers could tell seemingly dissimilar accounts of the same event. He implied that New Testament authors misconstrued or intentionally misrepresented Old Testament writings.

Up to that time, I felt I'd already answered my own questions to my satisfaction. But the close quarters and his practiced arguments began to hem me in. His skepticism soon raised doubts in my mind.

These questions drove me to seek out my pastor, who directed me to the Word itself. He reminded me that the Bible, not my own arguments, contained the best and most logical answers to my questions. I learned that as I read and studied difficult passages, God's Spirit enabled me to understand their context and consistency.

The God who breathed the words of the Scriptures into the writers is able to defend himself and his Word. There are many convincing arguments for the accuracy of the Bible; yet one of the best ways to "stand firm" is to know God's Word so well and to let it work in us so thoroughly that its truth is proven time and again in our own lives.

A Deeper Look
2 Timothy 3:14–17; 2 Peter 1:19–21

Go to page 1359 for your next devotional reading.

you*a* to be saved through the sanctifying work of the Spirit and through belief in the truth. ¹⁴He called you to this through our gospel, that you might share in the glory of our Lord Jesus Christ. ¹⁵So then, brothers, stand firm and hold to the teachings*b* we passed on to you, whether by word of mouth or by letter.

¹⁶May our Lord Jesus Christ himself and God our Father, who loved us and by his grace gave us eternal encouragement and good hope, ¹⁷encourage your hearts and strengthen you in every good deed and word.

Request for Prayer

3 Finally, brothers, pray for us that the message of the Lord may spread rapidly and be honored, just as it was with you. ²And pray that we may be delivered from wicked and evil men, for not everyone has faith. ³But the Lord is faithful, and he will strengthen and protect you from the evil one. ⁴We have confidence in the Lord that you are doing and will continue to do the things we command. ⁵May the Lord direct your hearts into God's love and Christ's perseverance.

Warning Against Idleness

⁶In the name of the Lord Jesus Christ, we command you, brothers, to keep away from every brother who is idle and does not live according to the teaching*c* you received from us. ⁷For you yourselves know how you ought to follow our example. We were not idle when we were with you, ⁸nor did we eat anyone's food without paying for it. On the contrary, we worked night and day, laboring and toiling so that we would not be a burden to any of you. ⁹We did this, not because we do not have the right to such help, but in order to make ourselves a

model for you to follow. ¹⁰For even when we were with you, we gave you this rule: "If a man will not work, he shall not eat."

¹¹We hear that some among you are idle. They are not busy; they are busybodies. ¹²Such people we command and urge in the Lord Jesus Christ to settle down and earn the bread they eat. ¹³And as for you, brothers, never tire of doing what is right.

¹⁴If anyone does not obey our instruction in this letter, take special note of him. Do not associate with him, in order that he may feel ashamed. ¹⁵Yet do not regard him as an enemy, but warn him as a brother.

Final Greetings

¹⁶Now may the Lord of peace himself give you peace at all times and in every way. The Lord be with all of you.

¹⁷I, Paul, write this greeting in my own hand, which is the distinguishing mark in all my letters. This is how I write.

¹⁸The grace of our Lord Jesus Christ be with you all.

*a*13 Some manuscripts *because God chose you as his firstfruits* *b*15 Or *traditions* *c*6 Or *tradition*

POINT OF INTEREST   2 Thessalonians 3:1

Time and again Paul asked that his fellow believers support him in prayer. A commitment to consistently pray is one of the greatest gifts we can give to those who have been called to full-time professional ministry, or to anyone, for that matter!

If you learn to play a musical instrument, you'll likely learn to play that instrument with others. Christians are not solo instruments. They're called to harmonize with others in a group called the church. What you're about to read is like a conductor's handbook. This nitty-gritty wisdom offers practical help to believers in their relationships with each other, with church leaders and with the world around them. Look for the underlying principles. Though specific problems and answers might never be exactly duplicated, the principles of the gospel never change.

1 TIMOTHY

1 Paul, an apostle of Christ Jesus by the command of God our Savior and of Christ Jesus our hope,

2 To Timothy my true son in the faith:

Grace, mercy and peace from God the Father and Christ Jesus our Lord.

Warning Against False Teachers of the Law

3 As I urged you when I went into Macedonia, stay there in Ephesus so that you may command certain men not to teach false doctrines any longer 4 nor to devote themselves to myths and endless genealogies. These promote controversies rather than God's work—which is by faith. 5 The goal of this command is love, which comes from a pure heart and a good con-

science and a sincere faith. 6 Some have wandered away from these and turned to meaningless talk. 7 They want to be teachers of the law, but they do not know what they are talking about or what they so confidently affirm.

8 We know that the law is good if one uses it properly. 9 We also know that law*a* is made not for the righteous but for lawbreakers and rebels, the ungodly and sinful, the unholy and irreligious; for those who kill their fathers or mothers, for murderers, 10 for adulterers and perverts, for slave traders and liars and perjurers—and for whatever else is contrary to the sound doctrine 11 that conforms to

a9 Or that the law

the glorious gospel of the blessed God, which he entrusted to me.

The Lord's Grace to Paul

12I thank Christ Jesus our Lord, who has given me strength, that he considered me faithful, appointing me to his service. 13Even though I was once a blasphemer and a persecutor and a violent man, I was shown mercy because I acted in ignorance and unbelief. 14The grace of our Lord was poured out on me abundantly, along with the faith and love that are in Christ Jesus.

15Here is a trustworthy saying that deserves full acceptance: Christ Jesus came into the world to save sinners—of whom I am the worst. 16But for that very reason I was shown mercy so that in me, the worst of sinners, Christ Jesus might display his unlimited patience as an example for those who would believe on him and receive eternal life. 17Now to the King eternal, immortal, invisible, the only God, be honor and glory for ever and ever. Amen.

18Timothy, my son, I give you this instruction in keeping with the prophecies once made about you, so that by following them you may fight the good fight, 19holding on to faith and a good conscience. Some have rejected these and so have shipwrecked their faith. 20Among them are Hymenaeus and Alexander, whom I have handed over to Satan to be taught not to blaspheme.

Instructions on Worship

2 I urge, then, first of all, that requests, prayers, intercession and thanksgiving

---

FRIDAY

Read *1 Timothy 1:1–20*
Key Verses *1 Timothy 1:15–17*

Choosing to Love – Jenny Forsberg

Once again the noise of raucous laughter, loud music and the smell of stale smoke reached my bedroom. I started to seethe inside. I found myself thinking how much I really hated the people who were once again partying in the apartment building yard.

Part of me wanted to go outside and scream at them. I was tired of being inconvenienced. I was tired of their bad habits. After all, I didn't blow smoke into their windows and keep them up nights. I was above all that!

But the Holy Spirit interrupted my thoughts with a gentle reminder that I was being judgmental. I asked God for forgiveness for my anger. I reflected on my attitude and what had just occurred in my heart. I decided that I needed to change my attitude toward others and "not think of [myself] more highly than [I] ought" (Romans 12:3). The painful truth is that I don't deserve Jesus' love. Yet he chooses to love me anyway, not because of what I do or don't do, and in spite of the bad habits I've acquired. He *chooses* to love me. Period! He freely offers his grace and salvation to me because of a decision of his will.

This episode taught me a lesson that I can use every single day. God's command is that I love other people in the same way that he loves me (see John 13:34). Because I receive God's unconditional love and forgiveness, I can accept others without conditions. After all, Jesus' work on the cross was for all of us.

A Deeper Look
1 Corinthians 13:4–7; Philippians 2:3–4

Go to page 1361 for your next devotional reading.

be made for everyone— ²for kings and all those in authority, that we may live peaceful and quiet lives in all godliness and holiness. ³This is good, and pleases God our Savior, ⁴who wants all men to be saved and to come to a knowledge of the truth. ⁵For there is one God and one mediator between God and men, the man Christ Jesus, ⁶who gave himself as a ransom for all men—the testimony given in its proper time. ⁷And for this purpose I was appointed a herald and an apostle—I am telling the truth, I am not lying—and a teacher of the true faith to the Gentiles.

⁸I want men everywhere to lift up holy hands in prayer, without anger or disputing.

⁹I also want women to dress modestly, with decency and propriety, not with braided hair or gold or pearls or expensive clothes, ¹⁰but with good deeds, appropriate for women who profess to worship God.

¹¹A woman should learn in quietness and full submission. ¹²I do not permit a woman to teach or to have authority over a man; she must be silent. ¹³For Adam was formed first, then Eve. ¹⁴And Adam was not the one deceived; it was the woman who was deceived and became a sinner. ¹⁵But women*a* will be saved*b* through childbearing—if they continue in faith, love and holiness with propriety.

Overseers and Deacons

3 Here is a trustworthy saying: If anyone sets his heart on being an overseer,*c* he desires a noble task. ²Now the overseer must be above reproach, the husband of but one wife, temperate, self-controlled, respectable, hospitable, able to teach, ³not given to drunkenness, not violent but gentle, not quarrelsome, not a lover of money. ⁴He must manage his own family well and see that his children obey him with proper respect. ⁵(If anyone does not know how to manage his own family, how can he take care of God's church?) ⁶He must not be a recent convert, or he may become conceited and fall under the same judgment as the devil. ⁷He must also have a good reputation with outsiders, so that he will not fall into disgrace and into the devil's trap.

⁸Deacons, likewise, are to be men worthy of respect, sincere, not indulging in much wine, and not pursuing dishonest gain. ⁹They must keep hold of the deep truths of the faith with a clear con-

science. ¹⁰They must first be tested; and then if there is nothing against them, let them serve as deacons.

¹¹In the same way, their wives*d* are to be women worthy of respect, not malicious talkers but temperate and trustworthy in everything.

¹²A deacon must be the husband of but one wife and must manage his children and his household well. ¹³Those who have served well gain an excellent standing and great assurance in their faith in Christ Jesus.

¹⁴Although I hope to come to you soon, I am writing you these instructions so that, ¹⁵if I am delayed, you will know how people ought to conduct themselves in God's household, which is the church of the living God, the pillar and foundation of the truth. ¹⁶Beyond all question, the mystery of godliness is great:

He*e* appeared in a body,*f*
  was vindicated by the Spirit,
was seen by angels,
  was preached among the nations,
was believed on in the world,
  was taken up in glory.

Instructions to Timothy

4 The Spirit clearly says that in later times some will abandon the faith and follow deceiving spirits and things taught by demons. ²Such teachings come through hypocritical liars, whose consciences have been seared as with a hot iron. ³They forbid people to marry and order them to abstain from certain foods, which God created to be received with thanksgiving by those who believe and who know the truth. ⁴For everything God created is good, and nothing is to be rejected if it is received with thanksgiving, ⁵because it is consecrated by the word of God and prayer.

⁶If you point these things out to the brothers, you will be a good minister of Christ Jesus, brought up in the truths of the faith and of the good teaching that you have followed. ⁷Have nothing to do with godless myths and old wives' tales; rather, train yourself to be godly. ⁸For physical training is of some value, but godliness has value for all things, holding

---

*a*15 Greek *she*   *b*15 Or *restored*
*c*1 Traditionally *bishop*; also in verse 2   *d*11 Or *way, deaconesses*   *e*16 Some manuscripts *God*
*f*16 Or *in the flesh*

Read 1 Timothy 2:1–15
Key Verses 1 Timothy 2:3–6

Get the Picture?

"This is good, and pleases God." What is good? What pleases God? Try these on for size: interceding for others (not talking behind their backs), praying for authorities (not criticizing them), living peaceful and quiet lives in all godliness and holiness (no screaming fights, no wild nights), lifting up holy hands in prayer (not against each other), being circumspect in dress and behavior (not dressing for effect), humility (not showing off). In other words, living the faith, not just talking it.

Why are all these things "good"? When we do these things, others may see concrete evidence that God is our *Savior* and may ask Jesus Christ to become their personal mediator before God. They will have "knowledge of the truth"; they will know what Jesus looks like. Because they will see power, peace, fruitfulness and gentleness in us, they will want what we have. We are walking, talking, living pictures of what God can and will do. Scary, isn't it? Yet if we *don't* do these things, how will they ever know that he wants all of them to be saved?

Digging Into the Word
1. What do these passages say about being a living example of the Good News?—*1 Corinthians 10:31—11:1; 1 Timothy 4:15–16*
2. The gospel is meant to be shared with others. What is said in the following passages about sharing Christ with others?—*Romans 10:9–15; 2 Corinthians 5:17–21; Philippians 1:27–30*

Action Challenge
Consider writing a note to a friend who doesn't know the Good News. In your letter include the following: how knowing Jesus has changed your life, what specific joy you are experiencing in your faith and why the message of Jesus is the best news in human history.

One Step Deeper
Acts 20:24; Ephesians 6:19–20

Go to page 1362 for your next devotional reading.

promise for both the present life and the life to come.

⁹This is a trustworthy saying that deserves full acceptance ¹⁰(and for this we labor and strive), that we have put our hope in the living God, who is the Savior of all men, and especially of those who believe.

¹¹Command and teach these things. ¹²Don't let anyone look down on you because you are young, but set an example for the believers in speech, in life, in love, in faith and in purity. ¹³Until I come, devote yourself to the public reading of Scripture, to preaching and to teaching. ¹⁴Do not neglect your gift, which was given you through a prophetic message when the body of elders laid their hands on you.

¹⁵Be diligent in these matters; give yourself wholly to them, so that everyone may see your progress. ¹⁶Watch your life and doctrine closely. Persevere in them, because if you do, you will save both yourself and your hearers.

Advice About Widows, Elders and Slaves

5 Do not rebuke an older man harshly, but exhort him as if he were your father. Treat younger men as brothers, ²older women as mothers, and younger women as sisters, with absolute purity.

³Give proper recognition to those widows who are really in need. ⁴But if a widow has children or grandchildren, these should learn first of all to put their religion into practice by caring for their own family and so repaying their parents and grandparents, for this is pleasing to God. ⁵The widow who is really in need and left all alone puts her hope in God and continues night and day to pray and to ask God for help. ⁶But the widow who lives for pleasure is dead even while she lives. ⁷Give the people these instructions, too, so that no one may be open to blame. ⁸If anyone does not provide for his relatives, and especially for his immediate family,

---

MONDAY

Read 1 Timothy 4:1–16
Key Verse 1 Timothy 4:12

So What If We're Young! —Lisa Lorimor

On my thirteenth birthday I received a ring from my parents. In it were five stones—one for each of the characteristics mentioned in 1 Timothy 4:12. Since then I've seen God make these aspects of the Christian life evident in my own life and in the lives of other young people around me:

A student set an example in *speech* as he shared Jesus with others on campus. While determining God's will concerning which college I should attend, I was able to be an example in *life* to my younger sisters. As I went to school, a close friend exemplified *love* as she poured her life into mine, helping me learn how to follow Jesus Christ. Yet another student set an example in *faith* as she trusted completely in God to provide financial support for a missions trip only a few weeks away. And an engaged couple I knew set an example in *purity* as they waited until marriage to have sexual intercourse.

I often feel my example isn't important and that I can't possibly influence older Christians. But in light of this verse, I've realized that even a young Christian can set an example by being faithful to Jesus Christ.

A Deeper Look
Matthew 5:16; 1 Corinthians 11:1; Titus 2:6–8,11–15

Go to page 1364 for your next devotional reading.

he has denied the faith and is worse than an unbeliever.

⁹No widow may be put on the list of widows unless she is over sixty, has been faithful to her husband,ᵃ ¹⁰and is well known for her good deeds, such as bringing up children, showing hospitality, washing the feet of the saints, helping those in trouble and devoting herself to all kinds of good deeds.

¹¹As for younger widows, do not put them on such a list. For when their sensual desires overcome their dedication to Christ, they want to marry. ¹²Thus they bring judgment on themselves, because they have broken their first pledge. ¹³Besides, they get into the habit of being idle and going about from house to house. And not only do they become idlers, but also gossips and busybodies, saying things they ought not to. ¹⁴So I counsel younger widows to marry, to have children, to manage their homes and to give the enemy no opportunity for slander. ¹⁵Some have in fact already turned away to follow Satan.

¹⁶If any woman who is a believer has widows in her family, she should help them and not let the church be burdened with them, so that the church can help those widows who are really in need.

¹⁷The elders who direct the affairs of the church well are worthy of double honor, especially those whose work is preaching and teaching. ¹⁸For the Scripture says, "Do not muzzle the ox while it is treading out the grain,"ᵇ and "The worker deserves his wages."ᶜ ¹⁹Do not entertain an accusation against an elder unless it is brought by two or three witnesses. ²⁰Those who sin are to be rebuked publicly, so that the others may take warning.

²¹I charge you, in the sight of God and Christ Jesus and the elect angels, to keep these instructions without partiality, and to do nothing out of favoritism.

²²Do not be hasty in the laying on of hands, and do not share in the sins of others. Keep yourself pure.

²³Stop drinking only water, and use a little wine because of your stomach and your frequent illnesses.

²⁴The sins of some men are obvious, reaching the place of judgment ahead of them; the sins of others trail behind them. ²⁵In the same way, good deeds are obvious, and even those that are not cannot be hidden.

6 All who are under the yoke of slavery should consider their masters worthy of full respect, so that God's name and our teaching may not be slandered. ²Those who have believing masters are not to show less respect for them because they are brothers. Instead, they are to serve them even better, because those who benefit from their service are believers, and dear to them. These are the things you are to teach and urge on them.

Love of Money

³If anyone teaches false doctrines and does not agree to the sound instruction of our Lord Jesus Christ and to godly teaching, ⁴he is conceited and understands nothing. He has an unhealthy interest in controversies and quarrels about words that result in envy, strife, malicious talk, evil suspicions ⁵and constant friction between men of corrupt mind, who have been robbed of the truth and who think that godliness is a means to financial gain.

⁶But godliness with contentment is great gain. ⁷For we brought nothing into the world, and we can take nothing out of it. ⁸But if we have food and clothing, we will be content with that. ⁹People who want to get rich fall into temptation and a trap and into many foolish and harmful desires that plunge men into ruin and destruction. ¹⁰For the love of money is a root of all kinds of evil. Some people, eager for money, have wandered from the faith and pierced themselves with many griefs.

Paul's Charge to Timothy

¹¹But you, man of God, flee from all this, and pursue righteousness, godliness, faith, love, endurance and gentleness. ¹²Fight the good fight of the faith. Take hold of the eternal life to which you were called when you made your good confession in the presence of many witnesses. ¹³In the sight of God, who gives life to everything, and of Christ Jesus, who while testifying before Pontius Pilate made the good confession, I charge you ¹⁴to keep this command without spot or blame until the appearing of our Lord Jesus Christ, ¹⁵which God will bring about in his own time—God, the blessed and only Ruler, the King of kings and

---

ᵃ9 Or *has had but one husband*   ᵇ18 Deut. 25:4
ᶜ18 Luke 10:7

Lord of lords, ¹⁶who alone is immortal and who lives in unapproachable light, whom no one has seen or can see. To him be honor and might forever. Amen.

¹⁷Command those who are rich in this present world not to be arrogant nor to put their hope in wealth, which is so uncertain, but to put their hope in God, who richly provides us with everything for our enjoyment. ¹⁸Command them to do good, to be rich in good deeds, and to be gener-ous and willing to share. ¹⁹In this way they will lay up treasure for themselves as a firm foundation for the coming age, so that they may take hold of the life that is truly life.

²⁰Timothy, guard what has been en-trusted to your care. Turn away from godless chatter and the opposing ideas of what is falsely called knowledge, ²¹which some have professed and in so doing have wandered from the faith.

Grace be with you.

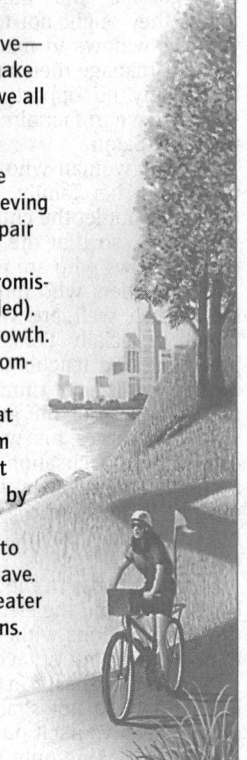

TUESDAY

Read 1 Timothy 6:1–21
Key Verses 1 Timothy 6:6–11

Truly Content — Ellen B. Susman

Sailboats. Laser discs. Sports cars. Designer clothes.

Isn't it great to dream? Think of all the things one could have—the best the world has to offer. There's so much out there to make our lives more comfortable, more exciting, more attractive. If we all just had more money . . .

Paul lets us in on a little secret in this passage: The love of money leads to *destruction*. This message contradicts what the world screams at us every day. It's a struggle to keep from believing the ads that tell us we need *something* to be content—a new pair of shoes, new clothes, a new bike, a new VCR—you name it!

God wants us to be content no matter what we have. He promis-es to provide for "*all [our] needs*" (Philippians 4:19, italics added). We are to be consumed with spiritual growth, not monetary growth. I frequently wonder how the length of time I spend with God com-pares with time spent thinking about "stuff."

I've come to realize that buying clothes, or anything for that matter, is a spiritual issue. I always need to ask God for wisdom before I shop. Then I'm focusing on what he thinks is important rather than on buying stuff that won't satisfy. Most important, by letting go of my desire for things, I am truly content.

Look honestly into your heart. What are you seeking? Talk to God about what you have and ask him what he wants you to have. Give what you have to him and ask him to develop in you a greater desire for him and for his kingdom than for material possessions.

A Deeper Look

Ecclesiastes 5:10–15; Matthew 6:28–33; Hebrews 13:5–6

Go to page 1366 for your next devotional reading.

If you knew your life was about to end and you wanted to pass on your values to someone close to you, what would you say? Second Timothy offers a look at Paul's answer to this question. Languishing in a cold Roman dungeon, chained like a common criminal and realizing he is about to die, Paul attempts to pull together the wisdom of a lifetime of service to God. His words, forged in the crucible of life-threatening experiences, point to the hope that belongs to all of us in Jesus Christ.

2 TIMOTHY

Paul, an apostle of Christ Jesus by the will of God, according to the promise of life that is in Christ Jesus,

²To Timothy, my dear son:

Grace, mercy and peace from God the Father and Christ Jesus our Lord.

Encouragement to Be Faithful

³I thank God, whom I serve, as my forefathers did, with a clear conscience, as night and day I constantly remember you in my prayers. ⁴Recalling your tears, I long to see you, so that I may be filled with joy. ⁵I have been reminded of your sincere faith, which first lived in your grandmother Lois and in your mother Eunice and, I am persuaded, now lives in you also. ⁶For this reason I remind you to fan into flame the gift of God, which is in you through the laying on of my hands.

⁷For God did not give us a spirit of timidity, but a spirit of power, of love and of self-discipline.

⁸So do not be ashamed to testify about our Lord, or ashamed of me his prisoner. But join with me in suffering for the gospel, by the power of God, ⁹who has saved us and called us to a holy life—not because of anything we have done but because of his own purpose and grace. This grace was given us in Christ Jesus before the beginning of time, ¹⁰but it has now been revealed through the appearing of our Savior, Christ Jesus, who has destroyed death and has brought life and immortality to light through the gospel. ¹¹And of this gospel I was appointed a herald and an apostle and a teacher. ¹²That is why I am suffering as I am. Yet I am not ashamed, because I know whom I have believed, and am convinced that

he is able to guard what I have entrusted to him for that day.

¹³What you heard from me, keep as the pattern of sound teaching, with faith and love in Christ Jesus. ¹⁴Guard the good deposit that was entrusted to you—guard it with the help of the Holy Spirit who lives in us.

¹⁵You know that everyone in the province of Asia has deserted me, including Phygelus and Hermogenes.

¹⁶May the Lord show mercy to the household of Onesiphorus, because he often refreshed me and was not ashamed of my chains. ¹⁷On the contrary, when he was in Rome, he searched hard for me until he found me. ¹⁸May the Lord grant that he will find mercy from the Lord on that day! You know very well in how many ways he helped me in Ephesus.

2 You then, my son, be strong in the grace that is in Christ Jesus. ²And the things you have heard me say in the presence of many witnesses entrust to reliable men who will also be qualified to teach others. ³Endure hardship with us like a good soldier of Christ Jesus. ⁴No one serving as a soldier gets involved in civilian affairs—he wants to please his commanding officer. ⁵Similarly, if anyone competes as an athlete, he does not receive the victor's crown unless he competes according to the rules. ⁶The hardworking farmer should be the first to receive a share of the crops. ⁷Reflect on what I am saying, for the Lord will give you insight into all this.

⁸Remember Jesus Christ, raised from the dead, descended from David. This is my gospel, ⁹for which I am suffering even

---

Read *2 Timothy 1:1–18*
Key Verses *2 Timothy 1:7–8*

A Spirit of Power – Sheri Platt

I'd resolved to talk with my friend Vanessa about Jesus. As we rode in the car, I thought of different questions: "So, do you go to church? What do you believe about God?" But the words just would not come out! I dropped her off at her dorm without ever having found out about her spiritual life.

I really wanted to talk with her about Jesus, and we had a good relationship, but the time never seemed right. Actually, I think I was just too scared to bring it up.

A few days later, someone asked our Bible study group to pray, because she was going to share Jesus with a girl she knew. That girl turned out to be Vanessa, who accepted Jesus Christ that night. When I heard the news, I remembered how I had desired to share the gospel with her. But 2 Timothy 1:7–8 tells me I really hadn't needed to be scared to talk with Vanessa about Jesus, because I had God's love and power living through me.

Since then, Vanessa and I have become close friends. We've talked about her struggles with timidity in speaking openly about how God has changed her life. I remind her of that night in the car when I failed to speak what was on my mind. Many of us have a hard time speaking boldly about Jesus' love, but we have to remind one another that God has prepared the way for us by giving us a spirit of power—and that's power we can rely on.

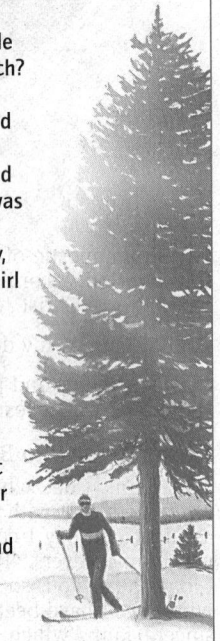

A Deeper Look
Luke 12:11; Colossians 4:3–6

Go to page 1367 for your next devotional reading.

to the point of being chained like a criminal. But God's word is not chained. [10]Therefore I endure everything for the sake of the elect, that they too may obtain the salvation that is in Christ Jesus, with eternal glory.
  [11]Here is a trustworthy saying:

If we died with him,
  we will also live with him;
[12]if we endure,
  we will also reign with him.
If we disown him,
  he will also disown us;
[13]if we are faithless,

Read 2 Timothy 2:1–26
Key Verse 2 Timothy 2:2

Exponential Growth – Ken Larson

In 1923, Russian leader Vladimir Lenin dispatched a man by the name of Michael Borodin to China to help strengthen the flagging Kuomintang (or KMT), China's nationalist party. Borodin's strategy was to form a small group of committed, reliable men, each instilled with Borodin's own vision for world government and a commitment to pass it on to others. He chose three men: Sun Yat-sen, Chinese statesman and revolutionary, founder of the Republic of China; Chiang Kai-shek, an ambitious and influential politician; and a young Vietnamese man who would later be known as Ho Chi Minh.

As history reveals, Borodin's plan worked. After Sun Yat-sen's death in 1925, Chiang Kai-shek, already a powerful Chinese military leader, ascended to the post of president of China (and later, Taiwan). Ho Chi Minh gained political power in China and later became president of North Vietnam.

The apostle Paul also used this method, instructing his spiritual "son" Timothy in this way: "And the things you have heard me say in the presence of many witnesses entrust to reliable men who will also be qualified to teach others." Notice the movement from *Paul* to *Timothy* to *reliable men* to *others*. In the interest of such spiritual multiplication, Paul recruited people who were spiritually hungry, highly committed to God's work. They in turn took the Good News to their world.

Dawson Trotman, founder of The Navigators, used to challenge people with this same vision by asking, "Where is your man?" or "Where is your woman?" In other words, "whom are you training to continue on in ministry for Jesus Christ?" Spiritual multiplication brings exponential, explosive growth to any ministry. Fostering a positive spiritual relationship with another person can have an enormous impact on the world around you. A few people who are totally committed to Jesus Christ could turn a campus or workplace upside down.

If you are a Paul, pray that God will give you a Timothy. If you are a Timothy, pray that God will give you reliable men and women who are willing to be the foundation of many generations of believers.

A Deeper Look
Exodus 18:13–26; Isaiah 60:22; Acts 2:42–47; 6:1–7

Go to page 1369 for your next devotional reading.

he will remain faithful,
for he cannot disown himself.

A Workman Approved by God

[14]Keep reminding them of these things. Warn them before God against quarreling about words; it is of no value, and only ruins those who listen. [15]Do your best to present yourself to God as one approved, a workman who does not need to be ashamed and who correctly handles the word of truth. [16]Avoid godless chatter, because those who indulge in it will become more and more ungodly. [17]Their teaching will spread like gangrene. Among them are Hymenaeus and Philetus, [18]who have wandered away from the truth. They say that the resurrection has already taken place, and they destroy the faith of some. [19]Nevertheless, God's solid foundation stands firm, sealed with this inscription: "The Lord knows those who are his,"[a] and, "Everyone who confesses the name of the Lord must turn away from wickedness."

[20]In a large house there are articles not only of gold and silver, but also of wood and clay; some are for noble purposes and some for ignoble. [21]If a man cleanses himself from the latter, he will be an instrument for noble purposes, made holy, useful to the Master and prepared to do any good work.

[22]Flee the evil desires of youth, and pursue righteousness, faith, love and peace, along with those who call on the Lord out of a pure heart. [23]Don't have anything to do with foolish and stupid arguments, because you know they produce quarrels. [24]And the Lord's servant must not quarrel; instead, he must be kind to everyone, able to teach, not resentful. [25]Those who oppose him he must gently instruct, in the hope that God will grant them repentance leading them to a knowledge of the truth, [26]and that they will come to their senses and escape from the trap of the devil, who has taken them captive to do his will.

Godlessness in the Last Days

3 But mark this: There will be terrible times in the last days. [2]People will be lovers of themselves, lovers of money, boastful, proud, abusive, disobedient to their parents, ungrateful, unholy, [3]without love, unforgiving, slanderous, without self-control, brutal, not lovers of the good, [4]treacherous, rash, conceited, lovers of pleasure rather than lovers of God— [5]having a form of godliness but denying its power. Have nothing to do with them.

[6]They are the kind who worm their way into homes and gain control over weak-willed women, who are loaded down with sins and are swayed by all kinds of evil desires, [7]always learning but never able to acknowledge the truth. [8]Just as Jannes and Jambres opposed Moses, so also these men oppose the truth—men of depraved minds, who, as far as the faith is concerned, are rejected. [9]But they will not get very far because, as in the case of those men, their folly will be clear to everyone.

Paul's Charge to Timothy

[10]You, however, know all about my teaching, my way of life, my purpose, faith, patience, love, endurance, [11]persecutions, sufferings—what kinds of things happened to me in Antioch, Iconium and Lystra, the persecutions I endured. Yet the Lord rescued me from all of them. [12]In fact, everyone who wants to live a godly life in Christ Jesus will be persecuted, [13]while evil men and impostors will go from bad to worse, deceiving and being deceived. [14]But as for you, continue in what you have learned and have become convinced of, because you know those from whom you learned it, [15]and how from infancy you have known the holy Scriptures, which are able to make you wise for salvation through faith in Christ Jesus. [16]All Scripture is God-breathed and is useful for teaching, rebuking, correcting and training in righteousness, [17]so that the man of God may be thoroughly equipped for every good work.

4 In the presence of God and of Christ Jesus, who will judge the living and the dead, and in view of his appearing and his kingdom, I give you this charge: [2]Preach the Word; be prepared in season and out of season; correct, rebuke and encourage—with great patience and careful instruction. [3]For the time will come when men will not put up with sound doctrine. Instead, to suit their own desires, they will gather around them a great number of teachers to say what their itching ears want to hear. [4]They will

---

[a]19 Num. 16:5 (see Septuagint)

turn their ears away from the truth and turn aside to myths. 5But you, keep your head in all situations, endure hardship, do the work of an evangelist, discharge all the duties of your ministry.

6For I am already being poured out like a drink offering, and the time has come for my departure. 7I have fought the good fight, I have finished the race, I have kept the faith. 8Now there is in store for me the crown of righteousness, which the Lord, the righteous Judge, will award to me on that day—and not only to me, but also to all who have longed for his appearing.

Personal Remarks

9Do your best to come to me quickly, 10for Demas, because he loved this world, has deserted me and has gone to Thessalonica. Crescens has gone to Galatia, and Titus to Dalmatia. 11Only Luke is with me. Get Mark and bring him with you, because he is helpful to me in my ministry. 12I sent Tychicus to Ephesus. 13When you come, bring the cloak that I left with Carpus at Troas, and my scrolls, especially the parchments.

14Alexander the metalworker did me a great deal of harm. The Lord will repay him for what he has done. 15You too

---

FRIDAY

Read 2 Timothy 3:1–4:8
Key Verses 2 Timothy 3:16–17

The Textbook For Life – Bill Gensky

Imagine you're being rolled into the operating room for brain surgery. Just before you receive your anesthetic, you look up and ask the surgeon, "Are you sure you know your way around the brain?"

"Sure do," he replies. Then he adds, "Well, I never actually studied the assigned textbooks on the brain, but I'm sure I can feel my way through it."

Like that surgeon, when we haven't spent time studying the Bible, we're left to "feel our way" through the Christian life—with similar, potentially disastrous, results. We may know in our heads certain things that are true about God—for instance, that he's all-powerful or that he's forgiving. Wouldn't it be good to be able to accept his forgiveness and rely on that power moment by moment? And on days when we don't particularly *feel* like Christians, wouldn't it be helpful to know Scripture passages that affirm who we are in Jesus Christ, regardless of how we feel?

Most important, we need to know the Good News and be able to demonstrate it to those who haven't heard. As Peter said, each of us must "always be prepared to give an answer to everyone who asks you to give the reason for the hope that you have" (1 Peter 3:15).

The God-breathed written Word is our guidebook for faith and life. It is abundantly useful for our instruction, and it is the one text that thoroughly equips us for living righteously. As God's Spirit educates us in the Word of God, we can learn to do much more than merely "feel our way" through life. As students of the Scriptures, we can know how to really *live*.

A Deeper Look
Luke 11:28; Hebrews 4:12

Go to page 1370 for your next devotional reading.

Read 2 Timothy 4:1–22
Key Verses 2 Timothy 4:9–10

Live for the World to Come!

Almost anyone can begin a marathon race. Very few people can finish one. In the same way, starting well in the Christian life, when
one is fresh and excited, is easy; it takes God's strength to finish
well. Demas learned this lesson in a big way. He had been one of
Paul's coworkers for several years (see Colossians 4:14; Philemon
24). But he got caught up with the things of the world and deserted Paul. He started living only for the here-and-now instead of for
the world to come.

Demas gave in to a temptation that faces each of us—we are
tempted to invest all our time and energy into the immediate
rather than the eternal, to put last things first and then find there
is no time left for first things—the things of God. Living for the
world to come means concentrating on things that make a difference for eternity.

Digging Into the Word
1. How do these passages challenge your views of success, money
   and fun?—*James 4:4–10; 1 John 2:15–16*
2. How do these passages give you hope for eternity?—*John
   14:1–4; 1 Peter 1:3–9*

Discussion Starter
Start up a conversation with these questions: What do you have in
this world that will last for eternity? How can we focus on eternal
things? What does that mean in daily life?

One Step Deeper
Matthew 16:26; Colossians 3:2

Go to page 1373 for your next devotional reading.

should be on your guard against him, because he strongly opposed our message. ¹⁶At my first defense, no one came to my support, but everyone deserted me. May it not be held against them. ¹⁷But the Lord stood at my side and gave me strength, so that through me the message might be fully proclaimed and all the Gentiles might hear it. And I was delivered from the lion's mouth. ¹⁸The Lord will rescue me from every evil attack and will bring me safely to his heavenly kingdom. To him be glory for ever and ever. Amen.

Final Greetings

¹⁹Greet Priscilla*ᵃ* and Aquila and the household of Onesiphorus. ²⁰Erastus stayed in Corinth, and I left Trophimus sick in Miletus. ²¹Do your best to get here before winter. Eubulus greets you, and so do Pudens, Linus, Claudia and all the brothers.

²²The Lord be with your spirit. Grace be with you.

ᵃ19 Greek *Prisca*, a variant of *Priscilla*

Like Timothy, Titus was a son in the faith to Paul. Paul expresses confidence in Titus, but he also gives Titus instructions about how to lead the troubled and argumentative church in Crete. Even with God's Spirit at work, church life means hard work and a lot of giving. Putting church difficulties in perspective, Paul offers Titus guidelines for a godly life—including successful relationships between family, friends and society—with an emphasis on faith that overcomes division and disharmony among believers.

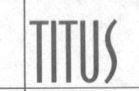

TITUS

1 Paul, a servant of God and an apostle of Jesus Christ for the faith of God's elect and the knowledge of the truth that leads to godliness— ²a faith and knowledge resting on the hope of eternal life, which God, who does not lie, promised before the beginning of time, ³and at his appointed season he brought his word to light through the preaching entrusted to me by the command of God our Savior,

⁴To Titus, my true son in our common faith:

Grace and peace from God the Father and Christ Jesus our Savior.

Titus's Task on Crete

⁵The reason I left you in Crete was that you might straighten out what was left unfinished and appoint*ᵃ* elders in every town, as I directed you. ⁶An elder must be blameless, the husband of but one wife, a man whose children believe and are not open to the charge of being wild and disobedient. ⁷Since an overseer*ᵇ* is entrusted with God's work, he must be blameless—not overbearing, not quick-tempered, not given to drunkenness, not violent, not pursuing dishonest gain. ⁸Rather he must be hospitable, one who loves what is good, who is self-controlled, upright, holy and disciplined. ⁹He must hold firmly to the trustworthy message as it has been taught, so that he can encourage others by sound doctrine and refute those who oppose it.

¹⁰For there are many rebellious people, mere talkers and deceivers, especially those of the circumcision group. ¹¹They must be silenced, because they

ᵃ5 Or *ordain*   *ᵇ7* Traditionally *bishop*

are ruining whole households by teaching things they ought not to teach—and that for the sake of dishonest gain. ¹²Even one of their own prophets has said, "Cretans are always liars, evil brutes, lazy gluttons." ¹³This testimony is true. Therefore, rebuke them sharply, so that they will be sound in the faith ¹⁴and will pay no attention to Jewish myths or to the commands of those who reject the truth. ¹⁵To the pure, all things are pure, but to those who are corrupted and do not believe, nothing is pure. In fact, both their minds and consciences are corrupted. ¹⁶They claim to know God, but by their actions they deny him. They are detestable, disobedient and unfit for doing anything good.

What Must Be Taught to Various Groups

2 You must teach what is in accord with sound doctrine. ²Teach the older men to be temperate, worthy of respect, self-controlled, and sound in faith, in love and in endurance.

Read *Titus 3:1–15*
Key Verses *Titus 3:5–8*

What Really Saves Us? —Lynn M. Hamilton

"I went to a funeral this week," said a young college student I'd just met.

"I'm so sorry," I replied. "Whose funeral was it?"

She didn't know. Out of the blue, she had called up a funeral parlor and asked if she could attend a funeral. She thought if she saw a dead person, it might scare her into being good.

She was searching for God but struggling with the concept of *grace*. She didn't realize, as this passage in Titus explains, that salvation is a *gift* from God, not something to be earned. She wanted to be good so God would accept her. I explained that, as a Christian, I desire to be good *because* God saved me, not because I believe my "goodness" might somehow save me.

To illustrate, I explained the following: "When you were born, you became your parents' daughter and they loved you very much. You did nothing to become their daughter. Nothing. And no matter what happens in life, you will always be their daughter. If you run away, you will still be their daughter. If you commit horrible crimes, you will still be their daughter. That fact cannot change. So if you don't have to be good to be their child, why do you want to please them?"

She thought for a moment, then replied, "I please them because I love them and I want to honor them."

That was the key! Although this young woman didn't *have* to please her parents in order to be their daughter, she *wanted* to because she loved and respected them. In the same way, when we decide to accept Jesus' claim on our lives, we are totally accepted by God "not because of righteous things we [have] done, but because of his mercy." We take our rightful position as God's children: "Yet to all who received him, to those who believed in his name, he gave the right to become children of God" (John 1:12).

A Deeper Look
Isaiah 53:4–6; Romans 5:8; 1 Peter 3:18

Go to page 1376 for your next devotional reading.

³Likewise, teach the older women to be reverent in the way they live, not to be slanderers or addicted to much wine, but to teach what is good. ⁴Then they can train the younger women to love their husbands and children, ⁵to be self-controlled and pure, to be busy at home, to be kind, and to be subject to their husbands, so that no one will malign the word of God.

⁶Similarly, encourage the young men to be self-controlled. ⁷In everything set them an example by doing what is good. In your teaching show integrity, seriousness ⁸and soundness of speech that cannot be condemned, so that those who oppose you may be ashamed because they have nothing bad to say about us.

⁹Teach slaves to be subject to their masters in everything, to try to please them, not to talk back to them, ¹⁰and not to steal from them, but to show that they can be fully trusted, so that in every way they will make the teaching about God our Savior attractive.

¹¹For the grace of God that brings salvation has appeared to all men. ¹²It teaches us to say "No" to ungodliness and worldly passions, and to live self-controlled, upright and godly lives in this present age, ¹³while we wait for the blessed hope—the glorious appearing of our great God and Savior, Jesus Christ, ¹⁴who gave himself for us to redeem us from all wickedness and to purify for himself a people that are his very own, eager to do what is good.

¹⁵These, then, are the things you should teach. Encourage and rebuke with all authority. Do not let anyone despise you.

Doing What Is Good

3 Remind the people to be subject to rulers and authorities, to be obedient, to be ready to do whatever is good, ²to slander no one, to be peaceable and considerate, and to show true humility toward all men.

³At one time we too were foolish, disobedient, deceived and enslaved by all kinds of passions and pleasures. We lived in malice and envy, being hated and hating one another. ⁴But when the kindness and love of God our Savior appeared, ⁵he saved us, not because of righteous things we had done, but because of his mercy. He saved us through the washing of rebirth and renewal by the Holy Spirit, ⁶whom he poured out on us generously through Jesus Christ our Savior, ⁷so that, having been justified by his grace, we might become heirs having the hope of eternal life. ⁸This is a trustworthy saying. And I want you to stress these things, so that those who have trusted in God may be careful to devote themselves to doing what is good. These things are excellent and profitable for everyone.

⁹But avoid foolish controversies and genealogies and arguments and quarrels about the law, because these are unprofitable and useless. ¹⁰Warn a divisive person once, and then warn him a second time. After that, have nothing to do with him. ¹¹You may be sure that such a man is warped and sinful; he is self-condemned.

Final Remarks

¹²As soon as I send Artemas or Tychicus to you, do your best to come to me at Nicopolis, because I have decided to winter there. ¹³Do everything you can to help Zenas the lawyer and Apollos on their way and see that they have everything they need. ¹⁴Our people must learn to devote themselves to doing what is good, in order that they may provide for daily necessities and not live unproductive lives.

¹⁵Everyone with me sends you greetings. Greet those who love us in the faith. Grace be with you all.

forgiveness is not always easy

to ask for or to give. Someone has to swallow the hurt.

Philemon is a case study in the cost of asking for forgive-

ness and of granting it. Writing from prison near the end

of his life, Paul writes to ask Philemon, a friend and broth-

er in Christ, to forgive and take back Onesimus, a run-

away slave. Most runaway slaves, if caught, faced harsh

punishment or even death. But Paul pleads with Philemon

to become a living illustration of the

grace Onesimus had already

received through Jesus Christ.

PHILEMON

¹Paul, a prisoner of Christ Jesus, and Timothy our brother,

To Philemon our dear friend and fellow worker, ²to Apphia our sister, to Archippus our fellow soldier and to the church that meets in your home:

³Grace to you and peace from God our Father and the Lord Jesus Christ.

Thanksgiving and Prayer

⁴I always thank my God as I remember you in my prayers, ⁵because I hear about your faith in the Lord Jesus and your love for all the saints. ⁶I pray that you may be active in sharing your faith, so that you will have a full understanding of every good thing we have in Christ. ⁷Your love has given me great joy and encouragement, because you, brother, have refreshed the hearts of the saints.

Paul's Plea for Onesimus

⁸Therefore, although in Christ I could be bold and order you to do what you ought to do, ⁹yet I appeal to you on the basis of love. I then, as Paul—an old man and now also a prisoner of Christ Jesus— ¹⁰I appeal to you for my son Onesimus,ᵃ who became my son while I was in chains. ¹¹Formerly he was useless to you, but now he has become useful both to you and to me.

¹²I am sending him—who is my very heart—back to you. ¹³I would have liked to keep him with me so that he could take your place in helping me while I am in chains for the gospel. ¹⁴But I did not want to do anything without your consent, so that any favor you do will be spontaneous and not forced. ¹⁵Perhaps the reason

ᵃ *10 Onesimus means useful.*

he was separated from you for a little while was that you might have him back for good— ¹⁶no longer as a slave, but better than a slave, as a dear brother. He is very dear to me but even dearer to you, both as a man and as a brother in the Lord.

¹⁷So if you consider me a partner, welcome him as you would welcome me. ¹⁸If he has done you any wrong or owes you anything, charge it to me. ¹⁹I, Paul, am writing this with my own hand. I will pay it back—not to mention that you owe me your very self. ²⁰I do wish, brother, that I may have some benefit from you in the Lord; refresh my heart in Christ. ²¹Confident of your obedience, I write to you, knowing that you will do even more than I ask.

²²And one thing more: Prepare a guest room for me, because I hope to be restored to you in answer to your prayers.

²³Epaphras, my fellow prisoner in Christ Jesus, sends you greetings. ²⁴And so do Mark, Aristarchus, Demas and Luke, my fellow workers.

²⁵The grace of the Lord Jesus Christ be with your spirit.

TUESDAY

Read Philemon 1–25
Key Verse Philemon 6

Every Good Thing in Christ — Jennifer Colquitt

"It just didn't feel like the right moment. The topic never came up." I was telling my husband of another failed attempt to witness to my friend Kristin. For almost a year, I had been praying for an opportunity to share my faith in Jesus with her. My husband said, "If you're convinced God has led you to share with her, just go for it. Quit waiting for the perfect moment; God has already told you what to do."

My husband was right. My delayed obedience was disobedience. When I saw Kristen the following week, I took my husband's advice to finally discuss with her what it means to be a Christian. What a great experience! Although she did not put her faith in Jesus at that time, we began to discuss spiritual things, and our friendship moved to a deeper level.

The activity of sharing my faith enabled me to experience "every good thing . . . in Christ," the very promise that Paul speaks of in this passage. It wasn't until I actually proclaimed Jesus' message that he graciously gave me the courage, strength, desire and even the words to say. He was faithful to help me act out of my convictions to bring about his will.

Witnessing for Jesus Christ enables Christians to enjoy the good things of God. Has God placed someone in your life for you to share with and experience this "good thing"? We can't know the joy of obedience until we obey. So don't delay—obey.

A Deeper Look
1 Corinthians 2:1–5; 1 Thessalonians 2:3–4

Go to page 1380 for your next devotional reading.

How would it feel to lose your

job or your car because you follow Jesus Christ? How

would it feel to lose the approval of your friends? This

kind of loss is what the audience of Hebrews faced. They

badly needed to be reminded that Jesus was sufficient to

meet their needs and to represent them before God. They

needed to hear the dangers of drifting from the faith. And

they needed to hear about the saints before them who

had lived by faith. As you read, allow the writer of

Hebrews to motivate you, as he did

the early church, to "fix [your]

eyes on Jesus" (12:2).

HEBREWS

The Son Superior to Angels

1 In the past God spoke to our forefathers through the prophets at many times and in various ways, **2** but in these last days he has spoken to us by his Son, whom he appointed heir of all things, and through whom he made the universe. **3** The Son is the radiance of God's glory and the exact representation of his being, sustaining all things by his powerful word. After he had provided purification for sins, he sat down at the right hand of the Majesty in heaven. **4** So he became as much superior to the angels as the name he has inherited is superior to theirs.

5 For to which of the angels did God ever say,

"You are my Son;
 today I have become your
 Father*a*"*b*?

Or again,

"I will be his Father,
 and he will be my Son"*c*?

6 And again, when God brings his first-born into the world, he says,

"Let all God's angels worship him."*d*

7 In speaking of the angels he says,

---

*a*5 Or *have begotten you*   *b*5 Psalm 2:7
*c*5 2 Samuel 7:14; 1 Chron. 17:13
*d*6 Deut. 32:43 (see Dead Sea Scrolls and Septuagint)

"He makes his angels winds,
    his servants flames of fire."[a]

8But about the Son he says,

"Your throne, O God, will last for
    ever and ever,
and righteousness will be the
    scepter of your kingdom.
9You have loved righteousness and
    hated wickedness;
therefore God, your God, has set
    you above your companions
by anointing you with the oil of
    joy."[b]

10He also says,

"In the beginning, O Lord, you laid
    the foundations of the earth,
and the heavens are the work of
    your hands.
11They will perish, but you remain;
    they will all wear out like a garment.
12You will roll them up like a robe;
    like a garment they will be changed.
But you remain the same,
    and your years will never end."[c]

13To which of the angels did God ever say,

"Sit at my right hand
until I make your enemies
    a footstool for your feet"[d]?

14Are not all angels ministering spirits sent to serve those who will inherit salvation?

Warning to Pay Attention

2 We must pay more careful attention, therefore, to what we have heard, so that we do not drift away. 2For if the message spoken by angels was binding, and every violation and disobedience received its just punishment, 3how shall we escape if we ignore such a great salvation? This salvation, which was first announced by the Lord, was confirmed to us by those who heard him. 4God also testified to it by signs, wonders and various miracles, and gifts of the Holy Spirit distributed according to his will.

Jesus Made Like His Brothers

5It is not to angels that he has subjected the world to come, about which we are speaking. 6But there is a place where someone has testified:

"What is man that you are mindful of
    him,
the son of man that you care for
    him?
7You made him a little[e] lower than
    the angels;
you crowned him with glory and
    honor
8   and put everything under his
    feet."[f]

In putting everything under him, God left nothing that is not subject to him. Yet at present we do not see everything subject to him. 9But we see Jesus, who was made a little lower than the angels, now crowned with glory and honor because he suffered death, so that by the grace of God he might taste death for everyone.

10In bringing many sons to glory, it was fitting that God, for whom and through whom everything exists, should make the author of their salvation perfect through suffering. 11Both the one who makes men holy and those who are made holy are of the same family. So Jesus is not ashamed to call them brothers. 12He says,

"I will declare your name to my
    brothers;
in the presence of the congregation
    I will sing your praises."[g]

13And again,

"I will put my trust in him."[h]

And again he says,

"Here am I, and the children God has
    given me."[i]

---

a7 Psalm 104:4   b9 Psalm 45:6,7
c12 Psalm 102:25-27   d13 Psalm 110:1
e7 Or him for a little while; also in verse 9
f8 Psalm 8:4-6   g12 Psalm 22:22
h13 Isaiah 8:17   i13 Isaiah 8:18

POINT OF INTEREST

Hebrews 1:3

Jesus said to Philip, "Anyone who has seen me has seen the Father" (John 14:9). Paul writes, "In Christ all the fullness of the Deity lives in bodily form" (Colossians 2:9). When we look at Jesus, we see God "with skin on." Jesus is everything that God is.

¹⁴Since the children have flesh and blood, he too shared in their humanity so that by his death he might destroy him who holds the power of death—that is, the devil— ¹⁵and free those who all their lives were held in slavery by their fear of death. ¹⁶For surely it is not angels he helps, but Abraham's descendants. ¹⁷For this reason he had to be made like his brothers in every way, in order that he might become a merciful and faithful high priest in service to God, and that he might make atonement for*a* the sins of the people. ¹⁸Because he himself suffered when he was tempted, he is able to help those who are being tempted.

Jesus Greater Than Moses

3 Therefore, holy brothers, who share in the heavenly calling, fix your thoughts on Jesus, the apostle and high priest whom we confess. ²He was faithful to the one who appointed him, just as Moses was faithful in all God's house. ³Jesus has been found worthy of greater honor than Moses, just as the builder of a house has greater honor than the house itself. ⁴For every house is built by someone, but God is the builder of everything. ⁵Moses was faithful as a servant in all God's house, testifying to what would be said in the future. ⁶But Christ is faithful as a son over God's house. And we are his house, if we hold on to our courage and the hope of which we boast.

Warning Against Unbelief

⁷So, as the Holy Spirit says:

"Today, if you hear his voice,
⁸   do not harden your hearts
as you did in the rebellion,
      during the time of testing in the desert,
⁹where your fathers tested and tried me
   and for forty years saw what I did.
¹⁰That is why I was angry with that generation,
   and I said, 'Their hearts are always going astray,
   and they have not known my ways.'
¹¹So I declared on oath in my anger,
   'They shall never enter my rest.' "*b*

¹²See to it, brothers, that none of you has a sinful, unbelieving heart that turns away from the living God. ¹³But encour-age one another daily, as long as it is called Today, so that none of you may be hardened by sin's deceitfulness. ¹⁴We have come to share in Christ if we hold firmly till the end the confidence we had at first. ¹⁵As has just been said:

"Today, if you hear his voice,
   do not harden your hearts
as you did in the rebellion."*c*

¹⁶Who were they who heard and re-belled? Were they not all those Moses led out of Egypt? ¹⁷And with whom was he angry for forty years? Was it not with those who sinned, whose bodies fell in the desert? ¹⁸And to whom did God swear that they would never enter his rest if not to those who disobeyed*d*? ¹⁹So we see that they were not able to enter, be-cause of their unbelief.

A Sabbath-Rest for the People of God

4 Therefore, since the promise of enter-ing his rest still stands, let us be careful that none of you be found to have fallen short of it. ²For we also have had the gos-pel preached to us, just as they did; but the message they heard was of no value to them, because those who heard did not combine it with faith.*e* ³Now we who have believed enter that rest, just as God has said,

"So I declared on oath in my anger,
   'They shall never enter my rest.' "*f*

And yet his work has been finished since the creation of the world. ⁴For some-where he has spoken about the seventh day in these words: "And on the seventh day God rested from all his work."*g* ⁵And again in the passage above he says, "They shall never enter my rest."

⁶It still remains that some will enter that rest, and those who formerly had the gospel preached to them did not go in, because of their disobedience. ⁷Therefore God again set a certain day, calling it To-day, when a long time later he spoke through David, as was said before:

"Today, if you hear his voice,
   do not harden your hearts."*c*

---

a17 Or *and that he might turn aside God's wrath, taking away*   *b11* Psalm 95:7-11
c15,7 Psalm 95:7,8   *d18* Or *disbelieved*
e2 Many manuscripts *because they did not share in the faith of those who obeyed*   *f3* Psalm 95:11; also in verse 5   *g4* Gen. 2:2

⁸For if Joshua had given them rest, God would not have spoken later about another day. ⁹There remains, then, a Sabbath-rest for the people of God; ¹⁰for anyone who enters God's rest also rests from his own work, just as God did from his. ¹¹Let us, therefore, make every effort to enter that rest, so that no one will fall by following their example of disobedience.

¹²For the word of God is living and active. Sharper than any double-edged sword, it penetrates even to dividing soul and spirit, joints and marrow; it judges the thoughts and attitudes of the heart. ¹³Nothing in all creation is hidden from God's sight. Everything is uncovered and laid bare before the eyes of him to whom we must give account.

Jesus the Great High Priest

¹⁴Therefore, since we have a great high priest who has gone through the heavens,ᵃ Jesus the Son of God, let us hold firmly to the faith we profess. ¹⁵For we do not have a high priest who is un-able to sympathize with our weaknesses, but we have one who has been tempted in every way, just as we are—yet was without sin. ¹⁶Let us then approach the throne of grace with confidence, so that we may receive mercy and find grace to help us in our time of need.

5 Every high priest is selected from among men and is appointed to represent them in matters related to God, to offer gifts and sacrifices for sins. ²He is able to deal gently with those who are ignorant and are going astray, since he himself is subject to weakness. ³This is why he has to offer sacrifices for his own sins, as well as for the sins of the people.

⁴No one takes this honor upon himself; he must be called by God, just as Aaron was. ⁵So Christ also did not take upon himself the glory of becoming a high priest. But God said to him,

"You are my Son;

ᵃ14 Or gone into heaven

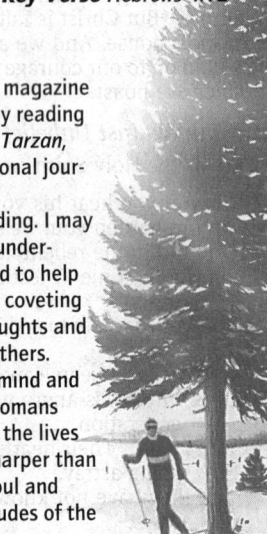

WEDNESDAY

Read Hebrews 4:1–16
Key Verse Hebrews 4:12

Penetrating Reading – Kent Walstrom

I love to read. In college I was required to read textbooks, magazine articles, term papers and great works of literature. Now my reading is wide and varied—the Sunday paper, *The Adventures of Tarzan*, my favorite on-line comics, nonfiction bestsellers, professional journals and commentaries that illuminate the Bible.

But when I read the Bible, it's like no other kind of reading. I may try to read God's Word for entertainment, information or understanding, but God has other plans for me. He uses his Word to help me see how to relate to a coworker, to point out when I'm coveting my neighbor's new car, to guard my mind from impure thoughts and to convict me when I repeat unflattering remarks about others.

In a way that no other book can, the Bible renews my mind and transforms me into the person God wants me to be (see Romans 12:2). Through God's living Word, the Holy Spirit works in the lives of its readers, "For the word of God is living and active. Sharper than any double-edged sword, it penetrates even to dividing soul and spirit, joints and marrow; it judges the thoughts and attitudes of the heart." Good reading—like nothing else!

A Deeper Look
Isaiah 55:10–11; 2 Corinthians 3:18

Go to page 1382 for your next devotional reading.

today I have become your Father.*a* " *b*

6And he says in another place,

"You are a priest forever,
   in the order of Melchizedek." *c*

7During the days of Jesus' life on earth, he offered up prayers and petitions with loud cries and tears to the one who could save him from death, and he was heard because of his reverent submission. 8Although he was a son, he learned obedience from what he suffered 9and, once made perfect, he became the source of eternal salvation for all who obey him 10and was designated by God to be high priest in the order of Melchizedek.

Warning Against Falling Away

11We have much to say about this, but it is hard to explain because you are slow to learn. 12In fact, though by this time you ought to be teachers, you need someone to teach you the elementary truths of God's word all over again. You need milk, not solid food! 13Anyone who lives on milk, being still an infant, is not acquainted with the teaching about righteousness. 14But solid food is for the mature, who by constant use have trained themselves to distinguish good from evil.

6 Therefore let us leave the elementary teachings about Christ and go on to maturity, not laying again the foundation of repentance from acts that lead to death,*d* and of faith in God, 2instruction about baptisms, the laying on of hands, the resurrection of the dead, and eternal judgment. 3And God permitting, we will do so.

4It is impossible for those who have once been enlightened, who have tasted the heavenly gift, who have shared in the Holy Spirit, 5who have tasted the goodness of the word of God and the powers of the coming age, 6if they fall away, to be brought back to repentance, because*e* to their loss they are crucifying the Son of God all over again and subjecting him to public disgrace. 7Land that drinks in the rain often falling on it and that produces a crop useful to those for whom it is farmed receives the blessing of God. 8But land that produces thorns and thistles is worthless and is in danger of being cursed. In the end it will be burned.

9Even though we speak like this, dear friends, we are confident of better things in your case—things that accompany salvation. 10God is not unjust; he will not forget your work and the love you have shown him as you have helped his people and continue to help them. 11We want each of you to show this same diligence to the very end, in order to make your hope sure. 12We do not want you to become lazy, but to imitate those who through faith and patience inherit what has been promised.

The Certainty of God's Promise

13When God made his promise to Abraham, since there was no one greater for him to swear by, he swore by himself, 14saying, "I will surely bless you and give you many descendants." *f* 15And so after waiting patiently, Abraham received what was promised. 16Men swear by someone greater than themselves, and the oath confirms what is said and puts an end to all argument. 17Because God wanted to make the unchanging nature of his purpose very clear to the heirs of what was promised, he confirmed it with an oath. 18God did this so that, by two unchangeable things in which it is impossible for God to lie, we who have fled to take hold of the hope offered to us may be greatly encouraged. 19We have this hope as an anchor for the soul, firm and secure. It enters the inner sanctuary behind the curtain, 20where Jesus, who went before us, has entered on our behalf. He has become a high priest forever, in the order of Melchizedek.

Melchizedek the Priest

7 This Melchizedek was king of Salem and priest of God Most High. He met Abraham returning from the defeat of the kings and blessed him, 2and Abraham gave him a tenth of everything. First, his name means "king of righteousness"; then also, "king of Salem" means "king of peace." 3Without father or mother, without genealogy, without beginning of days or end of life, like the Son of God he remains a priest forever.

4Just think how great he was: Even the patriarch Abraham gave him a tenth of the plunder! 5Now the law requires the descendants of Levi who become priests

*a*5 Or *have begotten you*   *b*5 Psalm 2:7
*c*6 Psalm 110:4   *d*1 Or *from useless rituals*
*e*6 Or *repentance while*   *f*14 Gen. 22:17

to collect a tenth from the people—that is, their brothers—even though their brothers are descended from Abraham. 6This man, however, did not trace his descent from Levi, yet he collected a tenth from Abraham and blessed him who had the promises. 7And without doubt the lesser person is blessed by the greater. 8In the one case, the tenth is collected by men who die; but in the other case, by him who is declared to be living. 9One might even say that Levi, who collects the tenth, paid the tenth through Abraham, 10because when Melchizedek met Abraham, Levi was still in the body of his ancestor.

Jesus Like Melchizedek

11If perfection could have been attained through the Levitical priesthood (for on the basis of it the law was given to the people), why was there still need for another priest to come—one in the order of Melchizedek, not in the order of Aaron? 12For when there is a change of the priesthood, there must also be a change of the law. 13He of whom these things are said belonged to a different tribe, and no one from that tribe has ever served at the altar. 14For it is clear that our Lord descended from Judah, and in regard to that tribe Moses said nothing about priests. 15And what we have said is even more clear if another priest like Melchizedek appears, 16one who has become a priest not on the basis of a regulation as to his ancestry but on the basis of the power of an indestructible life. 17For it is declared:

"You are a priest forever,
    in the order of Melchizedek."a

18The former regulation is set aside because it was weak and useless 19(for the law made nothing perfect), and a better

a17 Psalm 110:4

THURSDAY

Read Hebrews 6:1–20
Key Verse Hebrews 6:12

Butter, Faith and God's Promises – Dr. Tom Yeakley

Making fresh butter is one of our family's Thanksgiving traditions. We put cream in a jar, tighten down the lid and start shaking. We shake and shake that jar . . . until we're all worn out. It seems as though the cream will never turn to butter. But then, in the instance of one shake, what was cream suddenly becomes a lump of butter— and it tastes great!

In much the same way, walking by faith is like making butter. In Hebrews 6:12 we find that faith, patience and God's promises are all necessary in realizing answered prayer. Likewise when we make butter, we have a jar (faith), cream (God's promises) and lots of shaking (lots of patience). Though it seems to take forever, the end result is worth the effort.

A balanced, dynamic life in Jesus Christ must contain all three of these elements. Without faith, we will walk by sight, trusting only what is seen. Without patience, we will compromise and attempt to answer our own prayers. Without God's promises, we can easily presume God's will, which can lead to great hardship and error.

We have to have faith, patience and promises if we are to realize the blessings of God. Combine this strategic triangle in your walk with God and watch him do amazing things in and through you!

A Deeper Look
Psalm 119:140; 2 Corinthians 1:20; Colossians 1:9–14

Go to page 1386 for your next devotional reading.

hope is introduced, by which we draw near to God.

²⁰And it was not without an oath! Others became priests without any oath, ²¹but he became a priest with an oath when God said to him:

"The Lord has sworn
  and will not change his mind:
'You are a priest forever.' "ᵃ

²²Because of this oath, Jesus has become the guarantee of a better covenant.

²³Now there have been many of those priests, since death prevented them from continuing in office; ²⁴but because Jesus lives forever, he has a permanent priesthood. ²⁵Therefore he is able to save completelyᵇ those who come to God through him, because he always lives to intercede for them.

²⁶Such a high priest meets our need— one who is holy, blameless, pure, set apart from sinners, exalted above the heavens. ²⁷Unlike the other high priests, he does not need to offer sacrifices day after day, first for his own sins, and then for the sins of the people. He sacrificed for their sins once for all when he offered himself. ²⁸For the law appoints as high priests men who are weak; but the oath, which came after the law, appointed the Son, who has been made perfect forever.

The High Priest of a New Covenant

8 The point of what we are saying is this: We do have such a high priest, who sat down at the right hand of the throne of the Majesty in heaven, ²and who serves in the sanctuary, the true tabernacle set up by the Lord, not by man.

³Every high priest is appointed to offer both gifts and sacrifices, and so it was necessary for this one also to have something to offer. ⁴If he were on earth, he would not be a priest, for there are already men who offer the gifts prescribed by the law. ⁵They serve at a sanctuary that is a copy and shadow of what is in heaven. This is why Moses was warned when he was about to build the tabernacle: "See to it that you make everything according to the pattern shown you on the mountain."ᶜ ⁶But the ministry Jesus has received is as superior to theirs as the covenant of which he is mediator is superior to the old one, and it is founded on better promises.

⁷For if there had been nothing wrong with that first covenant, no place would have been sought for another. ⁸But God found fault with the people and saidᵈ:

"The time is coming, declares the Lord,
  when I will make a new covenant
with the house of Israel
  and with the house of Judah.
⁹It will not be like the covenant
  I made with their forefathers
when I took them by the hand
  to lead them out of Egypt,
because they did not remain faithful
  to my covenant,
and I turned away from them,
  declares the Lord.
¹⁰This is the covenant I will make with
  the house of Israel
after that time, declares the Lord.
I will put my laws in their minds
  and write them on their hearts.
I will be their God,
  and they will be my people.
¹¹No longer will a man teach his
  neighbor,
or a man his brother, saying,
  'Know the Lord,'
because they will all know me,
  from the least of them to the
  greatest.
¹²For I will forgive their wickedness
  and will remember their sins no
  more."ᵉ

¹³By calling this covenant "new," he has made the first one obsolete; and what is obsolete and aging will soon disappear.

Worship in the Earthly Tabernacle

9 Now the first covenant had regulations for worship and also an earthly sanctuary. ²A tabernacle was set up. In its first room were the lampstand, the table and the consecrated bread; this was called the Holy Place. ³Behind the second curtain was a room called the Most Holy Place, ⁴which had the golden altar of incense and the gold-covered ark of the covenant. This ark contained the gold jar of manna, Aaron's staff that had budded, and the stone tablets of the covenant. ⁵Above the ark were the cherubim of the Glory, overshadowing the atonement cover.ᶠ But we cannot discuss these things in detail now.

⁶When everything had been arranged

ᵃ21 Psalm 110:4   ᵇ25 Or *forever*
ᶜ5 Exodus 25:40   ᵈ8 Some manuscripts may be translated *fault and said to the people.*
ᵉ12 Jer. 31:31-34   ᶠ5 Traditionally *the mercy seat*

like this, the priests entered regularly into the outer room to carry on their ministry. ⁷But only the high priest entered the inner room, and that only once a year, and never without blood, which he offered for himself and for the sins the people had committed in ignorance. ⁸The Holy Spirit was showing by this that the way into the Most Holy Place had not yet been disclosed as long as the first tabernacle was still standing. ⁹This is an illustration for the present time, indicating that the gifts and sacrifices being offered were not able to clear the conscience of the worshiper. ¹⁰They are only a matter of food and drink and various ceremonial washings—external regulations applying until the time of the new order.

The Blood of Christ

¹¹When Christ came as high priest of the good things that are already here,ᵃ he went through the greater and more perfect tabernacle that is not man-made, that is to say, not a part of this creation. ¹²He did not enter by means of the blood of goats and calves; but he entered the Most Holy Place once for all by his own blood, having obtained eternal redemption. ¹³The blood of goats and bulls and the ashes of a heifer sprinkled on those who are ceremonially unclean sanctify them so that they are outwardly clean. ¹⁴How much more, then, will the blood of Christ, who through the eternal Spirit offered himself unblemished to God, cleanse our consciences from acts that lead to death,ᵇ so that we may serve the living God!

¹⁵For this reason Christ is the mediator of a new covenant, that those who are called may receive the promised eternal inheritance—now that he has died as a ransom to set them free from the sins committed under the first covenant.

¹⁶In the case of a will,ᶜ it is necessary to prove the death of the one who made it, ¹⁷because a will is in force only when somebody has died; it never takes effect while the one who made it is living. ¹⁸This is why even the first covenant was not put into effect without blood. ¹⁹When Moses had proclaimed every commandment of the law to all the people, he took the blood of calves, together with water, scarlet wool and branches of hyssop, and sprinkled the scroll and all the people. ²⁰He said, "This is the blood of the covenant, which God has commanded you to keep."ᵈ ²¹In the same way, he sprinkled with the blood both the tabernacle and everything used in its ceremonies. ²²In fact, the law requires that nearly everything be cleansed with blood, and without the shedding of blood there is no forgiveness.

²³It was necessary, then, for the copies of the heavenly things to be purified with these sacrifices, but the heavenly things themselves with better sacrifices than these. ²⁴For Christ did not enter a man-made sanctuary that was only a copy of the true one; he entered heaven itself, now to appear for us in God's presence. ²⁵Nor did he enter heaven to offer himself again and again, the way the high priest enters the Most Holy Place every year with blood that is not his own. ²⁶Then Christ would have had to suffer many times since the creation of the world. But now he has appeared once for all at the end of the ages to do away with sin by the sacrifice of himself. ²⁷Just as man is destined to die once, and after that to face judgment, ²⁸so Christ was sacrificed once to take away the sins of many people; and he will appear a second time, not to bear sin, but to bring salvation to those who are waiting for him.

Christ's Sacrifice Once for All

10 The law is only a shadow of the good things that are coming—not the realities themselves. For this reason it can never, by the same sacrifices repeated endlessly year after year, make perfect those who draw near to worship. ²If it could, would they not have stopped being offered? For the worshipers would have been cleansed once for all, and would no longer have felt guilty for their sins. ³But those sacrifices are an annual reminder of sins, ⁴because it is impossible for the blood of bulls and goats to take away sins.

⁵Therefore, when Christ came into the world, he said:

"Sacrifice and offering you did not desire,
    but a body you prepared for me;
⁶with burnt offerings and sin offerings you were not pleased.

ᵃ 11 Some early manuscripts *are to come*   ᵇ 14 Or *from useless rituals*   ᶜ 16 Same Greek word as *covenant*; also in verse 17   ᵈ 20 Exodus 24:8

[7]Then I said, 'Here I am—it is written
about me in the scroll—
I have come to do your will,
O God.' "[a]

[8]First he said, "Sacrifices and offerings,
burnt offerings and sin offerings you did
not desire, nor were you pleased with
them" (although the law required them
to be made). [9]Then he said, "Here I am,
I have come to do your will." He sets
aside the first to establish the second.
[10]And by that will, we have been made
holy through the sacrifice of the body of
Jesus Christ once for all.

[11]Day after day every priest stands and
performs his religious duties; again and
again he offers the same sacrifices, which
can never take away sins. [12]But when
this priest had offered for all time one
sacrifice for sins, he sat down at the right
hand of God. [13]Since that time he waits
for his enemies to be made his footstool,
[14]because by one sacrifice he has made
perfect forever those who are being made
holy.

[15]The Holy Spirit also testifies to us
about this. First he says:

[16]"This is the covenant I will make
with them
after that time, says the Lord.
I will put my laws in their hearts,
and I will write them on their
minds."[b]

[17]Then he adds:

"Their sins and lawless acts
I will remember no more."[c]

[18]And where these have been forgiven,
there is no longer any sacrifice for sin.

A Call to Persevere

[19]Therefore, brothers, since we have
confidence to enter the Most Holy Place
by the blood of Jesus, [20]by a new and
living way opened for us through the curtain, that is, his body, [21]and since we
have a great priest over the house of God,
[22]let us draw near to God with a sincere
heart in full assurance of faith, having
our hearts sprinkled to cleanse us from a
guilty conscience and having our bodies
washed with pure water. [23]Let us hold
unswervingly to the hope we profess, for
he who promised is faithful. [24]And let us
consider how we may spur one another
on toward love and good deeds. [25]Let us
not give up meeting together, as some are

in the habit of doing, but let us encourage
one another—and all the more as you see
the Day approaching.

[26]If we deliberately keep on sinning after we have received the knowledge of
the truth, no sacrifice for sins is left, [27]but
only a fearful expectation of judgment
and of raging fire that will consume the
enemies of God. [28]Anyone who rejected
the law of Moses died without mercy on
the testimony of two or three witnesses.
[29]How much more severely do you think
a man deserves to be punished who has
trampled the Son of God under foot, who
has treated as an unholy thing the blood
of the covenant that sanctified him, and
who has insulted the Spirit of grace? [30]For
we know him who said, "It is mine to
avenge; I will repay,"[d] and again, "The
Lord will judge his people."[e] [31]It is a
dreadful thing to fall into the hands of the
living God.

[32]Remember those earlier days after
you had received the light, when you
stood your ground in a great contest in
the face of suffering. [33]Sometimes you
were publicly exposed to insult and persecution; at other times you stood side
by side with those who were so treated.
[34]You sympathized with those in prison
and joyfully accepted the confiscation of
your property, because you knew that
you yourselves had better and lasting
possessions.

[35]So do not throw away your confidence; it will be richly rewarded. [36]You
need to persevere so that when you have
done the will of God, you will receive
what he has promised. [37]For in just a
very little while,

"He who is coming will come and
will not delay.
[38] But my righteous one[f] will live by
faith.
And if he shrinks back,
I will not be pleased with him."[g]

[39]But we are not of those who shrink
back and are destroyed, but of those who
believe and are saved.

By Faith

11 Now faith is being sure of what we
hope for and certain of what we do

---

[a]7 Psalm 40:6-8 (see Septuagint)   [b]16 Jer. 31:33
[c]17 Jer. 31:34   [d]30 Deut. 32:35
[e]30 Deut. 32:36; Psalm 135:14   [f]38 One early
manuscript *But the righteous*   [g]38 Hab. 2:3,4

not see. ²This is what the ancients were commended for.

³By faith we understand that the universe was formed at God's command, so that what is seen was not made out of what was visible.

⁴By faith Abel offered God a better sacrifice than Cain did. By faith he was commended as a righteous man, when God spoke well of his offerings. And by faith he still speaks, even though he is dead.

⁵By faith Enoch was taken from this life, so that he did not experience death; he could not be found, because God had taken him away. For before he was taken, he was commended as one who pleased God. ⁶And without faith it is impossible to please God, because anyone who comes to him must believe that he exists and that he rewards those who earnestly seek him.

⁷By faith Noah, when warned about things not yet seen, in holy fear built an ark to save his family. By his faith he condemned the world and became heir of the righteousness that comes by faith.

FRIDAY

Read Hebrews 10:1–31
Key Verses Hebrews 10:24–25

Real Fellowship — Bill Gensky

As I flipped through the television channels one day, I came across an old episode of "The Twilight Zone." This particular episode concerned a man who had decided that people were so annoying that he preferred to live totally alone. In line with the show's mysterious hallmark, "it was arranged" that he experience an entire day without human interaction of any kind.

Having decided he didn't like that, he opted for a day in which everyone he met—young and old, male and female—was exactly like him. There were no variations, no different ideas, nothing other than what he knew. That was just as bad, if not worse, than being by himself. The conclusion? People may be difficult to deal with at times, but life is definitely better with them than without them.

Is this true in the body of Christ? Absolutely. We've all been disappointed and hurt by Christian friends. But Hebrews 10:24–25 admonishes us not to neglect meeting together, even though we may have been hurt. These two verses speak of encouraging and being encouraged, considering new ways of serving and empowering each other to "hang in there" in our relationship with God.

Why continue in relationships that can be painful? What can we possibly get out of them? Those are honest questions, but the key to better fellowship with believers is found in Hebrews 10:19–23. We have a foundation of total freedom to enter into intimacy with God through Jesus Christ. With this opportunity comes complete acceptance, won for us by Jesus' sacrifice and shed blood. We can receive from him the ability and the motivation to encourage, love and serve together. We do this as we commit that we will "not give up meeting together."

When we do, we'll find, as did the character in "The Twilight Zone" episode, that it's a far better world with our brothers and sisters in Jesus Christ than without them.

A Deeper Look
Romans 15:1–7; 1 Corinthians 12:12–26

Go to page 1389 for your next devotional reading.

⁸By faith Abraham, when called to go to a place he would later receive as his inheritance, obeyed and went, even though he did not know where he was going. ⁹By faith he made his home in the promised land like a stranger in a foreign country; he lived in tents, as did Isaac and Jacob, who were heirs with him of the same promise. ¹⁰For he was looking forward to the city with foundations, whose architect and builder is God.

¹¹By faith Abraham, even though he was past age—and Sarah herself was barren—was enabled to become a father because he*a* considered him faithful who had made the promise. ¹²And so from this one man, and he as good as dead, came descendants as numerous as the stars in the sky and as countless as the sand on the seashore.

¹³All these people were still living by faith when they died. They did not receive the things promised; they only saw them and welcomed them from a distance. And they admitted that they were aliens and strangers on earth. ¹⁴People who say such things show that they are looking for a country of their own. ¹⁵If they had been thinking of the country they had left, they would have had opportunity to return. ¹⁶Instead, they were longing for a better country—a heavenly one. Therefore God is not ashamed to be called their God, for he has prepared a city for them.

¹⁷By faith Abraham, when God tested him, offered Isaac as a sacrifice. He who had received the promises was about to sacrifice his one and only son, ¹⁸even though God had said to him, "It is through Isaac that your offspring*b* will be reckoned."*c* ¹⁹Abraham reasoned that God could raise the dead, and figuratively speaking, he did receive Isaac back from death.

²⁰By faith Isaac blessed Jacob and Esau in regard to their future.

²¹By faith Jacob, when he was dying, blessed each of Joseph's sons, and worshiped as he leaned on the top of his staff.

²²By faith Joseph, when his end was near, spoke about the exodus of the Israelites from Egypt and gave instructions about his bones.

²³By faith Moses' parents hid him for three months after he was born, because they saw he was no ordinary child, and they were not afraid of the king's edict.

²⁴By faith Moses, when he had grown up, refused to be known as the son of Pharaoh's daughter. ²⁵He chose to be mistreated along with the people of God rather than to enjoy the pleasures of sin for a short time. ²⁶He regarded disgrace for the sake of Christ as of greater value than the treasures of Egypt, because he was looking ahead to his reward. ²⁷By faith he left Egypt, not fearing the king's anger; he persevered because he saw him who is invisible. ²⁸By faith he kept the Passover and the sprinkling of blood, so that the destroyer of the firstborn would not touch the firstborn of Israel.

²⁹By faith the people passed through the Red Sea*d* as on dry land; but when the Egyptians tried to do so, they were drowned.

³⁰By faith the walls of Jericho fell, after the people had marched around them for seven days.

³¹By faith the prostitute Rahab, because she welcomed the spies, was not killed with those who were disobedient.*e*

³²And what more shall I say? I do not have time to tell about Gideon, Barak, Samson, Jephthah, David, Samuel and the prophets, ³³who through faith conquered kingdoms, administered justice, and gained what was promised; who shut the mouths of lions, ³⁴quenched the fury of the flames, and escaped the edge of the sword; whose weakness was turned to strength; and who became powerful in battle and routed foreign armies. ³⁵Women received back their dead, raised to life again. Others were tortured and refused to be released, so that they might gain a better resurrection. ³⁶Some faced jeers and flogging, while still others were chained and put in prison. ³⁷They were stoned*f*; they were sawed in two; they were put to death by the sword. They went about in sheepskins and goatskins, destitute, persecuted and mistreated— ³⁸the world was not worthy of them. They wandered in deserts and mountains, and in caves and holes in the ground.

³⁹These were all commended for their faith, yet none of them received what had been promised. ⁴⁰God had planned some-

---

a 11 Or *By faith even Sarah, who was past age, was enabled to bear children because she*   *b 18* Greek *seed*   *c 18* Gen. 21:12   *d 29* That is, Sea of Reeds   *e 31* Or *unbelieving*   *f 37* Some early manuscripts *stoned; they were put to the test;*

thing better for us so that only together with us would they be made perfect.

God Disciplines His Sons

12 Therefore, since we are surrounded by such a great cloud of witnesses, let us throw off everything that hinders and the sin that so easily entangles, and let us run with perseverance the race marked out for us. ²Let us fix our eyes on Jesus, the author and perfecter of our faith, who for the joy set before him endured the cross, scorning its shame, and sat down at the right hand of the throne of God. ³Consider him who endured such opposition from sinful men, so that you will not grow weary and lose heart.

⁴In your struggle against sin, you have not yet resisted to the point of shedding your blood. ⁵And you have forgotten that word of encouragement that addresses you as sons:

> "My son, do not make light of the
>   Lord's discipline,
>   and do not lose heart when he
>   rebukes you,
> ⁶because the Lord disciplines those he
>   loves,
>   and he punishes everyone he
>   accepts as a son." ᵃ

⁷Endure hardship as discipline; God is treating you as sons. For what son is not disciplined by his father? ⁸If you are not disciplined (and everyone undergoes discipline), then you are illegitimate children and not true sons. ⁹Moreover, we have all had human fathers who disciplined us and we respected them for it. How much more should we submit to the Father of our spirits and live! ¹⁰Our fathers disciplined us for a little while as they thought best; but God disciplines us for our good, that we may share in his holiness. ¹¹No discipline seems pleasant at the time, but painful. Later on, however, it produces a harvest of righteousness and peace for those who have been trained by it.

¹²Therefore, strengthen your feeble arms and weak knees. ¹³"Make level paths for your feet," ᵇ so that the lame may not be disabled, but rather healed.

Warning Against Refusing God

¹⁴Make every effort to live in peace with all men and to be holy; without holiness no one will see the Lord. ¹⁵See to it that no one misses the grace of God and

that no bitter root grows up to cause trouble and defile many. ¹⁶See that no one is sexually immoral, or is godless like Esau, who for a single meal sold his inheritance rights as the oldest son. ¹⁷Afterward, as you know, when he wanted to inherit this blessing, he was rejected. He could bring about no change of mind, though he sought the blessing with tears.

¹⁸You have not come to a mountain that can be touched and that is burning with fire; to darkness, gloom and storm; ¹⁹to a trumpet blast or to such a voice speaking words that those who heard it begged that no further word be spoken to them, ²⁰because they could not bear what was commanded: "If even an animal touches the mountain, it must be stoned." ᶜ ²¹The sight was so terrifying that Moses said, "I am trembling with fear." ᵈ

²²But you have come to Mount Zion, to the heavenly Jerusalem, the city of the living God. You have come to thousands upon thousands of angels in joyful assembly, ²³to the church of the firstborn, whose names are written in heaven. You have come to God, the judge of all men, to the spirits of righteous men made perfect, ²⁴to Jesus the mediator of a new covenant, and to the sprinkled blood that speaks a better word than the blood of Abel.

²⁵See to it that you do not refuse him who speaks. If they did not escape when they refused him who warned them on

ᵃ6 Prov. 3:11,12   ᵇ13 Prov. 4:26
ᶜ20 Exodus 19:12,13   ᵈ21 Deut. 9:19

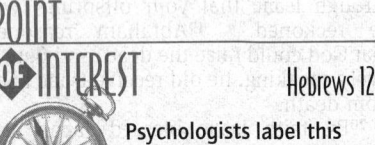

POINT OF INTEREST   Hebrews 12:2

Psychologists label this attitude "delayed gratification"—the ability to wait and to endure difficulties in the interest of attaining some future goal or benefit. The ability to delay gratification is said to be a sign of maturity. How might that concept apply to spiritual maturity? When things seem unbearable, ask God to help you look beyond your circumstances and ahead to what he's promised to those who love him.

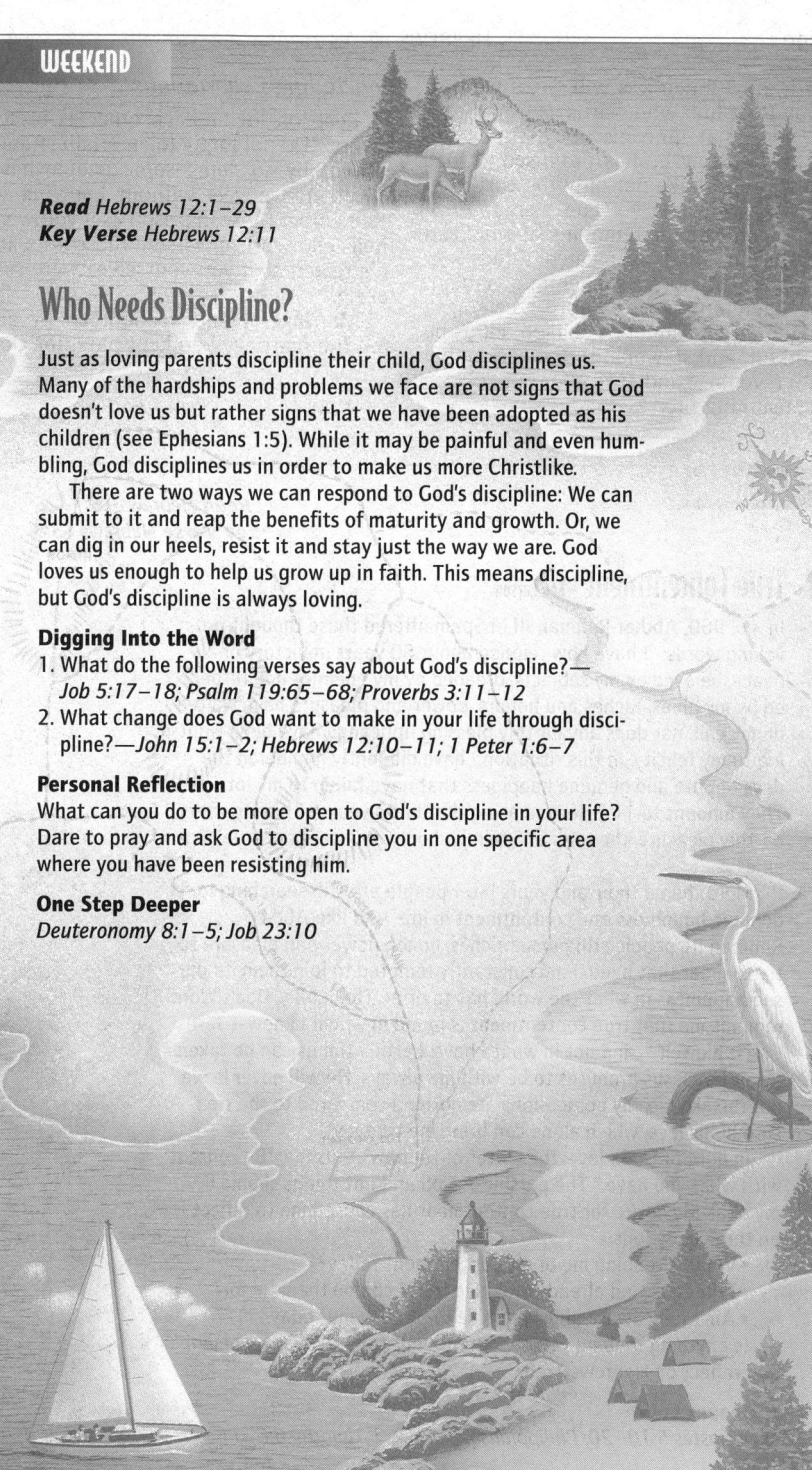

Read Hebrews 12:1–29
Key Verse Hebrews 12:11

Who Needs Discipline?

Just as loving parents discipline their child, God disciplines us.
Many of the hardships and problems we face are not signs that God
doesn't love us but rather signs that we have been adopted as his
children (see Ephesians 1:5). While it may be painful and even humbling, God disciplines us in order to make us more Christlike.

There are two ways we can respond to God's discipline: We can
submit to it and reap the benefits of maturity and growth. Or, we
can dig in our heels, resist it and stay just the way we are. God
loves us enough to help us grow up in faith. This means discipline,
but God's discipline is always loving.

Digging Into the Word
1. What do the following verses say about God's discipline?—
   Job 5:17–18; Psalm 119:65–68; Proverbs 3:11–12
2. What change does God want to make in your life through discipline?—*John 15:1–2; Hebrews 12:10–11; 1 Peter 1:6–7*

Personal Reflection
What can you do to be more open to God's discipline in your life?
Dare to pray and ask God to discipline you in one specific area
where you have been resisting him.

One Step Deeper
Deuteronomy 8:1–5; Job 23:10

Go to page 1390 for your next devotional reading.

earth, how much less will we, if we turn away from him who warns us from heaven? [26]At that time his voice shook the earth, but now he has promised, "Once more I will shake not only the earth but also the heavens."[a] [27]The words "once more" indicate the removing of what can be shaken—that is, created things—so that what cannot be shaken may remain.

[28]Therefore, since we are receiving a kingdom that cannot be shaken, let us be thankful, and so worship God acceptably with reverence and awe, [29]for our "God is a consuming fire."[b]

Concluding Exhortations

13 Keep on loving each other as brothers. [2]Do not forget to entertain strangers, for by so doing some people have entertained angels without knowing it. [3]Remember those in prison as if you were their fellow prisoners, and those who are mistreated as if you yourselves were suffering.

[4]Marriage should be honored by all, and the marriage bed kept pure, for God

[a]26 Haggai 2:6   [b]29 Deut. 4:24

MONDAY

Read Hebrews 13:1–25
Key Verse Hebrews 13:5

True Contentment – Ken Larson

In A.D. 960, Abd-er-Rahman III of Spain offered these thought-provoking words: "I have now reigned about 50 years in victory or peace, beloved by my subjects, dreaded by my enemies and respected by my allies. Riches and honors, power and pleasure have waited on my call, nor does any earthly blessing appear to have been wanting to my felicity. In this situation I have diligently numbered the days of pure and genuine happiness that have fallen to my lot: They amount to 14." How amazing that in 50 years of having every earthly pleasure, the ruler of Spain had only two weeks of true happiness!

More than a thousand years later people are still searching for genuine happiness and contentment in life. And like Abd-er-Rahman III, people still pursue riches, honor, power and pleasure to try to meet that need. I am constantly tempted to join them, to pursue happiness in what the world has to offer. Thankfully, God's Word reminds me that true contentment is found in whom I know—Jesus Christ himself—and not in what I have. Earthly things can be taken away, but Jesus promises to be with me always. He will never leave nor forsake me. My possessions are nothing compared to the treasure of his love, which alone can bring me true joy.

In light of God's love, the writer of Hebrews tells me, "Be content with what you have." The pursuit of God and not things should be my goal. My desire for true contentment has caused me to reflect on three questions:

• What is robbing me of my contentment today?
• What has God already provided that I can be thankful for?
• Am I fully aware of his promise to be with me today?

Is anything robbing you of contentment today? Take a moment and reflect on Hebrews 13:5.

A Deeper Look
Ecclesiastes 5:10–20; Philippians 4:11–12; 1 Timothy 6:6–11

Go to page 1394 for your next devotional reading.

will judge the adulterer and all the sexually immoral. ⁵Keep your lives free from the love of money and be content with what you have, because God has said,

"Never will I leave you;
never will I forsake you."ᵃ

⁶So we say with confidence,

"The Lord is my helper; I will not be afraid.
What can man do to me?"ᵇ

⁷Remember your leaders, who spoke the word of God to you. Consider the outcome of their way of life and imitate their faith. ⁸Jesus Christ is the same yesterday and today and forever.

⁹Do not be carried away by all kinds of strange teachings. It is good for our hearts to be strengthened by grace, not by ceremonial foods, which are of no value to those who eat them. ¹⁰We have an altar from which those who minister at the tabernacle have no right to eat.

¹¹The high priest carries the blood of animals into the Most Holy Place as a sin offering, but the bodies are burned outside the camp. ¹²And so Jesus also suffered outside the city gate to make the people holy through his own blood. ¹³Let us, then, go to him outside the camp, bearing the disgrace he bore. ¹⁴For here we do not have an enduring city, but we are looking for the city that is to come. ¹⁵Through Jesus, therefore, let us continually offer to God a sacrifice of praise—the fruit of lips that confess his name. ¹⁶And do not forget to do good and to share with others, for with such sacrifices God is pleased.

¹⁷Obey your leaders and submit to their authority. They keep watch over you as men who must give an account. Obey them so that their work will be a joy, not a burden, for that would be of no advantage to you.

¹⁸Pray for us. We are sure that we have a clear conscience and desire to live honorably in every way. ¹⁹I particularly urge you to pray so that I may be restored to you soon.

²⁰May the God of peace, who through the blood of the eternal covenant brought back from the dead our Lord Jesus, that great Shepherd of the sheep, ²¹equip you with everything good for doing his will, and may he work in us what is pleasing to him, through Jesus Christ, to whom be glory for ever and ever. Amen.

²²Brothers, I urge you to bear with my word of exhortation, for I have written you only a short letter.

²³I want you to know that our brother Timothy has been released. If he arrives soon, I will come with him to see you.

²⁴Greet all your leaders and all God's people. Those from Italy send you their greetings.

²⁵Grace be with you all.

ᵃ5 Deut. 31:6   ᵇ6 Psalm 118:6,7

How should I respond when I face hard times? How can I learn to control my temper—and my mouth? How do I find real wisdom? The book of James is loaded with straightforward advice for every-day life. The refreshing feature about this book is that James takes a no-nonsense approach to hypocrisy. He describes very real situations and offers hard-hitting, practical solutions. James shows that it's possible to believe the right things yet live the wrong way. But this book will also show you how to turn right doctrine into right living.

JAMES

James, a servant of God and of the Lord Jesus Christ,

To the twelve tribes scattered among the nations:

Greetings.

Trials and Temptations

²Consider it pure joy, my brothers, whenever you face trials of many kinds, ³because you know that the testing of your faith develops perseverance. ⁴Perseverance must finish its work so that you may be mature and complete, not lacking anything. ⁵If any of you lacks wisdom, he should ask God, who gives generously to all without finding fault, and it will be given to him. ⁶But when he asks, he must believe and not doubt, because he who doubts is like a wave of the sea, blown and tossed by the wind. ⁷That man should not think he will receive anything from the Lord; ⁸he is a double-minded man, unstable in all he does.

⁹The brother in humble circumstances ought to take pride in his high position. ¹⁰But the one who is rich should take pride in his low position, because he will pass away like a wild flower. ¹¹For the sun rises with scorching heat and withers the plant; its blossom falls and its beauty is destroyed. In the same way, the rich man will fade away even while he goes about his business.

¹²Blessed is the man who perseveres under trial, because when he has stood

the test, he will receive the crown of life that God has promised to those who love him.

[13]When tempted, no one should say, "God is tempting me." For God cannot be tempted by evil, nor does he tempt anyone; [14]but each one is tempted when, by his own evil desire, he is dragged away and enticed. [15]Then, after desire has conceived, it gives birth to sin; and sin, when it is full-grown, gives birth to death.

[16]Don't be deceived, my dear brothers. [17]Every good and perfect gift is from above, coming down from the Father of the heavenly lights, who does not change like shifting shadows. [18]He chose to give us birth through the word of truth, that we might be a kind of firstfruits of all he created.

Listening and Doing

[19]My dear brothers, take note of this: Everyone should be quick to listen, slow to speak and slow to become angry, [20]for man's anger does not bring about the righteous life that God desires. [21]Therefore, get rid of all moral filth and the evil that is so prevalent and humbly accept the word planted in you, which can save you.

[22]Do not merely listen to the word, and so deceive yourselves. Do what it says. [23]Anyone who listens to the word but does not do what it says is like a man who looks at his face in a mirror [24]and, after looking at himself, goes away and immediately forgets what he looks like. [25]But the man who looks intently into the perfect law that gives freedom, and continues to do this, not forgetting what he has heard, but doing it—he will be blessed in what he does.

[26]If anyone considers himself religious and yet does not keep a tight rein on his tongue, he deceives himself and his religion is worthless. [27]Religion that God our Father accepts as pure and faultless is this: to look after orphans and widows in their distress and to keep oneself from being polluted by the world.

Favoritism Forbidden

2 My brothers, as believers in our glorious Lord Jesus Christ, don't show favoritism. [2]Suppose a man comes into your meeting wearing a gold ring and fine clothes, and a poor man in shabby clothes also comes in. [3]If you show special attention to the man wearing fine clothes and say, "Here's a good seat for you," but say to the poor man, "You stand there" or "Sit on the floor by my feet," [4]have you not discriminated among yourselves and become judges with evil thoughts?

[5]Listen, my dear brothers: Has not God chosen those who are poor in the eyes of the world to be rich in faith and to inherit the kingdom he promised those who love him? [6]But you have insulted the poor. Is it not the rich who are exploiting you? Are they not the ones who are dragging you into court? [7]Are they not the ones who are slandering the noble name of him to whom you belong?

[8]If you really keep the royal law found in Scripture, "Love your neighbor as yourself,"[a] you are doing right. [9]But if you show favoritism, you sin and are convicted by the law as lawbreakers. [10]For whoever keeps the whole law and yet stumbles at just one point is guilty of breaking all of it. [11]For he who said, "Do not commit adultery,"[b] also said, "Do not murder."[c] If you do not commit adultery but do commit murder, you have become a lawbreaker.

[12]Speak and act as those who are going to be judged by the law that gives freedom, [13]because judgment without mercy will be shown to anyone who has not been merciful. Mercy triumphs over judgment!

Faith and Deeds

[14]What good is it, my brothers, if a man claims to have faith but has no deeds? Can such faith save him? [15]Suppose a brother or sister is without clothes and daily food. [16]If one of you says to him, "Go, I wish you well; keep warm and well fed," but does nothing about his physical needs, what good is it? [17]In the same way, faith by itself, if it is not accompanied by action, is dead.

[18]But someone will say, "You have faith; I have deeds."

Show me your faith without deeds, and I will show you my faith by what I do. [19]You believe that there is one God. Good! Even the demons believe that—and shudder.

[20]You foolish man, do you want evidence that faith without deeds is useless[d]? [21]Was not our ancestor Abraham

---

[a]8 Lev. 19:18　　[b]11 Exodus 20:14; Deut. 5:18　　[c]11 Exodus 20:13; Deut. 5:17　　[d]20 Some early manuscripts *dead*

considered righteous for what he did when he offered his son Isaac on the altar? ²²You see that his faith and his actions were working together, and his faith was made complete by what he did. ²³And the scripture was fulfilled that says, "Abraham believed God, and it was credited to him as righteousness,"ᵃ and he was called God's friend. ²⁴You see that a person is justified by what he does and not by faith alone.

²⁵In the same way, was not even Rahab the prostitute considered righteous for what she did when she gave lodging to the spies and sent them off in a different direction? ²⁶As the body without the spirit is dead, so faith without deeds is dead.

Taming the Tongue

3 Not many of you should presume to be teachers, my brothers, because you know that we who teach will be judged more strictly. ²We all stumble in many ways. If anyone is never at fault in what he says, he is a perfect man, able to keep his whole body in check.

³When we put bits into the mouths of horses to make them obey us, we can

ᵃ23 Gen. 15:6

TUESDAY

Read James 1:1–27
Key Verses James 1:22–25

Don't Be Deceived – Glen Hougen

"God did not give us the Bible to make us smarter sinners but to change our lives." I heard Walt Henrichsen, the keynote speaker at a collegiate conference, speak those words and they penetrated deep into my heart and soul. It was the exact message God wanted me to hear that day, and it came across loud and clear.

I grew up in a Christian family; we faithfully attended church week after week. Though I had heard many stories and truths taught from the Bible, I didn't live by them. Although I thought I was doing well, Henrichsen's words showed me that I was really deceiving myself. I looked okay on the outside but wasn't changing inside.

I was like the Pharisees in Matthew 23—men who *knew* but didn't *do*. They had knowledge of God in their heads, but it didn't change their hearts. I didn't want to stay that way. My heart began to change when I started making specific applications to my life from God's Word. As I studied the Bible, I looked for ways to apply it by using the acronym "MAP." I decided that to truly take hold, my goals for applying God's Word to my life needed to be Measurable, Applicable (to me personally) and Practical.

How are you doing with James's instruction in this passage? Are you making applications to your life from God's Word, or are you merely reading words? Are you allowing the Bible to change your life? Take a few minutes to write down some issues you are currently facing, then use a good subject index, commentary or concordance to find verses that relate to those issues. God wants to be involved in your life, and his Word is a living document, supported by the work of the Holy Spirit. Pray for his help as you start applying God's Word today.

A Deeper Look
Deuteronomy 32:46–47; Joshua 1:8; Matthew 7:24–27

Go to page 1396 for your next devotional reading.

turn the whole animal. ⁴Or take ships as an example. Although they are so large and are driven by strong winds, they are steered by a very small rudder wherever the pilot wants to go. ⁵Likewise the tongue is a small part of the body, but it makes great boasts. Consider what a great forest is set on fire by a small spark. ⁶The tongue also is a fire, a world of evil among the parts of the body. It corrupts the whole person, sets the whole course of his life on fire, and is itself set on fire by hell.

⁷All kinds of animals, birds, reptiles and creatures of the sea are being tamed and have been tamed by man, ⁸but no man can tame the tongue. It is a restless evil, full of deadly poison.

⁹With the tongue we praise our Lord and Father, and with it we curse men, who have been made in God's likeness. ¹⁰Out of the same mouth come praise and cursing. My brothers, this should not be. ¹¹Can both fresh water and salt*ᵃ* water flow from the same spring? ¹²My brothers, can a fig tree bear olives, or a grapevine bear figs? Neither can a salt spring produce fresh water.

Two Kinds of Wisdom

¹³Who is wise and understanding among you? Let him show it by his good life, by deeds done in the humility that comes from wisdom. ¹⁴But if you harbor bitter envy and selfish ambition in your hearts, do not boast about it or deny the truth. ¹⁵Such "wisdom" does not come down from heaven but is earthly, unspiritual, of the devil. ¹⁶For where you have envy and selfish ambition, there you find disorder and every evil practice.

¹⁷But the wisdom that comes from heaven is first of all pure; then peaceloving, considerate, submissive, full of mercy and good fruit, impartial and sincere. ¹⁸Peacemakers who sow in peace raise a harvest of righteousness.

Submit Yourselves to God

4 What causes fights and quarrels among you? Don't they come from your desires that battle within you? ²You want something but don't get it. You kill and covet, but you cannot have what you want. You quarrel and fight. You do not have, because you do not ask God. ³When you ask, you do not receive, because you ask with wrong motives, that you may spend what you get on your pleasures.

⁴You adulterous people, don't you know that friendship with the world is hatred toward God? Anyone who chooses to be a friend of the world becomes an enemy of God. ⁵Or do you think Scripture says without reason that the spirit he caused to live in us envies intensely?*ᵇ* ⁶But he gives us more grace. That is why Scripture says:

"God opposes the proud
    but gives grace to the humble."*ᶜ*

⁷Submit yourselves, then, to God. Resist the devil, and he will flee from you. ⁸Come near to God and he will come near to you. Wash your hands, you sinners, and purify your hearts, you doubleminded. ⁹Grieve, mourn and wail. Change your laughter to mourning and your joy to gloom. ¹⁰Humble yourselves before the Lord, and he will lift you up.

¹¹Brothers, do not slander one another. Anyone who speaks against his brother or judges him speaks against the law and judges it. When you judge the law, you are not keeping it, but sitting in judgment on it. ¹²There is only one Lawgiver and Judge, the one who is able to save and destroy. But you—who are you to judge your neighbor?

Boasting About Tomorrow

¹³Now listen, you who say, "Today or tomorrow we will go to this or that city, spend a year there, carry on business and make money." ¹⁴Why, you do not even

---

ᵃ 11 Greek *bitter* (see also verse 14)   *ᵇ 5* Or *that God jealously longs for the spirit that he made to live in us;* or *that the Spirit he caused to live in us longs jealously*   *ᶜ 6* Prov. 3:34

POINT OF INTEREST

James 3:6

James is not shy as he describes how we use words both to build up and tear down others. His ideas here echo the writer of Proverbs, who also had a lot to say about what we say. Skim the book of Proverbs and underline in red the verses that speak about speech.

know what will happen tomorrow. What is your life? You are a mist that appears for a little while and then vanishes. ¹⁵Instead, you ought to say, "If it is the Lord's will, we will live and do this or that." ¹⁶As it is, you boast and brag. All such boasting is evil. ¹⁷Anyone, then, who knows the good he ought to do and doesn't do it, sins.

Warning to Rich Oppressors

5 Now listen, you rich people, weep and wail because of the misery that is coming upon you. ²Your wealth has rotted, and moths have eaten your clothes. ³Your gold and silver are corroded. Their corrosion will testify against you and eat your flesh like fire. You have hoarded wealth in the last days. ⁴Look! The wages you failed to pay the workmen who mowed your fields are crying out against you. The cries of the harvesters have reached the ears of the Lord Almighty. ⁵You have lived on earth in luxury and self-indulgence. You have fattened yourselves in the day of slaughter.ᵃ ⁶You have condemned and murdered innocent men, who were not opposing you.

Patience in Suffering

⁷Be patient, then, brothers, until the Lord's coming. See how the farmer waits for the land to yield its valuable crop and how patient he is for the autumn and

ᵃ5 Or *yourselves as in a day of feasting*

WEDNESDAY

Read James 4:1–17
Key Verses James 4:7–8

Playing with Tarantulas – Dr. Jerry White

While visiting Sri Lanka, I stayed in a home with very few amenities. No hot water. No running water. I took my daily bath in a small, three-foot-square, cement-walled room with a pail of water in the corner. The first time I entered I spotted a large, tarantula-like spider, measuring about three inches across! I thought, "Live and let live," but I kept my eye on him at every bath time. A comfortable truce.

One day I came in and could not find him. I reached down to get the bucket of water to pour over myself. Suddenly, the spider dropped off the ceiling into the water by my hand! I nearly jumped out the door!

To me, this was a picture of sin. In one sense I was taunting the spider—taking the risk, playing a game, just like many do with sin. However, God commands us to resist sin and flee from it—not persist and play. We need to run from evil; there can be no middle ground.

The temptation to sin is often subtle. *I can handle it. It's just a small sin.* Yet God tells us to submit and resist: submit to God's life-plan and resist Satan's death-plan. Is that too extreme a view? Ask the thousands of believers with broken marriages and wounded lives.

Like the spider, unchecked sin will soon appear right in your face, where you least expect it. Then what will you do? Deal with it—today!

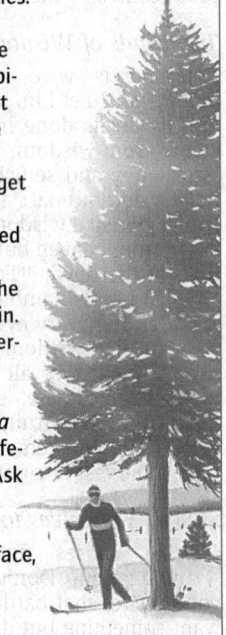

A Deeper Look
Ephesians 4:30; 1 John 1:9

Go to page 1397 for your next devotional reading.

spring rains. ⁸You too, be patient and stand firm, because the Lord's coming is near. ⁹Don't grumble against each other, brothers, or you will be judged. The Judge is standing at the door!

¹⁰Brothers, as an example of patience in the face of suffering, take the prophets who spoke in the name of the Lord. ¹¹As you know, we consider blessed those who have persevered. You have heard of Job's perseverance and have seen what the Lord finally brought about. The Lord is full of compassion and mercy.

¹²Above all, my brothers, do not swear—not by heaven or by earth or by anything else. Let your "Yes" be yes, and your "No," no, or you will be condemned.

The Prayer of Faith

¹³Is any one of you in trouble? He should pray. Is anyone happy? Let him sing songs of praise. ¹⁴Is any one of you sick? He should call the elders of the church to pray over him and anoint him with oil in the name of the Lord. ¹⁵And the prayer offered in faith will make the sick person well; the Lord will raise him up. If he has sinned, he will be forgiven. ¹⁶Therefore confess your sins to each other and pray for each other so that you may be healed. The prayer of a righteous man is powerful and effective.

¹⁷Elijah was a man just like us. He prayed earnestly that it would not rain,

---

THURSDAY

Read James 5:1–20
Key Verse James 5:16

Effective Prayer – Alison Ashmore

When I was five years old, I disliked talking to my grandmother on the telephone. I grew up in a small town in New Mexico, and my grandparents lived in Minnesota. I only got to see them once or twice a year, so my relationship with them was based on scary Saturday morning phone calls when Mom and Dad would make me say "hello." I would hold the phone near my ear and hear my grandmother's distant voice, but I couldn't remember her face. I sure didn't feel like I knew her!

Still, I loved visiting my grandmother when we'd travel to Minnesota on vacation. Soon after we'd arrive, I'd be sitting on her lap, listening to my grandfather's stories. I was close enough to feel her love.

When I was a young Christian, prayer was much like those scary phone conversations with my grandmother. When I talked to God, I felt that my words could never really reach him. Prayer was abstract and uncertain. Later, as I grew to know God better, promises like the one in James 5:16 took on new meaning. No longer was prayer fruitless and futile; it became my link to the One who knew me best.

Now I know what it means to pray an "effective prayer." Because of Jesus Christ, I know God personally in the same way that I could sit on my grandmother's lap and listen to my grandfather's stories. And confessing my sins, as James instructs me to do, helps me to know God more deeply. In a way even more powerful than physical closeness, through prayer I now can enjoy a personal, life-changing relationship with God.

A Deeper Look
Philippians 4:6–7; 1 John 5:14–15

Go to page 1402 for your next devotional reading.

and it did not rain on the land for three and a half years. [18]Again he prayed, and the heavens gave rain, and the earth produced its crops.

[19]My brothers, if one of you should wander from the truth and someone should bring him back, [20]remember this: Whoever turns a sinner from the error of his way will save him from death and cover over a multitude of sins.

Peter addresses this letter to Christians scattered throughout the Roman world. His readers were suffering because of the culture's fading tolerance of Christianity. Sound familiar? Peter's letter is as relevant now as the day he wrote it. The apostle poses some hard challenges. Rugged times require disciplined Christian living. There are no platitudes or easy answers here. But Peter's tough advice is gift wrapped in the language of hope: "These [sufferings] have come so that your faith—of greater worth than gold, which perishes even though refined by fire—may be proved genuine and may result in praise, glory and honor when Jesus Christ is revealed" (1:7).

1 PETER

1 Peter, an apostle of Jesus Christ,

To God's elect, strangers in the world, scattered throughout Pontus, Galatia, Cappadocia, Asia and Bithynia, ²who have been chosen according to the foreknowledge of God the Father, through the sanctifying work of the Spirit, for obedience to Jesus Christ and sprinkling by his blood:

Grace and peace be yours in abundance.

Praise to God for a Living Hope

³Praise be to the God and Father of our Lord Jesus Christ! In his great mercy he has given us new birth into a living hope through the resurrection of Jesus Christ from the dead, ⁴and into an inheritance that can never perish, spoil or fade—kept in heaven for you, ⁵who through faith are shielded by God's power until the coming of the salvation that is ready to be revealed in the last time. ⁶In this you greatly rejoice, though now for a little while

you may have had to suffer grief in all kinds of trials. ⁷These have come so that your faith—of greater worth than gold, which perishes even though refined by fire—may be proved genuine and may result in praise, glory and honor when Jesus Christ is revealed. ⁸Though you have not seen him, you love him; and even though you do not see him now, you believe in him and are filled with an inexpressible and glorious joy, ⁹for you are receiving the goal of your faith, the salvation of your souls.

¹⁰Concerning this salvation, the prophets, who spoke of the grace that was to come to you, searched intently and with the greatest care, ¹¹trying to find out the time and circumstances to which the Spirit of Christ in them was pointing when he predicted the sufferings of Christ and the glories that would follow. ¹²It was revealed to them that they were not serving themselves but you, when they spoke of the things that have now been told you by those who have preached the gospel to you by the Holy Spirit sent from heaven. Even angels long to look into these things.

Be Holy

¹³Therefore, prepare your minds for action; be self-controlled; set your hope fully on the grace to be given you when Jesus Christ is revealed. ¹⁴As obedient children, do not conform to the evil desires you had when you lived in ignorance. ¹⁵But just as he who called you is holy, so be holy in all you do; ¹⁶for it is written: "Be holy, because I am holy."ᵃ

¹⁷Since you call on a Father who judges each man's work impartially, live your lives as strangers here in reverent fear. ¹⁸For you know that it was not with perishable things such as silver or gold that you were redeemed from the empty way of life handed down to you from your forefathers, ¹⁹but with the precious blood of Christ, a lamb without blemish or defect. ²⁰He was chosen before the creation of the world, but was revealed in these last times for your sake. ²¹Through him you believe in God, who raised him from the dead and glorified him, and so your faith and hope are in God.

²²Now that you have purified yourselves by obeying the truth so that you have sincere love for your brothers, love one another deeply, from the heart.ᵇ ²³For you have been born again, not of perishable seed, but of imperishable, through the living and enduring word of God. ²⁴For,

"All men are like grass,
    and all their glory is like the
        flowers of the field;
the grass withers and the flowers fall,
²⁵   but the word of the Lord stands
        forever."ᶜ

And this is the word that was preached to you.

2 Therefore, rid yourselves of all malice and all deceit, hypocrisy, envy, and slander of every kind. ²Like newborn babies, crave pure spiritual milk, so that by it you may grow up in your salvation, ³now that you have tasted that the Lord is good.

The Living Stone and a Chosen People

⁴As you come to him, the living Stone—rejected by men but chosen by God and precious to him— ⁵you also, like living stones, are being built into a spiritual house to be a holy priesthood, offering spiritual sacrifices acceptable to God through Jesus Christ. ⁶For in Scripture it says:

"See, I lay a stone in Zion,
    a chosen and precious cornerstone,
and the one who trusts in him
    will never be put to shame."ᵈ

⁷Now to you who believe, this stone is

ᵃ16 Lev. 11:44,45; 19:2; 20:7   ᵇ22 Some early manuscripts *from a pure heart*   ᶜ25 Isaiah 40:6-8
ᵈ6 Isaiah 28:16

POINT OF INTEREST

1 Peter 1:4

Even if you're the wealthiest person on the block, chances are you've known economic uncertainty. Everybody, at one time or another, has had cash-flow problems. But Peter tells us that believers have an inheritance in heaven that will not change due to stock market fluctuations. It's not backed by the FDIC; God himself guards it. That treasure is eternal life—permanent, timeless and unchanging.

precious. But to those who do not believe,

"The stone the builders rejected
  has become the capstone,*a*"*b*

8and,

"A stone that causes men to stumble
  and a rock that makes them
  fall."*c*

They stumble because they disobey the message—which is also what they were destined for.

9But you are a chosen people, a royal priesthood, a holy nation, a people belonging to God, that you may declare the praises of him who called you out of darkness into his wonderful light. 10Once you were not a people, but now you are the people of God; once you had not received mercy, but now you have received mercy.

11Dear friends, I urge you, as aliens and strangers in the world, to abstain from sinful desires, which war against your soul. 12Live such good lives among the pagans that, though they accuse you of doing wrong, they may see your good deeds and glorify God on the day he visits us.

Submission to Rulers and Masters

13Submit yourselves for the Lord's sake to every authority instituted among men: whether to the king, as the supreme authority, 14or to governors, who are sent by him to punish those who do wrong and to commend those who do right. 15For it is God's will that by doing good you should silence the ignorant talk of foolish men. 16Live as free men, but do not use your freedom as a cover-up for evil; live as servants of God. 17Show proper respect to everyone: Love the brotherhood of believers, fear God, honor the king.

18Slaves, submit yourselves to your masters with all respect, not only to those who are good and considerate, but also to those who are harsh. 19For it is commendable if a man bears up under the pain of unjust suffering because he is conscious of God. 20But how is it to your credit if you receive a beating for doing wrong and endure it? But if you suffer for doing good and you endure it, this is commendable before God. 21To this you were called, because Christ suffered for you, leaving you an example, that you should follow in his steps.

22"He committed no sin,
  and no deceit was found in his
    mouth."*d*

23When they hurled their insults at him, he did not retaliate; when he suffered, he made no threats. Instead, he entrusted himself to him who judges justly. 24He himself bore our sins in his body on the tree, so that we might die to sins and live for righteousness; by his wounds you have been healed. 25For you were like sheep going astray, but now you have returned to the Shepherd and Overseer of your souls.

Wives and Husbands

3 Wives, in the same way be submissive to your husbands so that, if any of them do not believe the word, they may be won over without words by the behavior of their wives, 2when they see the purity and reverence of your lives. 3Your beauty should not come from outward adornment, such as braided hair and the wearing of gold jewelry and fine clothes. 4Instead, it should be that of your inner self, the unfading beauty of a gentle and quiet spirit, which is of great worth in God's sight. 5For this is the way the holy women of the past who put their hope in God used to make themselves beautiful. They were submissive to their own husbands, 6like Sarah, who obeyed Abraham and called him her master. You are her daughters if you do what is right and do not give way to fear.

*a*7 Or *cornerstone*   *b*7 Psalm 118:22
*c*8 Isaiah 8:14   *d*22 Isaiah 53:9

POINT OF INTEREST

1 Peter 2:2

Have you ever heard a hungry newborn cry? It's an intense, relentless kind of insistence that won't stop until the baby is satisfied. That's the kind of urgent desire Peter talks about here—a craving for God's Word that won't quit until it is satisfied, one that wakes us up and tugs at our souls until we fill it up with "pure spiritual milk."

⁷Husbands, in the same way be considerate as you live with your wives, and treat them with respect as the weaker partner and as heirs with you of the gracious gift of life, so that nothing will hinder your prayers.

Suffering for Doing Good

⁸Finally, all of you, live in harmony with one another; be sympathetic, love as brothers, be compassionate and humble. ⁹Do not repay evil with evil or insult with insult, but with blessing, because to this you were called so that you may inherit a blessing. ¹⁰For,

"Whoever would love life
    and see good days
must keep his tongue from evil
    and his lips from deceitful speech.

¹¹He must turn from evil and do good;
    he must seek peace and pursue it.
¹²For the eyes of the Lord are on the
        righteous
    and his ears are attentive to their
        prayer,
but the face of the Lord is against
    those who do evil."ᵃ

¹³Who is going to harm you if you are eager to do good? ¹⁴But even if you should suffer for what is right, you are blessed. "Do not fear what they fearᵇ; do not be frightened."ᶜ ¹⁵But in your hearts set apart Christ as Lord. Always be prepared to give an answer to everyone who asks you to give the reason for the

ᵃ12 Psalm 34:12-16   ᵇ14 Or *not fear their threats*   ᶜ14 Isaiah 8:12

FRIDAY

Read 1 Peter 2:1–25
Key Verse 1 Peter 2:23

The Strength to *Not* Retaliate – Doug Nuenke

Our idea began as a radical way to put the cross back in focus during Easter week. Five of us at the University of Kansas had decided to walk with a wooden cross down the main street of the university. We did it over the lunch hour, the busiest hour of the day, for three days, with our last walk taking place on Good Friday.

Even before the insults, name calling and mocking began, we started to understand in little ways what Jesus had gone through. "Man, this thing is heavy," said one guy. "Anyone have a towel I can put on my shoulder?" Each day we were mocked and insulted just as Jesus had been. As we walked through the noontime crowd, people yelled questions and made fun of us "out-of-touch" Christians. What a temptation to snap back at the hecklers!

Two thousand years ago, Jesus experienced mocking, insults and beatings for proclaiming that he was God. Our experience was contrived and temporary. We returned home. But the mocking he received was real and it must have penetrated deeply.

Jesus had the power to unleash the wrath of God. He could easily have disarmed the hecklers with a verbal or even physical blast. But he didn't retaliate. His life was marked by strength under control: "When they hurled their insults at him, he did not retaliate; when he suffered, he made no threats" (1 Peter 2:23).

Revenge and retaliation have no place in the Christian life. Jesus showed us a better way: "He entrusted himself to him who judges justly," and so should we.

A Deeper Look
Isaiah 53:4–9; Matthew 5:11–12; Romans 12:17–21

Go to page 1404 for your next devotional reading.

hope that you have. But do this with gentleness and respect, [16]keeping a clear conscience, so that those who speak maliciously against your good behavior in Christ may be ashamed of their slander. [17]It is better, if it is God's will, to suffer for doing good than for doing evil. [18]For Christ died for sins once for all, the righteous for the unrighteous, to bring you to God. He was put to death in the body but made alive by the Spirit, [19]through whom[a] also he went and preached to the spirits in prison [20]who disobeyed long ago when God waited patiently in the days of Noah while the ark was being built. In it only a few people, eight in all, were saved through water, [21]and this water symbolizes baptism that now saves you also—not the removal of dirt from the body but the pledge[b] of a good conscience toward God. It saves you by the resurrection of Jesus Christ, [22]who has gone into heaven and is at God's right hand—with angels, authorities and powers in submission to him.

Living for God

4 Therefore, since Christ suffered in his body, arm yourselves also with the same attitude, because he who has suffered in his body is done with sin. [2]As a result, he does not live the rest of his earthly life for evil human desires, but rather for the will of God. [3]For you have spent enough time in the past doing what pagans choose to do—living in debauchery, lust, drunkenness, orgies, carousing and detestable idolatry. [4]They think it strange that you do not plunge with them into the same flood of dissipation, and they heap abuse on you. [5]But they will have to give account to him who is ready to judge the living and the dead. [6]For this is the reason the gospel was preached even to those who are now dead, so that they might be judged according to men in regard to the body, but live according to God in regard to the spirit.

[7]The end of all things is near. Therefore be clear minded and self-controlled so that you can pray. [8]Above all, love each other deeply, because love covers over a multitude of sins. [9]Offer hospitality to one another without grumbling. [10]Each one should use whatever gift he has received to serve others, faithfully administering God's grace in its various forms. [11]If anyone speaks, he should do it as one speaking the very words of God. If anyone serves, he should do it with the strength God provides, so that in all things God may be praised through Jesus Christ. To him be the glory and the power for ever and ever. Amen.

Suffering for Being a Christian

[12]Dear friends, do not be surprised at the painful trial you are suffering, as though something strange were happening to you. [13]But rejoice that you participate in the sufferings of Christ, so that you may be overjoyed when his glory is revealed. [14]If you are insulted because of the name of Christ, you are blessed, for the Spirit of glory and of God rests on you. [15]If you suffer, it should not be as a murderer or thief or any other kind of criminal, or even as a meddler. [16]However, if you suffer as a Christian, do not be ashamed, but praise God that you bear that name. [17]For it is time for judgment to begin with the family of God; and if it begins with us, what will the outcome be for those who do not obey the gospel of God? [18]And,

"If it is hard for the righteous to be saved,
what will become of the ungodly and the sinner?"[c]

[19]So then, those who suffer according

[a] 18,19 Or *alive in the spirit,* [19]*through which*
[b] 21 Or *response*   [c] 18 Prov. 11:31

POINT OF INTEREST

1 Peter 4:12

"Bad people suffer. Good people don't. After all, it's only fair." Many Christians have assimilated this thinking; we expect that following God will be painless and carefree, that somehow, if we're doing things right, we should escape suffering and heartache. Those thoughts aren't new—first-century Christians were under the same illusion. But Peter told the early Christians that the opposite is true—that they could expect to share the sufferings of Jesus Christ. That's still true today. But there is a joyful (and just) caveat: If we share his suffering, we will also share in his glory (see Revelation 18:24—19:9).

Read 1 Peter 4:1—5:14
Key Verse 1 Peter 5:8

The Adversary

Did you ever read *Paradise Lost* for an English course? It tells the story of Satan, the powerful angel who led a rebellion in heaven against God. God put down the revolt and sentenced Satan and his rebellious angels to eternal punishment in the lake of fire. Though John Milton creates an almost romantic picture of the rebellious angel as a swashbuckling, sword-wielding guy, he is also cold, heartless, predatory, proud, lying and self-centered. In fact, he is like a snarling dog on a leash. Get too close and he can bite. But remember, God has him under control. We don't have to be afraid of him, we just have to stand firm—and well out of the vicinity of his teeth.

The devil—though he'd like us to believe he's as powerful as God—is a created being and as such his power is no match for his Creator's. For now, the devil is permitted limited freedom in the universe. But all of us who know Jesus Christ have the power from God to resist the devil and all his surly sidekicks, the evil spirits.

Digging Into the Word
1. Satan is out to destroy humankind. What do the following passages say about the devil?—*Genesis 3:1–20; Job 1:6–12; Revelation 20:7–10*
2. The devil is a defeated enemy. What is said in the following passages about our struggle with him?—*Hebrews 2:14–18; James 4:7*

Personal Reflection
What is one area in which you do battle against temptation? Read Ephesians 6:10–18 to see what kind of armor you can wear.

One Step Deeper
2 Corinthians 4:3–4; Ephesians 4:26–27

Go to page 1407 for your next devotional reading.

to God's will should commit themselves to their faithful Creator and continue to do good.

To Elders and Young Men

5 To the elders among you, I appeal as a fellow elder, a witness of Christ's sufferings and one who also will share in the glory to be revealed: ²Be shepherds of God's flock that is under your care, serving as overseers—not because you must, but because you are willing, as God wants you to be; not greedy for money, but eager to serve; ³not lording it over those entrusted to you, but being examples to the flock. ⁴And when the Chief Shepherd appears, you will receive the crown of glory that will never fade away.

⁵Young men, in the same way be submissive to those who are older. All of you, clothe yourselves with humility toward one another, because,

"God opposes the proud
    but gives grace to the humble."ᵃ

⁶Humble yourselves, therefore, under God's mighty hand, that he may lift you up in due time. ⁷Cast all your anxiety on him because he cares for you.

⁸Be self-controlled and alert. Your enemy the devil prowls around like a roaring lion looking for someone to devour. ⁹Resist him, standing firm in the faith, because you know that your brothers throughout the world are undergoing the same kind of sufferings.

¹⁰And the God of all grace, who called you to his eternal glory in Christ, after you have suffered a little while, will himself restore you and make you strong, firm and steadfast. ¹¹To him be the power for ever and ever. Amen.

Final Greetings

¹²With the help of Silas,ᵇ whom I regard as a faithful brother, I have written to you briefly, encouraging you and testifying that this is the true grace of God. Stand fast in it.

¹³She who is in Babylon, chosen together with you, sends you her greetings, and so does my son Mark. ¹⁴Greet one another with a kiss of love.

Peace to all of you who are in Christ.

ᵃ5 Prov. 3:34   ᵇ12 Greek *Silvanus*, a variant of *Silas*

Peter's second letter addresses four concerns: (1) the need to develop Christian character, (2) the importance of holding to the truth, (3) warnings against false teachers and (4) admonitions on how to live in view of the Lord's coming. As you read 2 Peter, consider how you would live if you knew Jesus Christ would return next year... next month... next week... or tomorrow.

2 PETER

1 Simon Peter, a servant and apostle of Jesus Christ,

To those who through the righteousness of our God and Savior Jesus Christ have received a faith as precious as ours:

²Grace and peace be yours in abundance through the knowledge of God and of Jesus our Lord.

Making One's Calling and Election Sure

³His divine power has given us everything we need for life and godliness through our knowledge of him who called us by his own glory and goodness. ⁴Through these he has given us his very great and precious promises, so that through them you may participate in the divine nature and escape the corruption in the world caused by evil desires.

⁵For this very reason, make every effort to add to your faith goodness; and to goodness, knowledge; ⁶and to knowledge, self-control; and to self-control, perseverance; and to perseverance, godliness; ⁷and to godliness, brotherly kindness; and to brotherly kindness, love. ⁸For if you possess these qualities in increasing measure, they will keep you from being ineffective and unproductive in your knowledge of our Lord Jesus Christ. ⁹But if anyone does not have them, he is nearsighted and blind, and has forgotten that he has been cleansed from his past sins.

¹⁰Therefore, my brothers, be all the more eager to make your calling and election sure. For if you do these things, you will never fall, ¹¹and you will receive a rich welcome into the eternal kingdom of our Lord and Savior Jesus Christ.

Prophecy of Scripture

¹²So I will always remind you of these things, even though you know them and are firmly established in the truth you now have. ¹³I think it is right to refresh your memory as long as I live in the tent of this body, ¹⁴because I know that I will soon put it aside, as our Lord Jesus Christ has made clear to me. ¹⁵And I will make

every effort to see that after my departure you will always be able to remember these things.

16We did not follow cleverly invented stories when we told you about the power and coming of our Lord Jesus Christ, but we were eyewitnesses of his majesty. 17For he received honor and glory from God the Father when the voice came to him from the Majestic Glory, saying, "This is my Son, whom I love; with him I am well pleased."*a* 18We ourselves heard this voice that came from heaven when we were with him on the sacred mountain.

19And we have the word of the prophets made more certain, and you will do well to pay attention to it, as to a light shining in a dark place, until the day dawns and the morning star rises in your hearts. 20Above all, you must understand that no prophecy of Scripture came about by the prophet's own interpretation. 21For prophecy never had its origin in the will of man, but men spoke from God as they were carried along by the Holy Spirit.

False Teachers and Their Destruction

2 But there were also false prophets among the people, just as there will be false teachers among you. They will secretly introduce destructive heresies, even denying the sovereign Lord who

a17 Matt. 17:5; Mark 9:7; Luke 9:35

MONDAY

Read 2 Peter 1:1–21
Key Verse 2 Peter 1:4

Hey, You Promised! – Kent Walstrom

"Dad, you promised to play Monopoly with me after supper."
"Mom, you promised you would read to me before bed."
"Do you promise we can go bike riding this weekend?"
"You promised we could stop at McDonald's for lunch."

As kids, we seek to extract promises from our parents, then hold them to those promises under threat of tantrums and whining. We act that way because we know that sometimes humans keep promises but also that they sometimes don't.

Eventually, we become cynical about the power of a promise. We no longer take people at their word, and we no longer expect that they'll keep a verbal promise; we want it in writing. With time, our lives become filled with broken promises—some are quickly forgotten while others linger in our minds.

Sadly, we often project this human failing—breaking promises—on to a perfect and holy God who is not a human and who does not lie (see Numbers 23:19). We shortchange ourselves when we refuse to take God at his word, and doubt that the promises he has revealed to us in the Bible will be fulfilled in our lives.

Next time you read one of the many universally applicable promises in the Bible, such as 2 Corinthians 1:20 ("For no matter how many promises God has made, they are 'yes' in Christ"), remind yourself that God is promising this to *you*—and that God does not lie.

A Deeper Look
Acts 2:38–39; 1 John 2:25

Go to page 1409 for your next devotional reading.

bought them—bringing swift destruction on themselves. ²Many will follow their shameful ways and will bring the way of truth into disrepute. ³In their greed these teachers will exploit you with stories they have made up. Their condemnation has long been hanging over them, and their destruction has not been sleeping.

⁴For if God did not spare angels when they sinned, but sent them to hell,ᵃ putting them into gloomy dungeonsᵇ to be held for judgment; ⁵if he did not spare the ancient world when he brought the flood on its ungodly people, but protected Noah, a preacher of righteousness, and seven others; ⁶if he condemned the cities of Sodom and Gomorrah by burning them to ashes, and made them an example of what is going to happen to the ungodly; ⁷and if he rescued Lot, a righteous man, who was distressed by the filthy lives of lawless men ⁸(for that righteous man, living among them day after day, was tormented in his righteous soul by the lawless deeds he saw and heard)— ⁹if this is so, then the Lord knows how to rescue godly men from trials and to hold the unrighteous for the day of judgment, while continuing their punishment.ᶜ ¹⁰This is especially true of those who follow the corrupt desire of the sinful natureᵈ and despise authority.

Bold and arrogant, these men are not afraid to slander celestial beings; ¹¹yet even angels, although they are stronger and more powerful, do not bring slanderous accusations against such beings in the presence of the Lord. ¹²But these men blaspheme in matters they do not understand. They are like brute beasts, creatures of instinct, born only to be caught and destroyed, and like beasts they too will perish.

¹³They will be paid back with harm for the harm they have done. Their idea of pleasure is to carouse in broad daylight. They are blots and blemishes, reveling in their pleasures while they feast with you.ᵉ ¹⁴With eyes full of adultery, they never stop sinning; they seduce the unstable; they are experts in greed—an accursed brood! ¹⁵They have left the straight way and wandered off to follow the way of Balaam son of Beor, who loved the wages of wickedness. ¹⁶But he was rebuked for his wrongdoing by a donkey—a beast without speech—who spoke with a man's voice and restrained the prophet's madness.

¹⁷These men are springs without water and mists driven by a storm. Blackest darkness is reserved for them. ¹⁸For they mouth empty, boastful words and, by appealing to the lustful desires of sinful human nature, they entice people who are just escaping from those who live in error. ¹⁹They promise them freedom, while they themselves are slaves of depravity— for a man is a slave to whatever has mastered him. ²⁰If they have escaped the corruption of the world by knowing our Lord and Savior Jesus Christ and are again entangled in it and overcome, they are worse off at the end than they were at the beginning. ²¹It would have been better for them not to have known the way of righteousness, than to have known it and then to turn their backs on the sacred command that was passed on to them. ²²Of them the proverbs are true: "A dog returns to its vomit,"ᶠ and, "A sow that is washed goes back to her wallowing in the mud."

The Day of the Lord

3 Dear friends, this is now my second letter to you. I have written both of them as reminders to stimulate you to wholesome thinking. ²I want you to recall the words spoken in the past by the holy prophets and the command given by our Lord and Savior through your apostles.

³First of all, you must understand that in the last days scoffers will come, scoffing and following their own evil desires. ⁴They will say, "Where is this 'coming' he promised? Ever since our fathers died, everything goes on as it has since the beginning of creation." ⁵But they deliberately forget that long ago by God's word the heavens existed and the earth was formed out of water and by water. ⁶By these waters also the world of that time was deluged and destroyed. ⁷By the same word the present heavens and earth are reserved for fire, being kept for the day of judgment and destruction of ungodly men.

⁸But do not forget this one thing, dear friends: With the Lord a day is like a thousand years, and a thousand years are like a day. ⁹The Lord is not slow in keep-

ᵃ4 Greek *Tartarus*   ᵇ4 Some manuscripts *into chains of darkness*   ᶜ9 Or *unrighteous for punishment until the day of judgment*   ᵈ10 Or *the flesh*   ᵉ13 Some manuscripts *in their love feasts*   ᶠ22 Prov. 26:11

ing his promise, as some understand slowness. He is patient with you, not wanting anyone to perish, but everyone to come to repentance.

[10]But the day of the Lord will come like a thief. The heavens will disappear with a roar; the elements will be destroyed by fire, and the earth and everything in it will be laid bare.[a]

[11]Since everything will be destroyed in this way, what kind of people ought you to be? You ought to live holy and godly lives [12]as you look forward to the day of God and speed its coming.[b] That day will bring about the destruction of the heavens by fire, and the elements will melt in the heat. [13]But in keeping with his promise we are looking forward to a new heaven and a new earth, the home of righteousness.

[14]So then, dear friends, since you are looking forward to this, make every effort to be found spotless, blameless and at peace with him. [15]Bear in mind that our Lord's patience means salvation, just as our dear brother Paul also wrote you with the wisdom that God gave him. [16]He writes the same way in all his letters, speaking in them of these matters. His letters contain some things that are hard to understand, which ignorant and unsta-

[a]10 Some manuscripts *be burned up*   [b]12 Or *as you wait eagerly for the day of God to come*

TUESDAY

Read *2 Peter 3:1–18*
Key Verses *2 Peter 3:10–13*

Tough Holiness – Mike Jordahl

He's at it again. He's really just your basic average-looking guy, and yet he's got another girl in his room. Another night, another woman. How does he do it? And why? My emotions are mixed—sadness, anger, even jealousy—but mostly I feel emptiness.

Some of the sadness is for her, because she doesn't know she doesn't mean anything to him. Then again, maybe he doesn't mean anything to her either. And after all, they're adults. Well, almost.

I'm angry, too, because I know he knows it's wrong! We've even talked about it! And he knows what I think, but he flaunts it in front of me. But then, what am I, the Moral Police of this hall?

This jealousy—that's a bit tougher. It's tough to watch someone living without restrictions, even though I know it'll hurt him in the long run. Sometimes I'm tempted to wish God would have brought me to himself just a bit later in my life—after I had had a chance for some "real fun" first. I know that's faulty reasoning, but I still have to sort through it. Then there's the loneliness and emptiness. I want to be with someone, but not that way.

I've made my choice. Because I follow Jesus Christ, I am determined to wait for the right woman—the one God has in mind for me. While my choice isn't easy, something in me knows it is best for my protection and welfare and is what God wants for me. One day I'll be more thankful than I feel right now.

O God, help me. I pour my heart out to you. Use me to be your light to them. Help them both to know your love. Please help me overcome this emptiness and loneliness. Help me to live the holy, pure life that you desire.

A Deeper Look
1 Corinthians 6:18–20; 2 Corinthians 7:1

Go to page 1412 for your next devotional reading.

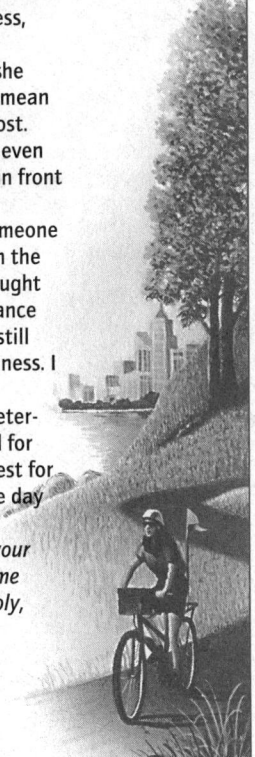

ble people distort, as they do the other Scriptures, to their own destruction. [17]Therefore, dear friends, since you already know this, be on your guard so that you may not be carried away by the error

of lawless men and fall from your secure position. [18]But grow in the grace and knowledge of our Lord and Savior Jesus Christ. To him be glory both now and forever! Amen.

Many of the world views spinning through cyberspace today run counter to Jesus' teachings. That's why 1 John is such a relevant book for us. The apostle John writes to correct a world view that denied that Jesus was both God and man. Though written to correct dangerous heresy, his letter is anything but dry. Instead it is a beautiful treatise on the love of God. He stresses that we are to walk in the light of God's love and to love others with the same love we have received from him, to love "with actions and in truth" (3:18).

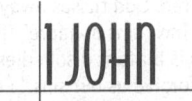

1 JOHN

The Word of Life

1 That which was from the beginning, which we have heard, which we have seen with our eyes, which we have looked at and our hands have touched—this we proclaim concerning the Word of life. ²The life appeared; we have seen it and testify to it, and we proclaim to you the eternal life, which was with the Father and has appeared to us. ³We proclaim to you what we have seen and heard, so that you also may have fellowship with us. And our fellowship is with the Father and with his Son, Jesus Christ. ⁴We write this to make our*ᵃ* joy complete.

Walking in the Light

⁵This is the message we have heard from him and declare to you: God is light; in him there is no darkness at all. ⁶If we claim to have fellowship with him yet walk in the darkness, we lie and do not live by the truth. ⁷But if we walk in the light, as he is in the light, we have fellowship with one another, and the blood of Jesus, his Son, purifies us from all*ᵇ* sin.

⁸If we claim to be without sin, we deceive ourselves and the truth is not in us. ⁹If we confess our sins, he is faithful and

ᵃ4 Some manuscripts *your*   *ᵇ7* Or *every*

just and will forgive us our sins and purify us from all unrighteousness. ¹⁰If we
claim we have not sinned, we make him
out to be a liar and his word has no place
in our lives.

2 My dear children, I write this to you so
that you will not sin. But if anybody
does sin, we have one who speaks to
the Father in our defense—Jesus Christ,
the Righteous One. ²He is the atoning
sacrifice for our sins, and not only for ours
but also for*a* the sins of the whole world.

³We know that we have come to know
him if we obey his commands. ⁴The man
who says, "I know him," but does not do
what he commands is a liar, and the truth
is not in him. ⁵But if anyone obeys his
word, God's love*b* is truly made complete in him. This is how we know we are
in him: ⁶Whoever claims to live in him
must walk as Jesus did.

⁷Dear friends, I am not writing you a

new command but an old one, which you
have had since the beginning. This old
command is the message you have
heard. ⁸Yet I am writing you a new command; its truth is seen in him and you,
because the darkness is passing and the
true light is already shining.

⁹Anyone who claims to be in the light
but hates his brother is still in the darkness. ¹⁰Whoever loves his brother lives in
the light, and there is nothing in him*c* to
make him stumble. ¹¹But whoever hates
his brother is in the darkness and walks
around in the darkness; he does not
know where he is going, because the
darkness has blinded him.

¹²I write to you, dear children,

*a*2 Or *He is the one who turns aside God's wrath,
taking away our sins, and not only ours but also*
*b*5 Or *word, love for God*   *c*10 Or *it*

WEDNESDAY

Read *1 John 1:1–10*
Key Verse *1 John 1:9*

No Exception – Jennifer Ranwez

Sometimes I feel as though I've sinned so much that I'm going to be
God's one exception. On judgment day, he'll turn to me and say, "You
know, Jenn, I can forgive everyone else who has asked me for forgiveness, but you—you've made a real mess of things. What you've
done is beyond my willingness to forgive."

What a relief it is to read 1 John 1:9 and know that this scenario
is not possible! Once I've repented, God tosses away my sins and
forgets them—he "remembers [my] sins no more" (Isaiah 43:25).

From lying to murder, all sin is blatant disobedience to God. Yet
with the promise that he "will forgive us our sins," I can be certain
of God's capability, his readiness and his faithfulness to forgive *anything*! Of course, I will often suffer the consequences of my actions,
but because of his grace I am purified in the most profound way.

I love the Biblical examples of how thrilled God is when his people are humble and repentant—stories of brother forgiving brother,
of father forgiving son, of the Son forgiving us all. Like the father of
the prodigal son (see Luke 15:11–32), God runs to meet us where
we are, embraces us and rejoices with us when we repent.

While God removes my sins "as far as the east is from the west"
(Psalm 103:12), he himself is never far away. And he will *always* forgive.

A Deeper Look
Psalm 103:8–14; Colossians 1:9–14

Go to page 1414 for your next devotional reading.

because your sins have been forgiven on account of his name.
13I write to you, fathers,
  because you have known him who is from the beginning.
I write to you, young men,
  because you have overcome the evil one.
I write to you, dear children,
  because you have known the Father.
14I write to you, fathers,
  because you have known him who is from the beginning.
I write to you, young men,
  because you are strong,
  and the word of God lives in you,
  and you have overcome the evil one.

Do Not Love the World

15Do not love the world or anything in the world. If anyone loves the world, the love of the Father is not in him. 16For everything in the world—the cravings of sinful man, the lust of his eyes and the boasting of what he has and does—comes not from the Father but from the world. 17The world and its desires pass away, but the man who does the will of God lives forever.

Warning Against Antichrists

18Dear children, this is the last hour; and as you have heard that the antichrist is coming, even now many antichrists have come. This is how we know it is the last hour. 19They went out from us, but they did not really belong to us. For if they had belonged to us, they would have remained with us; but their going showed that none of them belonged to us. 20But you have an anointing from the Holy One, and all of you know the truth.a 21I do not write to you because you do not know the truth, but because you do know it and because no lie comes from the truth. 22Who is the liar? It is the man who denies that Jesus is the Christ. Such a man is the antichrist—he denies the Father and the Son. 23No one who denies the Son has the Father; whoever acknowledges the Son has the Father also.
24See that what you have heard from the beginning remains in you. If it does, you also will remain in the Son and in the

Father. 25And this is what he promised us—even eternal life.
26I am writing these things to you about those who are trying to lead you astray. 27As for you, the anointing you received from him remains in you, and you do not need anyone to teach you. But as his anointing teaches you about all things and as that anointing is real, not counterfeit—just as it has taught you, remain in him.

Children of God

28And now, dear children, continue in him, so that when he appears we may be confident and unashamed before him at his coming.
29If you know that he is righteous, you know that everyone who does what is right has been born of him.
3 How great is the love the Father has lavished on us, that we should be called children of God! And that is what we are! The reason the world does not know us is that it did not know him. 2Dear friends, now we are children of God, and what we will be has not yet been made known. But we know that when he appears,b we shall be like him, for we shall see him as he is. 3Everyone who has this hope in him purifies himself, just as he is pure.
4Everyone who sins breaks the law; in fact, sin is lawlessness. 5But you know that he appeared so that he might take away our sins. And in him is no sin. 6No one who lives in him keeps on sinning. No one who continues to sin has either seen him or known him.
7Dear children, do not let anyone lead you astray. He who does what is right is righteous, just as he is righteous. 8He who does what is sinful is of the devil, because the devil has been sinning from the beginning. The reason the Son of God appeared was to destroy the devil's work. 9No one who is born of God will continue to sin, because God's seed remains in him; he cannot go on sinning, because he has been born of God. 10This is how we know who the children of God are and who the children of the devil are: Anyone who does not do what is right is not a child of God; nor is anyone who does not love his brother.

a20 Some manuscripts and you know all things
b2 Or when it is made known

Love One Another

[11]This is the message you heard from the beginning: We should love one another. [12]Do not be like Cain, who belonged to the evil one and murdered his brother. And why did he murder him? Because his own actions were evil and his brother's were righteous. [13]Do not be surprised, my brothers, if the world hates you. [14]We know that we have passed from death to life, because we love our brothers. Anyone who does not love remains in death. [15]Anyone who hates his brother is a murderer, and you know that no murderer has eternal life in him.

[16]This is how we know what love is: Jesus Christ laid down his life for us. And we ought to lay down our lives for our

---

THURSDAY

Read 1 John 2:1–29
Key Verses 1 John 2:15–17

Creeping Compromise – Mark Lewis

Three students, three issues. The first student had been taught by a religious leader, "A little pornography is not too harmful." After a few years of immersion, the pull seemed irresistible. The second student had acquired a credit card; with it he also quickly acquired some interest-heavy debt. A third struggled with anger that not only burned his heart but seared his relationships. Difficult struggles? Yes, but not all that bad, right? What's wrong with some soft porn, a few dollars' worth of debt or a little flare-up now and again? That's the deception!

We have to beware of creeping compromise. We tell ourselves, "Everyone is doing it," or "I can handle it," or "I have the right to . . . " We compromise, rationalize and justify actions or thoughts that we know are wrong. Little by little we slide into the world's patterns. Soon we find that we have embraced the world and that it has embraced us back with a crushing grip. Sin starts as a simple choice but soon seems to take on a life of its own. It grows, gets more possessive and becomes devastatingly destructive.

Sin's destructive nature bore fruit in the lives of the three students. The first kept sliding into adulterous relationships. Despite his love for his wife, unrestrained lust caused spells of temporary "sexual insanity." He grieved deeply for the lives he was destroying. The second became a millionaire but lost everything because he habitually spent money faster than he could make it. A third was finally arrested—his uncontrolled temper led him into physically abusing his wife and children. Choices that seemed small when these men were "young adults," left unchecked, had grown into obsessive, devastating patterns.

Those small, sinful actions that seem like "no big deal" can become obsessive behavioral patterns that become very hard to conquer; on our own we are just too weak. But Jesus Christ is strong, and can help us turn off the obsessive "self-destruct" mechanism; how much better, though, to rely on the Spirit to stop sinful actions and attitudes before "creeping compromise" lets them take root!

A Deeper Look
Romans 6:19–23; James 1:13–15; 2 Peter 2:18–19

Go to page 1416 for your next devotional reading.

brothers. [17]If anyone has material possessions and sees his brother in need but has no pity on him, how can the love of God be in him? [18]Dear children, let us not love with words or tongue but with actions and in truth. [19]This then is how we know that we belong to the truth, and how we set our hearts at rest in his presence [20]whenever our hearts condemn us. For God is greater than our hearts, and he knows everything.

[21]Dear friends, if our hearts do not condemn us, we have confidence before God [22]and receive from him anything we ask, because we obey his commands and do what pleases him. [23]And this is his command: to believe in the name of his Son, Jesus Christ, and to love one another as he commanded us. [24]Those who obey his commands live in him, and he in them. And this is how we know that he lives in us: We know it by the Spirit he gave us.

Test the Spirits

4 Dear friends, do not believe every spirit, but test the spirits to see whether they are from God, because many false prophets have gone out into the world. [2]This is how you can recognize the Spirit of God: Every spirit that acknowledges that Jesus Christ has come in the flesh is from God, [3]but every spirit that does not acknowledge Jesus is not from God. This is the spirit of the antichrist, which you have heard is coming and even now is already in the world.

[4]You, dear children, are from God and have overcome them, because the one who is in you is greater than the one who is in the world. [5]They are from the world and therefore speak from the viewpoint of the world, and the world listens to them. [6]We are from God, and whoever knows God listens to us; but whoever is not from God does not listen to us. This is how we recognize the Spirit[a] of truth and the spirit of falsehood.

God's Love and Ours

[7]Dear friends, let us love one another, for love comes from God. Everyone who loves has been born of God and knows God. [8]Whoever does not love does not know God, because God is love. [9]This is how God showed his love among us: He sent his one and only Son[b] into the world that we might live through him.

[10]This is love: not that we loved God, but that he loved us and sent his Son as an atoning sacrifice for[c] our sins. [11]Dear friends, since God so loved us, we also ought to love one another. [12]No one has ever seen God; but if we love one another, God lives in us and his love is made complete in us.

[13]We know that we live in him and he in us, because he has given us of his Spirit. [14]And we have seen and testify that the Father has sent his Son to be the Savior of the world. [15]If anyone acknowledges that Jesus is the Son of God, God lives in him and he in God. [16]And so we know and rely on the love God has for us.

God is love. Whoever lives in love lives in God, and God in him. [17]In this way, love is made complete among us so that we will have confidence on the day of judgment, because in this world we are like him. [18]There is no fear in love. But perfect love drives out fear, because fear has to do with punishment. The one who fears is not made perfect in love.

[19]We love because he first loved us. [20]If anyone says, "I love God," yet hates his brother, he is a liar. For anyone who does not love his brother, whom he has seen, cannot love God, whom he has not seen. [21]And he has given us this command: Whoever loves God must also love his brother.

Faith in the Son of God

5 Everyone who believes that Jesus is the Christ is born of God, and everyone

[a]6 Or *spirit*   [b]9 Or *his only begotten Son*
[c]10 Or *as the one who would turn aside his wrath, taking away*

POINT OF INTEREST

1 John 3:11–16

Love one another. Three simple words. Sounds easy, but it may be the hardest command of all. However, it is the only possible response to Jesus Christ's great love for us. It's the only possible response to his sacrifice. And it's the litmus test of our love for God. We are to serve others as Jesus Christ served us.

who loves the father loves his child as well. ²This is how we know that we love the children of God: by loving God and carrying out his commands. ³This is love for God: to obey his commands. And his commands are not burdensome, ⁴for everyone born of God overcomes the world. This is the victory that has overcome the world, even our faith. ⁵Who is it that overcomes the world? Only he who believes that Jesus is the Son of God.

⁶This is the one who came by water and blood—Jesus Christ. He did not come by water only, but by water and blood. And it is the Spirit who testifies, because the Spirit is the truth. ⁷For there are three that testify: ⁸the*a* Spirit, the water and the blood; and the three are in agreement. ⁹We accept man's testimony, but God's testimony is greater because it is the testimony of God, which he has given about his Son. ¹⁰Anyone who believes in the Son of God has this testimony in his heart. Anyone who does not believe God has made him out to be a liar, because he has not believed the testi-

a 7,8 Late manuscripts of the Vulgate *testify in heaven: the Father, the Word and the Holy Spirit, and these three are one. 8And there are three that testify on earth: the* (not found in any Greek manuscript before the sixteenth century)

FRIDAY

Read 1 John 5:1–21
Key Verses 1 John 5:11–13

Knowing Where We Stand — Greg Bryan

I was sitting in my psychology class with about a hundred other college students when suddenly the ground moved beneath me and the whole room began to shake. None of us knew how to react. We just sat and stared at each other for what seemed like minutes but actually was only seconds. It was an earthquake . . . but in *Ohio*?

We live in a very unstable world where strange things happen—like earthquakes in northeastern Ohio. But one thing that we can be sure about is our eternal standing with God. God doesn't want us to have an unstable faith. He wants us to know where we stand with him, and he has given us his word of assurance. Our standing with God is not dependent on what we *do*; it's dependent on what God has *done* for us through his Son.

I used to believe that if the good things I had done outweighed the bad, I would go to heaven. During that time I was never sure whether I was being quite good enough. Then I learned about what God had already done for me. He had sent his Son, Jesus Christ, to earth to die for my sins and the sins of the world. Through placing my trust in Jesus Christ rather than in my own feeble attempts at being "good," I'd have assurance that I would one day be with him in heaven. Once I made the decision to accept Jesus Christ as my Savior, my eternal destiny was set, for "he who has the Son has life."

What are you trusting in? Are you trusting in what you *do* or in what Jesus Christ has *done* for you? Put your trust in Jesus. Trust him as your Savior. Although the ground may sometimes shake under your feet, you can be sure of your standing with God.

A Deeper Look
Ephesians 2:8–10; Titus 3:3–7

Go to page 1419 for your next devotional reading.

mony God has given about his Son. [11]And this is the testimony: God has given us eternal life, and this life is in his Son. [12]He who has the Son has life; he who does not have the Son of God does not have life.

Concluding Remarks

[13]I write these things to you who believe in the name of the Son of God so that you may know that you have eternal life. [14]This is the confidence we have in approaching God: that if we ask anything according to his will, he hears us. [15]And if we know that he hears us—whatever we ask—we know that we have what we asked of him.

[16]If anyone sees his brother commit a sin that does not lead to death, he should pray and God will give him life. I refer to those whose sin does not lead to death. There is a sin that leads to death. I am not saying that he should pray about that. [17]All wrongdoing is sin, and there is sin that does not lead to death.

[18]We know that anyone born of God does not continue to sin; the one who was born of God keeps him safe, and the evil one cannot harm him. [19]We know

that we are children of God, and that the whole world is under the control of the evil one. [20]We know also that the Son of God has come and has given us understanding, so that we may know him who is true. And we are in him who is true— even in his Son Jesus Christ. He is the true God and eternal life.

[21]Dear children, keep yourselves from idols.

POINT OF INTEREST   1 John 4:1

How do we test the spirits? Have them take an exam? No, Acts 17:11 records that the Christians from Berea compared Paul's message to the Scriptures to see whether or not what Paul said was true. Any message from God will agree with what God has already said. Anything or anyone that doesn't agree with the Word of God isn't from God.

After reading 2 John, you *may think you've read the Cliff Notes to 1 John. While this letter was written for a different purpose, it returns to many of the same themes. In this second letter, John warns Christians to be certain of their beliefs so they can resist the efforts of false teachers. As you read, think about how you can stay on target spiritually. This book will challenge you to "watch out" (verse 8) and be certain about what you believe and how you live it.*

2 JOHN

¹The elder,

To the chosen lady and her children, whom I love in the truth—and not I only, but also all who know the truth— ²because of the truth, which lives in us and will be with us forever:

³Grace, mercy and peace from God the Father and from Jesus Christ, the Father's Son, will be with us in truth and love.

⁴It has given me great joy to find some of your children walking in the truth, just as the Father commanded us. ⁵And now, dear lady, I am not writing you a new command but one we have had from the beginning. I ask that we love one another. ⁶And this is love: that we walk in obedience to his commands. As you have heard from the beginning, his command is that you walk in love.

⁷Many deceivers, who do not acknowledge Jesus Christ as coming in the flesh, have gone out into the world. Any such person is the deceiver and the antichrist. ⁸Watch out that you do not lose what you have worked for, but that you may be rewarded fully. ⁹Anyone who runs ahead and does not continue in the teaching of Christ does not have God; whoever continues in the teaching has both the Father and the Son. ¹⁰If anyone comes to you and does not bring this teaching, do not take him into your house or welcome him. ¹¹Anyone who welcomes him shares in his wicked work.

¹²I have much to write to you, but I do not want to use paper and ink. Instead, I hope to visit you and talk with you face to face, so that our joy may be complete.

¹³The children of your chosen sister send their greetings.

Read 2 John 1–13
Key Verses 2 John 5–6

A New Song

When Moses received the Ten Commandments from the hand of God, the list was comprehensive and complete. They were perfect—the words to God's love song. But in Jesus Christ, God gave us the "music": "For the law was given through Moses; grace and truth came through Jesus Christ" (John 1:17). Jesus summed up the intent and the fulfillment of the law with the two "greatest" commandments: We are to love God and we are to love others (see Matthew 22:37–40). John plays the refrain again when he reiterates Jesus' command to "love one another" (John 13:34). Heaven only knows how much the world needs that kind of love song, and Jesus taught us and gave us the voices to sing it—to make it the score of our lives—in the same way he did.

The one and only source of that love is God, whose love moved him to send his Son to die for us—love that demonstrated both intense emotion and intentional action. Unexpected! Amazing! Extravagant! And God's love shines in us when we love each other with that same kind of boundless intensity.

Digging Into the Word

1. Why does God take this topic of love so seriously?—
   1 Corinthians 13:13; Galatians 5:6; Colossians 3:12–14
2. Why must love be seen in actions?—*John 15:13; Ephesians 5:1–2; James 2:14–19; 1 John 3:16–18*

Move Into Service

Identify one action of service you can perform in the next twenty-four hours. How will it show the love of Jesus Christ?

One Step Deeper

John 15:12; 1 Peter 1:22

Go to page 1421 for your next devotional reading.

What's the correct way to handle opposition to leadership, especially when that opposition comes from someone on an ego trip? Third John provides some insight. It seems that Diotrephes had rejected the itinerant teachers John sent to his church and alienated those who were trying to be hospitable. John commends his friend Gaius for his faithfulness and love for those traveling teachers. John doesn't avoid the problem but deals with it honestly and directly, a great example for leaders then and now!

3 JOHN

¹The elder,

To my dear friend Gaius, whom I love in the truth.

²Dear friend, I pray that you may enjoy good health and that all may go well with you, even as your soul is getting along well. ³It gave me great joy to have some brothers come and tell about your faithfulness to the truth and how you continue to walk in the truth. ⁴I have no greater joy than to hear that my children are walking in the truth.

⁵Dear friend, you are faithful in what you are doing for the brothers, even though they are strangers to you. ⁶They have told the church about your love.

You will do well to send them on their way in a manner worthy of God. ⁷It was for the sake of the Name that they went out, receiving no help from the pagans. ⁸We ought therefore to show hospitality to such men so that we may work together for the truth.

⁹I wrote to the church, but Diotrephes, who loves to be first, will have nothing to do with us. ¹⁰So if I come, I will call attention to what he is doing, gossiping maliciously about us. Not satisfied with that, he refuses to welcome the brothers. He also stops those who want to do so and puts them out of the church.

¹¹Dear friend, do not imitate what is evil but what is good. Anyone who does what is good is from God. Anyone who does what is evil has not seen God. ¹²De-

metrius is well spoken of by everyone—and even by the truth itself. We also speak well of him, and you know that our testimony is true.

¹³I have much to write you, but I do not want to do so with pen and ink. ¹⁴I

hope to see you soon, and we will talk face to face.

Peace to you. The friends here send their greetings. Greet the friends there by name.

MONDAY

Read *3 John 1–14*
Key Verses *3 John 6–8*

For the Sake of the Name – Greg Bryan

I did some pretty crazy things for God while I was in college—things like carrying a coffin around campus, performing a skit in a crowded lunchroom, witnessing at the largest fraternity party on campus and sharing my testimony with a guy who was trying to sell me drugs. I did these things because I wanted to make an eternal difference for Jesus Christ.

In this letter, the apostle John is urging another Christian brother, Gaius, to continue to make a difference for Jesus by lending support to traveling missionaries. John gives three good reasons to get involved in supporting missions: First, doing so demonstrates love. Second, missionaries look to believers for help as they obediently follow God's calling. Third, helping missionaries honors God and is a way believers can work together to witness to others and spread the truth.

You can increase your impact for Jesus Christ by collaborating with other believers. You don't have to carry a coffin around campus, but you can open your dorm room to host a Bible study led by your local campus missionary. You can support a missionary and your local pastor by writing letters of encouragement or by praying for them regularly. You can also begin giving regular financial support to those who work in full-time Christian service positions.

These are just a few ways you can make an eternal difference on your campus and in your world by supporting others who have gone out "for the sake of the Name." What's one thing you can do this week that will begin to make an eternal difference for Jesus Christ?

A Deeper Look
Romans 12:13; 2 Corinthians 1:3–11

Go to page 1423 for your next devotional reading.

*S*ometimes a slight variation of the truth is like a small spark of error that starts an inferno of heresy. Jude understood this, which is why he wrote this letter. Immoral men in the church were trying to convince believers that being saved by God's grace gave them freedom to sin. You can imagine what these men said: "Our sins are forgiven by grace and we are no longer under the law; go ahead and sin away because it doesn't matter." Jude's answer sounds a fire alarm that demands a response of unwavering faith.

JUDE

¹Jude, a servant of Jesus Christ and a brother of James,

To those who have been called, who are loved by God the Father and kept by*a* Jesus Christ:

²Mercy, peace and love be yours in abundance.

The Sin and Doom of Godless Men

³Dear friends, although I was very eager to write to you about the salvation we share, I felt I had to write and urge you to contend for the faith that was once for all entrusted to the saints. ⁴For certain men whose condemnation was written about*b* long ago have secretly slipped in among you. They are godless men, who change the grace of our God into a license for immorality and deny Jesus Christ our only Sovereign and Lord.

⁵Though you already know all this, I want to remind you that the Lord*c* delivered his people out of Egypt, but later destroyed those who did not believe. ⁶And the angels who did not keep their positions of authority but abandoned their own home—these he has kept in darkness, bound with everlasting chains for judgment on the great Day. ⁷In a similar way, Sodom and Gomorrah and the surrounding towns gave themselves up to sexual immorality and perversion. They serve as an example of those who suffer the punishment of eternal fire.

⁸In the very same way, these dreamers pollute their own bodies, reject authority and slander celestial beings. ⁹But even the archangel Michael, when he was dis-

*a*1 Or *for*; or *in*   *b*4 Or *men who were marked out for condemnation*   *c*5 Some early manuscripts *Jesus* puting with the devil about the body of Moses, did not dare to bring a slanderous accusation against him, but said, "The Lord rebuke you!" [10]Yet these men speak abusively against whatever they do not understand; and what things they do understand by instinct, like unreasoning animals—these are the very things that destroy them.

[11]Woe to them! They have taken the way of Cain; they have rushed for profit into Balaam's error; they have been destroyed in Korah's rebellion.

[12]These men are blemishes at your love feasts, eating with you without the slightest qualm—shepherds who feed only themselves. They are clouds without rain, blown along by the wind; autumn trees, without fruit and uprooted—twice dead. [13]They are wild waves of the sea, foaming up their shame; wandering stars, for whom blackest darkness has been reserved forever.

[14]Enoch, the seventh from Adam, prophesied about these men: "See, the Lord is coming with thousands upon thousands of his holy ones [15]to judge everyone, and to convict all the ungodly of

---

TUESDAY

Read Jude 1–25
Key Verse Jude 4

Traitors Among Us – John Carroll

When Linda's phone rang, she froze in terror. For several days she had been harassed by an unknown caller. This man seemed to know her schedule, timing the calls to coincide with her arrival from class and work. She shared her ordeal with Jerry, an old friend from high school, with whom she had a biology class.

Eventually, the police were able to trace the caller; it turned out to be Jerry. This was doubly devastating to Linda—the perpetrator was the very person she had trusted!

The believers to whom Jude wrote had experienced a similar betrayal by men who had "secretly slipped in among [them]." These phonies had gone undetected and were undermining the believers' faith. How could this happen?

First, the believers trusted a superficial evaluation of the traitors. Their message sounded familiar; they talked about the grace of God, but they changed the message slightly to allow new freedoms. This new spin appealed to the believers.

Second, the believers overlooked the inconsistency between the life and message of these men. A messenger who gives lip service to God but fails to demonstrate a godly lifestyle should immediately be suspect as one who is denying Jesus as the sovereign Lord in his or her life.

If we want to avoid being led away by false teachers, we have to evaluate any teaching based on God's Word and be alert to discrepancies between a person's life and message. In this way, false teachers and phony spiritual leaders will not easily catch us off guard. True spiritual leaders will encourage others to hold them accountable. They will encourage their Christian brothers and sisters to examine the Scriptures to test if the teaching and the teacher are genuine.

A Deeper Look
Acts 17:11; 2 Timothy 3:10–17; 1 John 4:1–3

Go to page 1429 for your next devotional reading.

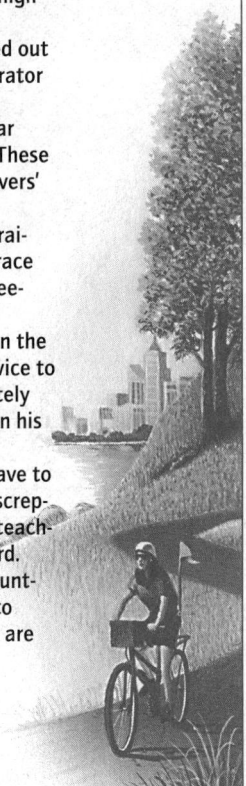

all the ungodly acts they have done in the ungodly way, and of all the harsh words ungodly sinners have spoken against him." [16]These men are grumblers and faultfinders; they follow their own evil desires; they boast about themselves and flatter others for their own advantage.

A Call to Persevere

[17]But, dear friends, remember what the apostles of our Lord Jesus Christ foretold. [18]They said to you, "In the last times there will be scoffers who will follow their own ungodly desires." [19]These are the men who divide you, who follow mere natural instincts and do not have the Spirit.

[20]But you, dear friends, build yourselves up in your most holy faith and pray in the Holy Spirit. [21]Keep yourselves in God's love as you wait for the mercy of our Lord Jesus Christ to bring you to eternal life.

[22]Be merciful to those who doubt; [23]snatch others from the fire and save them; to others show mercy, mixed with fear—hating even the clothing stained by corrupted flesh.

Doxology

[24]To him who is able to keep you from falling and to present you before his glorious presence without fault and with great joy— [25]to the only God our Savior be glory, majesty, power and authority, through Jesus Christ our Lord, before all ages, now and forevermore! Amen.

*S*even stars, seven lampstands

and seven bowls. The book of life. The mark of the beast.

It's tempting to get caught up in the symbolism and

prophecies we find in Revelation. But if we focus on these

things, we'll miss the point. God gave the apostle John

these visions to reassure Christians everywhere that God's

kingdom will ultimately prevail. What's more, John's

vision unfolds an awesome depiction of the return of Jesus

Christ as victorious Savior, resplendent in light and

beauty. As you read the final pages of this wonderful,

challenging book, be sure to add

your own assent: "Amen. Come,

Lord Jesus" (22:20).

REVELATION

Prologue

1 The revelation of Jesus Christ, which God gave him to show his servants what must soon take place. He made it known by sending his angel to his servant John, ²who testifies to everything he saw—that is, the word of God and the testimony of Jesus Christ. ³Blessed is the one who reads the words of this prophecy, and blessed are those who hear it and take to heart what is written in it, because the time is near.

Greetings and Doxology

⁴John,

To the seven churches in the province of Asia:

Grace and peace to you from him who is, and who was, and who is to come, and from the seven spirits*a* before his throne, ⁵and from Jesus Christ, who is the faithful witness, the firstborn from the dead, and the ruler of the kings of the earth.

To him who loves us and has freed us from our sins by his blood, ⁶and has made us to be a kingdom and priests to

a4 Or *the sevenfold Spirit*

serve his God and Father—to him be glory and power for ever and ever! Amen.

[7]Look, he is coming with the clouds,
    and every eye will see him,
even those who pierced him;
    and all the peoples of the earth
        will mourn because of him.
                So shall it be! Amen.

[8]"I am the Alpha and the Omega," says the Lord God, "who is, and who was, and who is to come, the Almighty."

One Like a Son of Man

[9]I, John, your brother and companion in the suffering and kingdom and patient endurance that are ours in Jesus, was on the island of Patmos because of the word of God and the testimony of Jesus. [10]On the Lord's Day I was in the Spirit, and I heard behind me a loud voice like a trumpet, [11]which said: "Write on a scroll what you see and send it to the seven churches: to Ephesus, Smyrna, Pergamum, Thyatira, Sardis, Philadelphia and Laodicea."

[12]I turned around to see the voice that was speaking to me. And when I turned I saw seven golden lampstands, [13]and among the lampstands was someone "like a son of man,"[a] dressed in a robe reaching down to his feet and with a golden sash around his chest. [14]His head and hair were white like wool, as white as snow, and his eyes were like blazing fire. [15]His feet were like bronze glowing in a furnace, and his voice was like the sound of rushing waters. [16]In his right hand he held seven stars, and out of his mouth came a sharp double-edged sword. His face was like the sun shining in all its brilliance.

[17]When I saw him, I fell at his feet as though dead. Then he placed his right hand on me and said: "Do not be afraid. I am the First and the Last. [18]I am the Living One; I was dead, and behold I am alive for ever and ever! And I hold the keys of death and Hades.

[19]"Write, therefore, what you have seen, what is now and what will take place later. [20]The mystery of the seven stars that you saw in my right hand and of the seven golden lampstands is this: The seven stars are the angels[b] of the seven churches, and the seven lampstands are the seven churches.

To the Church in Ephesus

[2] "To the angel[c] of the church in Ephesus write:

These are the words of him who holds the seven stars in his right hand and walks among the seven golden lampstands: [2]I know your deeds, your hard work and your perseverance. I know that you cannot tolerate wicked men, that you have tested those who claim to be apostles but are not, and have found them false. [3]You have persevered and have endured hardships for my name, and have not grown weary.

[4]Yet I hold this against you: You have forsaken your first love. [5]Remember the height from which you have fallen! Repent and do the things you did at first. If you do not repent, I will come to you and remove your lampstand from its place. [6]But you have this in your favor: You hate the practices of the Nicolaitans, which I also hate.

[7]He who has an ear, let him hear what the Spirit says to the churches. To him who overcomes, I will give the right to eat from the tree of life, which is in the paradise of God.

To the Church in Smyrna

[8]"To the angel of the church in Smyrna write:

These are the words of him who

---

[a]13 Daniel 7:13   [b]20 Or *messengers*   [c]1 Or *messenger*; also in verses 8, 12 and 18

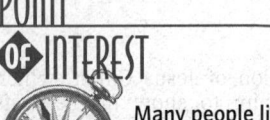

POINT OF INTEREST   Revelation 1:8

Many people like to say that Jesus wasn't God; he was merely a good teacher who lived a godly life. They say that if we follow him, we are to follow him only as a good example, not as Lord. That's a very old heresy. Don't fall for it. In this verse the Lord God declares that he is the "Alpha and the Omega." Compare it with John 8:58; 17:5; Hebrews 1:3; Revelation 22:13.

is the First and the Last, who died and came to life again. ⁹I know your afflictions and your poverty—yet you are rich! I know the slander of those who say they are Jews and are not, but are a synagogue of Satan. ¹⁰Do not be afraid of what you are about to suffer. I tell you, the devil will put some of you in prison to test you, and you will suffer persecution for ten days. Be faithful, even to the point of death, and I will give you the crown of life.

¹¹He who has an ear, let him hear what the Spirit says to the churches. He who overcomes will not be hurt at all by the second death.

To the Church in Pergamum

¹²"To the angel of the church in Pergamum write:

These are the words of him who has the sharp, double-edged sword. ¹³I know where you live—where Satan has his throne. Yet you remain true to my name. You did not renounce your faith in me, even in the days of Antipas, my faithful witness, who was put to death in your city—where Satan lives.

¹⁴Nevertheless, I have a few things against you: You have people there who hold to the teaching of Balaam, who taught Balak to entice the Israelites to sin by eating food sacrificed to idols and by committing sexual immorality. ¹⁵Likewise you also have those who hold to the teaching of the Nicolaitans. ¹⁶Repent therefore! Otherwise, I will soon come to you and will fight against them with the sword of my mouth.

¹⁷He who has an ear, let him hear what the Spirit says to the churches. To him who overcomes, I will give some of the hidden manna. I will also give him a white stone with a new name written on it, known only to him who receives it.

To the Church in Thyatira

¹⁸"To the angel of the church in Thyatira write:

These are the words of the Son of God, whose eyes are like blazing fire and whose feet are like burnished bronze. ¹⁹I know your deeds, your love and faith, your service and perseverance, and that you are now doing more than you did at first.

²⁰Nevertheless, I have this against you: You tolerate that woman Jezebel, who calls herself a prophetess. By her teaching she misleads my servants into sexual immorality and the eating of food sacrificed to idols. ²¹I have given her time to repent of her immorality, but she is unwilling. ²²So I will cast her on a bed of suffering, and I will make those who commit adultery with her suffer intensely, unless they repent of her ways. ²³I will strike her children dead. Then all the churches will know that I am he who searches hearts and minds, and I will repay each of you according to your deeds. ²⁴Now I say to the rest of you in Thyatira, to you who do not hold to her teaching and have not learned Satan's so-called deep secrets (I will not impose any other burden on you): ²⁵Only hold on to what you have until I come.

²⁶To him who overcomes and does my will to the end, I will give authority over the nations—

²⁷'He will rule them with an iron scepter;
he will dash them to pieces like pottery'ᵃ—

just as I have received authority from my Father. ²⁸I will also give him the morning star. ²⁹He who has an ear, let him hear what the Spirit says to the churches.

To the Church in Sardis

3 "To the angelᵇ of the church in Sardis write:

These are the words of him who holds the seven spiritsᶜ of God and the seven stars. I know your deeds; you have a reputation of being alive, but you are dead. ²Wake up! Strengthen what remains and is about to die, for I have not found your deeds complete in the sight of my God. ³Remember, therefore, what you have received and heard; obey it, and repent. But if you do

ᵃ27 Psalm 2:9   ᵇ1 Or messenger; also in verses 7 and 14   ᶜ1 Or the sevenfold Spirit not wake up, I will come like a thief, and you will not know at what time I will come to you.

⁴Yet you have a few people in Sardis who have not soiled their clothes. They will walk with me, dressed in white, for they are worthy. ⁵He who overcomes will, like them, be dressed in white. I will never blot out his name from the book of life, but will acknowledge his name before my Father and his angels. ⁶He who has an ear, let him hear what the Spirit says to the churches.

To the Church in Philadelphia

⁷"To the angel of the church in Philadelphia write:

These are the words of him who is holy and true, who holds the key of David. What he opens no one can shut, and what he shuts no one can open. ⁸I know your deeds. See, I have placed before you an open door that no one can shut. I know that you have little strength, yet you have kept my word and have not denied my name. ⁹I will make those who are of the synagogue of Satan, who claim to be Jews though they are not, but are liars—I will make them come and fall down at your feet and acknowledge that I have loved you. ¹⁰Since you have kept my command to endure patiently, I will also keep you from the hour of trial that is going to come upon the whole world to test those who live on the earth.

¹¹I am coming soon. Hold on to what you have, so that no one will take your crown. ¹²Him who overcomes I will make a pillar in the temple of my God. Never again will he leave it. I will write on him the name of my God and the name of the city of my God, the new Jerusalem, which is coming down out of heaven from my God; and I will also write on him my new name. ¹³He who has an ear, let him hear what the Spirit says to the churches.

To the Church in Laodicea

¹⁴"To the angel of the church in Laodicea write:

These are the words of the Amen,

the faithful and true witness, the ruler of God's creation. ¹⁵I know your deeds, that you are neither cold nor hot. I wish you were either one or the other! ¹⁶So, because you are lukewarm—neither hot nor cold—I am about to spit you out of my mouth. ¹⁷You say, 'I am rich; I have acquired wealth and do not need a thing.' But you do not realize that you are wretched, pitiful, poor, blind and naked. ¹⁸I counsel you to buy from me gold refined in the fire, so you can become rich; and white clothes to wear, so you can cover your shameful nakedness; and salve to put on your eyes, so you can see.

¹⁹Those whom I love I rebuke and discipline. So be earnest, and repent. ²⁰Here I am! I stand at the door and knock. If anyone hears my voice and opens the door, I will come in and eat with him, and he with me.

²¹To him who overcomes, I will give the right to sit with me on my throne, just as I overcame and sat down with my Father on his throne. ²²He who has an ear, let him hear what the Spirit says to the churches.'"

The Throne in Heaven

4 After this I looked, and there before me was a door standing open in heaven. And the voice I had first heard speaking to me like a trumpet said, "Come up here, and I will show you what must take place after this." ²At once I was in the Spirit, and there before me was a throne in heaven with someone sitting on it. ³And the one who sat there had the appearance of jasper and carnelian. A rainbow, resembling an emerald, encircled the throne. ⁴Surrounding the throne were twenty-four other thrones, and seated on them were twenty-four elders. They were dressed in white and had crowns of gold on their heads. ⁵From the throne came flashes of lightning, rumblings and peals of thunder. Before the throne, seven lamps were blazing. These are the seven spirits*a* of God. ⁶Also before the throne there was what looked like a sea of glass, clear as crystal.

In the center, around the throne, were

a5 Or the sevenfold Spirit

four living creatures, and they were covered with eyes, in front and in back. ⁷The first living creature was like a lion, the second was like an ox, the third had a face like a man, the fourth was like a flying eagle. ⁸Each of the four living creatures had six wings and was covered with eyes all around, even under his wings. Day and night they never stop saying:

"Holy, holy, holy
is the Lord God Almighty,
who was, and is, and is to come."

⁹Whenever the living creatures give glory, honor and thanks to him who sits on the throne and who lives for ever and ever, ¹⁰the twenty-four elders fall down before him who sits on the throne, and worship him who lives for ever and ever. They lay their crowns before the throne and say:

¹¹"You are worthy, our Lord and God,

to receive glory and honor and
power,
for you created all things,
and by your will they were created
and have their being."

The Scroll and the Lamb

5 Then I saw in the right hand of him who sat on the throne a scroll with writing on both sides and sealed with seven seals. ²And I saw a mighty angel proclaiming in a loud voice, "Who is worthy to break the seals and open the scroll?" ³But no one in heaven or on earth or under the earth could open the scroll or even look inside it. ⁴I wept and wept because no one was found who was worthy to open the scroll or look inside. ⁵Then one of the elders said to me, "Do not weep! See, the Lion of the tribe of Judah, the Root of David, has triumphed. He is able to open the scroll and its seven seals."

⁶Then I saw a Lamb, looking as if it had been slain, standing in the center of

---

WEDNESDAY

Read *Revelation 4:1—5:14*
Key Verse *Revelation 4:11*

Complimenting God – Tina Larson

I think the strangest compliment I ever received was, "Birds become you." At the time I was wearing a dress with a bird design in the fabric. My response was, "Maybe I should get a stuffed parrot and wear it on my shoulder!" Since that bizarre conversation, I've often thought about genuine compliments and expressions of praise and how best to express them.

Revelation 4:11 is a type of compliment directed to God himself: "You are worthy, our Lord and God, to receive glory and honor and power." As the creator and sustainer of all things, God is the only One worthy of this kind of worship. This awesome scene in Revelation is the crescendo and culmination of the praise of all God's saints.

Thinking of praise as a compliment to God has changed my prayer life. I used to begin praising him by reciting a list of his attributes. Nothing wrong with that, but it was a bit rote and impersonal. But now I try to phrase my prayer as I would to a dear friend: "God, you are so good! Everything you do is the best!" As I learn to praise God more genuinely, I can better acknowledge that he truly is worthy of all the praise I can give him.

A Deeper Look
1 Chronicles 29:10–13; Psalm 147:1–20; Ephesians 3:20–21

Go to page 1432 for your next devotional reading.

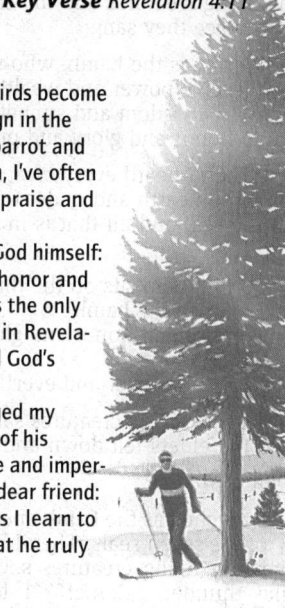

the throne, encircled by the four living creatures and the elders. He had seven horns and seven eyes, which are the seven spirits*a* of God sent out into all the earth. ⁷He came and took the scroll from the right hand of him who sat on the throne. ⁸And when he had taken it, the four living creatures and the twenty-four elders fell down before the Lamb. Each one had a harp and they were holding golden bowls full of incense, which are the prayers of the saints. ⁹And they sang a new song:

"You are worthy to take the scroll
    and to open its seals,
because you were slain,
    and with your blood you
        purchased men for God
    from every tribe and language and
        people and nation.
¹⁰You have made them to be a
        kingdom and priests to serve
        our God,
    and they will reign on the earth."

¹¹Then I looked and heard the voice of many angels, numbering thousands upon thousands, and ten thousand times ten thousand. They encircled the throne and the living creatures and the elders. ¹²In a loud voice they sang:

"Worthy is the Lamb, who was slain,
    to receive power and wealth and
        wisdom and strength
    and honor and glory and praise!"

¹³Then I heard every creature in heaven and on earth and under the earth and on the sea, and all that is in them, singing:

"To him who sits on the throne and
        to the Lamb
be praise and honor and glory and
        power,
        for ever and ever!"

¹⁴The four living creatures said, "Amen," and the elders fell down and worshiped.

The Seals

6 I watched as the Lamb opened the first of the seven seals. Then I heard one of the four living creatures say in a voice like thunder, "Come!" ²I looked, and there before me was a white horse! Its rider held a bow, and he was given a crown, and he rode out as a conqueror bent on conquest.

³When the Lamb opened the second seal, I heard the second living creature say, "Come!" ⁴Then another horse came out, a fiery red one. Its rider was given power to take peace from the earth and to make men slay each other. To him was given a large sword.

⁵When the Lamb opened the third seal, I heard the third living creature say, "Come!" I looked, and there before me was a black horse! Its rider was holding a pair of scales in his hand. ⁶Then I heard what sounded like a voice among the four living creatures, saying, "A quart*b* of wheat for a day's wages,*c* and three quarts of barley for a day's wages,*c* and do not damage the oil and the wine!"

⁷When the Lamb opened the fourth seal, I heard the voice of the fourth living creature say, "Come!" ⁸I looked, and there before me was a pale horse! Its rider was named Death, and Hades was following close behind him. They were given power over a fourth of the earth to kill by sword, famine and plague, and by the wild beasts of the earth.

⁹When he opened the fifth seal, I saw under the altar the souls of those who had been slain because of the word of God and the testimony they had maintained. ¹⁰They called out in a loud voice, "How long, Sovereign Lord, holy and true, until you judge the inhabitants of the earth and avenge our blood?" ¹¹Then each of them was given a white robe, and they were told to wait a little longer, until the number of their fellow servants and brothers who were to be killed as they had been was completed.

¹²I watched as he opened the sixth seal. There was a great earthquake. The sun turned black like sackcloth made of goat hair, the whole moon turned blood red, ¹³and the stars in the sky fell to earth, as late figs drop from a fig tree when shaken by a strong wind. ¹⁴The sky receded like a scroll, rolling up, and every mountain and island was removed from its place.

¹⁵Then the kings of the earth, the princes, the generals, the rich, the mighty, and every slave and every free man hid in caves and among the rocks of the mountains. ¹⁶They called to the mountains and the rocks, "Fall on us and hide us from the face of him who sits on the throne and from the wrath of the

---

*a*6 Or *the sevenfold Spirit* (probably about a liter)   *b*6 Greek *a choinix*   *c*6 Greek *a denarius*

Lamb! [17]For the great day of their wrath has come, and who can stand?"

144,000 Sealed

7 After this I saw four angels standing at the four corners of the earth, holding back the four winds of the earth to prevent any wind from blowing on the land or on the sea or on any tree. [2]Then I saw another angel coming up from the east, having the seal of the living God. He called out in a loud voice to the four angels who had been given power to harm the land and the sea: [3]"Do not harm the land or the sea or the trees until we put a seal on the foreheads of the servants of our God." [4]Then I heard the number of those who were sealed: 144,000 from all the tribes of Israel.

[5]From the tribe of Judah 12,000
were sealed,
from the tribe of Reuben 12,000,
from the tribe of Gad 12,000,
[6]from the tribe of Asher 12,000,
from the tribe of Naphtali 12,000,
from the tribe of Manasseh 12,000,
[7]from the tribe of Simeon 12,000,
from the tribe of Levi 12,000,
from the tribe of Issachar 12,000,
[8]from the tribe of Zebulun 12,000,
from the tribe of Joseph 12,000,
from the tribe of Benjamin 12,000.

The Great Multitude in White Robes

[9]After this I looked and there before me was a great multitude that no one could count, from every nation, tribe, people and language, standing before the throne and in front of the Lamb. They were wearing white robes and were holding palm branches in their hands. [10]And they cried out in a loud voice:

"Salvation belongs to our God,
who sits on the throne,
and to the Lamb."

[11]All the angels were standing around the throne and around the elders and the four living creatures. They fell down on their faces before the throne and worshiped God, [12]saying:

"Amen!
Praise and glory
and wisdom and thanks and honor
and power and strength
be to our God for ever and ever.
Amen!"

[13]Then one of the elders asked me, "These in white robes—who are they, and where did they come from?"

[14]I answered, "Sir, you know."

And he said, "These are they who have come out of the great tribulation; they have washed their robes and made them white in the blood of the Lamb. [15]Therefore,

"they are before the throne of God
and serve him day and night in his
temple;
and he who sits on the throne will
spread his tent over them.
[16]Never again will they hunger;
never again will they thirst.
The sun will not beat upon them,
nor any scorching heat.
[17]For the Lamb at the center of the
throne will be their shepherd;
he will lead them to springs of
living water.
And God will wipe away every tear
from their eyes."

The Seventh Seal and the Golden Censer

8 When he opened the seventh seal, there was silence in heaven for about half an hour.

[2]And I saw the seven angels who stand before God, and to them were given seven trumpets.

[3]Another angel, who had a golden censer, came and stood at the altar. He was given much incense to offer, with the prayers of all the saints, on the golden altar before the throne. [4]The smoke of the incense, together with the prayers of the saints, went up before God from the angel's hand. [5]Then the angel took the censer, filled it with fire from the altar, and hurled it on the earth; and there came peals of thunder, rumblings, flashes of lightning and an earthquake.

The Trumpets

[6]Then the seven angels who had the seven trumpets prepared to sound them.

[7]The first angel sounded his trumpet, and there came hail and fire mixed with blood, and it was hurled down upon the earth. A third of the earth was burned up, a third of the trees were burned up, and all the green grass was burned up.

[8]The second angel sounded his trumpet, and something like a huge mountain, all ablaze, was thrown into the sea. A

third of the sea turned into blood, ⁹a third of the living creatures in the sea died, and a third of the ships were destroyed.

¹⁰The third angel sounded his trumpet, and a great star, blazing like a torch, fell from the sky on a third of the rivers and on the springs of water— ¹¹the name of the star is Wormwood.ᵃ A third of the waters turned bitter, and many people died from the waters that had become bitter.

¹²The fourth angel sounded his trum-

ᵃ 11 That is, Bitterness

Read Revelation 7:1–17
Key Verse Revelation 7:9

Cosmic Replay – John Carroll

On one brisk fall Monday evening, a victorious football team gathered—bruised, but jubilant—in the film room of a campus stadium. As they watched the previous Saturday's hard-fought game, each player remembered how the team had struggled to make the winning field goal possible in the final seconds of the game. Each one recalled his discouragement when all had seemed lost. Each one relived the crushing impact of the blocks and tackles.

But watching the game on film was different from being on the playing field during the action. The players now knew the outcome; they knew that victory was theirs. This perspective shed a new light on the darkest moments of the game.

We can get discouraged when our efforts to share Jesus Christ with a roommate or some other friend seem to bring no results—or even a negative reaction. Often students feel that opposition to faith on campus is overwhelming. The name and cause of Jesus seem to mean little to others and at times are even ridiculed. While these things happen, we can sometimes feel as though we're part of a losing effort.

Or we might become discouraged in other ways. When our efforts to make inroads into ignorance, poverty or despair seem too small and too ineffective to make any difference. When our efforts to help others seem too weak to give them a boost. When our own efforts at living a Christlike life seem to fall far short. Knowing that events will turn out in our favor makes all the difference in moments of discouragement. This passage tells us ahead of time how the events surrounding Jesus' return and the world's end will turn out. We must still live out our lives and "future" history, but this glimpse of what is ahead gives us the same confidence the football players felt watching a game they had already won. We who are on God's side have already won.

Thankfully, the end of all things has been foretold, and this small glimpse of our celebration around God's throne implies ultimate victory. Efforts to reach lost people with the gospel will bear fruit "from every nation, tribe, people and language." We cannot lose, for Jesus has already won!

A Deeper Look
Psalm 60:12; 1 Corinthians 15:57–58; 1 John 5:4–5

Go to page 1436 for your next devotional reading.

pet, and a third of the sun was struck, a third of the moon, and a third of the stars, so that a third of them turned dark. A third of the day was without light, and also a third of the night.

¹³As I watched, I heard an eagle that was flying in midair call out in a loud voice: "Woe! Woe! Woe to the inhabitants of the earth, because of the trumpet blasts about to be sounded by the other three angels!"

9 The fifth angel sounded his trumpet, and I saw a star that had fallen from the sky to the earth. The star was given the key to the shaft of the Abyss. ²When he opened the Abyss, smoke rose from it like the smoke from a gigantic furnace. The sun and sky were darkened by the smoke from the Abyss. ³And out of the smoke locusts came down upon the earth and were given power like that of scorpions of the earth. ⁴They were told not to harm the grass of the earth or any plant or tree, but only those people who did not have the seal of God on their foreheads. ⁵They were not given power to kill them, but only to torture them for five months. And the agony they suffered was like that of the sting of a scorpion when it strikes a man. ⁶During those days men will seek death, but will not find it; they will long to die, but death will elude them.

⁷The locusts looked like horses prepared for battle. On their heads they wore something like crowns of gold, and their faces resembled human faces. ⁸Their hair was like women's hair, and their teeth were like lions' teeth. ⁹They had breastplates like breastplates of iron, and the sound of their wings was like the thundering of many horses and chariots rushing into battle. ¹⁰They had tails and stings like scorpions, and in their tails they had power to torment people for five months. ¹¹They had as king over them the angel of the Abyss, whose name in Hebrew is Abaddon, and in Greek, Apollyon.ᵃ

¹²The first woe is past; two other woes are yet to come.

¹³The sixth angel sounded his trumpet, and I heard a voice coming from the hornsᵇ of the golden altar that is before God. ¹⁴It said to the sixth angel who had the trumpet, "Release the four angels who are bound at the great river Euphrates." ¹⁵And the four angels who had been kept ready for this very hour and day and month and year were released to kill a third of mankind. ¹⁶The number of the mounted troops was two hundred million. I heard their number.

¹⁷The horses and riders I saw in my vision looked like this: Their breastplates were fiery red, dark blue, and yellow as sulfur. The heads of the horses resembled the heads of lions, and out of their mouths came fire, smoke and sulfur. ¹⁸A third of mankind was killed by the three plagues of fire, smoke and sulfur that came out of their mouths. ¹⁹The power of the horses was in their mouths and in their tails; for their tails were like snakes, having heads with which they inflict injury.

²⁰The rest of mankind that were not killed by these plagues still did not repent of the work of their hands; they did not stop worshiping demons, and idols of gold, silver, bronze, stone and wood—idols that cannot see or hear or walk. ²¹Nor did they repent of their murders, their magic arts, their sexual immorality or their thefts.

The Angel and the Little Scroll

10 Then I saw another mighty angel coming down from heaven. He was robed in a cloud, with a rainbow above his head; his face was like the sun, and his legs were like fiery pillars. ²He was holding a little scroll, which lay open in his hand. He planted his right foot on the sea and his left foot on the land, ³and he gave a loud shout like the roar of a lion. When he shouted, the voices of the seven thunders spoke. ⁴And when the seven thunders spoke, I was about to write; but I heard a voice from heaven say, "Seal up what the seven thunders have said and do not write it down."

⁵Then the angel I had seen standing on the sea and on the land raised his right hand to heaven. ⁶And he swore by him who lives for ever and ever, who created the heavens and all that is in them, the earth and all that is in it, and the sea and all that is in it, and said, "There will be no more delay! ⁷But in the days when the seventh angel is about to sound his trumpet, the mystery of God will be accomplished, just as he announced to his servants the prophets."

⁸Then the voice that I had heard from heaven spoke to me once more: "Go, take

---

ᵃ11 *Abaddon* and *Apollyon* mean *Destroyer*.
ᵇ13 That is, projections

the scroll that lies open in the hand of the angel who is standing on the sea and on the land."

9So I went to the angel and asked him to give me the little scroll. He said to me, "Take it and eat it. It will turn your stomach sour, but in your mouth it will be as sweet as honey." 10I took the little scroll from the angel's hand and ate it. It tasted as sweet as honey in my mouth, but when I had eaten it, my stomach turned sour. 11Then I was told, "You must prophesy again about many peoples, nations, languages and kings."

The Two Witnesses

11 I was given a reed like a measuring rod and was told, "Go and measure the temple of God and the altar, and count the worshipers there. 2But exclude the outer court; do not measure it, because it has been given to the Gentiles. They will trample on the holy city for 42 months. 3And I will give power to my two witnesses, and they will prophesy for 1,260 days, clothed in sackcloth." 4These are the two olive trees and the two lampstands that stand before the Lord of the earth. 5If anyone tries to harm them, fire comes from their mouths and devours their enemies. This is how anyone who wants to harm them must die. 6These men have power to shut up the sky so that it will not rain during the time they are prophesying; and they have power to turn the waters into blood and to strike the earth with every kind of plague as often as they want.

7Now when they have finished their testimony, the beast that comes up from the Abyss will attack them, and overpower and kill them. 8Their bodies will lie in the street of the great city, which is figuratively called Sodom and Egypt, where also their Lord was crucified. 9For three and a half days men from every people, tribe, language and nation will gaze on their bodies and refuse them burial. 10The inhabitants of the earth will gloat over them and will celebrate by sending each other gifts, because these two prophets had tormented those who live on the earth.

11But after the three and a half days a breath of life from God entered them, and they stood on their feet, and terror struck those who saw them. 12Then they heard a loud voice from heaven saying to them, "Come up here." And they went up to heaven in a cloud, while their enemies looked on.

13At that very hour there was a severe earthquake and a tenth of the city collapsed. Seven thousand people were killed in the earthquake, and the survivors were terrified and gave glory to the God of heaven.

14The second woe has passed; the third woe is coming soon.

The Seventh Trumpet

15The seventh angel sounded his trumpet, and there were loud voices in heaven, which said:

"The kingdom of the world has
    become the kingdom of our
        Lord and of his Christ,
    and he will reign for ever and
        ever."

16And the twenty-four elders, who were seated on their thrones before God, fell on their faces and worshiped God, 17saying:

"We give thanks to you, Lord God
    Almighty,
    the One who is and who was,
because you have taken your great
        power
    and have begun to reign.
18The nations were angry;
    and your wrath has come.
The time has come for judging the
        dead,
    and for rewarding your servants
        the prophets
and your saints and those who
        reverence your name,
    both small and great—
and for destroying those who destroy
        the earth."

19Then God's temple in heaven was opened, and within his temple was seen the ark of his covenant. And there came flashes of lightning, rumblings, peals of thunder, an earthquake and a great hailstorm.

The Woman and the Dragon

12 A great and wondrous sign appeared in heaven: a woman clothed with the sun, with the moon under her feet and a crown of twelve stars on her head. 2She was pregnant and cried out in pain as she was about to give birth. 3Then another sign appeared in heaven: an enormous red dragon with seven heads and ten

horns and seven crowns on his heads. ⁴His tail swept a third of the stars out of the sky and flung them to the earth. The dragon stood in front of the woman who was about to give birth, so that he might devour her child the moment it was born. ⁵She gave birth to a son, a male child, who will rule all the nations with an iron scepter. And her child was snatched up to God and to his throne. ⁶The woman fled into the desert to a place prepared for her by God, where she might be taken care of for 1,260 days.

⁷And there was war in heaven. Michael and his angels fought against the dragon, and the dragon and his angels fought back. ⁸But he was not strong enough, and they lost their place in heaven. ⁹The great dragon was hurled down—that ancient serpent called the devil, or Satan, who leads the whole world astray. He was hurled to the earth, and his angels with him.

¹⁰Then I heard a loud voice in heaven say:

"Now have come the salvation and
        the power and the kingdom
        of our God,
    and the authority of his Christ.
For the accuser of our brothers,
    who accuses them before our God
        day and night,
    has been hurled down.
¹¹They overcame him
    by the blood of the Lamb
    and by the word of their
        testimony;
they did not love their lives so much
    as to shrink from death.
¹²Therefore rejoice, you heavens
    and you who dwell in them!
But woe to the earth and the sea,
    because the devil has gone down
        to you!
He is filled with fury,
    because he knows that his time is
        short."

¹³When the dragon saw that he had been hurled to the earth, he pursued the woman who had given birth to the male child. ¹⁴The woman was given the two wings of a great eagle, so that she might fly to the place prepared for her in the desert, where she would be taken care of for a time, times and half a time, out of the serpent's reach. ¹⁵Then from his mouth the serpent spewed water like a river, to overtake the woman and sweep her away with the torrent. ¹⁶But the earth helped the woman by opening its mouth and swallowing the river that the dragon had spewed out of his mouth. ¹⁷Then the dragon was enraged at the woman and went off to make war against the rest of her offspring—those who obey God's commandments and hold to the testimony of Jesus. ¹And the dragon*a* stood on the shore of the sea.

The Beast out of the Sea

And I saw a beast coming out of the sea. He had ten horns and seven heads, with ten crowns on his horns, and on each head a blasphemous name. ²The beast I saw resembled a leopard, but had feet like those of a bear and a mouth like that of a lion. The dragon gave the beast his power and his throne and great authority. ³One of the heads of the beast seemed to have had a fatal wound, but the fatal wound had been healed. The whole world was astonished and followed the beast. ⁴Men worshiped the dragon because he had given authority to the beast, and they also worshiped the beast and asked, "Who is like the beast? Who can make war against him?"

⁵The beast was given a mouth to utter proud words and blasphemies and to exercise his authority for forty-two months. ⁶He opened his mouth to blaspheme God, and to slander his name and his dwelling place and those who live in heaven. ⁷He was given power to make war against the saints and to conquer them. And he was given authority over every tribe, people, language and nation. ⁸All inhabitants of the earth will worship the beast—all whose names have not been written in the book of life belonging to the Lamb that was slain from the creation of the world.*b*

⁹He who has an ear, let him hear.

¹⁰If anyone is to go into captivity,
    into captivity he will go.
If anyone is to be killed*c* with the
        sword,
    with the sword he will be killed.

This calls for patient endurance and faithfulness on the part of the saints.

*a*1 Some late manuscripts *And I*   *b*8 Or *written from the creation of the world in the book of life belonging to the Lamb that was slain*   *c*10 Some manuscripts *anyone kills*

The Beast out of the Earth

¹¹Then I saw another beast, coming out of the earth. He had two horns like a lamb, but he spoke like a dragon. ¹²He exercised all the authority of the first beast on his behalf, and made the earth and its inhabitants worship the first beast, whose fatal wound had been healed. ¹³And he performed great and miraculous signs, even causing fire to come down from heaven to earth in full view of men. ¹⁴Because of the signs he was given power to do on behalf of the first beast, he deceived the inhabitants of the earth. He ordered them to set up an image in honor of the beast who was wounded by the sword and yet lived. ¹⁵He was given power to give breath to the image of the first beast, so that it could speak and cause all who refused to worship the image to be killed. ¹⁶He also forced everyone, small and great, rich and poor, free and slave, to receive a mark on his right hand or on his forehead, ¹⁷so that no one could buy or sell unless he had the mark, which is the name of the beast or the number of his name.

FRIDAY

Read Revelation 12:1–17
Key Verse Revelation 12:17

Are You Battle-Ready? — Jack McQueeney

Imagine you're time-warped to the middle of a Civil War battlefield. Soldiers stagger in hand-to-hand combat; wounded men bleed at your feet; a wild-eyed soldier wheels around to face you. Panic grips your heart as he charges with bayonet raised.

This isn't an illusion—the truth is, a fierce battle does rage around you every day. Satan's declared purpose is to destroy anyone who believes in Jesus Christ and obeys God. His sworn intention is to demolish your faith into unrecognizable fragments. He is at war against *you*! Are you prepared to fight back? Check these three battle strategies.

First, we must know our enemy. It's Satan, and he's a liar. He schemes to convince us that the enemy is another person. If he can get us to blame each other for the disappointments in life, we waste our energy battling one another and leave him free to mock our faith and work on others. But Jesus' prayer in the garden showed his desire that believers maintain perfect unity with one another (see John 17:20–23).

Second, we must know our weapons. Through Jesus Christ we have many at our disposal, but God's Word is our most effective weapon. We can slice through Satan's deception with "the sword of the Spirit, which is the word of God" (Ephesians 6:17). If that sword doesn't feel very comfortable in our hands, we have available a wealth of teachers and resources to help us learn how to use it. With practice, we'll learn to handle that weapon with much more confidence.

Most important, we have to follow our Captain. His passion is to deny hell more prisoners. Under his banner, a soldier who is totally committed to him has power that will be felt in heaven, on earth and even in hell.

A Deeper Look
Ephesians 6:13–20; 1 Peter 5:8–10

Go to page 1444 for your next devotional reading.

¹⁸This calls for wisdom. If anyone has insight, let him calculate the number of the beast, for it is man's number. His number is 666.

The Lamb and the 144,000

14 Then I looked, and there before me was the Lamb, standing on Mount Zion, and with him 144,000 who had his name and his Father's name written on their foreheads. ²And I heard a sound from heaven like the roar of rushing waters and like a loud peal of thunder. The sound I heard was like that of harpists playing their harps. ³And they sang a new song before the throne and before the four living creatures and the elders. No one could learn the song except the 144,000 who had been redeemed from the earth. ⁴These are those who did not defile themselves with women, for they kept themselves pure. They follow the Lamb wherever he goes. They were purchased from among men and offered as firstfruits to God and the Lamb. ⁵No lie was found in their mouths; they are blameless.

The Three Angels

⁶Then I saw another angel flying in midair, and he had the eternal gospel to proclaim to those who live on the earth— to every nation, tribe, language and people. ⁷He said in a loud voice, "Fear God and give him glory, because the hour of his judgment has come. Worship him who made the heavens, the earth, the sea and the springs of water."

⁸A second angel followed and said, "Fallen! Fallen is Babylon the Great, which made all the nations drink the maddening wine of her adulteries."

⁹A third angel followed them and said in a loud voice: "If anyone worships the beast and his image and receives his mark on the forehead or on the hand, ¹⁰he, too, will drink of the wine of God's fury, which has been poured full strength into the cup of his wrath. He will be tormented with burning sulfur in the presence of the holy angels and of the Lamb. ¹¹And the smoke of their torment rises for ever and ever. There is no rest day or night for those who worship the beast and his image, or for anyone who receives the mark of his name." ¹²This calls for patient endurance on the part of the saints who obey God's commandments and remain faithful to Jesus.

¹³Then I heard a voice from heaven say, "Write: Blessed are the dead who die in the Lord from now on."

"Yes," says the Spirit, "they will rest from their labor, for their deeds will follow them."

The Harvest of the Earth

¹⁴I looked, and there before me was a white cloud, and seated on the cloud was one "like a son of man"ᵃ with a crown of gold on his head and a sharp sickle in his hand. ¹⁵Then another angel came out of the temple and called in a loud voice to him who was sitting on the cloud, "Take your sickle and reap, because the time to reap has come, for the harvest of the earth is ripe." ¹⁶So he who was seated on the cloud swung his sickle over the earth, and the earth was harvested.

¹⁷Another angel came out of the temple in heaven, and he too had a sharp sickle. ¹⁸Still another angel, who had charge of the fire, came from the altar and called in a loud voice to him who had the sharp sickle, "Take your sharp sickle and gather the clusters of grapes from the earth's vine, because its grapes are ripe." ¹⁹The angel swung his sickle on the earth, gathered its grapes and threw them into the great winepress of God's wrath. ²⁰They were trampled in the winepress outside the city, and blood flowed out of the press, rising as high as the horses' bridles for a distance of 1,600 stadia.ᵇ

Seven Angels With Seven Plagues

15 I saw in heaven another great and marvelous sign: seven angels with the seven last plagues—last, because with them God's wrath is completed. ²And I saw what looked like a sea of glass mixed with fire and, standing beside the sea, those who had been victorious over the beast and his image and over the number of his name. They held harps given them by God ³and sang the song of Moses the servant of God and the song of the Lamb:

"Great and marvelous are your deeds,
    Lord God Almighty.
Just and true are your ways,
    King of the ages.
⁴Who will not fear you, O Lord,
    and bring glory to your name?
For you alone are holy.
All nations will come

ᵃ14 Daniel 7:13   ᵇ20 That is, about 180 miles (about 300 kilometers)

and worship before you,
for your righteous acts have been
revealed."

⁵After this I looked and in heaven the
temple, that is, the tabernacle of the Testimony, was opened. ⁶Out of the temple
came the seven angels with the seven
plagues. They were dressed in clean,
shining linen and wore golden sashes
around their chests. ⁷Then one of the four
living creatures gave to the seven angels
seven golden bowls filled with the wrath
of God, who lives for ever and ever. ⁸And
the temple was filled with smoke from
the glory of God and from his power, and
no one could enter the temple until the
seven plagues of the seven angels were
completed.

The Seven Bowls of God's Wrath

16 Then I heard a loud voice from the
temple saying to the seven angels,
"Go, pour out the seven bowls of God's
wrath on the earth."

²The first angel went and poured out
his bowl on the land, and ugly and painful sores broke out on the people who
had the mark of the beast and worshiped
his image.

³The second angel poured out his bowl
on the sea, and it turned into blood like
that of a dead man, and every living thing
in the sea died.

⁴The third angel poured out his bowl
on the rivers and springs of water, and
they became blood. ⁵Then I heard the angel in charge of the waters say:

"You are just in these judgments,
    you who are and who were, the
        Holy One,
because you have so judged;
⁶for they have shed the blood of your
        saints and prophets,
    and you have given them blood to
        drink as they deserve."

⁷And I heard the altar respond:

"Yes, Lord God Almighty,
    true and just are your judgments."

⁸The fourth angel poured out his bowl
on the sun, and the sun was given power
to scorch people with fire. ⁹They were
seared by the intense heat and they
cursed the name of God, who had control
over these plagues, but they refused to
repent and glorify him.

¹⁰The fifth angel poured out his bowl

on the throne of the beast, and his kingdom was plunged into darkness. Men
gnawed their tongues in agony ¹¹and
cursed the God of heaven because of
their pains and their sores, but they refused to repent of what they had done.

¹²The sixth angel poured out his bowl
on the great river Euphrates, and its water was dried up to prepare the way for
the kings from the East. ¹³Then I saw
three evilᵃ spirits that looked like frogs;
they came out of the mouth of the dragon, out of the mouth of the beast and out
of the mouth of the false prophet. ¹⁴They
are spirits of demons performing miraculous signs, and they go out to the kings of
the whole world, to gather them for the
battle on the great day of God Almighty.

¹⁵"Behold, I come like a thief! Blessed
is he who stays awake and keeps his
clothes with him, so that he may not go
naked and be shamefully exposed."

¹⁶Then they gathered the kings together to the place that in Hebrew is called
Armageddon.

¹⁷The seventh angel poured out his
bowl into the air, and out of the temple
came a loud voice from the throne, saying, "It is done!" ¹⁸Then there came
flashes of lightning, rumblings, peals of
thunder and a severe earthquake. No
earthquake like it has ever occurred since
man has been on earth, so tremendous
was the quake. ¹⁹The great city split into
three parts, and the cities of the nations
collapsed. God remembered Babylon the
Great and gave her the cup filled with the
wine of the fury of his wrath. ²⁰Every island fled away and the mountains could
not be found. ²¹From the sky huge hailstones of about a hundred pounds each
fell upon men. And they cursed God on
account of the plague of hail, because the
plague was so terrible.

The Woman on the Beast

17 One of the seven angels who had the
seven bowls came and said to me,
"Come, I will show you the punishment
of the great prostitute, who sits on many
waters. ²With her the kings of the earth
committed adultery and the inhabitants
of the earth were intoxicated with the
wine of her adulteries."

³Then the angel carried me away in
the Spirit into a desert. There I saw a
woman sitting on a scarlet beast that was

ᵃ 13 Greek *unclean*

covered with blasphemous names and had seven heads and ten horns. ⁴The woman was dressed in purple and scarlet, and was glittering with gold, precious stones and pearls. She held a golden cup in her hand, filled with abominable things and the filth of her adulteries. ⁵This title was written on her forehead:

MYSTERY
BABYLON THE GREAT
THE MOTHER OF PROSTITUTES
AND OF THE ABOMINATIONS OF THE EARTH.

⁶I saw that the woman was drunk with the blood of the saints, the blood of those who bore testimony to Jesus.

When I saw her, I was greatly astonished. ⁷Then the angel said to me: "Why are you astonished? I will explain to you the mystery of the woman and of the beast she rides, which has the seven heads and ten horns. ⁸The beast, which you saw, once was, now is not, and will come up out of the Abyss and go to his destruction. The inhabitants of the earth whose names have not been written in the book of life from the creation of the world will be astonished when they see the beast, because he once was, now is not, and yet will come.

⁹"This calls for a mind with wisdom. The seven heads are seven hills on which the woman sits. ¹⁰They are also seven kings. Five have fallen, one is, the other has not yet come; but when he does come, he must remain for a little while. ¹¹The beast who once was, and now is not, is an eighth king. He belongs to the seven and is going to his destruction.

¹²"The ten horns you saw are ten kings who have not yet received a kingdom, but who for one hour will receive authority as kings along with the beast. ¹³They have one purpose and will give their power and authority to the beast. ¹⁴They will make war against the Lamb, but the Lamb will overcome them because he is Lord of lords and King of kings—and with him will be his called, chosen and faithful followers."

¹⁵Then the angel said to me, "The waters you saw, where the prostitute sits, are peoples, multitudes, nations and languages. ¹⁶The beast and the ten horns you saw will hate the prostitute. They will bring her to ruin and leave her naked; they will eat her flesh and burn her with fire. ¹⁷For God has put it into their hearts to accomplish his purpose by agreeing to give the beast their power to rule, until God's words are fulfilled. ¹⁸The woman you saw is the great city that rules over the kings of the earth."

The Fall of Babylon

18 After this I saw another angel coming down from heaven. He had great authority, and the earth was illuminated by his splendor. ²With a mighty voice he shouted:

"Fallen! Fallen is Babylon the Great!
  She has become a home for demons
and a haunt for every evil[a] spirit,
  a haunt for every unclean and detestable bird.
³For all the nations have drunk
  the maddening wine of her adulteries.
The kings of the earth committed adultery with her,
  and the merchants of the earth grew rich from her excessive luxuries."

⁴Then I heard another voice from heaven say:

"Come out of her, my people,
  so that you will not share in her sins,
  so that you will not receive any of her plagues;
⁵for her sins are piled up to heaven,
  and God has remembered her crimes.
⁶Give back to her as she has given;
  pay her back double for what she has done.
  Mix her a double portion from her own cup.
⁷Give her as much torture and grief

[a]2 Greek *unclean*

POINT OF INTEREST

Revelation 17:6

At the end of the age a world power will arise that will oppose the people of God, even to the point of shedding their blood. Persecution of God's people has occurred throughout history, but it will increase during that time.

as the glory and luxury she gave
herself.
In her heart she boasts,
'I sit as queen; I am not a widow,
and I will never mourn.'
⁸Therefore in one day her plagues will
overtake her:
death, mourning and famine.
She will be consumed by fire,
for mighty is the Lord God who
judges her.

⁹"When the kings of the earth who
committed adultery with her and shared
her luxury see the smoke of her burning,
they will weep and mourn over her.
¹⁰Terrified at her torment, they will stand
far off and cry:

" 'Woe! Woe, O great city,
O Babylon, city of power!
In one hour your doom has come!'

¹¹"The merchants of the earth will
weep and mourn over her because no
one buys their cargoes any more— ¹²car-
goes of gold, silver, precious stones and
pearls; fine linen, purple, silk and scarlet
cloth; every sort of citron wood, and articles of every kind made of ivory, costly
wood, bronze, iron and marble; ¹³cargoes
of cinnamon and spice, of incense, myrrh
and frankincense, of wine and olive oil,
of fine flour and wheat; cattle and sheep;
horses and carriages; and bodies and
souls of men.
¹⁴"They will say, 'The fruit you longed
for is gone from you. All your riches and
splendor have vanished, never to be recovered.' ¹⁵The merchants who sold
these things and gained their wealth from
her will stand far off, terrified at her torment. They will weep and mourn ¹⁶and
cry out:

" 'Woe! Woe, O great city,
dressed in fine linen, purple and
scarlet,
and glittering with gold, precious
stones and pearls!
¹⁷In one hour such great wealth has
been brought to ruin!'

"Every sea captain, and all who travel
by ship, the sailors, and all who earn
their living from the sea, will stand far
off. ¹⁸When they see the smoke of her
burning, they will exclaim, 'Was there
ever a city like this great city?' ¹⁹They will
throw dust on their heads, and with
weeping and mourning cry out:

" 'Woe! Woe, O great city,
where all who had ships on the
sea
became rich through her wealth!
In one hour she has been brought to
ruin!
²⁰Rejoice over her, O heaven!
Rejoice, saints and apostles and
prophets!
God has judged her for the way she
treated you.' "

²¹Then a mighty angel picked up a
boulder the size of a large millstone and
threw it into the sea, and said:

"With such violence
the great city of Babylon will be
thrown down,
never to be found again.
²²The music of harpists and musicians,
flute players and trumpeters,
will never be heard in you again.
No workman of any trade
will ever be found in you again.
The sound of a millstone
will never be heard in you again.
²³The light of a lamp
will never shine in you again.
The voice of bridegroom and bride
will never be heard in you again.
Your merchants were the world's
great men.
By your magic spell all the nations
were led astray.
²⁴In her was found the blood of
prophets and of the saints,
and of all who have been killed on
the earth."

Hallelujah!

19 After this I heard what sounded like
the roar of a great multitude in heav-
en shouting:

"Hallelujah!
Salvation and glory and power belong
to our God,
2   for true and just are his judgments.
He has condemned the great
prostitute
who corrupted the earth by her
adulteries.
He has avenged on her the blood of
his servants."

³And again they shouted:

"Hallelujah!
The smoke from her goes up for ever
and ever."

⁴The twenty-four elders and the four living creatures fell down and worshiped God, who was seated on the throne. And they cried:

"Amen, Hallelujah!"

⁵Then a voice came from the throne, saying:

"Praise our God,
　all you his servants,
you who fear him,
　both small and great!"

⁶Then I heard what sounded like a great multitude, like the roar of rushing waters and like loud peals of thunder, shouting:

"Hallelujah!
　For our Lord God Almighty reigns.
⁷Let us rejoice and be glad
　and give him glory!
For the wedding of the Lamb has
　come,
　and his bride has made herself
　　ready.
⁸Fine linen, bright and clean,
　was given her to wear."
(Fine linen stands for the righteous acts of the saints.)

⁹Then the angel said to me, "Write: 'Blessed are those who are invited to the wedding supper of the Lamb!'" And he added, "These are the true words of God."

¹⁰At this I fell at his feet to worship him. But he said to me, "Do not do it! I am a fellow servant with you and with your brothers who hold to the testimony of Jesus. Worship God! For the testimony of Jesus is the spirit of prophecy."

The Rider on the White Horse

¹¹I saw heaven standing open and there before me was a white horse, whose rider is called Faithful and True. With justice he judges and makes war. ¹²His eyes are like blazing fire, and on his head are many crowns. He has a name written on him that no one knows but he himself. ¹³He is dressed in a robe dipped in blood, and his name is the Word of God. ¹⁴The armies of heaven were following him, riding on white horses and dressed in fine linen, white and clean. ¹⁵Out of his mouth comes a sharp sword with which to strike down the nations. "He will rule them with an iron scep-

ter."ᵃ He treads the winepress of the fury of the wrath of God Almighty. ¹⁶On his robe and on his thigh he has this name written:

KING OF KINGS AND LORD OF LORDS.

¹⁷And I saw an angel standing in the sun, who cried in a loud voice to all the birds flying in midair, "Come, gather together for the great supper of God, ¹⁸so that you may eat the flesh of kings, generals, and mighty men, of horses and their riders, and the flesh of all people, free and slave, small and great."

¹⁹Then I saw the beast and the kings of the earth and their armies gathered together to make war against the rider on the horse and his army. ²⁰But the beast was captured, and with him the false prophet who had performed the miraculous signs on his behalf. With these signs he had deluded those who had received the mark of the beast and worshiped his image. The two of them were thrown alive into the fiery lake of burning sulfur. ²¹The rest of them were killed with the sword that came out of the mouth of the rider on the horse, and all the birds gorged themselves on their flesh.

The Thousand Years

20 And I saw an angel coming down out of heaven, having the key to the Abyss and holding in his hand a great chain. ²He seized the dragon, that ancient serpent, who is the devil, or Satan, and bound him for a thousand years. ³He threw him into the Abyss, and locked and sealed it over him, to keep him from deceiving the nations anymore until the thousand years were ended. After that, he must be set free for a short time.

⁴I saw thrones on which were seated those who had been given authority to judge. And I saw the souls of those who had been beheaded because of their testimony for Jesus and because of the word of God. They had not worshiped the beast or his image and had not received his mark on their foreheads or their hands. They came to life and reigned with Christ a thousand years. ⁵(The rest of the dead did not come to life until the thousand years were ended.) This is the first resurrection. ⁶Blessed and holy are those who have part in the first resurrection. The second death has no power

ᵃ15 Psalm 2:9

over them, but they will be priests of God and of Christ and will reign with him for a thousand years.

Satan's Doom

⁷When the thousand years are over, Satan will be released from his prison ⁸and will go out to deceive the nations in the four corners of the earth—Gog and Magog—to gather them for battle. In number they are like the sand on the seashore. ⁹They marched across the breadth of the earth and surrounded the camp of God's people, the city he loves. But fire came down from heaven and devoured them. ¹⁰And the devil, who deceived them, was thrown into the lake of burning sulfur, where the beast and the false prophet had been thrown. They will be tormented day and night for ever and ever.

The Dead Are Judged

¹¹Then I saw a great white throne and him who was seated on it. Earth and sky fled from his presence, and there was no place for them. ¹²And I saw the dead, great and small, standing before the throne, and books were opened. Another book was opened, which is the book of life. The dead were judged according to what they had done as recorded in the books. ¹³The sea gave up the dead that were in it, and death and Hades gave up the dead that were in them, and each person was judged according to what he had done. ¹⁴Then death and Hades were thrown into the lake of fire. The lake of fire is the second death. ¹⁵If anyone's name was not found written in the book of life, he was thrown into the lake of fire.

The New Jerusalem

21 Then I saw a new heaven and a new earth, for the first heaven and the first earth had passed away, and there was no longer any sea. ²I saw the Holy City, the new Jerusalem, coming down out of heaven from God, prepared as a bride beautifully dressed for her husband. ³And I heard a loud voice from the throne saying, "Now the dwelling of God is with men, and he will live with them. They will be his people, and God himself will be with them and be their God. ⁴He will wipe every tear from their eyes. There will be no more death or mourning or crying or pain, for the old order of things has passed away."

⁵He who was seated on the throne said, "I am making everything new!" Then he said, "Write this down, for these words are trustworthy and true."

⁶He said to me: "It is done. I am the Alpha and the Omega, the Beginning and the End. To him who is thirsty I will give to drink without cost from the spring of the water of life. ⁷He who overcomes will inherit all this, and I will be his God and he will be my son. ⁸But the cowardly, the unbelieving, the vile, the murderers, the sexually immoral, those who practice magic arts, the idolaters and all liars—their place will be in the fiery lake of burning sulfur. This is the second death."

⁹One of the seven angels who had the seven bowls full of the seven last plagues came and said to me, "Come, I will show you the bride, the wife of the Lamb." ¹⁰And he carried me away in the Spirit to a mountain great and high, and showed me the Holy City, Jerusalem, coming down out of heaven from God. ¹¹It shone with the glory of God, and its brilliance was like that of a very precious jewel, like a jasper, clear as crystal. ¹²It had a great, high wall with twelve gates, and with twelve angels at the gates. On the gates were written the names of the twelve tribes of Israel. ¹³There were three gates on the east, three on the north, three on the south and three on the west. ¹⁴The wall of the city had twelve founda-

POINT OF INTEREST

Revelation 20:15

How do our names come to be in this book? John wrote, "Whoever believes in the Son has eternal life" (John 3:36). Paul noted that his fellow workers' names were "in the book of life" (Philippians 4:3). As we trust in the One who died on the cross to take away our sin, he gives us eternal life and writes our names in this book; they'll never be erased or deleted (see Revelation 3:5). Those whose names are written in the book of life will be welcomed into the Holy City (see Revelation 21:27).

tions, and on them were the names of the twelve apostles of the Lamb.

¹⁵The angel who talked with me had a measuring rod of gold to measure the city, its gates and its walls. ¹⁶The city was laid out like a square, as long as it was wide. He measured the city with the rod and found it to be 12,000 stadia*a* in length, and as wide and high as it is long. ¹⁷He measured its wall and it was 144 cubits*b* thick,*c* by man's measurement, which the angel was using. ¹⁸The wall was made of jasper, and the city of pure gold, as pure as glass. ¹⁹The foundations of the city walls were decorated with every kind of precious stone. The first foundation was jasper, the second sapphire, the third chalcedony, the fourth emerald, ²⁰the fifth sardonyx, the sixth carnelian, the seventh chrysolite, the eighth beryl, the ninth topaz, the tenth chrysoprase, the eleventh jacinth, and the twelfth amethyst.*d* ²¹The twelve gates were twelve pearls, each gate made of a single pearl. The great street of the city was of pure gold, like transparent glass.

²²I did not see a temple in the city, because the Lord God Almighty and the Lamb are its temple. ²³The city does not need the sun or the moon to shine on it, for the glory of God gives it light, and the Lamb is its lamp. ²⁴The nations will walk by its light, and the kings of the earth will bring their splendor into it. ²⁵On no day will its gates ever be shut, for there will be no night there. ²⁶The glory and honor of the nations will be brought into it. ²⁷Nothing impure will ever enter it, nor will anyone who does what is shameful or deceitful, but only those whose names are written in the Lamb's book of life.

The River of Life

22 Then the angel showed me the river of the water of life, as clear as crystal, flowing from the throne of God and of the Lamb ²down the middle of the great street of the city. On each side of the river stood the tree of life, bearing twelve crops of fruit, yielding its fruit every month. And the leaves of the tree are for the healing of the nations. ³No longer will there be any curse. The throne of God and of the Lamb will be in the city, and his servants will serve him. ⁴They will see his face, and his name will be on their foreheads. ⁵There will be no more night. They will not need the light of a lamp or the light of the sun, for the Lord God will

give them light. And they will reign for ever and ever.

⁶The angel said to me, "These words are trustworthy and true. The Lord, the God of the spirits of the prophets, sent his angel to show his servants the things that must soon take place."

Jesus Is Coming

⁷"Behold, I am coming soon! Blessed is he who keeps the words of the prophecy in this book."

⁸I, John, am the one who heard and saw these things. And when I had heard and seen them, I fell down to worship at the feet of the angel who had been showing them to me. ⁹But he said to me, "Do not do it! I am a fellow servant with you and with your brothers the prophets and of all who keep the words of this book. Worship God!"

¹⁰Then he told me, "Do not seal up the words of the prophecy of this book, because the time is near. ¹¹Let him who does wrong continue to do wrong; let him who is vile continue to be vile; let him who does right continue to do right; and let him who is holy continue to be holy."

¹²"Behold, I am coming soon! My reward is with me, and I will give to everyone according to what he has done. ¹³I am the Alpha and the Omega, the First and the Last, the Beginning and the End. ¹⁴"Blessed are those who wash their

---

a16 That is, about 1,400 miles (about 2,200 kilometers)   *b17* That is, about 200 feet (about 65 meters)   *c17* Or *high*   *d20* The precise identification of some of these precious stones is uncertain.

POINT OF INTEREST   Revelation 22:13,20

Compare this verse with Revelation 1:8. Here Jesus claims the name "the Alpha and the Omega." It is linguistic nonsense to imagine there could be two Alphas and Omegas, two firsts, two lasts, two beginnings and two ends. Jesus and Almighty God are one and the same. He is unchanging, and his promises will be fulfilled.

Read *Revelation 21:1—22:6*
Key Verse *Revelation 22:5*

The Reality of Heaven

In the last two chapters of Revelation, John unfolds a vision of the fruition of God's kingdom, the eternal city, the new Jerusalem. The beauty of the Holy City seems beyond the words John uses to describe it. And the crowning promise is that "the throne of God and of the Lamb will be in the city" (Revelation 22:3) and we will be with God and will be his people. We will see his face . . . and will reign for ever and ever. We will have eternal bodies . . . there will be no more pain or suffering, nor tears of sorrow or sadness.

The new heavens and the new earth will come. John's vision of the new Jerusalem is not just wishful thinking. Revelation 1:3 tells us: "Blessed is the one who reads the words of this prophecy, and blessed are those who hear it and take to heart what is written in it, because the time is near." That time is not going to be pleasant for those who ignore the warnings (see Revelation 21:8). But for those who respond in the here-and-now—for those whose names are "written in the Lamb's book of life"—arriving in the Holy City will be coming home (Revelation 21:27). That's reality!

Digging Into the Word
1. How are you encouraged about your eternal destiny from these passages?—*Philippians 3:20–21; Revelation 7:9–17*
2. What do the following passages teach you about heaven?—*Romans 8:17; Revelation 21:4; Revelation 22:5*

Personal Reflection
Is the reality of heaven influencing how you live your life today? If it isn't, pray for a deeper understanding of the hope you have for eternity.

One Step Deeper
2 Corinthians 5:1; Hebrews 11:10

Go to page 3 for your next devotional reading.

robes, that they may have the right to the tree of life and may go through the gates into the city. [15]Outside are the dogs, those who practice magic arts, the sexually immoral, the murderers, the idolaters and everyone who loves and practices falsehood.

[16]"I, Jesus, have sent my angel to give you[a] this testimony for the churches. I am the Root and the Offspring of David, and the bright Morning Star."

[17]The Spirit and the bride say, "Come!" And let him who hears say, "Come!" Whoever is thirsty, let him come; and whoever wishes, let him take the free gift of the water of life.

[18]I warn everyone who hears the words of the prophecy of this book: If anyone adds anything to them, God will add to him the plagues described in this book. [19]And if anyone takes words away from this book of prophecy, God will take away from him his share in the tree of life and in the holy city, which are described in this book.

[20]He who testifies to these things says, "Yes, I am coming soon."

Amen. Come, Lord Jesus.

[21]The grace of the Lord Jesus be with God's people. Amen.

[a]16 The Greek is plural.

STUDY HELPS

Weights & Measures

Reading Plans

Indexes

Author Acknowledgments

	BIBLICAL UNIT		APPROXIMATE AMERICAN EQUIVALENT	APPROXIMATE METRIC EQUIVALENT
WEIGHTS	talent	(60 minas)	75 pounds	34 kilograms
	mina	(50 shekels)	1¼ pounds	0.6 kilogram
	shekel	(2 bekas)	⅖ ounce	11.5 grams
	pim	(⅔ shekel)	⅓ ounce	7.6 grams
	beka	(10 gerahs)	⅕ ounce	5.5 grams
	gerah		1/50 ounce	0.6 gram
LENGTH	cubit		18 inches	0.5 meter
	span		9 inches	23 centimeters
	handbreadth		3 inches	8 centimeters
CAPACITY				
Dry Measure	cor [homer]	(10 ephahs)	6 bushels	220 liters
	lethek	(5 ephahs)	3 bushels	110 liters
	ephah	(10 omers)	⅗ bushel	22 liters
	seah	(⅓ ephah)	7 quarts	7.3 liters
	omer	(1/10 ephah)	2 quarts	2 liters
	cab	(1/18 ephah)	1 quart	1 liter
Liquid Measure	bath	(1 ephah)	6 gallons	22 liters
	hin	(⅙ bath)	4 quarts	4 liters
	log	(1/72 bath)	⅓ quart	0.3 liter

The figures of the table are calculated on the basis of a shekel equaling 11.5 grams, a cubit equaling 18 inches and an ephah equaling 22 liters. The quart referred to is either a dry quart (slightly larger than a liter) or a liquid quart (slightly smaller than a liter), whichever is applicable. The ton referred to in the footnotes is the American ton of 2,000 pounds.

This table is based upon the best available information, but it is not intended to be mathematically precise; like the measurement equivalents in the footnotes, it merely gives approximate amounts and distances. Weights and measures differed somewhat at various times and places in the ancient world. There is uncertainty particularly about the ephah and the bath; further discoveries may shed more light on these units of capacity.

One Month Reading Plans

Old Testament Reading Plan

Read the Old Testament History in a Month!

DAY	READ
1	Genesis 1–11
2	Genesis 12–21
3	Genesis 22–29
4	Genesis 30–37
5	Genesis 38–45
6	Genesis 46–Exodus 4
7	Exodus 5–13
8	Exodus 14–22
9	Exodus 23–32
10	Exodus 33–40
11	Joshua 1–10
12	Joshua 11–20
13	Joshua 21–Judges 4
14	Judges 5–12
15	Judges 13–21
16	1 Samuel 1–11
17	1 Samuel 12–18
18	1 Samuel 19–28
19	1 Samuel 29–2 Samuel 6
20	2 Samuel 7–15
21	2 Samuel 16–22
22	2 Samuel 23–1 Kings 4
23	1 Kings 5–10
24	1 Kings 11–18
25	1 Kings 19–2 Kings 3
26	2 Kings 4–9
27	2 Kings 10–17
28	2 Kings 18–25
29	Ezra 1–10
30	Nehemiah 1–7
31	Nehemiah 8–13

New Testament Reading Plan

Read the New Testament in a Month!

DAY	READ
1	Matthew 1–8
2	Matthew 9–15
3	Matthew 16–22
4	Matthew 23–28
5	Mark 1–6
6	Mark 7–12
7	Mark 13–Luke 2
8	Luke 3–7
9	Luke 8–12
10	Luke 13–19
11	Luke 20–24
12	John 1–7
13	John 8–13
14	John 14–21
15	Acts 1–7
16	Acts 8–13
17	Acts 14–20
18	Acts 21–28
19	Romans 1–8
20	Romans 9–16
21	1 Corinthians 1–11
22	1 Corinthians 12–2 Corinthians 7
23	2 Corinthians 8–Galatians
24	Ephesians–Philippians
25	Colossians–2 Thessalonians
26	1 Timothy–Philemon
27	Hebrews 1–11
28	Hebrews 12–1 Peter
29	2 Peter–Jude
30	Revelation 1–11
31	Revelation 12–22

One Year Reading Plan

God's Word is full of promises, encouragement and guidance for you. This reading plan gives you a simple structure for reading through the entire Bible in one year.

January

DAY	READ
1	. . . Genesis 1–4
2	. . . Genesis 5–8
3	. . . Genesis 9–12
4	. . . Genesis 13–17
5	. . . Genesis 18–20
6	. . . Genesis 21–23
7	. . . Genesis 24–25
8	. . . Genesis 26–28
9	. . . Genesis 29–31
10	. . . Genesis 32–35
11	. . . Genesis 36–38
12	. . . Genesis 39–41
13	. . . Genesis 42–43
14	. . . Genesis 44–46
15	. . . Genesis 47–50
16	. . . Exodus 1–4
17	. . . Exodus 5–7
18	. . . Exodus 8–10
19	. . . Exodus 11–13
20	. . . Exodus 14–16
21	. . . Exodus 17–20
22	. . . Exodus 21–23
23	. . . Exodus 24–27
24	. . . Exodus 28–30
25	. . . Exodus 31–34
26	. . . Exodus 35–37
27	. . . Exodus 38–40
28	. . . Leviticus 1–4
29	. . . Leviticus 5–7
30	. . . Leviticus 8–10
31	. . . Leviticus 11–13

February

DAY	READ
1	. . . Leviticus 14–15
2	. . . Leviticus 16–18
3	. . . Leviticus 19–21
4	. . . Leviticus 22–23
5	. . . Leviticus 24–25
6	. . . Leviticus 26–27
7	. . . Numbers 1–2
8	. . . Numbers 3–4
9	. . . Numbers 5–6
10	. . . Numbers 7
11	. . . Numbers 8–10
12	. . . Numbers 11–13
13	. . . Numbers 14–15
14	. . . Numbers 16–18
15	. . . Numbers 19–21
16	. . . Numbers 22–24
17	. . . Numbers 25–26
18	. . . Numbers 27–29
19	. . . Numbers 30–32
20	. . . Numbers 33–36
21	. . . Deuteronomy 1–2
22	. . . Deuteronomy 3–4
23	. . . Deuteronomy 5–8
24	. . . Deuteronomy 9–11
25	. . . Deuteronomy 12–15
26	. . . Deuteronomy 16–19
27	. . . Deuteronomy 20–23
28	. . . Deuteronomy 24–27

March

DAY	READ
1	... Deuteronomy 28–29
2	... Deuteronomy 30–32
3	... Deuteronomy 33–34
4	... Joshua 1–4
5	... Joshua 5–7
6	... Joshua 8–10
7	... Joshua 11–13
8	... Joshua 14–17
9	... Joshua 18–20
10	... Joshua 21–22
11	... Joshua 23–24
12	... Judges 1–3
13	... Judges 4–5
14	... Judges 6–8
15	... Judges 9–10
16	... Judges 11–13
17	... Judges 14–16
18	... Judges 17–19
19	... Judges 20–21
20	... Ruth 1–4
21	... 1 Samuel 1–3
22	... 1 Samuel 4–7
23	... 1 Samuel 8–12
24	... 1 Samuel 13–14
25	... 1 Samuel 15–16
26	... 1 Samuel 17–18
27	... 1 Samuel 19–21
28	... 1 Samuel 22–24
29	... 1 Samuel 25–27
30	... 1 Samuel 28–31
31	... 2 Samuel 1–3

April

DAY	READ
1	... 2 Samuel 4–7
2	... 2 Samuel 8–11
3	... 2 Samuel 12–13
4	... 2 Samuel 14–16
5	... 2 Samuel 17–19
6	... 2 Samuel 20–22
7	... 2 Samuel 23–24
8	... 1 Kings 1–2
9	... 1 Kings 3–5
10	... 1 Kings 6–7
11	... 1 Kings 8–9
12	... 1 Kings 10–12
13	... 1 Kings 13–15
14	... 1 Kings 16–18
15	... 1 Kings 19–20
16	... 1 Kings 21–22
17	... 2 Kings 1–3
18	... 2 Kings 4–5
19	... 2 Kings 6–8
20	... 2 Kings 9–10
21	... 2 Kings 11–13
22	... 2 Kings 14–16
23	... 2 Kings 17–18
24	... 2 Kings 19–21
25	... 2 Kings 22–23
26	... 2 Kings 24–25
27	... 1 Chronicles 1–2
28	... 1 Chronicles 3–4
29	... 1 Chronicles 5–6
30	... 1 Chronicles 7–9

May

DAY	READ
1	... 1 Chronicles 10–12
2	... 1 Chronicles 13–16
3	... 1 Chronicles 17–19
4	... 1 Chronicles 20–23
5	... 1 Chronicles 24–26
6	... 1 Chronicles 27–29
7	... 2 Chronicles 1–4
8	... 2 Chronicles 5–7
9	... 2 Chronicles 8–11
10	... 2 Chronicles 12–16
11	... 2 Chronicles 17–20
12	... 2 Chronicles 21–24
13	... 2 Chronicles 25–28
14	... 2 Chronicles 29–31
15	... 2 Chronicles 32–34
16	... 2 Chronicles 35–36
17	... Ezra 1–4
18	... Ezra 5–7
19	... Ezra 8–10
20	... Nehemiah 1–3
21	... Nehemiah 4–7
22	... Nehemiah 8–9
23	... Nehemiah 10–11
24	... Nehemiah 12–13
25	... Esther 1–3
26	... Esther 4–7
27	... Esther 8–10
28	... Job 1–4
29	... Job 5–8
30	... Job 9–12
31	... Job 13–16

June

DAY	READ
1	... Job 17–20
2	... Job 21–24
3	... Job 25–30
4	... Job 31–34
5	... Job 35–38
6	... Job 39–42
7	... Psalms 1–8
8	... Psalms 9–17
9	... Psalms 18–21
10	... Psalms 22–27
11	... Psalms 28–33
12	... Psalms 34–37
13	... Psalms 38–42
14	... Psalms 43–49
15	... Psalms 50–55
16	... Psalms 56–61
17	... Psalms 62–68
18	... Psalms 69–72
19	... Psalms 73–77
20	... Psalms 78–80
21	... Psalms 81–88
22	... Psalms 89–94
23	... Psalms 95–103
24	... Psalms 104–106
25	... Psalms 107–111
26	... Psalms 112–118
27	... Psalm 119
28	... Psalms 120–133
29	... Psalms 134–140
30	... Psalms 141–150

July

DAY	READ
1	... Proverbs 1–3
2	... Proverbs 4–7
3	... Proverbs 8–11
4	... Proverbs 12–14
5	... Proverbs 15–17
6	... Proverbs 18–20
7	... Proverbs 21–23
8	... Proverbs 24–26
9	... Proverbs 27–29
10	... Proverbs 30–31
11	... Ecclesiastes 1–4
12	... Ecclesiastes 5–8
13	... Ecclesiastes 9–12
14	... Song of Songs 1–4
15	... Song of Songs 5–8
16	... Isaiah 1–3
17	... Isaiah 4–8
18	... Isaiah 9–11
19	... Isaiah 12–14
20	... Isaiah 15–19
21	... Isaiah 20–24
22	... Isaiah 25–28
23	... Isaiah 29–31
24	... Isaiah 32–34
25	... Isaiah 35–37
26	... Isaiah 38–40
27	... Isaiah 41–43
28	... Isaiah 44–46
29	... Isaiah 47–49
30	... Isaiah 50–52
31	... Isaiah 53–56

August

DAY	READ
1	... Isaiah 57–59
2	... Isaiah 60–63
3	... Isaiah 64–66
4	... Jeremiah 1–3
5	... Jeremiah 4–5
6	... Jeremiah 6–8
7	... Jeremiah 9–11
8	... Jeremiah 12–14
9	... Jeremiah 15–17
10	... Jeremiah 18–21
11	... Jeremiah 22–24
12	... Jeremiah 25–27
13	... Jeremiah 28–30
14	... Jeremiah 31–32
15	... Jeremiah 33–36
16	... Jeremiah 37–39
17	... Jeremiah 40–43
18	... Jeremiah 44–46
19	... Jeremiah 47–48
20	... Jeremiah 49
21	... Jeremiah 50
22	... Jeremiah 51–52
23	... Lamentations 1–2
24	... Lamentations 3–5
25	... Ezekiel 1–4
26	... Ezekiel 5–8
27	... Ezekiel 9–12
28	... Ezekiel 13–15
29	... Ezekiel 16–17
30	... Ezekiel 18–20
31	... Ezekiel 21–22

September

DAY	READ
1	... Ezekiel 23–24
2	... Ezekiel 25–27
3	... Ezekiel 28–30
4	... Ezekiel 31–32
5	... Ezekiel 33–35
6	... Ezekiel 36–38
7	... Ezekiel 39–40
8	... Ezekiel 41–43
9	... Ezekiel 44–46
10	... Ezekiel 47–48
11	... Daniel 1–3
12	... Daniel 4–5
13	... Daniel 6–8
14	... Daniel 9–12
15	... Hosea 1–4
16	... Hosea 5–9
17	... Hosea 10–14
18	... Joel 1–3
19	... Amos 1–4
20	... Amos 5–9
21	... Obadiah, Jonah 1–4
22	... Micah 1–4
23	... Micah 5–7
24	... Nahum 1–3
25	... Habakkuk 1–3
26	... Zephaniah 1–3
27	... Haggai 1–2
28	... Zechariah 1–5
29	... Zechariah 6–10
30	... Zechariah 11–14

October

DAY	READ
1	... Malachi 1–4
2	... Matthew 1–4
3	... Matthew 5–6
4	... Matthew 7–9
5	... Matthew 10–11
6	... Matthew 12–13
7	... Matthew 14–17
8	... Matthew 18–20
9	... Matthew 21–22
10	... Matthew 23–24
11	... Matthew 25–26
12	... Matthew 27–28
13	... Mark 1–3
14	... Mark 4–5
15	... Mark 6–7
16	... Mark 8–9
17	... Mark 10–11
18	... Mark 12–13
19	... Mark 14
20	... Mark 15–16
21	... Luke 1–2
22	... Luke 3–4
23	... Luke 5–6
24	... Luke 7–8
25	... Luke 9–10
26	... Luke 11–12
27	... Luke 13–15
28	... Luke 16–18
29	... Luke 19–20
30	... Luke 21–22
31	... Luke 23–24

November

DAY	READ
1	...John 1–2
2	...John 3–4
3	...John 5–6
4	...John 7–8
5	...John 9–10
6	...John 11–12
7	...John 13–15
8	...John 16–17
9	...John 18–19
10	...John 20–21
11	...Acts 1–3
12	...Acts 4–5
13	...Acts 6–7
14	...Acts 8–9
15	...Acts 10–11
16	...Acts 12–13
17	...Acts 14–15
18	...Acts 16–17
19	...Acts 18–19
20	...Acts 20–21
21	...Acts 22–23
22	...Acts 24–26
23	...Acts 27–28
24	...Romans 1–3
25	...Romans 4–7
26	...Romans 8–10
27	...Romans 11–14
28	...Romans 15–16
29	...1 Corinthians 1–4
30	...1 Corinthians 5–9

December

DAY	READ
1	...1 Corinthians 10–13
2	...1 Corinthians 14–16
3	...2 Corinthians 1–4
4	...2 Corinthians 5–9
5	...2 Corinthians 10–13
6	...Galatians 1–3
7	...Galatians 4–6
8	...Ephesians 1–6
9	...Philippians 1–4
10	...Colossians 1–4
11	...1 Thessalonians 1–5
12	...2 Thessalonians 1–3
13	...1 Timothy 1–6
14	...2 Timothy 1–4
15	...Titus 1–3, Philemon
16	...Hebrews 1–4
17	...Hebrews 5–8
18	...Hebrews 9–10
19	...Hebrews 11–13
20	...James 1–5
21	...1 Peter 1–5
22	...2 Peter 1–3
23	...1 John 1–5
24	...2, 3 John, Jude
25	...Revelation 1–3
26	...Revelation 4–7
27	...Revelation 8–11
28	...Revelation 12–14
29	...Revelation 15–17
30	...Revelation 18–19
31	...Revelation 20–22

Subject Index to Scripture

The Subject Index will lead you to key Scripture texts on a variety of subjects.

A

Aaron, Ex 4:10–12:50 (p. 65); 28—29 (p. 91); 32 (p. 95); Nu 17 (p. 162); 20:23–29 (p. 165)

Abandonment, Ezr 10:3 (p. 515)

Abuse (physical), Ge 16:9 (p. 17); Ex 20:4–5 (p. 82); Isa 50:4–6 (p. 814)

Abraham, Ge 11:26–12:20 (p. 13); 14:18–24 (p. 15); 15:18 (p. 16); 16 (p. 16); 18:16–33 (p. 18); 22 (p. 22); 25:1–11 (p. 27); Ro 4 (p. 1260); Gal 3:6–29 (p. 1317); Jas 2:20–24 (p. 1393)

Adam, Ge 1:26—5:5 (p. 2); Lk 3:23–38 (p. 1136); Ro 5:12–21 (p. 1262); 1 Co 15:21–22,42–57 (p. 1296)

Addiction, Pr 5:22–23 (p. 697); Jer 13:23 (p. 854); Mk 9:43–47 (p. 1117)

Adoption, Ge 15:2 (p. 16); 41:51–52 (p. 49); 48:5 (p. 56); 50:23 (p. 60); Ex 2:10 (p. 62); Dt 21:17 (p. 207); Eph 1:5 (p. 1323)

Adultery, Ge 35:22 (p. 41); Nu 5:31 (p. 146); Pr 2:22 (p. 693); 5:3–10 (p. 696); 5:22–23 (p. 697); 23:27 (p. 721); 31:3 (p. 730); Eze 23:25 (p. 935); Mt 19:1–9 (p. 1085); Mk 10:1–12 (p. 1117)

Advice, 1 Ch 21:3–4 (p. 452); Pr 15:22 (p. 710); Da 6:2 (p. 975)

Alcohol use, Ge 9:22–25 (p. 11); Lev 10:9 (p. 117); Est 1:8 (p. 536); Ps 104:14–15 (p. 658); 116:13 (p. 667); Pr 20:1 (p. 715); 23:29–35 (p. 721); Hos 4:11 (p. 988); Joel 1:5 (p. 997); Mt 26:17–30 (p. 1097); Lk 1:15 (p. 1131); Jn 2:1–11 (p. 1179); 1 Ti 5:23 (p. 1363)

Altars, Ge 12:7–8 (p. 13); 33:20 (p. 39); Jos 8:31 (p. 233); 2 Ki 16:10 (p. 413); Am 3:14 (p. 1005); Rev 6:9 (p. 1430); 16:7 (p. 1438)

Ambition, Ge 11:4 (p. 12); Nu 16:3 (p. 159); Jdg 18:20 (p. 277); Jer 45:5 (p. 890); Mt 20:20–21 (p. 1087); 1 Co 7:17,20,26 (p. 1286)

Angel of the Lord, Jdg 2:1,4 (p. 255); 6:11,14 (p. 261); Ps 34:7 (p. 606); Isa 31:8–9 (p. 789); Eze 40:3 (p. 955); Zec 12:8 (p. 1051)

Angels, Ex 23:20–23 (p. 87); 2 Ch 32:21 (p. 497); Job 33:23–24 (p. 573); Ps 29:1 (p. 602); Da 8:16 (p. 978); 10:12 (p. 981); Lk 1:19 (p. 1131); Ac 6:15 (p. 1221); 1 Co 6:2–3 (p. 1284); Heb 1:7 (p. 1377); 2 Pe 2:4 (p. 1408); Jude v. 6 (p. 1422)

   Guardian, Ps 91:11 (p. 649); Eze 9:1–2 (p. 919); Mt 18:8 (p. 1083); Ac 12:15 (p. 1230)

Anger, 1 Ch 13:11 (p. 445); Job 15:13 (p. 557); 32:2–5 (p. 572); 32:19 (p. 572); Pr 14:29 (p. 708); Da 2:5 (p. 968); Ac 15:39 (p. 1236); Eph 4:26 (p. 1328); Jas 1:19–20 (p. 1393)

Anointing, Ge 28:18 (p. 32); Ex 29:1,7 (p. 92); 40:9 (p. 105); Lev 8:12 (p. 114); Ru 3:3 (p. 286); 1 Sa 10:1 (p. 298); 12:3 (p. 300); 16:1,13 (p. 306); 26:9 (p. 319); 1 Ki 19:16 (p. 387); 2 Ch 6:42 (p. 471); Ps 2:2 (p. 582); 104:15 (p. 658); 105:15 (p. 659); Isa 61:1 (p. 827); Da 9:25 (p. 980); Mt 3:16 (p. 1062); Lk 10:34 (p. 1150); Jn 1:32 (p. 1178); 2:20,27 (p. 1179); 2 Co 1:21 (p. 1302); Jas 5:14 (p. 1397)

Antichrist, 2 Th 2:3–12 (p. 1355); 1 Jn 2:18 (p. 1413)

Anxiety, Mt 6:25–34 (p. 1067); Lk 12:22–34 (p. 1153); Php 4:4–9 (p. 1339)

Apostles, Lk 6:13 (p. 1141); Ac 1:26 (p. 1215); 8:1 (p. 1223); 15:19–21 (p. 1236); 1 Co 9:15 (p. 1288); 12:28 (p. 1293); 15:8 (p. 1296); 2 Co 12:12 (p. 1311); Gal 1:1 (p. 1314)

Arguments, Job 18:2 (p. 559); Ac 15:39 (p. 1236)

Ark of the covenant, Ex 16:34 (p. 79); 25:10–22 (p. 88); Nu 4:5 (p. 143); 7:89 (p. 150); Jos 6:9 (p. 230); 1 Sa 4:5,7,10 (p. 293); 2 Sa 6:7 (p. 331); 1 Ki 8:1–6 (p. 369); 8:9 (p. 369); 1 Ch 13:10,14 (p. 445); 13:9–10 (p. 445); 15:2 (p. 446); 2 Ch 35:3 (p. 501)

Armageddon, Jos 12:21 (p. 239); 17:11 (p. 244); Jdg 1:27 (p. 255); 5:19 (p. 261); 1 Ki 9:15 (p. 373); 2 Ki 9:27 (p. 406); 23:29 (p. 423); Zec 12:3 (p. 1051); Rev 16:14–16 (p. 1438); 19:19 (p. 1441)

Ascension, Ps 27 (p. 600); Lk 24:36–53 (p. 1175); Ac 1:1–11 (p. 1213); Jn 16:5–16 (p. 1202); Eph 4:7–13 (p. 1327)

Assurance of salvation, Ps 37 (p. 608); Ro 8 (p. 1265); 2 Ti 1:8–12 (p. 1365); 1 Jn 2:28—3:24 (p. 1413); 5:9–13 (p. 1416)

Atonement, Isa 27:8–9 (p. 783); 53:5 (p. 817); Eze 16:63 (p. 927); Jn 1:29 (p. 1178); Ro 3:25 (p. 1260)

Attitude, Ge 4:5–7 (p. 5); Ps 73:3–5 (p. 634); 77:12 (p. 638); 81:11 (p. 642); 86:11 (p. 645); Ecc 11:10 (p. 744); Isa 1:11–14 (p. 756); Jer 17:10 (p. 858); Joel 2:13 (p. 999); Php 4:8 (p. 1339); Col 3:2 (p. 1346)

B

Baptism, Mt 3:11 (p. 1062); 3:6 (p. 1062); Mk 1:4 (p. 1103); 1:8 (p. 1103); Lk 12:50 (p. 1155); Jn 3:23–25 (p. 1180); Ac 8:14–17 (p. 1224); 19:5 (p. 1242); Ro 6:3–5 (p. 1263); 1 Co 10:2 (p. 1290); Heb 10:22 (p. 1385); 1 Pe 3:21 (p. 1403)

Of the Holy Spirit, Mt 3:11 (p. 1062); 3:16 (p. 1062); Lk 3:16 (p. 1136); Jn 1:32–33 (p. 1178); 3:5 (p. 1180); Ac 1:5 (p. 1213); 2:1–4 (p. 1215); 2:38–39 (p. 1216); 8:12,14–17 (p. 1224); 9:17–18 (p. 1225); 10:44–48 (p. 1228); 19:1–6 (p. 1242); 1 Co 12:13 (p. 1292); Tit 3:5 (p. 1374)

Belonging, Ne 10:36 (p. 530)

Bethlehem, Ge 35:19–20 (p. 41); Jdg 12:8–10 (p. 270); Ru 1:1,19–22 (p. 283); Ru 4:11–13 (p. 287); 1 Sa 16:4–13 (p. 306); 2 Sa 23:14–17 (p. 355); 2 Ch 11:5–6 (p. 475); Mic 5:2 (p. 1021); Mt 2:16–18 (p. 1062); Lk 2:1–7 (p. 1133); 2:4,11 (p. 1133)

Betrayal, Ps 41:9 (p. 612); 109:1–3 (p. 663); Jer 40:16 (p. 886); 41:6 (p. 886); Ob v. 7 (p. 1012); Mt 26:14–16 (p. 1097); 26:49 (p. 1098); 26:75 (p. 1098); Mk 14:10–11 (p. 1124); 14:45 (p. 1125); 14:72 (p. 1127); Lk 22:47–48 (p. 1171); 22:61–62 (p. 1171)

Bitterness, Ru 1:13,20–21 (p. 284); Job 15:13 (p. 557); 38:2 (p. 577); Ps 140:10 (p. 684)

Blame

God, Ge 42:28 (p. 50); Ex 16:3 (p. 78); Ru 1:13,20–21 (p. 284); 2 Ki 3:10 (p. 395); Job 35:12–13 (p. 575); Ps 88:6 (p. 646); Pr 19:3 (p. 714); Ecc 5:19–20 (p. 739); Jer 2:29 (p. 838); 4:10 (p. 840)

Others, Ge 16:5 (p. 16); Jdg 19:25 (p. 278); 20:6 (p. 279); 1 Ki 17:18,20 (p. 383); Hos 4:4 (p. 987)

Blameless, 2 Sa 22:24 (p. 352); Ps 26:1 (p. 600); 84:11 (p. 644); 101:2 (p. 654); Pr 20:7 (p. 716); Tit 1:6 (p. 1372)

Blasphemy, Ex 20:7 (p. 82); Lev 24:13–23 (p. 134); Mt 9:1–8 (p. 1070); 26:57–67 (p. 1098); Mk 3:20–30 (p. 1108)

Blessed, Ps 32:1 (p. 604); Mt 5:3–10 (p. 1063); Eph 1:3 (p. 1323)

Blessings, Dt 7:12–16 (p. 192); Ps 32 (p. 604); 67 (p. 629); Eze 34:26–30 (p. 948); Jn 1:14–17 (p. 1177); Eph 1:3–14 (p. 1323); Mt 5:1–11 (p. 1063); Lk 6:20–22 (p. 1141)

Blood, Ge 9:4 (p. 10); Ex 24:6,8 (p. 88); 29:11–21 (p. 92); Lev 17:11 (p. 126); Heb 9:14 (p. 1384); 9:22 (p. 1384)

Born again, Jn 3:1–21 (p. 1179); Tit 3:4–8 (p. 1374)

Bread, Mt 14:13–21 (p. 1079); 15:29–38 (p. 1081); 26:26 (p. 1097); Mk 6:35–44 (p. 1112); 8:1–9 (p. 1114); 14:22 (p. 1125); Lk 9:12–17 (p. 1147); 11:5–8 (p. 1151); 22:19 (p. 1170); Jn 6:5–13 (p. 1185); 6:35,41,48,51 (p. 1186); 1 Co 10:16–17 (p. 1291); 11:23–24 (p. 1292)

Bribes, Pr 17:8 (p. 711); 21:14 (p. 718); 22:16 (p. 720)

C

Careers, Ex 7:7 (p. 67); Ac 18:3 (p. 1241)

Character, Dt 8:2 (p. 194); 2 Ch 32:31 (p. 498); Ps 35:11–16 (p. 607); 66:10 (p. 629); Pr 23:15 (p. 720); 24:10 (p. 721); 27:21 (p. 726); Jer 12:5–6 (p. 852); Mal 3:18 (p. 1056); Mt 11:18–19 (p. 1073); Lk 6:43–45 (p. 1142); 7:33–34 (p. 1144)

Children (importance), Ge 19:31–32 (p. 21); Ex 21:22–23 (p. 84); Dt 25:11–12 (p. 211); Ru 4:14–15 (p. 287); 1 Ch 2:32 (p. 430); Job 42:12–13 (p. 581); Ps 127:3–5 (p. 678); Jer 16:2 (p. 856); Mk 10:13 (p. 1117); Lk 18:15 (p. 1163)

Choice, Dt 31:16–21 (p. 217); 1 Ki 8:58 (p. 372); 12:15 (p. 377); 2 Ch 18:22 (p. 481); Job 14:5 (p. 556); Ps 25:12 (p. 599); 32:9 (p. 604); 103:19 (p. 656); 139:16 (p. 683); Isa 54:15 (p. 819); 63:17 (p. 830); Jer 4:10 (p. 840); 29:13 (p. 871); Eze 14:9 (p. 924); Mt 23:37 (p. 1093); Lk 15:11–32 (p. 1159); Ac 13:48 (p. 1234); Ro 9:8–33 (p. 1269); Eph 1:4–5 (p. 1323)

Christian fellowship, Ro 16:1–16 (p. 1276); 1 Co 11:20–22 (p. 1292); 2 Co 1:5 (p. 1300); Gal 6:10 (p. 1321)

Christian freedom, 1 Co 6:12 (p. 1284); Rev 2:20 (p. 1427)

Church, Mt 16:18 (p. 1082); Ac 1:8 (p. 1213); 5:5,10 (p. 1219); Eph 2:22 (p. 1325); 1 Pe 1:23 (p. 1400); 2 Jn v. 1 (p. 1418); Rev 11:12 (p. 1434); 12:1 (p. 1434)

Discipline, Eze 40:5—42:20 (p. 955); 1 Co 5:4 (p. 1284); 5:11 (p. 1284); 5:12 (p. 1284); 2 Th 3:14 (p. 1357); 1 Ti 1:20 (p. 1359); 5:20 (p. 1363)

Fighting, 1 Co 3:16–17 (p. 1283); 3:21 (p. 1283); 2 Co 10:10–11 (p. 1310); Php 1:15–18 (p. 1334); 1 Ti 5:17 (p. 1363); 2 Ti 2:24–25 (p. 1368); Tit 3:9 (p. 1374); 3 Jn v. 1–14 (p. 1419); Jude v. 3 (p. 1422)

Leaders, Ac 14:23 (p. 1235); 1 Th 5:12 (p. 1353); 1 Ti 3:2–7 (p. 1360); Tit 1:6 (p. 1372); 3 Jn v. 3,7 (p. 1419)

Structure, Tit 1:5 (p. 1372)

Unity, 1 Co 1:10 (p. 1279); 12:22 (p. 1293); Col 3:11 (p. 1346)

Circumcision, Ge 17:10 (p. 17); 34:24 (p. 40); Ex 4:24 (p. 65); 4:25 (p. 65); Jos 5:3 (p. 229); Ac 15:1 (p. 1235); 16:3 (p. 1237); 15:10–12 (p. 1235); Ro 2:25–27 (p. 1259); 1 Co 7:18 (p. 1286); Gal 5:2 (p. 1319)

Inner, Dt 10:16 (p. 196); Jer 4:4 (p. 840); Ro 2:28–29 (p. 1259); Col 2:11 (p. 1343)

Cleanness, Lev 11—15 (p. 117); Ps 51:1–9 (p. 619); Heb 10:19–22 (p. 1385); 1 Jn 1:5–10 (p. 1411)

Comfort, Job 4:1 (p. 547); Ps 23:4 (p. 597); 2 Co 1:5 (p. 1300)

Commitment, Ge 15:6 (p. 16); Dt 33:9 (p. 222); Ru 1:16–18 (p. 284); Ps 31:15 (p. 603); 40:6 (p. 611); 86:11 (p. 645); Pr 23:15 (p. 720); Isa 58:6–7 (p. 823); Jer 9:2 (p. 848); 26:10–16 (p. 869); Eze 20:3 (p. 930); Zec 13:3 (p. 1051); Lk 14:26 (p. 1157); Jn 6:51,53–58 (p. 1186); 2 Ti 3:7 (p. 1368); Rev 3:16 (p. 1428)

Compassion, Pr 24:11 (p. 721); Isa 21:3–4 (p. 776); Jer 4:19–26 (p. 841); 48:31–32,36 (p. 894); Mk 2:4 (p. 1105); Lk 5:19 (p. 1139); Gal 6:2,5 (p. 1320)

Competition, Ecc 4:4–6 (p. 737)

Complaining, Ex 16:7 (p. 78); 17:2 (p. 79); Nu 21:5–6 (p. 165); Job 6:5 (p. 549); Ps 3:1 (p. 583); Ecc 5:19–20 (p. 739); Isa 45:9 (p. 808); Jer 45:3 (p. 889); 2 Co 1:8 (p. 1300)

Confession, Jos 7:19 (p. 231); 2 Sa 12:13 (p. 338); Ne 1:6 (p. 517); Job 16:17 (p. 559); Pr 14:9 (p. 707); 28:13 (p. 727); Jn 9:41 (p. 1192); 1 Jn 1:9 (p. 1411)

Conscience, Ge 39:9 (p. 45); Dt 28:65 (p. 215); Jos 1:1 (p. 224); Job 13:25 (p. 556); Ps 19:13 (p. 594); Pr 20:27 (p. 717); Eze 38:22–23 (p. 953); Ac 24:25 (p. 1250); Ro 14:13 (p. 1274); 14:22–23 (p. 1274); 1 Co 8:10–11 (p. 1287)

Consecration, Ex 13:1–2 (p. 74); 19:14,22 (p. 81); Lev 8:10 (p. 114); 11:44–47 (p. 118); Nu 7:1 (p. 147); Jos 3:5 (p. 227)

Contentment, Ps 23:1 (p. 597); Ecc 1:6–8 (p. 733); 1 Co 7:17,20,26 (p. 1286); 1 Ti 6:6–8 (p. 1363)

Conversion, Jer 31:3–14 (p. 874); Jn 4:1–30,39–42 (p. 1181); Ac 8:26–40 (p. 1224); 9:1–25 (p. 1225); 16:11–15 (p. 1237); 16:22–34 (p. 1237); 2 Co 5:17–19 (p. 1305); Eph 2:1–10 (p. 1325)

Courage, Jos 1 (p. 224); 1 Sa 17:26–50 (p. 308); Da 3 (p. 970); Ac 4 (p. 1218); 5:17–42 (p. 1219)

Covenant

Abraham's, Ps 111:5–9 (p. 665); Jer 16:15 (p. 857)

David's, Ps 89:3 (p. 646)

Everlasting, Eze 16:60 (p. 927)

Israel's, Dt 28:16–19 (p. 213); Jos 24:25 (p. 253); Jdg 2:20–21 (p. 256); 2 Ki 21:9 (p. 420); Ne 9:5–38 (p. 526)

New, Isa 65:17 (p. 831); Eze 37:26–28 (p. 952); 39:29 (p. 954); Mt 17:3 (p. 1082); Mk 14:22–24 (p. 1125); Lk 9:30 (p. 1149); Ac 15:19–21 (p. 1236); Ro 2:25–27 (p. 1259); Heb 8:6–7 (p. 1383); 8:10–11 (p. 1383); Rev 21:1 (p. 1442)

New Testament, Ps 25:10 (p. 599); Isa 59:21 (p. 825); Jer 31:31 (p. 875)

Of nations, Ge 35:11 (p. 41)

Coveting, Ex 20:17 (p. 82); Jos 7 (p. 231); 1 Ki 21:1–14 (p. 389); Jas 4:1–10 (p. 1395)

Creation, Ge 1:5–31 (p. 1); 1—2 (p. 1); Job 37:14–16 (p. 577); 39:1–30 (p. 578); 39:17 (p. 579); Ps 19:1–6 (p. 594); 48:10 (p. 616); 74:13–14 (p. 636); 96:11–13 (p. 653); 104:6–9 (p. 658); 104:16–30 (p. 658); Pr 8:22–31 (p. 700); Ro 1:19–20 (p. 1257); Col 1:15,18 (p. 1342); 1 Ti 4:3–4 (p. 1360)

Criticism, Job 6:15–17 (p. 550); Ps 64:3–6 (p. 627); Pr 12:1 (p. 704); 27:6 (p. 725); 29:19 (p. 728); Ecc 10:20 (p. 743); Jer 18:19–23 (p. 860); Ro 14:4 (p. 1274); 2 Co 5:13 (p. 1304)

Cross, Mt 16:24 (p. 1082); Mk 8:31—9:1 (p. 1115); Lk 9:23 (p. 1147); 23:26–49 (p. 1172); Jn 3:14 (p. 1180); Gal 3:1–14 (p. 1317); 5:11 (p. 1319); Eph 2:11–18 (p. 1325); 1 Co 1:18—2:5 (p. 1280); 1 Pe 2:24 (p. 1401)

Crown

As a symbol, Ps 8:5 (p. 586); 103:4 (p. 656); 149:4 (p. 690); Pr 10:6 (p. 702); 12:4 (p. 704); 16:31 (p. 711); 17:6 (p. 711); 1 Th 2:19 (p. 1349); Php 4:1 (p. 1339)

Worn by leaders, Lev 8:9 (p. 114); 2 Sa 12:30 (p. 338); Est 1:11 (p. 536); 2:17 (p. 537); SS 3:11 (p. 749); Zec 6:9–11(p. 1046); Mt 27:29 (p. 1099); Jn 19:2,5 (p. 1207); Rev 14:14 (p. 1437); 19:12 (p. 1441)

Cults, Ge 9:25 (p. 11); 38:16 (p. 44); Ex 22:18–20 (p. 85); 2 Ki 1:2 (p. 393); Ps 77:12 (p. 638); Jer 2:8,27 (p. 837); Mt 6:23 (p. 1067); 2 Co 11:20 (p. 1311); 1 Jn 3:2 (p. 1413); Rev 2:24 (p. 1427)

D

David, 1 Sa 16 (p. 306); 17 (p. 307); 2 Sa 7 (p. 331); 11—12 (p. 335); Ps 51 (p. 619); Mt 1:1–18 (p. 1059); 21:41–45 (p. 1089); Lk 1:26–33 (p. 1131)

Day of the Lord, Isa 13:6 (p. 770); 34:4 (p. 792); Jer 25:33 (p. 868); Joel 1:15 (p. 998); Am 5:18 (p. 1008); Zep 1:7 (p. 1036); Zec 14:1 (p. 1052); 2 Co 1:14 (p. 1301); 1 Th 5:2 (p. 1352)

Deacon, Ac 6:1–4 (p. 1221); 1 Ti 3:8–13

Death, 2 Sa 22:6 (p. 352); Ps 116:15 (p. 667); Ecc 3:18 (p. 736); Isa 25:7 (p. 780); Mt 9:24 (p. 1071); Mk 5:39 (p. 1111); Lk 8:52 (p. 1146); 1 Th 4:14,16 (p. 1352)

> **Inevitable,** Job 21:23–26 (p. 562); Ecc 1:18 (p. 734); 2:13–16 (p. 734); 9:1–3 (p. 742); Lk 13:3–5 (p. 1155)
>
> **Spiritual,** Eph 2:1 (p. 1325)

Death penalty, Ge 4:15 (p. 5); 9:6 (p. 10); Nu 25:7–8 (p. 171); Dt 17:7 (p. 203); 19:13 (p. 205); Jos 20:3 (p. 247); Jdg 8:17 (p. 265); 1 Sa 15:33 (p. 305); 1 Ki 2:32 (p. 361); Ps 78:34 (p. 639); Ac 7:57–59 (p. 1223)

Debts, Ex 21:2 (p. 83); Dt 15:1 (p. 201); Ne 5:5 (p. 522); Pr 22:7 (p. 718); Mt 18:24–28 (p. 1085); 18:34 (p. 1085)

Deception, 2 Sa 13:6 (p. 339); 16:4 (p. 343); 2 Ch 18:29 (p. 481); Jer 41:6 (p. 886)

Decision making, Ge 4:7 (p. 5); Ex 10:1; 9:34 (p. 11); 1 Ch 19:3–5 (p. 451); 2 Ch 32:31 (p. 498); Pr 15:22 (p. 710); 16:1–9 (p. 710); 1 Co 2:15 (p. 1281); 10:27–30 (p. 1291)

Dedication, Lev 27:2 (p. 137); 27:26–28 (p. 138); Ne 12:27–43 (p. 532)

Demon possession, Mt 8:28–34 (p. 1070); Mk 1:23 (p. 1104); 5:1–10 (p. 1109); Lk 4:33 (p. 1138); Ac 16:16–19 (p. 1237); 1 Ti 4:1–10 (p. 1360)

Denial, Ps 32:3 (p. 604); Eze 33:32 (p. 947); Mk 16:7 (p. 1129)

Depending on God, Jos 24:19 (p. 252); Ps 62:3–6 (p. 626); 86:1 (p. 645); 104:16–30 (p. 658); Pr 27:1

(p. 725); Zec 10:1 (p. 1049); Mt 10:9–10 (p. 1071); Mk 6:8 (p. 1111); Lk 6:24–26 (p. 1141); Jn 15:4 (p. 1200); 2 Co 9:11 (p. 1309); 1 Ti 6:6–8 (p. 1363); 1 Jn 2:24 (p. 1413)

Depression, Job 17:15 (p. 559); Ps 61:2 (p. 625); 69:1–3 (p. 631); Pr 25:20 (p. 723); Ecc 4:1–3 (p. 736)

Despair, 1 Ki 11:10–12 (p. 375); Job 7:8–10 (p. 550); 7:15–16 (p. 551); 9:22–24 (p. 552); Ps 10:1 (p. 587); 142:6 (p. 685); Ecc 1:15 (p. 734); Isa 33:7–9 (p. 791); Jer 8:20 (p. 848); Eze 37:11 (p. 952); Hab 3:17–18 (p. 1034)

Disabilities, Ex 4:10 (p. 65); 4:11 (p. 65); Lev 21:17–23 (p. 130); Dt 27:18 (p. 212); 2 Sa 19:24 (p. 348); Ps 6:2–7 (p. 585); Lk 13:11 (p. 1156)

Discipleship, Mt 4:20 (p. 1063); 8:20 (p. 1069); 16:24 (p. 1082); 28:19 (p. 1102); Mk 1:16–17 (p. 1104); 8:34 (p. 1115); 10:21 (p. 1118); Lk 6:13 (p. 1141); 9:23 (p. 1147); 9:57–62 (p. 1149); 14:25–34 (p. 1157); Jn 1:40–42 (p. 1178); 8:51 (p. 1190); 15:1–17 (p. 1200); 21:15–19 (p. 1211); Ro 12:1 (p. 1272); Php 3:10 (p. 1339)

Discipline, Ps 6:1 (p. 585); 66:10 (p. 629); 94:12–13 (p. 651); 141:5 (p. 684); Pr 3:11–12 (p. 695); 19:18 (p. 715); 29:19 (p. 728); Jer 16:15 (p. 857); 30:11 (p. 873); 1 Co 9:27 (p. 1289); 1 Th 4:6 (p. 1351); Heb 12:5 (p. 1388)

Discouragement, 1 Ki 19:3 (p. 386); Ne 4:10 (p. 521); Hag 1—2 (p. 1040); 2 Ti 4:9–11 (p. 1369)

Discrimination, Ge 43:32 (p. 52); 1 Ch 1:5 (p. 427); Gal 3:28 (p. 1318); Col 3:11 (p. 1346); Phm v. 16 (p. 1376); Jas 2:1–7 (p. 1393)

Disobedience

> **God's response,** Ge 2:17 (p. 4); Lev 10:1 (p. 116); Nu 14:40–41 (p. 157); 20:12 (p. 164); Dt 1:37 (p. 185); 28:46 (p. 214); 1 Ki 20:36 (p. 388); 2 Ch 18:28 (p. 481); Ps 81:11 (p. 642); Pr 28:14 (p. 727); Jer 42:20 (p. 887); Eze 7:27 (p. 918)
>
> **Leaders' response,** 2 Sa 18:14 (p. 347)

Disrespect, 2 Ki 2:23–24 (p. 395)

Divorce, Dt 21:14 (p. 207); 24:1 (p. 209); 1 Ch 8:8 (p. 439); Ezr 10:17 (p. 515); Isa 50:1 (p. 814); Mal 2:14 (p. 1054); Mt 1:19 (p. 1060); 19:1–9 (p. 1085); Mk 10:1–12 (p. 1117); Jn 4:18 (p. 1182); 1 Co 7:15 (p. 1286)

Doubts, 1 Ki 17:24 (p. 383); Job 40:2 (p. 579); Ps 69:1–3 (p. 631); 73:3–5 (p. 634); Ecc 9:4–6 (p. 742); Jer 15:18 (p. 856); Mal 3:14–15 (p. 1056); Lk 7:19–23 (p. 1143); Jn 21:15–17 (p. 1211); Jas 1:6–8 (p. 1392)

Dreams (visions),
Ge 28:12–15 (p. 32); 31:11 (p. 35); Jdg 7:14 (p. 263);

7:15 (p. 263); 1 Ki 3:15 (p. 362); 1 Ch 17:2 (p. 449); Job 42:5 (p. 581); Isa 1:1 (p. 755); 6:1 (p. 761); Eze 1:1 (p. 913); 3:14 (p. 915); Zec 1:8 (p. 1043); Rev 1:19–20 (p. 1426); 4:2 (p. 1428)

E

Education, Jdg 5:1 (p. 260); 2 Ch 17:7 (p. 480); Pr 19:18 (p. 715)

   Religious, Jdg 2:10 (p. 256); 2 Ki 22:2 (p. 421); 2 Ch 29:3 (p. 493); 32:7–8 (p. 497); Ne 8:7 (p. 526); Job 3:3 (p. 546); Ps 22:9–10 (p. 596); 103:17–18 (p. 656)

Elder, Ac 5:17–42 (p. 1219); 14:21–25 (p. 1235); 20:13–38 (p. 1243); Tit 1:5–9 (p. 1372); 1 Ti 3:1–7 (p. 1360)

Elderly, Ps 92:14–15 (p. 651); Pr 16:31 (p. 711); Ecc 12:3–5 (p. 744)

Election, Ge 12:1–9 (p. 13); Ex 19:1–6 (p. 81); Dt 10:12–22 (p. 196); Isa 41:8–16 (p. 800); Jn 15:9–17 (p. 1200); Ro 9:6–13 (p. 1269); Eph 1:3–14 (p. 1323); 1 Pe 2:1–10 (p. 1400); 2 Pe 1:3–10 (p. 1406)

Elijah, 1 Ki 17–19,21 (p. 383); 2 Ki 2 (p. 394); Lk 9:28–36 (p. 1147)

Elisha, 1 Ki 19:16–21 (p. 387); 2 Ki 2—13 (p. 394)

Emotions (expressing), Ps 13:1–5 (p. 589); 88:5 (p. 646); 140:1–11 (p. 684); Pr 14:29 (p. 708); La 1:12 (p. 906)

Encouragement, 1 Sa 23:16 (p. 316); Job 4:1 (p. 547); Pr 25:20 (p. 723); Isa 12:1–6 (p. 768)

Enemies, Ps 27:2 (p. 600); 31:6 (p. 603); 35:11–16 (p. 607); Pr 25:21–22 (p. 723); Lk 6:27–36 (p. 1141); Ro 12:19–21 (p. 1273)

Envy, Ge 37 (p. 43); Mk 7:20–23 (p. 1114); Jas 3:13—4:10 (p. 1395)

Eternal life, Mt 19:16–30 (p. 1086); Jn 3:1–21 (p. 1179); Jn 6:46,57 (p. 1186); Ro 2:7 (p. 1258); Ro 6:15–23 (p. 1263); 1 Jn 5:1–13 (p. 1415); Rev 21:22–27 (p. 1443)

Eternity, Job 20:5–9 (p. 561); Ps 21:4 (p. 595); 30:9 (p. 602); Ecc 3:11 (p. 736)

Eve, Ge 1:26—5:2 (p. 2); 1 Co 11:2–16 (p. 1291); 1 Ti 2:8–15

Evil

   Destroyed, Mal 4:1 (p. 1056); 1 Co 15:24 (p. 1296); Col 2:15 (p. 1343)

   Fighting, Ps 94:16 (p. 651); Mt 5:39 (p. 1066); 18:10 (p. 1084); Lk 6:29–30 (p. 1141); Jas 4:7 (p. 1395); 1 Jn 5:4 (p. 1416); Rev 16:16 (p. 1438)

   Source, Ge 2:9 (p. 4); Ex 11:3 (p. 72); Dt 31:16–21 (p. 217); Jdg 9:23 (p. 266); 1 Ch 21:1 (p. 452); Job 19:8–12 (p. 560); Ps 71:20 (p. 633); Ecc 7:13–14 (p. 740); La 3:38 (p. 909); Am 9:4 (p. 1011); Jn 9:2 (p. 1190)

   Spirits, 1 Sa 16:14 (p. 307); 18:10 (p. 309); Mt 8:31–32 (p. 1070); Mk 1:23 (p. 1104); 5:13 (p. 1109); 9:18 (p. 1116); Lk 4:33 (p. 1138); 9:39 (p. 1149); 11:19 (p. 1152); Ac 16:17–18 (p. 1237); 19:13 (p. 1242); 1 Jn 4:1 (p. 1415); Rev 16:13 (p. 1438)

   Used by God, 1 Ki 22:20–22 (p. 391); Am 9:4 (p. 1011); Hab 1:6,13 (p. 1030); Jn 14:30 (p. 1200); Ac 2:23 (p. 1216)

Example, Jn 13:1–17 (p. 1198); 1 Co 10:1–13 (p. 1290); Php 2:1–11 (p. 1334); 2:14–15 (p. 1335); 1 Th 1 (p. 1348); Heb 11:4–40 (p. 1386); Jas 5:10–11 (p. 1397); 5:16–18 (p. 1397); 1 Pe 2:11–12 (p. 1401)

Exile, Isa 5:13 (p. 760); 2 Ki 17,25 (p. 414); 2 Ch 36 (p. 502)

Exodus

   God's deliverance, Ex 4:1–9 (p. 64); 5:1–5 (p. 65); 7:10—10:29 (p. 67); 11:1—12:39 (p. 72); 14:5–29 (p. 75)

   God's motive, Ge 15:13–16 (p. 16); Dt 7:8–9 (p. 192); Hos 11:1 (p. 993)

F

Failures, Jdg 14:4 (p. 271); Ps 106:7–43 (p. 660); Mt 26:75 (p. 1098); Mk 14:72 (p. 1127); Lk 22:61–62 (p. 1171)

Faith

   Abraham's, Ge 15:6 (p. 16); Ro 4:1–3 (p. 1260)

   Asking for proof, Mt 12:39 (p. 1075); Lk 11:29 (p. 1152)

   Beginning, Jos 9:9 (p. 234); 9:25 (p. 235); 2 Ki 5:17 (p. 399); Mt 17:20 (p. 1083); Lk 17:6 (p. 1161)

   Childlike, Ps 22:9–10 (p. 596); Mt 19:14 (p. 1086); Mk 10:14–15 (p. 1117)

   Cost of, Mt 10:35–37 (p. 1073); Lk 12:51–53 (p. 1155); 2 Ti 3:12 (p. 1368)

   Defending, Jude v. 3 (p. 1422)

   Defined, Heb 11:1 (p. 1385)

   During crisis, Ps 116:10 (p. 667); Isa 10:24 (p. 767); Jer 12:5–6 (p. 852); La 3:21–24 (p. 909); Hab 2:3 (p. 1032); Zep 3:15 (p. 1038); Mt 11:3 (p. 1073); 1 Pe 1:7 (p. 1400)

In action, Jos 2:4–5 (p. 226); Mt 25:35–36 (p. 1096); Lk 17:6 (p. 1161); Ac 3:6 (p. 1216); 2 Ti 2:15 (p. 1368); Heb 11:7 (p. 1386); Jas 2:14–24 (p. 1393)

Power of, Jn 14:12 (p. 1200)

Results of, 1 Ch 11:11 (p. 442); 2 Ch 27:6 (p. 492); Ps 106:31 (p. 661); Mk 11:22–24 (p. 1120)

Rewarded, Job 22:21–25 (p. 563); Jer 39:18 (p. 885); Mt 5:19 (p. 1064); 9:22 (p. 1071); Mk 5:34–36 (p. 1111); Lk 8:48 (p. 1146); 2 Co 5:10 (p. 1304); Eph 1:3 (p. 1323); 2 Jn v. 8 (p. 1418)

Signs of, Mt 3:6 (p. 1062); Lk 3:3 (p. 1135)

Ups and downs, Ge 26:7 (p. 28); Nu 21:5–6 (p. 165); 1 Ki 9:20–21 (p. 373); 2 Ki 13:18–19 (p. 410); 2 Ch 16:12 (p. 480); 24:18 (p. 487); Ps 13:1–5 (p. 589); Isa 54:1–17 (p. 819); Mt 8:10 (p. 1069); Mk 6:51–52 (p. 1113); Lk 8:13 (p. 1145); 17:5 (p. 1161)

Faithfulness, Ge 17:10 (p. 17); Job 36:7 (p. 576); Ps 78 (p. 638); 111 (p. 664); La 3:22–32 (p. 909); Lk 8:18 (p. 1145); Gal 5:16–26 (p. 1320); Heb 3 (p. 1379); Rev 2:8–11 (p. 1426)

False accusations, Job 19:29 (p. 561); 31:35 (p. 572)

False gods, Ac 17:23 (p. 1239)

Fame, Job 29:20 (p. 568); Mt 23:9 (p. 1092)

Family, Ge 2:24 (p. 4); Lev 20:9 (p. 128); Ps 127:3–5 (p. 678); Mal 4:6 (p. 1056); Mt 10:35–37 (p. 1073); Mk 10:29 (p. 1118); Lk 8:20–21 (p. 1145); 12:51–53 (p. 1155); 14:26 (p. 1157); Ac 16:15 (p. 1237)

Blessings, Ge 24:60 (p. 27); 27:38 (p. 30); 28:4 (p. 31); 48:20 (p. 57); Dt 33:1 (p. 220); Ru 4:12 (p. 287); 1 Ch 5:1 (p. 434); 16:43 (p. 449); 26:10 (p. 458)

Model, Ps 103:17–18 (p. 656); 1 Co 7:14 (p. 1286)

Name, Ge 15:2 (p. 16); 19:31–32 (p. 21); 38:14 (p. 44); Dt 25:5–9 (p. 210); Job 30:8 (p. 569)

Of God, Eph 1:5 (p. 1323); 1:13 (p. 1324)

Christ's, 2 Sa 7:16 (p. 332); 1 Ki 11:36 (p. 376); Ps 132:12 (p. 679); Mt 1:1–17 (p. 1059); Lk 2:48 (p. 1134); 3:23–38 (p. 1136); Jn 7:5 (p. 1187)

Famine, Ru 1:1 (p. 283); 1 Ki 17 (p. 383); 2 Ki 6:25—8:2 (p. 402)

Fasting, Lev 16:30 (p. 125); 23:27 (p. 133); Dt 9:18 (p. 195); 1 Ki 21:9 (p. 390); Isa 58:3 (p. 823); Joel 1:14 (p. 998); Zec 8:19 (p. 1048); Mt 6:18 (p. 1067); 9:14–15 (p. 1070); Mk 2:18–20 (p. 1106); Lk 5:35 (p. 1140); Ac 13:2–3 (p. 1232)

Fear, Ps 140:1–11 (p. 684); Mt 8:26 (p. 1070); Mk 4:40 (p. 1109); 5:17 (p. 1109); Lk 8:37 (p. 1146)

Consequences, Job 31:23 (p. 570)

Of death, Isa 38:10–14 (p. 796)

Of God, Ex 3:6 (p. 63); Nu 17:12 (p. 162); Dt 5:5 (p. 190); 2 Ch 26:5 (p. 490); Job 9:9 (p. 552); 28:28 (p. 568); Ps 14:5 (p. 589); 19:7–9 (p. 594); 25:14 (p. 599); 103:11 (p. 656); Pr 1:7 (p. 691)

Of the unknown, Ex 14:12 (p. 75)

Fellowship, Ac 2:42–47 (p. 1216); 4:24–35 (p. 1218); 2 Co 13:14 (p. 1313); Eph 4:17—5:21 (p. 1328); 1 Jn 1 (p. 1411)

Fights

Disputes, 2 Sa 19:26–27 (p. 348)

Feuds, Est 3:2–5 (p. 537); Isa 11:13 (p. 768); Eze 35:5 (p. 949); Lk 9:53 (p. 1149); Ac 23:9 (p. 1247)

Quarrels, Ge 45:24 (p. 54); Ne 5:1–5 (p. 521)

Financial planning, Pr 11:25–28 (p. 704); Ecc 11:2 (p. 743); Lk 12:33–34 (p. 1155); 16:8–11 (p. 1160)

Flood, Ge 7:19–20 (p. 8)

Forgiveness

Human, Ge 33:4 (p. 38); 50:15–21 (p. 60); Lk 15:17–24 (p. 1159); 23:34 (p. 1173); Ac 7:60 (p. 1223); 2 Ti 4:16 (p. 1371); Mt 18:35 (p. 1085); Lk 11:4 (p. 1151); Eph 4:32 (p. 1329); Col 3:13 (p. 1346)

God's, Ex 34:6–7 (p. 99); Ps 32:5 (p. 604); 51:1–2,7,9 (p. 619); 103:8,12 (p. 656); Isa 38:17 (p. 796); 43:25 (p. 806); 44:22 (p. 807); 55:7 (p. 820); Jer 31:34 (p. 876); Mk 2:1–11 (p. 1105); Lk 24:47 (p. 1175); Ac 2:38 (p. 1216); 3:19 (p. 1218); 10:43 (p. 1228); 13:38 (p. 1234); 1 Jn 1:9 (p. 1411)

Freedom, Jn 8:31–36 (p. 1189); Ro 6 (p. 1263); 8:1–17 (p. 1265); Gal 3:8–25 (p. 1317); 4:21—5:26 (p. 1319)

Friendship, 1 Sa 23:16 (p. 316); 2 Sa 1:26 (p. 326); Pr 17:17 (p. 713); 24:26 (p. 722); 27:10,17 (p. 725); Ecc 4:9–12 (p. 737)

With God, Ex 33:11 (p. 97); 33:12,17 (p. 97); Job 42:2 (p. 581); Ps 25:14 (p. 599); 119:57 (p. 670); 2 Co 5:19 (p. 1305)

Fruit of the Spirit, Lk 8:15 (p. 1145); Jn 15:4 (p. 1200); 1 Co 13:1–3 (p. 1294); Gal 5:16–26 (p. 1320)

G

Generosity, Ge 13:9 (p. 15); Dt 23:24–25 (p. 209); Pr 11:25–28 (p. 704); Mal 3:10 (p. 1056); Lk 16:9 (p. 1160); 2 Co 8:1,7 (p. 1307)

Gifts of the spirit, Ex 31:1–5 (p. 95); Ac 10:46 (p. 1228); 12:10,28–29 (p. 1230); 19:6 (p. 1242); Ro 12:6–8 (p. 1273); 1 Co 2:10,28–29 (p. 1281); 7:7–8 (p. 1286); 12:8–30 (p. 1292); 14:3–28 (p. 1295); Eph 4:11 (p. 1327); 1 Pe 4:1 (p. 1403)

Glory, Ex 40:34–38 (p. 106); 2 Ch 7:1–4 (p. 471); Ps 29,93,96 (p. 602); Jn 1:14–18 (p. 1177); 12:20–33 (p. 1196); 2 Co 3 (p. 1302); Ro 3:10–23 (p. 1259)

God, Ge 27:35 (p. 30); 45:8 (p. 53); Ex 4:11 (p. 65); 11:3 (p. 72); 1 Ch 1:1 (p. 427); Job 16:6 (p. 558); Ps 118:18 (p. 668); Jer 51:24 (p. 900); Eze 6:14 (p. 917); Hag 1:6,9 (p. 1040); Rev 10:7 (p. 1433)

God as creator, Ps 108:7–9 (p. 663)

God as father, Isa 64:8 (p. 830); Hos 11:1,4 (p. 993); Mk 14:36 (p. 1125); Ro 8:23 (p. 1267)

God as teacher, Job 38:21 (p. 578); 40:7 (p. 579); 42:4 (p. 581); Jnh 4:6–7 (p. 1017)

God's anger, Dt 1:34 (p. 185); Ezr 10:14 (p. 515); Job 16:9 (p. 558); Ps 2:12 (p. 583); 76:10 (p. 637); 79:5 (p. 641); Isa 6:5 (p. 761); 6:9–13 (p. 761); 12:1 (p. 768); 24:14–16 (p. 779); 47:6 (p. 810); Jer 17:4 (p. 858); 30:22–24 (p. 874); La 2:4–5 (p. 907); Eze 5:13 (p. 916); Ob v. 10–11 (p. 1013); Zec 1:2,15 (p. 1043); Mt 21:12 (p. 1088); Rev 14:19–20 (p. 1437); 15:1 (p. 1437); 16:1 (p. 1438)

God's appearance, Ps 23:3 (p. 597)

   In human form, Ge 18:10 (p. 18); 32:24,28 (p. 38); 32:30 (p. 38); 48:16 (p. 57); Jos 5:14 (p. 229); Jdg 2:1,4 (p. 255); 6:11,14 (p. 261); Job 36:26 (p. 576); Ps 13:1 (p. 589); 32:7 (p. 604); 34:9–10 (p. 606); 67:1 (p. 629); Jer 18:17 (p. 860); Da 3:25 (p. 971); Zec 4:10 (p. 1045); Lk 1:46–55 (p. 1132); 22:70–71 (p. 1172); Jn 1:1 (p. 1176); Heb 2:17 (p. 1379)

   Invisible spirit, Ge 3:8 (p. 4); Dt 5:4 (p. 190)

   Signs, 2 Ch 5:13–14 (p. 469); Job 38:1 (p. 577); 42:5 (p. 581); Ps 18:2 (p. 592); 27:1 (p. 600); 35:2 (p. 606); 61:2 (p. 625); 71:3 (p. 633); 84:11 (p. 644); 100:3 (p. 654); Isa 40:10–11 (p. 798); Eze 34:11 (p. 948); Mic 7:14 (p. 1025); Jn 10:1–15 (p. 1192)

God's call, Jer 1:5 (p. 835); 20:7–9 (p. 861); Eze 3:18 (p. 915); Am 1:1 (p. 1003); Jnh 1:10 (p. 1015); Lk 1:15 (p. 1131); 2 Co 10:12 (p. 1310); Gal 1:1,12 (p. 1314); 1:15–20 (p. 1315); 1 Ti 1:18 (p. 1359); 2 Ti 1:6 (p. 1365)

God's care, Ex 16:31 (p. 79); Nu 2:17 (p. 141); 33:49 (p. 181); Dt 14:23 (p. 200); Ezr 5:5 (p. 509); Job 10:13–14 (p. 553); 29:2 (p. 568); 39:1–30 (p. 578); Ps 23:3 (p. 597); 127:2 (p. 678); 131:2 (p. 678); 139:5 (p. 682); 145:14–16 (p. 687); Isa 49:16 (p. 813); Zec 11:7 (p. 1050)

   Physical needs, Ex 16:8 (p. 78); Jdg 15:19 (p. 273); Ne 3:1–32 (p. 519); Lk 6:35 (p. 1142); Php 4:19 (p. 1340)

God's character, Ex 34:6–7 (p. 99); 1 Sa 15:29 (p. 305); 2 Sa 7:15 (p. 332); 22:27 (p. 352); 1 Ch

21:15 (p. 453); Ne 8:9–11 (p. 526); Job 23:13–17 (p. 564); Ps 7:11 (p. 586); 18:25–26 (p. 593); 33:14–15 (p. 604); 90:11–14 (p. 648); 95:10 (p. 652); 102:25–26 (p. 656); 150:2 (p. 690); Isa 1:1 (p. 755); 43:25 (p. 806); 54:7 (p. 819); Jer 14:7 (p. 854); 14:21 (p. 855); 30:22–24 (p. 874); Eze 10:12 (p. 920); 45:13–25 (p. 961); Da 7:9 (p. 977); Na 1:7 (p. 1026); Zec 4:10 (p. 1045)

God's chosen people, Dt 4:33 (p. 189); Est 4:14 (p. 538); Ps 16:3 (p. 590); 78:67–68 (p. 640); 108:7–9 (p. 663); Eze 36:35–38 (p. 950); Zec 2:8 (p. 1044); Ro 11:22–32 (p. 1271); 2 Th 2:13 (p. 1356); 1 Pe 1:1 (p. 1399)

God's compassion, Ge 15:16 (p. 16); Jn 11:35 (p. 1195)

God's control, Dt 17:15 (p. 203); Jos 1:4 (p. 224); Ne 11:3–19 (p. 530); Est 4:16 (p. 538); 9:3–4 (p. 542); Job 9:13 (p. 552); Ps 46:8 (p. 615); 82:6 (p. 643); 103:19 (p. 656); 113:5 (p. 665); Isa 40:23 (p. 799); 55:11 (p. 820); Jer 29:13 (p. 871); Eze 1:5–6 (p. 913); Da (p. 965); Hab 2:20 (p. 1033); Zec 5:9 (p. 1046); Ro 9:22–23 (p. 1269)

   Over evil, Dt 31:16–21 (p. 217); Jos 6:21 (p. 230); Jdg 9:23 (p. 266); 1 Ki 15:34 (p. 381); Job 1:12 (p. 545); 2:3 (p. 545); 6:4 (p. 549); 16:10–11 (p. 558); 19:8–12 (p. 560); Hab 1:6,13 (p. 1030); Mt 6:10 (p. 1067); Jn 14:30 (p. 1200); Ac 13:48 (p. 1234); 2:23 (p. 1216); Ro 8:28 (p. 1267)

   Over humans, Ge 25:23 (p. 28); 50:20 (p. 60); Ex 11:3 (p. 72); Nu 23:11,25 (p. 168); Jdg 14:4 (p. 271); 1 Sa 2:25 (p. 291); 19:20 (p. 311); 2 Ch 10:15 (p. 474); 33:13 (p. 499); Job 3:23 (p. 547); 13:15 (p. 555); 40:8–14 (p. 580); Ps 33:10 (p. 604); 93:1–5 (p. 651); 118:6 (p. 668); Pr 16:1–9 (p. 710); Ecc 3:14 (p. 736); 7:13–14 (p. 740); Isa 28:11 (p. 784); 53:10 (p. 818); La 5:21 (p. 912); Eze 22:30 (p. 934); 38:16 (p. 953); Jnh 1:10 (p. 1015); Ro 4:17 (p. 1261); 8:29–30 (p. 1267); 9:8–33 (p. 1269); Eph 1:4–5 (p. 1323); 1 Ti 2:4 (p. 1360)

   Over nations, Ge 36:31 (p. 42); Dt 9:4 (p. 194); Jos 8:3–19 (p. 233); 1 Sa 8:21–22 (p. 297); 2 Ki 19:25 (p. 418); 1 Ch 17:9 (p. 450); 2 Ch 20:22–23 (p. 484); 28:5 (p. 492); Job 25:3 (p. 566); Ps 60:8 (p. 625); 108:7–9 (p. 663); Isa 10:5–6 (p. 766); 33:17–19 (p. 791); Jer 21:5 (p. 862); 51:24 (p. 900); Mt 23:37 (p. 1093)

   Over rulers, Ge 41:16 (p. 48); Ex 10:1 (p. 71); 2 Ki 18:25 (p. 417); 1 Ch 5:26 (p. 435); Ezr 7:12–15 (p. 511); Job 34:29–30 (p. 574); Ps 82:6 (p. 643); Isa 37:7 (p. 794); 44:28 (p. 807); Jer 27:6 (p. 869); Eze 29:20 (p. 943); Da 5:18 (p. 974)

God's emotions

   Hate, Mal 1:2–3 (p. 1053)

Jealousy, Hos 2:13–14 (p. 986); Joel 2:18 (p. 1000); Na 1:2 (p. 1026); Zec 8:2 (p. 1048)

Joy, Zep 3:17 (p. 1038)

Pain, Isa 5:1 (p. 759); 63:10 (p. 829); Eze 7:22 (p. 918); Jn 11:35 (p. 1195); Eph 4:30 (p. 1329)

God's faithfulness, Ex 16:34 (p. 79); Ps 18:31 (p. 593); 71:9–18 (p. 633); La 2:6 (p. 907)

God's glory, Ex 24:9–11 (p. 88); Lev 9:23 (p. 116); 1 Ki 8:10–13 (p. 369); 2 Ch 5:13–14 (p. 469); Job 37:21 (p. 577); Ps 26:8 (p. 600); Eze 9:3 (p. 919); Jn 9:3 (p. 1191); 17:1,5 (p. 1203); 1 Co 11:7 (p. 1291); 2 Pe 1:17 (p. 1407)

God's guidance, Ex 14:1–4 (p. 75); Ps 23:4 (p. 597); 25:12 (p. 599); 100:3 (p. 654); Zec 1:8 (p. 1043); Jn 16:13 (p. 1202); Ac 16:6–10 (p. 1237)

God's holiness, Ex 13:13 (p. 75); 30:20–21 (p. 94); Nu 1:51–53 (p. 141); 4:20 (p. 144); 17:12 (p. 162); 20:12–13 (p. 164); Dt 4:24 (p. 189); 9:4 (p. 194); Eze 25:3–7 (p. 938); 28:25 (p. 942); 40:22,26,34,37 (p. 955)

God's honor, Nu 14:13–16 (p. 156); Jdg 11:23–24 (p. 269); 2 Sa 12:14 (p. 338); 2 Ch 2:1 (p. 465); Ne 2:17 (p. 519); Job 1:8 (p. 544); Ps 74:20–23 (p. 636); Isa 5:15–16 (p. 760); 63:12,14 (p. 829); Jer 32:20–33 (p. 877); Eze 36:20 (p. 950)

God's house, Ex 35:4—37:29 (p. 100); 1 Ki 8:27,29 (p. 370); 2 Ch 3:3–17 (p. 467); Ps 114:2 (p. 666); Isa 57:15 (p. 822); La 2:1 (p. 907); Eze 43:9 (p. 958); Mic 1:3 (p. 1018); Eph 2:22 (p. 1325)

God's image, Ge 1:27 (p. 2); 9:6 (p. 10); Dt 19:13 (p. 205); Job 33:16–17 (p. 573); Ps 51:4 (p. 619); 103:14 (p. 656); Pr 19:17 (p. 715); Ecc 7:29 (p. 741); 1 Co 11:7 (p. 1291)

God's judgment, Nu 33:52–53 (p. 181); Dt 2:34; 3:2 (p. 142); Jos 6:21 (p. 230); 2 Ki 24:4 (p. 424); Job 20:23–29 (p. 561); Ps 98:9 (p. 653); Isa 24:1–6 (p. 779); 26:9–10 (p. 781); 66:15–16 (p. 834); Jer 9:25–26 (p. 850); Eze 7:2 (p. 917); Mal 4:1 (p. 1056); Mt 11:22 (p. 1074); Lk 10:14 (p. 1150); Rev 6:12–17 (p. 1430)

God's law, 2 Ki 11:12 (p. 408); 22:8 (p. 421); Ne 8:3 (p. 525); Ps 78:5–7 (p. 638); 93:5 (p. 651); 119:1–176 (p. 668); Isa 13:9–11 (p. 770); Mt 23:23 (p. 1092); Ro 5:20 (p. 1263); 6:14 (p. 1263); 7:10 (p. 1265)

　　After Christ, Dt 12:32 (p. 199); Mt 8:3 (p. 1069); Lk 16:16–17 (p. 1161); Ro 10:4 (p. 1270); 1 Co 10:3–4 (p. 1290); Eph 2:15 (p. 1325)

　　Keeping, Mt 5:17–18 (p. 1064); Gal 2:19 (p. 1317)

　　Misuse of, Isa 29:13 (p. 786)

　　Reason for, Lev 19:18–28 (p. 127); Dt 30:11 (p. 216); Ps 11:3 (p. 588); 19:7–9 (p. 594); 107:11 (p. 662); 2 Co 3:6 (p. 1303); Gal 3:1–25 (p. 1317); 1 Ti 1:9 (p. 1358)

God's love, Ex 34:14 (p. 99); Dt 4:24 (p. 189); 1 Ch 21:15 (p. 453); Ezr 2:2–61 (p. 505); Job 19:11 (p. 560); 23:14–15 (p. 564); 25:6 (p. 566); Ps 5:5 (p. 584); 33:5 (p. 604); 107:33–43 (p. 662); Isa 59:2 (p. 824); Jer 12:7–8 (p. 852); Mt 18:12 (p. 1084); Lk 15:3–7 (p. 1158)

God's name, Ge 4:26 (p. 6); 17:1 (p. 17); Ex 3:14 (p. 63); Nu 6:27 (p. 147); Dt 12:5 (p. 198); Jos 22:22 (p. 250); Ps 20:1 (p. 595); 25:11 (p. 599); Jer 14:7 (p. 854); Lk 1:31 (p. 1131); 2 Pe 1:17 (p. 1407)

God's patience, Isa 54:7 (p. 819); Jer 22:2–5 (p. 862); Eze 6:14 (p. 917); 14:20 (p. 924); Mic 3:4 (p. 1020)

God's presence

　　Everywhere, Lev 15:31 (p. 124); 1 Sa 16:18 (p. 307); Job 26:6 (p. 566); Ps 100:4 (p. 654); Eze 11:16 (p. 921); Ps 22:1–2 (p. 595)

　　Hidden, Job 9:13 (p. 552); 23:8–9 (p. 564); Ps 10:1 (p. 587); 32:6 (p. 604); Isa 45:15 (p. 808); Jer 14:8–9 (p. 854); La 2:1 (p. 907); Da 1:2 (p. 966); Hos 5:6 (p. 988); Mic 5:2 (p. 1021); Jn 12:36 (p. 1196)

　　Signs, Ge 15:17 (p. 16); Ex 13:21–22 (p. 75); Lev 6:12–13 (p. 112); Nu 9:15–16 (p. 151); 1 Ch 13:10,14 (p. 445); Ps 18:7–15 (p. 592); Isa 33:14 (p. 791); Jer 3:16 (p. 839); Am 4:13 (p. 1007); Mt 27:51 (p. 1100); Mk 9:2–3 (p. 1115); 15:38 (p. 1128)

　　Within people, Ps 26:8 (p. 600); Eze 43:9 (p. 958); Mt 28:20 (p. 1102); Col 1:27 (p. 1343); Heb 1:3 (p. 1377)

God's promises, Ge 22:16–17 (p. 23); Dt 4:40 (p. 189); Jos 1:8 (p. 224); 1:9 (p. 224); 2 Ch 7:14 (p. 471); 7:18 (p. 472); Ne 9:15 (p. 528); Ps 25:6 (p. 599); 89:39 (p. 648); Isa 54:1–17 (p. 819); 59:21 (p. 825); Jer 14:21 (p. 855); 2 Co 1:20 (p. 1302)

　　Fulfilled, Jos 14—21 (p. 240); Ps 138:2 (p. 682); Isa 40:3–5,9 (p. 798); Jer 31:33–34 (p. 876); Hab 2:3 (p. 1032)

God's protection, Dt 2:7 (p. 186); Ps 20:1 (p. 595); 37:3–25 (p. 608); 54:7 (p. 621); 57:1 (p. 623); 91:10 (p. 649); 97:10 (p. 653); Mk 16:18 (p. 1129); Lk 21:18 (p. 1169); Jn 17:11–12 (p. 1204); Rev 7:2 (p. 1431); 11:7 (p. 1434)

　　Using angels, Ge 32:1–2 (p. 37); 2 Ki 6:17 (p. 400); Eze 9:1–2 (p. 919)

God's record keeping, Ps 56:8 (p. 623); 130:3–4 (p. 678); Da 7:10 (p. 977); 10:21 (p. 981); Mal 3:16

(p. 1056); Rev 3:5 (p. 1428); 13:8 (p. 1435); 20:12 (p. 1442)

God's silence, 1 Sa 14:37 (p. 304); Job 19:7 (p. 560); 34:29 (p. 574); 42:2 (p. 581); Ps 10:1 (p. 587); 22:1–2 (p. 595); 74:9 (p. 636); 83:1 (p. 643); Isa 42:14 (p. 803)

God's timing, Ge 40:23 (p. 47); Ex 12:40 (p. 74); Dt 4:33 (p. 189); 2 Ch 33:1–2 (p. 499); 34:27–28 (p. 501); Ps 70:1,5 (p. 632); Hag 2:6 (p. 1042); Lk 21:32 (p. 1170); Jn 2:4 (p. 1179); Gal 4:4 (p. 1318); Eph 1:10 (p. 1323)

God's will

Accepting, 2 Ki 20:16–19 (p. 419); Job 1:20 (p. 545); 10:2 (p. 553); 23:2 (p. 564); 41:11 (p. 580); Ps 37:4 (p. 608); 88:10–12 (p. 646); Isa 39:5–8 (p. 798)

Asking for signs, Ge 24:14 (p. 25); 44:5,15 (p. 52); Jdg 6:37–40 (p. 263); 1 Sa 14:10–12 (p. 302); 2 Ki 20:8–11 (p. 419); Isa 7:11 (p. 763); 38:7–8 (p. 796)

Changing, Ex 32:14 (p. 96); Nu 23:19 (p. 168); Dt 9:19 (p. 195); 1 Sa 15:29 (p. 305); 2 Ki 20:5–6 (p. 419); Ps 106:23 (p. 660); Isa 38:1–5 (p. 796); Jer 26:3 (p. 868); Da 9:3 (p. 979); Hos 11:8 (p. 993); Am 7:3,6 (p. 1009); Mt 6:8 (p. 1066)

Resisting, Ex 10:1; Dt 2:30 (p. 187); Ecc 3:14 (p. 736); Isa 22:14 (p. 777); Jer 13:23 (p. 854); Lk 8:13 (p. 1145); Jn 12:39 (p. 1197); Ro 1:24,26,28 (p. 1258); 2 Th 2:11 (p. 1356)

Ways to know, Ge 24:14 (p. 25); Nu 34:13 (p. 181); Jdg 7:15 (p. 263); 1 Sa 6:9 (p. 295); 1 Ch 14:10,14 (p. 445); Ps 95:7 (p. 652); Jer 21:1–2 (p. 862); Eze 1:1 (p. 913); Ac 10:10–20 (p. 1227); Ro 12:2 (p. 1272); 1 Ti 4:1 (p. 1360)

God's word, 1 Ch 28:19 (p. 461)

Direction, Ps 95:7 (p. 652); 119:11 (p. 669); 119:105 (p. 672); Pr 14:12 (p. 707); Ac 10:10–20 (p. 1227); Eph 3:5 (p. 1327); 5:26 (p. 1331)

Love for, Ps 119:1–176 (p. 668)

Recognize, Ex 29:42–43 (p. 93); 2 Sa 2:1 (p. 326); 21:1 (p. 350); 1 Ch 28:12,19 (p. 461); 2 Ch 33:10 (p. 499); Da 1:17 (p. 968); Jnh 1:1 (p. 1015); Jn 1:1 (p. 1176); Ac 10:10–20 (p. 1227); 1 Th 2:13 (p. 1349); Heb 2:3–4 (p. 1378)

Good works, Ne 13:10 (p. 533); Mt 25:35–36 (p. 1096); Lk 14:12–14 (p. 1157); 16:9 (p. 1160); Php 2:12–13 (p. 1335); 3:6–8 (p. 1338); Col 1:29 (p. 1343); 2 Ti 2:15 (p. 1368); Heb 4:11 (p. 1380); 2 Pe 1:5 (p. 1406); 3 Jn v. 11 (p. 1419)

Gospel, Ac 8:1–4 (p. 1223); Ro 1:16–17 (p. 1257); 15:14–16 (p. 1276); Gal 1:6–9 (p. 1314); Eph 2:1–10 (p. 1325); Col 1:3–23 (p. 1341)

Gossip, Ps 94:20–23 (p. 652); 122:5 (p. 676); 125:3 (p. 677); Pr 10:18–21 (p. 703); 29:18 (p. 728); Ecc 8:2–6 (p. 741); 10:6 (p. 743); Ac 4:19 (p. 1218); Ro 13:1–7 (p. 1273); Tit 3:1–2 (p. 1374)

Grace, Ge 48:20 (p. 57); Ex 6:14–27 (p. 67); 1 Ki 8:58 (p. 372); Isa 26:9–10 (p. 781); Jer 12:14–16 (p. 853); Eze 36:26 (p. 950); Lk 17:7–10 (p. 1161); Ac 4:12 (p. 1218); Ro 6:14 (p. 1263); 2 Co 8:1,7 (p. 1307); 9:8 (p. 1308); Eph 4:7 (p. 1327); Tit 2:11 (p. 1374)

Overcomes sin, Ge 4:7 (p. 5); Ex 33:12 (p. 97); 2 Sa 12:13 (p. 338); Isa 65:1 (p. 831); Am 4:11 (p. 1007); Ro 3:8 (p. 1259); 5:18–19 (p. 1263)

Greed, Nu 11:33 (p. 154); 2 Sa 12:8 (p. 337); 1 Ki 20:34 (p. 388); Mic 2:1–2 (p. 1019); Hab 2:5 (p. 1032)

Grief, Lev 10:6 (p. 117); Dt 34:8 (p. 223); Jos 7:6–10 (p. 231); 2 Sa 13:19 (p. 339); Est 4:1–2 (p. 538); Eze 27:30 (p. 940)

Grudges, 2 Sa 14:24 (p. 341); Ps 95:10 (p. 652)

Guilt, Ge 44:16 (p. 52); Ex 20:24 (p. 83); Lev 4:2 (p. 110); 16:20–22 (p. 125); Dt 28:65 (p. 215); Job 25:4 (p. 566); Isa 6:6–7 (p. 761)

H

Happiness, Ps 100:2 (p. 654); Ecc 7:3 (p. 740); Ac 17:18 (p. 1239)

Hate, Ps 31:6 (p. 603); 139:21–22 (p. 684)

Healing

By God (faith), Nu 21:8 (p. 165); Mt 9:22 (p. 1071); Mk 5:34–36 (p. 1111); 6:13 (p. 1112); Lk 4:39 (p. 1138); 8:48 (p. 1146); Ac 5:15 (p. 1219); Jas 5:15–16 (p. 1397)

Relationships, Ge 42:7 (p. 49); Mk 9:12 (p. 1116)

Heart, 1 Sa 16:1–13 (p. 306); Ps 51 (p. 619); Pr 4:23 (p. 696); Jer 17:9–10 (p. 858); Mt 12:33–37 (p. 1075)

Heaven, Job 36:7 (p. 576); Mt 22:30 (p. 1090); Mk 12:25 (p. 1121); Jn 14:2 (p. 1199); Eph 2:6 (p. 1325); 4:10 (p. 1327); 1 Th 4:14,16 (p. 1352); Heb 1:3 (p. 1377); Rev 4:1 (p. 1428); 21:16 (p. 1443)

Hell, Isa 66:24 (p. 834); Mt 5:22 (p. 1065); Php 2:10 (p. 1335); 1 Th 4:14,16 (p. 1352); 2 Pe 2:4 (p. 1408); Rev 14:10–11 (p. 1437); 19:20 (p. 1441)

Herod, Mt 2 (p. 1060); 14:1–12 (p. 1078); Ac 12:1–23 (p. 1230)

Holiness (reasons for), Lev 19:2 (p. 127); Job 12:4 (p. 554); Jn 17:17,19 (p. 1204); Ro 1:4 (p. 1256); 3:8 (p. 1259); 1 Th 4:3–12 (p. 1351); 2 Ti 1:9 (p. 1365); Heb 12:14 (p. 1388); 1 Pe 1:15 (p. 1400)

Personal, Lev 5:2 (p. 111); 11:4–41 (p. 117); 2 Co 7:1 (p. 1307)

Priestly, Lev 22:32 (p. 131)

Holy Spirit, Ge 1:2 (p. 1); Mt 7:7–8 (p. 1067); Mk 1:8 (p. 1103); 3:29 (p. 1108); Jn 14:16,26 (p. 1200); 16:13 (p. 1202); 16:8 (p. 1202); Ac 19:2 (p. 1242); Ro 1:4 (p. 1256); 1 Co 2:13 (p. 1281); Eph 4:30 (p. 1329); 1 Th 5:19 (p. 1353); 1 Pe 1:15 (p. 1400)

Filling, Eph 5:18 (p. 1330)

Fruit of, Lk 8:15 (p. 1145); Gal 5:22–26 (p. 1320); Heb 12:14 (p. 1388)

Gifts of, Ac 21:9 (p. 1245); Ro 12:6 (p. 1273); 1 Co 12:1–31 (p. 1292); 14:2–4 (p. 1295); 14:20–25 (p. 1295)

Praying, Ro 8:27 (p. 1267); Eph 6:18 (p. 1331); Jude v. 20 (p. 1424)

Honesty, Pr 24:26 (p. 722)

Hope, Job 17:15 (p. 559); Isa 8:9–10 (p. 764); 40:31 (p. 799); La 3:21–24 (p. 909); Mic 7:8 (p. 1024); Zec 9:12 (p. 1049); 1 Pe 1:3–9 (p. 1399)

Hospitality, Ge 18:4–5 (p. 18); 19:2 (p. 20); 19:8 (p. 20); 24:20 (p. 25); Lev 3:1 (p. 109); Jdg 19:5–10 (p. 278); 1 Sa 25:8 (p. 317); 2 Sa 9:7 (p. 334); Ps 23:5 (p. 599); Lk 7:44–46 (p. 1144); 10:38–41 (p. 1151); Heb 13:2 (p. 1390)

Human nature, Ge 8:21 (p. 10); Jos 4:14 (p. 228); Ps 53:3 (p. 621); Ecc 1:9–10 (p. 733); Isa 64:6 (p. 830); Jer 24:7 (p. 866); 43:2 (p. 888); Zec 10:2 (p. 1049); Mk 9:33–37 (p. 1117); Lk 9:48 (p. 1149); Ac 15:39 (p. 1236)

Corrupt, Job 25:4 (p. 566); Ps 146:3–4 (p. 688); Ro 7:5–8 (p. 1265); Eph 4:22 (p. 1328); Col 3:5 (p. 1346)

Human sacrifice, Ge 22:2 (p. 23); Lev 18:21 (p. 126); Dt 12:31 (p. 199); 2 Ki 3:27 (p. 396); 16:3 (p. 413); 21:16 (p. 420); Jer 19:5 (p. 860); Hos 13:2 (p. 995)

Humility, 1 Sa 15:22 (p. 305); 2 Ki 17:14 (p. 414); Ps 25:9 (p. 599); 131:1–2 (p. 678); Pr 30:2–3 (p. 729); Mk 9:33–37 (p. 1117); Lk 2:9–12 (p. 1133); 9:48 (p. 1149); 14:11 (p. 1157); Jn 13:14–15 (p. 1198)

Hunger and thirst (spiritual), Dt 8:3 (p. 194); Am 8:11–12 (p. 1010); Isa 55:1–3 (p. 820); Mt 4:4 (p. 1062); 5:6 (p. 1063); Jn 4:13–14 (p. 1182); 6:35,48–58 (p. 1186); 7:37–38 (p. 1188); 1 Co 10:16 (p. 1291)

Hypocrisy, Ps 26:4–5 (p. 600); 66:18 (p. 629); Pr 15:8 (p. 708); Isa 5:18–19 (p. 760); Jer 17:10 (p. 858); 42:20 (p. 887); Am 5:21–23 (p. 1008); Mt 23:15 (p. 1092); 23:33 (p. 1093); Mk 7:11 (p. 1113); Lk 12:1 (p. 1153); Jn 8:7 (p. 1188); Ac 5:5,10 (p. 1219)

I

Idolatry, Dt 32:17 (p. 219); Jdg 16:23 (p. 274); 2 Ki 8:18 (p. 404); Isa 44:16–17 (p. 807); Jer 23:9–14 (p. 864)

Destruction, 2 Ch 15:16 (p. 478); Ps 115:4–7 (p. 666)

God's power over, Jdg 18:17 (p. 277); 1 Sa 5:6 (p. 294); 2 Ch 25:14 (p. 488); Isa 41:7 (p. 800); 43:10 (p. 805); 46:1 (p. 809)

Modern, Ps 97:7 (p. 653); Hos 4:12 (p. 988)

Political reasons, 2 Ki 10:29 (p. 407); Jer 44:8 (p. 888)

Punished, 1 Ki 11:10–12 (p. 375); 2 Ch 10:14–16 (p. 474); La 1:8 (p. 906)

Results, 2 Ch 27:2 (p. 492); Ps 115:8 (p. 667); Isa 65:5 (p. 831); Jer 17:1 (p. 858); Am 2:4 (p. 1004); 9:4 (p. 1011)

Illness, 2 Ki 5:1 (p. 398); 7:3 (p. 402); 2 Ch 16:12 (p. 480); 21:15 (p. 485); Job 2:7–8 (p. 545); Ps 38:3 (p. 610); 103:3 (p. 656)

Image of God, Ge 1:26–28 (p. 2); 5:1 (p. 6); 9:6 (p. 10); Ex 20:4 (p. 82); Ps 8:6–8 (p. 587); Jn 1:18 (p. 1177); 12:45 (p. 1197); 14:9 (p. 1200); Ac 17:29 (p. 1239); 1 Co 11:7 (p. 1291); 2 Co 4:4 (p. 1303); Col 1:15 (p. 1342); Heb 1:3 (p. 1377); Jas 3:9 (p. 1395)

Incarnation, Mt 1:18–25 (p. 1060); Lk 1—2 (p. 1130); Jn 1:1–18 (p. 1176)

Incest, Ge 4:17 (p. 5); 19:31–32 (p. 21); 35:22 (p. 41); Lev 20:17 (p. 129); Dt 27:22 (p. 212); 2 Sa 13:13 (p. 339); Am 2:7 (p. 1004)

Infertility, Ge 16:2 (p. 16); 25:2 (p. 27); 29:31 (p. 33); Nu 5:28 (p. 146); 1 Sa 1:5 (p. 289); Ps 113:7–9 (p. 665)

Injustice, Job 24:1–12 (p. 564); Ps 140:12 (p. 684); Ecc 8:14 (p. 741); Am 1—9 (p. 1003); Ob v. 1–21 (p. 1012)

In-laws, Ge 26:35 (p. 29); 31:2 (p. 35)

Integrity, Ex 8:28–32 (p. 70); Lev 19:36 (p. 128); Dt 25:15 (p. 211); 1 Ki 9:4–5 (p. 372); Ps 25:21 (p. 600); Pr 2:7 (p. 693); 10:9 (p. 702); 11:3 (p. 703); 16:11–13 (p. 710); 20:7 (p. 716); 28:6 (p. 727); Tit 2:7 (p. 1374)

Intercession, Ge 18:23–32 (p. 19); 1 Ki 8:33–51 (p. 370); Ezr 9:5–15 (p. 514); Da 9:3–19 (p. 979); Jn 17 (p. 1203); Ro 8:26–27,31–34 (p. 1267); 1 Ti 2:1–2 (p. 1359); Jas 5:16 (p. 1397); Heb 7:24–25 (p. 1383); 1 Jn 2:1 (p. 1412);

Isaac, Ge 18:1–15 (p. 18); 22:1–19 (p. 22); 24 (p. 25); 27 (p. 29); 35:16–29 (p. 41); Ro 9:6–9 (p. 1269); Gal 4:21–31 (p. 1319)

Israel, Nu 26:51 (p. 173); Jer 31:36,40 (p. 876); Eze 36:35–38 (p. 950); 47:15–20 (p. 963); Am 9:15 (p. 1011); Ro 11:22–32 (p. 1271)

J

Jacob, Ge 25:19–34 (p. 27); Ge 27 (p. 29); Ge 28:10–22 (p. 32); Ge 29–30 (p. 32); Ge 32 (p. 37)

Jealousy, Ge 43:34 (p. 52); Nu 12:1 (p. 154); 16:3 (p. 159); 1 Sa 18:12 (p. 310); Ps 73:22 (p. 636); Ecc 4:4–6 (p. 737); Lk 15:25–32 (p. 1159)

Jerusalem

Importance of, 2 Sa 5:9 (p. 330); 2 Ch 1:4 (p. 464); Ne 11:1–2 (p. 530); Ps 3:4 (p. 584); 46:4 (p. 615); 48:8 (p. 616); 76:2 (p. 637); 137:5–6 (p. 682); Isa 35:8 (p. 793); 58:12 (p. 823); Eze 16:8 (p. 925); 48:35 (p. 965); Joel 3:17 (p. 1001); Mic 1:13 (p. 1019); 4:2 (p. 1021); 7:8 (p. 1024)

New, Rev 21:2 (p. 1442); 21:22–27 (p. 1443)

Jesus Christ

Divinity, Jn 5:18 (p. 1183); 6:46,57 (p. 1186); 8:58–59 (p. 1190); 10:33 (p. 1192); 14:9–28 (p. 1200); Ac 1:9 (p. 1213); Ro 1:4 (p. 1256); 1 Co 15:28 (p. 1297); Col 1:19 (p. 1343); Heb 1:3 (p. 1377)

Enemies, Lk 5:17 (p. 1139); Heb 10:13 (p. 1385)

Glory, Mt 17:2 (p. 1082); Mk 9:2–3 (p. 1115); Jn 17:1,5 (p. 1203); 17:5,24 (p. 1203); 2 Co 4:17 (p. 1303)

Humanity, Mt 4:3–11 (p. 1062); 26:38–39 (p. 1097); Mk 13:32 (p. 1124); 14:33–35 (p. 1125); Lk 4:3–13 (p. 1137); 22:42–44 (p. 1171); Ro 8:29 (p. 1267); Heb 2:6–8 (p. 1378); 4:15 (p. 1380); 1 Jn 5:6 (p. 1416); 2 Jn v. 7 (p. 1418)

Humility, Php 2:6–7 (p. 1334)

Power, Mt 14:25 (p. 1079); Mk 3:22 (p. 1108); 5:11–13 (p. 1109); 5:25–29 (p. 1111); 6:48 (p. 1113); Lk 5:17 (p. 1139); 8:46 (p. 1146); Jn 6:19 (p. 1185); 1 Co 15:28 (p. 1297); Rev 9:17–19 (p. 1433)

Prayers, Mt 14:23 (p. 1079); Mk 6:46 (p. 1113); Heb 8:2 (p. 1383)

Purpose, Lk 13:32 (p. 1156); Heb 5:5,10 (p. 1380)

Reign, Zec 14:9 (p. 1052); Eph 1:10 (p. 1323); 1:20 (p. 1325); 4:10 (p. 1327); Php 2:10 (p. 1335); Rev 5:11–14 (p. 1430)

Second coming, Isa 35:1–2 (p. 793); Jer 23:5–8 (p. 864); Hos 14:5–7 (p. 996); Mt 24:29 (p. 1093); Mk 13:24 (p. 1124); Lk 17:22–37 (p. 1162); Ac 1:11 (p. 1214); Ro 13:11–12 (p. 1274); 1 Th 4:15 (p. 1352); 2 Th 2:3–12 (p. 1355); 2 Pe 3:12 (p. 1409); Rev 22:6,10 (p. 1443)

Jobs (attitude toward), Pr 18:9 (p. 714); 24:30–34 (p. 722); 28:19 (p. 727); 2 Th 3:10 (p. 1357)

Joy, Ps 100:2 (p. 654); Isa 12 (p. 768); 35 (p. 793); Mt 5:1–12 (p. 1063); Lk 15 (p. 1158); Jn 13:1–17 (p. 1198); Gal 5:16–26 (p. 1320); Php 4:4–9 (p. 1339); Col 1:24 (p. 1343); Jas 1:2–18 (p. 1392); 1 Pe 1:1–9 (p. 1399); 4:12–19 (p. 1403)

Judah, Dt 33:7 (p. 222); Nu 1:27 (p. 140); 26:22 (p. 172); Jos 15 (p. 242); Jdg 1:1–20 (p. 254); 2 Sa 2:1–4 (p. 326); 1 Ki 12:21–22 (p. 377); 14:21–22 (p. 380); 2 Ki 24:1–16 (p. 424); 1 Ch 28:2–4 (p. 460); Ezr 1:1–5 (p. 504); Eze 48:7 (p. 964); Mt 1:2–6 (p. 1059); Rev 7:5 (p. 1431)

Judging others, Lk 13:3–5 (p. 1155); Jn 5:22 (p. 1183); 8:7 (p. 1188); Ac 10:4 (p. 1227); Ro 14:1 (p. 1274); 1 Co 4:3 (p. 1283); Jas 2:13 (p. 1393)

Judgment

Attitude about, Mt 7:1–5 (p. 1067); 19:28 (p. 1086); Lk 22:30 (p. 1170); Ro 14:1–4,13 (p. 1274); 1 Co 4:5 (p. 1283); 10:29 (p. 1291); Gal 6:1–4 (p. 1320); Jas 4:11–12 (p. 1395)

God's, Ge 18:26 (p. 19); Dt 32:4 (p. 218); Job 34:10 (p. 574); Ps 94:2 (p. 651); Jn 5:22 (p. 1183); Ac 10:42 (p. 1228); 2 Th 1:5 (p. 1354); 2 Ti 4:1 (p. 1368)

Judgment day, Isa 13:10 (p. 770); Joel 2:30–32 (p. 1000); Ro 14:10 (p. 1274); Heb 10:25 (p. 1385)

Justice, Lev 24:20 (p. 134); 2 Ch 19:4–5 (p. 482); Job 24:18 (p. 565); Ps 122:5 (p. 676); Eze 38:22–23 (p. 953)

Delayed, Job 27:1–2 (p. 566); 34:19 (p. 574); 36:6 (p. 575); 36:9–11 (p. 576); Isa 11:4–5 (p. 768)

God's, Nu 14:20–35 (p. 156); Dt 28:58–59 (p. 214); 28:63 (p. 215); Job 1:13–19 (p. 545); Ps 78:34 (p. 639); Ecc 3:17 (p. 736); Jer 12:1 (p. 852); Eze 14:22–23 (p. 924); Na 2:13 (p. 1028); Zep 3:5 (p. 1037)

Justification, Lk 18:13–14 (p. 1163); Ac 13:39 (p. 1234); Ro 3:22–28 (p. 1259); 5:1–21 (p. 1261); 9:31–32 (p. 1270); 1 Co 1:30 (p. 1281); Gal 2:21 (p. 1317); 3:11 (p. 1317); Jas 2:14–26 (p. 1393); 1 Pe 2:22 (p. 1401)

K

Kindness, Ge 32:10 (p. 37); 39:21 (p. 46); Ru 2:20 (p. 285); 1 Ki 3:6 (p. 362); Ezr 9:9 (p. 514); Job 10:12 (p. 553); Isa 54:8 (p. 819); Gal 5:16–26 (p. 1320); Hos 11:4 (p. 993); Ac 14:17 (p. 1235); Tit 3:4 (p. 1374)

King, 1 Sa 8 (p. 296); 12 (p. 300); Ps 47 (p. 616); 99 (p. 653); Lk 1:26–38 (p. 1131); Eph 1:15–34 (p. 1324); 1 Ti 1:15–17 (p. 1359); Heb 1:1–12 (p. 1377)

Kingdom of God, 1 Ch 17:9 (p. 450); Jer 3:14–16 (p. 839); Mt 4:17 (p. 1063); 5:3–10 (p. 1063); 13:24 (p. 1076); Lk 3:4–6 (p. 1135); 16:16 (p. 1161); 17:20–21 (p. 1162)

Kings, Dt 17:15 (p. 203); 1 Sa 8:5–9 (p. 296); 10:24 (p. 299); 1 Ki 12:16 (p. 377); 2 Ki 11:12 (p. 408); 23:34 (p. 424); 25:30 (p. 426); 2 Ch 25:2 (p. 488); Eze 28:2 (p. 940); Da 3:13–14 (p. 970)

L

Last days, Isa 2:2 (p. 757); 24:18–20 (p. 779); Joel 2:30–32 (p. 1000); Mic 4:1 (p. 1020); Ac 2:19–20 (p. 1215); 1 Co 7:29 (p. 1286); 2 Th 2:2 (p. 1355); 2 Ti 3:1 (p. 1368); Heb 9:26 (p. 1384); 1 Pe 4:7 (p. 1403)

Lazarus, Jn 11:1–44 (p. 1194); Lk 16:19–31 (p. 1161)

Laziness, Pr 6:6–11 (p. 697); 2 Th 3:6–13 (p. 1357)

Leaders

　Ability, Jdg 6:25 (p. 262); 12:8,11,13 (p. 270); 13:25 (p. 271); 14:6 (p. 271); 1 Sa 10:9–11 (p. 298); 11:6 (p. 299); 2 Ki 2:9 (p. 394); Isa 45:1 (p. 808)

　Choosing, Ge 49:10–12 (p. 57); Ex 6:14–27 (p. 67); Dt 16:18 (p. 202); 31:3 (p. 217); Jdg 11:4–6 (p. 268); 1 Ch 5:2 (p. 434); 12:2 (p. 443); Isa 3:6 (p. 758); Hos 8:4 (p. 991); 1 Ti 3:2–7 (p. 1360); 5:24–25 (p. 1363)

　Preparation, Ex 17:9 (p. 79); Dt 34:9 (p. 223); 1 Ki 3:7 (p. 362); 19:19 (p. 387); Pr 30:21–23 (p. 729)

　Responsibility, Jer 23:1 (p. 864); Eze 44:20–23 (p. 960); Mal 2:3 (p. 1054); Jas 3:1 (p. 1394)

　Spiritual, Nu 27:18 (p. 174); 2 Ki 4:13 (p. 397); 6:21 (p. 402); 13:14 (p. 410); 16:15–16 (p. 413); 2 Ch 24:16 (p. 487); Ne 12:1 (p. 531); 13:28 (p. 534); Isa 29:9–10 (p. 785); 32:5–6 (p. 789); 56:10 (p. 821); Jer 29:21–23 (p. 871); Hos 6:9 (p. 990); Zep 3:4 (p. 1037); Mal 2:3 (p. 1054); Mt 20:26–28 (p. 1087); 23:33 (p. 1093); Lk 11:44 (p. 1152); Jn 21:15–17 (p. 1211); 1 Co 4:16 (p. 1283)

　Wicked, Job 34:29–30 (p. 574); Eze 11:3 (p. 920)

Life

　After death (Old Testament), Nu 20:24 (p. 165); 1 Sa 28:19 (p. 321); 2 Sa 12:23 (p. 338); Ps 6:5 (p. 585); 17:15 (p. 592); 30:9 (p. 602); 49:15 (p. 618); Pr 2:18 (p. 693); Ecc 9:10 (p. 742); 12:7 (p. 745)

　Principles, Pr 3:1–4 (p. 693)

　Source, Ge 2:7 (p. 3); Job 27:3 (p. 566); Ps 104:30 (p. 658); Ecc 12:7 (p. 745)

　Unfair, Ge 18:25 (p. 19); 2 Sa 21:6,9,14 (p. 350); Job 1:13–19 (p. 545); 34:19 (p. 574); Ps 73:3–5 (p. 634); Ecc 2:26 (p. 736); 4:13–16 (p. 738)

Value of, 2 Ki 11:1–2 (p. 407); Job 3:10–16 (p. 547); Ecc 12:6 (p. 745)

Without God, Ecc 1:2 (p. 733); 6:12 (p. 740)

Light, Ge 1:14–16 (p. 2); Ps 13:3 (p. 589); 112:4 (p. 665); 119:105 (p. 672); Isa 42:6 (p. 802); 58:8,10 (p. 823); 60:3 (p. 826); 1 Jn 1:5 (p. 1411)

Loneliness, Ps 42:3–4 (p. 612); 102:6–7 (p. 654); 102:16–18 (p. 655)

Lord's Supper, Mt 6:29 (p. 1067); 26:26,28 (p. 1097); Lk 22:17–20 (p. 1170); Jn 6:51–56 (p. 1186); 21:13 (p. 1211); Ac 1:4 (p. 1213); 2:42,46–47 (p. 1216); 20:7,11 (p. 1243); 1 Co 10:16–17 (p. 1291); 11:20–26 (p. 1292) 24:30,35,41–43 (p. 1292)

Love

　For God, Nu 30:2 (p. 177); Ps 37:4 (p. 608); 69:9 (p. 631); 112:2–8 (p. 665); 130:5–6 (p. 678); Lk 14:26 (p. 1157); Jn 21:15–17 (p. 1211); Ro 13:10 (p. 1273); Heb 10:6,8 (p. 1384); Rev 2:4 (p. 1426)

　For others, Mt 5:48 (p. 1066); Jn 13:34–35 (p. 1198); 15:12–14,17 (p. 1201); Ro 12:18 (p. 1273); 12:20 (p. 1273); 13:10 (p. 1273); 1 Co 1:7 (p. 1279); 3:2 (p. 1282); 13:1–3 (p. 1294); 1 Jn 4:16 (p. 1415)

Loyalty, 1 Ki 11:17–19 (p. 375); 2 Ch 11:13–14 (p. 475); 11:16 (p. 475); Ps 16:4 (p. 590); 84:11 (p. 644); Pr 17:17 (p. 713)

Lying, Ex 1:19–20 (p. 62); 1 Sa 21:2 (p. 314); 27:8–10 (p. 320); 2 Ki 8:10 (p. 403); 10:19 (p. 407); 2 Ch 18:22 (p. 481); Ps 62:4 (p. 626); Jer 38:27 (p. 884); Ac 5:5,10 (p. 1219)

M

Magic, witchcraft, and sorcery, Ex 22:18 (p. 85); Lev 19:26,31 (p. 128); 20:6,27 (p. 128); Dt 18:10–12,20–21 (p. 203); Isa 2:6 (p. 758); 47:10–14 (p. 810); Jer 27:9 (p. 869); Mic 5:12 (p. 1022); Mal 3:5 (p. 1056); Ac 8:9–24 (p. 1224); 13:6–12 (p. 1233); 16:16–18 (p. 1237); 19:13–19 (p. 1242); Gal 5:20 (p. 1320)

Marriage

　Choosing a spouse, Ru 3:10 (p. 287); 2 Ch 21:6 (p. 484); Pr 21:9 (p. 717)

　Customs, Ge 24:50–51 (p. 26); 24:67 (p. 27); 29:18 (p. 33); 29:23–25 (p. 33); 29:27 (p. 33); 31:15 (p. 36); 34:4 (p. 39); Ru 3:7–8,13–14 (p. 286); 1 Ch 2:21 (p. 430); 2:34–35 (p. 430)

　Interfaith, Ge 38:2 (p. 44); Dt 7:3–4 (p. 192); Jdg 12:9 (p. 270); 1 Ki 7:8 (p. 367); 11:1–4 (p. 375); 16:31 (p. 383); 2 Ch 8:11 (p. 472); 21:6 (p. 484); Ne 13:26 (p. 534); 13:28 (p. 534); 1 Co 7:14 (p. 1286)

Interracial, Lev 24:10 (p. 134); Ru 1:4 (p. 283); Jer 31:8 (p. 874)

Political, Ge 20:2 (p. 21); 41:45 (p. 48); 1 Ki 3:1 (p. 362); 2 Ch 18:1 (p. 480)

Relationship, Ge 2:24 (p. 4); 3:16 (p. 5); Pr 31:23 (p. 730); Jer 16:2 (p. 856); Mk 10:8 (p. 1117)

Remarriage, Dt 24:4 (p. 209); Mt 19:9 (p. 1085)

Martyrs, 1 Ki 18:4,13 (p. 384); 2 Ki 21:16 (p. 420); Ps 37:3–25 (p. 608); Isa 57:1–2 (p. 822); Da 6:22–23 (p. 976); Lk 21:18 (p. 1169); Php 3:10 (p. 1339); 1 Pe 1:6 (p. 1399); Rev 6:9 (p. 1430); 11:7 (p. 1434); 20:4–5 (p. 1441)

Materialism, Mt 5:3–12 (p. 1063); Lk 6:20–22 (p. 1141) 1 Co 3:3 (p. 1141); Eph 4:13 (p. 1327)

Meaning of life, Ps 73:13 (p. 635); 90:17 (p. 649); 102:9–10 (p. 655); Pr 1:7 (p. 691); Ecc 1:2 (p. 733); 2:3–11 (p. 734); 2:13–16 (p. 734); 8:16–17 (p. 742); 11:8 (p. 743); 2 Co 5:10 (p. 1304)

Mercy, Ps 7:11 (p. 586); 25:11 (p. 599); 39:13 (p. 611); 51:1 (p. 619); 78:39 (p. 640); 139:19 (p. 683); 143:1–2 (p. 685); Isa 30:18 (p. 787); Jer 3:1 (p. 839); 22:2–5 (p. 862); 24:7 (p. 866); Eze 3:7 (p. 915); 39:25 (p. 954); Hos 11:8 (p. 993); Na 2:13 (p. 1028); Jas 2:13 (p. 1393)

Messiah, Ps 110:4 (p. 664); Isa 16:5 (p. 773); 32:3 (p. 789); Jer 33:16 (p. 879); Na 1:15 (p. 1028); Zec 11:7 (p. 1050); Mt 16:20 (p. 1082); 17:2 (p. 1082); 20:30 (p. 1087); Mk 8:30 (p. 1115); 10:47 (p. 1118); 11:8 (p. 1120); Lk 2:32 (p. 1134); 18:34 (p. 1165); 20:41–44 (p. 1169); Jn 1:46 (p. 1178)

Other names for, Ps 2:2 (p. 582); 110:1 (p. 664); Zec 3:8 (p. 1045); 10:4 (p. 1049); Lk 2:25 (p. 1134); Jn 10:1–15 (p. 1192); Rev 5:5–6 (p. 1429)

Prophecy about, Isa 7:14–16 (p. 763); 9:4–6 (p. 764); 32:1 (p. 789); 53:2 (p. 817); Eze 34:11 (p. 948); Da 9:24–27 (p. 980); Zec 6:13 (p. 1046); 12:10 (p. 1051); Lk 3:4–6 (p. 1135)

Son of David, Ps 72:5 (p. 634); 132:12 (p. 679); Isa 11:1 (p. 768); Eze 17:22–24 (p. 927); 34:23–24 (p. 948); Hag 2:23 (p. 1042); Mk 12:35–37 (p. 1123); Lk 18:38 (p. 1165)

Miracles, Ex 4:1–9 (p. 64); 14:21 (p. 76); 16:31 (p. 79); Jos 3:16 (p. 227); 10:13–14 (p. 236); 2 Ki 20:11 (p. 419); Jnh 1:17 (p. 1016); Mk 8:12 (p. 1115); Lk 11:29 (p. 1152)

Moderation, Pr 25:16 (p. 723); Ecc 10:16–17 (p. 743)

Money, Dt 8 (p. 194); Ps 24 (p. 599); 62:10 (p. 626); Mt 6:19–34 (p. 1067); 1 Ti 6:3–19 (p. 1363) Jas 5:1–5 (p. 1363)

Moses, Ex 2—40 (p. 62); Nu 1—36 (p. 139); Dt 1—34 (p. 184); Mt 17:1–13 (p. 1082); Heb 11:24–28 (p. 1387)

Murder, Ge 9:6 (p. 10); Ex 2:12 (p. 62); Nu 35:24–25 (p. 182); Dt 19:13 (p. 205); 21:1–9 (p. 207); 2 Sa 20:10 (p. 349); 2 Ki 11:1–2 (p. 407); 2 Ch 22:10 (p. 486)

Mystery, 1 Co 15:50–58 (p. 1297); Eph 3 (p. 1327); Col 1:24—2:5 (p. 1343); 1 Ti 3:16 (p. 1360)

N

Natural disasters, Ge 7:11 (p. 8); 19:24 (p. 20); Isa 24:1–6 (p. 779); Jer 27:8–15 (p. 869); 36:3 (p. 881); Am 4:6–11 (p. 1006)

God's control, Ge 9:13 (p. 11); Dt 3:22 (p. 188); 4:26 (p. 189); Jos 10:11 (p. 236); 2 Ki 3:20 (p. 396); 20:11 (p. 419); Ps 148:1–10 (p. 689); Isa 38:7–8 (p. 796); Jnh 1:10 (p. 1015); Zec 10:1 (p. 1049); Lk 4:39 (p. 1138); 24:31 (p. 1175)

Lessons from, Ps 29:10 (p. 602); Pr 30:24–28 (p. 729)

Needs (spiritual), Ps 40:17 (p. 612); 63:1 (p. 626); 70:5 (p. 633); 86:1 (p. 645); Mt 5:20 (p. 1064)

Neighbor, Lev 19:18 (p. 127); Mt 22:37–40 (p. 1091); Lk 10:25–37 (p. 1150); Ro 13:8–10 (p. 1273)

O

Obedience

To God, Ex 4:13 (p. 65); Nu 15:3 (p. 158); Dt 6:3 (p. 191); Jdg 2:22 (p. 256); 1 Sa 15:22 (p. 305); 1 Ki 17:3 (p. 383); Pr 1:7 (p. 691); 10:27 (p. 703); Jer 36:8–9 (p. 882); Mic 6:8 (p. 1023); Hag 1—2 (p. 1040); Jn 13:34–35 (p. 1198); Heb 5:8 (p. 1381)

To the law, Dt 30:11 (p. 216); Mk 2:27 (p. 1106); Ac 16:21 (p. 1237); Tit 3:1–2 (p. 1374)

To leaders, 2 Ki 4:2–7 (p. 396); Jer 38:2–3 (p. 883); Da 3:13–14 (p. 970); Ac 4:19 (p. 1218); Tit 3:1–2 (p. 1374); 1 Pe 2:13–17 (p. 1401)

To parents, Ge 22:9 (p. 23); Jer 35:8–16 (p. 881); Eph 6:1 (p. 1331)

Rewards of, Ge 22:2 (p. 23); Ex 33:12 (p. 97); Lev 26:3–39 (p. 136); Jos 6:3 (p. 229); 1 Ki 11:4–8 (p. 375); 2 Ki 24:4 (p. 424); 2 Ch 25:2 (p. 488); Mt 6:10 (p. 1067)

Occult, 1 Sa 28:12 (p. 321); Job 31:24–28 (p. 570); Da 5:11 (p. 974); Mic 5:12 (p. 1022); Mt 2:2 (p. 1060); Ac 16:17–18 (p. 1237); 19:18–19 (p. 1242)

Astrology, 2 Ki 17:16 (p. 414); Isa 47:9,12–13 (p. 810); Jer 10:1–2 (p. 850); Mt 2:1 (p. 1060)

Black magic, Ge 41:8 (p. 47); Ex 7:11–12,22; 8:7 (p. 10); Eze 13:18 (p. 923); Rev 9:21 (p. 1433)

Fortune telling (divination), Ge 30:27 (p. 34); 44:5,15 (p. 52); Nu 22:7 (p. 167); Dt 18:14–15 (p. 203); 2 Ki 16:15 (p. 413); Eze 13:17 (p. 923); 21:21 (p. 932)

Sorcery, Ex 22:18 (p. 85); 2 Ki 9:22 (p. 405); Job 3:8 (p. 547); Isa 8:19 (p. 764); Ac 8:9–11 (p. 1224); 19:13 (p. 1242)

Offerings, Ex 23:15 (p. 87); 35:21 (p. 100); Lev 1:14 (p. 109); 3:3–5 (p. 109); 3:16 (p. 110); Dt 26:2 (p. 211); 1 Ch 21:26 (p. 453); Ezr 1:4–6 (p. 504); Ps 96:8 (p. 652); Pr 3:9–10 (p. 693); Eze 45:13–25 (p. 961); Mal 1:10 (p. 1054); Mt 26:10 (p. 1096); 2 Co 8:1,7 (p. 1307)

Oil, Lev 8:10 (p. 114); Dt 33:24 (p. 222); 1 Ki 1:39 (p. 360); Ps 45:7 (p. 615); 133:2 (p. 679); Isa 21:5 (p. 776); Mk 6:13 (p. 1112); Jas 5:14 (p. 1397)

Ordination, Lev 8:22 (p. 115); 1 Ki 19:19 (p. 387); 2 Ti 1:6 (p. 1365)

P

Pain, Job 16:6 (p. 558); 33:19 (p. 573); Jer 15:15–21 (p. 856); Hab 1—3 (p. 1030); Ro 5:1–5 (p. 1261); 8:28–39 (p. 1267); Rev 21:1–4 (p. 1442)

Parables, 2 Sa 14:2–3 (p. 340); 1 Ki 22:19–20 (p. 391); 2 Ch 18:18–21 (p. 481); 25:18–19 (p. 489); Mt 13:11–13 (p. 1076); Mk 4:10–12,21–25 (p. 1108); Lk 8:4–10 (p. 1145)

Parenting, Jdg 13:8 (p. 270); 2 Sa 18:33 (p. 347); Pr 19:18 (p. 715); 22:6 (p. 718); 31:1 (p. 730); Lk 2:44 (p. 1134); Eph 6:4 (p. 1331)

Passover, Mt 26:26–29 (p. 1097); Mk 14:22–24 (p. 1125); Lk 22:19–20 (p. 1170)

Patience, Ge 40:23 (p. 47); 1 Sa 13:11 (p. 301); Ps 27:14 (p. 601); Pr 14:29 (p. 708); 21:12 (p. 718); Jas 5:7–11 (p. 1396)

Paul, Ac 9:1–31 (p. 1225); 13:1—14:28 (p. 1232); 15:36—19:41 (p. 1236); 27:1—28:31 (p. 1252); Ro 1 (p. 1256)

Peace, Ps 85:10–11 (p. 645); 147:14 (p. 689); Ecc 11:10 (p. 744); Isa 11:6–9 (p. 768); Na 1:15 (p. 1028); Ro 12:18 (p. 1273)

Persecution, Ps 118:6 (p. 668); Da 11:35 (p. 983); Mt 5:11–12 (p. 1063); Lk 6:29–30 (p. 1141); 10:3 (p. 1150); Ac 7:51–53 (p. 1223); 14:22 (p. 1235); 28:22 (p. 1254); Php 3:10 (p. 1339); 2 Th 1:45 (p. 1354); 1 Pe 1:6 (p. 1399); Rev 7:14 (p. 1431); 13:17 (p. 1436)

Forms of, Ps 119:86 (p. 671); Lk 21:18 (p. 1169); Gal 6:17 (p. 1322); Php 1:29 (p. 1334); 2 Ti 3:12 (p. 1368)

Perseverance, Jn 10:27–30 (p. 1192); Ro 8:31–39 (p. 1267); Eph 6:10–20 (p. 1331); Php 1:1–11 (p. 1333); Heb 6:1–6 (p. 1381); 10:26–39 (p. 1385); Jas 1:1–12 (p. 1392); Rev 2—3 (p. 1426)

Perspective

God's, Ps 90:5–6 (p. 648); Hag 2:6 (p. 1042); Ac 5:38–39 (p. 1221); Ro 8:37 (p. 1267); 1 Co 1:2 (p. 1279)

Human, Pr 21:17 (p. 718); Ecc 6:12 (p. 740); 9:11–12 (p. 742); Zec 4:10 (p. 1045); Mt 6:22 (p. 1067); Ac 2:12–13 (p. 1215)

Pessimism, Ecc 1:2 (p. 733)

Peter, Mt 4:18–22 (p. 1063); 26:31–75 (p. 1097); Jn 21 (p. 1210); Ac 2:1—5:42 (p. 1215); 10:1—11:18 (p. 1227)

Pharisees, Mt 16:1–4 (p. 1081); 22:15–45 (p. 1090); 23 (p. 1092); Mk 7:1–23 (p. 1113); Lk 11:37–54 (p. 1152); 18:9–14 (p. 1163); Ac 23:6–11 (p. 1247); Php 3:2–7 (p. 1338)

Plagues, Ex 7:20–21 (p. 68); 8:18–19 (p. 69); 9:8–9 (p. 70); 9:19 (p. 71); 11:9–10 (p. 72); Nu 11:33 (p. 154); Jos 22:17 (p. 250); 2 Ki 19:35 (p. 419); Isa 37:36 (p. 796); Rev 16:2–4 (p. 1438)

Pleasure, Ecc 2:1–2 (p. 734); Isa 5:8 (p. 760)

Politicians, Ex 7:7 (p. 67); 2 Sa 19:13 (p. 348); 2 Ch 10:8–11 (p. 474); Ezr 1:1–2 (p. 504); Ps 26:4–5 (p. 600); 39:1 (p. 610); 82:1 (p. 643); Jer 10:21 (p. 851); 22:24 (p. 863); Hos 5:10 (p. 988); Ro 13:1–7 (p. 1273)

Ambition, 2 Ki 10:16 (p. 407); 25:25 (p. 425); 1 Ch 14:1–2 (p. 445); 2 Ch 21:4 (p. 484); 22:10 (p. 486); Ezr 4:1–2 (p. 508); Hos 7:6 (p. 990); 8:4 (p. 991)

Polygamy, Jdg 8:30 (p. 266); 2 Sa 5:13 (p. 330); 1 Ki 11:1–4 (p. 375); 1 Ch 14:3 (p. 445); 2 Ch 24:3 (p. 487); Pr 5:18–19 (p. 697); 31:3 (p. 730)

Poor (people)

God's love for, Ps 113:7–9 (p. 665); Pr 19:17 (p. 715)

Helping, Lev 25:36–37 (p. 135); Dt 15:1–11 (p. 201); Ru 2:2 (p. 285); 1 Sa 25:8 (p. 317); Ne 5:7 (p. 522); Ps 10:18 (p. 588); Mk 10:21 (p. 1118); 14:7 (p. 1124); Lk 16:19–31 (p. 1161); Jn 12:8 (p. 1196); 1 Co 16:1–4 (p. 1297)

Mistreated, Jer 5:27 (p. 843); Eze 24:7 (p. 937)

Power

Abuse of, 1 Sa 13:14 (p. 301); Da 4:27 (p. 973); Mic 2:9 (p. 1019)

God's, Ex 10:7 (p. 71); 17:11–12 (p. 80); Nu 24:1 (p. 170); Dt 2:25 (p. 186); Jdg 16:29–30 (p. 274); 1 Ki 18:46 (p. 386); 2 Ki 2:11 (p. 394); 1 Ch 4:9–10 (p. 432); 13:10,14 (p. 445); 2 Ch 14:14–15 (p. 478); Job 26:7–14 (p. 566); 41:10 (p. 580); Ps 46:8 (p. 615); 77:10 (p. 638); 93:1–5 (p. 651); Isa 41:7 (p. 800); 52:10 (p. 817); 64:1–3 (p. 830); Jer 46:25 (p. 892); 49:38 (p. 897); Mk 11:22–24 (p. 1120); Ac 5:15 (p. 1219); 8:39–40 (p. 1225); 1 Co 2:4 (p. 1281)

Man's, Ps 82:1 (p. 643); Da 4:35 (p. 973)

Of words, Ps 64:3–6 (p. 627); Pr 10:18–21 (p. 703); 25:11 (p. 723); Ecc 6:10–11 (p. 740); Mt 5:22 (p. 1065); 12:36–37 (p. 1075); Jas 3:8 (p. 1395)

Over others, Ps 101:4 (p. 654); Hag 2:13–14 (p. 1042); Mt 16:11–12 (p. 1081); Mk 8:15 (p. 1115); Lk 11:44 (p. 1152); Ac 27:36 (p. 1253)

Spiritual, Ex 15:6 (p. 77); 2 Ki 2:9 (p. 394); 2:23–24 (p. 395); Job 1:6 (p. 544); Mt 21:21 (p. 1089); 1 Th 1:5 (p. 1348)

Struggle, Ne 2:10,19 (p. 519); 6:17–18 (p. 524)

Praise (of God), Ps 3:1 (p. 583); 54:6–7 (p. 621); 63:4 (p. 626); 76:10 (p. 637); 96:1–3 (p. 652); 96:7–8 (p. 652); 150:1 2 (p. 690); Pr 27:2 (p. 725); 27:21 (p. 726)

Nature, Ps 148:1–10 (p. 689); 150:6 (p. 690); Isa 55:13 (p. 820)

People, Ps 22:30–31 (p. 597); 111:1 (p. 664); 112:2–8 (p. 665); 145:10 (p. 686); Isa 24:14–16 (p. 779); Hos 14:2 (p. 996); Hag 1:8 (p. 1040); Rev 4:9–10 (p. 1429)

Prayer, Ge 4:26 (p. 6); Jdg 3:15 (p. 257); 2 Ki 20:5–6 (p. 419); Ne 1:5–11 (p. 517); Ps 83:1 (p. 643); Isa 38:1–5 (p. 796); Jer 11:11 (p. 851); Mt 6:8 (p. 1066); Jn 15:7 (p. 1200); Ac 7:60 (p. 1223); Ro 15:31 (p. 1276)

Attitude, 1 Sa 12:23 (p. 300); 2 Ch 6:13 (p. 469); 30:27 (p. 496); Ne 4:4–5 (p. 521); Job 16:17 (p. 559); 27:7 (p. 567); Jer 10:23–24 (p. 851); Mt 6:7 (p. 1066); Jn 15:7 (p. 1200); Jas 4:3 (p. 1395); 1 Pe 3:7 (p. 1402)

Confession, Ps 19:12 (p. 594)

Delayed answers, Job 13:20–22 (p. 555); 30:20 (p. 569); Ps 10:1 (p. 587); 27:14 (p. 601); 102:1–2 (p. 654); Isa 62:7 (p. 828); 64:4 (p. 830); Hab 1:2 (p. 1030); 3 Jn v. 2 (p. 1419)

Effects, Ex 32:14 (p. 96); Dt 9:19 (p. 195); 1 Sa 30:6 (p. 322); Ps 106:23 (p. 660); Isa 37:21 (p. 795); Jer 15:1 (p. 855); Am 7:3,6 (p. 1009); Mt 7:7–8 (p. 1067); 21:21–22 (p. 1089); 26:41 (p. 1097); Mk 14:38 (p. 1125); Lk 11:9–13 (p. 1151); 22:40 (p. 1171); Rev 8:3 (p. 1431)

For others, Ge 18:17–19 (p. 18); 18:27–32 (p. 19); Est 4:16 (p. 538); Job 1:5 (p. 544); 42:8 (p. 581); Ps 20:9 (p. 595); Jer 29:7 (p. 871); 37:3 (p. 883); Eze 14:14 (p. 924); Ro 8:27 (p. 1267);

Group, Mt 18:19–20 (p. 1085)

Honest, 1 Sa 1:13 (p. 290); Job 13:3 (p. 555); 34:12 (p. 574); 35:12–13 (p. 575); Ps 6:8 (p. 585); 83:13–16 (p. 643); 88:5,10–12 (p. 646); 88:14 (p. 646); Isa 45:9 (p. 808); Hab 2:1 (p. 1032)

Ignored by God, Job 35:12–13 (p. 575); Ps 66:18 (p. 629); 102:1–2 (p. 654); Isa 59:2 (p. 824); Jer 11:11 (p. 851); 11:14 (p. 851); La 3:8 (p. 909); Mic 3:4 (p. 1020); Zec 7:13 (p. 1047); Jas 1:7–8 (p. 1392); 4:3 (p. 1395); 1 Jn 5:14 (p. 1417)

Need for, Lk 5:16 (p. 1139); Ro 8:27 (p. 1267); 15:31 (p. 1276); Col 4:18 (p. 1347)

Proper form, 2 Ch 6:13 (p. 469); Mt 6:7 (p. 1066); Ac 13:3 (p. 1232); 1 Ti 2:8 (p. 1360)

Public, 2 Ch 20:5–12 (p. 482); Ezr 9:6 (p. 514); Ne 9:5–38 (p. 526)

Thanks, Jnh 2:2 (p. 1016)

Preaching, Ps 119:43 (p. 670); Eze 3:1 (p. 914); Jnh 3:5 (p. 1016); Mt 13:3–23 (p. 1076); 16:19 (p. 1082); Mk 4:13–20 (p. 1108); Lk 4:15–20 (p. 1138); Ac 16:6–10 (p. 1237); 1 Th 2:13 (p. 1349); 2 Ti 4:3 (p. 1368); Tit 2:1 (p. 1373)

False, Eze 11:1 (p. 920); 12:24 (p. 922); Am 5:18 (p. 1008); Mic 2:11 (p. 1020); Zep 3:4 (p. 1037); 2 Co 6:14–15,17 (p. 1306); 1 Ti 1:3–4 (p. 1358); 2 Pe 1—3 (p. 1406)

Preachers, Mt 3:4 (p. 1062); Mk 1:6 (p. 1103); Ac 18:3 (p. 1241); 1 Co 9:15 (p. 1288); Gal 2:2 (p. 1315); Php 1:18 (p. 1334); 1 Ti 5:17 (p. 1363)

Prejudice, Ge 43:32 (p. 52); 46:34 (p. 55); Est 2:10 (p. 537); Am 1:13 (p. 1004); Jnh 4:3 (p. 1017); Mt 2:23 (p. 1062); Lk 9:53 (p. 1149); 20:16 (p. 1168); Jn 4:9 (p. 1181); Ac 6:1 (p. 1221); 1 Th 2:16 (p. 1349)

Pride (boasting), 2 Ki 17:14 (p. 414); 20:13 (p. 419); 2 Ch 32:25–26 (p. 498); Job 18:2 (p. 559); Ps 18:44–45 (p. 594); 25:9 (p. 599); Pr 21:4 (p. 717); Isa 16:6 (p. 773); Ob v. 10–11 (p. 1013); Lk 17:7–10 (p. 1161); 1 Co 5:2 (p. 1284); 14:18 (p. 1295); Gal 6:4 (p. 1321)

Examples of, 2 Ki 5:10–12 (p. 398); 20:13 (p. 419); 2 Ch 12:14 (p. 476); 26:18 (p. 490); Pr 27:2 (p. 725); Lk 14:11 (p. 1157); 15:25–32 (p. 1159); Jn 5:16 (p. 1183); Gal 6:1 (p. 1320)

Priests

Believers as, Isa 66:21 (p. 834); Jer 33:18 (p. 879); Eze 44:20–25 (p. 960)

Role of, Ex 28:12 (p. 91); 1 Ch 16:2 (p. 447); Heb 5:5,10 (p. 1380)

Salaries, Nu 5:10 (p. 145); 18:8 (p. 162); 2 Ki 12:6–8 (p. 408); 2 Ch 31:4 (p. 496); Eze 44:28 (p. 960)

Priorities, 1 Ki 7:1 (p. 367); Ne 10:36 (p. 530); Job 37:7 (p. 577); Ps 1:3–4 (p. 582); Mt 19:21 (p. 1086); Lk 10:38–41 (p. 1151); 14:18–20 (p. 1157); 18:22–30 (p. 1164); Jn 12:8 (p. 1196); 1 Co 7:29 (p. 1286); Col 3:2 (p. 1346); 1 Ti 6:9–11 (p. 1363)

Promises, Ge 42:37 (p. 51); Lev 5:4 (p. 111); Jos 9:19 (p. 234); Job 31 (p. 570); Isa 48:1 (p. 811); Jer 22:5 (p. 862); Mt 5:34–37 (p. 1066); 23:16–22 (p. 1092); Ac 23:14 (p. 1247); Heb 6:13 (p. 1381); Jas 5:12 (p. 1397)

Oaths and vows, Ge 28:20–22 (p. 32); Nu 6:2 (p. 146); 30:2 (p. 177); Jos 24:19 (p. 252); Jdg 11:29–31 (p. 269); 11:39 (p. 269); 13:5 (p. 270); 16:20 (p. 274); Ps 22:25 (p. 597); 116:14–18 (p. 667); Ecc 5:4–6 (p. 738)

Prophecy, Ezr 1:1 (p. 504); Isa 42:1 (p. 802); Mk 2:10 (p. 1105)

About Christ, Mt 17:10 (p. 1083); 21:7 (p. 1087); 1 Pe 1:10–11 (p. 1400)

About Christ's birth, Isa 9:2 (p. 764); 40:3–5,9 (p. 798); Mic 5:2 (p. 1021)

About Christ's death, Ps 22:16 (p. 597); 50:4–6 (p. 618); Isa 52:14 (p. 817); 53:1–12 (p. 817)

Examples of, 1 Ch 12:18 (p. 444); 25:1,6–7 (p. 456); 2 Ch 18:9 (p. 481); Isa 12:1–6 (p. 768); Jer 13:1–11 (p. 853); 28:10 (p. 870); 29:26 (p. 873); Hos 1:2 (p. 985); Mic 1:8 (p. 1019)

Fulfilled, Isa 49:2 (p. 814); Jer 31:8 (p. 874); 31:15 (p. 875); Eze 17:22–24 (p. 927); Da 2:31–45 (p. 969); 11:2–45 (p. 981); Ob v. 18–20 (p. 1013); Mt 1:1 (p. 1059); Lk 3:4–6 (p. 1135); 19:41–44 (p. 1167)

Future, 2 Ch 7:14 (p. 471); Isa 41:18 (p. 802); Jer 7:30–34 (p. 846); Eze 3:25 (p. 915); 4:3–6 (p. 915); 38:2–6 (p. 952); Da 7:24 (p. 978)

Purpose today, Isa 15:1–9 (p. 772); 21:1 (p. 776); Da 12:9–10 (p. 983); Hos 1:11 (p. 986); Am 9:11 (p. 1011); Zec 1:8 (p. 1043); Ac 11:27–30 (p. 1230); 1 Co 14:1 (p. 1295)

Understanding, Jer 23:5–8 (p. 864); Da 7:1 (p. 977); 8:27 (p. 979); Zep 1:2 (p. 1035); Zec 6:6 (p. 1046); Mt 24:15 (p. 1093); Mk 13:5–25 (p. 1123); Lk 18:34 (p. 1165); 24:45 (p. 1175); Rev 1:19–20 (p. 1426); 17:9–14 (p. 1439)

Warning, Jer 25:15–17 (p. 867); Jnh 3:4 (p. 1016); Ac 21:4,11–12 (p. 1245)

Prophets, 1 Sa 10:5 (p. 298); 1 Co 12:28 (p. 1293)

Mistreated, Jer 11:21 (p. 852); 20:1–2 (p. 861); 26:20–23 (p. 869); 32:3 (p. 876); 36:5 (p. 881); 37:16 (p. 883); Hos 9:7 (p. 991)

Reliable, Dt 18:21 (p. 204); 2 Ch 18:5–6 (p. 480)

Role, 2 Sa 12:1 (p. 337); 1 Ki 1:9–10 (p. 358); 12:24 (p. 377); 2 Ki 4:13 (p. 397); Jer 1:10 (p. 836); Jn 1:6 (p. 1176)

Test, 1 Ki 12:24 (p. 377); 22:6–7 (p. 390); Jer 23:18 (p. 865); 26:8–9 (p. 868); 28:8–9 (p. 870); 28:15–16 (p. 870); Da 1:17 (p. 968); Mt 7:15–16 (p. 1068); 1 Th 5:20–21 (p. 1353)

Prostitutes, Ge 19:4–5 (p. 20); 38:15 (p. 44); 38:21 (p. 45); 1 Ki 14:24 (p. 380); 2 Ki 23:7 (p. 422); Pr 7:4–5 (p. 698); 23:28 (p. 721); Jas 2:25 (p. 1394)

Providence of God, Ps 104 (p. 657); Mt 10:29–30 (p. 1072); Ac 14:14–17 (p. 1234)

Punishment, Ge 20:16 (p. 21); Ex 34:6–7 (p. 99); Nu 14:20–35 (p. 156); Mt 12:31–32 (p. 1075); Ac 13:46 (p. 1234); Ro 11:8 (p. 1271); 2 Th 1:8 (p. 1354)

Delayed, Nu 33:52–53 (p. 181); 2 Ki 23:24–26 (p. 423); 2 Ch 34:27–28 (p. 501); Ps 140:12 (p. 684)

Limits, Dt 25:3 (p. 210); Zec 1:15 (p. 1044); 9:1–6 (p. 1048)

Physical, Pr 26:3 (p. 723)

Substitute, Isa 53:5 (p. 817); 53:10 (p. 818); Ro 9:3 (p. 1267); Gal 3:13 (p. 1318)

Purity, Lev 6:10 (p. 112); Jos 5:15 (p. 229); Mal 3:2 (p. 1056); 1 Jn 3:3 (p. 1413)

Q

Quiet time, Ps 1:2 (p. 582); 16:7 (p. 591); 77:12 (p. 638); 119:11 (p. 669); 119:15 (p. 669); Mt 6:23 (p. 1067)

R

Racism, Ex 1:9–10 (p. 61); Est 2:10 (p. 537); Am 1:13 (p. 1004)

Rape, Ge 19:8 (p. 20); 34:26 (p. 40); Dt 22:19,29 (p. 208); Jdg 19:24 (p. 278); 2 Sa 13:13 (p. 339)

Rebellion (against God), Nu 15:30 (p. 159); Ps 85:4 (p. 645); 107:11 (p. 662); Isa 1:24 (p. 756); 57:17 (p. 822); Hos 4:4 (p. 987); Na 3:1–4 (p. 1028); Ac 26:14 (p. 1251); Rev 16:6 (p. 1438); 17:3 (p. 1438)

Reconciliation, Mt 5:23–26 (p. 1065); Php 4:2–3 (p. 1339); 2 Co 5:11—6:2 (p. 1304); Eph 2:11–22 (p. 1325); Col 1:15–23 (p. 1342)

Redemption, Ex 12:29 (p. 73); Nu 35:19 (p. 182); Ru 2:20 (p. 285); 3:12 (p. 287); 4:3–6 (p. 287); Job 19:25 (p. 560); Ps 54:7 (p. 621); 90:11–14 (p. 648); 130:7–8 (p. 678); Isa 35:10 (p. 793); Jer 17:9 (p. 858); Hos 13:14 (p. 995); Col 1:17 (p. 1342)

Rejection, Ps 88:14 (p. 646); Jn 9:22 (p. 1191)

Relationship (to God), Ps 5:5 (p. 584); 50:16 (p. 618); Ecc 12:13–14 (p. 746); Eze 43:10 (p. 958); Ac 17:30 (p. 1239); Ro 5:1 (p. 1261)

National, Isa 43:3 (p. 803); 59:18 (p. 825); Jer 18:7–10 (p. 859)

Personal, Ps 32:9 (p. 604); 107:33–43 (p. 662); Isa 37:14 (p. 795); 64:8 (p. 830); Jer 22:16 (p. 863); Hag 1:8 (p. 1040); Lk 18:22–30 (p. 1164); Mt 19:21 (p. 1086)

Repentance, Lev 26:41 (p. 137); 1 Ki 21:27 (p. 390); 2 Ki 6:30 (p. 402); 2 Ch 33:1–2 (p. 499); Ps 79:8 (p. 641); Joel 2:12–14 (p. 999)

National, Jdg 3:15 (p. 257); 1 Sa 7:6 (p. 296); Ne 8:9–11 (p. 526); La 5:21 (p. 912); Da 9:3 (p. 979); Hos 6:1–3 (p. 989)

Personal, Ps 38:4 (p. 610); 39:13 (p. 611); 143:1–2 (p. 685); Eze 11:19 (p. 921); Zec 1:3 (p. 1043); Mt 3:11 (p. 1062); Lk 7:29–30 (p. 1144); Jn 1:6 (p. 1176); Phm v. 12 (p. 1375); Rev 22:11 (p. 1443)

Respect

Elderly, Job 33:2–7 (p. 573)

God, Ex 3:5 (p. 63); 30:20–21 (p. 94); Lev 16:2 (p. 124); 1 Ch 13:9–10 (p. 445); 15:29 (p. 447); 2 Ch 27:2 (p. 492); Job 9:9 (p. 552); 28:28 (p. 568); Ps 103:11 (p. 656); Ecc 5:1 (p. 738); Isa 6:1–8 (p. 761); 54:5 (p. 819); Zec 2:13 (p. 1044); Mal 2:17 (p. 1054); Jn 12:3 (p. 1195); 2 Co 7:1 (p. 1307)

Leaders, 1 Sa 26:9 (p. 319); 2 Sa 1:6–10 (p. 325); 2 Ch 24:15–16 (p. 487); Ecc 10:20 (p. 743); Ro 13:4 (p. 1273); 1 Th 5:12 (p. 1353)

Parents, Ex 21:17 (p. 84); Pr 13:1 (p. 705); Jer 9:13–16 (p. 848); Mt 8:22 (p. 1069); 12:46–50 (p. 1075); Mk 3:31–35 (p. 1108); Jn 2:4 (p. 1179); Eph 6:1 (p. 1331)

Responsibility, 2 Ki 21:9 (p. 420); 1 Ti 4:14 (p. 1362)

Accepting, 2 Ki 6:5 (p. 400); Ps 104:14–15 (p. 658); 139:16 (p. 683); Isa 4:4 (p. 759); 2 Th 3:6–13 (p. 1357)

Resurrection, Eze 37:10 (p. 952); Da 12:2,13 (p. 983); Mt 28:17 (p. 1102); Lk 24:5–6 (p. 1173); 24:31,37–39

(p. 1175); Ac 10:41 (p. 1228); 23:9 (p. 1247); Ro 1:4 (p. 1256); 1 Co 15:2 (p. 1296)

Last days, Isa 26:19 (p. 783); Jn 20:17 (p. 1210); 1 Co 15:35–57 (p. 1297); Heb 11:35 (p. 1387); Rev 20:4–5 (p. 1441)

Revelation, Ps 19:1–6 (p. 594); Jn 1:1–18 (p. 1176); Ac 14:14–1 (p. 1234); Ro 1:18–23 (p. 1257); Heb 1 (p. 1377); 2 Ti 3:14–17 (p. 1368); 2 Pe 1:19–21 (p. 1407)

Revenge, Ex 21:23–25 (p. 84); Lev 24:20 (p. 134); 2 Sa 19:22 (p. 348); 1 Ki 2:6 (p. 360); Ps 58:6–8 (p. 624); 94:1–3 (p. 651); 149:6–9 (p. 690); Jer 46:10 (p. 891); Eze 25:3–7 (p. 938); Mt 5:39 (p. 1066); 2 Ti 4:14 (p. 1369)

Revival, 2 Ki 23:24–26 (p. 423); 2 Ch 15:12 (p. 478); 19:4–5 (p. 482); Ne 1:6 (p. 517); Ps 19:7 (p. 594); 80:18 (p. 642); Isa 19:19–25 (p. 775); Eze 37:10 (p. 952)

The rich and the poor, Ex 35:4–9 (p. 100); Dt 8:18 (p. 194); 1 Ch 29:3,12 (p. 461); Ps 62:10 (p. 626); 82:3–4 (p. 643); Hos 2:8 (p. 986); Mal 3:8–10 (p. 1056); Mt 6:19–25 (p. 1067); 19:16–21 (p. 1086); Eph 4:28 (p. 1328); 5:3 (p. 1329); Col 3:5 (p. 1346); 1 Ti 6:17–18 (p. 1364); 1 Pe 5:2 (p. 1405)

Righteousness, Ps 7 (p. 586); Jer 23:1–6 (p. 864); Mt 6:25–34 (p. 1067); Ro 4:6–8 (p. 1261); Gal 2:15–21 (p. 1317); Php 3:7–11 (p. 1338); 1 Ti 6:11–16 (p. 1363); 1 Pe 2:24–25 (p. 1401)

Role models, Est 4:16 (p. 538); Job 15:4 (p. 557); 2 Co 8:8 (p. 1307); Eph 5:1 (p. 1329); Php 4:9 (p. 1339); Heb 12:1 (p. 1388)

S

Sacrifices, Ex 20:24 (p. 83); 29:11–21 (p. 92); Lev 1:1 (p. 108); 17:11 (p. 126); Nu 7:41–80 (p. 148); Ps 40:6 (p. 611); 50:5 (p. 618); 50:8–15; 50:23 (p. 619); 51:19 (p. 619); 1 Pe 2:5 (p. 1400)

Sadducees, Mt 16:1–12 (p. 1081); Mk 12:18–23 (p. 1121); Ac 4:1–22 (p. 1218); 5:17–42 (p. 1219); 23:1–11 (p. 1247)

Salvation

Belief in Christ, Jn 3:16–18 (p. 1180); 6:29 (p. 1186); 8:37,40 (p. 1189); 8:51 (p. 1190); 13:8 (p. 1198); 17:2,6,9 (p. 1203); Ac 13:48 (p. 1234); 2 Co 13:5 (p. 1313); 2 Ti 2:19 (p. 1368)

By faith, Ge 15:6 (p. 16); Ps 106:31 (p. 661); 127:1–2 (p. 677); Isa 26:2 (p. 781); Eze 33:13 (p. 947); Mt 5:20 (p. 1064); 25:35–36 (p. 1096); Lk 19:9 (p. 1165); Ac 15:20 (p. 1236); Ro 10:3–7 (p. 1270); Heb 4:11 (p. 1380); Jas 2:14–24 (p. 1393)

For all people, Ge 35:11 (p. 41); Dt 4:33 (p. 189); Ru 4:22 (p. 288); 2 Ch 6:33 (p. 470); Est 13:1–3 (p. 543); Ps 22:27 (p. 597); 86:9 (p. 645); Isa 42:6 (p. 802); Jer 31:31 (p. 875); 48:47 (p. 894); Am 9:12 (p. 1011); Jnh 2:7–9 (p. 1016); Zep 2:11 (p. 1037); Zec 9:7 (p. 1049); Mt 2:2 (p. 1060); 15:23–26 (p. 1081); Lk 2:32 (p. 1134); Jn 10:16 (p. 1192); Ac 10:45 (p. 1228); 1 Ti 2:4 (p. 1360)

God's promise to Abraham, Ge 12:3 (p. 13); Dt 26:18 (p. 212); 1 Ki 8:43 (p. 371); Ps 47:9 (p. 616); Isa 19:19–25 (p. 775); Eph 3:3–4,6,9 (p. 1327)

Losing, Ro 11:21–22 (p. 1271); 1 Co 9:27 (p. 1289); Heb 6:6 (p. 1381); 2 Pe 2:20–22 (p. 1408)

Understanding, Ps 67:2 (p. 629); 87:4 (p. 646); 98:2–3 (p. 653); Pr 10:16 (p. 703); Isa 52:15 (p. 817); Jer 22:16 (p. 863); Mt 10:5 (p. 1071); 19:17 (p. 1086); Ac 4:12 (p. 1218); Ro 1:16 (p. 1257); Php 2:12–13 (p. 1335)

Sanctify, Jn 17:17,19 (p. 1204); 1 Co 1:2 (p. 1279); Php 1:6 (p. 1333); 1 Th 4:3–12 (p. 1351)

Satan

Limited by God, Job 1:12 (p. 545); 19:8–12 (p. 560); Lk 10:18 (p. 1150); Ro 16:20 (p. 1277); Col 2:15 (p. 1343); 1 Jn 5:18 (p. 1417)

Names for, 2 Sa 24:1 (p. 356); 2 Ki 1:2 (p. 393); Job 31:35 (p. 572); Zec 3:1 (p. 1044); Mt 4:1 (p. 1062); 4:1 (p. 1062); 4:3–4 (p. 1062); 10:25 (p. 1072); Mk 1:12–13 (p. 1104); 8:33 (p. 1115); Lk 4:3 (p. 1137); Jn 12:31 (p. 1196); Col 1:13 (p. 1342); Jas 4:7 (p. 1395); Rev 12:11 (p. 1435)

Power of, Job 1:13–19 (p. 545); Mt 4:8–9 (p. 1063); 7:22–23 (p. 1068); Lk 4:6 (p. 1137); 22:3 (p. 1170); Jn 13:27 (p. 1198); Ac 19:19 (p. 1242); 2 Co 2:11 (p. 1302); Eph 2:2 (p. 1325); 6:12 (p. 1331); 1 Th 2:18 (p. 1349); 1 Pe 5:8 (p. 1405); 1 Jn 1:8 (p. 1411); Rev 6:1–17 (p. 1430)

Scapegoat, Lev 16:20–22 (p. 125); 2 Ki 6:32–33 (p. 402); 1 Pe 1:6 (p. 1399)

Second chances, La 5:22 (p. 912)

Second coming, Mt 24—25 (p. 1093); Jn 14:1–4 (p. 1199); Ac 1:6–8 (p. 1213); 1 Co 15:12–28 (p. 1296); 1 Th 4:13–5:11 (p. 1352); 2 Th 2 (p. 1355); 2 Pe 3 (p. 1408); Rev 19—20 (p. 1440)

Self

Confidence, 1 Sa 10:22 (p. 299); Ps 22:6–7 (p. 596); Pr 12:9 (p. 705); Ro 12:3 (p. 1272); 1 Co 2:3 (p. 1281); Gal 6:4 (p. 1321)

Control, Pr 6:6–11 (p. 697); 25:28 (p. 723); Tit 2:2 (p. 1373)

Defense, Ex 22:3 (p. 85); 2 Sa 20:10 (p. 349)

Denial, Mt 7:13–14 (p. 1068)

Esteem, Ex 30:15 (p. 94); 1 Ch 4:9–10 (p. 432); Ezr 2:2–61 (p. 505); Job 25:6 (p. 566); Ps 8:5 (p. 586); 103:14 (p. 656); 139:13–16 (p. 682); Pr 22:2 (p. 718); Isa 41:14 (p. 801); 1 Pe 2:18–21 (p. 1401)

Reliance, 2 Ch 12:14 (p. 476); Isa 2:7–8 (p. 758); 26:18 (p. 781); 50:10–11 (p. 815)

Will, Jdg 16:17 (p. 274)

Service (to God and others), Nu 35:2 (p. 182); 1 Ch 23:7–23 (p. 454); Mt 25:26–27 (p. 1095); Jn 13:14–15 (p. 1198); 1 Ti 3:13 (p. 1360)

Servant, Isa 49:1–6 (p. 812); 50:4–9 (p. 814); 52:13—53:12 (p. 817); Mk 10:35–45 (p. 1118); Jn 13:1–17 (p. 1198); 1 Co 9:19–23 (p. 1289); Gal 5:13–26 (p. 1319); Php 2:6–11 (p. 1334); 1 Pe 2:18–25 (p. 1401)

Sex

Homosexuality, Ge 13:13 (p. 15); 19:4–5 (p. 20); Lev 18:22 (p. 127); Jdg 19:24 (p. 278); 2 Ki 23:7 (p. 422); Ro 1:26–27 (p. 1258)

In marriage, 1 Co 6:20 (p. 1284)

Pleasure, Pr 5:18–19 (p. 697)

Religious rituals, Nu 25:1 (p. 171); Jos 22:17 (p. 250); 1 Ki 14:24 (p. 380); 16:32 (p. 383); Hos 4:12 (p. 988); 4:14 (p. 988)

Rules about, Ex 19:15 (p. 81); 2 Sa 11:11 (p. 337)

Temptation, 2 Sa 11:2–3 (p. 335); Pr 5:3–10 (p. 696); 9:17 (p. 701); 23:28 (p. 721); 1 Co 6:18 (p. 1284)

Shame, Ezr 9:6–15 (p. 514); Ps 25 (p. 599); 34:1–7 (p. 605); Ro 1:16–17 (p. 1257); 2 Ti 1:8–14 (p. 1365)

Sin

Acceptance, Lev 26:41 (p. 137); Ps 38:4 (p. 610); Jn 9:41 (p. 1192)

Communal, Jos 7:11 (p. 231); 2 Sa 24:15 (p. 356); Ezr 9:6 (p. 514); Isa 59:12 (p. 825); Eze 21:4 (p. 932); Da 9:3 (p. 979); 9:5 (p. 979); Mal 4:6 (p. 1056)

Defeating, Ro 6:2–14 (p. 1263); 7:14–25 (p. 1265)

Development, 2 Ki 18:4 (p. 416)

Hated by God, Ps 5:5 (p. 584)

Individual, Lev 20:9 (p. 128); Nu 14:18 (p. 156); Dt 5:9 (p. 190); 23:2 (p. 209); Eze 18:2 (p. 928)

Punished, 1 Ch 21:14 (p. 453); 1 Th 4:6 (p. 1351)

Secret, 2 Ki 17:9 (p. 414); Ps 90:8 (p. 648)

Unforgivable, Mt 12:31–32 (p. 1075); Mk 3:29 (p. 1108)

Unintentional, Ps 19:12 (p. 594); Ac 3:14–15,17 (p. 1217); Jas 4:17 (p. 1396)

Sin's effects, Ge 12:17 (p. 13); 1 Sa 2:31–33 (p. 292); 2 Sa 12:9–10 (p. 337); 21:6,9,14 (p. 350); 1 Ch 21:14

(p. 453); Job 5:7 (p. 548); 15:20 (p. 558); Ps 7:13,16 (p. 586); 51:4 (p. 619); 103:10 (p. 656); Jer 17:9 (p. 858); Eze 7:27 (p. 918); 18:24 (p. 929); Mt 5:29–30 (p. 1065); Ro 1:24,26,28 (p. 1258); 5:13–14 (p. 1263); 6:1 (p. 1263); 2 Co 7:9 (p. 1307)

Church, 1 Co 5:7 (p. 1284); 8:12 (p. 1287)

Creation, Ge 9:2 (p. 10); Ps 107:33–34 (p. 662); Jer 7:20 (p. 846); Jn 9:2 (p. 1190); 9:3 (p. 1191); Ro 8:20–21 (p. 1267); Rev 8:7–11 (p. 1431)

Families, Ps 79:8 (p. 641); Jer 2:9 (p. 837); 31:29 (p. 875); 32:18 (p. 877); La 2:11–12 (p. 908); Eze 18:19–20 (p. 928); 18:19–20 (p. 928); Hos 2:4–5 (p. 986)

God, Job 35:6 (p. 575); Jer 12:7–8 (p. 852); Eze 33:11 (p. 947); Jn 11:35 (p. 1195)

Health, Ge 3:16 (p. 5); Jn 5:14 (p. 1183)

Nations, Ne 1:6 (p. 517); Ps 51:18 (p. 619); Jer 9:3–8 (p. 848); 18:7–10 (p. 859); 29:21–23 (p. 871); La 2:11–12 (p. 908); Eze 21:4 (p. 932); 22:30 (p. 934); Da 9:5 (p. 979)

Removed, Rev 22:2 (p. 1443)

Slander, Ps 12:5 (p. 588); Pr 10:18–21 (p. 703); Jas 4:11 (p. 1395)

Slavery, Ex 10:27–28 (p. 72); Lev 22:6,11 (p. 131); 25:44–46 (p. 135); Jos 16:10 (p. 243); Jdg 1:28 (p. 255); 1 Ki 12:18 (p. 377); 1 Ch 5:21 (p. 435); Mt 20:26–28 (p. 1087); Mk 10:43–45 (p. 1118); 1 Co 7:21–24 (p. 1286); 1 Pe 2:18–21 (p. 1401)

Son of God, Mt 16:18 (p. 1082); Lk 22:70–71 (p. 1172); Jn 1:18 (p. 1177); Heb 7:11 (p. 1382)

Son of man, Ps 80:17 (p. 642); Eze 2:1 (p. 914); Da 7:13 (p. 977); 8:17 (p. 978); Mk 2:10 (p. 1105); Heb 2:6–8 (p. 1378); Rev 1:13 (p. 1426); 14:14 (p. 1437)

Sorrow, Ex 3:1–9 (p. 63); Mt 26:36–46 (p. 1097)

Soul, Dt 6:1–5 (p. 191); 30:6 (p. 216); Ps 25:1 (p. 599); 42 (p. 612); 103 (p. 656); 130 (p. 678); Ecc 12:7 (p. 745); 1 Th 5:23 (p. 1353); Heb 4:12 (p. 1380); Rev 6:9–10 (p. 1430)

Spirit of God, Ge 6:3 (p. 7); Ex 24:2 (p. 87); 31:3 (p. 95); Jdg 13:25 (p. 271); 1 Sa 11:6 (p. 299); 16:14 (p. 307); 2 Sa 23:2 (p. 353); 1 Ch 12:18 (p. 444); 28:12,19 (p. 461); 2 Ch 20:14 (p. 483); Ps 104:30 (p. 658); Pr 20:27 (p. 717); Joel 2:28 (p. 1000); Zec 4:6 (p. 1045); Mk 1:10 (p. 1104)

Stealing, Ex 20:15 (p. 82); 22:1–15 (p. 85); Lev 19:11–13 (p. 127); Mal 3:8–10 (p. 1056); Eph 4:28 (p. 1328)

Stewardship, Mt 25:14–30 (p. 1095); Lk 12:35–48 (p. 1155); 16:10–12 (p. 1160); Eph 5:15–16 (p. 1330)

Stubbornness, Pr 29:1 (p. 728)

Submission

In marriage, Eph 5:24–33 (p. 1331); 1 Pe 3:5–6 (p. 1401)

To God, Isa 18:7 (p. 774); 19:18 (p. 775); Jer 27:8–15 (p. 869); 29:7 (p. 871)

To authority, Col 3:18–4:1 (p. 1346); 1 Pe 2:13–17 (p. 1401)

To others, Eph 5:21 (p. 1331)

Success, Dt 28:2–6 (p. 213); 2 Ch 26:5 (p. 490); Job 22:21–25 (p. 563); Ps 1:3–4 (p. 582); 90:17 (p. 649); Pr 6:6–11 (p. 697)

Suffering, Job 5:7 (p. 548); 6:24 (p. 550); 11:16 (p. 554); 34:37 (p. 575); Ps 88:3 (p. 646); Mk 8:34 (p. 1115); 15:23 (p. 1128); Ac 5:41 (p. 1221); Rev 13:10 (p. 1435)

Alone, Job 19:13–20 (p. 560); Ps 10:1 (p. 587); 12:1 (p. 588); 22:1 (p. 595); 88:6 (p. 646); 102:3–5 (p. 654); La 3:3 (p. 908); Mt 26:41 (p. 1097); 27:46 (p. 1100); Mk 14:38 (p. 1125); 14:51–52 (p. 1127); 15:34 (p. 1128); Lk 22:40 (p. 1171); 2 Ti 1:15 (p. 1366)

God's role, 2 Sa 12:14–15 (p. 338); 2 Ki 5:1 (p. 398); Ps 34:17 (p. 606); 71:20 (p. 633); 97:10 (p. 653); Rev 13:8 (p. 1435)

Purpose of, Job 32:14 (p. 572); 33:19 (p. 573); Ps 22:30–31 (p. 597); 102:9–10 (p. 655); Pr 22:4 (p. 718); Isa 45:7 (p. 808); 48:10 (p. 811); La 3:38 (p. 909); Eze 24:16–18 (p. 937); Jn 9:3 (p. 1191); 1 Th 3:3 (p. 1349)

Results, Job 3:10–16 (p. 547); 23:10 (p. 564); Ps 119:67–75 (p. 671); Pr 17:3 (p. 711); Ecc 11:8 (p. 743); La 3:38 (p. 909); Jn 11:4 (p. 1194); Ro 5:3 (p. 1261); 2 Co 4:12 (p. 1303); Rev 9:20–21 (p. 1433)

Understanding, Job 5:27 (p. 548); 9:22–24 (p. 552); 17:7–8 (p. 559); 23:10 (p. 564); 42:8 (p. 581); Isa 13:16 (p. 770); 53:9 (p. 817); Ro 8:17 (p. 1267); 2 Co 1:5 (p. 1300); 1 Pe 4:1 (p. 1403)

Suicide, 1 Sa 31:5 (p. 324); 2 Sa 17:23 (p. 346); Isa 57:1–2 (p. 822); Ac 1:18–19 (p. 1214); Ac 16:22–36 (p. 1237)

T

Talents, 1 Ch 22:8 (p. 454); Mt 25:26–27 (p. 1095); 1 Ti 4:14 (p. 1362)

Talking (with God), Ge 12:1 (p. 13); 18:10 (p. 18); Nu 1:1 (p. 139); 7:89 (p. 150); Jos 1:1 (p. 224); 1 Sa 3:21 (p. 292); 30:6 (p. 322); Job 38:1 (p. 577); Ps 95:7 (p. 652); Hab 2:1 (p. 1032); Mal 2:17 (p. 1054)

Temple, 2 Ch 3:1 (p. 467); 3:3–17 (p. 467); Mt 24:2–3 (p. 1093)

Employees, 1 Ch 23:26,28–32 (p. 455); 2 Ch 4:6–16 (p. 468); 23:8 (p. 486); Ne 12:29 (p. 532); Ps 134:1 (p. 679); Eze 44:16 (p. 960).

Finances, Lev 27:2 (p. 137); 27:13 (p. 138); Nu 5:10 (p. 145); 18:31 (p. 163); Jos 13:33 (p. 240); 2 Ki 12:6–8 (p. 408); 2 Ch 24:5 (p. 487); 31:4 (p. 496); Ezr 6:4 (p. 510).

Temptation, Dt 13:3 (p. 199); 1 Ch 21:1 (p. 452); Job 29:2 (p. 568); 31:1 (p. 570); Ps 81:7 (p. 642); Mt 4:1 (p. 1062); 4:3–4 (p. 1062); Mk 1:12–13 (p. 1104); Lk 4:3 (p. 1137); 1 Co 10:13 (p. 1290); Eph 6:14–17 (p. 1331); Heb 4:15 (p. 1380); Jas 1:13 (p. 1393); 1 Jn 5:4 (p. 1416).

Ten Commandments, Ex 3:1 (p. 63); 20:1–17 (p. 82); 31:18 (p. 95); Lev 16:13 (p. 124); Dt 5:1 (p. 190); 9:10 (p. 195); Jos 8:32 (p. 234); Mk 2:27 (p. 1106); Ro 10:4 (p. 1270).

Terrorism, 2 Ki 25:7–9 (p. 425); Jer 39:7 (p. 885).

Testing

By God, Dt 8:2 (p. 194); 13:3 (p. 199); 1 Ch 29:17 (p. 463); 2 Ch 32:31 (p. 498); Job 1:8 (p. 544); 7:18 (p. 551); 16:9 (p. 558); 23:10 (p. 564); Ps 66:10 (p. 629); 81:7 (p. 642); Mt 4:1 (p. 1062); 15:23–26 (p. 1081); Mk 7:26–27 (p. 1114); Ro 16:10 (p. 1276); 1 Th 3:3 (p. 1349); Jas 1:13 (p. 1393); 1 Pe 1:7 (p. 1400).

Of God, Ps 78:18 (p. 639).

Thanksgiving, Ex 23:15 (p. 87); 1 Sa 31:12 (p. 324); Ps 116:13 (p. 667); 116:17 (p. 667); Eph 5:20 (p. 1331).

Time, Ecc 3:1–8 (p. 736); Eph 5:15 (p. 1330); Col 4:5 (p. 1346).

Tithes, Ge 14:20 (p. 15); 28:22 (p. 32); Lev 27:30 (p. 138); Dt 12:17 (p. 198); 26:12 (p. 211); 1 Ch 6:54 (p. 436); 2 Ch 31:5 (p. 496); Pr 3:9–10 (p. 693); Mal 3:9–10 (p. 1056); 2 Co 9:7 (p. 1308).

Tongues, Ac 2:1–13 (p. 1215); 10:44–48 (p. 1228); 19:1–7 (p. 1242); 1 Co 12—14 (p. 1292).

Trinity, Ge 1:26 (p. 2); 11:7 (p. 12); Dt 6:4 (p. 191); Mt 28:16–20 (p. 1102); Jn 14:9–28 (p. 1200); 2 Co 13:14 (p. 1313); Tit 3:3–8 (p. 1374); Jude 20—21 (p. 1424).

Trust, Dt 28:65 (p. 215); Ps 77:2 (p. 637); Ecc 11:10 (p. 744); Mt 6:25 (p. 1067); Lk 12:22 (p. 1153).

In God, Ge 22:2 (p. 23); Ex 30:12 (p. 94); Jos 11:6 (p. 237); Jdg 7:5–6 (p. 263); 2 Ki 4:2–7 (p. 396); 18:14 (p. 416); 1 Ch 18:4 (p. 451); 2 Ch 28:5 (p. 492); Ne 6:13 (p. 523); Job 2:10 (p. 546); 12:15–16,22–23 (p. 555); 19:25 (p. 560); 23:14–15 (p. 564); Ps 11:1 (p. 588); 91:16 (p. 649); 112:6–7 (p. 665); 116:10 (p. 667); 142:6 (p. 685); Isa 30:18 (p. 787); Mic 7:7 (p. 1024); Hab 3:17 (p. 1034); Jas 1:2 (p. 1392); 1:7–8 (p. 1392).

In Idols, 2 Ch 25:14 (p. 488); Isa 27:10–11 (p. 783).

In military power, Jos 11:6 (p. 237); 1 Sa 12:12 (p. 300); 2 Sa 24:3,10 (p. 356); 1 Ch 21:1,6–7 (p. 452); Isa 20:5–6 (p. 776); 22:8–11 (p. 777); 30:1–2 (p. 786); 31:1 (p. 789); 34:1–3 (p. 792); Jer 2:36 (p. 838); Eze 16:26–29 (p. 925); 29:6–7 (p. 942); Hos 7:11 (p. 990); Hab 1:16 (p. 1032).

In money, Job 36:19 (p. 576); Ps 12:8 (p. 589); 97:7 (p. 653); Isa 2:7–8 (p. 758); 39:1–2 (p. 797).

In people, Ps 146:3–4 (p. 688).

Learning to, Ex 16:4 (p. 78); Ps 78:5–7 (p. 638); Isa 43:2 (p. 803).

Truth, Pr 22:17 (p. 720); 23:23 (p. 721); Isa 45:23 (p. 809); Jer 22:5 (p. 862); 38:2–3 (p. 883); Mt 5:34–37 (p. 1066); Ac 16:18 (p. 1237); 2 Ti 3:7 (p. 1368); Jas 5:12 (p. 1397); 2 Jn v. 1 (p. 1418); Rev 1:19–20 (p. 1426).

U

Unbelief, Nu 20:12 (p. 164); Dt 1:34 (p. 185); Ps 78:32 (p. 639); 95:11 (p. 652); 115:2 (p. 666); Isa 29:9–10 (p. 785); Mt 12:39 (p. 1075); Mk 6:5–6 (p. 1111); Lk 11:29 (p. 1152); Jn 6:29 (p. 1186); 10:26 (p. 1192).

Understanding God, Ge 14:18 (p. 15); 41:37–39 (p. 48); Ex 5:1–3 (p. 65); Dt 10:17 (p. 196); 29:4 (p. 215); 1 Ki 5:7 (p. 365); 10:1 (p. 374); 2 Ch 32:16–19 (p. 497); Ezr 6:10 (p. 510); Job 10:2 (p. 553); 41:11 (p. 580); Ps 65:8 (p. 628); 97:2–5 (p. 653); Pr 25:2 (p. 722); 30:2–3 (p. 729); Ecc 11:5 (p. 743); Eze 20:9 (p. 930); Jnh 2:7–9 (p. 1016); Lk 15:25–32 (p. 1159); Jn 6:46,57 (p. 1186).

Unity, Ps 133 (p. 679); Jn 17 (p. 1203); Ac 2:42–47 (p. 1216); 1 Co 1–4 (p. 1279); 10:16–17 (p. 1291); 11:17–34 (p. 1292); Gal 3:26–28 (p. 1318); Eph 4:1–16 (p. 1327).

Unity of believers, Ps 133:1 (p. 679); Jn 17:21–23 (p. 1204); Ac 15:20 (p. 1236); Ro 15:5–7 (p. 1274); Eph 4:13 (p. 1327); 5:21 (p. 1331); Php 2:2–5 (p. 1334).

V

Values (spiritual), Mt 5:3–10 (p. 1063); 5:19 (p. 1064).

Virgin birth, Mt 1:23 (p. 1060).

W

Wait (for God), Isa 64:4 (p. 830); Am 5:13 (p. 1008); Hab 2:1 (p. 1032)

Wars, Ge 49:24 (p. 58); Jos 11:23 (p. 238); Jdg 20:8–43 (p. 279)

  Atrocities, Jos 10:24–26 (p. 236); 1 Sa 27:9 (p. 320); 2 Ki 15:16 (p. 412); Ps 137:8–9 (p. 682); Isa 21:3–4 (p. 776)

  Destruction, 2 Ki 3:25 (p. 396)

  Spiritual, Job 1:13–19 (p. 545); Ps 70:2 (p. 632); 83:2,6–8 (p. 643); Isa 24:21–22 (p. 779); Da 10:12 (p. 981); Mt 11:12 (p. 1073); 2 Co 10:4 (p. 1310); Eph 6:14–17 (p. 1331); 6:12 (p. 1331); 2 Ti 2:3 (p. 1366)

Warning (others), Eze 3:17 (p. 915); 33:6–9 (p. 946)

Water, Jn 4:10–14 (p. 1181); 7:37–38 (p. 1188); Rev 22:1–2 (p. 1443)

Wealth, Nu 7:26–80 (p. 148); Ps 12:8 (p. 589); Pr 8:10–11 (p. 699); 11:25–28 (p. 704); 19:10 (p. 715); 22:2 (p. 718); Ecc 5:11 (p. 738); 10:19 (p. 743); Am 3:12 (p. 1005); Lk 6:24–26 (p. 1141); 16:19–31 (p. 1161); 18:25 (p. 1164); 1 Ti 6:9–11 (p. 1363); Jas 5:1–6 (p. 1396)

Widows, Dt 25:5–9 (p. 210); Isa 4:1 (p. 759); 54:1–6 (p. 819); Mic 2:9 (p. 1019); 1 Ti 5:9 (p. 1363)

Will of God, Mt 26:36–46 (p. 1097); Jn 4:34 (p. 1182); 6:38 (p. 1186); Ro 12:1–8 (p. 1272); Eph 1:3–14 (p. 1323); Php 2:5–11 (p. 1334); 1 Th 4:1–8 (p. 1351); Jas 4:13–15 1 Pe 4:12–19

Wisdom, Nu 27:18 (p. 174); Pr 1:2 (p. 691); 8:10–11 (p. 699); 21:5 (p. 717); 24:27 (p. 722); Ecc 1:18 (p. 734); Jas 4:13–15 (p. 1395)

  God's, 1 Ki 4:29–34 (p. 365); Job 2:10 (p. 546); 28:1–23 (p. 567); 1 Co 2:13 (p. 1281); 4:6 (p. 1283); Jas 1:5 (p. 1392)

  Using, 1 Ki 11:4–8 (p. 375); Pr 21:22 (p. 718)

  Worldly, 1 Ki 4:29–34 (p. 365)

Witchcraft, Lev 20:6–7 (p. 128); Dt 18:10–12 (p. 203); 1 Sa 28 (p. 320); Isa 8:19–22 (p. 764); 47:10–14 (p. 810); Ac 8:9–24 (p. 1224); 13:6–12 (p. 1233); 19:13–19 (p. 1242); Gal 5:19–21 (p. 1320)

Women

  As property, Ge 19:8 (p. 20); 30:3 (p. 33); 31:15 (p. 36); 38:14 (p. 44); Ex 21:7–11 (p. 84); Dt 20:14 (p. 206); Jdg 19:24 (p. 278); 2 Sa 3:7 (p. 328); 20:3 (p. 349); 1 Ki 2:22–23 (p. 361); Isa 13:16 (p. 770)

  Godly, Est 2:8 (p. 536); Pr 31:1 (p. 730); 31:10–31 (p. 730); 1 Ti 2:11 (p. 1360)

  Leadership, Ex 15:20 (p. 78); Jdg 4:4 (p. 257); 2 Ki 22:14 (p. 422); 1 Ch 7:24 (p. 438); 2 Ch 22:10 (p. 486); Ac 18:26 (p. 1241); Ro 16:1–2 (p. 1276)

  Roles of, Jdg 1:12–13 (p. 255); 2 Sa 20:16,22 (p. 350); Ne 3:12 (p. 520)

  Status, Ge 2:18–22 (p. 4); Ex 22:16–17 (p. 85); Nu 30:3–16 (p. 177); Ru 2:9 (p. 285); 2 Sa 11:4 (p. 335); Jer 44:19 (p. 889); Jn 4:7 (p. 1181)

Word of God, Ge 1 (p. 1); Ps 33:6–9 (p. 604); Mt 4:1–11 (p. 1062); Jn 1:1–18 (p. 1176); Eph 6:10–17 (p. 1331); Heb 4:12–13 (p. 1380); 11:1–3 (p. 1385); Jas 1:18 (p. 1393); 1 Pe 1:22–25 (p. 1400); Rev 9:13–16 (p. 1433)

Work

  Daily, Ne 4:6–9 (p. 521); Ps 90:17 (p. 649); 127:1–2 (p. 677); Isa 26:12 (p. 781); 1 Co 10:31 (p. 1291); 15:58 (p. 1297); Col 3:17 (p. 1346); 2 Th 3:10 (p. 1357)

  Nature of, Ge 1:28 (p. 2); 2:15,19–20 (p. 4); 3:17–19 (p. 5); Ex 20:9 (p. 82); Ecc 1:14 (p. 734); 2:11,17 (p. 734); 3:9–10 (p. 736); Eph 4:28 (p. 1328); 1 Th 4:11 (p. 1352)

  God's relationship to, Dt 5:13 (p. 190); Ps 104:23 (p. 658); Pr 6:6–11 (p. 697); 10:4–5 (p. 702); 14:23 (p. 708); 27:23–27 (p. 726)

Worship, Ex 39:2–7 (p. 104); Nu 7:12–83 (p. 147); 2 Ch 16:1 (p. 478); 2 Ch 29:30 (p. 494); Ps 96:8 (p. 652); 150:3–5 (p. 690); Jnh 3:7–9 (p. 1016)

  Attitude, 2 Ch 12:10 (p. 475); Ne 12:27–43 (p. 532); Ps 40:6 (p. 611); 51:19 (p. 619); 73:17 (p. 635); 99:5 (p. 654); Isa 29:13 (p. 786); 58:6–7 (p. 823); 66:3 (p. 832); Jer 6:20 (p. 844); Hos 6:6 (p. 989); 14:2 (p. 996); Am 5:21–23 (p. 1008); Zec 7:5–6 (p. 1046); Mal 1:10 (p. 1054); Ro 15:17 (p. 1276); Heb 10:6,8 (p. 1384)

  Idols, Jdg 17:1–4 (p. 274); 18:30–31 (p. 277); 1 Ki 3:3 (p. 362); 16:31 (p. 383); 2 Ki 12:3 (p. 408); 16:15–16 (p. 413); 17:41 (p. 416); 2 Ch 33:17 (p. 499); Ezr 4:3 (p. 508); 6:10 (p. 510); Ps 65:8 (p. 628); Eze 8:3 (p. 918); 20:3 (p. 930); Da 2:47 (p. 969); 6:26 (p. 976); 2 Co 11:4 (p. 1310)

  Jerusalem, 1 Ki 8:5 (p. 369); 2 Ki 18:22 (p. 416); 2 Ch 1:4 (p. 464); Ps 99:9 (p. 654); Ac 8:27 (p. 1224)

Many gods (polytheism), Ge 35:2 (p. 40); Jos
24:14,23 (p. 252); Jdg 6:25 (p. 262); 17:1–4
(p. 274); 1 Ki 11:5–8 (p. 375); 16:31 (p. 383); 2 Ki
12:3 (p. 408); 16:15–16 (p. 413); 17:41 (p. 416);
2 Ch 33:17 (p. 499); Ezr 1:1–2 (p. 504); 4:3
(p. 508); 6:10 (p. 510); Ps 65:8 (p. 628); 78:32
(p. 639); Jer 11:13 (p. 851); 12:2 (p. 852); 40:2
(p. 885); Eze 20:3 (p. 930); Da 2:47 (p. 969); 6:26
(p. 976);

Music, 2 Ki 3:15 (p. 396); 1 Ch 6:31 (p. 436); Ps 33:3
(p. 604); 90:9–10 (p. 648); 118:1–4 (p. 667)

Place, Ex 20:24 (p. 83); Lev 17:3–4 (p. 125); Dt 26:2
(p. 211); Jos 18:1 (p. 244); 22:10–12 (p. 250); 1 Sa
1:3 (p. 289); 1 Ki 8:5 (p. 369); 2 Ki 18:22 (p. 416);
1 Ch 16:39 (p. 449); 2 Ch 1:4 (p. 464); 3:3–17
(p. 467); 6:5–6 (p. 469); 11:16 (p. 475); 32:12
(p. 497); Ps 99:9 (p. 654); Am 4:4 (p. 1006)

Preparing for, Nu 8:7 (p. 150); Jer 7:1–2 (p. 845);
Eze 44:7–9 (p. 959)

Style, 2 Sa 6:14 (p. 331); Ps 63:4 (p. 626); 68:24–25
(p. 631); 95:11 (p. 652); 96:1–3 (p. 652); 118:1–4
(p. 667); 133:1 (p. 679); 143:6 (p. 685); 149:3
(p. 690); Mic 6:6–7 (p. 1022)

Y

Youth, Ecc 11:7–12:7 (p. 743); Joel 2:28–32 (p. 1000);
Ac 2:13–36 (p. 1215); 1 Ti 4:11–16 (p. 1362)

Z

Zion, 2 Sa 5:6–7 (p. 330); 2 Ki 19:31 (p. 419); 2 Ch 5:2
(p. 468); Ps 2:6 (p. 583); 9:7,11 (p. 587); 20:2 (p. 595);
48:1–2 (p. 616); 74:2 (p. 636); 78:68 (p. 640); 110:2
(p. 664); Isa 18:7 (p. 774); 28:16 (p. 784); 33:20
(p. 791); 51:16 (p. 816); 59:20 (p. 825); Joel 3:17,21
(p. 1001); Am 1:2 (p. 1003); Mic 4:7 (p. 1021); Heb
12:22 (p. 1388); Rev 14:1 (p. 1437)

Subject index to daily devotions and weekend bible studies

The subjects covered in the devotions are many and varied. This subject index will help you locate material on just about any topic or issue of interest, or about any problem confronting you.

Acceptance 1047
Accepting Christ 1177
Addiction 716
Advice. 476, 707
Alcohol 716
Ambition 890
Angels 197
Anger. 31, 971, 1084
Answers to Prayer 608
Apologetics 1356
Appearance 306, 565, 684
Application 1394
Arrogance 866
Assurance 1324, 1416
Atheism 590
Attitudes 31, 39, 160, 323, 491, 630, 713, 1336
Authenticity 1080
Authority 160, 303
Availability 399, 762, 827, 935
Beauty 306, 684
Betrayal 1423
Bible Study 512, 672, 687, 726, 1137, 1257
Biblical Accuracy 1356
Body of Christ 1293, 1386
Boundaries. 276
Busyness 389
Calling 1064, 1421
Career Decisions 228, 415
Celebration 527
Character 731, 1162, 1240
Cheating 76, 1335
Children 3
Choices. 232, 745, 1164, 1277, 1306, 1409
Christian Growth 1077
Christian Life. 1289
Christlikeness 1288
Commitment 169, 462, 1055, 1232
Communication 701, 1321, 1329
Compassion 951, 999, 1226
Complaining 1336
Compromise 1414

Confession 620, 845, 1249
Confidence. 64
Conflict 344, 483, 630, 1006, 1294, 1359
Confrontation 1084
Conscience 1249
Contentment 627, 1091, 1364, 1390
Convictions 1275, 1342, 1356
Counselors 476
Courage 206, 259, 498
Creation 401, 804
Credit Cards. 739
Cynicism 1013
Dating 556, 677
Death 19
Debt 719, 739
Deceit 709
Decisions. 605, 617, 788, 1068, 1158
Dependence on God. 833, 1330
Depending on God 989
Depression 1033
Despair 613, 782, 800
Diligence 702, 744
Direction 605
Discernment 605, 1275
Discipleship 726, 1101, 1140, 1143, 1148,
                                              1158, 1164, 1231
Discipline. 549, 724, 726, 1162,
                                                              1389
Divorce 596
Doubt 19
Emotions 623
Encouragement. 737
End Times 1432
Endurance 264
Envy 635
Eternal Life 1355
Eternity 1370
Ethics 225
Evangelism 813, 1061, 1072, 1101, 1107,
                                              1205, 1214, 1350, 1361
Evil 1396

Expectations 971, 1088, 1330
Failure. 1017
Faithfulness. 169, 780
Faith 206, 228, 259, 448, 613, 1262, 1382
False Teachers 1423
Family Issues 596
Fear. 498, 507, 623, 666, 782, 788, 790, 800, 801
Fellowship 1217
Finances. 1309
Following Jesus 1148
Forgiveness 39, 336, 630, 657, 999
Freedom from Sin 1190
Freedom. 1280
Friendship 313, 737, 1006, 1199, 1321
Friends 1217
Fruit of the Spirit 1320
Future. 24
Getting Even 1160
Gifts 1293, 1304
Giving. 694, 1309
God our Shepherd. 598
God's Care 797
God's Faithfulness. 910
God's Forgiveness. 50, 620, 657, 757, 845, 1184,
                         1211, 1260, 1412
God's Goodness. 1027
God's Grace 1312, 1412
God's Guidance 106, 221, 225, 448, 617, 677,
                      788, 872, 1201, 1203
God's Holiness. 371
God's Love 59, 994, 1038, 1229, 1229
God's Plan 836, 872
God's Power 483, 1122
God's Presence. 157, 498, 512, 1061
God's Promises 249, 827, 1382, 1407
God's Protection. 598, 644, 650, 1268
God's Provision. 384, 801, 1132, 1164, 1328
God's Purposes 546
God's Resources 401, 824
God's Strength. 800, 801
God's Timing. 9, 821, 1031
God's Will. 19, 35, 228, 556
God's Wisdom 235, 608
God's Word. 857, 866, 1137
Good Deeds. 1326, 1361
Good Shepherd 818
Gospel 1257
Grace 68, 323, 757, 1017, 1190, 1238,
               1260, 1264, 1280, 1373
Gratitude. 1280, 1344, 1390
Greatness. 890
Greed 232
Guilt. 50, 232, 1190, 1211
Happiness 1390
Hardships. 59, 644, 745
Hearing God's Voice. 1266
Heart. 951, 1166

Heaven. 1444
Hell. 1355
Helping Others 197, 824, 1226, 1282, 1301
Heroes 275
Holiness 549, 571, 655
Holy Spirit 106, 1266
Homosexuality 129
Honesty 655, 655, 1220, 1335
Hope. 3, 129, 627, 769, 872
Humility. . . 344, 421, 466, 491, 833, 1023, 1119, 1288
Hypocrisy 1080
Identity. 804
Illness 433, 713, 797
Injustice 35, 1031
Integrity. 275, 462, 655, 709, 976, 1220
Intercession. 935
Jesus Christ 765, 1316, 1342
Jesus our Shepherd. 1193
Joy. 1033, 1315, 1344
Justice 635
Kindness 286, 712, 1166
Kinsman-redeemer. 286
Knowing God. 98, 591, 1337
Knowing Jesus. 1337
Laziness 702
Leadership 303, 342, 687
Life Decisions 539
Lifestyle Evangelism. 1199
Lifestyle 1065, 1068, 1275, 1320, 1369
Listening to God. 293
Living Water. 1181
Lord's Supper. 527
Loss. 1268, 1298
Love 284, 1294, 1359
Loving God 83, 116, 1091
Loving Others 769, 1047, 1229, 1350, 1350
Loyalty 284, 313
Lying. 845
Making a Difference. 1421
Making Disciples 1282
Marriage 284, 556, 688, 753, 1055, 1285,
                            1306, 1330
Materialism 204, 739, 1088, 1094, 1154, 1364
Maturity. 421, 1272
Meaning. 735
Missions 14, 666, 813, 1064, 1232
Money. 204, 384, 719
Morality 282
Motivation. 466
Name of Jesus 1421
New Christians 1231
New Life 1316
Nurture. 1350
Obedience 14, 116, 762, 857, 1226
Obstacles 193, 241, 910
Ownership 546
Pain. 433, 1298, 1301

Parents 276
Patience 9, 1382
Peace 782, 790, 1110
Peer Pressure 86, 157, 476, 921
Permissiveness 276
Persecution 857, 1031, 1402
Perseverance 264
Perspective 635
Possessions 1158
Power 342
Praise 354, 1429
Prayer 98, 235, 333, 512, 518, 523, 585, 701,
879, 1105, 1105, 1328, 1338, 1397
Pregnancy 1305
Pressure 241
Pride 491, 866, 1013
Priorities 849, 1041
Procrastination 702
Promises 780, 1407
Punishment 1264
Purity 46, 336, 699, 967, 1351
Purpose 415, 804, 1244
Quiet Time 585, 1105
Relationships in the Church 680
Relationships 83, 688, 1306, 1352, 1386
Resources 258
Respect 1352
Responsibility 716, 744
Rest 132
Resurrection 1122, 1174, 1298
Revenge 1402
Reverence 371
Righteousness 1289
Rights 1143
Roommates 1006
Sacrifice 1272
Salvation 6, 286, 765, 1193, 1209, 1238,
1326, 1373, 1416
Satan 1404
Satisfaction 1094
Scripture Memorization 669
Security 601, 1110, 1262, 1268
Self-control 724, 1409
Self-discipline 193
Self-esteem 64, 565, 688, 1293
Self-image 306, 684

Self-talk 613
Self-worth 447
Servanthood 1119, 1336
Service 489, 824, 836, 935, 1166, 1304
Serving 1232
Sexual Immorality 129, 699
Sexual Pressure 336, 657, 967
Sexuality 46, 753, 1285, 1351, 1409
Shame 1017
Significance 415, 447, 735, 827, 1244
Singleness 333, 627
Sin 6, 68
Speech 712, 1329
Spiritual Growth 583, 1135, 1301, 1344, 1350
Spiritual Multiplication 1107, 1367
Spiritual Thirst 1181
Spiritual Warfare 1181
Starting a Job 989
Stewardship 204, 719
Stress 132, 241, 523
Struggling with Sin 1266
Studying 744, 1347
Submission 1197
Success 225, 1154
Suffering 433, 549, 666
Teamwork 323
Temptation 46, 76, 1290, 1396
Ten Commandments 83
Time Management 235, 389
Training 1162
Troubles 910
Trusting God 24, 565, 623, 1027, 1174
Trust 596, 790, 971
Truth 282, 675
Uniqueness 836
Unity 680
Unselfishness 762
Values 275, 1068, 1345
Wholeheartedness 303, 479, 489
Wisdom 489, 476, 672, 701, 707, 849, 1277
Witnessing 507, 539, 669, 687, 769, 821, 921,
984, 1023, 1061, 1205, 1238, 1366, 1376
Witness 1065, 1347, 1362
Word of God 583, 1094, 1290, 1369, 1380, 1394
Work 523
Youth 745, 1362

Author Acknowledgments

This index gives you information about each contributor and tells you where their devotions can be found.

Don Allen, and his wife, Kathy, are Navigator collegiate staff at California State University, Long Beach. *Devotions by this author can be found on pages 967, 1033, 1072, and 1320.*

Karen Allen is a Navigator collegiate staff serving at the University of Tennessee. *A devotion by this author can be found on page 1324.*

Eileen Anderson is a freelance writer for several Christian publications and lives with her family in Eagan, Minnesota. *Devotions by this author can be found on pages 275, 371, and 1160.*

Helene Ashker is a Navigator community staff serving in Denver, Colorado. *A devotion by this author can be found on page 1190.*

Alison Ashmore has completed a Bachelor's degree and is currently pursuing a teaching certificate at the University of Oklahoma. *A devotion by this author can be found on page 1397.*

Ward Ballard is a Navigator collegiate staff serving at Miami (Ohio) University. *A devotion by this author can be found on page 483.*

Margo Balsis and her husband, Glenn, are Navigator staff currently serving in the Development Department in Colorado Springs, Colorado. *A devotion by this author can be found on page 849.*

Larry Bauer and his wife, Brenda, are Navigator collegiate staff at Rutgers University. *Devotions by this author can be found on pages 801, 890, and 1201.*

Joe Bernardy and his wife, Ronni, are Navigator collegiate staff. Joe serves as the Regional Leader for Upper Midwest Region. Joe and his family currently live in Altoona, Wisconsin. *Devotions by this author can be found on pages 303, 476, 523, 737, 744, 1105, 1143, and 1244.*

Robert M. Bertrand is currently serving on staff at the Evangelical Free Church in Champaign, Illinois. *Devotions by this author can be found on pages 735 and 1065.*

Thomas Betts is a marketing director at Zondervan Publishing House. *A devotion by this author can be found on page 935.*

Lindy Black and her husband, Vic, are Navigator collegiate staff serving at Auburn University. *Devotions by this author can be found on pages 1084, 1177, and 1199.*

Vic Black and his wife, Lindy, are Navigator collegiate staff. Vic serves as the Regional Leader for the Southland Region. Vic and his family currently live in Auburn, Alabama. *A devotion by this author can be found on page 197.*

Bob Boardman and his wife, Jean, are Navigator military staff serving in Seattle, Washington. *A devotion by this author can be found on page 724.*

Jena Borah and her husband, Bernard, are Navigator collegiate staff at Eastern Illinois University. *Devotions by this author can be found on pages 106 and 206.*

Cathy Bowman and her husband, Dave, are Navigator collegiate staff serving at Penn State University. *Devotions by this author can be found on pages 228 and 1309.*

Dave Bowman and his wife, Cathy, are Navigator collegiate staff serving at Penn State University. *A devotion by this author can be found on page 1282.*

Kathy Brackman is a Navigator staff serving with the International Ministries Group. *A devotion by this author can be found on page 1064.*

Dr. Bill Bright is the founder and President of Campus Crusade for Christ International. He and his family currently live in Orlando, Florida. *A devotion by this author can be found on page 1205.*

Greg Bryan is a Navigator collegiate staff serving at Miami (Ohio) University. *Devotions by this author can be found on pages 701, 765, 1416, and 1421.*

Julie Bundt is a Navigator collegiate staff at the University of Northern Iowa. *Devotions by this author can be found on pages 19, 286, 344, 344, 384, and 1220.*

Tony Cammarota is working as a video editor in Denton, Texas. *A devotion by this author can be found on page 235.*

John Carroll is a former Navigator staff and is now a pastor at Central Presbyterian Church in Kingstree, South Carolina. *Devotions by this author can be found on pages 232, 1423, and 1432.*

Stefani Rae Carter and her husband, Chris, are Navigator collegiate staff at Marshall University. *A devotion by this author can be found on page 546.*

Stephanie Carter is a Navigator collegiate staff serving at

Dartmouth College. *Devotions by this author can be found on pages 1017 and 1351.*

Stephanie Choat grew up in Hong Kong and has recently earned a teaching degree from Colorado State University. *A devotion by this author can be found on page 1006.*

Jennifer Colquitt is a high school English teacher who lives with her family in Jacksonville, Arkansas. *Devotions by this author can be found on pages 1197 and 1376.*

Kirt Conroy is a Navigator staff serving with NavYouth and currently lives in Colorado Springs, Colorado. *A devotion by this author can be found on page 1231.*

Terry Cook is the US Collegiate Ministries Director for The Navigators. He lives with his wife, Sherry, and their family in Colorado Springs, Colorado. *Devotions by this author can be found on pages 193, 790, and 971.*

Catherine DeVries is an editor at Zondervan Publishing House. *A devotion by this author can be found on page 1305.*

Nancy Dorrell and her husband, Pete, are Navigator collegiate staff at Virginia Polytechnic Institute. *A devotion by this author can be found on page 780.*

Pete Dorrell and his wife, Nancy, are Navigator collegiate staff at Virginia Polytechnic Institute. *A devotion by this author can be found on page 813.*

Steve Draper and his wife, Sue, are Navigator collegiate staff at James Madison University. *Devotions by this author can be found on pages 284 and 921.*

Megan Dunham and her husband, Craig, are Navigator staff serving with NavYouth and currently live in Colorado Springs, Colorado. *Devotions by this author can be found on pages 489 and 1330.*

Mike Edsall and his wife, Stephanie, are Navigator collegiate staff at the University of Oregon. The Points of Interest were created by Mike and his team. *A devotion by this author can be found on page 157.*

LeRoy Eims and his wife, Virginia, are Navigator staff. LeRoy serves as Director of Public Ministry. He and his family currently live in Colorado Springs, Colorado. *A devotion by this author can be found on page 1290.*

Sherie Falkenstine and her husband, Mike, are Navigator collegiate staff at Colorado State University. *A devotion by this author can be found on page 116.*

Lynn Feldner is a Navigator staff serving with NavYouth and currently lives in Colorado Springs, Colorado. *Devotions by this author can be found on pages 169, 1158, and 1211.*

Joey Fiorino recently graduated from the University of Missouri. *A devotion by this author can be found on page 498.*

Jenny Forsberg is a Navigator collegiate staff serving at Penn State University. *Devotions by this author can be found on pages 627, 1038, 1174, 1203, and 1359.*

John Frese is a Navigator collegiate staff serving at the University of Nebraska. *A devotion by this author can be found on page 818.*

Shannon Gayk is a third year student at Duke University. *Devotions by this author can be found on pages 132 and 1260.*

Jessica Gengler is a third year student at the University of Minnesota. *A devotion by this author can be found on page 1132.*

Bill Gensky and his wife, Robyne, are Navigator collegiate staff at Texas A&M University. *Devotions by this author can be found on pages 86, 293, 601, 680, 1369, and 1386.*

Dawn Getz and her husband, Jay, are Navigator collegiate staff at the University of Illinois. *Devotions by this author can be found on pages 565, 845, 989, 1164, 1277, and 1306.*

Jay Getz and his wife, Dawn, are Navigator collegiate staff at the University of Illinois. *Devotions by this author can be found on pages 556, 699, 739, 1214, 1217, 1240, and 1356.*

Paula Gibson is an art director at Zondervan Publishing House. *Devotions by this author can be found on pages 1184, 1288, and 1344.*

Richard Gregg and his wife, Ruth, are Navigator collegiate staff at Western Michigan University. *A devotion by this author can be found on page 605.*

Sue Grindheim and her husband, Neil, are Navigator staff serving in the International Ministries Group. She and her family currently live in Colorado Springs, Colorado. *Devotions by this author can be found on pages 1110 and 1181.*

Christy Haley is a Navigator collegiate staff serving at Indiana University. *A devotion by this author can be found on page 64.*

Lynn M. Hamilton and her husband, Roger, are Navigator collegiate staff at the University of Wisconsin, Madison. *Devotions by this author can be found on pages 306, 1293, 1336, and 1373.*

Roger Hamilton and his wife, Lynn, are Navigator collegiate staff at the University of Wisconsin, Madison. *Devotions by this author can be found on pages 241, 821, 879, 1122, 1226, 1289, 1304, and 1342.*

Sjanna W. Hargrove currently leads a ministry to high school and collegiate women in Georgetown, Texas, called Women of Worth. *Devotions by this author can be found on pages 716 and 836.*

Dr. Stephen Hayner is President of InterVarsity Christian Fellowship and lives with his family in Madison, Wisconsin. *A devotion by this author can be found on page 857.*

Glen Hougen and his wife, Jeanne, are Navigator collegiate staff at the University of Colorado, Boulder. *Devotions by this author can be found on pages 512 and 1394.*

Jeanne Hougen and her husband, Glen, are Navigator collegiate staff at the University of Colorado, Boulder. *A devotion by this author can be found on page 824.*

Mistie Hutchison is a Navigator collegiate staff serving at Auburn University. *Devotions by this author can be found on pages 264, 507, and 684.*

Rich Jarvi and his wife, Lois, are Navigator collegiate staff. Rich serves as the Regional Leader for the Great Lakes Region. Rich and his family currently live in Columbus, Ohio. *Devotions by this author can be found on pages 591, 669, 827, and 1023.*

Chad Jeffreys and his wife, Wendy, are Navigator collegiate staff at California Polytechnic State University. *A devotion by this author can be found on page 389.*

Randy C. Johnson is pastor of the Denmark Baptist Church in Cutler, Illinois. *Devotions by this author can be found on pages 3, 1266, and 1316.*

Mike Jordahl and his wife, Nancy, are Navigator collegiate staff serving as the Regional Leader for the Northeastern Region. Mike and his family currently live in Sunderland, Massachusetts. *Devotions by this author can be found on pages 1335 and 1409.*

Kisa Kampfer is a Navigator collegiate staff serving at Texas A&M University. *A devotion by this author can be found on page 1321.*

Kyle Kelley and his wife, Kim, are Navigator staff serving in the National Collegiate Office in Colorado Springs, Colorado. *Devotions by this author can be found on pages 466 and 797.*

Bruce Knutson and his wife, Cindy, are Navigator collegiate staff at the University of Minnesota and Carleton College. *A devotion by this author can be found on page 1345.*

Ken Larson and his wife, Tina, are Navigator collegiate staff at Indiana University. *Devotions by this author can be found on pages 1154, 1367, and 1390.*

Tina Larson and her husband, Ken, are Navigator collegiate staff at Indiana University. *Devotions by this author can be found on pages 788 and 1429.*

Kyong A. Lee is a Navigator Edge Corps alumnus and graduate student at California State University, Long Beach. *A devotion by this author can be found on page 1091.*

Don Lenze and his wife, Janet, are Navigator collegiate staff at the University of Massachusetts. *A devotion by this author can be found on page 585.*

Jim Lett and his wife, Pam, are Navigator collegiate staff at Ohio State University. *Devotions by this author can be found on pages 83, 433, 549, 590, and 1135.*

Mark Lewis and his wife, Janet, are Navigator collegiate staff. Mark serves as the Regional Leader for Texas. He and his family currently live in Plano, Texas. *A devotion by this author can be found on page 613, 1355, and 1414.*

Phil Lewis has a doctorate in entomology and is a civilian pest management specialist at the Rock Island, Illinois, US Army base. *Devotions by this author can be found on pages 68.*

Darren Lindblom and his wife, Gina, are Navigator collegiate staff at California Polytechnic State University. *A devotion by this author can be found on page 702.*

John Littleton is a second year student at Wheaton College. *A devotion by this author can be found on page 769.*

Linda Llewelyn and her husband, Rich, are working in Indonesia. *Devotions by this author can be found on pages 623 and 1047.*

Lisa Lorimor is a second year student at Drake University. *A devotion by this author can be found on page 1362.*

Dale Magnusson and his wife, Sherrie, are Navigator collegiate staff at Michigan State University. *A devotion by this author can be found on page 399.*

Colette Magoon and her husband, Steve, are Navigator collegiate staff at the University of Idaho. *Devotions by this author can be found on pages 1013, 1068, 1315, and 1329.*

Deb Maschhoff and her husband, Lee, are Navigator collegiate staff serving at the University of Minnesota. *A devotion by this author can be found on page 1137.*

Jack McQueeney and his wife, Shaunda, are Navigator staff in Colorado Springs, Colorado, where he serves as the US Director for NavYouth and Eagle Lake Camp. *A devotion by this author can be found on page 1436.*

Shaunda McQueeney and her husband, Jack, are Navigator staff directing NavYouth and Eagle Lake Camp. She currently lives with her family in Colorado Springs, Colorado. *Devotions by this author can be found on pages 50, 1119, and 1272.*

Scott L. Moore and his wife, Jennifer, are Navigator collegiate staff at Ohio State University. *Devotions by this author can be found on pages 204, 719, and 1264.*

Bill Mowry and his wife, Peggy, are Navigator collegiate staff at Ohio State University. Bill also serves on The Navigators' People Resource Team. *A devotion by this author can be found on page 447.*

Michelle Murray is a second year student at Colorado College. *A devotion by this author can be found on page 910.*

Doug Nuenke and his wife, Pam, are Navigator collegiate staff at the University of Kansas. Doug also serves as the Navigators' Director for the Edge Corps. *A devotion by this author can be found on page 1402.*

Liesl Oberly is a third year student at Marshall University. *A devotion by this author can be found on page 596.*

Craig Parker and his wife, Nancy, are Navigator collegiate staff at Dartmouth College. *Devotions by this author can be found on pages 31 and 984.*

Sheri Platt is a Navigator staff serving with NavYouth and currently lives in Colorado Springs, Colorado. *Devotions by this author can be found on pages 14 and 1366.*

Jennifer Ranwez is an editor for a research company in the Washington, DC area and currently lives in Arlington,

Virginia. *A devotion by this author can be found on page 1412.*

Betsy Reinheimer is an editorial assistant working for Focus on the Family Publications and lives in Colorado Springs, Colorado. *A devotion by this author can be found on page 713.*

Eric Resler and his wife, Rachel are Navigator collegiate staff at the University of Wisconsin, Eau Claire. *Devotions by this author can be found on pages 421, 672, and 757.*

Jim Rinella and his wife, Linda, are Navigator collegiate staff at Illinois State University. *A devotion by this author can be found on page 1107.*

Jan Rodgers and her husband, Mike, are Navigator collegiate staff at Michigan State University. *A devotion by this author can be found on page 479.*

Inger Rudolph is a Navigator staff serving in the National Collegiate Office in Colorado Springs, Colorado. *Devotions by this author can be found on pages 448 and 1301.*

Carol Rugg and her husband, Steve, serve with the Navigators' Edge Corps Leadership Team. *Devotions by this author can be found on pages 635, 707, 1338, and 1352.*

Steve Rugg is an engineer as well as serving with his wife, Carol, in the Navigators' Edge Corps. They currently live in Columbus, Indiana. *Devotions by this author can be found on pages 46 and 415.*

Cheri Ruggles is a Navigator collegiate staff serving at California Polytechnic State University. *Devotions by this author can be found on pages 1088 and 1294.*

Vollie Sanders and her husband, Darrell, serve with the Navigators' US Leadership Team and currently live in Colorado Springs, Colorado. *Devotions by this author can be found on pages 39 and 342.*

Erica Searl and her husband, Chuck, are Navigator collegiate staff at Montana State University. *A devotion by this author can be found on page 745.*

Kathleen Selje and her husband, Chad, are Navigator collegiate staff at the University of Wisconsin, Eau Claire. *A devotion by this author can be found on page 1080.*

Doug Serven and his wife, Julie, are Navigator collegiate staff at the University of Nebraska. *Devotions by this author can be found on pages 655, 709, 726, 976, 1162, and 1280.*

Travis Stewart and his wife, Susan, are Navigator collegiate staff at the University of Kansas. They also serve with the Navigators' Edge Corps Leadership Team. *A devotion by this author can be found on page 762.*

Dennis Stokes and his wife, Ellen, are Navigator collegiate staff at the University of Colorado. *Devotions by this author can be found on pages 6, 336, 800, 1061, and 1275.*

Dean Storelli and his wife, Anne, are Navigator collegiate staff at Duke University. *Devotions by this author can be found on pages 35 and 608.*

Ellen B. Susman and her husband, Randy, are Navigator collegiate staff at Penn State University. *Devotions by this author can be found on pages 333, 617, 657, 999, and 1364.*

Tom Toomer and his wife, Linda, are Navigator collegiate staff at Colorado State University. *A devotion by this author can be found on page 1031.*

Kenneth G. Tussey is a fourth year student at Auburn University. *A devotion by this author can be found on page 129.*

Margery Van Zante and her husband, Brian, are Navigator collegiate staff at Illinois State University. *Devotions by this author can be found on pages 687 and 1257.*

Michael VanderKlipp is an editor at Zondervan Publishing House. *A devotion by this author can be found on page 688.*

Charla Vogelaar and her husband, Bob, are associate staff with NavYouth in Kansas City, Missouri. *Devotions by this author can be found on pages 539 and 1347.*

Kent Walstrom and his wife, Sharla, are Navigator collegiate staff at the University of Arkansas. *Devotions by this author can be found on pages 225, 866, 1380, and 1407.*

Sharla Walstrom and her husband, Kent, are Navigator collegiate staff at the University of Arkansas. *Devotions by this author can be found on pages 76, 518, 583, 630, 677, 1140, and 1328.*

Phil Ward and his wife, Lillian, are Navigator collegiate staff at Montana State University. *Devotions by this author can be found on pages 323, 644, and 1041.*

Dr. Jerry White is the General Director for The Navigators. He and his wife, Mary, currently live in Colorado Springs, Colorado. *Devotions by this author can be found on pages 1094, 1262, and 1396.*

Louise B. Wyly teaches writing at North Hennepin Community College in Minneapolis, Minnesota, and at Pima Community College in Tucson, Arizona. *A devotion by this author can be found on page 258.*

Dana Yeakley and her husband, Tom, are Navigator collegiate staff serving in The Navigators' Collegiate Ministries. She and her family currently live in Colorado Springs, Colorado. *Devotions by this author can be found on pages 259, 276, and 666.*

Dr. Tom Yeakley and his wife, Dana, are Navigator staff living in Colorado Springs, Colorado. Tom serves on the Navigators' Collegiate Ministries Leadership Team. He created the Weekend Bible studies. *Devotions by this author can be found on pages 9, 1232, 1238, and 1382.*

NOTES

NOTES

NOTES

NOTES

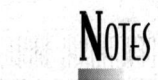

NOTES

COLLEGIATE DEVOTIONAL BIBLE, NIV

Daily devotions written by the Navigator US Campus Ministry staff and friends. Weekend Bible studies written by Dr. Tom Yeakley. Points of Interest written by Mike Edsall.

Navigator US Campus Ministry Editorial Staff

General Editor, Dr. Tom Yeakley

Karen Allen

Stefani Carter

Jay Getz

Katie Hubbard

Mistie Hutchison

Shaunda McQueeney

Julie Serven

Phil Ward

Dana Yeakley

Project management and editorial by Ruth A. DeJager

Interior design by Sharon Wright, Belmont, MI

Art direction by Paula Gibson

Interior and cover art by David Biedrzycki, Medfield, MA

Color insert pages designed by Chris Tobias, Grand Rapids, MI

Interior proofreading by Peachtree Editorial and Proofreading Service, Peachtree City, GA

Interior typesetting by Auto-Graphics, Pomona, CA

Printing and binding by R.R. Donnelley, Crawfordsville, IN

——— Guarantee ———

——— Care ———

We suggest loosening the binding of your new Bible by gently pressing on a small section of pages at a time from the center. To ensure against breakage of the spine, it is best not to bend the cover backward around the spine or to carry study notes, church bulletins, pens, and the like, inside the cover. Because a felt-tipped marker will "bleed" through the pages, we recommend use of a ball-point pen or pencil to underline favorite passages. Your Bible should not be exposed to excessive heat, cold or humidity. Protecting the gold or silver edges of the paper from moisture will avoid spotting, streaking or fading.

——— Definitions ———

Bonded leather: no less than 90% leather fibers with latex base.
Top-Grain leather: 100% pigskin
Cowhide: 100% cowhide

WORLD OF THE PATRIARCHS

→ Abraham's journeys

Possible location of Biblical "Ur of the Chaldeans," where Abraham's migration began

Possible location of Sodom and Gomorrah

© 1986 The Zondervan Corporation

Grid references:

A 1, A 2, A 3, A 4
B 1, B 2, B 3, B 4
C 1, C 2, C 3, C 4
D 1, D 2, D 3, D 4
E 1, E 2, E 3, E 4
F 1, F 2, F 3, F 4

**Map labels:**

Caspian Sea
CAUCASUS MTS.
Mt Ararat
Araxes R.
Lake Urmia
Black Sea
Troy
Aegean Sea
Mycenae
Knossos
Caphtor (Crete)
Kittim (Cyprus)
The Great Sea
HITTITES
Hattusha
TAURUS MTS.
Carchemish
Aleppo
Ugarit
Ebla
Byblos
Damascus
Hazor
Megiddo
Dothan
Shechem
Bethel
Ai
Beersheba
Hebron
Gerar
Zoar?
Kadesh Barnea
Zoan (Tanis)
Noph (Memphis)
On (Heliopolis)
EGYPTIANS
SINAI
Nile R.
Red Sea
ARABIA
PADDAN ARAM
Haran
Tadmor
Mari
Euphrates R.
Tigris R.
Nineveh
Asshur
Nuzi
BABYLONIANS
Babylon
Nippur
Erech (Uruk)
Ur
Persian Gulf

Scale:

300 mi.
0 100 200
0 100 200 300 400 km.

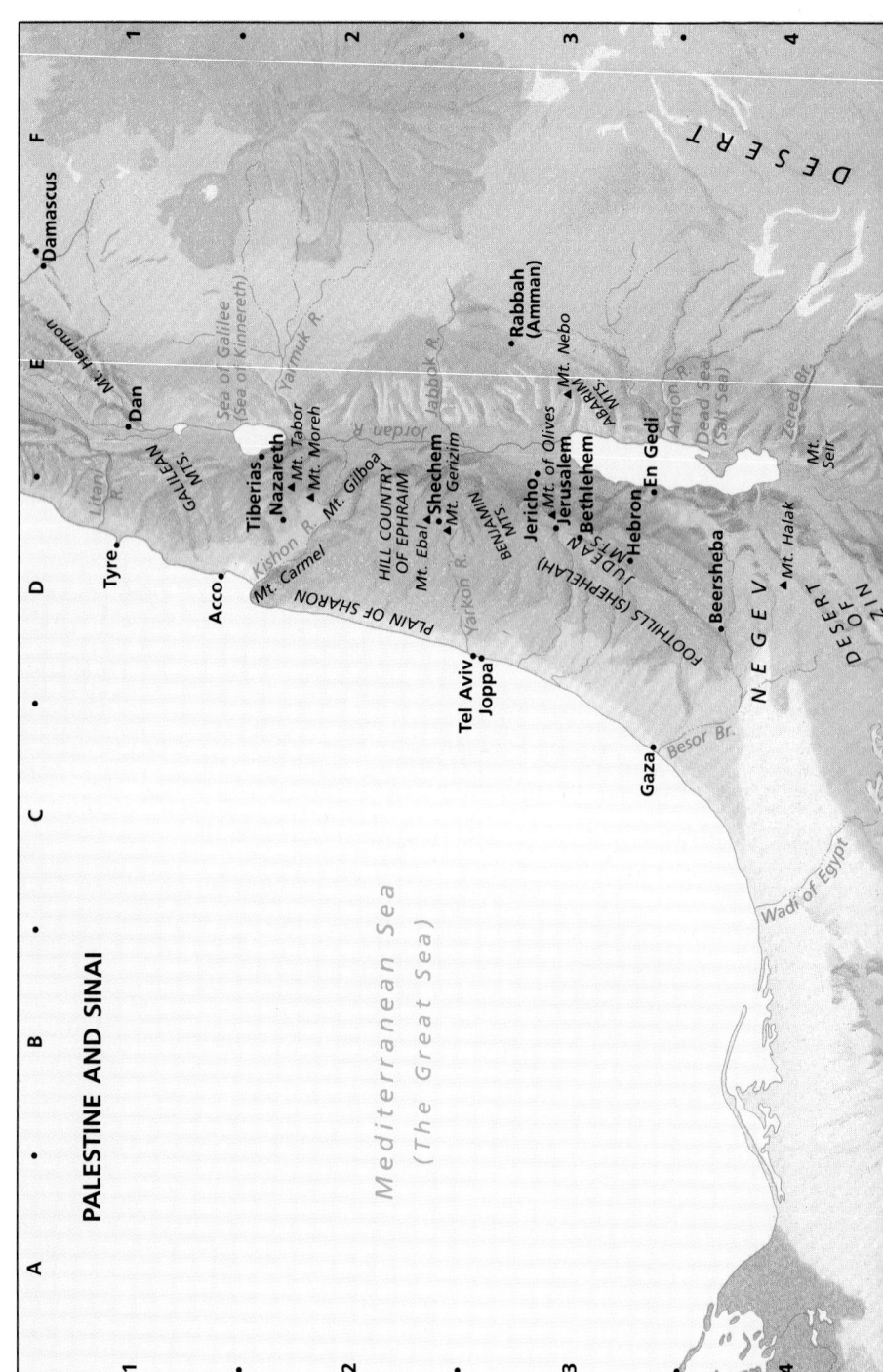

PALESTINE AND SINAI

Mediterranean Sea
(The Great Sea)

DESERT

Damascus

Mt. Hermon

Tyre

Dan

GALILEAN MT'S

Sea of Galilee
(Sea of Kinnereth)

Litani R.

Yarmuk R.

Jordan R.

Tiberias
Nazareth
Mt. Tabor
Mt. Moreh
Mt. Gilboa
Kishon R.

Acco

Mt. Carmel

PLAIN OF SHARON

HILL COUNTRY OF EPHRAIM

Shechem
Mt. Ebal
Mt. Gerizim

Jabbok R.

Rabbah
(Amman)

Tel Aviv
Joppa

Yarkon R.

BENJAMIN MT'S

Jericho
Mt. of Olives
Jerusalem
Bethlehem

Mt. Nebo
ABARIM MTS

FOOTHILLS (SHEPHELAH)

Hebron

JUDEAN MTS

En Gedi

Dead Sea
(Salt Sea)

Arnon R.

Gaza

Besor Br.

Beersheba

NEGEV

Mt. Halak

DESERT OF ZIN

Mt. Seir

Zered Br.

Wadi of Egypt

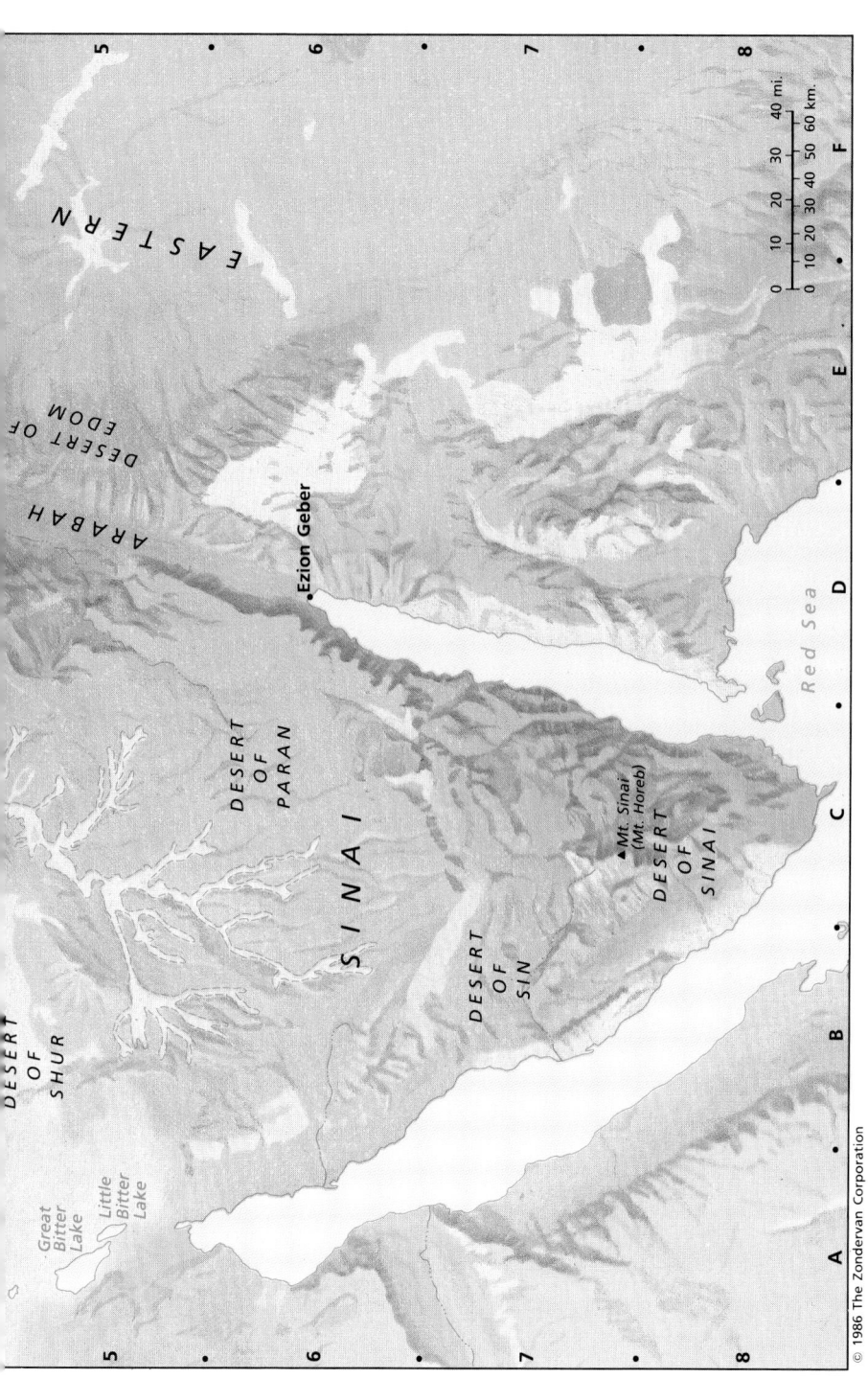

DESERT OF SHUR

Great Bitter Lake

Little Bitter Lake

SINAI

DESERT OF PARAN

DESERT OF SIN

▲Mt. Sinai (Mt. Horeb)

DESERT OF SINAI

ARABAH

DESERT OF EDOM

EASTERN

Ezion Geber

Red Sea

0 10 20 30 40 mi.
0 10 20 30 40 50 60 km.

Aleppo

Euphrates R.

Tiphsah

HAMATH

Hamath

Qatna

Arvad

Kadesh

Tadmor

Kittim (Cyprus)

The
Great Sea

Gebal
(Byblos)

Berothai

ARAMEAN
DESERT

Sidon

PHOENICIA

Litani R.

Damascus

Tyre

Kedesh

Dan

▲ Mt. Hermon

ARAM

Acco

Hazor

Sea of
Kinnereth

Megiddo

Beth

Ashtaroth

Taanach

▲ Shan

Edrei

Mt. Gilboa

Ramoth Gilead

EASTERN DESERT

Jordan R.

Shechem

Mahanaim?

AMMON

Joppa

Gezer

Rabbah

PHILISTIA

Gibeah

Ashdod

Gath

Medeba

Gaza

Jerusalem

Hebron

Ziklag

Salt
Sea

Beersheba

Kir Hareseth

Tamar

MOAB

Kadesh Barnea

EDOM

KINGDOM OF DAVID AND SOLOMON

Saul's kingdom

David and Solomon's kingdom

Territory under Solomon's control

SINAI

Wadi of Egypt

Ezion Geber

Gulf of
Aqaba

0   20   40   60   80 mi.

0 20 40 60 80 100 km.

JESUS' MINISTRY

International transportation artery
Regional roadway

0 10 20 30 mi.
0 10 20 30 40 km.

The Great Sea

PHOENICIA

Tyre

Heals Canaanite woman's daughter

Mt. Hermon

Transfiguration? (possible site)

Caesarea Philippi

Predicts his death

Sermon on the Mount?

Heals the centurion's servant, a paralytic, and Peter's mother-in-law; restores Jairus's daughter to life

Ptolemais (Acco)

GALILEE

Turns water to wine

Cana

Korazin

Bethsaida

Capernaum

Magdala

Sea of Galilee

Heals blind man; feeds 5,000?

Heals man with demons (Mk 5:1; Lk 8:26)

Khersa (Gergesa?)

Tiberias

Transfiguration? (traditional site)

Nazareth

Mt. Tabor

Walks on water; quiets storm

Yarmuk R.

Spends boyhood

Nain

Gadara

Heals men with demons (Mt 8:28)

Restores widow's son to life

Caesarea (Strato's Tower)

Bethany beyond Jordan?

DECAPOLIS

Baptism (possible site)

Salim?

Gerasa

SAMARIA

Jordan R.

Talks with woman at well

Sychar

Mt. Gerizim

Jabbok R.

PEREA

Raises Lazarus from dead; anointed in Simon the Leper's house

Tempted?

Ascends into heaven

Baptism (traditional site)

Clears temple

Jericho

Mt. of Olives

Bethany beyond Jordan?

Emmaus?

Bethany

Jerusalem

Heals blind Bartimaeus; calls Zacchaeus down from tree

Appears to two after resurrection

Bethlehem

JUDEA

Birth

Salt Sea

Crucifixion and resurrection

Machaerus

© 1986 The Zondervan Corporation

PAUL'S MISSIONARY JOURNEYS

First Missionary Journey (A.D. 46–48)

Second Missionary Journey (A.D. 49–52)

Third Missionary Journey (A.D. 53–57)

Trip to Rome (A.D. 59–60)

JERUSALEM IN JESUS' TIME

— City walls in Jesus' time
--- "City of David"
— The "Old City" (surviving walls, built in 16th century)

KIDRON VALLEY

Garden Tomb (alternate site of crucifixion)

Second Wall

Sheep Pool (Bethesda Pool)

Fish Gate

Israel Pool

Antonia Fortress

Sheep Gate

Jesus arrested

Preaching

Gethsemane

Golden Gate

Crucifixion and burial

Inner Court

Altar

Gate Beautiful

TEMPLE
Court of Women

Golgotha (traditional site)

SECOND QUARTER

TYROPOEON VALLEY

Mt. of Olives

Towers' Pool

Gennath Gate

First Wall

Bridge (Wilson's Arch)

Court of Men

Court of the Gentiles

Clearing of temple

Royal Porch

Tower of Phasael

Tower of Hippicus

Stairs (Robinson's Arch)

Pinnacle of the Temple (traditional location)

Tower of Mariamne

Herod's Palace

Herod Antipas's Palace

Huldah Gates

UPPER CITY

Theater

Valley Gate

Serpent's Pool

Jesus before high priests; Peter's denial

High Priest's House

ESSENE QUARTER

LOWER CITY
(Possibly part of Jerusalem in Jesus' time)

TYROPOEON VALLEY

Gihon Spring

KIDRON VALLEY

Upper Room (traditional site)

Last Supper

Hezekiah's Tunnel

Pool of Siloam

Water Gate

Essene Gate

HINNOM VALLEY

0   0.1   0.2 mi.
0   0.1   0.2   0.3 km.

© 1986 The Zondervan Corporation